DON'T . . . W9-BSQ-044

mope (*v.*) *pout, be dejected*
ache, be apathetic, be down in the mouth,
be gloomy, be in a funk, bleed, brood, chafe,
despair, despond, droop, eat one's heart out, fret,
grieve, grumble, grump, idle, lament, languish,
lose heart, moon, pine, pine away, regret,
repine, sink, stew over, sulk, sweat over, waste time,
wear a long face, yearn, SEE CONCEPTS *20,410*

DO . . .

FIND THE *EXACT* WORD OR PHRASE YOU NEED WITH . . .

**ROGET'S 21st CENTURY THESAURUS
in Dictionary Form**

THE MOST UP-TO-DATE AND USER-FRIENDLY THESAURUS
YOU CAN BUY

**TOMORROW'S CLASSIC
AVAILABLE TODAY—
AND IN PAPERBACK:**

"A book that provides a solid frame of reference, this new edition
combines the simplicity of a dictionary format with a concept index."
—*USA Today*

"Outstanding!"
—*American Bookseller*

ROGET'S
21ST CENTURY THESAURUS

ROGET'S
—21ST—
CENTURY THESAURUS

IN DICTIONARY FORM

The Essential Reference for Home, School, or Office

EDITED BY THE PRINCETON LANGUAGE INSTITUTE
BARBARA ANN KIPFER, PH.D., HEAD LEXICOGRAPHER

Produced by The Philip Lief Group, Inc.

A LAUREL BOOK

Published by
Dell Publishing
a division of
Bantam Doubleday Dell Publishing Group, Inc.
1540 Broadway
New York, New York 10036

If you purchased this book without a cover you should be aware that this book is stolen property. It was reported as "unsold and destroyed" to the publisher and neither the author nor the publisher has received any payment for this "stripped book."

Published by arrangement with
The Philip Lief Group, Inc.
6 West 20th Street
New York, New York 10011

Copyright © 1992, 1993 by The Philip Lief Group, Inc.

All rights reserved. No part of this book may be reproduced or transmitted in any form or by any means, electronic or mechanical, including photocopying, recording, or by any information storage and retrieval system, without the written permission of the Publisher, except where permitted by law. For information address: Delacorte Press, New York, New York.

The trademark Laurel® is registered in the U.S. Patent and Trademark Office.

The trademark Dell® is registered in the U.S. Patent and Trademark Office.

ISBN: 0-440-21555-2

Reprinted by arrangement with Delacorte Press

Printed in the United States of America

Published simultaneously in Canada

August 1993

10 9 8 7 6 5 4 3 2 1

CONTENTS

PREFACE

Language and our ideas about language change as rapidly and inevitably as the world around us. The "Information Age" we now live in has been made possible by the sophisticated technology of computers and the potential of databases for information storage and retrieval; we receive and process more information than ever before. These innovations did not exist even a generation ago. Further, the research and development of artificial intelligence systems has led to a new examination of the complex cognitive relationships human beings form between their ideas and the words they choose—how this process works, and how it can be recreated. Current lexicographical research must go beyond traditional methods and techniques to consider these new discoveries and applications in developing viable contemporary reference materials for students, linguists, and writers.

The results of recent studies on students' ability to develop reference skills show that most people learn a new word by guessing, based on context, what that word means. Combining this proven trend with the advanced theories of language gained through electronic media, I have arrived at an "onomasiological" approach to understanding American English. That is, the capability of traveling successfully from a meaning to a word instead of the only other practical method to date—the straight-forward dictionary approach of going from word to meaning. Onomasiologically, readers move from the concepts of "yellow" and "flower" to a selection of words that describe the combination, or from the notion of a "positive state of mind" to its qualities, actions, and conditions.

For the general public, we cannot believe that the printed book will go out of style within our lifetime. Indeed, its popularity is increasing. I have searched for a method of presenting this lexical theory in a format that provides diversified access within one resource. In *Roget's 21st Century Thesaurus*, the text is designed to do just that: allowing users to search both from word to meaning and from meaning to word. The dictionary format lends familiarity of use, while the Concept Index illustrates the language's semantic structure and displays links between words. The A to Z listings further amplify the resonances between words by specifying syntactic function through part-of-speech and sense division.

The result is the most complete and comprehensive selection of synonyms published in print media: *Roget's* for the 21st-century reader.

BARBARA ANN KIPFER, PH.D.

INTRODUCTION

In 1805, P. M. Roget, a British surgeon and inventor, took up a peculiar hobby: the classification of words according to ideas. His intention: to present those words in a kind of verbal catalogue that would assist writers and linguists in their search for the right manner of expression. As he worked, he perhaps had in mind the ancient Sanskrit *Amarakosha*, arguably the first arrangement of words by subject, or the French *Pasigraphie*, published in 1797, which was an attempt to order words so they could be understood universally, without translation. Roget called his own work a ''thesaurus''—a Latin word meaning ''treasury'' or ''storehouse of knowledge.''

Roget's pastime became a lifelong passion and in 1852, at the age of seventy-three, Roget published his *Thesaurus of English Words and Phrases, Classified and Arranged so as to Facilitate the Expression of Ideas and Assist in Literary Composition.* This new reference book became enormously popular and a second edition appeared only a year after the first. By the time of Roget's death in 1869, there had been over twenty-five editions and printings. Today, his name is synonymous with the thesaurus.

MAKING A BETTER THESAURUS

Because Roget's thesaurus assumes contemporary users share the compiler's ideas about language, Roget's 19th-century system is a difficult one for "21st-century" readers to use to advantage. Its abstruse classifications and indexes only present modern users with an agonizing labyrinth of possibility where each route dead-ends in a disappointing and many times inappropriate selection of synonyms. Synonyms are buried in the text in a way that is arcane and nearly impenetrable. All too often, the right word remains elusive and the thesaurus remains on the shelf.

While Roget's original idea was brilliant, his eccentrically organized hierarchy of the English language is demonstrably Victorian and outdated by today's standards. For over a century, thesaurus editors have strived to redefine the nature and function of the thesaurus, and to accomplish the primary objective of combining optimum accuracy with a highly usable format. Attempts to improve Roget's thesaurus began with Roget's own son, John Lewis, who expanded the selection of synonyms. Later, Thomas Y. Crowell acquired publishing rights to the thesaurus and his 1886 edition of Roget's provided a clearer page design and format that enhanced the book's readability. Subsequent generations of Crowells have added Americanisms, foreign expressions, slang and nonstandard speech, prefixes, suffixes, and quotations. However, Roget's structure of abbreviations, categories, cross-references, and indexes has only become further complicated by an elaborately conceived type design, boldface entries, numbered paragraphs, and a decimal system that requires an explanatory diagram.

Very few successful arrangements of lexical information have been devised to access words non-alphabetically. C. O. Sylvester Mawson was the first to attempt to simplify and reorganize Roget's thesaurus in dictionary form. In 1911, he issued his own alphabetical presentation of the famous Roget system. Twentieth-century editors quickly followed his lead, eager to arrive at an easier method for frustrated thesaurus users.

But because the dictionary-style thesauri do not suggest any relationships between words beyond the simple aggregation of synonyms listed with a main entry, adoption of a strict dictionary format is but a limited improvement. Although these thesauri do offer a more straightforward presentation than the old Roget's, they neither help users organize thoughts nor do they infer broad conceptual links between ideas as expressed through language in words.

INNOVATION ON A CLASSIC THEME

Until *Roget's 21st Century Thesaurus,* no other thesaurus has been able to proficiently combine the utility of a dictionary format with the sophistication made possible by arranging words according to ideas. This revolutionary design supersedes the traditional Roget and all other thesauri as the new standard for thesaurus users. It is, simultaneously, a fast and efficient handbook for writers and a medium to facilitate the expression of ideas—both of Roget's objectives brought forward and reinterpreted for the 21st-century user.

Electronically compiled using state-of-the-art techniques, *Roget's 21st Century Thesaurus* lists 17,000 main entries or headwords in alphabetical order that generate hundreds of thousands of synonyms—more than any other thesaurus in dictionary form.

Roget's 21st Century Thesaurus is the forerunner of the latest changes in the language. The editor's final selection of main entry words and synonyms reflects modern practices of speaking and writing, and appreciates contemporary linguistic sensitivities. Dialectic and obsolete terms have been replaced by timely words and phrases recently evolved from new technologies and disciplines including computers, video equipment, biotechnology, and environmental chemistry. A nonsexist approach to language replaces outmoded epithets. Foreign words and phrases that reflect our global consciousness have been included, as well as hundreds of Americanisms. Drawing upon computer technology and recent innovations in typesetting and design, the pages are printed in a highly readable and contemporary format for ease in making skillful and effective decisions.

The synonym lists contain no superfluous cross-references, compendious usage labels, or cumbersome abbreviations to come between users and the words themselves. Like main entries, the synonym lists are arranged in alphabetical order. This is done so as not to proscribe or suggest any particular preference to the wealth of synonym choices available, and also for the user's convenience.

Synonyms that represent nonstandard usage are marked with an unobtrusive asterisk. These include both informal words and colloquial phrases and expressions common to the language.

THE CONCEPT INDEX

Thesaurus entries are enriched by directing users to related concepts in *Roget's 21st Century Thesaurus*'s Concept Index. This unique index offers users an up-to-the-minute language hierarchy that stimulates the path of thought into expression by mirroring the cognitive process of the human brain. By considering subject and concept as well as presenting an agglomeration of synonyms, *Roget's 21st Century Thesaurus*'s Concept Index actually helps writers organize their thoughts and generates possibilities for millions of word choices—far beyond the capabilities of traditional thesauri.

The Index lists over 800 individual numbered concepts to which each of the book's 17,000 headwords is referenced. The words "SEE CONCEPT(s)" appear in small caps at the end of a main entry, followed by all relevant numerical assignments of concepts for that word. When an initial search does not yield adequate results, the Concept Index automatically provides users with alternative places to look when further exploration is desired.

For example, if none of the synonyms listed with the word "scintillating" seem appropriate, the Concept Index directs the writer to concepts #401, "attributes of behavior;" #529, "cognitive qualities;" and #617, "visual brightness." Each concept gathers together scores of headwords that share the same characteristics. Persistent writers or linguists can turn back in the A to Z listing to the synonym aggregates for any of these headwords again and again to accumulate a plethora of ideas for possible word choices.

In determining concept names and classifications, the most advanced theories of communication and learning available have been applied. The word hierarchies in *Roget's 21st Century Thesaurus* have been streamlined into categories that reflect contemporary ways of thinking. There are no misunderstandings or irksome inconsistencies about what concepts mean or confusion about how they are organized. Whether performing a speedy search through concepts referenced to a main entry in the A to Z listing, or entering the index with just a vague notion in mind, users will find the Concept Index to be a fast and reliable research tool.

HOW TO USE
ROGET'S 21st CENTURY THESAURUS

Roget's 21st Century Thesaurus's sensible format ensures swift access to the right alternatives. For quick identification, each main entry in the A to Z listing is printed in boldface; its part of speech follows in bracketed italics. Some headwords have more than one listing; separate entries are included for each different part of speech and are ordered in the following manner: noun forms, adjectives, verbs, adverbs, conjunctions, and prepositions. "Pass," for example, has 13 entries in *Roget's 21st Century Thesaurus*—four noun forms and nine verb forms. Each sense of the word "pass" is treated exclusively to help writers pinpoint the precise sense of the word desired.

Although no thesaurus is intended to replace a dictionary, concise definitions accompany main entries in order to supply users with a basic reference point and help them to evaluate synonym choices. Semicolons sometimes appear within definitions to denote fine points of sense for a word's particular usage when the discernments are too subtle to warrant a separate entry.

Remember that no two words mean *exactly* the same thing; no two words are directly interchangeable. It is the subtle nuance and flavor of particular words that give the English language its rich and various texture. While we turn to a thesaurus to find different, more expressive ways of speaking and writing, we must turn to a dictionary, a sophisticated semantic tool, to determine meaning. Always consider synonyms in their desired context and consult a dictionary if there remains any doubt about a word or phrase's application.

The Concept Index follows the alphabetical listing of headwords and begins with a reference key to its 837 concepts. The concepts appear in the index in numerical order and are divided into ten overarching categories of interest: Actions, Causes, Fields of Human Activity, Life Forms, Objects, The Planet, Qualities, Senses, States, and Weights and Measures. All main entry words grouped under a specific concept are ordered alphabetically. Headwords that denote different parts of speech appear together in these lists, allowing users to enhance their prose from more than one perspective—and to think more about the relationships between the words they choose.

TOMORROW'S CLASSIC FOR TODAY'S USER

In the minds of writers, Roget has always been the trademark of a dependable thesaurus. As we enter an era unimagined by P. M. Roget two hundred years ago, *Roget's 21st Century Thesaurus* secures that reputation. Adapting Roget's idea for his thesaurus to reflect today's concerns, this new text represents a living reference of American English.

ROGET'S
21ST CENTURY THESAURUS

A

abandon [n] *careless disregard for consequences*
disregard, freedom, impulse, licentiousness, recklessness, spontaneity, thoughtlessness, uninhibitedness, unrestraint, wantonness, wildness; SEE CONCEPTS 633,645

abandon [v1] *leave behind, relinquish*
abdicate, back out, bail out*, bow out*, chicken out*, cop out*, cut loose*, desert, discard, discontinue, ditch*, drop, drop out, duck*, dump*, dust*, flake out*, fly the coop*, give up the ship*, kiss goodbye*, leave, leg it*, let go, opt out, pull out, quit, run out on, screw*, ship out, stop, storm out*, surrender, take a powder*, take a walk*, throw over*, vacate, walk out on, wash hands of*, withdraw, yield; SEE CONCEPT 195

abandon [v2] *leave in troubled state*
back out, desert, disown, forsake, jilt, leave, leave behind, quit, reject, renounce, throw over*, walk out on; SEE CONCEPTS 7,19,195

abandoned [adj1] *left alone, deserted*
alone, cast aside, cast away, deserted, discarded, dissipated, dropped, dumped, eighty-sixed*, eliminated, empty, forgotten, forsaken, given up, godforsaken*, jilted, left, left in the cold*, left in the lurch*, neglected, on the rocks*, outcast, passed up*, pigeon-holed*, rejected, relinquished, shunned, sidelined*, side-tracked*, unoccupied, vacant, vacated; SEE CONCEPT 577

abandoned [adj2] *free from moral restraint; uninhibited*
corrupt, depraved, dissolute, immoral, incontinent, incorrigible, licentious, profligate, shameless, sinful, uncontrolled, unprincipled, unrestrained, wanton, wicked, wild; SEE CONCEPT 545

abase [v] *deprive of self-esteem, confidence*
belittle, debase, degrade, demean, diminish, disgrace, dishonor, humble, humiliate, lower, mortify, reduce, shame; SEE CONCEPTS 7,19

abashed [adj] *exhibiting mental discomfort, ill at ease*
ashamed, bewildered, bugged*, chagrined, confounded, confused, crushed, discombobulated*, disconcerted, embarrassed, fazed*, fuddled, humbled, humiliated, in a tizzy*, mortified, rattled, shamed, taken aback; SEE CONCEPT 403

abate [v] *lessen, grow or cause to grow less*
allay, chill out*, coast*, cool, cool it*, decline, decrease, diminish, dull, dwindle, ebb, go with the flow*, hang easy*, hang loose*, lay back*, let go, let it all hang out*, let up, mellow out*, moderate, quell, recede, reduce, slacken, slow, subdue, subside, take it easy*, taper, taper off, unlax*, wane; SEE CONCEPTS 240,698

abbey [n] *building that houses monks, nuns, or priests; church*
cloister, convent, friary, ministry, monastery, nunnery, priory, temple; SEE CONCEPTS 368,439

abbreviate [v1] *shorten*
abridge, abstract, boil down*, clip, compress, condense, contract, cut, cut back, cut down, cut off, cut out, digest, encapsulate, get to the meat*, pare, prune, put in a nutshell*, reduce, summarize, take out, trim; SEE CONCEPTS 236,247

abbreviate [v2] *cut short an activity*
abort, curtail, restrict, stop short, truncate; SEE CONCEPT 234

abbreviation [n] *something shortened*
abridgement, abstract, abstraction, clipping, compendium, compression, condensation, contraction, digest, outline, precis, reduction, sketch, summary, syllabus, synopsis; SEE CONCEPTS 283,652

abdicate [v] *give up a right, position, or power*
abandon, abjure, abnegate, bag it*, bail out*, cede, demit, drop, forgo, give up, leave, leave high and dry*, leave holding the bag*, leave in the lurch*, opt out*, quit, quitclaim, relinquish, renounce, resign, retire, sell out*, step down, surrender, vacate, waive, withdraw, yield; SEE CONCEPTS 133,298

abdomen [n] *the stomach and area directly below in an animate being*
bay window*, belly, bowels, breadbasket*, corporation, gut*, guts, intestines, middle, midriff, midsection, paunch, pot*, potbelly*, spare tire*, tummy, venter, viscera; SEE CONCEPT 393

abdominal [adj] *concerning the stomach and the area below it*
belly, duodenal, gastric, intestinal, stomachic, ventral, visceral; SEE CONCEPT 393

abduct [v] *take by force and without permission*
carry off, dognap*, grab, kidnap, make off with, put the snatch on*, remove, seize, shanghai*, snatch, sneeze*, spirit away*; SEE CONCEPT 139

aberrant [adj] *not normal; varying from the usual*
abnormal, atypical, bizarre, deviant, different, flaky*, mental*, nonstandard, odd, off-base, off-color, out of line*, peculiar, psycho*, strange, unusual, weird; SEE CONCEPT 547

aberration [n1] *state of abnormality*
delusion, eccentricity, oddity, peculiarity, quirk, strangeness, weirdness; SEE CONCEPT 647

aberration [n2] *different from that expected*
departure, deviation, difference, distortion, divergence, diversion, irregularity, lapse, straying, wandering; SEE CONCEPT 665

abet [v] *assist, help in wrongdoing*
advocate, back, condone, egg on*, encourage, endorse, goad, incite, instigate, prod, promote, provoke, sanction, spur, support, urge; SEE CONCEPTS 14,110

abeyance [n] *being inactive or suspended temporarily*
deferral, discontinuation, dormancy, inactivity, intermission, latency, postponement, quiescence, recess, remission, suspension, waiting; SEE CONCEPTS 681,705

abhor [v] *regard with contempt or disgust*
abominate, be allergic to*, be down on*, be grossed out by*, despise, detest, hate, have no use for*, loathe, scorn; SEE CONCEPT 29

abide [v1] *submit to, put up with*
accept, acknowledge, bear, bear with*, be big about*, concede, consent, defer, endure, hang in*, hang in there*, hang tough*, live with*, put up with*, receive, sit tight*, stand, stand for, stomach, suffer, swallow, take, tolerate, withstand; SEE CONCEPTS 23,35

abide [v2] *live in a certain place*
bide, bunk*, bunk out*, crash, dwell, hang out*, inhabit, lodge, nest, perch, reside, room, roost, settle, squat, stay; SEE CONCEPT 226

abide [v3] *remain or continue in a state*
continue, endure, keep on, last, persevere, persist, remain, survive; SEE CONCEPTS 23,239

abide [v4] *stop temporarily and wait for*
anticipate, bide, expect, linger, pause, remain, rest, sojourn, stay, stick around*, stop, tarry, wait; SEE CONCEPTS 119,681

abiding [adj] *continuing or existing for an indefinite time*
constant, continuing, enduring, eternal, everlasting, fast, indissoluble, lasting, permanent, perpetual, persistent, persisting, steadfast, steady; SEE CONCEPT 551

ability [n1] *power to act, perform*
aptitude, capability, capacity, competence, competency, comprehension, dexterity, endowment, facility, faculty, intelligence, might, potentiality, qualification, resourcefulness, skill, strength, talent, understanding; SEE CONCEPT 630

ability [n2] *natural or acquired power in a particular activity*
adeptness, adroitness, bent, capability, cleverness, command, craft, deftness, expertise, expertness, finesse, flair, genius, gift, handiness, ingenuity, knack, know-how, mastery, mind for, proficiency, savvy, skill, skillfulness, strength, talent, the goods*, the right stuff*, what it takes*; SEE CONCEPT 706

abject [adj] *hopeless and downtrodden*
base, contemptible, degraded, dejected, deplorable, dishonorable, fawning, forlorn, groveling, hangdog, humiliated, low, miserable, outcast, pitiable, servile, submissive, worthless, wretched; SEE CONCEPT 571

ablaze [adj1] *on fire*
afire, aflame, alight, blazing, burning, conflagrant, fiery, flaming, flaring, ignited, lighted; SEE CONCEPTS 485,605

ablaze [adj2] *very excited*
afire, angry, aroused, enthusiastic, fervent, frenzied, fuming, furious, heated, impassioned, incensed, intense, on fire, passionate, raging, stimulated, vehement; SEE CONCEPT 550

ablaze [adj3] *brightly illuminated*
aflame, aglow, brilliant, flashing, gleaming, glowing, incandescent, luminous, radiant, refulgent, sparkling; SEE CONCEPT 617

able [adj1] *capable of performing; having an innate capacity*
adept, adequate, adroit, agile, alert, apt, bright, capable, competent, cunning, deft, dexterous, easy, effortless, endowed, equipped, facile, fitted, good, intelligent, knowing, powerful, ready, smart, strong, worthy; SEE CONCEPTS 402,527

able [adj2] *able to perform well; having a proven capacity*
accomplished, adroit, agile, artful, au fait, brilliant, capable, clever, deft, dexterous, effective, effectual, efficient, equal to, experienced, expert, facile, gifted, ingenious, intelligent, keen, know backwards and forwards*, know one's onions*, know the ropes*, learned, masterful, masterly, powerful, practiced, prepared, proficient, qualified, responsible, savvy, sharp, skilled, skillful, smart, talented, there*, trained, up to it*, up to snuff*, up to speed*, with it*; SEE CONCEPTS 402,528

able-bodied [adj] *physically strong and capable*
firm, fit, hale, hardy, healthy, hearty, lusty, powerful, robust, staunch, stout, strapping*, sturdy, vigorous; SEE CONCEPTS 314,489

abnegation [n] *denial, renouncement of something*
abandonment, abstinence, eschewal, forbearance, giving up, nixing, refusal, rejection, relinquishment, renunciation, sacrifice, self-denial, stonewall*, surrender, temperance; SEE CONCEPTS 18,25

abnormal [adj] *different from standard or norm*
aberrant, anomalistic, anomalous, atypical, bizarre, curious, deviant, deviate, deviating, divergent, eccentric, exceptional, extraordinary, fantastic, funny, grody*, gross, heteroclite, heterodox, heteromorphic, irregular, odd, off-base, off-color, out of line, peculiar, preternatural, queer, screwy*, spastic*, strange, uncommon, unexpected, unnatural, unorthodox, unusual, weird; SEE CONCEPT 547

abnormality [n] *being different from standard or norm*
aberrancy, aberration, anomalism, anomaly, atypicalness, bizarreness, deformity, deviance, deviancy, deviation, eccentricity, exception, extraordinariness, flaw, irregularity, oddity, peculiarity, preternaturalness, singularity, strangeness, uncommonness, unnaturalness, unusualness, weirdness; SEE CONCEPT 647

aboard [adj] *on or in a transportation object*
boarded, consigned, embarked, en route, in transit, loaded, on, on board, traveling; SEE CONCEPT 583

abode [n] *building or place where one resides*
address, apartment, base, casa, condo, co-op, crash pad*, crib*, den, digs*, domicile, dwelling, flat, flop*, habitat, haunt, headquarters, hearth, hole*, home, homestead, house, joint*, lodging, pad, quarters, residence, roost*, sanctuary, seat; SEE CONCEPT 515

abolish [v] *do away with or put an end to*
abate, abrogate, annihilate, annul, call off, cancel, destroy, disestablish, dissolve, end, eradicate, erase, expunge, extinguish, extirpate, finish, inhibit, invalidate, kill, negate, nix, nullify, obliterate, overthrow, overturn, prohibit, put an end to, put kibosh on*, put the kibosh on*, quash, repeal, repudiate, rescind, revoke, scrub*, set aside, squelch, stamp out, subvert, supersede, suppress, terminate, undo, vacate, vitiate, void, wipe out, zap*; SEE CONCEPTS 121,252,298

abolition [n] *formal act of putting an end to, annulling*
abolishment, abrogation, annihilation, annulment, cancellation, destruction, dissolution, elimination, end, ending, eradication, extirpation, invalidation, negation, nullification, obliteration, overthrow, overturning, quashing, repeal, repudiation, rescinding, rescindment, rescission, revocation, subversion, suppression, termination, voiding, wiping out, withdrawal; SEE CONCEPTS 121,252,298

abominable [adj] *awful, detestable*
abhorrent, atrocious, awful, bad, base, beastly, contemptible, cursed, despicable, disgusting, foul, grim, grody*, gross*, hairy*, hateful, heinous, hellish, horrible, horrid, loathsome, lousy, nauseating, obnoxious, odious, offensive, repellent, reprehensible, repugnant, repulsive, revolting, rotten, sleazy*, stinking, terrible, vile, wretched; SEE CONCEPTS 29,544,571

abomination [n1] *object of extreme dislike, hate*
anathema, aversion, bother, curse, detestation, evil, horror, nuisance, plague, shame, torment; SEE CONCEPTS 29,666

abomination [n2] *wrongdoing*
crime, offense, wrong; SEE CONCEPT *691*

aboriginal [adj] *belonging to one, existing in a place since prehistory*
ancient, earliest, endemic, first, indigenous, native, original, primary, primeval, primitive, primordial; SEE CONCEPT *549*

abort [v1] *stop or cancel something*
arrest, break off, call it quits*, call off, check, cut off, drop, end, fail, halt, interrupt, knock it off*, lay off*, nullify, scrap, scratch, scrub*, terminate; SEE CONCEPT *121*

abort [v2] *terminate or fail to complete pregnancy*
miscarry; SEE CONCEPTS *121,304,308*

abortion [n] *failure*
disappointment, disaster, fiasco, misadventure, premature delivery; SEE CONCEPTS *304,308,674*

abortive [adj] *failing to achieve a goal*
failed, failing, fruitless, futile, ineffective, ineffectual, miscarried, unavailing, unproductive, unsuccessful, useless, vain, worthless; SEE CONCEPT *528*

abound [v] *exist in abundance*
be alive with, be all over the place*, be knee deep in*, be no end to*, be plentiful, be thick with*, be up to one's ears in*, crawl with*, crowd, flourish, flow, have a full plate*, infest, overflow, proliferate, swarm, swell, teem, thrive; SEE CONCEPT *141*

about [adv1] *in an opposite direction*
around, back, backward, in reverse, round; SEE CONCEPT *581*

about [adv2] *lying anywhere without order, arrangement*
anyhow, any which way*, around, here and there; SEE CONCEPT *583*

about [prep1] *near an amount, quantity*
almost, approximately, in general, in the ball park*, in the neighborhood*, nearly, practically, pretty nearly, roughly; SEE CONCEPT *771*

about [prep2] *concerning, relating to*
apropos, as concerns, as respects, dealing with, in connection with, in relation to, in respect to, referring to, regarding, relative to, touching, touching on; SEE CONCEPT *532*

about [prep3] *near or close to in position*
adjacent, beside, nearby; SEE CONCEPTS *586, 778*

about [prep4] *on every side, in every direction*
around, encircling, round, surrounding, through, throughout; SEE CONCEPT *586*

about-face [n] *change in direction*
changeabout, double, doubleback, reversal, reverse, turn, turnabout, volte-face; SEE CONCEPT *697*

above [prep1] *higher in position*
aloft, atop, beyond, high, on high, on top of, over, overhead, raised, superior, upon; SEE CONCEPT *752*

above [prep2] *more, higher in amount, degree*
beyond, exceeding, greater than, larger than, over; SEE CONCEPT *793*

above [prep3] *superior to*
before, beyond, exceeding, prior to, superior to, surpassing; SEE CONCEPT *567*

aboveboard [adj] *candid*
forthright, frank, honest, open, overt, right on*, square, straight, straightforward, straight from shoulder*, true, trustworthy, truthful, up front*, veracious; SEE CONCEPT *404*

aboveboard [adv] *candidly*
frankly, honestly, on the up and up*, openly, overtly, truly, truthfully, veraciously; SEE CONCEPT *404*

abrasion [n1] *scraped area*
chafe, injury, scrape, scratch, scuff; SEE CONCEPT *309*

abrasion [n2] *scraping or wearing down by friction*
abrading, chafing, erosion, grating, rubbing, scratching, scuffing; SEE CONCEPT *186*

abrasive [adj1] *irritating in manner*
annoying, biting, caustic, cutting, galling, hard to take*, hateful, hurtful, nasty, rough, rubbing the wrong way*, sharp, spiky*, unpleasant; SEE CONCEPT *404*

abrasive [adj2] *scraping or wearing*
cutting, erosive, grinding, polishing, rough, scratching, scratchy, scuffing, sharpening, smoothing; SEE CONCEPT *606*

abreast [adv1] *next to, alongside*
beside, equal, in alignment, in line, level, opposite, shoulder to shoulder, side by side; SEE CONCEPT *586*

abreast [adv2] *up-to-date*
acquainted, au courant, au fait, contemporary, familiar, informed, in touch, knowledgeable, up*, versed; SEE CONCEPT *402*

abridge [v] *shorten*
abbreviate, abstract, blue pencil*, chop, clip, compress, concentrate, condense, contract, curtail, cut, decrease, digest, diminish, downsize, lessen, limit, narrow, put in nutshell*, reduce, restrict, slash, snip*, summarize, trim, truncate; SEE CONCEPTS *236,247*

abridgement [n] *shortening, summary*
abbreviation, abstract, brief, compendium, condensation, conspectus, contraction, curtailment, cutting, decrease, digest, diminishment, diminution, lessening, outline, precis, reducing, reduction, synopsis; SEE CONCEPTS *283,652*

abroad [adj] *in a foreign country*
away, elsewhere, in foreign lands, in foreign parts, out of the country, overseas, touring, traveling; SEE CONCEPT *583*

abrogate [v] *formally put an end to*
abate, abolish, annul, cancel, dissolve, do in*, end, finish off*, invalidate, knock out*, negate, nix, nullify, quash, reject, renege, repeal, retract, revoke, scrub*, torpedo*, undo, vacate, vitiate, void; SEE CONCEPT *121*

abrupt [adj1] *rude or brief in manner*
blunt, brusque, crude, crusty, curt, direct, discourteous, gruff, impetuous, impolite, matter-of-fact, rough, short, snappy, snippy, uncivil, ungracious; SEE CONCEPT *542*

abrupt [adj2] *happening suddenly and unexpectedly*
hasty, hurried, jerky, precipitate, precipitous, quick, rushing, sudden, surprising, unanticipated, unceremonious, unexpected, unforeseen; SEE CONCEPT *820*

abscond [v] *run away, depart secretly*
beat it*, bolt*, break, clear out*, cut and run*, decamp, disappear, dog it*, duck out, escape, fade*, flee, fly the coop*, get, go AWOL*, go south*, hightail*, jump*, leave, make a break*, make off, make scarce*, pull out, quit, run off, scram*, skedaddle*, skip out*, slip, sneak away,

split*, steal away, take off*, vamoose*, vanish; SEE CONCEPTS *102,195*

absence [n1] *state of not being present*
absenteeism, AWOL*, cut*, French leave*, hooky*, nonappearance, nonattendance, no show*, truancy, vacancy; SEE CONCEPT *746*

absence [n2] *state of lacking something needed or usual*
dearth, deficiency, drought, inadequacy, insufficiency, lack, need, omission, privation, unavailability, void, want; SEE CONCEPT *646*

absent [adj1] *not present*
astray, away, AWOL*, elsewhere, ghost, gone, hooky*, missing, nobody home*, no-show*, removed, vanished; SEE CONCEPT *583*

absent [adj2] *deficient in something needed or usual*
bare, blank, devoid, empty, hollow, lacking, minus, missing, nonexistent, omitted, unavailable, vacant, vacuous, wanting; SEE CONCEPT *546*

absentee [adj] *not being present*
absent, distant, oblivious, remote; SEE CONCEPTS *403,583*

absenteeism [n] *state of not being present*
absence, defection, desertion, skipping, truancy; SEE CONCEPT *746*

absent-minded [adj] *unaware of events, surroundings*
absent, absorbed, abstracted, airheaded*, bemused, daydreaming, distracted, distrait, dreaming, dreamy, engrossed, faraway, forgetful, goofing off*, heedless, inattentive, inconscient, lost, mooning*, moony*, oblivious, out to lunch*, pipe dreaming*, preoccupied, remote, removed, space cadet*, spacey*, unconscious, unheeding, unmindful, unobservant, unthinking, withdrawn, woolgathering*; SEE CONCEPT *403*

absolute [adj1] *without limit*
complete, consummate, downright, entire, flat out*, free, full, infinite, no catch*, no fine print*, no holds barred*, no ifs ands or buts*, no joke*, no strings attached*, outright, plenary, pure, sheer, simple, straight out, supreme, thorough, total, unabridged, unadulterated, unconditional, unlimited, unqualified, unrestricted, utter; SEE CONCEPT *554*

absolute [adj2] *in control or complete authority*
absolutist, arbitrary, authoritarian, autocratic, autonomous, despotic, dictatorial, full, monocratic, preeminent, sovereign, supreme, totalitarian, tyrannical, tyrannous; SEE CONCEPT *536*

absolute [adj3] *certain*
actual, categorical, conclusive, consummate, decided, decisive, definite, exact, factual, fixed, genuine, infallible, positive, precise, sure, unambiguous, undeniable, unequivocal, unmitigated, unquestionable; SEE CONCEPT *535*

absolute [adj4] *excellent, perfect*
categorical, complete, faultless, flawless, ideal, impeccable, thorough, ultimate, unblemished, unflawed, untarnished; SEE CONCEPT *574*

absolutely [adv1] *certainly, without question*
actually, categorically, come hell or high water*, conclusively, decidedly, decisively, definitely, doubtless, easily, exactly, for sure*, no ifs ands or buts*, no strings attached*, on the button*, on the money*, on the nose*, positively*, precisely, really, right on*, straight out*, sure as can be*, sure as hell*, sure enough*, surely, sure thing*,

the very thing*, truly, unambiguously, unconditionally, unquestionably; SEE CONCEPT *535*

absolutely [adv2] *in a complete manner, degree*
completely, consummately, entirely, fully, thoroughly, utterly, wholly; SEE CONCEPT *531*

absolve [v] *free from responsibility, duty*
acquit, bleach, blink at, clear, discharge, exculpate, excuse, exempt, exonerate, forgive, free, go easy on, launder*, let off*, let off easy*, let off the hook*, let up on*, liberate, lifeboat*, loose, pardon, release, relieve, sanitize*, set free, spare, spring*, vindicate, whitewash, wink at*, wipe it off*, wipe the slate clean*, write off*; SEE CONCEPTS *83,317*

absorb [v1] *physically take in a liquid*
blot, consume, devour, drink in, imbibe, ingest, ingurgitate, osmose, soak up, sop up*, sponge up*, suck in*, swallow, take in; SEE CONCEPT *256*

absorb [v2] *mentally take in information*
assimilate, comprehend, digest, follow, get, get into*, grasp, incorporate, latch onto, learn, sense, soak up, take in, understand; SEE CONCEPT *31*

absorb [v3] *occupy complete attention*
captivate, concern, consume, employ, engage, engross, fascinate, fill, hold, immerse, involve, monopolize, obsess, preoccupy, rivet; SEE CONCEPT *17*

absorbed [adj] *being completely occupied mentally*
captivated, consumed, deep in thought, engaged, engrossed, fascinated, fixed, gone*, head over heels*, held, immersed, intent, involved, lost, preoccupied, rapt, really into*, up to here*, wrapped up*; SEE CONCEPT *403*

absorbent [adj] *capable of physically taking in a liquid*
absorptive, bibulous, dry, imbibing, penetrable, permeable, porous, pregnable, retentive, spongy, thirsty; SEE CONCEPT *603*

absorbing [adj] *holding one's attention*
arresting, captivating, consuming, engrossing, enthralling, exciting, fascinating, gripping, interesting, intriguing, monopolizing, preoccupying, riveting, spellbinding; SEE CONCEPT *403*

absorption [n1] *assimilation, incorporation*
consumption, digestion, drinking in, exhaustion, fusion, imbibing, impregnation, ingestion, inhalation, intake, osmosis, penetration, reception, retention, saturation, soaking up, suction, taking in; SEE CONCEPTS *169,256*

absorption [n2] *total attention toward something*
captivation, concentration, engagement, engrossment, enthrallment, fascination, hang-up*, holding, immersion, intentness, involvement, occupation, preoccupation, raptness; SEE CONCEPT *410*

abstain [v] *hold back from doing*
abjure, abnegate, avoid, cease, constrain, curb, decline, deny oneself, do without, eschew, evade, fast, fence-sit*, forbear, forgo, give the go by*, give up, go on the wagon*, keep from, pass, pass up, quit, refrain, refuse, renounce, shun, sit on one's hands*, sit on the fence*, sit out, spurn, starve, stop, take the cure*, take the pledge*, withhold; SEE CONCEPTS *25,121*

abstemious [adj] *restraining behavior or appetite*
abstinent, ascetic, austere, continent, frugal, moderate, moderating, restrained, self-denying, self-

restrained, sober, sparing, temperate; SEE CONCEPT 401

abstinence [n] *restraint from desires, especially physical desires*
abnegation, abstaining, abstemiousness, asceticism, avoidance, chastity, continence, fasting, forbearance, frugality, moderation, refraining, renunciation, self-control, self-denial, self-restraint, soberness, sobriety, teetotalism, temperance; SEE CONCEPT 633

abstract [n] *short document prepared from a longer one*
abridgment, brief, compendium, condensation, conspectus, digest, outline, precis, résumé, summary, synopsis; SEE CONCEPT 283

abstract [adj] *conceptual, theoretical*
abstruse, complex, deep, hypothetical, ideal, indefinite, intellectual, nonconcrete, philosophical, recondite, transcendent, transcendental, unreal; SEE CONCEPT 582

abstract [v1] *take away from*
detach, disconnect, disengage, dissociate, extract, isolate, part, remove, separate, steal, take out, uncouple, withdraw; SEE CONCEPTS 135,211

abstract [v2] *prepare short document from longer one*
abbreviate, abridge, condense, digest, outline, review, shorten, summarize; SEE CONCEPTS 79,236,247

abstraction [n] *state of being lost in thought*
absorption, aloofness, brooding, cogitation, consideration, contemplation, daydreaming, detachment, engrossment, entrancement, musing, pensiveness, pondering, preoccupation, reflecting, reflection, remoteness, reverie, ruminating, thinking, trance; SEE CONCEPT 410

abstruse [adj] *difficult to understand*
abstract, clear as dishwater*, complex, complicated, deep, enigmatic, esoteric, Greek to me*, heavy*, hidden, incomprehensible, intricate, involved, muddy, obscure, perplexing, profound, puzzling, recondite, subtle, unfathomable, vague; SEE CONCEPTS 402,562

absurd [adj] *ridiculous, senseless*
batty, campy, crazy, daffy, dippy*, flaky*, fooling around, foolish, for grins*, freaky, gagged up*, goofy*, idiotic, illogical, inane, incongruous, irrational, jokey, joshing, laughable, loony, ludicrous, nonsensical, nutty, off the wall*, preposterous, sappy*, screwy*, silly, stupid, tomfool, unreasonable, wacky; SEE CONCEPTS 544,552,558

absurdity [n] *ridiculous situation or behavior*
applesauce*, BS*, bull* crap*, craziness, farce, flapdoodle*, folly, foolishness, hot air*, idiocy, illogicality, illogicalness, improbability, inanity, incongruity, insanity, irrationality, jazz*, jive*, ludicrousness, ridiculousness, senselessness, silliness, stupidity, unreasonableness; SEE CONCEPTS 650,656

abundance [n] *great amount or supply*
affluence, ampleness, bounty, copiousness, fortune, myriad, opulence, plenitude, plenty, plethora, profusion, prosperity, prosperousness, riches, thriving, wealth; SEE CONCEPTS 710,767

abundant [adj] *plentiful, large in number*
abounding, ample, bounteous, bountiful, copious, crawling with*, cup runs over with*, eco-rich, exuberant, filled, full, generous, heavy, lavish, liberal, lousy with*, luxuriant, mucho*, no end

of*, overflowing, plate is full of*, plenteous, plenty, profuse, rich, rolling in*, stinking with*, sufficient, teeming; SEE CONCEPT 781

abuse [n1] *wrong use*
corruption, crime, debasement, delinquency, desecration, exploitation, fault, injustice, misapplication, misconduct, misdeed, mishandling, mismanage, misuse, offense, perversion, prostitution, sin, wrong, wrongdoing; SEE CONCEPT 156

abuse [n2] *physical hurting, injuring*
crime, damage, defilement, harm, hurt, impairment, injury, malevolence, maltreatment, manhandling, misdeed, offense, pollution, violation, wrongdoing; SEE CONCEPT 246

abuse [n3] *verbal attack*
bad-mouthing*, blame, castigation, censure, curse, curses*, defamation, derision, hosing*, insults, invective, kicking around*, knifing*, libel, obloquy, opprobrium, pushing around*, putdown, quinine*, reproach, revilement, scolding, signifying, slander, swearing, tirade, upbraiding, vilification, vituperation; SEE CONCEPT 54

abuse [v1] *physically hurt or injure*
bang up*, beat up, bung up*, corrupt, cut up*, damage, defile, deprave, desecrate, harm, hose*, ill-treat, impair, maltreat, mar, mess up*, mishandle, mistreat, misuse, molest, oppress, persecute, pollute*, roughhouse, rough up, ruin, shake up*, spoil, taint, total*, victimize, violate, wax*; SEE CONCEPT 246

abuse [v2] *use wrongly*
dissipate, exhaust, misemploy, mishandle, misuse, overburden, overtax, overwork, prostitute, spoil, squander, taint, waste; SEE CONCEPT 156

abuse [v3] *attack with words*
backbite, bad-mouth, bash, belittle, berate, blow off*, calumniate, cap*, castigate, cuss out*, cut down*, cut to the quick*, decry, defame, derogate, discount, do a number on*, dump on*, give a black eye*, hurl brickbat*, insult, knock*, minimize, nag, offend, oppress, persecute, pick on, put down*, rag on*, reproach, revile, ride*, rip up*, run down*, scold, signify, slam*, slap*, sling mud*, smear*, sound*, swear at*, tear apart*, trash*, upbraid, vilify, vituperate, zing*; SEE CONCEPTS 52,54

abuse [v4] *take advantage of*
do an injustice to, exploit, impose on, use, wrong; SEE CONCEPTS 156,384

abusive [adj] *exhibiting unkind behavior or words*
calumniating, castigating, censorious, contumelious, defamatory, derisive, disparaging, insolent, insulting, invective, libelous, maligning, obloquious, offensive, opprobrious, reproachful, reviling, rude, sarcastic, scathing, scolding, scurrilous, sharp-tongued, slanderous, traducing, upbraiding, vilifying, vituperative; SEE CONCEPT 267

abut [v] *touch or be next to something*
adjoin, be adjacent to, border on, butt against, join, neighbor; SEE CONCEPT 749

abysmal [adj1] *great extent; immeasurable*
bottomless, boundless, complete, deep, endless, extreme, illimitable, incalculable, infinite, profound, thorough, unending, unfathomable, vast; SEE CONCEPTS 772,793

abysmal [adj2] *extending deeply*
bottomless, fathomless, plumbless, plummetless; SEE CONCEPT 777

abyss [n] *something very deep, usually a feature of land*
abysm, chasm, crevasse, depth, fissure, gorge, gulf, hole, pit, void; SEE CONCEPTS *509,514*

academic [n] *scholar or university/college teacher*
academician, lecturer, professor, pupil, scholar, scholastic, student, tutor; SEE CONCEPT *350*

academic [adj1] *relating to schooling, learning*
bookish, book-learned, college, collegiate, erudite, intellectual, learned, pedantic, scholarly, scholastic, studious, university; SEE CONCEPT *536*

academic [adj2] *relating to theories, philosophy*
abstract, closet, conjectural, formalistic, hypothetical, notional, speculative, theoretical; SEE CONCEPTS *402,529*

academy [n1] *school, especially for higher education*
boarding school, brainery*, finishing school, halls of ivy*, institute, military school, preparatory school, prep school, secondary school, seminary; SEE CONCEPT *289*

academy [n2] *society or institution interested in learning*
alliance, association, circle, council, federation, foundation, fraternity, institute, league; SEE CONCEPT *288*

accede [v] *agree or consent*
accept, acquiesce, admit, allow, assent, be game for*, cave in*, comply, concede, concur, cooperate, cry uncle*, endorse, enter into, fold, give the go-ahead*, give the green light*, go along with, grant, let, okay, permit, play ball*, roll over and play dead*, subscribe, throw in the towel*, yield; SEE CONCEPTS *8,50,82,88*

accelerate [v] *increase speed, timing*
advance, drive, dust*, expedite, fire up*, forward, further, gun*, hammer on*, hasten, hurry, impel, lay a patch*, lay rubber*, make tracks*, nail it*, open up*, peel rubber*, precipitate, put on afterburners*, put pedal to metal*, quicken, railroad*, rev, rev up, roll*, speed up, spur, step on gas*, step up, stimulate, tool*; SEE CONCEPTS *234,242*

acceleration [n] *increasing speed, timing*
dispatch, expedition, hastening, hurrying, quickening, speeding up, spurring, stepping up, stimulation; SEE CONCEPT *234*

accent [n1] *importance, emphasis*
significance, stress, weight; SEE CONCEPT *668*

accent [n2] *stress or pitch in pronunciation*
accentuation, articulation, beat, cadence, emphasis, enunciation, force, inflection, intonation, meter, modulation, pronunciation, rhythm, stroke, timbre, tonality, tone; SEE CONCEPT *77*

accent [v] *place emphasis, importance*
accentuate, draw attention to, emphasize, highlight, intensify, stress, underline, underscore; SEE CONCEPTS *69,243*

accept [v1] *receive something given physically*
acquire, gain, get, obtain, secure, take, welcome; SEE CONCEPT *124*

accept [v2] *allow into group*
admit, receive, welcome; SEE CONCEPT *384*

accept [v3] *believe the goodness, realness of something*
acknowledge, affirm, approbate, approve, buy*, countenance, fancy, favor, go for*, hold, hold with, like, recognize, relish, swallow*, take as gospel truth*, take stock in*, trust; SEE CONCEPT *12*

accept [v4] *put up with*
acknowledge, acquiesce, agree, assent, bear, bear with, bow, capitulate, defer to, don't make waves*, don't rock the boat*, endure, fit in, go along with, live with, play the game*, recognize, respect, sit still for*, stand, stand for, stomach, submit to, suffer, swallow, take, tolerate, yield to; SEE CONCEPT *23*

accept [v5] *receive by agreeing, consenting*
accede, acknowledge, acquiesce, admit, adopt, affirm, agree to, approve, assent, assume, avow, bear, buy, check out*, comply, concur with, cooperate with, give stamp of approval*, give the go-ahead*, give the green light*, give the nod*, go for*, lap up*, okay, recognize, rubber-stamp*, set store by*, sign, sign off on*, take on*, take one up on*, thumbs up*, undertake; SEE CONCEPTS *8,82*

acceptable [adj] *satisfactory, agreeable*
adequate, admissible, all right, A-OK*, average, big*, common, cooking with gas*, cool*, copacetic, decent, delightful, fair, hep*, hip*, hunky-dory*, in the swim*, kosher*, large, okay, on the ball*, on the beam*, passable, peachy keen*, pleasant, pleasing, respectable, right on*, standard, sufficient, swell*, tolerable, trendy, unexceptional, unobjectionable, up to code*, up to snuff*, welcome; SEE CONCEPTS *533,558*

acceptance [n1] *agreement, taking*
accepting, acknowledgment, acquiring, admission, approval, assent, compliance, consent, cooperation, gaining, getting, go-ahead*, green light*, nod*, obtaining, okay, permission, receipt, receiving, reception, recognition, securing, taking on, undertaking, yes; SEE CONCEPTS *8,124*

acceptance [n2] *belief in goodness of something*
accedence, accession, acknowledgment, acquiescence, admission, adoption, affirmation, agreement, approbation, approval, assent, concession, concurrence, favor, recognition, seal of approval; SEE CONCEPTS *12,32*

accepted [adj] *generally agreed upon*
accustomed, acknowledged, allowed, approved, arrived at, authorized, card-carrying*, chosen, confirmed, conventional, credited, current, customary, endorsed, established, fashionable, in vogue, kosher*, legit*, normal, okayed, orthodox, passed, popular, preferred, received, recognized, regular, sanctioned, standard, straight*, time-honored, touted, universal, unopposed, usual, welcomed; SEE CONCEPTS *547,558*

access [n] *admission, means of entry, approach*
admittance, approach, avenue, connection, contact, course, door, entrance, entree, entry, in, ingress, introduction, key, open arms*, open door*, passage, path, road, route, way; SEE CONCEPTS *501,631*

accessible [adj] *approachable; ready for use*
attainable, available, door's always open*, employable, exposed, getatable, handy, near, obtainable, open, operative, possible, practicable, public, reachable, susceptible, unrestricted, usable; SEE CONCEPT *576*

accession [n1] *something that augments, adds to*
accretion, addition, augmentation, enlargement, extension, increase, increment, raise, rise; SEE CONCEPTS *700,775*

accession [n2] *coming to power*
assumption, attainment, inauguration, induction,

investment, succession, taking on, taking over; SEE CONCEPTS *133,298*

accession [n3] *agreement*
accedence, acceptance, acquiescence, assent, concurrence, consent; SEE CONCEPTS *8,410*

accessory [n1] *ornament; accompanying item; supplementary part*
accent, addition, adjunct, adornment, appendage, appendix, appliance, appurtenance, attachment, component, decoration, extension, extra, frill, help, supplement, trim, trimming; SEE CONCEPT *834*

accessory [n2] *person peripherally involved in illegal activity*
abettor, accomplice, aid, aide, assistant, associate, co-conspirator, colleague, confederate, conspirator, helper, insider, partner, plant*, ringer*, shill*, stall*, subordinate; SEE CONCEPT *412*

accident [n1] *unexpected, undesirable event; often physically injurious*
blow, calamity, casualty, collision, crack-up*, disaster, fender-bender*, fluke*, hazard, misadventure, misfortune, mishap, pileup*, rear ender*, setback, smash*, smashup*, stack-up*, total*, wrack-up*; SEE CONCEPT *674*

accident [n2] *chance event*
adventure, circumstance, contingency, fate, fluke*, fortuity, fortune, happening, luck, occasion, occurrence, turn; SEE CONCEPT *679*

accidental [adj] *happening unexpectedly*
adventitious, casual, chance, coincidental, contingent, fluky*, fortuitous, inadvertent, incidental, random, uncalculated, unexpected, unforeseen, unintended, unintentional, unplanned; SEE CONCEPTS *530,552*

acclaim [n] *expression of approval*
acclamation, acknowledgment, applause, approbation, celebration, cheering, clapping, commendation, eulogizing, exaltation, honor, kudos, pat on the back*, pat on the head*, plaudits, PR, praise, puff, pumping up*, rave, recognition, strokes*, stroking*; SEE CONCEPT *69*

acclaim [v] *give approval*
applaud, approve, blow horn*, boost, celebrate, cheer, clap, commend, complement, eulogize, exalt, extol, give a bouquet*, give a posy*, give kudos*, hail, hand it to*, hear it for*, honor, laud, praise, puff up*, push*, rave, recommend, root, salute, stroke*; SEE CONCEPT *69*

acclamation [n] *enthusiastic expression of approval*
acclaim, adulation, applause, approbation, big hand*, cheer, cheering, cheers, hand, honor, jubilation, laudation, ovation, plaudits, salutation, standing O*, tribute; SEE CONCEPTS *69,377*

acclimate [v] *make or become adjusted, adapted*
acclimatize, accommodate, acculture, accustom, climatize, conform, get used to, habituate, harden, season, toughen; SEE CONCEPTS *202,701*

accolade [n] *strong praise, recognition of achievement*
approval, award, badge, decoration, distinction, honor, kudos*, laurels; SEE CONCEPT *69*

accommodate [v1] *make room, lodging available*
board, contain, domicile, entertain, furnish, harbor, hold, house, put up*, quarter, receive, rent, shelter, supply, take in, welcome; SEE CONCEPT *226*

accommodate [v2] *make, become suitable for something*
accord, accustom, adapt, adjust, agree, attune, bend over backwards*, comply, compose, conform, coordinate, correspond, don't make waves*, don't rock the boat*, fit, go by the book*, go with the flow*, harmonize, integrate, make consistent, modify, play the game*, proportion, reconcile, settle, shape up, suit, tailor, tailor-make, tune; SEE CONCEPTS *23,126*

accommodate [v3] *perform service*
afford, aid, arrange, assist, avail, benefit, bow, comfort, convenience, defer, favor, furnish, gratify, help, humor, indulge, oblige, pamper, please, provide, serve, settle, submit, suit, supply, support, sustain, yield; SEE CONCEPT *136*

accommodating [adj] *willing to help*
considerate, cooperative, friendly, generous, handy, helpful, hospitable, kind, neighborly, obliging, on deck*, on tap*, polite, unselfish, user friendly*; SEE CONCEPTS *542,555*

accommodation [n] *adjustment for different situation, circumstances*
adaptation, compliance, composition, compromise, conformity, fifty-fifty deal*, fitting, modification, reconciliation, settlement; SEE CONCEPT *697*

accommodations [n] *place of residence, usually temporary*
apartment, board, boardinghouse, crash pad*, crib*, digs*, hotel, house, housing, lodging, motel, pad*, quarters, roof, room and board, rooming house, rooms, shelter; SEE CONCEPT *516*

accompaniment [n1] *necessary part or embellishment*
accessory, adjunct, appendage, appurtenance, attachment, attendant, attribute, augmentation, complement, concomitant, enhancement, enrichment, supplement; SEE CONCEPTS *834,835*

accompaniment [n2] *music that supports a theme or performer in a composition*
back, background, backing, back-up, harmony, instrument, part; SEE CONCEPT *262*

accompany [v1] *go or be with something*
associate with, attend, chaperon, come along, conduct, consort, convoy, date, dog*, draft*, drag*, escort, follow, go along, guard, guide, hang around with*, hang out*, keep company, lead, look after, shadow, shlep along*, show about, show around, spook, squire, stick to*, string along*, tag along*, tailgate*, take out, usher; SEE CONCEPTS *113,224*

accompany [v2] *occur with something*
add, appear with, append, be connected, belong to, characterize, coexist, coincide with, come with, complete, co-occur, follow, go together, happen with, join with, occur with, supplement, take place with; SEE CONCEPT *643*

accomplice [n] *helper, especially in committing a crime*
abettor, accessory, aid, aide, ally, assistant, associate, co-conspirator, collaborator, colleague, confederate, conspirator, insider, partner, plant*, stall*; SEE CONCEPT *412*

accomplish [v] *succeed in doing*
achieve, arrive, attain, bring about, bring off, carry out, conclude, consummate, do, do a bang-up job*, do justice*, do one proud*, do the trick*, effect, finish, fulfill, gain, get someplace*, get there*, hit*, make hay*, make it, manage, nail

it*, perform, produce, pull off*, put it over*, rack up*, reach, realize, score*, sew up*, take care of, win; SEE CONCEPTS *91,706*

accomplished [*adj*] *skilled in activity*
able, adept, brainy, consummate, cool*, cultivated, expert, gifted, hep*, hip*, masterly, polished, practiced, proficient, savvy, sharp, skillful, talented, wised up*, with it*; SEE CONCEPTS *326,528*

accomplishment [*n*] *something successfully done, completed*
ability, achievement, act, art, attainment, bringing about, capability, carrying out, completion, conclusion, consummation, coup, deed, effecting, effort, execution, exploit, feat, finish, fulfillment, performance, production, proficiency, realization, skill, stroke, talent, triumph; SEE CONCEPT *706*

accord [*n*] *agreement, mutual understanding (often written)*
accordance, concert, concord, concurrence, conformity, congruence, correspondence, deal, good vibes*, good vibrations*, harmony, okay, pact, rapport, reconciliation, sympathy, 10-4*, treaty, unanimity; SEE CONCEPT *684*

accord [*v1*] *give approval, grant*
accede, acquiesce, admit, allow, award, bestow, concede, confer, endow, give, present, render, tender, vouchsafe; SEE CONCEPTS *50,83,88*

accord [*v2*] *come to agreement*
affirm, agree, assent, be in tune, concur, conform, correspond, fit, harmonize, jibe, match, square, suit, tally; SEE CONCEPTS *8,664*

accordingly [*adv*] *in an appropriate, suitable way*
appropriately, as a consequence, as a result, consequently, correspondingly, duly, equally, ergo, fitly, hence, in consequence, in respect to, in that event, properly, proportionately, respectively, resultantly, so, subsequently, suitably, then, therefore, thus, under the circumstances; SEE CONCEPT *558*

accost [*v*] *approach for conversation or solicitation*
address, annoy, bother, brace*, buttonhole*, call, challenge, confront, cross, dare, entice, face, flag, greet, hail, proposition, run into, salute, welcome, whistle for*; SEE CONCEPTS *48,51*

account [*n1*] *written description of past events*
ABCs*, annal, blow by blow*, bulletin, chronicle, detail, explanation, history, lowdown*, make*, narration, narrative, play by play*, recital, report, run-down, score, story, tab, take, tale, the picture*, the whole picture*, version; SEE CONCEPT *282*

account [*n2*] *record of finances, fees, or charges*
bad news*, balance, bill, book, books, charge, check, computation, cuff*, grunt*, inventory, invoice, IOU*, ledger, reckoning, record, register, report, score, statement, tab, tally; SEE CONCEPTS *331,332*

account [*n3*] *basis or consideration for action*
cause, ground, grounds, interest, justification, motive, rationale, rationalization, reason, regard, sake; SEE CONCEPT *229*

accountable [*adj*] *responsible for having done*
answerable, charged with, culpable, liable, obligated, obliged, on the hook*; SEE CONCEPT *527*

accountant [*n*] *person who maintains financial accounts of a business*
actuary, analyst, auditor, bookkeeper, calculator, cashier, clerk, comptroller, CPA, examiner, public accountant, reckoner, teller; SEE CONCEPTS *348,353*

account for [*v*] *offer reason, explanation*
answer for, clarify, elucidate, explain, illuminate, justify, rationalize, resolve; SEE CONCEPT *57*

accredit [*v1*] *attribute responsibility or achievement*
ascribe, assign, charge, credit, refer; SEE CONCEPTS *49,69*

accredit [*v2*] *give authorization or control*
appoint, approve, authorize, certify, commission, empower, enable, endorse, entrust, guarantee, license, okay, recognize, sanction, vouch for; SEE CONCEPTS *50,88*

accretion [*n*] *gradual growth, addition*
accession, accumulation, augmentation, build-up, increase, increment, raise, rise; SEE CONCEPT *780*

accrue [*v*] *increase by addition or growth, often financial*
accumulate, amass, build up, collect, enlarge, flow, gather, grow, increase; SEE CONCEPTS *763,780*

accumulate [*v*] *gather or amass something*
accrue, acquire, add to, agglomerate, aggregate, amalgamate, assemble, bring together, cache, clean up*, collect, collocate, compile, concentrate, cumulate, draw together, expand, gain, gather, grow, heap, heap together, hoard, incorporate, increase, load up*, lump*, make a bundle*, make a killing*, mass, pile*, pile up*, procure, profit, rack up*, roll up*, round up*, scare up*, stack up, stockpile, store, store up, swell, unite; SEE CONCEPTS *236,245*

accumulation [*n*] *gathering or amassing*
accession, accretion, addition, agglomeration, aggrandizement, aggregation, amassment, augmentation, build-up, chunk, collecting, collection, conglomeration, enlargement, gob, growth, heap, hoarding, hunk, increase, inflation, intensification, mass, multiplication, pile, quantity, stack, stock, store, trove, up, upping; SEE CONCEPTS *432,780*

accuracy [*n*] *precision or correctness*
accurateness, carefulness, certainty, closeness, definiteness, definitiveness, definitude, efficiency, exactitude, exactness, faultlessness, incisiveness, mastery, meticulousness, preciseness, sharpness, skill, skillfulness, strictness, sureness, truthfulness, veracity, verity; SEE CONCEPTS *638,654*

accurate [*adj1*] *precise*
authentic, careful, close, concrete, correct, defined, definite, deft, detailed, discriminating, discriminative, distinct, exact, explicit, factual, faithful, genuine, judicious, just, literal, matter-of-fact, methodical, meticulous, on the button*, on the money*, on the nose*, particular, proper, punctilious, punctual, regular, right, rigid, rigorous, scientific, scrupulous, severe, sharp, skillful, solid, specific, strict, systematic, true, ultraprecise, unerring, unmistakable, veracious; SEE CONCEPT *535*

accurate [*adj2*] *correct, without error*
absolute, actual, authentic, authoritative, certain, conclusive, definite, definitive, errorless, exact, factual, faultless, final, flawless, genuine, infallible, irrefutable, official, perfect, right, straight, strict, true, truthful, undeniable, undisputed, unimpeachable, unquestionable, unrefuted, valid, veracious; SEE CONCEPT *557*

accusation [n] *charge of wrongdoing, fault*
allegation, arraignment, attribution, beef*, blast*, bum rap*, censure, citation, complaint, denunciation, dido, exposé, gripe, impeachment, imputation, incrimination, indictment, insinuation, recrimination, roar*, rumble*, slur, squawk*, stink*; SEE CONCEPT 54

accuse [v] *place blame for wrongdoing, fault*
allege, apprehend, arraign, arrest, attack, attribute, betray, blame, blow the whistle*, brand, bring charges, censure, charge, cite, complain, criminate, denounce, file claim, finger*, frame, hang something on*, hold accountable, impeach, implicate, impute, incriminate, inculpate, indict, lay at door*, let have it*, libel, litigate, lodge complaint, name, pin on*, point finger at*, prosecute, recriminate, serve summons, slander, slur, sue, summon, tax; SEE CONCEPT 44

accustomed [adj1] *be or become prepared, used to*
acclimatized, acquainted, adapted, addicted, confirmed, disciplined, familiar, familiarized, given to, grooved*, habituated, habituated in, in the habit, inured, seasoned, settled in, trained; SEE CONCEPT 98

accustomed [adj2] *normal, usual*
accepted, chronic, common, conventional, customary, established, everyday, expected, general, habitual, ordinary, orthodox, regular, routine, set, traditional, typical; SEE CONCEPT 547

ace [n] *expert in some activity*
champion, genius, master, pro, star, virtuoso, winner, wizard; SEE CONCEPT 416

ace [adj] *exhibiting expertise in some activity*
brilliant, champion, distinguished, excellent, expert, first-rate, great, master, outstanding, superb, virtuoso; SEE CONCEPT 528

acerbity [n1] *bitterness of taste*
acidity, asperity, astringency, mordancy, sourness, tartness; SEE CONCEPTS 462,613

acerbity [n2] *harsh speech, behavior*
acrimoniousness, causticity, ill temper, irritability, rancor, rudeness, sarcasm, sarcasticness, vitriolicism; SEE CONCEPTS 267,401

ache [n] *sore feeling; dull pain*
anguish, hurt, misery, pang, pounding, smarting, soreness, spasm, suffering, throb, throbbing, throe, twinge; SEE CONCEPTS 316,410,728

ache [v] *feeling soreness or dull pain, often physical*
be sore, hurt, pain, pound, smart, suffer, throb, twinge; SEE CONCEPTS 13,17,303,308,313

achieve [v] *bring to successful conclusion; reach a goal*
accomplish, acquire, actualize, attain, bring about, bring off*, bring to pass, cap, carry out, carry through, close, complete, conclude, consummate, deliver, discharge, dispatch, do, earn, earn wings*, effect, effectuate, enact, end, execute, finish, follow through, fulfill, gain, get, get done, manage, negotiate, obtain, perfect, perform, procure, produce, rack up*, reach, realize, resolve, score, seal, see through, settle, sign, solve, win, wind up, work out; SEE CONCEPT 706

achievement [n] *something completed successfully; goal reached*
accomplishment, acquirement, acquisition, act, actualization, attainment, completion, conquest, consummation, contrivance, creation, deed, effectuation, effort, enactment, encompassment, execution, exploit, feat, fulfillment, hit, masterpiece,

performance, production, realization, stroke, success, tour de force, triumph, victory; SEE CONCEPT 706

acid [adj1] *bitter, sour in taste*
acerbic, acidulous, biting, piquant, pungent, sharp, tart, vinegarish, vinegary; SEE CONCEPT 613

acid [adj2] *having acidic, corrosive properties*
acerbic, acidulous, acrid, anti-alkaline, biting, bleaching, corroding, disintegrative, dissolvent, eating away, eroding, erosive, oxidizing, rusting; SEE CONCEPT 485

acid [adj3] *bitter in words or behavior*
acerbic, biting, caustic, cutting, dry, harsh, hateful, hurtful, mordant, nasty, offensive, sarcastic, sharp, stinging, trenchant, vitriolic; SEE CONCEPTS 267,401

acidulous [adj1] *bitter, sour*
acerb, acerbic, acetose, dry, piquant, sharp, tart; SEE CONCEPT 613

acidulous [adj2] *bitter in speech*
biting, cutting, ironical, mocking, sarcastic; SEE CONCEPT 267

acknowledge [v1] *verbally recognize authority*
accede, accept, acquiesce, agree, allow, approve, attest to, certify, defend, defer to, endorse, grant, own, ratify, recognize, subscribe to, support, take an oath, uphold, yield; SEE CONCEPTS 8,50,88

acknowledge [v2] *admit truth or reality of something*
accede, accept, acquiesce, allow, avow, come clean*, come out of closet*, concede, confess, cop a plea*, crack*, declare, fess up*, get off chest*, grant, let on*, open up*, own, profess, recognize, yield; SEE CONCEPTS 12,49

acknowledge [v3] *verbally recognize receipt of something*
address, answer, greet, hail, notice, react, remark, reply, respond, return, salute, thank; SEE CONCEPTS 38,45,51,60

acknowledgment [n1] *act of recognizing authority or truth of something*
acceptance, accession, acquiescence, admission, admitting, affirmation, allowance, allowing, assent, assertion, asseveration, avowal, compliance, conceding, concession, concurrence, confession, confirmation, corroboration, declaration, profession, ratification, realization, recognition, yielding; SEE CONCEPTS 8,50,88

acknowledgment [n2] *physical symbol of recognition*
acclamation, addressing, answer, apology, applause, appreciation, bestowal, bow, card, confession, contract, credit, gift, gratitude, greeting, guarantee, hail, hailing, letter, nod, notice, reaction, receipt, reply, response, return, salutation, salute, signature, statement, support, thanks, token; SEE CONCEPTS 595,628

acme [n] *pinnacle of achievement or physical object*
apogee, capstone, climax, culmination, height, highest point, high point, meridian, optimum, peak, summit, top, ultimate, vertex, zenith; SEE CONCEPTS 706,836

acolyte [n] *attendant, usually in a church*
aid, assistant, follower, helper; SEE CONCEPT 361

acquaint [v] *inform oneself or another about something new*
accustom, advise, apprise, bring out, clue, come out with*, disclose, divulge, enlighten, familiar-

ize, fill in, fix up*, get together*, habituate, inform, intro*, introduce, knock down*, let know, make familiar, notify, post, present, reveal, tell, warn; SEE CONCEPTS 31,60

acquaintance [n1] *a person known informally*
associate, association, colleague, companion, contact, friend, neighbor; SEE CONCEPT 423

acquaintance [n2] *knowledge of something through experience*
awareness, cognizance, conversance, familiarity, fellowship, grasp, intimacy, ken, relationship, understanding; SEE CONCEPT 409

acquiesce [v] *agree with some reluctance*
accede, accept, accommodate, adapt, adjust, agree, allow, approve, bow to, buy, cave in*, come across, come around, comply, concur, conform, consent, cry uncle*, cut a deal*, ditto*, give in, give out, go along, jibe*, okay, pass, play ball*, reconcile, roll over and play dead*, say uncle*, set, shake on, submit, subscribe, yes, yield; SEE CONCEPTS 8,10,23,82

acquiescence [n] *reluctant agreement*
acceptance, accession, approval, assent, compliance, concurrence, conformity, consent, giving in, obedience, permission, resignation, submission, submissiveness, yielding; SEE CONCEPTS 8,10

acquire [v] *obtain or receive*
access, achieve, amass, annex, attain, bring in, buy, catch, collect, cop*, corral*, earn, gain, gather, get, get hands on, get hold of, grab, have, hustle, land, latch onto, lock up, pick up, procure, promote, rack up*, scare up*, secure, snag*, take, take possession of*, wangle*, win; SEE CONCEPTS 120,124,142

acquisition [n1] *obtaining or receiving*
accretion, achievement, acquirement, acquiring, addition, attainment, buy, gain, gaining, learning, obtainment, possession, prize, procuration, procurement, procuring, property, purchase, pursuit, recovery, redemption, retrieval, salvage, winning; SEE CONCEPTS 120,124,142

acquisition [n2] *something obtained, received*
accomplishment, achievement, allowance, annuity, award, benefit, bonus, commission, dividend, donation, earnings, fortune, gain, gift, grant, income, increment, inheritance, net, premium, prize, proceeds, profit, remuneration, return, reward, riches, salary, security, wages, wealth, winnings; SEE CONCEPTS 120,337,710

acquisitive [adj] *eager to obtain knowledge or things*
avaricious, avid, covetous, demanding, desirous, grabbing, grasping, greedy, predatory, prehensile, rapacious; SEE CONCEPT 542

acquit [v1] *announce removal of blame*
absolve, blink at*, clear, deliver, discharge, disculpate, exculpate, excuse, exonerate, free, let go, let off, let off the hook*, liberate, release, relieve, vindicate, whitewash*, wink at*, wipe off*; SEE CONCEPTS 50,83,88,317

acquit [v2] *behave some way*
act, bear, carry, comport, conduct, deport, perform; SEE CONCEPT 633

acquittal [n] *declaration removing blame*
absolution, acquitting, amnesty, clearance, deliverance, discharge, discharging, dismissal, dismissing, exculpation, exemption, exoneration, freeing, letting off, liberation, pardon, release, releasing, relief from, reprieve, vindication; SEE CONCEPTS 127,317,318

acre [n] *piece of land, unit of area*
acreage, bit, estate, grounds, manor, plot, property; SEE CONCEPT 792

acrid [adj1] *bitter, sour to taste*
acid, amaroidal, astringent, biting, burning, caustic, harsh, irritating, pungent, sharp, stinging; SEE CONCEPT 613

acrid [adj2] *nasty in behavior or words*
acrimonious, austere, biting, bitter, caustic, cutting, harsh, mordant, sarcastic, sharp, trenchant, vitriolic; SEE CONCEPTS 267,401

acrimonious [adj] *nasty in behavior, speech*
acerbic, acid, angry, astringent, belligerent, biting, bitter, caustic, censorious, churlish, crabby, cranky, cross, cutting, indignant, irascible, irate, ireful, mad, mordant, peevish, petulant, rancorous, sarcastic, sharp, spiteful, splenetic, tart, testy, trenchant, wrathful; SEE CONCEPTS 267,401

acrimony [n] *nasty behavior, speech*
acerbity, animosity, antipathy, asperity, astringency, belligerence, bitterness, churlishness, crankiness, harshness, ill will, irascibility, malevolence, malice, mordancy, peevishness, rancor, rudeness, sarcasm, spite, tartness, unkindness, virulence; SEE CONCEPTS 633,657

acrobat [n] *performer who does tricks, physical feats*
aerialist, artist, athlete, balancer, clown, contortionist, dancer, funambulist, gymnast, performer, stunt person, trapezist, tumbler; SEE CONCEPT 352

across [prep] *traversing a space, side to side*
athwart, beyond, cross, crossed, crosswise, opposite, over, transversely; SEE CONCEPT 581

act [n1] *something done*
accomplishment, achievement, action, deed, doing, execution, exploit, feat, move, operation, performance, step, thing, undertaking; SEE CONCEPT 1

act [n2] *legislative document*
amendment, announcement, bill, clause, code, commitment, decree, edict, enactment, judgment, law, measure, order, ordinance, resolution, statute, subpoena, summons, verdict, warrant, writ; SEE CONCEPTS 271,318

act [n3] *part of a performance*
bit*, curtain, epilogue, gag*, introduction, number, piece, prologue, routine, scene, schtick*, show, sketch, spot, turn; SEE CONCEPT 264

act [n4] *pretended behavior*
affectation, attitude, bit*, chaser*, dissimulation, fake, false front*, feigning, front, performance, phony, pose, posture, pretense, put-on, sham, show, shuck and jive*, simulation, soft soap*, stall, stance, stunt, sweet talk*; SEE CONCEPT 633

act [v1] *do something*
accomplish, achieve, begin, carry on, carry out, consummate, cook, create, develop, do, do a number*, do one's thing*, enforce, execute, function, get in there*, go about, go for broke*, go for it*, go in for*, go that route*, go to town*, intrude, knock off*, labor, make progress, maneuver, move, officiate, operate, percolate*, perk*, perpetrate, persevere, persist, practice, preside, pursue, respond, serve, take effect, take part, take steps, take up, transort, undertake, work out; SEE CONCEPTS 1,4

act [v2] *behave in a certain way*
appear, behave, carry, carry oneself, carry out,

ac
ac

comport, conduct, do, enact, execute, exert, function, give the appearance, go about, impress as, operate, perform, play part, react, represent oneself, seem, serve, strike, take on; SEE CONCEPT 633

act [v3] *entertain by playing a role*
be on*, bring down the house*, burlesque, characterize, do a turn*, dramatize, emote, enact, feign, go on, go over, ham*, ham it up*, impersonate, lay an egg*, make debut, mime, mimic, mug, parody, perform, personate, personify, play, play act, play gig, play part, play role, portray, pretend, put it over*, rehearse, represent, say one's piece*, simulate, star, stooge*, strut*, take part, tread the boards*; SEE CONCEPT 292

acting [n] *entertaining, performing*
assuming, characterization, depiction, dramatics, dramatizing, enacting, enactment, feigning, hamming*, histrionics, imitating, imitation, impersonation, improvisation, mime, mimicry, pantomime, performance, play acting, playing, portrayal, portraying, posing, posturing, pretending, pretense, putting, rendition, seeming, showing off, simulating, stagecraft, stooging*, theatre, theatricals; SEE CONCEPT 292

acting [adj] *substituting in a role*
ad interim, adjutant, alternate, assistant, delegated, deputy, interim, pro tem, pro tempore, provisional, surrogate, temporary; SEE CONCEPT 560

action [n1] *something done*
activity, agility, alacrity, alertness, animation, bag*, ballgame*, big idea*, bit*, business, bustle, commotion, dash, deal, energy, enterprise, flurry, force, functioning, game, going, happening, haste, hoopla*, hopper*, industry, in the works, life, liveliness, motion, movement, occupation, operation, plan, power, process, proposition, racket*, reaction, response, rush, scene, spirit, stir, stunt, trip, turmoil, vigor, vim, vitality, vivacity; SEE CONCEPT 1

action [n2] *individual deed*
accomplishment, achievement, act, blow, commission, dealings, doing, effort, enterprise, execution, exercise, exertion, exploit, feat, handiwork, maneuver, manipulation, move, operation, performance, procedure, step, stroke, thrust, transaction, undertaking; SEE CONCEPTS 91,706

action [n3] *a legal process*
case, cause, claim, lawsuit, litigation, proceeding, prosecution, suit; SEE CONCEPT 317

action [n4] *an aggressive military deed*
battle, combat, conflict, contest, encounter, engagement, fight, fighting, fray, skirmish, warfare; SEE CONCEPT 320

activate [v] *initiate something; start a function*
actify, actuate, arouse, call up, energize, impel, mobilize, motivate, move, prompt, propel, rouse, set in motion, start, stimulate, stir, switch on, take out of mothballs*, trigger, turn on; SEE CONCEPT 234

active [adj1] *having movement*
alive, astir, at work, bustling, effective, efficacious, exertive, flowing, functioning, going, hasty, impelling, in force, in play, in process, mobile, movable, moving, operating, operative, progressive, pushing, rapid, restless, rolling, running, rushing, rustling, shifting, simmering, speeding, speedy, streaming, swarming, traveling, turning, walking, working; SEE CONCEPT 542

active [adj2] *very involved in activity*
aggressive, agile, alert, alive, animated, assiduous, bold, brisk, bustling, busy, chipper, daring, dashing, determined, dexterous, diligent, dynamic, eager, energetic, engaged, enlivened, enterprising, enthusiastic, eventful, fireball*, forceful, forcible, fresh, frisky, hard-working, high-spirited, hyper*, industrious, intense, inventive, jumping, keen, lively, nimble, on the move, perky, persevering, purposeful, pushing, quick, rapid, ready, resolute, sharp, sprightly, spry, whiz*, zealous; SEE CONCEPTS 401,542

activity [n1] *state of being active*
action, activeness, animation, bustle, enterprise, exercise, exertion, hustle, labor, life, liveliness, motion, movement; SEE CONCEPTS 1,748

activity [n2] *special interest or pursuit*
act, avocation, bag*, ballgame*, bit*, deed, endeavor, enterprise, entertainment, game, hobby, job, labor, occupation, pastime, project, racket, scene*, scheme, stunt, task, trip, undertaking, venture, work, zoo*; SEE CONCEPT 32

actor [n] *person who performs, entertains by role-playing*
amateur, artist, barnstormer, bit player, character, clown, comedian, entertainer, extra, foil, ham*, hambone*, headliner, idol, impersonator, ingénue, lead, mime, mimic, pantomimist, performer, play-actor, player, soubrette, stand-in, star, stooge*, straight person, thesp*, thespian, trouper, understudy, ventriloquist, villain, walk-on; SEE CONCEPT 352

actual [adj1] *truly existing, real*
absolute, authentic, categorical, certain, concrete, confirmed, definite, factual, for real*, genuine, hard, honest injun*, honest to God*, indisputable, indubitable, kosher*, physical, positive, realistic, substantial, substantive, sure enough*, tangible, true, truthful, undeniable, unquestionable, verified; SEE CONCEPT 582

actual [adj2] *existing at the present time*
current, exact, existent, extant, live, living, original, prevailing; SEE CONCEPT 799

actuality [n] *something that truly exists, is real*
achievement, actualization, attainment, brass tacks*, fact, materiality, materialization, reality, real world*, straight stuff*, substance, substantiality, truth, what it is*; SEE CONCEPT 725

actually [adv] *truly real, existent*
absolutely, as a matter of fact, de facto, genuinely, indeed, in fact, in point of fact, in reality, in truth, literally, really, veritably, very; SEE CONCEPT 582

actuate [v] *start a function or action, motivate*
activate, animate, arouse, cause, drive, egg on*, energize, excite, fire up*, impel, incite, induce, influence, inspire, instigate, key up*, mobilize, motivate, move, prompt, propel, put up to*, quicken, rouse, spur, stimulate, turn on*, work into lather*, work up*; SEE CONCEPTS 221,234

acumen [n] *ability to understand and reason*
acuity, acuteness, astuteness, awareness, brains, brilliance, cleverness, comprehension, cunning, discernment, discrimination, farsightedness, good taste, grasp, guile, ingenuity, insight, intellect, intelligence, intuition, judgment, keenness, perception, percipience, perspicacity, perspicuity, refinement, sagacity, sensitivity, sharpness, shrewdness, smartness, smarts*, understanding, vision, wisdom, wit; SEE CONCEPT 409

acute [adj1] *deeply perceptive*
astute, canny, clever, discerning, discriminating, incisive, ingenious, insightful, intense, intuitive, judicious, keen, observant, penetrating, perspicacious, piercing, quick-witted, sensitive, sharp, smart, subtle; SEE CONCEPT *402*

acute [adj2] *very important*
afflictive, critical, crucial, dangerous, decisive, desperate, dire, essential, grave, serious, severe, sudden, urgent, vital; SEE CONCEPT *568*

acute [adj3] *severe, intense*
cutting, distressing, excruciating, exquisite, fierce, keen, overpowering, overwhelming, piercing, poignant, powerful, racking, severe, sharp, shooting, stabbing, sudden, violent; SEE CONCEPT *569*

acute [adj4] *having a sharp end or point*
acicular, aciculate, acuminate, acuminous, cuspate, cuspidate, knifelike, needle-shaped, peaked, piked, pointed, sharpened, spiked; SEE CONCEPT *485*

adage [n] *saying or proverb*
aphorism, apothegm, axiom, byword, dictum, maxim, motto, precept, saw; SEE CONCEPT *276*

adamant [adj1] *unyielding*
determined, firm, fixed, hanging tough*, hard-nosed, immovable, inexorable, inflexible, insistent, intransigent, obdurate, pat*, relentless, resolute, rigid, set, set in stone*, standing pat*, stiff, stubborn, unbendable, unbending, uncompromising, unrelenting, unshakable, unswayable; SEE CONCEPT *401*

adamant [adj2] *hard like rock*
adamantine, flinty, impenetrable, indestructible, rock-hard, tough, unbreakable; SEE CONCEPT *604*

adapt [v] *adjust to a different situation or condition*
acclimate, accommodate, accustom, alter, change, come around, comply, conform, familiarize, fashion, fit, get act together*, get used to, grow used to, habituate, harmonize, make, match, modify, play the game*, prepare, qualify, readjust, reconcile, remodel, revise, roll with punches*, shape, shape up*, square, suit, tailor; SEE CONCEPTS *232,697*

adaptable [adj] *able and usually willing to change*
AC-DC*, adjustable, all around, alterable, can-do*, changeable, compliant, conformable, convertible, ductile, easy-going, flexible, hanging loose*, malleable, modifiable, moldable, pliable, pliant, resilient, supple, switch-hitting, tractable, variable, versatile; SEE CONCEPTS *550,576*

adaptation [n1] *act of adapting*
adjustment, adoption, alteration, conversion, modification, refitting, remodeling, reworking, shift, transformation, variation; SEE CONCEPT *697*

adaptation [n2] *condition of something resulting from change*
acclimatization, accustomedness, agreement, compliance, correspondence, familiarization, habituation, naturalization; SEE CONCEPT *230*

add [v1] *simple arithmetical process of increase; accumulation*
calculate, cast, compute, count, count up, do addition, enumerate, figure, reckon, reckon up, sum, summate, tally, tot*, total, tote*, tot up*; SEE CONCEPT *764*

add [v2] *adjoin; increase; make further comment*
affix, annex, ante, append, augment, beef up*, boost, build up, charge up, continue, cue in*, figure in, flesh out*, heat up*, hike, hike up*, hitch on*, hook on*, hook up with*, include, jack up*, jazz up*, join together, pad, parlay, piggyback*, plug into*, pour it on*, reply, run up*, say further, slap on*, snowball*, soup up*, speed up, spike, step up, supplement, sweeten*, tack on*, tag; SEE CONCEPTS *51,113,236,245*

addendum [n] *something conjoined, added*
addition, adjunct, appendage, appendix, attachment, augmentation, codicil, extension, extra, postscript, rider, supplement; SEE CONCEPTS *270,827*

addict [n] *person who has compulsion toward activity, often injurious*
aficionado, buff, devotee, enthusiast, fan, fanatic, fiend, follower, freak*, habitué, hound*, junkie*, nut, practitioner, zealot; SEE CONCEPTS *412,423*

addicted [adj] *dependent on something, compulsive*
absorbed, accustomed, attached, dependent, devoted, disposed, fanatic, fond, given over to, given to, habituated, hooked, hyped*, imbued, inclined, obsessed, predisposed, prone to, spaced out*, strung out*, under the influence, used to, wedded to; SEE CONCEPT *542*

addiction [n] *a habit of activity, often injurious*
bag*, bent, craving, dependence, enslavement, fixation, hang-up*, hook, inclination, jones*, kick*, monkey*, monkey on back*, obsession, shot*, sweet tooth*, thing*; SEE CONCEPTS *20,316,709*

addition [n1] *process of conjoining, adding*
accession, adding, adjoining, affixing, annexation, attachment, augmentation, enlargement, extension, inclusion, increasing; SEE CONCEPTS *236,245*

addition [n2] *something conjoined to or enlargement of something*
accession, accessory, accretion, accrual, addendum, additive, adjunct, aggrandizement, annex, appendage, appendix, attachment, augmentation, bonus, boost, commission, dividend, enhancement, enlargement, expansion, extension, extra, gain, hike, increase, increment, option, profit, raise, reinforcement, rise, supplement, wing; SEE CONCEPTS *640,835*

addition [n3] *arithmetical process of augmentation*
accretion, accruing, adding, computing, counting, enlarging, expanding, increasing, reckoning, summation, summing, tabulating, totaling, toting*; SEE CONCEPT *764*

additional [adj] *extra, supplementary*
added, affixed, appended, further, increased, more, new, on the side, option, other, over-and-above, padding, perk, spare, supplementary; SEE CONCEPT *771*

addled [adj] *confused*
balled up*, befuddled, bewildered, fouled up*, gone*, mixed up, out of it, punchy, rattled, shaken, shook, shook up, slap-happy, thrown, unglued*, woozy*; SEE CONCEPT *403*

address [n1] *place of residence or business where one can be contacted*
abode, box number, direction, domicile, dwelling, headquarters, home, house, living quarters, location, lodging, number, place of business, place of residence, street, whereabouts, zip code; SEE CONCEPT *516*

address [n2] *speech given to formal gathering*
chalk talk*, discourse, dissertation, lecture, oration, pep talk*, pitch, sermon, soapbox*, spiel*, talk; SEE CONCEPT 278

address [v1] *write directions for delivery*
consign, dispatch, forward, inscribe, label, mark, postmark, remit, route, send, ship, superscribe, transmit; SEE CONCEPTS 60,79

address [v2] *speak to a formal gathering*
approach, bespeak, call, deliver speech, deliver talk, discourse, discuss, get on a soapbox*, give speech, give talk, greet, hail, lecture, memorialize, orate, pitch, pontificate, root for, sermonize, spiel*, spout, stump*, take the floor, talk; SEE CONCEPTS 60,266,285

address [v3] *devote effort to something*
apply oneself to, attend to, concentrate on, devote oneself to, dig, direct, engage in, focus on, give, go at*, go for*, hammer away*, have a go at*, have at*, knuckle down to*, peg away*, pitch into*, plug away at*, take care of, take up, throw oneself into, try, turn, turn to, undertake; SEE CONCEPT 100

adept [adj] *very able*
accomplished, ace*, adroit, brainy, capable, clean*, crack*, crackerjack*, deft, dexterous, expert, hot*, hotshot*, know stuff*, masterful, masterly, nobody's fool*, no dummy*, no slouch*, on the ball*, on the beam*, practiced, proficient, quick, savvy, sharp, sharp as a tack*, skilled, skillful, slick, smooth, there*, up to speed*, versed, whiz*, wizard; SEE CONCEPTS 402,527

adequacy [n] *ability, competency in some action*
capability, capacity, commensurateness, competence, enough, fairness, plenty, requisiteness, requisitioness, satisfactoriness, sufficiency, suitableness, tolerableness; SEE CONCEPTS 636,656

adequate [adj] *enough, able*
acceptable, all right, capable, comfortable, commensurate, competent, decent, equal, fair, passable, requisite, satisfactory, sufficient, sufficing, suitable, tolerable, unexceptional, unobjectionable; SEE CONCEPTS 533,558

adequately [adv] *sufficiently*
abundantly, acceptably, appropriately, capably, competently, copiously, decently, fairly well, fittingly, modestly, pleasantly enough, presentably, satisfactorily, sufficiently, suitably, to an acceptable degree, tolerably, well enough; SEE CONCEPTS 558,560

adhere [v1] *conform to or follow rules exactly*
abide by, be attached, be constant, be devoted, be devoted to, be faithful, be loyal, be true, cleave to, comply, follow, fulfill, heed, keep, maintain, mind, obey, observe, practice, respect, stand by, support; SEE CONCEPTS 87,636

adhere [v2] *stick or become stuck to, either physically or mentally*
attach, cement, cleave, cling like ivy*, cohere, fasten, fix, freeze to*, glue, hold fast, hold on like bulldog*, paste, stay put, stick like a barnacle*, stick like glue*, unite; SEE CONCEPTS 85,113,160

adhesive [adj] *sticking*
adherent, adhering, agglutinant, attaching, clinging, clingy, gelatinous, glutinous, gooey, gummed, gummy, holding, hugging, mucilaginous, pasty, resinous, sticky, tenacious, viscid, viscous, waxy; SEE CONCEPTS 488,606

adieu [n] *parting remark or action*
adios*, congé, farewell, goodbye, leave-taking,

parting, so long, valediction; SEE CONCEPT 276

ad infinitum [adj] *neverending*
ceaselessly, endlessly, forever, perpetually; SEE CONCEPT 798

adjacent [adj] *next to, abutting*
adjoining, alongside, beside, bordering, close, close by, contiguous, near, neighboring, next door, touching; SEE CONCEPT 586

adjective [n] *word that modifies a noun*
accessory, additional, adjunct, adnoun, attribute, attributive, dependent, descriptive, identifier, modifier, qualifier; SEE CONCEPT 275

adjoin [v1] *be next to*
abut, approximate, be adjacent to, border, butt, communicate, connect, join, lie, lie beside, link, neighbor, touch, verge; SEE CONCEPT 747

adjoin [v2] *attach*
add, affix, annex, append, combine, connect, couple, interconnect, join, link, unite; SEE CONCEPTS 85,113,160

adjoining [adj] *being next to*
abutting, adjacent, approximal, bordering on, connecting, conterminous, contiguous, coterminous, impinging, interconnecting, joined, joining, juxtaposed, near, neighboring, next door, touching, verging; SEE CONCEPT 586

adjourn [v] *stop a proceeding*
curb, defer, delay, discontinue, hold off, hold over, hold up, postpone, prorogue, put off, recess, restrain, shelve, stay, suspend; SEE CONCEPTS 121,234

adjournment [n] *discontinuation or delay of a proceeding*
break, deferment, deferral, intermission, interruption, pause, postponement, prorogation, putting off, recess, stay, suspension; SEE CONCEPTS 121,703

adjudicate [v] *formally judge*
adjudge, arbitrate, decide, determine, mediate, referee, settle, umpire; SEE CONCEPTS 18,317

adjunct [n] *addition; help*
accessory, addendum, appendage, appendix, appurtenance, associate, auxiliary, complement, detail, partner, subordinate, supplement; SEE CONCEPTS 484,835

adjust [v1] *become or make prepared, adapted*
acclimatize, accommodate, accustom, adapt, alter, arrange, compose, conform, dispose, do as Romans do*, doctor*, fiddle with*, fine-tune, fit, fix, fix up, get act together*, get it together*, grin and bear it*, habituate, harmonize, make conform, modify, order, quadrate, reconcile, rectify, redress, regulate, remodel, settle, suit, swim with the tide*, tailor, tailor-make, tune; SEE CONCEPTS 35,232,697

adjust [v2] *mechanically alter, especially to improve*
accommodate, align, balance, bring into line, calibrate, connect, correct, fine-tune, fit, fix, focus, grind, improve, mend, overhaul, polish, put in working order, readjust, rectify, regulate, renovate, repair, service, set, sharpen, square, tighten, troubleshoot, tune up; SEE CONCEPTS 202,212

adjust [v3] *bring into agreement or to a standard*
accord, allocate, arrange, clarify, conclude, conform, coordinate, doctor*, fiddle with*, fine-tune, fix up, grade, methodize, modify, organize, reconcile, regulate, settle, sort, standardize, straighten, systematize, tally; SEE CONCEPTS 84,117

adjustment [*n1*] *adaptation*
acclimation, acclimatization, alteration, arrangement, balancing, conformance, correcting, fitting, fixing, improvement, mending, modification, ordering, organization, organizing, orientation, readjustment, redress, regulating, regulation, repairing, setting, shaping, standardization, turning; SEE CONCEPT 697

adjustment [*n2*] *financial retribution, payment of claim*
agreement, allotment, apportionment, benefit, compensation, compromise, pay, reconciliation, reimbursement, remuneration, settlement, share, stake, stipulation; SEE CONCEPT 332

adjutant [*n*] *assistant*
aide, auxiliary, helper; SEE CONCEPT 348

ad-lib [*adj*] *improvised*
extemporaneous, extempore, extemporized, impromptu, made-up, off-the-cuff*, spontaneous, unprepared, unrehearsed; SEE CONCEPT 267

ad-lib [*v*] *improvise speech*
extemporize, invent, make up, speak extemporaneously, speak impromptu, speak off the cuff*; SEE CONCEPT 266

ad-lib [*adv*] *in an improvised manner*
extemporaneously, extempore, impromptu, off the cuff*, off the top of one's head*, spontaneously, without preparation, without rehearsal; SEE CONCEPT 267

administer [*v1*] *manage an organization or effort*
administrate, be in the driver's seat*, be in the saddle*, boss*, carry out, conduct, control, crack the whip*, direct, execute, govern, head, head up*, hold the reins*, oversee, pull the strings*, pull the wires*, render, ride herd on*, run, run the show*, sit on top of*, superintend, supervise; SEE CONCEPTS 117,298

administer [*v2*] *dispense something needed*
apply, apportion, authorize, bring, contribute, deal, deliver, disburse, distribute, dole out, execute, extend, furnish, give, impose, inflict, issue, measure out, mete out, offer, perform, portion, proffer, provide, regulate, serve, supply, tender; SEE CONCEPTS 108,136

administration [*n1*] *management of an organization or effort*
administering, agency, application, authority, charge, command, conduct, conducting, control, directing, direction, dispensation, disposition, distribution, enforcement, execution, governing, government, guidance, handling, jurisdiction, legislation, order, organization, overseeing, oversight, performance, policy, power, provision, regulation, rule, running, strategy, superintendence, supervision, surveillance; SEE CONCEPTS 117,298

administration [*n2*] *human or group who manages effort of an organization*
admiral, advisers, board, bureau, cabinet, chair, chairperson, chargé d'affaires, command, commander, committee, consulate, department, directors, embassy, executive, executives, feds*, front office*, general, governing body, headquarters, legislature, management, ministry, officers, officials, powers, presidency, president, presidium, stewards, superintendents, supervisors, top brass*, upstairs*; SEE CONCEPT 299

administration [*n3*] *period during which a particular human group is in power*
dynasty, incumbency, presidency, regime, reign, stay, tenure, term; SEE CONCEPTS 298,816

administrative [*adj*] *involved in managing or using power*
authoritative, bureaucratic, central, commanding, controlling, deciding, decisive, departmental, directing, directive, directorial, executive, governing, governmental, in charge, in control, jurisdictional, legislative, managerial, official, organizational, policy-making, presiding, regulative, regulatory, ruling, superintending, supervising, supervisory; SEE CONCEPTS 319,536

administrator [*n*] *person who manages organization*
ambassador, authority, boss, bureaucrat, captain, CEO, chair, chairperson, chief, commander, consul, controller, custodian, dean, director, exec*, executive, front office*, governor, head, head honcho*, head person*, inspector, judge, leader, manager, mayor, minister, officer, official, organizer, overseer, person upstairs*, premier, president, prez*, producer, superintendent, supervisor; SEE CONCEPTS 347,354

admirable [*adj*] *held in great respect*
ace*, A-OK*, A-1*, attractive, best ever, cat's pajamas*, choice, commendable, cool*, copacetic*, crackerjack*, deserving, dream*, estimable, excellent, exquisite, fine, good, great, greatest, hunky dory*, keen*, laudable, meritable, meritorious, neat*, out of sight*, out of this world*, peachy*, praiseworthy, rare, solid, super, superduper*, superior, unreal*, valuable, wicked*, wonderful, worthy, zero cool*; SEE CONCEPTS 572,574

admiration [*n*] *great respect*
account, adoration, affection, applause, appreciation, approbation, approval, deference, delight, esteem, estimation, favor, fondness, glorification, homage, honor, idolatry, idolization, liking, love, marveling, obeisance, pleasure, praise, prizing, recognition, regard, reverence, valuing, veneration, wonder, wonderment, worship; SEE CONCEPT 32

admire [*v*] *hold in high regard*
adore, applaud, appreciate, approve, be crazy about*, be crazy for*, be crazy over*, be mad about*, be nuts about*, be stuck on*, be sweet on*, be wild about*, cherish, commend, credit, delight in, esteem, eulogize, extol, fall for*, get high on*, glorify, go for*, groove on*, hail, hold in respect, honor, idolize, laud, look up to, marvel at, moon over*, pay homage to, praise, prize, rate highly, respect, revere, take pleasure in, think highly of, treasure, value, venerate, wonder at, worship; SEE CONCEPT 32

admirer [*n*] *person who holds someone in high regard*
adherent, beau, believer, booster, boyfriend, buff, bug*, cat*, devotee, disciple, enthusiast, fan, fancier, fiend*, follower, freak*, girlfriend, groupie*, hound*, junkie*, lover, nut*, partisan, patron, rooter*, suitor, supporter, swain, sweetheart, wooer, worshiper; SEE CONCEPT 423

admissible [*adj*] *able or deserving of consideration; allowable*
acceptable, allowed, applicable, appropriate, concedable, fair, fitting, just, justifiable, lawful, legal, legitimate, licit, likely, logical, not impossible, not unlikely, okay, passable, permissible, permitted, pertinent, possible, probable, proper, rational, reasonable, relevant, right, suit-

able, tolerable, tolerated, warranted, worthy; SEE
CONCEPT 533

admission [n1] *entering or allowing entry*
acceptance, access, admittance, certification, confirmation, designation, door, entrance, entree, ingress, initiation, introduction, permission, reception, recognition, way, welcome; SEE CONCEPTS 83,159

admission [n2] *confession or acknowledgment*
accession, admittance, affidavit, affirmation, allowance, assent, assertion, attestation, averment, avowal, concession, confirmation, declaration, deposition, disclosure, divulgence, profession, revelation, statement, testimonial, testimony; SEE CONCEPT 57

admit [v1] *allow entry or use*
accept, be big on*, bless, buy, concede, enter, entertain, give access, give the nod*, give thumbs up*, grant, harbor, house, initiate, introduce, let, let in, lodge, okay, permit, receive, shelter, sign*, sign off on*, suffer, take, take in; SEE CONCEPT 83

admit [v2] *confess, acknowledge*
accept, accord, acquiesce, adopt, affirm, agree, allow, approve, avow, bare, bring to light*, communicate, concede, concur, confide, confirm, consent, cop a plea*, credit, declare, disclose, divulge, enumerate, expose, go into details*, grant, indicate, let, let on, make known, narrate, number, open up, own, own up*, permit, proclaim, profess, recite, recognize, relate, reveal, spill*, subscribe to, talk, tell, tolerate, uncover, unveil, yield; SEE CONCEPTS 57,82

admonish [v] *warn, strongly criticize*
advise, berate, call down, call on the carpet*, censure, check, chide, come down hard on*, counsel, ding*, draw the line*, enjoin, exhort, forewarn, give a going over*, give a piece of one's mind*, glue*, growl*, hoist*, jack up*, notice, rap*, rap on knuckles*, rebuke, reprimand, reprove, scold, sit on, slap on wrist*, speak to, talk to, tell a thing or two*, tell off*, upbraid, warn; SEE CONCEPTS 52,78

adolescence [n] *state of puberty, preadulthood*
boyhood, girlhood, greenness, juvenility, minority, pubescence, spring, teens, youth, youthfulness; SEE CONCEPT 817

adolescent [n] *person in puberty, preadulthood*
juvenile, minor, stripling, sweet sixteen*, teen, teenager, teenybopper*, youngster, youth; SEE CONCEPT 424

adolescent [adj] *preadult or immature*
boyish, girlish, growing, juvenile, pubescent, puerile, teen, teenage, young, youthful; SEE CONCEPTS 401,578,797

adopt [v1] *choose or take something as one's own*
accept, adapt, affiliate, affirm, appropriate, approve, assent, assume, borrow, embrace, endorse, espouse, follow, go down the line*, go in for*, imitate, maintain, mimic, opt, ratify, seize, select, support, take on, take over, take up, tap, use, utilize; SEE CONCEPT 18

adopt [v2] *legally care for another's child*
choose, foster, naturalize, pick, raise, select, take in; SEE CONCEPT 317

adoption [n1] *choosing or taking something as one's own*
acceptance, approbation, appropriation, approval, assumption, choice, confirmation, embracement, embracing, enactment, endorsement, espousal,

following, maintenance, ratification, selection, support, taking on, taking over, taking up; SEE CONCEPT 18

adoption [n2] *legal taking of another's child*
adopting, fosterage, fostering, naturalizing, raising, taking in; SEE CONCEPT 317

adorable [adj] *cute, lovable*
ambrosial, appealing, attractive, captivating, charming, cute, darling, dear, delectable, delicious, delightful, dishy*, dreamy*, fetching, heavenly, hot*, luscious, pleasing, precious, sexy, suave; SEE CONCEPTS 579,589

adoration [n] *intense love*
admiration, amore, ardor, attachment, crush, devotion, esteem, estimation, exaltation, glorification, hankering, honor, idolatry, idolization, infatuation, pash*, passion, puppy love*, reverence, shine*, veneration, weakness*, worship, worshipping, yen*; SEE CONCEPT 32

adore [v] *love intensely*
admire, be crazy about*, be gone on*, be mad for*, be nuts about*, be serious about*, be smitten with*, be stuck on*, be sweet on*, be wild about*, cherish, delight in, dig*, dote on, esteem, exalt, fall for, flip over*, glorify, go for*, honor, idolize, prize, revere, reverence, treasure, venerate, worship; SEE CONCEPT 32

adorn [v] *decorate*
array, beautify, bedeck, deck, doll up*, dress up, embellish, enhance, enrich, fix up, furbish, garnish, grace, gussy up*, ornament, spruce up, trim; SEE CONCEPTS 162,177

adornment [n1] *decorating, enhancing*
beautification, decoration, embellishment, gilding, ornamentation, trimming; SEE CONCEPTS 162,177

adornment [n2] *a decoration*
accessory, dingbat, doodad, embellishment, fandangle*, floss*, frill, frippery, furbelow*, gewgaw*, jazz*, ornament, thing, trimming; SEE CONCEPTS 446,484

adrift [adv1] *floating out of control*
afloat, drifting, loose, unanchored, unmoored; SEE CONCEPT 488

adrift [adv2] *without purpose*
aimless, directionless, goalless, purposeless; SEE CONCEPT 542

adrift [adv3] *off course*
amiss, astray, erring, wrong; SEE CONCEPT 581

adroit [adj] *very able or skilled*
adept, apt, artful, clean, clever, crack*, crackerjack*, cunning, cute, deft, dexterous, expert, foxy*, good, handy, hot tamale*, ingenious, masterful, neat*, nifty*, nimble, on the ball*, on the beam*, proficient, quick on the trigger*, quick on the uptake*, quick-witted, savvy, sharp, skillful, slick, smart, up*, up to speed*, whiz*, wizard; SEE CONCEPT 527

adulation [n] *overenthusiastic praise*
applause, audation, blandishment, bootlicking*, commendation, fawning, flattery, sycophancy, worship; SEE CONCEPTS 32,69

adult [n] *a mature, fully grown person*
gentleperson, grownup, man, person, woman; SEE CONCEPTS 394,424

adult [adj] *being mature, fully grown*
developed, grown, grown-up, of age, ripe, ripened; SEE CONCEPT 406

adulterate [v] *alter or debase, often for profit*
alloy, amalgamate, attenuate, blend, cheapen,

commingle, contaminate, cook, corrupt, cut*, defile, degrade, denature, depreciate, deteriorate,
devalue, dilute, dissolve, doctor*, doctor up*, falsify, impair, infiltrate, intermix, irrigate, lace*,
make impure, mingle, mix, phony up*, plant*,
pollute, shave*, spike*, taint, thin, transfuse, vitiate, water down*, weaken; SEE CONCEPTS
240,254

adulterated [adj] debased or dirty
attenuated, blended, contaminated, corrupt, defiled, degraded, depreciated, deteriorated, devalued, diluted, dissolved, impaired, mixed,
polluted, tainted, thinned, vitiated, watered down,
weakened; SEE CONCEPT 485

adulterous [adj] unfaithful
cheating, double-crossing*, extracurricular*, fast
and loose*, illicit, immoral, moonlighting*,
speedy*, two-faced*, two-timing*, unchaste; SEE
CONCEPT 372

adultery [n] extramarital affair
affair, carrying on*, cheating, extracurricular activity*, fling, fornication, hanky-panky*, immorality, infidelity, matinee*, playing around*,
relationship, thing*, two-timing*; SEE CONCEPT
633

advance [n1] forward movement
advancement, headway, impetus, motion,
progress, progression; SEE CONCEPTS 152,208

advance [n2] improvement, progress in development
advancement, amelioration, betterment, boost,
break*, breakthrough, buildup, development, enrichment, furtherance, gain, go-ahead*, growth,
headway, increase, progress, promotion, rise,
step, up, upgrade, upping; SEE CONCEPTS
700,704

advance [n3] money given beforehand
accommodation, allowance, bite*, credit, deposit,
down payment, floater*, front money*, hike, increase, loan, prepayment, retainer, rise*, score,
stake, take*, touch*; SEE CONCEPTS 340,344

advance(s) [n4] desirous pursuit of someone
approach, move, overture, proposal, proposition,
suggestion; SEE CONCEPTS 20,384

advance [adj] ahead in position or time
beforehand, earlier, early, first, foremost,
forward, in front, in the forefront, in the lead,
leading, previously, prior; SEE CONCEPTS 583,
585,799

advance [v1] move something forward, often
quickly
accelerate, achieve, bring forward, come forward,
conquer, continue ahead, continue on, dispatch,
drive, elevate, forge ahead, gain ground, get
ahead, get green light*, get there*, get with it*,
go ahead, go forth, go forward, go great guns*, go
places*, go to town*, hasten, launch, make headway, make the scene*, march, move on, move
onward, move up, press on, proceed, progress,
promote, propel, push ahead, push on, quicken,
send forward, skyrocket*, speed, step forward,
storm; SEE CONCEPTS 152,208,704

advance [v2] promote or propose an idea
adduce, allege, ballyhoo, beat the drum for, benefit, boost, cite, encourage, foster, further, get ink
for*, hype*, introduce, lay forward, make a pitch
for*, offer, plug*, present, proffer, puff*, push,
put forward, put on the map*, serve, set forth,
splash, spot, submit, suggest, throw spotlight on*,
urge; SEE CONCEPTS 49,60,68

advance [v3] give money beforehand
furnish, lend, loan, pay, provide; SEE CONCEPT
341

advance [v4] increase in amount, number, or position
boost, break the bank*, develop, elevate, enlarge,
get fat*, get rich*, grade, grow, hit pay dirt*, hit
the jackpot*, improve, magnify, make a killing*,
make out*, multiply, pan out*, prefer, prosper,
raise, strike gold*, strike it rich*, thrive, up, upgrade, uplift; SEE CONCEPTS 236,244,245

advanced [adj] ahead in position, time, manner
avant-garde, breakthrough, cutting-edge*, excellent, exceptional, extreme, first, foremost, forward, higher, late, leading, leading-edge*, liberal,
precocious, progressive, radical, state-of-the-art*,
unconventional; SEE CONCEPTS 574,578,585,797

advancement [n1] promotion, progress
advance, amelioration, betterment, elevation,
gain, growth, headway, improvement, preference,
preferment, prelation, rise, upgrading; SEE CON-
CEPTS 700,704

advancement [n2] forward movement
advance, anabasis, gain, headway, march,
progress, progression; SEE CONCEPTS 152,208

advantage [n] benefit, favored position or circumstance
aid, ascendancy, asset, assistance, authority,
avail, blessing, boon, break, choice, comfort,
convenience, dominance, edge, eminence, expediency, favor, gain, good, gratification, help,
hold, improvement, influence, interest, lead, leeway, leg-up*, leverage, luck, mastery, odds, position, power, precedence, pre-eminence,
preference, prestige, prevalence, profit, protection, recognition, resources, return, sanction,
starting, superiority, support, supremacy, upper
hand*, utility, wealth; SEE CONCEPT 574

advent [n] beginning or arrival of something anticipated
appearance, approach, arrival, coming, entrance,
occurrence, onset, visitation; SEE CONCEPTS
119,159

adventure [n] risky or unexpected undertaking
chance, contingency, emprise, endangerment, enterprise, experience, exploit, feat, happening, hazard, incident, jeopardy, occurrence, peril, scene,
speculation, trip, undertaking, venture; SEE CON-
CEPTS 384,386

adventurer [n] person who takes risks
charlatan, daredevil, entrepreneur, explorer,
fortune-hunter, gambler, globetrotter, hero, heroine, madcap, mercenary, opportunist, pioneer, pirate, romantic, speculator, stunt person,
swashbuckler, traveler, venturer, voyager, wanderer; SEE CONCEPT 423

adventurous [adj] daring, risk-taking
adventuresome, audacious, bold, brave, courageous, dangerous, daredevil, enterprising, foolhardy, hazardous, headstrong, intrepid, rash,
reckless, risky, temerarious, venturesome, venturous; SEE CONCEPTS 404,542

adverb [n] word modifying a verb
limiter, modifier, qualifier; SEE CONCEPT 275

adversary [n] opponent
antagonist, attacker, bad person, bandit, competitor, contestant, enemy, foe, match, opposer, opposite number*, oppugner, rival; SEE CONCEPT
412

adverse [adj] unfavorable, antagonistic
allergic to*, conflicting, contrary, detrimental, disadvantageous, down on*, down side*, have no use for*, inimical, injurious, inopportune, negative, opposed, opposing, opposite, oppugning, ornery*, reluctant, repugnant, stuffy*, unfortunate, unfriendly, unlucky, unpropitious, unwilling; SEE CONCEPT 570

adversity [n] bad luck, situation
affliction, bad break*, bummer*, calamity, can of worms*, catastrophe, clutch, contretemps, crunch*, difficulty, disaster, distress, downer*, drag*, evil eye*, hard knocks*, hardship, hard times, hurting, ill fortune, jam, jinx, kiss of death*, misery, misfortune, mishap, on the skids*, pain in the neck*, poison*, reverse, sorrow, suffering, the worst*, tough luck*, trial, trouble; SEE CONCEPT 674

advertise [v] publicize for the purpose of selling or causing one to want
acquaint, advance, advise, announce, apprise, ballyhoo*, beat the drum for*, bill, blazon, boost*, build up, circularize, communicate, declare, disclose, display, divulge, drum*, endorse, exhibit, expose, flaunt, get on soapbox for*, hard sell, herald, hype*, inform, make a pitch*, make known, notify, pitch, plug, press agent*, proclaim, promote, promulgate, puff*, push, put on the map*, reveal, show, soft sell, splash*, sponsor, spot, tout, uncover, unmask; SEE CONCEPTS 60,324

advertisement [n] public notice of sale
ad, announcement, bill, blurb, broadcast, circular, classified ad, commercial, communication, declaration, display, endorsement, exhibit, exhibition, flyer, literature, notice, notification, placard, plug, poster, proclamation, promotion, promulgation, propaganda, publication, publicity, squib, throwaway, want ad; SEE CONCEPTS 270,277,278,280

advertising [n] public notice of sale; notices to increase consumer desire
announcement, announcing, ballyhoo*, billing, blasting*, broadcasting, buildup, displaying, exhibiting, exhibition, exposition, hard sell, hoopla*, hype*, pitch, plug, posting, PR, proclamation, promo*, promoting, promotion, publicity, puff*, screamer*, spread, squib; SEE CONCEPTS 97,138,324

advice [n] recommendation
admonition, advisement, advocacy, aid, bum steer*, caution, charge, consultation, counsel, directions, dissuasion, encouragement, exhortation, forewarning, guidance, help, information, injunction, input, instruction, judgment, lesson, news, opinion, persuasion, prescription, proposal, proposition, recommendation, steer, suggestion, teaching, telltale, tidings, tip, tip-off*, two cents' worth*, view, warning, word, word to the wise*; SEE CONCEPTS 75,274

advisable [adj] recommended, wise
appropriate, apt, commendable, desirable, expedient, fit, fitting, judicious, politic, prudent, seemly, sensible, sound, suggested, suitable, tactical; SEE CONCEPT 574

advise [v1] offer recommendation
admonish, advocate, caution, charge, commend, counsel, direct, dissuade, encourage, enjoin, exhort, forewarn, give a pointer*, give a tip*, guide, instruct, kibitz*, level with*, move, opine, point

out, preach, prepare, prescribe, prompt, put bug in ear*, put in two cents*, recommend, steer, suggest, tout, update, urge, warn; SEE CONCEPT 75

advise [v2] offer information
acquaint, apprise, clue*, clue in*, fill in, give the word*, inform, keep posted*, lay it out*, let in on*, make known, notify, post*, put next to*, put on the line*, put on to*, report, show, tell, tip off*, update, warn; SEE CONCEPT 60

advisedly [adv] with due consideration
carefully, cautiously, consciously, deliberately, discreetly, intentionally, prudently, thoughtfully; SEE CONCEPT 544

adviser/advisor [n] person who recommends, teaches, or otherwise helps
aide, attorney, authority, backseat driver*, buttinski*, clubhouse lawyer*, coach, confidant, consultant, counsel, counselor, director, doctor, Dutch uncle*, expert, friend, guide, helper, instructor, judge, kibitzer*, lawyer, mentor, monitor, partner, priest, quarterback*, referee, righthand person, second-guesser, teacher, tutor; SEE CONCEPTS 348,350

advisory [adj] able, authorized to recommend
advising, consultative, consultive, counseling, helping, recommending; SEE CONCEPT 537

advocacy [n] support for an idea or cause
advancement, aid, assistance, backing, campaigning for, championing, defense, encouragement, justification, pleading for, promotion, promulgation, propagation, proposal, recommendation, upholding, urging; SEE CONCEPT 689

advocate [n] person supporting an idea or cause publicly
apostle, attorney, backer, campaigner, champion, counsel, defender, exponent, expounder, lawyer, pleader, promoter, proponent, proposer, speaker, spokesperson, supporter, upholder; SEE CONCEPTS 359,423

advocate [v] support idea or cause publicly
advance, advise, argue for, back, be in corner*, bless, bolster, boost*, brace up*, build up, campaign for, champion, countenance, defend, encourage, favor, further, get on bandwagon*, give a leg up*, give a lift*, go for, go to bat for*, go with, hold with, justify, plead for, plug*, plump for*, press for, promote, propose, push, recommend, ride shotgun for*, root for*, run interference for*, say so*, side, speak for, spread around*, stump for*, support, tout, uphold, urge, vindicate; SEE CONCEPTS 10,49,75

aerial [adj] occurring in the air
aeriform, aeronautical, airy, atmospheric, birdlike, ethereal, flying, lofty, pneumatic, up above, vaporous; SEE CONCEPT 583

aerobics/aerobic [n/adj] exercise regime designed to increase heart and lung activity while toning muscles
aquarobics, dance workout, drill, exercise, high impact, low impact, slimnastics, step, warm-up, workout; SEE CONCEPT 363

aesthetic/esthetic [adj] beautiful or artful
artistic, creative, gorgeous, inventive; SEE CONCEPTS 485,579

afar [adv] a great distance away
distant, far away, far off, remote; SEE CONCEPT 778

affable [adj] friendly
amiable, amicable, approachable, benevolent, benign, breezy, civil, clubby*, congenial, cordial,

courteous, genial, gentle, good-humored, good-natured, gracious, kindly, mild, nice, obliging, pleasant, polite, sociable, urbane, warm; SEE CONCEPT 401

affair [n1] *matter or business to be taken care of; happening*

activity, assignment, avocation, calling, case, circumstance, concern, duty, employment, episode, event, hap, happening, incident, interest, job, mission, obligation, occupation, occurrence, office function, proceeding, profession, project, province, pursuit, question, realm, responsibility, subject, task, thing*, topic, transaction, undertaking; SEE CONCEPTS 2,349,362

affair [n2] *illicit sexual relationship*

affaire, amour, carrying on*, extracurricular activity*, fling, goings-on*, hanky-panky*, intimacy, intrigue, liaison, love, playing around*, relationship, rendezvous, romance, thing together*, two-timing*; SEE CONCEPTS 32,375

affair [n3] *party or celebration*

do, entertainment, function, gathering, reception, shindig, soiree; SEE CONCEPTS 377,383

affect [v1] *influence, affect emotionally*

act on, alter, change, disturb, impinge, impress, induce, influence, inspire, interest, involve, modify, move, overcome, perturb, prevail, regard, relate, stir, sway, touch, transform, upset; SEE CONCEPTS 7,19,22,228

affect [v2] *pretend, imitate*

act, adopt, aspire to, assume, bluff, contrive, counterfeit, do a bit*, fake, feign, lay it on thick, make out like*, playact, put on, put up a front*, sham*, simulate, take on; SEE CONCEPT 59

affectation [n] *pretended behavior to make an impression*

air, airs, appearance, artificiality, facade, false front*, front, going Hollywood*, imitation, insincerity, mannerism, pose, pretense, pretension, pretentiousness, put-on, putting on airs*, sham*, show, showing off, simulation; SEE CONCEPT 633

affected [adj1] *deeply moved or hurt emotionally*

afflicted, altered, changed, compassionate, concerned, damaged, distressed, excited, grieved, impaired, impressed, influenced, injured, overwhelmed, overwrought, sorry, stimulated, stirred, sympathetic, tender, touched, troubled, upset; SEE CONCEPT 403

affected [adj2] *changed in a bad or artificial way*

apish, artificial, assumed, awkward, campy*, chichi*, conceited, contrived, counterfeit, counterfeited, faked, false, feigned, fraud*, gone Hollywood*, ham*, hammy*, high falutin'*, hollow, imitated, insincere, melodramatic, ostentatious, overdone, pedantic, phony, playacting, pompous, precious, pretended, pretentious, put-on*, schmaltzy*, self-conscious, shallow, sham*, simulated, spurious, stiff, stilted, studied, superficial, theatrical, unnatural; SEE CONCEPTS 401,570

affection [n] *strong fondness*

amore, ardor, attachment, care, case*, closeness, concern, crush, desire, devotion, emotion, endearment, feeling, friendliness, friendship, good will, hankering*, heart, inclination, itch*, kindness, liking, love, passion, predilection, propensity, puppy love*, regard, sentiment, shine*, soft spot*, solicitude, tenderness, warmth, weakness*, yen*; SEE CONCEPT 32

affectionate [adj] *having or showing fondness*

all over*, attached, caring, crazy over*, dear, devoted, doting, fond, friendly, huggy*, kind, lovey-dovey*, loving, mushy*, nutty about*, partial, soft on*, sympathetic, tender, warm, warmhearted; SEE CONCEPTS 401,403

affective [adj] *concerning feelings and intuition*

emotional, emotive, feeling, intuitive, noncognitive, perceptual, visceral; SEE CONCEPT 529

affidavit [n] *written legal declaration*

affirmation, oath, sworn statement, testimony; SEE CONCEPTS 271,318

affiliate [n] *organization that is associated with another*

affil*, associate, branch, offshoot, partner, sibling; SEE CONCEPT 381

affiliate [v] *associate or be associated with a larger organization*

ally, amalgamate, annex, associate, band together, combine, come aboard, confederate, connect, form connection, go partners*, hook up*, incorporate, join, line up*, plug into*, relate*, team up, throw in with*, tie up, unite; SEE CONCEPTS 113,114

affiliation [n] *association with an organization*

alliance, amalgamation, banding together, bunch, cahoots*, clan, coalition, combination, confederation, conjunction, connection, crew, crowd, gang, hookup*, incorporation, joining, league, merging, mob, outfit, partnership, relationship, ring, syndicate, tie-in, union; SEE CONCEPT 381

affinity [n1] *liking or inclination toward something*

affection, attraction, closeness, compatibility, cotton*, cup of tea*, druthers*, fondness, good vibrations*, leaning, partiality, rapport, same wavelength, simpatico, sympathy, thing*, weakness*; SEE CONCEPTS 20,32,709

affinity [n2] *similarity*

alikeness, alliance, analogy, association, closeness, connection, correspondence, kinship, likeness, relation, relationship, resemblance, semblance, similitude; SEE CONCEPT 670

affirm [v] *declare the truth of something*

assert, asseverate, attest, aver, avouch, avow, certify, cinch, clinch, confirm, cross heart, declare, guarantee, have a lock on*, ice*, insist, lock up*, maintain, nail down*, okay, predicate, profess, pronounce, put on ice*, ratify, repeat, rubberstamp*, say so, set, state, swear, swear on bible*, swear up and down*, testify, vouch, witness; SEE CONCEPTS 49,50,88

affirmation [n] *declaration of the truth of something*

affidavit, assertion, asseveration, attestation, averment, avouchment, avowal, certification, confirmation, declaration, green light*, oath, okay, pronouncement, ratification, stamp of approval*, statement, sworn statement, testimonial, testimony; SEE CONCEPT 49

affirmative [adj] *being agreeable or assenting*

acknowledging, acquiescent, affirmatory, affirming, approving, complying, concurring, confirmative, confirmatory, confirming, consenting, corroborative, endorsing, favorable, positive, ratifying, supporting; SEE CONCEPTS 542,572

affix [v] *attach or stick*

add, annex, append, bind, fasten, glue, hitch on*, join, paste, put on, rivet, slap on*, subjoin, tack, tack on*, tag, tag on*; SEE CONCEPTS 85,113,160

afflict [v] *cause or become hurt*

agonize, annoy, beset, bother, burden, crucify, distress, grieve, harass, harrow, harry, irk, lacerate, martyr, oppress, pain, pester, plague, press, rack, smite, strike, torment, torture, trouble, try, vex, worry, wound; SEE CONCEPTS 7,19,246,313

affliction [n] *hurt condition; something that causes hurt*

adversity, anguish, calamity, cross, crux, depression, difficulty, disease, disorder, distress, grief, hardship, illness, infirmity, misery, misfortune, ordeal, pain, plague, plight, scourge, sickness, sorrow, suffering, torment, trial, tribulation, trouble, woe; SEE CONCEPTS 306,309,674,728

affluent [adj1] *wealthy*

flush*, loaded*, moneyed*, opulent, prosperous, rich, stinking rich*, upper class, upscale, well-off, well-to-do; SEE CONCEPT 334

affluent [adj2] *plentiful*

abundant, bountiful, copious, full, plenteous; SEE CONCEPT 771

afford [v1] *able to have or do; within financial means*

allow, be able to, bear, be disposed to, have enough for, have the means for, incur, manage, spare, stand, support, sustain; SEE CONCEPTS 335,713

afford [v2] *give, produce*

bestow, furnish, grant, impart, offer, provide, render, supply, yield; SEE CONCEPTS 108,143

affront [n] *an insult*

abuse, backhanded compliment*, brickbat*, dirty deed*, indignity, injury, left-handed compliment*, offense, outrage, provocation, put-down*, slap*, slap in the face*, slight, slur, vexation, wrong; SEE CONCEPTS 7,19,44,54

affront [v] *insult or involve in entanglement*

abuse, anger, annoy, confront, criticize, displease, dispraise, dump on*, encounter, face, give a zinger*, give the cold shoulder*, hit where one lives*, meet, offend, outrage, pique, provoke, put down*, slander, slight, taunt, vex; SEE CONCEPTS 7,19,44,54

afraid [adj1] *fearful*

abashed, aghast, alarmed, anxious, apprehensive, aroused, blanched, cowardly, cowed, daunted, discouraged, disheartened, dismayed, distressed, disturbed, faint-hearted, frightened, frozen, have cold feet*, horrified, in awe, intimidated, nervous, panic-stricken, perplexed, perturbed, petrified, rattled, run scared*, scared, scared stiff*, scared to death*, shocked, spooked, startled, stunned, suspicious, terrified, terror-stricken, timid, timorous, trembling, upset, worried; SEE CONCEPTS 403,690

afraid [adj2] *reluctant, regretful*

averse, backward, disinclined, hesitant, indisposed, loath, reluctant, sorry, uneager, unhappy, unwilling; SEE CONCEPT 529

afresh [adj] *new or repeated*

again, anew, de novo, lately, newly, of late, once again, once more, over, over again, recently; SEE CONCEPTS 578,797

after [adj] *following in position or time*

afterwards, back, back of, behind, below, ensuing, hind, hindmost, in the rear, later, next, posterior, postliminary, rear, subsequential, subsequently, succeeding, thereafter; SEE CONCEPTS 586,820

aftermath [n] *situation following an event, occurrence*

after-effects, causatum, chain reaction*, consequences, end, eventuality, flak*, impact, issue, outcome, payoff*, remainder, residual, residuum, results, upshot, waves*; SEE CONCEPT 230

afternoon [n] *period after 12 noon and before sunset*

cocktail hour, P.M., post meridian, siesta, teatime; SEE CONCEPTS 801,806,810

afterthought [n] *idea that occurs after it is timely*

reconsideration, review, second thought; SEE CONCEPT 529

afterward/afterwards [adv] *following a time, event*

after, another time, at a later time, a while later, behind, by and by, ensuingly, eventually, in a while, intra, late, later, latterly, next, on the next day, soon, subsequently, then, thereafter, thereon, ultimately; SEE CONCEPT 799

again [adv1] *another time; repeated*

afresh, anew, anon, bis, come again, encore, freshly, newly, once more, one more time, over, over and over, recurrently, reiteratively, repeatedly; SEE CONCEPTS 553,799

again [adv2] *in addition*

additionally, also, besides, further, furthermore, moreover, on the contrary, on the other hand, then; SEE CONCEPT 577

age [n1] *period of animate existence*

adolescence, adulthood, boyhood, childhood, dotage, elderliness, girlhood, infancy, life, lifetime, majority, maturity, middle age, milestone, old age, senility, seniority, wear and tear*, youth; SEE CONCEPTS 816,817

age [n2] *a period of time*

aeon, blue moon*, century, date, day, duration, epoch, era, generation, interim, interval, life, lifetime, millennium, span; SEE CONCEPT 807

age [v] *become older*

decline, deteriorate, develop, get along, grow, grow feeble, grow old, grow up, mature, mellow, push, put mileage on*, ripen, wane; SEE CONCEPT 105

aged [adj] *old*

age-old, ancient, antediluvian, antiquated, antique, been around*, creaky*, elderly, getting on*, gray, moth-eaten*, oldie*, over the hill*, passé*, rusty*, senescent, senior citizen, shot*, timeworn, venerable, worn, worse for wear*; SEE CONCEPTS 578,797

ageism [n] *age-based discrimination*

age bias, generation gap; SEE CONCEPT 689

agency [n1] *organization, often business-related*

bureau, company, department, firm, office; SEE CONCEPTS 325,381,441

agency [n2] *power, instrumentality*

action, activity, auspices, channel, efficiency, force, influence, instrument, instrumentality, intercession, intervention, means, mechanism, mediation, medium, operation, organ, vehicle, work; SEE CONCEPTS 376,658

agenda [n] *list of things to do*

calendar, card, diary, docket, lineup, plan, program, schedule, timetable; SEE CONCEPT 283

agent [n1] *person representing an organization or person in business*

abettor, actor, advocate, ambassador, assignee, assistant, attorney, broker, commissioner, delegate, deputy, doer, emissary, envoy, executor, factor, factotum, functionary, go-between, handler, intermediary, lawyer, mediary, middleperson, minister, mover, negotiator, officer, operative, operator, principal, proctor, promoter, proxy, representative, salesperson, servant, steward, substitute, surrogate, ten percenter*, worker; SEE CONCEPT 348

agent [n2] *power, instrument for achievement*
cause, channel, factor, force, means, medium, organ, power, vehicle; SEE CONCEPTS 376,658

aggrandize [v] *cause something to seem or be greater, bigger*
acclaim, applaud, augment, beef up*, boost, commend, dignify, distinguish, enlarge, ennoble, expand, extend, glorify, heighten, hike, hike up*, honor, hype, increase, intensify, jack up*, jump, magnify, multiply, parlay, praise; SEE CONCEPTS 50,69,88,236,245

aggravate [v1] *annoy*
be at*, be on the back of*, bother, bug, bum*, dog, drive up the wall*, exasperate, gall, get, get on one's nerves, get to, give a hard time, grate, hack, irk, irritate, nag, needle, nettle, peeve, pester, pick on, pique, provoke, tease, vex, wig*; SEE CONCEPTS 7,19

aggravate [v2] *cause to become worse*
complicate, deepen, enhance, exacerbate, exaggerate, heighten, increase, inflame, intensify, magnify, mount, rise, rouse, worsen; SEE CONCEPT 240

aggravation [n1] *annoyance*
affliction, aggro*, bother, botheration*, difficulty, distress, exasperation, hang-up*, headache*, irksomeness, irritation, pain, pain in the neck*, pet peeve*, provocation, teasing, vexation, worry; SEE CONCEPT 410

aggravation [n2] *worsening of a situation, condition*
deepening, exacerbation, exaggeration, heightening, increase, inflaming, inflammation, intensification, magnification, sharpening, strengthening, worsening; SEE CONCEPT 240

aggregate [n] *collection*
accumulation, agglomerate, agglomeration, all, amount, assemblage, body, bulk, combination, conglomerate, conglomeration, gross, heap, lump, mass, mixture, pile, quantity, sum, the works*, total, totality, whole, whole ball of wax*, whole enchilada*, whole schmear*, whole shooting match*; SEE CONCEPT 432

aggregate [adj] *forming a collection from separate parts*
accumulated, added, amassed, assembled, collected, collective, combined, composite, corporate, cumulative, heaped, mixed, piled, total; SEE CONCEPT 781

aggregate [v] *combine into a collection*
accumulate, add up, amass, amount, assemble, collect, combine, come, heap, mix, number, pile, sum, total; SEE CONCEPT 432

aggression [n1] *attack, often military*
assailment, assault, blitz, blitzkrieg, encroachment, injury, invasion, offense, offensive, onset, onslaught, push, raid; SEE CONCEPTS 86,320

aggression [n2] *hostile or forceful behavior, attitude*
aggressiveness, antagonism, belligerence, blitz, combativeness, destructiveness, fight, hostility, pugnacity, push; SEE CONCEPTS 29,411

aggressive [adj1] *belligerent, hostile*
advancing, antipathetic, assailing, attacking, barbaric, bellicose, combative, contentious, destructive, disruptive, disturbing, encroaching, hawkish, intruding, intrusive, invading, martial, militant, offensive, pugnacious, quarrelsome, rapacious, threatening, warlike; SEE CONCEPT 550

aggressive [adj2] *assertive*
assertory, bold, brassy*, cheeky*, cocky*, come on*, domineering, dynamic, energetic, enterprising, flip*, forceful, fresh*, get up and go*, go after, hard sell, imperious, masterful, militant, nervy*, pushing, pushy, sassy, shooting from the hip*, smart*, smart alecky*, strenuous, tough, vigorous, zealous; SEE CONCEPTS 404,542

aggrieved [adj] *very distressed*
afflicted, depressed, disturbed, grieving, harmed, hurt, injured, oppressed, pained, peeved, persecuted, saddened, unhappy, woeful, wronged; SEE CONCEPT 403

aghast [adj] *horrified; very surprised*
afraid, agape, agog, alarmed, amazed, anxious, appalled, astonished, astounded, awestruck, confounded, dismayed, dumbfounded, frightened, horror-struck, overwhelmed, shocked, startled, stunned, terrified, thunderstruck; SEE CONCEPTS 403,690

agile [adj] *physically or mentally nimble, deft*
active, acute, alert, athletic, brisk, buoyant, bustling, clever, dexterous, easy-moving, energetic, fleet, frisky, limber, lithe, lively, mercurial, prompt, quick, quick on the draw*, quick on the trigger*, quick-witted, rapid, ready, sharp, spirited, sportive, spright, sprightly, spry, stirring, supple, swift, twinkle toes*, vigorous, vivacious, winged, zippy; SEE CONCEPTS 485,527,588

agility [n] *physical or mental nimbleness, deftness*
activity, acuteness, adroitness, alacrity, alertness, briskness, celerity, cleverness, dexterity, dispatch, expedition, fleetness, friskiness, litheness, liveliness, promptitude, promptness, quickness, quick-wittedness, sharpness, sprightliness, spryness, suppleness, swiftness; SEE CONCEPTS 410,630,748

aging [n] *becoming older*
crumbling, declining, developing, fading, fermenting, getting along*, getting on*, maturing, mellowing, senescent, slumping, stale, waning, wearing out*; SEE CONCEPT 701

agitate [v1] *shake physically*
beat, churn, concuss, convulse, disturb, rock, rouse, stir, toss; SEE CONCEPT 152

agitate [v2] *disturb, trouble someone*
alarm, argue, arouse, bug*, bug up*, burn up*, confuse, craze*, debate, discompose, disconcert, discuss, dispute, disquiet, distract, disturb, egg on*, examine, excite, ferment, flurry, fluster, get to*, incite, inflame, make flip*, move, perturb, psych*, push buttons*, rouse, ruffle, spook, stimulate, stir, trouble, turn on*, unhinge*, upset, ventilate*, work up*, worry; SEE CONCEPTS 7,19,46

agitator [n] *person who disturbs, causes trouble*
adjy, advocate, agent, anarchist, champion, demagogue, disrupter, dissident, dogmatist, fighter, firebrand*, fomenter, heretic, incendiary, inciter, instigator, leftist, malcontent, mover, partisan, propagandist, provocateur, pusher, rabble-rouser, radical, reactionary, rebel, reformer, revisionist, revolutionary, ringleader, sparkplug*, troublemaker, wave maker*, zealot; SEE CONCEPT 412

agnostic [n] *person unsure that God exists*
doubter, freethinker, materialist, skeptic, unbeliever; SEE CONCEPT *361*

ago [adv] *in the past*
ages ago, back, back when, before, from way back, from year one*, gone, since, since God knows when*, time was; SEE CONCEPT *820*

agonize [v] *suffer or cause another to suffer*
afflict, bleed, carry on, crucify, distress, disturb, eat heart out*, excruciate, harrow, hurt, labor, lament, martyr, pain, rack, sing the blues*, squirm, stew over, strain, strive, struggle, take it badly*, torment, torture, try, wince, worry, writhe; SEE CONCEPTS *7,19,410*

agonizing [adj] *difficult and painful, suffering*
disturbing, excruciating, extreme, fierce, harrowing, intense, racking, struggling, tearing, tormenting, tortuous, torturing, vehement, violent; SEE CONCEPTS *403,565*

agony [n] *suffering, pain*
affliction, anguish, distress, dolor, misery, pangs, passion, throes, torment, torture, woe; SEE CONCEPTS *410,728*

agrarian [adj] *concerning land, farming*
agricultural, natural, peasant, rural, rustic, uncultivated, undomesticated; SEE CONCEPT *536*

agree [v1] *be in unison, assent with another*
accede, acknowledge, acquiesce, admit, allow, be of the same mind*, bury the hatchet*, buy into*, check, clinch the deal*, come to terms, comply, concede, concur, consent, cut a deal*, engage, give blessing*, give carte blanche*, give green light*, give the go-ahead*, go along with, grant, make a deal*, okay, pass on, permit, play ball*, recognize, see eye to eye*, set, settle, shake on*, side with, sign*, subscribe, take one up on*, yes*; SEE CONCEPTS *8,10,45,235*

agree [v2] *be similar or consistent*
accord, answer, attune, be in harmony, blend, click, cohere, coincide, concert, concord, concur, conform, consort, correspond, equal, fall in with*, fit, get along with, go hand in hand*, go together, go well with, harmonize, jibe, match, parallel, square, suit, synchronize, tally; SEE CONCEPTS *118,656,670*

agreeable [adj1] *pleasing*
acceptable, dandy, delicious, delightful, enjoyable, fair, fine, gratifying, hunky-dory*, mild, nice, peach*, peachy*, pleasant, pleasurable, pleasureful, pussycat*, ready, satisfying, spiffy*, swell*, to one's liking, to one's taste, welcome; SEE CONCEPT *572*

agreeable [adj2] *appropriate, in keeping*
befitting, compatible, congruous, consistent, consonant, fitting, proper; SEE CONCEPT *558*

agreeable [adj3] *willing to be in unison, assent*
acquiescent, amenable, approving, complying, concurring, congenial, consenting, favorable, grateful, in accord, responsive, sympathetic, well-disposed, willing; SEE CONCEPTS *401,542*

agreeably [adv] *willingly, assenting; pleasantly; in keeping*
affably, affirmatively, amiably, amicably, appropriately, benevolently, charmingly, cheerfully, convivially, favorably, genially, good-humoredly, good-naturedly, graciously, happily, kindly, mutually, obligingly, peacefully, pleasingly, politely, satisfactorily, sympathetically, well, wonderfully; SEE CONCEPTS *401,572*

agreement [n1] *concurrence*
acceding, accession, accommodation, accord, accordance, acknowledging, adjustment, affiliation, affinity, alliance, amity, approving, arbitration, arrangement, assenting, authorizing, bargaining, compatibility, compliance, complying, compromise, concert, concession, concord, concordance, concurring, conformity, congruity, consistency, correspondence, endorsing, granting, harmony, mediation, ratifying, reconciliation, similarity, suitableness, sympathy, understanding, union, unison, verification, verifying; SEE CONCEPT *684*

agreement [n2] *document of concurrence, contract*
acknowledgment, adjudication, affidavit, approval, arrangement, assent, avowal, bargain, bond, cartel, charter, codicil, compact, compromise, confirmation, covenant, deal, indenture, lease, negotiation, note, oath, okay, pact, piece of paper*, protocol, recognition, settlement, stipulation, the nod*, transaction, treaty, understanding, writ; SEE CONCEPTS *271,331*

agricultural [adj] *concerning farming, land*
aggie*, agronomical, arboricultural, floricultural, gardening, horticultural, ranch, rural, rustic; SEE CONCEPTS *536,583*

agriculture [n] *farming, crop production*
agronomics, agronomy, cultivation, culture, horticulture, husbandry, tillage; SEE CONCEPTS *205,257*

aground [adv] *on the bottom of*
ashore, beached, disabled, foundered, grounded, high and dry*, marooned, reefed, shipwrecked, stranded, stuck, swamped, wrecked; SEE CONCEPT *583*

ahead [adv] *in front or advance of*
advanced, advancing, ahead, along, ante, antecedently, at an advantage, at the head, before, beforehand, earlier, first, fore, foremost, forward, forwards, in the foreground, in the lead, leading, on, onward, onwards, precedent, precedently, preceding, previous, progressing, to the fore; SEE CONCEPTS *586,632,820*

aid [n1] *help, support*
advancement, advice, advocacy, alleviation, allowance, assist, assistance, attention, backing, backup, benefaction, benefit, benevolence, bounty, care, charity, comfort, compensation, cooperation, deliverance, encouragement, endowment, favor, furtherance, gift, giving, guidance, hand, handout, leg up*, lift, ministration, ministry, patronage, promotion, reinforcement, relief, rescue, reward, salvation, service, shot in the arm*, subsidy, sustenance, treatment; SEE CONCEPT *110*

aid/aide [n2] *person who helps*
abettor, adjutant, aide-de-camp, assistant, attendant, coadjutant, coadjutor, crew, deputy, helper, lieutenant, second, supporter; SEE CONCEPT *348*

aid [v] *help, support*
abet, alleviate, assist, bail out, befriend, benefact, encourage, favor, go to bat for*, go with*, lend a hand*, lighten, mitigate, open doors for*, promote, relieve, serve, stick up for*, straighten out*, subsidize, sustain; SEE CONCEPT *110*

ailing [adj] *not feeling well*
below par, debilitated, diseased, down, down with, enfeebled, feeble, feeling awful, ill, indisposed, rocky*, run down*, sick, sick as a dog*, sickly, under the weather*, unwell, wasting, weak; SEE CONCEPT *314*

ailment [n] *mild sickness*
ache, bug, complaint, condition, disease, disorder, dose*, flu, illness, indisposition, infirmity, malady, syndrome; SEE CONCEPTS *306,316*

aim [n] *goal*
ambition, aspiration, course, desideratum, design, desire, direction, end, intent, intention, mark, object, objective, plan, purpose, scheme, target, where one is heading*, wish; SEE CONCEPT *659*

aim [v] *point or direct at a goal*
address, angle, aspire, attempt, cast, concentrate, contemplate, covet, design, direct, endeavor, essay, fix, focus, intend, level, mean, plan, propose, purpose, set one's sights on*, sight, slant, steer, strive, target, train, try, want, wish, zero in on, zoom in; SEE CONCEPTS *20,41,201*

aimless [adj] *having no goal*
accidental, any which way*, bits-and-pieces*, blind, capricious, careless, casual, chance, desultory, directionless, drifting, erratic, fanciful, fickle, fits and starts*, flighty, fortuitous, frivolous, goalless, haphazard, heedless, hit-or-miss*, indecisive, indiscriminate, irresolute, objectless, pointless, purposeless, random, shiftless, stray, thoughtless, unavailing, undirected, unguided, unplanned, unpredictable, vagrant, wandering, wanton, wayward; SEE CONCEPTS *401,535,544*

air [n1] *gases forming the atmosphere*
blast, breath, breeze, draft, heavens, ozone, puff, sky, stratosphere, troposphere, ventilation, waft, whiff, wind, zephyr; SEE CONCEPT *437*

air [n2] *distinctive quality or character; style*
address, affectation, ambience, appearance, atmosphere, aura, bearing, comportment, demeanor, deportment, effect, feel, feeling, flavor, impression, look, manner, mannerism, mien, mood, pose, presence, property, quality, semblance, tone; SEE CONCEPTS *644,673*

air [n3] *musical tune*
aria, descant, lay, melody, song, strain, theme; SEE CONCEPTS *77,595*

air [v1] *put into the atmosphere; freshen*
aerate, aerify, air-condition, circulate, cool, eject, expel, expose, fan, open, oxygenate, purify, refresh, ventilate; SEE CONCEPT *255*

air [v2] *express opinion publicly*
broadcast, circulate, communicate, declare, disclose, display, disseminate, divulge, exhibit, expose, make known, make public, proclaim, publicize, publish, put, reveal, speak, state, tell, utter, ventilate, voice; SEE CONCEPTS *51,52*

airplane [n] *vehicle that transports cargo or passengers through the air*
aeroplane, airbus, aircraft, airliner, airship, cab*, crate*, jet, kite*, plane, ramjet*, ship*; SEE CONCEPT *504*

airport [n] *center for transportation by air*
aerodrome, airdrome, airfield, airstrip, hangar, helipad, heliport, home plate*, installation, landing strip, runway, strip; SEE CONCEPTS *325,439*

airs [n] *affectation; pretended behavior*
affectedness, arrogance, false front, front, haughtiness, hauteur, mannerism, ostentation, pomposity, pose, pretense, pretension, pretentiousness, put-on*, show, superciliousness; SEE CONCEPT *633*

airtight [adj1] *sealed*
closed, impenetrable, impermeable, shut; SEE CONCEPTS *483,490*

airtight [adj2] *certain*
incontestable, indisputable, invulnerable, irrefutable, unassailable; SEE CONCEPT *535*

airy [adj1] *open to the atmosphere*
aerial, atmospheric, blowy, breezy, drafty, exposed, fluttering, fresh, gaseous, gusty, light, lofty, out-of-doors, uncluttered, vaporous, ventilated, well-ventilated, windy; SEE CONCEPT *583*

airy [adj2] *delicate or ethereal*
dainty, diaphanous, flimsy, fragile, frail, frivolous, illusory, imaginary, immaterial, intangible, light, rare, rarefied, tenuous, thin, vaporous, visionary, volatile, weightless, wispy; SEE CONCEPTS *490,582*

airy [adj3] *buoyant, light, or lively in nature*
animated, blithe, bouncy, cheerful, cheery, effervescent, elastic, fanciful, flippant, frolicsome, gay, graceful, happy, high-spirited, jaunty, light, light-hearted, merry, nonchalant, resilient, sprightly, volatile, whimsical; SEE CONCEPTS *404,550*

aisle [n] *passageway dividing something*
alley, artery, avenue, clearing, corridor, course, egress, gangway, hallway, ingress, lane, opening, passage, path, walk, way; SEE CONCEPTS *440,513,830*

ajar [adj/adv] *slightly open*
open, unclosed, unlatched, unshut; SEE CONCEPT *586*

akin [adj] *related or connected*
affiliated, agnate, alike, allied, analogous, cognated, comparable, connate, consonant, corresponding, incident, kindred, like, parallel, similar; SEE CONCEPTS *487,563,573*

alacrity [n] *liveliness; promptness*
alertness, avidity, briskness, cheerfulness, dispatch, eagerness, enthusiasm, expedition, fervor, gaiety, hilarity, joyousness, promptitude, quickness, readiness, speed, sprightliness, willingness, zeal; SEE CONCEPTS *633,657*

alarm [n1] *feeling of sudden fear*
anxiety, apprehension, cold feet*, consternation, dismay, distress, dread, fright, horror, nervousness, panic, scare, strain, stress, tension, terror, trepidation, unease, uneasiness; SEE CONCEPTS *410,690*

alarm [n2] *warning, signaling device*
alert, bell, blast, buzzer, call, caution, clock, cry, drum, flap*, flash*, forewarning, gong, high sign*, horn, Mayday*, nod*, scramble*, scream, shout, sign, signal, siren, SOS, squeal, tip, tip off*, tocsin, trumpet, warning, whistle, wink*, yell; SEE CONCEPTS *269,463*

alarm [v] *upset*
amaze, astonish, chill, daunt, dismay, distress, frighten, give a turn*, make jump*, panic, scare, scare silly*, scare stiff*, scare to death*, spook, startle, surprise, terrify, unnerve; SEE CONCEPTS *7,14,19,42*

album [n] *blank book for collecting; holder*
anthology, collection, depository, index, memento, memory book, miscellany, notebook, portfolio, register, registry, scrapbook; SEE CONCEPTS *271,446*

alcohol [n] *intoxicating, flammable liquid*
alky*, booze*, canned heat*, cocktail, drink, ethanol, firewater*, hard stuff*, hootch*, intoxicant, liquor, methanol, moonshine*, palliative*, red-eye*, rotgut*, sauce*, smoke*, spirits, tipple*, toddy*; SEE CONCEPTS *454,467*

alcoholic [adj] *intoxicating*
brewed, distilled, fermented, hard, inebriant, inebriating, sprituous, vinous; SEE CONCEPT 462

alcove [n] *nook, secluded spot*
anteroom, bay, bower, compartment, corner, cubbyhole, cubicle, niche, recess, study; SEE CONCEPTS 440,448,513

ale [n] *intoxicating, fermented beverage*
beer, brew, hops, malt, suds*; SEE CONCEPT 454

alert [n] *warning*
admonition, alarm, flap*, high sign*, Mayday*, sign, signal, siren, SOS, tip off, wink*; SEE CONCEPTS 78,278,595,628

alert [adj] *attentive, lively*
active, all ears*, bright, cagey*, careful, circumspect, clever, fast on the draw*, good hands*, heads up*, heedful, hip, intelligent, jazzed*, observant, on guard*, on one's toes*, on the ball*, on the job*, on the lookout*, on the qui vive*, perceptive, psyched up*, quick, ready, sharp, spirited, switched on*, vigilant, wary, watchful, wide-awake, wired*, wise, with it*; SEE CONCEPTS 402,403

alert [v] *warn*
alarm, flag, forewarn, give the high sign*, inform, notify, put on guard, signal, tip, tip off, wave flag*; SEE CONCEPT 78

algae [n] *rootless, leafless plants living in water*
dulse, kelp, scum, seaweed; SEE CONCEPT 429

alias [n] *false name*
AKA, anonym, assumed name, handle*, moniker, nickname, nom de guerre, nom de plume, pen name, pseudonym, stage name, summer name*; SEE CONCEPT 683

alias [adv] *otherwise known as*
also called, also known as, otherwise; SEE CONCEPT 582

alibi [n] *defense against charges of wrongdoing; evidence of absence*
account, affirmation, airtight case*, allegation, answer, assertion, assurance, avowal, case, copout*, cover, declaration, excuse, explanation, fish story*, justification, plea, pretext, profession, proof, reason, reply, retort, song and dance*, stall, statement, vindication; SEE CONCEPT 661

alien [n] *foreign being*
blow in*, floater*, foreigner, greenhorn*, guest, immigrant, incomer*, interloper, intruder, invader, migrant, newcomer, noncitizen, outsider, refugee, settler, squatter, stranger, visitor, weed*; SEE CONCEPT 423

alien [adj] *foreign*
conflicting, contrary, estranged, exotic, extraneous, extrinsic, inappropriate, incompatible, incongruous, opposed, remote, separate, unusual; SEE CONCEPT 564

alienate [v] *cause unfriendliness, hostility*
break off, come between, disaffect, disunite, divide, divorce, estrange, make indifferent, part, separate, set against, turn away, turn off, wean, withdraw the affections of; SEE CONCEPTS 7,19,231

alienation [n] *unfriendliness*
breach, breaking off, coolness, disaffection, diverting, division, divorce, estrangement, indifference, remoteness, rupture, separation, setting against, turning away, variance, withdrawal; SEE CONCEPT 410

align [v1] *line up, arrange next to*
adjust, allineate, coordinate, even, even up, fix,
make parallel, order, range, regulate, straighten; SEE CONCEPT 158

align [v2] *join; bring to agreement*
affiliate, agree, ally, associate, cooperate, enlist, follow, join sides, sympathize; SEE CONCEPTS 8,114

alike [adj] *similar*
akin, allied, analogous, approximate, associated, carbon copy*, cognate, comparable, concurrent, correspondent, corresponding, dead ringer*, ditto*, double, duplicate, equal, equivalent, even, facsimile, identical, indistinguishable, kindred, like, look-alike, matched, matching, mated, parallel, proportionate, related, resembling, same, same difference*, similar, spitting image*, undifferentiated, uniform, Xerox*; SEE CONCEPTS 487,566,573

alike [adv] *similarly*
analogously, comparably, comparatively, consonantly, correspondingly, equally, equivalently, evenly, identically, in accordance with, in common, in the same degree, in the same manner, likewise, similarly, the same way, uniformly; SEE CONCEPTS 487,566,573

alimentary [adj] *digestive*
comestible, dietary, digestible, nourishing, nutrient, nutritional, nutritious, nutritive, peptic, salutary, sustaining, sustentative; SEE CONCEPTS 406,485

alimony [n] *money paid in support of a former spouse*
keep, livelihood, living, maintenance, provision, remittance, subsistence, sustenance, upkeep; SEE CONCEPT 344

alive [adj1] *being animately existent*
animate, around, awake, breathing, cognizant, conscious, dynamic, existing, extant, functioning, growing, knowing, live, living, mortal, operative, running, subsisting, viable, vital, working, zoetic; SEE CONCEPT 539

alive [adj2] *being active, full of life*
abounding, alert, animated, awake, brisk, bustling, cheerful, dynamic, eager, energetic, lively, overflowing, quick, ready, replete, rife, sharp, spirited, sprightly, spry, stirring, swarming, teeming, vigorous, vital, vivacious, zestful; SEE CONCEPTS 401,542

alkali [n] *soluble base; opposite of an acid*
antacid, caustic soda, salt; SEE CONCEPT 472

alkaline [adj] *being basic, not acid (chemically)*
acrid, alkalescent, alkali, antacid, bitter, caustic, neutralizing, salty, soluble; SEE CONCEPT 472

all [n] *whole; totality*
accumulation, across the board, aggregate, aggregation, collection, ensemble, entirety, everyone, everything, gross, group, integer, jackpot*, lock stock and barrel*, mass, quantity, sum, sum total, total, unit, utmost, wall to wall*, whole ball of wax*, whole enchilada*, whole nine yards*, whole schmear*, whole shooting match*, whole show*, works; SEE CONCEPTS 787,837

all [adj1] *whole quantity*
complete, entire, full, greatest, gross, outright, perfect, total, utter; SEE CONCEPT 771

all [adj2] *each; every one of a class*
any, bar none*, barring no one, complete, each and every, entire, every, every bit of, every single, sum, total, totality, whole; SEE CONCEPT 772

all [adj3] *exclusively*
alone, nothing but, only, solely; SEE CONCEPT 554

all [adv] *completely, without exception*
all in all, altogether, entirely, exactly, fully, just, purely, quite, totally, utterly, wholly; SEE CONCEPTS 771,772

allay [v] *reduce something, usually a pain or a problem*
abate, alleviate, assuage, calm, compose, cool out*, decrease, ease, lessen, lighten, make nice*, mitigate, moderate, mollify, pacify, play up to*, pour oil on*, quiet, square, take the bite out*, take the sting out*; SEE CONCEPTS 7,22,244

allegation [n] *assertion placing blame*
accusation, affirmation, asseveration, avowal, charge, claim, declaration, deposition, overment, plea, profession, statement; SEE CONCEPT 49

allege [v] *assert; claim*
adduce, advance, affirm, asseverate, aver, avouch, avow, charge, cite, declare, depose, lay, maintain, offer, plead, present, profess, put forward, recite, recount, state, testify; SEE CONCEPT 49

alleged [adj] *asserted, often doubtful*
averred, declared, described, dubious, ostensible, pretended, professed, purported, questionable, so-called, stated, supposed, suspect, suspicious; SEE CONCEPT 552

allegiance [n] *loyalty*
adherence, ardor, consecration, constancy, dedication, deference, devotion, duty, faithfulness, fealty, fidelity, homage, honor, obedience, obligation, piety; SEE CONCEPT 689

allegorical [adj] *symbolic*
emblematic, figurative, illustrative, metaphorical, parabolic, symbolizing, typifying; SEE CONCEPT 582

allegory [n] *indirect representation, storytelling*
apologue, emblem, fable, figuration, moral, myth, parable, story, symbol, symbolism, symbolization, tale, typification; SEE CONCEPT 282

alleviate [v] *relieve; lessen*
allay, assuage, ease, lighten, mitigate, mollify, pacify, pour oil on*, soft-pedal*, take the bite out*, take the edge off*, take the sting out*; SEE CONCEPTS 7,22,110,236,247

alley [n] *narrow passage*
alleyway, back street, lane, passageway, path, pathway, walk; SEE CONCEPT 501

alliance [n] *friendly association, agreement*
accord, affiliation, affinity, betrothal, bond, coalition, coherence, collaboration, collusion, combination, communion, compact, concord, concurrence, confederacy, confederation, congruity, conjunction, connection, consanguinity, cooperation, engagement, entente, federation, fraternization, friendship, interrelation, kinship, league, marriage, matrimony, membership, mutuality, pact, participation, partnership, relation, support, tie, treaty, union; SEE CONCEPTS 301,423,684

allied [adj] *friendly; united*
affiliated, agnate, akin, amalgamated, associated, bound, cognate, combined, confederate, connate, connected, incident, in league, joined, joint, kindred, linked, married, related, unified, wed; SEE CONCEPTS 555,563

allocate [v] *assign; divide among*
admeasure, allot, apportion, appropriate, budget, cut, designate, dish out*, divvy*, earmark, give,

mete, set aside, share, slice; SEE CONCEPTS 41,98,108,129

allot [v] *assign; give portion*
admeasure, allocate, appoint, apportion, appropriate, assign, budget, cut, cut the pie*, designate, distribute, divvy*, dole, earmark, mete, set aside, share, shell out*, slice, split up; SEE CONCEPTS 41,108

allotment [n] *portion assigned or given*
allocation, allowance, apportionment, appropriation, bite, chunk, cut, cut of pie*, end, grant, lot, measure, part, piece, piece of the action*, quota, rake off*, ration, share, slice, split, stint*; SEE CONCEPT 835

all-out [adj] *complete*
absolute, determined, entire, exhaustive, full, full-blown, full-fledged, full-scale, maximum, optimum, resolute, supreme, thorough, total, undivided, unlimited, utmost, utter; SEE CONCEPTS 531,772

allow [v1] *admit; acknowledge*
acquiesce, avow, concede, confess, grant, let on, own; SEE CONCEPTS 60,82

allow [v2] *permit an action*
accord, accredit, admit, approve, authorize, bear, be big*, be game for*, brook, certify, commission, consent, empower, endorse, endure, favor, free up*, give a blank check*, give carte blanche, give leave, give permission, give the go-ahead, give the green light*, go along with, grant permission, hear of, hold with, indulge, let, license, live with*, oblige, okay, pass, pass on, put up with, recognize, release, sanction, sit still for*, stand, suffer, support, take kindly to, tolerate, warrant; SEE CONCEPTS 83,99

allow [v3] *set aside*
admeasure, allocate, allot, apportion, assign, deduct, give, grant, lot, mete, provide, remit, spare; SEE CONCEPTS 41,108

allowance [n1] *amount of money or other supply*
aid, alimony, allocation, allotment, annuity, apportionment, bequest, bite*, bounty, commission, contribution, cut, endowment, fee, fellowship, gift, grant, honorarium, inheritance, interest, legacy, lot, measure, part, pay, pension, piece, portion, prize, quantity, quota, ration, recompense, remittance, salary, scholarship, share, slice, stint, stipend, subsidy, taste, wage; SEE CONCEPTS 337,340

allowance [n2] *discount; concession*
accommodation, adaptation, adjustment, admission, advantage, cut, deduction, rebate, reduction, sanction, sufferance, toleration; SEE CONCEPT 775

alloy [n] *mixture, usually of two metals*
admixture, adulterant, adulteration, amalgam, amalgamation, blend, combination, composite, compound, debasement, denaturant, fusion, hybrid, intermixture, reduction; SEE CONCEPTS 260,476

alloy [v1] *mix metals*
admix, amalgamate, blend, combine, compound, fuse, intermix, mix; SEE CONCEPTS 109,113

alloy [v2] *adulterate*
debase, denature, devalue, diminish, impair, reduce; SEE CONCEPT 240

all right [adj1] *satisfactory*
acceptable, adequate, appropriate, average, decent, fair, fit, fitting, good, hunky-dory*, okay, okey-dokey*, passable, proper, satisfying, stan-

dard, sufficient, swell*, tolerable, unexceptional, unobjectionable; SEE CONCEPTS 547,558

all right [adj2] *in good condition or health*
hale, healthy, safe, sound, unharmed, unhurt, unimpaired, well, whole; SEE CONCEPT 572

all right [adj3] *correct; excellent*
accurate, exact, good, great, precise, right; SEE CONCEPTS 557,574

all right [adv1] *satisfactorily*
acceptably, adequately, okay, passably, tolerably, unobjectionably, well enough; SEE CONCEPTS 547,558

all right [adv2] *yes*
agreed, certainly, definitely, of course, okay, positively, surely, very well, without a doubt; SEE CONCEPT 572

all-time [adj] *unsurpassed and permanent*
best, champion, enduring, everlasting, perpetual; SEE CONCEPTS 574,798

allude [v] *hint at*
advert, bring up, imply, insinuate, intimate, point, refer, suggest; SEE CONCEPTS 60,66

allure [n] *appeal*
attraction, bedroom eyes*, charisma, charm, come-hither look*, come-on*, enchantment, enticement, glamor, inveiglement, lure, magnetism, seductiveness, temptation, the jazz*; SEE CONCEPTS 673,720

allure [v] *entice*
attract, bait, beguile, bewitch, cajole, captivate, charm, coax, come on*, decoy, draw, enchant, entrap, fascinate, hook*, inveigle, lead on, lure, magnetize, persuade, pull, seduce, suck in*, sweep off feet*, tempt, turn on*, wile, win over; SEE CONCEPTS 7,22

allusion [n] *indirect reference; hint*
casual remark, charge, citation, connotation, denotation, figure of speech, implication, imputation, incidental mention, indication, inference, innuendo, insinuation, intimation, mention, play on words, quotation, remark, statement, suggestion; SEE CONCEPTS 60,274

ally [n] *something united with another, especially by treaty*
accessory, accomplice, associate, coadjutor, collaborator, colleague, confederate, co-worker, friend, helper, partner; SEE CONCEPTS 299, 322,354,359

alma mater [n] *school from which one has graduated*
academy, college, institution, old school, place of graduation, place of matriculation, university; SEE CONCEPTS 288,289

almanac [n] *document containing information for a year*
annual, calendar, chronicle, ephemeris, journal, record, register, registry, yearbook; SEE CONCEPTS 280,801,809,823

almighty [adj1] *having complete power, control*
absolute, all-powerful, invincible, mighty, omnipotent, puissant, supreme, unlimited; SEE CONCEPT 540

almighty [adj2] *godlike*
all-knowing, all-seeing, boundless, celestial, deathless, deific, divine, enduring, eternal, everlasting, godly, heavenly, illimitable, immortal, infinite, omnipotent, omnipresent, omniscient, pervading; SEE CONCEPT 539

almighty [adj3] *severe*
awful, desperate, enormous, excessive, extreme,

great, intense, loud, terrible; SEE CONCEPT 569

almost [adv] *nearly, very nearly*
about, about to, all but, approximately, around, as good as, bordering on, close to, close upon, essentially, for all practical purposes, for the greatest part, in effect, in the neighborhood of, in the vicinity of, just about, most, much, near to, nigh, not far from, not quite, on the brink of, on the edge of, on the point of, on the verge of, practically, pretty near, relatively, roughly, substantially, virtually, well-nigh, within sight of; SEE CONCEPTS 531,586,799

alone [adj1] *separate; apart*
abandoned, batching it*, by itself/oneself, companionless, deserted, desolate, detached, forlorn, forsaken, friendless, hermit, individual, in solitary*, isolated, lone, lonely, lonesome, me and my shadow*, me myself and I*, onliest*, only, on one's own, shag*, single, sole, solitary, solo, stag, traveling light*, unaccompanied, unaided, unassisted, unattached, unattended, unescorted, unmarried, widowed; SEE CONCEPTS 577,583

alone [adj2] *to the exclusion of; unique*
incomparable, matchless, peerless, singly, singular, solely, unequalled, unique, unmatched, unparalleled, unrivaled, unsurpassed; SEE CONCEPTS 556,653

along [adv1] *ahead*
forth, forward, on, onward; SEE CONCEPT 581

along [adv2] *together with*
accompanying, additionally, also, as companion, as well, at same time, besides, coupled with, furthermore, in addition to, likewise, moreover, side by side, simultaneously, too, with; SEE CONCEPT 577

along [adv3] *near*
adjacent, at, by; SEE CONCEPT 586

alongside [prep] *close, near side of*
along the side of, apace with, at the side of, beside, by, by the side of, close at hand, close by, equal with, in company with, next to, parallel to, side by side; SEE CONCEPT 586

aloof [adj] *remote*
above, apart, casual, chilly, cold, cold fish*, cool, detached, distant, forbidding, hard-boiled*, hardhearted, haughty, incurious, indifferent, laid back*, loner*, lone wolf*, offish*, on ice*, putting on airs*, reserved, secluded, solitary, standoffish*, stuck up*, supercilious, thick-skinned*, unapproachable, unconcerned, unfriendly, uninterested, unresponsive, unsociable, unsympathetic, uppity*, withdrawn; SEE CONCEPTS 401,542

aloud [adv] *in a spoken voice, usually not softly*
audibly, clearly, distinctly, intelligibly, loudly, lustily, noisily, out loud, plainly, vociferously; SEE CONCEPT 594

alphabet [n] *letters of a writing system*
ABCs, characters, elements, fundamentals, graphic representation, hieroglyphs, ideograph, morphemes, phonemes, pictograph, rune, signs, syllabary, symbols; SEE CONCEPT 276

alphabetical [adj] *in ascending order of a writing system*
A to Z, consecutive, graded, indexed, logical, ordered, progressive; SEE CONCEPT 585

alphabetize [v] *place in order of a writing system*
index, order, systematize; SEE CONCEPT 84

alpine [adj] *mountaintop; high altitude*
aerial, elevated, high, high-reaching, in the

clouds, lofty, montane, mountainous, rangy, snowcapped, soaring, towering; SEE CONCEPTS 779,836

already [adv] before expected time
as of now, at present, before, before now, but now, by now, by that time, by then, by the time mentioned, by this time, earlier, even now, formerly, heretofore, in the past, just now, now, once, previously, then, up to now; SEE CONCEPT 799

also [adv] in addition to
additionally, again, along, along with, and, as well as, besides, conjointly, further, furthermore, including, in conjunction with, in like manner, likewise, more, moreover, more than that, on top of, over and above, plus, still, to boot*, together with, too, withal; SEE CONCEPT 577

altar [n] church table, pedestal
chantry, font, reredos, retable, shrine, tabernacle; SEE CONCEPT 443

alter [v1] change
adapt, adjust, amend, change, convert, cook, correct mid-course*, develop, dial back*, diversify, doctor, fine tune*, make different, metamorphose, modify, mutate, phony up*, recalibrate, recast, reconstruct, refashion, reform, remodel, renovate, reshape, revamp, revise, shift, transform, transmute, turn, vary; SEE CONCEPT 232

alter [v2] sterilize animal
caponize, castrate, change, desexualize, emasculate, fix, geld, mutilate, neuter, spay, unsex; SEE CONCEPTS 310,375

alteration [n] change
about-face, accommodation, adaptation, adjustment, amendment, conversion, correction, difference, diversification, exchange, fixing, flip-flop*, metamorphosis, mid-course correction*, modification, mutation, reformation, remodeling, reshaping, revision, shift, switch, switch-over*, transformation, transmutation, turn, variance, variation; SEE CONCEPT 701

altercation [n] fight, often verbal
argument, beef*, bickering, blowup*, bone of contention*, brawl*, brush*, combat, contest, controversy, dispute, embroilment, flap*, fracas*, fuss, go*, hassle, quarrel, row, rumble*, run-in*, set-to*, squabbling, tiff*, words*, wrangle; SEE CONCEPTS 46,106

altered [adj] changed
adapted, adjusted, amended, converted, cooked, corrected, diversified, doctored, fitted, fixed, modified, qualified, redone, refitted, reformed, remade, remodeled, renovated, reshaped, retailored, revised, spiked, transformed, turned, updated; SEE CONCEPT 564

alter ego [n] other side to personality
doppelganger, evil twin*, second self; SEE CONCEPTS 410,423

alternate [n] substitute
backup, double, equivalent, fill-in, proxy, replacement, stand-in, sub*, surrogate; SEE CONCEPT 667

alternate [adj1] every other
alternating, every second, intermittent, periodic, recurrent, recurring, rotating; SEE CONCEPT 553

alternate [adj2] substitute
alternative, another, backup, different, interchanging, makeshift, second, surrogate, temporary; SEE CONCEPT 566

alternate [v] take turns, change back and forth
act reciprocally, alter, blow hot and cold*, change, come and go, exchange, fill in for, fluctuate, follow, follow in turn, interchange, intersperse, oscillate, relieve, rotate, seesaw, shift, shilly-shally*, substitute, sway, vacillate, vary, waver, yo-yo*; SEE CONCEPTS 13,104,232,701

alternative [n] possible choice
back-up, druthers*, opportunity, option, other, other fish in sea*, other fish to fry*, pick, preference, recourse, redundancy, selection, sub*, substitute, take it or leave it*; SEE CONCEPT 529

alternative [adj] other, alternate
another, back-up, different, flipside, other side, second, substitute, surrogate; SEE CONCEPT 564

although [conj] even though
admitting, albeit, despite, despite the fact, even if, even supposing, granting, granting all this, in spite of, much as, notwithstanding, still, supposing, though, when, whereas, while; SEE CONCEPT 544

altitude [n] height in the sky
apex, distance, elevation, eminence, loftiness, peak, summit; SEE CONCEPTS 739,752,791

altogether [adv1] as a whole
all, all in all, all things considered, all told, bodily, by and large, collectively, conjointly, en masse, everything considered, everything included, for the most part, generally, in all, in sum, in toto, on the whole, taken together; SEE CONCEPT 771

altogether [adv2] completely
absolutely, fully, perfectly, quite, thoroughly, totally, utterly, well, wholly; SEE CONCEPT 531

altruistic [adj] unselfish
all heart*, benevolent, big*, big-hearted*, bleeding heart*, charitable, considerate, generous, good, good scout, human, humane, humanitarian, kind, magnanimous, openhanded, philanthropic, Robin Hood*, self-sacrificing; SEE CONCEPT 404

alumnus/alumna [n] graduate
alum, old grad*, postgraduate; SEE CONCEPT 350

always [adv] forever; continually
consistently, constantly, eternally, ever, everlastingly, evermore, forevermore, for keeps, in perpetuum, invariably, perpetually, regularly, repeatedly, till blue in the face*, till cows come home*, till hell freezes over*, unceasingly, without exception; SEE CONCEPTS 551,798

amalgam [n] mixture
admixture, alloy, amalgamation, blend, combination, combo*, composite, compound, fusion, mishmash*, soup; SEE CONCEPT 432

amalgamate [v] blend
admix, alloy, ally, coalesce, combine, come together, compound, consolidate, fuse, hook up with*, incorporate, integrate, interface, intermix, join together, meld, merge, mingle, network, pool, team up*, tie in, tie up*, unite; SEE CONCEPT 113

amass [v] gather, accumulate
aggregate, assemble, clean up*, collect, compile, corral*, garner, heap*, hoard, lay up*, make a killing*, make a pile*, pile, round up*, scare up*, stockpile, store; SEE CONCEPTS 109,120

amateur [n] casual participant
abecedarian, apprentice, aspirant, beginner, bush leaguer*, dabbler, dilettante, greenhorn, ham*, hopeful, layperson, learner, neophyte, nonprofessional, novice, probationer, putterer, recruit, Sunday driver*, tenderfoot*, tyro; SEE CONCEPT 366

amatory [adj] *affectionate, desirous*
admiring, amorous, aphrodisiac, ardent, attracted, devoted, doting, erotic, fervent, fond, languishing, lovesick, loving, passionate, rapturous, romantic, sentimental, tender, wooing, yearning; SEE CONCEPTS 372,403

amaze [v] *surprise*
affect, alarm, astonish, astound, bewilder, blow away*, blow one's mind*, bowl over*, daze, dumbfound, electrify, flabbergast*, impress, move, perplex, put one away*, shock, stagger, startle, strike, stun, stupefy, touch*; SEE CONCEPT 42

amazement [n] *state of surprise*
admiration, astonishment, awe, bewilderment, confoundment, confusion, marvel, one for the books*, perplexity, shock, something else*, stopper*, stunner*, stupefaction, wonder, wonderment; SEE CONCEPTS 230,410

ambassador [n] *representative to a foreign country*
agent, consul, deputy, diplomat, emissary, envoy, minister, plenipotentiary; SEE CONCEPT 354

amber [n/adj] *gold-colored*
brown, golden, tan, yellowish; SEE CONCEPT 618

ambience [n] *environment*
ambient, atmosphere, climate, medium, surroundings; SEE CONCEPT 673

ambiguity [n] *uncertainty of meaning*
double-entendre, double meaning, doubt, doubtfulness, dubiety, dubiousness, enigma, equivocacy, equivocality, equivocation, incertitude, inconclusiveness, indefiniteness, indeterminateness, obscurity, puzzle, tergiversation, uncertainty, unclearness, vagueness; SEE CONCEPTS 638,682

ambiguous [adj] *having more than one meaning*
clear as dishwater*, cryptic, doubtful, dubious, enigmatic, enigmatical, equivocal, inconclusive, indefinite, indeterminate, inexplicit, muddy, obscure, opaque, puzzling, questionable, tenebrous, uncertain, unclear, unintelligible, vague; SEE CONCEPTS 267,535

ambition [n1] *strong desire for success*
appetite, ardor, aspiration, avidity, craving, desire, drive, eagerness, earnestness, emulation, energy, enterprise, enthusiasm, fire in belly*, get up and go*, hankering*, hope, hunger, initiative, itch*, keenness, longing, love, lust, moxie*, passion, pretension, push, right stuff*, spirit, striving, thirst, vigor, yearning, zeal; SEE CONCEPT 20

ambition [n2] *something desired*
aim, aspiration, desire, dream, end, enterprise, goal, hope, intent, mark, objective, purpose, target, wish; SEE CONCEPT 659

ambitious [adj1] *desiring success*
aggressive, anxious, ardent, aspiring, avid, ball of fire*, bent upon, climbing, come on, come on strong, designing, desirous, determined, driving, eager, eager beaver*, earnest, energetic, enterprising, enthusiastic, fireball*, get up and go*, goal-oriented, go-getter*, hard ball*, high-reaching, hopeful, hungry, industrious, inspired, intent, longing, power-loving, purposeful, pushing, pushy*, resourceful, self-starting, sharp, soaring, striving, thirsty, vaulting, zealous; SEE CONCEPTS 326,542

ambitious [adj2] *requiring great effort, ability*
arduous, bold, challenging, demanding, difficult, elaborate, energetic, exacting, formidable, gran-

diose, hard, impressive, industrious, lofty, pretentious, severe, strenuous, visionary; SEE CONCEPT 538

ambivalent [adj] *conflicting*
clashing, contradictory, debatable, doubtful, equivocal, fluctuating, hesitant, inconclusive, irresolute, mixed, opposed, uncertain, undecided, unresolved, unsure, vacillating, warring, wavering; SEE CONCEPTS 534,564

amble [v] *walk casually*
ankle*, boogie*, dawdle, drift, gander*, hoof it*, loiter, meander, mosey*, percolate*, ramble, sashay*, saunter, stroll, toddle*, wander; SEE CONCEPT 151

ambulance [n] *emergency vehicle*
EMS, hospital wagon, rescue, transport; SEE CONCEPT 505

ambulatory [adj] *changing position; able to move under own power*
ambulant, itinerant, nomadic, perambulant, perambulatory, peripatetic, roving, vagabond, vagrant; SEE CONCEPT 584

ambush [n] *lying in wait; concealed position*
ambuscade, ambushment, camouflage, concealment, deception, hiding, hiding place, lurking, pitfall, shelter, trap, trick*, waiting, waylaying; SEE CONCEPTS 86,188

ambush [v] *lie in wait; attack*
ambuscade, assail, assault, box in*, bushwhack*, decoy, dry gulch*, ensnare, entrap, hem in*, hide, hook*, jap*, jump, lay for, lurk, net, set trap, surprise, surround, trap, wait, waylay; SEE CONCEPTS 86,188

ameliorate [v] *make, become better*
alleviate, amend, help, improve, lighten, meliorate, mitigate, relieve, step up, upgrade; SEE CONCEPT 244

amenable [adj1] *willing, cooperative*
acquiescent, agreeable, biddable, docile, influenceable, manageable, obedient, open, persuadable, pliable, responsive, susceptible, tractable; SEE CONCEPT 404

amenable [adj2] *able to be judged; responsible*
accountable, answerable, chargeable, liable, subject; SEE CONCEPT 402

amend [v] *improve, correct*
alter, ameliorate, better, change, elevate, enhance, fix, help, lift, make up for, mend, modify, pay one's dues*, raise, rectify, reform, remedy, repair, revise, right, square*; SEE CONCEPTS 126,244

amendment [n1] *correction, improvement*
alteration, amelioration, betterment, change, correction, enhancement, improvement, mending, modification, rectification, reform, reformation, remedy, repair, revision; SEE CONCEPT 700

amendment [n2] *addition to a document*
act, addendum, adjunct, alteration, attachment, bill, clarification, clause, codicil, measure, modification, motion, revision, rider, suggestion, supplement; SEE CONCEPT 270

amends [n] *compensation*
apology, atonement, expiation, indemnification, indemnity, quittance, recompense, redress, reparation, reprisal, requital, restitution, restoration, satisfaction; SEE CONCEPTS 67,104,384

amenity [n1] *pleasant thing*
advantage, betterment, comfort, convenience, enhancement, enrichment, excellence, extravagance, facility, frill, improvement, luxury, merit,

quality, service, superfluity, virtue; SEE CONCEPT
712

amenity [n2] *pleasing, agreeable behavior*
affability, agreeableness, amiability, attention, attractiveness, charity, charm, complaisance, cordiality, courtesy, delightfulness, enjoyableness,
etiquette, gallantry, geniality, gentility, gratefulness, kindness, mildness, pleasantness, politeness, refinement, suavity, sweetness; SEE
CONCEPT 633

amiable [adj] *friendly, agreeable*
affable, amicable, attractive, benign, breezy,
buddy-buddy*, charming, cheerful, clubby*,
complaisant, cool*, copacetic*, cordial, cozy, delightful, downright neighborly*, easy, engaging,
friendly, genial, good-humored, good-natured,
gracious, home cooking*, kind, kindly, lenient,
lovable, mellow, mild, obliging, palsy-walsy*,
pleasant, pleasing, princely*, pussycat*, responsive, right, righteous, sociable, sweet-tempered,
swell*, tight*, warm, warmhearted, winning; SEE
CONCEPT 401

amicable [adj] *friendly, especially regarding an
agreement*
accordant, agreeing, amiable, civil, clubby*, concordant, cordial, courteous, cozy, empathic,
good-humored, harmonious, kind, kindly, like-
minded, mellow, neighborly, pacific, peaceable,
peaceful, polite, regular, right nice*, sociable,
square shooting*, sympathetic, understanding;
SEE CONCEPTS 529,542

amid/amidst [prep] *in middle of; among*
amongst, between, during, in the midst of, in the
thick of, mid, over, surrounded by, throughout;
SEE CONCEPTS 586,820

amiss [adj] *wrong; defective*
awry, bad, confused, crooked, erring, erroneous,
fallacious, false, faulty, flawed, foul, glitched
up*, haywire, imperfect, improper, inaccurate, inappropriate, incorrect, mistaken, out of order,
sick, unfair, unlawful, unsuitable, untoward; SEE
CONCEPT 570

amiss [adv] *wrongly; defectively*
afield, afoul, badly, erringly, erroneously, faultily, improperly, inappropriately, incorrectly, mistakenly, out of turn, unfavorably, unsuitably; SEE
CONCEPT 570

amity [n] *friendship*
amicableness, benevolence, comity, concord, cordiality, friendliness, good vibrations*, goodwill,
harmony, hitting it off*, kindliness, neighborliness, same wavelength*, simpatico*, togetherness*; SEE CONCEPT 388

ammonia [n] *pungent gas, liquid*
alkali, salts, spirits, vapor; SEE CONCEPT 472

ammunition [n] *projectiles for weaponry*
ammo*, armament, ball, bomb, buckshot, bullet,
cannonball, cartridge, charge, chemical, confet-
ti*, explosive, fuse, grenade, gunpowder, iron rations*, materiel, missile, munition, napalm,
powder, rocket, round, shell, shot, shrapnel, torpedo; SEE CONCEPTS 498,500

amnesty [n] *pardon, often by government*
absolution, condonation, dispensation, forgiveness, immunity, reprieve; SEE CONCEPTS 298,300

among [prep1] *in the middle of; between*
amid, amidst, betwixt, encompassed by, in dispersion through, in the midst of, in the thick of,
mid, surrounded by, with; SEE CONCEPT 586

among [prep2] *in a group*
by all of, by the whole of, in association with, in
connection with, in the class of, in the company
of, mutually, out of, together with, with, with one
another; SEE CONCEPT 785

amorous [adj] *loving, affectionate*
amative, amatory, aphrodisiac, ardent, attached,
boy crazy*, doting, enamored, erotic, fond, girl
crazy*, have a crush on*, horny*, hot, hot and
heavy*, impassioned, infatuated, in love,
lovesick, lovey dovey*, lustful, passionate, romantic, sexy, sweet for*, sweet on*, tender,
turned on*; SEE CONCEPTS 372,403,555

amorphous [adj] *without definite shape, character*
baggy, blobby, characterless, formless, inchoate,
indeterminate, irregular, nebulous, nondescript,
shapeless, unformed, unshaped, unstructured,
vague; SEE CONCEPTS 404,490

amount [n1] *quantity*
aplenty, bags*, bulk, bundle, chunk, expanse, extent, flock, gob*, heap, hunk, jillion*, load, lot,
magnitude, mass, measure, mess*, mint*, mucho*, number, oodles*, pack, passle, peck, pile,
scads*, score, slat*, slew*, supply, ton*, volume,
whopper*; SEE CONCEPTS 787,837

amount [n2] *total*
addition, aggregate, all, bad news*, body, budget, cost, damage*, entirety, expense, extent, list,
lot, net, outlay, output, price tag*, product, quantum, score, set-back*, sum, tab*, tidy sum*,
whole; SEE CONCEPTS 329,784,787

amount [n3] *whole effect*
body, burden, core, full value, import, matter,
purport, result, sense, significance, substance,
thrust, upshot, value; SEE CONCEPT 676

amount [v] *equal, add up to*
aggregate, approach, approximate, become, be
equivalent to, be tantamount to, check with, come
to, correspond, develop into, effect, extend, grow,
match, mean, number, purport, reach, rival, sum,
tally, total, touch; SEE CONCEPT 667

amour [n] *romance*
affair, entanglement, liaison, love, love affair,
passion, relationship; SEE CONCEPT 32

ample [adj] *more than necessary, sufficient*
abounding, abundant, big, bounteous, bountiful,
broad, capacious, commodious, copious, enough,
expansive, extensive, full, galore, generous,
great, heavy, large, lavish, liberal, no end, plenteous, plentiful, plenty, profuse, rich, roomy, spacious, spare, substantial, unrestricted,
voluminous, wide; SEE CONCEPTS 558,781

amplification [n] *increase in size or effect*
addition, augmentation, boost, boosting, buildup,
deepening, development, elaboration, enlargement, exaggeration, expansion, expatiation, extension, fleshing out, heightening, intensification,
lengthening, magnification, padding, raising,
strengthening, stretching, supplementing, upping,
widening; SEE CONCEPTS 236,245,780

amplify [v] *increase in size or effect*
add, augment, beef up*, boost, build up, deepen,
develop, elaborate, enlarge, exaggerate, expand,
expatiate, extend, flesh out*, heighten, hike up*,
inflate, intensify, jack up*, lengthen, magnify,
pad, pyramid, raise, soup up*, strengthen, stretch,
supplement, swell, up, widen; SEE CONCEPTS
236,245

amply [adv] *fully, sufficiently*
abundantly, acceptably, adequately, appropri-

ately, bountifully, capaciously, completely, copiously, enough, extensively, fittingly, generously, greatly, lavishly, liberally, plenteously, plentifully, profusely, properly, richly, rightly, satisfactorily, substantially, suitably, thoroughly, well; SEE CONCEPTS *558,771*

amputate [v] *remove a limb*
cut away, cut off, dismember, eliminate, excise, lop, separate, sever, truncate; SEE CONCEPTS *176,211*

amuck [adv] *crazily*
berserk, destructively, ferociously, frenziedly, in a frenzy, insanely, madly, maniacally, murderously, savagely, uncontrollably, violently, wildly; SEE CONCEPT *401*

amulet [n] *charm*
fetish, lucky piece, ornament, talisman; SEE CONCEPTS *260,446*

amuse [v] *entertain; make laugh*
break one up*, charm, cheer, crack up*, delight, divert, fracture*, gladden, grab*, gratify, interest, kill*, knock dead*, make roll in the aisles*, occupy, panic*, please, put away*, regale, slay*, tickle, wow*; SEE CONCEPTS *9,292,384*

amusement [n1] *entertaining, making someone laugh*
action, ball*, beguilement, cheer, delight, diversion, enjoyment, entertainment, field day*, fun, fun and games*, gladdening, gratification, grins*, high time*, hilarity, hoopla*, laughs*, laughter, merriment, merry go round*, mirth, picnic*, play, pleasing, pleasure, regalement, whoopee*; SEE CONCEPT *292*

amusement [n2] *game, pastime*
distraction, diversion, entertainment, hobby, interest, joke, lark, play, prank, recreation, sport; SEE CONCEPT *364*

amusing [adj] *entertaining, funny*
agreeable, boffo*, camp, campy, charming, cheerful, cheering, comical, cut up*, delightful, diverting, droll, enchanting, engaging, enjoyable, entertaining, for grins*, fun, gladdening, gratifying, gut-busting*, humorous, interesting, jocular, jokey*, joshing*, laughable, lively, merry, pleasant, pleasing, priceless, screaming*, sidesplitting*, too funny for words*, witty; SEE CONCEPTS *267,548*

anachronism [n] *error in time placement*
chronological error, metachronism, misdate, misplacement, postdate, prolepsis, solecism; SEE CONCEPT *818*

analgesic [n] *pain remover*
anesthetic, anodyne, painkiller, soother; SEE CONCEPT *307*

analogous [adj] *agreeing, similar*
akin, alike, comparable, consonant, convertible, correspondent, corresponding, equivalent, homologous, interchangeable, kindred, like, parallel, related, resembling, undifferentiated, uniform; SEE CONCEPTS *487,573*

analogy [n] *agreement, similarity*
affinity, alikeness, comparison, correlation, correspondence, equivalence, homology, likeness, metaphor, parallel, relation, relationship, resemblance, semblance, simile, similitude; SEE CONCEPTS *278,670*

analysis [n1] *examination and determination*
assay, breakdown, dissection, dissolution, division, inquiry, investigation, partition, reasoning,

resolution, scrutiny, search, separation, study, subdivision, test; SEE CONCEPTS *24,103*

analysis [n2] *statement of results from examination*
estimation, evaluation, finding, interpretation, judgment, opinion, outline, reasoning, report, study, summary; SEE CONCEPTS *271,274*

analyst [n] *person who examines and determines; psychoanalyst*
accountant, couch doctor*, examiner, guru*, head shrinker*, inquisitor, investigator, number cruncher*, psychiatrist, psychotherapist, questioner, shrink*, therapist; SEE CONCEPTS *348,357*

analytic/analytical [adj] *examining and determining*
cogent, conclusive, detailed, diagnostic, discrete, dissecting, explanatory, expository, inquiring, inquisitive, interpretive, investigative, judicious, logical, organized, penetrating, perceptive, perspicuous, precise, problem-solving, questioning, ratiocinative, rational, reasonable, scientific, searching, solid, sound, studious, subtle, systematic, testing, thorough, valid, well-grounded; SEE CONCEPT *402*

analyze [v1] *examine and determine*
assay, beat a dead horse*, chew over*, confab*, consider, estimate, evaluate, figure, figure out, get down to brass tacks*, hash*, inspect, interpret, investigate, judge, kick around*, rehash, resolve, scrutinize, sort out, spell out, study, talk game*, test, think through; SEE CONCEPTS *24,37,103*

analyze [v2] *break down to components*
anatomize, break up, cut up, decompose, decompound, determine, disintegrate, dissect, dissolve, divide, electrolyze, hydrolyze, lay bare, parse, part, resolve, separate, x-ray; SEE CONCEPTS *135,310*

anarchist [n] *person who opposes the idea of government and laws*
agitator, insurgent, insurrectionist, malcontent, mutineer, nihilist, rebel, revolter, revolutionary, terrorist; SEE CONCEPTS *359,412*

anarchy [n] *lawlessness; absence of government*
chaos, confusion, disorder, disorganization, disregard, hostility, misrule, mob rule, nihilism, nongovernment, rebellion, reign of terror, revolution, riot, turmoil, unrest; SEE CONCEPTS *29,674*

anathema [n1] *something hated*
abomination, bane, bugbear, detestation, enemy, hate, pariah; SEE CONCEPT *529*

anathema [n2] *denouncement*
ban, censure, commination, condemnation, curse, damnation, denunciation, excommunication, execration, imprecation, malediction, proscription, reprehension, reprobation, reproof, taboo; SEE CONCEPT *278*

anatomy [n1] *study of animal, plant structure*
analysis, biology, cytology, diagnosis, dissection, division, embryology, etiology, examination, genetics, histology, inquiry, investigation, medicine, morphology, physiology, zoology; SEE CONCEPT *349*

anatomy [n2] *physical structure of animals, plants*
build, composition, figure, form, frame, framework, makeup, physique, shape; SEE CONCEPT *733*

ancestor [n] *predecessor in family*
antecedent, antecessor, ascendant, forebear, forefather, foregoer, foremother, forerunner, founder, precursor, primogenitor, progenitor; SEE CONCEPT *414*

ancestral [adj] *related to previous family or family trait*
affiliated, born with, congenital, consanguine, consanguineous, familial, genealogical, inborn, inbred, inherited, innate, in the family, lineal, maternal, old, past, paternal, running in the family, totemic, tribal; SEE CONCEPT *549*

ancestry [n] *family predecessors; family history*
ancestor, antecedent, antecessor, blood, breed, breeding, derivation, descent, extraction, forebear, forefather, foregoer, foremother, forerunner, genealogy, heritage, house, kindred, line, lineage, origin, parentage, pedigree, precursor, primogenitor, progenitor, race, source, stock; SEE CONCEPTS *414,648*

anchor [n] *something used to hold another thing securely*
ballast, bower, comfort, defense, fastener, foothold, grapnel, grappling iron, grip, hold, hook, kedge, mainstay, mooring, mud hook, pillar, protection, safeguard, security, staff, stay, support; SEE CONCEPTS *464,502,731*

anchor [v] *hold, be held securely*
attach, berth, catch, dock, drop, fasten, fix, imbed, make port, moor, plant, secure, stay, tie, tie up; SEE CONCEPTS *85,160,190*

ancient [adj] *old, often very old*
aged, age-old, antediluvian, antiquated, antique, archaic, back number*, been around*, bygone, creaky*, early, elderly, few miles on*, fossil*, hoary, lot of mileage*, moth-eaten*, obsolete, older, old-fashioned, old goat*, oldie*, outmoded, out-of-date, primal, primeval, primordial, relic, remote, rusty, superannuated, timeworn, venerable, worse for wear*; SEE CONCEPTS *578,797*

ancillary [adj] *extra; supplementary*
accessory, accompanying, additional, adjuvant, appurtenant, attendant, attending, coincident, collateral, concomitant, contributory, incident, satellite, secondary, subordinate, subservient, subsidary; SEE CONCEPT *835*

and [conj] *in addition to; plus*
along with, also, as a consequence, as well as, furthermore, including, moreover, together with; SEE CONCEPT *577*

anecdote [n] *interesting or amusing story*
chestnut*, episode, fairy tale*, fish story*, gag*, incident, long and short of it*, narration, narrative, old chestnut*, recital, relation, reminiscence, short story, sketch, tale, tall story*, tall tale*, yarn; SEE CONCEPT *282*

anemic [adj] *weak and pale*
bloodless, feeble, frail, infirm, pallid, sickly, wan, watery; SEE CONCEPTS *314,483,618*

anesthesia/anaesthesia [n] *induced sleep; induced absence of feeling*
analgesia, insentience, numbness, stupor, unconsciousness; SEE CONCEPTS *313,315,728*

anesthetic/anaesthetic [n] *sleep-inducing or numbing drug*
analgesic, anodyne, dope*, gas, hypnotic, inhalant, narcotic, opiate, pain-killer, shot, soporific, spinal; SEE CONCEPT *307*

anew [adj/adv] *fresh; again*
afresh, another time, come again, de novo, from scratch, from the beginning, in a different way, in a new way, lately, new, newly, once again, once more, one more time, over, over again, recently; SEE CONCEPT *820*

angel [n1] *attendant of God*
archangel, celestial being, cherub, divine messenger, God's messenger, guardian, heavenly being, holy being, seraph, spirit, spiritual being, sprite, supernatural being; SEE CONCEPTS *361,370*

angel [n2] *sweet, kind person*
beauty, darling, dear, dream, gem, ideal, jewel, paragon, saint, treasure; SEE CONCEPT *416*

angelic [adj] *sweet, kind, and usually beautiful*
adorable, archangelic, beatific, beneficent, celestial, cherubic, devout, divine, entrancing, ethereal, godly, good, heavenly, holy, humble, innocent, lovely, otherworldly, pure, radiant, rapturous, righteous, saintly, self-sacrificing, seraphic, virtuous; SEE CONCEPT *572*

anger [n] *state of being mad, annoyed*
acrimony, animosity, annoyance, antagonism, blow up*, cat fit*, chagrin, choler, conniption, dander*, disapprobation, displeasure, distemper, enmity, exasperation, fury, gall, hatred, hissy fit*, huff, ill humor, ill temper, impatience, indignation, infuriation, irascibility, ire, irritability, irritation, mad, miff, outrage, passion, peevishness, petulance, pique, rage, rankling, resentment, slow burn*, soreness, stew, storm, tantrum, temper, tiff, umbrage, vexation, violence; SEE CONCEPTS *29,410*

anger [v] *make someone mad; become mad*
acerbate, affront, aggravate, agitate, annoy, antagonize, arouse, bait, blow up*, boil*, boil over*, bristle, burn, burn up, chafe, craze*, cross, displease, egg on*, embitter, enrage, exacerbate, exasperate, excite, fret, gall, get mad, get on one's nerves*, goad, incense, inflame, infuriate, irritate, lose one's temper, madden, make sore*, miff, nettle, offend, outrage, pique, provoke, raise hell*, rankle, rant, rave, rile, ruffle, seethe, steam up*, stew, stir up*, tempt, umbrage, vex; SEE CONCEPTS *7,19*

angle [n1] *shape formed by two lines meeting at a point*
bend, corner, crook, crotch, cusp, decline, divergence, dogleg, edge, elbow, flare, flection, flexure, fork, incline, intersection, knee, nook, notch, obliquity, point, slant, turn, turning, twist, V, Y; SEE CONCEPT *436*

angle [n2] *personal approach, purpose*
aim, approach, aspect, direction, hand, intention, outlook, perspective, plan, point of view, position, side, slant, standpoint, viewpoint; SEE CONCEPTS *660,661*

angle [v] *fish*
cast, dangle a line*, drop a line*; SEE CONCEPT *363*

angle for [v] *attempt to get*
aim for, be after, cast about for, connive, conspire, contrive, fish for, hint, hunt, invite, look for, maneuver, plan, plot, scheme, seek, solicit, strive, try for; SEE CONCEPTS *20,87*

angry [adj] *being mad, often extremely mad*
affronted, annoyed, antagonized, bitter, chafed, choleric, convulsed, cross, displeased, enraged, exacerbated, exasperated, ferocious, fierce, fiery, fuming, furious, galled, hateful, heated, hot, huffy, ill-tempered, impassioned, incensed, indignant, inflamed, infuriated, irascible, irate, ireful, irritable, irritated, maddened, nettled, offended, outraged, piqued, provoked, raging? resentful, riled, sore, splenetic, storming, sulky, sullen, tu-

multous/tumultuous, turbulent, uptight, vexed, wrathful; SEE CONCEPT *403*

anguish [n] *severe upset or pain*
affliction, agony, distress, dole, dolor, grief, heartache, heartbreak, hurting, misery, pang, rue, sorrow, suffering, throe, torment, torture, woe, wretchedness; SEE CONCEPT *410*

angular [adj1] *bent*
akimbo, bifurcate, cornered, crooked, crossing, crotched, divaricate, forked, intersecting, jagged, oblique, sharp-cornered, skewed, slanted, staggered, V-shaped, Y-shaped, zigzag; SEE CONCEPT *486*

angular [adj2] *thin, especially referring to people*
awkward, bony, gangling, gaunt, lank, lanky, lean, rangy, rawboned, scrawny, sharp, skinny, spare; SEE CONCEPT *773*

animal [n] *animate being; mammal*
beast, being, brute, bum*, creature, critter, invertebrate, living thing, mutt*, pet, stray, varmint*, vertebrate, wild thing; SEE CONCEPT *394*

animal [adj] *beastlike; carnal*
beastly, bestial, bodily, brute, brutish, corporeal, earthly, earthy, feral, fleshy, mammalian, muscular, natural, physical, sensual, untamed, wild, zoological; SEE CONCEPT *406*

animate [adj1] *alive*
breathing, live, living, mortal, moving, viable, vital, zoetic; SEE CONCEPT *539*

animate [adj2] *lively*
activated, active, alert, animated, dynamic, energized, gay, happy, spirited, vivacious; SEE CONCEPT *401*

animate [v] *bring to life*
activate, arouse, cheer, embolden, encourage, energize, enliven, exalt, excite, fire, gladden, hearten, impel, incite, inform, inspire, inspirit, instigate, invigorate, kindle, liven, make alive, move, quicken, revive, revivify, rouse, spark, spur, stimulate, stir, urge, vitalize, vivify; SEE CONCEPTS *231,241*

animated [adj] *lively*
activated, active, alert, animate, ardent, brisk, buoyant, dynamic, ebullient, elated, energetic, energized, enthusiastic, excited, fervent, gay, happy, passionate, peppy, quick, snappy, spirited, sprightly, vibrant, vigorous, vital, vitalized, vivacious, vivid, zealous, zestful, zingy, zippy; SEE CONCEPT *401*

animation [n] *liveliness; activity*
action, ardor, bounce, brio, briskness, buoyancy, dash, dynamism, ebullience, élan, elation, energy, enthusiasm, esprit, excitement, exhilaration, fervor, gaiety, high spirits, life, oomph*, passion, pep*, sparkle, spirit, sprightliness, verve, vibrancy, vigor, vim, vitality, vivacity, zap*, zeal, zest, zing*, zip*; SEE CONCEPT *657*

animosity [n] *extreme dislike, hatred*
acrimony, animus, antagonism, antipathy, bad blood, bitterness, displeasure, enmity, hate, hostility, ill will, malevolence, malice, malignity, rancor, resentment, virulence; SEE CONCEPT *29*

ankle [n] *joint between leg and foot*
anklebone, astragalus, bone, talus, tarsus; SEE CONCEPTS *392,418*

annal(s) [n] *history, records*
account, archive, chronicle, journal, memorial, record, register; SEE CONCEPTS *271,281*

annex [n] *something added; extension*
addendum, addition, adjunct, affix, appendix,

arm, attachment, ell, subsidiary, supplement, wing; SEE CONCEPTS *440,441,484*

annex [v] *join or add*
adjoin, affix, append, appropriate, associate, attach, connect, fasten, hitch on*, hitch up*, hook on*, hook up*, link, slap on*, subjoin, tack on*, tag, tag on*, take on, take over, unite; SEE CONCEPTS *85,113,160*

annexation [n] *adding, joining*
addition, annexing, appropriation, attachment, grab, incorporation, increase, increment, merger, takeover; SEE CONCEPTS *113,324*

annihilate [v] *destroy completely*
abate, abolish, abrogate, annul, blot out*, crush*, decimate, demolish, do in*, eradicate, erase, expunge, exterminate, extinguish, extirpate, finish off, invalidate, liquidate, massacre, murder, negate, nullify, obliterate, quash, quell, raze, root out*, rub out*, ruin, slaughter, take out*, undo, vitiate, wipe out*, wrack*, wreck; SEE CONCEPT *252*

anniversary [n] *yearly observance, celebration*
ceremony, commemoration, feast day, festival, holiday, jubilee, recurrence, red-letter day; SEE CONCEPTS *800,801,815,823*

annotate [v] *write explanatory notes*
comment, commentate, construe, define, elucidate, explain, expound, footnote, gloss, illustrate, interpret, note, remark; SEE CONCEPTS *51,57,79*

annotation [n] *explanatory note*
comment, commentary, definition, elucidation, exegesis, explanation, explication, footnote, gloss, glossary, illustration, interpretation, note, observation; SEE CONCEPTS *274,283*

announce [v1] *make a proclamation*
advertise, annunciate, blast, blazon, broadcast, call, communicate, declare, disclose, disseminate, divulge, drum*, give out, impart, intimate, issue, make known, make public, pass the word*, proclaim, promulgate, propound, publicize, publish, release, report, reveal, run off at mouth*, sound off*, spread around*, state, tell, trumpet; SEE CONCEPT *49*

announce [v2] *declare arrival*
augur, forebode, forecast, forerun, foreshow, foretell, harbinger, herald, indicate, portend, predict, presage, signal, signify; SEE CONCEPTS *60,70*

announcement [n] *proclamation, declaration*
advertisement, advice, briefing, broadcast, broadcasting, bulletin, communication, communiqué, disclosure, dissemination, divulgence, edict, exposing, exposition, expression, intimation, message, narration, news, notice, notification, prediction, promulgation, publication, publishing, recitation, release, report, reporting, revelation, statement; SEE CONCEPTS *49,274*

announcer [n] *media commentator*
anchorperson, broadcaster, communicator, deejay, disc jockey, DJ, leader of ceremonies, newscaster, reporter, rip and reader*, spieler*, talker, telecaster, veejay*, VJ; SEE CONCEPT *348*

annoy [v] *irritate, upset*
abrade, agitate, ask for it*, badger, be at*, bedevil, beleaguer, be on the back of*, bore, bother, break, bug, burn up, chafe, displease, distress, disturb, egg on*, exasperate, fire up*, gall, get, gnaw, harass, harry, heat up*, henpeck, hit where one lives*, irk, madden, make waves*, miff, nag, needle, nettle, nudge, peeve, perturb, pester,

plague, provoke, push button*, ride, rile, ruffle, tease, tick off*, T-off*, trouble, turn off*, vex, work on*, worry; SEE CONCEPTS 7,19

annual [n] *book produced once a year*
annuary, report, summary, yearbook; SEE CONCEPT 271

annual [adj1] *occurring, done yearly*
anniversary, each year, every year, once a year, year end; SEE CONCEPTS 541,823

annual [adj2] *lasting for a year*
a year's worth, yearlong; SEE CONCEPT 798

annually [adv] *occurring, done yearly*
by the year, each year, every year, per annum, per annum, year after year; SEE CONCEPTS 541,823

annul [v] *void an agreement*
abate, abolish, abrogate, annihilate, blot out, call off, cancel, countermand, declare, delete, discharge, dissolve, efface, erase, expunge, get off the hook*, invalidate, kill, negate, neutralize, nix, nullify, obliterate, quash, recall, render null and void, repeal, rescind, retract, reverse, revoke, scrub*, undo, vacate, vitiate, wipe out*; SEE CONCEPTS 252,297,317

annulment [n] *voiding an agreement*
abatement, abolition, abrogation, annihilation, breakup, cancellation, countermanding, dedomiciling, deletion, discharge, dissolution, erasing, going phfft*, invalidation, negation, neutralization, nullification, obliteration, recall, repeal, rescinding, rescindment, rescission, retraction, reversal, revocation, split*, split up*, undoing*, vitiation, voiding; SEE CONCEPTS 297,317,691

anoint [v] *bless, usually with oil or water*
bless, consecrate, daub, embrocate, grease, hallow, rub, sanctify, smear; SEE CONCEPT 367

anomalous [adj] *deviating from normal, usual*
aberrant, abnormal, atypical, bizarre, divergent, eccentric, exceptional, foreign, heteroclite, incongruous, inconsistent, irregular, odd, peculiar, preternatural, prodigious, rare, strange, unnatural, unorthodox, unrepresentative, untypical, unusual; SEE CONCEPT 547

anomaly [n] *deviation from normal, usual*
aberration, abnormality, departure, deviation, eccentricity, exception, incongruity, inconsistency, irregularity, oddity, peculiarity, rarity, unconformity, unorthodoxy; SEE CONCEPT 647

anonymous [adj] *unknown, usually by choice*
bearding*, incognito, innominate, Jane/John Doe*, nameless, pseudo, pseudonymous, secret, so and so*, such and such*, unacknowledged, unattested, unavowed, unclaimed, uncredited, undesignated, undisclosed, unidentified, unnamed, unsigned, unspecified, whatchamacallit*, what's his/her name*, whatsis*, X*, you know who*; SEE CONCEPT 683

another [n] *other person*
addition, a different person, one more, someone else, something else; SEE CONCEPT 423

another [prep/det] *additional, different*
added, a distinct, a further, a separate, else, farther, fresh, further, more, new, one more, other, some other, that; SEE CONCEPT 564

answer [n] *reply; reaction*
acknowledgment, antiphon, backcap*, back talk, band-aid*, close, comeback, comment, counter*, counterclaim, crack, defense, disclosure, echo, elucidation, explanation, feedback, guff*, interpretation, justification, key, lip*, observation,

parting shot*, pay dirt*, plea, quick fix*, rebuttal, refutation, rejoinder, remark, repartee, report, resolution, response, result, retort, return, riposte, sign, solution, statement, thank-you note*, the ticket*, topper*, vindication, wisecrack; SEE CONCEPTS 274,278

answer [v1] *reply, react*
acknowledge, answer back, argue, back at you*, back talk, be in touch*, claim, comeback, contest, counterclaim, defend, deny, disprove, dispute, echo, explain, feedback, field the question*, get back at*, get back to*, give a snappy comeback*, parry, plead, rebut, refute, rejoin, remark, resolve, respond, retaliate, retort, return, sass*, say, settle, shoot back*, solve, squelch, talk back, top*; SEE CONCEPTS 45,266

answer [v2] *solve; fulfill*
clarify, conform, correlate, correspond, crack*, deal with*, do*, dope, dope out*, elucidate, fill, fit*, lick*, measure up, meet, pass, qualify, satisfy, serve, suffice, suit, unzip*, work, work through; SEE CONCEPTS 87,664

answerable [adj] *responsible*
accountable, amenable, bound, chargeable, compelled, constrained, liable, obligated, obliged, subject, to blame; SEE CONCEPT 545

antagonism [n] *causing problem; opposition*
animosity, animus, antipathy, antithesis, clashing, competition, conflict, contention, contradistinction, contrariety, difference, disagreement, discord, dissension, enmity, friction, hatred, hostility, incongruity, oppugnancy, rancor, resistance, rivalry; SEE CONCEPT 29

antagonist [n] *person causing problem*
adversary, angries*, bad person*, bandit*, competitor, contender, crip*, enemy, foe, match, opponent, opposer, opposite number*, oppugnant, rival; SEE CONCEPT 412

antagonize [v] *cause problem; oppose*
alienate, anger, annoy, counteract, estrange, insult, irritate, neutralize, offend, repel, struggle, work against; SEE CONCEPTS 7,19,231

antecedent(s) [n] *predecessor(s) in family*
ancestor, ancestry, antecessor, blood, descent, extraction, forebears, forefather/mother, genealogy, line, primogenitor, progenitor, stock; SEE CONCEPT 414

antecedent [adj] *prior*
anterior, earlier, foregoing, former, past, precedent, preceding, precursory, preliminary, previous; SEE CONCEPT 820

antedate [v] *occur or cause to occur earlier*
accelerate, anachronize, antecede, backdate, date back, forerun, misdate, pace, precede, predate; SEE CONCEPT 84

antediluvian [adj] *out-of-date; prehistoric*
age-old, ancient, antiquated, antique, archaic, hoary, obsolete, old, old-fashioned, passé, primeval, primitive, primordial, timeworn, venerable; SEE CONCEPTS 578,797,799

antenna [n] *appendages for sensing, usually on insects or electronics*
aerial, bird snapper*, bullwhip*, ears*, feelers*, rabbit ears, receiver, sky wire*, whip*, wire; SEE CONCEPT 464

anterior [adj] *beginning, prior*
antecedent, foregoing, former, past, precedent, preceding, previous; SEE CONCEPT 799

anthem [n] *song*
canticle, chant, chorus, hymn, melody, paean; SEE CONCEPTS *263,595*

anthology [n] *literary collection*
album, analect, compendium, compilation, digest, garland, omnibus, selection, treasury; SEE CONCEPTS *280,432*

anthropology [n] *study of humans and their culture*
folklore, sociology; SEE CONCEPT *349*

antic [n] *funny act*
caper, dido, frolic, joke, lark, romp, shenanigan, tomfoolery, trick; SEE CONCEPT *292*

anticipate [v1] *expect; predict*
assume, await, bargain for*, be afraid*, conjecture, count chickens*, count on, cross the bridge*, divine, entertain*, figure, forecast, foresee, foretaste, foretell, have a hunch*, hope for, jump the gun*, look for, look forward to, plan on, prepare for, prevision, prognosticate, promise oneself, prophesy, see, see coming*, see in the cards*, suppose, visualize, wait, wait for; SEE CONCEPTS *26,70*

anticipate [v2] *act in advance of*
apprehend, beat someone to it*, be early, be one step ahead of*, block, delay, forestall, hinder, hold back, intercept, precede, preclude, prepare for, prevent, provide against; SEE CONCEPTS *100,121*

anticipation [n1] *expectation*
apprehension, awaiting, contemplation, expectancy, foresight, foretaste, high hopes, hope, impatience, joy, looking forward, outlook, preconception, premonition, preoccupation, prescience, presentiment, promise, prospect, trust; SEE CONCEPTS *26,689*

anticipation [n2] *readiness; forethought*
apprehension, awareness, foreboding, forecast, foreseeing, foresight, foretaste, forethought, inkling, intuition, preconception, premonition, prescience, presentiment, prevision, prior knowledge, realization; SEE CONCEPTS *409,410*

anticlimax [n] *ineffective conclusion*
bathos, comedown, decline, descent, disappointment, drop, letdown, slump; SEE CONCEPTS *230,674*

antidote [n] *counteracting agent*
antitoxin, antivenin, corrective, counteractant, counteragent, countermeasure, counterstep, cure, medicine, negator, neutralizer, nullifier, preventive, remedy; SEE CONCEPT *307*

antipathy [n] *strong dislike, disgust*
abhorrence, allergy, animosity, animus, antagonism, aversion, avoidance, bad blood*, contrariety, distaste, dyspathy, enmity, escape, eschewal, evasion, hate, hatred, hostility, ill will, incompatibility, loathing, opposition, rancor, repellency, repugnance, repulsion; SEE CONCEPT *29*

antiquarian [adj] *old, ancient*
aged, antique, archaic, hoary, obsolete, primitive, timeworn, venerable; SEE CONCEPTS *578,797*

antiquated [adj] *obsolete*
aged, ancient, antediluvian, antique, archaic, dated, elderly, fusty*, hoary, moldy, obsolescent, old, old-fangled, old-fashioned, old hat*, outmoded, out-of-date, outworn, superannuated; SEE CONCEPTS *530,578,797*

antique [n] *old object, often of great value*
antiquity, artifact, bygone, heirloom, monument, objet d'art, rarity, relic, ruin, vestige; SEE CONCEPTS *259,443*

antique [adj1] *old*
aged, ancient, elderly, obsolescent, obsolete, outdated, out-of-date, prehistoric, superannuated; SEE CONCEPTS *578,797*

antique [adj2] *old-fashioned*
antiquarian, archaic, classic, obsolete, olden, outdated, vintage; SEE CONCEPTS *530,578,797*

antiquity [n1] *old object*
antique, relic, ruin; SEE CONCEPT *259*

antiquity [n2] *oldness*
age, ancientness, antiqueness, archaicism, archaism, elderliness, hoariness, old age, venerableness; SEE CONCEPT *715*

antiquity [n3] *distant past*
ancient time(s), classical times, days of old, days of yore, former age, old days, olden days, remote time, time immemorial; SEE CONCEPT *807*

antiseptic [n] *decontaminating agent*
bactericide, detergent, disinfectant, germicide, preservative, preventative, preventive, prophylactic, purifier, sterilizer; SEE CONCEPTS *307,472,492*

antiseptic [adj] *completely clean, uncontaminated; decontaminating*
antibacterial, antibiotic, aseptic, bactericidal, clean, disinfectant, germ-destroying, germ-free, germicidal, hygienic, medicated, prophylactic, pure, purifying, sanitary, sterile, sterilized, sterilizing, unpolluted; SEE CONCEPT *485*

antisocial [adj] *nonparticipating; avoiding company*
alienated, ascetic, asocial, austere, cold, cynical, eremetic, hermitlike, introverted, misanthropic, reclusive, remote, reserved, retiring, solitary, standoffish, uncommunicative, unfriendly, unsociable, withdrawn; SEE CONCEPT *555*

antithesis [n1] *exact opposite*
antipode, antipole, contra, contradictory, contrary, contrast, converse, counter, flip side*, inverse, other side, reverse; SEE CONCEPT *665*

antithesis [n2] *contrast, opposition*
antagonism, contradiction, contradistinction, contraposition, contrariety, inversion, opposure, reversal; SEE CONCEPTS *633,665*

antitoxin [n] *agent for negating the effect of an infection or poison*
antibiotic, antibody, antipoison, antiseptic, antiserum, antivenin, counteractant, counteragent, medicine, neutralizer, preventive, serum, vaccine; SEE CONCEPT *307*

antonym [n] *word with opposite meaning to another word*
opposite, reverse; SEE CONCEPT *275*

anxiety [n] *worry, tension*
all-overs*, angst, ants in pants*, apprehension, botheration*, butterflies*, care, cold sweat*, concern, creeps*, disquiet, disquietude, distress, doubt, downer*, drag*, dread, fidgets*, flap*, foreboding, fretfulness, fuss, goose bumps*, heebie-jeebies*, jitters, jumps*, misery, misgiving, mistrust, nail-biting*, needles*, nervousness, panic, pins and needles*, restlessness, shakes*, shivers*, solicitude, suffering, suspense, sweat*, trouble, uncertainty, unease, uneasiness, watchfulness, willies*, worriment; SEE CONCEPTS *410,532,690*

anxious [adj1] *worried, tense*
afraid, aghast, antsy*, apprehensive, basket

case*, bugged*, butterflies, careful, choked*, clutched*, concerned, disquieted, distressed, disturbed, dreading, fearful, fidgety, fretful, hacked*, hyper*, in a state*, in a tizzy*, in suspense*, jittery, jumpy, nervous, nervy, overwrought, restless, scared, shaking, shaky, shivery, shook up*, shot to pieces*, solicitous, spooked*, strung out*, sweating bullets*, taut, troubled, uneasy, unglued*, unquiet, uptight*, watchful, wired*, worried sick*, wreck*; SEE CONCEPTS *403,690*

anxious [adj2] eager
agog, ardent, avid, breathless, desirous, enthusiastic, expectant, fervent, impatient, intent, itching*, keen, thirsty, yearning, zealous; SEE CONCEPTS *401,542*

any [det] one, some; unspecified, indiscriminate
a bit, a little, all, each, each and every, either, in general, part of, several, whatever; SEE CONCEPT *762*

anybody [n] one, some unspecified person or people
all, any of, anyone, anyone at all, any person, a person, each and every one, everybody, everyone, masses, one, public, whole world; SEE CONCEPT *417*

anyhow [adv] by any means
about, anyway, any which way, around, at any rate, at random, haphazard, haphazardly, helterskelter, however, in any case, in any respect, in any way, in either way, in one way or another, in whatever way, nevertheless, random, randomly, regardless, under any circumstances, whatever happens, willy-nilly; SEE CONCEPT *544*

anyone [n] one, some unspecified person
all, anybody, anybody at all, any of, any person, a person, each and every one, everybody, everyone, masses, one, public, whole world; SEE CONCEPT *417*

anyplace [n] unspecified area
all over, anywhere, everywhere, in any place, in whatever place, wherever; SEE CONCEPT *198*

anything [n] unspecified object or event
all, any one thing, anything at all, everything, whatever; SEE CONCEPTS *2,433*

anytime [n] unspecified moment, period
at all, at any moment, at one's convenience, every-time, no matter when, whenever, when one will; SEE CONCEPTS *807,819*

anyway [adv] by any means
anyhow, at all, at any rate, ever, however, in any case, in any event, in any manner, nevertheless, once; SEE CONCEPT *544*

anywhere [n] unspecified area
all over, anyplace, everywhere, in any place, in whatever place, wherever; SEE CONCEPT *198*

apart [adv] separate
afar, alone, aloof, aside, away, by itself, cut off*, disassociated, disconnected, distant, distinct, divorced, excluded, exclusively, freely, independent, independently, individually, isolated, lone wolf*, separated, separately, singly, special, to itself, to one side; SEE CONCEPTS *586,785*

apartment [n] set of rooms for rent
accommodation, cave*, chambers, cold-water*, condo, coop, cooperative, crash pad*, den*, digs*, dump*, flat, living quarters, lodging, pad*, penthouse, rental, residence, suite, walk-up; SEE CONCEPTS *448,516*

apathetic [adj] uncaring, disinterested
blah*, callous, cold, cool, could care less*, couldn't care less*, don't give a damn*, draggy*, emotionless, flat, impassive, indifferent, insensible, laid-back*, languid, moony*, passive, stoic, stolid, unconcerned, unemotional, unfeeling, uninterested, unmoved, unresponsive, untouched, what the hell*, wimpy*; SEE CONCEPTS *401,403*

apathy [n] uncaring attitude, lack of interest
aloofness, coldness, coolness, detachment, disinterest, dispassion, disregard, dullness, emotionlessness, halfheartedness, heedlessness, indifference, insensibility, insensitivity, insouciance, lassitude, lethargy, listlessness, passiveness, passivity, stoicism, unconcern, unresponsiveness; SEE CONCEPTS *410,633*

ape [v] mimic
affect, caricature, copy, counterfeit, ditto*, do*, do like*, echo, emulate, go like*, imitate, impersonate, make like*, mirror, mock, parody, parrot, take off*, travesty; SEE CONCEPTS *111,171*

aperture [n] hole
breach, break, chasm, chink, cleft, crack, cut, eye, fissure, gap, gash, interstice, opening, orifice, outlet, passage, perforation, pinhole, puncture, rift, rupture, slash, slit, slot, space, vent; SEE CONCEPT *757*

apex [n] top, high point
acme, apogee, climax, crest, crown, culmination, cusp, greatest, height, max*, maximum, meridian, most*, ne plus ultra, peak, pinnacle, point, roof, spire, sublimity, summit, tip, tops, up there*, vertex, zenith; SEE CONCEPTS *706,836*

aphorism [n] saying expressing a belief, often true
adage, apothegm, axiom, dictum, maxim, moral, precept, proverb, rule, saw, saying, truism; SEE CONCEPTS *275,278,689*

aphrodisiac [n/adj] seductive; inducing sex
amative, amatory, amorous, erotic, love drug, popper*, Spanish fly*, turn-on*, wampole*; SEE CONCEPTS *372,537*

apiece [adv] each
all, a pop*, aside, for each, from each, individually, one by one, per, respectively, separately, severally, singly, successively, to each; SEE CONCEPT *762*

apocryphal [adj] questionable; fake
counterfeit, doubtful, dubious, equivocal, false, fictitious, inaccurate, mythical, spurious, unauthenticated, ungenuine, unsubstantiated, untrue, unverified, wrong; SEE CONCEPTS *570,582*

apologetic [adj] expressing remorse, regret
atoning, attritional, compunctious, conciliatory, contrite, expiatory, explanatory, on one's knees*, penitent, penitential, propitiatory, regretful, remorseful, repentant, rueful, self-effacing, self-incriminating, sorry, supplicating; SEE CONCEPT *267*

apologize [v] express remorse, regret
admit guilt, ask forgiveness, ask pardon, atone, beg pardon, bow to*, clear oneself, confess, cop a plea*, cop out*, crawl*, excuse oneself, get down on knees*, give satisfaction*, make amends, make reparations, make up for, make up with, offer compensation, offer excuse, purge, retract, say one is sorry, square*, withdraw; SEE CONCEPTS *48,67*

apology [n] offering of remorse, regret
acknowledgment, admission, amends, atonement, concession, confession, defense, excuse, explana-

tion, extenuation, justification, mea culpa, mitigation, plea, redress, reparation, vindication; SEE CONCEPTS 48,67

apoplexy [n] *loss of consciousness from blockage in vein or artery*
occlusion, seizure, stroke, thrombosis; SEE CONCEPTS 316,720

apostate [n] *traitor*
backslider, defector, deserter, dissenter, heretic, nonconformist, rat*, recreant, renegade, turncoat; SEE CONCEPTS 359,412

apostle [n] *preacher; supporter*
advocate, champion, companion, converter, evangelist, follower, herald, messenger, missionary, pioneer, propagandist, proponent, proselytizer, witness; SEE CONCEPTS 359,361

appall/appal [v] *horrify*
alarm, amaze, astound, awe, consternate, daunt, disconcert, dishearten, dismay, faze, frighten, get to*, gross out*, insult, intimidate, outrage, petrify, scare, shake, shock, terrify, throw, unnerve; SEE CONCEPTS 7,19,42

appalling [adj] *horrifying*
alarming, astounding, awful, bad, daunting, dire, disheartening, dismaying, dreadful, fearful, formidable, frightening, frightful, ghastly, grim, grody*, gross*, harrowing, heavy*, hideous, horrible, horrid, horrific, intimidating, mean, petrifying, scaring, shocking, terrible, terrifying, the end*, unnerving; SEE CONCEPT 529

apparatus [n1] *equipment with a purpose*
accoutrement, appliance, black box*, contraption, device, dingbat, doodad*, doohickey*, furnishings, gaff*, gear, gimcrack*, gimmick, gizmo*, grabber*, habiliments, idiot box*, implement, jigger*, job*, machine, machinery, means, mechanism, outfit, paraphernalia, provisions, setup, stuff, supplies, tackle, thingamajig*, tools, utensils, whatchamacallit*, whatsis*, whosis*, widget*; SEE CONCEPTS 260,463,499

apparatus [n2] *organization or system*
bureaucracy, chain of command, hierarchy, network, setup, structure; SEE CONCEPTS 381,770

apparel [n] *clothing; covering*
accoutrement, array, attire, clothes, costume, drapery, dress, duds*, equipment, garb, garment, gear*, getup*, habiliment, habit, outfit, raiment, rig*, robe, suit, threads*, trapping, vestment; SEE CONCEPTS 451,473

apparent [adj1] *seeming, not proven real*
credible, illusive, illusory, likely, ostensible, outward, plausible, possible, probable, semblant, specious, superficial, supposed, suppositious; SEE CONCEPTS 552,582

apparent [adj2] *obvious*
barefaced, big as life*, clear, clear cut, conspicuous, crystal clear, discernible, distinct, evident, glaring, indubitable, make no bones*, manifest, marked, noticeable, observable, open, open and shut*, out in the open*, overt, palpable, patent, perceivable, plain, self-evident, transparent, unambiguous, under one's nose*, understandable, unequivocal, unmistakable, visible; SEE CONCEPTS 535,582

apparently [adv1] *seemingly*
allegedly, as if, as though, at a glance, at first sight, in all likelihood, intuitively, it appears that, it seems that, most likely, on the face of it, ostensibly, outwardly, plausibly, possibly, probably, professedly, reasonably, reputably, speciously,

superficially, supposedly, tangibly, to all appearances; SEE CONCEPTS 552,582

apparently [adv2] *obviously*
clearly, conspicuously, evidently, expressly, indubitably, in plain sight, manifestly, officially, openly, overtly, palpably, patently, perceptibly, plainly, transparently, unmistakably; SEE CONCEPT 535

apparition [n] *ghost*
bogeyman, bump in the night*, chimera, delusion, hallucination, haunt, illusion, phantasm, phantom, revenant, specter, spirit, spook, visitant; SEE CONCEPTS 370,689

appeal [n1] *request for help*
address, adjuration, application, bid, call, claim, demand, entreaty, imploration, importunity, invocation, overture, petition, plea, prayer, proposal, proposition, question, recourse, requisition, solicitation, submission, suit, supplication; SEE CONCEPT 48

appeal [n2] *power to attract, interest*
allure, attraction, attractiveness, beauty, charm, charmingness, engagingness, fascination, glamor, interestingness, pleasingness, seductiveness; SEE CONCEPTS 655,673

appeal [v1] *request*
address, adjure, advance, apply, ask, beg, beseech, bid, call, call upon, claim, contest, crave, demand, entreat, hit on, implore, importune, petition, plead, pray, propose, proposition, question, refer, require, resort to, solicit, strike, submit, sue, supplicate, urge; SEE CONCEPT 48

appeal [v2] *attract, interest*
allure, beguile, captivate, catch the eye, charm, enchant, engage, entice, fascinate, intrigue, invite, please, tantalize, tempt; SEE CONCEPTS 7,19,22,384

appear [v1] *come into sight*
arise, arrive, attend, be present, be within view, blow in*, bob up*, break through, breeze in*, check in*, clock in*, come, come forth, come into view, come out, come to light*, crop up*, develop, drop in*, emerge, expose, issue, loom, make the scene*, materialize, occur, pop in*, pop up*, present, punch in*, punch the clock*, recur, ring in*, rise, roll in*, show, show up, surface, time in*, turn out, turn up; SEE CONCEPTS 159,261

appear [v2] *seem*
have the appearance, look as if, look like, occur, resemble, sound, strike one as; SEE CONCEPTS 543,716

appear [v3] *be obvious, clear*
be apparent, be evident, be manifest, be patent, be plain; SEE CONCEPT 725

appear [v4] *be published; perform*
become available, be created, be developed, be invented, come into being, come into existence, come on, come on stage*, come out, enter, make an appearance, oblige, perform, play, play a part, present oneself, take part; SEE CONCEPTS 292,324

appearance [n1] *coming into sight*
actualization, advent, appearing, arrival, coming, debut, display, emergence, entrance, exhibition, introduction, manifestation, materialization, presence, presentation, representation, rise, showing up, turning up, unveiling; SEE CONCEPTS 159,261

appearance [n2] *outward aspect, characteristic*
air, attitude, bearing, blind, carriage, cast, character, condition, countenance, demeanor, dress,

expression, face, fashion, feature, figure, form, front, guise, image, look, looks, manner, mannerism, mien, mode, outline, pose, presence, presentation, screen, semblance, shape, stamp; SEE CONCEPTS 543,716

appearance [n3] *outward show; pretense*
aura, beard*, blind, countenance, dream, facade, front, guise, idea, illusion, image, impression, mirage, phenomenon, reflection, screen, seeming, semblance, sound, specter, vision; SEE CONCEPT 673

appease [v] *satisfy, pacify*
allay, alleviate, assuage, be enough, blunt, calm, compose, conciliate, content, diminish, do*, ease, gratify, lessen, lull, make matters up, meet halfway, mitigate, mollify, patch things up, placate, propitiate, quell, quench, quiet, serve, soften, soothe, subdue, sweeten, tranquilize; SEE CONCEPTS 7,22,126

appeasement [n] *satisfaction; pacification*
abatement, acceding, accommodation, adjustment, alleviation, amends, assuagement, blunting, compromise, concession, conciliation, easing, grant, lessening, lulling, mitigation, moderation, mollification, peace offering, placation, propitiation, quelling, quenching, quieting, reconciliation, reparation, restoration, settlement, softening, solace, soothing, tranquilization; SEE CONCEPTS 7,22,126

append [v] *add, join*
adjoin, affix, annex, attach, conjoin, fasten, fix, hang, subjoin, supplement, tack on*, tag on*; SEE CONCEPTS 85,113,160

appendage [n] *limb; accessory*
addendum, addition, adjunct, ancillary, annex, appendix, appurtenance, attachment, auxiliary, extremity, member, projection, protuberance, supplement; SEE CONCEPT 835

appendix [n] *added material at end of document*
addendum, addition, adjunct, appendage, appurtenance, attachment, codicil, excursus, index, notes, postscript, rider, sample, supplement, table, verification; SEE CONCEPT 270

appertain [v] *belong, be connected*
apply, bear, be characteristic of, be part of, be pertinent, be proper, be relevant, have to do with, pertain, refer, relate, touch upon; vest; SEE CONCEPT 532

appetite [n] *desire for food, worldly goods*
appetence, appetency, appetition, big eyes*, craving, demand, fondness, gluttony, greed, hankering, hunger, inclination, itch*, liking, longing, lust, passion, penchant, proclivity, propensity, ravenousness, relish, soft spot*, stomach, sweet tooth*, taste, thirst, urge, voracity, weakness, willingness, yearning, yen, zeal, zest; SEE CONCEPTS 20,32

appetizer [n] *snack before meal*
antipasto, aperitif, canapé, cocktail, dip, finger food, hors d'oeuvre, munchies*, relish, sample, spread, taste, tidbit; SEE CONCEPTS 457,828

appetizing [adj] *tasting very good*
aperitive, appealing, delectable, delicious, delish*, divine*, flavorsome, heavenly, inviting, luscious, mouthwatering, palatable, saporous, savory, scrumptious, succulent, sugar-coated*, sweetened, tantalizing, tasty, tempting, toothsome, yummy*; SEE CONCEPT 613

applaud [v] *clap for; express approval*
acclaim, approve, boost, cheer, commend, com-

pliment, encourage, eulogize, extol, give a hand*, give ovation, glorify, hail, hear it for*, kudize*, laud, magnify, plug, praise, rave, recommend, root*; SEE CONCEPTS 10,69,189

applause [n] *clapping; expression of approval*
acclaim, acclamation, accolade, approbation, big hand, bring down the house*, cheering, cheers, commendation, eulogizing, hand, hand-clapping, hurrahs, kudos, laudation, ovation, plaudits, praise, rooting, round, standing ovation; SEE CONCEPTS 69,189

appliance [n] *machine, usually with domestic purpose*
apparatus, device, gadget, implement, instrument, mechanism, tool; SEE CONCEPT 463

applicable [adj] *appropriate*
applicative, applicatory, apposite, apropos, apt, associable, befitting, felicitous, fit, fitting, germane, kosher, legit*, material, on target*, on the button*, on the nose*, pertinent, relevant, right on*, suitable, suited, that's the idea*, that's the ticket*, to the point, to the purpose, useful; SEE CONCEPTS 558,563

applicant [n] *person trying for position*
appellant, aspirant, candidate, claimant, hopeful, inquirer, petitioner, postulant, seeker, suitor, suppliant; SEE CONCEPTS 348,359

application [n1] *use*
appliance, appositeness, employment, exercise, exercising, function, germaneness, operation, pertinence, play, practice, purpose, relevance, usance, utilization, value; SEE CONCEPTS 680,694

application [n2] *request*
appeal, blank, claim, demand, draft, entreaty, form, inquiry, letter, paper, petition, requisition, solicitation, suit; SEE CONCEPT 48

application [n3] *hard work*
assiduity, attention, attentiveness, busyness, commitment, concentration, consideration, dedication, deliberation, diligence, effort, industry, perseverance, study, zeal; SEE CONCEPTS 91,410

application [n4] *putting substance on another*
administering, administration, applying, creaming, dosing, oiling, rubbing, treatment; SEE CONCEPT 200

applied [adj] *used*
activated, adapted, adjusted, brought to bear, correlated, devoted, enforced, exercised, practiced, related, tested, utilized; SEE CONCEPTS 538,546

apply [v1] *put into use*
administer, assign, bring into play, bring to bear, employ, engage, execute, exercise, exploit, handle, implement, practice, utilize; SEE CONCEPT 225

apply [v2] *be appropriate, relevant*
affect, allude, appertain, be applicable, bear upon, be pertinent, concern, connect, fit, involve, pertain, refer, regard, relate, suit, touch; SEE CONCEPT 532

apply [v3] *put substance on another*
administer, affix, anoint, bestow, cover, fasten, join, lay on, massage, paint, place, put on, rub, smear, spread, touch; SEE CONCEPT 200

apply [v4] *ask, request*
appeal, claim, demand, inquire, petition, put in, put in for, requisition, solicit, sue; SEE CONCEPT 48

apply [v5] *work hard*
address, bear down, be diligent, be industrious, bend, buckle down*, commit, concentrate, dedi-

ap
ap

cate, devote, dig, direct, give, give all one's got*, give best shot*, give old college try*, grind, hammer away*, hit the ball*, hustle*, knuckle down*, make effort, peg away*, persevere, plug*, pour it on*, pull out all stops*, scratch, study, sweat*, throw, try, turn; SEE CONCEPTS 87,100

appoint [v1] *assign responsibility; decide*
accredit, allot, assign, choose, command, commission, decree, delegate, designate, determine, direct, elect, enjoin, establish, finger, fix, install, name, nominate, ordain, select, set, settle, tap; SEE CONCEPTS 41,50,88

appoint [v2] *furnish*
arm, equip, fit, fit out, gear, outfit, provide, rig, supply, turn out; SEE CONCEPT 140

appointment [n1] *arrangement for meeting; prearranged meeting*
assignation, assignment, blind date*, consultation, date, engagement, errand, gig, interview, invitation, meet, rendezvous, session, tryst, zero hour*; SEE CONCEPTS 324,384

appointment [n2] *assignment of responsibility*
allotment, approval, assigning, authorization, certification, choice, choosing, commissioning, delegation, deputation, designation, election, empowering, installation, naming, nomination, ordination, promotion, selection; SEE CONCEPTS 41,50,88

appointment [n3] *job, position of responsibility*
appointee, assignment, berth, candidate, delegate, employment, nominee, office, officeholder, place, post, representative, situation, station, work; SEE CONCEPT 349

appointment [n4] *furnishing(s)*
accoutrement, appurtenance, equipage, fitting, fixture, gear, outfit, paraphernalia, trappings; SEE CONCEPT 475

apportion [v] *divide into shares*
accord, admeasure, administer, allocate, allot, assign, bestow, cut, cut up, deal, dispense, distribute, divvy, divvy up, dole out, give, lot, measure, mete, parcel, part, partition, piece up, prorate, ration, slice, split, split up; SEE CONCEPTS 98,108

appraisal [n] *judgment, estimation*
appraisement, assessment, estimate, evaluation, opinion, pricing, rating, reckoning, stock, survey, valuation; SEE CONCEPTS 18,328,766

appraise [v] *judge, estimate*
adjudge, assay, assess, audit, calculate, check, check out*, deem, evaluate, examine, eye*, figure, figure in, figure out, gauge, guesstimate*, have one's number*, inspect, look over, peg, price, rate, read, review, set at, size, survey, take account of, valuate, value; SEE CONCEPTS 18,764

appreciable [adj] *easily noticed; considerable*
apparent, ascertainable, clear-cut, definite, detectable, discernible, distinguishable, estimable, evident, goodly, good-sized, healthy, large, manifest, marked, material, measurable, noticeable, observable, obvious, perceivable, perceptible, plain, pronounced, recognizable, sensible, significant, sizable, substantial, tangible, visible; SEE CONCEPTS 619,781

appreciate [v1] *be grateful, thankful*
acknowledge, be appreciative, be indebted, be obliged, enjoy, flip over*, freak out on*, get high on*, give thanks, groove on*, welcome; SEE CONCEPTS 12,32,76

appreciate [v2] *increase in worth*
enhance, gain, grow, improve, inflate, raise the value of, rise; SEE CONCEPT 763

appreciate [v3] *recognize worth*
acknowledge, apprehend, be aware of, be cognizant of, be conscious of, catch the drift, comprehend, dig, fathom, grasp, know, perceive, read, realize, recognize, savvy, see daylight*, sympathize with, take account of, understand; SEE CONCEPT 15

appreciate [v4] *value highly*
admire, adore, applaud, apprise, cherish, enjoy, esteem, extol, honor, like, look up to, love, praise, prize, rate highly, regard, relish, respect, savor, treasure; SEE CONCEPTS 10,32

appreciation [n1] *thankfulness*
acknowledgment, gratefulness, gratitude, indebtedness, obligation, recognition, testimonial, thanks, tribute; SEE CONCEPTS 12,32

appreciation [n2] *increase in worth*
enhancement, gain, growth, improvement, inflation, rise; SEE CONCEPTS 346,763

appreciation [n3] *recognition of worth*
admiration, aesthetic sense, affection, appraisal, assessment, attraction, awareness, cognizance, commendation, comprehension, enjoyment, esteem, estimation, grasp, high regard, knowledge, liking, love, perception, realization, recognition, regard, relish, respect, responsiveness, sensibility, sensitiveness, sensitivity, sympathy, understanding, valuation; SEE CONCEPTS 15,409

appreciative [adj1] *thankful*
beholden, grateful, indebted, obliged, responsive; SEE CONCEPT 403

appreciative [adj2] *understanding, recognizing worth*
admiring, affectionate, alive, aware, cognizant, conscious, considerate, cooperative, cordial, enlightened, enthusiastic, favorable, friendly, generous, keen, kindly, knowledgeable, magnanimous, mindful, perceptive, pleased, receptive, regardful, respectful, responsive, satisfied, sensitive, supportive, sympathetic, understanding; SEE CONCEPT 402

apprehend [v1] *catch and arrest*
bag*, bust*, capture, collar, cop*, grab, nab, nail*, place under arrest, run in, seize, take in, take into custody, take prisoner; SEE CONCEPTS 90,191,317

apprehend [v2] *understand*
absorb, accept, appreciate, believe, catch, comprehend, conceive, digest, fathom, get, get the picture*, grasp, have, imagine, know, perceive, read, realize, recognize, sense, think; SEE CONCEPT 15

apprehension [n1] *anxiety, fear*
alarm, apprehensiveness, concern, disquiet, doubt, dread, foreboding, misgiving, mistrust, premonition, presage, presentiment, suspicion, trepidation, uneasiness, worry; SEE CONCEPTS 27,690

apprehension [n2] *catching and arresting*
booking, capture, collaring, detention, seizure, taking; SEE CONCEPTS 90,317

apprehension [n3] *understanding*
awareness, comprehension, grasp, idea, intellect, intelligence, judgment, ken, knowledge, notion, perception, perspicacity, thought; SEE CONCEPT 409

apprehensive [adj] anxious, fearful

afraid, alarmed, biting nails*, butterflies*, concerned, disquieted, doubtful, feel in bones*, foreboding, frozen*, get vibes*, have a hunch*, have cold feet*, have funny feeling*, have stage fright*, hung up*, in a cold sweat*, in a dither*, in a sweat*, jellyfish*, jittery, jumpy, lily-livered*, mistrustful, running scared*, scaredy-cat*, shaky*, stiff, suspicious, troubled, uncertain, uneasy, uptight, weak, worried, worried sick*; SEE CONCEPT 403

apprentice [n] novice/learner of a trade

amateur, beginner, flunky*, greenhorn*, heel*, neophyte, newcomer, new kid on block*, novitiate, probationer, pupil, rook*, rookie*, starter, student, tenderfoot*, tyro; SEE CONCEPTS 348,423

approach [n1] way, means of arriving

access, accession, advance, advent, avenue, coming, drawing near, entrance, gate, landing, nearing, passage, path, reaching, road, way; SEE CONCEPTS 159,501

approach [n2] request, suggestion

advance, appeal, application, offer, overture, proposal, proposition; SEE CONCEPT 278

approach [n3] plan of attack, resolution

attitude, concept, course, crack, dig*, idea, lick, manner, means, method, mode, modus operandi, new wrinkle*, offer, procedure, program, shot, stab, style, technique, way, whack*, wrinkle*; SEE CONCEPTS 655,660

approach [v1] come nearer

advance, approximate, bear, be comparable to, be like, belly up to*, border, buzz*, catch up, close in, come, come at, come close, compare with, contact, converge, correspond to, creep up, draw near, equal, gain on, go toward, impend, loom up, match, meet, move in on, move toward, near, progress, reach, resemble, surround, take after, threaten, verge upon; SEE CONCEPTS 159,198,701

approach [v2] make request, suggestion

accost, address, advise, appeal to, apply to, beseech, confer, consult, entreat, feel, feel one out*, give a play*, give a tumble*, greet, implore, make advance, make overture, make up to, plead, propose, sound out, speak to, supplicate, take aside, talk to, thumb, tumble; SEE CONCEPTS 48,75

approach [v3] begin

commence, embark, set about, start, undertake; SEE CONCEPT 234

approachable [adj1] accessible

attainable, come-at-able*, convenient, door's always open*, getable*, obtainable, reachable; SEE CONCEPT 576

approachable [adj2] friendly

affable, agreeable, congenial, cordial, open, receptive, sociable; SEE CONCEPT 404

approbation [n] praise

admiration, approval, bells*, consent, endorsement, esteem, favor, go-ahead*, high regard, okay, permission, recognition, sanction, support, the nod*; SEE CONCEPTS 10,69

appropriate [adj] suitable

adapted, applicable, appurtenant, apropos, apt, becoming, befitting, belonging, congruous, convenient, correct, deserved, desired, due, felicitous, fit, fitting, germane, good, just, on the button*, on the nose*, opportune, pertinent, proper, relevant, right, rightful, seemly, tailor-made, true, useful, well-suited, well-timed; SEE CONCEPT 558

appropriate [v1] set aside; allocate

allot, allow, appoint, apportion, assign, budget, devote, disburse, earmark, reserve, set apart; SEE CONCEPT 135

appropriate [v2] steal

annex, borrow, clap*, confiscate, cop, embezzle, filch, get fingers on*, get hands on*, glom on to*, grab, grab hold of*, hijack, liberate, lift, misappropriate, moonlight requisition*, pilfer, pocket, secure, snatch, swipe*, take over, usurp; SEE CONCEPT 139

appropriation [n1] allocation, setting aside

allotment, allowance, apportionment, assignment, budgeting, concession, donation, earmarking, endowing, funding, giving, grant, provision, setting apart, sponsoring, stipend, stipulation, subsidy; SEE CONCEPTS 135,340

appropriation [n2] stealing

confiscation, embezzlement, expropriation, grab, misappropriation, pilfering, seizure, takeover, taking, usurpation; SEE CONCEPT 139

approval [n1] authorization

acquiescence, assent, bells*, blessing, compliance, concurrence, confirmation, consent, countenance, endorsement, go-ahead*, green light*, leave, license, mandate, okay, permission, ratification, recommendation, sanction, support, the nod*, validation; SEE CONCEPTS 10,685

approval [n2] good opinion

acclaim, admiration, applause, appreciation, approbation, commendation, esteem, favor, liking, pat on the back*, pat on the head*, PR*, praise, puff, pumping up, regard, respect, strokes, stroking, wow*; SEE CONCEPT 32

approve [v1] agree something is good

accept, acclaim, admire, applaud, appreciate, approbate, be big on*, commend, countenance, esteem, face it, favor, go along with, grin and bear it*, handle, like, live with*, praise, put up with, regard highly, respect, roll with punches*, string along with*, take up on*, think highly of; SEE CONCEPT 10

approve [v2] allow, authorize

accede, accept, accredit, acquiesce, advocate, affirm, agree, assent, authorize, back*, bless*, boost, buy, buy into*, certify, charter, concur, confirm, consent, dig*, empower, encourage, endorse, establish, get behind, give go-ahead*, go along with, groove*, hats off to*, lap up*, license, maintain, make law, make valid, mandate, okay, permit, pronounce, push for, ratify, recommend, sanction, seal, second, sign, sign off on, stump for, subscribe to, support, thumbs up*, uphold, validate; SEE CONCEPTS 50,83,88

approximate [adj1] almost accurate, exact

almost, close, comparative, near, proximate, relative, rough; SEE CONCEPT 557

approximate [adj2] inexact

estimated, guessed, imperfect, imprecise, loose, rough, surmised, uncertain, unprecise, unscientific; SEE CONCEPT 557

approximate [adj3] similar

alike, analogous, close, comparable, like, matching, near, relative, resembling, verging on; SEE CONCEPTS 487,573

approximate [adj4] near

adjacent, bordering, close together, contiguous, nearby, neighboring; SEE CONCEPT 586

approximate [v] *come close*
approach, border on, come near, estimate, near, reach, resemble, touch, verge on; SEE CONCEPT 664

approximately [adv] *nearly*
about, almost, around, ballpark figure*, bordering on, circa, closely, close to, comparatively, generally, in the ballpark*, in the neighborhood of, in the region of, in the vicinity of, just about, loosely, more or less, most, much, not far from, not quite, proximately, relatively, roughly, upwards of*, very close; SEE CONCEPT 566

apropos [adj] *relevant, suitable*
applicable, apposite, appropriate, apt, befitting, belonging, correct, fit, fitting, germane, kosher*, legit*, material, on the button*, on the nose*, opportune, pertinent, proper, related, right, right on*, seemly; SEE CONCEPT 558

apropos [adv] *relevantly, suitably*
appropriately, aptly, opportunely, pertinently, suitably, timely; SEE CONCEPT 558

apropos [prep] *in respect of*
about, against, as for, as regards, as to, concerning, on the subject of, regarding, respecting, touching, toward, with reference to, with respect to; SEE CONCEPT 532

apt [adj1] *suitable*
applicable, apposite, appropriate, apropos, befitting, correct, felicitous, fit, fitting, germane, happy, just, pertinent, proper, relevant, seemly, suitable, timely; SEE CONCEPT 558

apt [adj2] *tending, inclined*
disposed, given, liable, likely, of a mind, prone, ready; SEE CONCEPT 542

apt [adj3] *quick to learn*
able, adept, astute, bright, clever, expert, gifted, ingenious, intelligent, nobody's fool*, no dummy*, not born yesterday*, prompt, quick on the trigger*, quick on the uptake*, ready, savvy, sharp, skilled, skillful, smart, talented, teachable; SEE CONCEPT 402

aptitude [n1] *inclination*
bent, disposition, drift, leaning, predilection, proclivity, proneness, propensity, tendency; SEE CONCEPT 657

aptitude [n2] *quickness at learning*
ability, capability, capacity, cleverness, competence, faculty, flair, gift, giftedness, intelligence, knack, proficiency, savvy, smarts, stuff*, talent, what it takes*; SEE CONCEPT 409

aquarium [n] *fish tank*
aquatic museum, fishbowl, marine exhibit; SEE CONCEPTS 396,438,514

aquatic [adj] *occurring in water*
amphibian, amphibious, floating, marine, maritime, natatory, oceanic, of the sea, sea, swimming, watery; SEE CONCEPTS 396,536

aqueduct [n] *canal*
channel, conduit, course, duct, pipeline, water passage, waterworks; SEE CONCEPT 514

arbiter [n] *person who settles dispute*
adjudicator, arbitrator, fixer, go-between, holdout, judge, maven, mediator, middleperson, moderator, referee, umpire; SEE CONCEPT 354

arbitrary [adj1] *whimsical, chance*
approximate, capricious, discretionary, erratic, fanciful, frivolous, inconsistent, injudicious, irrational, irresponsible, offhand, optional, random, subjective, supercilious, superficial, unaccountable, unreasonable, unscientific, wayward, willful; SEE CONCEPTS 534,542

arbitrary [adj2] *dictatorial*
absolute, autocratic, bossy, despotic, dogmatic, domineering, downright, flat out*, high-handed, imperious, magisterial, monocratic, no ifs ands or buts*, no joke*, overbearing, peremptory, straight out*, summary, tyrannical, tyrannous; SEE CONCEPT 401

arbitrate [v] *achieve settlement*
adjudge, adjudicate, adjust, bring to terms, come to school, come to terms, conciliate, decide, determine, hammer out a deal*, interpose, intervene, judge, make a deal, mediate, meet halfway, negotiate, parley, pass judgment, placate, play ball*, reconcile, referee, settle, smooth, soothe, step in, straighten out, strike happy medium*, trade off, umpire, work out a deal; SEE CONCEPTS 126,300

arbitration [n] *settlement of dispute*
adjudication, adjustment, agreement, compromise, decision, determination, judgment, mediation; SEE CONCEPTS 126,300

arbitrator [n] *settler of a dispute*
adjudicator, arbiter, fixer, go-between, holdout, judge, maven, mediator, middleperson, referee, umpire; SEE CONCEPTS 348,359

arc [n] *curve*
arch, bend, bow, crescent, curvation, curvature, half-moon, round; SEE CONCEPT 436

arcane [adj] *hidden, secret*
cabalistic, esoteric, impenetrable, mysterious, mystic, occult, recondite, unaccountable, unknowable; SEE CONCEPT 576

arch [n] *curve, curved structure*
arc, archway, bend, bow, curvature, dome, semicircle, span, vault; SEE CONCEPT 436

arch [adj1] *principal, superior*
accomplished, champion, chief, consummate, expert, finished, first, foremost, greatest, head, highest, leading, main, major, master, preeminent, premier, primary, top; SEE CONCEPT 574

arch [adj2] *knowing, coy*
artful, frolicsome, mischievous, pert, playful, roguish, saucy, sly, waggish, wily; SEE CONCEPT 401

arch [v] *curve*
arc, bend, bow, bridge, camber, extend, form, hook, hump, hunch, round, shape, span, stretch; SEE CONCEPT 184

archaeologist [n] *student of the physical remains of ancient cultures or eras*
archaeologian, classicist, excavator, paleologist, paleontologist, prehistorian; SEE CONCEPT 348

archaeology [n] *study of the physical remains of ancient cultures or eras*
antiquarianism, excavation, paleohistory, paleology, paleontology, prehistory; SEE CONCEPT 349

archaic [adj] *very old*
ancient, antiquated, antique, bygone, obsolete, olden, old-fashioned, outmoded, out of date, passé, primitive, superannuated; SEE CONCEPTS 578,797

archetype [n] *typical example*
classic exemplar, form, ideal, model, original, paradigm, pattern, perfect specimen, prime example, prototype, standard; SEE CONCEPTS 636,686

architect [n] *person who designs buildings*
artist, builder, creator, designer, draftsperson, engineer, inventor, maker, master builder, originator, planner, prime mover; SEE CONCEPT 348

architecture [n1] *design of buildings*
architectonics, building, construction, engineering, planning; SEE CONCEPTS 349,439

architecture [n2] *design, structure of something*
composition, constitution, construction, formation, framework, make-up, style; SEE CONCEPTS 660,733

archive [n] *collection, usually of records*
annals, chronicles, clippings, documents, excerpts, extracts, files, papers, registers, roll, scrolls, writings; SEE CONCEPTS 271,281,432

archives [n] *place where records are stored*
athenaeum, library, museum, office, registry, repository, storage, treasury, vault; SEE CONCEPT 439

archway [n] *curved opening*
entrance, passage; SEE CONCEPT 440

arctic [adj] *very cold*
chill, chilly, cool, freezing, frigid, frosty, frozen, gelid, glacial, icy, nippy, polar; SEE CONCEPT 605

ardent [adj1] *very enthusiastic*
agog, avid, blazing, burning, desirous, eager, fervent, fervid, fierce, fiery, horny*, hot*, hungry, impassioned, intense, keen, lovey-dovey*, lusty, passionate, spirited, thirsty, vehement, warm, zealous; SEE CONCEPTS 401,404

ardent [adj2] *loyal*
allegiant, constant, devoted, faithful, resolute, steadfast, true; SEE CONCEPT 404

ardor [n] *enthusiasm*
avidity, devotion, eagerness, earnestness, feeling, fervor, fierceness, fire, gusto, heat, intensity, jazz*, keenness, oomph*, passion, pep talk*, spirit, turn on*, vehemence, verve, warmth, weakness*, zeal, zest, zing; SEE CONCEPT 411

arduous [adj] *difficult, hard to endure*
backbreaking, burdensome, exhausting, fatiguing, formidable, grueling, harsh, heavy, labored, laborious, murder, no picnic*, onerous, painful, punishing, rigorous, rough, severe, strenuous, taxing, tiring, toilsome, tough, troublesome, trying, uphill; SEE CONCEPT 565

area [n1] *extent, scope of a surface*
breadth, compass, distance, expanse, field, operation, range, size, space, sphere, stretch, width; SEE CONCEPTS 651,792

area [n2] *region, district*
belt, block, city, county, division, domain, dominion, enclosure, field, kingdom, locality, neck of the woods*, neighborhood, parcel, patch, plot, precinct, principality, quarter, section, sector, sphere, square, state, stretch, territory, township, tract, turf, vicinity, ward, zone; SEE CONCEPT 508

arena [n1] *building or enclosure for entertainment or sports*
amphitheatre, boards*, bowl*, circus, coliseum, course, diamond, field, gridiron, ground, gym, gymnasium, hippodrome, ice, park, pit, platform, ring, rink, square, stadium, stage; SEE CONCEPT 438

arena [n2] *area of activity*
battlefield, battleground, domain, field, province, realm, scene, sector, sphere, territory, theatre; SEE CONCEPT 198

argue [v1] *verbally fight*
altercate, bandy, battle, bicker, break with, buck, bump heads, contend, cross, cross swords, disagree, dispute, face down, face off, feud, gang up on, get in one's face*, go one on one, hammer, hammer away, hash, hash over, hassle, have at

each other, have at it, jump, jump on, knock around, lock horns*, mix it up*, pettifog, pick an argument, put up a fight, put up a struggle, quarrel, quibble, rehash, row, sass, set to, sock it to*, squabble, stick to it, talk back, wrangle; SEE CONCEPT 46

argue [v2] *try to convince; present support*
appeal, assert, attest, claim, contend, controvert, defend, demonstrate, denote, display, elucidate, establish, evince, exhibit, explain, hold, imply, indicate, justify, maintain, manifest, persuade, plead, present, prevail upon, reason, show, suggest, talk into, testify, vindicate, warrant, witness; SEE CONCEPT 68

argue [v3] *discuss*
agitate, canvass, clarify, debate, dispute, expostulate, hold, maintain, question, reason, remonstrate, talk about; SEE CONCEPTS 46,56

argument [n1] *verbal fight*
altercation, beef, bickering, blowup, bone, bone of contention, bone to pick*, brannigan*, brawl, brush, clash, controversy, crusher*, debate, difference of opinion, disagreement, dispute, donnybrook, dustup*, exchange, face-off, falling, feud, finisher*, flap, fuss, gin*, go*, hassle, knockdown*, knock down and drag out*, out, quarrel, rhubarb*, romp, row, ruckus, ruction, rumpus, run-in, scene, scrap, set-to, shindy*, spat, squabble, static*, stew*, talking heads*, tiff, words, wrangle; SEE CONCEPT 46

argument [n2] *effort to convince; presentation of support*
argumentation, assertion, case, claim, contention, debate, defense, discussion, exchange, expostulation, grounds, line of reasoning, logic, plea, pleading, polemic, proof, questioning, reason, reasoning, remonstrance, remonstration; SEE CONCEPT 68

argumentative [adj] *wanting to quarrel*
belligerent, combative, contentious, contrary, controversial, disputatious, factious, fire-eating, having a chip on one's shoulder*, litigious, opinionated, pugnacious, quarrelsome, salty, scrappy, spiky, touchy; SEE CONCEPT 401

aria [n] *operatic solo*
descant, hymn, song; SEE CONCEPTS 263,595

arid [adj1] *dry*
barren, bone-dry, desert, dry as a bone, dry as dust, dusty, moistureless, parched, thirsty, waterless; SEE CONCEPT 603

arid [adj2] *uninterested, spiritless*
boring, colorless, drab, dreary, dry, dull, flat, insipid, lackluster, lifeless, tedious, unanimated, uninspired, vapid, wearisome; SEE CONCEPT 542

arise [v1] *come into being; proceed*
appear, begin, come to light, commence, crop up, derive, emanate, emerge, ensue, flow, follow, happen, head, issue, occur, originate, result, rise, set in, spring, start, stem; SEE CONCEPT 105

arise [v2] *get, stand, or go up*
ascend, climb, jump, mount, move upward, pile out*, rise, rise and shine*, roll out*, soar, stand, tower, turn out, wake up; SEE CONCEPTS 154,166

aristocracy [n] *privileged class, government*
elite, gentility, gentry, haut monde, high society, nobility, noblesse, patricians, patriciate, peerage, society, upper class, upper crust*; SEE CONCEPTS 296,423

aristocrat [n] *privileged person*
blueblood, gentleperson, lace curtain*, noble, pa-

trician, peer, silk stocking, swell*, upper cruster*; SEE CONCEPT *423*

aristocratic [*adj*] *privileged, elegant*
aloof, blue-blooded, courtly, dignified, elegant, elite, fine, haughty, noble, patrician, polished, refined, snobbish, stylish, upper-class, well-born, well-bred; SEE CONCEPT *555*

arithmetic [*n*] *mathematics*
addition, calculation, computation, division, estimation, figuring, multiplication, reckoning, subtraction; SEE CONCEPTS *349,764*

arm [*n1*] *limb, appendage*
bender, bough, bow, branch, fin, flapper, flipper, handle, hook, member, offshoot, projection, prong, rod, stump, wing; SEE CONCEPTS *392,471*

arm [*n2*] *subdivision, annex*
affiliate, authority, block, branch, command, department, detachment, division, ell, extension, force, offshoot, power, projection, section, sector, wing; SEE CONCEPTS *824,835*

arm [*n3*] *narrow body of water*
branch, brook, channel, creek, estuary, firth, fjord, inlet, rivulet, sound, strait, stream, subdivision, tributary; SEE CONCEPT *514*

arm [*v*] *equip with weapon or power*
accouter, appoint, array, deck, equalize, fortify, furnish, gear, gird, guard, heel*, heel up*, issue, load, load up, lug iron*, make ready, mobilize, outfit, pack, pack a rod*, prepare, prime, protect, provide, rig, rod up*, strengthen, supply, tote; SEE CONCEPTS *50,88,182*

armada [*n*] *group of ships or aircraft*
fleet, flotilla, force, navy, squadron; SEE CONCEPTS *432,504,506*

armament(s) [*n*] *weapon(s)*
ammunition, arms, defense, gun, hardware, heat*, material, materiel, munitions, ordnance, protection, security, weaponry; SEE CONCEPT *500*

armistice [*n*] *peace-establishing agreement*
ceasefire, suspension, treaty, truce; SEE CONCEPTS *230,684*

armor [*n*] *protective covering, often made of metal*
bulletproof vest, defense, guard, mail, plate, protection, security, sheath, shield; SEE CONCEPTS *451,476*

armory [*n*] *military building, usually for storing weapons*
arsenal, center, depot, dump, factory, headquarters, magazine, plant, range; SEE CONCEPTS *321,439*

arms [*n1*] *weaponry*
accoutrements, armaments, artillery, equipment, firearms, guns, munitions, ordnance, panoply, weapons; SEE CONCEPT *500*

arms [*n2*] *family crest*
blazonry, coat, emblazonry, emblem, ensign, escutcheon, heraldry, insignia, shield, signet; SEE CONCEPTS *284,625*

army [*n1*] *military force, usually for land*
armed force, artillery, battalion, battery, brigade, cavalry, column, command, company, corps, detail, division, flight, formation, infantry, legion, outfit, patrol unit, platoon, regiment, soldiers, soldiery, squad, troops, wing; SEE CONCEPT *322*

army [*n2*] *group resembling military force*
array, cloud, company, crowd, division, flock, horde, host, legion, mob, multitude, outfit, pack, regiment, scores, swarm, throng, unit; SEE CONCEPT *417*

aroma [*n*] *distinctive smell*
balm, bouquet, fragrance, incense, odor, perfume, redolence, scent, spice; SEE CONCEPT *599*

aromatic [*adj*] *distinctive smelling*
ambrosial, balmy, fragrant, odoriferous, perfumed, pungent, redolent, savory, scented, spicy, sweet, sweet-smelling; SEE CONCEPT *598*

around [*adv1*] *situated on sides, circumference, or in general area*
about, all over, any which way, encompassing, everywhere, in the vicinity, in this area, neighboring, over, throughout; SEE CONCEPT *581*

around [*adv2*] *close to a place*
about, almost, approximately, close at hand, near, nearby; SEE CONCEPT *586*

arouse [*v*] *excite, entice*
agitate, alert, animate, awaken, call, challenge, electrify, enliven, fire up, foment, foster, goad, heat up, incite, inflame, instigate, kindle, move, provoke, rally, rouse, send, spark, spur, stimulate, stir, thrill, turn on, waken, wake up, warm, whet, whip up, work up; SEE CONCEPTS *7,19,22*

arraign [*v*] *accuse*
blame, charge, criminate, hang on, incriminate, inculpate, indict, lay at one's door*, pin it on*, point the finger at*, summon; SEE CONCEPTS *44,317*

arrange [*v1*] *put in an order*
align, array, class, classify, clear the decks, dispose, file, fix up, form, group, line up, methodize, organize, police, police up, position, put in good shape*, put in order*, put to rights*, range, rank, regulate, sort, spruce, spruce up, systematize, tidy, whip into shape*; SEE CONCEPTS *84,158*

arrange [*v2*] *make plans, often involving agreement*
adapt, adjust, agree to, blueprint, chart, come to terms, compromise, concert, construct, contrive, decide, design, determine, devise, direct, draft, establish, frame*, get act together*, get ready, hammer out a deal*, harmonize, iron out*, lay out, line up, make a connection, make ready, manage, map out, negotiate, organize, prepare, project, promote, provide, pull a wire, pull things together, quarterback*, resolve, schedule, scheme, set stage, settle, shape up, tailor, work out, work out a deal; SEE CONCEPTS *36,84*

arrange [*v3*] *prepare musical composition differently*
adapt, instrument, orchestrate, score; SEE CONCEPT *292*

arrangement [*n1*] *an understanding*
adjustment, agreement, compact, compromise, deal, frame-up*, game plan*, layout*, organization, package*, package deal*, plan, preparation, provision, schedule, settlement, setup, terms; SEE CONCEPT *684*

arrangement [*n2*] *something that has been ordered*
alignment, array, classification, combination, composition, design, display, disposition, distribution, form, grouping, lineup, method, ordering, organization, pattern, pecking order*, ranging, rank, sequence, setup, structure, system; SEE CONCEPTS *84,727*

arrangement [*n3*] *musical adaptation*
chart, composition, instrumentation, interpretation, lead sheet, orchestration, score, version; SEE CONCEPTS *262,595*

array [*n1*] *collection, considerable group*
arrangement, batch, body, bunch, bundle, clump, cluster, design, display, disposition, exhibition, formation, host, lineup, lot, multitude, order, parade, pattern, set, show, supply, throng; SEE CONCEPTS 432,769,787

array [*n2*] *fine clothes*
apparel, attire, drapes*, dress, duds*, finery, full dress, garb, garments, getup*, rig*, threads*; SEE CONCEPT 451

array [*v1*] *arrange in collection or order*
align, display, exhibit, form, group, line up, methodize, organize, parade, range, set, show, systematize; SEE CONCEPT 84

array [*v2*] *dress in fine clothes*
attire, bedeck, clothe, deck, deck out, decorate, dog out*, drape, dud, dude up*, fit, fit out, garb, outfit, suit up, tog, try on, turn out, wrap; SEE CONCEPT 167

arrears [*n*] *debt*
back payment, balance due, claim, debit, deficiency, deficit, liability, obligation, unpaid bill; SEE CONCEPTS 332,335

arrest [*n1*] *taking into custody*
accommodation, apprehension, appropriation, bag*, booby trap*, bust, captivity, capture, collar, commitment, confinement, constraint, crimp*, detention, drop*, fall*, gaff*, glom*, grab*, heat*, hook*, imprisonment, incarceration, jailing, mitt*, nab*, nail*, nick*, nip*, pickle*, pick up*, pinch*, preventive custody, protective custody, pull*, pull in*, restraining, run in*, sequestering, snare, sweep*; SEE CONCEPTS 90,317

arrest [*n2*] *slowing or stopping*
blockage, cessation, check, checking, delay, end, halt, hindrance, inhibition, interruption, obstruction, prevention, restraining, restraint, stalling, stay, staying, stoppage, suppression, suspension; SEE CONCEPTS 121,234

arrest [*v1*] *take into authorized custody*
apprehend, bag*, book, brace*, bust, capture, catch, collar, detain, drop*, gaff*, get*, glom*, grab*, hook*, imprison, incarcerate, jail, kick*, nab*, nail*, net*, nick*, pick up*, pinch*, pull*, pull in*, put the arm on*, put the cuffs on*, round up*, roust*, run in*, secure*, seize*, sidetrack*, snag*, tab*, tag*, take in, take prisoner, toss in jail*; SEE CONCEPTS 90,317

arrest [*v2*] *stop or slow*
block, can, check, delay, drop, end, freeze, halt, hinder, hold, inhibit, interrupt, knock off, obstruct, prevent, restrain, restrict, retard, scrub*, shut down, stall, stay, suppress; SEE CONCEPTS 121,234

arrest [*v3*] *get someone's attention*
absorb, catch, engage, engross, fascinate, grip; SEE CONCEPTS 7,19,22

arrival [*n1*] *coming to a destination*
accession, advent, alighting, appearance, approach, arriving, debarkation, disembarkation, dismounting, entrance, happening, homecoming, influx, ingress, landing, meeting, occurrence, return; SEE CONCEPT 159

arrival [*n2*] *something that makes it to a destination*
addition, arriver, caller, cargo, comer, conferee, delegate, delivery, entrant, envoy, freight, guest, mail, newcomer, package, parcel, passenger, representative, shipment, tourist, traveler, visitant, visitor; SEE CONCEPTS 337,423,712

arrive [*v1*] *come to a destination*
access, alight, appear, attain, barge in, blow in, bob up*, breeze in*, bust in*, buzz*, check in*, clock in*, disembark, dismount, drop anchor, drop in, enter, fall by, fall in, get to, hit*, hit town*, land*, make it*, make the scene*, pop in*, pop up*, pull in*, punch the clock*, reach, report, roll in*, show, show up, sign in, sky in*, take place, turn up, visit, wind up at; SEE CONCEPT 159

arrive [*v2*] *achieve recognition*
accomplish, become famous, flourish, make good, make it, make the grade, prosper, reach the top, score, succeed, thrive; SEE CONCEPT 706

arrogance [*n*] *exaggerated self-opinion*
airs, aloofness, audacity, bluster, braggadocio, brass*, cheek*, chutzpah*, conceit, conceitedness, contemptuousness, crust*, disdain, disdainfulness, ego, egotism, gall, haughtiness, hauteur, high-handedness, hubris, imperiousness, insolence, loftiness, nerve, ostentation, overbearance, pomposity, pompousness, presumption, pretension, pretentiousness, pride, priggishness, scornfulness, self-importance, self-love, smugness, superciliousness, swagger, vanity; SEE CONCEPTS 411,633

arrogant [*adj*] *having exaggerated self-opinion*
aloof, assuming, audacious, autocratic, biggety*, bossy, bragging, cavalier, cheeky, cocky, cold-shoulder*, conceited, contemptuous, cool*, disdainful, domineering, egotistic, haughty, high and mighty*, high-handed, imperious, insolent, know-it-all*, lordly, on an ego trip*, overbearing, peremptory, pompous, presumptuous, pretentious, proud, puffed up*, scornful, self-important, smarty, smug, sniffy*, snippy*, snooty*, snotty*, stuck up*, supercilious, superior, swaggering, uppity*, vain, wise guy*; SEE CONCEPTS 401,404

arrogate [*v*] *claim without justification*
accroach, appropriate, assume, commandeer, confiscate, demand, expropriate, preempt, presume, seize, take, usurp; SEE CONCEPTS 142,266

arsenal [*n*] *storage of weapons*
armory, depository, depot, dump, factory, magazine, ordnance, plant, repository, stock, stockpile, store, storehouse, supply, warehouse; SEE CONCEPTS 432,439

arson [*n*] *intentional burning*
firing, incendiarism, pyromania, setting fire, torching, touching off; SEE CONCEPT 249

art [*n1*] *skill, creativity*
adroitness, aptitude, artistry, craft, craftsmanship, dexterity, expertise, facility, imagination, ingenuity, inventiveness, knack, know-how, knowledge, mastery, method, profession, trade, virtuosity; SEE CONCEPT 706

art [*n2*] *cunning*
artfulness, artifice, astuteness, canniness, craftiness, deceit, duplicity, guile, slyness, trickery, wiliness; SEE CONCEPT 411

art [*n3*] *creation meant to communicate or appeal to senses or mind*
abstraction, carving, description, design, illustration, imitation, modeling, molding, painting, pictorialization, portrayal, representation, sculpting, shaping, simulation, sketching, symbolization; SEE CONCEPT 349

artery [*n*] *channel*
avenue, boulevard, canal, conduit, corridor, course, duct, highway, line, passage, pathway,

road, route, sewer, thoroughfare, track, tube, way; SEE CONCEPT *501*

artful [*adj*] *skillful; cunning*
adept, adroit, clever, crafty, designing, dexterous, foxy*, ingenious, masterly, politic, proficient, resourceful, scheming, sharp, shrewd, slick*, sly, smart, smooth*, tricky, wily; SEE CONCEPTS *404,528*

article [*n1*] *item, object*
commodity, dojigger*, gizmo*, piece, substance, thing, thingamabob*, thingamajig*, unit; SEE CONCEPT *433*

article [*n2*] *piece of writing*
beat*, blurb*, column, commentary, composition, discourse, editorial, essay, exposition, feature, item, paper, piece, scoop*, spread, story, theme, think piece*, treatise, write-up; SEE CONCEPTS *270,271,280*

article [*n3*] *section of document*
branch, chapter, clause, detail, division, element, head, heading, item, matter, paragraph, part, passage, piece, point, portion, provision; SEE CONCEPTS *270,318*

articulate [*adj*] *clearly, coherently spoken*
clear, coherent, comprehensible, definite, distinct, eloquent, expressive, fluent, intelligible, lucid, meaningful, understandable, well-spoken; SEE CONCEPT *267*

articulate [*v1*] *say clearly, coherently*
enunciate, express, mouth, pronounce, say, sound off*, speak, state, talk, utter, verbalize, vocalize, voice; SEE CONCEPTS *47,55*

articulate [*v2*] *connect*
concatenate, couple, fit together, hinge, integrate, join, link; SEE CONCEPT *113*

articulation [*n1*] *clear, coherent speech*
delivery, diction, enunciation, expression, pronunciation, saying, speaking, statement, talking, utterance, verbalization, vocalization, voicing; SEE CONCEPT *55*

articulation [*n2*] *connection*
coupling, hinge, joining, joint, junction, juncture, unification, union; SEE CONCEPT *113*

artifice [*n1*] *hoax; clever act*
con, contrivance, device, dodge, expedient, gambit, gimmick*, machination, maneuver, play, ploy, racket*, ruse, savvy, scam*, stratagem, subterfuge, tactic, wile; SEE CONCEPT *59*

artifice [*n2*] *cunning; deception*
artfulness, chicanery, craftiness, dishonesty, duplicity, guile, scheming, slyness, trickery, wiliness; SEE CONCEPT *411*

artifice [*n3*] *skill, cleverness*
ability, adroitness, deftness, facility, finesse, ingenuity, invention, inventiveness, know-how*, skill; SEE CONCEPT *630*

artificial [*adj1*] *fake; imitation*
bogus, counterfeit, ersatz, fabricated, factitious, faked, false, falsie*, hyped up*, manufactured, mock, phony*, plastic, sham, simulated, specious, spurious, substitute, synthetic, unnatural, unreal; SEE CONCEPT *582*

artificial [*adj2*] *pretended; affected*
assumed, contrived, false, feigned, forced, hollow, insincere, labored, mannered, meretricious, phony*, put-on, spurious, theatrical, unnatural; SEE CONCEPT *401*

artillery [*n*] *weaponry or military unit*
arms, battery, bazooka, big guns*, cannon, cannonry, force, gunnery, heavy stuff*, munitions, ordnance, rainmakers*, stovepipe, weapons; SEE CONCEPTS *322,500*

artist [*n*] *person skilled in creative activity*
artisan, artiste, authority, composer, craftsperson, creator, expert, handicrafter, inventor, painter, virtuoso, whiz*; SEE CONCEPT *352*

artistic [*adj1*] *beautiful, satisfying to senses*
aesthetic, creative, cultivated, cultured, decorative, dramatic, elegant, exquisite, fine, graceful, grand, harmonious, ideal, imaginative, musical, ornamental, pictorial, picturesque, pleasing, poetic, refined, rhythmical, sensitive, stimulating, stylish, sublime, tasteful; SEE CONCEPT *579*

artistic [*adj2*] *being skilled in creative activity*
accomplished, artful, artsy-craftsy*, arty, crafty, discriminating, gifted, imaginative, inventive, skillful, talented; SEE CONCEPT *527*

artistry [*n*] *great skill in creative endeavors*
ability, accomplishment, artfulness, brilliance, craftship, creativity, finesse, flair, genius, mastery, proficiency, style, talent, taste, touch, virtuosity, workmanship; SEE CONCEPTS *630,655*

artless [*adj*] *simple*
direct, genuine, guileless, honest, ingenuous, innocent, naive, natural, open, plain, pure, sincere, straight, straightforward, talking turkey*, true, unadorned, unaffected, uncontrived, unpretentious, unsophisticated, up front*; SEE CONCEPTS *267,562*

arty [*adj*] *pretended expertise in art; affected interest*
affected, deceptive, ephemeral, false, flaunting, illusory, imitative, overblown, popular, popularized, pretentious, pseudo, tasteless; SEE CONCEPT *582*

as [*conj1*] *while, when*
at the time that, during the time that, in the act of, in the process of, just as, on the point of; SEE CONCEPT *544*

as [*conj2*] *in the way that; to a degree*
acting as, being, by its nature, comparatively, equally, essentially, for instance, functioning as, in the manner that, in the same manner with, just as, just for, like, serving as, similarly, such as; SEE CONCEPT *544*

as [*conj3*] *because*
as long as, being, cause, considering, for, for the reason that, inasmuch as, now, seeing that, since, whereas; SEE CONCEPT *544*

as [*prep*] *in the role of*
being, in the character of, under the name of; SEE CONCEPT *544*

ascend [*v*] *go up*
arise, climb, escalate, float, fly, lift off, mount, move up, rise, scale, soar, sprout, take off, tower; SEE CONCEPTS *149,166*

ascendancy/ascendency [*n*] *domination*
advantage, authority, command, control, dominance, dominion, edge, influence, jump*, leg up*, mastery, on top, power, predominance, preeminence, prepotence, prevalence, reign, rule, sovereignty, superiority, supremacy, sway, upper hand*, whip hand*; SEE CONCEPTS *376,671*

ascension [*n*] *going up*
ascent, climbing, escalating, flying, mounting, rise, rising, scaling, soaring, towering; SEE CONCEPTS *149,166*

ascent [*n1*] *upward movement*
ascendance, ascending, ascension, clambering,

climb, climbing, lift, mounting, rise, rising, scaling, spring, take off; SEE CONCEPT 166

ascent [n2] *upward slope*
acclivity, grade, gradient, incline, ramp, rise; SEE CONCEPTS 738,757

ascertain [v] *make sure*
catch on, check, check out*, check up on*, confirm, determine, dig*, discover, divine, double-check*, establish, eye*, eyeball*, find out, fix, get down cold*, get down pat*, get hold of*, get it down*, get the hang of*, identify, learn, learn the ropes*, look-see*, make certain, make sure, peg*, pick up*, pick up on*, read, see, settle, size, size up*, tell, verify; SEE CONCEPTS 31,34,38

ascribe [v] *assign to source*
accredit, attribute, charge, credit, hang on, impute, lay, pin on*, put down, refer, reference, set down; SEE CONCEPTS 39,49

ash(es) [n] *remains of burning*
charcoal, cinders, dust, embers, powder, relics, remains, ruins, slag, soot; SEE CONCEPT 260

ashamed [adj] *regretting, remorseful*
abashed, apologetic, bashful, blushing, chagrined, compunctious, conscience-stricken, contrite, crestfallen, debased, demeaned, discomfited, disconcerted, distraught, distressed, embarrassed, flustered, guilty, hesitant, humble, humbled, humiliated, meek, mortified, muddled, penitent, regretful, reluctant, repentant, shamed, shamefaced, sheepish, shy, sorry, stammering, stuttering, submissive; SEE CONCEPT 550

ashore [adv] *toward, onto land from water*
aground, beached, on dry land, on land, on shore, shorewards; SEE CONCEPT 583

aside [n] *confidential statement*
departure, digression, discursion, interpolation, interposition, parenthesis, tangent, throwaway*; SEE CONCEPT 51

aside [adv] *away from; to the side*
abreast, afar, alone, alongside, apart, away, beside, by oneself, down, in isolation, in reserve, near, nearby, neck and neck, out, out of the way, privately, separately, sidewise; SEE CONCEPT 586

ask [v1] *question*
buzz*, canvass, catechize, challenge, cross-examine, demand, direct, enjoin, examine, give the third degree*, go over, grill*, hit*, hunt for*, inquire, institute, interrogate, investigate, needle*, pick one's brains*, pop the question*, pry into, pump, put the screws to*, put through the wringer*, query, quiz, request, roast*, sweat*; SEE CONCEPT 48

ask [v2] *request*
angle, appeal, apply, beg, beseech, bite*, bum*, call for, charge, claim, command, contend for, crave, demand, entreat, file for, hit*, hustle*, implore, impose, knock*, levy, mooch*, order, petition, plead, pray, promote*, request, requisition, seek, solicit, sue, supplicate, touch*, urge; SEE CONCEPT 53

ask [v3] *invite*
bid, call upon, propose, suggest, summon, urge; SEE CONCEPT 75

askew [adj] *crooked*
askance, askant, aslant, awry, bent, buckled, catawampus*, cockeyed*, crookedly, curved, knotted, lopsided, oblique, obliquely, off-center, slanted, slanting, to one side, topsy-turvey*,

turned, twisted, yaw ways*, zigzag*; SEE CONCEPT 586

asleep [adj] *unconscious*
catching some zzz's*, comatose, conked*, crashed*, dormant, dozing, dreaming, flaked out*, getting shut-eye*, hibernating, inactive, in dreamland*, inert, in repose, napping, on the kip*, out*, out cold*, out like a light*, out of it*, reposing, resting, sacked out*, sleeping, slumbering, snoozing, snoring, somnolent, taking forty winks*; SEE CONCEPTS 210,315,681

aspect [n1] *visible feature*
air, appearance, attitude, bearing, condition, countenance, demeanor, expression, face, facet, form, look, manner, mien; SEE CONCEPTS 434,628,673

aspect [n2] *element to consider*
angle, bearing, direction, facet, feature, gimmick, hand, outlook, perspective, phase, point of view, position, prospect, regard, scene, side, situation, slant, switch, twist, view, vista; SEE CONCEPT 668

asperity [n] *harshness; bad temper*
acerbity, acrimony, bitterness, churlishness, crabbiness, crossness, difficulty, disagreeableness, irascibility, irritability, meanness, moroseness, peevishness, roughness, sharpness, sourness, sullenness, tartness; SEE CONCEPT 633

aspersion [n] *verbal exhibition of bad temper*
abuse, animadversion, backbiting, backhanded compliment, black eye*, calumny, defamation, detraction, dirty dig*, hit*, invective, knock*, libel, obloquy, put-down*, rap*, slam*, slander, smear*, vituperation; SEE CONCEPTS 52,54,58

asphyxiate [v] *cut off air*
choke, drown, smother, stifle, strangle, strangulate, suffocate; SEE CONCEPTS 121,246

aspiration [n] *goal, hope*
aim, ambition, ambitiousness, craving, desire, direction, dream, eagerness, endeavor, fire in the belly*, hankering, inclination, longing, object, objective, passion, pursuit, push, right stuff*, urge, vocation, wish, work, yearning; SEE CONCEPTS 20,659

aspire [v] *aim, hope*
be ambitious, be eager, crave, desire, dream, hanker, long, pursue, seek, strive, struggle, try, want, wish, yearn; SEE CONCEPT 20

aspiring [adj] *hopeful*
ambitious, aspirant, eager, eager beaver*, endeavoring, enthusiastic, impassioned, longing, on the make*, striving, wishful, would-be, zealous; SEE CONCEPT 403

ass [n] *stupid person*
blockhead*, dolt, donkey*, dope, dunce, fool, idiot, imbecile, jackass*, jerk*, nitwit*, numbskull*, simpleton*, twit*; SEE CONCEPT 412

assail [v] *attack, usually with words*
abuse, assault, bash, berate, beset, blast, blister, bust, charge, come at, criticize, encounter, have at*, impugn, invade, lambaste, lay into*, malign, maltreat, molest, revile, set upon*, trash*, vilify, work over; SEE CONCEPTS 52,86

assailant [n] *attacker*
aggressor, antagonist, assaulter, bushwhacker*, enemy, foe, goon*, hit person, invader, mugger, opposite number*, trigger person; SEE CONCEPT 412

assassin [n] *murderer of prominent or important person*
butcher*, clipper*, dropper*, eliminator, en-

forcer, executioner, guerrilla*, gun*, gun person, hatchet person, hit person, killer, liquidator, piece person*, plugger*, slayer, soldier, torpedo*, trigger person; SEE CONCEPT 412

assassinate [v] *murder prominent or important person*

bump off*, do in*, eliminate, execute, gun down, hit, kill, knock off*, liquidate, slaughter, slay; SEE CONCEPT 252

assault [n] *attack*

advance, aggression, charge, incursion, invasion, offensive, onset, onslaught, rape, storm, storming, strike, violation; SEE CONCEPT 86

assault [v] *attack*

abuse, advance, assail, bash, beset, blast, blitz, bushwhack, charge, come down on*, go for, haul off on*, invade, jump, jump down one's throat*, jump on one's case*, lay into, let have it*, light into*, rape, ruin, set upon, shoot down, slam, slap around, storm, strike, trash, violate, work over, zap*; SEE CONCEPTS 52,86

assay [n] *analysis*

appraisal, assessment, estimation, evaluation, examination, inspection, investigation, measurement, rating, survey, test, trial, valuation; SEE CONCEPTS 24,103,290

assay [v] *analyze*

appraise, apprise, assess, check, check out, estimate, evaluate, examine, eyeball*, inspect, investigate, measure, peg*, prove, rate, read, see, size, size up*, survey, test, try, valuate, value, weigh; SEE CONCEPTS 24,103

assemblage [v] *gathering of people*

aggregation, assembly, association, collection, company, congregation, convergence, crowd, group, throng; SEE CONCEPT 417

assemble [v1] *congregate*

accumulate, agglomerate, amass, bring together, bunch, bunch up, call, call together, capture*, collect, come together, convene, convoke, corral*, flock, gang up*, gather, group, hang around*, hang out*, huddle, lump, make the scene*, meet, meet up, mobilize, muster, rally, reunite, round up, scare up*, summon, unite; SEE CONCEPT 114

assemble [v2] *put together*

compile, connect, construct, contrive, erect, fabricate, fashion, fit, form, join, make, manufacture, model, mold, piece together, produce, set up, shape, unite, weld; SEE CONCEPT 113

assembly [n1] *congregation*

accumulation, aggregation, assemblage, association, band, body, bunch, clambake*, cluster, coffee klatch*, collection, company, conclave, confab*, conference, convocation, council, crew, crowd, faction, flock, gathering, get-together*, group, huddle, mass, meet*, meeting, multitude, rally, sit-in*, throng, turnout*; SEE CONCEPTS 381,432

assembly [n2] *putting together*

adjustment, attachment, building, collection, connecting, construction, erection, fabrication, fitting together, joining, manufacture, manufacturing, modeling, molding, piecing together, setting up, shaping, welding; SEE CONCEPT 113

assent [n] *agreement*

acceptance, accession, accord, acknowledgment, acquiescence, admission, affirmation, approval, authorization, compliance, concurrence, consent, nod, permission, sanction; SEE CONCEPTS 8,684

assent [v] *agree*

accede, accept, accord, acquiesce, adopt, allow, approve, buy, cave in*, comply, concur, conform, consent, cut a deal*, defer, ditto*, embrace, espouse, give five*, give in, go along with, grant, knuckle under*, okay*, pass on*, permit, recognize, sanction, say uncle*, shake on*, subscribe; SEE CONCEPT 8

assert [v] *insist, declare, maintain*

advance, affirm, allege, argue, asservate, attest, aver, avouch, avow, butt in*, cite, claim, contend, defend, horn in, justify, mouth off*, pop off*, predicate, press, proclaim, profess, pronounce, protest, put forward, say, shoot off one's mouth*, shoot one's wad*, stand up for, state, stress, swear, uphold, vindicate, warrant; SEE CONCEPT 49

assertion [n] *declaration, positive statement*

affirmation, allegation, asseveration, attestation, avowal, contention, defense, insistence, maintenance, mouthful, okay, predication, profession, pronouncement, report, say so*, stamp of approval, stressing, two cents' worth*, vindication; SEE CONCEPTS 49,278

assertive [adj] *aggressive*

absolute, assured, certain, confident, decided, decisive, demanding, dogmatic, domineering, emphatic, firm, forceful, forward, insistent, militant, overbearing, positive, pushy, self-assured, self-confident, strong-willed, sure; SEE CONCEPT 404

assess [v1] *evaluate, determine*

appraise, apprise, assay, check*, check out*, compute, determine, dig it*, estimate, figure*, fix, gauge, guess, judge, nick*, peg*, rate, reckon, set, size*, size up, survey, take measure*, valuate, value, weigh; SEE CONCEPT 24

assess [v2] *assign fee, amount*

charge, demand, evaluate, exact, fix, impose, levy, rate, tax, value; SEE CONCEPT 330

assessment [n1] *evaluation*

appraisal, computation, determination, estimate, estimation, judgment, rating, reckoning, valuation, value judgment; SEE CONCEPT 24

assessment [n2] *assignment of fee, amount*

appraisal, charge, demand, duty, estimate, fee, levy, rate, rating, tariff, tax, taxation, toll, valuation; SEE CONCEPT 332

asset [n1] *advantage*

aid, benefit, blessing, boon, credit, distinction, help, resource, service, treasure; SEE CONCEPT 661

asset(s) [n2] *property or money possessed*

ace in the hole*, ace up sleeve*, backing, bankroll, budget, capital, credit, equity, estate, funds, goods, holdings, kitty*, mattress*, means, nest egg*, nut*, possessions, rainy day*, reserve(s), resources, riches, sock*, something put aside, something put away, stake, stash*, stuff, valuables, wealth; SEE CONCEPTS 332,340,710

assiduous [adj] *hard-working*

active, attentive, busy, constant, diligent, eager beaver*, exacting, grinding, indefatigable, industrious, laborious, persevering, plugging, scrupulous, sedulous, steady, studious, unflagging, untiring, whiz, zealous; SEE CONCEPTS 538,542

assign [v1] *select and give a responsibility*

accredit, allow, appoint, ascribe, attach, attribute, authorize, cast, charge, choice, commission, commit, credit, delegate, deputize, designate, downlink, download, draft, elect, empower, enroll, entrust, hang on*, hire, hold responsible, impute, name, nominate, ordain, pin on*, refer, reference, select, slot, tab, tag; SEE CONCEPTS *41,50,88*

assign [v2] *set apart for a reason*
allocate, allot, appoint, apportion, appropriate, consign, designate, detail, determine, dish out*, distribute, divide, earmark, fix, fork out*, give, grant, hand out*, hand over, indicate, mete, prescribe, relegate, shell out*, specify, stipulate; SEE CONCEPTS *129,135*

assignation [n] *clandestine meeting*
affair, appointment, date, engagement, heavy date*, illicit meeting, love nest*, one-night stand*, quickie*, rendezvous, secret meeting, tryst; SEE CONCEPTS *375,386*

assignment [n1] *responsibility, task*
appointment, beat, charge, chore, commission, drill, duty, homework, job, mission, position, post, practice, stint; SEE CONCEPT *362*

assignment [n2] *selecting or setting apart*
allocation, allotment, appointment, apportionment, appropriation, ascription, assignation, attribution, authorization, choice, consignment, delegation, designation, determination, distribution, giving, grant, nomination, selection, specification, stipulation; SEE CONCEPTS *41,129*

assimilate [v1] *absorb mentally*
comprehend, digest, grasp, incorporate, ingest, learn, osmose, sense, soak up, take in, take up, understand; SEE CONCEPT *15*

assimilate [v2] *become adjusted; adjust*
acclimatize, accommodate, acculturate, accustom, adapt, become like, become similar, blend in, conform, fit, go native*, homogenize, homologize, intermix, match, mingle, parallel, standardize; SEE CONCEPT *232,701*

assist [n] *help*
abetment, aid, assistance, backing, benefit, boost, collaboration, comfort, compensation, cooperation, facilitation, furtherance, hand, helping hand, lift, reinforcement, relief, service, support; SEE CONCEPT *110*

assist [v] *help*
abet, aid, back, bail out, benefit, boost, collaborate, cooperate, do for*, expedite, facilitate, further, give a boost*, give a leg up*, give a lift*, go down the line for*, go for, go to bat for*, go with, grease the wheels*, hype*, lend a hand*, make a pitch for*, open doors*, plug*, puff*, push*, put on the map*, reinforce, relieve, ride shotgun*, root for*, run interference for*, serve, stand up for, stump*, support, sustain, take care of, thump*, work for, work with; SEE CONCEPT *110*

assistance [n] *help*
abetment, aid, assist, backing, benefit, boost, collaboration, comfort, compensation, cooperation, facilitation, furtherance, hand, help, helping hand, lift, reinforcement, relief, service, support, sustenance; SEE CONCEPT *110*

assistant [n] *helper*
abettor, accessory, accomplice, adherent, adjunct, aide, ally, appointee, apprentice, associate, attendant, auxiliary, backer, backup*, coadjutant, co-adjutor, collaborator, colleague, companion, confederate, cooperator, deputy, fellow worker, flunky*, follower, friend, gofer*, help, helpmate, mate, partner, patron, peon*, representative, right-hand person, secretary, subordinate, supporter, temp*, temporary worker; SEE CONCEPTS *348,423*

associate [n] *colleague*
accessory, accomplice, affiliate, aid, ally, assistant, auxiliary, branch, buddy, chum, clubber*, cohort, collaborator, companion, compatriot, comrade, confederate, consort, cooperator, co-worker, crony, fellow, friend, helper, joiner, kissing cousin, mate, offshoot, one of the folks*, pal, pard*, partner, peer, playmate, sidekick; SEE CONCEPTS *348,423*

associate [v1] *connect in the mind*
affiliate, blend, bracket, combine, concord, conjoin, correlate, couple, group, identify, join, league, link, lump together, mix, pair, relate, think of together, unite, yoke; SEE CONCEPT *39*

associate [v2] *befriend*
accompany, amalgamate, be friends, be in cahoots*, buddy up, bunch up, come together, confederate, consort, fraternize, gang up, get in on, get into, get in with, get together, go along with, go partners*, hang around, hang out, hang out with*, hobnob, join, join up with, line up with, mingle, mix, pal up, play footsie with*, pool, run around with, run with, string along with, swing with, take up with, team up, throw in together, tie in, tie up, truck with, work with; SEE CONCEPTS *114,384*

association [n1] *group with common interest or pursuit*
affiliation, alliance, band, bunch, circle, clan, clique, club, coalition, combination, combo, company, confederacy, confederation, congress, cooperative, corporation, crew, crowd, family, federation, fellowship, fraternity, gang, guild, hookup*, league, mob, order, organization, outfit, partnership, pool, rat pack*, ring, society, sodality, sorority, syndicate, tie-in, tie-up, tribe, troops, troupe, union, zoo*; SEE CONCEPTS *323,325,387*

association [n2] *friendship*
acquaintance, acquaintanceship, affiliation, agreement, assistance, camaraderie, companionship, comradeship, conjunction, cooperation, familiarity, fellowship, fraternization, frequenting, friendliness, hookup*, intimacy, membership, participation, partnership, relation, relationship; SEE CONCEPTS *387,388*

association [n3] *mental connection*
bond, combination, concomitance, concordance, connotation, correlation, identification, impression, joining, juxtaposition, linkage, linking, lumping together, mixing, mixture, pairing, recollection, relation, remembrance, tie, train of thought, union; SEE CONCEPT *39*

assorted [adj] *various*
different, diverse, diversified, heterogeneous, hybrid, indiscriminate, miscellaneous, mixed, motley, sundry, varied, variegated; SEE CONCEPT *564*

assortment [n] *variety*
array, choice, collection, combination, combo, diversity, garbage, group, hodgepodge, jumble, kind, medley, mélange, miscellany, mishmash, mixed bag, mixture, potpourri, selection, sort; SEE CONCEPTS *432,665*

assuage [v] *soothe, relieve*
allay, alleviate, appease, calm, compose, conciliate, cool*, ease, fill, lessen, lighten, lull, make nice*, mitigate, moderate, mollify, pacify, palliate, placate, pour oil on*, propitiate, quench, quiet, sate, satisfy, soften, still, surfeit, sweeten,

take the edge off*, take the sting out*, temper, tranquilize; SEE CONCEPTS 7,22,244

assume [v1] *believe, take for granted*
accept, ascertain, be afraid, be inclined to think, conclude, conjecture, consider, count upon, deduce, deem, divine, estimate, expect, fall for, fancy, find, gather, get the idea*, guess, have a hunch*, have sneaking suspicion, hypothesize, imagine, infer, judge, posit, postulate, predicate, presume, presuppose, speculate, suppose, surmise, suspect, theorize, think, understand; SEE CONCEPTS 12,26

assume [v2] *take, undertake*
accept, acquire, appropriate, arrogate, attend to, begin, confiscate, don, embark upon, embrace, enter upon, seize, set about, take on, take over, take up; SEE CONCEPTS 87,142

assume [v3] *pretend*
act, adopt, affect, bluff, counterfeit, fake, feign, imitate, impersonate, mimic, pretend, put on, simulate; SEE CONCEPT 59

assume [v4] *adopt, acquire*
annex, appropriate, arrogate, borrow, clap hands on*, commandeer, confiscate, expropriate, get fingers on*, get hands on*, glom onto*, grab, grab hold of*, hijack, kipe*, liberate, moonlight requisition*, preempt, seize, snatch, swipe, take over, usurp; SEE CONCEPTS 139,142

assumed [adj1] *pretended*
affected, artificial, bogus, counterfeit, fake, false, feigned, fictitious, imitation, made-up, make-believe, phony, pretended, put-on, sham, simulated, spurious; SEE CONCEPT 582

assumed [adj2] *expected*
accepted, conjectured, connoted, counted on, given, granted, hypothesized, hypothetical, inferred, postulated, presumed, presupposed, supposed, suppositional, surmised, tacit, taken as known, taken for granted, understood; SEE CONCEPTS 403,689

assuming [adj] *presumptuous, arrogant*
bold, conceited, disdainful, domineering, egotistic, forward, haughty, imperious, overbearing, pushy, rude; SEE CONCEPT 404

assumption [n1] *taking something for granted; something expected*
acceptance, accepting, assuming, belief, conjecture, expectation, fancy, guess, hunch, hypothesis, inference, posit, postulate, postulation, premise, presumption, presupposition, shot*, shot in the dark*, sneaking suspicion, stab, supposal, supposition, surmise, suspicion, theorization, theory; SEE CONCEPT 689

assumption [n2] *assuming possession, power*
acceptance, accepting, acquisition, adoption, appropriation, arrogation, assuming, embracing, grab, seizure, shouldering, takeover, taking, taking on, taking up, undertaking, usurpation; SEE CONCEPTS 129,142

assumption [n3] *arrogance*
brass*, chutzpah*, cockiness, conceit, imperiousness, insolence, nerve, presumption, pride, sass*, self-importance; SEE CONCEPT 411

assurance [n1] *statement to relieve doubt*
affirmation, assertion, declaration, guarantee, insurance, lock*, lock on*, oath, pledge, profession, promise, rain or shine*, security, shoo-in*, support, sure thing*, vow, warrant, warranty, word, word of honor; SEE CONCEPTS 71,278

assurance [n2] *confidence*
aggressiveness, aplomb, arrogance, assuredness, audacity, boldness, bravery, certainty, certitude, conviction, coolness, courage, effrontery, faith, firmness, impudence, nerve, poise, positiveness, presumption, security, self-confidence, self-reliance, sureness, surety, temerity, trust; SEE CONCEPT 410

assure [v1] *convince, relieve doubt*
bag*, bet on*, comfort, encourage, hearten, inspire, persuade, reassure, satisfy, sell*, sell on*, soothe; SEE CONCEPT 68

assure [v2] *promise*
affirm, attest, aver, brace up, buck up, certify, confirm, give one's word, guarantee, pledge, swear, vouch for, vow; SEE CONCEPT 71

assure [v3] *make certain*
cinch, clinch, complete, confirm, ensure, guarantee, have a lock on*, ice*, insure, lock, lock on, lock up, make sure, nail down*, put on ice*, seal, secure, set; SEE CONCEPTS 36,91

assured [adj1] *absolutely certain*
beyond doubt, cinched, clear-cut, clinched, confirmed, decided, definite, dependable, ensured, fixed, guaranteed, indubitable, insured, in the bag*, irrefutable, made certain, nailed down*, on ice*, pronounced, racked*, sealed, secure, set, settled, sewed up*, sure, surefire, undoubted, unquestionable; SEE CONCEPT 535

assured [adj2] *confident*
assertive, audacious, bold, brazen, certain, cocksure*, collected, complacent, composed, confident, cool, gung ho*, gutsy*, high*, imperturbable, overconfident, poised, positive, puffed up*, pumped up*, pushy, rosy*, sanguine, secure, self-assured, self-confident, self-possessed, sure, unflappable, unhesitating, upbeat*; SEE CONCEPTS 401,404

astern [adv] *backward*
abaft, aft, rear, rearward; SEE CONCEPT 581

astonish [v] *surprise*
amaze, astound, bewilder, blow away*, blow one's mind*, boggle, bowl over*, confound, daze, dumbfound, flabbergast, floor*, knock over*, overwhelm, put one away*, shock, spring on, stagger, startle, stun, stupefy, take aback, throw a curve*; SEE CONCEPT 42

astonishing [adj] *surprising*
amazing, astounding, bewildering, breathtaking, extraordinary, impressive, marvelous, miraculous, spectacular, staggering, startling, striking, stunning, stupefying, stupendous, wonderful, wondrous; SEE CONCEPTS 547,572

astonishment [n] *state of surprise*
amazement, astoundment, awe, bewilderment, confusion, consternation, dumbfoundment, one for the books*, shock, something else*, stunner, stupefaction, wonder, wonderment; SEE CONCEPTS 230,410

astound [v] *amaze*
astonish, bewilder, blow away, bowl over*, confound, confuse, daze, dumbfound, flabbergast, knock over with feather*, overwhelm, shock, stagger, startle, stun, stupefy, surprise, take aback; SEE CONCEPT 42

astray [adj] *off the path or right direction*
adrift, afield, amiss, awry, gone, lost, off, off course, off the mark, roaming, straying, vanished, wandering, wrong; SEE CONCEPTS 545,581

astride [*adj*] *with a leg on either side*
astraddle, athwart, on the back of, piggyback, sitting on, straddling; SEE CONCEPT *583*

astringent [*adj*] *harsh*
acetic, acrid, biting, bitter, cutting, sharp, tonic; SEE CONCEPTS *598,613*

astrology [*n*] *prophesy of the future by observation of stars and planets*
astrometry, horoscope; SEE CONCEPT *70*

astronaut [*n*] *space explorer*
cosmonaut, moonwalker, pilot, rocketeer, rocket scientist, space person, star person; SEE CONCEPT *348*

astronomy [*n*] *study of the stars and planets other than Earth*
astrochemistry, astrography, astrolithology, astrometry, astrophysics, selenology, sky-watching, stargazing, uranology; SEE CONCEPT *349*

astute [*adj*] *perceptive*
adroit, brainy, bright, calculating, canny, clever, crafty, discerning, foxy, insightful, intelligent, keen, knowing, not born yesterday*, on the ball*, perspicacious, quick on the uptake*, sagacious, savvy, sharp, sharp as a tack*, shrewd, sly; SEE CONCEPT *402*

asunder [*adv*] *apart; into pieces*
disconnected, disjoined, divided, in half, loose, separated, split, torn, to shreds; SEE CONCEPT *785*

asylum [*n1*] *refuge*
cover, den, harbor, haven, hideaway, hideout, hole, ivory tower*, port, preserve, refuge, retreat, safe house, safety, sanctuary, security, shelter; SEE CONCEPTS *435,515*

asylum [*n2*] *psychiatric hospital*
institution, loony bin*, madhouse*, mental hospital, mental institution, sanatorium; SEE CONCEPTS *312,439,516*

at [*prep*] *about; in the direction of*
appearing in, by, found in, in the vicinity of, near to, on, placed at, situated at, through, toward; SEE CONCEPTS *581,583,799*

atheism [*n*] *belief that no God exists*
disbelief, doubt, freethinking, godlessness, heresy, iconoclasm, impiety, infidelity, irreligion, irreverence, nihilism, nonbelief, paganism, skepticism, unbelief; SEE CONCEPT *689*

athlete [*n*] *person involved in sports*
amateur, animal, challenger, competitor, contender, contestant, games player, gorilla*, iron person*, jock, jockey, muscle person*, player, professional, shoulders, sport, sportsperson, superjock*; SEE CONCEPT *366*

athletic [*adj1*] *agile; prepared to participate in sports*
able-bodied, active, brawny, energetic, fit, lusty, muscular, powerful, robust, strapping, strong, sturdy, vigorous; SEE CONCEPTS *406,489*

athletic [*adj2*] *relating to sports*
competitive, contesting, exercise-related, recreational, sporting, team; SEE CONCEPT *536*

athletics [*n*] *sports*
contest, drill, events, exercises, games, practice, races, recreation, workout; SEE CONCEPT *363*

atmosphere [*n1*] *gases around the earth*
air, envelope, heavens, pressure, sky, substratosphere, troposphere; SEE CONCEPT *437*

atmosphere [*n2*] *general feeling or mood*
air, ambience, aura, background, character, climate, color, environment, feel, feeling, flavor, impression, local color, medium, mood, place, property, quality, scene, semblance, sense, space, spirit, surroundings, taste, tone; SEE CONCEPT *673*

atom [*n*] *smallest part of something*
bit, crumb, dot, fragment, grain, iota, jot, minimum, mite, modicum, molecule, morsel, mote, ounce, particle, scintilla, scrap, shred, smidgen, speck, spot, tittle, trace, whit; SEE CONCEPT *831*

atom bomb [*n*] *nuclear weapon*
A-bomb, backpack nuke*, doomsday machine*, fission bomb, H-bomb, hydrogen bomb, neutron bomb, nuclear bomb, nuke*, thermonuclear weapon; SEE CONCEPT *500*

atomic [*adj1*] *tiny*
diminutive, fragmentary, granular, microscopic, minute; SEE CONCEPT *773*

atomic [*adj2*] *nuclear*
atom-powered, fissionable, thermonuclear; SEE CONCEPT *485*

atone [*v*] *compensate; make amends for former misdoing*
absolve, answer, apologize, appease, balance, correct, counterbalance, do penance, expiate, make amends, make redress, make reparation, make up for, offset, outweigh, pay, pay one's dues*, propitiate, recompense, reconcile, redeem, redress, repair, set off, square, take one's medicine*; SEE CONCEPTS *108,126*

atonement [*n*] *compensation*
amends, expiation, indemnification, payment, penance, propitiation, recompense, redemption, redress, reparation, restitution, satisfaction; SEE CONCEPTS *126,337*

atrocious [*adj1*] *outrageous; widely condemned*
awful, bad, barbaric, beastly, desperate, diabolical, fiendish, flagrant, godawful*, grody*, gross*, hairy*, heinous, lousy, monstrous, nefarious, rotten, scandalous, shocking, villainous, wicked; SEE CONCEPTS *545,571*

atrocious [*adj2*] *offensive*
appalling, awful, bad, beastly, detestable, disgusting, dreadful, execrable, foul, godawful*, grody*, gross*, horrible, horrid, horrifying, icky*, loathsome, noisome, obscene, repulsive, rotten, sickening, terrible; SEE CONCEPTS *548,571*

atrocity [*n1*] *outrageous behavior*
atrociousness, barbarity, barbarousness, enormity, fiendishness, heinousness, horror, monstrousness, nefariousness, shockingness, villianousness, wickedness; SEE CONCEPTS *411,657*

atrocity [*n2*] *cruelness, offensiveness; widely condemned action*
abomination, barbarity, brutality, crime, enormity, evil, horror, infamy, inhumanity, iniquity, monstrosity, offense, outrage, ruthlessness, savagery, viciousness, wrong; SEE CONCEPTS *29,645*

atrophy [*n*] *wasting away; disintegration*
decline, degeneracy, degeneration, deterioration, diminution, downfall, downgrade; SEE CONCEPTS *674,698*

attach [*v1*] *join, fasten*
add, adhere, affix, annex, append, bind, connect, couple, fix, hitch on, hitch up, hook on, hook up, latch onto, link, make fast, prefix, rivet, secure, slap on*, stick, tag on*, tie, unite; SEE CONCEPTS *85,113,160*

attach [*v2*] *socially join*
accompany, affiliate, associate, become associated with, combine, enlist, join forces with, latch

onto*, sign on with, sign up with, unite with; SEE CONCEPT *114*

attach [*v3*] *attribute, ascribe*
allocate, allot, appoint, assign, associate, connect, consign, designate, detail, earmark, impute, invest with, lay, name, place, put, second, send; SEE CONCEPTS *62,73*

attachment [*n1*] *fastening*
adapter, bond, clamp, connection, connector, coupling, fastener, joint, junction, link, tie; SEE CONCEPT *471*

attachment [*n2*] *something joined, fastened to another*
accessory, accoutrement, adapter, addition, adjunct, annex, appendage, appurtenance, auxiliary, extension, extra, fitting, fixture, part, supplement; SEE CONCEPT *824*

attachment [*n3*] *affection, high regard*
affinity, amour, attraction, bond, case, crush, devotion, fidelity, fondness, friendship, hankering*, liking, love, loyalty, partiality, possessiveness, regard, shine*, tenderness, weakness, yen*; SEE CONCEPT *32*

attack [*n1*] *physical assault*
advance, aggression, assailing, assailment, barrage, blitz, blitzkrieg, charge, defilement, dirty deed*, drive, encounter, encroachment, foray, incursion, initiative, inroad, intervention, intrusion, invasion, irruption, mugging, offense, offensive, onrush, onset, onslaught, push, raid, rape, rush, skirmish, storming, strike, thrust, violation, volley; SEE CONCEPT *86*

attack [*n2*] *verbal assault*
abuse, aggression, belligerence, blame, calumny, censure, combativeness, criticism, denigration, denunciation, impugnment, libel, pugnacity, slander, vilification; SEE CONCEPTS *52,54*

attack [*n3*] *sudden dysfunction or disorder*
access, ailment, bout, breakdown, convulsion, disease, failure, fit, illness, paroxysm, relapse, seizure, spasm, spell, stroke, throe; SEE CONCEPT *308*

attack [*v1*] *assault physically*
advance, aggress, ambush, assail, assault, bash, bat, bean*, beat, beset, besiege, biff*, blast, blister, boff*, bombard, boot*, bop*, brain*, bust, charge, chop down, clip, clock*, club, combat, cook*, harm, hit, hurt, infiltrate, invade, jump, kick, knock block off*, knock cold*, knock for a loop*, larrup*, lay siege to, light into*, molest, mug, overwhelm, pounce upon, punch, raid, rush, set upon, slog, soak, stab, storm, strike, take the offensive, turn on, wallop*, whop*; SEE CONCEPT *86*

attack [*v2*] *assault verbally*
abuse, berate, blame, blitz, censure, criticize, impugn, jump down one's throat*, jump on one's case*, lay into, malign, refute, reprove, revile, shoot down*, stretch, vilify; SEE CONCEPTS *52,54*

attack [*v3*] *set to work*
buckle down*, deal with, dive into, plunge into, set to, start in on, tackle, take up, tear into*; SEE CONCEPT *112*

attain [*v*] *achieve, accomplish*
accede to, acquire, arrive, arrive at, bring off, come through, complete, cop*, earn, effect, fulfill, gain, get*, get fat*, get hands on, get there, glom onto*, grasp, hit, latch onto, make it, obtain, procure, promote, pull off*, rack up, reach,

realize, reap, score, secure, snag, succeed, unzip*, win; SEE CONCEPTS *120,706*

attainable [*adj*] *within reach; achievable*
accessible, accomplishable, at hand, available, cherry pie*, duck soup*, easy, feasible, gettable, likely, no problem*, no sweat*, obtainable, piece of cake*, possible, potential, practicable, probable, procurable, reachable, realizable, securable; SEE CONCEPTS *528,552*

attainment [*n*] *achievement, accomplishment*
acquirement, acquisition, arrival, completion, feat, finish, fulfillment, gaining, getting, obtaining, procurement, reaching, realization, reaping, securing, succeeding, winning; SEE CONCEPT *706*

attempt [*n*] *try, effort*
all one's got*, attack, bid*, crack*, dry run*, endeavor, exertion, experiment, fling, go, header*, lick*, one's all, one's darnedest*, one's level best*, pursuit, shot, stab, striving, struggle, trial, try, tryout, undertaking, venture, whack*, workout; SEE CONCEPT *87*

attempt [*v*] *try, make effort*
aim, attack, do level best*, endeavor, essay, exert oneself, experiment, give a fling*, give a whirl*, give best shot*, give it a go*, give it a try*, give old college try*, go the limit*, have a crack*, have a go at*, make a run at*, pursue, push, seek, shoot the works*, solicit, strive, tackle, take a stab at*, take best shot*, take on, try one's hand at*, undertake, venture; SEE CONCEPT *87*

attend [*v1*] *be present at*
appear, be a guest, be at, be present, be there, bob up*, catch, check in, clock in*, come to light*, drop in, frequent, go to, haunt, make an appearance, make it*, make the scene*, pop up*, punch in*, punch the clock*, ring in*, show, show up, sit in on, time in, turn up, visit; SEE CONCEPT *114*

attend [*v2*] *care for*
be in the service of, doctor, do for, look after, mind, minister to, nurse, serve, take care of, tend, wait upon, watch, work for; SEE CONCEPT *110*

attend [*v3*] *pay attention; apply oneself*
catch, concentrate on, devote oneself, follow, get a load of*, hear, hearken, heed, keep one's eye on*, lend an ear*, listen, listen up*, look after, look on, mark, mind, note, notice, observe, occupy oneself with, pay heed, pick up, regard, see to, watch; SEE CONCEPTS *34,596,623*

attend [*v4*] *accompany*
bear, be associated with, be connected with, catch, follow, issue from, make the scene, occur with, result from; SEE CONCEPT *714*

attend [*v5*] *escort*
accompany, chaperon, companion, consort, convoy, escort, guard, squire, usher; SEE CONCEPTS *114,714*

attendance [*n1*] *being present*
appearance, attending, being in evidence, being there, participation, presence; SEE CONCEPT *388*

attendance [*n2*] *people present at event*
assemblage, assembly, audience, box office, company, congregation, crowd, draw, gate, gathering, gross, house, observers, onlookers, patrons, public, spectators, turnout, witnesses; SEE CONCEPT *417*

attendant [*n*] *person who serves others*
aide, alarm clock*, assistant, auxiliary, baby sitter, bird dog, chaperon, companion, custodian, domestic, escort, follower, guide, helper, lackey,

nurse, orderly, secretary, servant, understudy, usher, waitperson; SEE CONCEPT *348*

attendant [*adj*] *being present or related*
accessory, accompanying, ancillary, associated, attending, coincident, concomitant, consequent, incident; SEE CONCEPT *577*

attention [*n1*] *concentration*
absorption, application, assiduity, consideration, contemplation, debate, deliberation, diligence, engrossment, heed, heedfulness, immersion, industry, intentness, mind, scrutiny, study, thinking, thought, thoughtfulness; SEE CONCEPT *409*

attention [*n2*] *consideration, care*
awareness, big rush*, brace, concern, consciousness, looking after, ministration, notice, observation, recognition, regard, spotlight, tender loving care, TLC*, treatment; SEE CONCEPTS *32,410*

attention(s) [*n3*] *courtesy*
amenity, assiduities, care, civility, compliment, consideration, deference, gallantry, mindfulness, politeness, regard, respect, service; SEE CONCEPT *644*

attentive [*adj1*] *concentrating*
alert, all ears*, awake, aware, conscientious, enrapt, enthralled, fascinated, glued, hanging on every word*, heedful, hooked, immersed, intent, interested, listening, mindful, observant, on one's toes*, on the ball*, on the job*, on the lookout*, on the qui vive*, preoccupied, regardful, studious, vigilant, watchful; SEE CONCEPT *403*

attentive [*adj2*] *considerate*
accommodating, civil, courteous, devoted, gallant, gracious, kind, obliging, polite, respectful, solicitous, thoughtful; SEE CONCEPT *401*

attenuate [*v*] *weaken*
abate, constrict, contract, cripple, debilitate, deflate, disable, dissipate, enfeeble, extenuate, lessen, mitigate, sap, shrink, thin, undermine, vitiate; SEE CONCEPT *240*

attest [*v*] *affirm, vouch for*
adjure, announce, argue, assert, asserverate, authenticate, aver, bear out, bear witness, certify, confirm, corroborate, countersign, declare, demonstrate, display, exhibit, give evidence, indicate, prove, ratify, seal, show, substantiate, support, sustain, swear, testify, uphold, verify, warrant, witness; SEE CONCEPT *49*

attic [*n*] *space under the roof of a house*
garret, loft, sky parlor*, top floor; SEE CONCEPTS *440,448*

attire [*n*] *clothing*
accoutrements, apparel, array, bib and tucker*, clothes, costume, drapes, dress, duds*, garb, garments, gear, getup, habiliments, habit, outfit, raiment, things, threads*, togs, uniform, vestment, wear; SEE CONCEPT *451*

attire [*v*] *clothe*
accoutre, array, clad, costume, deck, deck out*, doll up*, drape, dress, dud*, dude up*, equip, fit out, outfit, suit up, tog, turn out; SEE CONCEPT *167*

attitude [*n1*] *mental outlook*
air, angle, approach, belief, bent, bias, character, demeanor, disposition, frame of mind, headset*, inclination, leaning, like it is*, mental state, mindset*, mindtrip*, mood, notion, opinion, perspective, philosophy, point of view, position, posture, predilection, prejudice, proclivity, reaction, routine, say so*, sensibility, sentiment, set, slant, stance, stand, standing, standpoint, temper, temperament, twist, view, where one is at*; SEE CONCEPTS *410,689*

attitude [*n2*] *stance*
aspect, bearing, carriage, manner, mien, pose, position, posture, stand; SEE CONCEPT *757*

attorney [*n*] *lawyer*
advocate, ambulance chaser*, barrister, counsel, counselor, DA, fixer, front, legal beagle*, legal eagle*, lip*, mouthpiece*, pleader*, proxy, spieler*; SEE CONCEPT *355*

attract [*v*] *draw attention*
allure, appeal to, bait, beckon, beguile, bewitch, bring, captivate, charm, come on*, court, drag, draw, enchant, endear, engage, enthrall, entice, entrance, exert influence, fascinate, freak out*, give the come-on*, go over big, grab, hook, induce, interest, intrigue, inveigle, invite, kill, knock dead*, knock out*, lure, magnetize, make a hit with*, mousetrap*, pull, rope in*, score, seduce, send*, slay*, solicit, spellbind, steer, suck in*, sweep off one's feet*, tempt, turn on, vamp, wile, wow*; SEE CONCEPTS *7,11,22*

attraction [*n*] *ability to draw attention; something that draws attention*
allure, allurement, appeal, attractiveness, bait, captivation, charm, chemistry, come-on*, courting, draw, drawing power, enchantment, endearment, enthrallment, enticement, fascination, gravitation, inclination, inducement, interest, invitation, it*, lure, magnetism, pull, seduction, solicitation, temptation, tendency; SEE CONCEPTS *14,676*

attractive [*adj*] *appealing, drawing attention*
adorable, agreeable, alluring, beautiful, beckoning, bewitching, captivating, charming, comely, enchanting, engaging, enthralling, enticing, fair, fascinating, fetching, glamorous, good-looking, gorgeous, handsome, hunky*, interesting, inviting, looker*, lovely, luring, magnetic, mesmeric, pleasant, pleasing, prepossessing, pretty, provocative, seductive, stunning, taking, tantalizing, teasing, tempting, winning, winsome; SEE CONCEPTS *529,579*

attribute [*n*] *feature*
aspect, character, characteristic, facet, idiosyncrasy, indication, mark, note, particularity, peculiarity, point, property, quality, quirk, sign, speciality, symbol, trait, virtue; SEE CONCEPTS *411,673,834*

attribute [*v*] *ascribe, assign to source*
account for, accredit, apply, associate, blame, charge, connect, credit, fix upon, hang on, hold responsible, impute, lay, pin on, refer, reference, trace; SEE CONCEPT *73*

attrition [*n1*] *wearing down or away*
abrasion, attenuation, debilitation, depreciation, disintegration, erosion, grinding, rubbing, thinning, weakening, wear; SEE CONCEPTS *469,776*

attrition [*n2*] *regret*
contriteness, penance, penitence, remorse, remorsefulness, repentance; SEE CONCEPTS *410,689*

attune [*v*] *adjust*
acclimatize, accommodate, accord, accustom, adapt, balance, compensate, conform, coordinate, counterbalance, familiarize, harmonize, integrate, make agree, proportion, reconcile, regulate, tune; SEE CONCEPT *232*

atypical [*adj*] *nonconforming*
aberrant, abnormal, anomalous, deviant, differ-

ent, divergent, exceptional, heteroclite, irregular, odd, peculiar, preternatural, strange, unnatural, unrepresentative; SEE CONCEPTS 547,564

auburn [n] *reddish-brown color*
chestnut, copper, hazel, henna, nut, russet, rust, tawny, titian; SEE CONCEPT 622

auction [n] *competitive sale; sale by bid*
bargain, jam*, sell-off; SEE CONCEPTS 324,345

audacious [adj1] *reckless, daring*
adventurous, aweless, bold, brassy, brave, cheeky*, courageous, daredevil, dauntless, enterprising, fearless, foolhardy, gutty*, intrepid, nervy, rash, resolute, risky, smart ass*, unafraid, uncurbed, undaunted, ungoverned, valiant, venturesome; SEE CONCEPT 401

audacious [adj2] *arrogant, presumptuous*
assuming, bantam, bold, brash, brassy, brazen, cheeky*, defiant, disrespectful, forward, impertinent, impudent, insolent, nervy, rude, saucy, shameless; SEE CONCEPTS 401,404

audacity [n1] *recklessness, daring*
adventurousness, audaciousness, boldness, bravery, courage, dauntlessness, enterprise, fearlessness, guts, intrepidity, nerve, rashness, valor, venturesomeness; SEE CONCEPT 633

audacity [n2] *arrogance, presumptuousness*
assurance, audaciousness, brass, cheek*, chutzpah*, cockiness*, crust, defiance, disrespectfulness, effrontery, forwardness, gall, guts*, gutsiness, hardiness, impertinence, impudence, insolence, moxie, nerve, rudeness, shamelessness, spunk, stuff*, temerity; SEE CONCEPTS 411,633

audible [adj] *able to be heard*
aural, auricular, clear, deafening, detectable, discernible, distinct, hearable, loud, loud enough, perceptible, plain, resounding, roaring, sounding, within earshot; SEE CONCEPTS 591,594

audience [n1] *group observing an entertainment or sporting event*
admirers, assemblage, assembly, congregation, crowd, devotees, fans, following, gallery, gathering, hearers, house, listeners, market, moviegoers, onlookers, patrons, playgoers, public, showgoers, spectators, theatergoers, turnout, viewers, witnesses; SEE CONCEPT 417

audience [n2] *hearing*
audition, conference, consideration, consultation, conversation, discussion, interview, meeting, reception; SEE CONCEPT 266

audit [n] *inspection of financial records*
analysis, balancing, check, checking, examination, investigation, report, review, scrutiny, survey, verification, view; SEE CONCEPT 330

audit [v] *inspect financial records*
analyze, balance, check, examine, go over, go through, investigate, report, review, scrutinize, sit in, survey, verify; SEE CONCEPTS 103,330

audition [n] *test of ability*
audience, demo, hearing, reading, trial, try on, tryout; SEE CONCEPT 290

auditor [n] *person who inspects financial records*
accountant, actuary, bookkeeper, cashier; SEE CONCEPT 348

auditorium [n] *room, building for entertainment events*
amphitheater, assembly hall, barn*, concert hall, hall, movie house, music hall, opera house, playhouse, reception hall, theater; SEE CONCEPTS 293,439,448

augment [v] *make greater; improve*
add to, aggrandize, amplify, beef up*, boost, build, build up, compound, develop, enhance, enlarge, expand, extend, grow, heighten, increase, inflate, intensify, magnify, mount, multiply, pad, piggyback*, progress, raise, reinforce, strengthen, sweeten, swell, tag on; SEE CONCEPTS 236,244,245

augmentation [n] *making greater; improving*
accession, accretion, addition, amplification, beefing up*, boost, buildup, development, enhancement, enlargement, enrichment, expansion, extension, fleshing out, growth, heightening, hike, increase, increment, inflation, intensification, magnification, multiplication, raise, reinforcement, rise, strengthening, swelling, up, upping; SEE CONCEPTS 244,245

augur [n] *predictor*
diviner, forecaster, harbinger, herald, oracle, prognosticator, prophet, seer, soothsayer; SEE CONCEPT 423

augur [v] *predict; be an omen of*
adumbrate, bespeak, bode, call it*, call the shots*, crystal-ball, figure out, forecast, foreshadow, foretell, harbinger, have a hunch, herald, portend, presage, prognosticate, promise, prophesy, psych out*, read, signify, soothsay; SEE CONCEPT 70

augury [n1] *omen*
auspice, boding, forerunner, foretoken, forewarning, harbinger, herald, portent, precursor, presage, prognostication, promise, prophecy, sign, token, warning; SEE CONCEPT 284

augury [n2] *prediction*
divination, prediction, prophecy, soothsaying; SEE CONCEPT 70

august [adj] *dignified, noble*
baronial, brilliant, eminent, exalted, glorious, grand, grandiose, highfalutin'*, high-minded, high-ranking, honorable, imposing, impressive, lofty, lordly, magnificent, majestic, monumental, pompous, regal, resplendent, stately, superb, venerable; SEE CONCEPTS 404,567

aura [n] *air, character*
ambience, appearance, aspect, atmosphere, background, emanation, feel, feeling, mood, quality, scent, semblance, suggestion, tone; SEE CONCEPT 673

auspices [n] *protection; support*
advocacy, aegis, authority, backing, care, charge, control, countenance, guidance, influence, patronage, sponsorship, supervision; SEE CONCEPTS 94,376

auspicious [adj] *encouraging; favorable*
advantageous, bright, favorable, felicitous, fortunate, golden, halcyon, happy, hopeful, lucky, opportune, promising, propitious, prosperous, rosy, timely, well-timed; SEE CONCEPT 572

austere [adj1] *severe in manner*
ascetic, astringent, cold, earnest, exacting, forbidding, formal, grave, grim, hard, harsh, inexorable, inflexible, obdurate, rigid, rigorous, serious, sober, solemn, somber, stern, stiff, strict, stringent, unfeeling, unrelenting; SEE CONCEPT 550

austere [adj2] *refraining; abstinent*
abstemious, ascetic, chaste, continent, economical, puritanical, self-denying, self-disciplined, sober, straightlaced, strict, subdued, unrelenting; SEE CONCEPT 401

austere [adj3] *grim, barren*
bald, bare, bare-bones, bleak, clean, dour, plain,

primitive, rustic, severe, simple, spare, spartan, stark, subdued, unadorned, unembellished, vanilla*; SEE CONCEPT 485

austerity [n1] *severity*
acerbity, asperity, astringence, coldness, exactingness, exactness, formality, formalness, gravity, grimness, hardness, harshness, inclemency, inflexibility, obduracy, rigidity, rigor, seriousness, solemnity, sternness, stiffness, strictness, stringency; SEE CONCEPT **644**

austerity [n2] *refraining; abstinence*
abstemiousness, asceticism, chasteness, chastity, continence, determination, economy, prudence, puritanism, self-denial, self-discipline, sobriety, stoicism, strictness, temperance; SEE CONCEPT **633**

austerity [n3] *grimness, barrenness*
baldness, bareness, dourness, economy, plainness, primitiveness, rusticism, severity, simplicity, spareness, spartanism, starkness, unadornment; SEE CONCEPT **723**

authentic [adj] *real, genuine*
accurate, actual, authoritative, bona fide, certain, convincing, credible, creditable, dependable, factual, faithful, for real*, legit*, legitimate, official, original, pure, reliable, sure, true, trustworthy, trusty, twenty-four carat*, valid, veritable; SEE CONCEPT **582**

authenticate [v] *establish as real, genuine*
accredit, attest, authorize, bear out, certify, confirm, corroborate, endorse, guarantee, justify, prove, substantiate, validate, verify, vouch, warrant; SEE CONCEPTS **12,103**

author [n] *composer of written work*
biographer, columnist, composer, creator, essayist, ghost, ghostwriter, ink slinger*, journalist, originator, playwright, poet, producer, prose writer, reporter, scribbler*, scribe, scripter, word slinger*, wordsmith, work-for-hire*, writer; SEE CONCEPT **348**

authoritarian [n] *domineering person*
absolutist, autocrat, despot, dictator, disciplinarian, tyrant; SEE CONCEPTS **354,412**

authoritarian [adj] *domineering*
absolute, authoritative, autocratic, despotic, dictatorial, disciplinarian, doctrinaire, dogmatic, harsh, imperious, magisterial, rigid, severe, strict, totalitarian, tyrannical, unyielding; SEE CONCEPTS **319,401**

authoritative [adj1] *recognized as true, valid*
accurate, attested, authentic, authenticated, circumstantiated, confirmed, definitive, dependable, documented, factual, faithful, learned, legit*, proven, reliable, righteous, scholarly, sound, straight from horse's mouth*, supported, trustworthy, truthful, validated, verified, veritable; SEE CONCEPT **582**

authoritative [adj2] *domineering*
assertive, authoritarian, autocratic, commanding, confident, decisive, dictatorial, doctrinaire, dogmatic, dominating, imperative, imperious, imposing, masterly, officious, peremptory, self-assured; SEE CONCEPT **550**

authoritative [adj3] *official, authorized*
administrative, approved, bureaucratic, canonical, departmental, ex cathedra, executive, ex officio, imperial, lawful, legal, legitimate, magisterial, mandatory, ruling, sanctioned, sovereign, supreme; SEE CONCEPTS **319,536**

authority [n1] *power, control*
ascendancy, authorization, beef*, charge, clout*, command, credit, domination, dominion, edge, esteem, force, goods*, government, guts*, influence, juice*, jump, jurisdiction, leg up*, license, mastery, might, might and main*, permission, permit, pizzazz*, pow*, powerhouse, prerogative, prestige, punch, right, ropes*, rule, say, say-so*, steam, strength, strong arm*, stuff*, supremacy, sway, upper hand*, warrant, weight, what it takes*, whip hand*, word, zap*; SEE CONCEPTS **376,685,688**

authority [n2] *expert, animate or inanimate*
arbiter, aristocrat, bible, big cheese*, big shot*, big wig*, boss, brains*, brass*, buff*, CEO, city hall*, connoisseur, czar, egghead*, establishment*, exec*, executive, expert, feds*, front office*, governor, guru, ivory dome*, judge, kingfish*, kingpin*, law*, power elite, pro, professional, professor, pundit, scholar, specialist, textbook*, top brass*, top dog*, top hand*, upstairs*, veteran, virtuoso, whiz, wizard; SEE CONCEPTS **280,348,354**

authorize [v1] *give power or control*
accredit, bless, commission, empower, enable, entitle, give authority, give the go-ahead*, give the green light*, give the word*, invest, license, okay, rubber-stamp*, say the word*, vest; SEE CONCEPTS **50,88**

authorize [v2] *permit, allow*
affirm, approve, confirm, countenance, endorse, give leave, let, license, qualify, ratify, sanction, suffer, tolerate, warrant; SEE CONCEPTS **10,83**

autobiography [n] *written account of one's own life*
adventures, bio, biography, confession, diary, experience, journal, letter, letters, life, life story, memoir, personal history, reminiscences, self-portrayal; SEE CONCEPT **280**

autocracy [n] *government by one*
absolutism, czarism, despotism, dictatorship, monarchy, monocracy, oppression, totalitarian government, tyranny; SEE CONCEPTS **354,691**

autocratic [adj] *holding power exclusively*
absolute, all-powerful, arbitrary, bossy, czarlike, despotic, dictatorial, domineering, driving, imperious, monocratic, pushing, tyrannical, tyrannous; SEE CONCEPTS **319,536**

autograph [n] *handwritten signature*
endorsement, handwriting, inscription, John Hancock*, seal, token, undersignature, writing; SEE CONCEPT **284**

autograph [v] *write signature*
endorse, engross, handwrite, ink, inscribe, pen, sign, signature, subscribe, write by hand; SEE CONCEPT **79**

automated [adj] *made or done by a machine*
automatic, computerized, electrical, electronic, mechanical, mechanized, motorized, programmed, robotic; SEE CONCEPTS **538,549**

automatic [adj1] *done or made by machine*
automated, electric, electronic, mechanical, mechanized, motorized, robotic, self-moving, self-regulating, self-starting; SEE CONCEPTS **538,549**

automatic [adj2] *done by habit*
autogenetic, habitual, impulsive, instinctive, instinctual, intuitive, involuntary, knee-jerk, mechanical, natural, perfunctory, reflex, routine, spontaneous, unconscious, unforced, uninten-

tional, unmeditated, unthinking, unwilled; SEE
CONCEPTS *403,538*

automatic [*adj3*] *occurring as natural consequence*
assured, certain, inescapable, inevitable, necessary, routine, unavoidable; SEE CONCEPTS *530,535*

automation [*n*] *machine control*
computerization, industrialization, mechanization; SEE CONCEPT *770*

automobile [*n*] *land vehicle; car*
auto, bucket of bolts*, bug*, buggy*, bus, clunker*, compact, convertible, crate*, four-wheeler*, gas guzzler*, go-cart*, hardtop, hatchback, heap*, jalopy*, junker*, lemon*, limousine, motor car, oil burner*, passenger car, pickup truck, ride*, sedan, sports car, station wagon, subcompact, taxi, transportation, truck, tub*, van, wheels*, wreck*; SEE CONCEPT *505*

autonomous [*adj*] *independent*
free, self-determining, self-governing, self-ruling, sovereign, uncontrolled; SEE CONCEPT *554*

autonomy [*n*] *independence*
freedom, liberty, self-determination, self-government, self-rule, sovereignty; SEE CONCEPT *652*

autopsy [*n*] *examination of dead body*
dissection, necropsy, pathological examination, postmortem; SEE CONCEPTS *103,310*

autumn [*n*] *season between summer and winter*
autumnal equinox, fall, harvest; SEE CONCEPT *814*

auxiliary [*n*] *helper*
accessory, accomplice, adjutant, ally, assistant, associate, companion, confederate, crutch*, partner, reserve, subordinate, supporter; SEE CONCEPT *423*

auxiliary [*adj*] *supplementary*
abetting, accessory, adjuvant, ancillary, appurtenant, backup, complementary, contributory, extra, reserve, secondary, spare, subordinate, subservient, subsidiary, supporting; SEE CONCEPTS *546,824*

avail [*n*] *use*
account, advantage, applicability, appropriateness, fitness, service, usefulness; SEE CONCEPT *680*

avail [*v*] *be of use; use*
account, advantage, answer, be adequate, benefit, fill, fulfill, meet, profit, satisfy, serve, suffice, work; SEE CONCEPTS *91,225*

available [*adj*] *ready for use*
accessible, achievable, applicable, at hand, at one's disposal*, attainable, come-at-able*, convenient, derivable from, feasible, free, getatable*, handy, obtainable, on deck*, on hand*, on tap*, open to, possible, prepared, procurable, purchasable, reachable, ready willing and able*, realizable, securable, serviceable, up for grabs*, usable, vacant; SEE CONCEPT *576*

avalanche [*n*] *falling large mass; sudden rush of large quantity*
barrage, deluge, flood, inundation, landslide, landslip, snowslide, torrent; SEE CONCEPTS *509,524,787*

avant-garde [*adj*] *unconventional, forward-looking*
beat*, experimental, head*, hip*, innovative, lead, leading-edge*, liberal, new, new wave, pioneering, progressive, radical, state-of-the-art, vanguard*; SEE CONCEPTS *564,585*

avarice [*n*] *extreme greed*
avidity, close-fistedness*, covetousness, cupidity, frugality, grabbiness, greediness, miserliness, niggardliness, parsimony, penny-pinching*, penuriousness, rapacity, stinginess, thrift; SEE CONCEPTS *335,410*

avenge [*v*] *retaliate*
chasten, chastise, come back at, even the score, get back at, get even, payback, punish, redress, repay, requite, retribute, revenge, stick it to, take satisfaction, take vengeance, venge, vindicate; SEE CONCEPTS *122,126*

avenue [*n*] *street; path*
access, alley, approach, boulevard, channel, course, drive, entrance, entry, exit, outlet, parkway, passage, pathway, promenade, road, route, thoroughfare, way; SEE CONCEPT *501*

average [*n*] *normal, typical amount*
mean, median, medium, middle, midpoint, norm, par, rule, standard, usual; SEE CONCEPTS *647,787*

average [*adj1*] *normal, typical*
boilerplate*, common, commonplace, customary, dime a dozen*, everyday, fair, fair to middling*, familiar, garden*, garden-variety*, general, humdrum*, intermediate, mainstream, mediocre, medium, middle of the road*, middling, moderate, nowhere*, ordinary, passable, plastic*, regular, run of the mill*, so-so*, standard, tolerable, undistinguished, unexceptional, usual; SEE CONCEPT *547*

average [*adj2*] *numerical mean*
intermediate, median, medium, middle; SEE CONCEPT *762*

average [*v*] *obtain numerical mean*
balance, equate, even out; SEE CONCEPT *764*

averse [*adj*] *opposing*
afraid, allergic, antagonistic, antipathetic, contrary, disinclined, disliking, having no use for*, hesitant, hostile, ill-disposed, indisposed, inimical, loath, nasty, perverse, reluctant, uneager, unfavorable, unfriendly, unwilling; SEE CONCEPTS *403,564*

aversion [*n*] *dislike; opposition*
abhorrence, abomination, allergy, animosity, antagonism, antipathy, detestation, disfavor, disgust, disinclination, disliking, displeasure, dissatisfaction, distaste, dread, hate, hatred, having no use for*, horror, hostility, indisposition, loathing, odium, reluctance, repugnance, repulsion, revulsion, unwillingness; SEE CONCEPT *29*

avert [*v*] *thwart; avoid by turning away*
avoid, deflect, deter, divert, fend off, foil, forestall, frustrate, halt, look away, preclude, prevent, rule out, shove aside, shunt, stave off, turn, turn aside, turn away, ward off; SEE CONCEPTS *121,623*

aviation [*n*] *flying an aircraft; study of flying aircraft*
aerodynamics, aeronautics, flight, navigation, piloting; SEE CONCEPTS *148,187,324*

aviator [*n*] *person who flies aircraft*
ace, aeronaut, airperson, barnstormer, bird legs*, eagle*, flier, hotshot*, jockey*, navigator, pilot; SEE CONCEPTS *348,366*

avid [*adj*] *enthusiastic*
ardent, athirst, avaricious, breathless, covetous, desirous, devoted, dying to*, eager, fanatical, fervent, gotta have*, grasping, greedy, hungry, im-

patient, insatiable, intense, keen, passionate, rapacious, ravenous, thirsty, voracious, zealous; SEE CONCEPTS 20,401,403

avocation [n] *hobby*
amusement, diversion, kick*, occupation, pastime, recreation, schtick*, shot*, side interest, sideline, thing*; SEE CONCEPT 364

avoid [v] *refrain or stay away from; prevent*
abstain, avert, bypass, circumlocute, circumvent, deflect, desist, ditch, divert, dodge, duck, elude, escape, eschew, evade, fake out*, fend off, flee, give the slip*, hide, hold off, jump, keep clear, lay low*, obviate, recoil, run for cover*, shake, shake and bake*, shake off, shirk, shrink from, shuffle off, shun, shy, sidestep, skip*, skip out on*, skip town*, skirt*, stay away, stay out, steer clear of*, step aside, turn aside, ward off, weave, withdraw; SEE CONCEPTS 102,121

avoidance [n] *eluding; preventing*
absention, circumvention, delay, departure, dodge, dodging, elusion, escape, escapism, eschewal, evasion, flight, forbearance, nonparticipation, parry, passive resistance, prevention, recession, recoil, restraint, retreat, run-around, self-restraint, shirking, shunning, steering clear of*; SEE CONCEPTS 102,121

avow [v] *state; profess*
acknowledge, admit, affirm, allow, assert, aver, avouch, concede, confess, cross one's heart*, declare, grant, maintain, own up, proclaim, swear, swear on bible*, swear up and down*; SEE CONCEPTS 49,60,71

await [v] *wait with expectation*
anticipate, attend, be prepared for, be ready for, cool one's heels*, count on, hang around*, hang in*, hang out*, hope, look for, look forward to, stay, sweat*, sweat it out*; SEE CONCEPT 26

awake [adj] *conscious; alert*
alive, aroused, attentive, awakened, aware, cognizant, excited, heedful, knowing, observant, on guard, roused, vigilant, wakeful, waking, watchful; SEE CONCEPTS 402,406

awake [v1] *become alert or cause to rise from sleep*
arise, awaken, call, gain consciousness, get up, roll out*, rouse, stir, wake, wake up; SEE CONCEPTS 250,315

awake [v2] *become or make aware*
activate, alert, animate, arouse, awaken, call forth, enliven, excite, incite, kindle, provoke, revive, stimulate, stir up, vivify; SEE CONCEPT 231

awaken [v] *make conscious or alert*
activate, animate, arouse, awake, call, enliven, excite, fan, incite, kindle, pile up*, provoke, rally, revive, rise and shine*, roll out*, rouse, show a leg*, stimulate, stir up, turn out*, vivify, wake; SEE CONCEPTS 7,19,22,105,231

awakening [n] *making conscious or alert*
activation, animating, arousal, awaking, birth, enlivening, incitement, kindling, provocation, rebirth, renewal, revival, rousing, stimulation, stirring up, vivication, waking, waking up; SEE CONCEPTS 13,105,231

award [n] *prize or reward*
accolade, adjudication, allotment, bestowal, citation, conferment, conferral, decision, decoration, decree, distinction, donation, endowment, feather in cap*, gift, gold, gold star*, grant, honor, order, presentation, scholarship, trophy, verdict; SEE CONCEPT 337

award [v] *give prize or reward*
accord, adjudge, allocate, allot, apportion, assign, bestow, concede, confer, decree, dish out*, distribute, donate, endow, fork out*, gift, grant, hand out, present, render, reward, shell out*, sweeten the kitty*; SEE CONCEPT 132

aware [adj] *knowledgeable*
acquainted, alert, alive, appraised, appreciative, apprehensive, apprised, attentive, au courant, awake, cognizant, conscious, cool*, enlightened, familiar, go-go*, groovy*, grounded*, heedful, hip*, informed, in the know*, in the picture*, into*, know-how, knowing, know the score*, know what's what*, latched on*, mindful, on the beam*, on to*, perceptive, plugged in*, receptive, savvy, sensible, sentient, sharp, tuned in, up on; wise, wised up*, wise to*, with it*; SEE CONCEPT 402

awareness [n] *knowledge*
acquaintance, acquaintanceship, alertness, aliveness, appreciation, apprehension, attention, attentiveness, cognizance, comprehension, consciousness, discernment, enlightenment, experience, familiarity, information, keenness, mindfulness, perception, realization, recognition, sensibility, sentience, understanding; SEE CONCEPT 409

away [adv1] *in another direction; at a distance*
abroad, absent, afar, apart, aside, beyond, distant, elsewhere, far afield, far away, far off, far remote, forth, from here, hence, not present, off, out of, out of the way, over, to one side; SEE CONCEPTS 581,778

away [adv2] *continuously*
endlessly, forever, incessantly, interminably, on and on, relentlessly, repeatedly, tirelessly, unremittingly, without break, without end, without rest, without stopping; SEE CONCEPT 553

awe [n] *amazement*
admiration, apprehension, astonishment, consternation, dread, esteem, fear, fright, horror, regard, respect, reverence, shock, stupefaction, terror, veneration, wonder, wonderment, worship; SEE CONCEPTS 230,410

awe [v] *amaze*
alarm, appall, astonish, blow away*, cow*, daunt, dazzle, flabbergast, frighten, grandstand, horrify, hotdog*, impress, intimidate, knock socks off*, overawe, scare, showboat*, startle, strike, stun, stupefy, terrify; SEE CONCEPTS 7,19,22,42

awesome [adj] *amazing*
alarming, astonishing, awe-inspiring, awful, beautiful, breathtaking, daunting, dreadful, exalted, fearful, fearsome, formidable, frantic, frightening, grand, hairy*, horrible, horrifying, imposing, impressive, intimidating, magnificent, majestic, mean, mind-blowing*, moving, nervous, overwhelming, real gone*, shocking, something else*, striking, stunning, stupefying, terrible, terrifying, wonderful, wondrous, zero cool*; SEE CONCEPTS 537,572

awful [adj] *very bad; terrible*
abominable, alarming, appalling, atrocious, deplorable, depressing, dire, disgusting, distressing, dreadful, fearful, frightful, ghastly, grody*, gross*, gruesome, grungy*, harrowing, hideous, horrendous, horrible, horrific, horrifying, nasty, offensive, raunchy, repulsive, shocking, stinking,

synthetic, tough, ugly, unpleasant, unsightly; SEE CONCEPTS *570,571*

awfully [*adv1*] *badly*
clumsily, disgracefully, disreputably, dreadfully, inadequately, incompletely, poorly, reprehensibly, shoddily, unforgivably, unpleasantly, wickedly, wretchedly; SEE CONCEPTS *570,571*

awfully [*adv2*] *very*
badly, dreadfully, excessively, extremely, greatly, hugely, immensely, indeed, much, quite, terribly, truly, very much; SEE CONCEPT *569*

awhile [*adv*] *for a short period*
briefly, for a bit, for a little while, for a moment, for a spell, for a while, for the moment, momentarily, not for long, temporarily, transiently; SEE CONCEPT *798*

awkward [*adj1*] *clumsy, inelegant*
all thumbs*, amateurish, artless, blundering, bulky, bumbling, bungling, butterfingers*, coarse, floundering, gawky, graceless, green*, having two left feet*, having two left hands*, incompetent, inept, inexpert, klutzy*, lumbering, maladroit, oafish, rude, stiff, stumbling, uncoordinated, uncouth, unfit, ungainly, ungraceful, unhandy, unpolished, unrefined, unskilled, unskillful; SEE CONCEPTS *406,480,527*

awkward [*adj2*] *difficult to handle*
annoying, bulky, chancy, cramped, cumbersome, dangerous, disagreeable, discommodious, hard to use, hazardous, incommodious, inconvenient, perilous, risky, troublesome, uncomfortable, unhandy, unmanageable, unwieldy; SEE CONCEPTS *558,565*

awkward [*adj3*] *embarrassing*
compromising, delicate, difficult, embarrassed, ill at ease, inconvenient, inopportune, painful, perplexing, sticky*, thorny*, ticklish*, troublesome, trying, uncomfortable, unpleasant, untimely; SEE CONCEPT *555*

awkwardness [*n1*] *clumsiness; inelegance*
amateurishness, artlessness, boorishness, cloddishness, coarseness, crudeness, gawkiness, gracelessness, greenness*, ignorance, inability, incompetence, ineptitude, ineptness, inexpertness, maladroitness, oafishness, rudeness, tactlessness, uncoordination, uncouthness, ungainliness, unskillfulness; SEE CONCEPTS *405,630,717*

awkwardness [*n2*] *difficulty*
bulkiness, chanciness, cumbersomeness, danger, hazardousness, inconvenience, peril, perilousness, risk, troublesomeness, uncomfortableness, unhandiness, unmanageability, unwieldiness, SEE CONCEPTS *656,666*

awkwardness [*n3*] *embarrassment*
delicacy, difficulty, discomfort, inconvenience, inopportuneness, painfulness, stickiness*, thorniness*, ticklishness*, trouble, uncomfortableness, unpleasantness, untimeliness; SEE CONCEPT *388*

awning [*n*] *canopy*
covering, door cover, marquee, protection, shade, shelter, sunshade, tent; SEE CONCEPTS *440,473*

awry [*adj*] *off course; amiss*
afield, askance, askew, aslant, astray, badly, bent, cockeyed, crooked, curved, slanting, turned, wrong, zigzag; SEE CONCEPTS *537,581*

ax/axe [*n*] *large cutting tool*
adz, chopper, hatchet, tomahawk; SEE CONCEPT *499*

ax/axe [*v1*] *cut with large blade*
chop, cut, cut down, fell, hew; SEE CONCEPT *176*

ax/axe [*v2*] *dismiss from service*
boot*, bounce*, can*, cancel, cut back, discharge, dispense with, eliminate, fire, get rid of, give a pink slip*, give the boot*, kick out, lay off, remove, sack*, terminate, throw out; SEE CONCEPT *351*

axiom [*n*] *principle*
adage, aphorism, apothegm, device, dictum, fundamental, law, maxim, moral, postulate, precept, proposition, proverb, saying, theorem, truism, truth; SEE CONCEPTS *278,688,689*

axiomatic [*adj*] *understood; aphoristic*
absolute, accepted, aphoristic, apothegmatic, assumed, certain, fundamental, given, indubitable, manifest, obvious, presupposed, proverbial, self-evident, unquestioned; SEE CONCEPT *529*

axis [*n*] *point around which something revolves*
arbor, axle, hinge, pivot, pole, shaft, spindle, stalk, stem, support, turning point; SEE CONCEPT *830*

axle [*n*] *shaft around which wheels rotate*
arbor, axis, gudgeon, mandrel, pin, pivot, pole, rod, shaft, spindle, stalk, stem, support; SEE CONCEPTS *464,830*

B

babble [*n*] *trivial talk, often incessant*
blubbering, burble, chatter, clamor, drivel, gab, gabble, gibberish, gossip, gushing, idle talk, jabber, jabbering, jargon, murmur, muttering, prattle, ranting, tattling; SEE CONCEPTS *266,278*

babble [*v*] *talk trivially, often incessantly*
blab, blubber, blurt, burble, cackle, chat, chatter, gibber, go on, gossip, gush, jabber, mumble, murmur, mutter, patter, prate, prattle, rant, rave, run off at the mouth*, run on, spill the beans*, squeal*, talk foolishly, talk incoherently, talk nonsensically, tattle, trivialize, yak*, yakkety yak*; SEE CONCEPTS *51,266*

babe [*n*] *baby*
bairn, child, infant, little one, newborn, suckling; SEE CONCEPTS *414,424*

baby [*n*] *infant*
angelface*, babe, bairn, bambino, bundle, buttercup*, button, cherub, chick, child, crawler*, deduction*, dividend*, dumpling*, kid, little angel*, little darling*, little doll*, little one*, newborn, nipper*, nursling, papoose, preemie*, suckling, tad*, toddler, tot, write-off*, youngster; SEE CONCEPTS *414,424*

baby [*adj*] *miniature*
babyish, diminutive, dwarf, little, midget, mini*, minute, petite, small, tiny, wee, youthful; SEE CONCEPT *773*

baby [*v*] *treat like a child*
cater to, cherish, coddle, cosset, cuddle, dandle, dote on, foster, humor, indulge, nurse, overindulge, pamper, pet, please, satisfy, serve, spoil; SEE CONCEPTS *110,295*

babyhood [*n*] *period of infancy*
childhood, diaper days*, infanthood; SEE CONCEPT *817*

babyish [adj] *acting like an infant*
baby, childish, foolish, immature, infantile, juvenile, kid stuff, puerile, silly, sissy, spoiled; SEE CONCEPTS 401,550

baby-sit [v] *care for a child*
guard, sit, take care, tend, watch; SEE CONCEPT 295

bachelor [n] *unmarried man or woman*
available*, celibate, single*, single person, stag*, unattached; SEE CONCEPTS 415,419,423

back [n] *end part*
aft, back end, backside, extremity, far end, hindpart, hindquarters, posterior, rear, reverse, stern, tail, tail end, tailpiece; SEE CONCEPTS 392, 471,827,833

back [adj1] *end*
aback, abaft, aft, after, astern, back of, backward, behind, final, following, hind, hindmost, in the wake of, posterior, rear, rearmost, rearward, tail; SEE CONCEPTS 827,833

back [adj2] *from earlier time*
delayed, elapsed, former, overdue, past, previous; SEE CONCEPT 820

back [v1] *support*
abet, abide by, advocate, ally, angel*, assist, bankroll, boost, champion, countenance, encourage, endorse, favor, finance, give a boost, give a leg up*, give a lift*, go to bat for*, grubstake, sanction, second, side with, sponsor, stake, stand behind, stick by, stick up for, subsidize, sustain, underwrite, uphold; SEE CONCEPTS 8,50,88

back [v2] *put in reverse direction*
backtrack, drive back, fall back, recede, regress, repel, repulse, retire, retract, retreat, reverse, turn tail, withdraw; SEE CONCEPTS 195,208

backbiting [n] *hateful talk*
abuse, aspersion, backstabbing*, belittlement, calumniation, calumny, cattiness, defamation, denigration, depreciation, detraction, disparagement, gossip, invective, lie, malice, obloquy, scandal, slander, spite, spitefulness, tale, traducement, vilification, vituperation; SEE CONCEPTS 54,58,63

backbone [n1] *strength of character*
courage, determination, firmness, fortitude, grit, guts, hardihood, heart, intestinal fortitude*, mettle, moral fiber, nerve, pluck, resolution, resolve, spunk, stamina, steadfastness, tenacity, toughness, will, willpower; SEE CONCEPT 411

backbone [n2] *spinal column of vertebrate*
base, basis, foundation, spine, support, vertebrae, vertebral column; SEE CONCEPTS 420,442

back down [v] *withdraw from agreement or statement*
abandon, accede, admit, back off, back out, back pedal*, backtrack, balk, beg off*, cancel, chicken out*, concede, cop out*, demur, give in, give up, go back on, hold back, recant, recoil, renege, resign, retreat, surrender, take back, withdraw, yield; SEE CONCEPTS 266,697

backer [n] *supporter*
advocate, ally, angel*, benefactor, champion, endorser, follower, grubstaker, meal ticket*, money, patron, promoter, protagonist, sponsor, staker, underwriter, well-wisher; SEE CONCEPT 359

backfire [v] *have an opposite effect*
backlash, boomerang, bounce back, disappoint, fail, flop, miscarry, rebound, recoil, ricochet, spring back; SEE CONCEPTS 42,701

background [n] *experience or circumstances*
accomplishments, acquirement, actions, atmosphere, attainment, aura, backdrop, breeding, capacity, credentials, cultivation, culture, deeds, education, environment, framework, grounding, history, practice, preparation, qualification, rearing, seasoning, tradition, training, upbringing; SEE CONCEPTS 673,678,706

backing [n] *support*
abetment, accompaniment, adherence, advocacy, aegis, aid, assistance, auspices, championing, championship, encouragement, endorsement, funds, grant, help, patronage, reinforcement, sanction, secondment, sponsorship, subsidy; SEE CONCEPTS 110,332

backlash [n] *adverse reaction*
backfire, boomerang, counteraction, kickback, reaction, recoil, repercussion, resentment, resistance, response, retaliation, retroaction, tangle; SEE CONCEPT 230

backlog [n] *uncompleted work; accumulation*
excess, hoard, inventory, quantity, reserve(s), reservoir, resources, stock, stockpile, store, supply; SEE CONCEPTS 432,787

backpack [n] *sack carried on the back*
haversack, knapsack, pack, rucksack; SEE CONCEPT 446

backside [n] *rear end*
behind, bottom, butt*, buttocks, derrière, fanny*, posterior, rear, rump*, seat*, tail*, tush*; SEE CONCEPT 392

back talk [n] *nasty reply*
cheek, guff, lip, mouth, sass; SEE CONCEPTS 46,278

backward [adj1] *toward the rear*
astern, behind, inverted, rearward, regressive, retrograde; SEE CONCEPT 581

backward [adj2] *bashful*
afraid, averse, demure, diffident, disinclined, hesitant, hesitating, humble, indisposed, late, loath, modest, reluctant, reserved, retiring, shy, sluggish, tardy, timid, uneager, unwilling, wavering; SEE CONCEPT 401

backward [adj3] *slow in growth*
arrested, behind, checked, delayed, dense, dull, feeble-minded, imbecile, late, moronic, stupid, subnormal, underdeveloped, underprivileged, undeveloped; SEE CONCEPTS 402,562

backward [adv] *toward the rear*
aback, abaft, about, astern, back, behind, in reverse, inverted, rearward, turned around; SEE CONCEPT 581

backwash [n] *repercussion*
aftermath, result, wake; SEE CONCEPTS 230,674

backwoods [n/adj] *forests; land distant from settled area*
backcountry, boondocks*, frontier, hinterland, interior, isolation, outback, rural area, sticks*, timberland, woodland; SEE CONCEPT 509

backyard [n] *expanse behind house*
courtyard, garden, grass, lawn, patio, play area, terrace, yard; SEE CONCEPT 513

bacteria [n] *microorganisms*
bacilli, germs, microbes, organisms, pathogens; SEE CONCEPTS 306,393

bad [adj1] *poor quality*
abominable, amiss, atrocious, awful, bad news*, beastly, blah*, bottom out, bummer*, careless, cheap, cheesy*, crappy*, cruddy*, crummy*, defective, deficient, diddly*, dissatisfactory, downer*, dreadful, erroneous, fallacious, faulty, garbage, godawful*, grody*, gross*, grungy*,

icky*, imperfect, inadequate, incorrect, inferior, junky*, lousy*, not good, off, poor, raunchy*, rough, sad, slipshod, stinking, substandard, synthetic, the pits*, unacceptable, unsatisfactory; SEE CONCEPT 571

bad [adj2] *harmful*
damaging, dangerous, deleterious, detrimental, hurtful, injurious, ruinous, unhealthy; SEE CONCEPTS 537,570

bad [adj3] *immoral*
base, corrupt, criminal, delinquent, evil, iniquitous, mean, reprobate, sinful, vicious, vile, villainous, wicked, wrong; SEE CONCEPT 545

bad [adj4] *mischievous*
disobedient, ill-behaved, misbehaving, naughty, unruly, wrong; SEE CONCEPT 401

bad [adj5] *decayed*
moldy, off, putrid, rancid, rotten, sour, spoiled; SEE CONCEPTS 485,613

bad [adj6] *severe*
disastrous, distressing, grave, harsh, intense, painful, serious, terrible; SEE CONCEPT 569

bad [adj7] *sick*
ailing, diseased, ill, in pain, unwell; SEE CONCEPT 314

bad [adj8] *sorry*
apologetic, conscience-stricken, contrite, crestfallen, dejected, depressed, disconsolate, down, downcast, downhearted, guilty, low, regretful, remorseful, sad, upset, woebegone; SEE CONCEPT 403

bad [adj9] *distressing*
adverse, disagreeable, discouraged, discouraging, displeasing, distressed, gloomy, grim, melancholy, troubled, troubling, unfavorable, unfortunate, unhappy, unpleasant; SEE CONCEPTS 403,529

badge [n] *emblem worn*
brand, cordon, device, identification, insignia, mark, marker, medallion, motto, pin, ribbon, scepter, shield, sign, stamp, symbol, token; SEE CONCEPTS 260,284,476

badger [v] *nag, bother*
annoy, bait, bug, bully, cat*, give the business*, goad, harass, harry, hassle, heckle, hound, importune, insist on, needle, nudge, pester, plague, ride, tease, torment, work on; SEE CONCEPTS 14,51

badly [adv1] *inadequately*
abominably, awkwardly, blunderingly, carelessly, clumsily, crudely, defectively, erroneously, faultily, feebly, haphazardly, imperfectly, incompetently, ineffectively, ineptly, maladroitly, negligently, poorly, shoddily, stupidly, unfavorably, unfortunately, unsatisfactorily, unskillfully, unsuccessfully, weakly, wrong, wrongly; SEE CONCEPT 571

badly [adv2] *immorally*
criminally, evilly, improperly, naughtily, shamefully, unethically, wickedly; SEE CONCEPT 545

badly [adv3] *very much; desperately*
acutely, deeply, exceedingly, extremely, gravely, greatly, hard, intensely, painfully, roughly, seriously, severely; SEE CONCEPT 569

baffle [v1] *perplex*
addle, amaze, astound, befuddle, bewilder, buffalo*, confound, confuse, daze, disconcert, dumbfound, elude, embarrass, faze, floor*, get, mix up, muddle, mystify, nonplus, puzzle, rattle,

stick*, stump*, stun, throw; SEE CONCEPTS 7,19,42

baffle [v2] *hinder*
beat, block, check, circumvent, dash, defeat, disappoint, foil, frustrate, impede, obstruct, prevent, ruin, thwart, upset; SEE CONCEPT 121

bag [n1] *container for one's possesions*
attaché, backpack, briefcase, carryall, carry-on, case, duffel, gear, handbag, haversack, holdall, kit, knapsack, pack, packet, pocket, pocketbook, poke, pouch, purse, rucksack, sac, sack, saddlebag, satchel, suitcase, tote; SEE CONCEPTS 339,450,494

bag [n2] *special interest*
expertise, favorite activity, hobby, preference, speciality, thing*; SEE CONCEPTS 32,529

bag [v1] *catch*
acquire, apprehend, capture, collar, gain, get, hook, kill, land, nab, nail, net, seize, shoot, take, trap; SEE CONCEPT 90

bag [v2] *droop*
balloon, billow, bulge, flap, flop, hang, lop, sag, swell; SEE CONCEPTS 754,757

baggage [n] *gear*
accoutrements, bags, belongings, carry-on, effects, equipment, fortnighter, gear, impedimenta, luggage, overnighter*, paraphernalia, parcels, slough, suitcases, things, tote, tote bag, trappings, two-suiter; SEE CONCEPT 494

baggy [adj] *drooping*
billowing, bulging, droopy, flabby, floppy, ill-fitting, loose, oversize, roomy, sagging, slack, unshapely; SEE CONCEPTS 486,490

bail [n] *money for assurance*
bond, collateral, guarantee, pawn, pledge, recognizance, security, surety, warrant, warranty; SEE CONCEPTS 318,332

bail out [v1] *help*
aid, deliver, release, relieve, rescue, spring; SEE CONCEPT 110

bail out [v2] *escape*
flee, quit, retreat, withdraw; SEE CONCEPT 102

bait [n] *something for luring*
allurement, attraction, bribe, come-on*, drag, enticement, inducement, lure, seducement, shill, snare, temptation, trap; SEE CONCEPT 709

bait [v1] *lure*
allure, attract, bedevil, beguile, draw, entice, fascinate, lead on, seduce, tempt; SEE CONCEPTS 9,14

bait [v2] *needle*
anger, annoy, badger, bother, gall, harass, heckle, hound, irk, irritate, nag, persecute, provoke, tease, torment; SEE CONCEPTS 7,19

bake [v] *cook in oven*
heat, melt, scorch, simmer, stew, warm; SEE CONCEPT 170

baked [adj] *cooked in oven*
dried, heated, melted, scorched, simmered, stewed, warmed; SEE CONCEPT 462

baker [n] *person who cooks baked goods*
chef, cook, dough puncher*, pastry maker; SEE CONCEPT 348

bakery [n] *cooking business where baked goods are produced*
bake shop, confectionery, pastry shop, pâtisserie; SEE CONCEPTS 325,439,449

balance [n1] *equilibrium*
antithesis, correspondence, counterbalance, equity, equivalence, evenness, even-steven*, hang,

ba
ba

harmony, parity, proportion, stasis, symmetry, tension; SEE CONCEPTS *664,667*

balance [n2] *composure*
equanimity, poise, self-control, self-possession, stability, steadfastness; SEE CONCEPT *633*

balance [n3] *money remaining in account*
difference, dividend, excess, profit, remainder, residue, rest, surplus; SEE CONCEPT *332*

balance [v1] *make equal; cause to have equilibrium*
accord, adjust, attune, cancel, collate, come out, come out even, compensate, correspond, counteract, counterbalance, equalize, equate, even, harmonize, level, make up for, match, neutralize, nullify, offset, oppose, pair off, parallel, poise, readjust, redeem, set, square, stabilize, steady, tie, weigh; SEE CONCEPTS *197,697*

balance [v2] *compare*
assess, consider, deliberate, estimate, evaluate, weigh; SEE CONCEPT *17*

balance [v3] *make equal numerically*
adjust, audit, calculate, compute, count, enumerate, equate, estimate, figure, settle, square, sum up, tally, total; SEE CONCEPT *764*

balanced [adj1] *equalized*
counterbalanced, equitable, equivalent, evened, fair, just, offset, proportional, stabilized, symmetrical, uniform; SEE CONCEPT *566*

balanced [adj2] *settled financially*
certified, confirmed, validated; SEE CONCEPT *334*

balance sheet [n] *financial statement including gains and losses for a period*
account, annual report, assets and liabilities, budget, ledger, report; SEE CONCEPTS *271,332*

balcony [n] *porch or structure above the ground*
balustrade, box*, catwalk, gallery, mezzanine, piazza, platform, porch, portico, stoop, terrace, veranda; SEE CONCEPT *440*

bald [adj1] *having no covering*
baldheaded, bare, barren, depilated, exposed, glabrous, hairless, head*, naked, shaven, skin head*, smooth, stark, uncovered; SEE CONCEPT *485*

bald [adj2] *simple, unadorned*
austere, bare, blunt, direct, downright, forthright, outright, plain, severe, straight, straightforward, unembellished; SEE CONCEPTS *485,589*

bale [n] *bunch*
bundle, package, parcel; SEE CONCEPT *432*

baleful [adj] *menacing*
calamitous, deadly, dire, evil, foreboding, harmful, hurtful, injurious, malevolent, malignant, noxious, ominous, pernicious, ruinous, sinister, threatening, venomous, vindictive, woeful; SEE CONCEPTS *537,570*

balk [v1] *stop short*
cramp, crimp, demur, desist, dodge, evade, flinch, hesitate, recoil, refuse, resist, shirk, shrink from, shy, turn down, upset apple cart*; SEE CONCEPTS *119,121,188*

balk [v2] *thwart*
baffle, bar, beat, check, circumvent, counteract, cramp, cramp one's style*, dash, defeat, disappoint, disconcert, foil, forestall, frustrate, hinder, obstruct, prevent, ruin, stall, stop, throw a curve*, throw monkey wrench in*, upset the apple cart*; SEE CONCEPT *121*

balky [adj] *uncooperative*
averse, contrary, hesitant, immovable, indisposed, inflexible, intractable, loath, negative, negativistic, obstinate, ornery, perverse, reluctant, stubborn, unbending, unmanageable, unpredictable, unruly; SEE CONCEPT *401*

ball [n1] *dance party*
hoedown, hoodang, hop, jump, mingle, prom, promenade, reception, shindig; SEE CONCEPT *386*

ball [n2] *globe, sphere*
apple, balloon, drop, globule, orb, pellet, pill, round, spheroid; SEE CONCEPT *436*

ballad [n] *narrative song*
carol, chant, ditty, serenade; SEE CONCEPT *595*

ballast [n] *something giving balance*
balance, brace, bracket, counterbalance, counterweight, equilibrium, sandbag, stability, stabilizer, support, weight; SEE CONCEPT *712*

ballet [n] *graceful, expressive dancing*
choreography, dance, toe dancing; SEE CONCEPT *263*

ballet dancer [n] *person who performs graceful dance*
company, coryphee, dancer, danseur, danseuse, figurant, figurante, hoofer*, prima ballerina; SEE CONCEPT *352*

balloon [n] *inflated material or vehicle*
airship, bladder, blimp, dirigible, zeppelin; SEE CONCEPTS *293,504*

balloon [v] *billow out; bloat*
belly, blow up, bulge, dilate, distend, enlarge, expand, inflate, puff out, swell; SEE CONCEPTS *208,756*

ballot [n1] *voting; recording of vote*
election, franchise, plebiscite, poll, polling, referendum, slate, tally, ticket; SEE CONCEPTS *300,301*

ballot [n2] *candidates from political party*
choice, lineup, slate, ticket; SEE CONCEPT *301*

balm [n1] *oily substance*
analgesic, application, balsam, cerate, compound, cream, demulcent, dressing, embrocation, emollient, formula, lotion, medicine, ointment, potion, poultice, preparation, prescription, salve, soother, soothing agent, unction, unguent; SEE CONCEPTS *307,466*

balm [n2] *something soothing*
alleviation, anodyne, assuagement, comfort, consolation, curative, cure, easement, mitigation, palliative, refreshment, relief, remedy, restorative, solace, soother; SEE CONCEPTS *337,529*

balmy [adj1] *comfortable with respect to weather*
mild, moderate, moist, pleasant, refreshing, summerlike, summery, temperate, tropical; SEE CONCEPTS *603,605*

balmy [adj2] *insane*
absurd, bugged out*, cracked*, crazed, crazy, daft, deranged, dotty*, foolish, harebrained*, idiotic, loony, mentally incompetent, moronic, nuts*, nutty*, odd, potty*, preposterous, silly, stupid, wacky; SEE CONCEPT *403*

bamboozle [v] *fool; cheat*
baffle, befuddle, bilk, con, confound, confuse, deceive, defraud, delude, dupe, flimflam*, hoax, hoodwink*, hornswoggle*, mystify, perplex, puzzle, stump, swindle, trick; SEE CONCEPT *59*

ban [n] *official forbiddance*
a thou-shalt-not*, boycott, censorship, don't*, embargo, injunction, interdiction, limitation, no-no*, off limits*, out of bounds*, prohibition, proscription, refusal, restriction, stoppage, suppression, taboo; SEE CONCEPTS *50,88,121,688*

ban [v] *officially forbid*
banish, bar, blackball*, close down, close up,

curse, declare illegal, disallow, enjoin, exclude, halt, ice out*, illegalize, inhibit, interdict, outlaw, pass by, pass up, prevent, prohibit, proscribe, restrict, shut out, suppress; SEE CONCEPTS 50,88,121

banal [adj] *commonplace*
blah*, bland, bromidic, clichéd, common, conventional, cornball*, cornfed*, corny, dull as dishwater*, dumb, everyday, flat, hackneyed, ho hum*, hokey*, humdrum*, insipid, mundane, nonplace, nothing, nowhere, old hat*, ordinary, pabulum*, pedestrian, platitudinous, square, stale, stereotyped, stock, stupid, tired, tripe, trite, unimaginative, unoriginal, vapid, watery, wishywashy*, zero*; SEE CONCEPT 530

banality [n] *common saying*
adage, boiler*, buzzword, chestnut*, cliché, corn*, dullsville*, familiar tune*, high camp*, hokum*, old chestnut*, old saw*, plate*, platitude, prosaicism, prosaism, saw*, trite phrase, trivia, triviality, truism; SEE CONCEPT 275

band [n1] *something which encircles*
bandage, bandeau, belt, binding, bond, braid, cable, chain, circle, circuit, copula, cord, fillet, harness, hoop, ligature, line, link, manacle, ribbon, ring, rope, sash, scarf, shackle, snood, stay, strap, string, strip, tape, tie, truss; SEE CONCEPTS 470,751

band [n2] *group of people with same interest*
assembly, association, bevy, body, bunch, clique, club, cluster, collection, company, corps, coterie, covey, crew, gang, gathering, horde, menagerie, outfit, party, society, troop, troupe; SEE CONCEPTS 387,391,417

band [n3] *musical group*
combo, ensemble, orchestra, philharmonic, symphony, troupe; SEE CONCEPT 294

band [v] *group or join group*
affiliate, ally, amalgamate, belt, coadjute, combine, conjoin, consolidate, federate, gather, league, merge, team, unite; SEE CONCEPTS 113,114

handage [n] *covering for wound*
cast, compress, dressing, gauze, plaster; SEE CONCEPT 311

bandage [v] *cover a wound*
bind, dress, swathe, truss, wrap; SEE CONCEPT 310

bandanna [n] *colorful scarf*
handkerchief, kerchief, neckerchief, silk; SEE CONCEPT 450

bandit [n] *thief*
brigand, criminal, crook, desperado, forager, gangster, gunperson, highwayperson, hijacker, holdup person, hooligan, marauder, mobster, outlaw, pillager, pirate, plunderer, racketeer, raider, ravager, robber, villain; SEE CONCEPT 412

bane [n] *cause of misery*
affliction, bête noir, blight, burden, calamity, curse, despair, destruction, disaster, downfall, fatal attraction, misery, nuisance, pest, plague, poison, ruin, ruination, scourge, torment, trial, trouble, undoing, venom, woe; SEE CONCEPTS 529,674

baneful [adj] *ruinous, injurious*
baleful, calamitous, deadly, deleterious, destructive, disastrous, evil, fatal, harmful, hurtful, malefic, noxious, pernicious, pestilent, pestilential, poisonous, venomous, wicked; SEE CONCEPTS 537,570

bang [n1] *explosive noise*
blast, boom, burst, clang, clap, clash, crack, detonation, discharge, howl, peal, pop, report, roar, roll, rumble, salvo, shot, slam, smash, sound, thud, thump, thunder, wham; SEE CONCEPT 595

bang [n2] *loud hit or knock*
bash, bat, belt, blow, box, bump, collide, crack, cuff, punch, slam, smack, smash, sock, stroke, wallop, whack, whop; SEE CONCEPT 189

bang [n3] *thrilling situation*
enjoyment, excitement, kick*, pleasant feeling, smash, wallop, wow*; SEE CONCEPT 230

bang [v1] *hit or knock loudly*
boom, burst, clang, clatter, crash, detonate, drum, echo, explode, make noise, peal, rattle, resound, sound, thump, thunder; SEE CONCEPTS 65,189

bang [v2] *moving by hitting hard*
bash, beat, bump, clatter, collide, crash, hammer, hit, knock, pound, pummel, rap, slam, smash, strike, thump, whack; SEE CONCEPT 189

bang [adv] *suddenly, with force*
abruptly, hard, headlong, head on, noisily, precisely, smack, straight, suddenly; SEE CONCEPT 540

banish [v] *expel from place or situation*
ban, cast out, deport, discard, discharge, dislodge, dismiss, dispel, drive away, eject, eliminate, eradicate, evict, exclude, excommunicate, exile, expatriate, expulse, extradict, get rid of, isolate, ostracize, oust, outlaw, proscribe, relegate, remove, rusticate, sequester, shake off, shut out, transport; SEE CONCEPTS 121,217

banister [n] *railing of stairs*
baluster, balustrade, handrail, rail, support; SEE CONCEPT 443

bank [n1] *financial institution*
coffer, countinghouse, credit union, depository, exchequer, fund, hoard, investment firm, repository, reserve, reservoir, safe, savings, stock, stockpile, store, storehouse, thrift, treasury, trust company, vault; SEE CONCEPTS 333,339,439

bank [n2] *ground bounding waters*
beach, cay, cliff, coast, edge, embankment, lakefront, lakeshore, lakeside, ledge, levee, oceanfront, reef, riverfront, riverside, seabank, seaboard, seafront, shore, strand, streamside, waterfront; SEE CONCEPT 509

bank [n3] *row or tier of objects*
array, dashboard, group, line, rank, row, sequence, series, succession; SEE CONCEPT 464

bank [v1] *collect money or advantage*
amass, deposit, heap, hill, hoard, invest, lay aside, lay away, mass, mound, pile, put by, salt away, save, sock away, speculate, squirrel, stash; SEE CONCEPTS 109,330

bank [v2] *lean or tilt*
bend, camber, cant, incline, pitch, slant, slope; SEE CONCEPTS 148,213

banker [n] *professional in financial institution*
broker, capitalist, croupier, dealer, financier, house, investor, manager, money-lender, officer, teller, treasurer, usurer; SEE CONCEPTS 347, 348,353

bank on [v] *depend upon*
assume, believe in, be sure about, bet on, build on, count on, gamble on, lean on, look to, reckon on, rely on, stake, trust, venture, wager; SEE CONCEPT 12

bankrupt [adj] *unable to pay debts*
broke, depleted, destitute, exhausted, failed, im-

poverished, in Chapter 11*, insolvent, lacking, lost, out of business, ruined, spent, tapped out; SEE CONCEPT *334*

bankruptcy [*n*] *inability to pay debts*
Chapter 11*, defalcation, default, destituteness, destitution, disaster, exhaustion, failure, indebtedness, indigence, insolvency, lack, liquidation, loss, nonpayment, overdraft, pauperism, privation, repudiation, ruin, ruination; SEE CONCEPT *335*

banner [*n*] *flag, usually with message*
banderole, burgee, colors, emblem, ensign, gonfalon, heading, headline, pennant, pennon, standard, streamer; SEE CONCEPTS *270,277,278*

banquet [*n*] *formal dinner, usually ceremonial*
feast, festivity, fete, meal, reception, regale, repast, spread, treat; SEE CONCEPTS *377,459*

bantam [*adj*] *small*
diminutive, little, petite, tiny; SEE CONCEPTS *491,773*

banter [*n*] *teasing*
badinage, chaff, chaffing, chitchat, derision, dissing*, exchange, fun, gossip, jeering, jesting, joking*, joshing, kidding, mockery, persiflage, play, raillery, repartee, ribbing, ridicule, small talk; SEE CONCEPTS *59,278*

banter [*v*] *tease*
chaff, deride, fool, fun, jeer, jest, jive*, joke, josh, kid, make fun of, mock, rag*, razz*, rib, ridicule, satirize, taunt; SEE CONCEPTS *59,273*

baptism [*n*] *church rite; initiation*
ablution, baptismal, christening, debut, dedication, dunking, immersion, introduction, launching, lustration, purgation, purge, purification, rite of passage, ritual, sanctification, sprinkling; SEE CONCEPTS *367,377*

baptize [*v*] *initiate in church rite*
admit, asperse, besprinkle, call, christen, cleanse, denominate, dip, dub, entitle, immerse, name, purify, regenerate, sprinkle, term, title; SEE CONCEPT *367*

bar [*n1*] *rod; straight length of material*
batten, billet, boom, crossbar, crosspiece, ingot, lever, paling, pig, pole, rail, rib, rule, shaft, slab, spar, spoke, stake, stick, streak, strip, stripe, stroke; SEE CONCEPTS *470,471*

bar [*n2*] *barrier; blockage*
barricade, blank wall, block, clog, deterrent, encumbrance, fence, hindrance, hurdle, impediment, obstacle, obstruction, pale, rail, railing, restraint, road block, snag, stop, stumbling block, traverse, wall; SEE CONCEPTS *470,652,680*

bar [*n3*] *establishment serving alcohol*
alehouse, barroom, beer garden, bistro, canteen, cocktail lounge, drinkery, inn, lounge, pub, public house, rathskeller, saloon, tap, taproom, tavern, watering hole*; SEE CONCEPTS *325,439*

bar [*n4*] *legal system*
attorneys, barristers, bench, counsel, counselors, court, courtroom, dock, judgment, judiciary, jurists, law, law court, law practice, lawyers, legal profession, solicitors, tribunal; SEE CONCEPTS *318,381*

bar [*v1*] *secure, usually with a length of material*
barricade, block, blockade, bolt, caulk, clog, close, dam, deadbolt, dike, fasten, fence, jam, latch, lock, plug, seal, secure, trammel, wall; SEE CONCEPTS *121,130*

bar [*v2*] *prohibit*
ban, boycott, circumvent, condemn, debar, deny, disallow, discountenance, discourage, eliminate, enjoin, except, exclude, exile, forbid, freeze out, frustrate, hinder, interdict, interfere, keep out, limit, obstruct, ostracize, outlaw, override, preclude, prevent, refuse, reject, restrain, rule out, segregate, shut out, stop, suspend; SEE CONCEPTS *50,61,88*

barb [*n1*] *point*
arrow, bristle, dart, prickle, prong, quill, shaft, spike, spur, thistle, thorn; SEE CONCEPTS *434,836*

barb [*n2*] *pointed comment*
affront, criticism, cut, dig, gibe, insult, rebuff, sarcasm, scoff, sneer; SEE CONCEPTS *52,54*

barbarian [*n*] *crude, savage person*
beast, bigot, boor, brute, cannibal, clod, hooligan, hun, ignoramus, lout, monster, philistine, rascal, ruffian, troglodyte, vandal; SEE CONCEPT *412*

barbarian [*adj*] *crude, savage*
barbaric, barbarous, boorish, brutal, coarse, cruel, inhuman, lowbrow, merciless, philistine, primitive, rough, rude, uncivil, uncivilized, uncouth, uncultivated, uncultured, unsophisticated, untamed, vicious, vulgar, wild; SEE CONCEPT *401*

barbaric [*adj*] *crude, savage*
barbarian, barbarous, boorish, brutal, coarse, cruel, fierce, graceless, inhuman, lowbrow, primitive, rough, rude, tasteless, uncivilized, uncouth, vulgar, wild; SEE CONCEPT *401*

barbarism [*n*] *crudity, savagery, especially in speech*
atrocity, barbarity, brutality, catachresis, coarseness, corruption, cruelty, impropriety, inhumanity, localism, malapropism, misusage, misuse, primitive culture, provincialism, solecism, uncivilizedness, vernacularism, vernacularity, vulgarism; SEE CONCEPTS *275,633*

barbarity [*n*] *crudity, savagery*
boorishness, brutality, crudeness, cruelty, inhumanity, ruthlessness, savageness, viciousness, vulgarity; SEE CONCEPT *633*

barbarous [*adj*] *crude, savage*
atrocious, barbarian, barbaric, brutal, brutish, coarse, cruel, ferocious, heartless, ignorant, inhuman, inhumane, monstrous, primitive, rough, rude, ruthless, sadistic, truculent, uncivil, uncivilized, uncouth, uncultured, unsophisticated, vicious, vulgar, wicked, wild, wolfish; SEE CONCEPT *401*

barbecue [*n1*] *meal cooked on grill*
bake, clam bake, cookout, party, picnic, weinie roast; SEE CONCEPT *459*

barbecue [*n2*] *grill for cookout*
broiler, charcoal grill, fireplace, gas grill, griddle, pit of coals, roaster, spit; SEE CONCEPT *493*

barbecue [*v*] *cook outside, usually on a grill*
broil, charcoal, fry, grill, rotisserie, sear; SEE CONCEPT *170*

barber [*n*] *hair cutter*
beautician, coiffeur, coiffeuse, cosmetologist, hairdresser, hair stylist, shaver, tonsorial artist; SEE CONCEPT *348*

bare [*adj1*] *without clothing*
bald, bareskinned, denuded, disrobed, divested, exposed, in one's birthday suit*, naked, nude, peeled, shorn, stripped, unclad, unclothed, uncovered, undressed, unrobed; SEE CONCEPT *485*

bare [*adj2*] *without covering or content*
arid, barren, blank, bleak, clear, desert, desolate, empty, lacking, mean, open, poor, scanty, scarce,

stark, unfurnished, vacant, vacuous, void, wanting; SEE CONCEPT *490*

bare [*adj3*] *simple, unadorned*
austere, bald, basic, blunt, chaste, cold, essential, hard, literal, meager, mere, modest, scant, severe, sheer, simple, spare, stark, unembellished, unornamented; SEE CONCEPT *562*

bare [*v*] *reveal*
disclose, divulge, exhibit, expose, publish, show, uncover, unroll, unveil; SEE CONCEPTS *60,138*

barefaced [*adj*] *shameless; open*
apparent, arrant, audacious, blatant, blunt, bold, brash, brassy, brazen, candid, clear, flagrant, frank, glaring, immodest, impudent, insolent, manifest, naked, obvious, palpable, temerarious, transparent, unabashed, unconcealed; SEE CONCEPT *401*

barefoot [*adj*] *wearing no shoes*
barefooted, discalceate, discalced, shoeless, unshod; SEE CONCEPT *406*

barely [*adj*] *not quite*
almost, hardly, just, only just, scantily, scarcely; SEE CONCEPT *772*

bareness [*n*] *state of being unclothed*
dishabille, nakedness, nudity, starkness, unadornment, undress; SEE CONCEPT *453*

bargain [*n1*] *agreement*
arrangement, bond, business, compact, contract, convention, covenant, deal, engagement, negotiation, pact, pledge, promise, stipulation, transaction, treaty, understanding; SEE CONCEPT *684*

bargain [*n2*] *something bought at cheap price*
budget price, buy, closeout, deal, discount, giveaway, good buy, good deal, good value, low price, markdown, nominal price, reduction, steal, value; SEE CONCEPTS *332,338*

bargain [*v*] *negotiate terms of sale or agreement*
agree, arrange, barter, buy, compromise, confer, contract, convene, deal, dicker, do business, haggle, make terms, palter, promise, sell, stipulate, trade, traffic, transact; SEE CONCEPTS *56,330*

bargain for [*v*] *expect*
aim for, anticipate, contemplate, count on, foresee, imagine, look for, plan on, reckon on; SEE CONCEPT *26*

barge [*n*] *large work boat*
ark, canal boat, dory, flatboat, freight ship, lighter, raft, scow; SEE CONCEPT *506*

barge in/barge into [*v*] *charge*
break in, burst in, collide, infringe, interrupt, intrude, muscle in, push, shove, stumble; SEE CONCEPTS *150,208*

bark [*n1*] *plant covering*
case, casing, coat, cortex, crust, husk, peeling, rind, shell, skin; SEE CONCEPT *428*

bark [*n2*] *animal yelp*
bay, growl, grunt, howl, roar, snarl, woof, yap, yip; SEE CONCEPT *64*

bark [*v1*] *yelp*
arf, bay, cry, gnarl, growl, howl, snap, snarl, woof, yap, yip; SEE CONCEPT *64*

bark [*v2*] *shout*
bawl, bellow, clamor, cry, growl, grumble, mutter, roar, snap, snarl, yell; SEE CONCEPT *77*

barn [*n*] *animal shelter*
farm building, outbuilding, shed; SEE CONCEPTS *439,517*

baroque [*adj*] *decorative, especially architecture*
bizarre, convoluted, elaborate, embellished, extravagant, flamboyant, florid, gilt, grotesque, ornamented, ornate, overdecorated, rich, rococo; SEE CONCEPTS *562,589*

barracks [*n*] *shelter for military*
billet, bivouac, camp, cantonment, dormitory, encampment, enclosure, garrison, headquarters, hut, prefab, quarters, Quonset hut, tent; SEE CONCEPTS *321,516*

barrage [*n1*] *weapon fire*
battery, blast, bombardment, broadside, cannonade, crossfire, curtain of fire, discharge, enfilade, fire, fusillade, gunfire, hail, salvo, shelling, shower, storm, volley; SEE CONCEPT *320*

barrage [*n2*] *profusion of something*
assault, attack, blast, bombardment, burst, deluge, hail, mass, onslaught, plethora, rain, shower, storm, stream, surge, torrent; SEE CONCEPT *787*

barrel [*n*] *cylindrical container*
butt, cask, cylinder, drum, firkin, hogshead, keg, pipe, receptacle, tub, tun, vat, vessel; SEE CONCEPT *494*

barren [*adj1*] *unable to support growth*
arid, depleted, desert, desolate, dry, effete, empty, fallow, fruitless, impotent, impoverished, infecund, infertile, parched, sterile, unbearing, uncultivable, unfertile, unfruitful, unproductive, waste; SEE CONCEPTS *485,527*

barren [*adj2*] *unprofitable*
dull, flat, fruitless, futile, lackluster, profitless, stale, uninspiring, unproductive, unrewarding, useless, vain, vapid; SEE CONCEPT *560*

barricade [*n*] *blocking object*
bar, barrier, blank wall, block, blockade, bulwark, fence, obstruction, palisade, rampart, roadblock, stockade, stop, wall; SEE CONCEPT *470*

barricade [*v*] *block, usually to protect*
bar, blockade, defend, fortify, obstruct, shut in; SEE CONCEPTS *130,201*

barrier [*n1*] *obstruction*
bar, barricade, blank wall, blockade, bound, boundary, confines, curtain, ditch, enclosure, fence, fortification, gully, hurdle, impediment, limit, moat, obstacle, pale, palisade, railing, rampart, roadblock, stop, trench, wall; SEE CONCEPTS *435,470,513*

barrier [*n2*] *obstruction to goal*
bar, check, difficulty, drawback, encumbrance, handicap, hindrance, hurdle, impediment, limitation, obstacle, pale, preventive, restraint, restriction, stumbling block; SEE CONCEPT *532*

barter [*v*] *trade goods or services*
bargain, exchange, haggle, swap, trade, traffic, truck; SEE CONCEPT *104*

base [*n1*] *foundation*
basement, basis, bed, bedrock, bottom, foot, footing, ground, groundwork, infrastructure, pedestal, rest, root, seat, seating, stand, substratum, substructure, support, underpinning; SEE CONCEPT *442*

base [*n2*] *fundamental part*
authority, backbone, basis, chief constituent, core, essence, essential, evidence, foundation, fundamental, groundwork, heart, important part, infrastructure, key, origin, primary element, principal, principle, root, source, underpinning; SEE CONCEPT *826*

base [*n3*] *headquarters*
camp, center, depot, dock, field, garrison, hangar, harbor, home, port, post, settlement, site, starting point, station, strip, terminal; SEE CONCEPTS *435,449*

base [*adj*] *vulgar, low*
abject, abominable, cheap, coarse, common, contemptible, corrupt, depraved, despicable, disgraceful, dishonorable, disreputable, foul, grovelling, humble, ignoble, immoral, indelicate, loathsome, lowly, mean, menial, offensive, paltry, pitiful, plebeian, poor, scandalous, servile, shameful, shoddy, sleazy, sordid, sorry, squalid, trashy, ugly, unworthy, vile, worthless, wretched; SEE CONCEPTS 542,570

base [*v*] *build plan or opinion on*
construct, depend, derive, establish, found, ground, hinge, locate, plant, predicate, prop, rest, set up, station, stay; SEE CONCEPT 36

baseless [*adj*] *without substantiation*
bottomless, flimsy, foundationless, gratuitous, groundless, reasonless, unconfirmed, uncorroborated, unfounded, ungrounded, unjustifiable, unjustified, unsubstantiated, unsupported, untenable, unwarranted; SEE CONCEPT 582

basement [*n*] *room on lower floor of building*
bottom, cellar, crypt, excavation, furnace room, storage, substructure, subterranean room, underbuilding, understructure, vault; SEE CONCEPT 440

bashful [*adj*] *shy*
abashed, backward, blushful, blushing, chary, confused, constrained, coy, demure, diffident, embarrassed, humble, modest, nervous, overmodest, recoiling, reserved, reticent, retiring, self-conscious, self-effacing, shamefaced, sheepish, shrinking, silent, timid, timorous, unassertive; SEE CONCEPT 404

bashing [*n*] *abuse against a group or individual based on identity or ideological beliefs*
assault, attack, beating, beating up, bias crime, censure, charge, condemnation, criticism, denigration, harassment, hate crime, hounding, jumping, offensive, persecution, strike, torment; SEE CONCEPT 86

basic [*adj*] *elementary, fundamental*
basal, capital, central, chief, elemental, essential, indispensable, inherent, intrinsic, key, main, necessary, primary, primitive, principal, radical, substratal, underlying, vital; SEE CONCEPT 568

basically [*adv*] *fundamentally*
at heart, at the bottom, essentially, firstly, in essence, inherently, in substance, intrinsically, mostly, primarily, radically; SEE CONCEPT 568

basin [*n*] *container or area where water is held*
bay, bowl, concavity, depression, dip, ewer, gulf, hole, hollow, lagoon, pan, pool, pot, sag, sink, sinkage, sinkhole, tub, valley, vessel, watershed; SEE CONCEPTS 494,509,514

basis [*n1*] *physical foundation*
base, bed, bottom, foot, footing, ground, groundwork, rest, resting place, seat, substructure, support; SEE CONCEPT 442

basis [*n2*] *foundation for belief, action*
antecedent, assumption, authority, axiom, backbone, background, backing, base, bedrock, cause, center, chief ingredient, core, crux, data, dictum, essence, essential, evidence, explanation, footing, fundamental, hard fact, heart, infrastructure, justification, keynote, keystone, law, nexus, nucleus, postulate, premise, presumption, presupposition, principal element, principle, proof, reason, root, rudiment, sanction, security, source, substratum, support, theorem, theory, underpinning, warrant; SEE CONCEPTS 661,688,689

bask [*v1*] *lie in sunlight*
laze, loll, lounge, relax, sun, sunbathe, swim in, toast oneself*, warm oneself; SEE CONCEPTS 162,210

bask [*v2*] *lie in glory*
delight in, derive pleasure, enjoy, indulge, luxuriate, relish, revel, rollick, savor, take comfort, take pleasure, wallow, welter; SEE CONCEPT 32

basket [*n*] *woven container*
bassinet, bin, box, bushel, cradle, crate, creel, hamper, nacelle, pannier; SEE CONCEPT 494

bastard [*adj*] *illegitimate*
adulterated, baseborn, counterfeit, fake, false, imperfect, impure, inferior, irregular, misbegotten, misborn, mixed, mongrel, natural, phony, sham, spurious, suppositious, ungenuine; SEE CONCEPT 549

bastardize [*v*] *debase*
adulterate, bestialize, brutalize, corrupt, debauch, declare illegitimate, degrade, demoralize, deprave, pervert, vitiate, warp; SEE CONCEPT 44

baste [*v1*] *moisten during cooking*
brush with liquid, drip, grease, lard, season; SEE CONCEPT 170

baste [*v2*] *sew temporarily*
catch, fasten, stitch, tack; SEE CONCEPT 218

baste [*v3*] *pummel, thrash*
batter, beat, berate, blister, clobber, club, drub, lambaste, lash, maul, pelt, revile, scold, trounce, wallop, whip, whomp; SEE CONCEPTS 52,189

bastion [*n*] *support; fortified place*
breastwork, bulwark, citadel, defense, fortification, fortress, mainstay, parapet, prop, protection, rock, stronghold, support, tower of strength; SEE CONCEPT 712

bat [*n/v*] *a hit with a solid object*
bang, belt, blow, bop, crack, knock, rap, slam, smack, sock, strike, swat, thump, thwack, wallop, whack, whomp; SEE CONCEPT 189

batch [*n*] *group of same objects*
accumulation, aggregation, amount, array, assemblage, assortment, bunch, bundle, clump, cluster, clutch, collection, crowd, group, lot, pack, parcel, quantity, set, shipment, volume; SEE CONCEPTS 432,787

bath [*n1*] *washing with water and, usually, soap*
ablution, cleansing, dip, douche, dousing, gargle, laving, scrubbing, shower, soak, soaking, soaping, sponging, tub, wash; SEE CONCEPTS 161,165

bath [*n2*] *room for bathing*
bathroom, lavatory, powder room, restroom, sauna, shower, shower room, spa, steam room, toilet, washroom; SEE CONCEPT 448

bathe [*v*] *wash with water and, usually, soap*
bath, clean, cleanse, dip, douse, dunk, flood, hose, imbathe, imbue, immerse, moisten, rinse, scour, scrub, shower, soak, soap, sponge, steep, submerge, suffuse, tub, water, wet; SEE CONCEPTS 161,165

bathing suit [*n*] *clothing for swimming, sunning*
bathing costume, beach costume, bikini, maillot, one-piece, swimsuit, trunks, two-piece; SEE CONCEPT 451

bathroom [*n*] *room for bathing, toilet use*
bath, lavatory, powder room, restroom, sauna, shower, shower room, spa, steam room, toilet, washroom, water closet; SEE CONCEPT 448

baton [*n*] *stick used for conducting or for protection*
billy, billy club, blackjack, club, cudgel, mace,

nightstick, rod, staff, truncheon, wand; SEE CONCEPTS 262,470,500

battalion [n] *military division*
army, brigade, company, contingent, corps, force, horde, host, legion, multitude, regiment, squadron, throng, unit; SEE CONCEPT 322

batten [v1] *fasten securely*
board up, clamp down, cover up, fix, nail down, secure, tie, tighten; SEE CONCEPTS 85,160

batten [v2] *grow fat*
burgeon, feed on, grow, prosper, thrive, wax; SEE CONCEPT 704

batter [n] *mixture before baking*
concoction, dough, mix, mush*, paste, preparation, recipe; SEE CONCEPTS 457,466

batter [v] *strike and damage*
assault, bash, beat, break, bruise, buffet, clobber, contuse, cripple, crush, dash, deface, demolish, destroy, disable, disfigure, drub, hurt, injure, lacerate, lambaste, lame, lash, mangle, mar, maul, mutilate, pelt, pommel, pound, pummel, punish, ruin, shatter, smash, thrash, wallop, wreck; SEE CONCEPTS 189,246,252

battery [n1] *series of similar things*
array, batch, body, bunch, bundle, chain, clot, clump, cluster, group, lot, ring, sequence, set, suite; SEE CONCEPT 432

battery [n2] *physical abuse*
assault, attack, beating, mayhem, mugging, onslaught, thumping, violence; SEE CONCEPTS 189,246

battery [n3] *group of weapons*
artillery, cannon, cannonry, gunnery unit, guns; SEE CONCEPTS 321,500

battle [n1] *military fight*
action, assault, attack, barrage, blitzkreig, bloodshed, bombing, brush, campaign, carnage, clash, combat, conflict, contention, crusade, encounter, engagement, fighting, fray, havoc, hostility, onset, onslaught, press, ravage, scrimmage, significant contact, skirmish, sortie, strife, struggle, war, warfare; SEE CONCEPT 106

battle [n2] *struggle*
agitation, campaign, clash, conflict, contest, controversy, crusade, debate, disagreement, dispute, strife; SEE CONCEPTS 46,106

battle [v] *fight, struggle*
agitate, argue, clamor, combat, contend, contest, dispute, feud, oppugn, skirmish, strive, tug, war, wrestle; SEE CONCEPTS 46,106

battlefield [n] *location of military fights*
arena, Armageddon, battleground, combat zone, field, front, front line, salient, theater of operations, theater of war; SEE CONCEPTS 198,321

bawdy [adj] *vulgar, dirty*
blue, cheap, coarse, erotic, gross, indecent, indecorous, indelicate, lascivious, lecherous, lewd, libidinous, licentious, lustful, obscene, off-color, prurient, ribald, risqué, rude, salacious, suggestive; SEE CONCEPT 545

bawl [v1] *yell*
bark, bellow, bluster, call, cheer, clamor, holler, howl, roar, rout, scream, screech, shout, shriek, vociferate; SEE CONCEPT 77

bawl [v2] *cry*
blubber*, boohoo*, howl, shed tears, sob, squall, wail, weep, yowl; SEE CONCEPTS 77,185

bay [n1] *shoreline indentation*
anchorage, arm, basin, bayou, bight, cove, estuary, fiord, firth, gulf, harbor, inlet, lagoon, loch, mouth, narrows, sound, strait; SEE CONCEPTS 509,514

bay [n2] *alcove in wall*
bow window, compartment, niche, nook, opening, oriel, recess; SEE CONCEPT 440

bay [n3] *howl*
bark, bellow, clamor, cry, growl, howl, ululation, wail, yelp; SEE CONCEPT 64

bazaar [n] *fair; sale place*
exchange, exposition, fete, market, marketplace, mart; SEE CONCEPTS 345,438,449

be [v1] *exist*
abide, act, be alive, breathe, continue, do, endure, go on, have being, have place, hold, inhabit, last, live, move, obtain, persist, prevail, remain, rest, stand, stay, subsist, survive; SEE CONCEPT 407

be [v2] *happen*
befall, come about, come to pass, occur, take place, transpire; SEE CONCEPT 2

beach [n] *sandy area by body of water*
bank, coast, lakeshore, lakeside, littoral, margin, oceanfront, seaboard, seafront, seashore, seaside, shingle, shore, strand, waterfront; SEE CONCEPTS 509,514

beached [adj] *grounded*
abandoned, aground, ashore, deserted, high and dry, marooned, stranded, wrecked; SEE CONCEPT 583

beacon [n] *light used as signal, guide*
alarm, alert, balefire, beam, bonfire, flare, guidepost, heliograph, lamp, lantern, lighthouse, lodestar, pharos, radar, rocket, sign, signal fire, smoke signal, warning signal, watchtower; SEE CONCEPT 628

bead [n] *droplet, blob*
bean, bubble, dab, dot, driblet, drop, globule, grain, particle, pea, pellet, pill, shot, speck, spherule, stone; SEE CONCEPT 436

beads [n] *string of small, often round, objects*
chaplet, choker, necklace, necklet, pearls, pendant, rosary, wampum; SEE CONCEPTS 368,446

beak [n] *nose of animal*
bill, mandible, muzzle, neb, nib, nozzle, pecker, proboscis, projection, prow, snout; SEE CONCEPT 392

beam [n1] *length of material used as support*
axle, bail, balk, bolster, boom, brace, cantilever, column, crossbar, crosspiece, girder, jamb, joist, lath, lintel, pile, piling, pillar, plank, pole, post, prop, rafter, reach, scaffolding, scantling, shaft, sill, spar, stanchion, stay, stringer, strip, strut, stud, timber, transverse, trestle, two-by-four; SEE CONCEPTS 471,479

beam [n2] *ray of light*
bar, beacon, chink, column, dartle, emission, finger, flicker, glare, gleam, glimmer, glint, glow, laser, radiation, ray, shaft, shimmer, shoot, sparkle, streak, stream, twinkle; SEE CONCEPTS 624,628

beam [v1] *broadcast on air waves*
emit, give off, give out, glare, glimmer, glow, radiate, send, shed, shine, throw off, transmit; SEE CONCEPTS 519,624

beam [v2] *smile broadly*
gleam, glow, grin, laugh, radiate, shine, smirk; SEE CONCEPT 185

beam [v3] *shine, as a light*
burn, emit, glare, gleam, glitter, glow, radiate, yield; SEE CONCEPT 624

ba
be

beaming [*adj1*] *radiant; beautiful*
bright, brilliant, effulgent, flashing, fulgent, gleaming, glistening, glittering, glowing, incandescent, lambent, lucent, luminous, refulgent, scintillating, sparkling; SEE CONCEPT *617*

beaming [*adj2*] *very happy*
animated, cheerful, genial, grinning, joyful, radiant, shining, smiling, sparkling, sunny; SEE CONCEPT *401*

bear [*v1*] *bring*
buck, carry, convey, deliver, ferry, fetch, lug, move, pack, take, tote, transfer, transport; SEE CONCEPTS *108,143*

bear [*v2*] *support mentally*
cherish, entertain, exhibit, harbor, have, hold, hold up, maintain, possess, shoulder, sustain, uphold, weigh upon; SEE CONCEPTS *8,12*

bear [*v3*] *endure*
abide, admit, allow, brook, encounter, experience, permit, put up with, stomach, suffer, tolerate, undergo; SEE CONCEPTS *23,239*

bear [*v4*] *give birth*
be delivered of, beget, breed, bring forth, create, develop, engender, form, fructify, generate, invent, make, parturitate, produce, propagate, provide, reproduce, yield; SEE CONCEPTS *173, 251,302,373*

bearable [*adj*] *endurable*
acceptable, admissible, allowable, livable, manageable, passable, satisfactory, sufferable, supportable, sustainable, tolerable; SEE CONCEPT *529*

beard [*n1*] *facial hair on human*
bristles, brush, five-o'clock shadow*, fuzz, goatee, imperial, muttonchops, Santa Claus*, stubble, Vandyke*; SEE CONCEPT *418*

beard [*n2*] *decoy*
false face, front, mask; SEE CONCEPT *716*

beard [*v*] *confront*
brave, face, oppose, stand up to; SEE CONCEPTS *46,96*

bearded [*adj*] *having facial hair*
barbate, beardy, bewhiskered, bristly, bushy, goateed, hairy, hirsute, shaggy, stubbled, stubbly, unshaven, whiskered; SEE CONCEPTS *406,485*

bearer [*n1*] *person who carries messages or delivery*
agent, beast of burden*, carrier, conveyor, courier, drogher, emissary, envoy, internuncio, messenger, porter, runner, servant, shipper, transporter; SEE CONCEPT *348*

bearer [*n2*] *person who requests payment of bill*
beneficiary, casher, collector, consignee, payee; SEE CONCEPT *353*

bearing [*n1*] *person's conduct, posture*
address, air, aspect, attitude, behavior, carriage, comportment, demeanor, deportment, display, front, look, manner, mien, poise, port, pose, presence, set, stand; SEE CONCEPTS *411,633*

bearing [*n2*] *significance*
application, connection, import, meaning, pertinence, reference, relation, relevance, weight; SEE CONCEPT *668*

bearing/bearings [*n3*] *position, usually of water vehicle*
aim, course, direction, location, orientation, point of compass, position, situation, track, way, whereabouts; SEE CONCEPTS *739,746*

bear on/bear upon [*v*] *concern*
affect, appertain to, apply, belong to, involve, per-

tain to, refer to, relate to, touch upon; SEE CONCEPT *532*

bear out [*v*] *substantiate*
authenticate, confirm, corroborate, endorse, justify, prove, substantiate, support, uphold, validate, verify, vindicate; SEE CONCEPTS *50,88,97*

bear with [*v*] *tolerate*
be patient, endure, forbear, make allowance, put up with, suffer, wait; SEE CONCEPT *23*

beast [*n*] *large wild animal; brute*
barbarian, beastie*, creature, critter*, fiend, gargoyle, glutton, lower animal, monster, monstrosity, pig, quadruped, swine, varmint*; SEE CONCEPT *394*

beastly [*adv1*] *savage; vulgar*
abominable, animal, barbarous, base, bestial, boorish, brutal, brute, brutish, carnal, coarse, cruel, degraded, depraved, disgusting, feral, ferine, foul, gluttonous, gross, inhuman, irrational, loathsome, low, monstrous, obscene, piggish, prurient, repulsive, sadistic, swinish, unclean, vile; SEE CONCEPT *401*

beastly [*adv2*] *offensive*
awful, disagreeable, disgusting, foul, gross, mean, nasty, revolting, rotten, terrible, unpleasant, vile; SEE CONCEPTS *537,542*

beat [*n1*] *throbbing*
cadence, cadency, flow, flutter, measure, meter, oscillation, palpitation, pound, pressure, pulsation, pulse, quake, quiver, rhyme, rhythm, ripple, shake, surge, swell, swing, throb, thump, tick, undulation, vibration; SEE CONCEPTS *150,185*

beat [*n2*] *blow, stroke*
hit, lash, punch, shake, slap, strike, swing, thump; SEE CONCEPT *189*

beat [*n3*] *area of responsibility*
circuit, course, march, path, patrol, precinct, rounds, route, walk, way; SEE CONCEPTS *513,532*

beat [*adj*] *very tired*
dog tired*, exhausted, fatigued, kaput*, wearied, weary, worn out; SEE CONCEPTS *316,720*

beat [*v1*] *injure by striking*
bang, bash, bat, batter, belt, box, break, bruise, buffet, cane, castigate, clout, club, collide, crush, cudgel, drub, flagellate, flail, flog, hammer, hit, knock, lambaste*, lash, lick*, maltreat, mash, maul, pelt, pound, pummel, punch, punish, ram, rap, slap, slug, smack, spank, strike, swat, thrash, thresh, thump, thwack, trounce, wallop, whale*, whip; SEE CONCEPTS *189,246*

beat [*v2*] *defeat, surpass*
best, better, be victorious, conquer, exceed, excel, outdo, outplay, outrival, outrun, outshine, outstrip, overcome, overtake, overwhelm, shoot ahead of, subdue, top, transcend, triumph, vanquish, whip; SEE CONCEPTS *95,141*

beat [*v3*] *forge*
fashion, form, hammer, malleate, model, pound, shape, work; SEE CONCEPTS *137,175*

beat [*v4*] *throb*
agitate, alternate, bob, bounce, buffet, flap, flicker, fluctuate, flutter, heave, jerk, jounce, oscillate, palpitate, pitch, pound, pulsate, pulse, quake, quaver, quiver, ripple, shake, shiver, swing, thrill, throb, thump, tremble, twitch, undulate, vibrate, writhe; SEE CONCEPTS *150,185*

beat [*v5*] *mix*
stir, whip; SEE CONCEPT *170*

beaten [*adj1*] *defeated*
baffled, bested, circumvented, conquered, cowed,

crushed, disappointed, discomfited, disheartened, frustrated, humbled, licked, mastered, overcome, overpowered, overthrown, overwhelmed, routed, ruined, subjugated, surmounted, thwarted, trounced, undone, vanquished, worsted; SEE CONCEPTS *403,674*

beaten [*adj2*] *forged*
formed, hammered, milled, pounded, rolled, shaped, stamped, tamped, tramped, tramped down, trodden, worked; SEE CONCEPTS *486,490*

beaten [*adj3*] *mixed*
aerated, blended, bubbly, churned, creamy, foamy, frothy, meringued, stirred, whipped, whisked; SEE CONCEPTS *491,606*

beatnik [*n*] *unconventional, free-sprited person*
beat, Bohemian, demonstrator, dropout, flower child*, hippie, iconoclast, maverick, nonconformist, peacenik*, protester, radical; SEE CONCEPT *423*

beau [*n*] *boyfriend*
admirer, beloved, cavalier, escort, fiancé, flame, gentleman caller, gentleman friend, honey, inamorato, love, lover, paramour, squire, steady, suitor, swain, sweetheart, true love; SEE CONCEPT *423*

beautiful [*adj*] *physically attractive*
admirable, alluring, angelic, appealing, beauteous, bewitching, charming, classy, comely, cute, dazzling, delicate, delightful, divine, elegant, enticing, excellent, exquisite, fair, fascinating, fine, foxy*, good-looking, gorgeous, graceful, grand, handsome, ideal, lovely, magnificent, marvelous, nice, pleasing, pretty, pulchritudinous, radiant, ravishing, refined, resplendent, shapely, sightly, splendid, statuesque, stunning, sublime, superb, symmetrical, taking, well-formed, wonderful; SEE CONCEPTS *485,579,589*

beautifully [*adv*] *in an attractive or pleasing manner*
alluringly, appealingly, attractively, bewitchingly, celestially, charmingly, cutely, delightfully, divinely, elegantly, entrancingly, excellently, exquisitely, gorgeously, gracefully, handsomely, ideally, magnificently, prettily, seductively, splendidly, sublimely, superbly, tastefully, wonderfully; SEE CONCEPT *544*

beautify [*v*] *make more physically attractive*
adorn, array, bedeck, deck, decorate, dress up, embellish, enhance, garnish, gild, glamorize, grace, improve, make up, ornament, prettify, set off, trim; SEE CONCEPT *162*

beauty [*n1*] *physical attractiveness*
adorableness, allure, allurement, artistry, attraction, bloom, charm, class, comeliness, delicacy, elegance, exquisiteness, fairness, fascination, glamor, good looks, grace, handsomeness, loveliness, polish, pulchritude, refinement, shapeliness, style, symmetry, winsomeness; SEE CONCEPT *718*

beauty [*n2*] *good-looking person*
Adonis*, Apollo*, beaut*, charmer, dream, dreamboat*, enchanter, eyeful*, good-looker*, head turner*, looker*, ornament*, stunner*, Venus*, vision; SEE CONCEPT *424*

beauty [*n3*] *advantage*
asset, attraction, benefit, blessing, boon, excellent, feature, good thing, importance, merit, value, worth; SEE CONCEPT *668*

because [*conj/prep*] *on account of*
as, as a result of, as long as, as things go, being,

by cause of, by reason of, by virtue of, considering, due to, for, for the reason that, for the sake of, in as much as, in behalf of, in that, in the interest of, in view of, now that, on the grounds that, over, owing to, seeing, since, thanks to, through, whereas; SEE CONCEPT *676*

beckon [*v*] *call, signal, or lure*
allure, ask, attract, bid, coax, command, demand, draw, entice, gesticulate, gesture, invite, motion, nod, pull, sign, summon, tempt, wave; SEE CONCEPTS *7,22,53,74*

become [*v1*] *evolve into*
alter to, assume form of, be converted to, be reduced to, be reformed, be remodeled, be transformed into, change into, come, come to be, convert, develop into, emerge as, eventually be, grow into, incline, mature, metamorphose, pass into, ripen into, shift, turn into, turn out, wax; SEE CONCEPT *701*

become [*v2*] *enhance*
accord, adorn, agree, augment, be appropriate, belong to, display, embellish, enrich, fit, flatter, garnish, go together, go with, grace, harmonize, heighten, make handsome, match, ornament, set off, suit; SEE CONCEPT *244*

becoming [*adj1*] *flattering*
acceptable, agreeable, attractive, beautiful, comely, cute, effective, enhancing, excellent, fair, graceful, handsome, neat, nice, presentable, pretty, seemly, tasteful, welcome, well-chosen; SEE CONCEPTS *579,589*

becoming [*adj2*] *suitable; appropriate*
befitting, comme il faut, compatible, conforming, congruous, correct, decent, decorous, fit, fitting, in keeping, nice, proper, right, seemly, worthy; SEE CONCEPT *558*

bed [*n1*] *furniture for sleeping*
bassinet, bedstead, berth, bunk, chaise, cot, couch, cradle, crib, davenport, divan, mattress, pallet, platform, sack, trundle; SEE CONCEPT *443*

bed [*n2*] *patch of ground for planting*
area, border, frame, garden, piece, plot, row, strip; SEE CONCEPTS *509,513*

bed [*n3*] *base, foundation*
basis, bedrock, bottom, ground, groundwork, rest, seat, substratum, understructure; SEE CONCEPT *442*

bed [*v*] *plant*
base, embed, establish, fix, found, implant, insert, settle, set up; SEE CONCEPTS *234,257*

bedazzle [*v*] *captivate*
astound, bewilder, blind, confuse, daze, dazzle, dumbfound, enchant, overwhelm, stagger, stun; SEE CONCEPTS *7,22,42*

bedding [*n*] *covering for sleeping furniture*
bedclothes, bed linen, bedspread, blanket, comforter, cover, coverlet, eiderdown, electric blanket, linen, pillow, pillowcase, quilt, sheet, spread, thermal blanket; SEE CONCEPTS *444,473*

bedlam [*n*] *chaotic situation*
chaos, clamor, commotion, confusion, din, disquiet, disquietude, furor, hubbub, madhouse, maelstrom, noise, pandemonium, racket, shambles, tumult, turmoil, uproar; SEE CONCEPTS *230,674*

bedraggled [*adj*] *unkempt*
decrepit, dilapidated, dirty, disheveled, disordered, dowdy, drenched, dripping, faded, messy, muddied, muddy, run-down, seedy, shabby, sloppy, slovenly, sodden, soiled, stained, sullied,

tacky, tattered, threadbare, untidy, wet; SEE CONCEPT 589

bedroom [n] *place for sleeping*
bedchamber, bunk room, chamber, cubicle, guest room; SEE CONCEPT 448

bedspread [n] *thick, often quilted, covering for bed*
bedcover, blanket, counterpane, cover, coverlet, spread; SEE CONCEPT 444

bee [n1] *honey-making, stinging insect*
bumblebee, drone, honey bee, killer bee, queen bee; SEE CONCEPT 398

bee [n2] *collective task*
communal gathering, harvest, party, social, work party; SEE CONCEPTS 362,386

beef [n1] *strong physical makeup*
arm, brawn, flesh, force, heftiness, meat, might, muscle, physique, power, robustness, sinew, steam, strength, thew, vigor; SEE CONCEPT 757

beef [n2] *complaint*
bickering, criticism, dispute, grievance, gripe, grouse, grumble, objection, protestation, quarrel, rhubarb*, squabble; SEE CONCEPT 52

beer [n] *alcoholic beverage made from malted grain*
ale, amber brew*, barley pop*, brew, brewski*, brown bottle*, chill*, cold coffee*, cold one*, hops, lager, malt, malt liquor, oil*, stout*, suds*; SEE CONCEPT 455

befall [v] *happen to; take place*
action, bechance, betide, break, chance, come down, come off, come to pass, cook*, cook up a storm*, cook with gas*, develop, ensue, fall, fall out, follow, gel, go, go down, hap*, happen, jell*, materialize, occur, shake*, smoke*, supervene, transpire; SEE CONCEPT 4

befitting [adj] *appropriate -*
according to Hoyle*, apt, becoming, behooving, beseeming, comme il faut, conforming, correct, decent, decorous, felicitous, fit, fitting, happy, just, kosher*, nice, on the button*, on the nose*, proper, right, right on*, seemly, suitable, what the doctor ordered*; SEE CONCEPTS 533,558

before [adv] *earlier*
afore, aforetime, ahead, ante, antecedently, anteriorly, back, before present, ere, fore, former, formerly, forward, gone, gone by, heretofore, in advance, in days of yore, in front, in old days, in the past, past, precendently, previous, previously, since, sooner, up to now; SEE CONCEPT 820

before [prep] *earlier than*
ahead of, ante, antecedent to, anterior to, ere, in advance of, in front of, preceding, previous to, prior to, since; SEE CONCEPT 820

beforehand [adj/adv] *early*
advanced, ahead, ahead of time, already, ante, antecedently, before, before now, earlier, fore, in advance, in anticipation, precedently, precocious, previous, previously, sooner; SEE CONCEPT 820

befriend [v] *make social acquaintance; support*
advise, aid, assist, back, benefit, buddy up*, case out*, come on to*, cotton to*, encourage, favor, get chummy with, get in with*, help, hit it off*, patronize, side with, stand by, sustain, take under one's wing*, take up with, uphold, welcome; SEE CONCEPTS 110,384

befuddle [v] *confuse*
addle, baffle, ball up*, bewilder, bother, daze, disorient, distract, dumbfound, fluster, inebriate, intoxicate, make punchy*, mix up, muddle, puz-

zle, shake, stupefy, throw off*; SEE CONCEPTS 7,19,42

beg [v1] *request*
abjure, advocate, apply to, ask, beseech, besiege, call to, canvass, conjure, crave, desire, entreat, impetrate, implore, importune, invoke, nag, obsecrate, obtest, petition, plead, pray, press, requisition, solicit, sue, supplicate, urge, woo, worry; SEE CONCEPT 48

beg [v2] *seek charity*
ask alms, benefit, bite*, brace, bum*, burn*, buzz*, cadge*, call on, call upon, chisel*, clamor for, dime up*, ding*, freeload*, hit up*, hustle, knock, live hand to mouth*, mendicate, mooch*, nick*, nickel up*, panhandle, pass the hat*, put the bite on*, put the touch on*, score*, scrounge, solicit charity, sponge*, sponge on*, tap, touch, want; SEE CONCEPT 53

beget [v] *create, bear*
afford, breed, bring, bring about, cause, effect, engender, father, generate, get, give rise to, multiply, occasion, procreate, produce, progenerate, propagate, reproduce, result in, sire; SEE CONCEPTS 173,251,374

beggar [n1] *person asking for charity*
asker, borrower, bum, deadbeat, hobo, mendicant, panhandler, rustler, scrounger, supplicant, supplicator, tramp, vagabond; SEE CONCEPTS 412,423

beggar [n2] *person in financial trouble*
alms person, bankrupt, dependent, down-and-out*, guttersnipe*, indigent, mendicant, pauper, poor person, poverty-stricken person, street person*, suppliant, vagrant, ward of state; SEE CONCEPT 423

begin [v1] *start*
activate, actualize, break ground, break the ice*, bring about, bring to pass, cause, commence, create, do, drive, effect, embark on, enter on, enter upon, establish, eventuate, found, generate, get going, give birth to, give impulse, go ahead, go into, impel, inaugurate, induce, initiate, instigate, institute, introduce, launch, lay foundation for, lead, make, make active, motivate, mount, occasion, open, originate, plunge into, prepare, produce, set about, set in motion, set up, trigger, undertake; SEE CONCEPTS 234,241

begin [v2] *come into being; become functional*
appear, arise, be born, bud, come forth, come into existence, come out, commence, crop up, dawn, derive from, emanate, emerge, enter, germinate, get going, get show on road*, get under way, grow out of, happen, issue forth, kick off, make tick*, occur, originate, proceed from, result from, rise, sail, send off, set, spring, sprout, start, stem from, take off; SEE CONCEPTS 105,680

beginner [n] *person unskilled in something*
abecedarian, amateur, apprentice, buckwheater*, catechumen, colt, fish*, fledgling, greenhorn, greenie*, initiate, learner, neophyte, newcomer, new kid on the block*, new person, novice, novitiate, probationer, recruit, starter, student, tenderfoot*, trainee, tyro; SEE CONCEPTS 423,424

beginning [n1] *start of an event or action*
alpha, basis, birth, blastoff*, commencement, creation, dawn, dawning, day one*, genesis, inauguration, inception, induction, infancy, initiation, installation, introduction, kickoff, onset, opener, opening, origin, origination, outset, point of departure, preface, prelude, presentation, rise, root,

rudiment, source, spring, square one*, starting point, takeoff, threshold, top; SEE CONCEPTS **815,833**

beginning [n2] *origin, cause*
antecedent, birth, conception, egg, embryo, font, fount, fountain, fountainhead, generation, genesis, germ, heart, principle, resource, root, seed, stem, well; SEE CONCEPT **229**

begrudge [v] *wish that someone did not have*
be jealous, be reluctant, be stingy, covet, eat one's heart out, envy, grudge, pinch, resent, stint; SEE CONCEPTS **17,21**

beguile [v1] *fool*
betray, bluff, burn*, cheat, chisel, con, deceive, delude, double-cross, dupe, entice, exploit, finesse, flimflam*, gyp*, have, hoodwink*, impose on, jockey, juggle, lure, manipulate, mislead, play, play for a sucker*, rook*, rope in*, scam, seduce, shave*, snow*, stick*, string along, suck in*, take, take in, trick; SEE CONCEPT **59**

beguile [v2] *charm*
amuse, attract, cheer, delight, distract, divert, engross, entertain, entice, knock dead, knock out, lure, occupy, seduce, send, slay, solace, sweep off one's feet, tickle, tickle pink*, tickle to death*, turn on, vamp, wow*; SEE CONCEPTS **7,19,22**

behalf [n] *personal interest*
account, advantage, aid, assistance, benefit, cause, concern, countenance, defense, encouragement, favor, furtherance, good, help, part, place, profit, recommendation, representation, sake, service, side, stead, support, welfare; SEE CONCEPTS **410,532**

behave [v1] *function*
act, operate, perform, react, run, take, work; SEE CONCEPTS **1,4**

behave [v2] *act reasonably, properly*
act correctly, act one's age, act with decorum, be civil, be good, be nice, be on best behavior*, be orderly, comport oneself, conduct oneself properly, control, demean oneself, deport oneself, direct, discipline oneself, keep one's nose clean*, keep the peace, live up to, manage, manage oneself, mind one's manners*, mind one's p's and q's*, observe golden rule*, observe the law, play fair, shape up, toe the mark*, watch one's step*; SEE CONCEPT **633**

behavior [n] *manner of conducting oneself*
act, action, address, air, attitude, bag*, bearing, carriage, code, comportment, conduct, convention, course, dealings, decency, decorum, deed, delivery, demeanor, deportment, ethics, etiquette, expression, form, front, guise, habits, management, mien, mode, morals, nature, observance, performance, practice, presence, propriety, ritual, role, routine, savoir-faire, seemliness, social graces, speech, style, tact, talk, taste, tenue, tone, way, way of life, ways, what's done*; SEE CONCEPTS **633,655**

behead [v] *decapitate*
bring to the block, decollate, execute, guillotine, head, kill, neck; SEE CONCEPT **176**

behest [n] *order; personal decree*
bidding, charge, command, commandment, demand, dictate, direction, expressed desire, injunction, instruction, mandate, order, precept, prompting, request, solicitation, wish, word; SEE CONCEPTS **20,53**

behind [n] *buttocks*
backside, bottom, breech, can*, derrière, fanny*, fundament, posterior, rear, rump, seat, tail, tush*; SEE CONCEPT **392**

behind [adv1/prep1] *position farther back; following*
abaft, after, afterwards, at the heels of*, at the rear of, back of, bringing up the rear*, eating the dust*, in the background, in the wake, later than, next, off the pace, subsequently, trailing; SEE CONCEPTS **586,820**

behind [adv2] *in debt; late*
backward, behindhand, behind schedule, behind time, belated, delayed, dilatory, have to play catch up*, in arrears, laggard, overdue, slow, sluggish, tardy; SEE CONCEPTS **334,799**

behind [prep2] *being the reason for*
at the bottom of, causing, concerning the circumstances, initiating, instigating, responsible for; SEE CONCEPT **532**

behind [prep3] *in support*
backing, for, in agreement, on the side of, supporting; SEE CONCEPT **388**

behold [v] *regard; look at*
catch, consider, contemplate, descry, discern, distinguish, earmark, eye, eyeball*, feast one's eyes*, flash*, lay eyes on*, note, notice, observe, perceive, regard, scan, see, spot, spy, survey, view, watch, witness; SEE CONCEPTS **34,626**

beholden [adj] *indebted*
bound, grateful, in hock, into, obligated, obliged, on a string*, on the arm*, on the cuff*, on the tab*, owe one, owing, responsible, under obligation; SEE CONCEPT **403**

behoove [v] *be necessary, proper*
be expected, befit, be fitting, be incumbent upon, be needful, be one's obligation, be required, be requisite, be right, beseem, owe it to, suit; SEE CONCEPT **646**

beige [n/adj] *light brown color*
biscuit, buff, café au lait, camel, cream, ecru, fawn, khaki, mushroom, neutral, oatmeal, off-white, sand, tan, taupe; SEE CONCEPTS **618,622**

being [n1] *existence*
actuality, animation, journey, life, living, presence, reality, subsistence, vitality, world; SEE CONCEPT **407**

being [n2] *essential nature*
character, entity, essence, essentia, essentiality, individuality, marrow, personality, quintessence, self, soul, spirit, substance, texture; SEE CONCEPTS **411,673**

being [n3] *animate object*
animal, beast, body, conscious thing, creature, entity, human, human being, individual, living thing, mortal, organism, person, personage, soul, thing; SEE CONCEPT **389**

belated [adj] *late, slow*
behindhand, behind time, delayed, long-delayed, overdue, remiss, tardy, unpunctual; SEE CONCEPT **820**

belch [v] *burp; spew*
discharge, disgorge, emit, eruct, eructate, erupt, give off, gush, hiccup, irrupt, repeat, ventilate, vomit; SEE CONCEPT **185**

beleaguer [v] *harass, besiege*
annoy, badger, bedevil, beset, blockade, bother, gnaw, harry, nag, persecute, pester, plague, put upon, set upon, siege, storm, tease, vex, worry; SEE CONCEPTS **7,19**

belfry [n] *tower; part of tower*
bell tower, campanile, carillon, clocher, cupola,

be
be

dome, head, minaret, spire, steeple, turret; SEE CONCEPT *440*

belie [*v1*] *disprove*

confute, contradict, contravene, controvert, deny, disaffirm, disagree, explode, gainsay, negate, negative, oppose, repudiate; SEE CONCEPTS *54,58*

belie [*v2*] *deceive*

color, conceal, disguise, distort, falsify, garble, give the lie to, gloss over, hide, miscolor, mislead, misrepresent, misstate, pervert, trump up, twist, warp; SEE CONCEPT *63*

belief [*n1*] *putting regard in as true*

acceptance, admission, assent, assumption, assurance, avowal, axiom, certainty, conclusion, confidence, conjecture, conviction, credence, credit, deduction, divination, expectation, faith, fancy, feeling, guess, hope, hypothesis, idea, impression, intuition, judgment, knowledge, mind, mindset, notion, opinion, persuasion, position, postulation, presumption, presupposition, profession, reliance, supposition, surmise, suspicion, theorem, theory, thesis, thinking, trust, understanding, view; SEE CONCEPTS *410,529*

belief [*n2*] *something regarded as true, trustworthy*

assumption, concept, credence, credo, creed, doctrine, dogma, faith, fundamental, gospel, gospel truth*, hypothesis, idea, ideology, law, opinion, postulate, precept, principle, say-so*, tenet, theorem, theory; SEE CONCEPT *689*

believable [*adj*] *trustworthy*

aboveboard, acceptable, authentic, colorable, conceivable, convincing, credential, credible, creditable, fiduciary, honest-to-God*, imaginable, impressive, likely, persuasive, plausible, possible, presumable, presumptive, probable, rational, reasonable, reliable, satisfying, straight, supposable, tenable, tried, trusty, unquestionable, up front*; SEE CONCEPTS *403,582*

believe [*v1*] *trust, rely on*

accept, accredit, admit, affirm, attach weight to, be certain of, be convinced of, be of the opinion, buy*, conceive, conclude, consider, count on, credit, deem, fall for*, give credence to, have, have faith in, have no doubt, hold, keep the faith, lap up*, place confidence in, posit, postulate, presume true, presuppose, reckon on, regard, rest assured, suppose, swallow*, swear by, take as gospel*, take at one's word, take for granted, take it, think, trust, understand; SEE CONCEPT *12*

believe [*v2*] *assume or suppose*

conjecture, consider, credit, deem, expect, feel, gather, guess, hold, imagine, judge, maintain, postulate, presume, reckon, sense, speculate, suppose, suspect, take, think, understand; SEE CONCEPT *28*

believer [*n*] *person who has trust, faith in something*

acceptor, adherent, apostle, canonist, convert, devotee, disciple, doctrinaire, dogmatist, follower, freak, orthodox, prophet, proselyte, religionist, religious person, supporter, upholder, zealot; SEE CONCEPTS *361,423*

belittle [*v*] *detract*

bad-mouth, blister, criticize, cut down to size*, cut to the quick*, decry, deprecate, depreciate, deride, derogate, diminish, discount, discredit, disparage, dispraise, downgrade, downplay, dump on*, knock*, lower, minimize, pan, pooh pooh*, poor mouth*, put down, rip*, roast*, run down, scoff at, scorch*, scorn, shoot down*, shoot full

of holes*, slam*, smear, sneer at, sour grapes*, squash*, squelch, take a swipe at*, take down, take down a peg*, tear down*, underestimate, underrate, undervalue, write off; SEE CONCEPTS *52,54*

bell [*n*] *signaling object or sound*

alarm, buzz, buzzer, carillon, chime, clapper, curfew, ding-dong*, dinger*, gong, peal, ringer, siren, tintinnabulum, tocsin, toll, vesper; SEE CONCEPT *595*

belligerent [*adj*] *nasty, argumentative*

aggressive, antagonistic, ardent, at loggerheads*, battling, bellicose, cantankerous, combative, contentious, fierce, fighting, flip, have a bone to pick*, have chip on shoulder*, have it in for*, hostile, hot, hot-tempered, mean, militant, on the outs*, ornery, pugnacious, quarrelsome, scrappy, truculent, warlike; SEE CONCEPTS *401,404*

bellow [*v*] *holler*

bark, bawl, bay, beller, blare, bluster, bray, call, clamor, cry, howl, low, roar, rout, scream, shout, shriek, wail, whoop, yawp, yell, yelp; SEE CONCEPT *77*

belly [*n*] *stomach*

abdomen, bay window*, beer belly*, breadbasket*, corporation*, front porch*, gut, insides, intestines, paunch, pelvis, pot*, pot belly*, solar plexus, spare tire*, tank, tummy, venter; SEE CONCEPT *393*

belong [*v1*] *be part of, be in proper place*

accord, agree, appertain, apply, associate, attach to, be a component, be a constituent, be akin to, be an adjunct of, be a part, bear, bear upon, become, be connected with, befit, be fitting, be linked with, be related, be relevant, chime, concern, correlate, correspond, exist, fit, go, go with, harmonize, have relationship to, have respect to, have to do with, inhere, match, permeate, pertain, refer, regard, reside, set, suit, touch, vest; SEE CONCEPTS *532,543*

belong [*v2*] *be affiliated with*

be allied to, be a member, be a member of, be associated with, be classified among, be contained in, be included in, be one of, be one of the family, be part of, fit in, have a place, in, in with, owe allegiance, owe support, run with*, swing*, swing with*, take one's place with; SEE CONCEPTS *114,388*

belonging [*n*] *sense of security in friendship*

acceptance, affinity, association, attachment, inclusion, kinship, loyalty, rapport, relationship; SEE CONCEPTS *388,410*

belongings [*n*] *personal possessions*

accouterments, appurtenances, assets, chattels, effects, gear, goods, paraphernalia, personal property, property, stuff, things; SEE CONCEPTS *446,710*

beloved [*n*] *someone adored*

baby*, beau, boyfriend, darling, dear, dearest, fiancé, flame, girlfriend, heartbeat*, heartthrob, honey, idol, inamorato, love, love of my life*, lover, number one*, numero uno*, object of affection, one and only, pet*, prize, rave*, significant other, steady, sugar*, sweetheart, tootsie*, treasure, true love; SEE CONCEPT *423*

beloved [*adj*] *adored*

admired, cared for, cherished, darling, dear, dearest, doted on, endeared, esteemed, fair-haired, favorite, hallowed, highly regarded, highly valued, idolized, loved, near to one's heart*, pet*, pleasing, popular, precious, prized, respected, revered, sweet, treasured, venerated, well-liked, worshiped; SEE CONCEPTS 568,572

below [adv/prep] lower
beneath, down, down from, under, underneath; SEE CONCEPTS 581,586,735

below [prep2] less than; beneath
inferior, lesser, lower, subject, subordinate, unworthy; SEE CONCEPTS 567,771

belt [n1] supporting band
cincture, cummerbund, girdle, ribbon, ring, sash, strap, string, waistband; SEE CONCEPT 450

belt [n2] strip of land with characteristic feature
area, district, layer, region, stretch, territory, tract, zone; SEE CONCEPTS 513,517

belt [v] hit hard
bash, bat, biff, blast, blow, bop, clobber, slam, slug, smack, smash, sock, strap, switch, wallop, whip, whop; SEE CONCEPT 189

bemoan [v] express sorrow
beat one's breast*, bewail, complain, cry over spilled milk*, deplore, grieve for, lament, moan over, mourn, regret, rue, sing the blues*, weep for; SEE CONCEPTS 49,51

bemuse [v] confuse
addle, amaze, bewilder, daydream, daze, gather wool*, moon, muddle, overwhelm, paralyze, perplex, pipe dream*, puzzle, stun, stupefy; SEE CONCEPTS 7,19,22

bench [n1] furniture for sitting
bank, chair, form, lawn seat, pew, seat, settee, settle, stall; SEE CONCEPT 443

bench [n2] large table
board, counter, desk, easel, ledge, shelf, trestle, workbench, work table; SEE CONCEPT 443

bench [n3] group of judges
court, courtroom, judiciary, magistrate, the bar, tribunal, your honors; SEE CONCEPTS 318,355

benchmark [n] reference point
criterion, gauge, measure, standard, touchstone, yardstick; SEE CONCEPT 688

bend [n] curve
angle, arc, bending, bow, corner, crook, curvation, curvature, deflection, deviation, flection, flexure, hook, lean, loop, round, sag, shift, tack, tilt, turn, twist, yaw, zigzag; SEE CONCEPT 436

bend [v1] form or cause a curve
angle away, angle off, arch, bow, buckle, camber, careen, circle, contort, crimp, crinkle, crook, crouch, curl, deflect, deform, detour, double, droop, flex, genuflect, hook, incline, incurvate, lean, loop, pervert, round, spiral, stoop, swerve, tilt, turn, twist, veer, verge, warp, waver, wilt, wind, yaw, zigzag; SEE CONCEPTS 149,184

bend [v2] persuade; influence
change mind, compel, direct, mold, shape, subdue, submit, sway, yield; SEE CONCEPT 68

beneath [adv] in a lower place
below, underneath; SEE CONCEPT 586

beneath [prep] inferior
below, lesser, less than, lower than, subject, subordinate, unbefitting, under, underneath, unworthy of; SEE CONCEPT 586

benediction [n] closing prayer
amen, approbation, approval, beatitude, benedictus, benison, blessing, consecration, favor, grace, gratitude, invocation, laying on of hands, okay, orison, praise, sanctification, thanks, thanksgiving; SEE CONCEPT 69

benefactor [n] donor
aid, altruist, angel, assistant, backer, contributor, fairy godparent*, fan, good Samaritan, grubstaker, helper, humanitarian, mark*, patron, philanthropist, promoter, protector, Santa Claus*, sponsor, subscriber, subsidizer, supporter, wellwisher; SEE CONCEPTS 416,423

beneficial [adj] advantageous
benign, constructive, favorable, favoring, gainful, good, good for what ails you*, healthful, helpful, profitable, propitious, salubrious, salutary, serviceable, toward, useful, valuable, what the doctor ordered*, wholesome, worthy; SEE CONCEPTS 567,572

beneficiary [n] person who gains, benefits
almsperson, assignee, devisee, donee, grantee, heir, heiress, inheritor, legatee, payee, possessor, receiver, recipient, stipendiary, successor; SEE CONCEPTS 355,423

benefit [n1] advantage, profit
account, aid, asset, assistance, avail, benediction, betterment, blessing, boon, cream*, egg in one's beer*, extras, favor, gain, godsend*, good, gravy*, help, interest, perk*, profit, prosperity, use, welfare, worth; SEE CONCEPTS 337,346,661

benefit [n2] event to raise money
ball, bazaar, charitable affair, charity performance, concert, dance, dinner, exhibit, exhibition, fair, pancake breakfast, raffle; SEE CONCEPT 386

benefit [v] help, enhance
advance, advantage, aid, ameliorate, assist, avail, be good for, better, build, contribute to, do for one, do the trick, favor, fill the bill*, further, improve, make a killing*, make it*, pay, pay off*, profit, promote, relieve, serve, succor, work for; SEE CONCEPTS 110,244

benevolence [n] charity
altruism, amity, comity, compassion, feeling, friendliness, friendship, generosity, gift, goodness, good will, humanity, kindheartedness, kindness, sympathy; SEE CONCEPT 633

benevolent [adj] charitable, kind
all heart, altruistic, beneficent, benign, big, bighearted, bounteous, bountiful, caring, chivalrous, compassionate, considerate, generous, helpful, humane, humanitarian, kindhearted, liberal, magnanimous, philanthropic, tenderhearted, warmhearted, well-disposed; SEE CONCEPT 401

benign [adj1] kindly
amiable, beneficent, benevolent, benignant, complaisant, congenial, favorable, friendly, generous, genial, gentle, good, goodhearted, gracious, kind, liberal, merciful, mild, obliging, sympathetic; SEE CONCEPT 542

benign [adj2] mild, especially describing weather
auspicious, balmy, bright, favorable, fortunate, gentle, healthful, propitious, refreshing, temperate, warm; SEE CONCEPT 605

benign [adj3] advantageous
auspicious, beneficent, benevolent, bright, charitable, dexter, encouraging, favorable, fortunate, good, lucky, merciful, propitious, salutary, smiling; SEE CONCEPTS 537,572

benign [adj4] not cancerous
curable, early stage, harmless, limited, remediable, slight, superficial; SEE CONCEPT 314

bent [n] inclination; talent
ability, aim, aptitude, bag*, disposition, druthers*, facility, faculty, flair, forte, genius, gift,

be
be

head-set*, inclining, knack, leaning, mind-set*, nose, penchant, predilection, predisposition, preference, proclivity, propensity, set, tack, tendency, thing for*, tilt, turn, weakness for; SEE CONCEPTS 409,630

bent [adj1] *curved*
angled, arced, arched, arciform, bowed, contorted, crooked, curvilinear, doubled over, drooping, droopy, hooked, humped, hunched, inclined, limp, looped, round, rounded, sinuous, slouchy, slumped, stooped, twined, twisted, warped, wilted; SEE CONCEPT 486

bent [adj2] *determined*
bound, decided, decisive, dedicated, disposed, firm, fixed, inclined, insistent, intent, leaning, predisposed, resolute, resolved, set, settled, tending; SEE CONCEPT 403

bequeath [v] *give in a will*
bestow, commit, devise, endow, entrust, grant, hand down, hand on, impart, leave, leave to, legate, pass on, transmit, will; SEE CONCEPTS 108,317

bequest [n] *something given in will*
bequeathal, bequeathment, bestowal, devisal, devise, dower, endowment, estate, gift, heritage, inheritance, legacy, settlement, trust; SEE CONCEPTS 318,337

berate [v] *criticize hatefully*
bawl out*, blister, call down, castigate, censure, chew*, chew out*, chide, cuss out*, eat out*, give one hell*, give what for*, jaw*, jump all over*, rail at*, rake over the coals*, rate, rebuke, reprimand, reproach, revile, scold, scorch, tell off, tongue-lash, upbraid, vituperate; SEE CONCEPT 52

bereavement [n] *death; loss*
affliction, deprivation, distress, misfortune, sorrow, tribulation; SEE CONCEPTS 230,674

bereft [adj] *lacking; missing*
beggared, bereaved, cut off, deprived, destitute, devoid, dispossessed, divested, fleeced, impoverished, left without, minus, naked, parted from, robbed, shorn, stripped, wanting, without; SEE CONCEPTS 546,576

berry [n] *small fruit*
bean, drupe, drupelet, grain, haw, hip, kernel, pome, seed; SEE CONCEPT 426

berth [n1] *harbor; bunk*
anchorage, bed, bedroom, billet, compartment, cot, dock, hammock, haven, jetty, levee, pier, port, quay, slip, wharf; SEE CONCEPTS 513,516

berth [n2] *position of responsibility*
appointment, billet, capacity, connection, employment, job, living, office, place, post, profession, situation, spot; SEE CONCEPTS 362,668

beseech [v] *beg*
adjure, appeal, ask, call upon, crave, entreat, implore, importune, invoke, petition, plead, pray, solicit, sue, supplicate; SEE CONCEPT 48

beset [v] *plague; hem in*
aggress, assail, attack, badger, bedevil, beleaguer, besiege, bug*, circle*, compass, dog*, drive up the wall*, embarrass, encircle, enclose, encompass, entangle, environ, fall on, fall upon, girdle, give a bad time*, give a hard time*, give one the business*, give the needle*, harass, harry, hassle, infest, invade, jump on one's case*, nag, nudge, overrun, perplex, pester, pick on, put the squeeze on*, ride, ring, start in on, storm, strike, surround; SEE CONCEPTS 7,19

beside [adv/prep] *next to*
abreast of, adjacent to, adjoining, alongside, aside, a step from, at one's elbow, at the edge of, at the side of, bordering on, by, cheek by jowl*, close at hand, close to, close upon, connected with, contiguous to, forment, in juxtaposition, near, nearby, neck and neck*, neighboring, next door to, nigh, opposite, overlooking, round, side by side, verging on, with; SEE CONCEPT 586

besides [adv] *in addition; as well*
added to, additionally, along with, also, and all, apart from, aside from, as well as, beyond, conjointly, else, exceeding, exclusive of, extra, further, furthermore, in conjunction with, in distinction to, in excess of, in other respects, likewise, more, moreover, more than, not counting, on the side*, on top of everything, other than, otherwise, over and above, plus, secondly, supplementary to, to boot*, together with, too, what's more*, with the exception of, yet; SEE CONCEPT 772

besides [prep1] *apart from*
aside from, bar, barring, beside, but, except, excepting, excluding, exclusive of, in addition to, other than, outside of, over and above, save, without; SEE CONCEPT 772

besides [prep2] *in addition to*
added to, along with, as well as, beside, beyond, in excess of, more than, on top of, other than, over and above, plus, supplementary, together with; SEE CONCEPT 772

besiege [v1] *surround; assault*
assail, attack, beleaguer, beset, blockade, come at from all sides, confine, congregate, encircle, encompass, environ, hem in, invest, lay siege to, shut in, trap, work on, work over; SEE CONCEPTS 86,90

besiege [v2] *bother*
badger, beleaguer, bug*, buttonhole*, harass, harry, hound*, importune, nag, pester, plague, trouble; SEE CONCEPTS 7,19

best [n1] *most outstanding thing in class*
choice, cream, cream of the crop*, elite, fat, favorite, finest, first, flower, gem, model, nonpareil, paragon, pick, prime, prize, select, top; SEE CONCEPT 668

best [n2] *highest personal effort*
all one's got, best shot, hardest, highest endeavor, level best*, Sunday best*, utmost; SEE CONCEPT 411

best [adj1] *most excellent*
ace, A-1*, bad*, beyond compare, boss*, capital, champion, chief, choicest, cool*, culminating, finest, first, first-class, first-rate, foremost, greatest, highest, incomparable, inimitable, leading, matchless, nonpareil, number 1*, optimum, out-of-sight*, outstanding, paramount, peerless, perfect, preeminent, premium, prime, primo*, principal, sans pareil, second to none, super, superlative, supreme, 10*, terrific, tops, tough, transcendent, unequaled, unparalleled, unrivaled, unsurpassed; SEE CONCEPTS 568,572

best [adj2] *correct, right*
advantageous, apt, desirable, golden, most desirable, most fitting, preferred, presentable; SEE CONCEPT 558

best [adj3] *most*
biggest, bulkiest, greatest, largest; SEE CONCEPT 771

best [v] *defeat; gain advantage*
beat, beat up*, better, blank*, blast*, bulldoze*, clobber*, conquer, cream*, deck*, drub*, excel, flax*, floor*, get the better of, knock off*, KO*, lambaste, let have it*, lick*, master, outclass, outdo, outshine, outstrip, overcome, prevail, put away, shoot down*, shut down*, surpass, take care of, take down*, tan*, thrash*, top, total, transcend, trash*, triumph, triumph over, trounce, wallop, waste*, wax*, whip*, whomp*, whop*, wipe*, wipe out, wipe the floor with*, zap*; SEE CONCEPT 95

best [adv] *most excellently*
advantageously, attractively, creditably, extremely, gloriously, greatly, honorably, illustriously, magnanimously, most deeply, most fortunately, most fully, most highly, sincerely; SEE CONCEPTS 568,572

bestow [v] *give, allot*
accord, apportion, award, bequeath, come through, commit, confer, devote, donate, entrust, favor, gift, give away, grant, hand out, honor with, impart, kick in, lavish, offer, present, put out, render to; SEE CONCEPTS 98,108

bet [n] *game of chance; money gambled*
action, ante, betting, chance, down on, hazard, long shot, lot, lottery, odds, odds on, parlay, play, pledge, plunge, pot, raffle, random shot, risk, shot, shot in the dark*, speculation, stake, sweepstakes, uncertainty, venture, wager; SEE CONCEPTS 28,293,329

bet [v] *gamble*
ante, buy in on, chance, dice, game, hazard, lay down, lay odds, play against, play for, play the ponies*, pledge, pony up*, put, put money on, risk, set, speculate, tempt fortune*, toss up, trust, venture, wager; SEE CONCEPTS 292,330

betray [v1] *be disloyal*
abandon, be unfaithful, bite the hand that feeds you*, blow the whistle*, bluff, break faith, break promise, break trust, break with, commit treason, cross, deceive, deliver up*, delude, desert, double-cross, finger*, forsake, go back on, inform against, inform on, jilt, knife*, let down, mislead, play false*, play Judas*, seduce, sell down the river*, sell out, stab in the back*, take in*, trick, turn in, turn informer, turn state's evidence, walk out on; SEE CONCEPT 384

betray [v2] *divulge, expose information*
blurt out, dime*, disclose, evince, fink on*, give away, inform, lay bare, let slip, make known, manifest, rat on*, reveal, show, sing*, snitch*, spill, squeal*, stool*, tattle, tell, tell on, turn in, uncover, unmask; SEE CONCEPTS 44,60

betrayal [n1] *exhibition of disloyalty*
deception, dishonesty, double-crossing, double-dealing, duplicity, falseness, giveaway, Judas kiss*, let-down, perfidy, sellout, treachery, treason, trickery, unfaithfulness; SEE CONCEPT 633

betrayal [n2] *divulgence of information*
blurting out, diming*, disclosure, giving away, ratting*, revelation, snitching*, spilling*, squealing*, tattling, telling; SEE CONCEPTS 44,60

betroth [v] *marry*
affiance, become engaged, bind, commit, contract, engage, espouse, give one's hand, make compact, plight faith, plight troth, promise, tie oneself to, vow; SEE CONCEPT 297

betrothal [n] *marriage*
affiancing, betrothing, engagement, espousal,

plight, promise, troth, vow; SEE CONCEPT 297

better [adj1] *excelling, more excellent*
bigger, choice, exceeding, exceptional, finer, fitter, greater, higher quality, improved, larger, more appropriate, more desirable, more fitting, more select, more suitable, more useful, more valuable, preferable, preferred, prominent, sharpened, sophisticated, souped up*, superior, surpassing, worthier; SEE CONCEPTS 568,572

better [adj2] *improved in health*
convalescent, cured, fitter, fully recovered, healthier, improving, less ill, mending, more healthy, on the comeback trail*, on the mend, on the road to recovery*, out of the woods*, over the hump*, progressing, recovering, stronger, well; SEE CONCEPT 314

better [adj3] *larger*
bigger, greater, longer, more, preponderant, weightier; SEE CONCEPTS 771,773

better [v] *improve performance; outdo*
advance, ameliorate, amend, beat, best, cap, correct, enhance, exceed, excel, forward, further, help, meliorate, mend, outshine, outstrip, promote, raise, rectify, refine, reform, revamp, surpass, top, transcend; SEE CONCEPTS 141,244

better [adv] *in a more excellent manner*
finer, greater, in a superior way, more, more advantageously, more attractively, more competently, more completely, more effectively, more thoroughly, preferably, to a greater degree; SEE CONCEPTS 568,572

betterment [n] *improvement*
advancement, amelioration, mastery, melioration, progress, prosperity, upgrading; SEE CONCEPT 244

between [adv/prep] *middle from two points*
amid, amidst, among, at intervals, betwixt, bounded by, centrally located, enclosed by, halfway in, inserted, interpolated, intervening, in the middle, in the midst of, in the seam, in the thick of, medially, mid, midway, separating, surrounded by, 'tween, within; SEE CONCEPTS 586,820

beverage [n] *liquid refreshment*
cooler, draft, drink, drinkable, libation, liquor, potable, potation; SEE CONCEPT 454

bevy [n] *swarm*
assembly, band, bunch, cluster, collection, company, covey, crew, crowd, flight, flock, gathering, group, pack, party, troupe; SEE CONCEPT 432

bewail [v] *cry over, lament*
bemoan, deplore, eat heart out*, express sorrow, grieve for, moan, mourn, regret, repent, rue, sing the blues*, take on, wail, weep over; SEE CONCEPT 266

beware [v] *be careful*
attend, avoid, be cautious, be wary, guard against, heed, keep eyes open*, keep one's distance, keep on one's toes*, look out, mind, mind p's and q's*, notice, refrain from, shun, steer clear of*, take care, take heed, walk on eggs*, watch one's step, watch out; SEE CONCEPT 34

bewilder [v] *confuse*
addle, baffle, ball up*, befuddle, bemuse, confound, daze, disconcert, distract, floor*, fluster, mess with one's head*, mix up, muddle, mystify, perplex, puzzle, rattle, snow*, stump, stupefy, throw, upset; SEE CONCEPTS 14,42

bewildered [adj] *confused*
addled, agape, aghast, agog, appalled, astonished,

be
be

astounded, awed, awe-struck, baffled, befuddled, bowled over*, dazed, dazzled, disconcerted, dizzy, dumbfounded, dumbstruck, flabbergasted, flipped out*, floored*, flustered, giddy, in a dither*, lost, misled, muddled, mystified, perplexed, punchy*, puzzled, rattled, reeling, shocked, shook up, speechless, staggered, startled, stumped, stunned, stupefied, surprised, taken aback, thrown, thunderstruck*, uncertain, unglued*; SEE CONCEPTS 402,403

bewitch [v] *charm*
allure, attract, bedevil, beguile, captivate, capture, control, dazzle, draw, enchant, enrapture, enthrall, entrance, fascinate, hex, hypnotize, knock dead*, knock out, put horns on*, put the whammy on*, put under magic spell*, send*, slay*, spell*, spellbind, sweep off one's feet*, take, tickle*, tickle pink*, tickle to death*, trick, turn on*, vamp, voodoo, wile, wow*; SEE CONCEPTS 7,22

bewitched [adj] *charmed*
captivated, enamored, enchanted, enraptured, ensorcelled, entranced, fallen for*, fascinated, gaga about*, have a bug in one's ear*, have a thing about*, head over heels*, hooked*, hung up*, mad about, mesmerized, possessed, spellbound, transformed, turned on*, under a spell; SEE CONCEPTS 32,403

beyond [adv/prep] *further; outside limits*
above, after, ahead, apart from, as well as, at a distance, away from, before, behind, besides, beyond the bounds, clear of, farther, free of, good way off, hyper, in addition to, in advance of, long way off, moreover, more remote, on the far side, on the other side, out of range, out of reach, outside, over, over and above, over there, past, remote, superior to, without, yonder; SEE CONCEPTS 554,772,778

bias [n1] *belief in one way; partiality*
bent, bigotry, chauvinism, disposition, favoritism, flash, head-set*, illiberality, inclination, intolerance, leaning, mind-set*, mind trip*, narrowmindedness, one-sidedness, penchant, preconception, predilection, predisposition, preference, prejudice, prepossession, proclivity, proneness, propensity, spin, standpoint, tendency, tilt, turn, unfairness, viewpoint; SEE CONCEPT 689

bias [n2] *diagonal weave of fabric*
angle, cant, cross, incline, oblique, slant; SEE CONCEPT 606

bias [v] *cause to favor*
distort, incline, influence, make partial, prejudice, prepossess, slant, sway, twist, warp, weight; SEE CONCEPTS 7,19

bible [n] *holy book; authoritative book*
authority, creed, doctrine, guide, guidebook, handbook, manual, sacred writ, sacred writings, scripture, testament, text, the good news; SEE CONCEPTS 280,368

bicker [v] *nastily argue*
altercate, brawl, caterwaul, cause a scene*, cavil, dig, disagree, dispute, fall out, fight, hassle, pick at, quarrel, quibble, row, scrap, scrape, spar, spat, squabble, tiff, trade zingers*, wrangle; SEE CONCEPT 46

bicycle [n] *pedal-driven recreational vehicle*
bike, cycle, tandem, two-wheeler, velocipede, wheels; SEE CONCEPTS 364,505

bid [n1] *offering of money or services*
advance, amount, declaration, feeler, hit, invitation, offer, pass, price, proffer, proposal, proposition, request, submission, suggestion, sum, summons, tender; SEE CONCEPTS 67,330

bid [n2] *endeavor*
attempt, crack, effort, essay, try, venture; SEE CONCEPT 87

bid [v1] *offer money or services*
present, proffer, propose, render, submit, tender, venture; SEE CONCEPTS 67,330

bid [v2] *say*
call, greet, tell, wish; SEE CONCEPT 266

bid [v3] *ask for; command*
call, charge, demand, desire, direct, enjoin, instruct, invite, make a pass at*, make a pitch*, make a play for*, order, proposition, request, require, solicit, summon, tell, warn; SEE CONCEPT 53

bidding [n1] *command*
behest, call, charge, demand, dictate, direction, injunction, instruction, invitation, mandate, order, request, summons, word; SEE CONCEPT 53

bidding [n2] *offering of money, services*
advance, auction, invitation, offer, proffering, proposal, proposition, request, submission, suggestion, tender; SEE CONCEPTS 67,330

bide [v] *wait*
abide, attend, await, continue, dwell, hang around, hang in*, hang out*, hold the phone*, lie in wait*, linger, live, remain, reside, sit tight*, stay, stick around, sweat it*, tarry, watch for; SEE CONCEPT 681

big [adj1] *large, great*
ample, awash, a whale of a*, brimming, bulky, bull*, burly, capacious, chock-full*, colossal, commodious, considerable, copious, crowded, enormous, extensive, fat, full, gigantic, heavyduty*, heavyweight, hefty, huge, hulking, humongous*, husky, immense, jumbo, mammoth, massive, mondo*, monster*, oversize, packed, ponderous, prodigious, roomy, sizable, spacious, strapping, stuffed, substantial, super colossal*, thundering, tremendous, vast, voluminous, walloping, whopper, whopping; SEE CONCEPTS 771,773

big [adj2] *important*
big league*, big-time*, consequential, considerable, eminent, heavy-duty*, heavyweight, influential, leading, main, major league*, material, meaningful, momentous, paramount, popular, powerful, prime, principal, prominent, serious, significant, substantial, super, super colossal*, valuable, weighty; SEE CONCEPT 568

big [adj3] *grown*
adult, elder, full-grown, grown-up, mature, tall; SEE CONCEPTS 578,797

big [adj4] *generous*
altruistic, benevolent, bighearted, chivalrous, considerate, free, gracious, greathearted, heroic, liberal, lofty, magnanimous, noble, princely, unselfish; SEE CONCEPT 404

big [adj5] *arrogant*
arty, boastful, bragging, conceited, flamboyant, haughty, high-sounding, imperious, imposing, inflated, overblown, pompous, presumptuous, pretentious, proud; SEE CONCEPT 401

bigot [n] *intolerant, prejudiced person*
chauvinist, diehard, doctrinaire, dogmatist, enthusiast, extremist, fanatic, fiend, maniac, monoma-

niac, opinionated person, partisan, persecutor, puritan, racist, sectarian, segregationist, sexist, stickler, superpatriot, zealot; SEE CONCEPTS 359,423

bigoted [adj] *intolerant, prejudiced*
biased, chauvinistic, conservative, dogmatic, illiberal, narrow, narrow-minded, obstinate, opinionated, partial, partisan, sectarian, slanted, small-minded, twisted, unfair, warped; SEE CONCEPTS 403,555

bigotry [n] *intolerance, prejudice*
bias, conservatism/conservativism, discrimination, dogmatism, fanaticism, injustice, Jim Crowism*, narrow-mindedness, partiality, provincialism, racialism, racism, sectarianism, sexism, unfairness; SEE CONCEPTS 388,410

bilateral [adj] *having two sides*
mutual, reciprocal, respective, two-sided; SEE CONCEPT 562

bilk [v] *cheat*
bamboozle*, beat, circumvent, con, deceive, defraud, disappoint, do*, fleece*, flimflam*, foil, frustrate, gyp*, overreach, rook*, ruin, snow*, swindle, thwart, trick; SEE CONCEPTS 59,139

bill [n1] *account of charges; money owed*
bad news*, check, chit, damage*, debt, invoice, IOU, itemized account, knock*, note, reckoning, request for payment, score, statement, statement of indebtedness, tab; SEE CONCEPTS 329,332

bill [n2] *list; circular*
advertisement, affiche, agenda, bulletin, card, catalogue, flyer, handbill, handout, inventory, leaflet, listing, notice, placard, playbill, poster, program, roster, schedule, syllabus; SEE CONCEPTS 280,283

bill [n3] *piece of legislation*
act, draft, measure, projected law, proposal, proposed act; SEE CONCEPTS 271,318

bill [n4] *piece of paper money*
bank note, buck, certificate, currency, dollar, greenback*, long green*, skin*; SEE CONCEPT 340

bill [n5] *beak of animal*
mandible, neb, nib, pecker, projection; SEE CONCEPT 399

bill [v1] *charge money for goods, services*
bone, chase, debit, draw upon, dun, figure, invoice, put the arm on*, put the bite on*, put the squeeze on*, reckon, record, render, solicit; SEE CONCEPTS 330,342

bill [v2] *advertise*
announce, book, give advance notice, post; SEE CONCEPTS 60,292

billow [n] *surging mass*
beachcomber, breaker, crest, roller, surge, swell, tide, wave; SEE CONCEPTS 437,514

billow [v] *surge*
balloon, belly, bloat, bounce, bulge, ebb and flow, heave, pitch, puff up, ripple, rise and fall, rise up, rock, roll, swell, toss, undulate, wave; SEE CONCEPTS 159,208

billowy [adj] *surging*
bouncing, bouncy, bulgy, distended, ebbing and flowing, heaving, puffy, rippled, rippling, rising, rising and falling, rolling, swelling, swirling, swollen, undulating, waving, wavy; SEE CONCEPTS 486,584

bind [n] *predicament*
between a rock and a hard place*, crunch*, difficulty, dilemma, hot water*, no-win situation*,

nuisance, pickle*, predicament, quandary, sticky situation*, tight situation, tight spot*; SEE CONCEPTS 230,674

bind [v1] *fasten, secure*
adhere, attach, bandage, border, chain, cinch, clamp, connect, constrict, cover, dress, edge, encase, enchain, enfetter, fetter, finish, fix, fold, furl, glue, hamper, handcuff, hem, hitch, hitch on, hobble, hook on, hook up, lace, lap, lash, leash, manacle, moor, muzzle, paste, peg down, pin, pin down, pinion, put together, restrain, restrict, rope, shackle, stick, strap, swathe, tack on, tether, tie, tie up, trammel, trim, truss, unite, wrap, yoke; SEE CONCEPTS 85,160

bind [v2] *obligate; restrict*
compel, confine, constrain, detain, engage, enslave, force, hamper, hinder, hogtie*, indenture, lock up, necessitate, oblige, prescribe, put half nelson on*, put lock on*, require, restrain, restrict, yoke; SEE CONCEPTS 14,130

binding [n] *cover; something which fastens*
adhesive, belt, fastener, jacket, tie, wrapper; SEE CONCEPT 475

binding [adj1] *necessary*
bounden*, compulsory, conclusive, counted upon, essential, imperative, incumbent on, indissoluble, irrevocable, mandatory, obligatory, required, requisite, unalterable; SEE CONCEPT 546

binding [adj2] *confining*
attached, enslaved, fastened, indentured, limiting, restraining, tied, tying; SEE CONCEPT 554

binge [n] *spree*
affair, bender, blind*, bout*, carousal, compotation, drunk*, fling, jag*, orgy*, toot*; SEE CONCEPT 386

biography [n] *account of person's life*
adventures, autobiography, bio, blog, close-up, confessions, diary, experiences, journal, letters, life, life history, life story, memoir, personal account, personal anecdote, personal narrative, personal record, picture, profile, résumé, saga, sketch, vita; SEE CONCEPTS 280,282

bird [n] *flying animal*
feathered creature, fowl, game; SEE CONCEPT 395

birth [n1] *becoming alive*
act of God, bearing, beginning, birthing, blessed event*, childbearing, childbirth, creation, delivery, labor, nascency, natality, nativity, parturition, producing, travail, visit from stork*; SEE CONCEPTS 302,373

birth [n2] *beginning*
commencement, dawn, dawning, emergence, fountainhead, genesis, onset, opening, origin, outset, rise, source, start; SEE CONCEPT 119

birth [n3] *heritage*
ancestry, background, blood, breeding, derivation, descent, extraction, forebears, genealogy, heritance, legacy, line, lineage, parentage, pedigree, position, race, rank, station, status, stock, strain; SEE CONCEPTS 296,648

birth control [n] *method of preventing pregnancy*
abstinence, condom, contraception, contraceptive, diaphragm, IUD, pill, planned parenthood, rhythm method, rubber, safety*, tied tubes, vasectomy; SEE CONCEPTS 121,375

bisect [v] *divide in two*
bifurcate, branch off, cleave, cross, cut across, cut in half, cut in two, dichotomize, dimidiate, divaricate, divide in two, fork, furcate, halve, he-

be
bi

misect, intersect, separate, split, split down the middle; SEE CONCEPTS *98,137,176*

bisexual [*adj*] *having relations with either gender*
AC-DC*, androgynous, bi*, epicene, gynandrous, hermaphroditic, intersexual, monoclinous, swings both ways*; SEE CONCEPT *372*

bit [*n1*] *tiny piece*
atom, butt, chicken feed*, chip, chunk, crumb, dab, dash, division, dollop, dose, dot, driblet, droplet, end, excerpt, flake, fraction, fragment, grain, iota, item, jot, lick*, lump, mite, modicum, moiety, molecule, morsel, niggle, parcel, part, particle, peanuts*, pinch, portion, sample, scale, scintilla, scrap, section, segment, shard, share, shaving, shred, slice, sliver, smidgen, snatch, snip, snippet, specimen, speck, splinter, sprinkling, stub, stump, taste, tittle, trace, trickle; SEE CONCEPTS *831,835*

bit [*n2*] *short period of time*
instant, jiffy, little while, minute, moment, second, space, spell, stretch, tick, while; SEE CONCEPT *807*

bite [*n1*] *injury from gripping, tearing*
chaw*, chomp*, gob*, itch*, laceration, nip, pain, pinch, prick, smarting, sting, tooth marks*, wound; SEE CONCEPT *309*

bite [*n2*] *mouthful of food*
brunch, drop, light meal, morsel, nibble, nosh*, piece, refreshment, sample, snack, sop*, taste; SEE CONCEPTS *457,459*

bite [*n3*] *pungency; stinging sensation*
burn, edge, guts*, kick, piquancy, punch, spice, sting, zap*, zip*; SEE CONCEPT *614*

bite [*n4*] *allotment*
allowance, cut, lot, part, piece, portion, quota, share, slice; SEE CONCEPT *835*

bite [*v1*] *grip or tear with teeth*
champ, chaw, chaw on, chew, chomp, clamp, crunch, crush, cut, eat, gnaw, hold, lacerate, masticate, munch, nibble, nip, pierce, pinch, rend, ruminate, seize, sever, snap, take a chunk out of*, taste, tooth, wound; SEE CONCEPTS *185,616*

bite [*v2*] *corrode, eat away*
burn, consume, decay, decompose, deteriorate, dissolve, eat into, engrave, erode, etch, oxidize, rot, rust, scour, sear, slash, smart, sting, tingle, wear away; SEE CONCEPTS *215,250*

bite [*v3*] *take a chance*
be victim, get hooked*, nibble, risk, volunteer; SEE CONCEPT *384*

biting [*adj1*] *piercing, sharp*
bitter, bleak, blighting, cold, crisp, cutting, freezing, harsh, nipping, penetrating, raw; SEE CONCEPTS *569,605*

biting [*adj2*] *sarcastic*
acerbic, acrimonious, bitter, caustic, cutting, incisive, mordant, scathing, severe, sharp, stinging, trenchant, withering; SEE CONCEPT *267*

bitter [*adj1*] *pungent, sharp*
absinthal, absinthian, acerb, acerbic, acid, acrid, amaroidal, astringent, harsh, sour, tart, unsweetened, vinegary; SEE CONCEPT *613*

bitter [*adj2*] *hostile, nasty*
acrimonious, alienated, antagonistic, begrudging, biting, caustic, crabby, divided, embittered, estranged, fierce, freezing, hateful, intense, irreconcilable, morose, rancorous, resentful, sardonic, severe, sore, sour, stinging, sullen, virulent, vitriolic, with chip on shoulder*; SEE CONCEPTS *267,404*

bitter [*adj3*] *painful, distressing*
afflictive, annoying, bad, brutal, calamitous, cruel, dire, disagreeable, displeasing, distasteful, disturbing, galling, grievous, hard, harsh, heartbreaking, hurtful, inclement, intemperate, intense, merciless, offensive, poignant, provoking, rigorous, rugged, ruthless, savage, severe, sharp, stinging, unpalatable, unpleasant, vexatious, woeful; SEE CONCEPT *537*

bitterness [*n1*] *sourness*
acerbity, acidity, acridity, astringency, brackishness, brininess, piquancy, pungency, sharpness, tartness, vinegariness; SEE CONCEPT *614*

bitterness [*n2*] *agony*
acrimoniousness, anguish, asperity, distress, grievousness, harshness, hostility, mordancy, pain, painfulness, sarcasm, venom, virulence; SEE CONCEPTS *410,633*

bizarre [*adj*] *strange, wild*
bugged out*, camp*, comical, curious, eccentric, extraordinary, fantastic, far-out*, freakish, grody*, grotesque, kooky, ludicrous, odd, oddball, offbeat, off the wall*, outlandish, outré, peculiar, queer, ridiculous, singular, unusual, way-out*, weird; SEE CONCEPTS *547,564*

blab [*v*] *gossip*
babble, betray, blather, blurt out, chatter, disclose, divulge, gab, gabble, give away, go on, jabber, let out, let slip, mouth, peach*, prattle, reveal, run off at the mouth*, run on, shoot the breeze*, spill*, spill the beans*, squeal*, talk through one's hat*, tattle, tell, tell on, yak*, yakkety-yak*; SEE CONCEPTS *55,60*

black [*n*] *African-American*
African, Afro-American, Negro.

black [*adj1*] *dark, inky*
atramentous, brunet, charcoal, clouded, coal, dingy, dusky, ebon, ebony, inklike, jet, livid, melanoid, murky, obsidian, onyx, piceous, pitch, pitch-dark, raven, sable, shadowy, slate, sloe, somber, sombre, sooty, starless, stygian, swart, swarthy; SEE CONCEPT *618*

black [*adj2*] *hopeless*
atrocious, bleak, depressing, depressive, dismal, dispiriting, distressing, doleful, dreary, foreboding, funereal, gloomy, horrible, lugubrious, mournful, ominous, oppressive, sad, sinister, sombre, threatening; SEE CONCEPTS *529,570*

black [*adj3*] *dirty*
dingy, filthy, foul, grimy, grubby, impure, nasty, soiled, sooty, spotted, squalid, stained, unclean, uncleanly; SEE CONCEPT *589*

black [*adj4*] *angry*
enraged, fierce, furious, hostile, menacing, resentful, sour, sullen, threatening; SEE CONCEPT *403*

black [*adj5*] *evil*
bad, diabolical, iniquitous, mean, nefarious, villainous, wicked; SEE CONCEPT *545*

blacken [*v1*] *darken*
befoul, begrime, blot, cloud, deepen, ebonize, grow dark, grow dim, ink, make dark, shade, smudge, soil; SEE CONCEPT *250*

blacken [*v2*] *malign; smear*
asperse, attack, bad-mouth*, blot, blotch, calumniate, decry, defame, defile, denigrate, dishonor, do a number on*, give a black eye*, knock*, libel, malign, rip*, rip up and down*, slander, slur, smudge, stain, sully, taint, tarnish, traduce, vilify; SEE CONCEPT *54*

blacklist [v] *ban*

banish, bar, blackball, boycott, debar, exclude, expel, hit list*, ostracize, preclude, proscribe, put on hit list*, reject, repudiate, snub, thumbs down*, vote against; SEE CONCEPT 25

black magic [n] *sorcery*

diabolism, magic, necromancy, voodoo, witchcraft, wizardry; SEE CONCEPTS 370,689

blackmail [n] *intimidation for money; money to quiet informer*

bribe, bribery, exaction, extortion, hush money*, milking*, payoff, protection, ransom, slush fund*, tribute; SEE CONCEPTS 123,192

blackmail [v] *intimidating for money*

badger, bleed, coerce, compel, demand, exact, extort, force, hold to ransom, milk*, put the shake on*, ransom, shake*, shake down*, squeeze*, threaten; SEE CONCEPTS 192,342

black out [v1] *delete; cover*

batten, conceal, cover up, cross out, cut off, darken, eclipse, eradicate, erase, hold back, make dark, obfuscate, rub out, shade, squash, squelch; SEE CONCEPT 250

black out [v2] *faint*

collapse, crap out*, draw a blank*, go out like a light*, lose consciousness, pass out*, slip into coma, swoon*, zone out*; SEE CONCEPT 303

blade [n] *cutting tool*

brand, cutlass, edge, épée, knife, shank, sword; SEE CONCEPTS 495,499

blah [adj] *dull, lifeless*

banausic, bland, boring, dim, dreary, humdrum, monotone, monotonous, pedestrian, plodding, yawn producing*; SEE CONCEPT 544

blame [n1] *condemnation*

accusation, animadversion, arraignment, attack, attribution, castigation, censure, charge, chiding, complaint, criticism, denunciation, depreciation, diatribe, disapprobation, disapproval, disfavor, disparagement, expostulation, exprobation, impeachment, implication, imputation, incrimination, inculpation, indictment, invective, objurgation, obloquy, opposition, rebuke, recrimination, remonstrance, reprehension, reprimand, reproach, reprobation, reproof, repudiation, slur, tirade; SEE CONCEPT 54

blame [n2] *responsibility*

accountability, answerability, burden, culpability, fault, guilt, incrimination, liability, onus, rap*; SEE CONCEPTS 639,661

blame [v] *accuse; place responsibility*

admonish, ascribe, attribute, blast, blow the whistle on*, censure, charge, chide, climb all over*, condemn, criticize, denounce, denunciate, disapprove, express disapproval, find fault with, finger*, frame, hold responsible, impute, indict, jump all over*, jump down one's throat*, knock*, lay a bad trip on*, lay at one's door*, lay to*, let one have it*, lower the boom*, pass the buck*, point the finger*, rap, rebuke, reprehend, reproach, reprove, roast*, saddle, skin*, stick it to*, tax, upbraid; SEE CONCEPT 44

blameless [adj] *not responsible*

above suspicion, clean, clean-handed, clear, crimeless, exemplary, faultless, good, guilt-free, guiltless, immaculate, impeccable, inculpable, innocent, in the clear*, irreprehensible, irreproachable, not guilty, perfect, pure, righteous, stainless, unblemished, unimpeachable, unoffending, unspotted, unsullied, untarnished, upright, virtuous; SEE CONCEPT 555

blanch [v] *become afraid*

flinch, pale, recoil, shrink, start, wince; SEE CONCEPT 27

bland [adj1] *tasteless; undistinctive*

banal, blah*, boring, dull, dull as dishwater*, flat, flavorless, ho hum*, humdrum, insipid, milk-and-water*, monotonous, nerdy*, nothing, pabulum*, sapless*, tame, tedious, unexciting, uninspiring, uninteresting, unstimulating, vanilla*, vapid, waterish, watery, weak, wimpy*, wishy-washy*, zero*; SEE CONCEPTS 589,613

bland [adj2] *friendly, gracious*

affable, amiable, civilized, congenial, courteous, gentle, good-natured, ingratiating, oily, pleasant, smooth, suave, unctuous, unemotional, urbane; SEE CONCEPT 401

bland [adj3] *mild, temperate*

balmy, calm, calmative, clear, lenient, mollifying, nonirritant, nonirritating, smooth, soft, soothing; SEE CONCEPTS 485,605

blank [n] *empty space*

abyss, cavity, chasm, emptiness, gap, gulf, hiatus, hole, hollow, hollowness, interstice, interval, lacuna, nihility, nothingness, nullity, omission, opening, preterition, pretermission, skip, tabula rasa, vacancy, vacuity, vacuum, void, womb; SEE CONCEPT 513

blank [adj1] *clear*

bare, barren, clean, empty, fresh, new, pale, plain, spotless, uncompleted, unfilled, unmarked, untouched, unused, vacant, vacuous, virgin, virginal, void, white; SEE CONCEPTS 485,562

blank [adj2] *expressionless*

deadpan, dull, empty, fruitless, hollow, immobile, impassive, inane, inexpressive, inscrutable, lifeless, masklike, meaningless, noncommittal, poker-faced, stiff, stupid, uncommunicative, unexpressive, vacant, vacuous, vague; SEE CONCEPT 406

blank [adj3] *dumbfounded*

at a loss, awestruck, bewildered, confounded, confused, dazed, disconcerted, muddled, nonplussed, stupefied, uncomprehending, wonderstruck; SEE CONCEPT 402

blank [adj4] *absolute, utter*

complete, downright, out-and-out, outright, perfect, regular, sheer, straight-out, thorough, total, unconditional, unqualified; SEE CONCEPT 531

blanket [n] *cover, covering*

afghan, carpet, cloak, coat, coating, comforter, covering, coverlet, envelope, film, fleece, layer, mat, puff, quilt, rug, sheath, sheet, throw, wrapper; SEE CONCEPTS 473,475

blanket [adj] *comprehensive*

absolute, across-the-board, all-inclusive, overall, powerful, sweeping, unconditional, wide-ranging; SEE CONCEPT 772

blanket [v] *cover*

bury, cloak, cloud, coat, conceal, crown, eclipse, envelop, hide, mask, obscure, overcast, overlay, overspread, suppress, surround; SEE CONCEPT 172

blare [v] *make loud noise*

bark, bellow, blast, boom, bray, clamor, clang, honk, hoot, peal, resound, roar, scream, shout, shriek, sound out, toot, trumpet; SEE CONCEPTS 65,77

bi
bl

blarney [n] *flattery*
adulation, a line*, baloney*, blandishment, cajolery, coaxing, compliments, exaggeration, eyewash*, fawning*, honey*, incense, ingratiation,
inveiglement, oil*, overpraise, soft soap*, soft
words, sweet talk*, wheedling; SEE CONCEPT 69

blasé [adj] *nonchalant*
apathetic, been around twice*, bored, cloyed,
cool*, disenchanted, disentranced, done it all*,
fed up*, glutted, indifferent, jaded, knowing, laid-
back*, lukewarm*, mellow*, mundane, offhand,
satiated, sick of, sophisticate, sophisticated, surfeited, unconcerned, unexcited, uninterested, unmoved, weary, worldly, world-weary; SEE
CONCEPT 404

blasphemous [adj] *irreverent*
cursing, disrespectful, godless, impious, insulting, irreligious, profanatory, profane, sacrilegious, swearing, ungodly; SEE CONCEPT 545

blasphemy [n] *irreverence*
abuse, curse, cussing, desecration, execration,
heresy, impiety, impiousness, imprecation, indignity, lewdness, profanation, profaneness, profanity, reviling, sacrilege, scoffing, scurrility,
swearing, vituperation; SEE CONCEPT 645

blast [n1/v1] *loud sound; make loud sound*
bang, blare, blow, burst, clang, clap, crack, din,
honk, peal, roar, scream, slam, smash, toot, trumpet, wail, wham; SEE CONCEPTS 65,521,595

blast [n2] *explosion*
bang, blow-up, burst, crash, detonation, discharge, dynamite, eruption, outbreak, outburst,
salvo, volley; SEE CONCEPTS 179,521

blast [n3] *gust of wind*
blow, draft, gale, squall, storm, strong breeze,
tempest; SEE CONCEPTS 437,524

blast [n4] *fun time*
amusement, bash*, blow out*, excitement, good
time, great time, party, riot*; SEE CONCEPT 386

blast [v2] *explode*
annihilate, blight, blow up, bomb, break up, burst,
damage, dash, demolish, destroy, detonate, dynamite, injure, kill, ruin, shatter, shrivel, spoil,
stunt, torpedo, wither, wreck; SEE CONCEPTS
86,179

blast [v3] *lambaste; defeat mentally*
attack, beat, castigate, clobber*, criticize, drub*,
flay, lash out at, lick*, rail at, shellac*, whip*;
SEE CONCEPT 52

blatant [adj1] *obvious; brazen*
arrant, bald, barefaced, brassy, clear, conspicuous, crying, flagrant, flashy, flaunting, garish,
gaudy, glaring, glitzy, impudent, loud, meretricious, naked, obtrusive, ostentatious, outright,
overbold, overt, plain, prominent, pronounced,
protrusive, screaming, shameless, sheer, showy,
snazzy, unabashed, unblushing, unmitigated; SEE
CONCEPTS 540,569

blatant [adj2] *deafening*
boisterous, clamorous, crying, ear-splitting,
harsh, loud, loudmouthed, noisy, obstreperous,
obtrusive, piercing, screaming, scurrilous, strident, vociferant, vociferous, vulgar; SEE CON-
CEPTS 592,594

blaze [n1] *fire*
bonfire, burning, combustion, conflagration,
flame, flames, holocaust, wildfire; SEE CONCEPTS
478,521

blaze [n2] *flash of light*
beam, brilliance, burst, flare, glare, gleam, glitter, glow, radiance; SEE CONCEPT 628

blaze [n3] *torrent*
blast, burst, eruption, flare-up, flash, fury, outbreak, outburst, rush, storm; SEE CONCEPT 673

blaze [v] *burn brightly*
beam, burst out, coruscate, explode, fire, flame,
flare, flash, flicker, fulgurate, glare, gleam, glow,
illuminate, illumine, incandesce, jet, light, radiate, scintillate, shimmer, shine, sparkle; SEE CON-
CEPT 249

bleach [v] *whiten*
achromatize, blanch, blench, decolor, decolorize,
etiolate, fade, grow pale, lighten, make pale, per-
oxide, wash out; SEE CONCEPT 250

bleachers [n] *seating for watching event*
benches, boxes, grandstand, Ruthville*, seats,
stands; SEE CONCEPTS 440,443

bleak [adj1] *barren*
austere, bare, blank, blighted, bombed, bull-
dozed, burned, chilly, cleared, cold, deforested,
desert, deserted, desolate, dreary, exposed, flat,
gaunt, grim, open, raw, scorched, stripped, un-
populated, unsheltered, weather-beaten, wild,
windswept; SEE CONCEPT 490

bleak [adj2] *depressing*
black, cheerless, comfortless, dark, discouraging,
disheartening, dismal, drear, dreary, funereal,
gloomy, grim, hard, harsh, hopeless, joyless,
lonely, melancholy, mournful, oppressive, sad,
somber, unpromising; SEE CONCEPTS 403,537

bleed [v1] *cause blood to flow*
drain, exude, gush, hemorrhage, leech, ooze,
open vein, phlebotomize, run, seep, shed, spurt,
trickle, weep; SEE CONCEPT 185

bleed [v2] *extort*
blackmail, confiscate, deplete, drain, exhaust, extract, fleece, impoverish, leech*, milk*, mulct,
overcharge, pauperize, put the screws to*, rook*,
sap*, skin*, squeeze*, steal, stick*, strong-arm;
SEE CONCEPTS 192,342

bleed [v3] *grieve*
ache, agonize, be in pain, feel for, pity, suffer,
sympathize; SEE CONCEPTS 12,17

blemish [n] *flaw*
beauty spot, birthmark, blackhead, blister,
bloom*, blot, blotch, blot on the landscape*, blur,
brand, bruise, bug*, catch, chip, cicatrix, defacement, defect, deformity, dent, discoloration, disfigurement, disgrace, dishonor, eyesore, fault,
freckle, hickey*, imperfection, impurity, lentigo,
lump, macula, maculation, mark, mole, nevus,
nodule, patch, pimple, pock, pockmark, scar, second, sight, smudge, snag, speck, speckle, spot,
stain, stigma, taint, tarnish, vice, wart, whitehead,
zit*; SEE CONCEPT 580

blemish [v] *flaw, disfigure*
blot, blotch, blur, damage, deface, distort, harm,
hurt, impair, injure, maim, mangle, mar, mark,
mutilate, pervert, prejudice, scar, smudge, spoil,
spot, stain, sully, taint, tarnish, twist, vitiate,
wrench; SEE CONCEPTS 54,246

blend [n] *composite, mix*
alloy, amalgam, amalgamation, brew, combination, commixture, composite, compound, concoction, fusion, interfusion, intermixture, mixture,
synthesis, union; SEE CONCEPT 432

blend [v1] *mix*
amalgamate, cement, coalesce, combine, com-

mingle, commix, compound, fuse, integrate, interblend, intermix, meld, merge, mingle, synthesize, unite, weld; SEE CONCEPT 109

blend [v2] *harmonize*
arrange, complement, fit, go well, go with, integrate, orchestrate, suit, symphonize, synthesize, unify; SEE CONCEPT 656

bless [v1] *sanctify*
absolve, anoint, baptize, beatify, canonize, commend, confirm, consecrate, cross, dedicate, enshrine, eulogize, exalt, extol, give thanks to, glorify, hallow, honor, invoke benefits, invoke happiness, laud, magnify, make holy, offer, offer benediction, ordain, panegyrize, praise, pray for, pronounce holy, sacrifice, sign, sprinkle, thank; SEE CONCEPTS 69,367

bless [v2] *grant, bestow*
celebrate, endow, favor, give, glorify, grace, laud, magnify, praise, provide; SEE CONCEPTS 50,88

blessed [adj1] *sanctified*
adored, among the angels, beatified, consecrated, divine, enthroned, exalted, glorified, hallowed, holy, inviolable, redeemed, resurrected, revered, rewarded, sacred, sacrosanct, saved, spiritual, unprofane; SEE CONCEPTS 536,568

blessed [adj2] *happy*
blissful, content, contented, endowed, favored, fortunate, glad, granted, joyful, joyous, lucky; SEE CONCEPT 404

blessing [n1] *sanctification*
absolution, benedicite, benediction, benison, commendation, consecration, dedication, divine sanction, grace, invocation, laying on of hands, thanks, thanksgiving; SEE CONCEPT 367

blessing [n2] *good wishes, approval*
approbation, backing, concurrence, consent, favor, Godspeed, leave, okay*, permission, regard, sanction, support, valediction; SEE CONCEPTS 10,50,88

blessing [n3] *advantage*
asset, benediction, benefit, boon, bounty, break, favor, gain, gift, godsend, good, good fortune, good luck, help, kindness, luck break, manna from heaven*, miracle, profit, service, stroke of luck*, windfall; SEE CONCEPTS 230,679

blight [n] *disease; plague*
affliction, bane, blot on the landscape*, canker, contamination, corruption, curse, decay, dump, evil, eyesore, fungus, infestation, mildew, pest, pestilence, pollution, rot, scourge, sight, withering, woe; SEE CONCEPTS 306,674

blight [v] *ruin, destroy*
annihilate, blast, crush, damage, dash, decay, disappoint, foul up*, frustrate, glitch up*, injure, mar, mess up*, nip in the bud*, nullify, shrivel, spoil, taint, trash*, wither, wreck; SEE CONCEPT 252

blind [n] *screen, covering*
blinder, blindfold, blinker, camouflage, cloak, cover, curtain, facade, front, mask, trap, veil; SEE CONCEPT 716

blind [adj1] *sightless*
amaurotic, blind as a bat*, dark, destitute of vision, eyeless, groping, in darkness, purblind, typhlotic, undiscerning, unseeing, unsighted, visionless; SEE CONCEPT 619

blind [adj2] *indifferent*
careless, heedless, ignorant, imperceptive, inattentive, inconsiderate, indiscriminate, injudicious,

insensitive, myopic, nearsighted, neglectful, oblivious, thoughtless, unaware, unconscious, undiscerning, unmindful, unobservant, unperceiving, unreasoning, unseeing; SEE CONCEPT 402

blind [adj3] *uncontrolled*
hasty, heedless, impetuous, inconsiderate, irrational, mindless, rash, reckless, senseless, shortsighted, thoughtless, unseeing, unthinking, violent, wild; SEE CONCEPT 544

blind [adj4] *hidden or covered*
blocked, closed, closed at one end, concealed, dark, dead-end, dim, disguised, impassable, leading nowhere, obscured, obstructed, secluded, unmarked, without egress, without exit; SEE CONCEPTS 490,576

blindly [adv1] *without direction, purpose*
aimlessly, at random, confusedly, frantically, in all directions, indiscriminately, instinctively, madly, pell-mell, purposelessly, wildly; SEE CONCEPT 542

blindly [adv2] *carelessly*
foolishly, heedlessly, impulsively, inconsiderately, obtusely, passionately, purblindly, recklessly, regardlessly, senselessly, thoughtlessly, tumultuously, unreasonably, unreasoningly, willfully, without rhyme or reason*; SEE CONCEPT 401

blindness [n] *sightlessness*
amaurosis, anopsia, astigmatism, cataracts, darkness, defect, myopia, presbyopia, purblindness, typhlosis; SEE CONCEPT 629

blink [v1] *wink of eye; twinkle*
bat, flash, flicker, flutter, glimmer, glitter, nictate, nictitate, scintillate, shimmer, sparkle, squint; SEE CONCEPTS 185,624

blink [v2] *ignore*
bypass, condone, connive, cushion, discount, disregard, fail, forget, neglect, omit, overlook, overpass, pass by, slight, turn a blind eye*; SEE CONCEPT 30

bliss [n] *ecstasy*
beatitude, blessedness, cool*, euphoria, felicity, gladness, gone*, happiness, heaven*, joy, paradise, rapture; SEE CONCEPTS 32,230

blissful [adj] *happy*
beatific, cool*, crazy, delighted, dreamy, ecstatic, elated, enchanted, enraptured, euphoric, floating*, flying*, gone*, heavenly, in ecstasy, in seventh heaven*, in the twilight zone*, joyful, joyous, mad*, on cloud nine*, rapturous, sent*, spaced-out*, turned-on*; SEE CONCEPT 403

blister [n] *swelling*
abscess, blain, bleb, boil, bubble, bulla, burn, canker, carbuncle, cyst, furuncle, pimple, pustule, sac, sore, ulcer, vesication, vesicle, wale, weal, welt, wheal; SEE CONCEPT 309

blithe [adj] *happy*
animated, buoyant, carefree, cheerful, cheery, chirpy, gay, gladsome, gleeful, jaunty, jocund, jolly, jovial, joyful, lighthearted, merry, mirthful, sprightly, sunny, vivacious; SEE CONCEPT 404

blitz [n] *heavy attack*
assault, blitzkrieg, bombardment, bombing, lightning attack, offensive, onslaught, raid, shelling, strike; SEE CONCEPTS 86,320

blizzard [n] *snow storm*
blast, gale, precipitation, snowfall, squall, tempest, whiteout; SEE CONCEPT 526

bloat [v] *blow up like a balloon*
balloon, belly, bilge, billow, dilate, distend, en-

block [n1] *mass of material*
bar, brick, cake, chunk, cube, hunk, ingot, loaf, lump, oblong, piece, section, segment, slab, slice, solid, square; SEE CONCEPTS *470,471*

block [n2] *obstruction*
bar, barrier, blank wall, blockage, chunk, clog, hindrance, impediment, jam, mass, obstacle, obstruction, roadblock, snag, stop, stoppage, wall; SEE CONCEPTS *470,652*

block [v] *obstruct*
arrest, bar, barricade, blockade, block out, brake, catch, charge, check, choke, clog, close, close off, close out, congest, cut off, dam, deter, fill, halt, hang up*, hinder, hold up, impede, intercept, interfere with, occlude, plug, prevent, shut off*, shut out, stall, stonewall, stop, stopper, stop up*, stymie, tackle, take out of play*, thwart; SEE CONCEPTS *121,130*

blockade [n] *barrier*
bar, barricade, blank wall, clog, closure, embolus, encirclement, hindrance, impediment, infarct, infarction, obstacle, obstruction, restriction, roadblock, siege, snag, stop, stoppage, wall; SEE CONCEPTS *470,652*

block out [v1] *plan course*
arrange, chart, map out, outline, prepare, sketch; SEE CONCEPT *36*

block out [v2] *try to forget*
close, conceal, cover, hide, obscure, obstruct, screen, shroud, shut off, shut out; SEE CONCEPT *40*

blond/blonde [adj] *having light-colored hair*
albino, auricomous, bleached, champagne, fair, fair-haired, flaxen, golden-haired, light, pale, pearly, platinum, sallow, sandy-haired, snowy, straw, strawberry, towheaded*, washed-out, yellow-haired; SEE CONCEPT *618*

blood [n1] *red body fluid*
claret, clot, cruor, gore, hemoglobin, juice, plasma, sanguine fluid, vital fluid; SEE CONCEPTS *393,420*

blood [n2] *ancestry*
birth, consanguinity, descendants, descent, extraction, family, kindred, kinship, line, lineage, origin, pedigree, relations, stock; SEE CONCEPT *296*

bloodless [adj1] *unfeeling*
anesthetic, cold, coldhearted, dull, impassive, indolent, insensible, insensitive, languid, lazy, lifeless, listless, passionless, slow, sluggish, spiritless, torpid, unemotional, unkind; SEE CONCEPT *404*

bloodless [adj2] *pale*
anemic, ashen, cadaverous, chalky, colorless, ghostly, lifeless, pallid, pasty, sallow, sickly, wan, watery; SEE CONCEPT *618*

bloody [adj1] *bleeding*
blood-soaked, blood-spattered, bloodstained, crimson, ensanguined, gaping, gory, grisly, hematic, hemic, imbrued, open, raw, sanguinary, sanguine, unstaunched, unstopped, wounded; SEE CONCEPT *485*

bloody [adj2] *hard-fought*
bloodthirsty, cruel, cutthroat, decimating, ferocious, fierce, gory, grim, heavy, homicidal, murderous, sanguinary, sanguine, savage, slaughterous; SEE CONCEPTS *540,569*

bloom [n] *flower*
blossom, blossoming, bud, efflorescence, floret, flourishing, flower, floweret, opening; SEE CONCEPT *425*

bloom [v] *flower; flourish*
bear fruit, be in flower, blossom, blow, bud, burgeon, burst, develop, effloresce, fare well, fructify, germinate, grow, open, prosper, sprout, succeed, tassel out, thrive, wax; SEE CONCEPTS *427,706*

blooper [n] *blunder*
boner*, boo-boo*, bungle, error, faux pas, fluff*, gaffe, impropriety, indecorum, lapse, mistake, slip, solecism, trip*; SEE CONCEPTS *384,674*

blossom [n] *flower*
bloom, bud, efflorescence, floret, floweret, inflorescence, posy, spike; SEE CONCEPT *425*

blossom [v1] *flower*
bloom, blow, burgeon, burst, effloresce, leaf, open, outbloom, shoot, unfold; SEE CONCEPT *427*

blossom [v2] *flourish*
batten, bloom, develop, grow, mature, progress, prosper, succeed, thrive; SEE CONCEPT *706*

blot [n] *mark; flaw*
black eye*, blemish, blotch, blur, brand, defect, discoloration, disgrace, fault, odium, onus, patch, slur, smear, smudge, speck, spot, stain, stigma, taint; SEE CONCEPTS *230,580*

blot [v1] *disgrace, disfigure*
bespatter, blemish, dirty, discolor, mark, smudge, smut, soil, spoil, spot, stain, sully, tarnish; SEE CONCEPT *240*

blot [v2] *soak up*
absorb, dry, take up; SEE CONCEPT *211*

blotch [n] *smudge*
acne, blemish, blot, breakout, eruption, mark, mottling, patch, splash, spot, stain, stigma; SEE CONCEPT *580*

blouse [n] *shirt for woman*
bodice, bodysuit, middy, pullover, shell, slipover, T-shirt, turtleneck, V-neck; SEE CONCEPT *451*

blow [n1] *blast, rush of air, wind*
draft, flurry, gale, gust, hurricane, puff, squall, strong breeze, tempest, typhoon; SEE CONCEPT *526*

blow [n2] *hard hit*
bang, bash, bat, belt, biff, blindside, bop*, buffet, bump, clip, clout, clump, collision, concussion, crack, cut, ding*, impact, jab, jar, jolt, kick, knock, knockout, knuckle sandwich*, KO*, lick, percussion, poke, pound, punch, rap, shock, slam, slap, slug, smack, smash, sock, strike, stroke, swat, swing, swipe, thrust, thump, thwack*, uppercut, wallop, whack, whomp*, zap*; SEE CONCEPT *189*

blow [n3] *catastrophe*
affliction, balk, bolt from the blue*, bombshell*, calamity, casualty, chagrin, comedown, debacle, disappointment, disaster, disgruntlement, frustration, jolt, letdown, misadventure, misfortune, mishap, reverse, setback, shock, tragedy, upset; SEE CONCEPT *674*

blow [v1] *blast, rush of air, wind*
breathe, buffet, drive, exhale, fan, flap, flow, flutter, gasp, heave, huff, inflate, pant, puff, pump, ruffle, rush, stream, swell, swirl, waft, wave, whiff, whirl, whisk, whisper, whistle; SEE CONCEPTS *185,526*

large, expand, inflate, puff up, swell; SEE CONCEPTS *184,208*

blow [v2] *make sound, usually with instrument*
blare, blast, honk, mouth, pipe, play, sound, toot, trumpet, vibrate; SEE CONCEPT 65

blow [v3] *leave suddenly*
depart, go, hit the road*, split*, take a hike*, take a powder*; SEE CONCEPT 195

blow [v4] *ruin chance*
fail, flounder, goof*, miscarry, miss; SEE CONCEPT 699

blow [v5] *use up money*
dissipate, lay out, pay out, spend, squander, waste; SEE CONCEPT 341

blowout [n1] *explosion; something exploded*
blast, break, burst, detonation, eruption, escape, flat tire, leak, puncture, rupture, tear; SEE CONCEPT 179

blowout [n2] *wild party*
bash, binge, feast, riot*, shindig, spree; SEE CONCEPT 383

blow up [v1] *inflate*
billow, bloat, distend, enlarge, expand, fill, inflate, puff up, pump up, swell; SEE CONCEPTS 208,236,245

blow up [v2] *explode*
blast, bomb, blast, detonate, dynamite, erupt, go off, mushroom, rupture, shatter; SEE CONCEPTS 179,320

blow up [v3] *magnify importance*
enlarge, exaggerate, heighten, overstate; SEE CONCEPTS 49,59

blow up [v4] *burst with anger*
become angry, become enraged, erupt, go off the deep end*, hit the roof*, lose control, lose temper, rage, rave; SEE CONCEPTS 29,44

blue [adj1] *sky, sea color*
azure, beryl, cerulean, cobalt, indigo, navy, royal, sapphire, teal, turquoise, ultramarine; SEE CONCEPT 618

blue [adj2] *sad*
dejected, depressed, despondent, disconsolate, dismal, dispirited, downcast, downhearted, down in the dumps*, fed up*, gloomy, glum, low, melancholy, moody, unhappy, woebegone; SEE CONCEPT 403

blue [adj3] *vulgar*
bawdy, dirty, indecent, lewd, naughty, obscene, off-color, racy, risqué, salty, shady, smutty, spicy, suggestive, wicked; SEE CONCEPT 545

blues [n] *depression*
dejection, despondency, doldrums, dumps*, gloom, gloominess, glumness, heavy heart*, low spirits, melancholy, moodiness, mournfulness, sadness, the dismals*, the mopes*, unhappiness; SEE CONCEPT 410

bluff [n1] *boast; deceit*
bluster, braggadocio, bragging, bravado, deception, delusion, facade, fake, false colors, false front, feint, fraud, front, humbug*, jiving*, lie, pretense, pretext, ruse, sham, show, snow*, stall, subterfuge, trick; SEE CONCEPTS 58,59

bluff [n2] *precipice*
bank, cliff, crag, escarpment, headland, hill, mountain, peak, promontory, ridge, rock; SEE CONCEPT 509

bluff [adj] *abrupt*
barefaced, bearish, blunt, blustering, breviloquent, brief, brusque, candid, crusty, curt, direct, downright, forthright, frank, gruff, hearty, honest, laconic, no-nonsense, open, outspoken, plain-spoken, rough, rude, short, short-spoken, sincere,

snippety, snippy, straightforward, tactless, tart, terse, unceremonious; SEE CONCEPT 267

bluff [v] *deceive*
affect, beguile, betray, bunco*, con, counterfeit, defraud, delude, double-cross, fake*, fake out*, feign, fool, humbug*, illude, jive*, juggle, lie, mislead, pretend, psych out*, put on*, sham*, shuck*, simulate, snow*, take in*, trick; SEE CONCEPTS 58,59

blunder [n] *mistake*
blooper*, boner*, boo-boo*, bungle, dumb move*, dumb thing to do*, error, fault, faux pas, flub*, flub-up*, fluff*, gaffe, goof*, howler*, impropriety, inaccuracy, indiscretion, lapse, muff*, oversight, slip, slip-up, solecism, trip*; SEE CONCEPTS 101,230

blunder [v] *make mistake*
ball up*, blow, bobble, botch, bumble, bungle, confuse, drop the ball*, err, flounder, flub*, foul up, fumble, gum up*, louse up, mess up, misjudge, screw up*, slip up, stumble; SEE CONCEPT 101

blunt [adj1] *not sharp*
dull, dulled, edgeless, insensitive, obtuse, pointless, round, rounded, unsharpened; SEE CONCEPTS 485,486

blunt [adj2] *straightforward*
abrupt, bluff, brief, brusque, candid, crusty, curt, discourteous, explicit, forthright, frank, gruff, impolite, matter-of-fact, outspoken, plain-spoken, rude, short, snappy, snippy, tactless, trenchant, unceremonious, uncivil, unpolished; SEE CONCEPT 267

blunt [v] *make dull*
attenuate, benumb, cripple, dampen, deaden, debilitate, desensitize, disable, enfeeble, numb, obtund, sap, soften, take the edge off, undermine, water down, weaken; SEE CONCEPT 240

blur [v1] *cloud, fog*
becloud, bedim, befog, blear, blind, darken, daze, dazzle, dim, glare, make hazy, make indistinct, make vague, mask, muddy, obscure, shade, soften; SEE CONCEPT 627

blur [v2] *make dirty*
besmear, blemish, blot, discolor, smear, smudge, spot, stain, taint, tarnish; SEE CONCEPT 254

blush [n] *pink coloring*
bloom, blossom, burning, color, flush, flushing, glow, glowing, mantling, pink tinge, reddening, redness, rosiness, rosy tint, ruddiness, scarlet; SEE CONCEPT 622

blush [v] *become colored, pinken*
color, crimson, flush, glow, have rosy cheeks, mantle, redden, rouge, turn red, turn scarlet; SEE CONCEPT 250

bluster [n] *bullying, intimidation*
bluff, boasting, boisterousness, bombast, braggadocio, bragging, bravado, crowing, rabidity, rampancy, swagger, swaggering; SEE CONCEPT 633

bluster [v] *bully, intimidate*
badger, boast, brag, brazen, browbeat, bulldoze*, cow*, crow*, domineer, gloat, hector, rant, rave, ride the high horse*, roar, roister, shoot off one's mouth*, show off, storm, strut, swagger, swell, talk big*, vapor*, vaunt, yap*; SEE CONCEPTS 49,78

board [n1] *piece of wood*
lath, panel, plank, slat, strip, timber; SEE CONCEPT 479

board [n2] *meal*
daily bread*, eats*, fare, food, keep*, mess, provisions, victuals; SEE CONCEPT *459*

board [n3] *group of advisers*
advisers, advisory group, brass, cabinet, committee, conclave, council, directorate, directors, execs*, executives, executive suite, front office*, jury, panel, trustees, upstairs*; SEE CONCEPTS *323,333,417*

board [v1] *embark on vehicle*
catch, climb on, embus, emplane, enter, entrain, get on, hop on, mount; SEE CONCEPTS *159,195*

board [v2] *provide food and sleeping quarters*
accommodate, bed, canton, care for, feed, harbor, house, let crash*, lodge, put up, quarter, room; SEE CONCEPT *136*

boast [n] *brag; source of pride*
avowal, bluster, bombast, braggadocio, bravado, exaggeration, gasconade, grandiloquence, heroics, joy, pretension, pride, pride and joy, self-satisfaction, swank, treasure, vaunt; SEE CONCEPTS *410,710*

boast [v1] *brag*
advertise, aggrandize, attract attention, blow, blow one's own horn*, blow smoke*, bluster, bully, cock-a-doodle-doo*, con, congratulate oneself, crow, exaggerate, exult, fake, flatter oneself, flaunt, flourish, gasconade, give a good account of oneself, gloat, glory, grandstand*, hug oneself*, jive*, lay on thick*, prate, preen, psych*, puff*, shoot*, shovel*, showboat*, show off, shuck*, sling*, sound off, strut, swagger, talk big*, triumph, vapor*; SEE CONCEPT *49*

boast [v2] *to have advantage*
be proud of, claim, exhibit, have in keeping, own, possess, pride oneself on, show off; SEE CONCEPT *261*

boastful [adj] *bragging*
arrogant, big, big-headed, bombastic, cocky, conceited, crowing, egotistic, egotistical, exultant, full of hot air*, hifalutin*, hot stuff*, know-it-all, loudmouth, on ego trip*, pompous, pretentious, puffed-up, self-aggrandizing, self-applauding, smart-alecky*, snooty, strutting, stuck-up, swaggering, swanky, swollen-headed, too big for one's britches*, vainglorious, vaunting, windbag*; SEE CONCEPTS *267,404*

boat [n] *vehicle for water travel*
ark, barge, bark, bateau, bottom, bucket, canoe, catamaran, craft, dinghy, dory, hulk, ketch, launch, lifeboat, pinnace, raft, sailboat, schooner, scow, ship, skiff, sloop, steamboat, tub, yacht; SEE CONCEPT *506*

boating [n] *travel, recreation in water*
canoeing, cruising, drifting, paddling, rowing, sailing, sculling, trawling, yachting; SEE CONCEPT *363*

bob [v] *bounce up and down*
bow, duck, genuflect, hop, jerk, jounce, leap, nod, oscillate, quaver, quiver, ricochet, seesaw, skip, waggle, weave, wobble; SEE CONCEPT *147*

bodily [adj] *concerning animate structure*
actual, animal, carnal, corporal, corporeal, fleshly, gross, human, material, natural, normal, organic, physical, sensual, somatic, substantial, tangible, unspiritual; SEE CONCEPT *406*

bodily [adv] *totally*
absolutely, altogether, as a body, as a group, collectively, completely, en masse, entirely, fully, wholly; SEE CONCEPTS *531,772*

body [n1] *physique*
anatomy, bag of bones*, beefcake*, bod*, boody*, build, carcass, chassis, constitution, embodiment, figure, form, frame, makeup, mortal part, protoplasm, shaft, shape, tenement, torso, trunk; SEE CONCEPT *405*

body [n2] *corpse*
ashes, bones, cadaver, carcass, carrion, clay, corpus delicti, dead body, deceased, dust, relic, remains, stiff*; SEE CONCEPT *390*

body [n3] *human being*
being, creature, human, individual, mortal, party, person, personage, soul; SEE CONCEPT *389*

body [n4] *bulk; central portion*
assembly, basis, bed, box, chassis, core, corpus, crux, essence, frame, fuselage, gist, gravamen, groundwork, hull, main part, majority, mass, material, matter, pith, skeleton, staple, substance, substructure, sum, tenor, total, trunk, whole; SEE CONCEPT *829*

body [n5] *crowd*
array, batch, bunch, bundle, clump, cluster, group, horde, lot, majority, mass, mob, multitude, parcel, party, set, society, throng; SEE CONCEPTS *417,432*

body [n6] *main part of written work*
argument, burden, core, discourse, dissertation, evidence, exposition, gist, heart, material, meat, pith, sense, substance, text, thesis, treatise, upshot; SEE CONCEPT *270*

bog [n] *swamp*
fen, lowland, marsh, marshland, mire, morass, moss, peat, quag, quagmire, slough, sump, wetlands; SEE CONCEPT *509*

bog down [v] *stick; become stuck*
decelerate, delay, detain, halt, hang up, impede, retard, set back, sink, slacken, slow down, slow up, stall; SEE CONCEPT *121*

bogus [adj] *counterfeit*
artificial, dummy, ersatz, fake, false, fictitious, forged, fraudulent, imitation, not what it is cracked up to be*, phony, pretended, pseudo, sham, simulated, spurious; SEE CONCEPT *582*

boil [n] *blister*
abscess, blain, blister, carbuncle, excrescence, furuncle, pimple, pustule, sore, tumor, ulcer; SEE CONCEPT *309*

boil [v1] *heat to bubbling*
agitate, bubble, churn, coddle, cook, decoct, effervesce, evaporate, fizz, foam, froth, parboil, poach, seethe, simmer, smolder, steam, steep, stew; SEE CONCEPTS *170,255*

boil [v2] *be angry*
be indignant, blow up, bristle, burn, flare, foam at the mouth*, fulminate, fume, rage, rave, sputter, storm; SEE CONCEPT *29*

boiling [adj1] *very hot*
baking, blistering, broiling, burning, fiery, hot, red-hot, roasting, scalding, scorching, sizzling, torrid, tropical, warm; SEE CONCEPT *605*

boiling [adj2] *angered*
angry, enraged, fuming, furious, incensed, indignant, infuriated, mad, raging; SEE CONCEPT *403*

boisterous [adj] *noisy and mischievous*
bouncy, brawling, clamorous, disorderly, effervescent, impetuous, loud, obstreperous, rambunctious, raucous, riotous, rollicking, rowdy, strident, tumultous/tumultuous, unrestrained, unruly, uproarious, vociferant, vociferous, wild; SEE CONCEPT *401*

bold [adj1] brave
adventurous, assuming, audacious, aweless, bantam, courageous, daring, dauntless, enterprising, fearless, forward, gallant, heroic, intrepid, resolute, unafraid, undaunted, valiant, valorous; SEE CONCEPT 401

bold [adj2] brazen, insolent
assuming, audacious, barefaced, brash, brassy, cheeky, coming on strong*, confident, forward, fresh, gritty, gutsy, immodest, impudent, insolent, nervy, pert, presumptuous, rude, sassy, saucy, shameless, smart, smart-alecky*, spunky; SEE CONCEPTS 401,404

bold [adj3] bright, striking
clear, colorful, conspicuous, definite, evident, eye-catching, flashy, forceful, lively, loud, manifest, plain, prominent, pronounced, showy, spirited, strong, vivid; SEE CONCEPTS 589,617,618

bolster [v] help
aid, assist, bear up, boost, brace, buck up, bulwark, buoy, buttress, carry, cushion, help, hold up, maintain, pick up, pillow, prop, reinforce, shore up, stay, strengthen, support, sustain, uphold; SEE CONCEPT 110

bolt [n1] lock; part of lock
bar, brad, catch, coupling, dowel, fastener, lag, latch, lock, nut, padlock, peg, pin, pipe, rivet, rod, screw, skewer, sliding bar, spike, stake, staple, stud; SEE CONCEPTS 470,471,680

bolt [n2] flash; projectile
arrow, dart, fulmination, missile, shaft, thunderbolt, thunderstroke; SEE CONCEPTS 624,687

bolt [n3] large roll of material
coil, curl, cylinder, package, spindle, spiral, twist; SEE CONCEPT 432

bolt [v1] run quickly away
abscond, bail out*, bound, cop out*, cut loose*, cut out*, dart, dash, ditch*, drop out*, dump*, escape, flee, flight, fly, hightail*, hotfoot*, hurtle, jump, kiss goodbye*, leap, leave flat*, leave high and dry*, leave holding the bag*, leave in the lurch*, make a break for it*, make off*, make tracks*, opt out*, run like scared rabbit*, run out on, rush, scamper, scoot, skedaddle*, skip, split*, spring, sprint, start, startle, step on it*, take flight, take off*, walk out on; SEE CONCEPTS 150,195

bolt [v2] fasten securely
bar, deadbolt, latch, lock, secure; SEE CONCEPT 225

bolt [v3] eat very fast
consume, cram, devour, englut, gobble, gorge, gulp, guzzle, ingurgitate, inhale, scarf*, slop, slosh, stuff, swallow whole, wolf*; SEE CONCEPT 169

bomb [n] exploding weapon
atom bomb, bombshell, charge, device, explosive, grenade, hydrogen bomb, mine, missile, Molotov cocktail, nuclear bomb, projectile, rocket, shell, ticker*, torpedo; SEE CONCEPT 500

bomb [v1] detonate weapon
attack, blast, blitz, blow up, bombard, cannonade, destroy, napalm, prang, raid, rain destruction*, rake, shell, strafe, torpedo, wipe out*, zero in*; SEE CONCEPTS 86,252

bomb [v2] fail miserably
blow it*, flop, flummox, go out of business, lose, wash out*, wipe out*; SEE CONCEPT 699

bombard [v] assault, attack
assail, barrage, batter, beset, besiege, blast, blitz, bomb, cannonade, catapult, fire upon, harass,

hound, launch, open fire, pester, pound, shell, strafe, strike; SEE CONCEPTS 7,19,86

bombastic [adj] pompous, grandiloquent
aureate, balderdash, big-talking*, declamatory, euphuistic, flowery, full of hot air*, fustian, grandiose, highfalutin*, high-flown, histrionic, inflated, loudmouthed, magniloquent, orotund, ostentatious, overblown, ranting, rhapsodic, rhetorical, sonorous, stuffed shirt*, swollen, tumid, turgid, verbose, windbag*, windy, wordy; SEE CONCEPT 267

bond [n1] binder or fastener
band, binding, chain, connection, cord, fastening, fetter, gunk, handcuff, hookup, irons, ligature, link, linkage, manacle, network, nexus, rope, shackle, stickum*, tie, tie-in, wire; SEE CONCEPT 497

bond [n2] association, relation
affiliation, affinity, attachment, connection, connective, friendship, hookup, interrelationship, liaison, link, marriage, network, obligation, relationship, restraint, tie, tie-in, union; SEE CONCEPT 388

bond [n3] guarantee; contract
agreement, bargain, certificate, collateral, compact, convention, covenant, debenture, guaranty, obligation, pact, pledge, promise, security, transaction, warrant, warranty, word; SEE CONCEPTS 318,684

bond [v] fasten; stick
bind, connect, fix, fuse, glue, gum, paste, stickum*; SEE CONCEPTS 85,160

bondage [n] slavery
chains, enslavement, helotry, peonage, serfage, serfdom, servility, servitude, subjection, subjugation, thrall, thralldom, villenage, yoke; SEE CONCEPTS 136,652

bone [n] piece of animate skeleton
bony process, cartilage, ossein, osseous matter; SEE CONCEPTS 393,420

bonus [n] unexpected extra
additional compensation, benefit, bounty, commission, dividend, fringe benefit, frosting*, gift, golden parachute*, goody*, gratuity, gravy*, hand-out*, honorarium, ice*, perk*, plus*, premium, prize, reward, special compensation, tip; SEE CONCEPT 337

book [n1] published document
album, atlas, bestseller, bible, booklet, brochure, codex, compendium, copy, dictionary, dissertation, edition, encyclopedia, essay, fiction, folio, handbook, hardcover, leaflet, lexicon, magazine, manual, monograph, nonfiction, novel, octavo, offprint, omnibus, opus, opuscule, pamphlet, paperback, periodical, portfolio, preprint, primer, publication, quarto, reader, reprint, roll, scroll, softcover, speller, text, textbook, thesaurus, tome, tract, treatise, vade mecum, volume, work, writing; SEE CONCEPT 280

book [n2] account; diary
agenda, album, list, notebook, pad, record, register, roster; SEE CONCEPTS 271,331

book [v1] register, arrange for
bespeak, bill, charter, engage, enroll, enter, hire, line up*, make reservation, order, organize, pencil in*, preengage, procure, program, reserve, schedule, set up, sew up*; SEE CONCEPT 36

book [v2] arrest
accuse, charge, prefer charges, take into custody; SEE CONCEPT 317

boom [n1] *loud sound; crash*
bang, barrage, blare, blast, burst, cannonade, clap, crack, drumfire, explosion, reverberation, roar, rumble, slam, smash, thunder, wham; SEE CONCEPTS 521,595

boom [n2] *prosperity*
advance, boost, development, expansion, gain, growth, improvement, increase, inflation, jump, prosperousness, push, rush, spurt, upsurge, up-swing, upturn; SEE CONCEPTS 230,335,700

boom [v1] *crash; make loud sound*
bang, blast, burst, clap, crack, drum, explode, resound, reverberate, roar, roll, rumble, slam, smash, sound, thunder, wham; SEE CONCEPT 65

boom [v2] *prosper*
appreciate, bloom, develop, enhance, expand, flourish, flower, gain, grow, increase, intensify, rise in value, spurt, strengthen, succeed, swell, thrive; SEE CONCEPTS 700,704

boomerang [v] *backfire*
backlash, bounce back, come back, come home to roost*, kick back, react, rebound, recoil, return, reverse, ricochet; SEE CONCEPTS 242,695

boon [n] *advantage*
benefaction, benefit, benevolence, blessing, break, compliment, donation, favor, gift, god-send, good, good fortune, grant, gratuity, help, largess, present, windfall; SEE CONCEPTS 337,661

boor [n] *clod*
barbarian, bear, boob*, brute, buffoon, cad, churl, dork*, goon*, lout, oaf, peasant, philistine, rube*, vulgarian; SEE CONCEPT 423

boorish [adj] *crude, awkward*
bad-mannered, barbaric, bearish, cantankerous, churlish, cloddish, clodhopping*, clownish, clumsy, coarse, countrified, gross*, gruff, ill-bred, ill-mannered, impolite, inurbane, loud, lout-ish, lowbred, oafish, ornery, out-of-line, out-of-order, provincial, rough, rude, rustic, swinish, tasteless, ugly, uncivilized, uncouth, uncultured, uneducated, ungracious, unpoised, unpolished, unrefined, vulgar; SEE CONCEPT 404

boost [n1] *increase*
addition, advance, breakthrough, expansion, hike, improvement, increment, jump, lift, raise, rise, step-up, up, upgrade, wax; SEE CONCEPTS 700,780

boost [n2] *encouragement*
aid, assistance, backup, buildup, goose*, hand*, handout, help, helping hand, improvement, leg*, leg up*, lift, praise, promotion, shot in the arm*, support; SEE CONCEPT 110

boost [n3] *push, usually up*
advance, goose*, heave, hoist, lift, raise, shove, thrust; SEE CONCEPTS 196,208

boost [v1] *further, improve*
advance, advertise, assist, encourage, foster, in-spire, plug, praise, promote, push, support, sus-tain; SEE CONCEPT 244

boost [v2] *push, usually up*
advance, elevate, heave, heighten, hoist, lift, raise, shove, thrust, upraise, uprear; SEE CON-CEPTS 196,208

boost [v3] *increase*
add to, aggrandize, amplify, augment, beef up*, develop, enlarge, expand, extend, heighten, hike, jack up*, jump, magnify, multiply, put up, raise, up; SEE CONCEPTS 236,245

boot [n] *heavy, often tall, shoe*
brogan, footwear, galoshes, mukluk, oxford,

snow shoes, waders, waters*; SEE CONCEPT 450

boot [v] *kick; oust*
ax, bounce, can*, chase, chuck*, cut, discharge, dismiss, drive, dropkick*, eighty-six*, eject, evict, expel, extrude, fire, heave, kick out, knock, punt*, sack*, shove, terminate, throw out; SEE CONCEPTS 180,189

booth [n] *small enclosure or building*
berth, box, carrel, compartment, coop, corner, cote, counter, cubbyhole, cubicle, dispensary, hut, hutch, nook, pen, pew, repository, shed, stall, stand; SEE CONCEPTS 439,440,443

border [n1] *outermost edge, margin*
bound, boundary, bounds, brim, brink, circum-ference, confine, end, extremity, fringe, hem, limit, line, lip, outskirt, perimeter, periphery, rim, selvage, skirt, trim, trimming, verge; SEE CON-CEPTS 484,827

border [n2] *boundary; frontier*
beginning, borderline, door, edge, entrance, line, march, marchland, outpost, pale, perimeter, side-line, threshold; SEE CONCEPTS 484,513

border [v] *bound on; be on the edge*
abut, adjoin, be adjacent to, bind, circumscribe, communicate, contour, decorate, define, deline-ate, edge, encircle, enclose, flank, frame, fringe, hem, join, line, march, margin, mark off, neigh-bor, outline, rim, set off, side, skirt, surround, touch, trim, verge; SEE CONCEPT 747

borderline [adj] *inexact*
ambiguous, ambivalent, doubtful, dubitable, equivocal, indecisive, indefinite, indeterminate, marginal, open, problematic, uncertain, unclassi-fiable, unclear, undecided, unsettled; SEE CON-CEPT 534

border on [v] *come close to; approximate*
abut, adjoin, approach, be like, be similar to, come near, compare, connect, contact, echo, im-pinge, join, lie near, lie next to, march, match, near, neighbor, parallel, resemble, touch, verge on; SEE CONCEPTS 667,749

bore [n] *nuisance*
bother, bromide, bummer*, creep*, deadhead*, downer*, drag*, drip*, dull person, flat tire*, headache, nag, nudge, pain, pain in the neck*, pest, pill*, soporific, stuffed shirt*, tedious per-son, tiresome person, wet blanket*, wimp*, yawn*; SEE CONCEPT 423

bore [v1] *drill hole*
burrow, gouge out, mine, penetrate, perforate, pierce, pit, prick, punch, puncture, ream, riddle, sink, tunnel; SEE CONCEPT 178

bore [v2] *cause weariness, disinterest*
afflict, annoy, bend one's ear*, be tedious, bother, burn out, cloy, discomfort, drag, exhaust, fatigue, irk, irritate, jade, pall, pester, put to sleep*, send to sleep*, talk one's ear off*, tire, trouble, turn one off*, vex, wear, wear out, weary, worry; SEE CONCEPTS 7,19

boredom [n] *disinterest; weariness*
apathy, detachment, disgust, distaste, doldrums, dullness, ennui, fatigue, flatness, incuriosity, in-difference, irksomeness, jadedness, lack of inter-est, lassitude, lethargy, listlessness, monotony, pococurantism, sameness, taedium vitae, tedious-ness, tedium, tiresomeness, unconcern, world-weariness, yawn; SEE CONCEPT 410

boring [adj] *uninteresting*
arid, bomb*, bromidic, bummer*, characterless, cloying, colorless, commonplace, dead*, drab,

drag*, drudging, dull, flat*, ho hum*, humdrum, insipid, interminable, irksome, lifeless, monotonous, moth-eaten*, mundane, nothing, nowhere, platitudinous, plebeian, prosaic, repetitious, routine, spiritless, stale, stereotyped, stodgy, stuffy, stupid, tame, tedious, threadbare, tiresome, tiring, trite, unexciting, uninteresting, unvaried, vapid, wearisome, well-worn, zero*; SEE CONCEPT 529

born [adj] *innate*
built-in, congenital, constitutional, deep-seated, essential, inborn, inbred, ingenerate, inherent, intrinsic, natural; SEE CONCEPTS 549,550

borrow [v1] *take for temporary use*
accept loan of, acquire, beg, bite, bum, cadge*, chisel*, give a note for*, hire, hit up*, lift, mooch*, negotiate, obtain, pawn, pledge, raise money, rent, run into debt, scrounge, see one's uncle*, soak, sponge, take on loan, tap, touch, use temporarily; SEE CONCEPT 89

borrow [v2] *adopt from another source; appropriate*
acquire, adopt, assume, copy, filch, imitate, make one's own, obtain, pilfer, pirate, plagiarize, simulate, steal, take, use, usurp; SEE CONCEPT 225

bosom [n1] *breast*
bust, chest, rib cage, teats; SEE CONCEPT 418

bosom [n2] *heart; core*
affections, center, circle, conscience, emotions, feelings, inside, interior, sentiments, soul, spirit, sympathies; SEE CONCEPTS 410,826

boss [n] *manager over other employees*
administrator, big cheese*, big gun*, big person*, chief, chieftain, controller, director, dominator, employer, exec*, executive, foreperson, head, head honcho*, helmer, honcho*, leader, overseer, owner, person in charge, superintendent, supervisor, taskperson, top dog*, wheel*; SEE CONCEPT 347

boss [adj] *great*
awesome*, bang-up*, capital, champion, excellent, fine, first-rate, fly*, top, whiz-bang*, wonderful; SEE CONCEPT 572

boss [v] *control; command*
administer, administrate, chaperon, direct, employ, manage, overlook, oversee, quarterback*, run, superintend, supervise, survey, take charge; SEE CONCEPT 117

botany [n] *study of plants*
anatomy, cytology, dendrology, ecology, floristics, genetics, horticulture, morphology, natural history, paleobotany, pathology, physiology, phytogeography, phytology, pomology, study of flora, study of vegetation, taxonomy; SEE CONCEPT 349

botch [v] *blunder*
blow*, bobble*, boggle*, bollix*, boot, bumble, bungle, butcher*, distort, err, fall down*, flounder, flub*, fumble, goof up*, gum up*, louse up*, mar, mend, mess, mess up*, misapply, miscalculate, miscompute, misconjecture, misconstrue, mishandle, misjudge, mismanage, muck up*, muddle, muff, mutilate, patch, pull a boner*, ruin, screw up*, spoil, stumble, wreck; SEE CONCEPT 101

both [det] *two together*
one and the other, the couple, the pair, the two, twain; SEE CONCEPT 714

bother [n] *trouble, inconvenience*
ado, aggravation, annoyance, anxiety, bellyache*,

botheration, bustle, care, concern, difficulty, distress, drag*, exasperation, flurry, fuss, headache*, irritant, irritation, molestation, nudge, nuisance, pain, pain in the neck*, perplexity, pest, plague, pother*, pressure, problem, strain, to-do*, trial, trouble, vexation, worriment, worry; SEE CONCEPT 532

bother [v1] *harass, annoy; give trouble*
afflict, aggravate, agitate, alarm, badger, bedevil, bore, browbeat, carp at, concern, cross, discommode, disconcert, disgust, dismay, displease, disquiet, distress, disturb, eat, embarrass, exacerbate, exasperate, goad, grate on, grieve, harry, hinder, hurt, impede, inconvenience, insult, intrude upon, irk, irritate, molest, nag, needle, nudge, pain, perplex, perturb, pester, pick on, plague, provoke, pursue, put out, ride, scare, spite, tantalize, taunt, tease, torment, trouble, upset, vex, worry; SEE CONCEPTS 7,19

bother [v2] *take the trouble*
be concerned about, concern oneself, exert oneself, fuss over, go out of one's way*, make a fuss about*, make an effort, put oneself out*, take pains, try, worry about; SEE CONCEPT 87

bothersome [adj] *troubling*
aggravating, annoying, distressing, disturbing, exasperating, incommodious, inconvenient, irritating, rebarbative, remote, tiresome, troublesome, vexatious, vexing; SEE CONCEPT 529

bottle [n] *container, usually for liquids*
canteen, carafe, cruet, dead soldier*, decanter, ewer, flagon, flask, glass, jar, jug, phial, soldier, urn, vacuum bottle, vial; SEE CONCEPT 494

bottle up [v] *keep feeling inside oneself*
box up, check, collar, contain, coop up, corner, cramp, curb, keep back, restrain, restrict, shut in, suppress, trap; SEE CONCEPT 35

bottom [n1] *foundation*
base, basement, basis, bed, bedrock, belly, deepest part, depths, floor, foot, footing, ground, groundwork, lowest part, nadir, nether portion, pedestal, pediment, rest, seat, sole, substratum, substructure, support, terra firma, underbelly, underneath, underside; SEE CONCEPT 442

bottom [n2] *base, core*
basis, bottom line, cause, essence, essentiality, ground, heart, mainspring, marrow, origin, pith, principle, quintessence, root, soul, source, stuff, substance, virtuality; SEE CONCEPTS 648,826

bottom [n3] *rear end*
backside, behind, breech, bum*, butt*, buttocks, derriere, fanny*, fundament, posterior, rear, rump, seat, tail, tush*; SEE CONCEPT 418

bottom [adj] *lowest; fundamental*
basal, base, basement, basic, foundational, ground, last, lowermost, lowest, meat-and-potatoes*, nethermost, primary, radical, rock-bottom, underlying, undermost; SEE CONCEPTS 585,586,735,799

bottom line [n] *conclusion*
determination, final decision, income, last word, loss, main point, net, profit; SEE CONCEPT 230

bough [n] *branch*
arm, fork, limb, offshoot, shoot, sprig, sucker; SEE CONCEPT 428

boulevard [n] *street, often lined with trees*
artery, avenue, drag, highway, passage, path, road, thoroughfare, track, way; SEE CONCEPT 501

bounce [n] *spring*
animation, bound, dynamism, elasticity, energy,

bo
bo

give, go, life, liveliness, pep, rebound, recoil, resilience, springiness, vigor, vitality, vivacity, zip;
SEE CONCEPTS *150,411*

bounce [*v1*] *spring up; rebound*
backlash, bob, boomerang, bound, buck, bump,
carom, fly back, glance off, hop, hurdle, jerk up
and down*, jounce, jump, kick back, leap, rebound, recoil, resile, ricochet, saltate, snap back,
spring back, thump, vault; SEE CONCEPTS
150,194

bounce [*v2*] *evict*
ax*, boot out*, can*, discharge, dismiss, eighty-
six*, eject, fire, give one notice, give the heave
ho*, heave*, kick out*, oust, sack*, terminate,
throw; SEE CONCEPTS *211,351,384*

bound/bounds [*n*] *farthest limit*
boundary, compass, confine, edge, end, environs,
extremity, fringe, limit, limitation, line, march,
margin, pale, periphery, precinct, purlieus, rim,
term, termination, verge; SEE CONCEPTS *484,788*

bound [*adj*] *obligated; destined*
apprenticed, articled, bent, bounden, certain, coerced, compelled, constrained, contracted,
doomed, driven, duty-bound, enslaved, fated,
firm, forced, having no alternative, impelled, indentured, intent, made, necessitated, obligated,
obliged, pledged, pressed, required, restrained,
sure, under compulsion, under necessity, urged;
SEE CONCEPT *554*

bound [*v1*] *jump, bounce*
bob, caper, frisk, gambol, hop, hurdle, leap,
pounce, prance, recoil, ricochet, saltate, skip,
spring, vault; SEE CONCEPT *194*

bound [*v2*] *restrict*
circumscribe, confine, define, delimit, delimitate,
demarcate, determine, encircle, enclose, hem in,
limit, mark, mark out, measure, restrain, restrict,
surround, terminate; SEE CONCEPT *130*

boundary [*n*] *outer limit*
abuttals, ambit, barrier, beginning, border, borderland, borderline, bounds, brink, circumference, circumscription, compass, confines, edge,
end, environs, extent, extremity, frame, fringe,
frontier, hem, horizon, limits, line, line of demarcation, march, margin, mark, mere, mete, outline, outpost, pale, perimeter, periphery, precinct,
purlieus, radius, rim, side, skirt, terminal, termination, terminus, verge; SEE CONCEPTS *5,484,745*

bounded [*adj*] *limited, confined*
belted, bordered, boundaried, circumscribed,
compassed, contiguous, defined, definite, delimited, determinate, edged, encircled, enclosed, encompassed, enveloped, fenced, finite, flanked,
fringed, girdled, hedged, hog-tied*, limitary, restricted, rimmed, ringed, surrounded, walled; SEE
CONCEPTS *554,772*

boundless [*adj*] *endless, without limit*
great, illimitable, immeasurable, immense, incalculable, indefinite, inexhaustible, infinite, limitless, measureless, no catch*, no end of, no end to,
no holds barred*, no strings*, no strings attached*, tremendous, unbounded, unconfined, unending, unlimited, untold, vast, wide open; SEE
CONCEPTS *554,772*

bountiful [*adj*] *abundant*
ample, aplenty, bounteous, copious, crawling
with*, dime a dozen*, exuberant, free, galore*,
generous, handsome, lavish, liberal, luxuriant,
magnanimous, munificent, no end of*, plenteous,

plentiful, plenty, prolific, stink with*, unsparing;
SEE CONCEPT *771*

bounty [*n*] *bonus; compensation*
donation, gift, grant, gratuity, largess, pay, premium, present, prize, recompense, reward; SEE
CONCEPTS *337,344*

bouquet [*n1*] *flower arrangement*
boutonniere, buttonhole, corsage, festoon, garland, lei, nosegay, posy, pot, spray, vase, wreath;
SEE CONCEPTS *425,429*

bouquet [*n2*] *aroma*
aura, balm, fragrance, incense, odor, perfume,
redolence, savor, scent, smell, spice; SEE CON-
CEPT *599*

bourgeois [*adj*] *commonplace*
common, conservative, conventional, hidebound,
illiberal, materialistic, middle-class, old-line, Philistine, traditional, Victorian; SEE CONCEPTS
530,589

bout [*n1*] *period of time in which something occurs*
course, fit*, go*, round, run, session, shift, spell,
stint, stretch, tear, term, tour, trick*, turn; SEE
CONCEPT *807*

bout [*n2*] *competitive fight*
bat, battle, boxing match, competition, contest,
encounter, engagement, go, match, round, set-to,
struggle; SEE CONCEPTS *92,106*

bow [*n1*] *bend from waist*
angle, arc, arch, bend, bending, bob, curtsy, curvation, curvature, curve, flection, flexure, genuflection, inclination, kowtow*, nod, obeisance,
round, salaam, turn, turning; SEE CONCEPTS
154,201

bow [*n2*] *front of boat*
beak, bowsprit, fore, forepart, head, nose, prow,
stem; SEE CONCEPT *502*

bow [*v1*] *bend over*
arch, bob, cower, crook, curtsy, curve, debase,
dip, do obeisance, droop, duck, genuflect, hunch,
incline, nod, round, stoop; SEE CONCEPT *213*

bow [*v2*] *submit, concede*
accept, acquiesce, bend, be servile, capitulate,
cave, comply, defer, give in, knuckle*, knuckle
under*, kowtow*, relent, succumb, surrender,
yield; SEE CONCEPT *23*

bowels [*n*] *insides*
belly, core, deep, depths, entrails, guts, hold, innards, interior, intestines, penetralia, recesses,
viscera, vitals; SEE CONCEPTS *393,830*

bowl [*n*] *hollow, concave container*
basin, boat, casserole, crock, deep dish, dish, porringer, pot, saucer, tureen, urn, vessel; SEE CON-
CEPTS *493,494*

bowl [*v*] *roll a ball down a lane*
fling, hurl, pitch, play duckpins, play tenpins, revolve, rotate, spin, throw, trundle, whirl; SEE
CONCEPT *363*

box [*n*] *container, often square or rectangular*
bin, carton, case, casket, chest, coffer, crate,
pack, package, portmanteau, receptacle, trunk;
SEE CONCEPT *494*

box [*v1*] *place in square or rectangular container*
case, confine, crate, encase, pack, package, wrap;
SEE CONCEPT *209*

box [*v2*] *punch competitively*
buffet, clout, cuff, duke*, exchange blows, hit,
mix, scrap, slap, slug, sock, spar, strike, wallop,
whack*; SEE CONCEPTS *106,189*

boxing [*n*] *punching competition*
battle, glove game*, mill*, prelim*, prizefight-

ing, pugilism, slugfest*, sparring, the ring*; SEE CONCEPTS 92,363

boy [n] *young man*
buck, cadet, chap, child, dude*, fellow, gamin, guy, half-pint*, junior, lad, little gentleman, little guy*, little shaver*, master, punk*, puppy*, runt*, schoolboy, shaver*, small fry*, sonny*, sprout*, squirt*, stripling, tadpole*, whippersnapper*, youngster, youth; SEE CONCEPTS 419,424

boycott [v] *ban; refrain from using*
avoid, bar, blackball*, blacklist, brush off, cut off, embargo, exclude, hold aloof from, ice out*, ostracize, outlaw, pass by*, pass up*, prohibit, proscribe, refuse, reject, shut out*, snub, spurn, strike, withhold patronage; SEE CONCEPTS 25,130

boyfriend [n] *male acquaintance or romantic companion*
admirer, beau, companion, confidant, date, escort, fiancé, flame*, follower, friend, intimate, partner, soul mate, steady, suitor, swain, sweetheart, young man; SEE CONCEPTS 419,423

brace [n] *support*
arm, band, bar, bearing, block, bolster, boom, bracer, bracket, buttress, cantilever, clamp, girder, grip, guy, lever, mainstay, peg, prop, rafter, reinforcement, rib, shore, skid, splice, splint, staff, stanchion, stave, stay, stirrup, strengthener, strut, sustainer, truss, underpinning, vice; SEE CONCEPTS 470,475,499

brace [v] *support*
bandage, bind, bolster, buttress, fasten, fortify, gird, hold up, prepare, prop, ready, reinforce, shove, steady, steel, strap, strengthen, support, tie, tighten, uphold; SEE CONCEPT 191

bracelet [n] *wrist jewelry*
arm band, armlet, bangle, circlet, manacle, ornament, trinket, wristlet; SEE CONCEPT 446

bracing [adj] *brisk; exhilarating*
animating, chilly, cool, crisp, energizing, exhilarative, fortifying, fresh, invigorating, lively, quickening, refreshing, restorative, reviving, rousing, stimulating, stimulative, tonic, vigorous; SEE CONCEPTS 537,605

brag [v] *talk boastingly*
blow one's own horn*, bluster*, boast, crow*, exult, gasconade, gloat, grandstand*, hotdog*, jive*, mouth*, pat oneself on the back*, prate, puff*, rodomontade, showboat*, shuck*, swagger, vaunt; SEE CONCEPTS 49,51

braggart [n] *person who talks boastingly*
bag of wind*, bigmouth, big talker*, big-timer*, blowhard*, blusterer, boaster, brag, braggadocio, bragger, egotist, exhibitionist, gasbag*, gascon*, grandstander*, hotshot*, know-it-all, peacock*, ranter, raver, show-off, strutter, swaggerer, swashbuckler*, swelled head*, trumpeter*, windbag*; SEE CONCEPTS 412,423

braid [n] *interwoven hair style*
pigtail, plait, ponytail, queue; SEE CONCEPTS 418,716

braid [v] *interweave*
complect, cue, entwine, interknit, interlace, intertwine, lace, mesh, pigtail, plait, ravel, twine, twist, weave; SEE CONCEPTS 184,202

brain [n1] *very smart person*
academician, doctor, egghead*, Einstein*, genius, highbrow, intellect, intellectual, mastermind, prodigy, pundit, sage, scholar; SEE CONCEPT 350

brain [n2] *mind, intelligence*
cerebellum, cerebrum, encephalon, gray matter*, head, intellect, medulla oblongata, mentality, upper story*, wit; SEE CONCEPTS 393,409,420

brainwash [v] *force to believe or do things*
alter, catechize, condition, convert, convince, educate, indoctrinate, influence, instill, persuade, proselytize, teach; SEE CONCEPT 14

brake [n] *stopping device; check*
anchor, binders, cinchers, constraint, control, curb, damper, deterrent, discouragement, hamper, hindrance, hurdle, obstacle, rein, restraint, retarding device; SEE CONCEPTS 130,463

brake [v] *check; stop*
bar, block, dam, decelerate, halt, hinder, impede, moderate, obstruct, reduce speed, slacken, slow, slow down, stop; SEE CONCEPT 121

bramble [n] *thorny bush*
brier, burr, catch weed, cleaver, furze, goose grass, gorse, hedge, nettle, prick, prickly shrub, shrub, spray, thistle, thistle sage, thorn; SEE CONCEPT 429

branch [n1] *department*
annex, arm, bureau, category, chapter, classification, connection, dependency, derivative, division, extension, local, member, office, outpost, part, portion, section, subdivision, subsection, subsidiary, tributary, wing; SEE CONCEPTS 325,378

branch [n2] *arm, limb*
bough, branchlet, bug, detour, divergence, extension, fork, growth, offshoot, prong, scion, shoot, spray, sprig, wing; SEE CONCEPTS 392,428, 471,835

branch off/branch out [v] *extend beyond main part*
add to, develop, diverge, diversify, divide, enlarge, expand, extend, fork, grow, increase, multiply, part, proliferate, ramify, separate, spread out; SEE CONCEPT 756

brand [n1] *type, kind*
cast, character, class, description, grade, make, quality, sort, species, variety; SEE CONCEPT 378

brand [n2] *distinctive label, mark*
brand name, emblem, hallmark, heraldry, imprint, logo, logotype, marker, sign, stamp, symbol, trademark, welt; SEE CONCEPT 284

brand [n3] *stigma*
bar sinister, black eye, blot, blur, disgrace, infamy, mark, mark of Cain, odium, onus, reproach, slur, smirch, spot, stain, stigma, taint; SEE CONCEPT 388

brandish [v] *flaunt, swing around*
come on strong*, display, disport, exhibit, expose, flash, gesture, parade, raise, shake, show, show off, swing, threaten, throw weight around*, trot out*, warn, wield; SEE CONCEPT 261

brash [adj] *impulsive, brazen*
audacious, bold, brazenfaced, cheeky*, cocksure, cocky*, effervescent, flip, foolhardy, forward, hasty, headlong, heedless, hotheaded, ill-advised, impertinent, impetuous, impolitic, impudent, incautious, inconsiderate, indiscreet, insolent, madcap, maladroit, nervy, precipitate, presuming, presumptuous, pushing, rash, reckless, rude, self-asserting, self-assertive, tactless, thoughtless, undiplomatic, untactful, uppity, vivacious; SEE CONCEPTS 401,404

bo
br

brass [n] *impulsiveness; nerve*
assumption, audacity, brashness, cheek*, chutzpah*, confidence, effrontery, gall, impertinence, impudence, insolence, presumption, rudeness; SEE CONCEPT 633

brassy [adj] *vulgar, loud to the senses*
arrant, barefaced, blaring, blatant, bold, brash, brazen, flashy, flirtatious, forward, garish, gaudy, grating, hard, harsh, impudent, insolent, jarring, jazzy, loudmouthed, noisy, obtrusive, overbold, pert, piercing, rude, saucy, shameless, showy, shrill, strident, unabashed, unblushing; SEE CONCEPTS 401,589,592,594

brat [n] *spoiled child*
devil*, enfant terrible*, holy terror*, impudent child, kid, punk*, rascal, unruly child, urchin, whippersnapper*, wild one*, youngster; SEE CONCEPT 424

bravado [n] *boastfulness*
blowing, bluff, bluster, boasting, bombast, braggadocio, bragging, bullying, crowing*, fancy talk*, fuming*, gasconade, grandiosity, guts*, hot air*, pomposity, pretension, raging, railing, rant, self-glorification, storming, swaggering, swelling, talk, tall talk*; SEE CONCEPTS 49,51

brave [adj] *bold*
adventurous, audacious, chin-up*, chivalrous, confident, courageous, daring, dashing, dauntless, defiant, doughty, fearless, firm, foolhardy, forward, gallant, game, gritty, gutsy, hardy, heroic, herolike, imprudent, indomitable, intrepid, lionhearted, militant, nervy, plucky, reckless, resolute, spirited, spunky, stalwart, stout, stouthearted, strong, unabashed, unafraid, unblenching, undauntable, undaunted, undismayed, unfearful, valiant, valorous, venturesome; SEE CONCEPT 401

brave [v] *endure bad situation*
bear, beard, challenge, confront, court, dare, defy, face, face off, fly in the face of*, go through, outdare, risk, stand up to, suffer, support, take on, venture, withstand; SEE CONCEPT 23

bravery [n] *boldness*
courage, daring, dauntlessness, fearlessness, fortitude, gallantry, grit, guts, hardiness, heroism, indomitability, intrepidity, mettle, pluck, pluckiness, spirit, spunk, valor; SEE CONCEPTS 411,633

brawl [n] *nasty fight*
affray, altercation, argument, battle, battle royal*, bickering, broil, clash, disorder, dispute, donnybrook, duke out*, feud, fight, fracas, fray, free-for-all*, fuss, hassle, melee, quarrel, rhubarb*, riot, row, ruckus*, rumble*, rumpus, scrap, scuffle, squabble, tumult, uproar, wrangle; SEE CONCEPTS 46,106

brawl [v] *fight nastily*
altercate, argue, battle, bicker, buck*, caterwaul, dispute, kick up a row*, quarrel, raise Cain*, roughhouse*, row, rumble*, scrap, scuffle, spat, squabble, tussle, wrangle, wrestle; SEE CONCEPTS 46,106

brawn [n] *muscular strength and breadth*
beef, beefiness, clout, energy, flesh, kick, meat, might, moxie*, muscle, muscularity, power, punch, robustness, sinews, sock, steam, thew, vigor; SEE CONCEPTS 723,732

brawny [adj] *muscular, strong*
able-bodied, athletic, beefy, bulky, burly, fleshy, hardy, hefty, husky, powerful, robust, sinewy,

stalwart, strapping, sturdy, thewy, tough, vigorous, vital; SEE CONCEPTS 485,489

brazen [adj] *brash, unashamed*
audacious, barefaced, blatant, bold, brassy, cheeky, cocky, contumelious, defiant, flashy, flip, forward, gritty, gutsy, hotshot*, immodest, impertinent, impudent, indecent, insolent, loud, meretricious, nervy, overbold, pert, saucy, shameless, smart-alecky*, smart-ass*, spunky, tawdry, unabashed, unblushing; SEE CONCEPTS 267,401

breach [n1] *gap*
aperture, break, chasm, chip, cleft, crack, discontinuity, fissure, hole, opening, rent, rift, rupture, slit, split; SEE CONCEPT 513

breach [n2] *violation of a law*
contravention, delinquency, dereliction, disobedience, disregard, infraction, infringement, neglect, noncompliance, nonobservance, offense, transgression, trespass, violation; SEE CONCEPT 192

breach [n3] *change from friendly to unfriendly relationship*
alienation, break, difference, disaffection, disagreement, discord, disharmony, dissension, disunity, division, estrangement, falling-out, fissure, fracture, parting of the ways*, quarrel, rent, rift, rupture, schism, secession, separation, severance, split, strife, variance, withdrawal; SEE CONCEPT 388

bread [n1] *daily food*
aliment, bed and board, comestibles, diet, fare, feed, grub*, necessities, nourishment, nurture, nutriment, provender, provisions, shingle*, staff of life*, subsistence, sustenance, viands, victuals; SEE CONCEPT 457

bread [n2] *money*
cabbage*, cash, coin, dollars, dough*, finance, funds, greenbacks*, mazuma*, scratch*; SEE CONCEPT 340

breadth [n1] *width*
broadness, diameter, distance across, latitude, span, spread, wideness; SEE CONCEPT 760

breadth [n2] *extent*
amplitude, area, compass, comprehensiveness, dimension, expanse, extensiveness, fullness, gamut, greatness, inclusiveness, largeness, magnitude, measure, orbit, range, reach, scale, scope, size, space, spread, stretch, sweep, vastness; SEE CONCEPTS 651,756,788

break [n] *fissure, opening*
breach, cleft, crack, discontinuity, disjunction, division, fracture, gap, gash, hole, rent, rift, rupture, schism, split, tear; SEE CONCEPTS 230, 757

break [n2] *interruption of activity*
blow, breather, breathing space, caesura, coffee break, cutoff, downtime*, halt, hiatus, interlude, intermission, interval, lacuna, layoff*, letup*, lull, pause, recess, respite, rest, suspension, ten*, time off, time out; SEE CONCEPT 807

break [n3] *change from friendly to unfriendly relationship*
alienation, altercation, breach, clash, difference of opinion, disaffection, dispute, divergence, estrangement, fight, misunderstanding, rift, rupture, schism, separation, split, trouble; SEE CONCEPT 388

break [n4] *lucky happening*
accident, advantage, chance, favorable circumstances, fortune, good luck, luck, occasion, open-

ing, opportunity, shot, show, stroke of luck, time; SEE CONCEPT *679*

break [*v1*] *destroy; make whole into pieces*
annihilate, batter, burst, bust, bust up, crack, crash, crush, damage, demolish, disintegrate, divide, eradicate, finish off, fracture, fragment, make hash of*, make mincemeat of*, part, pull to pieces, rend, separate, sever, shatter, shiver, smash, snap, splinter, split, tear, torpedo, total, trash*; SEE CONCEPT *252*

break [*v2*] *violate law*
breach, contravene, disobey, disregard, infract, infringe, offend, renege on, transgress, violate; SEE CONCEPT *192*

break [*v3*] *weaken, cause instability*
bankrupt, bust, confound, confute, controvert, cow, cripple, declass, degrade, demerit, demoralize, demote, disconfirm, dispirit, disprove, downgrade, enervate, enfeeble, humiliate, impair, impoverish, incapacitate, pauperize, rebut, reduce, refute, ruin, subdue, tame, undermine; SEE CONCEPT *240*

break [*v4*] *stop an action*
abandon, cut, discontinue, give up, interrupt, pause, rest, suspend; SEE CONCEPT *121*

break [*v5*] *tell news*
announce, come out, communicate, convey, disclose, divulge, impart, inform, let out, make public, pass on, proclaim, reveal, tell, transmit; SEE CONCEPT *60*

break [*v6*] *better a performance*
beat, cap, exceed, excel, go beyond, outdo, outstrip, surpass, top; SEE CONCEPT *141*

break [*v7*] *emerge, happen*
appear, befall, betide, burst out, chance, come forth, come off, come to pass, develop, erupt, go, occur, transpire; SEE CONCEPT *4*

break [*v8*] *run away*
abscond, bust out*, clear out*, cut and run*, dash, decamp, escape, flee, fly, get away, get out; SEE CONCEPTS *102,195*

break [*v9*] *cushion something's effect*
diminish, lessen, lighten, moderate, reduce, soften, weaken; SEE CONCEPT *110*

breakable [*adj*] *easily hurt or destroyed*
brittle, crisp, crispy, crumbly, delicate, flimsy, fracturable, fragile, frail, frangible, friable, shatterable, shattery, splintery, vitreous, weak; SEE CONCEPTS *489,606*

breakdown [*n1*] *nervous collapse*
basket case*, crackup*, disintegration, disruption, failure, mishap, nervous prostration, neurasthenia, neurosis, psychasthenia; SEE CONCEPT *410*

breakdown [*n2*] *account of finances or other business*
analysis, categorization, classification, detailed list, diagnosis, dissection, itemization, resolution; SEE CONCEPT *283*

break in [*v1*] *intrude*
barge in, breach, break and enter, burglarize, burgle, burst in*, butt in*, interfere, interject, interrupt, intervene, invade, meddle, raid, rob, steal, trespass; SEE CONCEPTS *139,192*

break in [*v2*] *train in new skill*
accustom, condition, educate, gentle, get used to, habituate, initiate, instruct, prepare, tame; SEE CONCEPT *285*

break off [*v1*] *snap off something*
detach, disassemble, divide, part, pull off, separate, sever, splinter, take apart; SEE CONCEPT *211*

break off [*v2*] *end activity*
cease, desist, discontinue, end, finish, halt, pause, stop, suspend, terminate; SEE CONCEPT *234*

break out [*v1*] *happen, emerge*
appear, arise, begin, burst forth, commence, erupt, explode, occur, set in, spring up, start; SEE CONCEPT *701*

break out [*v2*] *escape*
abscond, bolt, break loose, burst out, bust out*, depart, flee, get free, leave; SEE CONCEPTS *102,195*

breakthrough [*n*] *advance, progress*
boost, development, discovery, find, finding, gain, hike, improvement, increase, invention, leap, progress, quantum leap*, rise, step forward; SEE CONCEPT *704*

breakup [*n*] *end of relationship*
breakdown, breaking, crackup*, disintegration, dispersal, dissolution, divorce, ending, parting, rift, separation, split, splitsville*, splitting, termination, wind-up; SEE CONCEPT *385*

break up [*v*] *end relationship, activity*
adjourn, disassemble, disband, dismantle, disperse, disrupt, dissolve, divide, divorce, end, halt, part, put an end to, scatter, separate, sever, split, stop, sunder, suspend, take apart, terminate; SEE CONCEPT *234*

breast [*n1*] *front of upper body*
bosom, bust, chest, front, mammary glands, mammilla, nipple, teat, udder; SEE CONCEPT *418*

breast [*n2*] *feelings, conscience*
being, bosom, character, core, emotions, essential nature, heart, mind, psyche, seat of affections, sentiments, soul, spirit, thoughts; SEE CONCEPTS *410,529*

breath [*n1*] *respiration*
animation, breathing, eupnea, exhalation, expiration, gasp, gulp, inhalation, inspiration, insufflation, pant, wheeze; SEE CONCEPT *163*

breath [*n2*] *wind or something in the air*
aroma, faint breeze, flatus, flutter, gust, odor, puff, sigh, smell, vapor, waft, whiff, zephyr; SEE CONCEPTS *437,599*

breath [*n3*] *respite, break*
blow*, breather, breathing space*, instant, moment, pause, rest, second, ten*; SEE CONCEPT *807*

breath [*n4*] *hint, suggestion*
dash, murmur, shade, soupçon, streak, suspicion, touch, trace, undertone, whiff, whisper; SEE CONCEPTS *278,831*

breathe [*v1*] *take air in and let out*
draw in, exhale, expire, fan, gasp, gulp, inhale, insufflate, open the floodgates*, pant, puff, respire, scent, sigh, sniff, snore, snort, use lungs, wheeze; SEE CONCEPTS *163,601*

breathe [*v2*] *inspire action*
imbue, impart, infuse, inject, instill, transfuse; SEE CONCEPT *242*

breathe [*v3*] *tell information*
articulate, confide, express, murmur, say, sigh, utter, voice, whisper; SEE CONCEPT *60*

breathless [*adj1*] *unable to respire normally*
asthmatic, blown, choking, emphysematous, exhausted, gasping, gulping, out of breath, panting, short of breath, short-winded, spent, stertorous, wheezing, winded; SEE CONCEPT *406*

breathless [*adj2*] *astounded*
agog, anxious, avid, eager, excited, flabbergasted, open-mouthed, thunderstruck, with bated breath; SEE CONCEPT *403*

breathtaking [adj] *beautiful, awesome*
amazing, astonishing, awe-inspiring, exciting, hair-raising, heart-stirring, heart-stopping, impressive, magnificent, moving, overwhelming, spine-tingling, stunning, thrilling; SEE CONCEPT 529

breed [n] *kind, class*
brand, character, extraction, family, feather, genus, ilk, likes, line, lineage, lot, nature, number, pedigree, progeny, race, sort, species, stamp, stock, strain, stripe, type, variety; SEE CONCEPT 378

breed [v1] *generate, bring into being*
bear, beget, bring about, bring forth, cause, create, deliver, engender, give birth to, give rise to, hatch, impregnate, induce, make, multiply, originate, procreate, produce, progenerate, propagate, reproduce; SEE CONCEPTS 173,251,302,373

breed [v2] *raise, nurture*
bring up, cultivate, develop, discipline, educate, foster, instruct, nourish, rear; SEE CONCEPTS 285,295

breeding [n] *cultivation of person*
ancestry, civility, conduct, courtesy, culture, development, gentility, grace, lineage, manners, nurture, polish, raising, rearing, refinement, schooling, training, upbringing, urbanity; SEE CONCEPT 388

breeze [n] *light wind*
air, airflow, breath, current, draft, flurry, gust, puff, waft, whiff, zephyr; SEE CONCEPTS 437,524

breeze [v] *work quickly through task*
cruise, flit, glide, hurry, move, pass, sail, sally, skim, slide, slip, sweep, trip, waltz, zip; SEE CONCEPT 704

breezy [adj1] *windy*
airy, blowing, blowy, blusterous, blustery, drafty, fresh, gusty, squally, stormy; SEE CONCEPT 525

breezy [adj2] *easy, lighthearted*
airy, animated, blithe, buoyant, carefree, casual, cheerful, debonair, easy-going, effervescent, free and easy*, gay, informal, jaunty, light, lively, low-pressure, peppy, racy, relaxed, sparkling, spicy, spirited, sprightly, sunny, unconstrained, vivacious; SEE CONCEPT 544

brevity [n] *shortness, briefness*
conciseness, concision, condensation, crispness, curtness, economy, ephemerality, impermanence, pithiness, pointedness, succinctness, terseness, transience, transitoriness; SEE CONCEPTS 730,804

brew [n] *concoction*
beverage, blend, broth, compound, distillation, drink, fermentation, hash, hodgepodge*, infusion, instillation, liquor, melange, miscellany, mishmash*, mixture, potpourri, preparation; SEE CONCEPTS 260,454,457

brew [v1] *prepare by boiling*
boil, concoct, cook, ferment, infuse, mull, seethe, soak, steep, stew; SEE CONCEPT 170

brew [v2] *plan, devise*
breed, compound, concoct, contrive, develop, excite, foment, form, gather, hatch, impend, loom, mull, plot, project, scheme, start, stir up, weave; SEE CONCEPT 36

bribe [n] *payoff to influence illegal or wrong activity*
allurement, bait, blackmail, buyoff, compensation, contract, corrupting gift, corrupt money, enticement, envelope*, feedbag*, fringe benefit, gift, goody*, graft, gratuity, gravy*, grease*, hush money*, ice*, incentive, inducement, influence peddling, kickback, lagniappe, lure, payola*, perk*, perquisite, present, price, protection*, remuneration, reward, sop*, sweetener*, sweetening*, take; SEE CONCEPTS 192,329

bribe [v] *request silence, action, or inaction for money*
approach, buy, buy back, buy off, coax, corrupt, do business*, entice, fix*, get at, get to, grease palm*, influence, instigate, lubricate, lure, make a deal, oil palm*, pay off, pervert, reward, seduce, soap*, square, suborn, sugar, sweeten the pot*, take care of, tamper, tempt, tip; SEE CONCEPTS 53,192

bridal [adj] *concerning marriage*
conjugal, connubial, epithalamic, espousal, hymeneal, marital, matrimonial, nubile, nuptial, prewedding, prothalamic, spousal; SEE CONCEPT 536

bride [n] *female marriage partner*
helpmate, mate, newly married woman, newlywed, old woman*, spouse, wife; SEE CONCEPTS 296,415

bridegroom [n] *male marriage partner*
benedict, groom, helpmate, husband, mate, newlywed, old man* spouse; SEE CONCEPTS 296,419

bridge [n] *structure or something that makes connection*
arch, bond, branch, catwalk, connection, extension, gangplank, link, overpass, platform, pontoon, scaffold, span, tie, transit, trestle, viaduct, wing; SEE CONCEPTS 501,721

bridge [v] *connect, extend*
arch over, attach, bind, branch, couple, cross, cross over, go over, join, link, reach, span, subtend, traverse, unite; SEE CONCEPTS 113,756

bridle [n] *restraining device*
check, control, curb, deterrent, hackamore, halter, headstall, leash, rein, restraint, trammels; SEE CONCEPT 497

bridle [v] *check, hold back*
constrain, control, curb, govern, inhibit, keep in check, master, moderate, repress, restrain, rule, subdue, suppress, withhold; SEE CONCEPT 121

brief [n] *abridgment*
abstract, argument, boildown*, case, condensation, conspectus, contention, data, defense, digest, epitome, outline, précis, sketch, summary, synopsis; SEE CONCEPTS 283,318

brief [adj1] *short, compressed*
abrupt, bluff, blunt, boiled down*, breviloquent, brusque, compendiary, compendious, concise, crisp, curt, hasty, laconic, limited, little, pithy, sharp, short and sweet*, skimpy, small, snippy, succinct, surly, terse, to the point; SEE CONCEPTS 267,773

brief [adj2] *short in time*
concise, curtailed, ephemeral, fast, fleeting, hasty, instantaneous, little, meteoric, momentary, passing, quick, short-lived, short-term, swift, temporary, transient, transitory; SEE CONCEPT 798

brief [v] *inform of facts*
abridge, advise, apprise, edify, enlighten, epitomize, explain, fill in, give pointers*, give the lowdown*, inform, initiate, instruct, let in on*, orient, prepare, prime, recapitulate, show the lay of the land*, show the ropes*, summarize, tip off*, update; SEE CONCEPT 60

briefcase [n] *carrier for work papers*
attaché, bag, baggage, case, dispatch, folder, portfolio, valise; SEE CONCEPTS *446,494*

briefing [n] *preparation by informing of facts*
background meeting, conference, directions, discussion, guidance, information, initiation, instruction, meeting, preamble, priming, rundown, update; SEE CONCEPT *60*

brigade [n] *fleet of trained people*
army, band, body, company, contingent, corps, crew, detachment, force, group, organization, outfit, party, posse, squad, team, troop, unit; SEE CONCEPTS *322,381*

bright [adj1] *shining, glowing in appearance*
ablaze, aglow, alight, argent, auroral, beaming, blazing, brilliant, burning, burnished, coruscating, dazzling, effulgent, flashing, fulgent, fulgid, glaring, gleaming, glistening, glittering, glossy, golden, illuminated, illumined, incandescent, intense, irradiated, lambent, light, lighted, limpid, luminous, lustrous, mirrorlike, moonlit, phosphorescent, polished, radiant, relucent, resplendent, scintillating, shimmering, shiny, silvery, sparkling, sunlit, sunny, twinkling, vivid; SEE CONCEPT *617*

bright [adj2] *sunny, clear (weather)*
clement, cloudless, fair, favorable, limpid, lucid, mild, pellucid, pleasant, translucent, transparent, unclouded; SEE CONCEPT *525*

bright [adj3] *intelligent*
acute, advanced, alert, astute, aware, brainy, brilliant, clear-headed, clever, discerning, eggheaded*, Einstein*, having smarts*, ingenious, inventive, keen, knowing, precocious, quick, quick-witted, sharp, smart, whiz kid*, wideawake; SEE CONCEPT *402*

bright [adj4] *hopeful, promising*
airy, auspicious, benign, breezy, cheering, encouraging, excellent, favorable, golden, good, optimistic, palmy, propitious, prosperous, rosy; SEE CONCEPT *537*

bright [adj5] *cheerful*
alert, animated, gay, genial, glad, happy, jolly, joyful, joyous, keen, lighthearted, lively, merry, optimistic, sanguine, spirited, sprightly, vivacious; SEE CONCEPT *404*

bright [adj6] *famous, outstanding*
distinguished, eminent, glorious, illustrious, magnificent, prominent, remarkable, splendid; SEE CONCEPT *568*

bright [adj7] *vivid in color*
brave, brilliant, clear, colored, colorful, deep, flashy, fresh, gay, glitzy*, hued, intense, psychedelic, razzle-dazzle, rich, ruddy, sharp, showy, tinged, tinted; SEE CONCEPT *618*

brighten [v1] *make shine or glow*
buff up, burnish, clear up, enliven, gleam, grow sunny, illuminate, illumine, intensify, kindle, lighten, light up, polish, punch up*, spiff up*; SEE CONCEPTS *244,250*

brighten [v2] *make happy, feel better*
become cheerful, buck up, buoy up, cheer, cheer up, clear up, encourage, enliven, gladden, hearten, improve, look up, perk up; SEE CONCEPTS *7,22*

brilliant [adj1] *shining, glowing in appearance*
ablaze, bright, coruscating, dazzling, effulgent, flashy, fulgent, gleaming, glittering, glossy, incandescent, intense, lambent, lucent, luminous, lustrous, radiant, refulgent, resplendent, scintillating, showy, sparkling, vivid; SEE CONCEPT *617*

brilliant [adj2] *famous, outstanding*
celebrated, distinguished, eminent, excellent, exceptional, glorious, illustrious, magnificent, prominent, splendid, superb; SEE CONCEPT *568*

brilliant [adj3] *very intelligent*
accomplished, acute, astute, brainy, bright, clever, discerning, eggheaded*, Einstein*, expert, genius, gifted, ingenious, intellectual, inventive, knowing, knowledgeable, masterly, penetrating, profound, quick, quick-witted, sharp, smart, talented, whip, whiz kid*; SEE CONCEPT *402*

brim [n] *edge of object, usually the top*
border, brink, circumference, fringe, hem, lip, margin, perimeter, periphery, rim, skirt, verge; SEE CONCEPT *836*

brim [v] *flow over the top*
fill, fill up, hold no more, overflow, run over, spill, swell, teem, well over; SEE CONCEPT *740*

brimming/brimful [adj] *overflowing; up to the top*
awash, chock-full, crammed, crowded, filled, flush, full, full to the top, jammed, level with, loaded, overfull, packed, running over, stuffed, topfull; SEE CONCEPTS *481,771,774*

brine [n] *salt solution*
alkali, blue, brackish water, deep, drink, marinade, ocean, pickling solution, preservative, saline, salt water, sea water, sodium chloride solution, vinegar; SEE CONCEPT *514*

bring [v1] *transport or accompany*
attend, back, bear, buck*, carry, chaperon, companion, conduct, consort, convey, deliver, escort, fetch, gather, guide, gun*, heel*, import, lead, lug, pack, pick up, piggyback*, ride, schlepp*, shoulder, take, take along, tote, transfer, transport, truck, usher; SEE CONCEPT *143*

bring [v2] *cause; Influence*
begin, compel, contribute to, convert, convince, create, dispose, effect, engender, force, induce, inflict, lead, make, move, occasion, persuade, prevail on, prevail upon, produce, prompt, result in, sway, wreak; SEE CONCEPT *242*

bring [v3] *command a price*
afford, bring in, draw, earn, fetch, gross, net, produce, return, sell for, take, yield; SEE CONCEPTS *330,335*

bring [v4] *file charges in court*
appeal, arraign, cite, declare, indict, initiate legal action, institute, prefer, serve, sue, summon, take to court; SEE CONCEPT *317*

bring about [v] *cause success*
accomplish, achieve, beget, bring to pass, compass, create, do, draw on, effect, effectuate, engender, generate, give rise to, make happen, manage, occasion, produce, realize, secure, succeed; SEE CONCEPTS *244,706*

bring around [v] *convince, induce*
argue, convert, draw, get, indoctrinate, persuade, prevail upon, prompt, prove, talk into, win over; SEE CONCEPT *68*

bring down [v] *reduce or hurt*
abase, cut down, damage, drop, fell, floor, injure, knock down, KO*, lay low, level, lower, mow down, murder*, overthrow, overturn, prostrate, pull down, shoot down, slay*, throw down, tumble, undermine, upset, wound; SEE CONCEPTS *7,19,252*

bring in [v] *make a profit*
accrue, acquire, bear, be worth, bring, cost, earn,

fetch, gain, get, gross, make, pay, produce, realize, return, sell, yield; SEE CONCEPTS *124,330*

bring off [*v*] *accomplish*
achieve, bring home the bacon*, bring to pass,
carry off, carry out, discharge, effect, effectuate,
execute, perform, pull off, realize, succeed; SEE
CONCEPTS *704,706*

bring up [*v1*] *raise youngster*
breed, cultivate, develop, discipline, educate,
feed, form, foster, nourish, nurture, provide for,
rear, school, support, teach, train; SEE CONCEPT
295

bring up [*v2*] *initiate, mention in conversation*
advance, advert, allude to, broach, discuss, introduce, moot, move, offer, point out, propose, put
forward, raise, raise a subject, refer, submit, tender, touch on, ventilate*; SEE CONCEPT *51*

brink [*n*] *edge of an object or area*
border, boundary, brim, fringe, frontier, limit, lip,
margin, perimeter, periphery, point, rim, skirt,
threshold, verge; SEE CONCEPTS *484,513*

brisk [*adj1*] *fast-moving; active*
adroit, agile, alert, animated, bustling, busy, energetic, lively, nimble, quick, speedy, sprightly,
spry, vigorous, vivacious, zippy; SEE CONCEPTS
542,584

brisk [*adj2*] *chilly, refreshing (weather)*
biting, bracing, crisp, exhilarating, fresh, invigorating, keen, nippy, sharp, snappy, stimulating;
SEE CONCEPT *605*

bristle [*n*] *short, prickly hair*
barb, feeler, fiber, point, prickle, quill, spine,
stubble, thorn, vibrissa, whisker; SEE CONCEPT
418

bristle [*v*] *become upset, excited*
be angry, be infuriated, be maddened, blow up*,
boil, boil over, bridle, flare, flare up, fume, get
one's dander up*, rage, rise, ruffle, see red*,
seethe, spit*, stand on end*, swell; SEE CONCEPT
410

brittle [*adj1*] *fragile*
breakable, crisp, crumbling, crumbly, delicate,
frail, frangible, friable, inelastic, shatterable,
shivery, vitreous, weak; SEE CONCEPTS *488,606*

brittle [*adj2*] *tense*
curt, edgy, irritable, nervous, prim, short, stiff,
stilted; SEE CONCEPT *401*

broach [*v1*] *bring up a topic*
advance, approach, bring up, hint at, interject,
interpose, introduce, mention, moot, move, offer,
open up, propose, raise subject, speak of, submit,
suggest, talk of, touch on, ventilate*; SEE CON-
CEPT *51*

broach [*v2*] *open, pierce*
begin, crack, decant, draw off, puncture, start,
tap, uncork; SEE CONCEPTS *142,225*

broad [*adj1*] *wide physically*
ample, capacious, deep, expansive, extended, extensive, full, generous, immense, large, latitudi-
nous, outspread, outstretched, roomy, spacious,
splay, squat, thick, vast, voluminous, widespread;
SEE CONCEPTS *773,796*

broad [*adj2*] *extensive*
all-embracing, all-inclusive, comprehensive, copious, encyclopedic, expansive, extended, far-
flung, far-reaching, general, inclusive,
nonspecific, scopic, sweeping, ubiquitous, undetailed, universal, unlimited, wide, wide-ranging,
widespread; SEE CONCEPT *772*

broad [*adj3*] *full, obvious*
apparent, clear, explicit, open, plain, straightforward, undisguised, unequivocal; SEE CONCEPT
576

broad [*adj4*] *liberal-minded*
advanced, cultivated, experienced, open, open-
minded, permissive, progressive, radical, tolerant,
unbiased, wide; SEE CONCEPT *403*

broad [*adj5*] *vulgar*
blue, coarse, dirty, gross, improper, indecent, indelicate, low-minded, off-color, purple, racy, risqué, salty, saucy, smutty, spicy, suggestive,
unrefined, unrestrained, wicked; SEE CONCEPT
545

broadcast [*n*] *information on electronic media*
advertisement, air time, announcement, newscast,
performance, program, publication, radiocast,
show, simulcast, telecast, transmission; SEE CON-
CEPTS *274,293*

broadcast [*v1*] *put forth on electronic media*
air, announce, beam, be on the air, cable, circulate, colorcast, communicate, get out*, go on the
air, go on the airwaves, put on the air, radio,
radiograph, relay, send, show, simulcast, telecast,
telegraph, telephone, televise, transmit; SEE CON-
CEPTS *60,292*

broadcast [*v2*] *make public*
advertise, announce, annunciate, blare, blazon,
circulate, communicate, declare, disseminate, distribute, proclaim, promulgate, publish, report,
sow, spread, strew, troll; SEE CONCEPT *60*

broadcasting [*n*] *informing via electronic media*
airing, air time, announcing, auditioning, news-
casting, performing, posting online, putting on
program, radio, reporting, telecasting, television,
transmission, transmitting; SEE CONCEPTS
263,293

broaden [*v*] *extend, supplement*
augment, breadthen, develop, enlarge, expand,
fatten, grow, increase, open up, ream, spread,
stretch, swell, widen; SEE CONCEPT *239*

broad-minded [*adj*] *liberal*
advanced, catholic, cosmopolitan, dispassionate,
flexible, free-thinking, indulgent, liberal, open,
open-minded, permissive, progressive, radical, receptive, responsive, tolerant, unbiased, unbigoted, undogmatic, unprejudiced, wide; SEE
CONCEPT *403*

brochure [*n*] *short, printed document*
advertisement, booklet, circular, flyer, folder,
handbill, handout, leaflet, pamphlet; SEE CON-
CEPT *280*

broil [*v*] *cook under direct heat*
burn, melt, roast, scorch, sear, swelter; SEE CON-
CEPT *170*

broiling [*adj*] *very hot*
baking, burning, fiery, on fire, red-hot, roasting,
scalding, scorching, sizzling, sweltering, torrid;
SEE CONCEPT *605*

broke [*adj*] *without money*
bankrupt, beggared, bust*, cleaned out*, destitute, dirt poor*, flat broke*, impoverished, in
Chapter 11*, in debt, indebted, indigent, insolvent, needy, penniless, penurious, poor, ruined,
stone broke*, strapped*, tapped out; SEE CON-
CEPT *334*

broken [*adj1*] *destroyed; made into pieces from a
whole*
burst, busted, collapsed, cracked, crippled, crumbled, crushed, damaged, defective, demolished,

disintegrated, dismembered, fractured, fragmentary, fragmented, hurt, injured, in pieces, mangled, mutilated, pulverized, rent, riven, ruptured, separated, severed, shattered, shivered, shredded, slivered, smashed, split; SEE CONCEPT 485

broken [adj2] *discontinuous*
disconnected, disturbed, erratic, fragmentary, incomplete, intermittent, interrupted, irregular, spasmodic, spastic; SEE CONCEPT 482

broken [adj3] *mentally defeated*
beaten, browbeaten, crippled, crushed, defeated, demoralized, depressed, discouraged, disheartened, heartsick, humbled, oppressed, overpowered, subdued, tamed, vanquished; SEE CONCEPT 403

broken [adj4] *not working*
busted, coming unglued, coming unstuck, defective, disabled, down, exhausted, fallen apart, faulty, feeble, gone, gone to pieces*, gone to pot*, haywire, imperfect, in disrepair, in need of repair, inoperable, in the shop*, kaput*, not functioning, on the blink*, on the fritz*, on the shelf*, out, out of commission*, out of kilter*, out of order, out of whack*, ruined, run-down, screwed up*, shot, spent, unsatisfactory, weak, wracked*, wrecked; SEE CONCEPTS 485,560

broken [adj5] *forgotten, ignored (promise)*
abandoned, dishonored, disobeyed, disregarded, ignored, infringed, isolated, retracted, traduced, transgressed, violated; SEE CONCEPT 544

broken [adj6] *stuttering in speech*
disjointed, halting, hesitant, hesitating, imperfect, incoherent, mumbled, muttered, stammering, unintelligible, weak; SEE CONCEPT 267

brokenhearted [adj] *devastated*
crestfallen, crushed, desolate, despairing, despondent, disappointed, disconsolate, grief-stricken, grieved, heartbroken, heartsick, heartsore, inconsolable, miserable, mournful, prostrated, sorrowful, wretched; SEE CONCEPT 403

broker [n] *financial expert*
agent, business person, dealer, entrepreneur, factor, financier, go-between, interagent, interceder, intercessor, intermediary, intermediate, mediator, merchant, middleperson, negotiator, stockbroker; SEE CONCEPTS 348,353

bronze [adj] *coppery-brown color*
brownish, burnished, chestnut, copper, copper-colored, metallic brown, reddish-brown, reddish-tan, russet, rust, tan; SEE CONCEPT 618

brooch [n] *ornamental pin*
bar pin, breastpin, clip, cluster, jewelry; SEE CONCEPT 446

brood [n] *cluster of children*
begats, breed, chicks, clutch, descendants, family, flock, hatch, infants, issue, litter, offspring, posterity, progeniture, progeny, scions, seed, young; SEE CONCEPT 296

brood [v] *agonize over*
be in brown study*, bleed, chafe inwardly*, consider, daydream, deliberate, despond, dream, dwell upon, eat one's heart out*, fret, gloom, grieve, lament, languish, meditate, mope, mull over, muse, ponder, reflect, repine, ruminate, sigh, speculate, stew over*, sulk, sweat out*, sweat over*, think about, think upon, worry; SEE CONCEPT 17

brook [n] *stream of water*
beck, branch, burn, creek, rill, rindle, river, riv-

ulet, run, runnel, streamlet, watercourse; SEE CONCEPT 514

brook [v] *endure, accept*
abide, allow, bear, be big*, countenance, go, hang in, hang in there*, hear of, live with, put up with, sit tight*, stand, stomach, suffer, support, swallow, take, tolerate, withstand; SEE CONCEPT 23

broom [n] *device for cleaning floors*
besom, carpet sweeper, feather duster, floor brush, mop, swab, sweeper, whisk; SEE CONCEPT 499

broth [n] *soup, usually clear*
borscht, bouillon, bowl, brew, chowder, concoction, consommé, decoction, dishwater*, distillation, elixir, fluid, gumbo, hodge-podge*, liquor, olio, porridge, potage, potpourri, pottage, puree, splash, stock, vichyssoise, water; SEE CONCEPTS 457,467

brothel [n] *house of prostitution*
bagnio, bawdy house*, bordello, call house*, cathouse*, den of iniquity*, house of assignation, house of ill repute, house with red doors*, massage parlor, red-light district, whorehouse; SEE CONCEPT 449

brother [n] *male sibling*
blood brother, kin, kinsperson, relation, relative, twin; SEE CONCEPTS 414,419

brow [n] *forehead*
countenance, eyebrow, face, frons, front, mien, temple, top; SEE CONCEPT 418

browbeat [v] *castigate, nag*
badger, bludgeon, bluster, bulldoze*, bully, coerce, cow, despotize, domineer, dragoon, frighten, harass, hector, intimidate, lean on*, lord it over*, oppress, overawe, overbear, put heat on*, put the chill on*, put through the wringer*, threaten, tyrannize; SEE CONCEPTS 14,52

brown [adj] *dark, burnished color*
amber, auburn, bay, beige, bister, brick, bronze, buff, burnt sienna, chestnut, chocolate, cinnamon, cocoa, coffee, copper, drab, dust, ecru, fawn, ginger, hazel, henna, khaki, mahogany, nut, ochre, puce, russet, rust, sepia, snuff-colored, sorrel, tan, tawny, terra-cotta, toast, umber; SEE CONCEPT 618

browse [v] *look around; look through*
check over, dip into*, examine cursorily, feed, flip through, get the cream*, give the once over*, glance at, graze, hit the high spots*, inspect loosely, leaf through, nibble*, once over lightly*, pass an eye over*, peruse, read, read here and there, riffle through, riff through, run through, scan, skim, skip through, survey, thumb through, wander; SEE CONCEPT 623

bruise [n] *black and blue mark under skin*
abrasion, black eye, black mark, blemish, booboo*, contusion, discoloration, injury, mark, mouse*, swelling, wale, wound; SEE CONCEPT 309

bruise [v] *break blood vessel; discolor*
bang up, batter, beat, black, blacken, blemish, bung up*, contuse, crush, damage, deface, do a number on*, injure, mar, mark, pound, pulverize, wound, zing*; SEE CONCEPTS 137,246,250

brunette/brunet [adj] *dark hair and/or skin*
bistered, brown, dusky, pigmented, swart, swarthy, tanned, tawny; SEE CONCEPTS 406,618

brunt [n] *bad end of a situation*
burden, force, full force, impact, pressure, shock,

strain, stress, tension, thrust, violence; SEE CON-
CEPT 674

brush [n1] *tool with bristles for cleaning*
besom, broom, hairbrush, mop, polisher,
sweeper, toothbrush, waxer, whisk; SEE CONCEPT
499

brush [n2] *fight*
clash, conflict, confrontation, encounter, engagement, fracas, rub, run-in, scrap, set-to, skirmish,
tap, touch, tussle; SEE CONCEPT 106

brush [n3] *scrappy bushes*
boscage, bracken, brushwood, chaparral, coppice,
copse, cover, dingle, fern, gorse, grove, hedge,
scrub, sedge, shrubbery, spinney, thicket, undergrowth, underwood; SEE CONCEPT 429

brush [v1] *touch lightly*
caress, contact, flick, glance, graze, kiss, scrape,
shave, skim, smooth, stroke, sweep, tickle; SEE
CONCEPT 612

brush [v2] *clean, prepare by whisking*
buff, clean, paint, polish, sweep, wash, whisk,
wipe; SEE CONCEPTS 165,202

brush aside/brush off [v] *ignore; refuse*
boycott, cold-shoulder*, contradict, cut, deny,
disclaim, dismiss, disown, disregard, get rid of,
have no time for*, ostracize, override, rebuff, reject, repudiate, scorn, send away, slight, snub,
spurn, sweep aside; SEE CONCEPT 30

brush up [v] *improve condition*
clean up, cram, go over, look over, polish up,
read up, refresh one's memory, refurbish, relearn,
renovate, reread, retouch, review, revise, study,
touch up; SEE CONCEPTS 202,244

brusque [adj] *curt, surly*
abrupt, bluff, blunt, brief, crusty, discourteous,
gruff, hasty, impolite, sharp, short, snappy,
snippy, tart, terse, unmannerly; SEE CONCEPTS
267,401

brutal [adj1] *cruel, remorseless*
barbarous, bloodthirsty, callous, ferocious, gruff,
hard, harsh, heartless, impolite, inhuman, insensitive, merciless, pitiless, remorseless, rough,
rude, ruthless, savage, severe, uncivil, uncivilized, unfeeling, unmannerly, unmerciful, vicious;
SEE CONCEPT 401

brutal [adj2] *crude, rough*
animal, bearish, beastly, bestial, brute, brutish,
carnal, coarse, feral, ferine, inhuman, inhumane,
rude, savage, swinish, unfeeling; SEE CONCEPT
544

brutality [n] *cruel treatment*
atrocity, barbarism, barbarity, bloodthirstiness,
brutishness, choke hold*, cruelty, ferocity, fierceness, grossness, inhumanity, ruthlessness, sadism,
savageness, savagery, third degree*, unfeelingness, viciousness; SEE CONCEPTS 14,86

brutally [adv] *cruelly, without remorse*
atrociously, barbarically, barbarously, brutishly,
callously, demoniacally, diabolically, ferally, ferociously, fiercely, hardheartedly, heartlessly, in
cold blood, inexorably, inhumanely, inhumanly,
meanly, mercilessly, murderously, pitilessly, relentlessly, remorselessly, ruthlessly, savagely,
something fierce, something terrible, unkindly,
unrelentingly, viciously; SEE CONCEPT 544

brute [n] *barbarian*
animal, beast, cannibal, creature, critter*, degenerate, devil, fiend, lout, monster, ogre, ruffian,
sadist, savage, swine, wild animal; SEE CONCEPTS
394,423

brute [adj] *very strong; animallike*
animal, beastly, bestial, bodily, carnal, feral, ferine, fleshly, instinctive, mindless, physical, senseless, swinish, unthinking; SEE CONCEPTS 489,540

bubble [n] *globule of air*
air ball*, balloon, barm, bead, blister, blob, drop,
droplet, effervescence, foam, froth, lather, sac,
spume, vesicle; SEE CONCEPT 437

bubble [v] *foam, froth up, especially with sound*
boil, burble, churn, eddy, effervesce, erupt, fester, fizz, gurgle, gush, issue, moil, murmur, percolate, ripple, seep, seethe, simmer, smolder,
sparkle, spume, stir, swash, trickle, well; SEE
CONCEPTS 179,469

buck [n] *male animal*
bull, stag; SEE CONCEPTS 394,419

buck [v] *resist, kick off*
bound, combat, contest, dispute, duel,
fight, jerk, jump, leap, oppose, prance, repel,
start, throw, traverse, trip, unseat, vault, withstand; SEE CONCEPTS 180,222

bucket [n] *container, often for liquids, with handle*
brazier, can, canister, cask, hod, kettle, pail, pot,
scuttle, vat; SEE CONCEPT 494

buckle [n] *fastener with long pin*
catch, clamp, clasp, clip, fastening, fibula, harness, hasp; SEE CONCEPT 450

buckle [v] *contort, warp*
bend, bulge, cave in, collapse, crumple, distort,
fold, twist, yield; SEE CONCEPT 702

buckle down [v] *concentrate on*
address, apply oneself, attend to, bend, dedicate
oneself to, devote oneself to, exert oneself, give,
give oneself over to, keep close to, keep one's
mind on, launch into, occupy oneself with, pitch
in, set to, throw, turn; SEE CONCEPTS 17,87

bud [n] *new sprout on plant*
bloom, blossom, embryo, floret, germ, incipient
flower, nucleus, shoot, spark; SEE CONCEPT 428

bud [v] *sprout*
burgeon, burst forth, develop, grow, pullulate,
shoot; SEE CONCEPT 427

budding [adj] *developing, flowering*
beginning, blossoming, burgeoning, bursting
forth, embryonic, fledgling, fresh, germinal, ger-
minating, growing, incipient, maturing, nascent,
opening, potential, promising, pubescent, pullulating, shooting up, sprouting, vegetating, young;
SEE CONCEPT 490

buddy [n] *friend*
associate, chum, co-mate, companion, comrade,
confidant, co-worker, crony, intimate, mate, pal,
peer, sidekick; SEE CONCEPT 423

budge [v] *dislodge from staid position*
bend, change, change position, convince, give
way, inch, influence, locomote, move, persuade,
propel, push, remove, roll, shift, slide, stir, sway,
yield; SEE CONCEPTS 68,147

budget [n] *financial plan*
account, aggregate, allocation, allowance, bulk,
cost, estimated expenses, finances, fiscal estimate,
funds, means, planned disbursement, quantity,
quantum, resources, spending plan, statement, total; SEE CONCEPT 332

budget [v] *plan money or action*
allocate, apportion, calculate, compute, cost, estimate, predict, ration; SEE CONCEPTS 36,330

buff [n] *enthusiast*
addict, admirer, aficionado, connoisseur, devotee,

expert, fan, fiend*, freak*, habitué, hound, lover, votary; SEE CONCEPTS *352,423*

buff [adj] *sandy color*
bare, blonde, canary, ecru, lemon, light brown, nude, ochre, straw, tan, tawny, yellow-brown, yellowish; SEE CONCEPT *618*

buff [v] *polish to a shine*
brush, burnish, furbish, glaze, gloss, pumice, rub, sandpaper, scour, shine, smooth; SEE CONCEPTS *202,215*

buffer [n] *safeguard*
bulwark, bumper, cushion, defense, fender, intermediary, screen, shield, shock absorber; SEE CONCEPTS *484,729*

buffet [n] *meal set out on table for choosing*
café, cafeteria, cold table, counter, cupboard, lunch wagon, salad bar, shelf, sideboard, smorgasbord, snack bar; SEE CONCEPTS *443,459*

buffet [v] *hit repeatedly*
bang, batter, beat, blow, box, bump, clobber, cuff, flail, jolt, knock, pound, pummel, push, rap, shove, slap, smack, spank, strike, thrash, thump, wallop; SEE CONCEPT *189*

buffoon [n] *clownlike person*
antic, bozo*, clown, comedian, comic, droll, fool, harlequin, jester, joker, merry-andrew, wag, zany; SEE CONCEPT *423*

bug [n1] *bacterium, microorganism*
bacillus, disease, germ, infection, microbe, virus, SEE CONCEPT *306*

bug [n2] *insect*
ant, beetle, cootie, flea, gnat, louse, pest, vermin; SEE CONCEPT *398*

bug [n3] *obsession*
craze, enthusiasm, fad, mania, rage, zeal, SEE CONCEPT *532*

bug [v1] *bother, disturb*
abrade, annoy, badger, chafe, gall, get on someone*, harass, irk, irritate, needle, nettle, pester, plague, provoke, vex; SEE CONCEPTS *7,19*

bug [v2] *listen to without permission*
eavesdrop, listen in, overhear, spy, tap, wiretap; SEE CONCEPTS *192,596*

bugle [n] *musical horn*
clarion, cornet, misery pipe*, trumpet; SEE CONCEPT *262*

build [n] *physical structure, form*
body, conformation, constitution, figure, frame, habit, habitus, physique, shape; SEE CONCEPT *757*

build [v1] *construct structure*
assemble, bring about, carpenter, cast, compile, compose, contrive, engineer, erect, evolve, fabricate, fashion, fit together, forge, form, frame, jerry-build, knock together*, make, manufacture, model, prefabricate, produce, put together, put up, raise, rear, reconstruct, sculpture, set up, superstruct, synthesize, throw together*, throw up*; SEE CONCEPT *168*

build [v2] *initiate, found*
base, begin, constitute, establish, formulate, inaugurate, institute, originate, set up, start; SEE CONCEPT *234*

build [v3] *increase, accelerate*
aggrandize, amplify, augment, boost, compound, develop, enlarge, escalate, expand, extend, heighten, improve, intensify, magnify, mount, multiply, strengthen, swell, wax; SEE CONCEPTS *236,245*

builder [n] *construction worker*
architect, artisan, constructor, contractor, craftsperson, erector, fabricator, framer, inventor, maker, manufacturer, mason, originator, producer; SEE CONCEPT *348*

building [n] *constructed dwelling*
architecture, construction, domicile, edifice, erection, fabric, framework, home, house, hut, pile, superstructure; SEE CONCEPTS *439,441*

buildup [n] *development; accumulation*
accretion, advertising, enlargement, escalation, expansion, gain, growth, heap, hype, increase, load, mass, plug, promotion, publicity, puff*, stack, stockpile, store; SEE CONCEPTS *230,704,787*

build up [v] *amplify, advertise*
add to, boost, develop, enhance, expand, extend, fortify, heighten, hype, improve, increase, intensify, plug*, promote, publicize, puff*, reinforce, spotlight, strengthen; SEE CONCEPTS *236,245,266*

built-in [adj] *included*
congenital, constitutional, deep-seated, essential, implicit, inborn, inbred, in-built, incorporated, indwelling, ingrained, inherent, innate, inseparable, integral, part and parcel*; SEE CONCEPT *549*

bulb [n] *globular object*
ball, bunch, corm, corn, globe, head, knob, nodule, nub, protuberance, swelling, tube, tumor; SEE CONCEPT *436*

bulge [n] *swollen object*
appendage, bagginess, blob, bump, bunch, bunching, convexity, dilation, distention, excess, excrescence, gibbosity, growth, hump, intumescence, jut, lump, nodulation, nodule, outgrowth, outthrust, projection, prominence, promontory, protrusion, protuberance, sac, sagging, salience, salient, superfluity, swelling, tuberosity, tumefaction, tumor, wart; SEE CONCEPTS *436,470*

bulge [v] *project outward*
bag, balloon, beetle, belly, bilge, billow, bloat, blob, bug out, dilate, distend, enlarge, expand, extrude, jut, overhang, poke, pop out, pouch, protrude, protuberate, puff out, sag, stand out, stick out, swell; SEE CONCEPTS *208,780*

bulk [n1] *size, largeness*
aggregate, amount, amplitude, bigness, dimensions, extent, immensity, magnitude, mass, massiveness, quantity, quantum, substance, total, totality, volume, weight; SEE CONCEPT *730*

bulk [n2] *main part, most*
best part, better part, biggest share, body, generality, greater number, greater part, gross, lion's share*, majority, major part, mass, nearly all, plurality, predominant part, preponderance, principal part; SEE CONCEPTS *635,829*

bulky [adj] *huge*
awkward, beefy, big, colossal, cumbersome, cumbrous, enormous, gross, heavy, hefty, high, hulking, immense, large, long, mammoth, massive, ponderous, substantial, unhandy, unmanageable, unwieldy, voluminous, weighty; SEE CONCEPT *781*

bulldoze [v1] *demolish*
drive, elbow, flatten, force, jostle, level, press, propel, push, raze, shove, thrust; SEE CONCEPTS *208,252*

bulldoze [v2] *bully, intimidate*
bludgeon, bluster, browbeat, coerce, cow, dragoon, harass, hector; SEE CONCEPT *14*

bullet [n] *small missile*
ammo*, ammunition, ball, bolt, cap, cartridge, dose*, lead, love letter*, pellet, projectile, rocket,

br
bu

round, shot, slug, trajectile; SEE CONCEPT *500*

bulletin [*n*] *message, notification*
account, announcement, break, calendar, communication, communiqué, dispatch, flash*, handout, hot wire*, item, list, news, news flash*, notice, program, publication, release, report, scoop*, skinny*, statement, the dope*, what's going down*, what's happening*; SEE CONCEPTS *271,274*

bully [*n*] *domineering person*
annoyer, antagonizer, browbeater, bulldozer, coercer, harrier, hector, insolent, intimidator, oppressor, persecutor, pest, rascal, rowdy, ruffian, tease, tormenter, tough; SEE CONCEPT *423*

bully [*v*] *intimidate, push around*
bludgeon, bluster, browbeat, buffalo, bulldoze, coerce, cow, despotize, domineer, dragoon, enforce, harass, hector, lean on, menace, oppress, overbear, persecute, ride roughshod*, showboat*, swagger, terrorize, threaten, torment, torture, turn on the heat*, tyrannize, walk heavy*; SEE CONCEPT *14*

bulwark [*n*] *fortification, support*
barrier, bastion, buffet, buttress, citadel, defense, embankment, fort, fortress, guard, mainstay, outwork, parapet, partition, protection, rampart, redoubt, safeguard, security, stronghold, vallation; SEE CONCEPTS *96,729*

bum [*n*] *beggar*
bindle*, black sheep*, derelict, drifter, floater, gutterpup*, guttersnipe*, hobo, stiff*, tramp, transient, vagabond, vagrant; SEE CONCEPTS *412,423*

bump [*v1*] *collide, hit, usually with sound*
bang, bounce, box, buck, bunt, butt, carom, clap, clatter, crack, crash, impinge, jar, jerk, jolt, jostle, jounce, knock, pat, plop, plunk, pound, punch, rap, rattle, shake, slam, smack, smash into, strike, thud, thump, thunder, thwack, whack; SEE CONCEPT *189*

bump [*v2*] *move over, dislodge*
budge, displace, remove, shift; SEE CONCEPT *213*

bump into [*v*] *happen upon*
chance upon, come across, encounter, hit, light, light upon, luck, meet, meet up with, run across, run into, stumble, tumble; SEE CONCEPT *114*

bun [*n*] *baked roll*
bread, cruller, Danish, doughnut, eclair, muffin, pastry, scone, sweet roll; SEE CONCEPT *457*

bunch [*n*] *collection of something*
agglomeration, assemblage, assortment, band, batch, bevy, blob, bouquet, bundle, caboodle*, chunk, clump, cluster, covey, crew, crowd, fascicle, flock, galaxy, gang, gathering, group, heap, host, hunk, knot, lot, mass, mess, mob, multitude, number, oodles*, pack, parcel, party, passel*, pile, quantity, sheaf, shebang*, shock, shooting match*, spray, stack, swarm, team, thicket, troop, tuft; SEE CONCEPT *432*

bunch [*v*] *gather in group*
assemble, bundle, cluster, collect, congregate, cram, crowd, flock, group, herd, huddle, mass, pack; SEE CONCEPT *109*

bundle [*n*] *accumulation, package of something*
array, assortment, bag, bale, batch, box, bunch, carton, clump, cluster, collection, crate, group, heap, lot, mass, pack, package, packet, pallet, parcel, pile, quantity, roll, set, stack, wad; SEE CONCEPTS *432,787*

bundle [*v*] *accumulate, package*
bale, bind, clothe, fasten, pack, palletize, tie, truss, wrap; SEE CONCEPTS *158,202*

bungle [*v*] *blunder, mess up*
ball up*, boggle, botch, butcher*, drop the ball*, err, flub, foul up*, fudge*, fumble, goof up*, gum up*, louse up*, make a mess of, mar, mess up, miscalculate, mishandle, mismanage, muff*, ruin, screw up*, spoil; SEE CONCEPT *101*

bungler [*n*] *person who blunders*
addlebrain*, blockhead*, blunderer, bonehead*, botcher*, bumbler, butcher*, butterfingers*, clod, clumsy oaf*, dolt, donkey*, duffer*, dunce, featherbrain*, fool, foul-up*, fumbler*, goofball*, goof off*, harebrain*, idiot, ignoramus, incompetent, klutz*, mismanager, muddler, muffer*, numskull*, screw up*, spoiler; SEE CONCEPTS *412,423*

bunk [*n1*] *nonsense*
applesauce*, balderdash, baloney*, bilge*, claptrap, eyewash*, flimflam*, garbage*, hogwash*, hooey*, horsefeathers*, jazz*, piffle*, poppycock, rot*, rubbish, tomfoolery*, tommyrot*, trash*, twaddle*; SEE CONCEPTS *63,278*

bunk [*n2*] *twin bed, usually stacked; place to sleep*
berth, cot, doss, hay, kip, pallet, sack; SEE CONCEPT *443*

bunt [*v*] *hit half-heartedly*
butt, lay it down*, meet, sacrifice, throw, toss; SEE CONCEPTS *189,363*

buoy [*n*] *floating device*
beacon, drift, float, guide, marker, signal; SEE CONCEPT *628*

buoy (up) [*v*] *make light, encourage*
bolster, boost, buck up, cheer, cheer up, encourage, hearten, keep afloat, lift, prop, raise, support, sustain, uphold; SEE CONCEPTS *7,22*

buoyancy/buoyance [*n1*] *lightness in weight*
airiness, ethereality, floatability, levity, weightlessness; SEE CONCEPT *734*

buoyancy/buoyance [*n2*] *lightness in spirit*
animation, bounce, cheerfulness, cheeriness, ebullience, effervescence, exuberance, gaiety, good feeling, good humor, happiness, high spirits, jollity, liveliness, pep, spiritedness, sunniness, vim and vigor*, zing*, zip; SEE CONCEPTS *410,411*

buoyant [*adj1*] *light in weight*
afloat, airy, bouncy, floatable, floating, resilient, supernatant, unsinkable, weightless; SEE CONCEPT *491*

buoyant [*adj2*] *light in spirit*
animated, blithe, bouncy, breezy, bright, carefree, cheerful, debonair, effervescent, elastic, expansive, full of zip, gay, happy, invigorated, jaunty, jovial, joyful, laid back*, lighthearted, lively, peppy, resilient, sunny, supple, vivacious; SEE CONCEPTS *403,404*

burden [*n*] *mental weight; stress*
accountability, affliction, albatross*, anxiety, ball and chain*, blame, care, charge, clog, concern, deadweight, difficulty, duty, encumbrance, excess baggage*, grievance, hardship, Herculean task, hindrance, load, millstone, misfortune, mishap, obstruction, onus, punishment, responsibility, sorrow, strain, task, tax, thorn in one's side*, trial, trouble, weary load, work, worry; SEE CONCEPTS *532,690*

burden [*v*] *encumber, strain*
afflict, bear down on, bother, crush, cumber, de-

press, dish it out*, dish out*, dump on*, encumber, give it to, hamper, handicap, hinder, impede, lade, load, make heavy, obligate, oppress, overcharge, overload, overwhelm, pile, press, saddle with, snow*, snow under*, stick it to, strain, tax, trouble, try, vex, weigh down, worry; SEE CONCEPTS 7,14,19

burdensome [adj] troublesome
carking, crushing, demanding, difficult, disturbing, exacting, exigent, heavy*, irksome, onerous, oppressive, superincumbent, taxing, tough, trying, wearing, wearying, weighty; SEE CONCEPT 529

bureau [n1] branch of an organization
agency, authority, board, commission, committee, department, division, front office*, office, salt mines*, service, setup, shop, store; SEE CONCEPTS 325,441,449

bureau [n2] chest of drawers
chiffonier, commode, desk, dresser, highboy, sideboard, writing desk; SEE CONCEPT 443

bureaucracy [n] system which controls organization
administration, authority, beadledom*, city hall*, civil service, directorate, government, management, ministry, officialdom, officials, powers that be*, red tape*, regulatory commission, the Establishment*, the system*; SEE CONCEPTS 325,770

burglar [n] person who steals
cat burglar, crook, filcher*, housebreaker, midnighter*, owl*, picklock*, pilferer*, porch-climber*, prowler, robber, safecracker, sneakthief*, thief; SEE CONCEPT 412

burglary [n] stealing from residence, business
break-in, breaking and entering, caper, crime, filching, heist, housebreaking, larceny, owl job*, pilferage, prowl, robbery, safecracking, second-story work*, sting, theft, thieving; SEE CONCEPT 139

burial [n] laying in of dead body
burying, deep six*, deposition, entombment, exequics, funeral, inhumation, interment, last rites, obsequies, sepulture; SEE CONCEPT 367

burlesque [n] bawdy show; vaudeville
burly*, caricature, farce, lampoon, lampoonery, mock, mockery, parody, pastiche, peep show, revue, satire, send-up, spoof, strip, takeoff, travesty, vaudeville; SEE CONCEPT 263

burlesque [adj] farcical
caricatural, comic, ironical, ludicrous, mock, mocking, parodic, satirical, travestying; SEE CONCEPT 555

burly [adj] husky
able-bodied, athletic, beefcake*, beefy*, big, brawny, bruising, bulky, gorillalike, hefty, hulking, hulky, hunk, muscular, portly, powerful, stocky, stout, strapping, strong, sturdy, thickset, well-built; SEE CONCEPT 773

burn [v1] be on fire; set on fire
bake, be ablaze, blaze, brand, broil, calcine, cauterize, char, combust, conflagrate, cook, cremate, enkindle, flame, flare, flash, flicker, glow, heat, ignite, incinerate, kindle, light, melt, parch, reduce to ashes, rekindle, roast, scald, scorch, sear, set a match to, singe, smoke, smolder, toast, torch, wither; SEE CONCEPT 249

burn [v2] feel stinging pain
bite, hurt, pain, smart, sting, tingle; SEE CONCEPT 590

burn [v3] be excited about; yearn for
be angry, be aroused, be inflamed, be passionate, be stirred up, blaze, boil, breathe fire*, bristle, desire, eat up*, fume, lust, rage, seethe, simmer, smoulder, tingle, yearn; SEE CONCEPTS 20,29,34

burn [v4] cheat
beat, bilk, chisel, cozen, deceive, defraud, gyp, overreach, ream, swindle, take, trick, use; SEE CONCEPTS 59,142

burning [adj1] blazing, flashing
afire, aflame, alight, blistering, broiling, conflagrant, enkindled, fiery, flaming, flaring, gleaming, glowing, heated, hot, ignited, illuminated, incandescent, in flames, kindled, on fire, oxidizing, red-hot*, scorching, searing, sizzling, smoking, smouldering, torrid, white-hot*; SEE CONCEPTS 485,605

burning [adj2] fervent, excited
all-consuming, ardent, blazing, eager, earnest, fervid, feverish, frantic, frenzied, heated, hectic, impassioned, intense, passionate, red-hot*, vehement, white-hot*, zealous; SEE CONCEPT 403

burning [adj3] stinging, painful
acrid, biting, caustic, irritating, painful, piercing, prickling, pungent, reeking, sharp, smarting, tingling; SEE CONCEPTS 314,537

burning [adj4] important
acute, clamant, clamorous, compelling, critical, crucial, crying, dire, essential, exigent, imperative, importunate, instant, pressing, significant, urgent, vital; SEE CONCEPT 568

burnish [v] polish, brighten
buff, furbish, glance, glaze, gloss, luster, patina, put on a finish, rub, sheen, shine, smooth, wax; SEE CONCEPTS 202,215

burrow [n] hole dug by animal
couch, den, hovel, lair, retreat, shelter, tunnel; SEE CONCEPT 517

burrow [v] dig a hole
delve, excavate, hollow out, scoop out, tunnel, undermine; SEE CONCEPT 178

burst [n] blow-up, blast
access, bang, barrage, blowout, bombardment, breach, break, cannonade, crack, discharge, eruption, explosion, fit, flare, fusillade, gush, gust, outbreak, outpouring, round, rupture, rush, sally, salvo, shower, spate, split, spurt, storm, surge, torrent, volley; SEE CONCEPTS 86,179,208

burst [v] blow up, break out
barge, blow, break, crack, detonate, discharge, disintegrate, erupt, explode, fly open, fracture, fragment, gush forth, perforate, pierce, pop, prick, puncture, rend asunder, run, rupture, rush, shatter, shiver, splinter, split, spout, tear apart; SEE CONCEPTS 179,252

bury [v1] lay to rest after death
consign to grave, cover up, deposit, embalm, ensepulcher, enshrine, entomb, hold last rites for*, hold services for, inearth, inhume, inter, inurn, lay out, mummify, plant*, put away*, put six feet under*, sepulcher, sepulture, tomb; SEE CONCEPT 367

bury [v2] conceal, cover
cache, cover up, ensconce, enshroud, hide, occult, plant, screen, secrete, shroud, stash, stow away; SEE CONCEPTS 172,188

bury [v3] plant in ground
drive in, embed, engulf, implant, sink, submerge; SEE CONCEPTS 172,257

bu
bu

bury [v4] *engross oneself*
absorb, concentrate, engage, immerse, interest, occupy, rivet, throw oneself into; SEE CONCEPT 24

bush [n] *shrubs; woodland*
backcountry, backwoods, boscage, bramble, briar, brush, chaparral, creeper, forest, hedge, hinterland, jungle, outback, plant, scrub, scrubland, shrubbery, the wild, thicket, vine, wilderness; SEE CONCEPT 429

bushy [adj] *shaggy, unkempt*
bristling, bristly, disordered, feathery, fluffy, fringed, full, furry, fuzzy, hairy, heavy, hirsute, leafy, luxuriant, nappy, prickly, rough, rumpled, spreading, stiff, thick, tufted, unruly, wiry, woolly; SEE CONCEPTS 406,606

busily [adv] *actively; intently*
agilely, animatedly, ardently, arduously, assiduously, briskly, carefully, diligently, eagerly, earnestly, energetically, enthusiastically, expeditiously, fervently, hastily, hurriedly, indefatigably, industriously, laboriously, like all get out*, like the devil*, like the dickens*, nimbly, painstakingly, perseveringly, persistently, purposefully, restlessly, seriously, speedily, spiritedly, strenuously, studiously, unremittingly, unweariedly, vigilantly, vigorously, vivaciously, zealously; SEE CONCEPT 544

business [n1] *job, profession*
bag*, biz*, calling, career, craft, dodge*, employment, field, function, game, line, livelihood, métier, occupation, pursuit, racket*, specialty, trade, vocation, what one is into*, work; SEE CONCEPT 360

business [n2] *company, enterprise*
cartel, concern, corporation, establishment, factory, firm, fly-by-night operation*, house, institution, market, megacorp*, mill, Mom and Pop*, monopoly, organization, outfit, partnership, setup, shoestring operation*, shop, store, syndicate, trust, venture; SEE CONCEPTS 325,449

business [n3] *commerce, trade*
affairs, bargaining, barter, buying and selling, capital and labor, commercialism, contracts, deal, dealings, exchange, free enterprise, game, industrialism, industry, manufacturing, market, merchandising, production and distribution, racket*, sales, selling, trading, traffic, transaction, undertaking; SEE CONCEPTS 325,770

business [n4] *personal concern*
affair, assignment, beeswax*, carrying on, duty, function, goings-on*, hanky-panky*, happening, interest, issue, lookout, matter, palaver, point, problem, question, responsibility, subject, task, topic; SEE CONCEPT 532

businesslike [adj] *efficient, professional*
accomplished, careful, concentrated, correct, diligent, direct, disciplined, earnest, effective, enterprising, expeditious, hardworking, industrious, intent, matter-of-fact, methodical, orderly, organized, painstaking, practical, practiced, purposeful, regular, routine, sedulous, serious, skillful, systematic, thorough, well-ordered, workaday; SEE CONCEPTS 326,544

businessperson [n] *professional working person*
baron, big-time operator*, big wheel*, capitalist, dealer, employer, entrepreneur, executive, financier, franchiser, gray flannel suit*, industrialist, manager, merchandiser, merchant, operator, organization person, small potatoes*, storekeeper,

suit*, the bacon*, tradesperson, trafficker, tycoon, wheeler-dealer*; SEE CONCEPTS 347,348

bust [n1] *chest of human*
bosom, breast, chest, front; SEE CONCEPT 392

bust [n2] *arrest for illegal action*
apprehension, arrest, capture, cop, detention, nab, pickup, pinch, raid, search, seizure; SEE CONCEPTS 298,317

bust [v1] *ruin, impoverish*
become insolvent, break, crash, fail, fold up, go bankrupt, go into Chapter 11*, pauperize; SEE CONCEPT 330

bust [v2] *arrest for illegal action*
apprehend, catch, collar, cop*, detain, nab, pick up, pinch, pull in, raid, run in, search; SEE CONCEPTS 298,317

bust [v3] *physically break*
burst, fold, fracture, rupture; SEE CONCEPT 252

bustle [n] *quick and busy activity*
ado, agitation, clamor, commotion, do*, excitement, flurry, furor, fuss, haste, hubbub, hurly-burly*, hurry, pother, rumpus, stir, to-do*, tumult, turmoil, uproar, whirl, whirlpool, whirlwind; SEE CONCEPT 386

bustle [v] *move around quickly, busily*
bestir, dash, dust, flit, flutter, fuss, hasten, hum, hurry, hustle, run, rush, scamper, scramble, scurry, scuttle, stir, tear, whirl, whisk; SEE CONCEPT 150

busy [adj1] *engaged, at work*
active, already taken*, assiduous, at it*, buried, diligent, employed, engaged, engrossed, having a full plate*, having enough on one's plate*, having fish to fry*, having many irons in the fire*, hustling, in a meeting, in conference, industrious, in someone else's possession*, in the field, in the laboratory, occupied, on assignment, on duty, on the go, overloaded, persevering, slaving, snowed*, swamped*, tied up, unavailable, up to one's ears*, with a customer, working; SEE CONCEPTS 326,544,555

busy [adj2] *active, on the go*
bustling, busy as a beaver*, energetic, full, fussy, hectic, humming*, hustling, lively, popping*, restless, strenuous, tireless, tiring; SEE CONCEPT 542

busy [adj3] *nosy, impertinent*
butting in, curious, forward, inquisitive, interfering, intrusive, meddlesome, meddling, nebby, obtrusive, officious, prying, pushy, snoopy, stirring, troublesome; SEE CONCEPT 404

busybody [n] *nosy, impertinent person*
backseat driver*, butt-in*, buttinsky*, eavesdropper, fink*, fussbudget, gossip, intermeddler, intruder, meddler, newsmonger*, nosey parker*, rubberneck*, scandalmonger*, sidewalk superintendent*, snoop, snooper, tattletale, troublemaker, yenta*; SEE CONCEPT 423

butcher [n] *meat killer, seller*
boner*, meatmarket person, meat person, processor, skinner*, slaughterer, slayer*; SEE CONCEPT 348

butcher [v1] *slay and prepare animal for meat*
beef up, carve, clean, cure, cut, cut down, dress, joint, liquidate, salt, slaughter, smoke, stick; SEE CONCEPTS 170,252

butcher [v2] *ruin*
bollix up*, botch, destroy, goof up*, louse up*, make a mess of*, mutilate, screw up*, spoil, wreck; SEE CONCEPT 101

butt [n1] *end, shaft*
base, bottom, edge, extremity, fag end, foot, fundament, haft, handle, hilt, shank, stock, stub, stump, tail, tip; SEE CONCEPT 827

butt/buttocks [n2] *animate rear end*
back end, backside, behind, bottom, bum*, derrière, fanny*, fundament, gluteus maximus, haunches, hindquarters, posterior, rear, rump, seat, tush*; SEE CONCEPT 392

butt [n3] *object of joking*
chump*, clay pigeon*, derision, dupe*, easy mark*, fall guy, fool, goat, jestee*, joke, laughingstock, mark, patsy, pigeon*, sap, setup*, sitting duck*, softie*, subject, sucker, target, turkey, victim; SEE CONCEPT 423

butt [v1] *bang up against with head*
batter, buck, buffet, bump, bunt, collide, gore, hook, horn, jab, knock, poke, prod, punch, push, ram, run into, shove, smack, strike, thrust, toss; SEE CONCEPT 189

butt [v2] *touch, adjoin*
abut, border, bound, communicate, join, jut, meet, neighbor, project, protrude, verge; SEE CONCEPTS 113,747

buttress [n] *brace, support*
abutment, column, mainstay, pier, prop, reinforcement, shore, stanchion, stay, strut, underpinning; SEE CONCEPT 440

buttress [v] *support, bolster*
back up, beef up*, brace, build up, bulwark, carry, jack up, jazz up*, prop, reinforce, shore, step up, strengthen, sustain, uphold; SEE CONCEPT 250

buxom [adj] *bosomy*
ample, built, busty, chubby, comely, curvaceous, curvy, full-bosomed, full-figured, healthy, hearty, lusty, plump, robust, shapely, stacked*, voluptuous, well-made, well-proportioned, well-rounded, zaftig*; SEE CONCEPT 406

buy [n] *something purchased*
acquisition, bargain, closeout, deal, good deal, investment, purchase, steal, value; SEE CONCEPT 710

buy [v1] *purchase*
acquire, bargain for, barter for, contract for, get, get in exchange, go shopping, invest in, market, obtain, pay for, procure, purchase, redeem, score, secure, shop for, sign for, take; SEE CONCEPT 327

buy [v2] *bribe*
corrupt, fix, grease palm*, have, land, lubricate, oil palm*, ransom, reach, redeem, sop*, square, suborn, tamper; SEE CONCEPTS 192,341

buyer [n] *someone who purchases*
client, consumer, customer, easy make*, emptor, end user, patron, prospect, purchaser, representative, shopper, sucker*, user, vendee; SEE CONCEPT 348

buzz [n1] *droning sound*
drone, fizz, fizzle, hiss, hum, murmur, purr, ring, ringing, sibilation, whir, whisper; SEE CONCEPT 595

buzz [n2] *gossip*
comment, cry, grapevine*, hearsay, news, report, rumble*, rumor, scandal, scuttlebutt, talk, whisper; SEE CONCEPT 274

buzz [v1] *make droning sound*
bombinate, bumble, drone, fizz, fizzle, hum, murmur, reverberate, ring, sibilate, whir, whisper, whiz; SEE CONCEPT 65

buzz [v2] *gossip*
call, chatter, inform, natter, rumor, tattle; SEE CONCEPT 60

buzzword [n] *popular word or phrase*
argot, cant, doublespeak, fuzzword, jargon, lingo, mediaspeak, phraseology, policyspeak, slang; SEE CONCEPT 275

by [adv] *near*
aside, at hand, away, beyond, close, handy, in reach, over, past, through, to one side; SEE CONCEPT 586

by [prep1] *next to*
along, alongside, beside, by way of, close to, near, nearby, nigh, over, past, round, via; SEE CONCEPT 586

by [prep2] *by means of*
at the hand of, in the name of, on, over, supported by, through, through the agency of, through the medium of, under the aegis of, with, with the assistance of; SEE CONCEPT 544

bygone [adj] *in the past*
ancient, antiquated, archaic, belated, dated, dead, defunct, departed, down memory lane*, erstwhile, extinct, forgotten, former, gone, gone by, in oblivion, late, lost, of old, of yore, olden, oldfangled, old-fashioned, old-time, one-time, out-of-date, previous, quondam, sometime, vanished, water over the dam*, water under the bridge*; SEE CONCEPT 820

bypass [v] *avoid*
blink at, burke, circumnavigate, circumvent, depart from, detour, deviate from, finesse, get around, go around, go around the barn*, ignore, let go, neglect, omit, outflank, pass around, sidestep, skirt, take back road*, wink at; SEE CONCEPTS 30,102

bystander [n] *person who watches*
eyewitness, gaper*, kibitzer*, looker-on, observer, onlooker, passerby, spectator, viewer, watcher, witness; SEE CONCEPT 423

byword [n] *saying*
adage, aphorism, apophthegm, axiom, catchphrase, catchword, dictum, epithet, gnome, gnomic saying, handle, maxim, motto, nickname, precept, proverb, saw, shibboleth, slogan, standing joke; SEE CONCEPT 275

C

cab [n] *car for hire*
carriage, hack, hackney, jitney, taxi, taxicab, tourist car; SEE CONCEPT 505

cabaret [n] *nightclub with musical performances*
after-hours joint*, bar, café, disco, discothèque, dive, hideaway, hot spot*, nightery, night spot, speakeasy, supper club, tavern, watering hole*; SEE CONCEPTS 447,449

cabin [n] *tiny house; lodging*
berth, box, caboose, camp, chalet, compartment, cot, cottage, crib, deckhouse, home, hovel, hut, lodge, log house, quarters, room, shack, shanty, shed, shelter; SEE CONCEPT 516

cabinet [n1] *cupboard for storage*
case, chiffonier, closet, commode, container, depository, dresser, escritoire, locker, repository, wardrobe; SEE CONCEPTS 443,494

bu
ca

cabinet [n2] *executives serving a leader*
administration, administrators, advisers, assembly, assistants, authority, brain trust*, bureau, bureaucracy, committee, council, counselors, department heads, governing body, government, kitchen cabinet*, ministry, official family; SEE CONCEPT 299

cache [n] *hidden supply*
accumulation, assets, drop, drop joint, drop-off, fund, hideout, hiding place, hoard, kitty*, nest egg*, plant, repository, reserve, shade, stake, stash, stockpile, store, storehouse, supplies, treasure, treasury, wealth; SEE CONCEPTS 446,710

cache [v] *hide a supply of something*
accumulate, bury, conceal, cover, ditch, duck, ensconce, lay away, maintain, park, plant, put away, put in the hole*, save, screen, secrete, squirrel*, squirrel away*, stash, stash away, store; SEE CONCEPT 188

cackle [n] *a loud laugh*
chortle, chuckle, cluck, crow, gibber, giggle, gobble, guffaw, quack, snicker, snigger, titter; SEE CONCEPT 77

cackle [v] *laugh irritatingly*
babble, blather, burble, chortle, chuckle, cluck, crow, gibber, giggle, gobble, jabber, quack, snicker, snigger, titter; SEE CONCEPT 77

cacophonous [adj] *harsh sounding*
clinking, discordant, disharmonic, dissonant, grating, ill-sounding, immusical, inharmonious, jangly, jarring, noisy, raucous, sour, strident, unmusical; SEE CONCEPTS 592,594

cad [n] *sly, dastardly person*
boor, bounder*, clown, creep, cur*, dog*, heel, louse, lout, rake, rascal, rat*, rotter*, rounder*, scoundrel, stinker, worm; SEE CONCEPT 412

cadaver [n] *dead body*
body, cage, carcass, corpse, deceased, mort*, remains, skeleton, stiff*; SEE CONCEPT 390

cadaverous [adj] *pale, corpselike*
ashen, bag of bones, blanched, bloodless, consumptive, dead, deathlike, deathly, emaciated, exsanguinous, gaunt, ghastly, ghostly, haggard, pallid, peaked, peaky, sallow, shadowy, sick, skeletal, skeletonlike, skin and bones*, spectral, thin, wan, wasted; SEE CONCEPTS 406,491,618

cadence [n] *rhythm*
accent, beat, count, inflection, intonation, lilt, measure, meter, modulation, pulse, rhythmus, swing, tempo, throb; SEE CONCEPT 65

cadre [n] *nucleus of effort*
core, force, framework, infrastructure, key group, officers, organization, personnel, staff; SEE CONCEPTS 417,432

café [n] *small, informal restaurant*
bistro, burger joint, cafeteria, cake shop, chophouse, coffee bar, coffee shop, diner, eating house, grease joint*, greasy spoon*, hash house*, luncheonette, lunchroom, noshery*, pit stop*, quick-lunch, snack bar, soup house, tearoom; SEE CONCEPT 449

cage [n] *enclosure with bars*
coop, corral, crate, enclosure, fold, jail, mew, pen, pinfold, pound; SEE CONCEPT 494

cage [v] *hold in enclosure*
close in, confine, coop up, enclose, envelop, fence in, hem, immure, impound, imprison, incarcerate, jail, lock up, mew, pen, restrain, shut in, shut up; SEE CONCEPT 191

cajole [v] *attempt to coax; flatter*
apple polish*, argue into, banter, beguile, blandish, bootlick*, brownnose*, build up, butter up*, con, crowd, deceive, decoy, delude, dupe, entice, entrap, get around, get next to*, hand a line*, induce, influence, inveigle, jolly, lay it on thick*, lure, make up to, maneuver, massage, mislead, oil*, play up to, push, rub the right way*, seduce, snow*, soap*, soften, soft-soap*, spread it on*, stroke, suck up to*, sweeten up*, sweet-talk*, tantalize, tempt, urge, wheedle, work on, work over*; SEE CONCEPTS 59,68,75

cake [n] *bar of something*
block, brick, loaf, lump, mass, slab; SEE CONCEPT 470

calamitous [adj] *disastrous; tragic*
adverse, afflicting, blighting, cataclysmic, catastrophic, deadly, deplorable, devastating, dire, fatal, grievous, harmful, heartbreaking, lamentable, messy, pernicious, regrettable, ruinous, unfavorable, unfortunate, woeful; SEE CONCEPT 537

calamity [n] *disaster; tragedy*
adversity, affliction, blue ruin*, cataclysm, catastrophe, collapse, cross, curtains, distress, downfall, hardship, holy mess*, misadventure, mischance, misfortune, mishap, reverse, ruin, scourge, the worst*, trial, tribulation, unholy mess*, visitation, waterloo*, woe, wreck, wretchedness; SEE CONCEPTS 674,675

calculable [adj] *able to be computed or estimated*
accountable, ascertainable, computable, countable, discoverable, estimable, foreseeable, measurable, predictable, reckonable; SEE CONCEPTS 402,762

calculate [v1] *compute or estimate amount*
account, add, adjust, appraise, assay, cast, cipher, consider, count, determine, divide, dope out*, enumerate, figure, forecast, foretell, gauge, guess, judge, keep tabs*, measure, multiply, number, rate, reckon, size up, subtract, sum, take account of, tally, tot, tote up*, value, weigh, work out; SEE CONCEPT 764

calculate [v2] *plan on*
aim, anticipate, assume, bank on, build, count on, depend on, design, intend, judge, plan, reckon, rely on, suppose, think likely, trust; SEE CONCEPTS 26,36

calculating [adj] *scheming to manipulate*
artful, canny, careful, cautious, chary, circumspect, considerate, contriving, crafty, cunning, designing, devious, discreet, gingerly, guarded, guileful, intelligent, Machiavellian, manipulative, politic, premeditating, safe, scheming, sharp, shrewd, sly, wary, wily; SEE CONCEPTS 401,403

calculation [n1] *computing, estimating amount*
adding, arithmetic, ciphering, computation, counting, dividing, estimate, estimation, figuring, forecast, judgment, multiplying, prediction, reckoning, subtracting, summation, totaling; SEE CONCEPTS 28,764

calculation [n2] *computed or estimated amount*
answer, computation, divination, estimate, estimation, figuring, forecast, judgment, prediction, prognosis, prognostication, reckoning, reply; SEE CONCEPT 787

calculation [n3] *forethought*
canniness, caution, circumspection, contrivance, deliberation, discretion, foresight, planning, precaution, prudence, thought; SEE CONCEPT 660

calendar [n] *schedule of events*
agenda, almanac, annal, bulletin, card, chronology, daybook, diary, docket, journal, lineup, list, log, logbook, menology, pipeline, program, record, register, sked, system of reckoning, tab, table, time, timetable; SEE CONCEPTS 274,281,809

calf [n1] *leg between knee and ankle*
foreleg, shin; SEE CONCEPT 392

calf [n2] *baby cow*
dogie, freemartin, heifer, maverick, veal, yearling, young bull, young cow; SEE CONCEPT 394

caliber [n1] *capacity; character*
ability, appetency, capability, competence, constitution, dignity, distinction, endowment, essence, faculty, force, gifts, habilitation, merit, nature, parts, power, quality, scope, stature, strength, talent, value, virtue, worth, worthiness; SEE CONCEPT 411

caliber [n2] *size of ammunition*
bore, class, diameter, gauge, grade, length, measure, measurement, quality, striking power, weight; SEE CONCEPT 730

call [n1] *yelled statement*
alarm, calling, command, cry, hail, holler*, scream, shout, signal, whoop, yawp, yell; SEE CONCEPT 278

call [n2] *demand, announcement*
appeal, bidding, command, invitation, notice, order, plea, proposal, request, solicitation, subpoena, summons, supplication, visit; SEE CONCEPT 53

call [n3] *need, cause for action*
claim, excuse, grounds, justification, necessity, obligation, occasion, reason, right, urge; SEE CONCEPT 709

call [n4] *normal sound of animal*
cheep, chirp, cry, note, peep, roar, shriek, song, tweet, twitter, warble; SEE CONCEPT 64

call [v1] *yell declaration*
announce, arouse, awaken, bawl, bellow, cry, cry out, exclaim, hail, holler*, hoot, howl, proclaim, roar, rouse, scream, screech, shout, shriek, vociferate, waken, whoop, yawp*, yoo hoo*, yowl; SEE CONCEPTS 47,266

call [v2] *arrange meeting*
ask, assemble, bid, collect, contact, convene, convoke, gather, invite, muster, phone*, rally, request, ring up, subpoena, summon, telephone; SEE CONCEPT 114

call [v3] *entitle*
address, baptize, christen, denominate, describe as, designate, dub, label, name, style, term, title; SEE CONCEPT 62

call [v4] *demand or announce action*
appeal to, appoint, ask, challenge, charge, claim, command, declare, decree, elect, entreat, exact, ordain, order, postulate, pray to, proclaim, require, requisition, set apart, solicit, summon; SEE CONCEPT 53

call [v5] *estimate, consider*
adumbrate, approximate, augur, forecast, foretell, guess, judge, make rough guess, place, portend, predict, presage, prognosticate, prophesy, put, reckon, regard, think, vaticinate; SEE CONCEPTS 28,70

call [v6] *attempt to communicate by telephone*
beep, blast*, bleep, buzz, contact, get back to*, phone, ring, telephone; SEE CONCEPTS 74,266

call [v7] *visit at residence or business*
come by, come over, crash, drop by, drop in, fall by, fall down, hit, look in on, look up, play, pop in*, run in, see, stop by, stop in, swing by; SEE CONCEPT 227

call for [v] *demand; entail*
ask for, inquire, involve, lack, necessitate, need, occasion, request, require, suggest, want; SEE CONCEPT 646

calling [n] *chosen profession*
art, business, career, craft, day gig*, do*, dodge*, employment, gig*, go*, handicraft, hang*, life's work, lifework, line, métier, mission, nine-to-five*, occupation, play, province, pursuit, racket*, rat race*, slot*, swindle*, trade, vocation, walk of life, work; SEE CONCEPT 360

callous [adj] *cruel, insensitive*
apathetic, blind to, careless, case-hardened, cold, cold-blooded, deaf to, hard, hard-bitten, hard-boiled, hardened, hardhearted, heartless, impassive, impenitent, indifferent, indurated, inflexible, insensate, insensible, insensitive, insentient, inured, obdurate, soulless, spiritless, stiff, stony, stubborn, thick-skinned, torpid, tough, toughened, unaffected, unbending, uncaring, uncompassionate, unconcerned, unfeeling, unimpressionable, unresponsive, unsusceptible, unsympathetic; SEE CONCEPT 404

callow [adj] *immature*
crude, green, guileless, inexperienced, infant, jejune, jellybean*, juvenile, kid, low tech*, naive, not dry behind ears*, puerile, raw, sophomore, tenderfoot, unbaked, unfledged, unripe, unsophisticated, untrained, untried, young; SEE CONCEPTS 578,678,797

calm [n] *quietness, composure*
calmness, dispassion, doldrums, hush, impassivity, imperturbation, lull, patience, peace, peacefulness, peace of mind, placidity, quiet, repose, rest, restraint, serenity, silence, stillness, stoicism, tranquility; SEE CONCEPTS 388,411,720

calm [adj1] *peaceful, quiet (inanimate)*
at a standstill, at peace, bland, bucolic, cool, halcyon, harmonious, hushed, inactive, in order, low-key, mild, motionless, pacific, pastoral, placid, quiescent, reposeful, reposing, restful, rural, serene, slow, smooth, soothing, still, stormless, tranquil, undisturbed, unruffled, waveless, windless; SEE CONCEPTS 544,705

calm [adj2] *composed, cool (animate)*
aloof, amiable, amicable, civil, collected, cool as cucumber*, cool-headed, detached, disinterested, dispassionate, equable, gentle, impassive, imperturbable, inscrutable, kind, laid-back*, level-headed, listless, moderate, neutral, patient, placid, pleased, poised, relaxed, restful, satisfied, sedate, self-possessed, serene, still, temperate, unconcerned, undisturbed, unemotional, unexcitable, unexcited, unflappable, unimpressed, unmoved, unruffled, untroubled; SEE CONCEPTS 401,404

calm [v] *make composed, quiet*
allay, alleviate, appease, assuage, balm, becalm, compose, cool, cool it*, cool out*, hush, lay back*, lull, mitigate, mollify, pacify, placate, quiet, quieten, relax, relieve, sedate, settle, simmer down, soft-pedal*, soothe, steady, still, stroke, take it easy*, take the edge off*, tranquilize; SEE CONCEPT 231

ca
ca

camaraderie [n] *friendship*
cheer, companionability, companionship, comradeship, conviviality, esprit de corps, fellowship, gregariousness, intimacy, jollity, sociability, togetherness; SEE CONCEPT *388*

camouflage [n] *disguise*
beard*, blind, cloak, concealment, cover, coverup, deceit, deceptive marking, dissimulation, faking, false appearance, front, guise, mask, masking, masquerade, mimicry, paint, plain brown wrapper*, protective coloring, red herring*, screen, shade, shroud, smokescreen, veil; SEE CONCEPT *260*

camouflage [v] *disguise, cover*
beard*, becloud, befog, cloak, conceal, cover up, deceive, dim, dissemble, dissimulate, dress up, hide, mask, obfuscate, obscure, screen, throw on makeup, veil; SEE CONCEPTS *172,188*

camp [n] *site for outdoor living*
bivouac, campfire, campground, camping ground, caravansary, chalet, cottage, encampment, hut, lean-to, lodge, log cabin, shack, shanty, shed, summer home, tent, tent city, tepee, tilt, wigwam; SEE CONCEPTS *198,516*

camp [adj] *consciously affecting the unfashionable, weird, or bizarre*
affected, arch, artificial, avant-garde, Daliesque*, far out*, in*, mannered, mod, ostentatious, pop, posturing, wild; SEE CONCEPT *544*

campaign [n] *attempt to win; attack*
crusade, drive, expedition, fight, movement, offensive, operation, push, warfare; SEE CONCEPTS *87,320*

campaign [v] *attempt to win political election*
agitate, barnstorm, canvass, contend for, contest, crusade, electioneer, go to grass roots*, hit the trail*, lobby, mend fences*, muckrake, mudsling*, politick, press the flesh*, ring doorbells*, run, run for, shake hands and kiss babies*, solicit votes, stand for, stump*, tour, whistle-stop*; SEE CONCEPT *300*

can [n1] *container, usually metallic*
aluminum, bottle, bucket, canister, cannikin, gunboat*, gutbucket*, jar, package, pop top*, receptacle, tin, vessel; SEE CONCEPTS *476,494*

can [n2] *toilet*
head*, john*, johnny*, latrine, lavatory, litter box*, outhouse, pot*, potty*, privy, restroom, sandbox*, throne*, washroom, water closet; SEE CONCEPT *443*

can [n3] *buttocks*
backside, behind, butt*, derrière, fanny*, fundament, gluteus maximus, hind end, posterior, rump, seat, tush*, tush*; SEE CONCEPT *418*

can [v1] *preserve fruit, vegetable*
bottle, keep, put up; SEE CONCEPT *170*

can [v2] *be able*
be capable of, be equal to, be up to, be within one's area, be within one's control, can do*, commit, could, cut the mustard*, have it made*, lie in one's power, make it*, make out, make the grade*, manage, may, take care of; SEE CONCEPT *630*

can [v3] *fire from job*
ax*, boot*, bounce*, cashier, discharge, dismiss, expel, give the heave ho*, kick out*, let go, sack*, terminate; SEE CONCEPT *351*

canal [n] *waterway*
aqueduct, bottleneck, channel, choke point, conduit, course, cove, ditch, duct, estuary, firth,

trench, water, watercourse; SEE CONCEPT *514*

cancel [v1] *call off; erase*
abolish, abort, abrogate, annul, ax, black out, blot out, break, break off, countermand, cross out, cut, deface, delete, destroy, do away with, do in, efface, eliminate, eradicate, expunge, finish off*, go back on one's word*, kill, obliterate, off*, omit, quash, remove, render invalid, repeal, repudiate, rescind, revoke, rub out, scratch out, scrub*, sink*, smash, squash, stamp across, strike out, torpedo*, total*, trash*, trim*, undo, wash out*, wipe out*, wipe slate clean*, X-out*, zap*; SEE CONCEPTS *18,211,234*

cancel [v2] *equal out*
abort, abrogate, annul, balance out, call off, compensate for, counteract, counterbalance, countercheck, countermand, counterpoise, declare invalid, discard, discharge, frustrate, ignore, invalidate, make up for, negate, neutralize, nullify, offset, overthrow, put an end to, recall, recant, redeem, redress, refute, render inert, render null and void, repeal, repudiate, rescind, retract, revoke, rule out, set aside, suppress, vacate, void; SEE CONCEPTS *232,667*

cancellation [n] *calling off; erasure*
abandoning, abandonment, abolishing, abolition, abrogation, annulment, canceling, deletion, dissolution, dissolving, elimination, invalidating, invalidation, nullification, overruling, quashing, recall, recalling, repeal, repudiation, retirement, retracting, retraction, reversal, reversing, revocation, revoking, undoing, withdrawing; SEE CONCEPT *119*

cancer [n] *malignant growth*
big C*, C*, canker, carcinoma, corruption, disease, long illness, malignancy, sickness, tumor; SEE CONCEPT *306*

candid [adj] *honest*
aboveboard, bluff, blunt, equal, equitable, fair, forthright, frank, free, frontal, genuine, guileless, impartial, ingenuous, just, objective, open, outspoken, plain, right up front*, scrupulous, sincere, straightforward, talking turkey*, telling it like it is*, truthful, unbiased, uncolored, unequivocal, unprejudiced, unpretended, up front*, upright; SEE CONCEPT *267*

candidate [n] *person desiring political office, job*
applicant, aspirant, bidder, claimant, competitor, contender, contestant, dark horse*, entrant, favorite son*, handshaker*, hopeful, job-hunter, nominee, office-seeker, petitioner, possibility, possible choice, pothunter*, runner, seeker, solicitant, stumper*, successor, suitor, whistle-stopper*, write-in*; SEE CONCEPT *359*

candlestick [n] *holder for candles*
candelabra, candelabrum, menorah, pricket, sconce, taper holder; SEE CONCEPT *444*

candor [n] *complete honesty*
artlessness, directness, fairness, forthrightness, frankness, glasnost, guilelessness, honesty, impartiality, ingenuousness, naïveté, openness, outspokenness, probity, simplicity, sincerity, straightforwardness, truthfulness, unequivocalness, uprightness, veracity; SEE CONCEPT *411*

candy [n] *confection*
bonbon, confectionery, confit, hokum*, jawbreaker*, sweet, sweetmeat; SEE CONCEPT *457*

cane [n] *stick to aid walking of disabled*
pikestaff, pole, rod, staff, vade mecum, walking stick; SEE CONCEPT *479*

canker [n] *blistered infection*
bane, blight, blister, boil, cancer, corrosion, corruption, lesion, rot, scourge, smutch, sore, ulcer; SEE CONCEPT 306

canker [v] *blight, corrupt*
animalize, bestialize, consume, corrode, debase, debauch, demoralize, deprave, embitter, envenom, inflict, pervert, poison, pollute, rot, ruin, scourge, sore, stain, ulcer, vitiate; SEE CONCEPT 240

cannibal [n] *beast, beastlike human*
aborigine, anthrophagite, anthropophaginian, anthropophagus, brute, bush dweller, cruel person, head-hunter, ogre, ogress, primitive, ruffian, savage; SEE CONCEPT 412

canny [adj] *clever, artful*
able, acute, adroit, astute, cagey, careful, cautious, circumspect, cunning, dexterous, discreet, foxy*, frugal, having fancy footwork*, hep*, ingenious, intelligent, judicious, knowing, nimble-witted, perspicacious, prudent, quick, quick-witted, sagacious, shrewd, skillful, slick, slippery*, sly, smart, smooth*, street smart*, streetwise*, subtle, wary, watchful, wise, with it*, worldly-wise; SEE CONCEPT 402

canoe [n] *light, paddled boat*
coracle, dugout, kayak, outrigger, piragua, pirogue; SEE CONCEPT 506

canon [n1] *rule, edict*
assize, catalogue, command, commandment, criterion, declaration, decree, decretum, dictate, doctrine, dogma, formula, law, list, maxim, order, ordinance, precept, principle, regulation, roll, screed, standard, statute, table, tenet, touchstone, yardstick; SEE CONCEPTS 318,688

canon [n2] *a body of the most important, influential or superior works in music, literature, or art*
ana, analects, anthology, chrestomathy, classics, collected works, delectus, library, miscellanea, oeuvre, works; SEE CONCEPTS 280,432

canonical [adj] *accepted, recognized*
approved, authoritative, authorized, lawful, legal, official, orthodox, received, sanctioned, sound, statutory; SEE CONCEPTS 319,535

canonize [v] *sanctify; idolize*
apotheosize, beatify, besaint, bless, consecrate, dedicate, deify, glorify, idolatrize, love, put on a pedestal*, saint, worship; SEE CONCEPTS 32,367

canopy [n] *overhanging covering*
awning, baldachin, cover, marquee, shade, sunshade, umbrella; SEE CONCEPTS 440,444

cant [n1] *hypocritical statement*
affected piety, deceit, dishonesty, humbug, hypocrisy, hypocriticalness, insincerity, lip service*, pecksniffery, pharisaicalness, pious platitudes, pomposity, pretense, pretentiousness, sanctimoniousness, sanctimony, sham holiness, show; SEE CONCEPT 63

cant [n2] *jargon*
argot, dialect, diction, idiom, language, lingo, patois, patter, phraseology, slang, vernacular, vocabulary; SEE CONCEPTS 275,278

cant [v] *lean, slant*
angle, bevel, careen, grade, heel, incline, list, recline, rise, slope, tilt, tip; SEE CONCEPTS 154,201

cantankerous [adj] *difficult, crabby*
bad-tempered, bearish, captious, choleric, contrary, cranky, critical, cross, crotchety*, crusty*, disagreeable, dour, grouchy*, grumpy*, huffy*, ill-humored, ill-natured, irascible, irritable, mo-

rose, obstinate, ornery*, peevish, perverse, petulant, prickly, quarrelsome, snappish, sour, stuffy*, testy, vinegarish, vinegary; SEE CONCEPT 401

canteen [n1] *portable kitchen*
chuck wagon, mobile kitchen, snack bar, snack shop; SEE CONCEPT 449

canteen [n2] *container for liquids, used in travels*
bota, bottle, flacon, flask, flasket, jug, thermos, water bottle; SEE CONCEPT 494

canvas [n1] *coarse material*
awning cloth, duck, fly, sailcloth, shade, tarp, tarpaulin, tenting; SEE CONCEPT 473

canvas [n2] *painting on coarse material*
art, artwork, oil, picture, piece, portrait, still life, watercolor; SEE CONCEPT 259

canvass [v] *poll; discuss issues*
agitate, analyze, apply, argue, campaign, check, check over, consult, debate, dispute, electioneer, examine, inspect, investigate, review, run, scan, scrutinize, sift, solicit, study, survey, ventilate; SEE CONCEPTS 24,48,56,300

canyon [n] *gulf in mountain area*
coulee, glen, gorge, gulch, gully, ravine, valley; SEE CONCEPTS 509,513

cap [n] *small hat*
beanie*, beret, bonnet, dink*, fez, pillbox, skull-cap, tam, tam o'shanter; SEE CONCEPT 450

cap [v] *outdo a performance*
beat, best, better, button down*, button up*, can*, clinch*, cob*, complete, cover, crest, crown, do to a T*, eclipse, exceed, excel, finish, outshine, outstrip, pass, put the lid on*, surmount, surpass, top, top it off*, transcend, trump, wrap up*; SEE CONCEPT 141

capability [n] *ability to perform*
adequacy, aptitude, art, capacity, competence, craft, cunning, effectiveness, efficacy, efficiency, facility, faculty, means, might, potency, potential, potentiality, power, proficiency, qualification, qualifiedness, skill, wherewithal; SEE CONCEPT 630

capable [adj] *able to perform*
able, accomplished, adapted, adept, adequate, apt, au fait, clever, competent, dynamite, efficient, experienced, fireball*, fitted, gifted, good, green thumb*, has what it takes*, having know how*, having the goods*, having the right stuff*, intelligent, knowing the ropes*, knowing the score*, like a one-man band*, like a pistol*, masterly, old hand*, old-timer*, on the ball*, proficient, proper, qualified, skillful, suited, talented, there*, up*, up to it*, up to snuff*, up to speed*, veteran; SEE CONCEPT 527

capacious [adj] *ample, extensive*
abundant, broad, comfortable, commodious, comprehensive, dilatable, distensible, expandable, expansive, extended, generous, liberal, plentiful, roomy, sizable, spacious, substantial, vast, voluminous, wide; SEE CONCEPTS 481,772,773,774

capacity [n1] *volume; limit of volume held*
accommodation, amplitude, bulk, burden, compass, contents, dimensions, expanse, extent, full, holding ability, holding power, latitude, magnitude, mass, measure, proportions, quantity, range, reach, retention, room, scope, size, space, spread, standing room only*, sufficiency, sweep; SEE CONCEPTS 481,736,774,794

capacity [n2] *ability; competency*
adequacy, aptitude, aptness, bent, brains, caliber,

capability, cleverness, compass, competence, efficiency, facility, faculty, forte, genius, gift, inclination, intelligence, knack, might, power, qualification, readiness, skill, stature, strength, talent, the goods*, up to it*, what it takes*; SEE CONCEPTS 409,630

cape [n1] *promontory into water*
arm, beak, bill, chersonese, finger, foreland, head, headland, jetty, jutty, mole, naze, neck, ness, peninsula, point, tongue; SEE CONCEPTS 509,514

cape [n2] *sleeveless coat*
bertha, capote, cardinal, cloak, cope, dolman, fichu, gabardine, manteau, mantelletta, mantilla, mantle, overdress, paletot, pelerine, pelisse, poncho, shawl, tabard, talma, tippet, Vandyke, victorine, wrap, wrapper; SEE CONCEPT 451

caper [n] *antic, lark*
escapade, gag*, gambol, high jinks*, hop, hot foot*, jest, joke, jump, leap, mischief, monkeyshines*, practical joke, prank, put on*, revel, rib*, rollick, shenanigan*, sport, stunt, tomfoolery*, trick; SEE CONCEPT 386

caper [v] *frolic, cavort*
blow the lid off*, bounce, bound, cut capers*, cut loose*, dance, frisk, gambol, go on a tear*, hop, horse around*, jump, kick up one's heels*, leap, let loose*, play, raise hell*, rollick, romp, skip, spring, whoop it up*; SEE CONCEPT 384

capital [n1] *financial assets*
business, cash, CD, estate, finances, financing, fortune, funds, gold, interests, investment, IRA, kitty*, means, money, nest egg*, principal, property, resources, savings, stake, stock, substance, treasure, ways and means*, wealth, wherewithal; SEE CONCEPTS 332,710

capital [n2] *city of governmental seat*
control, county seat, metropolis, municipality, political front, principal city, the Hill*; SEE CONCEPTS 507,512

capital [n3] *upper case written symbol*
cap, initial, majuscule, small cap, uncial; SEE CONCEPT 284

capital [adj1] *main, essential*
basic, cardinal, central, chief, controlling, dominant, first, foremost, fundamental, important, leading, major, number one*, outstanding, overruling, paramount, predominant, preeminent, primary, prime, principal, prominent, underlying, vital; SEE CONCEPTS 546,568,829

capital [adj2] *superior*
best, champion, choice, crack, dandy, delightful, deluxe, excellent, famous, fine, first, first-class*, first-rate*, five-star*, fly, great, prime, splendid, superb, top, top-notch*, world-class*; SEE CONCEPT 574

capitalism [n] *economic system of private ownership*
commercialism, competition, democracy, free enterprise, free market, industrialism, laissez faire economics, mercantilism, private enterprise; SEE CONCEPTS 299,689,770

capitalist [n] *person engaged in private ownership of business*
backer, banker, bourgeois, businessperson, entrepreneur, financier, investor, landowner, moneybags*, one who signs the checks*, plutocrat, the boss*, the money*; SEE CONCEPT 347

capitalize [v] *benefit from situation*
avail oneself of, exploit, gain, make capital of, obtain, profit, realize, subsidize, take advantage of; SEE CONCEPT 120

capitol [n] *building or buildings housing chief governmental offices*
Capitol Hill, center, dome, legislative hall, political scene*, seat of government, statehouse; SEE CONCEPTS 299,449

capitulate [v] *give in*
bow, buckle under, cave in, cede, come across, come to terms, concede, defer, fold, give away the store*, give out, give up, knuckle under, put out, relent, submit, succumb, surrender, yield; SEE CONCEPTS 35,83

capitulation [n] *giving in*
accedence, bowing, buckling, conceding, giving up, knuckling under, relenting, resignation, submission, succumbing, surrender, yielding; SEE CONCEPTS 83,410

caprice [n] *sudden change of behavior*
bee*, caper*, changeableness, contrariety, crotchet, fad, fancy, fickleness, fitfulness, fool notion*, freak, gag*, humor, impulse, inconsistency, inconstancy, jerk, kink, mood, notion, peculiarity, perversity, put on*, quirk, rib*, temper, thought, vagary, vein, whim, whimsy; SEE CONCEPTS 13,410

capricious [adj] *given to sudden behavior change*
any way the wind blows*, arbitrary, blowing hot and cold*, careless, changeful, contrary, crotchety, effervescent, erratic, every which way*, fanciful, fickle, fitful, flaky*, flighty, freakish, gaga*, helter-skelter*, humorsome, impulsive, inconstant, kinky*, lubricious, mercurial, moody, mutable, notional, odd, picky*, punchy*, queer, quirky, temperamental, ticklish, unpredictable, unreasonable, unstable, up and down*, vagarious, variable, volatile, wayward, whimsical, yo-yo*; SEE CONCEPT 401

capsize [v] *overturn*
invert, keel over, roll, tip over, turn over, turn turtle*, upset; SEE CONCEPTS 150,152

capsule [n] *tablet, usually medicine*
bolus, cap, dose, lozenge, pellet, pill, troche; SEE CONCEPTS 260,307

capsule [adj] *shortened form*
abridged, canned, condensed, epitomized, pocket, potted, tabloid; SEE CONCEPTS 531,773

captain [n] *chief of vehicle, effort*
authority, boss, cap, CEO, CFO, chieftain, commander, director, exec*, executive, four-striper*, guide, head, head honcho*, higher up*, leader, master, mistress, number one*, officer, operator, owner, pilot, royalty, skip*, skipper*, top*, top dog*; SEE CONCEPT 347

caption [n] *heading; short description*
explanation, head, inscription, legend, rubric, subtitle, title, underline; SEE CONCEPT 283

captious [adj] *very critical*
acrimonious, cantankerous, carping, caviling, cavillous, censorious, contrary, crabby, cross, demanding, deprecating, disparaging, exacting, exceptive, fault-finding, finicky, hypercritical, irritable, nagging, nit-picking, overcritical, peevish, perverse, petulant, sarcastic, severe, testy, touchy; SEE CONCEPTS 267,404

captivate [v] *attract, enchant*
allure, beguile, bewitch, charm, dazzle, delight, draw, enamour, enrapture, enslave, ensnare, entertain, enthrall, entrance, fascinate, gratify, grip, hold, hook, hypnotize, infatuate, intrigue, lure,

magnetize, make a hit with*, mesmerize, please, rope in*, seduce, spellbind, sweep off one's feet*, take, turn one on, vamp, wile, win; SEE CONCEPTS *7,22*

captive [*n*] *person held physically*
bondman, bondservant, bondwoman, con, convict, detainee, hostage, internee, prisoner, prisoner of war, slave; SEE CONCEPTS *412,423*

captive [*adj1*] *physically held by force*
bound, caged, confined, enslaved, ensnared, imprisoned, incarcerated, incommunicado, in custody, jailed, locked up, penned, restricted, subjugated, under lock and key*; SEE CONCEPTS *536,554*

captive [*adj2*] *mentally enchanted, held*
beguiled, bewitched, charmed, delighted, enraptured, enthralled, fascinated, hypnotized, infatuated; SEE CONCEPT *403*

captivity [*n*] *physical detention by force*
bondage, committal, confinement, constraint, custody, durance, duress, enslavement, enthrallment, entombment, impoundment, imprisonment, incarceration, internment, jail, limbo, restraint, serfdom, servitude, slavery, subjection, thralldom, vassalage; SEE CONCEPTS *191,652*

capture [*n*] *catching, forceful holding*
abduction, acquirement, acquisition, apprehension, appropriating, appropriation, arrest, bag*, bust*, catch, collar, commandeering, confiscation, drop*, ensnaring, fall, gaining, grab*, grasping, hit the jackpot*, hook*, imprisonment, knock off*, laying hold of*, nab*, nail*, obtaining, occupation, pick up*, pinch*, pull*, run in*, securing, seizing, seizure, snatching*, sweep*, taking, taking captive, taking into custody, trapping, trip, winning; SEE CONCEPT *90*

capture [*v*] *catch and forcefully hold*
apprehend, arrest, bag*, bust*, catch, collar, conquer, cop, gain control, get, grab*, hook*, land, nab*, nail*, net, occupy, overwhelm, pick up*, pinch*, prehend, pull in, put the cuffs on*, round up*, run in*, secure, seize, snare, snatch, take, take captive, take into custody, take prisoner, trap, tumble; SEE CONCEPT *90*

car [*n*] *vehicle driven on streets*
auto, automobile, bucket*, buggy*, bus, clunker*, compact, convertible, conveyance, coupe, gas guzzler*, hardtop, hatchback, heap*, jalopy*, jeep, junker*, limousine, machine, motor, motorcar, pickup, ride*, roadster, sedan, station wagon, subcompact, touring car, truck, van, wagon, wheels*, wreck*; SEE CONCEPT *505*

caravan [*n*] *group traveling together*
band, camel train, campers, cavalcade, convoy, expedition, procession, safari, train, troop; SEE CONCEPTS *432,503*

carbohydrate [*n*] *organic compound composed of carbon, hydrogen, and oxygen*
cellulose, dextrin, dextrose, disaccharide, fructose, galactose, glucose, glycogen, lactose, maltose, monosaccharide, polysaccharide, starch, sucrose, sugar; SEE CONCEPT *478*

carcass/carcase [*n*] *dead body; framework, base structure*
body, cadaver, corpse, framework, hulk, mort*, remains, shell, skeleton, stiff*; SEE CONCEPTS *390,434*

card [*n*] *piece of paper, often with purposeful writing*
agenda, badge, billet, calendar, cardboard, check,

docket, fiberboard, identification, label, pass, poster, program, schedule, sheet, square, tally, ticket, timetable, voucher; SEE CONCEPTS *260,271*

cardinal [*adj*] *important, key*
basal, basic, central, chief, constitutive, essential, first, foremost, fundamental, greatest, highest, indispensable, leading, main, overriding, overruling, paramount, pivotal, preeminent, primary, prime, principal, ruling, vital; SEE CONCEPTS *568,574*

care [*n1*] *personal interest, concern*
affliction, aggravation, alarm, anguish, annoyance, anxiety, apprehension, bother, burden, chagrin, charge, consternation, discomposure, dismay, disquiet, distress, disturbance, encumbrance, exasperation, fear, foreboding, fretfulness, handicap, hardship, hindrance, impediment, incubus, load, misgiving, nuisance, onus, oppression, perplexity, pressure, responsibility, solicitude, sorrow, stew, strain, stress, sweat, tribulation, trouble, uneasiness, unhappiness, vexation, woe, worry; SEE CONCEPTS *410,532*

care [*n2*] *carefulness, attention to detail*
alertness, caution, circumspection, concentration, concern, conscientiousness, consideration, diligence, direction, discrimination, effort, enthusiasm, exactness, exertion, fastidiousness, forethought, heed, interest, management, meticulousness, nicety, pains, particularity, precaution, prudence, regard, scrupulousness, solicitude, thought, trouble, vigilance, wariness, watchfulness; SEE CONCEPT *657*

care [*n3*] *custody of person, usually child*
administration, aegis, auspices, charge, control, direction, guardianship, keeping, management, ministration, protection, safekeeping, superintendence, supervision, trust, tutelage, ward, wardship; SEE CONCEPTS *285,295,388*

care [*v1*] *tend to*
attend, baby sit, consider, foster, keep an eye on*, keep tabs on*, look after, mind, mind the store*, minister, mother, nurse, nurture, pay attention to, protect, provide for, ride herd on*, sit, take pains, tend, treasure, wait on, watch, watch over; SEE CONCEPTS *110,295*

care [*v2*] *regard highly*
be crazy about*, be fond of*, cherish, desire, enjoy, find congenial, hold dear, like, love, prize, respect, take to, want; SEE CONCEPTS *20,32*

careen [*v*] *tilt; move wildly down path*
bend, lean, lurch, pitch, sway, tilt; SEE CONCEPT *147*

career [*n1*] *occupation*
bag*, calling, course, dodge*, employment, field, game*, job, lifework, livelihood, number*, pilgrimage, profession, pursuit, racket*, specialty, thing*, vocation, work; SEE CONCEPTS *349,360*

career [*n2*] *course, path*
course, orbit, passage, pilgrimage, procedure, progress, race, walk; SEE CONCEPTS *501,678,692*

carefree [*adj*] *lighthearted, untroubled*
airy, at ease, blithe, breezy, buoyant, calm, careless, cheerful, cheery, cool, easy, easy-going, feelgood*, happy, happy-go-lucky, insouciant, jaunty, jovial, laid back*, radiant, secure, sunny, unanxious, unbothered; SEE CONCEPT *404*

careful [*adj*] *cautious; painstaking*
accurate, alert, apprehensive, assiduous, attentive, chary, choosy, circumspect, concerned, conscien-

tious, conservative, cool, deliberate, discreet, exacting, fastidious, finicky, fussy, going to great lengths*, guarded, heedful, judicious, leery, meticulous, mindful, observant, particular, playing safe*, precise, prim, protective, provident, prudent, punctilious, regardful, religious, rigorous, scrupulous, self-disciplined, shy, sober, solicitous, solid, thorough, thoughtful, vigilant, wary; SEE CONCEPTS 326,542

carefully [adv] *cautiously; painstakingly*
anxiously, attentively, circumspectly, concernedly, conscientiously, correctly, deliberately, delicately, dependably, discreetly, exactly, faithfully, fastidiously, fully, gingerly, guardedly, heedfully, honorably, in detail, laboriously, meticulously, particularly, precisely, providently, prudently, punctiliously, regardfully, reliably, rigorously, scrupulously, solicitously, thoroughly, thoughtfully, trustily, uprightly, vigilantly, warily, watchfully, with forethought, with reservations; SEE CONCEPT 542

careless [adj 1] *without sufficient attention*
absent-minded, abstracted, casual, cursory, disregardful, forgetful, hasty, heedless, improvident, imprudent, inaccurate, inadvertent, incautious, inconsiderate, indifferent, indiscreet, indolent, injudicious, irresponsible, lackadaisical, lax, loose, mindless, napping, negligent, nonchalant, oblivious, offhand, perfunctory, pococurante, reckless, regardless, remiss, slipshod, sloppy, thoughtless, uncircumspect, unconcerned, unguarded, unheeding, unmindful, unobservant, unreflective, unthinking, wasteful; SEE CONCEPT 542

careless [adj2] *artless*
casual, modest, naive, natural, nonchalant, simple, unstudied; SEE CONCEPT 557

caress [n] *loving touch*
cuddle, embrace, endearment, feel, fondling, hug, kiss, pat, pet, petting, snuggle, squeeze, stroke; SEE CONCEPTS 375,590

caress [v] *touch lovingly*
bear hug*, brush, buss, clinch, clutch, coddle, cosset, cuddle, dandle, embrace, feel, fondle, graze, handle, hug, kiss, make love, massage, mug, neck, nestle, nuzzle, pat, pet, play around*, rub, squeeze, stroke, toy; SEE CONCEPTS 375,612

caretaker [n] *person who maintains something*
baby sitter, concierge, curator, custodian, housesitter, janitor, keeper, porter, sitter, super*, superintendent, supervisor, warden, watchperson; SEE CONCEPT 348

cargo [n] *baggage; something to be delivered*
burden, consignment, contents, freight, goods, haul, lading, load, merchandise, payload, shipload, shipment, tonnage, ware; SEE CONCEPTS 338,446

caricature [n] *exaggerated description in writing, drawing*
burlesque, cartoon, distortion, farce, imitation, lampoon, libel, mimicry, mockery, parody, pasquinade, pastiche, put-on*, ridicule, satire, sendup*, sham, takeoff*, travesty; SEE CONCEPTS 271,386,625

carillon [n] *set of bells*
angelus, chimes, glockenspiel, gong, lyra, peal, tintinnabulation, tocsin; SEE CONCEPT 595

carnage [n] *massacre*
annihilation, blitz, blood, blood and guts*, blood bath*, bloodshed, butchering, butchery, crime, extermination, gore, havoc, hecatomb, holocaust, homicide, killing, liquidation, manslaughter, mass murder, murder, offing*, rapine, search and destroy*, shambles, slaughter, slaying, taking out*, warfare, wasting; SEE CONCEPT 252

carnal [adj] *erotic, sensual*
animal, bodily, corporal, corporeal, earthly, fleshly, genital, impure, lascivious, lecherous, lewd, libidinous, licentious, lustful, physical, prurient, salacious, sensuous, temporal, unchaste, venereal, voluptuous, vulgar, wanton, worldly; SEE CONCEPTS 372,403

carnival [n] *outdoor celebration*
amusement park, bacchanal, carny*, carousal, circus, conviviality, exposition, fair, feasting, festival, fete, fiesta, frolic, gala, grind show*, heyday, jamboree, jollification, jubilee, Mardi Gras, masquerade, merrymaking, orgy, ragbag*, revelry, rout, saturnalia, side show, spree, street fair; SEE CONCEPTS 377,386

carnivorous [adj] *eating animal flesh*
cannibal, flesh-eating, hungry, omnivorous, predatory, rapacious; SEE CONCEPT 401

carol [n] *joyful hymn*
ballad, canticle, canzonet, chorus, Christmas song, ditty*, lay, madrigal, noel, song, strain; SEE CONCEPTS 263,595

carouse [v] *make merry, often with liquor*
booze, drink, frolic, go on a spree*, have fun, imbibe, paint the town*, paint the town red*, play, quaff, raise Cain*, revel, riot, roister, wassail, whoop it up*; SEE CONCEPT 384

carp [v] *nag*
bother, cavil, censure, complain, criticize, find fault, fuss, grumble, hypercriticize, knock, nitpick*, objurgate, pan, peck*, pick at, quibble, reproach; SEE CONCEPT 52

carpenter [n] *person who works with wood*
artisan, builder, cabinetmaker, carps*, chips*, craftsperson, joiner, laborer, mason, woodworker, worker; SEE CONCEPT 348

carpet [n] *nappy floor covering*
carpeting, matting, rug, runner, tapestry, throw rug, wall-to-wall*; SEE CONCEPT 473

carriage [n1] *delivery of freight*
carrying, conveyance, conveying, delivering, freight, transit, transport, transportation; SEE CONCEPTS 148,217

carriage [n2] *posture, physical and mental*
air, aspect, attitude, bearing, behavior, cast, comportment, conduct, demeanor, deportment, gait, look, manner, mien, pace, positure, presence, stance, step; SEE CONCEPTS 633,720

carry [v1] *transport physical object*
backpack*, bear, bring, cart, channel, conduct, convey, convoy, displace, ferry, fetch, freight, funnel, give, haul, heft, hoist, import, lift, lug*, move, pack, pipe, portage, relay, relocate, remove, schlepp*, shift, shoulder*, sustain, take, tote, traject, transfer, transmit, transplant, truck, waft; SEE CONCEPTS 148,217

carry [v2] *win; accomplish*
affect, be victorious, capture, drive, effect, gain, get, impel, impress, influence, inspire, move, prevail, secure, spur, strike, sway, touch, urge; SEE CONCEPTS 68,706

carry [v3] *broadcast electronically*
air, bear, communicate, conduct, convey, display, disseminate, give, offer, pass on, publish, relay, release, send, transfer, transport; SEE CONCEPTS 217,266

carry on [v1] *continue activity*
achieve, endure, hang on, keep going, last, maintain, perpetuate, persevere, persist, proceed; SEE CONCEPT *239*

carry on [v2] *manage operations*
administer, conduct, direct, engage in, keep, operate, ordain, run; SEE CONCEPT *117*

carry on [v3] *lose control emotionally*
act up, be indecorous, blunder, cut up, lose it*, make a fuss*, misbehave, rage, raise Cain*; SEE CONCEPT *633*

carry out [v] *complete activity*
accomplish, achieve, carry through, consummate, discharge, effect, effectuate, execute, finalize, fulfill, implement, meet, perform, realize; SEE CONCEPT *706*

cart [n] *small attachment for transporting*
barrow, buggy, curricle, dolly, dray, gig, gurney, handcart, palanquin, pushcart, rickshaw, tilbury, truck, tumbrel, two-wheeler, wagon, wheelbarrow; SEE CONCEPTS *499,505*

cart [v] *carry*
bear, bring, convey, ferry, haul, move, schlepp*, take, tote; SEE CONCEPTS *148,217*

carte blanche [n] *full power, authority*
blank check, freedom, free hand, free rein, license, permission, power of attorney, prerogative, sanction, say, say so, unconditional right; SEE CONCEPT *376*

cartel [n] *group which shares business interest*
bunch*, chain, combine, conglomerate, consortium, corporation, crew*, crowd*, gang*, holding company, megacorp*, mob*, monopoly, multinational*, outfit*, plunderbund*, pool, ring*, syndicate, trust; SEE CONCEPTS *323,325*

carton [n] *box for holding items*
bin, case, casket, chest, coffer, container, corrugated box, crate, pack, package, packet; SEE CONCEPT *494*

cartoon [n] *funny drawing, often with dialogue or caption*
animation, caricature, comic strip, drawing, lampoon, parody, representation, satire, sketch, takeoff; SEE CONCEPTS *280,625*

cartoonist [n] *person who draws cartoons*
artist, caricaturist, comic artist, gag person*, gagster*, illustrator, social critic; SEE CONCEPT *348*

carve [v] *cut carefully with sharp instrument*
block out, chip, chisel, cleave, dissect, dissever, divide, engrave, etch, fashion, form, grave, hack, hew, incise, indent, insculpt, model, mold, mould, pattern, rough-hew, sculpt, shape, slash, slice, stipple, sunder, tool, trim, whittle; SEE CONCEPTS *137,176,184*

cascade [n] *something falling, especially water*
avalanche, cataract, chute, deluge, downrush, falls, flood, force, fountain, outpouring, precipitation, rapids, shower, spout, torrent, watercourse, waterfall; SEE CONCEPTS *514,787*

cascade [v] *fall in a rush*
descend, disgorge, flood, gush, heave, overflow, pitch, plunge, pour, spew, spill, spit up, surge, throw up, tumble, vomit; SEE CONCEPT *179*

case [n1] *container; items in container*
bag, baggage, basket, bin, box, cabinet, caddy, caisson, canister, capsule, carton, cartridge, casing, casket, chamber, chassis, chest, coffer, compact, cover, covering, crate, crating, crib, drawer, envelope, folder, grip, holder, integument, jacket, receptacle, safe, scabbard, sheath, shell, suitcase, tray, trunk, wallet, wrapper, wrapping; SEE CONCEPT *494*

case [n2] *circumstance, conditions*
context, contingency, crisis, dilemma, event, eventuality, fact, incident, occurrence, plight, position, predicament, problem, quandary, situation, state, status; SEE CONCEPT *696*

case [n3] *example*
case history, exemplification, illustration, instance, occasion, occurrence, representative, sample, sampling, specimen; SEE CONCEPT *686*

case [n4] *matter brought before a court*
action, argument, cause, claim, dispute, evidence, lawsuit, litigation, petition, proceedings, process, proof, suit, trial; SEE CONCEPT *318*

case [v] *check something in detail*
canvass, check out, check over, check up, examine, inspect, scrutinize, study, view; SEE CONCEPT *103*

cash [n] *money; assets*
banknote, bread*, buck*, bullion, cabbage*, chicken feed*, coin, coinage, currency, dinero*, dough*, funds, green stuff*, investment, legal tender, lot, mazuma*, note, payment, pledge, principal, ready assets, refund, remuneration, reserve, resources, riches, savings, scratch*, security, skins*, stock, supply, treasure, wampum*, wherewithal; SEE CONCEPTS *340,710*

cash [v] *exchange for real money*
acknowledge, break a bill*, change, discharge, draw, honor, liquidate, make change, pay, realize, redeem; SEE CONCEPT *330*

cashier [n] *bank worker*
accountant, banker, bursar, clerk, collector, paymaster, purser, receiver, teller, treasurer; SEE CONCEPT *348*

cashier [v] *discard, expel*
ax*, boot*, bounce, break, can*, cast off, discharge, dismiss, displace, drum out*, fire, give a pink slip*, give the heave ho*, heave*, remove, sack*, terminate; SEE CONCEPTS *211,324*

casino [n] *gambling establishment*
bank, betting house, big store*, club, clubhouse, dance hall, dice joint*, dive, gambling den, hall, honky-tonk, house, joint, Monte Carlo, pool hall, roadhouse, rotunda, saloon, track; SEE CONCEPT *447*

cask [n] *rounded container for liquids*
barrel, barrelet, butt, firkin, hogshead, keg, pipe, tun, vat; SEE CONCEPT *494*

casket [n] *burial box*
bin, carton, case, chest, coffer, crate, funerary box, pine box, pinto, sarcophagus, wood overcoat*; SEE CONCEPTS *368,494*

casserole [n] *dish consisting of a combination of cooked food*
covered dish, goulash, hash, meat pie, pot pie, pottage, stew, stroganoff; SEE CONCEPT *457*

cast [n1] *a throw to the side*
casting, ejection, expulsion, fling, flinging, heave, heaving, hurl, hurling, launching, lob, lobbing, pitch, pitching, projection, propulsion, shooting, sling, slinging, thrust, thrusting, toss, tossing; SEE CONCEPT *222*

cast [n2] *appearance; shade of color*
air, complexion, countenance, demeanor, embodiment, expression, face, hue, look, manner, mien, semblance, stamp, style, tinge, tint, tone, turn, visage; SEE CONCEPTS *622,716*

ca
ca

cast [n3] *actors in performance*
actors, actresses, artists, characters, company, dramatis, list, parts, personae, players, roles, troupe; SEE CONCEPT *294*

cast [n4] *molded structure*
conformation, copy, duplicate, embodiment, facsimile, figure, form, mold, plaster, replica, sculpture, shape; SEE CONCEPTS *470,475*

cast [v1] *throw aside*
boot, bung*, chuck*, drive, drop, fire*, fling, heave, hurl, impel, launch, lob, peg, pitch, project, shed, shy, sling, thrust, toss; SEE CONCEPT *222*

cast [v2] *emit, give*
aim, bestow, deposit, diffuse, direct, distribute, point, radiate, scatter, shed, spatter, spray, spread, sprinkle, strew, train; SEE CONCEPTS *108,624*

cast [v3] *calculate*
add, compute, count, figure, foot, forecast, number, reckon, sum, summate, tot, total; SEE CONCEPT *764*

cast [v4] *select for activity*
allot, appoint, arrange, assign, blueprint, chart, choose, decide upon, delegate, design, designate, detail, determine, devise, give parts, name, pick, plan, project; SEE CONCEPT *41*

caste [n] *social class*
cultural level, degree, estate, grade, lineage, order, position, race, rank, social order, species, sphere, standing, station, status, stratum; SEE CONCEPTS *378,388*

castigate [v] *criticize severely*
baste, bawl out*, beat, berate, blister, cane, censure, chasten, chastise, chew out*, come down on*, correct, criticize, discipline, drag over the coals*, dress down*, drub, excoriate, flay, flog, jump down one's throat*, lambaste, lash, lay out*, lean on*, penalize, pummel, punish, rail, rate, read the riot act*, ream, rebuke, reprimand, scarify, scathe, scold, scorch, scourge, thrash, tonguelash*, upbraid, whip; SEE CONCEPT *52*

castle [n] *magnificent home, often for royalty*
acropolis, alcazar, château, citadel, donjon, estate house, fasthold, fastness, fort, fortification, fortress, hold, keep, manor, mansion, palace, peel, safehold, seat, stronghold, tower, villa; SEE CONCEPT *516*

castrate [v] *remove sexual organs*
alter, asexualize, caponize, change, cut, deprive of virility, desexualize, emasculate, eunuchize, fix, geld, mutilate, neuter, spay, sterilize, unsex; SEE CONCEPT *310*

casual [adj1] *chance, random*
accidental, adventitious, by chance, contingent, erratic, extemporaneous, extempore, fluky, fortuitous, impromptu, improvised, impulsive, incidental, infrequent, irregular, occasional, odd, offhand, serendipitous, spontaneous, uncertain, unexpected, unforeseen, unintentional, unplanned, unpremeditated; SEE CONCEPTS *541,544*

casual [adj2] *nonchalant, relaxed in manner*
aloof, apathetic, blasé, breezy, cool*, cursory, detached, down home*, easygoing, folksy*, homey*, incurious, indifferent, informal, insouciant, lackadaisical, laid-back*, loose*, low-pressure, mellow, offhand, perfunctory, pococurante, purposeless, remote, unconcerned, unfussy, uninterested, withdrawn; SEE CONCEPTS *401,542,589*

casualty [n1] *accident*
blow, calamity, catastrophe, chance, contingency, debacle, disaster, misadventure, misfortune, mishap; SEE CONCEPT *674*

casualty [n2] *victim*
dead, death toll, fatality, injured, killed, loss, missing, prey, sufferer, wounded; SEE CONCEPTS *407,423*

casuistry [n] *overgeneral reasoning*
chicanery, deception, deceptiveness, delusion, equivocation, evasion, fallacy, lie, oversubtleness, sophism, sophistry, speciousness, spuriousness, trick; SEE CONCEPT *54,63*

cat [n] *feline animal, sometimes a pet*
bobcat, cheetah, cougar, grimalkin, jaguar, kitten, kitty, leopard, lion, lynx, malkin, mouser, ocelot, panther, puma, puss, pussy, tabby, tiger, tom, tomcat; SEE CONCEPTS *394,400*

cataclysm [n] *disaster*
calamity, cataract, catastrophe, collapse, convulsion, crunch*, curtains*, debacle, deluge, disturbance, double trouble*, flood, flooding, holy mess*, inundation, misadventure, ruin, torrent, tragedy, unholy mess*, upheaval, waterloo*, woe; SEE CONCEPTS *674,675*

catalog/catalogue [n] *written or printed matter featuring a selection of objects*
archive, brief, bulletin, calendar, cartulary, charts, classification, compendium, directory, docket, draft, enumeration, gazette, gazetteer, hit list*, index, inventory, list, prospectus, record, register, roll, roster, schedule, slate, specification, syllabus, synopsis, table; SEE CONCEPTS *271,280*

catalyst [n] *something which incites activity*
adjuvant, agitator, enzyme, goad, impetus, impulse, incendiary, incentive, incitation, incitement, motivation, radical stimulus, reactant, reactionary, spark plug*, spur, stimulant, synergist, wave maker*; SEE CONCEPT *712*

catapult [n] *implement for shooting weapon*
arbalest, ballista, heaver, hurler, pitcher, propeller, shooter, sling, slingshot, tosser, trebuchet; SEE CONCEPTS *463,500*

catastrophe [n] *calamity; unhappy conclusion*
accident, adversity, affliction, alluvion, bad luck, bad news*, blow, calamity, casualty, cataclysm, contretemps, crash, culmination, curtains*, debacle, denouement, desolation, devastation, disaster, emergency, end, failure, fatality, fiasco, finale, grief, hardship, havoc, ill, infliction, letdown*, misadventure, mischance, misery, misfortune, mishap, reverse, scourge, stroke, termination, the worst*, tragedy, trial, trouble, upshot, waterloo*, wreck; SEE CONCEPT *674*

catch [n1] *fastener*
bolt, buckle, clamp, clasp, clip, hasp, hook, hook and eye, latch, snap; SEE CONCEPT *497*

catch [n2] *trick, hidden disadvantage*
Catch-22, conundrum, deception, decoy, drawback, fly in the ointment*, hitch, joke, puzzle, puzzler, snag, stumbling block, trap; SEE CONCEPTS *674,679*

catch [v1] *ensnare, apprehend*
arrest, bag, bust*, capture, clasp, claw, clench, clutch, collar, cop, corral, entangle, entrap, get one's fingers on*, glom, glove, grab, grasp, grip, hook, lasso, lay hold of, nab, nail, net, pick, pluck, pounce on, prehend, secure, seize, snag, snare, snatch, take, take hold of, trap; SEE CONCEPT *90*

catch [v2] *find out, discover*
descry, detect, encounter, expose, hit upon, meet with, spot, surprise, take unawares, turn up, unmask; SEE CONCEPT 31

catch [v3] *contract an illness*
become infected with, break out with, come down with, develop, fall ill with, fall victim to, get, incur, receive, sicken, succumb to, suffer from, take; SEE CONCEPTS 93,308

catch [v4] *come from behind and grab*
board, climb on, come upon, cotch, get, go after, grab, hop on, jump, make, overhaul, overtake, pass, ram, reach, run down, take; SEE CONCEPT 164

catch [v5] *hear and understand*
accept, apprehend, comprehend, discern, feel, follow, get, grasp, perceive, recognize, see, sense, take in, understand; SEE CONCEPT 15

catching [adj] *contagious (disease)*
communicable, dangerous, endemic, epidemic, epizootic, infectious, infective, miasmatic, pandemic, pestiferous, pestilential, taking, transferable, transmittable; SEE CONCEPT 314

catchword [n] *motto*
byword, catchphrase, household word, maxim, password, refrain, shibboleth, slogan, watchword; SEE CONCEPTS 275,278

catchy [adj] *captivating, addictive*
fetching, haunting, having a good hook*, memorable, popular; SEE CONCEPT 544

catechize [v] *instruct and question*
ask, cross-examine, drill, educate, examine, grill, inquire, interrogate, query, quiz, teach, train; SEE CONCEPTS 48,285

categorical [adj] *explicit, unconditional*
absolute, all out*, certain, clear-cut, definite, definitive, direct, downright, emphatic, express, flat out*, forthright, no holds barred*, no strings attached*, positive, specific, straight out, sure, ultimate, unambiguous, unequivocal, unmitigated, unqualified, unreserved; SEE CONCEPT 535

categorize [v] *sort by type, classification*
assort, button down*, class, classify, group, identify, peg*, pigeonhole*, put down as, rank, tab, typecast; SEE CONCEPT 39

category [n] *classification, type*
class, department, division, grade, group, grouping, head, heading, kind, league, level, list, order, pigeonhole*, rank, section, sort, tier; SEE CONCEPT 378

cater [v] *provide, help*
baby, coddle, cotton, furnish, gratify, humor, indulge, minister to, outfit, pamper, pander to, procure, provision, purvey, spoil, supply, victual; SEE CONCEPT 136

caterwaul [v] *make screeching, crying noise*
bawl, bicker, howl, quarrel, scream, screech, shriek, squall, wail, yell, yowl; SEE CONCEPT 77

catharsis [n] *purging, purification*
ablution, abreaction, cleansing, expurgation, lustration, purgation, purification, release; SEE CONCEPTS 13,165,230

cathedral [n] *large church*
basilica, bishop's seat, chancel, holy place, house of God, house of prayer, house of worship, minster, place of worship, sanctuary, temple; SEE CONCEPTS 368,439

catholic [adj] *all-embracing, general*
all-inclusive, broad-minded, charitable, comprehensive, cosmic, cosmopolitan, diffuse, eclectic, ecumenical, extensive, generic, global, inclusive, indeterminate, large-scale, liberal, open-minded, planetary, receptive, tolerant, unbigoted, universal, unprejudiced, unsectarian, whole, wide, world-wide; SEE CONCEPTS 557,772

cattle [n] *bovine animals*
beasts, bovid mammals, bulls, calves, cows, dogies*, herd, livestock, longhorn*, moo cows*, oxen, shorthorns, stock, strays; SEE CONCEPT 394

catty [adj] *nasty, malicious*
backbiting, evil, hateful, ill-natured, malevolent, mean, rancorous, spiteful, venomous, vicious, wicked; SEE CONCEPT 404

caucus [n] *group gathered to make decision*
assembly, conclave, convention, council, gathering, get-together, meeting, parley, session; SEE CONCEPTS 301,417

cause [n1] *agent, originator*
account, agency, aim, antecedent, author, basis, beginning, causation, consideration, creator, determinant, doer, element, end, explanation, foundation, genesis, ground, grounds, incitement, inducement, instigation, leaven, mainspring, maker, matter, motivation, motive, object, occasion, origin, prime mover, principle, producer, purpose, root, source, spring, stimulation; SEE CONCEPTS 229,661

cause [n2] *belief; undertaking for belief*
attempt, conviction, creed, enterprise, faith, goal, ideal, intention, movement, object, objective, plan, principles, purpose; SEE CONCEPT 689

cause [v] *bring into being; bring about*
be at the bottom of*, begin, brainstorm*, break in*, break the ice*, breed, bring to pass, come out with*, compel, cook up*, create, dream up*, effect, elicit, engender, evoke, fire up*, generate, get things rolling*, give rise to, hatch, incite, induce, introduce, kickoff*, kindle, lead to, let, make, make up, motivate, muster, occasion, open, originate, precipitate, produce, provoke, result in, revert, secure, sow the seeds, start the ball rolling*, think up, work up; SEE CONCEPTS 228,231,241

caustic [adj1] *burning, corrosive*
abrasive, acerbic, acid, acrid, alkaline, astringent, biting, corroding, erosive, keen, mordant, pungent, tart; SEE CONCEPT 485

caustic [adj2] *sarcastic*
acerb, acerbic, acrimonious, bitter, cutting, harsh, incisive, pithy, pungent, rough, salty, satiric, scathing, severe, sharp, stinging, trenchant, virulent; SEE CONCEPT 267

caution [n1] *alertness, carefulness*
attention, canniness, care, circumspection, deliberation, discreetness, discretion, Fabian policy, foresight, forethought, heed, heedfulness, providence, prudence, vigilance, watchfulness; SEE CONCEPT 410

caution [n2] *warning*
admonition, advice, bug in one's ear*, caveat, commonition, counsel, forewarning, hint, injunction, monition, notice, omen, premonition, sign, tip*, tip-off*; SEE CONCEPTS 78,274

caution [v] *warn, advise*
admonish, alert, exhort, flag, forewarn, give the high sign*, give the lowdown on*, pull one's coat*, put one wise*, tip*, tip off*, urge, wave a red flag*, wise one up*; SEE CONCEPT 78

cautious [adj] *careful, guarded*
alert, all ears*, cagey, calculating, chary, circum-

ca
ca

spect, considerate, discreet, forethoughtful, gingerly, hedging one's bets*, heedful, judicious, keeping on one's toes*, leery, on the lookout*, playing it cool*, playing safe*, politic, provident, prudent, pussyfoot*, safe, shrewd, taking it easy, taking it slow*, tentative, thinking twice*, vigilant, walking on eggs*, wary, watchful, watching one's step*, watching out, with one's eyes peeled*; SEE CONCEPTS 401,403

cavalcade [n] *parade*
array, drill, march-past, procession, promenade, review, spectacle, train; SEE CONCEPT 432

cavalier [adj] *arrogant*
condescending, curt, disdainful, haughty, high-and-mighty*, insolent, lofty, lordly, offhand, overbearing, proud, scornful, snooty*, snotty*, supercilious, superior; SEE CONCEPT 401

cavalry [n] *troops riding horses*
army, bowlegs*, chasseurs, cuirassiers, dragoons, horse, horse soldiers, hussars, lancers, mounted troops, Mounties, rangers, squadron, uhlans; SEE CONCEPT 322

cave [n] *hole in land formation*
cavern, cavity, den, grotto, hollow, pothole, rock shelter, subterrane, subterranean area; SEE CONCEPT 509

caveat [n] *warning*
admonition, alarm, caution, commonition, forewarning, monition, sign; SEE CONCEPTS 78,274

cavern [n] *hollow in land formation*
cave, grotto, hole, pothole, subterrane, subterranean area; SEE CONCEPT 509

cavernous [adj] *hollow and large*
alveolate, broad, chambered, chasmal, commodious, concave, curved inward, deep, deep-set, echoing, gaping, huge, resonant, reverberant, roomy, sepulchral, socketed, spacious, sunken, vast, wide, yawning; SEE CONCEPTS 490,773,796

cavity [n] *sunken or decayed area*
atrium, basin, bursa, caries, chamber, crater, decay, dent, depression, gap, hole, hollow, pit, pocket, sinus, socket, vacuity, void; SEE CONCEPT 513

cavort [v] *frolic, prance*
caper, caracole, carry on*, cut loose*, cut up*, dance, fool around*, frisk, gambol, go places and do things*, horse around*, horseplay, monkey around*, play, revel, rollick, romp, roughhouse*, sport; SEE CONCEPTS 114,384

cease [v] *stop, conclude*
back off, break off, bring to an end, call it a day*, call it quits*, close, close out, come to an end, culminate, cut it out*, desist, die, discontinue, drop, end, fail, finish, give over, halt, intermit, knock off*, leave off, pack in*, quit, quit cold turkey*, refrain, shut down, stay, surcease, terminate, wind up*; SEE CONCEPT 234

ceaseless [adj] *never-ending*
amaranthine, constant, continual, continuous, day and night*, endless, eternal, everlasting, incessant, indefatigable, interminable, nonstop, on a treadmill*, perennial, perpetual, round the clock*, unceasing, unending, uninterrupted, unremitting, untiring, world-without-end*; SEE CONCEPT 798

cede [v] *abandon, surrender*
abalienate, abdicate, accord, alien, alienate, allow, capitulate, come across with*, communicate, concede, convey, deed, drop, fold*, fork over*, give in*, give up, grant, hand over*, leave, make over, part with, relinquish, remise, renounce, re-

sign, sign over, throw in the sponge*, throw in the towel*, transfer, vouchsafe, waive, yield; SEE CONCEPTS 108,127

ceiling [n1] *top of a room*
baldachin, beam, canopy, covert, dome, fan vaulting, groin, highest point, housetop, plafond, planchement, plaster, roof, roofing, timber, topside covering; SEE CONCEPT 440

ceiling [n2] *maximum*
legal price, record, superiority, top; SEE CONCEPT 836

celebrate [v] *commemorate occasion, achievement*
beat the drum*, bless, blow off steam*, carouse, ceremonialize, commend, consecrate, dedicate, drink to, eulogize, exalt, extol, feast, fete, glorify, hallow, have a ball*, honor, jubilate, keep, kick up one's heels*, laud, let loose*, lionize, live it up*, make merry, make whoopee*, mark with a red letter*, memorialize, observe, paint the town red*, party*, perform, praise, proclaim, publicize, raise hell*, rejoice, revel, revere, ritualize, signalize, solemnize; SEE CONCEPT 377

celebrated [adj] *distinguished, famous*
acclaimed, big*, eminent, famed, glorious, great, high-powered, illustrious, immortal, important, large, laureate, lionized, notable, number one*, numero uno*, outstanding, popular, preeminent, prominent, renowned, revered, storied, up there*, well-known, w.k.*; SEE CONCEPT 568

celebration [n] *commemoration of occasion, achievement*
anniversary, bash*, birthday, blast*, blowout*, carousal, ceremony, conviviality, festival, festivity, fete, frolic, gaiety, gala, glorification, hilarity, honoring, hoopla, hullabaloo*, jollification, joviality, jubilation, jubilee, keeping, magnification, memorialization, merriment, merrymaking, observance, party, performance, recognition, remembrance, revelry, saturnalia, solemnization, spree, triumph, wingding*; SEE CONCEPT 377

celebrity [n1] *dignitary*
ace, big cheese*, big deal*, big gun*, big name*, big shot*, big stuff*, bigwig*, celeb*, cynosure, famous person, figure, heavyweight, hero, hotshot*, immortal, lion*, luminary, magnate, mahatma, major leaguer*, name, notable, personage, personality, somebody, someone, star, superstar, the cheese*, VIP, worthy; SEE CONCEPT 423

celebrity [n2] *fame, notoriety*
distinction, éclat, eminence, glory, honor, notability, popularity, preeminence, prestige, prominence, renown, reputation, repute, stardom; SEE CONCEPTS 388,668

celerity [n] *swiftness*
alacrity, briskness, dispatch, expedition, expeditiousness, fleetness, gait, haste, hurry, hustle, legerity, promptness, quickness, rapidity, speed, speediness, swiftness, velocity, vivacity; SEE CONCEPT 755

celestial [adj] *heavenly*
angelic, astral, beatific, blessed, divine, elysian, empyral, empyrean, eternal, ethereal, godlike, hallowed, holy, immortal, Olympian, otherworldly, seraphic, spiritual, sublime, supernal, supernatural, transcendental, transmundane; SEE CONCEPTS 536,673

celibacy [n] *abstinence from sexual activity*
abstention, chastity, continence, frigidity, impotence, maidenhood, purity, singleness, virginity, virtue; SEE CONCEPT 388

celibate [adj] *abstaining from sexual activity*
chaste, continent, pure, virgin, virginal, virtuous; SEE CONCEPT 372

cell [n1] *smallest living organism*
bacterium, cellule, corpuscle, egg, embryo, follicle, germ, haematid, microorganism, spore, unit, utricle, vacuole; SEE CONCEPTS 389,478

cell [n2] *small room, container*
alcove, antechamber, apartment, bastille, booth, burrow, cage, cavity, chamber, cloister, closet, compartment, coop, crib, crypt, cubicle, den, dungeon, hold, hole, keep, lockup, nook, pen, receptacle, recess, retreat, stall, tower, vault; SEE CONCEPTS 448,494,513

cellar [n] *underground story of building*
apartment, basement, subbasement, subterrane, underground room, vault; SEE CONCEPTS 440,448

cement [n] *gluing, binding material*
adhesive, binder, birdlime, bond, concrete, epoxy, glue, grout, gum, gunk*, lime, lute, mortar, mucilage, mud*, paste, plaster, putty, rubber cement, sand, sealant, size, solder, stickum*, tar; SEE CONCEPT 475

cement [v] *attach securely, often with sticky material*
bind, blend, bond, cohere, combine, connect, fasten, fuse, glue, gum, join, merge, mortar, paste, plaster, seal, solder, stick together, unite, weld; SEE CONCEPTS 85,160

cemetery [n] *burial ground*
boot hill*, catacomb, charnel, charnel house, churchyard, city of the dead*, crypt, eternal home*, funerary grounds, garden, God's acre*, Golgotha, grave, graveyard, marble town*, memorial park, mortuary, necropolis, ossuary, polyandrium, potter's field, resting place, sepulcher, tomb, vault; SEE CONCEPTS 305,368

censor [v] *forbid; ban; selectively remove*
abridge, blacklist, black out*, bleach, bleep*, blue-pencil*, bowdlerize, clean up, conceal, control, cork*, criticize, cut, decontaminate, delete, drop the iron curtain*, edit, examine, excise, expurgate, exscind, inspect, launder*, narrow, oversee, prevent publication, purge, purify, put the lid on*, refuse transmission, repress, restrain, restrict, review, revile, sanitize, scissor out*, squelch, sterilize, strike out, supervise communications, suppress, withhold; SEE CONCEPTS 121,266

censorious [adj] *very critical*
accusatory, captious, carping, caviling, cavillous, chiding, complaining, condemnatory, condemning, critical, culpatory, denouncing, disapproving, disparaging, fault-finding, hypercritical, overcritical, reprehending, reproaching, severe; SEE CONCEPT 267

censorship [n] *forbiddance; ban*
blackout*, blue pencil*, bowdlerization, control, forbidding, hush up*, infringing on rights, iron curtain*, restriction, suppression, thought control*; SEE CONCEPTS 376,388

censure [n] *severe criticism*
admonishment, admonition, blame, castigation, condemnation, disapproval, dressing down, objection, obloquy, rebuke, remonstrance, reprehension, reprimand, reproach, reproof, stricture; SEE CONCEPTS 52,410

censure [v] *condemn; criticize severely*
abuse, admonish, animadvert, asperse, attack, backbite, berate, blame, carp at, castigate, cavil,

chastise, chide, contemn, cut up*, denigrate, denounce, deprecate, disapprove, discipline, disparage, exprobate, find fault with, get after, impugn, incriminate, judge, knock, lecture, look askance, ostracize, pick apart, pull apart, read out*, rebuff, rebuke, remonstrate, reprehend, reprimand, reproach, reprove, scold, take to task*, tear apart*, tell off, upbraid; SEE CONCEPT 52

center [n1] *middle point*
axis, bull's-eye, centrality, centriole, centrum, core, cynosure, equidistance, essence, focal point, focus, gist, heart, hotbed, hub, inside, interior, intermediacy, kernel, mainstream*, marrow, middle of the road*, midpoint, midst, nave, navel, nucleus, omphalos, pith, pivot, place, polestar, quick, radial point, root, seat; SEE CONCEPT 830

center [n2] *point of attraction for visitors, shoppers, travelers*
capital, city, club, concourse, crossroads, focal point, focus, heart, hub, mall, market, marketplace, mart, meeting place, metropolis, nerve center, plaza, polestar, shopping center, social center, station, town, trading center; SEE CONCEPTS 435,438,507

center [adj] *middle*
at halfway point, centermost, deepest, equidistant, inmost, inner, innermost, inside, interior, intermediary, intermediate, internal, mean, medial, mid, middlemost, midpoint, midway; SEE CONCEPTS 583,585,830

center [v] *concentrate, draw together*
attract, bring to a focus, bring together, centralize, close on, collect, concenter, consolidate, converge upon, focalize, focus, gather, intensify, join, medialize, meet, unify; SEE CONCEPTS 35,84

central [adj] *main, principal; in the middle*
axial, basic, cardinal, center, centric, centroidal, chief, dominant, equidistant, essential, focal, foremost, fundamental, important, inmost, inner, interior, intermediate, key, leading, master, mean, median, mid, middle, middlemost, midmost, midway, nuclear, outstanding, overriding, paramount, pivotal, predominant, primary, prime, radical, ruling, salient, significant, umbilical; SEE CONCEPTS 567,583,830

centralize [v] *concentrate, draw toward a point*
accumulate, amalgamate, assemble, compact, concenter, condense, consolidate, converge, focus, gather, incorporate, integrate, organize, rationalize, streamline, systematize, unify; SEE CONCEPTS 35,84

centrifugal [adj] *radiating from a central point*
deviating, diffusive, divergent, diverging, eccentric, efferent, outward, radial, spiral, spreading; SEE CONCEPTS 581,584

ceremonial [adj] *ritual, formal*
august, conventional, imposing, liturgical, lofty, mannered, ritualistic, solemn, stately, studied, stylized; SEE CONCEPT 548

ceremonious [adj] *ritual, formal*
civil, courteous, courtly, decorous, deferential, dignified, exact, grandiose, impressive, majestic, moving, precise, proper, punctilious, seemly, solemn, starchy, stately, stiff, striking; SEE CONCEPT 548

ceremony [n1] *ritual; celebratory observation*
ceremonial, commemoration, custom, formality, function, liturgy, observance, ordinance, parade, rite, sacrament, service, show, solemnity, tradition; SEE CONCEPT 386

ca
ce

ceremony [n2] *etiquette*
ceremonial, conformity, decorum, form, formal courtesy, formalism, formality, nicety, politeness, pomp, preciseness, prescription, propriety, protocol, strictness, usage; SEE CONCEPT *388*

certain [adj1] *confident*
assertive, assured, believing, calm, cocksure, convinced, positive, questionless, sanguine, satisfied, secure, self-confident, sure, unconcerned, undisturbed, undoubtful, undoubting, unperturbed, untroubled; SEE CONCEPT *403*

certain [adj2] *undoubtable, valid*
absolute, ascertained, authoritative, clear, conclusive, confirmable, definite, demonstrable, destined, determined, establishable, evident, firm, fixed, genuine, guaranteed, having down pat*, incontrovertible, indubitable, infallible, in the bag*, irrefutable, known, on ice*, plain, positive, predestined, provable, real, reliable, safe, salted away*, set, sound, supreme, sure, sure thing*, true, trustworthy, unambiguous, undeniable, undoubted, unequivocal, unerring, unmistakable, verifiable; SEE CONCEPTS *535,582*

certain [adj3] *fixed*
assured, bound, certified, concluded, decided, definite, determined, ensured, established, guaranteed, insured, set, settled, stated, stipulated, sure, warranted; SEE CONCEPT *535*

certain [adj4] *referring to a specifically known amount*
a couple, a few, defined, divers, express, individual, many, marked, numerous, one, particular, precise, regular, several, singular, some, special, specific, specified, sundry, upwards of, various; SEE CONCEPT *557*

certainly [adv] *without doubt*
absolutely, assuredly, cert*, exactly, for a fact, of course, positively, posolutely*, right on*, surely, unquestionably, without fail; SEE CONCEPT *535*

certainty [n1] *positive assurance*
all sewn up*, authoritativeness, belief, certitude, cinch, confidence, conviction, credence, definiteness, dogmatism, faith, firmness, indubitableness, inevitability, lock*, lockup*, open and shut case*, positiveness, positivism, rain or shine*, setup, shoo-in*, staunchness, steadiness, stock, store, sure bet*, surefire*, sureness, sure thing*, surety, trust, validity, wrap-up; SEE CONCEPTS *638,725*

certainty [n2] *fact, resulting truth*
consequence, foregone conclusion, inevitable result, reality, sure thing*, surety; SEE CONCEPT *230*

certificate [n] *authorizing document*
affidavit, affirmation, attestation, authentication, authorization, certification, coupon, credential, deed, diploma, docket, documentation, endorsement, guarantee, license, paper, pass, permit, receipt, record, sheepskin*, shingle, testament, testification, testimonial, testimony, ticket, voucher, warrant, warranty; SEE CONCEPTS *271,685*

certify [v] *declare as true*
accredit, approve, ascertain, assure, attest, authenticate, authorize, aver, avow, commission, confirm, corroborate, endorse, guarantee, license, notify, okay, profess, reassure, rubber-stamp*, sanction, show, state, swear, testify, validate, verify, vouch, witness; SEE CONCEPTS *50,88*

cessation [n] *ending*
abeyance, arrest, break, break-off*, breather*, cease, ceasing, close, conclusion, cutoff*, desistance, discontinuance, downtime*, end, finish, freeze*, grinding halt, halt, halting, hiatus, intermission, interruption, interval, layoff*, let-up*, pause, recess, remission, respite, rest, screaming halt*, standstill, stay, stop, stoppage, suspension, termination, time off, time-out*; SEE CONCEPT *119*

chafe [v1] *rub, grind against*
abrade, bark, corrode, damage, erode, excoriate, gall, grate, graze, hurt, impair, inflame, irritate, peel, ruffle, scrape, scratch, skin, wear; SEE CONCEPT *215*

chafe [v2] *annoy*
abrade, anger, annoy, bother, exasperate, exercise, fret, fume, gall, grate, harass, incense, inflame, irk, irritate, itch, offend, provoke, rage, rasp, rub, ruffle, scrape, scratch, vex, worry; SEE CONCEPTS *7,19*

chaff [n] *waste*
crust, debris, dregs, husks, pod, refuse, remains, rubbish, shard, shell, trash; SEE CONCEPT *679*

chaff [v] *joke, ridicule*
banter, deride, fun, jeer, jolly, josh, kid, mock, rag*, rally, razz*, rib*, scoff, taunt, tease; SEE CONCEPT *273*

chagrin [n] *displeasure*
annoyance, balk, blow, crushing, discomfiture, discomposure, disgruntlement, dismay, disquiet, dissatisfaction, embarrassment, fretfulness, frustration, humiliation, ill-humor, irritation, letdown, mortification, peevishness, shame, spleen, upset, vexation; SEE CONCEPTS *410,674*

chagrin [v] *cause displeasure*
abash, annoy, confuse, crush, discomfit, discompose, disconcert, disgrace, dismay, displease, disquiet, dissatisfy, embarrass, humiliate, irk, irritate, mortify, peeve, perturb, shame, upset, vex; SEE CONCEPTS *7,19*

chain [n1] *succession, series*
alternation, catena, concatenation, conglomerate, consecution, continuity, group, order, progression, row, sequence, set, string, syndicate, train, trust; SEE CONCEPTS *432,727,769*

chain [n2] *connected metal links; jewelry made of such links*
bond, bracelet, cable, clinker*, connection, coupling, fetter, iron, lavaliere, link, locket, manacle, pendant, shackle, trammel; SEE CONCEPTS *446,476,499*

chain [v] *manacle in metal*
attach, bind, confine, connect, enslave, fetter, handcuff, hold, moor, restrain, shackle, tether, tie up, trammel; SEE CONCEPTS *85,160*

chair [n1] *single-seat furniture*
armchair, bench, cathedra, recliner, rocker, sling*; SEE CONCEPT *443*

chair [n2] *person in or position of authority*
captain, chairperson, director, fellowship, helm, instructorship, leader, monitor, position of control, principal, professorate, professorship, throne, tutor, tutorship; SEE CONCEPTS *348,376*

chairperson [n] *person in charge of proceedings*
administrator, captain, chair, director, introducer, leader, moderator, monitor, president, presider, principal, prolocutor, speaker, spokesperson, symposiarch; SEE CONCEPTS *348,376*

challenge [n] *dispute, question*
claiming, confrontation, dare, defiance, demanding, demur, interrogation, objection, protest,

provocation, remonstrance, summons to contest, test, threat, trial, ultimatum; SEE CONCEPTS 53,532

challenge [v] *dispute, question*
accost, arouse, ask for, assert, beard, brave, call for, call out, claim, confront, cross, dare, defy, demand, denounce, exact, face down, face off, face the music*, fly in the face of*, hang in*, impeach, impose, impugn, inquire, insist upon, investigate, invite competition, make a point of, make a stand, object to, provoke, query, reclaim, require, search out, stand up to, stick it out, stimulate, summon, tax, test, throw down the gauntlet*, try, vindicate; SEE CONCEPT 53

chamber [n1] *small compartment, room*
alcove, antechamber, apartment, bedchamber, bedroom, box, case, cavity, cell, chest, container, cubicle, enclosure, flat, hall, hollow, lodging, pocket, room, socket; SEE CONCEPTS 448,494

chamber [n2] *legislative body*
assembly, council, legislature, organization, representatives; SEE CONCEPT 299

champion [n] *defeater in competition; preeminent supporter*
advocate, ally, backer, challenger, champ, conqueror, defender, endorser, exponent, expounder, guardian, hero, heroine, medalist, nonpareil, number one*, numero uno*, paladin, partisan, patron, proponent, protector, supporter, sympathizer, the greatest*, titleholder, top dog*, upholder, vanquisher, victor, vindicator, warrior, winner; SEE CONCEPT 366

champion [adj] *best, excellent*
blue-ribbon, boss*, capital, chief, choice, cool, dandy, distinguished, first, greatest, head, illustrious, out of sight*, out of this world*, outstanding, premier, prime, principal, prize-winning, splendid, super, superior, tip top*, top drawer*, topflight*, top-notch*, tops*, unbeaten, undefeated, world class*; SEE CONCEPT 574

champion [v] *advocate, support*
back, battle, contend, defend, espouse, fight for, go to bat for*, patronize, plead for, promote, put in a good word for*, ride shotgun for*, side with, stand behind, stand up for, support, thump for, uphold; SEE CONCEPTS 10,69

chance [n1] *possibility, probability*
break, contingency, fair shake*, fighting chance*, indications, liability, likelihood, long shot*, look-in, occasion, odds, opening, opportunity, outlook, prospect, scope, shot*, show, squeak, time, wager; SEE CONCEPT 650

chance [n2] *fate, luck*
accident, advantage, adventure, bad luck, break, cast, casualty, coincidence, contingency, destination, destiny, doom, even chance, fluke, fortuity, fortune, future, gamble, good luck, hap*, haphazard, happening, hazard, heads or tails*, hit*, in the cards*, kismet, lot, lottery, luck out*, lucky break, misfortune, occurrence, odds, outcome, peradventure, peril, providence, risk, stroke of luck*, throw of the dice*, toss-up*, turn of the cards*, way the cookie crumbles*, wheel of fortune*; SEE CONCEPT 679

chance [n3] *gamble, risk*
bet, craps game*, fall of the cards*, hazard, jeopardy, lottery, raffle, speculation, stake, throw of the dice*, try, venture, wager; SEE CONCEPT 363

chance [adj] *accidental, unforeseeable*
adventitious, at random, casual, contingent, fluky,

fortuitous, fortunate, happy, inadvertent, incidental, lucky, odd, offhand, unforeseen, unintentional, unlooked for, unplanned; SEE CONCEPT 552

chance [v1] *risk, endanger*
attempt, cast lots, draw lots, gamble, go out on a limb, have a fling at, hazard, jeopardize, play with fire*, plunge, put eggs in one basket*, put it on the line*, roll the dice*, run the risk, skate on thin ice*, speculate, stake, stick one's neck out*, take shot in the dark*, tempt fate*, tempt fortune*, toss up*, try, venture, wager, wildcat; SEE CONCEPT 87

chance [v2] *happen*
arrive, befall, be one's fate, betide, blunder on, break, bump, come, come about, come off, come to pass, fall out, fall to one's lot, go, hap*, hit upon, light, light upon, luck, meet, occur, stumble, stumble on, transpire, tumble, turn up; SEE CONCEPT 4

chancy [adj] *dangerous, risky*
capricious, contingent, dicey, erratic, fluctuant, fluky, hazardous, iffy*, incalculable, precarious, problematic, problematical, rocky, speculative, ticklish, touchy, tricky, uncertain, unpredictable, unsound, whimsical; SEE CONCEPTS 552,587

chandelier [n] *light hanging from ceiling*
candelabrum, candleholder, corona, crown, electrolier, gasolier, light fixture, luster; SEE CONCEPT 444

change [n1] *something made different; alteration*
about-face*, addition, adjustment, advance, break, compression, contraction, conversion, correction, development, difference, distortion, diversification, diversity, innovation, metamorphosis, modification, modulation, mutation, novelty, permutation, reconstruction, refinement, remodeling, reversal, revision, revolution, shift, surrogate, switch, tempering, transformation, transition, transmutation, turn, turnover, variance, variation, variety, vicissitude; SEE CONCEPTS 230,260,701

change [n2] *substitution; replacement*
conversion, exchange, flip-flop*, interchange, swap, switch, trade, turnaround; SEE CONCEPT 128

change [n3] *smaller currency in exchange for larger*
chicken feed*, coins, copper, dimes, nickels, pennies, pin money*, pocket money, quarters, silver, spending money; SEE CONCEPT 340

change [v1] *make or become different*
accommodate, adapt, adjust, alter, alternate, commute, convert, diminish, diverge, diversify, evolve, fluctuate, make innovations, make over, merge, metamorphose, moderate, modify, modulate, mutate, naturalize, recondition, redo, reduce, reform, regenerate, remake, remodel, renovate, reorganize, replace, resolve, restyle, revolutionize, shape, shift, substitute, tamper with, temper, transfigure, transform, translate, transmute, transpose, turn, vacillate, vary, veer, warp; SEE CONCEPTS 228,232,235,701

change [v2] *substitute, replace*
alternate, barter, convert, displace, exchange, interchange, invert, remove, reverse, shift, supplant, swap, switch around, trade, transmit, transpose; SEE CONCEPT 128

changeable [adj] *erratic*
agitated, capricious, changeful, commutative,

ce
ch

convertible, fickle, fitful, flighty, fluctuating, fluid, impulsive, inconstant, indecisive, irregular, irresolute, irresponsible, kaleidoscopic, mercurial, mobile, movable, mutable, permutable, protean, restless, reversible, revocable, shifting, skittish, spasmodic, transformable, transitional, uncertain, unpredictable, unreliable, unsettled, unstable, unsteady, vacillating, vagrant, variable, variant, varying, versatile, volatile, wavering, whimsical; SEE CONCEPT *534*

channel [*n1*] *pathway, usually containing water*
approach, aqueduct, arroyo, artery, avenue, canal, canyon, carrier, chamber, chase, conduit, course, dig, ditch, duct, fluting, furrow, gouge, groove, gully, gutter, main, means, medium, pass, passage, pipe, raceway, route, runway, sewer, slit, sound, strait, tideway, trough, tube, tunnel, vein, watercourse, way; SEE CONCEPTS *501,514*

channel [*n2*] *means*
agency, agent, approach, avenue, course, instrument, instrumentality, instrumentation, medium, ministry, organ, route, vehicle, way; SEE CONCEPTS *6,660,770*

channel [*v*] *direct, guide*
carry, conduct, convey, funnel, pipe, route, send, siphon, traject, transmit, transport; SEE CONCEPTS *187,217*

chant [*n*] *chorus of song*
carol, croon, hymn, incantation, intonation, lilt, melody, psalm, shout, singing, song, trill, tune, warble; SEE CONCEPTS *263,595*

chant [*v*] *sing simple song or song part*
cantillate, carol, chofus, croon, descant, doxologize, drone, intone, recite, shout, tune, vocalize, warble; SEE CONCEPTS *65,77*

chaos [*n*] *utter confusion*
anarchy, ataxia, bedlam, clutter, disarray, discord, disorder, disorganization, entropy, free-for-all*, holy mess*, lawlessness, misrule, mix-up, mobocracy, muddle, pandemonium, rat's nest*, snarl, topsy-turviness*, tumult, turmoil, unruliness; SEE CONCEPTS *230,674*

chaotic [*adj*] *utterly confused*
anarchic, deranged, disordered, disorganized, every which way*, harum-scarum*, helter-skelter*, lawless, purposeless, rampageous, riotous, topsy-turvy*, tumultuous, turbid, turbulent, uncontrolled; SEE CONCEPT *548*

chaperon [*n*] *person who accompanies for supervision*
alarm clock*, babysitter*, bird dog*, companion, escort; SEE CONCEPT *423*

chaperon [*v*] *accompany for supervision*
attend, carry, conduct, consort with, convoy, escort, guide, oversee, protect, safeguard, shepherd, supervise, watch over; SEE CONCEPTS *114,714*

chaplain [*n*] *minister in church*
cleric, member of clergy, pastor, preacher, priest, rabbi, turn-around collar*; SEE CONCEPT *361*

chapter [*n*] *section of book or group of items*
affiliate, branch, clause, division, episode, member, offshoot, part, period, phase, stage, topic, unit, wing; SEE CONCEPTS *270,382,832*

char [*v*] *scorch, sear*
burn, carbonize, cauterize, singe; SEE CONCEPT *249*

character [*n1*] *individuality*
appearance, aspect, attribute, badge, bent, caliber, cast, complex, complexion, constitution, cra-

sis, disposition, emotions, estimation, ethos, frame, frame of mind, genius, grain, habit, humor, kind, makeup, mettle, mood, morale, mystique, nature, personality, quality, record, reputation, repute, sense, set, shape, singularity, sort, specialty, spirit, standing, streak, style, temper, temperament, tone, trait, turn, type, vein; SEE CONCEPT *411*

character [*n2*] *integrity*
courage, fame, honor, intelligence, mind, name, place, position, rank, rectitude, rep, report, reputation, repute, standing, station, status, uprightness; SEE CONCEPT *668*

character [*n3*] *odd person*
card*, case*, clown, crank*, customer*, duck*, eccentric, figure, freak, nut, oddball, oddity, original*, personage, personality, queer, spook*, wack*, weirdo, zombie*; SEE CONCEPTS *412,423*

character [*n4*] *written symbol*
cipher, device, emblem, figure, hieroglyph, letter, logo, mark, monogram, number, numeral, rune, sign, type; SEE CONCEPT *284*

character [*n5*] *portrayal of another*
impersonation, part, personification, role; SEE CONCEPTS *263,352*

characteristic [*n*] *typical feature, trait*
affection, aspect, attribute, badge, bag, bearing, bent, caliber, cast, complexion, component, differentia, disposition, distinction, earmark, endowment, essence, essential, faculty, flavor, frame, idiosyncrasy, inclination, individuality, lineament, mannerism, mark, mood, nature, originality, particularity, peculiarity, personality, point, property, quality, singularity, specialty, streak, stripe, style, symptom, temperament, tendency, thing, thumbprint, tinge, tone, trademark, turn, virtue; SEE CONCEPT *411*

characteristic [*adj*] *typical; distinguishing*
appropriate, diagnostic, differentiating, discriminating, discriminative, distinctive, distinguishing, emblematic, especial, essential, exclusive, fixed, idiosyncratic, inborn, inbred, indicative, individual, individualistic, individualizing, ingrained, inherent, innate, local, marked, native, normal, original, particular, peculiar, personal, private, proper, regular, representative, singular, special, specific, symbolic, symptomatic, unique; SEE CONCEPTS *542,547,550*

characterize [*v*] *typify, distinguish*
belong to, brand, button down*, constitute, define, delineate, describe, designate, differentiate, discriminate, feature, identify, indicate, individualize, individuate, inform, make up, mark, outline, peculiarize, peg, personalize, pigeonhole*, portray, represent, signalize, singularize, stamp, style, symbolize, tab, typecast; SEE CONCEPT *644*

charade [*n*] *pretense*
deception, disguise, fake, farce, make-believe, mimicry, pageant, pantomime, parody, pretension, pretentiousness, put-on, travesty, trick; SEE CONCEPT *59*

charge [*n1*] *accusation*
allegation, beef*, complaint, gripe, imputation, indictment, plaint, stink*; SEE CONCEPTS *44,317*

charge [*n2*] *attack*
assault, blitz, blitzkrieg, invasion, mugging, onset, onslaught, outbreak, push, rush, sortie; SEE CONCEPT *86*

charge [*n3*] *burden*
care, commitment, committal, concern, custody,

deadweight, duty, millstone, must, need, obligation, office, onus, ought, responsibility, right, safekeeping, task, tax, trust, ward, weight; SEE CONCEPTS 532,709

charge [n4] *price asked for something*
amount, bad news*, bite, cost, damage, expenditure, expense, nick, outlay, payment, price, price tag, rate, squeeze, tab, tariff, tick; SEE CONCEPT 329

charge [n5] *command*
behest, bidding, dictate, direction, exhortation, injunction, instruction, mandate, order, precept, word; SEE CONCEPTS 53,274

charge [n6] *supervisory responsibility*
care, conduct, custody, handling, intendance, management, oversight, running, superintendence, superintendency, supervision, ward; SEE CONCEPT 117

charge [v1] *accuse*
arraign, blame, blow the whistle on*, censure, criminate, drag into court*, finger*, hang something on*, impeach, impugn, impute, incriminate, inculpate, indict, involve, peg, point the finger at*, reprehend, reproach, tax, turn on, whistleblow*; SEE CONCEPTS 44,317

charge [v2] *attack*
assail, assault, blindside, bolt, buck, bushwhack*, chase, dash, invade, jump on, lunge, mug, rush, smash, stampede, storm, tear; SEE CONCEPT 86

charge [v3] *load, tax*
afflict, burden, choke, clog, commit, cram, crowd, cumber, encumber, entrust, fill, heap, impregnate, instill, lade, pack, penetrate, permeate, pervade, pile, ram, saddle, saturate, suffuse, transfuse, weigh; SEE CONCEPTS 107,156,740

charge [v4] *order something done*
adjure, ask, bid, command, direct, enjoin, entrust, exhort, instruct, request, require, solicit, tell, warn; SEE CONCEPTS 53,78

charge [v5] *ask a price*
demand, fix price at, impose, levy, price, require, sell for; SEE CONCEPTS 330,345

charge [v6] *pay with credit card*
book, buy on credit, chalk up, cuff, debit, encumber, go into hock*, incur debt, nick*, paste*, put on account, put on one's card, put on the cuff, put on the tab, receive credit, run up; SEE CONCEPTS 327,330

charisma [n] *great personal charm*
allure, animal magnetism*, appeal, dazzle, drawing power, fascination, flash, glamour, it*, magnetism, pizzazz*, something*, star quality, witchcraft, witchery; SEE CONCEPT 411

charitable [adj1] *giving, generous*
accommodating, all heart, altruistic, beneficent, benevolent, benign, big*, bighearted*, bountiful, eleemosynary, good, helpful, humane, humanitarian, kind, kindly, lavish, liberal, obliging, philanthropic, sympathetic; SEE CONCEPTS 334,542

charitable [adj2] *kind, lenient*
all heart*, benevolent, big*, bighearted*, broadminded, clement, considerate, easy, favorable, forbearing, forgiving, gracious, humane, indulgent, kindly, lenient, magnanimous, merciful, sympathetic, thoughtful, tolerant, understanding; SEE CONCEPT 404

charity [n1] *generosity, gift*
alms, alms-giving, assistance, benefaction, beneficence, contribution, dole, donation, endowment, fund, gifting, hand*, hand-out, helping hand*,

largesse, oblation, offering, philanthropy, relief, write-off; SEE CONCEPTS 337,657

charity [n2] *kindness, compassion*
affection, agape, altruism, amity, attachment, benevolence, benignity, bountifulness, bounty, caritas, clemency, fellow feeling, generosity, goodness, goodwill, grace, humaneness, humanity, indulgence, kindliness, lenity, love, magnanimity, mercy, tenderheartedness; SEE CONCEPTS 32,411

charm [n1] *enchantment, allure*
agreeableness, allurement, appeal, attraction, attractiveness, beauty, bewitchery, charisma, chemistry, conjuration, delightfulness, desirability, fascination, glamour, grace, it*, lure, magic, magnetism, pizzazz*, something*, sorcery, spell, star quality, witchery; SEE CONCEPTS 411,673

charm [n2] *talisman*
amulet, fetish, good-luck piece, juju, lucky piece, madstone, mascot, phylactery, rabbit's foot, trinket, zemi; SEE CONCEPTS 284,446

charm [v] *enchant*
allure, attract, beguile, bewitch, cajole, captivate, delight, draw, enamor, enrapture, ensorcell, enthrall, entrance, fascinate, grab, hex, hypnotize, inveigle, kill*, knock dead*, knock out*, magnetize, mesmerize, please, possess, put under a spell*, send*, slay*, spell*, sweep off feet*, take*, tickle, tickle pink*, transport, turn on*, vamp, voodoo, wile, win, win over, wow*; SEE CONCEPTS 7,22

charming [adj] *captivating*
absorbing, alluring, amiable, appealing, attractive, bewitching, charismatic, choice, cute, dainty, delectable, delicate, delightful, desirable, electrifying, elegant, enamoring, engaging, engrossing, enthralling, entrancing, eye-catching, fascinating, fetching, glamorous, graceful, infatuating, inviting, irresistible, likable, lovable, lovely, magnetizing, nice, pleasant, pleasing, provocative, rapturous, ravishing, seducing, seductive, sweet, tantalizing, tempting, titillating, winning, winsome; SEE CONCEPT 404

chart [n] *map, plan*
blueprint, diagram, graph, outline, plat, plot, rough draft, scheme, sketch, table, tabulation; SEE CONCEPTS 625,660

chart [v] *plan, map out*
arrange, block out, blueprint, cast, delineate, design, devise, draft, graph, lay out, outline, plot, project, shape, sketch; SEE CONCEPTS 36,174

charter [n] *treaty, agreement*
allotment, bond, code, concession, constitution, contract, conveyance, deed, document, endowment, franchise, grant, indenture, license, pact, patent, permit, prerogative, privilege, right, settlement; SEE CONCEPTS 684,685

charter [v] *reserve, commission*
allow, authorize, borrow, contract, employ, engage, hire, lease, let, license, permit, rent, sanction; SEE CONCEPTS 48,50,88,89

chary [adj] *careful, cautious*
cagey, calculating, canny, circumspect, considerate, constrained, discreet, economical, fastidious, frugal, gingerly, guarded, heedful, hesitant, inhibited, leery, loath, miserly, particular, prudent, reluctant, restrained, safe, scrupulous, sparing, stingy, suspicious, thrifty, uneasy, wary, watchful; SEE CONCEPTS 401,587

ch
ch

chase [n] *pursuit*

hunt, hunting, quest, race, venery; SEE CONCEPT 207

chase [v] *run after, pursue*

bird-dog*, charge, chivy, course, drive, drive away, expel, follow, go after, hound, hunt, run down, rush, seek, shag*, speed, take off after*, tear, track, track down, trail; SEE CONCEPT 207

chasm [n] *gap, abyss*

abysm, alienation, arroyo, blank, breach, cavity, cleavage, cleft, clough, clove, crater, crevasse, fissure, flume, gorge, gulch, gulf, hiatus, hole, hollow, omission, opening, oversight, preterition, ravine, rent, rift, schism, skip, split, void, yawn; SEE CONCEPT 513

chaste [adj] *pure, incorrupt*

austere, celibate, clean, continent, controlled, decent, decorous, elegant, immaculate, impotent, inexperienced, innocent, intemerate, modest, monogamous, moral, neat, platonic, proper, prudish, quiet, refined, restrained, simple, spotless, stainless, subdued, unaffected, unblemished, uncontaminated, undefiled, unstained, unsullied, unwed, vestal, virginal, virtuous, wholesome; SEE CONCEPTS 372,404

chasten [v] *correct, humiliate*

abase, admonish, afflict, berate, call down, castigate, chastise, chide, cow, curb, discipline, exprobate, fulminate against, have on the carpet*, humble, objurgate, penalize, punish, rake over the coals*, rebuke, reprehend, repress, reprimand, reproach, reprove, restrain, scold, scourge, soften, subdue, take to task, tame, tongue-lash*, try, upbraid; SEE CONCEPTS 52,122

chastise [v] *scold, discipline*

baste, beat, berate, castigate, censure, chasten, chew out*, climb all over*, correct, ferule*, flog*, lash*, lay into*, lean on*, pummel, punish, ream, scourge, skelp, slap down*, spank, thrash, upbraid, whip; SEE CONCEPTS 52,122

chastity [n] *celibacy, purity*

abstemiousness, abstinence, chasteness, cleanness, continence, decency, demureness, devotion, honor, immaculacy, innocence, integrity, modesty, monogamy, morality, naïveté, restraint, singleness, sinlessness, spotlessness, temperance, uprightness, virginity, virtue; SEE CONCEPT 633

chat [n] *talk, often short*

babble, bull session, chatter, conversation, converse, gab*, gas*, gossip, heart-to-heart*, hot air*, jabber*, palaver, prattle*, rap*, rap session*, tête-à-tête, visit, yak*; SEE CONCEPT 278

chat [v] *talk, gossip*

babble, blab*, burble, cackle, chatter, chew the fat*, chew the rag*, converse, gab*, go on*, jaw*, prate, prattle*, run on*, shoot the breeze*, yap*; SEE CONCEPT 266

chatter [n] *constant or rapid talk*

babble, blather, chat, chitchat, gas*, gossip, jabber*, palaver, prattle*, twaddle, yakking*; SEE CONCEPTS 266,278

chatter [v] *speak fast and non-stop*

babble, blab*, blather, cackle, chat, chitchat, clack, gab*, gabble, gas*, gibber, go on and on, gossip, jabber, jaw*, natter, palaver, prate, prattle*, tattle, twaddle, twiddle, yak*; SEE CONCEPT 266

chatty [adj] *talkative*

colloquial, communicative, conversational, familiar, friendly, gabby, garrulous, gossipy, informal,

intimate, loose-lipped, loquacious, multieloquent, spontaneous, talky; SEE CONCEPT 267

chauvinism [n] *extreme devotion to a belief or nation*

bellicism, ethnocentricity, fanatical patriotism, fanaticism, jingoism, narrowness, nationalism, zealotry; SEE CONCEPT 689

cheap [adj1] *inexpensive*

at a bargain, bargain, bargain-basement*, bargain-counter, bought for a song*, budget, buy, cheapo*, competitive, cost next to nothing*, cut-price, cut-rate, depreciated, dime a dozen*, easy on the pocketbook*, economical, half-priced, irregular, low-cost, lowered, low-priced, low tariff, marked down, moderate, nominal, on sale, popularly priced, real buy*, reasonable, reduced, sale, slashed, standard, steal, uncostly, undear, utility, worth the money*; SEE CONCEPT 334

cheap [adj2] *inferior, low in quality*

bad, base, bogus, catchpenny, cheesy, common, commonplace, crappy*, cruddy, dud, flashy, garbage, garish, glitzy*, junky*, lousy, mangy, mean, mediocre, meretricious, no bargain*, no good, ordinary, paltry, poor, ratty, raunchy, rinky-dink*, rotten, rubbishy, scroungy, second-rate, shoddy, sleazy, small-time*, tatty, tawdry, terrible, trashy, trumpery, two-bit, valueless, white elephant*, worthless; SEE CONCEPT 589

cheap [adj3] *low, vulgar*

abject, base, beggarly, contemptible, despicable, dirty, dishonest, mean, pitiable, scurvy, shabby, sordid, sorry, tawdry, vile; SEE CONCEPT 542

cheap [adj4] *concerned with saving money*

mean, mingy, miserly, penny-pinching, stingy, thrifty, tight*, tight-wad*; SEE CONCEPT 332

cheapen [v] *diminish worth*

abase, beat down, belittle, corrupt, damage, debase, decline, decry, degrade, demean, denigrate, depreciate, derogate, devalue, discredit, disparage, downgrade, drop, fall, lose value, lower, mar, mark down, minimize, reduce, render worthless, ruin, spoil, undervalue, write off; SEE CONCEPT 240

cheat [n1] *person who fools others*

bluff, charlatan, chiseler, con artist, confidence operator, conniver, cozener, crook, deceiver, decoy, defrauder, dodger, double-crosser*, double-dealer*, enticer, fake, hypocrite, impostor, inveigler, jockey, masquerader, pretender, quack, rascal, rogue, scammer*, shark, sharper, shyster, swindler, trickster; SEE CONCEPT 412

cheat [n2] *trick*

artifice, baloney, bamboozlement*, bill of goods*, bunco, chicanery, con, con game, cover up, cozening, deceit, deception, dirty pool*, dirty trick*, dodge, double-dealing*, fake, fast one, fast shuffle*, fix, flimflam, frame, fraud, gyp, hanky-panky*, hoax, hoaxing, humbug, hustle, imposture, jazz, jive, plant, put-on, racket, rip-off, run around, scam, sell, shady deal, sham, shell game, snow job*, spoof, sting, stunt, swindle, trickery, whitewash, wrong; SEE CONCEPT 59

cheat [v1] *defraud, fool*

bamboozle*, beat, beguile, bilk, bleed, bunco, burn, caboodle, chisel, con, cozen, crib, cross, deceive, defraud, delude, diddle*, do*, do a number on*, double-cross, double-deal, dupe, fast talk, finagle, fleece, flimflam, fudge*, give bum steer*, gouge, gyp*, hoodwink, hose, jerk around, milk, mislead, pull one's leg*, ream*, rip off*, rook*, rope in*, sandbag, scam, screw, shaft, short, shuck, skin, snow, stiff, sucker, swindle, take, take for a ride*, take in, take out, trick, trim, two-time, victimize; SEE CONCEPTS 59,139,192

cheat [v2] *frustrate, thwart*
baffle, check, defeat, deprive, foil, prevent; SEE CONCEPT 121

check [n1] *inspection, examination*
analysis, audit, checkup, control, inquiry, investigation, poll, rein, research, review, scrutiny, test; SEE CONCEPT 103

check [n2] *restraint, hindrance*
blow, constraint, control, curb, damper, disappointment, frustration, grunt, harness, holdup, impediment, inhibition, limitation, obstruction, rebuff, rejection, restrainer, reversal, reverse, setback, stoppage, trouble; SEE CONCEPTS 121,130,230

check [n3] *symbol for ticking off*
cross, dot, line, mark, score, sign, stroke, tick, X*; SEE CONCEPT 284

check [n4] *pattern of squares*
checkerboard, patchwork, plaid, quilt, tartan; SEE CONCEPT 436

check [v1] *inspect, examine*
analyze, ascertain, audit, balance account, candle, case, compare, confirm, correct, count, enquire about, eyeball*, find out, frisk, go through, investigate, keep account, look at, look over, look see*, make sure, monitor, note, overlook, probe, prove, quiz, review, scout out, scrutinize, study, take stock, tell, test, try, verify; SEE CONCEPTS 24,103

check [v2] *hinder, restrain*
arrest, baffle, bar, bit, bottleneck*, bridle, checkmate, choke, circumvent, constrain, control, counteract, curb, cut short, delay, discourage, foil, frustrate, halt, harness, hold, hold back, hold down, hold in, impede, inhibit, interrupt, keep back, limit, moderate, neutralize, nip in the bud*, obstruct, obviate, pause, play for time, preclude, prevent, rebuff, reduce, rein in, repress, repulse, retard, slacken pace, slow down, snub, squelch, stay, stop, suppress, tame, terminate, thwart, withhold; SEE CONCEPTS 121,130

checkered [adj] *patterned*
checky, diversified, motley, mutable, patchwork, plaid, quilted, spotted, variegated; SEE CONCEPT 486

cheek [n1] *side of human face*
chop*, choppers*, gill, jowl; SEE CONCEPT 418

cheek [n2] *audacity, boldness*
brashness, brass*, brazenness, chutzpah*, confidence, disrespect, effrontery, gall, impertinence, impudence, insolence, lip*, nerve*, presumption, rudeness, sauce*, temerity; SEE CONCEPT 633

cheep [v] *vocalize as a bird*
chip, chipper, chirp, chirrup, peek, tweedle, tweet, twitter; SEE CONCEPT 64

cheer [n1] *happiness*
animation, buoyancy, cheerfulness, cheeriness, comfort, delight, encouragement, exuberance, gaiety, geniality, gladness, glee, good cheer, hilarity, hopefulness, jauntiness, jocundity, joy, joyousness, lightheartedness, liveliness, merriment, merry-making, mirth, optimism, solace; SEE CONCEPT 410

cheer [n2] *applause, supportive yell*
acclamation, approbation, approval, cry, encour-

agement, hurrah, hurray, huzzah, ovation, plaudits, roar, shout; SEE CONCEPTS 69,77

cheer [v1] *make someone feel happier*
animate, brace up, brighten, buck up*, buoy, comfort, console, elate, elevate, embolden, encourage, enliven, exhilarate, give a lift*, gladden, hearten, help, incite, inspirit, let the sun shine in*, perk up, pick up, put on cloud nine*, put on top of the world*, snap out of it*, solace, steel, strengthen, uplift, upraise, warm; SEE CONCEPTS 7,22

cheer [v2] *encourage in activity*
acclaim, applaud, clap, hail, hurrah, plug*, rise to, root, salute, sound off for, support, yell; SEE CONCEPT 69

cheerful [adj] *happy*
airy, animated, blithe, bouncy, bright, bucked, buoyant, cheery, chipper, chirpy, contented, effervescent, enlivening, enthusiastic, full of pep, gay, glad, gladsome, good-humored, goodnatured, hearty, high, hilarious, hopeful, in good spirits, in high spirits, jaunty, jocund, jolly, joyful, lighthearted, lively, merry, optimistic, peppy, perky, pleasant, roseate, rosy, sanguine, snappy, sparkling, sprightly, sunny, sunny side up*, up*, upbeat, vivacious, winsome, zappy, zingy, zippy; SEE CONCEPTS 403,404

cheering [adj] *encouraging*
auspicious, bright, comforting, heartening, hopeful, promising, propitious; SEE CONCEPT 529

cheerless [adj] *depressing, unhappy*
austere, black, bleak, blue, comfortless, dark, dejected, dejecting, depressed, desolate, despondent, disconsolate, dismal, dispiriting, dolorous, drab, draggy, drearisome, dreary, dull, forlorn, funereal, gloomy, grim, in the dumps*, jarring, joyless, melancholy, miserable, mopey, mournful, oppressive, sad, somber, sorrowful, sullen, tenebrific, uncomfortable, wintry, woebegone, woeful; SEE CONCEPT 403

chemical [adj] *concerned with atom and molecule change*
actinic, alchemical, enzymatic, synthesized, synthetic, synthetical; SEE CONCEPT 536

cherish [v] *care about deeply*
admire, adore, appreciate, apprize, care for, clasp, cleave to, cling to, coddle, comfort, cosset, cultivate, defend, dote on, embrace, encourage, enshrine, entertain, fancy, fondle, foster, guard, harbor, hold dear, hold in high esteem, honor, hug, idolize, like, love, nourish, nurse, nurture, pet, preserve, prize, revere, reverence, safeguard, shelter, shield, support, sustain, treasure, value, venerate, worship; SEE CONCEPT 32

cherry [adj] *bright red color*
blooming, blushing, bright red, cerise, claret, crimson, dark red, erubescent, incarnadine, reddish, rosy, rubescent, rubicund, ruddy; SEE CONCEPT 618

chest [n1] *box for storage*
bin, bureau, cabinet, carton, case, casket, chiffonier, coffer, commode, crate, exchequer, pyxis, receptacle, reliquary, strongbox, treasury, trunk; SEE CONCEPT 494

chest [n2] *upper front of body*
bosom, breast, bust, heart, mammary glands, peritoneum, pulmonary cavity, rib cage, ribs, thorax, upper trunk; SEE CONCEPT 392

chew [v1] *grind with teeth*
bite, champ, chaw, chomp, crunch, dispatch, feast

ch
ch

upon, gnaw, gulp, gum, manducate, masticate, munch, nibble, rend, ruminate, scrunch; SEE CONCEPTS 169,185

chew [v2] *think about deeply*
consider, deliberate, meditate, mull, mull over, muse on, ponder, reflect upon, ruminate, weigh; SEE CONCEPT 24

chew out [v] *scold*
bawl out, carpet*, criticize, dress down, jaw, revile, tell off, tongue-lash*, vituperate, wig, yell at; SEE CONCEPT 52

chic [adj] *fashionable*
chichi*, clean*, current, dap*, dapper, dashing, elegant, exclusive, faddish, last word*, latest thing*, mod*, modern, modish, natty, sharp, smart, stylish, swank, trendy, voguish, with-it*; SEE CONCEPT 589

chicanery [n] *deception, trickery*
artifice, cheating, chicane, deviousness, dishonesty, dodge, double-crossing, double-dealing*, duplicity, feint, fourberie, fraud, furtiveness, gambit, hanky-panky*, intrigue, machination, maneuver, plot, ploy, ruse, sharp practice, skullduggery, sophistry, stratagem, subterfuge, surreptitiousness, underhandedness, wiles; SEE CONCEPTS 59,660

chicken [n1] *person afraid to try something*
coward, craven, dastard, funk, poltroon, quitter, recreant, scaredy cat*, yellow belly*; SEE CONCEPT 423

chicken [n2] *farm fowl*
banty, barnyard fowl, biddy, capon, chick, cock, cock-a-doodle-do*, cockalorum, cockerel, gump*, heeler, hen, poultry, pullet, rooster; SEE CONCEPTS 394,395

chide [v] *criticize, lecture*
admonish, berate, blame, call down*, call on the carpet*, castigate, censure, check, condemn, exprobate, find fault, flay, give a hard time*, lesson, monish, rate, rebuke, reprehend, reprimand, reproach, reprove, scold, slap on the wrist*, speak to, take down*, take down a peg*, talk to, tell off, tick off*, upbraid; SEE CONCEPT 52

chief [n] *person in charge*
big cheese*, big gun*, big wheel*, bigwig*, boss, captain, chieftain, commander, dictator, director, foreperson, general, governor, head, head honcho*, head person*, honcho*, key player*, leader, manager, monarch, overlord, overseer, president, principal, proprietor, ringleader, ruler, sovereign, superintendent, supervisor, suzerain, top brass*, top cat*; SEE CONCEPTS 347,376

chief [adj] *most important, essential*
arch, capital, cardinal, central, champion, consequential, controlling, crucial, effective, especial, first, foremost, grand, head, highest, key, leading, main, major, momentous, number one*, outstanding, paramount, potent, predominant, preeminent, premier, primal, primary, prime, principal, significant, star, stellar, superior, supreme, telling, uppermost, vital, weighty; SEE CONCEPTS 568,574,829

chiefly [adv] *most importantly*
above all, especially, essentially, in general, in the first place, in the main, largely, mainly, mostly, on the whole, overall, predominantly, primarily, principally, usually; SEE CONCEPTS 567,772

child [n] *very young person*
adolescent, anklebiter*, babe, baby, bairn, bambino, brat, cherub, chick, cub, descendant, dickens*, imp, infant, innocent, issue, juvenile, kid, kiddie*, lamb*, little angel*, little darling*, little doll*, little one, minor, mite, moppet, neonate, nestling, newborn, nipper, nursling, offspring, preteen, progeny, pubescent, shaver, small fry*, sprout, squirt, stripling, suckling, tadpole, teen, teenager, teenybopper*, toddler, tot, tyke, urchin*, whippersnapper*, young one, youngster, youth; SEE CONCEPTS 414,424

childbirth [n] *giving birth*
accouchement, bearing children, blessed event*, childbed, confinement, delivering, delivery, labor, lying-in, nativity, parturience, parturition, procreation, producing, propagation, reproduction, travail, visit from the stork*; SEE CONCEPTS 302,373

childhood [n] *period of being young*
adolescence, babyhood, cradle, immaturity, infancy, juniority, juvenility, minority, nonage, nursery, puberty, pupilage, schooldays, teens, tender age, youth; SEE CONCEPTS 816,817

childish [adj] *immature, silly*
adolescent, baby, babyish, callow, childlike, foolish, frivolous, green, infantile, infantine, innocent, jejune, juvenile, kid stuff*, naive, puerile, unsophisticated, young, youthful; SEE CONCEPTS 401,402,424,578,797

childlike [adj] *innocent, naive*
artless, childish, credulous, guileless, immature, ingenuous, natural, simple, spontaneous, trustful, trusting, unaffected, unfeigned; SEE CONCEPT 404

chill [n] *cold conditions*
bite, coldness, coolness, crispness, frigidity, gelidity, iciness, nip, rawness, rigor, sharpness; SEE CONCEPT 524

chill [adj1] *cold, raw*
arctic, biting, bleak, brisk, chilly, cool, freezing, frigid, frosty, gelid, glacial, icy, nippy, sharp, wintry; SEE CONCEPT 605

chill [adj2] *unfriendly, aloof*
cool, depressing, discouraging, dismal, dispiriting, distant, emotionless, formal, frigid, glacial, hateful, hostile, icy, indifferent, reserved, solitary, standoffish, stony, uncompanionable, unemotional, ungenial, unhappy, unresponsive, unwelcoming, wintry, withdrawn; SEE CONCEPTS 401,404

chill [v1] *make cold*
air-condition, congeal, cool, freeze, frost, ice, refrigerate; SEE CONCEPTS 255,521

chill [v2] *discourage*
cloud, dampen, dash, deject, demoralize, depress, dishearten, dismay, disparage, dispirit; SEE CONCEPTS 7,19

chilly [adj1] *cold*
arctic, biting, blowy, breezy, brisk, cool, crisp, drafty, freezing, fresh, frosty, glacial, hawkish, icebox, icy, nippy, penetrating, sharp, snappy, wintry; SEE CONCEPT 605

chilly [adj2] *unfriendly, aloof*
cold, frigid, hostile, unfriendly, unresponsive, unsympathetic, unwelcoming; SEE CONCEPT 404

chime [v] *ring, peal*
bell, bong, boom, clang, dong, jingle, knell, sound, strike, tinkle, tintinnabulate, toll; SEE CONCEPT 65

chimera [n] *dream, fantasy*
bogy, bubble, delusion, fabrication, fancy, fata morgana, figment, fool's paradise*, hallucination,

ignis fatuus, illusion, mirage, monster, monstrosity, pipe dream*, rainbow*, snare, specter, virtual reality; SEE CONCEPT 529

chimney [n] *smokestack for building*
chase, chimney pot, chimney stack, fireplace, flue, funnel, furnace, hearth, pipe, smokeshaft, stack, vent, ventilator; SEE CONCEPT 440

chin [n] *area under mouth*
button, jaw, jawbone, mandible, mentum, point; SEE CONCEPT 399

china [n] *dishes, often valuable*
ceramics, crockery, porcelain, pottery, service, stoneware, tableware, ware; SEE CONCEPT 493

chip [n] *shard, flaw*
dent, flake, fragment, gobbet, nick, notch, paring, part, scrap, scratch, shaving, slice, sliver, wafer, wedge; SEE CONCEPTS 580,831

chip [v] *knock a piece out of*
break, chisel, chop, clip, crack, crack off, crumble, cut away, cut off, damage, flake, fragment, gash, hack, hackle, hew, incise, nick, notch, shape, shear, slash, slice, sliver, snick, snip, splinter, split, whack, whittle; SEE CONCEPTS 137,189,246,250

chip in [v] *contribute*
ante up*, break in*, chime in*, come through*, conate, go Dutch*, interpose, interrupt, pay, pitch in, subscribe; SEE CONCEPT 110

chipper [adj] *happy*
alert, animate, animated, bright, brisk, gay, in good spirits, keen, lively, spirited, sprightly, vivacious; SEE CONCEPT 403

chips [n] *substitute for money; money*
coin, currency, markers, play money, scratch; SEE CONCEPT 340

chirp [v] *peep, cheep*
call, chip, chipper, chirrup, lilt, pipe, purl, quaver, roll, sing, sound, trill, tweedle, tweet, twitter, warble; SEE CONCEPT 64

chisel [n] *shaping tool*
adze, blade, edge, gouge, knife; SEE CONCEPTS 495,499

chisel [v] *cut, wear away*
carve, hew, incise, roughcast, roughhew, sculpt, sculpture, shape; SEE CONCEPTS 137,176,184

chivalrous [adj] *valiant*
benevolent, big, bold, brave, considerate, courageous, courteous, courtly, gallant, gentlemanlike, great-hearted, heroic, high-minded, honorable, intrepid, lofty, magnanimous, manly, nobleminded, polite, quixotic, spirited, sublime, true, valorous; SEE CONCEPT 401

chivalry [n] *valor, gallantry*
courage, courtesy, courtliness, fairness, politeness, valiance; SEE CONCEPT 633

choice [n] *power to select; selection*
alternative, appraisal, choosing, cull, cup of tea*, decision, determination, discretion, discrimination, distinction, druthers*, election, evaluation, extract, favorite, finding, free will, judgment, opportunity, option, pick, preference, rating, say, substitute, variety, verdict, volition, vote, weakness; SEE CONCEPTS 41,376

choice [adj] *best, superior*
A-1*, elect, elite, excellent, exceptional, exclusive, exquisite, fine, first-class, hand-picked, nice, popular, precious, preferential, preferred, prime, prize, rare, select, solid gold*, special, 10*, top-drawer*, 24-karat*, uncommon, unusual, valuable, winner; SEE CONCEPT 574

choke [v] *smother, block*
asphyxiate, bar, check, clog, close, congest, constrict, dam, die, drown, fill, gag, garrote, gasp, gibbet, kill, noose, obstruct, occlude, overpower, retard, squeeze, stifle, stop, stopper, strangle, strangulate, stuff, stunt, suffocate, suppress, throttle, wring; SEE CONCEPTS 121,219

choose [v] *pick, select*
accept, adopt, appoint, call for, cast, commit oneself, co-opt, crave, cull, decide on, designate, desire, determine, discriminate between, draw lots, elect, embrace, espouse, excerpt, extract, fancy, favor, feel disposed to, finger, fix on, glean, judge, love, make choice, make decision, make up one's mind, name, opt for, predestine, prefer, see fit, separate, set aside, settle upon, sift out, single out, slot, sort, tab, tag, take, take up, tap, want, weigh, will, winnow, wish, wish for; SEE CONCEPT 41

choosy [adj] *fussy, discriminating*
dainty, eclectic, exacting, fastidious, finical, finicky, nice, overparticular, particular, persnickety*, picky, prissy, select, selective; SEE CONCEPT 404

chop [v] *cut up with tool*
axe, cleave, clip, cube, dice, divide, fell, fragment, hack, hackle, hash, hew, lop, mangle, mince, sever, shear, slash, truncate, whack; SEE CONCEPT 176

choppy [adj] *wavy*
inclement, ripply, rough, uneven, violent, wild; SEE CONCEPT 488

chore [n] *task*
assignment, burden, devoir, duty, effort, errand, grind, housework, job, KP*, routine, scutwork, stint, trial, tribulation, workout; SEE CONCEPT 362

chortle [v] *laugh gleefully*
cackle, chuckle, crow, giggle, guffaw, hee-haw*, snicker, sniggle, snort, teehee*, titter; SEE CONCEPT 77

chorus [n1] *group of singers*
carolers, choir, chorale, choristers, ensemble, glee club, singing group, vocalists, voices; SEE CONCEPT 294

chorus [n2] *refrain*
bob, burden, chorale, main section, melody, motif, music, recurrent verse, response, ritornelle, song, strain, theme, tune, undersong; SEE CONCEPT 264

chorus [n3] *agreement*
accord, concert, concord, consonance, harmony, tune, unison; SEE CONCEPTS 673,684

chosen [adj] *preferred*
called, conscript, elect, exclusive, got the nod*, named, pegged, pick, picked, popular, preferential, select, selected, tabbed; SEE CONCEPTS 546,567,574

christen [v] *named in religious rite*
asperse, baptize, bless, call, dedicate, denominate, designate, dub, entitle, godparent, immerse, sprinkle, style, term, title; SEE CONCEPTS 62,367

chronic [adj] *incessant, never-ending*
abiding, ceaseless, confirmed, constant, continual, continuing, continuous, deep-rooted, deep-seated, enduring, ever-present, fixed, habitual, inborn, inbred, incurable, ineradicable, ingrained, inveterate, lasting, lifelong, lingering, long-lived, long-standing, obstinate, perennial, persistent, persisting, prolonged, protracted, recurrent, recur-

ch
ch

ring, rooted, routine, settled, stubborn, sustained, tenacious, unabating, unmitigated, unyielding, usual; SEE CONCEPTS *534,551,798*

chronicle [*n*] *account, narrative*
annals, archives, diary, history, journal, narration, prehistory, recital, record, recountal, register, report, story, version; SEE CONCEPTS *271,282*

chronicle [*v*] *report, recount*
enter, narrate, record, register, relate, set down, tell; SEE CONCEPTS *60,79*

chronological [*adj*] *in consecutive time order*
archival, chronographic, chronologic, chronometric, chronometrical, chronoscopic, classified, dated, historical, horological, horometrical, in due course, in due time, in order, in sequence, junctural, ordered, progressive, sequent, sequential, tabulated, temporal; SEE CONCEPTS *548,585*

chubby [*adj*] *slightly fat*
ample, bearish, big, butterball*, buxom, chunky, fatty, flabby, fleshy, full-figured, hefty, husky, pleasingly plump*, plump, plumpish, podgy, portly, pudgy, roly-poly*, rotund, round, stout, tubby, zaftig*; SEE CONCEPTS *491,773*

chuck [*v*] *throw aside, throw away, throw out*
abandon, can, cast, desert, discard, ditch, eighty-six*, eject, fire, fling, flip, forsake, give the heave ho*, heave, hurl, jettison, junk, launch, pitch, quit, reject, relinquish, renounce, scrap, shed, shy, sling, slough, toss; SEE CONCEPTS *180,222*

chuckle [*v*] *giggle*
cackle, chortle, crow, exult, guffaw, hee-haw*, laugh, smile, snicker, snigger, sniggle, teehee*, titter; SEE CONCEPT *77*

chum [*n*] *friend*
associate, bro*, buddy, co-mate, companion, comrade, crony, mate, pal, playmate, sis*; SEE CONCEPT *423*

chummy [*adj*] *friendly*
affectionate, buddy-buddy*, close, confidential, constant, cozy, familiar, intimate, pally*, palsy-walsy*, thick*; SEE CONCEPTS *401,555*

chunk [*n*] *mass, slab of something*
block, clod, dollop, glob, gob, hunk, lump, nugget, part, piece, portion, wad; SEE CONCEPT *471*

chunky [*adj*] *fat, plump*
beefy, chubby, dumpy, heavyset, husky, rotund, scrub, squat, stocky, stout, stubby, thick-bodied, thickset; SEE CONCEPTS *491,773*

church [*n1*] *religious institution, building*
abbey, basilica, bethel, cathedral, chancel, chantry, chapel, fold, house of God, house of prayer, house of worship, Lord's house, minster, mission, mosque, oratory, parish, sacellum, sanctuary, shrine, synagogue, tabernacle, temple; SEE CONCEPTS *368,449*

church [*n2*] *religious belief, group*
affiliation, body, chapter, communion, congregation, connection, creed, cult, denomination, doctrine, faction, faith, gathering, ism, order, persuasion, religion, schism, sect, society; SEE CONCEPTS *369,689*

churl [*n*] *rude and ill-bred, a boor; person overly concerned with saving money*
beast, chuff, clodhopper*, miser, mucker*, niggard*, oaf, peasant, provincial, rustic, tightwad, yokel; SEE CONCEPT *423*

churlish [*adj*] *crude, boorish*
base, blunt, brusque, cantankerous*, cloddish, clodhopping*, crabbed, crude, crusty, curt, cussed*, discourteous, dour, grouchy, gruff, grumpy, harsh, ill-tempered, impolite, loutish, lowbred, mean, miserly, morose, oafish, ornery*, rude, rustic, snippy*, sullen, surly, touchy*, ugly, uncivil, uncivilized, uncultured, unmannerly, unneighborly, unpolished, unsociable, vulgar; SEE CONCEPT *404*

churn [*v*] *mix up, beat*
agitate, boil, bubble, convulse, ferment, foam, froth, jolt, moil, seethe, simmer, stir up, swirl, toss; SEE CONCEPTS *147,170*

chute [*n*] *ramp, slope*
channel, course, fall, gutter, incline, rapid, runway, slide, trough; SEE CONCEPTS *440,471*

cinder [*n*] *hot ash*
clinker, ember, hot coal, soot; SEE CONCEPT *260*

cinema [*n*] *movie industry; movie arena*
big screen*, bijou, cine, drive-in, film, flicks*, motion pictures, movie house, movie theater, moving pictures, nabes*, photoplay, pictures, picture show, playhouse, show, silver screen*; SEE CONCEPTS *293,349*

cipher [*n*] *zero; nothingness*
blank, diddly squat*, goose egg*, insignificancy, nada*, naught, nil, nobody, nonentity, nothing, nought, nullity, squat, zilch, zip, zippo*, zot*; SEE CONCEPTS *668,787*

cipher [*v*] *figure out code*
break, calculate, clear up, compute, count, decipher, estimate, figure, reckon, resolve, solve, unravel; SEE CONCEPT *37*

circa [*prep*] *approximately*
about, around, close on, in the region of, near, nearby, nigh, roughly; SEE CONCEPT *820*

circle [*n1*] *orb, loop, round figure*
amphitheater, aureole, band, belt, bowl, bracelet, circlet, circuit, circumference, circus, cirque, coil, colure, compass, cordon, corona, crown, cycle, disc, disk, ecliptic, enclosure, equator, full turn, globe, halo, hoop, horizon, lap, meridian, orbit, parallel of latitude, perimeter, periphery, record, revolution, ring, ringlet, round, sphere, stadium, tire, turn, vortex, wheel, wreath, zodiac; SEE CONCEPT *756*

circle [*n2*] *group of close friends, associates*
assembly, bunch, cabal, camarilla, camp, clan, class, clique, club, companions, company, comrades, coterie, crew, cronies, crowd, crush, fraternity, gang, in-group, insiders, intimates, lot, Mafia, mob, outfit, party, posse, ring, school, set, society, sorority; SEE CONCEPTS *387,417*

circle [*v*] *go around, circumnavigate*
begird, belt, cincture, circuit, circulate, circumduct, circumscribe, coil, compass, curve, embrace, encircle, enclose, encompass, ensphere, envelop, gird, girdle, gyrate, gyre, hem in, loop, mill around, pivot, revolve, ring, roll, rotate, round, spiral, surround, tour, wheel, whirl, wind about; SEE CONCEPT *758*

circuit [*n*] *revolution, track, boundary*
ambit, area, bounds, circle, circling, circulation, circumference, circumnavigation, circumscription, circumvolution, compass, course, cycle, district, gyration, journey, lap, limit, line, orbit, perambulation, perimeter, periphery, range, region, round, route, tour, tract, turn, turning, twirl, way, wheel, whirl, wind, winding, zone; SEE CONCEPTS *484,501,770*

circuitous [*adj*] *going around, indirect*
back road*, by way of, circular, collateral, complicated, devious, labyrinthine, long way*, long

way around*, meandering, oblique, rambling, roundabout, tortuous, winding around; SEE CONCEPTS *544,581*

circular [n] *handbill*
advertisement, booklet, broadside, brochure, flyer, handout, insert, leaflet, literature, notice, pamphlet, poster, publication, throwaway*; SEE CONCEPT *271*

circular [adj] *going around*
annular, circling, disklike, indirect, oblique, orbicular, round, rounded, spheroid; SEE CONCEPT *486*

circulate [v1] *make known*
bring out, broadcast, diffuse, disperse, disseminate, distribute, exchange, interview, issue, promulgate, propagate, publicize, publish, radiate, report, spread, strew, troll; SEE CONCEPTS *60,138*

circulate [v2] *flow*
actuate, circle, fly about, get about, get around, go about, gyrate, mill around, mobilize, move around, radiate, revolve, rotate, set off, travel, wander; SEE CONCEPT *147*

circulation [n1] *distribution*
apportionment, currency, dissemination, spread, transmission; SEE CONCEPTS *631,651*

circulation [n2] *moving circularly*
circling, circuit, circumvolution, current, flow, flowing, gyration, gyre, motion, revolution, rotation, round, turn, twirl, wheel, whirl; SEE CONCEPTS *147,738*

circumference [n] *edge, perimeter*
ambit, border, boundary, bounds, circuit, compass, confines, extremity, fringe, girth, limits, lip, margin, outline, periphery, rim, verge; SEE CONCEPT *484*

circumlocution [n] *indirect speech*
beating around the bush*, circumambages, diffuseness, discursiveness, euphemism, gassiness, indirectness, periphrase, periphrasis, pleonasm, prolixity, roundabout, tautology, verbal evasion, verbality, verbiage, wordiness; SEE CONCEPTS *51,266*

circumscribe [v] *mark off, delimit*
bar, bound, confine, define, delineate, demarcate, encircle, enclose, encompass, environ, girdle, hamper, hem in*, limit, nail down*, outline, prelimit, restrain, restrict, surround, trammel; SEE CONCEPTS *18,130*

circumspect [adj] *cautious, discreet*
attentive, cagey, calculating, canny, careful, chary, considerate, deliberate, discriminating, gingerly, guarded, heedful, judicious, meticulous, observant, politic, prudent, punctilious, safe, sagacious, sage, scrupulous, vigilant, wary, watchful; SEE CONCEPTS *403,544*

circumstance [n] *situation, condition*
accident, action, adjunct, affair, article, case, cause, coincidence, concern, contingency, crisis, destiny, detail, doom, element, episode, event, exigency, fact, factor, fate, feature, fortuity, go, happening, happenstance, incident, intervention, item, juncture, kismet, lot, matter, Moira, occasion, occurrence, particular, phase, place, point, portion, proviso, respect, scene, status, stipulation, supervention, thing, time, where it's at*; SEE CONCEPT *696*

circumstances [n] *state of affairs in one's life*
assets, capital, chances, class, command, degree, dowry, financial status, footing, income, lifestyle, lot, means, net worth, outlook, position, prece-

dence, prestige, property, prospects, prosperity, rank, rating, resources, situation, sphere, standing, state, station, status, substance, times, way of life, worldly goods; SEE CONCEPTS *335,388*

circumstantial [adj] *incidental*
amplified, coincidental, concomitant, concurrent, conjectural, contingent, detailed, environmental, fortuitous, inconclusive, indirect, inferential, presumptive, provisional, uncertain; SEE CONCEPTS *556,582,653*

circumvent [v] *fool, mislead*
avoid, beat, beguile, bilk, bypass, circumnavigate, cramp, crimp, deceive, detour, disappoint, dodge, dupe, elude, ensnare, entrap, escape, evade, foil, frustrate, get around, hoodwink, outflank, outwit, overreach, prevent, queer, ruin, shun, sidestep, skirt, stave off, steer clear of*, stump, stymie, thwart, trick, ward off; SEE CONCEPTS *59,102,121*

circus [n] *fair with entertainment*
bazaar, big top, festival, gilly*, hippodrome, kermis, show, spectacle, three-ring*; SEE CONCEPT *293*

citadel [n] *top, tower*
bastion, blockhouse, castle, fastness, fort, fortification, fortress, keep, manor, redoubt, stronghold; SEE CONCEPTS *321,836*

citation [n1] *excerpt*
example, illustration, mention, passage, quotation, quote, quoting, reference, saying, source; SEE CONCEPT *283*

citation [n2] *award*
bidding, charge, commendation, encomium, mention, panegyric, reward, salutation, summons, tribute; SEE CONCEPTS *69,337*

cite [v1] *note, quote*
adduce, advance, allege, allude to, appeal to, enumerate, evidence, excerpt, exemplify, extract, get down to brass tacks*, give as example, illustrate with, indicate, instance, lay, mention, name, number, offer, point out, present, recite, recount, reference, refer to, rehearse, remember, reminisce, repeat, specify, spell out, tell; SEE CONCEPT *57*

cite [v2] *subpoena*
arraign, call, command, name, order, summon; SEE CONCEPT *317*

citizen [n] *person native of country*
aborigine, burgess, burgher, civilian, commoner, cosmopolite, denizen, dweller, freeman/woman, householder, inhabitant, John/Jane Q. Public*, member of body politic, member of community, national, native, naturalized person, occupant, resident, settler, subject, taxpayer, townsperson, urbanite, villager, voter; SEE CONCEPT *413*

city [n] *large town*
apple*, boom town, borough, burg, capital, center, conurbation, downtown, megalopolis, metropolis, metropolitan area, municipality, place, polis, port, urban place, urbs*; SEE CONCEPT *507*

city [adj] *metropolitan*
burghal, citified, civic, civil, interurban, intraurban, megalopolitan, municipal, urban; SEE CONCEPT *536*

civic [adj] *community*
borough, civil, communal, local, metropolitan, municipal, national, public, urban; SEE CONCEPTS *536,583*

civil [adj1] *civic, community*
civilian, domestic, governmental, home, interior,

local, municipal, national, political, public; SEE
CONCEPTS *536,583*

civil [adj2] *obliging, kind*
accommodating, affable, civilized, complaisant,
cordial, courteous, courtly, cultivated, diplomatic,
formal, genteel, gracious, mannerly, polished, polite, politic, refined, suave, urbane, well-bred,
well-mannered; SEE CONCEPT *401*

civilian [n] *nonmilitary person*
citizen, civ*, civvie*, commoner, noncombatant,
private citizen, subject; SEE CONCEPT *423*

civilian [adj] *nonmilitary*
noncombatant, noncombative, nonmilitant, not in
armed forces, pacificist, private, unhostile; SEE
CONCEPT *555*

civilization [n1] *culture, sophistication*
acculturation, advancement, breeding, civility,
cultivation, development, edification, education,
elevation, enlightenment, illumination, polish,
progress, refinement, social well-being; SEE CON-
CEPT *388*

civilization [n2] *society*
civilized life, community, customs, literate society, modern humanity, mores, nation, people, polity, way of life; SEE CONCEPTS *388,417*

civilize [v] *make cultured; develop*
acculturate, acquaint, advance, better, cultivate,
edify, educate, elevate, enlighten, ennoble, enrich, ethnicize, foster, help forward, humanize, idealize, improve, indoctrinate, inform, instruct,
polish, promote, reclaim, refine, sophisticate,
spiritualize, tame, uplift; SEE CONCEPTS *244,385*

claim [n] *property, right demanded or reserved*
affirmation, allegation, application, assertion,
birthright, call, case, counterclaim, declaration,
demand, dibs, due, entreaty, interest, lien, part,
petition, plea, postulation, prerogative, pretense,
pretension, privilege, profession, protestation,
reclamation, request, requirement, requisition,
suit, title, ultimatum; SEE CONCEPTS
278,318,376,709

claim [v] *demand, maintain property or right*
adduce, advance, allege, ask, assert, believe, call
for, challenge, collect, declare, defend, exact,
have dibs on something*, hit, hit up*, hold, hold
out for*, insist, justify, knock, lay claim to, need,
pick up, pop the question*, postulate, pretend,
profess, pronounce, require, requisition, solicit,
stake out, take, uphold, vindicate; SEE CONCEPTS
53,129

clairvoyance [n] *intuition*
acumen, discernment, ESP*, feeling, foreknowledge, insight, omen, penetration, perception, precognition, premonition, psyche, sixth sense*,
telepathy; SEE CONCEPTS *409,410*

clairvoyant [n] *person who is psychic*
augur, channeller, diviner, fortune-teller, haruspex, horoscopist, medium, oracle, palm reader,
prophet, seer, sibyl, soothsayer, telepath, tele-
pathist, visionary, voodoo doctor*; SEE CONCEPT
423

clairvoyant [adj] *intuitive, psychic*
clear-sighted, discerning, extrasensory, farseeing,
far-sighted, fey, judicious, long-sighted, new
age*, oracular, penetrating, perceptive, prescient,
prophetic, second-sighted, sibylline, spiritualistic,
telepathic, vatic, visionary; SEE CONCEPTS
402,403

clam [n] *bivalve living in ocean*
cherrystone, littleneck, mollusk, quahog; SEE
CONCEPT *394*

clammy [adj] *damp*
close, dank, drizzly, moist, mucid, mucous, mu-
culent, pasty, slimy, soggy, sticky, sweating,
sweaty, wet; SEE CONCEPT *603*

clamor [n] *loud cry; commotion*
agitation, babel, blare, brouhaha*, bustle, buzz,
clinker, complaint, convulsion, din, discord, exclamation, ferment, hassle, hoo-ha*, hubba-
hubba*, hubbub, hullabaloo*, hurly-burly*,
lament, noise, outcry, pandemonium, protesting,
racket, remonstrance, row, ruckus, shout, shouting, to-do, tumult, turmoil, upheaval, uproar, vociferation; SEE CONCEPTS *386,595,674*

clamor [v] *cry out, make commotion*
agitate, bark, bawl, bellow, bluster, claim, debate, demand, dispute, holler, put up a howl*,
raise Cain*, raise the roof*, roar, rout, shout; SEE
CONCEPTS *77,106*

clamp [n] *fastener*
bracket, catch, clasp, grip, hold, lock, nipper,
press, snap, vice; SEE CONCEPT *499*

clamp [v] *fasten*
brace, clench, clinch, fix, impose, make fast, secure; SEE CONCEPTS *85,160*

clan [n] *family, clique*
association, band, bunch, club, coterie, crew,
crowd, crush, faction, folks, gang, group, house,
insiders, kinfolks, mob, moiety, organization,
outfit, race, ring, sect, set, society, sodality,
stock, tribe; SEE CONCEPTS *296,387*

clandestine [adj] *secret, sly*
artful, cloak-and-dagger, closet, concealed, covert, foxy, fraudulent, furtive, hidden, hush-
hush*, illegitimate, illicit, in holes and corners*,
on the Q.T.*, on the quiet, private, sneaky,
stealthy, surreptitious, undercover, underground,
underhand, under-the-counter*, under wraps*;
SEE CONCEPTS *555,576*

clank [n] *metallic noise*
bang, bong, clash, clink, jangle, ring; SEE CON-
CEPT *595*

clank [v] *clang, clatter*
bong, clash, clink, jangle, make noise, resound,
reverberate, ring, toll; SEE CONCEPT *65*

clannish [adj] *exclusive, select*
akin, alike, associative, cliquish, close, insular,
like, narrow, related, reserved, restricting, restrictive, sectarian, unfriendly, unreceptive; SEE CON-
CEPT *555*

clap [n] *loud hitting noise*
applause, bang, blast, boom, burst, crack, crash,
handclap, pat, slam, slap, smash, strike, thrust,
thunder, thunderclap, thwack, wallop, whack,
wham; SEE CONCEPT *189,595*

clap [v] *applaud; slap with approbation*
acclaim, approve, bang, cheer, give a big hand*,
give a hand*, hear it for*, pat, praise, slap, strike
gently, thwack, whack; SEE CONCEPTS *185,189*

clarification [n] *explanation*
description, elucidation, exposition, illumination,
interpretation, resolution, simplification, solution,
unravelment, vivification; SEE CONCEPTS *57,274*

clarify [v1] *explain, make clear*
analyze, break down, clear up, define, delineate,
draw a picture, elucidate, formulate, illuminate,
illustrate, interpret, make perfectly clear, make
plain, resolve, settle, shed light on*, simplify,

spell out*, straighten out, throw light on; SEE CONCEPT 57

clarify [v2] *purify*
clean, cleanse, depurate, distill, filter, rarefy, refine; SEE CONCEPT 165

clarion [adj] *clear, stirring sound*
blaring, definite, inspiring, loud, ringing, sharp, shrill, strident; SEE CONCEPTS 562,592,594

clarity [n] *clearness*
accuracy, articulateness, brightness, certainty, cognizability, comprehensibility, conspicuousness, decipherability, definition, directness, distinctness, evidence, exactitude, exactness, explicability, explicitness, intelligibility, legibility, limpidity, limpidness, lucidity, manifestness, obviousness, openness, overtness, palpability, penetrability, perceptibility, perspicuity, plainness, precision, prominence, purity, salience, simplicity, tangibility, transparency, unambiguity, unmistakability; SEE CONCEPTS 409,638

clash [n1] *disagreement or fight, often brief*
affray, argument, battle, brawl, break, broil, brush, bump, collision, concussion, conflict, confrontation, crash, difference of opinion, discord, discordance, disharmony, dispute, donnybrook*, embroilment, encounter, engagement, fracas, fray, have a go at each other*, impact, jam, jar, jolt, jump, melee, misunderstanding, mix up, opposition, rift, riot, row, rumpus, run-in, rupture, scrap, scrimmage, set-to, shock, showdown, skirmish, smash, wallop; SEE CONCEPTS 46,106

clash [v1] *hit with a loud noise*
bang, bump, clang, clank, clatter, collide, crash, grate, grind, jangle, jar, jolt, prang, rattle, scrap, scrimmage, shock, smash, wallop; SEE CONCEPTS 65,189

clash [v2] *fight about, often verbally*
argue, bang heads*, battle, brawl, buck, combat, conflict, contend, cross swords, differ, disagree, encounter, feud, fret, gall, grapple, grate, mix it up*, quarrel, raise Cain*, row, try, war, wrangle; SEE CONCEPTS 46,106

clash [v3] *do not match*
be dissimilar, conflict, contrast, differ, disaccord, discord, disharmonize, mismatch, not go with; SEE CONCEPTS 655,664

clasp [n] *fastener; hold on something*
brooch, buckle, catch, clamp, clench, clinch, clip, clutch, embrace, fastening, fibula, grapple, grasp, grip, hasp, hold, hook, hug, pin, safety pin, snap; SEE CONCEPTS 497,641

clasp [v] *grab tightly*
attack, bear hug*, buckle, clamp, clinch, clip, clutch, coil, concatenate, connect, embrace, enfold, fasten, glom onto*, grapple, grasp, grip, hold, hug, pin, press, seize, snatch, squeeze, take; SEE CONCEPTS 85,160,191,219

class [n1] *kind, sort, category*
branch, brand, breed, cast, caste, character, classification, collection, color, degree, denomination, department, description, designation, distinction, division, domain, estate, family, feather, frame, genre, genus, grade, grain, grouping, hierarchy, humor, ilk, kidney, league, make, mold, name, nature, order, origin, property, province, quality, range, rank, rate, school, sect, section, selection, set, source, species, sphere, standing, status, stripe, style, suit, temperament, value, variety; SEE CONCEPT 378

class [n2] *societal group, background*
ancestry, birth, bourgeoisie, breed, caliber, caste, circle, clan, clique, club, company, condition, connection, coterie, cultural level, degree, derivation, descent, estate, extraction, family, genealogy, grade, hierarchy, influence, intelligentsia, league, lineage, moiety, nobility, origin, pecking order*, pedigree, pigeonhole*, place, position, prestige, quality, sect, social rank, source, sphere, standing, state, station, status, stock, strain, stratum, the right stuff*, tier, title; SEE CONCEPTS 296,387,388,417

class [n3] *group in school*
academy, colloquium, course, course of study, division, form, grade, homeroom, lecture group, line, quiz group, recitation, room, round table, section, seminar, seminary, session, study, study group, subdivision, subject; SEE CONCEPTS 286,287,288,289

class [adj] *stylish; with panache*
chic, classy, dashing, fashionable, fine, fly*, foxy*, sharp; SEE CONCEPT 589

class [v] *categorize*
account, allot, appraise, assess, assign, assort, brand, classify, codify, consider, designate, divide, evaluate, gauge, grade, group, hold, identify, judge, mark, part, pigeonhole*, rank, rate, reckon, regard, score, separate; SEE CONCEPTS 39,135

classic [n] *model*
chef d'oeuvre, exemplar, magnum opus, paradigm, prototype, standard, tour de force; SEE CONCEPTS 259,655,686

classic/classical [adj1] *best, model*
archetypal, capital, champion, consummate, definitive, distinguished, esthetic, excellent, exemplary, famous, fine, finest, first-rate, flawless, ideal, master, masterly, paradigmatic, paramount, perfect, prime, quintessential, ranking, standard, superior, top, top-notch, vintage, well-known; SEE CONCEPT 574

classic [adj2] *characteristic, regular*
prototypal, prototypical, representative, simple, standard, time-honored, typical, usual, vintage; SEE CONCEPTS 533,547

classical [adj1] *concerning ancient culture*
academic, Attic, Augustan, belletristic, bookish, canonic, canonical, classic, classicistic, Doric, Grecian, Greek, Hellenic, Homeric, humanistic, Ionic, Latin, Roman, scholastic, Virgilian; SEE CONCEPTS 536,549

classical [adj2] *simple, chaste*
classic, elegant, harmonious, pure, refined, restrained, symmetrical, understated, well-proportioned; SEE CONCEPT 589

classicism [n] *simple style; regularity, restraint*
aesthetic principle, Atticism, balance, Ciceronianism, clarity, class, classicalism, conventional formality, dignity, elegance, excellence, finish, formality, formal style, grandeur, grand style, Hellenism, high art, lucidity, majesty, neoclassicism, nobility, objectivity, polish, proportion, propriety, pure taste, purity, rationalism, refinement, rhythm, severity, simplicity, sobriety, sublimity, symmetry; SEE CONCEPT 655

classification [n] *categorization*
allocation, alloting, allotment, analysis, apportionment, arrangement, assignment, assortment, cataloguing, categorizing, codification, collocation, consignment, coordination, denomination,

ci
cl

department, designation, disposal, disposition, distributing, distribution, division, echelon, gradation, grade, grading, graduation, group, grouping, kind, order, ordering, ordination, organization, pigeonholing*, regulation, sizing, sorting, systematization, tabulating, taxonomy, typecasting; SEE CONCEPTS *18,39,135,378*

classify [v] *categorize*
allocate, allot, alphabetize, analyze, arrange, assort, brand, break down, button down*, catalogue, class, codify, collocate, coordinate, correlate, dispose, distinguish, distribute, divide, docket, embody, file, grade, group, incorporate, index, label, match, name, number, order, organize, peg*, pigeonhole*, put away, put down as, put down for, range, rank, rank out, rate, regiment, segregate, size, size up, sort, systematize, tab, tabulate, tag, take one's measure, ticket, type, typecast; SEE CONCEPTS *18,39,135*

classy [adj] *stylish, having panache*
chic, dashing, elegant, exclusive, fashionable, high-class, in, in vogue, mod, modish, posh, select, sharp, superior, swank, swanky, tony, uptown; SEE CONCEPT *589*

clatter [n] *loud noise*
ballyhoo*, bluster, clack, clangor, hullabaloo*, pandemonium, racket, rattle, rumpus, shattering, smashing; SEE CONCEPTS *181,189,595*

clatter [v] *crash; make racket*
bang, bluster, bump, clang, clank, clash, hurtle, noise, rattle, roar, shatter, smash; SEE CONCEPTS *65,181,189*

clause [n] *provision in document*
article, catch*, chapter, codicil, condition, fine print*, heading, item, joker*, kicker*, limitation, paragraph, part, passage, point, provision, proviso, requirement, rider, section, small print*, specification, stipulation, string attached to something*, ultimatum; SEE CONCEPTS *270,275*

claw [n] *nail of animal; tool shaped like nail of an animal*
barb, cant hook, clapperclaw, crook, fang, fingernail, grapnel, grappler, hook, manus, nail claw, nipper, paw, pincer, retractile, spur, talon, tentacle, unguis, ungula; SEE CONCEPT *392*

claw [v] *using sharp nail*
break, dig, graze, hurt, itch, lacerate, mangle, maul, open, rip, scrabble, scrap, scrape, scratch, tear; SEE CONCEPTS *178,214,220*

clay [n] *workable earth material*
adobe, argil, argillaceous earth, bole, brick, china material, clunch, earth, kaolin, loam, loess, marl, mud, porcelain material, pottery, slip, terra cotta, till, wacke; SEE CONCEPT *509*

clean [adj1] *not dirty; uncluttered*
apple-pie order*, blank, bright, cleansed, clear, delicate, dirtless, elegant, faultless, flawless, fresh, graceful, hygienic, immaculate, laundered, neat, neat as a button*, neat as a pin*, orderly, pure, sanitary, shining, simple, snowy, sparkling, speckless, spic and span*, spotless, squeaky, stainless, taintless, tidy, trim, unblemished, unpolluted, unsmudged, unsoiled, unspotted, unstained, unsullied, untarnished, vanilla*, washed, well-kept, white; SEE CONCEPT *485*

clean [adj2] *sterile*
antiseptic, aseptic, clarified, decontaminated, disinfected, hygienic, pure, purified, sanitary, sterilized, unadulterated, uncontaminated, uninfected,
unpolluted, unsullied, wholesome; SEE CONCEPTS *314,485*

clean [adj3] *chaste, virtuous*
blameless, crimeless, decent, exemplary, faultless, good, guiltless, honorable, inculpable, innocent, modest, moral, respectable, sinless, undefiled, unguilty, unsullied, upright, wholesome; SEE CONCEPT *404*

clean [adj4] *precise, sharp*
clear, clear-cut, correct, definite, distinct, legible, neat, plain, readable, simple, trim, uncluttered; SEE CONCEPT *535*

clean [adj5] *complete, thorough*
absolute, conclusive, decisive, entire, final, perfect, total, unimpaired, whole; SEE CONCEPT *531*

clean [v] *make undirty, uncluttered*
absterge, bath, bathe, blot, brush, cauterize, clarify, cleanse, clear the decks*, clear up, deodorize, depurate, deterge, disinfect, do up*, dredge, dust, edulcorate, elutriate, erase, expunge, expurgate, flush, hackle, launder, lave, mop, neaten, pick, pick up, polish, purge, purify, rake, rasp, refine, rinse, rout out, sanitize, scald, scour, scrape, scrub, shake out, shampoo, soak, soap, sponge, spruce up*, sterilize, straighten up, swab, sweep, tidy up, vacuum, wash, whisk, winnow, wipe; SEE CONCEPTS *161,165*

clean-cut [adj] *neat, clearly outlined*
categorical, chiseled, clear, definite, definitive, etched, explicit, express, sharp, specific, unambiguous, well-defined; SEE CONCEPTS *490,535*

cleanse [v] *make undirty; wash*
absolve, clarify, clean, clear, depurate, disinfect, expurgate, launder, lustrate, purge, purify, refine, restore, rinse, sanitize, scour, scrub, sterilize; SEE CONCEPT *165*

cleanser [n] *strong disinfectant, solvent*
abrasive, abstergent, antiseptic, cathartic, deodorant, detergent, fumigant, lather, polish, purgative, purifier, scourer, soap, soap powder, suds; SEE CONCEPT *492*

clear [adj1] *cloudless, bright*
clarion, crystal, fair, fine, halcyon, light, luminous, pleasant, rainless, shining, shiny, sunny, sunshiny, unclouded, undarkened, undimmed; SEE CONCEPTS *525,617,627*

clear [adj2] *understandable, apparent*
apprehensible, audible, clear-cut, coherent, comprehensible, conspicuous, crystal, definite, distinct, evident, explicit, express, graspable, incontrovertible, intelligible, knowable, legible, loud enough, lucent, lucid, manifest, obvious, open and shut*, palpable, patent, perceptible, perspicuous, plain, precise, pronounced, readable, recognizable, sharp, simple, spelled out*, straightforward, transparent, transpicuous, unambiguous, unblurred, uncomplicated, unequivocal, unmistakable, unquestionable; SEE CONCEPTS *402,562*

clear [adj3] *open, unhindered*
bare, empty, free, smooth, stark, unhampered, unimpeded, unlimited, unobstructed, vacant, vacuous, void; SEE CONCEPT *490*

clear [adj4] *transparent*
apparent, cloudless, crystal, crystal clear, crystalline, glassy, limpid, pellucid, pure, see-through, thin, tralucent, translucent, translucid; SEE CONCEPTS *618,619*

clear [adj5] *not guilty*
absolved, blameless, clean, cleared, discharged,

dismissed, exculpated, exonerated, guiltless, immaculate, innocent, pure, sinless, stainless, unblemished, uncensurable, undefiled, untarnished, untroubled; SEE CONCEPTS 319,404

clear [*adj6*] *certain in one's mind*
absolute, confirmed, convinced, decided, definite, positive, resolved, satisfied, sure; SEE CONCEPT 403

clear [*v1*] *clean, clear away*
ameliorate, break up, brighten, burn off, clarify, cleanse, disencumber, disengage, disentangle, eliminate, empty, erase, extricate, free, lighten, loosen, lose, meliorate, open, purify, refine, rid, rule out, shake off, sweep, throw off, tidy, unblock, unburden, unclog, unload, unloose, unpack, untie, vacate, void, wipe; SEE CONCEPTS 165,211

clear [*v2*] *liberate; free from uncertainty*
absolve, acquit, clarify, defog*, discharge, disculpate, emancipate, exculpate, exonerate, explain, find innocent, let go, let off, let off the hook*, release, relieve, set free, vindicate; SEE CONCEPTS 7,22,127

clear [*v3*] *pass over, often by jumping*
hurdle, leap, miss, negotiate, overleap, surmount, vault; SEE CONCEPT 194

clear [*v4*] *profit*
accumulate, acquire, clean up*, earn, gain, gather, get, glean, make, net, obtain, pick up, realize, reap, receive, secure, win; SEE CONCEPTS 129,342

clearance [*n1*] *permission for activity*
approval, authorization, consent, endorsement, go-ahead*, green light*, leave, okay, sanction, say-so*; SEE CONCEPT 376

clearance [*n2*] *gap above something*
allowance, assart, defoliated area, empty space, expanse, gap, headroom, margin, opening, open space; SEE CONCEPT 513

clear-cut [*adj*] *definite*
assured, categorical, crystalline, decided, definitive, distinct, evident, explicit, express, indubitable, lucent, lucid, obvious, plain, precise, pronounced, sharp-cut, specific, straightforward, unambiguous, undisputed, undoubted, unequivocal, unquestioned, well-defined; SEE CONCEPT 535

clearing [*n*] *gap in area*
allowance, assart, clearance, defoliated area, dell, empty space, expanse, gap, glade, headroom, margin, opening, open space; SEE CONCEPT 513

clearly [*adv*] *without any doubt*
acutely, apparently, audibly, beyond doubt, certainly, conspicuously, decidedly, definitely, discernibly, distinctly, evidently, incontestably, incontrovertibly, indubitably, lucidly, manifestly, markedly, noticeably, obviously, openly, overtly, patently, penetratingly, perceptibly, plainly, positively, precisely, prominently, purely, recognizably, seemingly, sharply, sonorously, surely, translucently, transparently, undeniably, undoubtedly, unmistakably; SEE CONCEPTS 535,552

clear out [*v1*] *empty something*
clean out, dispose of, eliminate, exhaust, get rid of, remove, sort, tidy up; SEE CONCEPT 211

clear out [*v2*] *leave, often quickly*
beat it*, begone, decamp, depart, go, hightail*, kite*, make oneself scarce*, remove oneself, retire, scram, skedaddle*, split*, take a hike*, take off, vamoose*, withdraw; SEE CONCEPT 195

clear up [*v1*] *explain; resolve*
answer, cipher, clarify, decipher, dissolve, elucidate, figure out, illuminate, illustrate, make plausible, make reasonable, puzzle out, resolve, solve, straighten out, tidy, unfold, unravel; SEE CONCEPTS 37,57

clear up [*v2*] *become improved*
become fair, become sunny, blow over, brighten, die away, die down, improve, lapse, lift, pick up, run its course*; SEE CONCEPT 700

cleavage [*n*] *gap*
break, chasm, cleft, discontinuity, divide, division, fracture, hole, rift, schism, separation, severance, split, valley; SEE CONCEPT 513

cleave [*v1*] *divide, split*
carve, chop, crack, cut, dissect, dissever, disunite, divorce, hack, hew, open, part, pierce, rend, rip, rive, separate, sever, slice, stab, sunder, tear asunder, whack; SEE CONCEPTS 98,137,176

cleave [*v2*] *stand by, stick together*
abide by, adhere, agree, associate, attach, be devoted to, be tight with*, be true*, cling, cohere, combine, freeze to*, hold, join, link, remain, stay put, unite; SEE CONCEPTS 8,113

cleft [*n*] *break, gap*
aperture, arroyo, breach, canyon, chasm, chink, cleavage, clough, cleave, crack, cranny, crevasse, crevice, fissure, fracture, gorge, gulch, opening, ravine, rent, rift, rima, rimation, rime, schism, slit; SEE CONCEPT 513

cleft [*adj*] *separated, split*
broken, cloven, cracked, crannied, crenelated, parted, perforated, pierced, rent, riven, ruptured, separated, sundered, torn; SEE CONCEPT 490

clemency [*n*] *forgiveness*
caritas, charity, compassion, endurance, equitableness, fairness, forbearance, gentleness, grace, humanity, indulgence, justness, kindness, lenience, leniency, lenity, lifesaver, mercifulness, mercy, mildness, moderation, soft-heartedness, sufferance, tenderness, tolerance, toleration; SEE CONCEPTS 410,644

clement [*adj1*] *calm, mild (weather)*
balmy, clear, fair, fine, moderate, peaceful, temperate, warm; SEE CONCEPT 525

clement [*adj2*] *forgiving*
benevolent, benign, benignant, charitable, compassionate, easy, forbearing, gentle, humane, humanitarian, indulgent, kind, kind-hearted, kindly, lenient, merciful, mild, soft-hearted, sympathetic, tender, tolerant; SEE CONCEPTS 404,550

clench [*v*] *grasp*
clamp, clasp, clinch, clutch, constrict, contract, double up, draw together, grapple, grip, hold; SEE CONCEPT 191

clergy [*n*] *ministry of church*
canonicate, canonry, cardinalate, churchpersons, clerics, conclave, deaconry, diaconate, ecclesiastics, first estate, holy order, pastorate, prelacy, priesthood, rabbinate, the cloth, the desk, the pulpit; SEE CONCEPT 369

clergyperson [*n*] *minister of church*
abbey, archbishop, bishop, blackcoat*, cardinal, cassock, chaplain, churchperson, cleric, clerk, curate, dean, divine, ecclesiast, ecclesiastic, evangelist, father, missionary, monsignor, padre, parson, pastor, person of God, person of the cloth, pontiff, preacher, predicant, priest, primate, pulpitarian, pulpiteer, rabbi, rector, reverend, sermonizer, shepherd, vicar; SEE CONCEPT 361

cl
cl

clerical [adj 1] secretarial
accounting, bookkeeping, clerkish, clerkly, office, pink collar*, scribal, stenographic, subordinate, typing, white collar*, written; SEE CONCEPT 536

clerical [adj 2] concerning clergy
apostolic, canonical, churchly, cleric, ecclesiastic, ecclesiastical, episcopal, holy, ministerial, monastic, monkish, papal, parsonical, parsonish, pastoral, pontifical, prelatic, priestly, rabbinical, sacerdotal, sacred, theocratical; SEE CONCEPT 536

clerk [n] assistant
agent, amanuensis, auditor, bookkeeper, cashier, copyist, counter jumper*, counterperson, employee, notary, office helper, operator, paper pusher*, paper shuffler*, pencil pusher*, pen pusher*, receptionist, recorder, registrar, salesperson, secretary, seller, shopperson, stenographer, teller, transcriber, white collar*, worker; SEE CONCEPT 348

clever [adj] bright, ingenious
able, adept, adroit, alert, apt, astute, brainy, brilliant, cagey, canny, capable, competent, crackerjack*, cunning, deep, dexterous/dextrous, discerning, egghead*, expert, foxy*, gifted, good, handy, intelligent, inventive, keen, knowing, knowledgeable, many-sided, nimble, nobody's fool*, pretty, pro, qualified, quick, quick on trigger*, quick-witted, rational, resourceful, sagacious, savvy, sensible, sharp, shrewd, skilled, skillful, slick, sly, smart, sprightly, talented, versatile, wise, witty; SEE CONCEPT 402

cleverness [n] brightness, ingenuity
ability, adroitness, astuteness, brains, calculation, canniness, dexterity, discernment, flair, gift, gumption, intelligence, quickness, quick wit, resourcefulness, sagacity, sense, sharpness, shrewdness, skill, smartness, talent, wisdom, wit; SEE CONCEPT 409

cliché [n] overused, hackneyed phrase
adage, banality, boiler plate*, bromide, buzzword, chestnut*, commonplace, corn*, counterword, familiar tune, motto, old story*, platitude, potboiler, prosaism, proverb, rubber stamp*, saying, shibboleth, slogan, stale saying, stereotype, threadbare phrase, triteness, trite remark, triviality, truism, vapid expression; SEE CONCEPTS 275,278

click [n/v 1] metallic sound
bang, beat, clack, snap, tick; SEE CONCEPTS 65,595

click [v 2] fall into place
become clear, be compatible, be on same wavelength*, come off*, feel a rapport*, get on*, go, go off well*, go over, hit it off*, make a hit*, make sense, match, meet with approval, pan out*, prove out, succeed, take to each other*; SEE CONCEPT 704

client [n] customer
applicant, believer, buyer, chump, consumer, dependent, disciple, follower, front, habitué, head, mark, patient, patron, protégé, protégée, purchaser, shopper, walk-in, ward; SEE CONCEPT 348

clientele [n] customers of business
audience, business, clientage, clientry, clients, constituency, cortege, dependents, following, market, patronage, patrons, public, regulars, trade; SEE CONCEPTS 325,417

cliff [n] overhang on hill or mountain
bluff, crag, escarpment, face, precipice, rock face, rocky height, scar, scarp, steep rock, wall; SEE CONCEPT 509

climactic/climacteric [adj] decisive
acute, climactical, critical, crucial, desperate, dire, paramount, peak; SEE CONCEPT 567

climate [n 1] weather of region
altitude, aridity, atmospheric conditions, characteristic weather, clime, conditions, humidity, latitude, meteorological character, meteorologic conditions, temperature; SEE CONCEPT 524

climate [n 2] mood of situation
ambience, ambient, atmosphere, disposition, environment, feeling, medium, milieu, mise-en-scène, mood, surroundings, temper, tendency, trend; SEE CONCEPT 673

climax [n] peak, culmination
acme, apex, apogee, ascendancy, capsheaf, capstone, climacteric, crest, crowning point, extremity, head, height, highlight, high spot, intensification, limit, maximum, meridian, ne plus ultra, orgasm, payoff*, pinnacle, pitch, summit, tiptop, top, turning point, utmost, zenith; SEE CONCEPTS 706,836

climax [v] come to top; culminate
accomplish, achieve, break the record*, cap, come, come to a head*, conclude, content, crown, end, finish, fulfill, hit high spot, orgasm, peak, please, reach a peak, reach the zenith, rise to crescendo*, satisfy, succeed, terminate, top, tower; SEE CONCEPTS 375,704,706

climb [v] crawl, move up
ape up*, ascend, clamber, escalade, escalate, go up, mount, rise, scale, soar, top; SEE CONCEPT 166

clinch [v 1] secure a goal
assure, cap, conclude, confirm, decide, determine, seal, seize, set, settle, sew up, verify; SEE CONCEPT 706

clinch [v 2] hold securely; grab
bolt, clamp, clasp, clench, clutch, cuddle, embrace, enfold, fasten, fix, grab hold of, grapple, grasp, grip, hug, lay hands on, make fast, nail, press, rivet, secure, seize, snatch, squeeze; SEE CONCEPTS 191,219

cling [v] attach to
adhere, be true to, cherish, clasp, cleave to, clutch, cohere, continue, embrace, endure, fasten, freeze to, grasp, grip, hang in, hang onto, hold fast, hug, last, linger, squeeze, stay put, stick, stick like glue*; SEE CONCEPTS 85,160,190

clinic [n] medical center
dispensary, hospital, infirmary, sick bay, surgery center; SEE CONCEPTS 312,439,449

clinical [adj] dispassionate
analytic, antiseptic, cold, detached, disinterested, emotionless, impersonal, objective, scientific, unemotional; SEE CONCEPT 404

clink [n/v] bang against, ring
chink, clang, jangle, jingle, sound, tingle, tinkle; SEE CONCEPTS 65,595

clip [v 1] cut short
bob, crop, curtail, cut, cut back, decrease, dock, lower, mow, pare, prune, reduce, shave, shear, shorten, skive, slash, snip, trim, truncate; SEE CONCEPTS 137,176

clip [v 2/n] punch
blow, box, clout, cuff, knock, punch, smack, sock, thump, wallop, whack; SEE CONCEPT 189

clique [n] group of friends
bunch, cabal, camarilla, camp, circle, clan, club,

coterie, crew, crowd, crush, faction, gang, in-group, insiders, lobby, Mafia, mob, organization, outfit, pack, posse, ring, set, society; SEE CONCEPTS 387,417

cloak [n] *cover; coat*
beard, blind, camouflage, cape, capote, disguise, facade, face, front, guise, manteau, mantle, mask, pretext, semblance, shawl, shield, show, veneer, wrap; SEE CONCEPTS 451,475,680

cloak [v] *disguise*
blanket, camouflage, coat, conceal, cover, curtain, dissemble, dissimulate, dress up, hide, mask, obscure, pretext, screen, shroud, veil; SEE CONCEPT 188

clobber [v] *hit, beat*
belt, blast, drub, lambaste*, lick, shellac*, slam, slug, smash, smear, smother, thrash, trim, wallop, whip; SEE CONCEPTS 189,252

clock [n] *timekeeping device*
alarm, Big Ben*, chroniker*, chronograph, chronometer, digital watch, hourglass, pendulum, stopwatch, sundial, tattler, ticker*, tick-tock*, timekeeper, timemarker, timepiece, timer, turnip*, watch; SEE CONCEPTS 463,819

clockwork [n] *being on time; precision*
accuracy, consistency, perfect timing, regularity, smoothness; SEE CONCEPT 818

clod [n] *stupid person*
blockhead*, boor, chump, clown, dimwit*, dolt, dope*, dumbbell, dummy, dunce, fool, imbecile, lame-brain*, lout, oaf, simpleton; SEE CONCEPTS 412,423

clog [n] *blockage*
bar, block, blockade, burden, cumbrance, dead weight, drag, encumbrance, hindrance, impedance, impediment, obstruction, snag; SEE CONCEPTS 121,674

clog [v] *block, hinder*
burden, choke, close, congest, curb, dam up, encumber, entrammel, fetter, fill, glut, hamper, impede, jam, leash, obstruct, occlude, plug, seal, shackle, stopper, stop up, stuff, tie, trammel; SEE CONCEPTS 121,130,190

cloister [n] *secluded religious place*
abbey, cell, chapter house, convent, friary, hermitage, house, lamasery, monastery, nunnery, order, priorate, priory, religious community, retreat, sanctuary; SEE CONCEPTS 368,516

cloistered [adj] *secluded*
cloistral, confined, hermitic, hidden, insulated, recluse, reclusive, restricted, secluse, seclusive, sequestered, sheltered, shielded, shut off, withdrawn; SEE CONCEPTS 554,583

close [n] *ending*
adjournment, cease, cessation, completion, conclusion, culmination, denouement, desistance, end, finale, finish, period, stop, termination, windup; SEE CONCEPTS 119,832

close [adj1] *near, nearby*
abutting, across the street, adjacent, adjoining, approaching, around the corner, at hand, contiguous, convenient, give or take a little*, handy, hard by, immediate, imminent, impending, in spitting distance*, in the ball park*, near-at-hand, nearest, nearly, neighboring, next, nigh, proximate, under one's nose*, warm; SEE CONCEPT 586

close [adj2] *dense, cramped*
circumscribed, close-grained, compact, confined, confining, congested, consolidated, cropped, crowded, firm, impenetrable, impermeable, jam-

packed, narrow, packed, restricted, short, solid, substantial, thick, tight; SEE CONCEPTS 481,483,774

close [adj3] *accurate, precise*
conscientious, exact, faithful, lifelike, literal, resembling, similar, strict; SEE CONCEPTS 535,563

close [adj4] *intimate*
attached, buddy-buddy*, chummy, confidential, cozy with, dear, devoted, familiar, inseparable, kissing cousins*, loving, making it with*, on top of each other*, palsy-walsy*, private, related, thick*, thick as thieves*, thick with*; SEE CONCEPTS 372,555

close [adj5] *oppressive, humid*
airless, breathless, choky, confined, fusty, heavy, moldy, motionless, muggy, musty, stagnant, stale, stale-smelling, sticky, stifling, stuffy, suffocating, sultry, sweltering, sweltry, thick, tight, uncomfortable, unventilated; SEE CONCEPTS 525,605

close [adj6] *secret, reserved*
buttoning one's lip*, buttoning up*, clamming up*, close-lipped, closemouthed, hidden, hush-hush*, mum's the word*, on the Q.T.*, private, reticent, retired, secluded, secretive, silent, taciturn, tight chops*, tight-lipped*, uncommunicative, unforthcoming, zipping one's lips*; SEE CONCEPTS 267,576

close [adj7] *stingy*
chintzy*, closefisted, illiberal, mean, mingy, miserly, narrow, niggardly, parsimonious, penny-pinching, penurious, skimpy, skinflint*, tight, tight-fisted, ungenerous; SEE CONCEPTS 334,404

close [v1] *obstruct, seal*
bang, bar, block, bolt, button, caulk, choke, clap, clench, clog, combine, congest, cork, dam, exclude, fasten, fill, lock, occlude, plug, prevent passage, put to, retard flow, screen, secure, shut, shut off, shutter, slam, stopper, stop up, stuff, turn off; SEE CONCEPTS 113,121,201

close [v2] *complete, finish, stop*
button down*, button up*, call it a day*, call off, cap, cease, clear, clinch, conclude, consummate, culminate, cut loose, determine, discontinue, do, drop the curtain*, end, fold, fold up, halt, pack it in*, put a lid on*, put to bed*, sew up*, shut down, shutter, terminate, ultimate, wind down*, wind up*, wrap up*; SEE CONCEPT 234

close [v3] *join, unite*
agree, bind, chain, coalesce, come together, connect, couple, encounter, fuse, grapple, inclose, meet, put together, tie, tie up; SEE CONCEPT 113

closed [adj1] *shut, out of service*
bankrupt, dark, fastened, folded, gone fishing*, locked, not open, out of business*, out of order*, padlocked, sealed, shut down; SEE CONCEPT 576

closed [adj2] *finished, terminated*
concluded, decided, ended, final, over, resolved, settled; SEE CONCEPT 548

closed [adj3] *exclusive, independent*
restricted, self-centered, self-contained, self-sufficient, self-sufficing, self-supported, self-supporting, self-sustained, self-sustaining; SEE CONCEPT 113

closely [adv] *approximately, carefully*
by the skin of one's teeth*, exactly, firmly, hard, heedfully, in conjunction with, intently, intimately, jointly, meticulously, mindfully, minutely, nearly, punctiliously, scrupulously,

cl
cl

searchingly, sharply, similarly, strictly, thoughtfully; SEE CONCEPTS 487,557,573

closemouthed [adj] silent, reserved
buttoned up*, clammed up*, close, close-lipped, dummied up, have tight chops*, hush-hush, on the Q.T.*, quiet, reticent, sedate, taciturn, tight-lipped, uncommunicative, zipped one's lips*; SEE CONCEPT 267

closet [n] storage cupboard, usually tall
ambry, bin, buffet, cabinet, chest of drawers, clothes room, cold storage, container, depository, locker, receptacle, recess, repository, room, safe, sideboard, vault, walk-in, wardrobe; SEE CONCEPT 440

closure [n1] conclusion
cease, cessation, close, closing, desistance, end, ending, finish, stop, stoppage, termination; SEE CONCEPT 119

closure [n2] plug, seal
blockade, bolt, bung, cap, cork, fastener, latch, lid, obstruction, occludent, occlusion, padlock, stop, stopper, stopple, tampon, tap; SEE CONCEPTS 471,680

clot [n] blockage, mass of coagulation
array, batch, battery, body, bulk, bunch, bundle, clotting, clump, cluster, coagulum, coalescence, conglutination, consolidation, curd, curdling, embolism, embolus, glob, gob, group, grume, lump, occlusion, precipitate, set, thickness, thrombus; SEE CONCEPTS 432,466,470

clot [v] coagulate
clabber, coalesce, congeal, curdle, gel, gelate, gelatinize, glop up*, jell, jellify, jelly, lopper*, lump, set, solidify, thicken; SEE CONCEPT 469

cloth [n] fabric
bolt, calico, cotton, dry goods, goods, material, stuff, synthetics, textiles, tissue, twill, weave, yard goods; SEE CONCEPT 473

clothe [v] cover with apparel
accouter, apparel, array, attire, bedizen, bedrape, breech, bundle up, caparison, cloak, coat, costume, dandify, deck, disguise, dizen, do up*, drape, dress, dress up, dud*, endow, endue, enwrap, equip, fit, fit out, garb, gown, guise, habilitate, habit, invest, jacket, livery, mantle, outfit, primp, raiment, rig, robe, spruce, suit up, swaddle, swathe, tog, turn out, vest; SEE CONCEPT 167

clothes/clothing [n] personal attire
accouterment, apparel, array, caparison, civvies*, costume, covering, drag*, drapery, dress, duds*, ensemble, equipment, finery, frippery, frock, full feather*, garb, garments, gear, get-up*, habiliment, habit, hand-me-downs, livery, mufti, outfit, overclothes, panoply, rags*, raiment, regalia, rigging*, sack*, sportswear, Sunday best*, tailleur, tatters*, things*, threads*, toggery*, togs, tout ensemble, trappings, trousseau, underclothes, vestment, vesture, vines*, wardrobe, wear, weeds*, zoot suit*; SEE CONCEPT 451

cloud [n1] mass of water particles in air
billow, brume, darkness, dimness, film, fog, fogginess, frost, gloom, haze, haziness, mare's tail*, mist, murk, nebula, nebulosity, obscurity, ol' buttermilk sky*, overcast, pea soup*, pother, puff, rack, scud, sheep, smog, smoke, smother, steam, thunderhead, vapor, veil, woolpack; SEE CONCEPTS 437,524

cloud [n2] crowd
army, dense mass, flock, horde, host, legion, multitude, rout, scores, shower, swarm, throng; SEE CONCEPTS 417,432

cloud [v1] become foggy or obscured
adumbrate, becloud, befog, blur, darken, dim, eclipse, envelop, fog, gloom, mist, obfuscate, overcast, overshadow, shade, shadow, veil; SEE CONCEPTS 469,526

cloud [v2] confuse
addle, becloud, befuddle, disorient, distort, distract, impair, muddle, muddy, obscure, perplex, puzzle; SEE CONCEPTS 7,19

cloudy [adj] hazy; darkened
blurred, confused, dark, dense, dim, dismal, dull, dusky, emulsified, foggy, gloomy, heavy, indefinite, indistinct, leaden, lowering, misty, mucky, muddy, murky, mushy, nebulous, nontranslucent, nontransparent, not clear, nubilous, obscure, opaque, overcast, somber, sullen, sunless, vaporous; SEE CONCEPT 525

clown [n1] joking person
antic, buffoon, comedian, comic, cut-up*, dolt, droll, farceur, fool, funnyperson, funster, gagman*, gagster*, harlequin, humorist, jester, joker, jokesmith, jokester, life of the party*, madcap, merry-andrew, merrymaker, mime, mountebank, mummer, picador, pierrot, prankster, punch, punchinello*, quipster, ribald, wag, wisecracker, wit*, zany*; SEE CONCEPT 423

clown [n2] stupid, ignorant person
blockhead*, boor, bucolic, buffoon, bumpkin*, chuff, churl, clodhopper*, gawk, hayseed*, hick*, hind, jake, lout, mucker*, oaf, peasant, rube, rustic, swain, yahoo*, yokel; SEE CONCEPTS 412,423

clown [v] joke
act crazy, act the fool*, bug out*, cut up*, fool around, have fun, jest, kid around; SEE CONCEPT 386

cloy [v] overfill
disgust, fill, glut, gorge, jade, nauseate, pall, sate, satiate, satisfy, sicken, stall, stodge, suffice, surfeit, weary; SEE CONCEPT 740

club [n1] bat, stick
baton, billy*, blackjack, bludgeon, business*, conk buster*, convincer*, cosh, cudgel, hammer, hickory, mace, mallet, nightstick, persuader*, quarterstaff, rosewood, sap, shill, shillelagh, staff, swatter, truncheon, works*; SEE CONCEPTS 470,499

club [n2] social organization
affiliation, alliance, association, bunch, circle, clique, company, crew, faction, gang, guild, hangout*, league, lodge, meeting, mob, order, outfit, ring, set, society, sodality, stamping ground*, union; SEE CONCEPTS 387,439

club [n3] golfing tool
brassie, cleek, driver, iron, mashie, midiron, niblick, putter, spoon, stick, wedge, wood; SEE CONCEPT 364

club [v] hit hard with object
bash, baste, batter, beat, blackjack, bludgeon, clobber, clout, cosh, cudgel, fustigate, hammer, pommel, pound, pummel, strike, whack; SEE CONCEPT 189

clue [n] hint, evidence
cue, dead giveaway*, hot lead*, indication, inkling, intimation, key, lead, mark, notion, pointer, print, proof, sign, solution, suggestion, suspicion, telltale, tip, tip-off*, trace, track, wind; SEE CONCEPT 274

clue [v] *give information*
acquaint, advise, apprise, fill in, give the low-down*, give the skinny on*, hint, indicate, inform, intimate, lead to, leave evidence, leave trace, leave tracks, notify, point to, post, suggest, tell, warn, wise up; SEE CONCEPT 60

clump [n1] *mass of something*
array, batch, blob, body, bunch, bundle, chunk, cluster, clutter, gob, group, hodgepodge, hunk, jumble, knot, lot, lump, nugget, parcel, set, shock, wad; SEE CONCEPTS 432,470

clump [n2] *thumping noise*
clatter, clomp, galumph, scuff, stomp, stumble, thud; SEE CONCEPT 595

clump [v] *make thumping noise*
barge, bumble, clatter, clomp, galumph, hobble, limp, lumber, plod, scuff, stamp, stomp, stump, thud, thump, tramp; SEE CONCEPTS 65,595

clumsy [adj] *not agile; awkward*
all thumbs*, blundering, blunderous, bulky, bumbling, bungling, butterfingered*, clownish, crude, elephantine, gauche, gawkish, gawky, graceless, ham-handed*, heavy, heavy-handed, helpless, hulking, ill-shaped, incompetent, inelegant, inept, inexperienced, inexpert, lubberly, lumbering, lumpish, maladroit, oafish, ponderous, splay, stumbling, unable, unadept, uncoordinated, uncouth, undexterous, uneasy, ungainly, unhandy, unskillful, untactful, untalented, untoward, unwieldy, weedy; SEE CONCEPTS 401,402,584

cluster [n] *group of something*
array, assemblage, band, batch, bevy, blob, body, bunch, bundle, chunk, clump, clutch, collection, covey, crew, gathering, hunk, knot, lot, pack, party, set; SEE CONCEPT 432

cluster [v] *assemble, group*
accumulate, aggregate, associate, bunch, bunch up, bundle, collect, crowd around, cumulate, flock, gang around, gather, package, parcel, round up; SEE CONCEPT 109

clutch [n] *strong hold*
clamp, clasp, clench, clinch, connection, coupling, grapple, grasp, grip, gripe, link; SEE CONCEPT 190

clutch [v] *grab, snatch*
catch, cherish, clasp, clench, clinch, cling to, collar, embrace, fasten, glom*, grapple, grasp, grip, harbor, hold, hook, keep, nab, nail*, put the snare on*, seize, snag, snatch, take; SEE CONCEPTS 190,191

clutches [n] *personal power*
claws, control, custody, grasp, grip, hands, keeping, possession, sway; SEE CONCEPTS 388,641,710

clutter [n] *disarray, mess*
ataxia, chaos, confusion, derangement, disorder, hodgepodge, huddle, jumble, litter, medley, melange, muddle, rummage, scramble, shuffle, tumble, untidiness; SEE CONCEPTS 432,674

clutter [v] *cause mess, disarray*
dirty, jumble, litter, muddle, scatter, snarl, strew; SEE CONCEPT 254

coach [n1] *instructor, usually in recreation*
drill instructor, educator, mentor, physical education instructor, skipper, teacher, trainer, tutor; SEE CONCEPTS 350,366

coach [n2] *carriage*
bus, car, chaise, charabanc, fourwheeler, gocart, perambulator, stage, tallyho*, train, vehicle, victoria; SEE CONCEPT 505

coach [v] *instruct, usually in recreation*
break in*, cram, drill, educate, hone, lay it out for*, lick into shape*, prepare, pull one's coat*, put through the grind*, put through the mill*, ready, school, teach, train, tutor; SEE CONCEPTS 285,363

coagulate [v] *clot*
clabber, coalesce, compact, concentrate, concrete, condense, congeal, consolidate, curdle, dry, gel, gelate, gelatinize, glop up*, harden, inspissate, jell, jellify, jelly, lopper*, set, solidify, thicken; SEE CONCEPT 469

coagulation [n] *clotting*
agglomeration, caseation, concentration, concretion, condensation, congelation, consolidation, curdling, embolism, gelatination, incrassation, inspissation, jellification, thickening; SEE CONCEPT 469

coalesce [v] *blend, come together*
adhere, amalgamate, associate, bracket, cleave, cling, cohere, combine, commingle, commix, conjoin, connect, consolidate, fuse, hook up with*, incorporate, integrate, join, join up with, link, merge, mingle, mix, relate, stick, tie in with*, unite, wed; SEE CONCEPTS 112,113

coalition [n] *allied group, association*
affiliation, alliance, amalgam, amalgamation, anschluss, bloc, coadunation, combination, combine, compact, confederacy, confederation, conjunction, consolidation, conspiracy, faction, federation, fusion, integration, league, melding, mergence, merger, merging, party, ring, unification, union; SEE CONCEPT 381

coarse [adj1] *not fine, rude*
base, bawdy, blue*, boorish, brutish, cheap, common, crass, crude, dirty, earthy, filthy, foul, foul-mouthed, gross, gruff, immodest, impolite, improper, impure, incult, indelicate, inelegant, loutish, low, lowbred, lowdown and dirty*, mean, nasty, obscene, off-color, offensive, raffish, raunchy, raw, ribald, rough, roughneck*, rude, scatological, smutty*, tacky, uncivil, uncouth, uncultivated, uncultured, unrefined, vulgar, vulgarian; SEE CONCEPTS 401,545

coarse [adj2] *rough, unrefined*
chapped, coarse-grained, crude, grainy, granular, harsh, homespun, impure, inferior, loose, lumpy, mediocre, particulate, poor quality, rough-hewn, rugged, unfinished, unpolished, unprocessed, unpurified; SEE CONCEPTS 574,606

coarseness [n] *rudeness, vulgarity*
bawdiness, boorishness, callousness, crassness, crudity, earthiness, harshness, indelicacy, offensiveness, poor taste, rawness, ribaldry, roughness, smut*, smuttiness*, uncouthness, unevenness, unrefinement; SEE CONCEPTS 633,645

coast [n] *border by water*
bank, beach, coastline, littoral, margin, seaboard, seacoast, seashore, seaside, shore, shoreline, strand; SEE CONCEPTS 509,514

coast [v] *glide along without much effort*
cruise, drift, float, freewheel, get by*, ride on current, sail, skate, slide, smooth along*, taxi; SEE CONCEPTS 150,704

coastal [adj] *bordering the water*
along a coast, littoral, marginal, marshy, riverine, seaside, skirting; SEE CONCEPT 583

cl
co

coat [n1] *animal hair*
crust, ectoderm, epidermis, felt, fleece, fur, hide, husk, integument, leather, membrane, pelage, pellicle, pelt, peltry, protective covering, rind, scale, scarfskin, shell, skin, wool; SEE CONCEPT 399

coat [n2] *covering*
bark, coating, crust, finish, glaze, gloss, lacquer, lamination, layer, overlay, painting, plaster, priming, roughcast, set, tinge, varnish, wash, whitewashing; SEE CONCEPTS 259,475

coat [n3] *personal outerwear*
cape, cloak, cutaway, flogger, frock, greatcoat, jacket, mackinaw, mink, overcoat, pea, raincoat, slicker, suit, tails, threads, topcoat, trench, tux, tuxedo, ulster, windbreaker, wrap; SEE CONCEPT 451

coat [v] *cover with layer of material*
apply, cover, crust, enamel, foil, glaze, incrust, laminate, paint, plaster, plate, smear, spread, stain, surface, varnish; SEE CONCEPTS 172,202

coating [n] *covering*
blanket, bloom, coat, crust, dusting, encrustation, film, finish, glaze, lamination, layer, membrane, patina, sheet, skin, varnish, veneer; SEE CONCEPT 475

coax [v] *persuade*
allure, argue into, arm-twist*, barter, beguile, blandish, blarney, butter up*, cajole, come on, con, decoy, entice, flatter, get, hook, importune, induce, influence, inveigle, jawbone*, lure, pester, plague, press, prevail upon, rope in*, softsoap*, soothe, sweet-talk, talk into, tease, tempt, urge, wangle, wheedle, work on, worm; SEE CONCEPT 68

cobweb [n] *entanglement; filament*
fiber, gossamer, labyrinth, mesh, net, network, snare, tissue, toil, web, webbing; SEE CONCEPTS 517,674

cock [n] *rooster*
capon, chanticleer, chicken, cock-a-doodle-doo*, cockalorum, cockerel; SEE CONCEPT 394

cock [v] *aim up toward*
erect, hump, perk up, pile, prick, raise, stack, stand erect, stand up, stick up; SEE CONCEPT 201

cockeyed [adj] *crooked, askew*
absurd, askance, askant, asymmetrical, awry, cam, canted, crazy, crooked, cross-eyed, lopsided, ludicrous, nonsensical, preposterous, squint, strabismic; SEE CONCEPT 586

cocky/cocksure [adj] *self-assured, full of oneself*
arrogant, brash, bumptious, certain, conceited, confident, egotistical, hotdogging*, hotshot*, hubristic, know-it-all*, lordly, nervy, overconfident, overweening, positive, presumptuous, selfconfident, smart aleck*, smart guy*, smarty*, smarty pants*, sure, swaggering, swollen-headed, vain, wise guy*; SEE CONCEPTS 401,404

cocoon [v] *protect with covering*
cushion, encase, envelop, insulate, pad, swaddle, swathe, truss, wrap; SEE CONCEPTS 130,134

coddle [v1] *indulge, pamper*
baby, caress, cater to, cosset, cotton, favor, humor, make much of, make over, mollycoddle, nurse, pet, play up to, spoil; SEE CONCEPTS 110,295

coddle [v2] *boil lightly, usually eggs*
brew, cook, poach, simmer, steam; SEE CONCEPT 170

code [n1] *secret language system*
cipher, cryptograph; SEE CONCEPTS 276,284

code [n2] *law, rule*
canon, charter, codex, constitution, convention, custom, digest, discipline, ethics, etiquette, manners, maxim, method, regulation, system; SEE CONCEPTS 318,688

co-dependent [adj] *unhealthy psychological reliance of one person on another*
addicted, attached, hooked, interconnected, interdependent, mutually dependent, slavish trust, unhealthy confidence; SEE CONCEPTS 404,542

codicil [n] *added part to document*
addendum, addition, appendix, postscript, rider, supplement; SEE CONCEPT 270

codify [v] *systematize*
arrange, catalogue, classify, code, collect, condense, digest, order, organize, summarize, tabulate; SEE CONCEPTS 39,84

coerce [v] *compel, press*
beset, browbeat, bulldoze*, bully, concuss, constrain, cow, dragoon, drive, force, high pressure*, hinder, impel, intimidate, lean on, make, make an offer they can't refuse*, menace, oblige, pressurize, push, put the squeeze on*, repress, restrict, shotgun*, strong-arm, suppress, terrorize, threaten, twist one's arm*, urge; SEE CONCEPTS 14,68

coercion [n] *compulsion, pressure*
browbeating, bullying, constraint, duress, force, intimidation, menace, menacing, persuasion, restraint, strong-arm tactic*, threat, threatening, violence; SEE CONCEPTS 14,68

coexistence [n] *happening or being at same time, place*
accord, coetaneousness, coevality, coincidence, concurrence, conformity, conjunction, contemporaneousness, harmony, order, peace, simultaneousness, synchronicity; SEE CONCEPT 407

coffee [n] *hot beverage made from beans of a tree*
battery acid*, brew, café, café au lait, café noir, cappuccino, decaf, decoction, demitasse, espresso, forty weight*, hot stuff*, ink*, jamocha*, java*, joe*, mocha*, mud*, perk*, varnish remover*; SEE CONCEPT 454

coffer [n] *large box*
case, casket, chest, exchequer, repository, strongbox, treasure chest, treasury, war chest*; SEE CONCEPT 494

coffin [n] *box for dead person*
casket, catafalque, crate, funerary box, pall, pine box, pine drape*, sarcophagus; SEE CONCEPTS 368,479,494

cog [n] *main part of device*
cogwheel, differential, fang, gear, pinion, prong, rack, ratchet, tine, tooth, transmission, tusk, wheel; SEE CONCEPT 464

cogency [n] *effectiveness*
bearing, concern, connection, conviction, convincingness, force, forcefulness, pertinence, point, potency, power, punch, relevance, strength, validity, validness; SEE CONCEPTS 376,676

cogent [adj] *effective*
apposite, apt, compelling, conclusive, consequential, convictive, convincing, fitting, forceful, forcible, inducing, influential, irresistible, justified, meaningful, momentous, persuasive, pertinent, potent, powerful, puissant, relevant, satisfactory, satisfying, significant, solid, sound, strong, suasive, telling, urgent, valid, weighty, wellgrounded; SEE CONCEPT 537

cogitate [v] *think deeply about*
brainstorm*, cerebrate, chew the cud*, conceive, consider, contemplate, deliberate, envisage, envision, figure, flash on*, imagine, kick around*, meditate, mull over, muse, noodle around*, ponder, reason, reflect, ruminate, speculate, stew over*; SEE CONCEPTS 17,24

cogitation [n] *deep thought*
brainwork, cerebration, consideration, contemplation, deliberation, meditation, reflection, rumination, speculation; SEE CONCEPT 410

cognate [adj] *alike, associated*
affiliated, agnate, akin, allied, analogous, comparable, connate, connatural, connected, consanguine, general, generic, incident, kindred, like, related, same, similar, universal; SEE CONCEPTS 487,573

cognizance/cognition [n] *understanding*
acknowledgment, apprehension, attention, awareness, comprehension, discernment, insight, intelligence, knowledge, mind, need, note, notice, observance, observation, perception, percipience, reasoning, recognition, regard; SEE CONCEPT 409

cognizant [adj] *aware*
acquainted, alive, apprehensive, au courant, awake, conscious, conversant, down with, familiar, grounded, hep to*, hip to*, informed, in on, in the know, in the picture*, judicious, knowing, knowledgeable, observant, on the beam*, on to*, perceptive, plugged in, savvy, sensible, sentient, tuned in*, up on*, versed, wise to*, with it*, witting; SEE CONCEPT 402

cohabit [v] *live together*
be roommates with, conjugate, couple, have relations, live illegally, live with, mingle, play house*, room together, shack up*, share address, take up housekeeping*; SEE CONCEPTS 226,375,384

cohere [v1] *stick to, cling*
adhere, associate, bind, blend, cleave, coalesce, combine, connect, consolidate, fuse, glue, hold, join, merge, unite; SEE CONCEPTS 85,113,160

cohere [v2] *agree, conform*
accord, be connected, be consistent, check, check out, comport, conform, correspond, dovetail, fit in, go, hang together, harmonize, hold, hold water, make sense, relate, square; SEE CONCEPTS 8,636,667

coherence [n] *agreement*
adherence, attachment, bond, cementation, cling, clinging, comprehensibility, concordance, conformity, congruity, connection, consistency, consonance, construction, continuity, correspondence, inseparability, inseparableness, integrity, intelligibility, rationality, relations, solidarity, stickage, tenacity, union, unity; SEE CONCEPTS 388,684

coherent [adj] *understandable*
articulate, comprehensible, consistent, identified, intelligible, logical, lucid, meaningful, orderly, organized, rational, reasoned, sound, systematic; SEE CONCEPT 402

cohort [n] *partner in activity*
accomplice, adherent, aide, ally, assistant, associate, companion, company, comrade, confrere, consociate, contingent, disciple, follower, friend, hand, legion, mate, myrmidon, pal, partisan, regiment, satellite, sidekick, stall, supporter; SEE CONCEPT 423

coiffure [n] *hairstyle*
afro, beehive, blow dry*, braids, corn rows, crew

cut, DA*, dreadlocks, dreads, flip, fuzz cut*, hair, hair-comb, haircut, hairdo, permanent, pigtails, plait, ponytail, razor cut*, tail, tease, trim, wave; SEE CONCEPTS 418,718

coil [n] *thread that curls*
bight, braid, circle, convolution, corkscrew, curlicue, gyration, helix, involution, lap, loop, ring, roll, scroll, spiral, tendril, turn, twine, twirl, twist, whorl, wind; SEE CONCEPT 436

coil [v] *curl around, entwine*
convolute, convolve, corkscrew, fold, intertwine, intervolve, lap, loop, make serpentine, rotate, scroll, sinuate, snake, spiral, spire, turn, twine, twist, wind, wrap around, wreathe, writhe; SEE CONCEPTS 201,758

coin [n] *metallic money*
bread*, cash, change, chicken feed*, chips*, coinage, copper, currency, dough, gold, jack*, legal tender, meter money*, mintage, money, piece, scratch*, silver, small change*, specie; SEE CONCEPT 340

coin [v] *create, invent*
brainstorm*, compose, conceive, contrive, counterfeit, dream up, fabricate, forge, formulate, frame, head trip*, make up, make up off the top of one's head*, manufacture, mint, mold, originate, spark, spitball*, stamp, strike, think up, trump up*; SEE CONCEPTS 36,173

coincide [v] *go along with; coexist*
accompany, accord, acquiesce, agree, be concurrent, befall, be the same, come about, concert, concur, correspond, equal, eventuate, harmonize, identify, jibe, match, occur simultaneously, quadrate, square, sync, synchronize, tally; SEE CONCEPTS 667,714

coincidence [n1] *agreement; coexistence*
accompaniment, accord, accordance, collaboration, concomitance, concurrence, conformity, conjunction, consonance, correlation, correspondence, parallelism, synchronism, union; SEE CONCEPTS 667,684,714

coincidence [n2] *accidental happening*
accident, chance, eventuality, fate, fluke, fortuity, happening, happy accident, incident, luck, stroke of luck; SEE CONCEPTS 4,230

coincident [adj] *concurring, happening together*
ancillary, attendant, attending, coinciding, collateral, concomitant, consonant, contemporaneous, contemporary, coordinate, correspondent, incident, satellite, simultaneous, synchronous; SEE CONCEPTS 548,820

coincidental [adj] *accidental*
casual, chance, circumstantial, fluky, fortuitous, incidental, unintentional, unplanned; SEE CONCEPT 548

cold [n] *frigid conditions*
ague, algidity, algor, chill, chilliness, coldness, congelation, draft, freeze, frigidity, frost, frostbite, frostiness, frozenness, gelidity, gelidness, glaciation, goose flesh, iciness, inclemency, rawness, refrigeration, shivering, shivers, snow, wintertime, wintriness; SEE CONCEPTS 524,610

cold [adj1] *chilly, freezing*
algid, arctic, below freezing, below zero, benumbed, biting, bitter, blasting, bleak, boreal, brisk, brumal, chill, chilled, cool, crisp, cutting, frigid, frore, frosty, frozen, gelid, glacial, have goose bumps*, hawkish, hiemal, hyperborean, icebox, iced, icy, inclement, intense, keen, nipping, nippy, numbed, numbing, one-dog night*,

penetrating, piercing, polar, raw, rimy, severe, sharp, shivery, Siberian, sleety, snappy, snowy, stinging, two-dog night*, wintry; SEE CONCEPT 605

cold [adj2] *aloof, unresponsive*
apathetic, cold-blooded, cool, dead, distant, emotionless, frigid, frosty, glacial, icy, impersonal, imperturbable, indifferent, inhibited, inhospitable, joyless, lukewarm, matter-of-fact, passionless, phlegmatic, reserved, reticent, spiritless, standoffish, stony, unconcerned, undemonstrative, unenthusiastic, unfeeling, unimpassioned, unmoved, unresponsive, unsympathetic; SEE CONCEPT 404

cold-blooded [adj] *cruel, heartless*
barbarous, brutal, callous, cold, dispassionate, hard-boiled, hardened, hard-hearted, imperturbable, inhuman, matter-of-fact, merciless, obdurate, pitiless, relentless, ruthless, savage, steely, stony-hearted, uncompassionate, unemotional, unfeeling, unmoved; SEE CONCEPT 542

coliseum [n] *arena for events*
amphitheater, bowl, hippodrome, open-air theater, stade, stadium, theater; SEE CONCEPT 438

collaborate [v] *work together*
be in cahoots*, coact, cofunction, collude, come together, concert, concur, conspire, cooperate, co-produce, do business with, get together, glue oneself to*, go partners*, hook on, hook up*, interface, join forces, join together, join up with, participate, team up, throw in together*, throw in with*, tie in, work with; SEE CONCEPTS 100,351,384

collaborator [n] *person who works with another*
assistant, associate, colleague, confederate, co-worker, fellow traveller, helper, partner, quisling, running dog, teammate, team player*; SEE CONCEPTS 348,423

collage [n] *mixture of pictures*
abstract composition, found art, photomontage; SEE CONCEPT 259

collapse [n] *downfall, breakdown*
bankruptcy, basket case*, cataclysm, catastrophe, cave-in, conk out*, crackup*, crash, debacle, destruction, disintegration, disorganization, disruption, exhaustion, failure, faint, flop, prostration, ruination, ruining, smash, smashup, subsidence, undoing, wreck; SEE CONCEPTS 230,316,410,674

collapse [v] *fall apart, break down*
belly up*, bend, break, cave in, conk out*, crack up*, crumple, deflate, disintegrate, droop, drop, exhaust, fail, faint, fall down, flag, flake out, fold, founder, give, give in, give out, give way, go*, go to pieces*, keel over, languish, shatter, subside, succumb, tire, topple, weaken, weary, wilt, yield; SEE CONCEPTS 252,469,702

collar [n] *neck attire*
bertha, choker, dicky, Eton, fichu, fraise, frill, jabot, neckband, ruff, torque, Vandyke; SEE CONCEPTS 450,452

collar [v] *apprehend*
abduct, appropriate, arrest, bag, capture, catch, cop*, corner, get, grab, hook, lay hands on, nab, nail*, prehend, secure, seize, take, tree; SEE CONCEPTS 90,317

collate [v] *sort collection*
adduce, analogize, assemble, bracket, collect, compare, compose, contrast, examine, gather, group, match, order, relate, verify; SEE CONCEPTS 84,158

collateral [n] *monetary deposit*
assurance, bond, endorsement, guarantee, pledge, promise, security, surety, warrant, wealth; SEE CONCEPT 344

collateral [adj] *indirect, secondary*
accessory, accompanying, added, adjunctive, adjuvant, ancillary, appurtenant, attendant, auxiliary, circuitous, coincident, complementary, concomitant, concurrent, confirmatory, coordinate, corresponding, corroborative, dependent, incident, lateral, not lineal, parallel, related, roundabout, satellite, side, sub, subordinate, subservient, subsidiary, supporting, tributary, under; SEE CONCEPTS 546,567,831

colleague [n] *associate, fellow worker*
aide, ally, assistant, auxiliary, buddy, chum, co-adjutor, cohort, collaborator, companion, compatriot, compeer, comrade, confederate, confrere, co-worker, crony, friend, helper, pal, partner, teammate, workmate; SEE CONCEPTS 348,423

collect [v1] *accumulate, come together*
aggregate, amass, array, assemble, cluster, compile, congregate, congress, convene, converge, convoke, corral, flock, flock together, gather, get hold of, group, heap, hoard, muster, rally, rendezvous, round up, save, scare up, stockpile; SEE CONCEPTS 109,114

collect [v2] *obtain (money)*
acquire, dig up, muster, pass the hat*, raise, requisition, secure, solicit; SEE CONCEPT 342

collected [adj] *composed, calm*
confident, cool, easy, easygoing, levelheaded, nonchalant, peaceful, placid, poised, possessed, quiet, sanguine, self-possessed, serene, still, sure, temperate, together, tranquil, unflappable, unperturbable, unperturbed, unruffled; SEE CONCEPT 401

collection [n] *group, accumulation*
accumulating, acquiring, acquisition, agglomeration, amassing, amassment, anthology, assemblage, assembling, assembly, assortment, batch, bringing together, caboodle, clump, cluster, collation, combination, company, compilation, congeries, congregation, convocation, crowd, cumulation, digest, gathering, heap, hoard, kit, levy, lot, mass, medley, mess, miscellany, mobilization, muster, number, obtaining, omnibus, pile, quantity, securing, selection, set, stack, stock, stockpile, store; SEE CONCEPTS 109,432

collective [adj] *composite*
aggregate, assembled, collated, combined, common, compiled, concentrated, concerted, conjoint, consolidated, cooperative, corporate, cumulative, gathered, grouped, heaped, hoarded, joint, massed, mutual, piled, shared, unified, united; SEE CONCEPT 585

college [n] *institution of higher education*
alma mater, association, brainery*, halls of ivy*, halls of knowledge*, institute, lyceum, organization, seminary, university; SEE CONCEPTS 287,288,289

college student [n] *person studying at institution of higher education*
first year student, grad student*, graduate student, junior, senior, sophomore, undergrad*, undergraduate student; SEE CONCEPT 350

collide [v] *slam into*
bang, beat, break up, bump, clash, conflict, crash, crunch*, disagree, fender-bend*, fragment, hit, jolt, meet head-on*, pile up*, plow into*, pulver-

collision [n] *accident*

blow, bump, butt, concussion, contact, crash, demolishment, destruction, dilapidation, encounter, fender bender*, head-on*, hit, impact, jar, jolt, knock, percussion, pileup*, rap, ruin, shock, sideswipe, slam, smash, strike, thud, thump, wreck; SEE CONCEPTS *189,230,674*

collocate [v] *compile*

accumulate, assemble, collect, collimate, gather, parallel; SEE CONCEPT *84*

colloquial [adj] *particular, familiar to an area, informal*

chatty, common, conversational, demotic, dialectal, everyday, idiomatic, jive*, popular, street*, vernacular; SEE CONCEPT *267*

colloquy [n] *conversation, debate*

buzz session, chat, chinfest*, chitchat, clambake*, colloquium, confab*, confabulation, conference, converse, dialogue, discourse, discussion, flap*, gab fest*, gam*, groupthink*, huddle*, palaver, parley, powwow*, rap*, rap session*, seminar, talk, talkfest*; SEE CONCEPT *266*

collusion [n] *secret understanding, often with intent to defraud*

bait and switch*, bill of goods*, bunco*, cahoots*, complicity, con game*, connivance, conspiracy, craft, deceit, diddling*, dodge, doublecross, fast shuffle, flam*, flimflam*, fraudulent artifice, graft, guilt, guiltiness, gyp, intrigue, plot, racket, scam, scheme, shell game*, skunk*, sting*, trick, whitewash; SEE CONCEPTS *114,660*

colonial [adj] *pioneering, relating to a nonindependent or new territory*

crude, dependent, dominion, early American, emigrant, frontier, immigrant, new, outland, pilgrim, pioneer, prerevolutionary, primitive, provincial, puritan, territorial, transplanted, uncultured, unsettled, unsophisticated, wild; SEE CONCEPTS *549,799*

colonization [n] *settlement of area*

clearing, establishment, expanding, expansion, founding, immigration, migration, opening up, peopling, pioneering, populating, settlement, settling, squatting, transplanting; SEE CONCEPTS *198,298*

colony [n] *community*

antecedents, clearing, dependency, dominion, mandate, new land, offshoot, outpost, possession, protectorate, province, satellite, settlement, subject state, swarm, territory; SEE CONCEPTS *379,512*

color [n1] *pigment, shade*

blush, cast, chroma, chromaticity, chromatism, chromism, colorant, coloration, coloring, complexion, dye, glow, hue, intensity, iridescence, luminosity, paint, pigmentation, polychromasia, saturation, stain, tinct, tincture, tinge, tint, undertone, value, wash; SEE CONCEPT *622*

color [n2] *deceptive appearance*

deception, disguise, excuse, facade, face, false show, front, guise, mask, plea, pretense, pretext, put-on, semblance, show; SEE CONCEPTS *59,716*

color [v1] *make pigmented; shade*

adorn, blacken, bloom, blush, burn, chalk, crayon, crimson, darken, daub, dye, embellish, emblazon, enamel, enliven, flush, fresco, gild, glaze, gloss, illuminate, imbue, infuse, lacquer, paint, pigment, pinken, redden, rouge, stain, stipple, suffuse, tinge, tint, tone, variegate, wash; SEE CONCEPTS *250,469*

color [v2] *distort, exaggerate*

angle*, belie, cook up*, disguise, doctor*, embroider*, fake, falsify, fudge*, garble, gloss over, magnify, misrepresent, misstate, overstate, pad*, pervert, prejudice, slant*, taint, twist*, warp*; SEE CONCEPTS *49,63*

colored [adj1] *not white*

dyed, flushed, glowing, hued, shaded, stained, tinged, tinted, washed; SEE CONCEPT *618*

colored [adj2] *distorted*

angled, biased, false, falsified, jaundiced, misrepresented, one-sided, partial, partisan, perverted, prejudiced, prepossessed, tampered with, tendentious, warped; SEE CONCEPT *582*

colorful [adj1] *brilliant, intensely hued*

bright, chromatic, flashy, florid, gaudy, gay, hued, intense, jazzy, kaleidoscopic, loud, motley, multicolored, picturesque, prismatic, psychedelic, rich, showy, splashy, variegated, vibrant, vivid; SEE CONCEPTS *617,618*

colorful [adj2] *full of life, interesting*

brave, characterful, distinctive, flaky*, gay, glamorous, graphic, jazzy, lively, picturesque, rich, stimulating, unusual, vivid; SEE CONCEPT *404*

colorless [adj1] *without hue*

achromatic, achromic, anemic, ashen, ashy, blanched, bleached, cadaverous, doughy, drab, dull, faded, flat, ghastly, livid, lurid, neutral, pale, sickly, uncolored, wan, washed out, waxen, white; SEE CONCEPT *618*

colorless [adj2] *unlively, uninteresting*

characterless, dreary, dull, insipid, lackluster, lifeless, prosaic, run-of-the-mill*, tame, unmemorable, unpassioned, vacuous, vapid; SEE CONCEPT *404*

colossal [adj] *very large*

barn door*, behemothic, blimp*, cyclopean, elephantine, enormous, gargantuan, giant, gigantic, huge, humongous*, immense, jumbo, mammoth, mondo*, monstrous, mountainous, super, titanic, vast; SEE CONCEPT *781*

colt [n] *young horse*

filly, fledgling, foal, rookie, sapling, yearling, youngling, youngster; SEE CONCEPT *394*

column [n1] *line, procession*

cavalcade, company, file, list, platoon, queue, rank, row, string, train; SEE CONCEPTS *432,727*

column [n2] *pillar*

brace, buttress, caryatid, colonnade, cylinder, mast, minaret, monolith, monument, obelisk, pedestal, peristyle, pier, pilaster, post, prop, pylon, shaft, standard, stay, stele, support, totem, tower, underpinning, upright; SEE CONCEPT *440*

coma [n] *deep unconsciousness*

blackout, dullness, faint, hebetude, insensibility, lethargy, oblivion, sleep, slumber, somnolence, stupor, swoon, syncope, torpidity, torpor, trance; SEE CONCEPT *315*

comatose [adj] *unconscious*

cold, dead, dead to the world*, dopey, drowsy, drugged, hebetudinous, inconscious, insensible, lethargic, out, out cold*, out to lunch*, senseless, sleepy, sluggish, slumberous, somnolent, soporose, stupefied, stupid, stuporous, torpid, vegged out*; SEE CONCEPT *539*

comb [v] *arrange hair*

adjust, card, cleanse, curry, disentangle, dress,

CO CO

groom, hackle, hatchet, lay smooth, rasp, scrape, separate, smooth, sort, straighten, tease, untangle; SEE CONCEPT 162

comb [v2] *search by ransacking*
beat, beat the bushes*, examine, finecomb*, forage, go through with fine-tooth comb*, grub, hunt, inspect, investigate, leave no stone unturned*, look high and low*, probe, rake, ransack, rummage, scour, screen, scrutinize, search high heaven*, sift, sweep, turn inside out*, turn upside down*; SEE CONCEPT 216

combat [n] *battle*
action, affray, battle royal*, brush, brush-off, conflict, contest, encounter, engagement, fight, flap, fray, jackpot*, mix-up*, run-in*, service, shoot-out*, skirmish, struggle, war, warfare; SEE CONCEPTS 86,106

combat [v] *fight*
battle, buck, clash, contend, contest, cope, cross swords with*, defy, dispute, do battle with, duel, engage, fight, go up against, oppose, put up a fight*, repel, resist, shoot it out*, strive, struggle, traverse, war, withstand; SEE CONCEPTS 86,106

combative [adj] *aggressive*
antagonistic, bellicose, belligerent, cantankerous, contentious, cussed, energetic, fire-eating*, gladiatorial, hawkish, militant, ornery*, pugnacious, quarrelsome, ructious, scrappy, strenuous, trigger-happy*, truculent, warlike, warring; SEE CONCEPTS 401,404

combination [n1] *mixture, blend*
aggregate, amalgam, amalgamation, blending, brew, coalescence, combo, composite, compound, connection, consolidation, everything but kitchen sink*, fusion, junction, medley, merger, miscellany, mishmash*, mix, olio, order, sequence, solution, soup, stew, succession, synthesis, unification, union; SEE CONCEPT 432

combination [n2] *alliance, association*
affiliation, bloc, cabal, cahoots, camarilla, cartel, circle, clique, club, coadunation, coalition, combine, compound, confederacy, confederation, conjunction, connection, consolidation, consortium, conspiracy, coterie, faction, federation, gang, guild, hookup*, mafia, melding, mergence, merger, merging, partnership, party, pool, ring, set, syndicate, tie-up*, trust, unification, union; SEE CONCEPT 381

combine [v] *connect, integrate*
amalgamate, associate, band, bind, blend, bond, bracket, bunch up, coadjute, coalesce, commingle, compound, conjoin, cooperate, couple, dub, fuse, get together, glue oneself to, hitch on*, hook on*, incorporate, interface, join, league, link, marry, merge, mingle, mix, network, plug into, pool, put together, relate, slap on*, stand in with, synthesize, tack on*, tag on*, team up with*, throw in together*, tie up with*, unify, unite, wed; SEE CONCEPT 113

combustible [adj] *able to be exploded*
burnable, comburent, combustive, explosive, fiery, firing, flammable, ignitable, incendiary, inflammable, kindling, volatile; SEE CONCEPTS 485,537

combustion [n] *explosion; on fire*
agitation, candescence, disturbance, flaming, ignition, kindling, oxidization, thermogenesis, tumult, turmoil; SEE CONCEPTS 521,676,724

come [v1] *advance, approach*
appear, arrive, attain, be accessible, be at disposal, become, be convenient, be handy, be obtainable, be ready, blow in*, bob up, breeze in*, burst, buzz*, check in*, clock in*, close in, draw near, drop in, enter, fall by, fall in, flare*, get, get in, happen, hit, hit town*, make it, make the scene*, materialize, move, move toward, near, occur, originate, pop in*, pop up*, punch in*, punch the clock*, reach, ring in*, roll in*, show, show up, sign in, sky in*, spring in, turn out, turn up, wind up at; SEE CONCEPT 159

come [v2] *happen*
befall, betide, break, chance, come to pass, develop, fall, hap*, occur, take place, transpire, turn out; SEE CONCEPT 4

come [v3] *extend, reach*
add up, aggregate, amount, become, come over, develop, expand, get, go, grow, join, mature, number, run, run into, spread, stretch, sum to, total, turn, wax; SEE CONCEPTS 239,701

come about [v] *happen*
arise, befall, come to pass, occur, result, take place, transpire; SEE CONCEPT 701

come across [v] *encounter, find*
bump into, chance upon, discover, happen upon, hit upon, light upon, meet, notice, stumble upon, uncover, unearth; SEE CONCEPTS 38,183

come along [v] *progress, develop*
do well, get on, improve, mend, perk up, pick up, rally, recover, recuperate, show improvement; SEE CONCEPT 700

come at [v1] *reach, attain*
accomplish, achieve, discover, feel for, find, grasp, succeed, touch, win; SEE CONCEPTS 34,706

come at [v2] *attack*
assail, assault, charge, fall upon, fly at, go for, invade, light into*, rush; SEE CONCEPT 86

comeback [n1] *recovery, triumph*
improvement, rally, rebound, resurgence, return, revival, victory, winning; SEE CONCEPT 706

comeback [n2] *snappy retort*
answer back, quip, rejoinder, repartee, reply, response, retaliation, riposte; SEE CONCEPT 278

come back [v] *return*
come again, do better, reappear, recover, recur, re-enter, remigrate, resume, triumph; SEE CONCEPT 239

come between [v] *alienate*
divide, estrange, interfere, interpose, interrupt, intervene, meddle, part, put at odds, separate; SEE CONCEPTS 14,386

come by [v1] *acquire*
get, lay hold of, obtain, procure, secure, take possession of, win; SEE CONCEPTS 124,129

come by [v2] *visit someone*
call, come over, drop by, drop in, look in, look up, meet, pay a call, pop in, run in, see, step in, stop by, visit; SEE CONCEPT 227

come clean [v] *acknowledge information*
admit, confess, explain, make clean breast*, own up, reveal; SEE CONCEPTS 49,57

comedian [n] *funny person, often professional*
actor, banana*, card*, clown, comic, cutup, droll, entertainer, farceur, humorist, jester, joker, jokester, laugh, merry-andrew, million laughs*, quipster, stand-up comic, stooge*, top banana*, wag, wisecracker, wit*, zany*; SEE CONCEPTS 352,423

comedown [n] *letdown, blow*
anticlimax, blow, collapse, comeuppance, crash,

cropper*, decline, defeat, deflation, demotion, descent, disappointment, discomfiture, dive, down, downfall, failure, fall, flop*, humiliation, pratfall*, reverse, ruin, setback, undoing, wreck; SEE CONCEPTS 674,699

come down [v] *worsen*
decline, decrease, degenerate, descend, deteriorate, fail, fall, go downhill, reduce, suffer; SEE CONCEPT 698

come down on [v] *criticize strongly*
attack, dress down, jump on, land on, rebuke, reprimand, scold; SEE CONCEPT 52

come down with [v] *contract illness*
be stricken with, catch, contract, fall ill, fall victim to, sicken, take, take sick; SEE CONCEPTS 93,303

comedy [n] *funny entertainment*
ball*, burlesque, camp, chaffing, comicality, comicalness, comic drama, drollery, drollness, facetiousness, farce, field day*, fun, fun and games*, funnies*, funniness, gag show, grins, high camp*, high time, hilarity, hoopla, humor, humorousness, interlude, jesting, joking, laughs, light entertainment, merry-go-round*, picnic, play on, satire, schtick*, send-up, sitcom*, slapstick, takeoff, travesty, vaudeville, wisecracking, witticism, wittiness; SEE CONCEPTS 263,293

come forward [v] *volunteer services*
appear, make proposal, offer services, present oneself, proffer oneself; SEE CONCEPT 67

come from [v] *arise, emanate*
accrue, derive from, ejaculate, emerge, end up, flow, hail from, issue, originate, proceed, result, rise, spring, stem, turn out; SEE CONCEPTS 105,179

come in [v] *enter place*
alight, appear, arrive, cross threshold, disembark, finish, immigrate, intrude, land, pass in, reach, set foot in, show up; SEE CONCEPT 159

come in for [v] *be eligible for something*
acquire, bear brunt, endure, get, receive, suffer; SEE CONCEPTS 23,124

comely [adj] *beautiful*
a ten*, attractive, beauteous, becoming, blooming, buxom, fair, fine, good-looking, gorgeous, graceful, handsome, nice, pleasing, pretty, pulchritudinous, stunning, wholesome, winsome; SEE CONCEPT 579

come off [v] *transpire*
befall, betide, break, chance, click, come about, develop, go, go off, go over, hap*, happen, occur, pan out, prove out, succeed, take place; SEE CONCEPT 4

come on [v1] *advance, progress*
develop, gain, improve, increase, make headway, proceed; SEE CONCEPT 704

come on [v2] *appear, enter*
begin, come across, come into, come upon, encounter, meet, pass in, set foot in*, take place; SEE CONCEPT 119

come out [v1] *make public*
appear, be announced, be brought out, be disclosed, be divulged, be exposed, be issued, be made known, be promulgated, be published, be released, be reported, be revealed, break*, debut, get out, leak*, out, transpire; SEE CONCEPT 60

come out [v2] *conclude*
end, result, terminate, transpire; SEE CONCEPT 119

come out with [v] *disclose information*
acknowledge, bring out, chime in*, come clean, declare, deliver, divulge, lay open, own, own up, say, state, tell, throw out, utter; SEE CONCEPT 60

come through [v1] *accomplish goal*
achieve, be successful, be victorious, carry out, chip in, contribute, kick in, pitch in, prevail, score, succeed, triumph, win; SEE CONCEPT 706

come through [v2] *survive bad situation*
endure, live through, persist, pull through, ride, ride out, survive, weather storm*, withstand; SEE CONCEPT 23

come up [v] *happen suddenly*
arise, crop up, occur, rise, spring up, turn up; SEE CONCEPT 119

come up to [v] *meet expectations*
admit of comparison with, approach, arrive, bear comparison with, come near, compare with, equal, extend, get near, match, measure up to, rank with, reach, resemble, rival, stand comparison with; SEE CONCEPT 667

come up with [v] *suggest, create*
advance, bring forth, compose, detect, discover, find, furnish, invent, offer, originate, present, produce, propose, provide, recommend, stumble upon, submit, uncover; SEE CONCEPTS 75,173

comfort [n1] *good feeling; ease*
abundance, alleviation, amenity, assuagement, bed of roses*, cheer, cheerfulness, complacency, contentment, convenience, coziness, creature comforts*, enjoyment, exhilaration, facility, gratification, happiness, luxury, opulence, peacefulness, pleasure, plenty, poise, quiet, relaxation, relief, repose, rest, restfulness, satisfaction, snugness, succor, sufficiency, warmth, well-being; SEE CONCEPTS 230,410,720

comfort [n2] *aid, help*
alleviation, assist, compassion, compensation, consolation, encouragement, hand, lift, pity, relief, secours, solace, succor, support, sympathy; SEE CONCEPTS 337,712

comfort [v] *make to feel better*
abate, aid, allay, alleviate, ameliorate, assist, assuage, bolster, buck up*, calm, cheer, commiserate with, compose, condole, confirm, console, delight, divert, ease, encourage, enliven, free, gladden, grant respite, hearten, help, inspirit, invigorate, lighten burden, make well, mitigate, nourish, put at ease, quiet fears, reanimate, reassure, refresh, relieve, remedy, revitalize, revive, salve, soften, solace, soothe, strengthen, stroke, succor, support, sustain, sympathize, uphold, upraise; SEE CONCEPTS 7,22,572

comfortable [adj1] *good feeling*
adequate, agreeable, appropriate, at rest, cared for, cheerful, complacent, contented, convenient, cozy, delightful, easy, enjoyable, gratified, hale, happy, healthy, hearty, loose, loose-fitting, made well, pleasant, pleased, protected, relaxed, relaxing, relieved, rested, restful, restored, satisfactory, satisfying, serene, sheltered, snug, snug as a bug in a rug*, soft, soothed, strengthened, untroubled, useful, warm, well-off; SEE CONCEPT 572

comfortable [adj2] *affluent, wealthy*
ample, easy, enough, prosperous, substantial, sufficient, suitable, well-heeled*, well-off, well-to-do; SEE CONCEPT 334

comfortable [adj3] more than adequate
ample, commodious, cushy, luxurious, palatial, rich, roomy, spacious; SEE CONCEPT *485*

comforting [adj] cheering
abating, allaying, alleviating, analeptic, assuaging, consolatory, consoling, curing, encouraging, freeing, health-giving, heart-warming, inspiriting, invigorating, lightening, mitigating, reassuring, refreshing, relieving, remedying, restoring, revitalizing, revivifying, softening, solacing, soothing, succoring, sustaining, tranquilizing, upholding, warming; SEE CONCEPT *529*

comic [n] funny person, often professional
banana*, buffoon*, card*, clown, comedian, droll, humorist, jester, joker, jokester, life of the party*, million laughs*, quipster, stand-up comic, stooge*, top banana*, wag*, wit*; SEE CONCEPTS *352,423*

comic/comical [adj] amusing
absurd, batty, boffo*, camp*, comical, crazy, dippy, diverting, dizzy, droll, entertaining, facetious, farcical, flaky*, fool, foolheaded, for grins*, freaky, funny, gelastic, goofus*, goofy, gump*, horse's tail*, humorous, ironic, jerky, jocular, joking, joshing, laughable, light, loony, ludicrous, Mickey Mouse*, nutty, off the wall*, priceless, ridiculous, risible, schtick*, screwy, side-splitting, silly, wacky, waggish, whimsical, witty; SEE CONCEPTS *401,529*

coming [n] arrival
accession, advent, approach, landing, reception; SEE CONCEPTS *119,159*

coming [adj] approaching, promising
about to happen, advancing, almost on one, anticipated, aspiring, at hand, certain, close, converging, deserving, docking, drawing near, due, en route, eventual, expected, fated, foreseen, forthcoming, future, gaining upon, getting near, immediate, imminent, impending, in prospect, instant, in store, in the offing, in the wind*, in view, marked, near, nearing, next, nigh, oncoming, ordained, predestined, preparing, progressing, prospective, pursuing, running after, subsequent, to be, up-and-coming; SEE CONCEPTS *537,799*

command [n1] directive, instruction
act, adjuration, ban, behest, bidding, call, canon, caveat, charge, citation, commandment, decree, demand, devoir, dictate, dictation, dictum, direction, duty, edict, enactment, exaction, fiat, imperative, imposition, injunction, interdiction, law, mandate, notification, obligation, order, ordinance, precept, prescript, proclamation, prohibition, proscription, regulation, request, requirement, requisition, responsibility, rule, subpoena, summons, ultimatum, warrant, will, word, writ; SEE CONCEPTS *274,662*

command [n2] rule, power
ability, absolutism, aplomb, authority, authorization, charge, coercion, compulsion, constraint, control, despotism, domination, dominion, expertise, expertism, expertness, government, grasp, grip, hold, jurisdiction, know-how*, leadership, management, might, prerogative, primacy, restraint, right, royalty, skill, sovereignty, strings*, supervision, supremacy, sway, tyranny, upper hand*; SEE CONCEPT *376*

command [v1] demand
adjure, appoint, authorize, ban, bar, beckon, bid, call, call for, call on, call the signals*, call upon, charge, check, cite, compel, debar, dictate, direct, enact, enjoin, exact, forbid, force upon, give directions, give orders, grant, impose, inflict, inhibit, instruct, interdict, lay down the law, mark out, oblige, ordain, order, ordinate, proclaim, prohibit, put foot down*, require, requisition, restrain, rule out, send for, set, subpoena, summon, take charge, take lead, task, tell, warn; SEE CONCEPT *53*

command [v2] rule, have power
administer, boss, charge, check, coach, coerce, compel, conduct, conquer, constrain, control, curb, determine, dictate, direct, dominate, domineer, exact, exercise power, force, govern, guide, have authority, head, hinder, hold office, influence, lead, manage, officiate, oppress, overbear, override, predominate, prescribe, preside over, prevail, push, regulate, reign, reign over, repress, restrain, run, stop, subdue, superintend, supervise, sway, take over, tyrannize, wield; SEE CONCEPTS *133,298*

commandeer [v] seize, take over
accroach, activate, annex, appropriate, arrogate, assume, confiscate, conscript, draft, enslave, expropriate, grab, hijack, liberate, moonlight requisition*, preempt, requisition, sequester, sequestrate, snatch, take, usurp; SEE CONCEPTS *90,142*

commander [n] leader of military or other organization
administrator, big cheese*, boss, captain, chief, CO*, czar, commandant, czar, director, don, exec, guru, head, head honcho*, head person, higher up, high priest/priestess*, kingfish*, kingpin*, lead-off person*, mastermind, officer, point person*, ruler, skipper, top banana*, top brass*, top dog*; SEE CONCEPTS *347,358*

commanding [adj] superior, authoritative
advantageous, arresting, assertive, autocratic, bossy, compelling, controlling, decisive, dictatorial, dominant, dominating, forceful, imperious, imposing, impressive, in charge, lofty, peremptory, striking; SEE CONCEPTS *536,574*

commemorate [v] honor, observe occasion
admire, celebrate, immortalize, keep, memorialize, monument, monumentalize, observe, pay tribute to, perpetuate, remember, salute, solemnize; SEE CONCEPTS *69,377,384*

commemoration [n] honoring, observance
celebration, ceremony, custom, memorial service, monumentalization, recognition, remembrance, tribute; SEE CONCEPT *377*

commemorative [adj] in honor of something
celebratory, commemoratory, dedicatory, in memory of, in remembrance, memorial, observing; SEE CONCEPT *555*

commence [v] start action
arise, begin, come into being, come into existence, embark on, enter upon, get cracking*, get going, get one's feet wet*, get show on road*, hit the ground running*, inaugurate, initiate, jump into, kick off*, launch, lead off, open, originate, start the ball rolling*, take up, tear into; SEE CONCEPTS *119,234*

commencement [n] ceremony marking the beginning of stage
admission, alpha, birth, bow, celebration, convocation, countdown, curtain-raiser*, dawn, dawning, genesis, graduation, initiation, kickoff*, onset, opener, opening, outset, proem, services, start, starting point, tee off*; SEE CONCEPT *377*

commend [v1] *recommend, praise*
acclaim, accredit, advocate, applaud, approve, boost, build, build up, compliment, countenance, endorse, eulogize, extol, give a posy*, gold star*, hail, hand it to*, hats off to*, hear it for*, kudize, laud, pat on the back*, puff up, sanction, speak highly of, stroke, support; SEE CONCEPTS *69,75*

commend [v2] *hand over with confidence*
assign, commit, confer, confide, consign, deliver, entrust, proffer, relegate, resign, tender, trust, turn over, yield; SEE CONCEPTS *108,132*

commendable [adj] *praiseworthy*
admirable, creditable, deserving, estimable, excellent, exemplary, laudable, meritable, meritorious, praisable, thankworthy, worthy; SEE CONCEPTS *527,572*

commendation [n] *giving of praise; acclaim*
acclamation, approbation, approval, award, bouquet, Brownie points*, credit, encomium, encouragement, good opinion, honor, panegyric, pat on the back*, pay, plum, points*, posy, PR*, puff, pumping up*, rave, recommendation, shot in the arm*, stroke, stroking, tribute; SEE CONCEPTS *69,337*

commensurate [adj] *adequate, corresponding*
appropriate, coextensive, comparable, compatible, consistent, due, equal, equivalent, fit, fitting, in accord, proportionate, sufficient, symmetrical; SEE CONCEPTS *563,566*

comment [n] *statement of opinion; explanation*
animadversion, annotation, backtalk*, buzz*, comeback*, commentary, crack*, criticism, dictum, discussion, editorial, elucidation, exposition, footnote, gloss, hearsay, illustration, input, judgment, mention, mouthful, note, obiter, observation, opinion, remark, report, review, two cents' worth*, wisecrack*; SEE CONCEPTS *51,278*

comment [v] *make statement of opinion, explanation*
affirm, animadvert, annotate, assert, bring out, clarify, commentate, conclude, construe, criticize, disclose, elucidate, explain, explicate, expound, express, gloss, illustrate, interject, interpose, interpret, mention, note, notice, observe, opine, pass on, point out, pronounce, reflect, remark, say, state, touch upon; SEE CONCEPTS *51,57*

commentary [n] *analysis*
annotation, appreciation, comment, consideration, criticism, critique, description, discourse, exegesis, explanation, exposition, gloss, narration, notes, obiter dictum, observation, remark, review, treatise, voice-over; SEE CONCEPTS *51,278*

commentator [n] *reporter*
analyst, annotator, announcer, correspondent, critic, expositor, interpreter, observer, pundit, reviewer, sportscaster, writer; SEE CONCEPT *356*

commerce [n] *buying and selling*
business, dealing, dealings, economics, exchange, industry, marketing, merchandising, merchantry, retailing, trade, traffic, truck, wholesaling; SEE CONCEPTS *325,770*

commercial [adj1] *concerning business, marketing*
across the counter*, bartering, commissary, economic, exchange, financial, fiscal, for sale, in demand, in the market, market, marketable, mercantile, merchandising, monetary, pecuniary, popular, profitable, profit-making, retail, retailing, saleable, sales, supplying, trade, trading, wholesale, wholesaling; SEE CONCEPT *536*

commercial [adj2] *intended for financial gain*
exploited, for profit, investment, materialistic, mercenary, monetary, money-making, pecuniary, profitmaking, venal, Wall Street*; SEE CONCEPT *334*

commercialize [v] *prepare for saleability*
advertise, cheapen, degrade, depreciate, develop as business, lessen, lower, make bring returns, make marketable, make pay, make profitable, make saleable, market, sell; SEE CONCEPT *324*

commingle [v] *blend*
amalgamate, combine, commix, compound, inmix, integrate, intermingle, intermix, join, merge, mingle, unite; SEE CONCEPT *109*

commiserate [v] *listen to woes of another*
ache, compassionate, condole, console, feel, feel for, have mercy, pity, share sorrow, sympathize; SEE CONCEPTS *110,596*

commission [n1] *task, duty*
agency, appointment, authority, brevet, certificate, charge, consignment, delegation, deputation, diploma, embassy, employment, errand, function, instruction, legation, mandate, mission, obligation, office, permit, power of attorney, proxy, trust, warrant, work; SEE CONCEPT *362*

commission [n2] *share of a profit*
allowance, ante, bite*, bonus, brokerage, chunk, compensation, cut, cut-in*, discount, end*, factorage, fee, indemnity, juice, pay, payment, percentage, piece, piece of the action*, rake-off*, remuneration, royalty, salary, slice*, stipend, taste, vigorish; SEE CONCEPTS *329,344*

commission [n3] *group working together toward goal*
board, commissioners, committee, delegation, deputation, representative; SEE CONCEPT *381*

commission [v] *authorize or delegate task*
accredit, appoint, assign, bespeak, bid, charge, command, commit, confide to, consign, constitute, contract, crown, depute, deputize, dispatch, employ, empower, enable, engage, enlist, enroll, entrust, hire, inaugurate, induct, instruct, invest, license, name, nominate, ordain, order, select, send; SEE CONCEPTS *50,88,324,351*

commit [v1] *perform an action*
accomplish, achieve, act, carry out, complete, contravene, do, effectuate, enact, execute, go for broke*, go in for*, go out for*, offend, perpetrate, pull, pull out*, scandalize, sin, transgress, trespass, violate, wreak; SEE CONCEPTS *6,87*

commit [v2] *deliver, entrust*
allocate, allot, apportion, authorize, charge, commend, commission, confer trust, confide, consign, convey, delegate, deliver, depend upon, deposit, depute, deputize, destine, dispatch, employ, empower, engage, give, give to do, grant authority, hand over, hold, ice, imprison, institutionalize, intrust, invest, leave to, make responsible for, move, offer, ordain, promise, put away, put in the hands of, relegate, rely upon, remove, send, shift, submit, transfer, turn over to, vest; SEE CONCEPTS *108,143,217*

commitment [n] *assurance; obligation*
charge, committal, devoir, duty, engagement, guarantee, liability, must, need, ought, pledge, promise, responsibility, undertaking, vow, word; SEE CONCEPTS *71,271,274*

committee [n] *group working on project*
board, bureau, cabinet, chamber, commission, consultants, convocation, council, investigators, jury, panel, representatives, task force, trustees; SEE CONCEPT *381*

commodious [adj] *ample, spacious*
big, capacious, comfortable, convenient, expansive, extensive, large, loose, roomy, wide; SEE CONCEPTS *773,781*

commodity [n] *merchandise, possession*
article, asset, belonging, chattel, goods, line, material, object, produce, product, property, specialty, stock, thing, vendible, ware; SEE CONCEPTS *338,710*

common [adj1] *average, ordinary*
accepted, banal, bourgeois, casual, characteristic, colloquial, comfortable, commonplace, conventional, current, customary, daily, everyday, familiar, frequent, general, habitual, hackneyed, homely, humdrum, informal, mediocre, monotonous, natural, obscure, passable, plain, prevailing, prevalent, probable, prosaic, regular, routine, run-of-the-mill*, simple, stale, standard, stereotyped, stock, trite, trivial, typical, undistinguished, universal, unvaried, usual, wearisome, workaday, worn-out; SEE CONCEPT *547*

common [adj2] *generally known; held in common*
accepted, coincident, collective, communal, communistic, community, commutual, congruous, conjoint, conjunct, constant, corporate, correspondent, customary, general, generic, in common, intermutual, joint, like, mutual, popular, prevailing, prevalent, public, reciprocal, shared, social, socialistic, united, universal, usual, well-known, widespread; SEE CONCEPT *530*

common [adj3] *low, coarse*
baseborn, characterless, cheap, colorless, crass, declassé, hack, hackneyed, impure, inferior, low-grade, mean, middling, nondescript, passable, pedestrian, Philistine, plebeian, poor, prosy, raffish, second-class, second-rate, shoddy, sleazy, stale, trite, undistinguished, vulgar; SEE CONCEPTS *401,545*

commonly [adv] *usually*
as a rule, by ordinary, frequently, generally, more often than not, ordinarily, regularly; SEE CONCEPTS *530,541*

commonplace [n] *clichéd saying or idea*
banality, bromide*, chestnut*, cliché, corn*, inanity, motto, platitude, prosaicism, prosaism, prose, rubber stamp*, shallowness, shibboleth, stereotype, tag, triteness, truism, triviality; SEE CONCEPTS *278,689*

commonplace [adj] *usual, everyday*
boiler plate*, characterless, clichéd, colorless, conventional, corny*, customary, dime-a-dozen*, familiar, familiar tune, garden variety*, hackneyed, humdrum, lowly, mainstream, matter-of-course, mediocre, middle-of-the-road*, middling, mundane, natural, normal, obvious, ordinary, pedestrian, plebeian, prevalent, prosaic, run-of-the-mill*, stale, starch, stereotyped, threadbare, trite, typical, uneventful, unexceptional, uninteresting, unnoteworthy, vanilla*, widespread, workaday, worn-out; SEE CONCEPT *530*

common sense [n] *good reasoning*
acumen, cool, good sense, gumption, horse sense*, intelligence, levelheadedness, practicality, prudence, reasonableness, sense, sound judgment, soundness, wisdom, wit; SEE CONCEPT *409*

common-sense [adj] *reasonable*
astute, commonsensical, cool, down-to-earth, hard-headed, judicious, levelheaded, matter-of-fact, practical, rational, realistic, sane, sensible, shrewd, sound; SEE CONCEPT *402*

commonwealth [n] *political or geographic area*
body politic, citizenry, citizens, commonality, democracy, federation, nation, people, polity, republic, society; SEE CONCEPTS *301,512*

commotion [n] *clamor, uproar*
ado, agitation, annoyance, backwash, ballyhoo*, bedlam, big scene*, big stink*, brouhaha, bustle, clatter, combustion, confusion, convulsion, discomposure, disquiet, dither, excitement, ferment, fermentation, flap, flurry, furor, fuss, hell broke loose*, hubbub, hurly-burly, insurgence, insurrection, lather*, mutiny, outcry, pandemonium, perturbation, pother, racket, rebellion, revolt, riot, rumpus, stew, stir, to-do, tumult, turbulence, upheaval, uprising, upset, upturn, vexation, welter, whirl; SEE CONCEPTS *388,674*

communal [adj] *collective; shared*
common, communistic, community, conjoint, conjunct, cooperative, general, intermutual, joint, mutual, neighborhood, public; SEE CONCEPTS *536,708*

commune [n] *group living together*
collective, commonage, commonality, community, cooperative, family, kibbutz, municipality, neighborhood, rank and file, village; SEE CONCEPT *379*

commune [v] *communicate, experience with another*
confer, confide in, contemplate, converse, discourse, discuss, mediate, muse, parley, ponder, reflect; SEE CONCEPTS *17,266*

communicable [adj] *able to be contracted*
catching, communicative, contagious, expansive, infectious, pandemic, taking, transferable, transmittable; SEE CONCEPT *314*

communicate [v1] *give or exchange information, ideas*
acquaint, advertise, advise, announce, be in touch, betray, break, broadcast, carry, connect, contact, convey, correspond, declare, disclose, discover, disseminate, divulge, enlighten, get across, get through, hint, impart, imply, inform, interact, interface, keep in touch, let on, let out, make known, network*, pass on, phone, proclaim, publicize, publish, raise, reach out, relate, report, reveal, ring up, signify, spread, state, suggest, tell, touch base*, transfer, transmit, unfold, write; SEE CONCEPT *266*

communicate [v2] *mutually exchange information*
answer, associate with, be close to, be in touch, be near, buzz, cable, chat, commune with, confabulate, confer, converse, correspond, discourse, drop a line*, drop a note*, establish contact, get on the horn*, give a call, give a ring*, have confidence of, hear from, reach, reply, talk, telephone, wire, write; SEE CONCEPTS *56,266*

communication [n1] *giving, exchanging information, ideas*
advice, advisement, announcing, articulation, assertion, communion, connection, contact, conversation, converse, correspondence, corresponding, declaration, delivery, disclosing, dissemination, elucidation, expression, intelligence, interchange, intercommunication, intercourse, link, making known, mention, notifying, publication, reading,

reception, revelation, talk, talking, telling, transfer, translating, transmission, utterance, writing; SEE CONCEPT 266

communication [n2] *information transmitted*
account, advice, announcement, briefing, bulletin, communiqué, conversation, converse, declaration, directive, disclosure, dispatch, excerpt, goods*, hot story*, ideas, info*, information, inside story*, intelligence, language, lowdown, message, missive, news, note, pipeline, poop*, precis, prophecy, publicity, report, revelation, scoop*, skinny*, speech, statement, summary, tidings, translation, utterance, warning, word, work; SEE CONCEPT 274

communications [n] *systems of information exchange*
information technology, means, media, publicity, public relations, route, telecommunications, transport, travel; SEE CONCEPTS 349,770

communicative [adj] *informative*
candid, chatty, communicable, conversable, conversational, demonstrative, effusive, enlightening, expansive, forthcoming, frank, garrulous, gushing, loquacious, open, outgoing, talkative, unreserved, voluble; SEE CONCEPT 267

communion [n1] *affinity, agreement*
accord, association, closeness, close relationship, communing, concord, contact, converse, fellowship, harmony, intercommunication, intercourse, intimacy, participation, rapport, sympathy, togetherness, unity; SEE CONCEPT 684

communion [n2] *sacrament in church; body of believers sharing a sacrament*
breaking of bread, church, creed, denomination, Eucharist, faith, Lord's Supper, Mass, persuasion, religion, sacrament; SEE CONCEPT 367

communism [n] *socialist government*
Bolshevism, collectivism, Leninism, Marxism, rule of the proletariat, socialism, state ownership, totalitarianism; SEE CONCEPT 301

community [n1] *society, area of people*
association, body politic, center, colony, commonality, commonwealth, company, district, general public, hamlet, locality, nation, neck of the woods*, neighborhood, people, populace, public, residents, society, state, stomping ground*, territory, turf; SEE CONCEPTS 379,512

community [n2] *agreement, similarity*
affinity, identity, kinship, likeness, sameness, semblance; SEE CONCEPTS 664,670

commute [v1] *travel to work*
drive, go back and forth, take the bus/subway/train; SEE CONCEPT 224

commute [v2] *reduce punishment*
alleviate, curtail, decrease, mitigate, modify, remit, shorten, soften; SEE CONCEPTS 236,247,317

commute [v3] *exchange, trade*
barter, change, convert, interchange, metamorphose, substitute, switch, transfer, transfigure, transform, translate, transmogrify, transmute, transpose; SEE CONCEPTS 104,232

commuter [n] *daily traveler, usually for work*
city worker, driver, straphanger*, suburbanite, traveler; SEE CONCEPT 348

compact [n] *agreement*
alliance, arrangement, bargain, bond, concordat, contract, convention, covenant, deal, engagement, entente, indenture, pact, settlement, stipulation, transaction, treaty, understanding; SEE CONCEPTS 271,684

compact [adj1] *condensed*
appressed, bunched, close, compressed, crowded, dense, firm, hard, impenetrable, impermeable, packed, pressed, solid, thick, tight; SEE CONCEPTS 481,483,774

compact [adj2] *short, brief*
boiled down, compendious, concise, epigrammatic, in a nutshell*, laconic, make a long story short*, marrowy, meaty, pithy, pointed, short and sweet*, succinct, terse, to the point; SEE CONCEPTS 773,798

compact [v] *make condensed*
combine, compress, concentrate, condense, consolidate, contract, cram, integrate, pack, set, solidify, stuff, unify, unite; SEE CONCEPTS 137,208,250

compact disc [n] *recording of music or speech*
album, CD, cut*, cylinder, demo, digital recording, disk, laser disk, record, release, track; SEE CONCEPT 262

companion [n] *helper, friend*
accompaniment, accomplice, aide, ally, assistant, associate, attendant, buddy, chaperon, colleague, comate, complement, comrade, concomitant, confederate, consort, convoy, counterpart, cousin, co-worker, crony, cuz*, double, escort, guide, match, mate, nurse, pal, pard*, partner, playmate, protector, roomie*, safeguard, sidekick; SEE CONCEPT 423

companionable [adj] *friendly*
affable, amicable, buddy buddy*, clubby*, complacent, congenial, conversable, convivial, cordial, cozy, cozy with, familiar, genial, good-natured, gregarious, intimate, mellow, neighborly, outgoing, pally, palsy*, sociable, social, tight, tight with*; SEE CONCEPT 555

companionship [n] *friendship, accompaniment*
affiliation, alliance, amity, camaraderie, company, comradeship, conviviality, esprit de corps, rapport, society, togetherness, union; SEE CONCEPT 388

company [n1] *crowd of people*
aggregation, assemblage, assembly, association, band, body, circle, clan, clique, club, collection, community, concourse, congregation, convention, corps, cortege, coterie, crew, ensemble, gang*, gathering, group, horde, jungle*, league, mob*, muster, order, outfit, pack, party, retinue, ring, ruck, set, team, throng, troop, troupe, turnout, zoo*; SEE CONCEPT 417

company [n2] *business concern*
association, business, concern, corporation, enterprise, establishment, firm, house, megacorp*, multinational, outfit, partnership, syndicate; SEE CONCEPT 325

company [n3] *social friend, guest*
boarder, caller, companionship, cortege, party, presence, retinue, society, visitor; SEE CONCEPTS 417,423

comparable [adj1] *worthy of comparison*
a match for, as good as, commensurable, commensurate, equal, equipollent, equipotential, equivalent, in a class with, on a par, proportionate, tantamount; SEE CONCEPT 566

comparable [adj2] *corresponding, similar*
agnate, akin, alike, analogous, cognate, consonant, corresponding, like, parallel, related, relative, undifferenced, uniform; SEE CONCEPTS 487,573

CO
CO

comparative [adj] approximate, close to
allusive, analogous, approaching, by comparison, comparable, conditional, connected, contingent, contrastive, correlative, corresponding, equivalent, in proportion, like, matching, metaphorical, near, not absolute, not positive, parallel, provisional, qualified, related, relative, restricted, rivaling, similar, vying, with reservation; SEE CONCEPTS 487,566,573

compare [v1] examine in contrast
analyze, approach, balance, bracket, collate, confront, consider, contemplate, contrast, correlate, divide, equal, examine, hang, hold a candle to*, inspect, juxtapose, match, match up, measure, observe, oppose, parallel, place in juxtaposition, ponder, rival, scan, scrutinize, segregate, separate, set against, set side by side, size up, stack up against*, study, touch, weigh, weigh against another; SEE CONCEPTS 24,103

compare [v2] liken, equate
allegorize, approach, approximate to, assimilate, balance, bear comparison, be in the same class as*, be on a par with*, bring near, come up to, compete with, connect, correlate, distinguish between, draw parallel, equal, equate, hold a candle to*, identify with, link, make like, match, notice similarities, parallel, put alongside, relate, resemble, show correspondence, stack up with*, standardize, tie up, vie; SEE CONCEPT 39

comparison [n] contrasting; corresponding
allegory, analogizing, analogy, analyzing, association, balancing, bringing together, collating, collation, comparability, connection, contrast, correlation, discrimination, distinguishing, dividing, estimation, example, exemplification, identification, illustration, juxtaposition, likeness, likening, measuring, metaphor, observation, opposition, paralleling, ratio, relating, relation, resemblance, segregation, separation, similarity, testing, weighing; SEE CONCEPTS 24,39,529

compartment [n] section, subdivision
alcove, area, bay, berth, booth, carrel, carriage, category, cell, chamber, corner, cubbyhole, cubicle, department, division, hole, locker, niche, nook, part, piece, pigeonhole, place, portion, slot, stall; SEE CONCEPT 434

compass [n] boundary, periphery
ambit, area, bound, circle, circuit, circumference, circumscription, confines, domain, enclosure, environs, expanse, extent, field, limit, limitation, orbit, perimeter, precinct, purlieus, purview, radius, range, reach, realm, restriction, round, scope, sphere, stretch, sweep, zone; SEE CONCEPTS 484,651,788

compass [v1] enclose
beset, besiege, blockade, circle, circumscribe, encircle, encompass, environ, gird, girdle, hem in, ring, round, surround; SEE CONCEPT 758

compass [v2] achieve, get
accomplish, annex, attain, bring about, effect, execute, fulfill, gain, have, land, obtain, perform, procure, realize, secure, win; SEE CONCEPTS 142,706

compassion [n] tender feeling
benevolence, charity, clemency, commiseration, compunction, condolence, consideration, empathy, fellow feeling, grace, heart, humaneness, humanity, kindness, lenity, mercy, softheartedness, softness, sorrow, sympathy, tenderheartedness, tenderness, yearning; SEE CONCEPTS 410,633

compassionate [adj] having tender feelings
all heart, being big*, benevolent, bleeding heart*, charitable, commiserative, forbearing, going easy on*, humane, humanitarian, indulgent, kindhearted, kindly, lenient, living with, merciful, old softie*, piteous, pitying, responsive, softhearted, soft shell*, sparing, sympathetic, tender, tenderhearted, understanding, warm, warmhearted; SEE CONCEPTS 401,403

compatibility [n] harmony in relationship
affinity, agreeableness, agreement, amity, congeniality, congruity, consonance, empathy, fit, likemindedness, rapport, single-mindedness, sympathy, unity; SEE CONCEPT 388

compatible [adj] agreeable, in harmony
accordant, adaptable, appropriate, congenial, congruent, congruous, consistent, consonant, cooperative, cotton to*, fit, fitting, getting along with, harmonious, having good vibes*, hitting it off*, in keeping, in sync with*, in the groove*, like-minded, meet, on the same wavelength*, proper, reconcilable, simpatico, suitable, sympathetic, together; SEE CONCEPT 555

compel [v] force to act
bulldoze*, coerce, concuss, constrain, crack down, dragoon, drive, enforce, exact, hustle, impel, make, make necessary, necessitate, oblige, put the arm on*, put the chill on*, restrain, shotgun*, squeeze, throw weight around*, turn on the heat*, urge; SEE CONCEPTS 14,384

compendious [adj] abridged
abbreviated, breviloquent, brief, close, compact, compendiary, comprehensive, concise, condensed, contracted, curt, inclusive, laconic, short, short and sweet*, succinct, summarized, summary, synoptic; SEE CONCEPTS 773,789

compendium [n] abridgment
abstract, aperçu, brief, conspectus, digest, epitome, essence, guide, handbook, manual, overview, pandect, precis, sketch, summary, survey, syllabus, sylloge; SEE CONCEPT 283

compensate [v1] make restitution
atone, come down with*, commit, guerdon, indemnify, make good*, pay, pay up, plank out*, pony up*, recompense, recoup, refund, reimburse, remunerate, repay, requite, reward, satisfy, shell out*, take care of, tickle the palm*; SEE CONCEPTS 108,126,341

compensate [v2] offset, make up for
abrogate, annul, atone for, balance, better, cancel out, counteract, counterbalance, counterpoise, countervail, fix, improve, invalidate, make amends, negate, negative, neutralize, nullify, outweigh, redress, repair, set off; SEE CONCEPTS 126,212

compensation [n] repayment; rectification
advantage, allowance, amends, atonement, benefit, bonus, bread*, consideration, counterclaim, coverage, damages, defrayal, deserts*, earnings, fee*, gain, honorarium, indemnification, indemnity, meet, pay, payment, payoff, premium, profit, quittance, reciprocity, reckoning, recompense, recoupment, redress, reimbursement, remittal, remittance, remuneration, reparation, reprisal, requital, restitution, reward, salary, salt, satisfaction, scale, settlement, shake, stipend, take*, take-home*, wage; SEE CONCEPTS 337,344

compete [v] go up against in contest
attempt, bandy, battle, be in the running*, bid, challenge, clash, collide, contend, contest, cope

with, emulate, encounter, essay, face, fence, fight, go after, go for*, go for broke*, go for the gold*, grapple, in the hunt*, jockey for position*, joust, lock horns*, match strength, match wits*, oppose, participate in, pit oneself against*, play, rival, run for, scramble for*, seek prize, spar, strive, struggle, take on, take part, tilt, try, tussle, vie, wrestle; SEE CONCEPT 92

competence [n] *ability*
adequacy, appropriateness, capability, capacity, competency, cutting it*, cutting the mustard*, expertise, fitness, hacking it*, know-how, makings, making the grade*, might, moxie, proficiency, qualification, qualifiedness, savvy, skill, suitability, the goods*, the right stuff*, what it takes*; SEE CONCEPT 630

competent [adj] *able*
adapted, adequate, all around, appropriate, au fait, being a pistol*, capable, clever, complete, crisp, decent, dynamite, efficient, endowed, enough, equal, fireball*, fit, fool, good, know ins and outs*, know one's business*, know one's stuff*, know the answers*, know the ropes*, know the score*, no slouch*, on the ball*, paid one's dues*, pertinent, polished, proficient, qualified, satisfactory, savvy, skilled, sufficient, suitable, there*, up to it, up to snuff*, up to speed*, wicked*; SEE CONCEPT 527

competition [n] *contest*
antagonism, athletic event, bout, candidacy, championship, clash, concours, contention, controversy, counteraction, dog eat dog*, do or die*, emulation, encounter, engagement, event, fight, game, go for it, go for the gold*, horse race*, jungle*, match, matchup, meeting, one on one*, one-upping, opposition, pairing off, puzzle, quiz, race, racing, rat race*, rivalry, run, sport, strife, striving, struggle, tilt, tournament, trial, tug-of-war, warfare; SEE CONCEPTS 92,363

competitive [adj] *willing to oppose*
aggressive, ambitious, antagonistic, at odds, combative, competing, cutthroat, dog-eat-dog*, emulous, killer*, killer instinct*, opposing, rival, streetwise, vying; SEE CONCEPT 542

competitor [n] *person willing to enter contest*
adversary, antagonist, challenger, competition, contestant, corival, dark horse*, emulator, favorite, opponent, opposition, rival; SEE CONCEPTS 366,423

compilation [n] *assemblage*
accumulating, accumulation, aggregating, anthology, assembling, assortment, collecting, collection, collocating, combining, compiling, consolidating, garner, garnering, gathering, incorporating, joining, treasury, unifying; SEE CONCEPTS 109,432

compile [v] *assemble, accumulate*
abridge, amass, anthologize, arrange, assemble, bring together, collate, collect, colligate, collocate, compose, concentrate, congregate, consolidate, cull, draw together, edit, garner, gather, get together, glean, group, heap up, marshal, muster, organize, put together, recapitulate, unite; SEE CONCEPTS 79,84,109

complacent [adj] *contented*
conceited, confident, easy-going, egoistic, egotistic, gratified, happy, obsequious, pleased, satisfied, self-assured, self-contented, self-pleased, self-possessed, self-righteous, self-satisfied, serene, smug, unconcerned; SEE CONCEPTS 401,403

complain [v] *grumble about*
accuse, ascribe, attack, beef*, bellyache*, bemoan, bewail, bitch, carp, cavil, charge, contravene, criticize, defy, demur, denounce, deplore, deprecate, differ, disagree, disapprove, dissent, expostulate, find fault, fret, fuss, gainsay, grieve, gripe, groan, grouse, growl, grumble, impute, indict, kick up a fuss*, lament, lay, look askance, make a fuss, moan, nag, object, oppose, protest, refute, remonstrate, repine, reproach, snivel, sound off, take exception to, wail, whimper, whine, yammer; SEE CONCEPT 52

complaint [n1] *statement of disagreement, discontent*
accusation, annoyance, beef*, cavil, CC*, charge, clamor, criticism, dissatisfaction, expostulation, fault-finding, grievance, gripe, grouse, grumble, guff*, jeremiad, kick, lament, moan, objection, plaint, protest, protestation, rap, remonstrance, remonstration, representation, reproach, rumble*, squawk, stink, trouble, wail, whine; SEE CONCEPTS 52,689

complaint [n2] *illness, affliction*
affection, ailment, condition, disease, disorder, ill, indisposition, infirmity, malady, sickness, syndrome, upset; SEE CONCEPTS 306,316

complaisance [n] *agreeableness*
accommodativeness, acquiescence, compliance, courtesy, deference, friendliness, kindness, obligingness, politeness, respect; SEE CONCEPT 633

complaisant [adj] *agreeable*
accommodating, amiable, compliant, conciliatory, deferential, easy, easy-going, friendly, generous, good-humored, good-natured, good-tempered, indulgent, lenient, mild, obliging, polite, solicitous, submissive, SEE CONCEPT 401

complement [n] *companion, counterpart*
accompaniment, addition, aggregate, augmentation, balance, capacity, completion, consummation, correlate, correlative, counterpart, enhancement, enrichment, entirety, filler, finishing touch, makeweight, pendant, quota, remainder, rest, rounding-off*, supplement, total, totality; SEE CONCEPTS 635,824

complement [v] *complete*
accomplish, achieve, cap, clinch, conclude, consummate, crown, finish, fulfill, integrate, perfect, round off, top off; SEE CONCEPTS 91,119,234

complementary [adj] *filling, completing*
commutual, complemental, completing, completory, conclusive, correlative, correspondent, corresponding, crowning, equivalent, fellow, integral, integrative, interconnected, interdependent, interrelated, interrelating, matched, mated, paired, parallel, reciprocal; SEE CONCEPTS 577,824

complete [adj1] *total, not lacking*
all, entire, exhaustive, faultless, full, full-dress, gross, hook line and sinker*, imperforate, intact, integral, integrated, lock stock and barrel*, organic, outright, plenary, replete, the works*, thorough, thoroughgoing, unabbreviated, unabridged, unbroken, uncondensed, uncut, undiminished, undivided, undocked, unexpurgated, unimpaired, unitary, unreduced, whole, whole enchilada*, whole-hog*, whole-length, whole nine yards*; SEE CONCEPT 531

complete [adj2] *finished*
accomplished, achieved, all-embracing, all-inclusive, all over, all over but the shouting*, at-

tained, compassed, concluded, consummate, done, done with, down, effected, ended, entire, executed, fini*, finished off, full, full-fledged, home free*, perfect, plenary, realized, sweeping, terminated, that's it*; SEE CONCEPT *528*

complete [adj3] *utter, absolute*
blank, blanket, categorical, consummate, downright, dyed-in-the-wool*, flawless, impeccable, out-and-out, outright, perfect, positive, sheer, thorough, thoroughgoing, total, unblemished, unconditional, unmitigated, unqualified, whole; SEE CONCEPTS *531,535*

complete [v] *carry out action*
accomplish, achieve, actualize, bring to fruition, bring to maturity, call it a day*, cap, carry off, close, conclude, consummate, crown, determine, develop, discharge, do, do thoroughly, effect, effectuate, elaborate, end, equip, execute, fill, finalize, finish, fulfill, furnish, get through, go the limit*, go through with, go whole hog*, halt, make good*, make up, perfect, perform, put to bed*, realize, refine, round off, round out, settle, sew up*, supplement, terminate, ultimate, wind up*, wrap up*; SEE CONCEPT *91*

completely [adv] *entirely*
absolutely, all the way*, altogether, competently, comprehensively, conclusively, effectively, en masse, exclusively, exhaustively, extensively, finally, from A to Z*, from beginning to end*, fully, heart and soul*, hook line and sinker*, in all, in entirety, in full, in toto*, on all counts*, painstakingly, perfectly, quite, solidly, thoroughly, totally, to the end, to the limit, to the max*, to the nth degree*, ultimately, unabridged, unanimously, unconditionally, undividedly, utterly, wholly, without omission; SEE CONCEPT *531*

completion [n] *accomplishment, finishing*
achievement, attainment, close, conclusion, consummation, culmination, curtains*, dispatch, end, expiration, finalization, finis, finish, fruition, fulfillment, hips*, integration, perfection, realization, swan song*, windup*, wrap-up; SEE CONCEPTS *119,706*

complex [n1] *composite, aggregate*
association, compound, conglomerate, ecosystem, entanglement, group, network, organization, scheme, structure, syndrome, synthesis, system, totality; SEE CONCEPTS *432,770*

complex [n2] *psychological problem*
anxiety, a thing about something*, exaggerated reaction, fear, fixation, fixed idea, hang-up*, idée fixe, insanity, mania, neurosis, obsession, phobia, preoccupation, repression; SEE CONCEPT *410*

complex [adj1] *involved, intricate*
circuitous, complicated, composite, compound, compounded, confused, conglomerate, convoluted, elaborate, entangled, heterogeneous, knotty, labyrinthine, manifold, mingled, miscellaneous, mixed, mixed-up, mosaic, motley, multifarious, multiform, multiple, multiplex, tangled, tortuous, variegated; SEE CONCEPT *562*

complex [adj2] *difficult to understand*
abstruse, bewildering, Byzantine, circuitous, complicated, confused, convoluted, crabbed, cryptic, Daedalean, discursive, disordered, disturbing, enigmatic, entangled, excursive, Gordian, hidden, impenetrable, inscrutable, interwoven, intricate, involved, jumbled, knotted, knotty, labyrinthine, mazy, meandering, mingled,

mixed, muddled, obscure, paradoxical, perplexing, puzzling, rambling, recondite, round-about, sinuous, snarled, sophisticated, tangled, tortuous, undecipherable, unfathomable, winding; SEE CONCEPTS *402,529*

complexion [n1] *skin coloring, appearance*
cast, color, coloration, coloring, flush, front, glow, hue, looks, mug*, phiz*, pigmentation, skin, skin tone, texture, tinge, tint, tone; SEE CONCEPTS *405,622*

complexion [n2] *someone's character*
appearance, aspect, cast, countenance, disposition, guise, humor, ilk, individualism, individuality, kind, light, look, make-up, nature, personality, seeming, semblance, sort, stamp, style, temper, temperament, type; SEE CONCEPT *411*

complexity [n] *complicatedness*
complication, convolution, elaboration, entanglement, intricacy, involvement, multiplicity, ramification; SEE CONCEPT *663*

compliance [n] *agreement*
acquiescence, amenability, assent, complaisance, concession, concurrence, conformity, consent, deference, docility, obedience, observance, passivity, resignation, submission, submissiveness, tractibility, yielding; SEE CONCEPTS *411,684*

complicate [v] *confuse, make difficult*
add fuel to fire*, bedevil, clog, combine, confound, convolute, derange, disarrange, disorder, elaborate, embroil, entangle, fold, foul up*, handicap, impede, infold, interfuse, interrelate, interweave, involve, jumble, make intricate, make waves*, mix up, muck up*, muddle, multiply, obscure, open can of worms*, perplex, ravel, render unintelligible, screw up*, snafu*, snag, snarl up*, tangle, twist, upset; SEE CONCEPTS *7,19*

complicated [adj] *difficult, complex*
abstruse, arduous, Byzantine, can of worms*, convoluted, Daedalean, difficult, elaborate, entangled, fancy, gasser*, Gordian, hard, hi-tech*, interlaced, intricate, involved, knotty, labyrinthine, mega factor*, mixed, perplexing, problematic, puzzling, recondite, sophisticated, troublesome, various, wheels within wheels*; SEE CONCEPTS *562,565*

complication [n] *difficult situation*
aggravation, complexity, confusion, development, difficulty, dilemma, drawback, embarrassment, entanglement, factor, intricacy, obstacle, problem, snag, web; SEE CONCEPTS *230,674*

complicity [n] *conspiracy*
abetment, agreement, collaboration, collusion, complot, concurrence, confederacy, connivance, engineering, guilt, guiltiness, implication, intrigue, involvement, machination, manipulation, partnership; SEE CONCEPTS *388,660*

compliment [n] *praise, flattery*
acclaim, acclamation, admiration, adulation, applause, appreciation, approval, blessing, bouquet*, buttering up*, cajolery, commendation, comp, confirmation, congratulations, courtesy, encomium, endorsement, eulogy, favor, felicitation, good word, homage, honor, kudo, laud, laudation, laurels, notice, orchid*, ovation, panegyric, pat on the back*, posy*, regard, respects, sanction, sentiment, tribute, veneration, warm fuzzy*; SEE CONCEPTS *69,278*

compliment [v] *praise, flatter*
acclaim, adulate, applaud, butter up*, cajole, cel-

ebrate, charm, cheer, commemorate, commend, congratulate, endorse, eulogize, exalt, extol, fawn upon, felicitate, give bouquet*, glorify, hail, hand it to*, honor, ingratiate oneself with, kudize*, laud, magnify, make much of, panegyrize, pat on the back*, pay respects, pay tribute to, please, puff up*, recommend, roose, salute, sanction, satisfy, sing praises of, soothe, speak highly of, take off hat to*, toast, trade last*, wish joy to, worship; SEE CONCEPT 69

complimentary [adj1] *flattering*
adulatory, appreciative, approbative, approbatory, approving, celebrating, commendatory, congratulatory, courtly, encomiastic, encomiastical, eulogistic, fair-spoken, fawning, highly favorable, honeyed, honoring, laudatory, panegyrical, plauditory, polite, praiseful, respectful, sycophantic, unctuous, well-wishing, with highest recommendation, with high praise; SEE CONCEPT 267

complimentary [adj2] *free*
as a perk*, chargeless, comp, costless, courtesy, donated, free lunch*, free of charge, gratis, gratuitous, honorary, on the house*; SEE CONCEPT 334

comply [v] *abide by, follow agreement or instructions*
accede, accord, acquiesce, adhere to, agree to, cave in, come around, conform to, consent to, cry uncle*, defer, discharge, ditto*, don't make waves*, don't rock the boat*, fit in, fold, fulfill, give in, give out, give up, go along with, go with the flow*, keep, knuckle to*, knuckle under*, mind, obey, observe, perform, play ball*, play the game*, put out, quit, respect, roll over and play dead*, satisfy, shape up, stay in line*, straighten up, submit, throw in towel*, toss it in*, yes one*, yield; SEE CONCEPTS 8,35,91

component [n] *part, element*
constituent, factor, fixings, ingredient, item, making, makings, peripheral, piece, plug-in, segment, unit; SEE CONCEPTS 831,834

component [adj] *constituent*
basic, composing, elemental, fundamental, inherent, integral, intrinsic, part and parcel of*, part of; SEE CONCEPTS 546,567

compose [v1] *be part of construction*
be an adjunct, be an element of, belong to, be made of, build, compound, comprise, consist of, constitute, construct, enter in, fashion, form, go into, make, make up, merge in; SEE CONCEPTS 168,642

compose [v2] *create writing, artwork, or music*
author, bang out*, cast, clef*, coin a phrase, comp, conceive, contrive, cook up*, design, devise, discover, draw up, dream up, fabricate, forge, form, formulate, frame*, fudge together*, ghost*, ghostwrite, imagine, indite, invent, knock off*, knock out*, make up, note down, orchestrate, originate, pen, poetize, produce, push pencil*, put down, put pen to paper*, score, scribble, script, set type, set up, time, turn out, whip up*, write; SEE CONCEPTS 79,173,174

compose [v3] *calm, bring under control*
adjust, allay, appease, arrange, assuage, balm, becalm, check, collect, comfort, console, contain, control, cool, ease, ease up, hold in, lessen, let up, lull, mitigate, moderate, modulate, pacify, placate, quell, quiet, re-collect, reconcile, regulate, rein, relax, repress, resolve, restrain, settle, simmer down, slacken, smother, soften, solace,

soothe, still, suppress, temper, tranquilize, tune down; SEE CONCEPTS 7,22,117

composed [adj] *calm, collected*
at ease, calmed, clearheaded, commonsensical, confident, cool, cool as cucumber*, disimpassioned, dispassionate, easy, easygoing, have one's act together*, imperturbable, keeping a stiff upper lip*, keeping one's shirt on*, levelheaded, nonchalant, not turn a hair*, placid, poised, possessed, quieted, relaxed, repressed, sedate, self-assured, self-possessed, sensible, serene, serious, soothed, staid, suppressed, sure of oneself, temperate, together, tranquil, unflappable, unruffled, untroubled; SEE CONCEPTS 401

composite [n] *combination, mixture*
amalgam, amalgamation, blend, combo, commixture, complex, compost, compound, conglomerate, fusion, immixture, intermixture, medley, mix, olio, pasteup*, stew*, synthesis, union; SEE CONCEPTS 260,432

composite [adj] *combined, mixed*
blended, complex, compound, conglomerate, melded, synthesized; SEE CONCEPT 490

composition [n1] *structure, arrangement*
agreement, architecture, balance, beauty, combination, concord, configuration, consonance, constitution, content, design, distribution, form, formation, harmony, layout, make-up, placing, proportion, relation, rhythm, spacing, style, symmetry, weave; SEE CONCEPTS 733,757

composition [n2] *written or musical creation*
arrangement, article, chart, concerto, dissertation, drama, essay, exercise, exposition, fiction, get-up*, literary work, manuscript, melody, music, novel, number, opus, paper, piece, play, poetry, rhapsody, romance, score, setup*, short story, song, stanza, study, symphony, theme, thesis, tune, verse, work, writing; SEE CONCEPTS 259,260,263,271

compost [n] *organic material*
admixture, blend, commixture, composition, compound, fertilizer, fusion, humus, manure, mix, mixture, mulch, ordure, pile; SEE CONCEPT 509

composure [n] *calmness, collectedness*
accord, aplomb, assurance, balance, calm, contentment, control, cool*, cool head*, coolheadedness, coolness, dignity, dispassion, ease, equanimity, equilibrium, evenness, even temper, fortitude, harmony, imperturbability, inexcitability, levelheadedness, moderation, nonchalance, peace of mind, placidity, poise, polish, presence of mind, quiet, quietude, repose, sang-froid, sedateness, self-assurance, self-control, self-possession, serenity, sobriety, stability, tranquility; SEE CONCEPT 410

compound [n] *combination, mixture*
admixture, aggregate, alloy, amalgam, amalgamation, blend, combo, commixture, composite, composition, compost, conglomerate, fusion, goulash, medley, mishmash*, soup, stew, synthesis, union; SEE CONCEPTS 260,432

compound [v1] *mix, combine*
admix, amalgamate, associate, blend, bracket, co-agment, coalesce, commingle, commix, concoct, connect, couple, fuse, immix, intermingle, join, link, make up, meld, mingle, synthesize, unite; SEE CONCEPTS 109,113

compound [v2] *make difficult; complicate*
add to, aggravate, augment, confound, confuse,

CO
CO

exacerbate, extend, heighten, intensify, magnify, make complex, make intricate, multiply, worsen; SEE CONCEPTS 231,240

comprehend [v1] *understand*
appreciate, apprehend, assimilate, capiche*, catch, click, cognize, conceive, dig*, discern, envisage, envision, fathom, get*, get the picture*, gotcha*, grasp, have, know, make out*, perceive, read, savvy*, see, take in, tumble*; SEE CONCEPT 15

comprehend [v2] *include*
comprise, contain, embody, embrace, enclose, encompass, have, involve, subsume, take in; SEE CONCEPT 118

comprehensible [adj] *understandable*
apprehensible, clear, coherent, comprehendible, conceivable, explicit, fathomable, graspable, intelligible, knowable, lucid, luminous, plain; SEE CONCEPTS 402,529

comprehension [n] *understanding*
aha*, apperception, apprehension, awareness, capacity, cognizance, conception, discernment, double take*, grasp, intelligence, judgment, ken, knowledge, perception, prehension, realization, sense, slow take*, take*; SEE CONCEPT 409

comprehensive [adj] *inclusive*
absolute, across the board*, all-embracing, all-inclusive, blanket, broad, catholic, compendious, complete, comprising, containing, discursive, encircling, encyclopedic, exhaustive, expansive, extensive, far-reaching, full, general, global, in depth, infinite, lock stock and barrel*, of great scope, overall, sweeping, synoptic, the big picture*, the whole shebang*, the works*, thorough, umbrella, wall-to-wall*, whole, wide, widespread; SEE CONCEPTS 531,772

compress [v] *compact, condense*
abbreviate, abridge, abstract, bind, boil down, coagulate, concentrate, consolidate, constrict, contract, cram, cramp, crowd, crush, decrease, dehydrate, densen, densify, epitomize, force into space, make brief, narrow, pack, press, press together, ram, reduce, restrict, shorten, shrink, shrivel, squash, squeeze, stuff, summarize, syncopate, telescope, tighten, wedge, wrap; SEE CONCEPTS 208,236,247

comprise [v] *make up, consist of*
add up to, amount to, be composed of, be contained in, compass, compose, comprehend, constitute, contain, cover, embody, embrace, encircle, enclose, encompass, engross, form, hold, include, incorporate, involve, span, subsume, sum up, take in; SEE CONCEPT 643

compromise [n] *agreement, give-and-take*
accommodation, accord, adjustment, arrangement, bargain, compact, composition, concession, contract, copout*, covenant, deal, fifty-fifty*, half and half, half measure, happy medium*, mean, middle course, middle ground, pact, sellout, settlement, trade-off, understanding, win-win situation*; SEE CONCEPTS 230,684

compromise [v1] *give and take*
adjust, agree, arbitrate, compose, compound, concede, conciliate, find happy medium*, find middle ground*, go fifty-fifty*, make a deal, make concession, meet halfway, negotiate, play ball with*, settle, split the difference*, strike balance, trade off; SEE CONCEPT 8

compromise [v2] *put in jeopardy*
blight, cop out*, discredit, dishonor, embarrass,

endanger, explode, expose, give in, hazard, imperil, implicate, jeopardize, mar, menace, peril, prejudice, put under suspicion, risk, ruin, sell out, spoil, weaken; SEE CONCEPTS 101,240

compulsion [n] *drive, obligation*
coercion, constraint, demand, drive, driving, duress, duty, engrossment, exigency, force, hang-up, have on the brain*, monkey*, necessity, need, obsession, preoccupation, prepossession, pressure, tiger by the tail*, urge, urgency; SEE CONCEPTS 410,532

compulsive [adj] *driving, obsessive*
besetting, compelling, enthusiastic, irresistible, overwhelming, passionate, uncontrollable, urgent; SEE CONCEPT 401

compulsory [adj] *binding*
compulsatory, de rigueur, forced, imperative, imperious, mandatory, necessary, obligatory, required, requisite; SEE CONCEPT 546

compunction [n] *regret, sorrow*
attrition, conscience, contrition, misgiving, penitence, penitency, pity, punctiliousness, qualm, reluctance, remorse, repentance, rue, ruth, second thoughts, shame, stab of conscience, sympathy; SEE CONCEPT 410

computation [n] *performing arithmetic*
calculation, ciphering, computing, counting, data processing, estimating, estimation, figuring, gauge, guess, reckoning, summing, totalling; SEE CONCEPT 764

compute [v] *calculate, estimate*
add up, cast up, cipher, count, count heads, count noses, cut ice*, dope out*, enumerate, figure, figure out, gauge, keep tabs*, measure, rate, reckon, run down, size up, sum, take account of, take one's measure, tally, tot*, total, tote*, tote up*; SEE CONCEPT 764

computer [n] *calculating, data processing machine*
abacus, adding machine, analog, artificial intelligence, brain*, calculator, clone, CPU, data processor, digital, electronic brain*, laptop*, MAC, mainframe, micro*, microcomputer, mini*, minicomputer, number cruncher*, PC, personal computer, thinking machine*; SEE CONCEPTS 269,463

comrade [n] *ally*
associate, bosom buddy, buddy, chum, colleague, comate, companion, compatriot, compeer, confederate, confidant, confidante, co-worker, crony, friend, intimate, mate, pal, partner, sidekick; SEE CONCEPT 423

con [n] *trick*
bluff, cheat, crime, deception, double-cross, dupe, fraud, gold brick*, graft, mockery, swindle, take in; SEE CONCEPT 59

con [v] *deceive, defraud*
bamboozle*, bilk, cajole, cheat, chicane, coax, double-cross, dupe, flimflam*, fool, hoax, hoodwink, hornswoggle*, humbug, inveigle, mislead, rip off*, rook, sweet-talk*, swindle, trick, wheedle; SEE CONCEPT 59

concatenation [n] *connection, sequence*
chain, connecting, continuity, integration, interlocking, link, linking, nexus, series, succession, uniting; SEE CONCEPTS 721,727

concave [adj] *curved, depressed*
biconcave, cupped, dented, dimpled, dipped, excavated, hollow, hollowed, incurvate, incurvated, incurved, indented, round, rounded, sagging, scooped, sinking, sunken; SEE CONCEPT 486

conceal [v] *hide, disguise*
beard, burrow, bury, cache, camouflage, cloak, couch, cover, cover up, dissemble, ditch, duck, ensconce, enshroud, harbor, hole up*, keep dark, keep secret, lie low*, lurk, mask, masquerade, obscure, plant*, put in a hole*, screen, secrete, shelter, skulk, slink, sneak, stash, stay out of sight, stow, tuck away, veil, wrap; SEE CONCEPT **188**

concealed [adj] *hidden, secret*
buried, cached, camouflaged, covered, covered up, covert, enshrouded, guarded, holed up, hushed up, hush-hush*, incog*, incognito, inconspicuous, masked, obscure, obscured, on the Q.T.*, perdu, planted, privy, put in the hole*, recondite, screened, secreted, shrouded, stashed, tucked away, ulterior, under wraps*, unseen, veiled; SEE CONCEPTS **576,619**

concealment [n] *hiding, secrecy*
beard, blind, camouflage, cover, covering, cover-up, curtain, disguise, dissimulation, fig leaf*, front, hideaway, hide-out, laundromat, mask, obliteration, obscuration, occultation, privacy, red herring*, secretion, smoke screen*, veil, wraps*; SEE CONCEPTS **188,631**

concede [v] *acknowledge, give in*
accept, accord, admit, allow, avow, award, bury the hatchet*, capitulate, cave in, cede, confess, cry uncle*, ditto*, fess up*, fold, give up, go along with, go with the flow*, grant, hand over, knuckle under, let on, own, own up, play ball with*, quit, relinquish, say uncle*, surrender, throw in the towel*, waive, yes one*; yield; SEE CONCEPTS **35,57,82,235**

conceit [n] *egotism*
amour-propre, arrogance, complacence, complacency, consequence, immodesty, narcissism, outrecuidance, pomposity, pride, self-admiration, self-exaltation, self-importance, self-love, self-regard, smugness, snottiness, stuffiness, swagger, swelled head*, vainglory, vainness, vanity; SEE CONCEPT **411**

conceited [adj] *egotistical*
arrogant, bigheaded*, big talking, cocky, conceity, full of hot air*, gall, ham*, hot stuff*, immodest, know-it-all, loudmouth, narcissistic, overweening, phony, puffed up*, self-important, smart-alecky*, snotty*, stuck up*, swollen-headed*, vain, vainglorious, windbag*; SEE CONCEPT **404**

conceivable [adj] *reasonable, easy to understand*
believable, convincing, credible, earthly, imaginable, likely, mortal, possible, probable, supposable, thinkable; SEE CONCEPTS **529,552**

conceive [v1] *understand*
accept, appreciate, apprehend, assume, believe, catch, compass, comprehend, deem, dig, envisage, expect, fancy, feel, follow, gather, get, grasp, imagine, judge, perceive, realize, reckon, suppose, suspect, take, twig; SEE CONCEPT **15**

conceive [v2] *create*
become pregnant, brainstorm, cogitate, consider, contrive, cook up*, depicture, design, develop, devise, dream up, envisage, envision, fancy, feature, form, formulate, head trip*, image, imagine, make up, meditate, originate, ponder, produce, project, purpose, realize, ruminate, spark, speculate, spitball, think up, trump up*, visualize; SEE CONCEPTS **35,173,251**

concentrate [v1] *think about closely*
apply, attend, be engrossed in, bring to bear, brood over, center, consider closely, contemplate, crack one's brains*, direct attention, establish, examine, fixate, fix attention, focus, focus attention, get on the beam*, give attention, hammer*, hammer away at*, head trip*, intensify, knuckle down, meditate, muse, need, occupy thoughts, peruse, ponder, pour it on*, put, put mind to, rack one's brains*, rivet, ruminate, scrutinize, set, settle, study, sweat, think hard, weigh; SEE CONCEPT **17**

concentrate [v2] *gather, collect*
accumulate, agglomerate, aggregate, amass, assemble, bunch, center, centralize, cluster, coalesce, collect, combine, compact, compress, congest, conglomerate, congregate, consolidate, constrict, contract, converge, cramp, crowd, draw together, eliminate, embody, focalize, focus, forgather, garner, get to the meat*, heap, heap up, hoard, huddle, integrate, intensify, localize, mass, muster, narrow, pile, reduce, salt away, store, strengthen, swarm, unify, zero in*; SEE CONCEPTS **84,109**

concentrated [adj1] *condensed, reduced*
boiled down, complete, crashed*, entire, evaporated, fixed, full-bodied, lusty, potent, rich, robust, straight, strong, stuffed*, telescoped*, thick, thickened, total, unadulterated, undiffused, undiluted, unmingled, unmixed, whole; SEE CONCEPTS **483,554**

concentrated [adj2] *intense*
all-out, deep, desperate, exquisite, fierce, furious, hard, intensive, terrible, vehement, vicious; SEE CONCEPTS **326,569**

concentration [n1] *consolidation of effort*
absorption, amassing, application, assembly, bringing to bear, centering, centralization, close attention, clustering, coalescing, combination, compacting, compression, concern, congregation, consolidation, convergence, converging, debate, deliberation, fixing, flocking, focusing, heed, huddling, intensification, massing, narrowing, need, single-mindedness, study, unity; SEE CONCEPT **677**

concentration [n2] *aggregation*
accumulation, army, array, audience, band, cluster, collection, company, concourse, convergence, flock, group, herd, horde, mass, miscellany, mob, party; SEE CONCEPT **432**

concept [n] *idea*
abstraction, apprehension, approach, big idea*, brainchild*, brain wave*, conceit, conception, conceptualization, consideration, fool notion*, hypothesis, image, impression, intellection, notion, perception, slant, supposition, theory, thought, twist, view, wrinkle; SEE CONCEPTS **532,689**

conception [n1] *understanding; idea*
apperception, appreciation, apprehension, clue, cogitating, cognition, communing, comprehension, conceit, concentrating, concept, consideration, considering, deliberating, design, dreaming, envisaging, explanation, exposition, fancy, fancying, image, imagining, impression, inkling, intellection, interpretation, meditating, meditation, mental grasp, musing, notion, perception, philosophizing, picture, plan, realization, representation, speculating, speculation, thought, version; SEE CONCEPTS **409,410,689**

CO
CO

conception [n2] *beginning, birth*
fertilization, formation, germination, impregnation, inception, initiation, insemination, invention, launching, origin, outset, start; SEE CONCEPTS *119,302,373,375*

concern [n1] *business, responsibility*
affair, burden, care, charge, company, corporation, deportment, entanglement, enterprise, establishment, field, firm, house, interest, involvement, job, jungle*, matter, megacorp*, mission, multinational, occupation, organization, outfit, shooting match*, task, thing, transaction, worry, zoo*; SEE CONCEPTS *325,362,532*

concern [n2] *interest; anxiety*
apprehension, attention, bearing, care, carefulness, concernment, consideration, disquiet, disquietude, distress, heed, heedfulness, important matter, matter, reference, regard, relation, relevance, solicitude, tender loving care, unease, worry; SEE CONCEPTS *410,690*

concern [v1] *affect personally*
apply to, bear on, become involved, be relevant to, bother, disquiet, distress, disturb, interest, involve, make anxious, make uneasy, pertain to, perturb, regard, take pains, touch, trouble, worry; SEE CONCEPTS *7,19,22*

concern [v2] *relate to, have reference to*
answer to, appertain to, apply to, be about, be applicable to, bear on, bear upon, be connected with, be dependent upon, be interdependent with, belong to, be pertinent to, be well taken, deal with, depend upon, have a bearing on, have connections with, have implications for, have relation to, have significance for, have to do with, involve, pertain to, refer to, regard; SEE CONCEPT *532*

concerned [adj1] *worried*
anxious, biting one's nails*, bothered, butterflies in stomach*, distressed, disturbed, exercised, in a stew*, on pins and needles*, perturbed, tied up in knots*, troubled, uneasy, upset, uptight, worried sick*; SEE CONCEPT *403*

concerned [adj2] *involved with*
active, affected, attentive, caring, down with, implicated, in on, interested, mixed up, privy to, solicitous; SEE CONCEPTS *401,403*

concert [n1] *musical performance*
gig, jam session, musical, musicale, recital, rockfest, selections, show; SEE CONCEPT *263*

concert [n2] *agreement, harmony*
accord, chorus, collaboration, concord, concordance, consonance, joint, league, togetherness, tune, unanimity, union, unison; SEE CONCEPTS *388,684*

concerted [adj] *coordinated*
agreed upon, collaborative, combined, joint, mutual, planned, prearranged, united; SEE CONCEPT *538*

concession [n] *yielding, adjustment*
acknowledgment, admission, allowance, assent, authorization, boon, buyback, compromise, confession, copout*, deal, giveback, giving in, grant, indulgence, permission, permit, privilege, rollback, sellout, surrender, trade-off, warrant; SEE CONCEPTS *13,50,67,88*

conciliatory [adj] *placid, yielding*
appeasing, assuaging, calm, civil, disarming, irenic, mollifying, pacific, peaceable, placating, placatory, propitiative, quiet, willing; SEE CONCEPT *401*

concise [adj] *short, to the point*
abridged, boiled down*, breviloquent, brief, compact, compendiary, compendious, compressed, condensed, curt, epigrammatic, in a nutshell*, laconic, lean, marrowy, meaty, pithy, short and sweet*, succinct, summary, synoptic, terse; SEE CONCEPTS *773,798*

conclave [n] *secret meeting*
assembly, buzz session*, cabinet*, confab*, conference, council, encounter, gathering, get-together, huddle, meet, parley, powwow*, private meeting, session; SEE CONCEPTS *324,384*

conclude [v1] *finish, come to an end*
achieve, bring down curtain*, call it a day*, cease, cinch, clinch, close, close out, complete, consummate, crown, desist, draw to close, end, halt, knock off, put the lid on*, put to bed*, round off, stop, terminate, top off, ultimate, wind up, wrap up; SEE CONCEPTS *119,234*

conclude [v2] *decide, deduce*
add up to, adjudge, analyze, assume, be afraid, boil down to*, collect, derive, draw, figure, gather, have a hunch*, infer, intuit, judge, make, make out, presume, ratiocinate, reason, reckon, sum up, suppose, surmise, the way one sees it*; SEE CONCEPTS *18,37*

conclude [v3] *settle, resolve*
accomplish, achieve, bring about, carry out, clinch, confirm, decide, determine, effect, establish, fix, pull off, rule, work out; SEE CONCEPTS *18,91,126*

conclusion [n1] *end*
cease, cessation, close, closure, completion, consequence, culmination, denouement, desistance, development, ending, end of the line*, eventuality, finale, finish, issue, outcome, payoff, period, result, stop, termination, upshot, windup, wrap; SEE CONCEPTS *119,832*

conclusion [n2] *judgment, decision*
agreement, conviction, corollary, deduction, determination, illation, inference, opinion, ratiocination, resolution, resolve, sequitur, settlement, verdict; SEE CONCEPT *689*

conclusive [adj] *definite, final*
absolute, all out*, clear, clinching, cogent, compelling, convincing, deciding, decisive, demonstrative, determinant, determinative, flat out*, incontrovertible, indisputable, irrefragable, irrefrangible, irrefutable, irrevocable, litmus test*, precise, resolving, revealing, settling, straight out, telling, ultimate, unambiguous, unanswerable, unarguable, unconditional, undeniable, unmistakable, unquestionable, what you see is what you get*; SEE CONCEPT *535*

concoct [v] *formulate, think up*
ad lib, batch*, brew*, compound, contrive, cook up, create, design, devise, discover, dream up, envisage, envision, fabricate, frame*, hatch, invent, make up, mature, originate, plan, plot, prefab*, prepare, project, scheme, slap together*, throw together*, vamp; SEE CONCEPTS *36,173,251*

concoction [n] *creation, blend*
brew, combination, compound, contrivance, intention, medley, mixture, plan, preparation, project, solution; SEE CONCEPTS *260,432,660*

concomitant [adj] *contributing, accompanying*
accessory, adjuvant, agreeing, ancillary, associated with, associative, attendant, attending, belonging, coefficient, coetaneous, coeval,

coexistent, coincident, coincidental, collateral, complementary, concordant, concurrent, conjoined, conjoined with, connected, contemporaneous, contemporary, coordinate, corollary, coterminous, coupled with, fellow, incident, in tempo, in time, isochronal, isochronous, joint, satellite, synchronal, synchronous, synergetic; SEE CONCEPT 577

concord [n1] *unity, harmony*
accord, agreement, amity, calmness, chime, comity, concert, concordance, consensus, consonance, friendship, goodwill, peace, placidity, rapport, serenity, tranquility, tune, unanimity, understanding, unison; SEE CONCEPT 388

concord [n2] *agreement, treaty*
compact, concordat, contract, convention, entente, pact, protocol; SEE CONCEPTS 271,684

concourse [n1] *passageway*
avenue, boulevard, entrance, foyer, hall, highway, lobby, lounge, meeting place, path, rallying point*, road, street; SEE CONCEPTS 440,501

concourse [n2] *crowd, group*
assemblage, assembly, collection, concursion, confluence, convergence, crush, gang, gathering, joining, junction, linkage, meeting, mob, multitude, rout, throng; SEE CONCEPT 432

concrete [adj1] *actual, factual*
accurate, corporeal, definite, detailed, explicit, material, objective, particular, precise, real, sensible, solid, specific, substantial, tangible; SEE CONCEPTS 535,582

concrete [adj2] *hardened*
caked, calcified, cemented, compact, compressed, congealed, conglomerated, consolidated, dried, firm, indurate, monolithic, petrified, poured, precast, set, set in stone*, solid, solidified, steeled, strong, unyielding; SEE CONCEPT 604

concur [v] *agree, approve*
accede, accord, acquiesce, assent, band, be consonant with, be in harmony, coadjute, coincide, collaborate, combine, come together, consent, cooperate, cut a deal*, equal, harmonize, jibe*, join, league*, meet, okay*, pass on*, shake on*, unite; SEE CONCEPTS 8,10,82

concurrent [adj1] *simultaneous*
circumstantial, coeval, coexisting, coincident, concerted, concomitant, contemporaneous, incidental, in sync, parallel, synchronal, synchronous; SEE CONCEPT 799

concurrent [adj2] *agreeing, converging*
allied, at one, centrolineal, coinciding, compatible, concerted, confluent, consentient, consistent, convergent, cooperating, coterminous, harmonious, in agreement, in rapport, joined, like-minded, meeting, mutual, of the same mind, unified, uniting; SEE CONCEPT 563

concussion [n] *collision, shaking*
blast, blow, buffeting, bump, clash, clout, crack, crash, hit, impact, injury, jar, jarring, jolt, jolting, jounce, pounding, punch, shock, trauma; SEE CONCEPTS 189,309,521

condemn [v] *blame, convict*
adjudge, belittle, blow whistle on*, call down*, castigate, censure, chide, come down on*, criticize, damn, decry, denounce, denunciate, deprecate, depreciate, disapprove, disparage, doom, find fault with, find guilty, frame, hang something on*, judge, knock, lay at one's door*, let have it*, name, pass sentence on*, pin it on*, point finger at*, pronounce, proscribe, punish, put away, put down, reprehend, reproach, reprobate, reprove, send up, send up the river*, sentence, skin, thumbs down on*, upbraid; SEE CONCEPTS 44,52,317

condemnation [n] *blaming, conviction*
accusation, blame, censure, damnation, denouncement, denunciation, disapproval, doom, judgment, proscription, reproach, reprobation, reproof, sentence, stricture; SEE CONCEPTS 44,52,317

condensation [n1] *abridgment*
abstract, boildown*, breviary, brief, compendium, compression, concentration, consolidation, conspectus, contraction, curtailment, digest, epitome, essence, précis, reduction, summary, synopsis; SEE CONCEPTS 283,730

condensation [n2] *water buildup*
condensate, crystallization, deliquescence, dew, distillation, liquefaction, precipitate, precipitation, rainfall; SEE CONCEPT 514

condense [v] *abridge*
abbreviate, blue pencil*, boil down, chop, coagulate, compact, compress, concentrate, constrict, contract, curtail, cut, cut down, decoct, densen, digest, edit, encapsulate, epitomize, inventory, precipitate, précis, press together, put in a nutshell*, reduce, shorten, shrink, snip, solidify, sum, summarize, summate, synopsize, telescope, thicken, trim; SEE CONCEPTS 236,247

condescend [v] *stoop, humble oneself*
accommodate, accord, acquiesce, agree, be courteous, bend, come down off high horse*, comply, concede, degrade oneself, deign, demean oneself, descend, favor, grant, high hat*, lower oneself, oblige, see fit, submit, talk down to, toss a few crumbs*, unbend, vouchsafe, yield; SEE CONCEPT 633

condescending [adj] *snobby, lordly*
arrogant, complaisant, disdainful, egotistic, la-dee-da*, lofty, patronizing, snobbish, snooty*, snotty*, supercilious, superior, uppish, uppity*; SEE CONCEPT 401

condescension [n] *disdain, superiority*
airs, civility, deference, haughtiness, loftiness, lordliness, patronage, patronizing attitude, superciliousness, toleration; SEE CONCEPT 633

condition [n1] *circumstances*
action, ballgame*, case, estate, happening, how it goes*, how things are*, how things stack up*, lay of the land*, like it is*, mode, order, plight, position, posture, predicament, quality, rank, repair, reputation, riff, scene, shape, situation, size of it*, sphere, spot, standing, state, state of affairs, status, status quo, trim, way things are*, way things shape up*, where it's at*; SEE CONCEPTS 639,696

condition [n2] *requirement, limitation*
arrangement, article, catch, codicil, contingency, demand, essential, exception, exemption, fine print*, kicker*, modification, must, necessity, postulate, precondition, prerequisite, provision, proviso, qualification, requisite, reservation, rule, sine qua non, small print*, stipulation, strings*, terms; SEE CONCEPTS 270,688

condition [n3] *physical shape, fitness*
appearance, aspect, build, constitution, fettle, form, health, kilter, mint, order, phase, repair, state, status, tone, trim; SEE CONCEPTS 316,757

condition [n4] *illness*
affection, ailment, complaint, disease, ill, infir-

CO
CO

mity, malady, predicament, problem, syndrome, temper, weakness; SEE CONCEPT *306*

condition [v] *adapt, prepare*
accustom, brainwash, build up, educate, equip, habituate, inure, loosen up, make ready, modify, practice, program, ready, shape up, sharpen, tone up, toughen up, train, warm up, whip into shape*, work out, work over; SEE CONCEPTS *35,202*

conditional [adj] *dependent*
codicillary, contingent, depending on, fortuitous, granted on certain terms, guarded, iffy*, incidental, inconclusive, limited, modified, not absolute, obscure, provisional, provisory, qualified, relative, reliant, relying on, restricted, restrictive, subject to, tentative, uncertain, with grain of salt*, with reservations, with strings attached*; SEE CONCEPT *554*

condolence [n] *sympathy*
comfort, commiseration, compassion, condolement, consolation, fellow feeling, solace; SEE CONCEPT *633*

condominium [n] *tenant-owned apartment house*
apartment, condo, co-op, timeshare, townhouse; SEE CONCEPT *516*

condone [v] *make allowance for*
buy*, disregard, excuse, forget, forgive, give green light*, go along with, ignore, lap up*, let it come*, let it go by*, let pass*, look the other way*, nod at*, okay, overlook, pardon, pass over, remit, wink at*; SEE CONCEPTS *10,23*

conducive [adj] *favorable for*
accessory, calculated to produce, contributive, contributory, helpful, leading, productive of, promotive, tending, useful; SEE CONCEPT *542*

conduct [n1] *administration*
care, carrying on*, channels, charge, control, direction, execution, guidance, handling, intendance, leadership, management, manipulation, organization, oversight, plan, policy, posture, red tape*, regimen, regulation, rule, running, strategy, superintendence, supervision, tactics, transaction, treatment, wielding; SEE CONCEPT *117*

conduct [n2] *behavior*
address, attitude, bearing, carriage, comportment, demeanor, deportment, manner, manners, mien, posture, stance, tenue, ways; SEE CONCEPT *633*

conduct [v1] *administer*
accompany, attend, call the tune*, carry on*, chair, chaperon, control, convey, direct, engineer, escort, govern, guide, handle, head, keep, lead, manage, operate, ordain, order, organize, oversee, pilot, preside over, regulate, ride herd on*, rule, run, run things, shepherd, steer, supervise, trailblaze*, usher, wield baton*; SEE CONCEPT *117*

conduct [v2] *comport oneself*
acquit, act, bear, behave, carry, demean, deport, go on, quit; SEE CONCEPT *384*

conduct [v3] *transport*
accompany, attend, bring, carry, chaperon, companion, convoy, escort, guide, lead, move, pass on, pilot, route, send, shepherd, show, steer, transfer; SEE CONCEPT *187*

conduit [n] *passage*
aqueduct, cable, canal, channel, conductor, course, culvert, duct, flow, flume, gully, gutter, lead-in, lead-out, main, pipe, pipeline, race, sewer, spout, trough, tube, watercourse; SEE CONCEPTS *499,501*

cone [n] *circular-shaped object with pointed end*
conoid, pyramid, raceme, strobile, strobiloid; SEE CONCEPT *436*

confection [n] *sweet food*
cake, candy, dainty, jam, pastry, sweet; SEE CONCEPT *457*

confederacy [n] *coalition*
alliance, anschluss, bond, compact, confederation, conspiracy, covenant, federation, government, league, organization, union; SEE CONCEPTS *299,301*

confederate [n] *abettor*
accessory, accomplice, ally, associate, coconspirator, collaborator, colleague, conspirator, fellow, fellow traveler, partner; SEE CONCEPT *412*

confederate [adj] *allied*
amalgamated, associated, combined, corporate, federal, federated, in alliance, incorporated, leagued, organized, syndicated, unionized; SEE CONCEPT *536*

confer [v1] *discuss, deliberate*
advise, argue, bargain, blitz*, brainstorm*, breeze*, collogue, confab*, confabulate, consult, converse, deal, debate, discourse, flap*, gab*, get heads together*, give meeting*, groupthink*, huddle, jaw, kick ideas around*, negotiate, parley, pick one's brain*, powwow*, speak, talk, toss ideas around*; treat; SEE CONCEPT *56*

confer [v2] *giving honor, award*
accord, allot, award, bestow, donate, gift with, give, grant, lay on, present, provide, sweeten the kitty*, vouchsafe; SEE CONCEPT *132*

conference [n1] *convention, colloquium*
appointment, argument, chat, colloquy, confabulation, conferring, congress, consultation, conversation, convocation, deliberation, discussion, forum, gabfest*, groupthink*, huddle, interchange, interview, meeting, palaver, parley, powwow*, round robin, round table, seminar, symposium, talk, think-in*, ventilation; SEE CONCEPTS *56,324,386*

conference [n2] *league of athletic teams*
association, athletic union, circuit, league, loop, organization, ring; SEE CONCEPT *365*

confess [v] *admit, confirm*
acknowledge, affirm, allow, assert, attest, aver, avow, blow, blurt out, chirp, clue in, come clean*, come out, concede, confide, declare, disclose, divulge, dump on*, evince, finger*, fink*, grant, humble oneself, leak*, let on*, level with, make clean breast of*, manifest, narrate, open one's heart*, own, own up, post, profess, prove, rat on*, recognize, relate, reveal, sing*, snitch*, sound off*, spill the beans*, spit out*, squeal*, tip hand*, unload*, vent, weasel*; SEE CONCEPT *60*

confession [n] *admittance of information*
acknowledgment, admission, affirmation, allowance, assenting, assertion, avowal, concession, declaration, disclosing, disclosure, divulgence, enumeration, exposé, exposure, making public, narration, owning up, proclamation, profession, publication, recitation, relation, revealing, revelation, song*, squawk*, squeal*, statement, story, telling, unbosoming, utterance; SEE CONCEPTS *60,274*

confidant [n] *close friend*
acquaintance, adherent, adviser, alter ego, bosom buddy, companion, crony, familiar, intimate, mate, pal; SEE CONCEPT *423*

confide [v1] *divulge information*
admit, bend an ear*, breathe, buzz*, confess, crack to, disclose, hint, impart, insinuate, intimate, lay it on*, lay the gaff*, let in on*, reveal, spill to*, suggest, tell, unload on*, whisper; SEE CONCEPT *57*

confide [v2] *entrust*
bestow, charge, commend, commit, consign, delegate, hand over, present, relegate, trust; SEE CONCEPT *108*

confidence [n1] *belief in oneself*
aplomb, assurance, backbone, boldness, brashness, certainty, cool, courage, daring, dash, determination, elan, faith in oneself, fearlessness, firmness, fortitude, grit, hardihood, heart, impudence, intrepidity, mettle, morale, nerve, pluck, poise, presumption, reliance, resoluteness, resolution, self-possession, self-reliance, spirit, spunk, sureness, tenacity; SEE CONCEPT *411*

confidence [n2] *belief in something*
assurance, credence, dependence, faith, hope, reliance, stock, store, sure bet*, trust; SEE CONCEPT *689*

confident [adj1] *certain, assured*
bet on*, bold, brave, cocksure, convinced, counting on, courageous, dauntless, depending on, expectant, expecting, fearless, having faith in, high*, hopeful, intrepid, positive, presuming, presumptuous, puffed up*, pushy, racked, sanguine, satisfied, secure, self-assured, self-reliant, self-sufficient, sure, trusting, unafraid, undaunted, upbeat, uppity*, valiant; SEE CONCEPTS *403,404*

confidential [adj] *secret*
arcane, backdoor, classified, closet, hushed, hush-hush*, inside, intimate, off the record*, private, privy, SEE CONCEPTS *267,576*

confidentially [adv] *in secret*
behind closed doors*, between ourselves, between us, between you and me*, covertly, don't breathe a word*, hushedly, in confidence, in on the ground floor*, off the cuff*, off the record*, personally, privately, sub rosa; SEE CONCEPTS *267,576*

confine [v] *enclose, limit*
bar, bind, bound, cage, circumscribe, constrain, cool, cool down, cramp, delimit, detain, enslave, fix, hem in, hinder, hog-tie*, hold back, ice*, immure, imprison, incarcerate, intern, jail, keep, put a lid on*, put away, put on ice*, repress, restrain, restrict, send up, shorten, shut up; SEE CONCEPTS *121,130*

confined [adj] *limited, enclosed*
bedfast, bedridden, bottled up, bound, chilled, circumscribed, compassed, cooped up, cramp, cramped, detained, flattened out, grounded, hampered, held, hog-tied*, iced*, immured, imprisoned, incarcerated, in chains, incommodious, indisposed, in jail, invalided, jailed, laid up, locked up, on ice*, pent, restrained, restricted, sealed up, shut in, sick; SEE CONCEPT *554*

confinement [n1] *imprisonment; restriction*
bonds, bounding, bounds, check, circumscription, coercion, constrainment, constraint, control, cramp, curb, custody, delimitation, detention, immuration, incarceration, internment, jail, keeping, limitation, repression, safekeeping, trammels; SEE CONCEPTS *90,191*

confines [n] *boundaries*
borders, bounds, circumference, compass, country, dimension, edge, end, environs, extent, limits, orbit, periphery, precinct, proportions,

purlieus, purview, radius, range, reach, region, scope, sweep, term, terrain, territory; SEE CONCEPTS *484,745,788*

confirm [v1] *ratify, validate, prove*
affirm, approve, attest, authenticate, back, bear out, bless, buy, certify, check, check out, circumstantiate, corroborate, debunk, double-check, endorse, establish, explain, give green light*, give high sign*, give stamp of approval*, give the go-ahead*, give the nod*, justify, lap up, make good*, make sure, okay, rubber-stamp*, sanction, settle, sign, sign off on*, size up, subscribe, substantiate, support, thumbs up*, underpin, uphold, verify, vouch, warrant, witness; SEE CONCEPTS *57,103*

confirm [v2] *reinforce*
assure, buttress, clinch, establish, fix, fortify, invigorate, make firm, settle, strengthen; SEE CONCEPTS *244,250*

confirmation [n] *ratification, validation, proof*
acceptance, accepting, accord, admission, affirmation, affirming, agreement, approval, assent, attestation, authenticating, authentication, authorization, authorizing, avowal, consent, corroborating, corroboration, endorsement, evidence, go ahead*, green light*, nod, okay, passage, passing, proving, recognition, sanction, sanctioning, stamp of approval*, substantiation, support, supporting, testament, testimonial, testimony, validating, verification, verifying, visa, witness; SEE CONCEPTS *661,685*

confirmed [adj] *habitual; rooted*
accepted, accustomed, chronic, deep-rooted, deep-seated, dyed-in-the-wool*, entrenched, firmly established, fixed, habituated, hardened, hard-shell*, ingrained, inured, inveterate, long-established, proved, seasoned, settled, staid, valid, worn; SEE CONCEPTS *542,798*

confiscate [v] *steal; seize*
accroach, annex, appropriate, arrogate, assume, commandeer, confisticate, expropriate, glom on to*, grab, hijack, impound, liberate, moonlight requisition*, possess oneself of, preempt, sequester, sequestrate, swipe, take, take over, usurp; SEE CONCEPTS *139,142*

conflagration [n] *large fire*
blaze, bonfire, burning, flaming, holocaust, inferno, rapid oxidation, up in smoke*, wildfire; SEE CONCEPTS *249,478*

conflict [n1] *fight, warfare*
battle, clash, collision, combat, competition, contention, contest, emulation, encounter, engagement, fracas, fray, rivalry, set-to, strife, striving, struggle, tug-of-war, war; SEE CONCEPTS *106,320*

conflict [n2] *disagreement, discord*
affray, animosity, antagonism, bad blood*, brush, competition, concours, contention, contest, dance, difference, disaccord, dispute, dissension, dissent, dissidence, disunity, divided loyalties, faction, factionalism, flap, fray, friction, fuss, hassle, hostility, interference, meeting, opposition, row, ruckus, run-in, set-to, strife, variance; SEE CONCEPTS *106,388,674*

conflict [v] *be at odds*
brawl, bump heads with*, clash, collide, combat, contend, contest, contrast, cross swords with, differ, disaccord, disagree, discord, disharmonize, disturb, fight, interfere, jar, lock horns with*, mismatch, oppose, romp, run against tide*, scrap,

slug, square off with, strive, struggle, tangle, vary; SEE CONCEPTS *46,106*

conflicting [*adj*] *contradictory*
adverse, antagonistic, antipathetic, at odds with, clashing, contrarian, contrary, disconsonant, discordant, discrepant, dissonant, incompatible, incongruent, incongruous, inconsistent, inconsonant, opposed, opposing, paradoxical, unfavorable, unmixable; SEE CONCEPTS *542,570*

confluence [*n*] *coming together*
assemblage, assembly, concourse, concurrence, concursion, conflux, convergence, crowd, gathering, host, junction, meeting, mob, multitude, union; SEE CONCEPTS *109,114*

conform [*v1*] *adjust, adapt*
accommodate, attune, be guided by, clean up act*, comply, coordinate, don't make waves*, don't rock the boat*, fall in with, fit, follow, follow beaten path*, follow the crowd, go by the book*, go with the flow*, harmonize, integrate, keep, make room, meet halfway, mind, move over, obey, observe, play the game*, proportion, quadrate, reconcile, reconciliate, roll with punches*, run with the pack*, shape up, square, straighten up, suit, tailor, tailor-make*, toe the line*, tune, yield; SEE CONCEPT *13*

conform [*v2*] *correspond, match*
accord, agree, assimilate, be regular, dovetail, fit in, fit the pattern, go, harmonize, jibe, square, suit, tally; SEE CONCEPT *664*

conformable [*adj*] *appropriate; matching*
adapted, agreeable, alike, amenable, applicable, assorted, comparable, compliant, consistent, docile, fitted, fitting, harmonious, in agreement, like, matched, obedient, orderly, proper, regular, resembling, similar, submissive, suitable, suited, tractable, unified, useable, well-regulated; SEE CONCEPTS *487,558,563,573*

conformation [*n*] *shape*
anatomy, arrangement, build, cast, configuration, figure, form, formation, frame, framework, outline, structure, symmetry, type; SEE CONCEPTS *754,757*

conformity [*n1*] *compliance*
acquiescence, allegiance, assent, consent, conventionality, docility, obedience, observance, orthodoxy, resignation, submission, willingness; SEE CONCEPTS *13,689*

conformity [*n2*] *correspondence, harmony*
accord, affinity, agreement, coherence, conformance, congruity, consistency, consonance, likeness, resemblance, similarity; SEE CONCEPT *664*

confound [*v*] *confuse*
abash, amaze, astonish, astound, baffle, befog, bewilder, blend, bug*, commingle, confute, discombobulate*, discomfit, discountenance, dumbfound, embarrass, faze, fiddle, flabbergast, jumble, metagrobolize, misidentify, mix, mix up*, mystify, nonplus, perplex, pose, puzzle, rattle, screw up*, startle, surprise, throw*; SEE CONCEPTS *16,42*

confront [*v*] *challenge*
accost, affront, beard, brave, call one's bluff*, come up against*, dare, defy, encounter, face down*, face up to*, face with*, flout, front, go one-on-one*, go up against*, make my day*, meet, meet eyeball-to-eyeball*, oppose, repel, resist, scorn, stand up to, tell off, withstand; SEE CONCEPTS *46,52,54*

confrontation [*n*] *conflict*
affray, battle, contest, crisis, dispute, encounter, fight, meeting, set-to, showdown, strife; SEE CONCEPTS *46,106*

confuse [*v1*] *bewilder someone*
abash, addle, amaze, astonish, baffle, becloud, bedevil, befuddle, bemuse, cloud, clutter, complicate, confound, darken, daze, demoralize, discomfit, discompose, disconcert, discountenance, disorient, distract, embarrass, faze, fluster, fog, frustrate, fuddle, involve, lead astray, mess up*, misinform, mislead, mortify, muddle, mystify, nonplus, obscure, perplex, perturb, puzzle, rattle, render uncertain, shame, stir up, stump, throw off, throw off balance*, trouble, unhinge, unsettle, upset, worry; SEE CONCEPT *16*

confuse [*v2*] *mix up; involve*
bedlamize, blend, clutter, confound, disarrange, disarray, discombobulate*, discreate, disorder, disorganize, embroil, encumber, entangle, intermingle, involve, jumble, litter, mess up*, mingle, mistake, muddle, muss up, rumple, snarl up, tangle, tousle, tumble; SEE CONCEPT *112*

confused [*adj1*] *disoriented mentally*
abashed, addled, at a loss*, at sea*, at sixes and sevens*, baffled, befuddled, bewildered, come apart*, dazed, discombobulated*, disconcerted, disorganized, distracted, flummoxed, flustered, fouled up*, glassy-eyed*, gone*, misled, mixed up, muddled, nonplussed, not with it*, out to lunch*, perplexed, perturbed, punch-drunk*, punchy*, puzzled, screwy*, shook up*, shot to pieces*, slaphappy, spaced out*, stumped, taken aback, thrown, thrown off balance*, unglued*, unscrewed*, unzipped*; SEE CONCEPT *403*

confused [*adj2*] *mixed up, disordered*
anarchic, blurred, chaotic, disarranged, disorderly, disorganized, haywire, in a muddle, in disarray, involved, jumbled, messy, miscalculated, miscellaneous, mistaken, misunderstood, obscured, out of order, snafu*, snarled, topsy-turvy, unsettled, untidy; SEE CONCEPT *585*

confusion [*n1*] *disorientation*
abashing, abashment, addling, agitation, befuddlement, befuddling, bemusement, bewilderment, blurring, chagrin, cluttering, commotion, confounding, demoralization, disarranging, discomfiting, discomfiture, disorientation, distraction, disturbing, dither, dumbfounding, embarrassing, embarrassment, embroiling, flap, fluster, lather, mixup mystification, obscuring, perplexing, perplexity, perturbation, pother, puzzlement, stew, stirring up, tangling, tumult, turbulence, turmoil, unsettling, upsetting; SEE CONCEPT *14*

confusion [*n2*] *disoriented state*
abashment, ado, anarchy, astonishment, bustle, chaos, clutter, commotion, complexity, complication, consternation, daze, difficulty, disarray, discomposure, dislocation, disorganization, distraction, emotional upset, ferment, fog, fracas, haze, hodge-podge, imbroglio, intricacy, jumble, labyrinth, mess, mistake, muddle, mystification, pandemonium, perturbation, racket, riot, row, shambles, stir, stupefaction, surprise, tangle, trouble, tumult, turmoil, untidiness, upheaval, uproar, wilderness; SEE CONCEPTS *410,727*

confute [*v*] *disprove, refute*
blow sky high*, break, bring to naught, confound, contradict, controvert, defeat, demolish, dismay, disprove, expose, invalidate, knocks props out

from under*, negate, oppugn, overcome, overthrow, overturn, overwhelm, parry, prove false, prove wrong, put down, rebut, set aside, shut up, silence, subvert, tap, upset, vanquish; SEE CONCEPTS *46,95*

congeal [v] *coagulate*
cake, clabber, clot, concrete, condense, curdle, dry, freeze, gel, gelate, gelatinate, gelatinize, glob up*, harden, indurate, jell, jellify, jelly, refrigerate, set, solidify, stiffen, thicken; SEE CONCEPTS *250,469*

congenial [adj] *friendly, compatible*
adapted, affable, agreeable, amical, clubby, companionable, compatible, complaisant, congruous, consistent, consonant, conversable, convivial, cooperative, cordial, delightful, favorable, fit, genial, good-humored, gracious, happy, harmonious, jovial, kindly, kindred, like-minded, mellow, pleasant, pleasing, regular fellow, right neighborly, sociable, social, suitable, sympathetic, well-suited; SEE CONCEPT *555*

congenital [adj] *inborn*
complete, connate, connatural, constitutional, inbred, indigenous, indwelling, ingrained, inherent, inherited, innate, intrinsic, inveterate, latent, native, natural, thorough, unacquired, utter; SEE CONCEPTS *314,549*

congested [adj] *blocked, clogged*
chock-full, choked, closed, crammed, crowded, filled, glutted, gorged, gridlocked, jam-full, jammed, jam-packed, massed, mobbed, obstructed, occluded, overcrowded, overfilled, overflowing, packed, packed like sardines*, plugged, stopped, stoppered, stuffed, stuffed-up, teeming, up to the rafters*, SEE CONCEPTS *481,483,774*

congestion [n] *blockage*
bottleneck*, clogging, crowdedness, crowding, excess, jam, mass, overcrowding, overdevelopment, overpopulation, press, profusion, rubber-necking*, snarl-up*, surfeit, surplus, traffic jam; SEE CONCEPTS *230,432*

conglomerate [n] *composite organization*
agglomerate, agglomeration, aggregate, aggregation, cartel, chain, combine, conglomeration, group, multinational, pool, syndicate, trust; SEE CONCEPTS *323,325*

conglomerate [adj] *composite*
amassed, assorted, blended, clustered, heterogeneous, indiscriminate, massed, melded, miscellaneous, mixed, motley, multifarious, promiscuous, varied, variegated; SEE CONCEPTS *490,589*

conglomeration [n] *accumulation, potpourri*
agglomeration, aggregate, aggregation, amassment, assortment, collection, combination, combo*, composite, cumulation, everything but the kitchen sink*, hoard, hodge-podge, mass, medley, miscellany, mishmash*, mixed bag*, trove; SEE CONCEPT *432*

congratulate [v] *compliment on achievement, luck*
applaud, bless, boost, felicitate, give a big cigar*, give bouquet*, give regards, gold star*, hand it to*, hear it for*, laud, pat on back, praise, rejoice with, salute, stroke*, toast, wish happy returns*, wish joy to, wish one well; SEE CONCEPTS *51,69*

congratulations [n] *complimentation on achievement, luck*
best wishes, compliments, felicitations, give a "hear-hear"*, good going*, good wishes, good work, greetings, hail; SEE CONCEPTS *69,278*

congregate [v] *assemble, come together*
besiege, bunch up*, collect, concentrate, congress, convene, converge, convoke, corral, flock*, forgather, gang around, gang up, gather, hang out*, make the scene*, mass, meet, meet up, muster, pack, raise, rally, rendezvous, round up, swarm, teem, throng; SEE CONCEPTS *109,114*

congregation [n] *assembled group, especially concerned with church-going*
aggregation, assemblage, assembly, audience, churchgoers, collection, company, confab*, crowd, disciples, flock, following, gathering, get-together, group, host, laity, meet, meeting, multitude, muster, parish, parishioners, public, sit-in, throng, turnout; SEE CONCEPTS *369,387,417*

congress [n] *delegation of representatives*
assembly, association, caucus, chamber, club, committee, conclave, conference, convention, convocation, council, delegates, government, guild, league, legislative body, legislature, meeting, order, parliament, senate, society, the Hill, the house, union; SEE CONCEPTS *299,387*

congruent [adj] *agreeable, harmonious*
coinciding, compatible, concurring, conforming, consistent, corresponding, identical, in agreement; SEE CONCEPT *563*

congruous [adj] *corresponding, suitable*
accordant, appropriate, apt, becoming, coincidental, compatible, concordant, congruent, consistent, consonant, correspondent, fit, fitting, harmonious, meet, proper, seemly, sympathetic; SEE CONCEPTS *558,563*

conical/conic [adj] *shaped cylindrically and with a point*
coned, cone-shaped, conoid, conoidal, funnel-shaped, pointed, pyramidal, sharp, strobilate, strobiloid, tapered, tapering; SEE CONCEPT *486*

conjectural [adj] *speculative*
academic, assumed, doubtful, figured, guessing, guesstimated*, hypothetical, on a hunch*, on a long shot*, putative, reputed, supposed, suppositional, suppositious, suppositive, surmised, surmising, suspect, tentative, theoretical, uncertain, unresolved; SEE CONCEPT *582*

conjecture [n] *speculation, assumption*
conclusion, fancy, guess, guesstimate*, guesswork, hunch, hypothesis, inference, notion, opinion, perhaps, presumption, shot in the dark*, sneaking suspicion, stab in the dark*, supposition, surmise, theorizing, theory; SEE CONCEPTS *28,274,689*

conjecture [v] *speculate*
assume, believe, conceive, conclude, deem, estimate, expect, fancy, feel*, figure, gather, glean, guess, guesstimate*, hazard a guess*, hypothesize, imagine, infer, judge, presume, pretend, suppose, surmise, suspect, take a shot*, take a stab*, take for granted, theorize, think; SEE CONCEPTS *28,51*

conjugal [adj] *marital*
bridal, connubial, hymeneal, married, matrimonial, nuptial, spousal, wedded; SEE CONCEPT *555*

conjunction [n] *combination*
affiliation, agreement, alliance, association, cahoots, coincidence, concomitance, concurrence, congruency, conjointment, hookup*, juxtaposition, parallelism, partnership, tie-up*, union; SEE CONCEPTS *388,714*

conjure [v1] *appeal to, implore*
adjure, ask, beg, beseech, brace, crave, entreat,

importune, pray, supplicate, urge; SEE CONCEPT 48

conjure [v2] *cast spell*
bewitch, call upon, charm, enchant, ensorcel, entrance, exorcise, fascinate, invoke, levitate, play tricks, raise, rouse, summon, voodoo; SEE CONCEPT 14

conjure up [v] *bring to mind*
call, contrive, create, evoke, materialize, produce as by magic, recall, recollect, remember, review, summon, urge; SEE CONCEPT 38

connect [v] *combine, link*
affix, ally, associate, attach, bridge, cohere, come aboard, conjoin, consociate, correlate, couple, equate, fasten, get into, hitch on, hook on, hook up, interface, join, join up with, marry, meld with, network with, plug into, relate, slap on, span, tack on, tag, tag on, tie in, tie in with, unite, wed, yoke; SEE CONCEPTS 85,113,160

connected [adj] *related, affiliated*
akin, allied, applicable, associated, banded together, bracketed, coherent, combined, consecutive, coupled, in on with*, joined, linked, pertinent, undivided, united; SEE CONCEPTS 482,577

connection [n1] *person who aids another in achieving goal*
acquaintance, agent, ally, associate, association, contact, friend, go-between, intermediary, kin, kindred, kinship, mentor, messenger, network, reciprocity, relation, relative, sponsor; SEE CONCEPTS 348,423

connection [n2] *something that connects, links*
affiliation, alliance, association, attachment, bond, combination, conjointment, conjunction, coupling, fastening, hookup, joining, joint, junction, juncture, link, linkage, network, partnership, seam, tie, tie-in, tie-up, union; SEE CONCEPTS 499,720

connection [n3] *something that communicates, relates*
affinity, application, association, bearing, bond, commerce, communication, correlation, correspondence, intercourse, interrelation, kinship, link, marriage, nexus, partnership, reciprocity, relation, relationship, relevance, tie-in, togetherness; SEE CONCEPTS 388,664

connive [v] *plot, scheme*
angle, be in cahoots with*, cabal, cogitate, collude, conspire, contrive, cook up, devise, diddle*, finagle, frame, frame up, intrigue, machinate, operate, promote, wangle, wire, work hand in glove*; SEE CONCEPT 36

connoisseur [n] *authority*
adept, aesthete, aficionado, appreciator, arbiter, bon vivant, buff*, cognoscente, critic, devotee, dilettante, expert, fan, freak*, gourmet, judge, maven*, nut*, one into*, savant, specialist; SEE CONCEPTS 352,376

connotation [n] *implication*
association, coloring, essence, hint, meaning, nuance, overtone, significance, suggestion, undertone; SEE CONCEPTS 682,689

connote [v] *imply*
add up to, betoken, denote, designate, evidence, express, hint at, import, indicate, insinuate, intend, intimate, involve, mean, signify, spell, suggest; SEE CONCEPTS 75,118

connubial [adj] *marital*
conjugal, hymeneal, married, matrimonial, nuptial, spousal, wedded; SEE CONCEPT 555

conquer [v1] *defeat, overcome*
beat, bring to knees*, checkmate, circumvent, clobber, control, cream*, crush, discomfit, drub, foil, frustrate, get the better of*, humble, lick, master, outwit, overmaster, overpower, override, overthrow, prevail, quell, reduce, rout, shut down, subdue, subjugate, succeed, surmount, throw, thwart, total*, trample underfoot, trash, triumph, vanquish, whip, wipe off map*, worst, zap*; SEE CONCEPT 95

conquer [v2] *win; obtain*
achieve, acquire, annex, best, master, occupy, overcome, overrun, prevail, seize, succeed, triumph; SEE CONCEPTS 90,141,706

conqueror [n] *champion*
conquistador, defeater, hero, subduer, subjugator, vanquisher, victor, winner; SEE CONCEPTS 354,358

conquest [n1] *defeat, victory*
acquisition, annexation, appropriation, big win*, clean sweep*, conquering, coup, defeating, discomfiture, grand slam*, invasion, killing*, occupation, overthrow, rout, routing, score, splash*, subdual, subjection, subjugation, success, takeover, triumph, vanquishment, win; SEE CONCEPTS 95,706

conquest [n2] *enchantment; person enchanted*
acquisition, adherent, admirer, captivation, catch, enthralment, enticement, fan, feather in cap*, follower, prize, seduction, supporter, worshiper; SEE CONCEPTS 410,423

consanguinity [n] *family relationship*
affiliation, affinity, agnate, blood-relationship, brotherhood, cognate, connection, family tie, filiation, kin, kindred, kindredship, kinship, lineage, race, sisterhood, strain; SEE CONCEPTS 296,388

conscience [n] *moral sense*
censor, compunction, demur, duty, inner voice, morals, principles, qualms, right and wrong, scruples, shame, small voice*, squeam, still small voice*, superego; SEE CONCEPTS 645,689

conscientious [adj1] *thorough, careful*
complete, diligent, exact, exacting, faithful, fastidious, fussy, hanging in*, hanging tough*, heart and soul into*, heedful, meticulous, minding p's and q's*, painstaking, particular, playing safe, punctilious, punctual, reliable, tough, walking on eggs*; SEE CONCEPTS 531,538

conscientious [adj2] *moral, upright*
conscionable, high-minded, high-principled, honest, honorable, incorruptible, just, pious, principled, responsible, right, scrupulous, straightforward, strict, true; SEE CONCEPT 545

conscious [adj1] *alert, aware*
able to recognize, acquainted, aesthetic, alive to, apperceptive, apprised, assured, attentive, au courant, aware, certain, cognizant, conversant, discerning, felt, hep to*, informed, in on*, in right mind, keen, knowing, known, mindful, noticing, noting, observing, on to*, perceiving, percipient, recognizing, remarking, responsive, seeing, sensible, sensitive to, sentient, supraliminal, sure, understanding, vigilant, watchful, wise to*, with it*, witting; SEE CONCEPTS 402,539

conscious [adj2] *intentional*
affected, calculated, deliberate, knowing, mannered, premeditated, rational, reasoning, reflec-

tive, responsible, self-conscious, studied, willful; SEE CONCEPTS 403,535

consciousness [n] *knowledge*
alertness, apprehension, awareness, care, carefulness, cognizance, concern, heed, heedfulness, mindfulness, realization, recognition, regard, sensibility; SEE CONCEPT 409

consecrate [v] *hold in high religious regard*
anoint, beatify, bless, dedicate, devote, exalt, hallow, honor, ordain, sanctify, set apart, venerate; SEE CONCEPTS 69,367

consecutive [adj] *in sequence*
after, chronological, connected, constant, continuing, continuous, ensuing, following, going on, increasing, in order, in turn, later, logical, numerical, one after another, progressive, running, sequent, sequential, serial, serialized, seriate, seriatim, succedent, succeeding, successional, successive, understandable, uninterrupted; SEE CONCEPTS 585,799

consensus [n] *general agreement*
accord, concord, concurrence, consent, harmony, unanimity, unison, unity; SEE CONCEPTS 684,689

consent [n] *agreement; concession*
accord, acquiescence, allowance, approval, assent, authorization, blank check*, blessing, carte blanche*, compliance, concurrence, go-ahead*, green light*, leave, okay*, permission, permit, right on*, sanction, say so*, stamp of approval*, sufferance, understanding, yes; SEE CONCEPTS 684,685

consent [v] *agree*
accede, accept, acquiesce, allow, approve, assent, bless, comply, concede, concur, fold, give in, give the nod*, give up, knuckle under, let, make a deal, okay*, permit, roll over, sanction, say uncle*, say yes, sign off on*, subscribe, throw in the towel*, yes*, yield; SEE CONCEPTS 8,50,88

consequence [n1] *result, outcome of action*
aftereffect, aftermath, bottom line*, can of worms*, chain reaction*, effect, end, event, fallout, follow through, follow-up, issue, outgrowth, payback, reaction, repercussion, sequel, sequence, spin-off, upshot, waves*; SEE CONCEPT 230

consequence [n2] *importance, significance*
account, concern, exigency, fame, honor, import, interest, magnitude, moment, momentousness, need, note, pith, portent, renown, reputation, repute, signification, value, weight, weightiness; SEE CONCEPT 668

consequence [n3] *person's status*
cachet, dignity, distinction, eminence, notability, position, prestige, rank, repute, standing, state, stature, status; SEE CONCEPT 388

consequent [adj] *resultant*
consistent, ensuing, following, indirect, inferable, intelligent, logical, rational, reasonable, resulting, sensible, sequential, sound, subsequent, successive, understandable; SEE CONCEPTS 537,548

consequential [adj] *significant*
big, considerable, eventful, far-reaching, grave, important, material, meaningful, momentous, serious, substantial, weighty; SEE CONCEPT 568

conservation [n] *preservation*
attention, care, cherishing, conservancy, conserving, control, custody, directing, economy, governing, guardianship, guarding, keeping, maintenance, management, managing, preserval, preserving, protecting, protection, safeguarding,

safekeeping, salvation, saving, stewardship, storage, supervising, supervision, sustentation, upkeep; SEE CONCEPTS 134,257

conservative [n] *person who is cautious, moderate; an opponent of change*
bitter-ender*, classicist, conserver, conventionalist, diehard, hard hat*, middle-of-the-roader*, moderate, moderatist, obstructionist, old guard*, old liner*, preserver, reactionary, redneck*, right, rightist, right-winger, silk-stocking*, standpat, stick-in-the-mud*, Tory*, traditionalist, unprogressive; SEE CONCEPT 359

conservative [adj] *cautious, moderate, tending to preserve the status quo*
bourgeois, constant, controlled, conventional, diehard, fearful, firm, fogyish*, fuddy-duddy*, guarded, hard hat*, hidebound, holding to, illiberal, in a rut*, inflexible, middle-of-the-road*, not extreme, obstinate, old guard*, old line*, orthodox, quiet, reactionary, redneck*, right, right of center*, right-wing, sober, stable, steady, timid, Tory*, traditional, traditionalistic, unchangeable, unchanging, uncreative, undaring, unimaginative, unprogressive, white bread*; SEE CONCEPT 542

conservatory [n] *greenhouse*
cold frame, glasshouse, hot house, nursery; SEE CONCEPTS 439,449,517

conserve [v] *save, protect*
cut back, cut down on, go easy on*, hoard, keep, maintain, nurse, preserve, safeguard, scrimp, skimp, sock away*, squirrel*, squirrel away*, stash, steward, store up, support, sustain, take care of, use sparingly; SEE CONCEPT 134

consider [v1] *turn over in one's mind*
acknowledge, allow for, assent to, chew over*, cogitate, concede, consult, contemplate, deal with, deliberate, dream of, envisage, examine, excogitate, favor, flirt with*, grant, inspect, keep in mind, look at, meditate, mull over, muse, perpend, ponder, provide for, reason, reckon with, recognize, reflect, regard, revolve, ruminate, scan, scrutinize, see, see about, speculate, study, subscribe to, take into account, take under advisement, take up, think out, think over, toss around*; SEE CONCEPTS 17,24

consider [v2] *regard a certain way*
analyze, appraise, bear in mind, believe, care for, count, credit, deem, estimate, feel, hold, hold an opinion, judge, keep in view, look upon, make allowance for, reckon with, reflect, remember, respect, sense, set down, suppose, take for, take into account, think, think of, view; SEE CONCEPT 12

considerable [adj1] *abundant, large*
ample, appreciable, astronomical, big, bountiful, comfortable, commodious, extensive, goodly, great, hefty, huge, large-scale, lavish, major, marked, much, noticeable, plentiful, pretty, reasonable, respectable, sizable, substantial, tidy, tolerable; SEE CONCEPT 781

considerable [adj2] *important*
big, consequential, distinguished, doozie*, dynamite, essential, fab*, fat, influential, material, meaningful, momentous, mondo*, noteworthy, renowned, significant, solid gold*, something, something else*, substantial, super, super-duper*, to the max*, unreal*, venerable, weighty; SEE CONCEPT 568

considerably [adv] *significantly*
appreciably, far, greatly, markedly, noticeably,

CO
CO

quite, rather, remarkably, somewhat, substantially, very much, well; SEE CONCEPT *569*

considerate [*adj*] *respectful of others*
accommodating, amiable, attentive, benevolent, big, charitable, chivalrous, circumspect, compassionate, complaisant, concerned, cool, discreet, forbearing, generous, kind, kindly, like a sport*, magnanimous, mellow, mindful, obliging, patient, polite, solicitous, sympathetic, tactful, tender, thoughtful, unselfish, warmhearted; SEE CONCEPT *401*

consideration [*n1*] *mental analysis*
application, attention, cogitation, concentration, contemplation, debate, deliberation, discussion, examination, forethought, heed, reflection, regard, review, scrutiny, study, thinking, thought; SEE CONCEPT *24*

consideration [*n2*] *concern; something mentally examined*
development, difficulty, emergency, estate, evidence, exigency, extent, factor, fancy, idea, incident, issue, items, judgment, magnitude, minutiae, notion, occasion, occurrence, particulars, perplexity, plan, point, problem, proposal, puzzle, scope, situation, state, thought, trouble; SEE CONCEPT *532*

consideration [*n3*] *high regard*
attentiveness, awareness, concern, considerateness, esteem, estimation, favor, forbearance, friendliness, heed, heedfulness, kindliness, kindness, mercy, mindfulness, respect, solicitude, tact, thoughtfulness, tolerance; SEE CONCEPTS *32,410*

consideration [*n4*] *payment*
baksheesh, commish*, commission, fee*, payback, percentage, perk, perquisite, recompense, remuneration, reward, salary, something to sweeten pot*, tip, wage; SEE CONCEPT *344*

considered [*adj*] *deliberate, thought-out*
advised, aforethought, contemplated, designed, designful, examined, express, given due consideration, gone into, intentional, investigated, mediated, premeditated, prepense, studied, studious, thought-about, thought-through, treated, voluntary, weighed, well advised, well chosen, willful; SEE CONCEPTS *402,529*

considering [*adj*] *taking everything in mind*
all in all, all things considered, as, as long as, because, everything being equal, for, forasmuch as, inasmuch as, in consideration of, in light of, insomuch as, in view of, now, pending, seeing, since, taking into account; SEE CONCEPT *529*

consign [*v*] *entrust, hand over for care*
address, appoint, assign, authorize, commend to, commission, commit, confide, convey, delegate, deliver, deposit with, dispatch, forward, give, issue, put in charge of, relegate, remit, route, send, ship, transfer, transmit, turn over; SEE CONCEPTS *108,143,217*

consignment [*n1*] *entrusting, handing over*
assignment, committal, dispatch, distribution, relegation, sending shipment, transmittal; SEE CONCEPTS *108,143,217*

consignment [*n2*] *something entrusted to another's care*
batch, delivery, goods, shipment; SEE CONCEPT *338*

consist [*v*] *exist, reside*
abide, be, be contained in, be expressed by, be found in, dwell, inhere, lie, repose, rest, subsist; SEE CONCEPT *539*

consistency [*n1*] *thickness*
bendability, bendableness, compactness, density, elasticity, fabric, firmness, flexibility, frangibility, hardness, limberness, moldability, organization, plasticity, pliability, softness, solidity, suppleness, texture, viscidity, viscosity, viscousness; SEE CONCEPTS *611,722*

consistency [*n2*] *constancy, regularity*
accord, agreement, apposition, appropriateness, aptness, coherence, cohesion, compatibility, concord, concurrence, conformability, congruity, consonance, correspondence, evenness, fitness, harmony, homogeneity, invariability, likeness, proportion, similarity, stability, steadfastness, steadiness, suitability, symmetry, uniformity, union, unity; SEE CONCEPTS *637,656,670*

consistent [*adj1*] *constant, regular*
dependable, even, expected, homogeneous, invariable, logical, of a piece, persistent, rational, same, steady, true, true to type, unchanging, undeviating, unfailing, uniform, unvarying; SEE CONCEPT *534*

consistent [*adj2*] *agreeing, compatible*
accordant, according to, agreeable, all of a piece, coherent, conforming with, congenial, congruous, consonant, equable, harmonious, like, logical, matching, sympathetic; SEE CONCEPT *563*

consist of [*v*] *made up of*
amount to, be composed of, comprise, contain, embody, include, incorporate, involve; SEE CONCEPT *643*

consolation [*n*] *relief, comfort*
alleviation, assuagement, cheer, comfort, compassion, ease, easement, encouragement, fellow feeling, help, lenity, pity, solace, succour, support, sympathy; SEE CONCEPTS *32,410*

console [*v*] *relieve, comfort*
animate, assuage, buck up*, calm, cheer, condole with, encourage, express sympathy, gladden, inspirit, lift, solace, soothe, tranquilize, untrouble, upraise; SEE CONCEPTS *7,22*

consolidate [*v*] *combine; make firm*
add to, amalgamate, amass, band, bind, blend, build up, bunch up, cement, centralize, compact, compound, concatenate, concentrate, condense, conjoin, connect, densen, develop, federate, fortify, fuse, harden, hitch, hitch on, hook up with, incorporate, join, league, mass, meld, mix, plug into, pool, reinforce, render solid, secure, set, slap on, solidify, stabilize, strengthen, tack on, tag on, team up with*, thicken, throw in together*, tie in, tie up with, unify; SEE CONCEPTS *109,250*

consolidation [*n*] *combination, fortification*
alliance, amalgamation, association, coadunation, coalition, compression, concentration, condensation, federation, fusion, incorporation, melding, mergence, merger, merging, reinforcement, solidification, strengthening, unification; SEE CONCEPTS *109,469*

consonance [*n*] *agreement, consistency*
accord, chime, chorus, concert, concord, conformity, congruence, congruity, correspondence, harmony, suitableness, tune; SEE CONCEPT *664*

consonant [*adj*] *agreeing, consistent*
accordant, according, agnate, akin, alike, analogous, blending, coincident, comfortable, comparable, compatible, concordant, congenial, congruous, correspondent, corresponding, harmo-

nious, in agreement, in rapport, like, parallel, similar, suitable, sympathetic, uniform; SEE CONCEPT *563*

consort [*n*] *associate, partner*
accompaniment, companion, concomitant, friend, husband, mate, spouse, wife; SEE CONCEPT *423*

consort [*vl*] *be friendly with; fraternize*
accompany, associate, attend, bear, befriend, bring, carry, chaperon, chum together*, chum with*, clique with, company, conduct, convoy, gang up with*, go around with*, hang around with*, hang out with*, hang with*, join, keep company, mingle, mix, pal, pal around with, pal with, run around with*, run with, take up with, tie up with; SEE CONCEPTS *114,384*

consort [*v2*] *agree*
accord, coincide, comport, concur, conform, correspond, dovetail, harmonize, march, square, tally; SEE CONCEPT *664*

conspicuous [*adj1*] *obvious, easily seen*
apparent, clear, discernible, distinct, evident, manifest, noticeable, open-and-shut*, patent, perceptible, plain, visible; SEE CONCEPT *619*

conspicuous [*adj2*] *important, prominent*
arresting, arrestive, blatant, celebrated, commanding, distinguished, eminent, famed, famous, flagrant, flashy, garish, glaring, glitzy*, illustrious, influential, jazzy, loud, marked, notable, noted, notorious, outstanding, pointed, rank, remarkable, renowned, salient, screaming, showy, signal, splashy, stick out like sore thumb*, striking, tony*, well-known; SEE CONCEPTS *542,567*

conspiracy [*n*] *collusion in plan*
cabal, complot, confederacy, connivance, countermine, counterplot, covin, disloyalty, fix, frame*, game, hookup*, intrigue, league, little game*, machination, perfidy, plot, practice, put-up job*, scheme, sedition, treacherousness, treachery, treason, trick, trickery; SEE CONCEPT *660*

conspire [*vl*] *plot, scheme with someone*
be in cahoots*, cabal, cogitate, collogue, collude, confederate, connive, contrive, cook up*, cooperate, devise, get in bed with*, hatch, intrigue, machinate, maneuver, operate, promote, put out a contract*, wangle, wire, work something out*; SEE CONCEPTS *36,192*

conspire [*v2*] *agree, concur*
cabal, colleague, combine, complot, conduce, consort, contribute, cooperate, join, tend, unite, work together; SEE CONCEPT *8*

constancy [*n*] *fixedness*
abidingness, adherence, allegiance, ardor, attachment, certainty, decision, dependability, determination, devotedness, devotion, doggedness, eagerness, earnestness, endurance, faith, fealty, fidelity, firmness, honesty, honor, integrity, love, loyalty, permanence, perseverance, principle, regularity, resolution, stability, staunchness, steadfastness, steadiness, surety, tenacity, trustiness, trustworthiness, truthfulness, unchangeableness, unfailingness, uniformity, zeal; SEE CONCEPTS *32,410,637*

constant [*adj1*] *fixed*
connected, consistent, continual, equable, even, firm, habitual, homogeneous, immutable, invariable, like the Rock of Gibralter*, monochrome, monophonic, monotonous, nonstop, of a piece, permanent, perpetual, regular, regularized, solid as rock*, stabile, stable, standardized, steadfast,

steady, together, unalterable, unbroken, unchanging, unflappable, unfluctuating, uniform, uninterrupted, unvarying; SEE CONCEPT *534*

constant [*adj2*] *neverending*
abiding, ceaseless, chronic, continual, continuous, endless, enduring, eternal, everlasting, incessant, interminable, lasting, nonstop, perpetual, persistent, persisting, relentless, sustained, unending, uninterrupted, unrelenting, unremitting; SEE CONCEPTS *649,798*

constant [*adj3*] *loyal, determined*
allegiant, attached, dependable, devoted, dogged, faithful, fast, persevering, resolute, staunch, tried-and-true, true, trustworthy, trusty, unfailing, unflagging, unshaken, unwavering; SEE CONCEPT *542*

consternation [*n*] *dismay, distress*
alarm, amazement, anxiety, awe, bewilderment, confusion, distraction, dread, fear, fright, horror, muddle, muddlement, panic, perplexity, shock, stupefaction, terror, trepidation, trepidity, wonder; SEE CONCEPT *230*

constituency [*n*] *voting public*
balloters, body of voters, body politic, citizenry, city, county, district, electorate, electors, faction, nation, people, precinct, state, system, voters, voting area, ward; SEE CONCEPT *379*

constituent [*n*] *element*
board, component, division, essential, factor, fixins*, fraction, ingredient, makings, part, part and parcel*, plug-in*, portion, principle, unit; SEE CONCEPTS *826,834*

constituent [*adj1*] *component, part*
basic, combining, composing, constituting, division, elemental, essential, factor, forming, fraction, fundamental, ingredient, integral, portion; SEE CONCEPTS *826,834,835*

constituent [*adj2*] *voting*
balloter, citizen, electing, electoral, official, overruling; SEE CONCEPT *536*

constitute [*vl*] *comprise, form*
aggregate, complement, complete, compose, compound, construct, cook up*, create, develop, dream up*, embody, enact, establish, fill out, fix, flesh out*, found, frame, fudge together*, incorporate, integrate, make, make up, set up; SEE CONCEPTS *173,184,251*

constitute [*v2*] *authorize*
appoint, commission, decree, delegate, depute, deputize, designate, draft, empower, enact, establish, legislate, make, name, nominate, ordain, order; SEE CONCEPTS *50,88*

constitution [*n1*] *physical make-up and health*
architecture, build, character, composition, construction, content, contents, design, disposition, essence, form, formation, frame, habit, habitus, nature, physique, structure, temper, temperament, type, vitality; SEE CONCEPT *757*

constitution [*n2*] *establishment*
charter, code, composition, custom, formation, lawmaking, legislation, organization, written law; SEE CONCEPTS *271,318*

constitutional [*n*] *walk*
airing, ambulation, footwork, legwork, perambulation, ramble, saunter, stroll, turn, walk; SEE CONCEPT *149*

constitutional [*adj1*] *inherent*
built-in, congenital, deep-seated, essential, inborn, inbred, ingrained, innate, intrinsic, natural, organic, vital; SEE CONCEPT *549*

CO
CO

constitutional [adj2] *provided for by law*
approved, chartered, democratic, ensured, lawful, legal, representative, statutory, vested; SEE CONCEPT 319

constrain [v] *force; restrain*
ban, bar, bind, bottle up, bridle, chain, check, coerce, compel, concuss, confine, constrict, cool off*, cork, curb, deny, deprive, disallow, drive, hem in*, hog-tie*, hold back, hold down, hold in, immure, impel, imprison, incarcerate, inhibit, intern, jail, keep lid on*, make, necessitate, oblige, pressure, pressurize, put half nelson on*, shotgun*, stifle, urge, withhold; SEE CONCEPTS 14,121,130

constraint [n1] *force*
a must*, coercion, compulsion, driving, duress, goad, hang-up*, impelling, impulsion, monkey*, motive, necessity, no-no*, pressure, repression, restraint, spring, spur, suppression, violence; SEE CONCEPTS 14,121

constraint [n2] *shyness*
bashfulness, diffidence, embarrassment, hang-up*, humility, inhibition, modesty, repression, reservation, reserve, restraint, timidity; SEE CONCEPT 411

constraint [n3] *restriction*
arrest, captivity, check, circumscription, confinement, constrainment, cramp, curb, damper, detention, deterrent, hindrance, limitation, restraint; SEE CONCEPTS 130,652

constrict [v] *inhibit*
astringe, choke, circumscribe, clench, compress, concentrate, condense, confine, constringe, contract, cramp, curb, draw together, limit, narrow, pinch, restrain, restrict, shrink, squeeze, strangle, strangulate, tauten, tense, tighten, tuck; SEE CONCEPTS 130,191,219

constriction [n] *blockage*
binding, choking, compression, constraint, contraction, cramp, impediment, limitation, narrowing, pressure, reduction, restriction, squeezing, stenosis, stricture, tightness; SEE CONCEPTS 130,191,219

construct [v] *assemble, build*
build up, cobble up*, compose, compound, constitute, cook up*, create, design, dream up*, elevate, engineer, envision, erect, establish, fabricate, fashion, forge, form, formulate, found, frame, fudge together*, hammer out*, hoke up*, imagine, invent, make, manufacture, organize, prefab*, produce, put out, put together, put up, raise, rear, set up, shape, throw together, throw up*, trump up*, uprear, whip up*; SEE CONCEPTS 168,173,251

construction [n1] *creation, building*
architecture, arrangement, assembly, build, cast, composition, conception, constitution, contour, cut, development, disposition, edifice, elevation, erecting, erection, fabric, fabricating, fabrication, figuration, figure, form, format, formation, foundation, improvisation, invention, makeup, making, manufacture, mold, origination, outline, plan, planning, prefab, prefabrication, putting up, raising, rearing, roadwork, shape, structure, system, systematization, turn, type; SEE CONCEPTS 168,439,757

construction [n2] *explanation*
apprehension, construal, definition, exegesis, explication, exposé, exposition, inference, interpretation, reading, rendering, rendition, translation, version; SEE CONCEPT 274

constructive [adj] *helpful*
effective, positive, practical, productive, useful, valuable; SEE CONCEPT 401

construe [v] *deduce; explain*
analyze, decipher, define, explicate, expound, figure it to be*, infer, interpret, one's best guess*, parse, read, render, spell out, take, translate, understand; SEE CONCEPTS 37,57

consul [n] *representative*
delegate, emissary, envoy, lawyer, legate; SEE CONCEPTS 354,355

consulate [n] *embassy*
consular office, government office, ministry; SEE CONCEPTS 439,449

consult [v] *ask, confer*
argue, ask advice of, be closeted with, brainstorm*, call in, cogitate, collogue, commune, compare notes, confab, confabulate, consider, debate, deliberate, discuss, examine, flap*, groupthink*, huddle, interrogate, interview, kick ideas around*, negotiate, parlay, pick one's brains*, powwow*, put heads together*, question, refer to, regard, respect, review, seek advice, seek opinion of, take account of, take a meeting*, take counsel, talk over, toss ideas around*, treat, turn to; SEE CONCEPTS 17,48,56

consultation [n] *asking, conference*
appointment, argument, buzz session*, clambake*, confab*, conference, council, deliberation, dialogue, discussion, examination, groupthink*, hearing, huddle, interview, meeting, powwow*, second opinion*, session; SEE CONCEPTS 48,114,324

consume [v1] *use up*
absorb, apply, avail oneself of, deplete, devour, dissipate, dominate, drain, drivel, eat up, employ, engross, exhaust, expend, finish, finish up, fritter away, frivol away, go, go through, have recourse to, lavish, lessen, monopolize, obsess, preoccupy, profit by, put away, run to use, run out of, run through, spend, squander, throw away, trifle, utilize, vanish, wash up, waste, wear out; SEE CONCEPT 225

consume [v2] *eat, drink*
absorb, bolt, chow down*, devour, down, eat up, feed, gobble*, gorge, gulp, guzzle, hoover*, ingest, ingurgitate, inhale, meal, mow*, nibble, partake, polish off*, punish, put away*, put down*, scarf*, snack, stuff one's face*, swallow, swill, take, toss down*, wolf*; SEE CONCEPT 169

consume [v3] *destroy*
annihilate, crush, decay, demolish, devastate, eat up, exhaust, expend, extinguish, lay waste, overwhelm, ravage, raze, ruin, suppress, waste, wreck; SEE CONCEPT 252

consumer [n] *person who buys merchandise, services*
buyer, customer, end user, enjoyer, purchaser, shopper, user; SEE CONCEPT 348

consummate [adj] *ultimate, best*
able, absolute, accomplished, complete, conspicuous, downright, faultless, finished, flawless, gifted, ideal, impeccable, inimitable, matchless, out-and-out*, peerless, perfect, perfected, polished, positive, practiced, ripe, skilled, superb, superlative, supreme, talented, thoroughgoing, total, trained, transcendent, unmitigated, unquali-

fied, unsurpassable, utter, virtuosic, whole; SEE CONCEPTS *528,572*

consummate [v] *achieve, finish*
accomplish, button down*, call a day*, can*, carry out, clean up, clinch, close, come, come through, compass, complete, conclude, crown, drop curtain*, effectuate, end, fold up, get it together*, go the distance*, halt, knock off, mop up, perfect, perform, polish off*, put away*, put finishing touch on*, put lid on*, put to bed*, sew up, sign, take care of, terminate, top it off, ultimate, wind up, wrap, wrap up; SEE CONCEPTS *234,704,706*

consummation [n] *achievement, fulfillment*
cleanup, completion, culmination, doing it to a T*, end, mop-up, payoff, perfection, realization, to a finish, wind-up*, wrap, wrap-up*; SEE CONCEPT *706*

consumption [n] *devouring; use*
burning, consuming, damage, decay, decrease, depletion, desolation, destruction, devastation, diminution, dispersion, dissipation, drinking, eating, exhaustion, expenditure, loss, misuse, ruin, swallowing, using up, utilization, waste, wear and tear; SEE CONCEPTS *156,169,225,252*

contact [n1] *form of communication*
acquaintance, association, channel, commerce, communion, companionship, connection, influence, intercourse, junction, meeting, network, touch, union, unity; SEE CONCEPTS *278,388,687*

contact [n2] *touching*
approximation, closeness, collision, connection, contiguity, contingence, hit, impingement, junction, juxtaposition, nearness, propinquity, proximity, relation, strike, taction, touch, union; SEE CONCEPT *747*

contact [v] *communicate with*
approach, be in touch with, buzz*, call, check with, connect, get, get ahold of, get in touch with, interact, interface, network*, phone, reach, reach out, relate, speak to, talk, telephone, touch base*, visit, write to; SEE CONCEPT *266*

contagion [n] *infection*
bane, contamination, corruption, illness, miasma, pestilence, plague, poison, pollution, taint, transmission, venom, virus; SEE CONCEPT *306*

contagious [adj] *communicable*
catching, deadly, endemic, epidemic, epizootic, impartible, infectious, inoculable, pestiferous, pestilential, poisonous, spreading, taking, transmissible, transmittable; SEE CONCEPT *314*

contain [v1] *include, hold*
accommodate, be composed of, comprehend, comprise, consist of, embody, embrace, enclose, encompass, have, have capacity for, hold, incorporate, involve, seat, subsume, take in; SEE CONCEPTS *112,736,742*

contain [v2] *hold back, control*
bottle up*, check, collect, compose, cool*, cork*, curb, harness, hog-tie*, hold in, keep back, keep lid on*, put half nelson on*, rein, repress, restrain, restrict, simmer down, smother, stifle, stop; SEE CONCEPTS *94,191*

container [n] *holder for physical object*
alembic, bag, beaker, bin, bottle, bowl, box, bucket, bunker, caisson, can, canister, canteen, capsule, carafe, carton, cask, casket, cauldron, chamber, chest, churn, cistern, cradle, crate, crock, dish, ewer, firkin, flask, hamper, hod, hopper, humidor, hutch, jar, jeroboam, jug, kettle,

magnum, package, packet, pail, pit, pod, poke, pot, pottery, pouch, purse, receptacle, reliquary, repository, sac, sack, scuttle, stein, storage, tank, tub, utensil, vase, vat, vessel, vial; SEE CONCEPT *494*

contaminate [v] *adulterate*
alloy, befoul, corrupt, debase, debauch, defile, deprave, desecrate, dirty, harm, infect, injure, muck up, pervert, poison, pollute, profane, radioactivate, soil, spoil, stain, sully, taint, tarnish, vitiate; SEE CONCEPTS *252,254*

contamination [n] *adulteration*
contagion, corruption, decay, defilement, dirtying, disease, epidemic, filth, foulness, impurity, infection, pestilence, plague, poisoning, pollution, radioactivation, rottenness, spoliation, taint; SEE CONCEPTS *230,306,674*

contemplate [v1] *think about seriously; plan*
aim, aspire to, brood over, chew over, consider, cool out*, deliberate, design, envisage, excogitate, expect, foresee, intend, kick around*, mean, meditate on, mind, mull over, muse over, observe, percolate, perpend, ponder, propose, purpose, reflect upon, ruminate, size up, speculate, study, take in, think of, weigh; SEE CONCEPTS *17,36*

contemplate [v2] *gaze at*
audit, behold, consider, examine, eye, inspect, notice, observe, peer, penetrate, peruse, pierce, pore over, probe, pry, regard, scan, scrutinize, see, stare at, study, survey, view, witness; SEE CONCEPT *623*

contemplation [n1] *deep thought; planning*
ambition, cogitation, consideration, deliberation, design, intention, meditation, musing, plan, pondering, purpose, reflection, reverie, rumination, study; SEE CONCEPT *410*

contemplation [n2] *gazing at*
examination, inspection, looking at, observation, scrutiny, survey, viewing; SEE CONCEPT *623*

contemplative [adj] *deep in thought*
attentive, cogitative, in brown study*, intent, introspective, lost, meditative, musing, pensive, pondering, rapt, reflecting, reflective, ruminative, speculative, thinking, thoughtful; SEE CONCEPTS *402,403*

contemporary [adj1] *modern*
abreast, à la mode*, au courant, contempo*, current, existent, extant, hot off press*, in fashion, instant, in vogue, just out*, latest, leading-edge*, mod*, new, newfangled, now, present, present-day, recent, red-hot*, state-of-the-art*, today*, topical, ultramodern, up*, up-to-date, up-to-the-minute, voguish, with it*; SEE CONCEPTS *578,589,797*

contemporary [adj2] *existing, occurring at same time*
accompanying, associated, attendant, coetaneous, coeval, coexistent, coexisting, coincident, concomitant, concurrent, connected, contemporaneous, current, linked, present, related, simultaneous, synchronal, synchronic, synchronous; SEE CONCEPT *820*

contempt [n1] *disdain, disrespect*
antipathy, audacity, aversion, condescension, contumely, defiance, derision, despisal, despisement, despite, disesteem, disregard, distaste, hatred, indignity, malice, mockery, neglect, recalcitrance, repugnance, ridicule, scorn, slight, snobbery, stubbornness; SEE CONCEPT *29*

CO
CO

contempt [n2] *state of disgrace*
discredit, disesteem, disfavor, dishonor, disrepute, humiliation, ignominy, infamy, insignificancy, opprobrium, shame, stigma; SEE CONCEPTS *388,674*

contemptible [adj] *despicable, shameful*
abhorrent, abject, abominable, bad, base, beggarly, cheap, crass, currish, degenerate, despisable, detestable, dirty, disgusting, hateful, heel, ignoble, ignominious, inferior, low, low-down*, lowest, mean, odious, outcast, paltry, pitiable, pitiful, poor, sad, scummy*, scurvy*, shabby, sordid, sorry*, swinish, unworthy, vile, worthless, wretched; SEE CONCEPT *550*

contemptuous [adj] *arrogant, insolent*
audacious, bold, cavalier, cheeky, cold-shoulder, condescending, contumelious, cool, derisive, derisory, disdainful, disrespectful, dog it*, hard, hard-nosed, haughty, high and mighty*, high hat*, insulting, in high horse*, opprobrious, sardonic, scornful, sneering, snippy, snobbish, snooty*, snotty*, supercilious, temperamental, uppity, upstage; SEE CONCEPT *401*

contend [v1] *compete, fight*
argue, battle, clash, confront, contest, controvert, cope, dispute, emulate, encounter, face, give all one's got*, give one's all*, go after, go for, go for broke*, go for it*, go for jugular*, grapple, have at*, jockey for position*, jostle, knock oneself out*, litigate, lock horns*, make play for*, meet, mix it up with*, oppose, oppugn, push, push for, resist, rival, scramble for, shoot at, shoot for, skirmish, stand, strive, struggle, tangle with, tug, vie, withstand; SEE CONCEPTS *92,106*

contend [v2] *argue*
affirm, allege, assert, aver, avow, blast, charge, claim, come at, cross, debate, defend, dictate, dispute, enjoin, fly in face of*, gang up on, go at, have at*, have bone to pick*, hold, insist, jump on, justify, lace into*, lay into*, let have it*, light into*, lock horns with*, maintain, mix, mix it up*, prescribe, put up argument, report, rip*, say, set to, sock it to one*, stick it to*, take on, tell, urge, vindicate, warrant, zap*; SEE CONCEPT *46*

content [n1] *comfort, happiness*
contentment, ease, gratification, peace, peace of mind, pleasure, satisfaction; SEE CONCEPT *410*

content [n2] *essence, meaning*
burden, composition, constitution, gist, idea, matter, significance, subject, subject matter, substance, text, thought; SEE CONCEPT *682*

content [n3] *capacity, volume*
filling, load, measure, packing, size; SEE CONCEPTS *719,740*

content [adj] *happy, agreeable*
appeased, at ease, can't complain*, comfortable, complacent, contented, fat dumb and happy*, fulfilled, gratified, pleased as punch*, satisfied, smug, tickled pink*, willing; SEE CONCEPT *403*

content [v] *please*
appease, bewitch, captivate, charm, delight, enrapture, gladden, gratify, humor, indulge, make happy, mollify, placate, reconcile, satisfy, suffice, thrill, tickle; SEE CONCEPTS *7,22*

contented [adj] *at ease; happy*
at peace, cheerful, comfortable, complacent, content, glad, gratified, pleased, satisfied, serene, thankful; SEE CONCEPT *403*

contention [n1] *competition*
altercation, argument, battle, beef*, belligerency, bone of contention*, bone to pick*, combat, conflict, contest, controversy, difference, disaccord, discord, dispute, dissension, dissent, dissidence, disunity, enmity, feuding, fight, flak*, hassle, hostility, quarrel, rivalry, run-in, scene, scrap, set-to*, squabble, static, strife, struggle, variance, war, wrangle, wrangling; SEE CONCEPTS *92,106*

contention [n2] *argument for idea*
advancement, affirmation, allegation, assertion, asseveration, avowal, belief, charge, claim, contestation, declaration, demurrer, deposition, discussion, explanation, ground, hurrah, hypothesis, idea, maintaining, opinion, plea, position, predication, profession, rumpus, stand, thesis, view; SEE CONCEPTS *46,278,689*

contentment [n] *comfort, happiness*
complacency, content, contentedness, ease, equanimity, fulfillment, gladness, gratification, peace, pleasure, repletion, satisfaction, serenity; SEE CONCEPT *410*

contents [n] *elements of larger object*
capacity, cargo, chapters, connotation, constituents, details, divisions, essence, filling, freight, furnishing, gist, guts, implication, ingredients, innards, inside, lading, load, meaning, nub, packing, shipment, significance, size, space, stuffing, subject matter, subjects, substance, sum, text, themes, topics, volume; SEE CONCEPT *835*

contest [n1] *competition*
challenge, concours, discussion, game, match, meet, meeting, proving, rencounter, sport, testing, tournament, trial, trying; SEE CONCEPTS *92,363*

contest [n2] *fight, struggle*
action, affray, altercation, battle, battle royal*, beef*, brawl, brush, combat, conflict, controversy, debate, discord, dispute, emulation, encounter, engagement, fray, go*, hassle, rivalry, row, rumble*, run-in, scrap, set-to*, shock, skirmish, static, strife, striving, tug-of-war, warfare, wrangle; SEE CONCEPTS *106,320*

contest [v1] *argue, challenge*
blast, call in question, debate, dispute, doubt, give it one's all*, go for it*, go for jugular*, jockey for position*, jump on, litigate, mix it up with*, object to, oppose, push, question, scramble for, shoot for*, stand up for, tangle; SEE CONCEPT *46*

contest [v2] *fight*
altercate, attack, battle, brawl, break with, buck, compete, conflict, contend, cross, defend, duel, feud, fight over, gang up on, hassle, knuckle with, lay a finger on*, lay out, put on gloves*, put up dukes*, quarrel, repel, rival, row, rumpus, scrap, scuffle, set to, sock*, square off, strike, struggle, take on, tilt, traverse, vie, withstand, wrangle; SEE CONCEPT *106*

contestant [n] *competitor*
adversary, antagonist, aspirant, battler, candidate, challenger, combatant, contender, contester, dark horse*, disputant, entrant, favorite, hopeful, member, participant, player, rival, scrapper*, team member, warrior; SEE CONCEPT *366*

context [n] *framework, circumstances*
ambience, background, conditions, connection, frame of reference, lexicon, relation, situation, substance, text, vocabulary; SEE CONCEPTS *682,696*

contiguous [adj] *adjacent, in contact*
abutting, adjoining, approximal, beside, bordering, close, contactual, conterminous, juxtaposed,

juxtapositional, meeting, near, near-at-hand, nearby, neighboring, next, next door to, next to, touching; SEE CONCEPTS *586,778*

continent [*adj*] *chaste, pure*
abstemious, abstentious, abstinent, ascetic, austere, bridled, celibate, curbed, inhibited, modest, restrained, self-restrained, sober, temperate; SEE CONCEPT *550*

contingency [*n*] *chance happening; possibility*
accident, break, chance, crisis, crossroads, emergency, event, eventuality, exigency, fortuity, happening, if it's cool*, incident, juncture, likelihood, occasion, odds, opportunity, pass, pinch, predicament, probability, strait, turning point, uncertainty, zero hour*; SEE CONCEPTS *650,679,693*

contingent [*n*] *group of followers*
batch, body, bunch, deputation, detachment, disciples, mission, quota, sect, section, set; SEE CONCEPT *417*

contingent [*adj*] *conditional; possible*
accidental, casual, chance, controlled by, dependent, fluky, fortuitous, haphazard, incidental, likely, odd, probable, probably, random, subject to, unanticipated, uncertain, unexpected, unforeseeable, unforeseen, unpredictable; SEE CONCEPT *552*

continual [*adj*] *constant, incessant*
aeonian, around-the-clock, ceaseless, connected, consecutive, continuous, dateless, endless, enduring, eternal, everlasting, frequent, interminable, oft-repeated, permanent, perpetual, persistent, persisting, recurrent, regular, relentless, repeated, repetitive, running, staying, steady, timeless, unbroken, unceasing, unchanging, unending, unfailing, unflagging, uninterrupted, unremitting, unvarying, unwaning; SEE CONCEPTS *534,798*

continuance [*n*] *duration*
constancy, continuation, endurance, extension, guts*, longevity, period, permanence, perpetuation, protraction, run, survival, term, vitality; SEE CONCEPTS *637,804,807*

continuation [*n*] *addition; maintenance*
assiduity, augmenting, continuance, continuing, continuity, duration, endurance, enduring, extension, furtherance, going on, increase, increasing, line, maintaining, perpetuating, perpetuation, persisting, postscript, preservation, preserving, producing, production, prolongation, prolonging, propagation, protracting, protraction, sequel, succession, supplement, sustaining, sustenance, tenacity; SEE CONCEPTS *640,651,804*

continue [*v1*] *persist, carry on*
abide, advance, carry forward, draw out, endure, extend, forge ahead, get on with it*, go on, hang in*, keep at, keep on, keep on truckin'*, keep the ball rolling*, keep up, last, lengthen, linger, live on, loiter, maintain, make headway, move ahead, never cease, outlast, outlive, perdure, persevere, persist in, press on, progress, project, prolong, promote, pursue, push on, reach, remain, rest, ride, run on, stand, stay, stay on, stick at, stick to, survive, sustain, uphold; SEE CONCEPT *239*

continue [*v2*] *begin again; resume*
begin over, begin where one left off, carry on, carry over, go on with, pick up, proceed, recapitulate, recommence, reestablish, reinstate, reinstitute, renew, reopen, restart, restore, return to, take up; SEE CONCEPT *234*

continuity [*n*] *progression*
chain, cohesion, connection, constancy, continuance, continuousness, continuum, dovetailing, durability, duration, endurance, extension, flow, interrelationship, linking, perpetuity, persistence, prolongation, protraction, sequence, stability, stamina, succession, survival, train, uniting, unity, vitality, whole; SEE CONCEPT *721*

continuous [*adj*] *constant, unending*
connected, consecutive, continued, day and night*, endless, everlasting, extended, for ever and ever, interminable, looped, no end of*, no end to, on a treadmill*, perpetual, prolonged, regular, repeated, stable, steady, timeless, unbroken, unceasing, undivided, unfaltering, uninterrupted; SEE CONCEPTS *482,798*

contort [*v*] *disfigure, distort*
bend, convolute, curve, deform, gnarl, knot, misshape, torture, twist, warp, wind, wrench, writhe; SEE CONCEPTS *147,184*

contortion [*n*] *distortion, mutilation*
anamorphosis, crookedness, deformation, deformity, dislocation, grimace, malformation, misproportion, misshapement, pout, twist, ugliness, unsightliness, wryness; SEE CONCEPTS *436,580*

contour [*n*] *outline, profile*
curve, delineation, figure, form, lineament, lines, relief, shape, silhouette; SEE CONCEPT *436*

contraband [*n*] *black-market production*
bootlegging, counterfeiting, crime, dealing, goods*, moonshine*, piracy, plunder, poaching, rum-running*, smuggling, stuff, swag, theft, trafficking, violation, wetbacking*; SEE CONCEPTS *192,338*

contraband [*adj*] *black-market; unlawful*
banned, bootleg, bootlegged, disapproved, excluded, forbidden, hot*, illegal, illicit, interdicted, prohibited, proscribed, shut out, smuggled, taboo, unauthorized, verboten; SEE CONCEPTS *319,545*

contraceptive [*n*] *birth control method*
armor, barrier method, coil, condom, diaphragm, foam, hormone, intrauterine device, IUD, jelly, loop, pill, planned parenthood, preventative, preventive medicine, prophylactic, rhythm method, ring, rubber, safety, shield, spermicidal cream, sponge, vaginal suppository; SEE CONCEPTS *307,446*

contract [*n*] *agreement, deal*
arrangement, bargain, bond, commission, commitment, compact, concordat, convention, covenant, deposition, dicker*, engagement, evidence, guarantee, handshake*, indenture, liability, mise, obligation, pact, paper, pledge, promise, proof, record, settlement, stipulation, treaty, understanding; SEE CONCEPTS *271,684*

contract [*v1*] *condense*
abate, abbreviate, abridge, become smaller, clench, compress, confine, constrict, consume, curtail, decline, decrease, deflate, draw in, dwindle, ebb, edit, epitomize, evaporate, fall away, fall off, grow less, lessen, lose, narrow, omit, purse, recede, reduce, shrink, shrivel, subside, syncopate, take in, tighten, wane, waste, weaken, wither, wrinkle; SEE CONCEPTS *169,236,247*

contract [*v2*] *come to terms*
accept offer, adjust, agree, arrange, assent, bargain, become indebted, bound, buy, circumscribe, clinch, close, come around, commit, consent,

covenant, dicker*, engage, enter into, firm a deal*, give one's word, go along with*, hammer out deal*, initial*, ink*, it's a deal*, limit, make terms, negotiate, obligate, owe, pact, pledge, promise, put in writing, set, settle, shake hands on it*, sign for, sign papers, sign up, stipulate, swear to, undertake, work out details*; SEE CONCEPTS 8,50,88

contract [v3] *catch disease*
acquire, afflict, be afflicted with, become infected with, be ill with, bring on, cause, come down with, decline, derange, develop, disorder, fall, fall victim to, get, go down with, incur, indispose, induce, obtain, sicken, sink, succumb to, take, take one's death, upset, weaken; SEE CONCEPTS 93,308

contraction [n] *drawing in; shortening*
abbreviating, abbreviation, abridging, abridgment, compression, condensation, condensing, confinement, confining, constriction, curtailing, curtailment, cutting down, decrease, decreasing, deflating, deflation, diminishing, diminution, drawing together, dwindling, elision, evaporating, evaporation, lessening, lopping, narrowing, omission, omitting, receding, recession, reducing, reduction, shrinkage, shrinking, shrivelling, tensing, tightening, withdrawal, withdrawing; SEE CONCEPTS 469,776

contradict [v] *be at variance with*
belie, buck, call in question*, challenge, confront, contravene, controvert, counter, counteract, cross, dare, deny, differ, disaffirm, disclaim, disprove, dispute, fly in the face of*, gainsay, have bone to pick*, impugn, negate, negative, oppose, refuse to accept, repudiate, take on, thumbs down*, traverse; SEE CONCEPTS 46,54,665

contradiction [n] *variance to something*
bucking, conflict, confutation, contravention, defiance, denial, difference, disagreement, discrepancy, dispute, dissension, gainsaying, incongruity, inconsistency, negation, opposite, opposition; SEE CONCEPTS 46,278,665

contradictory [adj] *antagonistic*
adverse, against, agin, anti, antipodal, antipodean, antithetic, antithetical, con, conflicting, contrary, converse, counter, counteractive, diametric, discrepant, incompatible, incongruous, inconsistent, irreconcilable, negating, no go*, nullifying, opposing, opposite, ornery*, paradoxical, polar, repugnant, reverse; SEE CONCEPT 542

contrary [adj] *antagonistic; opposite*
adverse, anti, antipathetic, antipodal, antipodean, antithetical, balky, clashing, conflicting, contradictory, contrariant, contumacious, converse, counter, diametric, discordant, dissentient, dissident, froward, headstrong, hostile, inconsistent, inimical, insubordinate, intractable, negative, nonconforming, nonconformist, obstinate, opposed, ornery*, paradoxical, perverse, rebellious, recalcitrant, recusant, refractory, restive, reverse, stubborn, unruly, wayward, wrongheaded; SEE CONCEPT 401

contrast [n] *difference*
adverse, antithesis, comparison, contradiction, contradistinction, contraposition, contrariety, converse, differentiation, disagreement, disparity, dissimilarity, dissimilitude, distinction, divergence, diversity, foil, heterogeneity, incompatibility, incongruousness, inconsistency, inequality,

inverse, oppositeness, opposition, reverse, unlikeness, variance, variation; SEE CONCEPTS 561,665

contrast [v] *compare, differ*
balance, be a foil to*, be contrary to, be dissimilar, be diverse, be unlike, be variable, bracket, collate, conflict, contradict, depart, deviate, differentiate, disagree, distinguish, diverge, hang, hold a candle to*, match up, mismatch, oppose, separate, set in opposition, set off, stack up against*, stand out, vary, weigh; SEE CONCEPTS 39,561,665

contravene [v] *go against, contradict*
abjure, breach, break, combat, conflict with, counteract, cross, defy, disaffirm, disobey, encroach, exclude, fight, gainsay, hinder, impugn, infract, infringe, interfere, interpose, intrude, negate, offend, oppose, overstep, refute, reject, repudiate, resist, spurn, thwart, transgress, traverse, trespass, violate; SEE CONCEPTS 46,106,121,192

contribute [v1] *donate, provide*
accord, add, afford, ante up, assign, bequeath, bequest, bestow, chip in, come through, commit, confer, devote, dispense, dole out*, dower, endow, enrich, furnish, give, give away, go Dutch*, grant, hand out, kick in*, pitch in*, pony up*, present, proffer, sacrifice, share, subscribe, subsidize, supply, sweeten the kitty*, tender, will; SEE CONCEPTS 108,140

contribute [v2] *be partly responsible for*
add to, advance, aid, assist, augment, be conducive, be instrumental, conduce, do one's bit*, finger in the pie*, fortify, get in the act*, have a hand in*, help, lead, put in two cents*, redound, reinforce, sit in on, strengthen, supplement, support, tend, uphold; SEE CONCEPTS 83,110,244

contribution [n] *gift, offering*
addition, a hand, alms, augmentation, benefaction, beneficence, bestowal, charity, donation, do one's part*, gifting, grant, handout, helping hand, improvement, increase, input, present, significant addition, subscription, supplement, write-off*; SEE CONCEPTS 337,340

contrite [adj] *regretful*
apologetic, attritional, chastened, compunctious, conscience-stricken, humble, penitent, penitential, remorseful, repentant, sorrowful, sorry; SEE CONCEPT 403

contrition [n] *regret*
attrition, compunction, contriteness, humiliation, penance, penitence, penitency, remorse, repentance, rue, ruth, self-reproach, sorrow; SEE CONCEPT 410

contrivance [n1] *plan, fabrication*
angle, artifice, brainchild, coinage, design, dodge, expedient, formation, gimmick, intrigue, invention, inventiveness, machination, measure, plot, project, ruse, scheme, slant, stratagem, switch, trick, twist; SEE CONCEPT 660

contrivance [n2] *gadget*
apparatus, appliance, brainchild, coinage, contraption, convenience, creation, device, discovery, engine, equipment, gear, gimcrack*, harness, implement, instrument, invention, machine, material, mechanism, tackle, thingamabob*, thingamajig*, tool, utensil, whatsis*, widget*; SEE CONCEPTS 260,463,499

contrive [v1] *invent, design*
come up with, concoct, construct, cook up, create, devise, dream up*, engineer, fabricate, fashion, forge, form, formulate, frame*, handle,

hatch, improvise, make, make up*, manipulate, manufacture, move, plan, plot, project, rig*, scheme, throw together*, trump up*, vamp, wangle, whip up*; SEE CONCEPTS 36,173

contrive [v2] *bring about, succeed with difficulty*
achieve, angle, arrange, carry out, cogitate, collude, compass, concoct, connive, develop, devise, effect, elaborate, engineer, execute, finagle*, hatch, hit upon, intrigue, jockey*, machinate, manage, maneuver, manipulate, mastermind, negotiate, pass, plan, play games*, plot, project, scheme, shift, swing, work out, wrangle; SEE CONCEPTS 36,91,94

control [n] *command, mastery*
ascendancy, authority, bridle, charge, check, clout, containment, curb, determination, direction, discipline, domination, dominion, driver's seat*, force, government, guidance, inside track, juice, jurisdiction, limitation, management, manipulation, might, oversight, predomination, qualification, regimentation, regulation, restraint, restriction, ropes, rule, strings*, subjection, subordination, superintendence, supervision, supremacy, sway, upper hand*, weight, wire pulling*; SEE CONCEPT 376

control [v1] *have charge of*
administer, administrate, advise, be in saddle*, boss, bully, call, call the signals*, command, conduct, deal with, direct, discipline, dominate, domineer, govern, guide, handle, head, head up*, hold purse strings*, hold sway over*, hold the reins*, instruct, lead, manage, manipulate, overlook, oversee, pilot, predominate, push buttons*, quarterback*, regiment, regulate, reign over, rule, run*, run the show*, run things*, steer, subject, subjugate, superintend, supervise; SEE CONCEPT 117

control [v2] *curb, hold back*
adjust, awe, bridle, check, collect, compose, constrain, contain, cool, corner, cow, limit, monopolize, quell, regulate, rein in, repress, restrain, simmer down*, smother, subdue; SEE CONCEPT 130

controversial [adj] *at issue*
arguable, argumentative, contended, contentious, contestable, controvertible, debateable, disputable, disputatious, disputed, doubtable, doubtful, dubious, dubitable, in dispute, litigious, moot, open to discussion*, open to question*, polemical, questionable, suspect, uncertain, under discussion; SEE CONCEPTS 535,546

controversy [n] *debate, dispute*
altercation, argument, beef*, bickering, brush, contention, difference, discussion, disputation, dissension, embroilment, falling-out*, flak, fuss, hurrah, miff, polemic, quarrel, row, rumpus, scene, scrap, squabble, strife, tiff*, words, wrangle, wrangling; SEE CONCEPTS 46,278,665

controvert [v] *oppose, argue*
break, challenge, confound, confute, contest, contradict, counter, debate, deny, disconfirm, discuss, disprove, dispute, oppugn, question, rebut, refute, wrangle; SEE CONCEPTS 21,46

contumacious [adj] *headstrong, obstinate*
alienated, contrary, disaffected, estranged, factious, froward, haughty, inflexible, insubordinate, insurgent, intractable, intransigent, irreconcilable, mutinous, obdurate, perverse, pig-headed, rebellious, recalcitrant, refractory, seditious, stubborn, unyielding; SEE CONCEPT 401

contusion [n] *bruise, injury*
bang, bump, cut, discoloration, knock, mouse, swelling, wale, wound; SEE CONCEPT 309

conundrum [n] *puzzle*
brain-teaser, closed book*, enigma, mystery, mystification, poser*, problem, puzzlement, riddle, why*; SEE CONCEPTS 532,666,690

convalescent [adj] *improving, recuperating*
ambulatory, discharged, dismissed, gaining strength, getting better, getting over something*, getting well, healing, mending, on the mend*, past crisis, perked up*, rallying, recovering, rejuvenated, rejuvenating, released, restored, strengthening; SEE CONCEPT 314

convene [v] *bring together; meet*
assemble, call, call in, collect, come together, congregate, convoke, corral, gather, get together, hold meeting, muster, open, rally, round up, scare up*, sit, summon, unite; SEE CONCEPTS 60,114,324

convenience [n1] *availability, usefulness; useful thing*
accessibility, accessory, accommodation, advancement, advantage, agreeableness, aid, amenity, appliance, appropriateness, assistance, avail, benefit, comfort, comforts, contribution, cooperation, decency, ease, enjoyment, facility, fitness, furtherance, handiness, help, life, luxury, means, ministration, ministry, openness, opportuneness, promotion, receptiveness, relief, satisfaction, service, serviceability, succor, suitability, suitableness, support, time saver, use, utility; SEE CONCEPTS 658,712

convenience [n2] *spare time*
chance, freedom, hour, leisure, liberty, occasion, one's own sweet time*, opportunity, place, preference, spare moment*, suitable time, whenever; SEE CONCEPT 807

convenient [adj1] *appropriate, useful*
acceptable, accommodating, adaptable, adapted, advantageous, agreeable, aiding, assisting, available, beneficial, comfortable, commodious, conducive, contributive, decent, favorable, fit, fitted, good, handy, helpful, in public interest, opportune, proper, ready, roomy, seasonable, serviceable, suitable, suited, timely, time-saving, user-friendly*, well-planned; SEE CONCEPT 560

convenient [adj2] *nearby*
accessible, adjacent, adjoining, all around, at elbows*, at fingertips*, at hand, available, central, close, close at hand, close-by, contiguous, easy to reach, handy, immediate, in neighborhood, next, next door, nigh, on deck*, on tap*, under one's nose*, within reach; SEE CONCEPT 586

convent [n] *nunnery*
abbey, cloister, monastery, religious community, retreat, school; SEE CONCEPTS 368,516

convention [n1] *conference*
assemblage, assembly, clambake, confab*, congress, convocation, council, delegates, delegation, get together, meet*, meeting, members, powwow*, rally, representatives, show; SEE CONCEPTS 114,324,417

convention [n2] *practice, tradition*
canon, code, covenance, custom, etiquette, fashion, form, formality, habit, law, percept, precept, propriety, rule, understanding, usage; SEE CONCEPT 688

convention [n3] *agreement*
bargain, bond, compact, concord, concordat, con-

CO
CO

tract, covenant, pact, protocol, stipulation, transaction, treaty; SEE CONCEPTS 271,684

conventional [adj1] *common, normal*
accepted, accustomed, button-down, commonplace, correct, current, customary, decorous, everyday, expected, fashionable, formal, general, habitual, in established usage, ordinary, orthodox, plain, popular, predominant, prevailing, prevalent, proper, regular, ritual, routine, square, standard, stereotyped, straight, traditional, tralatitious, typical, usual, well-known, wonted; SEE CONCEPTS 530,547

conventional [adj2] *unoriginal*
bigoted, bourgeois, commonplace, conforming, conservative, demure, doctrinal, dogmatic, drippy, hackneyed, hidebound, humdrum, illiberal, inflexible, in rut, insular, isolationist, lame, literal, moderate, moral, narrow, narrow-minded, not heretical, obstinate, parochial, pedestrian, prosaic, puritanical, rigid, routine, rube*, run-of-the-mill, sober, solemn, square, stereotyped, straight, straight-laced, strict, stuffy, uptight; SEE CONCEPT 550

converge [v] *gather*
assemble, coincide, combine, come together, concenter, concentrate, concur, encounter, enter in, focalize, focus, join, meet, merge, mingle, rally, unite; SEE CONCEPTS 113,114

conversant [adj] *experienced, familiar with*
abreast, acquainted, alive, apprehensive, au courant, au fait, aware, cognizant, comprehending, conscious, cool*, down with*, hep*, hip*, informed, into, kept posted, knowing, knowledgeable, learned, on the beam*, perceptive, percipient, plugged in*, practiced, proficient, sensible, sentient, skilled, up*, up-to-date, versant, versed, well-informed, witting; SEE CONCEPT 402

conversation [n] *dialogue, discourse*
chat, colloquy, comment, communication, communion, confab*, confabulation, conference, consultation, converse, debate, discussion, exchange, expression, gab*, gossip, hearing, intercourse, jive*, observation, palaver, parley, pillow talk*, powwow*, questioning, remark, repartee, speech, talk, talkfest*, tête-à-tête*, ventilation*, visit, yak*; SEE CONCEPT 266

converse [n] *opposite*
antipode, antipole, antithesis, contra, contrary, counter, counterpole, inverse, obverse, other side, reverse; SEE CONCEPT 665

converse [adj] *opposite*
antipodal, antipodean, antithetical, contradictory, contrary, counter, counterpole, different, reverse, reversed, transposed; SEE CONCEPT 564

converse [v] *talk*
chat, chew the fat*, chitchat*, commune, confer, discourse, exchange, gab*, parley, rap*, schmooze*, speak, use, yak*; SEE CONCEPT 266

conversion [n] *change, adaptation*
about-face*, alteration, born again*, change of heart*, changeover, exchange, flip-flop*, flux, growth, innovation, metamorphosis, metanoia, metasis, modification, novelty, passage, passing, permutation, progress, proselytization, qualification, reclamation, reconstruction, reformation, regeneration, remodelling, reorganization, resolution, resolving, reversal, see the light*, switch, transfiguration, transformation, translation, transmogrification, transmutation, turning, turning around; SEE CONCEPTS 232,701

convert [n] *new believer*
catechumen, disciple, follower, neophyte, novice, novitiate, proselyte; SEE CONCEPT 361

convert [v1] *change; adapt*
alter, apply, appropriate, commute, downlink, download, interchange, make, metamorphose, modify, remodel, reorganize, restyle, revise, switch, switch over, transfigure, transform, translate, transmogrify, transmute, transpose, turn; SEE CONCEPTS 232,701

convert [v2] *change belief, especially regarding religion*
actuate, alter conviction, assimilate to, baptize, be born again*, bend, bias, brainwash, bring, bring around, budge, cause to adopt, change into, change of heart*, convince, create anew, impel, incline, lead, lead to believe, make over, move, persuade, proselyte, proselytize, redeem, reform, regenerate, save, see the light*, sway, turn; SEE CONCEPTS 12,14,35

convex [adj] *rounded, curving outward*
arched, bent, biconvex, bulged, bulging, bulgy, gibbous, outcurved, protuberant, raised; SEE CONCEPT 486

convey [v1] *transport*
back, bear, bring, carry, channel, conduct, dispatch, ferry, fetch, forward, funnel, grant, guide, hump, lead, lug, move, pack, pipe, ride, schlepp*, send, shoulder, siphon, support, tote, traject, transfer, transmit, truck; SEE CONCEPTS 187,217

convey [v2] *express message*
break, carry, communicate, conduct, disclose, impart, make known, pass on, project, put across, relate, reveal, send, tell, transmit; SEE CONCEPT 60

conveyance [n] *transport*
car, carriage, carrying, communication, machine, movement, transfer, transference, transmission, transportation, vehicle; SEE CONCEPTS 143,501, 503

convict [n] *criminal*
captive, con, culprit, felon, jailbird*, longtermer*, loser*, malefactor, prisoner, repeater*; SEE CONCEPT 412

convict [v] *find guilty*
adjudge, attaint, bring to justice, condemn, declare guilty, doom, frame, imprison, pass sentence on, pronounce guilty, put away, put the screws to*, rap*, send up*, send up the river*, sentence, throw the book at*; SEE CONCEPTS 18,317

conviction [n1] *belief, opinion*
confidence, creed, doctrine, dogma, eye, faith, feeling, judgment call, mind, persuasion, principle, reliance, say so*, sentiment, slant, tenet, view; SEE CONCEPT 689

conviction [n2] *guilty sentence; assurance*
assuredness, certainty, certitude, condemnation, condemning, confidence, determining guilt, earnestness, fall, fervor, firmness, rap, reliance, sureness, surety, unfavorable verdict; SEE CONCEPTS 317,410

convince [v] *gain the confidence of*
argue into, assure, brainwash, bring around, bring home to*, bring to reason*, change, demonstrate, draw, effect, establish, get, hook*, induce, make a believer*, overcome, persuade, prevail upon, prompt, prove, put across, refute, satisfy, sell*, sell one on*, sway, talk into, turn, twist one's arm*, win over; SEE CONCEPT 68

convincing [adj] *persuasive*
acceptable, authentic, believeable, cogent, conclusive, credible, dependable, faithful, hopeful, impressive, incontrovertible, likely, moving, plausible, possible, powerful, presumable, probable, rational, reasonable, reliable, satisfactory, satisfying, solid, sound, swaying, telling, trustworthy, trusty, valid; SEE CONCEPTS 267,537,552

convivial [adj] *fun-loving*
back-slapping*, cheerful, clubby*, companionable, conversible, entertaining, festal, festive, friendly, gay, genial, glad-handering*, happy, hearty, hilarious, holiday, jocund, jolly, jovial, lively, merry, mirthful, pleasant, sociable, vivacious; SEE CONCEPTS 401,404

convocation [n] *assembly*
assemblage, conclave, concourse, confab*, conference, congregation, congress, convention, council, diet, get-together, meet, meeting, powwow*, synod, turnout; SEE CONCEPT 114

convolution [n] *loop, spiral*
coil, coiling, complexity, contortion, curlicue, flexing, gyration, helix, intricacy, involution, serpentine, sinuosity, sinuousness, snaking, swirl, tortuousness, twist, undulation, winding; SEE CONCEPT 436

convoy [n] *guard, escort*
attendance, attendant, companion, protection; SEE CONCEPT 423

convoy [v] *protect, escort*
accompany, attend, bear, bring, chaperon, companion, company, conduct, consort, defend, guard, pilot, safeguard, shepherd, shield, usher, watch; SEE CONCEPTS 96,110

convulsion [n1] *muscle spasm*
algospasm, attack, contortion, contraction, cramp, epilepsy, fit, paroxysm, seizure, throe, tremor; SEE CONCEPT 308

convulsion [n2] *disturbance*
agitation, cataclysm, clamor, commotion, disaster, ferment, furor, outcry, quaking, rocking, seism, shaking, shock, tottering, trembling, tumult, turbulence, upheaval, upturn; SEE CONCEPTS 152,748

cook [n] *person who prepares food*
baker, chef, hash slinger*, mess sergeant, servant, sous chef; SEE CONCEPT 348

cook [v] *prepare food, usually using heat*
bake, barbecue, blanch, boil, braise, brew, broil, brown, burn, coddle, curry, decoct, deep fry, devil, doctor*, escallop, fix, French fry, fricassee, fry, griddle, grill, heat, imbue, melt, microwave, mull, nuke*, panfry, parboil, parch, percolate, poach, pressure-cook, reduce, roast, ruin*, sauté, scald, scorch, sear, seethe, simmer, sizzle, spoil*, steam, steep, stew, toast, warm up; SEE CONCEPT 170

cook up [v] *devise*
arrange, concoct, contrive, dream up, fabricate, falsify, formulate, frame, hatch, improvise, invent, make up, plan, plot, prepare, scheme, vamp; SEE CONCEPTS 17,36

cool [adj1] *cold, nippy*
air-conditioned, algid, arctic, biting, chill, chilled, chilling, chilly, coldish, frigid, frore, frosty, gelid, hawkish, nipping, refreshing, refrigerated, shivery, snappy, wintry; SEE CONCEPT 605

cool [adj2] *calm, collected*
assured, composed, coolheaded, deliberate, detached, dispassionate, impassive, imperturbable, levelheaded, nonchalant, philosophical, phlegmatic, placid, quiet, relaxed, self-controlled, self-possessed, serene, stolid, together, tranquil, unagitated, unemotional, unexcited, unflappable, unruffled; SEE CONCEPT 401

cool [adj3] *aloof, disapproving*
annoyed, apathetic, distant, frigid, impertinent, impudent, incurious, indifferent, insolent, lukewarm, offended, offhand, offish, procacious, reserved, solitary, standoffish, unapproachable, uncommunicative, unenthusiastic, unfriendly, uninterested, unresponsive, unsociable, unwelcoming, withdrawn; SEE CONCEPT 404

cool [adj4] *excellent*
boss*, dandy, divine, glorious, hunky-dory*, keen, marvelous, neat, nifty, sensational, swell; SEE CONCEPT 572

cool [v1] *chill*
abate, air-condition, air-cool, ally, calm, freeze, frost, infrigidate, lessen, lose heat, mitigate, moderate, reduce, refrigerate, temper; SEE CONCEPT 255

cool [v2] *take a break; abate*
allay, assuage, calm, calm down, chill, compose, control, dampen, lessen, mitigate, moderate, quiet, reduce, rein, repress, restrain, simmer down, suppress, temper; SEE CONCEPTS 240,384

cooperate [v] *aid, assist*
abet, advance, agree, back up, band, befriend, be in cahoots*, chip in, coadjute, coincide, collaborate, combine, comply with, concert, concur, conduce, conspire, contribute, coordinate, espouse, forward, further, go along with, help, join forces, join in, league*, lend a hand*, participate, partner, pitch in*, play ball*, pool resources, pull together, second, share in, show willingness, side with, stick together, succor, take part, unite, uphold, work side by side, work together; SEE CONCEPTS 110,112

cooperation [n] *mutual effort*
aid, alliance, assistance, cahoots*, coaction, coadjuvancy, coalition, collaboration, combination, combined effort, communion, company, concert, concurrence, confederacy, confederation, conjunction, conspiracy, doing business with, esprit de corps, federation, fusion, give-and-take, harmony, help, helpfulness, logrolling*, participation, partisanship, partnership, playing ball*, reciprocity, responsiveness, service, society, symbiosis, synergism, synergy, teaming, teamwork, unanimity, union, unity; SEE CONCEPTS 110,112,388,677

cooperative [adj1] *joint, unified*
agreeing, coacting, coactive, coadjuvant, coefficient, collaborating, collaborative, collective, collegial, collusive, combined, combining, common, concerted, concurring, coordinated, hand in glove*, harmonious, in league, interdependent, joining, participating, reciprocal, shared, symbiotic, synergetic, synergic, team, united, uniting; SEE CONCEPT 538

cooperative [adj2] *helpful*
accommodating, companionable, obliging, responsive, sociable, supportive, useful; SEE CONCEPTS 538,555

co-opt [v] *to assimilate in order to take over or appropriate*
absorb, accept, admit, adopt, bring in, bring into line, bring into the fold, connaturalize, convert, draw in, elect, embrace, encompass, enfold, ho-

mogenize, homologize, include, incorporate, make one's own, take in, take over; SEE CONCEPTS *232,701*

coordinate [*adj*] *equivalent*
alike, coequal, correlative, correspondent, counterpart, equal, equalized, like, parallel, same, tantamount; SEE CONCEPT *566*

coordinate [*v*] *match, relate*
accommodate, adjust, agree, atune, combine, conduce, conform, correlate, get it together*, get one's act together*, harmonize, integrate, mesh, organize, pool, proportion, pull together, quarterback*, reconcile, reconciliate, regulate, shape up, synchronize, systematize, team up; SEE CONCEPTS *36,84,158*

cope [*v*] *manage, contend*
battle with, buffet, carry on, confront, deal, dispatch, encounter, endure, face, get a handle on*, get by, grapple, hack*, hack it*, handle, hold one's own*, live with, make go of it*, make it*, make out*, make the grade*, pit oneself against*, rise to occasion, struggle, struggle through, suffer, survive, tangle, tussle, weather, wrestle; SEE CONCEPTS *23,35*

copious [*adj*] *abundant*
alive with, a mess of*, ample, aplenty, bounteous, bountiful, coming out of ears*, crawling with*, extensive, exuberant, full, galore, generous, heavy, lavish, liberal, lush, luxuriant, no end*, overflowing, plenteous, plentiful, plenty, profuse, prolix, replete, rich, superabundant, thick with, verbose, wordy; SEE CONCEPT *771*

copiousness [*n*] *abundance*
affluence, amplitude, bountifulness, bounty, cornucopia, exuberance, fullness, horn of plenty*, lavishness, luxuriance, plentifulness, plenty, richness, superabundance; SEE CONCEPT *767*

cop out [*v*] *abandon, quit*
back down, back off, back out, backpedal, desert, dodge, excuse, give the slip*, have alibi, rationalize, renege, renounce, revoke, skip, use pretext, welsh, withdraw; SEE CONCEPTS *121,156*

copulate [*v*] *have sexual relations*
be carnal, bed, breed, cohabit, conjugate, couple, do it*, fool around*, fornicate, go all the way*, go to bed*, have coition, have relations, have sex, lay*, lie with, make it*, make love, make out*, mate, sleep together, sleep with, unite; SEE CONCEPT *375*

copy [*n*] *duplicate, imitation*
archetype, carbon, carbon copy*, cast, clone, counterfeit, counterpart, ditto*, ectype, effigy, ersatz, facsimile, forgery, hard copy, image, impersonation, impression, imprint, likeness, microfiche, mimeograph, miniature, mirror, model, offprint, parallel, pattern, photocopy, photograph, photostat, portrait, print, reflection, replica, replication, representation, reprint, reproduction, rubbings, similarity, simulacrum, simulation, study, tracing, transcript, transcription, type, Xerox*; SEE CONCEPTS *269,667,716*

copy [*v1*] *duplicate*
carbon, cartoon, clone, counterfeit, delineate, depict, ditto, draw, dupe, engrave, engross, fake, forge, imitate, knock off*, limn, manifold, mimeo, mirror, mold, paint, paraphrase, photocopy, photostat, picture, plagiarize, portray, reduplicate, reflect, repeat, replicate, represent, reproduce, rewrite, sculpture, simulate, sketch, stat, trace, transcribe, Xerox*; SEE CONCEPT *171*

copy [*v2*] *imitate*
act like, ape, burlesque, do, do a take-off*, do like*, echo, embody, emulate, epitomize, fake, follow, follow example, follow suit, go like*, illustrate, incarnate, knock off*, make like*, mimic, mirror, mock, model, parody, parrot, personify, phony, pirate, play a role, prefigure, repeat, sham, simulate, steal, take leaf out of book*, take off*, travesty, typify; SEE CONCEPTS *59,139,242*

coquet [*v*] *tease*
dally, flirt, fool, gold-dig*, lead on, make eyes at*, operate, philander, string along, titillate, toy, trifle, vamp, wanton, wink at*; SEE CONCEPTS *375,384*

cord [*n*] *rope*
bond, connection, cordage, fiber, line, link, string, tendon, tie, twine; SEE CONCEPTS *470,680*

cordial [*adj*] *friendly, sociable*
affable, affectionate, agreeable, amicable, buddy-buddy*, cheerful, clubby, companionable, congenial, convivial, cozy, earnest, genial, glowing, gracious, happy, heartfelt, heart-to-heart, hearty, invigorating, jovial, mellow, neighborly, palsy-walsy*, polite, red-carpet*, responsive, sincere, social, sympathetic, tender, warm, warmhearted, welcoming, wholehearted; SEE CONCEPT *401*

cordiality [*n*] *friendliness, sociability*
affability, agreeability, agreeableness, amenity, amiability, approbation, approval, earnestness, enjoyableness, favor, geniality, gratefulness, heartiness, mutuality, pleasantness, reciprocity, responsiveness, sincerity, sweetness and light*, sympathy, understanding, warmth, wholeheartedness; SEE CONCEPT *633*

core [*n*] *center, gist*
amount, base, basis, body, bottom line, bulk, burden, consequence, corpus, crux, essence, focus, foundation, heart, import, importance, kernel, main idea, mass, meat*, meat and potatoes*, middle, midpoint, midst, nitty gritty*, nub, nucleus, origin, pith, pivot, purport, quick, root, significance, staple, substance, thrust, upshot; SEE CONCEPTS *442,668,826*

corner [*n1*] *angle*
bend, branch, cloverleaf, crook, crossing, edge, fork, intersection, joint, junction, projection, ridge, rim, shift, V*, veer, Y*; SEE CONCEPTS *436,484,513*

corner [*n2*] *niche*
angle, cavity, compartment, cranny, hideaway, hide-out, hole, indentation, nook, recess, retreat; SEE CONCEPTS *440,471,513*

corner [*n3*] *predicament*
box, difficulty, dilemma, distress, fix, hole, impasse, impediment, jam, knot, pickle, plight, scrape, tight spot; SEE CONCEPTS *674,675*

corner [*v*] *trap*
bottle, bring to bay, capture, catch, collar*, fool, get on ropes*, have up a tree*, mousetrap*, nab, put out, seize, tree, trick, trouble; SEE CONCEPTS *59,90*

corny [*adj*] *trite, clichéd*
banal, commonplace, dull, feeble, hackneyed, mawkish, melodramatic, old-fashioned, old hat*, sentimental, shopworn, stale, stereotyped, stupid, tired, warmed-over; SEE CONCEPT *550*

corollary [*n*] *conclusion, deduction*
aftereffect, analogy, consequence, culmination, effect, end, end product, induction, inference, is-

sue, precipitate, result, sequel, sequence, upshot; SEE CONCEPTS 230,410,529

corporal [adj] *bodily, physical*
anatomical, carnal, corporeal, fleshly, fleshy, gross, human, material, objective, phenomenal, sensible, somatic, substantial, tangible; SEE CONCEPT 542

corporation [n] *business organization, usually large*
association, bunch, business, clan, company, corporate body, crew, crowd, enterprise, gang, hookup*, jungle*, legal entity, megacorp*, mob, multinational, octopus*, outfit, partnership, ring, shell, society, syndicate, zoo*; SEE CONCEPT 325

corporeal [adj] *bodily, physical*
anatomical, carnal, corporal, fleshly, fleshy, human, material, mortal, objective, phenomenal, sensible, somatic, substantial, tangible; SEE CONCEPT 542

corps [n] *group trained for action*
band, body, brigade, company, contingent, crew, detachment, division, outfit, party, posse, regiment, squad, squadron, team, troop, troupe, unit; SEE CONCEPTS 294,322,417

corpse [n] *dead body*
body, bones*, cadaver, carcass, carrion, deceased, departed, mort*, remains, stiff*; SEE CONCEPTS 390,417

corpulent [adj] *fat, chubby*
baby elephant*, beefy*, blimp*, bulky, burly, embonpoint, fat, fleshy, gross, having a bay window*, having a spare tire*, heavy, hefty, husky, large, lusty, obese, overblown, overweight, plump, portly, roly-poly*, rotund, stout, tubby, weighty, well-padded*; SEE CONCEPTS 406,491, 773

corpus [n] *body of text*
bulk, collection, compilation, complete works, core, entirety, extant works, mass, oeuvre, opera omnia, staple, substance, whole; SEE CONCEPT 271

correct [adj 1] *accurate, exact*
according to Hoyle*, actual, amen*, appropriate, cooking with gas*, dead on*, equitable, factual, faithful, faultless, flawless, for sure, free of error, impeccable, just, legitimate, nice, okay, on target*, on the ball*, on the beam*, on the button*, on the money*, on the nose*, on track*, perfect, precise, proper, regular, right, right as rain*, righteous, right on*, right stuff*, rigorous, stone, strict, true, undistorted, unmistaken, veracious, veridical; SEE CONCEPTS 542,557,574

correct [adj 2] *proper, appropriate*
acceptable, becoming, careful, comme il faut, conforming, conventional, decent, decorous, diplomatic, done, fitting, meticulous, nice, okay, punctilious, right, right stuff*, scrupulous, seemly, standard, suitable; SEE CONCEPTS 401,558

correct [v 1] *fix, adjust*
alter, ameliorate, amend, better, change, clean up, clean up act*, cure, debug*, doctor*, do over, edit, emend, fiddle with, fix up, get with it*, go over, help, improve, launder, make over, make right, make up for, mend, pay dues*, pick up, polish, put in order, reclaim, reconstruct, rectify, redress, reform, regulate, remedy, remodel, reorganize, repair, retouch, review, revise, right, scrub*, set right, set straight, shape up, straighten out, touch up, turn around, upgrade; SEE CONCEPT 126

correct [v 2] *discipline, chastise*
administer, admonish, castigate, chasten, chide, penalize, punish, reprimand, reprove; SEE CONCEPTS 52,122

correction [n 1] *adjustment; fixing*
alteration, amelioration, amending, amendment, changing, editing, emendation, improvement, indemnification, mending, modification, rectification, redress, reexamination, remodeling, repair, reparation, rereading, revisal, revising, righting; SEE CONCEPTS 126,700

correction [n 2] *discipline*
admonition, castigation, chastisement, punishment, punition, reformation, reproof, rod; SEE CONCEPT 122

corrective [adj] *healing, curing*
antidotal, counteracting, curative, disciplinary, palliative, penal, punitive, reformatory, rehabilitative, remedial, restorative, therapeutic; SEE CONCEPT 537

correctly [adv] *right*
accurately, befittingly, decently, decorously, fitly, fittingly, justly, nicely, perfectly, precisely, properly, rightly, to a T*, well; SEE CONCEPT 558

correctness [n 1] *accuracy*
definiteness, definitiveness, definitude, exactitude, exactness, faultlessness, fidelity, preciseness, precision, regularity, truth; SEE CONCEPTS 638,654

correctness [n 2] *propriety*
bon ton, civility, correctitude, decency, decorousness, decorum, fitness, good breeding, order, orderliness, properness, rightness, seemliness; SEE CONCEPTS 633,656

correlate [v] *equate, compare*
associate, be on same wavelength*, connect, coordinate, correspond, have good vibes*, interact, parallel, relate mutually, tie in*, tune in on*; SEE CONCEPT 39

correlation [n] *equating, equivalence*
alternation, analogue, complement, correspondence, correspondent, counterpart, interaction, interchange, interconnection, interdependence, interrelation, interrelationship, match, parallel, pendant, reciprocity, relationship; SEE CONCEPTS 388,667

correspond [v 1] *agree, complement*
accord, amount, approach, assimilate, be consistent, be identical to, be similar to, coincide, compare, conform, correlate, dovetail, equal, fit, harmonize, lip sync, match, partake of, reciprocate, resemble, rival, square, tally, touch; SEE CONCEPT 664

correspond [v 2] *communicate in writing*
answer, drop a kite*, drop a line*, drop a note*, epistolize, exchange letters, have pen pal, hear from, keep in touch, pen, put pen to paper*, reply, scribble, send letter, send word, write; SEE CONCEPTS 79,266

correspondence [n 1] *agreement*
accord, analogy, coherence, coincidence, comparability, comparison, concurrence, conformity, congruity, consistency, correlation, equivalence, fitness, harmony, likeness, match, regularity, relation, resemblance, similarity, symmetry; SEE CONCEPT 664

CO
CO

correspondence [n2] *communication by writing*
exchange of letters, letters, mail, messages, post, reports, writing; SEE CONCEPTS *79,277,278*

correspondent [n] *person communicating in writing*
contributor, epistler, epistolarian, freelancer, gazetteer, journalist, letter writer, pen pal, reporter, stringer*, writer; SEE CONCEPTS *348,423*

corresponding [adj] *equivalent, matching*
agnate, akin, alike, analogous, answering, comparable, complementary, consonant, correlative, correspondent, coterminous, identical, interrelated, kin, kindred, like, parallel, reciprocal, similar, synonymous, undifferentiated; SEE CONCEPT *566*

corridor [n] *hallway*
aisle, couloir, entrance hall, entranceway, foyer, hall, ingress, lobby, passage, passageway; SEE CONCEPT *440*

corroborate [v] *back up information, story*
approve, authenticate, bear out, certify, check on, check out, check up, confirm, declare true, document, double check, endorse, establish, give nod*, justify, okay, prove, ratify, rubber-stamp*, strengthen, substantiate, support, sustain, validate, verify; SEE CONCEPTS *49,57*

corrode [v] *wear away; eat away*
bite, canker, consume, corrupt, destroy, deteriorate, erode, gnaw, impair, oxidize, rot, rust, scour, waste; SEE CONCEPTS *156,169,186,250*

corrosive [adj] *consuming, wearing; bitter*
acerb, acerbic, acrid, biting, caustic, corroding, cutting, destructive, erosive, incisive, sarcastic, strongly acid, trenchant, venomous, virulent, wasting; SEE CONCEPT *537*

corrugated [adj] *ridged, grooved*
channelled, creased, crinkled, crumpled, flexed, fluted, folded, furrowed, puckered, roughened, rumpled, wrinkled; SEE CONCEPTS *485,606*

corrupt [adj1] *dishonest*
base, bent, bribable, crooked, debauched, double-dealing, exploiting, extortionate, faithless, fast and loose*, fixed, foul, fraudulent, gone to the dogs*, inconstant, iniquitous, knavish, mercenary, nefarious, on the take*, open, padded*, perfidious, praetorian, profiteering, racket up*, reprobate, rotten, shady, snide, suborned, tainted, treacherous, two-faced, underhanded, unethical, unfaithful, unprincipled, unscrupulous, untrustworthy, venal, wide open*; SEE CONCEPT *545*

corrupt [adj2] *debased, vicious*
abandoned, abased, baneful, boorish, degenerate, degraded, deleterious, depraved, dishonored, dissolute, evil, flagitious, infamous, loose, low, miscreant, monstrous, nefarious, perverse, profligate, rotten, villainous; SEE CONCEPTS *401,545*

corrupt [adj3] *adulterated, rotten*
altered, contaminated, decayed, defiled, distorted, doctored, falsified, foul, infected, noxious, polluted, putrescent, putrid, tainted; SEE CONCEPTS *485,613*

corrupt [v] *pervert; pollute*
abase, abuse, adulterate, animalize, bastardize, blemish, blight, bribe, contaminate, damage, debase, debauch, decay, decompose, deface, defile, deform, degrade, demean, demoralize, deprave, depreciate, despoil, disfigure, disgrace, dishonor, fix, grease palm*, harm, hurt, ill-treat, impair, infect, injure, lower, lure, maltreat, mar, mistreat, misuse, outrage, pull down, putrefy, ravage, reduce, rot, ruin, spoil, square, stain, suborn, sub-

vert, taint, undermine, violate, vitiate, warp, waste; SEE CONCEPTS *14,240*

corruption [n1] *dishonesty*
breach of trust, bribery, bribing, crime, crookedness, demoralization, exploitation, extortion, fiddling, fraud, fraudulency, graft, jobbery, malfeasance, misrepresentation, nepotism, on the take*, payoff, payola*, profiteering, racket*, shadiness*, shady deal*, shuffle, skimming, squeeze*, unscrupulousness, venality; SEE CONCEPT *645*

corruption [n2] *baseness*
atrocity, decadence, degeneration, degradation, depravity, evil, immorality, impurity, infamy, iniquity, looseness, lubricity, perversion, profligacy, sinfulness, turpitude, vice, viciousness, vulgarity, wickedness; SEE CONCEPTS *633,645*

corruption [n3] *adulteration*
debasement, decay, defilement, distortion, doctoring, falsification, foulness, infection, noxiousness, pollution, putrefaction, putrescence, rot, rottenness; SEE CONCEPT *723*

cosmetic [adj] *beautifying; relating to appearance*
corrective, gooky*, improving, makeup, nonessential, painted, remedial, restorative, superficial, surface, touching-up; SEE CONCEPT *579*

cosmic [adj] *limitless; universal*
catholic, cosmogonal, cosmogonic, cosmopolitan, ecumenical, empyrean, global, grandiose, huge, immense, infinite, measureless, planetary, vast, worldwide; SEE CONCEPT *772*

cosmopolitan [adj] *worldly-wise*
catholic, cultivated, cultured, ecumenical, global, gregarious, metropolitan, planetary, polished, public, smooth, sophisticated, universal, urbane, well-travelled, worldly, worldwide; SEE CONCEPT *589*

cosmos [n1] *universe*
creation, galaxy, macrocosm, macrocosmos, megacosm, nature, solar system, star system, world; SEE CONCEPTS *511,770*

cosmos [n2] *ordered system*
harmony, order, organization, scheme, structure; SEE CONCEPTS *727,770*

cost [n1] *expense; price paid*
amount, arm and a leg*, bad news*, bite*, bottom dollar*, bottom line*, charge, damage*, disbursement, dues, expenditure, figure, line, nick*, nut*, outlay, payment, price, price tag, rate, score*, setback*, squeeze*, tab, tariff, ticket, toll, top dollar*, value, worth; SEE CONCEPTS *328,336*

cost [n2] *penalty, sacrifice*
damage, deprivation, detriment, expense, forfeit, forfeiture, harm, hurt, injury, loss, suffering; SEE CONCEPTS *676,679*

cost [v1] *command a price of*
amount to, be asked, be demanded, be given, be marked at, be needed, be paid, be priced at, be received, be valued at, be worth, bring in, come to, mount up, move back, nick*, rap*, require, sell at, sell for, set back, take, to the tune of*, yield; SEE CONCEPTS *328,336*

cost [v2] *harm; exact a penalty*
do disservice to, expect, hurt, infuriate, lose, necessitate, obligate, require; SEE CONCEPT *246*

costly [adj] *expensive*
an arm and leg*, cher*, dear, excessive, executive, exorbitant, extortionate, extravagant, fancy, high, highly priced, high-priced, inordinate, pre-

cious, premium, pricey, steep, stiff*, top, valuable; SEE CONCEPT 334

costly [adj2] *priceless*
gorgeous, inestimable, invaluable, lavish, luxurious, opulent, precious, rich, splendid, sumptuous, valuable; SEE CONCEPT 567

costly [adj3] *harmful, damaging*
catastrophic, deleterious, disastrous, loss-making, ruinous, sacrificial; SEE CONCEPT 537

costume [n] *set of clothes*
apparel, attire, clothing, dress, duds*, ensemble, fashion, garb, getup*, guise, livery, mode, outfit, rig*, robes*, style, suit, uniform, wardrobe; SEE CONCEPT 451

cot [n] *temporary bed*
army bed, berth, bunk, camp bed, folding bed, gurney, small bed, trundle; SEE CONCEPT 443

cottage [n] *tiny house; lodging*
box, bungalow, cabana, cabin, caboose, camp, carriage house, chalet, cot, home, hut, lean-to, lodge, ranch, shack, shanty, small house; SEE CONCEPT 516

couch [n] *sofa; long, upholstered furniture*
bed, chair, chaise longue, chesterfield, davenport, daybed, divan, lounge, love seat, ottoman, resting place, settee; SEE CONCEPT 443

couch [v] *express in particular way*
formulate, frame, phrase, put, set forth, utter, word; SEE CONCEPT 51

couch potato [n] *inactive person*
bystander, goof-off*, idler, laggard, lazy person, loafer, lotuseater*, lounger, observer, slouch, sluggard, spectator, televiewer*, TV viewer, viewer; SEE CONCEPT 423

cough [n] *expelled air with sound*
ahem, bark, cold, croup, frog in throat*, hack, hem, tickle in throat*, whoop; SEE CONCEPTS 65,316

cough [v] *expelling air with sound*
bark, choke, clear throat, convulse, expectorate, hack, hawk, hem, spit up, vomit, whoop; SEE CONCEPTS 65,308

council [n] *people assembled for purpose*
assembly, board, body, brain trust*, cabinet, chamber, clan, committee, conclave, confab*, conference, congregation, congress, convention, convocation, diet, directorate, gang, gathering, governing body, groupthink*, huddle*, kitchen cabinet*, meet, ministry, mob, official family, outfit, panel, parliament, powwow*, ring, senate, synod; SEE CONCEPTS 299,325,381

counsel [n1] *guidance*
admonition, advice, advisement, caution, consideration, consultation, deliberation, direction, forethought, information, instruction, kibitz*, recommendation, steer, suggestion, tip, tip-off*, two cents' worth*, warning, word to the wise*; SEE CONCEPTS 75,274

counsel [n2] *legal representative*
adviser, advocate, attorney, barrister, bomber*, counselor, legal adviser, legal beagle*, legal eagle*, lip*, mouthpiece*, patch*, shyster*, solicitor; SEE CONCEPT 355

counsel [v] *give advice*
admonish, advise, advocate, caution, charge, confab*, direct, enjoin, exhort, give pointer, give two cents*, guide, huddle*, inform, instruct, keep posted, kibitz*, order, prescribe, prompt, put bug in ear*, put heads together*, put on to, recommend, reprehend, show the ropes*, steer, suggest,

teach, tip, tip off*, tout, urge, warn, wise one up*; SEE CONCEPTS 75,317

counselor [n] *legal representative; adviser*
advocate, ambulance chaser*, attorney, counsel, front*, guide, instructor, legal beagle*, legal eagle*, lip*, mentor, mouthpiece*, pleader, solicitor, squeal*, teacher*; SEE CONCEPT 355

count [n] *tally; number*
calculation, computation, enumeration, numbering, outcome, poll, reckoning, result, sum, toll, total, whole; SEE CONCEPT 766

count [v1] *add, check in order*
add up, calculate, cast, cast up, cipher, compute, enumerate, estimate, figure, foot, keep tab, number, numerate, reckon, run down, score, sum, take account of, tally, tell, tick off, total, tot up; SEE CONCEPT 764

count [v2] *consider, deem*
await, esteem, expect, hope, impute, judge, look, look upon, rate, regard, think; SEE CONCEPTS 18,43

count [v3] *have importance*
carry weight, cut ice*, enter into consideration, import, matter, mean, militate, rate, signify, tell, weigh; SEE CONCEPT 668

count [v4] *include*
await, expect, hope, look, number among, take into account, take into consideration; SEE CONCEPTS 26,112

countenance [n1] *appearance, usually of the face*
aspect, biscuit*, cast, demeanor, expression, face, features, gills*, kisser*, look, looks, map*, mask, mien, mug*, phizog*, physiognomy, poker face*, potato*, puss*, visage; SEE CONCEPTS 716,718

countenance [n2] *self-control*
calmness, composure, presence of mind, self-composure; SEE CONCEPT 633

countenance [v] *approve, support*
abet, accept, advocate, aid, applaud, approbate, back, bear with, champion, commend, condone, confirm, cope, encourage, endorse, favor, get behind, give green light*, give stamp of approval*, give the nod*, go along with, go for, grin and bear it*, handle, help, hold with, invite, live with*, nod at, okay*, put John Hancock on*, put up with, sanction, sign off on*, sit still for*, smile on*, stand for, stomach something*, swallow*, thumbs up*, uphold; SEE CONCEPTS 10,50,88

counter [adj] *opposite, opposing*
adverse, against, antagonistic, anti, antipodal, antipodean, antithetical, conflicting, contradictory, contrary, contrasting, converse, diametric, hindering, impeding, obstructive, obverse, opposed, polar, reverse; SEE CONCEPTS 544,581

counter [v] *answer, respond in retaliation*
backtalk, beat, bilk, buck, circumvent, contravene, counteract, counterwork, cross, dash, disappoint, fly in the face of*, foil, frustrate, have bone to pick*, hinder, hit back, mash, meet, offset, oppose, parry, pit, play off, resist, respond, retaliate, return, ruin, take on, thumbs down*, vie, ward off; SEE CONCEPTS 45,121

counter [adv] *contrary, reverse*
against, at variance with, contrarily, contrariwise, conversely, in defiance of, opposite, versus; SEE CONCEPTS 544,581

counteract [v] *do opposing action*
annul, buck, cancel, cancel out, check, contravene, correct, counterbalance, countercheck, countervail, counterwork, cross, defeat, fix, foil,

frustrate, go against, halt, hinder, invalidate, negate, negative, neutralize, offset, oppose, prevent, rectify, redress, resist, right, thwart; SEE CONCEPTS 87,96,126

counterbalance [v] *offset an action*
amend, atone for, balance, cancel, compensate, correct, counteract, counterpoise, countervail, equalize, make up for, outweigh, rectify, redeem, set off; SEE CONCEPTS 87,96,126

counterfeit [n] *fake, forgery*
actor, bogus*, bum, copy, deceit, deception, dummy, facsimile, fraud, gyp, hoax, humbug, imitation, imposture, junque*, phony, pseudo, put-on*, reproduction, self*, sham, simulacrum; SEE CONCEPTS 648,725

counterfeit [adj] *fake, simulated*
affected, assumed, bent, bogus*, brummagem, copied, crock, deceptive, delusive, delusory, ersatz, faked, false, feigned, fictitious, fishy*, forged, framed, fraudulent, Hollywood*, imitation, misleading, mock, not genuine, not kosher*, phony*, pirate, plant*, pretended, pretentious, pseudo, put-on*, queer, sham, snide, soft shell*, spurious, supposititious, two-faced*, won't fly*, wrong; SEE CONCEPTS 549,582

counterfeit [v] *make deceitful imitation*
act like, affect, ape, assume, bluff, carbon, cheat, circulate bad money, clone, copy, copy, defraud, delude, ditto, do, do like*, dupe, fabricate, fake, feign, forge, go like*, imitate, impersonate, knock off*, make like*, make money, mimeo, mimic, mint, phony*, phony up*, pretend, put on*, sham, simulate, stat, Xerox*; SEE CONCEPTS 59,171

countermand [v] *annul, cancel a command*
override, recall, repeal, rescind, retract, retreat, reverse, revoke; SEE CONCEPTS 50,53,88

counterpart [n] *match; identical part or thing*
analogue, carbon copy*, complement, copy, correlate, correlative, correspondent, dead ringer*, ditto*, doppelganger, duplicate, equal, equivalent, fellow, like, look alike, mate, obverse, opposite, opposite number, peas in a pod*, pendant, ringer*, spit and image*, spitting image*, supplement, tally, twin, two of a kind*; SEE CONCEPTS 667,834

countless [adj] *innumerable*
bags of*, endless, gobs*, heap*, immeasurable, incalculable, infinite, innumerous, jillion*, legion, limitless, loads*, lots of, many, measureless, mess*, mint*, mucho*, multitudinous, myriad, numberless, oodles*, passel of*, peck, pile, raft*, scads*, slew*, stack*, tidy sum, umpteen*, uncountable, uncounted, untold, wad*, whole slew*, zillion*; SEE CONCEPTS 762,781

count on/count upon [v] *depend on; rely*
aim for, bank on, bargain for, believe, believe in, bet bottom dollar*, bet on, expect from, heed, lean on, pin faith on, place confidence in, plan on, reckon on, rest on, score, stake on, swear by, tab, take as gospel truth*, take for granted, take on trust, trust; SEE CONCEPTS 12,26

count out [v] *disregard, exclude*
bar, bate, debar, eliminate, except, get rid of, leave out, leave out of account, mark off, pass over, rule out, suspend; SEE CONCEPT 25

country [n1] *political territory; nation*
citizenry, citizens, commonwealth, community, constituents, electors, grass roots, homeland, inhabitants, kingdom, land, native land, patria, people, polity, populace, public, realm, region,

society, soil, sovereign state, state, terrain, voters; SEE CONCEPTS 379,508,510

country [n2] *rural area; area away from city*
back country, backwoods, boondocks*, boonies*, bush, countryside, cow country*, farmland, farms, forests, green belt*, hinterland, middle of nowhere*, outback, outdoors, province, sticks*, up country, wide open space*, wilderness, wilds, woodlands, woods; SEE CONCEPTS 508,513

country [adj] *rural, pastoral*
agrarian, agrestic, Arcadian, bucolic, campestral, countrified, georgic, homey, out-country, outland, provincial, rustic, uncultured, unpolished, unrefined, unsophisticated; SEE CONCEPTS 401,536, 589

county [n] *province or district of area*
canton, constituency, division, shire; SEE CONCEPTS 508,513

coup [n] *achievement, often by maneuver*
accomplishment, action, coup de maître, coup d'état, deed, exploit, feat, overthrow, plot, revolution, stratagem, stroke, stroke of genius*, stunt, successful stroke, tour de force, upset; SEE CONCEPT 706

coup de grâce [n] *finishing blow*
blow, clincher*, comeuppance, deathblow, defeat, final blow, final stroke, kill, knockout, mercy stroke, mortal blow, quietus; SEE CONCEPTS 95,252

coup d'état [n] *violent seizure*
coup, overthrow, palace revolution, power play*, putsch*, rebellion, revolt, revolution, takeover; SEE CONCEPTS 86,90,320

couple [n] *pair of things*
brace, couplet, deuce*, doublet, duo, dyad, husband and wife, item, newlyweds, set, span, team, twain, twosome, yoke; SEE CONCEPTS 432,766

couple [v] *join two things*
bracket, bring together, buckle, clasp, coalesce, cohabit, come together, conjoin, conjugate, connect, copulate, harness, hitch, hook up, link, marry, match, pair, unite, wed, yoke; SEE CONCEPTS 113,114,297,375

coupon [n] *discount ticket*
advertisement, box top*, card, certificate, credit slip, detachable portion, order blank, premium certificate, ration slip, redeemable part, redemption slip, slip, token, voucher; SEE CONCEPT 331

courage [n] *boldness, braveness*
adventuresomeness, adventurousness, audacity, backbone, bravery, bravura, daring, dash, dauntlessness, determination, élan, endurance, enterprise, fearlessness, firmness, fortitude, gallantry, gameness, grit, guts, hardihood, heroism, intrepidity, lion-heartedness, mettle, nerve, pluck, power, prowess, pugnacity, rashness, recklessness, resolution, spirit, spunk, stoutheartedness, temerity, tenacity, valor, venturesomeness; SEE CONCEPTS 411,633

courageous [adj] *brave, bold*
adventuresome, adventurous, assured, audacious, cool, daredevil, daring, dauntless, doughty, fearless, fiery, fire-eating*, gallant, game, gritty*, gutsy*, hardy, heroic, high-spirited, impavid, indomitable, intrepid, lionhearted, martial, nervy, plucky*, red-blooded*, resolute, Spartan, stalwart, stand tall*, stouthearted, strong, tenacious, tough, Trojan*, unafraid, undaunted, valiant, valorous, venturesome, venturous; SEE CONCEPTS 401,404

courier [n] *messenger*
bearer, carrier, dispatcher, emissary, envoy, express, go-between, gofer*, gopher*, herald, intelligencer, internuncio, runner; SEE CONCEPT 348

course [n1] *progress, advance*
advancement, chain, channels, consecution, continuity, development, flow, furtherance, line, manner, march, movement, order, plan, policy, polity, procedure, program, progression, red tape*, row, scheme, sequel, sequence, series, string, succession, system, unfolding, way; SEE CONCEPTS 704,727

course [n2] *path, channel*
aisle, aqueduct, boards, byway, canal, circuit, conduit, direction, duct, flow, groove, itinerary, lap, line, movement, orbit, passage, range, road, route, run, rut, scope, stream, tack, track, trail, trajectory, watercourse, way; SEE CONCEPTS 501,514

course [n3] *length of action*
duration, elapsing, lapse, passage, passing, progress, sweep, term, time; SEE CONCEPT 804

course [n4] *plan of study*
class, conference, curriculum, discussion group, interest, laboratory, lecture, matriculation, meeting, method, period, preparation, procedure, program, regimen, schedule, seminar, session, speciality, subject; SEE CONCEPT 287

course [v] *flow, run*
career, chase, dart, dash, follow, gallop, gush, hasten, hunt, hurry, hustle, pursue, race, rush, scamper, scoot, scurry, speed, spring, stream, surge, tumble; SEE CONCEPTS 150,152

court [n] *yard, garden of building*
cloister, close, compass, courtyard, curtilage, enclosure, forum, patio, piazza, plaza, quad, quadrangle, square, street; SEE CONCEPTS 509,513

court [n2] *ruler's attendants*
castle, cortege, entourage, hall, lords and ladies, palace, retinue, royal household, staff, suite, train; SEE CONCEPTS 296,348

court [n3] *judicial system*
bar, bench, court of justice, forum, judge, justice, kangaroo court*, law court, magistrate, seat of judgment, session, tribunal; SEE CONCEPTS 299,318

court [n4] *building for legal proceedings*
bar, bench, city hall, county courthouse, courthouse, courtroom, federal building, hall of justice, justice building, law court, municipal building, tribunal; SEE CONCEPTS 318,439

court [n5] *wooing*
address, attention, homage, love, respects, suit; SEE CONCEPT 32

court [v] *fawn over, pay attention to*
allure, ask in marriage, attract, beseech, bid, bootlick, captivate, charm, chase, cultivate, curry favor, date, entice, entreat, flatter, follow, gallant, go out with, go steady, go together, go with, grovel, importune, invite, keep company with, make love to, make overture, make time with*, pander to, pay addresses to, pay court to, please, pop the question*, praise, propose, pursue, run after*, seek, seek the hand of, serenade, set one's cap*, solicit, spark, spoon*, sue, sweetheart, take out, woo; SEE CONCEPTS 32,384

courteous [adj] *gentle, mannerly*
affable, attentive, ceremonious, civil, civilized, complaisant, considerate, courtly, cultivated, debonair, elegant, gallant, genteel, gracious, polished, polite, refined, respectful, soft-spoken, suave, thoughtful, urbane, well-behaved, well-bred, well-mannered, well-spoken; SEE CONCEPTS 267,401

courtesy [n1] *good manners*
address, affability, amenities, amiability, attentiveness, ceremony, chivalry, civility, comity, complaisance, consideration, cordiality, courteousness, courtliness, cultivation, culture, deference, elegance, familiarity, favor, friendliness, gallantness, gallantry, generosity, geniality, gentleness, good behavior, good breeding, graciousness, indulgence, kindness, polish, politeness, refinement, respect, reverence, solicitude, suavity, sympathy, tact, thoughtfulness, urbanity; SEE CONCEPTS 633,644

courtesy [n2] *favor, indulgence*
accommodation, benevolence, bounty, charity, chivalry, compassion, consent, consideration, dispensation, generosity, kindness, liberality, service, unselfishness; SEE CONCEPTS 337,388,633

courtly [adj] *refined manner*
adulatory, affable, aristocratic, august, ceremonious, chivalrous, civil, civilized, complimentary, conventional, cultured, decorous, dignified, elegant, flattering, formal, gallant, gracious, highbred, imposing, lofty, obliging, polished, polite, preux, prim, refined, stately, studied, urbane; SEE CONCEPT 401

courtship [n] *dating, romance*
courting, engagement, keeping company*, love, lovemaking, pursuit, suit, wooing; SEE CONCEPT 388

cove [n] *inlet, small niche*
anchorage, arm, bay, bayou, bight, cave, cavern, creek, estuary, firth, frith, gulf, harbor, hole, lagoon, nook, retreat, slough, sound, wash; SEE CONCEPT 509

covenant [n] *pact, promise*
agreement, arrangement, bargain, bond, commitment, compact, concordat, contract, convention, deal, deed, dicker*, handshake*, papers, stipulation, transaction, treaty, trust; SEE CONCEPT 684

covenant [v] *agree*
bargain, concur, contract, engage, pledge, plight, promise, stipulate, swear, undertake, vow; SEE CONCEPTS 8,71,317

cover [n1] *wrapping, cover-up*
awning, bark, binding, camouflage, canopy, canvas, cap, caparison, case, ceiling, cloak, clothing, coating, covering, coverlet, disguise, dome, dress, drop, envelope, facade, false front*, fig leaf, front, guise, hood, integument, jacket, lid, marquee, mask, masquerade, overlay, paint, parasol, polish, pretense, put-on*, roof, screen, seal, semblance, sheath, sheet, shroud, smoke screen*, spread, stopper, tarp, tarpaulin, tegument, tent, top, umbrella, varnish, veil, veneer, window-dressing, wrapper, wraps; SEE CONCEPTS 484,750

cover [n2] *hiding place*
asylum, camouflage, concealment, covert, defense, drop, front, guard, harbor, harborage, haven, port, protection, refuge, retreat, safety, sanctuary, screen, security, shelter; SEE CONCEPT 198

cover [v1] *wrap, hide*
blanket, board up, bury, bush up, cache, camouflage, canopy, cap, carpet, cloak, clothe, coat, conceal, cover up, crown, curtain, daub, disguise, do on the sly*, dress, eclipse, encase, enclose,

enfold, ensconce, enshroud, envelop, hood, house, invest, layer, mantle, mask, obscure, overcast, overlay, overspread, protect, put on, screen, secrete, set on, shade, shield, shroud, stash*, superimpose, superpose, surface, veil; SEE CONCEPTS 172,188

cover [v2] *protect, guard*
bulwark, defend, fend, house, reinforce, safeguard, screen, secure, shelter, shield, watch over; SEE CONCEPT 96

cover [v3] *include, contain*
be enough, comprehend, comprise, consider, deal with, embody, embrace, encompass, examine, incorporate, involve, meet, provide for, reach, refer to, suffice, survey, take account of; SEE CONCEPT 643

cover [v4] *describe in published writing*
broadcast, detail, investigate, narrate, recount, relate, report, tell of, write up; SEE CONCEPTS 60,79

cover [v5] *fill in for, compensate*
balance, counterbalance, double for, insure, make good, make up for, offset, relieve, stand in for*, substitute, take over, take the rap for*; SEE CONCEPTS 110,126

cover [v6] *travel across area*
cross, do, journey over, pass over, pass through, range, track, traverse, trek; SEE CONCEPT 224

covert [adj] *clandestine, underhanded*
buried, camouflaged, cloaked, concealed, disguised, dissembled, furtive, hidden, hush-hush*, incog*, incognito, masked, obscured, private, privy, QT*, secret, shrouded, stealthy, sub rosa, surreptitious, ulterior, undercover, underhand, under-the-table*, under wraps*, unsuspected, veiled; SEE CONCEPTS 544,548

covertly [adv] *clandestine, underhandedly*
by stealth, clandestinely, furtively, hush-hush*, in camera, in holes and corners*, on the QT*, on the quiet, on the sly, privately, secretly, slyly, stealthily, sub rosa, surreptitiously, undercover, under wraps*, wildcat*; SEE CONCEPTS 544,548

covet [v] *desire strongly*
aspire to, begrudge, choose, crave, desiderate, envy, fancy, hanker for*, have eye on*, have hots for*, itch for*, long for, lust after, spoil for, thirst for, want, wish for, yearn for, yen for*; SEE CONCEPT 20

covetous [adj] *greedy; very desirous*
acquisitive, avaricious, avid, close-fisted, eager, ensurient, envious, gluttonous, grabby, grasping, green-eyed*, grudging, hogging, itchy*, jealous, keen, mercenary, piggish*, prehensile, rapacious, ravenous, selfish, swinish*, voracious, yearning; SEE CONCEPT 401

cow [v] *browbeat, intimidate*
abash, appall, awe, bludgeon, bluster, buffalo, bulldoze, bully, daunt, discomfit, disconcert, dishearten, dismay, dragoon, embarrass, enforce, faze, frighten, hector, lean on*, overawe, push around*, rattle, scare, showboat*, strong-arm*, subdue, terrorize, turn on the heat*, unnerve, walk heavy*; SEE CONCEPTS 7,19,52

coward [n] *person who is scared, easily intimidated*
alarmist, baby*, caitiff, chicken*, chicken heart*, chicken liver*, craven, cur, dastard, deserter, faintheart, faint-of-heart, fraidy-cat*, funk, gutless*, invertebrate*, jellyfish*, lily liver, malingerer, mouse*, pessimist, poltroon, quitter, rabbit*, recreant, scaredy cat*, shirk, shirker,

skulker, sneak, weakling, white liver*, wimp*, yellow*, yellow belly*; SEE CONCEPT 423

cowardly [adj] *fearful*
afraid, anxious, apprehensive, backward, base, caitiff, chicken-hearted, cowering, cowhearted, craven, dastardly, diffident, dismayed, fainthearted, frightened, gutless, having the willies*, jittery, lacking courage, lily-livered*, nervous, no guts, panicky, paper tiger*, pigeonhearted*, pusillanimous, recreant, retiring, running scared*, scared, shrinking, shy, soft*, spineless*, timid, timorous, weak, weak-kneed*, worthless, yellow*, yellow-bellied*; SEE CONCEPT 401

cower [v] *hide, hover in fear*
apple-polish*, blench, bootlick*, brownnose*, cringe, crouch, draw back, fawn, flinch, grovel, honey*, kowtow*, quail*, recoil, shrink, skulk, sneak, toady*, tremble, truckle, wince; SEE CONCEPTS 188,384

coy [adj] *very modest*
backward, bashful, blushing, coquettish, demure, diffident, evasive, flirtatious, humble, kittenish, overmodest, prudish, rabbity, reserved, retiring, self-effacing, shrinking, shy, skittish, timid, unassertive; SEE CONCEPTS 401,404

cozy [adj] *comforting, soft, warm*
comfortable, comfy, cuddled up, cushy, easeful, in clover, intimate, in velvet*, on bed of roses*, restful, safe, secure, sheltered, snug, snug as bug in rug*, snuggled down, tucked up; SEE CONCEPTS 485,605,606

crabby/crabbed [adj] *in a bad mood*
acid, acrid, acrimonious, awkward, bad-tempered, blunt, brusque, captious, choleric, churlish, cranky*, cross, crotchety, crusty*, cynical, difficult, dour, fretful, gloomy, glum, grouchy*, harsh, huffy, ill-humored, ill-tempered, irascible, irritable, misanthropic, morose, nasty-tempered, peevish, perverse, petulant, prickly, saturnine, snappish, snappy, sour, splenetic, sulky, sullen, surly, tart, testy, tough, trying, unsociable; SEE CONCEPTS 401,403

crack [n1] *break, crevice*
breach, chink, chip, cleft, cranny, crevasse, cut, discontinuity, division, fissure, fracture, gap, hole, interstice, interval, rent, rift, rima, rimation, rime, split; SEE CONCEPTS 469,513

crack [n2] *loud sound, usually from hitting*
bang, bash, belt, blast, blow, boom, buffet, burst, clap, clip, clout, crash, cuff, explosion, go, noise, pop, report, shot, slam, slap, smack, smash, snap, splintering, splitting, stab, stroke, thump, thwack, wallop, whack, wham; SEE CONCEPTS 189,595

crack [n3] *attempt to do something*
fling, go, opportunity, pop, shot, stab, try, whack, whirl; SEE CONCEPT 87

crack [n4] *joke*
dig, funny remark, gag, insult, jest, jibe, quip, remark, return, smart remark, wisecrack, witticism; SEE CONCEPT 273

crack [adj] *super, first-rate*
able, ace, adept, best, capital, choice, crackerjack*, deluxe, elite, excellent, expert, first-class, handpicked, pro*, proficient, skilled, skillful, superior, talented; SEE CONCEPTS 528,542,574

crack [v1] *break, usually into parts*
burst, chip, chop, cleave, crackle, crash, damage, detonate, explode, fracture, hurt, impair, injure, pop, ring, rive, sever, shiver, snap, splinter, split; SEE CONCEPT 248

crack [v2] *lose self-control*
become deranged, become insane, blow one's mind*, blow up, break down, bug out*, collapse, flip*, give way*, go bonkers*, go crazy, go to pieces*, lose it*, succumb, yield; SEE CONCEPT 13

crack [v3] *hit very hard*
bash, buffet, clip, clout, cuff, slap, thump, thunder, wallop, whack; SEE CONCEPT 189

crack [v4] *discover meaning, answer*
break, cryptanalyze, decipher, decode, decrypt, fathom, figure out, get answer, solve, work out; SEE CONCEPTS 37,38

cracker [n] *hard, often salted, baked wafer*
biscuit, bun, cookie, hardtack, pretzel, rusk, saltine; SEE CONCEPT 457

crack up [v] *break down mentally*
become demented, become psychotic, blow a fuse*, collapse, come apart at seams*, decline, derange, deteriorate, fail, flip out*, freak out*, go bonkers*, go crazy, go nuts, go off deep end*, go off rocker*, go out of mind*, go to pieces*, have breakdown, schizz out*, sicken; SEE CONCEPT 13

cradle [n1] *small bed for baby*
baby bed, bassinet, cot, crib, hamper, Moses basket, pannier, trundle bed; SEE CONCEPT 443

cradle [n2] *early childhood; origins*
babyhood, beginning, birthplace, fount, fountain, fountainhead, infancy, nativity, nursery, origin, source, spring, ultimate cause, wellspring; SEE CONCEPTS 648,817

cradle [v] *hold in arms; nurture*
lull, nestle, nourish, nurse, rock, support, tend, watch over; SEE CONCEPTS 190,295

craft [n1] *expertise, skill*
ability, adeptness, adroitness, aptitude, art, artistry, cleverness, competence, cunning, dexterity, expertness, ingenuity, knack, know-how*, proficiency, technique; SEE CONCEPTS 409,706

craft [n2] *deceit, scheme*
art, artfulness, artifice, cageyness, canniness, contrivance, craftiness, cunning, disingenuity, duplicity, foxiness, guile, ruse, shrewdness, slyness, stratagem, strategy, subterfuge, subtlety, trickery, wiles, wiliness; SEE CONCEPTS 645,660

craft [n3] *business, discipline*
art, calling, career, employment, handicraft, line, métier, occupation, profession, pursuit, trade, vocation, work; SEE CONCEPT 360

craft [n4] *water or air vehicle*
aircraft, airplane, air ship, barge, blimp, boat, bottom, plane, ship, shipping, spacecraft, vessel, watercraft, zeppelin; SEE CONCEPTS 504,506

craftsperson [n] *person skilled in art*
artificer, artisan, journeyperson, machinist, maker, manufacturer, mechanic, skilled worker, smith, specialist, technician, wright; SEE CONCEPT 348

crafty [adj] *clever, scheming*
adroit, artful, astute, cagey, calculating, canny, crazy like fox*, cunning, deceitful, deep, designing, devious, disingenuous, duplicitous, foxy*, fraudulent, guileful, insidious, intelligent, keen, knowing, sharp, shrewd, slick, slippery*, sly, smart, smooth, street smart*, streetwise*, subtle, tricky, vulpine, wily; SEE CONCEPT 401

craggy [adj] *jagged*
asperous, broken, cragged, harsh, precipitous, rock-bound, rocky, rough, rugged, scabrous,

scraggy, stony, uneven, unlevel, unsmooth; SEE CONCEPTS 490,606

cram [v1] *fill to overflowing; compress*
charge, chock, choke, compact, crowd, crush, devour, drive, force, gobble, gorge, guzzle, heap, ingurgitate, jam, jam-pack*, load, overcrowd, overeat, overfill, pack, pack 'em in*, pack in, pack it in*, pack like sardines*, press, ram, sardine*, satiate, shove, slop, slosh, squash, squeeze, stive, stuff, tamp*, thrust, wedge, wolf*; SEE CONCEPTS 208,740

cram [v2] *study intensely*
burn midnight oil*, heavy booking*, hit the books*, megabook*, mug up*, read, review, revise; SEE CONCEPT 17

cramp [n] *muscle spasm*
ache, charley horse*, circumscription, confinement, constipation, contraction, convulsion, crick, hindrance, impediment, kink, obstruction, pain, pang, restriction, shooting pain, stiffness, stitch, stricture, twinge; SEE CONCEPTS 308,728

cramp [v] *hinder, restrain*
bottle up*, box up*, check, circumscribe, clamp, clasp, clog, confine, constrain, coop up*, encumber, fasten, grip, hamper, hamstring, handicap, impede, inhibit, limit, object, obstruct, restrict, shackle, stymie, thwart; SEE CONCEPTS 130,191

cramped [adj] *congested, overcrowded*
awkward, circumscribed, close, closed in, confined, crabbed, crowded, hemmed in*, illegible, incommodious, indecipherable, irregular, jammed in, little, minute, narrow, packed, pent, restricted, small, squeezed, tight, tiny, tucked up, two-by-four*, uncomfortable; SEE CONCEPTS 483,773

cranky [adj] *in bad mood*
bad-humored, bearish, cantankerous, choleric, crabby, cross, crotchety, cussed, disagreeable, got up on wrong side of bed*, grouchy, grumpy, hot-tempered, ill-humored, irascible, irritable, like a bear*, mean, ornery*, out of sorts, perverse, quick-tempered, ratty, snappish, tetchy, ugly, vincgary; SEE CONCEPTS 401,403

cranny [n] *nook, opening*
breach, byplace, chink, cleft, crack, crevice, fissure, gap, hole, interstice, niche; SEE CONCEPTS 440,513

crash [n1/v1] *bang; banging sound*
blast, boom, burst, clang, clap, clash, clatter, clattering, crack, din, peal, racket, slam, smash, smashing, sound, thunder, thunderclap, wham; SEE CONCEPTS 65,521,595

crash [n2] *collision, accidental hitting*
accident, bump, collapse, concussion, crack-up*, crunch, debacle, ditch, fender bender*, fender tag*, impact, jar, jolt, percussion, pileup, ram, rear-ender*, shock, sideswipe, smash, smashup*, splashdown*, stack-up*, thud*, thump*, total*, washout*, wreck; SEE CONCEPT 189

crash [v2] *break into pieces*
bang into, crack up, crunch, dash, disintegrate, fracture, fragment, pile up, shatter, shiver, sideswipe, smash, smash up, splinter, total*, wrack up*; SEE CONCEPT 248

crash [v3] *fall*
bite the dust*, bump, collapse, collide, crash-land, ditch, dive, drive into, drop, fall flat*, fall headlong, fall prostrate, give way, go in*, hurtle, lurch, meet, overbalance, overturn, pancake*, pitch, plough into*, plunge, prang, slip, smash,

splash down, sprawl, topple, tumble, upset, wash-out*; SEE CONCEPT *181*

crass [adj] *coarse, insensitive*
asinine, blundering, boorish, bovine, churlish, dense, doltish, gross, indelicate, inelegant, loutish, lowbrow, lumpish, oafish, obtuse, Philistine, raw, rough, rude, stupid, uncouth, unrefined, vulgar, witless; SEE CONCEPT *401*

crate [n] *wooden container*
box, cage, carton, case, chest, package; SEE CONCEPT *494*

crave [v1] *desire intensely*
ache for, covet, cry out for, die for*, dream, eat one's heart out*, fancy, give eyeteeth for*, hunger for*, itch for*, long for, lust after, need, pine for*, require, sigh for, spoil for, suspire, thirst for*, want, yearn for, yen for*; SEE CONCEPT *20*

crave [v2] *beg*
ask, beseech, call for, demand, entreat, implore, necessitate, petition, plead for, pray for, require, seek, solicit, supplicate, take; SEE CONCEPTS *48,53*

craven [n] *timid person*
caitiff, chicken*, coward, dastard, fraidy cat*, nebbish, poltroon, quitter, recreant, scaredy cat*, weakling, wheyface, wimp*, wuss*, yellow belly*; SEE CONCEPT *423*

craven [adj] *weak, timid*
chicken*, cowardly, dastardly, fearful, gutless, lily-livered*, mean-spirited, poltroonish, pusillanimous, scared, timorous, weak-kneed*, wimpish*, wimpy*, wussy*, yellow*, yellow-bellied*; SEE CONCEPTS *401,550*

craving [n] *strong desire*
appetite, appetition, hankering, hunger, hurting, itch*, longing, lust, munchies*, need, passion, thirst, urge, yearning, yen*; SEE CONCEPTS *20,709*

crawl [v1] *move very slowly*
clamber, creep, drag, drag oneself along, go on all fours, go on belly, grovel, hang back, inch, lag, loiter along, lollygag*, move at snail's pace*, move on hands and knees, plod, poke, pull oneself along, scrabble, slide, slither, squirm, worm, wriggle, writhe; SEE CONCEPT *151*

crawl [v2] *humble oneself*
abase oneself, apple-polish*, brownnose*, cringe, fawn, grovel, toady, truckle; SEE CONCEPTS *35,48*

craze [n] *fad, strong interest*
chic, cry, enthusiasm, fashion, fever, furor, infatuation, in thing*, kick*, mania, mode, monomania, newest wrinkle*, novelty, passion, preoccupation, rage, the last word*, the latest thing*, trend, vogue, wrinkle; SEE CONCEPTS *532,690*

craze [v] *make insane*
bewilder, confuse, dement, derange, distemper, distract, drive mad, enrage, frenzy, infatuate, inflame, madden, unbalance, unhinge; SEE CONCEPTS *7,19*

crazy [adj1] *mentally strange*
ape, barmy, batty, berserk, bonkers*, cracked, crazed, cuckoo, daft, delirious, demented, deranged, dingy*, dippy*, erratic, flaky, flipped*, flipped out*, freaked out*, fruity*, idiotic, insane, kooky, lunatic, mad, maniacal, mental*, moonstruck*, nuts, nutty, nutty as fruitcake*, of unsound mind, out of one's mind, out of one's tree*, out to lunch*, potty*, psycho*, round the bend*,

schizo*, screwball*, screw loose*, screwy*, silly, touched*, unbalanced, unglued*, unhinged*, unzipped*, wacky; SEE CONCEPT *403*

crazy [adj2] *unrealistic, fantastic*
absurd, balmy, beyond all reason, bizarre, cockeyed, derisory, eccentric, fatuous, foolhardy, foolish, goofy*, half-baked*, harebrained*, idiotic, ill-conceived, impracticable, imprudent, inane, inappropriate, insane, irresponsible, loony, ludicrous, nonsensical, odd, out of all reason, outrageous, peculiar, preposterous, puerile, quixotic, ridiculous, senseless, short-sighted, silly, strange, unworkable, weird, wild; SEE CONCEPT *529*

crazy [adj3] *infatuated, in love*
ardent, beside oneself*, devoted, eager, enamored, fanatical, hysterical, keen, mad, passionate, smitten, wild, zealous; SEE CONCEPT *403*

creak [v] *grind, grate with high noise*
chirr, crepitate, groan, rasp, scrape, scratch, screech, sound, squeak, squeal; SEE CONCEPTS *65,186,215*

cream [n1] *lotion, oil*
cerate, chrism, cosmetic, demulcent, emulsion, essence, jelly, liniment, moisturizer, ointment, paste, salve, unction, unguent; SEE CONCEPTS *466,467,483*

cream [n2] *the best*
choice, crème de la crème*, elite, fat, favorite, finest, flower, pick, pride, prime*, prize, skim*, top; SEE CONCEPT *668*

creamy [adj] *smooth, buttery*
creamed, feathery, fluffy, gloppy*, gooey, gooky*, goopy*, greasy, gunky, luscious, lush, milky, oily, rich, soft, velvety; SEE CONCEPT *606*

crease [n] *fold, wrinkle*
bend, bulge, cockle, corrugation, furrow, groove, line, overlap, pleat, plica, pucker, ridge, rimple, rivel, ruck, rugosity, tuck; SEE CONCEPTS *452,757*

crease [v] *fold, rumple*
bend, cockle, corrugate, crimp, crinkle, crumple, dog-ear*, double up, plait, pleat, pucker, purse, ridge, ruck up, screw up*, wrinkle; SEE CONCEPTS *158,219*

create [v] *develop in mind or physically*
actualize, author, beget, bring into being, bring into existence, bring to pass, build, cause to be, coin, compose, conceive, concoct, constitute, construct, contrive, design, devise, discover, dream up, effect, erect, establish, fabricate, fashion, father, forge, form, formulate, found, generate, give birth to, give life to, hatch, imagine, initiate, institute, invent, invest, make, occasion, organize, originate, parent, perform, plan, procreate, produce, rear, set up, shape, sire, spawn, start; SEE CONCEPTS *173,239,251*

creation [n1] *development of entity*
conception, constitution, establishment, formation, formulation, foundation, generation, genesis, imagination, inception, institution, laying down, making, nascency, nativity, origination, procreation, production, setting up, siring; SEE CONCEPT *173*

creation [n2] *all living things*
cosmos, life, living world, macrocosm, macrocosmos, megacosm, nature, totality, universe, world; SEE CONCEPTS *389,429*

creation [n3] *invention, concoction*
achievement, brainchild, chef-d'oeuvre, concept, handiwork, magnum opus, opus, piece, pièce de

résistance, production, work, work of genius; SEE CONCEPTS 259,260

creative [adj] artistic, imaginative
clever, cool*, demiurgic, deviceful, fertile, formative, gifted, hip*, ingenious, innovational, innovative, innovatory, inspired, inventive, leading-edge*, original, originative, productive, prolific, stimulating, visionary, way out*; SEE CONCEPT 402

creator [n] inventor; God
architect, author, begetter, brain, deity, designer, founder, framer, generator, initiator, maker, originator, prime mover, producer, sire; SEE CONCEPTS 348,352,361

creature [n] being, beast
animal, body, brute, creation, critter*, fellow, individual, living being, living thing, lower animal, man, mortal, party, person, personage, quadruped, soul, varmint*, woman; SEE CONCEPT 389

credence [n] trust, acceptance
accepting, admission, admitting, assurance, belief, certainty, confidence, credit, dependence, faith, reliance, stock, store; SEE CONCEPT 689

credentials [n] references, attestation
accreditation, authorization, card, certificate, character, deed, diploma, docket, document, documentation, endorsement, letter of credence, letter of introduction, license, missive, papers, passport, proof, recommendation, sanction, testament, testimonial, title, token, voucher, warrant; SEE CONCEPTS 271,685

credibility [n] believeableness
believability, chance, integrity, likelihood, plausibility, possibility, probability, prospect, reliability, satisfactoriness, solidity, solidness, soundness, tenability, trustworthiness, validity; SEE CONCEPTS 650,725

credible [adj] believable
aboveboard, colorable, conceivable, conclusive, creditable, dependable, determinative, honest, honest to God*, imaginable, likely, plausible, possible, probable, probably, rational, reasonable, reliable, satisfactory, satisfying, seeming, sincere, solid, sound, straight, supposable, tenable, thinkable, trustworthy, trusty, up front*, valid; SEE CONCEPTS 552,582

credit [n1] recognition; trust
acclaim, acknowledgment, approval, attention, belief, Brownie points*, commendation, confidence, credence, distinction, faith, fame, glory, honor, kudos*, merit, notice, pat on the back*, points*, praise, reliance, strokes*, thanks, tribute; SEE CONCEPTS 69,410

credit [n2] reputation, status
authority, character, clout, esteem, estimation, fame, good name, influence, position, prestige, regard, renown, repute, standing, weight; SEE CONCEPT 388

credit [n3] deferred payment arrangement; assets
balance, bond, capital outlay, continuance, debenture, extension, installment buying, installment plan, lien, loan, mortgage, on account, on the arm*, on the cuff*, plastic*, respite, securities, stock, surplus cash, tab, trust, wealth; SEE CONCEPT 335

credit [v1] believe, depend on
accept, bank on, buy, consider, deem, fall for*, feel, hand it to one, have faith in, hold, pat on back, rely on, sense, swallow*, take as gospel truth*, take stock in*, think, trust; SEE CONCEPT 12

credit [v2] accredit, assign to
ascribe to, attribute to, chalk up to, charge to, defer, impute, lay, refer; SEE CONCEPT 18

creditable [adj] praiseworthy
admirable, batting a thousand*, believeable, commendable, decent, deserving, estimable, excellent, exemplary, honest, honorable, laudable, meritorious, nasty*, not too shabby*, organic, palmary, reputable, reputed, respectable, salt of the earth*, satisfactory, suitable, well-thought-of, worthy; SEE CONCEPT 542

credulous [adj] gullible, naïve
accepting, believing, born yesterday*, dupable, easy mark*, falling for*, green, overtrusting, simple, swallow whole, taken in, trustful, trusting, uncritical, unquestioning, unsophisticated, unsuspecting, unsuspicious, unwary; SEE CONCEPT 404

creed [n] belief, principles
articles of faith, canon, catechism, church, confession, conviction, cult, doctrine, faith, ideology, persuasion, profession, religion, tenet, weltanschauung; SEE CONCEPTS 688,689

creek [n] stream of water
brook, brooklet, burn, crick, ditch, race, rill, rindle, river, rivulet, run, runnel, spring, streamlet, tributary, watercourse; SEE CONCEPT 514

creep [v] crawl along, usually on ground
approach unnoticed, crawl on all fours, edge, glide, grovel, gumshoe*, inch, insinuate, lurk, pussyfoot, scrabble, scramble, skulk, slink, slither, snake*, sneak, squirm, steal, tiptoe, worm, wriggle, writhe; SEE CONCEPT 151

creepy [adj] nasty, scary
awful, direful, disgusting, disturbing, dreadful, eerie, frightening, ghoulish, gruesome, hair-raising, horrible, itching, itchy, macabre, menacing, nightmarish, ominous, shuddersome, sinister, terrifying, threatening, unpleasant, weird; SEE CONCEPT 570

crescent [n] sickle-shaped object
bow, concave figure, convex figure, cresentoid, curve, demilune, half-moon, horned moon, lune, meniscus, new moon, old moon, sickle; SEE CONCEPT 436

crescent [adj] sickle-shaped
bowed, bow-shaped, concave, convex, crescentic, crescentiform, curved, falcate, semicircular; SEE CONCEPT 486

crest [n1] highest point
acme, apex, apogee, climax, crescendo, crown, culmination, fastigium, head, height, noon, peak, pinnacle, ridge, roof, summit, top, vertex; SEE CONCEPT 836

crest [n2] emblem, symbol
badge, bearings, charge, device, insignia; SEE CONCEPT 284

crest [n3] topknot on head of animal
aigrette, caruncle, chine, cockscomb, comb, crown, feather, hogback, mane, panache, plume, ridge, tassel, tuft; SEE CONCEPT 399

crestfallen [adj] disappointed
ass in a sling*, blue, cast down, chapfallen, dejected, depressed, despondent, disconsolate, discouraged, disheartened, dispirited, down, downcast, downhearted, down in the dumps*, in a funk*, inconsolable, low, sad, singing the blues*, taken down*; SEE CONCEPT 403

cr
cr

crevice/crevasse [n] *crack, gap*
abyss, chasm, chink, cleft, crack, cranny, cut, division, fissure, fracture, hole, interstice, opening, precipice, rent, rift, slit, split; SEE CONCEPTS **509,513**

crew [n] *group working together*
aggregation, assemblage, band, bevy, bunch, cluster, collection, company, complement, congregation, corps, covey, crowd, faction, gang, hands, herd, horde, lot, mob, organization, pack, party, posse, retinue, sailors, sect, set, squad, swarm, team, troop, troupe, workers, working party; SEE CONCEPTS **381,417**

crib [n] *baby bed*
bassinet, bin*, box*, bunk, cot, cradle, manger, Moses basket*, rack*, stall*, trundle bed; SEE CONCEPT **443**

crick [n] *muscle spasm*
ache, charley horse*, convulsion, cramp, jarring, kink, pain, stitch, twinge, wrench; SEE CONCEPTS **308,728**

crime [n] *offense against the law*
abomination, antisocial behavior, atrocity, breach, break, caper, case, corruption, criminality, delict, delictum, delinquency, depravity, dereliction, enormity, evil, evil behavior, fast one*, fault, felony, hit, illegality, immorality, infraction, infringement, iniquity, job, lawlessness, malefaction, malfeasance, misconduct, misdeed, misdemeanor, mortal sin, outrage, racket, scandal, sneak, tort, transgression, trespass, unlawful act, vice, villainy, violation, wickedness, wrong, wrongdoing; SEE CONCEPT **192**

criminal [n] *person who breaks the law*
bad actor*, blackmailer, black marketeer, con, convict, crook, culprit, delinquent, desperado, deuce, evildoer, ex-con, felon, fugitive, gangster, guerilla, heavy*, hood*, hoodlum, hooligan*, hustler, inside person*, jailbird, lawbreaker, malefactor, mobster, mug, muscle*, offender, outlaw, racketeer, repeater, scofflaw, sinner, slippery eel*, thug*, transgressor, trespasser, wrongdoer, yardbird*; SEE CONCEPT **412**

criminal [adj] *lawless, felonious*
bent, caught, corrupt, crooked, culpable, deplorable, dirty, heavy, hung up*, illegal, illegitimate, illicit, immoral, indictable, iniquitous, nefarious, off base*, out of line*, peccant, racket, racketous, senseless, shady*, smoking gun*, unlawful, unrighteous, vicious, villainous, wicked, wildcat*, wrong; SEE CONCEPT **545**

crimp [v] *fold or curl*
coil, crease, crimple, crinkle, crisp, crumple, flow, frizz, pleat, rimple, ruck, screw, scrunch, set, swirl, undulate, wave, wrinkle; SEE CONCEPTS **137,213,250**

cringe [v] *flinch, recoil from danger*
blench, cower, crawl, crouch, dodge, draw back, duck, eat dirt, grovel, kneel, quail, quiver, shrink, shy, start, stoop, tremble, wince; SEE CONCEPTS **188,195**

crinkle [v] *crumple, ruffle*
cockle, coil, crackle, crease, crimp, crimple, curl, fold, hiss, pucker, ruck, rumple, rustle, scallop, screw, scrunch, seam, swish, twist, whisper, wind, wreathe, wrinkle; SEE CONCEPTS **65,137,213,250**

cripple [v1] *disable; make lame*
attenuate, blunt, debilitate, disarm, dislimb, dismember, enfeeble, hamstring*, hurt, immobilize, incapacitate, injure, lame, maim, mangle, mutilate, palsy, paralyze, prostrate, sap, sideline*, stifle, undermine, unstrengthen, weaken; SEE CONCEPT **246**

cripple [v2] *hinder action, progress*
bring to standstill, cramp, damage, destroy, halt, hamstring*, impair, put out of action*, ruin, spoil, stifle, vitiate; SEE CONCEPT **121**

crippled [adj] *disabled*
bedridden, broken, damaged, defective, deformed, enfeebled, game, gimp*, halt, hamstrung*, handicapped, harmed, hog-tied*, housebound, impaired, incapacitated, laid up*, lame, maimed, mangled, marred, mutilated, out of commission*, paralyzed, sidelined*; SEE CONCEPTS **314,485**

crisis [n] *critical situation*
big trouble*, catastrophe, change, climacteric, climax, confrontation, contingency, corner, crossroad, crunch*, crux, culmination, deadlock, dilemma, dire straits*, disaster, embarrassment, emergency, entanglement, exigency, extremity, height, hot potato*, hour of decision*, imbroglio, impasse, juncture, mess, moment of truth*, necessity, pass, perplexity, pickle*, pinch*, plight, point of no return*, predicament, pressure, puzzle, quandary, situation, stew, strait, trauma, trial, trouble, turning point, urgency; SEE CONCEPT **674**

crisp [adj1] *brittle, dry*
crispy, crumbly, crunchy, crusty, firm, fresh, friable, green, plump, ripe, short, unwilted; SEE CONCEPT **606**

crisp [adj2] *fresh, chilly*
bracing, brisk, clear, cloudless, invigorating, refreshing, stimulating; SEE CONCEPTS **525,605**

crisp [adj3] *short, curt in presentation*
abrupt, biting, brief, brusque, clear, clear-cut, cutting, incisive, penetrating, piquing, pithy, provoking, stimulating, succinct, tart, terse; SEE CONCEPT **267**

crisp [adj4] *smart, snappy in appearance*
clean-cut, neat, orderly, spruce, tidy, well-groomed, well-pressed; SEE CONCEPT **579**

criterion [n] *test, gauge for judgment*
archetype, basis, benchmark, canon, example, exemplar, fact, foundation, law, measure, model, norm, opinion, original, paradigm, pattern, point of comparison, precedent, principle, proof, prototype, rule, scale, standard, touchstone, yardstick; SEE CONCEPTS **290,688**

critic [n1] *analyst, interpreter*
analyzer, annotator, arbiter, authority, caricaturist, cartoonist, commentator, connoisseur, diagnostic, evaluator, expert, expositor, judge, pundit, reviewer, sharpshooter; SEE CONCEPT **348**

critic [n2] *faultfinder, detractor*
aristarch, attacker, backseat driver*, belittler, blamer, carper, caviler, censor, censurer, complainant, complainer, defamer, disapprover, disparager, disputer, doubter, fretter, hypercritic, maligner, muckraker, mud-slinger*, nagger*, hit-picker*, panner*, quibbler, reviler, scolder, sidewalk superintendent*, slanderer, vilifier, worrier, zapper*; SEE CONCEPT **412**

critical [adj1] *fault-finding, detracting*
analytical, belittling, biting, calumniatory, captious, carping, caviling, cavillous, censorious, censuring, choleric, condemning, critic, cutting, cynical, demanding, demeaning, derogatory, diagnostic, disapproving, discerning, discriminat-

ing, disparaging, exacting, exceptive, finicky, fussy, hairsplitting, humbling, hypercritical, lowering, nagging, niggling, nit-picking*, overcritical, particular, penetrating, reproachful, sarcastic, satirical, scolding, severe, sharp, trenchant, withering; SEE CONCEPT 267

critical [adj2] *urgently important*
acute, all-important, climacteric, conclusive, consequential, crucial, dangerous, deciding, decisive, desperate, determinative, dire, exceptive, grave, hairy*, hazardous, high-priority, integral, momentous, perilous, pivotal, precarious, pressing, risky, serious, significant, strategic, urgent, vital, weighty; SEE CONCEPT 568

criticism [n1] *interpretation, analysis*
appraisal, appreciation, assessment, comment, commentary, critique, elucidation, essay, estimate, evaluation, examination, exposition, judgment, notice, observation, opinion, pan*, rating, rave*, review, reviewal, scorcher, sideswipe*, sleighride*, study, write-up; SEE CONCEPTS 271,277,278

criticism [n2] *verbal disapproval*
animadversion, aspersion, bad press*, blast, brickbats, Bronx cheer*, carping, cavil, caviling, censure, critical remarks, cut*, denunciation, disparagement, faultfinding, flak*, hit*, knock*, nit-picking*, objection, opprobrium, pan, panning, put down, quibble, rap on knuckles*, reproof, roast*, slam*, slap*, slap on wrist*, static, stricture, swipe*, vitriol, zapper*; SEE CONCEPT 52

criticize [v1] *disapprove, judge as bad*
animadvert on, bash, blame, blast, blister, carp, castigate, censure, chastise, chide, clobber, come down on, condemn, cut down*, cut to bits*, cut up*, denounce, denunciate, disparage, do a number on*, dress down*, excoriate, find fault, fluff*, fulminate against, fustigate, give bad press*, hit, jump on*, knock*, lambaste*, nag at, nit-pick, pan, pick at, rap*, reprehend, reprimand, reprobate, reprove, rip*, roast*, scathe, scorch*, skin*, skin alive*, slam*, slog*, slug*, take down*, trash*, trim*, zap*; SEE CONCEPT 52

criticize [v2] *analyze, interpret*
appraise, assess, comment upon, evaluate, examine, give opinion, judge, pass judgment on, probe, review, scrutinize, study; SEE CONCEPTS 37,103

critique [n] *analysis, essay*
appraisal, assessment, comment, commentary, criticism, editorial, examination, exposition, flak*, judgment, notice, pan*, putdown*, rap*, rave*, review, reviewal, slam*, slap*, study, takedown*, write-up, zapper*; SEE CONCEPTS 51,52,271

croak [v] *make husky, squawking noise*
caw, crow, gasp, grunt, quack, squawk, utter huskily, utter throatily, wheeze; SEE CONCEPT 77

crony [n] *ally, companion*
accomplice, acquaintance, associate, bosom buddy*, buddy, chum, colleague, comate, comrade, confidant, friend, good buddy*, intimate, mate, pal, partner, sidekick*; SEE CONCEPT 423

crook [n] *criminal, thief*
cheat, filcher, knave, pilferer, purloiner, racketeer, robber, rogue, scoundrel, shark*, shyster*, swindler, villain; SEE CONCEPT 412

crook [v] *bend, angle*
bow, curve, flex, fork, hook, meander, notch, round, slither, snake, wind, zigzag; SEE CONCEPTS 213,738

crooked [adj1] *bent, angled*
agee, anfractuous, angular, asymmetric, awry, bowed, catawampus*, circuitous, cockeyed*, contorted, crippled, curved, curving, deformed, deviating, devious, disfigured, distorted, errant, gnarled, hooked, incurving, indirect, irregular, kinky, knurly, lopsided, meandering, misshapen, not straight, oblique, out of shape, rambling, roundabout, screwy*, serpentine, sinuous, skewed, slanted, snaky, spiral, tilted, topsyturvy*, tortile, tortuous, twisted, twisting, uneven, warped, winding, zigzag; SEE CONCEPTS 486,490,581

crooked [adj2] *evil, corrupt*
crafty, criminal, deceitful, devious, dishonest, dishonorable, double-dealing, dubious, fraudulent, illegal, indirect, iniquitous, lying, nefarious, questionable, ruthless, shady, shifty, suborned, treacherous, underhand, unlawful, unprincipled, unscrupulous, untruthful; SEE CONCEPT 545

crop [n] *harvest of fruit, vegetable*
annual production, byproduct, crops, fruitage, fruits, gathering, gleaning, output, produce, product, reaping, season's growth, vintage, yield; SEE CONCEPT 429

crop [v] *cut, trim off*
chop, clip, curtail, detach, detruncate, disengage, hew, lop, mow, pare, pollard, prune, reduce, shave, shear, shorten, skive, slash, snip, top, truncate; SEE CONCEPT 176

cross [adj] *very angry; in a bad mood*
annoyed, cantankerous, captious, caviling, choleric, churlish, crabby*, cranky, crotchety*, crusty, disagreeable, faultfinding, fractious, fretful, grouchy, grumpy, ill-humored, ill-tempered, impatient, irascible, irritable, jumpy, out of humor, peeved, peevish, pettish, petulant, put out*, querulous, quick-tempered, ratty, short, snappy, splenetic, sullen, surly, testy, tetchy, touchy, vexed, waspish; SEE CONCEPTS 401,403

cross [v1] *traverse an area*
bridge, cruise, cut across, extend over, ford, go across, meet, move across, navigate, overpass, pass over, ply, sail, span, transverse, voyage, zigzag; SEE CONCEPTS 159,224

cross [v2] *intersect, lie across*
bisect, crisscross, crosscut, decussate, divide, intercross, intertwine, lace, lie athwart of, rest across; SEE CONCEPTS 738,747

cross [v3] *hybridize, mix*
blend, crossbreed, cross-fertilize, cross-mate, cross-pollinate, interbreed, intercross, mingle, mongrelize; SEE CONCEPTS 250,257

cross [v4] *betray, hinder*
backtalk, block, bollix, buck, crab, cramp, crimp, deny, double-cross, flummox, foil, foul up*, frustrate, have bone to pick*, impede, interfere, knock props out*, louse up*, obstruct, oppose, resist, sell*, sell out*, snafu*, stab in the back*, stonewall*, stump, stymie, take on, take wind out of sails*, thwart; SEE CONCEPTS 7,19,59,121

cross-examine [v] *ask pointed questions*
catechize, check, cross-question, debrief, examine, grill, interrogate, investigate, pump, put the screws to*, question, quiz, sweat, third-degree*; SEE CONCEPTS 48,53,317

crossing [n] *pathway to traverse larger path*
bridge, cloverleaf, crossroad, crosswalk, cross-

cr
cr

way, decussation, exchange, grade crossing, grating, gridiron, interchange, intersection, junction, loop, network, overpass, passage, screen, traversal, traverse, underpass; SEE CONCEPTS *501,513*

crosswise/crossways [*adj*] *across, at an angle*
angular, aslant, athwart, at right angles, awry, contrariwise, crisscross, cross, crossing, diagonally, from side to side, horizontally, longways, on the bias, over, perpendicular, sideways, thwart, transversal, transverse, transversely, traverse, vertically; SEE CONCEPT *581*

crotchety [*adj*] *irritable, often due to old age*
awkward, bad-tempered, bearish, cantankerous, contrary, crabby*, cranky, cross, cross-grained, crusty, curmudgeonly, difficult, disagreeable, eccentric, fractious, grouchy, grumpy, irritable, obstinate, obstreperous, odd, ornery*, peevish, queer, surly, testy, unusual, vinegary*, waspish, waspy; SEE CONCEPTS *401,403*

crouch [*v*] *stoop low; cringe*
bend, bend down, bow, cower, dip, duck, grovel, huddle, hunch, hunker down, kneel, quail, quat, scrooch down, squat, stoop, wince; SEE CONCEPT *213*

crow [*v*] *brag, exult*
babble, blow, bluster, boast, cackle, caw, cock-a-doodle-doo*, cry, flourish, gas, gloat, glory in, gurgle, jubilate, mouth, prate, puff, rodomontade, squawk, strut, swagger, triumph, vaunt, whoop; SEE CONCEPT *49*

crowd [*n1*] *large assembly*
army, array, blowout, bunch, cattle, circle, clique, cloud, cluster, company, concourse, confluence, conflux, congeries, congregation, coterie, crew, crush, deluge, drove, faction, flock, flood, gaggle, great unwashed*, group, herd, horde, host, jam, legion, lot, mass, masses, meet, mob, multitude, muster, organization, pack, party, people, posse, press, rabble, rank and file*, scores, sellout, set, stream, surge, swarm, throng, troupe, tumult; SEE CONCEPTS *381,417*

crowd [*n2*] *special group of friends*
bunch, circle, clique, coterie, faction, group, in-crowd, lot, posse, push, set; SEE CONCEPTS *387,417*

crowd [*v*] *cram, press into area*
bear, bunch, bundle, chock, cluster, congest, congregate, crush, deluge, elbow, flock, gather, huddle, jam, jam-pack*, justle, mass, muster, overcrowd, pack, pack 'em in*, pack like sardines*, pile, push, ram, sardine*, shove, squash, squeeze, squish*, stream, surge, swamp, swarm, throng, top off, troop; SEE CONCEPTS *208,740*

crowded [*adj*] *busy, congested*
awash, brimful, brimming, chock-full, clean, close, compact, crammed, cramped, crushed, dense, elbow-to-elbow*, filled to the rafters*, fit to bust*, full, full house*, full up*, huddled, jammed, jam-packed*, loaded, lousy with*, massed, mobbed, mob scene*, overflowing, packed, populous, sardined*, sold out, SRO*, standing room only*, stiff with*, stuffed, swarming, teeming, thick, thickset, thronged, tight, topped off, up to here*, up to the hilt*, wall-to-wall*; SEE CONCEPTS *481,483,774*

crown [*n1*] *top; best*
acme, apex, climax, crest, culmination, fastigium, head, meridian, peak, perfection, pinnacle, roof,

summit, tip, top, ultimate, vertex, zenith; SEE CONCEPTS *706,836*

crown [*n2*] *tiara for royalty*
chaplet, circlet, coronal, coronet, diadem, garland, headband, headdress, wreath; SEE CONCEPT *452*

crown [*n3*] *royalty*
crowned head, monarch, monarchy, potentate, ruler, sovereign, sovereignty, supreme ruler, the throne; SEE CONCEPT *422*

crown [*v1*] *reward, dignify*
adorn, arm, authorize, commission, coronate, delegate, determine, dower, enable, endow, endue, ennoble, enthrone, erect, establish, exalt, festoon, fix, heighten, honor, inaugurate, induct, install, invest, raise, sanction, settle, set up, stabilize, strengthen; SEE CONCEPTS *50,69,88*

crown [*v2*] *be the culmination of*
cap, climax, complete, consummate, crest, finish, fulfill, perfect, put finishing touch on, round off, surmount, terminate, top, top off; SEE CONCEPTS *234,706*

crown [*v3*] *hit, usually on head*
biff, box, cuff, knock, punch, smite, strike; SEE CONCEPT *189*

crowning [*adj*] *climactic*
consummate, culminating, excellent, final, paramount, principal, sovereign, supreme, ultimate; SEE CONCEPTS *531,548*

crucial [*adj*] *critical, important*
acute, central, clamorous, climacteric, climatic, compelling, deciding, decisive, desperate, dire, essential, hanging by thread*, high-priority, imperative, insistent, momentous, necessary, on thin ice*, pivotal, pressing, searching, showdown*, touch and go*, touchy, urgent, vital; SEE CONCEPT *568*

crucify [*v1*] *execute; torture near to death*
excruciate, hang, harrow, kill, martyr, martyrize, nail to cross, persecute, rack, torment, torture; SEE CONCEPT *252*

crucify [*v2*] *browbeat, destroy with words*
afflict, agonize, bedevil, bother, harrow, ill-treat, lampoon, pan, ridicule, smite, tear to pieces*, torment, torture, try, wipe the floor with*; SEE CONCEPTS *7,19,52*

crude [*adj1*] *vulgar, unpolished in manner*
awkward, backward, barnyard*, boorish, cheap, cloddish, clumsy, coarse, crass, dirty, earthy, filthy, foul, grody*, gross*, ignorant, ill-bred, indecent, indelicate, inelegant, insensible, lewd, loud, loud-mouthed, loutish, lowbred, oafish, obscene, raunchy*, raw, rough, rude, savage, smutty*, tacky*, tactless, uncouth, unenlightened, ungainly, unskillful; SEE CONCEPTS *267,401*

crude [*adj2*] *unrefined, natural*
amateurish, callow, coarse, green, harsh, homemade, homespun, immature, impure, inexpert, in the rough*, makeshift, outline, prentice, primitive, raw, rough, rough-hewn, rude, rudimentary, rustic, simple, sketchy, thick, undeveloped, unfinished, unformed, ungraded, unmatured, unmilled, unpolished, unprepared, unprocessed, unproficient, unsorted, untaught, untrained, unworked, unwrought; SEE CONCEPTS *562,578, 589,797*

cruel [*adj*] *vicious, pitiless; causing pain*
atrocious, barbarous, bestial, bitter, bloodthirsty, brutal, brutish, callous, cold-blooded, degenerate, demoniac, depraved, evil, excruciating, ferocious,

fierce, flinty, hard, hard-hearted, harsh, hateful, heartless, hellish, implacable, inexorable, inhuman, inhumane, malevolent, merciless, monstrous, painful, pernicious, poignant, rancorous, relentless, revengeful, ruthless, sadistic, sinful, spiteful, tyrannical, unfeeling, unkind, unnatural, unrelenting, vengeful, vicious, virulent, wicked; SEE CONCEPTS **401,570**

cruelty [n] *brutality, harshness*
animality, barbarism, barbarity, bestiality, bloodthirstiness, brutishness, callousness, coarseness, coldness, depravity, despotism, ferocity, fiendishness, fierceness, hard-heartedness, heartlessness, inhumanity, insensibility, insensitiveness, malice, malignity, masochism, mercilessness, murderousness, persecution, rancor, ruthlessness, sadism, savageness, savagery, severity, spite, spitefulness, torture, truculence, unfeelingness, unkindness, venom, viciousness, wickedness; SEE CONCEPT **633**

cruise [n] *sailing expedition*
boat trip, crossing, jaunt, journey, sail, sailing, sea trip, voyage; SEE CONCEPTS **224,292,363**

cruise [v] *sail*
boat, coast, drift, fare, gad, gallivant, go, hie, jaunt, journey, keep steady pace, meander, navigate, pass, proceed, push on, repair, travel, voyage, wander about, wend; SEE CONCEPTS **147,151,159,224**

crumb [n] *tiny bit, morsel*
atom, dab, dash, dram, drop, grain, iota, jot, mite, ounce, particle, pinch, scrap, seed, shred, sliver, smidgen, snippet, soupçon, speck; SEE CONCEPT **831**

crumble [v] *break or fall into pieces*
break up, collapse, crumb, crush, decay, decompose, degenerate, deteriorate, disintegrate, dissolve, fragment, go to pieces, granulate, grind, molder, perish, powder, pulverize, putrefy, triturate, tumble; SEE CONCEPTS **181,248,469**

crumbly [adj] *brittle*
breakable, corroded, crisp, crunchy, decayed, degenerated, deteriorated, deteriorating, disintegrated, eroded, fragile, frail, frangible, friable, oxidized, perishing, powdery, pulverizable, rotted, rotten, rusted, shivery, short, soft, worn; SEE CONCEPTS **485,606**

crumple [v] *make or become wrinkled*
break down, buckle, cave in, collapse, crease, crimp, crimple, crinkle, crush, fall, fold, give way, go to pieces, pucker, rimple, ruck, rumple, screw, scrunch, shrivel, wad, wrinkle; SEE CONCEPTS **184,208,252**

crunch [n] *crucial point*
crisis, critical point, crux, difficulty, emergency, hour of decision*, moment of truth*, problem, test, trouble, trying time*; SEE CONCEPTS **388,674,675**

crunch [v] *grind, chew*
beat, bite, champ, chaw, chomp, crush, gnaw, masticate, munch, ruminate, scrunch; SEE CONCEPTS **169,186**

crusade [n] *campaign for cause*
cause, demonstration, drive, evangelism, expedition, holy war, jihad, march, movement, push; SEE CONCEPT **300**

crush [n1] *crowd of animate beings*
drove, gathering, horde, huddle, jam, multitude, party, press, push, throng, tumult; SEE CONCEPTS **417,432**

crush [n2] *infatuation*
beguin, desire, flame, love affair, passion, puppy love*, torch; SEE CONCEPT **20**

crush [v1] *compress, smash*
beat, bray, break, bruise, buck, comminute, contriturate, contuse, crease, crowd, crumble, crunch, embrace, enfold, express, hug, jam, kablooey*, mash, pound, powder, press, pulverize, push, romp, rumple, squash, squeeze, squish, total*, trample, tread, triturate, wrinkle; SEE CONCEPTS **208,219,246,252**

crush [v2] *defeating soundly*
annihilate, bear down, beat, blot out*, blow away*, conquer, defeat, demolish, extinguish, force down, ice*, kill, obliterate, overcome, overpower, overwhelm, quelch, quell, reduce, ruin, squelch, stamp out*, strangle, subdue, subjugate, suppress, vanquish, wreck; SEE CONCEPTS **95,252**

crush [v3] *humiliate*
abash, browbeat, chagrin, dispose of, dump, hurt, mortify, overwhelm, put away*, put down*, quash, quell, shame, suppress; SEE CONCEPTS **7,19**

crust [n] *stiff outer layer; coating*
band, bloom, border, caking, coat, concretion, covering, edge, encrustation, film, hull, incrustation, integument, layer, outside, rind, scab, shell, skin, surface, verge; SEE CONCEPT **484**

crusty [adj1] *irritable, often due to old age*
abrupt, bluff, blunt, brief, brusque, cantankerous, captious, choleric, crabbed, crabby*, cranky, cross, curt, dour, gruff, harsh, ill-humored, irascible, peevish, prickly, sarcastic, saturnine, scornful, short, short-tempered, snappish, snarling, snippety, snippy, splenetic, surly, testy, touchy, vinegary*; SEE CONCEPT **401**

crusty [adj2] *brittle on outside*
crisp, crispy, crunchy, friable, hard, short, well-baked, well-done; SEE CONCEPTS **462,606**

crux [n] *most important part*
body, bottom line*, core, decisive point, essence, gist, heart, kernel, matter, meat*, meat and potatoes*, nitty-gritty, nub, pith, purport, substance, thrust; SEE CONCEPTS **668,826**

cry [n1] *weeping and making sad sounds*
bawl, bawling, bewailing, blubber, blubbering, howl, howling, keening, lament, lamentation, mourning, shedding tears, snivel, snivelling, sob, sobbing, sorrowing, tears, the blues*, wailing, weep, whimpering, yowl; SEE CONCEPTS **77,469**

cry [n2] *calling out; yelling*
acclamation, bark, bawl, bay, bellow, cackle, call, caw, chatter, cheer, clack, clamor, cluck, coo, crow, ejaculation, exclamation, expletive, fuss, gobble, groan, grunt, hiss, holler, hoot, howl, hullabaloo, hurrah, meow, mewling, moo, motto, nicker, note, outcry, pipe, quack, report, roar, ruckus, scream, screech, shout, shriek, song, squall, squawk, squeak, trill, uproar, vociferation, wail, whine, whinny, whistle, whoop, yammer, yawp*, yell, yelp, yoo-hoo; SEE CONCEPTS **47,77,278**

cry [v1] *weep and make sad sounds*
bawl, bemoan, bewail, blub, blubber, boohoo*, break down, burst into tears*, caterwaul, choke up, complain, crack up*, deplore, dissolve in tears*, fret, grieve, groan, howl, keen, lament, let go, let it all out*, mewl, moan, mourn, put on the weeps*, regret, ring the blues*, shed bitter tears*, shed tears, sigh, sniff, snivel, sob, sorrow, squall,

turn on waterworks*, wail, weep, whimper, whine, yammer, yowl; SEE CONCEPTS 77,469

cry [v2] *call out, yell*
bark, bawl, bay, bellow, bleat, cackle, call, caw, chatter, cheer, clack, clamor, cluck, coo, croak, crow, ejaculate, exclaim, gabble, growl, grunt, hail, hiss, holler, holler out, hoot, howl, low, meow, moo, nicker, pipe, quack, roar, scream, screech, shout, shriek, sing out, snarl, squawk, trill, tweet, twitter, vociferate, whinny, whistle, whoop, yawp*, yelp; SEE CONCEPTS 47,77

cry [v3] *advertise*
announce, bark*, broadcast, build up, hawk, hype*, press-agent*, proclaim, promulgate, publicize, publish, puff*, trumpet*; SEE CONCEPT 324

crypt [n] *burial place*
catacomb, cave, cavern, cell, chamber, compartment, grave, grotto, mausoleum, room, sepulcher, tomb, undercroft, vault; SEE CONCEPT 305

cryptic [adj] *secret; obscure in meaning*
abstruse, ambiguous, apocryphal, arcane, cabbalistic, dark, Delphian, Delphic, enigmatic, equivocal, esoteric, evasive, hidden, incomprehensible, inexplicable, murky, mysterious, mystic, mystical, mystifying, occult, opaque, oracular, perplexing, puzzling, recondite, secretive, strange, tenebrous, unclear, unfathomable, uninformative, vague, veiled; SEE CONCEPTS 267,576,682

crystal [adj] *clear, transparent*
clear-cut, limpid, lucent, lucid, luminous, pellucid, translucent, transpicuous, unblurred; SEE CONCEPTS 617,618

cuddle [v] *hold fondly, closely*
bundle, burrow, caress, clasp, cosset, curl up, dandle, embrace, enfold, feel up*, fondle, huddle, hug, kiss, love, nestle, nuzzle, pet, snug, snuggle, touch; SEE CONCEPTS 190,375

cuddly [adj] *huggable, embraceable*
caressible, cuddlesome, kissable, lovable, plump, snuggly, soft, warm; SEE CONCEPT 485

cudgel [n] *baton for hitting*
bastinado, bat, billy*, billyclub, birch, blackjack, bludgeon, cane, club, cosh*, ferule, mace, nightstick, paddle, rod, sap, shill, shillelagh, spontoon, stick, switch, truncheon; SEE CONCEPT 500

cue [n] *signal to act*
catchword, clue, hint, hot lead*, idea, indication, inkling, innuendo, in the wind*, intimation, job, key, lead, mnemonic, nod, notion, prod, prompt, prompting, reminder, sign, suggestion, telltale*, tip-off, warning; SEE CONCEPTS 278,284,628

cuff [n] *beating with hands*
belt, biff, box, buffet, chop, clip, clout, hit, knock, poke, punch, rap, slap, smack, sock, thump, wallop, whack; SEE CONCEPT 189

cuff [v] *beat with hands*
bat, belt, biff, box, buffet, clap, clobber*, clout, hit, knock, pummel, punch, slap, smack, spank, thump, whack; SEE CONCEPT 189

cull [v1] *pick out for reason*
choose, discriminate, elect, extract, glean, mark, optate, opt for, pluck, prefer, select, sift, single out, take, thin, thin out, winnow; SEE CONCEPTS 41,142

cull [v2] *gather*
accumulate, amass, collect, extract, garner, glean, pick up, round up; SEE CONCEPT 109

culminate [v] *come to a climax*
cap, climax, close, come to a head*, conclude,

crown, end, end up, finish, go over the mountain*, go the route*, rise to crescendo, round off, shoot one's wad*, terminate, top off*, wind up*; SEE CONCEPT 119

culmination [n] *conclusion; climactic stage*
acme, all the way*, apex, apogee, blow off*, capper*, climax, completion, consummation, critical mass, crown, crowning touch, finale, finish, height, limit, maximum, meridian, ne plus ultra, noon, payoff, peak, perfection, pinnacle, punch line*, summit, top, zenith; SEE CONCEPTS 230,635,676

culpable [adj] *responsible for action*
amiss, answerable, at fault, blamable, blameful, blameworthy, caught, caught in the act*, caught red-handed*, censurable, demeritorious, dirty, found wanting, guilty, hung up, impeachable, indictable, in the wrong, liable, off base, out of line*, punishable, reprehensible, responsible, sinful, smoking gun*, to blame, unholy, wrong; SEE CONCEPTS 404,545

culprit [n] *person responsible for wrongdoing*
con, convict, criminal, delinquent, evildoer, ex-con, felon, fugitive, guilty party, jailbird*, malefactor, miscreant, offender, rascal, sinner, transgressor, wrongdoer, yardbird*; SEE CONCEPT 412

cult [n1] *group sharing belief*
band, body, church, clan, clique, creed, denomination, faction, faith, following, party, persuasion, religion, school, sect; SEE CONCEPTS 369,387

cult [n2] *worship; form of ceremony*
admiration, ceremony, craze, creed, cultus, devotion, faddism, faith, idolization, liturgy, persuasion, religion, reverence, rite, ritual, veneration; SEE CONCEPTS 410,689

cultivate [v1] *develop land for growing*
breed, crop, dress, farm, fertilize, garden, harvest, labor, manage, mature, plant, plow, prepare, propagate, raise, ripen, seed, tend, till, work; SEE CONCEPTS 253,257

cultivate [v2] *enrich situation; give special attention*
advance, ameliorate, better, bolster, bring on, brownnose*, butter up*, cherish, civilize, court, develop, discipline, elevate, encourage, enrich, foster, further, get in with*, get next to*, get on good side of*, improve, nourish, nurse, nurture, play up to*, polish, promote, refine, run after, seek friendship, shine up to*, suck up to*, take pains with, train; SEE CONCEPTS 244,384

cultivate [v3] *nurture, take care of*
aid, ameliorate, better, cherish, devote oneself to, educate, encourage, forward, foster, further, help, improve, instruct, nurse, patronize, promote, pursue, raise, rear, refine, support, teach, train; SEE CONCEPTS 110,295

cultivation [n1] *development of land for growing*
agrology, agronomics, agronomy, farming, gardening, horticulture, planting, plowing, tillage, tilling, working; SEE CONCEPT 257

cultivation [n2] *culture, sophistication, education*
advancement, aesthetics, breeding, civility, civilization, delicacy, discernment, discrimination, enlightenment, gentility, good taste, grounding, improvement, learning, letters, manners, polish, progress, refined taste, refinement, schooling, taste; SEE CONCEPTS 411,655,673

cultivation [n3] *nurture, help*
advancement, advocacy, development, encouragement, enhancement, fostering, furtherance, patronage, promotion, support; SEE CONCEPTS 110,657

cultural [adj] *educational, enlightening*
adorning, advancing, artistic, beautifying, beneficial, broadening, civilizing, constructive, corrective, developmental, dignifying, disciplining, edifying, educative, elevating, ennobling, enriching, expanding, glorifying, helpful, humane, humanizing, influential, inspirational, instructive, learned, liberal, liberalizing, nurturing, ornamenting, polishing, promoting, raising, refined, refining, regenerative, socializing, stimulating, uplifting, widening; SEE CONCEPTS 537,555,589

culture [n1] *breeding, education, sophistication*
ability, accomplishment, address, aestheticism, art, capacity, civilization, class, courtesy, cultivation, delicacy, dignity, discrimination, dress, elegance, elevation, enlightenment, erudition, experience, fashion, finish, gentility, good taste, grace, improvement, kindness, learning, manners, nobility, perception, polish, politeness, practice, proficiency, refinement, savoir-faire, science, skill, tact, training, urbanity; SEE CONCEPTS 388,633,678

culture [n2] *ideas, values of a people*
arts and sciences, civilization, convention, customs, development, ethnology, folklore, folkways, grounding, habit, humanism, knowledge, lifestyle, mores, society, the arts, way of life; SEE CONCEPTS 388,689

culture [n3] *development of land*
agriculture, agrology, agronomics, agronomy, cultivation, farming, gardening, raising, tending; SEE CONCEPT 257

cultured [adj] *well-bred, experienced*
able, accomplished, advanced, aesthetic, appreciative, au courant, blue-stocking*, chivalrous, civilized, courteous, cultivated, distingue, educated, elegant, enlightened, erudite, gallant, genteel, highbrow*, high class, informed, intellectual, intelligent, knowledgeable, lettered, liberal, literary, literate, mannerly, polished, polite, refined, savant, scholarly, sensitive, sophisticated, tasteful, tolerant, traveled, understanding, up-to-date, urbane, versed, well-informed; SEE CONCEPT 550

culvert [n] *ditch for flow of water*
canal, channel, conduit, drain, duct, gutter, pipe, watercourse; SEE CONCEPT 509

cumbersome [adj] *clumsy, awkward*
bulky, burdensome, clunker, clunking, clunky, cumbrous, embarrassing, galumphing, heavy, hefty, incommodious, inconvenient, leaden, massive, oppressive, ponderous, tiresome, unhandy, unmanageable, unwieldy, wearisome, weighty; SEE CONCEPTS 544,773

cumulative [adj] *accruing; growing in size or effect*
accumulative, additive, additory, advancing, aggregate, amassed, augmenting, chain, collective, heaped, heightening, increasing, increscent, intensifying, magnifying, multiplying, snowballing*, summative; SEE CONCEPTS 540,548,786

cunning [adj1] *devious*
acute, artful, astute, cagey, canny, crafty, crazy like fox*, deep, fancy footwork*, foxy, guileful, insidious, keen, knowing, Machiavellian, sharp,

shifty, shrewd, slick, slippery, sly, sly boots*, smart, smarts, smooth, street-smart*, streetwise*, subtle, tricky, wary, wily; SEE CONCEPTS 401,545

cunning [adj2] *imaginative*
able, adroit, canny, clever, crackerjack*, deft, dexterous, ingenious, intelligent, masterful, skillful, slighty, sly, smart, smooth, subtle, well-laid, well-planned; SEE CONCEPT 402

cup [n] *container for drinking*
beaker, bowl, cannikin, chalice, cupful, demitasse, draught, drink, goblet, grail, mug, potion, stein, taster, teacup, tumbler, vessel; SEE CONCEPT 494

cupboard [n] *storage cabinet*
buffet, closet, depository, facility, locker, press, repository, sideboard, storeroom, wardrobe; SEE CONCEPT 443

cupidity [n] *greed, strong desire*
acquisitiveness, avarice, avariciousness, avidity, covetousness, craving, eagerness, graspingness, greediness, hunger, infatuation, itching*, longing, lust, passion, possessiveness, rapaciousness, rapacity, voracity, yearning; SEE CONCEPTS 20,709

cur [n1] *rotten, lowly animate being*
blackguard, black sheep*, bum, cad, coward, dog*, good-for-nothing*, heel*, hound*, ne'er-do-well*, rat*, riffraff*, scoundrel, scum*, skunk*, snake*, stinker*, toad*, villain, worm*, wretch, yellow dog*; SEE CONCEPTS 389,412

cur [n2] *animal of mixed breed*
crossbreed, hybrid, mongrel, mutt; SEE CONCEPT 394

curable [adj] *able to be improved, fixed*
amenable, capable, correctable, corrigible, healable, improvable, mendable, not hopeless, not too bad, reparative, restorable, subject to cure; SEE CONCEPTS 314,485

curative [adj] *healing, health-giving*
alleviative, beneficial, corrective, curing, healthful, helpful, invigorating, medicable, medicative, medicinal, pick-me-up*, remedial, remedying, restorative, salutary, sanative, shot in the arm*, therapeutic, tonic, vulnerary, what the doctor ordered*, wholesome; SEE CONCEPTS 314,537

curb [n] *restraining device; check*
barrier, border, brake, bridle, chain, control, deterrent, edge, harness, hindrance, ledge, limitation, lip, rein, restrainer, restraint, restriction, rim; SEE CONCEPTS 376,497,652,745

curb [v] *repress, restrict*
abstain, bit, bottle up*, box in, bridle, bring to screeching halt*, check, clog, constrain, contain, control, cook*, cool down, cool off, deny, entrammel, fetter, hamper, hinder, hobble, hog-tie*, hold back, hold down, hold in, ice*, impede, inhibit, keep lid on*, keep tight rein on*, leash, manacle, moderate, muzzle, refrain, rein in, restrain, retard, scrub*, send up, shackle, subdue, suppress, tame, tie, tie up, withhold; SEE CONCEPTS 121,130

curdle [n] *sour; change into coagulated substance*
acerbate, acidify, acidulate, clabber, clot, coagulate, condense, congeal, curd, ferment, go off, spoil, thicken, turn, turn sour; SEE CONCEPT 456

cure [n] *solution to problem, often health*
aid, alleviation, antidote, assistance, catholicon, corrective, counteractant, counteragent, countermeasure, drug, elixir, elixir vitae, fix, healing, healing agent, help, medicament, medicant, medication, medicine, nostrum, panacea, pharmacon,

cr
cu

physic, placebo, proprietary, quick fix*, recovery, redress, remedy, reparation, restorative, therapeutic, treatment; SEE CONCEPTS 110,307,311

cure [v1] heal, ease bad situation
alleviate, ameliorate, attend, better, cold turkey*, correct, doctor, dose, dress, dry out*, help, improve, kick, kick the habit*, make better, make healthy, make whole, medicate, mend, minister to, nurse, palliate, quit cold*, rectify, redress, rehabilitate, relieve, remedy, repair, restore, restore to health, right, shake, sweat it out*, treat; SEE CONCEPTS 126,244,310

cure [v2] cook, age food
dry, fire, harden, keep, kipper, pickle, preserve, salt, smoke, steel, temper; SEE CONCEPT 170

curio [n] knickknack
antique, bauble, bibelot, bygone, collectible, collector's item, objet d'art, toy, trifle, trinket, whatnot; SEE CONCEPT 446

curiosity [n1] intense desire to know, understand
concern, eagerness, inquiring mind, inquiringness, inquisitiveness, interest, interestingness, intrusiveness, investigation, meddlesomeness, meddling, mental acquisitiveness, nosiness, officiousness, prying, questioning, regard, searching, snoopiness, snooping, thirst for knowledge; SEE CONCEPTS 20,410

curiosity [n2] odd item
anomaly, bibelot, bygone, conversation piece, curio, exoticism, freak, knickknack, marvel, monstrosity, nonesuch, objet d'art, oddity, peculiar object, prodigy, rarity, singular object, trinket, unusual object, wonder; SEE CONCEPT 260

curious [adj1] desiring knowledge, understanding
analytical, disquisitive, examining, impertinent, inquiring, inquisitive, inspecting, interested, interfering, intrusive, investigative, meddlesome, meddling, nosy, peeping, peering, prurient, prying, puzzled, questioning, scrutinizing, searching, snoopy*, tampering; SEE CONCEPTS 403,542

curious [adj2] very odd
bizarre, exotic, extraordinary, marvelous, mysterious, novel, oddball, peculiar, puzzling, quaint, queer, rare, remarkable, singular, strange, unconventional, unexpected, unique, unorthodox, unusual, weird, wonderful; SEE CONCEPTS 547,564

curl [n] loop, ringlet, curve
coil, crimp, crispation, curlicue, flourish, frizz, kink, quirk, spiral, swirl, twist, wave, whorl; SEE CONCEPTS 418,436

curl [v] bend, loop
buckle, coil, contort, convolute, corkscrew, crimp, crinkle, crisp, crook, curve, entwine, fold, form into ringlets, frizz, indent, kink, lap, meander, ringlet, ripple, roll, scallop, snake, spiral, swirl, turn, twine, twirl, twist, undulate, wave, wind, wreathe, writhe, zigzag; SEE CONCEPTS 147,184,213

curly [adj] looping, forming ringlets
coiled, convoluted, corkscrew, crimped, crimpy, crinkling, crinkly, crisp, curled, curling, frizzed, frizzy, fuzzy, kinky, looped, permed, spiralled, waved, waving, wavy, winding, wound; SEE CONCEPTS 406,486

currency [n] paper and coin money of a country
almighty dollar*, bills, bread*, cabbage*, cash, chicken feed*, coinage, coins, cold cash*, dinero*, dough*, folding money, green stuff*, legal tender, medium of exchange, moolah*, notes,

piece of change*, roll*, specie, wad*; SEE CONCEPT 340

current [n] flow of something, usually water
course, draught, drift, ebb and flow, flood, flux, jet, juice, progression, river, run, rush, spate, stream, tidal motion, tide; SEE CONCEPTS 514,519,738

current [adj] contemporary; common
accepted, accustomed, afoot, circulating, common knowledge, customary, cutting-edge*, doing, existent, extant, fad, fashionable, general, going around, hot*, in, in circulation, in progress, instant, in the mainstream, in the news, in use, in vogue, leading-edge*, mod*, modern, now*, on front burner*, ongoing, popular, present, present-day, prevailing, prevalent, rampant, regnant, rife, ruling, state-of-the-art, swinging, topical, trendy, up-to-date, widespread; SEE CONCEPTS 530,820

curse [n1] hateful, swearing remark
anathema, ban, bane, blaspheming, blasphemy, commination, cursing, cussing*, cuss word*, damning, denunciation, dirty name*, dirty word*, double whammy*, execration, expletive, four-letter word*, fulmination, imprecation, malediction, malison, naughty words*, no-no*, oath, objuration, obloquy, obscenity, profanation, profanity, sacrilege, swearing, swear word, vilification, whammy*; SEE CONCEPTS 54,278

curse [n2] misfortune wished upon someone
affliction, bane, burden, calamity, cancer, cross, disaster, evil, evil eye*, hydra, jinx, ordeal, pestilence, plague, scourge, torment, tribulation, trouble, vexation, voodoo; SEE CONCEPTS 674,675

cursed [adj1] damned, doomed for bad ending
accursed, bedeviled, blankety-blank*, blasted, blessed, blighted, cast out, confounded, doggone*, excommunicate, execrable, fey, foredoomed, hell fire*, ill-fated, infernal, snakebit*, star-crossed, unholy, unsanctified, villainous, voodooed*; SEE CONCEPTS 548,571

cursed [adj2] detestable, hateful
abominable, accursed, atrocious, damnable, devilish, disgusting, execrable, fiendish, flatitous, heinous, infamous, infernal, loathsome, odious, pernicious, pestilential, vile; SEE CONCEPTS 404,571

cursory [adj] casual, hasty
brief, careless, depthless, desultory, fast, half-assed*, half-baked*, haphazard, hit or miss*, hurried, offhand, passing, perfunctory, quick, random, rapid, shallow, short, sketchy, slapdash, slight, sloppy, speedy, summary, superficial, swift, uncritical; SEE CONCEPTS 562,588,589

curt [adj] abrupt, rude
blunt, breviloquent, brief, brusque, churlish, compendiary, compendious, concise, crusty, gruff, imperious, laconic, offhand, peremptory, pithy, sharp, short, short and sweet, snappish, snippety, snippy, succinct, summary, tart, terse, unceremonious, uncivil, ungracious; SEE CONCEPT 267

curtail [v] cut short; abridge
abbreviate, boil down, chop, clip, contract, cramp, cut, cut back, decrease, diminish, dock, downsize, get to meat*, halt, lessen, lop, minify, pare down, put in nutshell*, reduce, retrench, roll back, shorten, slash, trim, truncate; SEE CONCEPTS 130,236,247

curtain [n] window covering
blind, decoration, drape, drapery, film, hanging,

jalousie, oleo, portiere, rag, roller, screen, shade, shield, shroud, shutter, valance, veil, Venetian blind; SEE CONCEPT **444**

curvaceous [adj] *voluptuous, full-figured*
bosomy, buxom, curvesome, curvilinear, curvy, rounded, shapely, statuesque, well-developed, well-proportioned, well-rounded, zaftig*; SEE CONCEPTS **406,490**

curvature [n] *rounded part of thing, usually body part*
arc, arch, arching, bend, bow, curve, curving, curvity, deflection, flexure, incurvation, round, shape; SEE CONCEPTS **754,757**

curve [n] *arched, rounded line or object*
ambit, arc, arch, bend, bight, bow, camber, catenary, chord, circle, circuit, circumference, compass, concavity, contour, crook, curlicue, curvation, curvature, ellipse, festoon, flexure, hairpin, half-moon, helix, horseshoe, hyperbola, incurvation, incurvature, loop, meniscus, ogee, parabola, quirk, rondure, round, sinuosity, sweep, swerve, trajectory, turn, vault, whorl; SEE CONCEPT **436**

curve [v] *bending in a shape or course*
arc, arch, bend, bow, buckle, bulge, coil, concave, convex, crook, crumple, curl, deviate, divert, gyrate, hook, incurve, inflect, loop, round, skew, snake, spiral, stoop, swerve, turn, twist, veer, wind, wreathe; SEE CONCEPTS **147,184, 213,738**

curved [adj] *bowed, bent*
arced, arched, arciform, arrondi, biflected, circular, compass, crooked, curly, curvaceous, curvilinear, declinate, elliptical, enbowed, humped, incurvate, incurved, looped, loopy, round, rounded, serpentine, sigmoid, sinuous, skewed, snaky, S-shaped, sweeping, swirly, turned, twisted, twisting, twisty, wreathed; SEE CONCEPTS **486,490**

cushion [n] *pillow, pad*
beanbag, bolster, buffer, bumper, fender, hassock, headrest, mat, rest, seat, sham, squab, woolsack; SEE CONCEPTS **444,464,484**

cushion [v] *pad, protect from blow*
bolster, buttress, cradle, dampen, deaden, insulate, muffle, pillow, seclude, soften, stifle, support, suppress; SEE CONCEPT **680**

custodian [n] *caretaker, maintenance person*
baby sitter, bodyguard, cerebus, claviger, cleaner, cleaning person, concierge, curator, escort, guardian, housesitter, keeper, maintenance person, manager, overseer, protector, sitter, steward, super*, superintendent, supervisor, swamper*, warden, watchdog, watchperson; SEE CONCEPT **348**

custody [n1] *supervision, charge of something*
aegis, auspices, care, conservation, custodianship, guardianship, keeping, management, observation, preservation, protection, safekeeping, salvation, superintendence, trusteeship, tutelage, ward, wardship, watch; SEE CONCEPTS **117,376,710**

custody [n2] *confinement, jailing*
arrest, detention, duress, imprisonment, incarceration, jail, keeping; SEE CONCEPTS **90,691**

custom [n1] *habitual action*
addiction, beaten path*, characteristic, consuetude, daily grind*, fashion, form, grind*, groove, habit, habitude, hang-up*, into*, manner, matter of course, mode, observance, practice, praxis, precedent, procedure, proprieties, routine, rule,

second nature*, shot, swim, thing, trick, usage, use, way, wont; SEE CONCEPT **633**

custom [n2] *ritual, traditional action*
attitude, canon, ceremony, character, convention, conventionalism, design, dictates, established way, etiquette, fashion, folkways, form, formality, inheritance, manner, matter of course, method, mode, mold, mores, observance, observation, pattern, performance, policy, practice, praxis, precedent, precept, rite, routine, rule, second nature*, style, system, taste, type, unwritten law, unwritten rule, usage, use, vogue, way; SEE CONCEPTS **644,688**

customarily [adv] *ordinarily; as a rule*
as a matter of course, as usual, commonly, consistently, conventionally, frequently, generally, habitually, naturally, normally, regularly, routinely, traditionally, usually, wontedly; SEE CONCEPTS **530,547**

customary [adj] *usual, established*
accepted, according to Hoyle*, accustomed, acknowledged, by the numbers*, chronic, common, confirmed, conventional, established, everyday, familiar, fashionable, frequent, general, habitual, household, in a rut*, in the groove*, normal, ordinary, orthodox, playing it safe*, popular, prescriptive, recognized, regular, regulation, routine, same old*, SOP*, standard, standard operating procedure*, stipulated, traditional, understood, universal, wonted; SEE CONCEPTS **530,547**

customer [n] *buyer of goods, services*
client, clientele, consumer, habitué, patron, prospect, purchaser, regular shopper; SEE CONCEPT **348**

cut [n1] *incision*
carving, chip, chop, cleavage, cleft, dissection, fissure, furrow, gash, graze, groove, intersection, kerf, laceration, mark, nick, nip, notch, opening, passage, penetration, pierce, prick, rabbet, rent, rip, scarification, sculpture, section, shave, slash, slit, slot, snip, stab, stroke, trench, trim, wound; SEE CONCEPT **309**

cut [n2] *reduction, diminution*
cutback, decrease, decrement, downsize, economy, fall, lessening, lowering, reduction, saving; SEE CONCEPTS **698,776**

cut [n3] *portion of profit*
allotment, allowance, bite, chop*, division, kickback*, lot, member, moiety, part, partage, percentage, piece, quota, section, segment, share, slice; SEE CONCEPT **344**

cut [n4] *style, shape of clothing*
configuration, construction, fashion, figure, form, look, mode; SEE CONCEPTS **655,754**

cut [n5] *insult*
abuse, hateful remark, indignity, offense; SEE CONCEPT **52**

cut [n6] *type, kind*
cast, description, feather, ilk, lot, mold, sort, stamp; SEE CONCEPT **378**

cut [v1] *sever, chop with sharp instrument; incise*
amputate, behead, bisect, bite, carve, chine, chip, chisel, cleave, clip, crop, curtail, decussate, dice, dissect, dissever, divide, facet, fell, flitch, gash, guillotine, hack, hash, hew, intersect, lacerate, lay open, lop, mince, mow, nick, notch, part, penetrate, perforate, pierce, prune, puncture, quarter, rabbet, reap, rend, rip, rive, saber, saw, scarify, scissor, score, scythe, separate, shave, shear, sickle, skive, slash, slice, slit, sliver, snip,

split, sunder, transect, truncate, whack; SEE CONCEPTS 137,176

cut [v2] *shorten, reduce*
abbreviate, abridge, bob, clip, condense, contract, crop, curtail, cut back, cut down, decrease, delete, dock, ease up, edit out, excise, lessen, lower, mark down, mow, pare, precis, ration, reduce, shave, slash, slim, trim, truncate; SEE CONCEPTS 236,247

cut [v3] *ignore, avoid*
cold-shoulder*, disregard, ditch*, duck, dump*, evade, freeze someone out*, grieve, hurt, insult, look straight through*, look the other way, neglect, ostracize, pain, play hooky*, play truant, shirk, skip, slam door on*, slight, snob, snub, spurn, stay away, sting, turn aside, turn one's back on, wound; SEE CONCEPTS 38,188,633

cut [v4] *dilute*
impair, thin, undermine, weaken; SEE CONCEPT 240

cutback [n] *reduction*
curtailment, cut, decrease, decrement, economy, lessening, retrenchment, shortening; SEE CONCEPTS 335,776

cut back [v] *economize*
abbreviate, abridge, check, clip, curb, curtail, cut, cut down, decrease, lessen, lower, mark down, mark off, pare, prune, reduce, retrench, shave, shorten, slash, trim; SEE CONCEPTS 236,247

cut down [v] *kill; fell*
dispatch, hew, level, lop, massacre, mow, mow down, raze, slaughter, slay; SEE CONCEPT 252

cute [adj] *perky, attractive*
adorable, beautiful, charming, dainty, delightful, pleasant, pretty; SEE CONCEPTS 404,579

cut in [v] *interrupt*
break in, butt in*, chisel in*, horn in*, interfere, interpose, intervene, intrude, move in, obtrude; SEE CONCEPT 234

cut off [v1] *prevent; interrupt*
block, break in, bring to end, catch, close off, disconnect, discontinue, halt, insulate, intercept, intersect, intervene, intrude, isolate, obstruct, renounce, segregate, separate, sequester, suspend; SEE CONCEPT 234

cut off [v2] *disinherit in will*
cut out of will, disown, renounce; SEE CONCEPT 317

cut out [v] *excise, remove*
carve, cease, delete, displace, eliminate, exclude, exsect, extirpate, extract, give up, oust, pull out, refrain from, sever, stop, supersede, supplant, usurp; SEE CONCEPT 211

cut out for [adj] *adapted*
adequate, competent, designed, equipped, fit, fitted, good for, qualified, suitable, suited; SEE CONCEPT 558

cut short [v] *bring to an end; leave unfinished*
abbreviate, abort, abridge, break off, check, diminish, end, finish, halt, hinder, intercept, interrupt, postpone, quit, shorten, stop, terminate; SEE CONCEPTS 121,234

cutting [adj] *nasty, hateful*
acerbic, acid, acrimonious, barbed, biting, bitter, caustic, clear-cut, crisp, hurtful, incisive, ingoing, malicious, penetrating, piercing, pointed, probing, raw, sarcastic, sardonic, scathing, severe, sharp, stinging, trenchant, wounding; SEE CONCEPT 267

cut up [v1] *make fun of; criticize*
censure, condemn, crucify, denounce, give a rough time*, knock, pan*, rap, reprehend, reprobate, ridicule, skin, vilify; SEE CONCEPT 52

cut up [v2] *be rowdy*
act up, caper, carry on*, cavort, clown, fool around, joke, misbehave, play, play jokes, romp, roughhouse, show off, whoop it up*; SEE CONCEPT 384

cut up [v3] *chop, mince*
carve, dice, divide, slice; SEE CONCEPT 176

cybernetics [n] *science studying brain function to design analagous mechanical systems*
artificial intelligence, automatic technology, automation, autonetics, electronic communication, radiodynamics, robotization, telemechanics; SEE CONCEPTS 274,349

cycle [n] *era, phase*
aeon, age, alternation, chain, circle, circuit, course, eon, isochronism, loop, orbit, period, periodicity, revolution, rhythm, ring, rotation, round, run, sequel, sequence, series, succession, wheel; SEE CONCEPTS 816,817

cynic [n] *nonbeliever*
carper, caviler, detractor, disbeliever, doubter, doubting Thomas*, egoist, egotist, flouter, misanthrope, misanthropist, misogamist, misogynist, mocker, pessimist, questioner, satirist, scoffer, skeptic, sneerer, unbeliever; SEE CONCEPTS 361,423

cynical [adj] *nonbelieving; doubtful*
contemptuous, derisive, ironic, misanthropic, misanthropical, mocking, pessimistic, sarcastic, sardonic, scoffing, scornful, skeptical, sneering, suspicious, unbelieving, wry; SEE CONCEPTS 267,403

cyst [n] *unusual growth*
bag, bleb, blister, injury, pouch, sac, sore, vesicle, wen; SEE CONCEPT 306

D

dab [n] *small quantity*
bit, blob, dollop, drop, fleck, flick, pat, peck, smidgen, smudge, speck, spot, stroke, tap, touch; SEE CONCEPT 835

dab [v] *blot up; touch lightly*
bedaub, besmear, daub, pat, peck, plaster, smear, smudge, stipple, swab, tap, wipe; SEE CONCEPT 612

dabble [v] *play at; tinker*
amuse oneself with, be amateur, dally, dilly-dally*, fiddle with*, flirt with*, horse around*, idle, kid around*, mess around*, monkey*, monkey around*, muck around*, not be serious*, play, play around*, play games with, toy with, trifle, trifle with, work superficially; SEE CONCEPT 87

dabbler [n] *amateur*
abecedarian, beginner, dilettante, loafer, nonprofessional, novice, potterer, pretender, smatterer, tinkerer, trifler, tyro, uninitiate; SEE CONCEPTS 348,366

daft [adj] *stupid; crazy*
absurd, asinine, bedlamite, bonkers, cracked*,

crackers*, daffy*, demented, deranged, dopey*, flaky*, foolish, fried*, giddy, half-baked*, idiotic, inane, insane, in the ozone*, lunatic, mad, mental*, nuts, nutty*, off the wall*, out of one's gourd*, ridiculous, screwy*, silly, simple, touched, unbalanced, unhinged*, unsound, wacky, whacko*, witless; SEE CONCEPT 403

daily [*adj*] *occurring every day; during the day*
circadian, common, commonplace, constantly, cyclic, day after day, day by day, day-to-day, diurnal, everyday, from day to day, often, once a day, once daily, ordinary, per diem, periodic, quotidian, regular, regularly, routine; SEE CONCEPTS 541,801

dainty [*adj1*] *delicate, fragile, fine*
airy, attractive, beautiful, bonny, charming, choice, comely, cute, darling, delectable, delicious, delightful, diaphanous, elegant, ethereal, exquisite, fair, feeble, frail, graceful, lacy, light, lovely, neat, nice, palatable, petite, pleasing, precious, pretty, rare, recherché, refined, savory, select, soft, subtle, superior, sweet, tasteful, tasty, tender, thin, toothsome, trim, well-made; SEE CONCEPTS 490,491,606

dainty [*adj2*] *finicky, particular*
acute, choosy, delicate, fastidious, finical, finicking, fussy, mincing, nice, perceptive, persnickety*, refined, scrupulous, tasteful; SEE CONCEPT 404

dairy [*n*] *producer of milk products*
buttery, cow barn, creamery, dairy farm, factory, farm, pasteurizing plant; SEE CONCEPTS 449,517

dalliance [*n1*] *dawdling*
dabbling, delay, delaying, dilly-dallying*, frittering, frivoling, idling, loafing, loitering, playing, poking*, procrastinating, procrastination, puttering, toying, trifling; SEE CONCEPTS 151,210,681

dalliance [*n2*] *love affair*
affair, a little on the side*, amorous play, carrying on*, fling, fooling around*, frolicking, hankypanky*, messing around*, relationship, seduction, toying*, working late at office*; SEE CONCEPTS 114,375,388

dally [*v1*] *dawdle, delay*
boondoggle*, drag, fool around, fool with, fritter away, hang about*, horse around*, idle, jerk off*, lag, linger, loiter, lollygag*, play around*, play games with*, procrastinate, put off, putter, tarry, trail, trifle with, waste time, while away; SEE CONCEPTS 151,210,681

dally/dally with [*v2*] *have love affair*
be insincere with, carry on, cosset, fool around*, frivol, frolic, gambol, have a fling, lead on, play around*, rollick, romp, tamper, wanton; SEE CONCEPTS 114,375

dam [*n*] *embankment, wall*
bank, barrage, barrier, dike, ditch, gate, grade, hindrance, levee, milldam, millpond, obstruction, weir; SEE CONCEPT 470

dam [*v*] *hold back; block*
bar, barricade, brake, check, choke, clog, close, confine, hinder, hold in, impede, obstruct, repress, restrain, restrict, retard, slow, stop up, suppress; SEE CONCEPTS 130,191

damage [*n1*] *injury, loss*
accident, adulteration, adversity, affliction, bane, blemish, blow, breakage, bruise, casualty, catastrophe, cave-in, contamination, corruption, debasement, depreciation, deprivation, destruction, deterioration, detriment, devastation, disservice,

disturbance, evil, hardship, harm, hurt, illness, impairment, infliction, knockout, marring, mischief, mishap, mutilation, outrage, pollution, ravage, reverse, ruin, ruining, spoilage, stroke, suffering, waste, wound, wreckage, wrecking, wrong; SEE CONCEPTS 309,674

damage(s) [*n2*] *cost for problem*
amends, bill, charge, compensation, expense, fine, forfeit, indemnity, reimbursement, reparation, satisfaction, total; SEE CONCEPTS 123,329

damage [*v*] *cause injury, loss*
abuse, bang up*, batter, bleach, blight, break, burn, contaminate, corrode, corrupt, crack, cripple, deface, defile, dirty, discolor, disfigure, disintegrate, dismantle, fade, gnaw, harm, hurt, impair, incapacitate, infect, injure, lacerate, maim, maltreat, mangle, mar, mutilate, pollute, ravage, rot, ruin, rust, scathe, scorch, scratch, smash, split, spoil, stab, stain, tamper with, tarnish, tear, undermine, vitiate, weaken, wear away, wound, wreak havoc on*, wreck, wrong; SEE CONCEPTS 246,252

damaged [*adj*] *broken, not working*
beat-up, bent, blemished, busted, dinged, down, flawed, flubbed*, fouled up, glitched*, gone, hurt, impaired, imperfect, injured, in need of repair, in poor condition, in smithereens*, kaput*, loused up*, marred, messed up*, mucked up*, no go*, on the blink*, on the fritz*, out of action*, out of kilter*, out of whack*, run-down, screwed up*, shot, snafued*, spoiled, sunk*, totaled*, unsound; SEE CONCEPTS 485,560

damaging [*adj*] *hurtful to reputation*
bad, deleterious, detrimental, disadvantageous, evil, harmful, injurious, mischievous, nocent, nocuous, prejudicial, ruinous; SEE CONCEPT 537

damn [*v*] *condemn, denounce*
abuse, anathematize, attack, ban, banish, blaspheme, blast, castigate, cast out, censure, complain of, confound, convict, criticize, cry down, curse, cuss*, darn, denunciate, doom, drat, excommunicate, excoriate, execrate, expel, flame, fulminate against, imprecate, inveigh against, jinx, object to, objurgate, pan*, penalize, proscribe, punish, revile, sentence, slam, swear, thunder against*; SEE CONCEPTS 52,54

damnable [*adj*] *atrocious, horrible*
abhorrent, abominable, accursed, blamed, blessed, culpable, cursed, dang*, darn, depraved, despicable, detestable, dratted, execrable, hateful, odious, offensive, outrageous, wicked; SEE CONCEPTS 545,570

damned [*adj*] *hateful, unwelcome*
accursed, all-fired*, anathematized, bad, blankety-blank*, blasted, blessed*, bloody*, blooming*, condemned, confounded, cursed, cussed*, damnable, dang*, darn*, darned*, despicable, detestable, doggone*, done for*, doomed, dratted*, execrable, gone to blazes*, infamous, infernal*, loathsome, lost, lousy, reprobate, revolting, unhappy, voodooed*; SEE CONCEPTS 545,570

damp [*adj*] *wet, humid*
clammy, cloudy, dank, dewy, drenched, dripping, drippy, drizzly, irriguous, misty, moist, muggy, oozy, saturated, soaked, soaking, sodden, soggy, sopping, steam bath*, steamy, sticky, vaporous, waterlogged, wettish; SEE CONCEPT 603

dampen [*v1*] *make wet*
bedew, besprinkle, dabble, humidify, moisten,

cu
da

rinse, spray, sprinkle, water, wet; SEE CONCEPT 256

dampen [v2] *spoil spirits*
allay, check, chill, cloud, cool, curb, dash, deaden, deject, depress, diminish, discourage, dismay, dispirit, dull, humble, inhibit, moderate, muffle, mute, restrain, stifle; SEE CONCEPTS 7,19

dance [n1/v] *moving feet and body to music*
bob*, boogie, boogie down*, bunny hop, caper, careen, cavort, Charleston, conga, cut a rug*, disco, flit*, foot it*, foxtrot, frolic, gambol, get down*, hoof it*, hop, hustle, jig, jitter*, jitterbug, jive*, jump, leap, one-step, prance, promenade, rhumba, rock, rock 'n' roll, samba, shimmy, skip, spin, step, strut, sway, swing, tango, tap, tread, trip, trip the light fantastic*, twist, two-step, waltz, whirl; SEE CONCEPTS 292,363

dance [n2] *party for moving to music*
ball, brawl, disco, formal, hoedown, hop, jump, masquerade, mingle, prom, promenade, shindig, social, sock hop; SEE CONCEPT 383

dandle [v] *caress, cuddle*
amuse, cosset, cradle, dance, fondle, love, nuzzle, pet, play, ride on knee, rock, toss, toy*, toy with*; SEE CONCEPTS 147,190

dandy [adj] *fine, excellent*
capital, cool*, exemplary, famous, first-class, first-rate, five-star*, fly*, glorious, grand, great, groovy*, hunky-dory*, keen, marvelous, model, neat, nifty, paragon, peachy*, prime, splendid, superior, swell, terrific; SEE CONCEPT 574

danger [n] *hazard, troublesome situation*
clouds, crisis, double trouble*, dynamite, emergency, endangerment, exigency, exposure, hot potato*, insecurity, instability, jeopardy, menace, peril, pitfall, possibility, precariousness, precipice, probability, risk, risky business*, slipperiness, storm, thin ice*, threat, uncertainty, venture, vulnerability; SEE CONCEPT 675

dangerous [adj] *hazardous, troubling*
alarming, bad, breakneck*, chancy, critical, dangersome, deadly, delicate, dynamite, exposed, fatal, formidable, hairy*, heavy*, hot*, impending, impregnable, insecure, jeopardous, loaded, malignant, menacing, mortal, nasty, on collision course*, parlous, perilous, portentous, precarious, pressing, queasy, risky, serious, serpentine, shaky, speculative, terrible, thorny*, threatening, ticklish*, touch-and-go*, touchy, treacherous, ugly*, unhealthy, unsafe, unstable, urgent, viperous, vulnerable, wicked; SEE CONCEPT 548

dangerously [adv] *precariously*
alarmingly, carelessly, critically, daringly, desperately, gravely, harmfully, hazardously, perilously, precariously, recklessly, riskily, seriously, severely, unsafely, unsecurely; SEE CONCEPT 548

dangle [v] *suspend*
brandish, depend, droop, entice, flap, flaunt, flourish, hang, hang down, lure, sling, sway, swing, tantalize, tempt, trail, wave; SEE CONCEPTS 153,190

dank [adj] *clammy*
chilly, close, damp, dewy, dripping, humid, moist, muggy, slimy, soggy, steamy, sticky, wet, wettish; SEE CONCEPT 603

dapper [adj] *well-groomed, neat*
bandbox, brisk, chic, chichi, classy, clean, dainty, dashing, doggy*, dressed to kill*, dressed to nines*, jaunty, natty, nice, nifty, nimble, nobby, posh, prim, rakish, ritzy, sassy, sharp, showy, smart, snazzy*, snug, spiff, spiffy, spruce, spry, stylish, swank, swanky, swell, trim, turned out, well turned out; SEE CONCEPT 579

dappled [adj] *mottled, freckled*
brindle, brindled, checkered, discolored, flecked, motley, multicolor, multicolored, multihued, parti-colored, piebald, pied, speckled, spotted, stippled, varicolored, variegated, versicolor, versicolored; SEE CONCEPT 618

dare [n] *challenge, defiance*
cartel, defy, provocation, stump, taunt; SEE CONCEPTS 53,87

dare [v1] *challenge, defy someone*
beard, brave, bully, call one's bluff, confront, cope, denounce, disregard, face, face off, front, goad, insult, knock chip off shoulder*, laugh at, make my day*, meet, mock, muster courage, oppose, outdare, provoke, resist, run the gauntlet, scorn, spurn, square off, step over the line, take one on, taunt, threaten, throw down gauntlet; SEE CONCEPTS 14,53

dare [v2] *take a risk; be courageous*
adventure, attempt, be bold, brave, endanger, endeavor, gamble, go ahead, hazard, make bold, pluck up, presume, risk, run the risk, speculate, stake, take a chance, take heart, try, try one's hand*, undertake, venture; SEE CONCEPTS 35,87

daring [adj] *adventurous*
adventuresome, audacious, bold, brassy*, brave, cheeky, cocky, courageous, crusty, fearless, fire eating*, foolhardy, forward, game, go for broke*, gritty, gutsy*, gutty*, hot shot*, impudent, impulsive, intrepid, nervy, obtrusive, out on a limb*, plucky, rash, reckless, salty*, smart, smart-alecky*, spunky*, temerarious, valiant, venturesome; SEE CONCEPT 401

dark [n1] *place, time without light*
caliginosity, darkness, dead of night, dimness, dusk, duskiness, evening, gloom, midnight, murk, murkiness, night, nightfall, nighttime, obscurity, opacity, semidarkness, shade, shadows, twilight, witching hour; SEE CONCEPTS 620,810

dark [n2] *ignorance; mystery*
concealment, denseness, inscrutability, seclusion, secrecy, thickness; SEE CONCEPTS 409,410

dark [adj1] *lack of light*
aphotic, atramentous, black, blackish, caliginous, Cimmerian, clouded, cloudy, crepuscular, darkened, dim, dingy, drab, dull, dun, dusk, dusky, faint, foggy, gloomy, grimy, ill-lighted, indistinct, inky, lightless, lurid, misty, murky, nebulous, obfuscous, obscure, overcast, pitch-black, pitch-dark, pitchy, rayless, shaded, shadowy, shady, somber, sooty, stygian, sunless, tenebrous, unlighted, unlit, vague; SEE CONCEPT 617

dark [adj2] *shaded complexion, hair*
adumbral, bistered, black, brunet, brunette, dark-complexioned, dark-skinned, dusky, ebon, ebony, sable, swart, swarthy, tan; SEE CONCEPTS 406,618

dark [adj3] *hidden, secret*
abstruse, anagogic, arcane, cabalistic, complicated, concealed, cryptic, deep, Delphian, enigmatic, esoteric, intricate, knotty, mysterious, mystic, mystical, mystifying, not known, obscure, occult, puzzling, recondite; SEE CONCEPTS 402,576,582

dark [adj4] grim, hopeless
bleak, cheerless, dismal, doleful, drab, foreboding, gloomy, joyless, morbid, morose, mournful, ominous, sinister, somber, unpropitious; SEE CONCEPT 548

dark [adj5] evil, satanic
atrocious, bad, corrupt, damnable, foul, hellish, horrible, immoral, infamous, infernal, nefarious, sinful, sinister, vile, wicked; SEE CONCEPT 545

dark [adj6] ignorant
benighted, uncultivated, unenlightened, unlettered, unread; SEE CONCEPT 402

dark [adj7] angry, upset
dour, forbidding, frowning, glowering, glum, ominous, scowling, sulky, sullen, threatening; SEE CONCEPT 401

darken [v] become shaded, unlit
becloud, bedim, blacken, cloud over, cloud up, deepen, dim, eclipse, fog, gray, haze, make dim, murk, obfuscate, obscure, overcast, overshadow, shade, shadow, tone down*; SEE CONCEPTS 250,469

darkness [n1] place, time that is unlit
black, blackness, blackout, brownout, caliginosity, Cimmerian shade, cloudiness, crepuscule, dark, dimness, dusk, duskiness, eclipse, gloom, lightlessness, murk, murkiness, nightfall, obscurity, pitch darkness, shade, shadiness, shadows, smokiness, tenebrosity, twilight; SEE CONCEPT 620

darkness [n2] ignorance; mystery
blindness, concealment, denseness, inscrutability, isolation, privacy, seclusion, secrecy, unawareness; SEE CONCEPTS 409,410

darling [n] sweetheart, favorite person
angel*, apple of one's eye*, baby*, beloved, boyfriend, dear, dearest, dearie*, dear one, fair-haired boy*, flame, friend, girlfriend, heart's desire*, honeybunch, lamb*, light of my life*, love, lover, one and only*, pet*, precious, sugar*, sweetie, treasure*, truelove; SEE CONCEPT 423

dart [v] race away; propel
bound, career, cast, course, dash, flash, fling, flit, float, fly, gallop, hasten, heave, hurry, hurtle, launch, move quickly, pitch, plunge, run, rush, sail, scamper, scoot, scud, scurry, shoot, skim, speed, spring, sprint, spurt, start, tear, throw, thrust, whiz; SEE CONCEPTS 150,195,222

dash [n1] fast race for short distance
birr, bolt, dart, haste, onset, run, rush, sortie, sprint, spurt, zip; SEE CONCEPT 150

dash [n2] flair, style
animation, birr, brio, éclat, élan, energy, esprit, flourish, force, impressiveness, intensity, life, might, oomph*, panache, power, spirit, strength, vehemence, verve, vigor, vim, vivacity, zing, zip; SEE CONCEPTS 411,655,673

dash [n3] small amount; suggestion
bit, drop, few drops, flavor, grain, hint, lick, little, part, pinch, scattering, seasoning, smack, smidgen, soupçon, sprinkle, sprinkling, squirt, streak, suspicion, taste, tincture, tinge, touch, trace, trifle, zest; SEE CONCEPT 831

dash [v1] run very fast for short distance
boil, bolt, bound, career, charge, chase, course, dart, fly, gallop, get on it*, haste, hasten, hurry, lash, make a run for it*, make it snappy*, race, rush, rush at, scamper, scoot, scurry, shoot, speed, spring, sprint, tear; SEE CONCEPT 150

dash [v2] break by hitting or throwing violently
beat, bludgeon, cast, charge, crash, cudgel, destroy, fling, hit, hurl, hurtle, lunge, plunge, shatter, shiver, slam, sling, smash, splash, splatter, splinter, throw; SEE CONCEPTS 189,222,248

dash [v3] discourage, frustrate
abash, baffle, balk, beat, bilk, blast, blight, chagrin, chill, circumvent, cloud, confound, dampen, disappoint, discomfort, dismay, dispirit, foil, nip, ruin, spoil, thwart; SEE CONCEPTS 7,19,121

dashing [adj] bold, flamboyant
adventurous, alert, animated, chic, dapper, daring, dazzling, debonair, elegant, exclusive, exuberant, fashionable, fearless, gallant, gay, jaunty, keen, lively, modish, plucky, rousing, showy, smart, spirited, sporty, stylish, swank, swashbuckling, swish, vivacious; SEE CONCEPTS 404,589

data [n] information in visible form
abstracts, brass tacks*, chapter and verse*, circumstances, compilations, conclusions, details, documents, dope, dossier, evidence, experiments, facts, figures, goods, info, input, knowledge, materials, measurements, memorandums, notes, picture, proof, reports, results, scoop, score, statistics, testimony, whole story*; SEE CONCEPT 274

date [n1] point in time; particular day or time
age, century, course, day, duration, epoch, era, generation, hour, juncture, moment, period, quarter, reign, span, spell, stage, term, time, while, year; SEE CONCEPTS 800,801,802,815

date [n2] social engagement
appointment, assignation, call, interview, meeting, rendezvous, tryst, visit; SEE CONCEPTS 114,386

date [n3] person accompanying another socially
blind date, boyfriend, companion, escort, friend, girlfriend, lover, partner, steady, sweetheart; SEE CONCEPT 423

date [v1] assign a time
affix a date to, belong to, carbon-date, chronicle, come from, determine, exist from, fix, fix the date of, isolate, mark, measure, originate in, put in its place, record, register; SEE CONCEPTS 18,37

date [v2] see person socially
associate with, attend, consort with, court, deuce it*, escort, fix up, go around together*, go around with*, go out with, go steady, go together, keep company, make a date, see, step around, take out, woo; SEE CONCEPT 114

date [v3] become obsolete
antiquate, archaize, obsolesce, obsolete, outdate, show one's age; SEE CONCEPT 105

daub [v] coat; make dirty
begrime, besmear, bespray, blur, cover, dab, deface, dirty, fleck, grime, paint, plaster, slap on, smear, smirch, smudge, spatter, speckle, splatter, spot, spread, stain, sully, variegate, varnish; SEE CONCEPTS 172,250

daunt [v] frighten, alarm
appall, baffle, browbeat, bully, consternate, cow, deter, discourage, dishearten, dismay, dispirit, foil, horrify, intimidate, overawe, put off*, scare, shake, subdue, terrify, thwart; SEE CONCEPTS 7,19

dauntless [adj] bold, courageous
aweless, brave, daring, doughty, fearless, gallant, game, heroic, indomitable, intrepid, invincible, lionhearted, resolute, stouthearted, unafraid, un-

da
da

conquerable, undaunted, unfearing, unflinching, valiant, valorous; SEE CONCEPT *401*

dawdle [v] *delay; waste time*
amble, bum around*, dally, diddle-daddle*, dilly-dally*, drag, fool around*, fritter away*, get no place fast*, goof off*, hang around*, hang out*, idle, lag, laze, lazy, loaf, loiter, loll, lounge, mosey*, poke*, procrastinate, put off, saunter, scrounge around, shlep along*, sit around*, sit on one's butt*, stay, stroll, tarry, toddle, trifle, wait, warm a chair*; SEE CONCEPTS *210,681*

dawn [n1] *beginning of day*
aurora, break of day, bright, cockcrow, crack of dawn, dawning, daybreak, daylight, day peep, early bright, first blush, first light, light, morn, morning, sunrise, sunup, wee hours*; SEE CONCEPTS *810,815*

dawn [n2] *a beginning*
advent, alpha, birth, commencement, dawning, emergence, foundation, genesis, head, inception, onset, opening, origin, outset, outstart, rise, source, start, unfolding; SEE CONCEPT *832*

dawn [v] *start*
appear, begin, develop, emerge, glimmer, initiate, lighten, loom, open, originate, rise, show itself, unfold; SEE CONCEPT *119*

day [n1] *light part of every 24 hours*
astronomical day, bright, dawn-to-dark, daylight, daytime, diurnal course, early bright, light, light of day, mean solar day, nautical day, sidereal day, sunlight, sunrise-to-sunset, sunshine, working day; SEE CONCEPTS *801,803,810,821*

day [n2] *era*
age, ascendancy, cycle, epoch, generation, height, heyday, period, prime, term, time, years, zenith; SEE CONCEPTS *802,816*

daybreak [n] *beginning of light hours*
aurora, break of day, bright, cockcrow, crack of dawn, dawn, dawning, daylight, day peep, dayspring, early bright, first light, first light, morn, morning, sunrise, sunup; SEE CONCEPTS *810,815*

daydream [n] *fantasy thought of when awake*
castle in the air*, conceiving, dream, fancy, fancying, figment of imagination, fond hope, fool's paradise*, head trip*, imagination, imagining, in a zone*, mind trip*, musing, phantasm, phantasy, pie in the sky*, pipe dream, reverie, stargazing, trip*, vision, wish, woolgathering; SEE CONCEPT *529*

daydream [v] *make up fantasy*
build castles in air*, conceive, dream, envision, fancy, fantasize, hallucinate, imagine, moon, muse, pipe dream*, stargaze, trip out*, woolgather; SEE CONCEPTS *17,36*

daylight [n] *light part of 24 hours*
aurora, dawn, day, daybreak, daytime, during the day, light, light of day, sunlight, sunrise, sunshine; SEE CONCEPT *810*

daze [n] *confusion*
befuddlement, bewilderment, distraction, gauze, glaze, haze, lala-land*, maze, muddledness, nadaville*, narcosis, shock, stupefaction, stupor, trance; SEE CONCEPT *410*

daze [v] *confuse, shock*
addle, amaze, astonish, astound, befog, befuddle, benumb, bewilder, blind, blur, confound, dazzle, disorder, distract, dizzy, dumbfound, flabbergast, fuddle, mix up, muddle, mystify, numb, overpower, overwhelm, paralyze, perplex, petrify,

puzzle, rock, stagger, startle, stun, stupefy, surprise; SEE CONCEPTS *16,42*

dazzle [v] *confuse, amaze*
astonish, awe, bedazzle, blind, blur, bowl over*, daze, excite, fascinate, glitz*, hypnotize, impress, overawe, overpower, overwhelm, razzle-dazzle, strike dumb*, stupefy, surprise; SEE CONCEPTS *16,42*

dead [adj1] *no longer alive*
asleep, bereft of life, bloodless, bought the farm*, breathless, buried, cadaverous, checked out*, cold, cut off, deceased, defunct, departed, done for*, erased, expired, extinct, gone, gone to meet maker*, gone to reward*, inanimate, inert, late, lifeless, liquidated, mortified, no more, not existing, offed*, out of one's misery*, passed away, perished, pushing up daisies*, reposing, resting in peace, spiritless, stiff, unanimated, wasted; SEE CONCEPT *539*

dead [adj2] *indifferent, cold*
anesthetized, apathetic, asleep, boring, callous, deadened, dull, flat, frigid, glazed, inert, insensitive, insipid, lukewarm, numb, numbed, paralyzed, senseless, spiritless, stagnant, stale, still, tasteless, torpid, unfeeling, uninteresting, unresponsive, vapid, wooden; SEE CONCEPT *550*

dead [adj3] *not working*
barren, bygone, defunct, departed, exhausted, extinct, gone, inactive, inoperable, inoperative, lost, obsolete, spent, stagnant, sterile, still, tired, unemployed, unprofitable, useless, vanished, wearied, worn, worn out; SEE CONCEPT *560*

dead [adj4] *complete, total*
absolute, bloody, downright, entire, final, out-and-out*, outright, perfect, sure, thorough, unconditional, unmitigated, unqualified, utter, whole; SEE CONCEPT *531*

dead [adv] *completely, totally*
absolutely, direct, directly, due, entirely, exactly, right, straight, straightly, undeviatingly, wholly; SEE CONCEPTS *531,772*

deaden [v] *diminish, muffle, quiet*
abate, alleviate, anesthetize, benumb, blunt, check, chloroform, consume, cushion, damp, dampen, depress, deprive, desensitize, destroy, devitalize, dim, dope, drown, dull, etherize, exhaust, freeze, frustrate, gas, hush, impair, incapacitate, injure, knock out, KO*, lay out, lessen, mute, numb, paralyze, put out of order*, put to sleep, quieten, reduce, repress, retard, slow, smother, soften, stifle, stun, stupefy, suppress, tire, tone down, unnerve, weaken; SEE CONCEPTS *130,240*

deadlock [n] *stalemate, impasse*
box*, Catch-22*, cessation, checkmate, corner, dead end, dead heat, dilemma, draw, full stop, gridlock, halt, hole, pause, pickle, plight, posture, predicament, quandary, standoff, standstill, tie, wall*; SEE CONCEPT *674*

deadly [adj1] *causing end of life*
baleful, baneful, bloodthirsty, bloody, cannibalistic, carcinogenic, cruel, dangerous, death-dealing, deathly, deleterious, destroying, destructive, fatal, grim, harmful, homicidal, injurious, internecine, killing, lethal, malignant, mortal, mortiferous, murderous, noxious, pernicious, pestiferous, pestilent, pestilential, poisonous, ruthless, savage, slaying, suicidal, toxic, unrelenting, venomous, violent, virulent; SEE CONCEPT *537*

deadly [adj2] *ghostly*
ashen, corpselike, dead, deadened, deathful, deathlike, deathly, ghastly, pallid, wan, white; SEE CONCEPT 539

deaf [adj1] *without hearing*
deafened, earless, hard of hearing, stone deaf*, unable to hear; SEE CONCEPT 591

deaf [adj2] *unwilling to listen*
blind, bullheaded*, headstrong, indifferent, intractable, mulish*, oblivious, obstinate, pertinacious, perverse, pigheaded*, self-willed, strong-willed, stubborn, unaware, unconcerned, unhearing, unmoved; SEE CONCEPT 401

deal [n1] *agreement, bargain*
accord, arrangement, buy, compromise, conception, contract, pact, pledge, prearrangement, transaction, understanding; SEE CONCEPT 684

deal [n2] *amount, share*
abundance, degree, distribution, extent, plenty, plethora, portion, quantity, shake, superabundance, transaction; SEE CONCEPTS 344,787,835

deal [n3] *distribution of playing cards*
appointment, chance, cut and shuffle*, fresh start, game, hand, opportunity, round; SEE CONCEPT 363

deal/deal with [v1] *handle, manage*
act, approach, attend to, behave, behave toward, clear, concern, conduct oneself, consider, control, cope with, direct, discuss, get a handle on something*, hack it*, handle, have to do with, take with*, make a go of it*, make it*, oversee, play, review, rid, see to, serve, take, take care of, treat, unburden, use; SEE CONCEPTS 94,117

deal [v2] *do business*
hargain, barter, bicker, buy and sell, dicker*, hammer out deal*, handle, horse trade*, knock down price*, negotiate, sell, stock, swap, trade, traffic, treat, work out deal; SEE CONCEPT 324

deal [v3] *distribute*
administer, allot, apportion, assign, bestow, come across with*, deliver, disburse, dish out*, dispense, disperse, disseminate, divide, divvy*, dole out*, drop, fork out*, fork over*, give, hand out, impart, inflict, measure, mete out, partake, participate, partition, render, reward, share, strike; SEE CONCEPTS 108,140

dealer [n] *business owner*
banker, bursar, businessperson, chandler, changer, dispenser, marketer, merchandiser, merchant, retailer, trader, tradesperson, trafficker, vendor, wholesaler; SEE CONCEPT 347

dealings [n] *business relations*
affairs, balls in air*, business, commerce, concerns, doings, intercourse, irons in fire*, matters, proceedings, ropes*, sale, strings*, things, trade, traffic, transactions, truck, wire pulling*, wires*; SEE CONCEPT 324

dean [n] *leader of institution*
administrator, authority, dignitary, doyen, ecclesiastic, guide, lead, legislator, pilot, president, principal, professor, senior, tack; SEE CONCEPT 350

dear [n] *beloved person*
darling, favorite, heartthrob, honey, love, loved one, lover, pet, precious, sweetheart, treasure; SEE CONCEPT 423

dear [adj1] *beloved, favorite*
cherished, close, darling, doll face, endeared, esteemed, familiar, intimate, loved, pet, precious,

prized, respected, treasured; SEE CONCEPTS 555,567

dear [adj2] *very expensive*
an arm and a leg*, at a premium, cher*, costly, fancy, high, high-priced, out of sight*, overpriced, pretty penny*, pricey*, prized, steep, stiff*, valuable; SEE CONCEPT 334

dearly [adv1] *extremely*
greatly, profoundly, to a great extent, very, very much; SEE CONCEPT 772

dearly [adv2] *lovingly*
affectionately, devotedly, fondly, tenderly, yearningly; SEE CONCEPT 403

dearth [n] *insufficiency, scarcity*
absence, default, defect, deficiency, exiguousness, famine, inadequacy, infrequency, lack, meagerness, miss, need, paucity, poverty, privation, rareness, scantiness, scantness, shortage, slim pickings*, sparsity, uncommonness, want; SEE CONCEPTS 646,674,709

death [n] *end of life*
afterlife, annihilation, bereavement, casualty, cessation, curtains*, darkness, decease, demise, departure, destruction, dissolution, downfall, dying, end, ending, eradication, eternal rest, euthanasia, exit, expiration, extermination, extinction, fatality, finis*, finish, grave, grim reaper*, heaven, loss, mortality, necrosis, obliteration, oblivion, paradise, parting, passing, passing over, quietus, release, repose, ruin, ruination, silence, sleep, termination, tomb; SEE CONCEPT 304

deathly [adj1] *suggesting end of life*
appalling, cadaverous, corpselike, deathlike, defunctive, dreadful, gaunt, ghastly, grim, gruesome, haggard, horrible, macabre, pale, pallid, wan, wasted; SEE CONCEPTS 579,618

deathly [adj2] *fatal*
deadly, extreme, intense, lethal, mortal, mortiferous, noxious, pestilent, pestilential, terrible; SEE CONCEPT 537

debacle [n] *catastrophe*
beating, blue ruin*, breakdown, collapse, crackup*, crash, defeasance, defeat, devastation, disaster, dissolution, downfall, drubbing, failure, fiasco, havoc, licking, overthrow, reversal, rout, ruin, ruination, shellacking*, smash, smashup, trouncing, vanquishment, washout, wreck; SEE CONCEPT 674

debase [v1] *degrade, shame*
abase, bemean, cast down, cheapen, corrupt, cripple, debauch, debilitate, demean, demoralize, deprave, devaluate, devalue, disable, disgrace, dishonor, drag down*, dump on*, enfeeble, fluff off*, humble, humiliate, lower, put away, put down, reduce, sap, shoot down, sink, take down*, take down a peg*, undermine, weaken; SEE CONCEPTS 7,19,52,54

debase [v2] *adulterate*
abase, animalize, bastardize, bestialize, contaminate, corrupt, damage, defile, depreciate, doctor, dope up*, impair, load, pervert, pollute, sophisticate, spoil, taint, vitiate, weight, worsen; SEE CONCEPTS 240,250

debatable [adj] *controversial*
arguable, between rock and hard place*, between sixes and sevens*, betwixt and between*, bone of contention*, borderline, chancy*, contestable, disputable, doubtful, dubious, iffy*, in dispute, moot, mootable*, open to question, problematic, problematical, questionable, the jury's out*, touch

and go*, uncertain, undecided, unsettled, up for discussion; SEE CONCEPTS 267,535

debate [n] *discussion of issues; consideration*
agitation, altercation, argument, argumentation, blah-blah*, cogitation, contention, contest, controversy, controverting, deliberation, dialectic, disputation, dispute, forensic, hassle, match, meditation, mooting, polemic, rebutting, reflection, refuting, tiff, words, wrangle; SEE CONCEPTS 56,532

debate [v] *argue, discuss*
agitate, altercate, answer, bandy, bicker, bump heads*, canvass, chew the fat*, cogitate, confab*, confute, consider, contend, contest, controvert, cross swords*, deliberate, demonstrate, differ, discept, disprove, dispute, hammer away at*, hash over*, hassle, have at it*, kick around*, knock around*, lock horns*, moot, oppose, pettifog, pick a bone*, prove, put up argument, question, reason, rebut, refute, rehash, set to, talk back*, talk game*, thrash out*, toss around*, wrangle; SEE CONCEPTS 24,56

debauch [v] *deprave, corrupt*
abuse, bastardize, bestialize, betray, brutalize, debase, defile, deflower, demoralize, fornicate, fraternize, go bad*, go to hell*, intrigue, inveigle, lead astray*, live in the gutter*, lure, pervert, pollute, ravish, ruin, seduce, subvert, tempt, violate, vitiate, warp; SEE CONCEPTS 14,240,375

debauched [adj] *violated, corrupted*
abandoned, corrupt, debased, defiled, degenerate, degraded, depraved, deteriorated, dissipated, dissolute, fast, gone bad*, gone to the dogs*, immoral, in the gutter*, licentious, perverted, profligate, reprobate, vitiate, vitiated, wanton, wicked; SEE CONCEPT 545

debauchery [n] *immoral self-indulgence*
bender*, binge, blowout*, burning candle at both ends*, bust, carousal, depravity, dissipation, dissoluteness, drunk*, excess, fast living*, fornication, gluttony, incontinence, indulgence, intemperance, intimacy, la dolce vita*, lasciviousness, lechery, lewdness, license, licentiousness, life in fast lane*, lust, orgy, overindulgence, revel, revelry, seduction, sensuality, sybaritism, tear*; SEE CONCEPTS 633,645

debilitate [v] *incapacitate*
attenuate, blunt, cripple, devitalize, disable, enervate, enfeeble, eviscerate, exhaust, extenuate, harm, hurt, injure, mar, prostrate, relax, sap, spoil, unbrace, undermine, unstrengthen, weaken, wear out; SEE CONCEPTS 240,246

debility [n] *incapacity, weakness*
decrepitude, disease, enervation, enfeeblement, exhaustion, faintness, feebleness, frailty, infirmity, languor, malaise, sickliness, unhealthiness; SEE CONCEPT 316

debonair [adj] *charming, elegant*
affable, buoyant, casual, cheerful, courteous, dashing, detached, happy, jaunty, lighthearted, nonchalant, pleasant, refined, smooth, sprightly, suave, urbane, well-bred; SEE CONCEPT 401

debris [n] *litter, waste*
bits, crap*, detritus, dregs, dross, fragments, garbage, junk, offal, pieces, refuse, remains, riffraff, rubbish, rubble, ruins, trash, wreck, wreckage; SEE CONCEPT 260

debt [n] *money owed to others*
albatross*, arrearage, arrears, bad news*, baggage*, below the line*, bill, bite*, capital, check,

chit*, claim, commitment, credit, cuff*, damage*, dead horse*, debenture, debit, deficit, due, dues, duty, encumbrance, indebtedness, in hock*, in the hole*, in the red*, invoice, IOU, liability, manifest, mortgage, note, obligation, outstandings*, price tag*, promissory note, receipt, reckoning, red ink*, responsibility, score, tab, tally, voucher; SEE CONCEPTS 329,344

debunk [v] *disprove, ridicule*
cut down to size*, deflate, demystify, discover, disparage, expose, lampoon, mock, puncture, show up*, uncloak, unmask, unshroud; SEE CONCEPTS 49,60

debut [n] *first public appearance*
admission, appearance, beginning, bow, coming out*, coming out party*, entrance, entree, first step*, graduating, graduation, inauguration, incoming, initiation, introduction, launching, opener, presentation; SEE CONCEPT 386

decadence [n] *perversion; deterioration of morality*
corruption, debasement, decay, declension, decline, degeneracy, degeneration, degradation, devolution, dissipation, dissolution, downfall, downgrade, evil, excess, fall, gluttony, incontinence, intemperance, lasciviousness, lechery, lewdness, licentiousness, regression, sensuality, sybaritism; SEE CONCEPT 645

decadent [adj] *corrupt, self-indulgent*
debased, debauched, decaying, declining, degenerate, degraded, depraved, dissolute, effete, evil, gone bad, gone to the dogs*, immoral, lost, moribund, overripe, perverted, wanton, wicked; SEE CONCEPT 545

decay [n] *breaking down, collapse*
adulteration, atrophy, blight, caries, cariosity, consumption, corrosion, crumbling, decadence, decline, decomposition, decrease, decrepitude, degeneracy, degeneration, depreciation, deterioration, dilapidation, disintegration, disrepair, dissolution, downfall, dying, extinction, fading, failing, gangrene, impairment, mortification, perishing, putrefaction, putrescence, putridity, putridness, rot, rotting, ruin, ruination, rust, senescence, spoilage, spoilation, wasting, wasting away, withering; SEE CONCEPTS 230,674,716

decay [v] *deteriorate, crumble*
atrophy, become contaminated, be impaired, blight, break up, collapse, corrode, curdle, decline, decompose, defile, degenerate, depreciate, discolor, disintegrate, dissolve, dry-rot, dwindle, fade, fail, get worse, go bad, go to seed*, go to the dogs*, hit rock bottom*, hit the skids*, lessen, mildew, mold, molder, mortify, pejorate, perish, pollute, putrefy, putresce, reach depths, rot, sap, shrivel, sicken, sink, slump, spoil, suppurate, turn, wane, waste away, weaken, wear away, wither; SEE CONCEPTS 240,246,469

decayed [adj] *rotten, falling apart*
addled, bad, carious, carrion, corroded, decomposed, effete, gangrenous, moldered, overripe, perished, putrefied, putrescent, putrid, rank, riddled, rotted, ruined, spoiled, wasted, withered; SEE CONCEPT 485

decease [n] *death*
buying the farm*, curtains*, defunction, demise, departure, dissolution, dying, grim reaper*, passing, passing away, passing over, quietus, release, silence, sleep, taps*, the end; SEE CONCEPT 304

decease [v] *pass away; expire*
buy a one-way ticket*, call off all bets*, cease, check out*, cool off*, croak*, deep six*, depart, die, drop, go, pass, pass away, pass on, pass over, perish, succumb; SEE CONCEPT *304*

deceased [adj] *dead*
asleep, bit the dust*, cold*, defunct, departed, exanimate, expired, extinct, finished, former, gave up the ghost*, gone, inanimate, kicked the bucket*, late, lifeless, lost, passed on, pushing up daisies*; SEE CONCEPT *539*

deceit [n1] *practice of misleading*
ambidexterity, ambidextrousness, artifice, cheating, chicane, chicanery, cozening, craft, craftiness, cunning, deceitfulness, deception, defrauding, dirty dealing*, dirty pool*, dishonesty, dissemblance, dissimulation, double-dealing, duplicity, entrapping, fraud, fraudulence, guile, hypocrisy, imposition, overreaching, pretense, slyness, smoke and mirrors*, trapping, treachery, trickery, two-facedness*, two-timing*, underhandedness; SEE CONCEPTS *59,633*

deceit [n2] *particular type of trick, misleading*
artifice, blind, cheat, chicanery, crocodile tears*, deception, dirty trick*, dirty work*, duplicity, fake, feint, flimflam*, fraud, fraudulence, hoax, humbug, imposture, misrepresentation, pretense, ruse, sell, sellout, sham, shift, smoke and mirrors*, snow job*, soft soap*, spoof, stratagem, subterfuge, sweet talk*, swindle, trick, whitewash*, wile; SEE CONCEPTS *59,660*

deceitful [adj] *dishonest, insincere*
artful, astucious, astute, beguiling, clandestine, counterfeit, crafty, cunning, deceiving, deceptive, delusive, delusory, designing, disingenuous, double-dealing, duplicitous, fallacious, false, feline, foxy, fraudulent, furtive, guileful, hypocritical, illusory, impostrous, indirect, insidious, knavish, lying, mendacious, misleading, rascal, roguish, shifty, slick, sly, sneaky, stealthy, subtle, treacherous, tricky, two-faced*, underhand, underhanded, untrustworthy, untruthful, wily; SEE CONCEPT *401*

deceive [v] *mislead; be dishonest*
bamboozle*, beat, beat out of, beguile, betray, bilk, buffalo*, burn, cheat, circumvent, clip, con, cozen, cross up, defraud, delude, disappoint, double-cross, dupe, ensnare, entrap, fake, falsify, fleece, fool, gouge, gull, hoax, hoodwink, hook*, humbug, impose upon, lead on, outwit, play joke on, pull fast one*, put on, rob, scam, screw, sell, skin, suck in*, swindle, take advantage of, take for, take for ride*, take in, take to cleaners*, trick, victimize; SEE CONCEPTS *7,19,59*

decency [n] *respectable behavior*
appropriateness, ceremoniousness, civility, conventionality, correctness, courtesy, decorum, dignity, etiquette, fitness, fittingness, formality, good form, good manners, honesty, modesty, propriety, respectability, righteousness, seemliness, virtue; SEE CONCEPT *633*

decent [adj1] *respectable, appropriate*
approved, becoming, befitting, chaste, clean, comely, comme il faut, conforming, continent, correct, decorous, delicate, ethical, fit, fitting, good, honest, honorable, immaculate, mannerly, modest, moral, nice, noble, on the up and up*, polite, presentable, proper, prudent, pure, reserved, right, seemly, spotless, stainless, standard, straight, straight arrow*, straight shooting*,

suitable, trustworthy, unblemished, undefiled, untarnished, upright, virtuous, worthy; SEE CONCEPTS *401,558*

decent [adj2] *kind, generous*
accommodating, courteous, friendly, gracious, helpful, obliging, thoughtful, virtuous; SEE CONCEPTS *404,542*

decent [adj3] *sufficient, tolerable*
acceptable, adequate, all right, ample, average, comfortable, common, competent, enough, fair, fair to middling*, good, mediocre, middling, moderately good, passable, presentable, reasonable, respectable, right, satisfactory, sufficing, unexceptional, unimpeachable, unobjectionable; SEE CONCEPTS *533,558,572*

deception [n1] *misleading; being dishonest*
beguilement, betrayal, blarney*, boondoggle*, cheat, circumvention, cozenage, craftiness, cunning, deceit, deceitfulness, deceptiveness, defraudation, dirt, disinformation, dissimulation, double-dealing, dupery, duplicity, equivocation, falsehood, fast one*, flimflam*, fraud, fraudulence, guile, hokum*, hypocrisy, imposition, insincerity, juggling, legerdemain, lying, mendacity, pretense, prevarication, snow job*, sophism, treachery, treason, trickery, trickiness, trumpery, untruth; SEE CONCEPTS *7,19,59*

deception [n2] *trick*
artifice, bilk, bluff, catch, cheat, chicane, con, confidence game, con game*, cover-up, crock, decoy, device, dodge, fallacy, fast one*, fast shuffle*, feint, fib, fraud, gimmick, hoax, hogwash*, hustle, illusion, imposture, jive*, lie, malarkey*, mare's-nest*, pretext, ride*, ruse, scam, sham, shift, shuck, snare, snow job*, stall, sting, story, stratagem, subterfuge, swindle, trap, trick, whitewash*, wile, wrinkle*; SEE CONCEPTS *59,230*

deceptive [adj] *dishonest*
ambiguous, astucious, beguiling, bum*, catchy, crafty, cunning, deceitful, deceiving, deluding, delusive, delusory, designing, disingenuous, fake, fallacious, false, fishy, foxy, fraudulent, illusory, imposturous, indirect, insidious, lying, misleading, mock, oblique, off*, phony, plausible, rascal, roguish, scheming, seeming, serpentine, shifty, slick, slippery, sly, sneaky, snide, specious, spurious, subtle, treacherous, tricky, two-faced*, underhand, underhanded, unreliable, wily; SEE CONCEPTS *401,582*

decide [v] *make a determination; settle an issue*
adjudge, adjudicate, agree, arrive at conclusion, award, call shots*, cast the die*, choose, cinch, clinch, come to agreement, come to conclusion, come to decision, commit oneself, conclude, conjecture, decree, determine, draw a conclusion, elect, end, establish, figure, fix upon, form opinion, gather, go down line*, guess, have final word*, judge, make a decision, make up mind, mediate, opt, pick, poll, purpose, reach decision, resolve, rule, select, set, surmise, take a stand, tap, vote, will; SEE CONCEPT *18*

decided [adj1] *certain, definite*
absolute, assured, categorical, cinched, clear, clear-cut, clinched, destined, determined, distinct, emphatic, explicit, express, fated, for sure*, indisputable, in the bag*, nailed*, on ice*, positive, prearranged, predetermined, pronounced, resolved, runaway*, settled, sure, unalterable, unambiguous, undeniable, undisputed, unequivocal, unmistakable, unquestionable; SEE CONCEPT *535*

de
de

decided [adj2] *determined, strong-willed*
assertive, bent, certain, cocksure, decisive, deliberate, earnest, emphatic, established, firm, fixed, inflexible, intent, iron-jawed*, mulish, positive, purposeful, resolute, resolved, serious, set, settled, strong-minded, sure, unbending, unfaltering, unhesitating, unwavering, unyielding; SEE CONCEPTS 401,403

decidedly [adv] *certainly*
absolutely, bloody*, by all means, clearly, decisively, determinedly, distinctly, downright, emphatically, flat out*, for a fact*, in spades*, no catch*, no holds barred*, no ifs ands or buts*, no mistake*, no strings attached*, of course, positively, powerful, real, really, right, straight out, strongly, sure, surely, terribly, terrifically, unequivocally, unmistakably; SEE CONCEPT 535

deciding [adj] *determining*
chief, conclusive, critical, crucial, decisive, important, influential, key, necessary, prime, principal, significant; SEE CONCEPTS 546,568

decipher [v] *figure out, understand*
analyze, break, break down, bring out, cipher, construe, crack, decode, deduce, disentangle, dope out, elucidate, encipher, explain, expound, find the key, interpret, make clear, make out, puzzle out, read, render, reveal, solve, spell, translate, unfold, unravel, unriddle; SEE CONCEPTS 15,31,37

decision [n1] *conclusion; resolution reached*
accommodation, accord, adjudication, adjudicature, adjustment, agreement, arbitration, arrangement, choice, compromise, declaration, determination, end, finding, judgment, opinion, outcome, prearrangement, preference, reconciliation, resolution, result, ruling, selection, sentence, settlement, showdown, the call, the nod, understanding, verdict; SEE CONCEPTS 278,689

decision [n2] *strength of mind or will*
backbone, decidedness, decisiveness, determination, doggedness, earnestness, firmness, fortitude, grit, iron will, obstinacy, obstinance, perseverance, persistence, pluck*, purpose, purposefulness, purposiveness, resoluteness, resolution, resolve, seriousness, spine, stubbornness, volition, will, will power; SEE CONCEPTS 410,411

decisive [adj] *definite*
absolute, all out*, assured, bent, certain, conclusive, crisp, critical, crucial, decided, definitive, determined, fateful, final, firm, flat out*, forceful, imperative, imperious, incisive, influential, intent, litmus test*, momentous, peremptory, positive, resolute, resolved, set, settled, significant, straight out*, strong-minded, trenchant; SEE CONCEPT 535

deck [v] *put on clothing, usually nice*
accouter, adorn, appoint, array, attire, beautify, bedeck, clothe, decorate, dress, dress up, embellish, festoon, garland, garnish, grace, gussy up*, ornament, prettify, primp, slick, trim; SEE CONCEPT 167

declaim [v] *proclaim; get on a soapbox*
attack, bloviate, blow hot air*, declare, decry, denounce, harangue, hold forth, inveigh, lecture, mouth, orate, perorate, pile it on*, proclaim, rail, rant, recite, soapbox*, speak, spiel*, spout*, talk big*; SEE CONCEPTS 49,51

declaration [n1] *assertion of belief or knowledge*
acknowledgment, admission, advertisement, affirmation, allegation, announcement, answer, attestation, averment, avowal, bomb*, broadcast, communication, deposition, disclosure, enunciation, explanation, exposition, expression, hot air*, information, notice, notification, oath, pitch, presentation, profession, promulgation, protestation, publication, remark, report, revelation, saying, say so*, spiel*, statement, story, testimony, two cents' worth*, utterance; SEE CONCEPTS 49,274,278

declaration [n2] *official proclamation*
acclamation, affidavit, allegation, announcement, article, attestation, bulletin, canon, charge, confirmation, constitution, credo, creed, denunciation, deposition, document, edict, gospel, indictment, manifesto, notice, notification, plea, proclamation, profession, promulgation, pronouncement, pronunciamento, resolution, testament, testimony, ultimatum; SEE CONCEPTS 271,274,278

declare [v1] *make known clearly or officially*
acknowledge, advance, advocate, affirm, allegate, allege, announce, argue, assert, asseverate, attest, aver, avow, be positive, blaze, bring forward, certify, cite, claim, confess, confirm, contend, convey, demonstrate, disclose, enunciate, give out, inform, insist, maintain, manifest, notify, pass, proclaim, profess, promulgate, pronounce, propound, publish, put forward, reaffirm, reassert, render, repeat, reveal, set forth, show, sound, state, stress, swear, tell, testify, validate, vouch; SEE CONCEPTS 49,60

declare [v2] *claim as possession*
acknowledge, admit, avouch, avow, confess, convey, disclose, divulge, impart, indicate, manifest, notify, own, profess, represent, reveal, state, swear; SEE CONCEPTS 57,60

decline [n1] *lessening*
abatement, backsliding, comedown, cropper*, decay, decrepitude, degeneracy, degeneration, descent, deterioration, devolution, diminution, dissolution, dive, downfall, downgrade, downturn, drop, dwindling, ebb, ebbing, enfeeblement, failing, failure, fall, falling off, flop, lapse, on the skids*, pratfall, recession, relapse, senility, skids*, slump, wane, waning, weakening, worsening; SEE CONCEPTS 674,698,699

decline [n2] *downward change in value, position*
declivity, decrease, depression, descent, dip, downslide, downswing, downtrend, downturn, drop, drop-off, fall-off, hill, incline, lapse, loss, lowering, pitch, sag, slide, slip, slope, slump; SEE CONCEPTS 336,346,738

decline [v1] *say no*
abjure, abstain, avoid, balk, beg to be excused, bypass, demur, deny, desist, disapprove, dismiss, don't buy*, forbear, forgo, gainsay, nix*, not accept, not hear of, not think of, pass on*, refrain, refuse, reject, renounce, reprobate, repudiate, send regrets, shy, spurn, turn down, turn thumbs down*; SEE CONCEPTS 45,51

decline [v2] *lessen, become less*
abate, backslide, cheapen, decay, decrease, degenerate, depreciate, deteriorate, diminish, disimprove, disintegrate, droop, drop, dwindle, ebb, fade, fail, fall, fall off, flag, go downhill*, go to pot*, go to the dogs*, hit the skids*, languish, lapse, lose value, lower, pine, recede, relapse, retrograde, return, revert, rot, sag, settle, shrink, sink, slide, subside, wane, weaken, worsen; SEE CONCEPTS 240,698

decline [v3] *descend*
dip, droop, drop, fall, go down, lower, sag, set, settle, sink, slant, slope; SEE CONCEPTS *151,181*

decompose [v1] *rot, break up*
break down, crumble, decay, disintegrate, dissolve, fall apart, fester, molder, putrefy, putresce, spoil, taint, turn; SEE CONCEPT *469*

decompose [v2] *analyze by taking apart*
anatomize, atomize, break down, break up, decompound, disintegrate, dissect, dissolve, distill, resolve, separate; SEE CONCEPTS *24,103*

decomposition [n] *rot, breakdown*
atomization, corruption, decay, disintegration, dissipation, dissolution, division, putrefaction, putrescence, putridity; SEE CONCEPTS *230,674*

deconstructionist [n/adj] *exposing a text's multiple meanings*
critical, debunking, demystifying, demythifying, hermeneutical, reinterpretive, revisionist; SEE CONCEPT *268*

decor [n] *colors, furnishings of a place*
adornment, color scheme, decoration, interior design, ornamentation; SEE CONCEPTS *622,723*

decorate [v1] *beautify, embellish*
add finishing touches, adorn, bedeck, bedizen, brighten, burnish, color, deck, do up*, dress out*, dress up*, enhance, enrich, festoon, finish, fix up, frill, furbish, garnish, gild, grace, gussy up*, idealize, illuminate, jazz up*, ornament, paint, perfect, prank, renovate, spruce up*, trim; SEE CONCEPTS *162,177*

decorate [v2] *honor and give medal*
cite, laureate, pin medal on, plume; SEE CONCEPT *132*

decoration [n1] *beautification, embellishment*
adornment, beautifying, bedecking, bedizenment, designing, elaboration, enhancement, enrichment, festooning, flounce, flourish, frill, furbelow, garnish, garnishing, illumination, improvement, ornament, ornamentation, redecorating, spangle, trimming; SEE CONCEPTS *162,177*

decoration [n2] *particular type of embellishment*
appliqué, arabesque, bauble, braid, color, curlicue, design, dingbat*, doodad*, extravagance, fandangle*, festoon, filigree, finery, flounce, flourish, fretwork, frill, frippery, furbelow, fuss, garbage*, garnish, garniture, gewgaws, gilt, gimcracks*, gingerbread, inlay, jazz*, lace, ornament, parquetry, plaque, ribbon, scroll, sequin, spangle, thing*, tinsel, tooling, trimming, trinket, wreath; SEE CONCEPTS *259,260*

decoration [n3] *medal of honor*
accolade, award, badge, bays, citation, colors, cross, distinction, emblem, garter, kudos, laurels, medal, mention, order, Purple Heart, ribbon, star; SEE CONCEPT *337*

decorative [adj] *beautifying*
adorning, cosmetic, embellishing, enhancing, fancy, florid, nonfunctional, ornamental, prettifying, pretty; SEE CONCEPT *579*

decorous [adj] *appropriate, suitable*
au fait, becoming, befitting, ceremonial, ceremonious, civilized, comely, comme il faut, conforming, conventional, correct, decent, demure, de rigueur, dignified, done, elegant, fit, fitting, formal, good, mannerly, meet, moral, nice, polite, prim, proper, punctilious, refined, respectable, right, seasonable, sedate, seemly, staid, well-behaved; SEE CONCEPTS *401,558*

decorum [n] *appropriate behavior, good manners*
breeding, civility, conduct, convenance, convention, correctitude, correctness, courtliness, decency, demeanor, deportment, dignity, etiquette, form, formality, gentility, good grace, gravity, habits, order, orderliness, politeness, politesse, propereness, propriety, protocol, punctilio, respectability, seemliness, tact, usage; SEE CONCEPT *633*

decoy [n] *bait, trap*
allurement, attraction, beard*, blind, blow off*, booster, camouflage, catch, chicane, chicanery, come-on, deception, drawing card, ensnarement, enticement, facade, fake, front, imitation, inducement, inveiglement, lure, nark, plant, pretense, seducement, shill, sitting duck*, snare, stick, stoolie*, stool pigeon*, temptation, trick, trickery; SEE CONCEPTS *59,230,680*

decoy [v] *bait, entrap*
allure, come on, con, deceive, delude, egg one on*, ensnare, ensorcell, entice, fascinate, inveigle, lead on*, lead up garden path*, lure, mislead, mousetrap*, rope in*, seduce, shill, steer, suck in*, tempt, toll, tout, trap, wile; SEE CONCEPTS *16,59*

decrease [n] *diminishing, lessening*
abatement, compression, condensation, constriction, contraction, cutback, decline, declining, decrescence, depression, diminution, discount, downturn, dwindling, ebb, falling off, loss, reduction, shrinkage, striction, subsidence, waning; SEE CONCEPT *698*

decrease [v] *grow less or make less*
abate, calm down, check, contract, crumble, curb, curtail, cut down, decay, decline, degenerate, depreciate, deteriorate, devaluate, die down, diminish, droop, drop, drop off, dry up, dwindle, ease, ebb, evaporate, fade, fall off, lessen, let up, lighten, lose edge, lower, modify, narrow down, peter out, quell, quiet, reduce, restrain, run low, settle, shrink, shrivel, sink, slacken, slack off, slash, slow down, slump, soften, subside, tail off, wane, waste, weaken, wear away, wear down, wither; SEE CONCEPTS *240,698*

decree [n] *mandate, legal order*
act, announcement, behest, bidding, charge, charging, command, commandment, declaration, decretum, dictum, direction, directive, edict, enactment, injunction, instruction, judgment, law, order, ordinance, precept, prescript, proclamation, promulgation, pronouncement, rap*, regulation, rule, ruling, say, statute, the riot act*, the word*, ukase; SEE CONCEPTS *318,685*

decree [v] *order rule or action*
announce, command, compel, constrain, decide, declare, demand, determine, dictate, enact, force, impose, lay down the law*, oblige, ordain, prescribe, proclaim, pronounce, put one's foot down*, read the riot act*, require, rule, set; SEE CONCEPTS *50,53,81,88,317*

decrepit [adj] *deteriorated, debilitated, especially as a result of age*
aged, anile, antiquated, battered, bedraggled, broken-down, creaky, crippled, dilapidated, doddering, effete, feeble, flimsy, fragile, frail, haggard, incapacitated, infirm, insubstantial, old, quavering, ramshackle, rickety, run-down, seedy, senile, shabby, shaking, superannuated, tacky, threadbare, tired, tottering, tumble-down, unsound, used, wasted, weak, weakly, weather-beaten, worn, worn-out; SEE CONCEPTS *406,485*

decry [v] *criticize, blame*
abuse, asperse, bad-mouth*, belittle, calumniate, censure, condemn, cry down, defame, denounce, depreciate, derogate, detract, devalue, diminish, discount, discredit, disgrace, disparage, do a number on*, downgrade, dump on*, hit*, knock*, lower, malign, mark down, minimize, opprobriate, pan*, poor-mouth*, put down, rail against, rap, reprehend, reprobate, run down, slam*, take away, take swipe at*, throw stones at*, traduce, underestimate, underrate, undervalue, vilify, write off; SEE CONCEPTS 44,52

dedicate [v1] *donate, set aside for special use*
address, allot, apply, apportion, appropriate, assign, commit, consign, devote, give, give over to, inscribe, offer, pledge, restrict, surrender; SEE CONCEPTS 18,50,88,135

dedicate [v2] *sanctify*
anoint, bless, consecrate, hallow, set apart; SEE CONCEPTS 69,367

dedicated [adj] *loyal, hard-working*
committed, devoted, enthusiastic, faithful, given over to, old faithful*, purposeful, single-hearted, single-minded, sworn, true blue*, true to the end*, wholehearted, zealous; SEE CONCEPTS 404,542

dedication [n1] *faithfulness, loyalty*
adherence, allegiance, commitment, devotedness, devotion, single-mindedness, wholeheartedness; SEE CONCEPTS 411,657

dedication [n2] *speech of praise; sanctification*
address, celebration, consecration, devotion, envoy, glorification, hallowing, inscription, message; SEE CONCEPTS 69,367

deduce [v] *figure out, understand*
add up, analyze, assume, be afraid, boil down, cogitate, collect, conceive, conclude, consider, deduct, deem, derive, draw, fancy, figure, gather, glean, have a hunch*, imagine, infer, judge, make, make out, presume, presuppose, ratiocinate, read into, reason, regard, surmise, take to mean; SEE CONCEPTS 15,24

deducible [adj] *understandable*
a priori, consequent, deductive, derivable, dogmatic, following, inferable, inferential, provable, reasoned, traceable; SEE CONCEPTS 402,529

deduct [v] *take away or out; reduce*
abstract, allow, bate, cut back, decrease by, diminish, discount, dock, draw back, knock off, lessen, rebate, reduce, remove, roll back, subtract, take, take from, take off, withdraw, write off; SEE CONCEPTS 236,247,330

deduction [n1] *conclusion, understanding*
answer, assumption, cogitation, concluding, consequence, consideration, contemplation, corollary, deliberation, derivation, finding, illation, inference, inferring, judgment, meditation, mulling, musing, opinion, pondering, ratiocination, reasoning, reflection, result, rumination, sequitur, speculation, thinking, thought; SEE CONCEPTS 15,24,689

deduction [n2] *something subtracted*
abatement, abstraction, allowance, credit, cut, decrease, decrement, depreciation, diminution, discount, dockage, excision, rebate, reduction, removal, subtraction, withdrawal, write-off; SEE CONCEPTS 763,776

deed [n1] *achievement*
accomplishment, act, action, adventure, ballgame, big idea*, bit, byplay, cause, commission, crusade, do, enterprise, exploit, fact, feat, follow

through, game, happenin'*, performance, plan, quest, reality, securing, stunt, thing*, tour de force, truth, winning; SEE CONCEPTS 4,706

deed [n2] *legal paper assigning property; contract*
agreement, bargain, certificate, charter, compact, conveyance, covenant, document, indenture, instrument, lease, papers, proof, record, release, security, title, transaction, voucher, warranty; SEE CONCEPTS 271,318

deem [v] *regard, consider*
account, allow, appraise, assume, be afraid, believe, calculate, conceive, conjecture, credit, daresay, divine, esteem, estimate, expect, feel, guess, hold, imagine, judge, know, presume, reckon, sense, set store by, suppose, surmise, suspect, think, understand, view; SEE CONCEPTS 12,28

deep [n] *the sea*
blue*, brine, briny*, Davy Jones's locker*, drink*, main, middle, ocean, Poseidon's realm*, the high seas; SEE CONCEPT 514

deep [adj1] *extending very far, usually down*
abysmal, abyssal, below, beneath, bottomless, broad, buried, deep-seated, distant, downreaching, far, fathomless, immersed, inmost, low, profound, rooted, subaqueous, submarine, submerged, subterranean, sunk, underground, unfathomable, wide, yawning; SEE CONCEPTS 737,777

deep [adj2] *abstract, complicated in meaning*
abstruse, acute, arcane, complex, concealed, Delphic, difficult, discerning, esoteric, hard to understand, heavy*, hermetic, hidden, incisive, intricate, learned, mysterious, obscure, occult, Orphic, penetrating, profound, recondite, sagacious, secret, serious, Sibylline, wise; SEE CONCEPTS 402,529

deep [adj3] *scheming, devious*
acute, artful, astute, canny, contriving, crafty, cunning, designing, foxy, guileful, insidious, intriguing, keen, knowing, plotting, sharp, shrewd, sly, tricky, wily; SEE CONCEPT 404

deep [adj4] *absorbed, engrossed in activity*
abstracted, centered, concentrated, enfolded, engaged, fixed, focused, immersed, intent, into, lost, musing, preoccupied, rapt, set, wrapped, wrapped up; SEE CONCEPT 542

deep [adj5] *intense in effect on senses*
bass, booming, dark, extreme, full-toned, grave, great, hard, low, low-pitched, low-toned, profound, resonant, rich, sonorous, strong, vivid; SEE CONCEPTS 537,594,618

deepen [v1] *make depth greater*
dig, dig out, dredge, excavate, expand, extend, hollow, scoop out, scrape out; SEE CONCEPT 250

deepen [v2] *make more intense*
aggravate, develop, enhance, expand, extend, grow, heighten, increase, intensate, intensify, magnify, mount, redouble, reinforce, rise, rouse, strengthen; SEE CONCEPTS 236,245,697

deeply [adv] *completely, intensely*
acutely, affectingly, distressingly, feelingly, genuinely, gravely, intensely, mournfully, movingly, passionately, profoundly, sadly, seriously, severely, surely, thoroughly, to the quick; SEE CONCEPTS 531,772

deface [v] *mar, mutilate*
blemish, contort, damage, deform, demolish, destroy, dilapidate, disfigure, distort, harm, impair, injure, mangle, misshape, obliterate, ruin,

scratch, spoil, sully, tarnish, trash*, vandalize, wreck; SEE CONCEPTS *246,252*

de facto [*adv*] *in reality*
actual, actually, existing, genuinely, in effect, in fact, real, really, tangible, truly, veritably; SEE CONCEPT *582*

defamation [*n*] *libel, slander*
aspersion, backbiting, backstabbing, belittlement, black eye*, calumny, character assassination, cheap shot*, denigration, depreciation, detraction, dirt, dirty laundry*, disparagement, dump*, dynamite, hit, knock, lie, low-down dirty*, mud, obloquy, opprobrium, scorcher, slam*, slap in face*, slime, slur, smear, tale, traducement, vilification; SEE CONCEPT *54*

defamatory [*adj*] *libelous, slanderous*
abusive, calumnious, contumelious, denigrating, derogatory, detracting, detractive, disparaging, injurious, insulting, maligning, opprobrious, traducing, vilifying, vituperative; SEE CONCEPTS *267,537*

defame [*v*] *inflict libel or slander*
asperse, bad-mouth*, belie, besmirch, blacken, blister, calumniate, cast aspersions on, cast slur on, denigrate, detract, discredit, disgrace, dishonor, disparage, do a number on*, knock, malign, pan*, put zingers on*, roast, scandalize, scorch, slam, smear, speak evil of*, stigmatize, throw mud at*, traduce, vilify, villainize, vituperate; SEE CONCEPTS *7,19,54*

default [*n*] *failure; want*
absence, blemish, blunder, dearth, defect, deficiency, delinquency, dereliction, disregard, error, fault, imperfection, inadequacy, insufficiency, lack, lapse, miss, neglect, nonpayment, offense, omission, overlooking, oversight, privation, shortcoming, slight, transgression, vice, weakness, wrongdoing; SEE CONCEPTS *335,699,709*

default [*v*] *dodge payment*
bilk, defraud, dishonor, evade, fail, leave town*, meet under arch*, neglect, put on the cuff*, rat*, repudiate, run out on*, see in the alley, shirk, skate*, skip, skip out on*, stiff*, swindle, welch, welsh; SEE CONCEPTS *59,63,330*

defeat [*n1*] *overthrow, beating*
ambush, annihilation, beating, blow, break, breakdown, check, collapse, conquest, count, debacle, defeasance, destruction, discomfiture, downthrow, drubbing*, embarrassment, extermination, failure, fall, insuccess, killing*, KO*, lacing, licking, loss, massacre, mastery, nonsuccess, paddling, rebuff, repulse, reverse, rout, ruin, scalping, setback, shellacking*, slaughter, subjugation, thrashing, trap, trashing, trimming, triumph, trouncing, vanquishment, waxing, whaling, whipping, whitewashing*; SEE CONCEPT *95*

defeat [*n2*] *frustration*
disappointment, discomfiture, downfall, failure, foil, loss, rebuff, repulse, reversal, reverse, setback, thwarting; SEE CONCEPT *410*

defeat [*v1*] *conquer in military manner*
ambush, annihilate, bar, bear down, beat, best, block, butcher, crush, decimate, demolish, discomfit, drown, entrap, finish off, halt, hinder, impede, lick, mow down, obliterate, obstruct, outflank, outmaneuver, overpower, overrun, overthrow, overwhelm, parry, prevail over, quell, reduce, repel, repress, repulse, roll back, rout, route, sack, scatter, shipwreck, sink, slaughter,

smash, subdue, subjugate, suppress, surmount, swamp, torpedo*, trample, trash, upset, vanquish, whip, wipe out; SEE CONCEPTS *95,320*

defeat [*v2*] *conquer in athletic contest*
beat, bust*, clobber*, cream*, deck*, drop*, drub*, edge, flax*, flog*, floor*, knock out*, KO*, lambaste*, lick, outhit, outjump, outplay, outrun, overpower, plow under*, pommel*, pound*, powder*, pulverize*, run roughshod over*, skin*, steamroll*, take, take it all*, take to cleaners*, tan*, thrash, total, trounce, wallop*, whack*, whomp*, win, work over*, zap*; SEE CONCEPTS *95,363*

defeat [*v3*] *frustrate*
baffle, balk, beat down*, beat the system*, blank, block, bury, cast down, cause setback, checkmate, circumvent, confound, contravene, cook*, counterplot, cross, disappoint, discomfit, disconcert, disprove, edge out*, foil, invalidate, neutralize, nonplus, nose out*, nullify, outwit, overturn, put end to*, puzzle, quell, reduce, refute, ruin, scuttle, shave*, shellac*, skunk*, spoil, squash, stump, subdue, subjugate, surmount, take wind out of sails*, throw for loop*, thwart, undo, victimize; SEE CONCEPTS *14,121*

defect [*n*] *blemish, imperfection*
birthmark, blot, blotch, break, bug, catch, check, crack, deficiency, deformity, discoloration, drawback, error, failing, fault, flaw, foible, frailty, gap, glitch, gremlin, hole, infirmity, injury, irregularity, kink, knot, lack, mark, marring, mistake, patch, rift, rough spot, scar, scarcity, scratch, seam, second, shortage, shortcoming, sin, speck, spot, stain, taint, unsoundness, vice, want, weakness, weak point; SEE CONCEPTS *309,580,646*

defect [*v*] *break from belief, faith*
abandon, abscond, apostatize, back out, break faith*, change sides, depart, desert, fall away from, forsake, go, go back on, go over, go over the fence*, lapse, leave, pull out, quit, rat*, rebel, reject, renege, renounce, revolt, run out, schism, sell out*, spurn, take a walk*, tergiversate, tergiverse, turn, turn coat*, walk out on, withdraw; SEE CONCEPTS *198,367*

defection [*n*] *abandonment*
alienation, apostasy, backsliding, deficiency, dereliction, desertion, disaffection, disloyalty, disownment, divorce, estrangement, failing, failure, faithlessness, forsaking, lack, parting, rebellion, recreancy, rejection, repudiation, retreat, revolt, separation, severance, sundering, tergiversation, withdrawal; SEE CONCEPTS *195,198,367*

defective [*adj*] *broken, not working*
abnormal, amiss, blemished, damaged, deficient, faulty, flawed, impaired, imperfect, inadequate, incomplete, injured, insufficient, lacking, on the bum*, out of order, poor, seconds, sick, subnormal, unfinished, unhealthy, unsound, wanting; SEE CONCEPTS *560,565*

defend [*v1*] *protect*
avert, battle, beat off, bulwark, care for, cherish, conserve, contend, cover, entrench, espouse, fend off, fight, fight for, fortify, foster, garrison, guard, guard against, hedge, hold, hold at bay, house, insure, keep safe, look after, maintain, mine, nourish, oppose, panoply, preserve, prevent, provide sanctuary, repel danger, resist, retain, safeguard, save, screen, secure, shelter, shield, stave off, sustain, take in, uphold, war, ward off, watch, watch over, withstand; SEE CONCEPTS *96,110*

defend [v2] *show support for*
advocate, aid, apologize for, argue, assert, back, back up, bear one out*, befriend, champion, come to defense of, cover for, endorse, espouse, exculpate, exonerate, explain, go to bat for*, guarantee, justify, maintain, plead, prove a case, put in a good word*, rationalize, recommend, ride shotgun for*, say in defense, second, speak up for, stand by, stand up for, stick up for, stonewall*, support, sustain, thump for, uphold, vindicate, warrant; SEE CONCEPTS 10,49

defense [n1] *armament; protection system*
aegis, armor, arms, barricade, bastille, bastion, bulwark, buttress, citadel, cover, deterrence, dike, embankment, fastness, fence, fort, fortification, fortress, garrison, guard, immunity, munitions, palisade, parapet, position, protection, rampart, redoubt, resistance, safeguard, security, shelter, shield, stockade, stronghold, trench, wall, ward, warfare, weaponry, weapons; SEE CONCEPTS 321,322,500

defense [n2] *explanation, justification*
answer, apologetics, apologia, apologizing, apology, argument, cleanup, copout*, exculpation, excuse, excusing, exoneration, explaining, extenuation, fish story*, jive, off-time*, plea, rationalization, rejoinder, reply, response, retort, return, song and dance*, story, vindication, whitewash*; SEE CONCEPTS 57,278

defenseless [adj] *powerless, vulnerable*
caught, endangered, exposed, hands tied*, helpless, indefensible, in line of fire*, like a clay pigeon*, like a sitting duck*, naked*, on the line*, on the spot*, open, out on limb*, pigeon*, poor, unarmed, unguarded, unprotected, up the creek*, weak, wide open*; SEE CONCEPTS 555,576

defensible [adj] *justifiable*
condonable, defendable, excusable, fit, logical, pardonable, permissible, plausible, proper, tenable, valid, vindicable, warrantable; SEE CONCEPT 528

defensive [adj] *protective, watchful*
arresting, averting, balking, checking, conservative, coping with, defending, foiling, forestalling, frustrating, guarding, in opposition, interrupting, opposing, preservative, preventive, protecting, resistive, safeguarding, thwarting, uptight*, warding off, withstanding; SEE CONCEPTS 401,550

defer [v1] *hold off, put off*
adjourn, block, delay, detain, extend, give rain check*, hang fire*, hinder, hold up, impede, intermit, lay over, lengthen, obstruct, postpone, procrastinate, prolong, prorogue, protract, put on back burner*, put on hold*, put on ice*, remit, retard, set aside, shelve, slow, stall, stay, suspend, table, waive; SEE CONCEPT 121,130

defer [v2] *yield*
accede, accommodate, acquiesce, adapt, adjust, admit, agree, assent, bow, buckle, capitulate, cave, comply, concede, cringe, fawn, give in to, knuckle*, knuckle under*, kowtow*, obey, submit, succumb, truckle; SEE CONCEPT 83

deference [n1] *obedience, compliance*
acquiescence, capitulation, complaisance, condescension, docility, obeisance, submission, yielding; SEE CONCEPT 633

deference [n2] *attention, homage*
acclaim, civility, consideration, courtesy, esteem, honor, obeisance, politeness, regard, respect, reverence, thoughtfulness, veneration; SEE CONCEPTS 10,410

deferential [adj] *respectful, considerate*
civil, complaisant, courteous, disarming, duteous, dutiful, ingratiating, ingratiatory, insinuating, insinuative, obedient, obeisant, obsequious, polite, regardful, reverential, saccharine, silken, silky, submissive; SEE CONCEPT 401

deferment/deferral [n] *postponement*
adjournment, delay, holdover*, moratorium, pause, putting off*, stay, suspension; SEE CONCEPTS 121,130

deferred [adj] *put off till a later time*
adjourned, assessed, charged, delayed, funded, held up, indebted, in waiting, negotiated, on hold*, on the shelf*, pigeonholed*, postponed, prolonged, protracted, remanded, renegotiated, retarded, scrubbed*, stalled, staved off, temporized; SEE CONCEPT 820

defiance [n] *disobedience, disregard*
affront, audacity, back talk*, big talk*, boldness, bravado, brazenness, call, cartel, challenge, command, confrontation, contempt, contrariness, contumacy, dare, defy, effrontery, enjoinder, factiousness, gas*, guts*, hot air*, impudence, impugnment, insolence, insubordination, insurgence, insurgency, intractableness, lip*, muster*, opposition, order, perversity, provocation, rebellion, rebelliousness, recalcitrance, revolt, sass*, spite, stump, summons, temerity, throwing of the gauntlet*, unruliness; SEE CONCEPTS 633,657

defiant [adj] *disobedient, disregardful*
aggressive, audacious, bold, challenging, contumacious, daring, gutsy*, insolent, insubmissive, insubordinate, mutinous, obstinate, provocative, rebellious, recalcitrant, reckless, refractory, resistant, resistive, sassy*, truculent; SEE CONCEPT 401

deficiency [n] *imperfection, inadequacy*
absence, bug*, dearth, defalcation, default, defect, deficit, demerit, dereliction, failing, failure, fault, flaw, frailty, glitch*, inability to hack it*, insufficiency, insufficiency, lack, loss, need, neglect, paucity, privation, scantiness, scarcity, shortage, shortcoming, sin, want, weakness; SEE CONCEPTS 635,666,674

deficient [adj] *imperfect, inadequate*
amiss, bad, damaged, defective, exiguous, faulty, flawed, found wanting, impaired, incomplete, inferior, infrequent, injured, insufficient, lacking, marred, meager, not cut out for*, not enough, not make it*, not up to scratch*, outta gas*, rare, scant, scanty*, scarce, second fiddle*, second string, short, shy, sketchy, skimpy, third string*, unassembled, unequal, unfinished, unsatisfactory, wanting, weak; SEE CONCEPTS 531,565

deficit [n] *shortage of something needed, required*
arrears, dead horse*, defalcation, default, deficiency, due bill, dues, inadequacy, in hock*, insufficiency, insufficiency, in the hole*, in the red, lack, loss, paucity, red ink*, scantiness, shortcoming, shortfall, underage; SEE CONCEPTS 335,646

deficit spending [n] *paying out in excess of income*
debt, debt explosion, deficit financing, in the red, megadebt, negative cash flow, no assets, overspending; SEE CONCEPTS 324,330,344

defile [v] *corrupt, violate*
abuse, adulterate, befoul, besmirch, contaminate, debase, deflower, degrade, desecrate, dirty, dis-

color, disgrace, dishonor, hurt, maculate, make foul, mess up*, molest, muck up*, pollute, profane, rape, ravish, scuzz up*, seduce, shame, smear, soil, stain, sully, taint, tar, tarnish, trash, vitiate; SEE CONCEPTS 54,156,246

defiled [adj] *corrupted, violated*
besmirched, common, cooked, desecrated, dirty, dishonored, exposed, impure, mucked up*, polluted, profaned, ravished, spoilt, tainted, trashed*, unclean, vitiated; SEE CONCEPT 570

define [v1] *give description*
ascertain, assign, call a spade a spade*, characterize, construe, decide, delineate, denominate, denote, describe, designate, detail, determine, dub, elucidate, entitle, etch, exemplify, explain, expound, formalize, illustrate, interpret, label, lay it out*, nail it down*, name, prescribe, represent, specify, spell out, tag, translate; SEE CONCEPTS 55,57,62

define [v2] *delimit, outline*
belt, border, bound, circumscribe, compass, confine, curb, delineate, demarcate, distinguish, edge, encircle, enclose, encompass, envelop, establish, fence in, fix, flank, gird, girdle, limit, mark, mark out, rim, set, set bounds to, settle, stake out, surround, verge, wall in; SEE CONCEPTS 18,60,758

definite [adj1] *exact, clear*
audible, bold, categorical, clean-cut, clear-cut, clearly defined, complete, crisp, definitive, determined, distinct, distinguishable, downright, explicit, express, fixed, forthright, full, graphic, incisive, marked, minute, not vague, obvious, palpable, particular, plain, positive, precise, pronounced, ringing, severe, sharp, silhouetted, specific, straightforward, tangible, unambiguous, undubitable, unequivocal, unmistakable, visible, vivid, well-defined, well-grounded, well-marked; SEE CONCEPT 557

definite [adj2] *fixed, certain, positive*
assigned, assured, beyond doubt, circumscribed, convinced, decided, defined, determinate, determined, established, guaranteed, limited, narrow, precise, prescribed, restricted, set, settled, sure; SEE CONCEPT 535

definitely [adv] *certainly*
absolutely, beyond any doubt, categorically, clearly, decidedly, doubtless, doubtlessly, easily, explicitly, expressly, far and away*, finally, indubitably, no ifs ands or buts about it*, obviously, plainly, specifically, surely, undeniably, unequivocally, unmistakably, unquestionably, without doubt, without fail, without question; SEE CONCEPTS 535,552

definition [n] *description*
analogue, annotation, answer, characterization, clarification, clue, comment, commentary, cue, delimitation, delineation, demarcation, denotation, determination, diagnosis, drift, elucidation, exemplification, explanation, explication, exposition, expounding, fixing, formalization, gloss, individuation, interpretation, key, outlining, rationale, rendering, rendition, representation, settling, signification, solution, statement of meaning, terminology, translation; SEE CONCEPTS 274,278,689

definitive [adj] *authoritative*
absolute, actual, categorical, clear-cut, closing, complete, completing, concluding, conclusive, decisive, definite, determining, downright*, end-

ing, exhaustive, express, final, finishing, flat out*, last, limiting, nailed down, perfect, plain, precise, real, reliable, settling, specific, straight out, terminal, terminating, ultimate, unambiguous; SEE CONCEPTS 531,535,574

deflate [v1] *reduce or cause to contract*
collapse, decrease, depreciate, depress, devalue, diminish, empty, exhaust, flatten, puncture, shrink, squash, void; SEE CONCEPTS 236,247,776

deflate [v2] *humiliate*
chasten, cut down to size*, dash, debunk, disconcert, dispirit, humble, kick in the teeth*, knock down*, let down easy*, let wind out of sails*, mortify, puncture balloon*, put down*, shoot down*, take down*; SEE CONCEPTS 7,19

deflect [v] *bounce off; turn aside*
avert, bend, cover up, curve, deviate, disperse, diverge, divert, fend, glance off, hold off, hook, keep off, parry, pivot, ricochet, sheer, shy, sidetrack, slew, slip, swerve, twist, veer, volte-face, wheel, whip, whirl, wind; SEE CONCEPTS 147,189,194

deflower [v] *ravish; take away beauty*
assault, defile, deflorate, depredate, desecrate, despoil, devour, force, harm, have, mar, molest, outrage, possess, ravage, ravish, ruin, seduce, spoil, violate; SEE CONCEPT 375

deform [v] *distort, disfigure*
batter, blemish, buckle, contort, cripple, damage, deface, flaw, gnarl, grimace, impair, injure, knot, maim, malform, mangle, mar, misshape, mutilate, ruin, skew, spoil, twist, warp, wince; SEE CONCEPTS 246,250

deformed [adj] *disfigured, distorted*
askew, awry, bent, blemished, bowed, buckled, contorted, cramped, crippled, crooked, curved, damaged, disjointed, gnarled, grotesque, humpbacked, hunchbacked, ill-made, irregular, knotted, maimed, malformed, mangled, marred, misproportioned, misshapen, out of shape, scarred, twisted, ugly, warped; SEE CONCEPTS 485,486

deformity [n] *disfigurement, distortion*
aberration, abnormality, asymmetry, buckle, contortion, corruption, crookedness, damage, defacement, defect, depravity, evil, grossness, hideousness, impairment, injury, irregularity, knot, malconformation, malformation, misproportion, misshape, misshapenness, repulsiveness, ugliness, unattractiveness, unnaturalness, unsightliness, warp; SEE CONCEPT 580

defraud [v] *cheat, bilk*
bamboozle, beguile, burn, chouse, circumvent, clip, con, cozen, deceive, delude, do, do number on*, do out of*, dupe, embezzle, fleece, flimflam, foil, hoax, jive*, milk*, outwit, pilfer, pull fast one*, rip off*, rob, shaft*, shuck*, stick*, sucker into*, swindle, take*, take in*, take to the cleaner's*, trick, victimize; SEE CONCEPT 59

deft [adj] *agile, clever*
able, adept, adroit, apt, crack, crackerjack*, cute, dexterous, expert, fleet, handy, having good hands, having know-how, ingenious, neat, nimble, proficient, prompt, quick, ready, skilled, skillful; SEE CONCEPT 527

defunct [adj] *extinct, not functioning*
asleep, bygone, cold, dead, deceased, departed, done for*, down the drain*, exanimate, expired, gone, had it*, inanimate, inoperative, invalid, kaput*, late, lifeless, lost, nonexistent, obsolete,

de
de

out of commission*, vanished; SEE CONCEPTS
539,560

defy [v] *challenge, frustrate*
baffle, beard, brave, confront, contemn, dare, defeat, deride, despise, disregard, elude, face, flout,
fly in face of*, foil, front, gibe*, hang tough*,
hurl defiance at, ignore, insult, make my day*,
mock, oppose, outdare, provoke, repel, repulse,
resist, ridicule, scorn, slight, spurn, stick*, stick
fast*, take one on*, thwart, venture, violate, withstand; SEE CONCEPTS *78,87*

degeneracy [n1] *corruption*
abasement, decadence, degradation, depravity,
dissoluteness, downfall, immorality, inferiority,
meanness, poorness; SEE CONCEPT *645*

degeneracy [n2] *decay, deterioration*
atrophy, debasement, declination, decline, decrease, depravation, devolution, downfall, downgrade; SEE CONCEPTS *230,469*

degenerate [adj] *corrupt, deteriorated*
base, debased, debauched, decadent, decayed, degenerated, degraded, demeaned, depraved, dissolute, effete, failing, fallen, flatitious, immoral,
infamous, low, mean, miscreant, nefarious, overripe, perverted, retrograde, retrogressive, rotten,
sinking, unhealthy, vicious, villainous, vitiated,
wicked, worsen; SEE CONCEPTS *545,570*

degenerate [v] *decay, deteriorate*
backslide, come apart at seams*, corrode, corrupt, decline, decrease, deprave, descend, die on
vine*, disimprove, disintegrate, fall off, go downhill*, go to pieces*, go to the dogs*, lapse, lessen,
regress, retrogress, return, revert, rot, sink, slip,
vitiate, worsen; SEE CONCEPTS *469,698,702*

degradation [n] *depravity, shame*
abasement, debasement, decadence, decline, degeneracy, degeneration, demotion, derogation,
deterioration, discredit, disgrace, dishonor, down-
grading, evil, humiliation, ignominy, mortification, perversion, reduction; SEE CONCEPTS
230,410

degrade [v] *shame, humiliate*
abase, belittle, bemean, bench, break, bump,
bust, canker, cast down, cheapen, corrupt, cut
down to size*, debase, debauch, declass, decry,
degenerate, demean, demote, depose, deprave,
derogate, deteriorate, detract, diminish, disbar,
discredit, disgrace, dishonor, disparage, downgrade, humble, impair, injure, lessen, lower,
mudsling*, pan*, pervert, put down, reduce, rule
out, run down*, shoot down*, sink, slam, take
down*, take down a peg*, tear down*, vitiate,
weaken; SEE CONCEPTS *7,19,240*

degree [n1] *unit of measurement*
amount, amplitude, caliber, dimension, division,
expanse, extent, gauge, gradation, grade, height,
intensity, interval, length, limit, line, link, mark,
notch, period, plane, point, proportion, quality,
quantity, range, rate, ratio, reach, rung, scale,
scope, severity, shade, size, space, stage, stair,
standard, step, stint, strength, tenor, term, tier;
SEE CONCEPTS *651,783,792*

degree [n2] *recognition of achievement; rank or
grade of position*
approbation, approval, baccalaureate, caliber,
class, compass, credentials, credit, dignification,
dignity, distinction, eminence, grade, height,
honor, level, magnitude, order, pitch, point, position, potency, qualification, quality, quantity,
range, rank, reach, scope, sheepskin, shingle,

sort, stage, standard, standing, station, status,
strength, testimonial, testimony; SEE CONCEPTS
388,706

dehydrate [v] *take moisture out of*
cotton-mouth, desiccate, drain, dry, dry out, dry
up, evaporate, exsiccate, parch, sear; SEE CON-
CEPTS *250,469*

deify [v] *elevate, glorify*
adore, apotheosize, consecrate, ennoble, enthrone, exalt, extol, idealize, idolize, immortalize, venerate, worship; SEE CONCEPTS *69,367*

deign [v] *lower oneself*
condescend, consent, deem worthy, patronize, see
fit*, stoop, think fit*, vouchsafe; SEE CONCEPT *35*

deity [n] *god, worshiped being*
celestial, celestial being, creator, divine being, divinity, goddess, godhead, idol, immortal, supreme being; SEE CONCEPTS *368,370*

dejected [adj] *depressed, blue*
abject, all torn up*, atrabilious, black, bleak,
broody, bummed out*, cast down, cheerless,
clouded, crestfallen, dampened, dashed, despondent, disconsolate, discouraged, disheartened, dismal, dispirited, doleful, down, downcast,
downhearted, down in the dumps*, down in the
mouth*, dragged, drooping, droopy, gloomy,
glum, heavyhearted, hurting*, in the pits*, low,
low-spirited, melancholy, miserable, moody,
mopey*, mopish*, morose, sad, sagging, shot
down*, spiritless, woebegone, wretched; SEE
CONCEPT *403*

delay [n] *deferment, interruption*
adjournment, bind, check, cooling-off period*,
cunctation, dawdling, demurral, detention, discontinuation, downtime*, filibuster, hangup*,
hindrance, holding, holding pattern*, hold-up*,
impediment, interval, jam, lag, lingering, log-
jam*, loitering, moratorium, obstruction, postponement, problem, procrastination, prorogation,
putting off*, remission, reprieve, retardation, re-
tardment, setback, showstopper*, stall, stay, stop,
stoppage, surcease, suspension, tarrying, tie-up,
wait; SEE CONCEPTS *121,130,666*

delay [v] *cause stop in action*
adjourn, arrest, bar, bide time, block, check,
choke, clog, confine, curb, dawdle, defer, detain,
deter, dilly-dally*, discourage, drag, encumber,
filibuster, gain time, hamper, hold, hold over, impede, inhibit, interfere, intermit, keep, keep back,
lag, lay over, linger, loiter, obstruct, postpone,
prevent, procrastinate, prolong, prorogue, protract, put off, remand, repress, restrict, retard,
shelve, slacken, stall, stave off, stay, suspend,
table, tarry, temporize, withhold; SEE CONCEPTS
121,130,237

delectable [adj] *delicious, enjoyable*
adorable, agreeable, ambrosial, appetizing,
charming, choice, dainty, darling, delicate, delightful, delish, divine, enticing, exquisite, gratifying, heavenly, inviting, luscious, lush,
palatable, pleasant, pleasurable, rare, sapid, satisfying, savory, scrumptious, tasty, toothsome,
yummy; SEE CONCEPTS *574,579,613*

delegate [n] *representative, often governmental*
agent, alternate, ambassador, appointee, catch-
pole*, commissioner, consul, deputy, emissary,
envoy, factor, front*, legate, member, member of
congress, minister, mouthpiece, nominee, people's choice, pinch hitter*, plenipotentiary, proxy,
regent, rep*, replacement, senator, spokesperson,

stand-in, substitute, surrogate, vicar, viceroy; SEE CONCEPT 354

delegate [v1] *give authority; empower*
accredit, appoint, assign, authorize, cast, charge, choose, commission, constitute, depute, deputize, designate, elect, give nod, invest, license, mandate, name, nominate, ordain, place trust in, select, swear in, warrant; SEE CONCEPTS 50,88

delegate [v2] *assign responsibility*
authorize, consign, devolve, entrust, give, hand over, hold responsible for, parcel out*, pass on*, relegate, send on errand, send on mission, shunt, transfer; SEE CONCEPTS 50,88,143

delegation [n1] *assignment of responsibility*
appointment, apportioning, authorization, charge, commissioning, committal, consigning, consignment, conveyance, conveying, deputation, deputization, deputizing, devolution, entrustment, giving over, installation, investiture, mandate, nomination, ordination, reference, referring, relegation, sending away, submittal, submitting, transferal, transference, transferring, trust; SEE CONCEPTS 50,88,143,685

delegation [n2] *group of representatives*
commission, contingent, deputation, embassy, envoys, gathering, legation, mission, organization; SEE CONCEPTS 299,301

delete [v] *erase, remove*
annul, black out, bleep, blot out, blue-pencil*, cancel, clean, clean up, cross out, cut, cut out, decontaminate, destroy, drop, edit, efface, eliminate, exclude, expunge, obliterate, omit, pass up, rub, rub out, rule out, sanitize, snip, squash, squelch, sterilize, strike out, trim, wipe out, X-out*; SEE CONCEPT 211

deleterious [adj] *harmful, damaging*
bad, destroying, destructive, detrimental, hurtful, injurious, mischievous, nocent, nocuous, pernicious, prejudicial, prejudicious, ruining, ruinous; SEE CONCEPTS 537,570

deliberate [adj] *intentional*
advised, aforethought, calculated, careful, cautious, cold-blooded, conscious, considered, cut-and-dried*, designed, designful, done on purpose, express, fixed, intended, judged, meticulous, planned, pondered, prearranged, predesigned, predeterminate, predetermined, premeditated, prepense, projected, provident, prudent, purposed, purposeful, purposive, reasoned, resolved, schemed, scrupulous, studied, studious, thoughtful, thought out, voluntary, wary, weighed, willful, with forethought, witting; SEE CONCEPTS 401,542

deliberate [v] *think about seriously; discuss*
argue, bat it around*, cerebrate, chew over*, cogitate, consider, consult, contemplate, debate, excogitate, hammer away at*, judge, kick around, knock around, meditate, mull over, muse, ponder, pour it on*, put on thinking cap*, rack brains*, reason, reflect, revolve, roll, ruminate, run up a flagpole*, speculate, stew over*, study, sweat over*, talk over, turn over, weigh; SEE CONCEPTS 17,24,56

deliberately [adv] *intentionally*
advisedly, after consideration, apurpose, by design, calculatingly, consciously, designed, determinedly, emphatically, freely, in cold blood, independently, knowingly, meaningfully, on purpose, pointedly, premeditatively, prepensely, purposely, purposively, resolutely, studiously, to that

end, voluntarily, willfully, with a view to, with eyes wide open*, with malice aforethought*, without qualms, wittingly; SEE CONCEPTS 401,542

deliberation [n] *serious thought, discussion*
application, attention, brainwork, calculation, care, carefulness, caution, cerebration, circumspection, cogitation, confabulation, conference, consideration, consultation, debate, forethought, heed, meditation, prudence, purpose, rap, ratiocination, reflection, speculation, study, ventilation, wariness; SEE CONCEPTS 17,24,56

delicacy [n1] *daintiness, fineness of structure*
airiness, debility, diaphaneity, elegance, etherealness, exquisiteness, fragility, frailness, frailty, gossameriness, infirmity, lightness, slenderness, smoothness, softness, subtlety, tenderness, tenuity, translucency, transparency, weakness; SEE CONCEPTS 611,733

delicacy [n2] *delicious, gourmet food*
ambrosia, banquet, bonne bouche, dainty, delight, dessert, feast, goody, indulgence, luxury, morsel, nectar, pleasure, rarity, regale, relish, savory, special, sweet, tidbit, treat; SEE CONCEPT 457

delicate [adj1] *dainty, weak*
aerial, balmy, breakable, choice, delectable, delicious, delightful, elegant, ethereal, exquisite, faint, filmy, fine, fine-grained, finespun, flimsy, fracturable, fragile, frail, frangible, gauzy, gentle, gossamery, graceful, hairline, mild, muted, nice, pale, pastel, rare, recherché, select, shatterable, shattery, slight, soft, subdued, subtle, superior, tender; SEE CONCEPTS 490,574,606

delicate [adj2] *sickly*
ailing, debilitated, decrepit, feeble, flimsy, fragile, frail, infirm, shatterable, shattery, slender, slight, susceptible, tender, unhealthy, weak; SEE CONCEPT 314

delicate [adj3] *fussy, discriminating*
alert, careful, critical, dainty, fastidious, finical, finicking, finicky, gentle, nice, particular, persnickety, prudish, pure, refined, scrupulous, sensitive, squeamish, thin-skinned; SEE CONCEPT 404

delicate [adj4] *difficult, sticky (situation)*
critical, hair-trigger*, precarious, sensitive, ticklish, touchy, tricky, uncertain, unpredictable, volatile; SEE CONCEPT 565

delicate [adj5] *careful, tactful*
accurate, adept, cautious, considerate, deft, detailed, diplomatic, discreet, expert, foresighted, heedful, masterly, minute, politic, precise, proficient, prudent, sensitive, skilled, tactical, wary; SEE CONCEPTS 401,542

delicately [adv] *carefully*
beautifully, cautiously, daintily, deftly, elegantly, exquisitely, fastidiously, finely, gracefully, lightly, precisely, sensitively, skillfully, softly, subtly, tactfully; SEE CONCEPTS 542,544

delicious [adj] *pleasing, especially to the taste*
adorable, ambrosial, appetizing, choice, dainty, darling, delectable, delightful, delish*, distinctive, divine, enjoyable, enticing, exquisite, fit for king*, good, gratifying, heavenly, luscious, lush, mellow, mouthwatering, nectareous, nice, palatable, piquant, pleasant, rare, rich, sapid, savory, scrumptious, spicy, sweet, tasteful, tasty, tempting, titillating, toothsome, well-prepared, well-seasoned, yummy*; SEE CONCEPTS 572,613

de
de

delight [n] *enjoyment, happiness*
contentment, delectation, ecstasy, enchantment, felicity, fruition, gladness, glee, gratification, hilarity, jollity, joy, joyance, mirth, pleasure, rapture, relish, satisfaction, transport; SEE CONCEPT *410*

delight [v] *make happy; experience happiness*
allure, amuse, arride, attract, be the ticket*, charm, cheer, content, delectate, divert, enchant, enrapture, entertain, exult, fascinate, freak out, gladden, glory, go over big*, gratify, groove*, hit the spot*, jubilate, knock dead*, knock out*, please, pleasure, ravish, rejoice, satisfy, score, send, slay, thrill, tickle pink*, tickle to death*, turn on, wow; SEE CONCEPTS *7,22*

delighted [adj] *very happy*
captivated, charmed, ecstatic, elated, enchanted, entranced, excited, fulfilled, gladdened, gratified, joyous, jubilant, overjoyed, pleasantly surprised, pleased, thrilled; SEE CONCEPT *403*

delightful [adj] *pleasant, charming*
adorable, agreeable, alluring, ambrosial, amusing, attractive, beautiful, captivating, cheery, clever, congenial, darling, delectable, delicious, enchanting, engaging, enjoyable, entertaining, fair, fascinating, gratifying, heavenly, ineffable, lovely, luscious, lush, pleasing, pleasurable, rapturous, ravishing, refreshing, satisfying, scrumptious, thrilling, yummy*; SEE CONCEPTS *401,404*

delight in [v] *take pleasure from*
admire, adore, amuse oneself, appreciate, be content, be pleased, cherish, dig*, eat up*, enjoy, feast on, get a kick out of*, get high on*, get off on*, glory in, groove on*, indulge in, like, live a little*, live it up*, love, luxuriate in, relish, revel in, savor; SEE CONCEPTS *32,410*

delinquency [n] *misconduct*
crime, default, dereliction, failure, fault, lapse, misbehavior, misdeed, misdemeanor, neglect, nonobservance, offense, oversight, weakness, wrongdoing; SEE CONCEPTS *192,645*

delinquent [n] *criminal, often young*
behind, blackguard, black sheep*, culprit, dawdler, deadbeat*, deadhead*, debtor, defaulter, derelict, desperado, evader, fallen angel*, felon, hoodlum*, jailbird*, JD*, juvenile delinquent, juvie*, lawbreaker, loafer, lounger, malefactor, miscreant, neglecter, no show*, offender, outlaw, punk*, recreant, reprobate, sinner, wrongdoer, young offender; SEE CONCEPT *412*

delinquent [adj] *irresponsible, defaulting*
behind, blamable, blameworthy, careless, censurable, criminal, culpable, defaultant, derelict, disregardful, faulty, guilty, lax, neglectful, negligent, offending, overdue, procrastinating, red-handed*, remiss, reprehensible, shabby, slack, tardy, unpaid; SEE CONCEPTS *401,570*

delirious [adj1] *mentally imbalanced*
aberrant, bewildered, confused, crazed, crazy, demented, deranged, deviant, deviate, disarranged, disordered, distracted, disturbed, flipped*, flipped out*, hallucinatory, incoherent, insane, irrational, lightheaded, lunatic, mad, maniac, maniacal, manic, off one's head*, out of one's head*, out of one's skull*, rambling, raving, unhinged, unreasonable, unsettled, wandering; SEE CONCEPTS *402,403*

delirious [adj2] *excited; very happy*
beside oneself*, carried away*, corybantic, crazy, delighted, drunk*, ecstatic, enthused, frantic, frenetic, frenzied, furious, hysterical, intoxicated, mad, overwrought, rabid*, rapturous, thrilled, transported, wild; SEE CONCEPTS *401,403*

delirium [n] *madness*
aberration, ardor, dementia, derangement, ecstasy, enthusiasm, fervor, fever, frenzy, furor, fury, hallucination, hysteria, insanity, lunacy, mania, passion, rage, raving, transport, zeal; SEE CONCEPT *410*

deliver [v1] *transfer, carry*
bear, bring, cart, come across with*, convey, dish out*, distribute, drop, fork over*, gimme*, give, hand, hand-carry, hand over, pass, put on, put out, remit, transport, truck; SEE CONCEPTS *108,217*

deliver [v2] *relinquish possession*
abandon, cede, commit, give up, grant, hand over, let go, resign, surrender, transfer, turn over, yield; SEE CONCEPTS *116,131*

deliver [v3] *free, liberate*
acquit, discharge, emancipate, loose, ransom, redeem, release, rescue, save, unshackle; SEE CONCEPT *127*

deliver [v4] *announce, proclaim*
address, bring out, broach, chime in, come out with, communicate, declare, express, give, give forth, impart, present, pronounce, publish, read, say, state, tell, throw out, utter, vent, voice; SEE CONCEPTS *51,60*

deliver [v5] *administer; throw*
aim, deal, direct, dispatch, fling, give, hurl, inflict, launch, pitch, send, strike, transmit; SEE CONCEPTS *217,222*

deliver [v6] *discharge, give forth*
accouch, bear, birth, born, dispense, feed, find, hand, hand over, produce, provide, release, supply, turn over; SEE CONCEPTS *179,374*

delivery [n1] *transfer, transmittal*
carting, commitment, consignment, conveyance, dispatch, distribution, drop, freighting, giving over, handing over, impartment, intrusting, mailing, parcel post, portage, post, rendition, shipment, surrender, transmission; SEE CONCEPTS *108,217*

delivery [n2] *articulation of message*
accent, diction, elocution, emphasis, enunciation, inflection, intonation, modulation, pronunciation, speech, utterance; SEE CONCEPTS *47,595*

delivery [n3] *childbirth*
accouchement, bearing, birth, birthing, bringing forth, Caesarian section, childbearing, confinement, geniture, labor, lying-in, parturition, travail; SEE CONCEPTS *302,373,374*

delivery [n4] *giving of freedom*
deliverance, emancipation, escape, freeing, liberation, pardon, release, rescue, salvage, salvation; SEE CONCEPT *127*

delude [v] *deceive, fool*
beguile, betray, bluff, caboodle*, cheat, con, cozen, disinform, do a number on*, double-cross, dupe*, gull*, hoax*, hoodwink*, illude, impose on, jive*, juggle*, lead up garden path*, misguide, mislead, mousetrap*, outfox, play trick on, snow*, string along, sucker*, take in, trick; SEE CONCEPT *59*

deluge [n] *downpour, flood of something*
avalanche, barrage, cataclysm, cataract, drencher, flux, inundation, niagara, overflowing, overrunning, pour, rush, spate, torrent; SEE CONCEPTS *432,524,787*

deluge [*v1*] *inundate with water*
douse, drench, drown, engulf, flood, flush, gush, overflow, overrun, overwhelm, pour, sluice, soak, sop, souse, stream, submerge, swamp, wet, whelm; SEE CONCEPT 256

deluge [*v2*] *overwhelm*
abound, crowd, engulf, flood, glut, inundate, overcome, overcrowd, overload, overrun, over-supply, snow*, snow under*, swamp, teem; SEE CONCEPTS 42,140

delusion [*n*] *misconception, misbelief*
apparition, blunder, casuistry, chicanery, day-dream, deception, deceptiveness, dream, eidolon, error, fallacy, false impression, fancy, fantasy, figment*, fool's paradise*, ghost, hallucination, head trip*, ignis fatuus, illusion, lapse, mirage, misapprehension, mistake, optical illusion, over-sight, phantasm, phantom, pipe dream*, self-deception, shade, speciousness, spuriousness, trickery, trip, vision; SEE CONCEPTS 409,410,689

delusive [*adj*] *deceptive*
apparent, beguiling, chimerical, deceiving, delud-ing, fallacious, false, fanciful, fantastic, illusive, illusory, imaginary, misleading, ostensible, quix-otic, seeming, specious, spurious, visionary; SEE CONCEPT 582

deluxe [*adj*] *superior, plush*
choice, costly, dainty, delicate, elegant, exclu-sive, expensive, exquisite, first-class, grand, lus-cious, lush, luxuriant, luxurious, opulent, palatial, posh, rare, recherché, rich, ritzy, select, special, splendid, sumptuous, super, swank, swanky; SEE CONCEPT 574

delve [*v*] *dig into task, action*
burrow, dig, dredge, examine, excavate, explore, ferret out*, go into, gouge out, inquire, investi-gate, jump into, leave no stone unturned*, look into, probe, prospect, ransack, really get into*, research, rummage, scoop out, search, seek, shovel, sift, spade, trowel, turn inside out*, un-earth; SEE CONCEPTS 87,103,216

demagogue [*n*] *agitating person*
agitator, fanatic, firebrand*, fomenter, haranger, hothead*, incendiary, inciter, inflamer, instigator, politician, rabble-rouser*, radical, rebel, revolu-tionary, soapbox orator*, troublemaker; SEE CON-CEPTS 359,412

demand [*n*] *question, request*
appeal, application, arrogation, bid, bidding, call, call for, charge, claim, clamor, command, coun-terclaim, entreatment, entreaty, exaction, impe-tration, imploration, importunity, imposition, inquiry, insistence, interest, interrogation, lien, necessity, need, occasion, order, petition, plea, prayer, pursuit, requirement, requisition, rush, sale, search, solicitation, stipulation, suit, suppli-cation, trade, ultimatum, use, vogue, want; SEE CONCEPT 662

demand [*v1*] *ask strongly for something*
abuse, appeal, apply, arrogate, badger, beg, be-seech, besiege, bid, challenge, charge, cite, claim, clamor for, coerce, command, compel, constrain, counterclaim, direct, dun, enjoin, en-treat, exact, expect, force, hit, hit up, impetrate, implore, importune, inquire, insist on, interrogate, knock, nag, necessitate, oblige, order, pester, pe-tition, postulate, pray, press, question, request, require, requisition, solicit, stipulate, sue for, summon, supplicate, tax, urge, whistle for; SEE CONCEPT 53

demand [*v2*] *require*
ask, call for, command, crave, cry out for, fail, involve, lack, necessitate, need, oblige, take, want; SEE CONCEPTS 26,646

demanding [*adj*] *challenging, urgent*
ambitious, backbreaker*, bothersome, clamorous, critical, dictatorial, difficult, exacting, exhausting, exigent, fussy, grievous, hard, imperious, impor-tunate, insistent, nagging, onerous, oppressive, pressing, querulous, strict, stringent, taxing, tough, troublesome, trying, wearing, weighty; SEE CONCEPTS 542,565

demarcation [*n*] *boundary, division*
bound, confine, delimitation, differentiation, dis-tinction, enclosure, limit, margin, separation, split, terminus; SEE CONCEPT 745

demean [*v*] *humble, humiliate*
abase, bad-mouth*, belittle, bemean, cast down, contemn, cut down to size*, cut rate, debase, de-cry, degrade, derogate, descend, despise, detract, dis*, disparage, dump on*, knock down*, lower, pan*, poor-mouth*, scorn, sink, stoop*; SEE CON-CEPTS 7,19,54

demeanor [*n*] *behavior, manner*
address, air, attitude, bearing, carriage, comport-ment, conduct, deportment, disposition, mien, poise, port, presence, set; SEE CONCEPTS 411,633

demented [*adj*] *crazy, insane*
bananas*, bemused, crackbrained*, daft, deliri-ous, deranged, distracted, distraught, flipped out*, foolish, frenzied, fruity*, hysterical, idiotic, in the ozone*, lunatic, mad, maniac, maniacal, manic, non compos mentis, nutty as a fruitcake*, out of one's gourd*, out of one's tree*, psycho, psycho-pathic, psychotic, schitzy*, schizoid*, unbal-anced, unglued*, unhinged*, unsound, whacko*; SEE CONCEPT 403

demise [*n*] *fate, usually death*
annihilation, collapse, curtains, decease, depar-ture, dissolution, downfall, dying, end, ending, expiration, extinction, failure, fall, final thrill*, last out*, last roundup*, lights out*, number's up*, passing, quietus, ruin, silence, sleep, termi-nation; SEE CONCEPTS 105,304,679

democracy [*n*] *government in which people par-ticipate*
commonwealth, egalitarianism, emancipation, equalitarianism, equality, freedom, justice, liberal government, representative government, republic, suffrage; SEE CONCEPTS 299,688,689

democratic [*adj*] *representative, self-governing*
autonomous, common, communal, constitutional, egalitarian, equal, free, friendly, individualistic, informal, just, libertarian, orderly, popular, pop-ulist, self-ruling, socialist; SEE CONCEPTS 319,536

demolish [*v*] *destroy; consume*
annihilate, break, bulldoze, burst, crack, crush, decimate, defeat, devastate, devour, dilapidate, dismantle, eat, flatten, gobble up, knock down, level, obliterate, overthrow, overturn, pulverize, put away, put in toilet*, raze, ruin, sink, smash, take apart, take out, tear down, torpedo*, total*, trash*, undo, wax*, wipe off map*, wrack, wreck; SEE CONCEPTS 169,252

demolition [*n*] *destruction*
annihilation, bulldozing, explosion, extermina-tion, knocking down, leveling, razing, wrecking; SEE CONCEPT 252

de
de

demon [n] *evil, devilish being or influence*
archfiend, beast, brute, fiend, goblin, hellion, imp, incubus, little devil*, malignant spirit, monster, rascal, rogue, Satan, succubus, vampire, villain; SEE CONCEPTS *370,412*

demonic/demoniac/demonical [adj] *evil*
aroused, crazed, devilish, diabolic, diabolical, fiendish, fired, frantic, frenetic, frenzied, hellish, impious, infernal, insane, inspired, mad, maniacal, manic, possessed, satanic, serpentine, unhallowed, violent, wicked; SEE CONCEPTS *404,545*

demonstrable [adj] *provable, evident*
ascertainable, attestable, axiomatic, certain, conclusive, deducible, evincible, incontrovertible, indubitable, inferable, irrefutable, obvious, palpable, positive, self-evident, undeniable, unmistakable, verifiable; SEE CONCEPTS *529,535*

demonstrate [v1] *display, show*
authenticate, determine, establish, evidence, evince, exhibit, expose, flaunt, indicate, make evident, make out, manifest, prove, roll out*, show and tell*, test, testify to, trot out*, try, validate; SEE CONCEPT *97*

demonstrate [v2] *explain, illustrate*
confirm, debunk, describe, express, give for instance, make clear, ostend, proclaim, set forth, show how, teach, testify to, walk one through*; SEE CONCEPT *57*

demonstrate [v3] *display or take public action for a cause*
exhibit, fast, lie in, manifest, march, march on, parade, picket, protest, rally, sit in, stage walkout, strike, walkout; SEE CONCEPTS *261,300*

demonstration [n1] *display of proof*
affirmation, confirmation, description, evidence, exhibition, explanation, exposition, expression, illustration, induction, manifestation, presentation, proof, show, spectacle, substantiation, test, testimony, trial, validation; SEE CONCEPT *261*

demonstration [n2] *display of belief in cause by taking public action*
fast, lie-in*, love-in*, march, mass lobby, parade, peace march, picket, picket line, protest, rally, sit-in*, strike, teach-in*, walkout; SEE CONCEPTS *261,300*

demonstrative [adj1] *expressive, communicative*
affectionate, candid, effusive, emotional, evincive, expansive, explanatory, expository, frank, gushing, histrionic, illustrative, indicative, loving, open, outgoing, outpouring, outspoken, plain, profuse, symptomatic, tender, unconstrained, unreserved, unrestrained, warmhearted; SEE CONCEPTS *267,401*

demonstrative [adj2] *conclusive*
authenticating, certain, convincing, decisive, definite, final, proving, showing, specific, validating; SEE CONCEPTS *531,537*

demoralize [v1] *depress, unnerve*
abash, blow out, blow up, chill, cripple, damp, dampen, daunt, debilitate, deject, disarrange, disconcert, discountenance, discourage, dishearten, disorder, disorganize, disparage, dispirit, disturb, embarrass, enfeeble, get to*, jumble, muddle, nonplus, psych out*, rattle, sap, send up*, shake, snarl, take apart*, take steam out*, undermine, unglue*, unman, unsettle, unzip*, upset, weaken; SEE CONCEPTS *7,19*

demoralize [v2] *corrupt, pervert*
bastardize, bestialize, brutalize, debase, debauch, deprave, lower, vitiate, warp; SEE CONCEPT *14*

demote [v] *downgrade, lower in rank*
bench*, break, bump, bust, declass, degrade, demean, demerit, dismiss, disrate, hold back, kick downstairs*, lower, reduce, relegate, set back; SEE CONCEPTS *233,351*

demur [v] *disagree*
balk, cavil, challenge, combat, complain, deprecate, disapprove, dispute, doubt, fight, hem and haw*, hesitate, object, oppose, pause, protest, pussyfoot*, refuse, remonstrate, resist, scruple, shy, stick, stickle, strain, take exception*, vacillate, wait and see*, waver; SEE CONCEPTS *46,54*

demure [adj] *reserved, affected*
backward, bashful, blushing, close, coy, decorous, diffident, earnest, humble, modest, nice, prim, prissy, proper, prudish, reticent, retiring, sedate, serious, shy, silent, skittish, sober, solemn, staid, strait-laced, timid, unassertive, unassuming, unassured; SEE CONCEPTS *401,404*

den [n1] *cavern, hideaway*
atelier, burrow, cave, cloister, couch, cubbyhole, haunt, hideout, hole, hotbed, lair, lodge, nest, retreat, sanctuary, sanctum, shelter, snuggery, study; SEE CONCEPTS *448,513*

den [n2] *room for relaxation or informal entertaining*
family room, library, media room, playroom, recreation room, rec room*, rumpus room, studio, TV room; SEE CONCEPTS *440,448*

denial [n] *dismissal, refusal of belief in statement*
abnegation, abstaining, adjuration, brush-off, cold shoulder*, contradiction, controversion, declination, disallowance, disapproval, disavowal, disclaimer, dismissing, disproof, dissent, forswearing, gainsaying, nay, negation, negative, nix*, nonacceptance, noncommittal, no way*, prohibition, protestation, rebuff, rebuttal, refraining, refusing, refutal, refutation, rejecting, rejection, renegement, renouncement, renunciation, repudiating, repudiation, repulse, retraction, turndown, veto; SEE CONCEPTS *45,54*

denigrate [v] *belittle, malign*
asperse, bad mouth*, besmirch, blacken, blister, calumniate, decry, defame, dis*, disparage, give black eye*, impugn, knock*, libel, mudsling*, put down*, revile, rip up*, roast*, run down*, scandalize, slander, tear down*, traduce, vilify; SEE CONCEPTS *52,54*

denizen [n] *resident*
citizen, dweller, habitant, indweller, inhabitant, inhabiter, liver, national, native, occupant, resider, subject; SEE CONCEPT *413*

denomination [n1] *religious belief*
church, communion, connection, creed, cult, faith, group, persuasion, religion, school, sect; SEE CONCEPTS *368,689*

denomination [n2] *classification*
body, category, class, grade, group, size, type, unit, value; SEE CONCEPT *378*

denomination [n3] *name*
appellation, appellative, brand, cognomen, compellation, designation, flag, handle, identification, label, moniker, nomen, slot, style, surname, tab, tag, term, title; SEE CONCEPT *683*

denotation [n] *meaning, description*
designation, explanation, implication, indication, signification, specification; SEE CONCEPTS *268, 682*

denote [v] *designate, mean*
add up, announce, argue, bespeak, betoken, con-

note, evidence, express, finger, flash, hang sign on*, imply, import, indicate, insinuate, intend, make, mark, peg, prove, put down for, put finger on*, show, signify, spell, stand for, symbol, symbolize, tab, tag, typify; SEE CONCEPTS 55,682

denounce [v] *condemn, attack*
accuse, adjudicate, arraign, blacklist, blame, boycott, brand, castigate, censure, charge, charge with, criticize, damn, declaim, decry, denunciate, derogate, dress down, excoriate, expose, finger*, hang something on*, impeach, implicate, impugn, incriminate, indict, inveigh against, knock, ostracize, proscribe, prosecute, rap, rat*, rebuke, reprehend, reprimand, reproach, reprobate, reprove, revile, scold, show up, skin*, smear, stigmatize, take to task, threaten, upbraid, vilify, vituperate; SEE CONCEPTS 44,52

dense [adj1] *compressed, thick*
close, close-knit, compact, condensed, crammed, crowded, heaped, heavy, impenetrable, jammed, jam-packed*, massed, opaque, packed, packed like sardines*, piled, solid, substantial, thickset; SEE CONCEPTS 483

dense [adj2] *slow, stupid*
blockheaded*, boorish, doltish, dull, dumb, fatheaded*, ignorant, imbecilic, impassive, lethargic, numskulled*, oafish, obtuse, phlegmatic, simple, slow-witted, sluggish, stolid, thick, torpid; SEE CONCEPT 402

density [n] *bulk, mass*
body, closeness, compactness, concretion, consistency, crowdedness, denseness, frequency, heaviness, impenetrability, massiveness, quantity, solidity, substantiality, thickness, tightness; SEE CONCEPT 722

dent [n] *depression, scrape, chip*
cavity, concavity, crater, crenel, cut, dimple, dint, dip, embrasure, furrow, hollow, impression, incision, indentation, nick, notch, pit, scallop, score, scratch, sink, trough; SEE CONCEPT 580

dent [v] *chip, scrape, depress*
dig, dimple, dint, furrow, gouge, hollow, imprint, indent, make concave, mark, nick, notch, perforate, pit, press in, push in, ridge, scratch; SEE CONCEPTS 176,189,208,246

denunciation [n] *condemnation, criticism*
accusation, arraignment, blame, castigation, censure, charge, cursing, damning, denouncement, derogation, dressing down*, fulmination, incrimination, indictment, invective, knock*, obloquy, rap*, reprehension, reprimand, reprobation, smearing, stigmatization, upbraidment, vilification; SEE CONCEPT 52

deny [v] *disagree, renounce, decline*
abjure, abnegate, ban, begrudge, call on, contradict, contravene, controvert, curb, disacknowledge, disallow, disavow, disbelieve, discard, disclaim, discredit, disown, disprove, doubt, enjoin from, eschew, exclude, forbid, forgo, forsake, gainsay, hold back, keep back, negate, negative, not buy, nullify, oppose, rebuff, rebut, recant, refuse, refute, reject, repudiate, restrain, revoke, sacrifice, say no to, spurn, taboo, take exception to, turn down, turn thumbs down*, veto, withhold; SEE CONCEPTS 46,49,52

deodorant [n] *something that freshens*
air freshener, antiperspirant, cleanser, cosmetic, deodorizer, disinfectant, fumigant, fumigator, smoke screen*; SEE CONCEPT 492

depart [v1] *leave, retreat*
abandon, abdicate, absent, beat it*, blast off*, cut and run*, cut out*, decamp, desert, disappear, emigrate, escape, evacuate, exit, get away, git*, go, go away, go forth, hit the bricks*, hit the road*, hit the trail*, make a break*, march out, migrate, move on, move out, part, perish, pull out, quit, remove, retire, sally forth*, say goodbye*, scram*, secede, set forth, shove off*, slip away*, split*, start, start out, take leave, tergiversate, troop*, vacate, vanish, withdraw; SEE CONCEPT 195

depart [v2] *diverge from normal, expected*
abandon, cast, desert, deviate, differ, digress, disagree, discard, dissent, excurse, forsake, ramble, reject, repudiate, stray, swerve, turn aside, vary, veer, wander; SEE CONCEPTS 665,697

department [n1] *section of organization, area*
administration, agency, area, arena, beat, board, branch, bureau, canton, circuit, commission, commune, constituency, division, force, office, parish, precinct, quarter, range, staff, station, subdivision, territory, tract, unit, ward; SEE CONCEPTS 381,440,508

department [n2] *area of interest, expertise*
activity, administration, assignment, avocation, bailiwick, berth, bureau, business, capacity, class, classification, domain, dominion, duty, field, function, incumbency, jurisdiction, line, niche, occupation, office, province, realm, responsibility, slot, specialty, sphere, spot, station, vocation, walk of life, wing; SEE CONCEPT 349

departure [n1] *leaving*
abandonment, adieu, bow out*, congé, decampment, desertion, egress, egression, embarkation, emigration, escape, evacuation, exit, exodus, expatriation, farewell, flight, getaway*, going, going away, goodbye*, hegira, migration, parting, passage, powder*, quitting, recession, removal, retirement, retreat, sailing, separation, setting forth, setting out, stampede, start, takeoff, taking leave, taking off, vacation, vanishing act*, walkout, withdrawal; SEE CONCEPT 195

departure [n2] *deviation from normal, expected*
aberration, branching off, branching out, change, declination, deflection, difference, digression, divergence, diversion, innovation, in thing*, last word*, latest thing*, new wrinkle*, novelty, rambling, shift, straying, turning, variance, variation, veering, wandering; SEE CONCEPTS 665,697

depend [v1] *count on, rely upon*
bank on*, bet bottom dollar on*, bet on*, build upon, calculate on, confide in, gamble on*, lay money on*, lean on*, reckon on, trust in, turn to; SEE CONCEPT 26

depend [v2] *be contingent on*
be at mercy of, be based on, be conditioned, be connected with, be determined by, be in control of, be in the power of, be subject to, be subordinate to, bottom, found, ground, hang, hang in suspense, hang on, hinge on, pend, rest, rest on, rest with, revolve around, revolve on, stand on, stay, trust to, turn on; SEE CONCEPT 711

dependable [adj] *reliable, responsible*
always there, carrying the load*, certain, constant, faithful, good as one's word*, loyal, rocklike*, secure, stable, staunch, steadfast, steady, sturdy, sure, to be counted on, tried, tried-and-true, true, trustworthy, trusty, unfailing; SEE CONCEPTS 542,560

de
de

dependence/dependency [n1] *confidence, reliance*
assurance, belief, credence, expectation, faith, hope, interdependence, responsibility, responsibleness, stability, steadiness, stock, trust, trustiness, trustworthiness; SEE CONCEPTS *410,689*

dependence/dependency [n2] *addiction, need*
attachment, contingency, habit, helplessness, hook, inability, security blanket, servility, subjection, subordination, subservience, vulnerability, weakness, yoke; SEE CONCEPTS *20,709*

dependent [adj1] *weak, helpless*
abased, clinging, counting on, debased, defenseless, humbled, immature, indigent, inferior, lesser, minor, poor, reliant, relying on, secondary, subordinate, tied to apron strings*, under, under thumb*, unsustaining, vulnerable; SEE CONCEPTS *404,574*

dependent [adj2] *contingent, determined by*
accessory to, ancillary, appurtenant, conditional, controlled by, counting, depending, incidental to, liable to, provisory, reckoning, regulated by, relative, reliant, relying, subject to, subordinate, subservient, susceptible, sustained by, trusting, under control of; SEE CONCEPT *546*

depict [v] *describe, render in drawing or writing*
characterize, delineate, design, detail, illustrate, image, interpret, limn, narrate, outline, paint, picture, portray, relate, report, represent, reproduce, sculpt, sketch, state; SEE CONCEPTS *79,174*

depiction [n] *description, rendering*
delineation, drawing, illustration, image, likeness, outline, picture, portraiture, portrayal, presentment, representation, sketch; SEE CONCEPTS *259,268*

deplete [v] *consume, exhaust supply*
bankrupt, bleed*, decrease, dig into, diminish, drain, draw, dry up, empty, evacuate, expend, finish, impoverish, lessen, milk*, reduce, sap, spend, squander, suck dry*, undermine, use up, wash up, waste, weaken; SEE CONCEPTS *142,169,225*

depleted [adj] *consumed, exhausted*
all in*, bare, bleary*, collapsed, decreased, depreciated, destitute, devoid of, drained, effete, emptied, far-gone*, in want, kaput*, lessened, out of, pooped out*, reduced, sapped, short of, sold, sold out, spent, sucked out*, used, used up, vacant, washed out, wasted, weakened, without resources, worn, worn out; SEE CONCEPTS *576,771*

deplorable [adj] *unfortunate, shameful*
afflictive, awful, blameworthy, bummer*, calamitous, dire, dirty, disastrous, disgraceful, dishonorable, disreputable, distressing, dolorous, downer*, dreadful, execrable, faulty, godawful*, grievous, grim, heartbreaking, heartrending, horrifying, intolerable, lamentable, lousy, melancholy, miserable, mournful, opprobrious, overwhelming, pitiable, poor, regrettable, reprehensible, rotten, sad, scandalous, sickening, stinking, terrible, tragic, unbearable, unsatisfactory, woeful, wretched; SEE CONCEPTS *529,570,574*

deplore [v] *regret; condemn*
abhor, be against, bemoan, bewail, carry on, censure, complain, cry, denounce, deprecate, disapprove of, eat one's heart out*, grieve for, hate, hurt, lament, moan, mourn, object to, repent, rue, sing the blues*, sorrow over, take on, weep; SEE CONCEPTS *21,29*

deploy [v] *redistribute, station troops or weapons*
arrange, display, dispose, expand, extend, fan out, form front, open, position, put out patrol, set out, set up, spread out, take battle stations, unfold, use, utilize; SEE CONCEPTS *158,213,320*

deport [v] *banish*
cast out, dismiss, displace, exile, expatriate, expel, expulse, extradite, oust, relegate, ship out, transport; SEE CONCEPTS *198,211,217*

deportation [n] *banishment*
displacement, eviction, exile, expatriation, expulsion, extradition, ostracism, relegation, removal, transportation; SEE CONCEPTS *198,211,217*

deportment [n] *carriage, manner of person*
actions, address, air, appearance, aspect, bearing, behavior, cast, comportment, conduct, demeanor, mien, port, posture, set, stance; SEE CONCEPT *633*

depose [v] *oust from position*
boot out, bounce, break, can*, cashier, chuck, degrade, demote, dethrone, discrown, dismiss, displace, downgrade, drum out, eject, freeze out*, give heave-ho*, impeach, kick out*, overthrow, remove from office, ride out on rail*, run out of town*, send packing*, subvert, throw out, throw out on ear*, uncrown, unfrock, unmake, unseat, upset; SEE CONCEPTS *133,298,320*

deposit [n1] *down payment; money saved*
drop, installment, money in the bank, partial payment, pledge, retainer, security, stake, warranty; SEE CONCEPTS *340,344*

deposit [n2] *accumulation of solid*
alluvium, delta, deposition, dregs, drift, grounds, lees, precipitate, precipitation, sediment, settlings, silt; SEE CONCEPTS *432,470,471*

deposit [v] *locate, put in place for safekeeping*
accumulate, amass, bank, collect, commit, deliver, ditch, drop, entrust, garner, give in trust, hoard, install, invest, keep, lay, lay away, park, place, plant*, plop*, plunk*, plunk down*, precipitate, put aside, put by, repose, rest, salt away*, save, settle, sit down, sock away*, squirrel away*, stash, stock up, store, stow, transfer, treasure; SEE CONCEPTS *134,201,330*

deposition [n1] *dethroning, ousting*
degradation, discharge, dismissal, displacement, ejection, impeachment, overthrow, removal, unfrocking; SEE CONCEPTS *133,298,320*

deposition [n2] *attestation of truth, especially in legal matters*
affidavit, affirmation, allegation, announcement, declaration, evidence, sworn statement, testimony; SEE CONCEPTS *271,318*

depository [n] *storage place*
archive, arsenal, bank, bunker, cache, collection, depot, gallery, magazine, museum, repertory, repository, safe, safe-deposit box, store, storehouse, tomb, vault, warehouse; SEE CONCEPT *435*

depot [n] *storage place; station*
annex, armory, base, depository, destination, garage, halting-place, haven, junction, loft, lot, magazine, office, repository, stopping-place, store, storehouse, storeroom, terminal, terminus, waiting room, warehouse, yard; SEE CONCEPTS *435,449*

deprave [v] *corrupt, lead astray*
bastardize, bestialize, brutalize, debase, debauch, degrade, demoralize, pervert, seduce, subvert, vitiate, warp; SEE CONCEPT *14*

depraved [adj] *corrupt, immoral*
abandoned, bad, base, debased, debauched, degenerate, degraded, dirty*, dirty-minded, dissolute, evil, fast*, filthy*, flagitious, gone to the

dogs*, kinky*, lascivious, lewd, licentious, low, mean, miscreant, nefarious, perverted, profligate, putrid, rotten, shameless, sinful, twisted, unhealthy, unnatural, vicious, vile, villainous, vitiate, vitiated, wanton, warped, wicked; SEE CONCEPT 545

depravity [n] *corruption, immorality*
abandonment, baseness, contamination, criminality, debasement, debauchery, degeneracy, degradation, depravation, evil, iniquity, lewdness, licentiousness, perversion, profligacy, sensuality, sinfulness, vice, viciousness, vitiation, wickedness; SEE CONCEPT 645

deprecate [v] *belittle, condemn*
cut down to size*, depreciate, derogate, detract, disapprove of, discommend, discountenance, disesteem, disfavor, disparage, expostulate, frown, mudsling*, not go for*, object, pooh-pooh*, poor mouth*, protest against, put down*, rip*, run down*, take dim view of, take down, take exception to; SEE CONCEPTS 7,19,52

depreciate [v1] *devalue, lose value*
abate, cheapen, decay, decrease, decry, deflate, depress, deteriorate, devalorize, diminish, downgrade, drop, dwindle, erode, fall, lessen, lower, mark down, reduce, soften, underrate, undervalue, worsen, write down, write off; SEE CONCEPTS 698,776

depreciate [v2] *belittle, ridicule*
abuse, asperse, attack, calumniate, censure, clamor against, condemn, contemn, decry, defame, denigrate, denounce, deprecate, deride, derogate, detract, discount, discountenance, discredit, disgrace, disparage, dispraise, fault, find fault with, humble, knock, look down on*, lower, malign, minimize, put down, rap, revile, roast*, run down*, scoff at, scorn, slam, slander, slight, slur, smear, sneer at, spurn, take down a peg*, traduce, underestimate, underrate, undervalue, vilify; SEE CONCEPTS 7,19,52

depredation [n] *devastation, destruction*
burglary, crime, desecration, desolation, despoiling, laying waste, marauding, pillage, plunder, ransacking, rapine, ravaging, robbery, sacking, spoliation, stealing, theft, wasting; SEE CONCEPTS 192,252

depress [v1] *deject, make despondent; exhaust*
abase, afflict, ail, bear down, beat, beat down*, bother, bug*, bum out*, cast down, chill*, cow*, damp, dampen, darken, daunt, debase, debilitate, degrade, desolate, devitalize, discourage, dishearten, dismay, dispirit, distress, disturb, drag*, drain, dull, enervate, faze, keep under, lower, mock, mortify, oppress, perturb, press, put down*, reduce, reduce to tears*, run down*, sadden, sap*, scorn, slow, throw cold water on*, torment, trouble, try, turn one off*, upset, weaken, weary, weigh down*; SEE CONCEPTS 7,19,240

depress [v2] *devalue*
cheapen, debase, depreciate, diminish, downgrade, impair, lessen, lower, reduce; SEE CONCEPTS 240,330

depress [v3] *push down*
couch, demit, dip, droop, flatten, let down, level, lower, press down, settle, sink, smoosh, squash; SEE CONCEPT 208

depressed [adj1] *discouraged*
bad, bleeding, blue*, bummed out*, cast-down, crestfallen, crummy*, dejected, despondent, destroyed, disconsolate, dispirited, down, down and out*, downcast, downhearted, down in the dumps*, down in the mouth*, dragged*, fed up*, glum, grim, hurting, in a blue funk*, in pain*, in the dumps*, in the pits*, in the toilet*, let down, low, low-down, low-spirited, lugubrious, melancholy, moody, morose, on a downer*, pessimistic, ripped, sad, sob story*, spiritless, taken down*, torn up*, unhappy, weeping, woebegone; SEE CONCEPT 403

depressed [adj2] *concave, pushed down*
hollow, indented, recessed, set back, sunken; SEE CONCEPT 490

depressed [adj3] *disadvantaged*
cheapened, depreciated, deprived, destitute, devalued, distressed, ghetto, ghost, impaired, needy, poor, poverty-stricken, run-down, shanty, skid row*, underprivileged, weakened; SEE CONCEPTS 334,555

depressing [adj] *discouraging, upsetting*
black, bleak, daunting, dejecting, disheartening, dismal, dispiriting, distressing, dreary, funereal, gloomy, heartbreaking, hopeless, joyless, melancholic, melancholy, mournful, oppressive, sad, saddening, somber; SEE CONCEPT 529

depression [n1] *low spirits; despair*
abasement, abjection, abjectness, blahs*, bleakness, blue funk*, bummer, cheerlessness, dejection, desolation, desperation, despondency, disconsolation, discouragement, dispiritedness, distress, dole, dolefulness, dolor, downheartedness, dreariness, dullness, dumps, ennui, gloom, gloominess, heaviness of heart, heavyheartedness, hopelessness, lowness, lugubriosity, melancholia, melancholy, misery, mortification, qualm, sadness, sorrow, the blues*, trouble, unhappiness, vapors*, woefulness, worry; SEE CONCEPT 410

depression [n2] *economic decline*
bad times*, bankruptcy, bear market*, big trouble*, bottom out*, bust, crash, crisis, deflation, dislocation, downturn, drop, failure, hard times*, inactivity, inflation, overproduction, panic, paralysis, rainy days*, recession, retrenchment, sag, slide, slowness, slump, stagflation, stagnation, unemployment; SEE CONCEPTS 324,330,335

depression [n3] *concavity, cavity*
basin, bowl, crater, dent, dimple, dip, excavation, hole, hollow, impression, indentation, pit, pocket, sag, scoop, sink, sinkage, sinkhole, vacuity, vacuum, valley, void; SEE CONCEPT 513

deprivation [n] *taking, keeping away; need*
denial, deprival, destitution, detriment, disadvantage, dispossession, distress, divestiture, divestment, expropriation, hardship, loss, privation, removal, seizure, want, withdrawal, withholding; SEE CONCEPTS 121,142,709

deprive [v] *keep or take away something wanted, needed*
bankrupt, bare, bereave, denude, despoil, disinherit, dismantle, dispossess, disrobe, divest, dock, expropriate, hold back, lose, oust, rob, seize, skim, stiff, strip, wrest; SEE CONCEPTS 121,142

depth [n1] *distance down or across*
base, bottom, declination, deepness, draft, drop, expanse, extent, fathomage, intensity, lower register, lowness, measure, measurement, pit, pitch, profoundness, profundity, remoteness, sounding; SEE CONCEPTS 737,790

depth [n2] *insight, wisdom*
acuity, acumen, astuteness, brain, discernment,

de
de

intellect, intelligence, keenness, penetration, profoundness, profundity, sagacity, sense, sharpness, weightiness; SEE CONCEPT *409*

deputy [n] *assistant, agent*
aide, ambassador, appointee, assembly member, backup, commissioner, councilor, delegate, dogcatcher*, factor, legate, lieutenant, minister, proxy, regent, replacement, representant, representative, second-in-command, sub, subordinate, substitute, surrogate; SEE CONCEPTS *348,354*

derange [v] *make crazy; confuse*
confound, craze*, dement, disarrange, disarray, discommode, discompose, disconcert, disorder, disorganize, displace, distract, disturb, drive mad, frenzy, madden, make insane, mess up*, misplace, muss*, perplex, ruffle, rummage, unbalance, unhinge*, unsettle, upset; SEE CONCEPTS *16,84*

deranged [adj] *crazy, insane*
ape*, baked*, bananas*, berserk, cracked*, crazed, delirious, demented, disarranged, disconcerted, disordered, displaced, distracted, dotty*, flipped*, flipped out*, frantic, frenzied, fried*, irrational, loco*, lunatic, mad, maddened, maniac, maniacal, nuts*, perplexed, schizzo*, unbalanced, unglued*, unhinged*, unscrewed*, unsettled, unsound, unzipped*, whacko*; SEE CONCEPT *403*

deregulate [v] *remove imposed controls on a system*
decontrol, denationalize, leave be, let alone, not interfere, not meddle, not tamper; SEE CONCEPTS *94,117*

deregulation [n] *the removal of imposed controls on a system*
disinvolvement, free competition, free enterprise, free trade, isolationism, laissez-faire, liberalism, noninterference, nonintervention, self-regulating market; SEE CONCEPT *299*

derelict [n] *destitute or down-and-out person*
beggar, bum, castaway, dawdler, drifter, floater, grifter, hobo, ne'er-do-well*, outcast, renegade, skidrow bum, stiff, stumblebum*, tramp, vagabond, vagrant; SEE CONCEPTS *412,423*

derelict [adj1] *careless, negligent*
behindhand, delinquent, disregardful, irresponsible, lax, regardless, remiss, slack, undependable, unreliable, untrustworthy; SEE CONCEPT *542*

derelict [adj2] *deserted, forsaken*
abandoned, castoff, desolate, dilapidated, dingy, discarded, faded, lorn, neglected, ownerless, relinquished, ruined, run-down, seedy, shabby, solitary, threadbare, uncouth; SEE CONCEPT *560*

deride [v] *make fun of; insult*
banter, chaff, contemn, detract, dis*, disdain, disparage, do a number on*, dump on*, flout, gibe, jeer, jolly, kid, knock, laugh at, lout, mock, pan, pooh-pooh*, put down*, quiz, rag*, rally, razz*, rib*, ridicule, roast*, scoff, scorn, slam, sneer, taunt, twit; SEE CONCEPTS *52,54*

de rigueur [adj] *proper, right*
au fait, becoming, comme il faut, conventional, correct, decent, decorous, done, fitting, necessary, required; SEE CONCEPT *558*

derision [n] *insult, disrespect*
backhanded compliment*, brickbat*, Bronx cheer*, butt*, comeback, contempt, contumely, crack, dig*, disdain, disparagement, dump*, jab, jest, joke, laughingstock, laughter, mockery, object of ridicule, parting shot; pilgarlic, put-down,

raillery, ridicule, satire, scoffing, scorn, slam*, slap, sneering; SEE CONCEPTS *52,278,689*

derisive [adj] *ridiculing*
cheeky*, cocky, contemptuous, crusty, disdainful, flip*, fresh, gally, insulting, jeering, mocking, nervy, out-of-line, rude, sarcastic, sassy, scoffing, scornful, smart*, smart-alecky*, taunting; SEE CONCEPT *267*

derivable [adj] *deducible*
a priori, attributable, available, determinable, dogmatic, extractable, inferable, likely, obtainable, reasoned, resultant, traceable; SEE CONCEPT *529*

derivation [n] *root, source*
ancestry, basis, beginning, descent, etymology, foundation, genealogy, inception, origin, provenance, provenience, spin-off, well, wellspring, whence it came; SEE CONCEPT *648*

derivative [n] *product, descendant*
by-product, offshoot, outgrowth, spin-off, wave; SEE CONCEPT *260*

derivative [adj] *borrowed, transmitted from source*
acquired, ancestral, caused, cognate, coming from, connate, copied, evolved, hereditary, imitative, inferential, inferred, not original, obtained, plagiaristic, plagiarized, procured, rehashed, secondary, secondhand, subordinate, uninventive, unoriginal; SEE CONCEPT *549*

derive [v] *deduce a conclusion*
acquire, arrive, assume, collect, determine, develop, draw, educe, elaborate, elicit, evolve, excogitate, extract, follow, formulate, gain, gather, get, glean, infer, judge, make, make out, obtain, procure, put together, reach, receive, trace, work out; SEE CONCEPTS *15,18*

derive from [v] *come from; arise*
descend, emanate, flow, head, issue, originate, proceed, rise, spring from, stem from; SEE CONCEPT *648*

derogatory [adj] *offensive, uncomplimentary*
aspersing, belittling, calumnious, censorious, contumelious, critical, damaging, decrying, defamatory, degrading, demeaning, deprecatory, depreciative, despiteful, detracting, disdainful, dishonoring, disparaging, fault-finding, humiliating, injurious, malevolent, malicious, maligning, minimizing, opprobrious, reproachful, sarcastic, scornful, slanderous, slighting, spiteful, unfavorable, unflattering, vilifying; SEE CONCEPTS *267,570*

descend [v1] *move down, lower*
alight, cascade, cataract, cave in*, coast, collapse, crash, crouch, decline, deplane, detrain, dip, disembark, dismount, dive, dribble*, drop, fall, fall prostrate, get down, get off, go down, gravitate, ground, incline, light, lose balance; penetrate, pitch, plop, plummet, plunge, prolapse, set, settle, sink, slant, slide, slip, slope, slough off, slump, stoop, stumble, submerge, subside, swoop, toboggan, topple, trickle, trip, tumble, weep; SEE CONCEPTS *147,181,213*

descend [v2] *condescend*
abase oneself, concede, degenerate, deteriorate, humble oneself, lower oneself, patronize, stoop; SEE CONCEPTS *23,35*

descend [v3] *trace ancestry from; be passed or handed down*
arise, derive, issue, originate, proceed, spring; SEE CONCEPT *108*

descendant [n] *person in line of ancestry*
brood, child, children, chip off old block*, get*, heir, issue, kin, offshoot, offspring, posterity, product, progenitor, progeny, scion, seed, spinoff*; SEE CONCEPTS 296,414

descent [n1] *moving down; lowering*
cave-in, coast, coming down, crash, declension, declination, decline, declivity, dip, downgrade, droop, drop, drop-off, fall, falling, grade, gradient, header, hill, inclination, incline, landslide, plummeting, plunge, plunging, precipitation, prolapse, sag, settlement, sinkage, sinking, slant, slide, slip, slope, swoop, tailspin, topple, tumble; SEE CONCEPTS 147,181,213,738

descent [n2] *line of ancestry*
blood, extraction, family, family tree, genealogy, heredity, lineage, origin, parentage, pedigree, relationship; SEE CONCEPT 296

descent [n3] *deterioration*
abasement, anticlimax, cadence, comedown, debasement, decadence, decline, degradation, discomfiture, down, downcome, downfall, lapse, pathos, slump; SEE CONCEPTS 230,674

descent [n4] *assault, attack*
advance, foray, incursion, invasion, pounce, raid, swoop; SEE CONCEPTS 86,320

describe [v] *explain in speech, writing*
call, characterize, chronicle, communicate, construe, convey image, define, delineate, depict, detail, distinguish, draw, elucidate, epitomize, exemplify, explicate, expound, express, illuminate, illustrate, image, impart, interpret, label, limn, make apparent, make clear, make sense of, make vivid, mark out, name, narrate, outline, paint, particularize, picture, portray, recite, recount, rehearse, relate, report, represent, sketch, specify, state, tell, term, trace, transmit, write up; SEE CONCEPT 55

description [n1] *account in speech, writing*
ABCs*, blow by blow, brief, characterization, chronicle, confession, declaration, definition, delineation, depiction, detail, explanation, explication, fingerprint, information, make, monograph, narration, narrative, picture, portraiture, portrayal, presentment, recital, recitation, record, recountal, rehearsal, report, representation, rundown, sketch, specification, statement, story, summarization, summary, tale, version, vignette, writeup, yarn; SEE CONCEPT 268

description [n2] *class, kind*
brand, breed, category, character, classification, feather, genre, genus, ilk, kidney, nature, order, sort, species, stripe, type, variety; SEE CONCEPT 378

descriptive [adj] *explanatory*
anecdotic, characteristic, characterizing, circumstantial, classificatory, clear, definitive, delineative, depictive, describing, designating, detailed, eloquent, explicative, expository, expressive, extended, graphic, identifying, illuminating, illuminative, illustrative, indicative, interpretive, lifelike, narrative, particularized, pictorial, picturesque, revealing, specific, true to life, vivid; SEE CONCEPTS 267,557

desecrate [v] *abuse, violate*
befoul, blaspheme, commit sacrilege, contaminate, defile, depredate, desolate, despoil, devastate, devour, dishonor, make lose face*, mess up*, pervert, pillage, pollute, profane, prostitute, ravage, sack*, spoil, spoliate, waste; SEE CONCEPTS 246,252

desecration [n] *violation, abuse*
blasphemy, debasement, defilement, impiety, irreverence, profanation, sacrilege; SEE CONCEPTS 246,252

desert [n] *wasteland; dry area*
arid region, badland, barren, barren land, flats, lava bed, Sahara, sand dunes, solitude, wild, wilderness, wilds; SEE CONCEPTS 508,517

desert [adj] *barren, uncultivated*
arid, bare, desolate, infertile, lonely, solitary, sterile, uninhabited, unproductive, untilled, waste, wild; SEE CONCEPT 560

desert [v] *abandon, defect*
abscond, apostatize, bail out*, beach, betray, bolt, check out*, chuck, cop out*, crawl out, decamp, depart, duck*, escape, flee, fly, forsake, give up, go, go AWOL*, go back on, go over the hill*, go west*, jilt, leave, leave high and dry*, leave in the lurch*, leave stranded, light, maroon, opt out, play truant, pull out, quit, relinquish, renounce, resign, run out on*, sneak off*, split*, strand, take a hike*, take off, tergiversate, throw over, vacate, violate oath, walk; SEE CONCEPTS 195,297

deserted [adj] *abandoned, unoccupied*
bare, barren, bereft, cast off, derelict, desolate, empty, forlorn, forsaken, godforsaken*, isolated, left, left in the lurch*, left stranded, lonely, lorn, neglected, relinquished, solitary, uncouth, uninhabited, vacant; SEE CONCEPTS 485,577

deserter [n] *fugitive from responsibility*
absconder, apostate, AWOL*, backslider, betrayer, criminal, defector, delinquent, derelict, escapee, escaper, hookey player*, lawbreaker, maroon, no-show*, recreant, refugee, renegade, runaway, shirker, slacker, traitor, truant; SEE CONCEPTS 358,412,423

desertion [n] *abandonment*
abrogation, absconding, apostasy, avoidance, backsliding, betrayal, castoff, defecting, departing, departure, derelict, dereliction, disaffection, disavowal, disavowing, divorce, elusion, escape, evasion, falling away, falseness, flight, forsaking, going back on*, leaving, marooning, perfidy, recreancy, rejection, relinquishment, renunciation, repudiation, resignation, retirement, retreat, running out on*, secession, tergiversation, treachery, truancy, withdrawal; SEE CONCEPTS 195,297

deserts [n] *what is due one*
chastening, chastisement, comeuppance, compensation, deserving, discipline, disciplining, due, get hers*, get his*, guerdon, lumps*, meed, merit, payment, penalty, punishment, recompense, requital, retribution, return, revenge, reward, right, talion, what is coming to one*, what one is asking for*; SEE CONCEPTS 129,710

deserve [v] *be entitled to*
be given one's due*, be in line for*, be worthy of, demand, earn, gain, get, get comeuppance*, get what is coming to one*, have it coming*, have the right to, justify, lay claim to, merit, procure, rate, warrant, win; SEE CONCEPT 129

deserving [adj] *worthy, meritorious*
admirable, commendable, due, estimable, fitting, laudable, needy, praisable, praiseworthy, righteous, rightful, thankworthy; SEE CONCEPT 404

desiccate [v] *take moisture out of*
anhydrate, dehydrate, deplete, devitalize, divest,

drain, dry, dry up, evaporate, exsiccate, parch, sear, shrivel, wither, wizen; SEE CONCEPTS 137,250

design [*n1*] *sketch, draft*
architecture, arrangement, blueprint, chart, comp, composition, conception, constitution, construction, delineation, depiction, diagram, doodle, drawing, dummy, form, formation, idea, layout, makeup, map, method, model, outline, paste-up, pattern, perspective, picture, plan, scheme, study, tracery, tracing, treatment; SEE CONCEPTS 268,625,660

design [*n2*] *artful conception*
arrangement, configuration, construction, depiction, device, doodle, drawing, figure, form, illustration, motif, motive, organization, painting, pattern, picture, portrait, shape, sketch, style; SEE CONCEPT 259

design [*n3*] *intention*
action, aim, angle, animus, big picture*, brainchild*, child*, conation, conspiracy, deliberation, end, enterprise, game plan*, gimmick, goal, intendment, intrigue, lay of the land*, machination, meaning, notion, object, objective, picture, pitch, plan, play, plot, point, project, proposition, purport, purpose, recipe, reflection, scenario, scene, schema, scheme, setup, story, target, thinking, thought, trick, undertaking, view, volition, what's cooking*, will; SEE CONCEPTS 410,660

design [*v1*] *plan, outline*
accomplish, achieve, arrange, block out, blueprint, cast, chart, construct, contrive, create, delineate, describe, devise, diagram, dope out, draft, draw, effect, execute, fashion, form, frame, fulfill, invent, lay out, perform, produce, project, set out, sketch, sketch out, trace, work out; SEE CONCEPT 36

design [*v2*] *create, conceive*
compose, contrive, cook up*, devise, dream up*, fabricate, fashion, form, frame, invent, make up, originate, produce, think up; SEE CONCEPTS 43,173

design [*v3*] *intend, mean to do*
aim, contemplate, contrive, destine, devise, make, mind, plan, prepare, project, propose, purpose, scheme, tailor; SEE CONCEPTS 35,36

designate [*v1*] *name, entitle*
baptize, call, christen, cognominate, denominate, dub, label, nickname, nominate, style, term, title; SEE CONCEPT 62

designate [*v2*] *specify as selection*
allocate, allot, appoint, apportion, appropriate, assign, authorize, button down*, characterize, charge, choose, commission, connote, constitute, define, delegate, denote, depute, deputize, describe, dictate, earmark*, elect, evidence, favor, finger*, indicate, individualize, make, mark, mete, name, nominate, opt, peg*, pick, pin down, pinpoint, prefer, put down for*, reserve, set apart, set aside, show, single, slot, stipulate, tab*, tag*, tap*; SEE CONCEPTS 41,129

designation [*n1*] *name, label, mark*
appellation, appellative, class, classification, cognomen, compellation, denomination, description, epithet, identification, key word, moniker, nickname, nomen, style, title; SEE CONCEPT 683

designation [*n2*] *delegation, selection*
appointment, classification, identification, indication, pigeonhole*, recognition, specification; SEE CONCEPT 41

designedly [*adv*] *intentionally*
apurpose, by design, calculatedly, deliberately, knowingly, on purpose, prepensely, purposedly, purposely, purposively, studiously, willfully, wittingly; SEE CONCEPTS 402,535

designing [*adj*] *plotting, crafty*
artful, astute, conniving, conspiring, crooked, cunning, deceitful, devious, heedful, intriguing, Machiavellian, observant, scheming, sharp, shrewd, sly, treacherous, tricky, unscrupulous, wily; SEE CONCEPT 542

desirable [*adj1*] *attractive, seductive*
adorable, alluring, beautiful*, charming, covetable, enticing, fascinating, fetching, sexy; SEE CONCEPTS 372,579

desirable [*adj2*] *advantageous, good*
acceptable, advisable, agreeable, beneficial, covetable, eligible, enviable, expedient, grateful, gratifying, helpful, pleasing, preferable, profitable, useful, welcome, worthwhile; SEE CONCEPTS 560,572

desire [*n1*] *want, longing*
admiration, ambition, appetite, ardor, aspiration, attraction, avidity, concupiscence, covetousness, craving, craze, cupidity, devotion, doting, eagerness, fancy, fascination, fervor, fondness, frenzy, greed, hankering*, hunger, inclination, infatuation, itch*, lasciviousness, lechery, libido, liking, love, lust, mania, motive, need, passion, predilection, proclivity, propensity, rapaciousness, rapture, ravenousness, relish, salacity, solicitude, thirst, urge, voracity, will, wish, yearning; SEE CONCEPTS 20,709

desire [*n2*] *request*
appeal, entreaty, hope, importunity, petition, solicitation, supplication, want, wish; SEE CONCEPT 662

desire [*v1*] *want, long for*
aim, aspire to, be smitten, be turned on by*, choose, cotton to, covet, crave, desiderate, die over*, enjoy, fall for*, fancy, give eyeteeth for*, go for*, hanker after*, have eyes for*, have the hots for*, hunger for, like, lust after, make advances to, partial to, pine, set heart on*, spoil for, sweet on*, take a liking to*, take a shine to*, take to*, thirst, wish for, yearn for; SEE CONCEPT 20

desire [*v2*] *ask, request*
beg, bespeak, entreat, importune, petition, seek, solicit; SEE CONCEPT 48

desirous [*adj*] *aspiring, hopeful*
acquisitive, ambitious, amorous, anxious, avid, covetous, craving, desiring, eager, enthusiastic, grasping, greedy, hot*, itchy*, keen, longing, lustful, passionate, prehensile, ready, stimulated, turned on*, willing, wishful, wishing, yearning; SEE CONCEPT 529

desist [*v*] *stop, refrain from*
abandon, abstain, avoid, break off, cease, discontinue, end, forbear, give over, give up, halt, have done with*, knock off*, leave off, not do, pause, quit, relinquish, resign, surcease, suspend, yield; SEE CONCEPTS 119,234

desktop publishing [*n*] *producing publications with computer software*
desktop*, electronic publishing, formatting, outputting, typesetting; SEE CONCEPT 277

desolate [*adj1*] *unused, barren*
abandoned, bare, bleak, derelict, desert, destroyed, dreary, empty, forsaken, godforsaken*, isolated, lonely, lonesome, lorn, ruined, solitary,

unfrequented, uninhabited, unoccupied, vacant, waste, wild; SEE CONCEPTS **485,560**

desolate [*adj2*] *depressed, despondent*
abandoned, acheronian, bereft, black, bleak, blue, cheerless, comfortless, companionless, dejected, disconsolate, dismal, dolorous, down, downcast, forlorn, forsaken, funereal, gloomy, hurting, in a blue funk*, inconsolable, joyless, lonely, lonesome, lorn, melancholy, miserable, somber, tragic, wretched; SEE CONCEPT **403**

desolate [*v*] *ravage, destroy*
depopulate, depredate, desecrate, despoil, devastate, devour, lay low, lay waste, pillage, plunder, ruin, sack, spoliate, waste; SEE CONCEPT **252**

desolation [*n1*] *uninhabitated area; barrenness*
bareness, bleakness, desert, devastation, dissolution, extinction, forlornness, isolation, loneliness, ruin, solitariness, solitude, waste, wildness, wreck; SEE CONCEPTS **517,710**

desolation [*n2*] *distress, unhappiness*
anguish, dejection, despair, gloom, gloominess, loneliness, melancholy, misery, mourning, sadness, sorrow, woe, wretchedness; SEE CONCEPT **410**

despair [*n*] *depression, hopelessness*
anguish, dashed hopes, dejection, desperation, despondency, discouragement, disheartenment, forlornness, gloom, melancholy, misery, ordeal, pain, sorrow, trial, tribulation, wretchedness; SEE CONCEPT **410**

despair [*v*] *give up hope*
abandon, be hopeless, despond, destroy, drop, flatten, give way, have heavy heart*, let air out*, lose faith, lose heart, relinquish, renounce, resign, surrender, take down, yield; SEE CONCEPT **21**

despairing [*adj*] *upset, despondent*
anxious, at end of one's rope*, blue, brokenhearted, can't win*, cynical, dejected, depressed, desperate, disconsolate, downcast, forlorn, frantic, grief-stricken, hopeless, inconsolable, in pain*, in the dumps*, in the pits*, in the soup*, melancholic, melancholy, miserable, not a prayer*, no-win*, oppressed, pessimistic, sad, shot down*, strabilious, suicidal, sunk*, weighed down*, wretched; SEE CONCEPT **403**

desperado [*n*] *criminal*
bandit, convict, cutthroat, gangster, hoodlum, lawbreaker, mugger, outlaw, ruffian, thug; SEE CONCEPT **412**

desperate [*adj1*] *reckless, outrageous*
atrocious, audacious, bold, careless, dangerous, daring, death-defying, determined, devil-may-care, foolhardy, frantic, frenzied, furious, hasty, hazardous, headlong, headstrong, heinous, impetuous, incautious, madcap, monstrous, precipitate, rash, risky, scandalous, shocking, venturesome, violent, wild; SEE CONCEPT **401**

desperate [*adj2*] *extreme, intense*
acute, climacteric, concentrated, critical, crucial, dire, drastic, exquisite, fierce, furious, great, terrible, urgent, vehement, very grave, vicious, violent; SEE CONCEPTS **537,540,569**

desperate [*adj3*] *hopeless*
at end of one's rope*, back to the wall*, can't win*, dead duck*, despairing, despondent, desponding, downcast, forlorn, futile, gone*, goner*, hard up*, inconsolable, in the soup*, in the toilet*, irrecoverable, irremediable, irretrievable, no-chance*, no-way*, no-win*, running out of

time*, sad, sunk*, up against it*, up the creek*, useless, vain, wretched; SEE CONCEPT **548**

desperately [*adv1*] *severely*
badly, carelessly, dangerously, dramatically, fiercely, gravely, greatly, harmfully, hysterically, like crazy*, like mad*, perilously, seriously; SEE CONCEPT **569**

desperately [*adv2*] *frightfully*
appallingly, fearfully, hopelessly, shockingly; SEE CONCEPT **403**

desperation [*n1*] *hopelessness*
agony, anguish, anxiety, concern, dejection, depression, desolation, despair, despondency, discomfort, disconsolateness, distraction, distress, fear, gloom, grief, heartache, melancholy, misery, pain, pang, sorrow, torture, trouble, unhappiness, worry; SEE CONCEPT **410**

desperation [*n2*] *rashness*
carelessness, defiance, foolhardiness, frenzy, heedlessness, impetuosity, madness, recklessness; SEE CONCEPT **633**

despicable [*adj*] *hateful; beyond contempt*
abject, awful, base, beastly, cheap, contemptible, degrading, detestable, dirty, disgraceful, disreputable, down, ignominious, infamous, insignificant, loathsome, low, low-life*, mean, no-good*, pitiful, reprehensible, shameful, slimy*, sordid, vile, worthless, wretched; SEE CONCEPTS **404,570**

despise [*v*] *look down on*
abhor, abominate, allergic to*, contemn, deride, detest, disdain, disregard, eschew, excuse, feel contempt for, flout, hate, have no use for*, loathe, look down nose at*, misprize, neglect, put down*, reject, renounce, repudiate, revile, scorn, shun, slight, snub, spurn, undervalue, wipe out*; SEE CONCEPT **29**

despite [*prep*] *in spite of, regardless of*
against, although, even though, even with, in contempt of, in defiance of, in the face of, notwithstanding, undeterred by; SEE CONCEPT **544**

despoil [*v*] *ravage, destroy*
denude, depopulate, depredate, deprive, desecrate, desolate, devastate, devour, dispossess, divest, loot, maraud, pillage, plunder, raid, rifle, rob, sack, spoil, spoliate, strip, vandalize, waste, wreak havoc, wreck; SEE CONCEPT **252**

despondent [*adj*] *depressed*
all torn up*, blue*, bummed-out*, cast-down, dejected, despairing, disconsolate, discouraged, disheartened, dispirited, doleful, down, downcast, downhearted, forlorn, gloomy, glum, grief-stricken, grieving, hopeless, in a blue funk*, in despair, in the pits*, low, low-spirited, melancholy, miserable, morose, mourning, sad, shot down*, sorrowful, woebegone, wretched; SEE CONCEPT **403**

despot [*n*] *dictator*
autocrat, Hitler*, monocrat, oppressor, slavedriver, tyrant; SEE CONCEPTS **354,412**

destination [*n*] *goal; place one wants to go*
aim, ambition, design, end, harbor, haven, intention, journey's end, landing-place, object, objective, purpose, resting-place, station, stop, target, terminal, terminus; SEE CONCEPTS **198,659**

destine [*v*] *predetermine, ordain*
allot, appoint, assign, consecrate, decide, decree, dedicate, design, determine, devote, doom, doom to, earmark*, fate, foreordain, intend, mark out, predestine, preform, preordain, purpose, reserve; SEE CONCEPT **18**

de
de

destined [adj1] *bound for, fated in near future*
at hand, brewing*, certain, closed, coming, compelled, compulsory, condemned, designed, directed, doomed, foreordained, forthcoming, hanging over*, impending, ineluctable, inescapable, inevitable, inexorable, in prospect, instant, in store, intended, in the cards*, in the wind*, looming, meant, menacing, near, ordained, overhanging, predesigned, predestined, predetermined, que sera sera*, sealed, settled, stated, that is to be, that will be, threatening, to come, unavoidable, way the ball bounces*; SEE CONCEPTS 537,820

destined [adj2] *en route, on the road to*
appointed, appropriated, assigned, bent upon, booked, bound for, chosen, consigned, delegated, designated, determined, directed, entrained, heading, ordered to, prepared, routed, scheduled, specified; SEE CONCEPT 584

destiny [n] *fate*
afterlife, break*, breaks*, certainty, circumstance, conclusion, condition, constellation, course of events, cup, design, divine decree, doom, expectation, finality, foreordination, fortune, future, happenstance, hereafter, horoscope, inevitability, intent, intention, karma, kismet*, lot, luck, Moirai, objective, ordinance, portion, predestination, predetermination, prospect, serendipity, the stars*, way the ball bounces*, way the cookie crumbles*, what is written*, wheel of fortune*, world to come*; SEE CONCEPT 679

destitute [adj] *down and out; wanting*
bankrupt, beggared, bereft, busted, dead broke*, deficient, depleted, deprived of, devoid of, dirt poor*, divested, drained, empty, exhausted, flat*, flat broke*, impecunious, impoverished, indigent, in need of, insolvent, lacking, moneyless, necessitous, needy, on the breadline*, on the rocks*, penniless, penurious, pinched, played out*, poor, poverty-stricken, stony, strapped, stripped, totaled, wiped out*, without; SEE CONCEPT 334

destroy [v] *demolish, devastate*
abort, annihilate, annul, axe*, blot out, break down, butcher*, consume, cream*, crush, damage, deface, desolate, despoil, dismantle, dispatch, end, eradicate, erase, exterminate, extinguish, extirpate, gut*, impair, kill, lay waste, level, liquidate, maim, mar, maraud, mutilate, nuke*, nullify, overturn, quash, quell, ravage, ravish, raze, ruin, sabotage, shatter, slay, smash, snuff out*, spoliate, stamp out, suppress, swallow up*, tear down, torpedo*, total, trash*, vaporize, waste, wax*, wipe out, wreck, zap*; SEE CONCEPT 252

destruction [n] *demolition, devastation*
abolishing, abolition, annihilation, assassinating, bane, carnage, crashing, crushing, disintegrating, disrupting, dissolving, downfall, elimination, end, eradication, extermination, extinction, extinguishing, extirpation, havoc, invalidating, invalidation, liquidation, loss, massacre, murder, overthrow, ravaging, ruin, ruination, sacking, shattering, slaughter, slaying, subjugation, subversion, subverting, undoing, wreckage, wrecking; SEE CONCEPTS 230,252

destructive [adj1] *injurious, devastating*
annihilative, baleful, baneful, calamitous, cancerous, cataclysmic, catastrophic, consumptive, cutthroat, damaging, deadly, deleterious, detrimental, dire, disastrous, eradicative, evil, ex-

tirpative, fatal, fell, harmful, hurtful, internecine, lethal, lethiferous, mortal, noisome, noxious, pernicious, pestiferous, pestilential, ruinous, slaughterous, suicidal, toxic, venomous, wrackful, wreckful; SEE CONCEPT 537

destructive [adj2] *hurtful, disparaging*
abrasive, adverse, antagonistic, cankerous, caustic, contrary, corrosive, deleterious, derogatory, detrimental, discouraging, discrediting, erosive, hostile, injurious, invalidating, negative, offensive, opposed, troublesome, undermining, vicious; SEE CONCEPTS 267,537

detach [v] *disconnect, cut off*
abstract, disaffiliate, disassemble, disassociate, disengage, disentangle, disjoin, dismount, dissociate, disunite, divide, divorce, free, isolate, loose, loosen, part, remove, segregate, separate, sever, sunder, take apart, tear off, uncouple, unfasten, unfix, unhitch, withdraw; SEE CONCEPT 135

detached [adj1] *disconnected*
alone, apart, discrete, disjoined, divided, emancipated, free, isolate, isolated, loose, loosened, removed, separate, severed, unaccompanied, unconnected; SEE CONCEPT 490

detached [adj2] *aloof, disinterested; neutral*
abstract, apathetic, casual, cool*, dispassionate, distant, impartial, impersonal, incurious, indifferent, laid-back*, objective, out of it*, pokerfaced*, remote, removed, reserved, spaced-out, spacey*, staid, stolid, unbiased, uncommitted, unconcerned, uncurious, uninvolved, unpassioned, unprejudiced, withdrawn; SEE CONCEPTS 401,404

detachment [n1] *disconnection*
disengagement, disjoining, dissolution, disunion, division, divorce, divorcement, partition, rupture, separation, severing, split-up; SEE CONCEPTS 388,747

detachment [n2] *aloofness*
brown study*, coldness, coolness, disinterestedness, dreaminess, impartiality, incuriosity, indifference, neutrality, nonpartisanship, objectivity, preoccupation, remoteness, reverie, unconcern, woolgathering*; SEE CONCEPT 633

detachment [n3] *military troop*
army, body, detail, division, force, organization, party, patrol, special force, squad, task force, troupe, unit; SEE CONCEPT 322

detail [n1] *feature, specific aspect*
ABCs*, accessory, article, brass tacks*, chapter and verse*, circumstantiality, component, count, cue, design, dope*, element, fact, factor, fine point, fraction, item, meat and potatoes*, minor point, minutia, nicety, nitty-gritty*, nuts and bolts*, part, particular, peculiarity, plan, point, portion, respect, schedule, singularity, specialty, specification, structure, technicality, thing, trait, trivia, triviality; SEE CONCEPT 831

detail [n2] *military troop*
army, assignment, body, detachment, duty, fatigue, force, kitchen police, KP*, organization, party, special force, squad, unit; SEE CONCEPT 322

detail [v1] *specify, make clear*
analyze, catalog, circumstantiate, communicate, delineate, depict, describe, designate, elaborate, embellish, enumerate, epitomize, exhibit, fly speck*, get down to brass tacks*, individualize, itemize, lay out, narrate, particularize, portray, produce, quote chapter and verse*, recapitulate,

recite, recount, rehearse, relate, report, reveal, set forth, show, specialize, spell out, spread, stipulate, summarize, sweat details*, tell, uncover; SEE CONCEPTS 55,57,60

detail [v2] *assign specific task*
allocate, appoint, charge, commission, delegate, detach, send; SEE CONCEPTS 50,88

detailed [adj] *itemized, particularized*
abundant, accurate, all-inclusive, amplified, at length, blow-by-blow*, circumstantial, circumstantiated, clocklike, complete, complicated, comprehensive, copious, definite, described, developed, disclosed, elaborate, elaborated, enumerated, exact, exhausting, exhaustive, finicky*, full, fussy*, individual, individualized, intricate, meticulous, minute, narrow, nice, point-by-point, precise, seriatim, specific, specified, thorough, unfolded; SEE CONCEPT 557

detain [v] *hold, keep back; arrest*
apprehend, bog down*, bust*, buttonhole*, check, confine, constrain, decelerate, delay, hang up*, hinder, hold up*, ice*, impede, inhibit, intern, jail, mire, nab*, pick up, pinch*, pull in*, put away*, reserve, restrain, retard, run in, send up, set back, slow down, slow up, withhold; SEE CONCEPTS 191,317

detect [v] *discover*
ascertain, catch, descry, dig up*, disclose, distinguish, encounter, espy, expose, find, hit on*, hit upon*, identify, meet, meet with, nose out*, note, notice, observe, recognize, reveal, scent, see, smell out*, smoke out*, spot, stumble on, track down, tumble into, turn up, uncover, unmask, wise up to*; SEE CONCEPTS 38,183

detection [n] *discovery*
apprehension, disclosure, espial, exposé, exposure, ferreting out, find, revelation, strike, tracking down, uncovering, unearthing, unmasking; SEE CONCEPTS 38,183

detective [n] *investigator of crime*
agent, analyst, bird dog*, bloodhound*, bull*, constable, cop, dick*, eavesdropper, eye*, fed*, fink*, flatfoot*, gumshoe*, informer, nark*, peeper*, P.I.*, plainclothes officer, police officer, private eye, private investigator, prosecutor, reporter, roper, scout, sergeant, shadow*, shamus*, Sherlock Holmes*, shoofly*, sleuth, slewfoot*, snoop*, spy, tail*; SEE CONCEPT 348

detention [n] *confinement, imprisonment*
apprehension, arrest, arrestation, bust*, custody, delay, detainment, hindrance, holding back, holding pen*, immurement, impediment, incarceration, internment, keeping in, nab, pen*, pickup, pinch*, quarantine, restraint, retention, time up the river*, withholding; SEE CONCEPTS 191,317

deter [v] *check, inhibit from action*
act like a wet blanket*, avert, block, caution, chill, cool, damp, dampen, daunt, debar, disadvise, discourage, dissuade, divert, forestall, forfend, frighten, hinder, impede, intimidate, obstruct, obviate, preclude, prevent, prohibit, put a damper on, put off, restrain, rule out, scare, shut out, stave off, stop, talk out of, throw cold water on*, turn off, warn; SEE CONCEPT 121

deteriorate [v] *decay, degenerate*
adulterate, alloy, become worse, be worse for wear*, break, corrode, corrupt, crumble, debase, debilitate, decline, decompose, degrade, deprave, depreciate, descend, disimprove, disintegrate, ebb, fade, fail, fall apart, flag, go downhill*, go to

pieces*, go to pot*, go to the dogs*, hit the skids*, impair, injure, languish, lapse, lessen, lose it, lose quality, lower, mar, pervert, regress, retrograde, retrogress, rot, sink, skid, slide, spoil, undermine, vitiate, weaken, wear away, worsen; SEE CONCEPT 698

deterioration [n] *decay, degeneration*
abasement, adulteration, atrophy, corrosion, crumbling, debasement, decadence, decaying, declension, declination, decline, decomposition, degradation, degringolade, depreciation, descent, devaluation, dilapidation, disintegration, dislocation, disrepair, downfall, downgrade, downturn, drop, fall, lapse, lessening, perversion, retrogression, rotting, ruin, slump, spoiling, vitiation, worsening; SEE CONCEPTS 230,698

determination [n1] *perseverance*
assurance, backbone*, boldness, bravery, certainty, certitude, constancy, conviction, courage, dauntlessness, decision, dedication, doggedness, dogmatism, drive, energy, fearlessness, firmness, fortitude, grit, guts*, hardihood, heart*, independence, indomitability, intrepidity, nerve*, obstinacy, persistence, pluck*, purpose, purposefulness, resoluteness, resolution, resolve, self-confidence, single-mindedness, spine*, spunk*, steadfastness, stiff upper lip*, stubbornness, tenacity, valor, willpower; SEE CONCEPTS 411,657

determination [n2] *conclusion*
decision, judgment, measurement, opinion, perception, purpose, resolution, resolve, result, settlement, solution, verdict, visualization; SEE CONCEPTS 685,689

determine [v1] *conclude, decide*
actuate, arbitrate, call the shots*, cinch, clinch, complete, dispose, drive, end, figure, finish, fix upon, halt, impel, incline, induce, move, nail down*, opt, ordain, persuade, pin down*, predispose, regulate, resolve, rule, settle, take a decision, tap, terminate, ultimate, wind up*, wrap up*; SEE CONCEPTS 18,35,234

determine [v2] *discover, find out*
add up to*, ascertain, boil down to*, catch on, certify, check, demonstrate, detect, divine, establish, figure, figure out, have a hunch*, hear, learn, make out, see, size up, tell, tumble, unearth, verify, work out; SEE CONCEPTS 15,31

determine [v3] *choose, decide*
destine, doom, elect, establish, fate, finger*, fix, foreordain, make up mind, predestine, predetermine, preform, preordain, purpose, resolve, settle; SEE CONCEPT 18

determine [v4] *dictate, govern, regulate*
affect, bound, circumscribe, command, condition, control, decide, delimit, devise, direct, impel, impose, incline, induce, influence, invent, lead, limit, manage, mark off, measure, modify, plot, rule, shape; SEE CONCEPT 94

determined [adj] *driven, persistent*
bent, bent on, buckled down*, constant, decided, decisive, dogged, earnest, firm, fixed, hard-as-nails*, hardboiled*, intent, mean business*, obstinate, on ice*, pat, persevering, purposeful, resolute, resolved, serious, set, set on, settled, single-minded, solid, steadfast, strong-minded, strong-willed, stubborn, tenacious, unfaltering, unflinching, unhesitating, unwavering; SEE CONCEPTS 404,542

de
de

deterrent [n] *impediment, restraint*
bridle, check, curb, defense, determent, discouragement, disincentive, hindrance, leash, obstacle, preventative, preventive, rein, shackle; SEE CONCEPT 680

detest [v] *hate; feel disgust toward*
abhor, abominate, be allergic to, despise, dislike intensely, down on, execrate, feel aversion toward, feel hostility toward, feel repugnance toward, have no use for*, loathe, recoil from, reject, repudiate; SEE CONCEPT 29

detestable [adj] *loathsome, abominable*
abhorred, abhorrent, accursed, atrocious, awful, despicable, disgusting, execrable, godawful*, grody*, gross*, hateable, hateful, heinous, horrid, lousy, low-down, maggot, monstrous, obnoxious, odious, offensive, outrageous, repugnant, repulsive, revolting, rotten, shocking, sorry, vile; SEE CONCEPTS 529,542

dethrone [v] *oust*
degrade, depose, discrown, dismiss, displace, uncrown, unmake; SEE CONCEPTS 298,320

detonate [v] *set off bomb*
bang, blast, blow up, burst, discharge, explode, fulminate, kablooey*, let go, mushroom*, push the button*, shoot off, touch off, va-voom*; SEE CONCEPT 179

detour [n] *indirect course*
alternate route, back road, branch, bypass, bypath, byway, circuit, circuitous route, circumbendibus*, circumnavigation, circumvention, crotch, deviation, divergence, diversion, fork, roundabout way, runaround, secondary highway, service road, substitute, temporary route; SEE CONCEPT 501

detract [v] *take away a part; lessen*
backbite*, belittle, blister, cheapen, cut rate, decrease, decry, depreciate, derogate, devaluate, diminish, discount, discredit, disesteem, draw away, knock*, laugh at, lower, minimize, misprize, reduce, subtract from, underrate, undervalue, vilipend, withdraw, write off; SEE CONCEPTS 52,54,236,247

detraction [n] *misrepresentation; slander*
abuse, aspersion, backbiting*, backstabbing*, belittlement, calumny, damage, defamation, denigration, deprecation, derogation, disesteem, disparagement, harm, hit, hurt, injury, injustice, innuendo, insinuation, knock*, libel, libeling, lie, maligning, minimization, muckraking*, obloquy, pejorative, revilement, ridicule, running down*, scandal, scandalmongering, scurrility, slam, smear campaign*, tale, traducement, traducing, vilification, vituperation, wrong; SEE CONCEPTS 52,54,63

detriment [n] *disadvantage*
damage, disability, disservice, drawback, handicap, harm, hurt, impairment, injury, liability, loss, marring, mischief, prejudice, spoiling; SEE CONCEPTS 309,674

detrimental [adj] *damaging, disadvantageous*
adverse, bad, baleful, deleterious, destructive, disturbing, evil, harmful, hurtful, ill, inimical, injurious, mischievous, negative, nocuous, pernicious, prejudicial, unfavorable; SEE CONCEPTS 537,570

devalue [v] *depreciate*
cheapen, cut rate, debase, decrease, decry, devalorize, devaluate, knock off, lower, mark down, nose dive, revalue, take down, underrate, under-

value, write down, write off; SEE CONCEPTS 330,335

devastate [v] *demolish, destroy*
depredate, desecrate, desolate, despoil, devour, do one in*, lay waste, level, pillage, plunder, raid, ravage, raze, ruin, sack, smash, spoil, spoliate, stamp out*, take apart, total*, trash*, waste, wipe off map*, wreck; SEE CONCEPTS 246,252

devastation [n] *destruction*
confusion, defoliation, demolition, depredation, desolation, havoc, loss, pillage, plunder, ravages, ruin, ruination, spoliation, waste; SEE CONCEPT 674

develop [v1] *cultivate, prosper*
advance, age, enroot, establish, evolve, expand, flourish, foster, grow, grow up, maturate, mature, mellow, progress, promote, ripen, thrive; SEE CONCEPTS 253,427,704

develop [v2] *expand, work out*
actualize, advance, amplify, augment, beautify, broaden, build up, cultivate, deepen, dilate, elaborate, enlarge, enrich, evolve, exploit, extend, finish, heighten, improve, intensify, lengthen, magnify, materialize, perfect, polish, promote, realize, refine, spread, strengthen, stretch, unfold, widen; SEE CONCEPTS 700,775

develop [v3] *begin; occur*
acquire, arise, befall, betide, break, break out, breed, chance, come about, come off, commence, contract, ensue, establish, follow, form, generate, go, happen, invest, originate, pick up, result, start, transpire; SEE CONCEPT 119

develop [v4] *unfold; be made known*
account for, acquire, actualize, disclose, disentangle, elaborate, evolve, exhibit, explain, explicate, foretell, form, materialize, produce, reach, realize, recount, state, uncoil, uncover, unfurl, unravel, unroll, untwist, unwind; SEE CONCEPTS 60,261

development [n1] *growth*
adding to, addition, adulthood, advance, advancement, advancing, augmentation, augmenting, boost, buildup, developing, elaborating, enlargement, evolution, evolvement, evolving, expansion, flowering, hike, improvement, increase, increasing, making progress, maturation, maturing, maturity, ongoing, perfecting, progress, progression, reinforcement, reinforcing, ripening, spread, spreading, unfolding, unraveling, upgrowth, upping; SEE CONCEPTS 700,704,775

development [n2] *happening, incident*
change, circumstance, conclusion, denouement, event, eventuality, eventuation, issue, materialization, occurrence, outcome, phenomenon, result, situation, transpiration, turn of events, upshot; SEE CONCEPT 3

deviant [adj] *abnormal, different*
aberrant, anomalous, atypical, bent, devious, divergent, freaky, heretical, heteroclite, irregular, kinky, off-key, perverse, perverted, preternatural, queer, twisted, unorthodox, unrepresentative, untypical, variant, varying, wandering, wayward, weird; SEE CONCEPT 564

deviate [v] *stray from normal path*
aberrate, angle off, avert, bear off, bend, bend the rules*, break pattern, circumlocate, contrast, deflect, depart, depart from, differ, digress, divagate, diverge, drift, edge off*, err, get around, go amiss, go haywire*, go off on tangent*, go out of control*, go out of way, leave beaten path*, not

conform, part, shy, swerve, swim against stream*, take a turn, turn, turn aside, vary, veer, wander; SEE CONCEPTS 195,665,697

deviation [n] *change, departure*
aberration, alteration, anomaly, breach, crotch, deflection, detour, difference, digression, discrepancy, disparity, divergence, diversion, fluctuation, fork, hereticism, inconsistency, irregularity, modification, shift, transgression, turning, variance, variation; SEE CONCEPTS 665,697,738

device [n1] *instrument, tool*
accessory, agent, apparatus, appliance, arrangement, article, construction, contraption, contrivance, creation, doohickey*, equipment, expedient, gadget, gear, gimmick, implement, invention, machine, makeshift, material, means, mechanism, medium, outfit, resort, resource, rigging*, Rube Goldberg invention*, shift, tackle, thingamabob*, utensil, whatchamacallit*, whatnot*, whatsit*; SEE CONCEPTS 463,499

device [n2] *ploy, scheme, maneuver*
artifice, cabal, chicanery, clever move, craft, craftiness, cunningness, design, dodge, evasion, expedient, fake, feint, finesse, gambit, game, gimmick, improvisation, loophole*, machination, method, pattern, plan, plot, project, proposition, purpose, racket, ruse, shift, stratagem, strategy, stunt, subterfuge, trap, trick, wile; SEE CONCEPT 660

device [n3] *symbol, emblem*
badge, colophon, crest, design, ensign, figure, insignia, logo, motif, motto, pattern, scroll, sign, slogan, token; SEE CONCEPT 284

devil [n] *demon*
adversary, archfiend, beast, Beelzebub, bête noire, brute, common enemy, dastard, diablo, djinn, dybbuk, enfant terrible*, evil one, fiend, genie, hellion, imp, knave, Lucifer, Mephistopheles, monster, ogre, Prince of Darkness, rogue, Satan, scamp, scoundrel, the dickens*, the Erinyes, the Furies, villain; SEE CONCEPTS 370,412

devilish [adj] *wicked*
accursed, atrocious, bad, brutish, cloven-footed, cursed, damnable, demoniac, demonic, detestable, diabolic, diabolical, evil, execrable, fiendish, hellborn, hellish, infernal, inhuman, iniquitous, Mephistophelian, nefarious, satanic, serpentine, unhallowed, villainous; SEE CONCEPT 545

devious [adj1] *dishonest, crafty*
artful, calculating, crooked, deceitful, double-dealing, duplicitous, errant, erring, evasive, faking one out*, fishy*, foxy*, fraudulent, guileful, indirect, insidious, insincere, not straightforward, oblique, obliquitous, playing games, playing politics*, put on, roundabout, scheming, shady, shifty, shrewd, sly, sneaking, sneaky, surreptitious, treacherous, tricky, underhanded, wily; SEE CONCEPTS 401,404

devious [adj2] *crooked; indirect*
ambiguous, bending, circuitous, confounding, confusing, curving, detouring, deviating, digressing, digressory, diverting, errant, erratic, excursive, flexuous, misleading, obscure, out-of-the-way, rambling, remote, removed, roundabout, serpentine, straying, tortuous, twisting, wandering; SEE CONCEPT 581

devise [v] *conceive, dream up*
ad-lib, arrange, blueprint*, brainstorm*, cast, chart, cogitate, come up with, concoct, construct, contrive, cook up*, craft, create, design, discover, dope out*, fake it, forge, form, formulate, frame*, get off*, hatch, head trip*, imagine, improvise, intrigue, invent, machinate, make up, mastermind*, plan, play it by ear*, plot, prepare, project, scheme, shape, spark, think up, throw together, trump up*, vamp, whip up*, work out; SEE CONCEPTS 36,43

devoid [adj] *empty, wanting*
bare, barren, bereft, deficient, denuded, destitute, free from, innocent, lacking, needed, sans*, unprovided with, vacant, void, without; SEE CONCEPTS 483,485

devote [v] *commit one's energies, thoughts*
allot, apply, apportion, appropriate, assign, bestow, bless, concern oneself, confide, consecrate, consign, dedicate, donate, enshrine, entrust, give, give away, hallow, hand out, occupy oneself, pledge, present, reserve, sanctify, set apart, vow; SEE CONCEPTS 17,108,112

devoted [adj] *committed, loyal*
adherent, affectionate, ardent, behind one, caring, concerned, consecrated, constant, crazy about*, dear, dedicated, devout, doting, dutiful, faithful, fervid, fond, gone on*, lovesome, loving, staunch, steadfast, stuck on*, thoughtful, true, true-blue*, wild about*, zealous; SEE CONCEPT 542

devotee [n] *ardent supporter; fan*
addict, adherent, admirer, aficionado, amateur, believer, booster, buff, disciple, enthusiast, fanatic, fancier, fiend, follower, groupie, habitué, junkie, lover, rooter, supporter, votarient, votary; SEE CONCEPT 423

devotion [n] *commitment; loyalty*
adherence, adoration, affection, allegiance, ardor, attachment, consecration, constancy, dedication, deference, devotedness, devotement, devoutness, earnestness, enthusiasm, faithfulness, fealty, fervor, fidelity, fondness, intensity, love, observance, passion, piety, reverence, sanctity, service, sincerity, spirituality, worship, zeal; SEE CONCEPTS 32,657

devour [v] *swallow, consume*
absorb, annihilate, appreciate, be engrossed by, be preoccupied, bolt, bolt down*, chow down*, cram*, delight in, destroy, dispatch, do compulsively, do voraciously, drink in, eat, enjoy, exhaust, feast on, feed on, gloat over, gobble, gorge*, go through, gulp, guzzle, hoover*, imbibe, ingest, inhale, partake of, pig out*, polish off*, ravage, rejoice in, relish, revel in, scarf down*, spend, stuff, take, take in, use up, waste, wipe out, wolf*, wolf down*; SEE CONCEPTS 169,225

devout [adj] *sincerely believing; devoted*
adherent, adoring, ardent, deep, earnest, faithful, fervent, fervid, genuine, godly, goody-goody*, goody two-shoes*, heart-and-soul, heartfelt, holy, intense, orthodox, passionate, pietistic, pious, prayerful, profound, religious, reverent, revering, serious, sincere, venerating, worshiping, zealous; SEE CONCEPT 542

dexterity [n] *aptitude, ability*
address, adroitness, aptness, art, artistry, cleverness, craft, cunning, deftness, effortlessness, expertise, expertness, facility, finesse, handiness, ingenuity, knack, know-how, mastery, neatness, nimbleness, proficiency, readiness, skill, skillful-

de
de

ness, smoothness, tact, touch; SEE CONCEPTS *409,630*

dexterous [*adj*] *ingenious, proficient*
able, active, acute, adept, adroit, agile, apt, artful, canny, clever, crack*, crackerjack*, deft, effortless, expert, facile, handy, having the know-how*, masterly, neat, nimble, nimble-fingered, prompt, quick, savvy, skilled, skillful, slick, sly, smooth; SEE CONCEPTS *402,527*

diabolic [*adj*] *evil, fiendish*
atrocious, cruel, damnable, demoniac, demonic, devilish, hellish, impious, infernal, Mephistophelian, monstrous, nasty, nefarious, satanic, serpentine, shocking, unhallowed, unpleasant, vicious, vile, villainous, wicked; SEE CONCEPT *545*

diagnose [*v*] *identify problem, disease*
analyze, determinate, determine, diagnosticate, distinguish, interpret, investigate, pinpoint, place, pronounce, recognize, spot; SEE CONCEPTS *38,310*

diagnosis [*n*] *identification of problem, disease*
analysis, conclusion, examination, interpretation, investigation, opinion, pronouncement, scrutiny, summary; SEE CONCEPTS *283,689*

diagonal [*adj*] *angled*
askew, bevel, beveled, bias, biased, cater-cornered, catty-cornered, cornerways, cross, crossways, crosswise, inclining, kitty-cornered*, oblique, skewing, slanted, slanting, transversal, transverse; SEE CONCEPT *581*

diagonally [*adv*] *at an angle*
askew, aslant, cater-corner, catty-corner, cornerwise, crosswise, kitty-corner*, obliquely, on a slant, on the bias, slantingways, slantways, slantwise, slaunchways; SEE CONCEPT *581*

diagram [*n*] *drawing, sketch of form or plan*
big picture*, blueprint, chart, description, design, draft, figure, floor plan, game, game plan, ground plan, layout, outline, perspective, representation, rough draft; SEE CONCEPTS *625,660*

dial [*v*] *tune to desired position*
punch, ring, rotate, turn, twist, wheel, zero in on*; SEE CONCEPT *201*

dialect [*n*] *local speech*
accent, argot, can, idiom, jargon, language, lingo, localism, patois, patter, pronunciation, provincialism, regionalism, slang, terminology, tongue, vernacular, vocabulary; SEE CONCEPT *276*

dialectic [*n*] *logic, reasoning*
argumentation, contention, debate, deduction, discussion, disputation, forensic, logical argument, mooting, persuasion, polemics, question-and-answer method, ratiocination; SEE CONCEPT *37*

dialectic [*adj*] *logical, rational*
analytic, argumentative, controversial, dialectical, persuasive, polemical, ratiocinative; SEE CONCEPT *529*

dialogue/dialog [*n*] *talk, exchange of ideas*
chat, colloquy, communication, confab*, confabulation, conference, conversation, converse, discourse, discussion, duologue, interlocution, lines*, parlance, parley, powwow, remarks, repartee, script, sides, small talk*; SEE CONCEPTS *56,278*

diameter [*n*] *measurement across object*
bore, breadth, broadness, caliber, module, width; SEE CONCEPT *760*

diametric/diametrical [*adj*] *opposed, conflicting*
adverse, antipodal, antipodean, antithetical, contradictory, contrary, contrasting, converse,

counter, facing, opposite, polar, reverse; SEE CONCEPT *564*

diaphanous [*adj*] *fine, see-through*
chiffon, clear, cobweblike, delicate, filmy, flimsy, gauzy, gossamer, light, pellucid, pure, sheer, thin, translucent, transparent; SEE CONCEPTS *490,606*

diary [*n*] *recounting of activities in writing*
account, agenda, appointment book, chronicle, daily record, daybook, engagement book, journal, log, minutes, notebook, record; SEE CONCEPT *283*

diaspora [*n*] *the spreading out of a group of people*
disbandment, dispersal, dispersion, dissolution, escape, exodus, mass exodus, refugee flow; SEE CONCEPT *195*

diatribe [*n*] *harangue, criticism*
abuse, castigation, denunciation, disputation, invective, jeremiad, objection, onslaught, philippic, reviling, screed, stricture, tirade, vituperation; SEE CONCEPT *52*

dicey [*adj*] *risky*
capricious, chancy, dangerous, difficult, erratic, fluctuant, iffy*, incalculable, ticklish, tricky, uncertain, unpredictable, whimsical; SEE CONCEPTS *535,552*

dicker [*v*] *bargain; argue about*
barter, buy and sell, chaffer, cut a deal*, haggle*, hammer out a deal*, huckster*, negotiate, palter, trade, work out a deal*; SEE CONCEPTS *46,330*

dictate [*n*] *command; rule*
behest, bidding, code, decree, dictum, direction, edict, fiat, injunction, law, mandate, order, ordinance, precept, principle, requirement, statute, ultimatum, word; SEE CONCEPTS *274,318,688*

dictate [*v1*] *command; give instructions*
bid, bulldoze*, call the play*, call the shots*, call the tune*, charge, control, decree, direct, enjoin, govern, guide, impose, instruct, lay down, lay down the law, lead, manage, ordain, order, prescribe, pronounce, put foot down*, read the riot act*, regiment, rule, set, take the reins*, walk heavy*; SEE CONCEPTS *53,60*

dictate [*v2*] *read out for the record*
compose, deliver, draft correspondence, emit, formulate, give account, give forth, interview, orate, prepare draft, say, speak, talk, transmit, utter, verbalize; SEE CONCEPTS *60,324*

dictator [*n*] *absolute ruler*
absolutist, adviser, authoritarian, autocrat, boss, chief, commander, despot, disciplinarian, fascist, Hitler*, leader, magnate, mogul, oligarch, oppressor, ringleader, slavedriver, totalitarian, tycoon, tyrant, usurper; SEE CONCEPT *354*

dictatorial [*adj*] *tyrannical, authoritarian*
absolute, arbitrary, arrogant, autocratic, bossy, clamorous, crack-the-whip*, despotic, dictative, doctrinaire, dogmatic, domineering, egotistic, firm, haughty, imperative, imperious, iron-handed, oppressive, overbearing, peremptory, pompous, proud, stern, throwing weight around, totalitarian, unlimited, unrestricted; SEE CONCEPT *542*

dictatorship [*n*] *absolute rule*
authoritarianism, autocracy, coercion, despotism, fascism, garrison state, Nazism, reign of terror*, totalitarianism, tyranny, unlimited rule; SEE CONCEPTS *133,299,641*

diction [*n*] *style of speech; articulation*
command of language, delivery, elocution, eloquence, enunciation, expression, fluency, gift of

gab*, inflection, intonation, language, line, lingo, locution, oratory, parlance, phrase, phraseology, phrasing, pronunciation, rhetoric, usage, verbalism, verbiage, vocabulary, wordage, wording; SEE CONCEPTS 47,276

dictionary [n] *book of word meanings*
concordance, cyclopedia, encyclopedia, glossary, language, lexicon, palaver, promptory, reference, terminology, vocabulary; SEE CONCEPT 280

dictum [n1] *saying; proverb*
adage, aphorism, apothegm, axiom, brocard, gnome, maxim, moral, motto, precept, rule, saw, truism; SEE CONCEPTS 278,689

dictum [n2] *decree, pronouncement*
affirmation, assertion, command, declaration, dictate, edict, fiat, order; SEE CONCEPT 278

didactic [adj] *educational*
academic, advisory, donnish, edifying, enlightening, exhortative, expository, homiletic, hortative, instructive, moral, moralizing, pedagogic, pedantic, preachy, preceptive, schoolmasterist, sermonic, sermonizing, teacherish, teacherly, teachy; SEE CONCEPT 548

die [v1] *pass away; stop living*
be no more*, be taken, breathe one's last*, cease to exist, croak*, croak*, decease, demise, depart, drop, drop off, drown, expire, finish, give up the ghost*, go way of all flesh*, kick the bucket*, perish, relinquish life, rest in peace, succumb, suffocate; SEE CONCEPT 304

die [v2] *wither, dwindle*
abate, bate, break down, crumble, decay, decline, degenerate, deteriorate, dilapidate, diminish, disappear, droop, ease off, ebb, end, expire, fade, fade away, fade out, fail, fall, fizzle out*, go bad*, go downhill*, halt, lapse, let up, lose power, melt away, moderate, molder, pass, peter out*, rankle, recede, retrograde, rot, run down, run low, run out, sink, slacken, stop, subside, vanish, wane, weaken, wear away, wilt; SEE CONCEPTS 469,698

diehard [n] *overenthusiastic person*
bitter ender*, Bourbon*, dyed-in-the-wool*, extremist, fanatic, fogy, fundamentalist, intransigent, mossback*, old liner*, praetorian, pullback*, reactionary, right, rightist, rightwinger, standpat, standpatter, stick-in-the-mud*, Tory*, true blue*, ultraconservative, zealot; SEE CONCEPTS 359,423

die-hard [adj] *uncompromising*
conservative, convinced, dyed-in-the-wool*, extremist, firm, fogyish, immovable, inflexible, intransigent, old line*, orthodox, Philistine, reactionary, right, standpat, Tory*, traditionalistic, ultraconservative, unreconstructed; SEE CONCEPTS 404,542

diet [n1] *abstinence from food*
dietary, fast, nutritional therapy, regime, regimen, restriction, starvation, weight-reduction plan; SEE CONCEPT 660

diet [n2] *daily intake of food*
aliment, bite, comestibles, commons, daily bread, edibles, fare, goodies, grubbery, menu, nourishment, nutriment, nutrition, provisions, rations, snack, subsistence, sustenance, viands, victuals; SEE CONCEPTS 457,459

diet [v] *abstain from food*
count calories*, eat sparingly, fall off, fast, go without, lose weight, reduce, skinny down*, slim, slim down, starve, tighten belt*, watch weight*; SEE CONCEPT 169

differ [v1] *be dissimilar, distinct*
alter, bear no resemblance, be distinguished from, be off the beaten path*, be unlike, clash with, conflict with, contradict, contrast, depart from, deviate from, digress, disagree, divaricate from, diverge, diversify, jar with, lack resemblance, modify, not conform, not look like, qualify, reverse, run counter to, show contrast, sing a different tune*, stand apart, take exception, turn, vary; SEE CONCEPT 665

differ [v2] *clash; hold opposing views*
bicker*, bump heads*, contend, debate, demur, disaccord, disagree, discept, discord, dispute, dissent, divide, fight, go after each other, go at it*, hit a clinker*, hit a sour note*, jar*, lock horns*, object, oppose, protest against, quarrel, squabble, take issue, vary, war; SEE CONCEPT 46

difference [n1] *dissimilarity, distinctness*
aberration, alteration, anomaly, antithesis, asymmetry, change, characteristic, contrariety, contrariness, contrast, departure, deviation, digression, discongruity, discrepancy, disparity, dissemblance, distinction, divergence, diversity, exception, heterogeneity, idiosyncrasy, inequality, irregularity, nonconformity, opposition, particularity, peculiarity, separateness, separation, singularity, unconformity, unlikeness, unorthodoxness, variance, variation, variety; SEE CONCEPT 665

difference [n2] *opposing views*
argument, beef*, blowup*, bone to pick*, brannigan, brawl, brush*, brush-off*, catamaran, clash, conflict, contention, contrariety, contretemps, controversy, debate, disaccord, disagreement, discord, discordance, dispute, dissension, dissent, dissidence, disunity, dustup*, estrangement, hassle, quarrel, row*, run-in*, scrap*, setto*, spat*, strife, tiff*, variance, words*, wrangle; SEE CONCEPTS 46,388

different [adj1] *dissimilar, unlike*
a far cry from*, altered, antithetic, at odds, at variance, changed, clashing, colorful, contradistinct, contradistinctive, contrary, contrasting, contrastive, deviating, differential, discrepant, disparate, distant, distinct, distinctive, divergent, divers, diverse, incommensurable, incomparable, inconsistent, individual, like night and day*, mismatched, mismated, offbeat, opposed, other, otherwise, particular, peculiar, poles apart*, single, unalike, unequal, unrelated, unsimilar, variant, various; SEE CONCEPTS 487,564,573

different [adj2] *separate, distinct*
another, another story, atypical, bizarre, discrete, diverse, especial, express, extraordinary, individual, novel, original, other, out of the ordinary, particular, peculiar, rare, several, singular, something else, special, specialized, specific, startling, strange, uncommon, unconventional, unique, unusual, various; SEE CONCEPT 564

different [adj3] *miscellaneous, various*
anthologized, assorted, asymmetrical, collected, disparate, dissonant, divergent, divers, diverse, diversified, diversiform, heterogeneous, incongruous, inconsistent, indiscriminate, jarring, manifold, many, multifarious, multiform, numerous, omnifarious, omniform, several, some, sundry, varicolored, varied, variegated, varietal, variform; SEE CONCEPT 772

differentiate [v1] *make a distinction*
antithesize, characterize, comprehend, contrast,

**de
di**

demarcate, discern, discrepate, discriminate, extricate, individualize, know, know what's what*, mark, mark off, redline*, separate, set apart, set off, sever, severalize, split hairs*, tell apart, understand; SEE CONCEPTS 15,38

differentiate [v2] *change; make different*
adapt, alter, assort, convert, diversify, mismatch, mismate, modify, transform, variegate, vary; SEE CONCEPT 232

differently [adv] *in another way; otherwise*
abnormally, adversely, antagonistically, antithetically, asymmetrically, conflictingly, contradictorily, contrarily, contrastingly, contrastively, discordantly, disparately, dissimilarly, distinctively, divergently, diversely, hostilely, in a different manner, incompatibly, incongruously, individually, negatively, nonconformably, on the contrary, on the other hand, oppositely, poles apart, separately, uniquely, unorthodoxly, unusually, variously, vice versa; SEE CONCEPT 564

difficult [adj1] *hard on someone; hard to do*
ambitious, arduous, backbreaker*, bothersome, burdensome, challenging, crucial, demanding, difficile, easier said than done*, effortful, exacting, formidable, galling, Gargantuan*, hard-won, heavy, Herculean*, immense, intricate, irritating, labored, laborious, no picnic*, not easy, onerous, operose, painful, problem, problematic, prohibitive, rigid, severe, stiff, strenuous, titanic, toilsome, tough, troublesome, trying, unyielding, uphill, upstream, wearisome; SEE CONCEPT 538

difficult [adj2] *complicated; hard to comprehend*
abstract, abstruse, baffling, bewildering, complex, confounding, confusing, dark, deep, delicate, enigmatic, enigmatical, entangled, esoteric, formidable, hard to explain, hard to solve, hidden, inexplicable, intricate, involved, knotty, labyrinthine, loose, meandering, mysterious, mystical, mystifying, nice, obscure, obstinate, paradoxical, perplexing, problematical, profound, puzzling, rambling, subtle, tangled, thorny, ticklish, troublesome, unclear, unfathomable, unintelligible, vexing; SEE CONCEPT 529

difficult [adj3] *unmanageable socially*
argumentative, bearish, boorish, dark, demanding, fastidious, finicky, fractious, fussy, grim, hard to please, impolite, intractable, irritable, oafish, obstreperous, perverse, picky, refractory, rigid, rude, tiresome, tough, troublesome, trying, unaccommodating, unamenable; SEE CONCEPTS 404,542,555

difficulty [n1] *problem; situation requiring great effort*
adversity, arduousness, awkwardness, barricade, check, complication, crisis, crux, dead end, deadlock, deep water*, dilemma, distress, emergency, exigency, fix*, frustration, hardship, hazard, hindrance, hitch*, hot water*, impasse, knot*, labor, laboriousness, mess, misfortune, muddle, obstacle, obstruction, pain, painfulness, paradox, perplexity, pickle*, predicament, quagmire, quandary, scrape*, snag*, stew*, strain, strait, strenuousness, struggle, stumbling block*, tribulation, trouble; SEE CONCEPTS 674,677

difficulty [n2] *mental burden*
ado, aggravation, annoyance, anxiety, bafflement, bother, care, charge, complication, crisis, depression, discouragement, distress, embarrassment, emergency, exigency, frustration, grievance, hangup, harassment, imbroglio, inconvenience, irritation, jam, maze, mess, millstone*, misery, oppression, perplexity, pickle*, pinch, predicament, pressure, puzzle, quandary, ramification, responsibility, scrape*, setback, strain, strait, stress, strife, struggle, to-do*, trouble, vicissitude, weight, worry; SEE CONCEPTS 410,532,690

difficulty [n3] *argument*
altercation, beef*, bickering, controversy, dispute, falling-out*, fight, hassle, misunderstanding, quarrel, squabble, strife, trouble; SEE CONCEPT 46

diffidence [n] *hesitancy; lack of confidence*
backwardness, bashfulness, constraint, doubt, fear, hesitation, humility, insecurity, meekness, modesty, mousiness, reluctance, reserve, self-consciousness, sheepishness, shyness, timidity, timidness, timorousness, unassertiveness; SEE CONCEPT 633

diffident [adj] *hesitant; unconfident*
backward, bashful, blenching, chary, constrained, coy, demure, distrustful, doubtful, dubious, flinching, humble, insecure, meek, modest, mousy, rabbity, reluctant, reserved, retiring, self-conscious, self-effacing, sheepish, shrinking, shy, suspicious, timid, timorous, unassertive, unassuming, unassured, unobtrusive, unpoised, unsure, withdrawn; SEE CONCEPT 401

diffuse [adj1] *spread out*
broadcast, catholic, circulated, diluted, dispersed, disseminated, distributed, expanded, extended, general, prevalent, propagated, radiated, scattered, separated, strewn, thin, unconcentrated, universal, widespread; SEE CONCEPTS 530,583, 772

diffuse [adj2] *wordy*
circumlocutory, copious, diffusive, digressive, discursive, dull, exuberant, lavish, lengthy, long, long-winded, loose, meandering, palaverous, profuse, prolix, rambling, random, redundant, vague, verbose, waffling, windy; SEE CONCEPT 267

diffusion [n] *spread; wide distribution*
circulation, dispersal, dispersion, dissemination, dissipation, expansion, propaganda, propagation, scattering; SEE CONCEPTS 634,651

dig [n] *insult*
crack, cut, cutting remark, gibe, innuendo, jeer, quip, slur, sneer, taunt, wisecrack; SEE CONCEPT 54

dig [v1] *delve into; hollow out*
bore, break up, bulldoze, burrow, cat, channel, clean, concave, deepen, depress, dig down, discover, dredge, drill, drive, enter, excavate, exhume, fork out, go into, gouge, grub, harvest, hoe, investigate, mine, penetrate, pierce, pit, probe, produce, quarry, root, root out, rout, sap, scoop, scoop out, search, shovel, sift, spade, till, tunnel, turn over, uncover, undermine, unearth; SEE CONCEPT 178

dig [v2] *thrust object into*
drive, gouge, jab, jog, nudge, plunge, poke, prod, punch, ram, sink, stab, stick; SEE CONCEPT 208

dig [v3] *investigate; discover*
bring to light*, come across, come up with, delve, dig down, expose, extricate, find, go into, inquire, look into, probe, prospect, research, retrieve, root, search, search high and low*, shake down*, sift*, turn inside out*, turn upside down*, uncover, unearth; SEE CONCEPTS 31,103,216

dig [v4] *enjoy, like*
appreciate, follow, go for*, groove*, love, mind, relish, understand; SEE CONCEPT 32

dig [v5] *understand*
accept, apprehend, catch, comprehend, follow, grasp, recognize, see, take, take in; SEE CONCEPT 15

digest [n] *abridgement of something written*
abstract, aperçu, brief, compendium, condensation, epitome, pandect, précis, résumé, short form, sketch, summary, survey, syllabus, sylloge, synopsis; SEE CONCEPT 271

digest [v1] *assimilate food*
absorb, chymify, consume, dissolve, eat, incorporate, macerate, swallow, take; SEE CONCEPT 169

digest [v2] *make shorter; abridge*
abbreviate, abstract, boil down, classify, codify, compress, condense, cut, cut down, cut to bone*, decrease, epitomize, get to the meat*, inventory, methodize, nutshell*, put in a nutshell*, reduce, shorten, sum, summarize, summate, sum up, survey, synopsize, systematize, tabulate, trim; SEE CONCEPTS 236,247

digest [v3] *come to understand*
absorb, analyze, assimilate, consider, contemplate, deliberate, grasp, master, meditate, ponder, study, take in, think about, think over; SEE CONCEPT 15

digest [v4] *tolerate, endure*
abide, bear, brook, go, stand, stomach, swallow, take; SEE CONCEPT 23

dig in [v] *begin with enthusiasm*
bite, burrow, chew, commence, consume, delve, eat, fall to, set about, spring, start eating; SEE CONCEPTS 100,169

digit [n1] *number*
arabic, chiffer, cipher, figure, integer, notation, numeral, symbol, whole number; SEE CONCEPTS 765,784

digit [n2] *small appendage of animate being*
claw, extremity, fang, feeler, finger, fork, hook, index finger, phalange, pinkie, pointer, ring finger, thumb, toe; SEE CONCEPT 392

dignified [adj] *honorable*
aristocratic, august, courtly, decorous, distingué, distinguished, eminent, formal, grand, grave, great, highbrow*, highfalutin'*, imperial, imperious, lofty, magisterial, magnificent, nifty*, noble, proud, refined, regal, reserved, respected, solemn, somber, stately, superior, upright; SEE CONCEPTS 404,555,574

dignify [v] *make honorable; glorify*
adorn, advance, aggrandize, distinguish, elevate, ennoble, erect, exalt, grace, honor, magnify, prefer, promote, raise, sublime, uprear; SEE CONCEPTS 244,700

dignity [n] *excellence, nobility*
address, cachet, character, consequence, courtliness, culture, decency, decorum, distinction, elevation, eminence, ethics, etiquette, glory, grace, grandeur, gravity, greatness, hauteur, honor, importance, loftiness, majesty, merit, morality, nobleness, perfection, poise, prestige, propriety, quality, rank, regard, renown, respectability, seemliness, self-respect, significance, solemnity, splendor, standing, state, stateliness, station, stature, status, sublimity, virtue, worth, worthiness; SEE CONCEPTS 388,411,668

digress [v] *stray, deviate*
aberrate, beat about the bush*, be diffuse, circumlocute, depart, divagate, drift, excurse, get off the point, get off the subject, get sidetracked, go by way of*, go off on a tangent*, long way*, meander, ramble, roam, swerve, turn aside, veer, wander, wander away; SEE CONCEPTS 195,266,697

digression [n] *deviation; straying*
apostrophe, aside, deflection, departure, detour, difference, discursion, divagation, divergence, diversion, drifting, episode, excursion, excursus, footnote, incident, note, obiter dictum, parenthesis, rambling, variation, wandering; SEE CONCEPTS 278,665,697

dilapidated [adj] *falling apart; in ruins*
battered, beat-up, broken-down, crumbling, crumbly, crummy*, damaged, decayed, decaying, decrepit, derelict, dingy, dog-eared*, faded, fallen-in, impaired, in a bad way*, injured, marred, neglected, old, ramshackle, ratty*, raunchy, rickety, rinky-dink*, run-down, seedy, shabby, shaky, slummy, tacky, threadbare, tumble-down, uncared for, unimproved, unkempt, used-up, worn-out; SEE CONCEPTS 485,560

dilate [v] *stretch, widen*
amplify, augment, be profuse, be prolix, broaden, develop, distend, enlarge, expand, expatiate, expound, extend, increase, inflate, lengthen, prolong, protract, puff out, spin off, swell; SEE CONCEPTS 57,236,245

dilatory [adj] *procrastinating*
backward, behindhand, dallying, delaying, deliberate, laggard, late, lax, lazy, leisurely, lingering, loitering, moratory, neglectful, negligent, putting off, remiss, slack, slow, sluggish, snail-like*, tardy, tarrying, time-wasting, unhasty, unhurried; SEE CONCEPTS 542,799

dilemma [n] *crisis*
bind*, box*, Catch-22*, corner, difficulty, double bind*, embarrassment, fix, hole, hooker*, impasse, jam, mess, mire, perplexity, pickle*, plight, predicament, problem, puzzle, quandary, scrape, spot, strait, tight corner*; SEE CONCEPTS 674,675

dilettante [n] *amateur*
abecedarian, aesthete, connoisseur, dabbler, dallier, greenhorn*, nonprofessional, rookie, smatterer, tenderfoot*, trifler, tyro, uninitiate; SEE CONCEPT 423

dilettante [adj] *amateurish*
artsy fartsy*, dabbling, green*, half-baked*, half-cocked*, rookie, tenderfoot*, unaccomplished, ungifted, unskilled; SEE CONCEPT 527

diligence [n] *perseverance in carrying out action*
activity, alertness, application, assiduity, assiduousness, attention, attentiveness, briskness, care, carefulness, constancy, earnestness, exertion, heed, heedfulness, industry, intensity, intent, intentness, keenness, laboriousness, pertinacity, quickness, sedulousness, vigor; SEE CONCEPTS 657,677

diligent [adj] *persevering, hard-working*
active, assiduous, attentive, busy, careful, conscientious, constant, eager, eager beaver*, earnest, grind*, indefatigable, industrious, laborious, occupied, operose, painstaking, persistent, persisting, pertinacious, plugging*, sedulous, steadfast, studious, tireless, unflagging, unrelenting, untiring; SEE CONCEPTS 326,538,542

di
di

dilute [v] *make thinner; weaken*
adulterate, alter, attenuate, cook, cut, decrease, deliquesce, diffuse, diminish, doctor*, doctor up*, irrigate, lace, lessen, liquefy, mitigate, mix, moderate, modify, needle*, phony up*, plant, qualify, reduce, shave*, spike, temper, water, water down; SEE CONCEPT 250

diluted/dilute [adj] *thinned, weakened*
adulterated, attenuated, cut, impaired, impoverished, laced, light, moderated, reduced, shaved*, spiked, tempered, washy, watered down, waterish, watery, wishy-washy*; SEE CONCEPTS 485,606

dim [adj1] *darkish*
blah, bleary, blurred, caliginous, cloudy, dark, dingy, dreary, dull, dusk, dusky, faded, faint, flat, fuzzy, gloomy, gray, ill-defined, indistinct, lackluster, lightless, mat, monotone, monotonous, murky, muted, obscured, opaque, overcast, pale, poorly lit, shadowy, sullied, tarnished, tenebrous, unclear, unilluminated, vague, weak; SEE CONCEPT 617

dim [adj2] *unfavorable with regard to opinion*
depressing, disapproving, discouraging, gloomy, skeptical, somber, suspicious, unpromising; SEE CONCEPT 542

dim [adj3] *not very intelligent*
boorish, dense, dim-witted, doltish, dull, dumb, oafish, obtuse, slow, slow on uptake*, stupid, thick*, weak-minded; SEE CONCEPT 402

dim [v] *darken; obscure*
becloud, bedim, befog, blear, blur, cloud, dull, eclipse, fade, fog, haze, lower, muddy, obfuscate, pale, tarnish, turn down; SEE CONCEPTS 250,627

dimensions/dimension [n] *proportions; range*
admeasurement, ambit, amplitude, bigness, bulk, capacity, compass, depth, dimensionality, extension, extensity, extent, greatness, height, importance, largeness, length, magnitude, measure, measurement, reach, scale, scope, size, volume, width; SEE CONCEPTS 730,792

diminish [v1] *become or cause to be less*
abate, abbreviate, attenuate, become smaller, close, contract, curtail, cut, decline, decrease, depreciate, die out, drain, dwindle, ebb, extenuate, fade away, lessen, lower, minify, moderate, peter out, recede, reduce, retrench, shrink, shrivel, slacken, subside, taper, temper, wane, weaken; SEE CONCEPTS 698,776

diminish [v2] *belittle*
abuse, bad-mouth*, cheapen, cut down to size*, decry, demean, depreciate, derogate, detract from, devalue, disparage, dump on*, give comeuppance*, knock off high horse*, minimize, pan*, poormouth*, put away*, put down*, run down*, tear down*; SEE CONCEPT 54

diminution [n] *lessening, reduction*
abatement, alleviation, contraction, curtailment, cut, cutback, decay, decline, decrease, deduction, retrenchment, weakening; SEE CONCEPTS 698, 776

diminutive [adj] *tiny, petite*
bantam, bitsy*, bitty*, button*, Lilliputian, little, midget, mini, miniature, minute, peewee*, pint-sized, pocket, pocket-sized, small, teensy*, teensy-weensy*, teeny*, teeny-weeny*, under-size, wee*, weeny*; SEE CONCEPT 789

din [n] *loud, continuous noise*
babel, bedlam, boisterousness, brouhaha, buzz,

clamor, clangor, clash, clatter, commotion, confusion, crash, disquiet, hoo-ha*, hubbub, hullabaloo*, hurly-burly*, jangle, music, outcry, pandemonium, percussion, racket, row, shout, sound, stridency, tintamarre*, tintinnabulation, tumult, uproar; SEE CONCEPT 595

dine [v] *eat, often formally*
banquet, breakfast, consume, do lunch*, eat out*, fall to*, feast, feed on, lunch, sup, supper; SEE CONCEPT 169

diner [n] *casual restaurant with varied menu*
Automat*, bistro, booth, café, canteen, chuck wagon*, coffee shop, concession, dump*, eatery*, eating house, facility, fast-food outlet, greasy spoon*, grill, hash house*, ice-cream parlor, lunch counter, lunchroom, lunch wagon, mess hall, quick-lunch, saloon, sandwich shop, snack bar, tearoom; SEE CONCEPT 449

dingy [adj] *soiled, tacky*
bedimmed, broken-down, colorless, dark, darkish, dilapidated, dim, dirty, discolored, drab, dreary, dull, dusky, faded, gloomy, grimy, muddy, murky, obscure, run-down, seedy, shabby, smirched, somber, sullied, tarnished, threadbare, tired; SEE CONCEPTS 485,617

dinky [adj] *tiny, small*
bush-league*, dainty, insignificant, lesser, Lilliputian, mini, miniature, minor, minor-league*, neat, petite, secondary, second rate*, small-fry*, small-time*, trim; SEE CONCEPT 789

dinner [n] *evening meal*
banquet, blowout*, chow*, collation, din-din*, eats*, feast, feedbag*, fete, main meal, major munch*, potluck, principal meal, refection, regale, repast, ribs*, spread*, supper, table d'hôte; SEE CONCEPT 459

dip [n1] *submersion in liquid*
bath, dive, douche, drenching, ducking, immersion, plunge, soak, soaking, swim; SEE CONCEPT 256

dip [n2] *something for dunking*
concoction, dilution, infusion, mixture, preparation, solution, suffusion, suspension; SEE CONCEPTS 260,466

dip [n3] *depression; decline*
basin, concavity, declivity, descent, downslide, downswing, downtrend, drop, fall, fall-off, hole, hollow, inclination, incline, lowering, pitch, sag, sink, sinkage, sinkhole, slip, slope, slump; SEE CONCEPTS 513,697,738

dip [v1] *put into liquid*
baptize, bathe, douse, drench, duck, dunk, immerse, irrigate, lave, lower, moisten, pitch, plunge, rinse, slop, slosh, soak, souse, splash, steep, submerge, submerse, wash, water, wet; SEE CONCEPTS 201,256

dip [v2] *lower, descend*
bend, decline, disappear, droop, drop down, fade, fall, go down, incline, nose-dive, plummet, plunge, reach, recede, sag, set, settle, sheer, sink, skew, skid, slant, slip, slope, slue, slump, spiral, subside, swoop, tilt, tumble, veer, verge; SEE CONCEPT 181

dip [v3] *scoop, ladle*
bail, bale, bucket, decant, dish, draft off, draw, draw out, dredge, handle, lade, lift, offer, reach into, shovel, spoon, strain; SEE CONCEPTS 196,225

dip into [v] *try, sample*
appropriate, browse, dabble, flip through, get,

glance at, glance over, leaf through, peruse, play at, rifle through*, run over, run through, scan, seize, skim, take, taste, thumb through*; SEE CONCEPTS 87,623

diploma [n] *certificate for achievement*
authority, award, charter, commission, confirmation, credentials, degree, honor, recognition, sheepskin, shingle, voucher, warrant; SEE CONCEPTS 271,337

diplomacy [n] *tact*
address, artfulness, craft, delicacy, delicatesse, discretion, expedience, finesse, negotiation, poise, politics, savoir-faire, skill, statecraft, subtlety; SEE CONCEPTS 388,633

diplomat [n] *politician, consul*
agent, ambassador, attaché, cabinet member, chargé d'affaires, conciliator, emissary, envoy, expert, go-between, legate, mediator, minister, moderator, negotiator, plenipotentiary, public relations person, representative, tactician; SEE CONCEPTS 354,359

diplomatic [adj] *politic, tactful*
adept, arch, artful, astute, bland, brainy, cagey, calculating, capable, clever, conciliatory, conniving, contriving, courteous, crafty, cunning, deft, delicate, dexterous, discreet, gracious, guileful, intriguing, opportunistic, polite, prudent, savvy, scheming, sensitive, sharp, shrewd, sly, smooth, strategic, suave, subtle, wily; SEE CONCEPTS 401,542

dire [adj1] *urgent; crucial*
acute, burning, clamant, clamorous, climacteric, critical, crying, desperate, drastic, exigent, extreme, immoderate, imperative, importunate, instant, pressing; SEE CONCEPTS 546,568,799

dire [adj2] *terrible, ominous*
afflictive, alarming, appalling, awful, black, calamitous, cataclysmic, catastrophic, cruel, deplorable, depressing, disastrous, dismal, distressing, dreadful, fearful, fierce, frightful, gloomy, grievous, grim, heartbreaking, horrible, horrid, lamentable, oppressing, portentous, redoubtable, regrettable, ruinous, scowling, shocking, terrific, ugly, unfortunate, woeful; SEE CONCEPTS 537,548,570

direct [adj1] *honest*
absolute, bald, blunt, candid, categorical, downright, explicit, express, forthright, frank, matter-of-fact, open, outspoken, person-to-person, plain, plainspoken, point-blank, sincere, straight, straightforward, straight from the shoulder*, talk turkey*, unambiguous, unconcealed, undisguised, unequivocal, unreserved; SEE CONCEPT 267

direct [adj2] *undeviating; uninterrupted*
beeline*, continuous, even, horizontal, in bee line*, in straight line, linear, nonstop, not crooked, point-blank, right, shortest, straight, straight ahead, straightaway, through, true, unbroken, unswerving; SEE CONCEPTS 482,581

direct [adj3] *face-to-face; next to*
contiguous, firsthand, head-on, immediate, lineal, next, personal, primary, prompt, proximate, resultant, succeeding; SEE CONCEPTS 585,586

direct [v1] *manage, oversee*
administer, advise, be in the driver's seat*, boss, call the shots*, carry on, conduct, control, control the affairs of, dispose, dominate, govern, guide, handle, have the say, head up*, influence, keep, lead, operate, ordain, preside over, quarterback*, regulate, rule, run, run the show*, run things*,

shepherd, superintend, supervise, take the reins*; SEE CONCEPTS 94,117

direct [v2] *give instructions; teach*
address, advise, bid, charge, command, deliver, dictate, enjoin, give directions, give orders, inform, instruct, lecture, order, read, tell, warn; SEE CONCEPTS 53,61

direct [v3] *point in a direction; guide*
address, aim, beam, cast, conduct, escort, fix, focus, head, incline, indicate, intend, lay, lead, level, mean, move in, pilot, point, point the way, present, route, see, set, shepherd, show, sight, sight on, slant, steer, target, train, turn, zero in; SEE CONCEPTS 187,201

direct [v4] *send, usually by mail system*
address, designate, inscribe, label, mail, mark, route, superscribe; SEE CONCEPT 217

direct [v5] *put all of efforts toward*
address, aim, apply, bend, buckle down, devote, endeavor, fix, give, set, settle, strive, throw, try, turn; SEE CONCEPTS 87,677

direction [n1] *management*
administration, charge, command, control, government, guidance, leadership, order, oversight, superintendence, supervision; SEE CONCEPTS 299,325

direction [n2] *course, route*
aim, angle, area, aspect, bearing, beeline*, bent, bias, current, drift, end, inclination, line, objective, orientation, outlook, path, point of compass, proclivity, range, region, road, set, side, slant, spot, standpoint, stream, tack, tendency, that-a-way*, tide, track, trajectory, trend, viewpoint, way; SEE CONCEPTS 657,738

direction(s) [n3] *instructions, guidance*
advice, advisement, assignment, briefing, directive, guidelines, indication, lowdown*, notification, plan, prescription, recommendation, regulation, sealed order, specification, specs*, steer*, summons, tip, word*; SEE CONCEPTS 271,274

directive [n] *command, instruction*
charge, communication, decree, dictate, edict, injunction, mandate, memo, memorandum, message, notice, order, ordinance, regulation, ruling, ukase, word; SEE CONCEPTS 271,274,662

directly [adv1] *the shortest route*
as a crow flies*, beeline*, dead, direct, due, exactly, plump, precisely, right, slam bang*, slap, smack, smack dab*, straight, straightly, undeviatingly, unswervingly, without deviation; SEE CONCEPTS 581,778

directly [adv2] *as soon as possible*
anon, at once, contiguously, dead*, due, first off, forthwith, immediately, in a second, instantaneously, instanter, instantly, presently, promptly, pronto*, quickly, right away, shortly, speedily, straightaway, straight off; SEE CONCEPT 820

directly [adv3] *straightforwardly*
candidly, face-to-face, honestly, in person, literally, openly, personally, plainly, point-black, truthfully, unequivocally, verbatim, without prevarication, word for word; SEE CONCEPT 267

director [n] *manager*
administrator, big person*, boss, chair, chief, controller, exec, executive, executive officer, governor, head, head honcho*, helmer, key player*, kingpin*, leader, organizer, overseer, person upstairs*, player, principal, producer, skipper*, su-

di
di

pervisor, top dog*, top person*; SEE CONCEPTS *347,352*

directory [*n*] *reference book; guide*
agenda, almanac, atlas, blue book, book, catalogue, charts, gazeteer, hit list*, index, laundry list*, lineup, list, little black book*, record, register, roster, scorecard, short list*, social register, syllabus, white pages*, who's who*, yellow pages*; SEE CONCEPTS *280,283*

direful [*adj*] *fearful; horrible*
apocalyptic, appalling, awful, baleful, baneful, calamitous, dreadful, fateful, ghastly, gloomy, horrid, ill-boding, inauspicious, ominous, shocking, terrible, terrific, unlucky, unpropitious; SEE CONCEPTS *537,570*

dirge [*n*] *sad song*
chant, coronach, cry, death march, death song, elegy, funeral song, hymn, jeremiad, keen, lament, march, monody, requiem, threnody; SEE CONCEPT *595*

dirt [*n1*] *grime, impurity*
crud*, dreck, dregs, excrement, feculence, filth, filthiness, gook*, ground, gunk*, mire, muck, mud, rottenness, scuz*, sleaze, slime, smudge, smut, soil, stain, tarnish; SEE CONCEPT *509*

dirt [*n2*] *obscenity; immorality*
chicanery, double-dealing, filth, fourberie, fraud, indecency, lubricity, pornography, smut; SEE CONCEPT *645*

dirt [*n3*] *soil*
clay, dust, earth, loam, real estate, terra firma; SEE CONCEPT *509*

dirty [*adj1*] *soiled, unclean*
bedraggled, begrimed, black, contaminated, cruddy*, crummy, defiled, disarrayed, dishabille, disheveled, dreggy, dungy, dusty, filthy, foul, fouled, greasy, grimy, grubby, grungy*, icky*, lousy, messy, mucky*, muddy, mung*, murky, nasty, pigpen*, polluted, raunchy, scummy*, scuzzy*, slatternly, slimy, sloppy, slovenly, smudged, smutty, sooty, spattered, spotted, squalid, stained, straggly, sullied, undusted, unhygienic, unkempt, unlaundered, unsanitary, unsightly, unswept, untidy, unwashed, yucky*; SEE CONCEPT *485*

dirty [*adj2*] *obscene, pornographic*
base, blue, coarse, contemptible, despicable, filthy, immoral, impure, indecent, lewd, low, mean, nasty, off-color, ribald, risqué, salacious, scatological, scurvy, smutty, sordid, squalid, unchaste, unclean, uncleanly, vile, vulgar; SEE CONCEPTS *542,545*

dirty [*adj3*] *violent, stormy with regard to weather*
blustering, blustery, coarse, dark, furious, gusty, lowering, raging, rainy, rough, squally, storming, tempestuous, wild; SEE CONCEPT *525*

dirty [*v*] *cause to be soiled*
begrime, besoil, blacken, blotch, blur, botch, coat, contaminate, corrupt, debase, decay, defile, discolor, draggle, encrust, foul, grime, make dusty, make impure, mess up, mold, muddy, pollute, rot, smear, smirch, smoke, smudge, smutch, spatter, spoil, spot, stain, sully, sweat, taint, tar, tarnish; SEE CONCEPT *254*

disability [*n*] *disadvantage, restriction*
affliction, ailment, defect, detriment, disqualification, drawback, impairment, inability, incapacity, incompetency, inexperience, infirmity, injury, invalidity, lack, unfitness, weakness; SEE CONCEPTS *309,316,410,720*

disable [*v*] *render inoperative; cripple*
attenuate, batter, blunt, damage, debilitate, disarm, disenable, disqualify, enervate, enfeeble, exhaust, hamstring*, handicap, harm, hock*, hogtie*, hurt, immobilize, impair, incapacitate, invalidate, kibosh*, knock out*, maim, mangle, mar, mutilate, muzzle, paralyze, pinion, prostrate, put out of action*, render incapable, ruin, sabotage, sap, shatter, shoot down*, spoil, take out*, throw monkey wrench in*, total*, unbrace, undermine, unfit, unstrengthen, weaken, wreck; SEE CONCEPTS *130,246*

disabled [*adj*] *incapacitated*
broken-down, confined, decrepit, disarmed, hamstrung*, handicapped, helpless, hurt, incapable, infirm, laid-up, lame, maimed, out-of-action*, out-of-commission*, paralyzed, powerless, rundown, sidelined, stalled, weakened, worn-out, wounded, wrecked; SEE CONCEPTS *314,527*

disadvantage(s) [*n1*] *difficulty, trouble*
adverse circumstance, bar, blocking, burden, defect, deficiency, deprivation, detriment, disability, discommodity, drawback, failing, fault, flaw, fly in the ointment*, hamper, handicap, hardship, hindrance, impediment, imperfection, imposition, inadequacy, inconvenience, inutility, lack, liability, limitation, minus, nuisance, objection, obstacle, privation, problem, restraint, snag, stumbling block*, weakness, weak point; SEE CONCEPTS *666,674*

disadvantage [*n2*] *hurt, loss*
damage, deprivation, detriment, disservice, harm, injury, prejudice; SEE CONCEPTS *230,309,679*

disadvantageous [*adj*] *detrimental, inconvenient*
adverse, contrary, damaging, debit-side, deleterious, depreciative, depreciatory, derogatory, detracting, disparaging, downside, dyslogistic, harmful, hurtful, ill-timed, inexpedient, injurious, inopportune, objectionable, on the debit side, pejorative, prejudicial, slighting, uncomplimentary, unfavorable, unprofitable; SEE CONCEPTS *334, 537,555*

disaffect [*v*] *lose affection for, estrange*
agitate, alienate, antagonize, discompose, disquiet, disturb, disunify, disunite, divide, repel, upset, wean; SEE CONCEPTS *7,19,135,384*

disaffected [*adj*] *alienated, estranged*
antagonistic, discontented, disloyal, dissatisfied, hostile, indifferent, mutinous, rebellious, seditious, uncompliant, unfriendly, unsubmissive; SEE CONCEPTS *403,555*

disaffection [*n*] *alienation, estrangement*
animosity, antagonism, antipathy, aversion, breach, disagreement, discontent, dislike, disloyalty, dissatisfaction, hatred, hostility, ill will, repugnance, resentment, unfriendliness; SEE CONCEPTS *388,410*

disagree [*v1*] *be different*
be discordant, be dissimilar, clash, conflict, contradict, counter, depart, deviate, differ, discord, disharmonize, dissent, diverge, run counter to, vary, war; SEE CONCEPT *665*

disagree [*v2*] *argue; hold differing opinion*
altercate, battle, bicker, brawl, break with, bring action, clash, contend, contest, controversialize, controvert, debate, differ, disaccord, discept, discord, dispute, dissent, divide, fall out*, feud, fight, go for the jugular*, haggle, have words*, jump on*, lay into*, let have it, logomachize, object, oppose, palter, quarrel, quibble, rip, row,

scrap, set to, skirmish, spar, spat, sue, take issue, take on, war, wrangle, zap*; SEE CONCEPTS 12,46

disagree [v3] *be injurious*
be distasteful, be disturbing, be sickening, be unsuitable, bother, discomfort, distress, go against the grain*, hurt, injure, make ill, nauseate, sicken, trouble, upset; SEE CONCEPT 246

disagreeable [adj1] *bad-tempered, irritable*
bellicose, brusque, cantankerous, churlish, contentious, contrary, cross, difficult, disobliging, disputatious, eristic, grouchy, ill-natured, nasty, obnoxious, offensive, out of sorts, peevish, pettish, petulant, querulous, rude, snappy, surly, ugly, unfriendly, ungracious, unlikable, unpleasant, uptight, waspish, whiny; SEE CONCEPT 401

disagreeable [adj2] *disgusting, offensive*
annoying, awful, bad, bothersome, displeasing, distasteful, distressing, drag, nasty, objectionable, obnoxious, pain, repellent, repugnant, repulsive, rotten, sour, unhappy, uninviting, unpalatable, unpleasant, unsavory, upsetting, woeful; SEE CONCEPTS 537,548

disagreement [n1] *dispute, quarrel*
altercation, animosity, antagonism, argument, atmospherics, bickering, breach, break, clash, clashing, conflict, contention, contest, controversy, cross-purposes, debate, difference, discord, dissent, dissidence, disunion, disunity, division, divisiveness, falling out, feud, fight, friction, hassle, hostility, ill feeling, ill will, jarring, misunderstanding, opposition, rupture, spat, split, squabble, strife, tension, variance, vendetta, words, wrangle; SEE CONCEPTS 46,388

disagreement [n2] *difference, unlikeness*
clash, disaccord, discordance, discrepancy, disharmonism, disharmony, disparity, dissimilarity, dissimilitude, divergence, divergency, diversity, incompatibility, incongruity, incongruousness, inconsistency, variance; SEE CONCEPT 665

disallow [v] *reject, prohibit*
abjure, cancel, censor, debar, deny, disacknowledge, disavow, disclaim, dismiss, disown, embargo, exclude, forbid, keep back, kill, nix*, pass on, proscribe, put down, rebuff, refuse, repudiate, shut out, taboo*, veto, withhold, zing*; SEE CONCEPTS 21,25,30

disappear [v] *vanish; cease*
abandon, abscond, be done for, be gone, be lost, be no more*, be swallowed up, cease to exist, clear, come to naught, decamp, dematerialize, depart, die, die out, disperse, dissipate, dissolve, drop out of sight*, ebb, end, end gradually, escape, evanesce, evanish, evaporate, exit, expire, fade, fade away, flee, fly, go, go south*, leave, leave no trace, melt, melt away, pass, pass away, perish, recede, retire, retreat, sink, take flight, vacate, vamoose*, wane, withdraw; SEE CONCEPTS 102,105,195

disappearance [n] *vanishing*
ceasing to exist, decline and fall, dematerialization, departure, desertion, disappearing act, disintegration, dispersal, dispersion, dissolution, ebbing, eclipse, escape, evanescence, evaporation, exit, exodus, fading, flight, going, loss, melting, passing, receding, recession, removal, retirement, wane, wearing away, withdrawal; SEE CONCEPTS 102,105,195

disappoint [v] *sadden, dismay; frustrate*
abort, baffle, balk, bring to naught, bungle, cast down, chagrin, circumvent, come to nothing,

dash, dash hopes*, deceive, delude, disconcert, disenchant, disgruntle, dishearten, disillusion, dissatisfy, dumbfound, embitter, fail, fall down on, fall flat, fall short of, foil, founder, hamper, hinder, leave in the lurch*, let down, miscarry, mislead, not show, put out, ruin prospects, stand up, tease, thwart, torment, vex; SEE CONCEPTS 7,19,699

disappointed [adj] *let down, saddened*
aghast, balked, beaten, chapfallen, complaining, crestfallen, defeated, depressed, despondent, disconcerted, discontented, discouraged, disenchanted, disgruntled, disillusioned, dissatisfied, distressed, down, downcast, downhearted, down in the dumps*, fooled, frustrated, hopeless, objecting, shot down, taken down, thwarted, unhappy, unsatisfied, upset, vanquished, worsted; SEE CONCEPT 403

disappointment [n1] *saddening situation; letdown*
bitter pill*, blind alley*, blow, blunder, bringdown, bummer, bust*, calamity, defeat, disaster, discouragement, downer*, downfall, drag, dud, error, failure, false alarm*, faux pas*, fiasco, fizzle, flash in the pan*, impasse, inefficacy, lemon*, miscalculation, mischance, misfortune, mishap, mistake, obstacle, old one-two*, setback, slip, washout; SEE CONCEPTS 230,674

disappointment [n2] *mental upset; displeasure*
adverse fate, adversity, bafflement, blow, chagrin, defeat, despondency, discontent, discouragement, disenchantment, disgruntlement, disillusion, disillusionment, dissatisfaction, distress, failure, frustration, lack of success, letdown, mortification, nonsuccess, regret, setback, the knocks*, unfulfillment; SEE CONCEPT 410

disapproval [n] *condemnation*
blackball*, black list*, blame, boo*, boycott, brickbat, call down, castigation, catcall*, censure, criticism, denunciation, deprecation, disapprobation, discontent, disfavor, dislike, disparagement, displeasure, dissatisfaction, hiss*, nix*, objection, opprobrium, ostracism, reproach, reproof, slap on wrist*, stricture, thumbs down*, vitriol, zing*; SEE CONCEPTS 278,689

disapprove [v] *condemn*
blame, censure, chastise, criticize, damn, decry, denounce, deplore, deprecate, detract, disallow, discommend, discountenance, disesteem, disfavor, dislike, dismiss, dispraise, expostulate, find fault with, find unacceptable, frown on, look askance at, look down on, nix*, object to, oppose, pan*, pass on, refuse, reject, remonstrate, reprehend, reprobate, reprove, set aside, slam, spurn, take dim view of, take exception to, turn down, veto, zing*; SEE CONCEPTS 18,21,52

disarm [v1] *render defenseless*
conciliate, cripple, deactivate, debilitate, deescalate, demilitarize, demobilize, disable, disband, disqualify, incapacitate, invalidate, neutralize, occupy, pacify, paralyze, prostrate, skin, strip, subdue, subjugate, unarm, weaken; SEE CONCEPTS 142,211,320

disarm [v2] *persuade*
allure, attract, bewitch, captivate, charm, coax, convince, enchant, fascinate, seduce, set at ease, unarm, urge, win over; SEE CONCEPTS 7,19,22,68

disarmament [n] *reduction of weapons*
arms limitation, arms reduction, conquest, crippling, de-escalation, demilitarization, demobilization, disablement, disqualification, freeze,

di
di

neutralizing, occupation, pacification, paralyzing, rendering powerless, subjugation; SEE CONCEPTS *142,211,320*

disarming [*adj*] *charming*
bewitching, convincing, deferential, ingratiating, ingratiatory, insinuating, insinuative, inveigling, irresistible, likable, persuasive, saccharine, seductive, silken, silky, winning; SEE CONCEPT *401*

disarray [*n*] *disorder, confusion, mess*
anarchy, ataxia, chaos, clutter, disarrangement, discomposure, disharmony, dishevelment, disorganization, holy mess*, indiscipline, jumble, muddle, shambles*, snarl, tangle, topsy-turviness*, unholy mess*, unruliness, untidiness, upset; SEE CONCEPTS *230,727*

disaster [*n*] *accident, trouble*
act of God*, adversity, affliction, bad luck, bad news*, bale, bane, blight, blow, bust, calamity, casualty, cataclysm, catastrophe, collapse, collision, crash, debacle, defeat, depression, emergency, exigency, failure, fall, fell stroke*, fiasco, flood, flop, grief, hard luck, harm, hazard, holocaust, hot water*, ill luck, misadventure, mischance, misfortune, mishap, reverse, rock, rough, ruin, ruination, setback, slip, stroke, the worst*, tragedy, undoing, upset, washout*, woe; SEE CONCEPTS *674,675*

disastrous [*adj*] *detrimental, devastating*
adverse, calamitous, cataclysmal, cataclysmic, catastrophic, destructive, dire, dreadful, fatal, fateful, hapless, harmful, ill-fated, ill-starred, luckless, ruinous, terrible, tragic, unfavorable, unfortunate, unlucky, unpropitious, untoward; SEE CONCEPTS *537,548*

disavow [*v*] *reject*
abjure, contradict, deny, disacknowledge, disallow, disclaim, disown, drop out, forswear, gainsay, go back on word*, impugn, negate, negative, refuse, renege, renig, repudiate, wash hands of*, weasel out of*, welsh, worm out of*; SEE CONCEPTS *18,25*

disbelief [*n*] *doubt, skepticism*
atheism, distrust, dubiety, incredulity, mistrust, nihilism, rejection, repudiation, spurning, unbelief, unbelievingness, unfaith; SEE CONCEPTS *21,689*

disbelieve [*v*] *doubt*
discount, discredit, distrust, eschew, give no credence to, mistrust, not accept, not buy, not credit, not swallow*, question, reject, repudiate, scoff at, scorn, scout, suspect, unbelieve; SEE CONCEPT *21*

disbelieving [*adj*] *suspicious, doubting*
aporetic, cagey, cynical, incredulous, leery, mistrustful, questioning, quizzical, show-me*, skeptical, unbelieving; SEE CONCEPT *403*

disburse [*v*] *spend money*
acquit, ante up*, come across, come through, come up with, contribute, cough up*, deal, defray, dispense, disperse, distribute, divide, divvy*, dole out*, expend, foot the bill*, give, lay out*, measure out, outlay, partition, pay out, pony up*, put out, shell out*, use; SEE CONCEPTS *108,341*

disbursement [*n*] *payment*
cost, disposal, expenditure, expense, outgoing, outlay, spending; SEE CONCEPT *344*

discard [*v*] *get rid of*
abandon, abdicate, abjure, adios*, banish, can*, cancel, cashier, cast aside, chuck, deep-six*, desert, dispatch, dispense with, dispose of, dispossess, ditch, divorce, do away with, drop, dump, eject, eliminate, expel, forsake, free of, give up, have done with, jettison, junk*, oust, part with, protest, put by, reject, relinquish, remove, renounce, repeal, repudiate, scrap, shake off, shed, sweep away, throw away, throw out, throw overboard*, toss aside, write off; SEE CONCEPT *180*

discern [*v*] *catch sight of; recognize and understand*
anticipate, apprehend, ascertain, behold, descry, detect, determine, difference, differentiate, discover, discrepate, discriminate, distinguish, divine, espy, extricate, figure out, find out, focus, foresee, get a load off*, get the picture*, get wise to, judge, know, make distinction, make out, note, notice, observe, perceive, pick out, read, remark, rubberneck*, secern, see the light*, see through, separate, severalize, spot, take in, view; SEE CONCEPTS *15,38*

discernible [*adj*] *recognizable; distinct*
apparent, appreciable, audible, clear, detectable, discoverable, distinguishable, noticeable, observable, obvious, palpable, perceivable, perceptible, plain, sensible, tangible, visible; SEE CONCEPTS *535,576,619*

discerning [*adj*] *discriminating*
acute, astute, bright, brilliant, clear-sighted, clever, critical, gnostic, ingenious, insighted, insightful, intelligent, judicious, knowing, knowledgeable, penetrating, perceptive, percipient, perspicacious, piercing, sagacious, sage, sensitive, sharp, shrewd, subtle, wise; SEE CONCEPT *402*

discharge [*n1*] *setting free*
acquittal, clearance, disimprisonment, exoneration, liberation, pardon, parole, probation, release, remittance; SEE CONCEPT *127*

discharge [*n2*] *dismissal from responsibility*
ax, bounce, bum's rush*, congé, demobilization, ejection, gate, old heave ho*, pink slip*, the boot*, the door*, walking papers*; SEE CONCEPTS *324,351*

discharge [*n3*] *detonation*
barrage, blast, burst, explosion, firing, fusillade, report, salvo, shot, shower, volley; SEE CONCEPT *521*

discharge [*n4*] *pouring forth*
elimination, emission, emptying, excretion, exudation, flow, ooze, pus, secretion, seepage, shower, suppuration, vent, voiding; SEE CONCEPTS *179,748*

discharge [*n5*] *unloading*
disburdening, emptying, unburdening, unlading; SEE CONCEPT *211*

discharge [*n6*] *carrying out of responsibility*
accomplishment, achievement, execution, fulfillment, observance, performance; SEE CONCEPT *706*

discharge [*n7*] *payment of debt*
acquittal, disbursement, liquidation, satisfaction, settlement; SEE CONCEPTS *341,344*

discharge [*v1*] *set free*
absolve, acquit, allow to go*, clear, disimprison, dismiss, emancipate, exonerate, expel, liberate, loose, loosen, manumit, oust, pardon, release, unbind, unchain, unshackle; SEE CONCEPT *127*

discharge [*v2*] *dismiss from responsibility*
absolve, ax, boot out*, bounce, bump, bust, can*, cashier, disburden, discard, disencumber, dis-

pense, displace, eject, excuse, exempt, expel, fire, freeze out*, give one notice, kick out, lay off, let go, let off, let one go, let out, lock out*, nix*, oust, privilege from, relieve, remove, replace, ride out on rail*, run out of town*, show the door*, spare, supersede, supplant, terminate, unload; SEE CONCEPTS 324,351

discharge [v3] *detonate weapon*
blast, explode, fire, let off, set off, shoot, shoot off; SEE CONCEPT 179

discharge [v4] *pour forth*
break out, disembogue, dispense, ejaculate, emit, empty, erupt, excrete, exude, give off, gush, leak, ooze, release, send forth, spew, void, vomit; SEE CONCEPTS 152,179

discharge [v5] *unload*
carry away, disburden, empty, off-load, remove, remove cargo, send, take away, take off, unburden, unlade, unpack, unship, unstow; SEE CONCEPT 211

discharge [v6] *carry out responsibility*
accomplish, achieve, do, execute, fulfill, meet, observe, perform; SEE CONCEPT 91

discharge [v7] *pay, settle debt*
clear, honor, liquidate, meet, pay up, quit, relieve, satisfy, square up; SEE CONCEPT 341

discharge [v8] *invalidate agreement*
abrogate, annul, cancel, dissolve, quash, render void, vacate, void; SEE CONCEPT 121

disciple [n] *believer, follower*
adherent, apostle, attendant, booster, buff, bug*, catechumen, cohort, convert, devotee, enthusiast, fan, fanatic, fiend, freak, groupie, hound*, junkie*, learner, nut*, partisan, proselyte, pupil, rooter*, satellite, sectary, sectator, student, supporter, votary, witness, zealot; SEE CONCEPTS 361,423

disciplinarian [n] *person who makes others work hard*
authoritarian, bully, despot, drill sergeant, enforcer, formalist, master, sergeant, stickler, strict teacher, sundowner, teacher, trainer, tyrant; SEE CONCEPTS 350,354,423

discipline [n1] *regimen, training*
conduct, control, cultivation, curb, development, domestication, drill, drilling, education, exercise, inculcation, indoctrination, limitation, method, orderliness, practice, preparation, regulation, restraint, self-command, self-control, self-government, self-mastery, self-restraint, strictness, subordination, will, willpower; SEE CONCEPTS 94,326,410

discipline [n2] *punishment*
castigation, chastisement, comeuppance, correction, getting yours*, hell to pay*, punition, rod; SEE CONCEPTS 122,123

discipline [n3] *field of study; subject of interest*
area, branch of knowledge, course, curriculum, specialty; SEE CONCEPT 349

disclaim [v] *deny*
abandon, abjure, abnegate, belittle, contradict, contravene, criticize, decline, deprecate, disacknowledge, disaffirm, disallow, disavow, discard, disown, disparage, divorce oneself from, forswear, gainsay, minimize, negate, recant, refuse, reject, renounce, repudiate, retract, revoke, spurn, traverse, turn back on, wash hands of*; SEE CONCEPT 54

disclose [v] *reveal, make public*
acknowledge, admit, avow, bare, betray, blab, bring to light*, broadcast, come out of the closet*, communicate, confess, discover, display, divulge, exhibit, expose, give away, impart, lay bare, leak, let slip, make known, mouth*, open, own, publish, relate, reveal, show, snitch*, spill, spill the beans*, squeal*, tell, uncover, unfurl, unveil, utter; SEE CONCEPT 60

disclosure [n] *announcement, revelation*
acknowledgment, admission, advertisement, betrayal, blow-by-blow*, broadcast, confession, declaration, discovery, divulgation, divulgence, enlightenment, exposal, exposé, exposure, handout, impartance, impartation, leak, make, picture, publication, revealing, revealment, rundown, snitch*, squeal*, tip*, tip-off*, uncovering, unveilment, ventilation; SEE CONCEPT 274

discolor [v] *fading, dirtying of hue*
besmear, besmirch, blot, defile, mar, mark, rust, smear, soil, stain, streak, sully, tar, tarnish, tinge; SEE CONCEPTS 250,469

discomfit [v] *defeat, frustrate; confuse*
abash, annoy, baffle, balk, beat, bother, checkmate, confound, demoralize, discompose, disconcert, discountenance, disturb, embarrass, faze, fluster, foil, irk, outwit, overcome, perplex, perturb, prevent, rattle, ruffle, take aback, thwart, trump, unsettle, upset, vex, worry, worst; SEE CONCEPTS 7,19,95

discomfiture [n] *embarrassment, frustration*
abashment, agitation, beating, chagrin, comedown, confusion, conquest, defeasance, defeat, demoralization, descent, disappointment, discomposure, disconcertion, disconcertment, disquiet, failure, humiliation, overthrow, perturbation, rout, ruin, shame, undoing, unease, uneasiness, upset, vanquishment, vexation; SEE CONCEPTS 410,674

discomfort [n] *irritation, pain*
ache, annoyance, discomfiture, discomposure, displeasure, disquiet, distress, embarrassment, hardship, hurt, inquietude, malaise, nuisance, soreness, trouble, uneasiness, unpleasantness, upset, vexation; SEE CONCEPTS 410,728

discomfort [v] *irritate; cause pain*
discomfit, discompose, disquiet, distress, disturb, embarrass, make uncomfortable, nettle, perturb, upset, vex; SEE CONCEPTS 7,19,246,313

discommode [v] *annoy*
bother, burden, disoblige, disquiet, disturb, fluster, harass, incommode, inconvenience, irk, molest, perturb, put out, trouble, upset, vex; SEE CONCEPTS 7,19

discompose [v] *provoke, agitate*
annoy, bewilder, bother, confuse, discombobulate, discomfit, disconcert, dismay, disorganize, displease, disquiet, disturb, embarrass, faze, flurry, fluster, harass, harry, irk, irritate, nettle, perplex, perturb, pester, plague, rattle, ruffle, unhinge, unsettle, upset, vex, worry; SEE CONCEPTS 7,19

disconcert [v] *shake up; confuse*
abash, agitate, baffle, balk, bewilder, bug, confound, demoralize, disarrange, discombobulate, discomfit, discompose, discountenance, disturb, embarrass, faze, fluster, foul up, frustrate, get to, hinder, nonplus, perplex, perturb, psych out*, put off, puzzle, rattle, ruffle, take aback, throw off balance, trouble, unbalance, undo, unsettle, upset, upset apple cart*, worry; SEE CONCEPTS 7,16,19

di

disconcerted [adj] confused; shaken
annoyed, bewildered, caught off balance, come
apart, distracted, disturbed, embarrassed, fazed,
flustered, in botheration, messed-up, mixed-up,
nonplussed, out of countenance, perturbed,
psyched-out*, rattled, ruffled, shook-up*, spaced-
out*, taken aback, thrown, troubled, unglued, unsettled, unzipped*, upset; SEE CONCEPT 403

disconnect [v] take apart; uncouple
abstract, break it off, break it up, cut off, detach,
disassociate, disengage, disjoin, dissever, dissociate, disunite, divide, drop it, part, separate,
sever, sideline, unfix; SEE CONCEPTS 98,135

disconnected [adj] confused; discontinuous
broken, detached, disjointed, disordered, garbled,
illogical, inchoate, incoherent, incohesive, interrupted, irrational, irregular, jumbled, loose,
mixed-up, muddled, rambling, separated, uncon-
tinuous, uncoordinated, unintelligible, wandering;
SEE CONCEPTS 267,482

disconsolate [adj] depressed, unhappy
bad, black, blue, cheerless, cold, comfortless,
crestfallen, crushed, dark, dejected, desolate, despairing, destroyed, dispirited, distressed, doleful, down, downcast, downhearted, dreary,
forlorn, gloomy, grief-stricken, heartbroken,
hopeless, hurting, inconsolable, in pain*, in the
pits*, low, melancholy, miserable, ripped*, sad,
somber, sorrowful, torn-up*, woebegone, woeful,
wretched; SEE CONCEPT 403

discontent [n] dissatisfaction
depression, discontentment, displeasure, envy,
fretfulness, regret, restlessness, uneasiness, unhappiness, vexation; SEE CONCEPT 410

discontented/discontent [adj] unhappy, dissatisfied
blue, complaining, crabby, disaffected, disgruntled, displeased, disquieted, disturbed, exasperated, fed up, fretful, griping, kvetching*,
malcontent, malcontented, miserable, perturbed,
picky, restless, ungratified, upset, vexed; SEE
CONCEPT 403

discontinuance [n] stop, suspension of activity
adjournment, alternation, cease, cessation, close,
closing, desistance, desuetude, discontinuation,
disjunction, disruption, ending, finish, intermission, interruption, separation, stopping, termination; SEE CONCEPT 119

discontinue [v] prevent activity from going on
abandon, bag it*, blow off*, break off*, call it
quits, cease, close, desist, disconnect, disjoin, dissever, disunite, drop, end, finish, give over, give
up, halt, interpose, interrupt, intervene, kill,
knock off*, leave off, part, pause, put an end to,
quit, refrain from, scrub, stall*, stop, surcease,
suspend, terminate; SEE CONCEPTS 121,234

discontinuous [adj] broken; intermittent
alternate, desultory, disconnected, disjointed, disordered, fitful, gaping, inchoate, incoherent, incohesive, interrupted, irregular, muddled,
spasmodic, unconnected, unorganized; SEE CON-
CEPT 482

discord [n1] conflict, disagreement
animosity, antagonism, antipathy, clash, clashing,
collision, contention, difference, disaccord, discordance, discrepancy, disharmony, dispute, dissension, dissent, dissidence, dissonance,
disunion, disunity, division, enmity, friction,
fuss, hassle, hostility, incompatibility, incongruity, inharmony, lack of concord, mischief, oppo-

sition, polarization, rancor, row, ruckus, rupture,
scene, spat, split, static, strife, variance, wrangling; SEE CONCEPT 388

discord [n2] noise
cacophony, clamor, clinker, din, disharmony, dissonance, harshness, jangle, jarring, racket, sour
note, tumult; SEE CONCEPT 595

discordant [adj] not in harmony; conflicting
antagonistic, antipathetic, at odds, cacophonous,
clashing, contradictory, contrarient, contrary, different, disagreeing, discrepant, dissonant, divergent, grating, harsh, incompatible, incongruous,
inconsistent, inconsonant, inharmonious, jangling, jarring, on a sour note*, opposite, quarrel-
ing, strident, uncongenial, unharmonious,
unmelodious, unmixable; SEE   CONCEPTS
558,564,592,594

discount [n] reduction in cost
abatement, allowance, commission, concession,
cut, cut rate, decrease, deduction, depreciation,
diminution, drawback, exemption, knock-off*,
markdown, modification, percentage, premium,
qualification, rebate, remission, rollback, salvage,
something off, subtraction, tare; SEE CONCEPTS
335,763

discount [v1] lower, reduce cost
abate, allow, deduct, depreciate, diminish, hold a
sale, knock off*, make allowance for, mark down,
modify, rebate, redeem, remove, sell at discount,
strike off, subtract, take away, take off, undersell;
SEE CONCEPTS 236,247,330

discount [v2] ignore; treat as insignificant
belittle, blink at*, brush off*, depreciate, derogate, detract from, disbelieve, discredit, dispraise,
disregard, doubt, fail, forget, minimize, mistrust,
neglect, omit, overlook, overpass, pass over,
question, reject, scoff at, scout, slight; SEE CON-
CEPTS 21,30

discountenance [v1] reject, oppose
condemn, count me out*, deprecate, disapprove,
discommend, discourage, disesteem, disfavor,
dispute, frown on*, hold no brief for*, not go
for*, not stand for*, object to, put down, resist,
take a dim view of*, take exception to*; SEE CON-
CEPT 21

discountenance [v2] embarrass, disconcert
abash, chagrin, confuse, discomfit, discompose,
faze, humiliate, rattle, shame; SEE CONCEPTS
7,19,54

discourage [v1] dishearten, dispirit
abash, afflict, alarm, appall, awe, beat down,
bother, break one's heart*, bully, cast down, chill,
confuse, cow, dampen, dash, daunt, deject, demoralize, deprecate, depress, dismay, disparage,
distress, droop, frighten, intimidate, irk, overawe,
prostrate, repress, scare, throw cold water on*,
trouble, try, unnerve, vex, weigh; SEE CONCEPT
14

discourage [v2] deter, dissuade; restrain
check, chill, control, curb, deprecate, disadvise,
discountenance, disfavor, disincline, divert,
frighten, hinder, hold back, hold off, impede, indispose, inhibit, interfere, keep back, obstruct,
prevent, put off, quiet, repress, scare, shake, talk
out of, throw cold water on*, turn aside, turn off,
warn, withhold; SEE CONCEPTS 68,121

discouraged [adj] disheartened
beat, beat-down, blue, caved-in, come-apart,
crestfallen, dashed, daunted, depressed, deterred,
dismayed, dispirited, down, downbeat, downcast,

down-in-mouth*, glum*, gone to pieces*, in a funk*, in blue funk*, in the dumps*, lost momentum, pessimistic, sad; SEE CONCEPT *403*

discouragement [*n1*] *despondency*
cold feet*, dejection, depression, despair, disappointment, discomfiture, dismay, downheartedness, hopelessness, loss of confidence, low spirits, melancholy, pessimism, sadness, the blues*; SEE CONCEPT *410*

discouragement [*n2*] *restraint*
bar, constraint, curb, damper, deterrent, disincentive, hindrance, impediment, obstacle, opposition, rebuff, setback; SEE CONCEPT *674*

discouraging [*adj*] *upsetting*
black, bleak, dampening, daunting, depressing, depressive, deterring, disadvantageous, disappointing, disheartening, dismal, dismaying, dispiriting, dissuading, dreary, gloomy, hindering, inopportune, off-putting, oppressive, repressing, unfavorable, unpropitious; SEE CONCEPTS *403,529*

discourse [*n*] *dialogue; dissertation*
address, article, chat, communication, conversation, converse, descant, discussion, disquisition, essay, gabfest*, homily, huddle, lecture, memoir, monograph, monologue, oration, paper, rhetoric, sermon, speaking, speech, talk, thesis, tractate, treatise, utterance, verbalization; SEE CONCEPT *266*

discourse [*v*] *discuss, speak about*
argue, chew*, comment, commentate, confab*, confer, converse, debate, declaim, descant, develop, dilate upon, dispute, dissert, dissertate, elaborate, enlarge, expand, expatiate, explain, expound, give a meeting, harangue, hold forth, lecture, modulate, orate, perorate, remark, sermonize, talk, treat, voice; SEE CONCEPTS *51,56*

discourteous [*adj*] *rude, impolite*
abrupt, bad-mannered, boorish, brusque, cavalier, cheeky*, churlish, contumelious, crude, crusty*, curt, disrespectful, flip, fresh, ill-bred, ill-mannered, impertinent, inaffable, indelicate, insolent, inurbane, oafish, offhand, rustic, sassy, smart-alecky*, uncivil, uncouth, ungenteel, ungracious, unmannerly, unrefined; SEE CONCEPT *401*

discover [*v*] *find, uncover*
ascertain, bring to light, catch, come across, come upon, conceive, contrive, debunk, design, detect, determine, devise, dig up, discern, disclose, distinguish, elicit, espy, explore, ferret out*, get wind of*, get wise to*, glimpse, hear, identify, invent, learn, light upon, locate, look up, nose out*, notice, observe, originate, perceive, pick up on*, pioneer, realize, recognize, reveal, see, sense, smoke out*, spot, think of, turn up, unearth; SEE CONCEPTS *31,183*

discovery [*n1*] *finding, uncovering*
analysis, ascertainment, authentication, calculation, certification, detection, determination, diagnosis, discernment, disclosure, distinguishing, empiricism, encounter, espial, experimentation, exploration, exposition, exposure, feeling, hearing, identification, introduction, invention, learning, locating, location, origination, perception, revelation, sensing, sighting, strike, unearthing, verification; SEE CONCEPTS *31,183*

discovery [*n2*] *treasure; invention*
algorithm, bonanza*, breakthrough, conclusion,

contrivance, coup, data, design, device, find, finding, formula, godsend*, innovation, law, luck, luck out*, machine, method, principle, process, result, secret, theorem, way; SEE CONCEPTS *260,532*

discredit [*v1*] *blame, detract from*
blow up*, bring into disrepute, bring to naught, censure, defame, degrade, destroy, disconsider, disesteem, disfavor, disgrace, dishonor, disparage, disprove, enfeeble, expose, frown upon*, knock bottom out of*, mudsling*, poke full of holes*, pooh-pooh*, puncture, put down, reflect on, reproach, ruin, run down, shoot, show up, slander, slur, smear, take rug out from under*, tear down*, vilify; SEE CONCEPTS *44,54*

discredit [*v2*] *doubt, question*
challenge, deny, disbelieve, discount, dispute, distrust, mistrust, put under suspicion, reject, scoff at; SEE CONCEPT *21*

discreet [*adj*] *cautious, sensible*
alert, attentive, awake, cagey, calculating, careful, chary, circumspect, civil, conservative, considerate, controlled, diplomatic, discerning, discriminating, gingerly, guarded, having foresight, heedful, intelligent, judicious, like a clam*, moderate, noncommittal, not rash, observant, on lookout*, politic, precautious, prudent, reasonable, reserved, restrained, safe, sagacious, strategic, tactful, temperate, thoughtful, vigilant, wary, watchful, wise, worldly-wise; SEE CONCEPT *401*

discrepancy [*n*] *conflict, disagreement*
alterity, contrariety, difference, discordance, disparity, dissemblance, dissimilarity, dissimilitude, dissonance, distinction, divergence, divergency, error, far cry*, incongruity, inconsistency, miscalculation, otherness, split, unlikeness, variance, variation; SEE CONCEPT *665*

discrepant [*adj*] *disagreeing*
at variance, conflicting, contradictory, contrary, different, differing, disconsonant, discordant, disparate, dissonant, divergent, diverse, incompatible, incongruent, incongruous, inconsistent, inconsonant, unmixable, varying; SEE CONCEPT *564*

discrete [*adj*] *individual*
detached, different, disconnected, discontinuous, distinct, diverse, separate, several, unattached, various; SEE CONCEPT *564*

discretion [*n*] *caution, judgment*
acumen, attention, calculation, canniness, care, carefulness, chariness, circumspection, concern, considerateness, consideration, deliberation, diplomacy, discernment, discrimination, foresight, forethought, good sense, gumption, heed, heedfulness, judiciousness, maturity, observation, perspicacity, precaution, presence of mind, providence, prudence, responsibility, sagacity, sense, shrewdness, solicitude, tact, thoughtfulness, vigilance, wariness, warning, watchfulness, wisdom; SEE CONCEPT *657*

discretionary [*adj*] *open to choice*
at the call*, elective, facultative, judge and jury, leftover, nonmandatory, nonobligatory, open, optional, unrestricted; SEE CONCEPT *546*

discriminate [*v1*] *show prejudice*
be bigot, be partial, contradistinguish, disfavor, favor, hate, incline, judge, segregate, separate, set apart, show bias, single out, treat as inferior, treat differently, victimize; SEE CONCEPTS *32,384*

di
di

discriminate [v2] *differentiate, distinguish*
assess, collate, compare, contradistinguish, contrast, difference, discern, discrepate, evaluate, extricate, judge, know, know what's what*, make out*, note, perceive, remark, segregate, separate, sever, severalize, sift, specify, split hairs*, tell apart, tell the difference; SEE CONCEPTS 15,38

discriminating [adj] *critical*
acute, astute, careful, choicy, choosy, cultivated, discerning, distinctive, eclectic, fastidious, finical, finicky, fussy, individualizing, judicious, keen, opinionated, particular, persnickety*, picky, prudent, refined, select, selective, sensitive, tasteful, wise; SEE CONCEPTS 404,542

discrimination [n1] *bias*
bigotry, favoritism, hatred, inequity, injustice, intolerance, partiality, prejudice, unfairness, wrong; SEE CONCEPTS 29,689

discrimination [n2] *particularity in taste*
acumen, acuteness, astucity, astuteness, bias, clearness, decision, difference, differentiation, discernment, distinction, judgment, keenness, penetration, perception, percipience, perspicacity, preference, refinement, sagacity, sense, separation, shrewdness, subtlety, taste, understanding; SEE CONCEPTS 32,410,655

discuss [v] *talk over with another*
altercate, argue, bounce off*, canvass, compare notes, confabulate, confer, consider, consult with, contend, contest, converse, debate, deliberate, descant, discept, discourse about, dispute, dissert, dissertate, examine, exchange views on*, explain, figure, get together, go into, groupthink*, hash over*, hold forth, jaw*, kick about*, knock around*, moot, put heads together*, reason about, review, sift, take up, thrash out*, toss around*, ventilate, weigh; SEE CONCEPT 56

discussion [n] *talk with another*
altercation, analysis, argument, argumentation, canvass, colloquy, confabulation, conference, consideration, consultation, contention, controversy, conversation, debate, deliberation, dialogue, discourse, disputation, dispute, dissertation, examination, exchange, excursus, groupthink*, huddle, interview, meet, meeting, powwow*, quarrel, review, scrutiny, symposium, ventilation, wrangling; SEE CONCEPT 56

disdain [n] *hate; indifference*
antipathy, arrogance, aversion, contempt, contumely, derision, despisal, despisement, despite, dislike, disparagement, hatred, haughtiness, hauteur, insolence, loftiness, pride, ridicule, scorn, sneering, snobbishness, superbity, superciliousness; SEE CONCEPT 29

disdain [v] *scorn*
abhor, be allergic to*, belittle, chill, contemn, deride, despise, disregard, hate, ignore, look down nose at*, look down on, misprize, pooh-pooh*, put down*, refuse, reject, scout, slight, sneer at, spurn, undervalue; SEE CONCEPTS 29,30

disdainful [adj] *scornful*
aloof, antipathetic, arrogant, averse, cavalier, contemning, contemptuous, cool, derisive, despising, egotistic, haughty, high-and-mighty*, hoity-toity*, indifferent, insolent, lordly, overbearing, proud, rejecting, repudiating, scouting, sneering, snooty*, supercilious, superior, toplofty, unsympathetic, uppity*; SEE CONCEPT 401

disease [n] *ailment, affliction*
ache, affection, attack, blight, breakdown, bug*,

cancer, canker, collapse, complaint, condition, contagion, contamination, convulsions, debility, decrepitude, defect, disorder, distemper, endemic, epidemic, feebleness, fever, fit, flu, hemorrhage, ill health, illness, indisposition, infection, infirmity, inflammation, malady, misery, pathosis, plague, seizure, sickliness, sickness, spell, stroke, syndrome, temperature, unhealthiness, unsoundness, upset, virus, visitation; SEE CONCEPT 306

diseased [adj] *unhealthy*
afflicted, ailing, indisposed, infected, infectious, infirm, rotten, sick, sickly, tainted, unsound, unwell, unwholesome; SEE CONCEPT 314

disembark [v] *get off transportation*
alight, anchor, arrive, come ashore, debark, deplane, detrain, dismount, go ashore, land, put in, step out of; SEE CONCEPT 159

disenchanted [adj] *let down*
blasé, cynical, disappointed, disenthralled, disentranced, disillusioned, embittered, indifferent, jaundiced, knowing, mondaine, out of love, sick of, sophisticate, sophisticated, soured, undeceived, worldly, worldly-wise; SEE CONCEPT 403

disengage [v] *free from connection*
abstract, back off, back out, cut loose, cut out, detach, disassociate, disconnect, disentangle, disjoin, dissociate, disunite, divide, drop out, ease, extricate, liberate, loose, loosen, opt out, pull the plug, release, separate, set free, unbind, uncouple, undo, unfasten, unfix, unloose, untie, weasel out*, withdraw; SEE CONCEPT 135

disentangle [v] *unwind, disconnect; solve*
bail one out*, clear up, detach, discumber, disembroil, disencumber, disengage, disinvolve, emancipate, expand, extricate, free, let go, let off, loose, open, part, resolve, separate, sever, simplify, sort out, sunder, unbraid, undo, unfold, unravel, unscramble, unsnarl, untangle, untie, untwine, untwist, work out; SEE CONCEPTS 127,135

disfavor [n] *dislike; disgrace*
aversion, disapprobation, disapproval, discredit, disesteem, dishonor, disinclination, displeasure, disregard, disrepute, disrespect, dissatisfaction, distaste, distrust, doghouse*, indisposition, mistrust, shame, thumbs down*, unpopularity; SEE CONCEPTS 29,388

disfigure [v] *make ugly*
blemish, damage, deface, defile, deform, disfashion, disfeature, distort, hurt, injure, maim, mangle, mar, mutilate, scar; SEE CONCEPTS 137,246,250

disgrace [n] *state of shame; bad reputation*
abasement, abuse, baseness, black eye*, blemish, blur, brand, comedown, contempt, contumely, corruption, culpability, debasement, debasing, defamation, degradation, derision, disbarment, discredit, disesteem, disfavor, dishonor, disrepute, disrespect, humbling, humiliation, ignominy, ill repute, infamy, ingloriousness, meanness, obloquy, odium, opprobrium, pollution, prostitution, put-down, reproach, scandal, scorn, slander, slight, slur, spot, stain, stigma, taint, tarnish, turpitude, venality; SEE CONCEPT 388

disgrace [v] *bring shame upon*
abase, attaint, besmirch, blot, debase, defame, defile, degrade, depress, deride, derogate, desecrate, discredit, disfavor, dishonor, disparage, disregard, disrespect, expel, give a black eye*, hum-

ble, humiliate, libel, lose face*, lower, mock, put down, reduce, reproach, ridicule, slander, slur, snub, stain, stigmatize, sully, taint, take down a peg*, tar and feather*, tarnish; SEE CONCEPTS 14,54,384

disgraceful [adj] *shameful, low*
blameworthy, contemptible, degrading, detestable, discreditable, dishonorable, disreputable, ignoble, ignominious, infamous, inglorious, mean, offensive, opprobrious, scandalous, shabby, shady, shocking, shoddy, unrespectable, unworthy; SEE CONCEPT 555

disgruntled [adj] *unhappy; critical*
annoyed, bad tempered, bellyaching*, crabbing*, crabby, cranky, disappointed, discontent, discontented, displeased, dissatisfied, griping, grouchy, grousing, grumpy, irritable, irritated, kicking*, kvetching*, malcontent, malcontented, peeved, peevish, petulant, put out, sulky, sullen, testy, uncontent, ungratified, vexed; SEE CONCEPTS 401,403

disguise [n] *covering, makeup for deception*
beard, blind, camouflage, charade, cloak, color, coloring, concealment, costume, counterfeit, cover-up, dissimulation, dress, facade, face, faking, false front*, fig leaf*, front*, get-up, guise, illusion, make-believe, mask, masquerade, pageant, pen name, pretense, pretension, pretentiousness, pseudonym, put-on, red herring*, screen, semblance, smoke screen*, trickery, veil, veneer; SEE CONCEPTS 446,451,680

disguise [v] *mask; misrepresent*
affect, age, alter, antique, assume, beard, belie, camouflage, change, cloak, color, conceal, counterfeit, cover, cover up, deceive, dissemble, dissimulate, doctor up*, dress up, fake, falsify, feign, front, fudge*, garble, gloss over, hide, make like, make up, masquerade, muffle, obfuscate, obscure, pretend, put on a false front*, put on a front*, put on an act*, put up a front*, redo*, screen, secrete, sham, shroud, simulate, touch up, varnish, veil, wear cheaters*, whitewash*; SEE CONCEPTS 59,137,172,188,202

disguised [adj] *unrecognizable*
camouflaged, changed, cloaked, covered, covert, fake, false, feigned, hidden, incog, masked, pretend, undercover; SEE CONCEPTS 547,619

disgust [n] *aversion; repulsion*
abhorrence, abomination, antipathy, detestation, dislike, distaste, hatefulness, hatred, loathing, nausea, nauseation, nauseousness, objection, repugnance, revolt, revulsion, satiation, satiety, sickness, surfeit; SEE CONCEPTS 410,720

disgust [v] *cause aversion; repel*
abominate, be repulsive, bother, cloy on, disenchant, displease, disturb, fill with loathing, gross out*, insult, irk, make one sick*, nauseate, offend, offend morals of, outrage, pall, pique, put off, reluct, repulse, revolt, scandalize, shock, sicken, surfeit, turn off, turn one's stomach*, upset; SEE CONCEPTS 7,19

disgusted [adj] *sickened; offended*
abhorred, appalled, displeased, fastidious, fed up*, full up*, grossed out*, had bellyful*, had enough*, had it*, nauseated, nauseous, outraged, overwrought, queasy, repelled, repulsed, revolted, satiated, scandalized, sick, sick and tired of*, sick of*, squeamish, teed off*, tired, turned off*, unhappy, up to here*, weary; SEE CONCEPT 403

disgusting [adj] *sickening; repulsive*
abominable, awful, beastly, cloying, creepy, detestable, distasteful, foul, frightful, ghastly, grody*, gross*, gruesome, hateful, hideous, horrid, horrific, icky*, loathsome, lousy, macabre, monstrous, nasty, nauseating, nerdy*, noisome, objectionable, obnoxious, odious, offensive, outrageous, repellent, repugnant, revolting, rotten, satiating, scandalous, scuzzy*, shameless, shocking, sleazeball*, sleazy*, stinking, surfeiting, vile, vulgar, yecchy*, yucky*; SEE CONCEPTS 485,548

dish [n1] *eating receptacle*
bowl, casserole, ceramic, china, container, cup, mug, pitcher, plate, platter, porringer, pot, pottery, salver, saucer, tray, vessel; SEE CONCEPT 494

dish [n2] *main part of meal*
course, eats*, entrée, fare, food, helping, recipe, serving; SEE CONCEPTS 457,460,461

disharmony [n] *conflict, discord*
clash, contention, difference, disaccord, dissension, dissonance, dissonancy, friction, inharmoniousness, strife, variance; SEE CONCEPTS 388,665

dishearten [v] *depress, ruin one's hopes*
cast down, chill*, crush, damp, dampen, dash, daunt, deject, demoralize, deter, discourage, disincline, dismay, disparage, dispirit, get down*, humble, humiliate, indispose, put a damper on*, put down, shake, throw a pall over*; SEE CONCEPTS 7,19

disheveled [adj] *wrinkled, unkempt in appearance*
bagged out*, beat up*, bedraggled, blowzy*, dirty, disarranged, disarrayed, disordered, frowzy*, grubby*, messed up, messy, mussed up*, mussy, ruffled, rumpled, scuzzy, slipshod, sloppy, slovenly, tousled, unbuttoned, uncombed, unfastidious, untidy, unzipped*; SEE CONCEPTS 485,579

dishonest [adj] *lying, untruthful*
backbiting*, bent, bluffing, cheating, corrupt, crafty, crooked, cunning, deceitful, deceiving, deceptive, designing, disreputable, double-crossing, double-dealing, elusive, false, fraudulent, guileful, hoodwinking*, mendacious, misleading, perfidious, recreant, shady, shifty, sinister, slippery*, sneaking, sneaky, swindling, traitorous, treacherous, tricky, two-faced*, two-timing*, unctuous, underhanded, unfair, unprincipled, unscrupulous, untrustworthy, villainous, wily; SEE CONCEPT 267

dishonesty [n] *lying; unwillingness to tell the truth*
artifice, bunk, cheating, chicane, chicanery, corruption, craft, criminality, crookedness, cunning, deceit, double-dealing, duplicity, faithlessness, falsehood, falsity, flimflam*, fourberie, fraud, fraudulence, graft, guile, hanky-panky*, hocuspocus*, improbity, infamy, infidelity, insidiousness, mendacity, perfidiousness, perfidy, racket, rascality, sharp practice*, slyness, stealing, swindle, treachery, trickery, trickiness, unscrupulousness, wiliness; SEE CONCEPTS 59,633,657

dishonor [n] *state of shame*
abasement, abuse, affront, blame, degradation, discourtesy, discredit, disesteem, disfavor, disgrace, disrepute, ignominy, indignity, infamy, insult, obloquy, odium, offense, opprobrium, outrage, reproach, scandal, slight; SEE CONCEPT 388

dishonor [v] *shame, degrade*
abase, attaint, blot, corrupt, debase, debauch, de-

fame, defile, disconsider, discredit, disgrace, disoblige, give a black eye*, libel, make lose face*, reflect on, slander, sully; SEE CONCEPT *54*

dishonorable [*adj*] *shameful, corrupt*
base, blackguardly, contemptible, crooked, deceitful, despicable, devious, discreditable, disgraceful, disreputable, fraudulent, ignoble, ignominious, infamous, inglorious, low, miscreant, offensive, opprobrious, putrid, scandalous, shabby, shady, treacherous, unprincipled, unrespectable, unscrupulous, untrustworthy; SEE CONCEPT *555*

dish out [*v*] *distribute*
allocate, deliver, dispense, dole out*, fork over*, furnish, give out, hand, hand out, hand over, inflict, ladle, mete out, present, produce, scoop, serve, serve up, spoon, supply, transfer, turn over; SEE CONCEPT *140*

disillusioned [*adj*] *disappointed*
blasé, broken, brought down to earth*, debunked, disabused, disenchanted, disenthralled, disentranced, embittered, enlightened, freed, indifferent, knowing, let-down, mondaine, out of love*, punctured, sadder and wiser*, shattered, sophisticated, undeceived, worldly, worldly-wise*; SEE CONCEPT *403*

disinclination [*n*] *unwillingness to do or believe something*
alienation, antipathy, aversion, demur, disfavor, dislike, disliking, displeasure, disrelish, dissatisfaction, distaste, hatred, hesitance, indisposition, lack of desire, lack of enthusiasm, loathness, objection, opposition, reluctance, repugnance, resistance; SEE CONCEPTS *29,410,657*

disinclined [*adj*] *unwilling*
afraid, antipathetic, averse, backward, balking, doubtful, dubious, hesitating, indisposed, loath, not in the mood*, objecting, opposed, protesting, reluctant, resistant, shy, shying, slow, sticking, uneager, unsympathetic; SEE CONCEPTS *403,542*

disinfect [*v*] *make clean, pure*
antisepticize, cleanse, decontaminate, deodorize, fumigate, purify, sanitize, sterilize; SEE CONCEPT *165*

disingenuous [*adj*] *insincere*
artful, crooked, cunning, deceitful, designing, dishonest, duplicitous, false, feigned, foxy, guileful, indirect, insidious, mendacious, oblique, shifty*, sly, tricky, two-faced*, uncandid, underhanded, unfair, unfrank, wily; SEE CONCEPTS *401,542*

disinherit [*v*] *cut off in will of bequeathal*
bereave, cut off without a cent*, deprive, disaffiliate, disown, dispossess, divest, evict, exclude, exheridate, neglect, oust, repudiate, rob; SEE CONCEPTS *25,317*

disintegrate [*v*] *fall apart; reduce to pieces*
atomize, break apart, break down, break up, come apart, crumble, decay, decline, decompose, degenerate, deliquesce, descend, detach, dilapidate, disband, disconnect, disimprove, dismantle, disorganize, disperse, disunite, divide, fade away, fall to pieces*, molder, pulverize, putrefy, rot, separate, sever, shatter, sink, splinter, spoil, taint, take apart, turn, turn to dust*, wash away, wash out, wither, worsen; SEE CONCEPTS *252,469*

disinterested [*adj*] *detached, uninvolved*
aloof, candid, casual, dispassionate, equitable, even-handed, impartial, impersonal, incurious, indifferent, just watching the clock*, lackadaisical, negative, neutral, nonpartisan, not giving a damn*, outside, perfunctory, remote, unbiased, unconcerned, uncurious, unprejudiced, unselfish, withdrawn; SEE CONCEPTS *401,403*

disjointed [*adj*] *loose, disconnected*
aimless, confused, cool, discontinuous, disordered, displaced, disunited, divided, far-out, fitful, fuzzy, inchoate, incoherent, incohesive, irrational, jumbled, muddled, out-of-it*, out-to-lunch*, rambling, separated, spaced-out*, spacey*, spasmodic, split, unattached, unconnected, unorganized; SEE CONCEPTS *267,482,585*

disk [*n*] *round object*
circle, disc, discoid, discoidal, discus, dish, flan, plate, platter, quoit, sabot, saucer, shell; SEE CONCEPT *436*

dislike [*n*] *antagonism, hatred toward something*
animosity, animus, antipathy, aversion, deprecation, detestation, disapprobation, disapproval, disesteem, disfavor, disgust, disinclination, displeasure, dissatisfaction, distaste, enmity, hostility, indisposition, loathing, objection, offense, opposition, prejudice, repugnance; SEE CONCEPT *29*

dislike [*v*] *be antagonistic toward something; hate*
abhor, abominate, antipathize, avoid, be allergic to*, bear malice toward, be averse to, be turned off to*, condemn, contemn, deplore, despise, detest, disapprove, disesteem, disfavor, disrelish, eschew, execrate, grossed out on*, have hard feelings*, have no stomach for*, have no taste for, loathe, look down on, lose interest in, make faces at*, mind, not appreciate, not care for, not endure, not feel like, not take kindly to, object to, regret, resent, scorn, shudder at, shun; SEE CONCEPT *29*

dislocate [*v*] *displace*
break, disarticulate, disconnect, disengage, disjoint, disorder, disrupt, disturb, disunite, divide, jumble, misplace, mix up, move, put out of joint, remove, rummage, separate, shift, transfer, unhinge, upset; SEE CONCEPTS *135,147,213*

dislocation [*n*] *displacement*
break, confusion, disarray, disarticulation, disconnection, discontinuity, disengagement, disorder, disorganization, disruption, disturbance, division, luxation, misplacement, unhinging; SEE CONCEPTS *316,720,727*

dislodge [*v*] *knock loose*
dig out, disentangle, dislocate, displace, disturb, eject, evict, extricate, force out, oust, remove, uproot; SEE CONCEPTS *147,213*

disloyal [*adj*] *unfaithful*
alienated, apostate, cheating, disaffected, double-crossing, estranged, faithless, false, perfidious, recreant, seditious, snaky*, subversive, traitorous, treacherous, treasonable, two-faced*, two-timing*, unloyal, unpatriotic, untrue, untrustworthy, wormlike*; SEE CONCEPT *401*

disloyalty [*n*] *unfaithfulness*
apostasy, bad faith, betrayal of trust, breach of trust, breaking of faith, deceitfulness, disaffection, double-dealing, faithlessness, falseness, falsity, inconstancy, infidelity, perfidiousness, perfidy, recreancy, sedition, seditiousness, subversive activity, treachery, treason, untrueness, violation; SEE CONCEPT *633*

dismal [*adj*] *bleak, dreary, gloomy*
afflictive, black, boring, cheerless, cloudy, dark, depressed, depressing, desolate, despondent, dim, dingy, disagreeable, discouraging, disheartening,

dispiriting, doleful, dolorous, dull, forlorn, frowning, funereal, ghastly, gruesome, hopeless, horrible, horrid, inauspicious, in the pits*, joyless, lonesome, lowering, lugubrious, melancholy, miserable, monotonous, morbid, murky, oppressive, overcast, sad, shadowy, somber, sorrowful, tedious, tenebrous, troublesome, unfortunate, unhappy; SEE CONCEPTS *525,536,548*

dismantle [v] *take apart*
annihilate, bankrupt, bare, break down, break up, decimate, demolish, denudate, denude, deprive, destroy, disassemble, dismember, dismount, disrobe, divest, fell, knock down, level, part out, pull down, raze, ruin, strike, strip, subvert, take down, take to pieces, tear down, undo, unrig, wrack, wreck; SEE CONCEPTS *135,168,252*

dismay [n] *disappointed feeling; distress*
agitation, alarm, anxiety, apprehension, blue funk*, blues*, bummer*, chagrin, cold feet*, consternation, discouragement, disheartenment, disillusionment, downer*, dread, dumps*, fear, fright, funk*, hassle, horror, letdown, panic, terror, the blahs*, trepidation, upset; SEE CONCEPTS *27,410,690*

dismay [v] *disappoint, fill with consternation*
abash, affright, agitate, alarm, appall, bewilder, bother, chill, confound, daunt, discomfit, discompose, disconcert, discourage, dishearten, disillusion, dispirit, disquiet, distress, disturb, dumbfound, embarrass, faze, flummox*, fluster, foul up*, frighten, get to, horrify, louse up*, mess up*, muck up*, mystify, nonplus, paralyze, perplex, put off, puzzle, rattle, scare, screw up*, shake, snafu*, take aback, terrify, terrorize, throw, throw into a tizzy*, unhinge*, unnerve, upset; SEE CONCEPTS *7,19*

dismember [v] *cut into pieces*
amputate, anatomize, cripple, disassemble, disjoint, dislimb, dislocate, dismantle, dismount, dissect, divide, maim, mutilate, part, rend, sever, sunder, take down; SEE CONCEPTS *98,135,176*

dismiss [v1] *send away, remove; free*
abolish, banish, boot*, brush off*, bundle, cast off*, cast out*, chase, chuck, clear, decline, deport, detach, disband, discard, dispatch, dispense with, disperse, dispose of, dissolve, divorce, do without, drive out, eject, expel, force out, have done with*, kick out*, let go, let out, lock out*, outlaw, push aside, push back, reject, release, relegate, relinquish, repel, repudiate, rid, send off, send packing*, shed, show out*, slough off, supersede, sweep away*, turn out; SEE CONCEPTS *127,217*

dismiss [v2] *remove from job, responsibility*
ax*, boot*, boot out*, bounce*, bump*, can*, cashier*, defrock, depone, depose, deselect, discharge, disemploy, disfrock, displace, disqualify, drop, fire, furlough, give notice to, give the ax*, give the gate*, give the heave-ho*, give walking papers*, give warning, impeach, kick out*, lay off, let go*, let out*, oust, pension, pink-slip*, put away*, recall, retire, sack*, send packing*, shelve*, shut out*, suspend, terminate, turn away, unfrock, unseat, wash out*; SEE CONCEPTS *324,351*

dismiss [v3] *put out of one's mind*
banish, contemn, deride, despise, discard, disdain, dispel, disregard, drop, flout, gibe, gird, jeer, kiss off*, laugh away*, lay aside, mock, pooh-pooh*, rally, reject, relegate, repudiate, repulse, ridicule, scoff, scorn, scout, set aside, shelve*, spurn, taunt, twit; SEE CONCEPT *35*

dismissal [n] *release*
adjournment, banishment, bounce, brush-off, cold shoulder*, congé, deportation, deposal, deposition, discharge, dislodgment, displacement, dispossession, dissolution, door*, end, eviction, exile, exorcism, expatriation, expulsion, freedom, freeing, housecleaning*, kiss-off*, layoff, liberation, marching orders*, notice, old heave-ho*, ostracism, ouster, permission, pink slip*, relegation, removal, suspension; SEE CONCEPTS *127,217,351*

dismount [v] *get off something higher*
alight, debark, deplane, descend, detrain, disembark, get down, light; SEE CONCEPT *195*

disobedience [n] *misbehavior; noncompliance with rules*
defiance, dereliction, disregard, indiscipline, infraction, infringement, insubmission, insubordination, insurgence, intractableness, mutiny, neglect, nonobservance, perversity, rebellion, recalcitrance, refractoriness, revolt, revolution, riot, sabotage, sedition, strike, stubbornness, transgression, unruliness, violation, waywardness; SEE CONCEPT *633*

disobedient [adj] *defiant, mischievous*
contrary, contumacious, disorderly, fractious, froward, headstrong, insubordinate, intractable, naughty, noncompliant, nonobservant, obstreperous, perverse, recalcitrant, refractory, resistive, uncompliant, undisciplined, unruly, wayward, willful; SEE CONCEPT *401*

disobey [v] *disregard rules; refuse to conform*
balk, be remiss, break rules, contravene, counteract, dare, decline, defy, desert, differ, disagree, evade, flout, fly in face of*, go counter to, ignore, infringe, insurrect, misbehave, mutiny, neglect, not heed, not listen, not mind, object, overstep, pay no attention to, rebel, recalcitrate, resist, revolt, revolution, revolutionize, riot, rise in arms*, run riot*, set aside, shirk, strike, take law into own hands*, transgress, violate, withstand; SEE CONCEPTS *30,192,384*

disoblige [v] *displease, annoy*
affront, bother, discommode, disturb, incommode, inconvenience, insult, offend, put about, put out, slight, trouble, upset, vex; SEE CONCEPTS *7,19*

disobliging [adj] *rude, annoying*
awkward, disagreeable, discourteous, ill-disposed, ill-natured, unaccommodating, unamiable, uncivil, uncongenial, uncooperative, unhelpful, unpleasant; SEE CONCEPT *401*

disorder [n1] *chaos, clutter*
anarchy, ataxia, confusion, derangement, disarrangement, disarray, discombobulation, disorderliness, disorganization, huddle, irregularity, jumble, mess, muddle, rat's nest*, shambles, snarl, topsy-turviness*, untidiness; SEE CONCEPT *230*

disorder [n2] *social commotion; mental confusion*
agitation, anarchism, anarchy, brawl, bustle, chaos, clamor, complication, convulsion, discombobulation*, discord, disorganization, distemper, disturbance, dither, entanglement, fight, flap, fracas, fuss, hubbub, hullabaloo*, imbroglio, insurrection, lawlessness, mayhem, misrule, mob rule*, quarrel, rebellion, reign of terror*, revolution, riot, rioting, ruckus, rumpus, static, strike, terrorism, tizzy*, trouble, tumult, turbulence, tur-

moil, unrest, unruliness, uproar; SEE CONCEPTS
388,410

disorder [n3] *illness*
affliction, ailment, cachexia, complaint, disease,
diseasedness, indisposition, infirmity, malady,
sickness, unhealth, upset; SEE CONCEPT *306*

disorder [v] *mix up, disarrange*
clutter, confound, confuse, derange, discompose,
discreate, dishevel, disjoint, dislocate, disorganize, disrupt, distemper, disturb, embroil, jumble,
mess up, muddle, muss up*, rummage, rumple,
scatter, shuffle, tumble, unsettle, upset; SEE CON-
CEPTS *240,250*

disordered [adj] *in a mess*
all over the place*, confused, deranged, disarranged, discombobulated, disconnected, discontinuous, disjointed, dislocated, disorganized, mis-
displaced, incoherent, in confusion, jumbled, mislaid, misplaced, molested, moved, muddled, out-
of-place, removed, roiled, ruffled, rumpled,
shifted, shuffled, stirred up, tampered-with, tangled, tossed, tousled, tumbled, unsettled, untidy;
SEE CONCEPTS *485,535*

disorderly [adj1] *messy, untidy*
all over the place*, chaotic, cluttered, confused,
dislocated, disorganized, heterogeneous, indiscriminate, irregular, jumbled, mixed up, out-
of-control*, out-of-line*, out-of-step*, out-of-
whack*, scattered, scrambled, slovenly,
topsy-turvy*, tumult, uncombed, undisciplined,
unkempt, unmethodical, unrestrained, unsystematic, untrained; SEE CONCEPTS *485,535*

disorderly [adj2] *causing trouble; unlawful*
boisterous, disobedient, disruptive, drunk, fractious, indisciplined, intemperate, noisy, obstreperous, off-base*, on-a-tear*, out-of-line*, out-of-
order*, raucous, rebellious, refractory, riotous,
rowdy, stormy, termagant, tumultous/tumultuous,
turbulent, uncompliant, uncontrollable, ungovernable, unmanageable, unruly, wayward; SEE CON-
CEPTS *401,545*

disorganization [n] *unordered situation or thing*
anarchy, chaos, confusion, derangement, disarray, disjointedness, disorder, disruption, dissolution, disunion, foul-up*, incoherence, mix-up,
rat's nest*, screw-up*, unconnectedness, unholy
mess*; SEE CONCEPTS *674,727*

disorganize [v] *disrupt arrangement; make shambles of*
break down, break up, clutter, complicate, confound, confuse, demobilize, derange, destroy, disarrange, disarray, disband, discompose, discreate,
dishevel, dislocate, disorder, disperse, disturb,
embroil, jumble, litter, mess up, mislay, misplace, muddle, perturb, put out of order, scatter,
scramble, shuffle, toss, turn topsy-turvy, unsettle,
upset; SEE CONCEPTS *250,252,384*

disorganized [adj] *unmethodical; messed up*
chaotic, confused, disordered, disorderly, haphazard, jumbled, mixed up, muddled, screwed up*,
shuffled, unsystematic; SEE CONCEPTS *485,585*

disoriented [adj] *confused, unstable*
adrift, all at sea*, astray, bewildered, discombobulated, lost, mixed-up, not adjusted, off-beam*,
off-course, out-of-joint*, perplexed, unbalanced,
unhinged, unsettled; SEE CONCEPT *403*

disown [v] *refuse to acknowledge*
abandon, abjure, abnegate, cast off, deny, disacknowledge, disallow, disavow, discard, disclaim,
divorce oneself from, refuse to recognize, reject,

renounce, repudiate, retract; SEE CONCEPTS
50,54,88

disparage [v] *criticize; detract from*
abuse, belittle, chill*, cry down, decry, defame,
degrade, deject, demoralize, denigrate, deprecate,
depreciate, deride, derogate, dis*, discourage,
discredit, disdain, dishearten, dismiss, dispirit,
dispraise, downcry, dump on*, lower, malign,
minimize, pan*, put down, put hooks in*, rap*,
ridicule, roast*, run down*, scorch, scorn, slam*,
slander, smear*, sour grapes*, tear down, traduce,
underestimate, underrate, undervalue, vilify, write
off; SEE CONCEPTS *7,19,52,54*

disparagement [n] *strong criticism; detraction*
aspersion, backbiting*, backstabbing*, belittlement, blame, calumny, censure, condemnation,
contempt, contumely, debasement, degradation,
denunciation, depreciation, derision, derogation,
discredit, disdain, impairment, lessening, lie,
prejudice, reproach, ridicule, scandal, scorn, slander, tale, underestimation; SEE CONCEPTS *52,54*

disparate [adj] *at odds, different*
at variance, contrary, contrasting, discordant, discrepant, dissimilar, distant, distinct, divergent, diverse, far cry, incommensurate, incompatible,
inconsistent, inconsonant, like night and day*,
poles apart, separate, unalike, unequal, unequivalent, uneven, unlike, unsimilar, various; SEE
CONCEPT *564*

disparity [n] *difference*
alterity, discrepancy, disproportion, dissemblance, dissimilarity, dissimilitude, distinction,
divergence, divergency, diverseness, gap, imbalance, imparity, incongruity, inequality, otherness,
unevenness, unlikeness, variation; SEE CONCEPT
665

dispassionate [adj] *unfeeling, impartial*
abstract, aloof, calm, candid, cold-blooded, cold-
fish*, collected, composed, cool, cool cat*,
couldn't care less*, detached, disinterested, fair,
iceberg*, impersonal, imperturbable, indifferent,
judicial, just, laid back, moderate, neutral, nondiscriminatory, nonpartisan, objective, poker-
faced*, quiet, serene, sober, temperate, tough,
unbiased, unemotional, unexcitable, unexcited,
unflappable, uninvolved, unmoved, unprejudiced,
unruffled; SEE CONCEPTS *401,404*

dispatch [n1] *speed in carrying out action*
alacrity, celerity, expedition, expeditiousness,
haste, hurry, hustle, precipitateness, promptitude,
promptness, quickness, rapidity, rustle, speediness, swiftness; SEE CONCEPTS *755,818*

dispatch [n2] *communication*
account, bulletin, communiqué, document, instruction, item, letter, message, missive, news,
piece, report, story; SEE CONCEPTS *271,277,278*

dispatch [v1] *hurry, send fast*
accelerate, address, consign, dismiss, express,
forward, hand-carry, hasten, issue, quicken, railroad*, remit, route, run with, run with ball*, ship,
speed, transmit, walk through; SEE CONCEPTS
152,217

dispatch [v2] *finish; consume*
conclude, devour, discharge, dispose of, eat up,
expedite, lay low, perform, polish off*, scarf
down*, settle; SEE CONCEPTS *169,234*

dispatch [v3] *kill*
assassinate, bump off*, butcher*, destroy, eliminate, execute, finish, finish off*, murder, put

away*, put end to, slaughter, slay, take out*; SEE
CONCEPTS 238,252

dispel [v] *drive away thought, belief*
allay, banish, beat off*, break it up*, break up*,
bust up*, cancel, chase away, crumble, deploy,
disband, disintegrate, dismiss, disperse, dissipate,
distribute, eject, eliminate, expel, oust, repel, resolve, rout, scatter, scramble, split up*; SEE CON-
CEPTS 14,35

dispensable [adj] *not necessary; able to be thrown
away*
disposable, excessive, expendable, minor, needless, nonessential, removable, superfluous, trivial, unimportant, unnecessary, unrequired,
useless; SEE CONCEPT 546

dispensation [n1] *allocation of supply*
allotment, appointment, apportionment, award,
bestowal, conferment, consignment, courtesy,
dealing out, disbursement, distribution, dole, endowment, favor, indulgence, kindness, part, portion, quota, service, share; SEE CONCEPTS
140,337

dispensation [n2] *management*
administration, direction, economy, plan, regulation, scheme, stewardship, system; SEE CON-
CEPTS 325,660,770

dispensation [n3] *permission*
exception, exemption, immunity, indulgence, license, privilege, relaxation, relief, remission, reprieve; SEE CONCEPT 685

dispense [v1] *dole out supply*
allocate, allot, apportion, assign, come across
with, deal, deal out, disburse, dish out*, distribute, divide, divvy*, fork out*, furnish, give, give
away, give with, hand out, hand over, lot, measure, mete out, partition, portion, prepare, prorate, share, shell out*; SEE CONCEPT 140

dispense [v2] *operate, administer*
apply, carry out, command, direct, discharge, enforce, execute, handle, implement, manage, maneuver, manipulate, swing, undertake, wield; SEE
CONCEPT 117

dispense [v3] *exempt from responsibility*
absolve, discharge, except, excuse, exonerate, let
off, privilege from, release, relieve, reprieve,
spare; SEE CONCEPT 110

dispense with [v] *omit; do away with*
abolish, abstain from, brush aside, cancel, dispose
of, disregard, do without, forgo, get rid of, give
up, ignore, pass over, relinquish, render needless,
shake off, waive; SEE CONCEPT 30

disperse [v] *distribute; scatter*
banish, besprinkle, break up, broadcast, cast
forth, circulate, deal, diffuse, disappear, disband,
disburse, discharge, dislodge, dismiss, dispel, disseminate, dissipate, dissolve, divvy*, dole out,
eject, intersperse, measure out, partition, propagate, radiate, rout, scatter, scramble, send off,
separate, shed, sow, split up, spray, spread, strew,
take off in all directions*, vanish; SEE CONCEPTS
135,217

dispirited [adj] *dejected, sad*
blue*, bummed-out*, crestfallen, depressed, despondent, disconsolate, discouraged, disheartened, down*, downbeat, downcast, downhearted,
dragged*, funky*, gloomy, glum, in the doldrums, low, melancholy, morose, shot-down*,
spiritless, woebegone; SEE CONCEPT 403

displace [v1] *move, remove from normal place*
change, crowd out, derange, disarrange, disestab-

lish, dislocate, dislodge, displant, dispossess, disturb, eject, evict, expel, expulse, force out, lose,
mislay, misplace, relegate, shift, transpose, unsettle, uproot; SEE CONCEPTS 147,213

displace [v2] *remove from position of responsibility*
banish, can*, cashier*, cut out*, deport, depose,
dethrone, discard, discharge, discrown, disen-
throne, dismiss, disthrone, exile, expatriate, fire,
oust, relegate, remove, replace, sack*, step into
shoes of*, succeed, supersede, supplant, take
over, take the place of, transport, uncrown, unmake, usurp; SEE CONCEPTS 133,298,300

display [n] *public showing; spectacle*
act, affectation, arrangement, array, arrayal,
blaze, bravura, dash, demonstration, example, exhibit, exhibition, expo*, exposition, exposure,
fanfare, flourish, for show, frame-up*, frippery,
front, grandstand play*, layout, manifestation, ostentation, ostentatiousness, pageant, panorama,
parade, pedantry, pomp, presentation, pretension,
pretentiousness, revelation, sample, scheme,
shine, showboat*, splash, splendor, splurge,
spread, unfolding, vanity; SEE CONCEPTS 261,386

display [v] *show for public viewing; effect*
advertise, arrange, bare, betray, boast, brandish,
bring to view, demonstrate, disclose, emblazon,
evidence, evince, exhibit, expand, expose, extend, feature, flash, flaunt, flourish, glaze, grandstand*, illustrate, impart, lay bare*, lay out, make
clear, make known, manifest, model, open, open
out, parade, perform, present, promote, promulgate, publish, represent, reveal, set out, showcase, show off, sport, spread out, stretch out, trot
out*, uncover, unfold, unfurl, unmask, unroll, unveil, vamp; SEE CONCEPT 261

displease [v] *make unhappy*
aggravate, anger, annoy, antagonize, bother, cap,
chagrin, cool, curdle*, cut to the quick*, disappoint, discontent, disgruntle, disgust, disoblige,
dissatisfy, enrage, exasperate, fret, frustrate, gall,
hurt, incense, irk, irritate, nettle, offend, perplex,
pique, play dirty, provoke, put out, repel, revolt,
rile, roil, sound, turn off*, upset, vex, wing*,
worry, zing*; SEE CONCEPTS 7,19

displeasure [n] *unhappiness, anger*
annoyance, aversion, disapprobation, disapproval, discontentment, disfavor, disgruntlement,
disinclination, dislike, disliking, disrelish, dissatisfaction, distaste, incensement, indignation, indisposition, irritation, offense, pique, resentment,
umbrage, vexation, wrath; SEE CONCEPT 410

disposal [n1] *parting with or throwing something
away*
auctioning, bartering, chucking, clearance, conveyance, demolishing, demolition, destroying, destruction, discarding, dispatching, dispensation,
disposition, dumping, ejection, jettison, jettison-
ing, junking, relegation, relinquishment, removal,
riddance, sacrifice, sale, scrapping, selling, trading, transfer, transference, vending; SEE CONCEPT
180

disposal [n2] *conclusion, settlement of situation*
action, allocation, arrangement, array, assignment, assortment, bequest, bestowal, consignment, control, conveyance, determination,
dispensation, disposition, distribution, division,
effectuation, end, gift, grouping, order, ordering,
placing, position, provision, sequence, transfer,
winding up; SEE CONCEPTS 119,230

di
di

dispose [v] *place, order; deal with*
actuate, adapt, adjust, arrange, array, bend, bias, call the tune*, condition, determine, distribute, fix, govern, group, incline, induce, influence, lay down the law*, lead, locate, make willing, marshal, methodize, motivate, move, organize, predispose, prepare, promote, prompt, put, put one's foot down*, put to rights, range, rank, read the riot act*, regulate, ride herd on*, set, set in order, settle, shepherd, stand, sway, systematize, tailor, tempt; SEE CONCEPTS 84,117,158,180

disposed [adj] *inclined to a type of behavior*
apt, at drop of hat*, biased, fain, game*, game for, given, liable, likely, minded, of a mind to*, partial, predisposed, prone, ready, subject, tending toward, willing; SEE CONCEPTS 542,552

dispose of [v1] *throw away*
adios*, bestow, chuck*, deep six*, destroy, discard, dump, eighty-six*, eliminate, file in circular file*, get rid of, give, jettison, junk*, kiss*, kiss off*, make over, part with, relinquish, scrap, sell, transfer, unload; SEE CONCEPT 180

dispose of [v2] *settle a matter*
chop, cut, cut off, deal with, decide, determine, do the trick*, end, finish, knock off*, polish off*, put away, take care of; SEE CONCEPTS 18,234

disposition [n1] *personal temperament*
bag*, being, bent, bias, cast, character, complexion, constitution, cup of tea*, druthers*, emotions, flash, frame of mind, groove*, habit, humor, identity, inclination, individualism, individuality, leaning, make-up, mind-set*, mood, nature, penchant, personality, predilection, predisposition, proclivity, proneness, propensity, readiness, spirit, stamp, temper, tendency, tenor, thing*, tone, type, vein; SEE CONCEPT 411

disposition [n2] *arrangement, management of a situation*
adjustment, classification, control, decision, direction, disposal, distribution, grouping, method, order, ordering, organization, placement, plan, regulation, sequence; SEE CONCEPTS 6,660

disproportion [n] *imbalance*
asymmetry, difference, discrepancy, disparity, imparity, inadequacy, inequality, insufficiency, irregularity, lopsidedness, unevenness, unsuitableness; SEE CONCEPTS 665,667

disproportionate [adj] *out of balance*
asymmetric, excessive, incommensurate, inordinate, irregular, lopsided, nonsymmetrical, out of proportion, overbalanced, superfluous, too much, unequal, uneven, unreasonable, unsymmetrical; SEE CONCEPTS 564,566,771

disprove [v] *prove false*
belie, blow sky high*, blow up*, break, confound, confute, contradict, contravene, controvert, deny, disconfirm, discredit, explode, expose, find unfounded, impugn, invalidate, knock bottom out of*, knock props out*, negate, negative, overthrow, overturn, poke holes in*, puncture, rebut, refute, set aside, shoot, shoot holes in*, tear down*, throw out, traverse, weaken; SEE CONCEPT 58

disputable [adj] *debatable; open to discussion*
arguable, controversial, doubtful, dubious, moot, mootable, problematic, questionable, uncertain; SEE CONCEPTS 529,535

disputation [n] *controversy*
argumentation, debate, dialectic, dispute, dissension, forensic, mooting, polemics; SEE CONCEPTS 278,532

disputatious [adj] *argumentative*
cantankerous, captious, caviling, contentious, controversial, dissentious, litigious, polemical, pugnacious, quarrelsome; SEE CONCEPTS 401,542

dispute [n] *argument*
altercation, beef*, bickering, bone of contention*, brawl, broil, brouhaha, commotion, conflict, contention, controversy, debate, difference of opinion, disagreement, discord, discussion, dissension, disturbance, embroilment, falling-out, feud, fireworks*, flare-up, fracas, friction, fuss, hubbub, miff*, misunderstanding, polemic, quarrel, row, rumpus*, squabble, squall, strife, tiff, uproar, variance, words, wrangle; SEE CONCEPTS 46,106,278

dispute [v] *argue*
agitate, altercate, bicker, brawl, bump heads*, canvass, challenge, clash, confute, contend, contest, contradict, controvert, debate, deny, disaffirm, discept, discuss, disprove, doubt, gainsay, hassle, have at*, impugn, jump on one's case*, kick around*, lock horns*, moot, negate, pick a bone*, quarrel, question, quibble, rebut, refute, squabble, take on, thrash out, toss around*, wrangle; SEE CONCEPT 46

disqualification [n] *disability; rejection for participation*
awkwardness, clumsiness, debarment, disenablement, disentitlement, elimination, exclusion, incapacitation, incapacity, incompetence, incompetency, ineligibility, ineptitude, lack, unfitness, unproficiency; SEE CONCEPT 630

disqualify [v] *be unfit for; be ineligible*
bar, bate, debar, disable, disenable, disentitle, disfranchise, eighty-six*, except, exclude, impair, incapacitate, invalidate, nix*, not make the cut*, paralyze, preclude, prohibit, rule out, suspend, unfit, weaken; SEE CONCEPTS 121,699

disquiet [n] *worry; mental upset*
ailment, alarm, angst, anxiety, care, concern, concernment, disquietude, distress, disturbance, fear, ferment, foreboding, fretfulness, inquietude, nervousness, restiveness, restlessness, solicitude, storm, trouble, turmoil, uneasiness, unrest; SEE CONCEPTS 410,532,690

disquiet [v] *worry; make uneasy*
agitate, annoy, bother, concern, discompose, distress, disturb, fluster, fret, harass, incommode, perplex, perturb, pester, plague, trouble, unhinge, unsettle, upset, vex; SEE CONCEPTS 7,19

disquieting [adj] *upsetting*
annoying, bothersome, disconcerting, distressing, disturbing, irritating, perplexing, perturbing, troublesome, troubling, unnerving, unsettling, vexing, worrying; SEE CONCEPT 529

disregard [n] *ignoring*
apathy, brush-off*, contempt, disdain, disesteem, disfavor, disinterest, disrespect, forgetting, heedlessness, inadvertence, inattention, indifference, insouciance, lassitude, lethargy, listlessness, neglect, neglecting, negligence, oblivion, omission, omitting, overlooking, oversight, scorn, slight, slighting. the cold shoulder*, unconcern, unmindfulness; SEE CONCEPTS 30,633

disregard [v] *ignore; make light of*
blink at*, brush aside, brush away, brush off, cold-shoulder*, contemn, despise, discount, disdain, disobey, disparage, fail, forget, have no use

for*, laugh off*, leave out of account, let go, let off easy*, let pass*, live with*, look the other way*, miss, neglect, omit, overlook, overpass, pass over, pay no attention to, pay no heed to, pay no mind*, pooh-pooh*, scorn, shut eyes to*, slight, snub, take no notice of, tune out*, turn a blind eye*, turn a deaf ear*, vilipend, wink at*; SEE CONCEPT 30

disrepair [n] *state of deterioration*
collapse, decay, decrepitude, dilapidation, ruination; SEE CONCEPTS 230,674

disrepair [adj] *broken; deteriorated*
busted*, damaged, dead, decayed, decrepit, down, kaput*, not functioning, on the blink*, on the fritz*, out of commission*, out of order, worn out, wracked*; SEE CONCEPT 485

disreputable [adj] *dishonorable, lowly*
abject, bad, base, beggarly, cheap, contemptible, derogatory, despicable, discreditable, disgraceful, disorderly, dissolute, ignominious, in bad, infamous, inglorious, in low esteem, in the doghouse*, lewd, libidinous, licentious, mean, no good*, notorious, opprobrious, pitiable, scandalous, scurvy, shabby, shady, shameful, shocking, shoddy, sordid, sorry, unprincipled, vicious, vile; SEE CONCEPT 404

disrepute [n] *dishonor, shame*
blemish, blot, brand, cloud, discredit, disesteem, disfavor, disgrace, ignominy, ill fame, ill favor, ill repute, infamy, ingloriousness, notoriety, obloquy, odium, opprobrium, reproach, scandal, scar, slur, smear, spot, stain, stigma, taint, unpopularity; SEE CONCEPT 411

disrespect [n] *disregard, rudeness toward someone*
boldness, coarseness, contempt, discourtesy, dishonor, flippancy, hardihood, impertinence, impiety, impoliteness, impudence, incivility, insolence, insolency, insolentness, irreverence, lack of respect, sacrilege, unmannerliness; SEE CONCEPTS 29,633

disrespectful [adj] *insulting, rude*
aweless, bad-mannered, blasphemous, bold, cheeky*, contemptuous, discourteous, disgracious, flip*, flippant, fresh, ill-bred, ill-mannered, impertinent, impious, impolite, impudent, insolent, irreverent, misbehaved, nervy*, out-of-line*, profanatory, profane, sacrilegious, sassy*, saucy*, smart-alecky*, snippy*, uncivil, unfilial, ungracious; SEE CONCEPTS 267,401

disrobe [v] *take off one's clothes*
bare, denudate, denude, deprive, dismantle, divest, doff, husk*, peel*, remove, shed, shuck*, slip out of, strip, take it off, unbutton*, unclothe, uncover, undress; SEE CONCEPT 167

disrupt [v1] *upset, disorganize*
agitate, bollix, confuse, disarray, discombobulate, discompose, disorder, disturb, mess up, mix up, muck up*, muddle, muddy the waters*, psych out*, put off, rattle, rattle one's cage*, rummage, screw up*, shake, spoil, throw, unsettle, upset the apple cart*; SEE CONCEPTS 16,84,234

disrupt [v2] *break, interrupt*
breach, break into, break up, fracture, hole, interfere with, intrude, obstruct, open, rupture, unsettle, upset; SEE CONCEPTS 98,135

disruptive [adj] *causing trouble, confusion*
disorderly, distracting, disturbing, obstreperous, off-base*, out-of-line*, out-of-order*, rowdy,

troublemaking, troublesome, unruly, unsettling, upsetting; SEE CONCEPTS 401,537

dissatisfaction [n] *discontent, unhappiness*
annoyance, anxiety, aversion, boredom, chagrin, complaint, desolation, disapproval, discomfort, discouragement, disfavor, disgruntlement, disinclination, dislike, disliking, dismay, displeasure, disquiet, disrelish, distaste, distress, ennui, envy, exasperation, fretfulness, frustration, heartburn, hopelessness, indisposition, irritation, jealousy, lamentation, malcontent, malcontentment, oppression, querulousness, regret, resentment, trouble, uneasiness, weariness, worry; SEE CONCEPTS 29,410

dissatisfied [adj] *discontented, unhappy*
annoyed, begrudging, bothered, complaining, crabby*, critical, disaffected, disappointed, disgruntled, displeased, ennuied, envious, faultfinding, fed-up*, fretful, fretting, frustrated, griping, grudging, grumbling, grumpy*, insatiable, irked, jaundiced, jealous, kvetching*, malcontent, malcontented, not satisfied, offended, picky, plaintive, put-out*, querulous, sniveling, sulky, sullen, unappeased, unassuaged, unfulfilled, ungratified, unsated, unsatisfied, vexed; SEE CONCEPT 403

dissect [v1] *cut up; take apart*
anatomize, break up, cut, dichotomize, disjoin, disjoint, dislimb, dismember, dissever, divide, exscind, exsect, lay open, operate, part, prosect, quarter, section, sever, slice, sunder; SEE CONCEPTS 98,176

dissect [v2] *analyze*
anatomize, break down, decompose, decompound, examine, explore, inquire about, inspect, investigate, resolve, scrutinize, study; SEE CONCEPT 24

dissection [n1] *cutting up, particularly of a dead body*
anatomization, anatomy, autopsy, dismemberment, examination, necropsy, operation, postmortem, vivisection; SEE CONCEPTS 176,310

dissection [n2] *thorough analysis*
breakdown, breakup, criticism, critique, examination, inquest, inspection, investigation, resolution, review, scrutiny, study; SEE CONCEPTS 24,290

dissemble [v] *disguise, pretend*
affect, camouflage, cloak, conceal, counterfeit, cover, cover up, dissimulate, doublespeak*, double-talk*, dress up, fake, falsify, feign, fourflush*, hide, let on*, make like*, mask, pass, play possum*, pussyfoot*, put on a false front*, put on a front*, put on an act*, put up a front*, put up a smoke screen*, sham*, shroud, shuck and jive*, signify, simulate, stonewall*, whitewash*; SEE CONCEPTS 59,188,716

disseminate [v] *distribute, scatter*
advertise, announce, annunciate, blaze, blazon, broadcast, circulate, declare, diffuse, disject, disperse, dissipate, proclaim, promulgate, propagate, publicize, publish, radiate, sow, spread, strew; SEE CONCEPTS 108,140,201,222

dissemination [n] *distribution*
airing, broadcasting, circulation, diffusion, dissipation, promulgation, propagation, publication, publishing, spread; SEE CONCEPTS 651,746

dissension [n] *conflict of opinion*
altercation, argument, bad vibes*, bickering, clinker*, contention, controversy, difference, disaccord, disagreement, discord, discordance, dispute, dissent, dissidence, disunity, faction, factional-

ism, flak*, friction, fuss, quarrel, scene, sour note*, static, strife, trouble, variance, wrangle; SEE CONCEPTS 46,278,665

dissent [n] *disagreement, disapproval*
bone*, bone of contention*, bone to pick*, clinker*, conflict, contention, denial, difference, disaccord, discord, dissension, dissidence, disunity, far cry*, flak*, hassle, heresy, heterodoxy, misbelief, nonagreement, nonconcurrence, nonconformism, nonconformity, nope*, objection, opposition, poles apart*, protest, refusal, resistance, schism, sour note*, spat, split, strife, unorthodoxy, variance; SEE CONCEPTS 29,665,689

dissent [v] *disagree*
argue, balk, break with, buck, contradict, decline, demur, differ, disaccord, discord, divide, fly in the face of*, object, oppose, pettifog, protest, put up a fight*, put up an argument, refuse, say not a chance*, say nothing doing*, say no way*, shy, stickle, vary, wrangle; SEE CONCEPTS 21,46

dissertation [n] *scholarly thesis*
argumentation, commentary, critique, discourse, disputation, disquisition, essay, exposition, memoir, monograph, tractate, treatise; SEE CONCEPTS 271,287

disservice [n] *unkindness*
bad turn, detriment, disfavor, harm, hurt, injury, injustice, insult, outrage, prejudice, wrong; SEE CONCEPTS 309,645,674

dissidence [n] *difference of opinion*
bad vibes*, contention, disaccord, disagreement, discordance, disharmony, dispeace, dispute, dissension, dissent, feud, heresy, heterodoxy, misbelief, nonconformism, nonconformity, rupture, schism, sour note*, strife, unorthodoxy; SEE CONCEPTS 278,633,689

dissident [n] *person who holds different belief*
agitator, dissenter, heretic, misbeliever, nonconformist, protester, rebel, recusant, schismatic, schismatist, sectary, separatist; SEE CONCEPTS 359,423

dissident [adj] *disagreeing, differing*
discordant, dissentient, dissenting, heretical, heterodox, nonconformist, schismatic, sectarian, unorthodox; SEE CONCEPT 403

dissimilar [adj] *not alike; not capable of comparison*
antithetical, antonymous, contradictory, contrary, different, disparate, distant, divergent, diverse, far cry*, heterogeneous, individual, like night and day*, march to a different drummer*, mismatched, mismated, not similar, offbeat, opposite, poles apart*, unequal, unique, unlike, unrelated, unsimilar, various, weird*; SEE CONCEPT 564

dissimilarity [n] *unlikeness*
alterity, contrast, difference, discord, discordance, discrepancy, disparity, dissemblance, dissimilitude, distance, distinction, divarication, divergence, divergency, diversity, heterogeneity, incomparability, incongruity, inconsistency, inconsonance, nonuniformity, offset, otherness, separation, severance, unrelatedness, variance, variation; SEE CONCEPT 665

dissimulate [v] *conceal, disguise*
beard*, camouflage, cloak, deceive, dissemble, dress up, fake, feign, hide, make-believe, mask, present a false face*, present a false front*, pretend; SEE CONCEPTS 59,172,188

dissipate [v1] *expend, spend*
be wasteful with, blow*, burn up*, consume, deplete, dump*, fritter away, indulge oneself, kiss goodbye*, lavish, misspend, misuse, run through, squander, throw away, trifle away, use up, waste; SEE CONCEPTS 156,169

dissipate [v2] *disappear*
dispel, disperse, dissolve, drive away, evanesce, evaporate, melt away, run dry, scatter, spread, vanish; SEE CONCEPTS 105,469

dissipated [adj1] *used up*
blown, burnt out*, consumed, destroyed, exhausted, kaput*, played out*, scattered, spent, squandered, wasted; SEE CONCEPTS 560,576

dissipated [adj2] *self-indulgent*
abandoned, corrupt, debauched, dissolute, gone bad*, gone to seed*, gone to the dogs*, hellbent*, intemperate, profligate, rakish, wicked; SEE CONCEPTS 401,545

dissipation [n1] *amusement, entertainment, occasionally to excess*
bender*, binge, blow-out, bust*, celebration, circus, distraction, diversion, divertissement, gratification, party, recreation, self-indulgence, tear*, toot*, wingding*; SEE CONCEPTS 363,386

dissipation [n2] *wantonness*
abandonment, debauchery, dissoluteness, dissolution, drunkenness, evil, excess, extravagance, free-living, high-living*, indulgence, intemperance, lavishness, life in the fast lane*, prodigality, profligacy, self-gratification, squandering, to hell in handbasket*, waste; SEE CONCEPT 633

dissipation [n3] *disappearance*
diffusion, disintegration, dispersal, dispersion, dissemination, dissolution, distribution, emission, extravagance, improvidence, radiation, scattering, spread, vanishing, wastage, waste; SEE CONCEPTS 230,651,720

dissociate [v] *part company with; separate*
abstract, alienate, break off, detach, disassociate, disband, disconnect, disengage, disjoin, disperse, disrupt, distance, dissunite, divide, divorce, estrange, isolate, quit, scatter, segregate, set apart, uncouple, unfix; SEE CONCEPTS 135,384

dissociation [n] *detachment, separation*
break, disconnection, disengagement, disjunction, distancing, disunion, division, divorce, isolation, segregation, severance; SEE CONCEPT 388

dissolute [adj] *lacking restraint, indulgent*
abandoned, corrupt, debauched, degenerate, depraved, dissipated, evil, fast*, fast and loose*, gone bad*, high living*, intemperate, in the fast lane*, lascivious, lax, lecherous, lewd, libertine, licentious, light, loose*, nighthawk*, night owl*, on the take*, open, player*, profligate, raffish, rakish, reprobate, slack, swift, sybaritic, unconstrained, unprincipled, unrestrained, vicious, wanton, wayward, wicked, wild; SEE CONCEPTS 401,545

dissolution [n1] *separation, rupture*
breaking up, detachment, disintegration, disunion, division, divorce, divorcement, parting, partition, resolution, split-up; SEE CONCEPTS 230,388

dissolution [n2] *death; destruction*
adjournment, conclusion, curtains, decay, decease, decomposition, defunction, demise, disappearance, disbandment, discontinuation, dismissal, dispersal, end, ending, evaporation, extinction, finish, liquefaction, melting, overthrow, passing, quietus, release, resolution, ruin, silence,

sleep, solution, suspension, termination; SEE CONCEPTS *105,304,469,703*

dissolve [v1] *melt from solid to liquid; mix in*
defront, deliquesce, diffuse, fluidify, flux, fuse, liquefy, liquesce, render, run, soften, thaw, waste away; SEE CONCEPTS *469,702*

dissolve [v2] *disappear, disintegrate*
break down, break into pieces, break up, crumble, decline, decompose, diffuse, dilapidate, disband, disperse, dissipate, dwindle, evanesce, evaporate, fade, melt away, perish, separate, unmake, vanish, waste away; SEE CONCEPTS *105,469*

dissolve [v3] *annul, discontinue*
abrogate, adjourn, annihilate, break up, cancel, collapse, decimate, demolish, destroy, destruct, discharge, dismiss, disorganize, disunite, divorce, do away with, end, eradicate, invalidate, loose, overthrow, postpone, put an end to, quash, render void, repeal, resolve into, ruin, separate, sever, shatter, shoot, suspend, terminate, unmake, vacate, void, wind up, wrack, wreck; SEE CONCEPTS *121,234,252*

dissonance [n1] *disagreement*
antagonism, conflict, contention, controversy, difference, disaccord, discord, discrepancy, disharmony, disparity, dissension, dissidence, incongruity, inconsistency, strife, variance; SEE CONCEPTS *278,665,689*

dissonance [n2] *noise, discord*
cacophony, harshness, jangle, jarring, unmelodiousness; SEE CONCEPT *595*

dissonant [adj1] *different, conflicting*
anomalous, at variance, differing, disagreeing, disconsonant, discordant, discrepant, dissentient, incompatible, incongruent, incongruous, inconsistent, inconsonant, irreconcilable, irregular, sour note*, unmixable; SEE CONCEPT *564*

dissonant [adj2] *unharmonious*
cacophonic, cacophonous, discordant, disharmonic, disharmonious, grating, harsh, inharmonic, inharmonious, jangling, jarring, out of tune, raucous, strident, tuneless, unmelodious, unmusical, SEE CONCEPTS *592,594*

dissuade [v] *talk out of*
advise against, caution against, chicken out*, counsel, cry out against, deprecate, derail, deter, disadvise, discourage, disincline, divert, exhort, expostulate, faze, hinder, lean on*, persuade not to, prevent, prick, put off, remonstrate, throw a wet blanket on*, throw cold water on*, throw off, thwart, turn off*, urge not to, warn; SEE CONCEPTS *68,78*

distance [n1] *interval, range*
absence, ambit, amplitude, area, bit, breadth, compass, country mile*, expanse, extension, extent, farness, far piece*, gap, good ways*, heavens, hinterland, horizon, lapse, length, objective, orbit, outpost, outskirts, provinces, purlieu, purview, radius, reach, remoteness, remove, scope, separation, size, sky, space, span, spread, stretch, sweep, way, width; SEE CONCEPTS *651,739,790*

distance [n2] *aloofness*
coldness, coolness, frigidity, reserve, restraint, stiffness; SEE CONCEPT *633*

distance [v] *dissociate oneself; leave behind*
break away from the pack, outdo, outpace, outrun, outstrip, pass, put in proportion, separate oneself; SEE CONCEPT *195*

distant [adj1] *faraway*
abroad, abstracted, apart, a piece, arm's length*,

asunder, away, backwoods, beyond range, far, far back, far-flung, far-off, farther, further, inaccessible, indirect, in the background, in the boonies*, in the distance, in the sticks*, isolated, middle of nowhere*, not home*, obscure, outlying, out of earshot*, out of range, out of reach, out-of-the-way, remote, removed, retired, secluded, secret, separate, sequestered, telescopic, unapproachable, ways*, wide of*, yonder*; SEE CONCEPTS *576,778*

distant [adj2] *aloof*
arrogant, ceremonious, cold, cool, formal, haughty, insociable, laid back, modest, offish, on ice*, proud, put on airs*, remote, reserved, restrained, reticent, retiring, shy, solitary, standoff, standoffish, stiff, stuck-up*, unapproachable, uncompanionable, unconcerned, unfriendly, unsociable, uppity*, withdrawn; SEE CONCEPTS *401,404*

distaste [n] *dislike, hate*
abhorrence, antipathy, aversion, detestation, disfavor, disgust, disinclination, displeasure, disrelish, dissatisfaction, hatred, horror, hostility, indisposition, loathing, repugnance, repulsion, revolt, revulsion; SEE CONCEPT *29*

distasteful [adj] *repulsive, unpleasant*
abhorrent, abominable, afflictive, bitter, detestable, disagreeable, dislikable, displeasing, flat, flavorless, galling, grievous, grody*, gross*, hateful, icky*, insipid, loathsome, nauseous, objectionable, obnoxious, odious, offensive, painful, repellent, repugnant, savorless, tasteless, unappetizing, undesirable, uninviting, unlikable, unpalatable, unsavory, yicky*, yucky*; SEE CONCEPTS *529,589,613*

distend [v] *bulge, swell*
amplify, augment, balloon, bloat, dilate, distort, enlarge, expand, increase, inflate, lengthen, puff, stretch, widen; SEE CONCEPTS *157,469,780*

distill [v] *make pure; draw out something*
boil down, brew, clarify, concentrate, condense, cook, cut, cut down, cut to the bone*, dribble, drip, drop, evaporate, express, extract, ferment, get to the meat*, infuse, precipitate, press, press out, purify, rarefy, rectify, refine, squeeze out, steam, sublimate, trickle, trim, vaporize, volatilize; SEE CONCEPTS *165,170,211,219*

distinct [adj1] *apparent, obvious*
audible, categorical, clean-cut, clear, clear-cut, decided, definite, enunciated, evident, explicit, express, incisive, lucid, manifest, marked, noticeable, palatable, patent, perspicuous, plain, prescribed, recognizable, sharp, sharp-cut, specific, transparent, trenchant, unambiguous, unequivocal, unmistakable, well-defined; SEE CONCEPTS *535,591,619*

distinct [adj2] *different; unconnected*
detached, discrete, disparate, dissimilar, distinctive, disunited, divergent, diverse, especial, individual, offbeat, particular, peculiar, poles apart*, separate, separated, several, single, sole, special, specific, unassociated, unattached, unique, various; SEE CONCEPT *564*

distinction [n1] *differentiation; feature*
acumen, acuteness, alterity, analysis, characteristic, clearness, contrast, diagnosis, difference, differential, discernment, discrepancy, discreteness, discretion, discrimination, dissemblance, dissimilarity, dissimilitude, divergence, divergency, division, earmark, estimation, individuality, judg-

ment, mark, marking, nicety, otherness, particularity, peculiarity, penetration, perception, qualification, quality, refinement, sensitivity, separation, sharpness, tact, unlikeness; SEE CONCEPTS 411,665

distinction [n2] *prominence; achievement*
accolade, account, award, badge, bays, celebrity, consequence, credit, decoration, eminence, excellence, fame, flair, greatness, illustriousness, importance, kudos, laurels, manner, merit, name, note, perfection, preeminence, prestige, quality, rank, renown, reputation, repute, style, superiority, worth; SEE CONCEPTS 388,671,706

distinctive [adj] *different, unique*
characteristic, cool, diacritic, diagnostic, discrete, distinguishing, excellent, extraordinary, far cry, gnarly*, idiosyncratic, individual, like night and day*, offbeat, original, outstanding, peculiar, perfect, poles apart*, proper, separate, single, singular, special, superior, typical, uncommon, unreal, weird, wicked; SEE CONCEPTS 564,574

distinguish [v1] *tell the difference*
analyze, ascertain, categorize, characterize, classify, collate, decide, demarcate, determinate, determine, diagnose, diagnosticate, differentiate, discriminate, divide, estimate, extricate, figure out, finger*, identify, individualize, individuate, judge, know, label, make out, mark, mark off, name, part, pinpoint, place, qualify, recognize, select, separate, set apart, set off, sift, signalize, single out, singularize, sort out, specify, spot, tag, tell apart, tell between, tell from; SEE CONCEPTS 15,18,38

distinguish [v2] *discern, identify*
beam*, catch, descry, detect, dig, discover, discriminate, eye, eyeball*, flash*, focus, get a load of*, get an eyeful*, know, make out, mark, note, notice, observe, perceive, pick out, pick up on*, read, recognize, remark, see, spot, spy, take in, tell, view; SEE CONCEPTS 38,626

distinguish [v3] *make famous*
acknowledge, admire, celebrate, dignify, honor, immortalize, pay tribute to, praise, signalize; SEE CONCEPT 69

distinguished [adj] *famous, outstanding*
acclaimed, aristocratic, arresting, big name*, brilliant, celebrated, conspicuous, dignified, distingué, eminent, especial, esteemed, extraordinary, famed, foremost, glorious, great, highly regarded, honored, illustrious, imposing, marked, memorable, name, noble, nonpareil, notable, noted, noteworthy, peerless, prominent, remarkable, renowned, reputable, royal, salient, shining, signal, singular, special, stately, striking, superior, talked of, unforgettable, venerable, well-known; SEE CONCEPT 574

distort [v] *deform; falsify*
alter, angle, belie, bend, bias, buckle, change, collapse, color, con, contort, crush, curve, deceive, decline, deteriorate, deviate, disfigure, doctor*, fake, fudge*, garble, gnarl, knot, lie, make out like, mangle, melt, misconstrue, misinterpret, misrepresent, misshape, pervert, phony up*, put one on, sag, scam*, slant, slump, snow*, torture, trump up*, twist, warp, whitewash*, wind, wrench, writhe; SEE CONCEPTS 63,137,232,250

distortion [n] *deformity; falsification*
baloney*, bend, bias, BS*, buckle, coloring, contortion, crock, crookedness, exaggeration, intorsion, jazz*, jive*, lie, line, malconformation,

malformation, misinterpretation, misrepresentation, misshape, misstatement, misuse, mutilation, perversion, slant, smoke*, story*, tall story*, torture, twist, twistedness, warp; SEE CONCEPTS 63,580

distract [v] *divert attention; confuse*
abstract, addle, agitate, amuse, befuddle, beguile, bewilder, call away, catch flies*, confound, derange, detract, discompose, disconcert, disturb, divert, draw away, engross, entertain, fluster, frenzy, harass, lead astray*, lead away, madden, mislead, mix up, occupy, perplex, puzzle, sidetrack, stall, throw off*, torment, trouble, turn aside, unbalance, unhinge*; SEE CONCEPTS 14,16

distraction [n] *having one's attention drawn away*
aberration, abstraction, agitation, amusement, beguilement, bewilderment, commotion, complication, confusion, disorder, dissipation, disturbance, diversion, divertissement, engrossment, entertainment, frenzy, game, interference, interruption, pastime, perplexity, preoccupation, recreation; SEE CONCEPTS 293,410,532,690

distraught [adj] *very upset, worked-up*
addled, agitated, anxious, beside oneself, bothered, concerned, confused, crazed*, crazy, discomposed, distracted, distrait, distressed, flustered, frantic, harassed, hysterical, in a panic, like a chicken with its head cut off*, mad, muddled, nonplussed, nuts*, out of one's mind*, overwrought, perturbed, rattled, raving, shook up, thrown*, tormented, troubled, unglued*, unscrewed*, unzipped*, wild, worried; SEE CONCEPTS 401,403,690

distress [n1] *pain, agony*
ache, affliction, anguish, anxiety, bad news*, blues*, care, concern, cross, dejection, desolation, disappointment, discomfort, disquietude, dolor, embarrassment, grief, headache, heartache, heartbreak, irritation, malaise, misery, mortification, ordeal, pang, perplexity, sadness, shame, sorrow, stew, suffering, throe, torment, torture, trial, tribulation, trouble, twinge, unconsolability, unhappiness, vexation, visitation, woe, worriment, worry, wretchedness; SEE CONCEPTS 410,532,690,720,728

distress [n2] *hardship, adversity*
bad luck, bummer*, calamity, can of worms*, catastrophe, crunch*, destitution, difficulty, disaster, downer*, drag*, exigency, hard knocks*, hard time*, holy mess*, hot water*, indigence, jam*, misfortune, need, pickle*, pinch*, poverty, privation, rigor, rotten luck*, scrape*, straits, throe, ticklish spot*, tough break*, tough luck*, trial, trouble, unholy mess*, vicissitude, want; SEE CONCEPT 674

distress [v] *worry, upset*
afflict, aggrieve, agonize, ail, be on one's case*, bother, break, bug, burn up, depress, desolate, discombobulate*, disquiet, disturb, do a number on*, dog*, eat*, get*, get to*, give a hard time*, grieve, harass, harry, hound, hurt, injure, irk, irritate, make it tough for*, miff, nag, needle, nitpick, oppress, pain, peeve, perplex, pester, pick on, plague, push, push buttons*, rack, sadden, strain, strap, stress, tick off*, torment, torture, trouble, try, vex, weigh, wound; SEE CONCEPTS 7,19,313

distressed [adj] *upset*
afflicted, agitated, all torn up*, antsy, anxious, basket case*, bothered, bugged, bummed out*,

bundle of nerves*, concerned, cut up*, discombobulated*, disconsolate, distracted, distrait, distraught, dragged, exercised, fidgety, harassed, hyper*, in a stew*, in a tizzy*, inconsolable, jittery, jumpy, miffed, peeved, perturbed, ripped*, saddened, shaky, shook*, shook up*, shot down*, spooked*, strung out*, tormented, troubled, unconsolable, unglued*, up the wall*, uptight*, wired, worried, wrecked*, wretched; SEE CONCEPT 403

distribute [v1] *allocate, deliver, spread*
administer, allot, apportion, appropriate, assign, bestow, circulate, consign, convey, cut up, deal, deal out, diffuse, disburse, dish out*, dispense, disperse, dispose, disseminate, divide, divvy up*, dole out*, donate, endow, fork out*, give, give away, hand out, issue, lot out, measure out, mete, parcel, partition, pass out, pay out, present, prorate, radiate, ration, scatter, share, shell out*, slice up, sow, strew; SEE CONCEPTS 98,140,217

distribute [v2] *classify*
arrange, assort, categorize, class, file, group, order; SEE CONCEPT 84

distribution [n1] *allocation, dispersion*
administration, alloting, allotment, apportioning, apportionment, assessment, assigning, circulating, circulation, dealing, delivery, diffusion, dispensation, dispersal, disposal, disposing, dissemination, dissipating, division, dole, handing out, handling, mailing, marketing, partition, partitioning, propagation, prorating, rationing, scattering, sharing, spreading, trading, transport, transportation; SEE CONCEPTS 98,140,217

distribution [n2] *classification*
arrangement, assortment, disposal, disposition, grouping, location, order, ordering, organization, placement, sequence; SEE CONCEPTS 109,727

district [n] *geographical area*
commune, community, department, locale, locality, neck of the woods*, neighborhood, parcel, parish, precinct, quarter, region, section, sector, stomping ground*, territory, turf*, vicinage, vicinity, ward; SEE CONCEPT 508

distrust [n] *lack of faith in something*
disbelief, doubt, misdoubt, misgiving, mistrust, qualm, question, skepticism, suspicion, wariness; SEE CONCEPTS 21,689

distrust [v] *be suspicious, skeptical of*
be wary of, disbelieve, discredit, doubt, misbelieve, mistrust, question, smell a rat*, suspect, wonder about; SEE CONCEPT 21

distrustful [adj] *disbelieving*
been hit before*, cagey, cautious, chary, cynical, doubtful, doubting, dubious, fearful, jealous, leery, mistrustful, skeptical, suspicious, uneasy, uptight, wary; SEE CONCEPTS 403,542

disturb [v1] *bother, upset*
afflict, agitate, ail, alarm, amaze, annoy, arouse, astound, badger, burn up*, complicate, confound, confuse, depress, discompose, dishearten, disrupt, distract, distress, excite, fluster, frighten, gall, grieve, harass, interfere, interrupt, intrude, irk, irritate, make uneasy, molest, muddle, outrage, pain, perplex, perturb, pester, pique, plague, provoke, puzzle, rattle, rouse, ruffle, shake, shake up*, startle, tire, trouble, unhinge*, unnerve, unsettle, vex, worry; SEE CONCEPTS 7,19

disturb [v2] *disorder; dislocate*
confuse, derange, disarrange, disarray, discompose, disorganize, displace, distort, foul up*, interfere, jumble, louse up*, mess up, mix up, move, muddle, remove, replace, shift, tamper, unsettle, upset; SEE CONCEPTS 84,137,250

disturbance [n] *commotion; upset*
agitation, annoyance, big scene*, big stink*, bother, brawl, brouhaha, clamor, confusion, convulsion, derangement, disarrangement, disorder, disruption, distraction, eruption, explosion, ferment, fisticuffs, flap, fracas, fray, fuss, hindrance, hubbub, hullabaloo*, insurrection, interruption, intrusion, molestation, perturbation, quake, quarrel, racket, rampage, restlessness, riot, ruckus, rumble, shock, spasm, stink*, stir*, storm, to-do*, tremor, tumult, turmoil, upheaval, uprising, uproar, violence; SEE CONCEPTS 388,410, 674,720

ditch [n] *gulley*
canal, channel, chase, cut, dike, drain, excavation, furrow, gutter, mine, moat, trench, watercourse; SEE CONCEPTS 509,513

ditch [v] *get rid of*
abandon, desert, discard, dispose of, drop, dump*, eighty-six*, forsake, jettison, junk*, leave, reject, scrap*, throw away, throw out, throw overboard*; SEE CONCEPT 180

dive [n1] *descent, usually underwater*
belly flop*, dash, dip, duck, ducking, fall, header* headlong* jump, leap, lunge, nosedive, pitch, plunge, spring, submergence, submersion, swoop; SEE CONCEPTS 147,181,194

dive [n2] *dirty, sleazy establishment*
bar, barroom, beer garden* cabaret, dump, flea trap*, flophouse*, hangout, hole, honky-tonk*, joint, lounge, night club, pool hall, pub, saloon, taproom, tavern; SEE CONCEPT 449

dive [v] *descend, usually going underwater*
belly flop*, dip, disappear, drop, duck, fall, go headfirst, gutter, header*, jump, leap, lunge, nose-dive, pitch, plumb, plummet, plunge, spring, submerge, swoop, vanish, vault; SEE CONCEPTS 147,181,194

diverge [v1] *go in different directions*
bend, bifurcate, branch, branch off, depart, deviate, digress, divagate, divaricate, divide, excurse, fork, part, radiate, ramble, separate, split, spread, stray, swerve, veer, wander; SEE CONCEPTS 195,738

diverge [v2] *be different from; be at odds*
argue, conflict, contrast, depart, deviate, differ, digress, disagree, disapprove, dissent, oppose, stray, swerve, turn aside, vary, wander; SEE CONCEPTS 46,665

divergence [n] *branching out; difference*
aberration, alteration, alterity, crotch, deflection, departure, detour, deviation, digression, disagreeing, discrepancy, disparity, dissemblance, dissimilarity, dissimilitude, distinction, divagation, divergency, diversity, division, fork, mutation, otherness, parting, radiation, ramification, separation, turning, unlikeness, variety, varying; SEE CONCEPTS 665,738

divergent [adj] *differing*
aberrant, abnormal, anomalous, antithetical, atypical, conflicting, contradictory, contrary, deviating, different, disagreeing, disparate, dissimilar, dissonant, distant, diverging, diverse, factional, factious, irregular, off-key, opposite, poles apart*, separate, unalike, unequal, unlike, unnatural, unsimilar, untypical, variant, various; SEE CONCEPT 564

di
di

diverse [*adj*] *different; various*
assorted, contradictory, contrary, contrasted, contrasting, contrastive, differing, discrete, disparate, dissimilar, distant, distinct, divergent, diversified, diversiform, incommensurable, like night and day*, manifold, miscellaneous, mixed bag*, multifarious, opposite, separate, several, sundry, unalike, unequal, unlike, varied, varying; SEE CONCEPTS *564,772*

diversify [*v*] *spread out; branch out*
alter, assort, change, expand, mix, modify, transform, variegate, vary; SEE CONCEPTS *232,697*

diversion [*n1*] *change in a course, path*
aberration, alteration, deflection, departure, detour, deviation, digression, divergence, fake out*, red herring*, turning, variation; SEE CONCEPTS *501,738*

diversion [*n2*] *entertainment, recreation*
amusement, ball, beguilement, delectation, delight, disport, dissipation, distraction, divertissement, enjoyment, field day*, frivolity, fun, fun and games*, game, gratification, grins*, high time*, hoopla*, laughs*, levity, merry-go-round*, pastime, picnic*, play, pleasure, relaxation, relish, sport, whoopee*; SEE CONCEPTS *292,363,386*

diversity [*n*] *variety, difference*
assortment, dissimilarity, distinction, distinctiveness, divergence, diverseness, diversification, heterogeneity, medley, mixed bag*, multeity, multifariousness, multiformity, multiplicity, range, unlikeness, variance, variegation, variousness; SEE CONCEPTS *651,665*

divert [*v1*] *turn a different direction*
alter, avert, change, deflect, modify, pivot, redirect, sheer, swerve, switch, turn aside, veer, volte-face, wheel, whip, whirl; SEE CONCEPTS *187,213*

divert [*v2*] *amuse, entertain*
beguile, break one up*, delight, fracture one*, get one's jollies*, gladden, knock 'em dead*, make happy, panic, please, put 'em away*, recreate, regale, relax, slay, tickle, wow; SEE CONCEPT *9*

divert [*v3*] *take attention away*
abstract, attract attention, bend the rules*, catch flies*, circumlocute, detach, deter, detract, disadvise, discourage, disengage, dissuade, distract, disturb, draw away, get around, lead astray, lead away, send on a wild-goose chase*, sidetrack, stall; SEE CONCEPTS *7,19,22*

divest [*v*] *dispossess; take off*
bankrupt, bare, bereave, bleed, denudate, denude, deprive, despoil, disinherit, dismantle, disrobe, ditch*, doff, dump, eighty-six*, lose, milk*, oust, plunder, remove, rob, seize, spoil, strip, take from, unclothe, uncover, undress, unload; SEE CONCEPTS *139,142,211*

divide [*v1*] *separate, disconnect*
abscind, bisect, branch, break, break down, carve, chop, cleave, cross, cut, cut up, demarcate, detach, dichotomize, disengage, disentangle, disjoin, dislocate, dismember, dissect, dissever, dissociate, dissolve, disunite, divorce, halve, intersect, isolate, loose, part, partition, pull away, quarter, rend, rupture, section, segment, segregate, sever, shear, split, subdivide, sunder, tear, unbind, undo; SEE CONCEPTS *98,135,137*

divide [*v2*] *distribute*
allocate, allot, apportion, articulate, cut, cut in*, cut one in*, cut up, deal, deal out, disburse, dish out*, dispense, disperse, divvy up*, dole out*, factor, fork out*, go fifty-fifty*, hand out, hand over, lot out, measure out, parcel, partition, piece up, portion, prorate, quota, ration, share, shell out*, shift, slice, slice up, split up; SEE CONCEPTS *98,140*

divide [*v3*] *put in order; classify*
arrange, categorize, grade, group, separate, sort; SEE CONCEPT *84*

divide [*v4*] *disagree, alienate*
break up, cause to disagree, come between, differ, disaccord, dissent, disunite, estrange, part, pit against, separate, set against, set at odds*, sow dissension*, split, vary; SEE CONCEPTS *46,266*

dividend [*n*] *one's share, profit*
allotment, allowance, appropriation, bonus, carrot*, check, coupon, cut*, dispensation, divvy*, extra, gain, gravy*, guerdon, interest, lagniappe*, meed, pay, portion, premium, prize, proceeds, remittance, returns, reward, surplus, taste*; SEE CONCEPTS *337,344*

divine [*adj*] *godlike, perfect*
all-powerful, almighty, ambrosial, angelic, anointed, beatific, beautiful, blissful, celestial, consecrated, deific, deistic, estrange, eternal, exalted, excellent, glorious, godly, hallowed, heavenly, holy, immaculate, magnificent, marvelous, mystical, omnipotent, omnipresent, omniscient, rapturous, religious, sacramental, sacred, sacrosanct, sanctified, spiritual, splendid, superhuman, superlative, supernatural, supreme, theistic, transcendent, transcendental, transmundane, unearthly, wonderful; SEE CONCEPTS *568,574*

divine [*v*] *prophesy*
anticipate, apprehend, conjecture, deduce, discern, forebode, forefeel, foreknow, foresee, foretell, go out on a limb*, guess, infer, intuit, perceive, predict, previse, prognosticate, see, see in the cards*, suppose, surmise, suspect, take a shot*, take a stab*, understand, visualize; SEE CONCEPT *28*

divinity [*n*] *absolute being; divine nature*
celestial, deity, genius, god, goddess, godhead, godhood, godliness, godship, guardian spirit, higher power, holiness, lord, prime mover, sanctity, spirit; SEE CONCEPTS *368,370,689*

division [*n1*] *separation, disconnection*
analysis, apportionment, autopsy, bisection, breaking, breaking down, breaking up, carving, contrasting, cutting up, demarcation, departmentalizing, detaching, detachment, diagnosis, disjuncture, dismemberment, disparting, disseverance, dissolution, distinguishing, distribution, disunion, disuniting, dividing, divorce, parceling, parting, partition, reduction, rending, rupture, segmentation, selection, separating, severance, splitting up, subdivision, vivisection; SEE CONCEPTS *98,135*

division [*n2*] *something produced from separating*
affiliate, associate, border, boundary, branch, category, chunk, class, compartment, cut, degree, demarcation, department, divide, dividend, divider, dividing line, divvy*, end, fraction, fragment, grouping, head, kind, lobe, lump, member, moiety, offshoot, parcel, partition, piece, piece of action*, portion, rake-off*, ramification, section, sector, segment, share, slice, sort, split, subdivision, wedge; SEE CONCEPTS *378,382,710,835*

division [n3] *breach, estrangement*
conflict, difference of opinion, difficulty, disaccord, disagreement, discord, disharmony, dispute, dissension, dissent, dissidence, dissonance, disunion, feud, rupture, split, trouble, variance, words; SEE CONCEPT 388

divorce [n] *split-up of marriage*
annulment, breach, break, breakup, decree nisi, dedomiciling, detachment, disparateness, dissociation, dissolution, disunion, division, divorcement, on the rocks*, parting of the ways*, partition, rupture, separate maintenance, separation, severance, split, splitsville*; SEE CONCEPT 297

divorce [v] *split up a marriage*
annul, break up, cancel, disconnect, disjoin, dissever, dissociate, dissolve, disunite, divide, nullify, part, put away, separate, sever, split, sunder, unmarry; SEE CONCEPT 297

divulge [v] *make known; confess*
admit, betray, blab, blow the whistle*, broadcast, communicate, cough up*, declare, disclose, discover, exhibit, expose, fess up*, give away, go public*, gossip, impart, leak, let hair down*, let slip*, mouth, open up*, own up*, proclaim, promulgate, publish, reveal, spill, spill the beans*, spring, tattle, tell, tip off*, uncover; SEE CONCEPT 60

dizzy [adj1] *light-headed, confused*
addled, befuddled, bemused, bewildered, blind, blinded, dazed, dazzled, distracted, disturbed, dumb, dumbfounded, faint, gaga*, giddy, groggy*, hazy, light, muddled, off balance*, out of control*, punch-drunk*, punchy*, puzzled, reeling, shaky, slap-happy*, staggered, staggering, swimming*, tipsy, unsteady, upset, vertiginous, weak in the knees*, weak-kneed*, whirling, wobbly, woozy; SEE CONCEPTS 314,480

dizzy [adj2] *flighty, scatterbrained*
capricious, changeable, crazy, empty-headed, fatuous, feather-brained, fickle, foolish, frivolous, giddy, harebrained, heady, inane, light-headed, silly, skittish, unstable; SEE CONCEPT 402

do [v1] *carry out*
accomplish, achieve, act, arrange, be responsible for, bring about, cause, close, complete, conclude, cook*, create, determine, discharge, do one's thing*, effect, end, engage in, execute, finish, fix, fulfill, get ready, get with it*, go for it*, look after, make, make ready, move, operate, organize, perform, prepare, produce, pull off*, see to, succeed, take care of business*, take on, transact, undertake, wind up*, work, wrap up*; SEE CONCEPT 91

do [v2] *be sufficient*
answer, avail, be adequate, be enough, be good enough for, be of use, be useful, give satisfaction*, pass muster*, satisfy, serve, suffice, suit; SEE CONCEPTS 646,656

do [v3] *figure out, solve*
adapt, decipher, decode, interpret, puzzle out, render, resolve, translate, transliterate, transpose, work out; SEE CONCEPTS 15,37

do [v4] *act, behave*
acquit oneself, appear, bear, carry, come on like*, comport, conduct, demean, deport, discourse, enact, fare, get along, get by, give, go on, impersonate, make out*, manage, muddle through*, operate, perform, personate, play, playact, portray, present, produce, put on*, quit, render the

role, seem, stagger along*; SEE CONCEPT 633

do [v5] *travel, visit*
cover, explore, journey, look at, pass through, stop in, tour, track, traverse; SEE CONCEPT 224

do [v6] *cheat*
beat, bilk, chouse, con, cozen, deceive, defraud, dupe, fleece*, flimflam*, gyp*, hoax, overreach, swindle, take for a ride*, trick; SEE CONCEPT 59

do away with [v] *get rid of; destroy*
abolish, bump off*, cancel, discard, discontinue, do in*, eliminate, exterminate, finish, kill, liquidate, murder, put an end to, put to death, remove, slaughter, slay, take away, wipe out*; SEE CONCEPTS 180,252

docile [adj] *compliant, submissive*
accommodating, acquiescent, adaptable, agreeable, amenable, biddable, childlike, complacent, cool, docious, ductile, easily influenced, easy, easygoing, gentle, governable, humble, laid-back, manageable, meek, mellow, mild, obedient, obliging, orderly, pliable, pliant, quiet, resigned, soft, tame, teachable, tractable, usable, weak-kneed*, well-behaved, willing, yielding; SEE CONCEPTS 401,404

dock [n] *waterfront*
berth, embarkment, harbor, jetty, landing, landing pier, levee, lock, marina, pier, quay, slip, wharf; SEE CONCEPT 439

dock [v] *land on the waterfront*
anchor, berth, drop anchor, hook up, join, link up, moor, put in, rendezvous, tie up, unite; SEE CONCEPT 159

docket [n] *program, agenda*
calendar, card, schedule, tab, tally, ticket, timetable; SEE CONCEPT 271

doctor [n] *medical practitioner*
bones*, doc*, expert, general practitioner, healer, intern, MD, medic, medical person, medico, physician, professor*, quack*, scientist, specialist, surgeon; SEE CONCEPT 357

doctor [v1] *fix up, treat*
administer, apply medication, attend, do up, fix, give treatment, medicate, mend, overhaul, patch up*, rebuild, recondition, reconstruct, repair, revamp, supply; SEE CONCEPTS 110,310

doctor [v2] *adulterate, pervert*
add to, alter, change, cut, deacon, debase, dilute, disguise, dope up*, falsify, fudge*, gloss, load, misrepresent, mix with, sophisticate, spike*, tamper with, water down, weight; SEE CONCEPT 240

doctrinaire [adj] *dogmatic, opinionated*
authoritarian, authoritative, biased, bigoted, bullheaded*, dictative, dictatorial, dogged, fanatical, impractical, inflexible, insistent, magisterial, mulish, obstinate, one-sided, pertinacious, pigheaded*, rigid, speculative, stiff-necked*, stubborn, unrealistic; SEE CONCEPTS 267,401

doctrine [n] *opinion; principle*
article, article of faith, attitude, axiom, basic, belief, canon, concept, convention, conviction, credenda, creed, declaration, dogma, fundamental, gospel, implantation, inculcation, indoctrination, instruction, position, precept, pronouncement, propaganda, proposition, regulation, rule, statement, teaching, tenet, tradition, universal law, unwritten rule; SEE CONCEPTS 688,689

document [n] *written communication*
archive, certificate, credentials, deed, diary, evidence, form, instrument, language, pages, paper,

di
do

record, report, script, testimony, token; SEE CON-
CEPT 271

doddering [adj] aged, feeble

anile, decrepit, dotard, faltering, floundering, infirm, senile, shaky, tottering, trembling, unsteady,
weak; SEE CONCEPTS 314,488,578,797

dodge [n] trick, feint

contrivance, device, machination, method, plan,
plot, ploy, ruse, scheme, stratagem, strategy, subterfuge, wile; SEE CONCEPT 660

dodge [v] avoid

circumlocute, dark, deceive, ditch, duck, elude,
equivocate, escape, evade, fence, fend off,
fudge*, get around, get out of, give the slip*,
hedge, juke, lurch, malinger, move to the side*,
parry, pussyfoot*, put the move on*, shake, shake
off*, shift, shirk, short-circuit, shuffle, sidestep,
skip out on*, skirt, slide, slip, swerve, tergiversate, tergiverse, trick, turn aside, weasel*; SEE
CONCEPTS 59,102

do for [v1] destroy

defeat, deprive, finish, kill, ruin, shatter, slaughter, slay; SEE CONCEPTS 238,252

do for [v2] help

abet, aid, assist, benefact, care for, help out, lend
a hand*, look after, provide for, steady, support;
SEE CONCEPT 110

dog [n] canine mammal

bitch, bowwow*, cur, doggy, fido*, flea bag*,
hound, man's best friend*, mongrel, mutt,
pooch*, pup, puppy, stray, tail-wagger*, tyke;
SEE CONCEPT 400

dog [v] chase after; bother

bedog, haunt, hound, plague, pursue, shadow,
tag, tail, track, trail, trouble; SEE CONCEPT 207

dogged [adj] determined, persistent

adamant, bullheaded*, firm, hanging tough*,
hardheaded*, hard-nosed*, indefatigable, inexorable, inflexible, insistent, mulish, obdurate, obstinate, perseverant, perseverative, persevering,
pertinacious, pigheaded*, relentless, resolute,
rigid, single-minded, staunch, steadfast, steady,
stubborn, tenacious, tough nut*, unbending, unflagging, unshakable, unyielding; SEE CONCEPTS
401,542

dogma [n] belief, principle

article, article of faith, canon, conviction, credenda, credo, creed, doctrine, gospel, opinion,
persuasion, precept, rule, teachings, tenet, view;
SEE CONCEPTS 688,689

dogmatic [adj1] dictatorial, opinionated

arbitrary, arrogant, assertive, bigoted, bullheaded*, categorical, cocksure*, confident, definite,
despotic, determined, dictative, doctrinaire, domineering, downright, egotistical, emphatic, fanatical, fascistic, formal, high and mighty*,
imperious, intolerant, magisterial, narrow-
minded, obdurate, obstinate, one-sided, overbearing, peremptory, pigheaded*, prejudiced, stiff-
necked, stubborn, tenacious, tyrannical,
unequivocal, wrong-headed; SEE CONCEPTS
267,542

dogmatic [adj2] based on absolute truth

a priori, as a matter of course, assertive, authoritarian, authoritative, axiomatic, by fiat, by natural
law, by nature, canonical, categorical, deducible,
deductive, derivable, doctrinaire, doctrinal, eternal, excathedra, formal, imperative, inevitable, on
faith, oracular, orthodox, peremptory, positive,
pragmatic, prophetic, reasoned, systematic, theo-

retical, unchangeable, unerring, unqualified; SEE
CONCEPTS 530,567,582

do in [v] destroy; exhaust

assassinate, bankrupt, bump off*, butcher*,
cool*, dilapidate, dispatch, do away with*, eliminate, execute, fatigue, finish, frazzle*, kill,
knock out*, liquidate, murder, put away*, ruin,
shatter, slaughter, slay, tire, wear out, weary,
wreck; SEE CONCEPTS 137,250,252

doing [n] achievement

accomplishing, accomplishment, achieving, act,
action, carrying out, deed, execution, exploit,
handiwork, implementation, performance, performing, thing; SEE CONCEPT 706

doldrums [n] depression

apathy, black mood*, blahs*, blue funk*, blues*,
boredom, bummer*, dejection, disinterest, dismals, downer, dullness, dumps*, ennui, funk*,
gloom, inactivity, indifference, inertia, lassitude,
letdown, listlessness, malaise, mopes*, slump,
stagnation, stupor, tedium, torpor, yawn*; SEE
CONCEPT 410

dole [n] allowance, allocation

allotment, alms, apportionment, benefit, charity,
dispensation, distribution, division, donation, gift,
grant, gratuity, handout, living wage, mite, modicum, parcel, pittance, portion, quota, relief,
share, subsistence, trifle; SEE CONCEPTS 337,344

doleful [adj] depressing

afflicted, cast down, cheerless, crestfallen, dejected, depressed, dirgeful, dismal, dispirited, distressing, dolent, dolorous, down, downcast,
downhearted, down in the mouth*, dreary, forlorn, funereal, gloomy, grieving, lamentable, lugubrious, melancholy, mournful, painful, piteous,
pitiful, plaintive, rueful, sad, somber, sorrowful,
woebegone, woeful, wretched; SEE CONCEPTS
403,529

dole out [v] allocate, distribute

administer, allot, apportion, assign, deal, deal out,
dispense, disperse, divide, divvy*, give, hand out,
lot, measure, mete, mete out, parcel, partition,
share, share out; SEE CONCEPTS 108,140

doll [n] toy person

baby, dolly, effigy, figure, figurine, manikin, marionette, model, moppet*, puppet; SEE CONCEPT
446

dollar [n] paper money

ace*, bank note, bill, buck*, certificate, clam*,
cucumber*, currency, folding money, greenback*, legal tender, note, one-spot*, single; SEE
CONCEPT 340

doll up [v] beautify oneself; dress up

deck out*, fix up, gussy up*, preen, primp, put on
best clothes, smarten up*, spiff*, spruce up*; SEE
CONCEPTS 162,167,202

dolor [n] misery, anguish

agony, distress, grief, heartache, heartbreak, passion, ruth, sadness, sorrow, suffering; SEE CON-
CEPT 410

dolorous [adj] miserable, anguished

afflicted, afflictive, calamitous, deplorable, dire,
distressing, doleful, dolent, dolesome, grievous,
harrowing, heart-rending, lamentable, lugubrious,
melancholy, mournful, painful, plaintive, regrettable, rueful, ruthful, sad, sorrowful, woebegone,
woeful, wretched; SEE CONCEPTS 401,403

dolt [n] stupid person

airhead*, blockhead*, boob*, chump*, dimwit*,
dodo*, dope, dork*, dumbbell*, dumdum*,

dunce, fool, goon*, idiot, ignoramus, lamebrain*, lunkhead*, meathead*, nitwit*, sap*, simpleton, stupid, yo-yo*; SEE CONCEPTS *412,423*

domain [*n*] *area of expertise, rule*
authority, bailiwick, concern, demesne, department, discipline, district, dominion, empire, estate, field, home park*, jurisdiction, land, neck of the woods*, occupation, orbit*, power, province, quarter, realm, region, scope, slot, specialty, sphere, stomping grounds*, terrain, territory, turf, walk, wing; SEE CONCEPTS *349,518,710*

dome [*n*] *arched part of ceiling*
arcade, arch, bubble, bulge, covering, cupola, mosque, roof, span, top, vault; SEE CONCEPT *440*

domestic [*adj1*] *household*
calm, devoted, domiciliary, family, home, homelike, home-loving, homey, indoor, pet, private, sedentary, settled, stay-at-home, subdued, submissive, tame, trained, tranquil; SEE CONCEPT *542*

domestic [*adj2*] *not foreign*
handcrafted, home-grown, homemade, indigenous, inland, internal, intestine, intramural, municipal, national, native; SEE CONCEPTS *536,549*

domesticate [*v*] *tame; habituate*
acclimatize, accustom, break, break in, breed, bring up, bust, corral, domiciliate, familiarize, gentle, herd, hitch, housetrain, naturalize, raise, reclaim, round up, subdue, teach, train, yoke; SEE CONCEPTS *202,285*

domestic partner [*n*] *live-in significant other*
beneficiary, cohabitant, companion, housemate, longtime companion, lover, partner, spouse; SEE CONCEPT *414*

domicile [*n*] *human habitat*
abode, accommodation, apartment, castle, commorancy, condo*, condominium, co-op, crash pad*, dump, dwelling, habitation, home, house, joint, legal residence, mansion, pad*, rack*, residence, residency, roof over head*, roost*, settlement; SEE CONCEPTS *439,516*

dominance [*n*] *supremacy*
ascendancy, authority, command, control, domination, dominion, government, influence, paramountcy, power, preeminence, preponderance, prepotence, prepotency, rule, sovereignty, sway, upper hand, whip hand; SEE CONCEPTS *376,668*

dominant [*adj1*] *superior, controlling*
ascendant, assertive, authoritative, bossy, chief, commanding, demonstrative, despotic, domineering, effective, first, foremost, governing, imperative, imperious, leading, main, obtaining, outweighing, overbalancing, overbearing, overweighing, paramount, powerful, predominant, predominate, preeminent, preponderant, presiding, prevailing, prevalent, principal, regnant, reigning, ruling, sovereign, supreme, surpassing, transcendent; SEE CONCEPT *574*

dominant [*adj2*] *main, primary*
capital, chief, influential, major, number one*, outstanding, paramount, predominant, preeminent, prevailing, prevalent, principal, prominent, stellar; SEE CONCEPT *568*

dominate [*v1*] *govern, rule*
boss, call the shots*, command, control, detract from, dictate, direct, domineer, eclipse, handle, have one's way*, have upper hand*, head, hold sway over*, influence, keep under thumb*, lay down the law*, lead, lead by the nose*, manage, monopolize, outshine, overbear, overrule, over-

shadow, play first fiddle*, predominate, preponderate, prevail, prevail over, reign, rule the roost*, run, run the show*, sit on top of*, subject, subjugate, superabound, sway, tyrannize; SEE CONCEPTS *94,117,298*

dominate [*v2*] *tower above*
bestride, look down upon, loom over, overlie, overlook, overtop, stand over, survey; SEE CONCEPTS *741,752*

domination [*n*] *control; subjection*
ascendancy, authority, command, despotism, dictatorship, dominance, dominion, influence, jurisdiction, might, oppression, power, preponderancy, prepotence, prepotency, repression, rule, sovereignty, strings*, subordination, superiority, suppression, supremacy, sway, tyranny; SEE CONCEPT *376*

domineer [*v*] *oppress; assume authority*
be in the saddle*, bend, bluster, boss around*, browbeat, bulldoze*, bully*, call the shots*, dominate, hector, henpeck*, in the driver's seat*, intimidate, keep under thumb*, kick around*, lead by the nose*, menace, overbear, predominate, preponderate, prevail, push the buttons*, reign, rule, rule the roost*, run the show*, run things*, swagger, threaten, throw weight around*, tyrannize; SEE CONCEPTS *14,94*

domineering [*adj*] *oppressive, authoritarian*
arrogant, autocratic, bossy, coercive, crack the whip*, despotic, dictatorial, egotistic, highhanded, imperative, imperial, imperious, in driver's seat*, insolent, iron-handed*, on high horse*, overbearing, peremptory, tyrannical; SEE CONCEPT *401*

dominion [*n*] *area of rule; authority*
ascendancy, authorization, bailiwick, command, commission, control, country, demesne, district, domain, dominance, domination, empire, enclave, field, government, jurisdiction, management, power, preeminence, prepotence, prepotency, prerogative, privilege, property, province, realm, regency, regiment, regimentation, region, reign, rule, seniority, sovereignty, sphere, state, stomping grounds*, supremacy, sway, terrain, territory, turf, walk; SEE CONCEPTS *198,376,710*

donate [*v*] *make a gift of*
accord, ante up*, award, bequeath, bestow, chip in*, confer, contribute, devote, dole out*, do one's part*, feed the kitty*, get in the act*, get it up*, give, give away, grant, hand out, lay on, pass the hat*, present, provide, subscribe, sweeten the pot*; SEE CONCEPT *108*

donation [*n*] *gift*
a hand*, aid, allowance, alms, appropriation, assistance, benefaction, beneficence, bequest, boon, charity, contribution, dole, do one's part*, endowment, gifting, grant, gratuity, handout, help, helping hand* largess, lump, offering, philanthropy, pittance, present, presentation, ration, relief, subscription, subsidy, subvention, write-off*; SEE CONCEPTS *337,340*

done [*adj1*] *accomplished, finished*
all in*, all over*, a wrap*, brought about, brought to pass, buttoned up*, compassed, complete, completed, concluded, consummated, depleted, down, drained, effected, effete, ended, executed, exhausted, fixed, fulfilled, over, perfected, performed, realized, rendered, set, spent, succeeded,

do
do

terminated, through, used up, wired, wrought;
SEE CONCEPTS *528,531*

done [*adj2*] *thoroughly cooked*
baked, boiled, brewed, broiled, browned, crisped,
fried, ready, stewed; SEE CONCEPTS *462,613*

done [*adj3*] *approved, agreed upon*
compacted, determined, okay, settled, you're on*;
SEE CONCEPT *558*

done for [*adj*] *beaten, defeated*
broken, conquered, dashed, destroyed, doomed,
finished, foiled, lost, ruined, through, undone,
vanquished, washed-up*, wrecked; SEE CON-
CEPTS *537,570*

done in [*adj*] *exhausted*
all in*, bushed*, dead, depleted, done, effete,
fagged, far-gone*, on last leg*, ready to drop*,
spent, tired, used up, washed-out*, weary, worn-
out; SEE CONCEPTS *314,485*

donkey [*n*] *small domestic horselike mammal*
ass, burro, horse, jackass, jennet, jenny, maud,
moke, mule, neddy, pony, Rocky Mountain canary*; SEE CONCEPT *400*

donor [*n*] *giver of gift*
almsgiver, altruist, angel*, backer, benefactor,
benefactress, bestower, conferrer, contributor, do-
nator, grantor, heavy hitter*, patron, philanthropist, presenter, Santa Claus*, savior, subscriber;
SEE CONCEPTS *359,423*

doom [*n*] *fate or decision, usually unpleasant*
annihilation, calamity, cataclysm, catastrophe,
circumstance, conclusion, condemnation, death,
decree, destination, destiny, destruction, disaster,
downfall, end, fixed future, foreordination, fortune, handwriting on wall*, judgment, Judgment
Day, karma, kismet, lap of the gods*, lot, Moira,
opinion, portion, predestination, predetermination, ruin, sentence, tragedy, verdict, way the ball
bounces*, way the cookie crumbles*; SEE CON-
CEPT *679*

doomed [*adj*] *condemned, hopeless*
bedeviled, bewitched, convicted, cursed, cut
down, damned, dead duck*, destroyed, done,
done for*, fated, foreordained, ill-fated, ill-
omened, in the cards*, kiss of death*, lost, luckless, menaced, overthrown, overwhelmed,
predestined, que sera sera*, reprobate, ruined,
sentenced, star-crossed, sunk, suppressed, threatened, thrown down, undone, unfortunate, unredeemed, wrecked; SEE CONCEPT *537*

door [*n*] *entrance to room, building*
aperture, egress, entry, entryway, exit, gate, gateway, hatch, hatchway, ingress, opening, portal,
postern, slammer; SEE CONCEPT *440*

do out of [*v*] *cheat*
balk, beat out of*, bilk, con, deceive, deprive,
steal, swindle, trick; SEE CONCEPTS *59,139*

dope [*n1*] *stupid person*
ass, blockhead*, dimwit*, dolt, donkey*, dunce,
fool, idiot, lame-brain*, simpleton; SEE CON-
CEPTS *412,423*

dope [*n2*] *drug*
narcotic, opiate, stimulant; SEE CONCEPT *307*

dope [*n3*] *inside news*
account, details, developments, facts, info*, information, knowledge, lowdown*, tip*; SEE CON-
CEPT *274*

dope [*v*] *drug someone*
adulterate, anesthetize, deaden, debase, inject,
knock out*, load, narcotize, put to sleep, sedate,

soak, sophisticate, stupefy; SEE CONCEPTS
156,310

dopey [*adj*] *stupid*
comatose, dense, dumb, foolish, heavy, hebetudinous, idiotic, lethargic, senseless, silly, simple,
slow, sluggish, slumberish, thick, torpid; SEE
CONCEPT *402*

dormant [*adj*] *inactive; sleeping*
abeyant, asleep, closed down, comatose, down,
fallow, hibernating, inert, inoperative, latent, lethargic, lurking, on the shelf*, out of action*,
passive, potential, prepatent, quiescent, sidelined,
slack, sluggish, slumbering, smoldering, suspended, torpid; SEE CONCEPT *539*

dose [*n*] *portion of drug or other consumable*
application, dosage, dram, draught, fill, fix*, hit*,
lot, measure, measurement, nip*, potion, prescription, quantity, share, shot*, slug*, spoonful;
SEE CONCEPTS *307,835*

dot [*n*] *tiny mark, drop*
atom, circle, dab, droplet, fleck, flyspeck, grain,
iota, jot, mite, mote, particle, period, pinpoint,
point, speck, spot, tittle; SEE CONCEPTS *284,831*

dot [*v*] *make spot(s)*
bespeckle, dab, dabble, fleck, freckle, pepper,
pimple, sprinkle, stipple, stud; SEE CONCEPTS
79,174

dotage [*n*] *feebleness, old age*
advanced age, decrepitude, elderliness, fatuity,
imbecility, infirmity, second childhood*, senectitude, senility, weakness; SEE CONCEPTS *405,715*

dote on/dote upon [*v*] *lavish affection on*
admire, adore, be fond of, be infatuated with, be
sweet on*, cherish, enjoy, fancy, hold dear, idolize, like, love, pet, prize, treasure, worship; SEE
CONCEPT *32*

doting [*adj*] *indulgent; serving*
adoring, affectionate, devoted, fascinated, fatuous, fond, foolish, lovesick, lovesome, loving,
silly, simple, struck; SEE CONCEPT *401*

double [*n*] *something which exactly resembles another*
angel, clone, companion, coordinate, copy, counterpart, dead ringer*, duplicate, image, impersonator, lookalike*, match, mate, picture, portrait,
reciprocal, replica, ringer*, simulacrum, spitting
image*, stand-in*, twin; SEE CONCEPTS *664,716*

double [*adj*] *in a pair*
as much again, bifold, binary, binate, coupled,
dual, dualistic, duple, duplex, duplicate, duplicated, geminate, paired, repeated, second, twice,
twin, twofold, two times; SEE CONCEPT *771*

double [*v*] *make two of: make twice as large*
amplify, augment, dualize, dupe, duplicate, du-
plify, enlarge, fold, grow, increase, infold, loop,
magnify, multiply, plait, pleat, plicate, redouble,
repeat, replicate, supplement; SEE CONCEPTS
236,245

double back [*v*] *reverse path*
backtrack, circle, dodge, loop, retrace one's steps,
return, turn; SEE CONCEPTS *224,232*

double-cross [*v*] *betray*
beguile, bluff, cheat, con, cross, deceive, defraud,
four-flush*, hoodwink*, humbug*, illude, juggle,
mislead, sell, sell out*, split, swindle, take in,
trick, two-time*; SEE CONCEPTS *7,19,59*

double-dealing [*n*] *betrayal, cheating*
bad faith, chicane, chicanery, deceit, deception,
dishonesty, duplicity, foul play*, fourberie, fraud,
hanky-panky*, hypocrisy, mendacity, perfidy,

sharp practice*, treachery, trickery, two-timing*; SEE CONCEPT 59

double-dealing [adj] cheating, deceitful
ambidextrous, crooked, dishonest, double, duplicitous, fraudulent, hypocritical, insincere, left-handed*, lying, perfidious, sneaky, swindling, treacherous, tricky, two-faced*, two-timing*, underhanded, untrustworthy, wily; SEE CONCEPT 401

double entendre [n] play on words
ambiguity, amphibiology, double meaning, equivocality, equivocation, equivoque, innuendo, joke, pun, tergiversation; SEE CONCEPTS 278,682

double-talk [n] nonsense communicated
amphibiology, balderdash, baloney*, bull*, drivel, equivocation, flimflam*, gibberish, jazz*, mumbo jumbo*, rigmarole; SEE CONCEPT 278

doubt [n] lack of faith, conviction; questioning
agnosticism, ambiguity, apprehension, confusion, demurral, difficulty, diffidence, dilemma, disbelief, discredit, disquiet, distrust, dubiety, dubiousness, faithlessness, faltering, fear, hesitancy, hesitation, incertitude, incredulity, indecision, irresolution, lack of confidence, misgiving, mistrust, perplexity, problem, qualm, quandary, rejection, reluctance, scruple, skepticism, suspense, suspicion, uncertainty, vacillation, wavering; SEE CONCEPTS 21,410,689,690

doubt [v] lack confidence in; question
be apprehensive of, be curious, be dubious, be in a quandary, be puzzled, be uncertain, be undetermined, call in question, challenge, demur, disbelieve, discredit, dispute, distrust, fear, fluctuate, give no credence, harbor suspicion, have qualms, hesitate, imagine, impugn, insinuate, misdoubt, misgive, mistrust, not buy*, query, read differently, scruple, shilly-shally*, skepticize, smell a rat*, surmise, suspect, take dim view of, vacillate, waver, wonder at; SEE CONCEPT 21

doubter [n] person who does not believe
agnostic, cynic, disbeliever, headshaker*, questioner, skeptic, unbeliever, zetetic; SEE CONCEPTS 361,423

doubtful [adj1] questionable, unclear
ambiguous, borderline, chancy, clouded, contingent, debatable, dicey, disreputable, doubtable, dubious, dubitable, equivocal, far-fetched, fat chance, fishy*, hazardous, hazy, iffy*, impugnable, inconclusive, indecisive, indefinite, indeterminate, indistinct, insecure, long shot*, obscure, on thin ice*, open, pending, precarious, problematic, shady, sneaky*, speculative, suspect, suspicious, touch-and-go*, touchy, uncertain, unconfirmed, undecided, uneasy, unsettled, unstable, unsure, up for grabs*; SEE CONCEPTS 529,535

doubtful [adj2] not believing
agnostic, baffled, confused, discomposed, disconcerted, distracted, distrustful, disturbed, doubting, dubious, equivocal, faithless, faltering, flustered, hesitant, hesitating, in a quandary, in clouds*, indecisive, in dilemma, irresolute, like doubting Thomas*, lost, not following, of two minds*, perplexed, puzzled, questioning, skeptical, suspicious, tentative, theoretical, troubled, uncertain, unconvinced, undecided, unresolved, unsettled, unsure, vacillating, wavering, without belief; SEE CONCEPTS 403,542

doubtless [adv] certainly; most likely
absolutely, apparently, assuredly, clearly, easily,

for sure, indisputably, no ifs ands or buts*, of course, ostensibly, positively, precisely, presumably, probably, seemingly, supposedly, surely, truly, undoubtedly, unequivocally, unquestionably, without doubt; SEE CONCEPTS 535,552

doughnut [n] sweet ring-shaped fried cake
bun, cruller, danish, dunker*, pastry, sinker*, sweet roll; SEE CONCEPTS 457,461

do up [v] physically prepare; fix
clean, doctor, enclose, finish, gift-wrap, launder, mend, overhaul, package, patch, rebuild, recondition, reconstruct, repair, revamp, wash, wrap; SEE CONCEPTS 126,165,182,202

dour [adj] gloomy, grim
bleak, crabbed, dismal, dreary, forbidding, glum, hard, harsh, morose, saturnine, severe, sour, stringent, sulky, sullen, surly, ugly, unfriendly; SEE CONCEPTS 401,542

douse [v] drench, extinguish with liquid
blow out, deluge, drown, duck, dunk, immerse, plunge, put out, quench, saturate, slop, slosh, smother, snuff, snuff out, soak, sop, souse, spatter, splash, splatter, squench, steep, submerge, submerse, wet; SEE CONCEPTS 250,256

dovetail [v] link, fit together
accord, agree, check out, coincide, conform, correspond, go, harmonize, interlock, jibe, join, match, mortise, square, sync*, sync up*, tally, tenon, unite; SEE CONCEPTS 113,664

dowdy [adj] poorly dressed; old-fashioned
antiquated, archaic, baggy, bedraggled, blowsy*, bygone, dated, dingy, drab, dull, frowzy*, frumpy*, homely, moldy, old hat*, outdated, outmoded, out-of-date, passé, plain, run-down, scrubby*, shabby, slatternly, sloppy, slovenly, stodgy, tacky, tasteless, unfashionable, unkempt, unseemly, unstylish, untidy, vintage, wrinkled; SEE CONCEPT 589

do without [v] get along without
abstain from, dispense, endure, forgo, give up; SEE CONCEPTS 23,646

down [adj/adv] below; physically lower
bottomward, cascading, declining, depressed, descending, downgrade, downhill, downward, dropping, earthward, falling, gravitating, groundward, inferior, nether, precipitating, sagging, sinking, sliding, slipping, slumping, subjacent, to the bottom, under, underneath; SEE CONCEPTS 583,586,735

down [adj2] unhappy
bad, blue*, cast down, chapfallen, crestfallen, dejected, depressed, disheartened, dispirited, downcast, downhearted, low, miserable, off, sad, slack, sluggish; SEE CONCEPT 403

down-and-out [adj] poverty-stricken
beaten, beggared, defeated, derelict, destitute, finished, impoverished, needy, outcast, penniless, ruined, vagabond, vagrant; SEE CONCEPT 334

downcast [adj] depressed, unhappy
bad, blue, brooding, bummed out*, cast down, chapfallen, cheerless, crestfallen, daunted, dejected, despondent, disappointed, disconsolate, discouraged, disheartened, dismayed, dispirited, distressed, doleful, down, downhearted, down in the dumps*, down-in-the-mouth*, dragged*, droopy, dull, forlorn, gloomy, glum, heartsick, in pain, listless, low, low-spirited, miserable, moody, mopey*, morose, oppressed, sad, shot down*, singing the blues*, sunk*, troubled, weighed down*, woebegone; SEE CONCEPT 403

downfall [n] *disgrace, ruin*
atrophy, bane, breakdown, cloudburst, collapse, comedown, comeuppance, debacle, decadence, declension, degeneracy, degeneration, deluge, descent, destruction, deterioration, devolution, discomfiture, down, drop, failure, fall, flood, on the rocks*, overthrow, rack and ruin*, road to ruin*, ruination, storm, the skids*, undoing; SEE CONCEPTS *674,679,699*

downgrade [n] *slope*
decline, declivity, descent, dip, hill, inclination, pitch; SEE CONCEPTS *509,738*

downgrade [v] *lower in opinion or rank*
abase, bench*, break*, bump*, bust*, declass, decrease, decry, degrade, demerit, demote, denigrate, depreciate, detract from, devalorize, devalue, disparage, disrate, humble, mark down, minimize, reduce, run down, set back, take down a peg*, undervalue, write off*; SEE CONCEPTS *7,19,54,240*

downhearted [adj] *depressed, unhappy*
blue*, chapfallen, crestfallen, dejected, despondent, disconsolate, discouraged, disheartened, dismayed, dispirited, down, downcast, low, low-spirited, sad, sorrowful, spiritless, woebegone; SEE CONCEPT *403*

downlink [n] *transmission path for data*
circuit, communications pathway, network, pathway, signal route; SEE CONCEPT *269*

download [v] *to transfer data from one computer system to another*
boot up, compute, computerize, crunch numbers*, digitize, initialize, input, keyboard, key in, load, log in, log out, program, run; SEE CONCEPTS *211,217*

downpour [n] *tremendous pouring of rain*
cloudburst, deluge, drencher, flood, inundation, monsoon, rainstorm, storm, torrential rain; SEE CONCEPT *526*

downright [adj] *thorough, absolute*
blatant, blunt, categorical, certain, clear, complete, damned, explicit, flat, gross, honest, indubitable, open, out-and-out, outright, plain, positive, simple, sincere, straight, straightforward, sure, thoroughgoing, total, undisguised, unequivocal, unmitigated, unqualified, unquestionable, utter, whole; SEE CONCEPT *531*

downside [n] *a negative aspect of a situation*
defect, disadvantage, drawback, fault, flaw, inconvenience, minus, problem, trouble; SEE CONCEPTS *666,674*

downsize [v] *to decrease in size, especially of a workforce*
curtail, cut, cut back, cut down, decrease, deduct, diminish, phase down, phase out, reduce, retrench, roll back, roll down, scale back, scale down, shrink, step down, trim, trim away, tune down; SEE CONCEPTS *236,240,247*

downtime [n] *time during which an activity is stopped*
break, breathing spell, freedom, free time, halt, interim, interlude, intermission, letup, lull, pause, recess, repose, respite, rest, spare time, spell, stay, suspension, time on one's hands, time out, time to burn, time to kill; SEE CONCEPT *807*

down-to-earth [adj] *reasonable, practical*
common, commonsense, easy, hard, hard-boiled, hardheaded, matter-of-fact, mundane, no-nonsense, plainspoken, pragmatic, rational, realistic, sane, sensible, sober, unfan-

tastic, unidealistic, unsentimental; SEE CONCEPTS *402,558*

downtrodden [adj] *afflicted, abused*
abject, a slave to*, at one's beck and call*, at one's feet*, at one's mercy*, destitute, distressed, exploited, have-not, helpless, in one's clutches*, in one's pocket*, in one's power*, led by the nose*, maltreated, mistreated, needy, oppressed, overcome, persecuted, subjugated, subservient, suppressed, tyrannized, underdog*, underfoot*, under one's thumb*; SEE CONCEPT *542*

downy [adj] *fluffy*
featherlike, feathery, fleecy, fuzzy, light, plumate, plumose, pubescent, silky, soft, velutinous, velvety, woolly; SEE CONCEPTS *604,606*

doze [n] *light sleep*
catnap, drowse, forty winks*, nap, shut-eye*, siesta, slumber, snooze*; SEE CONCEPTS *315,681*

doze [v] *take a nap*
catch a wink*, catnap, cop some z's*, drift off*, drop off*, drowse, nod off*, sleep, sleep lightly, slumber, snooze; SEE CONCEPTS *315,681*

drab [adj] *dull, colorless*
arid, blah*, bleak, boring, brown, characterless, cheerless, desolate, dingy, dismal, dreary, dry, dull as dishwater*, faded, flat, gloomy, gray, grungy, lackluster, lusterless, muddy, murky, run-down, same, shabby, somber, subfuse, unchanging, uninspired, vapid, zero*; SEE CONCEPTS *536,617,618*

draft [n1] *something formulated; plan*
abstract, blueprint, delineation, outline, preliminary form, rough sketch, version; SEE CONCEPTS *271,660*

draft [n2] *check for paying money*
bank draft, bill, bond, cheque, coupon, debenture, IOU, letter of credit, money order, order, promissory note, receipt, warrant; SEE CONCEPTS *332,344*

draft [n3] *gust of air*
breeze, current, eddy, puff, wind; SEE CONCEPT *437*

draft [n4] *military conscription*
allotment, assignment, call of duty, call-up*, greetings*, impressment, induction, letter from Uncle Sam*, levy, lottery, recruiting, registration, roll call*, selection, selective service; SEE CONCEPT *321*

draft [n5] *drink of beverage*
drag*, drain, drench, glass, peg*, quaff, swallow, swig*, swill*; SEE CONCEPTS *169,454*

draft [v1] *formulate*
adumbrate, block out, characterize, compose, concoct, contrive, delineate, design, devise, draw, draw up, fabricate, fashion, forge, form, frame, invent, make, manufacture, outline, plan, prepare, project, rough, shape, skeleton, sketch; SEE CONCEPTS *36,79,173*

draft [v2] *select for military force*
call up, choose, conscribe, conscript, dragoon, enlist, enroll, impress, indite, induct, muster, press, recruit, sign on, sign up; SEE CONCEPTS *8,320*

drag [n1] *bad situation*
annoyance, bore, bother, burden, encumbrance, hang-up, hindrance, impediment, nuisance, pain, pest, pill, sway, trouble; SEE CONCEPT *674*

drag [n2] *a puff while smoking*
breathing, draw, inhalation, pull, smoke; SEE CONCEPT *185*

drag [v1] *haul something to a new place*
draw, hale, lug, magnetize, move, pull, schlepp*, tow, trail, transport, truck, tug, yank; SEE CONCEPTS *206,213*

drag [v2] *move very slowly*
be delayed, be quiescent, crawl, creep, dally*, dawdle*, delay, encounter difficulty*, hang*, inch*, lag, lag behind, limp along, linger, loiter, mark time*, poke*, procrastinate, put off*, sag, shamble, shuffle, slow down, stagnate, straggle, tarry, trail behind*, traipse; SEE CONCEPTS *151,681*

dragging [adj] *tiresome, monotonous*
boring, drawn-out, dull, going slowly, humdrum, lengthy, long, overlong, prolonged, protracted, tedious, wearisome; SEE CONCEPTS *482,798*

drag on/drag out [v] *extend time of action*
continue, draw out, endure, extend, go on slowly, keep going, lengthen, persist, prolong, protract, spin out, stretch out; SEE CONCEPT *239*

drain [n] *channel through which liquid runs off*
cesspool, cloaca, conduit, culvert, ditch, duct, outlet, pipe, sewer, sink, trench, watercourse; SEE CONCEPT *501*

drain [v1] *remove liquid; remove supply*
abate, bankrupt, bleed, bleed dry*, catheterize, consume, debilitate, decrease, deplete, devitalize, diminish, dissipate, divert, draft, draw off, drink up, dry, empty, evacuate, exhaust, expend, fatigue, filter off, finish, free from, get last drop*, get rid of, gulp down, impoverish, lessen, milk*, pump, pump out, quaff, reduce, sap, siphon, spend, strain, suck, suck dry*, swallow, tap, tax, tire out, use up, waste, wear, wear down, weary, withdraw; SEE CONCEPTS *142,211,225*

drain [v2] *seep, discharge liquid*
abate, decline, decrease, diminish, dwindle, effuse, exude, filter off, flow, flow out, leak, leave dry, ooze, osmose, percolate, reduce, run off, taper off, trickle, well; SEE CONCEPTS *179,698*

drained [adj] *used up; exhausted*
all in*, beat*, bleary, burned out*, dead, dead tired*, depleted, dragging, effete, far-gone, hacked*, pooped*, spent, washed-out, weary, wiped-out*, worn-out; SEE CONCEPTS *485,560*

drama [n1] *theatrical piece; acting*
boards*, Broadway*, climax, comedy, dramatic art, dramatization, dramaturgy, farce, footlights, histrionic art, melodrama, play, production, scene, show, show business, showmanship, stagecraft, stage show, tear-jerker*, theater, theatricals, thespian art, tragedy, vehicle*; SEE CONCEPTS *263,271,293*

drama [n2] *turmoil in real life*
climax, comedy, crisis, dramatics, emotion, excitement, farce, histrionics, melodrama, scene, spectacle, tension, theatrics, tragedy; SEE CONCEPT *674*

dramatic [adj] *exciting, moving*
affecting, breathtaking, climactic, comic, effective, electrifying, emotional, expressive, farcical, histrionic, impressive, melodramatic, powerful, sensational, startling, striking, sudden, suspenseful, tense, theatrical, thespian, thrilling, tragic, vivid; SEE CONCEPTS *537,548*

dramatize [v] *make a performance of*
act, amplify, burlesque, enact, exaggerate, execute, farcialize, give color to, ham it up*, lay it on*, make a production of, melodramatize, overdo, overstate, perform, playact, play on heart-

strings*, play to gallery, play up, present, produce, show, splash, stage, tragedize; SEE CONCEPTS *49,59,292*

drape [v] *hang over, adorn*
array, cloak, clothe, cover, dangle, display, don, dress, droop, drop, enclose, enswathe, envelop, enwrap, fold, hang, lean over, let fall, line, model, roll, sprawl, spread, spread-eagle, suspend, swathe, wrap; SEE CONCEPT *172*

drastic [adj] *severe, extreme*
desperate, dire, exorbitant, extravagant, forceful, harsh, immoderate, radical, strong; SEE CONCEPTS *537,569*

draw [n] *tie in competition*
dead end*, dead heat*, deadlock, even steven*, photo finish*, stalemate, standoff, tie; SEE CONCEPT *706*

draw [v1] *move something by pulling*
attract, bring, carry, convey, cull, draft, drag, drain, educe, elicit, evoke, extract, fetch, gather, haul, hook, jerk, lug, magnetize, pick, pluck, pump, rake, siphon, tap, tow, trail, trawl, tug, wind in, wrench, yank; SEE CONCEPT *206*

draw [v2] *create a likeness in a picture*
caricature, chart, compose, crayon, delineate, depict, describe, design, draft, engrave, etch, express, form, formulate, frame, graph, limn, map out, mark, model, outline, paint, pencil, portray, prepare, profile, sketch, trace, write; SEE CONCEPTS *79,174*

draw [v3] *deduce*
collect, conclude, derive, gather, get, infer, judge, make, make out, take; SEE CONCEPT *15*

draw [v4] *allure, influence*
argue into, attract, bewitch, bring around, bring forth, call forth, captivate, charm, convince, elicit, enchant, engage, entice, evoke, fascinate, get, induce, invite, lure, magnetize, persuade, prompt, take, wile, win over; SEE CONCEPTS *7,19,22,68*

draw [v5] *take out, extend*
attenuate, choose, drain, elongate, extort, extract, lengthen, pick, pull out, respire, select, single out, stretch, suck, take; SEE CONCEPTS *142,163,239*

drawback [n] *disadvantage*
check, defect, deficiency, detriment, difficulty, disability, evil, failing, fault, flaw, fly in the ointment*, handicap, hindrance, hitch, ill, impediment, imperfection, inconvenience, lack, nuisance, obstacle, shortcoming, snag, stumbling block*, trouble, weakness; SEE CONCEPTS *666, 674*

draw back [v] *retract from position*
deduct, discount, pull back, recede, recoil, reel in, retreat, sheathe, shrink, start back, subtract, take away, withdraw; SEE CONCEPTS *195,213*

drawing [n] *illustration*
cartoon, commercial art, comp, delineation, depiction, design, doodle, etching, graphics, layout, likeness, outline, painting, picture, portrayal, representation, sketch, storyboard, study, tracing, work of art; SEE CONCEPT *625*

drawl [v] *lengthen, draw out*
chant, drag out, drone, extend, intone, nasalize, prolong, pronounce slowly, protract, utter; SEE CONCEPTS *77,239*

drawn [adj] *tense, fatigued*
fraught, haggard, harassed, harrowed, peaked, pinched, sapped, starved, strained, stressed, taut, thin, tired, worn; SEE CONCEPT *485*

do
dr

draw on [v] *use to advantage*
effect, employ, exploit, extract, fall back on, have recourse to, make use of, rely on, require, take from; SEE CONCEPT 225

draw out [v] *prolong*
attract, continue, drag, drag out, elongate, extend, lead on, lengthen, make longer, prolongate, protract, pull, spin, spin out*, stretch, string out*, tug; SEE CONCEPTS 236,239,245

draw up [v] *draft document*
compose, formulate, frame, indite, make, prepare, write, write out; SEE CONCEPT 79

dread [n] *fear*
affright, alarm, apprehension, aversion, awe, cold feet*, consternation, creeps*, dismay, fright, funk*, goose bumps*, horror, jitters, panic, phobia, stage fright, terror, trepidation, trepidity, worriment; SEE CONCEPT 27

dread [adj] *horrible, terrifying*
alarming, awe-inspiring, awful, creepy*, dire, frightening, frightful, shuddersome, terrible; SEE CONCEPT 537

dread [v] *anticipate with horror*
apprehend, be afraid, cringe, fear, have cold feet*, misdoubt, quake, shrink from, shudder, tremble; SEE CONCEPT 27

dreadful [adj] *horrible, frightening*
abominable, alarming, appalling, atrocious, awful, bad, beastly, creepy*, dire, distressing, fearful, formidable, frightful, frozen, ghastly, godawful*, grievous, grim, grody*, gross*, hideous, horrendous, horrific, icky*, lousy, mean, monstrous, rotten, shameful, shocking, shuddersome, spooky, terrible, terrific, tragic, tremendous, wicked; SEE CONCEPTS 537,550

dream [n1] *illusion, vision*
bubble*, castle in the air*, chimera, daydream, delusion, fancy, fantasy, hallucination, head trip*, idea, image, imagination, impression, incubus, mental picture, nightmare, pie in the sky*, pipe dream*, rainbow, reverie, specter, speculation, thought, trance, vagary, wraith; SEE CONCEPT 529

dream [n2] *goal*
ambition, aspiration, design, desire, flight of fancy*, hope, notion, pipe dream*, wish; SEE CONCEPT 659

dream [v] *conjure up scenario*
be delirious, be moonstruck, be up in clouds*, brainstorm, build castles in air*, conceive, concoct, cook up*, crave, create, daydream, devise, envisage, fancy, fantasize, formulate, hallucinate, hanker*, hatch*, have a flash*, have a nightmare*, have a notion*, have a vision, hunger, idealize, imagine, invent, long, lust, make up, picture, pine, search for pot of gold*, sigh, stargaze*, sublimate, think, think up, thirst, visualize; SEE CONCEPTS 17,529

dream up [v] *concoct plan*
contrive, cook up*, create, devise, frame, hatch*, imagine, invent, make up, spin*, think up; SEE CONCEPTS 17,36

dreamy [adj] *illusory, romantic*
abstracted, astral, calming, chimerical, daydreaming, excellent, fanciful, fantastic, gentle, idealistic, imaginary, immaterial, impractical, intangible, introspective, introvertive, lulling, marvelous, misty, musing, mythical, nightmarish, otherworldly, out of this world*, pensive, phantasmagoric, phantasmagorical, preoccupied, quixotic, relaxing, shadowy, soothing, speculative,

unreal, unsubstantial, utopian, vague, visionary, whimsical; SEE CONCEPT 582

dreary [adj] *gloomy, lifeless*
black, blah, bleak, boring, cheerless, colorless, comfortless, damp, depressing, depressive, dingy, dismal, dispiriting, doleful, downcast, drab, dull, forlorn, funereal, glum, humdrum, joyless, lonely, lonesome, melancholy, monotonous, mournful, oppressive, pedestrian, raw, routine, sad, somber, sorrowful, tedious, uneventful, uninteresting, wearisome, windy, wintry, wretched; SEE CONCEPTS 525,544

drench [v] *wet thoroughly*
deluge, dip, douse, drown, duck, dunk, flood, imbrue, immerse, impregnate, inundate, pour, saturate, seethe, soak, sodden, sop, souse, steep, submerge, teem; SEE CONCEPT 256

dress [n] *clothing; woman's garment*
accouterment, apparel, attire, attirement, civvies*, costume, covering, drape, dry goods, duds*, ensemble, evening clothes, frock, garb, gear, gown, guise, habiliment, habit, muumuu, outfit, raiment, robe, shift, skirt, smock, suit, Sunday best*, things*, threads*, tog, toga, toggery, trappings, uniform, vestment, wardrobe; SEE CONCEPT 451

dress [v1] *put on clothing*
adorn, apparel, array, attire, bedeck, bundle up, change, clad, clothe, costume, cover, deck, decorate, don, drape, embellish, fit out, furbish, garb, ornament, outfit, primp, put on, raiment, rig, robe, slip into, slip on, spruce up, suit up, trim, turn out, wear; SEE CONCEPT 167

dress [v2] *physically prepare; groom*
adjust, align, arrange, comb, decorate, dispose, do up, fit, make ready, ornament, set, straighten, trim; SEE CONCEPT 202

dress [v3] *cover a wound*
attend, bandage, bind, cauterize, cleanse, give first aid, heal, plaster, sew up, sterilize, treat; SEE CONCEPTS 172,310

dress down [v] *scold*
bawl out, berate, carpet, castigate, censure, chew out*, lash, rail, rake over coals*, ream, rebuke, reprimand, reprove, tear into*, tell off*, tongue-lash*, upbraid; SEE CONCEPT 52

dress up [v] *put on one's best clothes*
array, attire, beautify, clothe, deck out*, embellish, fit out*, fix up, gussy up*, improve, overdress, preen, prettify, primp, prink, slick, smarten, spiff up*, spruce up*, titivate; SEE CONCEPT 167

dressy [adj] *formal, fashionable*
chic, classy, dressed to kill*, dressed to the nines*, dressed up*, elaborate, elegant, fancy, in high feather*, looking sharp, ornate, ritzy, smart, stylish; SEE CONCEPTS 579,589

dribble [v] *trickle*
distill, drip, drivel, drizzle, drool, drop, fall in drops, leak, ooze, run, salivate, seep, slaver, slobber, spout, squirt, trill, weep; SEE CONCEPTS 179,185

drift [n1] *accumulation*
alluvion, bank, batch, bunch, bundle, clump, cluster, deposit, heap, hill, lot, mass, mound, mountain, parcel, pile, set, shock, stack; SEE CONCEPTS 432,524

drift [n2] *meaning, significance of communication*
aim, design, direction, end, gist, implication, import, intention, object, progress, progression, pur-

port, scope, significance, tendency, tenor; SEE CONCEPT *682*

drift [*v*] *move aimlessly*
accumulate, aim, amass, amble, be carried along, coast, dance, draw near, flicker, flit, flitter, float, flow, flutter, gad*, gallivant*, gather, go-that-a-way*, go with the tide*, gravitate, hover, kick around*, linger, malinger, meander, mosey*, muck*, ride, sail, saunter, scud, skim, slide, stray, stroll, tend, waft, wander, wash*; SEE CONCEPT *147*

drill [*n1*] *practice, exercise*
assignment, call, conditioning, constitutional, daily dozen*, discipline, dress, drilling, dry run*, gym, homework, instruction, learning by doing, maneuvers, marching, preparation, repetition, run-through*, shakedown*, training, tryout, warm-up, workout; SEE CONCEPTS *87,290*

drill [*n2*] *tool for boring*
auger, awl, bit, borer, corkscrew, countersink, dibble, gimlet, implement, jackhammer, punch, riveter, rotary tool, trepan, trephine, wimble; SEE CONCEPT *499*

drill [*v1*] *train, discipline*
accustom, break, break in, exercise, get into shape, habituate, hone, instruct, lick into shape, practice, rehearse, teach, tune up, walk through, work out; SEE CONCEPTS *117,285*

drill [*n3*] *bore hole*
dig, penetrate, perforate, pierce, prick, punch, puncture, sink in; SEE CONCEPT *220*

drink [*n*] *beverage; alcoholic beverage*
alcohol, booze*, brew, cup, draft, glass, gulp, libation, liquid, liquor, potable, potation, potion, refreshment, shot, sip, slug*, spirits, spot*, swallow, swig, taste, thirst quencher*, toast; SEE CONCEPT *454*

drink [*v*] *take in liquid*
absorb, belt*, booze*, consume, dissipate, down, drain, gargle, gulp, guzzle*, hit the bottle*, imbibe, indulge, inhale, irrigate, lap*, liquor up*, nip*, partake of, put away, quaff, sip, slosh, slurp, soak up, sop, sponge, suck, sup, swallow, swig, swill, tank up*, thirst, tipple*, toast, toss off*, wash down*, wet whistle*; SEE CONCEPT *169*

drip [*v*] *drop, trickle*
dribble, drizzle, exude, filter, plop, rain, splash, sprinkle, trill, weep; SEE CONCEPT *181*

drive [*n1*] *journey by vehicle*
airing, commute, drive, excursion, expedition, hitch, jaunt, joyride, lift, outing, pickup, ramble, ride, run, spin, Sunday drive*, tour, trip, turn, whirl; SEE CONCEPT *224*

drive [*n2*] *campaign for cause*
action, advance, appeal, crusade, effort, enterprise, get-up-and-go*, initiative, push, surge; SEE CONCEPTS *87,300*

drive [*n3*] *person's will to achieve*
ambition, clout, effort, energy, enterprise, fire in belly*, get-up-and-go, goods*, gumption*, guts*, impellent, impetus, impulse, initiative, momentum, motivation, motive, moxie*, pep, pressure, punch*, push*, right stuff*, spunk*, steam*, stuff*, vigor, vitality, what it takes*, zip*; SEE CONCEPTS *411,706*

drive [*v1*] *move or urge on*
actuate, act upon, animate, arouse, bulldoze*, chase, coerce, compel, constrain, dog*, egg on*, encourage, force, goad, goose*, harass, hasten, herd, hound*, hurl, hurry, hustle, impel, induce, inspire, instigate, kick, lean on*, make, motivate, nag, oblige, overburden, overwork, pound, press, pressure, prod, prompt, propel, provoke, push, put up to*, railroad*, ride herd on*, rouse, rush, send, shepherd, shove, spirit up, spur, steamroll*, stimulate, work on, worry; SEE CONCEPTS *68,147,208*

drive [*v2*] *moving, controlling a vehicle*
actuate, advance, bear down, bicycle, bike, burn rubber*, burn up the road*, coast, cruise, cycle, dash, direct, drag, fire up*, floor it*, fly, guide, handle, impel, lean on it*, make sparks fly*, manage, mobilize, motor, operate, pour it on*, propel, push, ride, roll, run, send, speed, spin, start, steer, step on it*, step on the gas*, tailgate, tool*, transport, travel, turn, vehiculate*, wheel; SEE CONCEPTS *148,187*

drive [*v3*] *hit with heavy blow*
batter, beat, butt, dash, dig, hammer, jackhammer, knock, maul, plunge, pop, punch, ram, run, shoot, sink, smite, sock, stab, stick, strike, throw, thrust, thump, twack*, whack*, wham*; SEE CONCEPT *189*

drive at [*v*] *mean, suggest as meaning*
aim, allude to, contemplate, design, get at, have in mind, hint at, imply, indicate, intend, intimate, propose, refer to, signify; SEE CONCEPTS *73,682*

drivel [*n*] *foolish talk*
babble, balderdash*, blather, bunk*, double-talk, gibberish, gobbledygook*, Greek*, hogwash*, hooey*, jabber*, nonsense, poppycock*, prating, rot*, rubbish*, tripe*, twaddle*; SEE CONCEPT *278*

drivel [*v1*] *talk foolishly*
babble, blabber, blather*, blethe, gab, gabble, prate, prattle, ramble, twaddle*, waffle*; SEE CONCEPT *266*

drivel [*v2*] *drool*
dribble, salivate, slaver, slobber; SEE CONCEPTS *185,256*

driver [*n*] *person who engineers vehicle*
autoist, automobilist, cabbie, chauffeur, coach person, hack*, handler, jockey, leadfoot*, motorist, operator, road hog*, trainer, whip*; SEE CONCEPT *423*

driving [*adj*] *forceful*
active, compelling, dynamic, energetic, enterprising, galvanic, impellent, lively, propulsive, sweeping, urging, vigorous, violent; SEE CONCEPT *540*

drizzle [*v*] *fine rain*
dribble, drip, drop, mist, mizzle, shower, spit, spray, sprinkle; SEE CONCEPT *526*

droll [*adj*] *amusing, farcical*
absurd, camp, campy, clownish, comic, comical, crack-up, diverting, eccentric, entertaining, for grins*, funny, gagged up*, gelastic, humorous, jocular, joshing, laffer, laughable, ludicrous, odd, preposterous, quaint, queer, quizzical, ridiculous, riot, risible, waggish, whimsical; SEE CONCEPTS *267,548*

drone [*n1*] *person who is lazy*
idler, leech, loafer, lounger, parasite, slug, sluggard, sponger*; SEE CONCEPT *412*

drone [*n2*] *continuous noise*
buzz, hum, murmur, purr, sound, vibration, whirr; SEE CONCEPT *595*

drone [*v*] *making noise continuously*
bombinate, buzz, chant, drawl, hum, intone, na-

salize, purr, sound, strum, thrum, vibrate, whirr; SEE CONCEPTS 65,77

drool [v1] *salivate*
dribble, drivel, froth, ooze, run, slabber, slaver, slobber, spit, water, water at the mouth; SEE CONCEPTS 185,256

drool [v2] *desire, lust after*
dote on, enthuse, fondle, gush, lick chops*, make much of, pet, rave, rhapsodize, rhapsody, slobber over*, spoil, want; SEE CONCEPT 20

droop [v] *hang down; languish*
bend, dangle, decline, depress, diminish, drop, fade, fail, faint, fall down, flag, lean, let down, loll, lop, sag, settle, sink, sling, slouch, slump, subside, suspend, weaken, wilt, wither; SEE CONCEPTS 181,699

droopy [adj] *limp*
bent, drooping, flabby, floppy, languid, languorous, lassitudinous, pendulous, sagging, saggy, slouchy, stooped, wilting; SEE CONCEPT 485

drop [n1] *globule*
bead, bit, bubble, crumb, dab, dash, dewdrop, driblet, drip, droplet, iota, molecule, morsel, nip, ounce, particle, pearl, pinch, sip, smidgen, speck, splash, spot, taste, tear, teardrop, trace, trickle; SEE CONCEPTS 467,468,831,835

drop [n2] *steep decline; hole*
abyss, chasm, declivity, deepness, depth, descent, dip, fall, plunge, precipice, slope, tumble; SEE CONCEPTS 181,509

drop [n3] *decrease*
cut, decline, descent, deterioration, dip, downfall, downslide, downswing, downtrend, downturn, fall, fall-off, landslide, lapse, lowering, precipitation, reduction, sag, slide, slip, slump, tumble, upset; SEE CONCEPTS 698,776

drop [v1] *fall in globules*
bead, bleed, descend, distill, drain, dribble, drip, emanate, hail, leak, ooze, percolate, precipitate, seep, snow, splash, trickle, trill; SEE CONCEPT 179

drop [v2] *let go of; fall*
abandon, bring down, cave in, collapse, decline, depress, descend, dive, duck, dump, fell, floor, flop, give up, go down, ground, keel over*, knock, loosen, lower, nose-dive*, pitch, plummet, plump, plunge, release, relinquish, shed, shoot, sink, slide, slip, slump, topple, tumble, unload; SEE CONCEPTS 181,200

drop [v3] *abandon; ignore*
abort, adios*, be alienated from, break with, call off, cancel, cast off, cease, desert, discontinue, dismiss, disown, ditch*, divorce, dust off*, eighty-six*, end, forfeit, forget about, forsake, give up, have done with*, interrupt, jilt, kick*, leave, lose, part from, part with, quit, reject, relinquish, remit, renounce, repudiate, resign, sacrifice, scratch*, scrub*, separate, shake, stop, terminate, throw over, wash out*, waste one*, wipe out*, write off*; SEE CONCEPTS 30,121,195

drop in [v] *visit*
blow in*, call, call upon, come by, come over, go and see*, look in on, look up, pop in*, run in*, stop, stop by, stop in, turn up; SEE CONCEPT 227

drop off [v1] *decrease*
decline, diminish, dwindle, fall away, fall off, lessen, sag, slacken, slide, slip, slump; SEE CONCEPTS 698,776

drop off [v2] *deliver*
deposit, give, hand over, leave, let off, present, set down, unload; SEE CONCEPT 108

drop off [v3] *fall asleep*
catnap, doze, doze off*, drowse, have forty winks*, nod, nod off*, snooze; SEE CONCEPTS 210,315

drop out [v] *stop doing an activity*
abandon, back out, cease, forsake, give notice, give up, leave, quit, renege, retreat, withdraw; SEE CONCEPT 121

drought [n] *dryness; shortage of supply*
aridity, dearth, deficiency, dehydration, desiccation, dry spell, insufficiency, lack, need, parchedness, rainlessness, scarcity, want; SEE CONCEPTS 607,646

drove [n] *large gathering*
collection, company, crowd, crush, drive, flock, herd, horde, mob, multitude, pack, press, rout, run, swarm, throng; SEE CONCEPTS 397,432

drown [v] *submerge in liquid; submerge and die*
asphyxiate, deluge, dip, douse, drench, engulf, flood, go down, go under, immerse, inundate, knock over, obliterate, overcome, overflow, overpower, overwhelm, plunge, prostrate, sink, soak, sop, souse, stifle, suffocate, swamp, whelm, wipe out; SEE CONCEPTS 252,256

drowsy [adj] *sleepy*
comatose, dazed, dopy, dozing, dozy, dreamy, drugged, half asleep, heavy, indolent, lackadaisical, languid, lazy, lethargic, lulling, napping, nodding, out of it*, restful, sluggish, slumberous, snoozy, somnolent, soothing, soporific, tired, torpid; SEE CONCEPTS 406,539

drudge [n] *slave, very hard worker*
factotum, grind*, laborer, menial, nose to grindstone*, peon*, plodder*, servant, toiler, workaholic, worker, workhorse; SEE CONCEPT 348

drudge [v] *work very hard*
back to the salt mines*, dig, grind*, hammer*, keep nose to grindstone*, labor, muck*, perform, plod, plow, plug away*, pound*, schlepp*, slave, slog, sweat, toil, travail; SEE CONCEPTS 87,100,324

drudgery [n] *hard, tedious work*
backbreaker*, chore, daily grind*, elbow grease*, grind*, gruntwork*, labor, menial labor, rat race, slavery, struggle, sweat, toil, travail, workout; SEE CONCEPT 362

drug [n] *medication*
biologic, cure, depressant, dope, essence, medicament, medicinal, medicine, narcotic, opiate, pharmaceutic, pharmaceutical, physic, pill, poison, potion, prescription, remedy, sedative, stimulant, tonic; SEE CONCEPT 307

drug [v] *put under influence of medication*
analgize, anesthetize, benumb, blunt, deaden, desensitize, dope*, dope up, dose, dose up*, fix, hit, knock out*, medicate, narcotize, numb, poison, relax, sedate, stupefy, treat; SEE CONCEPT 310

drugged [adj] *under the influence of medication*
benumbed, blown away*, coked*, comatose, dazed, doped, dopey*, floating*, flying*, high*, junked-up*, loaded*, narcotized, on a trip*, out of it*, ripped*, smashed*, spaced-out*, stoned*, strung out*, stupefied, unconscious; SEE CONCEPT 314

drum [v] *beat, tap a beat*
boom*, pulsate, rap, reverberate, roar, strum, tat-

too, throb, thrum, thunder*; SEE CONCEPTS 65,189

drum into [v] *make a point strongly*
din into, drive home*, hammer away*, harp on*, instill, reiterate; SEE CONCEPTS 49,75

drum up [v] *gather support for something*
attract, bid for, canvass, discover, obtain, petition, round up, solicit, succeed in finding; SEE CONCEPTS 68,300

drunk/drunkard [n] *person who is inebriated*
alcoholic, boozer*, carouser*, dipsomaniac, drinker, guzzler*, inebriate, lush*, sot*, sponge*, wino*; SEE CONCEPT 423

drunk [adj] *intoxicated by alcohol*
bashed, befuddled, boozed up*, buzzed*, crocked*, feeling no pain*, flushed*, flying*, fuddled, glazed*, groggy, high*, inebriated, juiced*, laced*, liquored up*, lit*, lush, muddled, plastered*, potted*, seeing double*, sloshed*, stewed*, stoned*, tanked*, three sheets to the wind*, tight*, tipsy, totaled*, under the influence, under the table*, wasted*; SEE CONCEPTS 314,545

dry [adj1] *moistureless*
anhydrous, arid, athirst, baked, bald, bare, barren, dehydrated, depleted, desert, desiccant, desiccated, drained, dried-up, droughty, dusty, evaporated, exhausted, hard, impoverished, juiceless, not irrigated, parched, rainless, sapless, sapped, sear, shriveled, stale, thirsty, torrid, unmoistened, waterless; SEE CONCEPT 603

dry [adj2] *dull, uninteresting*
apathetic, blah, boring, bromidic, draggy, dreary, dull as dishwater*, dusty, ho hum* impassive, inelaborate, insipid, matter-of-fact, modest, monotonous, naked, phlegmatic, plain, simple, tedious, tiresome, trite, weariful, wearisome; SEE CONCEPT 529

dry [adj3] *sarcastic, sharp-tongued*
acerbic, arcane, biting, caustic, cutting, cynical, deadpan, droll, harsh, humorous, ironical, keen, low-key, restrained, salty, sardonic, satirical, sharp, sly, sour, subtle, tart; SEE CONCEPT 267

dry [v] *take moisture out of*
anhydrate, bake, blot, concentrate, condense, de humidify, dehydrate, deplete, desiccate, drain, empty, evaporate, exhaust, exsiccate, freeze-dry, harden, kiln, mummify, parch, scorch, sear, shrivel, soak up, sponge, stale, swab, torrefy, towel, wilt, wipe, wither, wizen; SEE CONCEPTS 250,469

dual [adj] *two-fold*
bifold, binal, binary, coupled, double, double-header, duple, duplex, duplicate, matched, paired, twin; SEE CONCEPTS 762,771

dub [v] *name, label something*
baptize, bestow, call, christen, confer, denominate, designate, entitle, knight, nickname, style, tag, term, title; SEE CONCEPT 62

dubious [adj1] *doubtful*
arguable, chancy, debatable, diffident, disputable, dubitable, equivocal, far-fetched, fishy*, fly-by-night*, hesitant, iffy*, improbable, indecisive, moot, mootable, open, perplexed, problematical, questionable, reluctant, shady, skeptical, suspect, suspicious, touch and go*, trustless, unassured, uncertain, unclear, unconvinced, undecided, undependable, unlikely, unreliable, unsure, untrustworthy, untrusty, wavering; SEE CONCEPT 552

dubious [adj2] *vague, unclear*
ambiguous, debatable, disinclined, doubtful, equivocal, indefinite, indeterminate, mistrustful, obscure, open, problematic, problematical, undecided, unsettled; SEE CONCEPTS 535,576

duck [v] *drop down; avoid*
bend, bob, bow, crouch, dip, dive, dodge, double, elude, escape, evade, fence, lower, lurch, move to side, parry, plunge, shirk, shun, shy, sidestep, stoop, submerge; SEE CONCEPTS 102,154,181

duct [n] *channel, pipe*
aqueduct, canal, conduit, course, funnel, passage, tube, vessel, watercourse; SEE CONCEPT 501

ductile [adj] *pliant, flexible*
adaptable, amenable, biddable, docile, extensile, malleable, manageable, moldable, plastic, pliable, responsive, submitting, supple, tractable, yielding; SEE CONCEPTS 488,490

dud [n] *failure*
bomb, bummer, bust, debacle, flop, lemon, loser, washout; SEE CONCEPT 674

due [n] *expected reward*
be in line for*, claim, comeuppance, compensation, deserts*, entitlement, guerdon, interest, merits, need, payment, perquisite, prerogative, privilege, rate, recompense, repayment, reprisal, retaliation, retribution, revenge, right, rights, satisfaction, title, vengeance, what is coming to one*; SEE CONCEPTS 337,710

due [adj1] *unpaid; owing money*
chargeable, collectible, expected, in arrears, IOU, mature, not met, outstanding, overdue, owed, payable, receivable, scheduled, to be paid, unliquidated, unsatisfied, unsettled; SEE CONCEPT 334

due [adj2] *appropriate, proper*
becoming, coming, condign, deserved, earned, equitable, fair, fit, fitting, good, just, justified, merited, obligatory, requisite, rhadamanthine, right, rightful, suitable; SEE CONCEPT 558

due [adv] *directly*
dead, direct, exactly, right, straight, straightly, undeviatingly; SEE CONCEPTS 581,799

dues [n] *payment for membership*
ante, arrearage, assessment, charge, charges, collection, contribution, custom, debit, debt, duty, fee, kickback, levy, liability, obligation, pay, protection, rates, tax, toll; SEE CONCEPTS 344,679

dull [adj1] *unintelligent*
addled, backward, besotted, boring, brainless, daffy, daft, dense, dim, dim-witted, dumb, feeble-minded, half-baked, ignorant, imbecilic, indolent, insensate, low, moronic, not bright, numskulled, obtuse, scatterbrained, shallow, simple, simple-minded, slow, sluggish, stolid, stupid, tedious, thick, unintellectual, vacuous, wearisome, witless; SEE CONCEPT 402

dull [adj2] *insensitive*
accustomed, apathetic, blank, boring, callous, colorless, dead, depressed, empty, even, flat, heavy, impassible, inactive, indifferent, inert, insensible, jejune, languid, lifeless, listless, lumpy, monotonous, passionless, placid, prosaic, quiet, regular, routine, slack, slow, sluggish, spiritless, stagnant, still, stolid, torpid, unexciting, unresponsive, unsympathetic, usual, vacuous; SEE CONCEPT 542

dull [adj3] *boring, uninteresting*
abused, archaic, arid, big yawn*, blah, colorless,

dr
du

common, commonplace, dead, dismal, dreary, driveling, dry, familiar, flat, hackneyed, heavy, hoary, ho hum*, humdrum*, insipid, jejune, long-winded, monotonous, oft-repeated*, ordinary, out-of-date, plain, pointless, prolix, prosaic, prosy, repetitious, repetitive, routine, run-of-the-mill*, soporific, stale, stock, stupid, tame, tedious, tired, tiresome, trite, unimaginative, uninspiring, usual, usual thing, vapid, worn-out; SEE CONCEPTS 529,530

dull [adj4] not sharp
blunt, blunted, edentate, edgeless, flat, not keen, obtuse, pointless, round, square, toothless, turned, unpointed, unsharpened; SEE CONCEPT 486

dull [adj5] uneventful
accustomed, apathetic, blah, boring, dead, depressed, draggy*, even, falling off, flat, inactive, inert, languid, lifeless, listless, monotonous, placid, quiet, regular, routine, sitting tight*, slack, slothful, slow, sluggish, stagnant, still, stolid, tight, torpid, unexciting, unresponsive, usual, without incident, yawn; SEE CONCEPT 548

dull [adj6] drab, lackluster in effect on senses
ashen, black, blind, cloudy, cold, colorless, dark, dead, dim, dingy, dismal, dun, dusky, faded, feeble, flat, grimy, hazy, indistinct, leaden, lifeless, low, matte, mousy, muddy, muffled, murky, muted, obscure, opaque, overcast, plain, shadowy, sober, soft, softened, somber, sooty, subdued, subfusc, toned-down, unlit; SEE CONCEPTS 594,617

duly [adv] accordingly, properly
appropriately, at the proper time, befittingly, correctly, decorously, deservedly, on time, punctually, rightfully, suitably; SEE CONCEPTS 558,799

dumb [adj1] unable to speak
at a loss for words*, inarticulate, incoherent, mousy*, mum, mute, quiet, silent, soundless, speechless, tongue-tied, uncommunicative, voiceless, wordless; SEE CONCEPT 593

dumb [adj2] stupid, unintelligent
dense, dim-witted, doltish, dull, feebleminded, foolish, moronic, simple-minded, thick*; SEE CONCEPT 402

dumbbell [n] stupid person
dodo*, dolt, dullard, dumbo*, dumdum*, dummy, dunce, idiot, ignoramus, moron, simpleton; SEE CONCEPTS 412,423

dumbfound [v] astound, confuse
amaze, astonish, bewilder, blow away*, blow one's mind*, boggle, bowl over*, confound, flabbergast, knock over with feather*, nonplus, overwhelm, puzzle, stagger, startle, stun, surprise, take aback, throw, throw into a tizzy*; SEE CONCEPTS 16,42

dumbfounded [adj] astounded, confused
agape, aghast, amazed, astonished, bamboozled*, beat, bewildered, blown away*, bowled over*, breathless, buffaloed*, confounded, dismayed, dumb, flabbergasted, floored, knocked, licked, nonplused, overcome, overwhelmed, puzzled, shocked, speechless, staggered, startled, stuck, stumped, stunned, surprised, taken aback, thrown, thunderstruck*; SEE CONCEPT 403

dummy [n1] mannequin
copy, counterfeit, duplicate, figure, form, imitation, manikin, model, ringer*, sham*, stand-in, sub, substitute; SEE CONCEPTS 436,716

dummy [n2] stupid person
blockhead*, dimwit*, dolt*, dullard*, dunce, fool, idiot, ignoramus, moron, numbskull, oaf, simpleton; SEE CONCEPTS 412,423

dump [n1] junkyard
ash heap*, cesspool, depot, dumping ground, garbage lot, junk pile*, magazine, refuse heap, rubbish pile, swamp; SEE CONCEPTS 438,449,680

dump [n2] slummy establishment
hole, hovel, joint*, mess*, pigpen*, pigsty*, shack, shanty, slum, sty; SEE CONCEPTS 449,673

dump [v] drop, throw away
cast, chuck, clear out, deep-six*, deposit, discard, discharge, dispose of, ditch, drain, eject, empty, evacuate, expel, exude, fling, fling down, get rid of, jettison, junk, leave, let fall, scrap, throw down, throw out, throw overboard*, tip, unload, unpack; SEE CONCEPTS 180,181

dunce [n] stupid person
ass, birdbrain*, blockhead*, bonehead*, buffoon, dimwit*, dolt, donkey*, dope, dork*, drip*, dullard, dunderhead*, fool, goof, goof ball*, half-wit, idiot, ignoramus, imbecile, jerk, knucklehead*, lame-brain*, lightweight*, moron, nerd*, nincompoop*, ninny*, nitwit, numskull, oaf, pinhead*, scatterbrain*, schnook*, simpleton, twit*; SEE CONCEPTS 412,423

dunk [v] dip in liquid
douse, duck, immerse, saturate, soak, sop, souse, submerge, submerse; SEE CONCEPT 256

duo [n] twosome
brace, couple, doublet, dyad, pair; SEE CONCEPT 787

dupe [n] person who is fooled
butt*, chump*, easy mark*, fish*, fool, mark*, patsy*, pigeon*, pushover*, sap*, sitting duck*, sucker, victim; SEE CONCEPT 423

dupe [v] fool someone
baffle, bamboozle*, beguile, betray, catch, cheat, chicane, circumvent, con, cozen, deceive, defraud, delude, double-cross, dust*, flimflam*, gull, hoax, hoodwink*, hornswoggle, jerk around*, kid, mislead, outwit, overreach, pull one's leg*, pull something*, rip off*, rook*, rope in*, shaft, spoof, swindle, trick, victimize; SEE CONCEPT 59

duplicate [n] copy, reproduction
analogue, carbon, carbon copy*, chip off the old block*, clone, companion, coordinate, copycat*, correlate, counterfeit, counterpart, counterscript, dead ringer*, ditto*, double, dupe*, duplication, facsimile, fake, fellow, germination, imitation, knockoff*, likeness, lookalike, match, mate, obverse, parallel, phony, photocopy, photostat, pirate, reciprocal, recurrence, repetition, replica, replication, repro*, ringer*, second, similarity, spitting image*, stat, twin, Xerox*; SEE CONCEPTS 664,667,716

duplicate [adj] matching
alike, corresponding, dualistic, duple, duplex, equal, equivalent, identic, identical, indistinguishable, same, self-same, tantamount, twin, twofold, very same; SEE CONCEPTS 563,566

duplicate [v] make a copy; repeat
act like, clone, copy, counterfeit, ditto*, do again, do a takeoff*, do like*, double, dualize, dupe, echo, fake, go like*, imitate, knock off*, make like*, make replica, make twofold, manifold, mimeo, mirror, multiply, phony, photocopy, photostat, pirate*, redo, redouble, reduplicate, re-

make, replicate, repro, reproduce, rework, stat, take off as*, trace, Xerox*; SEE CONCEPTS *91,171*

duplicity [n] *deception*
artifice, chicanery, cunning, deceit, dirty dealing*, dirty pool*, dirty trick, dirty work*, dishonesty, dissemblance, dissimulation, double-dealing, dualism, duality, faithlessness, falsehood, fraud, guile, hypocrisy, Judas kiss*, one-upmanship, perfidiousness, perfidy, skullduggery, stab in back*, treacherousness, treachery, two-facedness*, twoness; SEE CONCEPTS *59,63*

durability [n] *sturdiness over time*
backbone, constancy, durableness, endurance, grit, guts*, gutsiness, hard as nails*, heart*, imperishability, intestinal fortitude, lastingness, moxie*, permanence, persistence, stamina, starch*, staying power*, stick-to-itiveness*; SEE CONCEPTS *721,731,732*

durable [adj] *sturdy, long-lasting*
abiding, constant, dependable, diuturnal, enduring, fast, firm, fixed, impervious, lasting, long-continued, perdurable, perduring, permanent, persistent, reliable, resistant, sound, stable, stout, strong, substantial, tenacious, tough; SEE CONCEPTS *482,488,489*

duration [n] *length of action, event*
continuance, continuation, continuity, endurance, extent, period, perpetuation, persistence, prolongation, run, span, spell, stretch, term, tide, time; SEE CONCEPT *804*

duress [n] *threat, hardship*
bondage, captivity, coercion, compulsion, confinement, constraint, control, detention, discipline, force, imprisonment, incarceration, pressure, restraint, violence; SEE CONCEPTS *14,674*

during [prep] *concurrently with an activity, event*
all along, all the while, amid, as, at the same time, at the time, for the time being, in the course of, in the interim, in the meanwhile, in the middle of, in the time of, meanwhile, mid, midst, over, pending, the time between, the whole time, throughout, until, when, while; SEE CONCEPT *820*

dusk [n] *early evening*
dark, dimday, dimmet, eventide, gloaming, gloom, night, nightfall, sundown, sunset, twilight; SEE CONCEPT *810*

dusky [adj] *dark-hued; murky*
adusk, bistered, bleak, brunette, caliginous, cheerless, cloudy, crepuscular, dark, dark-complexioned, darkish, desolate, dim, dismal, dull, funereal, gloomy, joyless, lightless, obscure, overcast, sable, shadowy, shady, swart, swarthy, tenebrous, twilight, twilit, unilluminated, veiled; SEE CONCEPTS *617,618*

dust [n] *tiny particles in the air*
ashes, cinders, dirt, dust bunnies*, earth, filth, flakes, fragments, gilings, granules, grime, grit, ground, lint, loess, powder, refuse, sand, smut, soil, soot; SEE CONCEPT *437*

dust [v] *sprinkle tiny particles*
besprinkle, cover, dredge, powder, scatter, sift, spray, spread; SEE CONCEPTS *172,222*

dusty [adj] *filled with or covered with powdery particles*
arenaceous, arenose, chalky, crumbly, dirty, friable, granular, grubby, sandy, sooty, unclean, undusted, unswept, untouched; SEE CONCEPT *485*

dutiful [adj] *obedient*
binding, compliant, conscientious, deferential, devoted, docile, duteous, faithful, incumbent on,

obligatory, punctilious, regardful, respectful, reverential, submissive; SEE CONCEPT *542*

duty [n1] *responsibility, assignment*
burden, business, calling, charge, chore, commission, commitment, committal, contract, devoir, dues, engagement, function, hook*, job, load, millstone*, minding the store*, mission, must, need, obligation, occupation, office, onus, ought*, pains, part, province, role, service, station, string*, taking care of business*, task, trouble, trust, undertaking, weight, work; SEE CONCEPTS *362,376,679*

duty [n2] *tax on foreign goods*
assessment, custom, customs, due, excise, impost, levy, rate, revenue, tariff, toll; SEE CONCEPT *329*

duty [n3] *moral obligation*
accountability, accountableness, allegiance, amenability, answerability, burden, call of duty, charge, conscience, deference, devoir, faithfulness, good faith, honesty, integrity, liability, loyalty, obedience, pledge, respect, reverence; SEE CONCEPT *388*

dwarf [n] *very small person*
bantam, dwarfling, homunculus, Lilliputian*, midget, Tom Thumb*; SEE CONCEPT *424*

dwarf [adj] *miniature, tiny*
baby, diminutive, low, petite, pocket, small, undersized; SEE CONCEPT *773*

dwarf [v] *minimize*
belittle, check, detract from, dim, diminish, dominate, hinder, look down upon, lower, make small, micrify, minify, overshadow, predominate, retard, rise above, stunt, suppress, tower above, tower over; SEE CONCEPTS *7,19,698,741*

dwell [v] *live in*
abide, bide, bunk*, continue, crash*, establish oneself, exist, flop*, hang one's hat*, hang out*, hole up*, inhabit, keep house, locate, lodge, make one's home, nest, occupy, park*, perch*, pitch tent*, quarter, remain, rent, reside, rest, room, roost*, settle, sojourn, squat*, stay, stop, tarry, tenant, tent; SEE CONCEPT *226*

dwelling [n] *home*
abode, castle, commorancy, den, digs*, domicile, dump*, establishment, habitat, habitation, haunt, hole in the wall*, house, lodging, pad, quarters, residence, residency; SEE CONCEPT *516*

dwell on/dwell upon [v] *linger over; be engrossed in*
consider, continue, elaborate, emphasize, expatiate, harp on*, involve oneself, tarry over; SEE CONCEPTS *17,239*

dwindle [v] *waste away; taper off*
abate, bate, become smaller, close, contract, decay, decline, decrease, die away, die down, die out, diminish, drain, drop, ebb, fade, fall, grow less, lessen, peter out*, pine, shrink, shrivel, sink, slack off*, subside, taper, wane, weaken, wither; SEE CONCEPTS *698,776*

dye [n] *coloring agent*
color, colorant, dyestuff, pigment, stain, tincture, tinge, tint; SEE CONCEPT *259*

dye [v] *change color with mixture*
impregnate, pigment, stain, tincture, tinge, tint; SEE CONCEPT *250*

dying [adj] *failing, expiring*
at death's door*, at end of rope*, decaying, declining, disintegrating, done for*, doomed, ebbing, fading, fated, final, giving up the ghost*,

going, in extremis, moribund, mortal, one foot in grave*, on last leg*, passing, perishing, sinking, vanishing, withering; SEE CONCEPT 539

dynamic [adj] active, vital

activating, aggressive, changing, charismatic, coming on strong*, compelling, driving, effective, electric, energetic, energizing, enterprising, forceful, forcible, go-ahead*, go-getter*, go-getting*, high-powered, hyped-up, influential, intense, lively, lusty, magnetic, peppy*, play for keeps*, play hard ball*, potent, powerful, productive, progressive, red-blooded*, strenuous, vehement, vigorous, vitalizing, zippy*; SEE CONCEPTS 404,540,542

dynasty [n] area of rule

absolutism, ascendancy, dominion, empire, government, house, regime, sovereignty, sway; SEE CONCEPTS 435,508,710

dysfunctional [adj] socially impaired

broken, debilitated, decayed, defective, deteriorated, flawed, inhibited, maladjusted, malfunctional, sick, undermined, unfit, wounded; SEE CONCEPT 314

E

each [adj] every

all, any, exclusive, individual, one by one*, particular, personal, piece by piece*, respective, separate, several, single, specific, various, without exception; SEE CONCEPT 577

each [adv] apiece; for one

all, a pop*, a shot*, aside, a throw*, by the, every, individually, per, per capita, per head, per person, per unit, proportionately, respectively, separately, singly, without exception; SEE CONCEPT 577

each [prep] each one

each and every one*, each other, every last one, every one, one, one and all*, one another; SEE CONCEPT 577

eager [adj] anxious, enthusiastic

acquisitive, agog, ambitious, antsy, appetent, ardent, athirst, avid, breathless, champing at the bit*, covetous, craving, desiring, desirous, dying to, earnest, fervent, fervid, greedy, gung ho*, hankering, heated, hot*, hot to trot*, hungry*, impatient, intent, keen, longing, pining, rarin' to go*, ready and willing*, restive, restless, self-starting, solicitous, thirsty, vehement, voracious, warmblooded*, wild, wishful, yearning, zealous; SEE CONCEPTS 326,401,542

eagerness [n] enthusiasm, anxiousness

alacrity, ambition, anticipation, ardor, avidity, earnestness, excitement, fervor, greediness, gusto, heartiness, hunger, impatience, impetuosity, intentness, keenness, longing, promptness, quickness, solicitude, thirst, vehemence, voracity, yearning, zeal, zest, zing*; SEE CONCEPTS 20,633,657

ear [n] attention

appreciation, consideration, discrimination, hearing, heed, mark, mind, note, notice, observance, observation, perception, regard, remark, sensitivity, taste; SEE CONCEPT 532

early [adj1] in the beginning

a bit previous, aboriginal, ancient, antecedent, antediluvian, antiquated, brand-new, budding, early bird*, fresh, initial, new, original, preceding, premier, prevenient, previous, primal, prime, primeval, primitive, primordial, prior, pristine, proleptical, raw, recent, undeveloped, young; SEE CONCEPTS 799,828

early [adj2] sooner than expected

advanced, ahead of time, anticipative, anticipatory, before appointed time, beforehand, direct, immature, immediate, matinal, on short notice*, on the dot*, overearly, oversoon, preceding, precipitant, precocious, preexistent, premature, previous, prompt, pronto, punctual, quick, seasonable, soon, speedy, unanticipated, unexpected, untimely; SEE CONCEPT 820

early [adv1] sooner than expected

a bit previous, ahead of time, anon, beforehand, before long, betimes, briefly, bright and early*, directly, early bird*, ere long, far ahead, immediately, in advance, in good time*, in the bud*, in time, on short notice*, on the dot*, oversoon, prematurely, presently, previous, promptly, pronto, proximately, quick, shortly, soon, too soon, unexpectedly, with time to spare*; SEE CONCEPT 820

early [adv2] immediately

at once, betimes, directly, first, freshly, in a jiffy*, in an instant*, in no time*, instantaneously, instantly, newly, presto, primitively, promptly, recently, right away, seasonably, soon, straightaway, summarily, thereon, thereupon, timely, without delay; SEE CONCEPTS 799,828

earmark [n] signature characteristic

attribute, differential, distinction, feature, hallmark, label, marking, peculiarity, quality, stamp, tag, token, trademark, trait; SEE CONCEPT 644

earmark [v] reserve

allocate, designate, keep back, label, maintain, mark out, name, set aside, slot, tab, tag; SEE CONCEPT 129

earn [v1] make money

acquire, attain, be gainfully employed, be in line for*, bring home*, bring home the bacon*, bring home the groceries*, bring in, clean up*, clear*, collect, consummate, cop*, derive, draw, effect, gain, gather, get, gross, hustle, make, make fast buck*, make it big*, net, obtain, pay one's dues*, perform, pick up, procure, profit, pull*, pull down*, rate, realize, reap, receive, scare up*, score*, scrape together*, secure, snag*, sock*, turn, win, wrangle; SEE CONCEPTS 330,351

earn [v2] deserve a reward

acquire, attain, bag, be entitled to, be worthy of, come by, gain, harvest, merit, net, rate, reap, score, warrant, win; SEE CONCEPTS 120,129

earnest [adj1] very enthusiastic

ardent, busy, devoted, diligent, eager, fervent, fervid, heartfelt, impassioned, industrious, keen, passionate, perseverant, purposeful, sedulous, sincere, urgent, vehement, warm, wholehearted, zealous; SEE CONCEPTS 326,401,542

earnest [adj2] serious; very important

close, constant, determined, firm, fixed, for real, grave, intent, mean business, meaningful, no-fooling, no-nonsense, playing hard ball*, resolute, resolved, sedate, sincere, sober, solemn, somber, stable, staid, steady, thoughtful, weighty; SEE CONCEPT 568

earnestness [n] *determination; seriousness*

absorption, ardor, attentiveness, concentration, decision, deliberation, devotion, doggedness, eagerness, engrossment, enthusiasm, fervor, firmness, gravity, intensity, intentness, keenness, passion, perseverance, persistence, purposefulness, resolution, resolve, serious-mindedness, sincerity, sobriety, solemnity, stress, tenacity, urgency, vehemence, warmth, zeal; SEE CONCEPTS 633,657

earnings [n] *money for work performed*

balance, bottom line*, emolument, gain, gate, groceries*, income, in the black*, lucre, net, pay, payoff, piece of the pie*, proceeds, profit, receipts, remuneration, return, revenue, reward, salary, salt*, stipend, take-home*, takings, wages; SEE CONCEPT 344

Earth [n1] *the world*

apple*, big blue marble*, cosmos, creation, dust*, globe, macrocosm, orb, planet, sphere, star, sublunary world, terra, terra firma, terrene, terrestrial sphere, universe, vale; SEE CONCEPT 511

earth [n2] *ground, soil*

alluvium, clay, clod, coast, compost, deposit, dirt, dry land, dust, fill, glebe, gravel, humus, land, loam, marl, mold, muck, mud, peat moss, sand, shore, sod, subsoil, surface, terra firma, terrain, terrane, topsoil, turf; SEE CONCEPT 509

earthly [adj] *physically concerning land or its inhabitants*

alluvial, carnal, corporeal, geotic, global, human, in all creation, material, mortal, mundane, nonspiritual, physical, profane, secular, subastral, sublunary, tellurian, telluric, temporal, terraqueous, terrene, terrestrial, uncelestial, under the sun*, unspiritual, worldly; SEE CONCEPT 536

earthly [adj2] *conceivable*

feasible, imaginable, likely, mortal, possible, potential, practical, probable; SEE CONCEPT 552

earthquake [n] *tremor from inside the earth*

convulsion, fault, macroseism, microseism, movement, quake, quaker*, seismicity, seism, seismism, shake, shock, slip, temblor, trembler*, undulation, upheaval; SEE CONCEPTS 144,526

earthy [adj] *unsophisticated*

bawdy, coarse, crude, down, down home*, down-to-earth*, dull, easygoing, folksy, funky*, hard-boiled*, home folk*, homely, homey, indelicate, lowbred, lusty, mundane, natural, pragmatic, ribald, robust, rough, simple, unidealistic, uninhibited, unrefined; SEE CONCEPT 542

ease [n1] *peace, quiet; lack of difficulty*

affluence, ataraxia, bed of roses*, calm, calmness, comfort, content, contentment, easiness, enjoyment, gratification, happiness, idleness, inactivity, inertia, inertness, leisure, luxury, passivity, peace of mind*, prosperity, quietness, quietude, relaxation, repose, requiescence, rest, restfulness, satisfaction, security, serenity, supinity, tranquility; SEE CONCEPTS 388,410,673

ease [n2] *facility, freedom*

adroitness, affability, aplomb, breeze, child's play*, cinch, cleverness, composure, dexterity, dispatch, duck soup*, easygoingness, efficiency, effortlessness, expertise, expertness, familiarity, flexibility, fluency, informality, insouciance, knack, liberty, naturalness, nonchalance, poise, pushover, quickness, readiness, relaxedness, setup, simplicity, skillfulness, smoothness,

smooth sailing*, snap, unaffectedness, unconstraint, unreservedness; SEE CONCEPTS 376, 388,630

ease [v1] *alleviate, help*

abate, aid, allay, ameliorate, anesthetize, appease, assist, assuage, attend to, calm, cheer, clear the way*, comfort, cure, disburden, disengage, doctor, expedite, facilitate, forward, free, further, improve, lessen, let up on, lift, lighten, make easier, meliorate, mitigate, moderate, mollify, nurse, open the door*, pacify, palliate, promote, quiet, relax, release, relent, relieve, run interference for*, simplify, slacken, smooth, soften, soothe, speed, speed up, still, tranquilize, untighten; SEE CONCEPTS 110,310

ease [v2] *guide, move carefully*

disentangle, edge, extricate, facilitate, handle, inch, induce, insert, join, loose, loosen, maneuver, relax, remove, right, set right, slack, slacken, slide, slip, squeeze, steer, untighten; SEE CONCEPT 187

easily [adv1] *without difficulty*

calmly, comfortably, competently, conveniently, coolly, dexterously, efficiently, effortlessly, evenly, facilely, fluently, freely, handily, hand over fist*, hands down*, just like that*, lightly, like nothing*, no sweat*, nothing to it*, piece of cake*, plainly, quickly, readily, regularly, simply, smoothly, steadily, surely, swimmingly, uncomplicatedly, well, with ease, with no effort, without a hitch*, without trouble; SEE CONCEPT 565

easily [adv2] *without a doubt*

absolutely, actually, almost certainly, assuredly, beyond question, by far, certainly, clearly, decidedly, definitely, doubtless, doubtlessly, far and away, indeed, indisputably, indubitably, no doubt, plainly, positively, probably, really, surely, truly, undeniably, undoubtedly, unequivocally, unquestionably; SEE CONCEPTS 535,552

easy [adj1] *not difficult*

accessible, apparent, basic, child's play*, cinch, clear, easily done, effortless, elementary, evident, facile, inconsiderable, light, little, manageable, manifest, mere, no bother*, no problem*, no sweat*, not burdensome, nothing to it*, no trouble*, obvious, painless, paltry, picnic*, piece of cake*, plain, plain sailing*, pushover*, royal, simple, simple as ABC*, slight, smooth, snap, straightforward, uncomplicated, undemanding, uninvolved, untroublesome, wieldy, yielding; SEE CONCEPT 565

easy [adj2] *leisurely, relaxed*

at ease, calm, carefree, comfortable, comfy, commodious, composed, content, contented, cozy, cursive, cushy, easeful, effortless, flowing, fluent, forthright, gentle, in clover*, languid, light, mild, moderate, peaceful, pleasant, prosperous, quiet, running, satisfied, secure, serene, slow, smooth, snug, soft, spontaneous, substantial, successful, temperate, thriving, tranquil, undemanding, undisturbed, unexacting, unhurried, untroubled, unworried, well-to-do; SEE CONCEPTS 542,544

easy [adj3] *tolerant, permissive*

accommodating, amenable, benign, biddable, charitable, clement, compassionate, compliant, condoning, deceivable, deludable, dupable, easygoing, excusing, exploitable, fleeceable, flexible, forbearing, forgiving, gentle, gullible, humoring, indulgent, kindly, lax, lenient, liberal, light, merciful, mild, moderate, mollycoddling*, naive, pampering, pardoning, soft, spoiling, submissive, susceptible, sympathetic, temperate, tractable, trusting, unburdensome, unoppressive, unsuspicious; SEE CONCEPT 401

easy [adj4] good-humored
affable, amiable, at ease, carefree, casual, complaisant, diplomatic, familiar, friendly, gentle, good-natured, good-tempered, graceful, gracious, gregarious, informal, mild, natural, obliging, open, pleasant, polite, relaxed, secure, smooth, sociable, suave, tolerant, unaffected, unanxious, undemanding, unforced, unpretentious, urbane; SEE CONCEPT 404

easygoing [adj] complacent, permissive
amenable, breezy, calm, carefree, casual, collected, complaisant, composed, devil-may-care*, even-tempered*, flexible, free and easy*, hangloose*, happy-go-lucky*, indolent, indulgent, informal, insouciant, laid-back*, lazy, lenient, liberal, low-pressure, mild, moderate, nonchalant, offhand, outgiving, patient, placid, poised, relaxed, self-possessed, serene, tolerant, tranquil, unconcerned, uncritical, undemanding, unhurried, uninhibited; SEE CONCEPT 404

eat [v1] consume food
absorb, attack, banquet, bite, bolt*, break bread*, breakfast, chew, chow down*, cram*, devour, digest, dine, dispatch, dispose of, fall to, feast upon, feed, gobble up*, gorge, gormandize, graze*, have a bite*, have a meal, have for, ingest, inhale*, lunch, make pig of oneself*, masticate, munch, nibble, nosh*, partake of, peck at*, pick, pig out*, polish off*, pork out*, put away*, ruminate, scarf*, scoff, snack, sup, swallow, take food, take in, take nourishment, wolf; SEE CONCEPT 169

eat [v2] erode, wear away; use up
bite, condense, corrode, crumble, decay, decompose, disappear, disintegrate, dissipate, dissolve, drain, exhaust, gnaw, liquefy, melt, nibble, rot, run through, rust, spill, squander, vanish, waste away; SEE CONCEPTS 225,469

eatable [adj] able to be consumed
appetizing, comestible, culinary, delicious, delish*, dietary, digestible, edible, esculent, fit, good, harmless, kosher*, nutritious, nutritive, palatable, piquant, safe, satisfying, savory, scrumptious, succulent, tasty, tempting, wholesome, yummy*; SEE CONCEPTS 462,613

eating disorder [n] unhealthy disturbance in eating behavior
anorexia nervosa, bingeing, bulimarexia, bulimia, compulsive eating, hypheragia, pica, psychological disorder, purging; SEE CONCEPT 316

eavesdrop [v] listen without permission
be all ears*, bend an ear*, bug, ears into*, listen in, monitor, overhear, pry, snoop, spy, tap, tune in on*, wire, wiretap; SEE CONCEPTS 188,596

ebb [n] regression; decline
abatement, backflow, decay, decrease, degeneration, depreciation, deterioration, diminution, drop, dwindling, fading away, flagging, going out, lessening, low tide, low water, outward flow, petering out*, recession, refluence, reflux, retreat, retrocession, retroflux, shrinkage, sinking, slackening, subsidence, sweep, wane, waning, weakening, withdrawal; SEE CONCEPTS 195,698

ebb [v] subside; decline
abate, decay, decrease, degenerate, deteriorate,

die down, die out, diminish, drop, dwindle, ease off, fade away, fall, fall away, fall back, flag, flow back, go out, languish, lessen, let up, melt, moderate, peter out, recede, relent, retire, retreat, retrocede, shrink, sink, slacken, wane, weaken, withdraw; SEE CONCEPTS 195,698

ebullience [n] enthusiasm
agitation, animation, buoyancy, effervescence, effusiveness, elation, excitement, exhilaration, exuberance, exuberancy, ferment, gaiety, high-spiritedness, high spirits, liveliness, vitality, vivaciousness, vivacity, zest; SEE CONCEPT 633

ebullient [adj] enthusiastic
agitated, bouncy, brash, buoyant, chipper*, chirpy*, effervescent, effusive, elated, excited, exhilarated, exuberant, frothy*, gushing, high-spirited, in high spirits*, irrepressible, vivacious, zestful, zippy*; SEE CONCEPT 401

eccentric [n] person who is bizarre, unusual
beatnik, character, freak, hippie, kook, loner, maverick, nonconformist, nut*, oddball, oddity, odd person, original, queer duck*, rare bird*, three-dollar bill*, weirdo; SEE CONCEPT 423

eccentric [adj] bizarre, unusual
aberrant, abnormal, anomalous, beat*, bent*, bizarre, capricious, characteristic, cockeyed, crazy, curious, droll, erratic, far out*, flaky, freak, freakish, funky*, funny, idiosyncratic, irregular, kooky, nutty, odd, oddball, offbeat, off-center, off the wall*, out in left field*, outlandish, peculiar, quaint, queer, quirky, quizzical, singular, strange, uncommon, unconventional, unnatural, way out*, weird, whimsical, wild; SEE CONCEPTS 547,564

eccentricity [n] bizarreness, unusualness
aberration, abnormality, anomaly, caprice, capriciousness, foible, freakishness, hereticism, idiocracy, idiosyncrasy, irregularity, kink, nonconformity, oddity, oddness, outlandishness, peculiarity, queerness, quirk, singularity, strangeness, unconventionality, unorthodoxness, waywardness, weirdness, whimsicality, whimsicalness; SEE CONCEPTS 647,665

echelon [n] class, level
degree, file, grade, line, office, place, position, queue, rank, row, string, tier; SEE CONCEPTS 378,388

echo [n] repeat, copy
answer, imitation, mirror, mirror image, onomatopoeia, parallel, parroting, rebound, reflection, reiteration, repercussion, repetition, reply, reproduction, reverberation, ringing, rubber stamp*; SEE CONCEPTS 595,695,716

echo [v] repeat, copy
ape, ditto*, do like*, go like*, imitate, impersonate, make like*, mimic, mirror, parallel, parrot, react, recall, redouble, reflect, reiterate, reproduce, resemble, resound, respond, reverberate, ring, rubber-stamp*, second, vibrate; SEE CONCEPTS 91,171

eclectic [adj] comprehensive, general
all-embracing, assorted, broad, catholic, dilettantish, diverse, diversified, heterogeneous, inclusive, liberal, many-sided, mingled, mixed, multifarious, multiform, selective, universal, varied, wide-ranging; SEE CONCEPTS 537,772

eclipse [n] shadowing of the sun
concealment, darkening, decline, diminution, dimming, extinction, extinguishment, obliter-

tion, obscuration, occultation, penumbra, shading, shroud, veil; SEE CONCEPTS 522,624

eclipse [v1] *obscure, veil*
adumbrate, becloud, bedim, blot out, cloud, darken, dim, extinguish, murk, overshadow, shadow, shroud; SEE CONCEPT 250

eclipse [v2] *surpass achievement*
exceed, excel, outdo, outshine, overrun, surmount, tower above, transcend; SEE CONCEPT 141

economic [adj] *business-related; financial*
bread-and-butter*, budgetary, commercial, fiscal, industrial, material, mercantile, monetary, money-making, pecuniary, productive, profit-making, remunerative, solvent, viable; SEE CONCEPTS 334,536

economical [adj1] *conservative with resources; careful*
avaricious, canny, chary, circumspect, close, closefisted, cost-effective, curmudgeonly, efficient, frugal, meager, mean, methodical, miserly, money-saving, niggardly*, on the rims*, parsimonious, penny-pinching*, penny-wise*, penurious, practical, provident, prudent, prudential, saving, scrimping, skimping, spare, sparing, stingy, thrifty, tight, time-saving, unwasteful, watchful, work-saving; SEE CONCEPT 542

economical [adj2] *inexpensive*
bought for a song*, cheap, cost next to nothing*, cost nothing, cut rate, dime a dozen*, dirt cheap*, dog cheap*, fair, low, low-priced, low tariff, marked down, moderate, modest, on sale, quite a buy*, reasonable, reduced, sound, steal*; SEE CONCEPT 334

economize [v] *save money*
be frugal, be prudent, be sparing, conserve, cut back, cut corners*, cut down, keep within means, make ends meet*, manage, meet a budget, pay one's way*, pinch pennies*, retrench, run tight ship*, scrimp, shepherd, skimp, stint, stretch a dollar*, tighten one's belt*; SEE CONCEPT 330

economy [n] *saving, frugality*
abridgement, austerity, care, carefulness, caution, curtailment, cutback, decrease, deduction, direction, discretion, husbandry, layoff, meanness, miserliness, moratorium, niggardliness, parcity, parsimony, providence, prudence, recession, reduction, regulation; restraint, retrenchment, rollback, scrimping, shrinkage, skimping, sparingness, stinginess, supervision, thrift, thriftiness; SEE CONCEPTS 117,330,335

eco-rich [adj] *possessing an abundance of natural resources*
bountiful, clean, flowing, full, green, natural, plentiful, pure, rich; SEE CONCEPT 518

ecstasy [n] *bliss*
beatitude, blessedness, cool*, delectation, delight, delirium, ebullience, elation, enchantment, enthusiasm, euphoria, exaltation, felicity, fervor, frenzy, gladness, happiness, heaven, inspiration, intoxication, joy, joyfulness, paradise, rapture, ravishment, rhapsody, seventh heaven*, trance, transport, twilight zone*; SEE CONCEPT 410

ecstatic [adj] *very happy, blissful*
athrill, beatific, crazy, delirious, dreamy, elated, enraptured, enthusiastic, entranced, euphoric, fervent, floating, flying high*, frenzied, gone*, high*, in exaltation, in seventh heaven*, joyful, joyous, mad, on cloud nine*, out, overjoyed, pleased as punch*, rapturous, ravished, rhapsodic, sent*, sunny, thrilled, tickled pink*, tickled to

death*, transported*, turned on*, upbeat, wild; SEE CONCEPT 403

ecumenical [adj] *general*
all-comprehensive, all-inclusive, all-pervading, catholic, comprehensive, cosmic, cosmopolitan, global, inclusive, planetary, unifying, universal, worldwide; SEE CONCEPTS 537,772

edge [n1] *border, outline*
bend, berm, bound, boundary, brim, brink, butt, circumference, contour, corner, crook, crust, curb, end, extremity, frame, fringe, frontier, hem, hook, ledge, limb, limit, line, lip, margin, molding, mouth, outskirt, peak, perimeter, periphery, point, portal, rim, ring, shore, side, skirt, split, strand, term, threshold, tip, trimming, turn, verge; SEE CONCEPTS 484,513

edge [n2] *advantage*
allowance, ascendancy, bulge, dominance, draw, handicap, head start, lead, odds, start, superiority, upper hand*, vantage; SEE CONCEPT 712

edge [v1] *border, trim*
bind, bound, decorate, fringe, hem, margin, outline, rim, shape, skirt, surround, verge; SEE CONCEPTS 751,758

edge [v2] *defeat narrowly*
creep, ease, inch, infiltrate, nose out*, sidle, slip by, slip past, squeeze by*, squeeze past*, steal, worm*; SEE CONCEPT 95

edge [v3] *sharpen*
file, grind, hone, polish, sharpen, strop, whet; SEE CONCEPTS 137,250

edgy [adj] *nervous*
anxious, critical, excitable, excited, high-strung, ill at ease, impatient, irascible, irritable, keyed up*, overstrung, restive, restless, skittish, tense, touchy, uneasy, uptight; SEE CONCEPT 401

edible [adj] *able to be eaten*
comestible, digestible, eatable, esculent, fit, good, harmless, nourishing, nutritious, nutritive, palatable, savory, succulent, tasty, toothsome, wholesome; SEE CONCEPTS 462,613

edict [n] *pronouncement, order*
act, canon, command, commandment, decree, decretum, dictate, dictum, directive, enactment, fiat, injunction, instrument, judgment, law, mandate, manifesto, ordinance, precept, prescript, proclamation, pronunciamento, regulation, rule, ruling, statute, ukase, writ; SEE CONCEPTS 278,662,688

edification [n] *improvement, education*
betterment, elevation, elucidation, enhancement, enlightenment, guidance, illumination, information, instruction, irradiation, knowledge, learning, nurture, schooling, teaching, tuition, uplifting; SEE CONCEPTS 31,287,700

edifice [n] *structure*
building, construction, erection, habitation, house, monument, pile, rockpile*, skyscraper, towers; SEE CONCEPT 439

edit [v] *rewrite, refine*
adapt, alter, amplify, analyze, annotate, arrange, assemble, assign, blue-pencil*, boil down*, butcher, censor, check, choose, compile, compose, condense, correct, cut, delete, discard, doctor, draft, emend, excise, feature, fine-tune, finish, fly speck*, go over, make up, massage*, polish, prepare, prescribe, proofread, publish, put together, rearrange, recalibrate, rectify, redact, regulate, rehash, rephrase, report, revise, scrub*, select, set up, strike out, style, tighten, trim, write over; SEE CONCEPTS 79,126,203

ea
ed

edition [n] *issue of publication*
copy, impression, imprint, number, printing, program, publication, reissue, release, reprint, reprinting, version, volume; SEE CONCEPT *280*

educate [v] *teach information, experience*
brainwash*, brief, civilize, coach, cultivate, develop, discipline, drill, drum into, edify, enlighten, exercise, explain, foster, improve, indoctrinate, inform, instruct, let in on, mature, nurture, put hip*, put through the grind*, rear, school, show the ropes*, train, tutor; SEE CONCEPTS *61,285*

educated [adj] *learned, experienced*
accomplished, acquainted with, brainy, civilized, coached, corrected, cultivated, cultured, developed, enlightened, enriched, erudite, expert, finished, fitted, formed, informed, initiated, instructed, intelligent, knowledgeable, lettered, literary, literate, nurtured, polished, prepared, professional, refined, scholarly, schooled, scientific, shaped, skilled, tasteful, taught, trained, tutored, versed in, well-informed, well-read, well-taught, well-versed; SEE CONCEPT *402*

education [n] *instruction, development of knowledge*
apprenticeship, background, book learning*, brainwashing*, breeding, catechism, civilization, coaching, cultivation, culture, direction, discipline, drilling, edification, enlightenment, erudition, finish, guidance, improvement, inculcation, indoctrination, information, learnedness, learning, literacy, nurture, pedagogy, preparation, propagandism, proselytism, reading, rearing, refinement, scholarship, schooling, science, study, teaching, training, tuition, tutelage, tutoring; SEE CONCEPTS *285,287,409*

educe [v] *bring out, elicit*
come out, conclude, deduce, derive, develop, distill, drag, draw, draw out, evince, evoke, evolve, excogitate, extort, extract, gain, get, infer, milk*, obtain, procure, pull, reason, secure, think out, wrest, wring; SEE CONCEPTS *37,142*

eerie [adj] *spooky*
awesome, bizarre, crawly, creepy, fantastic, fearful, frightening, ghostly, mysterious, scary, spectral, strange, supernatural, superstitious, uncanny, unearthly, weird; SEE CONCEPT *537*

effect [n1] *result*
aftereffect, aftermath, backlash, backwash, can of worms*, causatum, chain reaction*, conclusion, consequence, corollary, denouement, development, end, end product, event, eventuality, fallout, flak*, follow through, follow-up, fruit, issue, outcome, outgrowth, precipitate, pursuance, ramification, reaction, reflex, repercussion, response, sequel, sequence, side effect, spin-off, upshot*, waves*; SEE CONCEPT *230*

effect [n2] *impact, impression*
action, clout, drift, effectiveness, efficacy, efficiency, enforcement, essence, execution, fact, force, implementation, import, imprint, influence, mark, meaning, power, purport, purpose, reality, sense, significance, strength, tenor, use, validity, vigor, weight; SEE CONCEPT *687*

effect [v] *carry out, accomplish*
achieve, actualize, actuate, begin, bring about, bring off, bring on, buy, carry through, cause, complete, conceive, conclude, consummate, create, do a number*, do one's thing*, do the job*, do the trick*, do to a T*, draw on, effectuate,

enact, enforce, execute, fulfill, generate, get across, get to, give rise to, implement, induce, initiate, invoke, make, make it*, make waves*, perform, procure, produce, pull it off*, put across, realize, render, secure, sell, turn out, turn the trick*, unzip*, yield; SEE CONCEPTS *91,706*

effective [adj1] *productive, persuasive*
able, active, adequate, capable, cogent, compelling, competent, convincing, direct, effectual, efficacious, efficient, emphatic, energetic, forceful, forcible, having lead in pencil*, impressive, live, moving, on the ball*, operative, playing hardball*, potent, powerful, powerhouse*, practical, producing, resultant, serviceable, serving, sound, striking, sufficient, telling, trenchant, useful, valid, virtuous, wicked*, yielding; SEE CONCEPTS *537,540*

effective [adj2] *in use at the time*
active, actual, current, direct, dynamic, in effect, in execution, in force, in operation, operative, real; SEE CONCEPTS *560,582,799*

effectiveness [n] *influence*
capability, clout, cogency, effect, efficacy, efficiency, force, forcefulness, performance, point, potency, power, punch, strength, success, use, validity, validness, verve, vigor, weight; SEE CONCEPTS *676,687*

effectual [adj] *influential; authoritative*
accomplishing, achieving, adequate, binding, capable, conclusive, decisive, determinative, effecting, effective, efficacious, efficient, forcible, fulfilling, in force, lawful, legal, licit, potent, powerful, practicable, productive, qualified, serviceable, sound, strong, successful, telling, useful, valid, virtuous, workable; SEE CONCEPTS *319,528,537*

effeminate [adj] *having female qualities*
epicene, feminine, womanish, womanlike, womanly; SEE CONCEPTS *401,404*

effervescence [n1] *fizz, foam*
bubbles, bubbling, ebullition, ferment, fermentation, froth, frothing, sparkle; SEE CONCEPTS *437,522*

effervescence [n2] *enthusiasm, vivacity*
animation, buoyancy, ebullience, excitedness, excitement, exhilaration, exuberance, exuberancy, gaiety, happiness, high spirits, joy, liveliness, vim, vitality, volatility, zing*; SEE CONCEPTS *633,657*

effervescent [adj1] *fizzing, foaming*
airy, boiling, bouncy, bubbling, bubbly, carbonated, elastic, expansive, fermenting, frothing, frothy, resilient, sparkling, volatile; SEE CONCEPTS *462,485*

effervescent [adj2] *enthusiastic, vivacious*
animated, bouncy, brash, bubbly, buoyant, ebullient, excited, exhilarated, exuberant, gleeful, happy, high-spirited, hilarious, in high spirits*, irrepressible, jolly, joyous, lively, merry, mirthful, sprightly, vital, zingy; SEE CONCEPTS *401,542*

effete [adj1] *spoiled, exhausted*
burnt out*, corrupt, debased, decadent, decayed, declining, decrepit, degenerate, dissipated, dissolute, drained, enervated, enfeebled, far-gone*, feeble, immoral, obsolete, overrefined, overripe, played out*, soft, spent, vitiated, washed-out*, wasted, weak, worn out; SEE CONCEPT *560*

effete [adj2] *unproductive*
barren, fruitless, impotent, infecund, infertile,

sterile, unfruitful, unprolific; SEE CONCEPT *527*

efficacious [*adj*] *efficient, productive*
active, adequate, capable, competent, effective, effectual, energetic, influential, operative, potent, powerful, puissant, serviceable, strong, successful, useful, virtuous; SEE CONCEPTS *528,537*

efficacy [*n*] *efficiency; productiveness*
ability, adequacy, capability, capableness, capacity, competence, effect, effectiveness, efficaciousness, energy, force, influence, performance, potency, power, strength, success, sufficiency, use, vigor, virtue, weight; SEE CONCEPTS *641,676,706*

efficiency [*n*] *adeptness, effectiveness*
ability, abundance, adaptability, address, adequacy, capability, capableness, competence, competency, completeness, economy, effectualness, efficacy, energy, expertise, facility, faculty, know-how, performance, potency, power, powerfulness, productiveness, productivity, proficiency, prowess, quantity, readiness, resourcefulness, response, skill, skillfulness, suitability, suitableness, talent, thoroughness; SEE CONCEPTS *409,630,658*

efficient [*adj*] *adept, effective*
able, accomplished, active, adapted, adequate, apt, businesslike, capable, clever, competent, conducive, decisive, deft, dynamic, economic, economical, effectual, effectual, efficacious, energetic, equal to, experienced, expert, familiar with, fitted, good at, good for, handy, masterly, organized, potent, powerful, practiced, productive, proficient, profitable, qualified, ready, saving, shrewd, skilled, skillful, systematic, talented, tough, useful, valuable, virtuous, well-organized; SEE CONCEPTS *402,527,560*

effigy [*n*] *dummy*
figure, icon, idol, image, likeness, model, picture, portrait, puppet, representation, statue; SEE CONCEPT *436*

effort [*n*] *work, exertion*
accomplishment, achievement, act, aim, application, aspiration, attempt, battle, crack*, creation, deed, discipline, drill, elbow grease*, endeavor, energy, enterprise, essay, exercise, feat, fling*, force, go*, industry, intention, job, labor, old college try*, pains, power, product, production, pull, purpose, push, resolution, shot*, spurt, stab*, strain, stress, stretch, strife, striving, struggle, sweat, tension, toil, training, travail, trial, trouble, try, tug*, undertaking, venture, whack*; SEE CONCEPTS *87,362,677,724*

effortless [*adj*] *easy*
child's play*, cursive, duck soup*, facile, flowing, fluent, light, no problem*, no sweat*, offhand, painless, picnic*, piece of cake*, royal, running, simple, smooth, snap*, uncomplicated, undemanding, untroublesome; SEE CONCEPT *565*

effrontery [*n*] *nerve, boldness*
arrogance, assurance, audacity, backtalk, brashness, brass*, brazenness, cheek*, cheekiness, chutzpah*, crust*, disrespect, face, gall, guff, hardihood, impertinence, impudence, incivility, insolence, lip*, presumption, rudeness, sass, sauce*, self-assurance, self-confidence, shamelessness, smart talk, temerity; SEE CONCEPTS *411,633*

effulgent [*adj*] *glowing, luminous*
beaming, blazing, bright, brilliant, dazzling, flaming, fluorescent, incandescent, lambent, lucent, lustrous, radiant, resplendent, shining, splendid, vivid; SEE CONCEPT *617*

effusion [*n*] *outpouring*
address, diffusion, discharge, effluence, effluvium, efflux, emanation, emission, exudate, gush, gushing, ooze, outflow, pouring, shedding, stream, verbosity, wordiness; SEE CONCEPTS *179,266*

effusive [*adj*] *gushing, profuse*
all jaw*, big mouthed*, demonstrative, ebullient, enthusiastic, expansive, extravagant, exuberant, free-flowing, fulsome, gabby*, gushy*, lavish, outpouring, overflowing, prolix, talkative, unconstrained, unreserved, unrestrained, verbose, windbag*, windy*, wordy; SEE CONCEPTS *267,542*

egg [*n*] *seed, cell; embryo of an animal*
bud, cackle*, cackleberry*, germ, nucleus, oospore, ovum, roe, rudiment, spawn, yellow eye*; SEE CONCEPTS *389,392*

egg on [*v*] *push to do something*
agitate, arouse, drive, encourage, excite, exhort, goad, incite, instigate, pique, prick, prod, prompt, propel, rally, sic, spur, stimulate, stir up, urge, whip up; SEE CONCEPT *68*

ego [*n*] *personality*
character, psyche, self, self-admiration, selfdom, self-pride; SEE CONCEPT *411*

egocentric [*adj*] *thinking very highly of oneself*
conceited, egoistic, egoistical, egomaniacal, egotistic, egotistical, individualist, individualistic, megalomaniac, narcissistic, pompous, self-absorbed, self-centered, self-concerned, self-indulgent, self-interested, selfish, self-loving, self-serving, stuck-up, vainglorious, wrapped up in oneself; SEE CONCEPT *404*

egoism/egotism [*n*] *self-centeredness*
arrogance, assurance, boastfulness, boasting, bragging, conceit, conceitedness, egocentricity, egomania, gasconade, haughtiness, insolence, megalomania, narcissism, ostentation, overconfidence, preoccupation with self, presumption, pride, self-absorption, self-admiration, self-confidence, self-importance, self-interest, selfishness, self-love, self-possession, self-regard, self-worship, superiority, swellheadedness, vainglory, vanity, vaunting; SEE CONCEPT *411*

egotistic/egoistic [*adj*] *thinking very highly of oneself*
affected, aloof, autocratic, boastful, boasting, bragging, conceited, egocentric, egomaniacal, haughty, individualistic, inflated, inner directed, intimate, intrinsic, introverted, isolated, narcissistic, obsessive, opinionated, personal, pompous, prideful, proud, puffed up*, self-absorbed, self-admiring, self-centered, self-important, snobbish, stuck on oneself*, stuck-up*, subjective, superior, swollen, vain, vainglorious; SEE CONCEPT *404*

egregious [*adj*] *outstandingly bad; outrageous*
arrant, atrocious, capital, deplorable, extreme, flagrant, glaring, grievous, gross*, heinous, infamous, insufferable, intolerable, monstrous, nefarious, notorious, outright, preposterous, rank, scandalous, shocking, stark; SEE CONCEPTS *545,548,570*

egress [*n*] *passage out*
departure, doorway, emanation, emergence, escape, exit, exiting, exodus, issue, opening, outlet, setting-out, vent, way out, withdrawal; SEE CONCEPTS *195,440*

ed
eg

eject [v] *throw or be thrown out*
banish, bounce*, bump, cast out, debar, disbar, discharge, disgorge, dislodge, dismiss, displace, dispossess, ditch, do away with*, drive off, dump*, eighty-six*, ejaculate, eliminate, emit, eradicate, eruct, erupt, evict, exclude, expel, expulse, extrude, fire, force out, get rid of, give the boot*, heave out*, irrupt, kick out*, kiss good-bye*, oust, reject, rout, sack, send packing*, show the gate to*, spew, spit out, spout, squeeze out, throw overboard*, turn out, unloose, vomit; SEE CONCEPTS *179,222*

eke out [v] *make something last*
barely exist, be economical with, be frugal with, be sparing with, economize on, get by*, stretch out; SEE CONCEPT *239*

elaborate [adj] *intricate; involved*
busy, careful, complex, complicated, decorated, detailed, elegant, embellished, exact, extensive, extravagant, fancy, fussy, garnished, highly wrought, high tech*, imposing, knotty, labored, labyrinthine, luxurious, many-faceted, minute, ornamented, ornate, ostentatious, overdone, overworked, painstaking, perfected, plush, posh, precise, prodigious, refined, showy, skillful, sophisticated, studied, thorough, with all the extras*, with all the options*, with bells and whistles*; SEE CONCEPT *562*

elaborate [v] *make detailed; expand*
amplify, bedeck, clarify, comment, complicate, deck, decorate, develop, devise, embellish, enhance, enlarge, evolve, expatiate, explain, expound, flesh out, garnish, improve, interpret, ornament, particularize, polish, produce, refine, specify, unfold, work out; SEE CONCEPT *57*

élan [n] *vivacity*
animation, ardor, brio, dash, esprit, flair, impetuosity, impetus, life, oomph*, panache, spirit, style, verve, vigor, vim, zest, zing*; SEE CONCEPT *411*

elapse [v] *go by; slip away*
expire, flow, glide by, lapse, pass, pass away, pass by, roll by, roll on, run out, transpire, vanish; SEE CONCEPTS *6,144,818*

elastic [adj1] *pliant, rubbery*
adaptable, bouncy, buoyant, ductile, extendible, extensible, flexible, irrepressible, limber, lithe, malleable, moldable, plastic, pliable, resilient, rubberlike, springy, stretchable, stretchy, supple, tempered, yielding; SEE CONCEPTS *490,606*

elastic [adj2] *adaptable, tolerant*
accommodating, adjustable, airy, animated, bouncy, buoyant, complaisant, compliant, ebullient, effervescent, expansive, flexible, gay, high-spirited, lively, recuperative, resilient, soaring, spirited, sprightly, supple, variable, vivacious, volatile, yielding; SEE CONCEPT *404*

elated [adj] *very happy*
animated, aroused, blissful, cheered, delighted, ecstatic, elevated, enchanted, enraptured, euphoric, exalted, excited, exhilarated, exultant, fired up*, flying*, flying high*, gleeful, high, hopped up*, in heaven*, in high spirits*, in seventh heaven*, intoxicated, joyful, joyous, jubilant, looking good*, on cloud nine*, overjoyed, proud, puffed up*, roused, set up, transported, turned-on*; SEE CONCEPTS *22,403*

elation [n] *extreme happiness*
bliss, buoyancy, buzz, charge, cloud nine*, delight, ecstasy, enthusiasm, euphoria, exaltation,

excitement, exhilaration, exultation, glee, high, high spirits, intoxication, jollies*, joy, joyfulness, joyousness, jubilation, kick*, kicks*, rapture, stars in one's eyes*, transport, triumph, up*, upper*; SEE CONCEPT *410*

elbow [n] *angular part of arm; angularly shaped item*
ancon, angle, bend, bow, corner, crazy bone*, crook, crutch, curve, fork, funny bone*, half turn, hinge, joint, turn; SEE CONCEPTS *418,436*

elbow [v] *push aside*
bend, bulldoze, bump, crowd, hook, hustle, jostle, knock, nudge, press, rough and tumble*, shoulder, shove; SEE CONCEPT *208*

elder [n] *older person*
ancestor, ancient, forebearer, golden ager*, matriarch, oldest, old fogey*, oldster*, patriarch, senior, senior citizen, superior, veteran; SEE CONCEPT *424*

elder [adj] *born earlier*
ancient, earlier, first-born, more mature, older, senior; SEE CONCEPTS *578,797*

elderly [adj] *in old age*
aged, aging, ancient, been around*, declining, gray*, hoary, long in tooth*, lot of mileage*, no spring chicken*, old, olden, on last leg*, over the hill*, retired, tired, venerable; SEE CONCEPTS *578,797*

elect [v] *select as representative; choose*
accept, admit, appoint, ballot, conclude, cull, decide upon, designate, determine, go down the line, judge, mark, name, nominate, optate, opt for, pick, pick out, prefer, receive, resolve, settle, settle on, single out, take, tap, vote, vote for; SEE CONCEPTS *41,300*

election [n] *choosing; voting*
alternative, appointment, ballot, balloting, choice, decision, determination, franchise, judgment, option, poll, polls, preference, primary, referendum, selection, ticket, vote-casting; SEE CONCEPTS *41,300*

elective [adj] *able to be chosen*
constituent, discretionary, electoral, facultative, nonobligatory, not compulsory, optional, selective, voluntary, voting; SEE CONCEPT *535*

electric/electrical [adj] *charged; energetic*
AC, DC, dynamic, electrifying, exciting, juiced*, magnetic, motor-driven, power-driven, rousing, stimulating, stirring, tense, thrilling, voltaic; SEE CONCEPT *540*

electricity [n] *energized matter, power*
AC, current, DC, electromagneticism, electron, galvanism, heat, hot stuff*, ignition, juice*, light, magneticism, service, spark, tension, utilities, voltage; SEE CONCEPT *520*

electrify [v] *thrill, stimulate*
amaze, animate, astonish, astound, charge, commove, disturb, dynamize, energize, enthuse, excite, fire, frenzy, galvanize, invigorate, jar, jolt, magnetize, power, provoke, rouse, send, shock, stagger, startle, stir, strike, stun, take one's breath away*, wire*; SEE CONCEPTS *7,22,42*

elegance [n] *cultivated beauty, taste*
breeding, charm, class, courtliness, cultivation, culture, delicacy, dignity, discernment, distinction, exquisiteness, felicity, gentility, good taste, grace, gracefulness, grandeur, hauteur, lushness, luxury, magnificence, nicety, nobility, noblesse, ornateness, polish, politeness, poshness, propriety, purity, refinement, restraint, rhythm, sophis-

tication, splendor, style, sumptuousness, symmetry, tastefulness; SEE CONCEPTS *655,671,718*

elegant [*adj*] *beautiful, tasteful*
affected, appropriate, apt, aristocratic, artistic, august, chic, choice, classic, clever, comely, courtly, cultivated, cultured, dainty, delicate, dignified, effective, exquisite, fancy, fashionable, fine, genteel, graceful, grand, handsome, ingenious, luxurious, majestic, modish, neat, nice, noble, opulent, ornamented, ornate, ostentatious, overdone, polished, rare, recherché, refined, rich, select, simple, stately, stuffy, stylish, stylized, sumptuous, superior, turgid, well-bred; SEE CONCEPTS *574,579,589*

element [*nl*] *essential feature*
aspect, basic, basis, bit, component, constituent, detail, drop, facet, factor, fundamental, hint, ingredient, item, material, matter, member, part, particle, particular, piece, portion, principle, root, section, stem, subdivision, trace, unit, view; SEE CONCEPTS *668,826,829*

element [*n2*] *place where one feels comfortable*
domain, environment, field, habitation, medium, milieu, sphere; SEE CONCEPTS *198,516*

elementary [*adj*] *simple, basic*
ABCs, abecedarian, basal, beginning, child's play*, clear, duck soup*, easy, elemental, essential, facile, foundational, fundamental, initial, introductory, meat and potatoes*, original, plain, prefatory, preliminary, primary, primitive, primo*, rudimentary, simplest, simplex, simplified, straightforward, substratal, uncomplex, uncomplicated, underlying; SEE CONCEPTS *546,562*

elevate [*v1*] *lift up*
erect, festoon up*, heighten, hike up*, hoist, jack up*, levitate, poise, pump, put up, pyramid*, raise, ramp, rear, shoot up*, stilt, take up, tilt, uphold, uplift, upraise; SEE CONCEPT *196*

elevate [*v2*] *promote; augment*
advance, aggrandize, appoint, boost, build up, dignify, enhance, ennoble, exalt, further, glorify, heighten, honor, increase, intensify, magnify, prefer, put up, skip, swell, upgrade; SEE CONCEPTS *69,351,700*

elevate [*v3*] *raise spirits*
animate, boost, brighten, bring up, buoy up*, cheer, elate, excite, exhilarate, glorify, hearten, inspire, lift up*, perk up*, refine, rouse, sublimate, uplift; SEE CONCEPTS *7,22*

elevated [*adj1*] *highly moral or dignified*
animated, big-time*, bright, elated, eloquent, eminent, ethical, exalted, exhilarated, formal, grand, grandiloquent, heavy, high, high-flown*, highminded, honorable, inflated, lofty, noble, righteous, stately, sublime, superb, upright, upstanding, virtuous; SEE CONCEPTS *402,545,567*

elevated [*adj2*] *raised up*
aerial, high, high-rise, lifted, raised, stately, tall, towering, upheaved, uplifted, upraised, uprisen; SEE CONCEPT *779*

elevation [*n1*] *height; high ground*
acclivity, altitude, ascent, boost, eminence, heave, hill, hillock, hoist, levitation, mount, platform, ridge, rise, roof, top, uplift, upthrow; SEE CONCEPTS *509,741*

elevation [*n2*] *advancement, promotion*
aggrandizement, apotheosis, boost, deification, eminence, ennoblement, exaltation, exaltedness, glorification, grandeur, immortalization, lionization, loftiness, magnification, nobility, nobleness, preference, preferment, prelation, raise, sublimity, upgrading; SEE CONCEPTS *69,351,668*

elf [*n*] *small, fairytale character*
brownie, elfin, fairy, fay, leprechaun, nisse, pixie; SEE CONCEPT *370*

elicit [*v*] *draw out*
arm-twist*, badger, bite*, bring, bring forth, bring out, bring to light*, call forth, cause, derive, educe, evince, evoke, evolve, exact, extort, extract, fetch, give rise to, milk*, obtain, put muscle on*, put the arm on*, rattle, shake, shake down*, squeeze, wrest, wring; SEE CONCEPTS *68,142*

eligible [*adj*] *fit, worthy*
acceptable, appropriate, becoming, capable of, desirable, discretionary, elective, employable, equal to, fitted, in line for*, in the running*, licensed, likely, preferable, privileged, proper, qualified, satisfactory, seemly, suitable, suited, trained, up to*, usable; SEE CONCEPTS *527,558*

eliminate [*v*] *remove, throw out*
annihilate, blot out*, bump off*, cancel, cast out, count out, cut out, defeat, discard, discharge, dismiss, dispense with, dispose of, disqualify, disregard, do away with, drive out, drop, eject, eradicate, erase, evict, exclude, expel, exterminate, get rid of, ignore, invalidate, kill, knock out*, leave out, liquidate, murder, omit, oust, phase out, put out, reject, rub out*, rule out, set aside, shut the door on*, slay, stamp out*, take out, terminate, waive, waste, wipe out*; SEE CONCEPTS *30,211*

elite [*n*] *high-class persons*
aristocracy, beautiful people*, best, blue blood*, carriage trade*, celebrity, choice, country club set*, cream, crème de la crème*, crowd, elect, establishment, fast lane*, fat*, flower, gentility, gentry, glitterati, high society*, in-crowd*, jetset*, main line*, nobility, old money*, optimacy, pride, prime, prize, quality, select, society, top, upper class, upper crust*; SEE CONCEPTS *387,388,417*

elite [*adj*] *best, first-class*
aristocratic, choice, cool*, crack*, elect, exclusive, gilt-edged, greatest, noble, out of sight*, out of this world*, pick, selected, super, tip-top*, top, top drawer*, topflight, top-notch, upper-class, world-class; SEE CONCEPTS *555,574*

elliptical [*adj*] *oval-shaped*
egg-shaped, ellipsoidal, oblong, ovoid; SEE CONCEPT *486*

elocution [*n*] *articulation*
declamation, delivery, diction, dramatic, eloquence, enunciation, expression, locution, oratory, pronunciation, public speaking, reading, rhetoric, speech, speechcraft, speechmaking, utterance, voice culture, voice production; SEE CONCEPT *47*

elongate [*v*] *make longer*
drag one's feet*, drag out, draw, draw out, extend, fill, lengthen, let out, pad*, prolong, prolongate, protract, put rubber in*, spin out, stretch; SEE CONCEPTS *137,239,250*

elope [*v*] *run away to be married*
abscond, bolt, decamp, disappear, escape, flee, fly, go secretly, go to Gretna Green*; leave, run off, skip*, slip away, slip out, steal away; SEE CONCEPT *297*

eloquence [*n*] *skillful way with words*
ability, appeal, articulation, command of lan-

ej
el

guage, delivery, diction, dramatic, expression, expressiveness, expressivity, facility, fervor, flow, fluency, force, forcefulness, gift of gab*, grandiloquence, loquacity, meaningfulness, mellifluousness, oration, oratory, passion, persuasiveness, poise, power, rhetoric, spirit, style, vigor, vivacity, volubility, wit, wittiness; SEE CONCEPTS *68, 278,630*

eloquent [*adj*] *having a skillful way with words*
affecting, ardent, articulate, expressive, facund, fervent, fervid, fluent, forceful, glib, grandiloquent, graphic, impassioned, impressive, indicative, magniloquent, meaningful, moving, outspoken, passionate, persuasive, poignant, potent, powerful, revealing, rhetorical, sententious, significant, silver-tongued*, smooth-spoken*, stirring, suggestive, telling, touching, vivid, vocal, voluble, well-expressed; SEE CONCEPT *267*

elsewhere [*adv*] *in another place*
abroad, absent, away, formerly, gone, hence, not here, not present, not under consideration, otherwhere, outside, remote, removed, somewhere, somewhere else, subsequently; SEE CONCEPT *586*

elucidate [*v*] *explain in detail*
annotate, clarify, clear, clear up, decode, demonstrate, draw a picture*, enlighten, exemplify, explicate, expound, get across*, gloss, illuminate, illustrate, interpret, make perfectly clear, make plain, make see daylight*, prove, shed light on*, spell out*, throw light on*, unfold; SEE CONCEPT *57*

elude [*v*] *avoid; escape*
baffle, beat around the bush*, be beyond someone*, bilk, circumvent, confound, cop out*, ditch, dodge, double, duck, eschew, evade, flee, fly, foil, frustrate, get around, get away from, give the runaround*, give the slip*, give wide berth to*, hem and haw*, not touch, outrun, outwit, pass the buck*, pass up, puzzle, run around, shirk, shuck, shun, shy, stall, stay shy of*, steer clear of*, stonewall*, stump, thwart; SEE CONCEPTS *30,38,59,102*

elusive [*adj*] *evasive, mysterious*
ambiguous, baffling, cagey, deceitful, deceptive, difficult to catch, elusory, equivocal, evanescent, fallacious, fleeting, fraudulent, fugacious, fugitive, greasy, illusory, imponderable, incomprehensible, indefinable, insubstantial, intangible, misleading, occult, phantom, puzzling, shifty, shy, slippery, stonewalling*, subtle, transient, transitory, tricky, unspecific, volatile; SEE CONCEPTS *529,542*

emaciated [*adj*] *undernourished; thin*
anorexic, atrophied, attenuate, attenuated, bony, cadaverous, consumptive, famished, gaunt, haggard, lank, lean, like a bag of bones*, meager, peaked, pinched, scrawny, skeletal, skeletonlike, skin-and-bones*, skinny, starved, thin as rail*, underfed, wasted, wizened; SEE CONCEPTS *490,491*

emanate [*v*] *come forth; give off*
arise, birth, derive, discharge, egress, emerge, emit, exhale, exit, exude, flow, initiate, issue, originate, proceed, radiate, rise, send forth, spring, stem; SEE CONCEPTS *179,221,648*

emanation [*n*] *emergence, discharge*
arising, beginning, derivation, drainage, effluence, effluent, efflux, effusion, ejaculation, emerging, emission, escape, exhalation, exudation, flow, flowing, gush, issuance, issuing, leak-

age, oozing, origin, origination, outflow, outpour, proceeding, radiation, springing, welling; SEE CONCEPTS *179,221,648*

emancipate [*v*] *set free*
affranchise, deliver, discharge, disencumber, disenthral, enfranchise, liberate, loose, loosen, manumit, release, unbind, unchain, unfetter, unshackle; SEE CONCEPT *127*

emasculate [*v*] *weaken, deprive of force*
alter, debilitate, devitalize, enervate, fix*, impoverish, vitiate; SEE CONCEPTS *240,250*

embalm [*v*] *preserve, immortalize*
anoint, cherish, consecrate, conserve, enshrine, freeze, lay out, mummify, prepare, process, store, treasure, wrap; SEE CONCEPT *202*

embargo [*n*] *prohibition, restriction*
ban, bar, barrier, blockage, check, hindrance, impediment, interdict, interdiction, proscription, restraint, stoppage; SEE CONCEPTS *119,130*

embark [*v*] *get on transportation object*
board, commence, emplane, enter, entrain, go aboard ship, launch, leave port, plunge into, put on board, set about, set out, set sail, take on board, take ship; SEE CONCEPTS *159,195,224*

embark on [*v*] *begin undertaking, journey*
broach, commence, engage, enter, get off, initiate, jump off, launch, open, plunge into, set about, set out, set to, start, take up, tee off*; SEE CONCEPTS *100,221*

embarrass [*v*] *cause mental discomfort*
abash, agitate, annoy, bewilder, bother, bug, catch one short*, chagrin, confuse, discombobulate*, discomfit, discompose, disconcert, discountenance, distract, distress, disturb, dumbfound, faze, fluster, give a bad time*, give a hard time*, hang up*, irk, let down*, make a monkey of*, mortify, nonplus, perplex, perturb, plague, put in a hole*, put in a spot*, put on the spot*, put out of countenance*, puzzle, rattle, shame, show up*, stun, tease, throw, throw into a tizzy*, upset; SEE CONCEPTS *7,19,54*

embarrassing [*adj*] *humiliating, shaming*
awkward, bewildering, compromising, confusing, delicate, difficult, disagreeable, discomfiting, discommoding, discommodious, disconcerting, distracting, distressing, disturbing, equivocal, exasperating, impossible, incommodious, inconvenient, inopportune, mortifying, perplexing, puzzling, rattling, sensitive, shameful, sticky, ticklish, touchy, tricky, troublesome, troubling, uncomfortable, uneasy, unpropitious, unseemly, upsetting, worrisome; SEE CONCEPTS *537,548*

embarrassment [*n*] *humiliation, shame*
awkwardness, awkward situation, bashfulness, bind, boo boo*, chagrin, clumsiness, complexity, confusion, destitution, difficulty, dilemma, discomfiture, discomposure, disconcertion, distress, egg on face*, faux pas, fix, hitch, hot seat*, hot water*, impecuniosity, indebtedness, indiscretion, inhibition, mess, mistake, mortification, pickle*, pinch, plight, poverty, predicament, puzzle, quandary, scrape, self-consciousness, shyness, snag, stew, strait, tangle, timidity, unease, uneasiness; SEE CONCEPTS *410,674*

embassy [*n*] *residence, offices of overseas representatives*
commission, committee, consular office, consulate, delegation, diplomatic office, legation, ministry, mission; SEE CONCEPTS *439,449,516*

embed [v] *sink, implant*
bury, deposit, dig in, drive in, enclose, fasten, fix, hammer in, impact, infix, ingrain, inlay, insert, install, lodge, pierce, plant, plunge, press, put into, ram in, root, set, stick in, stuff in, thrust in, tuck in; SEE CONCEPTS *178,188*

embellish [v] *make beautiful; decorate*
add bells and whistles*, adorn, amplify, array, beautify, bedeck, color, deck, dress up*, elaborate, emblaze, embroider, enhance, enrich, exaggerate, festoon, fix up*, fudge*, garnish, gild, give details, grace, gussy up*, magnify, ornament, overstate, spiff up*, spruce up*, trim; SEE CONCEPTS *49,162,177,700*

embellishment [n] *beautification; decorating*
adornment, coloring, decoration, doodad*, elaboration, embroidering, embroidery, enhancement, enrichment, exaggeration, fandangle*, floridity, flowery speech, frill, froufrou*, fuss*, garnish, gilding, gingerbread*, hyperbole, icing on the cake*, jazz*, ornament, ornamentation, ostentation, overstatement; SEE CONCEPTS *177,278, 700,718*

embers [n] *hot ashes from fire*
ash, brand, cinders, clinkers, coals, firebrand, live coals, slag, smoking remnants, smoldering remains; SEE CONCEPTS *260,478*

embezzle [v] *steal money, often from employer*
abstract, appropriate, defalcate, filch, forge, loot, misapply, misappropriate, misuse, peculate, pilfer, purloin, put hand in cookie jar*, put hand in till*, skim, thieve; SEE CONCEPT *139*

embezzlement [n] *stealing money, often from employer*
abstraction, appropriation, defalcation, filching, fraud, larceny, misapplication, misappropriation, misuse, peculation, pilferage, pilfering, purloining, skimming, theft, thieving; SEE CONCEPT *139*

embitter [v] *upset, alienate*
acerbate, acidulate, aggravate, anger, annoy, bitter, bother, disaffect, disillusion, envenom, exacerbate, exasperate, irritate, make bitter, make resentful, poison, sour, venom, worsen; SEE CONCEPTS *7,14,19*

emblem [n] *crest*
adumbration, arms, attribute, badge, banner, brand, character, coat of arms, colophon, colors, design, device, figure, flag, hallmark, identification, image, impress, insignia, logo, mark, marker, medal, memento, miniature, monogram, motto, pennant, regalia, reminder, representation, scepter, seal, sign, standard, symbol, token, trademark, type; SEE CONCEPTS *259,284,625*

embodiment [n] *representation, manifestation*
apotheosis, archetype, cast, collection, comprehension, conformation, embracement, encompassment, epitome, example, exemplar, exemplification, expression, form, formation, incarnation, inclusion, incorporation, integration, matter, organization, personification, prosopopoeia, quintessence, realization, reification, structure, symbol, systematization, type; SEE CONCEPTS *118,686*

embody [v1] *represent; materialize*
actualize, complete, concretize, demonstrate, emblematize, epitomize, evince, exemplify, exhibit, express, exteriorize, externalize, hypostatize, illustrate, incarnate, incorporate, manifest, mirror, objectify, personalize, personify, realize, reify,

show, stand for, substantiate, symbolize, typify; SEE CONCEPT *118*

embody [v2] *include, integrate*
absorb, amalgamate, assimilate, blend, bring together, codify, collect, combine, comprehend, comprise, concentrate, consolidate, contain, embrace, encompass, establish, fuse, have, incorporate, involve, merge, organize, subsume, systematize, take in, unify; SEE CONCEPTS *112,113*

embrace [v1] *hold tightly in one's arms*
bear hug*, clasp, clinch, cling, clutch, cradle, cuddle, encircle, enfold, entwine, envelop, fold, fondle, grab, grasp, grip, hug, lock, nuzzle, press, seize, snuggle, squeeze, take in arms*, wrap; SEE CONCEPTS *190,191*

embrace [v2] *include in one's beliefs; take into account*
accept, accommodate, admit, adopt, avail oneself of, comprehend, comprise, contain, cover, deal with*, embody, enclose, encompass, espouse, get into*, go in for*, grab, have, incorporate, involve, make use of, provide for, receive, seize, subsume, take advantage of, take in, take on, take up, welcome; SEE CONCEPTS *12,15,112*

embroider [v1] *add fancy stitching, adornment*
beautify, bedeck, braid, color, cross-stitch, deck, decorate, embellish, fix up, garnish, gild, gussy up*, knit, ornament, pattern, quilt, spruce up*, stitch, weave pattern, work; SEE CONCEPTS *177,218*

embroider [v2] *exaggerate information*
aggrandize, amplify, blow-up*, build up, color, distend, dramatize, elaborate, embellish, enhance, enlarge, expand, falsify, fudge*, heighten, hyperbolize, lie, magnify, make federal case*, make mountain out of molehill*, overdo, overelaborate, overembellish, overemphasize, overestimate, overstate, pad*, play up*, puff*, romanticize, spread on thick*, stretch, stretch the truth*, yeast*; SEE CONCEPTS *58,63*

embroidery [n] *fancy stitching*
adornment, appliqué, arabesque, bargello, brocade, crewel, crochet, cross-stitch, decoration, lace, lacery, needlepoint, needlework, quilting, sampler, tapestry, tatting, tracery; SEE CONCEPTS *218,259*

embroil [v] *involve in dispute; complicate*
cause trouble, compromise, confound, confuse, derange, disorder, disturb, disunite, encumber, enmesh, ensnare, entangle, implicate, incriminate, involve, mire, mix up, muddle, perplex, snarl, tangle, trouble; SEE CONCEPTS *7,19,86*

emend [v] *correct*
alter, amend, better, edit, emendate, improve, polish, rectify, redact, retouch, revise, right, touch up; SEE CONCEPT *126*

emerge [v] *come out, arise*
appear, arrive, become apparent, become known, become visible, come forth, come into view, come on the scene, come to light, come up, crop up, dawn, derive, develop, egress, emanate, flow, gush, issue, loom, make appearance, materialize, originate, proceed, rise, show, spring, spring up, spurt, steam, stem, surface, transpire, turn up; SEE CONCEPTS *105,118*

emergency [n] *crisis, danger*
accident, climax, clutch*, compulsion, crossroad, crunch*, depression, difficulty, distress, exigency, extremity, fix, hole, impasse, juncture,

el
em

meltdown*, misadventure, necessity, pass, pinch*, plight, predicament, pressure, push, quandary, scrape, squeeze, strait, tension, turning point, urgency, vicissitude, zero hour*; SEE CONCEPTS 674,675

emergent [adj] resulting
appearing, budding, coming, developing, efflorescent, emanant, emanating, issuing forth, outgoing, rising; SEE CONCEPT 537

emigrant [n] person who leaves his or her native country
alien, colonist, departer, displaced person, émigré, evacuee, exile, expatriate, fugitive, migrant, migrator, outcast, pilgrim, refugee, traveler, wanderer, wayfarer; SEE CONCEPTS 413,423

emigrate [v] move to new country
depart, migrate, move abroad, quit, remove, transmigrate; SEE CONCEPT 198

eminence [n1] importance, fame
authority, celebrity, credit, dignity, distinction, esteem, famousness, glory, greatness, honor, illustriousness, influence, kudos, loftiness, notability, note, power, preeminence, prepotency, prestige, prominence, prominency, rank, renown, reputation, repute, significance, standing, superiority, weight; SEE CONCEPTS 388,668,671

eminence [n2] high ground
altitude, elevation, height, highland, highness, hill, hillock, knoll, loftiness, peak, project, prominence, promontory, raise, ridge, rise, summit, upland; SEE CONCEPTS 509,741

eminent [adj] very important; famous
august, big-gun*, big-league*, big-name*, bigtime*, celeb*, celebrated, celebrious, conspicuous, distinguished, dominant, elevated, esteemed, exalted, famed, grand, great, high, high-ranking, illustrious, lionlike, lofty, name, noble, notable, noted, noteworthy, of note, outstanding, pageoner*, paramount, preeminent, prestigious, prominent, redoubted, renowned, star, superior, superstar, VIP*, well-known; SEE CONCEPTS 555,568

eminently [adv] exceptionally; well
conspicuously, exceedingly, extremely, greatly, highly, notably, outstandingly, prominently, remarkably, strikingly, suitably, surpassingly, very; SEE CONCEPT 574

emissary [n] deputy
agent, ambassador, bearer, carrier, consul, courier, delegate, envoy, front, go-between, herald, hired gun*, intermediary, internuncio, legate, messenger, rep*, representative, scout, spy; SEE CONCEPTS 348,423

emission [n] issuance, diffusion
discharge, ejaculation, ejection, emanation, exhalation, exudation, issue, radiation, shedding, transmission, utterance, venting; SEE CONCEPT 179

emit [v] diffuse, discharge
afford, beam, belch, breathe, cast out, disembogue, drip, eject, emanate, erupt, evacuate, excrete, exhale, expectorate, expel, expend, expire, extrude, exude, give off, give out, give vent to, gush, issue, jet, let off, loose, ooze, pass, perspire, pour, pronounce, purge, radiate, reek, secrete, send forth, send out, shed, shoot, speak, spew, spill, spit, squirt, throw out, transmit, utter, vent, voice, void, vomit, yield; SEE CONCEPTS 108,179,266

emotion [n] mental state
affect, affection, affectivity, agitation, anger, ardor, commotion, concern, desire, despair, despondency, disturbance, drive, ecstasy, elation, empathy, excitability, excitement, feeling, fervor, grief, gut reaction, happiness, inspiration, joy, love, melancholy, passion, perturbation, pride, rage, remorse, responsiveness, sadness, satisfaction, sensation, sensibility, sensitiveness, sentiment, shame, sorrow, sympathy, thrill, tremor, vehemence, vibes, warmth, zeal; SEE CONCEPT 410

emotional [adj] demonstrative about feelings
affecting, ardent, disturbed, ecstatic, emotive, enthusiastic, excitable, exciting, falling apart*, fanatical, feeling, fervent, fervid, fickle, fiery, heartwarming, heated, histrionic, hot-blooded*, hysterical, impassioned, impetuous, impulsive, irrational, moving, nervous, overwrought, passionate, pathetic, poignant, responsive, roused, sensitive, sentient, sentimental, spontaneous, stirred, stirring, susceptible, tear-jerking*, temperamental, tender, thrilling, touching, warm, zealous; SEE CONCEPTS 403,542

emotionless [adj] unfeeling, undemonstrative
blank, chill, cold, cold-blooded*, cold fish*, cool, cool cat*, deadpan, detached, dispassionate, distant, flat, frigid, glacial*, heartless, icy, immovable, impassive, impersonal, in cold blood*, indifferent, laid back*, matter-of-fact, nonemotional, nowhere*, poker face*, remote, reserved, stony-eyed*, thick-skinned*, toneless, unemotional, unimpassioned, with straight face; SEE CONCEPTS 401,403,542

empathy [n] understanding
affinity, appreciation, being on same wavelength*, being there for someone*, communion, community of interests, compassion, comprehension, concord, cottoning to*, good vibrations*, hitting it off*, insight, picking up on*, pity, rapport, recognition, responsiveness, soul, sympathy, warmth; SEE CONCEPTS 32,409,411

emphasis [n] importance, prominence
accent, accentuation, attention, decidedness, force, headline, highlight, impressiveness, insistence, intensity, moment, positiveness, power, preeminence, priority, significance, strength, stress, underlining, underscoring, weight; SEE CONCEPTS 668,682

emphasize [v] stress, give priority to
accent, accentuate, affirm, articulate, assert, bear down, charge, dramatize, dwell on, enlarge, enunciate, headline, highlight, hit*, impress, indicate, insist on, italicize, labor the point*, limelight*, maintain, make a point, make clear, make emphatic, make much of*, mark, pinpoint, play up*, point out*, point up*, press, pronounce, punctuate, put accent on*, reiterate, repeat, rub in*, spotlight*, underline, underscore, weight; SEE CONCEPTS 49,57

emphatic [adj] insistent, unequivocal
absolute, accented, assertive, assured, categorical, certain, cogent, confident, decided, definite, definitive, determined, direct, distinct, dogmatic, dynamic, earnest, energetic, explicit, express, flat, for a face*, forceful, forcible, important, impressive, marked, momentous, no mistake*, pointed, positive, potent, powerful, pronounced, resounding, significant, sober, solemn, stressed,

striking, strong, sure, telling, trenchant, unmistakable, vigorous; SEE CONCEPTS **267,535**

empire [*n*] *place ruled by sovereign; rule*
authority, command, commonwealth, control, domain, dominion, federation, government, people, power, realm, sovereignty, supremacy, sway, union; SEE CONCEPTS **198,299,376**

empirical /empiric [*adj*] *practical; based on experience*
experient, experiential, experimental, factual, observational, observed, pragmatic, provisional, speculative; SEE CONCEPTS **548,582**

employ [*v1*] *make use of*
apply, bestow, bring to bear*, engage, exercise, exert, exploit, fill, handle, keep busy*, manipulate, occupy, operate, put to use*, spend, take up*, use, use up*, utilize; SEE CONCEPT **225**

employ [*v2*] *give money in exchange for work performed*
bring on board*, come on board*, commission, contract, contract for, engage, enlist, hire, ink*, obtain, place, procure, put on*, retain, secure, sign on*, sign up*, take on, truck with*; SEE CONCEPT **351**

employed [*adj*] *working*
active, at it*, at work, busy, engaged, hired, in a job, in collar*, in harness*, inked*, in place, laboring, occupied, on board*, on duty*, on the job*, on the payroll*, operating, plugging away*, selected, signed*; SEE CONCEPTS **538,560**

employee [*n*] *person being paid for working for another or a corporation*
agent, apprentice, assistant, attendant, blue collar*, breadwinner*, clerk, cog*, company person, craftsperson, desk jockey*, domestic, hand, help, hired gun*, hired hand*, hireling, jobholder, laborer, member, operator, pink collar*, plug*, representative, sales help, salesperson, servant, slave, staff member, wage-earner, white collar*, worker, working stiff*; SEE CONCEPT **348**

employer [*n*] *person, business who hires workers*
big cheese*, big shot*, boss, businessperson, capitalist, CEO*, chief, CO*, company, corporation, director, entrepreneur, establishment, executive, firm, front office, head, head honcho*, juice*, kingpin*, management, manager, manufacturer, meal ticket*, organization, outfit, overseer, owner, patron, president, proprietor, slavedriver*, superintendent, supervisor; SEE CONCEPT **347**

employment [*n1*] *working for a living; engagement in activity*
application, assignment, avocation, awarding, business, calling, carrying, commissioning, contracting, craft, employ, engaging, enlistment, enrollment, exercise, exercising, exertion, field, function, game*, hire, hiring, job, line, métier, mission, number, occupation, occupying, office, position, post, profession, pursuit, racket*, recruitment, retaining, service, servicing, setup, signing on*, situation, taking on, thing*, trade, using, vocation, what one is into*, work; SEE CONCEPTS **349,351,360**

employment [*n2*] *using something*
adoption, appliance, application, disposition, exercise, exercising, exertion, exploitation, handling, operation, play, purpose, usage, usance, use, utilization; SEE CONCEPTS **225,658,694**

emporium [*n*] *market*
bazaar, boutique, chain, co-op, cut-rate store*, discount store, five-and-dime*, flea market, galleria, mall, mart, outlet, outlet store, shop, shopping center, shopping plaza, stand, store, supermarket, thrift shop; SEE CONCEPT **449**

empower [*v*] *authorize, enable*
accredit, allow, capacitate, charge, commission, delegate, entitle, entrust, grant, invest, legitimize, license, okay, permit, privilege, qualify, sanction, vest, warrant; SEE CONCEPTS **50,88**

emptiness [*n*] *void, bareness*
blank, blankness, chasm, depletedness, desertedness, desolation, destitution, exhaustion, gap, hollowness, inanition, vacancy, vacuity, vacuum, waste; SEE CONCEPTS **720,733**

empty [*adj1*] *containing nothing*
abandoned, bare, barren, blank, clear, dead, deflated, depleted, desert, deserted, desolate, despoiled, destitute, devoid, dry, evacuated, exhausted, forsaken, godforsaken*, hollow, lacking, stark, unfilled, unfurnished, uninhabited, unoccupied, vacant, vacated, vacuous, void, wanting, waste; SEE CONCEPTS **481,774,786**

empty [*adj2*] *fruitless, ineffective*
aimless, banal, barren, cheap, dead, deadpan, devoid, dishonest, dumb, expressionless, fatuous, flat, frivolous, futile, hollow, idle, ignorant, inane, ineffectual, inexpressive, insincere, insipid, jejune, meaningless, nugatory, otiose, paltry, petty, purposeless, senseless, silly, trivial, unintelligent, unreal, unsatisfactory, unsubstantial, vacuous, vain, valueless, vapid, worthless; SEE CONCEPTS **402,570,575**

empty [*adj3*] *hungry*
famished, ravenous, starving, unfed, unfilled; SEE CONCEPT **406**

empty [*v*] *remove contents*
clear, consume, decant, deplete, discharge, disgorge, drain, drink, dump, ebb, eject, escape, evacuate, exhaust, expel, flow out, gut, leak, leave, make void, pour out, purge, release, run out, rush out, tap, unburden, unload, use up, vacate, void; SEE CONCEPT **211**

empty-headed [*adj*] *flighty, scatterbrained*
brainless, dizzy, featherbrained, frivolous, giddy, harebrained, ignorant, illiterate, inane, knownothing, silly, skittish, stupid, uneducated, unschooled, untaught, vacant, vacuous; SEE CONCEPT **402**

emulate [*v*] *copy the actions of*
challenge, compete, compete with, contend, contend with, ditto*, do*, do like*, follow, follow in footsteps*, follow suit*, follow the example of*, go like*, imitate, make like*, mimic, mirror, outvie, pattern after*, rival, rivalize, take after*, vie with; SEE CONCEPTS **87,171**

enable [*v*] *allow, authorize*
accredit, approve, capacitate, commission, condition, empower, endow, facilitate, fit, give power, implement, invest, let, license, make possible, permit, prepare, provide the means*, qualify, ready, sanction, set up, warrant; SEE CONCEPTS **50,83,88,99**

enact [*v1*] *act out; accomplish*
achieve, appear as, depict, discourse, do, execute, go on*, perform, personate, play, playact, play the part of, portray, represent; SEE CONCEPTS **91,292**

enact [*v2*] *authorize, legislate*
accomplish, appoint, bring about, carry through, command, constitute, decree, determine, dictate, effect, effectuate, establish, execute, fix, formu-

late, get the floor*, institute, jam through*, make, make into law, make laws, ordain, order, pass, proclaim, put in force, put through, railroad*, railroad through*, ratify, sanction, set, steamroll*, transact, vote favorably*, vote in*; SEE CONCEPTS 50,88,298,317

enactment [n1] *playacting*
achievement, acting, depiction, execution, impersonation, performance, personation, personification, playing, portrayal, representation; SEE CONCEPTS 263,292

enactment [n2] *law; authorization*
command, commandment, decree, dictate, edict, execution, legislation, order, ordinance, proclamation, ratification, regulation, statute; SEE CONCEPTS 318,685

enamel [n] *paint, often shiny*
cloisonné, coating, finish, glaze, gloss, japan, lacquer, polish, stain, topcoat, varnish, veneer; SEE CONCEPTS 259,260,467

enamor [v] *fascinate, captivate*
attract, bewitch, charm, enchant, endear, enrapture, enthrall, entice, entrance, fall in love with*, grab, infatuate, make hit with*, please, slay*, sweep off feet*, turn on*; SEE CONCEPTS 7,22,375

enamored [adj] *in love*
amorous, attracted, besotted, bewitched, captivated, charmed, crazy about*, devoted, dotty, enchanted, enraptured, entranced, fascinated, fond, gone*, has a thing about*, hooked*, infatuated, loving, nuts about*, silly about*, smitten, stuck on*, swept off one's feet*, taken*, wild about*; SEE CONCEPTS 32,403

enchant [v] *delight, mesmerize*
allure, beguile, bewitch, captivate, carry away*, cast a spell on*, charm, delectate, draw, enamor, enrapture, ensorcell, enthrall, entice, entrance, fascinate, grab, gratify, hex, hypnotize, kill*, knock dead*, magnetize, make a hit with*, make happy*, please, send*, slay*, spell, spellbind, sweep off feet*, take, thrill, turn on*, voodoo*, wile, wow*; SEE CONCEPTS 7,22

enchanting [adj] *fascinating, delightful*
alluring, appealing, attractive, beguiling, bewitching, captivating, charming, delectable, endearing, enthralling, entrancing, exciting, glamorous, intriguing, lovely, pleasant, pleasing, ravishing, seductive, siren, sirenic, winsome; SEE CONCEPTS 404,529

encircle [v] *circumscribe*
band, begird, cincture, circle, circuit, compass, cover, enclose, encompass, enfold, enring, envelop, environ, gird in, girdle, halo, hem in*, inclose, invest, ring, surround, wreathe; SEE CONCEPT 758

enclose [v] *put inside, surround*
blockade, block off, bound, box up, cage, circle, circumscribe, close in, confine, coop, corral, cover, encase, encircle, encompass, enfold, enshroud, environ, fence, fence off*, hedge, hem in*, imbue, immure, implant, impound, imprison, include, induct, insert, intern, jail, limit, lock in*, lock up*, mew, mure, pen, restrict, set apart, shut in, veil, wall in, wrap; SEE CONCEPTS 112,209,758

enclosure [n1] *area bounded by something*
asylum, aviary, bowl, building, cage, camp, cell, close, coliseum, coop, corral, court, courtyard, den, dungeon, garden, ghetto, hutch, jail, pale,

park, patch, pen, place, plot, pound, precinct, prison, quad, quadrangle, region, room, stadium, stockade, sty, vault, walk, yard, zone; SEE CONCEPTS 439,448,513

enclosure [n2] *something included with a letter*
check, circular, copy, document, form, information, money, printed matter, questionnaire; SEE CONCEPT 271

encompass [v1] *surround, circumscribe*
beset, circle, compass, encircle, enclose, envelop, environ, gird, girdle, hem in, ring; SEE CONCEPT 758

encompass [v2] *include, contain*
admit, comprehend, comprise, cover, embody, embrace, have, hold, incorporate, involve, subsume, take in; SEE CONCEPT 112

encore [n] *another round of applause; repeat*
acclamation, cheers, number, plaudits, praise, reappearance, repeat performance, repetition, response, return; SEE CONCEPT 264

encounter [n1] *chance meeting*
appointment, brush, concurrence, confrontation, interview, rendezvous; SEE CONCEPT 384

encounter [n2] *fight, argument*
action, battle, bout, brush, clash, collision, combat, conflict, contention, contest, dispute, engagement, flap*, fray, hassle, quarrel, rumpus*, run-in*, scrap, set-to*, skirmish, velitation, violence; SEE CONCEPTS 46,86,106

encounter [v1] *happen upon*
alight upon, bear, bump into, chance upon, close, come across, come upon, confront, cross the path*, descry, detect, espy, experience, face, fall in with*, find, front, hit upon, meet, meet up with, rub eyeballs*, run across, run into, run smack into*, suffer, sustain, turn up, undergo; SEE CONCEPTS 38,384

encounter [v2] *fight, attack*
affront, battle, clash with, collide, combat, conflict, confront, contend, cross swords*, do battle*, engage, face, grapple, meet, strive, struggle; SEE CONCEPTS 86,106

encourage [v1] *stimulate spiritually*
animate, applaud, boost, brighten, buck up*, buoy, cheer, cheer up, comfort, console, embolden, energize, enhearten, enliven, excite, exhilarate, fortify, galvanize, give shot in arm*, gladden, goad, hearten, incite, inspire, inspirit, instigate, praise, prick, prop up*, psych up*, push, rally, reassure, refresh, restore, revitalize, revivify, rouse, spur, steel, stir, strengthen, sway; SEE CONCEPTS 7,22

encourage [v2] *give support; help*
abet, advance, advocate, aid, approve, assist, back, back up, befriend, bolster, boost, brace, comfort, console, countenance, develop, ease, egg on*, endorse, favor, fortify, forward, foster, further, get behind, give a leg up*, go for*, improve, instigate, invite, pat on the back, prevail, promote, pull for*, push, reassure, reinforce, relieve, root for*, sanction, second, serve, side with*, smile upon*, solace, spur, strengthen, subscribe to, subsidize, succor, support, sustain, uphold; SEE CONCEPTS 8,110

encouragement [n] *help, support*
advance, advocacy, aid, animation, assistance, backing, boost, cheer, comfort, confidence, consolation, consoling, easement, enlivening, faith, favor, firmness, fortitude, helpfulness, hope, incentive, incitement, inspiration, inspiriting, in-

vigoration, optimism, promotion, reassurance, reassuring, refreshment, relief, relieving, reward, shot in the arm*, softening, solacing, stimulation, stimulus, succor, supporting, trust, urging; SEE CONCEPTS 7,22,110,410

encroach [v] *invade another's property, business*
appropriate, arrogate, barge in*, butt in*, crash, elbow in*, entrench, horn in*, impinge, infringe, interfere, interpose, intervene, intrude, make inroads*, meddle, muscle in*, overstep, put two cents in*, squeeze in*, stick nose into*, trench, trespass, usurp, work in, worm in*; SEE CONCEPTS 7,19,86,159

encumber [v] *bother, burden*
block, charge, clog, cramp, discommode, embarrass, hamper, handicap, hang up, hinder, hogtie*, hold up, impede, incommode, inconvenience, lade, load, make difficult, obstruct, oppress, overburden, overload, retard, saddle, saddle with*, slow down, tax, trammel, weigh down, weight; SEE CONCEPTS 121,130

encyclopedic [adj] *comprehensive*
all-embracing, all-encompassing, all-inclusive, broad, catholic, complete, discursive, exhaustive, extensive, general, thorough, thorough-going, universal, vast, wide-ranging, widespread; SEE CONCEPTS 267,772

end [n1] *extreme, limit*
borderline, bound, boundary, butt end, confine, cusp, deadline, edge, extent, extremity, foot, head, heel, limitation, neb, nib, point, prong, spire, stub, stump, tail, tail end, term, terminal, termination, terminus, tip, top, ultimate; SEE CONCEPTS 745,827,833

end [n2] *completion, stop*
accomplishment, achievement, adjournment, attainment, bottom line*, cease, cessation, close, closing, closure, conclusion, consequence, consummation, culmination, curtain, denouement, desistance, desuetude, determination, discontinuance, execution, expiration, expiry, finale, finis, finish, fulfillment, issue, last word*, omega, outcome, payoff, perfection, realization, resolution, result, retirement, sign-off*, target, termination, terminus, upshot, windup, wrap-up*; SEE CONCEPTS 119,230,832

end [n3] *intention, aim*
aspiration, design, drift, goal, intent, mark, object, objective, point, purpose, reason, where one's heading*; SEE CONCEPT 659

end [n4] *leftover part*
bit, butt end, dregs, fragment, leaving, lees, particle, piece, portion, remainder, remnant, residue, scrap, share, side, stub, tag end; SEE CONCEPT 835

end [n5] *death, destruction*
annihilation, demise, dissolution, doom, expiration, extermination, extinction, finish, passing, ruin, ruination; SEE CONCEPT 304

end [v1] *bring to an end*
abolish, abort, accomplish, achieve, break off, break up, call it a day*, call off*, cease, close, close out, complete, conclude, consummate, crown, culminate, cut short, delay, determine, discontinue, dispose of, dissolve, drop, expire, finish, get done, give up, halt, interrupt, pack it in*, perorate, postpone, pull the plug*, put the lid on*, quit, relinquish, resolve, settle, sew up*, shut down*, stop, switch off*, terminate, top off*, ultimate, wind up*, wrap, wrap up*; SEE CONCEPT 234

end [v2] *die or kill*
abolish, annihilate, cease, depart, desist, destroy, die, expire, exterminate, extinguish, lapse, put to death, ruin, run out, wane; SEE CONCEPTS 252,304

endanger [v] *put in jeopardy*
be careless, chance, chance it*, expose, hazard, imperil, lay on the line*, lay open*, leave defenseless, leave in the middle*, make liable, menace, peril, play into one's hands*, put at risk, put in danger, put on the spot*, risk, stick one's neck out*, subject to loss, threaten, venture; SEE CONCEPTS 246,252,384

endear [v] *attract attention*
attach, bind, captivate, charm, cherish, engage, prize, treasure, value, win; SEE CONCEPTS 7,22,32

endeavor [n] *attempt to achieve something*
aim, all*, best shot*, crash project*, dry run*, effort, enterprise, essay, exertion, fling, full blast*, full court press*, full steam*, go, header*, labor, lick*, old college try*, one's all*, one's level best*, push, shot*, stab*, striving, struggle, toil, travail, trial, try, try-on*, undertaking, venture, whack*, whirl*, work; SEE CONCEPT 87

endeavor [v] *attempt to achieve something*
address, aim, apply, aspire, assay, bid for, buck, determine, dig, do one's best*, drive at, essay, go for*, go for broke*, grind, hammer away*, hassle, have a crack*, have a shot at*, have a swing at*, hump*, hustle, intend, labor, make an effort, make a run at*, offer, peg away*, plug, pour it on*, purpose, push, risk, scratch, seek, strain, strive, struggle, sweat, take on, take pains*, try, undertake, venture; SEE CONCEPT 87

ending [n] *conclusion*
catastrophe, cessation, close, closing, closure, completion, consummation, coup de grace, culmination, denouement, desistance, dissolution, epilogue, expiration, finale, finish, lapse, omega, outcome, period, resolution, stop, summation, swan song*, termination, terminus, upshot, wane, windup; SEE CONCEPTS 119,230,832

endless [adj] *not stopping, not finishing*
amaranthine, boundless, ceaseless, constant, continual, continuous, countless, deathless, enduring, eternal, everlasting, illimitable, immeasurable, immortal, incalculable, incessant, indeterminate, infinite, interminable, limitless, measureless, monotonous, multitudinous, never-ending, no end of, no end to, numberless, overlong, perpetual, self-perpetuating, unbounded, unbroken, undivided, undying, unending, unfathomable, uninterrupted, unlimited, unsurpassable, untold, without end; SEE CONCEPTS 482,551,798

endorse [v] *support, authorize*
accredit, advocate, affirm, approve, attest, authenticate, back, back up*, bless, boost, certify, champion, commend, confirm, countenance, defend, favor, give a boost to, give green light*, give one's word*, give the go-ahead*, give the nod*, go along with*, go to bat for*, go with, guarantee, lend one's name to, okay, praise, push, ratify, recommend, rubber-stamp*, sanction, second, stand behind, stand up for*, stump for*, subscribe to, sustain, underwrite, uphold, vouch for, warrant, witness; SEE CONCEPTS 10,50,69,88,300

en
en

endorse [v2] *countersign a check*
add one's name to, authenticate, autograph, co-sign, notarize, put John Hancock on*, put signature on, rubber-stamp*, say amen to*, sign, sign off on, sign on dotted line*, subscribe, superscribe, undersign, underwrite; SEE CONCEPTS *50,79,88,330*

endorsement [n] *support, authorization*
advocacy, affirmation, approbation, approval, backing, championing, commercial, confirmation, countersignature, favor, fiat, go-ahead*, green light*, hubba-hubba*, okay, pat on back*, permission, qualification, ratification, recommendation, sanction, seal of approval, signature, stroke, subscription to, superscription, the nod*, warrant; SEE CONCEPT *685*

endow [v] *give large gift*
accord, award, back, bequeath, bestow, come through with, confer, contribute, donate, empower, enable, endue, enhance, enrich, establish, favor, finance, found, fund, furnish, grant, heighten, invest, lay on*, leave, make over*, organize, promote, provide, settle on, sponsor, subscribe, subsidize, supply, support, vest in, will; SEE CONCEPTS *108,341*

endowment [n1] *large gift*
award, benefaction, benefit, bequest, bestowal, boon, bounty, dispensation, donation, fund, funding, gifting, grant, gratuity, income, inheritance, largess, legacy, nest egg, pension, presentation, property, provision, revenue, stake, stipend, subsidy, trust; SEE CONCEPTS *337,340*

endowment [n2] *personal talent, ability*
aptitude, attribute, capability, capacity, faculty, flair, genius, gift, habilitation, power, qualification, quality, turn; SEE CONCEPTS *411,630*

end up [v] *become eventually; come to a close*
arrive finally, cease, come to a halt, finish, finish as, finish up, stop, turn out to be, wind up; SEE CONCEPT *119*

endurable [adj] *tolerable*
bearable, livable, sufferable, supportable, sustainable; SEE CONCEPT *548*

endurance [n1] *bearing hardship; staying power*
ability, allowance, backbone, bearing, capacity, continuing, cool, coolness, courage, enduring, forebearance, fortitude, grit, guts, gutsiness, heart*, holding up*, intestinal fortitude, mettle, moxie*, patience, perseverance, persistence, pertinacity, pluck, resignation, resistance, resolution, restraint, spunk, stamina, standing, starch*, strength, submission, sufferance, suffering, tenacity, tolerance, toleration, undergoing, vitality, will, withstanding; SEE CONCEPTS *411,633*

endurance [n2] *continuity, lastingness*
continuance, continuation, durability, duration, immutability, longevity, permanence, persistence, stability; SEE CONCEPT *804*

endure [v1] *bear hardship*
abide, accustom, allow, bear the brunt*, be patient with, brave, brook, cope with, countenance, eat, encounter, experience, face, feel, go through, grin and bear it*, hang in*, keep up, know, live out, live through, meet with, never say die*, permit, put up with, repress feelings, resign oneself, ride out*, sit through, stand, stick, stick it out*, stomach*, subject to, submit to, suffer, support, sustain, swallow*, take, take it*, take patiently, tolerate, undergo, weather, withstand; SEE CONCEPT *23*

endure [v2] *continue; be durable*
abide, be, be left, be long lived, be timeless, bide, carry on, carry through, cling, exist, go on, hang on*, have no end, hold, hold on, hold out, keep on, last, linger, live, live on, never say die*, outlast, outlive, perdure, persist, prevail, remain, ride out*, run on, stand, stay, stay on, stick to*, superannuate, survive, sustain, wear, wear on, wear well*; SEE CONCEPTS *239,407,804*

enemy [n] *someone hated or competed against*
adversary, agent, antagonist, archenemy, asperser, assailant, assassin, attacker, backbiter, bad person*, bandit, betrayer, calumniator, competitor, contender, criminal, defamer, defiler, detractor, disputant, emulator, falsifier, fifth column*, foe, guerrilla, informer, inquisitor, invader, murderer, opponent, opposition, other side*, prosecutor, rebel, revolutionary, rival, saboteur, seditionist, slanderer, spy, terrorist, traducer, traitor, vilifier, villain; SEE CONCEPTS *322,412*

energetic [adj] *full of life; forceful*
active, aggressive, animated, ball of fire*, breezy, brisk, demoniac, driving, dynamic, enterprising, forcible, fresh, hardy, high-powered, indefatigable, industrious, kinetic, lively, lusty, peppy, potent, powerful, red-blooded*, rugged, snappy, spirited, sprightly, spry, stalwart, strenuous, strong, sturdy, tireless, tough, unflagging, untiring, vigorous, vital, vivacious, zippy*; SEE CONCEPTS *404,542*

energize [v] *activate; give more life*
actify, activize, animate, arm, build up, electrify, empower, enable, enliven, excite, fortify, goose*, innervate, inspirit, invigorate, jazz up*, juice up*, liven up, motivate, pep up, prime, pump up*, put zip into*, quicken, reinforce, start up, stimulate, strengthen, sustain, switch on, trigger, turn on, vitalize, work up, zap*; SEE CONCEPTS *7,22,231,700*

energy [n1] *person's spirit and vigor*
activity, animation, application, ardor, birr, dash, drive, effectiveness, efficacy, efficiency, élan, endurance, enterprise, exertion, fire, force, forcefulness, fortitude, get-up-and-go*, go, hardihood, initiative, intensity, juice, life, liveliness, might, moxie*, muscle, operativeness, pep, pizzazz, pluck, potency, power, puissance, punch, spirit, spontaneity, stamina, steam, strength, toughness, tuck, vehemence, verve, vim, virility, vitality, vivacity, zeal, zest, zing, zip*; SEE CONCEPT *411*

energy [n2] *generated power*
application, burn, conductivity, current, dynamism, electricity, force, friction, gravity, heat, horsepower, juice, kilowatts, magnetism, potential, pressure, radioactivity, rays, reaction, response, service, steam, strength, voltage, wattage; SEE CONCEPT *520*

enervate [v] *tire, wear out*
debilitate, devitalize, disable, enfeeble, exhaust, fatigue, incapacitate, jade, paralyze, sap, unnerve, vitiate, weaken, weary; SEE CONCEPTS *156, 225,250*

enervated [adj] *exhausted, worn out*
debilitated, deteriorated, devitalized, done in, enfeebled, fatigued, feeble, gone to seed*, incapacitated, lackadaisical, languid, languishing, languorous, limp, listless, on the ropes*, out of condition*, out of gas*, out of shape*, paralyzed, prostrate, prostrated, run-down, rusty, sapped, soft, spent, spiritless, tired, undermined, un-

nerved, vitiated, washed out, weak, weakened;
SEE CONCEPTS 485,560

enfeeble [v] *make very weak*
attenuate, blunt, cripple, debilitate, deplete, devitalize, diminish, disable, exhaust, fatigue, incapacitate, sap, undermine, unhinge, unnerve, weaken, wear out; SEE CONCEPTS 240,252

enfold [v] *embrace, hug*
bear hug, cinch, clasp, clinch, clutch, cover, drape, encase, enclose, encompass, enshroud, envelop, envelope, enwrap, fold, girdle, grab, hold, invest, press, shroud, squeeze, surround, swathe, veil, wrap, wrap up; SEE CONCEPTS 191,219

enforce [v] *put a rule, plan in force*
accomplish, administer, administrate, apply, carry out, coerce, commandeer, compel, constrain, crack down, demand, dictate, discharge, dragoon, drive, effect, egg on*, emphasize, exact, execute, exert, expect, extort, force upon, fortify, fulfill, goad, hound, impel, implement, impose, incite, insist on, invoke, lash, lean on, make, necessitate, oblige, perform, press, prosecute, put into effect, put screws to*, reinforce, require, sanction, spur, strain, stress, strong-arm, support, urge, whip, wrest; SEE CONCEPTS 50,88,133,298,317

enforcement [n] *requirement to obey; implementation of rule(s)*
administration, application, carrying out, coercion, compulsion, compulsory law, constraint, duress, enforcing, exaction, execution, fulfilling, imposition, impulsion, insistence, lash, martial law, necessitation, obligation, prescription, pressure, prosecution, reinforcement, spur, whip; SEE CONCEPTS 133,298,317,685

engage [v1] *hire for job, use*
appoint, bespeak, book, bring on board*, charter, come on board*, commission, contract, employ, enlist, enroll, ink*, lease, place, prearrange, put on, rent, reserve, retain, secure, sign on, sign up, take on, truck with*; SEE CONCEPTS 129,351

engage [v2] *occupy oneself; engross*
absorb, allure, arrest, bewitch, busy, captivate, catch, charm, draw, embark on, employ, enamor, enchant, enter into, enthrall, fascinate, give a try*, give a whirl*, go for broke*, go in for*, go out for*, grip*, have a fling at*, have a go at*, have a shot at*, imbue, immerse, interest, involve, join, keep busy, monopolize, partake, participate, pitch in, practice, preengage, preoccupy, set about, soak, tackle*, take part, tie up, try on for size*, undertake; SEE CONCEPTS 87,363

engage [v3] *promise to marry*
affiance, agree, betroth, bind, catch, commit, contract, covenant, give one's word*, guarantee, hook, obligate, oblige, pass, pledge, tie, troth, turn on*, undertake, vouch, vow; SEE CONCEPT 297

engage [v4] *start a fight; attack*
assail, assault, combat, do battle with, encounter, face, fall on, give battle to, join battle with, launch, meet, strike, take on; SEE CONCEPTS 86,106,320

engage [v5] *interconnect; bring into operation*
activate, apply, attach, dovetail, energize, fasten, get going, interact, interlace, interlock, intermesh, interplay, join, lock, mesh, switch on; SEE CONCEPTS 85,113,160,221

engaged [adj1] *promised to be married*
affianced, asked for, betrothed, bound, committed, contracted, future, given one's word*, going

steady*, hooked*, intended, matched, pinned, pledged, plighted, ringed, spoken for, steady; SEE CONCEPT 555

engaged [adj2] *operating; busy*
absorbed, at work, committed, connected with, dealing in, deep, doing, employed, engrossed, immersed, in place, intent, interested, in use, involved, occupied, performing, practicing, preoccupied, pursuing, rapt, signed, tied up, unavailable, working, wrapped up*; SEE CONCEPTS 542,555,576

engagement [n1] *pledge to marry*
assurance, betrothal, betrothing, betrothment, bond, commitment, compact, contract, espousal, match, oath, obligation, pact, plight, promise, troth, undertaking, vow, word; SEE CONCEPT 297

engagement [n2] *meeting; date*
appointment, arrangement, assignation, blind date*, commission, commitment, date, errand, get-together, gig, going out*, interview, invitation, meet, seeing one*, stint, tryst, visit; SEE CONCEPT 384

engagement [n3] *battle*
action, combat, conflict, confrontation, contest, encounter, fight, fray, skirmish; SEE CONCEPTS 106,320

engaging [adj] *charming*
agreeable, alluring, appealing, attractive, bewitching, captivating, enchanting, enticing, entrancing, fascinating, fetching, glamorous, interesting, intriguing, inviting, likable, lovable, magnetic, mesmeric, pleasant, pleasing, prepossessing, siren, sweet, winning, winsome; SEE CONCEPT 404

engender [v] *cause to happen; cause an action*
arouse, beget, breed, bring about, bring forth, create, develop, excite, foment, generate, give birth to, give rise to, hatch, incite, induce, instigate, lead to, make, muster, occasion, precipitate, procreate, produce, propagate, provoke, quicken, rouse, spawn, stimulate, stir, work up; SEE CONCEPTS 221,242

engine [n] *device that drives a machine*
agent, apparatus, appliance, barrel, contrivance, cylinder, diesel, dynamo, fan, generator, horses*, implement, instrument, means, mechanism, motor, piston, pot*, powerhouse, power plant, power train, putt-putt*, rubber band*, tool, transformer, turbine, weapon, what's under the hood*; SEE CONCEPTS 463,464

engineer [n] *person who puts together things*
architect, builder, contriver, designer, deviser, director, inventor, manager, manipulator, originator, planner, schemer, sights*, surveyor, techie*, technie*; SEE CONCEPT 348

engineer [v] *devise; bring about*
angle, arrange, cause, come up with, con, conceive, concoct, contrive, control, cook*, create, direct, doctor, effect, encompass, finagle*, jockey*, machinate, manage, maneuver, manipulate, negotiate, operate, organize, originate, plan, plant, play games*, plot, pull strings*, pull wires*, put one on*, put one over*, put over*, put through, rig*, scam, scheme, set up, superintend, supervise, swing, upstage, wangle, work; SEE CONCEPTS 36,173,251

engrave [v] *carve letters or designs into*
bite, burn, chase, chisel, crosshatch, cut, diaper, embed, enchase, etch, fix, grave, hatch, impress, imprint, infix, ingrain, initial, inscribe, instill, in-

taglio, lithograph, lodge, mezzotint, ornament, print, scratch, stipple; SEE CONCEPTS *79,174,176*

engraving [*n*] *carving of letters or design into something*
blocking, chasing, chiselling, cutting, dry point, enchasing, etching, illustration, impression, inscribing, inscription, intaglio, lithograph, mezzotint, photoengraving, photogravure, print, rotogravure, scratch, woodcut; SEE CONCEPTS *79,174,176,625*

engross [*v*] *hold one's attention*
absorb, apply, arrest, assimilate, attract, become lost, be hung*, bewitch, busy, captivate, consume, corner, engage, engulf, enrapture, enthrall, fascinate, fill, grip, hog*, immerse, involve, monopolize, occupy, preoccupy, sew up*, soak, take up, up on*; SEE CONCEPTS *14,17*

engrossed [*adj*] *preoccupied; attentive to*
absorbed, all wound up*, assiduous, bugged*, busy, captivated, caught up, caught up in, consumed, deep, diligent, engaged, enthralled, fascinated, fiend for*, gone*, gripped, head over heels*, heavily into*, hooked, hung up, immersed, industrious, intent, into*, intrigued, lost, monopolized, occupied, rapt, really into*, riveted, sedulous, submerged, taken up with, tied up, turned on*, up to here in*, wrapped up*; SEE CONCEPTS *403,542*

engrossing [*adj*] *very interesting*
absorbing, all-consuming, captivating, compelling, consuming, controlling, enthralling, exciting, fascinating, gripping, intriguing, monopolizing, obsessing, preoccupying, provoking, riveting, stimulating; SEE CONCEPT *529*

engulf [*v*] *absorb, overwhelm*
bury, consume, deluge, drown, encompass, engross, envelop, flood, imbibe, immerse, inundate, overflow, overrun, overwhelm, plunge, submerge, swallow up, swamp, whelm; SEE CONCEPTS *169,172,256*

enhance [*v*] *improve, embellish*
add to, adorn, aggrandize, amplify, appreciate, augment, beautify, boom, boost, build up, complement, elevate, embroider, enlarge, exaggerate, exalt, flesh out*, heighten, increase, intensify, lift, magnify, pad*, pyramid*, raise, reinforce, strengthen, swell, upgrade; SEE CONCEPTS *162, 177,244*

enigma [*n*] *mystery*
bewilderment, cliffhanger, conundrum, crux, cryptogram, Gordian knot*, grabber*, knot*, mind-boggler*, mind-twister*, mystification, parable, perplexity, problem, puzzle, puzzlement, puzzler, question, question mark, riddle, secret, sixty-four dollar question*, sphinx*, sticker, stickler, stumper, teaser, tough nut to crack*, twister, why*; SEE CONCEPT *532*

enigmatic/enigmatical [*adj*] *mysterious*
ambiguous, cryptic, dark, Delphian*, doubtful, equivocal, incomprehensible, indecipherable, inexplicable, inscrutable, obscure, occult, oracular, perplexing, puzzling, recondite, secret, Sibylline*, sphinxlike, stickling, stumping, teasing, uncertain, unfathomable, unintelligible; SEE CONCEPTS *529,576,582*

enjoin [*v1*] *order, command*
adjure, admonish, advise, appoint, bid, call upon, caution, charge, counsel, decree, demand, dictate, direct, forewarn, impose, instruct, ordain, prescribe, require, rule, tell, urge, warn; SEE CONCEPTS *53,78*

enjoin [*v2*] *forbid*
ban, bar, deny, disallow, inhibit, interdict, outlaw, place injunction on, preclude, prohibit, proscribe, restrain, taboo; SEE CONCEPTS *50,53,88,130*

enjoy [*v1*] *take pleasure in, from something*
adore, appreciate, be entertained, be fond of, be pleased, cotton to*, delight in, dig*, dote on*, drink in*, eat up*, fancy, flip over*, freak out on*, get a charge out of*, get a kick out of*, get high on*, go, have a ball*, have a good time, have fun, like, live a little*, live it up*, love, luxuriate in, mind, paint the town*, rejoice in, relish, revel in, savor, take joy in, thrill to; SEE CONCEPTS *32,384*

enjoy [*v2*] *have the benefit or use of*
be blessed, be favored, boast, command, experience, have, hold, maintain, occupy, own, possess, process, reap the benefits*, retain, use; SEE CONCEPT *710*

enjoyable [*adj*] *pleasing; to one's liking*
agreeable, amusing, clear sailing*, delectable, delicious, delightful, entertaining, fun, genial, gratifying, groovy*, just for grins*, just for kicks*, just for laughs*, just for the heck of it*, likable, lots of laughs*, pleasant, pleasurable, preferable, relishable, satisfying, welcome; SEE CONCEPTS *529,548*

enjoyment [*n1*] *delight in something*
amusement, delectation, diversion, enjoying, entertainment, fruition, fun, gladness, gratification, gusto, happiness, hedonism, indulgence, joy, loving, luxury, pleasure, recreation, rejoicing, relaxation, relish, satisfaction, savor, self-indulgence, sensuality, thrill, triumph, zest; SEE CONCEPTS *32,410*

enjoyment [*n2*] *possession; use of*
advantage, benefit, exercise, having, indulgence, ownership, spending, using; SEE CONCEPT *710*

enlarge [*v*] *make or grow bigger; increase*
add to, aggrandize, amplify, augment, beef up*, blow up*, boost, broaden, build, bulk, develop, diffuse, dilate, distend, elaborate, elongate, embroider, exaggerate, expand, expatiate, extend, give details, grow, grow larger, heighten, inflate, jack up*, jazz up*, lengthen, magnify, make larger, mount, multiply, pad*, pyramid*, rise, slap on*, snowball*, spread, stretch, swell, upsurge, wax, widen; SEE CONCEPTS *137,236, 245,780*

enlargement [*n*] *increase, expansion*
aggrandizement, amplification, augmentation, blow up, elongation, extension, growth, spread; SEE CONCEPT *780*

enlighten [*v*] *explain thoroughly; make aware*
acquaint, advise, apprise, brief, catechize, cause to understand, civilize, convert, counsel, direct, disclose, divulge, edify, educate, elucidate, give faith*, give the lowdown*, give the word*, guide, illume, illuminate, illumine, imitate, improve, inculcate, indoctrinate, inform, inspirit, instruct, let in on, open up, persuade, preach, put on to*, reveal, save, school, teach, tell, train, update, uplift; SEE CONCEPTS *57,60,75*

enlightened [*adj*] *informed, educated*
aware, broad-minded, civilized, cultivated, hip to*, instructed, in the picture*, knowing what's what*, knowledgeable, learned, liberal, literate,

open-minded, plugged in*, reasonable, refined, savvy, sharp, sophisticated, tuned in*, wised up*; SEE CONCEPT 402

enlightenment [n] *awareness, understanding*
broad-mindedness, civilization, comprehension, cultivation, culture, edification, education, information, insight, instruction, knowledge, learning, literacy, open-mindedness, refinement, sophistication, teaching, wisdom; SEE CONCEPT 409

enlist [v] *sign up for responsibility*
admit, appoint, assign, attract, call to arms, call up, conscribe, conscript, draft, embody, employ, engage, enroll, enter, enter into, gather, get, hire, hitch, incorporate, induct, initiate, inscribe, interest, join, join up, levy, list, mobilize, muster, oblige, obtain, place, press into service, procure, record, recruit, register, reserve, secure, serve, sign on, take on, volunteer; SEE CONCEPTS 8,320

enliven [v] *inspire, vitalize*
animate, brace up, brighten, buck up, buoy, cheer, cheer up, divert, entertain, excite, exhilarate, fire, fire up, galvanize, give a lift, give life to, gladden, hearten, inspirit, invigorate, jazz up*, juice up*, let sunshine in*, pep up*, perk up*, pick up, put pep into, quicken, recreate, refresh, rejuvenate, renew, restore, rouse, snap out of it*, spark, spice, spice up*, stimulate, vivificate, vivify, wake up, work up*, zap*; SEE CONCEPTS 7,22

en masse [adj] *all at once*
all in all, all together, altogether, as a body, as a group, as a whole, as one, bodily, by and large*, ensemble, generally, in a body, in a group, in a mass, jointly, on the whole, together; SEE CONCEPT 577

enmesh [v] *involve in a situation*
box in, catch, drag into*, draw in, embroil, ensnare, entangle, entrap, hook, implicate, incriminate, lay a trap for*, lay it for*, make party to*, net, snare, snarl, tangle, trammel, trap; SEE CONCEPTS 59,112

enmity [n] *hatred, animosity*
acrimony, alienation, animus, antagonism, antipathy, aversion, bad blood*, bitterness, daggers*, detestation, dislike, hate, hostility, ill will, loathing, malevolence, malice, malignancy, malignity, rancor, spite, spleen, uncordiality, unfriendliness, venom; SEE CONCEPT 29

ennui [n] *boredom*
apathy, blahs, blues, dejection, depression, dissatisfaction, doldrums, dumps*, fatigue, ho hums*, lack of interest, languidness, languor, lassitude, listlessness, melancholy, sadness, satiety, spiritlessness, surfeit, tedium, weariness, yawn*; SEE CONCEPT 410

enormity [n1] *horribleness*
abomination, atrociousness, atrocity, crime, depravity, disgrace, evil, evilness, flagrancy, grossness, heinousness, horror, monstrosity, monstrousness, nefariousness, outrage, outrageousness, rankness, turpitude, vice, viciousness, vileness, villainy, wickedness; SEE CONCEPTS 645,666

enormity [n2] *extreme largeness*
bigness, bulk, enormousness, greatness, hugeness, immensity, magnitude, massiveness, size, tremendousness, vastness; SEE CONCEPT 730

enormous [adj] *very large*
astronomic, barn door*, blimp*, colossal, excessive, gargantuan, gigantic, gross, huge, humongous, immense, jumbo*, mammoth, massive,

monstrous, mountainous, prodigious, stupendous, super-colossal*, titanic*, tremendous, vast, whopping; SEE CONCEPT 773

enough [n] *plenty*
abundance, adequacy, ampleness, ample supply, competence, plenitude, right amount, sufficiency, sufficient; SEE CONCEPTS 646,767

enough [adj] *plenty*
abundant, acceptable, adequate, all right already*, ample, bellyful*, bounteous, bountiful, comfortable, competent, complete, copious, decent, enough already*, fed up*, full, had it*, last straw*, lavish, plenteous, plentiful, replete, satisfactory, satisfying, sick and tired of*, sufficient, sufficing, suitable, unlimited, up to here*; SEE CONCEPTS 546,771

enough [adv] *adequately*
abundantly, acceptably, admissibly, amply, averagely, barely, commensurately, decently, fairly, moderately, passably, proportionately, rather, reasonably, satisfactorily, so-so*, sufficiently, tolerably; SEE CONCEPTS 546,558,771

enrage [v] *make very upset*
aggravate, anger, ask for it*, exasperate, get under skin*, hack*, incense, incite, inflame, infuriate, ire, irritate, madden, make blood boil*, make see red*, needle, provoke, rile, steam up*, T-off*, umbrage, whip up*; SEE CONCEPTS 7,14,19

enrapture [v] *captivate*
allure, attract, beguile, bewitch, charm, delight, elate, enamor, enchant, enthrall, entrance, fascinate, gladden, gratify, please, ravish, rejoice, score, send, spellbind, transport; SEE CONCEPTS 7,22

enrich [v] *improve, embellish*
adorn, aggrandize, ameliorate, augment, beef up*, better, build, build up, cultivate, decorate, develop, endow, enhance, figure in, flesh out*, grace, hike up*, hop up*, jack up*, jazz up*, make rich, ornament, pad, parlay, pour it on*, pyramid*, refine, run up*, soup up*, spike*, step up, supplement, sweeten*, up*, upgrade; SEE CONCEPTS 177,244

enroll [v1] *sign up for membership*
accept, admit, become student, call up, employ, engage, enlist, enter, join, join up, matriculate, muster, obtain, recruit, register, serve, sign on, subscribe, take course, take on; SEE CONCEPTS 114,129

enroll [v2] *list, record*
affix, bill, book, catalog, chronicle, engross, enlist, enter, file, fill out, index, inscribe, insert, inventorize, mark, matriculate, note, poll, register, schedule, slate; SEE CONCEPTS 79,125

enrollment [n] *registration for membership*
acceptance, accession, admission, conscription, engagement, enlistment, entrance, entry, induction, influx, listing, matriculation, rally, reception, record, recruitment, response, student body, students, subscription; SEE CONCEPTS 288, 388,417

en route [adj] *on the way to destination*
advancing, along the way, bound, driving, entrained, en voyage*, flying, heading toward, in passage, in transit, making headway*, midway, on the road*, pressing on, progressing, traveling; SEE CONCEPTS 577,586

ensconce [v] *hide; tuck away*
bury, cache, conceal, cover, curl up, ditch, establish, fix, install, locate, nestle, place, plant, pro-

en
en

tect, screen, seat, secrete, set, settle, shelter, shield, situate, snuggle up, stash, station; SEE CONCEPTS *188,201*

ensemble [*n1*] *collection*
aggregate, assemblage, band, cast, choir, chorus, company, composite, entirety, gathering, glee club, group, octet, orchestra, organization, outfit, quartet, quintet, set, sextet, sum, total, totality, trio, troupe, whole; SEE CONCEPTS *294,432*

ensemble [*n2*] *clothing outfit*
coordinates, costume, garb*, get-up*, suit, togs*; SEE CONCEPT *451*

ensemble [*adv*] *at the same time*
all at once, altogether, as a body, as a group, as a whole, as one, at once, en masse, in concert; SEE CONCEPT *577*

enshrine [*v*] *hold as sacred*
apotheosize, bless, cherish, consecrate, dedicate, embalm, exalt, hallow, idolize, preserve, revere, sanctify, treasure; SEE CONCEPTS *69,367*

enslave [*v*] *make someone a servant*
bind, capture, chain, check, circumscribe, coerce, compel, confine, deprive, disenfranchise, disfranchise, dominate, enchain, enclose, enthrall, fetter, get hooks into*, hobble, hold, immure, imprison, incarcerate, indenture, jail, keep under thumb*, oppress, put in irons*, reduce, restrain, restrict, secure, shackle, shut in, subdue, subject, subjugate, suppress, tether, tie, yoke; SEE CONCEPTS *14,90,130,191*

ensnare [*v*] *trap*
bag*, bat eyes at*, capture, catch, cheat, come on, deceive, decoy, embroil, enmesh, entangle, entice, entrap, hook, inveigle, lure, mislead, net, rope in, snag, snare, snarl, suck in*, tangle, trick; SEE CONCEPTS *59,90*

ensue [*v*] *start to happen; come to pass*
appear, arise, attend, be consequent on, befall, be subsequent to, come after, come next, come up, derive, develop, emanate, eventuality, eventuate, flow, follow, issue, occur, proceed, result, stem, succeed, supervene, turn out, turn up; SEE CONCEPTS *119,242*

ensuing [*adj*] *resultant*
after, coming, coming up, consequent, consequential, following, later, next, next off, posterior, postliminary, subsequent, subsequential; SEE CONCEPTS *548,820*

ensure [*v*] *guarantee; make secure*
arrange, assure, certify, cinch, clinch, confirm, effect, establish, guard, insure, lock on*, lock up*, make certain, make safe, make sure, nail down*, okay, protect, provide, put on ice*, safeguard, secure, set out, warrant; SEE CONCEPTS *71,96*

entail [*v*] *require; result in*
bring about, call for, cause, demand, encompass, entangle, evoke, give rise to, impose, involve, lead to, necessitate, occasion, require, tangle; SEE CONCEPTS *242,646*

entangle [*v*] *involve, mix up*
bewilder, burden, catch, clog, come on, complicate, compromise, confuse, corner, dishevel, duke in, embarrass, embrangle, embroil, enchain, enmesh, ensnare, entrap, fetter, hamper, hook, impede, implicate, intertangle, intertwine, interweave, jumble, knot, lead on, mat, muddle, perplex, puzzle, ravel, rope in, set up, snag, snare, snarl, swindle, tangle, trammel, trap, twist, unsettle; SEE CONCEPTS *59,90,112*

entanglement [*n*] *complication, predicament*
affair, association, cobweb, complexity, confusion, difficulty, embarrassment, embroilment, enmeshment, ensnarement, entrapment, imbroglio, intricacy, intrigue, involvement, jumble, knot, liaison, mesh, mess, mix-up, muddle, snare, tangle, tie-up, toil, trap, web; SEE CONCEPTS *666, 674*

enter [*v1*] *come, put into a place*
access, arrive, barge in*, blow in*, break in, breeze in*, burst in, bust in*, butt in*, come in, crack, crawl, creep, crowd in*, drive in, drop in, fall into, gain entree, get in, go in, horn in*, immigrate, infiltrate, ingress, insert, insinuate, introduce, intrude, invade, jump in, make an entrance, make way, move in, pass into, penetrate, pierce, pile in, pop in*, probe, rush in, set foot in, slip, sneak, work in, worm in*, wriggle; SEE CONCEPT *159*

enter [*v2*] *embark on; take part in*
become member, begin, commence, commit oneself, enlist, enroll, get oneself into*, inaugurate, join, join up, lead off, muster*, open, participate in, set about, set out on, set to, sign on, sign up, start, subscribe, take up, tee off*; SEE CONCEPTS *114,234*

enter [*v3*] *record, list*
admit, docket, inject, inscribe, insert, intercalate, interpolate, introduce, log, note, post, put in, register, set down, take down; SEE CONCEPT *125*

enterprise [*n1*] *adventure, undertaking*
action, activity, affair, attempt, baby*, bag*, ballgame*, biggie*, big idea*, bit*, business, campaign, cause, company, concern, crusade, deal, deed, do*, effort, endeavor, engagement, essay, establishment, firm, flier*, follow through*, game*, happening, hazard, house, move, operation, outfit, performance, pet project*, plan, plunge*, program, project, proposition, purpose, pursuit, risk, scheme, speculation, stake, striving, stunt, task, thing*, trade, try, venture, work; SEE CONCEPTS *87,324,325,362*

enterprise [*n2*] *resourcefulness, energy*
activity, adventurousness, alertness, ambition, audacity, boldness, courage, daring, dash, drive, eagerness, enthusiasm, force, foresight, get-up-and-go*, gumption, hustle, industry, initiative, inventiveness, pluck, push, readiness, resource, self-reliance, spirit, venturesomeness, vigor, zeal; SEE CONCEPTS *411,657*

enterprising [*adj*] *resourceful, energetic*
active, advancing, adventurous, aggressive, alert, ambitious, aspiring, audacious, bold, busy, coming on strong*, craving, daring, dashing, diligent, driving, eager, enthusiastic, go-ahead*, go-go*, gumptious, hard ball*, hardworking, hungry, hustling, industrious, intrepid, itching, keen, lively, lusting, peppy, progressive, pushing, ready, self-starting, snappy, spanking, spark plug*, spirited, stirring, take-over, up-and-coming*, venturesome, vigorous, yearning, zealous, zippy*; SEE CONCEPTS *326,404,542*

entertain [*v1*] *amuse*
absorb, beguile, captivate, charm, cheer, comfort, crack up*, delight, distract, divert, ecstasize, elate, engross, enliven, enthrall, gladden, grab, gratify, humor, indulge, inspire, inspirit, interest, knock dead*, make merry, occupy, pique, please, recreate, regale, relax, satisfy, slay, solace, stimulate, tickle; SEE CONCEPTS *9,292*

entertain [v2] *accommodate visitors*
admit, be host, board, chaperone, dine, do the honors*, feed, foster, give a party, harbor, have a do*, have a get-together*, have company, have guests, have visitors, house, invite, lodge, nourish, pick up the check*, pop for*, put up*, quarter, receive, recreate, regale, room, show hospitality, spring for*, throw a party*, treat, welcome, wine and dine*; SEE CONCEPTS 377,384

entertain [v3] *think about seriously*
cherish, cogitate on, conceive, consider, contemplate, deliberate, foster, harbor, heed, hold, imagine, keep in mind, maintain, muse over, ponder, recognize, support, think over; SEE CONCEPT 17

entertaining [adj] *amusing, pleasing*
absorbing, affecting, be a ball*, captivating, charming, cheerful, cheering, clever, compelling, delightful, diverting, droll, enchanting, engaging, engrossing, enjoyable, enthralling, enticing, entrancing, exciting, fascinating, fun, funny, gay*, gay, humorous, impressive, inspiring, interesting, lively, moving, piquant, pleasant, pleasurable, poignant, priceless, provocative, recreative, relaxing, restorative, riot, rousing, scream, sidesplitting, stimulating, stirring, striking, thrilling, witty; SEE CONCEPTS 529,537

entertainment [n] *amusement, pleasure*
ball*, baah*, big time*, blast*, blow out*, celebration, cheer, clambake*, delight, dissipation, distraction, diversion, divertissement, enjoyment, feast, frolic, fun, fun and games*, gaiety, game, good time*, grins*, high time*, laughs*, leisure activity, lots of laughs*, merriment, merrymaking, party, pastime, picnic, play, recreation, regalement, relaxation, relief, revelry, satisfaction, shindig*, sport, spree, surprise, treat, wingding*; SEE CONCEPTS 383,384,386,388

enthrall [v] *captivate*
absorb, beguile, bewitch, charm, enchant, engage, enrapture, enslave, entrance, fascinate, grab, grip, hold spellbound, hook, hypnotize, intrigue, mesmerize, preoccupy, rivet, spellbind, subduc, subject, subjugate; SEE CONCEPTS 7,19,22

enthusiasm [n] *keen interest, excitement*
activity, ardency, ardor, avidity, conviction, craze, dash, devotion, eagerness, earnestness, ecstasy, elan, emotion, energy, exhilaration, fad, fanaticism, feeling, fervor, fever, fieriness, fire, flame, flare, frenzy, fury, gaiety, glow, go*, heat, hilarity, hobby, impetuosity, intensity, interest, joy, joyfulness, keenness, life, mania, mirth, nerve, oomph*, orgasm, passion, pep, rapture, red heat*, relish, snap, spirit, transport, vehemence, verve, vim, vivacity, warmth, zeal, zealousness, zest; SEE CONCEPTS 633,657

enthusiast [n] *person active in interest*
addict, admirer, aficionado, believer, buff, bug*, bum*, devotee, eccentric, fan, fanatic, follower, freak, habitué, lover, maniac, monomaniac, nut*, optimist, participant, partisan, rooter, supporter, votary, worshiper, zealot; SEE CONCEPT 423

enthusiastic [adj] *interested, excited*
agog, animated, anxious, ardent, athirst, attracted, avid, bugged*, concerned, crazy about*, devoted, dying to*, eager, earnest, ebullient, exhilarated, exuberant, fanatical, fascinated, fervent, fervid, forceful, gaga*, gone on*, gung ho*, hearty, intent, keen, keyed up*, lively, nutty*, obsessed, passionate, pleased, rabid, red-hot*, rhapsodic,

spirited, tantalized, thrilled, titillated, unqualified, vehement, vigorous, wacky*, warm, wholehearted, willing, zealous; SEE CONCEPTS 401,542

entice [v] *allure; persuade*
attract, bait, bat eyes at*, beguile, cajole, coax, decoy, draw, entrap, inveigle, lead on, lure, prevail on, seduce, tempt, toll, turn on*, wheedle; SEE CONCEPTS 7,19,22,68

enticement [n] *allurement; persuasion*
attraction, bait, blandishment, cajolery, coaxing, come hither*, come-on*, decoy, fascination, inducement, inveiglement, lure, mousetrap*, promise, seduction, snare, sweetener*, sweetening, temptation, trap; SEE CONCEPTS 7,19,22,68

entire [adj] *complete, whole*
absolute, all, choate, consolidated, continuous, full, gross, intact, integral, integrated, outright, perfect, plenary, sound, thorough, total, unbroken, undamaged, undiminished, undivided, unified, unimpaired, uninjured, unmarked, unmarred, unmitigated, unreserved, unrestricted, untouched; SEE CONCEPTS 482,531

entirely [adv] *completely*
absolutely, alone, altogether, exclusively, fully, in every respect, only, perfectly, plumb, quite, reservedly, solely, thoroughly, totally, undividedly, uniquely, utterly, well, wholly, without exception, without reservation; SEE CONCEPTS 531,535

entirety [n] *wholeness, whole*
absoluteness, aggregate, all, allness, collectiveness, collectivity, completeness, complex, comprehensiveness, ensemble, entireness, everything, fullness, gross, intactness, integrality, integrity, omneity, omnitude, oneness, perfection, plenitude, sum, sum total, the works*, total, totality, undividedness, unity, universality, whole ball of wax*, whole bit*, whole enchilada*, whole nine yards*; SEE CONCEPTS 635,837

entitle [v1] *name, label*
baptize, call, characterize, christen, denominate, designate, dub, nickname, style, subtitle, term, title; SEE CONCEPT 62

entitle [v2] *hold right to*
accredit, allow, authorize, be in line for*, confer a right, empower, enable, enfranchise, fit for, have coming*, let, license, make eligible, permit, qualify for, rate, warrant; SEE CONCEPTS 50,83,88,129

entity [n1] *object that exists*
article, being, body, creature, existence, individual, item, material, matter, organism, presence, quantity, single, singleton, something, stuff, subsistence, substance, thing; SEE CONCEPT 433

entity [n2] *nature of a being*
actuality, essence, existence, integral, integrate, quiddity, quintessence, reality, subsistence, substance, sum, system, totality; SEE CONCEPTS 411,644

entourage [n] *followers*
associates, attendants, companions, company, cortege, court, courtiers, escort, following, groupies*, hangers-on*, retainers, retinue, staff, suite, sycophants, toadies*, train; SEE CONCEPTS 387,417

entrance [n1] *a way into a place*
access, approach, archway, avenue, corridor, door, doorway, entry, entryway, gate, gateway, hall, hallway, ingress, inlet, lobby, opening, passage, passageway, path, porch, port, portal, por-

en
en

tico, staircase, threshold, vestibule, way; SEE
CONCEPT *440*

entrance [*n2*] *coming into a place; introduction*
access, accession, adit, admission, admittance,
appearance, approach, arrival, baptism, beginning, commencement, debut, enlistment, enrollment, entree, entry, immigration, import,
importation, inception, incoming, ingoing, ingress, ingression, initiation, invasion, outset, passage, penetration, progress, start, trespass; SEE
CONCEPTS *119,159*

entrance [*v*] *captivate, hypnotize*
anesthetize, attract, bewitch, charm, delight, enchant, enrapture, enthrall, fascinate, gladden,
mesmerize, please, put in a trance, ravish, rejoice,
spellbind, transport; SEE CONCEPTS *7,14,22*

entrant [*n*] *person entering competition, starting
new activity*
aspirant, beginner, candidate, competitor, contestant, convert, entry, incomer, initiate, neophyte,
newcomer, new member, novice, participant, petitioner, player, probationer, rival, solicitor, tenderfoot*; SEE CONCEPTS *366,423*

entrap [*v*] *capture, involve*
allure, bag*, beguile, benet, box in*, catch, decoy, embroil, enmesh, ensnare, entangle, entice,
hook, implicate, inveigle, lay for*, lead on, lure,
net, reel in*, rope in*, seduce, set up, snare, suck
in*, tempt, trap, trick; SEE CONCEPTS *59,90,112*

entreat [*v*] *plead with*
appeal to, ask, beg, beseech, blandish, coax, conjure, crave, enjoin, exhort, implore, importune,
invoke, pester, petition, plague, pray, press, request, supplicate, urge, wheedle; SEE CONCEPTS
48,53

entreaty [*n*] *plea*
appeal, application, imploration, imprecation, petition, prayer, request, suit, supplication; SEE
CONCEPTS *318,662*

entrée [*n*] *admittance*
access, adit, admission, connection, contact, debut, door, entrance, entry, importation, in, incoming, induction, ingress, introduction, open arms*,
open door*, way; SEE CONCEPTS *388,685*

entrench [*v1*] *establish, make inroads*
anchor, confirm, define, dig in, embed, ensconce,
fence, fix, fortify, found, ground, hole up, implant, infix, ingrain, install, lodge, plant, protect,
root, seat, set, settle, strengthen; SEE CONCEPTS
518,710

entrench [*v2*] *trespass*
break in on, encroach, impinge, infringe, interfere, interlope, intervene, intrude, invade, make
inroads*, stick nose into*; SEE CONCEPT *192*

entrepreneur [*n*] *person who starts a business
alone*
administrator, backer, businessperson, contractor,
executive, founder, impressario, industrialist,
manager, organizer, producer, promoter, under-
taker; SEE CONCEPT *347*

entrust [*v*] *give custody, authority to*
allocate, allot, assign, authorize, bank, bend an
ear*, charge, commend, commit, confer, confide,
consign, count, delegate, deliver, depend, deposit
with, hand over, impose, invest, leave with,
reckon, relegate, rely, trust, turn over; SEE CON-
CEPTS *50,88,108*

entry [*n1*] *way in to a place*
access, adit, approach, avenue, door, doorway,
entrance, foyer, gate, hall, ingress, ingression, in-

let, lobby, opening, passage, passageway, portal,
threshold, vestibule; SEE CONCEPT *440*

entry [*n2*] *introduction; permission to enter*
access, adit, admission, admittance, appearance,
coming in, entering, entrance, entree, free passage*, ingress, initiation, introgression, way; SEE
CONCEPTS *388,685*

entry [*n3*] *person participating in competition; effort*
attempt, candidate, competitor, contestant, entrant, participant, player, submission; SEE CON-
CEPT *366*

entry [*n4*] *listing in a record*
account, item, jotting, memo, memorandum,
minute, note, registration; SEE CONCEPT *270*

entwine [*v*] *twist around*
braid, coil, corkscrew, curl, embrace, encircle,
enmesh, entangle, interlace, interplait, intertwine,
interweave, knit, lace, plait, spiral, surround,
twine, weave, wind, wreathe; SEE CONCEPTS
147,201,754

enumerate [*v*] *list, count*
add up, calculate, cite, compute, count noses*,
detail, figure, identify, inventory, itemize, keep
tabs*, mention, name, number, particularize,
quote, recapitulate, recite, reckon, recount, rehearse, relate, run down, run off*, specialize,
specify, spell out, sum, take account of, tally, tell,
tick off*, total; SEE CONCEPTS *57,125,764*

enunciate [*v*] *speak clearly*
affirm, announce, articulate, declare, deliver, develop, enounce, express, intone, lay down, modulate, outline, overspread, pen, protect, roll,
sheathe, shield, shroud, shut in, superimpose, surround, swaddle, swathe, veil, wrap, wrap up; SEE
CONCEPTS *172,188*

envelop [*v*] *encase, hide*
blanket, cage, cloak, conceal, contain, coop, corral, cover, drape, embrace, encircle, enclose, encompass, enfold, engulf, enshroud, enwrap,
fence, gird, girdle, guard, hem, immure, invest,
obscure, overlay, overspread, pen, protect, roll,
sheathe, shield, shroud, shut in, superimpose, surround, swaddle, swathe, veil, wrap, wrap up; SEE
CONCEPTS *172,188*

envelope [*n*] *wrapper*
bag, box, case, casing, cloak, coat, coating, container, cover, covering, enclosure, hide, jacket,
pocket, pouch, receptacle, sheath, shell, skin, vesicle, wrapping; SEE CONCEPT *494*

enviable [*adj*] *desired, blessed*
advantageous, covetable, desirable, excellent, favored, fortunate, good, lucky, privileged, superior, welcome; SEE CONCEPT *574*

envious [*adj*] *jealous, resentful*
appetent, aspiring, begrudging, coveting, covetous, craving, desiring, desirous, distrustful, fain,
grasping, greedy, green-eyed*, green with envy*,
grudging, hankering, invidious, jaundiced, longing for, malicious, spiteful, suspicious, umbrageous, watchful, wishful, yearning; SEE
CONCEPTS *401,403*

environment [*n*] *surroundings, atmosphere*
ambiance, aura, backdrop, background, circumstances, climate, conditions, context, domain, element, encompassment, entourage, habitat,
hood*, jungle*, locale, medium, milieu, neck of
the woods*, neighborhood, purlieus, scene, scenery, setting, situation, status, stomping ground*,

surroundings, terrain, territory, turf, zoo*; SEE CONCEPTS 515,673,696

environment [n2] *Earth's system of natural resources*
atmosphere, biosphere, ecosphere, ecosystem, environs, Gaia; SEE CONCEPTS 511,515

environs [n] *neighborhood*
bound, boundary, compass, confine, district, fringes*, limits, locality, outskirts, precinct, purlieus, suburb, surroundings, territory, turf, vicinity; SEE CONCEPT 516

envisage/envision [v] *picture in one's mind*
anticipate, behold, conceive, conceptualize, contemplate, externalize, fancy, feature, foresee, form mental picture of*, grasp, have a picture of*, image, imagine, look upon, materialize, objectify, predict, realize, regard, see, survey, think up, view, view in mind's eye*, vision, visualize; SEE CONCEPTS 17,43

envoy [n] *deputy*
agent, ambassador, attaché, bearer, carrier, chargé d'affaires, consul, courier, delegate, diplomat, emissary, intermediary, internuncio, legate, medium, messenger, minister, nuncio, plenipotentiary, representative, vicar; SEE CONCEPTS 348, 354

envy [n] *jealousy*
backbiting, coveting, covetousness, enviousness, evil eye*, green-eyed monster*, grudge, grudging, grudgingness, hatred, heartburn, ill will, invidiousness, jaundiced eye*, lusting, malevolence, malice, maliciousness, malignity, opposition, prejudice, resentfulness, resentment, rivalry, spite; SEE CONCEPT 410

envy [v] *be jealous of another*
be envious, begrudge, covet, crave, desire, die over*, eat one's heart out*, grudge, hanker, have hard feelings*, hunger, long, lust, object to, resent, thirst, turn green*, want, yearn; SEE CONCEPTS 10,20

ephemeral [adj] *momentary, passing*
brief, episodic, evanescent, fleeting, flitting, fugacious, fugitive, impermanent, short, short-lived, temporary, transient, transitory, unenduring, volatile; SEE CONCEPTS 798,801

epic [n] *long story*
heroic poem, legend, narrative, saga, tale; SEE CONCEPT 282

epicurean [n] *gourmet*
bon vivant, connoisseur, critic, epicure, gastronome, gastronomer, glutton, gourmand, hedonist, pleasure seeker, sensualist, specialist, sybarite; SEE CONCEPT 423

epicurean [adj] *loving food and finer things*
gluttonous, gourmandizing, gourmet, hedonistic, libertine, lush, luxurious, pleasure-seeking, self-indulgent, sensual, sensuous, sybaritic, voluptuous; SEE CONCEPT 401

epidemic [n] *widespread disease*
contagion, endemic, growth, outbreak, pest, pestilence, plague, rash, scourge, spread, upsurge, wave, what's going around*; SEE CONCEPTS 306,316

epidemic [adj] *widespread*
catching, communicable, contagious, endemic, general, infectious, pandemic, prevailing, prevalent, rampant, rife, sweeping, wide-ranging; SEE CONCEPTS 314,537

epigram [n] *witticism*
aphorism, bon mot, joke, motto, pithy saying, quip, quirk; SEE CONCEPT 278

epilogue [n] *afterword*
coda, concluding speech, conclusion, ending, finale, follow-up, peroration, postlude, postscript, sequel, summation, swan song*; SEE CONCEPTS 264,270,278

episode [n] *adventure; scene*
affair, business, chapter, circumstance, doings, event, experience, goings-on*, happening, incident, installment, interlude, matter, occasion, occurrence, part, passage, section, thing*, what's going down*; SEE CONCEPTS 3,4

episodic [adj] *intermittent; composed of several tales*
anecdotal, digressive, disconnected, discursive, disjointed, incidental, irregular, occasional, picaresque, rambling, roundabout, segmented, soap opera*, sporadic, wandering; SEE CONCEPT 482

epistle [n] *letter*
billet doux*, cannonball*, card, communication, dispatch, FYI*, get-well, invite, kite*, line*, love letter, memo, message, missive, note, poison pen*, postcard, scratch*, tab*, thank-you; SEE CONCEPT 271

epitaph [n] *inscription on a gravestone*
commemoration, elegy, epigraph, eulogy, hic jacet, legend, memorial, monument, remembrance, requiscat in pacem, sentiment; SEE CONCEPT 278

epithet [n] *nickname*
appellation, description, designation, name, sobriquet, tag, title; SEE CONCEPT 683

epitome [n1] *perfect example*
apotheosis, archetype, embodiment, essence, exemplar, exemplification, illustration, last word*, personification, quintessence, representation, type, typification, ultimate; SEE CONCEPT 686

epitome [n2] *abbreviation*
abridgment, abstract, brief, compendium, condensation, conspectus, contraction, digest, precis, recapitulation, résumé, summary, summation, syllabus, synopsis; SEE CONCEPT 283

equable [adj] *steady, calm*
agreeable, composed, consistent, constant, easygoing, even, even-tempered, imperturbable, levelheaded, methodical, orderly, placid, regular, serene, smooth, stabile, stable, systematic, temperate, tranquil, unchanging, unexcitable, unflappable, unfluctuating, unvarying; SEE CONCEPTS 401,542,544

equal [n] *peer*
alter ego, coequal, companion, compeer, competitor, complement, copy, counterpart, double, duplicate, equivalent, like, likeness, match, mate, parallel, rival, twin; SEE CONCEPT 423

equal [adj1] *alike*
according, balanced, break even, commensurate, comparable, coordinate, correspondent, corresponding, double, duplicate, egalitarian, equivalent, evenly matched, fifty-fifty*, homologous, identic, identical, indistinguishable, invariable, level, look-alike, matched, matching, one and the same, parallel, proportionate, same, same difference*, spit and image*, stack up with*, tantamount, to the same degree, two peas in pod*, uniform, unvarying; SEE CONCEPTS 487,566,573

equal [adj2] *fair, unbiased*
dispassionate, egalitarian, equable, even-handed,

impartial, just, nondiscriminatory, nonpartisan, objective, uncolored, unprejudiced, without distinction; SEE CONCEPTS *401,542*

equal [v] *make even, be even with*
agree, amount to, approach, balance, be commensurate, be identical, be level, be tantamount, break even, come up to, compare, comprise, consist of, coordinate, correspond, emulate, equalize, equate, equipoise, equiponderate, keep pace with*, level, live up to*, match, measure up, meet, parallel, partake of, rank with, reach, rise to, rival, run abreast, square with, tally, tie, touch; SEE CONCEPT *667*

equality [n] *similarity, balance; egalitarianism*
adequation, civil rights, commensurateness, coordination, correspondence, equal opportunity, equatability, equilibrium, equipoise, equivalence, evenness, fairness, fair play*, fair practice, fair shake*, homology, identity, impartiality, isonomy, likeness, par, parallelism, parity, sameness, tolerance, uniformity; SEE CONCEPTS *388,645,667*

equalize [v] *make the same; balance*
adjust, commeasure, communize, compare, coordinate, democratize, emulate, equal, equate, establish, even, even up, handicap, level, match, parallel, regularize, rival, smooth, socialize, square, standardize, trim; SEE CONCEPTS *126,232*

equanimity [n] *levelheadedness*
aplomb, assurance, ataraxia, ataraxy, calm, calmness, composure, confidence, cool, coolness, detachment, equability, imperturbability, patience, peace, phlegm, placidity, poise, presence of mind*, sangfroid, self-possession, serenity, steadiness, tranquillity; SEE CONCEPTS *410,633*

equate [v] *balance; think of together*
agree, assimilate, associate, average, be commensurate, compare, consider, correspond to, correspond with, equalize, even, hold, level, liken, make equal, match, offset, pair, paragon, parallel, regard, relate, represent, similize, square, tally, treat; SEE CONCEPTS *37,39,667*

equilibrium [n] *balance; evenness*
calm, calmness, composure, cool, coolness, counterbalance, counterpoise, equanimity, equipoise, poise, polish, rest, serenity, stability, stasis, steadiness, steadying, symmetry; SEE CONCEPTS *633,731*

equip [v] *make ready with supplies*
accouter, adorn, appoint, arm, array, attire, deck, deck out*, decorate, dress, endow, feather nest*, fit out, fix up, furnish, gear, gear up*, heel*, implement, line nest*, man, outfit, prep*, prepare, provide, qualify, ready, rig, set up, stake, stock, supply, turn out; SEE CONCEPTS *140,182*

equipment [n] *supplies, gear for activity*
accessories, accompaniments, accouterments, apparatus, appliances, appurtenances, articles, attachments, baggage, belongings, contraptions, contrivances, devices, equipage, facilities, fittings, fixtures, furnishings, furniture, gadgets, habiliments, impedimenta, kit and kaboodle*, machinery, material, materiel, miscellaneous, outfit, paraphernalia, provisioning, provisions, rig*, setup, shebang*, stock, store, stuff, tackle, things, tools, trappings, traps, utensils; SEE CONCEPTS *364,446,496*

equitable [adj] *impartial*
candid, cricket, decent, disinterested, dispassionate, due, ethical, even-handed, even-steven*, fair,

fair and square*, fair shake*, fair-to-middling*, honest, impersonal, just, level, moral, nondiscriminatory, nonpartisan, objective, proper, proportionate, reasonable, right, rightful, square, square deal*, stable, unbiased, uncolored, unprejudiced; SEE CONCEPTS *542,545*

equity [n1] *impartiality*
disinterestedness, equitableness, evenhandedness, fair-mindedness, fairness, fair play, honesty, integrity, justice, justness, nonpartisanship, piece, reasonableness, rectitude, righteousness, square deal*, uprightness; SEE CONCEPTS *645,657*

equity [n2] *money invested in possession*
capital, investment, outlay; SEE CONCEPTS *332,344*

equivalence [n] *sameness, similarity*
adequation, agreement, alikeness, compatibility, conformity, correlation, correspondence, equality, evenness, exchangeability, identity, interchangeability, interchangeableness, likeness, match, par, parallel, parity, synonym, synonymy; SEE CONCEPTS *667,670*

equivalent [n] *equal, counterpart*
carbon copy*, correspondent, dead ringer*, ditto, like, match, obverse, opposite, parallel, peer, reciprocal, same difference*, spitting image*, substitute, twin; SEE CONCEPTS *667,670*

equivalent [adj] *same, similar*
agnate, akin, alike, analogous, carbon*, commensurate, comparable, convertible, copy, correlative, correspondent, corresponding, ditto*, duplicate, equal, even, homologous, identical, indistinguishable, interchangeable, like, of a kind, parallel, proportionate, reciprocal, same difference*, substitute, synonymous, tantamount; SEE CONCEPTS *487,566,573*

equivocal [adj] *doubtful, uncertain*
ambiguous, ambivalent, amphibological, borderline, clear as mud*, clouded*, disreputable, dubious, evasive, fishy*, fuzzy*, hazy*, indefinite, indeterminate, indistinct, misleading, muddled, muzzy*, oblique, obscure, open, problematic, puzzling, questionable, suspect, suspicious, tenebrous, unclear, undecided, unexplicit, unintelligible, vague, with mixed feelings*; SEE CONCEPTS *529,535*

equivocate [v] *avoid an issue*
beat around the bush*, beg the question*, blow hot and cold*, cavil, cloud the issue*, con, cop a plea*, cop out*, cover up*, dodge, double-talk, elude, escape, eschew, evade, falsify, fence, fib, flip-flop*, fudge*, give run around*, hedge, hem and haw*, jive*, lie, mince words, palter, parry, pass the buck*, prevaricate, pussyfoot, quibble, run around, shuck, shuffle, sidestep, sit on the fence*, stonewall*, tell white lie*, tergiversate, tergiverse, waffle*, weasel*; SEE CONCEPTS *63,102*

equivocation [n] *avoidance of an issue*
ambiguity, amphibology, casuistry, coloring, con, cop out, cover, cover-up, deceit, deception, deceptiveness, delusion, dissimulation, distortion, double entendre, double meaning, double talk, doubtfulness, duplicity, equivocality, evasion, fallacy, fib, fibbing, hedging, lie, lying*, misrepresentation, prevarication, quibbling, routine, run-around, shuffling, song*, song and dance*, sophistry, speciousness, spuriousness, stall, stone-

wall*, tergiversation, waffle*; SEE CONCEPTS 63,278

era [n] *time period in history*
aeon, age, cycle, date, day, days, eon, epoch, generation, stage, term, time; SEE CONCEPTS 807,816

eradicate [v] *destroy; remove*
abate, abolish, annihilate, blot out*, demolish, deracinate, do away with, efface, eliminate, erase, expunge, exterminate, extinguish, extirpate, liquidate, mow down*, obliterate, off*, purge, raze, root out*, rub out*, scratch*, scrub, shoot down, squash, stamp out*, take out*, torpedo*, total, trash, unroot, uproot, wash out, waste, weed out*, wipe out*; SEE CONCEPTS 211,252

erase [v] *remove; rub out*
abolish, annul, black out, blank, blot, blue pencil*, cancel, cross out, cut, cut out, delete, disannul, dispatch, efface, eliminate, excise, expunge, extirpate, gut, kill, launder*, negate, nullify, obliterate, scratch out*, stamp out*, strike, strike out, take out, trim, wipe out*, withdraw, X-out*; SEE CONCEPTS 211,215

erect [adj] *straight up*
arrect, cocked, elevated, erectile, firm, perpendicular, raised, rigid, standing, stiff, upright, upstanding, vertical; SEE CONCEPTS 485,581,604

erect [v] *build; establish*
assemble, bring about, cobble up*, cook, compose, construct, create, effect, elevate, fabricate, fashion, fit together, forge, form, found, frame, fudge together*, heighten, hoist, initiate, institute, join, knock together*, lift, make, make up, manufacture, mount, organize, pitch, plant, prefabricate*, produce, put together, put up, raise, rear, run up, set up, shape, stand, stand up, throw together*, throw up, upraise, uprear; SEE CONCEPTS 168,221

ergo [adv] *for that reason*
accordingly, consequently, hence, in consequence, so, then, therefore, thereupon, thus, thusly; SEE CONCEPT 544

ergonomics [n] *human engineering*
comfort design, functional design, human factors, user-friendly systems, workplace efficiency; SEE CONCEPT 349

erode [v] *deteriorate; wear away*
abrade, bite, consume, corrode, crumble, destroy, disintegrate, eat, gnaw, grind down, scour, spoil, waste, wear down; SEE CONCEPTS 252,469

erosion [n] *deterioration; wearing away*
abrasion, attrition, consumption, corrosion, decrease, desedimentation, despoliation, destruction, disintegration, eating away, grinding down, spoiling, washing away, wear, wearing down; SEE CONCEPTS 252,257,698

erotic [adj] *sexy*
amative, amatory, amorous, aphrodisiac, bawdy, blue*, carnal, concupiscent, earthy, erogenous, fervid, filthy, fleshly, hot*, impassioned, kinky*, lascivious, lecherous, lewd, obscene, off-color*, prurient, purple*, raunchy, raw, romantic, rousing, salacious, seductive, sensual, sexual, spicy, steamy, stimulating, suggestive, titillating, venereal, voluptuous; SEE CONCEPTS 372,545

err [v] *make a mistake; do wrong*
be inaccurate, be incorrect, be in error, be mistaken, blow*, blunder, bollix*, boo-boo*, deviate, drop the ball*, fall, flub*, foul up*, go astray, goof*, go wrong, lapse, louse up*, make a mess

of*, mess up*, misapprehend, misbehave, miscalculate, misjudge, muff*, offend, screw up*, sin, slip up*, snafu*, snarl up, stray, stumble, transgress, trespass, wander; SEE CONCEPT 101

errand [n] *task*
assignment, charge, commission, duty, job, message, mission; SEE CONCEPT 362

errant [adj] *wrong; deviant*
aberrant, deviating, devious, drifting, errable, erratic, erring, fallible, heretic, meandering, misbehaving, mischievous, miscreant, naughty, offending, off straight and narrow*, rambling, ranging, roaming, roving, shifting, sinning, stray, straying, unorthodox, unreliable, wandering, wayward; SEE CONCEPTS 542,545,581

erratic [adj] *unpredictable; wandering*
aberrant, abnormal, anomalous, arbitrary, bizarre, capricious, changeable, desultory, devious, dicey, directionless, dubious, eccentric, fitful, flaky*, fluctuant, idiosyncratic, iffy*, incalculable, inconsistent, inconstant, irregular, meandering, mercurial, nomadic, oddball*, peculiar, planetary, rambling, roving, shifting, spasmodic, strange, stray, uncertain, undirected, unnatural, unreliable, unstable, unusual, vagarious, variable, volatile, wayward, weird, whimsical; SEE CONCEPTS 535,542,581

erroneous [adj] *wrong, incorrect*
all off*, all wet*, amiss, askew, awry, defective, fallacious, false, faulty, flawed, inaccurate, inexact, invalid, misguided, mistaken, off, specious, spurious, unfounded, unsound, untrue, way off, wrong number*; SEE CONCEPTS 267,570,582

error [n] *mistake; wrong*
absurdity, bad job*, blunder, boner*, boo-boo*, delinquency, delusion, deviation, erratum, failure, fall, fallacy, falsehood, falsity, fault, faux pas, flaw, glitch, goof*, howler*, inaccuracy, lapse, misapprehension, misbelief, miscalculation, misconception, miscue, misdeed, misjudgment, mismanagement, miss, misstep, misunderstanding, offense, omission, oversight, screamer*, screwup*, sin, slight, slip, slipup, solecism, stumble, transgression, trespass, untruth, wrongdoing, X*; SEE CONCEPTS 101,230,674,699

ersatz [adj] *artificial*
bogus, copied, counterfeit, fake, false, imitation, manufactured, phony, pretended, sham, simulated, spurious, substitute, synthetic; SEE CONCEPT 582

erstwhile [adj] *former*
bygone, ex, late, old, once, one-time, past, preceding, previous, quondam, sometime; SEE CONCEPT 820

erudite [adj] *well-educated, cultured*
brainy, cultivated, educated, highbrow, in the know, into*, knowledgeable, learned, lettered, literate, savvy, scholarly, scholastic, studious, well-read, wise up*; SEE CONCEPT 402

erudition [n] *higher education*
bookishness, brains, cultivation, culture, enlightenment, intellectuality, knowledge, learnedness, learning, letters, literacy, lore, pedantry, refinement, savvy, scholarliness, scholarship, science, studiousness; SEE CONCEPTS 287,409

erupt [v] *give forth, eject with force*
appear, belch, blow up, boil, break out, burst, cast out, detonate, discharge, emit, eruct, explode, extravasate, flare up*, go off*, gush, hurl, jet, pour forth, rupture, spew, spit, spout, spurt,

eq
er

throw off*, touch off*, vent, vomit; SEE CONCEPTS *179,222*

eruption [*n*] *ejection*
access, blast, blow-up, breakout, burst, discharge, explosion, flare-up, flow, gust, outbreak, outburst, sally, venting, vomiting; SEE CONCEPTS *179,467*

escalate [*v*] *increase, be increased*
amplify, ascend, broaden, climb, enlarge, expand, extend, grow, heighten, intensify, magnify, make worse, mount, raise, rise, scale, step up, widen; SEE CONCEPTS *236,245*

escapade [*n*] *adventure, usually lighthearted*
antic, caper, fling, folly, frolic, gag, high jinks, lark, mischief, monkeyshines*, prank, rib*, roguery, rollick, romp, scrape, shenanigans*, spree, stunt, trick, vagary; SEE CONCEPTS *384,386*

escape [*n*] *breaking away; getaway*
abdication, avoidance, AWOL*, beat, bolt, break, breakout, bypassing, circumvention, decampment, deliverance, departure, desertion, disappearance, dodging, ducking, elopement, elusion, elusiveness, eschewal, evasion, evasiveness, extrication, fadeout, flight, freedom, hegira, lam, leave, liberation, out, outbreak, powder, release, rescue, retreat, runaround, shunning, sidestepping, slip, spring, withdrawal; SEE CONCEPT *102*

escape [*v*] *break away from*
abscond, avoid, bail out*, bolt, burst out, circumvent, cut and run*; cut loose*, decamp, depart, desert, disappear, dodge, double, duck, duck out*, elope, elude, emerge, evade, flee, fly, fly the coop*, gafiate, get away with*, get off*, go scot-free*, leave, make getaway*, make off*, make oneself scarce*, pass, play hooky*, run, run away, run off*, run out on*, shun, skip, slip, slip away, steal away, take a powder*, take flight, take on the lam*, vanish, work out of, wriggle out*; SEE CONCEPT *102*

eschew [*v*] *have nothing to do with*
abandon, abjure, abstain, avoid, double, duck, elude, evade, forgo, forswear, give up, have no truck with*, let well enough alone*, not touch, refrain, renounce, sacrifice, shun, shy, shy away from, steer clear of*, swear off*; SEE CONCEPTS *30,102*

escort [*n*] *protection; accompaniment*
alarm clock*, attendant, beau, bird dog*, bodyguard, cavalier, chaperon, companion, company, consort, convoy, convoyer, cortege, date, entourage, fellow, friend, gallant, guard, guide, partner, protector, retinue, safeguard, squire, train, warden*; SEE CONCEPTS *419,423*

escort [*v*] *act as a companion, guard*
accompany, attend, bear, bring, carry, chaperon, company, conduct, consort with, convoy, date, direct, drag, go with, guide, lead, partner, pilot, protect, route, see, shepherd, show, squire, steer, take out, usher; SEE CONCEPTS *114,384,714*

esoteric [*adj*] *mysterious, obscure*
abstruse, acroamatic, arcane, cabbalistic, cryptic, deep, Delphic, heavy, hermetic, hidden, inner, inscrutable, mystic, mystical, occult, Orphic, private, profound, recondite, secret, Sibylline; SEE CONCEPTS *529,576,582*

especial [*adj*] *exceptional, particular*
chief, distinguished, dominant, exclusive, express, extraordinary, individual, marked, notable, noteworthy, outstanding, paramount, peculiar, personal, predominant, preeminent, preponderant,

principal, private, set, signal, singular, special, specific, supreme, surpassing, uncommon, unique, unusual; SEE CONCEPTS *535,564,574*

especially [*adv*] *exceptionally, particularly*
abnormally, above all, before all else, chiefly, conspicuously, curiously, eminently, exclusively, expressly, extraordinarily, in particular, in specie, mainly, markedly, notably, oddly, outstandingly, peculiarly, preeminently, primarily, principally, remarkably, signally, singularly, specially, specifically, strangely, strikingly, supremely, unaccountably, uncommonly, uncustomarily, uniquely, unusually, wonderfully; SEE CONCEPTS *535,564,574*

espouse [*v1*] *stand up for; support*
accept, adopt, advocate, approve, back, champion, defend, embrace, get into*, go in for*, maintain, stand behind*, take on, take up, uphold; SEE CONCEPT *10*

espouse [*v2*] *marry*
betroth, catch, take as spouse, unite, wed; SEE CONCEPT *297*

essay [*n1*] *written discourse*
article, composition, discussion, disquisition, dissertation, explication, exposition, manuscript, paper, piece, study, theme, thesis, tract, treatise; SEE CONCEPT *271*

essay [*n2*] *try, attempt*
aim, bid, dry run*, effort, endeavor, exertion, experiment, hassle, labor, one's all*, one's level best*, shot*, striving, struggle, test, toil, travail, trial, try on*, tryout, undertaking, venture, whack*, work; SEE CONCEPT *87*

essay [*v*] *try, attempt*
aim, assay, endeavor, have a crack*, have a go*, have a shot*, have at it*, labor, make a run at*, offer, put to the test*, seek, strive, struggle, take a stab at*, take a whack at*, take on, test, toil, travail, try out, undertake, venture, work; SEE CONCEPT *87*

essence [*n1*] *heart, significance*
aspect, attribute, backbone, base, basis, be-all and end-all*, being, bottom, bottom line*, burden, caliber, character, chief constituent, constitution, core, crux, element, entity, essentia, essentiality, fiber, form, fundamentals, germ, grain, kernel, life, lifeblood, main idea, marrow, meaning, meat*, name of game*, nature, nitty-gritty*, nub, nucleus, pith, point, principle, property, quality, quiddity, quintessence, reality, root, soul, spirit, structure, stuff, substance, timber, vein, virtuality; SEE CONCEPTS *411,661,668,688*

essence [*n2*] *distillate, concentrate*
balm, cologne, drug, effusion, elixir, extract, fragrance, juice, liquor, perfume, potion, scent, spirits, tincture; SEE CONCEPTS *260,467*

essential [*n*] *necessity, basic*
ABCs*, bottom line*, brass tacks*, condition, element, essence, fire and ice*, fundamental, proprieties*, guts*, heart, meat and potatoes*, must, name of the game*, nitty-gritty*, nuts and bolts*, part and parcel*, precondition, prerequisite, principle, quintessence, requirement, requisite, rudiment, sine qua non, stuff, substance, vital part, where one's at*; SEE CONCEPTS *646,661,826*

essential [*adj*] *important, vital*
capital, cardinal, chief, constitutive, crucial, foremost, fundamental, imperative, indispensable, leading, main, necessary, necessitous, needed,

needful, prerequisite, principal, required, requisite, right-hand, wanted; SEE CONCEPT *567*

essential [*adj2*] *basic, fundamental*
absolute, basal, cardinal, cold, complete, congenital, connate, constitutional, deep-seated, elemental, elementary, ideal, inborn, inbred, inherent, innate, intrinsic, key, main, material, meat and potatoes*, name of the game*, nitty-gritty*, nub, perfect, primary, prime, primitive, principal, quintessential, substratal, underlying; SEE CONCEPTS *546,549*

establish [*v1*] *set up, organize*
authorize, base, build, constitute, create, decree, domiciliate, enact, endow, ensconce, entrench, erect, fix, form, found, ground, implant, inaugurate, inculcate, install, institute, land, lay foundation, live, lodge, moor, originate, place, plant, practice, provide, put, ring in, rivet, root, secure, set down, settle, stabilize, start, start ball rolling*, station, stick; SEE CONCEPTS *168,173,221,251*

establish [*v2*] *authenticate; demonstrate*
ascertain, authorize, base, certify, circumstantiate, confirm, constitute, corroborate, decree, determine, discover, enact, find out, formulate, learn, legislate, make, make out, predicate, prescribe, prove, ratify, rest, show, stay, substantiate, validate, verify; SEE CONCEPTS *49,50,88,97*

establishment [*n1*] *organization; creation*
enactment, endowment, formation, formulation, foundation, founding, inauguration, installation, institution, setting up; SEE CONCEPTS *173,221*

establishment [*n2*] *business, institution*
abode, building, company, concern, corporation, enterprise, factory, firm, foundation, house, institute, office, organization, outfit, plant, quarters, residence, setup, structure, system, workplace; SEE CONCEPTS *323,325,449*

establishment [*n3*] *ruling class; bureaucracy*
authority, city hall*, conservatives, diehards*, established order, Old Guard*, powers that be*, them, the system*; SEE CONCEPTS *347,354*

estate [*n1*] *extensive manor and its property*
acreage, area, country home, country place, demesne, domain, dominion, farm, finca, freehold, grounds, holdings, lands, parcel, plantation, quinta, ranch, residence, rural seat, territory, villa; SEE CONCEPT *516*

estate [*n2*] *person's possessions, property, wealth*
assets, belongings, bequest, capital, chattels, devise, earthly possessions, effects, endowment, fortune, goods, heritage, inheritance, legacy, patrimony, substance; SEE CONCEPTS *340,710*

estate [*n3*] *class, rank*
bracket, caste, category, classification, condition, echelon, footing, form, grade, level, lot, order, period, place, position, quality, repair, shape, situation, sphere, standing, state, station, status, stratum; SEE CONCEPTS *378,388*

esteem [*v1*] *think highly of*
admire, appreciate, apprise, be fond of, cherish, consider, hold dear, honor, idolize, like, look up to*, love, prize, regard, regard highly, respect, revere, reverence, think the world of*, treasure, value, venerate, worship; SEE CONCEPT *32*

esteem [*v2*] *consider, believe*
account, calculate, deem, estimate, hold, judge, rate, reckon, regard, think, view; SEE CONCEPT *12*

estimable [*adj*] *honorable, worthy*
admirable, admired, appreciable, august, big

name*, big time*, commendable, decent, deserving, esteemed, excellent, good, high-powered, honored, in limelight*, laudable, major league*, meritorious, meritable, name, noble, palmary, praisable, praiseworthy, reputable, reputed, respectable, respected, sterling, valuable, valued, venerable, well-thought-of*; SEE CONCEPTS *567,572*

estimate [*n*] *approximate calculation; educated guess*
appraisal, appraisement, assay, assessment, ballpark figure*, belief, conclusion, conjecture, estimation, evaluation, gauging, guess, guesstimate*, impression, judgment, measure, measurement, mensuration, opinion, point of view, projection, rating, reckoning, sizing up*, stock, surmise, survey, thought, valuation; SEE CONCEPTS *28,37,689,784*

estimate [*v*] *guess, try to value*
account, appraise, assay, assess, believe, budget, calculate roughly, cast, cipher, class, classify, compute, conjecture, consider, count, decide, deduce, determine, enumerate, evaluate, examine, expect, figure, form opinion, gauge, guess, guesstimate*, judge, look into, look upon, number, outline, plan, predict, prophesy, rank, rate, reason, reckon, regard, run over*, scheme, set a figure*, size up*, sum, suppose, surmise, suspect, tax, think, think through*; SEE CONCEPTS *28,37,764*

estimation [*n*] *belief, guess*
admiration, appraisal, appreciation, arithmetic, assessment, calculating, ciphering, computation, consideration, considered opinion, credit, esteem, estimate, estimating, evaluation, favor, figuring, impression, judgment, opinion, predicting, reckoning, regard, respect, stock, valuation, veneration, view; SEE CONCEPTS *28,689*

estrange [*v*] *destroy the affections of*
alien, alienate, antagonize, break up, disaffect, disunify, disunite, divert, divide, divorce, drive apart, leave, make hostile, part, put on the outs*, separate, set at odds*, sever, split, sunder, turn off*, wean, withdraw, withhold; SEE CONCEPTS *7,19,297,384*

estrangement [*n*] *destruction of affections*
alienation, antagonization, breach, break-up, disaffection, disassociation, disunity, division, divorce, hostility, leave, leaving, parting, removal, schism, separation, split, withdrawal, withholding; SEE CONCEPTS *297,388*

et cetera [*adj*] *and so forth*
along with others, and all, and on and on, and others, and so on, and the like, and the rest, blah blah blah*, et al., whatever, whatnot; SEE CONCEPTS *267,577*

etch [*v*] *carve*
compose, corrode, cut, define, delineate, depict, describe, eat into, engrave, erode, execute, furrow, grave, impress, imprint, incise, ingrain, inscribe, outline, picture, portray, reduce, represent, set forth, stamp; SEE CONCEPTS *174,176*

etching [*n*] *art created by carving*
engraving, impression, imprint, inscription, mezzotint, photoengraving, photogravure, print, reproduction, rotogravure, transferring; SEE CONCEPT *259*

eternal [*adj*] *without pause; endless*
abiding, ageless, always, amaranthine, boundless, ceaseless, constant, continual, continued, continuous, dateless, deathless, enduring, everlasting,

er
et

forever, illimitable, immemorial, immortal, immutable, imperishable, incessant, indefinite, indestructible, infinite, interminable, lasting, never-ending, perdurable, perennial, permanent, perpetual, persistent, relentless, termless, timeless, unbroken, unceasing, undying, unending, unfading, uninterrupted, unremitting, without end; SEE CONCEPTS *482,798*

eternally [adv] *endlessly*
always, continually, ever, evermore, forever, forevermore, for ever so long*, for keeps, in perpetuum, perpetually, regularly, till cows come home*; SEE CONCEPT *798*

eternity [n] *forever*
aeon, afterlife, age, ages, blue moon*, dog's age*, endlessness, endless time, everlastingness, forever and a day*, future, immortality, imperishability, infiniteness, infinitude, infinity, kingdom come*, other world*, perpetuity, timelessness, time without end, wild blue yonder*, world without end*; SEE CONCEPTS *370,804,818*

ethereal [adj] *delicate, heavenly*
aerial, airy, celestial, dainty, divine, empyreal, empyrean, exquisite, fairy, filmy, fine, gaseous, ghostly, gossamer, impalpable, insubstantial, intangible, light, rarefied, refined, spiritual, sublime, subtle, supernal, tenuous, unearthly, unsubstantial, unworldly, vaporous, vapory; SEE CONCEPTS *491,549,582,606*

ethical [adj] *moral, righteous*
Christian, clean, conscientious, correct, decent, elevated, equitable, fair, fitting, good, high-principled, honest, honorable, humane, just, kosher*, moralistic, noble, principled, proper, respectable, right, right-minded, square, straight, true blue*, upright, upstanding, virtuous; SEE CONCEPT *545*

ethics/ethic [n] *moral philosophy, values*
belief, conduct, conscience, convention, conventionalities, criteria, descency, ethos, goodness, honesty, honor, ideal, imperative, integrity, moral code, morality, mores, natural law, nature, practice, principles, right and wrong, rules of conduct, standard, standards, the Golden Rule*; SEE CONCEPTS *645,688,689*

ethnic [adj] *racial, cultural*
indigenous, national, native, traditional, tribal; SEE CONCEPT *549*

etiquette [n] *manners, politeness*
amenities, civility, code, convention, courtesy, customs, decency, decorum, deportment, dignity, form, formalities, good behavior*, mores, politesse, proper behavior, propriety, protocol, p's and q's*, rules, seemliness, social graces, suavities, usage; SEE CONCEPT *633*

eulogize [v] *praise, glorify*
acclaim, applaud, bless, celebrate, commend, compliment, cry up, exalt, extol, flatter, give a bouquet*, give a posy*, hymn, idolize, laud, magnify, panegyrize, pay tribute to, sing praises; SEE CONCEPT *69*

eulogy [n] *praise, acclamation*
acclaim, accolade, adulation, applause, citation, commendation, compliment, encomium, exaltation, glorification, laudation, paean, panegyric, plaudit, salutation, tribute; SEE CONCEPTS *69,278*

euphemism [n] *nice way of saying something*
circumlocution, delicacy, floridness, grandiloquence, inflation, pomposity, pretense, purism; SEE CONCEPTS *275,278*

euphoria [n] *extreme happiness*
bliss, dreamland, ecstasy, elation, exaltation, exhilaration, exultation, frenzy, glee, health, high spirits, intoxication, joy, joyousness, jubilation, madness, rapture, relaxation, transport; SEE CONCEPT *410*

evacuate [v] *clear an area; empty*
abandon, bail out*, cut out, decamp, depart, desert, discharge, displace, eject, expel, forsake, hightail, leave, move out, pack up, pull out, quit, relinquish, remove, run for the hills*, skidaddle*, vacate, withdraw; SEE CONCEPTS *179,195*

evade [v] *get away from*
avoid, baffle, balk, beat around bush*, beg the question*, bypass, cavil, circumvent, conceal, confuse, cop out, deceive, decline, dodge, double, duck, elude, equivocate, escape, eschew, fence, fend off*, flee, fly, fudge*, get around, give the runaround*, hedge, hide, keep distance*, lay low*, lead on a merry chase*, lie, parry, pass up, pretend, prevaricate, pussyfoot, put off, shift, shirk, shuck, shuffle, shun, shy, sidestep, slip out, sneak away*, steer clear of*, tergiversate, trick, waffle*, weasel*; SEE CONCEPTS *30,102*

evaluate [v] *judge*
appraise, assay, assess, calculate, check, check out, class, classify, criticize, decide, estimate, figure out, future, gauge, grade, guesstimate*, look over, peg*, price out, rank, rate, read, reckon, set at, size, size up*, survey, take account of, take measure, valuate, value, weigh; SEE CONCEPTS *18,24,103*

evaluation [n] *judgment*
appraisal, appraisement, assessment, calculation, decision, estimate, estimation, guesstimation*, interpretation, opinion, rating, stock, take, valuation; SEE CONCEPTS *24,103,689*

evaporate [v] *dry up, dissolve*
clear, concentrate, dehumidify, dehydrate, dematerialize, desiccate, disappear, dispel, disperse, dissipate, evanesce, evanish, fade, fade away, melt, parch, pass, vanish, vaporize, weaken; SEE CONCEPTS *469,698*

evaporation [n] *drying up; dissolution*
dehydration, dematerialization, desiccation, disappearance, dispelling, dispersal, dissipation, escape, evanescence, fading, melting, vanishing, vaporescence, vaporization; SEE CONCEPTS *469, 607,698*

evasion [n] *escape, avoidance*
artifice, circumvention, cop-out*, cunning, ditch*, dodge*, dodging, elusion, equivocating, equivocation, eschewal, evading, evasiveness, excuse, fancy footwork*, fudging*, jive, lie, obliqueness, pretext, prevarication, quibble, routine, run-around, ruse, shift, shirking, shuffling, shunning, slip*, sophism, sophistry, stall, stonewall*, subterfuge, trick, trickery; SEE CONCEPTS *59,63,102*

evasive [adj] *deceitful, tricky*
ambiguous, cagey, casuistic, casuistical, cunning, deceptive, devious, dissembling, elusive, elusory, equivocating, false, fugitive, greasy, indirect, intangible, lying, misleading, oblique, prevaricating, shifty, shuffling, slippery, sly, sophistical, stonewalling*, unclear, vague; SEE CONCEPTS *267,401,542*

even [adj] *flat, uniform*
alike, balanced, consistent, constant, continual, continuous, direct, equal, flush, homogenous,

horizontal, level, matching, metrical, parallel, planate, plane, plumb, proportional, regular, right, same, smooth, square, stabile, stable, steady, straight, surfaced, true, unbroken, unchanging, undeviating, unfluctuating, uninterrupted, unvaried, unvarying, unwavering, unwrinkled; SEE CONCEPTS 480,490

even [adj2] *calm, undisturbed*
composed, cool, equable, equanimous, eventempered, imperturbable, peaceful, placid, serene, stable, steady, tranquil, unexcitable, unruffled, well-balanced; SEE CONCEPT 401

even [adj3] *commensurate; having no advantage*
balanced, coequal, comparable, coterminous, drawn, equal, equalized, equivalent, evensteven*, exact, fifty-fifty*, horse to horse*, identical, level, matching, neck and neck*, on a par*, parallel, proportional, proportionate, same, similar, smack in the middle*, square, tied, uniform; SEE CONCEPT 566

even [adj4] *fair, impartial*
balanced, disinterested, dispassionate, equal, equitable, fair and square*, honest, just, matching, nonpartisan, square, straightforward, unbiased, unprejudiced; SEE CONCEPTS 267,542

even [v] *balance, make smooth*
align, equal, equalize, flatten, flush, grade, lay, level, match, pancake*, plane, regularize, roll, square, stabilize, steady, symmetrize, uniform; SEE CONCEPTS 231,757

even [adv] *still, yet*
all the more, despite, disregarding, indeed, in spite of, much, notwithstanding, so much as; SEE CONCEPT 544

evening [n] *latter part of a day*
black, close, dark, decline, dim, dusk, duskiness, early black*, eve, even, eventide, late afternoon, nightfall, sundown, sunset, twilight; SEE CONCEPTS 801,806,810

event [n1] *occurrence, happening*
accident, act, action, advent, adventure, affair, appearance, business, calamity, case, catastrophe, celebration, ceremony, chance, circumstance, coincidence, conjuncture, crisis, deed, development, emergency, episode, experience, exploit, fact, function, holiday, incident, juncture, marvel, matter, milestone, miracle, misfortune, mishap, mistake, occasion, occurrence, pass, phase, phenomenon, predicament, proceeding, shift, situation, story, thing*, tide, transaction, triumph, turn, wonder; SEE CONCEPT 2

event [n2] *effect, result*
aftereffect, aftermath, case, causatum, chance, conclusion, consequence, end, end result, eventuality, fortuity, hap, happenstance, issue, offshoot, outcome, outgrowth, product, resultant, sequel, sequent, termination, upshot; SEE CONCEPT 230

event [n3] *performance, competition*
bout, contest, game, match, meet, tournament; SEE CONCEPTS 263,363

eventful [adj] *significant, busy*
active, consequential, critical, crucial, decisive, exciting, fateful, full, historic, important, lively, memorable, momentous, notable, noteworthy, outstanding, remarkable, signal; SEE CONCEPT 548

eventual [adj] *future, concluding*
closing, conditional, consequent, contingent, dependent, down the pike*, down the road*, ending, endmost, ensuing, final, hindmost, indirect, inevitable, in the cards*, last, later, latter, overall, possible, prospective, resulting, secondary, succeeding, terminal, ulterior, ultimate, vicarious; SEE CONCEPTS 552,820

eventuality [n] *something that probably will happen*
aftereffect, aftermath, any case, case, chance, consequence, contingency, effect, event, godown*, goings-on*, happening, issue, likelihood, outcome, possibility, probability, result, sequel, toss-up, upshot*; SEE CONCEPTS 230,650

eventually [adv] *in the course of time*
after all, at last, at the end of the day*, finally, hereafter, in future, in the end, in the long run*, one day, someday, sometime, sooner or later*, ultimately, when all is said and done*, yet; SEE CONCEPTS 552,820

eventuate [v] *be a consequence*
be consequent, befall, come about, come to pass, end, ensue, eventualize, follow, happen, issue, occur, result, stop, take place, terminate; SEE CONCEPTS 2,242

ever [adv] *always, at any time*
anytime, at all, at all times, at any point, by any chance*, consistently, constantly, continually, endlessly, eternally, everlastingly, evermore, forever, for keeps, in any case*, incessantly, in perpetuum, invariably, on any occasion*, perpetually, relentlessly, till cows come home*, to the end of time*, unceasingly, unendingly, usually; SEE CONCEPTS 798,799

everlasting [adj] *infinite, never-ending*
abiding, amaranthine, boundless, ceaseless, constant, continual, continuous, deathless, endless, eternal, immortal, imperishable, incessant, indestructible, interminable, lasting, limitless, perdurable, permanent, perpetual, termless, timeless, unceasing, undying, unending, uninterrupted, unremitting; SEE CONCEPT 798

every [adj] *each, all*
each one, whole, without exception; SEE CONCEPT 531

everybody/everyone [n] *all involved, all human beings; the whole world*
all, all and sundry*, anybody, each one, each person, every person, generality, masses, people, populace, the public, the whole, young and old*; SEE CONCEPT 417

everyday [adj] *common*
accustomed, average, commonplace, conventional, customary, daily, dime a dozen*, dull, familiar, frequent, garden variety*, habitual, informal, lowly, mainstream, middle-of-the-road*, mundane, normal, ordinary, per diem, plain, prosaic, quotidian,, regular, run-of-the-mill*, stock, unexceptional, unimaginative, unremarkable, usual, vanilla*, whitebread*, wonted, workaday; SEE CONCEPTS 530,547

everything [n] *entirety*
aggregate, all, all in all, all that, all things, business, complex, each thing, every little thing*, fixins'*, lock stock and barrel*, lot, many things, sum, the works*, total, universe, whole, whole ball of wax*, whole caboodle*, whole enchilada*, whole lot*, whole shebang*; SEE CONCEPTS 432,837

everywhere [adv] *in all places*
all around, all over, all over creation*, all over the map*, far and wide*, here and there*, here till Sunday*, high and low*, in all quarters, in each

et
ev

place, in every direction, in every place, inside and out, near and far*, omnipresent, overall, pole to pole*, the world over*, throughout, ubiquitous, ubiquitously, universally, wherever; SEE CONCEPT 583

evict [v] *throw out from residence*
boot out*, bounce*, chase, dislodge, dismiss, dispossess, eject, expel, extrude, force out, heaveho*, kick out*, oust, out, put out, remove, send packing*, show out, show the door*, shut out, toss out on ear*, turn out; SEE CONCEPTS 122,198,211

eviction [n] *throwing out of a residence*
boot*, bounce*, bum's rush*, clearance, dislodgement, dispossession, ejection, expulsion, kicking out*, ouster, removal, rush, the gate*, walking papers*; SEE CONCEPTS 123,198,211

evidence [n] *proof*
affirmation, attestation, averment, cincher*, clincher*, clue, confirmation, corroboration, cue, data, declaration, demonstration, deposition, documentation, dope*, goods*, gospel, grabber*, grounds, index, indication, indicia, info*, information, manifestation, mark, sign, significant, smoking gun*, substantiation, symptom, testament, testimonial, testimony, token, witness; SEE CONCEPTS 274,318

evidence [v] *prove*
attest, bespeak, betoken, confirm, connote, demonstrate, denote, designate, display, evince, exhibit, expose, illustrate, indicate, manifest, mark, ostend, proclaim, reveal, show, signify, testify to, witness; SEE CONCEPTS 57,97,317

evident [adj] *apparent, clear*
axiomatic, barefaced*, clear-cut, conspicuous, crystal clear*, distinct, fact, incontestable, incontrovertible, indisputable, logical, manifest, noticeable, obvious, open-and-shut*, palpable, patent, perceptible, plain, plain as day*, reasonable, straightforward, tangible, unambiguous, unmistakable, visible; SEE CONCEPTS 529,535

evidently [adv] *apparently, clearly*
doubtless, doubtlessly, incontestably, incontrovertibly, indisputably, it seems, it would seem, manifestly, obviously, officially, ostensibly, outwardly, patently, plainly, professedly, seemingly, to all appearances*, undoubtedly, unmistakably, without question; SEE CONCEPT 535

evil [n] *badness, immorality; disaster*
affliction, baseness, blow, calamity, catastrophe, corruption, crime, criminality, curse, debauchery, depravity, devilry, diabolism, harm, hatred, heinousness, hurt, ill, impiety, indecency, infamy, iniquity, injury, knavery, lewdness, licentiousness, looseness, malevolence, malignity, meanness, mischief, misery, misfortune, obscenity, outrage, pain, perversity, ruin, sin, sinfulness, sorrow, suffering, turpitude, vice, viciousness, vileness, villainy, wickedness, woe, wrong, wrongdoing; SEE CONCEPT 645

evil [adj] *sinful, immoral*
angry, atrocious, bad, baneful, base, beastly, calamitous, corrupt, damnable, depraved, destructive, disastrous, execrable, flagitious, foul, harmful, hateful, heinous, hideous, iniquitous, injurious, loathsome, low, maleficent, malevolent, malicious, malignant, nefarious, no good, obscene, offensive, pernicious, poison, rancorous, reprobate, repugnant, repulsive, revolting, spiteful, stinking, ugly, unpleasant, unpropitious, vi-

cious, vile, villainous, wicked, wrathful, wrong; SEE CONCEPTS 545,570

evoke [v] *induce, stimulate*
arouse, awaken, call, call forth, conjure, educe, elicit, evince, evolve, excite, extort, extract, give rise to, invoke, milk*, provoke, raise, rally, recall, rouse, stir up, summon, waken; SEE CONCEPTS 228,242

evolution [n] *development, progress*
change, enlargement, evolvement, expansion, flowering, growth, increase, maturation, natural process, progression, transformation, unfolding, working out; SEE CONCEPT 704

evolve [v] *develop, progress*
advance, derive, disclose, educe, elaborate, emerge, enlarge, excogitate, expand, get, grow, increase, mature, obtain, open, result, ripen, unfold, work out; SEE CONCEPTS 236,245,704

exacerbate [v] *infuriate; make worse*
add insult to injury*, aggravate, annoy, egg on*, embitter, enrage, envenom, exasperate, excite, fan the flames*, feed the fire*, go from bad to worse*, heat up*, heighten, hit on*, increase, inflame, intensify, irritate, madden, provoke, push one's button*, rattle one's cage*, rub salt in a wound*, vex, worsen; SEE CONCEPTS 7,19

exact [adj] *accurate, precise*
bull's-eye*, careful, clear, clear-cut, correct, dead on*, definite, distinct, downright, explicit, express, faithful, faultless, identical, literal, methodical, nailed down*, nice, on target*, on the button*, on the money*, on the numbers*, orderly, particular, perfect, right, right on*, rigorous, sharp, specific, true, unequivocal, unerring, veracious, verbal, verbatim; SEE CONCEPTS 535,557

exact [adj2] *careful, painstaking*
conscientious, conscionable, demanding, exacting, finicky, fussy, heedful, meticulous, punctilious, punctual, rigorous, scrupulous, severe, strict; SEE CONCEPT 542

exact [v] *demand, call for*
assess, bleed, call, challenge, claim, coerce, command, compel, constrain, extort, extract, force, gouge, impose, insist upon, lean on, levy, oblige, pinch, postulate, put on, require, requisition, shake down*, solicit, squeeze, wrench, wrest, wring; SEE CONCEPTS 53,142

exacting [adj] *demanding*
burdensome, by the book*, careful, critical, difficult, exigent, finicky, fussy, grievous, hard, harsh, hypercritical, imperious, nit-picking, onerous, oppressive, painstaking, particular, persnickety, picky, precise, rigid, rigorous, severe, stern, strict, stringent, taxing, tough, trying, unsparing, weighty; SEE CONCEPTS 401,404

exactly [adv] *accurately, particularly*
absolutely, altogether, bang*, carefully, completely, correctly, definitely, explicitly, expressly, faithfully, faultlessly, for a fact, for certain, for sure*, indeed, in every respect, just, literally, methodically, no mistake, on the dot*, on the money*, on the nail*, on the nose*, positively, precisely, quite, right, rigorously, scrupulously, severely, sharp, specifically, square, strictly, the ticket*, totally, truly, truthfully, unequivocally, unerringly, utterly, veraciously, wholly; SEE CONCEPTS 535,557

exactness [n] *accuracy, precision*
carefulness, correctness, definiteness, definitive-

ness, definitude, exactitude, faithfulness, fault-lessness, nicety, orderliness, painstakingness, preciseness, promptitude, regularity, rigor, rigorousness, scrupulousness, strictness, truth, unequivocalness, veracity; SEE CONCEPTS *638,654*

exaggerate [v] *overstate, embellish*
amplify, blow out of proportion*, boast, boost, brag, build up, caricature, color, cook up*, corrupt, distort, embroider, emphasize, enlarge, exalt, expand, fabricate, falsify, fudge*, go to extremes*, heighten, hike, hyperbolize, inflate, intensify, lay it on thick*, lie, loud talk*, magnify, make too much of*, misquote, misreport, misrepresent, overdo, overdraw, overemphasize, overestimate, pad*, pretty up*, puff, put on, pyramid*, romance, romanticize, scam, stretch, up*; SEE CONCEPT *63*

exaggerated [adj] *overstated, embellished*
a bit thick*, abstract, amplified, artificial, bouncing, caricatural, distorted, embroidered, exalted, excessive, extravagant, fabricated, fabulous, false, fantastic, farfetched, hammy, highly colored, histrionic, hyperbolic, impossible, inflated, magnified, melodramatic, out of proportion, overblown, overdone, overestimated, overkill, overwrought, preposterous, pretentious, schmaltzy, sensational, spectacular, steep, strained, stylized, tall, too much*, too-too*, unrealistic; SEE CONCEPTS *267,542,562*

exaggeration [n] *overstatement, embellishment*
aggrandizement, amplification, baloney*, boasting, caricature, coloring, crock*, elaboration, embroidery, emphasis, enlargement, exaltation, excess, extravagance, -fabrication, falsehood, fancy, fantasy, figure of speech, fish story*, flight of fancy*, hogwash*, hyperbole, inflation, jazz*, line*, magnification, misjudgment, misrepresentation, overemphasis, overestimation, pretension, pretentiousness, rant, romance, stretch, tall story*, untruth, whopper*, yarn*; SEE CONCEPTS *63,278,663*

exalt [v] *promote, praise*
acclaim, advance, aggrandize, apotheosize, applaud, bless, boost, build up*, commend, dignify, distinguish, ennoble, erect, eulogize, extol, glorify, halo, honor, idolize, intensify, laud, magnify, pay homage to, pay tribute to, raise, revere, set on pedestal*, sublime, transfigure, upgrade, uprear, worship; SEE CONCEPTS *10,69*

exaltation [n1] *promotion, praise*
acclaim, acclamation, advancement, aggrandizement, apotheosis, applause, blessing, dignity, elevation, eminence, ennoblement, extolment, glorification, glory, grandeur, high rank, homage, honor, idolization, laudation, lionization, loftiness, magnification, panegyric, plaudits, prestige, reverence, rise, tribute, upgrading, uplifting, worship; SEE CONCEPTS *69,278*

exaltation [n2] *great joy*
animation, bliss, delectation, delight, ecstasy, elation, elevation, euphoria, excitement, exhilaration, exultation, inspiration, intoxication, joyousness, jubilation, rapture, stimulation, transport, uplift; SEE CONCEPTS *32,410*

exalted [adj] *praised; held in high esteem*
astral, august, dignified, elevated, eminent, exaggerated, excessive, first, grand, high, highest, highest-ranking, high-minded, high-ranking, honorable, honored, ideal, illustrious, immodest, imposing, inflated, intellectual, leading, lofty,

magnificent, noble, number one, outstanding, overblown, pompous, prestigious, pretentious, proud, self-important, sublime, superb, superior, top-drawer*, top-ranking, uplifting; SEE CONCEPTS *404,529*

examination [n1] *test, analysis*
assay, audit, battery, blue book*, breakdown, canvass, catechism, checking, checkup, cross-examination, diagnosis, dissection, exam, experiment, exploration, final, grilling, inquest, inquiry, inquisition, inspection, interrogation, investigation, legwork*, make-up, observation, once-over*, oral, perlustration, perusal, probe, quest, questioning, questionnaire, quiz, raid, reconnaissance, research, review, scan, scrutiny, search, study, survey, the eye*, third degree*, trial, tryout, view, written; SEE CONCEPT *290*

examination [n2] *medical checkup*
autopsy, biopsy, exam, inquiry, observation, physical, postoperative, probe, test; SEE CONCEPTS *103,310*

examine [v1] *analyze, test*
appraise, assay, audit, canvass, case, check, check out, chew over*, consider, criticize, delve into, dig into, explore, eye*, finger*, frisk, go into, go over, go through, gun*, inquire, inspect, investigate, look over, look see*, parse, pat down, peruse, pick at, ponder, pore over, probe, prospect, prove, read, reconnoiter, research, review, scan, scope, screen, scrutinate, scrutinize, search into, sift, size up*, study, survey, sweep, take stock of*, try, turn over*, vet, view, weigh, winnow*; SEE CONCEPTS *24,103*

examine [v2] *ask questions pointedly*
catechize, check, cross-examine, experiment, give the third*, give the third degree*, grill, inquire, interrogate, judge, measure, pump, put through the wringer*, query, quiz, try, try out, weigh; SEE CONCEPT *48*

example [n] *instance, model*
archetype, case, case history, case in point, citation, copy, excuse, exemplar, exemplification, for instance, ideal, illustration, kind of thing, lesson, object, original, paradigm, paragon, part, pattern, precedent, prototype, quotation, representation, sample, sampling, specimen, standard, stereotype, symbol; SEE CONCEPT *686*

exasperate [v] *upset, provoke*
aggravate, agitate, anger, annoy, bug*, disturb, drive up the wall*, embitter, enrage, exacerbate, excite, gall, get*, get under one's skin*, incense, inflame, infuriate, irk, irritate, madden, make waves*, needle*, nettle, peeve, pique, rankle, rile, roil, rouse, T-off*, try the patience of, vex, work up; SEE CONCEPTS *7,19*

exasperation [n] *upset, provocation*
aggravation, anger, annoyance, besetment, bother, botheration, displeasure, exacerbation, fury, ire, irritant, irritation, nuisance, passion, pest, pique, plague, rage, resentment, vexation, wrath; SEE CONCEPTS *29,410*

excavate [v] *dig up*
burrow, cut, delve, empty, gouge, grub, hollow, mine, quarry, scoop, scrape, shovel, spade, trench, tunnel, uncover, unearth; SEE CONCEPT *178*

excavation [n] *site of digging; digging*
blasting, burrow, cavity, cut, cutting, dig, disinterring, ditch, dugout, exhuming, hole, hollow, mine, mining, pit, quarry, removal, scooping,

shaft, shoveling, trench, trough, unearthing; SEE
CONCEPTS *178,509,513*

exceed [v] *be superior to; surpass*
beat, best, better, break record*, cap, distance,
eclipse, excel, get upper hand*, go beyond, go
by, have advantage, have a jump on*, have it all
over*, out-distance, outdo, outpace, outreach,
outrun, outshine, outstrip, overstep, overtake,
overtax, pass, rise above*, run circles around*,
surmount, top, transcend; SEE CONCEPT *141*

exceedingly [adv] *very; exceptionally*
awfully, enormously, especially, excessively, extraordinarily, extremely, greatly, highly, hugely,
immoderately, in a marked degree, inordinately,
powerful, really, remarkably, strikingly, superlatively, surpassingly, terribly, too much, unusually, vastly, vitally; SEE CONCEPT *569*

excel [v] *be superior; surpass*
beat, be good, be master of, be proficient, be skillful, best, be talented, better, cap, come through,
eclipse, exceed, go beyond, go to town*, improve
upon, make it, outdo, outrival, outshine, outstrip,
pass, predominate, shine, show talent, surmount,
take precedence, top, transcend, wax*; SEE CON-
CEPTS *141,671,706*

excellence [n] *superiority*
arete, class, distinction, éclat, eminence, excellency, fineness, goodness, greatness, high quality,
merit, perfection, preeminence, purity, quality,
superbness, supremacy, transcendence, virtue,
worth; SEE CONCEPT *671*

excellent [adj] *superior, wonderful*
accomplished, admirable, A-1*, attractive, capital, certified, champion, choice, choicest, desirable, distinctive, distinguished, estimable,
exceptional, exemplary, exquisite, fine, finest,
first, first-class, first-rate, good, great, high, incomparable, invaluable, magnificent, meritorious,
notable, noted, outstanding, peerless, piked*, premium, priceless, prime, select, skillful, sterling,
striking, superb, superlative, supreme, tiptop*,
top-notch, transcendent, world-class; SEE CON-
CEPT *574*

except [v] *leave out*
ban, bar, bate, count out, debar, disallow, eliminate, exclude, exempt, expostulate, inveigh, object, omit, pass over, protest, reject, remonstrate,
rule out, suspend, taboo; SEE CONCEPTS
25,30,211

except [prep] *other than*
apart from, aside from, bar, barring, besides, but,
excepting, excluding, exclusive of, exempting, if
not, lacking, leaving out, minus, not for, omitting, outside of, rejecting, save, saving, short of,
without, with the exception of; SEE CONCEPT *577*

exception [n1] *leaving out*
barring, debarment, disallowment, excepting, exclusion, excusing, expulsion, noninclusion, omission, passing over, rejection, repudiation,
reservation; SEE CONCEPTS *25,30,211*

exception [n2] *special case; irregularity*
allowance, anomalism, anomaly, departure, deviation, difference, dispensation, eccentricity, exemption, freak, inconsistency, nonconformity,
oddity, peculiarity, perquisitor, privilege, privileged person, quirk; SEE CONCEPTS *423,665*

exceptional [adj1] *irregular*
aberrant, abnormal, anomalous, atypical, deviant,
distinct, extraordinary, inconsistent, infrequent,
notable, noteworthy, odd, peculiar, phenomenal,

rare, remarkable, scarce, singular, special,
strange, uncommon, uncustomary, unheard-of,
unimaginable, unique, unordinary, unprecedented, unthinkable, unusual; SEE CONCEPT *564*

exceptional [adj2] *excellent, wonderful*
brainy, extraordinary, fine, first-class, first-rate,
good, high, marvelous, outstanding, phenomenal,
premium, prodigious, remarkable, singular, special, superior, world-class; SEE CONCEPTS
572,574

excerpt [n] *citation; something taken from a whole*
extract, fragment, notation, note, part, passage,
pericope, piece, portion, quotation, quote, saying,
section, selection; SEE CONCEPTS *270,274,835*

excerpt [v] *take a part from a whole*
choose, cite, cull, extract, glean, note, pick, pick
out, quote, select, single out; SEE CONCEPTS
41,142,211

excess [n1] *overabundance of something*
balance, by-product, enough, exorbitance, exuberance, fat, fulsomeness, glut, inundation, lavishness, leavings, leftover, luxuriance, nimiety,
overdose, overflow, overkill, overload, overmuch, overrun, oversupply, overweight, plenty,
plethora, profusion, recrement, redundance, redundancy, refuse, remainder, residue, rest, spare,
superabundance, supererogation, superfluity, surfeit, surplus, the limit, too much*, too much of a
good thing*, waste, wastefulness; SEE CONCEPTS
787,824,835

excess [n2] *overindulgence in personal desires*
debauchery, dissipation, dissoluteness, exorbitance, extravagance, extreme, extremity, immod-
eracy, immoderation, indulgence, inordinateness,
intemperance, overdoing, prodigality, saturnalia,
self-indulgence, unrestraint; SEE CONCEPTS
633,645

excessive [adj] *too much; overdone*
boundless, disproportionate, dissipated, dizzying,
enormous, exaggerated, exorbitant, extra, extravagant, extreme, immoderate, indulgent, inordinate, intemperate, limitless, more, needless, over,
overboard, overkill, overmuch, plethoric, prodigal, profligate, recrementitious, redundant, self-
indulgent, sky-high*, steep, stiff, stratospheric*,
super, superabundant, superfluous, supernatural,
too many, towering, unbounded, unconscionable,
undue, unmeasurable, unreasonable, way out*;
SEE CONCEPTS *560,771,781*

exchange [n1] *trade; deal*
barter, buying and selling, castling, change, commerce, commutation, conversion, correspondence, dealing, interchange, interdependence,
interrelation, network, quid pro quo, rearrangement, reciprocation, reciprocity, replacement, revision, shift, shuffle, shuffling, substitution,
supplanting, supplantment, swap, switch, tit for
tat*, traffic, transaction, transfer, transposing,
transposition, truck*; SEE CONCEPTS *104,324*

exchange [n2] *place where stocks are bought, sold*
curb, market, net, network, over the counter,
stock exchange, store, the Big Board*, the
Street*, Wall Street*; SEE CONCEPTS *325,449*

exchange [v] *trade*
alternate, bandy, bargain, barter, buy and sell,
cash in, castle, change, change hands*, commute,
contact with, convert into, correspond, deal in,
displace, flip-flop*, give and take*, go over to*,
hook up, horse trade, interchange, invert, link up,
market, network, pass to, pay back, rearrange,

reciprocate, replace, return the compliment*, reverse, revise, seesaw, shift, shuffle, shuttle, substitute, swap, swap horses*, switch, traffic, transact, transfer, transpose, truck*, turn the tables*; SEE CONCEPT *104*

excise [n] *tax on goods*
customs, duty, import tax, levy, surcharge, tariff, toll; SEE CONCEPT *329*

excise [v] *remove, delete*
amputate, black out, blot out*, blue pencil*, cross out, cut, cut off, cut out, cut up, destroy, edit, elide, eradicate, erase, expunge, exscind, exsect, exterminate, extirpate, extract, gut, knock off*, launder*, lop off*, resect, scissor out, scratch out, slash, stamp out*, strike, trim, wipe out, X out*; SEE CONCEPT *211*

excitable [adj] *easily upset or inspired*
agitable, alarmable, demonstrative, edgy, emotional, enthusiastic, fidgety, fierce, fiery, galvanic, hasty, high-strung, hot-headed, hot-tempered, hysterical, impatient, impetuous, impulsive, inflammable, intolerant, irascible, mercurial, moody, nervous, neurotic, overzealous, passionate, peevish, quick, quick-tempered, rash, reckless, restless, sensitive, short fused, skittish, susceptible, temperamental, testy, touchy, uncontrolled, uneasy, vehement, violent, volatile, volcanic; SEE CONCEPTS *401,404*

excite [v] *inspire; upset*
accelerate, agitate, amaze, anger, animate, annoy, arouse, astound, awaken, bother, chafe, delight, discompose, disturb, electrify, elicit, energize, evoke, feed the fire*, fire, fluster, foment, galvanize, goad, incite, induce, inflame, infuriate, instigate, intensify, irritate, jar, jolt, kindle, madden, mock, move, offend, precipitate, provoke, quicken, rouse, start, stimulate, stir up, taunt, tease, thrill, titillate, touch off, vex, waken, wake up, warm, whet, work up, worry; SEE CONCEPTS *7,14,19,22*

excited [adj] *inspired; upset*
aflame, agitated, animated, annoyed, aroused, awakened, beside oneself*, charged, delighted, discomposed, disconcerted, disturbed, eager, enthusiastic, feverish, fired up*, frantic, high*, hot*, hot and bothered*, hyperactive, hysterical, in a tizzy*, inflamed, juiced up*, jumpy*, keyed up*, moved, nervous, on edge*, on fire*, overwrought, passionate, piqued, provoked, roused, ruffled, steamed up*, stimulated, stirred, thrilled, tumultuous/tumultuous, wild, wired*, worked up, zipped up*; SEE CONCEPTS *401,403*

excitement [n] *enthusiasm; incitement*
action, activity, ado, adventure, agitation, animation, bother, buzz*, commotion, confusion, discomposure, disturbance, dither*, drama, elation, emotion, excitation, feeling, ferment, fever, flurry, frenzy, furor, fuss, heat*, hubbub*, hullabaloo*, hurry, hysteria, impulse, instigation, intoxication, kicks*, melodrama, motivation, motive, movement, passion, perturbation, provocation, rage, stimulation, stimulus, stir, thrill, titillation, to-do*, trepidation, tumult, turmoil, urge, warmth, wildness; SEE CONCEPTS *388,410,633*

exciting [adj] *inspiring, exhilarating*
agitative, animating, appealing, arousing, arresting, astonishing, bracing, breathtaking, commoving, dangerous, dramatic, electrifying, exhilarant, eye-popping*, far-out*, fine, flashy, groovy*, hair-raising*, heady*, hectic, impelling, impres-

sive, interesting, intoxicating, intriguing, lively, melodramatic, mind-blowing, moving, neat, overpowering, overwhelming, provocative, racy, rip-roaring*, rousing, sensational, showy, spine-tingling*, stimulating, stirring, thrilling, titillating, wild, zestful; SEE CONCEPTS *529,542,548*

exclaim [v] *shout out*
assert, bellow, blurt, burst out, call, call aloud, call out, cry, cry out, declare, ejaculate, emit, figure, holler, proclaim, rend the air*, roar, say loudly, shout, state, utter, vociferate, yawp*, yell; SEE CONCEPTS *47,49*

exclamation [n] *shout; assertion*
bellow, call, clamor, cry, ejaculation, expletive, holler, interjection, outcry, roar, utterance, vociferation, yawp*, yell; SEE CONCEPTS *49,77*

exclude [v] *expel, forbid*
ban, bar, bate, blackball*, blacklist, block, bounce, boycott, close out, count out, debar, disallow, drive out, eject, eliminate, embargo, estop, evict, except, force out, get rid of, ignore, interdict, keep out, leave out, lock out, obviate, occlude, omit, ostracize, oust, pass over, preclude, prevent, prohibit, proscribe, put out, refuse, refuse admittance, reject, remove, repudiate, rule out, set aside, shut out, shut the door on*, sideline, suspend, throw out, veto, ward off; SEE CONCEPTS *25,30,121*

exclusion [n] *expulsion; forbiddance*
ban, bar, blackball*, blockade, boycott, coventry, cut, debarment, debarring, discharge, dismissal, ejection, elimination, embargo, eviction, exception, excommunication, interdict, interdicting, interdiction, keeping out, lockout, nonadmission, occlusion, omission, ostracism, ousting, preclusion, prevention, prohibition, proscription, refusal, rejection, relegation, removal, repudiation, segregation, separation, suspension, veto; SEE CONCEPTS *25,30,121*

exclusive [adj] *unshared, restricted*
absolute, aloof, aristocratic, chic, choice, chosen, circumscribed, clannish, classy, cliquish, closed, complete, confined, country club, discriminative, elegant, entire, exclusionary, exclusory, fashionable, full, independent, licensed, limited, narrow, only, particular, peculiar, posh, preferential, private, privileged, prohibitive, restrictive, ritzy, segregated, select, selfish, single, snobbish, socially correct, sole, swank, total, undivided, unique, upper crust*, whole; SEE CONCEPTS *554,567*

exclusively [adv] *particularly*
alone, but, completely, entirely, one and only, onliest, only, singularly, solely, wholly; SEE CONCEPT *554*

exclusive of [prep] *except for*
aside from, bar, barring, bating, besides, but, debarring, excepting, excluding, leaving aside, not counting, omitting, outside of, restricting, ruling out, save; SEE CONCEPT *554*

excogitate [v] *think about seriously*
conceive, consider, contemplate, contrive, deliberate, derive, develop, devise, educe, evolve, frame, invent, mind, mull over, perpend, ponder, ruminate, study, think out, think up, weigh, work out; SEE CONCEPTS *17,24*

excommunicate [v] *banish*
anathematize, ban, cast out, curse, denounce, dismiss, eject, exclude, expel, oust, proscribe, re-

move, repudiate, unchurch; SEE CONCEPTS 317,367

excoriate [v1] *scrape layers off*
abrade, chafe, flay, fret, gall, peel, rub, scarify, scratch, skin, strip; SEE CONCEPTS 211,215

excoriate [v2] *denounce, criticize*
attack, berate, blister, castigate, censure, chastise, condemn, flay, lambaste, lash, rebuke, reproach, reprove, revile, scathe, scold, scorch, slash, tear into, upbraid, vilify; SEE CONCEPT 52

excrete [v] *discharge, usually liquified substance*
defecate, egest, ejaculate, eject, eliminate, emanate, evacuate, exhale, expel, exudate, exude, give off, leak, pass, perspire, produce, remove, secrete, sweat, throw off, urinate, void; SEE CONCEPTS 179,185

excruciating [adj] *torturous, painful*
acute, agonizing, burning, chastening, consuming, exquisite, extreme, grueling, harrowing, insufferable, intense, piercing, punishing, racking, rending, searing, severe, sharp, shooting, stabbing, tearing, tormenting, torturesome, torturing, unbearable, unendurable, violent; SEE CONCEPTS 314,548,609

exculpate [v] *forgive*
absolve, acquit, amnesty, clear, condone, discharge, disculpate, dismiss, excuse, exonerate, explain, free, justify, let off*, pardon, rationalize, release, remit, vindicate, wipe slate clean*; SEE CONCEPTS 10,127,317

excursion [n] *journey*
circuit, cruise, day trip, digression, expedition, jaunt, junket, outing, picnic, pleasure trip, ramble, round trip, safari, tour, trek, trip, walk, wandering; SEE CONCEPTS 224,384

excusable [adj] *allowable*
all right, condonable, defensible, exculpatory, explainable, fair, forgivable, justifiable, minor, moderate, not too bad*, okay, pardonable, passable, permissible, plausible, reasonable, remittable, reprievable, slight, specious, temperate, tenable, trivial, understandable, venial, vindicable, vindicatory, warrantable, within limits; SEE CONCEPT 558

excuse [n] *reason, explanation*
alibi, apology, cleanup*, cop-out*, cover*, cover story*, coverup, defense, disguise, evasion, expedient, extenuation, fish story*, grounds, jive*, justification, makeshift, mitigation, plea, pretext, rationalization, regrets, routine, semblance, shift, song*, song and dance*, stall, stopgap*, story, substitute, subterfuge, trick*, vindication, whitewash*, why and wherefore*; SEE CONCEPTS 59,661

excuse [v] *forgive, absolve; justify*
acquit, alibi, apologize for, appease, bear with, clear, condone, cover, defend, discharge, dispense from, exculpate, exempt, exempt from, exonerate, explain, extenuate, forgive, free, give absolution, grant amnesty, indulge, let go*, let off*, liberate, make allowances for, mitigate, overlook, pardon, pass over*, plead ignorance, pretext, purge, rationalize, release, relieve, remit, reprieve, shrive, shrug off*, spare, take rap for*, tolerate, vindicate, whitewash*, wink at*; SEE CONCEPTS 10,57,83

execrable [adj] *horrible, sickening*
abhorrent, abominable, accursed, atrocious, confounded, cursed, damnable, defective, deplorable, despicable, detestable, disgusting, foul, hateful, heinous, horrific, loathsome, low, monstrous, nauseous, obnoxious, odious, offensive, repulsive, revolting, vile, wretched; SEE CONCEPT 542

execrate [v] *hate*
abhor, abominate, accurse, anathematize, censure, condemn, curse, damn, denounce, deplore, despise, detest, excoriate, imprecate, loathe, objurgate, reprehend, reprobate, reprove, revile, vilify; SEE CONCEPT 29

execration [n] *hating*
abhorrence, abomination, anathema, blasphemy, condemnation, contempt, curse, cursing, cussing, damnation, denunciation, detestation, detesting, execoriation, hatred, imprecation, loathing, malediction, odium, profanity, swearing, vilification; SEE CONCEPT 29

execute [v1] *kill*
assassinate, behead, bump off*, do in*, electrocute, eliminate, finish, gas, guillotine, hang, knock off*, liquidate, murder, purge, put away*, put to death, shoot; SEE CONCEPT 252

execute [v2] *carry out a task*
accomplish, achieve, act, administer, administrate, bring off, bring to fruition, cause, come through, complete, consummate, deal with, discharge, do, do the job*, do the trick*, do to a T*, earn wings*, effect, enact, enforce, finish, fulfill, get there*, govern, hack it*, hit*, implement, make it*, meet, percolate*, perform, play, polish off*, prosecute, pull off*, put into effect, put over*, put through, realize, render, sail through*, score*, take care of, take care of business*, transact; SEE CONCEPTS 91,706

execution [n1] *killing*
beheading, capital punishment, contract killing*, crucifixion, decapitation, electrocution, gassing, guillotining, hanging, hit, impalement, lethal injection, necktie party*, punishment, rub out*, shooting, strangling, strangulation; SEE CONCEPT 252

execution [n2] *carrying out of a task*
accomplishment, achievement, administration, completion, consummation, delivery, discharge, doing, effect, enactment, enforcement, fulfilling, implementation, nuts and bolts*, operation, performance, prosecution, realization, rendering, style; SEE CONCEPTS 91,706

executive [n] *person who manages an organization*
administration, administrator, big wheel*, boss, brass, businessperson, CEO*, chief, CO*, commander, director, directorate, entrepreneur, exec*, government, governor, head, head honcho*, head person*, heavyweight*, hierarchy, higher-up*, industrialist, key player*, leader, leadership, management, manager, officer, official, skipper*, supervisor, top brass*, tycoon, VIP*; SEE CONCEPTS 347,354

executive [adj] *administrative*
controlling, decision-making, directing, governing, managerial, managing, ruling; SEE CONCEPT 527

exemplar [n] *ideal*
archetype, copy, criterion, epitome, example, exemplification, illustration, instance, mirror, model, paradigm, paragon, pattern, prototype, specimen, standard, type; SEE CONCEPT 686

exemplary [adj] *ideal*
admirable, batting a thousand*, blameless, bueno*, characteristic, classic, classical, commendable, correct, estimable, excellent, good,

guiltless, honorable, illustrative, inculpable, innocent, irreprehensible, laudable, meritorious, model, neato*, not bad*, not too shabby*, paradigmatic, praiseworthy, prototypical, punctilious, pure, quintessential, representative, righteous, sterling, typical, virtuous, worthy; SEE CONCEPTS *404,572,574*

exemplify [v] *serve as an example*
body, cite, clarify, clear up, demonstrate, depict, display, elucidate, emblematize, embody, enlighten, epitomize, evidence, exhibit, illuminate, illustrate, instance, manifest, mirror, personify, quote, represent, show, spell out, symbolize, typify; SEE CONCEPTS *97,118*

exempt [adj] *freed from responsibility*
absolved, beat the rap*, clear, cleared, discharged, excepted, excluded, excused, favored, free, immune, let go*, let off*, liberated, not liable, not responsible, not subject, off the hook*, outside, privileged, released, set apart, spared, special, unbound, unchecked, unrestrained, unrestricted, unshackled, void of, walked*; SEE CONCEPTS *319,554*

exempt [v] *relieve, absolve*
clear, discharge, dispense, except, excuse, exonerate, free, go easy on*, grant immunity, let off*, let off the hook*, liberate, pass by, privilege from, release, spare, wipe the slate*, write off; SEE CONCEPTS *50,83,88,127*

exemption [n] *freedom from a responsibility*
absolution, discharge, dispensation, exception, exoneration, immunity, impunity, privilege, release; SEE CONCEPTS *652,685,691*

exercise [n1] *work, effort*
act, action, activity, calisthenics, constitutional*, daily dozen*, discharge, discipline, drill, drilling, examination, exercising, exertion, gym, labor, lesson, movement, occupation, operation, performance, problem, pursuit, recitation, schoolwork, study, task, test, theme, toil, training, warm-up, workout; SEE CONCEPTS *87,290,362,363*

exercise [n2] *accomplishment, use*
application, discharge, employment, enjoyment, exertion, fulfillment, implementation, operation, performance, practice, pursuit, utilization; SEE CONCEPTS *225,706*

exercise [v1] *put to use*
apply, bestow, bring to bear, devote, drill, employ, enjoy, execute, exert, exploit, handle, operate, practice, put into practice, rehearse, sharpen, use, utilize, wield; SEE CONCEPT *225*

exercise [v2] *do repeatedly, especially to improve*
break, break in, condition, cultivate, develop, discipline, drill, dry run*, exert, fix, foster, groom, habituate, hone, improve, inure, labor, lick into shape*, limber up, loosen up, maneuver, ply, practice, prepare, pump iron*, put out, put through grind*, put through mill*, rehearse, run through, set, strain, teach, train, tune up, walk through, warm up, work, work out; SEE CONCEPTS *87,363*

exercise [v3] *upset, worry*
abrade, afflict, agitate, annoy, bother, burden, chafe, distress, disturb, gall, irk, occupy, pain, perturb, preoccupy, provoke, trouble, try, vex; SEE CONCEPTS *7,19*

exert [v] *make use of*
apply, apply oneself, bring into play*, bring to bear*, dig*, employ, endeavor, exercise, expend, give all one's got*, give best shot*, labor, make

effort, peg away*, plug*, ply, pour it on*, push, put forth, put out, strain, strive, struggle, sweat it*, throw, toil, try hard, use, utilize, wield, work; SEE CONCEPTS *87,225*

exertion [n] *hard work*
action, activity, application, attempt, effort, elbow grease*, employment, endeavor, exercise, hard pull*, industry, labor, long pull*, operation, pains, strain, stretch, striving, struggle, toil, travail, trial, trouble, use, utilization; SEE CONCEPTS *87,362,677*

exhale [v] *breathe out*
breathe, discharge, eject, emanate, emit, evaporate, expel, give off, issue, let out, respire, steam, vaporize; SEE CONCEPT *163*

exhaust [v1] *tire or wear out*
bankrupt, burn out*, conk out*, cripple, debilitate, disable, do in*, drain, draw, enervate, enfeeble, fag, fatigue, frazzle, impoverish, overdo, overexert, overextend, overfatigue, overtire, overwork, peter out*, poop*, poop out*, prostrate, run ragged*, sap*, suck dry*, tucker*, use up, weaken, wear down, weary; SEE CONCEPTS *250,469*

exhaust [v2] *consume, use up*
bankrupt, bleed dry*, deplete, devour, dispel, disperse, dissipate, drain, draw, dry, eat, eat up*, empty, expend, finish, impoverish, run out, run through, spend, squander, strain, suck dry*, take last of, void, wash up, waste; SEE CONCEPTS *169,225*

exhausted [adj1] *extremely tired*
all in*, beat*, bleary, bone-weary, bushed, crippled, dead*, dead tired*, debilitated, disabled, dog-tired*, done for*, done in*, drained, effete, enervated, frazzled, had it*, kaput*, limp, out on one's feet*, outta gas*, prostrated, ready to drop*, run-down, sapped*, shot*, spent, tired out, wasted*, weak, weakened, wearied, worn, worn out; SEE CONCEPTS *406,485*

exhausted [adj2] *used up*
all gone, at an end, bare, consumed, depleted, dissipated, done, drained, dry, empty, expended, finished, gone, spent, squandered, void, washedout, wasted; SEE CONCEPTS *560,771*

exhaustion [n] *tiredness*
burnout*, collapse, consumption, debilitation, debility, enervation, expenditure, fatigue, feebleness, lassitude, prostration, weariness; SEE CONCEPTS *410,720*

exhaustive [adj] *all-inclusive, complete*
all-embracing, all-encompassing, all-out, catholic, comprehensive, embracive, encyclopedic, extensive, far-reaching, from A to Z*, full, fullblown, full-dress*, full-scale, in-depth, intensive, no stone unturned*, out-and-out*, profound, radical, sweeping, the word, thorough, thoroughgoing, total, whole-hog*; SEE CONCEPTS *531,772*

exhibit [n] *viewing; presentation*
display, exhibition, exposition, fair, illustration, model, performance, show; SEE CONCEPTS *259,261*

exhibit [v] *put on view; present*
advertise, air, brandish, demonstrate, disclose, display, disport, evidence, evince, expose, express, feature, flash, flaunt, illustrate, indicate, let it all hang out*, make clear, make plain, manifest, mark, offer, ostend, parade, parade wares*, proclaim, reveal, roll out, show, show and tell*,

ex
ex

showcase, show off, strut stuff*, trot out*, wave around*; SEE CONCEPT 261

exhibition [n] *showing, demonstration*
advertisement, airing, an act*, a scene*, carnival, display, exhibit, expo, exposition, fair, fireworks, flash*, front*, manifestation, offering, pageant, performance, presentation, representation, show, sight, spectacle; SEE CONCEPTS 261,386

exhilarate [v] *make very happy*
animate, boost, buoy, cheer, commove, delight, elate, enliven, exalt, excite, gladden, inspire, inspirit, invigorate, juice*, lift, pep up*, perk up*, pick up, put zip into*, quicken, rejoice, send, snap up*, stimulate, thrill, turn on*, uplift, vitalize; SEE CONCEPTS 7,22

exhilarating [adj] *stimulating, cheering*
animating, animative, bracing, breathtaking, electric, elevating, enlivening, exalting, exciting, exhilarant, exhilarative, exhilaratory, eye-popping*, gladdening, inspiring, inspiriting, intoxicating, invigorating, quickening, rousing, stimulative, stirring, thrilling, tonic, uplifting, vitalizing; SEE CONCEPTS 529,548

exhilaration [n] *great happiness, excitement*
animation, a rush*, cheerfulness, delight, elation, electrification, elevation, enlivenment, euphoria, exaltation, excitation, firing, gaiety, galvanization, gladness, gleefulness, head rush*, high spirits*, hilarity, inspiration, invigoration, joy, joyfulness, liveliness, mirth, quickening, sprightliness, stimulation, uplift, vitalization, vivacity, vivification; SEE CONCEPT 410

exhort [v] *urge, warn*
admonish, advise, beseech, bid, call upon, caution, counsel, egg on*, encourage, enjoin, entreat, goad, incite, insist, persuade, plead, preach, press, pressure, prick, prod, prompt, propel, spur, stimulate; SEE CONCEPTS 75,78

exhortation [n] *warning, urging*
admonition, advice, beseeching, bidding, caution, counsel, encouragement, enjoinder, entreaty, goading, incitement, instigation, lecture, persuasion, preaching, sermon; SEE CONCEPTS 75,78,274

exhume [v] *dig up, especially the dead*
disclose, disembalm, disentomb, disinhume, disinter, resurrect, reveal, unbury, uncharnel, unearth; SEE CONCEPT 178

exigency/exigence [n] *difficulty; demand*
acuteness, constraint, contingency, crisis, criticalness, crossroad, demandingness, dilemma, distress, duress, emergency, extremity, fix, hardship, imperativeness, jam, juncture, necessity, need, needfulness, pass, pickle*, pinch, plight, predicament, pressingness, pressure, quandary, requirement, scrape*, stress, turning point*, urgency, vicissitude, want, wont, zero hour*; SEE CONCEPTS 646,674,709

exigent [adj1] *urgent, pressing*
acute, burning, clamant, clamorous, constraining, critical, crucial, crying, imperative, importunate, insistent, instant, menacing, necessary, needful, threatening; SEE CONCEPTS 548,568

exigent [adj2] *difficult, taxing*
arduous, burdensome, demanding, exacting, grievous, hard, harsh, onerous, oppressive, rigorous, severe, stiff, strict, stringent, superincumbent, tough, weighty; SEE CONCEPTS 537,542

exiguous [adj] *scanty*
bare, confined, diminutive, inadequate, limited,

little, meager, narrow, negligible, paltry, petty, poor, restricted, skimpy, slender, slight, small, spare, sparse, tenuous, thin, tiny; SEE CONCEPTS 771,789

exile [n1] *deportation from a place*
banishment, diaspora, dispersion, displacement, exclusion, expatriation, expulsion, extradition, migration, ostracism, proscription, relegation, scattering, separation; SEE CONCEPT 298

exile [n2] *person deported from a place*
deportee, displaced person, DP*, émigré, expatriate, expellee, fugitive, nonperson*, outcast, outlaw, person without country*, refugee; SEE CONCEPTS 354,412,423

exile [v] *deport from place*
banish, cast out, displace, dispossess, drive out, eject, evacuate, expatriate, expel, expulse, extradite, ostracize, oust, outlaw, proscribe, relegate, transport, turn out; SEE CONCEPTS 122,198,298

exist [v1] *be living*
abide, be, be extant, be latent, be present, breathe, continue, endure, happen, last, lie, live, move, obtain, occur, prevail, remain, stand, stay, subsist, survive; SEE CONCEPT 407

exist [v2] *get along in life*
consist, dwell, eke out a living*, endure, get by*, go on, inhere, kick*, lie, live, make it*, reside, stay alive*, subsist, survive; SEE CONCEPTS 100,226

existence [n] *life*
actuality, animation, being, breath, continuance, continuation, duration, endurance, entity, essence, hand one is dealt*, individuality, journey, lifing, permanence, perseverance, presence, rat race*, reality, real world*, something, subsistence, survival, the big game*, world; SEE CONCEPTS 407,639

exit [n1] *way out of a place*
avenue, door, egress, fire escape, gate, hole, opening, outlet, passage out, vent; SEE CONCEPT 440

exit [n2] *leaving*
adieu, death, demise, departure, egress, egression, evacuation, exodus, expiration, expiry, farewell, going, goodbye, leave-taking, offgoing, retirement, retreat, stampede, withdrawal; SEE CONCEPT 195

exit [v] *leave a place*
bid farewell, blow*, depart, do vanishing act*, flake off*, get*, get away, get off, git*, go, go away, go out, issue, move, move out, quit, retire, retreat, say goodbye, split*, take a hike*, take one's leave*, withdraw; SEE CONCEPT 195

exodus [n] *leaving*
departure, egress, egression, emigration, evacuation, exit, exiting, flight, going out, journey, migration, offgoing, retirement, retreat, withdrawal; SEE CONCEPT 195

exonerate [v] *excuse, clear of responsibility or blame*
absolve, acquit, disburden, discharge, dismiss, except, exculpate, exempt, free, justify, let off*, let off hook*, liberate, pardon, release, relieve, sanitize, vindicate, whitewash*, wipe slate clean*; SEE CONCEPTS 10,127,317

exorbitant [adj] *extravagant, excessive*
absonant, dear, enormous, exacting, expensive, extortionate, extreme, high, highway robbery*, immoderate, inordinate, out of sight*, outrageous, overboard, overmuch, over one's head*, prepos-

terous, pricey, steep*, stiff*, towering, unconscionable, undue, unreasonable, unwarranted, up to here*, wasteful; SEE CONCEPTS *334,547,558*

exotic [adj] *not native or usual; mysterious*
alien, alluring, avant garde, bizarre, colorful, curious, different, enticing, external, extraneous, extraordinary, extrinsic, far out*, fascinating, foreign, glamorous, imported, introduced, kinky*, outlandish, outside, peculiar, peregrine, romantic, strange, striking, unfamiliar, unusual, way out*, weird*; SEE CONCEPTS *542,549*

expand [v1] *extend, augment*
aggrandize, amplify, beef up*, bloat, blow up*, bolster, broaden, bulk up*, burgeon, detail, develop, diffuse, dilate, distend, elaborate, embellish, enlarge, explicate, fan out*, fatten, fill out, grow, heighten, hike, increase, inflate, lengthen, magnify, mount, multiply, mushroom, open, open out, outspread, pad, piggyback*, prolong, protract, puff up*, pyramid*, slap on*, soup up*, spread, spread out, stretch, stretch out, swell, tack on*, thicken, unfold, unfurl, unravel, unroll, upsurge, wax*, widen; SEE CONCEPTS *236,245*

expand [v2] *go into detail*
amplify, beef up*, build up, develop, dilate, discourse, drag out*, elaborate, embellish, enlarge, expatiate, expound, extend, flesh out*, spell out, sweeten; SEE CONCEPT *57*

expanse [n] *large space, usually open*
amplitude, area, belt, breadth, compass, distance, domain, extension, extent, field, immensity, latitude, length, margin, orbit, plain, radius, range, reach, region, remoteness, room, scope, span, sphere, spread, stretch, sweep, territory, tract, uninterrupted space, width, wilderness; SEE CONCEPTS *509,513,651,788*

expansion [n] *growth*
amplification, augmentation, breadth, development, diffusion, dilation, distance, distension, enlargement, evolution, expanse, extension, increase, inflation, magnification, maturation, multiplication, opening out, space, spread, stretch, swelling, unfolding, unfurling; SEE CONCEPTS *700,704,780*

expansive [adj1] *broad, comprehensive*
all-embracing, ample, big, dilatant, elastic, expanding, expansile, extensive, far-reaching, great, inclusive, large, scopic, scopious, stretching, thorough, unrepressed, unsuppressed, voluminous, wide, wide-ranging, widespread; SEE CONCEPT *772*

expansive [adj2] *talkative*
affable, communicative, demonstrative, easy, effervescent, effusive, extroverted, free, friendly, garrulous, generous, genial, gregarious, gushy, lavish, liberal, loquacious, open, outgoing, sociable, unconstrained, uninhibited, unreserved, unrestrained, warm; SEE CONCEPT *267*

expatriate [n] *person thrown out of a country*
departer, deportee, displaced person, emigrant, émigré, evacuee, exile, expellee, migrant, outcast, refugee; SEE CONCEPTS *354,412,423*

expatriate [v] *throw out of a country*
banish, deport, displace, exile, expel, expulse, ostracize, oust, proscribe, relegate, transport; SEE CONCEPTS *130,198,211*

expect [v1] *believe strongly; anticipate*
apprehend, assume, await, bargain for, bargain on, be afraid, calculate, conjecture, contemplate, count on, divine, envisage, feel, figure, forecast, foreknow, foresee, gather, hope, hope for, imagine, in the cards*, look, look ahead to, look for, look forward to*, predict, presume, presuppose, reckon, see coming*, sense, suppose, surmise, suspect, take, think, trust, understand, wait for, watch for; SEE CONCEPTS *12,26*

expect [v2] *want, wish*
call for, count on, demand, exact, insist on, look for, rely upon, require; SEE CONCEPT *20*

expectancy [n] *anticipation*
assumption, assurance, belief, calculation, confidence, conjecture, expectation, hope, likelihood, looking forward, outlook, prediction, presentation, presentiment, presumption, probability, prospect, reliance, supposition, surmise, suspense, trust, view, waiting; SEE CONCEPTS *410,689*

expectant [adj1] *anticipating*
alert, anticipative, anxious, apprehensive, awaiting, breathless, eager, expecting, hopeful, hoping, in suspense, looking for, on edge*, on tenterhooks*, prepared, raring*, ready, vigilant, waiting, waiting on, watchful, with bated breath*; SEE CONCEPTS *403,406*

expectant [adj2] *preparing to give birth*
enceinte, expecting, gravid, parturient, pregnant, with child*; SEE CONCEPT *485*

expectation [n] *belief, anticipation*
apprehension, assumption, assurance, calculation, chance, confidence, conjecture, design, expectancy, fear, forecast, hope, intention, likelihood, looking forward, motive, notion, outlook, possibility, prediction, presumption, probability, promise, prospect, reliance, supposition, surmise, suspense, trust, view; SEE CONCEPTS *410,689*

expediency/expedience [n1] *appropriateness; worth*
advantage, advantageousness, advisability, appositeness, aptness, benefit, convenience, desirability, effectiveness, efficiency, fitness, helpfulness, judiciousness, meetness, opportunism, opportunity, order, policy, practicality, pragmatism, profitability, **profitableness**, properness, propitiousness, propriety, prudence, rightness, suitability, usefulness, utilitarianism, utility; SEE CONCEPTS *656,658*

expediency/expedience [n2] *resource*
band-aid*, contrivance, design, device, dodge, easy way out*, gimmick*, makeshift*, maneuver, means, measure, method, recourse, resort, scheme, shift, step, stopgap*, stratagem, strategy, substitute, surrogate, tactic, trick; SEE CONCEPTS *660,712*

expedient [n] *resource*
agency, contrivance, device, instrument, instrumentality, makeshift, maneuver, means, measure, medium, method, recourse, refuge, resort, scheme, shift, stopgap, stratagem, substitute; SEE CONCEPTS *660,712*

expedient [adj] *worthwhile, appropriate*
ad hoc, advantageous, advisable, beneficial, convenient, desirable, discreet, effective, feasible, fit, fitting, helpful, judicious, meet, opportune, politic, possible, practicable, practical, pragmatic, profitable, proper, prudent, seasonable, suitable, tactical, timely, useful, utilitarian, wise; SEE CONCEPTS *558,560*

expedite [v] *make happen faster*
accelerate, advance, assist, cut the red tape*, dispatch, facilitate, fast track*, forward, grease

wheels*, hand-carry, handle personally, hand-walk*, hasten, hurry, precipitate, press, promote, quicken, railroad*, run interference*, run with the ball*, rush, shoot through*, speed, speed up, urge, walk it through*; SEE CONCEPT 242

expedition [n1] *journey; people on a journey*
campaign, caravan, cavalcade, company, crew, crowd, cruise, crusade, enterprise, entrada, excursion, exploration, explorers, fleet, jaunt, junket, mission, outing, party, patrol, peregrination, picnic, posse, quest, safari, squadron, swing, team, tour, travel, travellers, trek, trip, undertaking, voyage, voyagers, wayfarers; SEE CONCEPTS 224,417

expedition [n2] *speed; speeding up*
alacrity, celerity, dispatch, expeditiousness, goodwill, haste, hurry, hustle, promptitude, promptness, punctuality, quickness, rapidity, readiness, swiftness; SEE CONCEPTS 242,755

expeditious [adj] *immediate, speedy*
active, alert, breakneck, brisk, diligent, effective, effectual, efficient, fast, fleet, hasty, instant, nimble, prompt, punctual, quick, rapid, ready, swift; SEE CONCEPTS 542,588

expel [v1] *discharge*
belch, blow out, cast out, disgorge, dislodge, drive out, ejaculate, eruct, erupt, evacuate, exhaust, exudate, exude, get rid of, irrupt, pass, remove, spew, throw out, vomit; SEE CONCEPT 179

expel [v2] *throw out, banish*
ban, bar, blackball*, bust, cast out, chase, deport, discharge, dismiss, displace, dispossess, drum out, eject, eliminate, evict, exclude, exile, expatriate, expulse, fire, give the boot*, give the hook*, give walking papers*, kick out, oust, proscribe, send packing*, show the door*, suspend, throw out on ear*, turn out; SEE CONCEPTS 122,130,198

expend [v] *exhaust; spend*
ante up*, blow*, consume, disburse, dish out*, dispense, dissipate, distribute, employ, finish, foot the bill*, fork out*, give, go through*, lay out, outlay, pay, pay out, put out*, shell out*, splurge*, spring for*, throw money at*, use up, wash up*; SEE CONCEPTS 225,341

expendable [adj] *not important*
dispensable, disposable, excess, inessential, nonessential, replaceable, superfluous, unimportant; SEE CONCEPTS 546,575

expenditure [n] *payment*
amount, application, bottom line*, cash on barrelhead*, charge, come to*, consumption, cost, disbursement, dissipation, expense, figure, investment, kickback*, outgo, outlay, output, payoff, price, rate, setback*, spending, splurge, squander, throw*, tune*, use, valuation, value, waste; SEE CONCEPT 344

expense [n] *cost, payment*
amount, assessment, bite*, bottom line*, budget, charge, consumption, debit, debt, decrement, deprivation, disbursement, duty, expenditure, forfeit, forfeiture, insurance, investment, liability, loan, loss, mortgage, obligation, outdo*, outlay, out of pocket*, output, overhead, payroll, price, price tag, rate, responsibility, risk, sacrifice, spending, sum, surcharge, tariff, toll, upkeep, use, value, worth; SEE CONCEPTS 328,329,336,344

expensive [adj] *high-priced*
an arm and a leg*, at a premium, big-ticket*, costly, dear, excessive, exorbitant, extravagant, fancy, high, highway robbery*, holdup*, immoderate, inordinate, invaluable, lavish, out of sight*, overpriced, plush, posh, pretty penny*, pricey*, rich, ritzy*, sky-high*, steep*, stiff*, swank*, too high, uneconomical, unreasonable, upscale*, valuable; SEE CONCEPT 334

experience [n1] *knowledge*
acquaintance, action, actuality, background, caution, combat, contact, doing, empiricism, evidence, existence, exposure, familiarity, forebearance, intimacy, involvement, inwardness, judgment, know-how*, maturity, observation, participation, patience, perspicacity, practicality, practice, proof, reality, savoir-faire, seasoning, sense, skill, sophistication, strife, struggle, training, trial, understanding, wisdom, worldliness; SEE CONCEPT 409

experience [n2] *happening, occurrence*
adventure, affair, encounter, episode, event, incident, ordeal, test, trial, trip; SEE CONCEPTS 2,696

experienced [adj] *knowledgeable, knowing*
accomplished, accustomed, adept, been around*, been there*, broken in*, capable, competent, cultivated, dynamite, expert, familiar, having something on the ball*, instructed, in the know*, knowing one's stuff*, knowing the score*, mature, matured, old, old hand*, practical, practiced, pro, professional, qualified, rounded, seasoned, skillful, sophisticated, sport, tested, the right stuff*, trained, tried, versed, vet, veteran, well-versed, wise, worldly, worldly-wise*; SEE CONCEPTS 402,527

experiment [n] *investigation, test*
agreement, analysis, assay, attempt, check, dissection, dry run*, enterprise, essay, examination, exercise, experimentation, fling*, measure, observation, operation, practice, probe, procedure, proof, quiz, R and D*, rehearsal, research, research and development, scrutiny, search, speculation, study, trial, trial and error*, trial run*, try, try-on, tryout, undertaking, venture, verification; SEE CONCEPTS 103,290

experiment [v] *investigate, test*
analyze, assay, diagnose, examine, explore, fool with*, futz around*, mess around*, play around with*, practice with, probe, prove, put to the test*, research, sample, scrutinize, search, shake down*, speculate, study, try, try on, try on for size*, try out, venture, verify, weigh; SEE CONCEPTS 24,87,103

experimental [adj] *exploratory*
beginning, developmental, empirical, experiential, first stage, laboratory, momentary, on approval, pilot, preliminary, preparatory, primary, probationary, provisional, speculative, temporary, tentative, test, trial, trial-and-error, unconcluded, under probation, unproved; SEE CONCEPT 535

expert [n] *master, specialist*
ace*, adept, artist, artiste, authority, buff, connoisseur, doyen, graduate, guru*, hot shot*, old hand*, old pro*, phenomenon, pro, professional, proficient, shark*, virtuoso, whiz*, wizard; SEE CONCEPTS 348,350,416

expert [adj] *knowledgeable, proficient*
able, adept, adroit, apt, big league*, clever, crack, crackerjack*, deft, dexterous, experienced, facile, handy, practiced, professional, qualified, savvy, schooled, sharp, skilled, skillful, slick, trained, virtuoso; SEE CONCEPTS 402,527

expertise/expertness [n] *knowledge, proficiency*
ability, ableness, adroitness, aptness, art, cleverness, command, competence, craft, cunning, deftness, dexterity, dodge*, facility, finesse, goods*, ingeniousness, judgment, knack*, know-how*, line*, makings*, oil*, one's thing*, prowess, readiness, savvy, sharpness, skill, skillfulness, stuff*; SEE CONCEPTS **409,630**

expiate [v] *make amends for*
absolve, amend, appease, atone, atone for, compensate, correct, do penance, excuse, forgive, pay one's dues*, rectify, redeem, redress, remedy, square things*; SEE CONCEPTS **67,126**

expiration [n] *finish, demise*
cessation, close, closing, conclusion, death, decease, departure, dying, elapsing, end, expiry, going, passing, termination, terminus; SEE CONCEPTS **119,304**

expire [v1] *come to an end*
bite the dust*, buy it*, cash in chips*, cease, close, conclude, croak*, decease, depart, die, elapse, end, finish, go, kick the bucket*, lapse, pass, pass away, pass on, pass over, perish, quit, run out, stop, strike out*, terminate, up and die*; SEE CONCEPTS **119,304**

expire [v2] *breathe out*
emit, exhale, expel; SEE CONCEPTS **163,185**

explain [v] *make clear; give a reason for*
account for, analyze, annotate, break down, bring out, clarify, clear up, construe, decipher, define, demonstrate, describe, diagram, disclose, elucidate, excuse, explicate, expound, get across*, go into detail, illustrate, interpret, justify, make plain*, manifest, paraphrase, point out, put across, put in plain English*, rationalize, read, refine, render, resolve, reveal, set right, solve, spell out*, teach, tell, throw light upon*, translate, unfold, unravel, untangle; SEE CONCEPT **57**

explanation [n] *clarification; reason*
account, annotation, answer, breakdown, brief, cause, comment, commentary, confession, definition, demonstration, description, details, display, elucidation, evidence, example, excuse, explication, exposition, expression, gloss, history, illustration, information, interpretation, justification, meaning, mitigation, motive, narration, note, recital, rendition, report, resolution, sense, showing, significance, specification, statement, story, summary, tale, talking, telling, vindication, writing; SEE CONCEPTS **271,274,661**

explanatory [adj] *descriptive*
allegorical, analytical, annotative, critical, declarative, demonstrative, diagrammatic, discursive, elucidatory, enlightening, exegetic, exegetical, explicative, expositional, expository, graphic, guiding, hermeneutic, illuminative, illustrative, informative, informing, instructive, interpretive, justifying, summary, supplementary; SEE CONCEPT **267**

expletive [n] *swear word; exclamation*
curse, cuss, cuss word, interjection, oath; SEE CONCEPT **275**

explicate [v] *clarify, expand*
amplify, clear up, construe, demonstrate, develop, dilate, elucidate, enlarge upon, enucleate, expatiate, explain, expound, give the big picture*, illustrate, interpret, make clear, make explicit, make plain*, run down, spell out*, tell why, unfold, untangle, work out; SEE CONCEPT **57**

explicit [adj] *specific, unambiguous*
absolute, accurate, categorical, certain, clean-cut, clear, clear-cut, correct, definite, definitive, direct, distinct, exact, express, frank, lucid, obvious, on the nose*, open, outspoken, patent, perspicuous, plain, positive, precise, stated, straightforward, sure, understandable, unequivocal, unqualified, unreserved; SEE CONCEPTS **267,529,535**

explode [v1] *blow up*
backfire, blast, blaze, blow to kingdom come*, break out, burst, collapse, convulse, detonate, discharge, erupt, flame up, flare up, fracture, jet, kablooey*, let go*, mushroom*, rupture, set off, shatter, shiver, split, thunder; SEE CONCEPTS **179,320**

explode [v2] *discredit*
belie, confute, debunk, deflate, discard, disprove, invalidate, puncture, refute, repudiate, shoot down*, shoot full of holes*; SEE CONCEPT **54**

exploit [n] *achievement*
accomplishment, adventure, attainment, coup, deed, do, effort, enterprise, escapade, feat, job, maneuver, performance, stroke, stunt, tour de force, venture; SEE CONCEPT **706**

exploit [v] *take advantage of; misuse*
abuse, apply, avail oneself of, bleed*, capitalize on, cash in on*, employ, exercise, finesse, fleece*, get mileage out of*, handle, impose upon, jockey*, make capital of, make use of, maneuver, manipulate, milk*, mine*, play*, play on, profit by, profit from, put to use, skin*, soak*, stick*, use, utilize, work; SEE CONCEPTS **156,225**

exploration [n] *investigation; survey*
analysis, examination, expedition, inquiry, inspection, probe, reconnaissance, research, scrutiny, search, study, tour, travel, trip; SEE CONCEPTS **216,224**

explore [v] *investigate; survey*
analyze, burrow, delve into, dig into, examine, go into*, have a look*, hunt, inquire into, inspect, leave no stone unturned*, look into, probe, prospect, question, reconnoiter, research, scout, scrutinize, search, seek, sift, test, tour, travel, traverse, try, turn inside out*; SEE CONCEPTS **103,216,224**

explosion [n] *eruption, discharge*
access, backfire, bang, blast, blowout, blowup, burst, clap, combustion, concussion, crack, detonation, firing, fit, flare-up, fulmination, gust, ignition, outbreak, outburst, paroxysm, percussion, pop, report, roar, salvo; SEE CONCEPTS **179,320,521**

explosive [n] *something that blows up*
ammunition, bomb, booby trap*, charge, detonator, dynamite, fireworks, grease*, grenade, gunpowder, mine, missile, mulligan, nitroglycerin, pineapple*, powder, propellant, shell, shot, soup*, TNT*; SEE CONCEPT **500**

explosive [adj] *volatile, dangerous*
at the boiling point*, bursting, charged, consequential, convulsive, detonating, detonative, ebullient, eruptive, fiery, forceful, frenzied, fulminant, fulminating, hazardous, impetuous, meteoric, overwrought, perilous, raging, rampant, stormy, tense, touchy, ugly, uncontrollable, unstable, vehement, violent, wild; SEE CONCEPT **542**

exponent [n1] *person who supports, advocates*
backer, booster, champion, defender, demonstrator, expositor, expounder, interpreter, partisan,

promoter, propagandist, proponent, protagonist, second, seconder, spokesperson, supporter, upholder; SEE CONCEPT 423

exponent [n2] *example*
denotation, exemplar, illustration, index, indication, model, representative, sample, sign, specimen, token, type; SEE CONCEPTS 284,686

export [v] *sell or trade abroad*
consign, convey, dump, find market, find outlet, freight, send out, ship, smuggle, transport, transship; SEE CONCEPTS 217,324

exposé [n] *disclosure*
betrayal, confession, construction, divulgence, exegesis, explanation, explication, exposal, exposition, exposure, interpretation, revelation, truth, uncovering; SEE CONCEPT 274

expose [v1] *reveal*
advertise, air, bare, betray, brandish, bring to light*, broadcast, crack, debunk, denude, dig up*, disclose, display, disport, divulge, exhibit, feature, flash, flaunt, give away, lay bare*, lay open*, leak, let cat out of bag*, let out*, make known, manifest, open, open to view, parade, present, prove, publish, put on view, report, show, show off, smoke out*, spill, streak, tip off*, trot out*, unclothe, uncover, unearth, unfold, unmask, unshroud, unveil; SEE CONCEPTS 60,261

expose [v2] *subject to danger*
endanger, hazard, imperil, jeopardize, lay open*, leave open*, make liable, make vulnerable, peril, put in harm's way*, risk; SEE CONCEPT 246

exposed [adj1] *made public*
apparent, bare, bared, brought to light*, caught, clear, debunked, defined, denuded, disclosed, discovered, divulged, dug up*, evident, exhibited, for show, found out, laid bare*, made manifest, manifest, naked, on display, on the spot*, on view, peeled, resolved, revealed, shown, solved, stripped, unconcealed, uncovered, unhidden, unmasked, unprotected, unsealed, unsheltered, unveiled, visible; SEE CONCEPT 576

exposed [adj2] *in danger*
accessible, in peril, laid bare*, laid open*, left open*, liable, menaced, open, prone, sensitive, subject, susceptible, threatened, unguarded, unprotected, vulnerable; SEE CONCEPTS 485,548

exposition [n1] *written description*
account, analysis, annotation, article, comment, commentary, composition, construal, construction, critique, delineation, details, discourse, discussion, disquisition, dissertation, editorial, elucidation, enucleation, enunciation, essay, exegesis, explanation, explication, exposé, expounding, history, illustration, interpretation, monograph, paper, piece, position paper, presentation, report, review, statement, story, study, tale, text, theme, thesis, tract, tractate, treatise; SEE CONCEPTS 268,271

exposition [n2] *fair*
bazaar, circus, county fair, demonstration, display, exhibition, expo, marketplace, mart, pageant, presentation, production, show, showing; SEE CONCEPT 386

expository [adj] *descriptive*
critical, disquisitional, elucidative, exegetic, explanatory, explicative, explicatory, hermeneutic, illustrative, informative, interpretive; SEE CONCEPT 267

expostulate [v] *reason with*
argue, dissuade, oppose, protest, remonstrate; SEE CONCEPT 46

exposure [n] *uncovering; putting in view or danger*
acknowledgment, airing, baring, betrayal, confession, defenselessness, denudation, denunciation, disclosure, display, divulgence, divulging, exhibition, exposé, giveaway, hazard, introduction, jeopardy, laying open, liability, manifestation, nakedness, openness, peril, presentation, publicity, revelation, risk, showing, susceptibility, susceptiveness, susceptivity, unfolding, unmasking, unveiling, vulnerability, vulnerableness; SEE CONCEPTS 60,261

expound [v] *talk about in great detail*
clarify, comment, construe, delineate, describe, discourse, elucidate, enucleate, exemplify, explain, explicate, express, illustrate, interpret, present, set forth, spell out, state, unfold; SEE CONCEPT 57

express [adj1] *certain, precise*
accurate, categorical, clean-cut*, clear, clear-cut, considered, definite, definitive, deliberate, designful, direct, distinct, especial, exact, explicit, expressed, individual, intended, intentional, out-and-out*, outright, particular, plain, pointed, premeditated, set, singular, special, specific, unambiguous, unconditional, unmistakable, unqualified, uttered, voiced, voluntary, willing, witting; SEE CONCEPTS 535,556,653

express [adj2] *direct, speedy*
accelerated, fast, high-speed, nonstop, quick, rapid, swift, velocious; SEE CONCEPTS 548,588

express [v1] *articulate; signify, mean*
add up to*, air, assert, asseverate, bespeak, broach, circulate, communicate, connote, convey, couch, declare, denote, depict, designate, disclose, divulge, embody, enunciate, evince, exhibit, formulate, frame*, give, hint, import, indicate, insinuate, intend, intimate, make known, manifest, phrase, pop off*, proclaim, pronounce, put, put across, put into words*, represent, reveal, say, show, speak, spell, stand for, state, suggest, symbolize, tell, testify, utter, vent, ventilate, verbalize, voice, word; SEE CONCEPTS 51,682

express [v2] *discharge by squeezing or force*
crush, dispatch, distill, expel, extract, force out, forward, press out, ship, squeeze out; SEE CONCEPT 179

expression [n1] *verbalization*
announcement, argument, articulation, assertion, asseveration, choice of words, commentary, communication, declaration, definition, delivery, diction, elucidation, emphasis, enunciation, execution, explanation, exposition, formulation, idiom, interpretation, intonation, issue, language, locution, mention, narration, phrase, phraseology, phrasing, pronouncement, remark, rendition, set phrase, speaking, speech, statement, style, term, turn of phrase, utterance, vent, voice, voicing, word, writ; SEE CONCEPTS 47,268,276

expression [n2] *facial appearance*
air, aspect, cast, character, contortion, countenance, face, grimace, grin, look, mien, mug*, pout*, simper, smile, smirk, sneer, visage; SEE CONCEPT 716

expressionless [adj] *having a blank look on face*
dead*, deadpan, dull, empty, fish-eyed*, impassive, inexpressive, inscrutable, lackluster, lusterless, nobody home*, poker-faced*, stolid,

straight-faced, stupid, unexpressive, vacant, vacuous, wooden; SEE CONCEPT 406

expressive [adj] *telling, revealing*
alive, allusive, articulate, artistic, brilliant, colorful, demonstrative, dramatic, eloquent, emphatic, energetic, forcible, graphic, indicative, ingenious, lively, masterly, meaningful, mobile, moving, passionate, pathetic, pictorial, picturesque, poignant, pointed, pregnant, representative, responsive, revelatory, showy, significant, silver-tongued*, spirited, stimulating, stirring, striking, strong, suggestive, sympathetic, tender, thoughtful, touching, understanding, vivid, warm; SEE CONCEPTS 267,537

expressly [adv1] *purposely*
especially, exactly, in specie, intentionally, on purpose, particularly, precisely, specially, specifically; SEE CONCEPT 556

expressly [adv2] *definitely, unambiguously*
absolutely, categorically, clearly, decidedly, directly, distinctly, explicitly, in no uncertain terms*, manifestly, outright, plainly, pointedly, positively, specifically, unequivocally, unmistakably; SEE CONCEPT 535

expressway [n] *large, well-travelled road*
freeway, interstate, parkway, superhighway, thruway, turnpike; SEE CONCEPT 501

expropriate [v] *seize*
accroach, annex, appropriate, arrogate, assume, commandeer, confiscate, deprive of property, dispossess, impound, preempt, requisition, sequester, take, take over; SEE CONCEPTS 90,142

expulsion [n] *banishing*
banishment, boot*, bounce, debarment, deportment, discharge, dislodgment, dismissal, displacement, dispossession, driving out, ejection, eviction, exclusion, exile, expatriation, extrusion, forcing out, ostracism, ouster, ousting, proscription, purge, relegation, removal, rush, suspension; SEE CONCEPTS 130,211,298

expunge [v] *destroy, obliterate*
abolish, annihilate, annul, black, black out*, blot out, blue pencil*, call all bets off*, call off, cancel, cut, delete, discard, drop, efface, eradicate, erase, exclude, exterminate, extinguish, extirpate, gut, kayo*, kill, knock off*, KO*, launder*, omit, raze, remove, scrub*, strike out, take out, trim, wipe out, X out*, zap*; SEE CONCEPTS 211,252

expurgate [v] *censor, cut*
bleep*, bleep out*, blip*, blue pencil*, bowdlerize, cleanse, clean up, decontaminate, lustrate, purge, purify, sanitize, screen, scrub*, squash, sterilize; SEE CONCEPTS 165,232

exquisite [adj1] *beautiful, excellent, finely detailed*
admirable, attractive, charming, choice, comely, consummate, cultivated, dainty, delicate, delicious, discerning, discriminating, elegant, errorless, ethereal, fastidious, fine, flawless, impeccable, incomparable, irreproachable, lovely, matchless, meticulous, outstanding, peerless, perfect, pleasing, polished, precious, precise, rare, recherché, refined, select, selective, splendid, striking, subtle, superb, superior, superlative; SEE CONCEPTS 574,579,589

exquisite [adj2] *intense*
acute, concentrated, consummate, desperate, excruciating, extreme, fierce, furious, keen, piercing, poignant, sharp, terrible, transcending, vehement, vicious, violent; SEE CONCEPT 569

extant [adj] *in existence*
actual, alive, around, being, contemporary, current, existent, existing, immediate, in current use, instant, living, not lost, present, present-day, real, remaining, subsisting, surviving, undestroyed; SEE CONCEPTS 539,582

extemporaneous/extemporary [adj] *unrehearsed, improvised*
ad hoc, ad lib, at first glance, automatic, by ear*, casual, expedient, extempore, free, immediate, impromptu, improv*, improvisatory, improviso, informal, jamming*, made-up, makeshift, offhand, off the cuff*, off the top of head*, on impulse, on-the-spot*, snap, spontaneous, spur-of-the-moment*, taking for ride*, thought out loud*, tossed off*, tossed out*, unplanned, unpremeditated, unprepared, unstudied, winging it*; SEE CONCEPTS 267,799

extemporize [v] *improvise*
ad-lib, dash out, devise, do offhand*, improvisate, invent, knock off*, make up, play by ear*, toss off*; SEE CONCEPT 51

extend [v1] *make larger, longer*
add to, aggrandize, amplify, augment, beef up*, boost, broaden, carry on, continue, crane, develop, dilate, drag one's feet*, drag out, draw, draw out, elongate, enhance, enlarge, expand, fan out, go on, heighten, increase, last, lengthen, let out, magnify, mantle, multiply, open, pad, prolong, prolongate, protract, run on, spin out, spread, spread out, stall, stretch, string out, supplement, take, unfold, unfurl, unroll, widen; SEE CONCEPTS 236,239,245

extend [v2] *offer*
accord, advance, allocate, allot, award, bestow, bring forward, confer, donate, give, grant, hold out, impart, place at disposal, pose, present, proffer, put forth, put forward, reach out, stretch out, submit, tender, yield; SEE CONCEPTS 66,67

extended [adj1] *lengthened*
continued, drawn-out, elongate, elongated, enlarged, lengthy, long, prolonged, protracted, spread, spread out, stretched out, unfolded, unfurled, very long; SEE CONCEPTS 782,798

extended [adj2] *widespread, comprehensive*
broad, enlarged, expanded, expansive, extensive, far-flung, far-reaching, large-scale, outspread, scopic, scopious, spread, sweeping, thorough, wide; SEE CONCEPT 772

extension [n] *enlargement, continuation*
addendum, addition, adjunct, amplification, annex, appendage, appendix, arm, augmentation, branch, broadening, compass, continuing, delay, development, dilatation, distension, drawing out, elongation, expansion, extent, increase, lengthening, orbit, postponement, production, prolongation, protraction, purview, radius, reach, scope, span, spread, spreading out, stretch, stretching, supplement, sweep, widening, wing; SEE CONCEPTS 236,245,824

extensive [adj] *far-reaching, thorough*
across the board*, all-encompassing, all-inclusive, big, blanket*, boundless, broad, capacious, commodious, comprehensive, comprising, considerable, expanded, extended, far-flung*, general, great, hefty, huge, inclusive, indiscriminate, large, large-scale, lengthy, long, major, pervasive, prevalent, protracted, roomy, scopic, scopious, sizable, spacious, sweeping, unexclusive, universal, unrestricted, vast, voluminous,

ex
ex

wall to wall*, wholesale, wide, wide-ranging, widespread; SEE CONCEPTS 772,773

extent [n] *range, magnitude*
admeasurement, ambit, amount, amplitude, area, bounds, breadth, bulk, capaciousness, compass, degree, dimensions, duration, elbowroom*, expanse, expansion, extension, intensity, leeway, length, limit, mass, matter, measure, neighborhood, orbit, order, period of time, play, proliferation, proportions, purview, quantity, radius, reach, scope, size, space, spaciousness, span, sphere, stretch, sweep, term, territory, time, tract, tune, vicinity, volume, wideness, width; SEE CONCEPTS 651,730,743,745,783,788,804

extenuating [adj] *serving as an excuse*
condoning, diminishing, justifying, lessening, mitigating, moderating, palliating, qualifying, reducing, sanitizing, softening, varnishing, whitewashing*; SEE CONCEPT 537

exterior [n] *visible part*
appearance, aspect, coating, cover, covering, exteriority, external, facade, face, finish, outside, polish, rind, shell, skin, superficies, superstratum, surface; SEE CONCEPT 484

exterior [adj] *outside*
exoteric, external, extraneous, extraterrestrial, extraterritorial, extrinsic, foreign, marginal, outdoor, outer, outermost, outlying, outmost, outward, over, peripheral, superficial, surface; SEE CONCEPT 583

exterminate [v] *kill*
abolish, annihilate, blot out*, decimate, destroy, do away with*, eliminate, eradicate, erase, execute, extinguish, extirpate, finish off, massacre, obliterate, put an end to*, rub out*, send to kingdom come*, slaughter, stamp out*, wipe out*; SEE CONCEPT 252

external [adj] *outside, extrinsic*
alien, apparent, exterior, extraneous, foreign, independent, out, outer, outermost, outmost, outward, over, peripheral, superficial, surface, visible; SEE CONCEPT 583

extinct [adj] *dead, obsolete*
abolished, archaic, asleep, bygone, cold*, dead and gone*, deceased, defunct, departed, disappeared, done for*, doused, ended, exanimate, exterminated, extinguished, fallen, gone, inactive, late, lifeless, lost, no longer known, out, outmoded, passé, passed on, snuffed out*, superseded, terminated, unknown, vanished, vanquished, void; SEE CONCEPT 539

extinguish [v1] *put out a fire*
blot out, blow out, choke, douse, drown, out, quench, smother, snuff out, stamp out, stifle, suffocate, trample; SEE CONCEPT 256

extinguish [v2] *kill; quash*
abate, abolish, annihilate, blot out*, check, crush, destroy, eliminate, end, eradicate, erase, expunge, exterminate, extirpate, obliterate, obscure, put down, put the lid on*, quell, remove, squash, stamp out, suppress, wipe out*; SEE CONCEPTS 95,252

extirpate [v] *destroy; uproot*
abate, abolish, annihilate, blot out*, cut out, demolish, deracinate, efface, eliminate, eradicate, erase, excise, expunge, exsect, exterminate, extinguish, kill, raze, remove, root out, wipe out*; SEE CONCEPTS 211,252

extol [v] *sing the praises of*
acclaim, applaud, bless, boost, brag about, celebrate, commend, cry up*, eulogize, exalt, give a boost to, give a bouquet*, glorify, hand it to*, hats off to*, hear it for*, hymn, laud, magnify, make much of, panegyrize, pay tribute to, praise, puff up*, push, rave, root, stroke*; SEE CONCEPT 69

extort [v] *cheat; blackmail*
bleed*, bully, clip, coerce, demand, educe, elicit, evince, exact, extract, fleece, force, get, gouge, hold up*, ice*, make pay through nose*, milk*, obtain, pinch, pull one's leg*, put screws to*, put the arm on*, secure, shake down*, skin*, soak, squeeze, stick, sting, wrench, wrest, wring; SEE CONCEPTS 53,59,139,342

extortion [n] *blackmail; cheating*
arm, badger, bite, coercion, compulsion, demand, exaction, force, fraud, oppression, payoff, payola*, pressure, protection, racket, rapacity, shake, shakedown*, squeeze, stealing, swindle, theft; SEE CONCEPTS 53,139,192,342

extra [n] *accessory*
addendum, addition, adjunct, affix, appendage, appurtenance, attachment, bonus, complement, extension, supernumerary, supplement; SEE CONCEPT 824

extra [adj] *accessory; excess*
added, additional, ancillary, another, auxiliary, beyond, button*, extraneous, extraordinary, fresh, further, fuss*, gingerbread*, gravy*, ice*, in addition, inessential, in reserve, in store, lagniappe*, leftover, more, needless, new, one more, optional, other, over and above*, perk*, plus, redundant, reserve, spare, special, superfluous, supernumerary, supplemental, supplementary, surplus, tip, unnecessary, unneeded, unused; SEE CONCEPTS 546,771

extra [adv] *particularly*
considerably, especially, exceptionally, extraordinarily, extremely, markedly, noticeably, rarely, remarkably, uncommon, uncommonly, unusually; SEE CONCEPTS 557,569

extract [n] *something condensed from whole*
abstract, citation, clipping, concentrate, cutting, decoction, distillate, distillation, elicitation, essence, excerpt, infusion, juice*, passage, quotation, selection; SEE CONCEPTS 270,835

extract [v1] *physically remove, draw out*
avulse, bring out, catheterize, cull, derive, distill, eke out, elicit, eradicate, evoke, evulse, exact, express, extirpate, extort, extricate, garner, gather, get, glean, obtain, pick up, pluck, press out, pry, pull, reap, secure, select, separate, siphon, squeeze, take, tear, uproot, weed out*, withdraw, wrest, wring, yank; SEE CONCEPTS 206,211

extract [v2] *select a quotation*
abridge, abstract, bring forth, choose, cite, condense, copy, cull, cut out, deduce, derive, educe, elicit, evolve, excerpt, glean, quote, shorten; SEE CONCEPTS 79,142,211

extraction [n1] *removal from whole; distillation*
abstraction, derivation, drawing, elicitation, eradication, evocation, evulsion, expression, extirpation, extrication, pulling, separation, taking out, uprooting, withdrawal, wrenching, wresting; SEE CONCEPT 211

extraction [n2] *ancestry, origin*
birth, blood, derivation, descent, family, lineage, parentage, pedigree, race, stock; SEE CONCEPTS 296,648

extradite [v] *send to another place by force*
abandon, apprehend, arrest, bring to justice, bring to trial, deliver, give up, release, surrender; SEE CONCEPTS *217,317*

extraneous [adj1] *unneeded; irrelevant*
accidental, additional, adventitious, beside the point, extra, foreign, immaterial, impertinent, inadmissible, inapplicable, inapposite, inappropriate, incidental, inessential, needless, nonessential, off the subject, peripheral, pointless, redundant, superfluous, supplementary, unconnected, unessential, unnecessary, unrelated; SEE CONCEPT *546*

extraneous [adj2] *foreign*
adventitious, alien, exotic, external, extrinsic, out of place, strange; SEE CONCEPT *549*

extraordinary [adj] *strange and wonderful*
amazing, bizarre, boss*, curious, exceptional, fab*, fantastic, flash*, gnarly*, heavy*, inconceivable, incredible, marvelous, odd, off beaten path*, out of the ordinary, outstanding, particular, peculiar, phenomenal, rare, remarkable, singular, special, strange, stupendous, surprising, terrific, uncommon, unfamiliar, unheard-of, unimaginable, unique, unprecedented, unthinkable, unusual, unwonted, weird, wicked*; SEE CONCEPTS *564,572*

extravagance [n] *indulgence; waste*
absurdity, amenity, dissipation, exaggeration, excess, exorbitance, expenditure, folly, frill, icing on the cake*, immoderation, improvidence, lavishness, luxury, outrageousness, overdoing, overindulgence, overspending, preposterousness, prodigality, profligacy, profusion, recklessness, squander, squandering, superfluity, unreasonableness, unrestraint, unthrift, wastefulness, wildness; SEE CONCEPTS *335,337,787*

extravagant [adj] *indulgent, wasteful*
absurd, bizarre, costly, crazy, exaggerated, excessive, exorbitant, expensive, extortionate, extreme, fanciful, fancy, fantastic, flamboyant, flashy, foolish, garish, gaudy, grandiose, immoderate, implausible, improvident, imprudent, inordinate, lavish, ludicrous, nonsensical, ornate, ostentatious, outrageous, overpriced, preposterous, pretentious, prodigal, profligate, reckless, ridiculous, showy, silly, spendthrift, steep, unbalanced, unconscionable, unreasonable, unrestrained; SEE CONCEPTS *334,560,771*

extravaganza [n] *spectacle*
caricature, display, divertissement, flight of fancy*, pageant, parody, show, spectacular; SEE CONCEPTS *263,293*

extreme [n] *ultimate; limit*
acme, apex, apogee, bitter end, boundary, ceiling, climax, consummation, crest, crown, culmination, depth, edge, end, excess, extremity, height, inordinacy, maximum, nadir, nth degree*, peak, pinnacle, pole, termination, top, utmost, uttermost, zenith; SEE CONCEPTS *484,706,745,836*

extreme [adj1] *very great*
acute, consummate, high, highest, intense, maximal, maximum, severe, sovereign, supreme, top, ultimate, utmost, uttermost; SEE CONCEPTS *569,771,781*

extreme [adj2] *beyond reason and convention*
absolute, desperate, dire, downright, drastic, egregious, exaggerated, exceptional, excessive, extraordinary, extravagant, fabulous, fanatical, flagrant, gross, harsh, immoderate, improper, imprudent, inordinate, intemperate, irrational, nonsensical, out-and-out*, out of proportion, outrageous, overkill, preposterous, rabid, radical, remarkable, rigid, severe, sheer, stern, strict, thorough, unbending, uncommon, uncompromising, unconventional, unreasonable, unseemly, unusual, utter, zealous; SEE CONCEPTS *547,558,569*

extreme [adj3] *faraway*
far-off, farthest, final, furthermost, last, most distant, outermost, outmost, remotest, terminal, ultimate, utmost, uttermost; SEE CONCEPT *778*

extremely [adv] *greatly, intensely*
acutely, almighty, awfully, drastically, exceedingly, exceptionally, excessively, exorbitantly, extraordinarily, highly, hugely, immensely, immoderately, inordinately, intensely, markedly, mortally, notably, over, overly, overmuch, parlous, plenty, powerful, prohibitively, quite, radically, rarely, remarkably, severely, strikingly, surpassingly, terribly, terrifically, to nth degree*, too, too much*, totally, ultra*, uncommonly, unduly, unusually, utterly, very*, violently, vitally; SEE CONCEPTS *569,771,781*

extremist [n] *person zealous about a belief*
agitator, die-hard, fanatic, radical, revolutionary, revolutionist, ultra, ultraist, zealot; SEE CONCEPTS *359,423*

extremity [n1] *ultimate; limit*
acme, acuteness, adversity, apex, apogee, border, bound, boundary, brim, brink, butt, climax, consummation, crisis, depth, dire straits, disaster, edge, end, excess, extreme, extremes, frontier, height, last, margin, maximum, nadir, outside, pinnacle, plight, pole, remote, rim, setback, terminal, termination, terminus, tip, top, trouble, verge, vertex, zenith; SEE CONCEPTS *484,706, 745,836*

extremity [n2] *animate being's appendage*
backside, finger, flipper, foot, hand, leg, limb, paw, posterior, toe; SEE CONCEPT *392*

extricate [v] *get out of a situation; relieve of responsibility*
bail out*, clear, deliver, detach, difference, differentiate, disburden, discumber, disembarrass, disencumber, disengage, disentangle, disinvolve, extract, free, get off the hook*, get out from under*, let go, let off*, liberate, loose, loosen, pull out, release, remove, rescue, resolve, save one's neck*, separate, sever, untie, withdraw, wriggle out of*; SEE CONCEPTS *102,127*

extrinsic [adj] *foreign*
acquired, alien, exotic, exterior, external, extraneous, gained, imported, outer, outside, outward, superficial; SEE CONCEPT *549*

extrovert [n] *sociable person*
character*, exhibitionist, gregarious person, life of the party*, showboat*, show-off*; SEE CONCEPT *423*

extrude [v] *force out*
boot*, chase, dismiss, eject, evict, expel, kick out, press, project, squeeze*, throw out, thrust; SEE CONCEPTS *208,222*

exuberance [n1] *energy, enthusiasm*
abandon, animation, ardor, bounce, buoyancy, cheerfulness, eagerness, ebullience, effervescence, excitement, exhilaration, fervor, friskiness, gayness, get up and go*, high spirits, juice*, life, liveliness, pep, pepper*, spirit, sprightliness, vigor, vitality, zap*, zest*, zip*; SEE CONCEPT *633*

ex
ex

exuberance [n2] *profusion*
abundance, affluence, copiousness, effusiveness, exaggeration, excessiveness, fulsomeness, lavishness, lushness, luxuriance, plenitude, plenty, prodigality, richness, superabundance, superfluity, teemingness; SEE CONCEPTS 710,767

exuberant [adj1] *energetic, enthusiastic*
animated, ardent, bouncy, brash, buoyant, cheerful, chipper, eager, ebullient, effervescent, elated, excited, exhilarated, feeling one's oats*, frolicsome, gay, high-spirited, lively, passionate, sparkling, spirited, sprightly, vigorous, vivacious, zappy*, zestful, zingy*, zippy*; SEE CONCEPT 401

exuberant [adj2] *profuse*
abundant, affluent, copious, diffuse, effusive, exaggerated, excessive, fecund, fertile, fruitful, fulsome, lavish, lush, luxuriant, opulent, overdone, overflowing, plenteous, plentiful, prodigal, prolific, rampant, rich, riotous, superabundant, superfluous, teeming; SEE CONCEPT 781

exude [v] *display, emit*
bleed, discharge, emanate, evacuate, excrete, exhibit, expel, flow out, give forth, give off, issue, leak, manifest, ooze, pass, percolate, radiate, secrete, seep, show, sweat, throw off, trickle, weep; SEE CONCEPTS 118,179

exult [v1] *be joyful*
be delighted, be elated, be happy, be in high spirits*, be jubilant, be overjoyed, celebrate, cheer, jubilate, jump for joy*, make merry*, rejoice; SEE CONCEPTS 32,266

exult [v2] *boast*
bluster, brag, bully, crow, gloat, glory, revel, show off, take delight in*, triumph, vaunt; SEE CONCEPT 49

exultant [adj] *very happy*
blown away*, delighted, ecstatic, elated, exulting, flipping, flushed, flying, gleeful, high, joyful, joyous, jubilant, overjoyed, rejoicing, revelling, transported, triumphant, turned on*, wowed*; SEE CONCEPT 403

exultation [n] *celebration, reveling*
crowing, delight, elation, glee, gloating, glory, happiness, high spirits, joy, joyousness, jubilance, jubilation, merriment, rejoicing, satisfaction, transport, triumph; SEE CONCEPTS 32,410

eye [n1] *judgment, opinion*
appreciation, belief, conviction, discernment, discrimination, eagle eye*, feeling, mind, perception, persuasion, point of view, recognition, scrutiny, sentiment, surveillance, tab, taste, view, viewpoint, watch; SEE CONCEPTS 411,689

eye [n2] *optical organ of an animate being*
baby blue*, blinder*, eyeball, headlight*, lamp*, ocular, oculus, optic, peeper*, pie*; SEE CONCEPT 392

eye [v] *gaze at, scrutinize*
check out, consider, contemplate, eyeball*, gape, give the eye*, glance at, have a look, inspect, keep eagle eye on*, leer, look at, ogle, peruse, regard, rubberneck*, scan, size up*, stare at, study, survey, take a look, take in, view, watch; SEE CONCEPTS 17,623,626

eyeful [n] *spectacular-looking person*
beauty, dazzler*, knockout*, looker, lovely, show, spectacle, stunner*, vision; SEE CONCEPT 424

eyesore [n] *mess, ugliness*
atrocity, blemish, blight, blot, blot on landscape*, deformity, disfigurement, disgrace, distortion, dump, horror, monstrosity, sight, ugly thing; SEE CONCEPTS 674,716

eyewitness [n] *person who sees an event occur*
beholder, bystander, looker-on, observer, onlooker, passer-by, spectator, viewer, watcher, witness; SEE CONCEPT 423

F

fable [n] *fantasy, story*
allegory, apologue, bestiary, bunk*, crock*, fabrication, fairy story, fairy tale, falsehood, fantasy, fib, fiction, figment, fish story*, hogwash*, invention, legend, lie, myth, old chestnut*, old saw*, one for the birds*, parable, romance, tale, tall story, untruth, white lie*, whopper*, yarn; SEE CONCEPT 282

fabled [adj] *legendary*
fabulous, famed, famous, fanciful, fictional, mythical, mythological, storied, unreal; SEE CONCEPT 568

fabric [n1] *cloth, material*
bolt, fiber, goods, stuff, textile, texture, web; SEE CONCEPT 473

fabric [n2] *structure*
building, consistency, constitution, construction, foundation, frame, framework, infrastructure, make-up, mold, organization, stamp, substance, texture; SEE CONCEPTS 733,757

fabricate [v1] *manufacture*
assemble, brainstorm, build, cobble up*, compose, concoct, construct, contrive, cook up*, create, devise, dream up, erect, fashion, fit together, form, formulate, frame, head trip*, invent, join, knock together*, make, make up, mix, organize, piece together, prefab*, produce, put together, shape, structure, think up, throw together*, throw up*, turn out, whip up*, whomp up*; SEE CONCEPTS 36,173,205,251

fabricate [v2] *falsify, make up a story*
coin, concoct, contrive, counterfeit, devise, fake, feign, fib, forge, form, fudge*, invent, jive*, lie, make like*, misrepresent, pretend, prevaricate, trump up*; SEE CONCEPTS 58,63

fabrication [n1] *lie*
artifact, concoction, deceit, fable, fairy story*, fake*, falsehood, fib, fiction, figment, forgery, hogwash*, invention, jazz*, jive*, line*, myth, opus, smoke*, song and dance*, untruth, work, yarn; SEE CONCEPTS 63,278

fabrication [n2] *something manufactured*
assemblage, assembly, building, construction, creation, erection, product, production; SEE CONCEPTS 205,260,338

fabulous [adj] *amazing, wonderful*
aces*, A-OK*, A-1*, astonishing, astounding, awesome, best, breathtaking, cool*, doozie*, extravagant, fab*, fantastic, fictitious, first-class, greatest, groovy*, immense, inconceivable, incredible, legendary, marvelous, mind-blowing*, out-of-sight*, out-of-this-world*, outrageous, peachy*, phenomenal, primo*, prodigious, rad*, remarkable, spectacular, striking, stupendous, super, superb, 10*, terrific, top drawer*, tops*, turn-

on*, unbelievable, unreal, wicked*; SEE CONCEPTS *529,572*

facade [n] *appearance, often deceptive*
beard*, bluff, color, disguise, exterior, face, fake, false colors*, false front*, front, frontage*, guise, look, mask, phony, pretense, put-on*, semblance, show, veneer, window dressing*; SEE CONCEPT *716*

face [n1] *front of something; expression, exterior*
air, appearance, aspect, cast, clock, countenance, dial*, disguise, display, facet, features, finish, frontage*, frontal, frontispiece, frown, glower, grimace, guise, kisser*, light*, lineaments, look, makeup, map*, mask, mug*, obverse, paint*, physiognomy, pout, presentation, profile, scowl, seeming, semblance, show, showing, silhouette, simulacrum, smirk, surface, top, visage; SEE CONCEPTS *484,716,836*

face [n2] *pretense, nerve*
air, audacity, boldness, brass*, cheek*, chutzpah*, cloak, confidence, cover, disguise, effrontery, facade, false front*, front, gall, impertinence, impudence, mask, presumption, semblance, show, veil; SEE CONCEPTS *633,657*

face [n3] *authority, status*
dignity, honor, image, prestige, reputation, self-respect, social position, standing; SEE CONCEPT *388*

face [v1] *come up against a situation*
abide, accost, affront, allow, bear, beard, be confronted by, bit the bullet*, brace, brave, brook, challenge, confront, contend, cope with, countenance, court, cross, dare, deal with, defy, encounter, endure, experience, eyeball*, fight, fly in face of*, go up against*, grapple with, make a stand*, meet, oppose, resist, risk, run into, square off*, stand, stomach*, submit, suffer, sustain, swallow*, take, take it, take on, take the bull by the horns*, tell off*, tolerate, venture, withstand; SEE CONCEPTS *23,35,117*

face [v2] *be opposite; look at*
be turned toward, border, confront, front, front onto, gaze, glare, meet, overlook, stare, watch; SEE CONCEPTS *623,637*

face [v3] *put paint or finish on*
clad, coat, cover, decorate, dress, finish, front, level, line, overlay, plaster, polish, redecorate, refinish, remodel, sheathe, shingle, side, skin, smooth, surface, veneer; SEE CONCEPTS *172,202*

facet [n] *surface; aspect*
angle, appearance, character, face, feature, front, hand, level, obverse, part, phase, plane, side, slant, switch, twist; SEE CONCEPT *835*

facetious [adj] *tongue-in-cheek, kidding*
amusing, blithe, capering, clever, comic, comical, droll, dry, fanciful, farcical, flip*, flippant, frivolous, funny, gay, humorous, indecorous, ironic, irreverent, jesting, jocose, jocular, joking, joshing, laughable, ludicrous, merry, not serious, playful, pleasant, pulling one's leg*, punning, putting one on*, ridiculous, salty, sarcastic, satirical, smart, sportive, sprightly, waggish, whimsical, wisecracking, witty, wry; SEE CONCEPT *267*

facile [adj] *easy; easily mastered*
accomplished, adept, adroit, apparent, articulate, breeze, child's play*, cursory, deft, dexterous, easy as pie*, effortless, fast talk*, flip*, fluent, glib, hasty, light, obvious, picnic*, practiced, proficient, pushover*, quick, ready, shallow, simple, skillful, slick*, smooth, superficial, uncompli-

cated, untroublesome, voluble; SEE CONCEPTS *527,565*

facilitate [v] *assist the progress of*
aid, ease, expedite, forward, further, grease the wheels*, hand-carry*, help, make easy, open doors*, promote, run interference for*, simplify, smooth, speed, speed up, walk through*; SEE CONCEPTS *110,242*

facility [n1] *ease; ability*
address, adroitness, aptitude, bent, child's play*, competence, dexterity, efficiency, effortlessness, expertness, fluency, knack, leaning, lightness, poise, proficiency, propensity, quickness, readiness, skill, skillfulness, smoothness, smooth sailing*, spontaneity, tact, turn, wit; SEE CONCEPTS *630,666*

facility [n2] *convenience*
accommodation, advantage, aid, amenity, appliance, comfort, equipment, fitting, material, means, opportunity, resource, tool; SEE CONCEPTS *693,712*

facsimile [n] *reproduction*
carbon, carbon copy*, chip off old block*, clone, copy, copycat*, dead ringer*, ditto*, double, dupe*, duplicate, knock-off*, likeness, lookalike, mimeo, miniature, mirror, photocopy, photostat, print, reduplication, replica, replication, repro*, ringer*, spitting image*, stat, transcript, twin, Xerox*; SEE CONCEPTS *271,625,716*

fact [n1] *verifiable truth; reality*
actuality, appearance, authenticity, basis, bottom line*, brass tacks*, case, certainty, certitude, concrete happening, dope*, evidence, experience, genuineness, gospel, gospel truth*, how it is*, intelligence, law, like it is*, matter*, naked truth*, palpability, permanence, scene, scripture, solidity, stability, substantiality, verity, what's what*; SEE CONCEPTS *688,725*

fact [n2] *event; detail of action*
accomplishment, act, action, actuality, adventure, affair, being, case, circumstance, conception, consideration, construction, creation, data, datum, deed, entity, episode, evidence, experience, factor, fait accompli, feature, happening, incident, information, item, manifestation, occurrence, organism, particular, performance, phenomenon, point, proceeding, specific, statistic, transaction, truism; SEE CONCEPTS *2,274,433*

faction [n1] *group sharing a belief or cause*
band, bloc, bunch, cabal, camp, caucus, cell, circle, clan, clique, club, coalition, combination, combine, combo, concern, conclave, confederacy, conspiracy, contingent, coterie, crew, crowd, design, division, entente, gang, guild, insiders, intrigue, junta, knot, lobby, machine, minority, mob, network, offshoot, outfit, partnership, party, pressure group, ring, schism, sect, section, sector, set, side, splinter group, team, unit, wing; SEE CONCEPTS *301,387*

faction [n2] *conflict, strife*
disagreement, discord, disharmony, dissension, disunity, division, divisiveness, friction, infighting, quarrelsomeness, rebellion, sedition, tumult, turbulence; SEE CONCEPTS *106,684*

factious [adj] *conflicting, warring*
alienated, belligerent, contending, contentious, contumacious, disaffected, disputatious, dissident, divisive, estranged, fighting, hostile, insubordinate, insurgent, insurrectionary, litigious, malcontent, mutinous, partisan, quarrelsome, re-

ex
fa

bellious, refractory, rival, sectarian, seditious, troublemaking, tumultous/tumultuous, turbulent; SEE CONCEPT 542

factor [n] *determinant*

agency, agent, aid, antecedent, aspect, board, cause, circumstance, component, consideration, constituent, element, fixin's*, influence, ingredient, instrument, instrumentality, item, makin's*, means, part, part and parcel*, point, portion, thing; SEE CONCEPTS 831,835

factory [n] *manufacturing plant*

branch, cooperative, firm, forge, foundry, industry, laboratory, machine shop, manufactory, mill, mint, salt mines*, shop, sweatshop*, warehouse, workroom, works, workshop; SEE CONCEPTS 439,441,449

facts [n] *inside information*

bottom line*, brass tacks*, certainty, clue, cue, data, details, dope*, gospel, info*, inside dope*, like it is*, lowdown*, numbers, poop*, reality, scoop*, score*, story, whole story*; SEE CONCEPT 274

factual [adj] *real, correct*

absolute, accurate, actual, authentic, card-carrying*, certain, circumstantial, close, credible, descriptive, exact, faithful, genuine, hard, kosher*, legit*, legitimate, literal, objective, on the level*, positive, precise, righteous, specific, straight from horse's mouth*, sure, sure-enough*, true, true-to-life*, unadorned, unbiased, undoubted, unquestionable, valid, veritable; SEE CONCEPTS 535,582

faculty [n1] *ability, skill*

adroitness, aptitude, aptness, bent, capability, capacity, cleverness, dexterity, facility, flair, forte, genius, gift, instinct, intelligence, knack, knowing way around*, leaning, nose*, peculiarity, penchant, pistol*, power, predilection, proclivity, propensity, property, quality, readiness, reason, right stuff*, sense, strength, talent, turn, what it takes*, wits; SEE CONCEPT 630

faculty [n2] *teachers in educational institution*

academics, advisers, body, clinic, college, corps, department, employees, institute, instructors, lecturers, literati, mentors, organization, pedagogues, personnel, professorate, professors, profs*, researchers, scholars, society, staff, tutors, university, workers; SEE CONCEPTS 288,350

fad [n] *craze*

affectation, amusement, caprice, chic, conceit, cry, custom, dernier cri, eccentricity, fancy, fantasy, fashion, fool notion*, frivolity, furor, hobby, humor, in, innovation, in thing*, kick, kink, latest word*, mania, mode, newest wrinkle*, new look*, passing fancy*, passion, quirk, rage, sport, style, thing, trend, vagary, vogue, whim, whimsy, wrinkle; SEE CONCEPT 655

fade [v1] *lose color*

achromatize, become colorless, blanch, bleach, blench, clear, decolorize, dim, disappear, discolor, dissolve, dull, etiolate, evanish, evaporate, grow dim, lose brightness, lose luster, muddy, neutralize, pale, tarnish, tone down, vanish, wash out; SEE CONCEPTS 250,469,622

fade [v2] *dwindle, die out*

abate, attenuate, clear, decline, deliquesce, deteriorate, die away, die on vine*, dim, diminish, disappear, disperse, dissolve, droop, ebb, etiolate, evanesce, evanish, evaporate, fag out*, fail, fall, flag, fold, hush, languish, lessen, melt, melt away, moderate, perish, peter out*, poop out*, quiet, rarefy, shrivel, sink, slack off*, taper, thin, tire, tucker out*, vanish, wane, waste away, weaken, wilt, wither; SEE CONCEPTS 105,698

faded [adj] *bleached; used*

achromatic, ashen, bedraggled, dim, dingy, discolored, dull, etiolated, indistinct, lackluster, lusterless, murky, not shiny, pale, pallid, run-down, seedy, shabby, shopworn, tacky, tattered, threadbare, tired, wan, washed out, wasted, worn; SEE CONCEPTS 560,617,618

fail [v1] *be unsuccessful*

abort, backslide, back wrong horse*, be defeated, be demoted, be found lacking*, be in vain*, be ruined, blunder, break down, come to naught, come to nothing, decline, deteriorate, fall, fall flat*, fall short*, fall through*, fizzle, flop, flounder, fold, founder, go astray*, go down*, go downhill*, go down swinging*, go up in smoke*, go wrong, hit bottom*, hit the skids*, lose control, lose out, lose status, meet with disaster, miscarry, miss, miss the boat*, play into, run aground*, slip, turn out badly; SEE CONCEPT 699

fail [v2] *abandon, forsake*

abort, back out, blink, break one's word, desert, disappoint, discount, disregard, fault, forget, funk, go astray, ignore, let down, miscarry, neglect, omit, overlook, overpass, slight, slip; SEE CONCEPTS 7,19

fail [v3] *lose money*

be cleaned out*, become insolvent, be in arrears, be ruined, be taken to the cleaners*, break, close, close down*, close one's doors*, crash, defalcate, default, dishonor, drop, drop a bundle*, end, finish, fold, go bankrupt, go belly up*, go broke*, go bust*, go into chapter 11*, go out of business*, go to the wall*, go under*, go up*, lose big*, lose one's shirt*, overdraw, repudiate, terminate; SEE CONCEPTS 330,335

failing [n] *lapse, shortcoming*

blind spot*, defect, deficiency, drawback, error, failure, fault, flaw, foible, frailty, imperfection, infirmity, miscarriage, misfortune, vice, weakness, weak point*; SEE CONCEPTS 411,674

failing [adj] *not well, weak*

declining, defeated, deficient, faint, feeble, inadequate, insufficient, scant, scanty, scarce, short, shy, unavailing, unprosperous, unsuccessful, unsufficient, unthriving, vain, wanting; SEE CONCEPTS 485,489

failure [n1] *lack of success*

abortion, bankruptcy, bomb, botch*, breakdown, bungle*, bust, checkmate, collapse, decay, decline, defeat, deficiency, deficit, deterioration, downfall, failing, false step*, faux pas, fiasco, flash in the pan*, flop*, frustration, implosion, inadequacy, lead balloon*, lemon*, loser, loss, mess, misadventure, miscarriage, misstep, nonperformance, nonsuccess, overthrow, rout, rupture, sinking ship*, stalemate, stoppage, total loss, turkey*, washout*, wreck; SEE CONCEPTS 699,706

failure [n2] *person who does not succeed*

also-ran*, bankrupt, beat*, born loser*, bum, castaway, deadbeat, defaulter, derelict, disappointment, dud*, flop, good-for-nothing*, has-been, incompetent, insolvent, loafer, loser, lumpy*, might-have-been*, moocher*, nobody, no-good, nonperformer, prodigal, turkey*, underachiever, washout*; SEE CONCEPTS 412,423

faint [n] *unconsciousness*
blackout, collapse, dizziness, grayout, insensibility, knockout, stupor, swoon, syncope, vertigo; SEE CONCEPTS 308,316

faint [adj1] *having little effect on senses*
aside, bated, bland, bleached, blurred, breathless, deadened, deep, delicate, dim, distant, dull, dusty, faded, faltering, far-off, feeble, gentle, hazy, hoarse, hushed, ill-defined, imperceptible, inaudible, indistinct, lenient, light, low, low-pitched, mild, moderate, muffled, murmuring, muted, muttering, obscure, out of earshot*, padded, pale, piano, quiet, remote, shadowy, slight, smooth, soft, softened, soothing, stifled, subdued, tenuous, thin, unclear, vague, wan, weak, whispered; SEE CONCEPTS 537,594,617

faint [adj2] *weak*
delicate, dizzy, drooping, enervated, exhausted, faltering, fatigued, feeble, fragile, languid, lethargic, lightheaded, slight, tender, unenthusiastic, woozy; SEE CONCEPTS 314,485

faint [v] *lose consciousness*
become unconscious, be overcome, black out, collapse, drop, fade, fail, fall, flicker, go out like light*, keel over, languish, pass out, succumb, swoon, weaken; SEE CONCEPTS 303,308

fair [n] *exposition, carnival*
bazaar, celebration, centennial, display, exhibit, exhibition, expo*, festival, fete, gala, market, observance, occasion, pageant, show, spectacle; SEE CONCEPTS 377,386

fair [adj1] *impartial, unprejudiced*
aboveboard, benevolent, blameless, candid, civil, clean, courteous, decent, disinterested, dispassionate, equal, equitable, even-handed, frank, generous, good, honest, honorable, impartial, just, lawful, legitimate, moderate, nonpartisan, objective, on the level*, on up-and-up*, open, pious, praiseworthy, principled, proper, reasonable, respectable, righteous, scrupulous, sincere, square, straight, straightforward, temperate, trustworthy, unbiased, uncolored, uncorrupted, upright, virtuous; SEE CONCEPT 542

fair [adj2] *light-complexioned, light-haired*
argent, blanched, bleached, blond, blonde, chalky, colorless, creamy, faded, fair-haired, fair-skinned, flaxen-haired, light, milky, neutral, pale, pale-faced, pallid, pearly, sallow, silvery, snowy, tow-haired, tow-headed, white, whitish; SEE CONCEPTS 406,618

fair [adj3] *mediocre, satisfactory*
adequate, all right, average, common, commonplace, decent, fairish, indifferent, intermediate, mean, medium, middling, moderate, not bad*, okay, ordinary, passable, pretty good*, reasonable, respectable, satisfactory, so-so*, tolerable, up to standard*, usual; SEE CONCEPT 530

fair [adj4] *beautiful*
attractive, beauteous, bonny, charming, chaste, comely, dainty, delicate, enchanting, exquisite, good-looking, handsome, lovely, pretty, pulchritudinous, pure; SEE CONCEPT 579

fair [adj5] *bright, cloudless (weather)*
balmy, calm, clarion, clear, clement, dry, favorable, fine, mild, placid, pleasant, pretty, rainless, smiling, sunny, sunshiny, tranquil, unclouded, undarkened, unthreatening; SEE CONCEPT 525

fairly [adv1] *somewhat*
adequately, averagely, enough, kind of, moderately, more or less, passably, pretty well, quite,

rather, ratherish, reasonably, some, something, sort of, so-so*, tolerably; SEE CONCEPT 786

fairly [adv2] *justly*
deservedly, equitably, honestly, honorably, impartially, objectively, properly, reasonably, without favor, without fear; SEE CONCEPT 542

fairness [n] *justice*
candor, charitableness, charity, civility, consideration, courtesy, decency, decorum, disinterestedness, due, duty, equitableness, equity, exactitude, fair-mindedness, fair shake*, give and take*, good faith, goodness, honesty, honor, humanity, impartiality, integrity, justness, legitimacy, moderation, open-mindedness, propriety, rationality, reasonableness, right, righteousness, rightfulness, rightness, seemliness, square deal*, suitability, tolerance, truth, uprightness, veracity; SEE CONCEPTS 645,657

fairy [n] *supernatural being*
bogie, brownie, elf, enchanter, fay, genie, gnome, goblin, gremlin, hob, imp, leprechaun, mermaid, nisse, nymph, pixie, puck, siren, spirit, sprite, sylph; SEE CONCEPT 370

faith [n1] *trust in something*
acceptance, allegiance, assent, assurance, belief, certainty, certitude, confidence, constancy, conviction, credence, credit, credulity, dependence, faithfulness, fealty, fidelity, hope, loyalty, reliance, stock, store, sureness, surety, troth, truth, truthfulness; SEE CONCEPT 689

faith [n2] *belief in a higher being; community of believers*
canon, church, communion, confession, connection, conviction, credo, creed, cult, denomination, doctrine, dogma, doxy, gospel, orthodoxy, persuasion, piety, piousness, principle, profession, religion, revelation, sect, teaching, tenet, theism, theology, worship; SEE CONCEPTS 368,689

faithful [adj1] *loyal, reliable*
affectionate, allegiant, ardent, attached, behind one, circumspect, confiding, conscientious, constant, dependable, devoted, dutiful, dyed-in-the-wool*, enduring, fast, firm, genuine, hard-core*, honest, honorable, incorruptible, loving, obedient, on the level*, patriotic, resolute, scrupulous, sincere, staunch, steadfast, steady, straight, string along with*, sure, tried, tried and true*, true, true-blue*, trustworthy, trusty, truthful, unchanging, unswerving, unwavering, upright, veracious; SEE CONCEPTS 401,545

faithful [adj2] *authentic, accurate*
close, credible, exact, just, lifelike, precise, right, similar, strict, true, trusty, undistorted, veracious, veridical; SEE CONCEPTS 487,573

faithfulness [n] *devotion*
adherence, adhesion, allegiance, ardor, attachment, care, constancy, dependability, duty, fealty, fidelity, loyalty, piety, trustworthiness, truth; SEE CONCEPTS 633,645,689

faithless [adj] *disloyal*
capricious, changeable, changeful, cheating, deceitful, dishonest, double-crossing*, double-dealing*, doubting, dubious, false, fickle, fluctuating, inconstant, perfidious, recreant, skeptical, traitorous, treacherous, two-faced*, two-timing*, unbelieving, unconverted, unfaithful, unloyal, unreliable, unstable, untrue, untrustworthy, untruthful, wavering; SEE CONCEPTS 401,545

faithlessness [n] *disloyalty*
betrayal, disbelief, dishonesty, doubt, falseness,

fa
fa

fickleness, fraud, inconstancy, infidelity, perfidiousness, perfidy, skepticism, treacherousness,
treachery, treason, unfaithfulness; SEE CONCEPTS
633,645

fake [*n*] *imposter, copy*
actor, bluffer, charlatan, cheat, counterfeit, deception, fabrication, faker, flimflam*, forgery,
four-flusher*, fraud, gold brick*, hoax, imitation,
imposition, imposture, junque, make-believe,
mountebank, phony, plant*, pretender, pretense,
pseudo*, put-on, reproduction, scam, sham*,
sleight, spoof, swindle, trick; SEE CONCEPTS
260,412

fake [*adj*] *false, imitation*
affected, artificial, assumed, bogus, concocted,
counterfeit, fabricated, fictitious, forged, fraudulent, invented, make-believe, mock, phony, pretended, pseudo*, reproduction, sham, simulated,
spurious; SEE CONCEPTS *401,582*

fake [*v*] *pretend*
act, affect, assume, bluff, copy, counterfeit, disguise, dissimulate, fabricate, feign, forge, put on,
put on an act*, sham, simulate, spoof; SEE CON-
CEPT *59*

fall [*n1*] *descent; lowering*
abatement, belly flop*, cut, decline, declivity, decrease, diminution, dip, dive, downgrade, downward slope, drop, dwindling, ebb, falling off,
header*, incline, lapse, lessening, nose dive*,
plummet, plunge, pratfall*, recession, reduction,
slant, slip, slope, slump, spill, tumble; SEE CON-
CEPTS *152,181,776*

fall [*n2*] *defeat, overthrow*
abasement, breakdown, capitulation, collapse,
death, degradation, destruction, diminution, disaster, dive, downfall, drop, failure, humiliation,
loss, resignation, ruin, surrender, tumble; SEE
CONCEPTS *116,230,674,699*

fall [*v1*] *descend; become lower*
abate, backslide, be precipitated, break down,
buckle, cascade, cave in, collapse, crash, decline,
decrease, depreciate, diminish, dip, dive, drag,
droop, drop down, dwindle, ease, ebb, flag, flop,
fold up, go down, gravitate, hit the dirt*, keel
over, land, lapse, lessen, nose-dive, pitch, plummet, plunge, recede, regress, relapse, settle, sink,
slip, slope, slump, spin, stumble, subside, take a
header*, tip over, topple, totter, trail, trip, tumble, wane; SEE CONCEPTS *152,181,776*

fall [*v2*] *be overthrown by an enemy; surrender*
back down, be casualty, be destroyed, be killed,
be lost, bend, be taken, capitulate, defer to, die,
drop, eat dirt*, fall to pieces*, give in, give up,
give way, go down, go under, lie down, obey,
pass into enemy hands*, perish, resign, slump,
submit, succumb, yield; SEE CONCEPTS *116,699*

fall [*v3*] *happen*
arrive, become, befall, chance, come about, come
to pass, occur, take place; SEE CONCEPT *119*

fallacious [*adj*] *false, wrong*
beguiling, deceiving, deceptive, deluding, delusive, delusory, erroneous, fictitious, fishy*, fraudulent, illogical, illusory, incorrect, invalid,
irrational, mad, misleading, mistaken, off*,
phony, reasonless, sophistic, sophistical, spurious, unfounded, ungrounded, unreal, unreasonable, unreasoned, unsound, untrue, way off*; SEE
CONCEPTS *267,570,582*

fallacy [*n*] *illusion, misconception*
aberration, ambiguity, artifice, bias, casuistry,

cavil, deceit, deception, deceptiveness, delusion,
deviation, elusion, equivocation, erratum, erroneousness, error, evasion, falsehood, faultiness,
flaw, heresy, illogicality, inconsistency, inexactness, invalidity, misapprehension, miscalculation,
misconstrual, misinterpretation, mistake, non sequitur, notion, paradox, perversion, preconception, prejudice, quibbling, quirk, solecism,
sophism, sophistry, speciousness, subterfuge, untruth; SEE CONCEPTS *410,689,725*

fall back [*v*] *retreat*
back, draw back, give back, recede, recoil, retire,
retrocede, retrograde, surrender, withdraw, yield;
SEE CONCEPT *195*

fallen [*adj1*] *disgraced, ruined*
collapsed, decayed, dishonored, immoral, loose,
ruinous, shaken, shamed, sinful, unchaste; SEE
CONCEPTS *539,555*

fallen [*adj2*] *dead*
casualty, killed, lost, perished, slain, slaughtered;
SEE CONCEPT *539*

fall for [*v*] *become infatuated with*
desire, fall in love with, flip over, go head over
heels*, lose one's head over*, succumb; SEE CON-
CEPT *32*

fallible [*adj*] *able or prone to err*
careless, deceptive, errable, errant, erring, faulty,
frail, heedless, human, ignorant, imperfect, in
question, liable, mortal, questionable, uncertain,
unreliable, untrustworthy, weak; SEE CONCEPT
542

fall out [*v1*] *argue*
altercate, bicker, clash, differ, disagree, fight,
quarrel, spar, squabble; SEE CONCEPT *46*

fall out [*v2*] *come to pass*
befall, chance, happen, occur, result, take place,
turn out; SEE CONCEPT *4*

fallow [*adj*] *inactive*
dormant, idle, inert, neglected, quiescent, resting,
slack, uncultivated, undeveloped, unplanted, un-
plowed, unproductive, unseeded, untilled, unused, vacant, virgin; SEE CONCEPTS *485,560*

fall to [*v*] *set about doing*
apply oneself to, begin, be up to, buckle down*,
commence, jump in, pitch in*, start, undertake,
wade into*; SEE CONCEPTS *100,221*

false [*adj1*] *wrong, made up*
apocryphal, beguiling, bogus, casuistic, concocted, contrary to fact, cooked-up*, counterfactual, deceitful, deceiving, delusive, dishonest,
distorted, erroneous, ersatz*, fake, fallacious, fanciful, faulty, fictitious, fishy, fraudulent, illusive,
imaginary, improper, inaccurate, incorrect, inexact, invalid, lying, mendacious, misleading, mis-
representative, mistaken, off the mark*, phony,
sham, sophistical, specious, spurious, trumped
up*, unfounded, unreal, unsound, untrue, untruthful; SEE CONCEPTS *267,570,582*

false [*adj2*] *dishonest, hypocritical*
apostate, base, beguiling, canting, corrupt,
crooked, deceitful, deceiving, deceptive, deluding, delusive, devious, dishonorable, disloyal,
double-dealing*, duplicitous, faithless, false-
hearted, forsworn, foul, lying, malevolent, malicious, mean, misleading, mythomaniac,
perfidious, perjured, rascally, recreant, renegade,
scoundrelly, traitorous, treacherous, treasonable,
two-faced*, underhanded, unfaithful, unscrupulous, untrustworthy, venal, villainous, wicked;
SEE CONCEPTS *267,401*

false [*adj3*] *fake, counterfeit*
adulterated, alloyed, artificial, assumed, bent, bogus*, brummagem, bum*, colored, contrived, copied, crock*, deceptive, disguised, ersatz*, fabricated, factitious, feigned, fishy*, forged, framed*, hollow, imitation, made-up, make-believe, manufactured, meretricious, mock, ostensible, phony, pretended, pseudo*, seeming, shady, sham*, simulated, snide, so-called*, spurious, substitute, synthetic, unreal, wrong; SEE CONCEPT **582**

falsehood [*n*] *lie*
canard, cover-up, deceit, deception, dishonesty, dissimulation, distortion, equivocation, erroneousness, error, fable, fabrication, fakery, fallaciousness, fallacy, falseness, falsity, feigning, fib, fibbery, fiction, figment, fraud, half truth, hogwash*, line, mendacity, misstatement, perjury, pretense, prevarication, sham*, story, tale, tall tale*, untruism, untruth, untruthfulness, whopper*, yarn; SEE CONCEPTS **63,278**

falsely [*adv*] *deceitfully*
basely, behind one's back*, crookedly, dishonestly, dishonorably, disloyally, faithlessly, falseheartedly, malevolently, maliciously, perfidiously, roguishly, traitorously, treacherously, underhandedly, unfaithfully, unscrupulously; SEE CONCEPTS **267,401**

falsify [*v*] *alter, misrepresent*
adulterate, belie, change, color, con, contort, contradict, contravene, cook, counterfeit, deacon, deceive, deny, distort, doctor, dress up*, embroider, equivocate, exaggerate, fake, fake it, fib, forge, four-flush*, frame up*, garble, gloss, lie, misquote, misstate, palter, pervert, phony up*, prevaricate, promote, put on an act*, salt*, tamper with, traverse, trump up*, twist, warp; SEE CONCEPT **63**

falsity [*n*] *dishonesty, deception*
canard, cheating, deceit, deceptiveness, disingenuousness, double-dealing, duplicity, erroneousness, error, faithlessness, fake, fallacy, falsehood, fib, fraud, fraudulence, hypocrisy, inaccuracy, infidelity, insincerity, lie, mendacity, misrepresentation, perfidiousness, perfidy, prevarication, sham*, story, tale, treachery, uncandidness, unfaithfulness, unreality, untruth; SEE CONCEPTS **278,645,725**

falter [*v*] *stumble, stutter*
be undecided, bobble, break, drop the ball*, flounder, fluctuate, fluff, halt, hem and haw*, hesitate, lurch, quaver, reel, rock, roll, scruple, shake, speak haltingly, stagger, stammer, stub toe*, teeter, topple, totter, tremble, trip up, vacillate, waver, whiffle, wobble; SEE CONCEPTS **18,147,266**

fame [*n*] *celebrity*
acclaim, acclamation, account, acknowledgment, character, credit, dignity, distinction, éclat, elevation, eminence, esteem, estimation, exaltation, favor, glory, greatness, heyday, honor, illustriousness, immortality, kudos, laurels, luster, majesty, name, nobility, note, notoriety, place, popularity, position, preeminence, prominence, public esteem, rank, recognition, regard, renown, rep*, report, reputation, repute, splendor, standing, stardom, station, superiority; SEE CONCEPT **388**

familiar [*adj1*] *common, well-known*
accustomed, commonplace, conventional, cus-

tomary, domestic, everyday, frequent, garden variety*, habitual, homespun, household, humble, informal, intimate, known, matter-of-fact, mundane, native, natural, old hat*, ordinary, plain, prosaic, proverbial, recognizable, repeated, routine, simple, stock, unceremonious, unsophisticated, usual, wonted, workaday; SEE CONCEPTS **530,547**

familiar [*adj2*] *knowledgeable*
abreast, acquainted, apprised, at home with*, au courant, au fait, aware, cognizant, conscious, conversant, grounded*, informed, in on*, in the know*, introduced, kept posted*, mindful, no stranger to*, plugged in*, savvy, tuned in*, up*, up on*, versant, versed in, well up in*, with it*; SEE CONCEPT **402**

familiar [*adj3*] *friendly, bold*
affable, amicable, buddy-buddy*, chummy*, close, comfortable, confidential, cordial, cozy, dear, easy, forward, free, free-and-easy*, fresh, genial, gracious, impudent, informal, intimate, intrusive, near, neighborly, nervy, obtrusive, officious, open, palsy, palsy-walsy*, presuming, presumptuous, relaxed, sassy*, smart, snug, sociable, thick, tight, unceremonious, unconstrained, unreserved, wise; SEE CONCEPT **555**

familiarity [*n1*] *friendliness*
acquaintance, acquaintanceship, boldness, closeness, ease, fellowship, forwardness, freedom, freshness, friendship, informality, intimacy, liberty, naturalness, openness, presumption, sociability, unceremoniousness; SEE CONCEPT **388**

familiarity [*n2*] *knowledgeableness*
acquaintance, awareness, cognition, comprehension, experience, feel, grasp, knowledge, sense, understanding; SEE CONCEPT **409**

familiarize [*v*] *make or become acquainted with, knowledgeable about*
accustom, adapt, adjust, awaken to, become adept in, become aware of, break the ice*, bring into use, case*, check out, coach, come to know, condition, enlighten, gain friendship, get in, get lay of land*, get lowdown on*, get together, get to know, get with it*, habituate, inform, instruct, inure, let down hair*, let know, let next to, make conversant, make used to, mix, naturalize, popularize, post, prime, put on to*, school, season, tip off*, train, use, wont; SEE CONCEPTS **15,38**

family [*n*] *kin, offspring; classification*
ancestors, ancestry, birth, blood, brood, children, clan, class, descendants, descent, dynasty, extraction, folk, forebears, genealogy, generations, genre, group, heirs and assigns, house, household, inheritance, in-laws, issue, kind, kindred, kith and kin, line, ménage, network, parentage, pedigree, people, progenitors, progeny, race, relations, relationship, relatives, siblings, strain, subdivision, system, tribe; SEE CONCEPTS **296,378,397**

famine [*n*] *hunger*
dearth, destitution, drought, misery, paucity, poverty, scarcity, starvation, want; SEE CONCEPTS **674,709**

famished [*adj*] *starving*
could eat a horse*, dog-hungry*, empty, flying light*, having the munchies*, hollow, hungering, hungry, ravening, ravenous, starved, starved to death*, voracious; SEE CONCEPTS **20,406,546**

famous [*adj*] *legendary, notable to many*
acclaimed, applauded, august, brilliant, cele-

fa
fa

brated, conspicuous, distinguished, elevated, eminent, exalted, excellent, extraordinary, foremost, glorious, grand, great, honored, illustrious, important, imposing, influential, in limelight*, in spotlight*, leading, lionized, memorable, mighty, much-publicized, noble, noted, noteworthy, notorious, of note, outstanding, peerless, powerful, preeminent, prominent, recognized, remarkable, renowned, reputable, signal, splendid, talked about*, well-known; SEE CONCEPT 568

fan [*n1*] *blower of air*
air conditioner, blade, draft, flabellum, leaf, palm leaf, propeller, thermantidote, vane, ventilator, windmill; SEE CONCEPT 463

fan [*n2*] *person enthusiastic about an interest*
addict, adherent, admirer, aficionado, amateur, buff, devotee, follower, freak*, groupie*, habitué, hound, lover, rooter, supporter, votary, zealot; SEE CONCEPTS 352,366,423

fan [*v1*] *blow on*
aerate, air-condition, air-cool, cool, refresh, ruffle, spread, ventilate, wind, winnow; SEE CONCEPTS 199,208

fan [*v2*] *provoke*
add fuel, agitate, arouse, enkindle, excite, expand, extend, impassion, increase, rouse, stimulate, stir up, whip up, work up; SEE CONCEPT 14

fanatic [*n*] *person overenthusiastic about an interest*
activist, addict, bigot, bug*, crank*, crazy, demon, devotee, enthusiast, extremist, fiend*, fool, freak, maniac, militant, monomaniac, nut*, radical, ultraist, visionary, zealot; SEE CONCEPTS 352,359,366

fanatical [*adj*] *overenthusiastic*
biased, bigoted, bugged*, burning*, contumacious, credulous, devoted, dogmatic, domineering, enthusiastic, erratic, extreme, fervent, feverish, fiery, frenzied, headstrong, high on*, immoderate, impassioned, impulsive, incorrigible, infatuated, mad, monomaniacal, narrow-minded, nuts for*, obsessed, obsessive, obstinate, opinionated, partial, partisan, passionate, possessed, prejudiced, rabid, radical, raving, single-minded, stubborn, turned on*, unruly, violent, visionary, wild, willful, zealous; SEE CONCEPT 401

fanaticism [*n*] *overenthusiasm*
abandonment, arbitrariness, bias, bigotry, contumacy, dedication, devotion, dogma, enthusiasm, extremism, faction, frenzy, hatred, illiberality, immoderation, incorrigibility, infatuation, injustice, intolerance, madness, monomania, obsessiveness, obstinacy, partiality, partisanship, passion, prejudice, rage, single-mindedness, stubbornness, superstition, tenacity, transport, unfairness, unreasonableness, unruliness, violence, willfulness, zeal, zealotry; SEE CONCEPTS 633,689

fanciful [*adj*] *imaginary, romantic*
absurd, aerial, bizarre, blue sky*, capricious, castles in the air*, chimerical, curious, dreamlike, extravagant, fabulous, fairy-tale, fancied, fantastic, fantastical, fictional, fictitious, fictive, flaky*, floating, ideal, illusory, imaginative, imagined, incredible, kinky*, legendary, mythical, notional, offbeat, on cloud nine*, pie in the sky*, pipe dream*, poetic, preposterous, shadowy, supposititious, unreal, visionary, whimsical, wild; SEE CONCEPTS 529,572

fancy [*n1*] *impulse, urge*
caprice, conceit, conception, contrariness, creation, cup of tea*, desire, druthers*, flash, fool's paradise*, groove*, humor, idea, image, imagination, impression, inclination, irrationality, liking, mind, notion, perverseness, pleasure, thing*, thought, vagary, velleity, visualization, weakness for, whim, will; SEE CONCEPTS 20,532

fancy [*n2*] *liking, dream*
big eyes*, chimera, conception, daydream, delusion, envisagement, envisioning, eyes for*, fabrication, fantasy, figment, fondness, hallucination, hankering, idea, illusion, imagination, imaginativeness, inclination, invention, itch*, mirage, nightmare, notion, partiality, penchant, phantasm, picture, pie in the sky*, pipe dream*, predilection, preference, relish, reverie, romancing, sweet tooth*, vision, yearning, yen; SEE CONCEPTS 20,32,409

fancy [*adj*] *extravagant, ornamental*
adorned, baroque, beautifying, chichi*, complicated, cushy, custom, decorated, decorative, deluxe, elaborate, elegant, embellished, fanciful, florid, frilly, froufrou*, garnished, gaudy, gingerbread*, intricate, lavish, ornate, ostentatious, resplendent, rich, rococo, showy, special, spiffy*, sumptuous, unusual; SEE CONCEPTS 562,579

fancy [*v1*] *imagine, create*
be inclined to think, believe, conceive, conjecture, dream up, envisage, envision, fantasize, feature*, guess, head trip*, image, infer, make up, make up off top of one's head*, phantom, picture, realize, reckon, spark, spitball*, suppose, surmise, think, think likely, think up, trump up*, vision, visualize; SEE CONCEPT 43

fancy [*v2*] *love, desire*
approve, be attracted to, be captivated by, be enamored of, be in love with, care for, crave, crazy about*, desire, dream of, endorse, fall for, favor, like, long for, lust after, mad for*, prefer, relish, sanction, set one's heart on*, take a liking to*, take to, wild for*, wish for, yearn for; SEE CONCEPTS 17,20,32

fanfare [*n*] *cheering*
alarum, array, ballyhoo*, demonstration, display, flourish, hullabaloo*, panoply, parade, pomp, shine, show, trump, trumpet call*; SEE CONCEPT 377

fantasize [*v*] *dream about desires*
build castles in air*, daydream, envision, hallucinate, head trip*, imagine, invent, live in a dream world*, moon, romance, trip out*, woolgather*; SEE CONCEPT 17

fantastic [*adj1*] *strange, different; imaginary*
absurd, artificial, capricious, chimerical, comical, crazy, eccentric, erratic, exotic, extravagant, extreme, fanciful, far-fetched, fictional, foolish, foreign, freakish, grotesque, hallucinatory, illusive, imaginative, implausible, incredible, insane, irrational, ludicrous, mad, misleading, nonsensical, odd, outlandish, out of sight*, peculiar, phantasmagorical, preposterous, queer, quaint*, ridiculous, singular, supposititious, unbelievable, unlikely, unreal, wacky*, weird, whimsical; SEE CONCEPTS 564,582

fantastic [*adj2*] *enormous*
cracking, extreme, great, huge, humongous, massive, monstrous, monumental, overwhelming, prodigious, severe, stupendous, towering, tremendous; SEE CONCEPT 781

fantastic [adj3] *wonderful, excellent*
A-1*, awesome, best, best ever, cat's meow*, delicious, far out*, first-class, first-rate, great, like wow*, marvelous, out of sight*, out of this world*, primo*, sensational, superb, unreal*; SEE CONCEPTS 572,574

fantasy [n] *imagination, dream*
air castle, apparition, appearance, Atlantis*, bubble*, chimera, conceiving, creativity, daydream, delusion, envisioning, externalizing, fabrication, fairyland*, fancy, fancying, fantasia, figment*, flight, flight of imagination, fool's paradise*, hallucination, head trip*, illusion, imaginativeness, imagining, invention, mind trip*, mirage, nightmare, objectifying, originality, rainbow*, reverie, trip, Utopia, vagary, vision; SEE CONCEPTS 20,529,689

far [adj/adv1] *at a great distance*
afar, a good way, a long way, bit, deep, distant, end of rainbow*, faraway, far-flung*, far-off, far piece*, far-removed, good ways*, long, middle of nowhere*, miles, outlying, out-of-the-way*, piece, remote, removed, stone's throw*, ways*; SEE CONCEPTS 586,778

far [adv2] *considerably*
decidedly, extremely, greatly, incomparably, much, notably, quite, significantly, somewhat, very, very much, well; SEE CONCEPTS 772,781

faraway [adj] *remote, distant*
absent, abstracted, beyond the horizon, distant, dreamy, far, far-flung*, far-off, far-removed, lost, outlying, preoccupied, quite a ways*, removed, well away; SEE CONCEPTS 586,778

farce [n] *nonsense, satire*
absurdity, broad comedy, buffoonery, burlesque, camp, caricature, comedy, high camp*, horseplay*, interlude, joke, low camp*, mock, mockery, parody, play, pratfall comedy, ridiculousness, sham*, skit, slapstick, travesty; SEE CONCEPTS 263,293

farcical [adj] *absurd*
amusing, camp, campy*, comic, comical, derisory, diverting, droll, for grins*, funny, gelastic, joshing, laughable, ludicrous, nonsensical, outrageous, preposterous, ridiculous, risible, slapstick, stupid; SEE CONCEPTS 267,542

fare [n1] *amount charged for transportation*
book, charge, check, expense, passage, price, slug, tariff, ticket, token, toll; SEE CONCEPT 329

fare [n2] *food served at meals*
commons, diet, eatables, eats*, edibles, meals, menu, provision, rations, slop*, sustenance, swill*, table, victuals; SEE CONCEPTS 457,459

fare [v] *get along; turn out*
advance, do, get by, get on, go, handle, happen, hie, journey, make headway, make out, manage, muddle through, pass, proceed, progress, prosper, prove, shift, stagger; SEE CONCEPTS 100,117,704

farewell [n] *departing saying; departure*
adieu, adieus, adieux, adios, bye-bye, cheerio, ciao, goodbye, hasta la vista, have a nice day, leave-taking, parting, salutation, sendoff, so long, ta-ta, valediction; SEE CONCEPTS 195,278

far-fetched [adj] *hard to believe*
bizarre, doubtful, dubious, eccentric, fantastic, fishy*, forced, hard to swallow*, illogical, implausible, improbable, incoherent, inconsequential, incredible, labored, preposterous, queer, recondite, strained, strange, suspicious, unbeliev-

able, unconvincing, unlikely, unnatural, unrealistic; SEE CONCEPTS 529,552,582

farm [n] *land for agriculture or animal breeding*
acreage, acres, arboretum, claim, demense, enclosure, estate, farmstead, field, freehold, garden, grange, grassland, holding, homestead, lawn, meadow, nursery, orchard, pasture, patch, plantation, ranch, soil, vineyard; SEE CONCEPTS 258,449,509,517

farm [v] *produce crops, raise animals*
bring under cultivation, crop, cultivate, direct, dress, garden, graze, grow, harrow, harvest, homestead, husband, landscape, look after, operate, pasture, plant, plow, ranch, reap, run, seed, sow, subdue, superintend, tend, till, till the soil, work; SEE CONCEPTS 117,253,324

farmer [n] *person who produces crops, raises animals*
agriculturalist, agriculturist, agronomist, breeder, clodhopper*, cob*, country person, cropper, cultivator, feeder, gardener, gleaner, grazer, grower, harvester, hired hand, homesteader, horticulturist, laborer, peasant, planter, plower, producer, rancher, reaper, sharecropper, sower, tender, tiller, villein; SEE CONCEPTS 347,348

farming [n] *producing crops, raising animals*
agriculture, agronomics, agronomy, breeding, crop-raising, cultivation, culture, feeding, fertilizing, gardening, geoponics, gleaning, grazing, growing, harvesting, homesteading, hydroponics, landscaping, operating, production, ranching, reaping, seeding, share-cropping, soil culture, threshing, tillage; SEE CONCEPTS 117,253,324

far-reaching [adj] *broad, widespread*
extensive, far-ranging, important, momentous, pervasive, significant, sweeping, wide; SEE CONCEPT 772

far-sighted [adj] *looking ahead wisely*
acute, canny, cautious, clairvoyant, commonsensical, cool-headed*, discerning, judicious, levelheaded, perceptive, politic, prescient, provident, prudent, sagacious, sage, shrewd, well-balanced, wise; SEE CONCEPT 402

farther [adv] *at a greater distance*
beyond, further, longer, more distant, more remote, remoter, yon, yonder; SEE CONCEPTS 586,778

farthest [adv] *most distant*
extreme, farthermost, furthermost, furthest, last, lattermost, outermost, outmost, remotest, ultimate, utmost, uttermost; SEE CONCEPTS 586,778

fascinate [v] *captivate, hold spellbound*
absorb, allure, animate, arouse, attach, attract, beguile, bewitch, charm, compel, delight, draw, enamor, enchant, engage, engross, enrapture, enslave, ensnare, enthrall, entice, entrance, excite, fire, gladden, hypnotize, infatuate, interest, intoxicate, intrigue, invite, kindle, lure, mesmerize, overpower, overwhelm, pique, please, provoke, ravish, rivet, seduce, spellbind, stimulate, stir, subdue, tantalize, tempt, thrill, titillate, transfix, transport, win; SEE CONCEPTS 7,11,22

fascinated [adj] *captivated, spellbound*
absorbed, aroused, attracted, beguiled, bewitched, charmed, dazzled, delighted, enamored, enchanted, engrossed, enraptured, enthralled, enticed, entranced, excited, fond of, hypnotized, infatuated, in love with, intoxicated, mesmerized, overpowered, seduced, sent, smitten, sold on*, stuck on*, tantalized, thrilled, titillated, trans-

fa
fa

fixed, transported, under a spell*; SEE CONCEPTS
32,403

fascinating [*adj*] *interesting, spellbinding*
alluring, appealing, attractive, bewitching, captivating, charming, compelling, delectable, delightful, enchanting, engaging, engrossing, enticing,
glamorous, gripping, intriguing, irresistible, ravishing, riveting, seducing, seductive, siren; SEE
CONCEPT *529*

fascination [*n*] *strong interest*
allure, appeal, attraction, bug*, charisma, charm,
enchantment, enthrallment, glamour, grabber*,
hang-up*, lure, magic, magnetism, obsession, piquancy, power, pull*, sorcery, spell, thing*, thing
for*, trance, witchcraft, witchery; SEE CONCEPTS
20,32,532,690

fascism [*n*] *political system of dictatorship*
absolutism, authoritarianism, autocracy, bureaucracy, despotism, Nazism, one-party system,
party government, racism, regimentation, totalitarianism; SEE CONCEPTS *299,301,689*

fashion [*n1*] *latest style, prevailing taste*
appearance, bandwagon*, chic, configuration,
convention, craze, cry, cultism, cultus, custom,
cut, dernier cri, fad, faddism, figure, form, furor,
in thing*, last word*, latest*, latest thing*, line*,
look, make, mode, model, mold, newest wrinkle*, pattern, rage, shape, thing*, tone, trend, usage, vogue; SEE CONCEPT *655*

fashion [*n2*] *attitude, manner*
convention, custom, demeanor, device, etiquette,
form, formality, formula, guise, method, mode,
modus operandi, mores, observance, order, practice, precedent, prescription, prevalence, procedure, sort, style, system, technique, tendency,
tone, trend, usage, vein, vogue, way; SEE CON-
CEPTS *644,657*

fashion [*v*] *adjust, design, create*
accommodate, adapt, build, carve, construct, contrive, cook up*, cut, devise, dream up*, erect,
fabricate, fit, forge, form, frame*, knock together*, make, manufacture, model, mold, plan, plot,
produce, sculpture, shape, suit, tailor, throw
together*, turn out*, work; SEE CONCEPTS
168,173,232

fashionable [*adj*] *stylish, up-to-date*
a go-go*, à la mode*, all the rage*, chic, chichi*,
contemporary, current, customary, dashing, faddy*, favored, fly*, genteel, hot*, in style, 'in-
thing'*, in vogue, last word*, latest*, latest thing*,
mod*, modern, modish*, natty*, new, newfangled, now, popular, prevailing, rakish, smart,
swank, trendsetting, trendy, upscale*, up-to-the-
minute*, usual, well-liked, with it*; SEE CON-
CEPTS *579,589*

fast [*n*] *abstention from eating*
abstinence, diet, fasting, xerophagy; SEE CON-
CEPT *169*

fast [*adj1*] *speedy*
accelerated, active, agile, blue streak*, breakneck*, brisk, chop-chop*, dashing, double-time*,
electric, expeditious, expedient, flashing, fleet,
fleeting, flying, hairtrigger*, hasty, hot, hurried,
hypersonic, in a jiffy*, in nothing flat*, lickety
split*, like a bat out of hell*, like all get out*, like
crazy*, like mad*, nimble, on the double*, PDQ*,
posthaste, presto, pronto, quick, racing, rapid,
ready, screamin'*, snap*, snappy*, speedball*,
supersonic, swift, velocious, winged; SEE CON-
CEPTS *588,799*

fast [*adj2*] *fixed, immovable*
adherent, ardent, attached, close, constant, constrained, durable, faithful, fastened, firm, fortified, glued, held, impregnable, indelible,
inextricable, lasting, loyal, permanent, resistant,
resolute, secure, set, sound, stable, staunch,
steadfast, stuck, sure, tenacious, tight, true, true
blue*, unwavering, wedged; SEE CONCEPTS
488,542

fast [*adj3*] *immoral, promiscuous*
bawdy, careless, debauched, depraved, devil-
may-care*, dissipated, dissolute, easy, extravagant, flirtatious, frivolous, gadabout*, giddy,
incontinent, indecent, intemperate, lascivious,
lecherous, lewd, libertine, libidinous, licentious,
light, loose, lustful, profligate, rakish, reckless,
salacious, self-gratifying, self-indulgent, sportive,
sporty, unchaste, wanton, wild; SEE CONCEPT *545*

fast [*v*] *go without food*
abstain, deny oneself, diet, famish, forbear, go
hungry, not eat, refrain, starve; SEE CONCEPT *169*

fast [*adv1*] *speedily*
apace, chop-chop*, expeditiously, flat-out*,
fleetly, full tilt*, hastily, hurriedly, in a flash*, in
haste, in nothing flat*, in short order*, like a
flash*, like a shot*, like greased lightning*, like
wildfire*, posthaste, presto, promptly, pronto,
quick, quickly, rapidly, soon, swift, swiftly; SEE
CONCEPTS *588,799*

fast [*adv2*] *fixedly*
deeply, firm, firmly, hard, securely, solidly,
soundly, steadfastly, tight, tightly; SEE CONCEPT
488

fasten [*v*] *make secure; join together*
adhere, affix, anchor, attach, band, bar, batten,
belt, bind, bolt, bond, brace, button, catch, cement, chain, cleave, close, cohere, connect, couple, embed, establish, fix, freeze to*, girth, glue,
grip, hitch, hitch on, hold, hook, hook up, implant, infix, jam, knot, lace, leash, link, lock,
lodge, make firm, moor, mortise, nail, rivet, rope,
screw, seal, set, settle, solder, stay put, stick,
strengthen, string, tack on, tag, tie, tighten, truss,
unite, wedge, weld; SEE CONCEPTS *85,113,160*

fastidious [*adj*] *very careful, meticulous*
captious, choosy, critical, dainty, demanding, difficult, discriminating, easily disgusted, exacting,
finical, finicky, fussbudgety*, fussy, hard to
please*, hypercritical, nice, nit-picky, overdeli-
cate, overnice, particular, persnickety*, picky,
punctilious, queasy, squeamish, stickling; SEE
CONCEPTS *542,550*

fat [*n*] *overweight, adipose tissue*
blubber, bulk, cellulite, corpulence, excess, fatness, flab, flesh, grease, lard, obesity, overabundance, overflow, paunch, plethora, suet,
superfluity, surfeit, surplus, tallow; SEE CON-
CEPTS *723,734*

fat [*adj1*] *overweight*
beefy*, big, blimp, bovine, brawny, broad, bulging, bulky, bull, burly, butterball*, chunky*, corpulent, distended, dumpy, elephantine, fleshy,
gargantuan, gross, heavy, heavyset*, hefty,
husky, inflated, jelly-belly*, lard, large, meaty*,
obese, oversize, paunchy, plump, plumpish, ponderous, porcine, portly, potbellied, pudgy*, roly-
poly*, rotund, solid, stout, swollen, thickset*,
weighty, whalelike*; SEE CONCEPT *491*

fat [adj2] *containing an oily substance*
adipose, fatlike, fatty, greasy, oleaginous, suety, unctuous; SEE CONCEPT 485

fat [adj3] *productive, rich*
affluent, cushy, fertile, flourishing, fruitful, good, lucrative, lush, profitable, prosperous, remunerative, thriving; SEE CONCEPT 334

fatal [adj1] *deadly, lethal*
baleful, baneful, calamitous, cataclysmic, catastrophic, deathly, destructive, disastrous, fateful, final, ill-fated, ill-starred, incurable, inevitable, killing, malefic, malignant, mortal, mortiferous, noxious, pernicious, pestilent, pestilential, poisonous, ruinous, terminal, virulent; SEE CONCEPTS 537,539

fatal [adj2] *critical, very important*
crucial, decisive, destined, determining, doomed, fateful, final, foreordained, inevitable, predestined, unlucky; SEE CONCEPTS 531,568

fatalism [n] *resignation to a fate*
acceptance, destinism, determinism, necessitarianism, passivity, predestinarianism, predestination, stoicism; SEE CONCEPT 689

fatality [n] *death, loss; ability to cause such*
accident, casualty, deadliness, destructiveness, disaster, dying, inevitability, lethality, lethalness, mortality, necrosis, noxiousness, poisonousness, virulence; SEE CONCEPTS 304,675

fate [n] *predetermined course*
break, chance, circumstance, consequence, cup*, destination, destiny, divine will*, doom, effect, end, ending, fortune, future, handwriting on the wall*, horoscope, inescapableness, issue, karma, kismet, lot, luck, Moirai, nemesis, outcome, portion, predestination, providence, stars*, termination, upshot, wheel of fortune*; SEE CONCEPT 679

fateful [adj1] *significant*
acute, apocalyptic, conclusive, critical, crucial, decisive, determinative, direful, doomful, eventful, important, inauspicious, momentous, ominous, portentous, resultful; SEE CONCEPT 568

fateful [adj2] *deadly*
calamitous, cataclysmic, catastrophic, destructive, disastrous, fatal, lethal, mortal, ominous, ruinous; SEE CONCEPT 537

father [n1] *male person who begets children*
ancestor, begetter, dad, daddy*, forebearer, origin, pa, padre, papa, parent, pop*, predecessor, procreator, progenitor, sire, source; SEE CONCEPTS 394,400,414,419,423

father/mother [n2] *founder, inventor*
administrator, architect, author, builder, creator, dean, elder, encourager, generator, initiator, introducer, leader, maker, matriarch, motor*, mover, organizer, originator, patriarch, patron, prime mover*, promoter, promulgator, publisher, sire, sponsor, supporter; SEE CONCEPTS 347,423

father [n3] *priest*
abbé, clergyman, confessor, curé, ecclesiastic, minister, padre, parson, pastor, preacher, reverend; SEE CONCEPT 361

fathom [v] *discern, understand*
appreciate, apprehend, catch, cognize, comprehend, dig, divine, estimate, figure out, follow, gauge, get, get to the bottom*, grasp, have, interpret, know, measure, penetrate, perceive, pierce, pinpoint, plumb, probe, recognize, savvy, sound, unravel; SEE CONCEPTS 15,38

fatigue [n] *tiredness*
brain fag*, burnout*, debility, dullness, enerva-

tion, ennui, exhaustion, faintness, fatigation, feebleness, heaviness, languor, lassitude, lethargy, listlessness, overtiredness, weakness, weariness; SEE CONCEPTS 316,405

fatigue [v] *tire, wear out*
bedraggle, burn out*, bush*, conk out*, debilitate, deplete, disable, drain, droop, drop, enervate, exhaust, fag, fizzle, flag, jade*, knock out*, languish, overtire, peter out*, poop*, poop out*, prostrate, sag, sink, succumb, take, tucker, weaken, wear down, weary; SEE CONCEPTS 137,225,240,250

fatigued [adj] *tired*
all in*, beat*, bedraggled, blasé, burned out*, bushed*, dead*, dead-beat*, dead-tired*, dog-tired*, dog-weary*, done in*, droopy, dropping, enervated, exhausted, fagged out*, jaded*, languid, languorous, lassitudinous, listless, out of gas*, overtired, played out*, pooped*, prostrate, ready to drop*, spent*, tuckered*, washed out*, wasted*, weary, worn, worn-out, zonked*; SEE CONCEPT 485

fatness [n] *overweight*
adiposity, breadth, bulkiness, corpulence, distension, flab*, flesh, fleshiness, girth, grossness, heaviness, heftiness, inflation, largeness, obesity, plumpness, portliness, protuberance, pudginess, rotundity, size, stoutness, tumidity, weight; SEE CONCEPT 734

fatten [v] *grow or make bigger; nourish*
augment, bloat, broaden, build up, coarsen, cram, distend, expand, feed, fill, gain weight, increase, overfeed, plump, put flesh on*, put on weight, round out, spread, stuff, swell, thicken, thrive, wax; SEE CONCEPTS 236,245,250

fatty [adj] *full of adipose tissue*
blubbery, fatlike, greasy, lardaceous, lardy, oily, oleaginous, rich, suety, unctuous; SEE CONCEPT 485

fatuous [adj] *stupid*
absurd, asinine, birdbrained*, boneheaded*, brainless*, dense, dull, foolish, idiotic, imbecile, inane, insensate, jerky*, lamebrained*, ludicrous, lunatic, mad, mindless, moronic, puerile, sappy, silly, simple, vacuous, witless; SEE CONCEPT 402

fault [n1] *blame, sin; mistake*
accountability, answerability, blunder, crime, culpability, defect, delinquency, dereliction, error, evil doing, failing, flaw, foible, frailty, guilt, impropriety, inaccuracy, indiscretion, infirmity, lapse, liability, loss of innocence, malfeasance, malpractice, misconduct, miscue, misdeed, misdemeanor, negligence, offense, omission, onus, oversight, peccancy, responsibility, slip, slip-up*, solecism, transgression, trespass, vice, weakness, wrong, wrongdoing; SEE CONCEPTS 101,192,699

fault [n2] *physical defect*
blemish, debility, deficiency, demerit, imperfection, infirmity, lack, pimple, shortcoming, weakness, weak point, zit*; SEE CONCEPT 580

faultless [adj] *having nothing wrong with it*
above reproach, accurate, blameless, classic, clean, correct, crimeless, errorless, exemplary, exquisite, faithful, flawless, foolproof, guiltless, ideal, immaculate, impeccable, inculpable, innocent, intact, irreproachable, model, on target*, perfect, pure, right on*, sinless, spotless, stainless, supreme, textbook*, unblemished, unguilty, unspotted, unsullied, whole; SEE CONCEPTS 545,572

faulty [adj] not working; incorrect
adulterated, amiss, awry, bad, below par, blamable, blemished, botched, broken, cracked, damaged, debased, defective, deficient, distorted, erroneous, fallacious, fallible, false, flawed, frail, impaired, imperfect, imprecise, inaccurate, inadequate, incomplete, inexact, injured, insufficient, invalid, lame, leaky, lemon, maimed, malformed, malfunctioning, marred, out of order, rank, sick, tainted, unfit, unreliable, unretentive, unsound, warped, weak, wrong; SEE CONCEPTS 560,570

faux pas [n] blunder in etiquette
blooper*, boo-boo*, breach, break, bungle, error, flop, flub*, gaffe*, goof*, impropriety, indecorum, indiscretion, mess-up, misconduct, misjudgment, misstep, mistake, oversight, solecism; SEE CONCEPTS 101,384

favor [n] approval, good opinion; help
accommodation, account, admiration, aid, approbation, assistance, backing, benediction, benefit, benevolence, benignity, bias, blessing, boon, championship, compliment, consideration, cooperation, courtesy, dispensation, encouragement, esteem, estimation, friendliness, gift, good turn*, good will*, grace, indulgence, kindness, largess, obligation, okay, partiality, patronage, present, regard, respect, service, support, token; SEE CONCEPTS 10,110,689

favor [v1] pamper, reward; help
abet, accommodate, advance, aid, assist, befriend, be partial to, do a kindness, do right by*, esteem, facilitate, further, gratify, humor, indulge, make exception, oblige, play favorites*, promote, pull strings*, show consideration, side with, smile upon*, spare, spoil, treat well, value; SEE CONCEPT 110

favor [v2] prefer, like
accept, advocate, appreciate, approbate, approve, back, be in favor of, be on one's side*, buck for*, champion, choose, commend, cotton to*, countenance, encourage, endorse, esteem, eulogize, fancy, flash on*, for, go for*, hold with, honor, incline, lean toward, look up to, opt for, patronize, pick, praise, prize, regard highly, root for, sanction, single out*, support, take a liking to*, take a shine to*, take to*, think well of, tilt toward*, value; SEE CONCEPT 32

favor [v3] look like
be the image of*, be the picture of*, feature, resemble, simulate, take after*; SEE CONCEPT 716

favorable [adj1] approving, friendly
acclamatory, affirmative, agreeable, amicable, approbative, approbatory, assenting, benevolent, benign, benignant, commending, complimentary, encouraging, enthusiastic, inclined, in favor of, kind, kindly, laudatory, okay, positive, praiseful, predisposed, reassuring, recommendatory, supportive, sympathetic, understanding, welcoming, well-disposed, well-intentioned; SEE CONCEPT 401

favorable [adj2] good, timely, advantageous
appropriate, auspicious, benefic, beneficial, benign, bright, cheering, convenient, encouraging, fair, fit, fortunate, full of promise, gratifying, happy, healthful, helpful, hopeful, kindly, lucky, nice, opportune, pleasant, pleasing, pleasurable, pleasureful, promising, propitious, prosperous, providential, reassuring, seasonable, suitable, toward, useful, welcome, well-timed, wholesome, worthy; SEE CONCEPTS 537,558,572

favorably [adv1] genially, in a kindly manner
agreeably, amiably, approvingly, cordially, courteously, enthusiastically, fairly, generously, graciously, heartily, helpfully, positively, receptively, usefully, willingly, with approbation, with approval, without prejudice; SEE CONCEPT 401

favorably [adv2] opportunely, advantageously
auspiciously, conveniently, fortunately, happily, profitably, prosperously, satisfyingly, successfully, swimmingly, to one's advantage, well; SEE CONCEPTS 537,558,572

favored [adj] popular
advantaged, best-liked, blessed, chosen, elite, fair-haired*, lucky, pet*, preferred, privileged, recommended, selected, singled out, sweetheart, well-liked; SEE CONCEPTS 529,568

favorite [n] something or someone cherished, prized
apple of eye*, beloved, chalk*, choice, darling, dear, fave*, front-runner*, ideal, idol, love, main, minion, number one*, paramour, pet*, pick, preference, shoo-in*, teacher's pet*; SEE CONCEPTS 423,446

favorite [adj] preferred
admired, adored, beloved, best-loved, cherished, choice, darling, dear, dearest, desired, especial, esteemed, favored, intimate, liked, main, number one*, personal, pet*, pleasant, popular, precious, prized, revered, sweetheart*, treasured, wished-for; SEE CONCEPTS 529,568

favoritism [n] bias, partiality
discrimination, inclination, inequity, nepotism, one-sidedness, partisanship, preference, preferential treatment, unfairness; SEE CONCEPTS 41, 388,645

fawn [n] baby deer
baby buck, baby doe, yearling; SEE CONCEPTS 394,400

fawn [v] ingratiate oneself to; serve
abase, apple-polish*, be at beck and call*, be obsequious, be servile, blandish, bow, brownnose*, buddy up*, butter up*, cajole, cater to, cave in to*, cotton*, court, cower, crawl, creep, cringe, crouch, curry favor*, debase, defer, fall all over, fall on one's knees*, flatter, grovel, honey up*, invite, jolly, kneel, kowtow*, lay it on*, lick boots*, make up to, massage*, oil*, pander, pay court*, play up to*, scrape, slaver, snow*, stoop, stroke*, submit, toady*, truckle*, woo*, yield; SEE CONCEPTS 110,384

fawning [adj] deferential, groveling
abject, adulatory, bootlicking*, bowing, brownnosing*, compliant, cowering, crawling, cringing, flattering, humble, ingratiating, kowtowing*, mealy-mouthed*, obsequious, parasitic, prostrate, scraping, servile, slavish, sniveling, spineless, submissive, subservient, sycophant, sycophantic; SEE CONCEPT 401

faze [v] embarrass
abash, annoy, appall, bother, confound, confuse, daunt, discomfit, disconcert, discountenance, dismay, dumbfound, horrify, irritate, muddle, mystify, nonplus, perplex, puzzle, rattle, vex; SEE CONCEPTS 7,19

fear [n] alarm, apprehension
abhorrence, agitation, angst, anxiety, aversion, awe, bête noire, chickenheartedness*, cold feet*, cold sweat*, concern, consternation, cowardice, creeps, despair, discomposure, dismay, disquietude, distress, doubt, dread, faintheartedness,

foreboding, fright, funk*, horror, jitters, misgiving, nightmare, panic, phobia, presentiment, qualm, recreancy, reverence, revulsion, scare, suspicion, terror, timidity, trembling, tremor, trepidation, unease, uneasiness, worry; SEE CONCEPT 27

fear [v] *feel alarm; be scared of*
anticipate, apprehend, avoid, be afraid, be anxious, be apprehensive, be disquieted, be frightened, be in awe, blanch, break out in a sweat*, cower, crouch, dare not, dread, expect, falter, feel concern, flinch, foresee, fret, have butterflies*, have qualms, lose courage*, quail, quaver, shrink, shudder, shun, shy, start, suspect, tremble, wilt, worry; SEE CONCEPT 27

fearful [adj1] *alarmed, apprehensive*
aflutter, afraid, aghast, agitated, anxious, chicken, chickenhearted*, diffident, discomposed, disquieted, disturbed, fainthearted, frightened, goosebumpy*, have cold feet*, hesitant, in a dither*, intimidated, jittery, jumpy, lily-livered*, mousy, nerveless, nervous, nervy, panicky, perturbed, phobic, pusillanimous, quivery, rabbity*, running scared*, scared, shaky, sheepish*, shrinking, shy, skittish, solicitous, spineless, tense, timid, timorous, tremulous, uneasy, unmanly, weak-kneed*, worried, yellow*; SEE CONCEPT 401

fearful [adj2] *horrifying*
appalling, astounding, atrocious, awful, baleful, bloodcurdling, creepy, dire, distressing, dreadful, eerie, formidable, frightful, ghastly, ghoulish, grievous, grim, grisly, gruesome, hair-raising*, hideous, horrendous, horrible, horrific, lurid, macabre, monstrous, morbid, overwhelming, redoubtable, shocking, shuddersome, sinister, strange, sublime, terrible, tremendous, unearthly, unspeakable; SEE CONCEPTS 529,537,570

fearless [adj] *brave, unafraid*
assured, aweless, bodacious, bold, brassy, cheeky, chesty*, cocky, confident, cool hand*, courageous, crack*, daring, dashing, dauntless, doughty, flip*, fresh*, gallant, game, gritty, gutsy, heroic, icy*, indomitable, intrepid, lion hearted, nervy, plucky, salty*, sanguine, sassy*, smart, spunky, sure, temerarious, unabashed, undaunted, unflinching, valiant, valorous, wise; SEE CONCEPT 401

feasible [adj] *possible, doable*
achievable, advantageous, appropriate, attainable, beneficial, breeze, cinch, dick soup*, easy as pie*, expedient, fit, fitting, likely, no sweat*, performable, pie*, piece of cake*, practicable, practical, probable, profitable, pushover, realizable, reasonable, simple as ABC*, snap, suitable, viable, workable, worthwhile; SEE CONCEPTS 528, 552,558

feast [n] *banquet and celebration*
barbecue, big feed*, blow*, blowout*, carnival, carousal, clambake, dinner, entertainment, fest, festival, festivity, fete, fiesta, gala, jollification, merrymaking, picnic, refreshment, regale, repast, spread, treat, wassail; SEE CONCEPTS 377,459

feast [v] *eat a great amount or very well*
banquet, dine, eat sumptuously, entertain, gorge, gormandize, indulge, overindulge, regale, stuff, stuff one's face*, treat, wine and dine*; SEE CONCEPT 169

feat [n] *achievement*
accomplishment, act, action, adventure, attainment, conquest, consummation, coup, deed, effort, enterprise, execution, exploit, performance, stunt, tour de force, triumph, venture, victory; SEE CONCEPTS 1,706

feather [n] *tuft of bird; plumage*
calamus, crest, down, fin, fluff, fringe, penna, pinion, pinna, plume, plumule, pompon, quill, shaft, spike, wing; SEE CONCEPT 399

feature [n1] *characteristic*
affection, angle, article, aspect, attribute, character, component, constituent, detail, differential, earmark*, element, facet, factor, gag*, gimmick, hallmark, idiosyncrasy, individuality, ingredient, integrant, item, mark, notability, particularity, peculiarity, point, property, quality, savor, slant*, speciality, specialty, trait, twist*, unit, virtue; SEE CONCEPTS 831,834,835

feature [n2] *highlight, special attraction*
big show*, crowd puller*, draw, drawing card*, headliner*, innovation, main item, peculiarity, prominent part, speciality, specialty; SEE CONCEPTS 386,829

feature [n3] *special article in publication*
column, comment, item, piece, report, story; SEE CONCEPT 270

feature [v] *give prominence to*
accentuate, advertise, blaze*, call attention to, emphasize, headline*, italicize, make conspicuous, mark, play up*, point up*, present, promote, set off*, spotlight*, star, stress, underline, underscore; SEE CONCEPT 60

features [n] *facial characteristics*
appearance, countenance, face, lineaments, looks, mien, mug*, physiognomy, puss*, visage; SEE CONCEPT 418

featuring [adj] *giving prominence to*
calling attention to, displaying, drawing attention to, giving center stage to*, headlining*, highlighting, making much of*, pointing up*, presenting, promoting, pushing, recommending, showing, showing off*, starring, turning, turning the spotlight on*; SEE CONCEPT 292

febrile [adj] *feverish*
delirious, fevered, fiery, flushed, hallucinatory, hot, inflamed, pyretic; SEE CONCEPTS 314,605

feckless [adj] *without purpose*
aimless, carefree, careless, feeble, fustian, futile, good-for-nothing*, hopeless, incautious, incompetent, ineffective, ineffectual, irresponsible, meaningless, reckless, shiftless, uncareful, useless, weak, wild, worthless; SEE CONCEPTS 404,542

fecund [adj] *productive*
breeding, fertile, fructiferous, fruitful, generating, pregnant, proliferant, prolific, propagating, reproducing, rich, spawning, teeming; SEE CONCEPT 537

federation [n] *partnership, organization*
alliance, amalgamation, association, bunch, coalition, combination, confederacy, crew, crowd, entente, family, federacy, gang, league, mob, outfit, pool, ring, syndicate, syndication, tribe, union; SEE CONCEPTS 323,381,417

fed up [adj] *disgusted with*
annoyed, blasé, blue*, bored, depressed, discontented, dismal, dissatisfied, down, gloomy, glum, jaded, sated, satiated, sick and tired*, surfeited, tired, up to here*, weary; SEE CONCEPT 403

fee [n] *charge for service or privilege*
account, ante*, bill, bite*, chunk*, commission, compensation, consideration, cost, cut*, emolu-

ment, end*, expense, gravy*, handle, hire, honorarium, house*, juice*, pay, payment, percentage, piece*, piece of the action*, price, rake-off*, recompense, remuneration, reward, salary, share, slice*, stipend, take*, take-in*, toll, wage; SEE CONCEPTS *329,344*

feeble [adj] *not strong; ineffective*
aged, ailing, chicken*, debilitated, decrepit, delicate, doddering, dopey*, effete, emasculated, enervated, enfeebled, etiolated, exhausted, failing, faint, flabby*, flat, fragile, frail, gentle, helpless, impotent, inadequate, incompetent, indecisive, ineffectual, inefficient, infirm, insubstantial, insufficient, lame, languid, low, out of gas*, paltry, poor, powerless, puny, sapless, sickly, slight, strengthless, tame, thin, unconvincing, vitiated, weak, weakened, weakly, wimpy*, woozy*, zero*; SEE CONCEPTS *267,489,527*

feebleness [n] *lack of strength; ineffectiveness*
debility, decrepitude, delicacy, disease, effeteness, enervation, etiolation, exhaustion, flimsiness, frailness, frailty, inability, inadequacy, incapacity, incompetence, ineffectualness, infirmity, infirmness, insignificance, insufficiency, lameness, languor, lassitude, malaise, senility, sickliness, unhealthiness, weakness; SEE CONCEPTS *630,676,732*

feed [v] *give nourishment; augment*
banquet, bolster, cater, cram, deliver, dine, dish out*, dispense, encourage, fatten, feast, fill, find, foster, fuel, furnish, give, gorge, hand, hand over, maintain, minister, nourish, nurse, nurture, provide, provision, regale, satisfy, stock, strengthen, stuff, supply, support, sustain, victual, wine and dine*; SEE CONCEPTS *107,140*

feed on [v] *consume*
devour, eat, exist on, fare, feast, graze, have a bite*, ingest, live on*, meal, munch, nibble, nurture, partake, pasture*, peck*, pig out*, prey on, scarf*, snack, sponge, subsist, take, take nourishment; SEE CONCEPT *169*

feel [n] *texture; air*
ambience, atmosphere, aura, feeling, finish, impression, mood, palpation, quality, semblance, sensation, sense, surface, tactility, taction, touch, vibes; SEE CONCEPTS *611,673*

feel [v1] *touch, stroke*
apperceive, caress, clasp, clutch, explore, finger, fondle, frisk, fumble, grapple, grasp, grip, grope, handle, manipulate, maul, palm, palpate, paw, perceive, pinch, ply, poke, press, run hands over*, sense, squeeze, test, thumb, tickle, try, twiddle, wield; SEE CONCEPT *612*

feel [v2] *experience*
accept, acknowledge, appear, appreciate, be affected, be aware of, be excited, be impressed, be sensible of, be sensitive, be turned on to*, comprehend, discern, encounter, endure, enjoy, exhibit, get*, get in touch*, get vibes*, go through*, have, have a hunch*, have funny feeling*, have vibes*, know, meet, note, notice, observe, perceive, receive, remark, resemble, savor, see, seem, sense, suffer, suggest, take to heart*, taste, undergo, understand, welcome; SEE CONCEPTS *15,34,38*

feel [v3] *believe*
assume, be convinced, be of the opinion, conclude, conjecture, consider, credit, deduce, deem, esteem, gather, guess, have a hunch*, have the impression*, hold, infer, intuit, judge, know, presume, repute, sense, suppose, surmise, suspect, think; SEE CONCEPT *12*

feeling [n1] *sensation, especially of touch*
activity, awareness, consciousness, enjoyment, excitability, excitation, excitement, feel, innervation, motility, motor response, pain, perceiving, perception, pleasure, reaction, receptivity, reflex, responsiveness, sense, sensibility, sensitivity, sensuality, tactility, tangibility, titillation; SEE CONCEPT *608*

feeling [n2] *idea, impression*
apprehension, belief, consciousness, conviction, eye*, hunch*, inclination, inkling, instinct, mind, notion, opinion, outlook, persuasion, point of view, presentiment, reaction, sense, sentiment, suspicion, thought, view; SEE CONCEPTS *532, 689,690*

feeling [n3] *a state of mind, often strong*
action, affection, appreciation, ardor, behavior, capacity, compassion, concern, cultivation, culture, delicacy, discernment, discrimination, emotion, empathy, faculty, fervor, fondness, heat, imagination, impression, intelligence, intensity, intuition, judgment, keenness, palpability, passion, pathos, pity, reaction, refinement, sensibility, sensitivity, sentiment, sentimentality, sharpness, spirit, sympathy, tangibility, taste, tenderness, understanding, warmth; SEE CONCEPTS *409,410*

feeling [n4] *ambience*
air, atmosphere, aura, impression, imprint, mood, quality, semblance; SEE CONCEPT *673*

feign [v] *pretend*
act, affect, assume, bluff*, counterfeit, devise, dissemble, dissimulate, do a bit*, fabricate, fake, forge, four-flush*, give appearance of, imagine, imitate, invent, make show of*, phony up*, play, play possum*, put on, put on act*, put up a front*, sham*, simulate, stonewall*; SEE CONCEPTS *59,63,292*

feigned [adj] *pretended*
affected, artificial, assumed, counterfeit, fabricated, fake, faked, false, fictitious, imaginary, imagined, imitation, insincere, phony, pretended, pseudo*, put-on*, sham*, simulated, spurious; SEE CONCEPTS *401,582*

feint [n] *pretense*
artifice, bait, blind, bluff, cheat, deceit, distraction, dodge, duck, expedient, fake, gambit, hoax, hoodwinking*, imposture, make-believe, maneuver, mock attack, play, ploy, pretension, pretext, ruse, sham*, shift, snare, stall, stratagem, subterfuge, trick, wile; SEE CONCEPTS *633,660,725*

felicitate [v] *congratulate*
commend, compliment, praise, recommend, rejoice with, salute, wish joy to; SEE CONCEPT *69*

felicitous [adj] *appropriate, suitable*
applicable, apposite, apropos, apt, convincing, fit, fitting, germane, happy, inspired, just, meet, neat, opportune, pat, pertinent, proper, propitious, relevant, seasonable, telling, timely, well-chosen, well-timed; SEE CONCEPTS *558,799*

fell [v] *chop down*
blow down, bowl over*, bring down, cause to fall, cleave, cut, cut down, dash, demolish, down, drop, flatten, floor*, gash, ground, hack, hew, knock down, knock over, lay low*, level, mangle, mow down*, prostrate, pull down, raze, rive, sever, shoot, shoot down*, slash, split, strike

fellow [n2] *male or female colleague, friend*
assistant, associate, cohort, companion, compeer, comrade, concomitant, confrere, consort, coordinate, counterpart*, coworker, double, duplicate, equal, instructor, lecturer, match, mate, member, partner, peer, professor, reciprocal, twin; SEE CONCEPTS 348,423

fellowship [n] *sociability, association*
acquaintance, affability, alliance, amity, camaraderie, club, communion, companionability, companionship, company, comradeship, conviviality, familiarity, friendliness, guild, intimacy, kindliness, league, order, society, sodality, togetherness; SEE CONCEPTS 387,388

felon [n] *criminal*
con, convict, delinquent, ex-con*, jailbird*, lawbreaker, lifer*, loser*, malefactor, offender, outlaw, yardbird*; SEE CONCEPT 412

female [n] *woman*
daughter, femme, gal, gentlewoman, girl, grandmother, lady, madam, matron, Miss/Mrs./Ms., mother, she, sister; SEE CONCEPT 415

female [adj] *having the qualities or characteristics of a woman*
effeminite, fecund, feminine, fertile, maternal, muliebrous, womanish, womanly; SEE CONCEPTS 371,408

femininity/feminine [n/adj] *womanly*
effeminate, effete, fertile, gender, gynic, womanhood, womanish, womanliness; SEE CONCEPTS 371,372,408,648

fence [n] *barrier used to enclose a piece of land*
backstop, balustrade, bar, barbed wire, barricade, block, boards, chains, Cyclone, defense, dike, guard, hedge, net, paling, palisade, pickets, posts, rail, railing, rampart, roadblock, shield, stakes, stockade, stop, wall; SEE CONCEPTS 260,476,479

fence [v1] *enclose or separate an area*
bound, cage, circumscribe, confine, coop, corral, defend, encircle, fortify, girdle, guard, hedge, hem, immure, mew, mure, pen, protect, rail, restrict, secure, surround, wall; SEE CONCEPT 758

fence [v2] *dodge; beat around the bush*
avoid, baffle, cavil, duck, equivocate, evade, feint, foil, hedge, maneuver, outwit, parry, prevaricate, quibble, shift, shirk, sidestep, stonewall*, tergiversate; SEE CONCEPTS 30,59

fend [v] *defend*
bulwark, cover, dodge, guard, oppose, parry, protect, repel, resist, safeguard, screen, secure, shield; SEE CONCEPT 96

fender [n] *piece protecting part of a vehicle*
apron, buffer, bumper, cover, curb, cushion, frame, guard, mask, mudguard*, protector, screen, shield, splashboard, ward; SEE CONCEPT 502

fend for [v] *take care of*
eke out existence*, look after, make do, make provision for, provide for, stay alive*, subsist, support, survive, sustain; SEE CONCEPTS 100,117

fend off [v] *keep at bay*
avert, avoid, beat off*, deflect, drive back*, hold at bay*, keep at a distance, keep at arm's length*, keep off, parry, rebuff, rebuke, rebut, refuse, reject, repel, repulse, resist, snub, spurn, stave off, turn aside, ward off; SEE CONCEPT 96

ferment [n1] *substance causing chemicals to split into simpler substances*
bacteria, bacterium, barm, ebullition, enzyme, fermentation agent, leaven, leavening, mold, seethe, simmer, yeast; SEE CONCEPT 478

ferment [n2] *agitation, uprising*
ailment, brouhaha, clamor, commotion, convulsion, disquiet, disquietude, disruption, disturbance, excitement, fever, flap, frenzy, furor, fuss, heat, hell broke loose*, hubbub, imbroglio, outcry, restiveness, restlessness, row, rumble, scene, state of unrest, stew*, stink*, stir, storm, to-do*, tumult, turbulence, turmoil, unrest, upheaval, uproar, upturn; SEE CONCEPTS 106,674

ferment [v] *split into simpler substances; be agitated*
acidify, be violent, boil, brew, bubble, churn, concoct, dissolve, effervesce, evaporate, excite, fester, fizz, foam, foment, froth, heat, incite, inflame, leaven, moil, overflow, provoke, ripen, rise, rouse, seethe, simmer, sour, sparkle, stir up, work; SEE CONCEPTS 7,19,22,250

ferocious [adj] *violent, barbaric*
barbarous, bloodthirsty, brutal, brutish, cruel, fell, feral, fierce, frightful, grim, implacable, inhuman, inhumane, lupine, merciless, murderous, pitiless, predatory, rapacious, ravening, ravenous, relentless, ruthless, sanguinary, savage, tigerish, truculent, unmerciful, unrestrained, untamed, vehement, vicious, voracious, wild, wolfish; SEE CONCEPTS 401,542

ferret out [v] *trace, search out*
ascertain, be on to, bring to light*, chase, determine, dig up*, disclose, discover, drive out, elicit, extract, follow, get at*, hunt, learn, nose out*, penetrate, pick up on, pierce, probe, pry, pursue, quest, root out*, seek, smell out*, smoke out*, track down, trail, unearth; SEE CONCEPTS 183,216

ferry [n] *transportation boat*
barge, ferryboat, packet, packet boat, passage boat; SEE CONCEPT 506

ferry [v] *carry across*
bear, buck, carry, chauffeur, convey, lug*, move across, pack, run, schlepp*, send, ship, shuttle, tote*, transport; SEE CONCEPTS 187,217

fertile [adj] *ready to bear, produce*
abundant, arable, bearing, black, bountiful, breeding, breedy, bringing forth, childing, fecund, feracious, flowering, flowing with milk and honey*, fruitful, generative, gravid, hebetic, loamy, lush, luxuriant, plenteous, plentiful, pregnant, procreant, producing, productive, proliferant, prolific, puberal, pubescent, rank, rich, spawning, teeming, uberous, vegetative, virile, with child*, yielding; SEE CONCEPTS 372,485

fertility [n] *readiness to bear, produce*
abundance, copiousness, fecundity, feracity, fruitfulness, generative capacity, gravidity, luxuriance, plentifulness, potency, pregnancy, productiveness, productivity, prolifacacy, prolificity, puberty, pubescence, richness, uberty, virility; SEE CONCEPTS 372,723

fertilize [v] *make ready to bear, produce*
beget, breed, compost, cover, dress, enrich, fecundate, feed, fructify, generate, germinate, impregnate, inseminate, lime, make fruitful, make pregnant, manure, mulch, pollinate, procreate, propagate, top-dress, treat; SEE CONCEPTS 257,374,375

fe
fe

fertilizer [*n*] *dressing to aid production of crops*
buffalo chips*, compost, cow chips*, dung, guano, humus, manure, maul*, mulch, peat moss, plant food, potash, top dressing*; SEE CONCEPTS 260,399,429

fervent/fervid [*adj*] *enthusiastic, excited*
animated, ardent, blazing, burning, devout, dying to*, eager, earnest, ecstatic, emotional, enthused, falling all over oneself*, fiery, glowing, go great guns*, heartfelt, hearty, hot*, hot-blooded*, impassioned, intense, passionate, perfervid, pious, religious, responsive, serious, sincere, unfeigned, vehement, warm, warmhearted, wholehearted, zealous; SEE CONCEPTS 401,542

fervor [*n*] *excitement, enthusiasm*
animation, ardency, ardor, devoutness, eagerness, earnestness, fervency, fire*, heartiness, heat*, hurrah, intensity, jazz*, love, oomph*, passion, pep talk*, piety, piousness, religiousness, seriousness, sincerity, solemnity, vehemence, warmth, weakness, wholeheartedness, zeal, zealousness; SEE CONCEPTS 633,657

fester [*v*] *intensify; become inflamed*
aggravate, blister, canker, chafe, decay, gall, gather, irk, maturate, putrefy, rankle, rot, smolder, suppurate, ulcer, ulcerate; SEE CONCEPTS 469,698

festival [*n*] *celebration*
anniversary, carnival, commemoration, competition, entertainment, fair, feast, festivities, fete, field day, fiesta, gala, holiday, jubilee, merrymaking, treat; SEE CONCEPT 377

festive [*adj*] *decorated, celebratory*
blithe, bouncy, carnival, cheery, chipper*, chirpy, convivial, festal, gala, gay, gleeful, go-go*, grooving, happy, hearty, holiday, jocund, jolly, jovial, joyful, joyous, jubilant, juiced up*, jumping, lighthearted, merry, mirthful, peppy*, perky, rocking*, snappy*, swinging, upbeat, zippy*; SEE CONCEPTS 403,548

festivity [*n*] *celebration, revelry*
amusement, bash*, blowout*, carousal*, clambake*, conviviality, do*, entertainment, festival, fun, fun and games*, gaiety, happiness, hilarity, hoopla, jamboree, jollity, joviality, joyfulness, levity, merriment, merrymaking, mirth, party, pleasure, revel, reveling, revelment, shindig*, sport, whoopee*, winging*; SEE CONCEPTS 377,383

fetch [*v*] *go get, bring in*
back, bear, be sold for, bring, bring back, bring to, buck, call for, carry, conduct, convey, deliver, draw forth, earn, elicit, escort, get, give rise to, go for, gun, heel, lead, lug*, make, obtain, pack, piggyback*, produce, realize, retrieve, ride, sell, sell for, shlep*, shoulder*, tote, transport, truck*, yield; SEE CONCEPTS 90,124,131

fetching [*adj*] *alluring, attractive*
beautiful, captivating, charming, cute, enchanting, enticing, fascinating, intriguing, luring, pleasing, sweet, taking, tempting, winsome; SEE CONCEPTS 537,579

fete [*n*] *celebration, party*
ball, banquet, bazaar, do*, fair, festival, fiesta, gala; SEE CONCEPT 377

fete [*v*] *throw a party for someone*
celebrate, entertain, feast, festival, hold reception for, holiday, honor, lionize, make much of*, roll out the red carpet*, treat, wine and dine*; SEE CONCEPT 384

fetid [*adj*] *foul, rancid*
corrupt, fusty, grody*, gross*, icky*, loathsome, lousy, malodorous, mephitic, noisome, noxious, offensive, putrid, rank, reeking, repugnant, repulsive, revolting, rotten, smelly, stenchy, stinking, stinky, strong, yecchy*, yucky*; SEE CONCEPT 598

fetish [*n1*] *obsession*
bias, craze*, desire, fixation, golden calf*, idée fixe, leaning, luck, mania, partiality, penchant, periapt, predilection, prejudice, preoccupation, prepossession, proclivity, propensity, stimulant, thing*; SEE CONCEPTS 529,689

fetish [*n2*] *object believed to have supernatural powers*
amulet, charm, cult object, idol, image, juju*, mascot, phylactery, superstition, talisman, voodoo doll*, zemi; SEE CONCEPTS 446,687

fetter [*v*] *tie up, hold*
bind, chain, check, clog, confine, cuff, curb, drag feet, encumber, hamper, hamstring*, handcuff, hang up, hinder, hobble, hog-tie*, hold captive, leash, manacle, put straitjacket on*, repress, restrain, restrict, shackle, throw monkey wrench in*, trammel; SEE CONCEPTS 130,191

fetters [*n*] *bindings; bondage*
bilboes, bonds, captivity, chains, check, cuffs, curb, handcuffs, hindrance, irons, manacles, obstruction, restraint, shackles, trammels; SEE CONCEPTS 130,191,500

feud [*n*] *major argument; estrangement*
altercation, bad blood*, bickering, broil*, combat, conflict, contention, contest, controversy, disagreement, discord, dispute, dissension, enmity, faction, falling out*, fight, fracas, grudge, hostility, quarrel, rivalry, row, run-in*, squabble, strife, vendetta; SEE CONCEPTS 46,106,388

feud [*v*] *fight bitterly; fall out*
be at daggers with*, be at odds*, bicker, brawl, clash, contend, dispute, duel, quarrel, row, squabble, war; SEE CONCEPTS 46,106

fever [*n*] *state of high temperature or agitation*
burning up*, delirium, ecstasy, excitement, febrile disease, ferment, fervor, fire, flush, frenzy, heat, intensity, passion, pyrexia, restlessness, running a temperature*, the shakes*, turmoil, unrest; SEE CONCEPTS 410,610

feverish [*adj1*] *having a high temperature*
above normal*, aguey, burning, burning up*, febrile, fevered, fiery, flushed, having the shakes*, hectic, hot, inflamed, on fire, pyretic, running a temperature*; SEE CONCEPT 605

feverish [*adj2*] *excited, agitated*
burning, distracted, fervid, fevered, frantic, frenetic, frenzied, furious, heated, hectic, highstrung*, impatient, keyed up*, nervous, obsessive, overwrought, passionate, restless; SEE CONCEPT 401

few [*adj*] *hardly any*
exiguous, few and far between*, imperceptible, inconsequential, inconsiderable, infrequent, insufficient, lean, less, meager, middling, minor, minority, minute, negligible, not many, not too many*, occasional, paltry, petty, piddling, rare, scant, scanty, scarce, scarcely any, scattered, scattering, seldom, semioccasional, short, skimpy, slender, slight, slim, some, sparse, sporadic, stingy, straggling, thin, trifling, uncommon, unfrequent, widely spaced; SEE CONCEPTS 771,789

few [*prep*] *scarcely any*
not many, not too many*, scattering, several, slim pickings*, small number, smatter, smattering, some, spattering, sprinkling; SEE CONCEPT *787*

fiancé/fiancée [*n*] *person engaged to marry*
affianced person, betrothed, engaged person, future*, husband-to-be, intended, prospective spouse, steady*, wife-to-be; SEE CONCEPTS *414,423*

fiasco [*n*] *catastrophe*
abortion, blunder, botched situation, breakdown, debacle, disaster, dumb thing to do*, dumb trick*, embarrassment, error, failure, farce, flap, flop, mess, miscarriage, route, ruin, screwup*, stunt, washout*; SEE CONCEPT *674*

fiat [*n*] *order, proclamation*
authorization, command, decree, dictate, dictum, edict, endorsement, mandate, ordinance, permission, precept, sanction, ukase, warrant; SEE CONCEPT *685*

fib [*n*] *undetailed lie*
canard, crock*, equivocation, evasiveness, fabrication, fairy tale*, falsehood, falsity, fiction, invention, jazz*, line*, mendacity, misrepresentation, prevarication, spinach*, story, tale, untruth, untruthfulness, white lie*, whopper*, yarn*; SEE CONCEPTS *278,282*

fib [*v*] *tell an undetailed lie*
concoct, create fiction, equivocate, fabricate, falsify, invent, jive*, make up, palter, plant, prevaricate, promote, shovel*, speak with forked tongue*, stretch the truth*, tell a little white lie*, trump up*; SEE CONCEPT *63*

fiber [*n1*] *strand of material*
cilia, cord, fibril, filament, footlet, grain, grit, hair, shred, staple, string, strip, tendril, thread, tissue, tooth, vein, warp, web, woof; SEE CONCEPTS *392,428,611,831*

fiber [*n2*] *texture*
essence, fabric, feel, hand, nap, nature, pile, spirit, substance; SEE CONCEPTS *411,682*

fibrous [*adj*] *stringy*
coarse, fibroid, hairy, muscular, pulpy, ropy, sinewy, stalky, threadlike, tissued, veined, wiry, woody; SEE CONCEPT *606*

fickle [*adj*] *vacillating, blowing hot and cold*
arbitrary, capricious, changeable, cheating, coquettish, double-crossing, faithless, fitful, flighty, frivolous, inconstant, irresolute, lubricious, mercurial, mutable, quicksilver, sneaking, temperamental, ticklish, two-timing, unfaithful, unpredictable, unstable, unsteady, untrue, variable, volatile, whimsical, yo-yo*; SEE CONCEPTS *401,534,545*

fiction [*n*] *made-up story*
anecdote, best seller, book, cliff-hanger*, clothesline*, concoction, crock*, drama, fable, fabrication, falsehood, fancy, fantasy, fib, figment of imagination*, fish story*, hooey*, imagination, improvisation, invention, legend, lie, misrepresentation, myth, narrative, novel, potboiler*, prevarication, romance, smoke*, storytelling, tale, tall story*, terminological inexactitude, untruth, whopper*, work of imagination, yarn*; SEE CONCEPTS *63,271,280,282*

fictitious [*adj*] *untrue, made-up*
apocryphal, artificial, assumed, bogus*, chimerical, concocted, cooked-up*, counterfeit, created, deceptive, delusive, delusory, dishonest, ersatz*, fabricated, factitious, fake, faked, false, fanciful,

fantastic, fashioned, feigned, fictional, fictive, figmental, hyped up*, illusory, imaginary, imagined, improvised, invented, made, make-believe, misleading, mock, mythical, phony, queer, romantic, sham*, simulated, spurious, supposititious, suppositional, synthetic, trumped-up*, unreal*; SEE CONCEPTS *267,582*

fiddle [*v*] *mess with, tinker*
dabble, doodle, feel, fidget, finger, fool, handle, interfere, mess, mess around*, monkey*, play, potter, puddle, putter, tamper, touch, toy, trifle, twiddle; SEE CONCEPTS *87,291*

fidelity [*n1*] *faithfulness in a relationship*
allegiance, ardor, attachment, constancy, dependability, devotedness, devotion, faith, fealty, integrity, loyalty, piety, reliability, staunchness, steadfastness, true-heartedness, trustworthiness; SEE CONCEPTS *32,388*

fidelity [*n2*] *conformity to a standard*
accuracy, adherence, adhesion, attachment, closeness, constancy, correspondence, exactitude, exactness, faithfulness, loyalty, naturalism, preciseness, precision, realism, scrupulousness, verism; SEE CONCEPTS *637*

fidget [*v*] *move restlessly*
be antsy*, be hyper*, be nervous, be on pins and needles*, be spooked*, be wired*, bustle, chafe, fiddle, fret, fuss, hitch, jiggle, jitter, joggle, jump, play, squirm, stir, toss, trifle, twiddle, twitch, wiggle, worry; SEE CONCEPT *147*

fidgety [*adj*] *restlessly moving*
antsy*, apprehensive, high-strung*, hyper*, impatient, jerky, jittery, jumpy, nervous, nervous wreck*, nervy, on edge*, on pins and needles*, restive, restless, spooked*, spooky*, twitchy, uneasy, unrestful, up the wall*, wired*; SEE CONCEPT *401*

field [*n1*] *open land that can be cultivated*
acreage, cropland, enclosure, farmland, garden, glebe, grassland, green, ground, lea, mead, meadow, moorland, pasture, patch, plot, ranchland, range, terrain, territory, tillage, tract, vineyard; SEE CONCEPTS *509,517*

field [*n2*] *persons taking part in competition*
applicants, candidates, competition, competitors, contestants, entrants, entries, nominees, participants, possibilities, runners; SEE CONCEPTS *325,365,417*

field [*n3*] *sphere of influence, activity, interest, study*
area, avocation, bailiwick, bounds, calling, champaign, circle, compass, confines, cup of tea*, demesne, department, discipline, domain, dominion, environment, job, jurisdiction, limits, line, long suit*, margin, métier, occupation, orbit, precinct, province, purview, racket, range, reach, region, scope, specialty, specialty, sweep, terrain, territory, thing, vocation, walk, weakness, work; SEE CONCEPT *349*

field [*n4*] *arena with special use, as athletics*
amphitheater, battlefield, circuit, course, court, diamond, fairground, golf course, green, gridiron, grounds, landing strip, lot, park, playground, playing area, racecourse, race track, range, rink, stadium, terrain, theater, track, turf; SEE CONCEPTS *364,438,449*

field [*v*] *catch a hit or thrown object*
cover, deal with, deflect, handle, hold, occupy, patrol, pick up, play, retrieve, return, stop, turn aside; SEE CONCEPT *164*

fe
fi

fiend [n1] *dastardly person*
barbarian, beast, brute, degenerate, demon, devil, diablo*, evil spirit, hellion, imp, little devil*, Mephistopheles, monster, ogre, Satan, savage, serpent, troll; SEE CONCEPT 412

fiend [n2] *person overenthusiastic about interest*
addict, aficionado, bigot, devotee, enthusiast, fan, fanatic, freak, maniac, monomaniac, nut*, votarist, votary, zealot; SEE CONCEPT 423

fierce [adj] *violent, menacing*
angry, animal, ape, awful, barbarous, bloodthirsty, blustery, boisterous, bold, brutal, brutish, cruel, cutthroat*, dangerous, enraged, fell, feral, ferocious, fiery, flipped*, frightening, furious, horrible, howling, impetuous, infuriated, intense, malevolent, malign, murderous, passionate, powerful, primitive, raging, raving, relentless, savage, stormy, strong, tempestuous, terrible, threatening, tigerish, truculent, tumultous/tumultuous, uncontrollable, untamed, vehement, venomous, vicious, wild; SEE CONCEPTS 525, 537,540

fiercely [adv] *violently, menacingly*
angrily, awfully, boldly, brutally, ferociously, forcefully, forcibly, frantically, frenziedly, frighteningly, furiously, hard, horribly, impetuously, in a frenzy, irresistibly, like cats and dogs*, madly, maleficiently, malevolently, malignly, mightily, monstrously, no holds barred*, passionately, riotously, roughly, savagely, severely, stormily, tempestuously, terribly, threateningly, tigerishly, tooth and nail*, turbulently, uncontrollably, vehemently, venomously, viciously, wildly, with bared teeth*; SEE CONCEPTS 525,537,540

fiery [adj] *passionate; on fire*
ablaze, afire, aflame, agitable, alight, blazing, burning, choleric, combustible, conflagrant, enthusiastic, excitable, febrile, fervid, fevered, feverish, fierce, flaming, flaring, flickering, flushed, glowing, heated, hot, hot-blooded, hot-headed*, hot-tempered*, igneous, ignited, impassioned, impetuous, impulsive, inflamed, in flames, intense, irascible, irritable, madcap, peppery, perfervid, precipitate, red-hot*, spirited, unrestrained, vehement, violent; SEE CONCEPTS 401,542,605

fiesta [n] *day of rest; religious celebration*
carnival, feast, festival, holiday, holy day, saint's day, vacation; SEE CONCEPTS 377,386

fight [n1] *physical encounter*
action, affray, altercation, argument, battle, battle royal*, bout, brawl, broil, brush, clash, combat, conflict, confrontation, contention, contest, controversy, difficulty, disagreement, dispute, dissension, dogfight, duel, engagement, exchange, feud, fisticuffs*, fracas, fray, free-for-all*, fuss, hostility, joust, match, melee, quarrel, riot, rivalry, round, row, ruckus, rumble, scrap*, scrimmage, scuffle, set-to*, skirmish, sparring match, strife, struggle, tiff, to-do*, tussle, war, wrangling; SEE CONCEPT 106

fight [n2] *courage, will to resist*
aggression, aggressiveness, attack, backbone, belligerence, boldness, combativeness, gameness, hardihood, mettle, militancy, pluck, pugnacity, resistance, spirit; SEE CONCEPT 411

fight [v1] *engage in physical encounter*
altercate, assault, attack, bandy with*, battle, bear arms, bicker, box, brawl, brush with*, buck, carry on war, challenge, clash, contend, cross swords, dispute, do battle, duel, exchange blows, feud, flare up, go to war, grapple, joust, meet, mix it up*, oppugn, ply weapons, protect, quarrel, repel, resist, rowdy, scrap, scuffle, skirmish, spar, strive, struggle, take all comers*, take the field*, take up the gauntlet*, tiff*, tilt*, traverse, tug, tussle, wage war, war, withstand, wrangle, wrestle; SEE CONCEPT 106

fight [v2] *oppose action, belief*
argue, bicker, buck*, buckle down*, carry on, combat, conduct, contest, continue, defy, dispute, effect, endure, engage in, exert oneself, fall out, force, further, hammer away*, hassle, lay into*, light into*, maintain, make a stand against*, oppose, persevere, persist, prosecute, push forward, put up an argument*, repel, resist, row, spare no effort*, squabble, stand up to*, strive, struggle, support, take on, take pains*, tangle with, toil on, travail, traverse, uphold, wage, withstand, wrangle; SEE CONCEPTS 46,100,384

fight back/fight off [v] *defend oneself*
beat off*, bottle up*, check, contain, control, curb, fend off, hold at bay*, hold back, keep at bay*, oppose, put up fight, repel, reply, repress, repulse, resist, restrain, retaliate, stave off, ward off; SEE CONCEPTS 96,106

fighter [n] *person engaged in hostile encounter*
aggressor, antagonist, assailant, battler, belligerent, boxer, brawler, bruiser*, bully, champion, combatant, competitor, contender, contestant, disputant, duelist, GI, gladiator, heavy*, jouster, mercenary, militant, opponent, person-at-arms, pugilist, punching bag*, rival, scrapper, serviceperson, slugger, soldier, tanker*, warrior, wildcat*; SEE CONCEPTS 358,366,412

fighting [n] *battle, encounter*
argument, battle royal*, beef*, bloodshed, blowup, bout, brannigan, brawling, brush, combat, conflict, contention, dispute, donnybrook*, exchange, flap*, fracas, free-for-all*, go, hassle, hell broke loose*, hostility, joust, match, melee, mix, punch out*, riot, roughhouse*, row, rowdy, rumble, rumpus, run-in*, scramble, scrap*, scrimmage, scuffle, set-to*, spat, strife, struggle, tiff, war, warfare, words, wrangle; SEE CONCEPT 106

fighting [adj] *aggressive, warlike*
angry, argumentative, battling, bellicose, belligerent, boxing, brawling, combative, contending, contentious, determined, disputatious, disputative, fencing, ferocious, hawkish, hostile, jingoistic, jousting, martial, militant, militaristic, pugnacious, quarrelsome, ready to fight, resolute, scrappy, skirmishing, sparring, tilting, truculent, unbeatable, under arms*, up in arms*, warmongering, wrestling; SEE CONCEPT 401

figment [n] *creation in one's mind*
bubble*, castle in the air*, chimera, daydream, dream, fable, fabrication, falsehood, fancy, fantasy, fiction, illusion, improvisation, invention, lie, nightmare, production; SEE CONCEPT 529

figurative [adj] *not literal, but symbolic*
allegorical, denotative, descriptive, emblematic, emblematical, fanciful, florid, flowery, illustrative, metaphoric, metaphorical, ornate, pictorial, poetical, representative, signifying, typical; SEE CONCEPTS 267,582

figure [n1] *numeral; numeric value*
amount, character, chiffer, cipher, cost, digit, in-

teger, number, price, quotation, rate, sum, symbol, terms, total, worth; SEE CONCEPTS *784,787*

figure [*n2*] *form, shape; physical structure*
anatomy, appearance, attitude, bod*, body, build, carriage, cast, chassis*, configuration, conformation, constitution, delineation, development, frame, mass, measurements, outline, physique, pose, posture, proportions, shadow, silhouette, substance, torso; SEE CONCEPTS *733,754,757*

figure [*n3*] *object with design; depiction*
cast, composition, decoration, device, diagram, drawing, effigy, embellishment, emblem, illustration, image, model, mold, motif, motive, ornamentation, pattern, piece, portrait, representation, sketch, statue; SEE CONCEPTS *259,625*

figure [*n4*] *famous person*
celebrity, character, dignitary, force, leader, notability, notable, personage, personality, presence, somebody, worthy; SEE CONCEPTS *354,423*

figure [*v1*] *calculate, compute*
add, cast, cipher, count, count heads*, count noses*, cut ice*, dope out*, enumerate, estimate, fix a price, foot*, guess, keep tabs*, number, reckon, run down, sum, summate, take account of, tally, tot*, total, totalize, tote*, tot up*, work out; SEE CONCEPTS *197,764*

figure [*v2*] *understand; decide, infer*
catch on to, cipher, clear up, comprehend, conclude, crack, decipher, decode, determine, discover, disentangle, dope out*, fathom, follow, get*, make heads or tails of*, make out*, master, opine, puzzle out, reason, resolve, rule, see, settle, solve, suppose, think, think out, unfold, unravel, unriddle, unscramble, untangle; SEE CONCEPTS *15,18,37*

figurehead [*n*] *person who is leader in name only*
cipher, front*, mouthpiece*, nominal head, nonentity, nothing, puppet*, straw boss*, straw person, titular head, token; SEE CONCEPTS *354,423*

figure in [*v*] *contribute to*
act, appear, be conspicuous, be featured, be included, be mentioned, have a place in, play a part*; SEE CONCEPT *112*

figure of speech [*n*] *communication that is not meant literally; stylistic device*
adumbration, allegory, alliteration, allusion, analogue, anaphora, anticlimax, antistrophe, antithesis, aposiopesis, apostrophe, asyndeton, bathos, comparison, conceit, echoism, ellipsis, euphemism, euphuism, exaggeration, hyperbole, image, imagery, irony, litotes, metaphor, metonymy, onomatopoeia, oxymoron, parable, paradox, parallel, personification, proteron, rhetoric, satire, simile, synecdoche, trope, tropology, turn of phrase, understatement; SEE CONCEPTS *275,278*

filch [*v*] *steal*
cop*, crib*, embezzle, hustle*, lift*, misappropriate, pilfer*, pinch*, purloin, rip off*, rob, scrounge, sneak, snipe, snitch*, swipe, take, thieve, walk off with*; SEE CONCEPTS *139,142*

file [*n1*] *system of order, placement for ease of use*
book, cabinet, case, census, charts, circular file*, data, directory, docket, documents, dossier, folder, index, information, list, notebook, pigeonhole*, portfolio, record, register, repository; SEE CONCEPTS *271,770*

file [*n2*] *line, queue*
column, echelon, list, parade, rank, row, string, tier, troop; SEE CONCEPT *727*

file [*v1*] *put in place, order*
alphabetize, arrange, catalog, catalogue, categorize, classify, deposit, docket, document, enter, index, list, pigeonhole*, record, register, slot, tabulate; SEE CONCEPTS *84,158*

file [*v2*] *rub down, grind*
abrade, burnish, erode, finish, furbish, grate, level, polish, rasp, raze, refine, scrape, shape, sharpen, smooth; SEE CONCEPTS *137,186, 215,250*

filibuster [*n*] *obstruction of progress, especially in verbal argument*
delay, hindrance, holding the floor*, interference, opposition, postponement, procrastination, stonewalling*, talkathon*; SEE CONCEPT *298*

fill [*n*] *capacity*
all one wants, ample, enough, filler, padding, plenty, satiety, stuffing, sufficiency, sufficient; SEE CONCEPTS *719,736,794*

fill [*v1*] *to put in and occupy the whole of*
block, blow up, brim over, bulge out, charge, choke, clog, close, congest, cram, crowd, distend, fulfill, furnish, glut, gorge, heap, impregnate, inflate, jam-pack, lade, load, meet, overflow, overspread, pack, pack like sardines*, permeate, pervade, plug, puff up*, pump up, ram, ram in*, replenish, sate, satiate, satisfy, saturate, shoal, stock, stopper*, store, stretch, stuff, supply, swell, take up, top, top off*; SEE CONCEPTS *107,209*

fill [*v2*] *execute, fulfill*
answer, assign, carry out, discharge, dispatch, distribute, elect, engage, fix, hold, meet, name, occupy, officiate, perform, satisfy, take up; SEE CONCEPT *91*

fill in [*v1*] *answer in writing*
advise, apprise, clue, complete, fill out, inform, insert, notify, post, sign, tell, warn, write in; SEE CONCEPTS *45,79*

fill in [*v2*] *act as substitute*
deputize, insinuate, interject, interpose, replace, represent, stand in, substract, take the place of, understudy; SEE CONCEPT *128*

filling/filler [*n*] *something that takes up capacity*
batting, bushing, cartridge, center, content, contents, cylinder, dressing, fill, guts*, impletion, inlay, innards, inside, layer, liner, mixture, pack, packing, pad, padding, refill, replenishment, shim, stuffing, wad, wadding; SEE CONCEPTS *826,830*

film [*n1*] *coating, tissue; mist*
blur, brume, cloud, coat, covering, dusting, fabric, foil, fold, gauze, haze, haziness, integument, layer, leaf, membrane, mistiness, nebula, obscuration, opacity, partition, pellicle, scum*, sheet, skin, transparency, veil, web; SEE CONCEPTS *478,524*

film [*n2*] *movie*
cinema, dailies*, flick*, footage, motion picture, moving picture, photoplay, picture, picture show, rushes, show, silent*, talkie*; SEE CONCEPT *293*

film [*v*] *take photographs*
photograph, put in the can*, record, roll, shoot, take, turn; SEE CONCEPTS *173,205*

filmy [*adj1*] *finespun, fragile*
chiffon, cobwebby*, dainty, delicate, diaphanous, fine, fine-grained, flimsy, floaty, gauzy, gossamer, insubstantial, see-through*, sheer, tiffany, transparent, wispy; SEE CONCEPT *606*

filmy [adj2] *covered with mist; blurry*
bleary, blurred, cloudy, dim, hazy, membranous, milky, misty, opalescent, opaque, pearly; SEE CONCEPTS 525,603

filter [v] *separate to refine; seep through*
clarify, clean, distill, drain, dribble, escape, exude, filtrate, leak, metastasize, ooze, osmose, penetrate, percolate, permeate, purify, refine, screen, sieve, sift, soak through, strain, trickle, winnow; SEE CONCEPTS 135,165

filth [n] *dirt, pollution*
carrion, contamination, corruption, crud*, defilement, dregs, dung, excrement, feces, feculence, filthiness, foul matter, foulness, garbage, grime, impurity, manure, mire, muck, mud, nastiness, ordure, putrefaction, putrescence, putridity, refuse, rottenness, sediment, sewage, silt, sleaze, slime, slop, sludge, slush, smut, trash, uncleanness; SEE CONCEPTS 260,674

filthy [adj1] *dirty, polluted*
begrimed, black, blackened, cruddy*, crummy*, disheveled, fecal, feculent, foul, grimy*, gross*, grubby*, grungy*, impure, loathsome, miry, mucky*, muddy, nasty, obscene, offensive, putrid, repulsive, revolting, scummy, sleazy, slimy, slipshod, sloppy, slovenly, smoky, soiled, sooty, sooty, squalid, unclean, uncleanly, unkempt, unwashed, verminous, vile, yecchy*; SEE CONCEPTS 485,570

filthy [adj2] *vulgar, obscene*
base, bawdy, blue*, coarse, contemptible, corrupt, depraved, despicable, dirty-minded*, foul, foul-mouthed, impure, indecent, lewd, licentious, low, mean, nasty, offensive, pornographic, raunchy, scatological, scurvy, smutty, suggestive, vicious, vile; SEE CONCEPTS 267,545

final [adj1] *ending, last*
closing, concluding, crowning, end, eventual, finishing, hindmost, lag, last-minute, latest, latter, supreme, terminal, terminating, ultimate; SEE CONCEPTS 531,820

final [adj2] *conclusive, definitive*
absolute, decided, decisive, definite, determinate, determinative, finished, incontrovertible, irrefutable, irrevocable, settled, unanswerable, unappealable; SEE CONCEPT 535

finale [n] *ending of an event*
afterpiece, blow-off*, button*, cessation, chaser*, climax, close, closer*, conclusion, consummation, crowning glory*, culmination, denouement, end, end piece, epilogue, finis, finish, last act, payoff*, peroration, summation, swan song*, termination, windup*; SEE CONCEPT 832

finality [n] *definiteness, conclusiveness*
certitude, completeness, decidedness, decisiveness, entirety, finish, inevitableness, intactness, integrity, irrevocability, perfection, resolution, terminality, totality, unavoidability, wholeness; SEE CONCEPTS 635,638,832

finalize [v] *finish, complete action*
agree, clinch*, conclude, consummate, decide, settle, sew up*, tie up*, work out, wrap up; SEE CONCEPT 91

finally [adv1] *beyond any doubt*
assuredly, beyond recall*, beyond shadow of doubt*, certainly, completely, conclusively, convincingly, decisively, definitely, determinately, done with, enduringly, for all time*, for ever, for good*, in conclusion, inescapably, inexorably, irrevocably, lastly, once and for all*, past regret*,

permanently, settled, with conviction; SEE CONCEPT 535

finally [adv2] *in the end; after period of time*
after all, after a while, already, as a sequel, at last, at length, at long last*, at the end, at the last moment, belatedly, despite delay*, eventually, in conclusion, in spite of all*, in the eleventh hour*, in the long run*, lastly, someday, sometime, sooner or later*, subsequently, tardily, ultimately, yet; SEE CONCEPT 799

finance [n] *economic affairs*
accounts, banking, business, commerce, economics, financial affairs, investment, money, money management; SEE CONCEPTS 360,770

finance [v] *offer loan money; set up in business*
back, bank, bankroll, capitalize, endow, float*, fund, go for*, grubstake*, guarantee, juice*, lay on one*, loan shark*, patronize, pay for, pick up the check*, pick up the tab*, prime the pump*, promote, provide funds, provide security, put up money, raise dough*, sponsor, stake, subsidize, support, underwrite; SEE CONCEPTS 108,115,341

finances [n] *person or corporation's money, property*
affairs, assets, balance sheet, budget, capital, cash, condition, funds, net, net worth, resources, revenue, wealth, wherewithal, worth; SEE CONCEPTS 340,710

financial [adj] *having to do with money*
banking, budgeting, business, commercial, economic, fiscal, monetary, numbers*, numeric, pecuniary, pocket; SEE CONCEPT 334

financier [n] *person who lends money, advises*
backer, banker, bankroller, broker, businessperson, capitalist, entrepreneur, fat cat*, grubstaker*, manipulator*, merchant, money, moneybags*, money lender, operator*, person who writes the checks*, rich person, Santa Claus*, speculator, sponsor, staker, stockbroker*, tycoon, usurer; SEE CONCEPTS 347,348,353

financing [n] *money for operating expenses*
costs, expenditure, funding, loan, matching funds, outgo, outlay, payment; SEE CONCEPTS 340,344

find [n] *discovery*
acquisition, asset, bargain, boast, bonanza, catch, gem, good buy, jewel, one in a million*, pride, treasure, treasure trove; SEE CONCEPTS 337,712

find [v1] *catch sight of, lay hands on*
arrive at, bring to light*, bump into*, chance upon, collar*, come across, come upon, come up with*, corral, descry, detect, dig up*, discern, discover, distinguish, encounter, espy, expose, fall in with*, ferret out, happen upon*, hit upon*, identify, lay fingers on, light upon*, locate, make out, meet, notice, observe, perceive, pinpoint, recognize, recover, run across, run into, scare up*, sight, smoke out*, spot, strike, stumble upon, track down, trip on*, turn up*, uncover, unearth; SEE CONCEPT 183

find [v2] *achieve, win*
acquire, attain, be one's lot*, earn, fall to the lot*, gain, get, meet, meet with, obtain, procure; SEE CONCEPTS 124,706

finding [n] *judgment, verdict*
award, conclusion, data, decision, decree, discovery, pronouncement, recommendation, sentence; SEE CONCEPT 685

find out [v] *discover, learn*
ascertain, catch, catch on, detect, determine, disclose, divine, expose, hear, identify, note, ob-

serve, perceive, realize, reveal, see, uncover, unearth, unmask; SEE CONCEPTS *31,183*

fine [n] *penalty in money*
amends, amercement, assessment, damages, forfeit, mulct, punishment, reparation, rip; SEE CONCEPT *123*

fine [adj1] *excellent, masterly*
accomplished, aces*, admirable, attractive, beautiful, capital, choice, cool*, crack*, dandy*, elegant, enjoyable, exceptional, expensive, exquisite, fashionable, first-class, first-rate, first-string, five-star*, gilt-edged*, gnarly*, good-looking, great, handsome, lovely, magnificent, mean, neat*, not too shabby*, ornate, outstanding, pleasant, rare, refined, select, showy, skillful, smart, solid, splendid, striking, subtle, superior, supreme, top, top-notch, unreal*, well-made, wicked*; SEE CONCEPTS *528,574,579*

fine [adj2] *cloudless, sunny*
balmy, bright, clarion, clear, clement, dry, fair, pleasant, rainless, undarkened; SEE CONCEPT *525*

fine [adj3] *dainty, delicate; sheer*
diaphanous, ethereal, exquisite. filmy, fine-drawn, fine-grained, fine-spun, flimsy, fragile, gauzy, gossamer, gossamery, granular, impalpable, light, lightweight, little, loose, minute, porous, powdered, powdery, pulverized, quality, slender, small, thin, threadlike, transparent; SEE CONCEPTS *491,606*

fine [adj4] *discriminating, exact*
abstruse, acute, clear, critical, cryptic, delicate, distinct, enigmatic, esoteric, fastidious, fine-spun, hairline, hairsplitting, intelligent, keen, minute, nice, obscure, petty, precise, pure, quick, recondite, refined, sensitive, sharp, sterling, strict, subtle, tasteful, tenuous, trifling, unadulterated, unpolluted; SEE CONCEPT *557*

fine [v] *penalize in monetary way*
alienate, amerce, confiscate, dock*, exact, extort, hit with*, levy, make pay, mulct, pay through the nose*, punish, sconce, seize, sequestrate, slap with*, tax, throw book at*; SEE CONCEPTS *122,342*

finery [n] *best clothing*
apparel, bib and tucker*, caparison, decoration, fancy dress, formals, frippery*, full dress, gear, regalia, splendor, suit, Sunday best* trappings, trimmings, trinkets; SEE CONCEPT *451*

finesse [n] *know-how, maneuver*
acumen, adeptness, adroitness, artfulness, artifice, big stick*, bluff, cleverness, competence, con, craft, craftiness, cunning, delicacy, diplomacy, discernment, discretion, feint, gimmick, grift, guile, polish, quickness, racket*, runaround*, ruse, savoir-faire, savvy, skill, sophistication, stratagem, subtlety, tact, trick, wile; SEE CONCEPTS *409,657*

finesse [v] *maneuver, manipulate*
angle, beguile, bluff, exploit, finagle*, jockey*, operate, play, play games*, pull strings*, pull wires*, rig*, wangle; SEE CONCEPTS *36,59*

finger [n] *appendage of hand*
antenna*, claw, digit, extremity, feeler*, hook*, pinky*, pointer*, ring finger, tactile member, tentacle*, thumb; SEE CONCEPT *392*

finger [v1] *touch lightly*
feel, fiddle, grope, handle, manipulate, maul, meddle, palpate, paw, play with, thumb, toy with; SEE CONCEPT *612*

finger [v2] *choose, designate*
appoint, determine, identify, indicate, locate, make, name, nominate, pin down*, point out, specify, tap; SEE CONCEPT *41*

finicky [adj] *overparticular*
choosy, critical, dainty, difficult, fastidious, finical, finicking, fussbudget*, fussy, hard to please, nice, nit-picking, overnice, persnickety*, picky, scrupulous, squeamish, stickling; SEE CONCEPTS *401,404,556*

finish [n1] *conclusion; completion*
accomplishment, achievement, acquirement, acquisition, annihilation, attainment, cease, cessation, close, closing, culmination, curtain*, curtains*, death, defeat, denouement, desistance, end, ending, end of the line*, end of the road*, finale, finis, last, last stage, ruin, stop, termination, terminus, winding-up*, wind-up, wrap, wrap-up*; SEE CONCEPTS *119,832*

finish [n2] *coating; perfecting*
appearance, beauty, burnish, cultivation, culture, elaboration, glaze, grace, grain, lacquer, luster, patina, perfection, polish, refinement, shine, smoothness, surface, texture, veneer; SEE CONCEPTS *611,655*

finish [v1] *bring to a conclusion; get done*
accomplish, achieve, bag it*, break up, bring to a close, carry through, cease, clinch, close, complete, conclude, crown*, culminate, deal with, determine, discharge, do, effect, end, execute, finalize, fold, fulfill, get out of the way*, halt, hang it up*, have done with*, make, make short work of*, mop up*, perfect, put finishing touches on*, round off*, round up*, scratch, scrub, settle, sew up*, shut down, shutter*, stop, terminate, top off*, ultimate, wind up*, wrap, wrap up*; SEE CONCEPTS *91,234,706*

finish [v2] *consume, use up*
deplete, devour, dispatch, dispose of, drain, drink, eat, empty, exhaust, expend, go, run through*, spend, use, wash up*; SEE CONCEPTS *169,225*

finish [v3] *defeat; kill*
annihilate, assassinate, best*, bring down*, carry off*, destroy, dispatch, dispose of, do in*, down, execute, exterminate, get rid of*, liquidate, overcome, overpower, put an end to, put away*, rout, rub out*, ruin, slaughter, slay, take off*, take out*, vaporize, worst*; SEE CONCEPTS *95,252*

finish [v4] *put a coating on; perfect*
coat, develop, elaborate, face, gild, lacquer, polish, refine, smooth, stain, texture, veneer, wax; SEE CONCEPTS *172,202*

finished [adj1] *cultivated, refined*
accomplished, all-around, classic, consummate, cultured, elegant, expert, exquisite, flawless, impeccable, many-sided, masterly, perfected, polished, professional, proficient, skilled, smooth, suave, urbane, versatile; SEE CONCEPTS *404,528*

finished [adj2] *complete, done*
accomplished, achieved, brought about, ceased, closed, come to an end, compassed, concluded, consummated, decided, discharged, dispatched, disposed of, done for, done with, effected, effectuated, elaborated, ended, entire, executed, final, finalized, fulfilled, full, in the past, lapsed, made, over, over and done*, perfected, performed, put into effect*, realized, resolved, satisfied, settled, sewn up*, shut, stopped, terminated, through, tied

up*, worked out*, wound up*, wrapped up*; SEE CONCEPTS 528,531

finished [adj3] *consumed, used up*
bankrupt, devastated, done, done for*, done in*, drained, empty, exhausted, gone, liquidated, lost, played out*, ruined, spent, through, undone, washed up*, wiped out*, wrecked*; SEE CONCEPTS 334,560

finite [adj] *subject to limitations*
bound, bounded, circumscribed, conditioned, confined, definable, definite, delimited, demarcated, determinate, exact, fixed, limited, precise, restricted, specific, terminable; SEE CONCEPTS 535,554

fire [n1] *burning*
blaze, bonfire, campfire, charring, coals, combustion, conflagration, devouring, element, embers, flame and smoke, flames, flare, glow, hearth, heat, holocaust, hot spot*, incandescence, inferno, luminosity, oxidation, phlogiston, pyre, rapid oxidation, scintillation, scorching, sea of flames*, searing, sparks, tinder, up in smoke*, warmth; SEE CONCEPTS 478,521

fire [n2] *barrage of projectiles*
attack, bombarding, bombardment, bombing, cannonade, cannonading, crossfire, explosion, fusillade, hail, round, salvo, shelling, sniping, volley; SEE CONCEPTS 86,320

fire [n3] *animation, vigor*
ardor, brio, calenture, dash, drive, eagerness, élan, energy, enthusiasm, excitement, exhilaration, fervency, fervor, force, ginger*, gusto, heartiness, heat, impetuosity, intensity, life, light, liveliness, luster, passion, pep*, punch*, radiance, red heat*, scintillation, snap*, sparkle, spirit, splendor, starch, verve, vim, virtuosity, vivacity, white heat*, zeal, zing, zip; SEE CONCEPT 411

fire [v1] *cause to burn*
enkindle, ignite, kindle, light, put a match to*, set ablaze, set aflame, set alight, set fire to, set on fire, start a fire, touch off*; SEE CONCEPT 249

fire [v2] *detonate or throw a weapon*
cast, discharge, eject, explode, fling, heave, hurl, launch, let off*, loose, pitch, pull trigger, set off*, shell, shoot, toss, touch off*; SEE CONCEPTS 179,222

fire [v3] *excite, arouse*
animate, electrify, enliven, enthuse, exalt, galvanize, heighten, impassion, incite, inflame, inform, inspire, inspirit, intensify, intoxicate, irritate, provoke, quicken, rouse, stir, thrill; SEE CONCEPT 14

fire [v4] *dismiss from responsibility*
-ax*, boot*, can*, discharge, drop, eject, expel, give bum's rush*, give marching orders*, give one notice*, give pink slip*, give the sack*, hand walking papers*, kick out*, lay off, let one go*, oust, pink slip*, sack*, terminate; SEE CONCEPTS 50,88,351

fireplace [n] *hearth for burning wood*
bed of coals, blaze, chimney, fireside, furnace, grate, hearthside, hob, ingle, inglenook, ingleside, settle, stove; SEE CONCEPTS 440,443

fireproof [adj] *resistant to burning*
asbestos, concrete, fire-resistant, incombustible, noncandescent, noncombustible, nonflammable, noninflammable; SEE CONCEPT 485

fireworks [n] *pyrotechnic display at celebrations*
bottle rockets, bursts, firecrackers, fire flowers, illuminations, rockets, Roman candles, sparklers; SEE CONCEPT 293

firm [n] *business*
association, bunch, company, concern, conglomerate, corporation, crew, crowd, enterprise, gang, house, megacorp, mob, multinational, organization, outfit, partnership, ring; SEE CONCEPTS 323,325

firm [adj1] *inflexible*
close, close-grained, compact, compressed, concentrated, concrete, condensed, congealed, dense, fine-grained, hard, hardened, heavy, impenetrable, impermeable, impervious, inelastic, jelled, nonporous, refractory, rigid, set, solid, solidified, stiff, sturdy, substantial, thick, tough, unyielding; SEE CONCEPTS 604,606

firm [adj2] *stable, unmoving*
anchored, bolted, braced, cemented, closed, durable, embedded, fast, fastened, fixed, immobile, immovable, motionless, mounted, nailed, petrified, riveted, robust, rooted, screwed, secure, secured, set, settled, soldered, solid, sound, spiked, stationary, steady, strong, sturdy, substantial, taut, tenacious, tight, tightened, unfluctuating, unshakable, welded; SEE CONCEPT 488

firm [adj3] *unalterable, definite*
abiding, adamant, bent, bound, consistent, constant, dead set on*, determined, enduring, established, exact, explicit, fixed, flat, going, hang tough*, inflexible, intent, never-failing, obdurate, persevering, persistent, prevailing, resolute, resolved, set, settled, specific, stable, stand pat*, stated, staunch, steadfast, steady, stipulated, strict, strong, sure, tenacious, true, unbending, unchangeable, undeviating, unflinching, unqualified, unshakable, unshaken, unwavering, unyielding; SEE CONCEPTS 267,403,542

firmament [n] *heaven*
empyrean, lid*, sky, the blue*, the skies, vault, welkin, wild blue yonder*; SEE CONCEPT 437

firmly [adv1] *immovably*
durably, enduringly, fast, fixedly, hard, inflexibly, like a rock*, motionlessly, rigidly, securely, solid, solidly, soundly, stably, steadily, stiffly, strongly, substantially, thoroughly, tight, tightly, unflinchingly, unshakeably; SEE CONCEPTS 488,489,604

firmly [adv2] *with determination*
adamantly, constantly, decisively, doggedly, indefatigably, intently, obdurately, obstinately, perseveringly, persistently, pertinaciously, purposefully, resolutely, staunchly, steadfastly, stolidly, strictly, stubbornly, tenaciously, through thick and thin*, unchangeably, unwaveringly, with heavy hand*; SEE CONCEPTS 534,542

firmness [n1] *stiffness*
compactness, density, durability, fixedness, hardness, impenetrability, impermeability, imperviousness, impliability, inelasticity, inflexibility, resistance, rigidity, solidity, temper, tensile strength, toughness; SEE CONCEPTS 722,726

firmness [n2] *immovability*
durability, solidity, soundness, stability, steadiness, strength, substantiality, tautness, tension, tightness; SEE CONCEPTS 731,732

firmness [n3] *resolution, resolve*
constancy, decidedness, decision, determination, fixedness, fixity, inflexibility, obduracy, obstinacy, purposefulness, purposiveness, staunch-

ness, steadfastness, strength, strictness; SEE CONCEPTS 410,633

first [adj1] *earliest in order*
aboriginal, ahead, antecedent, anterior, basic, beginning, cardinal, early, elementary, first off*, front, fundamental, head, headmost, inaugural, inceptive, incipient, initial, in the beginning, introductory, key, leading, lead off*, least, number one*, numero uno*, opening, original, pioneer, premier, primary, prime, primeval, primitive, primogenial, primordial, pristine, right up front*, rudimentary, slightest, smallest; SEE CONCEPTS 585,632,820

first [adj2] *highest in importance*
advanced, A-number-1*, arch, champion, chief, dominant, eminent, first-class, first-string*, foremost, greatest, head, head of the line*, leading, main, number one*, outstanding, paramount, predominant, preeminent, premier, primary, prime, primo*, principal, ranking, ruling, sovereign, supreme, top-flight*, top of the list; SEE CONCEPT 568

first [adv] *at the beginning*
at the outset, before all else, beforehand, initially, in the first place, originally, to begin with, to start with; SEE CONCEPTS 585,820

first-class/first-rate [adj] *superior, excellent*
capital, choice, dandy, fine, first-string*, five-star*, in class by itself*, prime*, shipshape, sound, supreme, tiptop*, top, top-notch*, very good; SEE CONCEPT 574

firsthand [adj] *direct*
eyewitness, immediate, primary, straight, straight from the horse's mouth*; SEE CONCEPT 267

fiscal [adj] *monetary*
budgetary, commercial, economic, financial, money, pecuniary, pocket; SEE CONCEPT 334

fish [v] *throwing bait to catch seafood*
angle, bait, bait the hook*, bob, cast, cast one's hook*, cast one's net*, chum, extract, extricate, find, go fishing, haul out*, net, produce, pull out, seine, trawl, troll; SEE CONCEPT 363

fish for [v] *look for, hint*
angle, angle for, elicit, hope for, hunt for, invite, search for, seek, solicit, try to evoke; SEE CONCEPTS 20,75

fishy [adj] *doubtful, suspicious*
ambiguous, doubtable, dubious, dubitable, equivocal, far-fetched, funny, implausible, improbable, odd, problematic, queer, questionable, shady, suspect, uncertain, unlikely; SEE CONCEPT 552

fit [n] *seizure; sudden emotion*
access, attack, blow, bout, burst, caprice, conniption*, convulsion, epileptic attack, frenzy, humor, jumps*, mood, outbreak, outburst, paroxysm, rage, rush, spasm, spate, spell, stroke, tantrum, throe, torrent, turn, twitch, whim, whimsy; SEE CONCEPTS 13,303

fit [adj1] *suitable, appropriate*
able, adapted, adequate, advantageous, apposite, apt, becoming, befitting, beneficial, capable, comely, comme il faut, competent, conformable, convenient, correct, correspondent, deserving, desirable, due, equipped, equitable, expedient, favorable, feasible, felicitous, fitted, fitting, good enough, happy, just, likely, meet, opportune, practicable, preferable, prepared, proper, qualified, ready, right, rightful, seasonable, seemly, tasteful, timely, trained, well-suited, wise, worthy; SEE CONCEPT 558

fit [adj2] *healthy, in good physical shape*
able-bodied, competent, fit as a fiddle*, hale, in good condition, muscled, robust, slim, sound, strapping*, toned, trim, up to snuff*, well, wholesome, wrapped tight*; SEE CONCEPTS 314,485

fit [v1] *belong, correspond*
accord, agree, answer, apply, be apposite, be apt, become, be comfortable, be consonant, befit, be in keeping, click*, concur, conform, consist, dovetail*, go, go together, go with, harmonize, have its place, interlock, join, match, meet, parallel, relate, respond, set, suit, tally; SEE CONCEPT 664

fit [v2] *equip*
accommodate, accoutre, arm, fix, furnish, get, implement, kit out*, make, make up, outfit, prepare, provide, ready, rig*; SEE CONCEPT 182

fit [v3] *adapt, change*
adjust, alter, arrange, conform, dispose, fashion, modify, place, position, quadrate, reconcile, shape, square, suit, tailor, tailor-make*; SEE CONCEPT 232

fitful [adj] *irregular, sporadic*
bits and pieces*, broken, capricious, catchy*, changeable, desultory, disturbed, erratic, flickering, fluctuating, haphazard, herky-jerky*, hit-or-miss*, impulsive, inconstant, intermittent, interrupted, on-again-off-again, periodic, random, recurrent, restive, restless, shifting, spasmodic, spastic*, spotty, unstable, variable; SEE CONCEPTS 482,534

fitness [n1] *good condition*
fettle*, good health, health, kilter*, repair, robustness, shape, strength, trim, vigor; SEE CONCEPTS 316,723

fitness [n2] *appropriateness*
accommodation, accordance, adaptation, adequacy, admissibility, agreeableness, applicability, appositeness, aptitude, aptness, assimilation, auspiciousness, compatibility, competence, concurrency, congeniality, congruousness, consistency, consonance, convenience, correspondence, decency, decorum, eligibility, expediency, harmony, keeping, order, patness, pertinence, preparedness, propriety, qualification, readiness, relevancy, rightness, seasonableness, seemliness, suitability, timeliness; SEE CONCEPT 656

fitted [adj1] *appropriate, right*
adapted, conformable, cut out for, equipped, matched, proper, qualified, suitable, suited, tailor-made; SEE CONCEPT 558

fitted [adj2] *equipped*
accoutered, appointed, armed, furnished, implemented, outfitted, provided, rigged out*, set up, supplied; SEE CONCEPTS 560,589

fitting [n] *accessory*
accouterment, appointment, attachment, component, connection, convenience, equipment, extra, furnishing, furniture, instrument, paraphernalia, part, piece, trimming, unit; SEE CONCEPT 824

fitting [adj] *appropriate, suitable*
applicable, apt, becoming, comme il faut, correct, decent, decorous, desirable, due, felicitous, happy, just, just what was ordered*, meet, on the button*, on the nose*, proper, right, right on*, seemly, that's the ticket*; SEE CONCEPT 558

fix [n] *difficult or ticklish situation*
box*, corner*, dilemma, embarrassment, hole*, hot water*, jam*, mess*, pickle*, plight, predic-

ament, quandary, scrape, spot*; SEE CONCEPT 674

fix [v1] *establish, make firm*
affix, anchor, attach, bind, catch, cement, congeal, connect, consolidate, couple, embed, entrench, fasten, freeze to*, glue, graft, harden, implant, inculcate, infix, ingrain, install, instill, link, locate, lodge, moor, nail down*, pin, place, plant, position, rigidify, rivet, root, secure, set, settle, solidify, stabilize, stay put, steady, stick, stiffen, thicken, tie; SEE CONCEPTS 85,113, 160,201

fix [v2] *determine, decide*
agree on, appoint, arrange, arrive at, conclude, define, establish, limit, name, resolve, set, settle, solve, specify, work, work out; SEE CONCEPT 18

fix [v3] *mend, repair*
adjust, amend, correct, debug, doctor, do up*, emend, face-lift*, fiddle with, overhaul, patch, put to rights*, rebuild, recondition, reconstruct, regulate, restore, retread, revamp, revise, set to*, sort, tune up; SEE CONCEPTS 126,212

fix [v4] *prepare, plan ahead*
arrange, dispose, frame, prearrange, precontrive, predesign, preorder, preplan, put up, rig*, set up, stack the deck*; SEE CONCEPT 36

fix [v5] *focus on*
concenter, concentrate, direct, fasten, fixate, level at, put, rivet; SEE CONCEPT 623

fix [v6] *cook a meal*
fit, get, get ready, heat, make, make up, microwave, prepare, ready, warm, whip up*; SEE CONCEPT 170

fix [v7] *manipulate, influence an event*
bribe, buy, buy off, corrupt, fiddle*, have, lubricate, maneuver, pull strings*, reach, square, suborn, tamper with; SEE CONCEPTS 192,232

fix [v8] *wreak vengeance on*
cook someone's goose*, get*, get even, get revenge, hurt, pay back, punish, take retribution; SEE CONCEPT 86

fixation [n] *obsession*
addiction, case, complex, craze, crush, fascination, fetish, hang-up*, idée fixe, infatuation, mania, preoccupation, thing; SEE CONCEPTS 532,690

fixed [adj1] *permanent, steady*
anchored, attached, established, fast, firm, hitched, hooked, immobile, immotile, immovable, located, locked, made fast, nailed*, quiet, rigid, rooted, secure, set, settled, situated, solid, stable, steadfast, stiff, still, tenacious, tight; SEE CONCEPTS 488,551,583,649

fixed [adj2] *intent, resolute; established*
abiding, agreed, arranged, certain, changeless, circumscribed, confirmed, decided, defined, definite, definitive, determinate, enduring, firm, inalterable, inflexible, in the bag*, inveterate, level, limited, narrow, never-failing, planned, prearranged, precise, resolved, restricted, rigged, rooted, set, settled, set-up, stated, steadfast, steady, still, stipulated, sure, unbending, unblinking, unchangeable, undeviating, unfaltering, unflinching, unmodifiable, unmovable, unqualified, unwavering; SEE CONCEPTS 535,554

fixed [adj3] *repaired*
back together, going, in order, in working order, mended, put right, rebuilt, refitted, sorted, whole; SEE CONCEPT 560

fix up [v] *prepare, beautify*
deck*, dress up, furnish, gussy up*, primp, provide, rehabilitate, repair, smarten, spiff*, spruce up*; SEE CONCEPTS 162,202

fizz [v] *bubble*
buzz, effervesce, fizzle, froth, hiss, seethe, sibilate, simmer, sparkle, sputter, whisper, whoosh; SEE CONCEPT 469

fizzle [v] *collapse, fall through*
abort, be a fiasco*, come to nothing*, die, end, end in defeat*, end in disappointment*, fail, fold, miscarry, misfire, miss the mark*, peter out*, wane; SEE CONCEPT 699

flabbergast [v] *surprise*
abash, amaze, astonish, astound, blow away*, bowl over*, confound, daze, disconcert, dumbfound, make speechless, nonplus, overcome, overwhelm, put away*, shock, stagger, stun, throw, throw for a loop*; SEE CONCEPT 42

flabby [adj] *baggy, fat*
drooping, enervated, flaccid, flexuous, floppy*, gone to seed*, hanging, irresilient, lax, limp, loose, out of condition*, out of shape*, pendulous, rusty, sagging, shapeless, slack, sloppy, soft, tender, toneless, unfit, yielding; SEE CONCEPTS 486,490

flaccid [adj] *drooping*
debilitated, emasculated, enervated, enfeebled, flabby, flimsy, inelastic, irresilient, lax, limp, loose, nerveless, quaggy, sapped, slack, soft, weak, weakened; SEE CONCEPTS 485,604

flag [n] *pennant, symbol*
banderole, banner, bannerol, burgee, colors, emblem, ensign, gonfalon, jack, pennon, standard, streamer; SEE CONCEPTS 284,473

flag [v1] *decline, fall off*
abate, deteriorate, die, droop, ebb, fade, fail, faint, languish, peter out*, pine, sag, sink, slump, succumb, taper off*, wane, weaken, weary, wilt; SEE CONCEPTS 698,699

flag [v2] *signal*
gesture, give a sign to, hail, indicate, motion, salute, warn, wave; SEE CONCEPT 74

flagrant [adj] *flaunting, blatant; without shame*
arrant, atrocious, awful, bare-faced*, bold, brazen, capital, conspicuous, crying, disgraceful, dreadful, egregious, enormous, flagitious, flaming, flashy*, glaring, grody*, gross*, hanging out*, heinous, immodest, infamous, noticeable, notorious, obvious, open, ostentatious, out-and-out*, outrageous, rank, scandalous, shameful, shameless, shocking, stick out like sore thumb*, striking, undisguised, wicked; SEE CONCEPTS 401,545,576

flair [n] *talent, style*
ability, accomplishment, aptitude, aptness, bent, chic, dash, elegance, faculty, feel, genius, gift, glamour, head, knack, mastery, panache, pizzazz*, presence, shine*, splash*, taste, turn, zip*; SEE CONCEPTS 630,706

flak [n] *complaint, criticism*
abuse, bad press*, brickbat*, censure, condemnation, disapprobation, disapproval, disparagement, fault-finding, hostility, knock*, opposition, pan*, rap*, swipe*; SEE CONCEPTS 52,278

flake [n] *scale, peel*
cell, disk, drop, foil, lamella, lamina, layer, leaf, membrane, pellicle, plate, scab, section, shaving, sheet, skin, slice, sliver, wafer; SEE CONCEPT 831

flake [v] *peel off*
blister, chip, delaminate, desquamate, drop, ex-

foliate, pare, scab, scale, shed, slice, sliver, trim, wear away; SEE CONCEPTS *157,469*

flamboyant [*adj*] *extravagant, theatrical*
baroque, bombastic, brilliant, camp, chichi*, colorful, dashing, dazzling, elaborate, exciting, flaky*, flaming, flashy, florid, gassy*, gaudy, glamorous, jazzy*, luscious, luxuriant, ornate, ostentatious, peacockish, pretentious, resplendent, rich, rococo, showy, splashy, sporty, swank*, swashbuckling*; SEE CONCEPTS *401,589*

flame [*n1*] *fire*
blaze, brightness, conflagration, flare, flash, holocaust, light, rapid oxidation, wildfire; SEE CONCEPTS *478,521*

flame [*n2*] *lover; passion*
affection, ardor, baby, beau, beloved, boyfriend, darling, dear, desire, enthusiasm, fervor, fire, girlfriend, heartthrob, honey, inamorata, inamorato, keenness, love, paramour, spark, steady, swain, sweetheart, sweetie, truelove; SEE CONCEPTS *32,423*

flame [*v*] *burn*
blaze, coruscate, fire, flare, flare up, flash, glare, glint, glow, ignite, kindle, light, oxidize, shine; SEE CONCEPT *249*

flaming [*adj1*] *burning*
ablaze, afire, aflame, alight, blazing, brilliant, conflagrant, fiery, flaring, glowing, ignited, in flames, raging, red, red-hot*; SEE CONCEPT *485*

flaming [*adj2*] *very angry, vehement*
ardent, aroused, blazing, bright, burning, fervent, frenzied, hot, hot-blooded*, impassioned, intense, passionate, raging, red-hot*, scintillating, vivid, white-hot*; SEE CONCEPTS *267,403*

flammable [*adj*] *easily set afire*
burnable, combustible, ignitable, incendiary, inflammable; SEE CONCEPT *485*

flank [*n*] *haunch of an animate being*
ham, hand, hip, loin, pleuron, quarter, side, thigh, wing; SEE CONCEPT *392*

flap [*n1*] *winged or extended part of an object*
accessory, adjunct, appendage, apron, cover, drop, fly, fold, hanging, lapel, lobe, lug, overlap, pendant, pendulosity, ply, queue, skirt, strip, tab, tag, tail, tippet; SEE CONCEPTS *471,824*

flap [*n2*] *commotion*
agitation, baby, brouhaha, confusion, dither, fluster, flutter, fuss, lather*, panic, pother*, state*, stew*, sweat*, tizzy, to-do, tumult, turbulence, turmoil, twitter*; SEE CONCEPTS *230,674*

flap [*v*] *flutter*
agitate, beat, dangle, flail, flash, flop, hang, lop, shake, swing, swish, thrash, thresh, vibrate, wag, wave; SEE CONCEPT *149*

flare [*v1*] *erupt, blow*
blaze, boil over, break out, burn, burn up, burst, dart, dazzle, explode, fire up, flash, flicker, flutter, fume, glare, glow, go off, lose control, rant, seethe, shimmer, shoot, waver; SEE CONCEPTS *13,179,249*

flare [*v2*] *spread*
broaden, grow, splay, widen; SEE CONCEPT *469*

flash [*n1*] *shimmer, flicker*
beam, bedazzlement, blaze, burst, coruscation, dazzle, flame, flare, glance, glare, gleam, glimmer, glint, glisten, glitter, glow, illumination, imprint, impulse, incandescence, luster, phosphorescence, quiver, radiation, ray, reflection, scintillation, shine, spark, sparkle, streak, stream,

twinkle, twinkling, vision; SEE CONCEPTS *521,624*

flash [*n2*] *instant, split second*
breathing, burst, jiffy, minute, moment, outburst, shake, show, trice, twinkling; SEE CONCEPTS *808,821*

flash [*n3*] *demonstration*
burst, display, manifestation, outburst, show, sign, splash, swank; SEE CONCEPT *261*

flash [*v1*] *shimmer, flicker*
beam, bedazzle, blaze, blink, coruscate, dazzle, flame, flare, glance, glare, gleam, glimmer, glint, glisten, glitter, glow, incandesce, light, phosphoresce, radiate, reflect, scintillate, shine, shoot out, spangle, spark, sparkle, twinkle; SEE CONCEPT *624*

flash [*v2*] *move fast and display*
bolt, brandish, dart, dash, disport, exhibit, expose, flaunt, flit, flourish, fly, parade, race, shoot, show, show off, speed, spring, streak, sweep, trot out, whistle, zoom; SEE CONCEPTS *150,261*

flashy [*adj*] *flamboyant, in poor taste*
blatant, brazen, catchpenny*, cheap, chintzy, flaunting, florid, garish, gaudy, glaring, glittering, glittery, glitzy, jazzy*, loud, meretricious, ornate, ostentatious, showy, snazzy, sparkling, tacky*, tasteless, tawdry, tinsel, vulgar; SEE CONCEPT *589*

flask [*n*] *small container for liquid*
alembic, ampulla, bag, beaker, bottle, canteen, carafe, caster, chalice, crock, cruel, crystal, decanter, demijohn, ewer, fiasco, flacon, flagon, flasket, glass, goblet, gourd, horn, jar, jug, noggin, phial, retort, tumbler, urn, vial; SEE CONCEPT *494*

flat [*n*] *apartment*
chambers, condo, co-op*, crash pad*, floorthrough, go-down, joint*, lodging, pad*, railroad apartment, rental, room, rooms, suite, tenement, walk-up; SEE CONCEPT *516*

flat [*adj1*] *level, smooth*
collapsed, complanate, decumbent, deflated, depressed, empty, even, extended, fallen, flush, horizontal, laid low, low, oblate, outstretched, pancake*, planar, planate, plane, procumbent, prone, prostrate, punctured, reclining, recumbent, splay, spread out, supine, tabular, unbroken; SEE CONCEPTS *486,490*

flat [*adj2*] *dull, lackluster to the senses*
banal, blah, bland, blind, boring, colorless, dead, dim, drab, draggy, flavorless, ho hum*, inane, innocuous, insipid, jejune, lead balloon*, lifeless, matte, monotonous, muted, pointless, prosaic, prosy, sapless, spiritless, stale, tasteless, tedious, uninteresting, unpalatable, unsavory, unseasoned, vanilla*, vapid, watery, weak, whitebread*; SEE CONCEPTS *529,537*

flat [*adj3*] *absolute, positive*
categorical, direct, downright, explicit, final, fixed, indubitable, out-and-out*, peremptory, plain, straight, unconditional, unequivocal, unmistakable, unqualified, unquestionable; SEE CONCEPT *535*

flatten [*v*] *level out*
abrade, beat down, compress, crush, debase, deflate, depress, even out, fell, floor, flush, grade, ground, iron out, knock down, lay, lay low, mow down, plane, plaster*, prostrate, raze, roll, smash, smooth, spread out, squash, straighten, subdue, trample; SEE CONCEPTS *137,250,469,702*

fi
fl

flatter [v1] *compliment excessively*
adulate, beslaver, blandish, bootlick*, brown-nose*, build up*, butter up*, cajole, cater to, charm, con, court, fawn*, get next to*, glorify, grovel, humor, inveigle, jolly, lay it on thick*, massage, oil*, overpraise, play up to*, praise, rub the right way*, salve, sell, snow*, soften*, soft-soap*, spread it on*, stroke, suck up to*, sweeten up*, sweet-talk*, toady*, wheedle, work on*, work over*; SEE CONCEPTS *59,69*

flatter [v2] *complement, enhance*
adorn, beautify, become, decorate, do something for*, embellish, enrich, finish, go with*, grace, ornament, perfect, put in best light*, set off, show to advantage, suit; SEE CONCEPTS *162,664*

flattery [n] *false praise, compliments*
adulation, applause, approbation, blandishment, blarney*, bootlicking*, cajolery, commendation, encomium, eulogy, eyewash*, fawning*, flattering, flummery, fulsomeness, gallantry, gratification, hokum*, honeyed words, incense, ingratiation, jive*, laud, mush*, obsequiousness, palaver, plaudits, pretty speech, puffery*, servility, smoke*, snow*, snow job*, soft-soap*, soft words, stroke*, sweet talk*, sycophancy, toadyism, tribute, truckling, unctuousness; SEE CONCEPTS *59,69*

flatulent [adj] *pretentious, long-winded*
bombastic, inflated, oratorical, overblown, pompous, prolix, shallow, superficial, swollen, tedious, tumescent, tumid, turgid, windy, wordy; SEE CONCEPTS *267,404*

flaunt [v] *make an exhibition, show off*
advertise, air, boast, brandish, break out, broadcast, declare, disclose, display, disport, divulge, expose, fan it*, flash, flash about, flourish, gasconade, grandstand*, hotdog*, let it all hang out*, make a scene*, parade, proclaim, put on an act*, reveal, roll out, show and tell, showcase, smack with*, sport, spring on*, streak, throw weight around*, trot out*, vaunt, wave around, whip out*; SEE CONCEPT *261*

flavor [n1] *odor and taste*
acidity, aroma, astringency, bitterness, essence, extract, gusto, hotness, piquancy, pungency, relish, saltiness, sapidity, sapor, savor, seasoning, smack, sourness, spiciness, sweetness, tang, tartness, twang, vim, wallop, zest, zing; SEE CONCEPT *614*

flavor [n2] *aura, essence*
aspect, character, feel, feeling, property, quality, soupçon, stamp, style, suggestion, tinge, tone, touch; SEE CONCEPT *673*

flavor [v] *add seasoning*
add zing, add zip, ginger, hot it up*, imbue, impart, infuse, lace, leaven, pepper, pep up*, salt, season, spice; SEE CONCEPT *170*

flavoring [n] *spice, extract added to food*
additive, condiment, distillation, essence, herb, quintessence, relish, sauce, seasoning, spirit, tincture, zest; SEE CONCEPT *428*

flaw [n] *imperfection*
blemish, bug, catch*, Catch-22*, defect, disfigurement, failing, fault, foible, glitch*, gremlin*, pitfall, slipup, speck, spot, stain, typo*, vice, wart*, weakness, weak spot; SEE CONCEPTS *580,674*

flawless [adj] *spotless, intact*
absolute, entire, faultless, immaculate, impeccable, irreproachable, perfect, sound, unblemished,

unbroken, undamaged, unimpaired, unmarred, unsullied, whole; SEE CONCEPTS *574,579*

fleck [n] *spot, pinpoint mark*
bit, dot, mite, mote, patch, pinpoint, speck, speckle, stipple, streak, stripe; SEE CONCEPTS *284,831*

fleck [v] *mark with spots*
bespeckle, besprinkle, dapple, dot, dust, maculate, mottle, speckle, stipple, streak, variegate; SEE CONCEPT *79*

fledgling [n] *beginner in activity*
apprentice, chick, colt, greenhorn*, learner, neophyte, nestling, newcomer, novice, rookie, tenderfoot*, trainee, tyro*; SEE CONCEPTS *352, 366,424*

flee [v] *run away to escape*
abscond, avoid, beat a hasty retreat*, blow*, bolt*, break, cut and run*, cut out*, decamp, depart, desert, elude, evade, fly, fly the coop*, get*, get away, get the hell out*, hotfoot*, jump, leave, make a getaway*, make off*, make oneself scarce*, make one's escape*, make quick exit*, make tracks*, retreat, scamper, scoot, scram*, skedaddle*, skip*, split*, step on it*, step on the gas*, take a hike*, take flight, take off, vamoose*, vanish; SEE CONCEPTS *102,150,195*

fleece [v] *plunder, steal*
bleed*, burn*, cheat*, clip*, con, cozen, defraud, despoil, flimflam*, gouge, hustle, jerk around*, milk*, mulct, overcharge, pluck, rifle, rip off*, rob, rook*, rope in*, run a game on*, sell a bill of goods*, shaft*, strip, swindle, take for a ride*, take to the cleaners*; SEE CONCEPTS *59,139,342*

fleecy [adj] *downy, woolly; like a lamb's coat*
floccose, flocculent, fluffy, hairy, hirsute, lanose, pileous, pilose, shaggy, soft, whiskered; SEE CONCEPT *606*

fleet [n] *group of ships*
argosy, armada, flotilla, formation, line, naval force, navy, sea power, squadron, tonnage, vessels, warships; SEE CONCEPTS *322,432,506*

fleet [adj] *quick in movement*
agile, barreling, breakneck*, brisk, expeditious, expeditive, fast, flying, hasty, in nothing flat*, like greased lightning*, lively, mercurial, meteoric, nimble, nimble-footed, on the double*, rapid, screaming, speedball*, speedy, swift, winged; SEE CONCEPTS *584,588*

fleeting [adj] *brief, transient*
cursory, ephemeral, evanescent, fading, flash in the pan*, flitting, flying, fugacious, fugitive, impermanent, meteoric, momentary, passing, short, short-lived, sudden, temporary, transitory, vanishing, volatile; SEE CONCEPTS *551,798*

flesh [n1] *body tissue, skin*
beef, brawn, cells, corpuscles, fat, fatness, flesh and blood, food, meat, muscle, plasm, plasma, protoplasm, sinews, thews, weight; SEE CONCEPT *392*

flesh [n2] *humankind*
animality, carnality, homo sapiens, humanity, human nature, human race, living creatures, mortality, people, physicality, physical nature, race, sensuality, stock, world; SEE CONCEPTS *407,417*

fleshly [adv1] *lecherous, desiring sex*
animal, animalistic, bodily, carnal, erotic, gross, lascivious, lewd, lustful, profane, sensual, venereal, voluptuous; SEE CONCEPTS *372,529,545*

fleshly [adv2] *bodily*
corporal, corporeal, earthly, human, material,

mundane, of this world, physical, secular, somatic, terrestrial, worldly; SEE CONCEPT 536

fleshy [adj] overweight
adipose, ample, beefy*, brawny, chubby*, chunky*, corpulent, fat, gross, heavy, hefty, husky, meaty*, obese, plump, porcine, portly, pudgy*, pulpy, sarcous, stout, tubby*, weighty, well-padded*, zaftig*; SEE CONCEPTS 406, 491,773

flex [v] bend
angle, contract, crook, curve, lean, mold, ply, spring, stretch, tighten, tilt, yield; SEE CONCEPTS 147,149

flexibility [n] elasticity, adaptability
adjustability, affability, complaisance, compliance, docility, extensibility, flaccidity, flexibleness, give, limberness, litheness, plasticity, pliability, pliancy, resilience, springiness, suppleness, tensility, tractability; SEE CONCEPTS 652,731

flexible [adj1] pliable, bendable
adjustable, bending, ductile, elastic, extensible, extensile, flexile, formable, formative, impressionable, like putty*, limber, lithe, malleable, moldable, plastic, pliant, soft, spongy, springy, stretch, stretchable, stretchy, supple, tensile, tractable, tractile, whippy*, willowy, yielding; SEE CONCEPTS 485,488

flexible [adj2] adaptable, responsive
acquiescent, adjustable, amenable, biddable, complaisant, compliant, discretionary, docile, gentle, going every which way*, hanging loose*, like putty in hands*, manageable, open, rolling with punches*, tractable, variable; SEE CONCEPTS 401,542

flicker [n] spark, glimmer
beam, flare, flash, gleam, oscillation, quivering, ray, scintillation, twinkle, vibration, SEE CONCEPTS 145,624,831

flicker [v] sparkle, flutter
blare, blaze, blink, burn, dance, flare, flash, flit, flitter, fluctuate, glance, gleam, glimmer, glint, glitter, glow, hover, oscillate, quaver, quiver, scintillate, shimmer, swing, tremble, twinkle, vibrate, waver; SEE CONCEPTS 152,624

flight [n1] flying; journey
aerial navigation, aeronautics, arrival, aviation, avigation, departure, gliding, hop, jump, mounting, navigation, shuttle, soaring, take-off, transport, trip, volitation, voyage, winging; SEE CONCEPT 224

flight [n2] fleeing; departure
beat*, break*, breakout, escape, escapement, escaping, exfiltration, exit, exodus, fugue, getaway, getaway car*, lam, out*, powder*, retreat, retreating, running away, slip*; SEE CONCEPTS 102,195

flightiness [n] irresponsibility
airheadedness*, capriciousness, changeability, dizziness, fickleness, flippancy, frivolity, giddiness, inconstancy, instability, levity, lightness, mercurialism, variability, volatility, whimsicality, whimsicalness; SEE CONCEPT 633

flighty [adj] fickle, irresponsible
airheaded*, birdbrained*, bubbleheaded*, capricious, changeable, dingbat*, dingdong*, dizzy*, effervescent, empty-headed, featherbrained*, frivolous, gaga*, giddy, harebrained*, impetuous, impulsive, inconstant, lightheaded, lively, mercurial, scatterbrained, silly, thoughtless, twit, unbal-

anced, unstable, unsteady, volatile, whimsical, wild; SEE CONCEPT 401

flimsy [adj1] not strong; light, thin
chiffon, cut-rate*, decrepit, defective, delicate, diaphanous, feeble, fragile, frail, gauzy, gossamer, house of cards*, inadequate, infirm, insubstantial, meager, papery, rickety, rinkydink*, shaky, shallow, sheer, slapdash*, sleazy, slight, superficial, tacky, transparent, unsound, unsubstantial, weak, wobbly; SEE CONCEPTS 489,606

flimsy [adj2] unconvincing, implausible
assailable, baseless, contemptible, controvertible, fallacious, false, feeble, frivolous, groundless, illogical, improbable, inadequate, inane, inconceivable, incredible, inept, lame, poor, puerile, superficial, thin, transparent, trifling, trivial, unbelievable, ungrounded, unpersuasive, unreasonable, unsatisfactory, unsubstantial, weak, weakly, wishful; SEE CONCEPT 267

flinch [v] shy away, wince
avoid, balk, blanch, blench, blink, cower, cringe, crouch, draw back, duck, elude, escape, eschew, evade, flee, quail, recede, recoil, retire, retreat, shirk, shrink, shun, start, swerve, withdraw; SEE CONCEPTS 102,150

fling [n1] casual throw
cast, chuck, firing, heave, hurl, launching, lob, peg, pitch, shot, slinging, toss; SEE CONCEPT 222

fling [n2] unrestrained behavior
affair, attempt, binge, celebration, crack*, essay, fun, gamble, go*, good time, indulgence, orgy, party, rampage, shot*, splurge, spree, stab*, trial, try, venture, whirl; SEE CONCEPT 386

fling [v] throw with abandon
cast, catapult, chuck*, dump, fire, heave, hurl, jerk, launch, let fly*, lob, peg*, pitch, precipitate, propel, send, shy*, sling, toss; SEE CONCEPT 222

flip [n/v] throw, jump with abandon
cast, chuck, flick, jerk, pitch, snap, spin, toss, twist; SEE CONCEPTS 194,222

flippancy [n] irreverence
archness, cheek, cheekiness, cockiness, disrespectfulness, flightiness, freshness, frivolity, impertinence, impishness, impudence, levity, lightness, mischievousness, pertness, playfulness, roguishness, rudeness, sauciness, volatility, waggishness; SEE CONCEPT 633

flippant [adj] irreverent
brassy, breezy, cheeky*, cocky, disrespectful, flighty, flip*, fresh, frivolous, glib, impertinent, impudent, insolent, lippy*, nervy*, offhand, pert, playful, rude, sassy*, smart*, smart-alecky*, superficial; SEE CONCEPT 401

flirt [n] person who makes advances
coquette, cruiser*, heartbreaker, operator*, philanderer, player, seducer, siren, swinger, tease, trifler, vamp, vixen, wanton, wolf*; SEE CONCEPT 423

flirt [v] make advances toward someone
banter, bat eyes at*, come hither*, come on*, coquet, dally, disport, eyeball*, fool, gam*, hit on*, lead on, linger with, make a move*, make a pass*, ogle, philander, pick up*, pitch*, proposition, tease, wink at*; SEE CONCEPTS 375,384

flirtation [n] amorous advance
amour, coquetry, courting, cruising, dalliance, flirting, intrigue, pickup*, romance, romancing, tease, teasing, toying*, trifling*; SEE CONCEPTS 32,375,384

fl
fl

flirtatious [*adj*] *provocative, teasing*
amorous, arch, come-hither*, come-on*, coquettish, coy, dallying, enticing, flirty, libidinous,
spoony*, sportive; SEE CONCEPTS **401,404**

flit [*v*] *flutter, move rapidly*
dance, dart, flash, fleet, flicker, float, fly, hover,
hurry, pass, run, rush, sail, scud*, skim, speed,
sweep, whisk, whiz, wing, zip; SEE CONCEPT **150**

float [*v*] *lie on the surface*
be buoyant, bob, drift, glide, hang, hover, move
gently, poise, rest on water, ride, sail, skim, slide,
slip along, smooth along, stay afloat, swim, waft,
wash; SEE CONCEPT **153**

flock [*n*] *congregation*
army, assembly, bevy, brood, cloud, collection,
colony, company, convoy, crowd, crush, drift,
drove, flight, gaggle, gathering, group, herd, host,
legion, litter, mass, multitude, pack, progeny,
rout, scores, skein, throng; SEE CONCEPTS
391,432

flock [*v*] *congregate*
collect, converge, crowd, gather, group, herd,
huddle, mass, throng, troop; SEE CONCEPTS
109,384

flog [*v*] *whip, lash*
beat, belt, cane, castigate, chastise, ferule, flagellate, flax, flay, give the cat o'nine tails*, hide, hit,
larrup, lather, leather*, paddle, scourge, spank,
strike, stripe, tan one's hide*, thrash, trounce,
wax*, whack, whale*, whomp*, whop*; SEE
CONCEPT **189**

flood [*n*] *overwhelming flow, quantity*
abundance, alluvion, bore, bounty, cataclysm,
cataract, current, deluge, downpour, drencher,
drift, eager, excess, flow, flux, freshet, glut, inundation, multitude, niagara, outgushing, outpouring, overflow, plenty, pour, profusion, rush,
spate, stream, superabundance, superfluity, surge,
surplus, tide, torrent, tsunami, wave; SEE CON-
CEPTS **179,524,787**

flood [*v*] *inundate or submerge*
brim over, choke, deluge, drown, engulf, fill,
flow, glut, gush, immerse, overflow, oversupply,
overwhelm, pour over, rush, saturate, surge,
swamp, swarm, sweep, whelm; SEE CONCEPTS
179,209,740

floor [*n*] *bottom of a room; level of a multistory
building*
basement, boards, canvas, carpet, cellar, deck,
downstairs, flat, flooring, ground, landing, lowest
point, mat, mezzanine, nadir, rug, stage, story,
tier, upstairs; SEE CONCEPT **440**

floor [*v*] *perplex, confound*
baffle, beat, bewilder, bowl over*, bring down*,
bring up short*, conquer, defeat, discomfit, disconcert, down, drop, dumbfound, fell, flatten,
ground, knock down, lay low*, level, nonplus,
overthrow, prostrate, puzzle, stump, throw; SEE
CONCEPTS **16,95**

flop [*n*] *miserable failure*
bomb, bust, debacle, disaster, dud*, fiasco, lemon*, loser, miscarriage, nonstarter, washout*;
SEE CONCEPTS **674,699**

flop [*v1*] *fall limply, collapse*
dangle, droop, drop, flag, flap, flounder, flutter,
hang, jerk, lop, quiver, sag, slump, stagger, teeter, topple, toss, totter, tumble, wave, wiggle;
SEE CONCEPTS **144,181**

flop [*v2*] *fail miserably*
bomb*, close, come apart*, come to nothing*,

fall flat*, fall short*, flummox, fold, founder, miscarry, misfire, wash out*; SEE CONCEPT **699**

floral [*adj*] *decorated with flowers*
blooming, blossoming, blossomy, botanic, decorative, dendritic, efflorescent, flower-patterned,
flowery, herbaceous, sylvan, verdant; SEE CON-
CEPT **589**

florid [*adj1*] *very elaborate*
aureate, baroque, busy, decorative, embellished,
euphuistic, figurative, flamboyant, flowery, fussy,
garnished, grandiloquent, high-flown, luscious,
magniloquent, ornamental, ornamented, ornate,
overblown, pretentious, rhetorical, rich, sonorous;
SEE CONCEPTS **267,589**

florid [*adj2*] *flushed, ruddy*
blowzy, flush, glowing, high-colored, pink, reddened, rubicund, sanguine; SEE CONCEPTS
406,618

flounce [*v*] *bounce; intermittently move*
fling, jerk, mince, nancy, prance, sashay, spring,
stamp, storm, strut, swish, throw, toss; SEE CON-
CEPT **149**

flounder [*v*] *struggle; be in the dark*
blunder, bobble, cast about, come apart at the
seams*, drop the ball*, fall down, flop, flummox,
foul up*, fumble, go at backwards*, go to pieces*,
grope, labor, lurch, make a mess of, miss one's
cue*, muddle, plunge, pratfall*, screw up*, slip
up*, snafu*, strive, stub one's toe*, stumble,
thrash, toil, toss, travail, trip up*, tumble, wallow, work at; SEE CONCEPTS **101,699**

flourish [*n*] *curlicue, decoration*
curl, embellishment, furbelow, garnish, ornamentation, plume, quirk, spiral, sweep, twist; SEE
CONCEPTS **259,284**

flourish [*v1*] *grow, prosper*
amplify, arrive, augment, batten, bear fruit, be on
top of heap*, bloom, blossom, boom, burgeon,
come along, develop, do well, expand, flower, get
ahead, get on*, go, go great guns*, hit it big*,
increase, live high on hog*, make out*, multiply,
score, succeed, thrive, wax; SEE CONCEPTS
141,704,706

flourish [*v2*] *wave about*
brandish, display, flaunt, flutter, shake, sweep,
swing, swish, twirl, vaunt, wag, wield; SEE CON-
CEPTS **147,152**

flourishing [*adj*] *prospering, going well*
blooming, burgeoning, doing well, expanding, exuberant, going strong, growing, in full swing*, in
the pink*, in top form*, lush, luxuriant, mush-
rooming, profuse, prosperous, rampant, rank,
rich, roaring, robust, successful, thriving, vigorous; SEE CONCEPT **528**

flout [*v*] *show contempt for*
affront, defy, deride, disregard, gibe, gird, insult,
jeer, laugh at, mock, outrage, quip, repudiate, ridicule, scoff, scorn, slight, sneer, spurn, taunt,
thumb nose at*; SEE CONCEPT **54**

flow [*n*] *issue, abundance*
breeze, continuance, continuation, continuity,
course, current, deluge, discharge, draft, draw,
dribble, drift, ebb, effusion, electricity, emanation, flood, flux, gush, juice, leakage, movement,
oozing, outflow, outpouring, plenty, plethora,
progress, progression, river, run, sequence, series, spate, spout, spurt, stream, succession, tide,
train, wind; SEE CONCEPTS **146,179,467,787**

flow [*v*] *issue, surge, run out*
abound, arise, brim, cascade, circulate, continue,

course, deluge, discharge, disembogue, dribble, ebb, emanate, emerge, emit, exudate, exude, flood, glide, gurgle, gush, inundate, jet, leak, move, ooze, overflow, pass, percolate, pour, proceed, progress, pullulate, regurgitate, result, ripple, roll, rush, slide, sluice, smooth along, spew, spill, splash, spring, spurt, sputter, squirt, stream, sweep, swell, swirl, teem, trickle, tumble, void, well forth; SEE CONCEPTS *146,179*

flower [n1] *bloom of a plant*
annual, blossom, bud, cluster, efflorescence, floret, floweret, head, herb, inflorescence, perennial, pompon, posy, shoot, spike, spray, vine; SEE CONCEPTS *425,428*

flower [n2] *best, choicest part*
cream, elite, finest point, freshness, greatest point, height, pick, pride, prime, prize, top; SEE CONCEPTS *668,829*

flower [v] *bloom, flourish*
batten, blossom, blow, burgeon, effloresce, mature, open, outbloom, prosper, thrive, unfold; SEE CONCEPTS *253,704*

flowery [adj] *ornate, especially referring to speech or writing*
aureate, baroque, bombastic, declamatory, diffuse, embellished, euphemistic, euphuistic, fancy, figurative, florid, grandiloquent, high-flown, magniloquent, ornamented, overwrought, prolix, purple, redundant, rhetorical, rococo, sonorous, swollen, verbose, windy, wordy; SEE CONCEPTS *267,589*

flowing [adj] *gushing, abounding*
brimming, continuous, cursive, easy, falling, flooded, fluent, fluid, fluidic, full, issuing, liquefied, liquid, overrun, pouring out, prolific, rich, rippling, rolling, running, rushing, sinuous, smooth, spouting, streaming, sweeping, teeming, tidal, unbroken, uninterrupted; SEE CONCEPTS *482,584*

fluctuate [v] *vacillate, change*
alter, alternate, be undecided, blow hot and cold*, ebb and flow, flutter, go up and down*, hem and haw*, hesitate, oscillate, vary, veer, vibrate, wave, waver, yo-yo*; SEE CONCEPTS *13,469,697*

fluent [adj] *articulate*
chatty, cogent, copious, cursive, declamatory, disputatious, easy, effortless, effusive, eloquent, facile, flowing, garrulous, glib, liquid, loquacious, mellifluent, mellifluous, natural, persuasive, prompt, quick, ready, running, silver-tongued*, smooth, smooth-spoken, talkative, verbose, vocal, voluble, well-versed, wordy; SEE CONCEPTS *267,529*

fluffy [adj] *soft, furry*
creamy, downy, featherlike, feathery, fleecy, flocculent, flossy, gossamer, linty, pile, silky, velutinous; SEE CONCEPT *606*

fluid [n] *liquid*
agua, broth, chaser, cooler, goo*, goop*, juice, liquor, solution, vapor; SEE CONCEPT *467*

fluid [adj1] *liquid*
aqueous, flowing, fluent, in solution, juicy, liquefied, lymphatic, melted, molten, running, runny, serous, uncongealed, watery; SEE CONCEPTS *603,757*

fluid [adj2] *adaptable, changeable*
adjustable, changeful, flexible, floating, fluctuating, indefinite, malleable, mercurial, mobile, mu-

table, protean, shifting, unsettled, unstable, unsteady, variable; SEE CONCEPTS *534,542*

fluke [n] *chance occurrence*
accident, blessing, break, contingency, fortuity, fortunate, fortune, good fortune*, good luck, incident, lucky break*, odd chance, quirk, stroke of luck*, windfall; SEE CONCEPTS *4,679,693*

fluky [adj] *chance*
accidental, casual, chancy, coincidental, contingent, fortuitous, incalculable, incidental, lucky, odd, uncertain, variable; SEE CONCEPT *552*

flurry [n] *commotion, burst*
ado, agitation, brouhaha, bustle, confusion, disturbance, excitement, ferment, flap*, flaw, fluster, flutter, furor, fuss, gust, haste, hurry, outbreak, pother, spell, spurt, squall, stir*, to-do, tumult, turbulence, turmoil, whirl, whirlwind; SEE CONCEPTS *230,524*

flurry [v] *agitate, confuse*
bewilder, bother, bustle, discombobulate*, discompose, disconcert, disquiet, distract, disturb, excite, fluster, flutter, frustrate, fuss, galvanize, hassle, hurry, hustle, perplex, perturb, provoke, quicken, rattle, ruffle, stimulate, unhinge, unsettle, upset; SEE CONCEPTS *7,19*

flush [n] *blush*
bloom, color, freshness, glow, pinkness, redness, rosiness, ruddiness; SEE CONCEPT *622*

flush [adj1] *flat*
even, horizontal, level, planate, plane, smooth, square, true; SEE CONCEPTS *486,490*

flush [adj2] *overflowing, abundant*
affluent, close, full, generous, lavish, liberal, opulent, prodigal, rich, wealthy, well-off; SEE CONCEPTS *334,771*

flush [v1] *become or make pink or red*
blush, burn, color, color up, crimson, flame, glow, go red, mantle, pink, pinken, redden, rose, rouge, suffuse; SEE CONCEPTS *250,469*

flush [v2] *inundate with liquid*
cleanse, douche, drench, eject, expel, flood, hose, rinse, swab, wash; SEE CONCEPTS *165,179*

flushed [adj] *pink, glowing*
ablaze, animated, aroused, blushing, burning, crimson, elated, embarrassed, enthused, exhilarated, feverish, florid, full-blooded, high, hot, inspired, intoxicated, red, rosy, rubicund, ruddy, sanguine, thrilled; SEE CONCEPTS *401,403,618*

fluster [n] *perturbation, upset*
agitation, brouhaha, commotion, disturbance, dither, flap*, flurry, flutter, furor, ruffle, state*, to-do*, turmoil; SEE CONCEPT *410*

fluster [v] *upset, perturb*
addle, agitate, bewilder, bother, confound, confuse, craze*, discombobulate*, discompose, disquiet, distract, disturb, excite, flip*, flurry, frustrate, fuddle*, get to*, hassle, heat*, hurry, make nervous, make waves*, muddle, mystify, nonplus, perplex, psych*, puzzle, rattle, ruffle, spook*, stir up*, throw off balance*, unhinge*, work up*; SEE CONCEPTS *7,16,19*

flutter [v] *wave rapidly, flap*
agitate, bat, beat, dance, drift, flicker, flit, flitter, flop, fluctuate, hover, lop, oscillate, palpitate, pulsate, quaver, quiver, ripple, ruffle, shake, shiver, swing, throb, tremble, vibrate, wiggle, wobble; SEE CONCEPTS *150,152*

flux [n] *state of constant change*
alteration, change, flow, fluctuation, fluidity, in-

stability, modification, motion, mutability, mutation, transition, unrest; SEE CONCEPT 697

fly [v1] *take to the air, usually employing wings*
aviate, barnstorm*, bend the throttle*, buzz*, circle, circumnavigate, climb, control, cross, dart, dash, dive, drift, flat-hat*, fleet, flit, float, flutter, glide, hop, hover, hurry, jet, jet out, jet over, maneuver, mount, operate, pilot, reach, remain aloft, rush, sail, scud*, seagull*, shoot, skim, skirt, sky out*, soar, speed, swoop, take a hop*, take flight, take off, take wing, travel, whisk*, whiz*, whoosh*, wing*, wing in*, zip*, zoom*; SEE CONCEPTS 148,150,224

fly [v2] *run or pass swiftly*
barrel, bolt, breeze, career, dart, dash, elapse, flee, flit, glide, go like the wind*, hasten, hurry, hustle, make off*, pass, race, roll, run its course*, rush, scamper, scoot, shoot, slip away*, speed, sprint, tear, whiz*, zoom*; SEE CONCEPTS 150,818

fly [v3] *escape, flee*
abscond, avoid, bolt, break, clear, clear out*, cut and run*, decamp, disappear, get away, hasten away, hide, hightail*, light out*, make a getaway*, make a quick exit*, make off, run*, run for it, run from, skedaddle*, skip, steal away, take flight, take off, withdraw; SEE CONCEPTS 102,195

fly-by-night [adj] *undependable*
brief, cowboy*, dubious, here-today-gone-tomorrow*, impermanent, questionable, shady, shifty, short-lived, slimy*, slippery*, treacherous, trustless, unreliable, unsure, untrustworthy; SEE CONCEPTS 542,551

flyer [n] *person who navigates an aircraft*
ace*, air person, aviator, flier, jet*, navigator, pilot; SEE CONCEPT 348

flying [adj] *in the air, winged*
aerial, aeronautical, airborne, avian, drifting, express, flapping, fleet, floating, fluttering, gliding, hovering, mercurial, mobile, on the wing, plumed, soaring, speedy, streaming, swooping, volant, volar, volitant, waving, winging, zooming; SEE CONCEPT 584

foam [n] *bubbles formed from a liquid*
cream, fluff, froth, head, lather, scum, spray, spume, suds, surf, yeast; SEE CONCEPT 260

foam [v] *become bubbly*
aerate, boil, burble, effervesce, ferment, fizz, froth, gurgle, hiss, lather, seethe, simmer, sparkle; SEE CONCEPTS 170,469

foamy [adj] *bubbly*
barmy, boiling, burbling, carbonated, creamy, ebullient, effervescent, fermented, fizzy, frothy, lathery, scummy*, seething, simmering, spumescent, spumous, spumy, sudsy, yeasty; SEE CONCEPT 485

focus [n] *center of attraction*
bull's eye*, center, core, cynosure, focal point, headquarters*, heart, hub, limelight*, locus, meeting place, nerve center*, point of convergence, polestar, seat, spotlight, target; SEE CONCEPTS 532,826,829

focus [v] *aim attention at*
adjust, attract, bring out, center, centralize, concenter, concentrate, convene, converge, direct, fasten, fix, fixate, get detail, home in*, home in on*, hone in*, join, key on*, knuckle down*, meet, move in, pinpoint, pour it on*, put, rivet,

sharpen, spotlight*, sweat*, zero in*, zoom in*; SEE CONCEPTS 17,623

foe [n] *person who is an opponent*
adversary, antagonist, anti*, enemy, hostile party, rival; SEE CONCEPT 412

fog [n1] *heavy mist that reduces visibility*
brume, cloud, effluvium, film, gloom, grease, ground clouds, haze, London fog, miasma, murk, murkiness, nebula, obscurity, pea soup*, smaze, smog, smoke, smother, soup*, steam, vapor, visibility zero-zero*, wisp; SEE CONCEPTS 524,627

fog [n2] *mental unclarity*
befuddlement, blindness, confusion, daze, haze, maze, mist, muddledness, muddlement, obscurity, perplexity, stupor, trance, vagueness; SEE CONCEPT 410

fog [v] *muddle, obscure*
addle, becloud, bedim, befuddle, bewilder, blind, blur, cloud, confuse, darken, daze, dim, eclipse, mist, muddy, mystify, obfuscate, perplex, puzzle, steam up, stupefy; SEE CONCEPTS 250,526

foggy [adj] *hazy, obscure*
blurred, ceiling zero*, closed in, clouded, cloudy, dark, dim, filmy, fogged in, fuzzy, gray, indistinct, misty, murky, mushy, nebulous, pea-soupy*, smazy, smoggy, socked in*, soupy*, unclear, vague, vaporous, vapory, zero-zero*; SEE CONCEPTS 403,525

foible [n] *personal imperfection*
characteristic, defect, eccentricity, failing, fault, frailty, idiosyncrasy, infirmity, kink, mannerism, oddity, peculiarity, quirk, shortcoming, singularity, vice, weakness, weak point; SEE CONCEPTS 411,644

foil [n] *contrast*
antithesis, background, complement, counterblow, defense, guard, setting; SEE CONCEPT 665

foil [v] *circumvent, nip in the bud*
baffle, balk, beat, bilk, bollix*, buffalo*, check, checkmate, counter, crab, cramp, crimp, curb, dash, defeat, disappoint, disconcert, ditch, dodge, duck, elude, faze, foul up*, frustrate, get around*, give the run-around*, give the slip*, hang up*, hinder, juke, nullify, outwit, prevent, rattle, restrain, run circles around*, run rings around*, shake, shake off, shuffle off, skip, stop, stymie, throw monkey wrench in*, thwart, upset the apple cart*; SEE CONCEPTS 121,130

fold [n] *double thickness*
bend, circumvolution, cockle, convolution, corrugation, crease, crimp, crinkle, dog's ear*, flection, flexure, furrow, gather, gathering, groove, knife-edge*, lap, lapel, layer, loop, overlap, plait, pleat, plica, plication, plicature, ply, pucker, ridge, rimple, rivel, ruche, ruck, ruffle, rumple, shirring, smocking, tuck, turn, wrinkle; SEE CONCEPT 754

fold [v1] *lay in creases*
bend, cockle, corrugate, crimp, crisp, crumple, curl, dog-ear*, double, double over, furrow, gather, groove, hem, intertwine, knit, lap, overlap, overlay, plait, pleat, plicate, pucker, purse, replicate, ridge, ruche, ruck, ruffle, telescope, tuck, turn under, wrinkle; SEE CONCEPT 184

fold [v2] *encase, enclose*
do up, enfold, entwine, envelop, involve, wrap, wrap up; SEE CONCEPT 209

fold [v3] *fail, close*
become insolvent, be ruined, break, bust, collapse, crash, crumple, give, go bankrupt, go bust,

go into Chapter 11*, go under*, impoverish, pauper, pauperize, shut down, yield; SEE CONCEPTS 324,699

folder [n] *paper envelope for holding items*
binder, case, file, pocket, portfolio, sheath, wrapper, wrapping; SEE CONCEPT 260

foliage [n] *leaves*
frondescence, greenness, growth, herbage, leafage, umbrage, vegetation, verdure; SEE CONCEPT 428

folk [n] *person's relations, acquaintances*
body politic, clan, community, confederation, culture group, ethnic group, family, general public, group, house, household, inhabitants, kin, kindred, lineage, masses, ménage, nation, nationality, people, population, proletariat, public, race, settlement, society, state, stock, tribe; SEE CONCEPTS 296,379

folklore [n] *tales from the past*
ballad, custom, fable, folk story, legend, myth, mythology, mythos, oral literature, superstition, tradition, wisdom; SEE CONCEPT 282

follow [v1] *take the place of*
be subsequent to, chase, come after, come from, come next, displace, ensue, go after, go next, postdate, proceed from, pursue, replace, result, spring from, succeed, supersede, supervene, supplant; SEE CONCEPTS 128,242,813

follow [v2] *trail, pursue physically*
accompany, attend, bring up the rear*, catenate, chase, come with, concatenate, convoy, dog*, dog the footsteps of*, draggle, escort, freeze, give chase, go after, go with, hound*, hunt, onto*, persecute, put a tail on*, run after, run down, schlepp along*, search, seek, shadow, shag*, spook*, stalk, stick to, string along*, tag, tag after*, tag along*, tail, tailgate*, take out after, track; SEE CONCEPT 207

follow [v3] *act in accordance with*
abide by, accord, adhere to, adopt, attend, be consistent with, be devoted to, be guided by, be in keeping, be interested in, comply, conform, copy, cultivate, do like, emulate, follow suit, give allegiance to, harmonize, heed, hold fast, imitate, keep, keep abreast of, keep an eye on, live up to, match, mimic, mind, mirror, model on, note, obey, observe, pattern oneself upon, reflect, regard, serve, string along*, support, take after, take as an example, watch; SEE CONCEPTS 8,91,171

follow [v4] *understand*
accept, appreciate, apprehend, catch*, catch on*, comprehend, dig*, fathom, get*, get the picture*, grasp, realize, see, take in*; SEE CONCEPT 15

follower [n] *person who believes or has great interest*
addict, adherent, admirer, advocate, apostle, attendant, backer, believer, bootlicker*, buff, client, cohort, companion, convert, copycat, devotee, disciple, fan, fancier, freak*, habitué, hanger-on*, helper, imitator, lackey*, member, minion, parasite, participant, partisan, patron, promoter, proselyte, protégé, pupil, representative, satellite, sectary, servant, sidekick, stooge*, supporter, sycophant, toady*, vassal, votary, worshiper, zealot; SEE CONCEPTS 352,366,423

following [n] *persons of an interest or belief*
adherents, audience, circle, clientage, clientele, cortege, coterie, dependents, entourage, fans, group, groupies*, hangers-on*, patronage, patrons, public, retinue, rout, suite, support, supporters, train; SEE CONCEPTS 294,387,417

following [adj] *happening, being next or after*
after a while, afterward, attendant, a while later, back, by and by, coming, coming after, coming next, consecutive, consequent, consequential, directly after, ensuing, henceforth, hinder, in pursuit, in search of, in the wake of, later, later on, latter, next, next off*, on the scent*, posterior, presently, proximate, pursuing, rear, resulting, sequent, sequential, serial, seriate, specified, subsequent, succeeding, successive, supervenient, then, trailing, when; SEE CONCEPTS 585,811,818,820

follow through [v] *bring to a conclusion*
complete, conclude, consummate, pursue, see through; SEE CONCEPT 91

follow up [v] *make inquiries*
check out, find out about, investigate, look into, make sure, pursue; SEE CONCEPT 103

folly [n] *nonsense, ridiculous idea*
absurdity, craziness, daftness, dottiness, dumb thing to do*, dumb trick*, fatuity, foolishness, idiocy, imbecility, impracticality, imprudence, inadvisability, inanity, indiscretion, irrationality, lunacy, madness, obliquity, preposterousness, rashness, recklessness, senselessness, silliness, stupidity, triviality, unsoundness, vice, witlessness; SEE CONCEPTS 410,633

foment [v] *instigate, provoke*
abet, agitate, clutch, arouse, brew, cultivate, encourage, excite, fan the flames*, foster, goad, incite, nurse, nurture, promote, quicken, raise, set, set on, sow the seeds*, spur, start, stimulate, stir up, whip up*; SEE CONCEPTS 14,221

fond [adj] *have a liking or taste for*
addicted, adoring, affectionate, amorous, attached, caring, devoted, doting, enamored, indulgent, keen on, lovesome, lovey-dovey*, loving, mushy*, partial, predisposed, responsive, romantic, sentimental, silly over, sympathetic, tender, warm; SEE CONCEPTS 32,542

fondle [v] *touch lovingly*
bear hug*, caress, clutch, cosset, cuddle, dandle, embrace, feel, fool around*, grab, grope, hug, love, make love to, neck, nestle, nuzzle, pat, paw, pet, play footsie*, snuggle, squeeze, stroke; SEE CONCEPTS 190,375

fondness [n] *liking or taste for*
affection, attachment, devotion, fancy, kindness, love, partiality, penchant, predilection, preference, soft spot, susceptibility, tenderness, weakness; SEE CONCEPT 32

food [n] *edible material*
aliment, bite*, board, bread, cheer, chow*, comestible, cookery, cooking, cuisine, diet, drink, eatable, eats*, entrée, fare, fast food, feed, fodder*, foodstuff, goodies*, grit*, groceries*, grub*, handout*, home cooking, keep, larder, meal, meat, menu, mess*, moveable feast, nourishment, nutriment, nutrition, pabulum, provision, ration, refreshment, slop*, snack, store, subsistence, support, sustenance, table, take out, tuck, viand, victual, vittles*; SEE CONCEPTS 457,460,461

food court [n] *public area where variety of food is sold*
cafe, counter, fast food, food festival, restaurant, smorgasbord; SEE CONCEPTS 439,448,449

fool [n] *stupid or ridiculous person*
ass, birdbrain*, blockhead*, bonehead*, boob*,

fl
fo

bore, buffoon, clod*, clown, cretin*, dimwit*, dolt*, dope*, dumb ox*, dunce, dunderhead*, easy mark*, fair game*, fathead*, goose*, halfwit, idiot, ignoramus, illiterate, imbecile, innocent, jerk*, lamebrain*, lightweight*, loon*, moron, nerd*, nincompoop*, ninny*, nitwit, numskull*, oaf, sap*, schlemiel*, silly, simpleton, stooge*, sucker*, turkey*, twerp*, twit*, victim; SEE CONCEPTS 412,423

fool [v] *trick, mislead*
bamboozle*, bluff, cheat, chicane, con, deceive, delude, diddle, dupe, fake out*, flimflam*, fox*, gull, hoax, hoodwink*, jive*, juke*, kid, lead on, make believe, outfox, play-act*, play a trick on, pretend, put on, put one over on*, scam*, snow*, spoof*, suck in*, take in*, trifle; SEE CONCEPT 59

fool around [v] *waste time*
dawdle, hang around*, idle, kill time*, lark, mess around*, play around*; SEE CONCEPT 681

fooled [adj] *tricked*
bamboozled*, conned, deceived, deluded, duped, flimflammed*, hornswoggled*, misled, outfoxed*, snowed*, sucked in*; SEE CONCEPT 537

foolhardy [adj] *impetuous, rash*
adventuresome, adventurous, audacious, bold, breakneck*, daredevil, daring, devil-may-care*, harebrained*, headstrong, imprudent, incautious, irresponsible, madcap, off deep end*, out on limb*, precipitate, reckless, temerarious, venturesome, venturous, wide open; SEE CONCEPT 401

fooling [n] *joking, tricks*
bluffing, buffoonery, clownishness, farce, frolicking, high jinks*, horseplay, jesting, joshing, kidding, making light*, mockery, nonsense, pretense, roughhouse*, roughhousing*, rowdiness, sham*, skylarking*, spoofing, teasing, trifling; SEE CONCEPT 59

foolish [adj] *nonsensical, idiotic*
absurd, asinine, brainless, cockamamy*, crazy, daffy*, daft, dippy*, doltish*, dotty*, fantastic, fatuous, feebleminded*, half-baked*, halfwitted*, harebrained*, ill-advised, ill-considered, imbecile, imprudent, incautious, indiscreet, injudicious, insane, irrational, jerky*, kooky*, loony*, ludicrous, lunatic, mad, moronic, nerdy*, nutty*, preposterous, ridiculous, senseless, shortsighted, silly, simple, stupid, unintelligent, unreasonable, unwise, wacky*, weak, witless, zany*; SEE CONCEPTS 401,542,544

foolishly [adv] *idiotic, without due consideration*
absurdly, ill-advisedly, imprudently, incautiously, indiscreetly, injudiciously, mistakenly, shortsightedly, stupidly, unwisely; SEE CONCEPTS 401,542,544

foolishness [n] *idiocy, nonsense*
absurdity, absurdness, bunk*, carrying-on*, claptrap*, craziness, dumb trick*, folly, foolery, fool trick, horse feathers*, impracticality, imprudence, inanity, indiscretion, insanity, insensibility, irrationality, irresponsibility, ludicrousness, lunacy, mistake, poppycock*, preposterousness, rubbish*, senselessness, silliness, stupidity, tommyrot*, twaddle, unreasonableness, unwiseness, weakness, witlessness; SEE CONCEPT 633

foot [n1] *extremity of an animate being*
hoof, pad, paw; SEE CONCEPT 392

foot [n2] *base of an object*
bottom, foundation, lowest point, nadir, pier; SEE CONCEPT 442

foot [n3] *twelve inches/30.48 centimeters measured*
cubic, square; SEE CONCEPTS 790,791

footing [n1] *foundation, basis*
basement, bedrock, bottom, establishment, foot, foothold, ground, groundwork, infrastructure, installation, resting place, seat, seating, settlement, substratum, substructure, underpinning, understructure, warrant; SEE CONCEPTS 442,661

footing [n2] *social status*
capacity, character, condition, grade, place, position, rank, relations, relationship, situation, standing, state, station, terms; SEE CONCEPT 388

for [conj] *in consequence of the fact that*
as, as long as, because, being, considering, inasmuch as, now, since, whereas; SEE CONCEPT 544

for [prep] *in consideration of*
after, as, beneficial to, concerning, conducive to, during, for the sake of, in contemplation of, in exchange for, in favor of, in furtherance of, in order to, in order to get, in place of, in pursuance of, in spite of, in the direction of, in the interest of, in the name of, notwithstanding, on the part of, on the side of, pro, supposing, to, to counterbalance, to go to, to the amount of, to the extent of, toward, under the authority of, with a view to, with regard to, with respect; SEE CONCEPT 544

forage [v] *search madly for*
beat, cast about, comb, explore, fine-toothcomb*, grub, hunt, pilfer, plunder, raid, rake, ransack, ravage, rummage, scour, scrounge, seek; SEE CONCEPT 216

foray [n] *incursion, attempt*
attack, depredation, descent, inroad, invasion, irruption, raid, reconnaissance, sally, sortie; SEE CONCEPTS 86,90,159

forbear [v] *resist the temptation to*
abstain, avoid, bridle, cease, curb, decline, desist, escape, eschew, evade, forgo, go easy*, hold back*, inhibit, keep, keep from, omit, pause, refrain, restrain, sacrifice, shun, stop, withhold; SEE CONCEPTS 35,121,130,681

forbearance [n] *resisting, avoidance*
abstinence, endurance, fortitude, going easy on*, living with*, longanimity, moderation, patience, patientness, refraining, resignation, restraint, self-control, temperance, tolerance; SEE CONCEPTS 410,633

forbearing [adj] *tolerant*
being big*, charitable, clement, considerate, easy, forgiving, gentle, going easy on*, going easy with*, humane, humanitarian, indulgent, lenient, living with*, longanimous, long-suffering, merciful, mild, moderate, patient, soft-shell*, thoughtful; SEE CONCEPTS 404,542

forbid [v] *outlaw, prohibit an action*
ban, block, cancel, censor, check, debar, declare illegal, deny, deprive, disallow, embargo, enjoin, exclude, forestall, forfend, freeze*, halt, hinder, hold up, impede, interdict, lock up, nix*, obstruct, obviate, oppose, preclude, prevent, proscribe, put the chill on*, restrain, restrict, rule out, say no*, shut down*, shut out*, spike*, stop, stymie*, taboo*, veto, withhold; SEE CONCEPT 121

forbidden [adj] *outlawed, prohibited*
banned, closed, closed-down*, closed-up*, contraband, no-no*, off limits, out of bounds, proscribed, refused, taboo*, verboten, vetoed; SEE CONCEPT 548

forbidding [adj] *ominous, daunting*

abhorrent, disagreeable, dour, foreboding, frightening, glowering, grim, hostile, menacing, odious, offensive, off-putting, repellent, repulsive, sinister, threatening, tough, ugly, unapproachable, unfriendly, unpleasant; SEE CONCEPTS 537,550

force [n1] *physical energy, power*

arm, brunt, clout, coercion, compulsion, conscription, constraint, draft, duress, dynamism, effort, enforcement, exaction, extortion, full head of steam*, fury, horsepower, impact, impetus, impulse, might, momentum, muscle, pains*, potency, potential, pow*, pressure, punch, push, sinew, sock*, speed, steam, stimulus, strain, strength, stress, strong arm*, stuff*, subjection, tension, trouble, velocity, vigor, violence, what it takes*; SEE CONCEPTS 641,724

force [n2] *mental power, energy*

ability, authority, bite*, capability, coercion, cogency, competence, determination, dominance, drive, duress, effect, effectiveness, efficacy, emphasis, fierceness, forcefulness, gumption, guts*, impressiveness, influence, intensity, intestinal fortitude, obligation, parent, persistence, persuasiveness, point, pressure, puissance, punch, push, requirement, sapience, stress, validity, validness, vehemence, vigor, willpower; SEE CONCEPTS 410,677

force [n3] *military organization*

armed forces, army, battalion, body, cell, corps, crew, detachment, division, guard, horses, host, legion, patrol, regiment, reserves, shop, soldiers, squad, squadron, troop, unit; SEE CONCEPTS 322,417

force [v1] *obligate to do something*

apply, bear down, bear hard on, bind, blackmail, bring pressure to bear upon*, burden, cause, charge, choke, coerce, command, compel, concuss, conscript, constrain, contract, demand, draft, drag, dragoon*, drive, enforce, enjoin, exact, extort, fix, impel, impose, impress, inflict, insist, limit, make, move, necessitate, oblige, obtrude, occasion, order, overcome, pin down, press, pressure, pressurize, put screws to*, put squeeze on*, require, restrict, sandbag*, shotgun*, strong-arm*, urge, wrest, wring; SEE CONCEPT 14

force [v2] *use violence upon*

assault, blast, break in, break open, burst, bust open, crack open, defile, extort, jimmy*, propel, pry, push, rape, ravish, spoil, squeeze, thrust, twist, undo, violate, wrench, wrest, wring; SEE CONCEPTS 156,208

forced [adj] *compulsory, strained*

affected, artificial, begrudging, binding, bound, coerced, coercive, compelled, conscripted, constrained, contrived, enforced, factitious, false, grudging, inflexible, insincere, involuntary, labored, mandatory, obligatory, peremptory, rigid, slave, stiff, stringent, unnatural, unwilling, wooden*; SEE CONCEPTS 542,548

forceful [adj] *effective, powerful*

ball of fire*, bullish*, cogent, coming on strong, commanding, compelling, constraining, convincing, dominant, dynamic, electric, elemental, energetic, forcible, gutsy*, mighty, persuasive, pithy, potent, powerhouse, puissant, punch, punchy*, steamroller*, stringent, strong, take-charge, take-over, telling, titanic, vehement, vigorous, violent, virile, weighty; SEE CONCEPTS 267,401,550

forcible [adj] *powerful, aggressive*

active, armed, assertive, coercive, cogent, compelling, compulsory, drastic, effective, efficient, energetic, forceful, impressive, intense, mighty, militant, persuasive, potent, puissant, strong, telling, valid, vehement, vigorous, violent, weighty; SEE CONCEPTS 267,537

forcibly [adv] *against one's will*

by force, coercively, compulsorily, effectively, energetically, hard, mightily, powerfully, strongly, under protest, vigorously; SEE CONCEPTS 544,548

fore [adv] *in the front*

ahead, ante*, antecedently, before, beforehand, forward, in advance, near, nearest, precedently, previous; SEE CONCEPTS 585,820

forebearer [n] *family predecessor*

ancestor, antecedent, ascendant, author, begetter, forerunner, founder, materfamilias, matriarch, originator, parent, paterfamilias, patriarch, precursor, primogenitor, procreator, progenitor, relative, sire; SEE CONCEPT 414

forebode [v] *predict, warn*

augur, betoken, bode, divine, forecast, foresee, foreshadow, foretell, foretoken, forewarn, indicate, omen, portend, premonish, presage, prognosticate, promise; SEE CONCEPTS 70,78

foreboding [n] *misgiving, bad omen*

anxiety, apprehension, apprehensiveness, augury, bad vibes*, chill, dread, fear, foreshadowing, foretoken, forewarning, funny feeling*, handwriting on the wall*, portent, prediction, premonition, prenotion, presage, presentiment, prognostic, prophecy, sinking feeling*, vibes*, warning, wind change*; SEE CONCEPTS 78,689,690

forecast [n] *prediction, often of weather or business*

anticipation, augury, budget, calculation, cast, conjecture, divination, estimate, foreknowledge, foreseeing, foresight, foretelling, forethought, foretoken, guess, outlook, planning, precognition, prescience, prevision, prognosis, prognostication, projection, prophecy; SEE CONCEPTS 28,37,70,78

forecast [v] *predict, guess*

adumbrate, anticipate, augur, calculate, call the turn*, conclude, conjecture, demonstrate, determine, divine, dope out*, estimate, figure, figure out*, foresee, foretell, gather, gauge, infer, in the cards*, plan, portend, predetermine, presage, prognosticate, prophesy, reason, see it coming*, soothsay, surmise, telegraph; SEE CONCEPTS 28,37,70,78

forefront/foreground [n] *prominence*

beginning, center, cutting-edge*, focus, fore, forepart, front, lead, leading-edge*, limelight*, on the line*, spearhead*, state-of-the-art, vanguard; SEE CONCEPT 668

foregoing [adj] *come before; previous*

above, aforementioned, aforesaid, aforestated, antecedent, anterior, former, past, precedent, preceding, prior; SEE CONCEPTS 585,820

foreign [adj] *from another country, experience*

adopted, alien, alienated, antipodal, barbarian, barbaric, borrowed, derived, different, distant, estranged, exiled, exotic, expatriate, external, extralocal, extraneous, extrinsic, far, faraway, far-fetched, far-off, from abroad, immigrant, imported, inaccessible, nonnative, nonresident,

fo
fo

not domestic, not native, offshore, outlandish, outside, overseas, remote, strange, transoceanic, unaccustomed, unexplored, unfamiliar, unknown; SEE CONCEPTS 536,549

foreign [adj2] *irrelevant*
accidental, adventitious, extraneous, extrinsic, heterogeneous, immaterial, impertinent, inapposite, incompatible, incongruous, inconsistent, inconsonant, irrelative, repugnant, unassimilable, uncharacteristic, unrelated; SEE CONCEPTS 267,537

foreigner [n] *person from another country*
alien, fresh off the boat*, greenhorn*, immigrant, incomer, newcomer, outlander, outsider, stranger; SEE CONCEPT 413

foremost [adj] *first in rank, order*
A-number-1*, A-1*, arch, at the cutting edge*, at the leading edge*, champion, chief, front, head, headmost, heavy, heavy stuff*, heavyweight*, highest, hotdog*, hotshot*, hot stuff*, inaugural, initial, leading, most important, number one*, original, paramount, preeminent, premier, primary, prime, primo*, principal, supreme; SEE CONCEPTS 568,585,799

forensic [adj] *judicial, legal*
argumentative, debatable, dialectic, dialectical, disputative, juridical, juristic, moot, polemical, rhetorical; SEE CONCEPTS 267,319

foreordain [v] *doom, fate*
destinate, destine, foredoom, foreshadow, foretell, prearrange, predestine, predetermine, preform, preordain, reserve; SEE CONCEPT 70

forerunner [n1] *messenger, herald*
advertiser, advocate, ancestor, announcer, author, envoy, forebearer, foregoer, harbinger, initiator, originator, pioneer, precursor, progenitor, prognostic, prototype; SEE CONCEPTS 414,423

forerunner [n2] *example, sign*
advertisement, announcement, antecedent, antecessor, augury, exemplar, foregoer, foreshadow, foretoken, forewarning, indication, mark, model, omen, pattern, portent, precursor, predecessor, premonition, presage, prognostic, prototype, sign, token, warning; SEE CONCEPT 529

foresee [v] *anticipate, predict*
apprehend, call the turn*, crystal ball it*, discern, divine, dope out*, envisage, espy, expect, forebode, forecast, forefeel, foreknow, foretell, have a hunch*, perceive, preknow, presage, previse, prevision, prognosticate, prophesy, psych out*, see, see it coming*, understand, visualize; SEE CONCEPTS 26,70

foreshadow [v] *indicate*
adumbrate, augur, be in the wind*, betoken, bode, forebode, foretell, hint, imply, omen, portend, predict, prefigure, presage, promise, prophesy, shadow, signal, suggest, telegraph; SEE CONCEPTS 70,75,261

foresight [n] *mental preparedness*
anticipation, canniness, care, carefulness, caution, circumspection, clairvoyance, discernment, discreetness, discretion, economy, far-sightedness, foreknowledge, forethought, insight, long-sightedness, perception, precaution, precognition, preconception, premeditation, premonition, prenotion, prescience, prospect, providence, provision, prudence, sagacity; SEE CONCEPTS 409,410

forest [n] *area with a large number of trees*
backwoods, brake, chase, clump, coppice, copse,

cover, covert, grove, growth, jungle, park, shelter, stand, thicket, timber, timberland, weald, wildwood, wood, woodland, woodlot, woods; SEE CONCEPTS 509,517

foretell [v] *predict, warn*
adumbrate, announce, anticipate, apprehend, augur, auspicate, betoken, bode, call, call it*, call the shot*, crystal ball it*, declare, disclose, divine, divulge, dope*, dope out*, figure, figure out*, forebode, forecast, foreknow, foreshadow, forewarn, make book*, portend, prefigure, presage, proclaim, prognosticate, prophesy, psych, read, reveal, see something coming*, signify, soothsay, tell; SEE CONCEPTS 70,78

forethought [n] *mental preparedness*
anticipation, canniness, caution, deliberation, discreetness, discretion, far-sightedness, foresight, gumption, judgment, planning, precaution, premeditation, providence, provision, prudence, sense; SEE CONCEPT 410

forever [adj1] *for all time; everlasting*
always, durably, endlessly, enduringly, eternally, evermore, everything considered*, for always, forevermore, for good*, for keeps*, for life*, immortally, infinitely, in perpetuity, in perpetuum, interminably, lastingly, now and forever*, on and on*, permanently, perpetually, till blue in the face*, till death do us part*, till Doomsday*, till the cows come home*, till the end of time*, unchangingly, world without end*; SEE CONCEPTS 551,649,798,799

forever [adj2] *not ceasing, continually*
all the time, constantly, endlessly, eternally, everlastingly, incessantly, interminably, perpetually, regularly, unendingly, unremittingly; SEE CONCEPTS 534,798

forewarn [v] *caution that something may happen*
admonish, advise, alarm, alert, apprise, dissuade, flag, forbode, give fair warning*, give the high sign*, portend, premonish, pull one's coat*, put a bug in one's ear*, put one wise*, put on guard*, telegraph, tip, tip off, wave a red flag*; SEE CONCEPT 78

foreword [n] *introduction to a document*
exordium, overture, preamble, preface, preliminary, prelude, prelusion, proem, prolegomenon, prologue; SEE CONCEPT 270

forfeit [n] *something given as sacrifice*
cost, damages, fine, loss, mulct, penalty, relinquishment; SEE CONCEPT 123

forfeit [v] *give up something in sacrifice*
abandon, be deprived of, be stripped of, drop, give over, lose, relinquish, renounce, sacrifice, surrender; SEE CONCEPT 116

forge [v1] *counterfeit*
coin, copy, design, duplicate, fabricate, fake, falsify, fashion, feign, frame, imitate, invent, make, phony up*, pirate*, produce, reproduce, scratch, trace, transcribe, trump up*; SEE CONCEPTS 59,171

forge [v2] *make something from scratch*
beat, build, construct, contrive, create, devise, fabricate, fashion, form, frame, hammer out*, invent, manufacture, mold, pound, put together, shape, turn out, work; SEE CONCEPTS 168, 173,175,205,251

forgery [n] *counterfeiting; counterfeit item*
bogus*, carbon*, carbon copy, cheat, coining, copy, fabrication, fake, faking, falsification, fraudulence, imitating, imitation, imposition, im-

posture, lookalike, phony, pseudo, sham*, twin, workalike*; SEE CONCEPTS 59,171,716

forget [v1] *not be able to remember*
blow, clean forget*, consign to oblivion*, dismiss from mind, disremember, draw a blank*, escape one's memory*, fail to remember, let slip from memory*, lose consciousness of, lose sight of*, misrecollect, obliterate, think no more of*; SEE CONCEPT 40

forget [v2] *leave behind*
blink, discount, disregard, drop, fail, ignore, lose sight of*, neglect, omit, overlook, overpass, pass over, skip, slight, transgress, trespass; SEE CONCEPTS 30,116

forgetful [adj] *tending to not remember*
absent, absent-minded, abstracted, airheaded*, amnemonic, amnesic, asleep on the job*, bemused, careless, distracted, dreamy, heedless, inattentive, lax, like an absent-minded professor*, looking out window*, mooning, moony*, neglectful, negligent, oblivious, on the job*, oblivious, out of it*, out to lunch*, pipe dreaming*, preoccupied, remiss, slack, sloppy, unmindful, unwitting, woolgathering*; SEE CONCEPTS 403, 550

forgetfulness [n] *consistent inability to remember*
absentmindedness, abstraction, amnesia, blackout, blank, blockout, carelessness, dreaminess, fugue, heedlessness, hypomnesia, inattention, lapse of memory, laxness, lethe, limbo, loss of memory, negligence, nirvana, oblivion, obliviousness, paramnesia, repression, short memory, suppression; SEE CONCEPTS 410,644

forgive [v] *stop blame and grant pardon*
absolve, accept apology, acquit, allow for, amnesty, bear no malice*, bear with, bury the hatchet*, clear, commute, condone, dismiss from mind, efface, exculpate, excuse, exempt, exonerate, extenuate, forget, kiss and make up*, laugh off*, let bygones be bygones*, let it go*, let off*, let off easy*, let pass*, let up on*, make allowance, overlook, palliate, pocket, purge, release, relent, remit, reprieve, respite, spring, think no more of*, turn other cheek*, wink at*, wipe slate clean*; SEE CONCEPTS 12,50,88

forgiveness [n] *pardon; end of blame*
absolution, acquittal, amnesty, charity, clemency, compassion, condonation, dispensation, exculpation, exoneration, extenuation, grace, immunity, impunity, indemnity, justification, lenience, lenity, mercy, overlooking, palliation, purgation, quarter, quittance, remission, remittal, reprieve, respite, vindication; SEE CONCEPTS 685,689

forgo [v] *give up, do without*
abandon, abdicate, abjure, abstain, cede, desist, eschew, forbear, forsake, give in, go on the wagon*, leave alone, leave out, pack in*, pass, pass on, pass up, quit, refrain, relinquish, renounce, resign, resist, sacrifice, sit out*, surrender, swear off*, take the cure*, take the oath*, waive, yield; SEE CONCEPTS 121,130,681

forgotten [adj] *out of one's mind*
abandoned, blanked out*, blotted out*, blown over*, buried, bygone, clean forgot*, consigned to oblivion*, disremembered*, drew a blank*, erased, fell between the cracks*, gone, lapsed, left behind, left out, lost, obliterated, omitted, past, past recollection, repressed, slipped one's mind*, suppressed, unrecalled, unremembered; SEE CONCEPTS 402,403,529

fork [v] *go separate ways*
angle, bifurcate, branch off, branch out, divaricate, diverge, divide, part, split; SEE CONCEPTS 98,738

forked [adj] *going separate ways*
angled, bifid, bifurcate, bifurcated, branched, branching, dichotomous, dichotonic, divaricate, divided, furcate, furcated, pronged, split, tined, tridented, zigzag; SEE CONCEPTS 485,581

forlorn [adj] *hopeless, inconsolable*
abandoned, alone, bereft, blue*, cheerless, comfortless, cynical, defenseless, depressed, deserted, desolate, despairing, desperate, despondent, destitute, destroyed, disconsolate, down and out*, dragging*, forgotten, forsaken, friendless, fruitless, futile, godforsaken*, helpless, homeless, in the dumps*, lonely, lonesome, lost, miserable, oppressed, pathetic, pessimistic, pitiable, pitiful, solitary, tragic, unhappy, vain, weighed down, woebegone, wretched; SEE CONCEPT 403

form [n1] *shape; arrangement*
anatomy, appearance, articulation, cast, configuration, conformation, construction, contour, cut, design, die, embodiment, fashion, figure, formation, framework, mode, model, mold, outline, pattern, plan, profile, scheme, silhouette, skeleton, structure, style, system; SEE CONCEPTS 184,660,754,757

form [n2] *animate body and its condition*
anatomy, being, build, condition, fettle*, figure, fitness, frame, health, object, outline, person, phenomenon, physique, shape, silhouette, thing, torso, trim*; SEE CONCEPTS 316,389,720

form [n3] *accepted procedure; ceremony*
behavior, by the book*, by the numbers*, canon, ceremonial, channels*, conduct, convenance, convention, custom, decorum, done thing*, etiquette, fashion, formality, habit, law, layout, manner, manners, method, mode, practice, precept, proceeding, process, propriety, protocol, regulation, rite, ritual, ropes*, rule, setup, style, usage, way; SEE CONCEPT 688

form [n4] *document that requires answers or information*
application, blank, chart, data sheet, letter, paper, questionnaire, sheet; SEE CONCEPT 271

form [n5] *type, kind*
arrangement, character, class, description, design, grade, guise, make, manifestation, manner, method, mode, order, practice, rank, semblance, sort, species, stamp, style, system, variety, way; SEE CONCEPTS 6,378

form [n6] *organization, arrangement*
format, framework, harmony, order, orderliness, placement, plan, proportion, scheme, structure, symmetry; SEE CONCEPT 727

form [v1] *bring into existence; make, produce*
arrange, assemble, block out, bring about, build, cast, complete, compose, conceive, concoct, constitute, construct, consummate, contrive, cook up*, create, cultivate, cut, design, develop, devise, dream up, erect, establish, fabricate, fashion, finish, fix, forge, found, frame, hammer out*, invent, knock off*, make up, manufacture, model, mold, organize, outline, pattern, perfect, plan, plot, project, put together, scheme, set, set up, shape, structure, throw together, trace, turn out*, work; SEE CONCEPTS 168,173,205,251

form [v2] *come into being; arise*
accumulate, acquire, appear, become a reality, be-

come visible, condense, crystallize, develop, eventuate, fall into place*, grow, harden, materialize, mature, rise, set, settle, shape up, show up, take on character, take shape*; SEE CONCEPTS 105,704

form [v3] *educate, discipline*
breed, bring up, give character, instruct, rear, school, teach, train; SEE CONCEPTS 285,295

form [v4] *comprise, be a part of*
act as, compose, constitute, figure in, make, make up, serve as; SEE CONCEPT 643

formal [adj] *established, orderly*
academic, approved, ceremonial, ceremonialistic, ceremonious, confirmed, conventional, decorous, directed, explicit, express, fixed, formalistic, lawful, legal, methodical, official, precise, prescribed, pro forma, proper, punctilious, regular, rigid, ritual, ritualistic, set, solemn, stately, stereotyped, stereotypical, strict, systematic; SEE CONCEPTS 533,547

formal [adj2] *stiff, affected, correct*
aloof, by the numbers*, ceremonious, conventional, decorous, distant, exact, nominal, playing the game*, polite, precise, prim, punctilious, reserved, seemly, sententious, starched*, stilted*, straight arrow*, stuffy*, unbending; SEE CONCEPT 401

formality [n1] *convention, custom*
academism, ceremony, convenance, conventionality, form, gesture, liturgy, matter of form*, officialism, procedure, red tape*, rite, ritual, rituality, rubric, rule, service, solemnity, solemnness, stereotype, tradition; SEE CONCEPT 688

formality [n2] *etiquette, protocol*
ceremoniousness, conventionalism, correctness, decorum, formalism, honors, mummery, politesse, propriety, p's and q's*, punctiliousness; SEE CONCEPT 633

formation [n] *composition, establishment*
accumulation, architecture, arrangement, compilation, configuration, constitution, construction, creation, crystallization, deposit, design, development, dispersal, disposition, embodiment, evolution, fabrication, figure, forming, generation, genesis, grouping, induction, makeup, manufacture, order, organization, pattern, production, rank, structure, synthesis; SEE CONCEPTS 173,260

formative [adj] *influential, impressionable*
determinative, developmental, immature, impressible, malleable, moldable, pliant, sensitive, shaping, susceptible; SEE CONCEPTS 534,537

former [adj] *previous in time or order*
above, aforementioned, aforesaid, ancient, antecedent, anterior, bygone, departed, earlier, erstwhile, ex-*, first, foregoing, late, long ago*, long gone, of yore*, old, once, one-time, past, preceding, prior, quondam, sometime, whilom; SEE CONCEPTS 585,820

formerly [adv] *previously in time or order*
aforetime, already, anciently, at one time, away back, a while back, back, back when*, before, before now, before this, down memory lane*, earlier, eons ago*, erewhile, erstwhile, heretofore, in former times, in the olden days*, in the past, lately, long ago, of old, of yore, olden days*, once, once upon a time*, radically, some time ago, time was*, used to be*, water under the bridge*; SEE CONCEPTS 585,820

formidable [adj1] *horrible, terrifying*
appalling, awful, dangerous, daunting, dire, dismaying, dreadful, fearful, fierce, frightful, horrific, imposing, impregnable, intimidating, menacing, redoubtable, shocking, terrible, terrific, threatening; SEE CONCEPT 537

formidable [adj2] *difficult, overwhelming*
all-powerful, arduous, awesome, ballbuster, challenging, colossal, dismaying, effortful, great, hard, impressive, indomitable, intimidating, labored, laborious, mammoth, mighty, murder*, onerous, overpowering, powerful, puissant, rough*, rough go*, staggering, strenuous, tall order*, toilsome, tough*, tough proposition*, tremendous, uphill*; SEE CONCEPT 565

formless [adj] *disorganized, vague*
amorphous, baggy*, blobby*, chaotic, crude, inchoate, incoherent, indefinite, indeterminate, indistinct, nebulous, obscure, orderless, raw, rough, rude, shapeless, unclear, undefined, unformed, unorganized; SEE CONCEPTS 485,535,589

formula [n] *set preparation; rule, recipe*
blueprint, canon, code, credo, creed, custom, description, direction, equation, form, formulary, maxim, method, modus operandi, precept, prescription, principle, procedure, rite, ritual, rote, rubric, specifications, theorem, way; SEE CONCEPTS 268,688

formulate [v] *plan, specify systematically*
codify, coin, compose, concoct, contrive, cook up, couch, define, detail, develop, devise, draft, draw up*, dream up*, evolve, express, forge, frame, give form to, hatch, indite, invent, make, make up*, map, originate, particularize, phrase, prepare, put, set down*, systematize, vamp, work, work out; SEE CONCEPTS 36,173,202

forsake [v] *abandon, turn one's back on*
abdicate, cast off, change one's tune*, desert, disclaim, disown, drift away*, forgo, forswear, give up, have done with, jettison, jilt, kiss goodbye*, leave, leave flat*, leave high and dry*, quit, relinquish, renounce, repudiate, resign, run out on*, set aside, show the door*, spurn, surrender, take the oath*, throw over*, walk out on*, wash one's hands of*, yield; SEE CONCEPTS 30,195,384

forsaken [adj] *abandoned*
cast off, derelict, deserted, desolate, destitute, disowned, forlorn, friendless, godforsaken*, ignored, isolated, jilted, left at the altar*, left behind, left in the lurch*, lonely, lorn, marooned, outcast, solitary, thrown over*; SEE CONCEPT 555

forswear [v] *abandon, disavow*
abjure, deny, disclaim, disown, drop, forgo, forsake, give up, recall, recant, reject, renege, renounce, repudiate, retract, swear off, take back, withdraw; SEE CONCEPTS 44,54

fort/fortress [n] *stronghold*
acropolis, blockhouse, camp, castle, citadel, fastness, fortification, garrison, redoubt, station; SEE CONCEPTS 321,439

forte [n] *person's strong point*
ability, ableness, aptitude, competence, effectiveness, efficiency, eminency, faculty, gift*, long suit*, medium, métier, oyster*, speciality, strength, strong suit*, talent, thing*; SEE CONCEPTS 409,411

forth [adv] *outward*
ahead, alee, along, away, first, forward, into, into the open*, on, onward, out; SEE CONCEPT 581

forthcoming [adj] *expected, imminent*
accessible, anticipated, approaching, at hand, available, awaited, coming, destined, fated, fu-

ture, impending, inescapable, in evidence, inevitable, in preparation, in prospect, in store*, in the cards*, in the wind*, nearing, obtainable, oncoming, on tap*, open, pending, predestined, prospective, ready, resulting, upcoming; SEE CONCEPTS 548,799

forthright [adj] straightforward, honest
aboveboard, bald, blunt, call a spade a spade*, candid, categorical, direct, directly, forward, frank, from the hip*, like it is*, no lie*, open, outspoken, plain, plainspoken, real, simple, sincere, straight, undisguised, up front*; SEE CONCEPT 267

forthwith [adv] immediately
abruptly, at once, away, directly, instantly, now, quickly, right away*, right now*, straightaway, suddenly, tout de suite, without delay; SEE CONCEPTS 544,820

fortification [n] reinforced position
barricade, barrier, bastion, battlement, block, blockhouse, breastwork, buffer, bulwark, castle, citadel, consolidation, defense, earthwork, embattlement, entrenchment, fastness, fort, fortress, garrison, keep, outpost, parapet, preparation, presidio, protection, reinforcement, stockade, strengthening, stronghold, support, wall; SEE CONCEPTS 439,729

fortify [v1] make strong and secure; add to
brace, build up, bulwark, buttress, charge up, consolidate, embattle, entrench, garrison, gird, prepare, prop, protect, punch up*, ready, reinforce, secure, shore up*, soup up*, steel*, step up, strengthen, support; SEE CONCEPT 202

fortify [v2] encourage, reassure
arouse, brace, buck up*, build up, cheer, confirm, embolden, energize, enliven, hearten, invigorate, pour it on*, punch up*, rally, refresh, reinforce, renew, restore, rouse, stiffen, stir, strengthen, sustain; SEE CONCEPTS 7,22

fortitude [n] strength of mind; guts
backbone*, boldness, braveness, bravery, constancy, courage, courageousness, dauntlessness, determination, endurance, fearlessness, firmness, grit*, gutsiness, hardihood, heart, intrepidity, mettle, moxie, nerve, patience, perseverance, pith, pluck, resoluteness, resolution, spine*, spirit, spunk, stamina, starch, staying power, stick-to-itiveness*, stomach, stoutheartedness, tenacity, true grit*, valiancy, valor, valorousness, what it takes*; SEE CONCEPTS 410,411

fortuitous [adj] lucky, accidental
arbitrary, casual, chance, contingent, fluke*, fluky*, fortunate, haphazard, happy, incidental, luck in*, luck out*, lucky-dog*, odd, providential, random, serendipitous, unforeseen, unplanned; SEE CONCEPTS 548,552

fortunate [adj] having good luck
advantageous, affluent, auspicious, blessed, born with a silver spoon*, bright, charmed, convenient, encouraging, favorable, favored, felicitous, flourishing, fortuitous, gaining, get a break*, golden, happy, healthy, helpful, hopeful, in luck*, in the gravy*, lucky, on a roll*, opportune, overcoming, profitable, promising, propitious, prosperous, providential, rosy, sitting pretty, successful, sunny side*, thriving, timely, triumphant, victorious, wealthy, well-off, well-to-do; SEE CONCEPTS 404,542,572

fortunately [adv] luckily
auspiciously, by good luck, by happy chance*,

favorably, happily, in good time*, in the nick of time*, opportunely, prosperously, providentially, satisfyingly, seasonably, successfully, swimmingly, well; SEE CONCEPTS 537,544,572

fortune [n1] wealth, possessions
affluence, capital, estate, gold mine*, inheritance, opulence, portion, property, prosperity, resources, riches, substance, treasure, worth; SEE CONCEPTS 335,710

fortune [n2] fate, lot in life
accident, break*, certainty, chance, circumstances, contingency, destiny, doom, expectation, experience, fifty-fifty*, fighting chance*, fluke*, fortuity, fortunateness, good break, hazard, history, karma*, kismet*, life, luck, lucked into*, lucked out*, luckiness, lucky break*, lucky hit*, Moirai, portion, providence, roll of the dice*, run of luck*, star, streak of luck, success, way the ball bounces*, way the cookie crumbles*, wheel of fortune*; SEE CONCEPT 679

fortune-teller [n] person attempting to tell the future
augur, clairvoyant, crystal ball gazer, diviner, medium, mind reader, oracle, palmist, palm reader, predicter, prophet, psychic, seer, soothsayer, spiritualist, tarot reader, tea-leaf reader; SEE CONCEPTS 348,423

forward [adj1] advancing, early
ahead, forth, forward-looking, in advance, leading, onward, precocious, premature, progressing, progressive, propulsive, well-developed; SEE CONCEPT 528

forward [adj2] in front, first
advance, anterior, facial, fore, foremost, front, head, leading, ventral; SEE CONCEPTS 581, 583,585

forward [adj3] brash, impertinent
aggressive, assuming, audacious, bantam, barefaced, bold, brazen, cheeky*, coming on strong*, confident, familiar, fresh, impudent, nervy*, overassertive, overweening, pert, presuming, presumptuous, pushing, pushy*, rude, sassy*, saucy*, self-assertive, smart, smart-alecky*, uppity*, wise; SEE CONCEPTS 401,404

forward [v1] aid, expedite
advance, assist, back, champion, cultivate, encourage, favor, foster, further, hasten, help, hurry, promote, serve, speed, support, uphold; SEE CONCEPTS 68,110

forward [v2] send, ship
address, consign, deliver, dispatch, express, freight, post, remit, route, transmit, transport; SEE CONCEPT 217

forward [adv] toward the front in order, time
ahead, alee, along, ante, antecedently, before, beforehand, fore, forth, in advance, into prominence, into view, on, onward, out, precedently, previous, to the fore*, vanward; SEE CONCEPTS 581,585,799

fossil [n] organic remains of a previous time
deposit, eolith, impression, neolith, paleolith, petrification, reconstruction, relic, skeleton, specimen, trace; SEE CONCEPTS 429,470,509

foster [v1] promote, support
advance, back, champion, cherish, cultivate, encourage, feed, foment, forward, further, harbor, nurse, nurture, serve, stimulate, uphold; SEE CONCEPT 110

foster [v2] give care or accommodation to
assist, bring up, care for, cherish, entertain, favor,

harbor, help, house, lodge, minister to, nourish, nurse, oblige, raise, rear, serve, shelter, sustain, take care of; SEE CONCEPTS *110,140,295*

foul [adj1] *disgusting, dirty*
abhorrent, abominable, base, contaminated, despicable, detestable, disgraceful, dishonorable, egregious, fetid, filthy, gross*, hateful, heinous, horrid, icky*, impure, infamous, iniquitous, loathsome, malodorous, mucky*, nasty, nauseating, nefarious, noisome, notorious, offensive, pigpen*, polluted, putrid, rank*, raunchy*, repellent, repulsive, revolting, rotten, scandalous, shameful, squalid, stinking*, sullied, tainted, unclean, vicious, vile, wicked, yecchy*, yucky*; SEE CONCEPTS *485,529*

foul [adj2] *vulgar, offensive*
abusive, blasphemous, blue*, coarse, dirty, filthy, foul-mouthed, gross*, indecent, lewd, low, nasty, obscene, profane, raunchy, scatological, scurrilous, smutty*; SEE CONCEPT *267*

foul [adj3] *corrupt, dishonest*
caitiff, crooked, dirty, fraudulent, inequitable, monstrous, shady, underhand, underhanded, unfair, unjust, unscrupulous, vicious; SEE CONCEPTS *537,548*

foul [v] *make or become dirty*
befoul, begrime, besmear, besmirch, block, catch, choke, clog, contaminate, defile, desecrate, discolor, ensnare, entangle, fill, jam, pollute, profane, smear, smudge, snarl, soil, spot, stain, sully, taint, tarnish, twist; SEE CONCEPTS *250,469*

foul up [v] *make a mess of*
botch, bungle, confuse, jumble, mismanage, mix up*, muck up*, muddle, screw up*, snafu*, snarl, tumble; SEE CONCEPTS *16,234*

found [v1] *bring into being*
begin, commence, constitute, construct, create, endow, erect, establish, fashion, fix, form, get going, inaugurate, initiate, institute, launch, organize, originate, plant, raise, ring in*, settle, settle up, start, start the ball rolling*, start up; SEE CONCEPT *221*

found [v2] *put on a base*
bottom, build, erect, establish, ground, predicate, raise, rear, rest, root, stay, support, sustain; SEE CONCEPTS *168,221*

foundation [n1] *basis for something physical or mental*
ABCs*, authority, base, basics, bed, bedrock, bottom, bottom line*, brass tacks*, foot, footing, ground, groundwork, guts*, heart*, infrastructure, justification, nitty-gritty*, nub*, nuts and bolts*, prop, reason, root, stay, substratum, substructure, support, underpinning, understructure; SEE CONCEPTS *442,826*

foundation [n2] *established institution*
association, charity, company, corporation, endowment, establishment, guild, inauguration, institute, organization, plantation, settlement, setup, society, trusteeship; SEE CONCEPT *381*

founder [n] *person who establishes an institution*
architect, author, beginner, benefactor, builder, constructor, creator, designer, establisher, forebearer, framer, generator, initiator, institutor, inventor, maker, organizer, originator, patron, planner, prime mover*; SEE CONCEPTS *347,423*

founder [v] *go under, fail*
abort, be lost, break down, collapse, come to nothing, fall, fall through, go down, go lame, go to bottom, lurch, miscarry, misfire, sink, sprawl,

stagger, stumble, submerge, submerse, trip; SEE CONCEPTS *181,699*

fountain [n] *source, often of liquid*
bubbler, cause, font, fount, geyser, gush, inception, inspiration, jet, lode, mainspring, mine, origin, play, provenance, provenience, pump, reservoir, root, spout, spray, spring, stream, well, wellhead, wellspring; SEE CONCEPTS *514,648*

fountainhead [n] *principal source; person who originates*
administrator, architect, author, builder, creator, father, fount, fountain, generator, initiator, leader, maker, mother, originator, spring, wellspring; SEE CONCEPTS *348,350*

foxy [adj] *shrewd*
artful, astute, canny, crafty, cunning, deceitful, deep, devious, dishonest, experienced, guileful, insidious, intelligent, knowing, retiary, sharp, slick, sly, subtle, tricky, vulpine, wily; SEE CONCEPTS *401,404*

foyer [n] *receiving area*
antechamber, anteroom, entrance hall, lobby, reception, vestibule; SEE CONCEPTS *440,441,448*

fracas [n] *disturbance, fight*
affray, altercation, battle, battle royal*, bickering, brawl, broil*, brouhaha, dispute, donnybrook*, feud, flap*, fray, free-for-all*, hassle, knockdown-drag-out*, melee, mix up*, quarrel, riot, row, ruction, ruffle, rumpus, run-in*, scrimmage, scuffle, set-to*, squabble, stew*, trouble, tumult, uproar, words*; SEE CONCEPTS *46,106*

fraction [n1] *part*
bite, chunk, cut, division, end, fragment, half, piece, portion, section, share, slice; SEE CONCEPT *835*

fraction [n2] *incomplete number*
bit, division, fragment, part, partial, piece, portion, quotient, ratio, section, segment, slice, subdivision; SEE CONCEPT *765*

fractional [adj] *partial*
apportioned, compartmental, compartmented, constituent, dismembered, dispersed, divided, fragmentary, frationary, incomplete, parceled, part, piecemeal, sectional, segmented; SEE CONCEPT *785*

fractious [adj] *grouchy, cross*
awkward, captious, crabby*, disorderly, fretful, froward, huffy*, indocile, indomitable, intractable, irritable, mean, ornery*, peevish, perverse, pettish, petulant, querulous, recalcitrant, refractory, restive, scrappy, snappish, testy, thin-skinned, touchy, uncompliant, undisciplined, unmanageable, unruly, wayward, wild; SEE CONCEPTS *267,401*

fracture [n] *break, rupture*
breach, cleavage, cleft, crack, discontinuity, disjunction, displacement, fissure, fragmentation, gap, mutilation, opening, rent, rift, schism, severance, splinter, split, wound; SEE CONCEPTS *309,513*

fragile [adj] *breakable, dainty*
brittle, crisp, crumbly, decrepit, delicate, feeble, fine, flimsy, fracturable, frail, frangible, friable, infirm, insubstantial, shatterable, shivery, slight, unsound, weak, weakly; SEE CONCEPTS *485,489*

fragment [n] *part, chip*
ace, atom, bit, bite, chunk, crumb, cut, end, fraction, gob*, grain, hunk, iota, job*, lump*, minim, morsel, particle, piece, portion, remnant, scrap,

share, shiver, shred, slice, sliver, smithereen*; SEE CONCEPT 835

fragment [v] *break into pieces*
burst, come apart, crumble, disintegrate, disunite, divide, rend, rive, shatter, shiver, smash, splinter, split, split up; SEE CONCEPTS 98,135, 137,246,469

fragmentary [adj] *broken, incomplete*
bitty, disconnected, discrete, disjointed, fractional, incoherent, part, partial, piecemeal, scattered, scrappy, sketchy, unsystematic; SEE CONCEPT 785

fragrance [n] *pleasant odor*
aroma, aura, balm, bouquet, incense, perfume, redolence, scent, smell, spice; SEE CONCEPT 600

fragrant [adj] *smelling pleasant*
ambrosial, aromal, aromatic, balmy, delectable, delicious, delightful, odoriferous, odorous, perfumed, perfumy, redolent, savory, spicy, sweet, sweet-scented, sweet-smelling; SEE CONCEPT 598

frail [adj] *breakable, weak*
brittle, dainty, decrepit, delicate, feeble, fishy, flimsy, fracturable, fragile, frangible, infirm, insubstantial, puny, sad, shatterable, shattery, sickly, slender, slight, slim, tender, tenuous, thin, unsound, unsubstantial, vulnerable, wimpy*, wishy-washy*, wispy; SEE CONCEPTS 485,489

frailty [n] *weakness, flaw*
Achilles heel*, blemish, daintiness, debility, decrepitude, defect, deficiency, delicacy, error, failing, fallibility, fault, feebleness, flimsiness, foible, foil, imperfection, infirmity, peccability, peccadillo, shortcoming, solecism, suscept, weak point*; SEE CONCEPTS 101,230,411,580

frame [n] *skeleton, casing*
anatomy, architecture, body, build, cage, carcass, construction, enclosure, fabric, flounce, form, framework, fringe, groundwork, hem, mount, mounting, outline, physique, scaffold, scaffolding, scheme, setting, shell, stage, structure, support, system, trim, trimming, truss, valance; SEE CONCEPTS 442,733,757

frame [v1] *build*
assemble, back, border, constitute, construct, encase, enclose, erect, fabricate, fashion, forge, form, institute, invent, lath, make, manufacture, mat, model, mold, mount, panel, produce, put together, raise, set up, shingle; SEE CONCEPTS 168,758

frame [v2] *compose, plan*
block out, conceive, concoct, contrive, cook up, design, devise, draft, draw up, dream up*, form, formulate, hatch, indite, invent, make, make up, map out, outline, prepare, shape, sketch, vamp, write; SEE CONCEPTS 36,173

framework [n] *foundation, core*
bare bones*, cage, fabric, frame, frame of reference*, groundwork, plan, schema, scheme, shell, skeleton, structure; SEE CONCEPTS 439,479,733

franchise [n] *authority, right*
authorization, ballot, charter, exemption, freedom, immunity, patent, prerogative, privilege, suffrage, vote; SEE CONCEPT 376

frank [adj] *completely honest*
aboveboard, apparent, artless, bare-faced*, blunt, bold, brazen, call a spade a spade*, candid, direct, downright, easy, familiar, flat-out*, forthright, free, from the hip*, guileless, heart-to-heart*, ingenuous, lay it on the line*, like it is*, matter-of-fact, naive, natural, open, outright, outspoken, plain, plain-spoken, real, saying what one thinks*, scrupulous, sincere, straight, straightforward, transparent, truthful, unconcealed, undisguised, uninhibited, unreserved, unrestricted, up front*, upright; SEE CONCEPTS 267,582

frankfurter [n] *cylindrical meat sausage*
bowwow*, Coney Island*, dog*, footlong*, frank, hot dog, link, weenie*, wiener, wienerwurst; SEE CONCEPTS 457,460

frankly [adv] *very honestly*
bluntly, candidly, dead level*, dead on*, directly, forthrightly, freely, from the hip*, in truth, laid on the line*, level, on the level*, on the line*, openly, plainly, straight, straightforwardly, without reserve; SEE CONCEPT 267

frantic [adj] *distressed, distracted*
agitated, angry, at wits' end*, berserk, beside oneself*, corybantic, crazy, delirious, deranged, distraught, excited, flipped out*, fraught, freaked out*, frenetic, frenzied, furious, hectic, hot and bothered*, hot under the collar*, hyper*, in a stew*, in a tizzy*, insane, keyed up*, mad, out of control, overwrought, rabid, raging, raving, shook up*, spazzed out*, unglued*, unscrewed*, unzipped*, violent, weird, weirded out*, wigged out*, wild, wired*, worked up*, zonkers*; SEE CONCEPTS 403,542

fraud [n1] *trickery, deception*
artifice, bamboozlement*, blackmail, cheat, chicane, chicanery, con, craft*, deceit, double-dealing*, dupery, duping, duplicity, extortion, fake, fast one*, fast shuffle*, flimflam*, fourberie, fraudulence, graft, guile, hanky-panky*, hoax, hocus-pocus*, hoodwinking*, hustle*, imposture, line, misrepresentation, racket, scam, sell, shakedown*, sham*, sharp practice*, skunk*, smoke*, song*, song and dance*, spuriousness, sting, string, swindle, swindling, treachery; SEE CONCEPTS 59,192,645

fraud [n2] *person who is false, deceitful*
bastard, bluffer, charlatan, cheat, counterfeit, crook, deceiver, double-dealer*, fake, forger, four-flusher*, hoaxer, horse trader*, impostor, mechanic*, mountebank, phony, play actor*, pretender, quack*, racketeer, sham*, shark*, swindler; SEE CONCEPT 412

fraudulent [adj] *deceptive, false*
bamboozling*, counterfeit, crafty, criminal, crooked, deceitful, devious, dishonest, dishonorable, double-dealing*, duplicitous, fake, forged, mock, phony, pseudo, sham*, spurious, swindling, treacherous, tricky; SEE CONCEPTS 545,582

fraught [adj] *full of*
abounding, attended, bristling, charged, filled, heavy, laden, replete, stuffed; SEE CONCEPTS 483,771

fray [n] *fight, battle*
affray, battle royal*, brawl, broil*, brouhaha*, clash, combat, conflict, contest, disturbance, donnybrook*, engagement, fracas, melee, quarrel, riot, row, ruckus, rumble, rumpus, scuffle, set-to*; SEE CONCEPTS 86,106

fray [v] *shred, come apart*
become ragged, become threadbare, chafe, erode, frazzle, fret, ravel, rip, rub, tatter, tear, unravel, wear, wear away, wear thin; SEE CONCEPT 214

frazzle [n] *exhaustion; something very worn*
collapse, enervation, lassitude, prostration, rag, remnant, shred; SEE CONCEPTS 410,720

fo
fr

frazzle [v] *wear out*
exhaust, fray, knock out, poop*, prostrate, rip, shred, tear, tire, tucker*, wear; SEE CONCEPTS 156,186

freak [n1] *something, someone very abnormal*
aberration, abortion, anomaly, chimera, curiosity, geek*, grotesque, malformation, miscreation, misshape, monster, monstrosity, mutant, mutation, oddity, queer, rarity, sport, weirdo*; SEE CONCEPTS 424,580

freak [n2] *irregularity, whim*
caprice, conceit, crochet, fad, fancy, folly, humor, megrim, quirk, turn, twist, vagary, whimsy; SEE CONCEPT 679

freak [n3] *person enthused about something*
addict, aficionado, buff, bug*, devotee, enthusiast, fan, fanatic, fiend*, maniac, nut*, zealot; SEE CONCEPTS 352,366,423

freak [v] *become extraordinarily upset*
flip out*, go beserk, go insane, go mad, lose control, rave, unhinge*, wig out*; SEE CONCEPTS 7,19,80

freakish [adj] *abnormal, unusual*
aberrant, arbitrary, bizarre, capricious, crazy, erratic, fantastic, far-out, freaky, grotesque, malformed, monstrous, odd, outlandish, outré, preternatural, queer, strange, unconventional, vagarious, wayward, weird, whimsical, wild; SEE CONCEPT 564

freckle [n] *small discoloration on skin*
blemish, blotch, daisy, dot, lentigo, macula, mole, patch, pepper, pigmentation, pit, pock, pockmark, speck, speckle, sprinkle, stipple; SEE CONCEPT 392

free [adj1] *without charge*
chargeless, comp*, complimentary, costless, for love*, for nothing*, freebie*, free of cost, free ride*, gratis, gratuitous, handout, on the cuff*, on the house*, paper*, unpaid, unrecompensed; SEE CONCEPT 334

free [adj2] *unrestrained personally*
able, allowed, at large, at liberty, casual, clear, disengaged, easy, escaped, familiar, fancy-free*, footloose*, forward, frank, free-spirited, freewheeling, independent, informal, lax, liberal, liberated, loose, off the hook*, on one's own*, on the loose*, open, permitted, relaxed, unattached, uncommitted, unconfined, unconstrained, unengaged, unfettered, unhampered, unimpeded, unobstructed, unregulated, unrestricted, untrammeled; SEE CONCEPTS 401,542

free [adj3] *unrestrained politically*
at liberty, autarchic, autonomic, autonomous, democratic, emancipated, enfranchised, freed, independent, individualistic, liberated, self-directing, self-governing, self-ruling, separate, sovereign, sui juris, unconstrained, unenslaved, unregimented; SEE CONCEPTS 319,536

free [adj4] *not busy; unoccupied*
at leisure, available, clear, empty, extra, idle, loose, not tied down*, spare, unemployed, unengaged, unhampered, unimpeded, uninhabited, unobstructed, unused, vacant; SEE CONCEPT 485

free [adj5] *generous, unsparing*
big, big-hearted*, bounteous, bountiful, charitable, eager, handsome, hospitable, lavish, liberal, munificent, open-handed*, prodigal, unstinging, willing; SEE CONCEPT 404

free [v1] *liberate, let go*
absolve, acquit, bail, bail out*, clear, cut loose*, deliver, demobilize, discharge, disengage, disenthrall, disimprison, dismiss, emancipate, enfranchise, extricate, let loose*, let off*, let off the hook*, let out, loose, loosen, manumit, pardon, parole, put on the street*, ransom, redeem, release, relieve, reprieve, rescue, save, set free, spring*, turn loose, turn out, unbind, uncage, unchain, undo, unfetter, unfix, unleash, untie; SEE CONCEPT 127

free [v2] *take burden from*
cast off, clear, cut loose, decontaminate, deliver, discharge, disembarrass, disencumber, disengage, disentangle, empty, excuse, exempt, extricate, put off, ransom, redeem, relieve, rescue, rid, unburden, undo, unlade, unload, unpack, unshackle; SEE CONCEPTS 110,211

freedom [n1] *independence, license to do as one wants*
abandon, abandonment, ability, bent, carte blanche, compass, discretion, elbowroom*, exemption, facility, flexibility, free rein*, full play*, full swing*, immunity, indulgence, laissez faire, latitude, laxity, leeway, liberty, margin, opportunity, own accord*, play, plenty of rope*, power, prerogative, privilege, profligacy, rampancy, range, rein, right, rope*, scope, sweep, swing, unrestraint; SEE CONCEPT 693

freedom [n2] *political independence*
abolition, abolitionism, autarchy, autonomy, citizenship, deliverance, delivery, democracy, discharge, disengagement, disimprisonment, emancipation, enfranchisement, exemption, extriction, franchise, home rule*, immunity, impunity, liberation, liberty, manumission, parole, prerogative, privilege, probation, redemption, release, relief, representative government, rescue, salvage, salvation, self-determination, self-government, sovereignty; SEE CONCEPT 691

freedom [n3] *easy attitude*
abandon, boldness, brazenness, candor, directness, disrespect, ease, facility, familiarity, forthrightness, forwardness, frankness, impertinence, informality, ingenuousness, lack of reserve, lack of restraint, laxity, license, openness, overfamiliarity, presumption, readiness, spontaneity, unconstraint; SEE CONCEPT 633

free-for-all [n] *fight*
affray, battle, brawl, broil*, brouhaha*, fracas, fray, knock-down-drag-out*, melee, riot, row, ruction; SEE CONCEPT 106

freely [adv1] *without restriction*
advisedly, as you please*, at one's discretion, at one's pleasure, at will, candidly, deliberately, designedly, fancy-free*, frankly, intentionally, of one's own accord*, of one's own free will*, openly, plainly, purposely, spontaneously, unchallenged, unreservedly, voluntarily, willingly, without hindrance, without prompting, without reserve, without restraint, without urging; SEE CONCEPT 401

freely [adv2] *easily, smoothly done*
abundantly, amply, as one pleases*, bountifully, cleanly, copiously, effortlessly, extravagantly, facilely, lavishly, liberally, lightly, like water*, loosely, open-handedly, readily, unhindered, unobstructedly, unstintingly, well, with a free hand*, without encumbrance*, without hindrance*, without restraint*, without stint*; SEE CONCEPT 544

free will [n] *person's full intent and purpose*
assent, choice, consent, desire, determination, discretion, free choice, freedom, inclination, intention, mind, option, own say so*, own sweet way*, pleasure, power, say so*, velleity, volition, voluntary decision, willingness, wish; SEE CONCEPTS 20,410

freeze [v1] *make cold enough to become solid*
benumb, bite, chill, chill to the bone*, congeal, frost, glaciate, harden, ice over, ice up, nip, pierce, refrigerate, solidify, stiffen; SEE CONCEPTS 255,521

freeze [v2] *stop*
dampen, depress, discourage, dishearten, fix, hold up, inhibit, peg, suspend; SEE CONCEPTS 14,121

freezing [adj] *very cold*
arctic, biting, bitter, chill, chilled, chilly, cutting, frigid, frost-bound, frosty, gelid, glacial, hawkish, icy, nippy, numbing, one-dog night*, penetrating, polar, raw, shivery, Siberian*, snappy*, two-dog night*, wintry; SEE CONCEPT 605

freight [n] *goods being shipped*
bales, ballast, bulk, burden, carriage, consignment, contents, conveyance, encumbrance, fardel, haul, lading, load, merchandise, pack, packages, payload, shipment, shipping, tonnage, transportation, wares, weight; SEE CONCEPT 338

frenetic [adj] *maniacal*
corybantic, delirious, demented, distraught, excited, fanatical, frantic, frenzied, furibund, furious, hyper*, in a lather*, insane, lost it*, mad, obsessive, overwrought, phrenetic, rabid, unbalanced, unscrewed*, weirded out*, wigged out*, wild, wired*; SEE CONCEPT 403

frenzied [adj] *uncontrolled*
agitated, berserk, convulsive, corybantic, delirious, distracted, distraught, excited, feverish, frantic, frenetic, furious, hysterical, mad, maniacal, nuts*, rabid, wild; SEE CONCEPTS 542,544

frenzy [n] *uncontrolled state or situation*
aberration, agitation, blow, blow a fuse*, blow one's cork*, blow one's stack*, blow one's top*, bout, burst, conniption*, convulsion, craze, delirium, derangement, distemper, distraction, dither*, excitement, ferment, fever, fit, flap*, flip one's lid*, free-for-all*, furor, fury, fuss, hell broke loose*, hysteria, insanity, lather, lunacy, madness, mania, outburst, paroxysm, passion, rage, row, ruckus, ruction, rumble, rumpus, seizure, spasm, stew, stir, to-do*, transport, turmoil, wingding*; SEE CONCEPTS 230,410,674

frequency [n] *commonness, repetitiveness*
abundance, beat, constancy, density, frequentness, iteration, number, oscillation, periodicity, persistence, prevalence, pulsation, recurrence, regularity, reiteration, repetition, rhythm; SEE CONCEPT 634

frequent [adj] *common, repeated*
a good many*, commonplace, constant, continual, customary, everyday, expected, familiar, general, habitual, incessant, intermittent, iterated, manifold, many, monotonous, numberless, numerous, periodic, perpetual, persistent, pleonastic, profuse, recurrent, recurring, redundant, reiterated, reiterative, successive, thick, ubiquitous, usual, various; SEE CONCEPT 530

frequent [v] *be a regular customer of*
affect, attend, attend regularly, be at home in*, be found at, be often in, drop in, go to, hang about*, hang around*, hang out at*, haunt*, hit*, infest,

overrun, patronize, play*, resort, revisit, visit often; SEE CONCEPTS 227,384

frequently [adv] *commonly, repeatedly*
again and again*, as a rule*, at regular intervals, at short intervals, at times, by ordinary, customarily, every now and then*, generally, habitually, in many instances*, in quick succession, intermittently, many a time*, many times, much, not infrequently, not seldom, oft, often, oftentimes, ofttimes, ordinarily, over and over, periodically, recurrently, regularly, spasmodically, successively, thick and fast*, time and again*, usually, very often; SEE CONCEPTS 530,544,799

fresh [adj1] *new, just produced*
beginning, brand-new*, comer, contemporary, crisp, crude, current, different, gleaming, glistening, green*, hot*, hot off the press*, immature, just out*, late, latest, mint*, modern, modernistic, natural, neoteric, newborn, newfangled*, novel, now, original, radical, raw, recent, sparkling, state-of-the-art, the latest*, this season's*, unconventional, unprocessed, unseasoned, untouched, unusual, up-to-date, virginal, what's happening*, young, youthful; SEE CONCEPTS 578,797

fresh [adj2] *additional*
added, another, auxiliary, else, extra, farther, further, increased, more, new, other, renewed, supplementary; SEE CONCEPTS 546,824

fresh [adj3] *refreshing to the senses*
bracing, bright, brisk, clean, clear, colorful, cool, crisp, definite, fair, invigorating, not stale, pure, quick, sharp, spanking, sparkling, stiff, stimulating, sweet, uncontaminated, unpolluted, vivid; SEE CONCEPT 537

fresh [adj4] *energetic, healthy*
active, alert, blooming, bouncing, bright, bright-eyed, bushy-tailed*, chipper*, clear, dewy, fair, florid, glowing, good, hardy, invigorated, keen, like new, lively, refreshed, rehabilitated, relaxed, relieved, rested, restored, revived, rosy, ruddy, sprightly, spry, stimulated, undimmed, unfaded, unused, unwearied, unwithered, verdant, vigorous, vital, wholesome, young; SEE CONCEPTS 485,542

fresh [adj5] *inexperienced*
artless, callow, green*, natural, new, raw, tender-footed*, uncultivated, unpracticed, unskilled, untrained, untried, unversed, young, youthful; SEE CONCEPT 404

fresh [adj6] *sassy, brazen*
bold, cheeky*, disrespectful, familiar, flip*, flippant, forward, impertinent, impudent, insolent, nervy*, pert, presumptuous, rude, saucy*, smart*, smart-alecky*, snippy*, wise; SEE CONCEPTS 267,401

freshen [v] *make like new; revitalize*
activate, air, cleanse, enliven, invigorate, purify, refresh, restore, revive, rouse, spruce up, sweeten, titivate, ventilate; SEE CONCEPT 244

freshness [n] *newness*
bloom, brightness, callowness, cleanness, clearness, dew, dewiness, glow, greenness, inexperience, innovativeness, inventiveness, novelty, originality, rawness, shine, sparkle, vigor, viridity, youth; SEE CONCEPT 715

fret [v1] *worry, be annoyed*
affront, agonize, anguish, bleed, bother, brood, carp, carry a heavy load*, chafe, chagrin, distress oneself, eat one's heart out*, fume, fuss, get into

a dither*, grieve, lose sleep over*, mope*, pother*, stew, sweat it out*, take on, torment, upset
oneself; SEE CONCEPT *410*

fret [*v2*] *upset someone*
abrade, agitate, bother, displease, distress, disturb, gall, get on nerves*, goad, harass, irk, irritate, nag, nettle, peeve, pique, provoke, rile,
ruffle, torment, trouble, vex; SEE CONCEPTS *7,19*

fret [*v3*] *rub hard*
abrade, chafe, corrode, erode, excoriate, fray,
gall, riffle, ripple, wear away, wear threadbare;
SEE CONCEPT *215*

fretful [*adj*] *irritable*
captious, carping*, caviling, complaining, contrary, crabby*, cranky*, critical, cross, crotchety*, edgy, faultfinding, fractious, huffy*, mean,
ornery*, out of sorts*, peevish, perverse, petulant, querulous, short-tempered, snappish*, splenetic, testy, touchy, uneasy, worried, wreck*;
SEE CONCEPTS *401,403*

friction [*n1*] *rubbing*
abrasion, agitation, attrition, chafing, erosion, filing, fretting, grating, grinding, irritation, massage, rasping, resistance, scraping, soreness,
traction, trituration, wearing away; SEE CONCEPT
215

friction [*n2*] *disagreement*
animosity, antagonism, bad blood*, bad feeling*,
bickering, bone to pick*, conflict, counteraction,
discontent, discord, disharmony, dispute, dissension, faction, factionalism, flak*, hassle, hatred,
hostility, impedance, incompatibility, interference, opposition, quarrel, resentment, resistance,
rivalry, row*, ruckus*, rumpus*, set-to*, sour
note*, strife, trouble, wrangling*; SEE CONCEPTS
46,106,674

friend [*n1*] *confidant, companion*
acquaintance, ally, alter ego, associate, bosom
buddy*, buddy, chum*, classmate, cohort, colleague, companion*, compatriot, comrade, consort, cousin, crony, familiar, intimate, mate, pal,
partner, playmate, roommate, schoolmate, sidekick, soul mate*, spare*, well-wisher; SEE CON-
CEPT *423*

friend [*n2*] *benefactor*
accomplice, adherent, advocate, ally, associate,
backer, partisan, patron, supporter, well-wisher;
SEE CONCEPT *348*

friendless [*adj*] *without companionship or confidant*
abandoned, adrift, alienated, all alone*, all by
one's self*, alone, cut off*, deserted, estranged,
forlorn, forsaken, isolated, lonely, lonesome, marooned*, ostracized, shunned, solitary, unattached, without ties; SEE CONCEPT *555*

friendliness [*n*] *companionability*
affability, amiability, amity, benevolence, camaraderie, comity, comradery, congeniality, conviviality, cordiality, friendship, geniality, goodwill,
kindliness, kindness, neighborliness, open arms*,
sociability, warmth; SEE CONCEPT *388*

friendly [*adj*] *intimate, companionable*
affable, affectionate, amiable, amicable, attached,
attentive, auspicious, beneficial, benevolent, benign, buddy-buddy*, chummy*, civil, close,
clubby, comradely, conciliatory, confiding, convivial, cordial, faithful, familiar, favorable, fond,
genial, good, helpful, kind, kindly, loving, loyal,
neighborly, on good terms*, outgoing, peaceable,
peaceful, propitious, receptive, sociable, solici-

tous, sympathetic, tender, thick, welcoming, well-
disposed*; SEE CONCEPT *555*

friendship [*n*] *companionship*
accord, acquaintanceship, affection, affinity,
agreement, alliance, amiability, amicability, amity, association, attachment, attraction, benevolence, closeness, coalition, comity, company,
concord, consideration, consonance, devotion,
empathy, esteem, familiarity, favor, favoritism,
fondness, friendliness, fusion, good will, harmony, intimacy, league, love, pact, partiality,
rapport, regard, sociability, society, sodality, solidarity, understanding; SEE CONCEPTS *388,714*

fright [*n1*] *extreme apprehension*
alarm, cold sweat*, consternation, dismay, dread,
fear, horror, panic, quaking, scare, shiver, shock,
terror, trepidation, trepidity; SEE CONCEPT *410*

fright [*n2*] *horrifying or unpleasant sight*
bother, eyesore*, frump*, mess, monstrosity, nuisance, scarecrow, ugliness; SEE CONCEPT *718*

frighten [*v*] *shock, scare*
affright, agitate, alarm, appall, astound, awe,
browbeat*, bulldoze*, chill, chill to the bone*,
cow, curdle the blood*, daunt, demoralize, deter,
disturb, discomfort, disconcert, discourage, dishearten, dismay, disquiet, faze, horrify, intimidate, make blood run cold*, make teeth chatter*,
panic, perturb, petrify, repel, scare away, scare
off, scare to death*, spook, startle, stiff, strike
terror into*, terrify, terrorize, unhinge*, unnerve;
SEE CONCEPTS *14,42*

frightened [*adj*] *very scared*
abashed, affrighted, afraid, aghast, alarmed, anxious, butterflies*, chicken*, chicken-hearted*,
cowed*, dismayed, fearful, frozen, have cold
feet*, having kittens*, hung up*, in a cold sweat*,
in a panic*, in a sweat*, jellyfish*, jittery, jumpy,
lily-livered*, mousy*, numb, panicky, petrified,
pushing the panic button*, rabbity*, running
scared*, scared stiff*, shaky, shivery, sissy*,
spooked, startled, terrified, terrorized, terror-
stricken, unnerved, uptight, yellow*; SEE CON-
CEPTS *403,690*

frightful/frightening [*adj1*] *scary, shocking*
alarming, appalling, atrocious, awesome, awful,
chilling, daunting, dire, direful, dismaying, disquieting, dread, dreadful, fearful, fearsome, formidable, ghastly, grabber, grim, grisly,
gruesome, hair-raising, hairy, harrowing, hideous, horrendous, horrible, horrid, horrifying, inconceivable, intimidating, lurid, macabre,
menacing, morbid, ominous, petrifying, portentous, repellent, spooky, terrible, terrifying, traumatic, unnerving, unspeakable; SEE CONCEPTS
529,537

frightful [*adj2*] *offensive*
annoying, awful, bad, calamitous, disagreeable,
dreadful, extreme, ghastly, great, hideous, horrible, insufferable, lewd, shocking, terrible, terrific,
unpleasant, vile, wicked, wrong; SEE CONCEPTS
529,545

frigid [*adj1*] *extremely cold*
antarctic, arctic, chill, chilly, cool, freezing, frost-
bound, frosty, frozen, gelid, glacial, hyperboreal,
icebox*, ice-cold, icy, refrigerated, Siberian*,
snappy, three-dog night*, wintry; SEE CONCEPT
605

frigid [*adj2*] *unresponsive*
aloof, austere, chilly, cold, cold-hearted*, cold-
shoulder*, cool, forbidding, formal, frosty, icy,

impotent, indifferent, lifeless, passionless, passive, repellent, rigid, stiff, unapproachable, unbending, unfeeling, unloving; SEE CONCEPT *404*

frill [*n*] *luxury, nice touch*
amenity, decoration, doodad*, extravagance, fandangle, flounce, foppery*, frippery*, fuss, garbage*, garnish, gathering, gimcrack*, gingerbread*, jazz*, lace, ruffle, superfluity, thing*, tuck; SEE CONCEPTS *646,655,824*

fringe [*n*] *border, trimming*
binding, borderline, brim, brink, edge, edging, flounce, hem, limit, mane, march, margin, outside, outskirts, perimeter, periphery, rickrack, ruffle, skirt, tassel, verge; SEE CONCEPTS *484,825*

frippery [*n*] *waste, nonsense*
adornment, bauble, decoration, fanciness, fandangle*, flashiness, frill, fussiness, gaudiness, knickknack, meretriciousness, ornament, ostentation, pretentiousness, showiness, tawdriness, toy, trinket; SEE CONCEPTS *655,824*

frisk [*v1*] *cavort*
bounce, caper, dance, frolic, gambol, hop, jump, lark, leap, play, prance, rollick, romp, skip, sport, trip; SEE CONCEPT *384*

frisk [*v2*] *search*
check, fan, inspect, run over, shake down; SEE CONCEPT *216*

frisky [*adj*] *full of spirit*
active, antic, bouncy, coltish*, dashing, feeling one's oats*, frolicsome, full of beans*, gamesome, high-spirited, in high spirits*, jumpy, kittenish*, larkish, lively, peppy, playful, prankish, rollicking, romping, spirited, sportive, wicked, zesty, zippy; SEE CONCEPTS *401,542,555*

fritter [*v*] *waste away*
be wasteful with, blow*, cast away, consume, dally, diddle away, dissipate, frivol, go through*, idle, lavish, misspend, run through*, spend like water*, squander, throw away, trifle; SEE CONCEPTS *156,341*

frivolity [*n*] *silliness, childishness*
coquetting, dallying, flightiness, flippancy, flirting, flummery, folly, fribble, frippery, frivolousness, fun, gaiety, game, giddiness, jest, levity, lightheartedness, lightness, nonsense, play, puerility, shallowness, sport, superficiality, toying, trifling, triviality, volatility, whimsicality, whimsy; SEE CONCEPTS *388,633*

frivolous [*adj*] *trivial, silly*
barmy, childish, dizzy*, empty-headed*, facetious, featherbrained*, flighty, flip, flippant, foolish, gay, giddy*, harebrained*, idiotic, idle, ill-considered, impractical, juvenile, light, lightminded, minor, niggling*, nonserious, not serious, paltry, peripheral, petty, playful, pointless, puerile, scatterbrained*, senseless, shallow, sportive, superficial, tongue-in-cheek*, unimportant, unprofound, volatile, whimsical; SEE CONCEPTS *402,575*

frock [*n*] *women's garment*
apron, clothing, dress, gown, habit, muumuu, robe; SEE CONCEPT *451*

frog [*n*] *jumping amphibian*
bullfrog, croaker*, polliwog, toad; SEE CONCEPT *394*

frolic [*n*] *amusement, revel*
antic, drollery, escapade, fun, fun and games*, gaiety, gambol, game, high jinks*, joke, joviality, lark, merriment, monkeyshines*, play, prank,

romp, shenanigan*, skylarking*, sport, spree, tomfoolery*, trick; SEE CONCEPTS *59,386*

frolic [*v*] *have fun, make merry*
caper, carouse, cavort, cut capers, cut loose*, fool around*, frisk, gambol, go on a tear*, kick up one's heels*, lark, let go*, let loose*, play, prance, raise hell*, revel, riot, rollick, romp, sport, spree, whoop it up*; SEE CONCEPTS *384,386*

frolicsome [*adj*] *playful*
antic, coltish, frisky, fun, gamesome, gay, gleeful, happy, impish, jocular, jovial, kittenish, lively, merry, mischievous, roguish, rollicking, sportive, sprightly; SEE CONCEPT *542*

from [*prep1*] *outside of, separating*
against, in distinction to, out of possession of, taken away; SEE CONCEPT *583*

from [*prep2*] *arising out of*
beginning at, coming out of, deriving out of, originating at, starting with; SEE CONCEPT *549*

front [*n1*] *forward, beginning part of something*
anterior, bow, breast, brow, exterior, facade, face, facing, fore, foreground, forehead, forepart, frontage, frontal, frontispiece, front line, head, lead, obverse, proscenium, top, van, vanguard; SEE CONCEPTS *833,835,836*

front [*n2*] *appearance put on for show*
air, aspect, bearing, blind, carriage, coloring, countenance, cover, cover-up*, demeanor, disguise, display, expression, exterior, facade, face, fake, figure, manner, mask, mien, phony, port, presence, pretext, put-on*, show, veil, window dressing*; SEE CONCEPT *716*

front [*adj*] *lead, beginning*
advanced, ahead, anterior, facial, first, fore, foremost, forward, frontal, head, headmost, in the foreground, leading, obverse, topmost, vanward, ventral; SEE CONCEPTS *567,583,585,632*

front [*v*] *look out on to*
border, confront, cover, encounter, face, look over, meet, overlay, overlook; SEE CONCEPT *746*

frontier [*n1*] *boundary*
borderland, borderline, bound, confines, edge, limit, march, perimeter, verge; SEE CONCEPTS *513,745*

frontier [*n2*] *unexplored, unoccupied area of land*
backcountry, backwater, backwoods, boondocks*, boonies*, bush, hinterland, outback, outskirts, sticks*, unknown*; SEE CONCEPT *509*

frost [*n*] *extreme cold*
blight, dip, drop, freeze, hoarfrost, ice, Jack Frost*, rime; SEE CONCEPTS *524,610*

frosty [*adj*] *very cold*
antarctic, arctic, chill, chilly, cool, frigid, frozen, gelid, glacial, hoar, ice-capped, icicled, icy, nippy*, rimy, shivery, wintry; SEE CONCEPT *605*

froth [*n*] *lather, bubbles*
barm, ebullition, effervescence, fizz, foam, head, scud, scum, spindrift, spray, spume, suds, yeast; SEE CONCEPTS *260,467,468*

frothy [*adj*] *bubbly*
barmy, bubbling, fermenting, fizzing, fizzy, foaming, foamy, soapy, spumescent, spumous, spumy, sudsy, with a head on*, yeasty; SEE CONCEPT *485*

frown [*v1*] *scowl*
cloud up*, do a slow burn*, give a dirty look*, give the evil eye*, glare, gloom, glower, grimace, knit brows*, look black*, look daggers*, look stern*, lower, pout, sulk; SEE CONCEPT *185*

frown [v2] *disapprove*
deprecate, discommend, discountenance, discourage, disesteem, disfavor, dislike, look askance at*, not take kindly to*, object, show displeasure, take a dim view of*; SEE CONCEPTS *21,29*

frozen [adj1] *very cold*
antarctic, arctic, chilled, frigid, frosted, icebound, ice-cold, ice-covered, iced, icy, numb, Siberian*; SEE CONCEPT *605*

frozen [adj2] *stopped*
fixed, pegged, petrified, rooted, stock-still, suspended, turned to stone; SEE CONCEPTS *534,584*

frugal [adj] *economical*
abstemious, canny, careful, chary, conserving, discreet, meager, meticulous, mingy*, niggardly*, parsimonious, penny-pinching*, pennywise*, preserving, provident, prudent, saving, scrimping, sparing, Spartan*, stingy, thrifty, tight, tightwad*, unwasteful, wary; SEE CONCEPT *334*

frugality [n] *economizing*
avarice, avariciousness, carefulness, conservation, economy, forehandedness, good management, miserliness, moderation, niggardliness, parsimoniousness, parsimony, penuriousness, providence, prudence, saving, scrimping, stinginess, thrift, thriftiness; SEE CONCEPTS *330,335*

fruit [n1] *edible part of vegetative growth developed after flowering*
berry, crop, drupe, grain, harvest, nut, pome, produce, product, yield; SEE CONCEPTS *426,428*

fruit [n2] *result of labor*
advantage, benefit, consequence, effect, outcome, pay, profit, result, return, reward; SEE CONCEPTS *230,337*

fruitful [adj] *productive*
abounding, abundant, advantageous, beneficial, blooming, blossoming, breeding, childing, conducive, copious, effective, fecund, fertile, flourishing, flush, fructiferous, gainful, plenteous, plentiful, profitable, profuse, proliferant, prolific, propagating, reproducing, rewarding, rich, spawning, successful, useful, well-spent, worthwhile; SEE CONCEPTS *528,537,560*

fruition [n] *achievement, maturation*
accomplishment, actualization, attainment, completion, consummation, enjoyment, fulfillment, gratification, materialization, maturity, perfection, pleasure, realization, ripeness, satisfaction, success; SEE CONCEPTS *704,706*

fruitless [adj] *bringing no advantage, product*
abortive, barren, empty, futile, gainless, idle, ineffective, ineffectual, infertile, in vain, pointless, profitless, spinning one's wheels*, sterile, to no avail*, to no effect*, unavailable, unavailing, unfruitful, unproductive, unprofitable, unprolific, unsuccessful, useless, vain, wild goose chase*; SEE CONCEPTS *528,537,560*

frustrate [v] *thwart, disappoint*
annul, arrest, baffle, balk, bar, beat, block, cancel, check, circumvent, confront, conquer, counter, counteract, cramp, cramp one's style*, crimp, dash, dash one's hope*, defeat, depress, discourage, dishearten, foil, forbid, forestall, foul up*, give the run around*, halt, hang up*, hinder, hold up, impede, inhibit, lick, negate, neutralize, nullify, obstruct, obviate, outwit, overcome, preclude, prevent, prohibit, render null and void*, ruin, stump*, stymie*, upset the applecart*; SEE CONCEPTS *7,19,121*

frustrated [adj] *disappointed, thwarted*
balked*, crabbed*, cramped, crimped, defeated, discontented, discouraged, disheartened, embittered, foiled, fouled up*, hung up on*, irked, resentful, stonewalled*, stymied*, through the mill*, ungratified, unsated, unslaked, up the wall*; SEE CONCEPT *403*

frustration [n] *disappointment, thwarting*
annoyance, bitter pill*, blocking, blow, bummer, chagrin, circumvention, contravention, curbing, defeat, disgruntlement, dissatisfaction, downer*, drag*, failure, fizzle, foiling, grievance, hindrance, impediment, irritation, letdown, nonfulfillment, nonsuccess, obstruction, old one-two*, resentment, setback, unfulfillment, vexation; SEE CONCEPTS *410,674*

fry [v] *cook in hot oil*
brown, french fry, fricassee, frizzle, pan fry, sauté, sear, singe, sizzle; SEE CONCEPT *170*

fudge [v] *fake, misrepresent*
avoid, color, cook up*, dodge, embellish, embroider, equivocate, evade, exaggerate, falsify, hedge, magnify, overstate, pad, patch, shuffle, slant, stall; SEE CONCEPTS *59,63*

fuel [n] *something providing energy*
ammunition, combustible, electricity, encouragement, food, gas, incitement, juice, material, means, nourishment, propellant, provocation; SEE CONCEPTS *467,520,523,661*

fuel [v] *give energy to*
charge, fan, feed, fill 'er up*, fill up, fire, gas, gas up*, incite, inflame, nourish, service, stoke up*, supply, sustain, tank up*; SEE CONCEPTS *107,140*

fugitive [n] *person escaping from law or other pursuer*
bolter, derelict, deserter, displaced person, dodger, émigré, escapee, escaper, evacuee, exile, fly-by-night*, hermit, hunted person, outcast, outlaw, recluse, refugee, runagate, runaway, stray, transient, truant, vagabond, waif, walkout; SEE CONCEPT *412*

fugitive [adj] *fleeing, transient*
avoiding, brief, criminal, elusive, ephemeral, errant, erratic, escaping, evading, evanescent, fleeting, flitting, flying*, fugacious, hot*, impermanent, lamster, momentary, moving, on the lam*, passing, planetary, running away*, short*, short-lived, temporary, transitory, unstable, volatile, wandering, wanted; SEE CONCEPTS *551,584,798*

fulfill [v] *bring to completion*
accomplish, achieve, answer, be just the ticket*, carry out, comply with, conclude, conform, discharge, do, effect, effectuate, execute, fill, fill the bill*, finish, hit the bull's-eye*, implement, keep, make it*, make the grade*, meet, obey, observe, perfect, perform, please, realize, render, satisfy, score*, suffice, suit; SEE CONCEPTS *7,22,91,706*

fulfilled [adj] *completed*
accomplished, achieved, actualized, attained, brought about, brought to a close, carried out, compassed, concluded, consummated, crowned, delighted, dispatched, effected, effectuated, executed, finished, gratified, made good*, matured, obtained, perfected, performed, pleased, put into effect, reached, realized, satisfied; SEE CONCEPTS *403,531*

fulfillment [n] *accomplishment, completion*
achievement, attainment, carrying out, carrying through, consummation, contentedness, content-

ment, crowning, discharge, discharging, effecting, end, gratification, implementation, just the ticket*, kick*, kicks* observance, perfection, realization, you got it*; SEE CONCEPTS 230,706

full [adj1] *brimming, filled*
abounding, abundant, adequate, awash, big, bounteous, brimful, burdened, bursting, chockablock, chock-full, competent, complete, crammed, crowded, entire, extravagant, glutted, gorged, imbued, impregnated, intact, jammed, jammed full*, jam-packed*, laden, lavish, loaded, overflowing, packed, packed like sardines, padded, plenteous, plentiful, plethoric, profuse, replete, running over, sated, satiated, satisfied, saturated, stocked, stuffed, sufficient, suffused, surfeited, teeming, voluminous, weighted; SEE CONCEPTS 481,483, 773,774,786

full [adj2] *thorough*
absolute, abundant, adequate, all-inclusive, ample, blow-by-blow*, broad, choate, circumstantial, clocklike, complete, comprehensive, copious, detailed, entire, exhaustive, extensive, generous, integral, itemized, maximum, minute, particular, particularized, perfect, plenary, plenteous, plentiful, unabridged, unlimited, whole; SEE CONCEPT 531

full [adj3] *deep in sound*
clear, distinct, loud, resonant, rich, rounded, throaty; SEE CONCEPT 594

full [adj4] *satiated in hunger*
glutted, gorged, jaded, lousy with*, sated, satiate, stuffed, surfeited, up to here*; SEE CONCEPTS 406,481,774

full-bodied [adj] *robust*
concentrated, fruity, full-flavored, heady*, heavy, lusty, mellow, potent, redolent, rich, strong, well-matured; SEE CONCEPTS 489,613

full-grown/full-fledged [adj] *developed, ripe, ready*
adult, full-blown*, grown, grown-up, in one's prime*, marriageable, mature, nubile, of age, perfected, prime, ripened; SEE CONCEPTS 358,578,797

fullness [n] *abundance, breadth*
adequateness, ampleness, amplitude, broadness, completeness, completion, comprehensiveness, congestion, copiousness, curvaceousness, dilation, distension, enlargement, entirety, extensiveness, fill, glut, plenitude, plenty, plenum, profusion, repletion, roundness, satiation, satiety, saturation, scope, sufficiency, surfeit, swelling, totality, tumescence, vastness, voluptuousness, wealth, wholeness, wideness; SEE CONCEPTS 635,730

full-scale [adj] *total, all-out*
all-encompassing, comprehensive, exhaustive, extensive, full-blown*, full-dress*, full-out*, in-depth, major, proper, sweeping, thorough, thoroughgoing, total, unlimited, wide-ranging; SEE CONCEPTS 531,772

fully [adv1] *completely, in all respects*
absolutely, all out*, all the way*, altogether*, entirely, every inch*, from A to Z*, from soup to nuts*, heart and soul*, intimately, outright, perfectly, positively, quite, royal*, thoroughly, through and through*, totally, utterly, wholly, without exaggeration; SEE CONCEPTS 531,772

fully [adv2] *sufficiently, adequately*
abundantly, amply, comprehensively, enough, plentifully, satisfactorily, well; SEE CONCEPT 558

fulminate [v] *criticize harshly*
animadvert, berate, blow up, bluster, castigate, censure, condemn, curse, declaim, denounce, denunciate, execrate, explode, fume, intimidate, inveigh against, menace, protest, rage, rail, reprobate, swear at, thunder, upbraid, vilify, vituperate; SEE CONCEPTS 52,54

fulmination [n] *tirade, condemnation*
blast, curse, denunciation, diatribe, discharge, explosion, intimidation, invective, obloquy, outburst, philippic, reprobation, warning; SEE CONCEPTS 52,54,278

fulsome [adj] *sickening or excessive behavior*
adulatory, bombastic, buttery*, canting, cloying, coarse, extravagant, fawning, flattering, glib, grandiloquent, hypocritical, immoderate, ingratiating, inordinate, insincere, magniloquent, mealy-mouthed*, nauseating, offensive, oily*, oleaginous, overdone, saccharine, sanctimonious, slick*, slimy*, smarmy*, smooth, suave, sycophantic, unctuous, wheedling*; SEE CONCEPTS 267,401

fumble [v] *bumble, mess up*
bollix*, botch*, bungle, err, feel, flounder, flub*, fluff*, goof*, grapple, grope, lose the handle*, louse up*, misfield, mishandle, mismanage, scrabble*, screw up*, spoil, stumble; SEE CONCEPTS 101,181

fume [v] *get very upset about*
anger, blow up*, boil, bristle, burn, chafe, chomp at the bit*, get hot*, get steamed up*, rage, rant, rave, seethe, smoke*, storm*; SEE CONCEPTS 21,29,410

fumes [n] *pollution, gas in air*
effluvium, exhalation, exhaust, haze, miasma, reek, smog, smoke, stench, vapor; SEE CONCEPTS 437,600

fun [n] *amusement, play*
absurdity, ball*, big time*, blast*, buffoonery, celebration, cheer, clowning, distraction, diversion, enjoyment, entertainment, escapade, festivity, foolery, frolic, gaiety, gambol, game*, good time*, grins*, high jinks*, holiday, horseplay*, jesting, jocularity, joke, joking, jollity, joy, junketing, laughter, living it up*, merriment, merry-making, mirth, nonsense, pastime, picnic*, playfulness, pleasure, recreation, rejoicing, relaxation, riot, romp, romping, solace, sport, tomfoolery*, treat, whoopee*; SEE CONCEPTS 386,388

fun [adj] *good, happy*
amusing, boisterous, convivial, diverting, enjoyable, entertaining, lively, merry, pleasant, witty; SEE CONCEPTS 537,572

function [n1] *capacity, job*
action, activity, affair, behavior, business, charge, concern, duty, employment, exercise, faculty, goal, mark, mission, object, objective, occupation, office, operation, part, post, power, province, purpose, raison d'être*, responsibility, role, service, situation, target, task, use, utility, work; SEE CONCEPTS 362,659

function [n2] *social occasion*
affair, celebration, do*, gathering, get-together*, meeting, party, reception; SEE CONCEPT 386

function [v] *perform, work*
act, act the part*, behave, be in action, be in commission, be in operation, be running, cook, do, do duty*, do one's thing*, get with it*, go, go to town*, move, officialize, officiate, operate, per-

fr
fu

colate*, react, run, serve, take, take care of business*; SEE CONCEPTS 87,362

functional [adj] *working*
handy, occupational, operative, practicable, practical, serviceable, useful, utile, utilitarian, utility; SEE CONCEPT 560

fund [n] *repository, reserve*
armamentarium, capital, endowment, foundation, hoard, inventory, kitty*, mine, pool*, reservoir, source, stock, store, storehouse, supply, treasury, trust, vein; SEE CONCEPTS 332,340,710

fund [v] *provide money for*
back, bankroll, capitalize, endow, finance, float, grubstake*, juice*, patronize, pay for, pick up the check*, pick up the tab*, promote, stake, subsidize, support; SEE CONCEPTS 115,341

fundamental [n] *basic, essential part*
ABCs*, axiom, basis, bottom line*, brass tacks*, coal and ice*, component, constituent, cornerstone, element, factor, foundation, guts*, heart, law, nitty-gritty*, principium, principle, rock bottom*, rudiment, rule, sine qua non*, theorem; SEE CONCEPTS 668,688,826,829

fundamental [adj] *basic, important*
axiological, axiomatic, basal, bottom, bottom-line*, cardinal, central, constitutional, constitutive, crucial, elemental, elementary, essential, first, foundational, grass-roots*, indispensable, integral, intrinsic, key, major, meat-and-potatoes*, necessary, organic, original, paramount, primary, prime, primitive, primordial, principal, radical, requisite, rudimentary, significant, structural, substratal, substrative, supporting, sustaining, theoretical, underived, underlying, vital; SEE CONCEPTS 546,567

funds [n] *cash reserve*
accounts receivable, affluence, assets, backing, bankroll, belongings, bread*, budget, capital, collateral, currency, dough*, earnings, finance, fluid assets, hard cash*, kitty*, lucre, means, money, money in the bank*, money on hand*, nest egg*, nut*, petty cash, pork barrel*, possessions, proceeds, profits, property, ready money*, resources, revenue, savings, scratch*, securities, specie, stakes*, store*, stuff*, substance, treasure, wealth, wherewithal*, winnings*; SEE CONCEPTS 340,710

funeral [n] *ceremony for the dead*
burial, cremation, entombment, exequies, funeration, inhumation, interment, last rites, obit, obsequies, planting, requiem, sepulture, services, solemnities; SEE CONCEPTS 172,386

funereal [adj] *depressing*
black, bleak, dark, deathlike, dirgelike, disheartening, dismal, doleful, dreary, elegiac, gloomy, grave, grim, lamenting, lugubrious, melancholy, mournful, oppressive, sad, sepulchral, serious, solemn, somber, woeful; SEE CONCEPTS 403,537,542

funk [n] *fear, depression*
alarm, cold sweat*, despondency, fright, gloom, misery, panic, trembling; SEE CONCEPTS 27,410

funnel [v] *direct down a path*
carry, channel, conduct, convey, filter, move, pass, pipe, pour, siphon, traject, transmit; SEE CONCEPTS 187,217

funny [adj1] *comical, humorous*
absurd, amusing, antic, blithe, capricious, clever, diverting, droll, entertaining, facetious, farcical, for grins*, gas*, gay, gelastic, good-humored, hilarious, humdinger, hysterical, jocose, jocular, joking, jolly, killing*, knee-slapper*, laughable, ludicrous, merry, mirthful, playful, priceless, rich, ridiculous, riot, riotous, risible, screaming, side-splitting*, silly, slapstick, sportive, waggish, whimsical, witty; SEE CONCEPTS 267,529,537

funny [adj2] *odd, peculiar*
bizarre, curious, dubious, fantastic, mysterious, perplexing, puzzling, queer, remarkable, strange, suspicious, unusual, weird; SEE CONCEPTS 552,564

fur [n] *hair on animals*
brush, coat, down, fluff, fuzz, hide, jacket, lint, pelage, pelt, pile, skin, wool; SEE CONCEPT 399

furbish [v] *polish; renovate*
brighten, buff, burnish, clean, deck out*, fix up, glaze, gloss, gussy up*, improve, recondition, refurbish, rehabilitate, renew, restore, rub, shine, smarten up*, spruce up*; SEE CONCEPTS 162,165,700

furious [adj1] *extremely angry, very mad*
bent*, bent out of shape*, beside oneself*, boiling*, browned off*, bummed out*, corybantic, crazed, demented, desperate, enraged, fierce, fit to be tied*, frantic, frenetic, frenzied, fuming, hacked, hopping mad*, incensed, infuriated, insane, irrational, livid, maddened, maniac, on the warpath*, rabid, raging, smoking*, steamed, unreasonable, up in arms*, vehement, vicious, violent, wrathful; SEE CONCEPT 403

furious [adj2] *stormy, turbulent*
agitated, blustering, blustery, boisterous, concentrated, excessive, exquisite, extreme, fierce, flaming, impetuous, intense, intensified, raging, rampageous, rough, savage, tempestuous, terrible, tumultuous/tumultuous, ungovernable, unrestrained, vehement, vicious, violent, wild; SEE CONCEPTS 525,537,548

furnace [n] *heating mechanism*
boiler, calefactor, cinerator, cremator, forge, Franklin stove, heater, heating system, incinerator, kiln, oil burner, smithy, stove; SEE CONCEPT 463

furnish [v1] *decorate, supply*
accoutre, apparel, appoint, arm, array, clothe, endow, equip, feather a nest*, fit, fit out*, fix up*, gear, line a nest*, make habitable, outfit, provide, provision, purvey, rig, stock, store, turn out; SEE CONCEPTS 140,177,182

furnish [v2] *give, reveal information*
afford, bestow, deliver, dispense, endow, feed, grant, hand, hand over, offer, present, provide, supply, transfer, turn over; SEE CONCEPTS 60,67,108

furniture [n] *household property*
appliance, appointment, bed, bookcase, buffet, bureau, cabinet, chair, chattel, chest, commode, couch, counter, cupboard, davenport, desk, dresser, effect, equipment, fittings, furnishing, goods, highboy, hutch, movables, possession, sideboard, sofa, stool, table, thing, wardrobe; SEE CONCEPT 443

furor [n] *disturbance, excitement*
ado*, agitation, big scene*, big stink*, bustle, commotion, craze, enthusiasm, fad, ferment, flap*, free-for-all*, frenzy, fury, fuss, hell broke loose*, hullabaloo*, hysteria, lunacy, madness*, mania, outburst, outcry, rage, row, ruckus, stir*, to-do*, tumult, uproar, whirl; SEE CONCEPTS 230,388,410

furrow [n] *ditch*

channel, corrugation, crease, crinkle, crow's-foot*, dike, fluting, fold, groove, gutter, hollow, line, plica, rabbet, ridge, rimple, rivel, ruck, rut, seam, trench, wrinkle; SEE CONCEPT *513*

further [adj] *additional*

added, another, else, extra, farther, fresh, in addition, more, new, other, supplementary; SEE CONCEPT *771*

further [v] *advance, lend support*

aid, assist, back up, bail out*, ballyhoo*, champion, contribute, encourage, engender, expedite, facilitate, forward, foster, generate, give a boost to*, go with, hasten, help, lend a hand*, open doors*, patronize, plug, promote, propagate, push, serve, speed, succor, take care of, work for; SEE CONCEPTS *69,87,110*

further [adv] *additionally*

again, also, as well as, besides, beyond, distant, farther, in addition, moreover, on top of*, over and above*, then, to boot, what's more*, yet, yonder; SEE CONCEPT *771*

furtherance [n] *advancement*

advocacy, backing, boosting, carrying-out, championship, progress, progression, promotion, prosecution, pursuit; SEE CONCEPTS *110,704*

furthermore [adv] *in addition*

additionally, along, as well, besides, likewise, moreover, not to mention, to boot, too, what's more*, withal, yet; SEE CONCEPTS *577,824*

furthest [adj] *most distant*

extreme, farthest, most remote, outermost, outmost, remotest, ultimate, uttermost; SEE CONCEPTS *586,778*

furtive [adj] *sneaky, secretive*

artful, calculating, cautious, circumspect, clandestine, cloaked, conspiratorial, covert, crafty*, creepy*, cunning, disguised, elusive, evasive, foxy, guileful, hidden, hush-hush*, insidious, masked, scheming, shifty*, skulking, slinking*, sly, stealthy, sub-rosa*, surreptitious, tricky*, undercover, underhand, underhanded, under-the-table*, under wraps*, wily; SEE CONCEPTS *548,576*

fury [n] *anger, wrath*

acerbity, acrimony, asperity, boiling point*, conniption, energy, ferocity, fierceness, fire, flare-up, force, frenzy, furor, impetuosity, indignation, intensity, ire, madness, might, passion, power, rabidity, rage, rampancy, rise, savagery, severity, slow burn*, sore, stew*, storm*, tempestuousness, turbulence, vehemence, violence; SEE CONCEPTS *29,410*

fuse [v] *meld, intermix*

agglutinate, amalgamate, bind, blend, cement, coalesce, combine, commingle, deliquesce, dissolve, federate, flux, integrate, interblend, interfuse, intermingle, join, liquefy, liquesce, melt, merge, mingle, run, run together, smelt, solder, thaw, unite, weld; SEE CONCEPT *113*

fusion [n] *melding; mixture*

admixture, alloy, amalgam, amalgamation, blend, blending, coadunation, coalescence, coalition, commingling, commixture, compound, federation, heating, immixture, integration, intermixture, junction, liquefaction, liquification, melting, merger, merging, smelting, soldering, synthesis, unification, union, uniting, welding; SEE CONCEPTS *113,260,432*

fuss [n] *disturbance, trouble*

ado, agitation, altercation, argument, bickering, bother, broil*, bustle, commotion, complaint, confusion, controversy, difficulty, display, dispute, excitement, falling-out*, fight, flap, flurry, flutter, fret, furor, hassle, kick-up*, objection, palaver, perturbation, quarrel, row, ruckus, scene, squabble, stew*, stink*, stir, storm, to-do*, turmoil, unrest, upset, winging*, worry; SEE CONCEPTS *46,106,388,633*

fussy [adj] *meticulous, particular*

careful, choosy, conscientious, conscionable, dainty, difficult, discriminating, exact, exacting, fastidious, finical, finicky, fretful, fuddy-duddy*, hard to please*, heedful, nit-picking*, overfastidious, painstaking, persnickety, picky, picky-picky*, punctilious, punctual, querulous, scrupulous, squeamish, stickling; SEE CONCEPTS *401,404*

futile [adj] *hopeless, pointless*

abortive, barren, bootless, delusive, empty, exhausted, forlorn, fruitless, hollow, idle, impracticable, impractical, ineffective, ineffectual, insufficient, in vain, no dice*, nugatory, on a treadmill*, otiose, out the window*, profitless, resultless, save one's breath*, sterile, to no avail*, to no effect*, to no purpose*, trifling, trivial, unavailing, unimportant, unneeded, unproductive, unprofitable, unreal, unsatisfactory, unsubstantial, unsuccessful, useless, vain, valueless, worthless; SEE CONCEPTS *528,548,560*

future [n] *time to come*

aftertime, afterward, by and by*, destiny, eternity, expectation, fate, futurity, hereafter, infinity, life to come, millennium, morrow, offing, outlook, posterity, prospect, subsequent time, to be*, tomorrow, world to come*; SEE CONCEPTS *679,807,811,818*

future [adj] *to come; expected*

approaching, booked, budgeted, close at hand*, coming, coming up, destined, down the line*, down the pike, down the road*, eventual, fated, final, forthcoming, from here in, from here on, from here to eternity*, from now on in*, imminent, impending, inevitable, in the cards*, in the course of time, in the offing*, just around the corner*, later, likely, looked toward, near, next, planned, prospective, scheduled, subsequent, to be*, ulterior, ultimate, unborn, unfolding, up; SEE CONCEPT *820*

fuzz [n] *fluff*

down, dust ball*, dust bunnies*, fiber, floss, fur, hair, lanugo, lint, nap, pile; SEE CONCEPT *260*

fuzzy [adj 1] *fluffy*

down-covered, downy, flossy, frizzy, furry, hairy, linty, napped, pilate, velutinous, woolly; SEE CONCEPT *606*

fuzzy [adj 2] *out of focus*

bleary, blurred, dim, distorted, faint, foggy, hazy, ill-defined, indefinite, indistinct, misty, muffled, murky, obscure, shadowy, unclear, unfocused, vague; SEE CONCEPT *619*

G

gab [n] *conversation*

blab*, blather*, chat, chitchat*, gossip, idle talk*, loquacity*, palaver*, prattle, small talk*, talk,

fu
ga

tête-à-tête, tongue-wagging*, yak*, yakkety-yak*; SEE CONCEPT 278

gab [v] *talk a lot*
blabber*, blather*, buzz*, chatter, gossip, jabber*, jaw*, prate, prattle, yak*, yakkety-yak*; SEE CONCEPT 266

gabby [adj] *talkative*
chattering, chatty, effusive, garrulous, glib, gossiping, gushing, jabbering, long-winded*, loose-lipped*, loquacious, mouthy*, prattling, prolix, talky, verbose, voluble, windy*, wordy; SEE CONCEPT 267

gad [v] *roam about*
cruise, gallivant, hit the road*, hit the trail*, jaunt, knock about*, knock around*, maunder, mooch*, ramble, range, rove, run around*, stray, traipse, wander; SEE CONCEPTS 149,224

gadget [n] *device, novelty*
apparatus, appliance, business, concern, contraption, contrivance, doodad*, doohickey*, gimmick, gizmo*, invention, object, thing*, thingamajig, tool, utensil, whatchamacallit*, widget*; SEE CONCEPTS 463,499

gaffe [n] *mistake, goof*
blooper*, blunder, boner*, boo-boo*, faux pas*, howler*, impropriety, indecorum, indiscretion, putting foot in mouth*, slip*, solecism; SEE CONCEPTS 101,230

gag [n] *practical joke*
crack, drollery, hoax, jest, quip, ruse, trick, wile, wisecrack, witticism; SEE CONCEPT 59

gag [v1] *silence, stop up*
balk, bottle up*, choke, constrain, cork*, cork up*, curb, deaden, demur, garrote, keep the lid on*, muffle, muzzle, obstruct, put the lid on*, quiet, repress, restrain, shut down, shy, squash*, squelch, stifle, still, stumble, suppress, tape up*, throttle*, tongue-tie*; SEE CONCEPTS 121,130

gag [v2] *vomit, choke*
be nauseated, disgorge, gasp, heave, nauseate, pant, puke*, retch, sicken, spew, strain, struggle, throw up; SEE CONCEPTS 179,308

gaiety [n] *happiness, celebration*
animation, blitheness, brightness, brilliance, cheer, color, colorfulness, conviviality, effervescence, elation, entertainment, exhilaration, festivity, frolic, fun, geniality, gladness, glee, glitter, good humor*, grins*, high spirits*, hilarity, joie de vivre, jollity, joviality, joyousness, lightheartedness, liveliness, merriment, merrymaking, mirth, pleasantness, radiance, revel, reveling, revelry, shindig*, showiness, sparkle, sport, sprightliness, vivacity, whoopee*, wingding*; SEE CONCEPTS 377,388

gaily [adv] *happily, brightly*
blithely, brilliantly, cheerfully, colorfully, flamboyantly, flashily, gleefully, glowingly, joyfully, laughingly, lightheartedly, merrily, showily, sparklingly, spiritedly, splendidly, vivaciously, with élan*, with spirit*; SEE CONCEPTS 542,589

gain [n] *acquisition, winnings*
accretion, accrual, accumulation, achievement, addition, advance, advancement, advantage, attainment, benefit, boost, buildup, cut, dividend, earnings, emolument, gravy*, growth, headway*, hike*, improvement, income, increase, increment, lucre, payoff, proceeds, produce, profit, progress, receipts, return, rise, share, take, up*, upping*, velvet*, yield; SEE CONCEPTS 337,344,706,710

gain [v] *acquire, win*
accomplish, achieve, advance, ameliorate, annex, attain, augment, benefit, boost, bring in, build up, capture, clear, collect, complete, consummate, earn, enlarge, enlist, expand, fulfill, gather, get, glean, grow, harvest, have, improve, increase, land, make, make a killing*, move forward, net, obtain, overtake, parlay, perfect, pick up, procure, produce, profit, progress, promote, rack up*, reach, realize, reap, score*, secure, succeed, win over; SEE CONCEPTS 120,124,129

gainful [adj] *very productive, profitable*
advantageous, beneficial, fat, fruitful, generous, going, going concern*, good, in the black*, lucrative, lush, moneymaking, paid off, paying, remunerative, rewarding, rich, satisfying, substantial, sweet*, useful, well-paying, worthwhile; SEE CONCEPT 334

gainsay [v] *contradict*
combat, contravene, controvert, cross, deny, disaffirm, disagree, disclaim, disprove, dispute, fight, impugn, negate, negative, oppose, refute, repudiate, resist, traverse, withstand; SEE CONCEPTS 52,54

gait [n] *way an animal or person moves, walks*
amble, bearing, canter, carriage, clip, gallop, get along, lick, march, motion, movement, pace, run, speed, step, stride, tread, trot, walk; SEE CONCEPT 149

gala [n] *festival*
affair, ball, bash, blast*, blowout*, carnival, celebration, clambake, dance, do, festivity, fete, fiesta, function, get-together*, hop, jamboree, moveable feast, pageant, party, prom, roast, shindig*, stag, to-do*, wingding*; SEE CONCEPTS 377,383

gala [adj] *celebratory*
bright, colorful, convivial, festal, festive, gay, happy, jovial, joyful, merry; SEE CONCEPT 548

gale [n] *violent storm*
blast, blow, burst, chinook, cyclone, hurricane, mistral, monsoon, outbreak, outburst, squall, tempest, tornado, typhoon, wind, windstorm; SEE CONCEPTS 524,526

gall [n] *nerve, brashness*
acrimony, animosity, arrogance, bitterness, brass, brazenness, cheek*, chutzpah*, conceit, confidence, crust, cynicism, effrontery, guts*, haughtiness, hostility, impertinence, impudence, insolence, malevolence, malice, overbearance, pomposity, presumption, rancor, sauciness, self-importance, spite, venom; SEE CONCEPTS 411,633

gall [v1] *upset, irritate*
aggravate, annoy, bedevil, bother, burn, chafe, chide, disturb, exasperate, fret, grate, harass, harry, inflame, irk, nag, peeve, pester, plague, provoke, rile, roil, rub, ruffle, scrape, torment, trouble, vex, worry; SEE CONCEPTS 7,19

gall [v2] *rub raw*
abrade, bark, burn, chafe, corrode, erode, excoriate, file, fray, frazzle, fret, grate, graze, irritate, scrape, scratch, scuff, skin, wear; SEE CONCEPT 215

gallant [adj] *brave, splendid*
attentive, bold, considerate, courageous, courteous, courtly, daring, dashing, dauntless, dignified, doughty, fearless, fire-eating*, game*, glorious, gracious, grand, gritty*, hairy*, heroic, honorable, intrepid, lionhearted*, lofty, magnan-

imous, noble, plucky*, polite, quixotic, stately, stouthearted, suave, thoughtful, urbane, valiant, valorous; SEE CONCEPTS 404,542

gallantry [n] *bravery, civility*
address, attentiveness, audacity, boldness, courage, courageousness, courteousness, courtesy, daring, dauntlessness, deference, derring-do*, duty, elegance, fearlessness, graciousness, honor, intrepidity, mettle, nerve, nobility, pluck*, poise, politeness, prowess, resolution, reverence, savoir-faire, spirit, tact, urbanity, valiance, valor; SEE CONCEPTS 411,657

gallery [n1] *balcony*
arcade, loggia, mezzanine, patio, porch, upstairs, veranda; SEE CONCEPT 440

gallery [n2] *showplace for wares*
exhibit, exhibition room, hall, museum, salon, showroom, studio, wing; SEE CONCEPTS 448,449

gallery [n3] *audience, usually seated high*
attendance, onlookers, peanut gallery*, public, spectators; SEE CONCEPTS 294,417

galling [adj] *very upsetting*
acid, afflictive, aggravating, annoying, bitter, bothersome, distasteful, exasperating, grievous, harassing, humiliating, irksome, irritating, nettlesome, painful, plaguing, provoking, rankling, unpalatable, vexatious, vexing; SEE CONCEPTS 7,19

gallivant [v] *run around, gad about*
cruise, jaunt, meander, mooch, ramble, range, roam, rove, stray, traipse, wander; SEE CONCEPTS 149,224

gallop [v] *bolt, race with slight jumping motion*
amble, canter, career, course, dart, dash, fly, hasten, hurdle, hurry, jump, leap, lope, pace, rack, run, rush, shoot, speed, spring, sprint, stride, tear along, trot, zoom; SEE CONCEPTS 150,194

galvanize [v] *inspire, stimulate*
animate, arouse, astonish, awaken, commove, electrify, energize, excite, fire*, frighten, innervate, invigorate, jolt, motivate, move, pique, prime, provoke, quicken, shock, spur, startle, stir, stun, thrill, vitalize, wake, zap*; SEE CONCEPTS 7,14,22

gambit [n] *plan, plot*
artifice, design, device, gimmick, jig, maneuver, play, ploy, ruse, trick; SEE CONCEPT 660

gamble [n] *chance, speculation*
action, bet, fling, leap*, long shot*, lottery, outside chance*, raffle, risk, shot in the dark*, spec*, stab*, throw of the dice*, toss up*, uncertainty, venture, wager; SEE CONCEPTS 28,363

gamble [v] *take a chance on winning*
back, bet, brave, buck the odds*, cast lots*, challenge, cut the cards, dare, defy, endanger, face, flip the coin*, game, go for broke*, hazard, imperil, jeopardize, lay money on*, lot, make a bet, play, plunge, put, put faith in, put trust in, risk, set, shoot the moon*, shoot the works*, speculate, stake, stick one's neck out*, take a flyer*, tempt fortune*, trust to luck, try one's luck, venture, wager; SEE CONCEPTS 28,363

gambol [v] *tumble playfully*
bound, caper, carry on, cavort, cut, cut a caper*, cut loose*, fool around*, frisk, frolic, hop, horse around*, jump, kibitz around*, kick up one's heels*, lark, leap, play, prance, revel, roister, rollick, romp, skip, sport, spring, whoop it up*; SEE CONCEPTS 149,194,363

game [n1] *entertainment*
adventure, amusement, athletics, business, distraction, diversion, enterprise, festivity, frolic, fun, jest, joke, lark, line, merriment, merrymaking, occupation, pastime, plan, play, proceeding, pursuit, recreation, romp, scheme, sport, sports, undertaking; SEE CONCEPTS 292,363

game [n2] *individual sporting event*
competition, contest, match, meeting, round, tournament; SEE CONCEPT 364

game [n3] *undomesticated animals chased for food*
chase, fish, fowl, kill, meat, prey, quarry, ravin, victim, wild animals; SEE CONCEPTS 394,457,460

game [n4] *plot, trick*
butt, derision, design, device, hoax, joke, object of ridicule, plan, ploy, practical joke, prank, scheme, stratagem, strategy, tactic; SEE CONCEPTS 59,660

game [adj1] *brave, willing*
bold, courageous, dauntless, desirous, disposed, dogged, eager, fearless, gallant, hardy, heroic, inclined, interested, intrepid, nervy*, persevering, persistent, plucky*, prepared, ready, resolute, spirited, spunky, unafraid, unflinching, up for*, valiant, valorous; SEE CONCEPT 404

game [adj2] *debilitated*
ailing, bad, crippled, deformed, disabled, incapacitated, injured, lame, maimed, weak; SEE CONCEPTS 314,485

gamut [n] *range*
area, catalogue, compass, diapason, extent, field, panorama, scale, scope, series, spectrum, sweep; SEE CONCEPTS 651,788

gang [n] *group, mob of people*
assemblage, band, bunch, circle, clan, clique, club, cluster, combo*, company, coterie, crew, crowd, herd, horde, knot, lot, organization, outfit, pack, party, posse, ring, set, shift, squad, syndicate, team, tribe, troop, troupe, workers, zoo*; SEE CONCEPT 387

gangster [n] *person involved in illegal activities*
bandit, bruiser*, criminal, crook, dealer, desperado, goon*, hit person, hood, hoodlum, hooligan*, Mafioso*, member of the family, mobster, pusher, racketeer, robber, ruffian, soldier*, thug, tough; SEE CONCEPT 412

gap [n] *break, breach*
aperture, arroyo, blank, caesura, canyon, chasm, cleft, clove, crack, cranny, crevice, cut, defile, difference, disagreement, discontinuity, disparity, divergence, divide, division, fracture, gorge, gulch, gully, hiatus, hole, hollow, inconsistency, interlude, intermission, interruption, interspace, interstice, interval, lacuna, lull, notch, opening, orifice, pause, ravine, recess, rent, respite, rest, rift, rupture, separation, slit, slot, space, vacuity, void; SEE CONCEPTS 513,665

gape [v1] *gawk*
beam, bore, eye, eyeball*, focus, get a load of*, get an eyeful*, give the eye*, glare, gloat, goggle*, look, ogle, peer, rubberneck*, size up*, stare, take in*, wonder, yawp*; SEE CONCEPT 623

gape [v2] *be wide open*
cleave, crack, dehisce, divide, frondesce, gap, part, split, yaw, yawn; SEE CONCEPT 135

gaping [adj] *wide open*
broad, cavernous, chasmal, great, vast, yawning; SEE CONCEPTS 485,490

garage [n] *storage building for vehicles, workplace*
barn, carport*, car stall*, parking lot, parking space, repair shop, shop, storage; SEE CONCEPTS 439,449

ga
ga

garb [n] *clothing*
apparel, appearance, array, attire, clothes, costume, dress, duds*, feathers*, form, garment, gear, guise, habiliment, habit, outfit, rags*, raiment, robes*, semblance, things*, threads*, uniform, vestments, wear; SEE CONCEPT *451*

garb [v] *fit with clothes*
apparel, array, attire, clad, clothe, cover, deck, deck out*, drape, dress, dud*, fit out*, garment, raiment, rig out*, rig up*, robe, suit up*, tog*, turn out*; SEE CONCEPT *167*

garbage [n] *refuse, litter*
bits and pieces*, debris, detritus, dreck, dregs, dross, filth, junk, muck, odds and ends*, offal, rubbish, rubble, scrap, scrapings, sewage, slop*, sweepings, swill, trash, waste; SEE CONCEPT *260*

garble [v] *mix up, misrepresent*
belie, color, confuse, corrupt, distort, doctor, falsify, jumble, misinterpret, mislead, misquote, misstate, mutilate, obscure, pervert, slant, tamper with, twist, warp; SEE CONCEPTS *59,63*

garden [n] *cultivated plants, flowers*
back yard, bed, cold frame, conservatory, enclosure, field, greenhouse, hothouse, nursery, oasis, patch, patio, plot, terrace; SEE CONCEPTS *509,517*

gargantuan [adj] *very large*
big, colossal, elephantine, enormous, giant, gigantic, heavyweight, huge, humongous, immense, jumbo, leviathan, mammoth, massive, monstrous, monumental, mountainous, prodigious, super-colossal*, super-duper*, titanic, towering, tremendous, vast, whopping*; SEE CONCEPTS *491,773*

gargle [v] *rinse the mouth with liquid*
irrigate, swish, trill, use mouthwash; SEE CONCEPTS *169,308,616*

garish [adj] *flashy, tasteless*
blatant, brassy, brazen, cheap, chintzy, flaunting, gaudy, glaring, glittering, kitschy*, loud, meretricious, ornate, ostentatious, overdone, overwrought, raffish, screaming*, showy, tawdry, tinsel, vulgar; SEE CONCEPT *589*

garland [n] *strand of material, usually hung*
bays, chaplet, coronal, crown, festoon, honors, laurel, palm, wreath; SEE CONCEPTS *260,429*

garment [n] *article of clothing*
apparel, array, attire, costume, covering, drapes*, dress, duds*, feathers*, garb, gear, get-up*, habiliment, habit, outfit, raiment, robe, things*, threads*, togs*, uniform, vestments, wear, weeds*; SEE CONCEPT *451*

garner [v] *collect, accumulate*
amass, assemble, cull, cumulate, deposit, extract, gather, glean, harvest, hive, hoard, lay in*, lay up*, pick up, put by*, reap, reserve, roll up*, save, stockpile, store, stow away, treasure; SEE CONCEPTS *109,135*

garnish [n] *embellishment, improvement*
adornment, decoration, enhancement, furbelow, gingerbread*, ornament, ornamentation, tinsel, trim, trimming; SEE CONCEPT *824*

garnish [v] *embellish, improve*
adorn, beautify, bedeck, deck, decorate, dress up, enhance, fix up, grace, gussy up*, ornament, set off*, spiff up*, spruce up*, trim; SEE CONCEPT *244*

garrulous [adj] *talkative*
babbling, blabbermouth*, chattering, chatty, effusive, flap jaw*, gabby, glib, gossiping, gushing, long-winded*, loose-lipped*, loose-tongued*, loquacious, motormouth*, mouthy, prating, prattling, prolix, prosy, running on at the mouth*, verbose, voluble, wind-bag*, windy*, wordy, yakkity*, yakky*; SEE CONCEPTS *267,404*

gas [n] *something not liquid or solid*
effluvium, fumes, miasma, smoke, stream, vapor, volatile substance; SEE CONCEPT *465*

gash [n] *cut made by slicing*
cleft, furrow, gouge, incision, laceration, mark, nip, notch, rent, slash, slit, split, tear, wound; SEE CONCEPT *309*

gash [v] *cut by slicing*
carve, cleave, furrow, gouge, incise, injure, lacerate, lance, mark, nip, notch, pierce, rend, slash, slit, split, tear, wound; SEE CONCEPTS *137,176*

gasp [n] *sharply drawn breath*
blow, ejaculation, exclamation, gulp, heave, pant, puff, wheeze, whoop; SEE CONCEPTS *163,595*

gasp [v] *draw breath in sharply*
blow, catch one's breath, choke, convulse, fight for breath, gulp, heave, inhale, inspire, pant, puff, respire, sniffle, snort, wheeze, whoop; SEE CONCEPT *163*

gate [n] *movable barrier at entrance*
access, bar, conduit, door, doorway, egress, exit, gateway, issue, lock, opening, passage, port, portal, revolving door, slammer*, turnstile, way, weir; SEE CONCEPTS *440,445*

gather [v1] *come or bring together*
accumulate, aggregate, amass, assemble, associate, bunch up, capture, choose, close with, cluster, collect, concentrate, congregate, convene, converge, corral, crowd, cull, draw, draw in, flock, forgather, gang up, garner, get together, group, hang around*, hang out*, heap, herd, hoard, huddle, make the scene*, marshal, mass, meet, muster, pick, pile up, pluck, poke*, pour in, punch*, rally, reunite, round up*, scare up*, scrape together*, show up, stack up, stockpile, swarm, throng, unite; SEE CONCEPTS *109,114*

gather [v2] *be led to believe; infer*
assume, conclude, deduce, draw, expect, find, hear, imagine, judge, learn, make, presume, reckon, suppose, surmise, suspect, take, think, understand; SEE CONCEPT *15*

gather [v3] *harvest, pick out*
crop, cull, draw, extract, garner, glean, heap, ingather, mass, pick up, pile, pluck, reap, select, stack, take in; SEE CONCEPT *257*

gather [v4] *gain, increase*
build, deepen, enlarge, expand, grow, heighten, intensify, rise, swell, thicken, wax; SEE CONCEPT *780*

gathering [n] *assemblage, accumulation*
acquisition, affair, aggregate, aggregation, association, band, body, bunch, caucus, clambake*, collection, company, concentration, conclave, concourse, conference, congregation, congress, convention, convocation, crowd, crush, drove, flock, function, gain, get-together*, group, heap, herd, horde, huddle, junction, knot, levy, mass, meet, meeting, muster, parley, party, pile, powwow*, rally, roundup, social function, society, stock, stockpile, swarm, throng, turnout, union; SEE CONCEPTS *324,386,417*

gauche [adj] *tactless, unsophisticated*
awkward, bumbling, clumsy, crude, graceless, green, halting, ham-handed*, heavy-handed, ignorant, ill-bred, ill-mannered, inelegant, inept, insensitive, lacking, maladroit, oafish, uncouth,

uncultured, unhappy, unpolished, wooden*; SEE CONCEPT 404

gaudy [adj] *bright and vulgar*

blatant, brazen, brilliant, catchpenny*, chichi*, chintzy, coarse, crude, flashy, flaunting, florid, frou-frou*, garish, gay, glaring, gross, gussied up*, jazzy, kitschy*, loud, meretricious, obtrusive, ostentatious, pizzazz*, pretentious, putting on the ritz*, raffish, ritzy, screaming*, showy, snazzy, splashy, splendiferous, tasteless, tawdry, tinsel; SEE CONCEPTS 589,618

gauge [n] *measure, standard*

barometer, basis, benchmark, bore, capacity, check, criterion, degree, depth, example, exemplar, extent, guide, guideline, height, indicator, magnitude, mark, meter, model, norm, pattern, rule, sample, scale, scope, size, span, test, thickness, touchstone*, type, width, yardstick; SEE CONCEPTS 647,680,688,792

gauge [v] *measure, judge*

adjudge, appraise, ascertain, assess, calculate, calibrate, check, check out, compute, count, determine, estimate, evaluate, eye*, figure, figure in, guess, guesstimate, have one's number*, look over, meter, peg*, quantify, quantitate, rate, reckon, scale, size, size up*, take account of, tally, value, weigh; SEE CONCEPTS 37,764

gaunt [adj] *skinny*

angular, anorexic, attenuated, bare, bleak, bony, cadaverous, desolate, dismal, dreary, emaciated, forbidding, forlorn, grim, haggard, harsh, lank, lean, like a bag of bones*, meager, peaked, peaky, pinched, rawboned, scraggy, scrawny, skeletal, skeleton, skin and bones*, spare, thin, wasted; SEE CONCEPTS 406,490,491

gauzy [adj] *see-through, gossamer in texture*

delicate, diaphanous, filmy, flimsy, insubstantial, light, lucid, pellucid, sheer, thin, tiffany, translucent, transparent; SEE CONCEPT 606

gawk [v] *stare at in amazement*

bore*, eyeball*, gape, gaze, glare, gloat, goggle*, look, ogle, peer, rubberneck*, yawp*; SEE CONCEPT 623

gawky [adj] *clumsy*

awkward, bumbling, clownish, gauche, loutish*, lumbering, lumpish*, lumpy, maladroit, oafish, rude, rustic, splay, uncouth, ungainly; SEE CONCEPTS 550,584

gay [adj1] *happy*

alert, animate, animated, blithe, blithesome, bouncy, brash, carefree, cheerful, cheery, chipper*, chirpy, confident, convivial, devil-may-care*, festive, forward, frivolous, frolicsome, fun-loving, gamesome, glad, gleeful, hilarious, insouciant, jocund, jolly, jovial, joyful, joyous, keen, lighthearted, lively, merry, mirthful, playful, pleasure-seeking, presuming, pushy, rollicking, self-assertive, sparkling, spirited, sportive, sprightly, sunny, vivacious, wild, zippy*; SEE CONCEPTS 403,542

gay [adj2] *colorful, vivid*

brave, bright, brilliant, flamboyant, flashy, fresh, garish, gaudy, intense, rich, showy; SEE CONCEPTS 589,618

gay [adj3] *homosexual*

homoerotic, homophile, lesbian, Sapphic; SEE CONCEPT 372

gaze [n] *long, fixed stare*

fish eye*, glaring, gun*, look, looking, ogling,

peek, peep, rubbernecking*, scrutiny, seeing, survey, watching; SEE CONCEPT 623

gaze [v] *stare at*

admire, beam*, bore*, contemplate, eye, eyeball*, gape, gawk, get a load of*, get an eyeful*, glare, gloat, inspect, lamp*, look, look fixedly, moon*, observe, ogle, peek, peep, peer, pin*, pipe*, regard, rubber*, rubberneck*, scrutinize, see, size up*, survey, take in*, view, watch, wonder; SEE CONCEPTS 623,626

gear [n1] *equipment*

accessory, accoutrement, adjunct, apparatus, appendage, appurtenance, baggage, belongings, contraption, effects, encumbrances, fittings, habiliment, harness, impedimenta, instrument, kit, kit and kaboodle*, luggage, machinery, material, materiel, means, outfit, paraphernalia, possessions, rigging, setup, stuff, supply, tackle, things, tools, trappings; SEE CONCEPT 496

gear [n2] *toothed part of wheel*

cog, cogwheel, gearwheel, pinion, ragwheel, sprocket, spurwheel; SEE CONCEPT 464

gear [n3] *clothing*

apparel, array, attire, clothes, costume, drapes*, dress, duds*, feathers*, garb, garments, habit, outfit, rags*, threads*, toggery*, togs*, wear; SEE CONCEPT 451

gear [v] *prepare, equip*

accouter, adapt, adjust, appoint, arm, blend, fit, fit out*, furnish, harness, match, organize, outfit, ready, regulate, rig*, suit, tailor, turn out; SEE CONCEPTS 182,202

gelatinous [adj] *coagulated*

gluey, glutinous, gummy, jelled, jellied, jelly-like, mucilaginous, pudding*, sticky, thick, viscid, viscous; SEE CONCEPT 606

gem [n] *precious stone; treasure*

bauble*, glass*, hardware*, jewel, jewelry, masterpiece, nonpareil, ornament, paragon, pearl, pick, prize, rock*, sparkler*, stone, trump*; SEE CONCEPTS 337,446,474

gender [n] *grammatical rules applying to nouns that connote sex or animateness*

common, feminine, gender-specific, masculine, neuter; SEE CONCEPT 408

genealogy [n] *person's family tree*

ancestry, blood line, derivation, descent, extraction, generation, genetics, heredity, history, line, lineage, parentage, pedigree, progeniture, stemma, stirps, stock, strain; SEE CONCEPT 296

general [adj1] *common, accepted*

accustomed, broad, commonplace, conventional, customary, everyday, extensive, familiar, generic, habitual, humdrum, inclusive, matter-of-course*, natural, normal, ordinary, popular, prevailing, prevalent, public, regular, routine, run-of-the-mill*, typical, uneventful, universal, usual, wide, widespread, wonted; SEE CONCEPTS 530,547

general [adj2] *inexact, approximate*

ill-defined, imprecise, inaccurate, indefinite, loose, not partial, not particular, not specific, uncertain, undetailed, unspecific, vague; SEE CONCEPT 557

general [adj3] *comprehensive*

across-the-board*, all-around*, all-embracing*, all-inclusive*, ample, blanket, broad, catholic, collective, comprehending, diffuse, ecumenical, encyclopedic, endless, extensive, far-reaching, generic, global, inclusive, indiscriminate, infinite, limitless, miscellaneous, overall, panoramic,

ga
ge

sweeping, taken as a whole, total, ubiquitous, unconfined, universal, unlimited, wide, worldwide; SEE CONCEPTS *537,772*

generality [*n*] *vague notion*
abstraction, abstract principle, generalization, half-truth, law, loose statement, observation, principle, sweeping statement, universality; SEE CONCEPTS *688,689*

generalize [*v*] *make a sweeping assumption, statement*
be metaphysical, conclude, derive, discern, discover, establish, hypothesize, induce, observe, philosophize, postulate, speculate, stay in the clouds*, theorize, vapor; SEE CONCEPTS *37,49*

generally [*adv*] *mainly, in most cases*
about, all in all, almost always, altogether, approximately, as a rule, broadly, by and large, chiefly, commonly, conventionally, customarily, en masse, extensively, for the most part, habitually, largely, mostly, normally, on average, on the whole, ordinarily, overall, popularly, practically, predominantly, primarily, principally, publicly, regularly, roughly, roundly, thereabouts, typically, universally, usually, widely; SEE CONCEPTS *530,547,772*

generate [*v*] *produce, create*
accomplish, achieve, bear, beget, breed, bring about, bring to pass, cause, develop, effect, engender, form, found, get up, give birth to, give rise to, hatch, inaugurate, induce, initiate, institute, introduce, make, multiply, muster, occasion, originate, parent, perform, procreate, propagate, provoke, reproduce, set up, spawn, whip up*, work up; SEE CONCEPTS *173,205,251,374*

generation [*n1*] *creation, production*
bearing, begetting, breeding, bringing forth, engenderment, formation, fructifying, genesis, multiplying, origination, procreation, propagation, reproduction, spawning; SEE CONCEPTS *173,205,374*

generation [*n2*] *era; age group*
aeon, breed, contemporaries, crop, day, days, eon, epoch, peers, period, rank, span, step, time, times; SEE CONCEPTS *807,816*

generic [*adj*] *common, general*
all-encompassing, blanket, collective, comprehensive, inclusive, nonexclusive, sweeping, universal, wide; SEE CONCEPT *530*

generosity [*n*] *spirit of giving*
all heart*, alms-giving, altruism, beneficence, benevolence, bounteousness, bounty, charitableness, charity, free giving, goodness, heart, high-mindedness, hospitality, kindness, largesse, liberality, magnanimity, munificence, nobleness, openhandedness, philanthropy, profusion, readiness, unselfishness; SEE CONCEPTS *411,657*

generous [*adj1*] *giving, big-hearted*
acceptable, altruistic, beneficent, benevolent, big, bounteous, bountiful, charitable, considerate, easy, equitable, excellent, fair, free, good, great-hearted, helpful, high-minded, honest, honorable, hospitable, just, kind, kindhearted, kindly, lavish, liberal, lofty, loose, magnanimous, moderate, munificent, noble, open-handed, philanthropic, prodigal, profuse, reasonable, soft-touch*, thoughtful, tolerant, ungrudging, unselfish, unsparing, unstinting, willing; SEE CONCEPTS *404,542*

generous [*adj2*] *plentiful*
abundant, affluent, ample, aplenty, bounteous, bountiful, copious, dime a dozen*, full, galore,

handsome, large, lavish, liberal, luxuriant, no end*, no end in sight*, overflowing, plenteous, rich, stinking with*, unstinting, wealthy; SEE CONCEPTS *334,589,781*

genesis [*n*] *beginning, creation*
alpha, birth, commencement, dawn, dawning, engendering, formation, generation, inception, opening, origin, outset, propagation, provenance, provenience, root, source, start; SEE CONCEPTS *119,832*

genetic [*adj*] *coming from heredity*
abiogenetic, ancestral, digenetic, eugenic, genesiological, genital, hereditary, historical, matriclinous, patrimonial, phytogenetic, sprogenous, xenogenetic; SEE CONCEPTS *314,549*

genial [*adj*] *extremely nice and happy*
affable, agreeable, amiable, amicable, blithe, cheerful, cheering, cheery, chipper*, chirpy*, congenial, convivial, cordial, easygoing, enlivening, favorable, friendly, gentle, glad, good-natured, gracious, hearty, high, jocund, jolly, jovial, joyous, kind, kindly, merry, neighborly, perky, pleasant, sociable, sunny*, sunny side up*, up*, upbeat, upper*, warm, warm-hearted; SEE CONCEPTS *401,404*

geniality [*n*] *extreme niceness*
affability, agreeability, agreeableness, amenity, amiability, cheerfulness, cheeriness, congenialness, conviviality, cordiality, enjoyableness, friendliness, gladness, good cheer, good nature, gratefulness, happiness, heartiness, jollity, joviality, joy, joyousness, kindliness, kindness, mirth, pleasance, pleasantness, sunniness*, sweetness and light*, warmheartedness, warmth; SEE CONCEPTS *411,633*

genius [*n*] *gift of high intellect*
ability, accomplishment, acumen, acuteness, adept, aptitude, aptness, astuteness, bent, brain, brilliance, capability, capacity, creativity, discernment, Einstein*, endowment, expert, faculty, flair, grasp, head, imagination, inclination, ingenuity, inspiration, intelligence, inventiveness, knack, mature, originality, percipience, perspicacity, power, precocity, prodigy, propensity, prowess, reach, sagacity, superability, talent, turn, understanding, virtuoso, wisdom; SEE CONCEPTS *350,409,416*

genre/genus [*n*] *type, class*
brand, category, character, classification, fashion, group, kind, school, sort, species, style; SEE CONCEPTS *378,388,655*

genteel [*adj*] *sophisticated, cultured*
affected, aristocratic, artificial, chivalrous, civil, confined, courteous, courtly, cultivated, distingué, elegant, fashionable, formal, graceful, hollow, intolerant, la-di-da*, mannerly, noble, ostentatious, polished, polite, pompous, precious, pretentious, priggish, prim, prissy, prudish, refined, respectable, straitlaced, stuffy*, stylish, urbane, well-behaved, well-bred, well-mannered; SEE CONCEPTS *401,404*

gentility [*n*] *sophistication, cultivation*
aristocracy, blue blood*, civility, courtesy, courtliness, culture, decorum, elegance, elite, etiquette, flower*, formality, gentle birth*, gentlefolk, gentry, good breeding*, good family*, good manners*, high birth*, mannerliness, nobility, optimacy, polish, politeness, propriety, quality, rank, refinement, respectability, ruling class*,

society, upper class, upper crust*, urbanity; SEE CONCEPTS **388,411**

gentle [adj1] *having a mild or kind nature*

affable, agreeable, amiable, benign, biddable, bland, compassionate, considerate, cool*, cultivated, disciplined, docile, domesticated, dovelike*, easy, genial, humane, kindly, laid back*, lenient, manageable, meek, mellow, merciful, moderate, pacific, peaceful, placid, pleasant, pleasing, pliable, polite, refined, quiet, soft, softhearted, sweet-tempered, sympathetic, tame, taught, temperate, tender, tractable, trained, warmhearted; SEE CONCEPTS **404,542**

gentle [adj2] *mild, temperate in effect on senses*

balmy, bland, calm, clement, delicate, easy, faint, feeble, gradual, halcyon, hushed, imperceptible, lenient, light, low, low-pitched, low-toned, mellow, mild, moderate, muted, peaceful, placid, quiet, sensitive, serene, slight, slow, smooth, soft, soothing, subdued, tender, tranquil, untroubled; SEE CONCEPTS **525,537,594**

gentle [adj3] *of noble birth*

aristocratic, blue-blooded*, Brahmin*, courteous, cultured, elegant, genteel, high-born, highbred, noble, polished, polite, refined, upper-class, well-born, well-bred; SEE CONCEPT **555**

gentleperson [n] *polite, well-mannered person*

aristocrat, brick*, good egg*, good person, nice person, noble, scholar; SEE CONCEPT **423**

genuine [adj1] *authentic, real*

18-carat*, 24-carat*, absolute, accurate, actual, authenticated, bona fide, certain, certified, demonstrable, exact, existent, factual, for real*, good, hard, honest, honest-to-goodness*, indubitable, in the flesh*, kosher*, legit, legitimate, literal, natural, official, original, palpable, plain, positive, precise, proved, pure, real stuff*, sound, sterling, sure-enough*, tested, true, unadulterated, unalloyed, undoubted, unimpeachable, unquestionable, unvarnished, valid, veritable, very, whole; SEE CONCEPT **582**

genuine [adj2] *unaffected; honest*

actual, artless, candid, earnest, frank, heartfelt, known, natural, open, positive, real, reliable, righteous, sincere, true, trustworthy, undesigning, unfeigned, unimpeachable, unpretended, unquestionable, up front*, valid, well-established; SEE CONCEPTS **267,542**

geography [n] *the earth's features; study of land*

cartography, chorography, earth science, geology, geopolitical study, geopolitics, physiographics, physiography, topography, topology; SEE CONCEPTS **349,509**

germ [n1] *microscopic organism, often causing illness*

antibody, bacterium, bug*, disease, microbe, microorganism, parasite, pathogen, plague, virus, what's going around*; SEE CONCEPTS **306,392**

germ [n2] *beginning*

bud, cause, egg, embryo, inception, nucleus, origin, ovule, ovum, root, rudiment, seed, source, spark, spore, sprig, sprout; SEE CONCEPTS **392,648,826,832**

germane [adj] *appropriate*

ad rem, akin, applicable, applicative, applicatory, apposite, apropos, apt, cognate, connected, fitting, kindred, kosher*, legit*, material, on target*, on the button*, on the nose*, pertinent, proper, related, relating, relevant, right on*,

suitable, that's the ticket*, to the point, to the purpose; SEE CONCEPT **558**

germinate [v] *grow*

bud, develop, generate, live, originate, pullulate, shoot, sprout, swell, vegetate; SEE CONCEPT **427**

gestation [n] *process of early development*

evolution, fecundation, gravidity, growth, incubation, maturation, pregnancy, reproduction, ripening; SEE CONCEPTS **316,704,809**

gesture [n] *motion as communication*

action, body language, bow, curtsy, expression, genuflection, gesticulation, high sign, indication, intimation, kinesics, mime, nod, pantomime, reminder, salute, shrug, sign, signal, sign language, token, wave, wink; SEE CONCEPTS **74,185**

gesture/gesticulate [v] *make signs, motions to communicate*

act out, flag, indicate, mime, pantomime, signal, signalize, use one's hands, use sign language, wave; SEE CONCEPT **74**

get [v1] *come into possession of; achieve*

access, accomplish, acquire, annex, attain, bag*, bring, bring in, build up, buy into, buy off, buy out, capture, cash in on*, chalk up*, clean up*, clear, come by, compass, cop*, draw, earn, educe, effect, elicit, evoke, extort, extract, fetch, gain, get hands on*, glean, grab, have, hustle*, inherit, land, lock up, make, make a buy, make a killing*, net, obtain, parlay, pick up, procure, pull, rack up*, realize, reap, receive, score, secure, snag*, snap up*, snowball*, succeed to, take, wangle*, win; SEE CONCEPTS **120,706,710**

get [v2] *fall victim to*

accept, be afflicted with, become infected with, be given, be smitten by, catch, come down with*, contract, get sick, receive, sicken, succumb, take; SEE CONCEPT **93**

get [v3] *seize*

apprehend, arrest, bag*, beat, capture, catch, collar*, defeat, grab, lay hold of*, lay one's hands on*, nab*, nail*, occupy, overcome, overpower, secure, take, trap; SEE CONCEPT **90**

get [v4] *come to be*

achieve, attain, become, come over, develop into, effect, go, grow, realize, run, turn, wax*; SEE CONCEPTS **697,706**

get [v5] *understand*

acquire, catch, catch on to, comprehend, fathom, figure out, follow, gain, get into one's head*, hear, know, learn, look at, memorize, notice, perceive, pick up*, receive, see, take in, work out; SEE CONCEPTS **15,31**

get [v6] *arrive*

advance, blow in*, come, come to, converge, draw near, land, make it, reach, show, show up, turn up; SEE CONCEPT **159**

get [v7] *contact for communication*

get in touch, reach; SEE CONCEPT **266**

get [v8] *arrange, manage desired goal*

adjust, contrive, dispose, dress, fit, fix, make, make up, order, prepare, ready, straighten, succeed, wangle*; SEE CONCEPT **202**

get [v9] *convince, induce*

argue into, beg, bring around, coax, compel, draw, influence, persuade, press, pressure, prevail upon, prompt, provoke, sway, talk into, urge, wheedle, win over; SEE CONCEPT **68**

get [v10] *have an effect on*

affect, amuse, arouse, bend, bias, carry, dispose, entertain, excite, gratify, impress, influence, in-

spire, move, predispose, prompt, satisfy, stimulate, stir, stir up, strike, sway, touch; SEE CONCEPTS *7,22*

get [*v11*] *produce offspring*
beget, breed, generate, procreate, produce, propagate, sire; SEE CONCEPT *374*

get [*v12*] *irritate, upset*
aggravate, annoy, bother, bug*, burn, exasperate, gall, get someone's goat*, irk, nettle, peeve, pique, provoke, put out*, rile, rub the wrong way*, try, vex; SEE CONCEPTS *7,19*

get [*v13*] *confuse*
baffle, beat, bewilder, buffalo*, confound, discomfit, disconcert, distress, disturb, embarrass, mystify, nonplus, perplex, perturb, puzzle, stick*, stump, upset; SEE CONCEPT *16*

get across [*v*] *communicate an idea*
bring home*, convey, get through to, impart, make clear, make understood, pass on, put over, transmit; SEE CONCEPT *60*

get ahead [*v*] *excel, succeed*
advance, be successful, climb, do well, flourish, get on, leave behind, make good, outdo, outmaneuver, overtake, progress, prosper, surpass, thrive; SEE CONCEPTS *141,706*

get along [*v1*] *make progress*
cope, develop, do, fare, flourish, get by*, get on*, make out, manage, muddle through*, prosper, shift, succeed, thrive; SEE CONCEPTS *117,704*

get along [*v2*] *depart*
advance, be off, go, go away, leave, march, move, move off, move on, proceed, progress, push ahead, take a hike*; SEE CONCEPT *195*

get along [*v3*] *be compatible*
agree, be friendly, get on*, harmonize, hit it off*; SEE CONCEPT *388*

get at [*v1*] *attain*
access, achieve, acquire, arrive, ascertain, gain access, get hold of, reach; SEE CONCEPT *120*

get at [*v2*] *mean, intend*
aim, hint, imply, lead up to, purpose, suggest; SEE CONCEPT *75*

getaway [*n*] *escape*
break, breakout, decampment, flight, lam, slip; SEE CONCEPT *102*

get back [*v1*] *regain*
reclaim, recoup, recover, repossess, retrieve, salvage; SEE CONCEPT *120*

get back [*v2*] *return*
arrive home, come back, come home, reappear, revert, revisit, turn back; SEE CONCEPT *159*

get back at [*v*] *settle a score*
be avenged, get even, pay back, retaliate, revenge, take vengeance; SEE CONCEPTS *14,246*

get by [*v*] *manage, survive*
contrive, cope, do, do well enough, exist, fare, flourish, get along, get on, make ends meet*, make out, muddle through*, prosper, shift, subsist, succeed, thrive; SEE CONCEPT *117*

get down [*v*] *dismount*
alight, bring down, climb down, come down, descend, disembark, get off, lower, step down; SEE CONCEPT *154*

get in [*v*] *infiltrate; find a way in*
alight, appear, arrive, blow in*, come, embark, enter, gain ingress, get inside, include, insert, interpose, land, mount, penetrate, reach, show, show up, turn up; SEE CONCEPT *159*

get off [*v*] *depart*
alight, blow*, descend, disembark, dismount, escape, exit, go, go away, leave, light, pull out, quit, retire, withdraw; SEE CONCEPTS *154,195*

get on [*v1*] *mount*
ascend, board, climb, embark, enplane, entrain, go up, scale; SEE CONCEPTS *159,166*

get on [*v2*] *cope, progress*
advance, do, do well enough, fare, get along, get by, make out, manage, muddle through*, prosper, shift, succeed; SEE CONCEPTS *117,704*

get on [*v3*] *be compatible*
agree, be friendly, concur, get along, harmonize, hit it off; SEE CONCEPT *388*

get on [*v4*] *put clothing on*
assume, attire, don, draw on, dress, slip into, throw on, wear; SEE CONCEPT *167*

get out [*v*] *escape*
alight, avoid, beat it*, begone, be off, break out, bug off*, buzz off*, clear out, decamp, depart, dodge, duck, egress, evacuate, evade, exit, extricate oneself, flee, fly, free oneself, go, hightail*, kite*, leave, make tracks*, run away, scram*, shirk, shun, skedaddle*, split, take a hike*, take off, vacate, vamoose*, withdraw; SEE CONCEPTS *102,195*

get over [*v*] *recover*
come round, get better, mend, overcome, pull through, recuperate, shake off, survive; SEE CONCEPT *35*

get together [*v*] *gather, accumulate*
assemble, collect, congregate, convene, converge, join, meet, muster, rally, unite; SEE CONCEPTS *109,113*

get up [*v*] *mount; get out of bed*
arise, ascend, awake, awaken, climb, increase, move up, pile out*, rise, rise and shine*, roll out, scale, spring out, stand, turn out, uprise, upspring; SEE CONCEPT *154*

ghastly [*adj*] *horrifying, dreadful; pale*
abhorrent, anemic, appalling, ashen, awful, bloodless, cadaverous, corpselike, deathlike, dim, disgusting, faint, frightening, frightful, funereal, ghostly, ghoulish, grim, grisly, gruesome, haggard, hideous, horrendous, horrible, horrid, livid, loathsome, lurid, macabre, mortuary, nauseating, offensive, pallid, repellent, repulsive, sepulchral, shocking, sickening, spectral, supernatural, terrible, terrifying, uncanny, unearthly, unnatural, unpleasant, wan, weak, wraithlike; SEE CONCEPTS *485,529,537*

ghost [*n*] *spirit of the dead*
apparition, appearance, banshee, daemon, demon, devil, eidolon, ethereal being, haunt, incorporeal being, kelpie, manes, phantasm, phantom, poltergeist, revenant, shade, shadow, soul, specter, spook, vampire, vision, visitor, wraith, zombie; SEE CONCEPT *370*

ghostly [*adj*] *spooky*
apparitional, cadaverous, corpselike, deathlike, divine, eerie, eidolic, ghastly, haunted, holy, illusory, insubstantial, pale, phantasmal, phantom, scary, shadowy, spectral, spiritual, supernatural, uncanny, unearthly, vampiric, wan, weird, wraithlike, wraithy; SEE CONCEPTS *485,537*

giant [*n*] *extremely large person*
behemoth, bulk, colossus, cyclops, elephant*, goliath, Hercules*, hulk, jumbo*, leviathan, mammoth, monster*, mountain*, ogre, polypheme, titan, whale*, whopper*; SEE CONCEPT *424*

giant [*adj*] *very large*
big, blimp*, brobdingnagian*, colossal, cyclo-

pean, elephantine*, enormous, gargantuan, gigantic, gross*, Herculean*, huge, hulking,
humongous*, immense, jumbo*, mammoth, monstrous*, mountainous, prodigious, super-duper*,
titanic, vast, whale of a*, whaling*; SEE CON-
CEPTS 491,773,779,781

gibberish [n] *nonsense talk*
babble, balderdash*, blah-blah*, blather, chatter,
claptrap*, double talk*, drivel, gobbledygook*,
hocus-pocus*, jabber*, jargon, mumbo jumbo*,
palaver*, prattle, scat*, twaddle*, yammer*; SEE
CONCEPT 278

gibe [n] *ridicule*
comeback, cutting remark, derision, dig*, dump*,
jab, jeer, joke, mockery, parting shot*, put-
down*, rank-out*, sarcasm, scoffing, slam*,
sneer, swipe, taunt; SEE CONCEPT 278

gibe [v] *ridicule*
deride, dis*, disrespect, flout, jeer, make fun of*,
mock, poke fun at*, scoff, scorn, sneer, taunt;
SEE CONCEPTS 52,54

giddy [adj] *silly, impulsive*
bemused, brainless, bubbleheaded*, capricious,
careless, changeable, changeful, ditzy*, dizzy,
empty-headed*, erratic, fickle, flighty*, flustered,
frivolous, gaga*, heedless, inconstant, irresolute,
irresponsible, lightheaded*, punchy*, reckless,
reeling, scatterbrained*, skittish*, slaphappy*,
swimming*, thoughtless, unbalanced, unsettled,
unstable, unsteady, vacillating, volatile, whimsical, whirling, wild, woozy*; SEE CONCEPTS
314,401

gift [n1] *something given freely, for no recompense*
allowance, alms, award, benefaction, benefit, bequest, bestowal, bonus, boon, bounty, charity,
contribution, courtesy, dispensation, donation, endowment, fairing, favor, giveaway, goodie, grant,
gratuity, hand, hand-me-down*, handout, honorarium, lagniappe, largesse, legacy, libation, oblation, offering, offertory, philanthropy, pittance,
premium, present, presentation, provision, ration,
relief, remembrance, remittance, reward, souvenir, subscription, subsidy, tip, token, tribute,
write-off*; SEE CONCEPT 337

gift [n2] *talent, aptitude*
ability, accomplishment, acquirement, aptness, attainment, attribute, bent, capability, capacity, endowment, faculty, flair, forte, genius, head*,
instinct, knack, leaning, nose*, numen, power,
propensity, set, specialty, turn; SEE CONCEPTS
409,630,706

gifted [adj] *talented, intelligent*
able, accomplished, adroit, brilliant, capable,
class act, clever, expert, got it*, have on the ball*,
have smarts*, have the goods*, hot*, hotshot, ingenious, mad, masterly, phenomenal, shining at*,
skilled, smart; SEE CONCEPTS 402,527,528

gigantic [adj] *very large*
blimp, brobdingnagian*, colossal, cyclopean*, elephantine, enormous, gargantuan, giant, gross*,
Herculean*, huge, immense, jumbo*, mammoth,
massive, Moby*, monster, monstrous, prodigious, stupendous, super-colossal*, titan, tremendous, vast, whopping*; SEE CONCEPTS
491,773,779,781

giggle [n/v] *snickering laugh*
cackle, chortle, chuckle, guffaw*, hee-haw*,
snicker, snigger, teehee*, titter, twitter; SEE CON-
CEPT 77

gild [v] *embellish, decorate*
adorn, aureate, aurify, beautify, bedeck, begild,
brighten, coat, deck, dress up, embroider, engild,
enhance, enrich, garnish, glitter, grace, ornament,
overlay, paint, plate, tinsel, varnish, wash, whitewash*; SEE CONCEPTS 172,177,202

gimmick [n] *contrived object; scheme*
aid, apparatus, artifice, catch, concern, counterfeit, deceit, device, dodge*, fake, feint, fixture,
fun, gadget, gambit, game, gizmo*, imposture,
instrument, jest, maneuver, means, method, ploy,
ruse, secret, shift, sport, stratagem, stunt, trick,
widget*, wile; SEE CONCEPTS 59,260,660

gingerly [adj] *careful*
calculating, cautious, chary, circumspect, considerate, dainty, delicate, discreet, fastidious,
guarded, hesitant, reluctant, safe, squeamish, suspicious, timid, wary; SEE CONCEPTS 542,550

gingerly [adv] *carefully*
cautiously, charily, circumspectly, daintily, delicately, discreetly, fastidiously, guardedly, hesi-
tantly, reluctantly, safely, squeamishly,
suspiciously, timidly, warily; SEE CONCEPTS
542,550

gird [v1] *encircle; strengthen*
band, belt, bind, block, blockade, bolster, brace,
buttress, cincture, circle, enclose, encompass, enfold, environ, fasten, fortify, girdle, hem in*,
make ready, pen, prepare, ready, reinforce, ring,
round, secure, steel, support, surround; SEE CON-
CEPTS 250,758

gird [v2] *make fun of*
deride, flout, fun at, gibe, jeer, jest, mock, poke,
quip, ridicule, scoff, scorn, sneer, taunt; SEE CON-
CEPTS 52,54

girl [n] *young female person*
adolescent, damsel, daughter, lady, lassie, made-
moiselle, Ms, schoolgirl, she, teenager, young
lady, young woman; SEE CONCEPTS 415,424

girlfriend [n] *female acquaintance or romantic
companion*
companion, confidante, date, fiancee, flame*,
friend, intimate, partner, soul mate, steady, sweetheart; SEE CONCEPTS 415,423

gist [n] *meaning, essence*
basis, bearing, bottom line*, burden, core, drift,
force, heart, idea, import, kernel*, keynote, marrow, matter, meat*, name of the game*, nature of
the beast*, nitty gritty*, nuts and bolts*, pith*,
point, punch line, quintessence, score, sense,
short, significance, soul, spirit, stuff*, subject,
substance, summary, tenor, theme, thrust, topic,
upshot*; SEE CONCEPT 682

give [v1] *contribute, supply, transfer*
accord, administer, allow, ante up, award, bequeath, bestow, cede, come across, commit, confer, consign, convey, deed, deliver, dish out*,
dispense, dispose of, dole out, donate, endow,
entrust, fork over*, furnish, gift, grant, hand
down, hand out, hand over, heap upon, lavish
upon, lay upon, lease, let have, make over*, parcel out, part with, pass down, pass out, permit,
pony up*, present, provide, relinquish, remit, sell,
shell out*, subsidize, throw in, tip, transmit, turn
over, vouchsafe, will; SEE CONCEPTS
108,223,243

give [v2] *communicate*
air, announce, be a source of, broadcast, carry,
deliver, emit, express, furnish, impart, issue, notify, present, pronounce, publish, put, read, ren-

ge
gi

der, state, supply, transfer, transmit, utter, vent, ventilate; SEE CONCEPTS *60,266*

give [*v3*] *demonstrate, proffer*
administer, bestow, confer, dispense, display, evidence, extend, furnish, hold out, indicate, issue, manifest, minister, offer, pose, present, produce, provide, put on, render, return, set forth, show, tender, yield; SEE CONCEPTS *97,118*

give [*v4*] *yield, collapse*
allow, bend, bow to, break, cave, cede, concede, contract, crumble, crumple, devote, fail, fall, flex, fold, fold up, give way, go, grant, hand over, lend, open, recede, relax, relent, relinquish, retire, retreat, sag, shrink, sink, slacken, surrender, weaken; SEE CONCEPTS *13,469*

give [*v5*] *perform action*
address, apply, bend, buckle down, cause, devote, direct, do, engender, lead, make, occasion, produce, throw, turn; SEE CONCEPT *100*

give away [*v1*] *reveal*
betray, blab*, disclose, discover, divulge, expose, inform, leak, let out, let slip, mouth*, spill, tell, uncover; SEE CONCEPT *60*

give away [*v2*] *unselfishly transfer*
award, bestow, devote, donate, hand out, present; SEE CONCEPT *108*

give in/give up [*v*] *admit defeat*
abandon, back down*, bail out*, bow out*, buckle under*, capitulate, cave in*, cease, cede, chicken out*, collapse, comply, concede, cry uncle*, cut out, desist, despair, drop, drop like a hot potato*, fold, forswear, hand over, leave off, pull out, quit, relinquish, resign, stop, submit, surrender, take the oath*, throw in the towel*, waive, walk out on, wash one's hands of*, yield; SEE CONCEPTS *8,45,119,385*

given to [*adj*] *likely to*
accustomed, addicted, apt, disposed, habituated, inclined, in the habit of, inured, liable, obsessed, prone; SEE CONCEPT *542*

give off/give out [*v*] *discharge*
beam, belch, effuse, emanate, emit, exhale, exude, flow, give forth, issue, pour, produce, radiate, release, send out, smell of, throw out, vent, void; SEE CONCEPT *179*

glacial [*adj1*] *extremely cold*
antarctic, arctic, biting, bitter, chill, chilly, cool, freezing, frigid, frosty, frozen, gelid, icy, nippy, piercing, polar, raw, wintry; SEE CONCEPT *605*

glacial [*adj2*] *unfriendly*
aloof, antagonistic, chill, cold, cool, distant, emotionless, frigid, hostile, icy, inaccessible, indifferent, inimical, remote, reserved, seclusive, standoffish, unapproachable, unemotional, withdrawn; SEE CONCEPTS *401,404*

glacier [*n*] *mountain of ice, snow*
berg, floe, glacial mass, iceberg, icecap, ice field, ice floe, snow slide; SEE CONCEPT *509*

glad [*adj*] *happy, delightful*
animated, beaming, beautiful, blithesome, bright, can't complain*, cheerful, cheering, cheery, contented, exhilarated, felicitous, floating on air*, gay, genial, gleeful, gratified, gratifying, hilarious, jocund, jovial, joyful, joyous, lighthearted, merry, mirthful, overjoyed, pleasant, pleased, pleased as punch*, pleasing, radiant, rejoicing, sparkling, tickled, tickled pink*, tickled to death*, up, willing; SEE CONCEPTS *403,529*

gladly [*adv*] *happily*
acquiescently, ardently, beatifically, blissfully, blithely, cheerfully, cheerily, contentedly, cordially, delightedly, delightfully, ecstatically, enchantedly, enthusiastically, felicitously, freely, gaily, genially, gleefully, gratefully, heartily, jocundly, jovially, joyfully, joyously, lovingly, merrily, paradisiacally, passionately, pleasantly, pleasingly, pleasurably, rapturously, readily, sweetly, warmly, willingly, with good grace, with pleasure, with relish, zealously, zestfully; SEE CONCEPTS *403,538,542*

gladness [*n*] *happiness*
animation, blitheness, cheer, cheerfulness, delight, felicity, gaiety, glee, high spirits*, hilarity, jollity, joy, joyousness, mirth, pleasure; SEE CONCEPT *410*

glamorous [*adj*] *sophisticated in style*
alluring, attractive, bewitching, captivating, charismatic, charming, classy, dazzling, drop-dead gorgeous*, elegant, enchanting, entrancing, exciting, fascinating, flashy, foxy*, glittering, glossy, looking like a million*, lovely, magnetic, nifty, prestigious, righteous, seductive, siren, smart; SEE CONCEPTS *579,589*

glamour [*n*] *sophisticated style*
allure, allurement, animal magnetism, appeal, attraction, beauty, bewitchment, charisma, charm, color, enchantment, fascination, interest, magnetism, prestige, ravishment, razzle-dazzle*, romance, star quality; SEE CONCEPTS *655,718*

glance [*n1*] *brief look*
eye*, eyeball*, flash*, fleeting look, gander, glimpse, lamp*, look, look-see*, peek, peep, quick look, sight, slant*, squint, swivel*, view; SEE CONCEPT *623*

glance [*n2*] *reflection of light*
coruscation, flash, gleam, glimmer, glint, glisten, shimmer, sparkle, twinkle; SEE CONCEPTS *624,628*

glance [*v1*] *look at briefly*
browse, check out, dip into*, flash*, flip through, gaze, get a load of*, glimpse, leaf through, peek, peep, peer, riffle through*, run over, run through, scan, see, skim through*, take a gander*, take in, thumb through*, view; SEE CONCEPT *623*

glance [*v2*] *reflect light*
coruscate, flash, gleam, glimmer, glint, glisten, glitter, shimmer, shine, sparkle, twinkle; SEE CONCEPT *624*

glance [*v3*] *ricochet, hit off of something*
bounce, brush, careen, carom, contact, dart, graze, kiss*, rebound, scrape, shave*, sideswipe, skim, skip, slant, slide, strike, touch; SEE CONCEPT *189*

glare [*n1*] *very bright light, shine*
blaze, blinding light, brilliance, dazzle, flame, flare, glow; SEE CONCEPT *628*

glare [*n2*] *dirty look*
angry stare, bad eye*, black look*, evil eye*, frown, glower, lower, scowl; SEE CONCEPTS *623,716*

glare [*v1*] *give a dirty look*
bore, do a slow burn*, fix, frown, gape, gawk, gaze, glower, look daggers*, lower, menace, peer, pierce, scowl, stare, stare angrily*, stare icily*, wither; SEE CONCEPT *623*

glare [*v2*] *shine very brightly*
beam, blare, blaze, blind, blur, daze, dazzle, flame, flare, glaze, glow, radiate; SEE CONCEPT *624*

glaring [adj1] *obvious, unconcealed*
audacious, blatant, brazen, capital, conspicuous, crying, egregious, evident, excessive, extreme, flagrant, gross, inordinate, manifest, noticeable, obtrusive, open, outrageous, outstanding, overt, patent, protrusive, rank, visible; SEE CONCEPTS 576,619

glaring [adj2] *bright, dazzling; flashy*
blatant, blazing, blinding, brazen, chintzy, florid, garish, gaudy, glowing, loud, meretricious, shining, tawdry; SEE CONCEPTS 589,617

glass [n1] *object that reflects an image*
looking glass, mirror, reflector, seeing glass; SEE CONCEPTS 260,470

glass [n2] *object used for drinking liquids*
beaker, bottle, chalice, cup, decanter, goblet, highball, jar, jigger, jug, mug, pilsener, pony, snifter, tumbler; SEE CONCEPT 494

glasses [n] *object worn to correct vision*
bifocals, blinkers*, cheaters*, contact lenses, eyeglasses, four eyes*, frames, goggles, lorgnette, pince-nez, rims*, shades*, specs*, spectacles, trifocals; SEE CONCEPT 446

glassy [adj1] *polished, smooth*
burnished, clear, glazed, glazy, glossy, hyaline, hyaloid, icy, lustrous, shiny, sleek, slick, slippery, transparent, vitreous, vitric; SEE CONCEPT 606

glassy [adj2] *expressionless, especially referring to eyes*
blank, cold, dazed, dull, empty, fixed, glazed, lifeless, stupid, vacant; SEE CONCEPTS 406,619

glaze [adj] *varnish, lacquer*
coat, enamel, finish, glint, gloss, luster, patina, polish, sheen, shine; SEE CONCEPTS 259,475

glaze [v] *varnish, lacquer*
buff, burnish, coat, cover, enamel, furbish, glance, glass, gloss, incrust, make lustrous, make vitreous, overlay, polish, rub, shine, vitrify; SEE CONCEPTS 172,202,215

gleam [n] *brightness, sparkle*
beam, brilliance, coruscation, flash, flicker, glance, glim, glimmer, glint, glitz, gloss, glow, luster, ray, scintillation, sheen, shimmer, splendor, twinkle; SEE CONCEPTS 620,624

gleam [v] *sparkle*
beam, burn, coruscate, flare, flash, glance, glimmer, glint, glisten, glister, glitter, glow, radiate, scintillate, shimmer, shine, twinkle; SEE CONCEPTS 620,624

glean [v] *pick out, collect*
accumulate, amass, ascertain, conclude, cull, deduce, extract, garner, gather, harvest, learn, pick, reap, select, sift, winnow; SEE CONCEPTS 31,135

glee [n] *extreme happiness*
blitheness, cheerfulness, delectation, delight, elation, enjoyment, exhilaration, exuberance, exultation, fun, gaiety, gladness, hilarity, jocularity, jollity, joviality, joy, joyfulness, joyousness, liveliness, merriment, mirth, pleasure, sprightliness, triumph, verve; SEE CONCEPT 410

gleeful [adj] *very happy*
blithe, blithesome, boon, cheerful, delighted, elated, exalted, exuberant, exultant, frolicsome, gay, gratified, hilarious, jocund, jolly, jovial, joyful, joyous, jubilant, lighthearted, merry, mirthful, overjoyed, pleased, triumphant; SEE CONCEPT 403

glen [n] *valley*
canyon, combe, dale, dell, glade, gorge, vale; SEE CONCEPT 509

glib [adj] *slick, smooth-talking*
artful, articulate, easy, eloquent, facile, fast-talking*, flip, fluent, garrulous, hot-air*, insincere, loquacious, plausible, quick, ready, silver-tongued*, slippery*, smooth operator*, smooth-spoken*, smooth-tongued*, suave, talkative, urbane, vocal, vocative, voluble; SEE CONCEPTS 267,404

glide [v] *move smoothly and quickly on a surface*
coast, decline, descend, drift, flit, float, flow, fly, glissade, roll, run, sail, scud, shoot, skate, skim, skip, skirr, slide, slink, slip, slither, smooth along, soar, spiral, stream, trip, waft, wing; SEE CONCEPT 150

glimmer [n] *flash, sparkle*
blink, coruscation, flicker, glance, gleam, glint, glow, grain, hint, inkling, ray, scintillation, shimmer, suggestion, trace, twinkle; SEE CONCEPTS 624,831

glimmer [v] *sparkle*
blink, coruscate, fade, flash, flicker, glance, gleam, glint, glisten, glister, glitter, glow, scintillate, shimmer, shine, twinkle; SEE CONCEPT 624

glimpse [n] *brief look*
eye, eyeball*, flash*, gander*, glance, glom*, gun*, impression, lamp*, look-see*, peek, peep, quick look, sight, sighting, slant, squint, swivel*; SEE CONCEPT 623

glimpse [v] *look briefly*
catch sight of, check out, descry, espy, eye, flash, get a load of*, get an eyeful*, peek, sight, spot, spy, take a gander*, take in*, view; SEE CONCEPT 623

glisten [v] *shimmer*
coruscate, flash, flicker, glance, glare, gleam, glimmer, glint, glister, glitter, glow, scintillate, shine, sparkle, twinkle; SEE CONCEPT 624

glitter [n] *brilliance, sparkle*
beam, brightness, coruscation, display, flash, gaudiness, glamour, glare, gleam, glint, glisten, glister, glitz, luster, pageantry, radiance, scintillation, sheen, shimmer, shine, show, showiness, splendor, tinsel, twinkle, zap*; SEE CONCEPTS 620,655

glitter [v] *sparkle*
coruscate, flash, glance, glare, gleam, glimmer, glint, glisten, glister, glow, scintillate, shimmer, shine, spangle, twinkle; SEE CONCEPT 624

gloat [v] *exclaim triumph*
celebrate, crow*, exult, glory, rejoice, relish, rub it in*, triumph, vaunt, whoop*; SEE CONCEPT 49

global [adj] *worldwide, all-encompassing*
all-around, all-inclusive, all-out, blanket, catholic, comprehensive, cosmic, cosmopolitan, earthly, ecumenical, encyclopedic, exhaustive, general, grand, international, mundane, overall, pandemic, planetary, spherical, sweeping, thorough, total, unbounded, universal, unlimited, world; SEE CONCEPTS 536,772

globe [n] *Earth, sphere*
apple*, ball, balloon*, big blue marble*, map, orb, planet, rondure, round, spheroid, terrene, world; SEE CONCEPTS 436,511

gloom [n1] *melancholy, depression*
anguish, bitterness, blue devils*, blue funk*, blues*, catatonia, chagrin, cheerlessness, dejec-

gi
gl

tion, desolation, despair, despondency, disconsolateness, discouragement, dismals, distress, doldrums, dolor, downheartedness, dullness, dumps*, foreboding, grief, heaviness, heavyheartedness, horror, low spirits*, malaise, misery, misgiving, mopes, morbidity, mourning, oppression, pensiveness, pessimism, sadness, saturninity, sorrow, unhappiness, vexation, weariness, woe; SEE CONCEPT 410

gloom [n2] *darkness, blackness*
bleakness, cloud, cloudiness, dimness, dullness, dusk, duskiness, gloominess, murk, murkiness, obscurity, shade, shadow, twilight; SEE CONCEPTS 620,622,810

gloomy [adj1] *dark, black*
bleak, caliginous, cheerless, clouded, cloudy, crepuscular, desolate, dim, dismal, dreary, dull, dusky, forlorn, funereal, lightless, murky, obscure, overcast, overclouded, sepulchral, shadowy, somber, tenebrous, unilluminated, unlit, wintry; SEE CONCEPTS 525,617,618

gloomy [adj2] *feeling down, blue*
blue funk*, broody, chapfallen, cheerless, crabbed*, crestfallen, dejected, depressed, desolate, despondent, disconsolate, dismal, dispirited, dour, downcast, downhearted, down in the dumps*, down in the mouth*, dragged, forlorn, glum, in low spirits*, in the dumps*, joyless, low, melancholy, mirthless, miserable, moody, moping, mopish, morose, mournful, oppressed, pessimistic, sad, saturnine, solemn, sulky, sullen, surly, ugly, unhappy, weary, woebegone, woeful; SEE CONCEPT 403

gloomy [adj3] *sad, depressing*
acheronian, acherontic, bad, black, bleak, cheerless, cold, comfortless, depressive, desolate, disconsolate, discouraging, disheartening, dismal, dispiriting, drab, dreary, dull, dusky, funereal, joyless, lugubrious, morose, oppressive, saddening, somber, tenebrific; SEE CONCEPTS 537,548

glorify [v1] *praise*
acclaim, bless, boost, build up, celebrate, commend, cry up, eulogize, exalt, extol, hike, honor, hymn, laud, lionize, magnify, panegyrize, put on a pedestal*, put up, sing the praises of*; SEE CONCEPT 69

glorify [v2] *adore, idolize*
adorn, aggrandize, apotheosize, augment, beatify, bless, canonize, deify, dignify, distinguish, elevate, enhance, ennoble, enshrine, erect, exalt, halo*, honor, illuminate, immortalize, lift up, magnify, pay homage to, raise, revere, sanctify, transfigure, uprear, venerate, worship; SEE CONCEPT 12

glorious [adj] *adored, idiolized; divine*
august, beautiful, bright, brilliant, celebrated, dazzling, delightful, distinguished, effulgent, elevated, eminent, enjoyable, esteemed, exalted, excellent, famed, famous, fine, gorgeous, grand, gratifying, great, heavenly, heroic, honored, illustrious, immortal, magnificent, majestic, marvelous, memorable, noble, notable, noted, pleasurable, preeminent, radiant, remarkable, renowned, resplendent, shining, splendid, sublime, superb, time-honored, triumphant, venerable, well-known, wonderful; SEE CONCEPTS 568,574,579

glory [n1] *fame, importance*
celebrity, dignity, distinction, eminence, exaltation, grandeur, greatness, honor, illustriousness,

immortality, kudos, magnificence, majesty, nobility, praise, prestige, renown, reputation, splendor, sublimity, triumph; SEE CONCEPTS 388,668

glory [n2] *great beauty*
brightness, brilliance, effulgence, fineness, gorgeousness, grandeur, luster, magnificence, majesty, pageantry, pomp, preciousness, radiance, resplendence, richness, splendor, sublimity, sumptuousness; SEE CONCEPTS 673,718

glory [v] *boast, exult*
crow, gloat, jubilate, pride oneself, relish, revel, take delight, triumph; SEE CONCEPTS 12,49

gloss [n1] *shine, sheen*
appearance, brightness, brilliance, burnish, facade, finish, front, glaze, gleam, glint, glossiness, luster, polish, shimmer, silkiness, sleekness, slickness, surface, varnish, veneer; SEE CONCEPTS 611,620

gloss [n2] *definition*
annotation, comment, commentary, elucidation, explanation, footnote, interpretation, note, translation; SEE CONCEPT 268

gloss [v1] *make shiny*
buff, burnish, finish, furbish, glance, glaze, lacquer, polish, rub, shine, varnish, veneer; SEE CONCEPTS 202,215

gloss [v2] *conceal truth*
belie, camouflage, cover up, deacon, disguise, doctor, explain, extenuate, falsify, hide, justify, mask, misrepresent, palliate, rationalize, smooth over, soft-pedal, sugarcoat*, varnish, veil, veneer, white, whiten, whitewash*; SEE CONCEPTS 49,63

gloss [v3] *define*
annotate, comment, construe, elucidate, explain, interpret, justify, translate; SEE CONCEPT 57

glossy [adj] *shiny*
bright, brilliant, burnished, glassy, glazed, gleaming, glistening, lustrous, polished, reflecting, silken, silky, sleek, slick, smooth; SEE CONCEPTS 606,617

glove [n] *hand covering for warmth, protection*
gage, gauntlet, mitt, mitten, muff; SEE CONCEPT 451

glow [n] *burning, brightness*
afterglow, bloom, blossom, blush, brilliance, effulgence, flush, glare, gleam, glimmer, glitter, gusto, heat, incandescence, intensity, lambency, light, luminosity, passion, phosphorescence, radiance, ray, splendor, vividness, warmth; SEE CONCEPTS 610,620,622,673

glow [v] *burn, radiate*
be suffused, blare, blaze, blush, brighten, color, crimson, fill, flame, flare, flush, gleam, glimmer, glisten, glitter, ignite, kindle, light, mantle, pink, pinken, redden, rose, rouge, shine, smolder, thrill, tingle, twinkle; SEE CONCEPTS 249,469,624

glower [v] *frown*
glare, gloom, look, look daggers*, lower, scowl, stare, sulk, watch; SEE CONCEPT 623

glowing [adj1] *burning, bright*
aglow, beaming, flaming, florid, flush, flushed, gleaming, lambent, luminous, lustrous, phosphorescent, red, rich, rubicund, ruddy, sanguine, suffused, vibrant, vivid, warm; SEE CONCEPTS 617,618

glowing [adj2] *very happy, enthusiastic*
adulatory, ardent, avid, blazing, burning, complimentary, desirous, eager, ecstatic, eulogistic, fervent, fervid, fierce, fiery, flaming, heated, hot-

blooded, impassioned, keen, laudatory, panegyrical, passionate, rave, rhapsodic, zealous; SEE CONCEPTS *267,401*

glue [n] *adhesive*
cement, gum, gunk*, mucilage, paste, plaster, spit*, stickum*; SEE CONCEPT *475*

glut [n] *overabundance*
excess, nimiety, oversupply, plenitude, saturation, superfluity, surfeit, surplus, too much*; SEE CONCEPTS *740,787*

glut [v] *choke; oversupply*
burden, clog, cloy, congest, cram, deluge, devour, feast, fill, flood, gorge, hog*, inundate, jade, load, make a pig of*, overfeed, overload, overstock, overwhelm, pack*, pall, raven, sate, satiate, saturate, stuff, surfeit, wolf*; SEE CONCEPTS *140,169,209,740*

glutton [n] *person who overeats*
epicure, gorger*, gormandizer, gourmand, hefty eater, hog*, pig*, sensualist, stuffer*; SEE CONCEPT *412*

gnarled [adj] *knotted*
bent, contorted, crooked, deformed, distorted, gnarly, knurled, leathery, out of shape, rough, rugged, tortured, twisted, weather-beaten, wrinkled; SEE CONCEPTS *485,486*

gnaw [v1] *bite, chew*
champ, chaw, chomp, consume, corrode, crunch, devour, eat, eat away, erode, gum, masticate, munch, nibble, wear; SEE CONCEPTS *169,185*

gnaw [v2] *be bothered, worried about*
annoy, bedevil, beleague, distress, eat at*, fret, harass, harry, haunt, irritate, nag, pester, plague, prey on one's mind*, rankle, tease, trouble, wear down; SEE CONCEPTS *17,34*

gnome [n] *troll*
elf, fairy; SEE CONCEPT *424*

go [n1] *spirit, vitality*
activity, animation, bang, birr*, drive, energy, force, get-up-and-go*, hardihood, life, moxie*, oomph*, pep, potency, push, snap*, starch*, tuck*, verve, vigor, vivacity, zest; SEE CONCEPT *411*

go [n2] *try, attempt*
bid, crack, effort, essay, fling, pop, shot, slap, stab, turn, whack, whirl; SEE CONCEPTS *87,677*

go [v1] *advance, proceed physically*
abscond, approach, beat it*, bug out*, cruise, decamp, depart, escape, exit, fare, flee, fly, get away, get going*, get lost, get off*, hie, hightail*, hit the road*, journey, lam, leave, light out*, make a break for it*, make for*, make one's way*, mosey*, move, move out, near, pass, progress, pull out, push off, push on, quit, repair, retire, run along, run away, set off, shove off*, skip out*, split*, take a hike*, take a powder*, take flight, take leave*, take off*, travel, vamoose*, wend, withdraw; SEE CONCEPTS *159,195*

go [v2] *operate, function*
act, carry on, click*, continue, flourish, maintain, make out, move, pan out*, perform, persist, prosper, run, score, succeed, thrive, work; SEE CONCEPTS *4,239*

go [v3] *span, stretch*
connect, cover, extend, fit, give access, lead, make, range, reach, run, spread, vary; SEE CONCEPTS *651,756*

go [v4] *contribute, work towards an end*
avail, befall, chance, come, concur, conduce, develop, eventuate, fall out, fare, happen, incline,

lead to, occur, persevere, persist, proceed, result, serve, tend, transpire, turn, turn out, wax*, work out; SEE CONCEPTS *87,704*

go [v5] *agree, harmonize*
accord, be adapted for, be designed for, belong, blend, chime, complement, conform, correspond, dovetail*, enjoy, fit, jibe*, like, match, mesh, relish, set, square, suit; SEE CONCEPTS *8,664,714*

go [v6] *die, collapse*
bend, break, cave, conclude, consume, crumble, decease, decline, demise, depart, deplete, devour, dissipate, drop, exhaust, expend, expire, fail, finish, fold up, fritter, give, pass away*, pass on*, perish, run through*, spend, squander, succumb, terminate, use up, waste, weaken, worsen, yield; SEE CONCEPTS *105,698,699*

go [v7] *elapse*
be spent, expire, flow, lapse, pass, pass away, slip away, transpire, waste away; SEE CONCEPT *804*

go [v8] *endure*
abide, allow, bear, brook, consent to, let, permit, put up with*, stand, stomach*, suffer, swallow*, take, tolerate; SEE CONCEPT *23*

go about [v] *undertake*
approach, be employed, begin, devote oneself to, engage in, get busy with, occupy oneself with, set about, tackle, work at; SEE CONCEPT *100*

goad [n] *stimulus*
catalyst, compulsion, desire, drive, impetus, impulse, impulsion, incentive, incitation, incitement, irritation, lash, lust, motivation, passion, pressure, prod, spur, urge, whip, zeal; SEE CONCEPTS *20,661*

goad [v] *egg on, incite*
animate, annoy, arouse, bully, coerce, drive, encourage, excite, exhort, fire up*, force, goose*, harass, hound, impel, inspirit, instigate, irritate, key up*, lash, move, needle*, press, prick*, prod, prompt, propel, provoke, push, put up to*, rowel, sic*, sound, spark*, spur, stimulate, sting*, tease, thrust, trigger, turn on*, urge, whip*, work up, worry; SEE CONCEPTS *14,68*

go ahead [v] *proceed*
advance, begin, continue, dash ahead, edge forward, go forward, go on, move on, progress, shoot ahead; SEE CONCEPTS *149,159,704*

go-ahead [n] *authorization*
assent, consent, green light*, leave, okay, permission; SEE CONCEPT *685*

go-ahead [adj] *progressive*
ambitious, enterprising, entrepreneurial, go-getting*, gumptious*, pioneering, up-and-coming*; SEE CONCEPTS *538,542*

goal [n] *aim, purpose of an action*
ambition, design, destination, duty, end, ground zero*, intent, intention, limit, mark, mission, object, objective, target, use, zero*; SEE CONCEPT *659*

go along/go along with [v] *agree, cooperate*
accompany, acquiesce, act jointly, assent, collaborate, concur, conspire, follow, share in, work together; SEE CONCEPTS *8,18*

goat [n1] *hollow-horned mammal*
billy, buck, kid; SEE CONCEPTS *394,400*

go back/go back on [v] *break promise; change one's mind*
abandon, betray, be unfaithful, desert, forsake, leave in the lurch*, renege, repudiate, retract, return, revert, run out on; SEE CONCEPTS *13,71*

gl
go

gobble [v] *eat hurriedly*
cram*, devour, gorge, gulp*, guzzle, ingurgitate, scarf*, stuff*, suck up*, swallow, wolf*; SEE CONCEPT 169

go-between [n] *person acting as an agent*
arbitrator, attorney, broker, dealer, delegate, deputy, emissary, entrepreneur, envoy, factor, interagent, interceder, intercessor, intermediary, intermediate, intermediator, liaison, matchmaker, mediator, medium, messenger, negotiator, proxy, referee, representative; SEE CONCEPTS 348,423

go by [v1] *elapse*
exceed, flow on, make one's way, move onward, pass, proceed; SEE CONCEPT 141

go by [v2] *adopt, conform*
abide by, adjust to, agree, be guided by, comply, cooperate, fall in with, follow, heed, judge from, observe, take as guide; SEE CONCEPTS 8,18

god [n] *supernatural being worshipped by people*
Absolute Being, Allah, All Knowing, All Powerful, Almighty, Creator, daemon, deity, demigod, demon, Divine Being, divinity, Father, God, holiness, Holy Spirit, idol, Infinite Spirit, Jah, Jehovah, King of Kings, Lord, Maker, master, numen, omnipotent, power, prime mover, providence, soul, spirit, totem, tutelary, universal life force, world spirit, Yahweh; SEE CONCEPT 370

godless [adj] *without a god or divine faith*
adiamorphic, agnostic, atheistic, freethinking, iconoclastic, irreligious, nonbelieving, skeptical, undogmatic; SEE CONCEPT 542

godly [adj] *religious*
angelic, born-again, celestial, charismatic, deific, devout, divine, god-fearing, good, holy, pietistic, pious, prayerful, righteous, saintlike, saintly, virtuous; SEE CONCEPT 542

go down [v] *lose, fall*
be beaten, be defeated, cave in, collapse, crumble, decline, decrease, descend, droop, drop, fold, founder, go under, keel, lessen, make less, pitch, plunge, reduce, sag, set, sink, slump, submerge, submerse, submit, succumb, suffer defeat, topple, tumble; SEE CONCEPTS 181,698,699

godsend [n] *gift, benefit*
advantage, benediction, blessing, boon, good, manna*, stroke of luck*, windfall; SEE CONCEPTS 337,679

go far [v] *be successful*
achieve, advance, do well, get ahead, get on, make a name*, move up in the world*, progress, rise, succeed; SEE CONCEPTS 704,706

go for [v1] *reach*
clutch at, fetch, obtain, outreach, seek, stretch for; SEE CONCEPT 149

go for [v2] *like, choose*
accept, admire, approbate, approve, be attracted to, be fond of, care for, countenance, fancy, favor, hold with, prefer; SEE CONCEPTS 10,32

go for [v3] *attack*
assail, assault, launch at, run at, rush, rush upon, set upon, spring at; SEE CONCEPT 86

go into [v1] *take an interest in; participate*
be absorbed in, begin, develop, engage in, enter, get involved with, take on*, take up*, take upon oneself*, undertake; SEE CONCEPT 100

go into [v2] *investigate*
analyze, consider, delve into, dig*, dig into*, discuss, examine, explore, inquire, look into, probe, prospect, pursue, review, scrutinize, sift, study; SEE CONCEPTS 24,103

gold/golden [adj1] *dark yellow*
aureate, auric, auriferous, aurous, aurulent, blond, blonde, caramel, dusty, flaxen, honeyed, mellow yellow, ochroid, straw, tan, tawny, wheat; SEE CONCEPT 618

golden [adj2] *beautiful, advantageous*
auspicious, best, blissful, bright, brilliant, delightful, excellent, favorable, flourishing, glorious, happy, joyful, joyous, opportune, precious, promising, propitious, prosperous, resplendent, rich, rosy, shining, successful, valuable; SEE CONCEPTS 529,574

gone [adj] *not present, no longer in existence*
absent, astray, away, AWOL*, burned up*, consumed, dead, decamped, deceased, defunct, departed, disappeared, disintegrated, displaced, dissipated, dissolved, done, down the drain*, dried up, elapsed, ended, extinct, finished, flown, lacking, left, lost, missing, moved, no more, nonextant, not a sign of*, not here, out the window*, over, passed, past, quit, removed, retired, run-off, shifted, spent, split, taken a powder*, taken leave*, transferred, traveling, turned to dust*, vanished, withdrawn; SEE CONCEPTS 407,586

good [n1] *advantage, benefit*
asset, avail, behalf, benediction, blessing, boon*, commonwealth, favor, gain, godsend, good fortune, interest, nugget*, plum*, prize, profit, prosperity, service, treasure, use, usefulness, welfare, well-being, windfall; SEE CONCEPTS 337,658,679

good [n2] *morality*
class, dignity, excellence, ideal, merit, prerogative, probity, quality, rectitude, right, righteousness, straight, uprightness, value, virtue, worth; SEE CONCEPT 645

good [adj1] *pleasant, fine*
acceptable, ace*, admirable, agreeable, bad, boss*, bully, capital, choice, commendable, congenial, crack*, deluxe, excellent, exceptional, favorable, first-class, first-rate, gnarly*, gratifying, great, honorable, marvelous, neat*, nice, pleasing, positive, precious, prime, rad*, recherché*, reputable, satisfactory, satisfying, select, shipshape*, sound, spanking*, splendid, sterling, stupendous, super, superb, super-eminent, superexcellent, superior, tip-top*, up to snuff*, valuable, welcome, wonderful, worthy; SEE CONCEPTS 529,572

good [adj2] *moral, virtuous*
admirable, blameless, charitable, dutiful, estimable, ethical, exemplary, guiltless, honest, honorable, incorrupt, inculpable, innocent, irreprehensible, irreproachable, lily-white*, obedient, praiseworthy, pure, reputable, respectable, right, righteous, sound, tractable, uncorrupted, untainted, upright, well-behaved, worthy; SEE CONCEPT 545

good [adj3] *competent, skilled*
able, accomplished, adept, adroit, au fait, capable, clever, dexterous, efficient, expert, first-rate, proficient, proper, qualified, reliable, satisfactory, serviceable, skillful, suitable, suited, talented, thorough, trustworthy, useful; SEE CONCEPT 527

good [adj4] *useful, adequate*
acceptable, advantageous, all right, ample, appropriate, approving, apt, auspicious, becoming, benefic, beneficial, benignant, brave, commendatory, commending, common, conformable, congruous, convenient, decent, desirable, favorable, favoring, fit, fitting, fruitful, healthful, healthy,

helpful, hygienic, meet, needed, opportune, profitable, proper, propitious, respectable, right, salubrious, salutary, satisfying, seemly, serviceable, suitable, tolerable, toward, unobjectionable, wholesome; SEE CONCEPTS 537,558,560

good [adj5] *reliable; untainted*
dependable, eatable, fit to eat, flawless, fresh, intact, loyal, normal, perfect, safe, solid, sound, stable, trustworthy, unblemished, uncontaminated, uncorrupted, undamaged, undecayed, unhurt, unimpaired, unspoiled, vigorous, whole; SEE CONCEPT 485

good [adj6] *kind, giving*
altruistic, approving, beneficent, benevolent, charitable, considerate, friendly, gracious, humane, humanitarian, kindhearted, merciful, obliging, philanthropic, tolerant, well-disposed; SEE CONCEPTS 404,542

good [adj7] *authentic, real*
bona fide, conforming, dependable, genuine, honest, justified, kosher*, legitimate, loyal, orthodox, proper, regular, reliable, sound, strict, true, trustworthy, valid, well-founded; SEE CONCEPT 582

good [adj8] *well-behaved*
considerate, decorous, dutiful, kindly, mannerly, obedient, orderly, polite, proper, respectful, seemly, thoughtful, tolerant, tractable, well-mannered; SEE CONCEPT 401

good [adj9] *considerable*
adequate, advantageous, ample, big, complete, entire, extensive, full, great, immeasurable, large, long, lucrative, much, paying, profitable, respectable, sizable, solid, substantial, sufficient, whole, worthwhile; SEE CONCEPTS 334,771,781

goodbye [n] *farewell statement*
adieu, adios, bye-bye, cheerio, ciao, godspeed*, leave-taking, parting, so long*, swan song*, toodle-oo*; SEE CONCEPTS 195,278

good-for-nothing [n] *person who is idle, worthless*
bad lot*, black sheep*, bum, loafer, ne'er-do-well*, no-good*, profligate, rapscallion, scalawag, scamp, tramp, vagabond, waster*, wastrel; SEE CONCEPT 412

good-humored [adj] *funny, happy*
affable, amiable, buoyant, cheerful, cheery, complaisant, congenial, easy, genial, good-natured, good-tempered, lenient, merry, mild, obliging, pleasant, smiling; SEE CONCEPT 404

good-looking [adj] *handsome*
attractive, beauteous, beautiful, clean-cut, comely, fair, impressive, lovely, pretty, pulchritudinous, righteous; SEE CONCEPT 579

good-natured [adj] *easygoing, easily pleased*
acquiescent, agreeable, altruistic, amiable, benevolent, bighearted, breezy, charitable, complaisant, compliant, cordial, easy, even-tempered, friendly, good-hearted, good-humored, gracious, helpful, kind, kindly, lenient, marshmallow*, mild, moderate, nice, obliging, softie*, tolerant, warmhearted, well-disposed, willing to please; SEE CONCEPT 404

goodness [n] *decency, excellence*
advantage, beneficence, benefit, benevolence, ethicality, friendliness, generosity, good will, grace, graciousness, honesty, honor, humaneness, integrity, kindheartedness, kindliness, kindness, mercy, merit, morality, nourishment, obligingness, probity, quality, rectitude, righteousness, rightness, superiority, uprightness, value, virtue, wholesomeness, worth; SEE CONCEPTS 411,645

goods [n1] *personal possessions*
appurtenances, belongings, chattels, effects, encumbrances, equipment, furnishings, furniture, gear, impedimenta, movables, paraphernalia, property, stuff, things, trappings; SEE CONCEPT 446

goods [n2] *merchandise*
bolt, cargo, commodities, fabric, freight, line, load, materials, seconds, stock, stuff, textile, vendibles, wares; SEE CONCEPT 338

good will/goodwill [n] *kindliness*
altruism, amity, benevolence, brownie points*, charity, comity, cordiality, favor, friendliness, friendship, generosity, good deed, good side of*, helpfulness, rapport, right side of*, sympathy, tolerance; SEE CONCEPTS 411,645

gooey [adj] *sticky, gummy*
adhesive, gluey, glutinous, mucilaginous, soft, tacky, viscous; SEE CONCEPT 606

go off [v1] *explode*
befall, blow, blow up, burst, detonate, discharge, fire, happen, mushroom, occur, pass, take place; SEE CONCEPT 179

go off [v2] *leave*
decamp, depart, exit, go away, move out, part, quit; SEE CONCEPT 195

go on [v] *continue*
act, advance, bear, behave, carry on, come about, comport, conduct, deport, endure, execute, go ahead, hang on, happen, hold on, keep on, last, occur, persevere, persist, proceed, ramble, stay, take place; SEE CONCEPTS 100,239

go out [v1] *become extinguished*
become dark, burn out, cease, darken, die, die out, dim, expire, fade out, flicker, stop shining; SEE CONCEPTS 105,469

go out [v2] *leave*
decamp, depart, exit, go on strike, walk out; SEE CONCEPT 195

go over [v1] *review*
analyze, examine, inspect, investigate, look at, peruse, practice, read, rehearse, reiterate, repeat, revise, riffle through*, scan, skim, study, thumb through*; SEE CONCEPTS 24,103

go over [v2] *succeed*
be impressive, be successful, click*, come off*, go, pan out*, prove; SEE CONCEPT 706

gorge [n] *valley*
abyss, arroyo, canyon, chasm, cleft, clough, clove, crevasse, fissure, flume, gap, glen, gulch, pass, ravine; SEE CONCEPT 509

gorge [v] *eat voraciously*
blimp out*, bolt*, cloy, congest, cram, devour, eat like a horse*, feed, fill, glut, gobble, gormandize, gulp, guzzle, hoover*, jade, jam, make a pig of*, overeat, overindulge, pack, sate, satiate, stuff*, surfeit, swallow, wolf*; SEE CONCEPT 169

gorgeous [adj] *beautiful, magnificent*
attractive, beaut*, bright, brilliant, centerfold*, colorful, dazzling, delightful, dream, drop-dead*, easy on the eyes*, elegant, enjoyable, exquisite, fine, flamboyant, foxy*, gaudy, glittering, glorious, good-looking, grand, handsome, imposing, impressive, knockout*, lavish, lovely, lulu*, luxuriant, luxurious, opulent, ostentatious, pleasing, plush, pulchritudinous, ravishing, resplendent, showy, splendid, splendiferous, stunning, sublime, sumptuous, superb; SEE CONCEPTS 579,589

gory [adj] *bloody, horrible*
bleeding, blood-soaked, bloodstained, imbrued,

go
go

murderous, offensive, sanguinary, sanguine; SEE CONCEPTS *314,537*

gospel [n] *fact, doctrine*
actuality, authority, belief, certainty, credo, creed, dogma, faith, last word, scripture, testament, truism, truth, veracity, verity; SEE CONCEPT *689*

gossamer [adj] *gauzy, thin*
airy, cobweb, delicate, diaphanous, fibrous, fine, flimsy, light, sheer, silky, tiffany, translucent, transparent; SEE CONCEPT *606*

gossip [n1] *talk about others; rumor*
account, babble, back-fence talk*, blather, blether, buzz*, calumny, chatter, chitchat*, chronicle, clothesline*, conversation, cry, defamation, dirty laundry*, dirty linen*, dirty wash*, earful*, grapevine*, hearsay, idle talk, injury, malicious talk, meddling, news, prate, prattle, report, scandal, scuttlebutt*, slander, small talk*, story, tale, talk, whispering campaign*, wire*; SEE CONCEPTS *274,278*

gossip [n2] *person who talks a lot, spreads rumors*
babbler*, blabbermouth*, busybody, chatterbox, chatterer, circulator, flibbertigibbet*, gossipmonger, informer, meddler, newsmonger, parrot*, prattler, rumormonger*, scandalizer*, scandalmonger*, snoop*, talebearer, tattler, telltale; SEE CONCEPT *412*

gossip [v] *talk about others; spread rumors*
babble, bad-mouth*, bend one's ear*, blab, blather, blether, chat, chatter, cut to pieces*, cut up*, dish, hint, imply, insinuate, intimate, jaw*, prate, prattle, rattle on*, repeat, report, rumor, schmooze*, spill the beans*, spread*, suggest, talk, talk idly, tattle, tell secrets*, tell tales*, wiggle-waggle*; SEE CONCEPTS *56,60*

go through [v1] *endure*
bear, brave, experience, suffer, support, survive, swallow, tolerate, undergo, withstand; SEE CONCEPT *23*

go through [v2] *use up*
consume, deplete, exhaust, pay out, spend, squander; SEE CONCEPT *169*

go through [v3] *search*
audit, check, examine, explore, hunt, inspect, investigate, look, pass through; SEE CONCEPT *103*

go together/go with [v1] *agree, match*
accompany, accord, become, befit, be suitable, blend, complement, concur, correspond, fit, go, harmonize, make a pair*, not clash, suit; SEE CONCEPT *664*

go together/go with [v2] *accompany socially*
attend, be with, court, date, escort, go out with*, go steady with*, keep company with*; SEE CONCEPT *384*

go under [v] *fail, submerge*
bankrupt, default, die, drown, fall, fold, founder, go down, sink, submerse, submit, succumb, suffocate, surrender; SEE CONCEPTS *181,699*

gourmet [n] *person who likes, knows about food*
bon vivant, connoisseur, critic, epicure, epicurean, gastronome, gastronomer, gastronomist, gourmand; SEE CONCEPTS *348,423*

govern [v1] *take control; rule*
administer, assume command, be in power, be in the driver's seat*, call the shots*, call the signals*, captain*, carry out, command, conduct, control, dictate, direct, execute, exercise authority, guide, head, head up, hold dominion, hold office, hold sway, lay down the law*, lead, man-

age, occupy throne, order, overrule, oversee, pilot, pull the strings*, regulate, reign, render, run, serve the people*, steer, superintend, supervise, sway, tyrannize, wear the crown*; SEE CONCEPT *133*

govern [v2] *influence; hold in check*
boss, bridle, check, contain, control, curb, decide, determine, direct, directionalize, discipline, dispose, dominate, get the better of*, guide, handle, incline, inhibit, manage, predispose, regulate, restrain, rule, shepherd, steer, subdue, sway, tame, underlie; SEE CONCEPTS *7,19,22,130*

government [n] *management, administration*
authority, bureaucracy, command, control, direction, domination, dominion, empire, execution, executive, governance, guidance, influence, jurisdiction, law, ministry, patronage, political practice, politics, polity, power, powers-that-be*, predominance, presidency, regency, regime, regimentation, regulation, restraint, rule, sovereignty, state, statecraft, superintendence, superiority, supervision, supremacy, sway, the feds*, Uncle Sam*, union, Washington*; SEE CONCEPT *299*

governor [n] *person administrating government*
administrator, boss, chief, chief of state, commander, comptroller, controller, director, executive, gubernatorial leader, guv*, head, head honcho*, leader, manager, overseer, presiding officer, ruler, superintendent, supervisor; SEE CONCEPT *354*

go without [adj] *deny or be denied*
abstain, be deprived of, do without, fall short*, go short*, lack, need, want; SEE CONCEPT *646*

gown [n] *robe, dress*
clothes, costume, frock, garb, garment, habit; SEE CONCEPT *451*

grab [v] *latch on to*
capture, catch, catch hold of, clutch, collar*, corral*, get one's fingers on*, get one's hands on*, glom*, grapple, grasp, grip, hook, land, lay one's hands on*, nab, nail, pluck, seize, snag, snap up, snatch, take, take hold of*; SEE CONCEPTS *90,190*

grace [n1] *charm, loveliness*
address, adroitness, agility, allure, attractiveness, balance, beauty, breeding, comeliness, consideration, cultivation, decency, decorum, dexterity, dignity, ease, elegance, etiquette, finesse, finish, form, gracefulness, lissomeness, lithesomeness, mannerliness, manners, nimbleness, pleasantness, pliancy, poise, polish, propriety, refinement, shapeliness, smoothness, style, suppleness, symmetry, tact, tastefulness; SEE CONCEPTS *633,655,718*

grace [n2] *mercy, forgiveness*
benefaction, beneficence, benevolence, caritas, charity, clemency, compassion, compassionateness, favor, forbearance, generosity, goodness, good will, indulgence, kindliness, kindness, leniency, lenity, love, pardon, quarter, reprieve, responsiveness, tenderness; SEE CONCEPTS *278,657,685*

grace [n3] *prayer*
benediction, blessing, invocation, petition, thanks, thanksgiving; SEE CONCEPTS *278,368*

grace [v] *beautify, embellish*
adorn, bedeck, crown, deck, decorate, dignify, distinguish, elevate, enhance, enrich, favor, garnish, glorify, honor, laureate, ornament, set off; SEE CONCEPTS *202,700*

graceful [adj] agile, charming, lovely
adroit, aesthetic, artistic, balletic, beautiful, becoming, comely, controlled, curvaceous, dainty, decorative, delicate, dexterous, easy, elastic, elegant, exquisite, fair, fine, flowing, handsome, harmonious, limber, lissome, lithe, natural, neat, nimble, pleasing, pliant, poised, practiced, pretty, refined, rhythmic, seemly, shapely, skilled, slender, smooth, springy, statuesque, supple, symmetrical, tasteful, trim, willowy; SEE CONCEPTS 579,584,589

graceless [adj] clumsy, unsophisticated
awkward, barbarian, barbaric, barbarous, boorish, clunky*, coarse, corrupt, crude*, forced, gauche, gawky*, ill-mannered, improper, indecorous, inelegant, inept, infelicitous, klutzy*, loutish, oafish, outlandish, rough, rude, shameless, tasteless, two left feet*, uncouth, uncultured, unfortunate, ungainly, unhappy, unmannered; SEE CONCEPTS 401,584

gracious [adj] kind, giving
accommodating, affable, amiable, amicable, approachable, beneficent, benevolent, benign, benignant, big-hearted, bland, bonhomous, charitable, chivalrous, civil, compassionate, complaisant, congenial, considerate, cordial, courteous, courtly, easy, forthcoming, friendly, gallant, genial, good-hearted, good-natured, hospitable, indulgent, lenient, loving, merciful, mild, obliging, pleasing, polite, sociable, stately, suave, tender, unctuous, urbane, well-mannered; SEE CONCEPTS 401,542

gradation [n] classification, step
arrangement, calibration, change, degree, difference, distinction, divergence, grade, grouping, level, mark, measurement, modification, notch, nuance, ordering, place, point, position, progression, rank, scale, sequence, series, shade, sorting, stage, succession, variation; SEE CONCEPTS 378,665,727,744

grade [n1] rank, step
brand, caliber, category, class, classification, condition, degree, division, echelon, estate, form, gradation, group, grouping, league, level, mark, notch, order, pigeonhole*, place, position, quality, rung*, size, stage, standard, station, tier; SEE CONCEPTS 286,378,665,727,744

grade [n2] incline, slope
acclivity, ascent, bank, cant, climb, declivity, descent, downgrade, elevation, embankment, gradient, height, hill, inclination, inclined plane, lean, leaning, level, obliquity, pitch, plane, ramp, rise, slant, tangent, tilt, upgrade; SEE CONCEPTS 738,757

grade [v] evaluate, rank
arrange, assort, brand, class, classify, group, order, range, rate, sort, value; SEE CONCEPTS 103,291

gradient [n] slope
acclivity, angle, bank, cant, declivity, grade, hill, inclination, incline, lean, leaning, pitch, ramp, rise, slant, tilt; SEE CONCEPTS 738,757

gradual [adj] happening slowly, evenly
bit-by-bit*, by degrees, continuous, creeping, even, gentle, graduate, moderate, piecemeal, progressive, regular, slow, steady, step-by-step*, successive, unhurried; SEE CONCEPTS 544,588,799

gradually [adv] happening slowly, evenly
bit by bit*, by degrees, by installments, con-

stantly, continuously, deliberately, gently, imperceptibly, inch by inch*, increasingly, in small doses*, little by little*, moderately, perceptibly, piece by piece*, piecemeal, progressively, regularly, sequentially, serially, steadily, step by step*, successively, unhurriedly; SEE CONCEPTS 544,588,799

graduate [n] person who completes education, pursuit
alum*, alumnus, baccalaureate, bachelor, collegian, diplomate, doctor, former student, grad, holder, licentiate, master, Ph.D., product, recipient; SEE CONCEPT 350

graduate [v1] complete education, pursuit
be commissioned, certify, confer degree, earn, finish, get a degree, get out*, give sheepskin*, grant diploma, take a degree, win; SEE CONCEPT 234

graduate [v2] classify, grade
arrange, calibrate, class, group, mark off, measure, measure out, order, proportion, range, rank, regulate, sort; SEE CONCEPTS 84,103

graft [n1] transplant
bud*, hybridization, implant, jointure, scion, shoot, slip, splice, sprout, union; SEE CONCEPTS 113,257

graft [n2] payoff for fraud
bribe, corruption, gain, hat*, hush money*, juice*, money, money under the table*, pay, payola*, peculation, shake*, share, skimming*, squeeze*, thievery; SEE CONCEPTS 192,344

graft [v] transplant, splice
affix, implant, ingraft, insert, join, plant, propagate, unite; SEE CONCEPTS 113,257

grain [n1] seed, piece
atom, bit, cereal, corn, crumb, drop, fragment, granule, grist, iota, jot, kernel, mite, modicum, molecule, morsel, mote, ounce, particle, pellet, scintilla, scrap, scruple, smidgen, spark, speck, tittle, trace, whit; SEE CONCEPTS 428,831

grain [n2] texture of fabric
character, current, direction, fiber, make-up, nap, pattern, staple, striation, surface, tendency, tissue, tooth, warp and woof, weave, weft; SEE CONCEPT 611

grammar [n] language rules
ABCs*, accidence, alphabet, elements, fundaments, linguistics, morphology, principles, rudiments, sentence structure, stratification, structure, syntax, tagmemics; SEE CONCEPTS 275,276,770

grand [adj1] impressive, great
admirable, ambitious, august, awe-inspiring, dignified, dynamite, elevated, eminent, exalted, excellent, fab*, fine, first-class, first-rate, glorious, grandiose, haughty, illustrious, imposing, large, lofty, luxurious, magnificent, majestic, marvelous, monumental, noble, opulent, ostentatious, outstanding, palatial, pompous, pretentious, regal, rich, smashing, something else*, splendid, stately, striking, sublime, sumptuous, super, superb, terrific, unreal, very good; SEE CONCEPTS 574,589,773

grand [adj2] most important
chief, dignified, elevated, exalted, grave, head, highest, leading, lofty, main, majestic, mighty, noble, preeminent, principal, regal, supreme, transcendent; SEE CONCEPT 568

grandeur [n] great importance
amplitude, augustness, beauty, breadth, brilliance, celebrity, circumstance, dignity, distinc-

go
gr

tion, elevation, eminence, expansiveness, fame, fineness, glory, grandiosity, gravity, greatness, handsomeness, immensity, impressiveness, inclusiveness, loftiness, luxuriousness, magnificence, majesty, might, nobility, opulence, pomp, preeminence, richness, splendor, state, stateliness, sublimity, sumptuousness, superbity, sway, transcendency, vastness; SEE CONCEPT 668

grandiloquent [adj] pretentious, flowery (communication)
aureate, big-talking*, bombastic, declamatory, euphistic, fustian, high-flown, histrionic, inflated, magniloquent, oratorical, orotund, overblown, pompous, purple*, rhetorical, sonorous, swollen, tall-talking*, verbose, windbag*, windy*; SEE CONCEPT 267

grandiose [adj] theatrical, extravagant
affected, ambitious, august, bombastic, cosmic, egotistic, flamboyant, fustian, grand, high-falutin'*, high-flown, imposing, impressive, lofty, lordly, magnificent, majestic, monumental, noble, ostentatious, overwhelming, pompous, pretentious, purple*, royal, showy, splashy, stately, unfathomable, vast; SEE CONCEPTS 401,542,589

grange [n] farm
acreage, farmstead, hacienda, manor, plantation, ranch; SEE CONCEPTS 258,516,517

grant [n] allowance, gift
admission, allocation, allotment, alms, appropriation, assistance, award, benefaction, bequest, boon, bounty, charity, concession, contribution, dole, donation, endowment, fellowship, gratuity, handout, lump, present, privilege, reward, scholarship, stipend, subsidy; SEE CONCEPTS 337,344

grant [v] authorize, allow
accede, accept, accord, acknowledge, acquiesce, admit, agree to, allocate, allot, assign, assume, avow, award, bestow, bless, cede, come across, come around, come through, concede, confer, consent to, convey, donate, drop, gift with*, give, give in, give out, give the nod*, give thumbs-up*, go along with*, impart, invest, own, own up*, permit, present, profess, relinquish, shake on*, sign off on*, sign on*, stake, suppose, surrender, transfer, transmit, vouchsafe, yield; SEE CONCEPTS 8,50,82,83,88

granted [adv] allowed, accepted
acknowledged, admitted, assumed, indeed, just so, yes; SEE CONCEPT 558

granulate [v] crush into tiny pieces
atomize, comminute, crumble, crystallize, disintegrate, grate, grind, make coarse, make grainy, pound, powder, pulverize, triturate; SEE CONCEPT 186

graphic [adj1] clear, explicit
colorful, compelling, comprehensible, concrete, convincing, definite, descriptive, detailed, distinct, eloquent, expressive, figurative, forcible, illustrative, incisive, intelligible, lively, lucid, moving, perspicuous, picturesque, precise, realistic, stirring, striking, strong, telling, unequivocal, vivid; SEE CONCEPTS 267,535,562

graphic [adj2] pictorial, visible
blocked-out, delineated, depicted, descriptive, diagrammatic, drawn, engraved, etched, iconographic, illustrated, illustrational, illustrative, marked-out, outlined, painted, photographic, pictoric, pictured, portrayed, representational, seen, sketched, traced, visual; SEE CONCEPTS 576,589,619

grapple [v] grab, wrestle
attack, battle, catch, clash, clasp, close, clutch, combat, confront, contend, cope, deal with, do battle*, encounter, engage, face, fasten, fight, grasp, grip, hold, hook, hug, nab, nail, scuffle, seize, snatch, struggle, tackle, take, take on*, tussle; SEE CONCEPTS 106,191

grasp [n1] hold, grip
butt, cinch, clamp, clasp, clench, clinch, clutches, embrace, grapple, lug, possession, purchase, tenure; SEE CONCEPTS 191,710

grasp [n2] understanding
awareness, comprehension, ken, knowledge, mastery, perception, realization; SEE CONCEPT 409

grasp [v1] grab
bag*, catch, clasp, clinch, clutch, collar*, corral, enclose, glom*, grapple, grip, hold, hook, land, seize, snatch, take, take hold of; SEE CONCEPTS 90,191

grasp [v2] understand
accept, appreciate, apprehend, catch, catch on*, cognize, compass, comprehend, dig*, envisage, fathom, follow, get, get the drift*, get the picture*, have, know, latch on*, make, perceive, pick up*, realize, see, take, take in*; SEE CONCEPT 15

grasping [adj] greedy
acquisitive, avaricious, avid, close-fisted, covetous, desirous, extorting, extortionate, grabby*, itchy*, mean, miserly, niggardly*, penny-pinching*, penurious, prehensile, rapacious, selfish, stingy*, tightfisted*, usurious, venal; SEE CONCEPTS 326,334,542

grate [v1] shred, grind down
abrade, bark, bray, file, fray, gall, mince, pound, pulverize, rasp, raze, rub, scrape, scratch, scuff, skin, triturate; SEE CONCEPTS 186,215

grate [v2] irritate
aggravate, annoy, burn, chafe, exasperate, fret, gall, get on one's nerves*, irk, nettle, peeve, pique, provoke, rankle, rile, rub the wrong way*, vex; SEE CONCEPTS 7,14,19

grateful [adj1] appreciative
beholden, gratified, indebted, obliged, pleased, thankful; SEE CONCEPT 403

grateful [adj2] pleasing, nice
acceptable, agreeable, comforting, congenial, consoling, delectable, delicious, delightful, desirable, favorable, good, gratifying, pleasant, pleasurable, pleasureful, refreshing, rejuvenating, renewing, restful, restorative, restoring, satisfactory, satisfying, solacing, welcome; SEE CONCEPTS 537,548,572

gratification [n] satisfaction
delight, enjoyment, fruition, fulfillment, glee, hit, indulgence, joy, kicks*, luxury, pleasure, recompense, regalement, relish, reward, sure shock*, thrill; SEE CONCEPT 410

gratify [v] give pleasure; satisfy
appease, arride, baby*, cater to, coddle, content, delectate, delight, do one proud*, do the trick*, enchant, favor, fill the bill*, fulfill*, get one's kicks*, gladden, hit the spot*, humor, indulge, make a hit*, make happy, oblige, pamper, please, recompense, requite, thrill; SEE CONCEPTS 7,22

grating [adj] irritating; scraping
annoying, disagreeable, discordant, displeasing, dissonant, dry, grinding, harsh, harsh-sounding, hoarse, irksome, jarring, offensive, rasping, raucous, rough, shrill, squeaky, strident, stridulent,

stridulous, unpleasant, vexatious; SEE CONCEPTS 529,592,594

gratis [adj] *free*
as a gift, chargeless, complimentary, costless, for love*, for nothing, freebie*, freely given, free of charge, free ride*, gratuitous, on someone*, on the house*, unpaid for, without charge, without recompense; SEE CONCEPT 334

gratitude [n] *appreciation*
acknowledgment, appreciativeness, grace, gratefulness, honor, indebtedness, obligation, praise, recognition, requital, response, responsiveness, sense of obligation, thankfulness, thanks, thanksgiving; SEE CONCEPTS 32,76,278,410

gratuitous [adj1] *free*
chargeless, complimentary, costless, for nothing, gratis, spontaneous, unasked-for, unpaid, voluntary, willing; SEE CONCEPTS 334,542

gratuitous [adj2] *not necessary*
assumed, baseless, bottomless, causeless, groundless, indefensible, inessential, needless, reasonless, supererogatory, superfluous, uncalled-for, unessential, unfounded, unjustified, unmerited, unprovoked, unsupportable, unwarranted, wanton; SEE CONCEPT 546

gratuity [n] *gift, tip*
alms, benefaction, bonus, boon, bounty, contribution, donation, fringe benefit, grease palm*, largesse, little something*, offering, perk*, perquisite, present, recompense, reward, salve*, sweetener*, token; SEE CONCEPTS 337,344

grave [n] *burial place*
catacomb, crypt, final resting place*, last home*, mausoleum, mound, permanent address*, place of interment, resting place, sepulcher, shrine, six feet under*, tomb, vault; SEE CONCEPT 305

grave [adj1] *serious; gloomy*
cold sober*, deadpan*, dignified, dour, dull, earnest, grim, grim-faced, heavy, leaden, long-faced, meaningful, muted, no-nonsense*, ponderous, quiet, sad, sage, saturnine, sedate, sober, solemn, somber, staid, strictly business*, subdued, thoughtful, unsmiling; SEE CONCEPT 401

grave [adj2] *crucial, dangerous*
acute, afflictive, consequential, critical, deadly, destructive, dire, exigent, fatal, fell, grievous, hazardous, heavy*, important, killing*, life-and-death*, major, momentous, of great consequence, ominous, perilous, pressing, serious, severe, significant, threatening, ugly, urgent, vital, weighty; SEE CONCEPTS 537,548,567

graveyard [n] *burial area*
boneyard*, burial ground, cemetery, charnel house, God's acre*, memorial park, necropolis; SEE CONCEPT 305

gravitate [v] *be drawn toward; fall to*
approach, be attracted, be influenced, be pulled, descend, drift, drop, incline, lean, move, precipitate, settle, sink, tend; SEE CONCEPTS 34,159

gravity [n1] *force of attraction*
force, heaviness, pressure, weight; SEE CONCEPT 641

gravity [n2] *seriousness, importance*
acuteness, concern, consequence, exigency, hazardousness, momentousness, perilousness, severity, significance, solemnity, urgency, weightiness; SEE CONCEPT 668

gray/grey [adj] *muted silver in color*
ash, ashen, battleship*, cineral, clouded, dingy, dove, drab, dusky, dusty, granite, heather, iron,

lead, leaden, livid, mousy, neutral, oyster, pearly, peppery, powder, sere, shaded, silvered, silvery, slate, smoky, somber, stone; SEE CONCEPT 618

graze [v1] *touch*
abrade, brush, carom, chafe, glance off, kiss*, ricochet, rub, scrape, scratch, shave*, skim, skip; SEE CONCEPT 612

graze [v2] *feed on*
bite, browse, champ, crop, crunch, eat, forage, gnaw, masticate, munch, nibble, pasture, ruminate, uproot; SEE CONCEPT 169

greasy [adj] *slippery, oily*
anointed, creamy, daubed, fatty, lubricated, lubricious, oleaginous, pomaded, salved, slick, slimy*, slithery, smeared, swabbed, unctuous; SEE CONCEPT 606

great [adj1] *very large*
abundant, ample, big, big league*, bulky, bull, colossal, considerable, decided, enormous, excessive, extended, extensive, extravagant, extreme, fat, gigantic, grievous, high, huge, humongous, husky, immense, inordinate, jumbo*, lengthy, long, major league*, mammoth, mondo*, numerous, oversize, prodigious, prolonged, pronounced, protracted, strong, stupendous, terrible, titanic*, towering, tremendous, vast, voluminous; SEE CONCEPTS 773,781

great [adj2] *important, celebrated*
august, capital, chief, commanding, dignified, distinguished, eminent, exalted, excellent, famed, famous, fine, glorious, grand, heroic, highly regarded, high-minded, honorable, idealistic, illustrious, impressive, leading, lofty, magnanimous, main, major, noble, notable, noted, noteworthy, outstanding, paramount, primary, principal, prominent, puissant, regal, remarkable, renowned, royal, stately, sublime, superior, superlative, talented; SEE CONCEPT 568

great [adj3] *excellent, skillful*
able, absolute, aces*, adept, admirable, adroit, awesome, bad*, best, brutal, cold*, complete, consummate, crack*, downright, dynamite, egregious, exceptional, expert, fab*, fantastic, fine, first-class*, first-rate*, good, heavy*, hellacious*, marvelous, masterly, number one*, out-and-out*, out of sight*, out of this world*, perfect, positive, proficient, super-duper*, surpassing, terrific, total, tough, transcendent, tremendous, unmitigated, unqualified, utter, wonderful; SEE CONCEPTS 527,528,574

greatly [adv] *considerably*
abundantly, by much, conspicuously, eminently, emphatically, enormously, exceedingly, exceptionally, extremely, famously, glaringly, highly, hugely, immeasurably, immensely, incalculably, incomparably, incredibly, indeed, infinitely, in great measure, inimitably, intensely, largely, markedly, mightily, most, much, notably, on a large scale, powerfully, remarkably, strikingly, superlatively, supremely, surpassingly, tremendously, vastly, very much; SEE CONCEPTS 537,569,772

greatness [n1] *large size*
abundance, amplitude, bigness, bulk, enormity, force, high degree, hugeness, immensity, infinity, intensity, length, magnitude, mass, might, potency, power, prodigiousness, sizableness, strength, vastness; SEE CONCEPTS 730,767

greatness [n2] *nobleness of character; eminence*
celebrity, chivalry, dignity, distinction, fame,

gr
gr

generosity, glory, grandeur, heroism, high-mindedness, idealism, illustriousness, importance, loftiness, magnanimity, majesty, merit, morality, nobility, note, prominence, renown, stateliness, sublimity, worthiness; SEE CONCEPTS 411,645,668

greed [n] *overwhelming desire for more*
acquisitiveness, avarice, avidity, covetousness, craving, cupidity, eagerness, edacity, esurience, excess, gluttony, gormandizing, graspingness, hunger, indulgence, insatiableness, intemperance, longing, piggishness*, rapacity, ravenousness, selfishness, swinishness*, the gimmies*, voracity; SEE CONCEPT 20

greedy [adj] *desiring excessively*
acquisitive, avaricious, avid, carnivorous, close, close-fisted*, covetous, craving, desirous, devouring, eager, edacious, esurient, gluttonous, gobbling, gormandizing, grabby, grasping, grudging, gulping, guzzling, hoggish*, hungry, impatient, insatiable, insatiate, intemperate, itchy*, miserly, niggardly, omnivorous, parsimonious, penny-pinching*, penurious, piggish*, prehensile, rapacious, ravening, ravenous, selfish, stingy, swinish, tight*, tight-fisted*, voracious; SEE CONCEPTS 326,403,542

green [n] *square or park in center of town*
common, field, grass, grassplot, lawn, plaza, sward, terrace, turf; SEE CONCEPTS 509,513

green [adj1] *young, new, blooming*
bosky, budding, burgeoning, callow, developing, flourishing, foliate, fresh, grassy, growing, half-formed, immature, infant, juvenile, leafy, lush, maturing, pliable, puerile, pullulating, raw, recent, sprouting, supple, tender, undecayed, undried, unfledged, ungrown, unripe, unseasoned, verdant, verduous, visculent, youthful; SEE CONCEPTS 485,578,790

green [adj2] *inexperienced*
callow, credulous, fresh, gullible, ignorant, immature, inexpert, ingenuous, innocent, naive, new, raw, tenderfoot*, unconversant, unpolished, unpracticed, unseasoned, unskillful, unsophisticated, untrained, unversed, wet behind the ears*, young, youthful; SEE CONCEPT 404

green [adj3] *emerald in color*
apple, aquamarine, beryl, chartreuse, fir, forest, grass, jade, kelly, lime, malachite, moss, olive, pea, peacock, pine, sage, sap, sea, spinach, verdigris, vert, viridian, willow; SEE CONCEPT 618

green [adj4] *referring to practices or policies that do not negatively affect the environment*
biodegradable, ecological, environmental, environmentally-safe, environment-friendly; SEE CONCEPT 485

greenhorn [n] *inexperienced person*
amateur, apprentice, babe*, beginner, colt*, hayseed*, ingénue, learner, naif, neophyte, newcomer, new hand, novice, recruit, rube*, simpleton, tenderfoot*, tyro*, virgin; SEE CONCEPT 423

greet [v] *welcome*
accost, acknowledge, address, approach, attend, bow, call to, compliment, curtsy, embrace, exchange greetings, extend one's hand, flag, hail, herald, highball*, high-five*, meet, move to, nod, pay respects, receive, recognize, roll out the red carpet*, salaam*, salute, say hello, say hi*, shake hands, shoulder, speak to, stop, tip one's hat*, usher in*, whistle for; SEE CONCEPT 51

greeting [n] *welcome; message of kindness*
accosting, acknowledgment, address, aloha*, attention, best wishes*, blow*, card*, ciao*, compellation, compliments, good wishes*, hail, hello, heralding, hi, highball*, high five*, how-do-you-do*, howdy*, letter*, nod, note, notice, ovation, reception, regards, respects, rumble, salaam*, salutation, salute, speaking to, testimonial, ushering in, what's happening*; SEE CONCEPT 51

gregarious [adj] *friendly*
affable, clubby*, companionable, convivial, cordial, fun, outgoing, sociable, social; SEE CONCEPT 404

grief [n] *mental suffering*
affliction, agony, anguish, bemoaning, bereavement, bewailing, care, dejection, deploring, depression, desolation, despair, despondency, discomfort, disquiet, distress, dole, dolor, gloom, grievance, harassment, heartache, heartbreak, infelicity, lamentation, lamenting, malaise, melancholy, misery, mortification, mournfulness, mourning, pain, purgatory, regret, remorse, repining, rue, sadness, sorrow, torture, trial, tribulation, trouble, unhappiness, vexation, woe, worry, wretchedness; SEE CONCEPTS 410,728

grievance [n] *complaint, gripe*
affliction, ax to grind*, beef*, bellyache*, big stink*, blast, case, cross*, damage, distress, flack*, grief, grouse*, hardship, holler*, hoo-ha*, howl*, injury, injustice, jeremiad*, kick, knock*, objection, outrage, pain, pain in the neck*, rap*, resentment, rigor, roar, rumble, sorrow, squawk*, stink*, trial, tribulation, trouble, unhappiness, violence, wrong, yell; SEE CONCEPTS 52,278,689

grieve [v1] *mourn, feel deep distress*
ache, bear, bemoan, bewail, carry on, complain, cry, cry a river*, deplore, eat one's heart out*, endure, hang crepe*, keen, lament, regret, rue, sing the blues*, sorrow, suffer, take it hard*, wail, weep; SEE CONCEPTS 17,410

grieve [v2] *upset, distress someone*
afflict, aggrieve, agonize, break the heart of*, constrain, crush, hurt, injure, pain, sadden, wound; SEE CONCEPTS 7,19

grievous [adj] *severe, painful; serious*
afflicting, agonizing, appalling, atrocious, calamitous, damaging, deplorable, dire, dismal, disquieting, distressing, disturbing, dreadful, egregious, flagrant, glaring, grave, harmful, heart-rending, heavy*, heinous, hurtful, injurious, intolerable, lamentable, monstrous, mournful, offensive, onerous, oppressive, outrageous, pathetic, pitiful, sad, shameful, sharp, shocking, sorrowful, taxing, tough, tragic, troublesome, unbearable, upsetting, villainous, weighty*, wounding; SEE CONCEPTS 537,544,548

grill [v1] *broil food*
barbecue, burn, charcoal-broil, cook, cook over an open pit, roast, rotisserie, sear; SEE CONCEPT 170

grill [v2] *ask questions aggressively*
catechize, cross-examine, give the third degree*, go over*, inquisition, interrogate, interview, put the pressure on*, put the screws to*, question, roast*, third degree*; SEE CONCEPTS 48,53

grim [adj] *hopeless, horrible in manner, appearance*
austere, barbarous, bleak, cantankerous, churlish, crabbed*, cruel, crusty, dogged, ferocious, fierce, forbidding, foreboding, formidable, frightful, fu-

nereal, ghastly, gloomy, glowering, glum, grisly, grouchy, gruesome, grumpy*, harsh, hideous, horrid, implacable, inexorable, intractable, merciless, morose, ominous, relentless, resolute, ruthless, scowling, severe, shocking, sinister, somber, sour, splenetic, stern, stubborn, sulky, sullen, surly, terrible, truculent, unrelenting, unyielding; SEE CONCEPTS 534,544,570

grimace [n] *scowling facial expression*
face, frown, moue, mouth, mouthing, mug*, scowl, smile, smirk, sneer, wry face; SEE CONCEPT 716

grimace [v] *make a pained expression*
contort, deform, distort, frown, make a face, make a wry face, misshape, mouth, mug*, scowl, screw up one's face*, smirk, sneer; SEE CONCEPT 185

grime [n] *dirt*
crud*, dust, film, filth, gook*, gunk*, muck*, smudge, smut*, soil, soot, tarnish; SEE CONCEPT 260

grimy [adj] *dirty*
begrimed, besmirched, cruddy*, dingy*, filthy, foul, grubby*, grungy*, messy, mucky*, nasty, scuzzy*, sleazy*, smeared, smutty*, soiled, sooty, sordid, squalid, unclean; SEE CONCEPTS 485,621

grin [n/v] *smile widely*
beam, crack, simper, smirk; SEE CONCEPTS 185,716

grind [n] *tedious job*
chore, drudgery, groove*, grubwork*, hard work, labor, moil, pace, rote, routine, rut*, sweat*, task, toil, travail, treadmill*; SEE CONCEPT 362

grind [v1] *crush, pulverize*
abrade, atomize, attenuate, beat, bray, chop up, comminute, crumble, crumple, disintegrate, file, granulate, grate, kibble*, levigate, mill, pestle, pound, powder, pulverize*, rasp, reduce, roll out*, scrape, shiver, triturate; SEE CONCEPTS 186,204

grind [v2] *sharpen*
abrade, file, give an edge to, gnash, grate, grit, polish, rub, sand, scrape, smooth, whet; SEE CONCEPTS 186,215

grind [v3] *oppress*
afflict, annoy, harass, hold down, hound, persecute, plague, trouble, tyrannize, vex; SEE CONCEPTS 14,130

grip [n1] *clasp, embrace*
anchor, brace, catch, cinch, cincture, clamp, clamping, clench, clinch, clutch, coercion, constraint, crushing, duress, enclosing, enclosure, fastening, fixing, grapnel, grapple, grasp, gripe, handclasp, handgrip, handhold, handshake, hold, hook, ligature, lug, purchase, restraint, snatch, squeeze, strength, tenure, vise, wrench; SEE CONCEPT 191

grip [n2] *perception, understanding*
clutches*, comprehension, control, domination, grasp, hold, influence, keeping, ken, possession, power, tenure; SEE CONCEPT 409

grip [v1] *hold tightly*
clap a hand on, clasp, clench, clinch, clutch, get one's hands on*, grasp, latch on to*, lay hands on, nab, seize, snag, snatch, take, take hold of; SEE CONCEPT 191

grip [v2] *entrance, enchant*
catch up, compel, engross, enthrall, fascinate, hold, hypnotize, involve, mesmerize, rivet, spellbind; SEE CONCEPTS 7,11,22

gripe [n1] *complaint*
ache, aching, affliction, disorder, distress, grievance, groan, grouse, grumble, illness, indisposition, infirmity, moan, objection, pain, pang; SEE CONCEPTS 52,278,313

gripe [n2] *strong hold*
clamp, clasp, clench, clinch, clutch, crunch, grab, grapple, grasp, grip, tenure; SEE CONCEPT 191

gripe [v1] *complain*
bellyache, blow off*, carp, crab*, fuss, groan, grouch, grouse, grumble, kvetch*, moan, murmur, mutter, nag, squawk, take on*, whine, yammer*, yawp*; SEE CONCEPTS 44,52

gripe [v2] *pain, annoy*
ache, bother, compress, cramp, disturb, hurt, irritate, pinch, press, squeeze, vex; SEE CONCEPTS 7,19,219,246

grisly [adj] *horrifying*
abominable, appalling, awful, blood-stained, bloody, disgusting, dreadful, eerie, frightful, ghastly, grim, grody*, gross*, gruesome, hideous, horrible, horrid, lurid, macabre, sanguine, shocking, sick, sickening, terrible, terrifying, yucky*; SEE CONCEPTS 537,544,570

grit [n1] *particles of dirt*
dust, foreign matter, gravel, lumps, pebbles, powder, sand; SEE CONCEPTS 260,831

grit [n2] *courage, determination*
backbone, daring, doggedness, fortitude, gameness, guts*, hardihood, intestinal fortitude*, mettle, moxie*, nerve, perseverance, pluck, resolution, spine*, spirit, spunk, steadfastness, tenacity, toughness; SEE CONCEPTS 411,633

gritty [adj1] *granular*
abrasive, branlike, calculous, crumbly, dusty, friable, grainy, gravelly, in particles, loose, lumpy, permeable, porous, powdery, pulverant, rasping, rough, sabulous, sandy, scratchy; SEE CONCEPT 606

gritty [adj2] *brave*
courageous, determined, dogged, game*, hardy, mettlesome, plucky*, resolute, spirited, steadfast, tenacious, tough; SEE CONCEPTS 401,404

groan [n] *moan, complaint*
cry, gripe, grouse, grumble, grunt, objection, sigh, sob, whine; SEE CONCEPTS 278,595

groan [v] *moan, complain*
bemoan, cry, gripe, grouse, grumble, keen, lament, mumble, murmur, object, sigh, whine; SEE CONCEPTS 44,52,77

groggy [adj] *dizzy, stunned*
befuddled, confused, dazed, dopey*, drunken, faint, hazy, out of it*, punch-drunk*, punchy*, reeling, shaky, slaphappy*, staggering, stupefied, swaying, tired, unsteady, weak, whirling, wobbly, woozy*; SEE CONCEPT 314

groom [n1] *man being married*
benedict, bridegroom, fiancé, husband, spouse, suitor; SEE CONCEPT 419

groom [n2] *stable attendant; servant*
equerry, hostler, stable person; SEE CONCEPTS 348,419

groom [v] *make ready, prepare physically*
brush, clean, coach, comb, curry, dress, drill, educate, lick into shape*, make attractive, make presentable, nurture, preen, prep*, pretty up*, prim, prime, primp, put through mill*, put through mill*, ready, refine, refresh, rub down, shape up, sleek, slick up*, smarten up*, spiff up*, spruce

gr
gr

up*, tend, tidy, train, turn out; SEE CONCEPTS 162,202,285

groove [n1] *channel, indentation*
canal, corrugation, crease, crimp, cut, cutting, depression, ditch, flute, fluting, furrow, gouge, gutter, hollow, incision, notch, pucker, rabbet, rut, scallop, score, scratch, slit, trench, valley; SEE CONCEPT 513

groove [n2] *daily routine*
daily grind*, grind, pace, rote, rut*, same old stuff*, schtick*, slot*; SEE CONCEPTS 362,677

grope [v] *feel about for*
cast about, examine, explore, feel blindly, finger*, fish*, flounder, fumble, grabble, handle, manipulate, poke, pry, root, scrabble, search, touch; SEE CONCEPTS 34,216,612

gross [n] *total, whole*
aggregate, all, entirety, sum, sum total, totality; SEE CONCEPTS 344,837

gross [adj1] *large, fat*
adipose, big, bulky, chubby*, corpulent, dense, fleshy, great, heavy, hulking, husky, lumpish, massive, obese, overweight, porcine, portly, stout, thick, unwieldy, weighty; SEE CONCEPTS 773,781

gross [adj2] *whole*
aggregate, all, before deductions, before tax, complete, entire, in sum, outright, total, whole ball of wax*, whole enchilada*, whole nine yards*, whole schmear*, whole shebang*; SEE CONCEPT 785

gross [adj3] *crude, vulgar*
barnyard*, boorish, breezy, callous, carnal, cheap, coarse, corporeal, crass, dull, fleshly, foul, ignorant, improper, impure, indecent, indelicate, inelegant, insensitive, in the gutter*, lewd, loudmouthed, low, low-minded, lustful, obscene, offensive, rank, raunchy, raw, ribald, rough, rude, scatological, sensual, sexual, sleazy*, smutty*, swinish*, tasteless, ugly, uncouth, uncultured, undiscriminating, unfeeling, unrefined, unseemly, unsophisticated, voluptuous; SEE CONCEPTS 267,542,545

gross [adj4] *obvious, apparent*
absolute, arrant, blatant, capital, complete, downright, egregious, excessive, exorbitant, extreme, flagrant, glaring, grievous, heinous, immoderate, inordinate, manifest, out-and-out*, outrageous, outright*, perfect, plain, rank, serious, shameful, sheer, shocking, unmitigated, unqualified, utter; SEE CONCEPTS 535,537

gross [v] *bring in as total*
earn, make, take in; SEE CONCEPTS 330,351

grotesque [adj] *ugly, misshapen*
aberrant, abnormal, absurd, antic, bizarre, deformed, distorted, eerie, extravagant, extreme, fanciful, fantastic, flamboyant, freakish, grody*, gross*, incongruous, ludicrous, malformed, monstrous, odd, outlandish, perverted, preposterous, queer, ridiculous, strange, surrealistic, uncanny, unnatural, weird, whimsical; SEE CONCEPTS 486,537,579

grouch [n] *person who complains a lot*
bear*, bellyacher*, bug*, crab*, crank, crosspatch*, curmudgeon, faultfinder, griper, grouser, growler, grumbler, grump*, kicker*, malcontent, moaner, sorehead*, sourpuss*, whiner; SEE CONCEPTS 412,423

grouch [v] *complain a lot*
bellyache*, carp, find fault, gripe, grouse, grumble, moan, murmur, mutter, scold, whine; SEE CONCEPT 52

grouchy [adj] *complaining, irritable*
cantankerous*, cross, crusty*, discontented, grumbling, grumpy*, ill-tempered, irascible, peevish, petulant, querulous, snappy, sulky, surly, testy; SEE CONCEPTS 267,401

ground [n] *earth, land*
arena, dirt, dust, field, landscape, loam, old sod, park, real estate, sand, sod, soil, terra firma, terrain, turf; SEE CONCEPT 509

ground [v1] *base, set; educate*
acquaint, bottom, coach, discipline, establish, familiarize, fit, fix, found, indoctrinate, inform, initiate, instruct, introduce, predicate, prepare, prime, qualify, rest, settle, stay, teach, train, tutor; SEE CONCEPTS 18,285

ground [v2] *restrict; drop in place*
bar, beach, bring down, dock, down, fell, floor, knock down, land, level, mow down*, prevent, strand; SEE CONCEPTS 130,181

groundless [adj] *without reason, justification*
baseless, bottomless, causeless, chimerical, empty, false, flimsy, foundationless, gratuitous, idle, illogical, illusory, imaginary, unauthorized, uncalled-for, unfounded, unjustified, unprovoked, unsupported, unwarranted; SEE CONCEPTS 267,552,582

grounds [n1] *estate, domain*
acreage, area, campus, country, district, environs, fields, gardens, habitat, holding, land, lot, premises, property, real estate, realm, sphere, spot, terrace, terrain, territory, tract, zone; SEE CONCEPTS 508,516

grounds [n2] *basis, premise*
account, antecedent, argument, base, bedrock*, call, cause, chapter and verse*, demonstration, determinant, dope*, evidence, excuse, factor, footing, foundation, goods*, groundwork, inducement, info*, information*; infrastructure, justification, motive, numbers, occasion, pretext, proof, rationale, reason, root*, seat, straight stuff*, substratum, test, testimony, trial, underpinning, wherefore, why, whyfor; SEE CONCEPTS 274,661

grounds [n3] *sediment*
deposit, dregs, grouts, leavings, lees, precipitate, precipitation, residue, settlings; SEE CONCEPT 260

groundwork [n] *basis, fundamentals*
ABCs*, background, base, bedrock*, cornerstone*, footing, foundation, ground, infrastructure, origin, preliminaries, preparation, root, substratum, underpinning, understructure; SEE CONCEPTS 274,442,660,661

group [n] *number of individuals collectively*
accumulation, aggregation, assemblage, assembly, association, assortment, band, batch, battery, bevy, body, bunch, bundle, cartel, category, chain, circle, class, clique, clot, club, clump, cluster, clutch, collection, combination, combine, company, conglomerate, congregation, coterie, covey, crew, crowd, faction, formation, gang, gathering, grade, league, lot, mess, organization, pack, parcel, party, passel, platoon, pool, posse, set, shooting match, society, sort, suite, syndicate, troop, trust; SEE CONCEPTS 391,432

group [v1] *bring together*
arrange, assemble, associate, band together, bracket, bunch, bunch up*, cluster, collect, congregate, consort, corral, crowd, gang around*, gang up*, gather, get together, hang out*, harmo-

nize, huddle, link, make the scene*, meet, organize, poke, punch*, round up*, scare up*, systematize; SEE CONCEPTS *109,114*

group [v2] *classify, sort*
arrange, assemble, associate, assort, bracket, categorize, class, dispose, file, gather, marshal, order, organize, pigeonhole*, put together, range, rank; SEE CONCEPTS *18,84,158*

grove [n] *cluster of trees*
brake, coppice, copse, covert, forest, orchard, plantation, spinney, stand, thicket, wood, woodland; SEE CONCEPTS *429,517*

grovel [v] *abase, demean oneself*
apple-polish*, beg, beg for mercy, beseech, blandish, bootlick*, bow and scrape*, brown-nose*, butter up*, cater to, court, cower, crawl, creep, cringe, crouch, eat crow*, eat dirt*, eat humble pie*, fall all over*, fawn*, flatter, humble oneself, humor, implore, kiss one's feet*, kneel, kowtow*, make much of*, make up to*, pamper, play up to*, prostrate*, revere, snivel, soft-soap*, stoop, suck up to*, truckle*, wheedle, yes*; SEE CONCEPTS *384,633*

grow [v] *become larger, evolve*
abound, advance, age, amplify, arise, augment, become, branch out, breed, build, burgeon, burst forth, come, come to be, cultivate, develop, dilate, enlarge, expand, extend, fill out, flourish, gain, germinate, get bigger, get taller, heighten, increase, issue, luxuriate, maturate, mature, mount, multiply, originate, pop up*, produce, propagate, pullulate, raise, ripen, rise, shoot*, spread, spring up, sprout, stem, stretch, swell, thicken, thrive, turn, vegetate, wax*, widen; SEE CONCEPTS *427,469,704,775*

growl [n/v] *animal-like sound*
bark, bellow, gnarl, gnarr, grumble, grunt, howl, moan, roar, roll, rumble, snarl, thunder; SEE CONCEPTS *77,595*

grown-up [n] *adult*
gentleman, grown person, lady, mam, man, Miss, mister, Mr., Mrs., Ms., woman; SEE CONCEPT *424*

growth [n1] *development, progress*
advance, advancement, aggrandizement, augmentation, beefing up*, boost, buildup, crop, cultivation, enlargement, evolution, evolvement, expansion, extension, fleshing out*, flowering, gain, germination, heightening, hike, improvement, increase, maturation, maturing, multiplication, produce, production, proliferation, prosperity, rise, sprouting, stretching, success, surge, swell, thickening, unfolding, up, upping, vegetation, waxing*, widening; SEE CONCEPTS *427,469,703,704,775*

growth [n2] *tumor*
cancer, cancroid, excrescence, fibrousness, fibrous tissue, fungus, lump, mole, outgrowth, parasite, polyp, swelling, thickening, wen; SEE CONCEPT *306*

grub [n1] *larva*
caterpillar, entozoon, maggot, worm; SEE CONCEPT *398*

grub [n2] *food*
chow*, comestibles, eats*, edibles, feed, nosh*, nurture, provisions, rations, sustenance, viands, victuals, vittles*; SEE CONCEPTS *457,460*

grub [v1] *dig, uncover*
beat, break, burrow, clean, clear, comb, delve, excavate, ferret, fine-tooth-comb*, forage, hunt,

poke, prepare, probe, pull up, rake, ransack, root, rummage, scour, search, shovel, spade, unearth, uproot; SEE CONCEPTS *178,216*

grub [v2] *work very hard*
drudge, grind, labor, moil, plod, slave, slog, sweat, toil; SEE CONCEPT *100*

grubby [adj] *dirty, disheveled*
besmeared, black, filthy, foul, frowzy*, grimy, grungy*, impure, messy, mucky*, nasty, scruffy, scuzzy*, seedy*, shabby, sloppy, slovenly, smutty*, soiled, sordid, squalid, unclean, uncleanly, unkempt, untidy, unwashed; SEE CONCEPTS *485,621*

grudge [n] *hard feelings*
animosity, animus, antipathy, aversion, bad blood*, bitterness, bone to pick*, dislike, enmity, grievance, hate, hatred, ill will, injury, injustice, malevolence, malice, maliciousness, malignancy, peeve, pet peeve*, pique, rancor, resentment, spite, spitefulness, spleen, venom; SEE CONCEPT *29*

grudge [v] *feel resentful; give unwillingly*
begrudge, be reluctant, be stingy*, complain, covet, deny, envy, hold back, mind, pinch, refuse, resent, stint; SEE CONCEPT *21*

grueling [adj] *difficult, taxing*
arduous, backbreaking, brutal, chastening, crushing, demanding, excruciating, exhausting, fatiguing, fierce, grinding, hairy*, hard, harsh, heavy*, laborious, punishing, racking, severe, stiff, strenuous, tiring, torturous, trying; SEE CONCEPT *565*

gruesome [adj] *horrible, awful*
abominable, appalling, daunting, fearful, frightful, ghastly, grim, grisly, grody*, gross*, hideous, horrendous, horrid, horrific, horrifying, loathsome, lurid, macabre, monstrous, morbid, offensive, repugnant, repulsive, shocking, sick*, spine-tingling*, terrible, terrifying, ugly, weird*; SEE CONCEPTS *485,548*

gruff [adj1] *bad-tempered, rude*
abrupt, bearish, blunt, boisterous, boorish, brusque, churlish, crabbed*, crabby*, crude, crusty*, curt, discourteous, dour, fierce, grouchy*, grumpy*, ill-natured, impolite, morose, nasty, offhand, rough, saturnine, short, snappy*, snippy*, sour, sullen, surly, truculent, uncivil, ungracious, unmannerly; SEE CONCEPTS *267,401*

gruff [adj2] *rasping in sound*
cracked, croaking, croaky, grating, guttural, harsh, hoarse, husky, low, rough, throaty; SEE CONCEPT *594*

grumble [v1] *complain*
bellyache*, carp, find fault, fuss, gripe, groan, grouch*, grouse, kick, kvetch*, moan, protest, pule, repine, scold, snivel*, squawk*, whine; SEE CONCEPTS *44,52*

grumble [v2] *murmur, rumble*
bark, croak, gnarl, gnarr, growl, grunt, gurgle, mumble, mutter, roar, roll, snap, snarl, snuffle, splutter, whine; SEE CONCEPTS *65,77*

grumpy [adj] *in a bad mood*
bad-tempered, cantankerous*, crabby*, cross, crotchety, disgruntled, dissatisfied, griping, grouchy*, grumbling, irritable, peevish, pettish, petulant, querulous, sulky, sullen, surly, testy, truculent; SEE CONCEPTS *401,403*

guarantee [n] *pledge, promise*
agreement, assurance, attestation, bail, bargain, bond, certainty, certificate, certification, charter,

gr
gu

collateral, contract, covenant, deposit, earnest, gage, guaranty, insurance, lock, oath, pawn, pipe, recognizance, security, sure thing*, surety, testament, token, undertaking, vow, warrant, warranty, word, word of honor; SEE CONCEPTS 71,271,685

guarantee [v] *pledge, promise*
affirm, angel, answer for, assure, attest, aver, back, bankroll, be surety for, bind oneself, certify, confirm, cosign, endorse, ensure, evidence, evince, get behind*, give bond, grubstake, guaranty, insure, juice*, maintain, make bail*, make certain, make sure, mortgage, pick up the check*, pick up the tab*, protect, prove, reassure, secure, sign for, stake, stand behind*, stand up for*, support, swear, testify, vouch for, wager, warrant, witness; SEE CONCEPTS 71,110

guaranteed [adj] *made certain*
affirmed, approved, ascertained, assured, attested, bonded, certified, confirmed, endorsed, for a fact, for sure, have a lock on*, insured, on ice*, pledged, plighted, protected, sealed, secured, sure, sure enough*, sure-fire*, warranted; SEE CONCEPT 535

guard [n1] *protector*
bouncer*, chaperon, chaperone, chaser*, convoyer, custodian, defender, escort, guardian, lookout, picket, sentinel, sentry, shepherd, shield, ward, warden, watch, watchperson; SEE CONCEPT 348

guard [n2] *defense*
aegis, armament, armor, buffer, bulwark, pad, protection, rampart, safeguard, screen, security, shield, ward; SEE CONCEPT 712

guard [v] *protect, watch*
attend, baby-sit, bulwark, chaperon, chaperone, conduct, convoy, cover, cover up, defend, escort, fend, keep, keep an eye on*, keep in view, keep under surveillance, look after, lookout, mind, observe, oversee, patrol, police*, preserve, ride shotgun for*, safeguard, save, screen, secure, see after, shelter, shepherd, shield, shotgun, stonewall*, superintend, supervise, tend; SEE CONCEPTS 96,134

guarded [adj] *suspicious*
attentive, cagey, calculating, canny, careful, cautious, chary, circumspect, discreet, gingerly, leery, noncommittal, on the lookout*, overcautious, prudent, reserved, restrained, reticent, safe, vigilant, wary, watchful, with eyes peeled*; SEE CONCEPT 542

guardian [n] *keeper, protector*
angel*, attendant, baby-sitter, bird dog*, cerberus, champion, chaperon, chaperone, conservator, cop*, curator, custodian, defender, escort, guard, keeper, nurse, overseer, paladin, patrol, preserver, safeguard, sentinel, shepherd, sitter, sponsor, superintendent, supervisor, trustee, vigilante, warden, watchdog*; SEE CONCEPTS 414,423

guess [n] *belief, speculation*
assumption, ballpark figure*, conclusion, conjecture, deduction, divination, estimate, fancy, feeling, guesstimate*, guesswork, hunch*, hypothesis, induction, inference, judgment, notion, opinion, postulate, postulation, prediction, presumption, presupposition, reckoning, shot*, shot in the dark*, sneaking suspicion*, stab*, supposal, supposition, surmisal, surmise, suspicion, theory, thesis, view; SEE CONCEPT 689

guess [v] *try to figure out; imagine*
believe, calculate, chance, conjecture, dare say, deduce, deem, divine, estimate, fancy*, fathom, go out on a limb*, guesstimate*, happen upon*, hazard*, hypothesize, infer, judge, jump to a conclusion*, lump it*, opine, penetrate, pick, postulate, predicate, predict, presume, pretend, reason, reckon, select, size up*, solve, speculate, suggest, suppose, surmise, survey, suspect, take a shot at*, take a stab at*, theorize, think, think likely, venture, work out*; SEE CONCEPT 28

guest [n] *person accommodated, given hospitality*
bedfellow, boarder, caller, client, companion, company, customer, frequenter*, habitué, inmate, lodger, mate, out-of-towner*, partaker, patron, recipient, renter, roomer, sharer, sojourner, tenant, transient, vacationer, visitant, visitor; SEE CONCEPT 423

guidance [n] *counseling*
advice, auspices, conduct, conduction, control, conveyance, direction, government, help, instruction, intelligence, leadership, management, navigation, supervision, teaching; SEE CONCEPTS 75,274,278

guide [n1] *something that or someone who leads*
adviser, attendant, captain, chaperon, cicerone, conductor, controller, convoy, counselor, criterion, design, director, docent, escort, example, exemplar, exhibitor, genie, genius, guiding spirit, guru, ideal, inspiration, lead, leader, lodestar, mentor, model, monitor, paradigm, pathfinder, pattern, pilot, pioneer, rudder, scout, standard, superintendent, teacher, usher, vanguard; SEE CONCEPTS 348,423,686

guide [n2] *information, instructions*
ABCs*, beacon*, bellwether*, bible, catalog, chapter and verse*, clue, compendium, directory, enchiridion, guidebook, guiding light*, handbook, hot lead*, key, landmark, lodestar, manual, mark, marker, no-no's*, pointer, print, sign, signal, signpost, telltale, the book*, the numbers*, tip-off*, vade mecum; SEE CONCEPT 274

guide [v] *direct, lead*
accompany, advise, attend, beacon*, chaperon, command, conduct, contrive, control, convoy, counsel, coxswain, educate, engineer, escort, govern, handle, have a handle on*, influence, instruct, manage, maneuver, marshal, navigate, oversee, pilot, quarterback*, regulate, route, rule, see, shepherd, show, show the way, spearhead*, steer, superintend, supervise, sway, teach, trailblaze*, train, usher; SEE CONCEPTS 75,110,117,187

guild [n] *association, fellowship*
club, company, corporation, federation, group, interest group, league, lodge, order, organization, profession, society, sodality, trade, union; SEE CONCEPTS 381,387

guile [n] *slyness, cleverness*
artfulness, artifice, chicanery, craft, craftiness, cunning, deceit, deception, dirty dealing*, dirty pool*, dirty trick*, dirty work*, dishonesty, dissemblance, dissimulation, double-cross*, duplicity, foul play*, jive*, run-around*, ruse, sellout*, sharp practice*, stab in the back*, treachery, trickery, trickiness, wiliness; SEE CONCEPTS 645,657

guileless [adj] *honest*
aboveboard, artless, candid, frank, genuine, ingenuous, innocent, naive, natural, open, simple, simple-minded, sincere, straightforward, truthful,

unaffected, undesigning, unsophisticated, unstudied; SEE CONCEPTS 267,542,545

guilt [n] *blame: bad conscience over responsibility*
answerability, blameworthiness, contrition, crime, criminality, culpability, delinquency, dereliction, disgrace, dishonor, error, failing, fault, indiscretion, infamy, iniquity, lapse, liability, malefaction, malfeasance, malpractice, misbehavior, misconduct, misstep, offense, onus, peccability, penitence, regret, remorse, responsibility, self-condemnation, self-reproach, shame, sin, sinfulness, slip, solecism, stigma, transgression, wickedness, wrong; SEE CONCEPTS *101,532, 645,690*

guiltless [adj] *blameless, not responsible*
clean, clear, crimeless, exemplary, faultless, free, good, immaculate, impeccable, inculpable, innocent, irreproachable, pure, righteous, sinless, spotless, unimpeachable, unsullied, untainted, untarnished, virtuous; SEE CONCEPT 545

guilty [adj] *blameworthy; found at fault*
accusable, caught, censurable, censured, chargeable, condemned, conscience-stricken, contrite, convictable, convicted, criminal, culpable, damned, delinquent, depraved, doomed, erring, evil, felonious, hangdog*, impeached, incriminated, in error, iniquitous, in the wrong, judged, liable, licentious, offending, on one's head*, out of line*, proscribed, regretful, remorseful, reprehensible, responsible, rueful, sentenced, sheepish, sinful, sorry, wicked, wrong; SEE CONCEPT 545

guise [n] *appearance, pretense*
air, aspect, behavior, cloak, color, cover, demeanor, disguise, disguisement, dress, facade, face, false front*, false show*, fashion, form, front, mask, mien, mode, pose, posture, role, seeming, semblance, shape, show, showing, simulacrum; SEE CONCEPTS 645,716

gulf [n1] *sea inlet*
basin, bay, bayou, bight, cove, firth, harbor, slough, sound, whirlpool; SEE CONCEPTS 509,514

gulf [n2] *deep, gaping hole*
abyss, breach, cave, cavity, chasm, cleft, crevasse, depth, depths, distance, expanse, gap, gulch, hiatus, hollow, opening, pit, ravine, rent, rift, separation, shaft, split, void, well, whirlpool; SEE CONCEPTS 509,513

gullible [adj] *naive, trusting*
being a sucker*, believing, biting, credulous, easily taken in*, easy mark*, falling hook line and sinker*, foolish, green*, innocent, kidding oneself*, mark*, silly, simple, sucker, susceptible, swallowing whole*, taken in*, taking the bait*, trustful, tumbling for*, unskeptical, unsophisticated, unsuspecting, wide-eyed*; SEE CONCEPTS 402,542

gully [n] *ravine, ditch*
channel, chase, chasm, crevasse, culvert, gutter, notch, trench, watercourse; SEE CONCEPTS 509,513

gulp [n] *swallow*
choke, draught, gasp, mouthful, swig, swill; SEE CONCEPT 185

gulp [v] *eat, drink fast*
belt*, choke down*, chugalug*, consume, devour, dispatch, dispose, drop*, englut, gobble*, guzzle*, imbibe, ingurgitate, inhale*, pour, quaff, scarf down*, slop*, slosh*, stuff, swallow, swig, swill, take in, toss off*, wolf*, wolf down*; SEE CONCEPTS 169,185

gum [n] *sticky substance*
adhesive, amber, cement, cohesive substance, exudate, glue, mucilage, paste, pitch, plaster, resin, rosin, tar, wax; SEE CONCEPT 466

gumption [n] *nerve, initiative*
ability, acumen, astuteness, cleverness, commonsense, discernment, enterprise, get-up-and-go*, good sense, horse sense*, industry, judgment, perspicaciousness, perspicacity, resourcefulness, sagaciousness, sagacity, savvy, sense, shrewdness, spirit, wisdom, wit; SEE CONCEPT 411

gun [n] *weapon that shoots*
blaster*, cannon, difference*, equalizer*, flintlock, forty-five*, handgun, hardware*, howitzer, magnum, mortar, musket, 9 mm.*, ordnance, peashooter*, persuader*, piece*, pistol, revolver, rifle, rod*, Saturday-night special*, shotgun, thirty-eight*, Uzi*; SEE CONCEPT 500

gurgle [n/v] *burble, murmur*
babble, bubble, crow, lap, plash, purl, ripple, slosh, splash, wash; SEE CONCEPTS 65,595

guru [n] *mentor, guide*
authority, guiding light*, leader, master, sage, teacher, tutor; SEE CONCEPT 350

gush [n] *outpouring*
burst, cascade, flood, flow, flush, issue, jet, run, rush, spate, spout, spring, spurt, stream, surge; SEE CONCEPTS 467,687

gush [v1] *pour out*
burst, cascade, emanate, emerge, flood, flow, flush, issue, jet, pour, roll, run, rush, sluice, spew, spout, spring, spurt, stream, surge, well; SEE CONCEPT 179

gush [v2] *speak with overwhelming enthusiasm*
babble*, blather, carry on about*, chatter, effervesce, effuse, enthuse, fall all over*, go on about*, jabber, make a to-do over*, overstate, prate, prattle, rave; SEE CONCEPT 49

gust [n] *rush, eruption*
access, blast, blow, breeze, burst, explosion, fit, flare-up, flurry, gale, outburst, paroxysm, passion, puff, sally, squall, storm, surge; SEE CONCEPTS 524,707

gusto [n] *great enthusiasm*
appetite, appreciation, ardor, brio, delectation, delight, enjoyment, exhilaration, fervor, heart, liking, palate, passion, pleasure, relish, savor, taste, verve, zeal, zest; SEE CONCEPTS 411,657

gusty [adj] *windy*
airy, blowy, blustering, blustery, breezy, hearty, robust, squally, stormy, tempestuous; SEE CONCEPT 525

gut [n] *stomach and abdomen*
belly, bowels, duodenum, entrails, innards, intestines, paunch, tripes, tummy*, venter, viscera; SEE CONCEPT 393

gut [adj] *intuitive*
basic, deep-seated, emotional, heartfelt, innate, inner, instinctive, interior, internal, intimate, involuntary, natural, spontaneous, unthinking, visceral, viscerous; SEE CONCEPT 403

gut [v] *clean out, strip*
bowel, decimate, despoil, dilapidate, disembowel, draw, empty, eviscerate, exenterate, loot, pillage, plunder, ransack, ravage, rifle, sack; SEE CONCEPTS 165,211

gutless [adj] *timid*
abject, chicken*, chicken-hearted*, coward, cowardly, craven, faint-hearted*, feeble, irresolute, lily-livered*, pusillanimous, spineless*, submis-

gu
gu

sive, weak, wimpy*, yellow*, yellow-bellied*;
SEE CONCEPTS 404,542

guts [n] *nerve, boldness*
audacity, backbone*, courage, daring, dauntlessness, effrontery, forcefulness, fortitude, grit*, hardihood, heart*, intestinal fortitude*, mettle, moxie*, pluck, resolution, sand*, spine*, spirit, spunk*, willpower; SEE CONCEPTS 411,657

gutsy [adj] *bold, brave*
courageous, determined, gallant, game*, indomitable, intrepid, mettlesome, plucky, resolute, spirited, spunky*, staunch, unfearful, valiant; SEE CONCEPTS 404,542

gutter [n] *ditch*
channel, conduit, culvert, dike, drain, duct, eaves, fosse, funnel, gully, moat, pipe, runnel, sewer, sluice, spout, sulcation, trench, trough, tube, watercourse; SEE CONCEPTS 440,513

guttural [adj] *deep in sound*
glottal, grating, gravely, growling, gruff, harsh, hoarse, husky, inarticulate, low, rasping, rough, sepulchral, thick, throaty; SEE CONCEPT 594

guzzle [v] *drink down fast*
bolt*, booze*, carouse*, cram, devour, englut, gobble*, gorge, gormandize, imbibe, ingurgitate, knock back*, quaff, slop*, slosh*, soak, swig, swill, tipple; SEE CONCEPT 169

gymnasium [n] *arena for sports, recreation*
alley, amphitheater, athletic club, center, circus, coliseum, course, exercise room, field house, floor, gym, health club, hippodrome, pit, recreation center, ring, rink, spa, stadium, sweatshop*, theater; SEE CONCEPTS 364,438,439

gymnastics [n] *acrobatic exercise*
aerobics, balance beam, bars, body-building, calisthenics, floor exercise, free exercise, gym, horse, rings, trampoline, trapeze, tumbling, vaulting, workout; SEE CONCEPT 363

gyrate [v] *revolve*
circle, circulate, circumduct, gyre, pirouette, purl, roll, rotate, spin, spiral, turn, twirl, whirl, whirligig; SEE CONCEPTS 147,149

H

habit [n1] *tendency, practice*
addiction, bent, bias, constitution, consuetude, convention, custom, dependence, disposition, fashion, fixation, fixed attitude, frame of mind*, gravitation, groove, habitude, hangup, impulsion, inclination, make-up*, manner, mannerism, mode, nature, obsession, pattern, penchant, persuasion, praxis, predisposition, proclivity, proneness, propensity, quirk, routine, rule, rut, second nature*, set, style, susceptibility, thing*, turn, usage, use, way, weakness, wont; SEE CONCEPT 644

habit [n2] *dress, clothing, often for a particular purpose*
apparel, costume, garb, garment, habiliment, riding clothes, robe, vestment; SEE CONCEPT 451

habitat/habitation [n] *place where someone resides*
abode, accommodations, address, apartment, berth, biosphere, cave, commoracy, condo, condominium, co-op, den, digs*, domicile, dwelling, element, environment, fireside, flat, haunt*, haven, hearth, hole*, home, home plate*, homestead, house, housing, locale, locality, lodging, neck of the woods*, nest, nook, occupancy, occupation, pad*, place, quarters, range, residence, residency, roof*, roost*, seat*, settlement, site, stamping ground*, stomping ground*, surroundings, terrain, territory, turf; SEE CONCEPT 515

habitual [adj] *usual, established*
accepted, accustomed, addicted, addicting, automatic, chronic, common, confirmed, constant, continual, conventional, customary, cyclic, disciplined, familiar, fixed, frequent, hardened, ingrained, inveterate, iterated, iterative, mechanical, methodical, natural, normal, ordinary, perfunctory, permanent, perpetual, persistent, practiced, recurrent, regular, reiterative, repeated, repetitious, rooted, routine, seasoned, set, standard, steady, systematic, traditional, wonted; SEE CONCEPTS 530,547

habituate [v] *prepare, accustom*
acclimate, acclimatize, addict, adjust, break in, condition, confirm, devote, discipline, endure, familiarize, harden, inure, make used to, school, season, take to, tolerate, train; SEE CONCEPTS 35,202

hack [n1] *person who does easy work for money*
drudge*, greasy grind*, grind*, hireling, lackey*, old pro*, plodder*, pro*, servant, slave, workhorse*; SEE CONCEPT 348

hack [n2] *taxicab*
cab, carriage, coach, hackney, taxi, vehicle; SEE CONCEPT 505

hack [n3/v] *cut without care*
chop, clip, fell, gash, hackle, hew, lacerate, mangle, mutilate, notch, slash, whack; SEE CONCEPTS 137,176

hacker [n] *someone proficient at computers, especially a hobbyist*
application programmer, computer architect, computer designer, computer jock, key puncher, operator, programmer, systems analyst, systems engineer, system software specialist, systems programmer, technician; SEE CONCEPTS 360,366

hackneyed [adj] *clichéd, tired*
antiquated, banal, common, commonplace, conventional, corny*, everyday, familiar tune*, hokey*, moth-eaten*, obsolete, old, old-chestnut*, old-hat*, old-saw*, outdated, outmoded, out-of-date, overworked, pedestrian*, played-out*, quotidian, run-of-the-mill*, stale, stereotyped, stock, threadbare*, timeworn, tripe, trite, unoriginal, well-worn, worn-out*; SEE CONCEPTS 267,530

haggard [adj] *worn, weakened*
ashen, careworn, drawn, emaciated, exhausted, faded, fagged, fatigued, fretted, gaunt, ghastly, lank, lean, pale, pallid, pinched, scraggy, scrawny, shrunken, skinny, spare, starved, thin, tired, wan, wasted, weak, wearied, worn-down, wrinkled; SEE CONCEPTS 314,406,491

haggle [v] *bicker, quarrel*
argue, bargain, barter, beat down*, cavil, chaffer, deal, dicker*, dispute, hammer out a deal*, horse-trade*, make a deal*, palter, quibble, squabble, wrangle; SEE CONCEPT 46

hail [n] *torrent*
barrage, bombardment, broadside, cannonade, hailstorm, pelting, rain, salvo, shower, storm, volley; SEE CONCEPTS 189,524

hail [v1] *call to, yell for*
accost, address, flag, flag down*, greet, hello, holler*, salute, shoulder, shout, signal, sing out*, speak to, wave down, welcome, whistle down*, whistle for*, yawp*, yoo-hoo*; SEE CONCEPTS 47,74,77

hail [v2] *honor, salute*
acclaim, acknowledge, applaud, cheer, commend, compliment, exalt, glorify, greet, hear it for*, kudize, praise, recognize, recommend, root for*, welcome; SEE CONCEPT 69

hail [v3] *come from; originate*
be a native of, be born in, begin, claim as birth-place; SEE CONCEPT 648

hail [v4] *rain down on*
barrage, batter, beat down upon, bombard, pelt, shower, storm, volley; SEE CONCEPT 526

hair [n] *threadlike growth on animate being*
beard, bristle, cilium, coiffure, cowlick, cut, down, eyebrow, eyelash, feeler, fiber, filament, fluff, fringe, frizzies*, fur, grass, haircut, hair-style, lock, mane, mop*, moustache, quill, ruff, shock, sideburn, split ends, strand, thatch, tress, tuft, vibrissa, villus, whiskers, wig, wool; SEE CONCEPT 392

hairless [adj] *without growth on body part*
bald, baldheaded, beardless, clean-shaven, cue ball*, depilated, egghead*, glabrate, glabrescent, glabrous, shaved, shaven, shorn, skinhead*, smooth, smooth-faced, tonsured, whiskerless; SEE CONCEPT 406

hairstyle [n] *cut, style of a head of hair*
afro*, beehive*, blow dry*, bob*, bouffant, braid, brushcut, bubble*, bun, coiffure, crewcut, cut, do*, dreadlocks, ducktail, fade, feather cut, flat-top*, flip, haircut, hairdo, headdress, horse tail, mohawk, natural, pageboy, pigtails, pixie, pony-tail, razor cut; SEE CONCEPT 718

hairy [adj1] *having much hair*
bearded, bewhiskered, bristly, bushy, downy, fleecy, flocculent, fluffy, furry, fuzzy, hirsute, lanate, pileous, piliferous, pilose, pubescent, rough, shaggy, stubbly, tufted, unshaven, un-shorn, villous, whiskered, woolly; SEE CONCEPT 406

hairy [adj2] *dangerous*
chancy, difficult, hazardous, jeopardous, perilous, risky, scary, treacherous, uncertain, unhealthy, unsound, wicked; SEE CONCEPT 548

hale [adj] *strong and healthy*
able-bodied, alive and kicking*, blooming, fit, fit as a fiddle*, flourishing, healthy, hearty, husky, in fine fettle*, in the pink*, right, robust, sane, sound, stout, strapping, strong, trim, vigorous, well, well-conditioned, wholesome; SEE CONCEPTS 314,489

half [n] *one of two equal parts of a whole*
bisection, division, fifty percent, fraction, hemi-sphere, moiety; SEE CONCEPT 835

half [adj] *partial*
bisected, divided, even-steven*, fifty-fifty*, frac-tional, halved, incomplete, limited, moderate, partly; SEE CONCEPT 785

half-baked [adj] *stupid; not thought through*
backward, batty*, birdbrained*, blockheaded*, boneheaded*, brainless, crazy, dumb, feeble-minded, foolish, harebrained*, idiotic, ignorant, ill-conceived, imbecilic, impractical, indiscreet, moronic, poorly planned, retarded, senseless, short-sighted, silly, slow, sophomoric, underde-veloped, unformed, witless; SEE CONCEPTS 403,529,548

half-breed [n] *mixed creation*
amalgam, blend, combination, conglomeration, cross, cross-breed, hodgepodge*, hybrid, medley, melange, miscegnation, mishmash*, mule, mutt*; SEE CONCEPTS 260,394

halfhearted [adj] *without enthusiasm*
apathetic, cool, impassive, indifferent, irresolute, lackluster, listless, lukewarm, neutral, passive, perfunctory, spiritless, tame, tepid, unenthusias-tic, uninterested; SEE CONCEPTS 401,542

halfway [adj] *not complete; in the middle*
betwixt and between*, center, centermost, cen-tral, equidistant, imperfect, intermediate, medial, median, mid*, middlemost, midway, moderate, part, partial, part-way, smack dab*, smack in the middle*; SEE CONCEPTS 531,586

halfway [adv] *not complete; in the middle*
comparatively, compromising, conciliatory, half the distance, imperfectly, incompletely, in part, insufficiently, medially, middling, midway, mod-erately, nearly, partially, partly, pretty*, rather, restrictedly, to a degree, to some extent, to the middle, unsatisfactorily; SEE CONCEPTS 531,586

hall [n1] *corridor*
anteroom, entrance, entranceway, entry, foyer, gallery, hallway, lobby, pass, passage, passage-way, room, rotunda, vestibule; SEE CONCEPT 440

hall [n2] *room for large affairs*
amphitheater, arena, armory, assembly room, au-ditorium, ballroom, casino, chamber, church, gal-lery, gym, gymnasium, lounge, lyceum, mart, meeting place, refectory, salon, stateroom, the-ater; SEE CONCEPTS 438,439,441,448

hallmark [n] *symbol, authentication*
badge, certification, device, emblem, endorse-ment, indication, mark, ratification, seal, sign, signet, stamp, sure sign, telltale sign, trademark; SEE CONCEPTS 284,628

hallowed [adj] *holy, revered*
anointed, beatified, blessed, consecrated, dedi-cated, divine, enshrined, holy, honored, inviola-ble, sacred, sacrosanct, sanctified, unprofane; SEE CONCEPT 568

hallucinate [v] *imagine vividly*
blow one's mind*, daydream, envision, fantasize, freak out*, have visions, head trip*, hear voices*, trip*, visualize; SEE CONCEPT 34

hallucination [n] *dream, delusion*
aberration, apparition, fantasy, figment of the imagination*, head trip*, illusion, mirage, phan-tasm, phantasmagoria, phantom, trip*, vision, wraith; SEE CONCEPTS 529,532,690

halo [n] *ring of light*
aura, aureola, aureole, aurora, corona, crown of light, glory, halation, nimbus, radiance; SEE CON-CEPTS 624,628

halt [n] *end, stoppage*
arrest, break, break-off*, close, cutoff, freeze*, grinding halt, impasse, interruption, layoff, letup, pause, screaming halt*, screeching halt*, stand, standstill, stop, termination; SEE CONCEPT 119

halt [v1] *stop, cause to stop*
adjourn, arrest, balk, bar, block, blow the whistle on*, break off*, bring to an end, bring to stand-still, call it a day*, cease, cease fire, check, close down, come to an end, cool it*, curb*, cut short, desist, deter, draw up, drop anchor*, end, frus-trate, hamper, hold at bay*, hold back, impede,

gu
ha

intermit, interrupt, obstruct, pause, pull up*, punctuate, put a cork in*, rest, stall, stand still, stay, stem, stop, suspend, terminate, wait; SEE CONCEPTS 121,234

halt [v2] *hesitate, stutter*
be defective, dither, falter, hobble, limp, pause, shilly-shally*, stagger, stammer, stumble, vacillate, waver, whiffle*, wiggle-waggle*; SEE CONCEPTS 234,721,804

halting [adj] *hesitant*
awkward, bumbling, clumsy, doubtful, faltering, gauche, imperfect, indecisive, inept, irresolute, labored, limping, lumbering, maladroit, slow, stammering, stumbling, stuttering, tentative, uncertain, unhandy, vacillating, vacillatory, wavering, wooden*; SEE CONCEPTS 534,550

halve [v] *cut in half*
bisect, divide equally, reduce by fifty percent, share equally, split in two; SEE CONCEPT 98

hamburger [n] *ground beef sandwich*
beefburger, burger, cheeseburger, chopped beefsteak, ground chuck, ground round, ground sirloin, Salisbury steak; SEE CONCEPTS 457,460

hammer [v] *beat, hit*
bang, batter, bear down, clobber, defeat, drive, drub, fashion, forge, form, knock, make, pound, pummel, shape, strike, tap, thrash, trounce, wallop, whack, whomp; SEE CONCEPT 189

hammer away/hammer into [v] *work hard at*
continue, drive home*, drub into*, drudge, drum into*, endeavor, grind*, grind into*, impress upon, instruct, keep on, peg away*, persevere, persist, plug away*, pound away*, repeat, stick to*, try hard, try repeatedly, work; SEE CONCEPTS 68,87,239

hammer out [v] *bring to a conclusion*
accomplish, bring about, build, complete, construct, erect, establish, excogitate, fight through, finish, form, make, negotiate, produce, settle, set up, sort out, thrash out*, work out; SEE CONCEPTS 91,706

hamper [n] *basket for storage*
bassinet, carton, crate, creel, laundry basket, pannier; SEE CONCEPT 494

hamper [v] *impede, restrict*
baffle, balk, bar, bind, block, check, clog, cramp, cramp one's style*, cumber, curb, drag one's feet*, embarrass, encumber, entangle, fetter, foil, frustrate, get in the way*, hamstring*, handicap, hang up*, hinder, hobble, hog-tie*, hold up*, inconvenience, inhibit, interfere with, leash, obstruct, prevent, restrain, retard, shackle, slow down, stymie, thwart, tie, tie one's hands*, tie up, trammel; SEE CONCEPT 130

hand [n1] *appendage at end of human arm, including fingers*
duke*, extremity, fin*, fist, grasp, grip, ham*, hold, hook, metacarpus, mitt*, palm, paw*, phalanges, shaker*; SEE CONCEPT 392

hand [n2] *person who does labor*
aide, artificer, artisan, craftsperson, employee, help, helper, hired person, laborer, operative, roustabout, worker; SEE CONCEPT 348

hand [n3] *help, aid*
ability, agency, assistance, control, direction, guidance, influence, instruction, knack, lift, part, participation, relief, share, skill, succor, support; SEE CONCEPTS 110,630

hand [n4] *handwriting*
calligraphy, chirography, longhand, script; SEE CONCEPT 79

hand [n5] *round of applause*
clap, handclapping, ovation, thunderous reception; SEE CONCEPT 189

handbag [n] *person's carryall*
backpack, bag, clutch, evening bag, grip, hide, knapsack, leather, pocketbook, portmanteau, purse, reticule; SEE CONCEPT 446

handbook [n] *document giving instruction, information*
bible, compendium, directory, enchiridion, encyclopedia, fundamentals, guide, guidebook, instruction book, manual, text, textbook, vade mecum; SEE CONCEPT 280

handful [adj] *a small quantity*
few, scattering, small number, smattering, some, spattering, sprinkling; SEE CONCEPT 789

handicap [n1] *disadvantage*
affliction, baggage*, barrier, block, burden, detriment, disability, drawback, encumbrance, hangup*, hindrance, impairment, impediment, injury, limitation, load, millstone, obstacle, psychological baggage*, restriction, shortcoming, stumbling block*; SEE CONCEPTS 666,674

handicap [n2] *advantage*
bulge, edge*, favor, head start*, odds, penalty, points*, start, upper hand*, vantage; SEE CONCEPT 693

handicap [v] *give disadvantage*
burden, cripple, encumber, hamper, hamstring*, hinder, hog-tie*, hold back, impede, limit, put out of commission*, restrict, sideline*, take out*; SEE CONCEPTS 130,246

handicraft [n] *artwork, skill*
achievement, art, artifact, artisanship, calling, craft, craftship, creation, design, handiwork, invention, métier, product, production, profession, result, trade, vocation; SEE CONCEPTS 259,630

handle [n1] *something to grip*
arm, bail, crank, ear, grasp, haft, handgrip, helve, hilt, hold, holder, knob, shaft, stem, stock, tiller; SEE CONCEPTS 445,502,831

handle [n2] *nickname*
appellation, byname, byword, cognomen, denomination, designation, moniker, name, nomen, sobriquet, style, title; SEE CONCEPT 683

handle [v1] *touch*
check, examine, feel, finger*, fondle, grasp, hold, manipulate, maul, palpate, paw*, pick up, poke, test, thumb*, try; SEE CONCEPT 612

handle [v2] *manage, take care of*
administer, advise, apply, behave toward, bestow, call the signals*, command, conduct, control, cope with, cut the mustard*, deal with, direct, discuss, dispense, dominate, employ, exercise, exploit, get a handle on*, govern, guide, hack it*, make out*, make the grade*, maneuver, manipulate, operate, play, ply, run things, serve, steer, supervise, swing, take, treat, use, utilize, wield, work; SEE CONCEPTS 91,117

handle [v3] *carry as merchandise*
deal in, market, offer, retail, sell, stock, trade, traffic in; SEE CONCEPT 345

handling [n] *management*
administration, approach, care, charge, conduct, direction, manipulation, running, styling, superintendence, supervision, treatment; SEE CONCEPT 117

hand out [v] *give to others*
bestow, deal out, deliver, devote, disburse, dish out, dispense, disseminate, distribute, donate, give away, give out, hand over, mete, present, provide; SEE CONCEPTS *108,140*

hand over [v] *give back; release*
abandon, cede, commend, commit, consign, deliver, dispense, donate, entrust, feed, find, fork out*, fork up*, give up, hand, leave, present, provide, relegate, relinquish, supply, surrender, transfer, turn over, waive, yield; SEE CONCEPTS *108,131*

handsome [adj1] *attractive*
admirable, aristocratic, athletic, august, beautiful, becoming, clean-cut, comely, dapper, elegant, fair, fashionable, fine, good-looking, graceful, impressive, lovely, majestic, noble, personable, pulchritudinous, robust, sharp, smart, smooth, spruce, stately, strong, stylish, suave, virile, well-dressed, well-proportioned; SEE CONCEPT *579*

handsome [adj2] *abundant*
ample, bounteous, bountiful, considerable, extensive, full, generous, gracious, large, lavish, liberal, magnanimous, munificent, openhanded, plentiful, princely, sizable, unsparing; SEE CONCEPT *781*

handsomely [adv] *abundantly*
amply, bountifully, generously, lavishly, liberally, magnanimously, munificently, nobly, plentifully, richly; SEE CONCEPT *781*

handwriting [n] *the way a person writes*
autography, calligraphy, chicken scratch*, chirography, ductus, griffonage, hand, hieroglyphics, longhand, manuscript, manuscription, mark, pencraft, penscript, scratching*, scrawl, scribble, script, scription, scrivenery, scrivening, style, writing; SEE CONCEPTS *284,625,628*

handy [adj1] *nearby*
accessible, adjacent, at hand, available, close, close-at-hand, close by, convenient, near, near-at-hand, on hand, ready, within reach; SEE CONCEPT *586*

handy [adj2] *easy to use*
adaptable, advantageous, available, beneficial, central, convenient, functional, gainful, helpful, manageable, neat, practicable, practical, profitable, ready, serviceable, useful, utile, wieldy; SEE CONCEPT *560*

handy [adj3] *adept physically*
able, adroit, clever, deft, dexterous, expert, fit, ingenious, nimble, proficient, ready, skilled, skillful; SEE CONCEPT *527*

hang [v1] *suspend or be suspended*
adhere, attach, beetle, be fastened, be in mid-air, be loose, bend, be pendent, be poised, bow, cling, cover, dangle, deck, decorate, depend, drape, drift, droop, drop, fasten, fix, flap, float, flop, furnish, hold, hover, impend, incline, lean, loll, lop, lower, nail, overhang, pin, project, remain, rest, sag, stay up, stick, swing, tack, trail, wave; SEE CONCEPTS *144,201,746*

hang [v2] *kill by suspension from a rope*
execute, gibbet, hoist, lynch, noose, scrag, send to the gallows, stretch*, string up*, swing*; SEE CONCEPT *252*

hang [v3] *depend on future action*
await, be conditional upon, be contingent on, be dependent on, be determined by, be in limbo, be in suspense, cling, hinge, pend, rest, turn on; SEE CONCEPT *681*

hang about/hang around/hang out [v] *associate with; be residing in*
abide, affect, dally, frequent, get along with, haunt, have relations with, linger, live, loiter, reside, resort, roam, spend time, stand around, swell, tarry, waste time; SEE CONCEPTS *114,226*

hanger-on [n] *person who attends the powerful for status or benefit*
dependent, flunky*, follower, freeloader*, lackey*, leech*, nuisance, parasite, sponger*, sycophant, truckler*; SEE CONCEPT *423*

hang on [v] *continue, endure*
be tough, carry on, cling, clutch, go on, grasp, grip, hold fast, hold on, hold out, persevere, persist, remain; SEE CONCEPTS *23,239*

hangout [n] *place for socializing*
bar, den*, dive*, haunt*, home, honky-tonk*, joint*, purlieu, resort, stomping ground*, watering hole*; SEE CONCEPTS *439,447,449*

hangover [n] *result of heavy drinking*
aftereffect, big head*, delirium tremens, drunkenness, DTs*, headache, morning after*, shakes*, under the weather*, willies*, withdrawal; SEE CONCEPT *316*

hang-up [n] *preoccupation*
block, difficulty, dilemma, disturbance, impasse, inhibition, obsession, predicament, problem, reserve, restraint, thing; SEE CONCEPTS *532,674,690*

hanker after/hanker for [v] *desire strongly*
ache, covet, crave, hunger, itch, long, lust, partial to, pine, sigh, thirst, want, wish, yearn, yen; SEE CONCEPT *20*

hankering [n] *strong desire*
ache, craving, druthers*, fire in belly*, hunger, itch*, longing, munchies*, pining, thirst, urge, want, weakness, wish, yearning, yen; SEE CONCEPTS *20,709*

hanky-panky [n] *mischief*
chicane, chicanery, deception, devilry, double-dealing, fourberie, fraud, funny business*, knavery, machinations, monkey business*, sharp practice*, shenanigans*, skullduggery*, subterfuge, trickery; SEE CONCEPTS *59,384*

haphazard [adj] *without plan or organization*
accidental, aimless, all over the map*, any old way*, any which way*, arbitrary, careless, casual, chance, designless, desultory, devil-may-care*, disorderly, disorganized, erratic, fluke, helter-skelter*, hit-or-miss*, incidental, indiscriminate, irregular, loose, offhand, purposeless, random, reckless, slapdash, slipshod, spontaneous, sudden, unconcerned, unconscious, unconsidered, uncoordinated, unexpected, unmethodical, unorganized, unpremeditated, unsystematic, unthinking, willy-nilly*; SEE CONCEPTS *535,581*

hapless [adj] *unfortunate*
behind the eightball*, cursed, hexed, ill-fated, ill-starred, infelicitous, jinxed, jonah*, loser, luckless, miserable, poor fish*, sad sack*, snakebit*, star-crossed*, unhappy, unlucky, untoward, voodooed*, woeful, wretched; SEE CONCEPT *548*

happen [v] *come to pass; occur*
appear, arise, arrive, become a fact, become known, become of, befall, be found, betide, bump, chance, come about, come after, come into being, come into existence, come off, crop up*, develop, down, ensue, eventuate, fall, follow, go on, hit, issue, light, luck, materialize, meet, pass,

ha
ha

present itself, proceed, recur, result, shake, smoke*, spring, stumble, stumble upon, supervene, take effect, take place, transpire, turn out, turn up, what goes*; SEE CONCEPT 4

happening [n] *occurrence*
accident, adventure, affair, case, chance, circumstance, episode, event, experience, go*, incident, milestone, occasion, phenomenon, proceeding, scene, thing*; SEE CONCEPT 4

happily [adv1] *with joy, pleasure*
agreeably, blissfully, blithely, brightly, buoyantly, cheerfully, contentedly, delightedly, delightfully, devotedly, elatedly, enthusiastically, exhilaratingly, exultantly, freely, gaily, gladly, gleefully, graciously, heartily, hilariously, jovially, joyfully, joyously, laughingly, lightheartedly, lightly, lovingly, merrily, optimistically, peacefully, playfully, sincerely, smilingly, sportively, vivaciously, willingly, with relish, with zeal, zestfully; SEE CONCEPTS 403,542

happily [adv2] *successfully*
appropriately, aptly, auspiciously, favorably, felicitously, fortunately, gracefully, propitiously, prosperously, providentially, satisfyingly, seasonably, swimmingly, well; SEE CONCEPT 548

happiness [n] *high spirits, satisfaction*
beatitude, blessedness, bliss, cheer, cheerfulness, cheeriness, content, contentment, delectation, delight, delirium, ecstasy, elation, enchantment, enjoyment, euphoria, exhilaration, exuberance, felicity, gaiety, geniality, gladness, glee, good cheer, good humor, good spirits, hilarity, hopefulness, joviality, joy, jubilation, laughter, lightheartedness, merriment, mirth, optimism, paradise, peace of mind, playfulness, pleasure, prosperity, rejoicing, sanctity, seventh heaven*, vivacity, well-being; SEE CONCEPT 410

happy [adj1] *in high spirits; satisfied*
blessed, blest, blissful, blithe, can't complain*, captivated, cheerful, chipper, chirpy, content, contented, convivial, delighted, ecstatic, elated, exultant, flying high*, gay, glad, gleeful, gratified, intoxicated, jolly, joyful, joyous, jubilant, laughing, light, lively, looking good*, merry, mirthful, on cloud nine*, overjoyed, peaceful, peppy, perky, playful, pleasant, pleased, sparkling, sunny, thrilled, tickled, tickled pink*, up, upbeat, walking on air*; SEE CONCEPT 403

happy [adj2] *lucky*
accidental, advantageous, appropriate, apt, auspicious, befitting, casual, convenient, correct, effective, efficacious, enviable, favorable, felicitous, fitting, fortunate, incidental, just, meet, nice, opportune, promising, proper, propitious, providential, right, satisfactory, seasonable, successful, suitable, timely, well-timed; SEE CONCEPT 558

happy-go-lucky [adj] *carefree and untroubled*
blithe, casual, cheerful, cool, devil-may-care*, easy, easygoing, feckless, free-minded, heedless, improvident, insouciant, irresponsible, lackadaisical*, lighthearted, nonchalant, reckless, unconcerned; SEE CONCEPTS 404,542

harangue [n] *long lecture*
address, chewing out*, declamation, diatribe, discourse, exhortation, hassle, jeremiad, oration, philippic, reading out*, screed, sermon, speech, spiel*, spouting, tirade; SEE CONCEPTS 51,278

harangue [v] *give a long lecture*
accost, address, apostrophize, buttonhole*, chew out*, declaim, exhort, get on a soapbox*, go on

about*, hold forth, orate, perorate, rant, rave, soapbox*, spiel*, spout, stump, talk to, yell at; SEE CONCEPT 51

harass [v] *badger*
annoy, attack, bait, bedevil, beleaguer, bother, bug*, burn*, despoil, devil*, distress, disturb, eat*, exasperate, exhaust, fatigue, foray, get to*, give a bad time*, give a hard time*, gnaw*, harry, hassle, heckle, hound*, intimidate, irk, irritate, jerk around*, macerate, maraud, noodge*, pain*, perplex, persecute, pester, plague, raid, rattle one's cage*, ride, strain, stress, tease, tire, torment, trouble, try, vex, weary, work on*, worry; SEE CONCEPTS 7,14,19

harassment [n] *badgering*
aggravation, annoyance, bedevilment, bother, bothering, disturbance, exasperation, hassle, irking, irritation, molestation, nuisance, persecution, perturbation, pestering, provocation, provoking, torment, trouble, vexation, vexing; SEE CONCEPTS 14,313

harbinger [n] *indication*
augury, forerunner, foretoken, herald, messenger, omen, portent, precursor, sign, signal; SEE CONCEPTS 74,284,529

harbor [n1] *place for storing boats in the water*
anchorage, arm, bay, bight, breakwater, chuck, cove, dock, embankment, firth, gulf, haven, inlet, jetty, landing, mooring, pier, port, road, roadstead, wharf; SEE CONCEPTS 439,509,514

harbor [n2] *place for seclusion*
asylum, cover, covert, harborage, haven, port, refuge, retreat, sanctuary, sanctum, security, shelter; SEE CONCEPT 515

harbor [v1] *hide, protect*
accommodate, board, bunk, conceal, defend, domicile, entertain, guard, hold back, house, lodge, nurse, nurture, provide refuge, put up, quarter, relieve, safeguard, screen, secrete, secure, shelter, shield, suppress, withhold; SEE CONCEPTS 134,188

harbor [v2] *hold in imagination*
believe, brood over, cherish, cling to, consider, entertain, foster, hold, imagine, maintain, nurse, nurture, regard, retain; SEE CONCEPT 17

hard [adj1] *rocklike*
adamantine, callous, compact, compacted, compressed, concentrated, consolidated, dense, firm, hardened, impenetrable, indurate, indurated, inflexible, iron*, packed, rigid, rocky, set, solid, stiff, stony, strong, thick, tough, unyielding; SEE CONCEPT 604

hard [adj2] *difficult, exhausting*
arduous, backbreaking, bothersome, burdensome, complicated, demanding, difficile, distressing, effortful, exacting, fatiguing, formidable, grinding, hairy*, heavy*, Herculean*, intricate, involved, irksome, knotty*, labored, laborious, mean, merciless, murder, onerous, operose, rigorous, rough, rugged, scabrous, serious, severe, slavish, sticky, strenuous, terrible, tiring, toilful, toilsome, tough, troublesome, unsparing, uphill*, uphill battle*, wearing, wearisome, wearying; SEE CONCEPTS 529,538,565

hard [adj3] *cruel, ruthless*
acrimonious, angry, antagonistic, austere, bitter, bleak, brutal, callous, cold, cold-blooded*, cold fish*, dark, disagreeable, distressing, dour, exacting, grievous, grim, hard as nails*, hard-boiled*, harsh, hostile, inclement, intemperate, intolera-

ble, obdurate, painful, perverse, pitiless, rancorous, resentful, rigorous, rugged, severe, stern, strict, stringent, stubborn, thick-skinned*, tough, unfeeling, unjust, unkind, unpleasant, unrelenting, unsparing, unsympathetic, vengeful; SEE CONCEPTS 401,542

hard [adj4] *true, indisputable*
absolute, actual, bare, cold, definite, down-to-earth, genuine, plain, positive, practical, pragmatic, realistic, sure, undeniable, unvarnished, verified; SEE CONCEPTS 535,582

hard [adv1] *with great force*
actively, angrily, animatedly, boisterously, briskly, brutally, cruelly, earnestly, energetically, ferociously, fiercely, forcibly, frantically, furiously, heavily, intensely, keenly, like fury, madly, meanly, painfully, powerfully, relentlessly, rigorously, roughly, rowdily, savagely, seriously, severely, sharply, spiritedly, sprightly, stormily, strongly, tumultuously/tumultously, turbulently, uproariously, urgently, viciously, vigorously, violently, vivaciously, wildly, with all one's might; SEE CONCEPT 540

hard [adv2] *with determination*
assiduously, closely, diligently, doggedly, earnestly, exhaustively, industriously, intensely, intensively, intently, painstakingly, persistently, searchingly, sharply, steadily, strenuously, thoroughly, unremittingly, untiringly; SEE CONCEPT 538

hard [adv3] *with difficulty*
agonizingly, arduously, awkwardly, badly, burdensomely, carefully, cumbersomely, cumbrously, distressingly, exhaustingly, gruelingly, hardly, harshly, inconveniently, laboriously, painfully, ponderously, roughly, severely, strenuously, tiredly, toilsomely, unwieldily, vigorously, with great effort; SEE CONCEPT 565

hard [adv4] *with resentment*
bitterly, hardly, keenly, rancorously, reluctantly, slowly, sorely; SEE CONCEPT 403

hard [adv5] *in a fixed manner*
close, fast, firm, firmly, solidly, steadfastly, tight, tightly; SEE CONCEPTS 488,586

hard-core [adj] *dedicated*
determined, devoted, die-hard*, dyed-in-the-wool*, explicit, extreme, faithful, intransigent, obstinate, resolute, rigid, staunch, steadfast, stubborn, uncompromising, unwavering, unyielding; SEE CONCEPTS 535,542

harden [v1] *make or become solid*
amalgamate, anneal, bake, brace, buttress, cake, calcify, callous, cement, close, clot, coagulate, compact, congeal, consolidate, contract, crystallize, curdle, densify, dry, firm, fix, fortify, fossilize, freeze, gird, indurate, jell, nerve, ossify, petrify, precipitate, press, reinforce, set, settle, solidify, starch, steel, stiffen, strengthen, temper, thicken, toughen, vitrify; SEE CONCEPTS 250,469

harden [v2] *accustom*
acclimate, acclimatize, adapt, adjust, blunt, brutalize, callous, callus, case-harden, climatize, coarsen, conform, deaden, develop, discipline, dull, embitter, habituate, indurate, inure, make callous, numb, paralyze, render insensitive, roughen, season, steel, stiffen, strengthen, stun, stupefy, teach, train; SEE CONCEPTS 35,235

hardened [adj] *unfeeling*
accustomed, benumbed, callous, case-hardened, coldhearted*, contemptuous, cruel, disdainful,

habituated, hard-as-nails*, hard-bitten*, hard-boiled*, hardhearted*, heartless, impenetrable, impious, inaccessible, indurated, inured, irreverent, obdurate, obtuse, prepared, resistant, seasoned, steeled, toughened, unashamed, unbending, uncaring, uncompassionate, unemotional, unrepenting, unsubmissive; SEE CONCEPTS 404,542

hardhearted [adj] *cold, cruel*
brutish, callous, cold-blooded*, coldhearted*, hard, hard-boiled*, heartless, indifferent, inhuman, insensitive, intolerant, merciless, obdurate, pitiless, stony, uncaring, uncompassionate, unemotional, unfeeling, unkind, unsympathetic; SEE CONCEPTS 401,404

hardly [adv] *scarcely; with difficulty*
almost inconceivably, almost not, barely, by a hair, by no means, comparatively, detectably, faintly, gradually, imperceptibly, infrequently, just, little, no more than, not a bit, not at all, not by much, not likely, not markedly, not measurably, not much, not notably, not noticeably, not often, not quite, no way, once in a blue moon*, only, only just, perceptibly, practically, pretty near, rarely, scantly, seldom, simply, slightly, somewhat, sparsely, sporadically, with trouble; SEE CONCEPTS 541,552,771

hard-nosed/hardheaded [adj] *stubborn*
astute, bullheaded*, hard*, hard-boiled*, headstrong, intractable, levelheaded, locked in*, mulish, obstinate, pertinacious, perverse, pigheaded*, practical, pragmatic, rational, realistic, resolute, sensible, shrewd, sober, stand pat, tough, toughnut*, unsentimental, unyielding, willful; SEE CONCEPTS 404,542

hardship [n] *personal burden*
accident, adversity, affliction, asperity, austerity, calamity, case, catastrophe, curse, danger, destitution, difficulty, disaster, discomfort, distress, drudgery, fatigue, grief, grievance, hard knocks*, hazard, Herculean task*, injury, labor, mischance, misery, misfortune, need, oppression, peril, persecution, privation, rainy day*, rigor, rotten luck*, sorrow, suffering, toil, torment, tough break*, tough luck*, travail, trial, tribulation, trouble, uphill battle*, vicissitude, want, worry; SEE CONCEPTS 674,675

hardware [n] *tools; fittings, especially made of metal*
accouterments, appliances, fasteners, fixtures, household furnishings, housewares, implements, ironware, kitchenware, metalware, plumbing, utensils; SEE CONCEPTS 338,499

hardy [adj] *strong, tough*
able, able-bodied, acclimatized, brawny, burly, capable, enduring, firm, fit, fresh, hale, hardened, healthy, hearty, hefty, indefatigable, in fine fettle*, in good condition, in good shape, inured, lusty, mighty, muscular, physically fit, powerful, resistant, robust, rugged, seasoned, solid, sound, stalwart, staunch, stout, sturdy, substantial, tenacious, unflagging, vigorous, well; SEE CONCEPTS 314,485,489

harebrained [adj] *stupid, unthinking*
absurd, asinine, barmy, bizarre, careless, changeable, crazy, dizzy*, empty-headed*, feather-brained*, flighty, foolish, frivolous, giddy, half-baked*, heedless, inane, irresponsible, loony*, mindless, preposterous, rash, rattlebrained, reck-

ha
ha

less, scatterbrained*, unstable, unsteady, wacky*, wild; SEE CONCEPTS *402,529*

harm [*n*] *injury, evil*
abuse, banefulness, damage, deleteriousness, detriment, disservice, foul play*, hurt, ill, immorality, impairment, infliction, iniquity, loss, marring, mischance, mischief, misfortune, misuse, noxiousness, outrage, perniciousness, prejudice, ravage, ruin, ruination, sabotage, sin, sinfulness, vandalism, vice, violence, wear and tear*, wickedness, wrong; SEE CONCEPTS *309,674,728*

harm [*v*] *injure; cause evil*
abuse, blemish, bruise, cripple, crush, damage, dilapidate, discommode, disserve, do violence to, dump on*, get, hurt, ill-treat, impair, incommode, inconvenience, louse up*, maim, maltreat, mangle, mar, mess up*, misuse, molest, muck up*, mutilate, nick, outrage, prejudice, put down*, ruin, sabotage, sap*, scathe, shatter, shock, spoil, stab, tarnish, total, trample, traumatize, tweak*, undermine, vandalize, vitiate, wing*, wound, wreck, wrench, wrong, zing*; SEE CONCEPTS *7,19, 246,313*

harmful [*adj*] *injurious, hurtful*
adverse, bad, baleful, baneful, calamitous, cataclysmic, catastrophic, consumptive, corroding, corrupting, crippling, damaging, deleterious, destructive, detrimental, dire, disadvantageous, disastrous, evil, harassing, incendiary, inimical, internecine, malefic, malicious, malignant, menacing, mischievous, murderous, nocuous, noxious, painful, pernicious, pestiferous, pestilential, risky, ruinous, sinful, sinister, subversive, toxic, undermining, unhealthy, unsafe, unwholesome, virulent; SEE CONCEPT *537*

harmless [*adj*] *not injurious or dangerous*
controllable, disarmed, gentle, guiltless, hurtless, innocent, innocuous, innoxious, inoffensive, inoperative, kind, manageable, naive, nonirritating, nontoxic, painless, paper-tiger*, powerless, pussycat*, reliable, safe, sanitary, simple, soft*, softie*, sound, sure, trustworthy, unobjectionable, unoffensive; SEE CONCEPT *537*

harmonious [*adj*] *agreeable, corresponding; friendly*
accordant, adapted, amicable, balanced, compatible, concordant, congenial, congruous, consonant, coordinated, cordial, dulcet, euphonious, harmonic, harmonizing, in accord, in chorus, in concert, in harmony, in step, in tune, in unison, like, matching, mellifluous, melodic, melodious, mix, musical, of one mind*, on same wavelength*, peaceful, rhythmical, silvery, similar, simpatico, sonorous, suitable, sweet-sounding, symmetrical, sympathetic, symphonic, symphonious, tuneful; SEE CONCEPT *563*

harmonize [*v*] *correspond, match*
accord, adapt, adjust, agree, arrange, attune, be in unison, be of one mind*, blend, carol, chime with, cohere, combine, compose, cooperate, coordinate, correlate, fit in with*, integrate, orchestrate, proportion, reconcile, reconciliate, relate, set, sing, suit, symphonize, synthesize, tune, unify, unite; SEE CONCEPTS *77,664*

harmony [*n1*] *social agreement*
accord, affinity, amicability, amity, compatibility, concord, conformity, consensus, consistency, cooperation, correspondence, empathy, friendship, good will, kinship, like-mindedness, meeting of minds*, peace, rapport, sympathy, tranquility,

unanimity, understanding, unity; SEE CONCEPT *388*

harmony [*n2*] *correspondence, balance*
accord, agreement, articulation, chime, concord, concordance, conformance, conformity, congruity, consistency, consonance, fitness, form, integration, integrity, oneness, order, parallelism, proportion, regularity, suitability, symmetry, togetherness, tune, unity; SEE CONCEPT *664*

harmony [*n3*] *musical accordance*
arrangement, attunement, blend, blending, chime, chord, chorus, composition, concentus, concert, concinnity, concurrence, consonance, diapason, euphony, harmonics, mellifluousness, melodiousness, melody, organum, overtone, piece, polyphony, richness, symphony, triad, tune, tunefulness, unison, unity; SEE CONCEPTS *65,262,595*

harness [*n*] *gear for controlling an animal*
belt, equipment, strap, tack, tackle, trappings; SEE CONCEPT *496*

harness [*v*] *rein in; control*
accouter, apply, bind, bridle, channel, check, cinch, collar, constrain, couple, curb, domesticate, employ, equip, exploit, fasten, fetter, fit, furnish, gear, govern, hitch, hold, leash, limit, make productive, mobilize, muzzle, outfit, put in harness, render useful, rig, saddle, secure, strap, tackle, tame, tie, utilize, yoke; SEE CONCEPTS *94,130,191*

harrowing [*adj*] *dangerous, frightening*
agonizing, alarming, chilling, distressing, disturbing, excruciating, heartbreaking, heart-rending, nerve-racking, painful, racking, soaring, tearing, terrifying, tormenting, torturing, torturous, traumatic; SEE CONCEPTS *529,548*

harry [*v*] *pester, annoy*
attack, badger, bedevil, beleaguer, chivy, depredate, devastate, disturb, fret, gnaw, harass, hassle, irk, irritate, lay waste, molest, persecute, perturb, pillage, plague, plunder, ravage, sack, tease, torment, trouble, upset, vex, worry; SEE CONCEPTS *7,19*

harsh [*adj1*] *rough, crude (to the senses)*
acrid, asperous, astringent, bitter, bleak, cacophonous, caterwauling, clashing, coarse, cracked, craggy, creaking, croaking, disagreeing, discordant, dissonant, disturbing, earsplitting, flat, glaring, grating, grim, guttural, hard, hoarse, incompatible, jagged, jangling, jarring, noisy, not smooth, off-key*, out-of-key*, out-of-tune*, rasping, raucous, rigid, rugged, rusty, screeching, severe, sharp, sour, strident, stridulous, tuneless, uneven, unlevel, unmelodious, unmusical, unrelenting; SEE CONCEPTS *537,569*

harsh [*adj2*] *nasty, abusive*
austere, bitter, brutal, comfortless, cruel, cussed, discourteous, dour, grim, gruff, hairy*, hard, hard-boiled, hard-nosed*, hard-shell*, mean, pitiless, punitive, relentless, rude, ruthless, severe, sharp, stern, stringent, tough, uncivil, unfeeling, ungracious, unkind, unpleasant, unrelenting, wicked; SEE CONCEPTS *267,542*

harvest [*n*] *crops; taking in of crops*
autumn, by-product, consequence, cropping, effect, fall, fruitage, fruition, garnering, gathering, harvesting, harvest-time, ingathering, intake, output, produce, reaping, repercussion, result, return, season, storing, summer, yield, yielding; SEE CONCEPTS *257,338,429*

harvest [v] *gathering of produce*
accumulate, acquire, amass, bin, cache, collect, crop, cull, cut, garner, gather, get, glean, harrow, hoard, mow, pick, pile up, plow, pluck, reap, squirrel*, stash, store, stow, strip, take in; SEE CONCEPTS *142,257*

hash [n] *mess, mix-up*
assortment, clutter, confusion, hodgepodge*, hotchpotch*, jumble, litter, medley, melange, miscellany, mishmash*, muddle*, salmagundi*, shambles*, stew*; SEE CONCEPTS *260,432*

hassle [n] *problem, fight*
altercation, argument, bickering, bother, clamor, commotion, difficulty, disagreement, dispute, inconvenience, quarrel, row, run-in*, squabble, struggle, trial, trouble, try, tumult, turmoil, tussle, uproar, upset, whirl, wrangle; SEE CONCEPTS *46,106,674*

hassle [v] *bother, harass*
annoy, argue, argufy, badger, bedevil, beleaguer, bicker, dispute, dun, harry, hound, pester, plague, quibble, squabble, worry, wrangle; SEE CONCEPTS *14,16,46*

haste [n] *extreme speed, hurry*
alacrity, briskness, bustle, carelessness, celerity, dash, dispatch, drive, expedition, expeditiousness, fleetness, flurry, foolhardiness, hastiness, heedlessness, hurly-burly*, hurriedness, hustle, hustling, impatience, impetuosity, incautiousness, nimbleness, pace, precipitancy, precipitateness, prematureness, press, promptitude, promptness, quickness, rapidity, rapidness, rashness, recklessness, rush, scamper, scramble, scurry, scuttle, swiftness, urgency, velocity; SEE CONCEPTS *755,818*

hasten [v] *speed something; hurry*
accelerate, advance, bolt, bound, burn, bustle, clip*, cover ground*, dash, dispatch, expedite, express, flee, fly, gallop, get cracking*, get the lead out*, goad, haste, hie, hustle, leap, make haste, make tracks*, move quickly, not lose a minute*, pace, plunge, precipitate, press, push, quicken, race, run, rush, scamper, scoot, scurry, scuttle, shake a leg*, skip, sprint, spurt, step on it*, step up*, take wing*, tear, trot, urge, waste no time*, whip around*; SEE CONCEPTS *150,152*

hastily [adv] *with great speed*
agilely, apace, carelessly, double-quick, expeditiously, fast, flat-out*, heedlessly, hurriedly, impetuously, impulsively, lickety-split*, nimbly, on spur of the moment*, posthaste, precipitately, prematurely, promptly, quickly, rapidly, rashly, recklessly, speedily, straightaway, subito, suddenly, swiftly, thoughtlessly, too quickly, unpremeditatedly; SEE CONCEPTS *544,588*

hasty [adj] *speedy; without much thought*
abrupt, agile, brash, breakneck*, brief, brisk, careless, chop-chop*, cursory, eager, expeditious, fast, fiery, fleet, fleeting, foolhardy, harefooted*, headlong, heedless, hurried, ill-advised, impatient, impetuous, impulsive, incautious, inconsiderate, madcap*, on the double*, passing, PDQ*, perfunctory, precipitate, prompt, pronto*, quick, quickened, quickie, rapid, rash, reckless, rushed, short, slambang*, slapdash*, snappy*, sudden, superficial, swift, thoughtless, urgent; SEE CONCEPTS *542,588,799*

hat [n] *covering for the head*
boater, bonnet, bowler, bucket, chapeau, fedora, headgear, headpiece, helmet, lid*, millinery, Panama, sailor*, skimmer, sombrero, Stetson, stove pipe*, straw*, tam, tam o'shanter*, ten-gallon*, topper*; SEE CONCEPT *451*

hatch [v] *create, plan*
bear, brainstorm*, breed, bring forth, brood, cause, come up with, conceive, concoct, contrive, cook up*, design, devise, dream up*, engender, formulate, generate, get up, give birth, incubate, induce, invent, lay eggs, make, make up, occasion, originate, parent, plot, prepare, procreate, produce, project, provoke, scheme, set, sire, spawn, spitball*, think up*, throw together*, trump up*, whip up*, work up*; SEE CONCEPTS *36,173,251*

hate [n] *extreme dislike*
abhorrence, abomination, anathema, animosity, animus, antagonism, antipathy, aversion, bête noire*, black beast*, bother, bugbear*, detestation, disgust, enmity, execration, frost*, grievance, gripe, hatred, horror, hostility, ill will, irritant, loathing, malevolence, malignity, mislike, nasty look, no love lost*, nuisance, objection, odium, pain, rancor, rankling, repugnance, repulsion, resentment, revenge, revulsion, scorn, spite, trouble, venom; SEE CONCEPT *29*

hate [v] *dislike very strongly*
abhor, abominate, allergic to*, anathematize, bear a grudge against, be disgusted with, be hostile to, be loath, be reluctant, be repelled by, be sick of, be sorry, can't stand*, contemn, curse, deprecate, deride, despise, detest, disapprove, disdain, disfavor, disparage, down on*, execrate, feel malice to, have an aversion to*, have enough of*, have no use for*, loathe, look down on, nauseate*, not care for*, object to, recoil from, scorn, shudder at, shun, spit upon*, spurn; SEE CONCEPT *29*

hateful [adj] *nasty, obnoxious*
abhorrent, abominable, accursed, awful, bitter, blasted, catty*, confounded, cursed, cussed, damnable, damned, despicable, despiteful, detestable, disgusting, evil, execrable, forbidding, foul, gross, heinous, horrid, infamous, invidious, loathsome, malevolent, malign, mean, odious, offensive, ornery*, pesky, pestiferous, repellent, repugnant, repulsive, resentful, revolting, shuddersome, spiteful, uncool*, undesirable, vicious, vile; SEE CONCEPTS *267,404*

hatred [n] *severe dislike*
abhorrence, abomination, acrimony, alienation, allergy to*, animosity, animus, antagonism, antipathy, aversion, bitterness, coldness, contempt, detestation, disapproval, disfavor, disgust, displeasure, distaste, enmity, envy, execration, grudge, hard feelings*, hate, horror, hostility, ignominy, ill will, invidiousness, loathing, malevolence, malice, malignance, militancy, no use for*, odium, pique, prejudice, rancor, repugnance, repulsion, revenge, revulsion, scorn, spite, spleen, venom; SEE CONCEPT *29*

haughtiness [n] *air of supremacy*
aloofness, arrogance, conceit, contempt, contemptuousness, disdain, disdainfulness, hauteur, insolence, loftiness, pomposity, pride, snobbishness, superbity, superciliousness; SEE CONCEPT *633*

haughty [adj] *arrogant*
assuming, cavalier*, conceited, contemptuous, detached, disdainful, distant, egotistic, egotistical, high, high and mighty*, hoity-toity*, imperious, indifferent, lofty, on high horse*,

ha
ha

overbearing, overweening, proud, reserved, scornful, sniffy*, snobbish, snooty*, snotty*, stuck-up*, supercilious, superior, uppity*; SEE CONCEPT **401**

haul [n] *something obtained or moved*
booty, burden, cargo, catch, find, freight, gain, harvest, lading, load, loot*, payload*, spoils, takings*, yield; SEE CONCEPTS **337,338**

haul [v] *move, pull to another spot*
back, boost, bring, buck, carry, cart, convey, drag, draw, elevate, gun, heave, heel, hoist, hump, jag, lift, lug, pack, piggy back*, raise, rake, remove, ride, shift, shlep*, shoulder, tote, tow, trail, transport, trawl, truck, tug; SEE CONCEPTS **147,148**

haunt [n] *place for socializing*
abode, bar, clubhouse, cubbyhole*, den, dwelling, gathering place, habitat, hangout*, headquarters, home, lair, living quarters, locality, meeting place, niche, place, purlieu, range, rendezvous, resort, retreat, site, stomping ground*, trysting place, watering hole*; SEE CONCEPTS **435,516**

haunt [v1] *visit as a spirit*
agitate, agonize, annoy, appall, appear, bedevil, be ever present, beset, besiege, come back, disquiet, dwell, float, frighten, harass, harrow, hound*, hover, infest, inhabit, intrude, madden, manifest, materialize, molest, nettle, obsess, overrun, permeate, pervade, pester, plague, possess, prey on, rack*, reappear, recur, return, rise, spook*, stay with, tease, terrify, terrorize, torment, trouble, vex, voodoo*, walk, weigh on, worry; SEE CONCEPT **14**

haunt [v2] *spend a lot of time at*
affect, frequent, habituate, hang about*, hang around*, hang out*, infest, repair, resort, tarry at, visit; SEE CONCEPT **384**

have [v1] *be in possession*
accept, acquire, admit, annex, bear, carry, chalk up, compass, corner, enjoy, gain, get, get hands on*, get hold of*, have in hand, hog*, hold, include, keep, land, latch on to*, lock up*, obtain, occupy, own, pick up, possess, procure, receive, retain, secure, sit on*, take, take in, teem with; SEE CONCEPTS **124,142,710**

have [v2] *endure, bear*
allow, become, be compelled to, be forced to, be one's duty to, be up to, consider, enjoy, entertain*, experience, fall on, feel, know, leave, let, meet with, must, need, ought, permit, put up with*, rest with, see, should, suffer, sustain, think about, tolerate, undergo; SEE CONCEPTS **23,83,646**

have [v3] *contain*
comprehend, comprise, embody, embrace, encompass, include, involve, subsume, take in; SEE CONCEPTS **642,742**

have [v4] *cheat, trick*
buy off*, deceive, dupe*, fix*, fool, outfox, outmaneuver, outsmart, outwit, overreach, swindle, take in*, tamper with, undo*; SEE CONCEPTS **59,192**

have [v5] *bring into the world*
bear, beget, bring forth, deliver, give birth; SEE CONCEPT **374**

haven [n] *refuge, port*
anchorage, asylum, cover, covert, harbor, harborage, retreat, roadstead, sanctuary, sanctum, shelter; SEE CONCEPTS **435,515**

havoc [n] *chaotic situation*
calamity, cataclysm, catastrophe, chaos, confusion, damage, desolation, despoiling, destruction, devastation, dilapidation, disorder, disruption, loss, mayhem, plunder, rack and ruin*, ravages, ruination, shambles*, vandalism, waste, wreck, wreckage; SEE CONCEPT **674**

hazard [n1] *danger*
double trouble*, dynamite, endangerment, hot potato*, imperilment, jeopardy, peril, risk, risky business*, thin ice*, threat; SEE CONCEPT **675**

hazard [n2] *luck, chance*
accident, adventure, coincidence, dynamite, fling*, fluke*, go*, hundred-to-one*, long shot, lucky break*, lucky hit*, misfortune, mishap, possibility, risk, risky business*, stroke of luck*, toss-up, venture, wager, way the ball bounces*, way the cookie crumbles*; SEE CONCEPT **693**

hazard [v] *take a chance; risk*
adventure, conjecture, dare, endanger, gamble, go for broke*, go out on limb*, guess, imperil, jeopardize, presume, proffer, skate on thin ice*, speculate, stake, submit, suppose, take a plunge*, throw out, try, venture, volunteer, wager; SEE CONCEPTS **28,87**

hazardous [adj] *dangerous, unpredictable*
chancy, dicey*, difficult, hairy*, haphazard, hot*, insecure, parlous, perilous, precarious, risky, touchy, uncertain, unhealthy, unsafe, unsound, venturesome, wicked; SEE CONCEPT **548**

haze [n] *cloudy air*
brume, cloud, dimness, film, fog, fumes, ground clouds, haziness, indistinctness, miasma, mist, murk, obscurity, smog, smokiness, smother, soup*, steam, vapor; SEE CONCEPT **524**

hazy [adj1] *cloudy*
bleared, bleary, blurred, blurry, clouded, crepuscular, dim, dull, dusky, faint, foggy, frosty, fuliginous, fumy, fuzzy, gauzy, indefinite, indistinct, misty, murky, mushy*, nebulous, obfuscated, obfuscous, obscure, opaque, overcast, rimy, screened, shadowy, smoggy, smoky, soupy*, steaming, thick, unclear, vague, vaporous, veiled; SEE CONCEPT **525**

hazy [adj2] *confused*
dazed, dizzy, dreamy, groggy, ill-defined, indefinite, indistinct, muddled, murky, nebulous, obscure, stuporous, tranced, uncertain, unclear, unintelligible, unsound, vague, whirling; SEE CONCEPTS **402,529**

head [n1] *top part of an animate body*
attic*, belfry*, brain, coconut*, cranium, crown, dome*, gray matter, noggin*, noodle*, pate, scalp, skull, thinker*, think tank*, top story*, upper story*, upstairs*; SEE CONCEPT **392**

head [n2] *leader*
boss, captain, chief, chieftain, commander, commanding officer, director, dominator, executive, honcho*, lead-off person*, manager, officer, president, principal, superintendent, supervisor, top dog*; SEE CONCEPT **347**

head [n3] *top*
apex, banner, beak, bill, cap, cork, crest, crown, heading, headline, height, peak, pitch, point, promontory, streamer, summit, tip, vertex; SEE CONCEPT **836**

head [n4] *front, beginning*
commencement, first place, fore, forefront, fountainhead, origin, rise, source, start, van, vanguard; SEE CONCEPTS **648,727**

head [n5] *ability, intelligence*
aptitude, aptness, bent, brains, capacity, faculty, flair, genius, gift, intellect, knack, mentality, mind, talent, thought, turn, understanding; SEE CONCEPTS 409,630

head [n6] *turning point*
acme, climax, conclusion, crisis, culmination, end; SEE CONCEPT 832

head [adj] *most important; chief*
arch, champion, first, foremost, front, highest, leading, main, pioneer, preeminent, premier, prime, principal, stellar, supreme, topmost; SEE CONCEPTS 568,574

head [v] *manage, oversee*
address, be first, be in charge, command, control, direct, dominate, go first, govern, guide, hold sway over*, lead, lead the way*, pioneer, precede, rule, run, supervise; SEE CONCEPT 117

headlong [adj] *dangerous, reckless*
abrupt, brash, breakneck, daredevil, daring, foolhardy, hasty, hurried, impetuous, impulsive, inconsiderate, precipitant, precipitate, rash, rough, rushing, sudden, tempestuous, thoughtless; SEE CONCEPTS 542,548

headstrong [adj] *stubborn*
bullheaded*, contrary, determined, foolhardy, froward, hard-core*, hard-nosed, hard-shell*, heedless, imprudent, impulsive, intractable, locked-in*, mule, mulish, murder, obstinate, perverse, pig-headed*, rash, reckless, refractory, self-willed, strong-minded, uncontrollable, ungovernable, unruly, unyielding, willful; SEE CONCEPTS 401,403

headway [n] *progress*
advance, advancement, anabasis, ground, improvement, increase, march, proficiency, progression, promotion, way; SEE CONCEPTS 230,704

heady [adj] *thrilling, intoxicating*
exciting, exhilarating, inebriating, overwhelming, potent, powerful, provocative, spirituous, stimulating, strong; SEE CONCEPT 529

heal [v] *cure, recover*
alleviate, ameliorate, attend, bring around, compose, conciliate, convalesce, doctor, dress, fix, free, get well, harmonize, improve, knit, make healthy, make sound, make well, make whole, medicate, meliorate, mend, minister to, patch up, physic, put on feet again*, reanimate, rebuild, reconcile, regenerate, rehabilitate, rejuvenate, remedy, renew, renovate, repair, restore, resuscitate, revive, revivify, salve, set, settle, soothe, treat; SEE CONCEPTS 308,310

health [n] *physical, mental wellness*
bloom*, clean bill*, complexion, constitution, energy, euepepsia, euphoria, fettle, fine feather*, fitness, form, good condition, haleness, hardihood, hardiness, healthfulness, healthiness, lustiness, pink*, prime*, robustness, salubriousness, salubrity, shape, soundness, stamina, state, strength, tone, tonicity, top form, verdure, vigor, wellbeing, wholeness; SEE CONCEPTS 316,410,720

healthful/healthy [adj1] *good for one's wellness*
advantageous, aiding, aseptic, beneficial, benign, body-building, bracing, cathartic, clean, compensatory, conducive, corrective, desirable, disease-free, energy-giving, fresh, harmless, healing, health-giving, helpful, hygienic, innocuous, invigorating, mitigative, nourishing, nutritious, nutritive, profitable, pure, restorative, salubrious, salutary, sanatory, sanitary, stimulating, sustain-

ing, tonic, unadulterated, unpolluted, untainted, useful, wholesome; SEE CONCEPT 537

healthy [adj2] *in good condition*
able-bodied, active, all right, athletic, blooming, bright-eyed*, bushy-tailed*, chipper*, firm, fit, flourishing, fresh, full of life*, hale, hardy, healthful, hearty, husky, in fine feather*, in fine fettle*, in good shape, in the pink*, lively, lusty, muscular, normal, physically fit, potent, restored, robust, rosy-cheeked*, safe and sound*, sound, stout, strong, sturdy, tough, trim, unimpaired, vigorous, virile, well, whole; SEE CONCEPTS 314,403

heap [n] *pile, accumulation*
abundance, agglomeration, aggregation, a lot*, amassment, assemblage, bank, batch, bulk, bunch, bundle, cargo, clump, cluster, collection, concentration, congeries, deposit, fullness, gathering, gobs*, great deal, harvest, haul, hill, hoard, jumble, load, lot, lots, lump, mass, million, mint, mound, mountain, much, ocean, oodles*, plenty, pot, profusion, quantity, scad*, stack, stock, stockpile, store, sum, thousand, ton, total, trillion, volume, whole; SEE CONCEPTS 432,787

heap [v] *amass, collect in pile*
accumulate, add, arrange, augment, bank, bunch, concentrate, deposit, dump, fill, fill up, gather, group, hoard, increase, load, lump, mass, mound, pack, stack, stockpile, store, swell; SEE CONCEPT 109

hear [v1] *detect by perceiving sound*
apprehend, attend, auscultate, be all ears*, become aware, catch, descry, devour, eavesdrop, get*, get an earful*, get wind of*, give an audience to*, give attention, give ears*, hark, hearken, heed, listen, make out*, overhear, pick up*, read, strain, take in*; SEE CONCEPTS 590,596

hear [v2] *become aware of information*
apperceive, ascertain, be advised, be informed, be led to believe, be told of, catch, catch on, descry, determine, discover, find out, gather, get the picture*, get wind of*, get wise to*, glean, have on good authority*, learn, pick up*, receive, see, tumble*, understand, unearth; SEE CONCEPTS 15,31

hearing [n1] *ability to perceive sound*
audition, auditory, auditory range, detecting, distinguishing, ear, earshot, effect, extent, faculty, hearing distance, listening, perception, range, reach, recording, sense; SEE CONCEPT 597

hearing [n2] *opportunity to present views, knowledge, or skill*
admittance, attendance, attention, audience, audit, audition, chance, conference, congress, consultation, council, discussion, inquiry, interview, investigation, meeting, negotiation, notice, parley, performance, presentation, reception, review, test, trial, tryout; SEE CONCEPTS 48,103,317,693

hearsay [n] *unsubstantiated information*
clothesline*, comment, cry, gossip, grapevine*, leak*, mere talk*, noise*, report, rumble*, rumor, scandal, scuttlebutt*, talk, talk of the town*, word of mouth*; SEE CONCEPTS 51,278

heart [n1] *person's emotions*
affection, benevolence, character, compassion, concern, disposition, feeling, gusto, humanity, inclination, love, nature, palate, pity, relish, response, sensitivity, sentiment, soul, sympathy, temperament, tenderness, understanding, zest; SEE CONCEPT 410

ha
he

heart [n2] *courage*
boldness. bravery. dauntlessness. fortitude. gallantry. guts*. mettle. mind. moxie*. nerve. pluck.
purpose. resolution. soul. spirit. spunk*. will: SEE
CONCEPT *411*

heart [n3] *essence, central part*
basic. bosom. bottom line*. center. coal and ice*.
core. crux. focal point. focus. gist. hub. kernel.
marrow. middle. nitty-gritty*. nub. nucleus. pith.
polestar*. quick*. quintessence. root. seat. soul:
SEE CONCEPT *826*

heart [n4] *blood-pumping organ in an animate being*
cardiac organ. clock*. ticker*. vascular organ:
SEE CONCEPTS *393,420*

heartbreak [n] *mental or emotional misery*
affliction. agony. anguish. bale. bitterness. broken
heart. care. desolation. despair. distress. grief.
heartache. heartsickness. heavy heart*. pain. regret. remorse: rue. sorrow. suffering. torment. torture. woe: SEE CONCEPTS *410,728*

heartbreaking [adj] *disappointing*
affecting. afflictive. agonizing. bitter. calamitous.
cheerless. deplorable. dire. distressing. grievous.
heart-rending. joyless. lamentable. moving. pitiful. poignant. regrettable. sad. touching. tragic.
unfortunate: SEE CONCEPTS *529,537*

hearten [v] *raise someone's spirits*
animate. arouse. assure. buck up. buoy. cheer.
comfort. console. embolden. encourage. energize.
enliven. incite. inspire. inspirit. rally. reassure.
revivify. rouse. steel. stimulate. stir. strengthen:
SEE CONCEPTS *7,22*

heartfelt [adj] *genuine*
ardent. bona fide. cordial. deep. devout. earnest.
fervent. heart-to-heart. hearty. honest. profound.
sincere. true. unfeigned. warm. wholehearted:
SEE CONCEPTS *267,582*

heartless [adj] *without feeling; cold*
brutal. callous. cold-blooded*. cold fish*. coldhearted*. cruel. hard. hard as nails*. hard-
boiled*. hard-hearted*. harsh. inhuman.
insensitive. merciless. obdurate. pitiless. ruthless.
savage. thick-skinned*. uncaring. uncompassionate. unemotional. unfeeling. unkind. unsympathetic: SEE CONCEPTS *401,542*

hearty [adj1] *energetic, enthusiastic*
affable. animated. ardent. avid. back-slapping*.
cheerful. cheery. cordial. deep. deepest. deep-felt.
devout. eager. earnest. ebullient. effusive. exuberant. frank. friendly. gay. generous. genial.
genuine. glad. gushing. heartfelt. honest. impassioned. intense. jolly. jovial. neighborly. passionate. profuse. real. responsive. sincere. true.
unfeigned. unreserved. unrestrained. vivacious.
warm. warmhearted. wholehearted. zealous: SEE
CONCEPTS *401,542*

hearty [adj2] *healthy, full*
active. ample. energetic. filling. glowing. good.
hale. hardy. nourishing. robust. sizable. solid.
sound. square. strong. substantial. vigorous. well:
SEE CONCEPTS *314,773*

heat [n1] *high temperature*
calefaction. calidity. dog days*. fever. fieriness.
heatwave. hotness. hot spell. hot weather. incalescence. incandescence. sultriness. swelter. tor-
ridity. torridness. warmness. warmth: SEE
CONCEPT *610*

heat [n2] *anger, passion*
agitation. ardor. desire. earnestness. excitement.

ferocity. fervor. fever. fury. impetuosity. intensity. rage. vehemence. violence. warmth. zeal:
SEE CONCEPTS *410,657*

heat [v] *make or become hot*
bake. bask. blaze. boil. broil. calorify. chafe.
char. enflame. enkindle. fire. flame. flush. frizzle.
fry. glow. grill. grow hot. grow warm. ignite.
incandesce. incinerate. inflame. kindle. melt. ox-
idate. oxidize. perspire. raise the temperature. re-
heat. roast. scald. scorch. sear. seethe. set on fire.
singe. smelt. steam. sun. swelter. tepefy. thaw.
toast. warm. warm up: SEE CONCEPTS *255,469*

heated [adj1] *angry*
acrimonious. ardent. avid. bitter. excited. fervent.
fervid. feverish. fierce. fiery. frenzied. furious.
hectic. impassioned. indignant. intense. irate. ireful. mad. passionate. raging. stormy. tempestuous. vehement. violent. wrathful: SEE CONCEPT
267

heated [adj2] *warmed*
baked. baking. boiling. broiled. broiling. burned.
burning. burnt. cooked. fiery. fired. fried. hot.
parched. scalding. scorched. scorching. sizzling.
toasted: SEE CONCEPT *605*

heathen [adj] *not believing in Christian god*
agnostic. atheistic. barbarian. godless. idolatrous.
infidel. irreligious. nonbeliever. pagan. profane.
skeptic: SEE CONCEPT *545*

heave [v1] *lift, throw with effort*
boost. cast. chuck. drag. elevate. fling. haul. heft.
hoist. hurl. launch. pitch. pull. raise. send. sling.
toss. tug: SEE CONCEPTS *196,222*

heave [v2] *discharge with force; expel from digestive system by mouth*
billow. breathe. cast. dilate. disgorge. exhale. expand. gag. groan. huff. palpitate. pant. puff.
puke*. retch. rise. sign. sob. spew. spit up. surge.
suspire. swell. throb. throw up. upchuck*. vomit:
SEE CONCEPTS *163,179*

heaven [n] *place where god lives; wonderful feeling*
afterworld. Arcadia. atmosphere. azure*. beyond.
bliss. Canaan. dreamland. ecstasy. Elysium. empyrean. enchantment. eternal home. eternal rest.
eternity. fairyland*. felicity. firmament. glory.
great unknown*. happiness. happy hunting
ground*. harmony. heights. hereafter. immortality. kingdom. kingdom come. life everlasting. life
to come. next world. nirvana. paradise. pearly
gates*. promised land*. rapture. Shangri-la*.
sky*. the blue*. transport. upstairs*. Utopia. wonderland*. Zion: SEE CONCEPTS *370,410,435*

heavenly [adj] *very pleasant*
adorable. alluring. ambrosial. angelic. beatific.
beautiful. blessed. blissful. celestial. cherubic.
darling. delectable. delicious. delightful. divine.
empyrean. enjoyable. entrancing. excellent. exquisite. extraterrestrial. glorious. godlike. holy.
immortal. lovely. luscious. lush. paradisaical. rapturous. ravishing. scrumptious. seraphic. sublime.
superhuman. supernal. supernatural. sweet. wonderful. yummy: SEE CONCEPTS *537,572*

heavy [adj1] *having great weight*
abundant. ample. awkward. beefy*. big. built.
bulky. burdensome. chunky*. considerable. copious. corpulent. cumbersome. cumbrous. elephantine. enceinte. excessive. expectant. fat. fleshy.
gravid. gross*. hefty. huge. laden. large. lead-
footed*. loaded. lumbering. massive. obese. oppressed. overweight. parturient. ponderous.

porcine, portly, pregnant, stout, substantial, top-heavy, two-ton*, unmanageable, unwieldy, weighted, weighty, zaftig*; SEE CONCEPT *491*

heavy [adj2] *difficult, severe*

abstruse, acroamatic, arduous, boisterous, burdensome, complex, complicated, confused, effortful, esoteric, formidable, grave, grievous, hard, harsh, intolerable, knotty*, labored, laborious, onerous, oppressive, profound, recondite, rough, serious, solemn, stormy, strenuous, tedious, tempestuous, toilsome, tough, troublesome, turbulent, vexatious, violent, wearisome, weighty, wild; SEE CONCEPTS *538,565,569*

heavy [adj3] *depressed, gloomy*

close, cloudy, crestfallen, damp, dark, dejected, despondent, disconsolate, dismal, downcast, dull, grieving, leaden, lowering, melancholy, oppressive, overcast, sad, sodden, soggy, sorrowful, stifling, wet; SEE CONCEPTS *403,525,548*

heavy [adj4] *listless, slow*

apathetic, comatose, dull, hebetudinous, indifferent, lethargic, sluggish, slumberous, torpid; SEE CONCEPT *584*

heckle [v] *jeer*

badger, bait, bother, bully, chivy, dis*, discomfit, disconcert, disrupt, disturb, embarrass, faze, gibe, hound*, interrupt, pester, plague, rattle, ride*, ridicule, shout at, taunt, tease, torment, worry; SEE CONCEPTS *44,47*

hectic [adj] *frantic, turbulent*

animated, boisterous, burning, chaotic, confused, disordered, excited, exciting, fervid, fevered, feverish, flurrying, flustering, frenetic, frenzied, furious, hassle, heated, hell broke loose*, jungle*, madhouse*, nutsy*, restless, riotous, rip-roaring, tumultuous, unsettled, wild, woolly*, zoolike*; SEE CONCEPT *548*

hedge [n] *boundary, obstacle, especially one made of plants*

barrier, bush, enclosure, fence, guard, hedgerow, hurdle, protection, quickset, screen, shrubbery, thicket, windbreak; SEE CONCEPTS *429,470*

hedge [v1] *avoid, dodge*

beat around the bush*, be noncommittal, blow hot and cold*, cop a plea*, cop out*, duck, equivocate, evade, flip-flop*, fudge*, give the run around*, hem and haw*, jive*, pass the buck*, prevaricate, pussyfoot*, quibble, run around, shilly-shally*, shuck*, shuffle, sidestep, sit on the fence*, stall, stonewall*, temporize, tergiversate, tergiverse, waffle*; SEE CONCEPTS *18,30*

hedge [v2] *enclose*

block, border, cage, confine, coop, corral, edge, fence, girdle, hem in, hinder, immure, obstruct, pen, restrict, ring, siege, surround; SEE CONCEPT *758*

hedonist [n] *person who seeks pleasure above other values*

bon vivant, debauchee, epicure, epicurean, glutton, gourmand, lecher, libertine, pleasuremonger, pleasureseeker, profligate, sensualist, sybarite, thrill-seeker, voluptuary; SEE CONCEPT *423*

heed [n] *care, thought*

application, attention, carefulness, caution, cognizance, concentration, concern, consideration, debate, deliberation, ear*, heedfulness, interest, listen up*, mark, mind*, note, notice, observance, observation, regard, remark, respect, spotlight*, study, tender loving care*, TLC*, watchfulness; SEE CONCEPTS *17,532*

heed [v] *give care, thought to*

attend, baby-sit, bear in mind, be aware, be guided by, catch, consider, dig*, do one's bidding*, follow, follow orders, get a load of*, give ear*, hark, hear, hearken, keep eye peeled*, keep tabs*, listen, mark, mind, mind the store*, note, obey, observe, pay attention, pick up, regard, ride herd on*, see, sit, spot, stay in line*, take notice of, take to heart*, toe the line*, watch, watch one's step*, watch out, watch over, watch the store*; SEE CONCEPTS *17,623*

heedless [adj] *careless*

asleep at the switch*, daydreaming, disregardful, fast and loose*, feckless, foolhardy, goofing off*, impetuous, imprudent, inadvertent, inattentive, incautious, inconsiderate, irreflective, neglectful, negligent, oblivious, out to lunch*, precipitate, rash, reckless, slapdash*, sloppy, thoughtless, uncaring, unmindful, unobservant, unthinking, unwary; SEE CONCEPT *401*

hefty [adj] *big, bulky*

ample, awkward, beefy*, brawny, burly, colossal, cumbersome, extensive, fat, forceful, heavy, hulking, husky, large, large-scale, major, massive, muscular, ponderous, powerful, robust, sizable, strapping*, strong, sturdy, substantial, thumping*, tremendous, unwieldy, vigorous, weighty; SEE CONCEPTS *491,773*

height [n1] *altitude, top part*

acme, apex, apogee, brow, ceiling, crest, crown, cusp, elevation, extent, highness, hill, loftiness, mountain, peak, pinnacle, pitch, prominence, rise, solstice, stature, summit, tallness, tip, tiptop, vertex, zenith; SEE CONCEPTS *741,743,791,836*

height [n2] *climax; importance*

acme, crest, crisis, crowning point, culmination, dignity, eminence, end, exaltation, extremity, grandeur, heyday*, high point, limit, loftiness, maximum, ne plus ultra*, prominence, sublimity, top, ultimate, utmost degree, uttermost; SEE CONCEPTS *388,668,832*

heinous [adj] *horrifying, monstrous*

abhorrent, abominable, accursed, atrocious, awful, bad, beastly, crying, cursed, evil, execrable, flagitious, flagrant, frightful, godawful*, grave, gross*, hateful, hideous, horrendous, infamous, iniquitous, nefarious, odious, offensive, outrageous, raunchy, revolting, scandalous, shocking, stinking*, unspeakable, vicious, villainous; SEE CONCEPTS *529,548,570*

heir [n] *person who inherits possessions*

beneficiary, crown prince/princess, devisee, grantee, heritor, inheritor, next in line, scion, successor; SEE CONCEPTS *355,414*

heirloom [n] *something inherited, often antique*

antique, bequest, birthright, gift, heritage, inheritance, legacy, patrimony, reversion; SEE CONCEPT *337*

hell [n] *place of the condemned; bad situation*

Abaddon*, abyss, affliction, agony, anguish, blazes*, bottomless pit*, difficulty, everlasting fire*, fire and brimstone*, Gehenna*, grave, Hades, hell-fire, infernal regions, inferno, limbo, lower world, misery, nether world, nightmare, ordeal, pandemonium, perdition, pit, place of torment, purgatory, suffering, torment, trial, underworld, wretchedness; SEE CONCEPTS *370,435,674*

help [n1] *assistance, relief*

advice, aid, assist, avail, balm*, benefit, comfort,

he
he

cooperation, corrective, cure, guidance, hand, helping hand*, lift*, maintenance, nourishment, remedy, service, succor, support, sustenance, use, utility; SEE CONCEPTS 658,694

help [n2] *employee*
abettor, adjutant, aide, ally, ancilla, assistant, attendant, auxiliary, collaborator, colleague, deputy, domestic, hand, helper, helpmate, mate, partner, representative, right-hand person*, servant, subsidiary, supporter, worker; SEE CONCEPT 348

help [v1] *aid, assist*
abet, accommodate, advocate, back, ballyhoo*, befriend, benefit, be of use, bolster, boost, buck up*, cheer, cooperate, do a favor, do a service, do one's part*, encourage, endorse, further, go to bat for*, go with, hype*, intercede, lend a hand*, maintain, open doors*, patronize, plug*, promote, prop, puff*, push, relieve, root for*, sanction, save, second, see through, serve, stand by, stick up for*, stimulate, stump for*, succor, support, sustain, take under one's wing*, uphold, work for; SEE CONCEPT 110

help [v2] *improve*
alleviate, ameliorate, amend, attend, better, cure, doctor, ease, facilitate, heal, meliorate, mitigate, nourish, palliate, relieve, remedy, restore, revive, treat; SEE CONCEPT 244

helpful [adj] *beneficial, beneficent*
accessible, accommodating, advantageous, applicable, benevolent, bettering, caring, conducive, considerate, constructive, contributive, convenient, cooperative, crucial, effectual, efficacious, essential, favorable, fortunate, friendly, good for, important, improving, instrumental, invaluable, kind, neighborly, operative, practical, pragmatic, productive, profitable, serendipitous, serviceable, significant, suitable, supportive, symbiotic, sympathetic, timely, usable, useful, utilitarian, valuable; SEE CONCEPTS 537,560

helping [n] *portion of food*
allowance, course, dollop, meal, order, piece, plateful, ration, serving, share; SEE CONCEPT 457

helpless [adj] *incapable, incompetent; vulnerable*
abandoned, basket-case*, debilitated, defenseless, dependent, destitute, disabled, exposed, feeble, forlorn, forsaken, friendless, handcuffed, impotent, inefficient, inexpert, infirm, invalid, over a barrel*, paralyzed, pinned*, powerless, prostrate, shiftless, tapped, tapped out*, unable, unfit, unprotected, up creek without paddle*, weak, with hands tied*; SEE CONCEPTS 401,542

helter-skelter [adv] *carelessly, confused*
about, anyhow, any which way*, anywise, around, at random, cluttered, disorderly, haphazard, hastily, headlong, higgledy-piggledy*, hit-or-miss*, hotfoot*, hurriedly, impetuously, incautiously, in confusion, incontinently, irregular, jumbled, muddled, pell-mell*, random, randomly, rashly, recklessly, topsy-turvy*, tumultous/tumultuous, unmindfully, wildly; SEE CONCEPT 544

hem [n] *border, edge*
brim, brink, define, edging, fringe, margin, perimeter, periphery, piping, rim, selvage, skirt, skirting, trimming, verge; SEE CONCEPTS 484,513

hem/hem in [v] *enclose, restrict*
begird, beset, border, bound, cage, circle, circumscribe, close in, confine, corral, define, edge, encircle, encompass, envelop, environ, fence,

fringe, girdle, hedge in, immure, margin, pen, rim, ring, round, shut, shut in, skirt, surround, verge; SEE CONCEPTS 130,758

hence [adv] *for that reason; therefore*
accordingly, as a deduction, away, consequently, ergo, forward, from here, from now on, henceforth, henceforward, hereinafter, in the future, it follows that, on that account, onward, out, so, then, thence, thereupon, thus, wherefore; SEE CONCEPT 799

herald [n] *omen, messenger*
adviser, bearer, courier, crier, forerunner, harbinger, indication, outrider, precursor, prophet, reporter, runner, sign, signal, token; SEE CONCEPTS 274,284,423

herald [v] *bring message*
advertise, announce, ballyhoo*, broadcast, declare, forerun, foretoken, harbinger, indicate, pave the way*, portend, precede, preindicate, presage, proclaim, promise, publicize, publish, show, tout, trumpet*, usher in*; SEE CONCEPT 60

herd [n] *large group*
assemblage, bevy, brood, clan, collection, covey, crowd, crush, drift, drove, flight, flock, gaggle, gathering, hoi polloi*, horde, lot, mass, mob, multitude, nest, pack, people, populace, press, rabble, school, swarm, throng; SEE CONCEPTS 397,432

herd [v] *gather; shepherd*
assemble, associate, collect, congregate, corral, drive, flock, force, goad, guide, huddle, lead, muster, poke, punch, rally, round up*, run, scare up*, spur; SEE CONCEPT 109

here [adv] *in this place*
attendant, attending, available, hereabouts, hither, hitherto, in this direction, on board, on deck, on hand, on-the-spot, on this spot, present, within reach; SEE CONCEPT 583

hereafter [n] *life after death*
afterlife, aftertime, afterward, afterworld, by-and-by*, future, future existence, future life, heaven, hell, next world, offing, otherworld, the beyond*, to-be*, underworld, world to come*; SEE CONCEPT 370

hereafter [adv] *from now on*
after this, eventually, hence, henceforth, henceforward, hereupon, in the course of time, in the future, ultimately; SEE CONCEPT 799

hereditary [adj] *inherited; transmitted at birth*
ancestral, bequeathed, family, genealogical, genetic, handed down, heritable, inborn, inbred, inheritable, inherited, lineal, maternal, paternal, patrimonial, traditional, transmissible, transmitted, willed; SEE CONCEPT 549

heredity [n] *transmission of traits from parents to offspring*
ancestry, congenital traits, constitution, eugenics, genesiology, genetic make-up, genetics, inborn character, inheritance; SEE CONCEPT 549

heresy [n] *unorthodox opinion, especially in religious matters*
agnosticism, apostasy, atheism, blasphemy, defection, disbelief, dissent, dissidence, divergence, error, fallacy, heterodoxy, iconoclasm, impiety, infidelity, misbelief, nonconformism, nonconformity, paganism, revisionism, schism, sectarianism, secularism, sin; SEE CONCEPT 689

heretical [adj] *unorthodox*
agnostic, apostate, atheistic, differing, disagreeing, dissenting, dissentive, dissident, freethink-

ing, heterodox, iconoclastic, idolatrous, impious, infidel, misbelieving, miscreant, nonconformist, revisionist, schismatic, sectarian, skeptical, unbelieving; SEE CONCEPTS *529,545*

heritage [*n*] *person's background, tradition*
ancestry, bequest, birthright, convention, culture, custom, dowry, endowment, estate, fashion, heirship, heritance, inheritance, legacy, lot, patrimony, portion, right, share, tradition; SEE CONCEPTS *296,648,678*

hermeneutical [*adj*] *interpretive*
critical, demonstrative, explanatory, explicative, expository, illustrative, investigative, revealing; SEE CONCEPT *268*

hermeneutics [*n*] *the science of searching for hidden meaning in texts*
exegetics, exploration, interpretation, investigation, literary criticism, psychoanalytic criticism, revealing, unmasking; SEE CONCEPT *349*

hermit [*n*] *person who chose to live alone outside of human society*
anchoret, anchorite, ascetic, eremite, misanthrope, pillarist, recluse, skeptic, solitaire, solitarian, solitary, stylite; SEE CONCEPTS *361,423*

hero/heroine [*n*] *brave person; champion*
ace, adventurer, celebrity, combatant, conqueror, daredevil, demigod, diva, exemplar, gallant, god, goddess, great person, heavy, ideal, idol, lead, leading person*, lion, martyr, model, paladin, person of the hour*, popular figure, prima donna*, principal, protagonist, saint, star, superstar, tin god*, victor, worthy; SEE CONCEPTS *352,416*

heroic [*adj*] *brave, champion*
bigger than life*, bold, classic, courageous, daring, dauntless, doughty, elevated, epic, exaggerated, fearless, fire-eating*, gallant, grand, grandiose, gritty, gutsy*, gutty*, high-flown, impavid, inflated, intrepid, lion-hearted, mythological, noble, stand tall*, stouthearted, unafraid, undaunted, valiant, valorous; SEE CONCEPTS *401,404*

heroism [*n*] *bravery*
boldness, courage, courageousness, daring, doughtiness, fearlessness, fortitude, gallantry, intrepidity, nobility, prowess, spirit, strength, valiance, valiancy, valor, valorousness; SEE CONCEPTS *411,633*

hesitant [*adj*] *uncertain, waiting*
afraid, averse, backward, dawdling, delaying, diffident, disinclined, doubtful, doubting, faltering, half-hearted, halting, hanging back, hesitating, indecisive, irresolute, lacking confidence, lazy, loath, reluctant, shy, skeptical, slow, tentative, timid, uneager, unpredictable, unsure, unwilling, vacillating, wavering; SEE CONCEPTS *534, 535,542*

hesitate [*v*] *wait; be uncertain*
alternate, balance, balk, be irresolute, be reluctant, be unwilling, blow hot and cold*, dally, debate, defer, delay, demur, dillydally*, dither, doubt, equivocate, falter, flounder, fluctuate, fumble, hang*, hang back, hedge, hem and haw*, hold back, hold off, hover, linger, oscillate, pause, ponder, pull back, pussyfoot*, scruple, seesaw*, shift, shrink, shy away, sit on fence*, stammer, stop, straddle, stumble, stutter, swerve, tergiversate, think about, think twice*, vacillate, waffle*, waver, weigh; SEE CONCEPTS *21,121, 681*

hesitation [*n*] *waiting; uncertainty*
averseness, dawdling, delay, delaying, demurral, doubt, dubiety, equivocation, faltering, fluctuation, fumbling, hemming and hawing*, hesitancy, indecision, indecisiveness, indisposition, irresolution, misgiving, mistrust, oscillation, pause, procrastination, qualm, reluctance, scruple, skepticism, stammering, stumbling, stuttering, unwillingness, vacillation, wavering; SEE CONCEPTS *21,121,410,681*

heterogeneous [*adj*] *assorted, miscellaneous*
amalgamate, composite, confused, conglomerate, contrary, contrasted, different, discordant, discrepant, disparate, dissimilar, divergent, diverse, diversified, incongruous, independent, inharmonious, jumbled, mingled, mixed, mongrel, mosaic, motley, multifarious, multiplex, odd, opposed, unallied, unlike, unrelated, variant, varied, variegated; SEE CONCEPT *564*

hiatus [*n*] *pause, interruption*
aperture, blank, breach, break, chasm, discontinuity, gap, interim, interval, lacuna, lapse, opening, rift, space; SEE CONCEPT *807*

hibernate [*v*] *lie dormant; sleep through cold weather*
hide, hole up, immure, lie torpid, sleep, vegetate, winter; SEE CONCEPT *315*

hidden [*adj*] *unseen, secret*
abstruse, buried, clandestine, cloaked, close, clouded, concealed, covered, covert, cryptic, dark, disguised, eclipsed, esoteric, hermetic, hermetical, imperceivable, indiscernible, in the dark, invisible, latent, masked, mysterious, mystic, mystical, obscure, occult, out of view, private, QT*, recondite, screened, secluded, sequestered, shadowy, shrouded, surreptitious, ulterior, undercover, underground, undetected, undisclosed, unexposed, unknown, unrevealed, veiled, withheld; SEE CONCEPT *576*

hide [*v*] *conceal; remain unseen*
adumbrate, blot out, bury, cache, camouflage, cloak, cover, curtain*, disguise, dissemble, ditch, duck, eclipse, ensconce, go into hiding, go underground, harbor, hold back, hole up*, hush up, keep from, keep secret, lie low*, lock up, mask, not give away, not tell, obscure, plant, protect, put out of the way, reserve, salt away*, screen, secrete, shadow, shelter, shield, shroud, smuggle, squirrel*, stash, stifle, stow away, suppress, take cover, tuck away, veil, withhold; SEE CONCEPTS *17,188*

hideous [*adj*] *grotesque, horrible*
abominable, animal, appalling, awful, beast, bestial, detestable, disgusting, dreadful, frightful, ghastly, grim, grisly, gross*, gruesome, hateful, horrendous, horrid, loathsome, macabre, monstrous, morbid, nasty, odious, offensive, repellent, repugnant, repulsive, revolting, shocking, sick, sickening, terrible, terrifying, ugly, uncomely, unsightly, weird; SEE CONCEPTS *537,579*

high [*adj1*] *tall; at a great distance aloft*
aerial, alpine, altitudinous, big, colossal, elevated, eminent, flying, formidable, giant, gigantic, grand, great, high-reaching, high rise, hovering, huge, immense, large, lofty, long, sky-high, sky-scraping, soaring, steep, towering, tremendous, uplifted, upraised; SEE CONCEPTS *779,782*

high [*adj2*] *extreme*
costly, dear, excessive, exorbitant, expensive,

extraordinary, extravagant, grand, great, high-priced, intensified, lavish, luxurious, precious, rich, sharp, special, steep, stiff, strong, unusual; SEE CONCEPTS *334,569*

high [adj3] *important*
arch, capital, chief, consequential, crucial, distinguished, eminent, essential, exalted, extreme, grave, influential, leading, necessary, noble, powerful, prominent, ruling, serious, significant, superior; SEE CONCEPT *567*

high [adj4] *very happy*
boisterous, bouncy, cheerful, elated, excited, exhilarated, exuberant, joyful, lighthearted, merry, psyched*, pumped*; SEE CONCEPT *403*

high [adj5] *intoxicated, drugged*
delirious, doped, drunk, euphoric, flying*, freaked out*, inebriated, on a trip*, potted*, spaced out*, stoned*, tanked*, tipsy; SEE CONCEPT *314*

high [adj6] *shrill, strong (on the senses)*
acute, high-pitched, loud, malodorous, penetrating, piercing, piping, putrid, rancid, rank, reeking, sharp, smelly, soprano, strident, treble; SEE CONCEPTS *406,594,598*

highlight [n] *memorable part*
best part, climax, feature, focal point, focus, high point, high spot, main feature, peak; SEE CONCEPT *832*

highly [adv] *very, well*
awful, awfully, bloody*, but good*, decidedly, deeply, eminently, exceedingly, exceptionally, extraordinarily, extremely, greatly, hugely, immensely, jolly, mighty, mucho*, notably, parlous, plenty, powerful, profoundly, real, really, remarkably, right, so, so much*, strikingly, supremely, surpassingly, terribly, terrifically, too much*, tremendously, vastly, very much; SEE CONCEPTS *537,569*

high-strung [adj] *nervous*
all shook up*, choked*, easily upset, edgy, excitable, fidgety, hyper*, impatient, irascible, irritable, jittery, jumpy, nervy, neurotic, on pins and needles*, on ragged edge, restless, sensitive, spooked*, stressed, taut, temperamental, tense, tight*, unrestful, uptight*, wired*, zonkers*; SEE CONCEPTS *401,404*

highway [n] *heavily traveled, capacious road*
artery, avenue, boulevard, drag*, four-lane*, freeway, interstate, parking lot*, parkway, path, pike*, roadway, skyway, street, superhighway, super slab*, thoroughfare, toll road, track, turnpike; SEE CONCEPT *501*

hike [n] *journey by foot*
backpack, constitutional, excursion, exploration, march, ramble, tour, traipse, tramp, trek, trip, walk, walkabout; SEE CONCEPTS *149,224,363*

hike [v1] *walk for recreation*
backpack, explore, hit the road*, hoof*, leg it*, ramble, rove, stroll, stump, tour, tramp, travel, tromp; SEE CONCEPTS *149,224,363*

hike [v2] *raise, increase*
advance, boost, jack, jump, lift, pull up, put up, up*, upgrade; SEE CONCEPTS *236,245*

hilarious [adj] *very funny*
amusing, comical, convivial, entertaining, exhilarated, frolicsome, gay, gleeful, gut-busting*, happy, humorous, jocular, jolly, jovial, joyful, joyous, laughable, lively, merry, mirthful, noisy, priceless, riot, rollicking, scream, side-splitting*, uproarious, witty; SEE CONCEPT *529*

hill [n] *uprising of earth's surface; pile*
acclivity, ascent, bluff, butte, cliff, climb, down, drift, dune, elevation, eminence, esker, fell, gradient, headland, heap, height, highland, hillock, hilltop, hummock, inclination, incline, knoll, mesa, mound, mount, precipice, prominence, promontory, protuberance, range, ridge, rise, rising ground, shock, slope, stack, summit, talus, tor, upland; SEE CONCEPT *509*

hinder [v] *prevent, slow down*
arrest, balk, bar, block, bottleneck, box in, burden, check, choke, clog, contravene, counteract, crab, cramp, crimp, cripple, curb, debar, delay, deter, encumber, fetter, frustrate, get in the way*, hamper, hamstring*, handicap, hog-tie*, hold back, hold up, impede, inhibit, interfere, interrupt, louse up*, muzzle, neutralize, obstruct, offset, oppose, preclude, prohibit, resist, retard, shut out, snafu*, stay, stop, stymie*, terminate, thwart, trammel; SEE CONCEPTS *121,130*

hindrance [n] *obstruction, difficulty*
albatross*, baggage*, ball and chain*, bar, barrier, catch, Catch-22*, check, clog, crimp, cumbrance, deterrent, drag, drawback, encumbrance, excess baggage*, foot dragging*, glitch*, gridlock, handicap, hang-up*, hitch, impedance, impediment, interference, interruption, intervention, jam-up*, joker, limitation, lock, millstone*, monkey wrench*, obstacle, restraint, restriction, snag, stoppage, stumbling block*, trammel; SEE CONCEPTS *666,674*

hinge [n] *pivot, turning point*
articulation, axis, ball-and-socket, butt, elbow, hook, joint, juncture, knee, link, pin, spring, swivel; SEE CONCEPTS *471,498*

hinge [v] *be contingent on*
be subject to, be undecided, depend, hang, pend, pivot, rest, revolve around, stand on, turn, turn on; SEE CONCEPT *711*

hint [n] *indication; suggestion*
adumbration, advice, allusion, announcement, clue, communication, connotation, denotation, evidence, flea in ear*, glimmering, help, idea, implication, impression, inference, information, inkling, innuendo, insinuation, intimation, iota, lead, mention, notice, notion, observation, omen, pointer, print, reference, reminder, scent, sign, signification, smattering, suspicion, symptom, taste, telltale, tinge, tip, tip-off*, token, trace, warning, whiff*, whisper, wink*, word to wise*, wrinkle*; SEE CONCEPT *274*

hint [v] *suggest; indicate*
acquaint, adumbrate, advise, allude to, angle, apprise, bring up, broach, coax, connote, cue, drop, expose, fish*, foreshadow, give an inkling*, impart, imply, infer, inform, insinuate, intimate, jog memory, leak*, let it be known, let out of bag*, make*, mention, point, prefigure, press, prompt, put flea in ear*, recall, refer to, remind, say in passing, shadow, signify, solicit, spring, tip off*, tip one's hand*, touch on*, whisper, wink*; SEE CONCEPTS *60,74,75*

hire [v] *commission for responsibility, use*
add to payroll, appoint, authorize, book, bring in, bring on board, carry, charter, contract for, delegate, draft, employ, empower, engage, enlist, exploit, fill a position, find help, give a break*, give job to, give work, ink*, lease, let, make use of, obtain, occupy, pick, place, pledge, procure, promise, put on*, put to work, rent, retain, se-

cure, select, sign on, sign up*, sublease, sublet, take on, truck with*, utilize; SEE CONCEPT 351

hiss [n] *buzzing sound; jeer*
boo, Bronx cheer*, buzz, catcall, contempt, derision, hoot, sibilance, sibilation; SEE CONCEPTS 278,595

hiss [v] *make buzzing sound; ridicule*
blow, boo, catcall, condemn, damn, decry, deride, disapprove, hoot, jeer, mock, rasp, revile, seethe, shout down, shrill, sibilate, siss, spit, wheeze, whirr, whisper, whistle, whiz; SEE CONCEPTS 52,77

historic [adj] *momentous, remarkable*
celebrated, consequential, extraordinary, famous, important, memorable, notable, outstanding, red-letter*, significant, well-known; SEE CONCEPTS 548,568

historical [adj] *recorded as actually having happened*
actual, ancient, archival, attested, authentic, chronicled, classical, commemorated, documented, factual, important, in truth, old, past, real, verifiable; SEE CONCEPTS 548,582,820

history [n1] *past events, experiences*
ancient times, antiquity, bygone times, days of old*, days of yore*, good old days*, old days*, olden days*, past, yesterday, yesteryear; SEE CONCEPTS 678,807

history [n2] *chronicle of events*
account, annals, autobiography, biography, diary, epic, journal, memoirs, narration, narrative, prehistory, recapitulation, recital, record, relation, report, saga, story, tale, version; SEE CONCEPTS 268,271

hit [n1] *strike, bump*
hang, bat, bell-ringer*, belt, blow, bonk, box*, buffet, butt, chop, clash, clip, clout, collision, cuff*, fisticuff, glance, impact, knock, lick*, one-two punch*, paste*, pat, plunk, punch, rap, roundhouse*, shock, shot, slap, slog, smack, smash, sock, spank, stroke, swat, swing, swipe, tap, uppercut, wallop, whammy*, whop, zap*, zinger*; SEE CONCEPTS 189,200

hit [n2] *entertainment success*
achievement, bang, click, favorite, knockout, masterstroke, sellout, sensation, smash, SRO*, triumph, winner, wow; SEE CONCEPT 706

hit [v1] *strike*
bang, bash, bat, batter, beat, belt, blast, blitz, box*, brain*, buffet, bump, clap, clip, clobber, clout, club, crack, cudgel, cuff*, dab, ding*, flail, flax, flog, give a black eye*, hammer*, hook, jab, kick, knock, knock around, knock out, KO*, lace, lambaste, larrup, lather, let fly*, let have it*, lob, nail*, pellet, pelt, percuss, pop, pound, punch, rap, ride roughshod*, slap, smack, sock, stone, swat, tap, thrash, thump, thwack, trash, uppercut, wallop, whack*, whang*; SEE CONCEPTS 189,200

hit [v2] *collide, bump into*
bang into, buffet, butt, carom, clash, crash, glance, jostle, knock, light, meet, meet head-on*, pat, rap, run into, scrape, sideswipe, smash, stumble, tap, thud, thump; SEE CONCEPTS 189,208

hit [v3] *accomplish*
achieve, affect, arrive at, attain, gain, influence, leave a mark, occur, overwhelm, reach, secure, strike, touch; SEE CONCEPTS 199,706

hitch [n] *problem, difficulty*
block, bug*, catch, check, delay, discontinuance, drawback, glitch*, hang-up, hindrance, hold-up,

impediment, interruption, joker, mishap, snafu*, snag, stoppage, stumbling block, tangle, trouble; SEE CONCEPTS 666,674

hitch [v] *join, fasten*
attach, chain, connect, couple, harness, hook, lash, make fast, moor, strap, tether, tie, unite, yoke; SEE CONCEPTS 85,113,160

hoard [n] *stockpile*
abundance, accumulation, agglomeration, aggregation, amassment, backlog, cache, collection, conglomeration, cumulation, fund, garner, heap, inventory, mass, nest egg*, pile, reserve, reservoir, riches, stock, store, supply, treasure, treasure-trove*, trove, wealth; SEE CONCEPT 712

hoard [v] *put away, accumulate*
acquire, amass, buy up, cache, collect, deposit, garner, gather, hide, keep, lay away, lay up, pile up, put aside for rainy day*, put by, save, scrimp, sock away*, squirrel*, stash, stockpile, store, stow away, treasure; SEE CONCEPTS 135,710

hoarse [adj] *raspy in voice*
blatant, breathy, cracked, croaking, croaky, croupy, discordant, dry, grating, gravelly, growling, gruff, guttural, harsh, husky, indistinct, jarring, piercing, ragged, raucous, rough, scratching, squawking, stertorous, strident, stridulous, thick, throaty, uneven, whispering; SEE CONCEPT 594

hoax [n] *trick*
cheat, cock-and-bull story*, con*, con game*, crock*, deceit, deception, dodge, fabrication, fake, falsification, fast one*, fast shuffle*, fib, flimflam*, fraud, gimmick, gyp*, hooey*, humbug*, hustle, imposture, joke, lie, practical joke, prank, put-on*, racket, ruse, scam, sell, shift, snow job*, spoof, sting, swindle, whopper*; SEE CONCEPTS 59,63

hoax [v] *trick*
bamboozle*, bluff, chicane, con, deceive, delude, dupe, fake out, fleece, flimflam*, fool, frame, gammon, gull, hoodwink*, Murphy*, play games with*, pull one's leg*, rook*, run a game on*, set up*, sting*, swindle, take for a ride*, take in*; SEE CONCEPT 59

hobble [v1] *limp*
clump, dodder, falter, halt, hitch, scuff, shuffle, stagger, stumble, totter; SEE CONCEPT 151

hobble [v2] *cripple, restrict*
clog, cramp, cramp one's style, crimp, curb, entrammel, fasten, fetter, gimp, hamper, hamstring*, hang up*, hinder, hog-tie*, leash, put a crimp in*, shackle, tie, trammel; SEE CONCEPT 130

hobby [n] *pleasurable pastime*
amusement, art, avocation, bag*, craft, craze, distraction, diversion, divertissement, fad*, fancy, favorite occupation, fun, game, interest, kick*, labor of love*, leisure activity, leisure pursuit, obsession, occupation, pet topic, play, quest, relaxation, schtick*, shot, sideline, specialty, sport, thing*, vagary, weakness, whim, whimsy; SEE CONCEPTS 363,364

hocus-pocus [n] *deception, magic*
abracadabra*, artifice, cant, chant, charm, cheating, chicanery, conjuring, deceit, delusion, flimflam*, fraud, gibberish, gobbledegook*, hoax, humbug, imposture, incantation, jargon, juggling, legerdemain, mumbo-jumbo*, mummery, nonsense, open-sesame*, rigmarole*, sleight of hand*, spell, swindle, trick, trickery; SEE CONCEPTS 59,278

hi
ho

hodgepodge [n] *mixture, mess*
collection, combination, goulash*, hash, jumble, medley, mélange, miscellany, mishmash*, mixed bag, olio, patchwork, potpourri, salmagundi*; SEE CONCEPTS 260,432

hogwash [n] *nonsense*
absurdity, balderdash*, baloney*, BS*, bull*, bunk*, debris, drivel*, foolishness, hokum, hooey*, horsefeathers*, poppycock*, refuse, ridiculousness, rot, rubbish, trash, twaddle*; SEE CONCEPT 278

hoist [v] *lift*
elevate, erect, heave, pick up, raise, rear, take up, uphold, uplift, upraise, uprear; SEE CONCEPT 196

hold [n] *grasp, possession*
authority, clasp, clench, clinch, clout, clutch, control, dominance, dominion, grip, influence, occupancy, occupation, ownership, pull, purchase, retention, sway, tenacity, tenure; SEE CONCEPTS 190,343,710

hold [v1] *have in one's hands, possession; grasp*
adhere, arrest, bind, bottle up, carry, catch, check, cherish, clasp, cleave, clench, clinch, cling, clutch, confine, contain, cork up*, cradle, detain, embrace, enclose, enjoy, fondle, freeze to*, grip, handle, hang on, have, hug, imprison, keep, keep close, keep out, lock up, maintain, not let go, nourish, occupy, own, palm, possess, press, put a lock on, restrain, retain, secure, seize, squeeze, stay put, stick, take, trammel, vise, wield, withhold, wring; SEE CONCEPTS 190,191,200,710

hold [v2] *believe*
assume, aver, bet bottom dollar*, buy*, consider, credit, cross one's heart*, deem, entertain, esteem, feel, have hunch*, have sneaking suspicion*, judge, lap up, lay money on, maintain, okay, presume, reckon, regard, sense, set store by*, swear by, swear up and down*, take as gospel truth*, take stock in*, think, view; SEE CONCEPT 12

hold [v3] *continue, endure*
apply, be in effect, be in force, be the case, be valid, exist, have bearing, hold good, hold true, last, operate, persevere, persist, remain, remain true, resist, stand up, stay, stay staunch, wear; SEE CONCEPT 239

hold [v4] *support*
bear, bolster, brace, buttress, carry, lock, prop, shore up, shoulder, stay, sustain, take, underpin, uphold; SEE CONCEPTS 110,190

hold [v5] *have a capacity for*
accommodate, be equipped for, carry, comprise, contain, include, seat, take; SEE CONCEPTS 719,742

hold [v6] *conduct meeting, function*
assemble, call, carry on, celebrate, convene, have, officiate, preside, run, solemnize; SEE CONCEPTS 324,384

hold back/hold off [v] *repress*
bit, bridle, check, control, curb, defer, delay, deny, forbear, hold down, hold in, inhibit, keep, keep back, keep out, postpone, prevent, put off, refrain, refuse, restrain, stop, suppress, withhold; SEE CONCEPTS 121,130

holdup [n1] *problem*
bottleneck*, delay, difficulty, gridlock*, hitch, obstruction, setback, snag, stoppage, traffic jam*, trouble, wait; SEE CONCEPTS 192,674

holdup [n2] *take goods illegally by force*
burglary, crime, mugging, robbery, stickup, theft; SEE CONCEPT 192

hold up [v1] *postpone*
delay, detain, hinder, hold off, impede, interfere, interrupt, pause, prorogue, retard, set back, slow down, stay, stop, suspend, waive; SEE CONCEPTS 121,130

hold up [v2] *rob*
burglarize, mug, steal from, stick up, waylay; SEE CONCEPTS 139,192

hole [n1] *opening in a solid object*
aperture, breach, break, burrow, cave, cavern, cavity, chamber, chasm, chink, cistern, cleft, covert, crack, cranny, crater, cut, den, dent, depression, dimple, dip, excavation, eyelet, fissure, foramen, fracture, gap, gash, gorge, hollow, hovel, keyhole, lacuna, lair, leak, mouth, nest, niche, nick, notch, orifice, outlet, passage, peephole, perforation, pit, pocket, pockmark, puncture, rent, retreat, scoop, shaft, shelter, space, split, tear, tunnel, vacuity, vent, void, window; SEE CONCEPT 513

hole [n2] *predicament*
box*, corner*, difficulty, dilemma, emergency, fix, imbroglio, impasse, jam, mess, pickle*, plight, quandary, scrape, spot, tangle; SEE CONCEPT 674

holiday [n] *celebratory day; time off*
anniversary, break, celebration, day of rest, feast, festival, festivity, fete, few days off*, fiesta, gala, gone fishing*, holy day, jubilee, layoff, leave, liberty, long weekend*, recess, red-letter day*, saint's day, vacation; SEE CONCEPTS 364,802

holiness [n] *religiousness*
asceticism, beatitude, blessedness, consecration, devotion, devoutness, divineness, divinity, faith, godliness, grace, humility, inviolability, piety, purity, religiosity, reverence, righteousness, sacredness, saintliness, sanctity, spirituality, unction, venerableness, virtuousness, worship; SEE CONCEPTS 368,645

hollow [n] *empty or dented area*
basin, bottom, bowl, cave, cavern, cavity, chamber, channel, cleft, concavity, crater, cup, dale, den, depression, dimple, dip, dish, excavation, groove, gulf, hole, indentation, notch, pit, pocket, sag, scoop, sinkage, sinkhole, socket, trough, vacuity, valley, void; SEE CONCEPTS 740,754

hollow [adj1] *empty, hollowed out*
alveolate, arched, carved out, cavernous, cleft, concave, cupped, cup-shaped, curved, deep-set, depressed, dimpled, excavated, incurved, indented, infundibular, notched, not solid, pitted, striated, sunken, troughlike, unfilled, vacant, vaulted, void; SEE CONCEPTS 483,490

hollow [adj2] *deep, resonant in sound*
cavernous, clangorous, dull, echoing, flat, ghostly, low, muffled, mute, muted, resounding, reverberant, ringing, roaring, rumbling, sepulchral, sounding, thunderous, toneless, vibrant, vibrating; SEE CONCEPT 594

hollow [adj3] *meaningless*
empty, fruitless, futile, idle, nugatory, otiose, pointless, specious, unavailing, useless, vain, worthless; SEE CONCEPT 560

hollow [adj4] *false, artificial*
cynical, deceitful, faithless, flimsy, hypocritical, insincere, treacherous, unsound, weak; SEE CONCEPT 267

hollow [v] *empty out; make concave*
channel, chase, corrugate, dent, dig, dish, ditch, excavate, furrow, gorge, groove, indent, notch, pit, rabbet, remove, rut, scoop, shovel, trench; SEE CONCEPTS 178,211

holy [adj] *religious, sacred*
angelic, believing, blessed, chaste, clean, consecrated, dedicated, devoted, devotional, devout, divine, faithful, faultless, glorified, god-fearing, godlike, godly, good, hallowed, humble, immaculate, innocent, just, moral, perfect, pietistic, pious, prayerful, pure, revered, reverent, righteous, sacrosanct, sainted, saintlike, saintly, sanctified, seraphic, spiritual, spotless, sublime, uncorrupt, undefiled, untainted, unworldly, upright, venerable, venerated, virtuous; SEE CONCEPTS 545, 567,574

homage [n] *devotion, admiration*
adoration, adulation, allegiance, awe, deference, duty, esteem, faithfulness, fealty, fidelity, genuflection, honor, kneeling, loyalty, obeisance, praise, respect, reverence, service, tribute, worship; SEE CONCEPTS 32,69

home [n1] *place where a human lives*
abode, address, apartment, asylum, boarding house, bungalow, cabin, castle, cave*, commorancy, condo, condominium, co-op, cottage, crash pad*, diggings*, digs*, domicile, dormitory, dump*, dwelling, farm, fireside*, flat, habitation, hangout*, haunt, hearth, hideout, hole in the wall*, home plate*, homestead, hospital, house, hut, joint*, living quarters, manor, mansion, nest*, orphanage, pad*, palace, parking place*, place, residence, resort, roof*, rooming house, roost*, shanty, shelter, trailer, turf, villa, where the hat is*; SEE CONCEPT 516

home [n2] *birthplace, environment*
abode, camping ground*, country, element, family, farm, fireside*, habitat, habitation, haunt, haven, hearth, hills, home ground, homeland, homestead, hometown, household, land, locality, neck of the woods*, neighborhood, range, roof, site, soil, stamping ground*, stomping ground*, territory; SEE CONCEPTS 510,515,648

home [adj] *domestic*
at ease, at rest, central, down home*, familiar, family, homey, homely, household, inland, in one's element*, internal, in the bosom*, local, national, native; SEE CONCEPT 536

homeless [adj] *displaced*
abandoned, banished, deported, derelict, desolate, destitute, disinherited, displaced, dispossessed, down-and-out*, estranged, exiled, forlorn, forsaken, friendless, houseless, itinerant, outcast, refugee, uncared-for, unhoused, unsettled, unwelcome, vagabond, vagrant, wandering, without a roof*; SEE CONCEPT 555

homely [adj1] *ordinary, comfortable*
comfy, cozy, domestic, everyday, familiar, friendly, homelike, homespun, homey, inelaborate, informal, modest, natural, plain, simple, snug, unaffected, unassuming, unostentatious, unpretentious, welcoming; SEE CONCEPTS 579,589

homely [adj2] *unattractive*
animal, disgusting, plain, ugly, unaesthetic, unalluring; SEE CONCEPT 579

homicide [n] *killing*
assassination, big chill*, bloodshed, bump-off*, butchery, carnage, crime, death, erase*, foul play, hit, manslaughter, murder, offing, ride, rubout*, slaying; SEE CONCEPT 252

homogenous [adj] *similar, comparable*
akin, alike, analogous, cognate, consistent, homologous, identical, kindred, like, uniform, unvarying; SEE CONCEPTS 487,573

homosexual [adj] *sexually attracted to the same sex*
gay, homoerotic, homophile, lesbian; SEE CONCEPT 372

honest [adj] *truthful, candid*
above-board, authentic, bona fide*, conscientious, decent, direct, equitable, ethical, fair, fair and square*, forthright, frank, genuine, high-minded*, honorable, impartial, ingenuous, just, law-abiding*, lay it on the line*, like it is*, no lie*, on the level*, on the up and up*, open, outright, plain, proper, real, reliable, reputable, scrupulous, sincere, straight, straightforward, true, true blue*, trustworthy, trusty, undisguised, unfeigned, upfront*, upright, veracious, virtuous, what you see is what you get*; SEE CONCEPTS 267,545

honesty [n] *truthfulness, candidness*
bluntness, candor, confidence, conscientiousness, equity, evenhandedness, fairness, faithfulness, fidelity, frankness, genuineness, goodness, honor, impeccability, incorruptibility, integrity, justness, loyalty, morality, openness, outspokenness, plainness, principle, probity, rectitude, reputability, responsibility, right, scrupulousness, self-respect, sincerity, soundness, straightforwardness, straightness, trustiness, trustworthiness, uprightness, veracity, virtue; SEE CONCEPTS 633,645

honor [n1] *respect*
account, adoration, adulation, aggrandizement, apotheosis, approbation, attention, canonization, celebration, confidence, consideration, credit, deference, deification, dignity, distinction, elevation, esteem, exaltation, faith, fame, fealty, glorification, glory, greatness, high standing, homage, immortalization, laud, laurel, lionization, notice, obeisance, popularity, praise, prestige, rank, recognition, renown, reputation, repute, reverence, tribute, trust, veneration, worship, wreath; SEE CONCEPTS 668,689

honor [n2] *integrity*
character, chastity, courage, decency, fairness, goodness, honestness, honesty, incorruption, incorruptness, innocence, modesty, morality, morals, principles, probity, purity, rectitude, righteousness, trustworthiness, truthfulness, uprightness, virtue; SEE CONCEPTS 411,645

honor [n3] *praise, award*
acclaim, accolade, adoration, badge, bays, commendation, compliment, credit, decoration, deference, distinction, favor, homage, kudos, laurels, pleasure, privilege, recognition, regard, respect, reverence, source of pride, tribute, veneration; SEE CONCEPTS 278,337,689

honor [v] *recognize, treat with respect*
acclaim, admire, adore, aggrandize, appreciate, be faithful, be true, celebrate, commemorate, commend, compliment, decorate, dignify, distinguish, ennoble, erect, esteem, exalt, give glad hand*, give key to city*, glorify, hallow, keep, laud, lionize, live up to, look up to, magnify, observe, praise, prize, revere, roll out red carpet*, sanctify, sublime, uprear, value, venerate, worship; SEE CONCEPTS 10,633

ho
ho

hook [n] *curved fastener*
angle, catch, clasp, crook, curve, grapnel, grapple, hasp, holder, link, lock, peg; SEE CONCEPTS 260,498

hook [v] *grab, catch*
angle, bag, clasp, crook, curve, enmesh, ensnare, entrap, fasten, fix, hasp, lasso, net, pin, secure, snare, trap; SEE CONCEPT 190

hop [n/v] *jump on one leg*
bounce, bound, caper, dance, hurdle, leap, lop, lope, skip, skitter, spring, step, trip, vault; SEE CONCEPT 194

hope [n] *longing; dream*
achievement, ambition, anticipation, aspiration, assumption, belief, bright side*, buoyancy, castles in air*, concern, confidence, daydream, dependence, desire, endurance, expectancy, expectation, faith, fancy, fool's paradise*, fortune, gain, goal, greedy glutton*, hopefulness, light at end of tunnel*, optimism, pipe dream*, promise, promised land*, prospect, reliance, reverie, reward, rosiness, sanguineness, security, stock, thing with feathers*, Utopia, wish; SEE CONCEPTS 20,410,709

hope [v] *long for, dream about*
anticipate, aspire, assume, await, believe, be sure of, cherish, contemplate, count on, deem likely, depend on, desire, expect, feel confident, foresee, hang in*, have faith, hold, keep fingers crossed*, knock on wood*, look at sunny side*, look forward to, pray, presume, promise oneself, rely, suppose, surmise, suspect, sweat*, sweat it*, sweat it out*, take heart*, think to, trust, watch for, wish; SEE CONCEPT 20

hopeful [adj1] *optimistic, expectant*
anticipating, anticipative, assured, at ease, blithe, buoyant, calm, cheerful, comfortable, confident, content, eager, elated, emboldened, enthusiastic, expecting, faithful, forward-looking*, high, hoping, inspirited, keeping the faith*, lighthearted, looking forward to, reassured, rose-colored*, rosy*, sanguine, satisfied, serene, trustful, trusting, unflagging, upbeat; SEE CONCEPT 403

hopeful [adj2] *promising, auspicious*
advantageous, arousing, beneficial, bright, cheerful, cheering, conducive, convenient, elating, encouraging, enlivening, exciting, expeditious, fair, favorable, fine, fit, flattering, fortifying, fortunate, golden, good, gracious, halcyon, heartening, helpful, inspiring, inspiriting, likely, lucky, opportune, pleasant, pleasing, probable, promiseful, propitious, providential, reasonable, reassuring, roseate, rosy*, rousing, stirring, suitable, sunny, timely, uplifting, well-timed; SEE CONCEPT 548

hopeless [adj] *futile, pessimistic*
bad, beyond recall, cynical, dejected, demoralized, despairing, desperate, despondent, disconsolate, discouraging, downhearted, fatal, forlorn, gone*, goner*, helpless, ill-fated, impossible, impracticable, incurable, in despair, irredeemable, irreparable, irretrievable, irrevocable, lost, menacing, no-win, past hope, pointless, sad, shot down*, sinister, sunk, threatening, tragic, unachievable, unavailing, unfortunate, unmitigable, up the creek*, useless, vain, woebegone, worsening; SEE CONCEPTS 529,548

horde [n] *uncontrolled throng, pack*
band, crew, crowd, crush, drove, everybody, gang, gathering, host, jam, mob, multitude, press, push, squash, swarm, troop, turnout, wall-to-wall*; SEE CONCEPTS 397,417

horizon [n] *skyline, extent*
border, boundary, compass, field of vision, ken, limit, perspective, prospect, purview, range, reach, realm, scope, sphere, stretch, vista; SEE CONCEPTS 484,509,529

horizontal [adj] *lying flat*
accumbent, aligned, even, flush, level, parallel, plane, recumbent, regular, smooth, straight, uniform; SEE CONCEPTS 581,583

horrible/horrendous/horrid [adj] *repulsive, very unpleasant*
abhorrent, abominable, appalling, awful, beastly, cruel, detestable, disagreeable, disgusting, dreadful, eerie, execrable, fearful, frightful, ghastly, grim, grisly, gross*, gruesome, heinous, hideous, loathsome, lousy, lurid, mean, nasty, obnoxious, offensive, repellent, revolting, scandalous, scary, shameful, shocking, terrible, terrifying, ungodly, unholy, unkind; SEE CONCEPTS 529,537

horrify [v] *scare*
affright, alarm, appall, chill off*, consternate, daunt, disgust, dismay, frighten, intimidate, outrage, petrify, scare to death*, shake, shock, sicken, terrify, terrorize; SEE CONCEPTS 7,14,19

horror [n] *fear, revulsion*
abhorrence, abomination, alarm, antipathy, apprehension, aversion, awe, chiller, consternation, detestation, disgust, dislike, dismay, dread, fright, hate, hatred, loathing, monstrosity, panic, repugnance, terror, trepidation; SEE CONCEPTS 27,29,532,690

hospitable [adj] *sociable, accommodating*
accessible, amenable, amicable, bountiful, charitable, companionable, convivial, cooperative, cordial, courteous, friendly, generous, genial, gracious, gregarious, kind, liberal, magnanimous, neighborly, obliging, open, open-minded, philanthropic, receptive, red-carpet treatment*, responsive, tolerant, welcoming; SEE CONCEPTS 542,555

hospital [n] *place where ill, injured are treated*
clinic, emergency room, health service, hospice, infirmary, institution, nursing home, rest home, sanatorium, sanitarium, sick bay*, surgery, ward; SEE CONCEPTS 312,439,449

hospitality [n] *neighborliness*
accommodation, affability, amiability, cheer, companionship, comradeship, consideration, conviviality, cordiality, entertainment, friendliness, generosity, geniality, good cheer, heartiness, hospitableness, obligingness, reception, sociability, warmth, welcome; SEE CONCEPTS 388,657

host [n1] *person who entertains, performs*
anchor, anchor person, emcee, entertainer, innkeeper, keeper, manager, moderator, owner, person of the house, presenter, proprietor; SEE CONCEPT 352

host [n2] *large group*
army, array, cloud, crowd, crush, drove, flock, gathering, horde, legion, multitude, myriad, rout, score, swarm, throng; SEE CONCEPTS 417,432

host [v] *entertain, accommodate*
do the honors*, introduce, pick up the check*, present, receive, spread oneself*, throw a party, treat, wine and dine*; SEE CONCEPTS 292,384

hostage [n] *person held captive until captor's demand is met*
captive, earnest, guaranty, pawn, pledge, pris-

oner, sacrificial lamb*, scapegoat*, security, surety, token, victim; SEE CONCEPTS 359,423

hostile [*adj*] *antagonistic, mean*
adverse, alien, allergic, anti*, argumentative, bellicose, belligerent, bitter, catty*, chill*, cold*, competitive, contentious, contrary, disapproving, dour, hateful, ill-disposed, inhospitable, inimical, malevolent, malicious, malignant, militant, nasty, opposed, opposite, oppugnant, ornery*, pugnacious, rancorous, scrappy*, sour*, spiteful, surly, unfavorable, unfriendly, unkind, unpropitious, unsociable, unsympathetic, unwelcoming, viperous, virulent, vitriolic, warlike; SEE CONCEPTS 401,542

hostility [*n*] *antagonism, meanness*
abhorrence, aggression, animosity, animus, antipathy, aversion, bad blood*, bellicosity, belligerence, bitterness, detestation, disaffection, enmity, estrangement, grudge, hatred, ill will, inimicality, malevolence, malice, opposition, rancor, resentment, spite, spleen, unfriendliness, venom, virulence, war, warpath; SEE CONCEPTS 633,657

hot [*adj1*] *very high in temperature*
baking, blazing, blistering, boiling, broiling, burning, calescent, close, decalescent, febrile, fevered, feverish, feverous, fiery, flaming, heated, humid, igneous, incandescent, like an oven*, on fire, ovenlike, parching, piping, recalescent, red*, roasting, scalding, scorching, searing, sizzling, smoking, steaming, stuffy, sultry, summery, sweltering, sweltry, thermogenic, torrid, tropic, tropical, very warm, warm, white*; SEE CONCEPT 605

hot [*adj2*] *spicy to taste*
acrid, biting, peppery, piquant, pungent, racy, sharp, spicy, zestful; SEE CONCEPT 613

hot [*adj3*] *passionate, vehement*
angry, animated, ardent, aroused, distracted, eager, enthusiastic, excited, fervent, fervid, fierce, fiery, furious, ill-tempered, impassioned, impetuous, indignant, inflamed, intense, irascible, lustful, raging, stormy, temperamental, touchy, violent; SEE CONCEPTS 401,403

hot [*adj4*] *new, in vogue*
approved, cool*, dandy, favored, fresh, glorious, groovy*, in demand, just out*, keen, latest*, marvelous, neat*, nifty*, peachy*, popular, recent, sought-after, super, trendy, up-to-the-minute*; SEE CONCEPT 589

hot [*adj5*] *sexually excited*
aroused, carnal, concupiscent, erotic, lascivious, lewd, libidinous, lustful, passionate, prurient, salacious, sensual; SEE CONCEPTS 372,555

hotel [*n*] *place where one pays for accommodation*
auberge, boarding house, caravansary, dump*, fleabag*, flophouse*, hospice, hostel, hostelry, house, inn, lodging, motel, motor inn, public house, resort, roadhouse, rooming house, spa, tavern; SEE CONCEPTS 439,449,516

hound [*n*] *dog*
afghan, airedale, akita, basset, beagle, bowwow*, canine, dachshund, man's best friend*, mongrel, mutt, pointer, pooch, poodle, retriever; SEE CONCEPTS 394,400

hound [*v*] *chase, badger*
annoy, bait, be at, beat the bushes*, be on one's back*, be on one's case*, be on one's tail*, birddog*, bother, bug, chivy, curdle, dog*, drive, give chase, goad, harass, harry, hassle, heckle, hector, hunt, hunt down, impel, leave no stone unturned*, persecute, pester, prod, provoke, pursue, rag*, rag on*, ride, scout, scratch, scratch around, search high heaven*, tail, take out after*, track down, turn inside out, turn upside down, yap at*; SEE CONCEPTS 7,19,207

house [*n1*] *human habitat*
abode, apartment, box*, building, bullpen, castle, cave*, commoracy, condo, condominium, co-op, coop, crash pad*, crib*, cubbyhole*, den, diggings*, digs*, domicile, dump*, dwelling, edifice, flat, flophouse*, habitation, hole in the wall*, home, home plate*, homestead, joint, kennel, layout, lean-to*, mansion, pad, pied-à-terre, pigpen*, pigsty*, rack*, residence, residency, roof, roost*, setup, shack, shanty, turf*; SEE CONCEPTS 439,516

house [*n2*] *family, ancestry*
clan, dynasty, family tree, folk, folks, household, kin, kindred, line, lineage, ménage, race, stock, tradition, tribe; SEE CONCEPT 296

house [*n3*] *business establishment*
company, concern, corporation, firm, organization, outfit, partnership; SEE CONCEPT 325

house [*n4*] *government body, sometimes elected, responsible for laws*
commons, congress, council, legislative body, legislature, parliament; SEE CONCEPT 299

household [*n*] *domestic establishment*
family, family unit, folks, home, house, ménage; SEE CONCEPTS 296,516

household [*adj*] *domestic*
domiciliary, everyday, family, home, homely, homey, ordinary, plain; SEE CONCEPT 536

housework [*n*] *cleaning, maintaining a home*
administration, bed-making, cooking, domestic art, domestic science, dusting, home economics, homemaking, housecraft, housekeeping, ironing, laundering, management, mopping, sewing, stewardship, sweeping, washing; SEE CONCEPTS 165,170,202

housing [*n*] *place of accommodation*
construction, digs*, dwelling, habitation, home, house, lodgment, quarter, quarterage, residence, roof, shelter, sheltering, stopping place; SEE CONCEPTS 388,516

hovel [*n*] *tiny unkempt house*
burrow, cabin, cottage, den, dump*, hole*, hut, hutch, lean-to, pigpen*, pigsty*, rathole*, rattrap*, shack, shanty, shed, stall, sty*; SEE CONCEPT 516

hover [*v*] *hang, float over*
be suspended, brood over, dance, drift, flicker, flit, flitter, flutter, fly, hang about, linger, poise, wait nearby, waver; SEE CONCEPT 154

how [*adv*] *in what way or manner*
according to what, after what precedent, by means of, by virtue of what, by what means, by what method, by whose help, from what source, through what agency, through what medium, to what degree, whence, whereby, wherewith; SEE CONCEPT 544

however [*adv*] *still, nevertheless*
after all, all the same, anyhow, be that as it may, but, despite, for all that, howbeit, in spite of, nonetheless, notwithstanding, on the other hand, per contra, though, withal, without regard to; yet; SEE CONCEPT 544

howl [*n/v*] *long, painful cry*
bark, bawl, bay, bellow, blubber, clamor, groan, growl, hoot, keen, lament, moan, outcry, quest, roar, scream, shout, shriek, ululate, wail, weep,

ho
ho

whimper, whine, yell, yelp, yip, yowl; SEE CONCEPTS *64,77,595*

hub [n] *center, focal point*
core, focus, heart, middle, nerve center*, pivot, polestar, seat; SEE CONCEPT *826*

hubbub [n] *commotion, disorder*
babel, bedlam, brouhaha*, clamor, confusion, din, disturbance, fuss, hassle, hell broke loose*, hue and cry*, hullabaloo*, hurly-burly*, jangle, noise, pandemonium, racket, riot, rowdydow*, ruckus, ruction, rumpus, to-do*, tumult, turmoil, uproar, whirl; SEE CONCEPTS *230,384,388*

huddle [n] *assemblage, crowd, often disorganized*
bunch, chaos, cluster, clutter, confab*, conference, confusion, disarray, discussion, disorder, gathering, group, heap, jumble, mass, meeting, mess*, muddle; SEE CONCEPTS *230,260,417,432*

huddle [v] *meet, discuss*
bunch, cluster, confer, consult, converge, crouch, crowd, cuddle, curl up, draw together, flock, gather, herd, hug, hunch up*, mass, nestle, parley, powwow*, press, press close, snuggle, throng; SEE CONCEPTS *56,114,154*

hue [n] *color, shade*
aspect, cast, chroma, complexion, dye, tincture, tinge, tint, tone, value; SEE CONCEPT *622*

huff [n] *bad mood*
anger, annoyance, dudgeon, miff, offense, passion, perturbation, pet*, pique, rage, snit*, stew*, temper, tiff, umbrage; SEE CONCEPT *410*

huff [v] *sigh, breathe out forcefully*
blow, expire, gasp, heave, pant, puff; SEE CONCEPT *163*

huffy [adj] *angry, in a bad mood*
angered, annoyed, crabbed, crabby, cross, crotchety, crusty, curt, disgruntled, exasperated, fractious, grumpy, huffish, hurt, insulted, irked, irritable, miffed, moody, moping, nettled, offended, peeved, peevish, pettish, petulant, piqued, provoked, put out*, querulous, resentful, riled, short, snappish, snappy, stewed, sulky, sullen, surly, testy, touchy, vexed, waspish; SEE CONCEPTS *401,403*

hug [n] *embrace*
affection, bear hug*, bunny hug*, caress, clasp, clinch, lock, squeeze, tight grip; SEE CONCEPTS *190,375*

hug [v] *hold close, cling to*
bear hug, be near to, cherish, clasp, clinch, cradle, cuddle, embrace, enbosom, enfold, envelop, fold in arms, follow closely, grasp, hold onto, keep close, lie close, lock, love, nestle, nurse, press, receive, retain, seize, squeeze, stay near, take in one's arms, welcome; SEE CONCEPTS *190,375*

huge [adj] *extremely large*
behemothic, bulky, colossal, cyclopean, elephantine, enormous, extensive, gargantuan, giant, gigantic, great, gross*, humongous, immeasurable, immense, jumbo, leviathan, lusty, magnificent, mammoth, massive, mighty, mondo*, monster*, monstrous*, monumental, mountainous, outsize, oversize, planetary, prodigious, stupendous, titanic*, towering, tremendous, vast, walloping, whopping*; SEE CONCEPTS *771,773*

hulk [n] *large piece, mass; remains*
blob, body, bulk, chunk, clod, clump, frame, hull, hunk, mass, ruins, shambles, shell, shipwreck, skeleton, wreck; SEE CONCEPT *829*

hull [n] *skeleton, body*
bark, case, casing, cast, covering, frame, framework, husk, mold, peel, peeling, pod, rind, shell, shuck, skin, structure; SEE CONCEPTS *484,829*

hum [v] *buzz, vibrate*
bombilate, bombinate, bum, bumble, croon, drone, moan, mumble, murmur, purr, rustle, sing, sing low, sound, strum, throb, thrum, trill, warble, whir, whisper, zoom; SEE CONCEPTS *65,77*

human [n] *person, homosapien*
being, biped, body, character, child, creature, homo sapien, individual, life, mortal, personage, soul, wight; SEE CONCEPT *417*

human [adj] *characteristic of people*
animal, anthropoid, anthropological, anthropomorphic, biped, bipedal, civilized, creatural, ethnologic, ethological, fallible, fleshly, forgivable, hominal, homonid, homonine, humanistic, individual, mortal, personal, vulnerable; SEE CONCEPTS *406,549*

humane [adj] *kind, compassionate*
accommodating, altruistic, amiable, approachable, benevolent, benign, benignant, broad-minded, charitable, clement, considerate, cordial, democratic, forbearing, forgiving, friendly, generous, genial, gentle, good, good-natured, gracious, helpful, human, humanitarian, indulgent, kindhearted, kindly, lenient, liberal, magnanimous, merciful, mild, natural, obliging, open-minded, philanthropic, pitying, righteous, sympathetic, tender, tenderhearted, tolerant, understanding, unselfish, warmhearted; SEE CONCEPTS *401,542*

humanitarian [n] *person who gives generously*
altruist, benefactor, bleeding heart*, do-gooder*, Good Samaritan*, good scout*, helper, patron, philanthropist; SEE CONCEPTS *416,423*

humanitarian [adj] *giving, compassionate*
altruistic, beneficent, benevolent, charitable, eleemosynary, generous, good, humane, idealistic, kindly, philanthropic, public-spirited; SEE CONCEPT *542*

humankind [n] *the human race*
community, flesh, Homo sapiens, human beings, humanity, human species, mortality, mortals, people, populace, society; SEE CONCEPT *417*

humble [adj1] *meek, unassuming*
apprehensive, backward, bashful, biddable, blushing, content, courteous, deferential, demure, diffident, docile, fearful, gentle, hesitant, lowly, manageable, mild, modest, obliging, obsequious, ordinary, polite, quiet, reserved, respectful, retiring, reverential, sedate, self-conscious, self-effacing, servile, sheepish, shy, simple, soft-spoken, standoffish, submissive, subservient, supplicatory, tentative, timid, timorous, tractable, unambitious, unobtrusive, unostentatious, unpretentious, withdrawn; SEE CONCEPTS *401,404*

humble [adj2] *poor, inferior*
base, beggarly, common, commonplace, contemptible, humdrum, ignoble, inglorious, insignificant, little, low, low-born, lowly, low-ranking, meager, mean, measly, menial, miserable, modest, obscure, ordinary, paltry, petty, pitiful, plebeian, proletarian, puny, rough, scrubby, seemly, servile, severe, shabby, simple, small, sordid, trivial, unassuming, uncouth, underprivileged, undistinguished, unfit, unimportant, unpretentious, unrefined, vulgar, wretched; SEE CONCEPTS *334,549,589*

humble [v] *shame, put down*
abase, abash, bemean, break, bring down*, cast down, chagrin, chasten, confound, confuse, crush*, cut to the quick*, debase, deflate, degrade, demean, demote, deny, discomfit, discredit, disgrace, embarrass, hide, humiliate, lower*, make eat dirt*, make one feel small*, mortify, overcome, pop one's balloon*, pull down*, put away*, put one away*, put to shame, reduce, silence, sink, snub, squash*, squelch, strike dumb, subdue, take down*, take down a peg*, upset; SEE CONCEPTS *14,16,44,52*

humdrum [adj] *boring, uneventful*
arid, banausic, blah, bromidic, common, commonplace, dim, dime a dozen*, drab, dreary, dull, everyday, garden-variety*, insipid, lifeless, monotone, monotonous, mundane, ordinary, pedestrian, plodding, prosy, repetitious, routine, tedious, tiresome, toneless, treadmill, uninteresting, unvaried, vanilla*, wearisome, white-bread*; SEE CONCEPT *548*

humid [adj] *very damp, referring to weather*
boiling, clammy, close, dank, irriguous, moist, mucky, muggy, oppressive, sodden, soggy, steamy, sticky, stifling, stuffy, sultry, sweaty, sweltering, watery, wet; SEE CONCEPTS *525,603*

humidity [n] *very damp weather*
clamminess, dampness, dankness, dew, dewiness, evaporation, fogginess, heaviness, humectation, humidness, moistness, moisture, mugginess, oppressiveness, sogginess, steam, steaminess, stickiness, sultriness, sweatiness, swelter, thickness, vaporization, wet, wetness; SEE CONCEPTS *524,607*

humiliate [v] *embarrass, put down*
abase, abash, base, bemean, blister, break, bring down*, bring low*, cast down, chagrin, chasten, confound, confuse, conquer, crush*, cut down to size*, debase, degrade, demean, denigrate, deny, depress, discomfit, discountenance, disgrace, dishonor, downplay, humble, lower, make a fool of*, make ashamed, mortify, put down*, put down out of countenance*, put to shame, rip*, run down*, shame, shoot down*, slam*, smear, snub, squash*, subdue, take down*, take down a peg*, tear down*, vanquish, wither; SEE CONCEPTS *14,44,52*

humiliation [n] *embarrassment*
abasement, affront, chagrin, comedown*, comeuppance, condescension, confusion, degradation, discomfiture, disgrace, dishonor, humbling, ignominy, indignity, loss of face*, mental pain, mortification, put-down, resignation, self-abasement, shame, submission, submissiveness, touché*; SEE CONCEPTS *388,410*

humility [n] *humbleness, modesty*
abasement, bashfulness, demureness, diffidence, docility, fawning, inferiority complex, lack of pride, lowliness, meekness, mortification, nonresistance, obedience, obsequiousness, passiveness, reserve, resignation, self-abasement, self-abnegation, servility, sheepishness, shyness, subjection, submissiveness, subservience, timidity, timorousness, unobtrusiveness, unpretentiousness; SEE CONCEPTS *633,657*

humor [n1] *comedy, funniness*
amusement, badinage, banter, buffoonery, clowning, comicality, comicalness, drollery, facetiousness, farce, flippancy, fun, gag, gaiety, happiness, high spirits, jest, jesting, jocoseness, jocularity, joke, joking, joyfulness, kidding, levity, lightness, playfulness, pleasantry, raillery, tomfoolery, whimsy, wisecrack, wit, witticism, wittiness; SEE CONCEPT *293*

humor [n2] *mood, temperament*
bee, bent, bias, caprice, character, complexion, conceit, disposition, fancy, frame of mind, individualism, individuality, makeup, mind, nature, notion, personality, propensity, quirk, spirits, strain, temper, tone, vagary, vein, whim; SEE CONCEPTS *9,410,411*

humorous [adj] *funny, comical*
amusing, campy*, campy*, comic, droll, entertaining, facetious, farcical, hilarious, jocose, jocular, jokey, joshing, laughable, ludicrous, merry, playful, pleasant, priceless, ribald, screaming*, sidesplitting*, too funny for words*, waggish, whimsical, witty; SEE CONCEPTS *267,529*

hump [n] *swelling, projection*
bulge, bump, convexedness, convexity, dune, elevation, eminence, excrescence, gibbosity, hill, hummock, hunch, knap, knob, knurl, kyphosis, mound, prominence, protrusion, protuberance, ridge, swell, tumescence; SEE CONCEPTS *471,513*

hunch [n] *feeling, idea*
anticipation, apprehension, auguration, augury, boding, clue, expectation, feeling in one's bones*, foreboding, forecast, foreknowledge, forewarning, forewisdom, funny feeling*, glimmer, hint, impression, inkling, instinct, intuition, misgiving, notion, omination, portent, preapprehension, precognition, preconceived notion, premonition, prenotation, prenotice, presage, presagement, prescience, presentiment, qualm, suspicion, thought; SEE CONCEPT *689*

hunch [v] *cower, crouch*
arch, bend, bow, curve, draw in, draw together, huddle, hump, lean, scrooch down, squat, stoop, tense; SEE CONCEPT *154*

hunger [n] *appetite for food, other desire*
ache, appetence, appetency, appetition, a stomach for*, big eyes*, bottomless pit*, craving, desire, emptiness, esurience, eyes for*, famine, famishment, gluttony, greed, greediness, hungriness, longing, lust, mania, munchies*, ravenousness, starvation, sweet tooth*, vacancy, void, voracity, want, yearning, yen; SEE CONCEPTS *20,709*

hungry [adj] *starving; desirous*
athirst, avid, carnivorous, could eat a horse*, covetous, craving, eager, edacious, empty, esurient, famished, famishing, flying light*, got the munchies*, greedy, hankering, hoggish, hollow, hungered, insatiate, keen, omnivorous, on empty stomach*, piggish*, rapacious, ravenous, starved, unfilled, unsatisfied, voracious, yearning; SEE CONCEPTS *20,406*

hunk [n] *chunk of solid material*
a lot*, batch, bit, block, bulk, bunch, clod, glob, gob*, large piece, loads*, loaf, lump, mass, morsel, nugget, piece, pile, portion, quantity, slab, slice, wad, wedge; SEE CONCEPTS *470,471*

hunt [n] *search, chase*
coursing, exploration, field sport, following, frisking, game, hounding, hunting, inquest, inquiry, inquisition, interrogation, investigation, looksee*, meddling, probe, prosecution, prying, pursuance, pursuing, pursuit, quest, race, raid, reconnaissance, research, rummage, scrutiny, seeking, sifting, snooping, sporting, steeplechase, study, tracing, trailing; SEE CONCEPTS *207,216*

hu
hu

hunt [v1] *chase for killing*
beat the bushes*, bird-dog*, capture, course, dog, drag, drive, fish, follow, give chase, grouse, gun*, gun for*, hawk, heel, hound, kill, look for, poach, press, pursue, ride, run, scent, scratch, scratch around, seek, shadow, shoot, snare, stalk, start, track, trail; SEE CONCEPTS *207,216,252,363*

hunt [v2] *look, search for*
be on the lookout*, cast about, delve, drag, examine, ferret out, fish for, forage, go after, grope, inquire, interrogate, investigate, look all over hell*, look high and low*, nose around*, probe, prowl, quest, question, ransack, rummage, run down, scour, scratch around*, search high heaven*, seek, sift, trace, trail, try to find, winnow; SEE CONCEPT *216*

hurdle [n] *barrier, obstacle*
bar, barricade, blockade, complication, difficulty, fence, hamper, handicap, hedge, hindrance, impediment, interference, mountain, obstruction, rub, snag, stumbling block, traverse, wall; SEE CONCEPTS *470,674*

hurdle [v] *jump over an obstacle*
bounce, bound, clear, conquer, down, hop, jump across, leap over, lick, lop, master, negotiate, over, overcome, saltate, scale, spring, surmount, vault; SEE CONCEPT *194*

hurl [v] *throw forcefully*
bung, cast, chuck, chunk, fire, fling, gun, heave, launch, let fly, lob, peg, pitch, project, propel, send, sling, toss; SEE CONCEPT *222*

hurricane [n] *violent windstorm*
blow, cyclone, gale, line storm, monsoon, storm, tempest, tornado, tropical cyclone, tropical storm, twister, typhoon, whirlwind; SEE CONCEPTS *524,526*

hurried [adj] *quick, rushed*
abrupt, breakneck, brief, cursory, fast, hasty, headlong, hectic, impetuous, perfunctory, precipitant, precipitate, precipitous, rushing, short, slapdash, speedy, subitaneous, sudden, superficial, swift; SEE CONCEPTS *548,588,799*

hurry [n] *speed in action, motion*
bustle, celerity, commotion, dash, dispatch, drive, expedition, expeditiousness, flurry, haste, precipitance, precipitateness, precipitation, promptitude, push, quickness, rush, rustle, scurry, speediness, swiftness, urgency; SEE CONCEPTS *657,748,755*

hurry [v] *act, move speedily*
accelerate, barrel, beeline*, be quick, bestir, breeze, bullet, burst, bustle, dash, dig in, drive, expedite, fleet, flit, fly, get a move on*, goad, go like lightning*, haste, hasten, hurry up, hustle, jog, lose no time, make haste, make short work of*, make time*, make tracks*, nip, push, quicken, race, rip, rocket, roll, run, rush, sally, scoot, scurry, shake a leg*, smoke, speed, speed up, spur, step on gas*, step on it*, turn on steam*, urge, whirl, whish, whisk, whiz, zip; SEE CONCEPTS *150,234*

hurt [n] *injury; damage*
ache, black and blue*, blow, boo-boo*, bruise, chop, detriment, disadvantage, disaster, discomfort, disservice, distress, down, gash, harm, ill, ill-treatment, loss, mark, mischief, misfortune, nick, ouch, outrage, pain, pang, persecution, prejudice, ruin, scratch, sore, soreness, suffering, wound, wrong; SEE CONCEPTS *316,728*

hurt [adj] *physically or mentally injured*
aching, aggrieved, agonized, all torn up*, battered, bleeding, bruised, buffeted, burned, busted up*, contused, crushed, cut, damaged, disfigured, distressed, disturbed, grazed, harmed, hit, impaired, indignant, in pain, lacerated, marred, mauled, miffed, mutilated, nicked, offended, pained, piqued, put away, resentful, rueful, sad, scarred, scraped, scratched, shook, shot, sore, stricken, struck, suffering, tender, tortured, umbrageous, unhappy, warped, wounded; SEE CONCEPTS *314,403*

hurt [v1] *cause physical pain; experience pain*
abuse, ache, afflict, ail, belt, be sore, be tender, bite, blemish, bruise, burn, cramp, cut, cut up, damage, disable, do violence, flail, flog, harm, impair, injure, kick, lacerate, lash, maltreat, mar, maul, mess up, nip, pierce, pinch, pommel, prick, pummel, punch, puncture, punish, rough up, shake up, slap, slug, smart, spank, spoil, squeeze, stab, sting, tear, throb, torment, torture, total, trouble, wax, whack, whip, wing, wound, wrack up, wring; SEE CONCEPTS *246,313*

hurt [v2] *cause mental pain*
abuse, afflict, aggrieve, annoy, burn, chafe, constrain, cut to the quick*, discomfit, discommode, displease, distress, excruciate, faze, give no quarter*, go for jugular*, grieve, hit where one lives*, injure, lambaste, lay a bad trip on*, lean on*, martyr, martyrize, prejudice, punish, put down, put out, sadden, sting*, thumb nose at*, torment, torture, try, upset, vex, vitiate, work over*, wound, zing*; SEE CONCEPTS *7,14,19*

hurtful [adj] *injurious, cruel*
aching, afflictive, bad, cutting, damaging, dangerous, deadly, deleterious, destructive, detrimental, disadvantageous, distressing, evil, harmful, hurting, malicious, mean, mischievous, nasty, nocuous, noxious, ominous, pernicious, poisonous, prejudicial, spiteful, unkind, upsetting, wounding; SEE CONCEPTS *537,542*

hurtle [v] *plunge, charge*
bump, collide, fly, lunge, push, race, rush, rush headlong, scoot, scramble, shoot, speed, spurt, tear; SEE CONCEPT *150*

husband [n] *married man*
bridegroom, companion, consort, groom, helpmate, hubby, mate, monogamist, monogynist, other half, partner, spouse; SEE CONCEPTS *414,419*

hush [n] *quiet*
calm, lull, peace, peacefulness, quietude, silence, still, stillness, tranquility; SEE CONCEPT *65*

hush [v] *attempt to make quiet*
burke, choke, gag, muffle, mute, muzzle, quiet, quieten, shush*, shut up, silence, stifle, still, stop, suppress; SEE CONCEPTS *65,87*

hush-hush [adj] *secret*
clandestine, classified, closet, confidential, covert, dark, private, restricted, sub-rosa*, surreptitious, undercover, under-the-table*; SEE CONCEPT *576*

hush up [v] *keep secret*
burke, conceal, cover, cover up, keep dark, sit on, smother, squash, stifle, suppress; SEE CONCEPT *266*

husk [n] *covering, case*
aril, bark, case, chaff, glume, hull, outside, pod, rind, shell, shuck, skin; SEE CONCEPTS *428,484*

husky [adj1] *deep, scratchy in sound*
croaking, croaky, growling, gruff, guttural, harsh, hoarse, loud, rasping, raucous, rough, throaty; SEE CONCEPT 594

husky [adj2] *big, burly*
brawny, gigantic, hefty, Herculean*, mighty, muscular, powerful, rugged, sinewy, stalwart, stocky, stout, strapping, strong, sturdy, thickset, well-built; SEE CONCEPT 773

hustle [v] *hurry; work hurriedly*
apply oneself, be conscientious, bulldoze*, bustle, elbow, fly, force, haste, hasten, hotfoot*, impel, jog, press, push, race, rush, shove, speed, thrust, use elbow grease*; SEE CONCEPTS 91,150

hut [n] *often roughly built, house*
box*, bungalow, cabana, cabin, camp, chalet, cot, cottage, crib*, den, dugout, dump*, hovel*, hutch, lean-to, lodge, log house, pigeonhole*, rathole*, refuge, shack, shanty, shed, shelter, summer house, tepee, wigwam; SEE CONCEPT 516

hybrid [n] *composite, mixture*
amalgam, bastard, combination, compound, cross, crossbreed, half-blood, half-breed, half-caste, incross, miscegenation, mongrel, mule, outcross; SEE CONCEPTS 260,394,414,429

hygiene [n] *cleanliness*
healthful living, hygienics, preventive medicine, public health, regimen, salutariness, sanitation, wholesomeness; SEE CONCEPTS 316,405

hygienic [adj] *clean*
aseptic, disinfected, germ-free, good, healthful, healthy, pure, salubrious, salutary, salutiferous, sanitary, sterile, uncontaminated, uninfected, wholesome; SEE CONCEPT 621

hymn [n] *religious song*
aria, canticle, carol, chant, choral, chorale, descant, ditty, evensong, hosanna, laud, lay, lied, littany, ode, oratorio, paean, psalm, shout, song of praise, worship song; SEE CONCEPTS 262,595

hype [n] *extensive publicity*
advertising, buildup*, plugging*, promotion; SEE CONCEPTS 292,324

hyperbole [n] *exaggeration*
amplification, big talk*, coloring*, distortion, embellishment, embroidering, enlargement, hype*, laying it on thick*, magnification, metaphor, mountain out of molehill*, overstatement, PR*, tall talk*; SEE CONCEPT 268

hyperinflation [n] *extremely high, rising economic inflation*
devaluation, overextension, run-away inflation, wheelbarrow economics; SEE CONCEPT 335

hypermedia [n] *system giving access to multimedia information on a single subject*
data base, information bank, information retrieval; SEE CONCEPT 274

hypnotic [adj] *spellbinding, sleep-inducing*
anesthetic, anodyne, calmative, lenitive, mesmeric, mesmerizing, narcotic, opiate, sleepy, somniferous, somnolent, soothing, soporific, soporose, trance-inducing; SEE CONCEPTS 529,537

hypnotize [v] *put in trance; spellbind*
anesthetize, bring under control, captivate, charm, drug, dull the will, entrance, fascinate, hold under a spell, induce, lull to sleep, magnetize, make drowsy, make sleepy, mesmerize, narcotize, put to sleep, soothe, stupefy, subject to suggestion; SEE CONCEPT 250

hypocrisy [n] *deceitfulness, pretense*
affectation, bad faith*, bigotry, cant, casuistry,

deceit, deception, dishonesty, display, dissembling, dissimulation, double-dealing, duplicity, false profession, falsity, fraud, glibness, imposture, insincerity, irreverence, lie, lip service*, mockery, pharisaicalness, pharisaism, phoniness, pietism, quackery, sanctimoniousness, sanctimony, speciousness, unctuousness; SEE CONCEPTS 63,633,657

hypocrite [n] *person who pretends, is deceitful*
actor, attitudinizer, backslider*, bigot, bluffer, casuist, charlatan, cheat, con artist, crook, deceiver, decoy, dissembler, dissimulator, fake, faker, four-flusher*, fraud, hook*, humbug, impostor, informer, lip server*, malingerer, masquerader, mountebank, Pharisee, phony, playactor*, poser, pretender, quack*, smoothie*, sophist, swindler, trickster, two-face*, two-timer*, wolf in sheep's clothing*; SEE CONCEPT 412

hypocritical [adj] *deceitful, pretending*
affected, artificial, assuming, bland, canting, captious, caviling, deceptive, deluding, dissembling, double, double-dealing, duplicitous, faithless, false, feigning, fishy*, fraudulent, glib, hollow, insincere, jivey, left-handed, lying, moralistic, oily, pharisaical, phony, pietistic, pious, sanctimonious, self-righteous, smooth, smooth-spoken, smooth-tongued*, snide, specious, spurious, two-faced*, unctuous, unnatural, unreliable; SEE CONCEPTS 267,401,542

hypothesis [n] *theory*
antecedent, apriority, assignment, assumption, attribution, axiom, basis, belief, conclusion, condition, conjecture, data, deduction, demonstration, derivation, explanation, foundation, ground, guess, inference, interpretation, layout, lemma, philosophy, plan, position, postulate, premise, presupposition, principle, proposal, proposition, rationale, reason, scheme, shot in the dark*, speculation, starting point, suggestion, supposition, surmise, system, tentative law, term, theorem, thesis; SEE CONCEPTS 661,689

hypothetical [adj] *guessed, assumed*
academic, assumptive, casual, concocted, conditional, conjecturable, conjectural, contestable, contingent, debatable, disputable, doubtful, equivocal, imaginary, imagined, indefinite, indeterminate, postulated, presumptive, presupposed, pretending, problematic, provisory, putative, questionable, refutable, speculative, stochastic, supposed, suppositional, suppositious, suspect, theoretic, theoretical, uncertain, unconfirmed, vague; SEE CONCEPTS 529,552,582

hysteria [n] *state of extreme upset*
agitation, delirium, excitement, feverishness, frenzy, hysterics, madness, mirth, nervousness, panic, unreason; SEE CONCEPT 410

hysterical [adj] *very upset, excited*
agitated, berserk, beside oneself, blazing, carried away*, convulsive, crazed, crazy, delirious, distracted, distraught, emotional, fiery, frantic, frenzied, fuming, furious, impassioned, impetuous, in a fit, incensed, irrepressible, mad, maddened, nervous, neurotic, overwrought, panic-stricken, passionate, possessed, rabid, raging, rampant, raving, seething, spasmodic, tempestuous, turbulent, uncontrollable, uncontrolled, unnerved, unrestrained, uproarious, vehement, violent, wild, worked up*; SEE CONCEPTS 403,542

hu
hy

I

ice [n] *frozen water*

chunk, crystal, cube ice, diamonds*, dry ice, floe, glacier, glaze, hail, hailstone, iceberg, ice cube, icicle, permafrost, sleet; SEE CONCEPTS *470,514*

icky [adj] *not pleasant*

disgusting, horrible, loathsome, nasty, noisome, offensive, repellent, revolting, sickening, vile; SEE CONCEPT *570*

icy [adj1] *frozen; slippery when frozen*

antarctic, arctic, biting, bitter, chill, chilled to the bone*, chilling, chilly, cold, freezing, frigid, frost-bound, frosty, frozen over, gelid, glacial, glaring, iced, polar, raw, refrigerated, rimy, shivering, shivery, sleeted, smooth as glass*; SEE CONCEPTS *605,606*

icy [adj2] *aloof*

chill, cold, distant, emotionless, forbidding, frigid, frosty, glacial, hostile, indifferent, steely, stony, unemotional, unfriendly, unwelcoming; SEE CONCEPTS *401,404*

idea [n] *something understood, planned, or believed*

abstraction, aim, approximation, belief, brainstorm*, clue, concept, conception, conclusion, conviction, design, doctrine, end, essence, estimate, fancy, feeling, flash*, form, guess, hint, hypothesis, import, impression, inkling, intention, interpretation, intimation, judgment, meaning, notion, object, objective, opinion, pattern, perception, plan, purpose, reason, scheme, sense, significance, solution, suggestion, suspicion, teaching, theory, thought, understanding, view, viewpoint; SEE CONCEPTS *529,660,661,689*

ideal [n] *model*

archetype, criterion, epitome, example, exemplar, goal, idol, jewel, last word*, mirror, nonesuch, nonpareil, paradigm, paragon, pattern, perfection, prototype, standard; SEE CONCEPTS *671,686*

ideal [adj1] *model, perfect*

absolute, archetypal, classic, classical, complete, consummate, excellent, exemplary, fitting, flawless, have-it-all*, indefectible, optimal, paradigmatic, pie-in-the-sky*, prototypical, quintessential, representative, Shangri-la*, supreme; SEE CONCEPTS *533,574*

ideal [adj2] *conceptual; impractical*

abstract, chimerical, dreamlike, extravagant, fanciful, fictitious, high-flown, hypothetical, imaginary, intellectual, in the clouds*, ivory-tower*, mental, mercurial, notional, out-of-reach*, quixotic, theoretical, transcendent, transcendental, unattainable, unearthly, unreal, Utopian*, visionary; SEE CONCEPTS *529,552*

idealist [n] *person who holds fancies in mind, who believes in perfection*

dreamer, enthusiast, escapist, optimist, Platonist, radical, romancer, romantic, romanticist, seer, stargazer, theorizer, transcendalist, Utopian, visionary; SEE CONCEPTS *359,416,423*

ideals [n] *moral beliefs*

ethics, goals, principles, standards, values; SEE CONCEPTS *645,689*

identical [adj] *alike, equal*

carbon copy*, corresponding, dead ringer*, ditto*, double, duplicate, equivalent, exact, identic, indistinguishable, interchangeable, like, like two peas in a pod*, look-alike, matching, same, same difference*, selfsame, spitting image*, tantamount, twin, very, very same, Xerox*; SEE CONCEPTS *487,566,573*

identification [n] *labeling; means of labeling*

apperception, assimilation, badge, bracelet, cataloging, classifying, credentials, description, dog tag, establishment, ID*, identity bracelet, letter of introduction, letter of recommendation, naming, papers, passport, recognition, tag, testimony; SEE CONCEPTS *268,271*

identify [v] *recognize; label*

analyze, button down*, card, catalog, classify, describe, determinate, determine, diagnose, diagnosticate, distinguish, establish, find, make out, name, peg*, pick out, pinpoint, place, put one's finger on*, select, separate, single out*, spot, tab*, tag*; SEE CONCEPTS *38,62*

identify with [v] *put oneself in the place of another*

ally, associate, empathize, feel for*, put in same category*, put oneself in another's shoes*, relate to, respond to, see through someone's eyes*, sympathize, think of in connection*, understand; SEE CONCEPTS *15,39*

identity [n1] *person's individuality*

character, circumstances, coherence, distinctiveness, existence, identification, integrity, ipseity, name, oneness, particularity, personality, self, selfdom, selfhood, selfness, singleness, singularity, status, uniqueness; SEE CONCEPT *411*

identity [n2] *similarity, correspondence*

accord, agreement, congruence, congruity, empathy, equality, equivalence, identicalness, likeness, oneness, rapport, resemblance, sameness, selfsameness, semblance, similitude, unanimity, uniformity, unity; SEE CONCEPTS *664,670*

ideology [n] *beliefs*

articles of faith*, credo, creed, culture, dogma, ideas, outlook, philosophy, principles, system, tenets, theory, view, Weltanschauung*; SEE CONCEPTS *688,689*

idiocy [n] *utter stupidity*

asininity, cretinism, derangement, fatuity, fatuousness, foolishness, imbecility, inanity, insanity, insipidity, lunacy, madness, senselessness, tomfoolery; SEE CONCEPTS *409,410*

idiom [n] *manner of speaking, turn of phrase*

argot, colloquialism, dialect, expression, idiosyncrasy, jargon, language, lingo*, localism, locution, parlance, patois, phrase, provincialism, set phrase, street talk*, style, talk, tongue, usage, vernacular, vernacularism, word; SEE CONCEPT *275*

idiosyncrasy [n] *oddity, quirk*

affectation, bit, characteristic, distinction, eccentricity, feature, habit, mannerism, peculiarity, singularity, trait, trick; SEE CONCEPTS *411,644*

idiot [n] *very stupid person*

blockhead, bonehead*, cretin, dimwit, dork, dumbbell, dunce, fool, ignoramus, imbecile, jerk, kook*, moron, nincompoop, ninny*, nitwit, out to lunch*, pinhead*, simpleton, stupid, tomfool, twit*; SEE CONCEPT *402*

idiotic [adj] *very stupid*

asinine, batty*, birdbrained*, crazy, daffy*, daft, dull, dumb, fatuous, foolhardy, foolish, harebrained*, imbecile, imbecilic, inane, insane, lunatic, moronic, senseless, silly, squirrelly*, thickwitted*, unintelligent; SEE CONCEPT *402*

idle [adj1] *not used; out of action*

abandoned, asleep, barren, closed down, dead,

deserted, down, dusty, empty, gathering dust*, inactive, inert, jobless, laid-off, leisured, mothballed, motionless, on the bench*, on the shelf*, out of operation, out of work*, passive, quiet, redundant, resting, rusty, sleepy, stationary, still, uncultivated, unemployed, unoccupied, untouched, unused, vacant, void, waste, workless; SEE CONCEPTS 542,560

idle [adj2] *lazy*
at rest, indolent, lackadaisical, resting, shiftless, slothful, sluggish, taking it easy*; SEE CONCEPTS 401,538

idle [adj3] *worthless, ineffective*
abortive, bootless, empty, frivolous, fruitless, futile, groundless, hollow, insignificant, irrelevant, not serious, nugatory, of no avail*, otiose, pointless, rambling, superficial, trivial, unavailing, unhelpful, unnecessary, unproductive, unsuccessful, useless, vain; SEE CONCEPTS 267,560

idleness [n] *laziness, inaction*
dawdling, dilly-dallying*, dormancy, droning, goof-off time*, hibernation, inactivity, indolence, inertia, joblessness, laze, lazing, leisure, lethargy, loafing, loitering, otiosity, own sweet time*, pottering, shiftlessness, sloth, slothfulness, slouch, slowness, sluggishness, stupor, time on one's hands*, time to burn*, time to kill*, time-wasting, torpidity, torpor, trifling, truancy, unemployment, vegetating; SEE CONCEPTS 657,677,681

idol [n] *person greatly admired*
beloved, darling, dear, deity, desire, eidolon, false god, favorite, fetish, god, goddess, golden calf*, graven image, hero, icon, image, inamorata, pagan symbol, simulacrum, superstar; SEE CONCEPTS 352,423

idolize [v] *think of very highly; worship*
admire, adore, apotheosize, bow down, canonize, deify, dote on, exalt, glorify, look up to*, love, put on a pedestal*, revere, reverence, venerate; SEE CONCEPTS 10,32

idyllic [adj] *perfect; extremely pleasant*
arcadian, bucolic, charming, comfortable, halcyon, heavenly, ideal, idealized, out-of-this-world*, pastoral, peaceful, picturesque, pleasing, rustic, unspoiled; SEE CONCEPTS 529,572

iffy [adj] *uncertain*
capricious, chancy, conditional, dicey, doubtful, erratic, fluctuant, incalculable, in lap of gods*, problematic, undecided, unpredictable, unsettled, up in the air*, whimsical; SEE CONCEPT 552

ignite [v] *set on fire*
burn, burst into flames, catch fire, enkindle, fire, flare up, inflame, kindle, light, put match to*, set alight, set fire to, start up, take fire, touch off; SEE CONCEPT 249

ignoble [adj] *lowly, unworthy*
abject, base, baseborn, coarse, common, contemptible, corrupt, craven, dastardly, degenerate, degraded, despicable, disgraceful, dishonorable, heinous, humble, infamous, inferior, lewd, low, mean, menial, modest, ordinary, peasant, petty, plain, plebeian, poor, rotten, scurvy, servile, shabby, shameful, simple, sordid, unwashed, vile, vulgar, wicked, wretched, wrong; SEE CONCEPTS 542,545,549

ignorance [n] *unintelligence, inexperience*
benightedness, bewilderment, blindness, callowness, crudeness, darkness, denseness, disregard, dumbness, empty-headedness*, fog*, half-knowledge, illiteracy, incapacity, incomprehension, innocence, inscience, insensitivity, lack of education, mental incapacity, naiveté, nescience, oblivion, obtuseness, philistinism, rawness, sciolism, shallowness, simplicity, unawareness, unconsciousness, uncouthness, unenlightenment, unfamiliarity, unscholarliness, vagueness; SEE CONCEPTS 409,678

ignorant [adj] *unaware, unknowing*
apprenticed, benighted, birdbrained*, blind to*, cretinous, dense, green*, illiterate, imbecilic, inexperienced, innocent, insensible, in the dark*, mindless, misinformed, moronic, naive, nescient, oblivious, obtuse, shallow, thick, unconscious, unconversant, uncultivated, uncultured, uneducated, unenlightened, uninformed, uninitiated, unintellectual, unknowledgeable, unlearned, unlettered, unmindful, unread, unschooled, unsuspecting, untaught, untrained, unwitting, witless; SEE CONCEPTS 402,542

ignore [v] *disregard on purpose*
avoid, be oblivious to, blink, brush off*, bury one's head in sand*, cold-shoulder*, discount, disdain, evade, fail, forget, let it go*, neglect, omit, overlook, overpass, pass over, pay no attention to, pay no mind*, pooh-pooh*, reject, scorn, shut eyes to*, slight, take no notice, tune out*, turn back on*, turn blind eye*, turn deaf ear; SEE CONCEPT 30

ill [n] *misfortune*
abuse, affection, affliction, ailment, badness, complaint, condition, cruelty, damage, depravity, destruction, disease, disorder, evil, harm, hurt, illness, indisposition, infirmity, injury, insult, malady, malaise, malice, mischief, misery, pain, sickness, suffering, syndrome, trial, tribulation, trouble, unpleasantness, wickedness, woe, wrong; SEE CONCEPTS 316,674,675

ill [adj1] *sick*
afflicted, ailing, a wreck*, below par*, bummed*, diseased, down, down with, feeling awful, feeling rotten, feeling terrible, got the bug*, indisposed, infirm, laid low*, off one's feet*, on sick list*, out of sorts*, peaked, poorly, queasy, rotten, run-down, running temperature, sick as a dog*, under the weather*, unhealthy, unwell, woozy*; SEE CONCEPT 314

ill [adj2] *bad, evil*
acrimonious, adverse, antagonistic, cantankerous, cross, damaging, deleterious, detrimental, disrespectful, disturbing, foreboding, foul, harmful, harsh, hateful, hostile, hurtful, ill-mannered, impertinent, inauspicious, inimical, iniquitous, injurious, malevolent, malicious, nocent, nocuous, noxious, ominous, ruinous, sinister, sullen, surly, threatening, unfavorable, unfortunate, unfriendly, ungracious, unhealthy, unkind, unlucky, unpromising, unpropitious, unwholesome, vile, wicked, wrong; SEE CONCEPTS 537,545,570

ill-advised [adj] *unwise, not thought out*
brash, confused, foolhardy, foolish, half-baked*, hotheaded*, ill-considered, ill-judged, impolitic, imprudent, inappropriate, incautious, inconsiderate, indiscreet, inexpedient, injudicious, madcap*, misguided, off the top of one's head*, overhasty, rash, reckless, short-sighted*, thoughtless, unseemly, wrong; SEE CONCEPTS 544,548

ill at ease [adj] *uncomfortable, nervous*
anxious, awkward, discomfited, disquieted, disturbed, doubtful, edgy, faltering, fidgety, hesitant, insecure, on edge*, on pins and needles*, on ten-

ic
il

terhooks*, out of place*, restless, self-conscious, shy, suspicious, tense, uneasy, unrelaxed, unsettled, unsure; SEE CONCEPTS 401,403

illegal [adj] *against the law*
actionable, banned, black-market*, bootleg*, contraband, criminal, crooked, extralegal, felonious, forbidden, heavy*, hot*, illegitimate, illicit, interdicted, irregular, lawless, not approved, not legal, outlawed, outside the law, prohibited, proscribed, prosecutable, racket, shady, smuggled, sub rosa, taboo, unauthorized, unconstitutional, under the table*, unlawful, unlicensed, unofficial, unwarrantable, unwarranted, verboten, violating, wildcat*, wrongful; SEE CONCEPTS 319,545

illegible [adj] *unreadable*
cacographic, crabbed, cramped, difficult to read, faint, hard to make out*, hieroglyphic, indecipherable, indistinct, obscure, scrawled, unclear, undecipherable, unintelligible; SEE CONCEPTS 535,576

illegitimate [adj] *not legal*
contraband, illegal, illicit, improper, invalid, misbegotten, spurious, supposititious, unauthorized, unconstitutional, unlawful, unsanctioned, wicked, wrong; SEE CONCEPTS 319,549

ill-fated/ill-starred [adj] *doomed*
blighted, catastrophic, destroyed, disastrous, hapless, ill-omened, inauspicious, luckless, misfortunate, ruined, star-crossed*, unfortunate, unhappy, unlucky, untoward; SEE CONCEPTS 537,548

illicit [adj] *not legal; forbidden*
adulterous, black-market*, bootleg*, clandestine, contraband, contrary to law, criminal, crooked, dirty*, felonious, furtive, guilty, heavy*, illegal, illegitimate, immoral, improper, in violation of law, lawless, out of line*, prohibited, racket, unauthorized, unlawful, unlicensed, wrong, wrongful; SEE CONCEPTS 319,545

illiterate [adj] *unable to read well; lacking education*
benighted, catachrestic, ignorant, inerudite, solecistic, uneducated, unenlightened, ungrammatical, uninstructed, unlearned, unlettered, unread, unschooled, untaught, untutored; SEE CONCEPT 402

ill-mannered [adj] *badly behaved*
bad-mannered, boorish, cheap, churlish, coarse, discourteous, disrespectful, ill-behaved, ill-bred, impertinent, impolite, insolent, loud, loudmouthed, loutish, raunchy*, raw, rough, roughneck*, rude, tacky*, uncivil, uncouth, ungracious, unmannerly, unrefined, vulgar; SEE CONCEPT 401

ill-natured [adj] *bad-tempered*
catty, churlish, crabbed, crabby, cross, crotchety, cussed*, dirty*, disagreeable, disobliging, dyspeptic, hot-tempered, ill-humored, irritable, malevolent, malicious, mean, nasty, ornery*, perverse, petulant, spiteful, sulky, sullen, surly, temperamental, tempersome, touchy, unfriendly, unkind, unpleasant; SEE CONCEPTS 401,404

illness [n] *disease; bad health*
affliction, ailing, ailment, attack, breakdown, bug*, collapse, complaint, confinement, convalescence, disability, diseasedness, disorder, disturbance, dose, failing health, fit, flu, ill health, indisposition, infirmity, malady, malaise, poor health, prostration, relapse, seizure, sickness, syndrome, unhealth, virus, what's going around*; SEE CONCEPT 306

illogical [adj] *not making sense*
absurd, casuistic, cockeyed*, fallacious, false, fatuous, faulty, groundless, hollow, implausible, inconclusive, incongruous, inconsequent, inconsistent, incorrect, invalid, irrational, irrelevant, mad, meaningless, not following, nutty*, off the wall*, preposterous, screwy*, self-contradictory, senseless, sophistic, sophistical, specious, spurious, unconnected, unproved, unreasonable, unscientific, unsound, unsubstantial, untenable, wacky, without basis, without foundation; SEE CONCEPTS 267,529

ill-timed [adj] *not occurring at a suitable time*
awkward, badly timed, improper, inappropriate, inconvenient, inept, inopportune, malapropos, mistimed, unbecoming, unbefitting, unfavorable, unseasonable, unseemly, unsuitable, untimely, unwelcome; SEE CONCEPT 548

illuminate [v1] *make light*
brighten, fire, flash, floodlight, highlight, hit with a light*, ignite, illume, illumine, irradiate, kindle, light, lighten, light up, limelight*, spot, spotlight; SEE CONCEPT 624

illuminate [v2] *make clear; educate*
better, clarify, clear up, construe, define, dramatize, edify, elucidate, enlighten, explain, expound, express, finish, give insight, gloss, illustrate, improve, instruct, interpret, perfect, polish, shed light on*, uplight; SEE CONCEPTS 57,285

illumination [n1] *light; making light*
beam, brightening, brightness, brilliance, flame, flash, gleam, lighting, lights, radiance, ray; SEE CONCEPTS 620,624

illumination [n2] *clear understanding*
awareness, clarification, edification, education, enlightenment, information, insight, inspiration, instruction, perception, revelation, teaching; SEE CONCEPTS 274,409

illusion [n] *false appearance; false belief*
apparition, bubble*, chimera, confusion, daydream, deception, déjà vu*, delusion, error, fallacy, false impression, fancy, fantasy, figment of imagination*, fool's paradise*, ghost, hallucination, head trip*, hocus-pocus*, idolism, ignus fatuus, image, invention, make-believe, mirage, misapprehension, misbelief, misconception, misimpression, mockery, myth, optical illusion, paramnesia, phantasm, pipe dream*, rainbow*, seeming, semblance, trip*, virtual reality; SEE CONCEPTS 689,716

illusory/illusive [adj] *deceptive, false*
apparent, blue-sky*, chimerical, deceitful, delusive, delusory, fake, fallacious, fanciful, fantastic, fictional, fictitious, fictive, hallucinatory, ideal, imaginary, misleading, mistaken, ostensible, pseudo*, seeming, semblant, sham*, supposititious, unreal, untrue, visionary, whimsical; SEE CONCEPTS 529,552,582

illustrate [v1] *demonstrate, exemplify*
allegorize, bring home*, clarify, clear, clear up, delineate, depict, disclose, draw a picture*, elucidate, emblematize, embody, emphasize, epitomize, evidence, evince, exhibit, explain, expose, expound, get across*, get over*, highlight, illuminate, imitate, instance, interpret, lay out*, limelight*, make clear, make plain, manifest, mark, mirror, ostend, personify, picture, point up*, portray, proclaim, represent, reveal, show, show and

tell*, spotlight*, symbolize, typify, vivify; SEE CONCEPTS *57,97*

illustrate [*v2*] *explain by drawing, decorating*
adorn, delineate, depict, embellish, illuminate, limn, ornament, paint, picture, portray, represent, sketch; SEE CONCEPTS *57,174*

illustration [*n1*] *demonstration, exemplification*
analogy, case, case history, case in point, clarification, elucidation, example, explanation, for instance, instance, interpretation, model, representative, sample, sampling, specimen; SEE CONCEPTS *268,686*

illustration [*n2*] *drawing, artwork that assists explanation*
adornment, cartoon, decoration, depiction, design, engraving, etching, figure, frontispiece, halftone, image, line drawing, painting, photo, photograph, picture, plate, sketch, snapshot, tailpiece, vignette; SEE CONCEPT *259*

illustrative [*adj*] *explanatory*
allegorical, clarifying, comparative, corroborative, delineative, descriptive, diagrammatic, emblematic, exemplifying, explicatory, expository, figurative, graphic, iconographic, illuminative, illustrational, illustratory, imagistic, indicative, interpretive, metaphoric, pictorial, pictoric, representative, revealing, sample, specifying, symbolic, typical; SEE CONCEPT *267*

illustrious [*adj*] *famous, prominent*
big league*, brilliant, celeb*, celebrated, distinguished, eminent, esteemed, exalted, famed, glorious, great, heavy, lofty, monster*, name*, noble, notable, noted, outstanding, remarkable, renowned, resplendent, signal, splendid, star, sublime, superstar, well-known; SEE CONCEPT *568*

ill will [*n*] *hatred; hard feelings*
acrimony, animosity, animus, antagonism, antipathy, aversion, bad blood*, bad will, blame, despite, dislike, enmity, envy, feud, grudge, hate, hostility, malevolence, malice, maliciousness, no love lost*, objection, rancor, resentment, spite, spitefulness, spleen, unfriendliness, venom; SEE CONCEPT *29*

image [*n1*] *representation; counterpart*
angel*, appearance, carbon*, carbon copy, carved figure, chip off old block*, copy, dead ringer*, double, drawing, effigy, equal, equivalent, facsimile, figure, form, icon, idol, illustration, likeness, match, model, photocopy, photograph, picture, portrait, reflection, replica, reproduction, similitude, simulacre, simulacrum, spitting image*, statue; SEE CONCEPTS *259,667,716*

image [*n2*] *concept*
apprehension, conceit, conception, construct, figure, idea, impression, intellection, mental picture, notion, perception, phantasm, thought, trope, vision; SEE CONCEPTS *529,689*

imaginable [*adj*] *believable, possible*
apprehensible, calculable, comprehensible, conceivable, conjectural, convincing, credible, likely, plausible, sensible, supposable, thinkable, under the sun*; SEE CONCEPTS *529,552*

imaginary [*adj*] *fictitious, invented*
abstract, apocryphal, apparitional, assumed, chimerical, deceptive, delusive, dreamed-up*, dreamlike, dreamy, fabulous, fancied, fanciful, fantastic, fictional, figmental, fool's paradise*, hallucinatory, hypothetical, ideal, illusive, illusory, imaginative, imagined, legendary, made-up*, mythological, nonexistent, notional, phantasmal,

phantasmic, quixotic, shadowy, spectral, supposed, supposititious, theoretical, trumped up*, unreal, unsubstantial, visionary, whimsical; SEE CONCEPTS *529,582*

imagination [*n*] *power to create in one's mind*
acuteness, artistry, awareness, chimera, cognition, conception, creation, creative thought, creativity, enterprise, fabrication, fancy, fantasy, flight of fancy*, idea, ideality, illusion, image, imagery, ingenuity, insight, inspiration, intelligence, invention, inventiveness, mental agility, notion, originality, perceptibility, realization, resourcefulness, sally, supposition, thought, thoughtfulness, unreality, verve, vision, visualization, wit, wittiness; SEE CONCEPTS *409,410*

imaginative [*adj*] *creative, inventive*
artistic, avant-garde, blue-sky*, brain wave, breaking ground, clever, dreamy, enterprising, extravagant, fanciful, fantastic, fertile, fictive, high-flown*, ingenious, inspired, offbeat, original, originative, pie-in-the-sky*, poetic, poetical, productive, quixotic, romantic, utopian, visionary, vivid, way out*, whimsical; SEE CONCEPTS *529,542*

imagine [*v1*] *dream up, conceive*
brainstorm, build castles in air*, conceptualize, conjure up, cook up*, create, depict, devise, envisage, envision, fabricate, fancy, fantasize, fantasy, feature, figure, form, frame, harbor, image, invent, make up, nurture, perceive, picture, plan, project, realize, scheme, see in one's mind*, spark, think of, think up, vision, visualize; SEE CONCEPT *43*

imagine [*v2*] *assume, deduce*
apprehend, believe, conjecture, deem, expect, fancy, gather, guess, infer, presume, realize, reckon, suppose, surmise, suspect, take for granted, take it, think, understand; SEE CONCEPTS *12,26*

imbecile [*n*] *very stupid person*
birdbrain, dimwit, dolt, dummy, dunce, fool, idiot, jerk, lamebrain*, moron, pinhead*, simpleton; SEE CONCEPT *412*

imbecile [*adj*] *stupid, foolish*
asinine, backward, deranged, dim-witted, dull, fatuous, feeble-minded, idiotic, imbecilic, inane, ludicrous, moronic, simple, simple-minded, slow, thick, witless; SEE CONCEPT *402*

imbibe [*v*] *drink, often heavily*
absorb, assimilate, belt*, consume, down, gorge, guzzle*, ingest, ingurgitate, irrigate, partake, put away*, quaff, raise a few*, sip, swallow, swig*, swill*, toss*; SEE CONCEPT *169*

imbroglio [*n*] *misunderstanding; fight*
altercation, argument, bickering, brawl, broil*, brouhaha*, complexity, complication, dispute, embarrassment, embroilment, entanglement, falling-out*, flack*, involvement, knock-down-drag-out*, miff*, quandary, quarrel, row, run-in*, soap opera*, spat, squabble; SEE CONCEPTS *46,106*

imbue [*v*] *infuse, saturate*
bathe, diffuse, impregnate, inculcate, infix, ingrain, inoculate, instill, invest, leaven, permeate, pervade, steep, suffuse; SEE CONCEPTS *209, 236,245*

imitate [*v*] *pretend to be; do an impression of*
act like, affect, ape, assume, be like, borrow, burlesque, carbon*, caricature, clone, copy, counterfeit, ditto*, do like*, do likewise, duplicate, echo,

il
im

emulate, falsify, feign, follow, follow in footsteps*, follow suit*, forge, impersonate, look like, match, mime, mimic, mirror, mock, model after, parallel, parody, pattern after, personate, play a part, pretend, put on*, reduplicate, reflect, repeat, replicate, reproduce, resemble, send up*, sham, simulate, spoof, take off*, travesty, Xerox*; SEE CONCEPTS 87,111,171

imitation [n] *simulation, substitution*

apery, aping, carbon copy, clone, copy, counterfeit, counterfeiting, counterpart, ditto*, dupe*, duplicate, duplication, echoing, ersatz*, fake, forgery, image, impersonation, impression, likeness, match, matching, mime, mimicry, mirroring, mockery, parallel, paralleling, paraphrasing, parody, parroting, patterning, phony, picture, reflection, replica, representing, reproduction, resemblance, ringer, semblance, sham*, simulacrum, takeoff*, transcription, travesty, Xerox*; SEE CONCEPTS 171,260,716

imitative [adj] *simulated, unoriginal*

artful, copied, copycat, copying, counterfeit, deceptive, derivative, echoic, emulative, emulous, following, forged, mimetic, mimic, mimicking, mock, onomatopoeic, parrot*, plagiarized, pseudo*, put-on*, reflecting, reflective, secondhand, sham*, simulant; SEE CONCEPT 582

immaculate [adj1] *very clean; unspoiled*

bright, clean, errorless, exquisite, faultless, flawless, impeccable, irreproachable, neat, pure, snowy*, spick-and-span*, spotless, spruce, stainless, taintless, trim, unexceptionable, unsoiled, unsullied; SEE CONCEPT 621

immaculate [adj2] *innocent, uncorrupted*

above reproach, chaste, clean, decent, faultless, flawless, guiltless, incorrupt, modest, perfect, pure, sinless, spotless, stainless, unblemished, uncontaminated, undefiled, unpolluted, unsullied, untarnished, virtuous; SEE CONCEPTS 404,545

immaterial [adj1] *irrelevant*

extraneous, foreign, impertinent, inapplicable, inapposite, inappropriate, inconsequential, inconsiderable, inconsiderate, inessential, insignificant, irrelative, matter of indifference, meaningless, no big deal*, no never mind*, of no account*, of no consequence*, of no importance*, trifling, trivial, unimportant, unnecessary; SEE CONCEPT 575

immaterial [adj2] *not existing in physical form*

aerial, airy, apparitional, asomatous, bodiless, celestial, disbodied, discarnate, disembodied, dreamlike, dreamy, ethereal, ghostly, heavenly, impalpable, imponderable, incorporate, incorporeal, insensible, intangible, metaphysical, nonmaterial, nonphysical, psychic, shadowy, spectral, spiritlike, spiritual, subjective, supernatural, unearthly, unembodied, unfleshly, unsubstantial, unworldly, wraithlike; SEE CONCEPT 539

immature [adj] *young, inexperienced*

adolescent, baby, babyish, callow, childish, crude, green*, half-grown, imperfect, infantile, infantine, jejune, juvenile, kid, kidstuff*, premature, puerile, raw, sophomoric, tender*, tenderfoot*, underdeveloped, undergrown, undeveloped, unfinished, unfledged, unformed, unripe, unseasonable, unseasoned, unsophisticated, untimely, wet behind ears*, youthful; SEE CONCEPTS 485,578,797

immeasurable [adj] *infinite, incalculable*

alive with, bottomless, boundless, countless, crawling with, endless, extensive, illimitable, immense, indefinite, inestimable, inexhaustible, jillion*, large, limitless, measureless, no end of*, no end to*, umpteen*, unbounded, uncountable, unfathomable, unlimited, unmeasurable, unreckonable, vast, zillion*; SEE CONCEPTS 762, 773,781

immediate [adj1] *instantaneous; without delay*

actual, at once, at present time, at this moment, critical, current, existing, extant, first, hairtrigger*, instant, live, next, now, on hand*, paramount, present, pressing, prompt, up-to-date*, urgent; SEE CONCEPTS 567,585,812,820

immediate [adj2] *near, next*

adjacent, close, contiguous, direct, firsthand, near-at-hand, nearby, nearest, nigh, primary, proximal, proximate, recent; SEE CONCEPTS 586,778

immediately [adv] *at once, right away*

anon, at short notice, away, directly, double-time*, forthwith, hereupon, in a flash*, in a jiffy*, in a New York minute*, in nothing flat*, instantaneously, instanter, instantly, like now*, now, now or never*, on the dot*, on the double*, on the spot*, PDQ*, promptly, pronto*, rapidly, right now, shortly, soon, soon afterward, straight away*, straight off*, summarily, thereupon, this instant, this minute, tout de suite*, unhesitatingly, urgently, without delay, without hesitation; SEE CONCEPTS 544,820

immemorial [adj] *ancient, old*

age-old, archaic, fixed, forever, long-standing, of yore, olden, prehistoric, primeval, rooted, time-honored, traditional; SEE CONCEPTS 578,797,799

immense [adj] *extremely large*

barn door*, boundless, Brobdingnagian*, colossal, elephantine, endless, enormous, eternal, extensive, giant, gigantic, great, gross, huge, humongous, illimitable, immeasurable, infinite, interminable, jumbo*, limitless, mammoth, massive, measureless, mighty, monstrous, monumental, prodigious, stupendous, super, titanic*, tremendous, unbounded, vast; SEE CONCEPT 773

immerse [v1] *submerge in liquid*

asperse, baptize, bathe, bury, christen, dip, douse, drench, drown, duck, dunk, merge, plunge, saturate, sink, slop, soak, souse, sprinkle, steep, submerse; SEE CONCEPT 256

immerse [v2] *become deeply involved*

absorb, busy, engage, engross, interest, involve, occupy, soak, take up; SEE CONCEPTS 17,100

immersed [adj] *deeply involved with*

absorbed, bound-up*, buried*, busy, consumed, deep, eat sleep and breathe*, engaged, engrossed, intent, into*, mesmerized, occupied, preoccupied, rapt, spellbound, taken up*, tied up*, turned on*, wrapped up*; SEE CONCEPT 542

immigrant [n] *person from a foreign land*

adoptive citizen, alien, colonist, documented alien, foreigner, incomer, migrant, naturalized citizen, newcomer, outsider, pioneer, settler, undocumented alien; SEE CONCEPT 413

immigrate [v] *enter a foreign area intending to live there*

arrive, colonize, come in, go in, migrate, settle; SEE CONCEPT 159

imminent [adj] *at hand, on the way*

about to happen, approaching, brewing*, close, coming, expectant, fast-approaching, following, forthcoming, gathering, handwriting-on-the-wall*, immediate, impending, ineluctable, inescapable, inevasible, inevitable, in store*, in the air*, in the cards*, in the offing*, in the wind*, in view*, likely, looming, menacing, near, nearing, next, nigh, on its way, on the horizon, on the verge, overhanging, possible, probable, see it coming*, threatening, to come, unavoidable, unescapable; SEE CONCEPTS 548,820

immobile [adj] *motionless, fixed*
anchored, at a standstill, at rest, frozen, immobilized, immotile, immovable, nailed, nailed down, pat, quiescent, rigid, riveted, rooted, stable, stagnant, static, stationary, steadfast, stiff, still, stock-still, stolid, unmovable, unmoving; SEE CONCEPTS 488,584

immoderate [adj] *excessive, extreme*
dizzying, egregious, enormous, exaggerated, exorbitant, extravagant, inordinate, intemperate, overindulgent, profligate, steep, too much*, too-too*, towering, unbalanced, unbridled, uncalled-for*, unconscionable, uncontrolled, undue, unjustified, unmeasurable, unreasonable, unrestrained, unwarranted, wanton; SEE CONCEPTS 544,569

immoral [adj] *evil, degenerate*
abandoned, bad, corrupt, debauched, depraved, dishonest, dissipated, dissolute, fast*, graceless, impure, indecent, iniquitous, lewd, licentious, loose*, nefarious, obscene, of easy virtue*, pornographic, profligate, rakish, reprobate, saturnalian, shameless, sinful, speedy, unchaste, unclean*, unethical, unprincipled, unscrupulous, vicious, vile, villainous, wicked, wrong, X-rated*; SEE CONCEPT 545

immortal [adj1] *death-defying, imperishable*
abiding, amaranthine, ceaseless, constant, deathless, endless, enduring, eternal, evergreen, everlasting, incorruptible, indestructible, indissoluble, interminable, lasting, never-ceasing, never-ending, perdurable, perennial, permanent, perpetual, phoenixlike, sempiternal, timeless, undying, unfading; SEE CONCEPTS 539,798

immortal [adj2] *famous*
celebrated, eminent, epic, genius, glorious, heroic, illustrious, laureate, paragon, storied; SEE CONCEPT 568

immovable [adj] *fixed, stubborn*
adamant, constant, dead set on*, dug in, fast, firm, hard-nosed, immobile, immotile, immutable, impassive, inflexible, intransigent, locked in*, motionless, obdurate, quiescent, resolute, rooted, secure, set, set in concrete*, set in stone*, solid, stable, stand pat*, stationary, steadfast, stick to guns*, stuck, tough nut*, unalterable, unchangeable, uncompromising, unmodifiable, unshakable, unwavering, unyielding; SEE CONCEPTS 404,488,534

immune [adj] *invulnerable*
allowed, clear, exempt, favored, free, hardened to, insusceptible, irresponsible, licensed, not affected, not liable, not subject, privileged, protected, resistant, safe, unaffected, unanswerable, unliable, unsusceptible; SEE CONCEPTS 314,552

immunity [n] *privilege, exemption*
amnesty, charter, exoneration, franchise, freedom, impunity, indemnity, invulnerability, liberty, license, prerogative, protection, release, resistance, right; SEE CONCEPTS 316,376,388

immutable [adj] *unchangeable*
abiding, ageless, changeless, constant, enduring, fixed, immovable, inflexible, invariable, perma-

nent, perpetual, sacrosanct, stable, steadfast, unalterable, unmodifiable; SEE CONCEPT 534

imp [n] *mischievous child, small person*
brat, demon, devil, deviling, devilkin, elf, fiend, gamin, gnome, gremlin, hellion, minx, pixie, puck, rascal, rogue, scamp, sprite, troll, tyke, urchin, villain; SEE CONCEPT 412

impact [n1] *collision, force*
appulse, bang, blow, bounce, brunt, buffet, bump, clash, concussion, contact, crash, crunch, crush, encounter, hit, impingement, jar, jolt, jounce, kick, knock, meeting, percussion, pound, punch, quake, quiver, ram, rap, rock, shake, shock, slap, smash, smashup, strike, stroke, thump, tremble, tremor, wallop; SEE CONCEPTS 189,641

impact [n2] *effect*
brunt, burden, consequences, full force, impression, imprint, influence, mark, meaning, power, repercussion, significance, thrust, weight; SEE CONCEPT 230

impact [v] *hit with force*
bang into, clash, collide, crack up, crash, crush, jolt, kick, register, smash, smash up, strike, wrack up*; SEE CONCEPT 189

impair [v] *harm, hinder*
blemish, blunt, cheapen, debase, debilitate, decrease, destroy, deteriorate, devaluate, devalue, diminish, ding*, disqualify, enervate, enfeeble, hurt, injure, invalidate, lessen, lose strength, make useless, mar, prejudice, queer, reduce, rough up*, spoil, tarnish, total, tweak, undermine, unfit, vitiate, weaken, worsen; SEE CONCEPTS 130,240,246

impaired [adj] *injured, faulty*
broken, busted, damaged, debilitated, defective, down*, flawed, harmed, hurt, imperfect, kaput*, marred, on the blink*, on the fritz*, spoiled, unsound; SEE CONCEPTS 485,560

impale [v] *stab*
lance, perforate, pierce, prick, punch, puncture, run through, skewer, skiver, spear, spike, stick, transfix; SEE CONCEPT 220

impalpable [adj] *intangible, unsubstantial*
airy, delicate, disembodied, fine, imperceptible, imponderable, imprecise, inappreciable, incorporeal, indiscernible, indistinct, insensible, insubstantial, nebulous, shadowy, tenuous, thin, unapparent, unobservable, unperceivable, vague; SEE CONCEPTS 485,529,619

impart [v1] *make known*
admit, announce, break, communicate, convey, disclose, discover, divulge, expose, inform, pass on, publish, relate, reveal, tell, transmit; SEE CONCEPT 60

impart [v2] *give*
accord, afford, allow, bestow, cede, confer, contribute, grant, lead, offer, part with, present, relinquish, render, yield; SEE CONCEPT 108

impartial [adj] *fair, unprejudiced*
candid, detached, disinterested, dispassionate, equal, equitable, evenhanded, fair-minded, impersonal, just, middle-of-the-road*, neutral, nondiscriminating, nondiscriminatory, nonpartisan, objective, on-the-fence, open-minded, unbiased, unbigoted, uncolored, unslanted, without favor; SEE CONCEPTS 403,542

impasse [n] *stalemate*
box*, Catch-22*, cessation, corner*, cul-de-sac*, dead end, deadlock, dilemma, fix, gridlock, jam, mire*, morass*, pause, pickle*, plight, predica-

ment, quandary, rest, scrape*, standoff, standstill;
SEE CONCEPT *674*

impassioned [*adj*] *excited, vehement*
animated, ardent, blazing, burning, deep, fervent,
fervid, fierce, fiery, fired up*, flaming, furious,
glowing, heated*, hot-blooded*, inflamed, inspired, intense, melodramatic, moving, mushy,
overemotional, passionate, perfervid, powerful,
profound, red-hot*, romantic, rousing, sentimental, starry-eyed*, steamed up*, stirring, torrid, violent, vivid, warm, white-hot*, wild about,
worked up*, zealous; SEE CONCEPT *403*

impassive [*adj*] *aloof, cool*
apathetic, callous, cold, cold-blooded*, collected,
composed, dispassionate, dry, emotionless, hardened, heartless, imperturbable, indifferent, indurated, inexplicable, inexpressive, inscrutable,
insensible, insusceptible, matter-of-fact, nonchalant, passionless, phlegmatic, placid, poker-
faced*, reserved, reticent, sedate, self-contained,
serene, spiritless, stoic, stoical, stolid, taciturn,
unconcerned, unemotional, unexcitable, unfeeling, unflappable, unimpressible, unmoved, unruffled, wooden; SEE CONCEPTS *404,542*

impatience [*n*] *inability, unwillingness to wait*
agitation, anger, annoyance, ants in pants*,
anxiety, avidity, disquietude, eagerness, edginess,
excitement, expectancy, fretfulness, haste, hastiness, heat*, impetuosity, intolerance, irritability,
irritableness, nervousness, quick temper, rashness, restiveness, restlessness, shortness, snappi-
ness, suspense, uneasiness, vehemence, violence;
SEE CONCEPTS *633,657*

impatient [*adj*] *unable, unwilling to wait*
abrupt, agog, antsy, anxious, appetent, ardent,
athirst, avid, breathless, brusque, chafing, choleric, curt, demanding, dying to*, eager, edgy,
feverish, fretful, hasty, having short fuse*, headlong, hot-tempered, hot under collar*, impetuous,
indignant, intolerant, irascible, irritable, itchy,
keen, on pins and needles*, quick-tempered, racing one's motor*, restless, ripe*, snappy, straining, sudden, testy, thirsty, unforbearing,
unindulgent, vehement, violent; SEE CONCEPTS
401,542

impeach [*v*] *denounce, censure*
accuse, arraign, blame, bring charges against, call
into question, call to account, cast aspersions on,
cast doubt on, challenge, charge, criminate, criticize, discredit, disparage, hold at fault, impugn,
incriminate, inculpate, indict, query, question,
reprehend, reprimand, reprobate, tax, try; SEE
CONCEPTS *44,52,317*

impeccable [*adj*] *above suspicion; flawless*
accurate, aces, A-okay*, apple-pie*, clean, correct, errorless, exact, exquisite, faultless, fleck-
less, immaculate, incorrupt, infallible, innocent,
irreproachable, nice, note-perfect, on target*, perfect, precise, pure, right, sinless, stainless, ten*,
unblemished, unerring, unflawed, unimpeachable;
SEE CONCEPTS *535,574,621*

impecunious [*adj*] *poverty-stricken*
beggared, broke*, cleaned out*, destitute, dirt
poor*, homeless, impoverished, indigent, insolvent, necessitous, needy, penniless, penurious,
poor, strapped*, unprosperous; SEE CONCEPT *334*

impede [*v*] *obstruct, hinder*
bar, block, blow whistle on*, brake, check, clog,
close off, cramp one's style*, curb, cut off, dam,
delay, deter, discomfit, disconcert, disrupt, em-

barrass, faze, flag one*, freeze, hamper, hang up,
hold up, interfere, oppose, rattle, restrain, retard,
saddle with*, shut down, shut off, slow, slow
down, stonewall*, stop, stymie, thwart; SEE CON-
CEPTS *121,130*

impediment [*n*] *obstruction, hindrance*
bar, barricade, barrier, block, blockage, bottleneck*, burden, catch*, Catch-22*, chain, check,
clog, cramp, curb, dead weight*, defect, delay,
deterrent, detriment, difficulty, disadvantage,
drag*, drawback, encumbrance, fault, flaw, handicap, hazard, hitch, holdup, hurdle, inhibition,
load, manacle, millstone*, obstacle, prohibition,
red tape*, restraint, restriction, retardation, retard-
ment, road block*, rub*, setback, shackle, snag,
stoppage, stricture, stumbling block*, tie, trammel, wall; SEE CONCEPT *666*

impel [*v*] *prompt, incite*
actuate, boost, compel, constrain, drive, excite,
foment, force, goad, induce, influence, inspire,
instigate, jog, lash, mobilize, motivate, move,
oblige, poke, power, press, prod, propel, push,
require, set in motion, shove, spur, start, stimulate, thrust, urge; SEE CONCEPTS *14,68,221,242*

impending [*adj*] *forthcoming*
approaching, at hand, brewing, coming, gathering, handwriting-on-the-wall*, hovering, imminent, in the cards*, in the offing*, in the wind*,
looking to*, looming, menacing, near, nearing,
ominous, on the horizon*, overhanging, portending, proximate, see it coming*, threatening, waiting to; SEE CONCEPTS *548,820*

impenetrable [*adj1*] *dense*
bulletproof, close, compact, firm, hard, hermetic,
impassable, impermeable, impervious, inviolable,
solid, substantial, thick, unpierceable; SEE CON-
CEPTS *483,604*

impenetrable [*adj2*] *incomprehensible*
arcane, baffling, cabalistic, dark, Delphic, enigmatic, enigmatical, hidden, incognizable, indiscernible, inexplicable, inscrutable, mysterious,
mystic, obscure, sibylline, unaccountable, unfathomable, ungraspable, unintelligible, unknowable;
SEE CONCEPTS *529,576*

imperative [*adj1*] *necessary*
acute, burning, clamant, clamorous, compulsory,
critical, crucial, crying, essential, exigent, immediate, important, importunate, indispensable, inescapable, insistent, instant, no turning back*,
obligatory, pressing, urgent, vital; SEE CONCEPT
546

imperative [*adj2*] *authoritative*
aggressive, autocratic, bidding, bossy, commanding, dictatorial, dominant, domineering, harsh,
high-handed, imperial, imperious, ordering, overbearing, peremptory, powerful, stern; SEE CON-
CEPTS *267,574*

imperceptible [*adj*] *hard to sense; faint*
ephemeral, evanescent, fine, gradual, impalpable,
imponderable, inappreciable, inaudible, inconsiderable, inconspicuous, indiscernible, indistinct,
indistinguishable, infinitesimal, insensible, insignificant, invisible, microscopic, minute, momentary, shadowy, slight, small, subtle, tiny, trivial,
undetectable, unnoticeable, vague; SEE CONCEPTS
406,537

imperfect [*adj*] *flawed*
amiss, below par, bottom-of-barrel*, broken,
damaged, defective, deficient, disfigured, dud*,
faulty, few bugs*, garbage*, immature, impaired,

incomplete, inexact, injured, junk*, lemon*, limited, low, marred, minus, partial, patchy, rudimentary, schlocky*, sick, sketchy, two-bit*, undeveloped, unfinished, unsound, vicious, warped; SEE CONCEPTS 570,574,579

imperfection [n] *flaw*

blemish, bug*, catch, defect, deficiency, deformity, demerit, disfigurement, failing, fallibility, fault, foible, frailty, glitch*, gremlin*, inadequacy, incompleteness, infirmity, insufficiency, peccadillo, problem, shortcoming, sin, stain, taint, weakness, weak point; SEE CONCEPTS 230,671,718

imperil [v] *cause to be in danger*

chance it, compromise, endanger, expose, hazard, jeopard, jeopardize, jeopardy, menace, peril, risk; SEE CONCEPT 240

imperious [adj] *bossy, overbearing*

arrogant, authoritative, autocratic, commanding, compulsory, despotic, dictatorial, domineering, exacting, haughty, high-handed, imperative, imperial, mandatory, obligatory, oppressive, overweening, peremptory, required, tyrannical, tyrannous; SEE CONCEPTS 267,574

impersonal [adj] *cold, unfriendly*

abstract, bureaucratic, businesslike, candid, cold-blooded*, cold turkey*, colorless, cool, detached, disinterested, dispassionate, emotionless, equal, equitable, fair, formal, impartial, indifferent, inhuman, neutral, nondiscriminatory, objective, poker-faced*, remote, straight, strictly business*, unbiased, uncolored, unpassioned; SEE CONCEPTS 401,542,544

impersonate [v] *pretend to be another*

act, act a part, act like, act out, ape, assume character, ditto*, do, do an impression of, double as, dress as, enact, fake, imitate, make like*, masquerade as, mimic, mirror, pass oneself off as*, perform, personate, play, playact, play a role, portray, pose as, put on an act*, represent, take the part of; SEE CONCEPTS 59,292

impertinence [n] *boldness*

assurance, audacity, backchat, back talk*, brazenness, cheek*, chutzpah*, come-back*, crust*, disrespect, disrespectfulness, effrontery, forwardness, freshness, gall, guff, hardihood, impropriety, impudence, incivility, insolence, insolency, lip*, nerve, pertness, presumption, rudeness, sass*, smart mouth*, wisecrack*, wise guy*; SEE CONCEPT 633

impertinent [adj] *bold, disrespectful*

arrogant, brash, brassy*, brazen, contumelious, discourteous, disgracious, flip*, forward, fresh, ill-mannered, impolite, impudent, inappropriate, incongruous, inquisitive, insolent, interfering, intrusive, lippy*, meddlesome, meddling, nosy*, off base*, offensive, out of line*, pert, presumptuous, procacious, prying, rude, sassy*, smart, smart alecky*, uncalled-for*, uncivil, ungracious, unmannerly, unsuitable; SEE CONCEPT 401

imperturbable [adj] *calm, collected*

assured, complacent, composed, cool, cool as cucumber*, dispassionate, equanimous, hard as nails*, immovable, nerveless, nonchalant, roll with punches*, sedate, self-possessed, self-satisfied, smug, stiff upper lip*, stoical, thick-skinned, tranquil, unaffected, undisturbed, unexcitable, unflappable, unmoved, unruffled, untouched; SEE CONCEPT 404

impervious [adj] *unable to be penetrated*

closed to, hermetic, immune, impassable, impassive, impenetrable, impermeable, imperviable, inaccessible, invulnerable, resistant, sealed, tight, unaffected, unapproachable, unmoved, unpierceable, unreceptive, watertight; SEE CONCEPTS 485,534,604

impetuous [adj] *acting without thinking*

abrupt, ardent, eager, fervid, fierce, furious, going off deep end*, hasty, headlong, hurried, impassioned, impulsive, passionate, precipitant, precipitate, precipitous, rash, restive, rushing, spontaneous, spur-of-the-moment, subitaneous, sudden, swift, unbridled, unexpected, unplanned, unpremeditated, unreflecting, unrestrained, unthinking, vehement, violent; SEE CONCEPTS 404,542

impetus [n] *stimulus, force*

catalyst, energy, goad, impulse, impulsion, incentive, incitation, incitement, momentum, motivation, power, pressure, push, spur, stimulant, urge; SEE CONCEPTS 641,661

impinge [v] *trespass*

affect, bear upon, disturb, encroach, influence, infringe, intrude, invade, make inroads, meddle, obtrude, pry, touch, violate; SEE CONCEPTS 14,156

impious [adj] *not religious*

agnostic, apostate, atheistic, blasphemous, canting, contrary, deceitful, defiling, desecrating, desecrative, diabolic, disobedient, disrespectful, godless, hardened, hypocritical, iconoclastic, immoral, iniquitous, irreligious, irreverent, perverted, pietistical, profane, recusant, reprobate, sacrilegious, sanctimonious, satanic, scandalous, sinful, unctuous, undutiful, unethical, unfaithful, ungodly, unhallowed, unholy, unregenerate, unrighteous, unsanctified, wayward, wicked; SEE CONCEPT 545

impish [adj] *mischievous*

casual, devilish, devil-may-care*, elfin, elvish, fiendish, flippant, free and easy*, fresh, frolicsome, giddy, jaunty, naughty, offhand, pert, pixieish, playful, prankish, puckish, rascally, saucy*, sportive, waggish; SEE CONCEPT 401

implacable [adj] *merciless, cruel*

grim, inexorable, inflexible, intractable, iron-fisted, mortal, pitiless, rancorous, relentless, remorseless, ruthless, unappeasable, unbending, uncompromising, unflinching, unforgiving, unrelenting, unyielding, vindictive; SEE CONCEPT 542

implausible [adj] *not likely*

doubtful, dubious, farfetched, far out*, fishy*, flimsy, for the birds*, full of holes*, impossible, improbable, inconceivable, incredible, obscure, problematic, puzzling, reachy, suspect, thin*, too much*, unbelievable, unconvincing, unreasonable, unsubstantial, weak, won't hold water*, won't wash*; SEE CONCEPT 552

implement [n] *agent, tool*

apparatus, appliance, contraption, contrivance, device, equipment, gadget, instrument, machine, utensil; SEE CONCEPT 499

implement [v] *start, put into action*

achieve, actualize, bring about, carry out, complete, effect, enable, enforce, execute, fulfill, invoke, make good*, make possible, materialize, perform, provide the means, put into effect, realize, resolve; SEE CONCEPTS 91,99,221

im
im

implicate [v] *imply, involve*
accuse, affect, associate, blame, charge, cite, compromise, concern, connect, embroil, entangle, frame, hint, impute, include, incriminate, inculpate, insinuate, lay at one's door*, link, mean, mire, name, pin on*, point finger at*, relate, stigmatize, suggest, tangle*; SEE CONCEPTS **44,112**

implication [n] *association, suggestion*
assumption, conclusion, connection, connotation, entanglement, guess, hint, hypothesis, incrimination, indication, inference, innuendo, intimation, involvement, link, meaning, overtone, presumption, ramification, reference, significance, signification, undertone, union; SEE CONCEPTS **28,39,278**

implicit [adj] *included without question, inherent, absolute*
accurate, certain, complete, constant, constructive, contained, definite, entire, firm, fixed, full, implicative, implied, inarticulate, inevitable, inferential, inferred, latent, practical, steadfast, tacit, taken for granted, total, undeclared, understood, unexpressed, unhesitating, unqualified, unquestioned, unreserved, unsaid, unshakable, unspoken, unuttered, virtual, wholehearted; SEE CONCEPTS **267,535,549**

implied [adj] *hinted at*
adumbrated, alluded to, allusive, connoted, constructive, figured, foreshadowed, hidden, implicit, indicated, indicative, indirect, inferential, inferred, inherent, insinuated, intended, involved, latent, lurking, meant, occult, parallel, perceptible, potential, significative, signified, suggested, symbolized, tacit, tacitly assumed, undeclared, understood, unexpressed, unsaid, unspoken, unuttered, wordless; SEE CONCEPTS **267,535**

implore [v] *beg*
appeal, beseech, conjure, crave, entreat, go on bended knee*, importune, plead, pray, solicit, supplicate, urge; SEE CONCEPT **48**

imply [v] *indicate, mean*
betoken, connote, denote, designate, entail, evidence, give a hint, hint, import, include, insinuate, intend, intimate, involve, mention, point to, presuppose, refer, signify, suggest; SEE CONCEPTS **75,97,682**

impolite [adj] *having bad manners*
bad-mannered, boorish, churlish, crude, discourteous, disgracious, disrespectful, ill-bred, ill-mannered, indecorous, indelicate, insolent, irritable, loutish, moody, oafish, rough, rude, sullen, uncivil, ungracious, unmannered, unmannerly, unrefined; SEE CONCEPT **401**

impolitic [adj] *unwise, careless*
brash, ill-advised, ill-judged, imprudent, inadvisable, inconsiderate, indiscreet, inexpedient, injudicious, maladroit, misguided, rash, stupid, tactless, undiplomatic, untimely; SEE CONCEPTS **401,544**

import [n1] *meaning*
acceptation, bearing, bottom line*, construction, drift*, gist*, heart*, implication, intendment, intention, interpretation, meat*, message, name of the game*, nature of beast*, nuts and bolts*, point, punch line*, purport, score*, sense, significance, significancy, signification, stuff*, thrust, understanding; SEE CONCEPT **682**

import [n2] *significance, weight*
consequence, design, emphasis, importance, intent, magnitude, moment, momentousness, object, objective, pith, purpose, signification, stress, substance, value, weightiness, worth; SEE CONCEPTS **346,668**

importance [n1] *significance, weight*
accent, attention, bearing, caliber, concern, concernment, consequence, denotation, distinction, drift*, effect, emphasis, force, gist*, gravity, import, influence, interest, materiality, moment, momentousness, notability, paramountcy, point, precedence, preponderance, preponderancy, priority, purport, relevance, sense, seriousness, signification, standing, stress, substance, tenor, usefulness, value, weightiness; SEE CONCEPTS **346,668,682**

importance [n2] *prominence, standing*
consequence, conspicuousness, distinction, eminence, esteem, fame, greatness, influence, lionization, mark, notability, note, noteworthiness, rank, reputation, salience, status, usefulness, worth; SEE CONCEPTS **388,671**

important [adj1] *valuable, substantial*
big, big-league*, chief, considerable, conspicuous, critical, crucial, decisive, determining, earnest, essential, esteemed, exceptional, exigent, extensive, far-reaching, foremost, front-page*, grave, great, heavy, imperative, importunate, influential, large, marked, material, mattering much, meaningful, momentous, necessary, of moment, of note, of substance, paramount, ponderous, pressing, primary, principal, relevant, salient, serious, signal, significant, something, standout, urgent, vital, weighty; SEE CONCEPT **567**

important [adj2] *eminent, influential, outstanding*
aristocratic, big-time*, distinctive, distinguished, effective, esteemed, extraordinary, famous, first-class*, foremost, four-star*, front-page*, grand, heavy*, high-level, high profile, high-ranking, high-up, honored, illustrious, imposing, incomparable, leading, majestic, major-league*, noble, notable, noted, noteworthy, of note, page-one*, potent, powerful, preeminent, prominent, remarkable, seminal, signal, solid, superior, talented, top-drawer*, top-notch*, upper-class, VIP*, well-known; SEE CONCEPTS **555,574**

imported [adj] *brought in from another place*
alien, carried, choice, exotic, ferried, foreign, introduced, rare, sent, shipped, transported, trucked; SEE CONCEPT **549**

importunate [adj] *demanding, insistent*
burning, clamant, clamorous, crying, disturbing, dogged, earnest, exigent, harassing, imperative, instant, overly solicitous, persevering, persistent, pertinacious, pressing, solicitous, troublesome, urgent; SEE CONCEPTS **267,401**

importune [v] *demand, insist*
appeal, ask, badger, beg, beseech, beset, besiege, con*, crave, dun, egg on*, entreat, goose*, harass, hound*, implore, invoke, nag, persuade, pester, plague, plead, pray, press, sell, solicit, supplicate, urge, work on*; SEE CONCEPT **53**

impose [v] *set, dictate*
appoint, burden, charge, command, compel, constrain, decree, demand, encroach, enforce, enjoin, establish, exact, fix, foist, force, force upon, horn in, inflict, infringe, institute, introduce, intrude, lade, lay, lay down, lay down the law, levy, move in on, oblige, obtrude, ordain, order, place, prescribe, presume, promulgate, put, put foot down*, read riot act*, require, saddle*, take advantage,

trespass, visit, wish, wreak, wreck; SEE CONCEPTS 18,53,133

imposing [adj] *impressive*

august, big, commanding, dignified, effective, exciting, grand, grandiose, imperial, magnificent, majestic, massive, mega*, mind-blowing*, monumental, moving, noble, ominous, one for the book*, overblown, overwhelming, pretentious, regal, royal, something else*, something to write home about*, stately, stirring, striking, towering; SEE CONCEPTS 537,574,773

imposition [n1] *deception*

artifice, cheating, con, craftiness, dissimulation, fraud, hoax, hocus-pocus*, hypocrisy, illusion, imposture, stratagem, trick, trickery; SEE CONCEPTS 59,645

imposition [n2] *burden*

charge, command, constraint, demand, drag, duty, encroachment, encumbrance, intrusion, levy, pain, pain in the neck*, pressure, presumption, restraint, tax; SEE CONCEPTS 14,130

impossible [adj1] *beyond the bounds of possibility*

absurd, beyond, contrary to reason, cureless, futile, hardly possible, hopeless, hundred-to-one*, impassable, impervious, impracticable, impractical, inaccessible, inconceivable, inexecutable, infeasible, insurmountable, irrealizable, irreparable, no go*, not a prayer*, no-way*, no-win*, out of the question*, preposterous, too much, unachievable, unattainable, uncorrectable, unfeasible, unimaginable, unobtainable, unreasonable, unrecoverable, unthinkable, unworkable, useless, visionary, way out; SEE CONCEPT 552

impossible [adj2] *intolerable, ungovernable*

absurd, egregious, hopeless, improper, incongruous, ludicrous, objectionable, offensive, outrageous, preposterous, unacceptable, unanswerable, undesirable, unreasonable, unsuitable; SEE CONCEPT 401

impostor [n] *person pretending to be something else*

actor, beguiler, bluffer, charlatan, cheat, con artist, deceiver, empiric, fake, faker, four-flusher*, fraud, hypocrite, imitator, impersonator, masquerader, mimic, mocker, mountebank, pettifogger, phony, pretender, pseudo, quack, scorner, sham, sharper, shyster, trickster; SEE CONCEPT 412

imposture [n] *fraud, trick*

artifice, cheat, con, copy, counterfeit, deceit, deception, fabrication, fake, feint, fiddle, flimflam*, forgery, gambit, hoax, hocus-pocus*, illusion, imitation, impersonation, imposition, make-believe, maneuver, masquerade, phony, ploy, pretense, pretension, put-on*, quackery, ruse, sell*, sham, sleight, spoof, stratagem, swindle, wile; SEE CONCEPTS 59,192,645,674

impotent [adj] *disabled; unable to perform action*

barren, crippled, dud, effete, enervated, enfeebled, feeble, forceless, frail, gutless, helpless, inadequate, incapable, incapacitated, incompetent, ineffective, ineffectual, inept, infecund, infirm, nerveless, paper tiger*, paralyzed, powerless, prostrate, sterile, unfruitful, unproductive, weak; SEE CONCEPT 485

impoverished [adj] *poor, exhausted*

bankrupt, barren, beggared, broke, clean, depleted, destitute, distressed, drained, empty, flat*, flat broke*, have-not*, hurting, impecunious, indigent, insolvent, necessitous, needy, penurious,

played out*, poverty-stricken, reduced, ruined, spent, sterile, strapped; SEE CONCEPTS 334,560

impractical/impracticable [adj] *unrealistic*

abstract, absurd, chimerical, idealistic, illogical, impossible, impracticable, improbable, inapplicable, inefficacious, infeasible, inoperable, irrealizable, ivory-tower*, no-go*, nonfunctional, nonviable, not a prayer*, otherworldly, out of the question*, quixotic, romantic, speculative, starry-eyed*, theoretical, unattainable, unbusinesslike, unfeasible, unreal, unserviceable, unusable, unwise, unworkable, useless, visionary, wild, won't fly*; SEE CONCEPT 552

impregnate [v] *infuse, fill; make pregnant*

charge, conceive, drench, fecundate, fertilize, imbrue, implant, inoculate, inseminate, leaven, overflow, percolate, permeate, pervade, procreate, produce, reproduce, saturate, seethe, soak, sodden, souse, steep, suffuse, transfuse; SEE CONCEPTS 179,375

impress [v1] *influence*

affect, arouse, awe, be conspicuous, blow away*, buffalo*, bulldoze*, carry, electrify, enforce, enthuse, excite, faze, galvanize, get*, grab, grandstand*, inspire, kill*, knock out*, make a hit*, make an impression, make splash*, move, overawe, pique, provoke, push around*, register, score, show off, slay*, stimulate, stir, strike, sway, thrill, touch*; SEE CONCEPTS 7,19,22,261

impress [v2] *press down to make design*

carve, dent, emboss, engrave, etch, imprint, indent, inscribe, mark, print, stamp; SEE CONCEPT 174

impress [v3] *emphasize*

bring home*, drive home*, establish, fix, get into head*, inculcate, instill, press, set, stress; SEE CONCEPT 49

impression [n1] *influence*

consequence, effect, feeling, impact, reaction, response, result, sway; SEE CONCEPT 230

impression [n2] *feeling, idea*

apprehension, belief, conceit, concept, conception, conjecture, conviction, fancy, feel, hunch, image, inkling, intellection, memory, notion, opinion, perception, recollection, sensation, sense, supposition, suspicion, theory, thought, view; SEE CONCEPTS 529,689

impression [n3] *design made by pressing*

brand, cast, dent, depression, dint, fingerprint, footprint, form, hollow, impress, imprint, indentation, mark, matrix, mold, outline, pattern, print, sign, spoor, stamp, stamping, trace, track, vestige; SEE CONCEPTS 284,625

impression [n4] *pretending to be somebody*

imitation, impersonation, masquerade, parody, sendup, takeoff; SEE CONCEPT 263

impressionable [adj] *easily taught; gullible*

affectable, affected, feeling, impressible, influenceable, ingenuous, open, perceptive, plastic*, receptive, responsive, sensible, sensile, sensitive, sentient, suggestible, susceptive, vulnerable, wax-like; SEE CONCEPTS 402,403

impressive [adj] *powerful, influential*

absorbing, affecting, arresting, august, awe-inspiring, consequential, cool*, deep*, dramatic, effective, eloquent, excited, exciting, extraordinary, forcible, grand, impassioned, important, imposing, inspiring, intense, lavish, luxurious, majestic, massive, momentous, monumental, moving, noble, notable, penetrating, prime*, pro-

im
im

found, remarkable, rousing, splendid, stately, stirring, striking, sumptuous, superb, thrilling, touching, towering, vital, well-done; SEE CONCEPTS 574,773

imprint [n] *impression; symbol*
banner, dent, design, effect, emblem, heading, impress, indentation, influence, mark, name, print, sign, signature, stamp, trace, trademark; SEE CONCEPTS 284,625

imprint [v] *stamp*
designate, engrave, establish, etch, fix, impress, inscribe, mark, offset, print; SEE CONCEPT 174

imprison [v] *confine; put in jail*
apprehend, bastille, bottle up*, cage, check, circumscribe, closet, commit, constrain, curb, detain, fence in, hold, hold captive, hold hostage, hold in custody, ice*, immure, impound, incarcerate, intern, jail, keep, keep captive, keep in custody, limit, lock in, lock up, nab*, occlude, pen, put away, put behind bars, rail in, remand, restrain, send to prison, send up*, shut in, stockade, take prisoner, trammel; SEE CONCEPTS 90,191,317

improbable [adj] *not likely*
doubtful, dubious, fanciful, far-fetched, flimsy*, hundred-to-one*, iffy*, implausible, inconceivable, not expected, outside chance*, questionable, rare, slim, slim and none*, unbelievable, uncertain, unconvincing, unheard of, unimaginable, unlikely, unsubstantial, weak; SEE CONCEPT 552

impromptu [adj/adv] *unrehearsed, improvised*
ad-lib*, dashed off, extemporaneous, extempore, extemporized, fake, faked, improv*, improviso, offhand, off the cuff*, played by ear*, shot from the hip*, spontaneous, spur-of-the-moment, thrown off*, tossed off*, unpremeditated, unprepared, unscripted, unstudied, vamped, whipped up*, winged*; SEE CONCEPT 267

improper [adj1] *not suitable*
abnormal, at odds, awkward, bad form, discordant, discrepant, erroneous, false, ill-advised, ill-timed, imprudent, inaccurate, inadmissible, inadvisable, inapplicable, inapposite, inappropriate, inapt, incongruous, incorrect, inexpedient, infelicitous, inharmonious, inopportune, irregular, ludicrous, malapropos, odd, off-base*, out-of-place*, out-of-season*, preposterous, unapt, unbefitting, uncalled-for*, uncomely, undue, unfit, unfitting, unseasonable, unsuitable, unsuited, untimely, unwarranted, wrong; SEE CONCEPT 558

improper [adj2] *vulgar, immoral*
blue*, dirty, impolite, indecent, indecorous, indelicate, lewd, malodorous, naughty, risqué, rough, salacious, suggestive, unbecoming, unconventional, unequitable, unethical, ungodly, unjust, unrighteous, unright ful, unseemly, untoward, wrong, wrongful; SEE CONCEPTS 542,545

impropriety [n] *bad taste, mistake*
barbarism, blunder, faux pas, gaffe, gaucherie, goof*, immodesty, impudence, incongruity, incorrectness, indecency, indecorum, inelegance, rudeness, slip*, solecism, unseemliness, unsuitability, vulgarism, vulgarity; SEE CONCEPTS 101,278,674

improve [v] *make or become better*
advance, ameliorate, amend, augment, better, boost, civilize, come around*, convalesce, correct, cultivate, develop, doctor up*, edit, elevate, emend, enhance, gain ground*, help, increase, lift, look up*, make strides, meliorate, mend, perk

up*, pick up*, polish, progress, promote, purify, raise, rally, recover, rectify, recuperate, refine, reform, revamp, revise, rise, set right*, shape up*, sharpen, skyrocket*, straighten out*, take off*, touch up*, turn the corner*, update, upgrade; SEE CONCEPTS 244,700

improvement [n] *bettering; something bettered*
advance, advancement, amelioration, amendment, augmentation, betterment, change, civilization, correction, cultivation, development, elevation, enhancement, enrichment, furtherance, gain, growth, increase, preferment, progress, progression, promotion, rally, reclamation, recovery, rectification, reformation, regeneration, renovation, revision, rise, upbeat, upgrade, upswing; SEE CONCEPTS 230,700

improvident [adj] *careless, spendthrift*
extravagant, heedless, imprudent, inconsiderate, lavish, negligent, prodigal, profligate, profuse, reckless, shiftless, shortsighted, thoughtless, thriftless, uneconomical, unthrifty, wasteful; SEE CONCEPTS 334,542

improvise [v] *make up*
ad-lib, brainstorm, coin, concoct, contrive, dash off*, devise, do offhand, do off top of head*, dream up, extemporize, fake, fake it, improv*, improvisate, invent, jam*, knock off*, make do*, slapdash*, spark, speak off the cuff*, throw together*, wing it*; SEE CONCEPTS 173,266

improvised [adj] *made-up*
ad-lib, autoschediastic, Band-Aid*, extemporaneous, extempore, extemporized, fly-by-night*, hit-or-miss*, impromptu, improviso, makeshift, offhand, spontaneous, spur-of-the-moment*, unprepared, unrehearsed, unstudied; SEE CONCEPTS 267,589

imprudent [adj] *without much thought*
brash, careless, foolhardy, foolish, heedless, ill-advised, ill-considered, ill-judged, impolitic, improvident, incautious, inconsiderate, indiscreet, inexpedient, injudicious, irresponsible, leaving self wide open*, off the deep end*, overhasty, playing with fire*, rash, reckless, temerarious, thoughtless, unadvisable, unthinking, unwise; SEE CONCEPTS 267,542

impudent [adj] *bold, shameless*
arrant, audacious, barefaced, blatant, boldfaced, brassy, brazen, bumptious, cheeky*, cocky*, contumelious, cool*, flip*, forward, fresh, immodest, impertinent, insolent, nervy*, off-base*, overbold, pert, presumptuous, procacious, rude, sassy*, saucy*, smart*, smart-alecky*, unabashed, unblushing, wise*; SEE CONCEPT 401

impugn [v] *criticize, challenge*
assail, attack, blast, break, call into question, cast aspersions upon, cast doubt upon, come down on*, contradict, contravene, cross, cut to shreds*, deny, disaffirm, dispute, gainsay, knock*, negate, negative, oppose, pin something on*, put down*, question, resist, run down, skin alive*, slam*, smear*, stick it to*, swipe at*, tar*, throw doubt on, throw the book at*, thumb nose at*, traduce, trash, traverse, zap*, zing*; SEE CONCEPTS 52,58

impulse [n1] *drive, resolve*
actuation, appeal, bent, caprice, catalyst, desire, disposition, excitant, extemporization, fancy, feeling, flash*, goad, hunch, impellent, impulsion, incitation, incitement, inclination, influence, inspiration, instinct, itch*, lash, lust, mind, motivation, motive, notion, passion, spontaneity,

spur, thought, urge, vagary, whim, whimsy, wish, yen; SEE CONCEPTS 20,410

impulse [n2] *throb, stimulus*
augmentation, beat, bump, catalyst, drive, force, impetus, impulsion, lash, momentum, movement, pressure, propulsion, pulsation, pulse, push, rush, shock, shove, stroke, surge, thrust, vibration; SEE CONCEPT 641

impulsive [adj] *tending to act without thought*
abrupt, ad-lib*, automatic, careless, devil-may-care*, emotional, extemporaneous, flaky*, gone off deep end*, hasty, headlong, hot-and-cold*, impetuous, instinctive, intuitive, involuntary, jumping the gun*, mad, offhand, passionate, precipitate, quick, rash, spontaneous, sudden, swift, unconsidered, unexpected, unmeditated, unpredictable, unpremeditated, unprompted, up-and-down*, violent, winging it*; SEE CONCEPTS 401,542

impunity [n] *freedom*
dispensation, exception, exemption, immunity, liberty, license, nonliability, permission, privilege, security; SEE CONCEPT 376

impure [adj] *not clean mentally, physically; mixed*
admixed, adulterated, alloyed, carnal, coarse, common, contaminated, corrupt, debased, defiled, desecrated, diluted, dirty, doctored*, filthy, foul, gross*, grubby*, immodest, immoral, indecent, infected, lewd, nasty, not pure, obscene, polluted, profaned, smutty*, squalid, sullied, tainted, unchaste, unclean, unrefined, unwholesome, vile, vitiated, weighted, wicked; SEE CONCEPTS 545,621

impute [v] *attribute*
accredit, accuse, adduce, ascribe, assign, blame, brand, censure, charge, credit, hang something on*, hint, indict, insinuate, intimate, lay, pin on*, refer, reference, stigmatize; SEE CONCEPTS 44,49

inability [n] *disabling lack of talent, skill*
disqualification, failure, frailty, impotence, inadequacy, inaptitude, incapability, incapacitation, incapacity, incompetence, ineffectiveness, ineffectualness, inefficacy, inefficiency, ineptitude, ineptness, insufficiency, inutility, lack, necessity, powerlessness, shortcoming, unfitness, weakness; SEE CONCEPT 630

inaccessible [adj] *out of reach*
aloof, away, beyond, distant, elusive, far, far-away, far-off, impassable, impervious, impracticable, insurmountable, not at hand*, out-of-the-way*, remote, unachievable, unapproachable, unattainable, unavailable, unfeasible, ungettable, unobtainable, unreachable, unrealizable, unworkable; SEE CONCEPT 576

inaccuracy [n] *error, erroneousness*
blunder, corrigendum, deception, defect, erratum, exaggeration, fault, howler*, imprecision, incorrectness, inexactness, miscalculation, mistake, slip*, solecism, typo*, unfaithfulness, unreliability, wrong; SEE CONCEPTS 101,230

inaccurate [adj] *erroneous*
all wet*, careless, counterfactual, defective, discrepant, doesn't wash*, fallacious, false, faulty, imprecise, incorrect, in error, inexact, mistaken, off, off base*, out*, specious, unfaithful, unreliable, unsound, untrue, way-off*, wide*, wild*, wrong; SEE CONCEPTS 565,582

inactive [adj] *not engaged in action; inert, lazy*
abeyant, asleep, blah*, disengaged, do-nothing*, dormant, down, draggy, dull, idle, immobile, indolent, in holding pattern*, inoperative, jobless, latent, lax, lethargic, limp, low-key, mothballed*, motionless, on hold, ossified, out of action, out of commission*, out of service, out of work*, passive, quiescent, quiet, sedentary, slack, sleepy, slothful, slow, sluggish, somnolent, stable, static, still, torpid, unemployed, unoccupied, unused; SEE CONCEPTS 401,560,584

inadequacy [n] *shortage, defect, inability*
blemish, dearth, defalcation, defectiveness, deficiency, deficit, drawback, failing, faultiness, flaw, imperfection, inadequateness, inaptness, incapacity, incompetence, incompetency, incompleteness, ineffectiveness, ineffectualness, inefficacy, inefficiency, ineptitude, insufficiency, lack, meagerness, paucity, poverty, scantiness, shortcoming, skimpiness, underage, unfitness, unsuitableness, weakness; SEE CONCEPTS 335,674,709

inadequate [adj] *defective, insufficient, incompetent*
bare, barren, bush-league*, deficient, depleted, dry, failing, faulty, feeble, found wanting, glitch*, imperfect, impotent, inappreciable, inapt, incapable, incommensurate, incompetent, incomplete, inconsiderable, insubstantial, junk*, lacking, lame*, lemon*, lousy, low, meager, minus, miserly, niggardly, not enough, parsimonious, poor, scanty, scarce, short, shy*, sketchy*, skimpy*, small, spare, sparse, sterile, stinted, stunted*, thin*, too little, unequal, unproductive, unqualified, weak; SEE CONCEPTS 546,570,771

inadmissible [adj] *not appropriate*
exceptionable, ill-favored, ill-timed, immaterial, improper, inappropriate, inapt, incompetent, inept, irrelevant, malapropos, objectionable, unacceptable, unallowable, unbecoming, undesirable, unfit, unqualified, unreasonable, unsatisfactory, unseemly, unsuited, unwanted, unwelcome; SEE CONCEPTS 319,558

inadvertent [adj] *accidental*
careless, chance, feckless, heedless, irreflective, negligent, not on purpose, reckless, thoughtless, uncaring, unconcerned, undesigned, undevised, unheeding, unintended, unintentional, unmindful, unplanned, unpremeditated, unthinking, unthought, unwitting; SEE CONCEPTS 542,544

inadvisable [adj] *not recommended*
careless, foolhardy, foolish, harebrained*, ill-advised, impolitic, improper, imprudent, inappropriate, incautious, inconvenient, indiscreet, inexpedient, injudicious, pointless, rash, undesirable, unsensible, unsuitable, unwise, wrong; SEE CONCEPTS 529,558

inalienable [adj] *absolute, inherent*
basic, entailed, inbred, inviolable, natural, nonnegotiable, nontransferable, sacrosanct, unassailable, untransferable; SEE CONCEPT 535

inane [adj] *stupid*
absurd, asinine, daft, empty, fatuous, flat, foolish, frivolous, futile, harebrained*, idiotic, illogical, imbecilic, innocuous, insipid, jejune, laughable, meaningless, mindless, pointless, puerile, ridiculous, sappy*, senseless, silly, trifling, unintelligent, vacant, vacuous, vain, vapid, weak, wishy-washy*, worthless; SEE CONCEPTS 542, 548

inanimate [adj] *not alive, not organic*
azoic, cold, dead, defunct, dull, exanimate, extinct, idle, inactive, inert, inoperative, insensate,

im
in

insentient, lifeless, mineral, motionless, nonanimal, nonvegetable, quiescent, soulless, spiritless; SEE CONCEPT 539

inapplicable [adj] not relevant
extraneous, foreign, garbage*, immaterial, impertinent, inapposite, inappropriate, inappurtenant, inapropos, inapt, inconsistent, irrelative, irrelevant, remote, unsuitable, unsuited; SEE CONCEPTS 546,558

inappropriate [adj] not proper, suitable
bad form, disproportionate, foot-in-mouth*, garbage*, ill-fitted, ill-suited, ill-timed, improper, inapplicable, inapropos, incongruous, inconsonant, incorrect, indecorous, inept, irrelevant, left-field*, malapropos, off*, out of line, out of place, tasteless, unbecoming, unbefitting, undue, unfit, unfitting, unmeet, unseasonable, unseemly, unsuitable, untimely, way off*, wrong, wrong-number*; SEE CONCEPT 558

inapt [adj] incompetent; not suitable
awkward, banal, clumsy, dull, flat, gauche, ill-adapted, ill-fitted, ill-suited, improper, inadept, inapposite, inappropriate, incongruous, inept, inexperienced, inexpert, infelicitous, insipid, jejune, maladroit, malapropos, slow, stupid, unable, undexterous, unfacile, unfit, unhandy, unmeet, unproficient, unskilled, unsuitable, unsuited, untimely; SEE CONCEPTS 527,558

inarticulate [adj] unable to speak well
blurred, dumb, faltering, halting, hesitant, hesitating, inaudible, incoherent, incomprehensible, indistinct, maundering, muffled, mumbled, mumbling, mute, obscure, reticent, silent, speechless, stammering, tongue-tied, unclear, unintelligible, unspoken, unuttered, unvocal, unvoiced, vague, voiceless, wordless; SEE CONCEPT 267

inattentive [adj] negligent, not paying attention
absent, absentminded, apathetic, blind, bored, careless, distracted, distrait, distraught, diverted, dreamy, faraway, heedless, inadvertent, indifferent, inobservant, listless, lost*, musing, neglectful, oblivious, off-guard*, out to lunch*, preoccupied, rapt, regardless, remiss, removed, scatterbrained*, thoughtless, unconscious, undiscerning, unheeding, unmindful, unnoticing, unobservant, unobserving, unperceiving, unthinking, unwatchful, vague; SEE CONCEPTS 403,542

inaugurate [v] begin; install
bow, break in, break the ice*, commence, commission, dedicate, get things rolling*, get under way*, induct, initiate, instate, institute, introduce, invest, jump, kick off*, launch, make up, open, ordain, originate, set in motion*, set up, start, usher in; SEE CONCEPT 221

inauguration [n] installation of newcomers
commencement, inaugural, induction, initiation, institution, investiture, launch, launching, opening, setting up; SEE CONCEPT 386

inauspicious [adj] ominous, unpromising
bad, baleful, baneful, black, dire, discouraging, evil, fateful, foreboding, ill-boding, ill-omened, impending, inopportune, sinister, threatening, unfavorable, unfortunate, unlucky, unpromising, unpropitious, untimely, untoward; SEE CONCEPTS 548,570

inborn/inbred [adj] coming from birth; natural
congenital, connate, connatural, constitutional, deep-seated, essential, hereditary, inbred, indigenous, indwelling, ingenerate, ingrained, inherent,

inherited, innate, instinctive, intrinsic, intuitive, native, unacquired; SEE CONCEPTS 406,549

incalculable [adj] countless, limitless
boundless, capricious, chancy, enormous, erratic, fluctuant, iffy*, immense, incomputable, inestimable, infinite, innumerable, jillion*, measureless, no end of*, no end to*, numberless, uncertain, uncountable, unfixed, unforeseen, unpredictable, unreckonable, untold, vast, whimsical, without number, zillion*; SEE CONCEPTS 535,773,781

incandescent [adj] glowing
beaming, brilliant, effulgent, fulgent, intense, lambent, lucent, luminous, phosphorescent, radiant, red-hot*, refulgent, shining, white-hot*; SEE CONCEPT 617

incantation [n] spell, magic
abracadabra*, ala kazam*, bewitchment, black magic, chant, charm, conjuration, conjuring, enchantment, formula, hex, hocus-pocus*, hoodoo*, hymn, invocation, mumbo-jumbo*, necromancy, open sesame*, rune, sorcery, voodoo*, witchcraft, wizardry; SEE CONCEPTS 370,689

incapable [adj] not adequate; helpless
butterfingers*, disqualified, feeble, impotent, inadequate, incompetent, ineffective, ineligible, inept, inexperienced, inexpert, inproficient, insufficient, losing, naive, not equal to, not up to*, poor, powerless, unable, uncool*, unequipped, unfit, unqualified, unskilled, unskillful, unsuited, weak; SEE CONCEPT 527

incapacitate [v] put out of action
clip wings*, cripple, damage, disable, disarm, disenable, disqualify, hamstring*, hinder, hogtie*, hurt, immobilize, lame, lay up*, maim, paralyze, prostrate, put out of commission*, take out, undermine, weaken; SEE CONCEPTS 121,246

incarcerate [v] put in jail, confinement
bastille, book*, cage*, commit, confine, constrain, coop up*, detain, hold, immure, impound, imprison, intern, jail, lock up, put away, put on ice*, put under lock and key*, railroad*, restrain, restrict, send up the river*, settle, slough, take away, throw book at*; SEE CONCEPTS 90,191,317

incarnate [adj] in bodily form
embodied, exteriorized, externalized, human, in human form, in the flesh*, made flesh, manifested, materialized, personified, physical, real, substantiated, tangible, typified; SEE CONCEPTS 490,539

incautious [adj] not careful
any old way*, bold, brash, careless, caught napping*, devil-may-care*, fast-and-loose*, foot-in-mouth*, hasty, heedless, hotheaded*, ill-advised, ill-judged, impetuous, improvident, imprudent, impulsive, inconsiderate, indiscreet, injudicious, madcap*, neglectful, negligent, off guard*, pay no mind*, playing with fire*, precipitate, rash, reckless, regardless, sticking one's neck out*, thoughtless, unalert, unguarded, unmindful, unthinking, unvigilant, unwatchful, wary, wide open*; SEE CONCEPTS 542,544

incendiary [n] person who causes fire, trouble
agitator, arsonist, criminal, demagogue, demonstrator, firebrand*, insurgent, pyromaniac, rabble-rouser*, rebel, revolutionary, rioter; SEE CONCEPT 412

incendiary [adj] causing trouble, damage
dangerous, demagogic, dissentious, inflamma-

tory, malevolent, provocative, rabble-rousing*, seditious, subversive, treacherous, wicked; SEE CONCEPTS 537,570

incense [n] *strongly fragrant smoke*
aroma, balm, bouquet, burnt offering, essence, flame, frankincense, fuel, myrrh, odor, perfume, punk, redolence, scent, spice; SEE CONCEPTS 599,600

incense [v] *make very angry*
anger, ask for it*, bother, disgust, egg on*, enrage, exasperate, excite, fire up*, get a rise out of*, get under one's skin*, inflame, infuriate, ire, irritate, mad, madden, make blood boil*, make see red*, provoke, rile, umbrage; SEE CONCEPT 14

incensed [adj] *very angry*
at end of one's rope*, buffaloed*, bugged*, bummed out*, burned up*, dogged, enraged, exasperated, fuming, furious, hacked, hot and bothered*, huffy*, indignant, infuriated, irate, ireful, mad, maddened, miffed, on the warpath*, peeved, riled, rousted, rubbed the wrong way*, steamed up*, up in arms*, uptight*, wrathful; SEE CONCEPT 403

incentive [n] *lure, inducement*
allurement, bait, carrot*, catalyst, come-on*, consideration, determinant, drive, encouragement, enticement, excuse, exhortation, goad, ground, impetus, impulse, incitement, influence, insistence, inspiration, instigation, motivation, motive, persuasion, provocation, purpose, rationale, reason, reason why, spring, spur, stimulant, stimulation, stimulus, temptation, urge, whip; SEE CONCEPT 661

inception [n] *beginning*
birth, commencement, dawn, derivation, fountain, inauguration, initiation, kickoff, origin, outset, provenance, provenience, rise, root, source, start, well, wellspring; SEE CONCEPTS 648,832

incessant [adj] *never-ending, persistent*
ceaseless, constant, continual, continuous, day-and-night*, endless, eternal, everlasting, interminable, interminate, monotonous, nonstop, perpetual, relentless, round-the-clock*, timeless, unbroken, unceasing, unending, unrelenting, unremitting; SEE CONCEPTS 534,798

inch [n] *one-twelfth of a foot/2.54 centimeters measured*
fingerbreadth, one thirty-sixth of a yard, square; SEE CONCEPTS 790,791

inchoate [adj] *undeveloped, beginning*
amorphous, elementary, embryonic, formless, immature, imperfect, inceptive, incipient, just begun, nascent, preliminary, rudimentary, shapeless, unfinished, unformed, unshaped; SEE CONCEPTS 485,578,797

incident [n] *occurrence*
adventure, circumstance, episode, event, fact, happening, matter, milestone, occasion, scene, trip; SEE CONCEPT 2

incidental [adj] *related; minor*
accidental, accompanying, adventitious, ancillary, attendant, by-the-way*, casual, chance, circumstantial, coincidental, concomitant, concurrent, contingent, contributing, contributory, fluke*, fortuitous, irregular, nonessential, occasional, odd, random, secondary, subordinate, subsidiary; SEE CONCEPTS 547,548,577

incidentally [adv] *by chance*
accidentally, as a by-product, as side effect, by the

bye*, by the way, casually, fortuitously, in passing, in related manner, not by design, obiter, parenthetically, remotely, subordinately, unexpectedly; SEE CONCEPT 544

incipient [adj] *developing*
basic, beginning, commencing, elementary, embryonic, fundamental, inceptive, inchoate, initial, initiative, initiatory, introductory, nascent, originating, start; SEE CONCEPT 585

incisive [adj1] *intelligent*
acute, bright, clever, concise, keen, penetrating, perspicacious, piercing, profound, sharp, trenchant; SEE CONCEPT 402

incisive [adj2] *sarcastic*
acerb, acerbic, acid, biting, caustic, clear-cut, concise, crisp, cutting, drilling, laconic, mordant, penetrating, sardonic, satirical, scathing, severe, sharp, slashing, succinct, tart, terse, trenchant; SEE CONCEPT 267

incite [v] *encourage, provoke*
abet, activate, actuate, agitate, animate, arouse, coax, craze, drive, egg on*, encourage, excite, exhort, fan the fire*, foment, force, forward, further, get to*, goad, impel, induce, inflame, influence, inspire, inspirit, instigate, juice*, key up*, motivate, persuade, prick, promote, prompt, provoke, psych*, push, put up to*, raise, rouse, set, set off*, solicit, spur, stimulate, stir up*, talk into, taunt, trigger, urge, whip up*, work up*; SEE CONCEPTS 14,221,242

inclement [adj1] *bitter, nasty (weather)*
brutal, cold, foul, hard, harsh, intemperate, raw, rigorous, rough, rugged, severe, stormy, tempestuous, violent, wintry; SEE CONCEPT 525

inclement [adj2] *cruel, merciless*
callous, draconian, harsh, intemperate, pitiless, rigorous, ruthless, savage, severe, tyrannical, unfeeling, unkind, unmerciful; SEE CONCEPT 401

inclination [n1] *tendency, bent*
affection, appetite, aptitude, aptness, attachment, attraction, bias, capability, capacity, cup of tea*, desire, disposition, drift, druthers*, fancy, fondness, groove*, idiosyncrasy, impulse, leaning, liking, mind, movement, partiality, penchant, persuasion, pleasure, predilection, predisposition, preference, prejudice, proclivity, proneness, propensity, slant*, soft spot*, stomach*, susceptibility, taste, temperament, thing*, trend, turn*, type, urge, velleity, weakness, whim, will, wish; SEE CONCEPTS 20,411,630

inclination [n2] *slant, angle*
acclivity, bank, bend, bending, bevel, bow, bowing, cant, declivity, deviation, direction, downgrade, grade, gradient, hill, incline, lean, leaning, list, pitch, ramp, slope, tilt; SEE CONCEPT 738

incline [n] *slope*
acclivity, approach, ascent, cant, declivity, descent, dip, grade, gradient, inclination, lean, leaning, plane, ramp, rise, slant, tilt; SEE CONCEPT 738

incline [v1] *tend toward*
affect, be disposed, bend, be partial, be predisposed, be willing, bias, drive, favor, govern, gravitate toward, impel, induce, influence, lean to, look, make willing, move, not mind, persuade, predispose, prefer, prejudice, prompt, sway, turn, verge; SEE CONCEPT 657

incline [v2] *bend, lean*
aim, bevel, bow, cant, cock, deviate, diverge, heel, lay, level, list, lower, nod, point, recline,

skew, slant, slope, stoop, tend, tilt, tip, train, turn, veer, yaw; SEE CONCEPT 738

include [v] *contain, involve*
accommodate, add, admit, allow for, append, bear, be composed of, be made up of, build, build in, carry, combine, comprehend, comprise, consist of, constitute, count, cover, cut in on, embody, embrace, encircle, enclose, encompass, entail, enter, have, hold, implicate, incorporate, inject, insert, interject, interpolate, introduce, make allowance for, make room for, number, number among, receive, subsume, take in, take into account, teem with, work in; SEE CONCEPTS *112,532,643*

including [adj] *containing*
along with, among other things, as well as, containing, counting, in addition to, inclusive of, in conjunction with, made up of, not to mention, plus, together with, with; SEE CONCEPT 577

inclusion [n] *addition*
admittance, composition, comprisal, embodiment, embracement, encompassment, formation, incorporation, insertion, involvement, subsumption; SEE CONCEPT 642

inclusive [adj] *all-encompassing, all-embracing*
across-the-board*, all-around, all the options*, all together, ball-of-wax*, blanket*, broad, catch-all*, comprehensive, encyclopedic, full, general, global, in toto*, overall, sweeping, umbrella*, wall-to-wall*, whole, without exception; SEE CONCEPT 772

incognito [adj] *in disguise*
anonymous, bearded, camouflaged, concealed, disguised, hidden, incog*, isolated, masked, masquerading, obscure, under assumed name, unknown, unrecognized; SEE CONCEPTS *576,589*

incoherent [adj] *unintelligible*
breathless, confused, disconnected, discontinuous, discordant, disjointed, disordered, dumb, faltering, inarticulate, incohesive, incomprehensible, incongruous, inconsistent, indistinct, indistinguishable, irrational, jumbled, maundering, muddled, muffled, mumbling, mute, muttered, puzzling, rambling, stammering, stuttering, tongue-tied*, uncommunicative, unconnected, uncoordinated, uneven, unvocal, wandering, wild; SEE CONCEPT 267

income [n] *money earned by work or investments*
assets, avails, benefits, bottom line*, cash, cash flow, commission, compensation, dividends, drawings, earnings, gains, gravy*, gross, harvest, honorarium, interest, in the black*, livelihood, means, net, pay, payoff, proceeds, profit, receipts, returns, revenue, royalty, salary, take home, wage; SEE CONCEPTS *340,344*

incomparable [adj] *superlative*
beyond compare, excellent, exceptional, ideal, inimitable, matchless, paramount, peerless, perfect, preeminent, second to none, sovereign, superior, supreme, surpassing, towering, transcendent, ultimate, unequalled, unmatchable, unmatched, unparalleled, unrivalled, unsurpassable; SEE CONCEPT 574

incompatible [adj] *antagonistic, contradictory*
adverse, antipathetic, antipodal, antithetical, clashing, conflicting, contrary, counter, disagreeing, discordant, discrepant, disparate, factious, inadmissible, inappropriate, incoherent, inconformable, incongruous, inconsistent, inconsonant, inconstant, irreconcilable, jarring, marching to a

different drummer*, mismatched, night and day*, offbeat*, opposed, opposite, poles apart*, unadapted, uncongenial, unsuitable, unsuited, warring, whale of difference*; SEE CONCEPT 564

incompetent [adj] *unskillful, unable*
amateur, amateurish, awkward, bungling, bush-league*, clumsy, disqualified, floundering, helpless, inadequate, incapable, ineffectual, inefficient, ineligible, inept, inexperienced, inexpert, insufficient, maladroit, not cut out for*, not equal to, not have it*, out to lunch*, raw, unadapted, unequipped, unfit, unfitted, unhandy, uninitiated, unproficient, unqualified, unskilled, untrained, useless; SEE CONCEPT 527

incomplete [adj] *unfinished, wanting*
abridged, broken, crude, defective, deficient, expurgated, fractional, fragmentary, garbled, half-done, immature, imperfect, inadequate, incoherent, insufficient, lacking, meager, part, partial, rough, rude, rudimentary, short, sketchy, unaccomplished, unconsummated, under construction, undeveloped, undone, unexecuted, unpolished; SEE CONCEPT 531

incomprehensible [adj] *not understandable*
baffling, beats me*, beyond comprehension, beyond one's grasp*, clear as mud*, cryptic, Delphic*, enigmatic, fathomless, Greek*, impenetrable, incognizable, inconceivable, inscrutable, mysterious, mystifying, obscure, opaque, over one's head*, perplexing, puzzling, sibylline, unclear, unfathomable, ungraspable, unimaginable, unintelligible, unknowable; SEE CONCEPTS *402,529*

inconceivable [adj] *beyond reason, belief*
extraordinary, fantastic, imcomprehensible, implausible, impossible, improbable, incogitable, incredible, insupposable, mind-boggling*, phony, rare, reachy, staggering, strange, thin*, unbelievable, unconvincing, unheard-of, unimaginable, unknowable, unlikely, unsubstantial, unthinkable, weak*, won't fly*, won't wash*; SEE CONCEPTS *529,552*

inconclusive [adj] *up in the air*
ambiguous, deficient, incomplete, indecisive, indeterminate, lacking, open, uncertain, unconvincing, undecided, uneventful, unfateful, unfinished, unsatisfactory, unsettled, vague; SEE CONCEPTS *537,548*

incongruous [adj] *out of place; absurd*
alien, bizarre, conflicting, contradictory, dissonant, discordant, disparate, distorted, divergent, extraneous, fantastic, fitful, foreign, illogical, improper, inappropriate, inapropos, inapt, incoherent, incompatible, incongruent, inconsistent, irreconcilable, irregular, jumbled, lopsided, mismatched, out of keeping*, rambling, shifting, twisted, unavailing, unbalanced, unbecoming, unconnected, uncoordinated, uneven, unintelligible, unpredictable, unrelated, unsuitable, unsuited; SEE CONCEPTS *547,558*

inconsequential/inconsiderable [adj] *of no significance*
casual, dinky*, entry-level*, exiguous, immaterial, inadequate, inappreciable, inconsequent, insignificant, insufficient, light, little, measly, minor, negligible, paltry, petty, picayune, puny, runt, scanty, shoestring*, skimpy, small, small potatoes*, small-time*, trifling, trivial, two-bit*, unconsidered, unimportant, wimpy*, worthless; SEE CONCEPT 575

inconsiderate [adj] insensitive to others
boorish, brash, careless, discourteous, hasty, impolite, incautious, indelicate, intolerant, reckless, rude, self-centered, selfish, sharp, short, tactless, thoughtless, unceremonious, uncharitable, ungracious, unkind, unthinking; SEE CONCEPT 401

inconsistent [adj] contradictory, irregular
at odds, at variance, capricious, changeable, conflicting, contrary, discordant, discrepant, dissonant, erratic, fickle, illogical, incoherent, incompatible, in conflict, incongruent, incongruous, inconstant, irreconcilable, lubricious, mercurial, out of step*, temperamental, uncertain, unpredictable, unstable, variable, warring; SEE CONCEPTS 534,564

inconsolable [adj] brokenhearted
comfortless, dejected, dim, desolate, despairing, disconsolate, discouraged, distressed, forlorn, heartbroken, heartsick, sad, unconsolable; SEE CONCEPT 403

inconspicuous [adj] hidden, unnoticeable
camouflaged, concealed, dim, faint, hidden, indistinct, insignificant, low-key*, low-profile*, modest, muted, ordinary, plain, quiet, retiring, secretive, shy, soft-pedalled*, subtle, tenuous, unassuming, unemphatic, unobtrusive, unostentatious; SEE CONCEPTS 485,576

incontrovertible [adj] beyond dispute
accurate, authentic, certain, established, incontestable, indisputable, indubitable, irrefutable, nailed down*, no mistake*, no two ways about it*, positive, sure, surefire*, sure thing*, uncontestable, undeniable, unequivocable, unquestionable, unshakable; SEE CONCEPT 535

inconvenience [n] bother, trouble
aggravation, annoyance, awkwardness, bothersomeness, cumbersomeness, difficulty, disadvantage, disruption, disturbance, drawback, exasperation, fuss, hindrance, nuisance, pain*, stew*, trial, troublesomeness, uneasiness, unfitness, unhandiness, unsuitableness, untimeliness, unwieldiness, upset, vexation; SEE CONCEPT 674

inconvenience [v] bother, trouble
aggravate, discombobulate, discommode, discompose, disoblige, disrupt, disturb, exasperate, give a hard time*, give trouble*, hang up*, interfere, irk, make it tough*, meddle, put in a spot*, put on the spot*, put to trouble*, try, upset; SEE CONCEPTS 14,242

inconvenient [adj] bothersome, troublesome
annoying, awkward, cumbersome, detrimental, difficult, disadvantageous, discommoding, discommodious, disturbing, embarrassing, incommodious, inexpedient, inopportune, pestiferous, prejudicial, remote, tiresome, troublesome, unhandy, unmanageable, unseasonable, unsuitable, untimely, unwieldy, vexatious; SEE CONCEPTS 537,548

incorporate [v] include, combine
absorb, add to, amalgamate, assimilate, associate, blend, charter, coalesce, consolidate, cover, dub, embody, form, fuse, gang up*, hook in*, imbibe, integrate, join, link, merge, mix, organize, pool, put together, start, subsume, tie in*, unite; SEE CONCEPTS 112,113,324

incorrect [adj] wrong
counterfactual, erroneous, false, faulty, flawed, imprecise, improper, inaccurate, inappropriate, inexact, mistaken, not trustworthy*, out*, specious, unfitting, unreliable, unseemly, unsound,

unsuitable, untrue, way off*, wide of the mark*, wrong number*; SEE CONCEPTS 558,570

incorrigible [adj] bad, hopeless
abandoned, beastly, hardened, incurable, intractable, inveterate, irredeemable, irreparable, loser, recidivous, uncorrectable, unreformed, useless, wicked; SEE CONCEPT 570

incorruptible [adj] honest, honorable
above suspicion, imperishable, indestructible, inextinguishable, just, loyal, moral, perpetual, persistent, pure, reliable, straight, trustworthy, unbribable, undestroyable, untouchable, upright; SEE CONCEPTS 485,545

increase [n] addition, growth
access, accession, accretion, accrual, accumulation, aggrandizement, augmentation, boost, breakthrough, burgeoning, cumulation, development, elaboration, enlargement, escalation, exaggeration, expansion, extension, gain, hike, incorporation, increment, inflation, intensification, maximization, merger, multiplication, optimization, raise, rise, spread, step-up, surge, swell, swelling, upgrade, upsurge, upturn, waxing; SEE CONCEPTS 763,780

increase [v] add or grow
advance, aggrandize, aggravate, amplify, annex, augment, boost, broaden, build, build up, deepen, develop, dilate, distend, double, enhance, enlarge, escalate, exaggerate, expand, extend, further, heighten, inflate, intensify, lengthen, magnify, mark up, mount, multiply, pad*, progress, proliferate, prolong, protract, pullulate, raise, redouble, reinforce, rise, sharpen, slap on*, snowball*, spread, step up, strengthen, supplement, swarm, swell, tack on*, teem, thicken, triple, wax, widen; SEE CONCEPTS 236,245,780

increasingly [adv] to a greater extent
more, more and more, progressively, with acceleration; SEE CONCEPT 772

incredible [adj1] beyond belief
absurd, far-fetched, fishy*, flimsy*, implausible, impossible, improbable, incogitable, inconceivable, insupposable, outlandish, out of the question*, phony, preposterous, questionable, ridiculous, rings phony*, suspect, thin*, unbelievable, unconvincing, unimaginable, unsubstantial, untenable, unthinkable; SEE CONCEPT 552

incredible [adj2] marvellous
ace*, amazing, astonishing, astounding, awe-inspiring, awesome, extraordinary, fabulous, glorious, great, prodigious, superhuman*, unreal*, wonderful; SEE CONCEPTS 529,572

incredulous [adj] unbelieving
disbelieving, distrustful, doubtful, doubting, dubious, hesitant, mistrustful, questioning, quizzical, show-me*, skeptical, suspect, suspicious, uncertain, unconvinced, unsatisfied, wary; SEE CONCEPTS 403,529

increment [n] small step toward gain
accession, accretion, accrual, accrument, addition, advancement, augmentation, enlargement, increase, profit, raise, rise, supplement; SEE CONCEPTS 763,780

inculcate [v] implant, infuse information
brainwash*, break down, communicate, drill, drum into*, educate, hammer into*, impart, impress, indoctrinate, inseminate, instill, instruct, plant, program, shape up, teach, work over*; SEE CONCEPTS 14,285

in
in

incur [v] *bring upon oneself*
acquire, arouse, be subjected to, bring down on*, catch, contract, draw, earn, expose oneself to, gain, get, induce, meet with, obtain, provoke; SEE CONCEPT 93

incurable [adj] *unfixable, unchangeable*
cureless, deadly, fatal, hopeless, immedicable, impossible, inoperable, irrecoverable, irremediable, irreparable, nowhere to go*, out of time*, remediless, serious, terminal, uncorrectable, unrecoverable; SEE CONCEPTS 485,548

incursion [n] *invasion*
aggression, attack, foray, infiltration, inroad, intrusion, irruption, penetration, raid; SEE CONCEPTS 86,320

indebted [adj] *under an obligation*
accountable, answerable for, appreciative, beholden, bound, bounden, chargeable, duty-bound, grateful, honor-bound, hooked*, in debt, in hock*, liable, obligated, obliged, owed, owing, responsible, thankful; SEE CONCEPTS 334,546

indecency [n] *obscenity, vulgarity*
bawdiness, coarseness, crudity, drunkenness, evil, foulness, grossness, immodesty, impropriety, impurity, incivility, indecorum, indelicacy, lewdness, licentiousness, offense, outrageousness, pornography, ribaldry, smuttiness, unseemliness, vileness; SEE CONCEPTS 633,645

indecent [adj] *obscene, vulgar; offensive*
blue*, coarse, crude, dirty*, filthy, foul, foul-mouthed, gross*, ill-bred, immodest, immoral, improper, impure, in bad taste, indecorous, indelicate, lewd, licentious, malodorous, off-color*, outrageous, pornographic, raunchy*, raw, ridiculous, rough, salacious, scatological, shameless, shocking, smutty*, tasteless, unbecoming, undecorous, unseemly, untoward, vile, wicked, X-rated*; SEE CONCEPT 545

indecisive [adj] *uncertain, indefinite*
astraddle, changeable, doubtful, faltering, halting, hemming and hawing*, hesitant, hesitating, hot and cold*, inconclusive, indeterminate, irresolute, of two minds*, on the fence*, tentative, unclear, undecided, undetermined, uneventful, unsettled, unstable, vacillating, waffling, wavering, weak-kneed*, wishy-washy*; SEE CONCEPTS 534,535

indeed [adv] *actually*
absolutely, amen*, certainly, doubtlessly, easily, even, for real, in point of fact, in truth, much, naturally, of course, positively, really, strictly, surely, sure thing*, to be sure, truly, undeniably, undoubtedly, verily, veritably, very, very much, well; SEE CONCEPT 535

indefatigable [adj] *untiring*
active, assiduous, bound and determined*, dead set on*, determined, diligent, dogged, energetic, hell-bent*, industrious, inexhaustible, ironclad, nose to grindstone*, painstaking, patient, persevering, persistent, pertinacious, relentless, sedulous, steadfast, stop at nothing*, strenuous, tireless, unfaltering, unflagging, unflinching, unremitting, unwavering, unwearied, unwearying, vigorous; SEE CONCEPT 542

indefensible [adj] *inexcusable*
bad, faulty, inexpiable, insupportable, unforgivable, unjustifiable, unpardonable, untenable, unwarrantable, wrong; SEE CONCEPTS 545,548

indefinite [adj] *ambiguous, vague*
broad, confused, doubtful, dubious, equivocal, evasive, general, ill-defined, imprecise, indeterminable, indeterminate, indistinct, inexact, inexhaustible, infinite, innumerable, intangible, loose, obscure, shadowy, uncertain, unclear, undefined, undependable, undetermined, unfixed, unknown, unlimited, unsettled, unspecific, unsure, wide; SEE CONCEPT 535

indefinitely [adv] *continually*
considerably, endlessly, forever, frequently, regularly, sine die, without end; SEE CONCEPT 798

indelible [adj] *not able to be erased, indestructible*
enduring, ineffaceable, ineradicable, inerasable, inexpungible, inextirpable, ingrained, lasting, memorable, permanent, rememberable, stirring, unforgettable; SEE CONCEPTS 482,529

indelicate [adj] *obscene, vulgar*
base, brash, brutish, callow, coarse, crude, earthy, embarrassing, immodest, improper, indecent, indecorous, lewd, low, lowbred, off-color*, offensive, outrageous, risqué, rude, suggestive, tasteless, unbecoming, unblushing, uncouth, unseemly, untactful, untoward; SEE CONCEPTS 544,545

indent [v] *make a space; push in slightly*
bash, cave in, cut, dent, depress, dint, hollow, jag, mark, nick, notch, pink, pit, rabbet, rut, scallop, score, serrate; SEE CONCEPTS 158,201,208

independence [n] *liberty, freedom*
ability, aptitude, autarchy, autonomy, home rule*, license, qualification, self-determination, self-government, self-reliance, self-rule, self-sufficiency, separation, sovereignty; SEE CONCEPTS 376,691

independent [adj] *liberated, free*
absolute, autarchic, autarchical, autonomous, freewheeling, individualistic, nonaligned, nonpartisan, on one's own, self-contained, self-determining, self-governing, self-reliant, self-ruling, self-sufficient, self-supporting, separate, separated, sovereign, unaided, unallied, unconnected, unconstrained, uncontrolled, unregimented; SEE CONCEPT 554

independently [adv] *alone*
all by one's self, apart, autonomously, by oneself, exclusive of, freely, individually, of one's own volition, one at a time, on one's own, on one's own, separately, severally, singly, solo, unaided, unrestrictedly, unsupervised, without regard to, without support; SEE CONCEPT 554

indescribable [adj] *beyond words*
impossible, incommunicable, indefinable, ineffable, inexpressible, nondescript, sublime, subtle, unspeakable, untellable, unutterable; SEE CONCEPT 267

indestructible [adj] *lasting, unable to be destroyed*
abiding, deathless, durable, enduring, everlasting, immortal, immutable, imperishable, incorruptible, indelible, indissoluble, inexterminable, inextinguishable, inextirpable, irrefragable, irrefrangible, nonperishable, permanent, perpetual, unalterable, unbreakable, unchangeable, undestroyable, undying, unfading; SEE CONCEPTS 489,534

indeterminate [adj] *uncertain, vague*
borderless, general, imprecise, inconclusive, indefinite, indistinct, inexact, undefined, undetermined, unfixed, unspecified, unstipulated; SEE CONCEPT 535

index [n] *indication*
basis, clue, evidence, formula, guide, hand, indicant, indication, indicator, indicia, mark, model,

needle, pointer, ratio, rule, sign, significant, symbol, symptom, token; SEE CONCEPTS *284,290*

index [v] *arrange, order*
alphabetize, catalogue, docket, file, list, record, tabulate; SEE CONCEPT *84*

indicate [v] *signify, display*
add up to, announce, argue, attest, augur, bespeak, be symptomatic, betoken, button down*, card, connote, demonstrate, denote, designate, evidence, evince, express, finger, hint, illustrate, imply, import, intimate, make, manifest, mark, mean, name, peg*, pin down*, pinpoint*, point out, point to, prove, read, record, register, reveal, show, sign, signal, slot, specify, suggest, symbolize, tab, tag, testify, witness; SEE CONCEPTS *74,118,266*

indication [n] *evidence, clue*
adumbration, attestation, augury, auspice, cue, earnest, explanation, expression, forewarning, gesture, hint, implication, index, indicia, inkling, intimation, manifestation, mark, nod, note, notion, omen, pledge, portent, preamble, prefiguration, prognostic, prolegomenon, proof, reminder, show, sign, signal, significant, signifier, suggestion, symptom, telltale, token, trace, vestige, warning, wind*, wink*; SEE CONCEPTS *74,278,284*

indicative [adj] *exhibitive*
apocalyptic, augural, auspicious, characteristic, connotative, demonstrative, denotative, denotive, designative, diagnostic, emblematic, evidential, evincive, expressive, inauspicious, indicatory, indicial, ominous, pointing to, prognostic, significant, significatory, suggestive, symbolic, symptomatic, testatory, testimonial; SEE CONCEPT *267*

indict [v] *accuse*
arraign, censure, charge, criminate, face with charges, finger*, frame*, impeach, incriminate, inculpate, prosecute, summon, tax; SEE CONCEPTS *44,317*

indictment [n] *accusation*
allegation, arraignment, bill, blame, censure, charge, citation, detention, findings, impeachment, incrimination, presentment, prosecution, statement, summons, warrant, writ; SEE CONCEPTS *44,317,318*

indifference [n] *absence of feeling, interest*
alienation, aloofness, apathy, callousness, carelessness, cold-bloodedness, coldness, cold shoulder*, coolness, detachment, disdain, disinterest, disinterestedness, dispassion, disregard, equity, heedlessness, immunity, impartiality, impassiveness, impassivity, inattention, inertia, insensitivity, insouciance, isolationism, lack, lethargy, listlessness, negligence, neutrality, nonchalance, noninterference, objectivity, stoicism, torpor, unconcern, unmindfulness; SEE CONCEPTS *410,657*

indifferent [adj] *unfeeling, uninterested*
aloof, apathetic, blasé, callous, cold, cool, detached, diffident, disinterested, dispassionate, distant, equitable, haughty, heartless, heedless, highbrow, impartial, impervious, inattentive, listless, neutral, nonchalant, nonpartisan, objective, passionless, phlegmatic, regardless, scornful, silent, stoical, supercilious, superior, unaroused, unbiased, uncaring, uncommunicative, unconcerned, unemotional, unimpressed, uninvolved, unmoved, unprejudiced, unresponsive, unsocial, unsympathetic; SEE CONCEPTS *403,542*

indigenous [adj] *native, inborn*
aboriginal, autochthonous, chthonic, congenital, connate, domestic, endemic, homegrown, inbred, inherent, inherited, innate, natural, original, primitive, unacquired; SEE CONCEPT *549*

indigent [adj] *poor*
beggared, busted, destitute, down and out*, flat broke*, hard up*, homeless, impecunious, impoverished, in want, necessitous, needy, penniless, penurious, poverty-stricken; SEE CONCEPT *334*

indigestion [n] *upset stomach*
acid indigestion, acidosis, digestive upset, dyspepsia, dyspepsy, flatulence, flu, gas, gaseous stomach, heartburn, nausea, pain; SEE CONCEPT *306*

indignant [adj] *angry*
acrimonious, annoyed, bent out of shape*, boiling*, bugged*, burned up*, disgruntled, displeased, exasperated, fuming, furious, heated, huffy*, in a huff*, incensed, irate, livid, mad, miffed, peeved, piqued, p.o.'d*, provoked, resentful, riled, scornful, seeing red*, up in arms*, upset, wrathful; SEE CONCEPTS *403,542*

indignation [n] *anger*
animus, boiling point*, danger, displeasure, exasperation, fury, huff*, ire, mad, miff*, pique, rage, resentment, rise, scorn, slow burn*, umbrage, wrath; SEE CONCEPTS *29,657*

indignity [n] *embarrassment, humiliation*
abuse, affront, backhanded compliment*, contumely, discourtesy, dishonor, disrespect, grievance, injury, injustice, insult, obloquy, opprobrium, outrage, put-down*, reproach, slap*, slight, slur, snub, take-down*, taunt; SEE CONCEPTS *278,410*

indirect [adj] *roundabout; unintended*
ambiguous, ancillary, circuitous, circular, circumlocutory, collateral, complicated, contingent, crooked, devious, discursive, duplicitous, erratic, eventual, implied, incidental, long, long-drawn-out*, long way home*, long-winded*, meandering, oblique, obscure, out-of-the-way, periphrastic, rambling, secondary, serpentine*, sidelong, sinister, sinuous, snaking*, sneaking, sneaky, subsidiary, tortuous, twisting, underhand, vagrant, wandering, winding, zigzag; SEE CONCEPTS *544,581*

indiscretion [n] *mistake*
bumble, crudeness, dropping the ball*, dumb move*, error, excitability, faux pas, folly, foolishness, fool mistake*, foul-up, gaffe, gaucherie, goof*, hastiness, imprudence, indiscreetness, ingenuousness, lapse, miscue, misjudgment, misspeak, naïveté, rashness, recklessness, screw-up*, simple-mindedness, slip*, slip of the tongue*, slip-up*, stumble, stupidity, tactlessness, thoughtlessness, unseemliness; SEE CONCEPTS *101,633,674*

indiscriminate [adj] *random, chaotic*
aimless, assorted, broad, careless, confused, designless, desultory, extensive, general, haphazard, heterogeneous, hit-or-miss*, imperceptive, jumbled, mingled, miscellaneous, mixed, mongrel, motley*, multifarious, promiscuous, purposeless, shallow, spot, superficial, sweeping, unconsidered, uncritical, undiscriminating, unmethodical, unplanned, unselective, unsystematic, varied, variegated, wholesale*, wide; SEE CONCEPTS *403,542,585,772*

in
in

indispensable [*adj*] *necessary*
basal, basic, cardinal, crucial, essential, fundamental, imperative, key, necessitous, needed, needful, prerequisite, primary, required, requisite, vital; SEE CONCEPT *546*

indisposed [*adj1*] *not well*
ailing, below par, confined, down, down with*, feeling rotten*, got a bug*, ill, infirm, laid up*, on sick list*, out of action*, poorly, sick, sickly, under the weather*, unwell; SEE CONCEPT *314*

indisposed [*adj2*] *unwilling*
afraid, antagonistic, antipathetic, averse, backward, disinclined, hesitant, hostile, inimical, loath, reluctant, uncaring, uneager, uninclined; SEE CONCEPT *542*

indisputable [*adj*] *beyond doubt*
absolute, accurate, actual, certain, double-checked, evident, incontestable, incontrovertible, indubitable, irrefutable, no ifs ands or buts about it*, no mistake*, open and shut*, positive, real, sure, that's a fact*, true, unassailable, undeniable, undoubted, unfabled, unquestionable, veridical; SEE CONCEPTS *535,582*

indistinct [*adj*] *obscure, ambiguous*
bleared, bleary, blurred, confused, dark, dim, doubtful, faint, fuzzy, hazy, ill-defined, inaudible, inconspicuous, indefinite, indeterminate, indiscernible, indistinguishable, inexact, misty, muffled, murky, out of focus, shadowy, unclear, undefined, undetermined, unheard, unintelligible, vague, weak; SEE CONCEPTS *485,535*

indistinguishable [*adj*] *alike*
duplicate, equivalent, identic, identical, like, same, tantamount, twin; SEE CONCEPT *566*

individual [*n*] *singular person, thing*
being, body, character, child, creature, dude*, entity, existence, human being, man, material, matter, mortal, number, party, person, personage, self, singleton, somebody, something, soul, stuff, substance, type, unit, woman; SEE CONCEPTS *389,433*

individual [*adj*] *distinctive, exclusive*
alone, characteristic, definite, diacritic, diagnostic, different, discrete, distinct, especial, express, idiosyncratic, indivisible, lone, odd, only, original, own, particular, peculiar, personal, personalized, proper, reserved, respective, secluded, select, separate, several, single, singular, sole, solitary, special, specific, uncommon, unique, unitary, unusual; SEE CONCEPTS *404,564*

individuality [*n*] *personality*
air, character, complexion, difference, discreteness, disposition, dissimilarity, distinction, distinctiveness, eccentricity, habit, humor, identity, idiosyncrasy, independence, individualism, ipseity, makeup, nature, oddity, oneness, originality, particularity, peculiarity, rarity, seity, selfdom, selfhood, selfness, separateness, singleness, singularity, singularness, temper, temperament, uniqueness, unity, unlikeness, way; SEE CONCEPT *411*

individually [*adv*] *separately*
alone, apart, by oneself, distinctively, exclusively, independently, one at a time, one by one, personally, restrictedly, severally, singly, without help; SEE CONCEPT *544*

indoctrinate [*v*] *brainwash*
break down, convince, drill, ground, imbue, implant, inculcate, influence, initiate, instill, instruct, plant, program, school, teach, train, work over; SEE CONCEPTS *14,285*

indolent [*adj*] *lazy*
drony, easygoing, fainéant, idle, inactive, inert, lackadaisical, languid, lax, lazy, lethargic, listless, resting, shiftless, slothful, slow, slow-going, sluggish, torpid; SEE CONCEPTS *538,542,584*

indomitable [*adj*] *steadfast, unyielding*
dogged, impassable, impregnable, insuperable, insurmountable, invincible, invulnerable, obstinate, pertinacious, resolute, ruthless, staunch, stubborn, unassailable, unbeatable, unconquerable, undefeatable, unflinching, willful; SEE CONCEPTS *404,489,534*

induce [*v*] *cause to happen; encourage*
abet, activate, actuate, argue into, breed, bring about, bring around, bulldoze*, cajole, cause, coax, convince, draw, draw in, effect, engender, generate, get*, get up, give rise to, goose*, impel, incite, influence, instigate, lead to, make, motivate, move, occasion, persuade, press, prevail upon, procure, produce, promote, prompt, sell one on*, set in motion, soft-soap*, squeeze, steamroll*, suck in*, sway, sweet-talk*, talk into*, twist one's arm*, urge, wheedle, win over*; SEE CONCEPTS *14,68,242*

inducement [*n*] *incentive, motive*
attraction, bait, brainwash*, carrot*, cause, come-on*, con*, consideration, desire, encouragement, hard sell*, hook*, impulse, incitement, influence, leader, lure, reward, snow job*, soft soap*, spur, stimulus, sweet talk*, temptation, twist, urge; SEE CONCEPTS *68,661*

induct [*v*] *take into an organization*
conscript, draft, enlist, inaugurate, initiate, install, instate, introduce, invest, recruit, sign on, sign up, swear in; SEE CONCEPTS *50,88,320,384*

induction [*n1*] *taking in, initiation*
consecration, draft, entrance, greetings, inaugural, inauguration, installation, instatement, institution, introduction, investiture, ordination, selection; SEE CONCEPTS *320,384,685*

induction [*n2*] *inference*
conclusion, conjecture, deducement, generalization, judgment, logical reasoning, ratiocination, rationalization, reason; SEE CONCEPTS *37,689*

indulge [*v1*] *treat oneself or another to*
allow, baby, cater, coddle, cosset, delight, entertain, favor, foster, give in, give rein to*, go along, go easy on*, gratify, humor, mollycoddle*, nourish, oblige, pamper, pander, pet, please, regale, satiate, satisfy, spoil, spoil rotten*, take care of*, tickle, yield; SEE CONCEPT *110*

indulge [*v2*] *luxuriate in*
bask in, ego trip*, enjoy, go in for*, live it up*, look out for number one*, revel in, rollick*, take part, wallow in; SEE CONCEPT *20*

indulgence [*n*] *luxury; gratification*
allowance, appeasement, attention, babying*, coddling*, courtesy, endurance, excess, extravagance, favor, favoring, fondling, fondness, forbearance, fulfillment, goodwill, gratifying, hedonism, immoderation, intemperance, intemperateness, kindness, kowtowing*, lenience, leniency, pampering, partiality, patience, permissiveness, petting, placating, pleasing, privilege, profligacy, profligateness, satiation, satisfaction, service, spoiling, toadying*, tolerance, toleration, treating, understanding; SEE CONCEPTS *337,657,712*

indulgent [adj] lenient, giving
able to live with*, big*, charitable, clement, compassionate, complaisant, compliant, considerate, easy, easygoing, favorable, fond, forbearing, gentle, going along with*, going easy on*, gratifying, kind, kindly, liberal, merciful, mild, overpermissive, permissive, soft-shelled*, tender, tolerant, understanding; SEE CONCEPTS 404,542

industrial [adj] related to manufacturing
automated, business, factory-made, industrialized, in industry, machine-made, manufactured, manufacturing, mechanical, mechanized, modern, smokestack, streamlined, technical; SEE CONCEPT 536

industrious [adj] hardworking
active, assiduous, ball of fire*, burning, busy, conscientious, diligent, dynamic, eager, energetic, grind*, in full swing*, intent, involved, jumping, laborious, on the go*, operose, perky*, persevering, persistent, plugging, productive, psyched up on*, purposeful, sedulous, spirited, steady, tireless, zealous; SEE CONCEPT 538

industry [n1] manufacturing
big business*, business, commerce, commercial enterprise, corporation, management, manufactory, megacorp*, mob, monopoly, multinational, outfit*, production, trade, traffic; SEE CONCEPTS 323,325

industry [n2] hard work
activity, application, assiduity, attention, care, determination, diligence, dynamism, effort, energy, enterprise, intentness, inventiveness, labor, pains, patience, perseverance, persistence, tirelessness, toil, vigor, zeal; SEE CONCEPT 677

inebriated [adj] drunk
blind drunk*, bombed, boozy, high*, inebriate, intoxicated, loaded*, plastered*, smashed*, tight*, tipsy, under the influence, wasted*; SEE CONCEPT 314

ineffable [adj] too great for words
beyond words, celestial, divine, empyreal, empyrean, ethereal, heavenly, holy, ideal, impossible, incommunicable, incredible, indefinable, indescribable, inexpressible, nameless, sacred, spiritual, too sacred for words*, transcendent, transcendental, unspeakable, untellable, unutterable; SEE CONCEPTS 267,574

ineffective/ineffectual [adj] weak, useless
abortive, anticlimactic, barren, bootless, defeasible, feckless, feeble, forceless, fruitless, futile, idle, impotent, inadequate, incompetent, indecisive, inefficacious, inefficient, inept, inferior, innocuous, inoperative, invertebrate, lame, limited, neutralized, nugatory, null, null and void*, paltry, powerless, spineless, unable, unavailing, unfruitful, unproductive, unprofitable, unsuccessful, vain, void, withered, worthless; SEE CONCEPTS 537,560

inefficient [adj] not working well; wasteful
can't hack it*, careless, disorganized, extravagant, faulty, feeble, half-baked*, improficient, improvident, incapable, incompetent, ineffective, ineffectual, inefficacious, inept, inexpert, not cut out for*, prodigal, shooting blanks*, slack, slipshod, sloppy, slovenly, unfit, unprepared, unqualified, unskilled, unskillful, untrained, weak; SEE CONCEPTS 402,527,560

inelegant [adj] clumsy, crude
awkward, coarse, crass, gauche, graceless, gross, indelicate, labored, oafish, raw, rough, rude,

stiff*, uncouth, uncultivated, uncultured, ungainly, ungraceful, unpolished, unrefined, vulgar, wooden*; SEE CONCEPTS 267,542,555

ineligible [adj] not qualified
disqualified, inappropriate, incompetent, objectionable, ruled out, unacceptable, unavailable, undesirable, unequipped, unfit, unqualified, unsuitable; SEE CONCEPTS 402,558

inept [adj1] clumsy, unskilled; incompetent
all thumbs*, artless, awkward, bumbling, bungling, butterfingers*, gauche, halting, inadept, incapable, incompetent, inefficient, inexpert, loser, maladroit, unapt, undexterous, unfacile, ungraceful, unhandy, unproficient, unskillful, wooden*; SEE CONCEPTS 402,527

inept [adj2] not suitable; improper
absurd, ill-timed, inappropriate, inapt, infelicitous, malapropos, meaningless, not adapted, out of place*, pointless, ridiculous, undue, unfit, unseasonable, unseemly, unsuitable; SEE CONCEPT 558

inequality [n] prejudice; lack of balance
asperity, bias, contrast, difference, discrimination, disparity, disproportion, dissimilarity, dissimilitude, diversity, imparity, incommensurateness, injustice, irregularity, one-sidedness, partisanship, preferentiality, roughness, unequivalence, unevenness, unfairness, unjustness, variation; SEE CONCEPT 665

inert [adj] not moving; lifeless
apathetic, asleep, dead, dormant, down, dull, idle, immobile, impassive, impotent, inactive, inanimate, indolent, languid, languorous, lazy, leaden, listless, motionless, numb, paralyzed, passive, phlegmatic, powerless, quiescent, quiet, slack, sleepy, slothful, sluggard, sluggish, slumberous, static, still, stolid, torpid, unmoving, unreactive, unresponsive; SEE CONCEPTS 542,584

inertia [n] disinclination to move; lifelessness
apathy, deadness, drowsiness, dullness, idleness, immobility, immobilization, inactivity, indolence, languor, lassitude, laziness, lethargy, listlessness, oscillancy, paralysis, passivity, sloth, sluggishness, stillness, stupor, torpidity, torpor, unresponsiveness; SEE CONCEPTS 657,681

inevitable [adj] certain; cannot be avoided
all locked up*, assured, binding, compulsory, decided, decreed, destined, determined, doomed, fated, fateful, fixed, for certain, foreordained, imminent, impending, ineluctable, ineludible, inescapable, inexorable, inflexible, in the bag*, irresistible, irrevocable, necessary, no ifs ands or buts*, obligatory, ordained, pat*, prescribed, settled, sure, unalterable, unavoidable, undeniable, unpreventable, without recourse; SEE CONCEPTS 535,552

inexcusable [adj] not forgivable
blamable, blameworthy, censurable, criticizable, impermissible, indefensible, inexpiable, intolerable, outrageous, reprehensible, unallowable, unforgivable, unjustifiable, unpardonable, unpermissible, untenable, unwarrantable, wrong; SEE CONCEPTS 545,570

inexorable [adj] cruel, pitiless
adamant, adamantine, bound, bound and determined*, compulsory, dead set on*, dogged, hard, harsh, hell bent on*, immobile, immovable, implacable, ineluctable, inescapable, inflexible, ironclad, like death and taxes*, locked in*, mean business*, merciless, necessary, no going back*,

in
in

obdurate, obstinate, relentless, remorseless, resolute, rigid, set in stone*, severe, single-minded, stubborn, unappeasable, unbending, uncompromising, unmovable, unrelenting, unyielding; SEE CONCEPTS 401,534

inexpensive [adj] not high priced
bargain, budget, buy, cheap, cost next to nothing*, cut-rate, dime a dozen*, dirt-cheap*, economical, for a song*, half-price, low, low-cost, low-priced, marked down, modest, nominal, popular, popularly priced, real buy*, real steal*, reasonable, reduced, steal, thrifty; SEE CONCEPT 334

inexperienced [adj] unskilled, unfamiliar
amateur, callow, fresh, green*, ignorant, immature, inept, inexpert, innocent, kid*, naive, new, prentice, raw*, rookie, rude, sophomoric, spring chicken*, tenderfoot*, unaccustomed, unacquainted, unconversant, undisciplined, unfamiliar with, unfledged, unpracticed, unschooled, unseasoned, unsophisticated, untrained, untried, unused, unversed, unworldly, verdant, wet behind ears*, young; SEE CONCEPTS 402,404,527

inexplicable [adj] beyond comprehension, explanation
baffling, enigmatic, incomprehensible, indecipherable, indescribable, inexplainable, inscrutable, insoluble, mysterious, mystifying, obscure, odd, peculiar, puzzling, strange, unaccountable, undefinable, unexplainable, unfathomable, unintelligible, unsolvable; SEE CONCEPTS 267,529

infallible [adj] unerring, dependable
acceptable, accurate, agreeable, apodictic, authoritative, certain, correct, effective, effectual, efficacious, efficient, exact, faultless, flawless, foolproof, handy, helpful, impeccable, incontrovertible, inerrable, inerrant, omniscient, perfect, positive, reliable, satisfactory, satisfying, sure, surefire, true, trustworthy, unbeatable, undeceivable, unfailing, unimpeachable, unquestionable, useful; SEE CONCEPTS 535,560,574

infamous [adj] shameful, bad in reputation
abominable, atrocious, base, caitiff, contemptible, corrupt, degenerate, despicable, detestable, disgraceful, dishonorable, disreputable, egregious, evil, flagitious, foul, hateful, heinous, ignominious, ill-famed, iniquitous, loathsome, miscreant, monstrous, nefarious, notorious, odious, offensive, opprobrious, outrageous, perverse, questionable, rotten, scandalous, scurvy, shady, shocking, sorry, unhealthy, vicious, vile, villainous, wicked*; SEE CONCEPTS 404,545,570

infamy [n] shameful, bad reputation
abomination, atrocity, disapprobation, discredit, disesteem, disgrace, dishonor, disrepute, enormity, evil, ignominy, immorality, impropriety, notoriety, notoriousness, obloquy, odium, opprobrium, outrageousness, scandal, shame, stigma, villainy, wickedness; SEE CONCEPTS 411,645

infant [n] baby
babe, bairn, bambino, bantling, bundle, child, kid, little one, neonate, newborn, small child, suckling, toddler, tot; SEE CONCEPTS 414,424

infant/infantile [adj] very young
baby, babyish, callow, childish, childlike, dawning, developing, early, emergent, green*, growing, immature, infantine, initial, juvenile, kid, naive, nascent, newborn, puerile, tender, unfledged, unripe, weak, youthful; SEE CONCEPTS 542,578,797,820

infatuated [adj] in love with; obsessed
beguiled, besotted, bewitched, captivated, carried away*, charmed, crazy about*, enamored, enraptured, far gone on*, fascinated, foolish, inflamed, intoxicated, possessed, seduced, silly*, smitten, spellbound, under a spell*; SEE CONCEPTS 32,403

infect [v] pollute, contaminate
affect, blight, corrupt, defile, disease, influence, poison, spoil, spread among, spread to, taint, touch, vitiate; SEE CONCEPTS 143,246

infection [n] contamination
bug*, communicability, contagion, contagiousness, corruption, defilement, disease, epidemic, flu, germs, impurity, insanitation, poison, pollution, septicity, virus, what's going around*; SEE CONCEPTS 230,306

infectious [adj] catching, spreading
communicable, contagious, contaminating, corrupting, defiling, diseased, epidemic, infective, mephitic, miasmic, noxious, pestilent, pestilential, poisoning, polluting, toxic, transferable, transmittable, virulent, vitiating; SEE CONCEPTS 314,559

infer [v] conclude
arrive at, ascertain, assume, believe, collect, conjecture, construe, deduce, derive, draw, draw inference, figure, figure out, gather, glean, guess, induce, interpret, intuit, judge, presume, presuppose, reach conclusion, read between lines*, read into*, reason, reckon, speculate, suppose, surmise, think, understand; SEE CONCEPTS 12,15,37

inferior [n] person of lesser rank, importance
adherent, attendant, auxiliary, deputy, disciple, follower, hanger-on, hireling, junior, menial, minion, minor, peon, satellite, second banana*, subaltern, subject, subordinate, sycophant, underling; SEE CONCEPTS 348,423

inferior [adj] 1 less in rank, importance
back seat*, bottom, bottom-rung*, entry-level, junior, less, lesser, lower, menial, minor, minus, nether, peon, second, secondary, second-banana*, second-fiddle*, second-string*, smaller, subjacent, subordinate, subsidiary, under, underneath; SEE CONCEPT 567

inferior [adj] 2 poor, second-rate
average, bad, base, common, déclassé, fair, good-for-nothing*, hack*, imperfect, indifferent, junk*, lemon*, lousy, low-grade, low-rent*, mean, mediocre, middling, ordinary, paltry, poorer, sad, second-class, sorry*, substandard, tawdry, two-bit*, worse, wretched; SEE CONCEPT 574

infernal [adj] damned; underworld
accursed, blamed, blasted, chthonian, confounded, cursed, cussed, damnable, demonic, devilish, diabolical, execrable, fiendish, hellish, lower, malevolent, malicious, monstrous, nether, satanic, subterranean, sulphurous, wicked; SEE CONCEPTS 536,545

infertile [adj] not bearing fruit, young
barren, depleted, drained, effete, exhausted, impotent, impoverished, infecund, nonproductive, sterile, unbearing, unfertile, unfruitful, unproductive; SEE CONCEPTS 406,560

infest [adj] flood, overrun
abound, annoy, assail, beset, crawl, crowd, defile, fill, flock, harass, harry, infect, invade, overspread, overwhelm, pack, penetrate, pester, plague, pollute, press, ravage, swarm, teem, throng, worry; SEE CONCEPTS 14,86,179

infidelity [n] *disloyalty to an obligation*
adultery, affair, bad faith, betrayal, cheating, duplicity, extramarital relations, faithlessness, falseness, falsity, inconstancy, lewdness, perfidiousness, perfidy, treacherousness, treachery, treason, two-timing*, unfaithfulness; SEE CONCEPTS *388,645*

infiltrate [v] *creep in*
access, crack*, edge in, filter through, foist, impregnate, insinuate, penetrate, percolate*, permeate, pervade, saturate, sneak in, tinge, work into, worm into*; SEE CONCEPTS *159,179*

infinite [adj] *limitless, without end*
absolute, all-embracing, bottomless, boundless, enduring, enormous, eternal, everlasting, illimitable, immeasurable, immense, incalculable, incessant, inestimable, inexhaustible, interminable, measureless, million, never-ending, no end of, no end to, numberless, perdurable, perpetual, sempiternal, stupendous, supertemporal, supreme, total, unbounded, uncounted, unending, untold, vast, wide, without limit, without number; SEE CONCEPTS *762,781,798*

infinitesimal [adj] *small*
atomic, imperceptible, inappreciable, inconsiderable, insignificant, little, microscopic, miniature, minuscule, minute, negligible, teeny*, tiny, unnoticeable; SEE CONCEPTS *773,789*

infinity [n] *endlessness*
beyond, boundlessness, continuity, continuum, endless time, eternity, expanse, extent, immeasurability, immensity, infinitude, limitlessness, myriad, perpetuity, sempiternity, space, ubiquity, unlimited space, vastitude, vastness; SEE CONCEPTS *730,807*

infirm [adj] *sick, weak*
ailing, anemic, anile, debilitated, decrepit, delicate, enfeebled, failing, faint, faltering, feeble, flimsy, fragile, frail, halting, ill, insecure, irresolute, laid low*, lame, sensile, shaky, unsound, unstable, unsubstantial, vacillating, wavering, wobbly; SEE CONCEPTS *314,485,489*

infirmity [n] *weakness, sickness*
affliction, ailing, ailment, confinement, debilitation, debility, decay, decrepitude, defect, deficiency, disease, diseasedness, disorder, failing, fault, feebleness, flu, frailty, ill health, imperfection, indisposition, malady, malaise, shortcoming, sickliness, unhealth, unhealthiness, unwellness, vulnerability; SEE CONCEPTS *306,674,732*

inflame [v] *anger, aggravate*
agitate, annoy, arouse, burn, disturb, embitter, enrage, exacerbate, exasperate, excite, fan, fire, fire up, foment, gall, get*, grate, heat, heat up, ignite, impassion, incense, increase, infuriate, intensify, intoxicate, irritate, kindle, light, madden, provoke, put out*, rile, roil, rouse, steam up, stimulate, vex, worsen; SEE CONCEPTS *7,14, 19,22,249*

inflammable [adj] *ready to burn*
burnable, combustible, dangerous, flammable, hazardous, ignitable, incendiary, risky, unsafe; SEE CONCEPT *485*

inflammatory [adj] *instigative, angering*
anarchic, demagogic, exciting, explosive, fiery, incendiary, incitive, inflaming, insurgent, intemperate, provocative, rabble-rousing*, rabid, rebellious, revolutionary, riotous, seditionary, seditious; SEE CONCEPTS *537,542*

inflate [v] *blow up, increase*
aerate, aggrandize, amplify, augment, balloon*, beef up*, bloat, boost, build up, cram*, dilate, distend, enlarge, escalate, exaggerate, exalt, expand, flesh out*, magnify, maximize, overestimate, pad*, puff up*, pump up*, pyramid, raise, spread, stretch, surcharge, swell up*, widen; SEE CONCEPTS *236,245,780*

inflated [adj] *exaggerated*
aggrandized, amplified, augmented, aureate, bloated, bombastic, diffuse, dilated, distended, dropsical, enlarged, euphuistic, extended, filled, flatulent, flowery, fustian, grandiloquent, grown, magnified, magniloquent, ostentatious, overblown, overestimated, pompous, pretentious, prolix, puffed, pumped up, ranting, rhapsodical, rhetorical, showy, spread, stretched, surcharged, swollen, tumescent, tumid, turgid, verbose, windy, wordy; SEE CONCEPTS *267,773*

inflation [n] *increase, swelling*
aggrandizement, blowing up, boom, boost, buildup, distension, enhancement, enlargement, escalation, expansion, extension, hike, intensification, prosperity, puffiness, rise, spread, tumefaction; SEE CONCEPTS *335,763,780*

inflection [n] *accent, intonation*
articulation, change, emphasis, enunciation, modulation, pitch, pronunciation, sound, timbre, tonality, tone, tone of voice, variation; SEE CONCEPTS *65,595*

inflexible [adj 1] *stubborn*
adamant, adamantine, determined, dogged, dyed-in-the-wool*, firm, fixed, hard, hard-and-fast*, immovable, immutable, implacable, indomitable, inexorable, intractable, iron, obdurate, obstinate, relentless, resolute, rigid, rigorous, set, set in one's ways*, single-minded, stand one's ground*, staunch, steadfast, steely, stiff, strict, stringent, unadaptable, unbending, unchangeable, uncompliant, uncompromising, unrelenting, unswayable, unyielding; SEE CONCEPT *404*

inflexible [adj 2] *hardened, stiff*
hard, immalleable, impliable, inelastic, nonflexible, rigid, set, starched, taut, unbending; SEE CONCEPT *604*

inflict [v] *impose something*
administer, apply, bring upon, command, deal out, deliver, dispense, exact, expose, extort, force, force upon, give, give it to*, lay down the law*, levy, mete out, require, stick it to*, strike, subject, visit, wreak; SEE CONCEPTS *50,53, 88,242*

influence [n] *power, authority*
access, agency, ascendancy, character, clout, command, connections, consequence, control, credit, direction, domination, dominion, drag, effect, esteem, fame, fix, force, grease*, guidance, hold, impact, importance, imprint, in, juice*, leadership, leverage, magnetism, mark, moment, money, monopoly, network, notoriety, predominance, prerogative, pressure, prestige, prominence, pull, repercussion, reputation, ropes*, rule, significance, spell, supremacy, sway, weight*; SEE CONCEPT *687*

influence [v] *lead to believe, do*
act upon, affect, alter, argue into, arouse, be recognized, bias, brainwash*, bribe, bring to bear, carry weight, change, channel, compel, control, count, determine, direct, dispose, form, get at*, guide, have a part in, impact on, impel, impress,

in
in

incite, incline, induce, instigate, manipulate, modify, mold, move, persuade, predispose, prejudice, prevail, prompt, pull strings*, regulate, rouse, rule, seduce, sell, shape, snow*, sway, talk into, train, turn, urge, work upon; SEE CONCEPTS 18,68,242

influential [adj] *effective, powerful*
affecting, authoritative, big-gun*, big-wheel*, controlling, dominant, efficacious, famous, forcible, governing, guiding, hot-dog*, important, impressive, inspiring, instrumental, leading, major-league*, meaningful, momentous, moving, name, persuasive, potent, prominent, significant, strong, substantial, telling, touching, weighty; SEE CONCEPTS 537,568

influx [n] *flow, rush*
arrival, coming in, convergence, entrance, incursion, inflow, inpouring, inrush, introduction, inundation, invasion, penetration; SEE CONCEPTS 159,179,786

infomercial [n] *full-length television program existing solely to market a product*
advertorial, commercial, demonstration, docutainment, infotainment, paid announcement; SEE CONCEPT 277

inform [v] *communicate knowledge, information*
acquaint, advise, apprise, betray, blab*, brief, caution, clue, edify, educate, endow, endue, enlighten, familiarize, fill in, forewarn, give a pointer, give a tip, give away, give two cents*, illuminate, inspire, instruct, invest, leak, let in on*, let know, level, make conversant with, notify, post, relate, send word, show the ropes*, snitch, squeal, tattle, teach, tell, tell on, tip, tout, update, warn, wise; SEE CONCEPT 60

informal [adj] *casual, simple*
breezy, colloquial, congenial, cool*, democratic, down home*, easy, easygoing, everyday, extempore, familiar, folksy, frank, free, free-and-easy*, homey, improv*, inconspicuous, intimate, laid back*, loose, low-pressure, mellow, mixed, motley, natural, off-the-cuff*, open, ordinary, relaxed, spontaneous, sporty, straightforward, throwaway*, unceremonious, unconstrained, unconventional, unfussy, unofficial, unrestrained, urbane, without ceremony; SEE CONCEPTS 548, 589

informant/informer [n] *person who delivers news*
accuser, adviser, announcer, betrayer, blabbermouth*, canary*, crier, deep throat*, double-crosser, herald, interviewer, journalist, messenger, newscaster/newsperson, notifier, preacher, propagandist, rat*, reporter, sneak, source, stool pigeon*, tattler, tattletale; SEE CONCEPTS 348,354,423

information [n] *facts, news*
advice, ammo*, break*, chapter and verse*, clue, confidence, counsel, cue, data, dirt*, dope*, dossier, earful*, enlightenment, erudition, illumination, info*, inside story*, instruction, intelligence, knowledge, leak, learning, lore, lowdown*, material, message, network, notice, notification, orientation, propaganda, report, science, scoop, score, tidings, tip, what's what*, whole story*, wisdom, word*; SEE CONCEPT 274

informative [adj] *educational*
advisory, chatty, communicative, descriptive, edifying, educative, elucidative, enlightening, explanatory, forthcoming, gossipy, illuminating, informational, instructional, instructive, newsy,

revealing, revelatory, significant; SEE CONCEPT 267

informed [adj] *cognizant, conversant*
abreast, acquainted, apprized, au courant*, au fait*, briefed, enlightened, erudite, expert, familiar, in the know*, into*, knowledgeable, know the score*, know what's what*, learned, on top of*, posted*, primed*, reliable, savvy*, tuned in*, up*, up on*, up-to-date, versant, versed, well-read, wise to*; SEE CONCEPT 402

infraction [n] *violation*
breach, breaking, contravention, crime, error, faux pas, infringement, lapse, offense, sin, slip*, transgression, trespass; SEE CONCEPTS 192,645

infrequent [adj] *not happening regularly*
exceptional, few, few and far between*, isolated, limited, meager, occasional, odd, rare, scant, scanty, scarce, scattered, seldom, semioccasional, sparse, spasmodic, sporadic, stray, uncommon, unusual; SEE CONCEPT 530

infringe [v] *violate*
borrow, breach, break, contravene, crash, disobey, encroach, entrench, impose, infract, intrude, invade, lift, meddle, obtrude, offend, pirate, presume, steal, transgress, trespass; SEE CONCEPTS 192,384

infuriate [v] *make angry*
aggravate, anger, enrage, exasperate, incense, ire, irritate, madden, make blood boil*, provoke, rile, T-off*, umbrage; SEE CONCEPT 14

infuse [v] *introduce; soak*
animate, breathe into, imbue, impart, implant, impregnate, inculcate, indoctrinate, ingrain, inoculate, inspire, instill, intersperse, invest, leaven, permeate, pervade, plant, saturate, steep, suffuse; SEE CONCEPTS 140,179,187

ingenious [adj] *clever; brilliant*
able, adroit, artistic, bright, canny, crafty, creative, cunning, deviceful, dexterous, gifted, imaginative, innovational, innovative, innovatory, intelligent, inventive, original, ready, resourceful, shrewd, skillful, sly, subtle; SEE CONCEPT 402

ingenuous [adj] *honest, trustful*
artless, candid, childlike, frank, green*, guileless, innocent, like a babe in the woods*, naive, natural, open, outspoken, plain, simple, sincere, square, straightforward, trusting, unaffected, unartful, unartificial, undisguised, unreserved, unschooled, unsophisticated, unstudied, up front*; SEE CONCEPTS 267,542,589

ingrained [adj] *deep-rooted*
built-in, chronic, confirmed, congenital, constitutional, deep-seated, fixed, fundamental, hereditary, implanted, inborn, inbred, inbuilt, indelible, indwelling, ineradicable, inherent, innate, in the blood*, intrinsic, inveterate, rooted; SEE CONCEPTS 535,549

ingratiate [v] *get on the good side of someone*
attract, blandish, brownnose*, captivate, charm, crawl, flatter, get in with*, grovel, hand a line*, insinuate oneself, kowtow*, play up to*, seek favor, truckle; SEE CONCEPTS 7,22,68

ingratiating [adj] *fawning, servile*
charming, crawling, deferential, disarming, flattering, humble, insinuating, obsequious, saccharine, serving, silken, smarmy, soft, sycophantic, toadying*, unctuous; SEE CONCEPT 401

ingredient [n] *component of concoction*
additive, constituent, element, factor, fixing, fundamental, innards, integral, integrant, making,

part, part and parcel*, piece; SEE CONCEPT 835

inhabit [v] take up residence in
abide, crash, dwell, indwell, live, locate, lodge, make one's home, occupy, park, people, perch, populate, possess, reside, roost, settle, squat, stay, tenant; SEE CONCEPT 226

inhabitant [n] person who is resident of habitation
aborigine, addressee, autochthon, boarder, citizen, colonist, denizen, dweller, householder, incumbent, indweller, inmate, lessee, lodger, native, neighbor, occupant, occupier, renter, resider, roomer, settler, squatter, suburbanite, tenant, urbanite; SEE CONCEPTS 354,413

inhale [v] breathe in
drag, draw in, gasp, inspire, insufflate, puff, pull, respire, smell, sniff, snort, suck in; SEE CONCEPTS 163,601

inherent [adj] basic, hereditary
built-in, characteristic, congenital, connate, constitutional, deep-rooted, deep-seated, distinctive, elementary, essential, fixed, fundamental, genetic, immanent, implicit, inborn, inbred, inbuilt, indigenous, indispensable, individual, indwelling, ingrained, inherited, innate, inner, instinctive, integral, integrated, internal, in the grain, intimate, intrinsic, inward, latent, native, natural, original, part and parcel*, resident, running in the family*, subjective, unalienable; SEE CONCEPTS 404,549

inherit [v] gain as possession from someone's death
accede, acquire, be bequeathed, be granted, be left, come in for, come into, derive, fall heir, get, obtain, receive, succeed, take over; SEE CONCEPTS 124,551

inheritance [n] possession gained through someone's death
bequest, birthright, devise, estate, gift, heirloom, heritage, heritance, legacy, primogeniture; SEE CONCEPT 337

inhibit [v] restrict, prevent
arrest, avert, bar, bit, bridle, check, constrain, cramp, curb, discourage, enjoin, faze, forbid, frustrate, hang up*, hinder, hog-tie*, hold back, hold down, hold in, impede, interdict, keep in, obstruct, outlaw, prohibit, put on brakes*, repress, restrain, sandbag*, stop, stymie, suppress, taboo*, ward, withhold; SEE CONCEPTS 121,130

inhibited [adj] shy
bottled up*, cold, constrained, frustrated, guarded, hung up*, passionless, repressed, reserved, reticent, self-conscious, subdued, undemonstrative, unresponsive, uptight, withdrawn; SEE CONCEPTS 404,542

inhibition [n] restriction, hindrance
bar, barrier, blockage, check, embargo, hangup, interdict, interference, obstacle, prevention, prohibition, reserve, restraint, reticence, self-consciousness, shyness, sublimation, suppression; SEE CONCEPTS 411,657

inhospitable [adj] unfriendly
brusque, cold, cool, hostile, rude, short, uncongenial, unfavorable, ungenerous, unkind, unreceptive, unsociable, unwelcoming; SEE CONCEPT 401

inhuman/inhumane [adj] animal, savage
barbaric, barbarous, bestial, brutal, cannibalistic, cold-blooded, cruel, devilish, diabolical, fell, ferocious, fiendish, fierce, grim, hateful, heartless, implacable, malicious, malign, malignant, mean, merciless, pitiless, relentless, remorseless, ruthless, truculent, uncompassionate, unfeeling, unkind, unrelenting, unsympathetic, vicious; SEE CONCEPTS 401,545

inimical [adj] antagonistic, contrary
adverse, antipathetic, destructive, disaffected, harmful, hostile, hurtful, ill, ill-disposed, inimicable, injurious, noxious, opposed, oppugnant, pernicious, repugnant, unfavorable, unfriendly, unwelcoming; SEE CONCEPTS 401,537

inimitable [adj] incomparable
consummate, matchless, nonpareil, peerless, perfect, supreme, unequalled, unexampled, unique, unmatched, unparalleled, unrivalled, unsurpassable; SEE CONCEPT 574

iniquity [n] sin, evil
abomination, baseness, crime, evildoing, heinousness, immorality, infamy, injustice, miscreancy, misdeed, offense, sinfulness, unfairness, unrighteousness, wickedness, wrong, wrongdoing; SEE CONCEPT 645

initial [adj] beginning, primary
antecedent, basic, commencing, earliest, early, elementary, embryonic, first, foremost, fundamental, germinal, headmost, inaugural, inceptive, inchoate, incipient, infant, initiative, initiatory, introductory, leading, nascent, opening, original, pioneer, virgin; SEE CONCEPTS 585,799,828

initiate [v1] start, introduce
admit, begin, break the ice*, come out with, come up with, commence, dream up, enter, get ball rolling*, get feet wet*, get under way, inaugurate, induct, install, instate, institute, intro*, invest, kick off*, launch, make up, open, originate, pioneer, set in motion, set up, take in, take up, trigger, usher in; SEE CONCEPT 221

initiate [v2] teach
brief, coach, edify, enlighten, familiarize, indoctrinate, induct, inform, instate, instruct, introduce, invest, train; SEE CONCEPT 285

initiation [n] start, introduction
admission, baptism, beginning, commencement, debut, enrollment, entrance, inaugural, inauguration, inception, indoctrination, induction, installation, instatement, investiture, preliminaries; SEE CONCEPTS 221,386

initiative [n] eagerness to do something
action, ambition, drive, dynamism, energy, enterprise, enthusiasm, get-up-and-go*, gumption*, inventiveness, leadership, moxie*, originality, punch, push, resource, resourcefulness, spunk*, steam*, vigor; SEE CONCEPTS 411,657

inject [v1] put in, introduce
add, drag in, force into, imbue, implant, impregnate, include, infuse, insert, instill, interjaculate, interject, place into, squeeze in, stick in, throw in; SEE CONCEPTS 187,208,209

inject [v2] introduce into bloodstream by use of a needle
give a shot, inoculate, jab, mainline*, shoot, vaccinate; SEE CONCEPTS 179,310

injection [n] introduction into bloodstream
booster, dose, dram, enema, inoculation, needle, vaccine; SEE CONCEPT 311

injunction [n] decree
admonition, ban, bar, behest, bidding, charge, command, demand, dictate, embargo, enjoinder, exhortation, instruction, mandate, order, precept, prohibition, ruling, word, writ; SEE CONCEPTS 271,318

injure [v] *hurt, harm*
abuse, aggrieve, batter, blemish, blight, break, contort, cripple, cut up, damage, deface, deform, disable, disfigure, distort, distress, do in*, draw blood*, foul, foul up, grieve, hack up, impair, maim, maltreat, mangle, mar, mutilate, pain, pique, prejudice, ruin, shake up, spoil, sting, tarnish, torment, torture, total, undermine, vitiate, wax, weaken, wound, wrong; SEE CONCEPT 246

injurious [adj] *hurtful*
abusive, adverse, bad, baneful, corrupting, damaging, dangerous, deadly, deleterious, destructive, detrimental, disadvantageous, evil, harmful, iniquitous, insulting, libeling, mischievous, nocent, nocuous, noxious, opprobrious; pernicious, poisonous, prejudicial, ruinous, slanderous, unconducive, unhealthy, unjust, wrongful; SEE CONCEPTS 537,570

injury [n] *hurt, harm*
abrasion, abuse, affliction, affront, agony, bad, bite, blemish, boo-boo*, bruise, burn, chop, cramp, cut, damage, deformation, detriment, discomfiture, disservice, distress, evil, fracture, gash, grievance, hemorrhage, ill, impairment, indignity, injustice, insult, laceration, lesion, libel, loss, mischief, misery, mutilation, nick, ouch*, outrage, pang, ruin, scar, scratch, shock, slander, sore, sprain, stab, sting, suffering, swelling, trauma, twinge, wound, wrong; SEE CONCEPTS 309,728

injustice [n] *unfair treatment; bias*
abuse, breach, crime, crying shame*, damage, dirty deal*, discrimination, encroachment, favoritism, grievance, inequality, inequity, infraction, infringement, iniquity, malfeasance, malpractice, maltreatment, miscarriage, mischief, negligence, offense, onesidedness, oppression, outrage, partiality, partisanship, prejudice, railroad*, ruin, sellout*, transgression, trespass, unfairness, unjustness, unlawfulness, villainy, violation, wrong, wrongdoing; SEE CONCEPTS 192,645,674

inkling [n] *idea, clue*
conception, cue, faintest idea*, foggiest idea*, glimmering, hint, hot lead*, hunch*, impression, indication, innuendo, intimation, lead, notion, sneaking suspicion*, suggestion, suspicion, tip, tipoff, whisper; SEE CONCEPT 689

inlet [n] *arm of the sea*
basin, bay, bayou, bight, canal, channel, cove, creek, delta, entrance, estuary, firth, fjord, gulf, harbor, ingress, loch, narrows, passage, slew, slough, sound, strait; SEE CONCEPTS 509,514

inn [n] *accommodation for travellers*
auberge, hospice, hostel, hostelry, hotel, lodge, motel, public house, resort, roadhouse, saloon, tavern; SEE CONCEPTS 439,449,516

innate [adj] *inherited, native*
congenital, connate, connatural, constitutional, deep-seated, elemental, essential, hereditary, inborn, inbred, indigenous, ingrained, inherent, instinctive, intrinsic, intuitive, natural, normal, regular, standard, typical, unacquired; SEE CONCEPTS 406,549

inner [adj1] *central, middle physically*
close, constitutional, essential, familiar, focal, inherent, innermore, inside, interior, internal, intestinal, intimate, intrinsic, inward, nuclear; SEE CONCEPTS 826,830

inner [adj2] *mental, private*
central, concealed, deep-rooted, deep-seated,

emotional, esoteric, essential, focal, gut*, hidden, individual, inherent, innate, inside, interior, internal, intimate, intrinsic, intuitive, inward, personal, psychological, repressed, secret, spiritual, subconscious, unrevealed, visceral, viscerous; SEE CONCEPTS 529,576

innocence [n1] *blamelessness*
chastity, clean hands*, clear conscience*, guiltlessness, immaculateness, impeccability, incorruptibility, incorruption, inculpability, probity, purity, righteousness, sinlessness, stainlessness, uprightness, virtue; SEE CONCEPT 645

innocence [n2] *harmlessness, naïveté*
artlessness, candidness, credulousness, forthrightness, frankness, freshness, guilelessness, gullibility, ignorance, inexperience, ingenuousness, innocuousness, innoxiousness, inoffensiveness, lack, nescience, plainness, purity, simplicity, sincerity, unaffectedness, unawareness, unfamiliarity, unknowingness, unsophistication, unworldliness, virtue; SEE CONCEPTS 409,411

innocent [adj1] *blameless*
above suspicion, angelic, chaste, clean, cleanhanded, clear, crimeless, exemplary, faultless, free of, good, guilt-free, guiltless, honest, immaculate, impeccable, impeccant, inculpable, in the clear*, irreproachable, lawful, legal, legitimate, licit, not guilty, pristine, pure, righteous, safe, sinless, spotless, stainless, unblemished, uncensurable, uncorrupt, unimpeachable, uninvolved, unoffending, unsullied, untainted, upright, virginal, virtuous; SEE CONCEPT 545

innocent [adj2] *harmless, naive*
artless, childlike, credulous, frank, fresh, guileless, gullible, hurtless, ignorant, inexperienced, ingenuous, innocuous, innoxious, inobnoxious, inoffensive, offenseless, open, raw, safe, simple, soft, square, unacquainted, unartificial, uncool, unfamiliar, unhurtful, uninjurious, unmalicious, unobjectionable, unoffensive, unschooled, unsophisticated, unstudied, unsuspicious, unworldly, well-intentioned, well-meant, wide-eyed, youthful; SEE CONCEPTS 404,542

innocuous [adj] *harmless*
banal, bland, flat, innocent, innoxious, inobnoxious, inoffensive, insipid, jejune, kind, painless, safe, sapless, unobjectionable, unoffending, weak; SEE CONCEPTS 401,572

innovation [n] *change, novelty*
addition, alteration, contraption, cutting edge*, departure, deviation, introduction, last word*, latest thing*, leading edge*, modernism, modernization, modification, mutation, newness, notion, permutation, shift, variation, vicissitude, wrinkle*; SEE CONCEPTS 260,529,660,665

innovative [adj] *creative*
avant-garde, breaking new ground*, contemporary, cutting-edge*, deviceful, ingenious, innovational, innovatory, inventive, just out*, leading-edge*, new, newfangled*, original, originative, state-of-the-art; SEE CONCEPTS 529,578,589,797

innuendo [n] *suggestion*
allusion, aside, aspersion, hint, implication, imputation, insinuation, intimation, overtone, reference, whisper; SEE CONCEPTS 75,278

innumerable [adj] *many, infinite*
alive with*, beyond number, countless, frequent, incalculable, multitudinous, myriad, numberless, numerous, uncountable, unnumbered, untold; SEE CONCEPT 762

inoffensive [adj] not obnoxious; harmless
calm, clean, friendly, humble, innocent, innocuous, innoxious, mild, neutral, nonprovocative, peaceable, pleasant, quiet, retiring, safe, unobjectionable, unobtrusive, unoffending; SEE CONCEPTS 267,542

inopportune [adj] not appropriate or suitable
contrary, disadvantageous, disturbing, ill-chosen, ill-timed, inappropriate, inauspicious, inconvenient, malapropos, mistimed, troublesome, unfavorable, unfortunate, unpropitious, unseasonable, unsuitable, untimely; SEE CONCEPT 558

inordinate [adj] excessive, extravagant
disproportionate, dizzying, exorbitant, extortionate, extreme, gratuitous, immoderate, intemperate, irrational, outrageous, overindulgent, overmuch, preposterous, supererogatory, superfluous, surplus, too much, towering, uncalled-for, unconscionable, uncurbed, undue, unmeasurable, unreasonable, unrestrained, untempered, unwarranted, wanton, wasteful; SEE CONCEPTS 570,781

inquest [n] investigation
delving, examination, hearing, inquiry, inquisition, probe, probing, quest, research, trial; SEE CONCEPTS 48,290,318

inquire [v] ask; look into
analyze, catechize, examine, explore, feel out, go over, grill, hit, hit up, inspect, interrogate, investigate, knock, probe, prospect, pry, query, question, request information, roast, scrutinize, search, seek, seek information, sift, study, test the waters*; SEE CONCEPTS 24,48

inquiring [adj] wondering, curious
analytical, catechistic, doubtful, examining, fact-finding, heuristic, inquisitive, interested, interrogative, investigative, investigatory, nosy, outward-looking, probing, prying, questioning, quizzical, searching, Socratic, speculative, studious; SEE CONCEPTS 402,542

inquiry [n] asking; looking into
analysis, audit, catechizing, check, cross-examination, delving, disquisition, examination, exploration, fishing expedition*, grilling, hearing, inquest, inquisition, inspection, interrogation, interrogatory, investigation, legwork*, poll, probe, probing, pursuit, Q and A*, query, quest, question, questioning, quizzing, request, research, scrutiny, search, study, survey, third degree*, trial balloon*; SEE CONCEPTS 24,48,290

inquisitive [adj] curious
analytical, big-eyed*, challenging, forward, impertinent, inquiring, inquisitorial, interested, intrusive, investigative, meddlesome, meddling, nosy, peering, personal, poking, presumptuous, probing, prying, questioning, scrutinizing, searching, sifting, snooping, speculative; SEE CONCEPT 402

inroad [n] advance, foray
encroachment, impingement, incursion, intrusion, invasion, irruption, onslaught, raid, trespass; SEE CONCEPTS 86,704

insane [adj] mentally ill; foolish
batty*, bizarre, cracked*, crazed, crazy, cuckoo*, daft, demented, derailed, deranged, fatuous, frenzied, idiotic, impractical, irrational, irresponsible, loony*, lunatic, mad, maniacal, mental, moonstruck*, nuts*, nutty*, off one's rocker*, of unsound mind, out of one's mind*, paranoid, preposterous, psychopathic, psychotic, rabid, raging, raving, schizophrenic, screwy, senseless,

touched, unhinged, unsettled, wild; SEE CONCEPTS 314,403,548

insanely [adv] extremely
crazily, ferociously, fiercely, furiously, idiotically, irrationally, stupidly, violently, wildly; SEE CONCEPT 569

insanity [n] mental illness; foolishness
aberration, absurdity, alienation, craziness, delirium, delusion, dementia, derangement, distraction, dotage, folly, frenzy, hallucination, hysteria, illusion, inanity, irrationality, irresponsibility, lunacy, madness, mania, mental disorder, neurosis, phobia, preposterousness, psychopathy, psychosis, senselessness, unbalance, unreasonableness, witlessness; SEE CONCEPTS 316,410

insatiable [adj] voracious, wanting
clamorous, crying, demanding, desiring, exigent, gluttonous, greedy, importunate, insatiate, insistent, intemperate, pressing, quenchless, rapacious, ravenous, unappeasable, unquenchable, unsatisfiable, unsatisfied, urgent, yearning; SEE CONCEPTS 20,403,546

inscribe [v] imprint, write
book, carve, cut, engrave, engross, etch, impress, indite, list, record, register, scribe; SEE CONCEPT 79

inscrutable [adj] hidden, mysterious; blank
ambiguous, arcane, cabalistic, deadpan*, difficult, enigmatic, impenetrable, incomprehensible, inexplicable, mysterial, mystic, poker-faced*, secret, sphinxlike, unaccountable, undiscoverable, unexplainable, unfathomable, unintelligible, unknowable, unreadable; SEE CONCEPTS 529,576

insecure [adj1] uncertain, worried
afraid, anxious, apprehensive, choked, Delphic, diffident, hanging by thread*, hesitant, jumpy, on thin ice*, questioning, shaky, touch and go*, touchy*, troubled, unassured, unconfident, unpoised, unsure, up in the air*, uptight*, vague; SEE CONCEPTS 403,542

insecure [adj2] dangerous, precarious
defenseless, exposed, fluctuant, frail, hazardous, immature, insubstantial, loose, open to attack*, perilous, rickety, rocky, rootless, shaky, unguarded, unprotected, unreliable, unsafe, unshielded, unsound, unstable, unsteady, vacillating, vulnerable, wavering, weak, wobbly; SEE CONCEPTS 488,570

insensitive [adj1] indifferent, callous
aloof, bloodless*, coldhearted*, crass, feelingless, hard, hard as nails*, hard-boiled*, hardened, hardhearted*, heartless, imperceptive, incurious, obtuse, stony, tactless, thick-skinned*, tough, uncaring, unconcerned, unfeeling, unkind, unresponsive, unsusceptible; SEE CONCEPT 401

insensitive [adj2] numb
anesthetized, asleep, benumbed, dead, deadened, immune to, impervious to, insensible, nonreactive, senseless, unfeeling; SEE CONCEPT 406

inseparable [adj] unable to be divided
as one, attached, conjoined, connected, entwined, inalienable, indissoluble, indivisible, inseverable, integral, integrated, intertwined, interwoven, molded, secure, tied up, unified, united, whole; SEE CONCEPT 531

insert [v] put, tuck in
admit, drag in, embed, enter, fill in, imbed, implant, include, infix, infuse, inject, inlay, insinuate, instill, intercalate, interject, interlope, interpolate, interpose, introduce, intrude, lug in,

in
in

obtrude, place, pop in*, root, set, shoehorn*, shove in, squeeze in, stick, work in; SEE CONCEPTS 201,209

inside [*n*] *middle, lining*
belly, bowels, breast, center, contents, gut, heart, innards, inner portion, interior, recess, soul, stuffing, womb; SEE CONCEPT 830

inside [*adj*] *in the middle; interior*
central, indoors, inner, innermost, internal, intramural, inward, surrounded, under a roof; SEE CONCEPTS 583,830

inside [*adj2*] *secret*
classified, closet, confidential, esoteric, exclusive, hushed, internal, limited, private, restricted; SEE CONCEPTS 529,576

inside [*adv*] *within*
indoors, under a roof, under cover, within doors, within walls; SEE CONCEPT 583

insidious [*adj*] *sneaky, tricky*
artful, astute, corrupt, crafty, crooked, cunning, dangerous, deceitful, deceptive, deep, designing, dishonest, disingenuous, duplicitous, ensnaring, false, foxy, guileful, intriguing, like a snake in the grass*, Machiavellian, perfidious, perilous, secret, slick, sly, smooth, snaky*, sneaking, stealthy, subtle, surreptitious, treacherous, wily, wormlike*; SEE CONCEPTS 401,542,545

insight [*n*] *intuitiveness, awareness*
acumen, click*, comprehension, discernment, divination, drift*, intuition, judgment, observation, penetration, perception, perceptivity, perspicacity, sagaciousness, sagacity, sageness, sapience, shrewdness, understanding, vision, wavelength*, wisdom; SEE CONCEPTS 409,410

insignia [*n*] *emblem*
badge, coat of arms, crest, decoration, earmark, ensign, mark, paraphernalia, regalia, symbol; SEE CONCEPTS 259,284

insignificant [*adj*] *not important; of no consequence*
casual, immaterial, inappreciable, inconsequential, inconsiderable, infinitesimal, irrelevant, lesser, light, lightweight*, little, meager, meaningless, minim, minimal, minor, minuscule, minute, negligible, nondescript, nonessential, not worth mentioning*, nugatory, paltry, petty, pointless, purportless, scanty, secondary, senseless, small, trifling, trivial, unimportant, unsubstantial; SEE CONCEPT 575

insincere [*adj*] *dishonest, pretended*
ambidextrous, backhanded, deceitful, deceptive, devious, disingenuous, dissembling, dissimulating, double, double-dealing, duplicitous, evasive, faithless, fake, false, hollow, hypocritical, lying, mendacious, perfidious, phony, pretentious, put-on*, shifty, slick, sly, snide, two-faced*, unfaithful, untrue, untruthful; SEE CONCEPTS 267, 542,545

insinuate [*v1*] *hint, suggest*
allude, ascribe, connote, imply, impute, indicate, intimate, mention, propose, purport, refer, signify; SEE CONCEPTS 49,75

insinuate [*v2*] *force one's way into*
curry favor*, edge in, fill in, foist, get in with*, horn in*, infiltrate, infuse, ingratiate, inject, insert, instill, intercalate, interject, interpose, introduce, muscle in*, slip in, wedge in, work in, worm in*; SEE CONCEPTS 159,208,384

insipid [*adj1*] *dull, uninteresting*
anemic, arid, banal, beige, blah*, bland, charac-

terless, colorless, commonplace, dead*, drab, driveling, dry, feeble, flat, ho-hum*, inane, innocuous, jejune, lifeless, limp, mild, mundane, nebbish, nothing, ordinary, plain, pointless, prosaic, prosy, slight, soft*, spiritless, stale, stupid, subdued, tame, tedious, tenuous, thin, tired, trite, unimaginative, vapid, watery, weak, weariful, wearisome, wishy-washy*; SEE CONCEPTS 402, 404,537

insipid [*adj2*] *tasteless*
bland, distasteful, flat, flavorless, jejune, mild, savorless, stale, unappetizing, unpalatable, unsavory, vapid, watered-down, watery; SEE CONCEPT 613

insist [*v*] *order and expect; claim*
assert, asseverate, aver, be firm, contend, demand, hold, importune, lay down the law*, maintain, persist, press, reiterate, repeat, request, require, stand firm, swear, take a stand*, urge, vow; SEE CONCEPTS 49,53

insistent [*adj*] *demanding*
assertive, burning, clamant, clamorous, continuous, crying, dire, dogged, emphatic, exigent, forceful, imperative, imperious, importunate, incessant, obstinate, peremptory, perseverant, persevering, persistent, pressing, reiterative, resolute, resounding, unrelenting, urgent; SEE CONCEPTS 267,534,540

insolence [*n*] *boldness, disrespect*
abuse, arrogance, audacity, back talk, brass*, brazenness, cheek*, chutzpah*, contempt, contemptuousness, contumely, effrontery, gall, guff*, hardihood, impertinence, impudence, incivility, insubordination, lip*, offensiveness, pertness, presumption, rudeness, sass*, sauce*, uncivility; SEE CONCEPT 633

insolent [*adj*] *bold, disrespectful*
abusive, arrogant, barefaced, brassy*, brazen, breezy, contemptuous, contumelious, dictatorial, discourteous, disdainful, flip*, fresh, imperative, impertinent, impolite, impudent, insubordinate, insulting, magisterial, nervy, off-base*, offensive, out-of-line*, overbearing, peremptory, pert, procacious, put down, rude, sassy*, saucy*, smart, smart-alecky*, uncivil, ungracious; SEE CONCEPTS 267,401

insoluble [*adj*] *mysterious, unable to be solved or answered*
baffling, difficult, impenetrable, indecipherable, inexplicable, inextricable, irresolvable, mystifying, obscure, unaccountable, unconcluded, unfathomable, unresolved, unsolvable, unsolved; SEE CONCEPTS 529,576

insolvent [*adj*] *financially ruined*
bankrupt, broke*, broken, busted*, failed, foreclosed, in Chapter 11*, in Chapter 13*, indebted, in receivership, in the red*, lost, on the rocks*, out of money, strapped*, taken to the cleaners*, unbalanced, undone, wiped out*; SEE CONCEPT 334

insomnia [*n*] *inability to sleep soundly*
indisposition, insomnolence, restlessness, sleeplessness, stress, tension, vigil, vigilance, wakefulness; SEE CONCEPT 315

insouciant [*adj*] *easygoing, casual*
airy, breezy, buoyant, carefree, careless, free and easy*, gay, happy-go-lucky*, heedless, jaunty, lighthearted, nonchalant, sunny*, thoughtless, unconcerned, untroubled, unworried; SEE CONCEPTS 404,542

inspect [v] *examine, check*
audit, canvass, case, catechize, check out, clock*, eye*, give the once-over*, go over, go through, inquire, interrogate, investigate, kick the tires*, look over, notice, observe, oversee, probe, question, review, scan, scope, scout, scrutinize, search, study, superintend, supervise, survey, vet, view, watch; SEE CONCEPTS *103,623*

inspection [n] *examination, check*
analysis, checkup, frisk, inquest, inquiry, inquisition, inventory, investigation, look-over, maneuvers, once-over*, pageant, parade, perlustration, probe, read, research, review, scan, scrutiny, search, superintendence, supervision, surveillance, survey, view; SEE CONCEPTS *103,290*

inspiration [n] *idea, stimulus*
afflatus, animus, approach, arousal, awakening, brainchild*, brainstorm*, creativity, deep think*, elevation, encouragement, enthusiasm, exaltation, fancy, flash*, genius, hunch*, illumination, impulse, incentive, inflatus, influence, insight, motivation, motive, muse, notion, revelation, rumble, spark, spur, stimulation, thought, vision, whim; SEE CONCEPTS *529,661*

inspire [v] *encourage, stimulate*
affect, animate, arouse, be responsible for, carry, cause, commove, elate, embolden, endue, enkindle, enliven, exalt, excite, exhilarate, fire up*, galvanize, get*, give impetus, give one an idea*, give rise to, hearten, imbue, impress, infect, inflame, influence, inform, infuse, inspirit, instill, invigorate, motivate, occasion, produce, provoke, quicken, reassure, set up, spark, spur, start off, stir, strike, sway, touch, trigger, urge, work up; SEE CONCEPTS *7,22,221,242*

instability [n] *imbalance, inconstancy*
alternation, anxiety, capriciousness, changeability, changeableness, disequilibrium, disquiet, fickleness, fitfulness, flightiness, fluctuation, fluidity, frailty, hesitation, immaturity, impermanence, inconsistency, inquietude, insecurity, irregularity, irresolution, mutability, oscillation, pliancy, precariousness, restlessness, shakiness, transience, uncertainty, unfixedness, unpredictability, unreliability, unsteadiness, vacillation, variability, volatility, vulnerability, wavering, weakness; SEE CONCEPTS *410,637,731*

install [v] *set up, establish*
build in, ensconce, fix, fix up, furnish, inaugurate, induct, instate, institute, introduce, invest, lay, line, lodge, place, plant, position, put in, settle, station; SEE CONCEPTS *201,221*

installation [n1] *establishment, inauguration*
accession, coronation, fitting, furnishing, inaugural, induction, installment, instatement, investiture, investment, launching, ordination, placing, positioning, setting up; SEE CONCEPTS *201,221,832*

installation [n2] *equipment*
base, establishment, fort, fortification, furnishings, lighting, machinery, plant, post, power, station, system, wiring; SEE CONCEPTS *439,463,496*

installment [n] *part, section*
chapter, division, earnest, episode, partial payment, payment, portion, repayment, token; SEE CONCEPTS *14,835*

instance [n] *case, situation*
case history, case in point, detail, example, exemplification, exponent, ground, illustration, item, occasion, occurrence, particular, precedent, proof, reason, representative, sample, sampling, specimen, time; SEE CONCEPTS *686,696,815*

instance [v] *name*
adduce, cite, exemplify, illustrate, mention, quote, refer, show, specify; SEE CONCEPT *73*

instant [n] *moment*
bat of the eye*, breath, crack, flash, jiffy*, juncture, minute, nothing flat*, occasion, point, sec*, second, shake*, short while, split second*, tick, time, trice, twinkling*, while, wink*; SEE CONCEPTS *802,808*

instant [adj] *immediate, urgent*
burning*, clamant, contemporary, crying*, current, dire, direct, exigent, existent, extant, fast, imperative, importunate, insistent, instantaneous, on-the-spot*, present, present-day, pressing, prompt, quick, split-second*; SEE CONCEPTS *544,588,799*

instantaneous [adj] *immediate*
direct, fast, hair-trigger*, in a flash*, instant, momentary, quick, rapid, spontaneous, transitory; SEE CONCEPT *820*

instantly [adv] *right now*
at once, away, directly, double-time*, first off*, forthwith, immediately, in a flash*, instantaneously, instanter, now, on a dime*, PDQ*, pronto*, right, right away, spontaneously, straight away*, there and then*, this minute, tout de suite*, without delay; SEE CONCEPTS *544,588,799*

instead [adv] *alternatively*
alternately, alternative, as a substitute, in lieu, in place of, in preference, on behalf of, on second thought, preferably, rather, rather than; SEE CONCEPT *560*

instigate [v] *influence, provoke*
abet, actuate, add fuel, bring about, egg on*, encourage, fire up*, foment, goad, hint, impel, incite, inflame, initiate, insinuate, kindle, make waves*, move, needle*, persuade, plan, plot, prompt, put up to, rabble-rouse*, raise, rouse, scheme, set on, spur, start, steam up, stimulate, stir up, suggest, turn on, urge, whip up*, work up; SEE CONCEPTS *7,19,22,221,242*

instill [v] *implant, introduce*
brainwash*, catechize, diffuse, disseminate, engender, engraft, force in, imbue, impart, impregnate, impress, inculcate, indoctrinate, infiltrate, infix, infuse, inject, inoculate, inseminate, insert, insinuate, inspire, interject, intermix, program, propagandize, put in head*, suffuse, transfuse; SEE CONCEPTS *14,221,285*

instinct [n] *gut feeling, idea*
aptitude, faculty, feeling, funny feeling*, gift, gut reaction*, hunch, impulse, inclination, intuition, knack, know-how*, nose*, predisposition, proclivity, savvy*, sense, sentiment, sixth sense*, talent, tendency; SEE CONCEPTS *529,689*

instinctive [adj] *reflex, automatic*
accustomed, by seat of one's pants*, congenital, habitual, impulsive, inborn, ingrained, inherent, innate, instinctual, intrinsic, intuitional, intuitive, involuntary, knee-jerk*, mechanical, native, natural, normal, regular, rooted, second-nature*, spontaneous, typical, unlearned, unmeditated, unpremeditated, unprompted, unthinking, visceral; SEE CONCEPT *544*

in
in

institute/institution [n1] *organization, usually educational*

academy, association, asylum, business, clinic, college, company, conservatory, establishment, fixture, foundation, guild, hospital, orphanage, school, seminar, seminary, society, system, think tank, university; SEE CONCEPTS 288,381,439

institute [n2] *law; custom*

convention, decree, decretum, doctrine, dogma, edict, establishment, fixture, habit, maxim, ordinance, practice, precedent, precept, prescript, principle, regulation, rite, ritual, rule, statute, tenet, tradition; SEE CONCEPTS 318,688

institute [v] *begin; put into operation*

appoint, bow, break in, bring into being, come out with, come up with, commence, constitute, create, enact, establish, fix, found, inaugurate, induct, initiate, install, introduce, invest, launch, make up, open, open up, ordain, organize, originate, pioneer, rev*, set in motion, settle, set up, start, usher in*; SEE CONCEPTS 173,221,242

instruct [v1] *inform, teach*

acquaint, advise, apprise, brainwash*, break in, break it to, brief, clue in, coach, counsel, discipline, disclose, drill, drum into*, educate, engineer, enlighten, give lessons, ground, guide, keep posted*, lead, lecture, level, notify, pilot, reveal, school, steer, tell, train, tutor, update, wise up*; SEE CONCEPTS 60,285

instruct [v2] *order, command*

assign, bid, charge, define, direct, enjoin, prescribe, tell, warn; SEE CONCEPTS 53,61

instruction [n1] *education*

apprenticeship, chalk talk*, coaching, direction, discipline, drilling, edification, enlightenment, grounding, guidance, information, lesson, preparation, schooling, teaching, training, tuition, tutelage; SEE CONCEPTS 274,285

instruction [n2] *demand, command*

advice, briefing, direction, directive, information, injunction, mandate, order, plan, ruling; SEE CONCEPTS 274,278

instructor [n] *person who educates*

adviser, coach, demonstrator, exponent, guide, lecturer, mentor, pedagogue, preceptor, professor, teacher, trainer, tutor; SEE CONCEPT 350

instrument [n1] *tool, implement*

apparatus, appliance, contraption, contrivance, device, doodad*, equipment, gadget, gear, gizmo*, machine, machinery, mechanism, paraphernalia, tackle, utensil; SEE CONCEPTS 463,499

instrument [n2] *means, agent*

agency, channel, factor, force, instrumentality, material, mechanism, medium, ministry, organ, vehicle, wherewithal; SEE CONCEPTS 6,687

instrumental [adj] *influential, assisting*

active, auxiliary, conducive, contributory, helpful, helping, involved, of help, of service, partly responsible, serviceable, subsidiary, useful; SEE CONCEPT 560

insubordinate [adj] *rebellious*

contrary, contumacious, defiant, disaffected, disobedient, disorderly, dissentious, factious, fractious, insurgent, intractable, mutinous, naughty, perverse, recalcitrant, refractory, riotous, seditious, treacherous, turbulent, uncompliant, uncomplying, undisciplined, ungovernable, unruly; SEE CONCEPT 401

insubstantial [adj] *weak, imaginary*

aerial, airy, chimerical, decrepit, ephemeral, false, fanciful, feeble, flimsy, fly-by-night*, fragile, frail, idle, illusory, immaterial, imponderable, incorporeal, infirm, intangible, metaphysical, petty, poor, puny, slender, slight, tenuous, thin, too little too late*, unreal, unsound, unsubstantial; SEE CONCEPT 485

insufferable [adj] *horrible, intolerable*

detestable, distressing, dreadful, destitute, insupportable, outrageous, painful, unacceptable, unbearable, unendurable, unspeakable; SEE CONCEPTS 529,537

insufficient [adj] *not enough; lacking*

bereft, defective, deficient, destitute, devoid, drained, dry, failing, faulty, imperfect, inadequate, incapable, incommensurate, incompetent, incomplete, infrequent, meager, minus, out of, poor, rare, scant, scarce, short, short of, shy, thin*, too little too late*, unample, unfinished, unfitted, unqualified, unsatisfactory, wanting; SEE CONCEPTS 546,771

insular [adj] *narrow-minded*

bigoted, circumscribed, closed, confined, contracted, cut off, detached, illiberal, inward-looking, isolated, limited, narrow, parochial, petty, prejudiced, provincial, restricted, secluded, separate, separated, sequestered; SEE CONCEPTS 403,583

insulate [v] *protect; close off*

coat, cocoon, cushion, cut off, inlay, island, isolate, keep apart, line, seclude, separate, sequester, set apart, shield, tape, treat, wrap; SEE CONCEPT 172

insult [n] *hateful communication*

abuse, affront, aspersion, black eye*, blasphemy, cheap shot*, contempt, contumely, derision, despite, discourtesy, disdainfulness, disgrace, disrespect, ignominy, impertinence, impudence, incivility, indignity, insolence, invective, libel, mockery, obloquy, offense, opprobrium, outrage, put-down, rudeness, scorn, scurrility, shame, slam, slanger, slap, slap in the face*, slight, snub, superciliousness, taunt, unpleasantry, vilification, vituperation; SEE CONCEPTS 52,54,278

insult [v] *abuse, offend*

abase, affront, aggravate, annoy, blister, curse, cut to the quick*, debase, degrade, deride, dishonor, disoblige, dump on*, flout, gird, humiliate, injure, irritate, jeer, libel, mock, outrage, pan*, provoke, put down*, revile, ridicule, roast*, scoff, slam*, slander, slight, sneer, snub, step on one's toes*, taunt, tease, underestimate, vex; SEE CONCEPTS 52,54

insurance [n] *protection, security*

allowance, assurance, backing, cover, coverage, guarantee, indemnification, indemnity, provision, safeguard, support, warrant, warranty; SEE CONCEPTS 318,332

insure [v] *protect, secure*

assure, cinch, cover, guarantee, guard, hedge, indemnify, register, safeguard, shield, underwrite, warrant; SEE CONCEPTS 317,330

insurgent [n] *rebel*

agitator, anarch, anarchist, demonstrator, frondeur, insurrectionist, malcontent, mutineer, radical, resister, revolter, revolutionary, revolutionist, rioter; SEE CONCEPTS 359,412

insurgent [adj] *rebellious*

anarchical, contumacious, disobedient, factious, insubordinate, insurrectionary, mutinous, revolting, revolutionary, riotous, seditious; SEE CONCEPT 401

insurmountable [adj] *impossible*
forget it, hopeless, impassable, impregnable, inaccessible, indomitable, ineluctable, insuperable, invincible, not a prayer*, no way*, no-win*, overwhelming, unbeatable, unconquerable, unmasterable; SEE CONCEPTS 552,565

insurrection [n] *rebellion*
coup, disorder, insurgence, insurgency, mutiny, revolt, revolution, riot, rising, sedition, uprising; SEE CONCEPTS 86,320

intact [adj] *undamaged; all in one piece*
complete, entire, flawless, imperforate, indiscrete, perfect, scatheless, sound, together, unblemished, unbroken, uncut, undefiled, unharmed, unhurt, unimpaired, uninjured, unmarred, unscathed, untouched, unviolated, whole; SEE CONCEPTS 485,531

intangible [adj] *indefinite, obscured*
abstract, abstruse, airy, dim, eluding, elusive, ethereal, evading, evanescent, evasive, hypothetical, impalpable, imperceptible, imponderable, inappreciable, incorporeal, indeterminate, insensible, invisible, rare, shadowy, slender, slight, unapparent, uncertain, unobservable, unreal, unsubstantial, unsure, vague; SEE CONCEPTS 535,582

integral [adj1] *necessary, basic*
component, constituent, elemental, essential, fundamental, indispensable, intrinsic, requisite; SEE CONCEPT 546

integral [adj2] *complete*
aggregate, choate, elemental, entire, full, indivisible, intact, part-and-parcel*, perfect, unbroken, undivided, whole; SEE CONCEPT 531

integrate [v] *mix, merge*
accommodate, amalgamate, arrange, articulate, assimilate, associate, attune, blend, coalesce, combine, come together, compact, concatenate, concentrate, conform, conjoin, consolidate, coordinate, desegregate, embody, fuse, get together, harmonize, incorporate, interface, intermix, join, knit, link, meld with, mesh, orchestrate, organize, proportion, reconcile, reconciliate, symphonize, synthesize, systematize, throw in together, tune, unify, unite, wed; SEE CONCEPTS 113,114

integrity [n1] *honor, uprightness*
candor, forthrightness, goodness, honestness, honesty, honorableness, incorruptibility, incorruption, principle, probity, purity, rectitude, righteousness, sincerity, straightforwardness, virtue; SEE CONCEPT 411

integrity [n2] *completeness*
absoluteness, coherence, cohesion, entireness, perfection, purity, simplicity, soundness, stability, totality, unity, wholeness; SEE CONCEPT 635

intellect [n] *capability of the mind; someone with capable mind*
ability, acumen, brains*, cerebration, comprehension, egghead*, genius, intellectual, intellectuality, intelligence, intuition, judgment, mentality, mind, psyche, pundit, reason, savvy, sense, smarts, thinker, understanding, what it takes*, wits; SEE CONCEPTS 409,416

intellectual [n] *very smart person*
academic, academician, avant-garde, brain*, braintruster*, doctor, egghead*, Einstein*, genius, highbrow*, intelligentsia, philosopher, pundit, sage, scholar, thinker, whiz*, wizard; SEE CONCEPTS 350,416

intellectual [adj] *very smart*
bookish, brainy*, cerebral, creative, highbrow*, highbrowed*, intellective, intelligent, inventive, learned, mental, phrenic, psychological, rational, scholarly, studious, subjective, thoughtful; SEE CONCEPT 402

intelligence [n1] *ability to perceive, understand*
acuity, acumen, agility, alertness, aptitude, brainpower, brains*, brightness, brilliance, capacity, cleverness, comprehension, coruscation, discernment, gray matter*, intellect, IQ*, judgment, luminosity, mentality, mind, penetration, perception, perspicacity, precocity, quickness, quotient, reason, sagacity, savvy, sense, skill, smarts, subtlety, the right stuff*, trenchancy, understanding, what it takes*, wit; SEE CONCEPT 409

intelligence [n2] *secret information*
advice, clue, data, dirt, disclosure, facts, findings, hot tip*, info*, inside story*, knowledge, leak, lowdown*, news, notice, notification, picture, report, rumor, tidings, tip-off*, word*; SEE CONCEPT 274

intelligent [adj] *very smart*
able, acute, alert, alive, all there*, apt, astute, brainy*, bright, brilliant, calculating, capable, clever, comprehending, creative, deep*, discerning, enlightened, exceptional, highbrow*, imaginative, ingenious, instructed, inventive, keen, knowing, knowledgeable, original, penetrating, perceptive, perspicacious, profound, quick, quick-witted, rational, ready, reasonable, resourceful, responsible, sage, sharp, smart, thinking, together*, understanding, well-informed, whiz*, wise, witty; SEE CONCEPT 402

intelligible [adj] *understandable*
apprehensible, clear, comprehensible, distinct, fathomable, graspable, knowable, lucid, luminous, obvious, open, plain, unambiguous, unequivocal, unmistakable; SEE CONCEPT 529

intend [v] *have in mind; determine*
add up, aim, appoint, aspire to, attempt, be determined, be resolved, connote, contemplate, decree, dedicate, denote, design, designate, destine, devote, endeavor, essay, expect, express, figure on, have in mind, hope to, import, indicate, look forward, mean, meditate, ordain, plan, plot, propose, purpose, reserve, resolve, scheme, set apart, set aside, signify, spell, strive, think, try; SEE CONCEPTS 18,36,73,129

intended [adj] *engaged; destined*
accidentally on purpose*, advised, affianced, aforethought, asked for, betrothed, calculated, contemplated, contracted, designed, expected, future, intentional, meant, pinned, planned, plighted, prearranged, predestined, predetermined, promised, proposed, set, steady; SEE CONCEPT 552

intense [adj] *forceful, severe; passionate*
acute, agonizing, all-consuming, ardent, biting, bitter, burning, close, concentrated, consuming, cutting, deep, diligent, eager, earnest, energetic, exaggerated, exceptional, excessive, exquisite, extraordinary, extreme, fanatical, fervent, fervid, fierce, forcible, full, great, hard, harsh, heightened, impassioned, intensified, intensive, keen, marked, piercing, powerful, profound, protracted, pungent, sharp, shrill, stinging, strained, strong,

in
in

supreme, undue, vehement, violent, vivid, zealous; SEE CONCEPT *569*

intensify [*v*] *make more forceful, severe*
accent, accentuate, add fuel*, add to, aggrandize, aggravate, augment, beef up*, boost, brighten, build up, concentrate, darken, deepen, emphasize, enhance, escalate, exacerbate, exalt, heat up*, heighten, increase, intensate, lighten, magnify, point, pour it on*, quicken, raise, redouble, reinforce, rise, rouse, set off, sharpen, spike*, step up, strengthen, stress, tone up, whet; SEE CONCEPTS *233,250*

intensity [*n*] *passion, force*
acuteness, anxiety, ardor, concentration? deepness, depth, earnestness, emotion, emphasis, energy, excess, excitement, extreme, extremity, fanaticism, ferment, ferociousness, ferocity, fervency, fervor, fierceness, fire, force, forcefulness, fury, high pitch*, intenseness, keenness, magnitude, might, nervousness, potency, power, severity, sharpness, strain, strength, tenseness, tension, vehemence, vigor, violence, volume, weightiness, wildness; SEE CONCEPTS *641,669*

intensive [*adj*] *exhaustive*
accelerated, all-out*, complete, comprehensive, concentrated, deep, demanding, fast, hard, in-depth, out-and-out*, profound, radical, severe, speeded-up*, thorough, thoroughgoing; SEE CONCEPT *531*

intent/intention [*n*] *aim, purpose*
acceptation, animus, bottom line*, conation, design, desire, drift, end, goal, heart, hope, idea, import, intendment, meaning, meat*, name of the game*, nature, notion, nub, nuts and bolts*, object, objective, plan, point, project, purport, scheme, score, sense, significance, significancy, signification, target, understanding, volition, will, wish; SEE CONCEPT *659*

intent [*adj*] *determined, resolute*
absorbed, alert, attending, attentive, bent, bound, committed, concentrated, concentrating, decided, decisive, deep, eager, earnest, engaged, engrossed, enthusiastic, firm, fixed, hell-bent*, immersed, industrious, intense, minding, occupied, piercing, preoccupied, rapt, resolved, riveted*, set, settled, steadfast, steady, watchful, watching, wrapped up*; SEE CONCEPTS *403,542*

intentional [*adj*] *deliberate*
advised, aforethought, calculated, considered, designed, designful, done on purpose, intended, meant, meditated, planned, prearranged, premeditated, proposed, purposed, studied, unforced, voluntary, willful, willing, witting; SEE CONCEPT *544*

intently [*adv*] *with concentration*
attentively, closely, fixedly, hard, keenly, searchingly, sharply, steadily, watchfully; SEE CONCEPTS *403,544*

inter [*v*] *bury*
cover up, entomb, inhume, inurn, lay to rest, plant, put away, sepulcher, sepulture, tomb; SEE CONCEPTS *172,178,367*

interact [*v*] *communicate*
collaborate, combine, connect, contact, cooperate, get across*, get the message*, interface, interplay, interreact, join, keep in touch, merge, mesh, network, reach out, relate, touch, touch base*, unite; SEE CONCEPT *266*

intercede [*v*] *mediate*
advocate, arbitrate, barge in, butt in*, intermedi-

ate, interpose, intervene, intrude, mix in, monkey with*, negotiate, plead, reconcile, speak, step in; SEE CONCEPTS *56,110*

intercept [*v*] *head off; interrupt*
ambush, appropriate, arrest, block, catch, check, curb, cut in, cut off, deflect, head off at pass*, hijack, hinder, interlope, interpose, make off with, obstruct, prevent, seize, shortstop*, stop, take, take away; SEE CONCEPTS *121,164*

interchange [*n*] *switch, exchange*
altering, alternation, barter, change, crossfire, give-and-take*, intersection, junction, mesh, networking, reciprocation, shift, trade, transposition, variation, varying; SEE CONCEPTS *104,697*

interchange [*v*] *switch, exchange*
alternate, bandy, barter, commute, connect, contact, convert, interact, interface, mesh, network, reciprocate, relate, reverse, substitute, swap, trade, transpose; SEE CONCEPTS *56,104*

interchangeable [*adj*] *identical, transposable*
changeable, commutable, compatible, converse, convertible, correspondent, equivalent, exchangeable, fungible, interconvertible, mutual, reciprocal, reciprocative, same, substitutable, synonymous, workalike; SEE CONCEPTS *487,573*

intercourse [*n1*] *sexual act*
carnal knowledge, coition, coitus, copulation, fornication, intimacy, love-making, relations, sex, sexual relations; SEE CONCEPT *375*

intercourse [*n2*] *communication; business exchange*
association, commerce, communion, connection, contact, converse, correspondence, dealings, give-and-take, interchange, intercommunication, mesh, networking, team play, teamwork, trade, traffic, transactions; SEE CONCEPTS *266,324*

interest [*n1*] *attraction, curiosity*
absorption, activity, affection, attentiveness, care, case, concern, concernment, consequence, diversion, engrossment, enthusiasm, excitement, game, hobby, importance, interestedness, into, leisure activity, matter, moment, note, notice, passion, pastime, preoccupation, pursuit, racket, recreation, regard, relaxation, relevance, significance, sport, suspicion, sympathy, thing; SEE CONCEPTS *20,532,690*

interest [*n2*] *advantage*
benefit, gain, good, profit, prosperity, welfare, well-being; SEE CONCEPT *693*

interest [*n3*] *share, investment*
accrual, authority, bonus, claim, commitment, credit, discount, due, earnings, gain, influence, involvement, participation, percentage, piece, points, portion, premium, right, stake, title; SEE CONCEPTS *332,344,835*

interest [*v*] *hold the attention of*
affect, amuse, appeal, appeal to, arouse, attract, be interesting to, concern, divert, engage, engross, entertain, enthrall, excite, fascinate, grab, hook, intrigue, involve, lure, move, perk up, pique, please, pull, sit up, snare, tantalize, tempt, titillate, touch, turn on; SEE CONCEPTS *7,11,22*

interested [*adj*] *concerned, curious*
absorbed, affected, attentive, attracted, awakened, biased, caught, drawn, eat sleep and breathe*, engrossed, excited, fascinated, fired*, gone*, hooked*, implicated, impressed, inspired, inspirited, intent, into*, involved, keen, lured, moved, obsessed, occupied, on the case*, open, partial, partisan, predisposed, prejudiced, respon-

sive, roused, sold, stimulated, stirred, struck, sympathetic, taken, touched); SEE CONCEPT *403*

interesting [adj] *appealing, entertaining*
absorbing, affecting, alluring, amusing, arresting, attractive, beautiful, captivating, charismatic, compelling, curious, delightful, elegant, enchanting, engaging, engrossing, enthralling, entrancing, exceptional, exotic, fascinating, fine, gracious, gripping, impressive, intriguing, inviting, lovely, magnetic, pleasing, pleasurable, prepossessing, provocative, readable, refreshing, riveting, stimulating, stirring, striking, suspicious, thought-provoking, unusual, winning; SEE CONCEPTS *529,572*

interfere [v] *meddle, intervene*
baffle, balk, barge in, busybody*, butt in*, conflict, discommode, foil, fool with, frustrate, get in the way*, get involved, hamper, handicap, hang up*, hinder, hold up, horn in*, impede, incommode, inconvenience, inhibit, intercede, interlope, intermeddle, intermediate, intermit, interpose, intrude, jam, make*, mix in, obstruct, obtrude, oppose, poke nose in*, prevent, remit, step in, stop, suspend, tamper, thwart, trammel, trouble; SEE CONCEPTS *121,384*

interference [n] *meddling, impedance*
arrest, background, backseat driving*, barging in*, barring, blocking, checking, choking, clashing, clogging, conflict, hampering, hindrance, intermeddling, interposition, intervention, intrusion, meddlesomeness, obstruction, opposition, prying, resistance, retardation, tackling, tampering, trespassing; SEE CONCEPTS *121,384*

interim [n] *interval*
breach, break, breather, breathing spell, coffee break, cutoff, downtime*, gap, hiatus, interlude, interregnum, interruption, lacuna, layoff, letup*, meantime, meanwhile, pause, take*, ten*, time*, time-out; SEE CONCEPTS *807,822*

interim [adj] *temporary*
acting, ad interim, caretaker*, improvised, intervening, makeshift, pro tem, pro tempore, provisional, stopgap, thrown together*; SEE CONCEPT *560*

interior [n] *center, core*
belly, bosom, contents, heart, heartland, innards, inner parts, inside, internals, intrinsically, lining, marrow, midst, pith, pulp, soul, substance, viscera, within; SEE CONCEPTS *742,826,830*

interior [adj] *inside, central*
autogenous, domestic, endogenous, gut, home, in-house, inland, inner, innermost, internal, intimate, inward, private, remote, secret, visceral, viscerous, within; SEE CONCEPTS *583,826,830*

interject [v] *throw in; interrupt*
add, fill in, force in, implant, import, include, infiltrate, infuse, ingrain, inject, insert, insinuate, intercalate, interpolate, interpose, intersperse, introduce, intrude, parenthesize, put in, splice, squeeze in; SEE CONCEPTS *14,51*

interloper [n] *person who intrudes, meddles*
alien, busybody, intermeddler, intruder, meddler, obtruder, trespasser, uninvited guest, unwanted visitor; SEE CONCEPTS *412,423*

interlude [n] *pause, break*
breathing space*, delay, episode, halt, hiatus, idyll, interim, intermission, interregnum, interruption, interval, lull, meantime, meanwhile, parenthesis, recess, respite, rest, spell, stop, stoppage, wait; SEE CONCEPT *807*

intermediary [n] *person who negotiates*
agent, broker, channel, connection, cutout, delegate, emissary, entrepreneur, fixer, go-between*, influence, instrument, interagent, interceder, intercessor, intermediate, mediator, medium, middle person, negotiator, organ, vehicle; SEE CONCEPTS *348,354*

intermediate [adj] *middle, in-between*
average, between, center, central, common, compromising, fair, halfway, indifferent, intermediary, interposed, intervening, mean, medial, median, mediocre, medium, mid, middling, midway, moderate, neutral, so-so*, standard, transitional; SEE CONCEPTS *585,830*

interminable [adj] *infinite*
boring, boundless, ceaseless, constant, continuous, day-and-night*, dragged out*, dull, endless, eternal, everlasting, immeasurable, incessant, interminate, limitless, long, long-drawn-out*, longwinded, looped, never-ending, no end of*, no end to*, on a treadmill*, permanent, perpetual, protracted, spun out*, strung out*, timeless, unbound, unceasing, uninterrupted, unlimited, wearisome; SEE CONCEPT *798*

intermingle [v] *blend, mix*
amalgamate, associate, combine, come together, commingle, commix, fuse, immingle, interblend, interfuse, interlace, intermix, interweave, join, merge, mesh, network, pool, throw in with, throw together, wed; SEE CONCEPTS *113,114*

intermission [n] *break, recess*
abeyance, abeyancy, break-off, breather, breathing spell, cessation, doldrums, dormancy, downtime*, interim, interlude, interregnum, interruption, interval, latency, layoff, let-up*, lull, parenthesis, pause, quiescence, quiescency, respite, rest, spell, stop, stoppage, suspense, suspension, time, time-out, wait; SEE CONCEPT *807*

intermittent [adj] *irregular, sporadic*
alternate, arrested, broken, by bits and pieces*, checked, cyclic, cyclical, discontinuing, discontinuous, epochal, every other, fitful, here and there*, hit-or-miss*, infrequent, interrupted, isochronal, isochronous, iterant, iterative, metrical, now and then*, occasional, on and off*, periodic, periodical, punctuated, recurrent, recurring, rhythmic, rhythmical, seasonal, serial, shifting, spasmodic, stop-and-go*; SEE CONCEPTS *482,534,799*

internal [adj] *within*
centralized, circumscribed, civic, constitutional, domestic, enclosed, gut, home, indigenous, inherent, in-house, innate, inner, innermore, inside, interior, intestine, intimate, intramural, intrinsic, inward, municipal, national, native, private, subjective, visceral, viscerous; SEE CONCEPTS *536,585,826,830*

international [adj] *worldwide*
all-embracing, cosmopolitan, ecumenical, foreign, global, intercontinental, universal, world; SEE CONCEPTS *536,772*

interplay [n] *interaction*
coaction, exchange, give-and-take*, mesh, meshing, networking, reciprocation, reciprocity, team play*, teamwork, tit for tat*, transaction; SEE CONCEPT *266*

interpolate [v] *add*
admit, annex, append, enter, fill in, include, inject, insert, insinuate, intercalate, interjaculate, in-

in
in

terject, interlope, interpose, introduce, intrude, throw in; SEE CONCEPTS 112,201,209

interpret [v] *make sense of; define*
adapt, annotate, clarify, comment, commentate, construe, decipher, decode, delineate, depict, describe, elucidate, enact, exemplify, explain, explicate, expound, gather, gloss, illustrate, image, improvise, limn, make of, mimic, paraphrase, perform, picture, play, portray, read, reenact, render, represent, solve, spell out, take*, throw light on*, translate, understand, view; SEE CONCEPTS 57,292

interrogate [v] *ask pointed questions*
catechize, cross-examine, cross-question, examine, give the third degree*, go over*, grill, inquire, investigate, pump, put the screws to*, put through the wringer*, query, question, quiz, roast*, sweat out*, work over*; SEE CONCEPTS 48,53

interrupt [v] *bother, interfere*
arrest, barge in, break, break in, break off, break train of thought*, bust in*, butt in*, check, chime in*, come between, crash, crowd in, cut, cut in on*, cut off*, cut short*, defer, delay, disconnect, discontinue, disjoin, disturb, disunite, divide, edge in, get in the way, halt, heckle, hinder, hold up, horn in, impede, in, infringe, inject, insinuate, intrude, lay aside, obstruct, prevent, punctuate, put in, separate, sever, shortstop*, stay, stop, suspend, work in; SEE CONCEPTS 51,121,384

interruption [n] *break; interference*
abeyance, abeyancy, arrest, blackout, breach, break-off, cessation, check, cutoff, delay, disconnection, discontinuance, disruption, dissolution, disturbance, disuniting, division, doldrums, dormancy, gap, halt, hiatus, hindrance, hitch, impediment, interim, intermission, interval, intrusion, lacuna, latency, layoff, letup*, obstacle, obstruction, parenthesis, pause, quiescence, rift, rupture, separation, severance, split, stop, stoppage, suspension; SEE CONCEPTS 807,832

intersect [v] *cut across; cross at a point*
bisect, break in two, come together, converge, crisscross, cross, crosscut, cut, decussate, divide, intercross, join, meet, separate, touch, traverse; SEE CONCEPTS 113,738,749

intersection [n] *crossroads*
circle, cloverleaf, crossing, crosswalk, crossway, interchange, junction, stop; SEE CONCEPT 501

intersperse [v] *scatter*
bestrew, diffuse, distribute, infuse, interfuse, interlard, intermix, intersow, intersprinkle, pepper, sprinkle; SEE CONCEPTS 201,222

interstice [n] *opening, crack*
aperture, chink, cleft, cranny, crevice, fissure, gap, hole, interval, slit, space; SEE CONCEPT 513

intertwine/interweave [v] *twist around*
associate, braid, connect, convolute, crisscross, cross, entwine, interknit, interlace, intertwist, intervolve, interwind, interwreathe, link, mesh, network, relate, reticulate, tangle, tat, weave; SEE CONCEPTS 113,114

interval [n] *break, pause*
breach, breathing space*, comma, delay, distance, downtime, five*, gap, hiatus, interim, interlude, intermission, interregnum, interruption, lacuna, layoff, letup, lull, meantime, opening, parenthesis, pausation, period, playtime, rest, season, space, spell, ten*, term, time, time-out, wait, while; SEE CONCEPTS 807,822

intervene [v1] *mediate*
arbitrate, barge in, butt in*, come between, divide, horn in*, intercede, interfere, intermediate, interpose, interrupt, intrude, involve, meddle, mix in, muscle in*, negotiate, obtrude, part, put in two cents*, reconcile, separate, settle, sever, step in, take a hand*; SEE CONCEPTS 110,234,266

intervene [v2] *happen*
bedevil, befall, come to pass, ensue, occur, succeed, supervene, take place; SEE CONCEPTS 4,242

interview [n] *questioning and evaluation*
account, audience, call, call back, cattle call*, communication, conference, consultation, conversation, dialogue, examination, hearing, meeting, oral, parley, press conference, record, statement, talk; SEE CONCEPTS 48,351

interview [v] *ask questions and evaluate*
consult, converse, examine, get for the record, get opinion, give oral examination, hold inquiry, interrogate, question, quiz, sound out, talk, talk to; SEE CONCEPTS 48,351

intestinal/intestine [adj] *pertaining to digestive organs*
abdominal, alimentary, bowel, celiac, duodenal, gut, inner, inside, interior, internal, inward, rectal, stomachic, ventral, visceral; SEE CONCEPT 406

intimacy [n] *closeness between people*
acquaintance, affection, affinity, close relationship, communion, confidence, confidentiality, experience, familiarity, friendship, inwardness, understanding; SEE CONCEPT 388

intimate [n] *a close friend; familiar person*
associate, bosom buddy*, chum, companion, comrade, confidant, confidante, crony, familiar, family, lover, mate, pal; SEE CONCEPTS 416,423

intimate [adj1] *friendly, devoted*
affectionate, bosom, buddy-buddy*, cherished, chummy*, close, clubby*, comfy, confidential, cozy, dear, dearest, faithful, fast, fond, loving, mellow, mix, near, nearest, next, nice, regular, roommate, snug, warm; SEE CONCEPT 555

intimate [adj2] *private, personal*
confidential, deep, deep-seated, detailed, elemental, essential, exhaustive, experienced, firsthand, guarded, gut*, immediate, inborn, inbred, indepth, indwelling, ingrained, inherent, inmost, innate, innermost, interior, internal, intrinsic, penetrating, privy, profound, secret, special, thorough, trusted, uptight, visceral, viscerous; SEE CONCEPTS 529,549

intimate [v] *suggest; tip off*
affirm, air, allude, announce, assert, aver, avouch, communicate, connote, declare, drop a hint*, expose, express, hint, impart, imply, indicate, infer, insinuate, leak, let cat out of bag*, let it be known, make known, make noise*, profess, remind, spill the beans*, spring, state, utter, vent, voice, warn; SEE CONCEPTS 49,60,75

intimation [n] *clue, hint*
allusion, announcement, breath, communication, cue, declaration, implication, indication, inkling, innuendo, insinuation, notice, notion, reminder, shade, shadow, strain, streak, suggestion, suspicion, telltale, tinge, tip, trace, warning, wind; SEE CONCEPTS 274,689

intimidate [v] *frighten, threaten*
alarm, appall, awe, badger, bait, bludgeon, bluster, bowl over*, browbeat*, buffalo*, bulldoze*, bully, chill, coerce, compel, constrain, cow*,

intolerable [adj] *unacceptable; beyond bearing*
a bit much, enough already*, excruciating, extreme, impossible, insufferable, insupportable, last straw*, offensive, painful, unbearable, undesirable, unendurable; SEE CONCEPT *529*

intolerant [adj] *impatient; prejudiced*
antipathetic, averse, biased, bigoted, chauvinistic, communist, conservative, contemptuous, dictatorial, disdainful, dogmatic, fanatical, fractious, hateful, illiberal, indignant, individualistic, inflexible, irate, irritable, jaundiced, narrow, narrow-minded, obdurate, one-sided, outraged, racialist, racist, short-fuse*, small-minded*, snappy, stuffy, tilted, uncharitable, unfair, unforbearing, unindulgent, unsympathetic, unwilling, upset, waspish, worked-up*, xenophobic; SEE CONCEPTS *403,404,542*

intoxicated [adj1] *drunk*
blind*, bombed*, boozed*, buzzed*, drunken, high*, inebriated, loaded*, looped*, muddled, potted*, sloppy, smashed*, tanked*, three sheets to the wind*, tied one on*, tight*, tipsy, under the influence, unsober; SEE CONCEPT *406*

intoxicated [adj2] *extremely happy*
absorbed, affected, beside oneself, captivated, concerned, delirious, dizzy, drunk, ecstatic, elated, enraptured, euphoric, excited, exhilarated, galvanized, high*, infatuated, interested, moved, piqued, quickened, sent*, stimulated, turned-on*; SEE CONCEPT *403*

intoxicating [adj] *causing great happiness*
exciting, exhilarant, exhilarating, exhilarative, eye-popping, heady, inspiring, provocative, rousing, stimulating, stirring, thrilling; SEE CONCEPT *537*

intractable /intransigent [adj] *difficult, stubborn*
awkward, bullheaded*, cantankerous, contrary, hang tough*, hard-line*, headstrong, immovable, incompliant, incurable, indocile, indomitable, insoluble, locked in*, mulish, obdurate, obstinate, pat, pertinacious, perverse, pigheaded*, recalcitrant, refractory, resolute, self-willed, set in stone, tenacious, tough, tough-nut*, unbending, uncompromising, uncooperative, undisciplined, ungovernable, unmanageable, unpliable, unruly, unyielding, wayward, wild, willful; SEE CONCEPTS *401,534,542*

intrepid [adj] *brave, nervy*
audacious, bodacious*, bold, courageous, daring, dauntless, doughty, fearless, gallant, game, gritty, gutsy*, heroic, impavid, lionhearted, nerveless, plucky, resolute, spunky*, stalwart, unafraid, undaunted, unflinching, valiant, valorous; SEE CONCEPT *401*

intricate [adj] *complicated, elaborate*
abstruse, baroque, Byzantine*, can of worms*, complex, convoluted, Daedal*, difficult, entangled, fancy, hard, high-tech*, involved, labyrinthine, obscure, perplexing, rococo, sophisticated, tangled, tortuous, tricky; SEE CONCEPT *562*

intrigue [n1] *scheme*
artifice, cabal, chicanery, collusion, complication, conspiracy, contrivance, deal, design, dodge, double-dealing*, fix, frame-up*, fraud, game, graft, hookup, little game*, machination, maneuver, manipulation, plan, plot, ruse, stratagem, trickery, wile; SEE CONCEPTS *192,660*

intrigue [n2] *love affair*
affair, amour, attachment, case, flirtation, infatuation, interlude, intimacy, liaison, romance; SEE CONCEPT *388*

intrigue [v1] *arouse curiosity*
appeal, attract, bait, captivate, charm, con, delight, draw, enchant, entertain, excite, fascinate, grab, hook, interest, lead on*, mousetrap*, pique, please, pull, rivet, tickle, titillate, tout; SEE CONCEPTS *7,11,22*

intrigue [v2] *plot*
angle, be in cahoots*, cogitate, collude, connive, conspire, contrive, cook up*, devise, finagle, frame up*, machinate, maneuver, operate, plan, promote, scheme, set up*, work hand in glove*; SEE CONCEPT *36*

intrinsic [adj] *basic, inborn*
built-in, central, congenital, connate, constitutional, constitutive, deep-seated, elemental, essential, fundamental, genuine, hereditary, inbred, indwelling, inherent, inmost, innate, intimate, material, native, natural, particular, peculiar, real, true, underlying; SEE CONCEPTS *404,406,546*

introduce [v1] *make known; present*
acquaint, advance, air, announce, bring out, bring up, broach, come out with, do the honors*, familiarize, fix up, get things rolling*, get together, give introduction, harbinger*, herald, kick off, knock down, lead into, lead off, moot, offer, open, open up, originate, pave the way*, precede, preface, propose, put forward, recommend, set forth, spring with, start ball rolling*, submit, suggest, usher, ventilate; SEE CONCEPTS *60,384*

introduce [v2] *begin, institute*
admit, bring forward, bring in, commence, enter, establish, found, inaugurate, induct, initiate, innovate, install, invent, kick off*, launch, organize, pioneer, plan, preface, present, set up, start, unveil, usher in; SEE CONCEPT *221*

introduce [v3] *add, insert*
carry, enter, fill in, freight, import, include, infix, inject, inlay, inlet, inset, insinuate, instill, intercalate, interject, interpolate, interpose, put in, send, ship, throw in, transport, work in; SEE CONCEPTS *112,113,209*

introduction [n] *something new; something that begins*
addition, admittance, awakening, baptism, basic principles, basic text, beginning, commencement, debut, essentials, establishment, exordium, first acquaintance, first taste, foreword, inauguration, inception, induction, influx, ingress, initiation, insertion, installation, institution, interpolation, intro*, launch, lead, lead-in, opening, opening remarks, overture, pioneering, preamble, preface, preliminaries, prelude, presentation, primer, proem, prolegomenon, prologue, survey; SEE CONCEPTS *270,727,828*

introductory [adj] *preliminary, first*
anterior, basic, beginning, early, elementary, inaugural, incipient, inductive, initial, initiatory, opening, original, precursory, prefatory, prelusive, preparative, preparatory, primary, prior, proemial, provisional, rudimentary, starting; SEE CONCEPTS *546,585*

introspection [n] *self-analysis*
brooding, contemplation, deep thought, egoism,

in
in

heart-searching, introversion, meditation, reflection, rumination, scrutiny, self-absorption, self-examination, self-observation, self-questioning, soul-searching; SEE CONCEPTS *24,410*

introvert [n] *person who retreats mentally*
autist, brooder, egoist, egotist, loner*, narcissist, self-observer, solitary, wallflower*; SEE CONCEPT *423*

intrude [v] *trespass, interrupt*
barge in, bother, butt in*, chisel in*, cut in, disturb, encroach, entrench, go beyond, hold up, horn in*, infringe, insinuate, intercalate, interfere, interject, interlope, intermeddle, interpolate, interpose, introduce, invade, meddle, obtrude, overstep, pester, push in, thrust, violate; SEE CONCEPTS *14,159,208,266*

intruder [n] *person who trespasses*
burglar, criminal, gate-crasher*, infiltrator, interferer, interloper, interrupter, invader, meddler, nuisance, obtruder, prowler, raider, snooper, squatter, thief, trespasser; SEE CONCEPTS *412,423*

intuition [n] *insight*
clairvoyance, discernment, divination, ESP*, feeling*, foreknowledge, gut reaction*, hunch*, innate knowledge, inspiration, instinct, intuitiveness, nose*, penetration, perception, perceptivity, premonition, presentiment, second sight*, sixth sense*; SEE CONCEPTS *409,689*

intuitive [adj] *instinctive*
automatic, direct, emotional, habitual, immediate, inherent, innate, instinctual, involuntary, natural, perceptive, spontaneous, understood, unreflecting, untaught, visceral; SEE CONCEPT *402*

inundate [v] *drown, overwhelm*
deluge, dunk, engulf, flood, glut, immerse, overflow, overrun, pour down on, snow*, submerge, swamp, whelm; SEE CONCEPTS *172,179*

invade [v] *attack and encroach*
access, assail, assault, breach, burglarize, burst in, crash, descend upon, entrench, fall on, foray, go in, infect, infest, infringe, inroad, interfere, loot, make inroads*, maraud, meddle, muscle in*, occupy, overrun, overspread, overswarm, penetrate, permeate, pervade, pillage, plunder, raid, ravage, storm, swarm over, trespass, violate; SEE CONCEPTS *86,159,320*

invalid [n] *sick person*
consumptive, convalescent, incurable, patient, shut-in, sufferer; SEE CONCEPT *424*

invalid [adj1] *worthless; unfounded*
bad, baseless, fallacious, false, ill-founded, illogical, inoperative, irrational, mad, not binding, not working, nugatory, null, null and void*, reasonless, sophistic, unreasonable, unreasoned, unscientific, unsound, untrue, void, wrong; SEE CONCEPTS *552,560*

invalid [adj2] *sickly*
ailing, bedridden, below par, debilitated, disabled, down, feeble, frail, ill, infirm, laid low*, on the sick list*, out of action*, peaked, poorly, run-down, sick, weak; SEE CONCEPT *314*

invalidate [v] *render null and void*
abate, abolish, abrogate, annihilate, annul, blow sky-high*, cancel, circumduct, counteract, counterbalance, disannul, discredit, disqualify, impair, negate, negative, neutralize, nix, nullify, offset, overrule, overthrow, quash, refute, revoke, shoot full of holes*, undermine, undo, unfit, weaken, X-out*; SEE CONCEPTS *121,234*

invaluable [adj] *priceless*
beyond price, costly, dear, expensive, helpful, inestimable, precious, serviceable, valuable; SEE CONCEPTS *334,568*

invariable [adj] *not changing*
changeless, consistent, constant, fixed, immovable, immutable, inalterable, inflexible, monotonous, perpetual, regular, rigid, same, set, static, unalterable, unchangeable, unchanging, undiversified, unfailing, uniform, unmodifiable, unrelieved, unvarying, unwavering; SEE CONCEPT *534*

invasion [n] *attack, encroachment*
aggression, assault, breach, entrenchment, foray, forced entrance, incursion, infiltration, infraction, infringement, inroad, intrusion, irruption, maraud, offense, offensive, onslaught, overstepping, raid, transgression, trespass, usurpation, violation; SEE CONCEPTS *86,159,320*

invective [n] *verbal abuse*
accusation, berating, billingsgate, blame, blasphemy, castigation, censure, condemnation, contumely, denunciation, diatribe, epithet, jeremiad, obloquy, philippic, reproach, revilement, sarcasm, scurrility, tirade, tongue-lashing*, vilification, vituperation; SEE CONCEPTS *44,52,54,278*

inveigh [v] *blame, denounce*
admonish, berate, blast, castigate, censure, condemn, crack down on*, except, expostulate, go after*, have at*, jump down one's throat*, kick, lambaste, lay into, lay out, let have it, object, protest, rail, read out*, recriminate, remonstrate, reproach, rip into, roast, scold, scorch, sound off, tongue-lash, trash*, upbraid, vituperate, work over*; SEE CONCEPTS *44,52,54*

inveigle [v] *entice, manipulate*
allure, bait, bamboozle, beguile, blandish, butter*, cajole, charm, coax, con*, decoy, egg on*, ensnare, entrap, get around*, honey*, hook, influence, jolly, lay it on thick*, lead on*, lure, maneuver, massage, oil*, overdo it, persuade, play up to, rope in*, seduce, snow*, soap*, soften up*, string along*, stroke*, sweet talk*, tempt, toll, urge, wheedle, work over*; SEE CONCEPTS *11,14,59*

invent [v1] *create, think up*
ad-lib, author, bear, bring into being, coin, come upon, come up with, compose, conceive, contrive, cook up*, design, devise, discover, dream up, envision, execute, fake, fashion, find, forge, form, formulate, frame, hatch, imagine, improve, improvise, inaugurate, initiate, jam*, knock off*, make, make up, mint, off-the-cuff*, originate, plan, produce, project, toss off*, turn out, wing*; SEE CONCEPTS *36,173,221*

invent [v2] *fabricate*
concoct, conjure up, create out of thin air*, equivocate, fake, falsify, feign, fib, forge, lie, make believe, make up, misrepresent, misstate, pretend, prevaricate, simulate, tell a white lie*, tell untruth, think up, trump up*, vamp; SEE CONCEPTS *59,63*

invention [n1] *creation, creativeness*
apparatus, black box*, brainchild*, coinage, concoction, contraption, contrivance, creativity, design, development, device, discovery, doodad*, gadget, genius, gimmick, gizmo*, imagination, ingenuity, innovation, inspiration, inventiveness, novelty, opus, original, originality, resourcefulness; SEE CONCEPTS *260,409,660*

invention [n2] *fabrication, lie*
deceit, fake, falsehood, fancy, fantasy, fib, fiction, figment, forgery, prevarication, sham*, story, tall story*, untruth, yarn*; SEE CONCEPTS 63,278

inventive [adj] *creative*
adroit, artistic, avant-garde, breaking new ground, causative, constructive, demiurgic, deviceful, fertile, forgetive, formative, fruitful, gifted, imaginative, ingenious, innovational, innovative, innovatory, inspired, original, originative, poetical, productive, resourceful, teeming; SEE CONCEPTS 402,542

inventor [n] *person who comes up with idea*
administrator, architect, artist, author, authority, brain, brains*, director, engineer, expert, genius, intellect, philosopher, planner; SEE CONCEPTS 348,350

inventory [n] *list of stock; stock*
account, backlog, catalogue, file, fund, hoard, index, itemization, record, register, reserve, reservoir, roll, roster, schedule, stock book, stockpile, store, summary, supply, table, tabulation; SEE CONCEPTS 283,338

inverse [adj] *opposite*
changed, contrary, converse, flipped, inverted, reverse, reversed, reverted, transposed, turned, turned over; SEE CONCEPT 564

invert [v] *reverse; turn upside down*
alter, backtrack, capsize, change, convert, double back, evert, flip, flip-flop*, introvert, inverse, modify, overturn, renege, revert, tip, transplace, transpose, turn, turn down, turn inside out, turn over, turn the tables*, upend, upset, upturn; SEE CONCEPTS 213,232

invest [v1] *contribute money to make money*
advance, back, bankroll, buy into, buy stock, devote, endow, endue, get into, go in for, imbue, infuse, intrust, lay out, lend, loan, pick up the tab*, plow back into*, plunge, provide, put in, put up dough*, salt away*, sink, spend, stake, supply; SEE CONCEPTS 115,330,341

invest [v2] *give power or authority*
adopt, authorize, bequeath, charge, consecrate, empower, endow, endue, enthrone, establish, honor, inaugurate, induct, initiate, install, instate, license, ordain, sanction, vest; SEE CONCEPTS 50,88

investigate [v] *check into thoroughly*
be all ears*, bug, case*, check out, check over, check up, consider, delve, dig, examine, explore, eyeball*, feel out, frisk, give the once over*, go into, inquire, inquisite, inspect, interrogate, listen in, look into, look over, look-see, make inquiry, muckrake, nose around*, poke, probe, prospect, pry, put to the test*, question, read, reconnoiter, research, review, run down, scout, scrutinize, search, sift, spy, stake out, study, tap, wiretap; SEE CONCEPTS 48,103,216

investigation [n] *thorough check*
analysis, case, delving, examination, exploration, fact-finding, gander, hearing, hustle, inquest, inquiry, inquisition, inspection, legwork, observation, observing, pike, probe, probing, quest, quiz, research, review, scrutiny, search, sounding, study, survey, surveying; SEE CONCEPTS 48,103,216,290

investigator [n] *person who checks thoroughly*
agent, analyst, attorney, auditor, detective, examiner, gumshoe*, hound*, inquirer, inspector,

plainclothes officer, police, private detective, private eye, prosecutor, researcher, reviewer, Sherlock Holmes*, sleuth, snooper, spy, tester, undercover cop; SEE CONCEPTS 348,355

investment [n] *something given, lent for a return*
advance, ante, asset, backing, bail, contribution, endowment, expenditure, expense, finance, financing, flutter, grant, hunch, inside, interests, investing, loan, money, piece, plunge, property, purchase, smart money*, spec*, speculation, stab*, stake, transaction, venture, vested interests; SEE CONCEPTS 330,332,340

inveterate [adj] *long-standing, established*
abiding, accustomed, addicted, chronic, confirmed, continuing, customary, deep-rooted, deep-seated, dyed-in-the-wool*, enduring, entrenched, fixed, habitual, habituated, hard-core*, hardened, inbred, incorrigible, incurable, indurated, ineradicable, ingrained, innate, lifelong, long-lasting, long-lived, obstinate, old, perennial, permanent, persistent, persisting, set, settled, stubborn, sworn, usual; SEE CONCEPTS 404,534,798

invidious [adj] *hateful*
abominable, calumnious, defamatory, detestable, detracting, detractive, detractory, discriminatory, envious, envying, green-eyed*, jealous, libelous, maligning, obnoxious, odious, offensive, repugnant, scandalous, slanderous, slighting, undesirable, vilifying; SEE CONCEPTS 401,403

invigorate [v] *stimulate*
activate, animate, brace, buck up, energize, enliven, excite, exhilarate, fortify, freshen, galvanize, harden, inspirit, liven up, nerve, pep up, perk up, pick up, quicken, rally, refresh, reinforce, rejuvenate, renew, restore, revitalize, rouse, snap up*, stir, strengthen, trigger, turn on*, vitalize, vivify, zap; SEE CONCEPTS 7,14,22,110

invigorating [adj] *stimulating*
aesthetic, bracing, brisk, charged, energizing, exhilarating, exhilarative, fascinating, fresh, healthful, high*, hyper*, interesting, lively, quickening, refreshing, rejuvenating, rejuvenative, restorative, salubrious, tonic, uplifting, vitalizing; SEE CONCEPT 537

invincible [adj] *indestructible*
bulletproof, impassable, impregnable, indomitable, insuperable, inviolable, invulnerable, irresistible, powerful, strong, unassailable, unattackable, unbeatable, unconquerable, undefeatable, unsurmountable, untouchable, unyielding; SEE CONCEPTS 489,540,551

invisible [adj] *unable to be seen; hidden*
concealed, covert, deceptive, disguised, ethereal, gaseous, ghostly, ideal, impalpable, imperceptible, imponderable, inappreciable, inconspicuous, indiscernible, infinitesimal, insensible, intangible, masked, microscopic, not in sight, obliterated, obscured, occult, out of sight, perdu, screened, supernatural, ulterior, unapparent, undisclosed, ungraspable, unnoticeable, unobservable, unperceivable, unreal, unseeable, unseen, unviewable, vaporous, veiled, wraithlike; SEE CONCEPTS 485,582,619

invitation [n] *proposal; asking*
allurement, appeal, attraction, begging, bid, bidding, call, challenge, compliments, coquetry, date, encouragement, enticement, feeler*, ground, hit, incitement, inducement, invite, lure, motive, offer, open door*, overture, paper, pass, petition, pressure, proffer, prompting, proposi-

tion, provocation, rain check*, reason, request, solicitation, suggestion, summons, supplication, temptation, urge; SEE CONCEPTS *48,384*

invite [v] *ask to do something socially*
allure, appeal to, attract, beg, bid, bring on, call, command, countenance, court, draw, encourage, entice, entreat, give invitation, have in, have over, include as guest, insist, inveigle, invitation, issue, lead, lure, persuade, petition, ply, pray, press, prevail on, propose, provoke, request, send invitation, solicit, suggest, summon, supplicate, tempt, toll, urge, vamp, welcome, woo; SEE CONCEPTS *48,68,384*

inviting [adj] *alluring, captivating*
agreeable, appealing, attractive, beguiling, bewitching, charming, cordial, delightful, encouraging, engaging, enticing, fascinating, intriguing, magnetic, mouthwatering, open, persuasive, pleasing, provocative, seductive, tempting, warm, welcoming, winning, winsome; SEE CONCEPTS *404,529,537*

invocation [n] *prayer*
abracadabra*, appeal, beseeching, calling, command, conjuration, entreaty, hocus-pocus*, hoodoo*, mumbo-jumbo*, petition, rune, summons, supplication, voodoo*; SEE CONCEPTS *48, 278,368*

invoke [v1] *call upon*
adjure, appeal to, beg, beseech, call forth, conjure, crave, entreat, implore, importune, petition, plead, pray, request, send for, solicit, summon, supplicate; SEE CONCEPT *48*

invoke [v2] *put into effect*
apply, call in, effect, enforce, have recourse to, implement, initiate, resort to, use; SEE CONCEPTS *50,88*

involuntary [adj] *automatic; not done willingly*
automatic, begrudging, blind, compulsory, conditioned, forced, grudging, habitual, impulsive, instinctive, instinctual, knee-jerk*, obligatory, reflex, reflexive, reluctant, spontaneous, uncalculated, unconscious, uncontrolled, unintended, unintentional, unmeditated, unpremeditated, unprompted, unthinking, unwilling, unwitting, will-less; SEE CONCEPT *544*

involve [v] *draw in; include*
absorb, affect, argue, associate, bind, catch, commit, complicate, comprehend, comprise, compromise, concern, connect, contain, cover, denote, embrace, embroil, engage, engross, enmesh, entail, entangle, grip, hold, hook, implicate, imply, incorporate, incriminate, inculpate, link, mean, mire, mix up*, necessitate, number, point to, preoccupy, presuppose, prove, relate, require, rivet, rope in, snarl up, suggest, take in, tangle, touch, wrap up in*; SEE CONCEPT *112*

involved [adj1] *complicated*
Byzantine*, complex, confusing, convoluted, difficult, elaborate, Ghordian*, high-tech*, intricate, knotty*, labyrinthine, mazy, muddled, ramified, sophisticated, tangled, tortuous, winding; SEE CONCEPT *562*

involved [adj2] *implicated in action*
affected, caught, concerned, eat sleep and breathe*, embarrassed, embroiled, enmeshed, entangled, hooked, immersed in, incriminated, interested, into, knee-deep in*, mixed up in*, mixed up with*, occupied, participating, taking part in, tangled, up to here in*, up to one's neck in*; SEE CONCEPTS *542,545*

inward [adj1] *ingoing*
entering, inbound, incoming, infiltrating, inflowing, inpouring, penetrating, through; SEE CONCEPT *581*

inward [adj2] *private*
confidential, hidden, inmost, inner, innermost, inside, intellectual, interior, internal, intimate, personal, privy, psychological, religious, secret, spiritual; SEE CONCEPT *529*

iota [n] *small bit*
atom, crumb, grain, hint, infinitesimal, jot, mite, molecule, nucleus, ounce, particle, ray, scintilla, scrap, smidgen, speck, trace, whit; SEE CONCEPT *831*

irascible [adj] *crabby*
angry, bearish, bristly, cantankerous, choleric, crabbed, cranky, cross, feisty, fractious, grouchy, hasty, hot-tempered, huffy, ireful, irritable, ogre, passionate, peevish, petulant, querulous, quick-tempered, short-tempered, snappish, surly, testy, thin-skinned*, touchy, uptight; SEE CONCEPT *401*

irate [adj] *angry*
angered, annoyed, blown a gasket*, enraged, exasperated, fuming, furious, incensed, indignant, infuriated, irritated, livid, mad, piqued, provoked, riled, steamed*, ticked off*, up in arms*, worked up*, wrathful, wroth; SEE CONCEPTS *403,542*

ire [n] *anger*
annoyance, boiling point*, conniption, conniption fit*, displeasure, exasperation, fury, indignation, more heat than light*, passion, rage, slow burn*, wrath; SEE CONCEPT *410*

iridescent [adj] *rainbow-colored*
irised, lustrous, many-colored, nacreous, opalescent, opaline, pearly, polychromatic, prismatic, rainbowlike, shimmering; SEE CONCEPT *618*

irk [v] *aggravate; rub the wrong way*
abrade, annoy, bother, bug*, discommode, disturb, eat*, fret, gall, get on nerves*, get to*, give a hard time*, harass, incommode, inconvenience, irritate, make waves*, miff, nettle, peeve, provoke, put out*, rasp, rile, ruffle, trouble, vex; SEE CONCEPTS *7,19*

iron [n1] *hard, ferrous metal*
cast, coke, pig; SEE CONCEPT *476*

iron [n2] *restraint made of metal*
bond, chain, cuffs, fetter, handcuffs, leg irons, manacles, shackles; SEE CONCEPT *476*

iron [adj] *hard, tough; inflexible*
adamant, adamantine, cruel, dense, ferric, ferrous, firm, heavy, immovable, implacable, indomitable, inexorable, insensible, obdurate, relentless, rigid, robust, steel, steely, strong, stubborn, thick, unbending, unyielding; SEE CONCEPTS *534,604*

ironic/ironical [adj] *sarcastic*
acrid, alert, arrogant, backbiting, biting, bitter, burlesque, caustic, chaffing, clever, contemptuous, contradictory, critical, cynical, defiant, derisive, disparaging, double-edged, exaggerated, implausible, incisive, incongruous, jibing, keen, mocking, mordant, paradoxical, pungent, quick-witted, ridiculous, sardonic, satiric, satirical, scathing, scoffing, sharp, sneering, spicy, trenchant, twisted, uncomplimentary, witty, wry; SEE CONCEPTS *267,548*

iron out [v] *reconcile a situation*
agree, arbitrate, clear up*, compromise, eliminate, eradicate, erase, expedite, get rid of*, harmonize, negotiate, put right*, reach agreement,

irony [n] *sarcasm*

banter, burlesque, contempt, contrariness, criticism, derision, humor, incongruity, jibe, mockery, mordancy, paradox, quip, raillery, repartee, reproach, ridicule, sardonicism, satire, taunt, twist, wit; SEE CONCEPTS *230,278*

irrational [adj] *illogical, senseless*

aberrant, absurd, brainless, cockamamie*, crazy, delirious, demented, disconnected, disjointed, distraught, fallacious, flaky*, foolish, freaky, incoherent, injudicious, insane, invalid, kooky*, loony*, mad, mindless, nonsensical, nutty*, off-the-wall*, preposterous, raving, reasonless, ridiculous, silly, sophistic, specious, stupid, unreasonable, unreasoning, unsound, unstable, unthinking, unwise, wacky*, wild, wrong; SEE CONCEPTS *402,403,529*

irreconcilable [adj] *hostile, conflicting*

clashing, diametrically opposed, discordant, discrepant, dissonant, hard-line, implacable, incompatible, incongruous, inconsistent, inexorable, inflexible, inharmonious, intransigent, opposed, reluctant, unappeasable, uncompromising, unfriendly; SEE CONCEPTS *401,564*

irrefutable [adj] *beyond question*

accurate, apodictic, can bet on it*, certain, double-checked, evident, final, inarguable, incontestable, incontrovertible, indisputable, indubitable, invincible, ironclad, irrebuttable, irrefragable, irresistible, nof ifs ands or buts*, obvious, odds-on*, positive, proven, set, sure, unanswerable, unassailable, undeniable, unimpeachable, unquestionable; SEE CONCEPTS *529,535,582*

irregular [adj1] *random, variable*

aberrant, aimless, capricious, casual, changeable, designless, desultory, disconnected, discontinuous, eccentric, erratic, faltering, fitful, fluctuating, fragmentary, haphazard, hit-or-miss*, inconstant, indiscriminate, infrequent, intermittent, jerky, nonuniform, occasional, out of order*, patchy, purposeless, recurrent, shaky, shifting, spasmodic, sporadic, uncertain, unconsidered, uneven, unmethodical, unpunctual, unreliable, unsettled, unsteady, unsystematic, up and down*, weaving; SEE CONCEPTS *534,799*

irregular [adj2] *abnormal, peculiar*

aberrant, anomalous, atypical, capricious, deviant, different, disorderly, divergent, eccentric, exceptional, extraordinary, immoderate, improper, inappropriate, inordinate, odd, off-key*, queer, quirky, singular, strange, unconventional, unique, unnatural, unofficial, unorthodox, unsuitable, unusual; SEE CONCEPT *547*

irregular [adj3] *bumpy, uneven*

aberrant, amorphous, asymmetrical, bent, broken, cockeyed*, craggy, crooked, devious, disproportionate, eccentric, elliptic, elliptical, hilly, jagged, lopsided, lumpy, meandering, notched, not uniform, off-balance, off-center, out of proportion, pitted, protuberant, rough, scarred, serrate, serrated, unaligned, unbalanced, unequal, unsymmetrical, variable, wobbly, zigzagged; SEE CONCEPTS *490,606*

irregularly [adv] *intermittently*

anyhow, any which way*, at intervals, by fits and starts*, by turns, disconnectedly, eccentrically, erratically, fitfully, haphazardly, helter-skelter*, infrequently, in snatches*, jerkily, now and again, occasionally, off and on*, out of sequence, periodically, slapdash, spasmodically, sporadically, uncertainly, uncommonly, unevenly, unmethodically, unpunctually, willy-nilly*; SEE CONCEPTS *544,548,799*

irrelevant [adj] *beside the point*

extraneous, foreign, garbage, immaterial, impertinent, inapplicable, inapposite, inappropriate, inappurtenant, inapropos, inapt, inconsequent, inconsequential, insignificant, not connected with, not germane, not pertaining to, off the point, off the topic, out of order, out of place, outside, pointless, remote, trivial, unapt, unconnected, unimportant, unnecessary, unrelated, without reference; SEE CONCEPTS *560,575*

irreparable [adj] *unable to be fixed*

beyond repair, broken, cureless, destroyed, hopeless, impossible, incorrigible, incurable, irrecoverable, irredeemable, irremediable, irremedial, irreplaceable, irretrievable, irreversible, ruined, uncorrectable, unrecoverable; SEE CONCEPTS *314,485*

irrepressible [adj] *effervescent, vivacious*

boisterous, bubbling, buoyant, ebullient, enthusiastic, insuppressible, rebellious, rhapsodical, tumultuous/tumultuous, unconstrained, uncontainable, uncontrollable, unmanageable, unquenchable, unrestrainable, unrestrained, unruly, unstoppable; SEE CONCEPT *401*

irreproachable [adj] *innocent*

beyond reproach, blameless, exemplary, faultless, good, guiltless, impeccable, inculpable, innocent, irreprehensible, irreprovable, perfect, pure, reproachless, righteous, unblamable, unblemished, unimpeachable, virtuous; SEE CONCEPTS *545,574*

irresistible [adj] *compelling; inescapable*

alluring, beckoning, charming, enchanting, fascinating, glamorous, imperative, indomitable, ineluctable, inevitable, inexorable, invincible, lovable, overpowering, overwhelming, potent, powerful, ravishing, scrumptious, seductive, stunning, tempting, unavoidable, unconquerable, urgent; SEE CONCEPTS *529,574,579*

irresolute [adj] *indecisive*

changing, doubtful, doubting, faltering, fearful, fickle, fluctuating, halfhearted*, halting, hesitant, hesitating, hot-and-cold*, infirm, on-the-fence*, shaky, tentative, timid, uncertain, undecided, undetermined, unsettled, unstable, unsteady, vacillating, waffling*, wavering, weak, weak-kneed*, wimpy*, wishy-washy*, wobbly; SEE CONCEPTS *403,535*

irresponsible [adj] *careless, reckless*

capricious, carefree, devil-may-care*, feckless, fickle, flighty, fly-by-night*, giddy, harebrained, ill-considered, immature, immoral, incautious, lax, loose*, no-account*, rash, scatterbrained*, shiftless, thoughtless, unaccountable, unanswerable, uncareful, undependable, unpredictable, unreliable, unstable, untrustworthy, wild; SEE CONCEPTS *404,544*

irreverence [n] *disrespect*

blasphemy, cheek, derision, discourtesy, flippancy, heresy, impertinence, impiety, impudence, insult, mockery, profanity, ridicule, rudeness, sauciness*, sin, sinfulness; SEE CONCEPT *633*

irreverent [adj] *disrespectful*

aweless, cheeky*, cocky*, contemptuous, crusty*, derisive, flip*, flippant, fresh, iconoclas-

resolve, settle, settle differences, simplify, smooth over*, sort out*, straighten out*, unravel; SEE CONCEPT *126* tic, impertinent, impious, impudent, insolent, ir-reverential, mocking, out-of-line*, profane, rude, sacrilegious, sassy*, saucy*, tongue-in-cheek*, ungodly, unhallowed, unholy; SEE CONCEPT *401*

irrevocable [*adj*] *fixed, unchangeable*
certain, changeless, constant, doomed, estab-lished, fated, final, immutable, indelible, inevita-ble, invariable, irremediable, irretrievable, irreversible, lost, permanent, predestined, prede-termined, settled, unalterable, unrepealable, unre-versible; SEE CONCEPTS *534,551*

irritable [*adj*] *bad-tempered, crabby*
annoyed, bearish, brooding, cantankerous, carp-ing, choleric, complaining, contentious, crabbed, cross, crotchety, disputatious, dissatisfied, dys-peptic, easily offended, exasperated, fiery, frac-tious, fretful, fretting, gloomy, grouchy, grumbling, hasty, hot, huffy, hypercritical, ill-humored, irascible, moody, morose, out of hu-mor, oversensitive, peevish, petulant, plaintive, prickly, querulous, quick-tempered, resentful, sensitive, snappy, snarling, surly, tense, testy, touchy; SEE CONCEPTS *401,403*

irritate [*v1*] *upset, anger*
abrade, affront, aggravate, annoy, bother, bug*, burn*, chafe, confuse, distemper, disturb, drive up the wall*, enrage, exasperate, fret, gall, get, get on nerves*, get under skin*, grate, harass, incense, inflame, infuriate, irk, madden, needle*, nettle, offend, pain, peeve, pester, pique, pro-voke, put out, rankle, rasp, rattle, rile, roil, rub the wrong way*, ruffle, sour, try, vex; SEE CON-CEPTS *7,19*

irritate [*v2*] *hurt, chafe*
aggravate, burn, erupt, fret, inflame, intensify, itch, pain, redden, rub, sensitize, sharpen, sting, swell; SEE CONCEPT *246*

island [*n*] *land surrounded by body of water*
archipelago, atoll, bar, cay, enclave, haven, isle, islet, key, peninsula, reef, refuge, retreat, sanctu-ary, shelter; SEE CONCEPT *509*

isolate [*v*] *cut off, set apart*
abstract, block off, close off, confine, detach, dis-connect, disengage, divide, divorce, insulate, is-land, keep apart, part, quarantine, remove, seclude, segregate, separate, sequester, sever, sunder; SEE CONCEPTS *188,201*

isolated [*adj*] *unique; private*
abandoned, abnormal, alone, anomalous, apart, backwoods*, confined, deserted, detached, excep-tional, far-out, forsaken, hidden, incommunica-do*, lonely, lonesome, off beaten track*, outlying, out-of-the-way*, random, remote, re-tired, screened, secluded, segregated, seques-tered, single, solitary, special, stranded, unaccompanied, unfrequented, unrelated, untypi-cal, unusual, withdrawn; SEE CONCEPTS *577,583*

issue [*n1*] *point in question*
affair, argument, concern, contention, contro-versy, matter, matter of contention, point, point of departure, problem, puzzle, question, subject, topic; SEE CONCEPTS *278,532*

issue [*n2*] *result*
causatum, conclusion, consequence, culmination, effect, end, end product, eventuality, finale, fruit, outcome, payoff, sequel, termination, upshot; SEE CONCEPT *230*

issue [*n3*] *edition of publication*
copy, impression, installment, number, printing; SEE CONCEPT *280*

issue [*n4*] *distribution*
circulation, delivery, dispersion, dissemination, granting, issuance, issuing, publication, sending out, supply, supplying; SEE CONCEPT *140*

issue [*n5*] *children*
brood, descendants, get, heirs, offspring, poster-ity, progeniture, progeny, scions, seed; SEE CON-CEPTS *296,414*

issue [*v1*] *distribute*
air, allot, announce, assign, bring out, broadcast, circulate, consign, declare, deliver, dispatch, dis-pense, emit, get out, give out, promulgate, pub-lish, put in circulation, put out, release, send, send out, transmit; SEE CONCEPTS *60,140,292*

issue [*v2*] *emit, emerge; come from*
appear, arise, be a consequence, birth, come forth, derive from, emanate, exude, flow, give off, give out, ooze, originate, proceed, release, rise, send forth, spring, spurt, stem, throw off, vent, well; SEE CONCEPTS *179,648*

itch [*n1*] *scratching; tingling*
crawling, creeping, irritation, itchiness, prickling, psoriasis, rawness, tickle; SEE CONCEPTS *608,728*

itch [*n2*] *strong desire*
aphrodisia, appetite, appetition, concupiscence, craving, eroticism, hankering, hunger, impulse, longing, lust, lustfulness, motive, passion, pruri-ence, restlessness, urge, yearning, yen; SEE CON-CEPTS *20,529*

itch [*v1*] *scratch; tingle*
crawl, creep, irritate, prick, prickle, sting, tickle, titillate; SEE CONCEPTS *185,313,612*

itch [*v2*] *desire strongly*
ache, be impatient, burn, chafe, crave, hanker, have a yen for, hunger, long, lust, pant, pine, sigh, thirst, want, yearn; SEE CONCEPT *20*

item [*n*] *part, article*
account, aspect, bit, blurb*, bulletin, column, component, consideration, conversation piece, de-tail, dispatch, element, entry, feature, incidental, information, matter, minor point, minutia, news, note, notice, novelty, paragraph, particular, piece, point, report, scoop*, scrap, specific, story, thing, write-up; SEE CONCEPTS *270,831,835*

itemize [*v*] *keep detailed record*
catalog, circumstantiate, cite, count, detail, doc-ument, enumerate, individualize, instance, inven-tory, lay out, list, mention, number, particularize, quote, recite, record, recount, rehearse, relate, set out, specify, spell out, tally; SEE CONCEPTS *57,125*

itinerant [*adj*] *roaming*
afoot, ambulant, ambulatory, floating, gypsy, journeying, migratory, moving, nomadic, on foot, peripatetic, ranging, riding the rails*, roving, shifting, travelling, unsettled, vagabond, vagrant, wandering, wayfaring; SEE CONCEPTS *536,584*

itinerary [*n*] *plan of travel*
beat, circuit, course, guide, guidebook, journey, line, outline, path, program, route, run, schedule, tour, way; SEE CONCEPTS *281,660*

J

jab [*n/v*] *poke*
blow, buck, bump, bunt, dig, hit, jog, lunge,

nudge, prod, punch, push, stab, tap, thrust; SEE CONCEPT *189*

jabber [*v*] *talk incessantly and trivially*
babble, blather*, chatter, drivel, gab, go on and on*, jaw, mumble, murmur, mutter, prate, ramble, run off at mouth*, shoot the breeze*, talk, tattle, utter, yak, yap; SEE CONCEPTS *51,56*

jacket [*n*] *covering*
case, casing, coat, envelope, folder, fur, hide, parka, pelt, sheath, skin, threads, tunic, wrapper, wrapping; SEE CONCEPTS *451,484*

jaded [*adj*] *exhausted, indifferent*
been around, blah*, blasé, bored, cool*, done it all*, dulled, fagged, fatigued, fed up*, had it*, mellow, sated, satiated, sick of*, spent, surfeited, tired, tired-out*, up to here*, wearied, weary, worn, worn-down, worn-out; SEE CONCEPTS *401,406*

jagged [*adj*] *ragged, notched*
asperous, barbed, broken, cleft, craggy, denticulate, harsh, indented, irregular, pointed, ridged, rough, rugged, scabrous, serrated, snaggy, spiked, toothed, uneven, unlevel, unsmooth; SEE CONCEPTS *490,606*

jail [*n*] *place for incarceration*
bastille, black hole*, brig, bullpen*, can*, cell, clink*, cooler*, detention camp, dungeon, house of correction, inside*, jailhouse, joint*, lockup, pen, penal institution, penitentiary, pound, prison, rack*, reformatory, slammer*, solitary*, stir*, stockade, up the river*; SEE CONCEPTS *439, 449,516*

jail [*v*] *incarcerate*
bastille, book, cage, can*, confine, constrain, detain, hold, immure, impound, imprison, lock up, prison, put away*, put behind bars*, put on ice*, railroad*, send up*, sentence, take away*, throw away the keys*, throw in dungeon, throw the book at*; SEE CONCEPT *317*

jam [*n*] *troublesome situation*
bind, box, corner, difficulty, dilemma, fix, hole, hot water*, pickle*, plight, predicament, problem, quandary, scrape, spot, strait, trouble; SEE CONCEPT *674*

jam [*v*] *squeeze in; compress*
bear, bind, block, cease, clog, congest, cram, crowd, crush, elbow, force, halt, jam-pack, jostle, obstruct, pack, press, push, ram, squash, squish, stall, stick, stuff, tamp, throng, wad, wedge; SEE CONCEPTS *121,208*

jangle [*n*] *cacophony of noises*
babel, babble, clangor, clash, din, dissonance, hubbub*, hullabaloo*, jar, pandemonium, racket, rattle, reverberation, roar, tumult, uproar; SEE CONCEPT *595*

jangle [*v*] *make clinking noises*
chime, clank, clash, clatter, conflict, disaccord, discord, disharmonize, hit a sour note*, jar, jingle, mismatch, rattle, vibrate; SEE CONCEPT *65*

janitor [*n*] *person who cleans and maintains*
attendant, caretaker, cleaning person, concierge, custodian, doorkeeper, doorperson, gatekeeper, house sitter, porter, sitter, super, superintendent, sweeper, watchperson; SEE CONCEPT *348*

jar [*n1*] *container*
basin, beaker, bottle, burette, can, chalice, crock, cruet, decanter, ewer, flagon, flask, jug, pitcher, pot, tun, urn, vase, vat, vessel; SEE CONCEPT *494*

jar [*n2*] *shocking hit*
bump, clash, collision, concussion, crash, impact, jolt, jounce, rock, smash, succussion, thud, thump; SEE CONCEPT *189*

jar [*v1*] *shock, jolt*
agitate, bang, bounce, bump, clash, convulse, crash, disturb, grate, grind, hit, irritate, jerk, jiggle, jounce, jump, offend, quake, rasp, rattle, rock, shake, slam, thump, tremor, vibrate, wiggle, wobble; SEE CONCEPTS *65,189*

jar [*v2*] *clash, disharmonize*
annoy, bicker, contend, disaccord, disagree, discompose, discord, grate, grind, interfere, irk, irritate, jangle, mismatch, nettle, oppose, outrage, quarrel, shock, wrangle; SEE CONCEPTS *7,19*

jargon [*n*] *specialized language; dialect*
abracadabra*, argot, balderdash*, banality, bombast, bunk*, buzzwords*, cant, cliché, colloquialism, commonplace term, doublespeak, drivel, fustian, gibberish, hackneyed term, idiom, insipidity, lexicon, lingo*, mumbo jumbo*, neologism, newspeak, nonsense, overused term, palaver, parlance, patois, patter, rigmarole, shoptalk, slang, slanguage*, speech, stale language, street talk*, tongue, trite language, twaddle*, usage, vernacular, vocabulary; SEE CONCEPTS *275,276*

jaundiced [*adj*] *tainted, prejudiced*
biased, bigoted, bitter, colored, cynical, disapproving, distorted, envious, grudging, hostile, intolerant, jealous, one-sided, opprobrious, partial, partisan, preconceived, prepossessed, resentful, skeptical, spiteful, suspicious, tendentious, unfair, unfriendly, unindifferent, warped, yellow; SEE CONCEPTS *401,403,542*

jaunt [*n*] *expedition*
adventure, airing, amble, beat, canter, circuit, constitutional, course, cruise, drive, excursion, frolic, gallop, hike, jog, journey, junket, march, outing, patrol, peregrination, picnic, promenade, prowl, ramble, ride, round, roundabout, run, safari, sally, saunter, stroll, tour, tramp, travel, trek, trip, turn, voyage, walk; SEE CONCEPTS *159,195,224*

jaunty [*adj*] *lively*
airy, animated, bold, brash, breezy, buoyant, carefree, careless, cocky, dapper, dashing, debonair, devilish, devil-may-care*, easy, exhilarated, flip*, flippant, forward, free, fresh, frisky, frolicsome, gamesome, gay, high-spirited, hilarious, impetuous, impish, impudent, jocose, joking, jolly, jovial, light, natty, nervy, perky, playful, prankish, provocative, reckless, rollicking, self-confident, showy, smart, sportive, sporty, sprightly, spruce, swaggering, trim, venturesome, vivacious; SEE CONCEPTS *401,404*

jaw [*n*] *bones of chin*
bone, chops*, jowl, mandible, maxilla, mouth, muzzle*, orifice; SEE CONCEPT *392*

jaw [*v1*] *talk a lot*
babble, chat, chatter, gab*, gossip, jabber, lecture, orate, prate, prattle, yak; SEE CONCEPTS *51,56*

jaw [*v2*] *criticize*
abuse, baste, berate, blame, call on the carpet*, censure, rail, rate, revile, scold, tongue-lash*, upbraid, vituperate; SEE CONCEPT *52*

jazzy [*adj*] *fancy*
animated, exciting, flashy, gaudy, lively, salacious, sexy, smart, snazzy*, spirited, vivacious, wild, zestful, zippy*; SEE CONCEPTS *537,589*

ir
ja

jealous [adj] *desirious; wary*
anxious, apprehensive, attentive, begrudging, covetous, demanding, doubting, emulous, envious, envying, grabby, grasping, green-eyed, grudging, guarded, intolerant, invidious, jaundiced, mistrustful, monopolizing, possessive, possessory, protective, questioning, resentful, rival, skeptical, solicitous, suspicious, vigilant, watchful, zealous; SEE CONCEPTS *403,542*

jeer [v] *heckle*
banter, comeback, contemn, deride, dig*, fleer, flout, gibe, hector, hoot, jab, jest, laugh at, make a crack*, mock, poke fun, put down, put on, quip, ridicule, scoff, sneer, snipe, taunt; SEE CONCEPT *54*

jell [v] *coagulate*
clot, cohere, come together, condense, congeal, crystallize, finalize, form, freeze, gel, gelate, gelatinize, harden, jellify, jelly, materialize, set, solidify, stick, stiffen, take shape, thicken; SEE CONCEPTS *250,469*

jeopardy [n] *danger, trouble*
accident, chance, double-trouble*, endangerment, exposure, hazard, insecurity, liability, on the line*, on the spot*, out on a limb*, peril, precariousness, risk, venture, vulnerability; SEE CONCEPT *675*

jerk [n1] *a lurching move*
bounce, bump, flick, flop, jolt, pull, quake, quiver, shiver, snag, thrust, tug, tweak, twitch, wiggle, wrench, wriggle, yank; SEE CONCEPTS *80,149,150*

jerk [n2] *stupid, bumbling person*
brute, fool, idiot, nincompoop, ninny, oaf, rascal; SEE CONCEPT *423*

jerk [v] *move with lurch*
bounce, bump, dance, flick, fling, flip, flop, grab, hook, hurtle, jolt, lug, pluck, pull, quake, quiver, seize, shiver, shrug, sling, snag, snatch, throw, thrust, tug, tweak, twitch, vellicate, whisk, wiggle, wrench, wrest, wriggle, wring, yank; SEE CONCEPTS *150,152*

jest [n] *joke*
banter, bon mot, crack, fun, funny, gag, game, hoax, jive, jolly, laugh, one-liner*, play, pleasantry, prank, quip, rib, rib-tickler*, ridicule, sally, spoof, sport, wisecrack, witticism; SEE CONCEPT *273*

jest [v] *joke*
banter, chaff, deride, flout, fool, fun*, gibe*, gird*, jeer, jive*, jolly*, josh*, kid, mock, needle*, put on, quip, rag*, razz*, rib*, roast*, scoff, sneer, spoof, tease; SEE CONCEPT *273*

jester [n] *person who jokes, plays jokes*
actor, antic, banterer, buffoon, card*, clown, comedian, comic, cutup*, droll, fool, harlequin, humorist, japer, joker, jokester, larker, life of the party*, madcap*, pantaloon, practical joker, prankster, quipster, standup comic, trickster, wag*, wisecracker*, wit; SEE CONCEPT *423*

jet [n1] *rush, gush of substance*
flow, fountain, spout, spray, spritz, spurt, squirt, stream; SEE CONCEPTS *465,467*

jet [n2] *vehicle propelled by ejection of pressurized gas or liquid*
airbus, airplane, plane, supersonic, supersonic transport, turbo; SEE CONCEPTS *463,503*

jet [adj] *black*
atramentous, coal-black, dark, ebon, ebony, inky,

midnight, obsidian, pitch-black, pitch-dark, raven, sable; SEE CONCEPT *618*

jet [v] *spurt, gush*
flow, fly, issue, pour, roll, rush, shoot, soar, spew, spout, spritz, squirt, stream, surge, travel, zoom; SEE CONCEPT *179*

jettison [v] *eject; throw overboard*
abandon, abdicate, cashier*, cast, cast off, deep-six*, discard, dump, expel, heave, hurl, junk*, maroon, reject, scrap*, shed, slough, throw away, unload*; SEE CONCEPTS *180,222*

jewel [n1] *precious stone*
baguette, bauble, bead, bijou, birthstone, brilliant, gem, gemstone, glass, gullion, hardware*, ornament, rock*, sparkler*, stone, trinket; SEE CONCEPTS *446,474,478*

jewel [n2] *something, someone precious*
charm, find, gem, genius, ideal, masterpiece, nonesuch, nonpareil, paragon, pearl*, phenomenon, phoenix*, prize, prodigy, rarity, specialty, treasure, wonder; SEE CONCEPT *671*

jewelry [n] *precious stones, metals worn as decoration*
adornment, anklet, band, bangle, bauble, beads, bijou, bracelet, brass, brooch, cameo, chain, charm, choker, costume, cross, crown, diamonds, earring, finery, frippery, gem, glass*, gold, ice*, jewel, junk*, knickknack, lavaliere, locket, necklace, ornament, pendant, pin, regalia, ring, rock, rosary, silver, solitaire, sparkler, stickpin, stone, tiara, tie pin, treasure, trinket; SEE CONCEPT *446*

jibe [v] *agree*
accord, conform, correspond, dovetail, fit, fit in, go, harmonize, match, resemble, square, tally; SEE CONCEPT *664*

jiffy [n] *instant*
breath, crack, flash, jiff*, minute, moment, second, shake*, split second*, trice, twinkling*; SEE CONCEPT *808*

jiggle [v] *bounce up and down*
agitate, bob, fidget, jerk, jig, jigger, jog, joggle, shake, shimmer, shimmy, twitch, vellicate, wiggle; SEE CONCEPTS *150,152*

jilt [v] *abandon, betray*
break off*, coquette, deceive, desert, disappoint, discard, ditch*, drop*, dump*, forsake, get rid of, leave, leave at the altar*, leave flat*, reject, throw over*; SEE CONCEPTS *195,297,384*

jingle [v] *make metallic clinking noise*
chime, chink, chinkle, clamor, clang, clatter, clink, ding, jangle, rattle, reverberate, ring, sound, tingle, tinkle, tintannabulate; SEE CONCEPT *65*

jinx [n] *curse*
black magic, charm, enchantment, evil eye*, hex, hoodoo*, kiss of death*, nemesis, plague, spell, voodoo*; SEE CONCEPTS *230,679*

jinx [v] *curse*
bedevil, bewitch, cast a spell on, charm, condemn, damn*, enchant, give the evil eye*, hex; SEE CONCEPTS *14,192*

jitters [n] *nervousness*
anxiety, dither, fidgets, heebie-jeebies*, jumps, nerves, shakes, shivers, tenseness, willies*; SEE CONCEPTS *230,410,690*

job [n1] *employment*
activity, appointment, assignment, berth, billet, business, calling, capacity, career, chore, connection, craft, daily grind*, engagement, faculty, function, gig*, grind*, handicraft, line, liveli-

hood, means, métier, niche, nine-to-five*, occupation, office, opening, operation, place, position, post, posting, profession, pursuit, racket*, rat race*, situation, spot, stint, swindle*, task, trade, vocation, work; SEE CONCEPTS 351,360

job [n2] *task*
act, action, affair, assignment, burden, business, care, charge, chore, commission, concern, contribution, deed, devoir, duty, effort, enterprise, errand, function, matter, mission, obligation, office, operation, project, province, pursuit, responsibility, role, stint, task, taskwork, thing*, tour of duty, undertaking, venture, work; SEE CONCEPT 362

jocular/jocose/jocund [adj] *funny, playful*
amusing, blithe, camp, cheerful, comic, comical, crazy, daffy, droll, facetious, flaky*, frolicsome, gay, gleeful, happy, humorous, jesting, jokey, joking, jolly, joshing, jovial, joyous, laughable, lighthearted, lively, ludicrous, merry, mischievous, pleasant, roguish, sportive, teasing, wacky, waggish, whimsical, witty; SEE CONCEPTS 267,529

jog [v1] *activate, push*
agitate, arouse, bounce, dig, hit, jab, jar, jerk, jiggle, joggle, jolt, jostle, jounce, nudge, press, prod, prompt, punch, remind, rock, shake, shove, stimulate, stir, suggest, whack; SEE CONCEPTS 14,208

jog [v2] *run for recreation*
amble, canter, dash, dogtrot, lope, pace, sprint, trot; SEE CONCEPT 151

join [v1] *unite*
accompany, add, adhere, affix, agglutinate, annex, append, assemble, associate, attach, blend, bracket, cement, clamp, clasp, clip, coadunate, coalesce, combine, compound, concrete, conjoin, conjugate, connect, copulate, couple, entwine, fasten, fuse, grapple, hitch on, incorporate, interlace, intermix, juxtapose, knit, leash, link, lock, lump together, marry, mate, melt, mix, pair, put together, slap on, span, splice, stick together, tack on, tag on, tie, tie up, touch, weave, wed, weld, yoke; SEE CONCEPT 113

join [v2] *affiliate with organization*
align, associate with, be in, come aboard*, consort, cooperate, enlist, enroll, enter, fall in with*, follow, go to, mingle with, pair with, plug into*, side with, sign on, sign up, take part in, take up with, team up with, throw in with*, tie up with; SEE CONCEPT 114

join [v3] *touch; border on*
abut, adjoin, be adjacent to, be at hand, be close to, be contiguous to, bound, butt, communicate, conjoin, extend, fringe, hem, lie beside, lie near, lie next to, line, march, meet, neighbor, open into, parallel, reach, rim, skirt, trench on, verge on; SEE CONCEPT 747

joint [n1] *intersection, juncture*
abutment, articulation, bend, bond, bracket, bridge, concourse, confluence, conjuncture, connection, copula, coupling, crux, elbow, hinge, hyphen, impingement, interconnection, junction, knot, link, meeting, nexus, node, point, seam, splice, suture, swivel, tangency, tie, union, vinculum; SEE CONCEPTS 393,830,831

joint [n2] *cheap hangout*
bar, club, dive*, hole in the wall*, honky-tonk*, juke joint*, roadhouse, tavern; SEE CONCEPTS 439,449

joint [adj] *shared, combined*
collective, common, communal, concerted, conjoint, conjunct, consolidated, cooperative, hand in hand, intermutual, joined, mutual, public, united; SEE CONCEPTS 577,708

jointly [adv] *as one*
accordingly, agreeably, alike, arm in arm*, coincidentally, collectively, combined, companionably, concomitantly, concurrently, conjointly, connectedly, cooperatively, en masse, hand in glove*, hand in hand*, harmoniously, in a group, in common, in company with, in concert, in conjunction, inextricably, in league, in partnership, inseparably, intimately, in unison, mutually, reciprocally, side by side*, similarly, simultaneously, synchronically, together, unitedly, with one another; SEE CONCEPT 577

joke [n1] *fun, quip*
antic, bon mot, buffoonery, burlesque, caper, caprice, chestnut*, clowning, drollery, epigram, escapade, farce, frolic, gag, gambol, game, ha-ha*, hoodwinking*, horseplay*, humor, jape, jest, lark, laugh, mischief, monkeyshine*, mummery, one-liner*, parody, payoff, play, pleasantry, prank, pun, put-on, quirk, raillery, repartee, revel, rib, sally, saw, shaggy-dog story*, shenanigan*, snow job*, sport, spree, stunt, tomfoolery, trick, vagary, whimsy, wisecrack, witticism, yarn; SEE CONCEPT 273

joke [n2] *person that is made fun of*
buffoon, butt, clown, derision, fool, goat, jackass, jestee, laughingstock, mockery, simpleton, sport, target; SEE CONCEPTS 412,423

joke [v] *kid, tease*
banter, chaff, deceive, deride, fool, frolic, fun, gambol, horse around*, jape, jest, jive*, jolly, josh, kid around, laugh, make merry, mock, needle, play, play the clown, play tricks, poke fun*, pull one's leg*, pun, put on, quip, rag, revel, rib, ridicule, roast*, spoof, sport, taunt, trick, wisecrack*; SEE CONCEPT 273

joker [n] *person who kids, teases*
actor, banana*, buffoon, card*, clown, comedian, comic, cutup*, droll, farceur, fool, funster*, gagster*, humorist, jester, jokesmith, jokester, josher*, kidder, life of the party*, prankster*, punster*, quipster*, second banana*, stand-up comic, stooge, straight person, top banana*, trickster*, wag, wisecracker*, wit; SEE CONCEPTS 352,423

jolly [adj] *laughing, joyful*
blithe, blithesome, bouncy, carefree, cheerful, chipper, chirpy, convivial, daffy, delightful, enjoyable, entertaining, festive, frolicsome, funny, gay, gladsome, gleeful, happy, hilarious, jocund, jokey, joshing, jovial, joyous, jubilant, larking, lighthearted, lots of laughs, merry, mirthful, playful, pleasant, sportive, sprightly, zippy*; SEE CONCEPTS 267,542,548

jolt [n] *surprise; sudden push*
blow, bombshell*, bounce, bump, clash, collision, concussion, double whammy*, impact, jar, jerk, jog, jounce, jump, kick, lurch, percussion, punch, quiver, reversal, setback, shake, shock, shot, start, surprise, thunderbolt; SEE CONCEPTS 42,208

jolt [v] *surprise; push suddenly*
astonish, bowl over*, bump, churn, convulse, discompose, disturb, floor, jar, jerk, jog, jostle, knock, knock over*, lay out*, perturb, rock,

je
jo

shake, shake up*, shock, shove, spring something on*, stagger, start, startle, stun, throw a curve*, upset; SEE CONCEPTS *42,208*

jostle [*v*] *bump, shake*
bang into, bulldoze*, bump heads*, butt*, crash, crowd, elbow, hustle, jab, jog, joggle, jolt, nudge, press, push, push around, push aside, rough and tumble*, scramble, shoulder, shove, squeeze, thrust; SEE CONCEPTS *152,189,208*

journal [*n*] *chronicle*
account, almanac, annals, annual, calendar, chronology, comic book, daily, daybook, diary, gazette, ledger, log, magazine, memento, memoir, minutes, monthly, newspaper, note, observation, organ, paper, periodical, publication, rag, record, register, reminder, reminiscence, review, scandal sheet*, statement, tabloid, weekly; SEE CONCEPTS *271,280,801*

journalist [*n*] *person who writes about factual events for a living*
announcer, broadcaster, columnist, commentator, contributor, correspondent, cub, editor, hack, media person, newspaper person, newsperson, pencil pusher*, press, publicist, reporter, scribe, scrivener, stringer, television commentator, writer; SEE CONCEPTS *348,356*

journey [*n*] *excursion*
adventure, airing, beat, campaign, caravan, circuit, constitutional, course, crossing, drive, expedition, exploration, hike, itinerary, jaunt, junket, march, migration, odyssey, outing, passage, patrol, peregrination, pilgrimage, progress, promenade, quest, ramble, range, roaming, round, route, run, safari, sally, saunter, sojourn, stroll, survey, tour, tramp, transit, transmigration, travel, traveling, traverse, trek, trip, vagabondage, vagrancy, venture, visit, voyage, wandering, wayfaring; SEE CONCEPT *224*

journey [*v*] *travel*
circuit, cruise, fare, fly, globe trot*, go, go places, hie, hop, jaunt, jet, junket, knock about*, pass, peregrinate, proceed, process, push on, ramble, range, repair, roam, rove, safari, take a trip, tour, traverse, trek, voyage, wander, wend; SEE CONCEPT *224*

jovial [*adj*] *happy*
affable, airy, amiable, animated, bantering, blithe, blithesome, bouncy, buoyant, chaffing, cheery, chipper, chirpy, companionable, conversable, convivial, cordial, daffy*, delightful, dizzy*, enjoyable, facetious, festal, festive, gay, glad, gleeful, good-natured, hilarious, humorous, jocose, jocund, jokey, jolly, jollying, joshing, jubilant, larking, lighthearted, loony, lots of laughs*, merry, mirthful, nutty*, off-the-wall*, pleasant, sociable; SEE CONCEPTS *401,403*

joy [*n*] *great happiness, pleasure*
alleviation, amusement, animation, bliss, charm, cheer, comfort, delectation, delight, diversion, ecstasy, elation, exultation, exulting, felicity, festivity, frolic, fruition, gaiety, gem, gladness, glee, good humor, gratification, hilarity, humor, indulgence, jewel, jubilance, liveliness, luxury, merriment, mirth, pride, pride and joy, prize, rapture, ravishment, refreshment, regalement, rejoicing, revelry, satisfaction, solace, sport, transport, treasure, treat, wonder; SEE CONCEPTS *410,529*

joyful/joyous [*adj*] *happy*
blithesome, cheerful, cheery, delighted, ecstatic, effervescent, elated, enjoyable, enraptured, expansive, festive, flying*, gay, glad, gladsome, gratified, heartening, high*, high as a kite*, jubilant, lighthearted, merry, overjoyed, pleased, pleasurable, popping*, rapturous, satisfied, sunny*, sunny-side up*, transported, upbeat; SEE CONCEPTS *403,542,548*

joyless [*adj*] *unhappy*
black, bleak, blue, cheerless, dejected, depressant, depressed, depressing, dismal, dispirited, dispiriting, doleful, downcast, down in the mouth*, dragged, dreary, droopy, gloomy, have the blahs*, heavy*, low, melancholic, melancholy, miserable, mopey, mournful, sad, saddening, somber; SEE CONCEPTS *403,542,548*

jubilant [*adj*] *happy*
celebrating, doing handsprings*, elated, enraptured, euphoric, excited, exuberant, exultant, exulting, flipping, flying*, glad, gleeful, joyous, overjoyed, pleased, rejoicing, rhapsodic, thrilled, tickled*, triumphal, triumphant; SEE CONCEPTS *401,403*

judge [*n*] *person who arbitrates*
adjudicator, appraiser, arbiter, assessor, authority, bench, chancellor, conciliator, court, critic, evaluator, expert, honor, inspector, intercessor, intermediary, interpreter, judiciary, justice, justice of peace, legal official, magister, magistrate, marshal, moderator, negotiator, peacemaker, reconciler, referee, umpire, warden; SEE CONCEPT *355*

judge [*v*] *make decision from evidence; deduce*
act on, adjudge, adjudicate, appraise, appreciate, approximate, arbitrate, arrive, ascertain, assess, check, collect, conclude, condemn, consider, criticize, decide, decree, deduct, derive, determine, discern, distinguish, doom, draw, esteem, estimate, evaluate, examine, find, gather, give a hearing, make, make out, mediate, pass sentence, place, pronounce sentence, put, rate, reckon, referee, resolve, review, rule, sentence, settle, sit, size up, suppose, test, try, umpire, value; SEE CONCEPTS *18,317*

judgment [*n1*] *common sense*
acumen, acuteness, apprehension, astuteness, awareness, brains, capacity, comprehension, discernment, discrimination, experience, genius, grasp, incisiveness, ingenuity, intelligence, intuition, keenness, knowledge, mentality, penetration, perception, percipience, perspicacity, prudence, quickness, range, rationality, reach, readiness, reason, reasoning, sagacity, sanity, sapience, savvy, sense, sharpness, shrewdness, sophistication, soundness, taste, understanding, wisdom, wit; SEE CONCEPTS *37,409*

judgment [*n2*] *decision about blame*
analysis, appraisal, appreciation, arbitration, assaying, assessment, award, belief, close study, conclusion, contemplation, conviction, decree, deduction, determination, estimate, estimation, evaluation, examination, exploration, finding, idea, inference, inquest, inquiry, inquisition, inspection, observation, opinion, order, probing, pursuit, quest, reconnaissance, regard, report, research, resolution, result, review, ruling, scrutiny, search, sentence, sifting, summary, verdict, view, weigh-in; SEE CONCEPTS *103,689*

judgment [*n3*] *doom, fate*
affliction, castigation, chastisement, correction, damnation, infliction, manifestation, misfortune,

mortification, punishment, retribution, visitation; SEE CONCEPT 679

judicial [adj] *legal*
administrative, authoritative, constitutional, discriminating, distinguished, equitable, forensic, impartial, judgelike, judiciary, juridical, jurisdictional, juristic, lawful, legalistic, magisterial, official, pontifical, principled, regular, statutory; SEE CONCEPT 319

judicious [adj] *wise, thoughtful*
accurate, acute, astute, calculating, careful, cautious, circumspect, clear-sighted, considerate, considered, diplomatic, discerning, discreet, discriminating, efficacious, enlightened, expedient, far-sighted, informed, judicial, keen, perceptive, perspicacious, politic, profound, prudent, quick-witted, rational, reasonable, sagacious, sage, sane, sapient, seasonable, seemly, sensible, sharp, shrewd, skillful, sober, sophisticated, sound, thorough, wary, well-advised, well-judged, worldly-wise; SEE CONCEPTS 402,403,542

jug [n] *container for liquid*
amphora, beaker, bottle, bucket, canteen, carafe, crock, cruet, decanter, ewer, flagon, flask, growler, hooker, jar, pitcher, pot, tub, urn, vase, vessel; SEE CONCEPT 494

juggle [v] *mislead, falsify; handle several things at once*
alter, beguile, betray, bluff, change, conjure, delude, disguise, doctor*, double cross, fix, humbug*, illude, maneuver, manipulate, misrepresent, modify, perform magic, prestidigitate, shuffle, take in, tamper with, trim; SEE CONCEPTS 59,63

juice [n] *liquid squeezed from fruit, plant*
abstract, alcohol, aqua vitae, distillation, drink, essence, extract, fluid, liquor, milk, nectar, oil, sap, sauce, secretion, serum, spirit, syrup, water; SEE CONCEPTS 428,467

juicy [adj1] *moist*
dank, dewy, dripping, humid, liquid, luscious, lush, mellow, oily, oozy, pulpy, sappy, saturated, sauced, slippery, slushy, soaked, sodden, succulent, syrupy, viscid, watery, wet; SEE CONCEPT 603

juicy [adj2] *exciting, interesting*
colorful, fascinating, intriguing, piquant, provocative, racy, risqué, sensational, spicy, suggestive, tantalizing, vivid; SEE CONCEPTS 537,548

jumble [n] *hodgepodge*
assortment, chaos, clutter, confusion, derangement, disarrangement, disarray, disorder, farrago, gallimaufry, garbage, goulash, hash*, litter, medley, mélange, mess, miscellany, mishmash, mixture, muddle, olio, pastiche, patchwork, potpourri, salmagundi, scramble, shuffle, snarl, tangle, tumble; SEE CONCEPT 432

jumble [v] *mix up, confuse*
clutter, confound, derange, disarrange, disarray, dishevel, disorder, disorganize, disturb, entangle, foul up, mess up, mistake, muddle, rummage, shuffle, snarl, tangle, tumble; SEE CONCEPTS 16,84

jumbo [adj] *gigantic*
colossal, cyclopean, elephantine, giant, huge, immense, large, mammoth, mighty, oversized, prodigious; SEE CONCEPT 781

jump [n1] *leap*
bob, bounce, bound, buck, canter, caper, capriole, dance, dive, drop, fall, gambade, gambol, hop, hopping, hurdle, jar, jerk, jolt, leapfrog, leapfrogging, leaping, lurch, nosedive, plummet, plunge, pounce, rise, saltation, shock, skip, skipping, spring, start, swerve, twitch, upspring, upsurge, vault, wrench; SEE CONCEPT 194

jump [n2] *increase, advantage*
advance, ascent, augmentation, boost, handicap, head start, increment, inflation, rise, spurt, start, upper hand, upsurge, upturn; SEE CONCEPTS 704,763

jump [n3] *obstacle*
bar, barricade, barrier, fence, hurdle, impediment, rail, stretch; SEE CONCEPTS 470,674

jump [v1] *leap, spring*
bail out, barge, bob, bounce, bound, buck, canter, caper, clear, curvet, dive, drop, fall, gambol, hop, hurdle, hurtle, jerk, jiggle, jounce, lollop, lop, lunge, lurch, parachute, plummet, pop, quiver, rattle, ricochet, saltate, shake, skip, sky, somersault, surge, take, top, trip, vault, waver, wobble; SEE CONCEPT 194

jump [v2] *recoil*
bob, bolt, bounce, carom, flinch, jerk, jounce, rebound, ricochet, spring, start, startle, wince; SEE CONCEPT 213

jump [v3] *omit, avoid*
abandon, cancel, clear out, cover, cross out, digress, evade, leave, miss, nullify, overshoot, pass over, skip, switch; SEE CONCEPT 25

jump [v4] *increase*
advance, ascend, boost, escalate, gain, hike, jack up, mount, put up, raise, rise, surge, up; SEE CONCEPTS 236,245,763

jumpy [adj] *nervous*
agitated, antsy*, anxious, apprehensive, creepy*, excitable, excited, fidgety, frisky, high-strung*, jittery, on edge*, on pins and needles*, restless, sensitive, shaky, skittish, spooked, tense, timorous, unrestful; SEE CONCEPTS 401,690

junction/juncture [n1] *link, connection*
alliance, annexation, articulation, assemblage, attachment, bond, coalition, coherence, collocation, combination, combine, concatenation, concourse, concursion, confluence, conjugation, consolidation, convergence, coupling, crossing, crossroads, dovetail, elbow, gathering, gore, hinge, hookup, interface, intersection, joining, joint, knee, linking, meeting, miter, mortise, node, pivot, plug-in, reunion, seam, splice, terminal, tie-in, tie-up, union, weld; SEE CONCEPTS 746,830

juncture [n2] *turning point*
choice, circumstance, condition, contingency, crisis, crossroad, crux, emergency, exigency, instant, meeting point, moment, occasion, pass, pinch, plight, point, position, posture, predicament, quandary, state, status, strait, time, zero hour*; SEE CONCEPTS 388,693,815

jungle [n] *wilderness full of plant and animal life*
boscage, bush, chaparral, forest, labyrinth, maze, morass, primeval forest, tangle, undergrowth, wasteland, web, wood, zoo; SEE CONCEPT 517

junior [adj] *subordinate, younger*
inferior, lesser, lower, minor, second, secondary, second-string*; SEE CONCEPTS 574,578,797

junk [n] *odds and ends; garbage*
clutter, collateral, debris, filth, hogwash*, litter, miscellany, offal, refuse, rubbish, rubble, rummage, salvage, scrap, trash, waste; SEE CONCEPTS 260,432

jo
ju

jurisdiction [n] *area of authority*
administration, arbitration, area, authority, bailiwick, bounds, circuit, command, commission, compass, confines, control, discretion, district, domination, dominion, empire, extent, field, hegemony, influence, inquisition, judicature, limits, magistracy, might, orbit, power, prerogative, province, purview, range, reach, reign, right, rule, say, scope, slot, sovereignty, sphere, stomping grounds*, supervision, sway, territory, turf*, zone; SEE CONCEPTS *198,376,651*

jury [n] *panel that hears legal matter*
board, judges, peers, tribunal; SEE CONCEPTS *299,318*

just [adj1] *fair, impartial*
aloof, blameless, condign, conscientious, decent, dependable, dispassionate, due, equal, equitable, ethical, evenhanded, fair-minded, good, honest, honorable, lawful, nondiscriminatory, nonpartisan, objective, pure, reliable, right, righteous, rightful, rigid, scrupulous, strict, tried, true, trustworthy, unbiased, uncolored, upright, virtuous; SEE CONCEPTS *319,545*

just [adj2] *accurate, precise*
cogent, correct, exact, faithful, good, justified, normal, proper, regular, right, sound, strict, true, undistorted, veracious, veridical, well-founded, well-grounded; SEE CONCEPTS *535,582*

just [adj3] *suitable, appropriate*
apt, befitting, condign, deserved, due, felicitous, fit, fitting, happy, justified, legitimate, meet, merited, proper, reasonable, requisite, right, rightful, well-deserved; SEE CONCEPT *558*

just [adv1] *definitely*
absolutely, accurately, completely, directly, entirely, exactly, expressly, perfectly, precisely, right, sharp, smack-dab*, square, squarely, unmistakably; SEE CONCEPT *535*

just [adv2] *only now*
almost, a moment ago, approximately, at this moment, barely, by very little, hardly, just a while ago, just now, lately, nearly, now, presently, recently, right now, scarce, scarcely; SEE CONCEPTS *544,820*

just [adv3] *merely*
at most, but, no more than, nothing but, only, plainly, simply, solely; SEE CONCEPT *557*

just about [adv] *almost*
about, all but, approximately, around, as good as, close to, nearly, nigh, not quite, practically, well-nigh; SEE CONCEPTS *762,771,799*

justice [n1] *lawfulness, fairness*
amends, appeal, authority, authorization, charter, code, compensation, consideration, constitutionality, correction, credo, creed, decree, due process, equity, evenness, fair play, fair treatment, hearing, honesty, impartiality, integrity, judicatory, judicature, justness, law, legality, legalization, legal process, legitimacy, litigation, penalty, reasonableness, recompense, rectitude, redress, reparation, review, right, rule, sanction, sentence, square deal*, truth; SEE CONCEPTS *376,645,691*

justice [n2] *person who oversees court of law*
chancellor, court, judge, magistrate, umpire*; SEE CONCEPT *354*

justifiable [adj] *reasonable, well-founded*
acceptable, admissible, allowable, condonable, defensible, excusable, fair, fit, forgivable, lawful, legit*, legitimate, licit, logical, pardonable, probable, proper, reasonable, remissible, right, right-ful, sound, suitable, tenable, understandable, valid, vindicable, warrantable; SEE CONCEPTS *545,558*

justification [n] *reason, excuse*
absolution, account, acquittal, advocacy, answer, apologia, apology, approval, argument, basis, confirmation, defense, exculpation, exoneration, explanation, extenuation, grounds, idea, mitigation, palliation, palliative, plea, pretext, raison d'être, rationale, rationalization, rebuttal, redemption, reply, response, salvation, sanctification, song and dance*, story, support, validation, vindication, warrant, whatfor*, wherefore*, whitewashing*, whole idea*, why and wherefore*; SEE CONCEPT *661*

justify [v] *legitimize, substantiate*
absolve, acquit, advocate, alibi*, answer for, apologize for, approve, argue for, assert, be answerable for, bear out, brief, claim, clear, condone, confirm, contend, cop a plea*, countenance, crawl, defend, do justice to, establish, exculpate, excuse, exonerate, explain, favor, legalize, maintain, make allowances, make good*, palliate, pardon, plead, rationalize, rebut, show cause, speak in favor, square, stand up for, support, sustain, uphold, validate, verify, vindicate, warrant; SEE CONCEPTS *49,57*

justly [adv] *fairly*
accurately, befittingly, beneficently, benevolently, benignly, candidly, charitably, correctly, decently, decorously, duly, duteously, dutifully, equally, equitably, evenhandedly, fitly, fittingly, frankly, helpfully, honestly, honorably, impartially, lawfully, legally, legitimately, moderately, nicely, piously, properly, reasonably, respectably, righteously, rightfully, rightly, straightforwardly, temperately, tolerantly, unreservedly, uprightly, virtuously, well; SEE CONCEPTS *544,545*

jut [v] *extend*
beetle, bulge, elongate, impend, lengthen, overhang, poke, pop, pouch, project, protrude, protuberate, stand out, stick out; SEE CONCEPT *201*

juvenile [n] *young person*
adolescent, boy, child, girl, infant, kid*, minor, youngster, youth; SEE CONCEPT *424*

juvenile [adj] *childish*
adolescent, babyish, beardless, blooming, boyish, budding, callow, childlike, developing, formative, fresh, girlish, green, growing, immature, inexperienced, infant, infantile, jejune, junior, kid stuff*, milk-fed*, naive, pubescent, puerile, teenage, tender, undeveloped, unfledged, unripe, unsophisticated, unweaned, vernal, young, younger, youthful; SEE CONCEPTS *401,578,797*

K

keel over [v] *fall, faint*
black out, capsize, collapse, drop, founder, go down, overturn, pass out, pitch, plunge, slump, swoon, topple, tumble, upset; SEE CONCEPTS *152,181*

keen [adj] *enthusiastic*
agog, alert, animate, animated, anxious, appetent, ardent, athirst, avid, breathless, devoted, dying

to*, eager, earnest, ebullient, fervent, fervid, fierce, fond of, gung ho*, impassioned, impatient, intense, intent, interested, lively, perfervid, spirited, sprightly, thirsty, vehement, vivacious, warm, zealous; SEE CONCEPTS *401,403*

keen [*adj2*] *sharp, piercing*
acid, acute, caustic, cutting, edged, extreme, fine, honed, incisive, intense, observant, penetrating, perceptive, pointed, quick-witted, razor-sharp*, sardonic, satirical, strong, tart, trenchant, unblunted; SEE CONCEPT *267*

keen [*adj3*] *intelligent*
astute, bright, brilliant, canny, clever, discerning, discriminating, Einstein*, nobody's fool*, perceptive, perspicacious, quick, sagacious, sapient, sensitive, sharp, sharp as a tack*, shrewd, whiz, wise; SEE CONCEPT *402*

keep [*v1*] *hold, maintain*
accumulate, amass, cache, care for, carry, conduct, conserve, control, deal in, deposit, detain, direct, enjoy, garner, grasp, grip, have, heap, hold back, manage, own, pile, place, possess, preserve, put, put up, reserve, retain, save, season, stack, stock, store, trade in, withhold; SEE CONCEPT *710*

keep [*v2*] *tend; provide for*
administer, attend, board, care for, carry on, command, conduct, continue, defend, direct, endure, feed, foster, guard, look after, maintain, manage, mind, minister to, nourish, nurture, operate, ordain, protect, provision, run, safeguard, shelter, shield, subsidize, support, sustain, victual, watch over; SEE CONCEPTS *110,140*

keep [*v3*] *prevent*
arrest, avert, block, check, constrain, control, curb, delay, detain, deter, hamper, hamstring, hinder, hold back, impede, inhibit, limit, obstruct, restrain, retard, shackle, stall, stop, withhold; SEE CONCEPT *121*

keep [*v4*] *commemorate; pay attention to*
adhere to, bless, celebrate, comply with, consecrate, fulfill, hold, honor, laud, obey, observe, perform, praise, regard, respect, ritualize, sanctify, solemnize; SEE CONCEPT *377*

keep at [*v*] *continue, endure*
be steadfast, carry on, complete, drudge, finish, grind, labor, last, maintain, persevere, persist, remain, slave, stay, stick, toil; SEE CONCEPTS *23,87*

keepsake [*n*] *something precious*
emblem, favor, memento, memorial, relic, remembrance, reminder, souvenir, symbol, token, trophy; SEE CONCEPT *446*

keep up [*v*] *maintain, sustain*
balance, compete, contend, continue, emulate, go on, hold on, keep pace, keep step, match, pace, persevere, preserve, rival, run with, vie; SEE CONCEPTS *23,87,363*

keg [*n*] *barrel*
butt, cask, container, drum, firkin, hogshead, pipe, tub, tun, vat; SEE CONCEPT *494*

kernel [*n*] *seed, essence*
atom, bit, center, core, crux, fruit, germ, gist, grain, heart, hub, keynote, marrow, matter, meat, morsel, nub, nubbin, nut, part, piece, pith, root, substance, upshot; SEE CONCEPTS *668,826*

key [*n1*] *item that unlocks*
latchkey, opener, passkey, screw*, skeleton; SEE CONCEPT *499*

key [*n2*] *answer, solution*
blueprint, brand, cipher, clue, code, core, crux,

cue, earmark, explanation, fulcrum, guide, hinge, index, indicator, interpretation, lead, lever, marker, means, nexus, nucleus, passport, password, pivot, pointer, root, sign, symptom, ticket, translation; SEE CONCEPTS *274,668*

key [*adj*] *essential, important*
basic, chief, crucial, decisive, fundamental, indispensable, leading, main, major, material, pivotal, primary, principal, vital; SEE CONCEPT *568*

keynote/keystone [*n*] *essence, theme*
basic idea, basis, center, core, cornerstone, criterion, crux, gist, heart, idea, kernel, linchpin, mainspring, marrow, measure, motive, nub, pith, principle, root, source, spring, standard, substance; SEE CONCEPTS *532,661,688*

kick [*n1*] *thrill, enjoyment*
bang*, buzz*, excitement, fun, gratification, hoot*, joy, pleasure, refreshment, sensation, stimulation, wallop*; SEE CONCEPTS *388,410*

kick [*n2*] *power, strength*
backlash, blow, boot*, force, intensity, jar, jolt, pep, punch, pungency, snap, sparkle, tang, verve, vitality, zest, zing*; SEE CONCEPTS *641,732*

kick [*v1*] *hit with foot*
boot, calcitrate, dropkick, give the foot, jolt, punt; SEE CONCEPT *189*

kick [*v2*] *complain*
anathematize, carp, combat, condemn, criticize, curse, damn, except, execrate, expostulate, fight, fuss, gripe, grumble, inveigh, mumble, object, oppose, protest, rebel, remonstrate, repine, resist, spurn, wail, whine, withstand; SEE CONCEPT *52*

kick [*v3*] *quit a habit*
abandon, desist, give up, go cold turkey*, leave off, stop; SEE CONCEPT *234*

kickback [*n*] *bribe*
cut, gift, graft, money under the table*, oil*, payment, payoff, payola, percentage, recompense, reward, share; SEE CONCEPTS *192,344*

kick out [*v*] *get rid of*
ax, boot*, bounce*, can*, cashier*, chase, chuck, discharge, dismiss, drop, eject, evict, expel, extrude, fire, oust, out, reject, remove, sack*, throw out, toss out; SEE CONCEPTS *180,351,384*

kid [*n*] *young person*
baby, bairn, boy, child, daughter, girl, infant, juvenile, lad, lass, little one*, son, teenager, tot, youngster, youth; SEE CONCEPTS *414,424*

kid [*v*] *fool, ridicule*
bamboozle*, banter, beguile, bother, cozen, delude, dupe, flimflam*, fun*, gull, hoax, hoodwink, jape, jest, joke, jolly, josh, make fun of, make sport of, mock, pretend, rag*, razz, rib, roast, spoof, tease, trick; SEE CONCEPTS *59,273*

kidnap [*v*] *abduct; hold for ransom*
bodysnatch*, bundle off, capture, carry away, carry off, coax, decoy, entice, grab, hijack, impress, inveigh, lay hands on, lure, make off with*, pirate, remove, run away with, seduce, seize, shanghai*, skyjack, snatch, spirit away*, steal, waylay; SEE CONCEPTS *90,139*

kill [*v1*] *deprive of existence; destroy*
annihilate, asphyxiate, assassinate, crucify, dispatch, do away with*, do in*, drown, dump, electrocute, eradicate, erase*, execute, exterminate, extirpate, finish, garrote, get*, guillotine, hang, hit*, immolate, liquidate, lynch, massacre, murder, neutralize, obliterate, off*, poison, polish off*, put away*, put to death, rub out*, sacrifice, slaughter, slay, smother, snuff, strangle, suffo-

cate, waste*, wipe out*, X-out*, zap*; SEE CONCEPT 252

kill [v2] *turn off; cancel*
annul, cease, counteract, deaden, defeat, extinguish, forbid, halt, negative, neutralize, nix*, nullify, prohibit, quash, quell, recant, refuse, revoke, ruin, scotch*, shut off, smother, stifle, still, stop, suppress, turn out, veto; SEE CONCEPTS 121,239

kin [n] *blood relative*
affinity, blood, clan, connection, consanguinity, cousin, extraction, family, folk, house, kindred, kinsfolk, kinship, kinsperson, kith, lineage, member, people, race, relation, relationship, sibling, stock, tribe; SEE CONCEPTS 296,414,421

kind [n1] *class, species*
brand, breed, classification, family, genus, ilk, kin, order, race, set, sort, type, variety; SEE CONCEPT 378

kind [n2] *type, character*
breed, complexion, connection, denomination, description, designation, essence, fiber, gender, habit, ilk, likes, lot, manner, mold, nature, number, persuasion, set, sort, stamp, stripe, style, temperament, tendency, tribe, variety, way; SEE CONCEPTS 411,673

kind [adj] *generous, good*
affectionate, all heart*, altruistic, amiable, amicable, beneficent, benevolent, benign, big, bleeding-heart*, bounteous, charitable, clement, compassionate, congenial, considerate, cordial, courteous, eleemosynary, friendly, gentle, good-hearted, gracious, heart in right place*, humane, humanitarian, indulgent, kindhearted, kindly, lenient, loving, mild, neighborly, obliging, philanthropic, propitious, softhearted, soft touch, sympathetic, tenderhearted, thoughtful, tolerant, understanding; SEE CONCEPTS 401,404,542

kindhearted [adj] *compassionate, helpful*
altruistic, amiable, amicable, considerate, generous, good, good-natured, gracious, humane, kind, merciful, responsive, softhearted, sympathetic, tender, tenderhearted, warm, warmhearted; SEE CONCEPTS 404,542

kindle [v1] *start a fire*
blaze, burn, fire, flame, flare, glow, ignite, inflame, light, set alight, set fire; SEE CONCEPT 249

kindle [v2] *excite, incite*
agitate, animate, arouse, awaken, bestir, burn up*, challenge, egg on*, enkindle, exasperate, fire up*, foment, get smoking*, induce, inflame, inspire, key up*, provoke, rally, rouse, sharpen, stimulate, stir, thrill, turn on*, wake, waken, whet, work up*; SEE CONCEPTS 7,14,22,221

kindly [adj] *compassionate, helpful*
attentive, beneficial, benevolent, benign, benignant, cool, cordial, favorable, friendly, genial, gentle, good, good-hearted, good-natured, gracious, hearty, humane, kind, kindhearted, mellow, merciful, mild, neighborly, pleasant, polite, sociable, sympathetic, thoughtful, warm; SEE CONCEPTS 404,542

kindly [adv] *with compassion*
affectionately, agreeably, benevolently, benignly, carefully, charitably, compassionately, considerately, cordially, courteously, delicately, generously, genially, good-naturedly, graciously, heedfully, helpfully, humanely, politely, solicitously, sympathetically, tenderly, thoughtfully, tolerantly, understandingly, well; SEE CONCEPTS 542,544

kindness [n1] *compassion, generosity*
affection, altruism, amiability, beneficence, benevolence, charity, clemency, consideration, cordiality, courtesy, decency, delicacy, fellow feeling, forbearance, gentleness, good intention, goodness, good will, grace, graciousness, heart, helpfulness, hospitality, humanity, indulgence, kindliness, magnanimity, mildness, patience, philanthropy, serviceability, solicitousness, solicitude, sweetness, sympathy, tact, tenderness, thoughtfulness, tolerance, understanding, unselfishness; SEE CONCEPTS 633,657

kindness [n2] *helping act; service*
accommodation, aid, alms, assistance, benediction, benefaction, benevolence, benison, blessing, boon, boost, bounty, charity, dispensation, favor, generosity, good deed, good turn, help, indulgence, lift, mercy, philanthropy, relief, succor; SEE CONCEPTS 110,657

kindred [n] *blood relative*
affinity, blood, clan, connection, consanguinity, cousin, family, flesh, folk, homefolk, house, kin, kinsfolk, kinsperson, lineage, race, relation, relationship, stock, tribe; SEE CONCEPTS 296,414,421

kindred [adj] *corresponding, matching*
affiliated, agnate, akin, alike, allied, analogous, cognate, congeneric, congenial, connate, connatural, consanguine, germane, homogeneous, incident, kin, likable, parallel, related, similar; SEE CONCEPT 563

kingdom [n] *historically, an area ruled by a monarch*
commonwealth, country, county, crown, division, domain, dominion, dynasty, empire, field, lands, monarchy, nation, possessions, principality, province, realm, reign, rule, scepter, sovereignty, sphere, state, suzerainty, sway, territory, throne, tract; SEE CONCEPTS 508,510

kink [n1] *bend, twist*
coil, corkscrew, crimp, crinkle, curl, curve, entanglement, frizz, knot, loop, tangle, wrinkle; SEE CONCEPT 436

kink [n2] *spasm of muscular tissue*
charley horse*, cramp, crick, knot, muscle spasm, pain, pang, pinch, stab, stitch, tweak, twinge; SEE CONCEPTS 185,728

kink [n3] *complication*
defect, difficulty, flaw, hitch, impediment, imperfection, knot, tangle; SEE CONCEPT 674

kink [n4] *person's idiosyncrasy*
eccentricity, fetish, foible, notion, peculiarity, quirk, singularity, vagary, whim; SEE CONCEPT 411

kinky [adj1] *twisted*
coiled, crimped, curled, curly, frizzled, frizzy, knotted, matted, matty, rolled, tangled; SEE CONCEPT 486

kinky [adj2] *bizarre, perverted*
degenerated, depraved, deviant, eccentric, far-out, licentious, odd, outlandish, outre, peculiar, queer, quirky, sick, strange, unconventional, unnatural, unusual, warped, weird; SEE CONCEPTS 372,542,589

kiss [n] *touching lips to another*
butterfly*, caress, embrace, endearment, osculation, peck, salutation, salute, smack*, smooch*; SEE CONCEPTS 185,375

kiss [v] *touch one's lips to another's*
blow, brush, butterfly*, French*, glance, graze, greet, lip*, make out*, mush*, neck*, osculate,

peck, pucker up*, salute, smack*, smooch*; SEE
CONCEPTS *185,375*

kit [n] *provisions, equipment*
accoutrements, apparatus, assortment, bag, collection, container, effects, gear, impedimenta, implements, material, outfit, pack, paraphernalia,
rig, satchel, selection, set, stock, stuff, suitcase,
supplies, tackle, things, tools, trappings, utensils;
SEE CONCEPTS *494,496*

kitchen [n] *room for cooking food*
canteen, cookery, cookhouse, cook's room, cuisine, eat-in, gallery, galley, kitchenette, mess,
scullery; SEE CONCEPT *448*

kittenish [adj] *frisky, playful*
childish, coquettish, coy, elvish, flirtatious, frolicsome, fun-loving, impish, jaunty, mischievous,
sportive; SEE CONCEPT *401*

knack [n] *ability, talent*
adroitness, aptitude, aptness, bent, capacity, command, dexterity, expertise, expertism, expertness,
facility, faculty, flair, forte, genius, gift, handiness, hang of it*, head*, ingenuity, know-how,
mastership, nose*, propensity, quickness, readiness, savvy*, set, skill, skillfulness, trick, turn;
SEE CONCEPTS *409,630*

knead [v] *mix by pressing*
acrate, alter, blend, form, manipulate, massage,
mold, ply, press, push, rub, shape, squeeze,
stroke, twist, work; SEE CONCEPTS *170,208*

kneel [v] *get down on one's knees*
bow, bow down, curtsey, do obeisance, genuflect,
kowtow, prostrate oneself, stoop; SEE CONCEPT
154

knickknack [n] *trinket; decorative piece*
bagatelle, bauble, bibelot, bric-a-brac, conversation piece, curio, curiosity, device, embellishment, flummery, frill, furbelow, gadget*,
miniature, notion, novelty, objet d'art, ornament,
plaything*, showpiece, souvenir, thingamajig*,
toy, trapping, trifle, whatnot*, whimsy; SEE CON-
CEPTS *259,260,446*

knife [n] *cutting tool*
bayonet, blade, bolo, cutlass, cutter, cutting edge,
dagger, edge, lance, lancet, machete, point, rip-
per, sabre, scalpel, scimitar, scythe, shank, shiv,
sickle, skewer, skiver, steel, stiletto, switchblade,
sword, tickler; SEE CONCEPTS *495,499*

knife [v] *stab with pointed tool*
brand, carve, chop down, clip, cut, hurt, impale,
jag, kill, lacerate, lance, open up, pierce, shank,
shiv, slash, slice, spit, stick, thrust, wound; SEE
CONCEPTS *176,220,246*

knit [v] *intertwine*
affiliate, affix, ally, bind, cable, connect, contract,
crochet, fasten, heal, interlace, intermingle, join,
link, loop, mend, net, purl, repair, secure, sew,
spin, tie, unite, weave, web; SEE CONCEPTS
113,202,218

knob [n] *lump, handle*
bulge, bulk, bump, bunch, doorknob, hump, knot,
knurl, latch, lever, nub, opener, projection, protrusion, protuberance, snag, stud, swell, swelling,
trigger, tumor; SEE CONCEPTS *445,471*

knock [n1] *pushing, striking*
beating, blow, box, clip, conk, cuff, hammering,
hit, injury, lick, rap, slap, smack, swat, swipe,
thump, whack; SEE CONCEPT *189*

knock [n2] *strong criticism*
blame, censure, condemnation, defeat, failure,

flak, pan, rap, rebuff, rejection, reversal, setback,
stricture, swipe; SEE CONCEPTS *52,278*

knock [v1] *push over; strike*
abuse, bash, batter, beat, beat up, bob, bruise,
buffet, clap, clout, cuff, damage, deck, drub*,
fell, flatten, floor, hit, hurt, KO*, level, maltreat,
manhandle, maul, mistreat, pound, punch, rap,
roughhouse, slap, smack, tap, thrash, thump,
thwack*, total, wallop, whack*, wound; SEE
CONCEPT *189*

knock [v2] *criticize harshly*
abuse, alive*, belittle, blame, carp, cavil, censure, condemn, denounce, denunciate, deprecate,
disparage, find fault, lambaste, reprehend, reprobate, run down*, skin*, slam; SEE CONCEPT *52*

knock about/knock around [v] *roam, wander*
drift, ramble, range, rove, traipse, travel, walk;
SEE CONCEPTS *151,224*

knock off [v1] *kill*
assassinate, do away with*, do in*, dust*, eliminate, execute, finish, liquidate, murder, rub out*,
shoot, slay, stab, waste; SEE CONCEPT *252*

knock off [v2] *steal*
filch, knock over, loot, pilfer, pinch, plunder, purloin, ransack, relieve, rifle, rip off*, rob, thieve;
SEE CONCEPTS *139,192*

knock off [v3] *stop action; accomplish*
achieve, cease, complete, conclude, desist, discontinue, eliminate, finish, give over, halt, leave
off, quit, stop work, succeed, surcease, terminate;
SEE CONCEPTS *119,234*

knot [n1] *bow, loop*
bond, braid, bunch, coil, connection, contortion,
entanglement, gnarl, helix, hitch, joint, kink, ligament, ligature, link, mat, nexus, perplexity, ro-
sette, screw, snag, snarl, spiral, splice, tangle, tie,
twirl, twist, vinculum, warp, whirl, whorl, yoke;
SEE CONCEPTS *436,471*

knot [n2] *lump; crowd*
aggregation, assemblage, assortment, band,
bunch, circle, clique, clump, cluster, collection,
company, crew, gang, gathering, group, heap,
mass, mob, pack, pile, set, squad, swarm, tuft;
SEE CONCEPT *432*

knot [v] *weave, complicate*
bind, cord, entangle, knit, loop, secure, tat, tether,
tie; SEE CONCEPTS *85,113,160*

knotty [adj] *troublesome*
baffling, complex, complicated, difficult, effortful, elaborate, formidable, Gordian*, hard, intricate, involved, labyrinthine, mazy, mystifying,
perplexing, problematical, puzzling, ramified, re-
ticular, rough, rugged, sophisticated, sticky*, terrible, thorny*, tough, tricky, uphill*; SEE CON-
CEPTS *529,565*

know [v1] *understand information*
apperceive, appreciate, apprehend, be acquainted,
be cognizant, be conversant in, be informed, be
learned, be master of, be read, be schooled, be
versed, cognize, comprehend, differentiate, discern, discriminate, distinguish, experience,
fathom, feel certain, get the idea*, grasp, have,
have down pat*, have information, have knowledge of, keep up on, ken, learn, notice, on top
of*, perceive, prize, realize, recognize, see, undergo; SEE CONCEPTS *15,38*

know [v2] *be familiar with*
associate, be acquainted with, be friends with, experience, feel, fraternize, get acquainted, have

ki
kn

dealings with, identify, savor, see, sustain, taste, undergo; SEE CONCEPT 384

know-how [n] *skill, talent*
ability, adroitness, aptitude, art, background, capability, command, craft, cunning, dexterity, experience, expertise, expertness, faculty, flair, ingenuity, knack, knowledge, proficiency, savoir-faire, wisdom; SEE CONCEPTS 409,630

knowing [adj] *experienced, aware*
alive, apprehensive, astute, awake, brainy, bright, brilliant, canny, clever, cognizant, competent, conscious, conversant, cool*, crack*, deliberate, discerning, expert, insightful, intelligent, intended, intentional, judicious, knowledgeable, observant, perceptive, percipient, qualified, quick, quick-witted, sagacious, sage, sensible, sentient, sharp, skillful, slick*, smart, sophic, sophisticated, tuned-in, vigilant, watchful, well-informed, wise, with-it, witting, worldly, worldly-wise; SEE CONCEPT 402

knowledge [n] *person's understanding; information*
ability, accomplishments, acquaintance, apprehension, attainments, awareness, cognition, comprehension, consciousness, dirt*, discernment, doctrine, dogma, dope*, education, enlightenment, erudition, expertise, facts, familiarity, goods*, grasp, inside story*, insight, instruction, intelligence, judgment, know-how*, learning, light*, lore, observation, philosophy, picture, power*, principles, proficiency, recognition, scholarship, schooling, science, scoop*, substance, theory, tuition, wisdom; SEE CONCEPTS 274,409,529

knowledgeable [adj] *aware, educated*
abreast, acquainted, alert, appreciative, apprised, au courant, au fait, brainy*, bright, brilliant, clever, cognizant, conscious, conversant, discerning, erudite, experienced, familiar, informed, insightful, intelligent, in the know, knowing, learned, lettered, omniscient, perceptive, plugged in*, posted, prescient, privy, quick-witted, sagacious, sage, savvy, scholarly, sensible, sharp, smart, sophic, sophisticated, tuned-in*, understanding, versed, well-informed, well-rounded, wise, with-it; SEE CONCEPT 402

known [adj] *famous, popular*
accepted, acknowledged, admitted, avowed, celebrated, certified, common, confessed, conscious, down pat*, established, familiar, hackneyed, manifest, noted, notorious, obvious, patent, plain, proverbial, published, received, recognized, well-known; SEE CONCEPTS 529,567,576

kook [n] *eccentric person*
crackpot, crank, crazy*, dingbat*, flake*, fruitcake*, lamebrain, lunatic, nut, screwball*, wacko*, weirdo; SEE CONCEPTS 412,423

kowtow [v] *grovel*
bow, brownnose*, cave in*, court, cower, cringe, fawn, flatter, fold, genuflect, give in, go along with, kneel, knuckle under, lie down and roll over*, pander, prostrate, say uncle*, stoop, toe the mark*; SEE CONCEPT 384

kudos [n] *praise, acclaim*
applause, credit, distinction, eminence, esteem, fame, flattery, glory, honor, illustriousness, laudation, notability, pat on the back*, plaudits, plum*, PR*, preeminence, prestige, prominence, puff*, pumping up*, raves*, regard, renown, repute, strokes*; SEE CONCEPTS 69,268

L

label [n] *marker, description; brand*
characterization, classification, company, design, epithet, hallmark, identification, insignia, logo, mark, number, price mark, stamp, sticker, tag, tally, ticket, trademark; SEE CONCEPTS 268,270,284

label [v] *mark, describe; brand*
call, characterize, class, classify, define, designate, identify, name, specify, stamp, sticker, tag, tally; SEE CONCEPTS 62,79

labor [n1] *work, undertaking*
activity, chore, daily grind, diligence, drudgery, effort, employment, endeavor, energy, exercise, exertion, grind*, gruntwork*, industry, job, moonlight*, operation, pains*, pull, push, strain, stress, struggle, sweat, toil, travail; SEE CONCEPTS 87,100,351,360,362

labor [n2] *person(s) performing service*
apprentice, blue collar, breadwinner, employee, hack*, hand*, hard hat*, help, helper, hireling, instrument, laborer, learner, operative, prentice, proletariat, rank and file*, toiler, worker, work force, working people; SEE CONCEPTS 325,348

labor [n3] *childbirth process*
birth, birth pangs, childbearing, contractions, delivery, giving birth, pains, parturition, throes, travail; SEE CONCEPT 374

labor [v] *work very hard*
bear down, cultivate, drive, drudge, endeavor, exert oneself, grind, plod, plug away*, pour it on*, slave, strain, strive, struggle, sweat, tend, toil, travail, work oneself to the bone*; SEE CONCEPTS 87,100

labored [adj] *difficult to understand, unclear*
affected, arduous, awkward, clumsy, contrived, effortful, forced, hard, heavy, inept, maladroit, operose, overdone, overwrought, ponderous, stiff, strained, strenuous, studied, toilsome, unnatural, uphill*, weighty; SEE CONCEPT 538

laborious [adj1] *hard, difficult*
arduous, backbreaking, burdensome, effortful, fatiguing, forced, heavy, herculean*, labored, onerous, operose, ponderous, rough go*, stiff, strained, strenuous, tiresome, toilsome, tough, tough job*, wearing, wearisome, wicked*; SEE CONCEPTS 538,565

laborious [adj2] *hardworking*
active, assiduous, diligent, indefatigable, industrious, operose, painstaking, persevering, sedulous, tireless, unflagging; SEE CONCEPTS 538,550

labyrinth [n] *maze, complexity*
coil, complication, convolution, entanglement, intricacy, jungle, knot, mesh, morass, perplexity, problem, puzzle, riddle, skein, snarl, tangle, web; SEE CONCEPTS 436,663,666

lace [n1] *netted material*
appliqué, banding, border, crochet, edging, filigree, mesh, net, netting, openwork, ornament, tatting, threadwork, tissue, trim, trimming; SEE CONCEPT 473

lace [n2] *string used to connect*
band, cord, rope, shoelace, thong, thread, tie; SEE CONCEPT 475

lace [v] *fasten, intertwine*
add, attach, bind, close, do up, fortify, interlace,

interweave, mix, plat, spike, strap, thread, tie, twine; SEE CONCEPT 113

lacerate [v] *tear, cut; wound*
claw, gash, harm, hurt, injure, jag, lance, maim, mangle, mutilate, puncture, rend, rip, score, serrate, slash, stab, torment, torture; SEE CONCEPTS 137,176,214,220,246

lack [n] *deficiency, need*
abridgement, absence, curtailment, dearth, decrease, default, defect, deficit, depletion, deprivation, destitution, distress, exigency, exiguity, inadequacy, inferiority, insufficience, insufficiency, loss, meagerness, miss, necessity, paucity, poverty, privation, reduction, retrenchment, scantiness, scarcity, shortage, shortcoming, shortfall, shortness, shrinkage, shrinking, slightness, stint, want; SEE CONCEPTS 707,709

lack [v] *do not have*
be deficient in, be short of, be without, have need of, hurting for*, minus, miss, need, not got* out, require, too little too late*, want; SEE CONCEPTS 20,646

lackadaisical [adj] *careless, indifferent*
abstracted, apathetic, daydreaming, disinterested, dreamy, dull, energyless, enervated, faineant, halfhearted, idle, inattentive, incurious, indolent, inert, laid-back, languid, languishing, languorous, lazy, lethargic, limp, listless, moony*, passive, romantic, sentimental, slothful, spiritless, spring fever*, unconcerned; SEE CONCEPTS 403,542,544

lacking [adj] *wanting, deficient*
can't cut it*, coming up short*, defective, deprived of, flawed, impaired, inadequate, incomplete, minus, missing, needed, needing, not hacking it*, not making it*, sans, short, without; SEE CONCEPTS 546,771

lackluster [adj] *dull, lifeless*
blah*, blind, boring, colorless, dark, dead, dim, drab, draggy*, dry, flat*, ho-hum*, laid-back*, leaden, lusterless, matte, muted, nothing*, obscure, pabulum*, prosaic, sombre, unimaginative, uninspired, vanilla*, vapid, zero*; SEE CONCEPTS 542,548,617

laconic [adj] *short, to the point*
breviloquent, brief, brusque, compact, compendiary, compendious, concise, crisp, curt, pithy, sententious, short and sweet*, succinct, terse; SEE CONCEPTS 267,773,798

lacy [adj] *delicate, netlike*
elegant, fancy, filigree, fine, frilly, gauzy, gossamer, lacelike, meshy, open, ornate, patterned, sheer, thin, transparent; SEE CONCEPT 606

lad [n] *young man*
boy, buddy, child, fellow, guy, half-pint*, juvenile, kid*, runt*, schoolboy, son, stripling, youngster, youth; SEE CONCEPTS 419,424

laden [adj] *loaded down*
burdened, charged, encumbered, fraught, full, hampered, oppressed, taxed, weighed down, weighted; SEE CONCEPTS 485,538

lag [v] *move slowly; delay*
be behind, dally, dawdle, decrease, dillydally*, diminish, drag, drag one's feet*, ebb, fail, fall off, falter, flag, get no place fast*, hang back, hobble, idle, inch, inch along*, jelly, limp, linger, loiter, lose strength, lounge, plod, poke, procrastinate, put off, retard, saunter, shuffle, slacken, slouch, slow, slow up, stagger, stay, straggle, tail, tarry, tool, trail, trudge, wane; SEE CONCEPTS 151,153

lair [n] *hideout, habitat*
burrow, cave, den, earth, form, hideaway, hole, nest, pen, refuge, resting place, retreat, sanctuary; SEE CONCEPT 515

laissez-faire [n] *free enterprise, for the most part unrestrained by law*
free trade, indifference, individualism, live and let live*, neutrality, nonintervention; SEE CONCEPTS 388,691

lake [n] *inland body of water*
basin, creek, inland sea, lagoon, lakelet, loch, mere, millpond, mouth, pond, pool, reservoir, sluice, spring, tarn; SEE CONCEPT 514

lambaste [v] *punish, beat*
assail, attack, berate, blister, bludgeon, castigate, censure, criticize, cudgel, denounce, excoriate, flay, flog, hammer, hit, lash into*, pan, pelt, pound, pummel, rake over the coals*, read the riot act*, rebuke, reprimand, rip into, roast, scathe, scold, scorch, scourge, shellac, slam, slap, slash, smear, smother, strike, thrash, trim, upbraid, wallop, whip; SEE CONCEPTS 52,54,86

lame [adj1] *unable to walk properly*
bruised, deformed, disabled, game, gimp, gimpy, halt, handicapped, hobbling, limping, pained, raw, sidelined, sore, stiff; SEE CONCEPTS 314,489

lame [adj2] *feeble, weak*
faltering, faulty, flabby, flimsy, inadequate, ineffective, inefficient, insufficient, poor, thin, unconvincing, unpersuasive, unpleasing, unsatisfactory, unsuitable; SEE CONCEPTS 558,570

lament/lamentation [n] *grief, complaint*
complaining, dirge, elegy, grieving, jeremiad, keen, keening, lament, moan, moaning, mourning, plaint, requiem, sob, sobbing, sorrow, tears, threnody, ululation, wail, wailing, weeping; SEE CONCEPTS 29,278,410

lament [v] *to mourn or grieve deeply*
bawl, beat one's breast*, bemoan, bewail, bleed, cry, deplore, eat one's heart out*, howl, hurt, kick self*, moan, rain, regret, repine, rue, sing, sob, sorrow, take it hard*, wail, weep; SEE CONCEPTS 53,51

lamentable [adj] *upsetting, miserable*
afflictive, awful, bad, calamitous, deplorable, dire, dirty, distressing, doleful, dolorous, godawful, grievous, grim, heartbreaking, hurting, lousy, low, lugubrious, meager, mean, melancholy, mournful, pitiful, plaintive, poor, regretful, rotten, rueful, sad, sorrowful, stinking, tragic, unfavorable, unfortunate, unsatisfactory, woeful, wretched; SEE CONCEPTS 529,537

laminate [v] *cover with veneer*
coat, exfoliate, face, flake, foil, foliate, layer, overlayer, plate, separate, split, stratify, veneer; SEE CONCEPT 172

lampoon [n] *parody, satire*
burlesque, caricature, invective, pasquil, pasquinade, pastiche, ridicule, roast*, send-up*, skit, squib, takedown, takeoff*; SEE CONCEPTS 263,273

lampoon [v] *ridicule, make fun of*
burlesque, caricature, jape, mock, parody, pasquinade, put on*, rail, roast*, satirize, send up*, squib, take off*, travesty; SEE CONCEPT 273

land [n] *earth's surface; ownable property*
acreage, acres, area, beach, continent, country, countryside, dirt, district, earth, estate, expanse, extent, farming, farmland, field, ground, grounds, holding, home, homeland, loam, mainland,

kn
la

manor, nation, old sod, parcel, plot, province, purlieu, quarry, quinta, ranch, real estate, realty, region, shore, sod, soil, stretch, sweep, terra firma, terrain, territory, tillage, tract; SEE CONCEPTS 508,509,510,515

land [v1] *arrive, come to rest on*
alight, berth, bring in, check in, come ashore, come down, come in, come to berth, debark, descend upon, disembark, ditch, dock, drop anchor, flatten out, get down, ground, level off, light on, make land, pilot, put down, put in, set down, set on deck, settle, sit down, splash down, steer, take down, thump, touch down; SEE CONCEPTS 159,181

land [v2] *achieve, acquire*
annex, bring in, gain, get, have, obtain, pick up, procure, secure, win; SEE CONCEPTS 120,706

landlord [n] *owner of property leased*
freeholder, hotelier, hotelkeeper, innkeeper, lessor, property owner, proprietor, saw, squire; SEE CONCEPT 347

landmark [n1] *historical or notable sight*
battleground, benchmark, bend, blaze, feature, fragment, guide, hill, mark, marker, memorial, milepost, milestone, monument, mountain, museum, promontory, remnant, ruins, souvenir, specimen, stone, survival, trace, tree, vantage point, vestige, waypost; SEE CONCEPTS 198, 284,447

landmark [n2] *turning point*
crisis, event, milepost, milestone, stage, watershed, waypost; SEE CONCEPTS 696,817

landscape [n] *countryside; picture of countryside*
mural, outlook, painting, panorama, photograph, prospect, scene, scenery, sketch, view, vista; SEE CONCEPTS 259,509

language [n] *system of words for communication*
accent, argot, articulation, brogue, cant, communication, conversation, dialect, diction, dictionary, discourse, doublespeak*, expression, gibberish, idiom, interchange, jargon, lexicon, lingua franca, palaver, parlance, patois, phraseology, prose, signal, slang, sound, speech, style, talk, terminology, tongue, utterance, verbalization, vernacular, vocabulary, vocalization, voice, word, wording; SEE CONCEPT 276

languid [adj] *drooping, dull, listless*
apathetic, blah*, blahs*, comatose, dopey, easy, energyless, enervated, faint, feeble, heavy, impassive, inactive, indifferent, inert, infirm, lackadaisical, laid-back, languishing, languorous, lazy, leaden, leisurely, lethargic, limp, moony*, nebbish, phlegmatic, pining, sickly, sleepyhead*, slow, sluggish, snoozy*, spiritless, supine, torpid, unconcerned, unenthusiastic, unhurried, uninterested, weak, weary, wimpy*; SEE CONCEPTS 403,542,584

languish [v] *droop; become dull, listless*
be disregarded, be neglected, brood, conk out*, decline, desire, despond, deteriorate, die on vine*, dwindle, ebb, fade, fag, fag out, fail, faint, fizzle out, flag, go soft*, go to pieces*, grieve, hanker, hunger, knock out, long, pine, repine, rot, sicken, sigh, snivel, sorrow, suffer, tucker, waste, waste away, weaken, wilt, wither, yearn; SEE CONCEPTS 20,105,469

lanky [adj] *tall and thin*
angular, attenuated, beanpole*, beanstalk*, bony, broomstick*, extenuated, gangling, gangly, gaunt, lean, meager, rangy, rawboned, scraggy,

scrawny, slender, spare, spindling, spindly, stilt, stringy, twiggy*, weedy; SEE CONCEPTS 491,779

lap [n] *orbit, circuit*
circle, course, distance, loop, round, tour; SEE CONCEPTS 364,436

lap [v1] *slosh, wash against*
bathe, bubble, burble, drink, gurgle, lave, lick, lip, plash, purl, ripple, sip, slap, splash, sup, swish; SEE CONCEPT 144

lap [v2] *overlap*
cover, enfold, envelop, fold, imbricate, overlie, override, ride, shingle, swaddle, swathe, turn, twist, wrap; SEE CONCEPTS 172,201

lapse [n1] *mistake*
blunder, breach, bungle, crime, error, failing, failure, fault, flub, foible, frailty, gaff, goof, goof-up*, indiscretion, miscue, negligence, offense, omission, oversight, screw-up*, sin, slip, slip-up, transgression, trespass, trip*, vice, violation; SEE CONCEPTS 101,674

lapse [n2] *break in action*
gap, intermission, interruption, interval, lacuna, lull, passage, pause; SEE CONCEPT 807

lapse [n3] *backsliding*
decadence, declension, decline, degeneration, descent, deterioration, devolution, drop, fall, recession, regression, relapse, retrogradation, retrogression; SEE CONCEPTS 230,316,388

lapse [v] *become void; fall back into previous pattern*
apostatize, backslide, become obsolete, cease, decline, degenerate, descend, deteriorate, die, elapse, end, expire, go by, pass, recede, recidivate, relapse, retrograde, return, revert, run out, slide, slip, subside, terminate, weaken; SEE CONCEPTS 119,698

larceny [n] *theft*
burglary, crime, lift, misappropriation, pilfering, pinch, purloining, robbery, steal, stealing, thievery, thieving, touch*; SEE CONCEPTS 139,192

large [adj] *big, abundant*
ample, barn door*, blimp*, booming, broad, bulky, capacious, colossal, comprehensive, considerable, copious, enormous, excessive, exorbitant, extensive, extravagant, full, generous, giant, gigantic, goodly, grand, grandiose, great, gross, hefty, huge, humongous*, immeasurable, immense, jumbo*, liberal, massive, monumental, mountainous, plentiful, populous, roomy, sizable, spacious, stupendous, substantial, super, sweeping, thumping, tidy, vast, voluminous, whopping*, wide; SEE CONCEPTS 773,781

largely [adv] *to a great extent*
abundantly, as a rule, broadly, by and large, chiefly, commodiously, comprehensively, considerably, copiously, expansively, extensively, extravagantly, generally, generously, grandly, immoderately, imposingly, in a big way, in a grand manner, lavishly, liberally, magnificently, mainly, mostly, on a large scale, overall, predominantly, primarily, principally, prodigally, prodigiously, voluminously, widely; SEE CONCEPTS 544,772

lascivious [adj] *sexually aroused; displaying excessive interest in sex*
bawdy, blue, bodily, carnal, coarse, crude, evil-minded, fast*, fleshly, gross*, hard-core*, hot*, immoral, incontinent, indecent, lecherous, lewd, libertine, libidinous, licentious, low-down*, lubricious, lustful, nasty, obscene, off-color*, of-

fensive, orgiastic, pornographic, prurient, randy, raunchy*, raw, ribald, rough, salacious, scurrilous, sensual, smutty*, soft-core*, steamy, suggestive, unchaste, voluptuous, vulgar, wanton, X-rated*; SEE CONCEPTS 372,403

lash [v1] *beat, whip*
baste, batter, buffet, chastise, dash, drum, flagellate, flay, flog, hammer, hide, hit, horsewhip, knock, lam, lather, pound, pummel, scourge, smack, strap, strike, thrash, wear out, whale*; SEE CONCEPT 189

lash [v2] *criticize harshly*
abuse, attack, baste, bawl out*, belabor, berate, blister, castigate, censure, chew out*, exprobate, flay, fulminate, jaw, lambaste, lampoon, ridicule, satirize, scold, tear into*, tell off*, tongue-lash*, upbraid; SEE CONCEPT 52

last [n] *end*
close, completion, conclusion, ending, finale, finis, finish, omega, termination; SEE CONCEPT 832

last [adj] *final; newest*
aftermost, antipodal, at the end, bitter end, climactic, closing, concluding, conclusive, crowning, curtains*, definitive, determinate, determinative, end, ending, eventual, extreme, far, far-off, farthest, finishing, furthest, hindmost, latest, least, lowest, meanest, most recent, once and for all*, outermost, rearmost, remotest, supreme, swan song*, terminal, ulterior, ultimate, utmost, uttermost; SEE CONCEPTS 585,778,799

lasting [adj] *enduring, unending*
abiding, constant, continual, continuing, deep-rooted, durable, endless, eternal, everlasting, forever, incessant, indelible, indissoluble, inexhaustible, inexpungible, in for the long haul*, lifelong, long-standing, long-term, old, perdurable, perennial, permanent, perpetual, persisting, stable, till the cows come home*, unceasing, undying, unremitting; SEE CONCEPTS 551,798

lastly/last [adv] *in the end*
after, after all, all in all, at last, at the end, behind, bringing up rear*, finally, in conclusion, in the rear, to conclude, to sum up, ultimately; SEE CONCEPTS 585,799

latch [n] *lock*
bar, bolt, catch, clamp, fastening, hasp, hook, padlock; SEE CONCEPTS 445,499

latch [v] *fasten with lock*
bar, bolt, cinch, close, close up, lock, make fast, secure; SEE CONCEPTS 85,160

late [adj1] *not on time*
backward, behind, behindhand, behind time, belated, blown*, delayed, dilatory, eleventh-hour*, gone, held up, hung up*, in a bind*, in the lurch*, jammed*, lagging, last-minute, missed the boat*, out of luck*, overdue, postponed, put off, remiss, slow, stayed, strapped*, tardy, too late, unpunctual; SEE CONCEPTS 548,799

late [adj2] *new*
advanced, fresh, just out, modern, recent; SEE CONCEPTS 578,797

late [adj3] *dead*
asleep, bygone, cold, deceased, defunct, departed, erstwhile, ex-*, exanimate, extinct, former, inanimate, lifeless, old, once, onetime, past, preceding, previous, quondam, sometime; SEE CONCEPT 539

late [adv] *at the last minute*
backward, behind, behindhand, behind time, be-

lately, dilatorily, slowly, tardily, unpunctual; SEE CONCEPT 799

lately [adv] *new, recently*
afresh, anew, a short time ago, in recent times, just now, latterly, newly, not long ago, of late; SEE CONCEPT 820

latent [adj] *dormant, hidden*
abeyant, between the lines, concealed, contained, covert, idle, immature, implied, in abeyance, inactive, inert, inferential, inferred, inherent, inoperative, intrinsic, invisible, involved, lurking, passive, possible, potential, quiescent, rudimentary, secret, sleeping, smoldering, suppressed, suspended, tacit, torpid, underdeveloped, underlying, undeveloped, unexposed, unexpressed, unrealized, unripe, unseen, veiled, vestigial; SEE CONCEPTS 404,576

later [adj] *coming after*
downstream, ensuing, following, more recent, next, posterior, postliminary, proximate, subsequent, subsequential, succeeding, ulterior; SEE CONCEPT 799

later [adv] *happening after*
after, afterward, again, at another time, behind, by and by*, come Sunday*, down the line*, down the road*, in a while, infra, in time, later on, latterly, more recent, next, subsequently, succeeding, thereafter; SEE CONCEPT 799

lateral [adj] *sideways*
crabwise, edgeways, flanking, oblique, side, side-by-side, sidelong, sideward, sidewise, skirting; SEE CONCEPTS 581,583

lather [n1] *bubbles*
cream, foam, froth, head, soap, soapsuds, spume, suds, yeast; SEE CONCEPTS 260,437

lather [n2] *commotion, fuss*
agitation, bustle, clamor, confusion, dither, fever, flap*, fluster, hassle, hoopla*, hubbub*, hullaballoo*, state, stew*, storm*, sweat*, tizzy*, tumult, turbulence, turmoil, twitter*; SEE CONCEPTS 230,388

lather [v] *cause to bubble*
beat, foam, froth, scrub, soap, wash, whip; SEE CONCEPT 165

latitude [n] *freedom, room to move; scope*
breadth, compass, elbow room, extent, independence, indulgence, laxity, leeway, liberty, license, margin, play, range, reach, room, run, run of, space, span, spread, sweep, swing, unrestrictedness, width; SEE CONCEPTS 651,739,756,788

latter [adj] *latest, concluding*
closing, eventual, final, following, hindmost, lag, last, last-mentioned, later, modern, rearmost, recent, second, terminal; SEE CONCEPTS 585,799

lattice [n] *mesh, trellis*
filigree, frame, fretwork, grating, grid, grill, latticework, net, network, openwork, reticulation, screen, structure, tracery, web; SEE CONCEPT 259

laud [v] *acclaim, praise*
admire, adore, approve, bless, boost, build up, celebrate, commend, compliment, cry up, eulogize, extol, flatter, glorify, hand it to*, honor, hymn, magnify, panegyrize, pat on the back*, revere, reverence, sing the praises of*, stroke, venerate, worship; SEE CONCEPT 69

laudable [adj] *admirable*
commendable, creditable, deserving, estimable, excellent, mean, meritable, meritorious, of note, praisable, praiseworthy, stellar, terrific, thankworthy, worthy; SEE CONCEPT 574

la
la

laudatory [adj] complimentary
acclamatory, adulatory, approbative, approbatory, approving, commendatory, encomiastic, eulogistic, flattering, laudative, panegyrical, praiseful; SEE CONCEPT 267

laugh/laughter [n] audible expression of amusement
amusement, cachinnation, cackle, chortle, chuckle, chuckling, crack-up*, crow, fit, gesture, giggle, giggling, glee, guffaw, hilarity, howling, merriment, mirth, peal, rejoicing, roar, shout, shriek, snicker, snigger, snort, sound, titter, yuck*; SEE CONCEPTS 77,185

laugh [v] expressing amusement, happiness with sound
be convulsed*, be in stitches*, break up*, burst*, cachinnate, chortle, chuckle, crack up*, crow, die laughing*, fracture*, giggle, grin, guffaw, howl, roar, roll in the aisles*, scream, shriek, snicker, snort, split one's sides*, titter, whoop*; SEE CONCEPTS 77,185

laughable [adj] easily made fun of
absurd, amusing, asinine, bizarre, camp, campy, comic, comical, derisive, derisory, diverting, droll, eccentric, entertaining, facetious, fantastic, farcical, funny, gelastic, har-har*, hilarious, humorous, inane, jocose, jocular, jokey, joshing, ludicrous, mirthful, mocking, nonsensical, preposterous, rich, ridiculous, riot, risible, scream, unusual, witty; SEE CONCEPTS 267,550

laugh at [v] ridicule
belittle, deride, hoot, jeer, lampoon, make fun of, mock, scoff, taunt; SEE CONCEPT 54

launch [v1] send off
barrage, bombard, bung, cast, catapult, discharge, dispatch, drive, eject, fire, fling, heave, hurl, lance, pitch, project, propel, send forth, set afloat, set in motion, shoot, sling, throw, toss; SEE CONCEPTS 179,222

launch [v2] begin, initiate
bow, break the ice*, break the seal*, commence, embark upon, get show on road*, inaugurate, instigate, institute, introduce, jump, kick off*, open, originate, set going, start, start ball rolling*, usher in*; SEE CONCEPT 221

laurels [n] credit, praise
acclaim, accolade, award, badge, bays, blue ribbon, commendation, crown, decoration, distinction, fame, feather in cap*, glory, gold, gold star*, kudos, prestige, recognition, renown, reward; SEE CONCEPTS 69,278,337

lavish [adj] profuse, splendid
abundant, bountiful, copious, effusive, exaggerated, excessive, extravagant, exuberant, first-class, free, generous, gorgeous, grand, immoderate, impressive, improvident, inordinate, intemperate, liberal, lush, luxuriant, luxurious, munificent, openhanded, opulent, plentiful, plush, posh, prodigal, profligate, profusive, prolific, riotous, ritzy, sumptuous, swanky, thriftless, unreasonable, unrestrained, unsparing, unstinting, wasteful, wild; SEE CONCEPTS 334,589,781

lavish [v] pamper, shower
be generous, be wasteful, deluge, dissipate, expend, fritter, give, go through, heap, pour, run through*, scatter, spend, spend money like water*, squander, thrust upon, waste; SEE CONCEPTS 110,327,341

law [n1] rules of a government, society
act, assize, behest, bidding, bylaw, canon, case,

caveat, charge, charter, code, command, commandment, constitution, covenant, decision, decree, decretum, demand, dictate, divestiture, due process, edict, enactment, equity, garnishment, injunction, institute, instruction, jurisprudence, legislation, mandate, measure, notice, order, ordinance, precedent, precept, prescript, prescription, reg, regulation, requirement, ruling, statute, subpoena, summons, warrant, writ; SEE CONCEPT 318

law [n2] standard, principle of behavior
assumption, axiom, base, canon, cause, criterion, exigency, formula, foundation, fundamental, generalization, ground, guide, maxim, origin, postulate, precept, principium, proposal, proposition, reason, regulation, rule, source, theorem, truth, usage; SEE CONCEPT 688

lawful [adj] allowable, legitimate
authorized, bona fide, canonical, card-carrying*, commanded, condign, constitutional, decreed, due, enacted, enforced, enjoined, established, innocent, judged, judicial, jural, juridical, jurisprudent, just, justifiable, kosher*, legal, legalized, legislated, legit*, legitimatized, licit, mandated, official, of right, on the level*, on the up and up*, ordained, ordered, passed, permissible, proper, protected, rightful, ruled, statutory, valid, vested, warrantable, warranted; SEE CONCEPTS 319,545

lawless [adj] reckless, ungoverned
anarchic, anarchical, anarchistic, bad, barbarous, chaotic, contumacious, criminal, despotic, disobedient, disordered, disorderly, evil, fierce, heterodox, infringing, insubordinate, insurgent, mutinous, nihilistic, noncompliant, nonconformist, piratical, rebellious, recusant, revolutionary, riotous, savage, seditious, tempestuous, terrorizing, traitorous, turbulent, tyrannous, uncivilized, uncultivated, unorthodox, unpeaceful, unrestrained, unruly, untamed, violent, warlike, wild; SEE CONCEPTS 319,545

lawn [n] cultivated area of green grass
backyard, garden, grass, grassplot, green, park, plot, terrace, yard; SEE CONCEPTS 509,513,517

lawsuit [n] case brought to court
accusation, action, argument, arraignment, assumpsit, bill, cause, claim, contest, dispute, impeachment, indictment, litigation, presentment, proceedings, prosecution, replevin, suit, trial; SEE CONCEPT 318

lawyer [n] person who is trained to counsel or argue in cases of law
advocate, attorney, attorney-at-law, barrister, counsel, counsellor, counselor, defender, jurisprudent, jurist, legal adviser, legal eagle*, legist, member of the bar, mouthpiece*, pleader, practitioner, proctor, procurator, solicitor; SEE CONCEPT 355

lax [adj] slack, remiss
any way*, asleep on job*, behindhand, broad, careless, casual, delinquent, derelict, devil-may-care*, disregardful, easygoing, flaccid, forgetful, general, imprecise, inaccurate, indefinite, indifferent, inexact, lenient, neglectful, negligent, nonspecific, oblivious, overindulgent, paying no mind*, regardless, shapeless, slipshod, sloppy, soft, unmindful, vague, yielding; SEE CONCEPTS 401,542,557

lay [adj] amateur, not trained in a religious or other profession
inexpert, nonclerical, nonprofessional, nonspe-

cialist, ordinary, secular, temporal, unsacred; SEE CONCEPT 530

lay [v1] *put, place*
arrange, deposit, dispose, establish, fix, leave, locate, order, organize, plant, posit, position, repose, rest, set, set down, set out, settle, spread, stick, systematize; SEE CONCEPTS 158,201

lay [v2] *produce, advance*
adduce, allege, bear, bring forth, bring forward, cite, deposit, generate, lodge, offer, present, put forward, submit, yield; SEE CONCEPTS 66,205

lay [v3] *credit, allocate*
accredit, address, aim, allot, apply, ascribe, assess, assign, attribute, burden, cast, charge, direct, encumber, impose, impute, incline, level, point, refer, saddle, tax, train, turn, zero in*; SEE CONCEPTS 49,50,88,187

lay [v4] *design, plan*
concoct, contrive, devise, hatch, plot, prepare, work out; SEE CONCEPT 36

lay [v5] *make smooth*
allay, alleviate, appease, assuage, calm, even, flatten, flush, iron, level, plane, press, quiet, relieve, steam, still, suppress; SEE CONCEPTS 235,250

lay [v6] *bet, wager*
gamble, game, give odds, hazard, play, risk, stake; SEE CONCEPT 363

layer [n] *coating, tier*
band, bed, blanket, coat, coping, couch, course, cover, covering, film, flag, flap, floor, fold, girdle, lamina, lamination, lap, mantle, overlap, overlay, panel, ply, row, seam, sheet, slab, story, stratum, stripe, substratum, thickness, zone; SEE CONCEPTS 744,835

lay into [v] *criticize, attack*
assail, battle, belabor, fire at*, invade, lambaste, let fly at*, set about; SEE CONCEPTS 52,86

layoff [n] *dismissal from job or responsibility*
cutback, discharge, early retirement, respite, unemployment; SEE CONCEPT 351

lay off [v1] *stop doing*
cease, desist, end, give a rest, give up, halt, leave alone, leave off, let up, lie by, quit, rest, spell; SEE CONCEPTS 119,234

lay off [v2] *relieve of responsibility*
discharge, dismiss, drop, fire, let go, oust, pay off, retire early; SEE CONCEPT 351

layout [n] *physical arrangement*
blueprint, chart, design, diagram, draft, formation, geography, map, organization, outline, plan, purpose; SEE CONCEPTS 625,660

lay out [v1] *spend money*
disburse, expend, give, invest, lend, outlay, pay, put out, put up, shell out*; SEE CONCEPTS 327,341

lay out [v2] *design, plan*
arrange, chart, diagram, display, exhibit, map, outline, set out, spread out; SEE CONCEPTS 36,158,174

layperson [n] *amateur person, not trained in religious or other profession*
believer, dilettante, follower, laic, member, neophyte, nonprofessional, novice, outsider, parishioner, proselyte, recruit, secular; SEE CONCEPTS 361,423

lay up/lay by [v1] *set aside, store*
accumulate, amass, build up, bury, conserve, cumulate, garner, hide, hoard, keep, lay in, pre-

serve, put away, roll up, salt away, save, spare, store up, treasure; SEE CONCEPTS 120,134

lay up [v2] *hurt, incapacitate*
beat up, confine, disable, harm, hospitalize, injure; SEE CONCEPT 246

laziness [n] *unwillingness to work, be active*
apathy, dilatoriness, do-nothingness, dormancy, dreaminess, drowsiness, dullness, faineance, faineancy, heaviness, idleness, inactivity, indolence, inertia, inertness, lackadaisicalness, languidness, languorousness, laxness, leadenness, leisureliness, lethargy, listlessness, neglectfulness, negligence, otioseness, otiosity, passivity, remissness, slackness, sleepiness, sloth, slothfulness, slowness, sluggishness, stolidity, supineness, tardiness, torpescence, torpidness, weariness; SEE CONCEPTS 411,633

lazy [adj] *inactive, sluggish*
apathetic, asleep on the job*, careless, comatose, dallying, dilatory, drowsy, dull, flagging, idle, inattentive, indifferent, indolent, inert, lackadaisical, laggard, lagging, languid, languorous, lethargic, lifeless, loafing, neglectful, out of it*, passive, procrastinating, remiss, shiftless, slack, sleepy, slothful, slow, slow-moving, snoozy*, somnolent, supine, tardy, tired, torpid, trifling, unconcerned, unenergetic, unindustrious, unpersevering, unready, weary; SEE CONCEPTS 401,404

lead [n1] *first place, supremacy*
advance, advantage, ahead, bulge, cutting edge*, direction, edge, example, facade, front rank, guidance, head, heavy, leadership, margin, model, over, pilot, point, precedence, primacy, principal, priority, protagonist, spark, star, start, title role, top, top spot, vanguard; SEE CONCEPTS 668,693,828

lead [n2] *clue*
evidence, guide, hint, indication, proof, sign, suggestion, tip, trace; SEE CONCEPTS 274,284

lead [v1] *guide physically*
accompany, attend, be responsible for, chaperone, assault, compel, conduct, convey, convoy, direct, drive, escort, find a way, force, get, go along with, guard, impel, induce, manage, pass along, persuade, pilot, point out, point the way, precede, prevail, protect, quarterback*, route, safeguard, see, shepherd, show, show around, show in, show the way, span, squire, steer, traverse, usher, watch over; SEE CONCEPT 187

lead [v2] *guide mentally; influence*
affect, bring, bring on, call the shots*, cause, command, conduce, contribute, convert, direct, dispose, draw, get the jump on*, go out in front*, govern, head, helm, incline, induce, introduce, manage, motivate, move, persuade, preside over, prevail, produce, prompt, quarterback*, result in, run things*, serve, shepherd, spearhead*, spur, supervise, tend, trail-blaze*; SEE CONCEPTS 68,117,221

lead [v3] *surpass*
be ahead, blaze a trail*, come first*, exceed, excel, outdo, outstrip, precede, preface, transcend, usher; SEE CONCEPT 141

lead (a life) [v4] *experience*
have, live, pass, spend, undergo; SEE CONCEPT 678

leader [n] *person who guides*
boss, captain, chief, chieftain, commander, conductor, controller, counsellor, dean, dignitary, director, doyen, eminence, exec, forerunner,

la
le

general, governor, guide, harbinger, head, herald, lead, lion*, luminary, manager, mistress, notability, notable, officer, pacesetter, pilot, pioneer, precursor, president, principal, rector, ringleader, ruler, shepherd, skipper, superintendent, superior; SEE CONCEPTS 347,354

leadership [n] *guidance*
administration, authority, capacity, command, conduction, control, conveyance, direction, directorship, domination, foresight, hegemony, influence, initiative, management, pilotage, power, preeminence, primacy, skill, superintendency, superiority, supremacy, sway; SEE CONCEPTS 376,687

leading [adj] *chief, superior*
arch, best, champion, dominant, dominating, famous, first, foremost, governing, greatest, headmost, highest, inaugural, initial, main, noted, notorious, number one*, outstanding, popular, preeminent, premier, primary, principal, prominent, ruling, stellar, top, well-known; SEE CONCEPTS 574,585

leaf [n1] *green foliage of plant*
blade, bract, flag, foliole, frond, leaflet, needle, pad, petal, petiole, scale, stalk, stipule; SEE CONCEPT 428

leaf [n2] *page of document*
folio, paper, sheet; SEE CONCEPT 270

leaf [v] *flip through*
browse, dip into, glance, riff, riffle, run through, scan, skim, thumb; SEE CONCEPTS 72,623

leafy [adj] *abundant in foliage*
abounding, abundant, covered, green, hidden, leafed, leaved, shaded, shady, umbrageous, verdant, wooded; SEE CONCEPTS 485,583

league [n1] *association, federation*
alliance, band, bunch, circle, circuit, club, coalition, combination, combine, compact, company, confederacy, confederation, conference, consortium, crew, gang, group, guild, loop, mob, order, organization, outfit, partnership, pool, ring, society, sodality, union, unit; SEE CONCEPTS 365,381,387

league [n2] *group of a certain ability*
category, circle, class, grade, grouping, level, pigeonhole*, rank, status, tier; SEE CONCEPTS 388,630

league [v] *associate*
ally, amalgamate, band, coadjute, collaborate, combine, concur, confederate, conjoin, consolidate, cooperate, federate, join forces, unite; SEE CONCEPTS 8,10,114

leak [n] *opening; seepage through opening*
aperture, chink, crack, crevice, decrease, destruction, detriment, drip, drop, escape, expenditure, exposure, fissure, flow, hole, leakage, leaking, loss, outgoing, percolation, pit, puncture, short circuit, slip; SEE CONCEPTS 116,513

leak [v] *seep; make known*
break, come out, discharge, disclose, divulge, drip, drool, escape, exude, get out, give away, let slip*, make public, ooze, out, pass, pass on, percolate, reveal, slip, spill, spill the beans, tell, transpire, trickle; SEE CONCEPTS 60,116,179

lean [adj] *bare, thin*
angular, anorexic, barren, beanpole*, bony, emaciated, gangling, gangly, gaunt, haggard, inadequate, infertile, lank, lanky, meager, no fat, pitiful, poor, rangy, rawboned, scanty, scraggy, scrawny, shadow*, sinewy, skinny, slender, slim,

spare, sparse, stick, stilt, stringy, svelte, sylphlike, twiggy*, unfruitful, unproductive, wasted, wiry, wizened, worn; SEE CONCEPTS 485,491

lean [v1] *bend, angle toward*
bear on, beetle, be off, be slanted, bow, cant, careen, cock, curve, decline, deflect, dip, divert, drift, droop, fasten on, hang on, heel, incline, jut, list, nod, overhang, pitch, place, prop, put weight on, recline, repose, rest, rest on, roll, sag, sheer, sink, slant, slope, tilt, tip, turn, twist, veer; SEE CONCEPTS 147,201,738

lean [v2] *be disposed*
be prone, be willing, favor, gravitate toward, have propensity, incline, look, not mind, prefer, tend; SEE CONCEPT 20

lean [v3] *count, depend on*
bank on*, believe in, bet bottom dollar*, bet on*, confide, gamble on*, have faith, hinge on*, lay money on*, put faith in, rely, trust; SEE CONCEPTS 12,26

leaning [n] *tendency, bias*
aptitude, bent*, cup of tea*, disposition, drift, favor, favoritism, inclination, inclining, liking, mindset, partiality, penchant, predilection, predisposition, proclivity, proneness, propensity, sentiment, taste, thing, weakness; SEE CONCEPTS 20,32,689

leap [n] *jump; increase*
bound, caper, escalation, frisk, hop, rise, skip, spring, surge, upsurge, upswing, vault; SEE CONCEPTS 194,780

leap [v] *jump, jump over; increase*
advance, arise, ascend, bounce, bound, caper, cavort, clear, escalate, frisk, hop, hurdle, lop, mount, rise, rocket, saltate, skip, soar, spring, surge, vault; SEE CONCEPTS 194,780

learn [v1] *acquire information*
apprentice, attain, become able, become versed, be taught, be trained, brush up on*, burn midnight oil*, commit to memory, con, crack the books*, cram*, determine, drink in*, enroll, gain, get, get down pat*, get the hang of*, get the knack of*, grasp, grind, imbibe, improve mind, lucubrate, major in, master, matriculate, memorize, minor in, peruse, pick up*, pore over, prepare, read, receive, review, soak up*, specialize in, study, take course*, take in, train in, wade through*; SEE CONCEPTS 31,33

learn [v2] *discover, find out*
ascertain, catch on, detect, determine, dig up*, discern, gain, gather, hear, see, smoke out*, stumble upon*, trip over, tumble, uncover, understand, unearth; SEE CONCEPTS 34,183

learned [adj] *well-informed*
abstruse, academic, accomplished, bookish, brainy*, conversant, cultivated, cultured, deep*, educated, erudite, esoteric, experienced, expert, grave, grounded, highbrow*, intellectual, in the know*, judicious, lettered, literary, literate, omniscient, pansophic, pedantic, philosophic, philosophical, polymath, posted, professorial, recondite, sage, sapient, scholarly, scientific, sharp, skilled, solemn, solid, sound, studied, studious, versed, well-educated, well-grounded, well-read, well-rounded; SEE CONCEPT 402

learner [n] *person who receives education*
abecedarian, apprentice, beginner, bookworm, catechumen, disciple, initiate, neophyte, novice, probationer, pupil, scholar, student, trainee; SEE CONCEPT 350

learning [n] *education, knowledge*
acquirements, attainments, culture, erudition, information, letters, literature, lore, research, scholarship, schooling, science, study, training, tuition, wisdom; SEE CONCEPTS 274,409

lease [v] *rent object, residence*
charter, hire, let, loan, rent out, sublease, sublet; SEE CONCEPTS 89,115

leash [n] *restraint*
bridle, chain, check, control, cord, curb, deterrent, hold, lead, restraint, rope, strap, tether; SEE CONCEPT 475

leash [v] *rein, hold*
bridle, check, clog, control, curb, entrammel, fasten, fetter, hamper, hobble, hog-tie*, hold back, restrain, secure, shackle, suppress, tether, tie, tie up, trammel; SEE CONCEPT 191

least [adj] *slightest, smallest*
atomic, bottom, entry-level, feeblest, fewest, finical, first, gutter, infinitesimal, last, lowest, meanest, microcosmic, microscopic, minimal, minimum, minute, minutest, molecular, most trivial, nadir, next to nothing*, niggling*, piddling*, poorest, second, short-end*, third*, tiniest, trivial, unimportant; SEE CONCEPTS 585,789

leathery [adj] *hard, durable*
coriaceous, hardened, leatherlike, rough, rugged, strong, tough, wrinkled; SEE CONCEPTS 489,606

leave [n1] *permission*
allowance, assent, authorization, concession, consent, dispensation, freedom, go-ahead*, green light*, liberty, okay, permit, sanction, sufferance, tolerance; SEE CONCEPTS 376,685

leave [n2] *holiday, time off*
adieu, departure, farewell, furlough, goodbye, leave of absence, liberty, parting, retirement, sabbatical, vacation, withdrawal; SEE CONCEPTS 802,807

leave [v1] *depart, abandon physically*
abscond, beat it*, break away, clear out*, come away, cut out, decamp, defect, desert, disappear, ditch*, elope, embark, emigrate, escape, exit, flee, flit, fly, forsake, give the slip*, go, go away, go forth, head out*, issue, migrate, move, move out, part, pull out*, push off*, quit, relinquish, remove oneself, retire, ride off*, run along*, sally, say goodbye*, scram, set out, slip out, split*, start, step down, take a hike*, take leave, take off, vacate, vamoose*, vanish, walk out, withdraw; SEE CONCEPT 195

leave [v2] *abandon, renounce*
back out*, cease, cede, desert, desist, drop, drop out*, evacuate, forbear, forsake, give notice, give up*, hand over, knock off, maroon, quit, refrain, relinquish, resign, stop, surrender, terminate, waive, yield; SEE CONCEPT 234

leave [v3] *forget, neglect*
allow, drop, have, lay down, leave behind, let, let be, let continue, let go, let stay, mislay, omit, permit, suffer; SEE CONCEPTS 30,83

leave [v4] *give, especially after death*
allot, apportion, assign, bequeath, bequest, cede, commit, confide, consign, demise, devise, entrust, give over, hand down, leave behind, legate, refer, transmit, will; SEE CONCEPTS 108,317

leave off [v] *stop*
abstain, break off, cease, desist, discontinue, end, give over, give up, halt, knock off*, quit, refrain, surcease; SEE CONCEPT 234

lecherous [adj] *lustful, lewd*
carnal, concupiscent, corrupt, fast*, hot and heavy*, incontinent, lascivious, libertine, libidinous, licentious, low-down*, lubricous, prurient, raunchy*, salacious, satyric, sensual, unchaste, wanton; SEE CONCEPTS 372,401

lecture [n1] *lesson, speech*
address, allocution, chalk talk*, discourse, disquisition, harangue, instruction, oration, pep talk*, pitch*, soapbox*, spiel*, talk; SEE CONCEPTS 60,278

lecture [n2] *speech of criticism*
castigation, censure, chiding, dressing-down*, going-over*, harangue, moralism, preaching, preachment, rebuke, reprimand, reproof, scolding, sermon, talking-to*, telling off*; SEE CONCEPTS 52,54

lecture [v1] *give a lesson, speech*
address, declaim, deliver, discourse, expound, get on a soapbox*, give a talk, harangue, hold forth, orate, prelect, recite, speak, spiel*, spout, talk, teach; SEE CONCEPTS 60,266

lecture [v2] *criticize lengthily*
admonish, berate, chide, exprobate, flay, give going-over*, give piece of mind*, moralize, preach, rank on, rate, reprimand, reprove, scold, sermonize, tell off; SEE CONCEPT 52

ledge [n] *shelf*
bar, bench, berm, bracket, console, edge, jut, mantle, offset, path, projection, reef, ridge, rim, route, sill, step, strip, tier, track, trail, walk, way; SEE CONCEPTS 445,513

leer [n/v] *look at longingly*
eye, eyeball*, gloat, goggle*, ogle, smirk, sneer, squint, stare, wink; SEE CONCEPT 623

leery [adj] *suspicious*
careful, cautious, chary, distrustful, doubting, dubious, on one's guard*, shy, skeptical, uncertain, unsure, wary; SEE CONCEPT 529

leeway [n] *room to move, grow*
elbow room*, extent, headway, latitude, margin, play, scope, space; SEE CONCEPT 739

left [adj1] *on west side when facing north*
hard to left, larboard, near, nigh side, port, port side, sinister, sinistral, south; SEE CONCEPTS 581,583

left [adj2] *politically radical*
leftist, left-wing, liberal, progressive, revolutionary, socialist; SEE CONCEPT 529

left [adj3] *abandoned*
continuing, departed, extra, forsaken, gone out, leftover, marooned, over, remaining, residual, split, staying; SEE CONCEPT 577

leftover [n] *remainder, remains*
debris, leavings, legacy, oddments, odds and ends*, orts, remnants, residue, scraps, surplus, survivor, trash; SEE CONCEPTS 260,457

leftover [adj] *remaining, excess*
extra, residual, surplus, unconsumed, uneaten, untouched, unused, unwanted; SEE CONCEPTS 560,771

leg [n] *appendage used for support*
brace, column, lap, limb, member, part, pile, pole, portion, post, prop, section, segment, shank, stage, stake, stilt, stretch, stump, support, upright; SEE CONCEPTS 392,471,832

legacy [n] *inheritance, heritage*
bequest, birthright, devise, endowment, estate, gift, heirloom, throwback, tradition; SEE CONCEPTS 337,710

le
le

legal [*adj*] *allowable, permissible*
acknowledged, allowed, authorized, card-carrying*, chartered, clean*, condign, constitutional, contractual, decreed, due, enforced, enforcible, enjoined, fair, forensic, granted, innocent, judged, judicial, juridical, just, justifiable, justified, lawful, legalized, legit*, legitimate, licit, on the level*, on the up and up*, ordained, passed, precedented, prescribed, proper, protected, right, rightful, sanctioned, sound, statutory, straight, sure enough, valid, warranted, within the law; SEE CONCEPT *319*

legalize [*v*] *allow, validate*
approve, authorize, clean up, codify, constitute, decree, decriminalize, enact, formulate, launder, legislate, legitimate, legitimatize, license, ordain, permit, regulate, sanction; SEE CONCEPTS *298,317*

legend [*n1*] *story of the past, often fictitious*
fable, fiction, folklore, folk story, folk tale, lore, myth, mythology, mythos, narrative, saga, tale, tradition; SEE CONCEPT *282*

legend [*n2*] *brief description in document*
cipher, code, device, epigraph, epitaph, head, heading, inscription, key, motto, rubric, table, underline; SEE CONCEPTS *268,270*

legendary [*adj1*] *fictitious but well known*
allegorical, apocryphal, created, customary, doubtful, dubious, fabled, fabricated, fabulous, fanciful, figmental, handed-down, imaginary, imaginative, improbable, invented, mythical, mythological, related, romantic, storied, told, traditional, unhistoric, unhistorical, unreal, unverifiable; SEE CONCEPTS *267,552*

legendary [*adj2*] *famous*
celebrated, famed, illustrious, immortal, renowned, well-known; SEE CONCEPT *568*

legible [*adj*] *easy to read*
clear, coherent, decipherable, distinct, easily read, intelligible, lucid, neat, plain, readable, sharp, understandable; SEE CONCEPTS *267,535,576*

legion [*n*] *mass, force of people*
army, body, brigade, cloud, company, division, drove, flock, group, horde, host, multitude, myriad, number, phalanx, rout, scores, throng, troop; SEE CONCEPTS *322,387,417*

legion [*adj*] *numerous*
countless, many, multifarious, multitudinal, multitudinous, myriad, numberless, populous, several, sundry, various, very many, voluminous; SEE CONCEPTS *762,781*

legislation [*n*] *law of a government*
act, bill, charter, codification, constitution, enactment, lawmaking, measure, prescription, regulation, ruling, statute; SEE CONCEPT *318*

legislative [*adj*] *lawmaking*
congressional, decreeing, enacting, jurisdictive, lawgiving, legislational, legislatorial, ordaining, parliamentarian, parliamentary, senatorial, statute-making, synodical; SEE CONCEPT *319*

legislator [*n*] *person in government who makes laws*
administrator, aldermember, assemblymember, council member, deputy, lawgiver, lawmaker, leader, member, member of Congress, parliamentarian, representative, senator; SEE CONCEPT *354*

legislature [*n*] *governmental body, most often elected, that makes laws*
assembly, body, chamber, congress, council, diet, house, house of representatives, lawmakers, parliament, plenum, senate, voice of the people; SEE CONCEPT *299*

legitimate [*adj*] *authentic, valid, legal*
accepted, accredited, acknowledged, admissible, appropriate, authorized, canonical, certain, cogent, consistent, correct, customary, fair, genuine, innocent, just, justifiable, lawful, licit, logical, natural, normal, official, on the level, on the up and up, orthodox, probable, proper, real, reasonable, received, recognized, regular, reliable, rightful, sanctioned, sensible, sound, statutory, sure, true, typical, usual, verifiable, warranted, well-founded; SEE CONCEPTS *319,558,582*

leisure [*n*] *free time and its activities*
chance, convenience, ease, freedom, holiday, idle hours, intermission, leave of absence, liberty, one's own sweet time*, opportunity, pause, quiet, range, recess, recreation, relaxation, repose, requiescence, respite, rest, retirement, sabbatical, scope, spare moments*, spare time, time, time off*, unemployment, vacant hour*, vacation; SEE CONCEPTS *363,681,807*

leisurely [*adj*] *casual, unhurried*
comfortable, delayed, deliberate, dilatory, easy, free, gentle, laggard, laid-back*, languid, lax, lazy, relaxed, restful, slack, slackened, slow, slow-moving, unhasty; SEE CONCEPTS *550,584,799*

leisurely [*adv*] *casually, unhurriedly*
at one's convenience*, at one's leisure, calmly, comfortably, composedly, deliberately, dilatorily, easily, gradually, inactively, indolently, laggardly, langorously, languidly, lazily, lethargically, lingeringly, listlessly, slowly, sluggishly, taking one's time*, tardily, torpidly, with delay, without haste; SEE CONCEPTS *544,584,799*

lend [*v*] *loan, accommodate*
add, advance, afford, allow, bestow, confer, contribute, entrust, extend, furnish, give, grant, impart, lay on one, lend-lease, let, loan shark*, oblige, permit, present, provide, shark, stake, supply, trust; SEE CONCEPTS *115,140*

length [*n*] *extent of object, distance, time*
breadth, compass, continuance, diameter, dimension, duration, elongation, endlessness, expanse, expansion, extensiveness, height, interval, lastingness, lengthiness, limit, linearity, loftiness, longitude, longness, magnitude, measure, mileage, orbit, panorama, period, piece, portion, protractedness, purview, quantity, radius, range, ranginess, reach, realm, remoteness, season, section, segment, space, spaciousness, span, stretch, stride, tallness, term, unit, width, year; SEE CONCEPTS *651,721,743,788,804*

lengthen [*v*] *extend*
amplify, augment, continue, dilate, distend, drag out, draw, draw out*, elongate, expand, increase, let out, make longer, pad, proceed, prolong, prolongate, protract, reach, spin out*, stretch, string out*; SEE CONCEPTS *236,239,245*

lengthy [*adj*] *extended*
diffuse, dragging, drawn-out, elongate, elongated, interminable, lengthened, long, longish, long-winded, overlong, padded, prolix, prolonged, protracted, tedious, tiresome, verbose, very long, wearisome, windy, wordy; SEE CONCEPTS *267,482,782*

lenient [*adj*] *permissive*
allowing, amiable, assuaging, assuasive, being

big*, benign, benignant, charitable, clement, compassionate, complaisant, compliant, condoning, easy, easygoing, emollient, excusing, favoring, forbearing, forgiving, gentle, going easy on*, good-natured, humoring, indulgent, kind, kindly, letting, live with*, loving, merciful, mild, mollycoddling*, obliging, pampering, pardoning, permitting, soft, softhearted, soft-shell*, sparing, spoiling, sympathetic, tender, tolerant, yielding; SEE CONCEPTS 401,542

less [adj] *smaller, inferior*
beneath, declined, deficient, depressed, diminished, excepting, fewer, lacking, lesser, limited, lower, minor, minus, negative, not as great, reduced, secondary, shortened, shorter, slighter, subordinate, subtracting, unsubstantial, without; SEE CONCEPTS 574,762,789

less [adv] *little*
barely, in a lower degree, meagerly, to a smaller extent; SEE CONCEPTS 530,544

lessen [v] *lower, reduce*
abate, abridge, amputate, attenuate, become smaller, clip, close, contract, crop, curtail, cut, cut back, decline, decrease, de-escalate, degrade, die down, dilute, diminish, downsize, drain, dwindle, ease, erode, grow less, impair, lighten, minify, minimize, mitigate, moderate, narrow, roll back, shrink, slacken, slack up, slow down, soft-pedal*, take the bite out*, take the edge off*, take the sting out*, taper, taper off, thin, truncate, weaken, wind down; SEE CONCEPTS 247,698,776

lesser [adj] *inferior, secondary*
a notch under*, bottom, bush, bush-league*, dinky*, insignificant, less important, low, lower, minor, minor-league*, nether, second-fiddle*, second-string*, slighter, small, small-fry*, small-time*, subjacent, subordinate, third-string*, undersized; SEE CONCEPTS 575,793

lesson [n1] *information taught*
assignment, chalk talk*, class, coaching, drill, education, exercise, homework, instruction, lecture, period, practice, quiz, reading, recitation, schooling, study, task, teaching, test, tutoring; SEE CONCEPTS 274,285,287

lesson [n2] *helpful example, communication*
admonition, censure, chiding, deterrent, exemplar, helpful word, message, model, moral, noble action, notice, precept, punishment, rebuke, reprimand, reproof, scolding, warning; SEE CONCEPTS 123,661,686

let [v1] *allow*
accredit, approve, authorize, be big*, cause, certify, commission, concede, enable, endorse, free up, give, give leave, give okay, give permission, grant, have, hear of, leave, license, live with, make, permit, sanction, sit still for*, suffer, tolerate, warrant; SEE CONCEPTS 50,83,88

let [v2] *rent out object, property*
charter, hire, lease, sublease, sublet; SEE CONCEPTS 89,115

letdown [n] *disappointment*
anticlimax, balk, bitter pill*, blow, chagrin, comedown, disgruntlement, disillusionment, frustration, setback, washout*; SEE CONCEPTS 410,728

let down [v] *disappoint*
abandon, depress, disenchant, disillusion, dissatisfy, fail, fall short, leave in lurch*, leave stranded*, lower, pull down, take down; SEE CONCEPTS 7,19

lethal [adj] *deadly*
baleful, dangerous, deathly, destructive, devastating, fatal, harmful, hurtful, malignant, mortal, mortiferous, mortuary, murderous, necrotic, noxious, pernicious, pestilent, pestilential, poisonous, virulent; SEE CONCEPT 537

lethargic [adj] *lazy, sluggish*
apathetic, blah*, comatose, debilitated, dilatory, dopey, dormant, draggy*, drowsy, dull, enervated, having spring fever*, heavy, idle, impassive, inactive, indifferent, inert, lackadaisical, laggard, laid-back*, languid, languorous, listless, moony*, nebbish, out of it*, passive, phlegmatic, sleepy, sleepyhead*, slothful, slow, slumberous, snoozy, somnolent, spiritless, stolid, stretchy, stupefied, supine, torpid, wimpy*; SEE CONCEPTS 401,403,584

lethargy [n] *laziness, sluggishness*
apathy, coma, disinterest, disregard, drowsiness, dullness, hebetude, heedlessness, idleness, impassivity, inaction, inactivity, inanition, indifference, indolence, inertia, inertness, insouciance, languor, lassitude, listlessness, passiveness, phlegm, sleep, sleepiness, sloth, slowness, slumber, stupor, supineness, torpidity, torpidness, torpor, unconcern, unmindfulness; SEE CONCEPTS 315,410,633,748

let off [v] *make not subject to punishment or action*
abandon, absolve, discharge, dispense, drop, excuse, exempt, exonerate, forgive, let go, pardon, privilege from, release, relieve, remove, spare; SEE CONCEPTS 50,83,88,317

let on [v] *acknowledge, admit*
allow, avow, betray, concede, confess, disclose, divulge, give away, grant, hint, imply, indicate, let out, make known, mouth*, own, own up*, reveal, say, spill*, suggest, tell, uncover, unveil; SEE CONCEPTS 57,60

letter [n1] *symbol of an alphabet*
ABCs*, alphabet, cap, capital, character, majuscule, minuscule, rune, sign, small letter, type, uncial; SEE CONCEPT 284

letter [n2] *written communication*
acknowledgment, answer, billet, dispatch, epistle, junk mail*, kite, line, memo, memorandum, message, missive, note, postcard, reply, report, thank you; SEE CONCEPTS 271,278

letup [n] *pause*
abatement, break, cessation, interval, lapse, lessening, lull, recess, remission, respite, slackening; SEE CONCEPT 807

let up [v] *pause*
abate, cease, decrease, die down, die out, diminish, ease, ease off, ease up, ebb, fall, moderate, release, relent, slacken, slow down, stop, subside, wane; SEE CONCEPTS 240,698

level [n1] *horizontal position or thing*
altitude, elevation, floor, height, layer, plain, plane, story, stratum, surface, zone; SEE CONCEPTS 738,744

level [n2] *rank, position*
achievement, degree, grade, stage, standard, standing, status; SEE CONCEPTS 286,388

level [adj] *smooth, balanced*
akin, aligned, alike, calm, commensurate, common, comparable, consistent, constant, continuous, equable, equivalent, even, exact, flat, flush, horizontal, identical, in line, leveled, like, lined up, matched, matching, of same height, on a line, on a par, on one plane, parallel, plain, planate,

le
le

plane, planed, polished, precise, proportionate, regular, rolled, same, stable, steady, straight, trim, trimmed, unbroken, unfluctuating, uniform, uninterrupted; SEE CONCEPTS *401,490,566*

level [v1] *make even*
equalize, equate, even, even off, even out, flatten, flush, grade, lay, make equal, make flat, mow, plane, press, roll, smooth, smoothen, straighten, surface; SEE CONCEPT *250*

level [v2] *destroy, demolish*
bring down, bulldoze*, devastate, down*, drop, equalize, fell, flatten, floor, ground, knock down, knock over, lay low, mow*, pull down, raze, ruin, smooth, tear down, waste*, wreck; SEE CONCEPTS *208,252*

level [v3] *be honest*
be above-board, be frank, be on the up and up*, be open, be straight, be straightforward, be upfront*, come clean*, come to terms*, keep nothing back*, talk straight*, tell the truth; SEE CONCEPT *49*

level [v4] *aim, direct*
address, beam, cast, focus, incline, lay, point, slant, train, turn, zero in on; SEE CONCEPT *187*

levelheaded [adj] *reasonable, calm*
all there*, balanced, collected, commonsensical, composed, cool, cool as cucumber*, coolheaded*, dependable, discreet, even-tempered, far-sighted, in one's right mind*, judicious, practical, prudent, rational, sane, self-possessed, sensible, steady, together, unflappable, wise, with all marbles*; SEE CONCEPTS *403,542*

leverage [n] *influence*
advantage, ascendancy, authority, bargaining chip*, break, clout, drag, edge, grease*, jump on*, power, pull, rank, ropes*, suction, weight; SEE CONCEPTS *687,693*

levity [n] *funniness, silliness*
absurdity, amusement, buoyancy, facetiousness, festivity, fickleness, flightiness, flippancy, folly, foolishness, frivolity, giddiness, happiness, high spirits, hilarity, jocularity, laughs, lightheartedness, mirth, picnic*, pleasantry, repartee, trifling, triviality, volatility, wit; SEE CONCEPTS *273,410*

levy [n] *assessment, tax*
burden, collection, custom, duty, exaction, excise, fee, gathering, imposition, impost, muster, tariff, toll; SEE CONCEPT *329*

levy [v] *assess, impose*
call, call up, charge, collect, demand, exact, extort, gather, lay on, place, put on, raise, set, summon, tax, wrest, wring; SEE CONCEPT *330*

lewd [adj] *vulgar, indecent*
bawdy, blue, coarse, erotic, fast*, filthy*, foulmouthed, gross*, hard-core*, immodest, immoral, improper, impure, in bad taste, incontinent, indelicate, lascivious, lecherous, libertine, libidinous, licentious, loose*, lustful, naughty, obscene, off-color*, pornographic, profligate, questionable, racy*, rakish, ribald, risqué, salacious, scandalous, scurrilous, shameless, smutty*, suggestive, taboo, unchaste, unclean, unconventional, unvirtuous, vile, wanton, wicked, X-rated*; SEE CONCEPTS *372,542,545*

lexicon [n] *collection of word meanings, usage*
dictionary, glossary, terminology, thesaurus, vocabulary, wordbook, wordlist, word stock; SEE CONCEPTS *276,280*

liability [n1] *answerability, responsibility*
accountability, accountableness, amenability,

amenableness, arrearage, blame, burden, compulsion, culpability, debt, duty, indebtedness, obligation, onus, owing, subjection, susceptibility; SEE CONCEPT *645*

liability [n2] *burden, debt*
account, arrear, arrearage, bad news*, baggage*, balance, bite*, chance, chit*, contingency, contract, damage, debit, disadvantage, drag*, drawback, due*, encumbrance, handicap, hindrance, impediment, inconvenience, indebtedness, indebtment, involvement, IOU*, lease, loan, millstone*, minus, misfortune, mortgage, nuisance, obligation, onus, pledge, possibility, remainder, responsibility, tab; SEE CONCEPTS *332,674*

liability [n3] *chance, probability*
exposure, likelihood, openness, proneness, susceptibility, tendency, vulnerability, vulnerableness; SEE CONCEPTS *650,657*

liable [adj1] *answerable, responsible*
accountable, amenable, bound, chargeable, obligated, subject, tied; SEE CONCEPT *545*

liable [adj2] *open, likely*
apt, assailable, attackable, beatable, conquerable, disposed, exposed, given, inclined, in danger, penetrable, prone, sensitive, subject, susceptible, tending, verisimilar, vincible, vulnerable; SEE CONCEPTS *542,552*

liaison [n1] *person who acts as go-between*
communication, connection, contact, fixer, hookup, in, interchange, interface, intermediary, link; SEE CONCEPTS *348,354,423*

liaison [n2] *love affair*
amour, encounter, entanglement, fling, illicit romance, interlude, intrigue, romance; SEE CONCEPTS *32,388*

liar [n] *person who tells falsehood*
cheat, con artist, deceiver, deluder, dissimulator, equivocator, fabler, fabricator, fabulist, false witness, falsifier, fibber, maligner, misleader, perjurer, phony, prevaricator, promoter, storyteller, trickster*; SEE CONCEPT *412*

libel [n] *purposeful lie about someone, often malicious*
aspersion, calumny, defamation, denigration, lying, malicious, obloquy, smear, vituperation; SEE CONCEPTS *63,318*

libel [v] *purposefully lie about someone*
asperse, bad-mouth*, blister, burlesque, calumniate, caricature, crack, defame, denigrate, derogate, drag name through mud*, give a black eye*, knock, malign, mark*, mark wrong, revile, roast, scandalize, scorch, sizzle, slur, smear, tear down, traduce, travesty, vilify; SEE CONCEPTS *63,192*

libelous [adj] *derogatory*
aspersive, backbiting, calumniatory, calumnious, contumelious, debasing, defamatory, depreciative, detracting, detractory, disparaging, false, injurious, invidious, malevolent, malicious, maligning, opprobrious, pejorative, sarcastic, scurrilous, traducing, untrue, vilifying, vituperative; SEE CONCEPT *267*

liberal [adj1] *progressive*
advanced, avant-garde, broad, broad-minded, catholic, enlightened, flexible, free, general, highminded, humanistic, humanitarian, indulgent, intelligent, interested, latitudinarian, left, lenient, libertarian, loose, magnanimous, permissive, radical, rational, reasonable, receiving, receptive, reformist, tolerant, unbiased, unbigoted,

unconventional, understanding, unorthodox, unprejudiced; SEE CONCEPTS *529,542*

liberal [*adj2*] *giving, generous*
altruistic, beneficent, benevolent, bighearted*, bounteous, bountiful, casual, charitable, eleemosynary, exuberant, free, free-and-easy, handsome, kind, lavish, loose, munificent, openhanded, openhearted, philanthropic, princely, prodigal, profuse, soft-touch, unselfish, unsparing, unstinging; SEE CONCEPTS *334,401,404*

liberal [*adj3*] *abundant, profuse*
ample, aplenty, bounteous, bountiful, copious, dime a dozen*, galore, generous, handsome, lavish, munificent, no end, plentiful, plenty, rich; SEE CONCEPT *771*

liberate [*v*] *give freedom*
bail one out*, deliver, detach, discharge, disembarrass, emancipate, free, free up*, get out from under*, let loose*, let out*, loose, loosen, manumit, redeem, release, rescue, save, save one's neck*, set free, unbind, unchain, unhook, unshackle; SEE CONCEPTS *83,110*

liberty [*n*] *freedom*
autarchy, authorization, autonomy, birthright, carte blanche, choice, convenience, decision, deliverance, delivery, dispensation, emancipation, enfranchisement, enlightenment, exemption, franchise, free speech, immunity, independence, leave, leisure, liberation, license, opportunity, permission, power of choice, prerogative, privilege, relaxation, release, rest, right, sanction, self-determination, self-government, sovereignty, suffrage, unconstraint; SEE CONCEPTS *388,691*

libidinous [*adj*] *lustful*
carnal, coarse, concupiscent, debauched, fast, hot*, impure, incontinent, lascivious, lecherous, libertine, loose*, obscene, passionate, prurient, salacious, satyric, sensual, unchaste, wanton, wicked; SEE CONCEPTS *372,545*

license [*n1*] *authority, permission*
authorization, carte blanche*, certificate, charter, consent, dispensation, entitlement, exemption, freedom, go-ahead* grant, green light*, immunity, independence, latitude, leave, liberty, okay*, permit, privilege, right, self-determination, ticket, unconstraint, warrant; SEE CONCEPT *685*

license [*n2*] *abandon, indulgence*
anarchy, animalism, arrogance, audacity, boldness, complacency, debauchery, disorder, effrontery, excess, forwardness, gluttony, immoderation, impropriety, irresponsibility, lawlessness, laxity, looseness, presumptuousness, prodigality, profligacy, retractoriness, relaxation, relaxedness, sauciness*, self-indulgence, sensuality, slackness, temerity, unrestraint, unruliness, wantonness, wildness; SEE CONCEPTS *633,645*

license [*v*] *authorize*
accredit, allow, certify, commission, empower, enable, let, permit, privilege, sanction, suffer, warrant; SEE CONCEPTS *50,83,88*

licentious [*adj*] *immoral, uncontrolled*
abandoned, amoral, animal, carnal, corrupt, debauched, depraved, desirous, disorderly, dissolute, fast, fast and loose*, fleshly, impure, incontinent, in the fast lane*, lascivious, lax, lecherous, lewd, libertine, libidinous, lickerish, loose*, lubricious, lustful, oversexed, profligate, promiscuous, relaxed, reprobate, salacious, satyric, scabrous, sensual, swinging, unconstrained,

uncontrollable, uncurbed, unmoral, unprincipled, unruly, wanton; SEE CONCEPTS *372,401,545*

lick [*n*] *light touch; little amount*
bit, brush, cast, dab, dash, hint, sample, smack, speck, stroke, suggestion, taste, tinge, trace, whiff; SEE CONCEPTS *612,831*

lick [*v1*] *touch with tongue*
brush, calm, caress, fondle, glance, gloss, graze, lap, lap against, move over, osculate, pass over, play, quiet, ripple, rub, soothe, stroke, sweep, taste, tongue, touch, wash; SEE CONCEPTS *185,612*

lick [*v2*] *play over with fire*
blaze, burn, dart, flick, flicker, fluctuate, flutter, ignite, kindle, leap, palpitate, quiver, ripple, run over, shoot, touch, tremble, vacillate, vibrate, waver; SEE CONCEPTS *249,612*

lick [*v3*] *defeat, sometimes by hitting*
beat, best, clobber, conquer, down, excel, flog, hit, hurdle, lambaste, master, outdo, outstrip, overcome, overwhelm, rout, slap, smear, smother, spank, strike, surmount, surpass, thrash, throw, top, trim, trounce, vanquish, wallop, whip; SEE CONCEPTS *95,141,189*

lid [*n*] *top covering*
cap, cover, hood, roof, top; SEE CONCEPT *836*

lie [*n*] *untruth*
aspersion, backbiting, calumniation, calumny, deceit, deception, defamation, detraction, dishonesty, disinformation, distortion, evasion, fable, fabrication, falsehood, falseness, falsification, falsity, fib, fiction, forgery, fraudulence, guile, hyperbole, inaccuracy, invention, libel, mendacity, misrepresentation, misstatement, myth, obloquy, perjury, prevarication, revilement, reviling, slander, subterfuge, tale, tall story*, vilification, white lie*, whopper; SEE CONCEPTS *63,278*

lie [*v1*] *tell an untruth*
bear false witness, beguile, be untruthful, break promise, BS*, bull*, con, concoct, deceive, delude, dissemble, dissimulate, distort, dupe*, equivocate, exaggerate, fabricate, fake, falsify, fib, forswear, frame, fudge, go back on*, invent, make believe, malign, misguide, misinform, misinstruct, mislead, misrepresent, misspeak, misstate, overdraw, palter, perjure, pervert, phony, plant*, prevaricate, promote, put on*, put up a front*, snow*, soft-soap*, string along*, victimize; SEE CONCEPT *63*

lie [*v2*] *be prostrate, flat*
be prone, be recumbent, be supine, couch, go to bed*, laze, lie down, loll, lounge, nap, recline, repose, rest, retire, siesta, sleep, sprawl, stretch out, turn in; SEE CONCEPTS *154,201*

lie [*v3*] *be situated*
be, be beside, be buried, be established, be even, be fixed, be found, be interred, be level, be located, belong, be on, be placed, be seated, beset, be smooth, exist, extend, have its seat in, occupy, prevail, reach, remain, spread, stretch; SEE CONCEPT *746*

life [*n1*] *animation, spirit*
activity, being, breath, brio, dash, élan*, élan vital*, energy, enthusiasm, entity, esprit, essence, excitement, get-up-and-go*, go*, growth, heart, high spirits, impulse, lifeblood, liveliness, oomph*, sentience, soul, sparkle, verve, viability, vigor, vitality, vivacity, zest*, zing*; SEE CONCEPT *411*

le
li

life [n2] *existence, duration*

being, career, continuance, course, cycle, days, endurance, epoch, era, expectancy, extent, generation, history, length, life span, lifetime, longevity, orbit, period, pilgrimage, record, season, span, survival, time; SEE CONCEPTS 816,817

life [n3] *being*

animal, animateness, animation, body, breath, consciousness, continuance, creature, endurance, entity, essence, existence, flesh, flesh and blood*, growth, human, human being, individual, living, living being, living thing, man, metabolism, mortal being, organism, person, personage, presence, soul, subsistence, substantiality, survival, symbiosis, viability, vitality, vital spark*, wildlife, woman; SEE CONCEPT 389

life [n4] *history, biography*

autobiography, bio, career, confession, curriculum vitae, journal, life story, memoir, memorial, story; SEE CONCEPT 271

life [n5] *person's experiences*

attainment, behavior, circumstances, conduct, development, enjoyment, enlightenment, growth, hand one is dealt*, happiness, human condition, journey, knowledge, lifestyle, participation, personality, realization, suffering, trials and tribulations*, vicissitudes, way of life*, world; SEE CONCEPT 678

lifeless [adj1] *not living, not containing living things*

asleep, bare, barren, brute, cold, comatose, dead, deceased, defunct, departed, desert, empty, exanimate, extinct, faint, inanimate, inert, inorganic, insensate, insensible, late, out cold*, sterile, unconscious, uninhabited, waste; SEE CONCEPTS 485,539

lifeless [adj2] *dull, spiritless*

blah*, cold, colorless, drab, draggy*, flat, hollow, insipid, lackluster, lethargic, listless, lusterless, nothing*, pabulum*, passive, prosaic, prosy, slothful, slow*, sluggish, spent, static, stiff*, torpid, wooden*, zero*; SEE CONCEPTS 401,542,584

lifelong [adj] *lasting*

constant, continuing, deep-rooted, enduring, for life, inveterate, lifetime, livelong, long-lasting, long-lived, long-standing, old, perennial, permanent, persistent; SEE CONCEPT 798

lifetime [n] *span of animate being's existence*

all one's born days*, career, continuance, course, cradle to grave*, days, endurance, existence, life, life span, natural life, period, time; SEE CONCEPT 817

lifework [n] *person's calling*

business, career, interest, mission, occupation, profession, purpose, pursuit, vocation, work; SEE CONCEPTS 349,360

lift [n1] *transportation*

car ride, drive, journey, passage, ride, run, transport; SEE CONCEPT 155

lift [n2] *help, aid*

assist, assistance, boost, comfort, encouragement, hand, leg up*, pick-me-up*, reassurance, relief, secours, shot in the arm*, succor, support; SEE CONCEPTS 110,700

lift [v1] *move upwards; ascend*

arise, aspire, bear aloft, boost, bring up, build up, buoy up, climb, come up, disappear, disperse, dissipate, draw up, elevate, erect, goose*, heft, hike, hike up, hoist, jack up, jump up, mount, move up, pick up, put up, raise, raise high, rear,

rise, soar, take up, up, upheave, uphold, uplift, upraise, uprear, vanish; SEE CONCEPTS 196,200,236,245

lift [v2] *repeal, revoke*

annul, cancel, countermand, dismantle, end, recall, relax, remove, rescind, reverse, stop, terminate; SEE CONCEPTS 234,317

lift [v3] *steal*

abstract, appropriate, cop, copy, crib, filch, hook, nip, pilfer, pinch, pirate, plagiarize, pocket, purloin, snitch, swipe, take, thieve; SEE CONCEPTS 139,200

lift [v4] *promote, improve*

advance, ameliorate, boost, build up, dignify, elevate, enhance, exalt, hike, jack up, raise, support, upgrade; SEE CONCEPTS 110,244

ligature [n] *link*

band, bandage, binding, bond, connection, knot, ligament, nexus, rope, tie, yoke; SEE CONCEPTS 471,831

light [n1] *luminescence from sun or other source*

aurora, beacon, blaze, brightness, brilliance, brilliancy, bulb, candle, coruscation, dawn, daybreak, daylight, daytime, effulgence, emanation, flare, flash, fulgor, glare, gleam, glimmer, glint, glitter, glow, illumination, incandescence, irradiation, lambency, lamp, lantern, lighthouse, luminosity, luster, morn, morning, phosphorescence, radiance, radiation, ray, refulgence, scintillation, sheen, shine, sparkle, splendor, star, sun, sunbeam, sunrise, sunshine, taper, torch, window; SEE CONCEPTS 620,624,628,810

light [n2] *context, point of view; understanding*

angle, approach, aspect, attitude, awareness, comprehension, condition, education, elucidation, enlightenment, example, exemplar, explanation, illustration, information, insight, interpretation, knowledge, model, paragon, slant, standing, vantage point, viewpoint; SEE CONCEPTS 274, 409,682,686

light [adj1] *illuminated*

ablaze, aglow, bright, brilliant, burnished, clear, cloudless, flashing, fluorescent, glossy, glowing, lambent, lucent, luminous, lustrous, phosphorescent, polished, radiant, refulgent, resplendent, rich, scintillant, shining, shiny, sunny, unclouded, unobscured, vivid, well-lighted, well-lit; SEE CONCEPTS 617,618

light [adj2] *blond, fair*

bleached, faded, fair-skinned, light-hued, light-skinned, light-toned, pale, pastel, tow-headed; SEE CONCEPTS 406,618

light [adj3] *not heavy*

agile, airy, atmospheric, buoyant, crumbly, dainty, delicate, downy, easy, effervescent, ethereal, featherweight, feathery, filmy, flimsy, floatable, floating, fluffy, friable, frothy, gossamery, graceful, imponderous, inconsequential, insubstantial, light-footed, lightweight, lithe, little, loose, meager, nimble, petty, porous, portable, sandy, sheer, slender, slight, small, spongy, sprightly, sylphlike, thin, tissuelike, trifling, trivial, unheavy, unsubstantial, weightless; SEE CONCEPT 491

light [adj4] *small in amount, content*

casual, digestible, faint, fractional, fragmentary, frivolous, frugal, gentle, hardly any, hardly enough, inadequate, inconsequential, inconsiderable, indistinct, insignificant, insufficient, mild, minor, minuscule, minute, moderate, modest, not many, not much, not rich, puny, restricted, scanty, shoestring*, slight, soft, sparse, superficial, thin, tiny, trifling, trivial, unimportant, unsubstantial, weak, wee; SEE CONCEPTS 762,789

light [adj5] *simple, easy*
effortless, facile, manageable, moderate, smooth, undemanding, unexacting, untaxing, untroublesome; SEE CONCEPT 538

light [adj6] *funny, cheery*
airy, amusing, animated, blithe, carefree, cheerful, chipper*, chirpy, diverting, dizzy, entertaining, fickle, flighty, frivolous, gay, giddy, high, humorous, lighthearted, lively, merry, perky, pleasing, sunny, sunny-side up*, superficial, trifling, trivial, up, upbeat, witty; SEE CONCEPTS 401,542

light [v1] *illuminate*
animate, brighten, cast, fire, flood, floodlight, furnish with light, highlight, ignite, illume, illumine, inflame, irradiate, kindle, lighten, light up, limelight, make bright, make visible, put on, shine, spot, spotlight, switch on, turn on; SEE CONCEPTS 250,624

light [v2] *start on fire*
burn, enkindle, fire, flame, ignite, inflame, kindle, set fire to, set on fire, spark, strike a match; SEE CONCEPT 249

light [v3] *step down; land*
alight, arrive, come down, deplane, detrain, disembark, drop, fly down, get down, perch, rest, roost, set down, settle, settle down, sit, sit down, stop, touch down; SEE CONCEPTS 159,181

lighten [v1] *illuminate*
become light, brighten, flash, gleam, illume, irradiate, light, light up, make bright, shine; SEE CONCEPT 624

lighten [v2] *reduce weight, load*
allay, alleviate, ameliorate, assuage, attenuate, buoy, change, comfort, cut down, decrease, dilute, disburden, disencumber, ease, empty, eradicate, extenuate, facilitate, free, jettison, lessen, levitate, make less, make lighter, mitigate, mollify, pour out, put off, reduce, relieve, remove, shift, take, take a load off*, thin, throw out, unburden, unload, uplight, upraise; SEE CONCEPTS 110,244,250

lighten [v3] *cheer up; inspire*
brighten, buoy up, cheer, elate, encourage, gladden, hearten, lift, perk up, revive, take a load off; SEE CONCEPTS 7,22

light-headed [adj] *silly; feeling faint*
changeable, delirious, dizzy, empty, featherbrained*, fickle, flighty, flippant, foolish, frivolous, gaga*, giddy, harebrained*, hazy, punchy*, reeling, rocky, scatterbrained*, shallow, superficial, swimming, swimmy, tired, trifling, vertiginous, whirling, woozy*; SEE CONCEPTS 314,401

lighthearted [adj] *carefree, untroubled*
blithe, blithesome, bright, buoyant, cheerful, effervescent, expansive, feelgood*, frolicsome, gay, glad, gleeful, happy, happy-go-lucky*, high-spirited, insouciant, jocund, jolly, jovial, joyful, joyous, laid-back, lightsome, lively, merry, playful, resilient, spirited, sprightly, sunny, upbeat, vivacious, volatile; SEE CONCEPTS 404,542

lightly [adv] *gently, effortlessly*
agilely, airily, breezily, carelessly, casually, daintily, delicately, easily, ethereally, faintly, flippantly, freely, frivolously, gingerly, heedlessly, indifferently, leniently, mildly, moderately, nimbly, peacefully, quietly, readily, simply, slightingly, slightly, smoothly, softly, sparingly, sparsely, subtly, tenderly, tenuously, thinly, thoughtlessly, timidly, unsubstantially, well; SEE CONCEPTS 538,544,584

light out [v] *run away*
abscond, depart, escape, head, leave, make, make off, quit, set out, strike out, take a hike, take off; SEE CONCEPT 195

lightweight [adj] *inconsequential*
failing, featherweight, foolish, imponderous, incompetent, insignificant, of no account, paltry, petty, slight, trifling, trivial, unimportant, weightless, worthless; SEE CONCEPTS 491,575

likable [adj] *nice, pleasant*
agreeable, amiable, appealing, attractive, charismatic, charming, engaging, enjoyable, friendly, genial, good, good-natured, pleasing, preferable, relishable, sweet, sweet-natured, sympathetic, winning, winsome; SEE CONCEPT 404

like [adj] *similar*
according to, agnate, akin, alike, allied, allying, analogous, approximating, approximative, close, coextensive, cognate, commensurate, comparable, compatible, conforming, congeneric, congenerous, consistent, consonant, corresponding, double, equal, equaling, equivalent, homologous, identical, in the manner of, jibing, matching, much the same, near, not far from, not unlike, on the order of, parallel, related, relating, resembling, same, selfsame, such, twin, undifferentiated, uniform; SEE CONCEPTS 487,573

like [v1] *enjoy, be fond of*
admire, adore, appreciate, approve, be gratified by, be keen on, be partial to, be pleased by, be sweet on, care for, care to, cherish, delight in, derive pleasure from, dig*, dote on, esteem, exclaim, fancy, feast on, find appealing, get a kick out of*, go for*, hanker for, hold dear, indulge in, love, luxuriate in, prize, rejoice in, relish, revel in, savor, stuck on*, take an interest in, take delight in, take satisfaction in, take to; SEE CONCEPT 32

like [v2] *choose, feel inclined*
care to, desire, elect, fancy, feel disposed, feel like, have a preference for, incline toward, please, prefer, select, want, will, wish; SEE CONCEPTS 20,41

likelihood [n] *chance of something happening*
coin flip*, direction, even break, fair shake, fifty-fifty*, fighting chance*, good chance*, liability, likeliness, long shot*, outside chance*, plausibility, possibility, presumption, probability, prospect, reasonableness, shot at*, strong possibility, tendency, toss-up*, trend; SEE CONCEPT 650

likely [adj] *probable, apt, hopeful*
acceptable, achievable, anticipated, assuring, attainable, believeable, conceivable, conjectural, credible, destined, disposed, expected, fair, favorite, feasible, given to, imaginable, inclined, in favor of, inferable, in the cards*, in the habit of*, liable, odds-on*, on the verge of, ostensible, plausible, possible, practicable, predisposed, presumable, promising, prone, rational, reasonable, seeming, subject to, supposable, tending, thinkable, true, up-and-coming*, verisimilar, workable; SEE CONCEPT 552

likely [adv] *probably*
assumably, doubtless, doubtlessly, in all likelihood, in all probability, like as not, most likely,

no doubt, presumably, presumptively, prima facie, seemingly, to all appearances; SEE CONCEPT 552

likeness [n] *correspondence in appearance; something that corresponds*

affinity, agreement, alikeness, analogousness, analogy, appearance, carbon, clone, comparableness, comparison, conformity, copy, counterpart, dead ringer*, delineation, depiction, ditto*, double, effigy, equivalence, facsimile, form, guise, identicalness, identity, image, knock-off*, lookalike*, model, parallelism, photocopy, photograph, picture, portrait, replica, representation, reproduction, resemblance, sameness, semblance, similarity, simile, similitude, study, uniformity, Xerox*; SEE CONCEPTS 664,670,716

likewise [adj] *also, similarly*

additionally, along, as well, besides, correspondingly, further, furthermore, in addition, in like manner, in the same way, more, moreover, so, too, withal; SEE CONCEPT 563

liking [n] *fondness, taste*

affection, affinity, appetite, appreciation, attachment, attraction, bent, bias, desire, devotion, fancy, favoritism, inclination, love, mind, palate, partiality, passion, penchant, pleasure, predilection, preference, proneness, propensity, relish, soft spot*, stomach, sympathy, tendency, tooth, velleity, weakness, will; SEE CONCEPTS 20,32,529

limb [n] *appendage*

arm, bough, branch, extension, extremity, fin, gam*, leg, lobe, member, offshoot, part, pin, pinion, process, projection, spray, sprig, spur, stem, switch, unit, wheel, wing; SEE CONCEPTS 392,428

limber [adj] *flexible*

agile, deft, elastic, graceful, lissome, lithe, lithesome, loose, nimble, plastic, pliable, pliant, resilient, springy, spry, supple; SEE CONCEPTS 406,488

limbo [n] *state of uncertainty*

demilitarized zone, left field*, nothingness, nowhere, oblivion, out there*, Siberia*; SEE CONCEPTS 679,705

limit [n1] *greatest extent*

absolute, bitter end*, border, bottom line*, bound, bourne, breaking point*, brim, brink, cap, ceiling, check, circumscription, conclusion, confinement, confines, curb, cutoff point*, deadline, destination, edge, end, end point, extremity, far out, farthest point, farthest reach, fence, finality, goal, limitation, margin, maximum, obstruction, restraint, restriction, rim, termination, the max*, the most*, tops*, ultimate, utmost, verge; SEE CONCEPTS 529,548,832

limit [n2] *physical boundary*

border, borderland, compass, confines, edge, end, extent, extreme, extremity, frontier, perimeter, periphery, precinct, purlieu; SEE CONCEPTS 513,745

limit [v] *confine, restrict*

appoint, assign, bar, bottle up, bound, cap, check, circumscribe, constrict, contract, cork, cramp, curb, define, delimit, delimitate, demarcate, draw the line, fix, hem in, hinder, inhibit, keep the lid on*, lessen, narrow, prescribe, ration, reduce, restrain, set, specify; SEE CONCEPTS 5,130

limitation [n] *restraint, disadvantage*

bar, block, check, circumspection, condition, constraint, control, cramp, curb, definition, drawback, impediment, inhibition, injunction, modification, obstruction, qualification, reservation, restriction, snag, stint, stricture, taboo; SEE CONCEPTS 666,674

limited [adj1] *restricted, definite*

bound, bounded, checked, circumscribed, confined, constrained, controlled, curbed, defined, delimited, determinate, finite, fixed, hampered, hemmed in, local, modified, narrow, particular, precise, qualified, reserved, restrained, sectional, topical; SEE CONCEPTS 554,557

limited [adj2] *inadequate, short*

cramped, diminished, faulty, ineffectual, insufficient, little, mean, minimal, narrow, paltry, poor, reduced, restricted, set, small, unsatisfactory; SEE CONCEPT 771

limitless [adj] *never-ending, infinite*

bottomless, boundless, countless, endless, illimitable, immeasurable, immense, incomprehensible, indefinite, inexhaustible, innumerable, measureless, no end of*, no end to*, no holds barred*, no strings*, numberless, unbounded, uncalculable, undefined, unending, unfathomable, unlimited, untold, vast, wide-open; SEE CONCEPTS 762, 771,798

limp [n] *faltering walk*

bad wheel, falter, flat wheel, floppy, gimp, halt, hitch, hobble, lameness; SEE CONCEPT 151

limp [adj] *not stiff; weak*

bending, debilitated, drooping, droopy, ductile, enervated, exhausted, feeble, flabby, flaccid, flexible, flexuous, flimsy, floppy, impressible, infirm, languid, languishing, lax, lethargic, limber, listless, loose, plastic, pliable, pliant, relaxed, slack, soft, spent, spiritless, supple, tired, unsubstantial, weakened, wearied, worn out, yielding; SEE CONCEPTS 490,604

limp [v] *walk with faltering step*

clump, dodder, falter, flag, gimp, halt, hitch, hobble, hop, lag, scuff, shamble, shuffle, stagger, stumble, teeter, totter, waddle, walk lamely; SEE CONCEPT 151

limpid [adj] *clear, comprehensible*

bright, comprehensible, crystal-clear, crystalline, definite, distinct, filmy, intelligible, lucid, luculent, obvious, pellucid, perspicuous, pure, see-through, thin, translucent, transparent, transpicuous, unambiguous; SEE CONCEPT 535

line [n1] *mark, stroke; border*

band, bar, borderline, boundary, channel, configuration, contour, crease, dash, delineation, demarcation, edge, figuration, figure, frontier, furrow, groove, limit, lineament, lineation, outline, profile, rule, score, scratch, silhouette, streak, stripe, tracing, underline, wrinkle; SEE CONCEPTS 284, 436

line [n2] *row, succession; course*

arrangement, array, axis, band, block, border, catalogue, channel, column, concatenation, crack, direction, division, drain, echelon, file, fissure, formation, furrow, groove, group, lane, length, list, magazine, mark, order, path, progression, queue, rank, ridge, road, route, row, scar, seam, sequence, series, street, string, thread, tier, track, train, trajectory, trench, way; SEE CONCEPTS 501,727,738,744

line [n3] *cord, rope*

cable, filament, strand, string, thread, wire; SEE CONCEPT 475

line [*n4*] *belief, policy*
approach, avenue, course, course of action, ideology, method, polity, position, practice, principle, procedure, program, route, scheme, system; SEE CONCEPTS **688,689**

line [*n5*] *person's calling, interest*
activity, area, business, department, employment, field, forte, job, occupation, profession, province, pursuit, racket*, specialization, trade, vocation, work; SEE CONCEPTS **349,360**

line [*n6*] *ancestry*
breed, descent, family, heredity, lineage, pedigree, race, stock, strain, succession; SEE CONCEPT **296**

line [*n7*] *written communication*
card, letter, message, note, postcard, report, word; SEE CONCEPT **271**

line [*n8*] *hint; influential communication*
clue, indication, information, lead, patter, persuasion, pitch, prepared speech, song and dance*, spiel*; SEE CONCEPT **278**

line [*n9*] *merchandise carried by store*
commodity, goods, involvement, materials, produce, trade, vendibles, wares; SEE CONCEPT **338**

line [*v1*] *border, mark*
abut, adjoin, align, allineate, array, bound, butt against, communicate, crease, cut, delineate, draw, edge, fix, follow, fringe, furrow, group, inscribe, join, line up, march, marshal, neighbor, order, ordinate, outline, place, queue, range, rank, rim, rule, score, skirt, touch, trace, underline, verge; SEE CONCEPTS **79,84,753**

line [*v2*] *put covering inside object*
bush, ceil, cover, encrust, face, fill, incrust, interline, overlay, panel, quilt, reinforce, sheath, stuff, wad, wainscot; SEE CONCEPTS **172,218**

lineage [*n*] *ancestry*
birth, blood, breed, clan, descendants, descent, extraction, family, folk, forbears, genealogy, heredity, house, kin, kindred, line, offspring, origin, pedigree, progenitors, progeny, race, stirps, stock, succession, tribe; SEE CONCEPT **296**

linger [*v1*] *loiter, delay*
amble, be dilatory, be long, be tardy, crawl, dally, dawdle, dillydally*, drift, falter, fool around*, fritter away*, goof off*, hang around*, hang out*, hesitate, hobble, idle, lag, loll, lumber, mope, mosey, plod, poke, procrastinate, put off, putter, remain, saunter, shuffle, sit around, slouch*, stagger, stay, stick around, stop, stroll, take one's time*, tarry, tool, totter, trail, traipse, trifle, trudge, vacillate, wait, wait around; SEE CONCEPTS **151,681**

linger [*v2*] *continue, endure*
abide, bide, cling, hang on, last, persist, remain, stand, stay, stick around, survive, wait; SEE CONCEPTS **23,239**

lingo [*n*] *dialect spoken by a group*
argot, cant, idiom, jargon, language, patois, patter, slang, speech, talk, tongue, vernacular, vocabulary; SEE CONCEPT **276**

link [*n*] *component, connection*
articulation, association, attachment, bond, channel, connective, constituent, contact, copula, coupler, coupling, division, element, fastening, hitch, hookup, in, interconnection, interface, intersection, joining, joint, junction, knot, ligament, ligation, ligature, loop, member, network, nexus, part, piece, relationship, ring, seam, section, splice, tie, tie-up, vinculum, weld, yoke; SEE CONCEPTS **471,835**

link [*v*] *connect*
associate, attach, bind, bracket, combine, conjoin, conjugate, couple, fasten, group, hitch on, hook up, identify, incorporate, interface, join, meld with, network, plug into, relate, slap on, tack on, tag along, tag on, team up with, throw in with*, tie, tie in with, unite, yoke; SEE CONCEPTS **113,114,193**

lip [*n1*] *edge, brink*
border, brim, chops, flange, flare, labium, labrum, margin, nozzle, overlap, portal, projection, rim, spout; SEE CONCEPTS **392,484,513**

lip [*n2*] *insolence*
back talk, cheek*, effrontery, guff*, impertinence, jaw*, mouth*, rudeness, sass*, sauce*, sauciness*; SEE CONCEPTS **54,278**

liquid [*n*] *fluid*
aqua, aqueous material, broth, elixir, extract, flow, flux, goo*, goop*, juice, liquor, melted material, nectar, sap, secretion, slop*, solution, swill*; SEE CONCEPT **467**

liquid [*adj1*] *fluid, flowing, melting*
aqueous, damp, deliquescent, dissolvable, dissolved, dulcet, fluent, fluidic, fusible, ichorous, juicy, liquefied, liquescent, liquiform, luscious, mellifluent, mellifluous, mellow, meltable, melted, moist, molten, moving, pulpy, running, runny, sappy, serous, smooth, soft, solvent, splashing, succulent, thawed, thin, uncongealed, viscous, watery, wet; SEE CONCEPTS **485,584,603**

liquid [*adj2*] *readily available*
convertible, fluid, free, marketable, negotiable, quick, ready, realizable, usable; SEE CONCEPT **334**

liquidate [*v1*] *pay; change into cash*
cash, cash in, cash out, clear, convert, discharge, exchange, honor, pay off, quit, realize, reimburse, repay, satisfy, sell off, sell up, settle, square; SEE CONCEPT **330**

liquidate [*v2*] *destroy, dissolve*
abolish, annihilate, annul, cancel, dispatch, do away with*, do in*, eliminate, exterminate, finish off*, get rid of*, kill, murder, purge, remove, rub out*, silence, terminate, vaporize, wipe out*; SEE CONCEPT **252**

liquor [*n*] *drink; alcoholic beverage*
alcohol, aqua vitae, booze*, broth, decoction, drinkable, elixir, extract, firewater*, fluid, hard stuff*, inebriant, infusion, intoxicant, liquid, moonshine*, poison*, potable, sauce*, solvent, spirits, stock, the bottle*, whiskey; SEE CONCEPT **455**

list [*n*] *record, tabulation*
account, agenda, archive, arrangement, ballot, bill, brief, bulletin, calendar, canon, catalog, catalogue, census, checklist, contents, dictionary, directory, docket, draft, enumeration, file, gazette, index, inventory, invoice, lexicon, lineup, listing, loop, manifest, memorandum, menu, outline, panel, poll, program, prospectus, register, roll, roll call, row, schedule, screed, scroll, series, slate, statistics, syllabus, table, tally, thesaurus, ticket, timetable, vocabulary; SEE CONCEPT **281**

list [*v1*] *keep a record; tabulate*
arrange, bill, book, button down, calender, catalogue, census, chart, chronicle, classify, detail, docket, enroll, enter, enumerate, file, index, inscribe, insert, inventory, invoice, itemize, keep

count, manifest, note, numerate, particularize, peg, place, poll, post, put down as, put down for, record, register, run down, schedule, set down, specialize, specify, spell out, tab, tally, tick off, write down; SEE CONCEPTS 79,125

list [v2] *lean, slant*
cant, careen, heel, incline, pitch, recline, slope, tilt, tip; SEE CONCEPTS 154,201,738

listen [v] *hear and pay attention*
accept, admit, adopt, attend, audit, auscult, auscultate, be all ears*, be attentive, catch, concentrate, eavesdrop, entertain, get, get a load of*, give an audience to, give attention, give heed to, hang on words*, hark, harken, hearken, hear out, hear tell, lend an ear*, mind, monitor, obey, observe, overhear, pick up on*, prick up ears*, receive, take advice*, take into consideration*, take notice, take under advisement*, tune in, tune in on*, welcome; SEE CONCEPT 596

listless [adj] *spiritless, without energy*
absent, abstracted, apathetic, blah*, bored, careless, dormant, dreamy, drowsy, dull, easygoing, energyless, enervated, faint, heavy, heedless, impassive, inanimate, inattentive, indifferent, indolent, inert, insouciant, lackadaisical, lagging, laid-back*, languid, languishing, languorous, leaden, lethargic, lifeless, limp, lukewarm, lymphatic, mopish, neutral, out of it*, passive, phlegmatic, slack, sleepy, slow, sluggish, stupid, supine, thoughtless, torpid, uninterested, vacant; SEE CONCEPTS 401,584

litany [n] *recital of items, often part of religious services*
account, catalogue, enumeration, invocation, list, petition, prayer, recitation, refrain, repetition, supplication, tale; SEE CONCEPTS 278,368

literacy [n] *ability to read*
articulacy, articulateness, background, cultivation, education, knowledge, learning, proficiency, refinement, scholarship; SEE CONCEPTS 409,630

literal [adj] *word for word; exact, real*
accurate, actual, apparent, authentic, bona fide, close, critical, faithful, genuine, gospel, methodical, natural, not figurative, ordinary, plain, scrupulous, simple, strict, to the letter*, true, undeviating, unerring, unexaggerated, unvarnished, usual, veracious, verbal, verbatim, veritable, written; SEE CONCEPTS 267,557

literally [adv] *word for word; exactly*
actually, completely, correctly, direct, directly, faithfully, indisputably, letter by letter*, literatim, not figuratively, plainly, precisely, really, rightly, rigorously, sic*, simply, straight, strictly, to the letter*, truly, undeviatingly, undisputably, unerringly, unmistakably, verbatim, veritably; SEE CONCEPTS 267,557

literary [adj] *concerning books*
belletristic, bookish, classical, erudite, formal, learned, lettered, literate, scholarly, well-read; SEE CONCEPTS 267,536

literature [n] *written matter, both fictional and nonfictional*
abstract, article, belles-lettres, biography, books, brochure, classics, comment, composition, critique, discourse, discussion, disquisition, dissertation, drama, essay, exposition, findings, history, humanities, information, leaflet, letters, lit*, literary works, lore, novel, observation, pamphlet, paper, poetry, precis, prose, report, research, story, summary, theme, thesis, tract, treatise,

treatment, writings, written work; SEE CONCEPT 280

lithe [adj] *flexible, graceful and slender*
agile, lean, lightsome, limber, lissome, loose, nimble, pliable, pliant, slight, slim, spare, supple, thin; SEE CONCEPTS 488,491,584

litigate [v] *bring matter before court of law*
appeal, contest, dispute, drag into court*, file suit, go to court, go to law, institute legal proceedings, press charges, prosecute, see one in court*, sue, take the law on*; SEE CONCEPT 317

litigation [n] *matter coming before court of law*
action, case, cause, contention, dispute, lawsuit, process, prosecution, suit, trial; SEE CONCEPT 318

litter [n1] *mess, debris*
clutter, collateral, confusion, detritus, disarray, disorder, garbage, hash, hodgepodge, jumble, jungle, junk, mishmash, muck, muddle, offal, rash, refuse, rubbish, rummage, scattering, scramble, shuffle, trash, untidiness, waste; SEE CONCEPTS 260,432

litter [n2] *animal offspring*
brood, cubs, family, kittens, piglets, progeny, puppies, school, young; SEE CONCEPTS 394,397

litter [v] *make a mess*
clutter, confuse, derange, dirty, disarrange, disarray, disorder, jumble, mess up, scatter, strew; SEE CONCEPT 254

little [n] *small amount of something*
bit, dab, dash, fragment, hint, modicum, particle, pinch, snippet, soupçon, speck, spot, taste, touch, trace, trifle, whit; SEE CONCEPT 835

little [adj1] *small in size, amount*
babyish, bantam, brief, cramped, diminutive, dinky, elfin, embryonic, fleeting, hardly any, hasty, immature, imperceptible, inappreciable, inconsiderable, infant, infinitesimal, insufficient, junior, light, Lilliputian*, limited, meager, microscopic, mini, miniature, minute, not big, not large, peanut*, petite, scant, short, short-lived, shrimpy*, shriveled, skimpy, slight, snub, sparse, stubby, stunted, teeny, tiny, toy, truncated, undersized, undeveloped, wee, wizened, young; SEE CONCEPTS 773,789

little [adj2] *not important*
casual, inconsiderable, insignificant, light, minor, minute, negligible, paltry, petty, shoestring*, small, trifling, trivial, unimportant; SEE CONCEPT 575

little [adj3] *narrow-minded*
base, bigoted, cheap, contemptible, hidebound, illiberal, ineffectual, limited, mean, narrow, paltry, petty, provincial, self-centered, selfish, set, small, small-minded, vulgar, wicked; SEE CONCEPT 404

little [adv] *infrequently, not much*
a little, barely, hardly, hardly ever, not many, not often, not quite, only just, rarely, scarcely, seldom, somewhat; SEE CONCEPTS 530,544

liturgy [n] *worship, ceremony*
celebration, ceremonial, form, formality, formula, observance, rite, ritual, sacrament, service, services; SEE CONCEPT 368

livable [adj] *adequate, acceptable*
bearable, comfortable, cozy, endurable, fit, habitable, homey, inhabitable, lodgeable, passable, satisfactory, snug, sufferable, supportable, sustainable, tenantable, tolerable, worthwhile; SEE CONCEPTS 485,558

live [adj1] existent
alive, animate, aware, breathing, conscious, living, vital; SEE CONCEPT 539

live [adj2] energetic, vigorous
active, alert, brisk, burning, controversial, current, dynamic, earnest, effective, effectual, efficacious, efficient, functioning, hot*, lively, operative, pertinent, pressing, prevalent, running, topical, unsettled, vital, vivid, working; SEE CONCEPTS 542,560

live [v1] exist
abide, be, be alive, breathe, continue, draw breath, endure, get along, get by, have life, last, lead, maintain, make it, move, pass, persist, prevail, remain, remain alive, subsist, survive; SEE CONCEPT 407

live [v2] inhabit a dwelling
abide, bide, bunk*, crash*, dwell, hang one's hat*, hang out*, locate, lodge, nest, occupy, perch, reside, roost, settle; SEE CONCEPT 226

live [v3] enjoy being alive
be happy, delight, experience, flourish, love, luxuriate, make the most of, prosper, relish, savor, take pleasure, thrive; SEE CONCEPT 678

live [v4] make money to support living
acquire a livelihood, earn a living, earn money, fare, feed, get along*, get by*, maintain, make ends meet*, make it, profit, subsist, support; SEE CONCEPT 351

livelihood [n] occupation
alimentation, art, bread and butter*, business, circumstances, craft, employment, game*, grind*, income, job, keep*, living, maintenance, means, nine to five*, profession, racket*, rat race*, resources, slot, source of income, subsistence, support, sustenance, thing*, trade, vocation, what one is into*, work; SEE CONCEPTS 349,351,360

lively [adj] energetic, active, busy
agile, alert, animate, animated, astir, blithe, blithesome, bouncy, bright, brisk, buoyant, bustling, buzzing, cheerful, chipper*, chirpy*, complex, dashing, driving, effervescent, enjoyable, enterprising, entertaining, festive, frisky, frolicsome, full of pep*, gay, go-go*, happy, hyper*, industrious, involved, jocund, jumping, keen, merry, nimble, peppy*, perky, pert, provocative, quick, refreshing, rousing, snappy, sparkling, spirited, sprightly, spry, stimulating, stirring, vigorous, vivacious, zippy*; SEE CONCEPTS 401,542,548

livid [adj1] pale, ashen
ashy, blanched, bloodless, colorless, discolored, dusky, gloomy, greyish, grisly, leaden, lurid, murky, pallid, pasty, wan, waxen; SEE CONCEPT 618

livid [adj2] bruised
black-and-blue, contused, purple; SEE CONCEPT 618

livid [adj3] extremely angry
beside oneself, black*, boiling, enraged, exasperated, flaming, fuming, furious, hot*, incensed, indignant, infuriated, mad, offended, outraged; SEE CONCEPTS 403,542

living [n] lifestyle; source of income
alimentation, bread and butter*, existence, income, job, keep*, livelihood, maintenance, means, mode, occupation, salt*, subsistence, support, sustainment, sustenance, sustentation, way, work; SEE CONCEPTS 335,351

living [adj] existing, active
alert, alive, animated, around, awake, breathing, brisk, contemporary, continuing, current, developing, dynamic, existent, extant, in use, live, lively, ongoing, operative, persisting, strong, subsisting, ticking, vigorous, vital, warm; SEE CONCEPTS 539,560

load [n1] cargo, freight
amount, bale, bundle, capacity, charge, consignment, contents, encumbrance, goods, haul, heft, hindrance, lading, mass, pack, parcel, part, payload, shipment, shot, weight; SEE CONCEPTS 338,432

load [n2] burden, pressure
affliction, albatross, care, charge, cumber, deadweight*, drag, drain, duty, encumbrance, excess baggage*, incubus, liability, millstone*, obligation, onus, oppression, responsibility, task, tax, trouble, trust, weight, worry; SEE CONCEPT 674

load [v1] burden, saddle
arrange, ballast, bear, carry, charge, chock, choke, containerize, cram, fill, flood, freight, glut, gorge, heap, heap up, jam*, lade, lumber, mass, oversupply, pack, pile, pile it on, pile up, place, pour in, put aboard, ram in, stack, store, stow, stuff, surfeit, swamp, top, top off, weigh, weigh down, weight; SEE CONCEPT 209

load [v2] overburden, pressure
burden, charge, encumber, hamper, lade, oppress, saddle, task, tax, trouble, weigh down, weight, worry; SEE CONCEPT 14

loaf [n] block of something
bun, cake, cube, dough, lump, mass, pastry, roll, slab, twist; SEE CONCEPTS 436,457,460,461

loaf [v] be idle, lazy
be inactive, be indolent, be slothful, be unoccupied, bum*, bum around*, dally, dillydally*, dream, drift, evade, fool around*, fritter away*, goldbrick, hang out*, idle, kill time*, knock around*, laze, let down, lie, loiter, loll, lounge, lounge around, malinger, not lift a finger*, pass time, piddle, relax, saunter, shirk, sit around, slack, slow down, stall, stand around, stroll, take it easy, trifle, twiddle thumbs*, vegetate, waste time, while away hours*; SEE CONCEPTS 210,681

loafer [n] person who is idle, lazy
beachcomber, deadbeat, do-nothing, good-for-nothing*, goof-off*, idler, lazybones*, lounger, malingerer, ne'er-do-well*, shirker, slacker, slouch, sluggard, sponger, wanderer, waster, wastrel; SEE CONCEPT 412

loan [n] money given temporarily
accommodation, advance, allowance, credit, extension, floater, investment, mortgage, time payment, trust; SEE CONCEPT 332

loan [v] give money, possession temporarily
accommodate, advance, allow, credit, lay on one, lend, let out, provide, score, scratch, stake, touch; SEE CONCEPT 115

loath [adj] against, averse
afraid, counter, disinclined, hesitant, indisposed, opposed, reluctant, remiss, resisting, uneager, unwilling; SEE CONCEPTS 29,542

loathe [v] dislike strongly
abhor, abominate, be allergic to*, be down on, decline, despise, detest, execrate, feel repugnance, find disgusting, hate, have aversion to, have no use for*, refuse, reject, repudiate, revolt, spurn; SEE CONCEPT 29

li
lo

loathsome [adj] *hateful*
abhorrent, abominable, beastly, bitchy*, creepy, deplorable, detestable, disgusting, execrable, gross, hideous, horrible, invidious, lousy, nasty, nauseating, obnoxious, odious, offensive, pesky, pestiferous, repellent, repugnant, repulsive, revolting, sleazy*, slimy*, uncool*, vile; SEE CONCEPTS 485,529,570

lobby [n] *entrance hall*
antechamber, corridor, doorway, foyer, gateway, hall, hallway, passage, passageway, porch, vestibule, waiting room; SEE CONCEPTS 441,448

lobby [v] *press for political action*
advance, affect, alter, bill, billboard*, boost, bring pressure to bear*, build up, campaign for, change, drum, exert influence, further, hard sell*, high pressure, hype*, induce, influence, make a pitch for*, modify, persuade, pitch, plug, politick, press, pressure, procure, promote, pull strings*, push, put pressure on, request, sell, sell on*, soft-sell*, soft-soap*, solicit, solicit votes, splash, spot, sway, sweet-talk*, thump, urge; SEE CONCEPTS 68,300

local [n] *person deeply rooted in community*
character, inhabitant, native, resident; SEE CONCEPTS 413,423

local [adj] *of a community, restricted to immediate area*
bounded, civic, confined, district, divisional, geographical, insular, legendary, limited, narrow, neighborhood, parish, parochial, provincial, regional, sectarian, sectional, small-town, territorial, town, vernacular; SEE CONCEPT 536

locale/locality [n] *physical setting*
area, bailiwick, belt, district, domain, haunt, hole, home, location, locus, neck of the woods*, neighborhood, place, position, region, scene, sector, site, sphere, spot, stage, stomping ground*, territory, theater, tract, turf, venue, vicinity, zone; SEE CONCEPT 198

locate [v1] *find*
come across, come upon, detect, determine, discover, establish, ferret out*, get at, happen upon, hit upon, hook*, lay one's hands on*, light upon*, meet with, pick up on, pin down, pinpoint, place, position, read, search out, smell out, smoke out*, spot, station, strike, stumble on, track down, trip over*, uncover, unearth, zero in on*; SEE CONCEPT 183

locate [v2] *settle*
dig in, dispose, dwell, establish, fix, hang one's hat*, inhabit, park, place, put, reside, seat, set, situate, squat, stand; SEE CONCEPT 226

location [n] *place of residence or activity*
area, bearings, district, fix*, hole, locale, locality, locus, neck of the woods*, neighborhood, part, point, position, post, region, scene, section, site, situation, spot, station, tract, turf, venue, whereabouts; SEE CONCEPT 198

lock [n] *device that fastens and bars free passage*
bar, bolt, bond, catch, clamp, clasp, clinch, connection, fastening, fixture, grapple, grip, hasp, hook, junction, latch, link, padlock; SEE CONCEPT 499

lock [v] *fasten, clasp*
bar, bolt, button, button up, clench, close, clutch, embrace, encircle, enclose, engage, entwine, grapple, grasp, hug, join, latch, link, mesh, press, seal, secure, shut, turn the key, unite; SEE CONCEPTS 85,160

lodge [n] *cabin; vacation residence*
abode, auberge, burrow, camp, chalet, cottage, couch, country house, den, dormitory, dwelling, gatehouse, haunt, home, hospice, hostel, hostelry, hotel, house, hut, inn, motel, public house, retreat, roadhouse, shack, shanty, shelter, stopover, tavern, villa; SEE CONCEPT 516

lodge [v1] *become fixed or wedged*
abide, catch, come to rest, embed, entrench, fix, imbed, implant, infix, ingrain, install, plant, remain, root, stay, stick; SEE CONCEPT 201

lodge [v2] *stay at temporary residence*
abide, accommodate, bestow, board, bunk, canton, crash, domicile, dwell, entertain, harbor, hole up*, hostel, house, locate, nest, park*, perch*, put up, quarter, rent, reside, room, roost*, shelter, sojourn, squat, station, stay, stay over, stop; SEE CONCEPT 226

lodging [n] *accommodation for rent*
abode, address, apartment, bed and breakfast, boarding house, camp, castle, chambers, cover, domicile, dorm, dwelling, habitation, harbor, home, hostel, hotel, inn, lodge, lodgment, motel, palace, pied-à-terre, place, port, protection, quarters, residence, resort, roof, room, room and board, rooming house, shelter; SEE CONCEPT 516

loft [n] *room on upper floor*
apartment, attic, dormer, garret, storage, studio; SEE CONCEPT 448

lofty [adj1] *high, elevated*
aerial, airy, high-rise, lifted, raised, sky-high, skyscraping, skyward, soaring, spiring, tall, towering; SEE CONCEPT 779

lofty [adj2] *grand, stately*
arresting, benevolent, big, chivalrous, commanding, considerate, dignified, distinguished, elevated, exalted, generous, great, illustrious, imposing, magnanimous, majestic, noble, renowned, striking, sublime, superb, superior, utopian, visionary; SEE CONCEPT 574

lofty [adj3] *arrogant, high and mighty*
ambitious, cavalier, condescending, disdainful, grandiose, haughty, high-minded, immodest, insolent, overbearing, patronizing, pretentious, proud, snooty, supercilious; SEE CONCEPT 401

log [n1] *stump of tree*
block, bole, chunk, length, piece, stick, timber, trunk, wood; SEE CONCEPTS 428,479

log [n2] *record*
account, book, chart, daybook, diary, journal, listing, logbook, register, tally; SEE CONCEPT 271

logic [n] *science of reasoning*
antithesis and synthesis, argumentation, coherence, connection, course of thought, deduction, dialectic, good sense, induction, inference, linkage, philosophy, ratiocination, rationale, relationship, sanity, sense, sound judgment, syllogism, syllogistics, thesis, train of thought; SEE CONCEPTS 37,349,689

logical [adj] *probable, reasonable*
analytic, analytical, clear, cogent, coherent, commonsensical, compelling, congruent, consequent, consistent, convincing, deducible, discerning, discriminating, extensional, fair, germane, holding together, holding water*, inferential, intelligent, judicious, juridicious, justifiable, kosher*, legit*, legitimate, lucid, most likely, necessary, obvious, perceptive, perspicuous, pertinent, plausible, rational, relevant, sensible, sound, subtle, telling,

valid, well-organized, wise; SEE CONCEPTS 402,529,552

loiter [v] *hang around; stroll*
amble, dabble, dally*, dawdle, delay, diddle, drag, flag, fritter away, get no place fast*, halt, hover, idle, lag, linger, loaf, loll, lounge, pass time, pause, poke, procrastinate, put off, ramble, saunter, shamble, shuffle, slacken, slough, tarry, trail, traipse, wait, waste time; SEE CONCEPTS 151,210,681

loll [v] *lay sprawled*
bum, dangle, dawdle, droop, drop, flap, flop, goof off, hang, hang loose, idle, lag, lean, loaf, loiter, lounge, recline, relax, rest, sag, slouch, slump, sprawl; SEE CONCEPTS 154,210

lone [adj] *by oneself; only*
abandoned, alone, deserted, forsaken, isolated, lonely, lonesome, one, onliest, particular, secluded, separate, separated, single, singular, sole, solitary, solo, stag, unaccompanied, unique; SEE CONCEPT 577

lonely [adj1] *feeling friendless, forlorn*
abandoned, alone, apart, by oneself, comfortless, companionless, deserted, desolate, destitute, disconsolate, down, empty, estranged, forsaken, godforsaken, homeless, isolated, left, lone, lonesome, outcast, reclusive, rejected, renounced, secluded, single, solitary, troglodytic, unattended, unbefriended, uncherished, unsocial, withdrawn; SEE CONCEPTS 403,555

lonely [adj2] *out-of-the-way*
alone, deserted, desolate, godforsaken, isolated, obscure, off the beaten track*, private, quiet, remote, removed, retired, secluded, secret, sequestered, solitary, unfrequented, uninhabited; SEE CONCEPT 583

lonesome [adj] *forlorn, friendless*
alone, cheerless, companionless, deserted, desolate, dreary, gloomy, homesick, isolated, lone, lonely, solitary; SEE CONCEPTS 403,555

long [adj1] *extended in space or time*
continued, deep, distant, drawn out, elongate, elongated, enduring, enlarged, expanded, extensive, faraway, far-off, far-reaching, gangling, great, high, lanky, lasting, lengthened, lengthy, lingering, lofty, longish, outstretched, prolonged, protracted, rangy, remote, running, spread out, spun out, stretch, stretched, stretching, stringy, sustained, tall, towering; SEE CONCEPTS 482,779,798

long [adj2] *interminable, excessive in length*
boundless, delayed, diffuse, diffusive, dilatory, dragging, drawn-out, for ages*, forever and a day*, late, lengthy, limitless, lingering, long-drawn-out*, long-winded*, overlong, prolix, prolonged, protracted, slow, sustained, tardy, unending, verbose, without end, wordy; SEE CONCEPTS 482,779,798

long [v] *desire, crave*
ache, aim, aspire, covet, dream of, hanker, have a yen for, hunger, itch, lust, miss, pine, sigh, spoil for, suspire, thirst, want, wish, yearn; SEE CONCEPT 20

longing [n] *strong desire*
ambition, aspiration, coveting, craving, fire in the belly*, hankering, hunger, hungering, itch, pining, thirst, urge, wish, yearning, yen; SEE CONCEPTS 20,709

longing [adj] *desirous*
anxious, ardent, avid, craving, eager, hungry, languishing, pining, ravenous, wishful, wistful, yearning; SEE CONCEPT 403

look [n1] *visual examination*
attention, beholding, case, cast, contemplation, evil eye*, eye*, flash, gander, gaze, glance, glimpse, gun, inspection, introspection, keeping watch, leer, look-see*, marking, noticing, observation, once-over, peek, reconnaissance, regard, regarding, review, scrutiny, sight, slant, speculation, squint, stare, surveillance, survey, swivel, view, viewing; SEE CONCEPT 623

look [n2] *characteristic, stylish appearance*
air, aspect, bearing, cast, complexion, countenance, demeanor, effect, expression, face, fashion, guise, manner, mien, mug*, physiognomy, presence, seeming, semblance, visage; SEE CONCEPTS 655,673,716

look [v1] *examine visually*
admire, attend, behold, beware, consider, contemplate, eye, feast one's eyes*, flash, focus, gape, gawk, gaze, get a load of, glance, glower, goggle, heed, inspect, mark, mind, note, notice, observe, ogle, peep, peer, pore over, read, regard, rubberneck*, scan, scout, scrutinize, see, spot, spy, stare, study, survey, take a gander*, take in the sights*, tend, view, watch; SEE CONCEPT 623

look [v2] *appear, seem to be*
display, evidence, exhibit, express, indicate, look like, make clear, manifest, present, resemble, show, sound, strike as; SEE CONCEPTS 261,716

look [v3] *expect, anticipate*
await, count on, divine, forecast, foretell, hope, hunt, reckon on, search, seek; SEE CONCEPT 26

look [v4] *face*
front, front on, give onto, overlook; SEE CONCEPT 746

look down on [v] *hold in contempt*
abhor, contemn, despise, disdain, scorn, scout, sneer, spurn, turn nose up at*; SEE CONCEPT 29

look into [v] *check, research*
audit, check out, delve into, dig, examine, explore, follow up, go into, inquire, inspect, investigate, look over, make inquiry, probe, prospect, scrutinize, sift, study; SEE CONCEPT 103

lookout [n] *guard; place from which to guard*
anchor, beacon, belvedere, case, catbird seat*, citadel, crow's nest*, cupola, eagle eye*, hawk, observance, observation, observatory, outlook, overlook, panorama, patrol, post, scene, scout, sentinel, sentry, spotter, station, surveillance, tip, tower, view, vigil, vigilance, ward, watch, watcher, watch person watchtower*, weather eye*; SEE CONCEPTS 198,358,623

look out [v] *be wary*
be alert, be careful, be on guard, beware, check out, have a care, heads up*, hearken, keep an eye out*, keep tabs*, listen, mind, notice, pay attention, peg*, pick up on*, scope, shotgun*, size up, spot, spy, watch out; SEE CONCEPTS 35,623

look up [v1] *research*
come upon, confirm, discover, find, hunt for, peruse, scan, search for, seek, seek out, track down; SEE CONCEPTS 72,216

look up [v2] *improve*
advance, ameliorate, come along, convalesce, gain, get better, mend, perk up, pick up, progress, recuperate, shape up, show improvement; SEE CONCEPTS 303,700

loom [v] *appear, often imposingly*
approach, await, be at hand*, become visible, be

lo
lo

coming, be forthcoming, be imminent, be in the cards*, be in the wind*, be near, break through, brew, bulk, come forth, come into view, come on, come on the scene*, dawn, dominate, emanate, emerge, figure, gather, hang over, hover, impend, impress, issue, lower, make up, menace, mount, near, overhang, overshadow, overtop, portend, rear, rise, seem huge, seem large, show, soar, stand out, take shape, threaten, top, tower; SEE CONCEPTS 118,159,261

loop [n] *circle, spiral*
bend, circuit, circumference, coil, convolution, curl, curve, eyelet, hoop, kink, knot, loophole, noose, ring, twirl, twist, whorl, wreath; SEE CONCEPT 436

loop [v] *circle, spiral*
arc, arch, begird, bend, bow, braid, coil, compass, connect, crook, curl, curve, curve around, encircle, encompass, fold, gird, girdle, join, knot, ring, roll, surround, tie together, turn, twist, wind around; SEE CONCEPTS 147,201,754

loose [adj1] *not tight; unconstrained*
apart, asunder, at large, baggy, clear, detached, disconnected, easy, escaped, flabby, flaccid, floating, free, hanging, insecure, lax, liberated, limp, loosened, movable, not fitting, relaxed, released, separate, slack, slackened, sloppy, unattached, unbolted, unbound, unbuttoned, uncaged, unclasped, unconfined, unconnected, undone, unfastened, unfettered, unhinged, unhooked, unlatched, unlocked, unpinned, unrestrained, unrestricted, unsecured, unshackled, untied, wobbly; SEE CONCEPT 485

loose [adj2] *indefinite, vague*
detached, diffuse, disconnected, disordered, ill-defined, imprecise, inaccurate, indistinct, negligent, obscure, rambling, random, remiss; SEE CONCEPTS 267,529

loose [adj3] *promiscuous*
abandoned, capricious, careless, corrupt, debauched, disreputable, dissipated, dissolute, easy, fast, heedless, high living*, immoral, imprudent, inconstant, lax, lewd, libertine, licentious, light, negligent, out of control*, playing, profligate, rash, reckless, speeding, swinging, thoughtless, unchaste, unmindful, unrestrained, wanton; SEE CONCEPTS 372,401,545

loose/loosen [v] *set free; unbind*
alleviate, become unfastened, break up, deliver, detach, discharge, disconnect, disengage, disenthrall, disjoin, ease, ease off, emancipate, extricate, free, let go, let out, liberate, manumit, mitigate, relax, release, separate, slacken, unbar, unbolt, unbuckle, unbutton, unchain, unclasp, undo, unfasten, unfix, unhitch, unhook, unlace, unlash, unlatch, unleash, unlock, unloose, unpin, unscrew, unsnap, unstick, unstrap, untie, untighten, work free, work loose; SEE CONCEPTS 127,250

loot [n] *stolen goods*
booty, dough*, graft, haul, hot goods*, lift*, make*, money, pickings*, pillage, plunder, plunderage*, prize, seizure, spoils, squeeze, take*; SEE CONCEPTS 337,340

loot [v] *steal goods*
appropriate, boost, burglarize, despoil, grab, gut, liberate, lift, loft, make, moonlight requisition*, pillage, plunder, raid, ransack, ravage, relieve, requisition, rifle, rip off*, rob, sack, salvage,

smash and grab*, snatch, snitch*, stick up, swipe, take, thieve, tip over; SEE CONCEPTS 139,192

lopsided [adj] *leaning, falling to one side; larger on one side*
askew, asymmetrical, awry, cockeyed, crooked, disproportional, disproportionate, inclinatory, irregular, nonsymmetrical, off-balance, one-sided, out of shape, overbalanced, squint, tilting, top-heavy, unbalanced, unequal, uneven, unsteady, warped; SEE CONCEPT 480

loquacious [adj] *talkative*
babbling, chattering, chatty, fluent, gabby*, garrulous, gossipy, jabbering, long-winded*, loose-lipped*, motormouth*, multiloquent, prolix, verbose, voluble, wordy, yacking*; SEE CONCEPTS 267,401

lore [n] *myths, traditional wisdom*
adage, belief, custom, doctrine, enlightenment, erudition, experience, fable, folklore, information, knowledge, learning, legend, letters, mythology, mythos, saga, saw, saying, scholarship, science, superstition, tale, teaching, tradition; SEE CONCEPTS 274,282,287

lose [v1] *be deprived of; mislay*
be careless, become poorer, be impoverished, bereave, be reduced, capitulate, consume, default, deplete, disinherit, displace, dispossess, dissipate, divest, drain, drop, exhaust, expend, fail, fail to keep, fall short, forfeit, forget, give up, lavish, misplace, miss, misspend, oust, pass up, relinquish, rob, sacrifice, squander, suffer, suffer loss, surrender, use up, waste, yield; SEE CONCEPTS 116,156

lose [v2] *be defeated*
be humbled, be outdistanced, be sunk, be taken to cleaners*, be the loser, be worsted*, come up short, decline, drop, drop a bundle*, fall, kiss goodbye*, lose out, miss, succumb, suffer defeat, take a beating*, take the count*, take the heat*, yield; SEE CONCEPTS 384,674

lose [v3] *escape, avoid*
clear, dodge, duck, elude, evade, give the slip*, leave behind, outrun, rid, shake, shake off*, slip away, stray, throw off*, unburden, wander from; SEE CONCEPTS 30,102

loser [n] *person, thing that fails*
also-ran*, deadbeat*, defeated, disadvantaged, down-and-outer*, dud*, failure, flop*, flunkee*, has-been, underdog, underprivileged; SEE CONCEPTS 412,423,433

loss [n] *misfortune, deficit; something misplaced or lost*
accident, bad luck, bereavement, calamity, casualty, cataclysm, catastrophe, cost, damage, death, debit, debt, defeat, deficiency, depletion, deprivation, destitution, destruction, detriment, disadvantage, disappearance, disaster, dispossession, failure, fall, fatality, forfeiture, harm, hurt, impairment, injury, losing, misadventure, mishap, mislaying, misplacing, need, perdition, privation, retardation, ruin, sacrifice, shrinkage, squandering, trial, trouble, undoing, want, waste, wreckage; SEE CONCEPTS 407,674,707

lost [adj1] *missing, off-track*
absent, adrift, astray, at sea, cast away, disappeared, disoriented, down the drain*, fallen between cracks*, forfeit, forfeited, gone, gone astray, hidden, invisible, irrecoverable, irretrievable, irrevocable, kiss goodbye*, lacking, minus, mislaid, misplaced, missed, nowhere to be

found*, obscured, off-course, out the window*, strayed, unredeemed, vanished, wandering, wayward, without; SEE CONCEPT 576

lost [adj2] extinct, destroyed
abolished, annihilated, bygone, consumed, dead, demolished, devastated, dissipated, eradicated, exterminated, forgotten, frittered, gone, lapsed, misspent, missed, obliterated, obsolete, out-of-date, past, perished, ruined, squandered, unremembered, wasted, wiped out*, wrecked; SEE CONCEPTS 539,560

lost [adj3] distracted, dreaming
absent, absentminded, absorbed, abstracted, bemused, bewildered, distrait, dreamy, engrossed, entranced, faraway, feeble, going in circles*, ignorant, inconscient, musing, perplexed, preoccupied, rapt, spellbound, taken in*, taken up*, unconscious, wasted; SEE CONCEPT 403

lot [n1] piece of property
acreage, allotment, apportionment, area, block, clearing, division, field, frontage, parcel, part, patch, percentage, piece, plat, plot, plottage, portion, property, real estate, tract; SEE CONCEPTS 509,710

lot [n2] quantity, often large
abundance, aggregate, aggregation, amplitude, assortment, barrel, batch, body, bunch, bundle, circle, clump, cluster, clutch, collection, conglomerate, conglomeration, consignment, crowd, great deal, group, heap, load, mass, mess*, much, multiplicity, number, ocean, oodles, order, pack, pile, plenitude, plenty, push, reams, requisition, scores, set, stack, stacks*; SEE CONCEPTS 432,787

lot [n3] portion, share
allotment, allowance, bite, cut, parcel, part, percentage, piece, quota, ration, slice, take; SEE CONCEPTS 710,835

lot [n4] fate, destiny
accident, break, breaks, chance, circumstance, decree, doom, foreordination, fortune, hand one is dealt*, hazard, karma, kismet, Moirai, plight, portion, predestination, run of luck*, way cookie crumbles*, wheel of fortune*; SEE CONCEPT 679

lotion [n] creamy solution
balm, cosmetic, cream, demulcent, embrocation, lenitive, liniment, medicine, ointment, palliative, preparation, salve, unguent, wash; SEE CONCEPTS 311,446,466

loud [adj1] blaring, noisy
big, blatant, blustering, boisterous, booming, cacophonous, clamorous, crashing, deafening, deep, ear-piercing, ear-splitting, emphatic, forte, full, full-mouthed, fulminating, heavy, high-sounding, intense, loud-voiced, lusty, obstreperous, pealing, piercing, powerful, rambunctious, raucous, resonant, resounding, ringing, roaring, rowdy, sonorous, stentorian, strident, strong, thundering, tumultuous, turbulent, turned up, uproarious, vehement, vociferous, wakes the dead*; SEE CONCEPTS 592,594

loud [adj2] offensive, gaudy
brash, brassy, brazen, chintzy, coarse, crass, crude, flamboyant, flashy, garish, glaring, gross, lurid, meretricious, obnoxious, obtrusive, ostentatious, raucous, rude, showy, tasteless, tawdry, vulgar; SEE CONCEPTS 401,542,589

lounge [n] club, socializing place
bar, barroom, club room, cocktail lounge, dive*, drinkery, hideaway, lobby, mezzanine, parlor, pub, reception, saloon, spot, tap, taproom, watering hole*; SEE CONCEPTS 293,449

lounge [v] lie about, waste time
bum*, dawdle, fritter away, goldbrick*, goof off*, idle, kill time*, laze, loaf, loiter, loll*, pass time, recline, relax, repose, saunter, sprawl, take it easy*; SEE CONCEPTS 154,210,681

lousy [adj] very bad
awful, base, contemptible, despicable, dirty, disliked, execrable, faulty, harmful, hateful, horrible, inferior, low, mean, miserable, no good*, outrageous, poor, rotten, second-rate*, shoddy, slovenly, terrible, unpopular, unwelcome, vicious, vile; SEE CONCEPT 571

lovable [adj] very likable; endearing
adorable, agreeable, alluring, amiable, angelic, appealing, attractive, bewitching, captivating, charming, cuddly, delightful, desirable, enchanting, engaging, enthralling, entrancing, fascinating, fetching, friendly, genial, lovely, lovesome, pleasing, ravishing, seductive, sweet, winning, winsome; SEE CONCEPT 404

love [n1] adoration; very strong liking
adulation, affection, allegiance, amity, amorousness, amour, appreciation, ardency, ardor, attachment, case*, cherishing, crush, delight, devotedness, devotion, emotion, enchantment, enjoyment, fervor, fidelity, flame, fondness, friendship, hankering, idolatry, inclination, infatuation, involvement, like, lust, mad for, partiality, passion, piety, rapture, regard, relish, respect, sentiment, soft spot*, taste, tenderness, weakness, worship, yearning, zeal; SEE CONCEPT 32

love [n2] person who is loved by another
admirer, angel, beau, beloved, boyfriend, courter, darling, dear, dearest, dear one, flame, girlfriend, honey, inamorata, inamorato, Juliet*, loved one, lover, paramour, passion, Romeo*, spark, suitor, swain, sweet, sweetheart, truelove, valentine; SEE CONCEPT 423

love [v1] adore, like very much
admire, adulate, be attached to, be captivated by, be crazy about, be enamored of, be enchanted by, be fascinated with, be fond of, be in love with, canonize, care for, cherish, choose, deify, delight in, dote on, esteem, exalt, fall for, fancy, glorify, go for*, gone on*, have affection for, have it bad*, hold dear, hold high, idolize, long for, lose one's heart to*, prefer, prize, put on pedestal*, think the world of*, thrive with, treasure, venerate, wild for*, worship; SEE CONCEPT 32

love [v2] have sexual relations
caress, clasp, cling, cosset, court, cuddle, draw close, embrace, feel, fondle, hold, hug, kiss, lick, look tenderly, make love, neck*, pet*, press, shine, soothe, stroke, take into one's arms, tryst, woo; SEE CONCEPTS 375,384

love affair [n] sexual relationship outside of marriage
adultery, affair, amour, devotion, extracurricular activity*, flirtation, intrigue, liaison, love, menage à trois, passion, romance, thing, triangle; SEE CONCEPTS 375,388

lovely [adj] beautiful, charming; agreeable
admirable, alluring, amiable, attractive, beauteous, bewitching, captivating, comely, dainty, delectable, delicate, delicious, delightful, enchanting, engaging, enjoyable, exquisite, fair, good-looking, gorgeous, graceful, gratifying, handsome, knockout, lovesome, nice, picture,

lo
lo

pleasant, pleasing, pretty, pulchritudinous, rare, scrumptious, splendid, stunning, sweet, winning; SEE CONCEPTS 537,579,589

lover [n] *person having sexual relationship*
admirer, beau, beloved, boyfriend, companion, courter, darling, dear, dearest, escort, fiancé, fiancée, flame, girlfriend, idolizer, inamorata, inamorato, infatuate, Juliet*, paramour, petitioner, Romeo*, significant other, solicitor, steady, suitor, suppliant, swain, sweetheart, truelove, valentine, wooer; SEE CONCEPT 423

loving [adj] *expressing adoration*
admiring, affectionate, amatory, amiable, amorous, anxious, appreciative, ardent, attached, attentive, benevolent, bound up, caring, concerned, considerate, cordial, dear, demonstrative, devoted, doting, earnest, enamored, erotic, expressive, faithful, fervent, fond, friendly, generous, idolatrous, impassioned, infatuated, kind, liking, loyal, passionate, respecting, reverent, reverential, romantic, sentimental, solicitous, tender, thoughtful, valuing, warm, warm-hearted, worshipful, zealous; SEE CONCEPTS 372,401,542

low [adj1] *close to the ground; short*
below, beneath, bottom, bottommost, crouched, decumbent, deep, depressed, flat, ground-level, inferior, junior, lesser, level, little, lowering, low-hanging, low-lying, low-set, minor, nether, not high, profound, prostrate, rock-bottom, shallow, small, squat, squatty, stunted, subjacent, subsided, sunken, under, unelevated; SEE CONCEPTS 583,779,782,793

low [adj2] *close to; mediocre*
cheap, cut, cut-rate*, deficient, depleted, economical, inadequate, inexpensive, inferior, insignificant, little, low-grade, marked down, meager, moderate, modest, nominal, paltry, poor, puny, reasonable, scant, second-rate*, shoddy, slashed, small, sparse, substandard, trifling, uncostly, worthless; SEE CONCEPTS 334,574,789

low [adj3] *crude, vulgar*
abject, base, blue, coarse, common, contemptible, crass, crumby, dastardly, degraded, depraved, despicable, disgraceful, dishonorable, disreputable, gross*, ignoble, ill-bred, inelegant, mean, menial, miserable, nasty, obscene, off-color*, offensive, raw, rough, rude, scrubby, scruffy*, scurvy, servile, sordid, unbecoming, uncouth, undignified, unrefined, unworthy, vile, woebegone, woeful, wretched; SEE CONCEPTS 404,542

low [adj4] *living in, coming from poor circumstances*
base, baseborn, humble, ignoble, lowborn, lowly, mean, meek, obscure, plain, plebeian, poor, rude, simple, unpretentious, unwashed; SEE CONCEPT 549

low [adj5] *depressed*
bad, blue*, crestfallen, dejected, despondent, disheartened, down, down and out*, downcast, downhearted, down in the dumps*, down in the mouth*, dragged, fed up, forlorn, gloomy, glum, in the pits*, low-down*, miserable, moody, morose, sad, singing the blues*, spiritless, unhappy; SEE CONCEPT 403

low [adj6] *not feeling well*
ailing, debilitated, dizzy, dying, exhausted, faint, feeble, frail, ill, indisposed, poorly, prostrate, reduced, sick, sickly, sinking, stricken, unwell, weak; SEE CONCEPT 314

low [adj7] *not loud*
faint, gentle, hushed, muffled, muted, quiet, soft, subdued, whispered; SEE CONCEPT 594

lower [adj] *under, inferior*
bush-league*, curtailed, decreased, diminished, junior, lessened, lesser, low, lower rung, minor, nether, pared down, reduced, secondary, second-class, second-fiddle*, second-string*, smaller, subjacent, subordinate, under; SEE CONCEPTS 586,772

lower [v1] *let down; fall*
bring low, cast down, couch, demit, depress, descend, detrude, droop, drop, ground, let down, make lower, push down, reduce, set down, sink, submerge, take down; SEE CONCEPT 181

lower [v2] *reduce, minimize*
abate, clip, curtail, cut, cut back, cut down, decrease, decry, de-escalate, deflate, demote, depreciate, devaluate, devalue, diminish, downgrade, downsize, lessen, mark down, moderate, pare, prune, roll back, scale down, shave, slash, soften, tone down, undervalue, write off; SEE CONCEPTS 236,240,247

lower [v3] *belittle, disgrace*
abase, bemean, cast down, condescend, debase, degrade, deign, demean, depress, devalue, downgrade, humble, humiliate, stoop; SEE CONCEPTS 7,19

low-key [adj] *subdued*
easygoing, laid-back*, loose, low-pitched, muffled, muted, played down, quiet, relaxed, restrained, sober, softened, soft-sell*, subtle, toned down, understated; SEE CONCEPTS 542,544,548

lowly [adj] *inferior, plain*
average, base, baseborn, cast down, common, commonplace, docile, dutiful, everyday, gentle, humble, ignoble, low, lowborn, mean, meek, menial, mild, modest, mundane, obscure, obsequious, ordinary, plebeian, poor, proletarian, prosaic, retiring, reverential, servile, simple, submissive, subordinate, unassuming, unpretentious, withdrawing; SEE CONCEPTS 404,547,549

loyal [adj] *faithful, dependable*
allegiant, ardent, attached, behind one, believing, coming through, constant, devoted, dutiful, dyed-in-the-wool*, firm, on one's side*, patriotic, resolute, staunch, steadfast, steady, tried-and-true*, true, true-blue*, trustworthy, trusty, unfailing, unswerving, unwavering; SEE CONCEPTS 404,545

loyalty [n] *faithfulness, dependability*
adherence, allegiance, ardor, attachment, bond, conscientiousness, constancy, devotedness, devotion, duty, earnestness, faith, fealty, fidelity, homage, honesty, honor, incorruptibility, integrity, inviolability, obedience, patriotism, probity, reliability, resolution, scrupulousness, sincerity, single-mindedness, singleness, staunchness, steadfastness, subjection, submission, support, tie, troth, trueheartedness, trueness, trustiness, trustworthiness, truth, truthfulness, uprightness, zeal; SEE CONCEPTS 411,645

lubricate [v] *make slippery*
anoint, cream, grease, lard, lube, make, oil, oil the wheels*, slick, smear, smooth, tallow, wax; SEE CONCEPT 202

lucid [adj] *evident, obvious*
apprehensible, clear, clear-cut, comprehendible, comprehensible, crystal clear, distinct, explicit, fathomable, graspable, intelligible, knowable, limpid, luminous, pellucid, plain, translucent,

transparent, transpicuous, unambiguous, unblurred, understandable; SEE CONCEPT 529

lucid [adj2] *brilliant, shining*
beaming, bright, effulgent, gleaming, incandescent, lambent, luminous, lustrous, radiant, refulgent, resplendent; SEE CONCEPT 617

lucid [adj3] *clear, transparent*
clear, crystalline, diaphanous, gauzy, glassy, limpid, obvious, pellucid, pure, sheer, translucent, transpicuous, unblurred; SEE CONCEPTS 606,619

lucid [adj4] *clearheaded, sensible*
all there, compos mentis, cool, got head together*, in right mind, normal, rational, reasonable, right, sane, sober, sound, together; SEE CONCEPTS 402,403

luck [n1] *good fortune*
advantage, big break*, blessing, break*, fluke*, fortunateness, godsend*, good luck, happiness, health, in the cards*, karma*, kismet*, luckiness, lucky break*, occasion, opportunity, profit, prosperity, run of luck*, serendipity, smile*, streak of luck, stroke, success, triumph, victory, weal, wealth, win, windfall; SEE CONCEPT 693

luck [n2] *chance*
accident, break, destiny, fate, fifty-fifty*, fortuity, fortune, hap*, happenstance, hazard, occasion, occurrence, toss-up*, unforeseen event; SEE CONCEPT 679

luckily [adv] *happily*
by chance, favorably, fortuitously, fortunately, opportunely, propitiously, providentially; SEE CONCEPTS 544,572

lucky [adj] *fortunate, opportune*
advantageous, adventitious, all systems go*, auspicious, beneficial, benign, blessed, charmed, coming up roses*, everything going*, favored, felicitous, fortuitous, getting a break*, golden, happy, hit it big*, holding aces*, hopeful, hot*, in the groove*, into something, on a roll*, on a streak, promising, propitious, prosperous, providential, serendipitous, striking it rich*, successful, timely, well; SEE CONCEPTS 537,572

lucrative [adj] *productive, well-paid*
advantageous, cost effective, fatness, fruitful, gainful, good, high-income*, in the black*, money-making, paying, profitable, remunerative, sweet, worthwhile; SEE CONCEPT 334

ludicrous [adj] *absurd, ridiculous*
antic, bizarre, burlesque, comic, comical, crazy, droll, fantastic, farcical, foolish, funny, gelastic, grotesque, incongruous, laughable, nonsensical, odd, outlandish, preposterous, risible, silly, zany; SEE CONCEPT 548

lug [v] *drag something around*
bear, buck, carry, convey, draw, ferry, haul, heave, hump, jerk, lift, lurch, pack, pull, rake, schlepp*, snap, tote, tow, transport, trawl, tug, vellicate, yank; SEE CONCEPT 206

luggage [n] *bag, suitcase*
baggage, carry-on, case, fortnighter, gear, impedimenta, paraphernalia, suit bag, things*, tote bag, trunk, valise; SEE CONCEPTS 446,494

lukewarm [adj1] *slightly heated*
blood-warm, milk-warm, tepid, warm, warmish; SEE CONCEPT 605

lukewarm [adj2] *indifferent, unenthusiastic*
apathetic, chilly, cold, cool, halfhearted, hesitant, indecisive, irresolute, phlegmatic, tepid, uncertain, uncommitted, unconcerned, undecided, un-

interested, unresolved, unresponsive, wishy-washy*; SEE CONCEPTS 403,542

lull [n] *pause, calm*
abeyance, break, breather, breathing spell, calmness, coffee break, comma*, downtime*, hiatus, hush, layoff, letup, pausation, quiescence, quiet, respite, silence, stillness, stop, time-out*, tranquility; SEE CONCEPT 807

lull [v] *calm, ease off*
abate, allay, balm, becalm, cease, chill out*, compose, cool*, cool off*, decrease, die down, diminish, dwindle, ebb, fall, hush, lay back, let up, lullaby, moderate, pacify, put a lid on*, qualify, quell, quiet, quiet down, settle, slacken, softpedal*, soothe, still, stroke, subdue, subside, take it easy*, take the edge*, take the sting out*, temper, tranquilize, wane; SEE CONCEPTS 7,22, 210,698

lumber [v1] *walk heavily, clumsily*
barge, clump, galumph, lump, plod, shamble, shuffle, slog, stump, trudge, trundle, waddle; SEE CONCEPT 151

lumber [v2] *burden*
charge, cumber, encumber, impose upon, lade, land, load, saddle, tax, weigh; SEE CONCEPT 14

lumbering [adj] *clumsy, awkward*
blundering, bovine, bumbling, clodhopping*, clunking, elephantine, gauche, gawky, halting, heavy, heavy-footed, hulking, inept, klutzy*, lead-footed*, lumpish, maladroit, overgrown, ponderous, splay, two left feet*, ungainly, unhandy, unwieldy, wooden; SEE CONCEPTS 406,584

luminary [n] *very important person*
big name*, celeb*, celebrity, dignitary, eminence, leader, lion*, name, notability, notable, personage, personality, somebody*, star, superstar, VIP*, worthy; SEE CONCEPTS 352,423

luminescent [adj] *glowing, shining*
bright, effulgent, fluorescent, luminous, phosphorescent, radiant; SEE CONCEPT 617

luminous [adj1] *bright, glowing*
beaming, brilliant, clear, crystal, effulgent, fulgent, illuminated, incandescent, lambent, lighted, lit, lucent, lucid, luminescent, lustrous, radiant, refulgent, resplendent, shining, translucent, transparent, vivid; SEE CONCEPT 617

luminous [adj2] *obvious, understandable*
apprehensible, bright, brilliant, clear, comprehendible, comprehensible, evident, fathomable, graspable, intelligible, knowable, lucid, perspicacious, perspicuous; SEE CONCEPT 529

lump [n] *clump, mass*
agglomeration, ball, bit, block, bulge, bulk, bump, bunch, cake, chip, chunk, cluster, crumb, dab, gob, group, growth, handful, hunk, knot, knurl, lot, morsel, mountain, much, nugget, part, peck, piece, pile, portion, protrusion, protuberance, scrap, section, solid, spot, swelling, tumescence, tumor, wad, wedge; SEE CONCEPTS 432,470,471

lump [v] *tolerate, withstand*
abide, bear, brook, digest, endure, put up with, stand, stomach, suffer, swallow, take; SEE CONCEPT 23

lunacy [n] *craziness, madness*
aberration, absurdity, alienation, asininity, dementia, derangement, distraction, fatuity, folly, foolhardiness, foolishness, idiocy, imbalance, imbecility, inanity, ineptitude, insanity, mania, psy-

lo
lu

chopathy, psychosis, senselessness, silliness, stupidity; SEE CONCEPTS *410,633*

lunatic [n] *person who is crazy, mad*
crackpot*, crank, cuckoo*, demoniac, flake*, fruitcake*, kook*, lamebrain*, loon*, maniac, neurotic, nut*, paranoid, psycho*, psychopath, psychotic, scatterbrain, schizophrenic, sociopathic; SEE CONCEPTS *412,809*

lunatic [adj] *crazy, mad*
absurd, baked*, balmy*, bananas*, bonkers*, cracked, crazed, daft, demented, deranged, dippy*, flaky*, flipped out*, foolish, freaked out*, fried*, idiotic, insane, irrational, kooky*, loco, maniac, maniacal, nonsensical, nutty*, preposterous, psyched out*, psychotic, schizoid*, screwy*, stupid, unsound, whacko*, zany; SEE CONCEPTS *401,403*

lunge [n] *pounce*
charge, cut, jab, jump, pass, spring, stab, swing, swipe, thrust; SEE CONCEPTS *159,194*

lunge [v] *pounce, dive for*
bound, burst, charge, cut, dash, drive, fall upon, hit, jab, jump, leap, lurch, pitch, plunge, poke, push, set upon, stab, strike, surge, thrust; SEE CONCEPTS *159,194*

lurch [v] *move toward with jerk*
blunder, bumble, careen, dodge, duck, falter, flounder, heave, jerk, lean, list, move to the side, pitch, reel, rock, roll, seesaw, slide, slip, stagger, stumble, sway, swing, teeter, tilt, toss, totter, wallow, weave, wobble, yaw; SEE CONCEPTS *80,150,152,194*

lure [n] *bait*
allurement, ambush, appeal, attraction, bribe, call, camouflage, carrot*, come-on*, con game*, decoy, delusion, draw, enticement, fake, gimmick, hook, illusion, incentive, inducement, inveiglement, invitation, magnet*, mousetrap*, pull, seducement, seduction, siren song*, sitting duck*, snare, sweetener*, temptation, tout, trap, trick; SEE CONCEPTS *32,529*

lure [v] *attract, seduce*
allure, bag, bait, beckon, beguile, bewitch, cajole, captivate, capture, catch, charm, come on*, decoy, drag, draw, enchant, ensnare, entice, fascinate, grab, haul, hit on*, hook, inveigle, invite, lead on, pull, rope, steer, suck in*, sweep of one's feet*, tempt, train, turn on; SEE CONCEPT *11*

lurid [adj] *shocking, gruesome*
ashen, bloody, deep, disgusting, distinct, exaggerated, extreme, fiery, ghastly, gory*, graphic, grim, grisly, hideous, horrible, horrid, horrifying, livid, low-down, macabre, melodramatic, obscene, off-color*, offensive, purple*, racy, raunchy, revolting, rough, salty, sanguine*, savage, sensational, sinister, startling, terrible, terrifying, violent, vivid, yellow*; SEE CONCEPTS *267,537*

lurk [v] *hide; move stealthily*
conceal oneself, creep, crouch, go furtively, gumshoe, lie in wait, prowl, skulk, slide, slink, slip, snake, sneak, snoop, stay hidden, steal, wait; SEE CONCEPTS *151,188*

luscious [adj] *delicious, delectable*
adorable, ambrosial, appetizing, choice, darling, delish, deluxe, distinctive, divine, exquisite, flamboyant, flavorsome, heavenly, honeyed, juicy, lush, luxurious, mellow, mouth-watering, nectarious, opulent, ornate, palatable, palatial, piquant, rare, rich, savory, scrumptious, succulent, sump-

tuous, sweet, toothsome, voluptuous, yummy*; SEE CONCEPTS *574,613*

lush [adj] *profuse and delightful*
abundant, ambrosial, delectable, delicious, deluxe, dense, elaborate, extensive, extravagant, exuberant, flourishing, fresh, grand, green, heavenly, juicy, lavish, luscious, luxuriant, luxurious, opulent, ornate, overgrown, palatial, plush, prodigal, prolific, rank, rich, riotous, ripe, ritzy, scrumptious, sensuous, succulent, sumptuous, teeming, tender, verdant, voluptuous; SEE CONCEPTS *574,589,771*

lust [n] *appetite, passion*
animalism, aphrodisia, appetence, appetition, avidity, carnality, concupiscence, covetousness, craving, cupidity, desire, eroticism, excitement, fervor, greed, hunger; itch, lasciviousness, lechery, lewdness, libido, licentiousness, longing, prurience, pruriency, salaciousness, salacity, sensualism, sensuality, thirst, urge, wantonness, weakness, yen; SEE CONCEPTS *20,709*

lust [v] *desire strongly*
ache, be consumed with desire, be hot for*, covet, crave, hanker, hunger for, itch, long, need, pine, thirst, want, wish, yearn, yen; SEE CONCEPT *20*

luster [n] *gloss, shine*
afterglow, brightness, brilliance, brilliancy, burnish, candescence, dazzle, effulgence, glaze, gleam, glint, glitter, glow, incandescence, iridescence, lambency, luminousness, opalescence, polish, radiance, refulgence, resplendence, sheen, shimmer, sparkle; SEE CONCEPT *620*

lustrous [adj] *glossy, shining*
bright, burnished, dazzling, effulgent, fulgent, glacé, gleaming, glinting, glistening, glorious, glowing, incandescent, lambent, lucent, luminous, polished, radiant, refulgent, shimmering, shiny, sparkling, splendid, waxy; SEE CONCEPT *617*

lusty [adj] *energetic, healthy*
brawny, dynamic, hale, hearty, potent, powerful, red-blooded, robust, rugged, stalwart, stout, strapping, strenuous, strong, sturdy, tough, vigorous, vital; SEE CONCEPTS *314,485,489*

luxuriant [adj] *profuse, plush*
abundant, ample, copious, deluxe, dense, elaborate, excessive, extravagant, exuberant, fancy, fecund, fertile, flamboyant, flourishing, fruitful, lavish, luscious, lush, opulent, overflowing, palatial, plenteous, plentiful, prodigal, productive, profusive, prolific, rampant, rank, rich, riotous, sumptuous, superabundant, teeming, thriving; SEE CONCEPTS *574,771*

luxuriate [adj] *indulge, prosper*
abound, bask, be in clover*, bloom, burgeon, delight, eat up*, enjoy, feast, flourish, grow, increase, live extravagantly, live high on hog*, live in luxury*, live it up*, love, overdo, relish, revel, riot, roll, rollick, take it easy*, thrive, wallow, wanton; SEE CONCEPTS *539,544,589*

luxurious [adj] *affluent, indulgent*
comfortable, costly, deluxe, easy, elaborate, epicurean, expensive, extravagant, fancy, fit for a king/queen*, gorgeous, grand, grandiose, gratifying, hedonistic, immoderate, imposing, impressive, in the lap of luxury, lavish, luscious, lush, magnificent, majestic, opulent, ostentatious, palatial, pampered, pleasurable, pleasure-loving, plush, plushy, posh, pretentious, rich, ritzy*, self-indulgent, sensual, sensuous, splendid, stately,

sumptuous, sybaritic, upscale, voluptuous, well-appointed; SEE CONCEPTS 544,574,589

luxury [n] *great pleasure, indulgence*
affluence, bliss, comfort, delight, enjoyment, exorbitance, extravagance, frill, gratification, hedonism, high living, immoderation, intemperance, leisure, luxuriousness, opulence, rarity, richness, satisfaction, splendor, sumptuousness, treat, well-being; SEE CONCEPTS 337,388,712

lying [adj] *dishonest*
committing perjury, deceitful, deceptive, delusive, delusory, dissembling, dissimulating, double-crossing*, double-dealing*, equivocating, false, falsifying, fibbing, guileful, inventing, mendacious, misleading, misrepresenting, misstating, perfidious, prevaricating, shifty, treacherous, tricky, two-faced*, two-timing*, unreliable, untruthful, wrong; SEE CONCEPT 267

M

macabre [adj] *eerie; deathlike*
cadaverous, deathly, dreadful, frightening, frightful, ghastly, ghostly, ghoulish, grim, grisly, gruesome, hideous, horrible, horrid, lurid, morbid, offensive, scary, spookish, spooky, terrible, unearthly, weird; SEE CONCEPTS 537,547

machinate [v] *maneuver, plot*
cogitate, collude, come up with, connive, conspire, contrive, design, devise, engineer, finagle, hatch, intrigue, invent, plan, play games*, promote, pull strings*, scheme, trump up*, wangle; SEE CONCEPT 36

machination [n] *maneuver, plot*
artifice, cabal, conspiracy, design, device, dirty work*, dodge*, intrigue, monkey business*, on the make*, ploy, practice, ruse, scheme, sellout, skullduggery*, song and dance*, stratagem, trick; SEE CONCEPT 660

machine [n1] *device that performs a task*
apparatus, appliance, automaton, automobile, computer, contraption, contrivance, engine, gadget, implement, instrument, mechanism, motor, robot, thingamabob*, tool, vehicle, widget*; SEE CONCEPT 463

machine [n2] *well-run political organization*
agency, lineup, machinery, movement, party, ring, setup, structure, system; SEE CONCEPT 301

machine [n3] *person who acts automatically*
agent, automaton, clone, drudge, grind, laborer, mechanical, puppet, robot, zombie*; SEE CONCEPTS 348,423

machinery [n] *devices performing work*
accouterment, agency, agent, apparatus, appliance, channel, contraption, contrivance, engine, equipment, gadget, gear, habiliments, implement, instrument, materiel, means, mechanism, medium, method, motor, organ, outfit, paraphernalia, shifts, structure, system, tackle, tool, utensil, vehicle, works; SEE CONCEPTS 463,770

mad [adj1] *crazy, insane*
aberrant, absurd, bananas*, batty, crazed, cuckoo*, daft, delirious, demented, deranged, distracted, fantastic, foolhardy, foolish, frantic, frenetic, frenzied, illogical, imprudent, invalid, irrational, kooky*, loony*, ludicrous, lunatic, mental, non compos mentis, nonsensical, nutty*, off one's rocker*, of unsound mind, out of one's mind*, preposterous, psychotic, rabid, raving, senseless, unbalanced, unhinged, unreasonable, unsafe, unsound, unstable, wacky*; SEE CONCEPTS 403,529

mad [adj2] *angry*
abandoned, agitated, berserk, distracted, distraught, enraged, exasperated, excited, frantic, frenetic, fuming, furious, incensed, infuriated, irritated, livid, provoked, raging, resentful, seeing red*, uncontrolled, very upset, wild, wrathful; SEE CONCEPT 403

mad [adj3] *enthusiastic; in love*
ardent, avid, crazy, daft, devoted, enamoured, enthused, fanatical, fond, hooked*, impassioned, infatuated, keen, nuts*, wild, zealous; SEE CONCEPTS 32,403

madcap [adj] *crazy, impulsive*
brash, foolhardy, foolish, frivolous, harebrained*, heedless, hotheaded, ill-advised, imprudent, incautious, inconsiderate, lively, rash, reckless, stupid, thoughtless, wild; SEE CONCEPT 548

madden [v] *make angry*
anger, annoy, bother, craze, derange, distract, drive crazy, drive insane, drive out of mind*, drive to distraction*, enrage, exasperate, frenzy, incense, inflame, infuriate, ire, irritate, make see red*, pester, possess, provoke, shatter, steam up*, umbrage, unbalance, unhinge*, upset, vex; SEE CONCEPTS 7,19

made-up [adj] *invented mentally*
fabricated, false, fictional, imaginary, make-believe, mythical, prepared, specious, trumped-up, unreal, untrue; SEE CONCEPT 582

madhouse [n] *place where mentally ill live; place full of commotion*
asylum, bedlam, chaos, insane asylum, loony bin*, mental hospital, mental institution, pandemonium, psychiatric hospital, sanitarium, turmoil, uproar; SEE CONCEPTS 312,449,516,674

madly [adv] *wildly, fiercely*
absurdly, crazily, deliriously, dementedly, desperately, devotedly, distractedly, energetically, exceedingly, excessively, excitedly, extremely, foolishly, frantically, frenziedly, furiously, hard, hastily, hurriedly, hysterically, insanely, intensely, irrationally, like mad, ludicrously, nonsensically, passionately, psychotically, quickly, rabidly, rapidly, rashly, recklessly, senselessly, something fierce, speedily, stormily, to distraction, tumultously/tumultuously, turbulently, unreasonably, violently; SEE CONCEPTS 537,540,544

mad person [n] *person who is considered mentally ill*
bedlamite, crazy person, demented, deranged, idiot, imbecile, loon, lunatic, maniac, mental case*, patient, psycho*, psychopath, psychotic, raver*, schizophrenic, sociopath; SEE CONCEPTS 412,423

magazine [n1] *periodic publication*
annual, bimonthly, biweekly, booklet, broadside, brochure, circular, daily, digest, gazette, glossy, joint, journal, manual, monthly, newsletter, newspaper, organ, pamphlet, paper, periodical, pulp*, quarterly, rag*, review, semiweekly, sheet*, slick, throwaway*, weekly; SEE CONCEPT 280

magazine [n2] *arsenal of weapons*
ammunition dump, armory, cache, depository, de-

pot, munitions dump, repertory, repository, store, storehouse, warehouse; SEE CONCEPTS 321,500

magic [n] *supernatural power; appearance of impossible feats by tricks*
abracadabra*, alchemy, allurement, astrology, augury, bewitchment, black art, conjuring, conjury, devilry, diabolism, divination, enchantment, exorcism, fascination, foreboding, fortune-telling, hocus-pocus*, horoscopy, illusion, incantation, legerdemain, magnetism, necromancy, occultism, power, prediction, presage, prestidigitation, prophecy, rune, sleight of hand, soothsaying, sorcery, sortilege, spell, superstition, taboo, thaumaturgy, trickery, voodoo, voodooism, witchcraft, wizardry; SEE CONCEPTS 370,689

magic/magical [adj] *bewitching, charming*
bewitched, charismatic, clairvoyant, conjuring, demoniac, diabolic, eerie, enchanted, enchanting, ensorcelled, entranced, entrancing, extraordinary, fascinating, fiendish, ghostly, haunted, imaginary, magnetic, marvelous, miraculous, mysterious, mystic, mythical, necromantic, occult, otherworldly, parapsychological, runic, sorcerous, spectral, spellbinding, spellbound, spiritualistic, spooky, telekinetic, thaumaturgic, tranced, uncanny, unusual, weird, witching, witchlike, wizardly, wonderful; SEE CONCEPTS 537,548,582

magician [n] *person who performs supernatural feats or tricks*
archimage, charmer, conjurer, diabolist, diviner, enchanter, enchantress, exorciser, exorcist, fortune-teller, genie, genius, illusionist, marvel, medicine person, medium, miracle worker, necromancer, prophet, satanist, seer, shaman, siren, soothsayer, sorcerer, spellbinder, thaumaturge, theurgist, trickster, virtuoso, voodoo, warlock, witch, witch doctor, wizard; SEE CONCEPTS 352,361

magnanimous [adj] *giving and kind*
all heart, altruistic, beneficent, benevolent, big, bighearted, bountiful, charitable, considerate, forgiving, free, generous, great, greathearted, handsome, has heart in right place*, high-minded, kindly, knightly, liberal, lofty, loose, munificent, noble, openhanded, Santa Claus*, selfless, soft*, soft-touch*, ungrudging, unselfish, unstinting; SEE CONCEPTS 404,542

magnate [n] *important person, usually in business*
aristocrat, bigwig*, businessperson, capitalist, captain of industry, chief, figure, financier, industrialist, leader, lion*, merchant, mogul, name, noble, notable, peer, personage, plutocrat, tycoon, VIP*; SEE CONCEPT 347

magnetic [adj] *drawing, attractive*
alluring, appealing, arresting, bewitching, captivating, charismatic, charming, enchanting, entrancing, fascinating, hypnotic, inviting, irresistible, mesmerizing, pulling, seductive; SEE CONCEPTS 404,537

magnetism [n] *charm, attractiveness*
allure, appeal, attraction, captivatingness, charisma, draw, drawing power, enchantment, fascination, glamour, hypnotism, influence, lure, magic, mesmerism, power, pull, seductiveness, spell, witchcraft, witchery; SEE CONCEPTS 411,676

magnificent [adj] *glorious, wonderful*
arresting, august, brilliant, chivalric, commanding, elegant, elevated, exalted, excellent, fine, glittering, gorgeous, grand, grandiose, high-

minded, imperial, imposing, impressive, lavish, lofty, luxurious, magnanimous, magnific, majestic, noble, opulent, outstanding, palatial, plush, pompous, posh, proud, radiant, regal, resplendent, rich, royal, smashing, splendid, standout, stately, striking, sublime, sumptuous, superb, superior, superlative, swanky, towering, transcendent; SEE CONCEPTS 485,572

magnify [v1] *enlarge, intensify*
aggrandize, aggravate, amplify, augment, bless, blow up, boost, build up, deepen, dignify, dilate, distend, enhance, ennoble, eulogize, exalt, expand, extend, glorify, heighten, hike, hike up, increase, inflate, intensate, jack up, jump up, mount, multiply, pad, pyramid, redouble, rise, rouse, run up, step up, sweeten, swell; SEE CONCEPTS 236,244,245

magnify [v2] *exaggerate, blow out of proportion*
aggravate, blow up*, boost, color, dramatize, embellish, embroider, enhance, fudge*, inflate, make mountain of molehill*, overcharge, overdo, overdraw, overemphasize, overestimate, overplay, overrate, overstate, overstress, pad*, puff up*, pyramid; SEE CONCEPTS 49,69,266

magnitude [n1] *importance*
consequence, degree, eminence, grandeur, greatness, import, mark, moment, momentousness, note, pith, significance, signification, weight, weightiness; SEE CONCEPT 668

magnitude [n2] *size*
admeasurement, amount, amplitude, bigness, breadth, bulk, capacity, compass, dimension, dimensions, enormity, enormousness, expanse, extent, greatness, hugeness, immensity, intensity, largeness, mass, measure, measurement, proportion, proportions, quantity, range, reach, sizableness, space, strength, tremendousness, vastness, volume; SEE CONCEPT 730

maiden [adj] *earliest*
beginning, first, fresh, inaugural, initial, initiatory, intact, introductory, new, original, pioneer, primary, prime, unbroached, untapped, untried, unused; SEE CONCEPTS 548,585

mail [n] *written correspondence; system for sending correspondence*
air mail, communication, junk mail, letter, package, parcel, post, postal service, postcard, post office; SEE CONCEPTS 271,770

mail [v] *send through the postal system*
dispatch, drop, express, forward, post, send by mail, transmit; SEE CONCEPT 217

maim [v] *cripple, put out of action*
batter, blemish, break, castrate, crush, damage, deface, disable, disfigure, dismember, disqualify, gimp*, hack, hamstring*, harm, hog-tie*, hurt, impair, incapacitate, injure, lame, mangle, mar, massacre, maul, mayhem, mutilate, spoil, truncate, warp, wound; SEE CONCEPT 246

main [n] *pipe for system*
cable, channel, conduit, duct, line, trough, trunk; SEE CONCEPT 494

main [adj1] *principal, predominant*
capital, cardinal, central, chief, controlling, critical, crucial, essential, foremost, fundamental, head, leading, major, necessary, outstanding, paramount, particular, preeminent, premier, prevailing, primary, prime, special, star, stellar, supreme, vital; SEE CONCEPTS 546,567,829

main [adj2] *absolute, utter*
brute, direct, downright, entire, mere, only, pure,

sheer, simple, undisguised, utmost; SEE CONCEPT 535

mainly [adv] *for the most part*
above all, chiefly, essentially, first and foremost, generally, in general, in the main, largely, mostly, most of all, on the whole, overall, predominantly, primarily, principally, substantially, to the greatest extent, usually; SEE CONCEPTS 530,544,772

mainstay [n] *chief support*
anchor, backbone, brace, bulwark, buttress, crutch*, good right arm*, linchpin*, maintainer, pillar, prop, right-hand person*, sinew, staff, standby, stay, strength, supporter, sustainer, upholder; SEE CONCEPTS 646,712

maintain [v1] *care for, keep up*
advance, carry on, conserve, continue, control, cultivate, finance, go on with, guard, keep, keep going, look after, manage, nurture, perpetuate, persevere, preserve, prolong, protect, provide, renew, repair, retain, save, supply, support, sustain, take care of, uphold; SEE CONCEPTS 134,140

maintain [v2] *assert, claim; argue for*
advocate, affirm, allege, asseverate, attest, aver, avow, back, champion, contend, correct, declare, defend, emphasize, fight for, hold, insist, justify, persist, plead for, profess, protest, rectify, report, right, say, stand by, state, stress, uphold, vindicate; SEE CONCEPTS 46,49,68

maintenance [n] *perpetuation, support; sustenance*
aliment, alimentation, alimony, allowance, bacon*, bread, bread and butter*, care, carrying, conservation, continuance, continuation, food, keep, keeping, livelihood, living, nurture, preservation, prolongation, provision, repairs, resources, retainment, salt*, subsistence, supply, sustaining, sustainment, sustention, upkeep, wherewithal; SEE CONCEPTS 134,340,457,712

majestic [adj] *impressive, splendid*
august, awesome, ceremonious, cool, courtly, dignified, elevated, exalted, fab*, grand, grandiose, imperial, imposing, lofty, magnific, magnificent, marvelous, mind-blowing*, monumental, noble, out of this world*, pompous, regal, royal, smashing, sovereign, stately, stunning, sublime, sumptuous, superb; SEE CONCEPTS 567,572,574

major [adj1] *bigger*
above, better, big, chief, considerable, dominant, elder, exceeding, extensive, extreme, greater, hefty, higher, large, larger, large-scale, leading, main, most, oversized, primary, senior, sizable, superior, supreme, ultra, upper, uppermost; SEE CONCEPTS 574,773

major [adj2] *important*
big, chief, critical, crucial, dangerous, grave, great, grievous, heavyweight, influential, life and death*, main, major-league, meaningful, notable, outstanding, overshadowing, preeminent, principal, radical, serious, significant, star, stellar, top, vital, weighty; SEE CONCEPT 568

majority [n1] *plurality, most*
best part*, bulk, greater number, greater part, larger part, lion's share*, mass, max*, more, more than half*, preponderance, superiority; SEE CONCEPTS 766,809,835

majority [n2] *adulthood*
age of consent, drinking age, estate, full age, legal maturity, manhood, maturity, prime, prime of life*, ripe age*, seniority, voting age, womanhood; SEE CONCEPTS 715,817

make [v1] *create, build*
accomplish, adjust, arrange, assemble, beget, brew, bring about, cause, compose, conceive, constitute, construct, cook, cook up*, dash off*, draw on, dream up, effect, engender, fabricate, fashion, forge, form, frame, generate, get ready, give rise to, hatch, initiate, invent, knock off*, lead to, manufacture, mold, occasion, originate, parent, prepare, procreate, produce, put together, secure, shape, spawn, synthesize, tear off, throw together*, whip, whip out*; SEE CONCEPTS 168,173,205,221

make [v2] *induce, compel*
bring about, cause, coerce, concuss, constrain, dragoon, drive, effect, force, horn in*, impel, impress, initiate, interfere, meddle, oblige, press, pressurize, prevail upon, require, secure, shotgun, start, tamper; SEE CONCEPTS 14,221

make [v3] *designate, appoint*
advance, assign, constitute, create, delegate, elect, finger, install, invest, name, nominate, ordain, proffer, select, tap, tender; SEE CONCEPTS 50,88

make [v4] *enact, execute*
act, carry on, carry out, carry through, conduct, declare, decree, do, draft, draw up, effect, engage in, establish, fix, form, formulate, frame, legislate, pass, perform, practice, prepare, prosecute, wage; SEE CONCEPTS 91,100,242

make [v5] *add up to; constitute*
amount to, come to, compose, compound, comprise, construct, embody, equal, fabricate, form, make up, mix, organize, put together, represent, structure, synthesize, texture; SEE CONCEPTS 664,667

make [v6] *estimate, infer*
calculate, collect, conclude, deduce, deduct, derive, dope out, draw, figure, gather, gauge, judge, reckon, suppose, think; SEE CONCEPTS 15,37

make [v7] *earn, acquire*
bring home bacon*, bring in, clean up*, clear, gain, get, harvest, hustle, net, obtain, pull, pull down*, rate, realize, reap, receive, secure, sock*, take in; SEE CONCEPTS 120,124,351

make [v8] *arrive, aim at*
advance, arrive at, arrive in time, attain, bear, break for, catch, get to, go, head, light to, meet, move, proceed, progress, reach, set out, strike out, take off; SEE CONCEPTS 159,224

make believe [v] *pretend, dream*
act as if, act as though, counterfeit, enact, fantasize, feign, fool, imagine, play, playact*, simulate; SEE CONCEPTS 12,59

make-believe [n] *unreality*
charade, disguise, dissimulation, dream, fairy tale, fakery, fantasy, imagination, pageant, playacting, pretense, pretension, pretentiousness, sham; SEE CONCEPTS 689,725

make-believe [adj] *imagined, unreal*
acted, dream, false, fantasized, fantasy, fictional, fraudulent, imaginary, made-up, mock, pretend, pretended, sham, simulated; SEE CONCEPTS 529,582

make off [v] *flee, run away*
abscond, bolt*, clear, cut and run, decamp, depart, escape, fly*, go, leave, make away, quit, retire, run, run for it, run off, scamper, scoot, skedaddle*, skip*, withdraw; SEE CONCEPTS 102,150,195

ma
ma

make out [v1] *see, recognize*
detect, discern, discover, distinguish, espy, notice, observe, perceive, remark; SEE CONCEPT *626*

make out [v2] *understand*
accept, catch, collect, compass, comprehend, conclude, decipher, deduce, deduct, derive, dig,
fathom, follow, gather, grasp, infer, judge, perceive, realize, recognize, see, take in, work out;
SEE CONCEPTS *15,18*

make out [v3] *get by, succeed*
accomplish, achieve, do, do well enough, do with,
endure, fare, flourish, get along, get on, manage,
muddle through, prosper, score, thrive; SEE CON-
CEPTS *23,91,140*

makeshift [n] *temporary help*
expediency, expedient, last resort, pis aller, recourse, refuge, replacement, resort, resource,
shift, stopgap, substitute; SEE CONCEPTS *658,712*

makeshift [adj] *temporary*
alternative, Band-Aid*, expedient, hit-or-miss*,
make-do*, provisional, quick-and-dirty*, slapdash*, stopgap, substitute, temp, throwaway*;
SEE CONCEPTS *551,560*

makeup [n1] *cosmetics*
blush, face*, foundation, greasepaint, lipstick,
maquillage, paint, pancake, powder*; SEE CON-
CEPT *446*

makeup [n2] *structure, composition*
architecture, arrangement, assembly, configuration, constitution, construction, content, contents,
design, form, format, formation, layout, order,
ordering, organization, plan, scheme, setup,
shape, spread, style; SEE CONCEPT *757*

makeup [n3] *person's character*
build, cast, complexion, constitution, disposition,
fiber, figure, frame of mind, grain, humor, individualism, individuality, make, mold, nature, personality, stamp, stripe, temper, temperament,
vein; SEE CONCEPT *411*

make up [v1] *create*
ad-lib*, blend, coin, combine, compose, compound, concoct, construct, contrive, cook up*, devise, dream up, fabricate, fake it, fashion, fix,
formulate, frame, fuse, hatch, improv*, improvise, invent, join, knock off, make, meld, merge,
mingle, mix, originate, play by ear*, prepare, pretend, put together, ready, trump up, whip up*,
wing it*, write; SEE CONCEPTS *173,202*

make up [v2] *comprise, constitute*
complete, compose, consist, fill, form, furnish,
include, make, meet, provide, supply; SEE CON-
CEPT *643*

make up [v3] *compensate, reconcile*
accommodate, atone, balance, bury the hatchet*,
come to terms, compose, conciliate, counterbalance, counterpoise, countervail, forgive and forget, make amends, make peace, mend, offset,
outweigh, pacify, recompense, redeem, redress,
requite, set off, settle, shake hands; SEE CON-
CEPTS *126,384*

maladroit [adj1] *awkward, clumsy*
all thumbs*, blundering, bumbling, bungling,
clunky, floundering, gauche, halting, heavy-
handed, inept, inexpert, klutzy*, lumbering,
stumbling, two left feet*, ungraceful, unhandy,
unskillful; SEE CONCEPTS *401,584*

maladroit [adj2] *tactless*
brash, gauche, impolitic, inconsiderate, inelegant,
insensitive, thoughtless, undiplomatic, untactful,
untoward; SEE CONCEPT *401*

malaise [n] *depression, sickness*
angst, anxiety, debility, decrepitude, despair, discomfort, disquiet, distress, doldrums, enervation,
feebleness, illness, infirmity, infirmness, lassitude, melancholy, pain, sickliness, unease, uneasiness, unhealthiness, weakness; SEE CONCEPTS
316,410

male [n] *man*
boy, brother, father, fellow, gent*, gentleman,
grandfather, guy, he, husband, Mr., sir, son; SEE
CONCEPT *419*

male [adj] *masculine*
macho*, manful, manlike, manly, paternal, potent, virile; SEE CONCEPTS *371,408*

malediction [n] *curse*
anathema, commination, curse word, cuss, cuss
word, damn, damnation, damning, darn, denunciation, dirty name*, dirty word*, execration, expletive, four-letter word*, imprecation, jinx, no-
no*, oath, swear word, whammy*; SEE CONCEPT
278

malevolent [adj] *hateful*
bad-natured, baleful, catty*, despiteful, dirty,
evil, evil-minded, hellish, hostile, lousy, malicious, malign, malignant, murder, murderous,
pernicious, poison, rancorous, rough, sinister,
spiteful, tough, vengeful, vicious, vindictive,
waspish, wicked; SEE CONCEPTS *401,542*

malformed [adj] *distorted*
abnormal, contorted, crooked, deformed, grotesque, irregular, misshapen, twisted, warped;
SEE CONCEPT *486*

malfunction [n] *breakdown, failure*
bug*, defect, fault, flaw, glitch*, gremlin*, impairment, slip; SEE CONCEPTS *658,674*

malice [n] *hate, vengefulness*
acerbity, animosity, animus, antipathy, bad blood,
bane, bile, bitterness, despite, despitefulness, dirt,
dislike, down, enmity, evil, grudge, hatefulness,
hatred, hostility, ill will, implacability, malevolence, maliciousness, malignance, malignity,
meanness, mordacity, poison, rancor, repugnance, resentment, spite, spitefulness, spleen, umbrage, venom, viciousness, vindictiveness; SEE
CONCEPT *29*

malicious [adj] *hateful*
awful, bad-natured, baleful, beastly, bitter, catty*, cussed, deleterious, despiteful, detrimental,
envious, evil, evil-minded, green*, green-eyed*,
gross*, ill-disposed, injurious, jealous, low, malevolent, malign, malignant, mean, mischievous,
nasty, noxious, ornery, pernicious, petty, poisonous, rancorous, resentful, spiteful, uncool*,
vengeful, venomous, vicious, virulent, wicked;
SEE CONCEPTS *267,401,542*

malign [adj] *hurtful, injurious*
antagonistic, antipathetic, bad, baleful, baneful,
deleterious, despiteful, destructive, detrimental,
evil, harmful, hateful, hostile, inimical, malefic,
maleficent, malevolent, malignant, noxious, pernicious, rancorous, sinister, spiteful, vicious,
wicked; SEE CONCEPTS *267,537,542*

malign [v] *slander, defame*
abuse, accuse, asperse, backbite*, bad-mouth*,
befoul, besmirch, bespatter, blacken, calumniate,
cast aspersion, curse, decry, defile, denigrate, depreciate, derogate, detract, dirty*, disparage,
harm, injure, insult, misrepresent, mudsling, opprobriate, pollute, rap, revile, roast*, run down*,
scandalize, slur, smear, soil, spatter*, speak ill of,

stain, sully, taint, take a swipe at*, tarnish, tear down, traduce, vilify, villainize, vituperate; SEE CONCEPTS *44,52,54,63*

malignant [*adj*] *diseased*
cancerous, deadly, destructive, fatal, internecine, lethal, mortal, pestilential, poisonous; SEE CONCEPT *314*

mall [*n*] *commercial complex with many individual retail stores*
commercial center, market, mart, mini-mart, plaza, shopping center, shopping mall; SEE CONCEPTS *325,439,449*

malleable [*adj*] *pliable*
adaptable, compliant, ductile, flexible, governable, go-with-the-flow*, impressionable, manageable, moldable, plastic, pliant, putty in hands*, rolls with punches*, soft, submissive, supple, tractable, tractile, transformable, workable, yielding; SEE CONCEPTS *403,485*

malodorous [*adj*] *foul-smelling*
bad, decayed, decomposed, fetid, foul, frowzy, funky*, fusty, gamy*, high*, infested, lousy, mephitic, musty, nasty, nauseating, noisome, noxious, off*, offensive, pestilential, poisonous, polluted, putrid, rancid, rank, reeking, rotten, smelly, stale, stenchful, stinking, strong, tainted, vile; SEE CONCEPT *598*

malpractice [*n*] *abuse, misconduct*
carelessness, dereliction, malefaction, misbehavior, misdeed, mismanagement, negligence, offense, transgression, violation; SEE CONCEPTS *101,156,310,324*

mammoth [*adj*] *huge*
behemothic, colossal, elephantine, enormous, gargantuan, giant, gigantic, high, immense, jumbo, large, leviathan, long, massive, mighty, monstrous, monumental, mountainous, prodigious, stupendous, titanic, vast; SEE CONCEPT *773*

man [*n2*] *male human*
beau, boyfriend, brother, father, fellow, gentleman, grandfather, guy, he, husband, Mr., nephew, papa, sir, son, spouse, swain*, uncle; SEE CONCEPT *419*

manage [*v1*] *be in charge, control*
administer, advocate, boss, call the shots*, call upon, captain, care for, carry on, command, concert, conduct, counsel, designate, direct, disburse, dominate, engage in, engineer, execute, govern, guide, handle, head, hold down*, influence, instruct, maintain, manipulate, minister, officiate, operate, oversee, pilot, ply, preside, regulate, request, rule, run, run the show, steer, superintend, supervise, take care of, take over, take the helm*, train, use, watch, watch over, wield; SEE CONCEPTS *94,117*

manage [*v2*] *accomplish*
achieve, arrange, bring about, bring off, carry out, con*, contrive, cook*, cope with, deal with, doctor*, effect, engineer, execute, finagle, fix, jockey*, plant*, play games*, pull strings*, push around, put one over*, rig*, scam*, succeed, swing, upstage, wangle, work; SEE CONCEPTS *91,706*

manage [*v3*] *survive, get by*
bear up, carry on, cope, endure, fare, get along*, get on*, make do*, make out*, muddle, scrape by*, shift, stagger; SEE CONCEPTS *23,407*

management [*n1*] *persons running an organization*
administration, authority, board, bosses, brass, di-

rectorate, directors, employers, execs*, executive, executives, executive suite, front office*, head, mainframe*, management, micro management*, person upstairs*, top brass*, upstairs*; SEE CONCEPT *325*

management [*n2*] *running an organization*
administration, care, charge, command, conduct, control, direction, governance, government, guidance, handling, intendance, manipulation, operation, oversight, rule, superintendence, superintendency, supervision; SEE CONCEPTS *117,324*

manager [*n*] *person who runs organization*
administrator, boss, comptroller, conductor, controller, director, exec*, executive, governor, handler, head, head person, officer, official, organizer, overseer, producer, proprietor, slave-driver*, straw boss*, superintendent, supervisor, zookeeper*; SEE CONCEPT *347*

mandate [*n*] *authority, order*
authorization, behest, bidding, blank check*, carte blanche*, charge, command, commission, decree, dictate, directive, edict, fiat, go-ahead*, green light*, imperative, injunction, instruction, okay*, precept, sanction, warrant, word*; SEE CONCEPTS *318,685*

mandatory [*adj*] *required, necessary*
binding, commanding, compelling, compulsatory, compulsory, de rigueur, essential, forced, imperative, imperious, indispensable, involuntary, irremissible, needful, obligatory, requisite; SEE CONCEPT *546*

maneuver [*n1*] *move, tactic*
action, angle, artifice, contrivance, curveball, demarche, device, dodge, fancy footwork*, feint, finesse, gambit, game, gimmick, intrigue, jig*, machination, manipulation, measure, movement, plan, play, plot, ploy, procedure, proceeding, ruse, scheme, shenanigans*, shuffle*, step, stratagem, stunt, subterfuge, trick; SEE CONCEPTS *6,660*

maneuver [*n2*] *military practice, operation*
battle, deployment, drill, evolution, exercise, measure, movement, parade, plan, procedure, proceeding, stratagem, tactics, war games; SEE CONCEPT *320*

maneuver [*v1*] *plan, scheme*
angle, beguile, cheat, come up with, con*, conspire, contrive, cook, design, devise, doctor, engineer, exploit, fence, finagle, finesse, go around, intrigue, jockey, leave holding the bag*, machinate, manage, manipulate, move, navigate, operate, play, play games*, plot, proceed, pull strings*, push around, put one over*, rig, scam, sham, shift, trick, upstage, wangle, work; SEE CONCEPTS *36,59*

maneuver [*v2*] *direct physically*
deploy, dispense, drive, exercise, guide, handle, manipulate, move, navigate, negotiate, pilot, ply, steer, swing, wield; SEE CONCEPTS *187,225*

mangle [*v*] *mutilate, deform*
batter, break, bruise, butcher, carve, contort, crush, cut, damage, deface, destroy, disfigure, distort, flay, hack, hash, impair, injure, lacerate, maim, mar, maul, rend, ruin, separate, slash, slay, slice, slit, spoil, tear, wound, wreck; SEE CONCEPTS *176,246,252*

mangy [*adj*] *scruffy*
decrepit, dirty, impoverished, indigent, mean,

moth-eaten*, poor, ragtag*, shabby, shoddy, sick, sleazy*, squalid, tattered; SEE CONCEPTS *485,621*

manhood/womanhood [*n*] *physical maturity and strength of adult male or female*
adulthood, coming of age*, fecundity, femininity, fertility, manfulness, manliness, masculinity, mettle, potency, virility, womanliness, womanness; SEE CONCEPTS *633,715*

mania [*n*] *fixation, madness*
aberration, ax to grind*, bee*, bee in bonnet*, bug*, bug in ear*, compulsion, craving, craze, craziness, delirium, dementia, derangement, desire, disorder, enthusiasm, fad, fancy, fascination, fetish, fixed idea, frenzy, furor, grabber*, hangup*, idée fixe, infatuation, insanity, lunacy, monomania, obsession, on the brain*, partiality, passion, preoccupation, rage, thing, tiger*, tiger by the tail*; SEE CONCEPTS *20,32,410,529*

maniac [*n*] *person who is crazy, overenthusiastic*
bedlamite, bigot, crackpot*, enthusiast, fan, fanatic, fiend, flake*, freak, fruitcake*, kook*, loon, loony*, lunatic, madperson, nut*, nutcase*, psycho*, psychopath, schizoid*, screwball*, Section 8*, zealot; SEE CONCEPT *412*

manic/maniacal [*adj*] *overexcited, crazy*
berserk, crazed, demented, deranged, excited, flipped*, flipped out*, freaked out*, freaky*, frenzied, high*, insane, lunatic, mad, nutty*, psychotic, rabid, raving, turned-out, unbalanced, up*, wild; SEE CONCEPT *403*

manifest [*adj*] *clear, obvious*
apparent, big as life*, bold, clear-cut*, conspicuous, crystal clear*, disclosed, distinct, divulged, evidenced, evident, evinced, glaring, noticeable, open, palpable, patent, plain, prominent, revealed, shown, straightforward, told, unambiguous, unmistakable, visible; SEE CONCEPTS *529,576*

manifest [*v*] *exhibit, make plain*
confirm, declare, demonstrate, display, embody, establish, evidence, evince, expose, express, exteriorize, externalize, flash, illustrate, incarnate, let it all hang out*, mark, materialize, objectify, ostend, parade, personalize, personify, personize, proclaim, prove, reveal, set forth, show, show and tell*, showcase, signify, sport, strut, substantiate, suggest, utter, vent, voice, wave around*; SEE CONCEPTS *118,261*

manifestation [*n*] *exhibition, proof*
appearance, demonstration, disclosure, display, explanation, exposure, expression, indication, instance, mark, materialization, meaning, phenomenon, revelation, show, sign, symptom, token; SEE CONCEPTS *642,672*

manifold [*adj*] *abundant, many*
assorted, complex, copious, different, diverse, diversified, diversiform, multifarious, multifold, multiform, multiple, multiplied, multitudinous, multivarious, numerous, sundry, varied, various; SEE CONCEPTS *564,762,781*

manipulate [*v1*] *maneuver, handle physically*
employ, feel, finger*, form, manage, mold, operate, ply, shape, swing, thumb*, use, wield, work; SEE CONCEPTS *225,612*

manipulate [*v2*] *change to suit one's desire*
beguile, conduct, control, direct, engineer, exploit, finagle, finesse, guide, handle, influence, jockey, machinate, maneuver, massage, mold, negotiate, play, play games*, pull strings*, pull wires*, push around, shape, steer, upstage, use; SEE CONCEPTS *14,234*

manner [*n1*] *person's behavior, conduct*
address, affectation, affectedness, air, appearance, aspect, bearing, comportment, demeanor, deportment, idiosyncrasy, look, mannerism, mien, peculiarity, presence, style, tone, turn, way; SEE CONCEPTS *411,633,644*

manner [*n2*] *method, approach*
consuetude, custom, fashion, form, genre, habit, habitude, line, means, mode, modus, practice, procedure, process, routine, style, system, tack, technique, tenor, tone, trick, usage, use, vein, way, wise, wont; SEE CONCEPTS *6,660*

manner [*n3*] *class, category*
brand, breed, form, kind, nature, sort, type, variety; SEE CONCEPT *378*

mannered [*adj*] *affected, put-on*
airish*, apish*, artificial, artsy, campy*, chichi*, conscious, gone Hollywood*, highfaluting*, posed, pretentious, self-conscious, stilted, stuck up*, unnatural; SEE CONCEPT *401*

mannerism [*n*] *peculiarity of how someone behaves, acts*
affectation, air, characteristic, eccentricity, foible, habit, idiosyncrasy, oddness, pose, pretension, queerness, quirk, singularity, trait, trick; SEE CONCEPT *644*

mannerly [*adj*] *polite, well-behaved*
charming, civil, civilized, considerate, courteous, decorous, genteel, gracious, polished, refined, respectful, well-bred, well-mannered; SEE CONCEPT *401*

manners [*n*] *polite, refined social behavior*
amenities, bearing, behavior, breeding, carriage, ceremony, civilities, comportment, conduct, courtesy, culture, decorum, demeanor, deportment, dignity, elegance, etiquette, formalities, good breeding, good form, mien, mores, polish, politeness, politesse, propriety, protocol, p's and q's*, refinement, social graces, sophistication, taste, urbanity; SEE CONCEPT *633*

mansion [*n*] *very large house*
abode, building, castle, chateau, dwelling, estate, habitation, hall, home, manor, palace, residence, seat, villa; SEE CONCEPTS *439,516*

manslaughter [*n*] *killing without malicious forethought*
crime, foul play*, hit*, homicide, killing, murder; SEE CONCEPT *252*

manual [*n*] *book giving instruction*
bible, compendium, cookbook, enchiridion, guide, guidebook, handbook, primer, reference book, schoolbook, text, textbook, workbook; SEE CONCEPT *280*

manual [*adj*] *done by hand*
chiral, hand-operated, human, not automatic, physical, standard; SEE CONCEPT *544*

manufacture/manufacturing [*n*] *production of processed goods*
accomplishment, assembling, assembly, casting, completion, composing, composition, construction, creation, doing, erection, fabrication, finishing, forging, formation, making, mass-production, preparing, produce, tooling; SEE CONCEPT *324*

manufacture [*v1*] *build, produce*
accomplish, assemble, carve, cast, cobble*, complete, compose, construct, create, execute, fabricate, fashion, forge, form, frame, fudge

together*, machine, make, make up, mass-produce, mill, mold, prefab, process, put together, shape, synthesize, throw together, tool, turn out; SEE CONCEPT **205**

manufacture [v2] *concoct, invent*
contrive, cook up*, create, devise, fabricate, hatch, make up, produce, think up, trump up*; SEE CONCEPTS *35,36*

many [n] *abundance; a lot*
gobs*, heaps*, horde, jillion*, large numbers, mass, multitude, oodles*, piles*, plenty, scads*, scores, thousands, throng, tons, umpteen*, whole slew*; SEE CONCEPTS *432,787*

many [adj] *profuse, abundant*
abounding, alive with, bounteous, bountiful, copious, countless, crowded, divers, frequent, innumerable, legion, lousy with*, manifold, multifarious, multifold, multiplied, multitudinous, myriad, no end of*, numberless, numerous, plentiful, populous, prevalent, rife, several, sundry, teeming, umpteen, uncounted, varied, various; SEE CONCEPTS *762,771*

map [n] *chart of geographic area*
atlas, delineation, design, diagram, draft, drawing, elevation, globe, graph, ground plan, outline, picture, plan, plat, portrayal, print, projection, sketch, topographical depiction, tracing; SEE CONCEPT *625*

mar [v] *hurt, damage*
bend, blemish, blight, blot, break, bruise, deface, deform, detract, ding*, disfigure, foul up, harm, impair, injure, louse up, maim, mangle, mess up*, mutilate, queer*, rough up, ruin, scar, scratch, shake up, spoil, stain, sully, taint, tarnish, tweak, vitiate, warp, wreck; SEE CONCEPT *246*

maraud [v] *pillage and plunder*
despoil, forage, foray, harass, harry, loot, raid, ransack, ravage, sack; SEE CONCEPTS *86,139*

march [v] *walk with deliberation*
advance, boot, debouch, drill, file, forge ahead, go on, hoof it*, journey, mount, move, move out, pace, parade, patrol, pound, pound the pavement*, proceed, progress, promenade, range, space, stalk, step, step out, stomp, stride, strut, traipse, tramp, tread; SEE CONCEPT *150*

margin [n] *border; room around something*
allowance, bound, boundary, brim, brink, compass, confine, edge, elbowroom*, extra, field, frame, hem, latitude, leeway, limit, lip, perimeter, periphery, play, rim, scope, selvage, shore, side, skirt, space, surplus, trimming, verge; SEE CONCEPTS *270,484,513*

marginal [adj] *borderline; slight*
bordering, insignificant, low, minimal, minor, negligible, on the edge, peripheral, rimming, small, verging; SEE CONCEPTS *513,789*

marine/maritime [adj] *concerning the sea*
abyssal, aquatic, coastal, deep-sea, hydrographic, littoral, maritime, natatorial, nautical, naval, navigational, Neptunian, oceangoing, oceanic, oceanographic, of the sea, pelagic, saltwater, sea, seafaring, seagoing, seashore, seaside, shore; SEE CONCEPT *536*

mariner [n] *person who makes living on the sea*
bluejacket*, captain, crew, mate, navigator, sailor, salt*, sea dog*, seafarer, shipmate, swab*, yachtie*; SEE CONCEPTS *348,366*

marital [adj] *concerning marriage*
conjugal, connubial, married, matrimonial, nuptial, spousal, wedded; SEE CONCEPT *555*

mark [n1] *blemish; character*
autograph, blaze, blot, blotch, brand, brand name, bruise, check, cross, dent, dot, impression, imprint, ink, John Hancock*, John Henry*, label, line, logo, nick, pock, point, record, register, representation, scar, score, scratch, sign, signature, smudge, splotch, spot, stain, stamp, streak, stroke, symbol, tag, ticket, trace, trademark, underlining, X*; SEE CONCEPTS *79,284*

mark [n2] *characteristic, symptom*
affection, attribute, badge, blaze, brand, character, device, distinction, earmark, emblem, evidence, feature, hallmark, idiosyncrasy, image, impression, incision, index, indication, indicia, label, marking, note, particularity, peculiarity, print, proof, property, quality, seal, sign, significant, stamp, symbol, token, trait, type, virtue; SEE CONCEPTS *411,644,716*

mark [n3] *criterion, standard*
gauge, level, measure, norm, yardstick; SEE CONCEPTS *561,783*

mark [n4] *goal, target*
aim, ambition, bull's eye*, duty, end, function, object, objective, prey, purpose, use; SEE CONCEPT *659*

mark [n5] *importance*
consequence, dignity, distinction, effect, eminence, fame, influence, manifestation, notability, note, notice, prestige, quality, regard, result, standing, value; SEE CONCEPTS *346,668*

mark [v1] *blemish, stain*
autograph, blaze, blot, blotch, brand, bruise, chalk, check, dent, dot, impress, imprint, initial, ink, inscribe, label, letter, nick, pinpoint, point, print, scar, score, scratch, seal, sign, smudge, splotch, stamp, streak, stroke, trace, underline, write, X*; SEE CONCEPTS *79,250*

mark [v2] *characterize*
bespeak, betoken, brand, check off, demonstrate, denote, designate, distinguish, earmark, evidence, evince, exemplify, exhibit, feature, identify, illustrate, indicate, individualize, individuate, label, manifest, mark off, ostend, point out, point up*, proclaim, qualify, remark, set apart, show, show up, signalize, signify, singularize, stake out*, stamp; SEE CONCEPT *261*

mark [v3] *see, notice*
attend, behold, chronicle, discern, distinguish, eye, hearken, mind, note, observe, pay attention, pay heed, perceive, regard, register, remark, take notice of, view, watch, write down; SEE CONCEPTS *38,626*

marked [adj] *apparent, obvious*
arresting, clear, considerable, conspicuous, decided, distinct, evident, manifest, notable, noted, noticeable, outstanding, patent, pointed, prominent, pronounced, remarkable, salient, signal, striking; SEE CONCEPTS *485,535,589*

markedly [adv] *distinctly*
clearly, considerably, conspicuously, decidedly, especially, evidently, greatly, manifestly, notably, noticeably, obviously, outstandingly, particularly, patently, remarkably, signally, strikingly, to a great extent; SEE CONCEPTS *535,544*

market/mart [n] *place, venue for selling goods*
bazaar, bodega, booth, business, chain store, co-op, corner store, deli, delicatessen, department store, dimestore, drugstore, emporium, exchange, fair, general store, grocery store, mall, mart, outlet, shop, shopping mall, showroom, souk,

square, stall, stock exchange, store, supermarket, trading post, truck, variety store, warehouse; SEE CONCEPTS 323,333,449

market [v] *package and sell goods*
advertise, barter, display, exchange, merchandise, offer for sale, retail, vend, wholesale; SEE CONCEPTS 324,345

marketable [adj] *easily sold; in demand*
bankable, commercial, fit, for sale, good, hot*, merchandisable, merchantable, profitable, salable, sellable, selling, sought after, sound, trafficable, vendible, wanted; SEE CONCEPTS 334,546

maroon [v] *abandon*
beach, cast ashore, cast away, desert, forsake, isolate, leave, leave high and dry*, strand; SEE CONCEPTS 195,384

marriage [n] *legal joining of two people; a union*
alliance, amalgamation, association, confederation, conjugality, connubiality, consortium, coupling, espousal, holy matrimony, link, match, mating, matrimony, merger, monogamy, nuptials, pledging, sacrament, spousal, tie, tie that binds*, wedded bliss*, wedded state, wedding, wedding bells*, wedding ceremony, wedlock; SEE CONCEPTS 297,388

marrow [n] *heart, essence*
bottom, core, cream, essentiality, gist, kernel, meat, pith, quick, quintessence, quintessential, soul, spirit, stuff, substance, virtuality; SEE CONCEPT 826

marry [v] *become husband and wife in legal ceremony*
ally, associate, become one, bond, catch*, combine, conjoin, conjugate, contract, couple, drop anchor*, espouse, get hitched*, get married, join, knit, land*, lead to altar, link, match, mate, merge, one, pledge, plight one's troth, promise, relate, settle down*, take vows, tie, tie the knot*, unify, unite, walk down aisle*, wed, yoke; SEE CONCEPT 297

marsh [n] *swamp*
bog, estuary, everglade, fen, mire, morass, moss, quag, quagmire, slough, swampland, wetland; SEE CONCEPT 509

marshal [v] *organize, guide*
align, arrange, array, assemble, collect, conduct, deploy, direct, dispose, distribute, draw up, escort, gather, group, lead, line up, methodize, mobilize, muster, order, rally, rank, shepherd, space, systematize, usher; SEE CONCEPTS 84,117,187

martial [adj] *having to do with armed hostilities*
aggressive, bellicose, belligerent, combative, hostile, military, pugnacious, soldierly, warlike; SEE CONCEPT 401

martyrdom [n] *suffering endured for sake of a cause*
affliction, agonizing, agony, anguish, crucifixion, devotion, distress, mortification, ordeal, pain, persecution, sacrifice, self-immolation, self-sacrifice, torment, torture, unselfishness; SEE CONCEPTS 410,411

marvel [n] *wonder*
curiosity, genius, miracle, one for the books*, phenomenon, portent, prodigy, sensation, something else*, stunner, whiz; SEE CONCEPTS 529,671

marvel [v] *be amazed*
be awed, be surprised, feel surprise, gape, gaze, goggle, stand in awe, stare, wonder; SEE CONCEPT 17

marvelous [adj1] *hard to believe; amazing*
astonishing, astounding, awe-inspiring, awesome, awful, bewildering, breathtaking, confounding, difficult to believe, extraordinary, fabulous, fantastic, implausible, improbable, incomprehensible, inconceivable, incredible, miraculous, phenomenal, prodigious, remarkable, singular, spectacular, staggering, strange, striking, stunning, stupendous, supernatural, surprising, unbelievable, unimaginable, unlikely, unusual, wonderful, wondrous; SEE CONCEPTS 529,552

marvelous [adj2] *superb, great*
agreeable, astonishing, bad*, boss*, colossal, cool*, divine, dreamy*, enjoyable, excellent, fab*, fabulous, fantastic, glorious, greatest, groovy*, hot*, keen, magnificent, neat*, out of this world*, outrageous, peachy, pleasant, pleasurable, prime*, rewarding, satisfying, sensational, smashing, solid*, solid gold*, spectacular, splendid, stupendous, super, supreme, swell, terrific, wonderful; SEE CONCEPT 574

masculinity/masculine [n/adj] *manly*
andric, gender, macho*, male, manful, mannish, potent, virile; SEE CONCEPTS 371,372,408,648

mash [v] *smash, squash*
brew, bruise, chew, crush, decoct, grind, hash, infuse, macerate, masticate, mush up, pound, press, pulp, pulverize, push, reduce, scrunch, squeeze, squish, steep, triturate; SEE CONCEPTS 170,186,208

mask [n] *false face, cover*
affectation, air*, appearance, aspect, beard*, blind, camouflage, cloak*, concealment, cover-up, disguise, disguisement, dissembling, dissimulation, domino*, facade, fig leaf*, front, guise, hood, masquerade, pose, posture, pretense, pretext, put-on*, screen, semblance, show*, simulation, veil*, veneer, visage, visor, window dressing*; SEE CONCEPTS 450,716

mask [v] *disguise*
beard, camouflage, cloak, conceal, cover, cover up, defend, dissemble, dissimulate, dress up, front, guard, hide, obscure, protect, safeguard, screen, secrete, shield, veil; SEE CONCEPTS 172,188,384

masquerade [n] *disguise; social occasion for disguises*
carnival, circus, cloak, color, costume, costume ball, cover, cover-up, deception, dissimulation, domino*, facade, festivity, front, guise, impersonation, imposture, Mardi Gras*, mask, masked ball, masking, mummery, personation, pose, pretense, put-on, revel, screen, show, subterfuge, veil; SEE CONCEPTS 172,188,383,451

masquerade [v] *disguise*
attitudinize, dissemble, dissimulate, frolic, impersonate, mask, pass as, pass for, pass off, pose, posture, pretend, revel; SEE CONCEPT 59

mass [n1] *body of matter; considerable portion*
accumulation, aggregate, assemblage, band, batch, block, bulk, bunch, chunk, clot, coagulation, collection, combination, concretion, conglomeration, core, corpus, crowd, entirety, gob, great deal, greater part, group, heap, horde, host, hunk, knot, lion's share*, load, lot, lump, majority, mob, mound, mountain, much, number, object, peck, piece, pile, plurality, preponderance, pyramid, quantity, shock, stack, staple, stockpile, sum, sum total, throng, totality, troop, volume, wad, whole; SEE CONCEPTS 432,787,835

mass [n2] *bulk, measurement*
dimension, extent, greatness, magnitude, size, span, volume; SEE CONCEPT *792*

massacre [n] *killing of many*
annihilation, assassination, bloodbath, bloodshed, butchery, carnage, decimation, extermination, genocide, internecion, murder, slaughter, slaying; SEE CONCEPT *252*

massacre [v] *kill, often in great numbers*
annihilate, butcher, decimate, depopulate, exterminate, mass murder, murder, slaughter, slay; SEE CONCEPT *252*

massage [n] *kneading of body parts*
back rub, beating, chirapsia, manipulation, rolfing*, rubbing, rubbing-down, stroking; SEE CONCEPTS *308,310*

massage [v] *knead body parts*
caress, manipulate, pat, press, push, rolf*, rub, rub down, stimulate, stroke; SEE CONCEPTS *208,308,310*

masses [n] *public, crowd*
commonalty, common people, great unwashed*, hoi polloi*, lower class, mob, multitude, proletariat, rabble, rank and file*, riffraff*; SEE CONCEPT *417*

massive [adj] *large*
big, bulky, colossal, cracking, cumbersome, cumbrous, elephantine, enormous, extensive, gargantuan, gigantic, grand, great, gross, heavy, hefty, huge, hulking, immense, imposing, impressive, mammoth, mighty, monster, monumental, mountainous, ponderous, prodigious, solid, stately, substantial, titanic, towering, tremendous, unwieldy, vast, walloping, weighty, whopping*; SEE CONCEPTS *773,781*

master [n1] *person in charge, female or male*
administrator, boss, captain, chief, chieftain, commandant, commander, commanding officer, conqueror, controller, director, employer, general, governor, guide, guru, head, head person, instructor, judge, lord, manager, matriarch, overlord, overseer, owner, patriarch, pedagogue, preceptor, principal, pro, ruler, schoolmaster/mistress, skipper, slave driver*, spiritual leader, superintendent, supervisor, swami*, taskmaster, teacher, top dog*, tutor, wheel*; SEE CONCEPTS *347,350,354*

master [n2] *expert, skilled person, female or male*
ace*, adept, artist, artiste, authority, buff*, champion, connoisseur, conqueror, doctor, doyen, doyenne, genius, guru, maestro, maven, old hand*, old pro*, past master, prima donna*, pro, professional, proficient, pundit, real pro*, sage, savant, scientist, shark*, victor, virtuoso, whiz*, whizbang*, winner, wizard; SEE CONCEPTS *350,366,423*

master [adj1] *expert*
ace*, adept, crack*, crackerjack*, experienced, masterly, proficient, skilled, skillful; SEE CONCEPT *527*

master [adj2] *main*
ascendant, chief, controlling, foremost, grand, great, leading, major, original, overbearing, paramount, predominant, predominate, preponderant, prevalent, prime, principal, regnant, sovereign, supreme; SEE CONCEPT *568*

master [v1] *learn; become proficient*
acquire, beat the game*, beat the system*, bone up*, bury yourself in*, comprehend, cram, excel in, gain mastery, get down cold*, get down pat*, get hold of*, get the hang of*, get the knack of*, grasp, grind, hit the books*, learn the ropes*, megastudy*, pick up, study, swamp*, understand; SEE CONCEPTS *31,630*

masterful [adj1] *expert, skilled*
adept, adroit, clever, consummate, crack, crackerjack*, deft, dexterous, excellent, exquisite, fine, finished, first-rate, master, masterly, preeminent, proficient, skillful, superior, superlative, supreme, transcendent; SEE CONCEPT *527*

masterpiece [n] *respected work of art*
chef d'oeuvre, classic, cream*, cream of the crop*, flower, gem*, jewel*, magnum opus, masterstroke, master work, model, monument, perfection, pièce de résistance*, prize, showpiece, standard, tour de force*, treasure; SEE CONCEPT *259*

mastery [n1] *command, expertise*
ability, acquirement, adeptness, adroitness, attainment, capacity, cleverness, comprehension, cunning, deftness, dexterity, expertism, expertness, familiarity, finesse, genius, grasp, grip, ken, knack, know-how, knowledge, mastership, power, proficiency, prowess, skill, understanding, virtuosity, wizardry; SEE CONCEPT *630*

match [n1] *competition*
bout, contest, engagement, event, game, meet, race, rivalry, sport, test, trial; SEE CONCEPT *363*

match [n2] *counterpart, equal*
adversary, analogue, antagonist, approximation, companion, competitor, complement, copy, correlate, countertype, dead ringer*, double, duplicate, equivalent, like, lookalike, mate, opponent, parallel, peer, replica, ringer*, rival, spitting image*, twin; SEE CONCEPTS *664,667,716*

match [n3] *couple*
affiliation, alliance, combination, duet, espousal, marriage, mating, pair, pairing, partnership, union; SEE CONCEPTS *297,388*

matching [adj] *corresponding, equal*
analogous, comparable, coordinating, double, duplicate, equivalent, identical, like, paired, parallel, same, twin; SEE CONCEPT *566*

matchless [adj] *unequalled, unique*
alone, consummate, excellent, exquisite, incomparable, inimitable, nonpareil, only, peerless, perfect, superior, superlative, supreme, unapproached, unmatched, unparalleled, unrivaled; SEE CONCEPT *574*

mate [n] *one of a pair; partner*
acquaintance, alter ego, analog, assistant, associate, bedmate, bride, buddy*, chum*, classmate, cohort, colleague, companion, compeer, complement, comrade, concomitant, consort, coordinate, counterpart, coworker, crony, double, duplicate, familiar, friend, groom, helper, helpmate, intimate, match, pal*, peer, playmate, reciprocal, roommate, schoolmate, sidekick*, spouse, twin; SEE CONCEPTS *296,423,664*

mate [v] *marry and breed*
cohabit, copulate, couple, crossbreed, generate, join, land*, match, merge, pair, procreate, serve, tie, tie the knot*, wed, yoke; SEE CONCEPTS *297,375*

material [n1] *matter, fabric*
being, body, bolt, cloth, component, constituent, crop, element, entity, equipment, gear, goods, habiliments, individual, ingredient, machinery, materiel, object, outfit, paraphernalia, staple, stock,

stuff, substance, supply, tackle, textile, thing; SEE CONCEPTS *475,523*

material [n2] *written matter*
data, evidence, facts, information, notes, reading, text, work; SEE CONCEPTS *271,274*

material [adj1] *bodily, tangible*
actual, animal, appreciable, carnal, concrete, corporeal, earthly, fleshly, incarnate, nonspiritual, objective, palpable, perceptible, phenomenal, physical, real, sensible, sensual, substantial, true, worldly; SEE CONCEPT *485*

material [adj2] *important, relevant*
ad rem, applicable, applicative, apposite, apropos, big, cardinal, consequential, considerable, essential, fundamental, germane, grave, indispensable, intrinsic, key, meaningful, momentous, pertinent, pointful, primary, serious, significant, substantial, vital, weighty; SEE CONCEPT *567*

materialistic [adj] *thinking mainly about physical things*
acquisitive, banausic, carnal, earthly-minded, earthy, greedy, material, mundane, object-oriented, possessive, profane, secular, sensual, temporal, terrestrial, unspiritual; SEE CONCEPT *542*

materialize [v] *come into being*
actualize, appear, become concrete, become real, become visual, be incarnate, be realized, coalesce, come about, come to pass, corporealize, develop, embody, emerge, entify, evolve, exteriorize, externalize, happen, hypostatize, make real, manifest, metamorphose, objectify, occur, personalize, personify, personize, pragmatize, realize, reify, substantialize, substantiate, symbolize, take form, take place, take shape, turn up, typify, unfold, visualize; SEE CONCEPTS *105,173,184,231,251*

maternity [n] *period of being pregnant with child*
gestation, maternology, motherhood, parenthood; SEE CONCEPTS *316,817*

mathematical [adj] *concerning manipulation of numbers*
algebraic, algorithmic, analytical, arithmetical, computative, geometrical, math, measurable, numerical, scientific, trigonometric; SEE CONCEPT *762*

matriculate [v] *begin, enroll*
enter, join, register, sign up for; SEE CONCEPTS *114,119*

matrimonial [adj] *married*
betrothed, conjugal, connubial, engaged, epithalamic, espoused, marital, nuptial, spousal, wedded, wedding; SEE CONCEPT *555*

matrimony [n] *being joined in marriage*
alliance, bells*, conjugality, connubiality, marital rites, marriage, match, nuptials, shotgun wedding*, union, wedding, wedding bells*, wedding ceremony, wedlock; SEE CONCEPT *297*

matrix [n] *something from which another originates*
cast, forge, form, grid, model, mold, origin, pattern, source, womb; SEE CONCEPT *648*

matted [adj] *tangled*
disordered, kinky, knotted, rumpled, snarled, tousled, twisted, uncombed; SEE CONCEPT *606*

matter [n1] *substance*
amount, being, body, constituents, corporeality, corporeity, element, entity, individual, material, materialness, object, phenomenon, physical world, protoplasm, quantity, stuff, substantiality, sum, thing; SEE CONCEPTS *407,433,470*

matter [n2] *concern, issue*
affair, bag, business, circumstance, episode, event, goings-on*, incident, job, lookout, occurrence, proceeding, question, shooting match*, situation, subject, thing, topic, transaction, undertaking; SEE CONCEPTS *532,696*

matter [n3] *subject, thesis*
argument, context, focus, head, interest, motif, motive, point, purport, resolution, sense, subject matter, substance, text, theme, topic; SEE CONCEPTS *349,529*

matter [n4] *significance, meaning*
amount, body, burden, consequence, content, core, extent, gist*, import, importance, magnitude, meat, moment, neighborhood, note, order, pith, range, sense, substance, text, tune, upshot, vicinity, weight; SEE CONCEPTS *651,668*

matter [n5] *difficulty, problem*
circumstance, complication, distress, grievance, perplexity, predicament, to-do*, trouble, upset, worry; SEE CONCEPTS *666,674*

matter [n6] *secretion of a sore*
discharge, infection, maturation, purulence, pus, suppuration, ulceration; SEE CONCEPTS *311,467*

matter [v] *be of consequence, importance*
affect, be important, be of value, be substantive, carry weight, count, cut ice*, express, have influence, imply, import, involve, make a difference, mean, mean something, signify, value, weigh; SEE CONCEPTS *7,19,22,130,682*

matter-of-fact [adj] *realistic, unembellished*
apathetic, calm, cold, cold-blooded*, deadpan, down-to-earth*, dry, dull, earthy, emotionless, factual, feasible, flat, hard-boiled*, impassive, impersonal, lifeless, mundane, naked*, objective, phlegmatic, plain, practical, pragmatic, prosaic, prosy, serious, sober, stoic, stolid, unaffected, unidealistic, unimaginative, unimpassioned, unsentimental, unvarnished; SEE CONCEPTS *267,582*

mature [adj] *adult, grown-up*
complete, cultivated, cultured, developed, fit, full-blown, full-fledged, full-grown, fully grown, grown, in full bloom, in one's prime, matured, mellow, mellowed, of age, perfected, prepared, prime, ready, ripe, ripened, seasoned, settled, sophisticated; SEE CONCEPTS *485,578,797*

mature [v] *become adult, fully grown*
advance, age, arrive, attain majority, become experienced, become wise, bloom, blossom, come of age, culminate, develop, evolve, fill out, flower*, grow, grow up, maturate, mellow*, mushroom*, perfect, prime, progress, reach adulthood, reach majority, ripen, round, season, settle down*, shoot up*; SEE CONCEPT *704*

maturity [n] *adulthood, full growth*
ability, advancement, capability, civilization, completion, cultivation, development, experience, fitness, full bloom, fullness, majority, manhood, maturation, matureness, maturescence, mellowness, mentality, perfection, postpubescence, prime, prime of life, readiness, ripeness, sophistication, wisdom, womanhood; SEE CONCEPTS *678,715,720*

maudlin [adj] *teary, overemotional*
bathetic, befuddled, confused, cornball*, drippy*, gushing, insipid, lachrymose, mawkish, mushy*, romantic, schmaltzy*, sentimental, slush*, soap*, soapy*, soppy*, syrupy*, tearful, tear-jerking*, weak, weepy; SEE CONCEPTS *529,542*

maul [v] *mangle, abuse*
bang, bash, batter, beat, beat up, bludgeon, break face, buffet, claw, clean, drub, flagellate, flail, handle roughly, hit, hurt, ill-treat, knock about*, knock around*, lacerate, lash, lean on*, let have it*, maltreat, molest, mug, muscle, paste*, paw, pelt, pound, pummel, put in the hospital*, rough up, skin, take care of*, thrash, trample, wax, whip, work over*; SEE CONCEPTS *189,246*

mauve [adj] *purplish color*
lavender, lilac, plum, violaceous, violet; SEE CONCEPT *618*

maverick [n] *person who takes chances, departs from accepted course*
bohemian, dissenter, extremist, malcontent, non-conformist, radical; SEE CONCEPTS *348,423*

mawkish [adj] *sentimental, emotional*
bathetic, cloying, feeble, gooey*, gushing, gushy*, lovey-dovey*, maudlin, mushy*, nause-ating, romantic, sappy*, schmaltzy*, sickening, sloppy, tear-jerking*, teary; SEE CONCEPTS *401,542*

maxim [n] *saying*
adage, aphorism, apophthegm, axiom, belief, bro-card, byword, canon, commonplace, device, dic-tum, epithet, formula, law, moral, motto, platitude, precept, prescript, proverb, rule, saw, tenet, theorem, truism; SEE CONCEPTS *278,689*

maximum [n] *upper limit, greatest amount*
apex, apogee, ceiling, climax, crest, culmination, extremity, height, max*, maxi*, most, nonpareil, peak, pinnacle, preeminence, record, summit, su-premacy, the end*, top, utmost, uttermost, zenith; SEE CONCEPTS *706,776,836*

maximum [adj] *highest, utmost*
best, biggest, greatest, largest, maximal, most, mostest, outside, paramount, superlative, su-preme, top, topmost, ultimate; SEE CONCEPTS *574,762,781*

maybe [adv] *possibly*
as it may be, can be, conceivable, conceivably, could be, credible, feasible, imaginably, it could be, might be, obtainable, perchance, perhaps, weather permitting; SEE CONCEPT *552*

mayhem [n] *chaos, confusion*
anarchy, commotion, destruction, disorder, fra-cas, havoc, pandemonium, trouble, violence; SEE CONCEPTS *106,675*

maze [n] *labyrinth; confusion*
bewilderment, convolution, entanglement, hodge-podge, imbroglio, intricacy, jungle, knot, mean-der, meandering, mesh, miscellany, morass, muddle, network, perplexity, puzzle, quandary, skein, snarl, tangle, torsion, twist, uncertainty, web, winding; SEE CONCEPTS *436,529,674*

meadow [n] *grassy field*
bottoms*, carpet*, grassland, heath, lea, mead, pasturage, pasture, plain, prairie, rug*, steppe, veldt; SEE CONCEPT *509*

meager [adj1] *small, inadequate; poor*
bare, barren, deficient, exiguous, flimsy, inappre-ciable, inconsiderable, infertile, insubstantial, in-sufficient, little, mere, minimum, miserable, paltry, puny, scant, scanty, scrimp, scrimpy, shabby, short, skimp, skimpy, slender, slight, spare, sparse, subtle, tenuous, too little too late*, unfinished, unfruitful, unproductive, wanting, weak; SEE CONCEPTS *546,789*

meager [adj2] *very thin*
angular, bare, beanpole*, beanstalk*, bony,
broomstick*, emaciated, gangling, gangly, gaunt, hungry, lacking, lank, lanky, lean, lithe, little, narrow, rattleboned, rawboned, scraggy, scrawny, skin and bones*, skinny, slender, slim, spare, starved, stinted, stunted, tenuous, underfed, want-ing, willowy, withered; SEE CONCEPT *491*

meal [n] *food, often taken by several individuals together*
banquet, blue plate*, board, breakfast, brunch, carryout, chow*, chow time*, collation, cookout, dessert, din-din*, dinner, eats*, fare, feast, feed, grub*, lunch, luncheon, mess, munchies*, picnic, potluck, refection, refreshment, regalement, re-past, snack, special*, spread, square meal*, sup-per, table, tea; SEE CONCEPT *459*

mean [n] *average*
balance, center, compromise, happy medium, me-dian, middle, middle course, midpoint, norm, par; SEE CONCEPTS *727,830*

mean [adj1] *ungenerous*
close, greedy, mercenary, mingy, miserly, nig-gard, parsimonious, penny-pinching*, penurious, rapacious, scrimpy, selfish, stingy, tight, tight-fisted*; SEE CONCEPT *334*

mean [adj2] *hostile, rude*
bad-tempered, callous, cantankerous, churlish, contemptible, dangerous, despicable, difficult, dirty*, disagreeable, dishonorable, down*, evil, formidable, hard, hard-nosed*, ignoble, ill-tempered, infamous, knavish, liverish, lousy*, low-down and dirty*, malicious, malign, nasty, perfidious, pesky, rotten, rough, rugged, scurril-ous, shameless, sinking, snide, sour, the lowest*, touch, treacherous, troublesome, ugly, unfriendly, unpleasant, unscrupulous, vexatious, vicious, vile; SEE CONCEPTS *267,401,542*

mean [adj3] *poor; of or in inferior circumstances*
base, beggarly, common, contemptible, déclassé, down-at-heel*, hack, humble, ignoble, ineffec-tual, inferior, insignificant, limited, low, lowborn, lowly, mediocre, menial, miserable, modest, nar-row, obscure, ordinary, paltry, petty, pitiful, ple-beian, proletarian, run-down*, scruffy*, second-class*, second-rate, seedy*, servile, shabby*, sordid, squalid, tawdry, undistinguished, un-washed, vulgar, wretched; SEE CONCEPTS *334,485,589*

mean [adj4] *average*
common, conventional, halfway, intermediate, medial, median, mediocre, medium, middle, mid-dling, normal, popular, standard, traditional; SEE CONCEPTS *547,585*

mean [v1] *signify, convey*
add up, adumbrate, allude, allude to, argue, at-test, augur, betoken, connote, denote, designate, determine, drive at*, express, foreshadow, fore-tell, herald, hint at, imply, import, indicate, inti-mate, involve, name, point to, portend, presage, promise, purport, represent, say, speak of, spell, stand for, suggest, symbolize, tell the meaning of, touch on; SEE CONCEPTS *55,73,682*

mean [v2] *have in mind; intend*
aim, anticipate, aspire, contemplate, design, de-sire, destine, direct, expect, fate, fit, make, match, plan, predestine, preordain, propose, purpose, re-solve, set out, suit, want, wish; SEE CONCEPTS *26,36*

meander [v] *wander, zigzag*
be all over the map*, change, drift, extravagate, gallivant, get sidetracked, peregrinate, ramble,

range, recoil, roam, rove, snake, stray, stroll, traipse, turn, twine, twist, vagabond, wind; SEE CONCEPTS 151,738

meaning [n1] *message, signification*
acceptation, allusion, bearing, bottom line*, connotation, content, context, definition, denotation, drift, effect, essence, explanation, force, gist, heart*, hint, implication, import, interpretation, intimation, meat, name of the game*, nature of beast*, nitty-gritty*, nuance, nuts and bolts*, pith, point, purport, sense, significance, spirit, stuff, subject, subject matter, substance, suggestion, symbolization, tenor, thrust, understanding, upshot, use, value, worth; SEE CONCEPTS 278,661,682

meaning [n2] *intention, aim*
animus, design, end, goal, idea, intent, interest, object, plan, point, purpose, trend; SEE CONCEPT 659

meaningful [adj] *significant*
allusive, big, clear, concise, consequential, considerable, deep, eloquent, essential, exact, explicit, expressive, heavy, important, indicative, intelligible, material, momentous, pointed, pregnant, purposeful, relevant, sententious, serious, substantial, succinct, suggestive, useful, valid, weighty, worthwhile; SEE CONCEPTS 267,567

meaningless [adj] *without use, value, worth*
absurd, aimless, blank, doesn't cut it*, doublespeak*, double-talk*, empty, feckless, fustian, futile, good-for-nothing, hollow, hot air*, inane, inconsequential, insignificant, insubstantial, nonsensical, nothing, nugatory, pointless, purportless, purposeless, senseless, trifling, trivial, unimportant, unmeaning, unpurposed, useless, vacant, vague, vain, valueless, vapid, worthless; SEE CONCEPT 575

means [n1] *way, method*
agency, agent, aid, apparatus, auspices, avenue, channel, course, dodge*, equipment, expedient, factor, fashion, gimmick*, instrument, instrumentality, instrumentation, intermediary, machinery, manner, measure, mechanism, medium, ministry, mode, modus operandi, organ, organization, paraphernalia, path, power, process, road, route, step, stepping-stone, system, tactic, technique, trick, vehicle, ways and means*; SEE CONCEPT 6

means [n2] *wealth, resources*
ace in the hole*, affluence, assets, backing, bankroll, budget, bundle, capital, dough*, estate, finances, fortune, funds, holdings, income, intangibles, kitty*, money, nest egg*, nut*, pocket, possessions, property, purse, rainy day*, reserves, revenue, riches, savings, securities, sock*, stake, stuff, substance, ways and means*, wherewithal; SEE CONCEPTS 332,340

meantime [n/adv] *in the intervening time*
at the same time, concurrently, for now, for the duration, for the moment, for then, interim, interregnum, interruption, interval, in the interim, in the interval, in the meanwhile, meanwhile, recess, simultaneously, while; SEE CONCEPTS 799,807

meanwhile [adv] *at the same time*
ad interim, concurrently, during the interval, for now, for the duration, for the moment, for then, for the time being, in the interim, in the interval, in the intervening time, in the meantime, meantime, simultaneously, till, until, up to, when; SEE CONCEPT 799

measly [adj] *skimpy*
beggarly, contemptible, insignificant, meager, mean, miserable, miserly, niggling*, paltry, pathetic, petty, picayune, piddling*, pitiful, poor, puny, scanty, stingy, trifling, trivial, ungenerous, unimportant, valueless, worthless; SEE CONCEPT 789

measurable [adj] *determinable*
assessable, calculable, commensurate, computable, fathomable, gaugeable, material, mensurable, perceptible, quantifiable, quantitative, significant, surveyable, weighable; SEE CONCEPT 529

measure [n1] *portion, scope*
admeasurement, admensuration, allotment, allowance, amount, amplification, amplitude, area, bang, breadth, bulk, capacity, degree, depth, dimension, distance, duration, extent, fix, frequency, height, hit, magnitude, mass, meed, mensuration, nip, part, pitch, proportion, quantity, quantum, quota, range, ratio, ration, reach, share, shot, size, slug, span, strength, sum, volume, weight; SEE CONCEPTS 787,792,835

measure [n2] *standard, rule*
benchmark*, canon, criterion, example, gauge, meter, method, model, norm, pattern, scale, system, test, touchstone*, trial, type, yardstick; SEE CONCEPTS 686,688

measure [n3] *preventive or institutive action*
act, action, agency, bounds, control, course, deed, device, effort, expedient, limit, limitation, makeshift, maneuver, means, moderation, move, procedure, proceeding, project, proposal, proposition, resort, resource, restraint, shift, step, stopgap*, strategem; SEE CONCEPT 5

measure [n4] *bill, law*
act, enactment, project, proposal, proposition, resolution, statute; SEE CONCEPT 318

measure [n5] *beat, rhythm*
accent, cadence, cadency, division, melody, meter, rhyme, step, stress, stroke, swing, tempo, throb, time, tune, verse, vibration; SEE CONCEPTS 65,262

measure [v] *calculate, judge*
adapt, adjust, align, appraise, assess, average, beat, blend, bound, calibrate, caliper, check, check out, choose, compute, delimit, demarcate, determine, dope out*, estimate, evaluate, even, eye*, figure, fit, gauge, gradate, grade, graduate, level, limit, line, look over, mark, mark out, mete, pace off, peg*, plumb, portion, quantify, rank, rate, read, reckon, regulate, rhyme, rule, scale, shade, size, size up, sound, square, stroke, survey, tailor, take account, time, value, weigh; SEE CONCEPTS 103,197,764

measurement [n] *calculation*
altitude, amount, amplitude, analysis, appraisal, area, assessment, calibration, capacity, computation, degree, density, depth, determination, dimension, distance, estimation, evaluation, extent, frequency, height, judgment, length, magnitude, mass, measure, mensuration, metage, pitch, quantification, quantity, range, reach, scope, size, survey, thickness, time, valuation, volume, weight, width; SEE CONCEPTS 730,792

meat [n1] *flesh of animal consumed as food*
aliment, brawn, chow, comestible, eats*, edible, fare, food, foodstuff, grub*, muscle, nourishment, nutriment, provision, ration, subsistence, sustenance, victual; SEE CONCEPTS 399,457,460

meat [n2] *core, gist*
burden, essence, heart, kernel, marrow, matter, nub, nucleus, pith, point, sense, short, substance, thrust, upshot; SEE CONCEPTS 682,826

meaty [adj] *significant*
compact, epigrammatic, factual, full of content, interesting, meaningful, pithy, pointed, profound, rich, substantial, weighty; SEE CONCEPT 267

mechanical [adj] *done by machine; machinelike*
automated, automatic, cold, cursory, emotionless, fixed, habitual, impersonal, instinctive, involuntary, laborsaving, lifeless, machine-driven, matter-of-fact, monotonous, perfunctory, programmed, routine, spiritless, standardized, stereotyped, unchanging, unconscious, unfeeling, unthinking, useful; SEE CONCEPT 544

mechanism [n1] *machine, device*
apparatus, appliance, black box*, components, contrivance, doohickey*, gadget, gears, gimmick, innards, instrument, machinery, motor, structure, system, tool, workings, works; SEE CONCEPT 463

mechanism [n2] *means, method*
agency, execution, functioning, medium, operation, performance, procedure, process, system, technique, workings; SEE CONCEPT 6

medal [n] *decoration of honor*
badge, commemoration, gold, hardware*, laurel, medallion, reward, ribbon, wreath; SEE CONCEPTS 337,476

meddle [v] *intervene, interfere*
abuse rights, advance, barge in, break in on, busybody*, butt in*, chime in, come uninvited, crash the gates*, dabble in, encroach, encumber, fool with, hinder, horn in*, impede, impose, infringe, inquire, interlope, intermeddle, interpose, intrude, invade, kibitz*, mess around*, mix in, molest, obtrude, pry, push in, put two cents in*, sidewalk-superintend*, snoop*, stick nose in*, tamper, trespass, worm in*; SEE CONCEPTS 14,384

meddlesome [adj] *interfereing*
busy, busybody*, chiseling*, curious, encumbering, hindering, impeding, impertinent, intermeddling, interposing, interrupting, intruding, intrusive, kibitzing*, meddling, mischievous, nosy, obstructive, officious, prying, pushy, snooping*, snoopy*, tampering, troublesome; SEE CONCEPT 555

media [n] *communication by publication or broadcast*
announcement, announcing, cable, communications, correspondence, disclosure, expression, intelligence, news, publishing, radio, television; SEE CONCEPT 279

median [n/adj] *middle*
average, center, centermost, central, equidistant, halfway, intermediary, intermediate, mean, medial, mid, middlemost, midmost, midpoint, midway, par; SEE CONCEPTS 727,746,830

mediate [v] *try to bring to an agreement*
act as middle*, arbitrate, bring to terms, conciliate, deal, go fifty-fifty*, intercede, interfere, intermediate, interpose, intervene, make a deal, make peace, meet halfway*, moderate, negotiate, propitiate, reconcile, referee, resolve, restore harmony, settle, step in, strike happy medium*, trade off, umpire; SEE CONCEPTS 126,324,384

mediation [n] *attempt to bring to agreement*
arbitration, conciliation, intercession, interposition, intervention, negotiation, reconciliation; SEE CONCEPTS 126,324,384

mediator [n] *person who negotiates agreement*
advocate, arbiter, arbitrator, broker, conciliator, fixer, go-between*, interagent, interceder, intermediary, intermediator, judge, medium, middle person, moderator, negotiator, peacemaker, ref*, referee, rent-a-judge*, troubleshooter*, umpire; SEE CONCEPTS 348,423

medicine/medication [n] *substance that helps cure, alleviate, or prevent illness*
anesthetic, antibiotic, antidote, antiseptic, antitoxin, balm, biologic, capsule, cure, drug, elixir, injection, inoculation, liniment, lotion, medicament, ointment, pharmaceutical, pharmacon, physic, pill, potion, prescription, remedy, salve, sedative, serum, tablet, tincture, tonic, vaccination, vaccine; SEE CONCEPT 307

medieval [adj] *having to do with the Middle Ages; old*
antediluvian, antiquated, antique, archaic, feudal, Gothic, old, old-fashioned, primitive, unenlightened; SEE CONCEPTS 549,578,797

mediocre [adj] *average, commonplace*
characterless, colorless, common, conventional, decent, dull, fair, fairish, fair to middling*, humdrum*, indifferent, inferior, insignificant, intermediate, mainstream, mean, medium, middling, moderate, no great shakes*, of poor quality, ordinary, passable, pedestrian, run-of-the-mill*, second-rate, so-so*, standard, tolerable, undistinguished, unexceptional, uninspired, vanilla*; SEE CONCEPTS 533,547

meditate [v] *think deeply about*
brood over, cogitate, consider, contemplate, deliberate, design, devise, dream, entertain idea*, figure, have in mind*, intend, moon*, mull over, muse, plan, ponder, purpose, put on thinking cap*, puzzle over, reflect, revolve, roll, ruminate, say to oneself, scheme, speculate, study, think, think over, track, view, weigh; SEE CONCEPT 17

medium [n1] *means, mode*
agency, agent, avenue, channel, clairvoyant, factor, form, instrument, instrumentality, intermediate, measure, mechanism, ministry, organ, psychic, seer, tool, vehicle, way; SEE CONCEPTS 658,712

medium [n2] *atmosphere, setting*
ambience, ambient, climate, conditions, element, habitat, influences, milieu, surroundings; SEE CONCEPTS 673,696

medium [n3] *area of artistic expression*
art, drama, interpretation, manifestation, mark, music, painting, revelation, sculpture, speech, writing; SEE CONCEPTS 259,263,293

medium [adj] *midway, average*
common, commonplace, fair, fairish, intermediate, mean, medial, median, mediocre, middle, middling, moderate, neutral, normal, ordinary, par, passable, popular, run-of-the-mill*, so-so*, standard, tolerable; SEE CONCEPTS 533,547

medley [n] *miscellany*
assortment, brew, collection, combo, composition, confusion, conglomeration, farrago, hodgepodge, jumble, mélange, melee, mingling, mishmash, mixed bag, mixture, pasticcio, pastiche, patchwork, potpourri, salmagundi, variety; SEE CONCEPTS 262,432

meek [adj] *shy; compliant*
acquiescent, deferential, docile, forbearing, gentle, humble, lenient, longanimous, long-suffering, lowly, manageable, mild, milquetoast*, modest,

nothing, orderly, pabulum*, passive, patient, peaceful, plain, resigned, serene, soft, spineless, spiritless, subdued, submissive, tame, timid, tolerant, unassuming, unpretentious, unresisting, weak, weak-kneed*, wishy-washy*, yielding, zero*; SEE CONCEPT 401

meet [n] *sporting event involving several participants*
athletic event, competition, conflict, contest, event, match, meeting, tournament, tourney; SEE CONCEPT 363

meet [adj] *fitting*
accommodated, applicable, appropriate, apt, conformed, equitable, expedient, fair, felicitous, fit, good, happy, just, proper, reconciled, right, suitable, timely; SEE CONCEPT 558

meet [v1] *happen on*
accost, affront, brush against, bump into, chance on, clash, collide, come across, come up against, confront, contact, cross, dig up*, encounter, engage, experience, face, fall in with*, find, front, get together, grapple, greet, hit, light, luck*, make a meet, meet face to face, rendezvous with, rub eyeballs*, run across, run into, run up against, salute, see, strike, stumble, touch shoulders*, tumble, tussle, wrestle; SEE CONCEPTS 183,384,626

meet [v2] *connect, join*
abut, adhere, adjoin, border, coincide, connect, converge, cross, intersect, link, link up, reach, touch, unite; SEE CONCEPTS 612,759

meet [v3] *perform, carry out*
answer, approach, come up to, comply, cope with, discharge, equal, execute, fit, fulfill, gratify, handle, match, measure up, rival, satisfy, suffice, tie, touch; SEE CONCEPT 91

meet [v4] *come together, convene*
appear, assemble, be introduced, be present, be presented, collect, congregate, converge, enter in, flock, foregather, gather, get together, get to know, join, make acquaintance, muster, open, rally, rendezvous, show, sit; SEE CONCEPTS 114,324

meeting [n1] *gathering, conference*
affair, assemblage, assembly, assignation, audience, bunch, call, cattle call*, company, competition, conclave, concourse, concursion, confab*, conflict, confrontation, congregation, congress, contest, convention, convocation, date, encounter, engagement, gang, get-together, huddle, introduction, meet, one on one*, parley, powwow*, rally, rendezvous, reunion, session, showdown, talk, tryst, turnout*; SEE CONCEPTS 324,363,384

meeting [n2] *convergence, intersection*
abutment, agreement, apposition, concourse, confluence, conjunction, connection, contact, crossing, joining, junction, juxtaposition, unification, union; SEE CONCEPTS 113,684

melancholy [n] *depression, sadness*
blahs*, blue devils*, blue funk*, blues*, boredom, bummer*, dejection, despair, desperation, despondency, dismals, dolefuls, dolor, downer*, down trip*, dumps, ennui, funk, gloom, gloominess, grief, letdown, low spirits, miserableness, misery, mopes*, mournfulness, pensiveness, sorrow, tedium, unhappiness, wistfulness, woe, wretchedness; SEE CONCEPT 410

melancholy [adj] *depressed, sad*
blue*, dejected, despondent, destroyed, disconsolate, dismal, dispirited, doleful, dolorous, down*,

down and out*, downbeat, downcast, downhearted, down in the dumps*, down in the mouth*, dragged, droopy, funereal, gloomy, glum, grim, heavyhearted, in blue funk*, joyless, lachrymose, low, low-spirited, lugubrious, mirthless, miserable, moody, moony*, mournful, pensive, saddened, saddening, somber, sorrowful, sorry*, torn up, trite, unhappy, wet blanket*, wistful, woebegone, woeful; SEE CONCEPT 403

mélange [n] *mixture*
assortment, combo, confusion, farrago, gallimaufry, hodgepodge, jumble, medley, miscellany, mishmash, mix, mixed bag, pasticcio, pastiche, patchwork, potpourri, salmagundi, soup, stew; SEE CONCEPT 432

meld [v] *blend, bring together*
amalgamate, associate, compound, dissolve, feather in, fuse, interblend, interface, interfuse, intermingle, marry, merge, mingle, mix, unite; SEE CONCEPTS 113,193

melee [n] *battle, fight*
affray, battle royal*, brawl, broil, brouhaha*, brush, clash, donnybrook*, fracas, fray, free-for-all*, knock-down-drag-out*, row, ruckus, ruction, rumpus, scrimmage, scuffle, set-to*, skirmish, to-do*, tussle, words; SEE CONCEPT 106

mellow [adj] *ripe, mature; softened*
aged, cultured, cured, delicate, developed, dulcet, flavorful, full, full-flavored, fully developed, juicy, matured, mellifluent, mellifluous, melodious, perfect, perfected, rich, ripened, rounded, sapid, savory, seasoned, smooth, soft, soothing, sweet, tuneful; SEE CONCEPTS 462,578,594,797

mellow [v] *ripen, mature*
age, arrive, develop, grow, grow up, improve, maturate, milden, mollify, perfect, ripe, season, settle down, soften, sweeten; SEE CONCEPTS 678,704

melodious/melodic [adj] *harmonious, musical*
accordant, agreeable, assonant, canorous, clear, concordant, dulcet, euphonic, euphonious, harmonic, in tune, mellifluous, mellow, pleasing, resonant, silvery, soft, songful, sweet, sweet-sounding, symphonic, symphonious, tuned, tuneful, well-tuned; SEE CONCEPT 594

melodramatic [adj] *extravagant in speech, behavior*
artificial, blood-and-thunder*, cliff-hanging*, cloak-and-dagger*, exaggerated, ham*, hammy*, histrionic, hokey*, overdramatic, overemotional, sensational, spectacular, stagy, theatrical; SEE CONCEPT 542

melody [n] *harmony, tune*
air, aria, assonance, carillon, chant, chime, concord, consonance, descant, diapason, euphony, inflection, lay, lyric, measure, melodiousness, music, musicality, refrain, resonance, run, song, strain, theme, tunefulness, unison; SEE CONCEPTS 262,595

melt [v1] *liquefy; dissolve*
cook, deliquesce, diffuse, disappear, disintegrate, disperse, evanesce, evaporate, fade, flow, flux, fuse, go, heat, merge, pass away, render, run, smelt, soften, thaw, vanish, warm, waste away; SEE CONCEPTS 250,255

melt [v2] *give in, yield*
become lenient, disarm, forgive, mollify, relax, relent, show mercy, soften, touch; SEE CONCEPT 35

member [n1] *part of a group*
affiliate, associate, branch, chapter, component, comrade, constituent, cut, division, joiner, offshoot, parcel, piece, portion, post, representative, section, segment, unit; SEE CONCEPTS 417,834,835

member [n2] *appendage*
arm, component, constituent, element, extremity, feature, fragment, leg, limb, organ, part, portion, segment; SEE CONCEPT 392

membership [n] *belonging to organization; those belonging to a group*
associates, association, body, club, company, enrollment, fellows, group, members, participation, society; SEE CONCEPTS 388,417

membrane [n] *covering layer*
film, lamina, leaf, mucosa, sheath, sheet; SEE CONCEPT 484

memento [n] *souvenir*
keepsake, memorial, relic, remembrance, remembrancer, reminder, token, trace, trophy, vestige; SEE CONCEPTS 337,446

memoir [n] *record of experiences*
account, anecdote, annal, autobiography, bio*, biography, chronicle, confessions, diary, discourse, dissertation, essay, journal, life, life story, memory, monograph, narrative, note, recollection, register, reminiscence, thesis, tractate, transactions, treatise, vita; SEE CONCEPTS 271,280,282

memorable [adj] *noteworthy, significant*
A-1*, big-league*, bodacious, catchy, celebrated, critical, crucial, decisive, distinguished, doozie*, enduring, eventful, extraordinary, famous, great, heavy*, heavyweight*, historic, hot*, illustrious, important, impressive, indelible, interesting, lasting, major-league, meaningful, mind-blowing*, momentous, monumental, notable, observable, red-letter*, remarkable, rememberable, rubric, serious, signal, something, standout, striking, super, surpassing, terrible, terrific, top-drawer, unforgettable; SEE CONCEPTS 529,548

memorandum/memo [n] *written note*
announcement, chit, diary, directive, dispatch, epistle, jotting, letter, message, minute, missive, notation, notice, record, reminder, tickler; SEE CONCEPTS 271,277,278

memorial [n] *monument, testimonial in honor, praise*
cairn, ceremony, column, headstone, inscription, keepsake, mausoleum, memento, monolith, obelisk, pillar, plaque, record, relic, remembrance, reminder, shaft, slab, souvenir, statue, stele, tablet, token, tombstone, trophy; SEE CONCEPTS 337,386

memorial [adj] *commemorative*
canonizing, celebrative, commemoratory, consecrating, consecrative, dedicatory, deifying, enshrining, in tribute, memorializing, monumental, remembering; SEE CONCEPT 537

memory [n1] *ability to hold in the mind*
anamnesis, awareness, camera-eye*, cognizance, consciousness, dead-eye*, flashback, memorization, mind, mindfulness, mind's eye*, recall, recapture, recognition, recollection, reflection, remembrance, reminiscence, retention, retentiveness, retrospection, subconsciousness, thought; SEE CONCEPT 409

memory [n2] *specific thing remembered*
concept, cue, fantasy, hint, image, jog, memo, memoir, mnemonic, picture, prod, prompt, re-

minder, representation, suggestion, thought, vision; SEE CONCEPTS 529,678

menace [n] *danger; pest*
annoyance, caution, commination, hazard, intimidation, jeopardy, nuisance, peril, plague, risk, scare, threat, thunder, trouble, troublemaker, warning; SEE CONCEPTS 412,675

menace [v] *bother, frighten*
alarm, bad-eye*, browbeat, bully, chill, compromise, endanger, hazard, impend, imperil, intimidate, jeopardize, lean on, loom, lower, overhang, peril, portend, push around, put heat on*, risk, scare, scare hell out of*, spook, terrorize, threaten, torment, whip around*; SEE CONCEPTS 7,19

menacing [adj] *intimidating, ominous*
alarming, approaching, dangerous, frightening, imminent, impending, intimidatory, looming, louring, lowering, minacious, minatory, overhanging, threatening; SEE CONCEPTS 401,537,548

mend [v] *correct, improve, fix*
aid, ameliorate, amend, better, condition, convalesce, cure, darn, doctor, emend, fiddle with, gain, get better, get well, heal, knit, look up, overhaul, patch, perk up, ready, rebuild, recondition, reconstruct, recover, rectify, recuperate, redress, refit, reform, refurbish, rejuvenate, remedy, renew, renovate, repair, restore, retouch, revamp, revise, right, service, sew; SEE CONCEPTS 126,244,303,700

mendacious [adj] *dishonest*
deceitful, deceptive, duplicitous, equivocating, erroneous, fallacious, false, fibbing, fraudulent, insincere, lying, paltering, perfidious, perjured, prevaricating, shifty, spurious, untrue, untruthful, wrong; SEE CONCEPT 267

menial [adj] *lowly, low-status*
abject, base, baseborn, boring, common, degrading, demeaning, dull, fawning, grovelling, humble, humdrum, ignoble, ignominious, low, mean, obeisant, obsequious, routine, servile, slavish, sorry, subservient, sycophantic, unskilled, vile; SEE CONCEPTS 574,575

men's movement [n] *men's attempt to redefine gender roles*
gender revisionism, men's liberation, male reform, men's studies; SEE CONCEPT 388

mental [adj1] *concerning the mind*
brainy*, cerebral, clairvoyant, deep, heavy, ideological, imaginative, immaterial, inner, intellective, intellectual, mysterious, phrenic, psychic, psychical, psychological, rational, reasoning, spiritual, subconscious, subjective, subliminal, telepathic, thinking, thoughtful, unreal; SEE CONCEPTS 402,403

mental [adj2] *insane*
deranged, disturbed, fruity, loco*, lunatic, mad, maniac, mentally ill, mindless, non compos mentis, nuts*, nutsy*, psychiatric, psychotic, unbalanced, unstable; SEE CONCEPTS 314,403

mentality [n] *state of mind; intelligence*
attitude, brainpower, brains, cast, character, comprehension, disposition, frame of mind*, headset*, intellect, intelligence quotient, IQ, makeup, mental age, mind, mindset*, outlook, personality, psychology, rationality, reasoning, routine, sense, turn of mind*, understanding, way of thinking*, wit; SEE CONCEPTS 409,411

mention [n] *referral, observation*
acknowledgment, allusion, citation, comment,

footnote, indication, naming, note, notice, notification, recognition, reference, remark, specifying, tribute, utterance; SEE CONCEPTS 73,278

mention [v] *refer to*
acknowledge, acquaint, adduce, advert, allude to, bring up, broach, call attention to, cite, communicate, declare, designate, detail, disclose, discuss, divulge, enumerate, hint at, impart, infer, instance, intimate, introduce, make known, name, notice, notify, observe, point out, point to, quote, recount, remark, report, reveal, speak about, speak of, specify, state, suggest, tell, throw out, touch on; SEE CONCEPT 73

mentor [n] *person who advises*
adviser, coach, counsellor, guide, instructor, teacher, trainer, tutor; SEE CONCEPT 350

menu [n] *list from which to choose, often to choose food*
bill of fare, card, carte, carte du jour, cuisine, food, spread, table; SEE CONCEPT 283

mercenary [n] *person who fights, kills for money*
hireling, legionnaire, merc, professional soldier, slave, soldier of fortune, warrior; SEE CONCEPTS 358,412

mercenary [adj] *greedy for money*
acquisitive, avaricious, bribable, corrupt, covetous, grabby, grasping, miserly, money-grubbing, selfish, sordid, stingy, unethical, unprincipled, unscrupulous, venal; SEE CONCEPT 401

merchandise [n] *goods for sale*
commodity, effects, job lot, line, material, number, produce, product, seconds, staple, stock, stuff, truck, vendible, wares; SEE CONCEPT 338

merchandise [v] *sell goods*
advertise, buy and sell, deal in, distribute, do business in, market, promote, publicize, retail, trade, traffic in, vend, wholesale; SEE CONCEPT 345

merchant [n] *person who sells goods*
broker, businessperson, consigner, dealer, exporter, handler, jobber, marketer, operator, retailer, salesperson, seller, sender, shipper, shopkeeper, storekeeper, trader, tradesperson, trafficker, tycoon, vendor, wholesaler; SEE CONCEPT 347

merciful [adj] *kind, sparing*
all heart*, beneficent, benign, benignant, bleeding heart*, charitable, clement, compassionate, condoning, easygoing, feeling, forbearing, forgiving, generous, gentle, gracious, heart in right place*, humane, humanitarian, indulgent, kindly, lenient, liberal, mild, pardoning, pitiful, pitying, soft*, softhearted*, sympathetic, tender, tenderhearted, tolerant; SEE CONCEPTS 401,542

merciless [adj] *mean, heartless*
barbarous, callous, compassionless, cruel, cutthroat, dog-eat-dog*, fierce, gratuitous, grim, hard, hardhearted, harsh, hatchet job*, having a killer instinct*, implacable, inexorable, inhumane, iron-fisted, mean machine*, mortal, pitiless, relentless, ruthless, severe, unappeasable, uncalled-for, unfeeling, unflinching, unforgiving, unmerciful, unpitying, unrelenting, unsparing, unsympathetic, unyielding, wanton; SEE CONCEPTS 401,542

mercurial [adj] *flighty, temperamental*
blowing hot and cold*, bubbleheaded*, buoyant, capricious, changeable, effervescent, elastic, erratic, expansive, fickle, flaky, flip*, fluctuating, gaga*, gay, impulsive, inconstant, irregular, irrepressible, lighthearted, lively, lubricious, mad,

mobile, movable, quicksilver, resilient, short-fuse*, spirited, sprightly, ticklish, unpredictable, unstable, up-and-down*, variable, volatile, yo-yo*; SEE CONCEPTS 401,404

mercy [n] *kindness, compassion*
benevolence, benignancy, blessing, boon, charity, clemency, commiseration, favor, forbearance, forgiveness, generosity, gentleness, godsend, goodwill, grace, humanity, kindliness, lenience, leniency, lenity, lifesaver, luck, mildness, pity, quarter, relief, ruth, softheartedness, sympathy, tenderness, tolerance; SEE CONCEPTS 32,633

mere [adj] *nothing more; absolute*
bald, bare, blunt, common, complete, entire, insignificant, little, minor, plain, poor, pure, pure and simple, sheer, simple, small, stark, unadorned, unadulterated, unmitigated, unmixed, utter, very; SEE CONCEPTS 535,589

meretricious [adj] *gaudy, flashy*
blatant, bogus, brazen, chintzy, counterfeit, garish, glaring, insincere, loud, misleading, ornate, phony, plastic*, put-on*, sham, showy, spurious, superficial, tawdry, tinsel, trashy; SEE CONCEPTS 542,589

merge [v] *bring or come together*
absorb, amalgamate, assimilate, become lost in, become partners, be swallowed up*, blend, cement, centralize, coalesce, combine, come aboard*, compound, conglomerate, consolidate, converge, deal one in, fuse, hitch on*, hook up*, immerge, incorporate, interface, intermingle, intermix, join, join up, line up, marry, meet, meld, melt into, mingle, mix, network, plug into, pool, slap on, submerge, synthesize, tack on*, tag, team up*, throw in together*, tie in, unite; SEE CONCEPTS 113,193,324

merger [n] *consolidation*
alliance, amalgamation, cahoots*, coadunation, coalition, combination, fusion, hookup, incorporation, lineup, melding, mergence, merging, organization, pool, takeover, tie-in, tie-up, unification, union; SEE CONCEPTS 323,324,703

meridian [n] *summit, climax*
acme, apex, apogee, crest, culmination, extremity, high noon, high-water mark, peak, pinnacle, zenith; SEE CONCEPTS 832,836

merit [n] *advantage*
arete, asset, benefit, caliber, credit, desert, dignity, excellence, excellency, good, goodness, honor, integrity, perfection, quality, stature, strong point, talent, value, virtue, worth, worthiness; SEE CONCEPT 693

merit [v] *be entitled to*
be in line for, be worthy, deserve, earn, get one's comeuppance*, get one's due*, get one's just deserts*, get what is coming*, have a claim, have a right, have coming, incur, justify, rate, warrant; SEE CONCEPT 129

meritorious [adj] *honorable, commendable*
admirable, boss*, choice, creditable, deserving, estimable, excellent, exemplary, golden, good, laudable, meritable, noble, praisable, praiseworthy, right, righteous, thankworthy, top drawer*, virtuous, winner, world-beating*, worthy; SEE CONCEPTS 404,548,572

merriment/merrymaking [n] *enjoyment, amusement*
brawl, buffoonery, cheerfulness, conviviality, festivity, frolic, fun, fun and games*, gaiety, glee, happiness, hilarity, hoopla*, indulgence, jocular-

ity, jocundity, jollity, joviality, joy, laughs, laughter, levity, liveliness, mirth, picnic, recreation, revel, revelry, self-indulgence, shindig, sport, whoopee*, wingding*; SEE CONCEPTS *386,410*

merry [adj] *very happy; festive*
amusing, blithe, blithesome, boisterous, boon, carefree, cheerful, comic, comical, convivial, enjoyable, entertaining, facetious, frolicsome, fun-loving, funny, gay, glad, gleeful, grooving*, hilarious, humorous, jocund, jolly, joyful, joyous, jumping, larking, lighthearted, lively, mad, mirthful, perky, pleasant, riotous, rip-roaring*, rocking, rollicking, saturnalian, sportive, sunny, unconstrained, uproarious, vivacious, wild, winsome, zappy*, zingy*, zippy*; SEE CONCEPTS *403,548,572*

mesh [n] *netting, entanglement*
cobweb, jungle, knot, labyrinth, maze, morass, net, network, plexus, reticulation, screen, skein, snare, snarl, tangle, toils, tracery, trap, web; SEE CONCEPTS *611,733*

mesh [v] *entangle, connect*
agree, catch, coincide, combine, come together, coordinate, dovetail, engage, enmesh, ensnare, fit, fit together, harmonize, interlock, knit, net, snare, tangle, trap; SEE CONCEPTS *113,193*

mesmerize [v] *captivate*
catch up, control, deaden, drug, ensorcell, enthrall, entrance, fascinate, grip, hold spellbound, hypnotize, magnetize, numb, render unconscious, spellbind, stupefy; SEE CONCEPTS *11,14*

mess [n1] *disorder, litter*
botch, chaos, clutter, combination, compound, confusion, debris, dirtiness, disarray, discombubulation*, disorganization, every which way*, eyesore, fright, hash, hodgepodge, jumble, mayhem, mishmash, monstrosity, salmagundi, shambles, sight, turmoil, untidiness, wreck, wreckage; SEE CONCEPTS *230,260*

mess [n2] *difficulty, predicament*
dilemma, fix, imbroglio, jam, mix-up, muddle, perplexity, pickle*, plight, stew; SEE CONCEPT *674*

message [n1] *communication, often written*
bulletin, cannonball, communiqué, directive, dispatch, dope, earful, epistle, information, intelligence, intimation, letter, memo, memorandum, missive, news, note, notice, paper, report, tidings, wire, word; SEE CONCEPTS *271,274*

message [n2] *meaning, idea*
acceptation, import, intendment, moral, point, purport, sense, significance, significancy, signification, theme, understanding; SEE CONCEPTS *661,682*

mess around [v] *fiddle; goof off*
amuse oneself, dabble, dawdle, doodle, fool around, loiter, muck around*, play, play around, play the fool*, potter, puddle, putter, tinker, trifle; SEE CONCEPTS *87,363*

messenger [n] *person carrying information to another*
agent, ambassador, bearer, carrier, commissionaire, courier, crier, delegate, delivery person, detachment, detail, dispatcher, emissary, envoy, errand person*, flag-bearer, forerunner, go-between*, gofer*, harbinger, herald, intermediary, mediator, minister, post, precursor, prophet, runner, schlepper*; SEE CONCEPT *348*

mess up [v] *disorder, dirty*
befoul, besmirch, bobble, bollix*, botch, bungle, clutter, confuse, damage, derange, destroy, disarrange, discompose, dishevel, disorganize, disturb, foul, goof up*, gum up*, jumble, litter, louse up, muddle, pollute, ruin, rummage, scramble, screw up*, smear, soil, spoil, unsettle, upset; SEE CONCEPTS *158,252,254*

messy [adj] *cluttered, dirty*
blotchy*, careless, chaotic, confused, disheveled, disordered, disorganized, grimy, grubby*, littered, muddled, raunchy*, rumpled, slapdash*, slipshod*, sloppy, slovenly, unfastidious, unkempt, untidy; SEE CONCEPTS *485,621*

metal [n] *lustrous chemical element*
alloy, casting, deposit, foil, hardware, ingot, leaf, load, mail, mineral, native rock, ore, plate, solder, vein; SEE CONCEPT *476*

metamorphose [v] *convert, transform*
age, alter, be reborn, change, commute, develop, diverge, mature, mutate, remake, remodel, reshape, ripen, transfigure, translate, transmogrify, transmute, transubstantiate, vary; SEE CONCEPTS *469,697,701*

metamorphosis [n] *conversion, transformation*
alteration, change, changeover, evolution, mutation, rebirth, transfiguration, transfigurement, translation, transmogrification, transmutation, transubstantiation; SEE CONCEPTS *469,697,701*

metaphor [n] *figure of speech, implied comparison*
allegory, analogy, emblem, hope, image, metonymy, personification, similitude, symbol, trope; SEE CONCEPT *275*

metaphysical [adj] *not physical; without physical presence*
abstract, abstruse, bodiless, deep, difficult, discarnate, esoteric, eternal, fundamental, high-flown, ideal, immaterial, impalpable, incorporeal, insubstantial, intangible, intellectual, jesuitic, mystical, nonmaterial, nonphysical, numinous, oversubtle, philosophical, preternatural, profound, recondite, spiritual, superhuman, superior, supermundane, supernatural, suprahuman, supramundane, supranatural, theoretical, transcendental, unearthly, unfleshly, universal, unphysical, unreal, unsubstantial; SEE CONCEPTS *529,582*

mete [v] *administer, distribute*
admeasure, allocate, allot, allow, apportion, assign, deal, dispense, divide, dole, give, lot, measure, parcel, portion, ration, share; SEE CONCEPTS *98,108*

meteoric [adj] *brief, sudden*
dazzling, ephemeral, flashing, fleeting, momentary, overnight, rapid, spectacular, speedy, swift, transient; SEE CONCEPTS *548,798,799*

meter [n] *rhythm, beat*
cadence, cadency, feet, lilt, measure, mora, music, pattern, poetry, rhyme, structure, swing; SEE CONCEPTS *65,262*

method [n1] *means, procedure*
adjustment, approach, arrangement, channels, course, custom, design, disposal, disposition, fashion, form, formula, habit, line, manner, mechanism, method, mode, modus, modus operandi, nuts and bolts*, plan, practice, proceeding, process, program, receipt, recipe, red tape*, ritual, rote, routine, rubric, rule, rut, schema, scheme, shortcut, style, system, tack, tactics, technic, technique, tenor, the book*, usage, way,

ways and means*, wise, wrinkle*: SEE CONCEPTS *6,660*

method [n2] *order, pattern*
arrangement, classification, design, form, orderliness, organization, plan, planning, purpose, regularity, structure, system: SEE CONCEPTS *727,770*

methodical/methodic [adj] *organized, precise*
all together, analytical, businesslike, by the book*, by the numbers, careful, cut-and-dried*, deliberate, disciplined, efficient, exact, fixed, framed, in a groove*, logical, methodized, meticulous, neat, ordered, orderly, painstaking, planned, regular, scrupulous, set-up*, structured, systematic, tidy, together, well-regulated: SEE CONCEPTS *326,542,544,585*

meticulous [adj] *detailed, perfectionist*
accurate, cautious, conscientious, conscionable, crossing the t's*, dotting the i's*, exact, fastidious, fussy, heedful, microscopic, nitpicking*, painstaking, particular, persnickety*, picky, precise, punctilious, punctual, scrupulous, stickling, strict, thorough: SEE CONCEPTS *542,544,557*

metropolitan [adj] *concerning a city*
city, cosmopolitan, modern, municipal, urban, urbane: SEE CONCEPT *536*

mettle [n] *boldness, strength of character*
animation, ardor, backbone, bravery, caliber, courage, daring, dauntlessness, disposition, energy, fire, force, fortitude, gallantry, gameness, grit*, guts*, hardihood, heart*, indomitability, kidney*, life*, makeup, moxie, nature, nerve, pluck, quality, resolution, resolve, spirit, spunk, stamina, stamp*, starch, temper, temperament, valor, vigor, vitality: SEE CONCEPT *411*

microbe [n] *bacteria*
bacillus, bacterium, bug*, crud, germ, microorganism, pathogen, plague, virus: SEE CONCEPT *306*

microscopic [adj] *tiny, almost undetectable*
atomic, diminutive, imperceptible, infinitesimal, invisible, little, minuscule, minute, negligible, teeny*, wee*: SEE CONCEPTS *773,789*

middle [n] *center*
core, deep, focus, halfway, halfway point, heart, inside, marrow, mean, media, midpoint, midriff, midsection, midst, thick, waist: SEE CONCEPTS *746,761,830,833*

middle [adj] *central*
average, between, betwixt and between*, center, centermost, equidistant, halfway, inner, inside, intermediate, intervening, mainstream, mean, medial, median, medium, mezzo*, middlemost, middle of the road*, midmost, smack in the middle, straddling the fence*: SEE CONCEPTS *547,583,830*

middle person [n] *person who acts as intermediary*
agent, broker, connection, distributor, entrepreneur, fixer, go-between*, influence, interagent, interceder, intercessor, intermediate, intermediator, jobber*, mediator, representative, salesperson, wholesaler: SEE CONCEPT *348*

middling [adj] *adequate, okay*
all right, average, common, conventional, decent, fair, fairish, good, indifferent, intermediate, mean, mediocre, medium, moderate, modest, okay, ordinary, passable, run-of-the-mill*, so-so*, tolerable, traditional, unexceptional, unremarkable: SEE CONCEPT *547*

midget [n] *small person*
bantam, gnome, homuncule, homunculus, Lilli-

putian*, little person, manikin, midge, runt*: SEE CONCEPT *424*

midget [adj] *short, small*
baby, diminutive, knee-high*, Lilliputian, miniature, minikin, pocket, teensy*, teeny*, tiny: SEE CONCEPTS *773,779*

midst [n] *middle, core*
betwixt and between*, bosom, center, deep, depths, halfway, heart, hub, interior, mean, medium, midpoint, nucleus, thick: SEE CONCEPT *830*

mien [n] *person's presence, manner*
act, address, air, appearance, aspect, aura, bearing, carriage, countenance, demeanor, deportment, expression, front, image, look, mannerism, port, set, style: SEE CONCEPTS *411,644*

miff [v] *annoy*
aggrieve, bother, displease, hurt, irk, irritate, nettle, offend, pester, pique, provoke, put out, resent, upset, vex: SEE CONCEPTS *7,19*

might [n] *ability, power*
adequacy, arm, authority, capability, capacity, clout, command, competence, control, domination, efficacy, efficiency, energy, force, forcefulness, forcibleness, get-up-and-go*, jurisdiction, lustiness, mastery, moxie*, muscle*, potency, powerfulness, prowess, puissance, punch, qualification, qualifiedness, sinew*, steam, strength, strenuousness, strong arm*, sway, valor, vigor, vigorousness: SEE CONCEPTS *411,641,732*

mightily [adv1] *very much, extremely*
decidedly, exceedingly, greatly, highly, hugely, intensely, mighty, notably, surpassingly, very: SEE CONCEPT *569*

mightily [adv2] *forcefully*
arduously, energetically, forcibly, hard, hardly, laboriously, lustily, might and main*, powerfully, strenuously, strongly, vigorously, with all one's strength: SEE CONCEPTS *540,544*

mighty [adj1] *forceful, powerful*
boss*, doughty, hardy, indomitable, lusty, muscular, omnipotent, potent, powerhouse, puissant, robust, stalwart, steamroller*, stout, strapping, strengthy, strong, strong as ox*, sturdy, vigorous, wieldy: SEE CONCEPTS *489,540*

mighty [adj2] *gigantic, monumental*
august, bulky, colossal, considerable, dynamic, eminent, enormous, extensive, extraordinary, grand, great, heroic, high, huge, illustrious, immense, imposing, impressive, intense, irresistible, large, magnificent, majestic, massive, moving, notable, prodigious, renowned, stupendous, titanic, towering, tremendous, vast: SEE CONCEPTS *537,773,781*

migrant [n] *person who moves to a foreign place*
departer, drifter, emigrant, evacuee, expatriate, gypsy, immigrant, itinerant, migrator, mover, nomad, rover, tinker, transient, traveler, vagrant, wanderer: SEE CONCEPT *413*

migrant/migratory [adj] *moving, traveling*
casual, changing, drifting, emigrating, errant, gypsy, immigrant, immigrating, impermanent, itinerant, migrative, migratorial, mobile, nomad, nomadic, on the move, passing over, passing through, peripatetic, ranging, roving, seasonal, shifting, temporary, tramp, transient, transmigratory, unsettled, vagabond, vagrant, wandering: SEE CONCEPT *584*

migrate [v] *move, travel to another place*
drift, emigrate, immigrate, journey, leave, no-

madize, range, roam, rove, shift, transmigrate, trek, voyage, wander; SEE CONCEPTS *198,224*

mild [adj1] *gentle, temperate, nonirritating*
balmy, benign, benignant, blah*, bland, breezy, calm, choice, clear, clement, cool, dainty, delicate, demulcent, easy, emollient, exquisite, faint, fine, flat, genial, ho-hum*, lenient, lenitive, light, lukewarm, medium, mellow, moderate, mollifying, nothing, nothing much*, pabulum, pacific, peaceful, placid, smooth, soft, soothing, sunny, tempered, tepid, untroubled, vanilla*, warm, weak, wimpy*; SEE CONCEPTS *485,525,537*

mild [adj2] *easygoing, pleasant in personality*
amiable, balmy, bland, calm, clement, compassionate, complaisant, deferential, docile, dull, easy, equable, feeble, flat, forbearant, forbearing, forgiving, gentle, good-humored, good-natured, good-tempered, humane, indulgent, insipid, jejune, kind, lenient, meek, merciful, mild-mannered, moderate, obeisant, obliging, pacific, patient, peaceable, placid, serene, smooth, soft, spiritless, subdued, submissive, subservient, tame, temperate, tender, tranquil, unassuming, vapid, warm; SEE CONCEPTS *401,404*

mile [n] *5,280 feet/1.609 kilometers measured*
nautical, square, statute; SEE CONCEPTS *790,791*

milestone [n] *achievement*
anniversary, breakthrough, discovery, event, landmark, milepost, occasion, turning point, waypost; SEE CONCEPTS *2,706*

milieu [n] *environment, atmosphere*
ambience, ambient, background, bag, climate, element, locale, location, medium, mise-en-scène, nabe, neighborhood, place, scene, setting, space, sphere, surroundings, turf; SEE CONCEPT *673*

militant [n] *person who fights, is aggressive*
activist, belligerent, combatant, demonstrator, fighter, objector, partisan, protester, rioter, warrior; SEE CONCEPTS *358,359*

militant [adj] *aggressive, combative*
active, assertive, assertory, bellicose, belligerent, combating, contending, contentious, embattled, fighting, gladiatorial, in arms, martial, militaristic, military, offensive, pugnacious, pushy, quarrelsome, scrappy, self-assertive, truculent, up in arms, vigorous, warlike, warring; SEE CONCEPT *401*

military [n] *armed force*
air force, army, force, marines, navy, service, servicepeople, soldiery, troop; SEE CONCEPT *322*

military [adj] *soldierlike; concerning the armed forces*
aggressive, armed, army, combatant, combative, fighting, martial, militant, militaristic, noncivil, soldierly, warlike, warmongering; SEE CONCEPT *536*

milk [n] *liquid produced by mammals*
buttermilk, chalk*, condensed, cream, evaporated, formula, goat, half-and-half, homogenized, laiche, low fat, moo juice*, pasteurized, powdered, raw, skim, two-percent, whole; SEE CONCEPT *467*

milk [v] *tap; exploit*
bleed, drain, draw off, elicit, empty, evince, evoke, exhaust, express, extort, extract, fleece, impose on, let out, press, pump, siphon, suck, take advantage, take out, use, wring; SEE CONCEPTS *139,142,156,225*

milky [adj] *white, cloudy*
alabaster, clouded, frosted, lacteal, lacteous, lac-

tescent, milk-white, opalescent, opaline, opaque, pearly, whitish; SEE CONCEPT *618*

mill [n] *factory*
foundry, manufactory, plant, shop, sweatshop, works; SEE CONCEPTS *439,449*

mill [v] *grind*
comminute, crush, granulate, grate, pound, powder, press, pulverize; SEE CONCEPT *186*

mimic [n] *person who imitates*
actor, caricaturist, comedian, copycat, imitator, impersonator, impressionist, mime, mummer, parodist, parrot, performer, playactor, player, thespian, trouper; SEE CONCEPT *352*

mimic [v] *imitate, mock*
act, ape, burlesque, caricature, copy, copycat, ditto*, do, do like*, echo, enact, fake, go like*, impersonate, look like*, make believe, make fun of, make like*, mime, mirror, pantomime, parody, parrot, perform, personate, play, resemble, ridicule, sham, simulate, take off*, travesty; SEE CONCEPTS *54,59,111,171*

mince [v1] *chop up*
chip, crumble, cut, dice, divide, grind, hack, hash, whack; SEE CONCEPT *176*

mince [v2] *pose, put on airs*
attitudinize, flounce, posture, prance, sashay, strut; SEE CONCEPT *59*

mince [v3] *euphemize, hold back in communication*
alleviate, decrease, diminish, extenuate, lessen, minimize, moderate, palliate, soften, spare, tone down, weaken; SEE CONCEPT *266*

mincing [adj] *affected, pretentious*
artificial, dainty, delicate, effeminate, fastidious, finical, finicky, fussy, genteel, insincere, la-di-da*, nice, particular, persnickety, precious, sissy, squeamish, stilted, too-too*, unnatural; SEE CONCEPTS *401,404*

mind [n1] *intelligence*
apperception, attention, brain*, brainpower, brains*, capacity, cognizance, conception, consciousness, creativity, faculty, function, genius, head, imagination, ingenuity, instinct, intellect, intellectual, intellectuality, intuition, judgment, lucidity, marbles*, mentality, observation, perception, percipience, power, psyche, ratiocination, reason, reasoning, regard, sanity, sense, soul, soundness, spirit, talent, thinker, thought, understanding, wisdom, wits; SEE CONCEPTS *393,409*

mind [n2] *memory*
attention, cognizance, concentration, head, mark, note, notice, observance, observation, recollection, regard, remark, remembrance, subconscious, thinking, thoughts; SEE CONCEPTS *409,630*

mind [n3] *inclination, tendency; belief*
attitude, bent, conviction, desire, determination, disposition, eye, fancy, feeling, humor, impulse, intention, judgment, leaning, liking, mood, notion, opinion, outlook, persuasion, pleasure, point of view, purpose, sentiment, strain, temper, temperament, thoughts, tone, urge, vein, view, way of thinking, will, wish; SEE CONCEPTS *20,657,689*

mind [v1] *be bothered; care*
be affronted, be opposed, complain, deplore, disapprove, dislike, look askance at, object, resent, take offense; SEE CONCEPTS *21,29*

mind [v2] *comply, obey*
adhere to, attend, behave, do as told, follow, fol-

low orders, heed, keep, listen, mark, note, notice, observe, pay attention, pay heed, regard, respect, take heed, watch; SEE CONCEPTS 23,91

mind [v3] *attend, tend*
baby-sit, be attentive, behold, care for, discern, discipline, ensure, give heed to, govern, guard, have charge of, keep an eye on*, listen up, look, make certain, mark, mind the store*, note, notice, observe, oversee, perceive, regard, ride herd on*, see, sit, superintend, supervise, watch; SEE CONCEPTS 110,295,596,623

mind [v4] *be careful*
be cautious, be concerned, be on guard, be solicitous, be wary, have a care, mind one's p's and q's*, take care, tend, toe the line*, trouble, watch, watch one's step*, watch out*; SEE CONCEPT 34

mind [v5] *remember*
bethink, bring to mind, cite, recall, recollect, remind, reminisce, retain; SEE CONCEPT 40

mindful [adj] *attentive, aware*
alert, alive to, apprehensive, au courant, be up on*, cagey, careful, cautious, chary, cognizant, conscientious, conscious, conversant, heedful, in the know, know all the answers*, knowing, know ins and outs*, knowledgeable, observant, observative, observing, on one's toes*, on the ball*, on the job*, on to*, plugged in*, regardful, respectful, sensible, solicitous, thoughtful, tuned in*, vigilant, wary, watchful, with eyes peeled*; SEE CONCEPTS 402,403,542

mindless [adj] *oblivious, stupid; automatic*
asinine, brutish, careless, daydreaming, foolish, forgetful, gratuitous, heedless, idiotic, imbecilic, inattentive, mooning, moronic, neglectful, negligent, nitwitted, obtuse, out, out of it*, rash, senseless, silly, simple, spaced-out*, thoughtless, unaware, unintelligent, unmindful, unthinking, witless; SEE CONCEPTS 403,538

mine [n] *deposit, supply*
abundance, bed, bonanza, ditch, excavation, field, fount, fountain, fund, gold mine, hoard, lode, pit, quarry, reserve, shaft, source, spring, stock, store, treasure trove, treasury, trench, vein, wealth, well, wellspring; SEE CONCEPTS 449,509,712

mine [v] *dig up*
burrow, delve, dig for, drill, excavate, extract, hew, pan, quarry, sap, scoop, shovel, unearth, work; SEE CONCEPT 178

mingle [v1] *physically join*
admix, alloy, blend, coalesce, commingle, compound, intermingle, intermix, interweave, make up, marry, meld, merge, mix, unite, wed; SEE CONCEPT 193

mingle [v2] *socialize*
associate, circulate, consort, fraternize, gang up*, hang out*, hobnob, mix, network, pool, rub shoulders*, tie in, work the room*; SEE CONCEPT 384

miniature [n] *tiny thing*
baby, insignificancy, midget, model, pocket edition, toy; SEE CONCEPT 730

miniature [adj] *tiny*
baby, diminutive, itsy-bitsy*, itty-bitty*, Lilliputian*, little, midget, mini, minikin, minuscule, minute, mite, model, petite, pint-sized*, pocket, reduced, scaled-down, small, small-scale, teensy*, teeny*, toy, wee; SEE CONCEPTS 773,789

minimal [adj] *littlest, slightest*
basal, basic, essential, fundamental, least, least

possible, lowest, minimum, nominal, smallest, token; SEE CONCEPTS 762,773,789

minimize [v] *make smaller; underrate*
abbreviate, attenuate, belittle, cheapen, curtail, cut down to size, cut rate, decrease, decry, deprecate, depreciate, derogate, detract, diminish, discount, disparage, downplay*, dwarf*, knock*, knock down*, lessen, make light of*, make little of, miniaturize, pan, play down, pooh-pooh*, poor-mouth*, prune, put down, reduce, run down, shrink, underestimate, underplay; SEE CONCEPTS 54,240,247

minimum [n] *lowest amount*
atom, bottom, dab, depth, dot, gleam, grain, hair, iota, jot, least, lowest, margin, modicum, molecule, nadir, narrowest, particle, pittance, point, scintilla, scruple, shadow, slightest, smallest, smidgen, soupçon, spark, speck, trifle, whit; SEE CONCEPTS 787,831

minimum [adj] *least, lowest*
least possible, littlest, merest, minimal, slightest, smallest, tiniest; SEE CONCEPTS 762,789

minister [n1] *person in charge of church*
abbot, archbishop, archdeacon, bishop, chaplain, clergy, clergyperson, cleric, clerical, clerk, confessor, curate, deacon, dean, diocesan, divine, ecclesiastic, lecturer, missionary, monk, parson, pastor, preacher, prelate, priest, pulpiteer, rector, reverend, shepherd, vicar; SEE CONCEPT 361

minister [n2] *person high in government*
administrator, agent, aide, ambassador, assistant, cabinet member, consul, delegate, diplomat, envoy, executive, legate, liaison, lieutenant, officeholder, official, plenipotentiary, premier, prime minister, secretary; SEE CONCEPT 354

minister [v] *help, serve*
accommodate, administer, aid, answer, attend, be solicitous of, cater to, cure, doctor, do for, foster, heal, nurse, pander, pander to, remedy, succor, take care of, tend, treat, wait on, watch over; SEE CONCEPT 110

minor [n] *person under legal age of maturity*
adolescent, baby, boy, child, girl, infant, junior, juvenile, lad, little one, schoolboy, schoolgirl, teenager, underage, youngster, youth; SEE CONCEPT 424

minor [adj] *insignificant, small*
accessory, below the mark, bush-league*, casual, dependent, dinky*, inconsequential, inconsiderable, inferior, junior, lesser, light, low, minus, negligible, paltry, petty, piddling, secondary, second-string*, slight, smaller, small-fry*, smalltime, subordinate, subsidiary, tacky, trifling, trivial, two-bit*, unimportant, younger; SEE CONCEPTS 575,773,789

mint [n] *a lot of money*
boodle, bundle, fortune, heap, million, packet, pile, pot, roll, wad; SEE CONCEPTS 340,787

mint [adj] *brand-new*
excellent, first-class, fresh, intact, original, perfect, spanking-new*, spick-and-span*, unblemished, undamaged, unmarred, untarnished, virgin; SEE CONCEPTS 574,578,797

mint [v] *create, coin*
cast, construct, devise, fabricate, fashion, forge, invent, issue, make, make up, mold, monetize, produce, provide, punch, stamp, strike, think up; SEE CONCEPTS 43,173,205,251

minute [n] *brief time period*
bat of an eye*, breath, breathing, crack, flash,

mi
mi

instant, jiffy*, min*, mo*, moment, nothing flat*, sec*, second, shake, short time*, sixtieth of hour, sixty seconds, split second, twinkling*; SEE CONCEPTS 803,807,821

minute [adj1] *very small*
atomic, diminutive, exact, exiguous, fine, inconsiderable, infinitesimal, insignificant, invisible, little, microbic, microscopic, miniature, minim, minimal, minuscule, molecular, peewee*, piddling, peewee, puny, slender, teeny-weeny*, tiny, wee; SEE CONCEPTS 773,789

minute [adj2] *unimportant*
immaterial, inconsiderable, insignificant, light, little, minor, negligible, nonessential, paltry, petty, picayune, piddling, puny, slight, small, trifling, trivial; SEE CONCEPT 575

minute [adj3] *exact, precise*
blow-by-blow*, careful, circumstantial, clocklike, close, critical, detailed, elaborate, exhaustive, full, itemized, meticulous, painstaking, particular, particularized, punctilious, scrupulous, specialized, thorough; SEE CONCEPT 557

miracle [n] *wonderful, surprising event or thing*
marvel, phenomenon, portent, prodigy, rarity, revelation, sensation, stunner, supernatural occurrence, surprise, thaumaturgy, unusualness, wonder; SEE CONCEPTS 671,689,693

miraculous [adj] *surprisingly wonderful*
amazing, anomalous, astonishing, astounding, awesome, extraordinary, fabulous, freakish, heavy, incredible, inexplicable, magical, marvelous, monstrous, numinous, phenomenal, preternatural, prodigious, spectacular, staggering, strange, stupefying, stupendous, superhuman, superior, supermundane, supernatural, supranatural, thaumaturgic, the utmost, unaccountable, unbelievable, unearthly, unimaginable, unreal, wonderworking, wondrous; SEE CONCEPTS 529,548,572

mirage [n] *imaginary vision*
delusion, fantasy, hallucination, ignis fatuus, illusion, optical illusion, phantasm; SEE CONCEPTS 529,628

mire [n] *muck, morass*
bog, dirt, fen, glop*, goo*, gunk*, marsh, moss, mud, ooze*, quagmire, quicksand, slime*, swamp; SEE CONCEPTS 509,674

mire [v] *delay, catch up in*
bog down, cling, decelerate, detain, dirty, embroil, enmesh, ensnare, entangle, entrap, flounder, hang up, implicate, involve, retard, set back, sink, slow down, slow up, snare, soil, stick, tangle, trap; SEE CONCEPTS 112,121

mirror [n] *glass that reflects image*
cheval glass, gaper, hand glass, imager, looking glass, pier glass, polished metal, reflector, seeing glass, speculum; SEE CONCEPTS 443,470

mirror [v] *copy, reflect*
act like, depict, double, echo, embody, emulate, epitomize, exemplify, follow, glass, illustrate, image, imitate, make like*, mimic, personify, represent, show, simulate, symbolize, take off*, typify; SEE CONCEPTS 111,118,171

mirth [n] *great joy*
amusement, cheer, cheerfulness, convulsions, entertainment, festivity, frivolity, frolic, fun, gaiety, gladness, glee, happiness, hilarity, hysteria, hysterics, jocularity, jocundity, jollity, joviality, joyousness, kicks*, laughs, laughter, levity, lightheartedness, merriment, merrymaking, plea-

sure, rejoicing, revelry, sport, whoopee*; SEE CONCEPTS 388,410

misadventure [n] *bad luck, mishap*
accident, adversity, bad break*, blunder, calamity, casualty, cataclysm, catastrophe, debacle, disaster, error, failure, faux pas, ill fortune, lapse, mischance, misfortune, reverse, setback, slip, tragedy, woe; SEE CONCEPT 674

misanthrope [n] *person who hates others*
cynic, doubter, egoist, egotist, hater, isolate, loner, misanthropist, recluse, skeptic; SEE CONCEPT 412

misanthropic [adj] *unsociable, cynical*
antisocial, egoistic, egotistical, eremitic, hating, inhumane, malevolent, misanthropical, reclusive, reserved, sarcastic, selfish, solitary, standoffish, unfriendly; SEE CONCEPT 404

misapprehend [v] *get the wrong idea, impression*
blunder, confuse, err, misconceive, misconstrue, misinterpret, misread, miss, mistake, misunderstand; SEE CONCEPT 15

misappropriate [v] *use wrongly; steal*
abuse, appropriate, defalcate, embezzle, misapply, misspend, misuse, peculate, plunder, pocket, rob, swindle; SEE CONCEPTS 139,156,341

misbegotten [adj] *illegitimate, illicit*
baseborn, bastard, dishonest, disreputable, illegal, natural, poor, shady, spurious, stolen, supposititious, unlawful, unrespectable; SEE CONCEPTS 319,549

misbehave [v] *act in inappropriate manner*
act up, be at fault, be bad, be dissolute, be guilty, be immoral, be indecorous, be insubordinate, be mischievous, bend the law*, be out of line*, be out of order*, be reprehensible, carry on, cut up, deviate, do evil, do wrong, fail, fool around*, get into mischief, go astray, go wrong, make trouble, misconduct, offend, roughhouse*, sin, sow wild oats*, take a wrong turn*, transgress, trespass; SEE CONCEPTS 633,645

misbehavior [n] *naughty act, conduct*
acting up*, fault, immorality, impropriety, incivility, indiscipline, insubordination, mischief, misconduct, misdeed, misdemeanor, misdoing, monkey business*, naughtiness, rudeness, shenanigans*, transgression, wrongdoing; SEE CONCEPTS 633,645

miscalculate [v] *make a mistake*
blow*, blunder, discount, disregard, drop the ball*, err, get signals crossed*, get wrong, go wrong, mess up*, misconstrue, miscount, misinterpret, misjudge, misread, misreckon, miss by a mile*, misunderstand, mix up, overestimate, overlook, overrate, overvalue, slip up, stumble, underestimate, underrate, undervalue; SEE CONCEPT 101

miscarriage [n] *failure*
abortion, botch, breakdown, defeat, error, interruption, malfunction, misadventure, mischance, misfire, mishap, miss, mistake, nonsuccess, perversion, undoing; SEE CONCEPTS 230,699

miscellaneous [adj] *diversified, various*
assorted, confused, conglomerate, different, disordered, disparate, divergent, divers, diverse, heterogeneous, indiscriminate, jumbled, many, mingled, mixed, motley, muddled, multifarious, multiform, odd, promiscuous, scattered, scrambled, sundry, unmatched, unsorted, varied, variegated; SEE CONCEPT 564

miscellany [n] *varied collection*
accumulation, aggregation, anthology, assortment, brew, collectanea, combination, combo, compilation, conglomeration, cumulation, diversity, farrago, gallimaufry, garbage*, hash, hodgepodge, jumble, medley, mélange, melee, mess, mishmash, mix, mixed bag, mixture, muddle, odds and ends*, olio, pasticcio, pastiche, patchwork, potpourri, salad, salmagundi, smorgasbord, stew, variety; SEE CONCEPTS *432,665*

mischief [n] *trouble, damage*
atrocity, catastrophe, devilment, devilry, dirty trick*, evil, fault, friskiness, frolicsomeness, funny business*, gag, harm, high jinks*, hurt, ill, impishness, injury, misbehavior, mischievousness, misconduct, misdoing, misfortune, monkey business*, naughtiness, outrage, playfulness, prank, rascality, roguery, roguishness, sabotage, shenanigans, sportiveness, transgression, vandalism, waggery, waggishness, waywardness, wrong, wrongdoing; SEE CONCEPTS *192,633,645*

mischievous [adj] *devilish, wicked*
arch, artful, bad, bothersome, damaging, dangerous, deleterious, destructive, detrimental, dickens*, evil, exasperating, foxy*, frolicsome, harmful, hazardous, holy terror*, hurtful, ill, ill-behaved, impish, injurious, insidious, irksome, malicious, malignant, misbehaving, naughty, nocuous, perilous, pernicious, playful, precarious, puckish, rascal, rascally, risky, rude, sinful, sly, spiteful, sportive, teasing, tricky, troublesome, vexatious, vexing, vicious, wayward; SEE CONCEPTS *401,545*

misconception [n] *wrong idea, impression*
delusion, error, fallacy, fault, misapprehension, misconstruction, misinterpretation, mistake, mistaken belief, misunderstanding; SEE CONCEPTS *409,689*

misconduct [n] *bad or unethical behavior*
delinquency, dereliction, evil, immorality, impropriety, malfeasance, malpractice, malversation, misbehavior, mischief, misdemeanor, misdoing, mismanagement, naughtiness, offense, rudeness, transgression, wrongdoing; SEE CONCEPTS *192,633,645*

misconstrue [v] *get a wrong or false impression*
distort, exaggerate, misapprehend, misconceive, misinterpret, misjudge, misread, mistake, mistranslate, misunderstand, pervert, take the wrong way; SEE CONCEPT *15*

miscreant [n] *person who is very bad, immoral*
blackguard, black sheep*, bootlegger, bully, cad, caitiff, convict, criminal, culprit, delinquent, drunkard, evildoer, felon, fink*, heel*, hoodlum, jailbird, loafer, louse*, lowlife*, malefactor, outcast, outlaw, pickpocket, racketeer, rapscallion, rascal, rat*, reprobate, rowdy, ruffian, scalawag, scamp, scoundrel, scum*, sinner, sneak, vagabond, villain, wretch, wrongdoer; SEE CONCEPT *412*

miscreant [adj] *evil, immoral*
corrupt, criminal, degenerate, depraved, flagitious, infamous, iniquitous, nefarious, perverse, rascally, reprehensible, reprobate, unhealthy, unprincipled, vicious, villainous, wicked; SEE CONCEPTS *401,545*

misdeed/misdemeanor [n] *sin, crime*
breach of law, criminality, dirt*, dirty deed*, dirty pool*, fault, infringement, malefaction, misbehavior, misconduct, miscue, offense, peccadillo,

slipup, transgression, trespass, villainy, violation, wrong, wrongdoing; SEE CONCEPTS *192,633,645*

miser [n] *person who hoards money, possessions*
cheapskate*, churl, harpy*, hoarder, moneygrubber*, penny-pincher*, pinchfist*, pinchpenny*, Scrooge*, stiff*, tightwad*; SEE CONCEPTS *348,412,423*

miserable [adj 1] *unhappy, depressed*
afflicted, agonized, ailing, anguished, brokenhearted, crestfallen, dejected, desolate, despairing, despondent, destroyed, disconsolate, discontented, distressed, doleful, dolorous, down, downcast, down in the mouth*, forlorn, gloomy, heartbroken, hopeless, hurt, hurting, ill, injured, in pain, melancholy, mournful, on a downer*, pained, pathetic, pitiable, racked, rueful, ruthful, sad, sick, sickly, sorrowful, strained, suffering, tormented, tortured, tragic, troubled, woebegone, wounded, wretched; SEE CONCEPT *403*

miserable [adj 2] *destitute, shabby*
abject, bad, contemptible, deplorable, despicable, detestable, disgraceful, godforsaken, impoverished, indigent, inferior, lamentable, low, meager, mean, needy, paltry, pathetic, penniless, piteous, pitiable, poor, poverty-stricken, sad, scanty, scurvy, shameful, sordid, sorry, squalid, tragic, vile, worthless, wretched; SEE CONCEPTS *485,570*

miserly [adj] *greedy, stingy*
abject, avaricious, beggarly, cheapskate*, churlish, close, close-fisted, covetous, grasping, ignoble, illiberal, mean, parsimonious, pennypinching*, penurious, skinflint*, sordid, tightfisted*, ungenerous; SEE CONCEPTS *326,334, 401,404*

misery [n 1] *pain, mental or physical*
ache, agony, anguish, anvil chorus, bad news*, blues*, depression, desolation, despair, despondency, discomfort, distress, dolor, gloom, grief, hardship, headache, heartache, hurting, melancholy, pang, passion, sadness, sorrow, squalor, stitch, suffering, throe, torment, torture, twinge, unhappiness, woe, worriment, worry, wretchedness; SEE CONCEPT *728*

misery [n 2] *trouble, disaster*
adversity, affliction, anxiety, bitter pill*, burden, calamity, catastrophe, curse, destitution, difficulty, grief, indigence, load, misfortune, need, ordeal, penury, poverty, privation, problem, sordidness, sorrow, squalor, trial, tribulation, want, woe; SEE CONCEPTS *335,666,674*

misfortune/mishap [n] *bad luck; disaster*
accident, adversity, affliction, annoyance, anxiety, bad break*, bad news*, blow*, burden, calamity, casualty, cataclysm, catastrophe, contretemps, cross, crunch, debacle, disadvantage, disappointment, discomfort, dole, failure, hard luck*, hardship, harm, inconvenience, infelicity, loss, misadventure, mischance, misery, nuisance, reverse, rotten luck, setback, stroke of bad luck*, tough luck*, tragedy, trial, tribulation, trouble, unpleasantness, visitation, worry; SEE CONCEPTS *674,679*

misgiving [n] *uncertainty*
anxiety, apprehension, apprehensiveness, distrust, doubt, fear, foreboding, hesitation, mistrust, premonition, prenotion, presage, presentiment, qualm, reservation, scruple, suspicion, unbelief, unease, worry; SEE CONCEPTS *21,689,690*

misguided [adj] ill-advised, deluded
bearded, bum-steer*, confused, deceived, disinformed, erroneous, faked-out*, foolish, imprudent, indiscreet, inexpedient, injudicious, led up the garden path*, mislead, misplaced, mistaken, stonewalled*, uncalled for, unreasonable, unwarranted, unwise, wrong; SEE CONCEPTS *544, 548,570*

mishandle/mismanage [v] mess up
abuse, be incompetent, be inefficient, blow, blunder, botch*, bungle, confound, err, flub*, foul up, fumble, goof*, goof up*, gum up*, harm, make a hash of*, make a mess of*, maladminister, misapply, misconduct, misdirect, misemploy, misgovern, mistreat, misuse, muff*, overlook, pervert, prostitute, put foot in*, screw up*, shoot oneself in foot*; SEE CONCEPTS *101,156,384*

misinform [v] give wrong information intentionally
bait and switch*, cover up, deceive, disinform, doublespeak*, double-talk*, lead astray, lie, misdirect, misguide, mislead, misstate, mousetrap*, pervert, prevaricate, put on*, put on an act*, put on false front*, put up smoke screen*, signify, string along*, wrong steer*; SEE CONCEPT *63*

misjudge [v] get the wrong idea
bark up wrong tree*, be misled, be overcritical, be partial, be unfair, be wrong, come to hasty conclusion, dogmatize, drop the ball*, err, misapprehend, miscalculate, miscomprehend, misconceive, misconjecture, misconstrue, misdeem, misreckon, miss by a mile*, mistake, misthink, misunderstand, overestimate, overrate, prejudge, presume, presuppose, put foot in*, stumble, suppose, underestimate, underrate; SEE CONCEPTS *12,18,101*

mislead [v] give someone the wrong idea, information
bait, beguile, betray, bilk, bluff, bunk, cheat, cozen, deceive, defraud, delude, double-cross*, dupe, enmesh, ensnare, entangle, entice, fool, fudge*, gull, hoax, hoodwink*, hose*, illude, inveigle, juggle, lead astray, lead on*, lie, lure, misdirect, misguide, misinform, misrepresent, outwit, overreach, pervert, pull wool over eyes*, put on*, rip off*, rook, rope in*, scam, seduce, shaft, snow*, take in, tempt, trick, victimize; SEE CONCEPTS *59,63*

misleading [adj] deceptive, confusing
ambiguous, beguiling, bewildering, casuistical, catchy, confounding, deceitful, deceiving, deluding, delusive, delusory, demagogic, disingenuous, distracting, evasive, fallacious, false, inaccurate, perplexing, puzzling, sophistical, specious, spurious, tricky, wrong; SEE CONCEPTS *267,548*

misplace [v] lose; be unable to find
be unable to lay hands on*, confuse, disarrange, dishevel, disorder, disorganize, displace, disturb, forget whereabouts of, lose track of, misfile, mislay, miss, mix, muss, place unwisely, place wrongly, put in wrong place, remove, scatter, unsettle; SEE CONCEPTS *116,201*

misrepresent/misquote [v] lie, distort
adulterate, angle, beard*, belie, build up, cloak, color, con, confuse, cover up, disguise, distort, dress, embellish, embroider, equivocate, exaggerate, falsify, garble, give snow job*, mangle, mask, miscolor, misinterpret, misreport, misstate, overdraw, overstate, palter, pervert, phony up*, pirate*, prevaricate, promote, puff*, skew, slant,

snow*, spread it on*, stretch, take out of context*, throw a curve*, trump up*, twist, warp; SEE CONCEPT *63*

miss [n] failure
absence, blunder, default, defect, error, fault, loss, mishap, mistake, omission, oversight, slip, want; SEE CONCEPTS *101,699*

miss [v] fail, make a mistake
be late for, blow, blunder, botch, disregard, drop, drop the ball*, err, fall flat on face*, fall short, flub*, forget, fumble, ignore, juggle, let go, let slip, lose, miscarry, misfire, mislay, misplace, muff*, neglect, omit, overlook, overshoot, pass over, pass up, skip, slight, slip, trip, trip up, undershoot; SEE CONCEPTS *101,699*

miss [v2] want; feel a loss
crave, desire, long, need, pine, wish, yearn; SEE CONCEPT *20*

missile [n] projectile weapon
ammunition, arrow, bat, bird*, bolt, bomb, bullet, cartridge, dart, MX*, pellet, projectile, rocket, shot, stealth, trajectile; SEE CONCEPT *500*

missing [adj] gone, absent
astray, away, AWOL*, disappeared, lacking, left behind, left out, lost, mislaid, misplaced, not present, nowhere to be found*, omitted, removed, short, unaccounted for, wanting; SEE CONCEPTS *539,576*

mission [n] person's task, responsibility
aim, assignment, business, calling, charge, commission, duty, end, errand, goal, job, lifework, object, objective, office, operation, profession, purpose, pursuit, quest, sortie, trade, trust, undertaking, vocation, work; SEE CONCEPTS *360,362,659*

missionary [n] person who aids, does religious work
apostle, clergy, clergyperson, converter, evangelist, herald, messenger, minister, missioner, pastor, preacher, promoter, propagandist, proselytizer, revivalist, teacher; SEE CONCEPTS *361,416*

missive [n] written communication
dispatch, epistle, letter, line, memo, memorandum, message, note, report, word; SEE CONCEPTS *271,278*

misspent [adj] wasted
blown*, dissipated, down the drain*, idle, imprudent, misapplied, prodigal, profitless, squandered, thrown away; SEE CONCEPTS *544,560,570*

misstep [n] mistake, wrong move
bad move*, blunder, bungle, error, failure, false step, faux pas, fluff*, gaffe, indiscretion, lapse, miscue, miss, slip, slipup*, stumble, trip; SEE CONCEPTS *101,674,699*

mist [n] film, vapor
brume, cloud, condensation, dew, drizzle, fog, ground clouds, haze, moisture, rain, smog, soup*, spray, steam, visibility zero*; SEE CONCEPT *524*

mist [v] cloud, steam up
becloud, befog, blur, dim, drizzle, film, fog, haze, mizzle, murk, obscure, overcast, overcloud, rain, shower, sprinkle, steam; SEE CONCEPT *526*

mistake [n] error, misunderstanding
aberration, blooper*, blunder, boo-boo*, bungle, confusion, delusion, erratum, false move, false step, fault, faux pas, flub*, fluff*, gaffe, illusion, inaccuracy, inadvertence, lapse, misapplication, misapprehension, miscalculation, misconception, misinterpretation, misjudgment, misprint, mis-

statement, misstep, muddle, neglect, omission, overestimation, oversight, slight, slip, slip of tongue*, slipup*, snafu*, solecism, trip*, typographical error, underestimation; SEE CONCEPTS 101,230,410

mistake [v] *mix up, misunderstand*
addle, be off the mark*, be wrong, blunder, botch*, bungle, confound, confuse, deceive oneself, err, fail, get wrong, goof*, have wrong impression, jumble, lapse, make a mess*, misapprehend, miscalculate, misconceive, misconstrue, miscount, misdeem, misinterpret, misjudge, misknow, misread, miss, miss the boat*, not know, omit, overestimate, overlook, put foot in*, slip*, slip up*, snarl, take for*, tangle, underestimate; SEE CONCEPTS 15,101

mistaken [adj] *wrong, incorrect*
all wet*, at fault, barking up wrong tree*, confounded, confused, confused with, deceived, deluded, duped, erroneous, fallacious, false, faulty, fooled, ill-advised, illogical, inaccurate, inappropriate, misconstrued, misguided, misinformed, misinterpreting, misjudged, misled, misunderstanding, off base*, off track*, tricked, unadvised, under wrong impression, unfounded, unreal, unsound, untrue, warranted, way off*, wide of mark*, wrongly identified, wrong number*; SEE CONCEPTS 402,529

mistreat [v] *treat badly or wrongly*
abuse, backbite, bash, brutalize, bung up*, chop, do wrong, dump on*, give black eye*, handle roughly, harm, injure, kick around, knock around, maltreat, maul, mess up, misuse, molest, outrage, push around, rip, roughhouse*, rough up, shake up, total*, trash*, wax*, wound, wrong; SEE CONCEPTS 14,156,246

mistrust [n] *doubtfulness*
apprehension, chariness, concern, distrust, doubt, dubiety, dubiosity, fear, foreboding, incertitude, misgiving, presentiment, scruple, skepticism, suspicion, uncertainty, wariness, wonder; SEE CONCEPTS 21,27,690

mistrust [v] *doubt*
apprehend, beware, be wary, challenge, disbelieve, dispute, distrust, fear, have doubts, question, suspect, suspicion; SEE CONCEPT 21

misty [adj] *filmy, obscure*
bleary, blurred, closed in, clouded, cloudy, dark, dewy, dim, enveloped, foggy, fuzzy, hazy, indistinct, murky, mushy, nebulous, opaque, overcast, shrouded, socked in, soupy*, unclear, vague, vaporous; SEE CONCEPTS 525,603,617

misunderstand [v] *get the wrong idea*
be at cross purposes*, be bewildered, be confused, be perplexed, confound, confuse, fail, get signals crossed*, get signals mixed*, get wrong, get wrong impression*, misapply, misapprehend, miscalculate, miscomprehend, misconceive, misconstrue, misinterpret, misjudge, misknow, misread, misreckon, miss*, miss the point*, mistake, not register*, take amiss, take wrongly; SEE CONCEPT 15

misunderstanding [n1] *instance of having the wrong idea*
confounding, confusion, delusion, error, false impression, misapprehension, misconception, misconstruction, misinterpretation, misjudgment, misreckoning, mistake, mix-up; SEE CONCEPT 409

misunderstanding [n2] *argument, fight*
bad vibes*, blowup*, breach, break, clash, conflict, crossed wires*, debate, difference, difficulty, disagreement, discord, dissension, falling-out*, feud, fuss, quarrel, rift, row, run-in*, rupture, set-to, sour note*, spat, squabble, tiff*, variance, words*; SEE CONCEPTS 46,106

misuse [n] *abuse; wrong application*
abusage, barbarism, catachresis, corruption, cruel treatment, desecration, dissipation, exploitation, harm, ill-treatment, injury, malapropism, maltreatment, misapplication, misemployment, mistreatment, misusage, perversion, profanation, prostitution, rough handling, solecism, squandering, waste; SEE CONCEPT 156

misuse [v] *abuse; apply wrongly*
blow*, brutalize, corrupt, cut up, desecrate, dissipate, exploit, go through, handle roughly, ill-treat, maltreat, maul, mess up*, misapply, misemploy, mistreat, molest, outrage, pervert, profane, prostitute, run through*, shake up, squander, waste, wrong; SEE CONCEPT 156

mitigate [v] *check, diminish, lighten*
abate, allay, alleviate, appease, assuage, blunt, calm, come together, cool*, dull, ease, extenuate, lessen, meet halfway*, moderate, modify, mollify, pacify, palliate, placate, quiet, reduce, relieve, remit, soften, soothe, subdue, take the edge off*, temper, tone down, tranquilize, weaken; SEE CONCEPTS 233,240

mix/mixture [n] *assortment, combination*
admixture, adulteration, alloy, amalgam, amalgamation, assimilation, association, batter, blend, brew, combine, combo, commixture, composite, compound, concoction, confection, conglomeration, cross, crossing, dough, fusion, goulash, grab bag*, hodgepodge, hybrid, hybridization, incorporation, infiltration, interfusion, jumble, mash, medley, melange, merger, mingling, miscellany, mishmash, mixed bag, mosaic, package, patchwork, potpourri, salmagundi, saturation, soup*, stew*, transfusion, union, variety; SEE CONCEPTS 260,432

mix [v1] *combine, join*
admix, adulterate, alloy, amalgamate, associate, blend, braid, coalesce, commingle, commix, compound, conjoin, cross, embody, fuse, hybridize, incorporate, infiltrate, infuse, instill, interbreed, intermingle, interweave, jumble, knead, link, lump, make up, merge, mingle, mix up, put together, saturate, stir, suffuse, synthesize, tangle, transfuse, unite, weave, work in; SEE CONCEPTS 113,193

mix [v2] *socialize*
associate, come together, consort, get along, hang out, hobnob, join, mingle; SEE CONCEPT 114

mixed [adj] *assorted, combined*
alloyed, amalgamated, assimilated, assorted, blended, brewed, composite, compound, conglomerate, crossbred, crossed, different, disordered, diverse, diversified, embodied, fused, heterogeneous, hybrid, hybridized, incorporated, infused, interbred, interdenominational, joint, kneaded, married, merged, mingled, miscellaneous, mongrel, motley, multifarious, tied, transfused, united, varied, woven; SEE CONCEPTS 485,564,772

mix up [v] *confuse*
addle, befuddle, bewilder, confound, derange, disorder, disorganize, disrupt, distract, disturb,

dizzy, fluster, foul up*, jumble, mess up*, mistake, muddle, perplex, puzzle, snafu*, upset; SEE CONCEPTS 16,158

mix-up [n] *confusion, misunderstanding*
botch*, chaos, commotion, disorder, jumble, mess, mixture, muddle, shambles*, tangle, turmoil; SEE CONCEPTS 230,674

moan [n] *groan, complaint*
beef, cry, gripe, grouse, grumble, lament, lamentation, plaint, sigh, sob, wail, whine; SEE CONCEPTS 52,77

moan [v] *groan, complain*
bemoan, bewail, carp, deplore, grieve, gripe, grouse, grumble, keen, lament, mourn, sigh, sob, wail, whine; SEE CONCEPTS 52,77

mob [n] *large group of people*
assemblage, body, cabal, camp, canaille, cattle, circle, clan, class, clique, collection, commonality, company, coterie, crew, crowd, crush, drove, flock, gang, gathering, herd, horde, host, jam, lot, mass, masses, multitude, pack, populace, posse, press, proletariat, rabble, riffraff*, ring, riot, scum, set, swarm, throng, troop; SEE CONCEPTS 378,417,432

mob [v] *come upon by pushing; surround*
attack, cram, crowd, fill, hustle, jam, jostle, overrun, pack, riot, set upon, swarm, throng; SEE CONCEPTS 208,758

mobile [adj] *movable, travelling*
adaptable, ambulatory, changeable, fluid, free, itinerant, liquid, locomotive, loose, migrant, migratory, motile, motorized, moving, mutable, nomadic, peripatetic, portable, roaming, roving, unsettled, unstable, unstationary, unsteadfast, unsteady, versatile, wandering; SEE CONCEPTS 576,584

mobilize [v] *ready for action, movement*
activate, actuate, animate, assemble, call to arms, call up, catalyze, circulate, drive, gather, get ready, impel, make ready, marshal, muster, organize, prepare, propel, put in motion, rally, ready, set in motion, set off; SEE CONCEPTS 148,187,221,320

mock [adj] *artificial, fake*
apish*, bogus*, counterfeit, dummy, ersatz*, faked, false, feigned, forged, fraudulent, hokey*, imitation, imitative, make-believe, mimic, phony, pretended, pseudo*, put-on*, quasi*, sham*, simulated, so-called*, spurious, substitute, unreal; SEE CONCEPTS 566,582

mock [v1] *ridicule*
buffoon, burlesque, caricature, chaff, deride, flout, hoot, insult, jape, jeer, kid, laugh at, make fun of, needle, parody, poke fun at*, rally, rib*, scoff, scorn, show contempt, sneer, taunt, tease, thumb nose at*, travesty; SEE CONCEPTS 7,19,49

mock [v2] *mimic*
affect, ape, assume, burlesque, caricature, counterfeit, ditto*, do, fake, feign, hoke, imitate, lampoon, mime, mirror, parody, satirize, send up*, simulate, take off*, travesty; SEE CONCEPT 111

mock [v3] *deceive*
beguile, belie, betray, challenge, cheat, defeat, defy, delude, disappoint, double-cross*, dupe, elude, foil, fool, frustrate, juggle, let down*, mislead, sell out*, thwart; SEE CONCEPTS 59,63

mockery [n1] *joke, parody*
burlesque, butt*, caricature, deception, farce, imitation, jest, lampoon, laughingstock, mimicry,

mock, pretense, send-up*, sham*, spoof, sport*, take-off*, travesty; SEE CONCEPTS 111,278

mockery [n2] *insult, disrespect*
contempt, contumely, derision, disdain, disparagement, gibe, jeer, ridicule, scoffing, scorn, sport; SEE CONCEPTS 49,278

mode [n1] *manner, way*
approach, book, channels, condition, course, custom, fashion, form, mechanism, method, modus, nuts and bolts*, plan, posture, practice, procedure, process, quality, rule, situation, state, status, style, system, technique, tone, vein, wise; SEE CONCEPTS 6,644

mode [n2] *trend, fad*
chic, convention, craze, cry, dernier cri*, fashion, furor, last word*, latest thing*, latest wrinkle*, look, mainstream, now*, rage*, style, thing*, vogue; SEE CONCEPTS 529,655

model [n1] *imitation, replica*
cartoon, clone, copy, copycat, dead ringer*, ditto*, dummy, duplicate, effigy, engraving, facsimile, figure, figurine, game plan, illustration, image, knock-off, layout, look-alike, miniature, mock-up, painting, paste-up, photograph, picture, pocket, portrait, print, relief, representation, ringer*, setup, sketch, spitting image*, statue, statuette, tracing, visual; SEE CONCEPTS 259,625,628,667

model [n2] *example, standard*
apotheosis, archetype, beau ideal, criterion, design, emblem, embodiment, epitome, exemplar, gauge, hero, ideal, lodestar, mirror, mold, nonesuch, nonpareil, original, paradigm, paragon, pattern, prototype, quintessence, role model, saint, symbol, touchstone, type; SEE CONCEPTS 686,688

model [n3] *person, thing that poses*
dummy, manikin, mannequin, nude, sitter, subject; SEE CONCEPT 348

model [n4] *type, version*
configuration, design, form, kind, mark, mode, style, variety; SEE CONCEPTS 378,463,505,654

model [adj] *typical, ideal*
archetypal, classic, classical, commendable, copy, dummy, exemplary, facsimile, flawless, illustrative, imitation, miniature, paradigmatic, perfect, prototypical, quintessential, representative, standard, very; SEE CONCEPTS 566,574

model [v1] *form, shape*
base, carve, cast, create, design, fashion, mold, pattern, plan, sculpt; SEE CONCEPT 184

model [v2] *display, pose*
parade, represent, set example, show off, sit, sport, wear; SEE CONCEPT 138

moderate [adj1] *calm, temperate*
abstinent, balanced, bearable, careful, cautious, compromising, conservative, considerate, considered, controlled, cool, deliberate, disciplined, dispassionate, equable, even, gentle, impartial, inconsiderable, inexpensive, judicious, limited, low-key, measured, middle-of-the-road*, midway, mild, modest, monotonous, neutral, nonpartisan, not excessive, pacific, peaceable, pleasant, reasonable, reserved, restrained, sober, soft, steady, straight, tame, tolerable, tolerant, tranquil, untroubled; SEE CONCEPTS 533,563

moderate [adj2] *fair, average, so-so*
bland, fairish*, fair to middling*, inconsequential, inconsiderable, indifferent, intermediate, mean, mediocre, medium, middling*, ordinary,

paltry, passable, piddling*, trifling, trivial, unexceptional; SEE CONCEPTS 547,575

moderate [v1] *restrain, control*
abate, allay, alleviate, appease, assuage, calm, chasten, check, constrain, cool*, cool out*, curb, decline, decrease, die down, diminish, ease off, fall, lessen, let up, meet halfway, mitigate, modify, modulate, mollify, pacify, play down, qualify, quiet, reduce, regulate, relent, relieve, repress, slacken, slow, soften, soft-pedal, subdue, subside, tame, temper, tone down, wane; SEE CONCEPTS 94,130,240

moderate [v2] *mediate, arbitrate*
chair, judge, make peace*, negotiate, preside, referee, take the chair*, umpire; SEE CONCEPTS 18,317

moderately [adv] *to a degree, to some extent*
a little, averagely, enough, fairly, gently, in moderation, in reason, kind of, more or less*, more than not*, not exactly, passably, pretty, quite, quite a bit, rather, reasonably, slightly, some, something, somewhat, sort of, so-so*, temperately, tolerable, tolerably, tolerantly, within limits*, within reason*; SEE CONCEPTS 544,772

moderation [n] *temperance*
balance, calmness, composure, constraint, coolness, dispassionateness, equanimity, fairness, forbearance, golden mean, judiciousness, justice, justness, lenity, measure, mildness, moderateness, patience, poise, quiet, reasonableness, restraint, sedateness, sedation, sobriety, steadiness, toleration; SEE CONCEPTS 633,657

modern [adj] *new, up-to-date*
avant-garde, coincident, concomitant, concurrent, contempo, contemporary, current, cutting-edge*, fresh, last word*, late, latest, latter-day*, leading-edge*, modernistic, modernized, modish, neoteric, newfangled*, new-fashioned, novel, now, present, present-day, prevailing, prevalent, recent, state-of-the-art*, stylish, today, twenty-first century*, up-to-the-minute, with-it*; SEE CONCEPTS 578,589,797

modernize [v] *bring up to date; remodel*
improve, refresh, regenerate, rejuvenate, remake, renew, renovate, restore, revamp, revive, update; SEE CONCEPTS 168,177,202

modest [adj1] *shy*
bashful, blushing, chaste, coy, demure, diffident, discreet, humble, lowly, meek, moderate, nice, proper, prudent, quiet, reserved, resigned, reticent, retiring, seemly, self-conscious, self-effacing, sheepish, silent, simple, temperate, timid, unassertive, unassuming, unassured, unboastful, unobtrusive, unpresuming, unpretending, unpretentious, withdrawing; SEE CONCEPTS 401,404

modest [adj2] *limited, ordinary*
average, cheap, discreet, dry, economical, fair, humble, inelaborate, inexpensive, middling, moderate, natural, plain, reasonable, simple, small, unadorned, unaffected, unembellished, unembroidered, unexceptional, unexcessive, unextravagant, unextreme, unobtrusive, unornamented, unostentatious, unpretentious, unradical, unstudied; SEE CONCEPTS 334,547,562

modesty [n] *shyness*
bashfulness, celibacy, chastity, constraint, coyness, decency, delicacy, demureness, diffidence, discreetness, humbleness, humility, inhibition, innocence, lack of pretension, meekness, propriety, prudery, purity, quietness, reserve, reticence, self-effacement, simplicity, timidity, unobtrusiveness, unostentatiousness, unpretentiousness, virtue; SEE CONCEPT 633

modicum [n] *bit, small amount*
atom, crumb, dash, drop, fraction, fragment, grain, inch, iota, jot, little, minim, mite, molecule, ounce, particle, pinch, scrap, shred, smidge, speck, tinge, touch, trifle, whit; SEE CONCEPT 831

modify [v1] *alter, change*
adapt, adjust, become, convert, correct, customize, doctor, mutate, recast, redo, refashion, reform, remodel, reorganize, repair, reshape, revise, rework, shift gears*, switch over, transfigure, transform, transmogrify, transmute, turn, turn one around*, turn over new leaf*, turn the corner*, turn the tables*, tweak*, vary; SEE CONCEPT 232

modify [v2] *lessen, reduce*
abate, curb, decrease, limit, lower, mitigate, moderate, modulate, qualify, relax, remit, restrain, restrict, slacken, soften, temper, tone down; SEE CONCEPTS 236,240,247

modish [adj] *fashionable*
a la mode*, all the rage*, chic, contemporary, current, dashing, exclusive, faddy, fresh, happening, hip*, in*, in-thing*, last-word, latest, mod*, now*, smart, stylish, swank, swish*, trendy, up-to-date, up-to-the-minute, vogue, voguish, with-it*; SEE CONCEPTS 578,589,797

modulate [v] *adjust, harmonize*
attune, balance, fine-tune, inflect, regulate, restrain, revamp, switch, temper, tone, transmogrify, tune, tweak, vary; SEE CONCEPT 202

mogul [n] *person who has great power, many possessions*
executive, key player*, king, magnate, notable, personage, potentate, power, princess queen, royalty, top brass*, tycoon, VIP*; SEE CONCEPTS 347,354

moist [adj] *wet, wettish*
clammy, damp, dampish, dank, dewy, dripping, drippy, drizzly, humid, irriguous, muggy, not dry, oozy*, rainy, soggy, teary, watery; SEE CONCEPT 603

moisten [v] *make wet, damp*
bathe, bedew, dampen, dip, drench, humidify, lick, mist, moisturize, rain on, rinse, saturate, shower, soak, sog, sop, splash, splatter, spray, sprinkle, squirt, steam, steep, wash, water, water down, waterlog, wet; SEE CONCEPT 256

moisture [n] *dampness; liquid*
damp, dankness, dew, drizzle, fog, humidity, mist, perspiration, precipitation, rain, sweat, water, wateriness, wet, wetness; SEE CONCEPTS 467,524

mold [n] *form, pattern*
cast, cavity, character, class, depression, description, design, die, frame, image, impression, kind, lot, matrix, model, nature, shape, sort, stamp, type, womb; SEE CONCEPTS 378,411,436

mold [v] *form, give shape*
build, construct, devise, erect, fashion, forge, form, frame, make, pat, plan, plant, plot, put together, round, scheme, sculpt, whittle; SEE CONCEPTS 173,175,184,251

molecule [n] *smallest part*
bit, fragment, iota, jot, minim, mite, modicum, mote, ounce, particle, ray, speck, unit; SEE CONCEPTS 393,831

molest [v1] *physically abuse*

accost, assail, attack, disorganize, displace, disturb, encroach, fondle, harm, hinder, hurt, illtreat, injure, interfere, intrude, maltreat, meddle, misuse, rape; SEE CONCEPTS 246,375

molest [v2] *bother, annoy*

abuse, afflict, badger, bait, bedevil, beset, break in, bug*, confuse, discommode, discompose, disquiet, disturb, encroach, frighten, harass, harry, heckle, hector, interrupt, intrude, irk, irritate, obtrude, persecute, perturb, pester, plague, pother, pursue, scare, tease, terrify, torment, trouble, upset, vex, worry; SEE CONCEPTS 7,14,19

mollify [v] *pacify, soothe*

abate, allay, alleviate, ameliorate, appease, assuage, blunt, calm, compose, conciliate, cool, cushion, decrease, diminish, dulcify, ease, fix up, lessen, lighten, lull, mellow, mitigate, moderate, modify, pacify, patch things up*, placate, propitiate, quell, quiet, reduce, relieve, soften, sweeten, take sting out*, temper, tranquilize; SEE CONCEPTS 7,22,244,698

moment [n1] *brief time period*

bit, breathing, crack, date, flash, hour, instant, jiff*, jiffy*, juncture, minute, nothing flat*, no time*, occasion, point, point in time, sec*, second, shake, split second*, stage, three winks*, tick*, time, trice*, twinkle*, twinkling*, while, wink*; SEE CONCEPTS 807,808

moment [n2] *importance*

advantage, avail, concern, consequence, gravity, import, magnitude, momentousness, note, pith, profit, seriousness, significance, signification, substance, use, value, weight, weightiness, worth; SEE CONCEPT 668

momentarily [adv] *for a short time*

briefly, for a little while, for a minute, for a moment, for an instant, for a second, for a short time, for a short while, immediately, instantly, now, right now, temporarily; SEE CONCEPT 820

momentary [adj] *brief, fleeting*

cursory, dreamlike, ephemeral, evanescent, flashing, flitting*, flying, fugacious, fugitive, gone in flash*, hasty, impermanent, impulsive, instantaneous, in wink of an eye*, like lightning, passing, quick, shifting, short, short-lived, spasmodic, summary, temporary, transient, transitory, vanishing, volatile; SEE CONCEPT 798

momentous [adj] *important; serious*

big, chips are down*, consequential, considerable, critical, crucial, decisive, earth-shaking, earth-shattering, epochal, eventful, far-reaching, fateful, grave, heavy, heavy number, historic, material, meaningful, memorable, notable, of moment, outstanding, pivotal, significant, substantial, vital, weighty; SEE CONCEPT 568

momentum [n] *impetus, push*

drive, energy, force, impulse, power, propulsion, strength, thrust; SEE CONCEPTS 641,712

monarch [n] *ruler*

autocrat, crowned head, despot, emperor, empress, king, majesty, potentate, prince, princess, queen, sovereign; SEE CONCEPTS 354,422

monastery [n] *place where monks live*

abbey, cloister, friary, house, lamasery, priory, religious community; SEE CONCEPTS 368,439,516

monetary [adj] *concerning money, finances*

budgetary, capital, cash, commercial, financial, fiscal, pecuniary, pocket; SEE CONCEPT 334

money [n] *currency accepted as exchange for goods, services*

almighty dollar*, banknote, bankroll, bill, bread*, bucks*, capital, cash, check, chips, coin, coinage, dough*, finances, fund, funds, gold, gravy*, greenback*, hard cash*, legal tender, loot*, medium of exchange, pay, payment, pesos*, property, resources, riches, roll, salary, silver, specie, treasure, wad*, wage, wealth, wherewithal*; SEE CONCEPT 340

moneyed [adj] *rich*

affluent, fat-cat*, flush*, leisure-class*, loaded*, opulent, prosperous, upper-class, upscale, uptown, wealthy, well-heeled*, well-off*, well-to-do*; SEE CONCEPT 334

moneymaking [adj] *producing profit*

advantageous, gainful, going, good, lucrative, paying, profitable, remunerative, successful, thriving, well-paying; SEE CONCEPT 334

mongrel [n] *animal of mixed background*

bastard, cross, crossbreed, cur, half-blood, half-breed, hybrid, mixed breed, mixture, mule, mutt; SEE CONCEPT 394

monitor [n] *person who watches, oversees*

adviser, auditor, counselor, director, eavesdropper, guide, informant, invigilator, listener, overseer, supervisor, watchdog; SEE CONCEPTS 348,350

monitor [v] *listen, watch carefully*

advise, audit, check, control, counsel, follow, keep an eye on*, keep track of*, observe, oversee, record, scan, supervise, survey, track; SEE CONCEPTS 117,596,623

monk [n] *man who devotes life to contemplation of god*

abbot, anchorite, ascetic, brother, cenobite, eremite, friar, hermit, monastic, priest, recluse, religious, solitary; SEE CONCEPT 361

monkey [n] *primate*

anthropoid, ape, baboon, chimpanzee, gorilla, imp, lemur, monk, orangutan, rascal, scamp, simian; SEE CONCEPT 394

monkey [v] *fiddle, tamper with*

busybody, butt in*, fool, fool around*, fool with*, horn in*, interfere, interlope, intermeddle, make*, meddle, mess, play, pry, tinker, trifle; SEE CONCEPTS 87,612

monologue [n] *speech by one person*

address, descant, discourse, disquisition, harangue, lecture, sermon, soliloquy, speech, stand-up bit*, talk; SEE CONCEPTS 266,278

monopolize [v] *dominate, control*

absorb, acquire, bogart, consume, copyright, corner, corner the market*, devour, employ, engross, exclude, exercise control, have, hog*, hold, keep to oneself, lock up*, manage, own, own exclusively, patent, possess, restrain, sew up*, sit on*, syndicate, take over, take up, use, utilize; SEE CONCEPTS 94,324,710

monopoly [n] *something held, owned exclusively*

cartel, consortium, copyright, corner, holding, oligopoly, ownership, patent, pool, possessorship, proprietorship, syndicate, trust; SEE CONCEPT 710

monotonous [adj] *all the same, remaining the same*

banausic, blah*, boring, colorless, dreary, droning, dull, dull as dishwater*, flat, flat as pancake*, ho-hum*, humdrum*, monotone, nothing, pedestrian, plodding, prosaic, puts one to sleep*, recurrent, reiterated, repetitious, repetitive, samely, sing-song*, soporific, tedious, tiresome, toneless, treadmill, unchanged, unchanging, uniform, un-inflected, uninteresting, unrelieved, unvaried, un-varying, wearisome, wearying; SEE CONCEPTS 529,534,544

monotony [n] *boredom; sameness*
colorlessness, continuance, continuity, dreariness, dryness, dullness, ennui, equability, evenness, flatness, humdrum*, identicalness, invariability, levelness, likeness, monotone, monotonousness, oneness, repetitiousness, repetitiveness, routine, same old thing*, similarity, tediousness, tedium, tiresomeness, unchangeableness, uniformity, wearisomeness; SEE CONCEPTS 410,637,673

monster [n] *giant animal; supernatural being*
abnormality, barbarian, beast, behemoth, brute, centaur, colossus, demon, devil, dragon, fiend, Frankenstein, freak, giant, hellion, horror, levia-than, lusus naturae, mammoth, miscreation, mon-strosity, mutant, ogre, phoenix, savage, titan, villain, werewolf, whale; SEE CONCEPTS 370,394,412

monstrous [adj1] *unnatural, shocking*
aberrant, abnormal, atrocious, cruel, desperate, devilish, diabolical, disgraceful, dreadful, egre-gious, evil, fiendish, flagitious, foul, freakish, frightful, grotesque, gruesome, heinous, hellish, hideous, horrendous, horrible, horrifying, infa-mous, inhuman, intolerable, loathsome, macabre, miscreated, morbid, obscene, odious, ominous, outrageous, preposterous, rank, satanic, scandal-ous, teratoid, terrible, uncanny, unusual, vicious, villainous; SEE CONCEPTS 537,564,582

monstrous [adj2] *very large*
colossal, cracking, elephantine, enormous, fantas-tic, gargantuan, giant, gigantic, grandiose, great, huge, immense, impressive, magnificent, mam-moth, massive, monumental, prodigious, stupen-dous, titanic, towering, tremendous, vast, whopping; SEE CONCEPTS 773,781

monument [n] *memorial, remembrance*
cairn, cenotaph, column, commemoration, erec-tion, footstone, gravestone, headstone, ledger, magnum opus, marker, masterpiece, mausoleum, memento, monolith, obelisk, pile, pillar, record, reminder, shrine, slab, statue, stele, stone, tablet, testament, token, tomb, tombstone, tower, trib-ute, witness; SEE CONCEPTS 259,271,305,470

monumental [adj] *impressive, overwhelming*
awe-inspiring, awesome, classic, enduring, enor-mous, fantastic, gigantic, grand, great, historic, huge, immense, immortal, important, lasting, lofty, majestic, mammoth, massive, memorable, mighty, mortal, mountainous, outstanding, prodi-gious, significant, stupendous, towering, tremen-dous, unforgettable, vast; SEE CONCEPTS 568,773

mood [n] *state of mind*
affection, air, atmosphere, attitude, aura, bent*, blues*, caprice, character, color*, condition, crotchet, cue, depression, desire, disposition, dol-drums, dumps*, emotion, fancy, feel*, feeling, frame of mind*, high spirits, humor, inclination, individuality, low spirits, melancholy, mind, per-sonality, pleasure, propensity, response, scene, semblance, soul, spirit, strain, temper, tempera-ment, tendency, tenor, timbre, vagary, vein, whim, wish; SEE CONCEPTS 410,411,673

moody [adj] *crabby, temperamental*
angry, cantankerous, capricious, changeable, crabbed*, crestfallen, cross, dismal, doleful,

dour, downcast, down in the dumps*, down in the mouth*, erratic, fickle, fitful, flighty, frowning, gloomy, glum, huffy, ill-humored, ill-tempered, impulsive, in a huff*, in the doldrums, introspec-tive, irascible, irritable, lugubrious, melancholy, mercurial, miserable, moping, morose, offended, out of sorts*, pensive, petulant, piqued, sad, sat-urnine, short-tempered, splenetic, sulky, sullen, testy, touchy; SEE CONCEPT 403

moon [n] *Earth's satellite*
celestial body, crescent, full moon, half-moon, heavenly body, new moon, old moon, orb of night*, planetoid, pumpkin*, quarter-moon, sat-ellite; SEE CONCEPTS 511,809

moon [v] *dream about; desire*
daydream, idle, languish, mope, pine, waste time, yearn; SEE CONCEPT 20

moor [v] *anchor, fasten securely*
berth, catch, chain, dock, fix, lash, make fast, picket, secure, tether, tie, tie up; SEE CONCEPTS 85,160

moot [adj] *doubtful, arguable*
at issue, contestable, controversial, debatable, dis-putable, dubious, open, open to debate, problem-atic, questionable, suspect, uncertain, undecided, unresolved, unsettled; SEE CONCEPT 535

mop [n1] *tangle of material, often used to absorb liquid*
duster, sponge, squeegee, swab, sweeper, towel; SEE CONCEPTS 392,499

mop [n2] *thick mass of hair*
mane, shock, tangle, thatch, tresses; SEE CON-CEPT 399

mop [v] *clean by using water and cloth*
dab, dust, pat, polish, rub, soak up, sponge, squeegee, swab, towel off, wash, wipe; SEE CON-CEPT 165

mope [v] *pout, be dejected*
ache, be apathetic, be down in the mouth*, be gloomy, be in a funk*, bleed*, brood, chafe, de-spair, despond, droop, eat one's heart out, fret, grieve, grumble, grump, idle, lament, languish, lose heart, moon, pine, pine away*, regret, re-pine, sink, stew over*, sulk, sweat over*, waste time*, wear a long face*, yearn; SEE CONCEPTS 20,410

moral [n] *lesson, proverb*
adage, aphorism, apophthegm, axiom, dictum, epigram, gnome, maxim, meaning, message, moralism, motto, point, precept, rule, saw, say-ing, sermon, significance, truism; SEE CONCEPTS 278,283

moral [adj] *ethical, honest*
aboveboard, blameless, chaste, conscientious, correct, courteous, decent, decorous, dutiful, ele-vated, exemplary, good, high-minded, honorable, immaculate, incorruptible, innocent, just, kindly, kosher*, laudable, meet, meritorious, modest, moralistic, noble, praiseworthy, principled, proper, pure, respectable, right, righteous, saintly, salt of the earth*, scrupulous, seemly, square, straight, true-blue*, trustworthy, truthful, upright, upstanding, virtuous, worthy; SEE CONCEPT 545

morale [n] *confidence, self-esteem*
assurance, attitude, disposition, drive, esprit, es-prit de corps, heart, humor, mettle, mood, out-look, resolve, self-confidence, self-possession, spirit, temper, temperament, turn, vigor; SEE CONCEPTS 410,411

morality [n] *ethics, honesty*
chastity, conduct, decency, ethicality, ethicalness, gentleness, godliness, good habits, goodness, honor, ideals, incorruptibility, incorruption, integrity, justice, manners, moral code, morals, mores, philosophy, principle, principles, probity, purity, rectitude, righteousness, rightness, saintliness, standards, uprightness, virtue, worthiness; SEE CONCEPT 645

morals [n] *personal principles, standards*
behavior, beliefs, conduct, customs, dogmas, ethic, ethics, habits, ideals, integrity, manners, morality, mores, policies, scruples; SEE CONCEPTS 411,645,688

morass [n] *bog; mess*
chaos, confusion, fen, jam, jungle, knot, labyrinth, marsh, maze, mesh, mix-up, muddle, quagmire, skein, snarl, swamp, tangle, web; SEE CONCEPTS 230,509

morbid [adj] *gloomy, nasty, sickly*
aberrant, abnormal, ailing, brooding, dark, deadly, depressed, despondent, diseased, dreadful, frightful, ghastly, ghoulish, grim, grisly, gruesome, hideous, horrid, infected, irascible, macabre, malignant, melancholy, monstrous, moody, pessimistic, saturnine, sick, somber, sullen, unhealthy, unnatural, unsound, unusual, unwholesome; SEE CONCEPTS 314,403,537

more [adj] *additional, greater*
added, aggrandized, also, amassed, and, another, augmented, besides, bounteous, deeper, else, enhanced, exceeding, expanded, extended, extra, farther, fresh, further, heavier, higher, in addition, increased, innumerable, larger, likewise, major, massed, more than that, new, numerous, other, over and above, spare, supplementary, too many, wider; SEE CONCEPTS 762,771

more [adv] *to a greater extent*
additionally, along with, also, as well, besides, better, beyond, further, furthermore, in addition, likewise, longer, moreover, over, too, withal; SEE CONCEPTS 544,772

moreover [adv] *additionally*
also, as well, besides, by the same token*, further, furthermore, in addition, likewise, more, to boot*, too, what is more*, withal, yet; SEE CONCEPTS 544,772

morning [n] *first part of the day*
after midnight, AM, ante meridiem, aurora, before lunch, before noon, breakfast time*, break of day, cockcrow*, crack of dawn*, dawn, daybreak, daylight, dayspring, early bright*, first blush*, foreday, forenoon, morn*, morningtide, morrow, prime*, sunrise, sunup, wee hours*; SEE CONCEPTS 801,802,806,810

moron [n] *stupid person*
addlepate, blockhead*, boob*, dimwit, dingbat*, dolt, dope*, dork*, dumbbell*, dummy*, dunce, fool, halfwit, idiot, ignoramus, imbecile, lamebrain*, loony*, loser*, mental defective*, nerd*, simpleton; SEE CONCEPT 423

morose [adj] *depressed, pessimistic*
acrimonious, blue*, brusque, cantankerous, choleric, churlish, crabbed*, crabby*, cranky*, cross, dolorous, dour, down, down in the dumps*, down in the mouth*, frowning, gloomy, glum, grouchy, gruff, harsh, having blue devils*, having the blahs*, ill-humored, ill-tempered, in a bad mood*, in a blue funk*, irritable, low, melancholy, moody, moping, mournful, perverse, perversive, sad, saturnine, singing the blues*, snappish, sour, splenetic, sulky, sullen, surly, taciturn, testy, troubled, ugly; SEE CONCEPT 403

morsel [n] *tiny piece*
bait, bit, bite, chunk, crumb, cut, delicacy, drop, fraction, fragment, grain, hunk, lump, mouthful, nibble, nosh, part, sample, scrap, segment, slice, snack, soupcon, taste, tidbit, treat; SEE CONCEPTS 457,458,831,835

mortal [n] *human being*
animal, being, body, character, creature, earthling, human, individual, living soul, man, naked ape, party, person, personage, soul, woman; SEE CONCEPT 417

mortal [adj1] *deadly*
bitter, death-dealing, deathly, destructive, dire, ending, extreme, fatal, grave, great, grievous, grim, intense, killing, last, lethal, malignant, merciless, monstrous, mortiferous, murderous, noxious, pestilent, pestilential, poisonous, relentless, remorseless, ruthless, severe, terminal, terrible, unrelenting; SEE CONCEPT 537

mortal [adj2] *human*
animate, bipedal, corporeal, creatural, earthly, ecce homo, ephemeral, evanescent, fading, finite, frail, fugacious, impermanent, momentary, passing, perishable, precarious, sublunary, temporal, transient, weak, worldly; SEE CONCEPT 549

mortality [n1] *death*
bloodshed, carnage, deadliness, destruction, dying, extinction, fatality, killing, lethality, loss of life; SEE CONCEPT 407

mortality [n2] *humanness*
being, ephemerality, flesh, Homo sapiens, humanity, humankind, human race, impermanence, temporality, transience; SEE CONCEPTS 417,648

mortify [v] *embarrass*
abase, abash, affront, annoy, belittle, chagrin, chasten, confound, control, crush, deflate, deny, disappoint, discipline, discomfit, disgrace, displease, get one's comeuppance*, harass, humble, humiliate, put to shame, ridicule, shame, subdue, take down a peg*, take the wind out*, vex, worry; SEE CONCEPTS 7,19,52,54

most [adj] *best, greatest*
better, biggest, greater, highest, largest, lion's share*, max*, maximum, ultimate, utmost, uttermost; SEE CONCEPTS 771,772

most [adv] *nearly all; extremely*
about, all but, almost, approximately, close, eminently, exceedingly, in the majority, mightily, much, nearly, nigh, practically, remarkably, super, surpassingly, too, very, well-nigh; SEE CONCEPTS 544,569,771

mostly [adv] *generally, mainly*
above all, almost entirely, as a rule*, chiefly, customarily, essentially, for the most part*, frequently, in many instances*, largely, many times, most often, often, on the whole*, overall, particularly, predominantly, primarily, principally, regularly, usually; SEE CONCEPTS 544,548,772

motel [n] *temporary, short-term residence, often for travelers*
cabin, court, hotel, inn, lodge, motor court, resort, roadhouse; SEE CONCEPTS 439,449,516

mother [n] *female person who has borne children*
ancestor, child-bearer, creator, forebearer, mom*, mommy*, origin, parent, predecessor, procreator, progenitor, source; SEE CONCEPTS 394,400, 414,415,423

motion [n1] *movement, action*

act, advance, agitation, ambulation, body English*, change, changing, direction, drift, dynamics, flow, fluctuation, flux, full swing*, gesticulation, gesture, high sign*, inclination, kinetics, locomotion, mobility, motility, move, oscillation, passage, passing, progress, sign, signal, stir, stirring, stream, sway, sweep, swing, tendency, travel, wave, wavering; SEE CONCEPT 145

motion [n2] *formal suggestion in a meeting*

plan, proposal, proposition, recommendation, submission; SEE CONCEPTS 75,278

motion [v] *gesture, direct*

beckon, flag, gesticulate, guide, invite, move, nod, sign, signal, signalize, wave; SEE CONCEPT 149

motionless [adj] *calm, not moving*

apoplectic, at a standstill, at rest, becalmed, dead, deadlocked, deathly, firm, fixed, frozen, halted, immobile, immotile, inanimate, inert, lifeless, numb, palsied, paralyzed, petrified, quiescent, quiet, spellbound, stable, stagnant, stalled, standing, static, stationary, steadfast, still, stock-still, torpid, transfixed, unmovable, unmoved, unmoving; SEE CONCEPTS 488,584

motivate [v] *stimulate, instigate*

actuate, arouse, bring, cause, dispose, draw, drive, egg on*, excite, fire, galvanize, give incentive, goad, goose*, impel, incite, incline, induce, innervate, innerve, inspire, inspirit, lead, move, persuade, pique, predetermine, predispose, prevail upon, prompt, propel, provoke, quicken, rouse, set afoot, set astir, sound, spark, spur, suggest, sway, touch off, trigger, whet; SEE CONCEPTS 14,68,242

motivation [n] *ambition, inspiration*

action, actuation, angle, catalyst, desire, disposition, drive, encouragement, fire, get up and go*, gimmick, goose*, hunger, impetus, impulse, impulsion, incentive, incitation, incitement, inclination, inducement, instigation, interest, kick*, motive, persuasion, predetermination, predisposition, provocation, push, reason, right stuff*, spur, stimulus, suggestion, wish; SEE CONCEPTS 20,411,689

motive [n] *reason, purpose*

aim, antecedent, basis, cause, consideration, design, determinant, drive, emotion, end, feeling, grounds, idea, impulse, incentive, incitement, inducement, influence, inspiration, intent, intention, mainspring, motivation, object, occasion, passion, rationale, root, spring, spur, stimulus, thinking; SEE CONCEPTS 20,661,689

motley [adj] *mixed, varied*

assorted, conglomerate, dappled, discrepant, disparate, dissimilar, diversified, heterogeneous, indiscriminate, kaleidoscopic, mingled, miscellaneous, mixed, mottled, multicolor, multicolored, multiform, multihued, polychromatic, prismatic, rainbow, unlike, varicolored, variegated, various, versicolor; SEE CONCEPTS 564, 618,772

mottled [adj] *speckled*

blotchy, checkered, dappled, flecked, freckled, maculate, marbled, motley, piebald, pied, skewbald, spotted, streaked, tabby, variegated; SEE CONCEPTS 606,618

motto [n] *saying, slogan*

adage, aphorism, apothegm, battle cry, byword, catchphrase, cry, epigram, formula, maxim, precept, proverb, rallying cry, rule, saw, sentiment, shibboleth, war cry, watchword, word; SEE CONCEPT 278

mound [n] *heap, hill*

anthill, bank, drift, dune, embankment, hillock, knoll, mass, molehill, mountain, pile, rise, shock, stack, tumulus; SEE CONCEPTS 432,509

mount [v1] *climb*

arise, ascend, back, bestride, clamber up, climb onto, climb up on, escalade, escalate, get astride, get up on, go up, jump on, lift, rise, scale, soar, tower, up, vault; SEE CONCEPTS 149,154,166

mount [v2] *increase, grow*

accumulate, aggravate, augment, build, deepen, enhance, enlarge, escalate, expand, heighten, intensate, intensify, multiply, pile up, redouble, rise, rouse, swell, upsurge, wax; SEE CONCEPTS 704,780

mount [v3] *affix, frame*

emplace, exhibit, fit, install, place, position, prepare, produce, put in place, put on, set up, show, stage; SEE CONCEPTS 174,261

mountain [n] *very large hill*

abundance, alp, bank, bluff, butte, cliff, crag, dome, drift, elevation, eminence, glob, heap, height, hump, mass, mesa, mound, mount, palisade, peak, pile, pile, precipice, pyramid, range, ridge, shock, sierra, stack, ton, tor, volcano; SEE CONCEPTS 432,509

mourn [v] *be sad over loss*

ache, agonize, anguish, be brokenhearted*, bemoan, be sad, bewail, bleed, blubber, carry on, complain, cry, deplore, fret, grieve, hurt, keen, lament, languish, long for, miss, moan, pine, regret, repine, rue, sigh, sob, sorrow, suffer, take it hard*, wail, wear black*, weep, wring hands*, yearn; SEE CONCEPTS 23,410

mourning [n] *sadness, time of sadness*

aching, bereavement, blackness, crying, darkness, grief, grieving, keening, lamentation, lamenting, languishing, moaning, pining, repining, sorrowing, wailing, weeping, woe; SEE CONCEPTS 388,410

mousy [adj] *drab; quiet*

bashful, colorless, diffident, dull, indeterminate, ineffectual, pale, plain, self-effacing, shy, timid, timorous, unassertive, unassuming; SEE CONCEPTS 401,618

mouth [n1] *opening*

aperture, beak, box, cavity, chops*, clam, crevice, delta, door, embouchement, entrance, estuary, firth, fly trap, funnel, gate, gills, gob, harbor, inlet, jaws, kisser*, lips, mush*, orifice, portal, rim, trap*, yap*; SEE CONCEPTS 392,513

mouth [n2] *backtalk*

boasting, braggadocio, bragging, cheek, empty talk*, freshness, gas*, guff*, hot air*, idle talk, impudence, insolence, lip*, rudeness, sass*, sauce*; SEE CONCEPTS 54,278

movable [adj] *transportable*

adaptable, adjustable, ambulatory, conveyable, deployable, detachable, in parts, liftable, loose, mobile, motile, moving, not fastened, not fixed, on wheels, portable, portative, removable, separable, shiftable, transferable, turnable, unattached, unfastened, unstationary, unsteady; SEE CONCEPTS 488,584

move [n] *progress, deed*

act, action, alteration, change, maneuver, measure, modification, motion, movement, ploy, procedure, proceeding, shift, step, stir, stirring, stratagem, stroke, turn, variation; SEE CONCEPTS 2,660

move [v1] *be in motion, put in motion*
actuate, advance, blow, budge, bustle, carry, change, climb, crawl, cross, depart, dislocate, disturb, drift, drive, exit, flow, fly, get away, get going, get off, glide, go, go away, head for, hurry, impel, jump, leap, leave, locomote, march, migrate, off-load, position, proceed, progress, propel, pull out, push, quit, relocate, remove, roll, run, scram, shift, ship, shove, skip out, split, stir, switch, take off, transfer, transport, transpose, travel, traverse, walk, withdraw; SEE CONCEPTS 147,149,198

move [v2] *motivate, influence*
activate, actuate, advocate, affect, agitate, bring, bring up, budge, carry, cause, convert, draw up, drive, excite, get going, give rise to, impel, impress, incite, induce, inspire, inspirit, instigate, introduce, lead, operate, persuade, play on, prevail upon, prompt, propel, propose, push, put forward, quicken, recommend, rouse, shift, shove, start, stimulate, stir, strike, submit, suggest, sway, touch, tug at, turn, urge, work on; SEE CONCEPTS 7,19,22,75,242

movement [n1] *motion, activity*
act, action, advance, agitation, alteration, change, changing, deed, development, displacement, dynamism, evolution, evolving, exercise, flight, flow, flux, gesture, journey, journeying, locomotion, maneuver, migration, mobility, motility, movableness, move, moving, operation, operativeness, passage, progress, progression, regression, roaming, shift, shifting, steps, stir, stirring, transferal, transit, translating, transplanting, undertaking, velocity, voyaging, wandering; SEE CONCEPTS 2,145,697

movement [n2] *drive, campaign*
change, crusade, current, demonstration, displacement, drift, evolution, faction, flight, flow, front, group, grouping, march, mobilization, organization, party, patrol, shift, sweep, swing, tendency, transfer, transition, trend, unrest, withdrawal; SEE CONCEPTS 381,697

movie [n] *presentation of action on continuous film*
cine, cinema, cinematics, cinematograph, feature, film, flick*, motion picture, moving picture, photoplay, picture, screenplay, show, silent*, silver screen*, talkie*, talking picture, videotape; SEE CONCEPTS 263,293

moving [adj1] *affecting, exciting*
affective, arousing, awakening, breathless, dynamic, eloquent, emotional, emotive, expressive, facund, far-out*, felt in gut*, grabbed by*, gripping, hairy*, heartbreaking, heartrending, impelling, impressive, inspirational, inspiring, meaningful, mind-bending*, mind-blowing*, motivating, persuasive, poignant, propelling, provoking, quickening, rallying, rousing, sententious, significant, something*, stimulating, stimulative, stirring, stunning, touching, turned on by*; SEE CONCEPTS 529,537

moving [adj2] *mobile*
advancing, changing, climbing, evolving, flying, going, jumping, motile, movable, nomadic, portable, progressing, roaming, roving, running, shifting, traversing, unfixed, unstable, unsteadfast, unsteady, walking; SEE CONCEPTS 488,584

much [n] *a great deal*
abundance, all kinds of*, a lot*, amplitude, appreciable amount, barrel, breadth, completeness, copiousness, excess, exuberance, fullness, gobs*, great quantity, heaps*, loads*, lots*, lump, mass, mess*, mountain, multiplicity, oodles*, overage, oversupply, pack, peck, pile, plentifulness, plenty, plethora, profuseness, riches, scads*, sufficiency, superabundance, superfluity, thousands, tons*, very much, volume, wealth; SEE CONCEPT 771

much [adj] *plenty*
abundant, adequate, a lot of*, ample, complete, considerable, copious, countless, endless, enough, everywhere, extravagant, full, galore, generous, great, heaps*, immeasurable, jam-packed*, lavish, loads*, lotsa*, many, mega*, mucho*, no end*, plenteous, plentiful, profuse, satisfying, scads*, sizable, substantial, sufficient, very many, voluminous; SEE CONCEPTS 772,781

much [adv] *greatly, a lot*
again and again, a great deal*, considerably, decidedly, eminently, exceedingly, exceptionally, extremely, frequently, highly, hugely, indeed, notably, oft, often, over and over*, regularly, repeatedly, surpassingly, time and time again*, very; SEE CONCEPTS 530,544,548

muddle [n] *confused state*
ataxia, awkwardness, botch, chaos, clutter, complexity, complication, confusion, daze, difficulty, dilemma, disarrangement, disarray, disorder, disorganization, emergency, encumbrance, fog, foul-up*, hash, haze, intricacy, involvement, jumble, mess, mess and a half*, mix-up*, muss*, perplexity, plight, predicament, quandary, rat's nest*, screw-up*, shambles*, snarl, struggle, tangle, trouble; SEE CONCEPTS 230,410,666

muddle [v] *confuse, disorganize*
addle, befuddle, bewilder, blunder, botch, bungle, clutter, complicate, confound, daze, derange, disarrange, discombobulate*, disorder, disorient, disturb, entangle, fluster, foul, foul up*, jumble, louse up, make a mess of* mess, misarrange, mix, mix up*, muck, mumble, murmur, nonplus, perplex, perturb, psych out*, rattle, ravel, ruffle, scramble, shuffle, snafu*, snarl, spoil, stir up, stumble, stupefy, tangle, throw, throw off, tumble; SEE CONCEPTS 16,84,242

muddy [adj] *dark and cloudy*
addled, bemired, bespattered, black, blurred, boggy*, caked, confused, dingy, dirty, dull, filthy, flat, foul, fuzzy, gloomy, greasy, grimy, grubby*, gummy*, gunky*, hazy, impure, indistinct, marshy, miry, mucky*, obscure, opaque, roily, sloppy, slushy, smoky, sodden, soggy, soiled, subfuse, swampy, turbid, unclean, unclear; SEE CONCEPTS 485,606,618

muffle [v] *suppress, make quiet*
conceal, cover, cushion, dampen, deaden, decrease, drown, dull, envelop, gag, hide, hush, mellow, mute, muzzle, put the lid on*, quieten, shut down, silence, sit down on*, smother, soften, soft-pedal*, squelch, stifle, subdue, tone down*, wrap*; SEE CONCEPTS 65,121,240

muffled [adj] *quietened*
deadened, dim, dull, faint, flat, indistinct, mute, muted, obscure, silenced, stifled, strangled, subdued, suppressed; SEE CONCEPT 594

muggy [adj] *humid*
clammy*, close, damp, dampish, dank, moist,

mo
mu

mucky*, oppressive, soggy, sticky, stuffy, sultry; SEE CONCEPTS *525,603*

mull [v] *think about seriously*
brood over, chaw, consider, contemplate, delay, deliberate, examine, figure, hammer away at*, linger, meditate, moon*, muse on, ponder, pore over, procrastinate, rack one's brains*, reflect, review, revolve, ruminate, stew over*, study, sweat over*, think over, turn over, weigh, woolgather*; SEE CONCEPT *17*

multicolored [adj] *having various hues*
checkered, dappled, flecked, kaleidoscopic, marbled, motley, mottled, multicolor, particolored, piebald, pied, polychrome, prismatic, speckled, spotted, streaked, varicolored, veined, versicolor; SEE CONCEPT *618*

multiculturalism [n] *doctrine acknowledging contributions and interests of many cultures*
cross-culturalism, cultural diversity, diversity, ethnic inclusiveness, ethnic mosaic, multiracialism, pluralism; SEE CONCEPTS *665,689*

multimedia [n] *combined use of several media*
interactive media, intermedia, mixed media; SEE CONCEPT *274*

multiple/multifarious [adj] *diversified, miscellaneous*
assorted, collective, conglomerate, different, diverse, diversiform, heterogeneous, indiscriminate, legion, manifold, many, mixed, motley, multiform, multiplex, multitudinal, multitudinous, numerous, populous, several, sundry, varied, variegated, various, voluminous; SEE CONCEPTS *564,762,772*

multiply [v] *increase; reproduce*
accumulate, add, aggrandize, aggregate, augment, boost, breed, build up, compound, cube, double, enlarge, expand, extend, generate, heighten, magnify, manifold, mount, populate, procreate, produce, proliferate, propagate, raise, repeat, rise, spread, square; SEE CONCEPTS *171,374*

multitude [n] *large group*
aggregation, army, assemblage, assembly, collection, commonalty, concourse, congregation, crowd, crush, drove, great number, heap, herd, horde, host, infinitude, infinity, jam*, loads, lot, lots*, majority, mass, mob, much, myriad, number, numbers, ocean*, oodles*, people, plenitude, plurality, populace, proletariat, public, push*, quantity, scores*, sea, slew*, swarm, throng, turnout; SEE CONCEPTS *417,432*

multitudinous [adj] *many, considerable*
abounding, abundant, copious, countless, great, heaps*, infinite, innumerable, innumerous, legion, manifold, multifarious, myriad, numberless, numerous, populous, profuse, several, sundry, teeming, uncountable, uncounted, unnumbered, untold, various, voluminous; SEE CONCEPTS *762,781*

mumble [v] *say low and inarticulately*
grumble, maunder, murmur, mutter, ramble, rumble, say to oneself, speak, stammer, stutter, swallow, talk, utter, verbalize, vocalize, voice, whimper, whine, whisper; SEE CONCEPTS *47,77*

munch [v] *chew, eat*
bite, break up, champ, chomp, crunch, crush, grind, mash, masticate, press, reduce, ruminate, scrunch, smash, soften; SEE CONCEPTS *169,185*

mundane [adj] *ordinary*
banal, commonplace, day-to-day, earthly, everyday, humdrum*, lowly, normal, prosaic, routine,

workaday*, workday, worldly; SEE CONCEPT *547*

municipal [adj] *concerning cities*
borough, burghal, city, civic, civil, community, corporate, domestic, home, incorporated, internal, local, metropolitan, native, public, town, urban; SEE CONCEPT *536*

munificent [adj] *giving, generous*
beneficent, benevolent, big, big-hearted, bounteous, bountiful, charitable, free, handsome, kind, lavish, liberal, loose, magnanimous, openhanded, philanthropic, rich, unsparing, unstinting; SEE CONCEPTS *334,401*

murder [n] *killing*
annihilation, assassination, blood, bloodshed, butchery, carnage, crime, death, destruction, dispatching, felony, foul play*, hit*, homicide, knifing, liquidation, lynching, manslaughter, massacre, off*, offing*, one-way ticket*, rub out*, shooting, slaying, taking out*, terrorism, the business*, the works*; SEE CONCEPTS *192,252*

murder [v] *kill*
abolish, asphyxiate, assassinate, behead, blot out*, bump off*, butcher, chill*, cool*, decapitate, defeat, destroy, dispatch, do in*, drub*, dust off*, electrocute, eliminate, eradicate, execute, exterminate, extinguish, finish, garotte, guillotine, hang, hit*, knife, knock off*, liquidate, lynch, mangle, mar, massacre, misuse, off*, put away*, rub out*, ruin, shoot, slaughter, slay, smother, snuff, spoil, strangle, take a life, take for a ride*, take out*, thrash*, waste*; SEE CONCEPTS *192,252*

murderer [n] *person who kills*
assassin, butcher, criminal, cutthroat, enforcer, executioner, hit-and-run*, hit person*, homicide, killer, manslaughterer, perpetrator, slaughterer, slayer, soldier, trigger person*; SEE CONCEPT *412*

murderous [adj] *difficult*
arduous, brutal, criminal, cruel, dangerous, deadly, destroying, destructive, devastating, exhausting, fell, ferocious, harrowing, hellish, killing, lethal, ruinous, sapping, savage, strenuous, unpleasant; SEE CONCEPTS *538,548,565*

murky [adj] *gloomy, obscure*
black, caliginous, cheerless, cloudy, dark, darkened, dim, dingy, dirty, dismal, drab, dreary, dull, dun*, dusk, dusky, filthy, foggy, foul, fuzzy, glowering, gray, grubby*, impenetrable, lowering, misty, mucky, muddy, nasty, nebulous, nubilous, overcast, roily, sad, smoky, somber, squalid, stormy, tenebrous, turbid, unclean; SEE CONCEPTS *617,618*

murmur [n] *low, continuous sound*
babble, buzz, buzzing, drone, grumble, hum, humming, mumble, murmuration, mutter, muttering, purr, rumble, rumor, undertone, whisper, whispering; SEE CONCEPTS *65,595*

murmur [v] *make low, continuous sound*
babble, burble, buzz, drip, drone, flow, growl, gurgle, hum, meander, moan, mumble, mutter, purl, purr, ripple, rumble, stage-whisper, stammer, stutter, susurrate, tinkle, trickle, utter, verbalize, vocalize, voice, whisper; SEE CONCEPTS *65,77*

muscle [n1] *large fibers of animal body*
beef, brawn, flesh, meat, might, sinew, tendon, thew, tissue; SEE CONCEPTS *393,420*

muscle [n2] *power, influence*
brawn, clout, energy, force, forcefulness, might,

potency, sinew, stamina, strength, strong arm*, sturdiness, weight; SEE CONCEPTS *641,687*

muscular [adj] *powerfully built*
able-bodied, athletic, brawny, bruising, burly, fibrous, hefty, Herculean*, hulky, husky, lusty, mighty, muscled, powerful, powerhouse*, pumped up*, ripped*, robust, ropy, sinewy, stalwart, stout, strapping, stringy, strong, sturdy, tiger*, tough, vigorous, well-built, wiry; SEE CONCEPTS *485,489*

muse [v] *think about, dream*
be lost in thought*, brood, build castles in air*, chew over*, cogitate, consider, contemplate, deliberate, feel, meditate, moon*, mull over, percolate, ponder, puzzle over, reflect, revolve, roll, ruminate, speculate, think, think over, turn over, weigh; SEE CONCEPT *17*

museum [n] *place for viewing artifacts or exhibits*
archive, building, depository, exhibition, foundation, gallery, hall, institution, library, menagerie, repository, salon, storehouse, treasury, vault; SEE CONCEPTS *439,449*

mushroom [v] *sprout; grow quickly*
augment, blow up, boom, burgeon, burst, detonate, expand, explode, flourish, go off, grow, grow rapidly, increase, luxuriate, proliferate, shoot up, spread, spring up; SEE CONCEPTS *179,704*

mushy [adj1] *doughy, soft*
gelatinous, jelled, mashy*, muddy, pap*, pastelike, pulpous, pulpy, quaggy, semiliquid, semisolid, slushy, spongy, squashy*, squishy*; SEE CONCEPTS *604,606*

mushy [adj2] *romantic, corny*
bathetic, effusive, emotional, lovey-dovey*, maudlin, mawkish, saccharine, schmaltzy*, sentimental, sloppy*, slushy*, soppy*, sugary, syrupy, tear-jerking, weepy, wet; SEE CONCEPTS *267,542*

music [n] *sounds that are pleasant, harmonized*
a cappella, acoustic, air, bebop, bop, chamber, classical, folk, fusion, hard rock, harmony, heavy metal, hymn, instrumental, jazz, measure, melody, modern, opera, piece, plainsong, popular, ragtime, rap, refrain, rock, rock and roll, singing, song, soul, strain, swing, tune; SEE CONCEPTS *263,595*

musical [adj] *harmonic, lyrical*
agreeable, blending, chiming, choral, consonant, dulcet, euphonious, harmonious, lilting, mellow, melodic, melodious, operatic, orchestral, pleasing, rhythmic, silvery, songful, sweet, sweet-sounding, symphonic, symphonious, tuned, tuneful, vocal; SEE CONCEPT *594*

musician [n] *person who performs music*
artist, artiste, composer, conductor, diva, entertainer, instrumentalist, performer, player, session player, soloist, virtuoso, vocalist; SEE CONCEPT *352*

muss [n] *disorder*
chaos, confusion, disarrangement, hash, mess, mess-up, mix-up*, muddle, shambles, turmoil; SEE CONCEPTS *230,674*

muss [v] *dishevel, disorder*
clutter, crumple, disarrange, disarray, disorganize, disrupt, disturb, jumble, mess up, mix up*, muddle, ruffle, rummage, rumple, tangle, tousle, upset, wrinkle; SEE CONCEPT *158*

must [n] *necessity, essential*
charge, commitment, committal, condition, devoir, duty, fundamental, imperative, necessary, need, obligation, ought, precondition, prerequisite, requirement, requisite, right, sine qua non; SEE CONCEPTS *646,709*

must [v] *ought, should*
be compelled, be destined, be directed, be doomed*, be driven*, be made, be necessitated, be obliged, be one's fate, be ordered, be required, got to, have, have got to*, have no choice, have to, must needs*, need, pushed to the wall*; SEE CONCEPT *650*

muster [n] *gathering*
aggregation, assemblage, assembly, call-up*, collection, company, congeries, convocation, crowd, draft, group, head count*, meeting, mobilization, nose count*, rally, roll, roll call*, roster, round-up*; SEE CONCEPTS *417,432*

muster [v] *gather, come together*
assemble, call together, call up, collect, congregate, congress, convene, convoke, enroll, enter, group, join up, marshal, meet, mobilize, organize, raise, rally, rendezvous, round up, sign on, sign up, summon; SEE CONCEPT *109*

musty [adj1] *stuffy, aged*
airless, ancient, antediluvian, antique, crumbling, dank, decayed, decrepit, dirty, dried-out*, dry, fetid, filthy, frowzy*, malodorous, mildewed, mildewy, moldy, moth-eaten*, noisome, old, putrid, rotten, smelly, spoiled, squalid, stale, stuffy; SEE CONCEPTS *578,598,603,797*

musty [adj2] *worn-out, clichéd*
ancient, antiquated, banal, common, commonplace, dull, hackneyed, hoary, obsolete, old-fashioned, old hat*, shopworn*, stale, stereotypical, threadbare, timeworn*, tired, trite, warmed-over*, worn; SEE CONCEPTS *267,530,578,797*

mutation [n] *metamorphosis*
alteration, anomaly, change, deviant, deviation, evolution, innovation, modification, mutant, novelty, permutation, transfiguration, transformation, variation, vicissitude; SEE CONCEPTS *665,697*

mute [adj] *unable to speak*
aphasiac, aphasic, aphonic, muffled, mum, quiet, silenced, silent, speechless, tongueless, tongue-tied, unexpressed, unpronounced, unsounded, unspeaking, unspoken, voiceless, wordless; SEE CONCEPT *593*

mute [v] *muffle, tone down sound*
benumb, bottle up*, cork up*, dampen, deaden, decrease the volume, drown, gag, hush, keep it down*, lower, moderate, muzzle, pipe down*, put damper on*, put the lid on*, reduce, silence, soften, soft-pedal*, subdue, turn down; SEE CONCEPTS *65,240*

mutilate [v] *maim, damage*
adulterate, amputate, batter, bowdlerize, butcher, cripple, crush, cut to pieces, cut up, deface, disable, disfigure, dismember, distort, expurgate, hack*, hash up*, hurt, injure, lacerate, lame, mangle, mar, mess up*, ravage, scratch, spoil, weaken; SEE CONCEPTS *176,246*

mutiny [n] *defiance, resistance*
disobedience, insubordination, insurrection, refusal to obey, revolt, revolution, riot, rising, strike, uprising; SEE CONCEPTS *300,388,633*

mutiny [v] *defy, revolt*
be insubordinate, disobey, insurrect, kick over, rebel, refuse to obey, resist, rise against, rise up, strike; SEE CONCEPTS *300,384*

mutter [v] *grumble, mumble*
complain, croak, groan, grouch*, grouse, growl, grunt, moan, muddle, murmur, rumble, snarl, sputter, swallow, whisper; SEE CONCEPTS *52,77*

mutual [adj] *shared, common*
associated, bilateral, collective, communal, conjoint, conjunct, connected, convertible, correlative, dependent, give-and-take*, given and taken*, interactive, interchangeable, interchanged, interdependent, intermutual, joint, partaken, participated, public, reciprocal, reciprocated, related, requited, respective, returned, two-sided*, united; SEE CONCEPTS *563,708*

mutually [adv] *together*
all at once, as a group, by agreement, by contract, commonly, conjointly, cooperatively, en masse, in collaboration, in combination, in conjunction, jointly, reciprocally, respectively; SEE CONCEPTS *544,577*

muzzle [n] *covering for control*
cage, cover, envelope, gag, guard, sheath, wrap; SEE CONCEPT *172*

muzzle [v] *gag, quiet*
bottle up*, censor, check, choke, clamp down on*, cork, crack down on*, curb, dry up*, dummy up*, hush, ice*, muffle, prevent, quieten, repress, restrain, restrict, shush, shut down, silence, squash, squelch, stifle, still, stop, suppress, tongue-tie*, trammel; SEE CONCEPTS *121,250*

myopic [adj] *able only to see things near at hand*
astigmatic, biased, blind, halfsighted, nearsighted, presbyopic, shortsighted; SEE CONCEPT *619*

myriad [n] *a lot*
army, flood, heap, horde, host, loads*, mint, mountain*, multitude, oodles*, scores, slew, stacks*, swarm, thousands*; SEE CONCEPT *787*

myriad [adj] *innumerable*
countless, endless, gobs*, heaping, immeasurable, incalculable, infinite, multiple, multitudinous, no end of*, numberless, thousand-and-one*, uncounted, untold, variable; SEE CONCEPTS *762,781*

mysterious [adj] *secret, concealed*
abstruse, alchemical, arcane, astrological, baffling, cabalistic, covert, cryptic, curious, dark, difficult, enigmatic, enigmatical, equivocal, esoteric, furtive, hidden, impenetrable, incomprehensible, inexplicable, inscrutable, insoluble, magical, mystical, mystifying, necromantic, obscure, occult, oracular, perplexing, puzzling, recondite, secretive, sphinxlike, spiritual, strange, subjective, symbolic, transcendental, uncanny, unfathomable, unknowable, unknown, unnatural, veiled, weird; SEE CONCEPTS *529,576*

mystery [n] *puzzle, secret*
abstruseness, brainteaser*, braintwister*, charade, chiller, cliffhanger*, closed book*, conundrum, crux, cryptogram, difficulty, enigma, grabber, inscrutability, inscrutableness, mindboggler*, mystification, occult, oracle, perplexity, poser, problem, puzzlement, question, rebus, riddle, rune, secrecy, sixty-four-thousand-dollar question*, sphinx, stickler, stumper, subtlety, teaser, thriller, tough nut to crack*, twister, whodunit*, why*; SEE CONCEPTS *282,532,696*

mystic/mystical [adj] *secret, esoteric*
abstruse, anagogic, arcane, cabalistic, cryptic, enigmatical, hidden, imaginary, impenetrable, inscrutable, magic, magical, metaphysical, mysterial, mysterious, necromantic, nonrational, numinous, occult, otherworldly, paranormal, preternatural, quixotic, sorcerous, spiritual, supernatural, telestic, thaumaturgic, transcendental, unaccountable, unknowable, visionary, wizardly; SEE CONCEPTS *529,549,582*

mystify [v] *bewilder, confuse*
baffle, bamboozle*, beat*, befog*, buffalo*, confound, deceive, elude, escape, floor*, fog in*, hoodwink*, lick*, lie, perplex, puzzle, stump*, throw*, trick; SEE CONCEPT *16*

mystique [n] *person's strong impression*
attitude, awe, character, charisma, charm, complex, fascination, glamour, magic, nature, spell, temperament; SEE CONCEPT *411*

myth [n] *fictitious story, often ancient*
allegory, apologue, creation, delusion, fable, fabrication, fairy story, fancy, fantasy, fiction, figment, folk ballad, folk tale, illusion, imagination, invention, legend, lore, mythos, parable, saga, superstition, tale, tall story*, tradition; SEE CONCEPT *282*

mythical/mythological [adj] *make-believe, fairy-tale*
allegorical, chimerical, created, fabled, fabricated, fabulous, false, fanciful, fantasy, fictitious, fictive, folkloric, imaginary, invented, legendary, made-up, mythic, nonexistent, pretended, storied, supposititious, traditional, unreal, untrue, visionary, whimsical; SEE CONCEPTS *267,582*

mythology [n] *folklore*
belief, conviction, folk tales, legend, lore, mythicism, mythos, myths, stories, tradition; SEE CONCEPT *282*

N

nab [v] *seize*
apprehend, arrest, capture, catch, clutch, cop*, detain, grab, nail*, pick up*, run in*, snatch*, take*, take into custody; SEE CONCEPTS *90,317*

nag [v] *harass, bother*
annoy, badger, bait, berate, bug*, carp at, dog*, eat*, egg*, find fault, fuss, give a hard time*, goad, harry, heckle, hector, hound, importune, irk, irritate, needle, nudge*, pester, pick at, plague, prod, provoke, ride, scold, take it out on*, tease, torment, upbraid, urge, vex, work on*, worry; SEE CONCEPTS *7,19,52*

nail [v1] *fasten, fix with pointed object*
attach, beat, bind, drive, hammer, hit, hold, join, pin, pound, secure, sock*, spike, strike, tack, whack*; SEE CONCEPTS *85,160,189*

nail [v2] *capture, arrest*
apprehend, bag, catch, collar*, detain, get*, hook*, nab, pinch*, prehend, secure, seize, take*; SEE CONCEPTS *90,317*

naive [adj] *childlike, trusting*
aboveboard, artless, callow, candid, confiding, countrified, credulous, forthright, frank, fresh, green*, guileless, gullible, harmless, ignorant, impulsive, ingenuous, innocent, innocuous, instinctive, jejune, lamb*, like a babe in the woods*, natural, open, original, patsy*, plain, simple, simple-minded, sincere, spontaneous,

square, sucker*, unaffected, unjaded, unpretentious, unschooled, unsophisticated, unsuspecting, unsuspicious, untaught, unworldly, virgin, wide-eyed*; SEE CONCEPTS 401,542,678

naiveté [n] *innocence, gullibility*
artlessness, callowness, candor, childishness, credulity, frankness, guilelessness, inexperience, ingenuousness, naturalness, openness, simplicity; SEE CONCEPTS 633,657,678

naked [adj1] *without covering*
au naturel, bald, bare, bared, bare-skinned, barren, defenseless, denuded, disrobed, divested, exposed, helpless, in birthday suit*, in dishabille*, in the altogether*, in the buff*, in the raw*, leafless, natural, nude, open, peeled*, raw, stark-naked*, stripped, threadbare, unclad, unclothed, unconcealed, uncovered, undraped, undressed, unprotected, unveiled, vulnerable, without a stitch*; SEE CONCEPTS 485,589

naked [adj2] *manifest, evident*
artless, blatant, disclosed, discovered, dry, matter-of-fact, obvious, open, overt, palpable, patent, plain, pure, revealed, sheer, simple, stark, unadorned, undisguised, unexaggerated, unmistakable, unqualified, unvarnished; SEE CONCEPTS 267,529

name [n1] *title given to something, someone*
agname, agnomen, alias, appellation, autograph, autonym, brand, cognomen, compellation, denomination, designation, epithet, eponym, flag*, handle*, head, heading, label, matronymic, moniker, monogram, nickname, nom de guerre, nom de plume, nomen, patronymic, pen name, pet name, place name, prenomen, proper name, pseudonym, rubric, sign, signature, sobriquet, stage name, style, surname, tag, term, trade name; SEE CONCEPTS 268,683

name [n2] *fame, distinction*
character, credit, eminence, esteem, honor, note, praise, renown, rep*, report, reputation, repute; SEE CONCEPTS 388,668

name [n3] *celebrity*
big name*, celeb*, entertainer, headliner, hero, lion*, luminary, notability, notable, personality, somebody*, star, superstar; SEE CONCEPTS 352,366

name [v1] *give a title*
baptize, call, characterize, christen, classify, cognominate, define, denominate, designate, dub, entitle, give a handle*, identify, label, nickname, nomenclature, put tag on, style, tag, term, ticket, title; SEE CONCEPT 62

name [v2] *choose, designate*
announce, appoint, cite, classify, commission, connote, declare, delegate, denote, elect, identify, index, instance, list, make, mark, mention, nominate, peg*, pin down*, point to, put down for, put finger on*, recognize, refer to, remark, select, signify, single out, slot, specify, suggest, tab, tag, tap; SEE CONCEPTS 41,50,88

nameless [adj] *unknown, anonymous*
incognito, inconspicuous, innominate, obscure, pseudonymous, unacknowledged, uncelebrated, undesignated, undistinguished, unfamed, unheard-of, unnamed, unnoted, unsung, untitled, whatchamacallit*, X*; SEE CONCEPTS 267,576

namely [adv] *that is to say*
by way of explanation, especially, expressly, id est*, i.e., in other words, in plain English*, particularly, scilicet, specially, specifically, strictly

speaking, that is, to wit, videlicet, viz.; SEE CONCEPT 557

nap [n1] *short, light sleep*
break, catnap, doze, few z's*, forty winks*, interlude, intermission, microsleep*, nod, pause, respite, rest, shuteye*, siesta, snooze*, spot; SEE CONCEPT 315

nap [n2] *grain of material*
down, feel, fiber, grit, outside, pile, roughness, shag, smoothness, surface, tooth, wale, warp, weave, weft, woof; SEE CONCEPTS 473,611

nap [v] *take a short, light sleep*
catch forty winks*, catnap, doze, drop off*, drowse, get some shut-eye*, grab some z's*, nod, nod off, rack*, relax, rest, sleep, snooze, take a siesta*, take a snooze*; SEE CONCEPTS 210,315

narcissistic [adj] *concerned only with oneself*
conceited, egotistic, egotistical, self-centered, self-involved, self-loving, stuck-up*, vain, vainglorious; SEE CONCEPTS 401,404

narcotic [n] *powerful drug inducing anesthesia or sleep*
analgesic, anesthetic, anodyne, dope*, downer*, fix*, hard drug, hard stuff*, heroin, hypnotic, junk*, laudanum, lenitive, merchandise*, nepenthe, opiate, opium, painkiller, sedative, somnifacient, soporific, stuff*, stupefacient, tranquilizer; SEE CONCEPT 307

narcotic [adj] *dulling, painkilling*
analgesic, anesthetic, calming, deadening, hypnotic, numbing, opiate, sedative, somnifacient, somnific, somnolent, somnorific, soporiferous, soporific, stupefacient, stupefactive, stupefying; SEE CONCEPT 537

narrate [v] *describe, detail*
characterize, chronicle, delineate, depict, descant, disclose, discourse, enumerate, expatiate, give an account of, hold forth, make known, paint, picture, portray, proclaim, recite, recount, rehearse, relate, repeat, report, reveal, set forth, spin, state, tell, tell a story, unfold; SEE CONCEPTS 55,72

narration [n] *description, reading*
account, anecdote, explanation, narrative, recital, recountal, recounting, rehearsal, relation, report, story, storytelling, tale, telling, voice-over*, yarn*; SEE CONCEPTS 55,72,282

narrative [n] *story, tale*
account, anecdote, book, chronicle, chronology, description, detail, fiction, history, line, long and short of it*, narration, plot, potboiler*, recount, report, statement, version, yarn*; SEE CONCEPTS 271,282

narrative [adj] *storylike, chronological*
anecdotal, fictional, fictive, historical, narrated, recounted, reported, retold, sequential; SEE CONCEPT 267

narrow [adj1] *confined, restricted*
attenuated, circumscribed, close, compressed, confining, constricted, contracted, cramped, definite, determinate, exclusive, exiguous, fine, fixed, incapacious, limited, linear, meager, near, paltry, pent, pinched, precarious, precise, scant, scanty, select, set, shrunken, slender, slim, small, spare, strait, taper, tapered, tapering, thin, threadlike, tight; SEE CONCEPTS 554,773

narrow [adj2] *intolerant, small-minded*
biased, bigoted, conservative, conventional, dogmatic, hidebound, illiberal, inexorable, inflexible, narrow-minded, obdurate, parochial, partial, prejudiced, reactionary; SEE CONCEPTS 403,542

narrow [*adj3*] *cheap, stingy*
avaricious, close, mean, mercenary, scrimpy*,
tight*, ungenerous; SEE CONCEPT *334*

narrow [*v*] *reduce, simplify*
circumscribe, constrict, contract, diminish, limit,
taper, tighten; SEE CONCEPTS *130,236,247*

narrowly [*adv*] *just, closely*
almost, barely, by a hair*, by a whisker*, by narrow margin, carefully, close, nearly, only just,
painstakingly, scarcely, scrutinizingly; SEE CON-
CEPTS *544,799*

narrow-minded [*adj*] *biased, intolerant*
bigoted, conservative, conventional, hidebound,
illiberal, insular, narrow, opinionated, parochial,
petty, prejudiced, provincial, reactionary, short-
sighted, small-minded, strait-laced, unenlarged;
SEE CONCEPTS *403,542*

nasty [*adj1*] *disgusting, offensive*
awful, beastly, bum*, dirty, disagreeable, fierce,
filthy, foul, gross, grubby, hellish, horrible, horrid, icky*, impure, loathsome, lousy, malodorous, mephitic, murderous*, nauseating, noisome,
noxious, objectionable, obnoxious, obscene, odious, ornery, outrageous, poison, polluted, raunchy*, repellent, repugnant, repulsive, revolting,
rough, sickening, soiled, squalid, stinking, tough,
unappetizing, unclean, uncleanly, ungodly, unholy, unpleasant, vile, vulgar, yucky*; SEE CON-
CEPTS *485,548,571*

nasty [*adj2*] *indecent, smutty*
blue*, coarse, dirty, filthy, foul, gross, immodest,
immoral, improper, impure, indecorous, indelicate, lascivious, lewd, licentious, obscene, pornographic, raunchy*, ribald, scatological,
shameful, unseemly, vulgar, wicked, X-rated*;
SEE CONCEPTS *372,545*

nasty [*adj3*] *bad-tempered, mean*
abusive, annoying, beastly, critical, cruel, despicable, disagreeable, distasteful, evil, fierce, hateful, malevolent, malicious, malign, malignant,
ornery, ruthless, sarcastic, sordid, spiteful,
squalid, unkind, unpleasant, vicious, vile, wicked;
SEE CONCEPT *401*

nasty [*adj4*] *injurious, dangerous*
bad, critical, damaging, harmful, noxious, painful, poisonous, serious, severe, ugly; SEE CON-
CEPT *537*

nation [*n*] *country with its own government*
body politic, commonwealth, community, democracy, domain, dominion, empire, land, monarchy,
people, populace, population, principality, public, race, realm, republic, society, sovereignty,
state, tribe, union; SEE CONCEPT *510*

national [*adj*] *concerning a country with a government*
civic, civil, communal, countrywide, domestic,
ethnic, federal, general, governmental, home, imperial, inland, internal, interstate, nationwide, native, politic, political, public, royal, social,
societal, sovereign, state, sweeping, vernacular,
widespread; SEE CONCEPT *536*

nationality [*n*] *place of birth*
allegiance, body politic, citizenship, community,
country, ethnic group, nation, native land, origin,
political home, race, society; SEE CONCEPTS
380,510

native [*n*] *person born in the country in which
he/she dwells*
aboriginal, aborigine, ancient, autochthon, citi-

zen, dweller, home towner, indigene, inhabitant,
local, national; SEE CONCEPT *413*

native [*adj1*] *innate, inherent*
built-in, congenital, connate, connatural, constitutional, endemic, essential, fundamental, genuine, hereditary, implanted, inborn, inbred,
indigenous, ingrained, inherited, instinctive, intrinsic, inveterate, inwrought, natal, natural, original, real, unacquired, wild; SEE CONCEPTS
404,549

native [*adj2*] *domestic, home*
aboriginal, autochthonous, belonging, endemic,
from, homegrown, homemade, indigenous, inland, internal, local, municipal, national, original,
primary, primeval, primitive, regional, related,
vernacular; SEE CONCEPT *536*

natural [*adj1*] *normal, everyday*
accustomed, anticipated, characteristic, common,
commonplace, congenital, connatural, consistent,
constant, counted on, customary, essential, familiar, general, habitual, inborn, indigenous, ingenerate, inherent, innate, instinctive, intuitive,
involuntary, legitimate, logical, looked for,
matter-of-course, natal, native, ordinary, prevailing, prevalent, probable, reasonable, regular, re-
lied on, spontaneous, typic, typical, unacquired,
uncontrolled, uniform, universal, usual; SEE CON-
CEPTS *530,547*

natural [*adj2*] *open, unaffected*
artless, being oneself, candid, childlike, credulous, direct, easy, folksy, forthright, frank, genuine, homey*, ignorant, impulsive, inartificial,
ingenuous, innocent, instinctive, laid-back*, naive, plain, primitive, provincial, real, rustic,
simple, simplehearted, sincere, spontaneous,
straightforward, trusting, unassumed, uncontrived, undesigning, unembarrassed, unfeigned,
unforced, unlabored, unpolished, unpretentious,
unschooled, unsophisticated, unstudied, unworldly, up-front*; SEE CONCEPTS *267,401,404*

natural [*adj3*] *organic, unrefined*
agrarian, agrestal, crude, native, plain, pure, raw,
unbleached, uncultivated, undomesticated, unmixed, unpolished, unprocessed, whole, wild;
SEE CONCEPTS *462,485*

naturally [*adv*] *as anticipated*
artlessly, but of course*, by birth, by nature, candidly, casually, characteristically, commonly,
consistently, customarily, easily, freely, generally, genuinely, habitually, impulsively, informally, innocently, instinctively, normally,
openly, ordinarily, readily, simply, spontaneously, typically, unaffectedly, uniformly, unpretentiously, usually; SEE CONCEPT *544*

nature [*n1*] *character, disposition*
attributes, being, bottom line*, complexion, constitution, description, drift, essence, essentiality,
features, heart*, humor, individualism, individuality, like, makeup, meat*, mood, name of
game*, name of tune*, nature of beast*, outlook,
personality, point, quality, score, stuff, temper,
temperament, texture, traits, type; SEE CONCEPTS
411,682

nature [*n2*] *type, kind*
anatomy, brand, cast, category, character, color,
conformation, description, figure, framework, ilk,
shape, sort, species, stripe*, structure, style, variety, way; SEE CONCEPT *378*

nature [*n3*] *earth, creation*
cosmos, country, countryside, environment, for-

est, generation, landscape, macrocosm, mega-cosm, natural history, outdoors, scenery, seascape, setting, universe, view, world; SEE CONCEPTS 407,429,509,511

naughty [adj1] *bad, misbehaved*
annoying, badly behaved*, contrary, disobedient, disorderly, evil, exasperating, fiendish, fractious, froward, headstrong, impish, indecorous, insubordinate, intractable, mischievous, obstreperous, perverse, playful, rascally, raunchy, recalcitrant, refractory, rough, rowdy, sinful, teasing, tough, ungovernable, unmanageable, unruly, wanton, wayward, wicked, willful, worthless, wrong; SEE CONCEPT 401

naughty [adj2] *obscene, vulgar*
adult, bawdy, blue*, dirty*, hot*, improper, lascivious, lewd, loose*, off-color*, pornographic, purple*, ribald, risqué, steamy*; SEE CONCEPTS 372,545

nausea [n] *sickness in stomach; revulsion*
abhorrence, aversion, biliousness, disgust, hatred, loathing, offense, qualm, qualms, queasiness, regurgitation, rejection, repugnance, retching, squeamishness, vomiting; SEE CONCEPTS 316,410

nauseate [v] *make sick; disgust*
bother, disturb, horrify, offend, reluct, repel, repulse, revolt, sicken; SEE CONCEPTS 14,308

nauseous [adj] *disgusting*
abhorrent, brackish, detestable, distasteful, ill, loathsome, nauseated, nauseating, offensive, queasy, repugnant, repulsive, revolting, rocky*, seasick, sick, sick as dog*, sickening, squeamish; SEE CONCEPTS 314,529

nautical/naval [adj] *concerning ships, sea*
abyssal, aquatic, boating, cruising, deep-sea, marine, maritime, navigating, navigational, ocean-going, oceanic, oceanographic, pelagic, rowing, sailing, sailorly, salty, seafaring, seagoing, sea-loving, thalassic, yachting; SEE CONCEPT 536

navigate [v] *guide along route, often over water*
captain*, cross, cruise, direct, drive, handle, head out for*, helm, journey, lay the course*, maneuver, operate, pilot, plan, plot, ride out, sail, skipper*, steer, voyage; SEE CONCEPTS 148,187,224

navigation [n] *traveling, guiding along route, often over water*
aeronautics, boating, cruising, exploration, flying, helmsmanship, nautics, navigating, ocean travel, pilotage, piloting, plotting a course, sailing, seafaring, seamanship, shipping, steerage, steering, voyage, voyaging, yachting; SEE CONCEPTS 155,187,224

near [adj1] *close by physically*
abreast, abutting, adjacent, adjoining, alongside, along toward, approximal, around, at close quarters, available, beside, bordering, burning, close, close-at-hand, close-by, close shave*, contiguous, contiguous, convenient, hair's breadth*, handy, immediate, in close proximity*, near-at-hand*, nearby, neighboring, next door*, nigh*, not remote, practically, proximal, proximate, ready, side-by-side, touching, vincinal, warm*, within stone's throw*; SEE CONCEPTS 586,778

near [adj2] *close in time; forthcoming*
approaching, approximate, at hand, coming, comparative, expected, imminent, impending, in the offing*, looming, near-at-hand*, next, relative; SEE CONCEPTS 812,820

near [adj3] *familiar*
affecting, akin*, allied, attached, close, con-nected, dear, friendly, intimate, related, touching; SEE CONCEPT 555

nearby [adj] *adjoining*
adjacent, close, close-at-hand, close-by, contiguous, convenient, handy, immediate, neighboring, proximate, ready; SEE CONCEPTS 586,778

nearby [adv] *within reach*
about, at close quarters, close, close at hand, hard, near, near-at-hand*, nigh*, not far away; SEE CONCEPTS 586,778

nearing [adj] *approaching*
advancing, approximating, coming, forthcoming, imminent, impending, oncoming, threatening, upcoming; SEE CONCEPTS 548,820

nearly [adv] *almost*
about, all but*, approaching, approximately, as good as*, circa*, close but no cigar*, closely, give or take a little*, in effect, in essence, in substance, in the ballpark*, in the neighborhood*, just about, more or less, most, much, nearabout, not quite, practically, pretty near, roughly, round, roundly, some, somewhere, upwards of*, virtually, well-nigh*, within a little*; SEE CONCEPT 566

neat [adj1] *arranged well, uncluttered*
accurate, apple-pie order*, chic*, correct, dainty, dapper, elegant, exact, fastidious, finical, finicky, immaculate, in good order, in good shape, methodical, natty, neat as a pin*, nice, orderly, precise, prim, proper, regular, shipshape*, sleek, slick, smart, spick-and-span*, spotless, spruce, systematic, tidy, trim, well-groomed, well-kept; SEE CONCEPTS 485,589,621

neat [adj2] *clever, practiced*
able, adept, adroit, agile, apt, artful, deft, dexterous, efficient, effortless, elegant, expert, finished, graceful, handy, nimble, precise, proficient, quick, ready, skillful, speedy, stylish, well-judged; SEE CONCEPTS 527,542

nebulous [adj] *confused, obscure*
ambiguous, amorphous, cloudy, dark, dim, hazy, imprecise, indefinite, indeterminate, indistinct, misty, murky, shadowy, shapeless, uncertain, unclear, unformed, vague; SEE CONCEPTS 535,617

necessarily [adv] *inevitably, certainly*
accordingly, as a matter of course*, automatically, axiomatically, beyond one's control*, by definition, by its own nature*, cardinally, come what may*, compulsorily, consequently, exigently, from within*, fundamentally, incontrovertibly, indubitably, ineluctably, inescapably, inexorably, irresistibly, naturally, no doubt, of course, of necessity, perforce, positively, pressingly, significantly, undoubtedly, unpreventably, unquestionably, vitally, willy-nilly*, without fail*; SEE CONCEPTS 535,544

necessary [adj1] *essential*
all-important, basic, binding, bottom-line*, cardinal, chief, compelling, compulsory, crucial, decisive, de rigueur*, elementary, exigent, expedient, fundamental, imperative, incumbent on, indispensable, mandatory, momentous, name of game*, needed, needful, obligatory, paramount, prerequisite, pressing, prime, principal, quintessential, required, requisite, significant, specified, unavoidable, urgent, vital, wanted; SEE CONCEPTS 546,568

necessary [adj2] *inevitable*
assured, certain, fated, imminent, ineluctable, ineludible, inerrant, inescapable, inevisable, inexo-

rable, infallible, returnless, unavoidable, undeniable, unescapable; SEE CONCEPTS 535,548

necessitate [v] *call for, make necessary*
ask, behoove, cause, coerce, command, compel, constrain, crave, demand, drive, entail, force, impel, make, oblige, postulate, require, take; SEE CONCEPTS 53,242,646

necessity [n] *need, essentiality*
call, cause, claim, compulsion, demand, desideratum, duress, essence, essential, exaction, exigency, fundamental, godsend*, imperative, indispensability, inevitability, inexorableness, life or death*, must, necessary, needfulness, no alternative, no choice, obligation, pinch, precondition, prerequisite, privation, requirement, requisite, sine qua non, stress, undeniability, urgency, vital part, vitals, want; SEE CONCEPTS 646,709

need [n1] *want, requirement*
charge, commitment, committal, compulsion, demand, desideratum, devoir, duty, essential, exigency, extremity, longing, must, obligation, occasion, ought, requisite, right, the urge, urgency, use, weakness, wish; SEE CONCEPTS 20,709

need [n2] *poverty*
deprivation, destitution, distress, extremity, impecuniousness, impoverishment, inadequacy, indigence, insufficiency, lack, neediness, paucity, pennilessness, penury, poorness, privation, shortage, want; SEE CONCEPTS 335,709

need [n3] *emergency; pressing lack*
deficiency, exigency, inadequacy, insufficiency, necessity, obligation, shortage, urgency, want; SEE CONCEPTS 646,709

need [v] *want something*
be deficient, be deprived, be down and out*, be hard up*, be inadequate, be in need of, be in want, be needy, be poor, be short, be without, call for, claim, covet, crave, demand, desire, die for*, do without, drive for*, exact, feel a dearth of*, feel the necessity for, feel the pinch*, go hungry*, hanker, have occasion for, have occasion to, have use for*, hunger, hurt for, lack, long, lust, miss, necessitate, pine, require, suffer privation, thirst, wish, yearn, yen for; SEE CONCEPTS 20,646

needle [v] *tease, annoy*
aggravate, badger, bait, bedevil, bother, examine, gnaw, goad, harass, hector, irk, irritate, nag, nettle, pester, plague, prick, prod, provoke, question, quiz, ride*, rile, ruffle, spur, sting, taunt, tweak*, worry; SEE CONCEPTS 7,19,54

needless [adj] *unnecessary, groundless*
causeless, dispensable, excessive, expendable, gratuitous, inessential, nonessential, pointless, redundant, superfluous, uncalled-for, undesired, unrequired, unwanted, useless; SEE CONCEPTS 546,575

needy [adj] *deprived, impoverished*
beggared, dead broke*, destitute, dirt poor*, disadvantaged, down-and-out*, down at heel*, down to last cent*, flat*, impecunious, indigent, necessitous, penniless, penurious, poor, poverty-stricken, underprivileged, unprosperous; SEE CONCEPT 334

nefarious [adj] *bad, sinful*
abominable, atrocious, base, corrupt, criminal, degenerate, depraved, detestable, dreadful, evil, execrable, flagitious, flagrant, foul, glaring, gross, heinous, horrible, infamous, infernal, iniquitous, miscreant, monstrous, odious, opprobrious, out-rageous, perverse, putrid, rank, rotten, shameful, treacherous, vicious, vile, villainous, wicked; SEE CONCEPTS 401,545,548

negate [v] *contradict, countermand*
abate, abolish, abrogate, annihilate, annul, belie, blackball*, break with*, cancel, cancel out, controvert, countercheck, cross*, deny, ding*, disaffirm, disallow, disprove, dump*, fly in the face of*, frustrate, gainsay, impugn, invalidate, kill, negative, neutralize, nullify, oppose, put down, quash*, rebut, redress, refute, repeal, rescind, retract, reverse, revoke, stonewall*, traverse, turn down, turn thumbs down*, undo, vitiate, void; SEE CONCEPTS 46,50,88,121

negation [n] *contradiction, denial*
antithesis, antonym, blank, cancellation, contrary, converse, counterpart, disavowal, disclaimer, forget it*, gainsaying, inverse, negatory, neutralization, no, nonexistence, nothingness, nullification, nullity, opposite, opposition, proscription, refusal, rejection, renunciation, repudiation, reverse, vacuity, veto, void; SEE CONCEPTS 121,278,685

negative [n] *contradiction*
denial, disavowal, nay, refusal, refutation; SEE CONCEPT 278

negative [adj] *bad, contradictory*
abrogating, adverse, against, annulling, antagonistic, anti, balky, colorless, con, contrary, contravening, counteractive, cynical, denying, detrimental, disallowing, disavowing, dissentient, dissenting, gainsaying, gloomy, impugning, invalidating, jaundiced, naysaying, neutralizing, nugatory, nullifying, opposing, pessimistic, privative, recusant, refusing, rejecting, removed, repugnant, resisting, resistive, unaffirmative, unenthusiastic, unfavorable, uninterested, unwilling, weak; SEE CONCEPTS 267,403,570

neglect [n1] *disregard*
carelessness, coolness, delinquency, disdain, disregardance, disrespect, heedlessness, inadvertence, inattention, inconsideration, indifference, laxity, laxness, oversight, scorn, slight, thoughtlessness, unconcern; SEE CONCEPTS 410,657

neglect [n2] *failure, default*
carelessness, chaos, delay, delinquency, dereliction, dilapidation, forgetfulness, lapse, laxity, laxness, limbo, neglectfulness, negligence, omission, oversight, pretermission, remissness, slackness, slovenliness; SEE CONCEPTS 674,699

neglect [v1] *be indifferent, leave alone*
affront, brush aside, brush off, condemn, depreciate, despise, detest, discount, disdain, dismiss, disregard, have nothing to do with*, ignore, keep at arm's length*, keep one's distance*, laugh off*, let go*, live with*, make light of*, not care for*, overlook, pass by, pass over, pass up, pay no attention to, pay no mind*, pretermit, rebuff, reject, scant, scorn, shrug off*, slight, slur, spurn, tune out*, underestimate; SEE CONCEPTS 30,681

neglect [v2] *fail to do; forget*
be careless, be derelict, be irresponsible, be negligent, be remiss, bypass, defer, discard, dismiss, disregard, elide, evade, gloss over*, let pass*, let slide*, look the other way*, miss, neglect*, miss, not trouble oneself*, omit, overleap, overlook, overpass, pass over, postpone, procrastinate, shirk, skimp, skip, suspend, think little of*, trifle; SEE CONCEPTS 101,699

neglectful [adj] careless, failing
behindhand, delinquent, derelict, disregardful, heedless, inattentive, indifferent, lax, lazy, negligent, regardless, remiss, slack, thoughtless, uncaring, unmindful; SEE CONCEPTS 401,542

negligent [adj] careless, indifferent
asleep at switch*, behindhand, cursory, delinquent, derelict, discinct, disregardful, forgetful, heedless, inadvertent, inattentive, inconsiderate, incurious, lax, neglectful, nonchalant, offhand, regardless, remiss, slack, slapdash*, slipshod*, sloppy*, slovenly, thoughtless, unconcerned, unheedful, unmindful, unthinking; SEE CONCEPTS 401,542

negligible [adj] insignificant
imperceptible, inconsequential, minor, minute, off*, outside, petty, remote, slender, slight, slim, small, trifling, trivial, unimportant; SEE CONCEPTS 552,575,789

negotiate [v1] bargain, discuss
accommodate, adjudicate, adjust, agree, arbitrate, arrange, bring to terms*, come across with*, compose, concert, conciliate, confer, connect, consult, contract, covenant, cut a deal*, deal, debate, dicker*, haggle, hammer out a deal*, handle, horse trade*, intercede, make a deal, make peace*, make terms*, manage, mediate, moderate, network, parley*, referee, settle, step in*, stipulate, swap, transact, treat, umpire*, work out*, work out a deal; SEE CONCEPTS 8,56,68

negotiate [v2] traverse, cross
clear, get around, get over, get past, hurdle, leap over, overleap, pass, pass through, surmount, vault; SEE CONCEPTS 149,224

negotiation [n] bargaining
agreement, arbitration, colloquy, compromise, conference, consultation, debate, diplomacy, discussion, intervention, mediation, meeting, transaction; SEE CONCEPTS 56,68,684

negotiator [n] person who bargains, controls discussion
adjudicator, ambassador, arbitrator, broker, delegate, diplomat, fixer*, go-between*, interagent, intermediary, intermedium, judge, mediator, middleperson, moderator; SEE CONCEPTS 348,354,423

neighbor [n] person who lives close by
acquaintance, bystander, friend, homebody*, nearby resident, next-door neighbor; SEE CONCEPT 423

neighbor [v] be next to
abut, adjoin, be adjacent, be contiguous, be near, be nearby, border, butt against, communicate, connect, join, line, march, surround, touch, verge; SEE CONCEPT 759

neighborhood [n] community, surroundings
adjacency, area, block, closeness, confines, contiguity, district, environs, ghetto, hood, jungle*, locale, locality, nearness, neck of the woods*, parish, part, precinct, propinquity, proximity, purlieus, quarter, region, section, slum, stomping ground*, street, suburb, territory, tract, turf, vicinage, vicinity, ward, zone, zoo*; SEE CONCEPTS 198,379,516

neighborly [adj] friendly
amiable, civil, companionable, considerate, cooperative, cordial, genial, gracious, gregarious, harmonious, helpful, hospitable, kind, obliging, sociable, social, well-disposed; SEE CONCEPT 401

neologism [n] new word
buzz word*, coinage, neology, new phrase, slang, synthetic word*, vogue word*; SEE CONCEPT 275

nerve [n] daring, boldness
assumption, assurance, audacity, backbone, brass*, bravery, brazenness, cheek*, chutzpah*, confidence, coolness, courage, crust*, determination, effrontery, endurance, energy, face*, fearlessness, firmness, force, fortitude, gall*, gameness, grit*, guts*, hardihood, hardiness, heart*, impertinence, impudence, insolence, intestinal fortitude, intrepidity, mettle, might, moxie*, pluck*, presumption, resolution, sauce*, spirit, spunk*, starch*, steadfastness, stomach*, temerity, vigor, will; SEE CONCEPT 411

nerve [v] strengthen, hearten
animate, brace, cheer, embolden, encourage, enhearten, fortify, inspirit, invigorate, steel; SEE CONCEPTS 7,14,22

nerveless [adj1] calm, cool
collected, composed, controlled, impassive, imperturbable, intrepid, patient, self-possessed, tranquil, unemotional; SEE CONCEPT 542

nerveless [adj2] scared to death
afraid, cowardly, debilitated, enervated, fearful, feeble, nervous, petrified, spineless*, timid, weak, yellow-bellied*; SEE CONCEPTS 401,403

nerves [n] extreme anxiety
fretfulness, hysteria, imbalance, irritation, nervousness, neurasthenia, sleeplessness, strain, stress, tenseness, tension; SEE CONCEPT 410

nervous [adj] anxious, fearful
afraid, agitated, annoyed, apprehensive, basket case*, bothered, concerned, distressed, disturbed, edgy, excitable, fidgety, fitful, flustered, fussy*, hesitant, high-strung*, hysterical, irritable, jittery*, jumpy*, nervy*, neurotic, on edge*, overwrought, querulous, restive, ruffled, sensitive, shaky*, shrinking, shy, skittish, snappish, solicitous, spooked*, taut, tense, timid, timorous, troubled, twitchy*, uneasy, unrestful, unstrung*, upset, uptight, volatile, weak, wired*, worried; SEE CONCEPTS 403,542

nervousness [n] anxious state
agitation, all-overs*, anger, animation, butterflies*, cold sweat*, creeps*, delirium, discomfiture, disquiet, disquietude, dithers*, excitability, feverishness, fidgets*, flap*, fluster*, fuss*, impatience, jitters*, jumps*, moodiness, neurasthenia, neuroticism, perturbation, quivers, sensitivity, shakes, stage fright, stimulation, stress, tension, timidity, tizzy*, to-do*, touchiness, trembles*, tremulousness, turbulence, uneasiness, willies*, worry; SEE CONCEPTS 410,657

nervy [adj] bold, pushy
cheeky*, crass, crude, forward, fresh*, impudent, inconsiderate, pert, plucky*, rude, sassy*, smart, smart-alecky*, wise; SEE CONCEPT 401

nestle [v] curl up
bundle, burrow, cuddle, huddle, lie against, lie close, make snug*, move close, nuzzle, settle down, snug*, snuggle, take shelter; SEE CONCEPTS 154,612

net [n] mesh, web
cloth, fabric, lace, lacework, lattice, netting, network, openwork, reticulum, screen, tracery; SEE CONCEPTS 473,770

net [adj] profiting
after deductions, after taxes, clear, excluding, ex-

clusive, final, irreducible, pure, remaining, take-home, undeductible; SEE CONCEPT 334

net [v1] *capture*
bag*, catch, enmesh, ensnare, entangle, hook*, lasso*, nab*, trap; SEE CONCEPT 90

net [v2] *gain after expenses*
accumulate, bring in, clean up, clear, earn, make, profit, realize, reap; SEE CONCEPT 330

nettle [v] *provoke, upset*
annoy, chafe, disgust, disturb, exasperate, fret, get*, goad, harass, huff, incense, insult, irritate, miff, peeve*, pester, pet, pique, put out*, rile, roil, ruffle, snit*, stew*, sting*, tease, tiff*, vex; SEE CONCEPTS 7,14,19

network [n] *system of connections*
arrangement, artery, chain, checkerboard*, circuitry, complex, convolution, crisscross*, fabric, fiber, grid, grill*, grillwork, hookup, interconnections, jungle, labyrinth, maze, mesh, net, netting, nexus, organization, patchwork*, plexus, reticulation, reticule, screening, structure, system, tessellation, tracks, wattle, weave, web, wiring; SEE CONCEPTS 381,388,770

network [v] *to socialize for professional or personal gain*
associate, circulate, hobnob, make contacts, meet, meet and greet*, mingle, rub elbows*, schmooze*; SEE CONCEPT 384

neurosis [n] *mental disturbance, disorder*
aberration, abnormality, affliction, breakdown, compulsion, crack-up*, derangement, deviation, hysteria, inhibition, insanity, instability, madness, maladjustment, mental illness, neurasthenia, obsession, personality disorder, phobia, psychological disorder, psychopathy; SEE CONCEPTS 316,410

neurotic [adj] *mentally maladjusted*
aberrant, abnormal, anxious, basket case*, bundle of nerves*, choked*, clutched*, compulsive, deviant, disordered, disoriented, distraught, disturbed, erratic, hung up*, hysteric, inhibited, manic, nervous, nervous wreck*, obsessive, overwrought, psychoneurotic, unhealthy, unstable, upset, uptight, wired*; SEE CONCEPTS 314,403

neuter [v] *remove sex organs*
alter, castrate, change, desexualize, doctor, dress, fix, geld, make barren, make impotent, make infertile, make sexless, mutilate, spay, sterilize, unsex; SEE CONCEPTS 157,250

neutral [adj1] *impartial, noncommittal*
aloof, bystanding, calm, clinical, collected, cool, detached, disengaged, disinterested, dispassionate, easy, evenhanded, fair-minded, impersonal, inactive, indifferent, inert, middle-of-road*, nonaligned, nonbelligerent, nonchalant, noncombatant, nonparticipating, nonpartisan, on sidelines*, on the fence*, pacifistic, poker-faced*, relaxed, unaligned, unbiased, uncommitted, unconcerned, undecided, uninvolved, unprejudiced; SEE CONCEPTS 403,542

neutral [adj2] *flat, dull to senses*
abstract, achromatic, colorless, drab, expressionless, indeterminate, indistinct, indistinguishable, intermediate, toneless, undefined, vague, vanilla; SEE CONCEPTS 485,537,618

neutralize [v] *counteract*
abrogate, annul, balance, cancel, compensate for, conquer, counterbalance, countercheck, counterpoise, countervail, defeat, frustrate, invalidate, negate, negative, nullify, offset, overcome, over-

ride, overrule, redress, subdue, undo; SEE CONCEPTS 121,232

never [adv] *not at any time*
at no time, don't hold your breath*, forget it, nevermore, not at all, not ever, not in any way, not in the least, not on your life*, not under any condition, no way*; SEE CONCEPT 799

never-ending [adj] *continual, unceasing*
amaranthine, boundless, ceaseless, constant, continuous, endless, eternal, everlasting, immortal, incessant, interminable, nonstop, perpetual, persistent, relentless, timeless, unbroken, unchanging, uninterrupted, unremitting; SEE CONCEPTS 482,798

nevertheless [adv] *however*
after all, although, but, even so, even though, howbeit, nonetheless, not the less, notwithstanding, regardless, still, still and all, though, withal, yet; SEE CONCEPT 544

new [adj1] *recent, fresh*
advanced, au courant, brand-new, contemporary, current, cutting-edge*, dewy, different, dissimilar, distinct, fashionable, inexperienced, just out*, late, latest, modern, modernistic, modish*, neoteric, newfangled*, novel, now*, original, recent, spick-and-span*, state-of-the-art, strange, topical, ultramodern, unaccustomed, uncontaminated, unfamiliar, unique, unknown, unlike, unseasoned, unskilled, unspoiled, untouched, untrained, untried, untrodden, unused, unusual, up-to-date, virgin, youthful; SEE CONCEPTS 564,578,797

new [adj2] *additional*
added, another, else, extra, farther, fresh, further, increased, more, other, supplementary; SEE CONCEPTS 771,824

new [adj3] *modernized, restored*
altered, changed, improved, redesigned, refreshed, regenerated, renewed, revived; SEE CONCEPT 589

new [adv] *recently*
afresh, anew, freshly, lately, newly, of late; SEE CONCEPT 820

new age [adj] *of a broad-ranging consciousness-raising movement*
Age of Aquarius*, alternative, astrological, balanced, crystal healing, holistic, mystic, occult, planetary, spiritual, supernaturalist; SEE CONCEPTS 403,529

newcomer [n] *person who has just arrived in area*
alien, arrival, beginner, blow-in*, colt*, foreigner, greenhorn*, immigrant, incomer, Johnny-come-lately*, late arrival, latecomer, maverick, neophyte, new kid on the block*, novice, novitiate, outsider, rookie, settler, stranger, tenderfoot*; SEE CONCEPTS 413,423

newfangled [adj] *quite recent*
contemporary, fashionable, fresh, gimmicky*, in vogue, modern, modernistic, neoteric, new, new-fashioned, novel, popular, unique; SEE CONCEPTS 578,589,797

newly [adv] *recently*
anew, freshly, just, lately, latterly, of late; SEE CONCEPT 820

news [n] *information, revelation*
account, advice, announcement, broadcast, bulletin, cable, cognizance, communication, communiqué, copy, data, description, disclosure, discovery, dispatch, enlightenment, exposé, eye-opener*, front-page news*, headlines, hearsay, intelligence, itemization, knowledge, leak, low-

down, message, narration, news flash, particularization, recital, recognition, release, report, rumor, scandal, scoop*, specification, statement, story, telecast, telegram, telling, the goods*, tidings*, word*; SEE CONCEPTS *268,274,293*

newspaper [n] *regular, continuous publication containing information*
biweekly, bulldog*, community, daily, extra, gazette, journal, magazine, metropolitan, organ, paper, periodical, press, rag*, record, review, scandal sheet*, sheet, tabloid, trade, weekly; SEE CONCEPTS *279,280*

next [adj] *coming immediately after in space, time, order*
abutting, adjacent, adjoining, after, alongside, attached, back-to-back, beside, close, closest, coming, consequent, co-terminous, ensuing, following, hard by*, later, meeting, nearest, neighboring, on the side, proximate, side-by-side, subsequent, succeeding, touching; SEE CONCEPTS *585,586,799*

next [adv] *immediately after in time, space, order*
after, afterward, afterwhile, behind, by and by, closely, coming up, following, later, latterly, next off, subsequently, thereafter; SEE CONCEPTS *585,586,799*

nibble [n] *morsel, bite*
crumb, peck, snack, soupçon, taste, tidbit; SEE CONCEPTS *458,831*

nibble [v] *bite, pick at*
crop, eat, eat like a bird*, gnaw, munch, nip*, nosh on*, peck*, snack; SEE CONCEPT *169*

nice [adj1] *likable, agreeable*
admirable, amiable, approved, attractive, becoming, charming, commendable, considerate, copacetic, cordial, courteous, decorous, delightful, ducky, fair, favorable, fine and dandy*, friendly, genial, gentle, good, gracious, helpful, ingratiating, inviting, kind, kindly, lovely, nifty*, obliging, okay*, peachy*, pleasant, pleasurable, polite, prepossessing, seemly, simpatico, superior, swell, unpresumptuous, welcome, well-mannered, winning, winsome; SEE CONCEPTS *404,548,572*

nice [adj2] *precise, neat, refined*
accurate, becoming, befitting, careful, choosy, conforming, correct, critical, cultured, dainty, decent, delicate, discerning, discriminating, distinguishing, exact, exacting, fastidious, fine, finespun, finical, finicking, finicky*, fussy*, genteel, hairsplitting*, meticulous, minute, particular, persnickety*, picky*, proper, respectable, right, rigorous, scrupulous, seemly, squeamish, strict, subtle, tidy, trim, trivial*, virtuous, well-bred; SEE CONCEPTS *542,557,558*

niche [n] *place all one's own*
alcove, byplace, calling, compartment, corner, cranny*, cubbyhole*, hole, hollow, indentation, nook, opening, pigeonhole*, position, recess, slot, vocation; SEE CONCEPTS *440,513,630*

nick [n/v] *chip, scratch*
cut, damage, dent, dint, indent, jag, knock, mark, mill, notch, scar, score, slit; SEE CONCEPTS *137,176,208*

nickname [n] *informal title*
appellation, byname, byword, denomination, diminutive, epithet, familiar name, handle*, label, moniker, pet name*, sobriquet, style, tag*; SEE CONCEPTS *268,683*

nifty [adj] *marvelous*
chic, clever, cool*, dandy, enjoyable, excellent,

groovy*, keen, neat, peachy*, pleasing, quick, sharp, smart, spruce, stylish, super, swell, terrific; SEE CONCEPT *572*

night [n] *part of day after sundown and before sunrise*
after dark, after hours*, bedtime, before dawn, black*, blackness, dark, dark hours, darkness, dead of night*, dim, duskiness, dusk to dawn, evening, eventide, gloom, midnight, nightfall, nighttide, nighttime, obscurity*, pitch dark, twilight, witching hour*; SEE CONCEPTS *620,801,806,810*

nightclub [n] *place for evening entertainment*
bar, bistro, cabaret, café, casino, disco*, discotheque, dive*, hideaway*, honky-tonk*, joint*, nightery, night spot, nitery, restaurant, roadhouse, saloon, speakeasy*, spot, supper club, tavern, theatre, watering hole*; SEE CONCEPTS *293,439,449*

nightfall [n] *beginning of darkness*
black*, crepuscule, dim, dusk, eve, eventide, sundown, sunset, twilight, vespers; SEE CONCEPT *810*

nightgown [n] *dress in which to sleep*
bedgown, lingerie, negligee, nightdress, nightie*, nightrobe, nightshirt, pajamas, PJs*, sleeper*; SEE CONCEPT *451*

nightly [adj/adv] *each evening; after dark*
at night, by night, every night, in the night, night after night, nights, nighttime, nocturnal, nocturnally; SEE CONCEPTS *541,799,801*

nightmare [n] *bad dream or experience*
dream, fancy, fantasy, hallucination, horror, illusion, incubus, ordeal, phantasm, succubus, torment, trial, tribulation, vision; SEE CONCEPTS *315,674*

nihilism [n] *refusal to believe*
abnegation, agnosticism, anarchy, atheism, denial, disbelief, disorder, lawlessness, mob rule*, nonbelief, rejection, renunciation, repudiation, skepticism, terrorism; SEE CONCEPT *689*

nil [adj] *nonexistent*
naught, nihil, nix*, none, nothing, nought, zero; SEE CONCEPTS *539,762,771*

nimble [adj] *dexterous, smart*
active, adept, adroit, agile, alert, bright, brisk, clever, deft, handy, light, lissome, lithe, lively, proficient, prompt, quick, quick-witted, ready, skillful, sprightly, spry, swift, vigilant, wide-awake; SEE CONCEPTS *402,527,584*

nip [n] *swallow, taste*
bite, catch, dram, drop, finger, jolt, morsel, mouthful, nibble, pinch, portion, shot*, sip, slug*, snifter, soupçon, toothful; SEE CONCEPTS *458,831*

nip [v1] *bite; take small part*
catch, clip, compress, grip, munch, nab at*, nibble, pinch, sink teeth into*, snag, snap*, snip*, squeeze*, take a chunk out of*, tweak, twinge, twitch; SEE CONCEPTS *142,169,190*

nip [v2] *stop, thwart*
arrest, balk, blight, check, dash, end, frustrate; SEE CONCEPTS *121,234*

nobility [n] *aristocracy; eminence*
dignity, elevation, elite, ennoblement, exaltation, excellence, generosity, gentry, glorification, grandeur, greatness, high society, honor, illustriousness, incorruptibility, integrity, loftiness, magnanimity, magnificence, majesty, nobleness, patricians, peerage, royalty, ruling class, society, stateliness, sublimity, superiority, upper class, up-

rightness, virtue, worthiness; SEE CONCEPTS *378,388,668*

noble [*n*] *member of royal or important family*
archduchess, archduke, aristocrat, blue blood*, count, countess, duchess, duke, emperor, empress, gentleman, gentlewoman, lady, lord, patrician, peer, prince, princess, royalty, silk stocking*; SEE CONCEPTS *422,423*

noble [*adj1*] *aristocratic*
gentle, highborn, imperial, kingly, nobiliary, patrician, queenly, titled, wellborn; SEE CONCEPTS *549,555*

noble [*adj2*] *dignified, excellent*
august, beneficent, benevolent, benign, big, bounteous, brilliant, charitable, courtly, cultivated, dignified, distinguished, elevated, eminent, extraordinary, first-rate, generous, gracious, grand, great, great-hearted, high-minded, honorable, humane, imposing, impressive, liberal, lofty, magnanimous, magnificent, meritorious, preeminent, refined, remarkable, reputable, splendid, stately, sublime, supreme, sympathetic, tolerant, upright, virtuous, worthy; SEE CONCEPTS *401,404,572*

nobody/nonentity [*n*] *person of little importance*
cipher, insignificancy, lightweight*, menial, nix*, nothing, parvenu*, small potato*, squirt*, upstart, wimp*, zero*, zip; SEE CONCEPT *423*

nocturnal [*adj*] *happening at night*
after dark, late, night, night-loving, nightly, nighttime; SEE CONCEPTS *799,801*

nod [*n*] *gesture of the head*
acceptance, acknowledgment, affirmative, beckon, bow, dip, greeting, inclination, indication, permission, salute, sign, signal, yes; SEE CONCEPTS *74,185,685*

nod [*v1*] *gesture with head*
acknowledge, acquiesce, agree, approve, assent, beckon, bend, bow, concur, consent, curtsy, dip, duck, greet, indicate, recognize, respond, salute, say yes, sign, signal; SEE CONCEPTS *10,50,74,88,185*

nod [*v2*] *fall asleep*
become inattentive, be sleepy, doze, drift, drift off, droop, drowse, nap, sleep, slump; SEE CONCEPTS *210,315,681*

node/nodule [*n*] *knot, growth*
bud, bulge, bump, burl, clot, knob, lump, protuberance, swelling, tumor; SEE CONCEPTS *471,831*

noise [*n*] *sound that is loud or not harmonious*
babble, babel, bang, bedlam, bellow, bewailing, blare, blast, boisterousness, boom, buzz, cacophony, caterwauling, clamor, clang, clatter, commotion, crash, cry, detonation, din, discord, disquiet, disquietude, drumming, eruption, explosion, fanfare, fireworks, fracas*, fuss*, hoo-ha*, hubbub*, hullabaloo*, jangle, lamentation, outcry, pandemonium, peal, racket, ring, roar, row, shot, shouting, sonance, squawk, stridency, talk, thud, tumult, turbulence, uproar, uproariousness, yelling, yelp; SEE CONCEPTS *521,595*

noiseless [*adj*] *quiet*
hushed, hushful, inaudible, mute, muted, silent, soundless, speechless, still, voiceless, wordless; SEE CONCEPT *594*

noisome [*adj*] *immoral, bad, offensive*
baneful, dangerous, deadly, deleterious, disgusting, fetid, foul, harmful, horrid, hurtful, injurious, insalubrious, insalutary, loathsome, malodorous, mephitic, mischievous, nauseating, noxious, pernicious, pestiferous, pestilential, poisonous, putrid, rank, reeking, repulsive, sickening, sickly, smelly, stinking, unhealthful, unhealthy, unwholesome, vile, yucky*; SEE CONCEPTS *537,571,598*

noisy [*adj*] *very loud and unharmonious in sound*
blatant, blusterous, boisterous, booming, cacophonous, chattering, clamorous, clangorous, clattery, deafening, disorderly, ear-popping*, ear-splitting*, jumping, loudmouth, obstreperous, piercing, rackety, raising Cain*, raising the roof*, rambunctious, raspy, riotous, rowdy, screaming, strepitous, strident, tumultous/tumultuous, turbulent, turned up, uproarious, vociferous; SEE CONCEPTS *592,594*

nomad [*n*] *person who wanders from place to place*
hobo, itinerant, migrant, pilgrim, rambler, roamer, rover, vagabond, wanderer, wayfarer; SEE CONCEPT *413*

nomadic [*adj*] *itinerant*
drifting, gypsy, itinerate, migrant, migratory, pastoral, perambulant, perambulatory, peripatetic, roaming, roving, traveling, vagabond, vagrant, wandering, wayfaring; SEE CONCEPTS *401,536,584*

nomenclature [*n*] *vocabulary*
classification, codification, glossary, locution, phraseology, taxonomy, terminology; SEE CONCEPTS *275,276,683*

nominal [*adj1*] *supposed, theoretical*
alleged, apparent, as advertised, formal, given, honorary, in effect only, in name only, mentioned, named, ostensible, pretended, professed, puppet, purported, seeming, self-styled, simple, so-called, stated, suggested, titular; SEE CONCEPT *582*

nominal [*adj2*] *insignificant*
cheap, inconsiderable, inexpensive, low, low-priced, meaningless, minimal, small, symbolic, token, trifling, trivial, unnecessary; SEE CONCEPTS *334,575,789*

nominate [*v*] *designate, select*
appoint, assign, call, choose, cognominate, commission, decide, denominate, draft, elect, elevate, empower, intend, make, mean, name, offer, present, proffer, propose, purpose, put down for, put up, recommend, slate, slot, specify, submit, suggest, tab, tap, tender, term; SEE CONCEPTS *41,50,75,88,300*

nomination [*n*] *appointment for responsibility*
choice, designation, election, naming, proposal, recommendation, selection, suggestion; SEE CONCEPTS *41,50,75,88,300*

nonchalant [*adj*] *easygoing, laid back*
airy, aloof, apathetic, blasé, calm, careless, casual, cold, collected, composed, cool, detached, disimpassioned, disinterested, dispassionate, easy, effortless, happy, impassive, imperturbable, incurious, indifferent, insouciant, lackadaisical, light, listless, loose, lukewarm, mellow, neglectful, negligent, neutral, offhand, placid, serene, smooth, trifling, uncaring, unconcerned, unemotional, unexcited, unfeeling, unflappable, unimpressible, unperturbed, unruffled, untroubled; SEE CONCEPTS *401,404,542*

noncommittal [*adj*] *unwilling to decide*
ambiguous, buttoned up*, careful, cautious, circumspect, clammed up*, constrained, discreet, equivocal, evasive, even-steven*, guarded, hush-hush*, incommunicable, indefinite, judicious, middle-ground*, middle-of-the-road*, neutral, on-the-fence*, politic, reserved, restrained, tact-

ful, temporizing, tentative, unrevealing, vague, wary, zipped*; SEE CONCEPTS 267,403,542

noncompliant [adj] unwilling to go along with something

belligerent, contumacious, declinatory, declining, divergent, impatient, irregular, negative, objecting, rebellious, recalcitrant, refractory, refusing, restive, truculent; SEE CONCEPTS 401,542

nonconformist [n] person who goes against normal behavior, beliefs

beatnik*, bohemian*, demonstrator, different breed*, dissenter, dissentient, dissident, dropout, eccentric, fish out of water*, freak*, heretic, iconoclast, individualist, liberal, malcontent, maverick, misbeliever, night person, oddball, offbeat, original, protester, radical, rebel, sectary, separatist, swinger, weirdo*; SEE CONCEPTS 359,423

nonconformist [adj] unwilling to behave, believe as most do

beatnik*, bohemian*, dissident, freak*, heretical, heterodox, hippie*, iconoclastic, maverick, oddball, offbeat, original, rebel, schismatic*, sectarian, swinger, unorthodox, weird*; SEE CONCEPTS 401,542

nonconformity [n] belief, behavior different from most

bohemianism, breach, contumaciousness, denial, disaffection, disagreement, disapprobation, disapproval, discordance, disobedience, dissent, eccentricity, exception, heresy, heterodoxy, iconoclasm, insubordination, lawlessness, mutinousness, negation, nonacceptance, nonagreement, noncompliance, nonconsent, objection, opposition, originality, recalcitrance, recusance, recusancy, rejection, strangeness, transgressiveness, unconventionality, uniqueness, unorthodoxy, unruliness, veto, violation; SEE CONCEPTS 633,657,689

nondescript [adj] undistinguished, commonplace characterless, colorless, common, dull, empty, featureless, garden*, indescribable, indeterminate, mousy*, ordinary, unclassifiable, unclassified, unexceptional, uninspiring, uninteresting, unmemorable, unremarkable, vague; SEE CONCEPTS 529,537,547

none [pron] not one thing

nil, nobody, no one, no one at all, no part, not a bit, not any, not anyone, not anything, not a soul, not a thing, nothing, not one, zero, zilch*; SEE CONCEPT 407

nonessential [adj] not needed or important

deadwood*, dispensable, excess baggage*, excessive, expendable, extraneous, inessential, insignificant, peripheral, petty, superfluous, trivial, unimportant, unnecessary; SEE CONCEPTS 546,575

nonexistent [adj] fictional, not real

absent, airy, baseless, blank, chimerical, dead, defunct, departed, dreamlike, dreamy, empty, ethereal, extinct, extinguished, fancied, flimsy, gone, gossamery, groundless, hallucinatory, hypothetical, illusory, imaginary, imagined, immaterial, imponderable, insubstantial, legendary, lost, missing, mythical, negative, null, null and void*, passed away, passed on, perished, shadowy, tenuous, ungrounded, unreal, unsubstantial, vacant, vague, vaporous, void, without foundation; SEE CONCEPTS 539,582

nonpartisan [adj] impartial; not political

detached, equitable, fair, free-wheeling*, independent, indifferent, just, middle-of-the-road*, neutral, nonaligned, nondiscriminatory, objective, on one's own*, on-the-fence*, playing it cool*, unaffected, unaffiliated, unbiased, unbigoted, uncolored, unimplicated, uninfluenced, uninvolved, unprejudiced; SEE CONCEPT 542

nonplus [v] confuse, perplex

astonish, astound, baffle, balk, beat, bewilder, boggle, buffalo*, confound, daze, discomfit, disconcert, discountenance, dismay, dumbfound, embarrass, faze, floor*, flurry, fluster, frustrate, get*, mess with one's head*, muddle, mystify, overcome, paralyze, puzzle, rattle, rattle one's cage*, stagger, stick, stump, stun, stymie*, take aback, throw*, throw into tizzy*, thwart; SEE CONCEPTS 14,16

nonsense [n] craziness, ridiculousness

absurdity, babble, balderdash*, baloney*, bananas*, bombast, bull*, bunk*, claptrap*, drivel, fatuity, flightiness, folly, foolishness, fun, gibberish, giddiness, hogwash*, hooey*, hot air*, imprudence, inanity, irrationality, jazz, jest, jive*, joke, ludicrousness, madness, mumbo jumbo*, palaver, poppycock*, prattle, pretense, ranting, rashness, rot, rubbish, scrawl, scribble, senselessness, silliness, soft soap*, stupidity, thoughtlessness, trash*, tripe*; SEE CONCEPTS 230,388,633

nonstop [adj] continuous, direct

ceaseless, constant, endless, incessant, interminable, relentless, round-the-clock*, steady, unbroken, unending, unfaltering, uninterrupted, unremitting; SEE CONCEPTS 482,584,798

nonviolent [adj] peaceful

irenic, nonbelligerent, pacifist, passive, peaceable, quiet, resistant, without violence; SEE CONCEPT 401

nook [n] corner, cubbyhole

alcove, byplace, cavity, compartment, cranny, crevice, den, hideout, hole, inglenook, niche, opening, quoin, recess, retreat; SEE CONCEPTS 440,513

noon [n] the middle of a day

apex, high noon, meridian, midday, noonday, noontide, noontime, twelve noon, twelve o'clock; SEE CONCEPTS 801,802,806

norm [n] average, standard

barometer, benchmark*, criterion, gauge, mean, measure, median, medium, model, par, pattern, rule, scale, touchstone*, type, yardstick; SEE CONCEPTS 647,686,688

normal [adj1] common, usual

accustomed, acknowledged, average, commonplace, conventional, customary, general, habitual, mean, median, methodical, natural, orderly, ordinary, popular, prevalent, regular, routine, run-of-the-mill*, standard, traditional, typic, typical, unexceptional; SEE CONCEPT 547

normal [adj2] sane, rational

all there*, compos mentis*, cool*, healthy, in good health, in one's right mind*, lucid, reasonable, right, right-minded, sound, together, well-adjusted, whole, wholesome; SEE CONCEPTS 314,403

normally [adv] usually

as a rule, commonly, habitually, in accordance with, ordinarily, regularly, typically; SEE CONCEPT 547

north [adj/adv] toward the top pole of the earth

arctic, boreal, cold, frozen, hyperborean, north-

no
no

bound, northerly, northern, northmost, north-
ward, polar, septentrional, toward North Pole,
tundra; SEE CONCEPTS *581,583*

nose [*n*] *smelling organ of animate being*
adenoids, beak*, bill*, horn*, muzzle*, nares,
nostrils, olfactory nerves, proboscis, schnoz*,
smeller*, sneezer*, sniffer*, snoot*, snout*,
snuffer*, whiffer*; SEE CONCEPTS *392,601*

nose [*v*] *detect, search*
busybody*, examine, inspect, meddle, mouse*,
pry, scent, smell, sniff, snoop*; SEE CONCEPTS
103,216

nostalgia [*n*] *pleasant remembrances*
fond memories*, hearts and flowers*, homesick-
ness, longing, pining, reminiscence, remorse,
schmaltz*, sentimentality, tear-jerker*, wistfulness, yearning; SEE CONCEPTS *20,410*

nostalgic [*adj*] *longingly remembering*
cornball*, down memory lane*, drippy*, homesick, like yesterday*, lonesome, longing, mushy*,
regretful, sappy*, sentimental, sloppy, syrupy*,
wistful, yearning; SEE CONCEPTS *403,529*

nostrum [*n*] *cure-all, often ineffective*
catholicon, cure, drug, elixir, fix, formula, home
remedy, medicine, panacea, patent medicine, potion, quack medicine*, quick fix*, remedy, treatment; SEE CONCEPTS *307,311*

nosy [*adj*] *curious; prying*
eavesdropping, inquisitive, inquisitorial, inquisi-
tory, interested, interfering, intermeddling, intrusive, meddlesome, personal, searching, snooping,
snoopy; SEE CONCEPT *401*

notable [*n*] *person who is famous, important*
big name*, big shot*, big-time operator*, big
wheel*, celebrity, chief, dignitary, eminence, executive, figure*, heavyweight, high-up, hotdog*, leader, lion*, luminary, magnate, mogul,
name, notability, personage, personality, pooh-
bah*, power, somebody*, star, superstar, VIP*,
worthy; SEE CONCEPTS *347,352,423*

notable [*adj*] *important; famous*
big-league*, bodacious*, celebrated, celebrious,
conspicuous, distingué, distinguished, eminent,
eventful, evident, extraordinary, famed, great,
heavy*, high-profile*, illustrious, major-league*,
manifest, marked, memorable, momentous,
nameable, noteworthy, noticeable, notorious, observable, outstanding, preeminent, prominent,
pronounced, rare, red-letter*, remarkable, renowned, rubric, serious, something else*, striking, top-drawer*, uncommon, unusual, well-
known; SEE CONCEPT *568*

notably [*adv*] *especially*
conspicuously, distinctly, exceedingly, exceptionally, extremely, greatly, highly, hugely, markedly, noticeably, outstandingly, particularly,
prominently, remarkably, reputably, signally,
strikingly, uncommonly, very; SEE CONCEPT *569*

notation [*n*] *written remarks*
characters, chit, code, documentation, figures, jotting, memo, memorandum, note, noting, record,
representation, script, signs, symbols, system;
SEE CONCEPTS *268,284*

notch [*n1*] *indentation*
cleft, cut, gap, gash, groove, incision, indent, indenture, mark, mill, nick, nock, rabbet, rut, score,
scratch; SEE CONCEPT *513*

notch [*n2*] *level within classification*
cut, degree, grade, rung, stage, step; SEE CON-
CEPTS *388,744*

notch [*v*] *indent*
chisel, cleave, crenelate, crimp, cut, dent, gash,
incise, jag, mark, mill, nick, scallop, score,
scratch; SEE CONCEPTS *137,176,208*

note/notes [*n1*] *written communication*
agenda, annotation, calendar, comment, commentary, datum, definition, diary, dispatch, entry,
epistle, gloss, inscription, jotting, journal, letter,
line, marginalia, mark, memo, memorandum,
message, minute, missive, obiter dictum, observation, record, remark, reminder, scratch, scrawl,
scribble, summary, thank-you, word; SEE CON-
CEPT *271*

note [*n2*] *symbol, often used in reference to music*
character, degree, figure, flat, indication, interval,
key, lick*, mark, natural, pitch, representation,
scale, sharp, sign, step, token, tone; SEE CON-
CEPTS *262,284*

note [*n3*] *attention, heed*
cognizance, mark, mind, notice, observance, observation, regard, remark; SEE CONCEPT *529*

note [*v*] *observe, perceive*
catch, clock, denote, descry, designate, dig, discern, discover, distinguish, document, enter, get a
load of*, get an eyeful*, heed, indicate, jot down,
mark, mention, notice, pick up on*, put down,
record, register, remark, see, set down, spot, take
in*, transcribe, view, write, write down; SEE CON-
CEPTS *34,626*

noted [*adj*] *famous, eminent*
acclaimed, celeb, celebrated, conspicuous, distinguished, esteemed, illustrious, leading, name, notable, notorious, of note, popular, prominent,
recognized, redoubted, renowned, somebody,
star, well-known; SEE CONCEPT *568*

noteworthy [*adj*] *important*
boss*, conspicuous, cool*, evident, exceptional,
extraordinary, heavy*, high-profile*, hot*, major-
league*, manifest, meaningful, memorable, mind-
blowing*, murder, nameable, notable, noticeable,
observable, outstanding, patent, prominent, red-
letter*, remarkable, serious, significant, something else*, splash*, stand-out*, super, terrific,
the end*, underlined*, unique, unusual, utmost;
SEE CONCEPTS *567,568*

nothing/nothingness [*n*] *emptiness, nonexistence*
annihilation, aught, blank, cipher, extinction, fly
speck*, insignificancy, naught, nihility, nobody,
nonbeing, nonentity, not anything, nought, nullity, obliteration, oblivion, shutout*, trifle, void,
wind*, zero*, zilch*, zip; SEE CONCEPTS *407,707*

nothingness [*n2*] *insignificance*
pettiness, smallness, unimportance, worthless-
ness; SEE CONCEPT *668*

notice [*n1*] *observation*
apprehension, attention, care, cognizance, concern, consideration, ear, grasp, heed, mark, mind,
note, observance, regard, remark, respect,
thought, understanding; SEE CONCEPTS *34,532*

notice [*n2*] *announcement, information*
admonition, advertisement, advice, caution, caveat, circular, clue, comment, comments, communication, criticism, critique, cue, declaration,
directive, enlightenment, goods*, handbill, info*,
instruction, intelligence, intimation, know*, low-
down*, manifesto, memo, memorandum, news,
note, notification, order, picture, poster, proclamation, remark, review, score, sign, squib*,
story, tip, warning, whole story*, write-up; SEE
CONCEPTS *271,274,278*

notice [v] *observe, perceive*
acknowledge, advert, allude, catch, clock, descry, detect, dig*, discern, distinguish, espy, flash on*, get a load of*, heed, look at, make out*, mark, mind, note, pick up on, recognize, refer, regard, remark, see, spot, take in; SEE CONCEPTS 34,626

noticeable [adj] *conspicuous, evident*
apparent, appreciable, arresting, arrestive, big as life*, can't miss it*, clear, distinct, eye-catching, manifest, marked, notable, noteworthy, observable, obvious, open and shut*, outstanding, palpable, patent, perceptible, plain, pointed, prominent, remarkable, salient, sensational, signal, spectacular, striking, under one's nose*, unmistakable; SEE CONCEPTS 529,537,567

notify [v] *inform*
acquaint, advise, air, alert, announce, apprise, assert, blazon, brief, broadcast, cable, caution, circulate, clue in, convey, cue, debrief, declare, disclose, disseminate, divulge, enlighten, express, fill in, give, herald, hint, let in on, let know, make known, mention, pass out, post, proclaim, promulgate, publish, radio, report, reveal, send word, speak, spread, state, suggest, talk, teach, telephone, tell, tip off, vent, warn, wire, wise up*, write; SEE CONCEPTS 60,79

notion [n1] *belief, idea*
angle, apprehension, approach, assumption, awareness, clue, comprehension, conceit, concept, conception, consciousness, consideration, cue, discernment, flash, hint, image, imagination, impression, inclination, indication, inkling, insight, intellection, intimation, intuition, judgment, knowledge, opinion, penetration, perception, sentiment, slant, spark, suggestion, telltale, thought, twist, understanding, view, wind, wrinkle; SEE CONCEPTS 529,532,689

notion [n2] *whim, desire*
caprice, conceit, fancy, humor, imagination, impulse, inclination, wish; SEE CONCEPT 20

notoriety [n] *reputation*
ballyhoo*, celebrity, center stage*, dishonor, disrepute, éclat*, fame, flak*, infamy, ink*, name*, obloquy, opprobrium, renown, rep*, scandal, splash*, spotlight*, wise*; SEE CONCEPTS 388,411

notorious [adj] *known for a trait, often an unadmirable one*
belled, blatant, crying, dishonorable, disreputable, flagrant, glaring, ill-famed, infamous, leading, noted, obvious, open, opprobrious, overt, patent, popular, prominent, questionable, scandalous, shady, shameful, undisputed, wanted, well-known, wicked; SEE CONCEPT 404

notwithstanding [adv/prep] *although, however*
after all, against, at any rate, but, despite, for all that, howbeit, in any case, in any event, in spite of, nevertheless, nonetheless, on the other hand, regardless of, though, to the contrary, withal, yet; SEE CONCEPT 544

nourish [v] *feed, care for*
attend, cherish, comfort, cultivate, encourage, foster, furnish, maintain, nurse, nurture, promote, provide, supply, support, sustain, tend; SEE CONCEPTS 140,295

nourishing [adj] *healthful*
alimentative, beneficial, health-giving, healthy, nutrient, nutrimental, nutritious, nutritive, wholesome; SEE CONCEPTS 462,537

nourishment [n] *food*
aliment, diet, feed, foodstuff, home cooking*, maintenance, nutriment, nutrition, pabulum, pap*, provender, support, sustenance, viands, victuals, vittles*; SEE CONCEPT 457

novel [n] *fictional book*
best-seller, cliff-hanger, fiction, narrative, novelette, novella, paperback, potboiler*, prose, romance, story, tale, yarn*; SEE CONCEPT 280

novel [adj] *new, original*
at cutting edge*, atypical, avant-garde, breaking new ground*, contemporary, different, far cry*, fresh, funky*, innovative, just out*, modernistic, neoteric, newfangled, new-fashioned, now*, odd, offbeat, peculiar, rare, recent, singular, strange, uncommon, unfamiliar, unique, unusual; SEE CONCEPTS 564,578,797

novelty [n1] *newness, originality*
change, crazy*, creation, dernier cri*, freshness, innovation, last word*, modernity, mutation, newfangled contraption, oddball, oddity, original, origination, permutation, recentness, sport*, strangeness, surprise, unfamiliarity, uniqueness, vicissitude, weird*; SEE CONCEPTS 665,697,715

novelty [n2] *trinket, gadget*
bagatelle*, bauble, bibelot*, conversation piece, curio, curiosity, gewgaw*, gimcrack*, gimmick, item, knick-knack, memento, objet d'art*, oddity, souvenir, trifle, whatnot*; SEE CONCEPTS 260,446

novice [n] *person just learning something*
amateur, apprentice, beginner, colt*, convert*, cub*, first of May*, fledgling, greenhorn, gremlin, know from nothing*, learner, mark*, neophyte, newcomer, new kid on the block*, novitiate, plebe, postulant, prentice, probationer, proselyte, punk*, pupil, recruit, rookie, starter, student, tenderfoot*, trainee; SEE CONCEPTS 348,350,423

now [adv] *presently*
any more, at once, at the moment, at this moment, at this time, away, directly, first off, forthwith, here and now, immediately, in a minute, in a moment, in nothing flat, instanter, instantly, just now, like now*, momentarily, nowadays, on the double*, PDQ*, promptly, pronto*, right away, right now, soon, straightaway, these days, this day, today; SEE CONCEPTS 812,820

noxious [adj] *deadly, injurious*
baneful, corrupting, dangerous, deleterious, destructive, detrimental, fetid, foul, harmful, hurtful, insalubrious, insalutary, noisome, pernicious, pestiferous, pestilent, pestilential, poisonous, putrid, sickly, spoiled, stinking, toxic, unhealthful, unhealthy, unwholesome, venomous, virulent; SEE CONCEPTS 485,537

nuance [n] *slight difference; shading*
dash, degree, distinction, gradation, hint, implication, nicety, refinement, shade, shadow, soupçon, subtlety, suggestion, suspicion, tinge, touch, trace; SEE CONCEPT 665

nub [n1] *core, gist*
basic, bottom line*, crux, essence, heart*, kernel, meat*, meat and potatoes*, nitty-gritty*, nubbin, nucleus, pith, point, short, substance, upshot; SEE CONCEPTS 661,682,826

nub [n2] *bump, knot*
bulge, knob, lump, node, protuberance, swelling; SEE CONCEPT 471

nuclear weapon [n] *explosive driven by nuclear energy*
A-bomb, atomic bomb, atomic weapon, doomsday machine*, H-bomb, hydrogen bomb, mininuke*, mirv*, MX*, neutron bomb, nuke*; SEE CONCEPT 500

nucleus [n] *core; basis for something's beginning*
bud, center, crux, embryo, focus, foundation, germ, heart, hub, kernel, matter, nub, pivot, premise, principle, seed, spark; SEE CONCEPTS 393,826,828

nude [adj] *without clothes, covering*
au naturel*, bald, bare, bare-skinned, buck naked*, dishabille*, disrobed, exposed, garmentless, in birthday suit, in one's skin*, in the altogether*, naked, peeled*, raw, skin, stark, stark-naked*, stripped, unattired, unclad, unclothed, uncovered, undraped, undressed, wearing only a smile*, without a stitch*; SEE CONCEPT 485

nudge [n/v] *bump, elbow*
dig, jab, jog, poke, prod, punch, push, shove, tap, touch; SEE CONCEPTS 208,612

nugget [n] *lump, solid piece; often of metal ore*
asset, bullion, chunk, clod, clump, gold, hunk, ingot, mass, plum, rock, treasure, wad*; SEE CONCEPT 471

nuisance [n] *annoyance; annoying person*
besetment, blister, bore, bother, botheration, botherment, bum*, creep, drag*, drip*, exasperation, frump, gadfly, headache*, inconvenience, infliction, insect*, irritant, irritation, louse, nag*, nudge*, offense, pain, pain in the neck*, pest, pester, pesterer, pill*, plague, poor excuse*, problem, terror, trouble, vexation; SEE CONCEPTS 412,674

null [adj] *ineffectual, valueless*
absent, bad, barren, characterless, imaginary, ineffective, inefficacious, inoperative, invalid, negative, nonexistent, nothing, null and void*, powerless, unavailing, unreal, unsanctioned, useless, vain, void, worthless; SEE CONCEPTS 560,570

nullify [v] *cancel, revoke*
abate, abolish, abrogate, annihilate, annul, ax, blue pencil*, bring to naught*, call all bets off*, compensate, confine, counteract, counterbalance, countervail, disannul, forget it*, invalidate, kill*, limit, negate, neutralize, nig*, offset, quash*, render null and void*, renege, renig*, repeal, rescind, restrict, scratch*, scrub*, squash*, stamp out*, take out*, torpedo*, trash*, undo, veto, vitiate, void, wash out*, wipe out*, zap*; SEE CONCEPTS 50,88,121,234

numb [adj] *deadened, insensitive*
aloof, anesthetized, apathetic, asleep, benumbed, callous, casual, comatose, dazed, dead, detached, disinterested, frozen, immobilized, incurious, indifferent, insensate, insensible, insentient, lethargic, listless, numbed, paralyzed, phlegmatic, remote, senseless, stupefied, stuporous, torpid, unconcerned, unconscious, uncurious, unfeeling, uninterested; SEE CONCEPTS 403,609

numb [v] *deaden*
anesthetize, benumb, blunt, chill, desensitize, dull, freeze, frost, immobilize, obtund, paralyze, stun, stupefy; SEE CONCEPTS 250,255

number [n1] *unit of the mathematical system*
cardinal, character, chiffer, cipher, count, decimal, denominator, digit, emblem, figure, folio, fraction, googol, integer, numeral, numerator, ordinal, prime, representation, sign, statistic, sum, symbol, total, whole number; SEE CONCEPTS 765,784

number [n2] *aggregate, bunch*
abundance, amount, caboodle*, collection, company, conglomeration, crowd, estimate, flock, horde, jillion*, lot, manifoldness, many, multitude, plenitude, plenty, product, quantity, slew*, sum, throng, total, totality, umpteen*, volume, whole, zillion*; SEE CONCEPTS 432,787

number [v] *count, calculate*
account, add, add up, aggregate, amount, come, computer, count heads*, count noses*, count off, enumerate, estimate, figure in, figure out, include, keep tabs, numerate, reckon, run, run down, run into, run to, sum, take account of, tale, tally, tell, tick off*, total, tote*, tote up*; SEE CONCEPT 764

numbered [adj] *limited in number*
categorized, checked, contained, counted, designated, doomed, enumerated, fated, fixed, included, indicated, marked, specified, told, totalled; SEE CONCEPT 554

numberless [adj] *infinite*
countless, endless, heaps*, incalculable, innumerable, jillion, many, multitudinous, myriad, no end of*, no end to*, numerous, umpteen*, uncountable, uncounted, unnumbered, untold, zillion*; SEE CONCEPTS 482,762,781

numeral [n] *symbol of mathematical system*
character, chiffer, cipher, digit, figure, integer, number; SEE CONCEPTS 284,784

numeric/numerical [adj] *concerning mathematics*
algebraic, algorithmic, arithmetic, arithmetical, binary, differential, digital, exponent, exponential, fraction, fractional, integral, logarithm, logarithmic, mathematical, numeral, numerary, statistical; SEE CONCEPT 762

numerous [adj] *many, abundant*
big, copious, diverse, great, infinite, large, legion, lousy with*, multifarious, multitudinal, multitudinous, plentiful, populous, profuse, rife, scads*, several, sundry, thick, umpteen*, various, voluminous, zillion*; SEE CONCEPTS 762,781

nun [n] *woman in religious order*
abbess, anchorite, canoness, mother superior, postulant, prioress, religious woman, sister, vestal; SEE CONCEPT 361

nuptial [adj] *concerning marriage*
bridal, conjugal, connubial, espousal, marital, married, matrimonial, spousal, wedded, wedding; SEE CONCEPT 555

nuptials [n] *marriage ceremony*
bridal, espousal, marriage, matrimony, spousal, wedding; SEE CONCEPT 297

nurse [n] *person who tends to sick, cares for someone*
assistant, attendant, baby sitter, caretaker, foster parent, medic, minder, nurse practitioner, practical nurse, registered nurse, RN, sitter, therapist, wet nurse; SEE CONCEPTS 357,414

nurse [v] *care for, tend*
advance, aid, attend, baby-sit, cherish, cradle, cultivate, encourage, father, feed, forward, foster, further, harbor, humor, immunize, indulge, inoculate, irradiate, keep alive, keep an eye on*, keep tabs on*, look after, medicate, minister to, mother, nourish, nurture, pamper, preserve, promote, see to, serve, sit, succor, support, take care

of, take charge of, treat, vaccinate, wait on, watch out for, watch over; SEE CONCEPTS *110,140*

nurse [v2] *give milk, usually from breast*
bottle-feed, breast-feed, cradle, dry-nurse, feed, give suck, lactate, nourish, nurture, suck, suckle, wet-nurse; SEE CONCEPTS *140,295*

nurture [n] *development, nourishment*
breeding, care, diet, discipline, edibles, education, feed, food, instruction, nutriment, provender, provisions, rearing, subsistence, sustenance, training, upbringing, viands, victuals; SEE CONCEPTS *457,712*

nurture [v] *feed, care for*
back, bolster, bring up, cherish, cultivate, develop, discipline, educate, foster, instruct, nourish, nurse, nursle, provide, raise, rear, school, support, sustain, tend, train, uphold; SEE CONCEPTS *110,140,295*

nut [n1] *seed of fruit, vegetable*
achene, caryopsis, kernel, stone, utricle; SEE CONCEPT *428*

nut [n2] *crazy, overenthusiastic person*
bedlamite, bigot, crackpot, crank, dement, eccentric, fanatic, fiend, freak, harebrain*, loony*, lunatic, maniac, non compos mentis, screwball*, zealot; SEE CONCEPTS *412,423*

nutrition [n] *food*
diet, menu, nourishment, nutriment, subsistence, sustenance, victuals; SEE CONCEPT *457*

nutritious [adj] *healthy*
alimental, alimentative, balanced, beneficial, good, healthful, health-giving, invigorating, nourishing, nutrient, nutrimental, nutritive, salubrious, salutary, strengthening, wholesome; SEE CONCEPT *462*

nuts/nutty [adj] *mentally deranged*
absurd, batty*, bedlamite, cracked*, crazy, daffy, daft, demented, eccentric, enthusiastic, foolish, gung ho*, harebrained*, insane, irrational, keen, kooky, loony, lunatic, mad, out of one's mind*, ridiculous, touched, unusual, wacky*, warm, zealous; SEE CONCEPT *403*

nuzzle [v] *cuddle*
bundle, burrow, caress, fondle, nestle, nudge, pet, snug, snuggle; SEE CONCEPTS *190,612*

nymph [n] *female nature spirit*
dryad, fairy, goddess, mermaid, naiad, nymphet, spirit, sprite, sylph; SEE CONCEPTS *415,424*

O

oaf [n] *person who is clumsy, stupid*
beast, blunderer, bruiser, brute, chump*, clod, clown, dolt, dumb ox*, dunce, fool, goon*, idiot, imbecile, klutz*, loser, lout*, moron, nincompoop*, ox*, sap*, simpleton; SEE CONCEPT *412*

oasis [n] *refuge*
haven, resting place, retreat, sanctuary, sanctum, spot, tract; SEE CONCEPT *515*

oath [n1] *promise*
adjuration, affidavit, affirmation, avowal, bond, contract, deposition, pledge, profession, sworn declaration, sworn statement, testimony, vow, word, word of honor; SEE CONCEPTS *71,278*

oath [n2] *curse*
blasphemy, cuss*, cuss word*, dirty name*, dirty

word*, expletive, four-letter word*, imprecation, malediction, no-no*, profanity, strong language, swearword; SEE CONCEPTS *54,278*

obdurate [adj] *pigheaded, stubborn*
adamant, bullhead*, callous, cold fish*, dogged, firm, fixed, hanging tough*, hard, hard-boiled*, hard-hearted*, hard-nosed*, harsh, heartless, immovable, implacable, indurate, inexorable, inflexible, iron*, mean, mulish*, obstinate, perverse, relentless, rigid, set in stone*, stiff-necked*, thick-skinned*, tough, tough nut to crack*, unbending, uncompassionate, uncompromising, uncooperative, unemotional, unfeeling, unimpressible, unrelenting, unshakable, unsympathetic, unyielding; SEE CONCEPTS *401,542*

obedience [n] *good behavior; submissiveness*
accordance, acquiescence, agreement, compliance, conformability, conformity, deference, docility, duteousness, dutifulness, duty, manageability, meekness, observance, orderliness, quietness, respect, reverence, servility, submission, subservience, tameness, tractability, willingness; SEE CONCEPTS *411,633*

obedient [adj] *well-behaved; submissive*
acquiescent, amenable, at one's beck and call*, attentive, biddable, complaisant, compliant, controllable, deferential, devoted, docile, docious, duteous, dutiful, faithful, governable, honoring, in one's clutches*, in one's pocket*, in one's power*, law-abiding, loyal, obelsant, obliging, observant, on a string*, pliant, regardful, resigned, respectful, reverential, sheeplike*, subservient, tame, tractable, under control, venerating, well-trained, willing, wrapped around finger*, yielding; SEE CONCEPTS *401,404*

obeisance [n] *salutation*
allegiance, bending of the knee*, bow, curtsy, deference, fealty, genuflection, homage, honor, kowtow*, loyalty, praise, respect, reverence, salaam*; SEE CONCEPTS *154,384*

obese [adj] *very overweight*
adipose, avoirdupois, corpulent, fat, fleshy*, gross*, heavy, outsize, paunchy, plump, porcine, portly, pudgy, rotund, stout; SEE CONCEPT *491*

obey [v] *conform, give in*
abide by, accede, accept, accord, acquiesce, act upon, adhere to, agree, answer, assent, be loyal to, be ruled by, bow to*, carry out, comply, concur, discharge, do as one says, do one's bidding, do one's duty, do what is expected, do what one is told, embrace, execute, follow, fulfill, get in line*, give way*, heed, hold fast*, keep, knuckle under*, live by, mind, observe, perform, play second fiddle*, respond, serve, submit, surrender, take orders, toe the line*; SEE CONCEPTS *91,136*

obituary [n] *notice of person's death*
announcement, death notice, eulogy, mortuary tribute, necrology, obit, register; SEE CONCEPTS *268,270*

object [n1] *thing able to be seen/felt/perceived*
article, body, bulk, commodity, doodad*, doohickey*, entity, fact, gadget, gizmo*, item, mass, matter, phenomenon, reality, something, substance, thingamajig*, volume, whatchamacallit*, widget*; SEE CONCEPT *433*

object [n2] *purpose, use*
aim, design, duty, end, end in view, end purpose, function, goal, idea, intent, intention, mark, mission, motive, objective, point, reason, target, view, wish; SEE CONCEPT *659*

nu
ob

object [n3] *aim, recipient*
butt*, focus, ground zero*, receiver, target, victim, zero*; SEE CONCEPTS 124,532

object [v] *disagree, argue against*
balk, be displeased, challenge, complain, crab*, criticize, cross, demur, deprecate, disapprove, disavow, discommend, discountenance, disesteem, dispute, dissent, except, expostulate, frown, go-one-on-one*, gripe, grouse, inveigh, kick*, make a stink*, mix it up with*, oppose, protest, rail, raise objection, rant, rave, remonstrate, sound off*, spurn, squawk*, storm, take exception, take on, tangle*; SEE CONCEPTS 12,21,46

objection [n] *argument, disagreement*
cavil, censure, challenge, counter-argument, criticism, declination, demur, demurral, demurring, difficulty, disapprobation, disapproval, discontent, disesteem, disinclination, dislike, displeasure, dissatisfaction, doubt, exception, grievance, gripe, hesitation, kick*, niggle*, odium, opposition, protest, protestation, question, rejection, reluctance, remonstrance, remonstration, repugnancy, revilement, scruple, shrinking, squawk*, stink*, unwillingness; SEE CONCEPTS 21,46,410,689

objectionable [adj] *not nice; unpleasant*
abhorrent, censurable, deplorable, disagreeable, dislikable, displeasing, distasteful, exceptionable, ill-favored, inadmissible, indecorous, inexpedient, insufferable, intolerable, invidious, loathsome, lousy, murder, noxious, obnoxious, offensive, opprobrious, poison, regrettable, repellent, reprehensible, repugnant, repulsive, revolting, unacceptable, undesirable, unfit, unpalatable, unsatisfactory, unseemly, unsuitable, unwanted, unwelcome; SEE CONCEPTS 548,558,570

objective [n] *aim, goal*
ambition, aspiration, design, end, end in view*, ground zero*, intention, mark, mission, object, purpose, target, zero*; SEE CONCEPT 659

objective [adj] *fair, impartial*
cold, cool, detached, disinterested, dispassionate, equitable, evenhanded, impersonal, judicial, just, like it is*, nondiscriminatory, nonpartisan, open-minded*, straight, strictly business*, unbiased, uncolored, unemotional, uninvolved, unprejudiced, unpossessed; SEE CONCEPTS 403,542

objectively [adv] *impartially*
consideratedly, detachedly, disinterestedly, dispassionately, equitably, evenhandedly, indifferently, justly, neutrally, on the up and up*, open-mindedly*, soberly, squarely, with an open mind*, with impartiality, with objectivity, without favor, without prejudice; SEE CONCEPTS 542,544

obligate [v] *require*
astrict, bind, constrain, force, indebt, make indebted, oblige, restrain, restrict; SEE CONCEPTS 53,130,646

obligation [n] *responsibility*
accountability, accountableness, agreement, bond, burden, business, call, cause, charge, chit*, commitment, committal, compulsion, conscience, constraint, contract, debit, debt, devoir, due bill, dues, duty, engagement, IOU*, liability, must, necessity, need, occasion, onus, ought, part, place, promise, requirement, restraint, right, trust, understanding; SEE CONCEPTS 329,335,388,645

obligatory [adj] *essential, required*
binding, coercive, compulsative, compulsory, de rigueur, enforced, imperative, imperious, mandatory, necessary, requisite, unavoidable; SEE CONCEPT 546

oblige [v1] *require*
bind, coerce, command, compel, constrain, force, impel, make, necessitate, obligate, shotgun*; SEE CONCEPTS 14,242,646

oblige [v2] *do a favor or kindness*
accommodate, aid, assist, avail, bend over backward*, benefit, come around, contribute, convenience, don't make waves*, favor, fill the bill*, fit in, go fifty-fifty*, gratify, grin and bear it*, help, indulge, make a deal*, make room*, meet halfway*, please, profit, put oneself out*, roll with it*, serve, swim with the tide*, take it*, toe the mark*; SEE CONCEPTS 110,136,384

obliging [adj] *friendly, helpful*
accommodating, agreeable, amiable, cheerful, civil, complaisant, considerate, cooperative, courteous, eager to please, easy, easygoing, good-humored, good-natured, hospitable, kind, lenient, mild, polite, willing; SEE CONCEPTS 401,404

oblique [adj1] *slanting; at an angle*
angled, askance, askew, aslant, asymmetrical, awry, bent, cater-cornered, crooked, diagonal, distorted, diverging, inclined, inclining, leaning, on the bias, pitched, pitching, sideways, skew, slanted, sloped, sloping, strained, tilted, tilting, tipped, tipping, turned, twisted; SEE CONCEPTS 485,490

oblique [adj2] *indirect, evasive*
backhanded, circuitous, circular, circumlocutory, collateral, devious, implied, obliquitous, obscure, roundabout, sidelong, vague; SEE CONCEPT 267

obliterate [v] *destroy*
annihilate, ax*, black out*, blot out*, blue pencil*, bog, cancel, cover, cut, defeat, delete, do in*, efface, eliminate, eradicate, erase, expunge, exterminate, extirpate, finish, finish off*, kill, knock off*, knock out*, KO*, level*, liquidate, mark out, nix*, obscure, off, ravage, root out*, rub off*, rub out*, scratch, scrub, shoot down, sink, smash, squash, take apart, take out*, torpedo*, total*, trash*, wash out*, waste, wipe off face of earth*, wipe out*, X-out*, zap*; SEE CONCEPT 252

oblivion [n1] *mental blankness*
abeyance, amnesia, carelessness, disregard, forgetfulness, inadvertence, indifference, insensibility, insensibleness, Lethe*, neglect, nirvana*, obliviousness, unawareness, unconcern, unconsciousness, unmindfulness; SEE CONCEPTS 410,633

oblivion [n2] *nothingness, obscurity*
blackness, darkness, eclipse, emptiness, extinction, limbo, nihility, nirvana*, nonexistence, nothing, nowhere*, nullity, out there*, void; SEE CONCEPTS 407,672,679

oblivious [adj] *unaware, ignorant*
absent, absentminded, absorbed, abstracted, amnesic, blind*, blundering, careless, deaf*, disregardful, distracted, dreamy, forgetful, forgetting, gone, heedless, inattentive, incognizant, inconversant, insensible, neglectful, negligent, not all there*, out to lunch*, overlooking, preoccupied, regardless, spacey*, strung out*, unacquainted, unconcerned, unconscious, undiscerning, unfamiliar, uninformed, uninstructed, unknowing, un-

mindful, unnoticing, unobservant, unrecognizing, unwitting, zonked*; SEE CONCEPTS 402,403,542

oblong [*adj*] *elongated and rounded*
egg-shaped, ellipsoidal, elliptical, elongate, long, oval, ovaliform, ovaloid, ovate, ovated, ovoid, rectangular; SEE CONCEPT 486

obnoxious [*adj*] *offensive, repulsive*
abhorrent, abominable, annoying, awful, beastly*, big mouth*, detestable, disagreeable, disgusting, dislikable, displeasing, foul, gross*, hateable, hateful, heel, horrid, insufferable, invidious, loathsome, mean, nasty, nauseating, objectionable, odious, off-color*, ornery, pain in the neck*, pesky*, pestiferous, pill*, repellent, reprehensible, repugnant, revolting, rotten, sickening, stinking, unpleasant; SEE CONCEPTS 267,401,542

obscene [*adj*] *indecent, offensive, immoral*
atrocious, barnyard*, bawdy, blue*, coarse, crude, dirty*, disgusting, evil, filthy, foul, gross, heinous, hideous, horrible, immodest, improper, impure, lascivious, lewd, licentious, loathsome, loose*, lustful, nasty, noisome, outrageous, porno*, pornographic, profane, prurient, rank*, raunchy*, raw, repellent, repugnant, ribald, salacious, scabrous, scatological, scurrilous, shameless, shocking, sickening, smutty*, suggestive, unchaste, unclean, unwholesome, vile, wanton, wicked, X-rated*; SEE CONCEPTS 267,372,545

obscenity [*n*] *indecency, immorality; vulgarism*
abomination, affront, atrocity, bawdiness, blight, blueness*, coarseness, curse, dirtiness, dirty name*, dirty word*, evil, filthiness, foulness, four letter word*, immodesty, impropriety, impurity, indecency, indelicacy, lewdness, licentiousness, lubricity, offense, outrage, porn*, pornography, profanity, prurience, salacity, scatology, scurrility, sleaze*, smut*, smuttiness, suggestiveness, swearword, vileness, vulgarity, wrong, X-rating*; SEE CONCEPTS 278,645

obscure [*adj*] *not easily understood*
abstruse, ambiguous, arcane, clear as mud*, complicated, concealed, confusing, cryptic, dark, deep, dim, doubtful, enigmatic, enigmatical, esoteric, far-out, hazy, hidden, illegible, illogical, impenetrable, incomprehensible, inconceivable, incredible, indecisive, indefinite, indeterminate, indistinct, inexplicable, inscrutable, insoluble, intricate, involved, mysterious, occult, opaque, recondite, unaccountable, unbelievable, unclear, undefined, unfathomable, unintelligible, vague; SEE CONCEPT 529

obscure [*adj2*] *cloudy, shadowy*
blurred, caliginous, clouded, dark, dense, dim, dusk, dusky, faint, fuliginous, gloomy, indistinct, lightless, murky, obfuscated, shady, somber, tenebrous, umbrageous, unilluminated, unlit, veiled; SEE CONCEPT 617

obscure [*adj3*] *out-of-the-way, little-known*
abstruse, arcane, blind, cabalistic, close, covered, cryptic, dark, deep, devious, distant, enigmatic, esoteric, far, far-off, hidden, humble, inaccessible, inconspicuous, inglorious, invisible, irrelevant, lonesome, lowly, minor, mysterious, nameless, odd, oracular, orphic, rare, recondite, remote, removed, reticent, retired, secluded, secret, secretive, seldom seen, sequestered, solitary, undisclosed, undistinguished, unheard-of, unhonored, unimportant, unknown, unnoted, unseen, unsung; SEE CONCEPT 576

obscure [*v*] *conceal, hide*
adumbrate, becloud, bedim, befog, belie, blear, blind, block, block out, blur, camouflage, cloak, cloud, cloud the issue*, con, confuse, cover, cover up, darken, dim, disguise, double-talk*, eclipse, equivocate, falsify, fog, fuzz, gloom, gray, haze, mask, misrepresent, mist, muddy, muddy the waters*, murk, obfuscate, overcast, overcloud, overshadow, pettifog*, screen, shade, shadow, shroud, stonewall*, throw up smoke screen*, veil, wrap; SEE CONCEPTS 16,63,172,188

obsequious [*adj*] *groveling, submissive*
abject, beggarly, brownnosing*, complacent, compliable, compliant, cringing, crouching, deferential, enslaved, fawning, flattering, ingratiating, kowtowing*, menial, obeisant, oily*, parasitic, parasitical, prostrate, respectful, servile, slavish, sneaking, sniveling, spineless*, stipendiary, subject, submissive, subordinate, subservient, sycophantic, toadying*, unctuous; SEE CONCEPTS 401,404

observable [*adj*] *apparent*
appreciable, clear, detectable, discernible, discoverable, evident, noticeable, obvious, open, palpable, patent, perceivable, perceptible, recognizable, sensible, tangible, visible; SEE CONCEPTS 529,576

observance [*n1*] *attention to, knowledge of something*
acknowledgment, acquittal, acquittance, adherence, awareness, carrying out, celebration, cognizance, compliance, discharge, fidelity, fulfillment, heed, heeding, honoring, keeping, mark, mind, note, notice, obedience, observation, performance, regard, remark, satisfaction; SEE CONCEPTS 409,410,633

observance [*n2*] *ceremony, rite*
celebration, ceremonial, custom, fashion, form, formality, liturgy, performance, practice, ritual, rule, service, tradition; SEE CONCEPTS 377,384,688

observant [*adj*] *alert, watchful*
advertent, alive, attentive, bright, clear-sighted*, comprehending, considering, contemplating, correct, deducing, detecting, discerning, discovering, discriminating, eager, eagle-eyed*, heedful, intelligent, intentive, interested, keen, mindful, not missing a trick*, obedient, observative, on one's toes*, on the ball*, penetrating, perceptive, questioning, quick, regardful, searching, sensitive, sharp, sharp-eyed*, surveying, understanding, vigilant, wide-awake*; SEE CONCEPTS 402,403

observation [*n1*] *attention, scrutiny*
ascertainment, check, cognition, cognizance, conclusion, consideration, detection, estimation, examination, experience, heedfulness, information, inspection, investigation, knowledge, mark, measurement, mind, monitoring, note, notice, noticing, once-over*, overlook, perception, probe, recognizing, regard, remark, research, review, search, study, supervision, surveillance, view, watching; SEE CONCEPTS 409,410

observation [*n2*] *comment on something scrutinized*
annotation, catch phrase, comeback, commentary, crack*, finding, mention, mouthful*, note, obiter dictum, opinion, pronouncement, reflection, remark, saying, say so*, thought, utterance, wisecrack; SEE CONCEPTS 51,278

ob
ob

observe [v1] *see, notice*

beam, behold, catch, contemplate, detect, dig, discern, discover, distinguish, eagle-eye*, espy, examine, eyeball*, flash*, get a load of*, get an eyeful of*, inspect, keep one's eye on*, lamp*, look at, make out*, mark, mind, monitor, note, pay attention to, perceive, pick up on*, read, recognize, regard, scrutinize, spot, spy, study, survey, take in*, view, watch, witness; SEE CONCEPTS 24,34,103,265,626

observe [v2] *comment, remark*

animadvert, commentate, declare, mention, mouth off*, note, opine, say, state, wisecrack; SEE CONCEPT 51

observe [v3] *celebrate, commemorate*

dedicate, hold, honor, keep, remember, respect, revere, reverence, solemnize, venerate; SEE CONCEPT 377

observe [v4] *abide by, obey*

adhere, adopt, comply, comply with, conform, follow, fulfill, heed, honor, keep, mind, perform, respect; SEE CONCEPTS 91,384

obsessed [adj] *consumed, driven about belief, desire*

bedeviled, beset, bewitched, captivated, controlled, dogged*, dominated, eat sleep and breathe*, engrossed, fiendish, fixated, gripped, harassed, haunted, have on the brain*, held, hooked, hung up on*, immersed in, infatuated, into*, overpowered, plagued*, possessed, preoccupied, prepossessed, really into*, seized, taken over, tied up*, tormented, troubled, turned on, up to here in*, wound up with*, wrapped up in*; SEE CONCEPTS 403,404

obsession [n] *fixation; consumption with belief, desire*

attraction, ax to grind*, bug in ear*, case*, complex, compulsion, concrete idea, craze*, crush, delusion, enthusiasm, fancy, fascination, fetish, hang-up*, idée fixe, infatuation, mania, monkey*, must, neurosis, one-track mind*, passion, phantom, phobia, preoccupation, something on the brain*, thing*, tiger by the tail*; SEE CONCEPTS 20,410,529,689,690

obsolete [adj] *no longer in use, in vogue*

anachronistic, ancient, antediluvian, antiquated, antique, archaic, bygone, dated, dead, dead and gone*, dinosaur*, discarded, disused, done for*, dusty, extinct, fossil, gone, had it*, has-been*, horse and buggy*, kaput*, moldy*, moth-eaten*, old, old-fashioned, old-hat, old-school, out*, outmoded, out-of-date, out-of-fashion, outworn, passé, stale, superannuated, superseded, timeworn, unfashionable; SEE CONCEPTS 539,560,589

obstacle [n] *impediment, barrier*

bar, block, booby trap*, bump*, catch, Catch-22*, check, clog*, crimp*, difficulty, disincentive, encumbrance, hamper, handicap, hang-up*, hardship, hindrance, hitch*, hurdle, interference, interruption, joker*, monkey wrench*, mountain, obstruction, restriction, rub*, snag, stumbling block*, traverse, vicissitude; SEE CONCEPTS 470,532,666,674

obstinate [adj] *stubborn, determined*

adamant, cantankerous, contradictory, contrary, contumacious, convinced, dead set on*, dogged, dogmatic, firm, hard, hardened, headstrong, heady, immovable, indomitable, inflexible, intractable, intransigent, locked in*, mulish*, obdurate, opinionated, opinionative, persistent, pertina-

cious, perverse, pigheaded*, recalcitrant, refractory, relentless, resolved, restive, self-willed, steadfast, strong-minded, tenacious, unalterable, unflinching, unmanageable, unyielding, willful; SEE CONCEPTS 401,542

obstruct [v] *prevent, restrict*

arrest, bar, barricade, block, check, choke, clog, close, congest, crab, curb, cut off, drag one's feet*, fill, foul up, frustrate, get in the way*, hamper, hamstring*, hang up*, hide, hinder, hold up, impede, inhibit, interfere, interrupt, mask, monkey with*, obscure, occlude, plug, restrain, retard, sandbag*, shield, shut off, slow down, stall, stonewall*, stop, stopper, stymie*, terminate, throttle, thwart, trammel, weigh down; SEE CONCEPTS 5,121,130

obstruction [n] *obstacle, impediment*

bar, barricade, barrier, block, blockage, blocking, booby trap*, check, checkmate*, circumvention, difficulty, gridlock*, hamper, hindrance, hurdle, interference, jam*, lock, monkey wrench*, mountain*, restraint, roadblock*, snag, stop, stoppage, stumbling block*, trammel, trouble, wall; SEE CONCEPTS 470,532,666,674

obtain [v] *get, acquire*

access, accomplish, achieve, annex, attain, beg borrow or steal*, capture, chalk up*, collect, come by, compass, cop*, corral, drum up*, earn, effect, fetch, gain, gather, get at, get hold of*, get one's hands on*, glean, gobble up*, grab, have, hoard, inherit, invade, lay up, make use of, nab*, occupy, pick up, pocket*, procure, purchase, reach, realize, reap, receive, recover, retrieve, salvage, save, score, scrape together, scrape up, secure, seize, snag, take, wangle, win; SEE CONCEPT 120

obtainable [adj] *achievable, available*

at hand*, attainable, derivable, duck soup*, gettable, in stock, no problem*, no sweat*, on deck*, on offer*, on tap*, piece of cake*, procurable, purchasable, pushover, ready, realizable, securable, there for the taking*, to be had*; SEE CONCEPTS 528,576

obtrusive [adj] *pushy, obvious*

bulging, busy, forward, impertinent, importunate, interfering, intrusive, jutting, meddlesome, meddling, nosy, noticeable, officious, presumptuous, projecting, prominent, protruding, protuberant, prying, sticking out*; SEE CONCEPTS 401,542

obtuse [adj1] *slow to understand*

dense, dopey*, dull*, dumb, imperceptive, insensitive, opaque, slow on uptake*, stolid, thick, uncomprehending, unintelligent; SEE CONCEPT 402

obtuse [adj2] *blunt, not sharp*

round, rounded; SEE CONCEPTS 485,486

obviate [v] *make unnecessary*

anticipate, avert, block, counter, counteract, deter, do away with, forestall, forfend, hinder, interfere, interpose, intervene, preclude, prevent, remove, restrain, rule out, stave off, ward; SEE CONCEPT 121

obvious [adj] *apparent, understandable*

accessible, barefaced, bright, clear, clear as a bell*, conclusive, conspicuous, discernible, distinct, distinguishable, evident, explicit, exposed, glaring, indisputable, in evidence, lucid, manifest, noticeable, observable, open, overt, palpable, patent, perceivable, perceptible, plain, precise, prominent, pronounced, public, recognizable, self-evident, self-explanatory, standing out,

straightforward, transparent, unconcealed, undeniable, undisguised, unmistakable, unsubtle, visible; SEE CONCEPTS 485,529

occasion [n1] *chance*
break*, convenience, demand, excuse, incident,
instant, moment, need, occurrence, opening, opportunity, possibility, season, shot*, show, time,
use; SEE CONCEPT 693

occasion [n2] *reason, cause*
antecedent, basis, call, circumstance, determinant, excuse, foundation, ground, grounds, incident, inducement, influence, justification,
motivation, motive, necessity, obligation, prompting, provocation, purpose, right, warrant; SEE
CONCEPT 661

occasion [n3] *event, happening*
affair, celebration, circumstance, episode, experience, go*, goings-on*, happening, incident, instant, milepost*, milestone, moment, occurrence,
scene, thing*, time, while; SEE CONCEPTS 2,386

occasion [v] *make happen, bring about*
breed, cause, create, do, effect, elicit, engender,
evoke, generate, give rise to, hatch, induce, influence, inspire, lead to, move, muster, originate,
persuade, produce, prompt, provoke, work up;
SEE CONCEPTS 68,242

occasional [adj] *irregular, sporadic*
casual, desultory, especial, exceptional, exclusive, few, incidental, infrequent, intermittent, not
habitual, odd, off and on*, particular, random,
rare, scarce, seldom, semioccasional, special, specific, uncommon, unfrequent, unusual; SEE CON-
CEPTS 530,541

occasionally [adv] *every now and then*
at intervals, at random, at times, every so often,
from time to time, hardly, infrequently, irregularly, now and again, once in a blue moon*, once
in a while, once or twice*, on occasion, periodically, seldom, sometimes, sporadically, uncommonly; SEE CONCEPTS 530,541

occlude [v] *block, prevent*
choke, clog, close, close out, congest, curb, fill,
hinder, impede, leave out, lock out, obstruct,
plug, seal, shut, stopper, stop up, throttle; SEE
CONCEPTS 121,201

occult [adj] *mysterious, secret; supernatural*
abstruse, acromatic, arcane, cabalistic, concealed, deep, eerie, esoteric, hermetic, hidden,
invisible, magic, magical, mystic, mystical, obscure, orphic, preternatural, profound, psychic,
recondite, transmundane, unearthly, unknown,
unrevealed, veiled, weird; SEE CONCEPTS
576,582

occupancy [n] *residence of place*
control, deed, habitation, holding, inhabitance, inhabitancy, occupation, ownership, possession, retention, settlement, tenancy, tenure, term, title,
use; SEE CONCEPTS 518,710

occupant [n] *person who resides in a place*
addressee, denizen, dweller, holder, householder,
incumbent, indweller, inhabitant, lessee, occupier, possessor, renter, resident, resider, tenant,
user; SEE CONCEPT 414

occupation [n1] *profession, business*
activity, affair, calling, chosen work, craft, daily
grind*, day gig*, do, dodge*, employment,
game*, grindstone*, hang*, job, lick*, line, line
of work, métier, moonlight*, nine-to-five*, play*,
post, pursuit, racket*, rat race*, slot*, thing*,
trade, vocation, walk of life*, what one is into*,
work; SEE CONCEPTS 349,351,360

occupation [n2] *control, possession*
habitation, holding, inhabitancy, inhabitation, occupancy, ownership, residence, settlement, tenancy, tenure, title, use; SEE CONCEPTS 518,710

occupation [n3] *seizure, takeover*
attack, capture, conquest, entering, foreign rule,
invasion, subjugation; SEE CONCEPTS 86,90,320

occupied [adj1] *busy*
active, clocked up*, employed, engaged, engrossed, head over heels*, tied up*, too much on
plate*, working; SEE CONCEPT 542

occupied [adj2] *inhabited; in use*
busy, engaged, full, leased, lived-in*, peopled*,
populated, populous, rented, settled, taken, unavailable, utilized; SEE CONCEPT 560

occupy [v1] *be busy with*
absorb, amuse, attend, be active with, be concerned with, busy, divert, employ, engage, engross, entertain, fill, hold attention, immerse,
interest, involve, keep busy, monopolize, preoccupy, soak, take up, tie up, utilize; SEE CONCEPTS
7,17,19,22

occupy [v2] *reside; use*
be established, be in command, be in residence,
cover, dwell, ensconce, establish, fill, hold, inhabit, involve, keep, live in, maintain, own, people, permeate, pervade, populate, possess,
remain, sit, stay, take up, tenant, utilize; SEE CON-
CEPTS 225,226

occupy [v3] *seize, take over*
capture, conquer, garrison, hold, invade, keep,
obtain, overrun, take possession; SEE CONCEPTS
86,90,320

occur [v1] *take place, happen*
action, appear, arise, befall, be found, be present,
betide, chance, come about, come off*, come to
pass, cook*, crop up, develop, ensue, eventualize, eventuate, exist, follow, go, jell*, manifest,
materialize, obtain, present itself, result, shake*,
show, smoke*, take place, transpire, turn out, turn
up; SEE CONCEPTS 4,742

occur [v2] *come to mind*
come to one*, cross one's mind*, dawn on*, expose, flash*, go through one's head*, hit, offer
itself, present itself, reveal, spring to mind*,
strike, suggest itself; SEE CONCEPTS 34,43

occurrence [n] *happening, development*
accident, adventure, affair, appearance, circumstance, condition, contingency, emergency, episode, event, exigency, existence, incidence,
incident, instance, juncture, manifestation, materialization, occasion, pass, piece, proceeding, routine, scene, situation, state, thing*, transaction,
transpiration; SEE CONCEPTS 3,4,230,696

ocean [n] *very large body of water*
blue*, bounding main*, brine, briny*, briny
deep*, Davy Jones's locker*, deep, drink*, high
seas*, main, pond, puddle, salt water, sea, sea-
way, Seven Seas, sink, tide; SEE CONCEPT 514

odd/oddball [adj1] *unusual, abnormal*
atypical, avant-garde, bizarre, character, crazy,
curious, deviant, different, eccentric, erratic, exceptional, extraordinary, fantastic, flaky*, freak*,
freakish*, freaky*, funny, idiosyncratic, irregular, kinky*, kooky*, offbeat, off-the-wall*, outlandish, out of the ordinary, peculiar, quaint,
queer, rare, remarkable, singular, spacey*,
strange, uncanny, uncommon, unconventional,

ob
od

unique, way out*, weird, weirdo*, whimsical; SEE CONCEPTS *404,542,564*

odd [*adj2*] *miscellaneous, various*
accidental, casual, chance, contingent, different, fluky*, fortuitous, fragmentary, incidental, irregular, occasional, odd-lot*, periodic, random, seasonal, sundry, varied; SEE CONCEPT *552*

odd [*adj3*] *single, unmatched; uneven*
additional, alone, exceeding, individual, irregular, left, leftover, lone, lonely, over, over and above, remaining, singular, sole, solitary, spare, surplus, unconsumed, unitary, unpaired; SEE CONCEPTS *480,577*

oddity [*n1*] *abnormality*
anomaly, bizarreness, characteristic, conversation piece, curiosity, eccentricity, extraordinariness, freak, freakishness, idiosyncrasy, incongruity, irregularity, kink, oddness, outlandishness, peculiarity, phenomenon, queerness, quirk, rarity, singularity, strangeness, unconventionality, unnaturalness; SEE CONCEPTS *260,411,665*

oddity/oddball [*n2*] *person who is very different*
case*, character, duck*, eccentric, fish out of water*, maverick, misfit, odd bird*, original*, rara avis, screwball*, weirdo*; SEE CONCEPT *423*

odds [*n1*] *advantage*
allowance, benefit, bulge, difference, disparity, dissimilarity, distinction, draw, edge, handicap, head start, lead, overlay, start, superiority, vantage; SEE CONCEPT *693*

odds [*n2*] *probability*
balance, chances, favor, likelihood, superiority, toss-up; SEE CONCEPT *650*

odds and ends [*n*] *miscellaneous paraphernalia*
assortment, bits, bits and pieces*, debris, etcetera*, hodgepodge, jumble, leavings, litter, medley, mélange, . melee, miscellany, motley, oddments, olio, particles, potpourri, remnants, rest, rubbish, rummage, scraps, sundry items, this and that*; SEE CONCEPTS *260,432,446*

odious [*adj*] *hateful, horrible*
abhorrent, abominable, creepy*, detestable, disgusting, execrable, foul, hateable, horrid, loathsome, mean, obnoxious, offensive, ornery, pain in the neck*, repellent, repugnant, repulsive, revolting, unpleasant, vile; SEE CONCEPTS *401,404*

odium [*n*] *shame, dishonor*
abhorrence, antipathy, aversion, bar sinister*, black eye*, blame, blot, blur, brand, censure, condemnation, detestation, disapproval, discredit, disesteem, disfavor, disgrace, dislike, disprobation, disrepute, enmity, execration, hate, hatred, ignominy, infamy, malice, obloquy, onus, opprobrium, rebuke, reprobation, resentment, slur, spot, stain, stigma; SEE CONCEPTS *29,388*

odor [*n*] *scent*
air, aroma, bouquet, effluvium, efflux, emanation, essence, exhalation, flavor, fragrance, musk, perfume, pungence, pungency, redolence, smell, snuff, stench, stink, tang, tincture, trail, whiff; SEE CONCEPT *599*

odorless [*adj*] *without fragrance*
deodorant, deodorizing, flat, inodorous, odorfree, unaromatic, unfragrant, unperfumed, unscented, unsmelling; SEE CONCEPT *598*

odorous [*adj*] *having fragrance*
aromatic, balmy, dank, effluvious, fetid, flavorsome, flowery, foul, fragrant, heady, honeyed, loud, malodorous, mephitic, miasmic, moldy, musty, nauseous, odoriferant, odoriferous, offensive, olfactive, olfactory, perfumatory, perfumed, perfumy, pungent, putrid, redolent, reeking, rotten, savorous, savory, scented, scentful, scentladen, skunky*, smelly, spicy, stagnant, stale, stinking, strong, sweet, sweet-scented, sweetsmelling, tumaceous, unsavory, whiffy*; SEE CONCEPT *598*

of course [*adv*] *as expected*
by all means, certainly, definitely, indeed, indubitably, naturally, obviously, surely, undoubtedly, without a doubt; SEE CONCEPT *544*

off [*adj1*] *gone; remote*
absent, canceled, finished, inoperative, negligible, not employed, not on duty, on vacation, outside, postponed, slender, slight, slim, small, unavailable; SEE CONCEPT *552*

off [*adj2*] *inferior; spoiled*
bad, decomposed, disappointing, disheartening, displeasing, low-quality, mortifying, not up to par*, not up to snuff*, poor, putrid, quiet, rancid, rotten, slack, sour, substandard, turned, unrewarding, unsatisfactory; SEE CONCEPT *570*

off [*adv*] *apart, away*
above, absent, afar, ahead, aside, away from, behind, below, beneath, beside, disappearing, divergent, elsewhere, far, farther away, gone away, in the distance, not here, out, over, removed, to one side, turning aside, up front, vanishing; SEE CONCEPTS *583,778*

offbeat [*adj*] *strange, very different*
bizarre, bohemian*, eccentric, far-out, freaky, fresh, idiosyncratic, novel, oddball, outré, uncommon, unconventional, unique, unorthodox, unusual, way-out*, weird; SEE CONCEPT *564*

off-color [*adj*] *risqué*
blue*, indelicate, purple*, racy*, salty*, shady, suggestive, vulgar, wicked; SEE CONCEPT *545*

offend [*v*] *displease, insult*
affront, aggrieve, anger, annoy, antagonize, be disagreeable, disgruntle, disgust, disoblige, distress, disturb, exasperate, fret, gall, horrify, hurt, irritate, jar, miff, nauseate, nettle, outrage, pain, pique, provoke, repel, repulse, rile, shock, sicken, sin, slight, slur, snub, sting, transgress, trespass, turn one off*, upset, vex, wound, zing*; SEE CONCEPTS *7,14,19*

offense [*n1*] *violation, trespass*
breach, crime, delinquency, fault, infraction, lapse, malfeasance, misdeed, misdemeanor, peccadillo, sin, transgression, wrong, wrongdoing; SEE CONCEPTS *192,691*

offense [*n2*] *insult, displeasure*
affront, aggression, assailment, assault, attack, battery, black eye*, blitz*, blitzkrieg*, dig*, dirty dig*, harm, hit*, hurt, indignation, indignity, injury, injustice, left-handed compliment*, mugging, offensive, onset, onslaught, outrage, push*, put-down*, slam*, slap in the face*, slight, snub, zinger*; SEE CONCEPTS *52,278*

offense [*n3*] *anger, hard feelings*
annoyance, conniption*, displeasure, explosion, fit, flare-up*, huff, indignation, ire, miff, needle*, outburst, pique, resentment, scene, tantrum, tizzy*, umbrage, wounded feelings, wrath; SEE CONCEPT *410*

offensive [*n*] *attack*
aggression, assailment, assault, drive, invasion, onset, onslaught, push; SEE CONCEPTS *86,320*

offensive [adj1] *disrespectful, insulting; displeasing*
abhorrent, abusive, annoying, biting, cutting, detestable, disagreeable, discourteous, distasteful, dreadful, embarrassing, evil, foul, ghastly, grisly, gross, hideous, horrible, horrid, impertinent, insolent, invidious, irritating, nauseating, objectionable, obnoxious, odious, off-color*, offending, opprobrious, outrageous, repellent, reprehensible, repugnant, repulsive, revolting, rotten, rude, shocking, stinking*, terrible, uncivil, unmannerly; SEE CONCEPTS 267,529,537

offensive [adj2] *attacking*
aggressive, assailing, assaulting, belligerent, invading; SEE CONCEPT 548

offer [n] *proposal, suggestion*
action, attempt, bid, endeavor, essay, feeler*, hit*, overture, pass*, pitch*, presentation, proposition, propoundment, rendition, submission, tender; SEE CONCEPTS 66,67,278

offer [v1] *present, propose for acceptance*
accord, advance, afford, allow, award, be at service, bid, come forward, display, donate, exhibit, extend, furnish, give, grant, hold out, lay at one's feet*, make available, move, place at disposal*, ply, pose, press, proffer, propound, provide, put forth, put forward, put on the market, put up, put up for sale, sacrifice, show, submit, suggest, tender, volunteer; SEE CONCEPT 67

offer [v2] *propose*
adduce, advance, advise, allege, cite, make a motion, make a pitch*, present, proposition, submit, suggest; SEE CONCEPT 66

offer [v3] *try*
assay, attempt, endeavor, essay, seek, strive, struggle, undertake; SEE CONCEPT 87

offering [n] *donation*
alms, atonement, benefaction, beneficence, charity, contribution, expiation, gift, oblation, present, sacrifice, subscription; SEE CONCEPTS 337,340

offhand [adj1] *abrupt, careless*
aloof, breezy, brusque, casual, cavalier, cool*, curt, easygoing, folksy, glib, informal, laid-back, mellow, perfunctory, unceremonious, unconcerned, uninterested; SEE CONCEPTS 267,401,542

offhand [adj2/adv] *ad-lib, extemporaneous*
extemporary, extempore, impromptu, improvised, informal, off the cuff*, off the hip*, off the top of head*, spontaneous, spur-of-the-moment*, throwaway*, unpremeditated, unprepared, unrehearsed, unstudied, without preparation; SEE CONCEPT 267

office [n1] *business, responsibility*
appointment, berth, billet, capacity, charge, commission, connection, duty, employment, function, job, obligation, occupation, performance, place, post, province, responsibility, role, service, situation, spot, station, trust, work; SEE CONCEPTS 351,362,376

office [n2] *place of business*
agency, building, bureau, cave*, center, department, facility, factory, foundry, room, salt mines*, setup, shop, store, suite, warehouse, workstation; SEE CONCEPTS 312,439,441,448,449

officer [n1] *person who has high position in organization*
administrator, agent, appointee, bureaucrat, chief, civil servant, deputy, dignitary, director, executive, functionary, head, leader, magistrate, manager, officeholder, official, president, public servant, representative; SEE CONCEPT 347

officer [n2] *person in law enforcement*
arm*, badge*, black and white*, captain, cop*, deputy, detective, flatfoot*, mounty, police, police officer, sergeant, sheriff; SEE CONCEPTS 354,355,358

official [n] *person representing organization*
administrator, agent, big shot*, boss, brains*, brass*, bureaucrat, CEO*, chancellor, civil servant, commissioner, comptroller, dignitary, director, exec*, executive, front office*, functionary, governor, head person, higher-up*, incumbent, leader, magistrate, manager, marshal, mayor, minister, officeholder, officer, panjandrum, premier, president, representative, secretary, top*, top brass*, top dog*, top drawer*, treasurer; SEE CONCEPTS 347,354

official [adj] *authorized, legitimate*
accredited, approved, authentic, authenticated, authoritative, bona fide, canonical, cathedral, ceremonious, certified, cleared, conclusive, correct, customary, decided, decisive, definite, endorsed, established, ex cathedra, ex officio, fitting, formal, legitimate, licensed, okay*, ordered, orthodox, positive, precise, proper, real, recognized, rightful, sanctioned, suitable, true, valid; SEE CONCEPT 535

officiate [v] *oversee, manage*
act, boss, chair, command, conduct, direct, do the honors*, emcee, function, govern, handle, preside, run, serve, superintend, umpire; SEE CONCEPT 117

officious [adj] *self-important, dictatorial*
busy, forward, impertinent, inquisitive, interfering, intrusive, meddlesome, meddling, obtrusive, opinionated, overzealous, pragmatic, pushy, rude; SEE CONCEPT 404

off-key [adj] *not harmonious*
abnormal, anomalous, clinker*, deviant, discordant, dissonant, divergent, inharmonious, irregular, jarring, out of keeping*, out of tune*, sour*, sour note*, unnatural; SEE CONCEPT 594

offset [v] *counterbalance, compensate*
account, allow for, atone for, balance, be equivalent, cancel out, charge, counteract, counterpoise, counterpose, countervail, equal, equalize, equipoise, make amends, make up for, negate, neutralize, outweigh, recompense, redeem, requite, set off; SEE CONCEPTS 126,232

offshoot [n] *development, product*
adjunct, appendage, branch, by-product, derivative, descendant, limb, outgrowth, spin-off, sprout; SEE CONCEPTS 260,824

offspring [n] *child, children*
baby, bambino*, brood, chip off old block*, cub, descendant, family, generation, heir, heredity, issue, kid*, lineage, offshoot, posterity, produce, progeniture, progeny, pup*, scion, seed, spawn, succession, successor, young; SEE CONCEPTS 296,414

often [adv] *frequently*
again and again, a number of times, generally, many a time, much, oftentimes, ofttimes, over and over, recurrently, regularly, repeatedly, time after time, time and again, usually; SEE CONCEPT 541

ogre [n] *nasty person*
demon, devil, fiend, giant, monster, monstrosity, specter, troll; SEE CONCEPT 412

od
og

oil [v] *lubricate*
anoint, coat, grease, lard, lube, pomade, slick, smear; SEE CONCEPTS *172,256*

oily [adj1] *fatty, greasy*
adipose, buttery, creamy, lardy, lubricant, lubricative, lubricous, lustrous, oiled, oil-soaked, oleaginous, polished, rich, saponaceous, sleek, slippery, smeary, smooth, soapy, soothing, swimming, unctuous, waxy; SEE CONCEPTS *603,606*

oily [adj2] *flattering*
bland*, cajoling, coaxing, compliant, fulsome, glib, gushing*, hypocritical, ingratiating, insinuating, obsequious, plausible, servile, slick, smarmy*, smooth, smooth-tongued*, suave, supple, unctuous; SEE CONCEPTS *267,401*

ointment [n] *cream for treatment*
balm, cerate, demulcent, dressing, embrocation, emollient, lenitive, liniment, lotion, medicine, salve, unguent; SEE CONCEPTS *311,466*

okay [n] *agreement*
acceptance, affirmation, approbation, approval, assent, authorization, benediction, blessing, consent, endorsement, favor, go-ahead*, green light*, permission, sanction, say-so*, seal of approval*, yes; SEE CONCEPTS *684*

okay [adj] *acceptable, satisfactory*
accurate, adequate, all right, approved, convenient, correct, fair, fine, good, in order, middling, not bad, passable, permitted, so-so*, surely, tolerable; SEE CONCEPT *558*

okay [v] *agree to*
accept, accredit, approve, authorize, certify, condone, confirm, consent to, endorse, give one's consent, give the go-ahead*, give the green light*, notarize, pass, rubber-stamp*, sanction, say yes to; SEE CONCEPTS *10,50,88*

old [adj] *advanced in age*
aged, along in years*, ancient, broken down*, debilitated, decrepit, elderly, enfeebled, exhausted, experienced, fossil*, geriatric, getting on*, gray, gray-haired*, grizzled*, hoary*, impaired, inactive, infirm, mature, matured, not young, olden, oldish, over the hill*, past one's prime*, seasoned, senile, senior, skilled, superannuated, tired, venerable, versed, veteran, wasted*; SEE CONCEPTS *578,797*

old [adj2] *obsolete, outdated*
aboriginal, age-old, antediluvian, antiquated, antique, archaic, bygone, cast-off, crumbling, dated, decayed, demode, done, early, erstwhile, former, hackneyed*, immemorial, late, moth-eaten*, of old, of yore, olden, oldfangled, old-fashioned, old-time, once, onetime, original, outmoded, out-of-date, passé, past, primeval, primitive, primordial, pristine, quondam, relic, remote, rusty, sometime, stale, superannuated, time-worn, traditional, unfashionable, unoriginal, venerable, worn-out; SEE CONCEPTS *558,560,799*

old [adj3] *traditional, long-established*
age-old, constant, continuing, enduring, established, experienced, familiar, firm, hardened, inveterate, lifelong, long-lasting, long-lived, of long standing, perennial, perpetual, practiced, skilled, solid, staying, steady, time-honored, versed, veteran, vintage; SEE CONCEPTS *482,530,798*

old age [n] *latter part of animate life*
advancing years*, age, agedness, autumn of life*, caducity, debility, declining years*, decrepitude, dotage, elderliness, evening of life*, feebleness, golden age*, golden years*, infirmity, second childhood*, senectitude, senescence, senility, years; SEE CONCEPTS *715,817*

older [adj] *most senior*
earlier, elder, eldest, first, first-born, former, lower, of a former period, of an earlier time, preceding, prior, senior; SEE CONCEPTS *578,585,797*

old-fashioned [adj] *outmoded, obsolete*
ancient, antiquated, antique, archaic, behind the times*, bygone, corny*, dated, dead*, demode, demoded, disapproved, dowdy*, extinct, grown old, moldy*, musty, neglected, not current, not modern, not with it*, obsolescent, odd*, of old, of olden days*, of the old school*, olden, old-fangled*, old-hat*, old-time, out*, outdated, out-of-date, out of it*, out-of-style, outworn, passé*, past, primitive, rococo*, superannuated, unfashionable, unstylish, vintage; SEE CONCEPTS *578,589,797,799*

old hand [n] *person experienced in something*
expert, longtimer, old guard*, old school*, old-timer*, pro*, vet*, veteran; SEE CONCEPT *423*

oligarchic [adj] *governed by small group*
cabalistic, cliquey*, elite, exclusive, select; SEE CONCEPTS *554,568*

omen [n] *sign of something to come*
augury, auspice, bodement, boding, foreboding, foretoken, harbinger, indication, portent, premonition, presage, prognostic, prognostication, prophecy, straw, warning, writing on the wall*; SEE CONCEPTS *74,278,689*

ominous [adj] *menacing, foreboding*
apocalyptic, augural, baleful, baneful, clouded, dangerous, dark, dire, direful, dismal, doomed, doomful, fateful, fearful, forbidding, gloomy, grim, haunting, hostile, ill-boding, ill-fated, impending, inauspicious, inhospitable, lowering, malefic, malificent, malign, minatory, perilous, portentous, precursive, premonitory, presaging, prescient, prophetic, sinister, suggestive, threatening, unfriendly, unlucky, unpromising, unpropitious; SEE CONCEPT *548*

omission [n] *something forgotten or excluded*
blank, breach, break, cancellation, carelessness, chasm, cutting out, default, disregard, disregardance, elimination, elision, excluding, exclusion, failing, failure, forgetfulness, gap, hiatus, ignoring, inadvertence, inadvertency, lack, lacuna, lapse, leaving out, missing, neglect, noninclusion, overlook, overlooking, oversight, passing over, preclusion, preterition, pretermission, prohibition, repudiation, skip, slighting, slip, withholding; SEE CONCEPTS *25,116,699*

omit [v] *exclude, forget*
bar, blink at*, bypass, cancel, cast aside, count out, cut, cut out, delete, discard, dismiss, disregard, drop, edit, eliminate, evade, except, fail, ignore, knock off, leave out, leave undone, let go, let slide*, miss, miss out, neglect, overlook, overpass, pass by, pass over, preclude, prohibit, reject, repudiate, skip, slight, snip, trim, void, withhold, X-out*; SEE CONCEPTS *25,121,211*

omnipotent [adj] *all-powerful*
almighty, divine, godlike, mighty, supreme, unlimited, unrestricted; SEE CONCEPT *574*

omniscient [adj] *all-knowing*
all-seeing, almighty, infinite, knowledgeable, pansophical, preeminent, wise; SEE CONCEPT *402*

on [adv] *in contact; ahead of*
about, above, adjacent, against, approaching, at, beside, close to, covering, forth, forward, held,

leaning on, near, next, on top of, onward, over, resting on, situated on, supported, touching, toward, upon, with; SEE CONCEPTS 585,586,750

once [adj/adv] *in the past; occurred one time only*
already, a single time, at one time, away back, back, back when, before, but once, bygone, earlier, erstwhile, formerly, heretofore, in the old days, in the olden days, in times gone by, in times past, late, long ago, old, once only, once upon a time, one, one time before, one time previously, only one time, on one occasion, previously, quondam, sometime, this time, time was, whilom; SEE CONCEPTS 799,820

oncoming [adj] *impending*
advancing, approaching, coming, expected, forthcoming, imminent, looming, nearing, onrushing, upcoming; SEE CONCEPTS 548,799

one [adj] *individual*
alone, definite, different, lone, odd, one and only, only, particular, peculiar, precise, separate, single, singular, sole, solitary, special, specific, uncommon, unique; SEE CONCEPTS 577,762,789

onerous [adj] *difficult; requiring hard labor*
arduous, austere, backbreaking, burdensome, crushing, cumbersome, demanding, difficult, distressing, embittering, exacting, excessive, exhausting, exigent, fatiguing, formidable, galling, grave, grinding, grueling, hard*, harsh, headache, heavy*, intolerable, irksome, laborious, merciless, oppressive, overpowering, overtaxing, painful, plodding, ponderous, pressing, responsible, rigorous, serious, severe, strenuous, taxing, tiresome, tiring, toilsome, troublesome, vexatious, weighty; SEE CONCEPTS 538,565

ongoing [adj] *continuous*
advancing, continuing, current, developing, evolving, extant, growing, heading, in process, in progress, marching, open-ended, progressing, successful, unfinished, unfolding; SEE CONCEPTS 482,798

onlooker [n] *person observing an event*
beholder, bystander, eyewitness, looker-on, observer, sightseer, spectator, viewer, watcher, witness; SEE CONCEPT 423

only [adj] *singular*
alone, apart, by oneself, exclusive, individual, isolated, lone, matchless, once in a lifetime, one, one and only, one shot, onliest, particular, peerless, single, sole, solitary, solo, unaccompanied, unequaled, unique, unparalleled, unrivaled; SEE CONCEPT 577

only [adv] *barely; exclusively*
alone, at most, but, entirely, hardly, just, merely, nothing but, particularly, plainly, purely, simply, solely, totally, uniquely, utterly, wholly; SEE CONCEPTS 535,772

onset [n] *beginning; attack*
access, aggression, assailment, assault, birth, charge, commencement, dawn, dawning, encounter, inception, incipience, kickoff*, offense, offensive, onfall, onrush, onslaught, opening, origin, outbreak, outset, outstart, rush, seizure, start; SEE CONCEPTS 86,221,832

onslaught [n] *attack*
aggression, assailment, assault, blitz, charge, incursion, invasion, offense, offensive, onfall, onrush, onset; SEE CONCEPT 86

onus [n] *burden*
bar sinister*, black eye*, blame, blot, blur, brand, charge, culpability, deadweight*, duty, encumbrance, fault, guilt, incubus, liability, load, millstone*, obligation, odium, oppression, responsibility, slur, spot, stain, stigma, task, tax, weight; SEE CONCEPTS 388,674

onward/onwards [adv] *ahead, beyond*
alee, along, forth, forward, in front, in front of, moving, on, on ahead; SEE CONCEPTS 585,778

ooze [n] *liquid emitted*
alluvium, fluid, glop*, goo*, gook*, gunk*, mire, muck*, mud, silt, slime*, sludge; SEE CONCEPTS 466,467

ooze [v] *emit liquid*
bleed, discharge, drain, dribble, drip, drop, escape, exude, filter, flow, issue, leach, leak, overflow, percolate, perspire, seep, spurt, strain, sweat, swelter, trickle, weep, well; SEE CONCEPT 179

opaque [adj1] *clouded, muddy*
blurred, cloudy, dark, darkened, dim, dirty, dull, dusky, filmy, foggy, frosty, fuliginous, gloomy, hazy, impenetrable, lusterless, misty, muddied, murky, nontranslucent, nontransparent, nubilous, obfuscated, shady, smoky, sooty, thick, turbid; SEE CONCEPTS 606,617,618

opaque [adj2] *hard to understand*
abstruse, amphibological, arcane, baffling, concealed, cryptic, difficult, enigmatic, equivocal, imperceptive, incomprehensible, nubilous, obscure, obtuse, perplexing, purblind, tenebrous, uncertain, unclear, unfathomable, unintelligible, vague; SEE CONCEPT 529

open [adj1] *unfastened, unclosed*
accessible, agape, airy, ajar, bare, clear, cleared, dehiscent, disclosed, emptied, expanded, expansive, exposed, extended, extensive, free, gaping, made passable, naked, navigable, passable, patent, patulous, peeled, removed, rent, revealed, ringent, rolling, spacious, spread out, stripped, susceptible, unbarred, unblocked, unbolted, unburdened, uncluttered, uncovered, unfolded, unfurled, unimpeded, unlocked, unobstructed, unplugged, unsealed, unshut, unstopped, vacated, wide, yawning; SEE CONCEPTS 485,576

open [adj2] *accessible; not forbidden*
admissible, agreeable, allowable, approachable, appropriate, attainable, available, employable, fit, free, general, getable*, nondiscriminatory, not posted, obtainable, on deck*, on tap*, open-door*, operative, permitted, practicable, proper, public, reachable, securable, suitable, to be had*, unconditional, unoccupied, unqualified, unrestricted, usable, vacant, welcoming, within reach; SEE CONCEPTS 560,576

open [adj3] *clear, obvious*
apparent, avowed, barefaced, blatant, conspicuous, downright, evident, flagrant, frank, manifest, noticeable, overt, plain, unconcealed, undisguised, visible, well-known; SEE CONCEPTS 267,535

open [adj4] *undecided*
ambiguous, arguable, controversial, debatable, doubtful, dubious, dubitable, equivocal, indecisive, in question, moot, problematic, questionable, uncertain, unresolved, unsettled, up for discussion*, up in the air*, yet to be decided*; SEE CONCEPTS 267,529

open [adj5] *honest, objective*
artless, candid, disinterested, fair, frank, free, guileless, impartial, ingenuous, innocent, lay it on the line*, mellow, natural, objective, on the lev-

el*, open-and-shut*, openhearted*, plain, receptive, sincere, straightforward, talking turkey*,
transparent, unbiased, uncommitted, unconcealed, undisguised, undissembled, unprejudiced,
unreserved, up-front*; SEE CONCEPTS 267,542

open [v1] begin
begin business, bow, commence, convene, embark, get things rolling*, inaugurate, initiate,
jump, kick off, launch, meet, raise the curtain*,
ring in*, set in motion, set up shop*, sit, start,
start the ball rolling*; SEE CONCEPT 221

open [v2] clear, expose; spread
bare, break in, break out, broach, burst, bust in,
come apart, crack, disclose, display, disrupt, expand, fissure, free, gap, gape, hole, jimmy, kick
in, lacerate, lance, penetrate, perforate, pierce,
pop, puncture, release, reveal, rupture, separate,
sever, slit, slot, split, tap, throw wide, unbar, unblock, unbolt, unclose, unclothe, uncork, uncover, undo, unfasten, unfold, unfurl, unlatch,
unlock, unroll, unseal, unshut, unstop, untie, unwrap, vent, ventilate, yawn, yawp; SEE CONCEPTS
135,250,469

opening [n1] gap, hole
aperture, breach, break, cavity, chink, cleft,
crack, cranny, crevice, cut, discontinuity, door,
fissure, hatch, interstice, mouth, orifice, outlet,
perforation, recess, rent, rift, rupture, scuttle, slit,
slot, space, split, spout, tear, vent, window; SEE
CONCEPT 513

opening [n2] chance
availability, big break*, connection, cut*, fling*,
go*, go-at*, in the running*, iron in the fire*,
look-in*, occasion, opportunity, place, possibility, run, scope, shot*, show, squeak*, time, vacancy, whack*; SEE CONCEPT 693

opening [n3] beginning
birth, coming out, commencement, curtain-
raiser*, dawn, inauguration, inception, initiation,
kickoff, launch, launching, onset, opener, outset,
start; SEE CONCEPT 832

openly [adv] honestly
aboveboard, artlessly, blatantly, brazenly, candidly, face to face, flagrantly, forthrightly,
frankly, fully, honestly, in broad daylight, in full
view, ingenuously, in public, in the open, naively,
naturally, plainly, publicly, readily, shamelessly,
simply, straight, unabashedly, unashamedly, under one's nose*, unhesitatingly, unreservedly,
wantonly, warts and all*, willingly, without pretense, without reserve; SEE CONCEPTS 267,544

operate [v1] perform, function
accomplish, achieve, act, act on, advance, behave, be in action, bend, benefit, bring about,
burn, carry on, click*, compel, complete, concern, conduct, contact, contrive, convey, cook*,
determine, direct, do, enforce, engage, exert, finish, fulfill, get results, go, hit*, hum, influence,
keep, lift, move, ordain, percolate, proceed, produce, produce a result, progress, promote, react,
revolve, roll, run, serve, spin, take, tick, transport, turn, work; SEE CONCEPTS 91,680,706

operate [v2] manage, use
administer, be in charge, be in driver's seat*, be
in saddle*, call the play*, call the shots*, call the
signals*, carry on, command, conduct, drive, handle, hold the reins*, keep, make go*, maneuver,
manipulate, ordain, pilot, play, ply, pull the
strings*, pull the wires*, run, run the show*, run

things*, sit on top of*, steer, wield, work; SEE
CONCEPTS 94,117,148

operate [v3] perform surgery
amputate, carve up, cut, excise, explore, open up,
remove, set, transplant, treat; SEE CONCEPT 310

operation [n1] movement, working
act, action, activity, affair, agency, application,
ballgame*, bit, carrying on, conveyance, course,
deal, deed, doing, effect, effort, employment, engagement, enterprise, exercise, exercising, exertion, exploitation, force, handiwork, happening,
influence, instrumentality, labor, manipulation,
motion, movement, performance, play, procedure, proceeding, process, progress, progression,
scene, service, transaction, transference, trip, undertaking, use, work, workmanship; SEE CON-
CEPTS 658,680

operation [n2] business concern
affair, deal, enterprise, proceeding, transaction,
undertaking; SEE CONCEPTS 324,325

operation [n3] surgical procedure
biopsy, excision, surgery; SEE CONCEPT 310

operative [adj] active, functioning; influential
accessible, alive, crucial, current, dynamic, effective, efficient, employable, functional, important,
indicative, in force, in operation, key, live, open,
operational, practicable, relevant, running, serviceable, significant, standing, usable, workable,
working; SEE CONCEPTS 560,567

opinion [n] belief
assessment, assumption, attitude, conception,
conclusion, conjecture, estimate, estimation,
eye*, fancy, feeling, guess, hypothesis, idea,
imagining, impression, inclination, inference,
judgment, mind, notion, persuasion, point of
view, postulate, presumption, presupposition, reaction, say-so*, sentiment, slant, speculation,
supposition, surmise, suspicion, take*, theorem,
theory, thesis, think*, thought, view, viewpoint;
SEE CONCEPT 689

opinionated [adj] believing very strongly and conveying it
adamant, arbitrary, assertive, biased, bigoted,
bossy, bullheaded*, cocksure*, cocky*, conceited, dictatorial, doctrinaire, dogmatic, hard-
line*, high-handed, inflexible, intransigent,
locked in*, obdurate, obstinate, one-sided, oracular, overbearing, pigheaded*, positive, pragmatic, pragmatical, prejudiced, self-assertive, set
in stone*, set-on, single-minded, stubborn, tilted,
uncompromising, unyielding, weighted; SEE CON-
CEPTS 267,404

opponent [n] person with whom one competes
adversary, antagonist, anti*, aspirant, assailant,
bandit*, bidder, candidate, challenger, competitor, con, contestant, counteragent, dark horse*,
disputant, dissentient, enemy, entrant, foe, litigant, match, opposer, opposition, oppugnant,
player, rival; SEE CONCEPT 366

opportune [adj] advantageous, lucky
appropriate, apt, auspicious, convenient, favorable, felicitous, fit, fitting, fortuitous, fortunate,
happy, helpful, pat, proper, propitious, seasonable, suitable, timely, timeous, well-timed; SEE
CONCEPTS 548,572

opportunity [n] lucky chance; favorable circumstances
befalling, break*, connection, contingency, convenience, cut*, event, excuse, fair shake*, fighting chance*, fitness, fling*, fortuity, freedom,

go*, good fortune, good luck, happening, hope, hour, iron in the fire*, juncture, leisure, liberty, moment, occasion, one's move*, one's say*, one's turn*, opening, pass, prayer*, probability, relief, room, run, scope, shot*, show, space, spell, squeak, stab, the hunt*, the running*, time, turn, whack*; SEE CONCEPT 693

oppose [v1] *fight, obstruct*
argue, assail, assault, attack, bar, battle, bombard, call in question, check, combat, confront, contradict, controvert, counter, counterattack, cross, debate, defy, deny, disagree, disapprove, dispute, encounter, expose, face, face down*, fight, fly in the face of*, frown at, gainsay, hinder, neutralize, not countenance, prevent, protest, resist, reverse, run counter to, search out, speak against, stand up to, take a stand, take issue, take on, taunt, thwart, turn the tables*, withstand; SEE CONCEPTS 21,54,106

oppose [v2] *compare, play off*
array, confront, contrast, counter, counterbalance, face, match, pit, set against, vie; SEE CONCEPTS 73,363

opposed/opposing [adj] *antagonistic, against*
against the grain*, allergic*, anti*, antipathetic, antithetical, anonymous, at cross-purposes, at odds, averse, battling, clashing, combating, conflicting, confronting, contrary, controverting, counter, crossing, defending, defensive, denying, disagreeing, disputed, disputing, dissentient, enemy, exposing, facing, gainsaying, hostile, incompatible, inimical, in opposition, irreconcilable, objecting, obstructive, opposite, protesting, repelling, restrictive, rival, up against, warring; SEE CONCEPTS 403,542,564

opposite [n] *something completely unlike another*
adverse, antilogy, antipode, antipole, antithesis, antonym, contra*, contradiction, contrary, contrast, converse, counterpart, foil, inverse, obverse, opposition, other extreme*, other side*, other side of coin*, paradox, reverse, vice versa; SEE CONCEPT 665

opposite [adj] *unlike, conflicting; completely different*
adverse, antagonistic, antipodal, antipodean, antithetical, contradictory, contrapositive, contrary, contrasted, corresponding, counter, crosswise, diametric, diametrically opposed, different, differing, dissimilar, diverse, facing, flip-side*, fronting, hostile, inconsistent, independent, inimical, inverse, irreconcilable, obverse, opposed, ornery*, paradoxical, polar, repugnant, retrograde, reverse, reversed, separate, unalike, unconnected, unrelated, unsimilar, violative, vis-à-vis; SEE CONCEPT 564

opposition [n1] *obstruction, antagonism*
action, antinomy, antithesis, aversion, brush, civil disobedience, clash, combat, competition, con, conflict, confronting, contention, contest, contradistinction, contraposition, contrariety, counteraction, counterattack, defense, defiance, disapproval, duel, encounter, engagement, fray, grapple, hostility, negativism, obstructiveness, opposure, oppugnancy, prevention, repugnance, repulsion, resistance, rivalry, skirmish, strife, struggle, unfriendliness, violation, war, warfare; SEE CONCEPTS 29,92,106,665

opposition [n2] *person, people competing*
adversary, antagonist, disputant, enemy, foe,

iconoclast, opponent, other side, rebel, rival; SEE CONCEPTS 348,366

oppress [v] *depress, subdue*
abuse, afflict, aggrieve, annoy, beat down*, burden, crush, despotize, dishearten, dispirit, distress, encumber, force, handicap, harass, harry, hound*, keep down, maltreat, outrage, overcome, overload, overpower, overthrow, overwhelm, persecute, pick on, plague, press, prey on, put down, put screws to*, put the squeeze on*, put upon, ride, rule, sadden, saddle*, smother, strain, subjugate, suppress, tax, torment, torture, trample, trouble, tyrannize, vex, weigh heavy upon, worry, wrong; SEE CONCEPTS 7,14,19,133

oppression [n] *misery, hardship*
abuse, abusiveness, autocracy, brutality, calamity, coercion, compulsion, conquering, control, cruelty, despotism, dictatorship, domination, fascism, force, forcibleness, hardness, harshness, injury, injustice, iron hand*, maltreatment, martial law, overthrowing, persecution, severity, subduing, subjection, suffering, torment, tyranny; SEE CONCEPTS 14,320,674

oppressive [adj1] *overwhelming, repressive*
backbreaking*, bleak, brutal, burdensome, confining, cruel, demanding, depressing, depressive, despotic, dictatorial, discouraging, disheartening, dismal, dispiriting, exacting, exigent, gloomy, grievous, grinding, harsh, headache*, heavy, heavy-handed*, hefty, inhuman, ironhanded*, mean, onerous, overbearing, rough going*, severe, somber, superincumbent, taxing, tough, troublesome, tyrannical, unjust, weighty; SEE CONCEPTS 537,548

oppressive [adj2] *hot and humid*
airless, close, heavy, muggy, overpowering, steam bath*, steamy, sticky, stifling, stuffy, suffocating, sultry, sweat box*, torrid; SEE CONCEPT 525

opprobrious [adj] *abusive, hateful*
abasing, calumniatory, contemptuous, contumelious, damaging, debasing, defamatory, defaming, denigrating, depreciative, derogatory, despicable, despiteful, detractive, disgracing, dishonoring, disparaging, humiliating, hurting, injuring, injurious, insolent, insulting, invective, libeling, malevolent, malign, malignant, maligning, notorious, offending, offensive, pejorative, reproaching, reviling, scandalous, scurrilous, shaming, spiteful, truculent, vile, vitriolic, vituperative, vulgar; SEE CONCEPTS 267,404,542

opt [v] *choose*
cull, decide, elect, exercise choice, go for*, make a selection, mark, pick, prefer, select, single out*, take; SEE CONCEPT 41

optimism [n] *state of having positive beliefs*
anticipation, assurance, brightness, buoyancy, calmness, certainty, cheer, cheerfulness, confidence, easiness, elation, encouragement, enthusiasm, exhilaration, expectation, good cheer, happiness, hopefulness, idealism, looking on bright side*, positivism, rose-colored glasses*, sanguineness, sureness, trust; SEE CONCEPTS 410,689

optimistic [adj] *believing positively*
assured, bright, buoyant, cheerful, cheering, confident, encouraged, expectant, happy, high, hopeful, hoping, idealistic, keeping the faith, merry, on cloud nine*, on top of world*, positive, promising, ray of sunshine*, rose-colored*, rosy, san-

op
op

guine, sunny*, trusting, upbeat, Utopian; SEE
CONCEPTS *404,542*

optimum [*adj*] *best*
24-carat*, A1*, ace, capital, choice, choicest, excellent, flawless, gilt-edge*, greatest, highest,
ideal, matchless, maximum, most advantageous,
most favorable, optimal, peak, peerless, perfect,
select, solid gold*, superlative, world class*; SEE
CONCEPT *574*

option [*n*] *alternative*
advantage, benefit, choice, claim, dibs*, dilemma, discretion, druthers, election, flipside*,
franchise, free will*, grant, license, opportunity,
other side of coin*, pickup, preference, prerogative, privilege, right, selection, take it or leave it*;
SEE CONCEPTS *376,712*

optional [*adj*] *possible; available as choice*
alternative, arbitrary, discretional, discretionary,
elective, extra, facultative, free, noncompulsory,
nonobligatory, no strings attached*, not required,
open, unforced, unrestricted, up to the individual,
volitional, voluntary; SEE CONCEPTS *552,576*

opulent [*adj*] *rich, luxurious, profuse*
abundant, affluent, copious, deluxe, extravagant,
exuberant, frilly*, lavish, luscious, luxuriant,
moneyed, ostentatious, palatial, plentiful, plush,
pretentious, prodigal, profusive, prolific, prosperous, rich, riotous, showy, sumptuous, swank, upholstered*, velvet*, wealthy, well-heeled*, well-
off*, well-to-do*; SEE CONCEPTS *334,589,781*

opus [*n*] *great work of writing or music*
composition, creation, magnum opus, music, oeuvre, piece, product, production; SEE CONCEPTS
263,271

oracle [*n*] *prophecy*
answer, apocalypse, augury, canon, commandment, divination, edict, fortune, law, prediction,
prognostication, revelation, vision; SEE CON-
CEPTS *70,278,689*

oracular [*adj*] *prophetic*
ambiguous, anticipating, apocalyptic, arcane, au-
guring, auspicious, authoritative, cabalistic, clairvoyant, cryptic, Delphian, discovering, divining,
divulging, dogmatic, fatidic, foreboding, forecasting, foretelling, imperious, interpretive, mantic,
mysterious, mystical, obscure, occult, ominous,
peremptory, portending, portentous, positive, predicting, presaging, prescient, proclaiming, prog-
nosticating, prophesying, sage, secret, sibylline,
significant, soothsaying, vague, vatic, venerable,
wise; SEE CONCEPT *267*

oral [*adj*] *spoken*
articulate, ejaculatory, lingual, narrated, pho-
nated, phonetic, phonic, recounted, related, said,
sonant, sounded, told, unwritten, uttered, verbal,
viva voce, vocal, voiced, word-of-mouth; SEE
CONCEPT *267*

orange [*n/adj*] *combination of red and yellow*
apricot, bittersweet, cantaloupe, carrot, coral,
peach, red-yellow, salmon, tangerine, titian; SEE
CONCEPTS *618,622*

oration [*n*] *speech*
address, chalk talk*, declamation, discourse, harangue, homily, lecture, pep talk*, pitch*, sermon, soapbox*, spiel*; SEE CONCEPTS *266,278*

orb [*n*] *globe*
ball, circle, eye*, lamp, ring, rondure, round,
sphere; SEE CONCEPT *436*

orbit [*n1*] *circuit, revolution*
apogee, circle, circumgyration, course, curve, cy-

cle, ellipse, lap, locus, path, pattern, perigee, rotation, round, track, trajectory; SEE CONCEPTS
436,738

orbit [*n2*] *influence, domain*
ambit, area, arena, boundary, bounds, career, circle, circumference, compass, course, department,
dominion, extension, extent, field, jurisdiction,
limit, pilgrimage, precinct, province, purview, radius, range, reach, realm, scope, sphere, sweep;
SEE CONCEPTS *349,673,687*

orchestrate [*v*] *organize; cause to happen*
arrange, blend, compose, concert, coordinate,
harmonize, integrate, manage, present, put together, score, set up, symphonize, synthesize,
unify; SEE CONCEPTS *117,242*

ordain [*v*] *establish, install*
anoint, appoint, bless, call, commission, consecrate, constitute, deal, deal with, decree, delegate, destine, dictate, elect, enact, enjoin, fix,
frock, impose, institute, invest, lay down the
law*, legislate, nominate, order, prescribe, pronounce, put foot down*, rule, set, walk heavy*,
will; SEE CONCEPTS *18,50,88,317*

ordeal [*n*] *trouble, suffering*
affliction, agony, anguish, calamity, calvary,
cross, crucible, difficulty, distress, nightmare,
test, torment, torture, trial, tribulation, visitation;
SEE CONCEPTS *674,728*

order [*n1*] *arrangement, organization*
adjustment, aligning, array, assortment, cast, categorization, classification, codification, composition, computation, disposal, disposition,
distribution, establishment, form, grouping, harmony, layout, line, lineup, management, method,
neatness, ordering, orderliness, pattern, placement, plan, procedure, procession, progression,
propriety, regularity, rule, scale,
scheme, sequence, series, setup, standardization,
structure, succession, symmetry, system, tidiness,
uniformity; SEE CONCEPT *727*

order [*n2*] *lawfulness*
calm, control, decorousness, decorum, discipline,
goodness, integrity, law, law and order, niceness,
orderliness, peace, peacefulness, probity, properness, propriety, quiet, rectitude, rightness, seemliness, suitability, tranquility, uprightness; SEE
CONCEPTS *633,691*

order [*n3*] *class, status*
bracket, branch, breed, cast, caste, degree, description, estate, family, feather, genre, genus,
grade, hierarchy, ilk, kidney, kind, line, nature,
pecking order*, pigeonhole*, place, position,
rank, set, slot, sort, species, station, stripe, subclass, taxonomic group, type; SEE CONCEPT *378*

order [*n4*] *command*
authorization, behest, bidding, charge, commandment, decree, dictate, direction, directive, injunction, instruction, law, mandate, ordinance,
permission, precept, regulation, rule, say-so*,
stipulation, ukase, word*; SEE CONCEPTS
53,278,685

order [*n5*] *request; purchase agreement*
amount, application, booking, bulk, commission,
engagement, goods, materials, purchase, quantity,
requisition, reservation, reserve, shipment, stipulation; SEE CONCEPTS *332,338,684*

order [*n6*] *organization*
association, brotherhood, club, community, company, fraternity, guild, league, lodge, sect, sister-

hood, society, sodality, sorority, union; SEE
CONCEPT *387*

order [*v1*] *command, authorize*
adjure, apply for, bid, book, buy, call for, call the
shots*, call the signals*, charge, contract for, decree, dictate, direct, enact, engage, enjoin, hire,
instruct, obtain, ordain, prescribe, pull strings*,
request, require, reserve, rule the roost*, secure,
send away for, tell, warn; SEE CONCEPTS
50,53,88,327

order [*v2*] *arrange, organize*
adapt, adjust, align, alphabetize, array, assign,
catalogue, class, classify, codify, conduct, control, dispose, distribute, establish, file, fix, formalize, furnish, group, index, lay out, line, line
up, locate, manage, marshal, methodize, neaten,
normalize, pattern, place, plan, put away, put to
rights*, range, regiment, regularize, regulate,
right, routine, set guidelines, set in order, settle,
sort out, space, standardize, streamline, systematize, tabulate, tidy; SEE CONCEPTS *84,158*

orderly [*adj1*] *methodical, organized*
alike, all together, arranged, businesslike, careful,
clean, conventional, correct, exact, fixed, formal,
framed, in apple-pie order*, in good shape, in
order, in shape, methodic, neat, neat as button*,
neat as pin*, precise, regular, regulated, scientific, set-up, shipshape*, slick, spick-and-span*,
systematic, systematized, thorough, tidy, together, to rights*, trim, uncluttered, uniform; SEE
CONCEPTS *326,485,585,589*

orderly [*adj2*] *well-behaved*
at peace, calm, controlled, decorous, disciplined,
docile, law-abiding, manageable, nonviolent, obedient, peaceable, quiet, restrained, submissive,
tranquil, well-mannered; SEE CONCEPT *401*

ordinance [*n*] *law, rule*
authorization, canon, code, command, decree,
dictum, direction, edict, enactment, fiat, mandate,
order, precept, prescript, reg, regulation, ruling,
statute, ukase; SEE CONCEPT *318*

ordinarily [*adv*] *usually*
as a rule, commonly, customarily, frequently,
generally, habitually, in general, normally, regularly; SEE CONCEPT *530*

ordinary [*adj1*] *common, regular*
accustomed, customary, established, everyday,
familiar, frequent, general, habitual, humdrum*,
natural, normal, popular, prevailing, public, quotidian, routine, run-of-the-mill*, settled, standard,
stock, traditional, typical, usual, wonted; SEE
CONCEPTS *533,547*

ordinary [*adj2*] *average; not distinctive*
characterless, common, commonplace, conventional, dull, fair, familiar, garden*, garden variety*, generic, habitual, homespun, household,
humble, indifferent, inferior, mean, mediocre,
modest, no great shakes*, normal, pedestrian,
plain, plastic, prosaic, quotidian, routine, run-
of-the-mill*, second-rate, simple, so-so*, stereotyped, undistinguished, uneventful, unexceptional, uninspired, unmemorable, unnoteworthy,
unpretentious, unremarkable, usual, vanilla*,
white-bread*, whitewash*; SEE CONCEPTS *530,575*

organ [*n*] *means, tool*
agency, agent, channel, device, element, forum,
implement, instrument, journal, magazine, medium, member, ministry, mouthpiece, newspaper,
paper, part, periodical, process, publication, re-

view, structure, unit, vehicle, voice, way; SEE
CONCEPTS *280,499,712*

organic [*adj*] *basic, natural*
amoebic, anatomical, animate, basal, biological,
biotic, cellular, constitutional, elemental, essential, fundamental, inherent, innate, integral, live,
living, necessary, nuclear, original, plasmic, primary, prime, primitive, principal, structural, vital; SEE CONCEPT *549*

organism [*n*] *living thing*
animal, being, body, creature, entity, morphon,
person, plant, structure; SEE CONCEPTS *389,429*

organization [*n1*] *arrangement, arranging*
alignment, assembling, assembly, chemistry,
composition, configuration, conformation, constitution, construction, coordination, design, disposal, format, formation, forming, formulation,
framework, grouping, harmony, institution,
make-up, making, management, method, methodology, organism, organizing, pattern, plan, planning, regulation, running, situation, standard,
standardization, structure, structuring, symmetry,
system, unity, whole; SEE CONCEPTS *84,117,727*

organization [*n2*] *group bound by interest/work/
goal*
affiliation, aggregation, alliance, association,
band, body, business, cartel, circle, clique, club,
coalition, combination, combine, company, concern, concord, confederation, consortium, cooperative, corporation, coterie, crew, establishment,
federation, fraternity, guild, house, industry, institute, institution, league, lodge, machine, monopoly, order, outfit, party, profession, set,
society, sodality, sorority, squad, syndicate, team,
trade, troupe, trust, union; SEE CONCEPT *381*

organize [*v*] *arrange, systematize*
adapt, adjust, be responsible for, catalogue, classify, codify, combine, compose, constitute, construct, coordinate, correlate, create, dispose,
establish, fashion, fit, form, formulate, frame, get
going*, get together, group, harmonize, lick into
shape*, line up, look after, marshal, methodize,
mold, pigeonhole*, put in order, put together,
range, regulate, run, see to, settle, set up, shape,
standardize, straighten, straighten out, tabulate,
tailor, take care of, whip into shape*; SEE CON-
CEPTS *36,84,158*

orgy [*n*] *celebration devoted to sensual enjoyment*
bacchanal, bacchanalia, bender*, binge*, blowout*, bout*, carousal, circus*, debauch, dissipation, excess, feast, fling*, indulgence, jag*,
merrymaking, overindulgence, party, rampage*,
revel, revelry, saturnalia, splurge, spree, surfeit,
tear*; SEE CONCEPTS *377,383*

orient [*v*] *familiarize*
acclimatize, adapt, adjust, align, conform, determine, direct, get one's bearings*, locate, orientate, turn; SEE CONCEPTS *35,202*

orientation [*n*] *introduction, adjustment*
acclimatization, adaptation, assimilation, bearings, breaking in*, coordination, direction, familiarization, fix*, lay of the land*, location,
position, sense of direction, settling in*; SEE CON-
CEPTS *31,832*

origin [*n1*] *cause, basis*
agent, ancestor, ancestry, antecedent, author,
base, causality, causation, connection, creator,
derivation, determinant, egg*, element, embryo,
fountain, generator, germ, horse's mouth*, impulse, inception, inducement, influence, inspira-

op
or

tion, mainspring, motive, nucleus, occasion, parent, parentage, principle, producer, progenitor, provenance, provenience, root, roots, seed, source, spring, stock, well, wellspring; SEE CONCEPTS 229,648,661

origin [n2] *beginning, inception*
alpha, birth, blast off, commencement, creation, dawn, dawning, day one*, early stage, embarkation, emergence, entrance, entry, forging, foundation, genesis, git go*, inauguration, ingress, initiation, introduction, launch, nativity, opener, origination, outbreak, outset, rise, square one*, start, starting point*; SEE CONCEPT 832

origin [n3] *family, heritage*
ancestry, beginnings, birth, blood, descent, extraction, lineage, maternity, parentage, paternity, pedigree, stock; SEE CONCEPT 296

original [n1] *standard, prototype*
archetype, coinage, creation, exemplar, forerunner, invention, model, novelty, paradigm, pattern, precedent, precursor, type; SEE CONCEPTS 260,686

original [n2] *person who is eccentric*
anomaly, card*, case*, character, eccentric, nonconformist, oddball, oddity, queer, weirdo*; SEE CONCEPT 423

original [adj1] *earliest*
aboriginal, archetypal, authentic, autochthonous, beginning, commencing, early, elementary, embryonic, first, first-hand, genuine, inceptive, infant, initial, introductory, opening, pioneer, primary, prime, primeval, primitive, primordial, pristine, prototypal, rudimental, rudimentary, starting, underivative, underived; SEE CONCEPTS 549,585

original [adj2] *fresh, new*
avant garde, breaking new ground*, causal, causative, conceiving, creative, demiurgic, devising, envisioning, fertile, formative, generative, imaginative, ingenious, innovational, innovative, innovatory, inspiring, inventive, novel, originative, productive, quick, ready, resourceful, seminal, sensitive, unconventional, unprecedented, untried, unusual; SEE CONCEPTS 578,589,797

originality [n] *creativeness*
boldness, brilliance, cleverness, creative spirit, creativity, daring, freshness, imagination, imaginativeness, individuality, ingeniousness, ingenuity, innovation, innovativeness, invention, inventiveness, modernity, new idea, newness, nonconformity, novelty, resourcefulness, spirit, unconventionality, unorthodoxy; SEE CONCEPTS 409,410

originally [adv] *initially*
at first, at the outset, at the start, basically, by birth, by origin, first, formerly, incipiently, in the beginning, in the first place, primarily, primitively, to begin with; SEE CONCEPTS 578,585,797,799

originate [v1] *begin; spring*
arise, be born, birth, come, come from, come into existence, commence, dawn, derive, emanate, emerge, flow, hail from, issue, proceed, result, rise, start, stem; SEE CONCEPTS 105,221

originate [v2] *create, introduce*
break the ice*, bring about, cause, coin, come up with, compose, conceive, develop, discover, evolve, form, formulate, found, generate, give birth to, hatch, inaugurate, initiate, innovate, institute, invent, launch, make, open up, parent,

pioneer, procreate, produce, set in motion, set up, spark, spawn, start, think up, usher in; SEE CONCEPTS 43,173,251

ornament [n] *decoration*
accessory, adornment, art, bauble, beautification, design, doodad*, embellishment, embroidery, flower, frill, frou frou*, garnish, gewgaw*, gimcrack*, gingerbread*, honor, jewel, knickknack*, pride, treasure, trimming, trinket; SEE CONCEPTS 259,476

ornament [v] *decorate*
adorn, array, beautify, bedeck, bedizen, brighten, deck, dress, dress up*, embellish, embroider, enrich, festoon, fix up*, garnish, gild, grace, ornamentalize, polish, prank, prettify, primp, prink, smarten*, spruce up*, trim; SEE CONCEPTS 162,167,177

ornamental [adj] *decorative*
accessory, adorning, attractive, beautiful, beautifying, decking, decorating, delicate, dressy, elaborate, embellishing, enhancing, exquisite, fancy, festooned, florid, for show*, furbishing, garnishing, heightening, luxurious, ornate, setting off*, showy; SEE CONCEPTS 579,589

ornate [adj] *fancily decorated*
adorned, aureate, baroque, beautiful, bedecked, bright, brilliant, busy, colored, convoluted, dazzling, elaborate, elegant, embroidered, fancy, fine, flamboyant, flashy, flaunting, florid, flowery, fussy, gaudy, gilded, glamorous, glitzy, glossy, high-wrought, jeweled, lavish, luscious, magnificent, meretricious, opulent, ornamented, ostentatious, overdone, overelaborate, pretentious, resplendent, rich, rococo, showy, sparkling, splashy, sumptuous, superficial, tawdry, variegated; SEE CONCEPTS 579,589

orphan [n] *child without parents*
foundling, ragamuffin*, stray, waif; SEE CONCEPT 414

orthodox [adj] *accepted, traditional*
according to the book*, acknowledged, admitted, approved, authoritative, buttoned-down*, by the numbers*, canonical, conformist, conservative, conventional, correct, customary, devout, diehard, doctrinal, established, in line*, legitimate, official, old-line*, pious, proper, punctilious, reactionary, received, recognized, religious, right, rightful, sanctioned, sound, square, standard, straight, straight arrow, traditional, traditionalistic, true, well-established; SEE CONCEPTS 533,558

oscillate [v] *change back and forth*
be unsteady, dangle, fishtail, flicker, fluctuate, librate, lurch, palpitate, pendulate, pitch, pivot, reel, ripple, rock, roll, seesaw, stagger, sway, swing, switch, swivel, teeter, teeter-totter*, thrash, toss, totter, undulate, vacillate, vary, vibrate, waddle, wag, waggle, waltz, wave, waver, whirl, wiggle, wobble; SEE CONCEPTS 13,147,697

ossify [v] *become hard from aging*
congeal, fossilize, freeze, harden, indurate, petrify, solidify, stiffen, thicken, turn to bone; SEE CONCEPT 469

ostensible [adj] *alleged, supposed*
apparent, avowed, colorable, demonstrative, exhibited, illusive, illusory, likely, manifest, notable, outward, plausible, pretended, professed, purported, quasi, seeming, semblant, so-called*, specious, superficial; SEE CONCEPTS 552,582

ostensibly [adv] apparently
at first blush*, evidently, externally, for all intents and purposes*, for show*, officially, on the face*, on the surface*, outwardly, professedly, seemingly, sensibly, superficially, supposedly, to the eye*; SEE CONCEPT 582

ostentation [n] exhibitionism, flashiness
affectation, array, boast, boasting, brag, braggadocio*, bragging, bravado, demonstration, display, exhibition, false front*, flamboyance, flash*, flaunting, flourish, fuss, garishness, grandstand play*, magnificence, pageant, pageantry, parade, parading, pomp, pomposity, pompousness, pretending, pretension, pretentiousness, put-on, shine*, show, showiness, showing off*, showoff*, spectacle, splendor, splurge, swagger*, swaggering, swank*, vainglory, vaunt*, vaunting*, window-dressing; SEE CONCEPTS 633,655

ostentatious [adj] flashy, showy
boastful, chichi*, classy, conspicuous, crass*, dashing, egotistic, exhibitionistic, extravagant, flamboyant, flatulent, flaunted, fussy, garish, gaudy, gay, glittery, grandiose, highfaluting*, jaunty, loud, obtrusive, peacocky, pompous, pretentious, spectacular, splashy, splurgy, sporty, swank, swanky*, theatrical, tinsel*, tony*, uptown*, vain, vulgar; SEE CONCEPTS 401,589

ostracize [v] exile, banish
avoid, blackball*, blacklist*, boycott, cast out, cold-shoulder*, cut, deport, displace, drop, exclude, excommunicate, expatriate, expel, expulse, leave in the cold, oust, reject, shun, shut out, snub, throw out; SEE CONCEPTS 25,384

other [adj1] additional, added
alternative, another, auxiliary, else, extra, farther, fresh, further, more, new, spare, supplementary; SEE CONCEPT 771

other [adj2] different
contrasting, disparate, dissimilar, distant, distinct, divergent, diverse, opposite, otherwise, remaining, separate, unalike, unequal, unlike, unrelated, variant; SEE CONCEPT 564

otherwise [adv] in another way; alternatively
any other way, contrarily, differently, diversely, elseways, if not, in different circumstances, on the other hand, or else, or then, under other conditions, variously; SEE CONCEPT 544

ounce [n] one-sixteenth of a pound/28.35 grams of weight
avoirdupois, troy, uncia; SEE CONCEPT 795

oust [v] expel, get rid of
banish, bereave, boot out*, bounce*, bundle off*, cast out, chase, depose, deprive, dethrone, discharge, disinherit, dislodge, displace, dispossess, divest, drive out, eject, evict, expulse, fire, force out, give the 1-2-3*, kick out, lay off, let go, lose, ostracize, pack off, pink slip*, relegate, remove, rob, sack, send packing*, show the door*, throw out, topple, transport, turn out, unseat; SEE CONCEPTS 25,211,351

out [adj] not possible; gone
absent, antiquated, at an end, away, behind the times*, cold, dated, dead, demode, doused, ended, exhausted, expired, extinguished, finished, impossible, not allowed, not on, old-fashioned, old-hat*, outmoded, outside, passé, ruled out, unacceptable, unfashionable, used up; SEE CONCEPTS 539,552,576

out [adv] outside, outdoors
out of doors, outward, without; SEE CONCEPT 583

outbreak [n] sudden happening
beginning, blowup, brawl, break, breaking, burst, bursting, commencement, commotion, convulsion, crack, crash, dawn, detonation, discharge, disorder, disruption, ebullition, effervescence, epidemic, eruption, explosion, fit, flare-up, flash, fury, gush, gushing, insurrection, irruption, mutiny, onset, outburst, outpouring, paroxysm, plague, rebellion, rending, revolution, roar, sally, sortie, spasm, spurt, storm, sundering, surge, thunder, tumult, uprising, volley; SEE CONCEPTS 2,86,179,832

outburst [n] fit of temper
access, attack, blow, burst, conniption*, discharge, eruption, explosion, flare, flare-up, frenzy, gush, gust, outbreak, outpouring, paroxysm, rapture, scene, spasm, storm, surge, tantrum, transport, upheaval; SEE CONCEPT 410

outcast [n] person who is unwanted, not accepted
bum*, castaway, deportee, derelict, displaced person, exile, expatriate, fugitive, gypsy, hobo*, persona non grata*, rascal, refugee, reprobate, tramp, untouchable, vagabond, vagrant, wretch; SEE CONCEPT 423

outcome [n] consequence, effect
aftereffect, aftermath, blowoff, causatum, chain reaction*, conclusion, end, end result*, event, fallout, issue, payback*, payoff*, reaction, result, score, sequel, upshot*; SEE CONCEPT 230

outcry [n] scream, exclamation
clamor, commotion, complaint, convulsion, cry, ferment, flak*, hoo-ha*, howl, hubba-hubba*, hullabaloo*, noise, objection, outburst, protest, screech, tumult, uproar, upturn, yell; SEE CONCEPTS 77,278

outdated/out-of-date [adj] old-fashioned
anachronous, antiquated, antique, archaic, back number*, behind the times*, dated, démodé, dusty, has-been*, moth-eaten*, musty, not with it*, obsolete, old, old-hat*, outmoded, out-of-style*, passé, square, tired, unfashionable, vintage; SEE CONCEPTS 578,589,797

outdo [v] better, overcome
beat, best, blow out of water*, bulldoze*, bury*, cook*, cream*, defeat, do in*, down*, eclipse, exceed, excel, fake out*, go one better*, leave behind*, lick*, outclass, outdistance, outfox, outgun, outjockey, outmaneuver, outrival, outshine, outsmart, outstrip, pull a fast one*, shake off*, shoot ahead*, snow*, surpass, top, transcend, trash*; SEE CONCEPTS 95,141

outdoor [adj/adv] in the open air
alfresco, casual, free, garden, healthful, hilltop, informal, in the open, invigorating, mountain, natural, nature-loving, out-of-doors, out of the house, outside, patio, picnic, rustic, unrestricted, woods, yard; SEE CONCEPT 583

outdoors [n] open air; nature
bucolic surroundings, country, countryside, environment, fresh air, garden, green earth*, hill, mountain, open, out-of-doors, patio, without, woods, yard; SEE CONCEPT 198

outer [adj] external, exposed
alien, beyond, exoteric, exterior, extraneous, extrinsic, outermost, outlying, outmost, outside, outward, over, peripheral, remote, superficial, surface, without; SEE CONCEPTS 484,583

outfit [n] set of clothes or equipment
accoutrements, apparatus, appliances, clothing, costume, ensemble, garb, gear, get-up*, guise,

or
ou

kit, machinery, materiel, outlay, paraphernalia, provisions, rig, rigging, suit, supplies, tackle, togs, trappings*, wardrobe; SEE CONCEPTS 451,496

outfit [n2] *large group; business*
band, clique, company, concern, corps, coterie, crew, enterprise, establishment, firm, house, organization, party, set, squad, team, troop, troupe, unit; SEE CONCEPTS 325,417

outfit [v] *clothe, equip*
accoutre, appoint, arm, deck out*, drape, fit out*, furnish, gear, prepare, provide, provision, rig up*, stock, suit, supply, tog*, turn out*; SEE CONCEPTS 167,182

outgoing [adj1] *demonstrative, extroverted*
approachable, civil, communicative, cordial, easy, expansive, extrovert, friendly, genial, gregarious, informal, kind, open, sociable, sympathetic, unconstrained, unreserved, unrestrained, warm; SEE CONCEPT 404

outgoing [adj2] *leaving*
departing, ex-*, former, last, migratory, outbound, outward-bound, past, retiring, withdrawing; SEE CONCEPTS 581,584

outgrowth [n1] *projection*
bulge, enlargement, excrescence, jut, node, offshoot, outcrop, process, prolongation, prominence, protuberance, shoot, sprout, swelling; SEE CONCEPTS 471,824

outgrowth [n2] *product, consequence*
aftereffect, branch, by-product*, derivative, descendant, development, effect, emergence, end, end result*, issue, member, offshoot, offspring, outcome, result, spin-off*, yield; SEE CONCEPTS 230,260

outing [n] *short trip*
airing, drive, excursion, expedition, jaunt, junket, long weekend, picnic, pleasure trip, roundabout, spin*, vacation, weekend; SEE CONCEPTS 224,386

outing [n2] *politically motivated exposure of another's secrets*
announcement, declaration, demystification, disclosure, proclamation, revealing, tossing, uncloseting, unmasking; SEE CONCEPT 60

outlandish [adj] *bizarre, strange*
alien, awkward, barbaric, barbarous, boorish, clumsy, curious, droll, eccentric, erratic, exotic, extravagant, fantastic, far-out*, foreign, freakish, gauche, graceless, grotesque, kinky*, odd, outrageous, outré, peculiar, preposterous, quaint, queer, ridiculous, rude, singular, tasteless, ultra, unconventional, uncouth, unheard-of*, unorthodox, unusual, weird, whimsical, wild; SEE CONCEPTS 401,548

outlast [v] *endure beyond another*
hang on, outlive, outstay, outwear, remain, survive; SEE CONCEPT 407

outlaw [n] *person who is running from the law*
bandit, brigand, con, criminal, crook, desperado, drifter, ex-con, fugitive, gangster, gunslinger*, hood*, hoodlum, hooligan*, jailbird, marauder, mobster, mug*, outcast, pariah, racketeer, robber, wrong number*; SEE CONCEPT 412

outlaw [v] *prohibit; make illegal*
ban, banish, bar, condemn, damn, disallow, embargo, enjoin, exclude, forbid, illegalize, inhibit, interdict, prevent, proscribe, stop, taboo; SEE CONCEPTS 121,317

outlay [n] *expenses*
bite*, bottom line*, charge, cost, damage, disbursement, expenditure, expense, highway robbery*, investment, price tag, secret*, setback*, spending, tab*, throw*, tune*; SEE CONCEPT 344

outlet [n1] *place or means of escape, release*
aperture, avenue, break, channel, crack, duct, egress, escape, exit, hole, nozzle, opening, orifice, porthole, release, safety valve, spout, tear, vent, way out; SEE CONCEPTS 513,693

outlet [n2] *store that sells discounted items*
factory store, market, mill store, seconds store, shop, showroom; SEE CONCEPTS 439,448,449

outline [n1] *plan, sketch*
bare facts*, blueprint, diagram, draft, drawing, floor plan, frame, framework, ground plan, layout, main features, recapitulation, résumé, rough draft, rough idea, rundown, skeleton, summary, synopsis, thumbnail sketch*, tracing; SEE CONCEPT 268

outline [n2] *form, tracing of an object*
configuration, conformation, contour, delineation, figuration, figure, profile, shape, silhouette; SEE CONCEPTS 436,625

outline [v] *sketch out; plan*
adumbrate, block out, characterize, chart, delineate, describe, draft, lay out, paint, plot, recapitulate, rough out, sketch, skeletonize, summarize, tell about, trace; SEE CONCEPTS 36,55,174

outlook [n1] *point of view*
angle*, attitude, direction, frame of mind*, headset*, mind-set*, perspective, routine, scope, side, size of it*, slant*, standpoint, viewpoint, views, vision; SEE CONCEPTS 410,689

outlook [n2] *probable future*
appearances, chance, expectation, forecast, law of averages*, likelihood, normal course, opening, opportunity, possibility, probability, prospect, prospects, risk; SEE CONCEPT 679

outlook [n3] *scene, view*
aspect, lookout, panorama, perspective, prospect, scape, sight, vista; SEE CONCEPTS 509,628

outlying [adj] *in rural area; remote*
afar, backwoods, distant, external, faraway, far-flung*, far-off, off-lying, outer, out-of-the-way*, peripheral, provincial, removed; SEE CONCEPT 583

outmoded [adj] *obsolete, old-fashioned*
anachronistic, antediluvian, antiquated, antique, archaic, behind the times*, bent, bygone, dated, dead, démodé, dinosaur*, disused, extinct, fossilized, has-been*, horse and buggy*, moldy*, moth-eaten*, musty*, obsolescent, obsolete, olden, old-hat*, old-time, out, out-of-date, out-of-style, outworn, passé*, superannuated, superseded, tired, unfashionable, unstylish, unusable, vintage; SEE CONCEPTS 560,578,589,797

output [n] *something produced*
achievement, amount, crop, gain, harvest, making, manufacture, manufacturing, producing, product, production, productivity, profit, take, turnout, yield; SEE CONCEPTS 205,260

outrage [n1] *atrocity, evil*
abuse, affront, barbarism, damage, desecration, enormity, evildoing, harm, hurt, indignity, inhumanity, injury, insult, mischief, misdoing, offense, profanation, rape, rapine, ravishing, ruin, shock, violation, violence, wrongdoing; SEE CONCEPTS 192,645,674

outrage [n2] *anger*
blowup, flare-up*, fury, huff*, hurt, indignation, resentment, ruckus*, shock*, stew*, storm*, wrath; SEE CONCEPT **29**

outrage [v] *wrong, offend, abuse*
affront, aggrieve, boil over*, burn up*, defile, deflower, desecrate, do violence to, fire up*, force, ill-treat, incense, infuriate, injure, insult, jar*, kick up a row*, madden, make hit the ceiling*, maltreat, mistreat, misuse, oppress, persecute, raise Cain*, rape, ravage, ravish, reach boiling point*, scandalize, shock, spoil, violate, whip up*; SEE CONCEPTS **7,19,29,246**

outrageous [adj1] *very bad*
abominable, atrocious, barbaric, beastly, brazen, contemptible, contumelious, corrupt, criminal, debasing, debauching, degenerate, depraving, disgraceful, disgracing, egregious, flagitious, flagrant, gross, heinous, horrendous, horrible, ignoble, infamous, inhuman, iniquitous, malevolent, monstrous, nefarious, notorious, odious, opprobrious, scandalous, scurrilous, shameless, shaming, shocking, sinful, unbearable, ungodly, unspeakable, villainous, violent, wanton, wicked; SEE CONCEPT **571**

outrageous [adj2] *beyond reasonable limits*
barbarous, crazy*, excessive, exorbitant, extortionate, extravagant, immoderate, inordinate, last straw*, offensive, out of bounds*, preposterous, scandalous, shocking, steep*, too much*, uncivilized, unconscionable, unreasonable; SEE CONCEPTS **569,771**

outright [adj] *complete, unconditional*
absolute, all, arrant, consummate, definite, direct, downright, entire, flat, gross, out-and-out*, perfect, positive, pure, straightforward, thorough, thoroughgoing, total, undeniable, unequivocal, unmitigated, unqualified, utter, whole, wholesale; SEE CONCEPTS **531,535**

outside [n] *exterior; out-of-doors*
appearance, covering, facade, face, front, integument, open, open air, outdoors, seeming, sheath, skin, surface, topside, without; SEE CONCEPTS **198,484**

outside [adj1] *external*
alfresco, alien, apart from, away from, exterior, extramural, extraneous, extreme, farther, farthest, foreign, furthest, open-air, out, outdoor, outer, outermost, outward, over, surface; SEE CONCEPTS **484,583**

outside [adj2] *slight, slim*
distant, faint, far, marginal, negligible, off, remote, slender, small, unlikely; SEE CONCEPTS **552,789**

outsider [n] *person who is foreign to something*
alien, floater*, foreigner, incomer*, interloper, intruder, newcomer, odd one out*, outlander, refugee, stranger; SEE CONCEPTS **413,423**

outskirts [n] *edge of a geographic area*
bedroom community*, border, boundary, edge, environs, limit, outpost, periphery, purlieu, purlieus, sticks*, suburb, suburbia, vicinity; SEE CONCEPTS **508,513**

outspoken [adj] *explicit, unreserved*
abrupt, artless, blunt, calling spade a spade*, candid, direct, forthright, frank, free, laying it on the line*, open, plain, plain-spoken, point-blank*, round, square, straightforward, strident, talking turkey*, unceremonious, unequivocal, unreticent, up front*, vocal; SEE CONCEPTS **267,404**

outstanding [adj1] *superior, excellent*
ace*, A-number-1*, A-1*, bad*, boss*, capital*, celebrated, chief, cool*, crack*, distinguished, dominant, eminent, eventful, exceptional, famous, far-out*, great, greatest, hundred-proof*, important, impressive, magnificent, main, major, meritorious, momentous, mostest, number one*, out-of-sight*, out-of-this-world*, phenomenal, predominant, preeminent, primo*, principal, special, standout, star, steller, super, superlative, tops*, well-known, world-class; SEE CONCEPTS **568,574**

outstanding [adj2] *noticeable, striking*
arresting, arrestive, conspicuous, distinguished, eye-catching, important, leading, marked, memorable, notable, noteworthy, prominent, pronounced, remarkable, salient, signal; SEE CONCEPTS **485,537**

outstanding [adj3] *referring to an unpaid debt*
due, mature, ongoing, open, overdue, owing, payable, pending, remaining, uncollected, unresolved, unsettled; SEE CONCEPT **334**

outward [adj] *visible; for appearances*
apparent, evident, exterior, external, from within, noticeable, observable, obvious, on the surface, open, ostensible, out, outer, outside, over, perceptible, superficial, surface, to the eye, toward the edge; SEE CONCEPTS **576,581,583**

outwardly [adv] *to all appearances*
apparently, as far as one can see, evidently, externally, for all intents and purposes*, in appearance, officially, on the face of it, on the surface, ostensibly, professedly, seemingly, superficially, to the eye; SEE CONCEPTS **544,576**

outweigh [v] *override, dominate*
atone for, balance, cancel out, compensate, counterbalance, counterpoise, countervail, eclipse, exceed, excel, make up for, offset, outbalance, outrival, outrun, overcome, overshadow, predominate, preponderate, prevail, set off, surpass, take precedence, tip the scales; SEE CONCEPT **141**

outwit/outsmart [v] *get the better of; figure out before another*
baffle, bamboozle*, beat*, bewilder, cap, cheat, circumvent, con*, confuse, deceive, defeat, defraud, dupe, end-run*, fake out*, finagle*, fox*, goose*, gull*, have*, hoax, hoodwink, lead astray*, make a fool of*, make a monkey of*, mislead, outdo, outfox, outgeneral, outguess, outjockey, outmaneuver, outthink, overreach, pull a fast one on*, put one over on*, run circles around*, swindle, take in*, top*, trick, worst*; SEE CONCEPTS **15,59**

oval [adj] *long and rounded in shape*
egg-shaped, ellipsoidal, elliptic, elliptical, oblong, ooid, ovaloid, ovate, oviform, ovoid; SEE CONCEPT **486**

ovation [n] *clapping and cheers*
acclaim, acclamation, applause, big hand*, bravos, cheering, hand, laudation, plaudits, praise, salvo, testimonial, tribute; SEE CONCEPTS **69,264**

over [adj1] *accomplished*
ancient history, at an end, by, bygone, closed, completed, concluded, done, done with, ended, finished, gone, past, settled, up; SEE CONCEPTS **531,548**

over [adj2/adv1] *in addition*
additionally, beyond, ever, excessively, extra, extremely, immensely, in excess, inordinately, left

over, more, over and above, overly, overmuch, remaining, superfluous, surplus, too, unduly, unused; SEE CONCEPTS *544,771*

over [*adv2*] *above*
aloft, beyond, covering, farther up, higher than, in heaven, in the sky, off, on high, on top of, overhead, overtop, straight up, traversely, upstairs; SEE CONCEPTS *583,793*

overabundance [*n*] *excess*
embarrassment of riches*, glut, nimiety, overflow, overkill, overmuch, oversupply, plethora, profusion, superabundance, superfluity, surfeit, surplus, surplusage, too much*; SEE CONCEPTS *767,787*

overall [*adj*] *complete, general*
all-embracing, blanket, comprehensive, global, inclusive, long-range, long-term, sweeping, thorough, total, umbrella; SEE CONCEPT *772*

overall [*adv*] *in general*
all over, chiefly, everyplace, everywhere, generally speaking, in the long run, largely, mainly, mostly, on the whole, predominantly, primarily, principally, throughout; SEE CONCEPTS *548,772*

overbearing [*adj*] *arrogant, domineering*
ascendant, autocratic, bossy, cavalier, cocky*, despotic, dictatorial, disdainful, dogmatic, egotistic, haughty, high-and-mighty*, high-handed*, imperative, imperial, imperious, insolent, magisterial, officious, oppressive, overweening, paramount, peremptory, predominant, preponderant, prevalent, proud, regnant, sniffy*, snotty*, sovereign, stuffy, supercilious, superior, tyrannical, uppity*; SEE CONCEPTS *401,404*

overblown [*adj*] *excessive, too much*
aureate, bombastic, disproportionate, euphuistic, flowery, fulsome, grandiloquent, hyped up*, immoderate, inflated, magniloquent, oratorical, overdone, pompous, pretentious, profuse, rhetorical, sonorous, superfluous, turgid, undue, verbose, windy; SEE CONCEPTS *267,548*

overcast [*adj*] *cloudy, darkened*
clouded, clouded over, dark, dismal, dreary, dull, gray, hazy, leaden, lowering, murky, nebulous, not clear, not fair, oppressive, somber, sunless, threatening; SEE CONCEPT *525*

overcome [*adj*] *overwhelmed; visibly moved*
affected, at a loss for words, beaten, blown-away*, bowled-over*, buried*, conquered, defeated, overthrown, run-over*, speechless, swamped, swept off one's feet*, taken*, unable to continue; SEE CONCEPT *403*

overcome [*v*] *beat, defeat*
best*, be victorious, come out on top*, conquer, crush, down*, drown, get around*, get the better of*, hurdle, knock over*, knock socks off*, lick*, master, outlive, overpower, overthrow, overwhelm, prevail, prostrate, reduce, render, rise above*, shock, stun, subdue, subjugate, surmount, survive, throw*, triumph over, vanquish, weather*, whelm*, win, worst*; SEE CONCEPT *95*

overconfident [*adj*] *overly sure of oneself*
brash, careless, cocksure*, cocky*, foolhardy, heading for a fall*, heedless, hubristic, impudent, overweening, presuming, presumptuous, pushy*, rash, reckless, self-assertive; SEE CONCEPTS *401,542*

overdo [*v*] *go to extremes; carry too far*
amplify, be intemperate, belabor, bite off too much*, do to death, drive oneself, exaggerate, fatigue, go overboard*, go too far*, hype, lay it

on*, magnify, make federal case*, not know when to stop*, overburden, overestimate, overindulge, overload, overplay, overrate, overreach, overstate, overtax, overtire, overuse, overvalue, overwork, pile on*, pressure, puff*, run into the ground*, run riot*, strain oneself, stretch, talk big*, wear down*, wear oneself out*; SEE CONCEPTS *87,112,156*

overdue [*adj*] *late, behind schedule*
behindhand, behind time, belated, delinquent, due, held up*, hung up*, jammed*, long delayed, mature, not punctual, outstanding, owing, payable, tardy, unpaid, unpunctual, unsettled; SEE CONCEPTS *334,548,799*

overflow [*n*] *flood, inundation*
advance, cataclysm, cataract, congestion, deluge, discharge, encroachment, enforcement, engorgement, excess, exuberance, flash flood, flooding, infringement, niagara, overabundance, overcrowding, overkill, overmuch, overproduction, plethora, pour, propulsion, push, redundancy, spate, spill, spillover, submergence, submersion, superfluity, surfeit, surplus, torrent; SEE CONCEPT *740*

overflow [*v*] *pour out, flood*
brim, bubble over, cascade, cover, deluge, discharge, drain, drown, engulf, fall over, gush, inundate, irrupt, issue, jet, leak, overbrim, overrun, overtop, pour, run over, rush, shed, shower, slop, slosh, soak, spill, spill over, spout, spray, spurt, squirt, submerge, surge, swamp, water, wave, well, well over, wet, whelm; SEE CONCEPTS *179,256,740*

overhang [*v*] *bulge, hang over*
beetle, be imminent, be suspended, cast a shadow, command, dangle over, droop over, endanger, extend, flap over, impend, jut, loom, menace, overtop, poke, portend, pouch, project, protrude, rise above, stand out, stick out, swing over, threaten, tower above; SEE CONCEPT *752*

overhaul [*v*] *redo, restore*
check, debug, doctor*, do up*, examine, fiddle with*, fix, give facelift*, improve, inspect, mend, modernize, patch, rebuild, recondition, reconstruct, reexamine, renew, repair, retread, revamp, service, survey; SEE CONCEPTS *126,202,212*

overhead [*n*] *general, continuing costs of operation*
budget, burden, cost, depreciation, expense, expenses, insurance, outlay, rent, upkeep, utilities; SEE CONCEPTS *329,332*

overhead [*adj/adv*] *up above*
above, aerial, aloft, atop, hanging, in the sky, on high, over, overhanging, roof, skyward, upper, upward; SEE CONCEPT *586*

overjoyed [*adj*] *extremely happy*
charmed, delighted, deliriously happy, elated, euphoric, happy as a clam*, happy as a lark*, joyful, jubilant, on cloud nine*, only too happy*, over the moon*, rapturous, ravished, thrilled, tickled pink*, transported; SEE CONCEPT *403*

overlap [*v*] *lie over something else*
extend along, flap, fold over, go beyond, imbricate, lap over, overhang, overlay, overlie, overrun, project, protrude, ride, run over, shingle; SEE CONCEPT *759*

overlook [*v1*] *disregard, neglect*
discount, disdain, fail to notice, forget, ignore, leave out, leave undone, let fall between the cracks*, let go, let slide*, make light of*, miss,

omit, overpass, pass, pass by, pay no attention, slight, slip up*; SEE CONCEPTS *30,101,699*

overlook [v2] *make allowances for*
bear with*, blink at*, condone, disregard, excuse, forgive, go along with, grin and bear it*, handle, ignore, let bygones be bygones*, let go, let pass*, live with*, look the other way, pay no mind*, play past*, put up with*, roll with punches*, stand for, stomach, swim with the tide*, take, tune out*, turn blind eye to*, whitewash*, wink at*, wipe slate clean*; SEE CONCEPTS *10,83*

overlook [v3] *have a view of something*
afford a view, command, command a view, dominate, front on, give on, give upon, have a prospect of, inspect, look down, look out, look out on, look over, mount, oversee, overtop, soar above, surmount, survey, top, tower over, view, watch over; SEE CONCEPT *752*

overlook [v4] *supervise*
boss, chaperon, control, oversee, quarterback*, superintend, survey; SEE CONCEPTS *94,117*

overly [adv] *excessively*
ever, exceedingly, extremely, immensely, immoderately, inordinately, over, overfull, overmuch, too, too much, too-too*, unduly, very much; SEE CONCEPT *544*

overplay [v] *be dramatic*
accent, accentuate, blow out of proportion*, dramatize, exaggerate, get carried away*, ham it up*, hyperbolize, labor at, lay it on thick*, magnify, maximize, mug*, overact, overdo, overdraw, overemphasize, overstate, overstress, overuse, overwork, point up*, show off*, stretch; SEE CONCEPTS *59,87,202*

overpower [v] *beat; get the upper hand*
bear down, beat down, blank, blow away*, bulldoze*, bury, clobber, conquer, cream*, crush, defeat, drown, drub*, immobilize, knock out*, lay one out*, murder*, overcome, overthrow, overwhelm, prostrate, put away*, quell, reduce, roll over*, rout, shellack*, shut off*, smash*, subdue, subjugate, swamp*, take care of*, take out*, torpedo*, total*, trash*, trounce, vanquish, waste*, wax*, whelm*; SEE CONCEPTS *95,191*

overrate [v] *assign too much value, importance*
assess too highly, build up, exaggerate, exceed, expect too much of, magnify, make too much of*, overassess, overesteem, overestimate, overpraise, overprize, overreckon, oversell, overvalue, rate too highly, think too highly of*, think too much of*; SEE CONCEPTS *12,49*

override/overrule [v] *cancel, reverse a decision*
alter, annul, bend to one's will*, control, countermand, direct, disallow, disregard, dominate, govern, ignore, influence, invalidate, make null and void*, make void, not heed, nullify, outvote, outweigh, overturn, prevail over, quash, recall, repeal, rescind, revoke, ride roughshod*, rule against, set aside, supersede, sway, take no account of, thwart, trample, upset, vanquish, veto; SEE CONCEPTS *50,88,121,298,317*

overriding [adj] *central, most important*
cardinal, compelling, determining, dominant, final, main, major, number one*, overruling, paramount, pivotal, predominant, prevailing, primary, prime, principal, ruling, supreme, ultimate; SEE CONCEPT *568*

overrun [v1] *defeat, invade*
beat, clobber, drub*, foray, inroad, lambaste, lick*, massacre, occupy, overwhelm, put to flight,

raid, rout, swamp*, thrash, trim, whip; SEE CONCEPTS *86,95*

overrun [v2] *infest, spread over; exceed*
beset, choke, deluge, go beyond, inundate, invade, overflow, overgrow, overshoot, overspread, overstep, overwhelm, permeate, ravage, run on, run over, spill, spread like wildfire*, surge, surpass, swarm, well over; SEE CONCEPTS *172,179,651*

overseas [adj] *across an ocean*
abroad, across, away, foreign, in foreign land, transatlantic, transoceanic, transpacific; SEE CONCEPT *583*

oversee [v] *manage, supervise*
baby-sit*, be in driver's seat*, boss, call the shots*, captain, chaperon, command, eye*, herd, inspect, keep one's eye on*, look after, overlook, quarterback*, ride herd on*, run the show*, shepherd, sit on top of*, skipper, superintend, survey, watch; SEE CONCEPT *117*

overseer [n] *person who supervises others' work*
executive, head, head honcho*, manager, pit boss*, straw boss*, superintendent, supervisor; SEE CONCEPT *347*

overshadow [v] *make obscure, dim, vague*
adumbrate, becloud, bedim, cloud, command, darken, dim, dominate, dwarf, eclipse, excel, govern, haze, leave in the shade*, obfuscate, outshine, outweigh, overcast, overcloud, overweigh, preponderate, rise above*, rule, shadow, steal spotlight*, surpass, take precedence, tower above*, veil; SEE CONCEPTS *620,668*

oversight [n1] *failure, omission*
blank*, blunder, carelessness, chasm, default, delinquency, dereliction, disregard, error, fault, inattention, lapse, laxity, misuse, mistake, neglect, overlook, overlooking, preterition, pretermission, skip, slip, slipup*; SEE CONCEPT *101*

oversight [n2] *care, supervision*
administration, aegis, charge, check, control, custody, direction, guard, guardianship, handling, inspection, intendance, keep, keeping, maintenance, management, superintendence, surveillance, tutelage; SEE CONCEPT *117*

overt [adj] *obvious, unconcealed*
apparent, clear, definite, manifest, observable, open, patent, plain, public, undisguised, visible; SEE CONCEPT *535*

overtake [v] *catch; pass*
beat, befall, better, catch up with, come upon, engulf, gain on, get past, get to, happen, hit, leave behind, outdistance, outdo, outstrip, overhaul, overwhelm, reach, strike, take by surprise; SEE CONCEPTS *95,141*

overthrow [v] *defeat, destroy*
abolish, beat, bring down, bring to ruin, conquer, crush, demolish, depose, dethrone, do away with, eradicate, exterminate, knock down, knock over, level, liquidate, oust, overcome, overpower, overrun, overturn, overwhelm, purge, put an end to, raze, ruin, subdue, subjugate, subvert, terminate, tip, topple, tumble, unseat, upend, upset, vanquish; SEE CONCEPTS *95,252,320*

overtone [n] *implication, hint*
association, connotation, flavor, inference, innuendo, intimation, meaning, nuance, sense, suggestion, tone, undercurrent, undertone; SEE CONCEPT *278*

overture [n] *introduction, approach*
advance, bid, conciliatory move, exordium, fore-

word, invitation, offer, opening, preamble, preface, prelude, prelusion, presentation, proem, prologue, proposal, proposition, signal, suggestion, tender; SEE CONCEPTS *278,384,828,832*

overturn [*v*] *flip over*
annul, bring down, capsize, countermand, down, invalidate, invert, keel over, knock down, knock over, nullify, overbalance, prostrate, repeal, rescind, reverse, roll, set aside, spill, tip over, topple, tumble, turn over, turn upside down, upend, upset, upturn, void; SEE CONCEPTS *147,232*

overweight [*adj*] *heavier than average*
ample, bulky, corpulent, fat, fleshy, gross, heavy, hefty, huge, massive, obese, outsize, overfed, overstuffed, plump, portly, pudgy, rotund, stout, upholstered*, weighty; SEE CONCEPT *491*

overwhelm [*v1*] *flood, beat physically*
bury, conquer, crush, defeat, deluge, destroy, drown, drub*, engulf, inundate, massacre, overcome, overflow, overpower, overrun, overthrow, rout, smother, submerge, swamp, thrash, total*, whip*, win*; SEE CONCEPTS *86,95*

overwhelm [*v2*] *astonish, devastate*
bewilder, blow out of the water*, bowl over*, confound, confuse, demoralize, destroy, disturb, do in*, downgrade*, drown, dumbfound, floor*, kill*, overcome, overpower, prostrate, puzzle, render speechless*, run circles around, shatter, shock, stagger, steamroller*, stun, subordinate, surprise, swamp, upset, wreck; SEE CONCEPTS *16,42*

overwrought [*adj*] *exhausted and excited*
affected, agitated, all shook up*, beside oneself*, crazy, distracted, emotional, excitable, fired-up*, flipped out*, frantic, freaked-out*, high*, hot-and-bothered*, hot under collar*, hyper*, in a state*, keyed-up*, nervous, neurotic, on edge*,overexcited, overstrung, overworked, spent, steamed up*, stirred*, strung-out*, tense, tired, uneasy, unstrung*, uptight*, weary, wired, worked-up, wound-up; SEE CONCEPTS *401,403,542*

owe [*v*] *have an obligation*
be beholden, be bound, be contracted, behind, be in arrears, be in debt, be indebted, be into one for, be obligated, be under obligation, feel bound, get on credit, have borrowed, incur, in hock*, lost, on the tab*, ought to, run up a bill*; SEE CONCEPT *335*

owing [*adj*] *unpaid*
attributable, comeuppance, due, in debt, mature, matured, outstanding, overdue, owed, payable, unsettled; SEE CONCEPT *334*

own [*adj*] *belonging to individual*
endemic, hers, his, individual, inherent, intrinsic, its, mine, owned, particular, peculiar, personal, private, resident, theirs, very own, yours; SEE CONCEPT *710*

own [*v1*] *possess; be responsible for*
be in possession of, be possessed of, boast, control, dominate, enjoy, fall heir to, have, have in hand, have rights, have title, hold, inherit, keep, occupy, reserve, retain; SEE CONCEPT *710*

own [*v2*] *acknowledge, admit*
allow, assent to, avow, come clean*, concede, confess, declare, disclose, grant, let on*, make clean breast of*, own up, recognize, tell the truth; SEE CONCEPT *57*

owner [*n*] *person who has possession of something*
buyer, governor, heir, heir-apparent, heiress, heritor, holder, keeper, landowner, legatee, partner, possessor, proprietor, purchaser, sharer, squire, titleholder; SEE CONCEPTS *343,347,414*

ownership [*n*] *possession of property*
buying, claim, control, cut, deed, dominion, end, hand, having, holding, occupancy, partnership, piece, possessorship, property, proprietary rights, proprietorship, purchase, purchasing, residence, slice, takeover, tenancy, tenure, title, use; SEE CONCEPT *710*

P

pace [*n1*] *steps in walking*
clip, footstep, gait, getalong, lick*, measure, step, stride, tread, walk; SEE CONCEPT *149*

pace [*n2*] *speed, tempo of motion*
beat, bounce, celerity, clip, downbeat, lick*, momentum, motion, movement, progress, quickness, rapidity, rapidness, rate, swiftness, time, velocity; SEE CONCEPTS *755,818*

pace [*v1*] *walk back and forth*
ambulate, canter, foot it*, gallop, hoof*, march, patrol, pound*, step, stride, traipse, tread, troop, trot, walk up and down; SEE CONCEPT *149*

pace [*v2*] *measure by footsteps*
count, determine, mark out, step, step off*; SEE CONCEPTS *291,764*

pacify [*v*] *make peaceful; appease*
allay, ameliorate, assuage, bury the hatchet*, butter up*, calm, chasten, compose, con, conciliate, cool, dulcify, fix up, grease*, kiss and make up*, lay back, lull, make peace, mitigate, moderate, mollify, pacificate, placate, propitiate, put the lid on*, qualify, quell, quiet, relieve, repress, silence, smooth over, soften, soft-pedal*, soothe, square, still, stroke, subdue, sweeten*, take the edge off*, tame, temper, tranquilize; SEE CONCEPTS *7,22,250*

pack [*n1*] *kit, package*
backpack, baggage, bale, bundle, burden, equipment, haversack, knapsack, load, luggage, outfit, parcel, rucksack, truss; SEE CONCEPTS *260,446,496*

pack [*n2*] *group, bunch*
assemblage, band, barrel, bundle, circle, collection, company, crew, crowd, deck, drove, flock, gang, great deal, heap, herd, horde, lot, lump, mess, mob, much, multiplicity, number, peck, pile, press, set, swarm, throng, troop; SEE CONCEPTS *397,417,432*

pack [*v1*] *make ready for transport*
batch, bind, brace, bunch, bundle, burden, collect, dispose, fasten, gather, get ready, load, package, put in order, store, stow, tie, warehouse; SEE CONCEPT *202*

pack [*v2*] *fill, compact*
arrange, bind, charge, chock, choke, compress, condense, contract, cram, crowd, drive in, heap, insert, jam, jam-pack*, lade, load, mob, pile, press, push, put away, ram, ram in*, sardine*, squeeze, stuff, tamp, throng, thrust in, top off, wedge; SEE CONCEPT *209*

pack [*v3*] *transport, carry*
bear, buck, convey, ferry, freight, gun, haul, heel,

hump, jag, journey, lug, piggyback*, ride, shlep*, shoulder, tote, trek, truck; SEE CONCEPTS 148,217

package [n] *bundle; whole*
amalgamation, assortment, bag, baggage, bale, batch, biddle, bottle, box, bunch, burden, can, carton, combination, container, crate, entity, kit, load, lot, luggage, pack, packet, parcel, pile, sack, sheaf, stack, suitcase, tin, trunk, unit; SEE CONCEPTS 432,494

packed [adj] *full*
arranged, awash, brimful, brimming, bundled, chock, chock-full*, compact, compressed, congested, consigned, crammed, crowded, filled, full to the gills*, jammed, jam-packed*, loaded, mobbed, overflowing, overloaded, packed like sardines*, seething, serried, stuffed, swarming, to the roof*, tumid, up to the hilt*, up to the rafters*, wall-to-wall*, wrapped; SEE CONCEPTS 481,483,740,774

packet [n] *small, often flat, bundle*
bag, carton, container, envelope, file, folder, package, parcel, wrapper, wrapping; SEE CONCEPT 494

pact [n] *agreement*
alliance, arrangement, bargain, bond, compact, concord, concordat, contract, convention, covenant, deal, league, paper, piece of paper, protocol, settlement, transaction, treaty, understanding; SEE CONCEPTS 271,684

pad/padding [n1] *protection*
buffer, cushion, filling, packing, stuffing, wad, wadding, waste; SEE CONCEPTS 473,475

pad [n2] *tablet of paper*
block, jotter, memorandum, notebook, notepad, paper, parchment, quire, ream, scratch, scratch pad, slips; SEE CONCEPTS 260,475

pad [v1] *protect with cushioning*
cushion, fill out, line, pack, protect, shape, stuff; SEE CONCEPTS 134,202

pad [v2] *elaborate, amplify*
augment, bulk, embellish, embroider, enlarge, exaggerate, expand, fill out, flesh out*, fudge*, increase, inflate, lengthen, magnify, overdraw, overstate, protract, spin, stretch; SEE CONCEPTS 63,244

pad [v3] *walk quietly; walk ploddingly*
creep, go barefoot, hike, march, patter*, pitter-patter*, plod, pussyfoot*, sneak, steal, traipse, tramp, trek, trudge; SEE CONCEPT 149

paddle [n] *item used for propelling object*
oar, paddlewheel, pole, propeller, pull, scull, sweep; SEE CONCEPTS 479,499

paddle [v] *propel with arms or tool*
boat, cruise, cut water*, drift, drive, navigate, oar, pull, row, run rapids*, scull, sky an oar*, slop, splash, stir, sweep, thrash, wade; SEE CONCEPT 147

pagan [n] *person who does not believe in an orthodox religion*
agnostic, atheist, doubter, freethinker, heathen, heretic, iconoclast, idolater, idolist, infidel, paganist, pantheist, polytheist, scoffer, skeptic, unbeliever; SEE CONCEPTS 361,423

pagan [adj] *irreligious*
agnostic, atheistic, heathen, idolatrous, impious, infidel, polytheistic, profane; SEE CONCEPT 542

page [n1] *sheet of paper*
folio, leaf, recto, side, signature, surface, verso; SEE CONCEPT 475

page [n2] *person who serves others*
attendant, bellhop, equerry, errand runner, servant, youth; SEE CONCEPTS 348,354

page [v1] *call for over communications system*
announce, beep, call, call out, call the name of, hunt for, preconize, seek, send for, summon; SEE CONCEPTS 74,78

page [v2] *mark sheets of document*
check, count, foliate, number, paginate; SEE CONCEPTS 79,764

pageant [n] *spectacle or contest*
celebration, charade, display, exhibition, exposition, extravaganza, fair, make-believe, motorcade, parade, pomp, procession, ritual, show, tableau; SEE CONCEPTS 292,377

pain [n1] *physical suffering*
ache, affliction, agony, burn, catch, convulsion, cramp, crick, discomfort, distress, fever, gripe, hurt, illness, injury, irritation, laceration, malady, misery, pang, paroxysm, prick, sickness, smarting, soreness, spasm, sting, stitch, strain, tenderness, throb, throe, tingle, torment, torture, trouble, twinge, wound; SEE CONCEPTS 316,728

pain [n2] *mental suffering*
affliction, agony, anguish, anxiety, bitterness, despondency, distress, grief, heartache, hurt, malaise, martyrdom, misery, rack, sadness, shock, suffering, torment, torture, travail, tribulation, woe, worry, wretchedness; SEE CONCEPTS 410,728

pain [n3] *problem*
aggravation, annoyance, bore, bother, drag, effort, exertion, irritation, nuisance, pest, trouble, vexation; SEE CONCEPT 532

pain [v] *bother, trouble*
ache, afflict, aggrieve, agonize, ail, anguish, annoy, bite, chafe, chasten, constrain, convulse, cut to the quick*, discomfort, disquiet, distress, exasperate, excruciate, gall, grieve, gripe, harass, harm, harrow, hit where one lives*, hurt, inflame, injure, irk, irritate, nick, prick, punish, rack, rile, sadden, smart, sting, strain, stress, suffer, throb, tingle, torment, torture, upset, vex, worry, wound; SEE CONCEPTS 7,19,246

painful [adj] *physically or mentally agonizing*
aching, afflictive, agonizing, arduous, awful, biting, burning, caustic, difficult, dire, disagreeable, distasteful, distressing, dreadful, excruciating, extreme, extremely bad, grievous, hard, harrowing, hurtful, hurting, inflamed, irritated, laborious, piercing, raw, saddening, sensitive, severe, sharp, smarting, sore, stinging, tedious, tender, terrible, throbbing, tormenting, troublesome, trying, uncomfortable, unpleasant, vexatious; SEE CONCEPTS 529,537

painstaking [adj] *meticulous, thorough*
assiduous, by the book*, by the numbers*, careful, conscientious, conscionable, diligent, earnest, exact, exacting, finicky, fussbudget*, fussy, hardworking, heedful, industrious, particular, persevering, persnickety*, picky, punctilious, punctual, scrupulous, sedulous, stickler*, strenuous, thoroughgoing; SEE CONCEPTS 326,538

paint [n] *tinted covering*
acrylic, chroma, color, coloring, cosmetic, dye, emulsion, enamel, flat, gloss, greasepaint, latex, makeup, oil, overlay, pigment, rouge, stain, tempera, varnish, veneer, wax; SEE CONCEPTS 467,475

ov
pa

paint [v] *apply colored tint, often to make design*
brush, catch a likeness, coat, color, compose, cover, cover up, daub, decorate, delineate, depict, design, draft, draw, dye, figure, fresco, gloss over, limn, ornament, outline, picture, portray, put on coats*, represent, shade, sketch, slap on*, slather, stipple, swab, tint, touch up, wash; SEE CONCEPTS 172,174

pair [n] *two of something*
brace, combination, combine, combo, couple, deuce, doublet, duality, duo, dyad, match, mates, span, team, twins, two, two of a kind, twosome, yoke; SEE CONCEPTS 432,784

pair [v] *make, become a twosome*
balance, bracket, combine, couple, join, marry, match, match up, mate, pair off, put together, team, twin, unite, wed, yoke; SEE CONCEPT 113

pajamas [n] *sleeping clothes*
jamas*, jammies*, jams*, loungewear, lounging robe, nightdress, nightie*, nightshirt, nightwear, PJ's*, sleeper, sleeping suit; SEE CONCEPT 451

pal [n] *person's friend*
amiga, amigo, associate, boon companion*, bosom buddy*, bro*, brother, buddy, chum, companion, comrade, connate, crony, cuz, good buddy*, homeboy, homegirl, mate, sidekick, sis*, sister; SEE CONCEPT 423

palace [n] *royal or enormous home*
alcazar, castle, chateau, dwelling, hall, manor, mansion, official residence, royal residence; SEE CONCEPT 516

palatable [adj] *delicious, agreeable*
acceptable, A-OK*, aperitive, appetizing, attractive, cool, copacetic, delectable, delightful, divine, enjoyable, fair, flavorsome, good-tasting, heavenly, home-cooking*, luscious, mellow, mouthwatering, peachy, pleasant, relishing, sapid, saporific, saporous, satisfactory, savory, scrumptious, sugar-coated*, sweetened, tasteful, tasty, tempting, toothsome, toothy*, yummy*; SEE CONCEPTS 529,613

palatial [adj] *grand, opulent*
deluxe, grandiose, illustrious, imposing, impressive, lush, luxuriant, luxurious, magnificent, majestic, monumental, noble, plush, regal, rich, silken, spacious, splendid, stately, sumptuous, upholstered; SEE CONCEPTS 334,485,589

pale [adj] *light in color or effect*
anemic, ashen, ashy, blanched, bleached, bloodless, cadaverous, colorless, deathlike, dim, doughy, dull, faded, faint, feeble, ghastly, gray, haggard, inadequate, ineffective, ineffectual, insubstantial, livid, lurid, pallid, pasty, poor, sallow, sick, sickly, spectral, thin, unsubstantial, wan, washed-out, waxen, waxlike, weak, white, whitish; SEE CONCEPTS 537,618

pale [v] *become, make lighter or weakened*
blanch, decrease, dim, diminish, dull, fade, faint, go white, grow dull, lessen, lose color, lose luster, muddy, tarnish, whiten; SEE CONCEPTS 240,250

pall [n] *cloud, gloom*
cloak, cloth, covering, damp, damper, dismay, mantle, melancholy, shadow, shroud, veil; SEE CONCEPTS 620,674

pall [v] *bore, tire*
become dull, become tedious, cloy, disgust, fill, glut, gorge, jade, sate, satiate, sicken, surfeit, weary; SEE CONCEPTS 7,19

palliate [v] *gloss over; cover up*
abate, allay, alleviate, apologize for, assuage, camouflage, cloak, conceal, condone, cover, diminish, disguise, dissemble, ease, exculpate, excuse, extenuate, gloze, hide, hush up*, justify, lessen, lighten, make light of*, mask, minimize, mitigate, moderate, mollify, prettify, put on a Band-Aid*, qualify, quick fix*, relieve, screen, soften, soothe, sugarcoat*, temper, varnish, veil, veneer, vindicate, white, whiten, whitewash*; SEE CONCEPTS 57,59,172,188

palpable [adj1] *clear, obvious*
apparent, appreciable, arresting, believable, blatant, certain, colorable, conspicuous, credible, detectable, discernible, distinct, evident, manifest, noticeable, observable, open, ostensible, patent, perceivable, perceptible, plain, plausible, positive, remarkable, seeming, sensible, straightforward, striking, sure, tangible, unequivocal, unmistakable, visible; SEE CONCEPTS 529,535

palpable [adj2] *concrete, real*
material, sensible, solid, substantial, tactile, tangible, touchable; SEE CONCEPTS 485,582

palpitate [v] *beat at a rapid pace, like a heart*
flutter, pitpat*, pitter-patter*, pound, pulsate, pulse, quiver, shiver, throb, tremble, vibrate; SEE CONCEPTS 152,308

palsied [adj] *crippled*
arthritic, atonic, debilitated, disabled, diseased, helpless, neurasthenic, paralytic, paralyzed, rheumatic, sclerotic, shaking, shaky, sick, spastic, trembling, tremorous, weak; SEE CONCEPTS 314,485

paltry [adj] *poor; worthless*
base, beggarly, cheap, common, contemptible, derisory, despicable, inconsiderable, ineffectual, insignificant, limited, low, low-down*, meager, mean, measly, minor, miserable, narrow, petty, picayune, piddling, pitiful, puny, set, shabby, shoddy, sleazy*, slight, small, sorry*, trashy, trifling, trivial, unconsequential, unimportant, vile, wretched; SEE CONCEPTS 334,485

pamper [v] *serve one's every need, whim*
baby, caress, cater to, coddle, cosset, dandle*, fondle, gratify, humor, indulge, mollycoddle*, overindulge, pet, please, regale, satisfy, spare the rod*, spoil, spoil rotten*, tickle, yield; SEE CONCEPTS 136,295

pamphlet [n] *booklet*
announcement, broadside, brochure, bulletin, circular, compilation, flyer*, folder, handout, leaflet, throwaway*, tract, tractate; SEE CONCEPTS 271,280

pan [n] *container for cooking food*
bucket, casserole, double boiler, frying pan, kettle, pail, pannikin, pot, roaster, saucepan, sheet, skillet, vessel; SEE CONCEPTS 493,494

pan [v1] *look, search for over a wide area*
follow, move, scan, separate, sift, sweep, swing, track, traverse, wash; SEE CONCEPT 216

pan [v2] *criticize strongly*
blame, censure, condemn, cut up, denounce, denunciate, disparage, flay, hammer, jeer at, knock, rap, reprehend, review unfavorably, roast, slam; SEE CONCEPT 52

panacea [n] *cure-all*
catholicon, cure, elixir, nostrum, patent medicine, relief, remedy; SEE CONCEPTS 307,311

panache [n] *person's flamboyant spirit*
brio, charisma, dash, élan, flair, flamboyance,

flourish, style, swagger, verve, vigor; SEE CONCEPT 411

pancake [n] *flat, round breakfast cake*
batter cake, blanket*, cake, crepe, flapjack, griddlecake, hot cake, johnnycake, jonnycake, sourdough, waffle, wheat*, wheat cake; SEE CONCEPTS 457,461

pandemonium [n] *craziness, commotion*
anarchy, babel, bedlam, bluster, brouhaha*, chaos, clamor, clatter, confusion, din, hassle, hubbub*, hue and cry*, hullabaloo*, jangle, noise, racket, riot, ruckus*, rumpus, tumult, turbulence, turmoil, uproar; SEE CONCEPTS 388,674

pander [v] *cater to, indulge*
brownnose*, cajole, fall all over*, gratify, lay it on*, massage, play the game*, play up to*, please, politic, satisfy, snow*, soap*, soften up, stroke, suck up to*; SEE CONCEPTS 59,136,384

pang [n] *ache, twinge*
agony, anguish, bite, discomfort, distress, gripe, misery, pain, prick, spasm, stab, sting, stitch, throb, throe, wrench; SEE CONCEPT 728

panic [n1] *extreme fright*
agitation, alarm, cold feet*, confusion, consternation, crush, dismay, dread, fear, frenzy, horror, hysteria, jam, rush, scare, stampede, terror, trepidation; SEE CONCEPTS 27,410,690

panic [n2] *sudden drop in value in financial markets*
Black Monday*, bust, crash, depression, rainy day*, slump; SEE CONCEPT 335

panic [v] *become, make afraid or distressed*
alarm, become hysterical, be terror-stricken, chicken out*, clutch, come apart, freeze up*, go to pieces*, have a fit*, lose it*, lose nerve*, overreact, push panic button*, run scared*, scare, shake in boots*, stampede, startle, terrify, unnerve; SEE CONCEPTS 14,27

panorama [n] *scene, horizon*
bird's-eye view*, compass, dimension, diorama, extent, orbit, overview, perspective, picture, prospect, purview, radius, range, reach, scenery, scenic view, scope, spectacle, survey, sweep, view, vista; SEE CONCEPTS 529,628,651

pan out [v] *come to pass; succeed*
click*, come out*, culminate, eventuate, go, go over*, happen, net*, prove out, result, turn out, work out, yield; SEE CONCEPT 706

pant [v1] *gasp for air*
be out of breath, blow, breathe, chuff, gulp, heave, huff, palpitate, puff, snort, throb, wheeze, whiff, wind; SEE CONCEPT 163

pant [v2] *long for*
ache, aim, aspire, covet, crave, desire, hunger, lust, pine, sigh, thirst, want, wish, yearn; SEE CONCEPT 20

pants [n] *clothing for legs, lower half of body*
Bermudas*, bloomers, blue jeans, boxer shorts, breeches, briefs, britches*, chaps*, chinos, clam diggers*, cords*, corduroys, denims, drawers, dungarees, jeans, jodhpurs, knickers, overalls, pantaloons*, panties*, pedal pushers*, shorts, slacks, trousers, underpants; SEE CONCEPT 451

paper/papers [n1] *legal document*
affidavit, archive, bill, certificate, certification, citation, contract, credentials, data, deed, diaries, diploma, documentation, dossier, file, grant, ID*, identification papers, indictment, instrument, letter, letters, order, passport, plea, record, subpoena, summons, testimony, token, visa,

voucher, warrant, will, writ, writings; SEE CONCEPTS 271,318

paper [n2] *newspaper*
daily, gazette, journal, news, organ, rag*, weekly; SEE CONCEPT 280

paper [n3] *thesis, article*
analysis, assignment, composition, critique, dissertation, essay, examination, monograph, report, script, study, theme, treatise; SEE CONCEPTS 271,280

paper [n4] *material upon which one writes*
card, filing card, letterhead, newsprint, note, note card, note pad, onion skin, pad, papyrus, parchment, poster, rag, sheet, stationery, tissue, vellum; SEE CONCEPTS 260,475

paper [adj] *thin, flimsy*
cardboard, disposable, insubstantial, paper-thin, papery, wafer-thin; SEE CONCEPT 606

paper [v] *line with material*
cover, hang, paste up, plaster, wallpaper; SEE CONCEPTS 172,177

par [n] *average, equilibrium*
adequation, balance, coequality, criterion, equal footing, equality, equatability, equivalence, equivalency, level, mean, median, model, norm, parity, sameness, standard, usual; SEE CONCEPTS 636,667

parade [n] *pageant, display*
array, autocade, cavalcade, ceremony, column, demonstration, exhibition, fanfare, flaunting, line, march, ostentation, panoply, pomp, procession, review, ritual, shine, show, spectacle, train, vaunting; SEE CONCEPTS 377,386

parade [v] *show off; march*
advertise, air, boast, brag, brandish, declare, demonstrate, disclose, display, disport, divulge, exhibit, expose, flash, flaunt, march in review, prance, proclaim, publish, reveal, sport, strut, swagger, trot out*, vaunt; SEE CONCEPT 261

paradigm [n] *example*
archetype, beau ideal*, chart, criterion, ensample, exemplar, ideal, mirror, model, original, pattern, prototype, sample, standard; SEE CONCEPT 686

paradise [n] *land, feeling of great pleasure; absence of evil*
Arcadia*, ballpark, bliss, cloud nine*, delight, divine abode*, Eden*, felicity, happy hunting ground*, heaven, heavenly kingdom, kingdom come*, next world*, pearly gates*, promised land, Shangri-la*, Utopia*, wonderland, Zion*; SEE CONCEPTS 370,410,515

paradox [n] *contradiction, puzzle*
absurdity, ambiguity, anomaly, catch, Catch-22*, enigma, error, inconsistency, mistake, mystery, nonsense, oddity, opposite, reverse; SEE CONCEPT 532

paragon [n] *outstanding example*
apotheosis, archetype, beau ideal*, beauty, best, champ, champion, crackerjack*, cream*, criterion, cynosure, epitome, essence, exemplar, gem, ideal, jewel*, love, lovely, model, nonesuch, nonpareil, original, paradigm, pattern, peach*, perfection, pick, prototype, quintessence, standard, sublimation, tops*, trump*, ultimate; SEE CONCEPTS 671,686

parallel [n] *complement, correlation*
analogue, analogy, comparison, corollary, correlate, correspondence, correspondent, counterpart, countertype, double, duplicate, duplication, equal, equivalent, homologue, kin*, likeness,

pa
pa

match, parallelism, resemblance, similarity, twin; SEE CONCEPTS *667,670*

parallel [*adj1*] *aligned, side-by-side*
alongside, coextending, coextensive, coordinate, equidistant, extending equally, in the same direction, lateral, laterally, never meeting, running alongside; SEE CONCEPTS *581,586*

parallel [*adj2*] *akin, similar*
agnate, like, analogous, comparable, complementary, conforming, consonant, correspondent, corresponding, equal, identical, like, matching, resembling, uniform; SEE CONCEPTS *487,573*

parallel [*v*] *be alike*
agree, assimilate, collimate, collocate, compare, complement, conform, copy, correlate, correspond, equal, equate, imitate, keep pace, liken, match, paragon, parallelize; SEE CONCEPTS *111,171,667*

paralytic [*adj*] *impaired in movement*
diplegic, disabled, immobile, immobilized, inactive, incapacitated, insensible, lame, numb, palsied, palsified, paralyzed, paraplegic, powerless, quadriplegic; SEE CONCEPTS *314,485*

paralyze [*v*] *immobilize*
anesthetize, appall, arrest, astound, bemuse, benumb, bring to grinding halt*, close, daunt, daze, deaden, debilitate, demolish, destroy, disable, disarm, enfeeble, freeze, halt, incapacitate, knock out, lame, make inert, make nerveless, nonplus, numb, palsy, petrify, prostrate, shut down*, stop dead*, stun, stupefy, transfix, weaken; SEE CONCEPTS *14,121,246,252*

parameter [*n*] *limit*
constant, criterion, framework, guideline, limitation, restriction, specification; SEE CONCEPT *688*

paramount [*adj*] *principal, superior*
ascendant, capital, cardinal, chief, commanding, controlling, crowning, dominant, eminent, first, foremost, headmost, leading, main, outstanding, overbearing, predominant, predominate, preeminent, premier, preponderant, prevalent, primary, prime, regnant, sovereign, supreme; SEE CONCEPTS *568,574*

paraphernalia [*n*] *equipment, belongings*
accoutrements, apparatus, appurtenances, baggage, effects, equipage, gear, habiliments, impedimenta, impediments, machinery, material, materiel, outfit, regalia, stuff, tackle, things, trappings; SEE CONCEPTS *446,496*

paraphrase [*n*] *translation, interpretation*
digest, explanation, rehash, rendering, rendition, rephrasing, restatement, rewording, summary, version; SEE CONCEPTS *55,57,268*

paraphrase [*v*] *interpret, translate*
express in other words, express in own words, recapitulate, rehash, render, rephrase, restate, reword, summarize, transcribe; SEE CONCEPTS *55,57*

parasite [*n*] *something that exists by taking from or depending on another*
barnacle, bloodsucker*, bootlicker*, deadbeat*, dependent, flunky, freeloader*, groupie*, hanger-on*, idler, leech, scrounger, sponge*, stooge*, sucker*, sycophant, taker*; SEE CONCEPTS *394,412*

parcel [*n1*] *container prepared to be sent*
bindle, bundle, carton, load, pack, package, packet; SEE CONCEPT *494*

parcel [*n2*] *group, bunch*
array, band, batch, body, clot, clump, cluster,

clutch, collection, company, crew, crowd, gang, lot, pack; SEE CONCEPT *432*

parcel [*n3*] *piece of land*
acreage, plat, plot, property, tract; SEE CONCEPTS *509,513*

parcel [*n4*] *part, piece*
bite, chunk, cut, division, lion's share*, member, moiety, piece of the action*, portion, rake-off*, section, segment, slice; SEE CONCEPTS *829,835*

parch [*v*] *dry, burn*
blister, brown, dehydrate, desiccate, dry up, evaporate, exsiccate, make thirsty, scorch, sear, shrivel, stale, wither; SEE CONCEPTS *249,255*

parched [*adj*] *dry*
arid, burned, cotton-mouth*, dehydrated, dried out, dried up*, dry as dust*, scorched, shriveled, thirsty, waterless, withered; SEE CONCEPT *603*

pardon [*n*] *forgiveness*
absolution, acquittal, allowance, amnesty, anchor, clemency, commute, conciliation, condonation, discharge, exculpation, excuse, exoneration, forbearance, freeing, grace, indemnification, indemnity, indulgence, justification, kindness, lifeboat*, lifesaver*, mercy, release, remission, reprieve, vindication; SEE CONCEPTS *10,318,685*

pardon [*v*] *forgive*
absolve, accept, acquit, amnesty, blink at*, bury the hatchet*, clear, condone, discharge, exculpate, excuse, exonerate, free, give absolution, grant amnesty, justify, let off*, let off easy*, liberate, lifeboat*, overlook, release, remit, reprieve, rescue, spring*, suspend charges, tolerate, wink at*, wipe slate clean*, write off*; SEE CONCEPTS *10,50,88,317*

pare [*v*] *peel, trim*
carve, clip, crop, cut, cut back, cut down, decorticate, decrease, dock, flay, knock off, lop, lower, mark down, prune, reduce, scalp, scrape, shave, shear, skin, skive, slash, strip, thin, uncover; SEE CONCEPTS *176,202,236,247*

parent [*n*] *person, source of product*
ancestor, architect, author, begetter, cause, center, creator, father, folks, forerunner, fountainhead, guardian, mother, origin, originator, procreator, progenitor, prototype, root, source, wellspring; SEE CONCEPTS *414,648*

parental [*adj*] *having the quality or nature of a parent*
affectionate, benevolent, benign, caring, comforting, devoted, fatherly, fond, forbearing, gentle, indulgent, kind, loving, maternal, matriarchal, motherly, paternal, patriarchal, protective, sheltering, supportive, tender, warm, watchful; SEE CONCEPTS *401,542*

parenthetical [*adj*] *incidental*
bracketed, by the way, episodic, explanatory, extraneous, extrinsic, incidental, in parenthesis, inserted, intermediate, interposed, qualifying, related, subordinate; SEE CONCEPTS *544,577*

parish [*n*] *congregation of a church*
archdiocese, bethel, church, churchgoers, community, flock*, fold*, parishioners, territory; SEE CONCEPT *369*

parity [*n*] *equality, balance*
adequation, affinity, agreement, analogy, approximation, closeness, coequality, conformity, congruity, consistency, correspondence, equal terms, equivalence, equivalency, likeness, nearness, par, parallelism, paraphernalia, resemblance, same-

ness, similarity, similitude, uniformity, unity;
SEE CONCEPTS 667,670

park [n] *land that is reserved for pleasure, recreation*
esplanade, estate, forest, garden, grass, green, grounds, lawn, lot, meadow, parkland, place, playground, plaza, pleasure garden, recreation area, square, tract, village green, woodland; SEE CONCEPTS 509,513

park [v] *place vehicle in a position*
deposit, leave, line up, maneuver, order, position, put, seat, stand, station, store; SEE CONCEPTS 148,201

parlor [n] *sitting room*
drawing room, front room, guest room, living room, lounge, reception, salon, waiting room; SEE CONCEPT 448

parochial [adj] *narrow-minded, restricted*
biased, bigoted, conservative, conventional, insular, inward-looking, limited, local, narrow, petty, prejudiced, provincial, regional, sectarian, sectional, shallow, small-minded, small-town; SEE CONCEPT 542

parody [n] *imitation, spoof*
apology, burlesque, caricature, cartoon, copy, derision, farce, irony, jest, joke, lampoon, mime, mimicry, misrepresentation, mockery, mock-heroic*, pastiche, play-on*, raillery, rib*, ridicule, roast*, satire, send-up*, skit, takeoff*, travesty; SEE CONCEPTS 59,273,292

parody [v] *imitate, spoof*
ape, burlesque, caricature, copy, deride, disparage, distort, do a takeoff of*, exaggerate, impersonate, jeer, jest, joke, lampoon, laugh at, mime, mimic, mock, poke fun at, put on*, ridicule, roast, satirize, send up, sheik*, take off*, travesty; SEE CONCEPTS 59,111,273

paroxysm [n] *seizure, spasm*
agitation, anger, attack, convulsion, eruption, excitement, explosion, fit, flare-up*, frenzy, frothing, fuming, furor, fury, hysterics, outbreak, outburst, passion, rage, violence; SEE CONCEPTS 308,316,410

parrot [v] *repeat*
ape, chant, copy, copycat, echo, imitate, mime, mimic, quote, recite, reiterate; SEE CONCEPTS 47,77,171

parry [v] *ward off, circumvent*
anticipate, avoid, block, bypass, deflect, dodge, duck*, elude, evade, fence*, fend off, forestall, hold at bay*, preclude, prevent, rebuff, rebuke, repel, repulse, resist, shirk, shun, sidestep, stave off; SEE CONCEPTS 25,30,121

parsimonious [adj] *penny-pinching*
avaricious, chintzy*, close, frugal, greedy, illiberal, mean, miserly, penurious, prudent, saving, scrimpy, selfish, skinflint*, sparing, stingy*, tight*, tightfisted*, tightwad*; SEE CONCEPTS 334,401

part [n1] *piece, portion of something*
allotment, any, apportionment, articulation, atom, bit, bite, branch, chip, chunk, component, constituent, cut, department, detail, division, element, extra, factor, fraction, fragment, helping, hunk, ingredient, installment, item, limb, lot, lump, measure, meed, member, module, moiety, molecule, organ, parcel, particle, partition, piece, quantum, quota, ration, scrap, section, sector, segment, share, side, slab, slice, sliver, splinter, subdivision, unit; SEE CONCEPT 834

part [n2] *person or group's interest, concern*
behalf, bit, business, capacity, cause, charge, duty, faction, function, involvement, office, party, place, responsibility, role, say, share, side, task, work; SEE CONCEPTS 362,532

part [n3] *theatrical role*
antagonist, bit, bit part, cameo, character, dialogue, hero, lead, leading role, lines, minor role, piece, principal character, protagonist, romantic lead, silent bit, stock character, straight part, supporting role, title role, villain, walk-on; SEE CONCEPT 263

part [v1] *break, disconnect*
articulate, break up, cleave, come apart, detach, dichotomize, disjoin, dismantle, dissever, disunite, divide, factor, itemize, particularize, partition, portion, rend, section, segment, separate, sever, slice, split, strip, subdivide, sunder, tear; SEE CONCEPTS 98,135

part [v2] *leave, go away from someone*
break, break off, break up, clear out*, cut and run*, dedomicile, depart, ease out, go, go separate ways*, hit the road*, leave flat*, part company, pull out*, push off, quit, quit the scene*, say goodbye, separate, ship out*, shove off*, split, split up*, take a hike*, take leave, take off, walk out on, withdraw; SEE CONCEPTS 195,297,384

partake [v] *eat, share*
be a party to, be in on, be into, consume, devour, divide, engage, enter into, feed, get in the act, have a finger in, ingest, participate, receive, sample, savor, sip, sit in, sit in on, take, take part, tune in; SEE CONCEPTS 169,225

partial [adj1] *incomplete*
fractional, fragmentary, half done, halfway, imperfect, limited, part, sectional, uncompleted, unfinished, unperformed; SEE CONCEPT 531

partial [adj2] *biased, prejudiced*
colored, discriminatory, disposed, favorably inclined, influenced, interested, jaundiced, minded, one-sided, partisan, predisposed, prepossessed, tendentious, unfair, unindifferent, unjust, warped; SEE CONCEPTS 403,542

partiality [n] *favoritism, fondness*
affinity, bias, cup of tea*, dish, druthers*, flash, inclination, inclining, leaning, liking, love, partisanship, penchant, predilection, predisposition, preference, prejudice, proclivity, propensity, taste, tendency, thing*, type, weakness; SEE CONCEPTS 32,709

partially [adv] *incompletely*
by degrees, by installments, fractionally, halfway, in part, in some measure, little by little, moderately, not wholly, partly, piece by piece, piecemeal, somewhat, to a certain degree, to a certain extent; SEE CONCEPTS 531,544

participant [n] *person who takes part in activity*
actor, aide, a party to, assistant, associate, attendant, colleague, contributor, helper, in, member, partaker, participator, partner, party, player, shareholder, sharer; SEE CONCEPTS 352,366,423

participate [v] *take part in activity*
aid, associate with, be a participant, be a party to, be into*, chip in*, come in, compete, concur, cooperate, engage, engage in, enter into, get in on*, get in on the act*, go into, have a hand in*, have to do with, join in, latch on*, lend a hand, partake, perform, play, share, sit in*, sit in on*,

strive, take an interest in, tune in*; SEE CONCEPT *100*

particle [n] *atom, piece*
bit, crumb, dot, dribble, drop, fleck, fragment, grain, hoot*, iota, jot, minim, mite, modicum, molecule, morsel, mote, ounce, ray, scrap, scruple, seed, shred, smidgen, smithereen, speck, spot, stitch, whit; SEE CONCEPT *831*

particular [n] *detail*
ABC's*, article, bottom line*, brass tacks*, case, chapter and verse*, circumstance, clue, cue, element, fact, facts of life, feature, gospel, item, know*, lowdown*, nitty-gritty*, nuts and bolts*, picture, point, rundown*, scoop*, score*, speciality, specific, specification, story, thing*, what's what*, whole story*; SEE CONCEPTS *274,532,832*

particular [adj1] *exact, specific*
accurate, appropriate, blow-by-blow*, circumstantial, clocklike, detailed, distinct, especial, express, full, individual, intrinsic, itemized, limited, local, meticulous, minute, painstaking, particularized, peculiar, precise, scrupulous, selective, singular, special, thorough, topical; SEE CONCEPT *557*

particular [adj2] *notable, uncommon*
especial, exceptional, exclusive, lone, marked, noteworthy, odd, one, only, peculiar, personal, remarkable, respective, separate, single, singular, sole, solitary, unique, unusual; SEE CONCEPT *564*

particular [adj3] *finicky, demanding*
careful, choosy, choicy, critical, dainty, discriminating, exacting, fastidious, finical, fussbudget*, fussy, hard to please, meticulous, nice, nitpicking*, persnickety*, picky*, rough, stickler*, tough; SEE CONCEPTS *404,542*

particularly [adv] *specifically*
decidedly, distinctly, especially, exceptionally, explicitly, expressly, individually, in particular, markedly, notably, outstandingly, peculiarly, principally, singularly, specially, surprisingly, uncommonly, unusually; SEE CONCEPT *557*

parting [n] *goodbye, separation*
adieu, bisection, break, breaking, breakup, crossroads*, departure, detachment, divergence, division, farewell, going, leave-taking, on the rocks*, partition, rift, rupture, severance, split, split-up, valediction; SEE CONCEPTS *195,297,384*

parting [adj] *farewell*
departing, final, goodbye, last, valedictory; SEE CONCEPT *267*

partisan [n] *person devoted to another or cause*
accessory, adherent, backer, champion, cohort, defender, devotee, disciple, follower, satellite, stalwart, supporter, sycophant, sympathizer, upholder, votary, zealot; SEE CONCEPTS *359,423*

partisan [adj] *interested, factional*
accessory, adhering, biased, bigoted, blind, cliquish, colored, conspiratorial, denominational, devoted, diehard*, exclusive, fanatic, jaundiced, one-sided, overzealous, partial, prejudiced, prepossessed, sectarian, sympathetic, tendentious, unjust, unreasoning, warped, zealous; SEE CONCEPTS *401,542,548*

partition [n] *divider, division*
allotment, apportionment, barrier, detachment, disconnection, dissolution, distribution, disunion, dividing, hindrance, obstruction, parting, portion, rationing, rupture, screen, segregation, separation, severance, share, splitting, wall; SEE CONCEPTS *98,440,443,470*

partition [v] *divide, separate*
apportion, cut, cut in, cut into, cut up, deal, disburse, dispense, disperse, distribute, divvy up*, dole out*, fence off*, measure out, parcel out, portion, screen, section, segment, separate, share, size into, slice, split, split up, subdivide, wall off*; SEE CONCEPTS *98,135*

partly [adv] *not completely*
at best, at least, at most, at worst, bit by bit, by degrees, carelessly, halfway, inadequately, in a general way, in bits and pieces*, incompletely, in part, in some measure, in some ways, insufficiently, little by little, measurably, notably, not entirely, not fully, noticeably, not strictly speaking, not wholly, partially, piece by piece, piecemeal, relatively, slightly, so far as possible, somewhat, to a certain degree, to a certain extent, up to a certain point, within limits*; SEE CONCEPT *531*

partner [n] *person who takes part with another*
accomplice, ally, assistant, associate, buddy, chum*, cohort, collaborator, colleague, companion, comrade, confederate, consort, coworker, crony*, date, friend, helper, helpmate, husband, mate, pal*, participant, playmate, sidekick*, spouse, teammate, wife; SEE CONCEPTS *348,414,423*

partnership [n] *alliance; participation*
affiliation, assistance, association, band, body, brotherhood, business, cahoots*, cartel, chumminess, clique, club, combination, combine, community, companionship, company, conglomerate, conjunction, connection, consociation, cooperation, cooperative, corporation, coterie, crew, faction, firm, fraternity, friendship, gang, help, hookup, house, interest, joining, lodge, mob, organization, ownership, party, ring, sharing, sisterhood, society, sorority, tie-up, togetherness, union; SEE CONCEPTS *325,381,388*

party [n1] *social gathering*
affair, amusement, at-home*, ball, banquet, barbecue, bash*, blowout*, carousal, carousing*, celebration, cocktails, coffee klatch, coming-out, dinner, diversion*, do*, entertainment, feast, festive occasion, festivity, fete, fun, function, gala, get-together, luncheon, movable feast*, orgy*, prom, reception, riot, shindig*, social, soiree, splurge*, spree*, tea; SEE CONCEPT *383*

party [n2] *gang, group*
assembly, band, bevy, body, bunch, cluster, company, corps, covey, crew, crowd, detachment, force, gathering, mob, multitude, outfit, squad, team, troop, troupe, unit; SEE CONCEPTS *417,432*

party [n3] *group supporting certain beliefs*
alliance, association, bloc, body, cabal, clique, coalition, combination, combine, confederacy, coterie, electorate, faction, grouping, junta, league, ring, sect, set, side, union; SEE CONCEPTS *301,381*

party [n4] *individual*
being, body, character, creature, human, man, mortal, part, person, personage, somebody, someone, woman; SEE CONCEPT *417*

party [n5] *person(s) involved in legal action*
actor, agent, cojuror, compurgator, confederate, contractor, defendant, litigant, partaker, participant, participator, plaintiff, plotter, sharer; SEE CONCEPT *355*

pass [n1] *opening through solid*
canyon, cut, gap, gorge, passage, passageway, path, ravine; SEE CONCEPTS 509,513

pass [n2] *authorization, permission*
admission, chit*, comp, free ride*, furlough, identification, license, order, paper, passport, permit, safe-conduct*, ticket, visa, warrant; SEE CONCEPTS 271,685

pass [n3] *sexual proposition*
advance, approach, overture, play, suggestion; SEE CONCEPTS 375,384

pass [n4] *predicament*
condition, contingency, crisis, crossroads*, emergency, exigency, juncture, pinch, plight, situation, stage, state, strait, turning point*, zero hour*; SEE CONCEPT 674

pass [v1] *go by, elapse; move onward*
befall, blow past, catch, come off, come to pass, come up, crawl, cross, cruise, depart, develop, drag, fall out, fare, flow, fly, fly by, get ahead, give, glide, glide by, go, go past, happen, hie, journey, lapse, leave, linger, move, occur, pass away, pass by, proceed, progress, push on, reach, repair, rise, roll, run, run by, run out, slip away, take place, transpire, travel, wend; SEE CONCEPTS 2,149,242

pass [v2] *surpass, beat*
exceed, excel, go beyond, go by, leave behind, outdistance, outdo, outgo, outrace, outshine, outstrip, shoot ahead of, surmount, top, transcend; SEE CONCEPT 141

pass [v3] *succeed, graduate*
answer, do, get through, matriculate, pass muster, qualify, suffice, suit; SEE CONCEPT 706

pass [v4] *give, transfer*
buck, convey, deliver, exchange, hand, hand over, kick, let have, reach, relinquish, send, shoot, throw, transmit; SEE CONCEPTS 108,217

pass [v5] *cease*
blow over*, cash in*, close, decease, demise, depart, die, disappear, discontinue, dissolve, drop, dwindle, ebb, end, evaporate, expire, fade, go, melt away, pass away, perish, peter out*, stop, succumb, terminate, vanish, wane; SEE CONCEPTS 105,119

pass [v6] *enact, legislate*
accept, adopt, approve, authorize, become law, become ratified, become valid, be established, be ordained, be sanctioned, carry, decree, engage, establish, ordain, pledge, promise, ratify, sanction, undertake, validate, vote in; SEE CONCEPTS 298,317

pass [v7] *express formally*
claim, declare, deliver, pronounce, state, utter; SEE CONCEPTS 49,60

pass [v8] *decide not to do*
decline, discount, disregard, fail, forget, ignore, miss, neglect, not heed, omit, overlook, pass on, pass up, refuse, skip, slight; SEE CONCEPTS 25,30

pass [v9] *rid of waste*
defecate, discharge, eliminate, emit, empty, evacuate, excrete, expel, exude, give off, send forth, void; SEE CONCEPT 179

passable [adj1] *acceptable, admissible*
adequate, allowable, all right, average, common, fair, fair enough, mediocre, middling, moderate, not too bad*, ordinary, presentable, respectable, so-so*, tolerable, unexceptional; SEE CONCEPT 558

passable [adj2] *clear and able to be traveled*
accessible, attainable, beaten, broad, crossable, easy, fair, graded, motorable, navigable, open, penetrable, reachable, travelable, traveled, traversable, unblocked, unobstructed; SEE CONCEPTS 559,576

passage/passageway [n1] *path for travel*
access, alley, alleyway, avenue, channel, corridor, course, doorway, entrance, entrance hall, exit, gap, hall, hallway, lane, line, lobby, opening, pathway, road, route, shaft, subway, thoroughfare, tunnel, vestibule, way; SEE CONCEPTS 440,501

passage [n2] *excerpt from document*
clause, extract, paragraph, piece, portion, quotation, reading, section, sentence, text, transition, verse; SEE CONCEPT 270

passage [n3] *travel*
advance, change, conversion, crossing, flow, journey, motion, movement, passing, progress, progression, tour, traject, transfer, transference, transit, transition, transmission, transmittal, transmittance, traverse, traversing, trek, trip, voyage; SEE CONCEPTS 145,217,224,704

passage [n4] *authorization; enactment*
acceptance, allowance, establishment, freedom, legalization, legislation, passing, passport, permission, ratification, right, safe-conduct, visa, warrant; SEE CONCEPTS 318,685

pass away [v] *die*
decease, demise, depart, drop, expire, perish, succumb; SEE CONCEPT 304

pass by [v] *neglect, forget*
abandon, disregard, fail, ignore, leave, miss, not choose, omit, overlook, overpass, pass over; SEE CONCEPTS 25,30

passé [adj] *old-fashioned*
antiquated, belated, dated, dead, démodé, disused, extinct, has-been*, obsolete, outdated, outmoded, out-of-date, outworn, superseded, unfashionable, yesterday; SEE CONCEPTS 578,589,797

passenger [n] *person who rides in vehicle conducted by another*
commuter, customer, excursionist, fare*, hitchhiker, patron, pilgrim, rider, tourist, traveler, voyager, wanderer, wayfarer; SEE CONCEPT 423

passing [n] *death*
decease, defunction, demise, dissolution, end, finish, loss, silence, sleep, termination; SEE CONCEPT 304

passing [adj] *brief, casual*
cursory, ephemeral, evanescent, fleeting, fugacious, fugitive, glancing, hasty, impermanent, momentary, quick, shallow, short, short-lived, slight, superficial, temporary, transient, transitory; SEE CONCEPTS 551,798

passion [n1] *strong emotion*
affection, affectivity, agony, anger, animation, ardor, dedication, devotion, distress, dolor, eagerness, ecstasy, excitement, feeling, fervor, fire, fit, flare-up, frenzy, fury, heat, hurrah, indignation, intensity, ire, joy, misery, outbreak, outburst, paroxysm, rage, rapture, resentment, sentiment, spirit, storm, suffering, temper, transport, vehemence, warmth, wrath, zeal, zest; SEE CONCEPT 410

passion [n2] *adoration, love*
affection, amorousness, amour, appetite, ardor, attachment, concupiscence, craving, crush*, de-

sire, emoting, eroticism, excitement, fondness, infatuation, keenness, lust, prurience, urge, weakness, yen; SEE CONCEPTS *32,372*

passion [n3] *strong interest*
craving, craze, drive, enthusiasm, fad*, fancy, fascination, idol, infatuation, jazz*, mania, obsession; SEE CONCEPTS *349,532,690*

passionate [adj1] *sensual, desirous*
amorous, ardent, aroused, concupiscent, desirous, erotic, heavy*, hot*, lascivious, libidinous, loving, lustful, prurient, romantic, sexy, steamy*, stimulated, sultry, turned-on*, wanton, wistful; SEE CONCEPT *372*

passionate [adj2] *excited; enthusiastic*
affecting, animated, ardent, blazing, burning, deep, dramatic, eager, eloquent, emotional, expressive, fervent, fervid, fierce, fiery, flaming, forceful, frenzied, glowing, headlong, heartfelt, heated, high-powered, high-pressure, hot*, hot-blooded*, impassioned, impetuous, impulsive, inspiring, intense, melodramatic, moving, poignant, precipitate, quickened, spirited, steamed up*, stimulated, stirring, strong, thrilling, vehement, violent, warm, wild, zealous; SEE CONCEPTS *401,542*

passionate [adj3] *angry*
all shook up*, choleric, enraged, fiery, frantic, furious, hotheaded*, hottempered*, inflamed, irascible, irritable, mean, peppery, quick-tempered, shaken, steamed-up*, stormy, tempestuous, testy, touchy*, vehement, violent; SEE CONCEPTS *401,542*

passive [adj] *lifeless, inactive*
acquiescent, apathetic, asleep, bearing, compliant, cool, docile, enduring, flat, forbearing, going through motions*, hands off*, idle, indifferent, inert, laid-back*, latent, long-suffering, moony, motionless, nonresistant, nonviolent, patient, phlegmatic, poker-faced*, quiescent, quiet, receptive, resigned, sleepy, static, stolid, submissive, tractable, unassertive, unflappable, uninvolved, unresisting, walking through it*, yielding; SEE CONCEPTS *542,584*

pass off [v] *give because one does not want it*
eject, foist, make a pretense of*, palm, palm off*, send forth, work off; SEE CONCEPT *108*

pass out [v] *become unconscious, usually from abusing a substance*
black out*, drop, faint, keel over*, lose consciousness, swoon; SEE CONCEPT *308*

pass over [v] *ignore, disregard*
dismiss, fail, forget, miss, neglect, not dwell on, omit, overlook, overpass, pass, pass by, skip, take no notice of*; SEE CONCEPTS *25,30*

passport [n] *identification of origin, country*
authorization, credentials, key, license, pass, permit, safe-conduct*, ticket, travel permit, visa, warrant; SEE CONCEPTS *271,685*

password [n] *secret word given for entry*
countersign, identification, key, key word, open sesame*, parole, phrase, signal, ticket, watchword, word; SEE CONCEPT *278*

past [n1] *time gone by*
antiquity, days gone by*, former times, good old days*, history, long ago, olden days*, old lang syne, old times*, time immemorial*, times past*, years ago*, yesterday, yesteryear, yore; SEE CONCEPTS *807,811,816,818*

past [adj1] *preceding, done*
accomplished, ago, antecedent, anterior, completed, elapsed, ended, extinct, finished, foregoing, forgotten, former, gone, gone by, over, over and done, precedent, previous, prior, spent; SEE CONCEPTS *531,585*

past [adj2] *olden, former*
ages ago*, ancient, ancient history*, back when*, behind one*, bygone, bypast, down memory lane*, earlier, early, erstwhile, ex-*, foregoing, gone-by*, good old days*, late, latter, latter-day, long-ago, old, olden days*, once, one-time, over, preceding, previous, prior, quondam, recent, retired, sometime, time was*, way back*, way back when*; SEE CONCEPT *820*

paste [n/v] *glue, adhesive*
cement, fasten, fix, gum, mucilage, patch, plaster, spit, stick, stickum*; SEE CONCEPTS *85,160,466*

pastel [adj] *muted in color*
delicate, light, pale, soft-hued, toned; SEE CONCEPT *618*

pastiche [n] *work of art formed from disparate sources*
assortment, collage, collection, compilation, copy, hodgepodge, imitation, mishmosh*, paste-up, patchwork, potpourri, reappropriation, reproduction, synthesis; SEE CONCEPT *260*

pastime [n] *leisure activity*
amusement, distraction, diversion, entertainment, fun, fun and games*, game, hobby, play, recreation, relaxation, sport; SEE CONCEPT *363*

pastor [n] *person who conducts church services*
cleric, divine, ecclesiastic, minister, parson, preacher, priest, rector, reverend, shepherd, vicar; SEE CONCEPT *361*

pastoral [adj] *peaceful, especially referring to the countryside*
agrarian, agrestic, Arcadian, bucolic, countrified, country, idyllic, outland, provincial, rural, rustic, simple, sylvan; SEE CONCEPT *583*

pastry [n] *baked product made with flour*
bread, cake, croissant, dainty, Danish, delicacy, doughnut, éclair, panettone, patisserie, phyllo, pie, strudel, sweet roll, tart, turnover; SEE CONCEPTS *457,461*

pasty [adj1] *sticky*
adhesive, doughy, gelatinous, gluelike, gluey, glutinous, gooey, mucilaginous, starchy; SEE CONCEPT *606*

pasty [adj2] *pale*
anemic, ashen, bloodless, dull, pallid, sallow, sickly, unhealthy, wan, waxen; SEE CONCEPT *618*

pat [n1/v] *tap, touch*
beat, caress, dab, fondle, form, hit, massage, mold, pet, punch, rub, slap, stroke, tip, whittle; SEE CONCEPTS *184,189,612*

pat [n2] *small slice or slab*
cake, dab, lump, piece, portion; SEE CONCEPTS *458,835*

pat [adj] *relevant, suitable*
apposite, apropos, apt, auspicious, felicitous, fitting, happy, meat, opportune, pertinent, propitious, rehearsed, timely, to the point; SEE CONCEPT *558*

pat [adv] *exactly, fittingly*
aptly, faultlessly, flawlessly, just right, opportunely, perfectly, plumb, precisely, relevantly, seasonably; SEE CONCEPTS *535,557*

patch [n1] *piece, spot, area*
bit, blob, chunk, fix, ground, hunk, land, lot, plat,

plot, scrap, shred, stretch, strip, tract; SEE CONCEPTS 452,471,513

patch [n2] *piece applied to cover a gap or lack*
application, appliqué, Band-Aid*, mend, reinforcement; SEE CONCEPTS 452,831

patch [v] *fix, mend*
cobble, cover, darn, do up, fiddle with, overhaul, rebuild, recondition, reconstruct, reinforce, repair, retread, revamp, sew; SEE CONCEPTS 212,218

patch up [v] *settle differences*
adjust, appease, bury the hatchet*, compensate, conciliate, make friends*, mediate, negotiate, placate, restore, settle*, smooth; SEE CONCEPT 384

patchwork [n] *mixture, hodgepodge*
check, confusion, disorder, hash*, jumble, medley, miscellany, mishmash, muddle, olio, pastiche, plaid, salad*, salmagundi, stew*, tartan; SEE CONCEPTS 260,432,475

patchy [adj] *spotty, not consistent*
erratic, fitful, irregular, random, sketchy, uneven, variable, varying; SEE CONCEPT 482

patent [n] *copyright on an invention*
charter, concession, control, franchise, license, limitation, privilege, protection; SEE CONCEPTS 271,318,685

patent [adj] *unconcealed, conspicuous*
apparent, barefaced*, blatant, clear, clear-cut, controlled, crystal clear*, distinct, downright, evident, exclusive, flagrant, glaring, gross*, indisputable, limited, manifest, obvious, open, open and shut*, palpable, plain, prominent, rank, straightforward, transparent, unequivocal, unmistakable; SEE CONCEPT 576

path [n] *course, way*
aisle, artery, avenue, beat, beaten path, boulevard, byway, crosscut, direction, drag, footpath, groove, highway, lane, line, pass, passage, pathway, procedure, rail, road, roadway, route, rut, shortcut, street, stroll, terrace, thoroughfare, track, trail, walk, walkway; SEE CONCEPTS 6,501

pathetic [adj] *sad, affecting*
commiserable, deplorable, distressing, feeble, heartbreaking, heartrending*, inadequate, lamentable, meager, melting, miserable, moving, paltry, petty, piteous, pitiable, pitiful, plaintive, poignant, poor, puny, rueful, sorry*, tender, touching, useless, woeful, worthless, wretched; SEE CONCEPTS 485,529

pathos [n] *deep sadness*
desolation, emotion, feeling, passion, pitiableness, pitifulness, plaintiveness, poignance, poignancy, sentiment; SEE CONCEPT 410

patience [n] *capacity, willingness to endure*
backbone*, bearing, calmness, composure, constancy, cool*, diligence, endurance, equanimity, even temper, forbearance, fortitude, grit*, guts*, gutsiness, heart, humility, imperturbability, intestinal fortitude*, legs*, leniency, longanimity, long-suffering, moderation, moxie*, nonresistance, passiveness, passivity, perseverance, persistence, poise, resignation, restraint, self-control, serenity, starch*, staying power*, stoicism, submission, sufferance, tolerance, toleration, yielding; SEE CONCEPTS 411,657

patient [n] *person being treated for medical problem*
case, convalescent, emergency, inmate, invalid, outpatient, shut-in, sick person, subject, sufferer, victim; SEE CONCEPT 357

patient [adj] *capable, willing to endure*
accommodating, calm, composed, easy-going, enduring, even-tempered, forbearing, forgiving, gentle, imperturbable, indulgent, lenient, long-suffering, meek, mild, mild-tempered, persevering, persistent, philosophic, philosophical, quiet, resigned, self-possessed, serene, stoical, submissive, tolerant, tranquil, uncomplaining, understanding, unruffled, untiring; SEE CONCEPTS 404,542

patrician [n] *person born to upper-class*
aristocrat, blue blood*, gentleperson, noble, nobleperson, peer, silk stocking*, upper cruster*; SEE CONCEPT 423

patrician [adj] *upper-class*
aristocratic, blue-blooded*, gentle, grand, highborn, high-class, noble, royal, well-born; SEE CONCEPTS 334,549

patriot [n] *person who loves his or her country*
flag-waver*, good citizen, jingoist*, loyalist, nationalist, partisan, patrioteer, statesperson, ultranationalist, volunteer; SEE CONCEPT 413

patrol [n] *guarding; guard*
convoying, defending, escorting, garrison, lookout, patroler, policing, protecting, protection, rounds, safeguarding, scouting, sentinel, spy, vigilance, watch, watching, watchperson; SEE CONCEPTS 134,354,358

patrol [v] *guard, protect*
cruise, inspect, keep guard, keep watch, make the rounds*, mount, police, pound, range, ride shotgun, safeguard, shotgun, walk the beat*, watch; SEE CONCEPTS 134,623

patron [n1] *person who supports a cause*
advocate, angel*, backer, benefactor, booster, champion, defender, encourager, fairy godparent*, fan, financer, friend, front*, guarantor, guardian, guide, head, helper, leader, partisan, patron saint*, philanthropist, protector, sponsor, supporter, surety, sympathizer, well-wisher; SEE CONCEPTS 348,359,423

patron [n2] *person who does business at establishment*
buyer, client, customer, frequenter, habitué, purchaser, shopper; SEE CONCEPT 348

patronage [n1] *support of a cause*
advocacy, aegis, aid, assistance, auspices, backing, benefaction, championship, encouragement, financing, grant, guardianship, help, promotion, protection, recommendation, sponsorship, subsidy, support; SEE CONCEPTS 110,332,341

patronage [n2] *business done at an establishment*
buying, clientage, clientele, commerce, custom, shopping, trade, trading, traffic; SEE CONCEPTS 323,324

patronage [n3] *condescension*
civility, cronyism, deference, deigning, disdain, insolence, patronization, patronizing, stooping, sufferance, toleration; SEE CONCEPTS 83,300

patronize [v1] *condescend*
be gracious to, be lofty, be overbearing, deign, favor, indulge, look down on*, pat on the back*, snub, stoop, talk down to*, toss a few crumbs*, treat as inferior, treat badly, treat like a child*; SEE CONCEPT 384

patronize [v2] *support a cause*
assist, back, befriend, foster, fund, help, maintain, promote, sponsor, subscribe to; SEE CONCEPTS 110,341

pa
pa

patronize [v3] *do business at an establishment*
be a client, be a customer, buy, buy from, deal with, frequent, give business to, habituate, purchase from, shop at, shop with, trade with; SEE CONCEPTS 324,327

patter [n1/v1] *light walk; soft beat*
chatter, pad, pat, pelt, pitapat*, pitter-patter*, rat-a-tat*, rattle, scurry, scuttle, skip, tap, tiptoe, trip; SEE CONCEPTS 65,149

patter [n2] *casual talk*
argot, cant, chatter, dialect, jabber*, jargon, jive*, line*, lingo, monologue, patois, pitch*, prattle*, slant*, spiel*, vernacular; SEE CONCEPTS 276,278

patter [v2] *gab, chatter*
babble, blab*, clack*, hold forth*, jabber, jaw*, prate, prattle, rattle, spiel*, spout, tattle, yak*, yakety-yak*; SEE CONCEPT 266

pattern [n1] *design, motif*
arrangement, decoration, device, diagram, figure, guide, impression, instruction, markings, mold, motive, original, ornament, patterning, plan, stencil, template, trim; SEE CONCEPTS 259,625

pattern [n2] *arrangement, order*
constellation, kind, method, orderliness, plan, sequence, shape, sort, style, system, type, variety; SEE CONCEPTS 6,727,770

pattern [n3] *model, example*
archetype, beau ideal*, copy, criterion, cynosure, ensample, exemplar, guide, mirror, norm, original, paradigm, paragon, prototype, sample, specimen, standard; SEE CONCEPT 686

pattern [v] *copy, imitate; decorate*
design, emulate, follow, form, model, mold, order, shape, style, trim; SEE CONCEPTS 111,171

paucity [n] *lack, scarcity*
absence, dearth, deficiency, famine, fewness, insufficiency, insufficiency, meagerness, paltriness, poverty, rarity, scantiness, scarceness, shortage, slenderness, slightness, smallness, sparseness, sparsity; SEE CONCEPTS 335,646,767

paunch [n] *large stomach*
abdomen, belly, bulge, epigastrium, fat, gut, potbelly*, spare tire*, tummy*; SEE CONCEPT 399

pauper [n] *person who is poor*
almsperson, bankrupt, beggar, bum, dependent, destitute, down-and-out*, have-not*, homeless person, indigent, insolvent, in the gutter*, lazarus*, mendicant, poor person, supplicant; SEE CONCEPT 423

pause [n] *wait, delay*
abeyance, break, break-off*, breathing space*, breathing spell*, caesura, cessation, coffee break*, comma, cutoff, deadlock, discontinuance, downtime*, freeze*, gap, gridlock*, halt, happy hour*, hesitancy, hesitation, hiatus, hitch*, hush*, interim, interlude, intermission, interregnum, interruption, interval, lacuna, lapse, layoff, letup*, lull, pausation, recess, respite, rest, rest period, stand, standstill, stay, stillness, stopover, stoppage, suspension, time out*; SEE CONCEPT 807

pause [v] *wait, delay*
break it up*, call time*, catch one's breath*, cease, come to standstill*, deliberate, desist, discontinue, drop, halt, hesitate, hold back, interrupt, put on hold, reflect, rest, shake, sideline, stop briefly, suspend, take a break*, take a breather*, take five*, take ten*, think twice*, waver; SEE CONCEPTS *119,121,234*

pave [v] *cover with asphalt, concrete*
brick, cobblestone, flagstone, gravel, lay asphalt, lay concrete, macadamize, surface, tar, tile; SEE CONCEPTS 168,172

pavilion [n] *domed building or tent*
awning, canopy, cover, covering, dome, structure; SEE CONCEPT 439

paw [v] *touch roughly*
clap, claw, clutch, dig, feel, finger, fondle, grab, grate, grope, handle, hit, maul, molest, palpate, pat, rake, rasp, rub, scratch, search, slap, smite, stroke; SEE CONCEPTS 375,612

pawn [n1] *security for a loan*
assurance, bond, collateral, earnest, forfeit, gage, gambit, guarantee, guaranty, pledge, security, token, warrant; SEE CONCEPT 332

pawn [n2] *person who is a fool*
creature, dupe*, instrument, mark*, patsy*, pigeon*, puppet, stooge*, sucker*, tool, toy, victim; SEE CONCEPT 412

pawn [v] *give as security for a loan*
deposit, give in earnest, hazard, hock*, hook*, mortgage, pledge; SEE CONCEPTS 115,330

pay [n] *earnings from employment*
allowance, bacon*, bread*, commission, compensation, consideration, defrayment, emoluments, fee, hire*, honorarium, income, indemnity, meed, payment, perquisite, pittance, proceeds, profit, reckoning, recompensation, recompense, redress, reimbursement, remuneration, reparation, requital, return, reward, salary, satisfaction, scale, settlement, stipend, stipendium, take-home*, takings*, wage, wages; SEE CONCEPTS 329,332, 340,344

pay [v1] *give money for goods, services*
adjust, bear the cost, bear the expense, bequeath, bestow, chip in*, clear, come through, compensate, confer, cough up*, defray, dig up*, disburse, discharge, extend, foot*, foot the bill*, grant, handle, hand over*, honor, kick in*, liquidate, make payment, meet, offer, plunk down*, prepay, present, proffer, put up*, recompense, recoup, refund, reimburse, remit, remunerate, render, repay, requite, reward, satisfy, settle, stake, take care of*; SEE CONCEPTS 327,341,351

pay [v2] *be advantageous*
benefit, be worthwhile, repay, serve; SEE CONCEPT 700

pay [v3] *make amends*
answer, atone, be punished, compensate, get just desserts*, suffer, suffer consequences; SEE CONCEPT 23

pay [v4] *profit, yield*
be profitable, be remunerative, bring in, kick back*, make a return, make money, pay dividends, pay off*, pay out*, produce, provide a living, return, show gain, show profit, sweeten*, yield profit; SEE CONCEPT 330

pay [v5] *get revenge*
avenge oneself, get even, make up for, pay back*, pay one's dues*, punish, reciprocate, recompense, repay, requite, retaliate, settle a score*, square, square things*; SEE CONCEPT 122

payable [adj] *to be paid*
due, mature, maturing, obligatory, outstanding, overdue, owed, owing, receivable, unpaid, unsettled; SEE CONCEPT 334

payment [n] *fee; installment of fee*
acquittal, advance, alimony, amends, amortization, amount, annuity, award, bounty, cash, de-

frayal, defrayment, deposit, disbursement, discharge, down, fee, hire, indemnification, outlay, part, paying, pay-off, pension, portion, premium, quittance, reckoning, recompense, redress, refund, reimbursement, remittance, remuneration, reparation, repayment, requital, restitution, retaliation, return, reward, salary, settlement, subsidy, sum, support, wage; SEE CONCEPT 344

payoff [n] *conclusion, climax*
adjustment, clincher*, consequence, culmination, day of reckoning*, finale, final reckoning*, judgment, moment of truth*, outcome, pay, payment, punch line*, result, retribution, reward, settlement, upshot*; SEE CONCEPTS 230,679

peace [n1] *harmony, agreement*
accord, amity, armistice, cessation, conciliation, concord, friendship, love, neutrality, order, pacification, pacifism, reconciliation, treaty, truce, unanimity, union, unity; SEE CONCEPTS 388,691

peace [n2] *calm, serenity*
amity, calmness, composure, concord, congeniality, contentment, equanimity, harmony, hush, lull, peacefulness, placidity, quiet, quietude, relaxation, repose, reserve, rest, silence, stillness, sympathy, tranquility; SEE CONCEPTS 410,705, 720

peaceable [adj] *friendly, serene*
amiable, amicable, calm, complacent, conciliatory, gentle, irenic, mild, neighborly, nonviolent, pacific, pacificatory, pacifist, peaceful, peace-loving, placid, quiet, restful, still, tranquil; SEE CONCEPT 548

peaceful [adj] *friendly, serene*
all quiet, amicable, at peace, bloodless, calm, collected, composed, constant, easeful, equable, free from strife*, gentle, halcyon, harmonious, irenic, level, mellow, neutral, neutralist, nonbelligerent, nonviolent, on friendly terms*, on good terms*, pacifistic, peaceable, peace-loving, placatory, placid, quiet, restful, smooth, sociable, steady, still, tranquil, undisturbed, unruffled, untroubled, without hostility; SEE CONCEPTS 485,542

peacemaker [n] *person who settles problem*
appeaser, arbitrator, conciliator, diplomat, makepeace, mediator, negotiator, pacificator, pacifier, pacifist, peacekeeper, peacemonger*, placater, statesperson; SEE CONCEPTS 354,416

peak [n1] *top of something*
aiguille, alp, apex, brow, bump, cope, crest, crown, hill, mount, mountain, pinnacle, point, roof, spike, summit, tip, vertex; SEE CONCEPTS 509,836

peak [n2] *maximum, zenith*
acme, apex, apogee, capstone, climax, crown, culmination, greatest, height, high point, meridian, ne plus ultra, pinnacle, summit, tip, top; SEE CONCEPTS 668,766,767,832

peak [v] *reach highest point*
be at height, climax, come to a head*, crest, culminate, reach the top, reach the zenith, top out*; SEE CONCEPTS 763,780

peaked [adj] *pale, sick*
ailing, bilious, emaciated, ill, in bad shape*, peaky, poorly, sickly, under the weather*, wan; SEE CONCEPTS 314,618

peal [n] *chime, clang*
blast, carillon, clamor, clap, crash, resounding, reverberation, ring, ringing, roar, rumble, sound, thunder, tintinnabulation*; SEE CONCEPT 595

peal [v] *chime, clang*
bell, bong, crack, crash, knell, resonate, resound, reverberate, ring, ring out, roar, roll, rumble, sound, strike, thunder, tintinnabulate*, toll; SEE CONCEPT 65

pearly [adj] *opalescent*
fair, frosted, iridescent, ivory, milky, nacreous, off-white, opaline, pearl, silver; SEE CONCEPT 618

peck [n/v] *bite*
beak, dig, hit, jab, kiss, mark, nibble, pick, pinch, poke, prick, rap, strike, tap; SEE CONCEPTS 169,189

peculiar [adj1] *characteristic, distinguishing*
appropriate, diacritic, diagnostic, distinct, distinctive, endemic, exclusive, idiosyncratic, individual, intrinsic, local, particular, personal, private, proper, restricted, special, specific, typical, unique; SEE CONCEPTS 404,557

peculiar [adj2] *bizarre, odd*
abnormal, bent*, creepy*, curious, eccentric, exceptional, extraordinary, flaky*, freakish, freaky, funny, idiosyncratic, kinky*, kooky*, oddball, offbeat, off-the-wall*, outlandish, quaint, queer, singular, strange, uncommon, unconventional, uncustomary, unusual, wacky*, way-out*, weird, wonderful; SEE CONCEPTS 404,564

peculiarity [n] *characteristic; oddity*
abnormality, affectation, attribute, bizarreness, character, distinctiveness, eccentricity, feature, foible, freakishness, gimmick, idiosyncrasy, kink*, mannerism, mark, odd trait, particularity, property, quality, queerness, quirk, savor, schtick*, singularity, slant*, specialty, trait, twist*, unusualness; SEE CONCEPTS 411,665

pedagogic [adj] *educational*
academic, dogmatic, instructive, learned, professorial, profound, scholastic, teaching; SEE CONCEPTS 529,536

pedantic [adj] *bookish, precise*
abstruse, academic, arid, didactic, doctrinaire, donnish, dry, dull, egotistic, erudite, formal, fussy, hairsplitting*, learned, nit-picking, ostentatious, overnice, particular, pedagogic, pompous, priggish*, punctilious, scholastic, schoolish, sententious, stilted; SEE CONCEPTS 401,529

peddle [v] *sell door to door*
canvas*, hawk*, huckster*, market, monger*, push, shove, solicit, trade, vend; SEE CONCEPT 345

pedestrian [n] *person traveling on foot*
ambler, hiker, jaywalker*, passerby, stroller, walker; SEE CONCEPT 366

pedestrian [adj] *everyday, dull*
banal, banausic, blah*, boring, commonplace, dim, dreary, flat, humdrum*, inane, jejune, mediocre, monotone, monotonous, mundane, ordinary, platitudinous, plodding, prosaic, run-of-the-mill*, stodgy, truistic, unimaginative, uninspired, uninteresting, wishy-washy*; SEE CONCEPTS 530,547

pedigree [n] *ancestry, heritage*
blood, breed, clan, derivation, descent, extraction, family, family tree, genealogy, heredity, line, lineage, origin, race, stirps, stock; SEE CONCEPT 296

pedigree [adj] *purebred*
full-blooded, pedigreed, pure-blood, thoroughbred; SEE CONCEPT 549

pa
pe

peek/peep [n] *sneaked look*
blink, gander*, glance, glimpse, look-see, sight; SEE CONCEPT *623*

peek/peep [v] *sneak a look*
blink, glance, glimpse, have a gander*, look, peer, snatch, snoop, spy, squint, stare, take a look; SEE CONCEPT *623*

peel [n] *skin, covering*
bark, cover, epicarp, exocarp, husk, peeling, pellicle, rind, shell, shuck; SEE CONCEPTS *428,484*

peel [v] *take off outer covering*
decorticate, delaminate, desquamate, excorticate, exfoliate, flake, flay, pare, pull off, scale, shave, skin, strip, tear off, uncover; SEE CONCEPTS *142,176,211*

peep [n2/v2] *chirp*
chatter, cheep, chirrup, chuck, churr, coo, cry, hoot, pipe, squeak, tweet, twitter; SEE CONCEPT *64*

peep/peer [v3/v2] *appear briefly*
become visible, crop up, emerge, open to view, peep out, peer out, show partially; SEE CONCEPT *261*

peer [n] *person who is another's equal*
associate, coequal, companion, compeer, like, match, rival; SEE CONCEPT *423*

peer [v1] *scan, scrutinize*
bore, eagle eye*, eye*, eyeball*, focus, gape, gawk, gaze, get a load of, glare, glim, gloat, inspect, look, peep, pin*, pry, rubberneck*, snoop, spy, squint, stare; SEE CONCEPTS *103,623*

peerless [adj] *having no equal; superior*
aces*, all-time, alone, best, beyond compare, champion, excellent, faultless, gilt-edge*, greatest, incomparable, matchless, most, nonpareil*, only, outstanding, perfect, second to none*, solid-gold*, super, superlative, supreme, tops*, unequaled, unexampled, unique, unmatched, unparagoned, unparalleled, unrivaled, unsurpassed, world class*; SEE CONCEPT *574*

peeve [n] *something strongly disliked*
annoyance, bother, gripe, nuisance, pest, sore point*, vexation; SEE CONCEPTS *532,690*

peeve [v] *bother, annoy*
aggravate, anger, bug*, bum*, burn*, disturb, drive up the wall*, exasperate, gall, get, get one's goat*, hack*, irk, irritate, miff*, nettle, pique, provoke, put out, rile, roil, rub the wrong way*, steam*, T-off*, vex; SEE CONCEPTS *7,19*

peevish [adj] *irritable, testy*
acrimonious, angry, bad-tempered, cantankerous, captious, carping, caviling, childish, churlish, complaining, crabbed*, cranky, critical, cross, crotchety*, crusty*, cussed, fault-finding, fractious, fretful, fretting, grouchy, grousing, growling, grumpy, huffy, ill-natured, mean, morose, obstinate, ogre, ornery, out-of-sorts*, pertinacious, petulant, querulous, short-tempered, snappy, splenetic, sulky, sullen, surly, tetchy, touchy, ugly, waspish, waspy, whining; SEE CONCEPTS *401,542*

peg [v] *attach*
clinch, fasten, fix, join, make fast, pin, secure, tighten; SEE CONCEPTS *85,160*

pejorative [adj] *negative, belittling*
debasing, deprecatory, depreciatory, derisive, derogatory, detracting, detractive, detractory, disadvantageous, disparaging, irreverent, rude, slighting, uncomplimentary, unpleasant; SEE CONCEPT *267*

pell-mell [n] *disorder*
anarchy, ataxia, chaos, clutter, confusion, disarray, ferment, helter-skelter, huddle, muddle, pandemonium, snarl, tumult, turmoil, upheaval; SEE CONCEPT *674*

pell-mell [adj] *disordered*
chaotic, confused, disarrayed, disorganized, haphazard, muddled, tumultous/tumultuous; SEE CONCEPTS *562,585*

pell-mell [adv] *hurriedly and carelessly*
foolishly, full tilt*, hastily, headlong, heedlessly, helter-skelter, impetuously, incontinently, indiscreetly, posthaste, precipitiously, rashly, recklessly, thoughtlessly; SEE CONCEPTS *544,799*

pelt [n] *animal fur*
coat, epidermis, fell, hair, hide, jacket, skin, slough, wool; SEE CONCEPT *399*

pelt [v] *beat; throw hard*
assail, batter, belabor, belt, bombard, career, cast, charge, dash, hammer, hurl, knock, lapidate, pepper, pound, pour, pummel, rain, rush, shoot, shower, sling, speed, stone, strike, swat, tear, thrash, wallop; SEE CONCEPTS *189,222*

pen [n1] *enclosure*
cage, coop, corral, fence, fold, hedge, hutch, jail, penitentiary, prison, sty, wall*; SEE CONCEPTS *439,443*

pen [n2] *writing instrument*
ball point, felt-tip, fountain pen, marker, nib, quill, reed, stick, stylograph; SEE CONCEPTS *277,499*

pen [v1] *enclose*
box, cage, case, close in, confine, coop, corral, fence in, hedge, hem in, mew*, shut in; SEE CONCEPTS *191,758*

pen [v2] *write*
autograph, commit to paper, compose, draft, draw up, engross, indict, jot down; SEE CONCEPT *79*

penal [adj] *disciplinary*
chastening, corrective, penalizing, punishing, punitive, punitory, reformatory, retributive; SEE CONCEPTS *548,583*

penalize [v] *punish*
amerce, castigate, chasten, chastise, condemn, correct, discipline, dock*, fine, handicap, hit with*, impose penalty, inflict handicap, judge, mulct, put at disadvantage, scold, slap with*, throw the book at*; SEE CONCEPT *122*

penalty [n] *punishment*
amends, amercement, cost, damages, disadvantage, discipline, dues, fall, fine, forfeit, forfeiture, handicap, mortification, mulct, price, rap*, retribution; SEE CONCEPTS *344,679*

penance [n] *reparation for wrong*
absolution, atonement, attrition, compensation, compunction, confession, contrition, expiation, forgiveness, hair shirt*, mortification, penalty, penitence, punishment, purgation, remorse, remorsefulness, repentance, retribution, rue, ruth, sackcloth and ashes*, self-flagellation*, shrift, sorrow, suffering; SEE CONCEPTS *126,367,384,410*

penchant [n] *fondness, inclination*
affection, affinity, attachment, bias, disposition, druthers*, inclining, itch*, leaning, liking, partiality, predilection, predisposition, proclivity, proneness, propensity, taste, tendency, tilt*, turn*, weakness, yen; SEE CONCEPTS *20,32,411,709*

pending [*adj*] *about to happen*
awaiting, continuing, dependent, forthcoming, hanging, imminent, impending, indeterminate, in line*, in the balance*, in the offing*, in the works*, ominous, on board*, on line*, pensile, undecided, undetermined, unsettled, up in the air*; SEE CONCEPT 548

pendulous/pendent [*adj*] *hanging*
dangling, dependent, drooping, pending, pendulant, pensile, suspended, swinging; SEE CONCEPTS 485,584

penetrate [*v1*] *pierce; get through physically*
access, barge in, bayonet, blow in, bore, break in, breeze in, bust in, charge, come, crack, diffuse, drill, drive, eat through, encroach, enter, filter in, force, get in, gore, go through, impale, infiltrate, ingress, insert, insinuate, introduce, invade, jab, knife, make a hole, make an entrance, pass through, percolate, perforate, permeate, pervade, pop in, prick, probe, puncture, ream, run into, saturate, seep, sink into, spear, stab, stick into, suffuse, thrust, trespass; SEE CONCEPTS 159,179,220

penetrate [*v2*] *understand or be understood*
affect, become clear, come across*, comprehend, decipher, discern, fathom, figure out, get across*, get over*, get through*, get to the bottom*, grasp, impress, perceive, put over*, see through*, sink in*, soak in*, touch, unravel, work out; SEE CONCEPT 15

penetrating [*adj1*] *stinging, harsh*
biting, carrying, clear-cut, crisp, cutting, edged, entering, forcing, going through, infiltrating, ingoing, intrusive, passing through, penetrant, permeating, pervasive, piercing, pointed, puncturing, pungent, sharp, shrill, strong, trenchant; SEE CONCEPTS 267,537

penetrating [*adj2*] *intelligent*
acute, astute, critical, discerning, discriminating, incisive, keen, penetrative, perceptive, perspicacious, profound, quick, quick-witted, sagacious, searching, sharp, sharp-witted, shrewd; SEE CONCEPT 402

penitence [*n*] *shame, sorrow*
anguish, attrition, compunction, contriteness, contrition, debasement, degradation, distress, grief, humbling, humiliation, penance, qualm, regret, remorse, remorsefulness, repentance, rue, ruefulness, ruth, sadness, scruple, self-castigation, self-condemnation, self-flagellation, self-punishment, self-reproach; SEE CONCEPT 410

penitent [*adj*] *shamed, sorrowful*
abject, apologetic, atoning, attritional, compunctious, conscience-stricken, contrite, penitential, regretful, remorseful, repentant, rueful, sorry; SEE CONCEPTS 403,542

penitentiary [*n*] *jail*
big house*, campus, can*, college, cooler*, correctional institution, inside*, joint*, lockup*, pen*, penal institution, prison, reformatory, slammer*, stockade; SEE CONCEPTS 439,449,516

pennant [*n*] *flag, banner*
banderole, bunting, burgee, color, decoration, emblem, ensign, jack, pennon, standard, streamer; SEE CONCEPTS 260,473

penniless [*adj*] *without any money*
bankrupt, broke*, clean*, cleaned out*, dead broke*, destitute, dirt poor*, down to last penny*, flat*, flat broke*, impecunious, impoverished, indigent, in the gutter*, lacking, moneyless, neces-

sitous, needy, on last leg*, over a barrel*, penurious, poor, poverty-stricken, ruined, strapped*, tapped out*, without a dime*; SEE CONCEPT 334

pension [*n*] *benefits paid after retirement*
allowance, annuity, gift, grant, IRA*, payment, premium, retirement account, reward, social security, subsidy, subvention, superannuation, support; SEE CONCEPTS 332,344

pensive [*adj*] *meditative, solemn*
absorbed, abstracted, attentive, cogitative, contemplative, dreamy, grave, musing, pondering, preoccupied, reflecting, reflective, ruminating, ruminative, serious, sober, speculative, thinking, thoughtful, wistful, withdrawn; SEE CONCEPT 403

pent-up [*adj*] *held within*
bottled-up, bridled, checked, constrained, curbed, held-back, held in check, inhibited, repressed, restrained, restricted, smothered, stifled, suppressed; SEE CONCEPTS 401,403

people [*n*] *human beings*
bodies, body politic*, bourgeois, cats*, citizens, clan, commonality, common people, community, crowd, family, folk, folks, general public, heads*, herd, hoi polloi*, horde, humanity, humankind, human race, humans, inhabitants, John/Jane Q. Public*, kin, masses, mob, mortals, multitude, nation, nationality, person in the street*, persons, plebeians, populace, population, proletariat, public, rabble, race, rank and file*, riffraff*, society, tribe; SEE CONCEPTS 296,379,380,417

pep [*n*] *vim, vigor*
animation, bang, birr, energy, get-up-and-go*, go, gusto, hardihood, high spirits, life, liveliness, moxie*, potency, punch*, push, snap*, spirit, starch*, tuck*, verve, vitality, vivacity, zip*; SEE CONCEPTS 411,633

peppery [*adj1*] *highly seasoned*
fiery, hot, piquant, poignant, pungent, racy, snappy, spicy, zestful, zesty; SEE CONCEPT 613

peppery [*adj2*] *irritable; sarcastic*
acute, angry, astringent, biting, caustic, choleric, cranky, cross, fiery, hot-tempered, incisive, irascible, keen, lively, passionate, quick-tempered, sharp, sharp-tempered, snappish, spirited, spunky, stinging, testy, touchy, trenchant, waspish; SEE CONCEPTS 267,401,542

peppy [*adj*] *lively, vigorous*
active, alert, animate, animated, bright, gay, keen, perky, sparkling, spirited, sprightly, vivacious; SEE CONCEPTS 401,404

pep up [*v*] *invigorate, inspire*
animate, enliven, exhilarate, jazz up*, quicken, stimulate, vitalize, vivify; SEE CONCEPTS 7,22

perceive [*v1*] *notice, see*
apperceive, apprehend, be aware of, behold, descry, discern, discover, distinguish, divine, espy, feel, grasp, identify, look, make out, mark, mind, note, observe, realize, recognize, regard, remark, seize, sense, spot, spy, take; SEE CONCEPTS 38,626

perceive [*v2*] *understand*
appreciate, apprehend, comprehend, conclude, copy, deduce, distinguish, feature, feel, flash*, gather, get, get the message*, get the picture*, grasp, know, learn, pin*, read, realize, recognize, see, sense, track; SEE CONCEPT 15

percentage [*n*] *portion, allotment*
allowance, bite, bonus, chunk, commission, corner*, cut, discount, division, duty, fee, holdout,

interest, juice*, payoff, percent, piece, piece of the action*, points*, proportion, quota, rate, ratio, section, slice*, split*, taste*, winnings; SEE CONCEPTS 766,784,835

perceptible [adj] *noticeable, obvious*
apparent, appreciable, audible, clear, cognizable, conspicuous, detectable, discernible, distinct, distinguishable, evident, lucid, observable, palpable, perceivable, perspicuous, recognizable, sensible, signal, tangible, understandable, visible; SEE CONCEPTS 529,576

perception [n] *understanding, idea*
acumen, apprehending, apprehension, approach, attention, attitude, awareness, big idea*, brainchild*, brain wave*, conceit, concept, conception, consciousness, discernment, feeling, flash, grasp, image, impression, insight, intellection, judgment, knowledge, light, notion, observation, opinion, perspicacity, picture, plan, realizing, recognition, sagacity, sensation, sense, study, taste, thought, viewpoint; SEE CONCEPTS 409,410,689

perceptive [adj] *alert, sensitive*
acute, astute, awake, aware, brainy*, conscious, discerning, discreet, ear to the ground*, gnostic, incisive, insighted, insightful, intuitive, judicious, keen, knowing, knowledgeable, knows what's what*, observant, penetrating, penetrative, percipient, perspicacious, quick, rational, responsive, sagacious, sage, savvy*, sharp, sophic, tuned in*, wise, wise to*; SEE CONCEPTS 402,542

perch [n] *object placed high for sitting on*
branch, landing place, lounge, pole, post, resting place, roost, seat; SEE CONCEPTS 443,479

perch [v] *sit atop of*
alight, balance, land, light, rest, roost, set down, settle, sit on, squat, touch down; SEE CONCEPT 154

percolate [v] *seep, drip (liquid)*
bleed, bubble, charge, drain, exude, filter, filtrate, impregnate, leach, ooze, pass through, penetrate, perk, permeate, pervade, saturate, strain, sweat, transfuse, transude, weep; SEE CONCEPTS 179,181

peremptory [adj] *overbearing, authoritative*
absolute, arbitrary, assertive, autocratic, binding, bossy, categorical, certain, commanding, compelling, decided, decisive, dictatorial, dogmatic, domineering, final, finished, firm, fixed, high-handed, imperative, imperial, imperious, incontrovertible, intolerant, irrefutable, magisterial, obligatory, obstinate, positive, rigorous, severe, stringent, tyrannical, uncompromising, undeniable; SEE CONCEPTS 535,537,542

perennial [adj] *enduring, perpetual*
abiding, annual, ceaseless, chronic, constant, continual, continuing, deathless, durable, eternal, everlasting, immortal, imperishable, incessant, inveterate, lasting, lifelong, long-lasting, long-lived, long-standing, never-ending, old, perdurable, permanent, persistent, recurrent, seasonal, sustained, unceasing, unchanging, undying, unfailing, uninterrupted, yearlong, yearly; SEE CONCEPTS 539,798

perfect [adj1] *flawless, superlative*
absolute, accomplished, aces*, adept, A-OK*, beyond compare, blameless, classical, consummate, crowning, culminating, defectless, excellent, excelling, experienced, expert, faultless, finished, foolproof, ideal, immaculate, impeccable, indefectible, matchless, out-of-this-world*, paradis-

iac, paradisiacal, peerless, pure, skilled, skillful, sound, splendid, spotless, stainless, sublime, superb, supreme, ten*, unblemished, unequaled, unmarred, untainted, untarnished, utopian; SEE CONCEPT 574

perfect [adj2] *whole, intact*
absolute, choate, complete, completed, consummate, downright, entire, finished, flawless, full, gross, integral, out-and-out*, outright, positive, rank, sheer, simple, sound, unadulterated, unalloyed, unblemished, unbroken, undamaged, unimpaired, unmitigated, unmixed, unqualified, utter; SEE CONCEPTS 482,485

perfect [adj3] *accurate, correct*
appropriate, bull's-eye*, certain, close, dead-on*, definite, distinct, exact, express, faithful, fit, ideal, model, needed, on target*, on the button*, on the money*, precise, proper, required, requisite, right, sharp, strict, suitable, textbook, to a T*, to a turn*, true, unerring, very; SEE CONCEPTS 535,557,558

perfect [v] *polish; achieve*
accomplish, ameliorate, carry out, complete, consummate, crown, cultivate, develop, effect, elaborate, finish, fulfill, hone, idealize, improve, perform, put finishing touch on, realize, refine, round, slick, smooth; SEE CONCEPTS 91,244,706

perfection [n] *achievement, completeness*
accomplishment, achieving, acme, arete, completion, consummation, crown, ending, entireness, evolution, exactness, excellence, excellency, exquisiteness, faultlessness, finish, finishing, fulfillment, ideal, idealism, impeccability, integrity, maturity, merit, paragon, perfectness, phoenix, precision, purity, quality, realization, ripeness, sublimity, superiority, supremacy, transcendence, virtue, wholeness; SEE CONCEPTS 671,706

perfectly [adv1] *absolutely*
altogether, completely, consummately, entirely, fully, quite, thoroughly, totally, utterly, well, wholly; SEE CONCEPTS 531,544

perfectly [adv2] *without flaw*
admirably, correctly, excellently, exquisitely, faultlessly, fitly, flawlessly, ideally, impeccably, superbly, superlatively, supremely, to perfection, wonderfully; SEE CONCEPT 574

perforate [v] *make a hole in*
bore, drill, drive, hole, honeycomb*, penetrate, permeate, pierce, pit, poke full of holes*, probe, punch, puncture, shoot full of holes*, slit, stab; SEE CONCEPT 220

perform [v1] *carry out, accomplish*
achieve, act, be engaged in, behave, bring about, bring off, carry through, carry to completion, complete, comply, deliver the goods*, discharge, dispose of, do, do justice to*, do to a turn*, effect, end, enforce, execute, finish, fulfill, function, go that route*, implement, meet, move, observe, operate, percolate, perk, pull off*, put through, react, realize, run with the ball*, satisfy, take, take care of business*, tick, transact, wind up, work; SEE CONCEPTS 91,199

perform [v2] *act, depict as entertainment*
act out, appear as, be on, bring down the house*, discourse, display, do a number*, do a turn*, dramatize, emote, enact, execute, exhibit, give, go on, ham*, ham it up*, impersonate, offer, personate, play, playact, present, produce, put on, render, represent, show, stage, tread the boards*; SEE CONCEPT 292

performance [n1] *accomplishment*
achievement, act, administration, attainment, carrying out, completion, conduct, consummation, discharge, doing, enforcement, execution, exploit, feat, fruition, fulfillment, pursuance, realization, work; SEE CONCEPT 706

performance [n2] *acting, depiction*
act, appearance, ballet, behavior, burlesque, business, ceremony, concert, custom, dance, display, drama, exhibition, gig*, interpretation, matinee, offering, opera, pageant, play, portrayal, presentation, production, recital, rehearsal, representation, review, revue, rigmarole, rite, set, show, special, spectacle, stage show, stunt, to-do*; SEE CONCEPT 263

performance [n3] *efficiency*
action, conduct, effectiveness, efficacy, exercise, functioning, operation, practice, pursuit, running, working; SEE CONCEPT 630

perfume [n] *scent, often manufactured and packaged for personal use*
aroma, attar, balm, balminess, bouquet, cologne, eau de cologne, essence, fragrance, incense, odor, oil, redolence, sachet, smell, spice, sweetness; SEE CONCEPTS 599,600

perfunctory [adj] *automatic, unthinking*
apathetic, careless, cool, cursory, disinterested, going through the motions*, heedless, impersonal, inattentive, indifferent, involuntary, lackadaisical, laid-back*, mechanical, negligent, offhand, phoning it in*, routine, sketchy, slipshod*, slovenly, standard, stereotyped, stock, superficial, unaware, unconcerned, uninterested, usual, walking through it*, wooden*; SEE CONCEPTS 542,544

perhaps [adv] *possibly*
as it may be, as the case may be, conceivably, feasibly, for all one knows, imaginably, it may be, maybe, perchance, reasonably; SEE CONCEPT 552

peril [n] *danger, risk*
cause for alarm*, double trouble*, endangerment, exposure, hazard, insecurity, jeopardy, liability, menace, openness, pitfall, risky business*, uncertainty, vulnerability; SEE CONCEPT 675

perilous [adj] *dangerous*
chancy, delicate, dicey*, dynamite, exposed, hairy*, hazardous, insecure, loaded*, on thin ice*, playing with fire*, precarious, risky, rugged, Russian roulette*, shaky, threatening, ticklish, touch and go*, touchy, treacherous, uncertain, unhealthy, unsafe, unsound, unstable, unsteady, unsure, vulnerable, wicked*; SEE CONCEPTS 548,587

perimeter [n] *circumference, border*
ambit, borderline, boundary, bounds, brim, brink, circuit, compass, confines, edge, fringe, hem, limit, margin, outline, periphery, skirt, verge; SEE CONCEPTS 484,745,792

period [n1] *extent of time*
aeon, age, course, cycle, date, days, duration, epoch, era, generation, interval, measure, season, space, span, spell, stage, stretch, term, time, while, years; SEE CONCEPTS 807,822

period [n2] *ending*
cessation, close, closing, closure, conclusion, discontinuance, end, limit, stop, termination; SEE CONCEPT 832

periodic [adj] *at fixed intervals*
alternate, annual, at various times, centennial, cyclic, cyclical, daily, epochal, every once in a while, every so often, fluctuating, hourly, infrequent, intermittent, isochronal, isochronous, monthly, occasional, on-again-off-again*, on certain occasions, orbital, perennial, periodical, recurrent, recurring, regular, repeated, rhythmic, routine, seasonal, serial, spasmodic, sporadic, weekly, yearly; SEE CONCEPTS 541,799

periodical [n] *regular publication*
journal, mag*, magazine, monthly, newspaper, number, paper, quarterly, rag*, review, serial, sheet*, slick*, throwaway*, weekly; SEE CONCEPT 280

peripatetic [adj] *constantly traveling*
ambulant, itinerant, itinerate, migrant, mobile, nomadic, perambulant, roaming, roving, vagabond, vagrant, wandering, wayfaring; SEE CONCEPTS 401,584

peripheral [adj] *minor, outside*
beside the point, borderline, exterior, external, incidental, inessential, irrelevant, minor, outer, outermost, perimetric, secondary, superficial, surface, tangential, unimportant; SEE CONCEPTS 575,583,831

periphery [n] *outskirts, outer edge*
ambit, border, boundary, brim, brink, circuit, circumference, compass, covering, edge, fringe, hem, margin, outside, perimeter, rim, skirt, verge; SEE CONCEPTS 484,745

perish [v] *die, decline, decay*
be destroyed, be killed, be lost, bite the dust*, break down, buy the farm*, cease, check out*, collapse, corrupt, croak, crumble, decease, decompose, demise, depart, disappear, disintegrate, end, expire, fall, give up the ghost*, go, go under, kick the bucket*, lose life, OD*, pass, pass away, pass on, rot, succumb, vanish, waste*, wither; SEE CONCEPTS 13,105,304

perishable [adj] *liable to spoil, rot*
decaying, decomposable, destructible, easily spoiled, short-lived, unstable; SEE CONCEPTS 462,485

perjure [v] *give false testimony*
bear false witness*, commit perjury, deceive, delude, equivocate, falsify, forswear, lie, lie under oath, mislead, prevaricate, swear falsely, trick; SEE CONCEPTS 63,317

perk [n] *benefit*
advantage, bonus, dividend, extra, fringe benefit, gratuity, gravy*, lagniappe, largess, perquisite, plus, tip; SEE CONCEPT 344

perk up [v] *cheer*
ameliorate, be refreshed, brighten, buck up*, cheer up, convalesce, gain, improve, invigorate, liven up, look up, mend, pep up, rally, recover, recuperate, refresh, renew, revive, shake, take heart*; SEE CONCEPTS 7,22,244,308

perky [adj] *animated, happy*
active, alert, aware, bouncy, bright, bright-eyed and bushy-tailed*, brisk, bubbly, buoyant, cheerful, cheery, gay, in fine fettle*, jaunty, lively, spirited, sprightly, sunny, vivacious; SEE CONCEPTS 401,404

permanent [adj] *constant, lasting*
abiding, changeless, continual, diurnal, durable, enduring, everlasting, fixed, forever, forever and a day*, for keeps*, immutable, imperishable, indestructible, in for the long haul*, invariable, long-lasting, perdurable, perduring, perennial, perpetual, persistent, set, set in concrete*, set in

stone*, stable, steadfast, unchanging, unfading; SEE CONCEPTS *551,649,798*

permeable [*adj*] *absorbent, penetrable*
absorptive, accessible, enterable, passable, pervious, porose, porous, spongelike, spongy; SEE CONCEPTS *576,604,606*

permeate [*v*] *filter, spread throughout*
charge, diffuse, drench, fill, go through, imbue, impregnate, infiltrate, infuse, ingrain, interfuse, invade, pass through, penetrate, percolate, pervade, pierce, saturate, seep, soak, stab, stalk, steep, suffuse, transfuse; SEE CONCEPTS *159,179,256*

permissible [*adj*] *allowable, legal*
acceptable, admissible, all right, approved, authorized, bearable, endorsed, kosher*, lawful, legalized, legit*, legitimate, licit, okay*, on the up and up*, permitted, proper, sanctioned, tolerable, tolerated, unforbidden, unprohibited; SEE CONCEPTS *319,548,554*

permission [*n*] *authorization, consent*
acceptance, acknowledgment, acquiescence, admission, agreement, allowance, approbation, approval, assent, avowal, canonization, carte blanche*, concession, concurrence, condonance, condonation, dispensation, empowerment, endorsement, freedom, imprimatur, indulgence, leave, letting, liberty, license, okay, permit, privilege, promise, recognition, rubber stamp*, sanctification, sanction, stamp of approval*, sufferance, tolerance, toleration, verification, warrant; SEE CONCEPTS *50,83,88,376,685*

permissive [*adj*] *lenient*
acquiescent, agreeable, allowing, approving, easy-going, forbearing, free, indulgent, latitudinarian, lax, liberal, open-minded, permitting, susceptible, tolerant; SEE CONCEPT *401*

permit [*n*] *authorization*
admittance, allowance, charter, concession, consent, empowering, favor, franchise, go-ahead*, grant, green light*, indulgence, leave, legalization, liberty, license, pass, passport, patent, permission, privilege, safe-conduct, sanction, sufferance, toleration, visa, warrant; SEE CONCEPTS *271,376,685*

permit [*v*] *allow participation*
abet, accede, accept, acquiesce, admit, agree, authorize, bless, blink at*, boost, buy, charter, concede, concur, condone, consent, empower, enable, endorse, endure, franchise, give leave, give permission, go for, grant, have, humor, indulge, leave, let, let pass, license, okay, pass, privilege, sanctify, sanction, say yes, shake on*, sign, sign off on*, suffer, take kindly to*, thumbs up*, tolerate, warrant, wink at*; SEE CONCEPTS *50,83,88*

pernicious [*adj*] *bad, hurtful*
baleful, damaging, dangerous, deadly, deleterious, destructive, detrimental, devastating, evil, fatal, harmful, iniquitous, injurious, killing, lethal, maleficent, malevolent, malicious, malign, malignant, miasmatic, miasmic, mortal, nefarious, noisome, noxious, offensive, pestiferous, pestilent, pestilential, poisonous, prejudicial, ruinous, sinister, toxic, venomous, virulent, wicked; SEE CONCEPTS *537,548,571*

perpendicular [*adj*] *at right angles to*
erect, horizontal, on end, plumb, sheer, standing, stand-up, steep, straight, straight-up, upright, vertical; SEE CONCEPTS *581,583*

perpetrate [*v*] *be responsible for*
act, bring about, carry out, commit, do, effect, enact, execute, inflict, perform, pull, up and do*, wreak; SEE CONCEPT *91*

perpetual [*adj*] *continual, lasting*
abiding, ceaseless, constant, continued, continuous, endless, enduring, eternal, everlasting, going on, immortal, imperishable, incessant, infinite, interminable, intermittent, never-ceasing, never-ending, perdurable, perennial, permanent, persistent, recurrent, recurring, reoccurring, repeated, repeating, repetitious, returning, sempiternal, unceasing, unchanging, undying, unending, unfailing, uninterrupted, unremitting, without end; SEE CONCEPTS *551,649,798,799*

perpetuate [*v*] *keep going*
bolster, conserve, continue, eternalize, eternize, immortalize, keep, keep alive, keep in existence, keep up, maintain, preserve, secure, support, sustain; SEE CONCEPT *239*

perplex [*v*] *confuse, mix up*
astonish, astound, baffle, balk, befuddle, beset, bewilder, buffalo*, complicate, confound, discombobulate*, discompose, dumbfound, encumber, entangle, fog, get to*, involve, jumble, muck, muddle, muddy the waters*, mystify, nonplus, perturb, pose, puzzle, rattle, ravel, snarl up, stumble, stump, surprise, tangle, thicken, thwart; SEE CONCEPTS *16,84*

per se [*adv*] *essentially*
alone, as such, by and of itself, by definition, by itself, by its very nature, fundamentally, independently, in essence, in itself, intrinsically, of itself, singularly, solely, virtually; SEE CONCEPTS *544,577*

persecute [*v*] *wrong, torment*
afflict, aggrieve, annoy, badger, bait, beat, be on one's case*, bother, crucify, distress, dog*, dragoon, drive up the wall*, exile, expel, harass, hector, hound*, hunt, ill-treat, injure, maltreat, martyr, molest, oppress, outrage, pester, pick on, plague, pursue, tease, torture, tyrannize, vex, victimize, worry; SEE CONCEPTS *7,19,44,246*

perseverance [*n*] *diligence, hard work*
backbone*, constancy, continuance, cool, dedication, determination, doggedness, drive, endurance, grit*, guts*, immovability, indefatigability, moxie*, persistence, pertinacity, pluck*, prolonging, purposefulness, pursuance, resolution, sedulity, spunk, stamina, steadfastness, stick-to-itiveness*, tenacity; SEE CONCEPTS *411,633*

persevere [*v*] *keep at; work hard*
be determined, be resolved, be stubborn, carry on, continue, endure, go for broke*, go for it*, go on, hang in*, hang tough*, hold fast*, hold on, keep driving*, keep going, keep on, leave no stone unturned*, maintain, persist, plug away*, press on, proceed, pursue, remain, see it through*, stand firm*, stay the course*, stick with it*; SEE CONCEPTS *87,239*

persist [*v*] *carry on, carry through*
abide, be resolute, be stubborn, continue, endure, follow through*, follow up*, go all the way*, go on, go the limit*, grind, hold on, insist, keep up*, last, leave no stone unturned*, linger, obtain, perdure, persevere, persevere, prevail, pursue, recur, remain, repeat, see through, stick it out*, stick to guns*, strive, tough it out*; SEE CONCEPTS *23,87,91,239*

persistent [*adj*] *determined; continuous*
assiduous, bound, bound and determined*, bull-dogged*, constant, continual, dogged, endless, enduring, firm, fixed, immovable, incessant, indefatigable, in for long haul*, insistent, interminable, like bad penny*, never-ending, obdurate, obstinate, perpetual, perseverant, persevering, persisting, pertinacious, relentless, repeated, resolute, steadfast, steady, sticky*, stubborn, tenacious, tireless, unflagging, unrelenting, unremitting, unshakable; SEE CONCEPTS *326,401, 404,538*

persnickety [*adj*] *fussy, particular*
careful, choosy, fastidious, finicky, nice, picky; SEE CONCEPT *404*

person [*n*] *human being*
being, body, character, creature, customer, gal, guy, human, identity, individual, individuality, joker*, life, living soul, man, mortal, party, personage, personality, self, somebody, soul, specimen, spirit, unit*, woman; SEE CONCEPT *417*

personable [*adj*] *friendly, sociable*
aces*, affable, agreeable, all heart*, all right*, amiable, attractive, charming, easygoing, good egg*, gregarious, likable, nice, okay, pleasant, pleasing, presentable, sweetheart*, white-hat*, winning; SEE CONCEPT *404*

personage/personality [*n/n2*] *celebrity, notable*
big shot*, bigwig*, brass*, celeb*, chief, cynosure, dignitary, distinguished person, eminence, face*, hot shot*, individual, luminary, monster*, name*, public figure, somebody, star, superstar, top dog*, VIP*, worthy; SEE CONCEPTS *352,354,423*

personal [*adj*] *private, individual*
claimed, exclusive, intimate, own, particular, peculiar, privy, retired, secluded, secret, special; SEE CONCEPT *536*

personality [*n1*] *person's character, traits*
charisma, charm, complexion, disposition, dynamism, emotions, identity, individuality, likableness, magnetism, makeup, nature, psyche, self, selfdom, selfhood, singularity, temper, temperament; SEE CONCEPT *411*

personally [*adv*] *independently*
alone, by oneself, directly, for oneself, for one's part, individualistically, individually, in one's own view, in person, in the flesh, narrowly, on one's own, privately, solely, specially, subjectively; SEE CONCEPTS *544,577*

personify [*v*] *represent some other being, character*
act out, body forth, contain, copy, emblematize, embody, epitomize, exemplify, express, exteriorize, externalize, hominify, humanize, illustrate, image, imitate, impersonate, incarnate, live as, make human, manifest, materialize, mirror, objectify, personize, substantiate, symbolize, typify; SEE CONCEPTS *261,716*

personnel [*n*] *employees of business or other enterprise*
cadre, corps, crew, faculty, group, helpers, human resources, members, men and women, office, organization, people, shop, staff, troop, troops, workers, work force; SEE CONCEPTS *325,417*

perspective [*n*] *view, outlook*
angle, aspect, attitude, broad view, context, frame of reference*, headset*, landscape, mindset*, objectivity, overview, panorama, proportion, prospect, relation, relative importance, relativity,

scene, size of it*, viewpoint, vista, way of looking; SEE CONCEPTS *410,629,689*

perspicacious [*adj*] *observant, perceptive*
acute, alert, astute, aware, clear-sighted, clever, discerning, heady*, judicious, keen, penetrating, percipient, sagacious, savvy*, sharp, sharp-witted, shrewd; SEE CONCEPT *402*

perspicuous [*adj*] *clear, obvious*
apparent, clear-cut, comprehensible, crystal*, crystal-clear*, distinct, easily understood, explicit, intelligible, limpid, lucent, lucid, luminous, pellucid, plain, self-evident, straightforward, transparent, unambiguous, unblurred, understandable; SEE CONCEPT *529*

perspire [*v*] *become wet with sweat*
be damp, be wet, break a sweat*, drip, exude, get in a lather*, glow, lather, pour, secrete, swelter; SEE CONCEPTS *185,469*

persuade [*v*] *cause to believe; convince to do*
actuate, advise, affect, allure, argue into, assure, blandish, brainwash*, bring around, bring to senses, cajole, coax, convert, counsel, draw, enlist, entice, exhort, gain confidence of, get, impel, impress, incite, incline, induce, influence, inveigle, lead, lead to believe, lead to do, move, prevail upon, prompt, propagandize, proselyte, proselytize, reason, satisfy, seduce, sell, stroke, sway, talk into, touch, turn on to, urge, wear down*, wheedle, win argument, win over, woo, work over; SEE CONCEPT *68*

persuasion [*n1*] *influencing to do, believe*
alignment, alluring, arm-twist*, blandishment, brainwashing*, cajolery, cogency, con*, conversion, enticement, exhortation, force, goose*, hard sell*, hook*, inducement, inveiglement, persuasiveness, potency, power, promote, pull*, seduction, sell*, snow job*, soft soap*, squeeze*, sweet talk*, wheedling, winning over, working over; SEE CONCEPTS *68,687*

persuasion [*n2*] *belief, religion*
bias, camp, certitude, church, communion, connection, conviction, credo, creed, cult, denomination, eye, faction, faith, feeling, mind*, opinion, partiality, party, predilection, prejudice, school, school of thought*, sect, sentiment, side, tenet, view; SEE CONCEPT *689*

persuasive [*adj*] *effective, influential*
actuating, alluring, cogent, compelling, conclusive, convictive, convincing, credible, effectual, efficacious, efficient, eloquent, energetic, enticing, forceful, forcible, impelling, impressive, inducing, inspiring, inveigling, logical, luring, moving, plausible, pointed, potent, powerful, seductive, slick, smooth, sound, stimulating, stringent, strong, swaying, telling, touching, unctuous, valid, weighty, wheedling, winning; SEE CONCEPTS *267,537,542*

pert [*adj*] *lively, bold*
animated, audacious, brash, brazen, breezy, bright, brisk, cheeky*, dapper, daring, dashing, disrespectful, flip*, flippant, forward, fresh, gay, impertinent, impudent, insolent, jaunty, keen, nervy, perky, presumptuous, sassy*, saucy*, smart, smart-alecky*, spirited, sprightly, vivacious, wise; SEE CONCEPTS *401,404*

pertain [*v*] *be relevant to*
affect, appertain, apply, associate, be appropriate, bear on, befit, belong, be part of, be pertinent, combine, concern, connect, inhere with, join, refer, regard, relate, touch, vest; SEE CONCEPT *532*

pertinent [*adj*] *relevant, suitable*
admissible, ad rem, applicable, apposite, appropriate, apropos, apt, connected, fit, fitting, germane, kosher*, legit*, material, on target*, on the button*, on the nose*, opportune, pat*, pertaining, proper, related, right on, to the point, to the purpose; SEE CONCEPT *558*

perturb [*v*] *upset, unsettle*
agitate, alarm, annoy, bewilder, bother, bug*, confound, confuse, disarrange, discompose, disconcert, discountenance, dismay, disorder, disquiet, disturb, flurry, fluster, irritate, make a scene*, make waves*, muddle, needle, perplex, pester, ruffle, stir up*, trouble, vex, worry; SEE CONCEPTS *7,16,19*

peruse [*v*] *check out; examine*
analyze, browse, glance over, inspect, look through, pore over, read, scan, scrutinize, skim, study; SEE CONCEPTS *72,103*

pervade [*v*] *affect strongly; spread through*
charge, diffuse, extend, fill, imbue, impregnate, infuse, overspread, penetrate, percolate, permeate, suffuse, transfuse; SEE CONCEPTS *172,179*

pervasive [*adj*] *extensive*
all over the place*, can't get away from*, common, general, inescapable, omnipresent, permeating, pervading, prevalent, rife, ubiquitous, universal, wall-to-wall*, widespread; SEE CONCEPT *772*

perverse [*adj*] *mean, ornery; troublesome*
abnormal, bad-tempered, cantankerous, capricious, contradictory, contrary, contumacious, corrupt, crabby*, cross, degenerate, delinquent, depraved, deviant, disobedient, dogged*, erring, fractious, hard-nosed*, headstrong, intractable, intransigent, irritable, miscreant, mulish*, nefarious, obdurate, obstinate, petulant, pigheaded*, rebellious, refractory, rotten*, self-willed, spiteful, stubborn, unhealthy, unmanageable, unreasonable, unyielding, villainous, wayward, wicked, willful; SEE CONCEPTS *401,542,571*

pervert [*n*] *person who lacks morals*
debauchee, degenerate, deviant, deviate, freak, weirdo*; SEE CONCEPT *412*

pervert [*v*] *twist, turn away from what is acceptable or correct*
abuse, adulterate, alloy, animalize, brainwash, color, corrupt, cut*, debase, debauch, demoralize, deprave, desecrate, distort, divert, doctor, doctor up*, fake, falsify, fudge*, garble, misconstrue, misinterpret, misrepresent, misstate, mistreat, misuse, outrage, phony up*, prostitute, ruin, salt*, seduce, spike, vitiate, warp, water*; SEE CONCEPTS *14,63,156,252*

perverted [*adj*] *immoral, evil*
abandoned, aberrant, abnormal, abused, contorted, corrupt, corrupted, debased, debauched, defiled, depraved, deviant, deviating, distorted, foreign, grotesque, impaired, kinky*, misguided, misused, monstrous, outraged, polluted, queer, sick, tainted, twisted, unhealthy, unnatural, vicious, vitiate, vitiated, warped, wicked; SEE CONCEPTS *485,545*

pesky [*adj*] *bothersome*
annoying, disturbing, irksome, mean, nettlesome, peeving, provoking, troublesome, ugly, vexatious, vexing, wicked; SEE CONCEPTS *529,537*

pessimism [*n*] *belief in bad outcome*
cynicism, dark side*, dejection, depression, despair, despondency, dim view*, distrust, dyspep-

sia, expectation of worst, gloom, gloominess, gloomy outlook, glumness, grief, hopelessness, low spirits, melancholy, sadness, unhappiness; SEE CONCEPTS *410,689*

pessimist [*n*] *person who expects bad outcome*
complainer, crepehanger*, cynic, defeatist, depreciator, downer, gloomy, killjoy*, misanthrope, party pooper*, prophet of doom*, sourpuss*, wet blanket*, worrier, worrywart*; SEE CONCEPTS *412,423*

pessimistic [*adj*] *expecting bad outcome*
bleak, cynical, dark, dejected, depressed, despairing, despondent, discouraged, distrustful, downhearted, fatalistic, foreboding, gloomy, glum, hopeless, melancholy, misanthropic, morbid, morose, resigned, sad, sullen, troubled, worried; SEE CONCEPTS *403,548*

pest [*n*] *person or thing that presents problem*
annoyance, badgerer, bane, besetment, blight, blister, bore, bother, botheration, bug*, contagion, crashing bore*, creep, curse, drag, drip, epidemic, exasperation, headache*, infection, irritant, irritation, nag, nudge, nuisance, pain*, pain in the neck*, pesterer, pestilence, pill*, plague*, scourge*, tease*, thorn in side*, tormentor, trial*, trouble, vexation, virus*; SEE CONCEPTS *306,398,412,674*

pester [*v*] *bother, harass*
annoy, badger, be at, bedevil, beleaguer, bug*, disturb, dog*, drive crazy, drive up the wall*, fret, get at*, get in one's hair*, get on one's nerves*, get to*, harry, hassle, hector, hound, importune, insist, irk, mess with*, nag, nudge, pick at*, plague, provoke, remind, ride*, tantalize, tease, torment, work on*, worry; SEE CONCEPTS *7,19,48*

pestilent/pestilential [*adj*] *dangerous, harmful*
baneful, contagious, contaminating, corrupting, deadly, deleterious, destructive, detrimental, diseased, evil, fatal, infectious, injurious, lethal, mortal, noxious, pernicious, pestiferous, ruinous, tainting, troublesome, vicious; SEE CONCEPTS *314,537*

pet [*n*] *favorite thing, person*
apple of eye*, beloved, cat, darling, dear, dog, evergreen*, idol, jewel*, love, lover, persona grata*, treasure*; SEE CONCEPTS *394,416*

pet [*adj*] *favorite*
affectionate, cherished, darling, dear, dearest, endearing, favored, loved, precious, preferred, special; SEE CONCEPTS *568,574*

pet [*v*] *stroke, kiss*
baby, caress, coddle, cosset, cuddle, dandle, embrace, fondle, grab, hug, love, make love, neck*, pamper, pat, smooch*, spoil, spoon*, touch; SEE CONCEPTS *375,612*

peter out [*v*] *dwindle, decrease*
abate, come to nothing*, die out*, diminish, drain, ebb, evaporate, fade, fail, give out, lessen, pall, rebate, recede, run dry, run out, stop, taper off, wane; SEE CONCEPTS *105,698*

petite [*adj*] *small*
baby, bantam, dainty, delicate, diminutive, elfin, little, miniature, minikin*, slight, smallish, tiny, wee*; SEE CONCEPTS *773,779,789*

petition [*n*] *appeal, plea*
address, application, entreaty, imploration, imprecation, invocation, memorial, prayer, request, round robin, solicitation, suit, supplication; SEE CONCEPTS *271,662*

petition [v] *plead, appeal for*
adjure, ask, beg, beseech, call upon, entreat, impetrate, implore, pray, press, put in for, request, seek, solicit, sue, supplicate, urge; SEE CONCEPTS 48,53

petrify [v1] *make hard*
calcify, clarify, fossilize, harden, lapidify, mineralize, set, solidify, turn to stone; SEE CONCEPT 250

petrify [v2] *frighten*
alarm, amaze, appall, astonish, astound, benumb, chill, confound, daze, dismay, dumbfound, horrify, immobilize, numb, paralyze, put chill on*, scare, scare silly*, scare stiff*, spook*, startle, stun, stupefy, terrify, transfix; SEE CONCEPTS 7,14,19,42

petty [adj] *trivial, insignificant*
base, casual, cheap, contemptible, frivolous, inconsequent, inconsiderable, inessential, inferior, irrelevant, junior, lesser, light, little, lower, measly, minor, narrow-minded, negligible, nickel-and-dime*, niggling*, paltry, peanut*, pennyante*, pettifogging*, picayune, piddling*, scratch, secondary, shabby, shallow, shoestring*, slight, small, small-minded, subordinate, trifling, two-bit*, unimportant; SEE CONCEPTS 403,575

petulant [adj] *crabby, moody*
bad-tempered, captious, caviling, complaining, cranky*, cross, crybaby*, displeased, fault-finding, fractious, fretful, grouchy, grumbling, huffy, ill-humored, impatient, irritable, mean, peevish, perverse, pouting, querulous, snappish, sour, sulky, sullen, testy, touchy, ungracious, uptight*, waspish, whining, whiny; SEE CONCEPTS 401,542

phantom [n] *ghost; figment of the imagination*
apparition, chimera, daydream, delusion, dream, eidolon, figment, hallucination, haunt, ignis fatuus, illusion, mirage, nightmare, phantasm, revenant, shade, shadow, specter, spirit, spook, vision, wraith; SEE CONCEPTS 370,529

phase [n] *period in life of something*
appearance, aspect, chapter, condition, development, facet, juncture, point, position, posture, stage, state, step, time; SEE CONCEPTS 816,834

phenomenal [adj] *astounding, exceptional*
extraordinary, fantastic, marvelous, miraculous, outstanding, preternatural, prodigious, rare, remarkable, sensational, singular, substantial, uncommon, unique, unparalleled, unusual, unwonted, wondrous; SEE CONCEPTS 564,574

phenomenology [n] *study of subject and objects of a person's experience*
intentionality, life-world, lived experience, meaning-making; SEE CONCEPTS 282,349

phenomenon [n] *rare occurrence; wonder*
abnormality, actuality, anomaly, appearance, aspect, circumstance, curiosity, episode, event, exception, experience, fact, happening, incident, marvel, miracle, nonpareil, one for the books*, paradox, peculiarity, portent, prodigy, rara avis*, rarity, reality, sensation, sight, something else*, spectacle, stunner*, uniqueness; SEE CONCEPTS 230,529,678

philanderer [n] *person who has many love affairs*
adulterer, chaser, cruiser, dallier, debaucher, flirt, gallant, lover, operator*, swinger; SEE CONCEPT 423

philanthropic [adj] *charitable, giving*
altruistic, beneficent, benevolent, benignant, big-hearted, bountiful, contributing, donating, eleemosynary, generous, good, gracious, helpful, humane, humanitarian, kind, kindhearted, liberal, magnanimous, munificent, openhanded, patriotic, public-spirited; SEE CONCEPTS 404,542

philosophical/philosophic [adj1] *thinking deeply, rationally*
abstract, cogitative, deep, erudite, judicious, learned, logical, pensive, profound, rational, reflective, sagacious, sapient, theoretical, thoughtful, wise; SEE CONCEPT 402

philosophical/philosophic [adj2] *calm, serene*
collected, commonsensical, composed, cool*, cool as cucumber*, enduring, impassive, imperturbable, patient, resigned, stoical, tranquil, unagitated, unflappable, unmoved, unruffled; SEE CONCEPT 401

philosophy [n] *principles, knowledge*
aesthetics, attitude, axiom, beliefs, conception, convictions, doctrine, idea, ideology, logic, metaphysics, ontology, outlook, rationalism, reason, reasoning, system, tenet, theory, thinking, thought, truth, values, view, viewpoint, wisdom; SEE CONCEPTS 349,688,689

phobia [n] *fear*
anxiety, aversion, avoidance, awe, detestation, disgust, dislike, distaste, dread, fear, hang-up*, hatred, horror, irrationality, loathing, neurosis, obsession, repulsion, resentment, revulsion, terror, thing*, thing about*; SEE CONCEPTS 27,29,529

phony [adj] *fake, false*
affected, artificial, assumed, bogus, counterfeit, forged, imitation, pseudo, put-on*, sham*, spurious, trick; SEE CONCEPT 582

photocopy [n/v] *mechanical image produced from a copier; making the image*
copy, duplicate, reproduce, stat, velox, Xerox; SEE CONCEPT 269

photograph [n] *a still picture taken with a camera*
blowup, close-up, image, Kodachrome*, Kodak*, likeness, microfilm, mug*, negative, photo, photostat, pic*, picture, pinup*, pix*, Polaroid*, portrait, positive, print, shot*, slide, snap, snapshot, transparency; SEE CONCEPT 265

photograph [v] *take a picture with a camera*
capture*, capture on film*, cinematize, close-up*, copy, film, get, get a likeness*, get a shot*, illustrate, lens*, make a picture*, microfilm, mug*, photo, photoengrave, photostat, picture, print, record, reproduce, roll, shoot, snap*, snapshot, take*, turn*, X-ray*; SEE CONCEPT 174

photographic [adj] *exact, retentive in detail*
accurate, cinematic, detailed, faithful, filmic, graphic, lifelike, minute, natural, pictorial, picturesque, precise, realistic, true-to-life*, visual, vivid; SEE CONCEPT 557

phrase [n] *group of words; way of speaking*
byword, catchphrase, catchword, diction, expression, idiom, locution, maxim, motto, parlance, phraseology, phrasing, remark, saying, shibboleth, slogan, styling, tag, terminology, utterance, verbalism, verbiage, watchword, wordage, wording; SEE CONCEPTS 275,278

phrase [v] *express in words carefully*
couch, formulate, frame, present, put, put into words, say, term, utter, voice, word; SEE CONCEPT 55

physical [adj1] *tangible, material*
concrete, corporeal, environmental, gross, mate-

pe
ph

rialistic, natural, objective, palpable, phenomenal, ponderable, real, sensible, solid, somatic, substantial, visible; SEE CONCEPT 582

physical [adj2] concerning the body
bodily, brute, carnal, corporal, corporeal, earthly, fleshly, incarnate, mortal, personal, somatic, unspiritual, visceral; SEE CONCEPT 485

physician [n] person trained in medical science
bones*, doc*, doctor, general practitioner, healer, intern, MD*, medic, medical practitioner, quack*, sawbones*, specialist, surgeon; SEE CONCEPT 357

physique [n] build of human body
anatomy, body, built, character, configuration, constitution, corpus, figure, form, frame, habit, habitus, makeup, muscles, nature, shape, structure, type; SEE CONCEPTS 405,757

pick [n] a chosen option, usually the choicest
aces, bag, best, choice, choosing, cream*, crème de la crème*, cup of tea*, decision, druthers*, elect, elite, flower*, preference, pride, prime, prize, select, selection, top, tops; SEE CONCEPTS 529,671

pick [v1] choose, select
cull, decide upon, elect, finger*, fix upon, go down the line*, hand-pick, mark, name, optate, opt for, pick and choose, pick out, prefer, say so, separate, settle on, sift out*, single out, slot, sort out, tab, tag, take, take it or leave it*, tap, winnow; SEE CONCEPT 41

pick [v2] gather, harvest
accumulate, choose, collect, cull, cut, draw, pluck, pull; SEE CONCEPTS 41,109,206

pick [v3] break into something closed, locked
break open, crack, dent, force, hit, indent, jimmy, open, pry, strike; SEE CONCEPT 192

pick at/pick on [v] nag, provoke
badger, bait, blame, bully, carp, cavil, criticize, find fault, foment, get at*, get to*, goad, hector, incite, instigate, quibble, start, tease, torment; SEE CONCEPTS 7,19,52

picket [n1] post of structure
pale, paling, palisade, panel, peg, pillar, rail, stake, stanchion, upright; SEE CONCEPTS 445,479

picket [n2] person who demonstrates for cause
demonstrator, picketer, protester, striker; SEE CONCEPTS 348,359

picket [n3] person acting as guard
guard, lookout, patrol, scout, sentinel, sentry, spotter, vedette, ward, watch, watchperson; SEE CONCEPT 348

picket [v] protest against, for cause
blockade, boycott, demonstrate, hit the bricks*, strike, walk out; SEE CONCEPTS 300,351

pickle [n] sticky situation
bind, box*, corner*, difficulty, dilemma, disorder, fix, hole*, hot water*, jam*, predicament, quandary, scrape, spot*, tight spot*; SEE CONCEPT 674

pickle [v] preserve fruit or vegetable
can, cure, keep, marinade, salt, souse, steep; SEE CONCEPT 170

pick up [v1] lift, raise
elevate, gather, grasp, hoist, rear, take up, uphold, uplift, upraise, uprear; SEE CONCEPT 196

pick up [v2] obtain, find
acquire, annex, buy, chalk up*, come across, compass, cull, extract, gain, garner, gather, get, get the hang of*, glean, happen upon*, have,

learn, procure, purchase, score, secure, take; SEE CONCEPTS 31,120,183

pick up [v3] improve
continue, gain, gain ground*, get better, get well, increase, make a comeback*, mend, perk up*, rally, recommence, recover, renew, reopen, restart, resume, swell, take up; SEE CONCEPTS 234,700

pick up [v4] call for socially
accompany, collect, drop in for*, get*, give a lift*, go for*, go to get*, invite, offer, proposition, stop for*; SEE CONCEPTS 224,384

pick up [v5] arrest for crime
apprehend, book*, bust*, collar*, detain, nab, pinch*, pull in*, run in*, take into custody; SEE CONCEPT 317

picky [adj] choosy, finicky
captious, critical, dainty, fastidious, fault-finding, fussy, nice, particular, persnickety; SEE CONCEPT 404

picnic [n1] outdoor meal
barbecue, clambake, cookout, dining alfresco, excursion, fish fry, outing, weiner roast; SEE CONCEPTS 386,459

picnic [n2] easy undertaking
breeze*, child's play*, cinch, duck soup*, kid stuff*, lark*, light work, no trouble, piece of cake*, pushover*, setup*, smooth sailing*, snap, sure thing, walkover*; SEE CONCEPTS 362,693

picture [n1] illustration, likeness of something
account, art, blueprint, canvas, cartoon, copy, delineation, depiction, description, doodle, double, draft, drawing, duplicate, effigy, engraving, figure, icon, image, impression, lookalike, outline, painting, panorama, photo, photograph, piece, portrait, portrayal, presentment, print, re-creation, replica, report, representation, ringer*, similitude, simulacrum, sketch, spectacle, spitting image*, statue, tableau, twin; SEE CONCEPTS 259,625

picture [n2] perfect example
archetype, embodiment, epitome, essence, idea, personification; SEE CONCEPT 686

picture [n3] entertainment film
cartoon, cinema, flick*, motion picture, movie, moving picture, photoplay, picture show, show; SEE CONCEPT 293

picture [v1] depict, describe
delineate, draw, illustrate, image, interpret, limn, paint, photograph, portray, render, represent, show, sketch; SEE CONCEPTS 79,174

picture [v2] form vision in one's mind
conceive of, create, daydream, dream, envision, fancy, fantasize, imagine, portray, see, see in the mind's eye*, visualize; SEE CONCEPTS 17,43

picturesque [adj] attractive, referring to scenery
arresting, artistic, beautiful, charming, colorful, graphic, photographic, pictorial, pleasant, pretty, quaint, scenic, striking, vivid; SEE CONCEPTS 579,589

piddling [adj] insignificant
derisory, little, measly*, niggling*, paltry, peanut*, pettifogging*, petty, picayune, puny, trifling, trivial, unimportant, useless, worthless; SEE CONCEPTS 575,789

piece [n1] part
allotment, bit, bite, chunk, cut, division, dole, end, example, fraction, fragment, gob, half, hunk, instance, interest, iota, item, length, lot, lump, member, moiety, morsel, parcel, percentage, portion, quantity, quota, sample, scrap, section, seg-

ment, share, shred, slice, smithereen*, specimen; SEE CONCEPTS *834,835*

piece [*n2*] *work of art, music, writing*
arrangement, article, bit, composition, creation, discourse, dissertation, engraving, exposition, icon, item, lines, painting, paper, part, photograph, print, production, sketch, song, statue, study, theme, thesis, treatise, treatment, vignette, work; SEE CONCEPTS *259,262,263,271*

piece [*v*] *put together*
assemble, combine, compose, create, fix, join, make, mend, patch, repair, restore, unite; SEE CONCEPTS *113,173,193,251*

piecemeal [*adj/adv*] *bit by bit*
at intervals, by degrees, by fits and starts*, fitfully, fragmentary, gradual, gradually, intermittent, intermittently, interrupted, little by little*, partial, partially, patchy, spotty, step by step*; SEE CONCEPTS *531,544*

pier [*n*] *support; place for boats*
berth, buttress, column, dam, dock, jetty, landing, levee, mole, pierage, pilaster, pile, piling, pillar, post, promenade, quay, slip, upright, wharf; SEE CONCEPTS *439,443,479*

pierce [*v*] *cut, penetrate*
bore, break, break in, break through, cleave, crack, crack open, drill, enter, gash, incise, intrude, pass through, perforate, plow, prick, probe, puncture, run through, slash, slice, slit, spike, stab, stick into, transfix; SEE CONCEPTS *137,159,176,220*

piercing [*adj*] *intense to the senses*
acute, agonizing, arctic, biting, bitter, blaring, cold, deafening, earsplitting, excruciating, exquisite, fierce, freezing, frosty, high, high-pitched, keen, knifelike, loud, numbing, painful, penetrating, powerful, racking, raw, roaring, severe, sharp, shattering, shooting, shrill, stabbing, stentorian, stentorious, thin, treble, wintry; SEE CONCEPTS *406,537,592,594*

piety [*n*] *devotion, religiousness*
allegiance, application, ardor, belief, devoutness, docility, dutifulness, duty, faith, fealty, fervor, fidelity, godliness, grace, holiness, loyalty, obedience, passion, religion, religiosity, reverence, sanctity, veneration, zeal; SEE CONCEPTS *633,689*

pig [*n*] *animal of swine family*
boar, cob roller*, hog, piggy*, piglet, porker*, porky, shoat, sow, swine; SEE CONCEPTS *394,400*

pigheaded [*adj*] *stubborn*
bullheaded, contrary, dense*, forward, headstrong, inflexible, insistent, intractable, mulish*, obstinate, perverse, recalcitrant, self-willed, stiffnecked, stupid*, unyielding, willful; SEE CONCEPTS *404,542*

pigment [*n*] *color, shade*
colorant, coloring, coloring matter, dye, dyestuff, oil, paint, stain, tincture, tint; SEE CONCEPTS *259,622*

pile [*n1*] *heap, collection*
accumulation, aggregate, aggregation, amassment, assemblage, assortment, bank, barrel, buildup, chunk, conglomeration, drift, gob, great deal, hill, hoard, hunk, jumble, lump, mass, mound, mountain, much, ocean, oodles*, pack, peck, pyramid, quantity, shock, stack, stockpile; SEE CONCEPTS *432,787*

pile [*n2*] *wealth*
affluence, boodle*, bundle*, dough*, fortune,

mint*, money, pot*, riches, wad*; SEE CONCEPTS *335,340*

pile [*v*] *gather, pack; put on top of another*
accumulate, amass, assemble, bank, bunch, collect, crowd, crush, fill, flock, heap, hill, hoard, jam, load, mass, mound, rush, stack, store; SEE CONCEPTS *84,109,201,750*

pilfer [*v*] *steal, embezzle*
annex, appropriate, borrow, cop*, crib*, filch*, liberate*, lift*, moonlight*, palm*, pinch*, pluck*, purloin, requisition, rip off*, rob, scrounge, snare, snatch, swipe, take, thieve, walk off with*; SEE CONCEPTS *139,142,192*

pilgrimage [*n*] *long journey*
crusade, excursion, expedition, mission, tour, travel, trip, wayfaring; SEE CONCEPT *224*

pill [*n1*] *capsule of medicine*
bolus, dose, lozenge, medicine, pellet, pilule, tablet, troche; SEE CONCEPTS *307,470*

pill [*n2*] *person who is annoying*
bore, drag*, nuisance, pain*, pain in the neck*, pest, trial*; SEE CONCEPTS *412,423*

pillage [*v*] *plunder, destroy*
appropriate, arrogate, confiscate, depredate, desecrate, desolate, despoil, devastate, devour, gut, invade, lay waste*, lift*, loot, maraud, nab*, pilfer, pinch*, purloin, raid, ransack, ravage, rifle*, rob, ruin, sack, spoil, spoliate, steal, strip, thieve, trespass, waste; SEE CONCEPTS *86,139,252*

pillar [*n1*] *column of building, or freestanding column*
colonnade, mast, obelisk, pedestal, pier, pilaster, piling, post, prop, shaft, stanchion, support, tower, upright; SEE CONCEPT *440*

pillar [*n2*] *mainstay; source of strength*
backbone*, guider, leader, light*, rock*, sinew, supporter, tower of strength*, upholder, worthy; SEE CONCEPTS *423,712*

pilot [*n*] *person who guides aircraft, ship, or other vehicle*
ace*, aerialist, aeronaut, aviator, bellwether*, captain, conductor, coxswain, dean, director, doyen/doyenne, eagle*, flier*, flyer, guide, helmsperson, jockey*, lead, leader, navigator, one at the controls, one at the wheel, scout*, steerer, steersperson, wheelperson; SEE CONCEPT *348*

pimple [*n*] *small swelling on the skin*
abscess, acne, beauty spot, blackhead, blemish, blister, boil, bump, carbuncle, caruncle, excrescence, furuncle, hickey*, inflammation, lump, papula, papule, pustule, spot, whitehead, zit*; SEE CONCEPT *306*

pin [*v*] *attach, hold in place*
affix, bind, clasp, close, fasten, fix, hold down, hold fast, immobilize, join, pinion, press, restrain, secure; SEE CONCEPTS *85,160,190*

pinch [*n1*] *tight pressing*
compression, confinement, contraction, cramp, grasp, grasping, hurt, limitation, nip, nipping, pressure, squeeze, torment, tweak, twinge; SEE CONCEPT *728*

pinch [*n2*] *small amount*
bit, dash, drop, jot, mite, small quantity, soupçon, speck, splash, splatter, taste; SEE CONCEPT *831*

pinch [*n3*] *predicament*
box*, clutch, contingency, crisis, crunch*, difficulty, emergency, exigency, hardship, juncture, necessity, oppression, pass, plight, pressure,

ph
pi

strait, stress, tight spot*, tight squeeze*, turning point*, zero hour*; SEE CONCEPT 674

pinch [v1] *press tightly*
chafe, compress, confine, cramp, crush, grasp, hurt, nip, pain, squeeze, tweak, twinge, wrench, wrest, wring; SEE CONCEPTS 219,313

pinch [v2] *be stingy*
afflict, distress, economize, oppress, pinch pennies*, press, scrape, scrimp, skimp, spare, stint; SEE CONCEPT 330

pinch [v3] *steal*
cop*, crib*, filch*, knock off*, lift*, nab*, pilfer, purloin, rob, snatch, swipe, take; SEE CONCEPT 139

pinch [v4] *arrest*
apprehend, bust*, collar*, detain, hold, nab*, pick up*, pull in*, run in*, take into custody; SEE CONCEPTS 90,317

pine [v] *long for*
ache, agonize, brood, carry a torch*, covet, crave, desire, dream, fret, grieve, hanker, languish for, lust after, mope*, mourn, sigh, spoil for*, thirst for, want, wish, yearn, yen for; SEE CONCEPT 20

pink [n1/adj] *rose color*
blush, coral, flush, fuchsia, rose, roseate, salmon; SEE CONCEPT 622

pink [n2] *best condition*
acme*, bloom*, fitness, good health, height*, peak, perfection, prime, summit, trim*, verdure; SEE CONCEPTS 316,388

pink [v] *cut in zigzag*
incise, notch, perforate, prick, punch, scallop, score; SEE CONCEPT 176

pinnacle [n] *top, crest*
acme, apex, apogee, climax, cone, crown, culmination, greatest, height, max*, most*, needle*, obelisk, peak, pyramid, spire, steeple, summit, tops, tower, vertex, zenith; SEE CONCEPTS 706,836

pinpoint [v] *define, locate*
determinate, diagnose, distinguish, finger*, get a fix on*, home in on*, identify, place, recognize, spot; SEE CONCEPTS 38,183

pioneer [n] *person who finds a new place, founds something*
colonist, colonizer, developer, explorer, founder, frontier settler, guide, homesteader, immigrant, innovator, leader, pathfinder, pilgrim, scout, settler, squatter, trailblazer; SEE CONCEPTS 348,413

pioneer [adj] *early, first*
avant-garde, brave, experimental, head, inaugural, initial, lead, original, primary, prime; SEE CONCEPT 585

pioneer [v] *invent; lay the groundwork*
begin, colonize, create, develop, discover, establish, explore, found, go out in front*, initiate, instigate, institute, launch, map out, open up, originate, prepare, show the way, spearhead*, start, take the lead, trailblaze*; SEE CONCEPTS 173,221,324

pious [adj] *dedicated, religious*
born-again*, clerical, devoted, devout, divine, ecclesiastical, godly, goody-goody*, orthodox, prayerful, priestly, reverent, righteous, sacred, saintly, sanctimonious, spiritual; SEE CONCEPT 401

pipe [n] *passage, tube*
aqueduct, canal, channel, conduit, conveyer, duct, hose, line, main, pipeline, sewer, spout, trough, vent, vessel; SEE CONCEPTS 475,499

pipe [v1] *conduct through tube, passage*
bring in, carry, channel, convey, funnel, siphon, supply, traject, transmit; SEE CONCEPT 217

pipe [v2] *make a sound; peep*
blubber*, boohoo*, cheep*, cry, play, say, shout, sing, sob, sound, speak, talk, toot*, trill, tweet, twitter, wail, warble, weep, whistle; SEE CONCEPTS 47,65,77

piquant [adj] *flavorful, biting*
highly-seasoned, interesting, lively, peppery, poignant, provocative, pungent, racy, savory, sharp, snappy, sparkling, spicy, spirited, stimulating, stinging, tangy, tart, well-flavored, with a kick*, zestful, zesty; SEE CONCEPTS 529,613

pique [n] *anger, irritation*
annoyance, blowup*, conniption*, dander*, displeasure, flare-up, grudge, huff, hurt, irk, miff*, offense, peeve, pet*, provocation, resentment, rise, ruckus*, slow burn*, snit, sore*, stew*, storm*, tiff*, umbrage, vexation; SEE CONCEPTS 29,410

pique [v] *offend, provoke*
absorb, affront, annoy, arouse, bother, bug*, displease, egg on*, exasperate, excite, fire up*, gall, galvanize, get*, get a rise out of*, get under skin*, give a hard time*, give the business*, goad, goose*, grab, ignite, incense, irk, irritate, kindle, make waves*, miff*, mortify, motivate, move, nettle, offend, peeve, prick, put out*, quicken, rile, rouse, spur, stimulate, sting*, stir, vex, whet, work up*, wound; SEE CONCEPTS 7,14,19,22

pit [n] *hole, cavity*
abyss, chasm, crater, dent, depression, dimple, excavation, grave, gulf, hell, hollow, indentation, mine, perforation, pockmark, pothole, puncture, shaft, tomb, trench, well; SEE CONCEPTS 509,513

pit [v] *oppose, play off*
contend, counter, match, put in opposition, set against, vie; SEE CONCEPTS 92,363

pitch [n1] *tilt*
angle, cant, degree, dip, gradient, height, incline, level, point, slant, slope, steepness; SEE CONCEPTS 692,738

pitch [n2] *tone of sound*
frequency, harmonic, modulation, rate, sound, timbre; SEE CONCEPT 65

pitch [n3] *talk to convince*
patter*, persuasion, sales talk, song and dance*, spiel*; SEE CONCEPTS 68,278

pitch [v1] *throw, hurl*
bung, cast, chuck*, fire, fling, gun, heave, launch, lob, peg, sling, toss, unseat; SEE CONCEPT 222

pitch [v2] *put up, erect*
fix, locate, place, plant, raise, settle, set up, station; SEE CONCEPT 168

pitch [v3] *dive, roll*
ascend, bend, bicker, careen, descend, dip, drive, drop, fall, flounder, go down, heave, lean, lunge, lurch, plunge, rise, rock, seesaw, slope, slump, stagger, tilt, topple, toss, tumble, vault, wallow, welter, yaw; SEE CONCEPTS 147,181,201

pitch in [v] *help; get busy*
aid, attack, begin, buckle down*, chip in*, come through, commence, contribute, cooperate, do, do one's bit*, fall to*, get cracking*, get going, go to it*, hop to it*, join in, jump in*, launch, lend a hand*, participate, plunge into*, set about, set to, subscribe, tackle, tee off*, volunteer, wade in; SEE CONCEPTS 100,110

piteous [adj] *miserable, pathetic*
beseeching, commiserable, deplorable, distressing, doleful, dolorous, entreating, grievous, heartbreaking, heart-rending, imploring, lamentable, melancholy, mournful, moving, pitiable, pitiful, plaintive, poignant, poor, rueful, ruined, sad, sorrowful, supplicating, woeful, wretched; SEE CONCEPTS *485,529*

pitfall [n] *hazard, trap*
booby trap*, catch*, danger, deadfall*, difficulty, downfall, drawback, entanglement, hook*, mesh*, mousetrap*, peril, pit*, quicksand*, risk, setup*, snag*, snare, swindle*; SEE CONCEPTS *674,679*

pithy [adj] *brief, to the point*
cogent, compact, concise, crisp, curt, down to brass tacks*, effective, epigrammatic, expressive, honed, laconic, meaningful, meaty*, pointed, short, short-and-sweet*, significant, succinct, terse, trenchant; SEE CONCEPT *267*

pitiful [adj] *in bad shape; poor*
abject, affecting, afflicted, arousing, base, beggarly, cheap, cheerless, comfortless, commiserative, compassionate, contemptible, deplorable, despicable, dismal, distressed, distressing, grievous, heartbreaking, heartrending, inadequate, insignificant, joyless, lamentable, low, mean, miserable, mournful, moving, paltry, pathetic, piteous, pitiable, sad, scurvy, shabby, sorrowful, sorry, stirring, suffering, tearful, touching, vile, woeful, worthless, wretched; SEE CONCEPTS *485,529*

pitiless [adj] *without mercy or care*
austere, barbarous, brutal, callous, cold*, coldblooded*, coldhearted*, cruel, cutthroat*, dog-eat-dog*, frigid, hardhearted*, harsh, hatchetjob*, heartless, implacable, indifferent, inexorable, inhuman, insensible, killer instinct*, mean, merciless, obdurate, relentless, remorseless, ruthless, satanic, savage, soulless*, stony*; SEE CONCEPT *401*

pittance [n] *small amount*
allowance, bit, chicken feed*, dribble*, drop*, drop in the bucket*, inadequacy, insufficiency, mite, modicum, peanuts*, pension, portion, ration, scrap*, slave wages*, smidgen, trace, trifle*; SEE CONCEPTS *344,787*

pity [n1] *feeling of mercy toward another*
benevolence, charity, clemency, comfort, commiseration, compassion, compunction, condolement, condolence, dejection, distress, empathy, favor, forbearance, goodness, grace, humanity, kindliness, kindness, lenity, melancholy, mercy, philanthropy, quarter, rue, ruth, sadness, solace, sorrow, sympathy, tenderness, understanding, warmth; SEE CONCEPTS *410,657*

pity [n2] *sad situation*
bad luck, catastrophe, crime, crisis, crying shame*, disaster, mischance, misfortune, mishap, regret, shame, sin; SEE CONCEPT *674*

pity [v] *feel sorry for; spare*
ache*, be sorry for, be sympathetic, bleed for*, comfort, commiserate, condole, console, feel for, feel with, forgive, give quarter*, grant amnesty, grieve with, have compassion, have mercy on, identify with, lament with, pardon, put out of one's misery*, relent, reprieve, show forgiveness*, show sympathy*, solace, soothe, sympathize, take pity on*, understand, weep for*; SEE CONCEPTS *10,34,83*

pivot [n] *center point about which something revolves*
axis, axle, center, focal point, fulcrum, heart, hinge, hub, kingpin, shaft, spindle, swivel, turning point; SEE CONCEPTS *445,464,498,830*

pivot [v] *revolve around center point*
be contingent, depend, hang, hinge, rely, rotate, sheer, spin, swivel, turn, twirl, veer, volte-face, wheel, whip, whirl; SEE CONCEPTS *147,532*

pivotal [adj] *important*
cardinal, central, climactic, critical, crucial, decisive, determining, essential, focal, middle, momentous, overriding, overruling, principal, ruling, vital; SEE CONCEPT *568*

placate [v] *soothe, pacify*
appease, assuage, calm, cheer, comfort, conciliate, humor, make peace*, make up*, mollify, pacify, play up to*, pour oil on*, propitiate, reconcile, satisfy, soft-pedal*, soothe, stroke*, sweeten, tranquilize, win over*; SEE CONCEPTS *7,22,126*

place [n1] *location with purpose, function*
abode, accommodation, apartment, area, berth, city, community, compass, corner, country, distance, district, domicile, dwelling, field, habitat, hamlet, hangout, hole*, home, house, joint, latitude, lay, locale, locality, locus, longitude, neighborhood, niche, nook, pad*, part, plant, point, position, property, quarter, region, reservation, residence, room, seat, section, site, situation, spot, station, stead, suburb, town, venue, vicinity, village, volume, whereabouts, zone; SEE CONCEPTS *435,515*

place [n2] *position, rank*
capacity, character, footing, grade, pecking order*, slot, standing, state, station, status; SEE CONCEPT *388*

place [n3] *job, employment*
appointment, berth, connection, occupation, office, position, post, profession, situation, spot, trade; SEE CONCEPT *360*

place [n4] *duty, role*
affair, charge, concern, function, prerogative, responsibility, right; SEE CONCEPT *532*

place [v1] *locate, situate*
allocate, allot, assign, deposit, distribute, establish, finger, fix, install, lay, lodge, nail, park, peg, plant, position, put, quarter, repose, rest, set, settle, spot, stand, station, stick, store, stow; SEE CONCEPT *201*

place [v2] *order, sort*
allocate, appoint, approximate, arrange, assign, call, charge, class, classify, commission, constitute, delegate, deputize, designate, entrust, estimate, fix, give, grade, group, judge, name, nominate, ordain, put, rank, reckon; SEE CONCEPTS *50,84,88,98*

place [v3] *identify, recognize*
associate, determinate, determine, diagnose, distinguish, figure out*, finger*, indicate, know, nail*, peg*, pinpoint, put one's finger on*, remember, set in context, spot, tell; SEE CONCEPT *38*

placid [adj] *calm, mild*
collected, composed, cool*, cool as a cucumber*, detached, easygoing, equable, even, eventempered, gentle, halcyon, hushed, imperturbable, irenic, peaceful, poised, quiet, restful, selfpossessed, serene, still, tranquil; SEE CONCEPTS *401,485*

pi
pl

plagiarism [n] *copying of another's written work*
appropriation, borrowing, counterfeiting, cribbing, falsification, fraud, infringement, lifting, literary theft, piracy, stealing, theft; SEE CONCEPTS *139,192*

plague [n1] *disease that is widespread*
affliction, contagion, curse, epidemic, hydra, infection, infestation, influenza, invasion, outbreak, pandemic, pestilence, rash, ravage, scourge; SEE CONCEPT *306*

plague [n2] *annoyance, curse*
affliction, aggravation, bane, besetment, blast, blight, bother, botheration, calamity, cancer, evil, exasperation, hydra, irritant, nuisance, pain, pest, problem, scourge, thorn in side, torment, trial, vexation; SEE CONCEPTS *674,679*

plague [v] *annoy, disturb*
afflict, badger, bedevil, beleaguer, bother, chafe, fret, gall, gnaw, harass, harry, hassle, haunt, hector, hound, infest, irk, molest, pain, persecute, pester, pursue, ride, tease, torment, torture, trouble, vex, worry; SEE CONCEPTS *7,14,19*

plain [n] *level land*
champaign, expanse, field, flat, flatland, grassland, heath, level, meadow, moor, moorland, open country, plateau, prairie, steppe, tundra; SEE CONCEPT *509*

plain [adj1] *clear, obvious*
apparent, audible, big as life*, broad, comprehensible, definite, distinct, evident, legible, lucid, manifest, open, open-and-shut*, palpable, patent, talking turkey*, transparent, understandable, visible; SEE CONCEPTS *529,535,576*

plain [adj2] *straightforward in speech*
abrupt, artless, blunt, candid, direct, forthright, frank, guileless, honest, impolite, ingenuous, open, outspoken, rude, sincere; SEE CONCEPT *267*

plain [adj3] *normal, everyday*
average, common, commonplace, conventional, dull, homely, lowly, modest, ordinary, quotidian, routine, simple, traditional, usual, vanilla*, whitebread*, workaday; SEE CONCEPT *547*

plain [adj4] *unembellished, basic*
austere, bare, bare bones*, clean, discreet, dry, modest, muted, pure, restrained, severe, simple, spartan, stark, stripped down, unvarnished, vanilla*; SEE CONCEPTS *485,589*

plain [adj5] *ugly*
deformed, hard on the eyes*, homely, not beautiful, ordinary, plain-featured; SEE CONCEPT *579*

plaintive [adj] *pathetic, woebegone*
beefing*, bellyaching*, cantankerous, crabby*, cranky*, disconsolate, doleful, grief-stricken, grievous, grousing, grumpy*, heartrending, lamenting, lugubrious, melancholy, mournful, out of sorts*, pathetic, piteous, pitiful, rueful, sad, saddening, sorrowful, wailing, wistful, woeful; SEE CONCEPTS *401,529*

plan [n1] *scheme, design, way of doing things*
aim, angle, animus, arrangement, big picture*, contrivance, course of action, deal, device, disposition, expedient, game plan, gimmick, ground plan, idea, intent, intention, layout, machination, meaning, means, method, orderliness, outline, pattern, picture, platform, plot, policy, procedure, program, project, projection, proposal, proposition, purpose, scenario, stratagem, strategy, suggestion, system, tactics, treatment, trick, undertaking; SEE CONCEPT *660*

plan [n2] *written description; diagram*
agenda, agendum, blueprint, chart, delineation, draft, drawing, form, illustration, layout, map, projection, prospectus, representation, road map, rough draft, scale drawing, sketch, time line, view; SEE CONCEPTS *268,271,625*

plan [v1] *think out; prepare in advance*
arrange, bargain for, block out, blueprint, brainstorm*, calculate, concoct, conspire, contemplate, contrive, cook up*, craft, design, devise, draft, engineer, figure on, figure out, fix to, form, formulate, frame, hatch*, intrigue, invent, lay in provisions, line up*, make arrangements, map, meditate, organize, outline, plot, project, quarterback*, ready, reckon on, represent, rough in*, scheme, set out, shape, sketch, steer, trace, work out; SEE CONCEPT *36*

plan [v2] *intend, mean*
aim, bargain for*, contemplate, count on, design, envisage, foresee, have every intention*, mind, propose, purpose, reckon on*; SEE CONCEPTS *26,35*

plane [n1] *flat surface; level*
condition, degree, extension, face, facet, footing, grade, horizontal, obverse, position, sphere, stratum; SEE CONCEPTS *744,757*

plane [n2] *aircraft*
airbus, airplane, airship, bird*, craft, crate, jet, ship, twin-engine; SEE CONCEPT *504*

plane [adj] *level, horizontal*
even, flat, flush, plain, planate, regular, smooth, uniform; SEE CONCEPTS *490,581*

planet [n] *celestial body orbiting a star*
apple*, asteroid, earth, globe, heavenly body, luminous body, marble, orb*, planetoid, sphere, terrene, wandering star*, world; SEE CONCEPT *511*

plant [n1] *organism belonging to the vegetable kingdom*
annual, biennial, bush, creeper*, cutting*, flower, grass, greenery, herb, perennial, seedling, shoot, shrub, slip, sprout, tree, vine, weed; SEE CONCEPT *429*

plant [n2] *factory and its buildings, equipment*
apparatus, forge, foundry, gear, machinery, manufactory, mill, shop, works, yard; SEE CONCEPTS *439,449,463,496*

plant [v1] *put in the ground for growing*
bury, cover, farm, grow, implant, pitch, pot, raise, scatter, seed, seed down, set out, sow, start, stock, transplant; SEE CONCEPTS *178,253*

plant [v2] *establish, set*
deposit, fix, found, imbed, insert, install, institute, lodge, park, plank, plank down, plop, plunk, root, settle, station; SEE CONCEPTS *18,201,221*

plaster [n] *thick, gooey material that hardens*
adhesive, binding, cement, coat, dressing, glue, gum, gypsum, lime, mortar, mucilage, paste, plaster of Paris, stucco; SEE CONCEPTS *466,475*

plaster [v] *spread, smear*
adhere, bedaub, besmear, bind, cement, coat, cover, daub, glue, gum, overlay, paste, smudge; SEE CONCEPT *202*

plastic [adj1] *flexible, soft; made of manufactured, treated compounds*
bending, ductile, elastic, fictile, formable, moldable, molded, pliable, pliant, resilient, shapeable, supple, workable; SEE CONCEPT *604*

plastic [adj2] *easily influenced*
amenable, bending, compliant, docile, ductile, flexible, giving, impressionable, influenceable,

malleable, manageable, moldable, pliable, pliant, receptive, responsive, suggestible, supple, susceptible, tractable, yielding; SEE CONCEPT 542

plastic [adj3] *artificial; made of manufactured compounds*
cast, chemical, ersatz, false, manufactured, phony, pseudo*, substitute, synthetic, unnatural; SEE CONCEPT 582

plate [n1] *dish or meal served*
bowl, casserole, course, helping, platter, portion, service, serving, trencher; SEE CONCEPTS 459,493

plate [n2] *sheet, panel*
coat, disc, flake, foil, lamella, lamina, layer, leaf, plane, print, scale, slab, slice, spangle, stratum; SEE CONCEPT 475

plate [v] *coat with metallic material*
anodize, bronze, chrome, cover, electroplate, enamel, encrust, face, flake, foil, gild, laminate, layer, nickel, overlay, platinize, scale, silver, stratify; SEE CONCEPTS 172,202

plateau [n] *level; flat, often high, land*
elevation, highland, mesa, plain, stage, table, tableland, upland; SEE CONCEPTS 509,744

platform [n1] *stand or stage*
belvedere, dais, floor, podium, pulpit, rostrum, scaffold, scaffolding, staging, terrace; SEE CONCEPTS 440,443

platform [n2] *political stance, promises*
manifesto, objectives, party line*, plank, policy, principle, program, soapbox*, stump*, tenets; SEE CONCEPTS 278,689

platitude [n] *dull, overused saying*
banality, boiler plate*, bromide*, buzzword, chestnut*, cliché, commonplace, corn*, evenness, familiar tune*, flatness, hackneyed saying, high camp*, hokum*, inanity, insipidity, monotony, motto, old chestnut*, old story*, potboiler*, prosaicism, proverb, saw*, shibboleth, stereotype, tag*, triteness, trite remark, triviality, truism, vapidity, verbiage; SEE CONCEPTS 278,388

platonic [adj] *expressing nonphysical love*
ideal, idealistic, intellectual, quixotic, spiritual, transcendent, Utopian, visionary; SEE CONCEPTS 403,555

platoon [n] *group of military people*
army, array, batch, battery, bunch, clump, cluster, company, detachment, lot, outfit, parcel, patrol, set, squad, squadron, team, troop, unit; SEE CONCEPTS 322,417

plausible [adj] *reasonable, believable*
conceivable, credible, creditable, like enough*, likely, logical, persuasive, possible, presumable, probable, smooth, sound, supposable, tenable, valid, very likely; SEE CONCEPT 552

play [n1] *theater piece*
comedy, curtain-raiser*, drama, entertainment, farce, flop*, hit*, mask*, musical, one-act*, opera, performance, potboiler*, show, smash*, smash hit*, stage show, theatrical, tragedy, turkey*; SEE CONCEPT 263

play [n2] *amusement, entertainment*
caper, dalliance, delight, disport, diversion, foolery, frisk, frolic, fun, gambol, game, gaming, happiness, humor, jest, joking, lark, match, pastime, pleasure, prank, recreation, relaxation, romp, sport, sportiveness, teasing; SEE CONCEPTS 292,363

play [n3] *latitude, range*
action, activity, elbowroom*, exercise, give, leeway, margin, motion, movement, operation,

room, scope, space, sweep, swing, working*; SEE CONCEPTS 651,745

play [v1] *have fun*
amuse oneself, be life of party*, caper, carouse, carry on, cavort, clown, cut capers, cut up*, dally, dance, disport, divert, entertain oneself, fool around, frisk, frolic, gambol, go on a spree*, horse around*, idle away, joke, jump, kibitz*, kick up heels*, let go*, let loose*, let one's hair down*, make merry, mess around*, rejoice, revel, romp, show off, skip, sport, toy, trifle; SEE CONCEPTS 292,384

play [v2] *compete in sport*
be on a team, challenge, contend, contest, disport, engage in, participate, recreate, rival, sport, take on, take part, vie; SEE CONCEPTS 92,363

play [v3] *act; take the part of*
act the part of, discourse, do*, enact, execute, ham*, ham it up*, impersonate, lay an egg*, perform, personate, playact, play a gig*, portray, present, read a part, represent, take the role of, tread the boards*; SEE CONCEPT 292

play [v4] *gamble, risk*
bet, chance, exploit, finesse, game, hazard, jockey*, lay money on*, maneuver, manipulate, put, set, speculate, stake, take, wager; SEE CONCEPTS 341,363

play [v5] *produce music*
blow, bow, drum, execute, fiddle, fidget, finger, operate, pedal, perform, render, tickle, work; SEE CONCEPT 65

play down [v] *pretend as if something were unimportant*
belittle, deemphasize, gloss over*, hold back*, make light of*, make little of*, minimize, mute, restrain, soften, soft-pedal*, underplay, underrate; SEE CONCEPTS 49,59,63

player [n1] *person participating in sport*
amateur, athlete, champ, competitor, contestant, jock*, member, opponent, participant, pro, professional, rookie, sportsperson, superjock*, sweat*, team player; SEE CONCEPT 366

player [n2] *person who acts in performance*
actor, bit player, entertainer, extra, ham*, hambone*, impersonator, lead, mime, mimic, performer, playactor, scene stealer*, stand-in, star, thespian, trouper, understudy, walk-on; SEE CONCEPT 352

player [n3] *person who produces music*
artist, instrumentalist, musician, music maker, performer, rocker, soloist, virtuoso; SEE CONCEPT 352

playful [adj] *funny, fun-loving*
antic, blithe, cheerful, coltish*, comical, elvish*, feeling one's oats*, flirtatious, frisky, frolicsome, full of pep*, gamesome, gay, good-natured, impish, jaunty, jesting, jocund, joking, joyous, lighthearted, lively, merry, mirthful, mischievous, prankish, puckish, rollicking, snappy, spirited, sportive, sprightly, teasing, tongue-in-cheek*, vivacious, waggish, whimsical, zippy*; SEE CONCEPTS 401,542

plaything [n] *toy*
amusement, bauble, doll, gadget, game, gimcrack, pastime, trifle, trinket; SEE CONCEPT 446

play up [v] *emphasize*
accentuate, bring to the fore*, call attention to, feature, highlight, italicize*, magnify, make a production of*, point up, stress, turn spotlight on*, underline, underscore; SEE CONCEPT 49

pl
pl

person who writes for the theater
...st, dramaturge, dramaturgist, li-
...t, scripter, tragedian, writer; SEE
...548

plaza [n] *central location, spot*
common, court, green, park, square, village
green; SEE CONCEPTS 509,513

plea [n1] *begging request*
appeal, application, entreaty, imploration, imprecation, intercession, orison, overture, petition,
prayer, round robin*, solicitation, suit, supplication; SEE CONCEPT 662

plea [n2] *excuse, defense*
action, alibi, allegation, apology, argument,
cause, claim, cop-out*, explanation, extenuation,
fish tale*, justification, mitigation, out, palliation,
pleading, pretext, rationalization, right, song and
dance*, story, vindication, whitewash*; SEE CON-
CEPTS 57,278,318

plead [v1] *beg, request*
appeal, ask, beseech, cop a plea*, crave, crawl,
entreat, entreaty, importune, importune, make up
for, petition, pray, solicit, square things*, supplicate; SEE CONCEPT 48

plead [v2] *present a defense*
adduce, advocate, allege, answer charges, argue,
assert, avouch, cite, cop a plea*, declare, give
evidence, maintain, plea bargain, present, put forward, respond, use as excuse, vouch; SEE CON-
CEPTS 49,317

pleasant [adj] *acceptable; friendly*
affable, agreeable, amiable, amusing, bland,
charming, cheerful, civil, civilized, congenial,
convivial, cool*, copacetic, cordial, delectable,
delightful, diplomatic, enchanting, engaging, enjoyable, fine, fine and dandy*, fun, genial, good-
humored, gracious, gratifying, homey, jolly,
jovial, kindly, likable, lovely, mild, mild-
mannered, nice, obliging, pleasing, pleasurable,
polite, refreshing, satisfying, social, soft, sweet,
sympathetic, urbane, welcome; SEE CONCEPTS
542,548,572

pleasantry [n] *nice remark*
badinage, banter, bon mot*, humor, jest, joke,
joking, levity, merriment, quip, quirk, repartee,
sally*, squib*, wit, witticism; SEE CONCEPTS
273,278

please [v1] *delight, make happy*
amuse, charm, cheer, content, enchant, entertain,
fill the bill*, gladden, go over big*, grab, gratify,
hit the spot*, humor, indulge, kill*, make the
grade*, overjoy, satisfy, score, suit, sweep off
feet*, tickle*, tickle pink*, titillate, turn on*,
wow*; SEE CONCEPTS 7,22

please [v2] *will, elect to do*
be inclined, choose, command, demand, desire,
like, opt, prefer, see fit, want, wish; SEE CONCEPT
20

pleasing/pleasurable [adj] *welcome, nice*
agreeable, amiable, amusing, charming, congenial, delightful, enchanting, engaging, enjoyable,
entertaining, favorable, good, grateful, gratifying,
likable, luscious, musical, palatable, pleasant, polite, satisfactory, satisfying, savory, suitable,
sweet, winning; SEE CONCEPTS 537,572

pleasure [n1] *delight, happiness*
amusement, bliss, buzz*, comfort, contentment,
delectation, diversion, ease, enjoyment, entertainment, felicity, flash*, fruition, game, gladness,
gluttony, gratification, gusto, hobby, indulgence,

joie de vivre, joy, joyride*, kick*, kicks*, luxury,
primrose path*, recreation, relish, revelry, satisfaction, seasoning, self-indulgence, solace, spice,
thrill, titillation, turn-on*, velvet*, zest; SEE CON-
CEPTS 388,410

pleasure [n2] *will, inclination*
choice, command, desire, fancy, liking, mind, option, preference, purpose, velleity, want, wish;
SEE CONCEPTS 20,659

plebeian [n] *person of lower class*
commonalty, commoner, common people, peasant, person in the street*, pleb*, plebe*, proletarian, rank and file*; SEE CONCEPTS 413,423

plebeian [adj] *base, lower-class*
banal, coarse, common, conventional, humble, ignoble, low, lowborn, lowly, mean, ordinary, pedestrian, popular, proletarian, traditional,
uncultivated, unrefined, unsophisticated, unwashed*, vulgar, working-class; SEE CONCEPT
549

pledge [n1] *word of honor*
agreement, assurance, covenant, guarantee,
health, oath, promise, toast, undertaking, vow,
warrant, word; SEE CONCEPTS 71,278

pledge [n2] *sign of good faith*
bail, bond, collateral, deposit, earnest, gage, guarantee, guaranty, pawn, security, surety, token,
warrant, warranty; SEE CONCEPTS 318,332,446

pledge [v] *guarantee; give word of honor*
contract, covenant, engage, give word*, hock*,
hook*, mortgage, pawn, plight, promise, sign for,
soak*, swear, undertake, vouch, vow; SEE CON-
CEPT 71

plenary [adj] *entire, whole*
absolute, complete, full, general, inclusive, open,
sweeping, thorough; SEE CONCEPT 531

plentiful/plenty [adj] *abundant, productive*
abounding, ample, bounteous, bountiful,
bumper*, chock-full*, complete, copious,
enough, excessive, extravagant, exuberant, fertile, flowing, flush*, fruitful, full, fulsome, generous, improvident, infinite, large, lavish, liberal,
lousy with*, lush, luxuriant, overflowing, plenteous, prodigal, profuse, prolific, replete, rife, sufficient, superabundant, superfluous, swarming,
swimming, teeming; SEE CONCEPTS 762,781

plenty [n] *much, abundance*
affluence, avalanche*, capacity, copiousness, cornucopia, deluge*, enough, flood*, fruitfulness,
full house*, fund, good deal*, great deal*,
heaps*, loads*, lots, luxury, mass, masses*,
mine*, mountains*, oodles*, opulence, peck*,
piles*, plethora, profusion, prosperity, quantity,
stacks*, store, sufficiency, torrent*, volume,
wealth; SEE CONCEPTS 767,787

plethora [n] *excess*
deluge, flood, glut, many, much, overabundance,
overflow, overkill, overmuch, plenty, profusion,
superabundance, superfluity, surfeit, surplus; SEE
CONCEPTS 767,787

pliable [adj] *bendable, adaptable*
compliant, docile, ductile, easily led, easy, flexible, impressionable, limber, lithe, malleable,
manageable, manipulable, moldable, obedient,
plastic, pliant, putty*, receptive, responsive, rolling with the punches*, spongy, submissive,
supple, susceptible, tractable, yielding; SEE CON-
CEPTS 404,488

plight [n] *dilemma, difficulty; situation*
bad news*, circumstances, condition, corner*,

double trouble*, extremity, fix*, hole*, impasse, jam, perplexity, pickle*, pinch*, predicament, quandary, scrape*, spot*, state*, straits, tight situation, trouble; SEE CONCEPTS *666,674*

plod [v1] *walk heavily*
clump*, drag, flounder, hike, lumber*, plug, schlepp*, slog*, stamp, stomp, toil, tramp, trample, tread, tromp, trudge, wallow; SEE CONCEPT *151*

plod [v2] *work slowly and under duress*
bear down*, buckle down*, drudge, grind, knuckle down*, labor, persevere, plough through*, plug away*, scratch*, slave, sweat*, toil; SEE CONCEPTS *87,677*

plot [n1] *plan, scheme*
artifice, booby trap*, cabal, collusion, complicity, connivance, conniving, conspiracy, contrivance, covin, design, device, fix, frame, frame-up*, game, intrigue, little game*, machination, maneuver, practice, ruse, scam, setup, stratagem, trick; SEE CONCEPT *660*

plot [n2] *story line*
action, design, development, enactment, events, incidents, movement, narrative, outline, picture, progress, scenario, scene, scheme, story, structure, subject, suspense, theme, thread, unfolding; SEE CONCEPTS *264,282*

plot [n3] *tract of land*
acreage, allotment, area, division, ground, land, lot, parcel, patch, piece, plat, spread; SEE CONCEPTS *509,513*

plot [v1] *plan, scheme*
angle, brew*, cabal, cogitate, collude, conceive, concoct, connive, conspire, contrive, cook up*, design, devise, draft, finagle, frame, hatch*, imagine, intrigue, lay*, machinate, maneuver, operate, outline, project, promote, rough out*, set up, sketch, wangle; SEE CONCEPT *36*

plot [v2] *map out; draw*
calculate, chart, compute, draft, lay out, locate, mark, outline, put forward; SEE CONCEPTS *36,79,174*

plow [v] *dig up ground for cultivation*
break, break ground, bulldoze, cultivate, farm, furrow, harrow, harvest, list, push, rake, reap, ridge, rush, shove, smash, till, trench, turn, turn over; SEE CONCEPT *178*

ploy [n] *game, trick*
artifice, contrivance, device, dodge, feint, gambit, maneuver, move, play, ruse, scheme, stratagem, subterfuge, tactic, wile; SEE CONCEPT *59*

pluck [n] *person's resolution, courage*
backbone, boldness, bravery, dauntlessness, determination, grit, guts*, hardihood, heart*, intestinal fortitude*, intrepidity, mettle, moxie*, nerve, resolution, spirit, spunk; SEE CONCEPT *411*

pluck [v] *grab, pull out; pick at*
catch, clutch, collect, cull, draw, finger, gather, harvest, jerk, plunk, pull at, snatch, strum, tug, tweak, yank; SEE CONCEPT *206*

plug [n1] *stopper*
bung, connection, cork, filling, fitting, occlusion, river, spigot, stopple, tampon, wedge; SEE CONCEPTS *471,836*

plug [n2] *publicity*
advertisement, blurb*, good word*, hype*, mention, push*, write-up; SEE CONCEPT *274*

plug [v1] *stop up*
block, bung, choke, clog, close, congest, cork, cover, drive in, fill, obstruct, occlude, pack, ram,

seal, secure, stop, stopper, stopple, stuff; SEE CONCEPT *209*

plug [v2] *publicize*
advertise, boost*, build up*, hype*, mention, promote, push*, write up; SEE CONCEPTS *49,60*

plum [n] *reward, prize*
asset, bonus, carrot*, catch*, cream*, dividend, find, meed, nugget*, pick, premium, treasure; SEE CONCEPTS *337,712*

plumb [adj] *vertical*
erect, perpendicular, sheer, straight, straight up, up and down, upright; SEE CONCEPT *581*

plumb [v] *probe, go into*
delve, explore, fathom, gauge, get to the bottom of*, measure, penetrate, search, sound, take soundings, unravel; SEE CONCEPTS *181,216,291*

plummet [v] *fall hard and fast*
collapse, crash, decline, decrease, descend, dip, dive, downturn, drop, drop down, dump, fall, nose-dive, plunge, precipitate, sink, skid, stoop, swoop, tumble; SEE CONCEPTS *181,698,763*

plump [adj] *chubby, fat*
beefy*, burly, buxom, chunky*, corpulent, filled, fleshy, full, obese, portly, pudgy*, rotund, round, stout, tubby*; SEE CONCEPT *491*

plunder [n] *something stolen*
booty*, goods*, graft, hot goods*, loot, make*, pickings*, pillage, plunderage, prey, prize, quarry, rapine, raven, spoil, stuff*, take*, trappings*, winnings*; SEE CONCEPT *710*

plunder [v] *ravage, steal*
appropriate, burn, depredate, despoil, devastate, fleece, forage, foray, grab, gut, kip, knock off*, knock over*, lay waste, liberate, lift, loot, loot, maraud, moonlight requisition*, pillage, prey, prowl, raid, ransack, relieve, requisition, rifle, rip off*, rob, sack, salvage, smash and grab*, snatch, spoil, stick up*, strip; SEE CONCEPTS *86,139,252*

plunge [n] *quick drop, enthusiastic attempt*
belly flop*, descent, dive, duck, dunk, fall, high dive, immersion, investment, jump, nose-dive, spree, submergence, submersion, swoop, venture; SEE CONCEPTS *100,150,152,181,194*

plunge [v] *dive or fall fast*
belly-flop*, career, cast, charge, dash, descend, dip, drive, drop, duck, fling, go down, go the limit, go whole hog*, hurtle, immerge, immerse, jump, keel, lunge, lurch, nose-dive, pitch, plummet, plunk, propel, rush, shoot the works*, sink, sound, submerge, submerse, swoop, take a flyer*, take a header*, tear, throw, throw oneself, thrust, topple, tumble; SEE CONCEPTS *100,150, 152,181,194*

plurality [n] *large part of a group*
advantage, bulk, greater part, lead, majority, mass, most, multiplicity, nearly all, numerousness, preponderance, profusion, variety; SEE CONCEPTS *382,829*

plus [n] *asset; something added*
advantage, benefit, bonus, extra, gain, good point, overage, overstock, oversupply, perk, surplus; SEE CONCEPT *693*

plus [adj] *added, extra*
additional, augmented, boosted, enlarged, expanded, increased, positive, supplementary, surplus; SEE CONCEPTS *762,771*

plush [adj] *luxurious, rich*
costly, deluxe, elegant, lavish, luscious, lush, luxury, opulent, palatial, ritzy, silken, sumptuous; SEE CONCEPTS *334,589*

ply [v] *use, work at*
carry on, dispense, employ, exercise, exert, follow, function, handle, maneuver, manipulate, practice, pursue, put out, swing, throw, utilize, wield; SEE CONCEPTS *100,225*

poach [v] *infringe upon; trespass*
appropriate, encroach, filch, fish illegally, hunt illegally, intrude, pilfer, plunder, rob, smuggle, steal; SEE CONCEPTS *139,192*

pocket [n] *cavity, pouch*
bag, chamber, compartment, hole, hollow, opening, receptacle, sack, socket; SEE CONCEPTS *452,513*

pocket [adj] *small, portable*
abridged, canned, capsule, compact, concise, condensed, diminutive, epitomized, itsy-bitsy*, little, midget, miniature, minute, peewee*, pint-sized*, potted, tiny, wee; SEE CONCEPT *773*

pocket [v] *help oneself to something*
abstract, appropriate, conceal, enclose, filch, hide, lift, nab, pilfer, pinch, purloin, shoplift, steal, swipe, take; SEE CONCEPTS *139,142*

pocketbook [n] *accessory for carrying personal items*
bag, clutch, frame, handbag, hide, leather, pouch, purse, reticule, suitcase, wallet; SEE CONCEPTS *446,450*

pod [n/v] *encasement of vegetable seeds*
capsule, case, covering, hull, husk, sheath, sheathing, shell, shuck, skin, vessel; SEE CONCEPTS *428,484*

podium [n] *structure from which speakers orate*
dais, platform, pulpit, rostrum, soapbox*, stage, stump*; SEE CONCEPT *443*

poem [n] *highly expressive, rhythmical literary piece*
ballad, beat, blank verse, composition, creation, epic, free verse, haiku, limerick, lines, lyric, ode, poesy, poetry, quatrain, rhyme, rime, rune, sestina, song, sonnet, verse, villanelle, words, writing; SEE CONCEPTS *268,282*

poet [n] *person who writes expressive, rhythmic verse*
artist, author, balladist, bard, dilettante, dramatist, librettist, lyricist, lyrist, maker, metrist, odist, parodist, poetaster, rhapsodist, rhymer, rimer, sonnetist, versifier, writer; SEE CONCEPTS *348,423*

poetic [adj] *with rhythm and beauty; related to poetic composition*
anapestic, dactylic, dramatic, elegiac, epic, epical, epodic, iambic, idyllic, imaginative, lyric, lyrical, melodious, metrical, odic, rhythmical, romantic, songlike, tuneful; SEE CONCEPT *267*

poetry [n] *expressive, rhythmic literary work*
balladry, doggerel, metrical composition, paean, poems, poesy, rhyme, rhyming, rime, rune, song, stanza, verse, versification; SEE CONCEPTS *268,282,349*

poignant [adj1] *affecting, painful*
agitating, agonizing, bitter, distressing, disturbing, emotional, heartbreaking, heartrending, impressive, intense, moving, passionate, pathetic, perturbing, piteous, pitiful, sad, sentimental, sorrowful, touching, upsetting; SEE CONCEPTS *529,548*

poignant [adj2] *sharp, bitter*
acrid, acute, biting, caustic, keen, penetrating, peppery, piercing, piquant, pointed, pungent, racy, sarcastic, severe, snappy, spicy, stinging, tangy, zesty; SEE CONCEPTS *267,613*

point [n1] *speck*
bit, count, dot, fleck, flyspeck, full stop, iota, mark, minim, mite, mote, notch, particle, period, scrap, stop, tittle, trace; SEE CONCEPTS *79,831*

point [n2] *specific location*
locality, locus, place, position, site, situation, spot, stage, station, where; SEE CONCEPT *198*

point [n3] *sharp end, top, end of extension*
apex, awn, barb, beak, bill, cape, claw, cusp, dagger, foreland, head, headland, jag, nib, pin point, prick, prickler, promontory, prong, snag, spike, spine, spire, spur, sticker, stiletto, summit, sword, thorn, tine, tip, tooth; SEE CONCEPTS *827,836*

point [n4] *circumstance, stage; limited time*
brink, condition, date, degree, duration, edge, extent, instant, juncture, limit, moment, period, point in time, position, threshold, time, verge, very minute; SEE CONCEPTS *696,815*

point [n5] *goal, aim*
appeal, attraction, bottom line*, charm, cogency, design, effectiveness, end, fascination, intent, intention, interest, motive, name of the game*, nitty-gritty*, nub, nuts and bolts*, object, objective, punch*, purpose, reason, significance, use, usefulness, utility, validity, validness; SEE CONCEPT *659*

point [n6] *meaning, essence*
argument, bottom line*, burden, core, crux, drift, force, gist, head, heart, idea, import, kicker*, main idea, marrow, matter, meat*, motif, motive, name of the game*, nitty-gritty*, nub, nuts and bolts*, pith, pointer, proposition, punch line*, question, score, stuff, subject, subject matter, text, theme, thrust, tip, tip-off*, topic; SEE CONCEPTS *274,682*

point [n7] *aspect, characteristic*
attribute, case, circumstance, circumstantial, constituent, detail, element, facet, feature, instance, item, material, nicety, part, particular, peculiarity, property, quality, respect, side, thing*, trait; SEE CONCEPTS *274,411,654*

point [n8] *scoring unit of sport competition*
count, mark, notch, score, tally; SEE CONCEPTS *364,784*

point [v1] *show as probable; call attention*
bespeak, button down*, denote, designate, direct, finger*, hint, imply, indicate, lead, make*, name, offer, peg*, pin down*, put down for*, put finger on*, signify, suggest, tab*, tag*; SEE CONCEPTS *118,138*

point [v2] *direct, lead*
aim, beam*, bring to bear, cast, face, guide, head, influence, lay, level, look, slant, steer, tend, train, turn, zero in*; SEE CONCEPTS *187,201,623*

pointed [adj1] *having a sharp end or part*
acicular, aciculate, acuminate, acuminous, acute, barbed, cornered, cuspidate, edged, fine, keen, mucronate, peaked, piked, pointy, pronged, sharp, sharp-cornered, spiked; SEE CONCEPTS *490,606*

pointed [adj2] *penetrating, biting*
accurate, acid, acute, barbed, boiled down, calling a spade a spade*, cutting, in a nutshell*, incisive, insinuating, keen, laid on the line*, legit, meaty*, on the button*, on the nose*, pertinent, pregnant, right-on*, right to it*, sarcastic, sharp,

pointer [n1] *indicator*
arrow, dial, director, gauge, guide, hand, index, mark, needle, register, rod, signal; SEE CONCEPTS *464,498*

pointer [n2] *hint, suggestion*
advice, caution, clue, information, recommendation, steer, tip, tip-off, warning; SEE CONCEPTS *75,274*

pointless [adj] *ridiculous, senseless*
absurd, aimless, around in circles*, fruitless, futile, going nowhere*, impotent, inane, inconsequential, ineffective, ineffectual, insignificant, in vicious circle*, irrelevant, meaningless, needle in haystack*, nongermane, nonsensical, not pertinent, on treadmill*, powerless, purportless, remote, silly, stupid, trivial, unavailing, uninteresting, unnecessary, unproductive, unprofitable, useless, vague, vain, worthless; SEE CONCEPTS *529,548*

point out [v] *call attention to*
advert, allude, bring up, denote, designate, identify, indicate, mention, refer, remind, reveal, show, specify; SEE CONCEPTS *49,73,261*

poise [n] *self-composure, dignity*
address, aplomb, assurance, balance, bearing, calmness, confidence, cool, coolness, delicatesse, diplomacy, elegance, equability, equanimity, equilibrium, ease, gravity, polish, presence, presence of mind, sangfroid, savoir-faire, self-assurance, self-possession, serenity, stasis, tact, tactfulness, tranquility; SEE CONCEPTS *633,717*

poise [v] *balance, suspend*
ballast, be ready, brood, float, hang, hold, hover, position, stabilize, stand, steady, support, wait; SEE CONCEPT *154*

poison [n] *substance that causes harm, death*
adulteration, bacteria, bane, blight, cancer, contagion, contamination, corruption, germ, infection, malignancy, miasma, toxicant, toxin, toxoid, venin, venom, virus; SEE CONCEPTS *307,475,674,675*

poison/poisonous [adj] *harmful*
bad, baleful, baneful, corrupt, corruptive, dangerous, deadly, deleterious, destructive, detrimental, evil, fatal, hurtful, infective, lethal, malicious, malignant, mephitic, miasmatic, morbid, mortal, noocuous, noisome, noxious, peccant, pernicious, pestiferous, pestilential, septic, toxic, toxicant, toxiferous, venomous, vicious, viperous, virulent; SEE CONCEPT *537*

poison [v] *contaminate, pollute*
adulterate, corrupt, debase, defile, deprave, destroy, envenom, fester, harm, infect, injure, kill, make ill, murder, pervert, stain, subvert, taint, undermine, vitiate, warp; SEE CONCEPTS *14,246, 252*

poke [n] *push, thrust*
blow, boost, bout, butt, dig, hit, jab, nudge, prod, punch, shove, stab; SEE CONCEPTS *189,208*

poke [v1] *push at; thrust*
arouse, awaken, bulge, butt*, crowd, dig, elbow*, goose*, hit, jab, jostle, jut, nudge*, overhang, prod, project, protrude, provoke, punch, ram, rouse, shoulder*, shove, stab, stand out, stick, stick out, stimulate, stir; SEE CONCEPTS *189,208,723*

poke [v2] *interfere, snoop*
busybody*, butt in*, intrude, meddle, nose*, peek, pry, tamper; SEE CONCEPT *384*

poke [v3] *move along slowly*
dally, dawdle, delay, drag, get no place fast*, idle, lag, loiter, mosey*, procrastinate, put off*, shlep along*, tarry, toddle*, trail; SEE CONCEPT *151*

polar [adj1] *cold*
arctic, extreme, farthest, freezing, frigid, frozen, glacial, icy, north, south, terminal; SEE CONCEPTS *583,605*

polar [adj2] *opposite, opposed*
antagonistic, antipodal, antipodean, antithetical, contradictory, contrary, converse, counter, diametric, reverse; SEE CONCEPT *564*

pole [n] *bar, post*
beam, extremity, flagpole, flagstaff, leg, mast, pile, plank, rod, shaft, spar, staff, stake, standard, stave, stick, stilt, stud, terminus; SEE CONCEPTS *440,470,475,479*

police/police officer [n] *person, people hired to uphold the laws*
arm of the law*, badge*, bear*, beat cop, black and white*, blue*, bluecoat*, bobby, constable, constabulary, cop*, copper*, corps*, detective, fed*, flatfoot*, force, gendarme, heat*, law, law enforcement, narc*, patrol; SEE CONCEPTS *299,354*

policy [n] *procedure, tactics*
action, administration, approach, arrangement, behavior, channels, code, course, custom, design, guideline, line, management, method, order, organization, plan, polity, practice, program, protocol, red tape*, rule, scheme, stratagem, strategy, tenet, the book*, the numbers*, theory; SEE CONCEPTS *6,271,660,688*

polish [n1] *shine, brightness*
brilliance, burnish, finish, glaze, glint, gloss, luster, sheen, smoothness, sparkle, varnish, veneer, wax; SEE CONCEPTS *492,611,620*

polish [n2] *cultivated look, performance*
breeding, class, cultivation, culture, elegance, finesse, finish, grace, politesse, refinement, style, suavity, urbanity; SEE CONCEPTS *388,633,655*

polish [v1] *shine, buff*
brighten, burnish, clean, finish, furbish, glaze, gloss, rub, scour, scrub, sleek, slick, smooth, wax; SEE CONCEPTS *202,215*

polish [v2] *improve performance, look*
amend, better, brush up, correct, cultivate, emend, enhance, finish, furbish, make improvement, mature, mend, perfect, refine, round, sleek, slick, smooth, touch up; SEE CONCEPT *244*

polish off [v] *finish using*
consume, devour, dispatch, dispose of, do away with*, down*, eat, eat up, eliminate, get rid of*, liquidate, put away*, swill*, use up, wolf*; SEE CONCEPTS *169,225*

polite [adj] *mannerly, civilized*
affable, amenable, amiable, attentive, bland, civil, complaisant, concerned, conciliatory, condescending, considerate, cordial, courteous, courtly, cultured, deferential, diplomatic, elegant, friendly, genteel, gentle, good-natured, gracious, mild, neighborly, nice, obliging, obsequious, pleasant, polished, politic, punctilious, refined, respectful, smooth, sociable, solicitous, sympathetic, thoughtful, urbane, well-behaved, well-bred, well-mannered; SEE CONCEPT *401*

pl
po

politic [*adj*] *wise, tactful*
adroit, advisable, canny*, cool, delicate, diplomatic, discreet, expedient, in one's best interests*, judicious, on the lookout*, perspicacious, prudent, sagacious, sensible, sharp, shrewd, smooth, tactical, tuned in*, urbane; SEE CONCEPT 401

politically correct [*adj*] *sensitive to all forms of oppression*
bias-free, dogmatic, gay/lesbian affirmative, gender-free, inclusive, liberal, multicultural, non-discriminatory, nonsexist, nonracist, PC*, respectful, revisionary; SEE CONCEPTS 529,542

politician [*n*] *person pursuing or occupying elective office*
baby-kisser*, boss, chieftain, congressperson, democrat, grandstander*, handshaker*, lawmaker, leader, legislator, member of Congress, member of parliament, officeholder, office seeker, orator, partisan, party member, president, public servant, republican, senator, speaker, statesperson, whistle-stopper*; SEE CONCEPT 359

politics [*n*] *art and science of administration of government*
affairs of state, backroom*, campaigning, civics, domestic affairs, electioneering, foreign affairs, government, government policy, hat in the ring*, internal affairs, jungle*, legislature, matters of state, political science, polity, smoke-filled room*, statecraft, stateship, zoo*; SEE CONCEPTS 300,301

poll [*n*] *census; tally of answers to questions of opinion*
ballot, canvass, count, figures, opinion, returns, sampling, survey, vote, voting; SEE CONCEPTS 48,300

poll [*v*] *take census; question*
ballot, canvass, enroll, examine, interview, list, register, sample, send up a balloon*, survey, tally, test the waters*, vote; SEE CONCEPTS 48,300

pollute [*v*] *make dirty; corrupt*
adulterate, alloy, befoul, besmirch, contaminate, debase, defile, deprave, desecrate, dirty, dishonor, foul, infect, make filthy, mar, poison, profane, soil, spoil, stain, sully, taint, violate; SEE CONCEPTS 246,254

pollution [*n*] *dirtiness, contamination*
abuse, adulteration, besmearing, besmirching, blight, corruption, decomposition, defilement, desecration, deterioration, dirtying, fouling, foulness, impairment, impurity, infection, misuse, polluting, profanation, rottenness, soiling, spoliation, taint, tainting, uncleanness, vitiation; SEE CONCEPT 720

pomp [*n*] *pageantry, display*
affectation, array, ceremonial, ceremony, fanfare, flourish, formality, grandeur, grandiosity, magnificence, ostentation, pageant, panoply, parade, pomposity, ritual, shine, show, solemnity, splendor, state, vainglory; SEE CONCEPTS 335,377,655

pompous [*adj*] *arrogant, egotistic*
affected, bloated, boastful, bombastic, conceited, flatulent, flaunting, flowery, fustian, grandiloquent, grandiose, high and mighty*, highfaluting*, high-flown*, imperious, important, inflated, magisterial, magniloquent, narcissistic, orotund, ostentatious, overbearing, overblown, pontifical, portentous, presumptuous, pretentious, puffed up*, puffy*, rhetorical, self-centered, self-important, selfish, showy, sonorous, stuck-up*,

supercilious, turgid, uppity*, vain, vainglorious, windy*; SEE CONCEPTS 267,401,542

pond [*n*] *small body of water*
basin, dew, duck pond, lagoon, lily pond, millpond, pool, puddle, small lake, splash; SEE CONCEPT 514

ponder [*v*] *think about seriously*
appraise, brood, build castles in air*, cerebrate, cogitate, consider, contemplate, daydream, debate, deliberate, dwell, evaluate, examine, excogitate, figure, give thought to, meditate, mind, moon*, mull, mull over, muse, noodle around*, perpend, pipe dream*, put on thinking cap*, puzzle over, reason, reflect, revolve, roll, ruminate, speculate, study, think out, think over, turn over, weigh, woolgather*; SEE CONCEPTS 17,24

ponderous [*adj1*] *heavy, cumbersome*
awkward, bulky, burdensome, clumsy, cumbrous, dull, elephantine, graceless, hefty, huge, laborious, lifeless, lumbering, massive, onerous, oppressive, substantial, troublesome, unhandy, unwieldy, weighty; SEE CONCEPTS 491,565

ponderous [*adj2*] *dreary, tedious*
arid, barren, cardboard*, dry, dull, heavy, humdrum*, labored, lifeless, long-winded*, monotonous, pedantic, pedestrian, plodding, prolix, stiff*, stilted, stodgy, stuffy*, vapid, verbose, wooden*; SEE CONCEPTS 267,529,542

pool [*n1*] *collection of liquid*
basin, bath, lagoon, lake, mere, millpond, mud puddle, natatorium, pond, puddle, splash, swimming pool, tank, tarn; SEE CONCEPTS 364,514

pool [*n2*] *supply of money, goods*
bank, combine, conglomerate, equipment, funds, group, jackpot, kitty*, pot, provisions, stakes; SEE CONCEPTS 340,432

pool [*v*] *combine*
amalgamate, blend, join forces, league, merge, put together, share; SEE CONCEPTS 113,193

poor [*adj1*] *lacking sufficient money*
bad off*, bankrupt, beggared, beggarly, behind eight ball*, broke*, destitute, dirt poor*, down-and-out*, empty-handed*, flat*, flat broke*, fortuneless, hard up*, impecunious, impoverished, indigent, in need, insolvent, in want, low, meager, moneyless, necessitous, needy, pauperized, penniless, penurious, pinched*, poverty-stricken, reduced*, scanty*, stone broke*, strapped*, suffering, truly needy, underprivileged, unprosperous; SEE CONCEPT 334

poor [*adj2*] *deficient, inadequate*
base, below par, common, contemptible, crude, diminutive, dwarfed, exiguous, faulty, feeble, humble, imperfect, incomplete, inferior, insignificant, insufficient, lacking, low-grade, lowly, meager, mean, mediocre, miserable, modest, niggardly*, ordinary, paltry, pitiable, pitiful, plain, reduced, rotten, scanty, second-rate*, shabby, shoddy, skimpy, slight, sorry*, sparse, subnormal, subpar, substandard, trifling, trivial, unsatisfactory, valueless, weak, worthless; SEE CONCEPTS 570,574

poor [*adj3*] *weak, unfertile*
bare, barren, depleted, exhausted, feeble, fruitless, impaired, imperfect, impoverished, indisposed, infertile, infirm, puny, sick, sterile, unfruitful, unproductive, worthless; SEE CONCEPT 314

poor [*adj4*] *unfortunate, unhappy*
commiserable, hapless, ill-fated, luckless, miser-

able, pathetic, piteous, pitiable, pitiful, rueful, unlucky, wretched; SEE CONCEPTS *542,548*

poorly [adj] *not well*
ailing, below par, failing, ill, indisposed, low,
mean, out of sorts*, rotten*, sick, sickly, under
the weather*, unwell; SEE CONCEPT *314*

poorly [adv] *unsatisfactorily*
badly, crudely, defectively, inadequately, incompetently, inexpertly, inferiorly, insufficiently,
meanly, shabbily, unsuccessfully; SEE CONCEPTS
544,571,574

pop [n] *bang*
burst, crack, explosion, jump, leap, report, snap,
strike, thrust, whack; SEE CONCEPT *595*

pop [v] *jump, burst*
appear, bang, blow, crack, dart, explode, go, go
off, hit, insert, leap, protrude, push, put, report,
rise, shove, snap, sock, stick, strike, thrust,
whack; SEE CONCEPT *145*

popular [adj] *well-known, favorite*
accepted, approved, attractive, beloved, caught
on*, celebrated, crowd-pleasing*, faddish*, famous, fashionable, favored, in*, in demand, in
favor, in the mainstream*, in vogue, leading, likable, liked, lovable, noted, notorious, now*,
okay*, pleasing, praised, preferred, prevailing,
prominent, promoted, right stuff*, run-after*,
selling, social, societal, sought, sought-after, stylish, suitable, the rage*, thing*, trendy, well-liked,
well-received; SEE CONCEPTS *555,589*

popular [adj2] *common, standard*
accepted, accessible, adopted, approved, conventional, current, demanded, embraced, familiar,
general, in demand, in use, ordinary, prevailing,
prevalent, proletarian, public, rampant, regnant,
rife, ruling, stock, ubiquitous, universal, widespread; SEE CONCEPT *530*

popularity [n] *recognition, celebrity*
acceptance, acclaim, adoration, approval, currency, demand, esteem, fame, fashion, fashionableness, favor, following, heyday, idolization,
lionization, prevalence, regard, renown, reputation, repute, universality, vogue; SEE CONCEPTS
388,655

popularize [v] *make widely popular, accessible*
catch on, disseminate, familiarize, generalize,
give currency, make available, promote, restore,
resurrect, revive, simplify, spread, universalize;
SEE CONCEPTS *324,384*

population [n] *inhabitants of a place*
citizenry, community, culture, denizens, dwell-
ers, folk, natives, people, populace, public, residents, society, state; SEE CONCEPT *379*

populous [adj] *packed with inhabitants*
crawling, crowded, dense, heavily populated,
jammed, legion, many, multifarious, multitudinal,
multitudinous, numerous, occupied, overpopu-
lated, peopled, populated, settled, several, swarming, teeming, thick, thronged, various, voluminous; SEE CONCEPT *583*

pore [n] *small aperture in skin*
foramen, opening, orifice, outlet, stoma, sweat
gland, vesicle; SEE CONCEPT *418*

pore [v] *go over carefully*
brood, contemplate, dwell on, examine, look
over, muse, peruse, ponder, read, regard, scan,
scrutinize, study; SEE CONCEPTS *24,72,103*

pornographic [adj] *obscene*
adult, immoral, indecent, lewd, off-color, offensive, porn*, porno*, prurient, purple*, raunchy*,

rough, salacious, sexy, smutty*, steamy*,
X-rated*; SEE CONCEPTS *267,372,545*

porous [adj] *having holes; absorbent*
absorptive, penetrable, permeable, pervious,
spongelike, spongy; SEE CONCEPT *606*

port [n] *place for boat docking, traffic, and storage*
anchorage, boatyard, dockage, docks, dockyard,
gate, harbor, harborage, haven, landing, piers,
refuge, retreat, roads, roadstead, sanctuary, sea-
port, shelter, wharf; SEE CONCEPTS *449,509*

portable [adj] *easily transported*
carriageable, cartable, compact, convenient, conveyable, easily carried, handy, haulable, light,
lightweight, manageable, movable, portative,
transportable, wieldy; SEE CONCEPTS *491,584,
773*

portal [n] *hole or door in vessel*
doorway, entrance, entry, entryway, gate, gateway, ingress, opening, way in; SEE CONCEPT *502*

portend [v] *foreshadow, indicate*
adumbrate, augur, be in the cards*, bespeak, betoken, bode, call*, crystal-ball*, forebode, forecast, foreshow, foretell, foretoken, forewarn,
harbinger, have a hunch, herald, hint, omen, point
to, predict, premonish, presage, prognosticate,
promise, prophesy, read, see coming*, threaten,
warn of; SEE CONCEPTS *71,78,261*

portent [n] *indication, forewarning*
augury, bodement, boding, caution, clue, foreboding, foreshadowing, foretoken, funny feeling*, handwriting on the wall*, harbinger, hunch,
omen, premonition, presage, presentiment, prognostic, prognostication, sign, sinking feeling*,
threat, vibes*, warning; SEE CONCEPT *278*

portent [n2] *miracle*
marvel, phenomenon, prodigy, sensation, stunner,
wonder; SEE CONCEPTS *230,529*

porter [n] *person who serves as attendant, caretaker*
baggage carrier, bearer, bellhop, carrier, concierge, doorkeeper, doorperson, gatekeeper, janitor, red cap*, sky cap*, transporter; SEE CONCEPT
348

portfolio [n] *flat case for transporting papers*
attaché case, bag, brief bag, briefcase, case, container, envelope, folder, notebook, valise; SEE
CONCEPT *494*

portion [n] *share, cut, ration*
allocation, allotment, allowance, apportionment,
bang, bit, chunk, division, divvy*, drag*, dram,
excerpt, extract, fix, fraction, fragment, gob,
helping, hit, hunk, lagniappe, lion's share*, lot,
lump, measure, meed, member, moiety, morsel,
parcel, part, piece, piece of action*, plum, quantity, quantum, quota, scrap, section, segment,
serving, shot*, slug*, smithereen*, taste; SEE
CONCEPT *835*

portion [n2] *fate, destiny*
circumstance, cup*, doom, fortune, kismet*, lot*,
luck; SEE CONCEPT *679*

portion [v] *divide into pieces*
administer, allocate, allot, apportion, assign, deal,
dispense, distribute, divvy up*, dole out*, mete
out*, parcel, part, partition, piece, prorate, quota,
ration, section, share, shift; SEE CONCEPTS
98,140

portly [adv] *bulky, fat*
ample, avoirdupois, beefy*, broad, burly, corpulent, fleshy, heavy, hefty, husky, large, obese,

po
po

overweight, plump, rotund, stout; SEE CONCEPT 491

portrait [n] *drawn representation; description*
account, characterization, depiction, figure, image, likeness, model, painting, photograph, picture, portraiture, portrayal, profile, silhouette, simulacrum, sketch, snapshot, spitting image*, vignette; SEE CONCEPTS 259,268,625

portray [v] *represent, imitate*
act like, characterize, copy, delineate, depict, describe, draw, duplicate, figure, illustrate, image, impersonate, interpret, limn, mimic, paint, parody, photograph, picture, render, reproduce, simulate, sketch; SEE CONCEPTS 55,174,265

pose [n] *artificial position*
act, affectation, air, attitude, attitudinizing, bearing, carriage, facade, fake, false show, front, guise, mannerism, masquerade, mien, positure, posture, posturing, pretense, pretension, role, stance, stand; SEE CONCEPTS 633,716

pose [v1] *sit, stand in place*
arrange, model, peacock, poise, position, posture, sit for, strike a pose, strut; SEE CONCEPTS 154,174

pose [v2] *pretend, fake*
act, affect, attitudinize, feign, grandstand*, impersonate, make believe, make out like*, masquerade, pass off*, peacock*, playact, posture, profess, purport, put on airs*, put up a front*, sham*, show off*, strike an attitude*, take off as*; SEE CONCEPTS 59,63,633

pose [v3] *offer, put forward idea*
advance, ask, extend, give, hold out, posit, prefer, present, proffer, propose, proposition, propound, put, query, question, set, state, submit, suggest, tender; SEE CONCEPTS 66,67,75

posh [adj] *luxurious, upper-class*
chic, classy, deluxe, elegant, exclusive, fashionable, grand, high-class, la-di-da*, luxury, modish*, opulent, rich, ritzy*, smart, swank, swanky*, swish*, trendy; SEE CONCEPTS 334,589

position [n1] *physical place*
area, bearings, district, environment, fix, geography, ground, locale, locality, location, locus, point, post, reference, region, scene, seat, setting, site, situation, space, spot, stand, station, surroundings, topography, tract, whereabouts*; SEE CONCEPT 198

position [n2] *posture, stance*
arrangement, attitude, ballgame*, bearing, carriage, circumstances, condition, deportment, disposition, form, habit, how things stack up*, like it is*, manner, mien, pass, plight, port, pose, predicament, situation, spot, stand, state, status, strait, the size of it*; SEE CONCEPT 696

position [n3] *belief, point of view*
angle, attitude, color, judgment, opinion, outlook, slant, stance, stand, standpoint, view, viewpoint; SEE CONCEPT 689

position [n4] *class, stature*
cachet, capacity, caste, character, consequence, dignity, footing, importance, place, prestige, rank, reputation, situation, sphere, standing, station, status; SEE CONCEPTS 378,388

position [n5] *responsibility in business or other enterprise*
berth, billet, capacity, connection, do*, duty, employment, function, job, nine-to-five*, occupation, office, place, post, profession, role, situation, slot*, spot*, trade; SEE CONCEPTS 324,349,360

position [v] *place physically in location*
arrange, array, dispose, fix, lay out, locate, put, set, settle, stand, stick; SEE CONCEPTS 158,201

positive [adj1] *definite, certain*
absolute, actual, affirmative, assured, categorical, clear, clear-cut, cocksure*, cold*, complete, conclusive, concrete, confident, consummate, convinced, decided, decisive, direct, downright, explicit, express, factual, firm, forceful, forcible, genuine, hard, inarguable, incontestable, incontrovertible, indisputable, indubitable, irrefutable, out-and-out*, outright, perfect, rank, real, specific, sure, thorough, thoroughgoing, unambiguous, undeniable, unequivocal, unmistakable, unmitigated; SEE CONCEPTS 535,582

positive [adj2] *beneficial, helpful*
affirmative, constructive, effective, efficacious, forward-looking, good, practical, productive, progressive, reasonable, sound, useful; SEE CONCEPT 572

positively [adv] *absolutely, definitely*
amen*, assuredly, categorically, certainly, doubtless, doubtlessly, easily, emphatically, firmly, flat*, flat out*, for a fact*, indubitably, no catch*, no holds barred*, no ifs ands or buts*, no kicker*, no strings attached*, on the money*, on the nose*, really truly*, right on*, sure, surely, the ticket*, to a tee*, undeniably, undoubtedly, unequivocally, unmistakably, unquestionably, with certainty, without qualification; SEE CONCEPTS 535,544,582

possess [v] *have or obtain*
acquire, bear, be blessed with, be born with, be endowed with, carry, control, corner*, corner the market*, dominate, get hands on*, get hold of*, grab, have to name*, hog*, hold, latch on to*, lock up, maintain, occupy, own, retain, seize, sit on, take over, take possession; SEE CONCEPTS 120,710

possessed [adj] *bewitched; under a spell*
bedeviled, berserk*, consumed, crazed*, cursed, demented, enchanted, enthralled, fiendish, frenetic, frenzied, gone*, haunted, hooked*, insane, into*, mad*, obsessed, raving*, taken over*, violent; SEE CONCEPT 401

possession [n1] *control, ownership*
custody, dominion, hold, occupancy, occupation, possessorship, proprietary, proprietary rights, proprietorship, retention, tenancy, tenure, title; SEE CONCEPTS 343,710

possession [n2] *something owned; property*
accessories, appointments, appurtenances, assets, baggage, belongings, chattels, effects, equipment, estate, fixtures, furnishings, furniture, goods, impedimenta, paraphernalia, province, real estate, settlement, tangibles, territory, things, trappings, tricks, wealth; SEE CONCEPTS 446,710

possibilities [n] *potential*
capabilities, potentiality, promise, prospects, talent; SEE CONCEPTS 411,650

possibility [n] *feasibility, likelihood; chance*
achievability, action, attainableness, break, circumstance, contingency, fair shake*, fifty-fifty*, fling*, fluke*, fortuity, happening, hazard, hope, incident, instance, liability, likeliness, occasion, occurrence, odds*, opportunity, outside chance*, plausibility, play*, potentiality, practicability, prayer*, probability, prospect, risk*, shot*, stab*, toss-up*, workableness; SEE CONCEPTS 650,693

possible [adj] *likely, attainable*

accessible, achievable, adventitious, advisable, available, breeze*, can do*, cinch, conceivable, credible, dependent, desirable, doable, dormant, duck soup*, easy as pie*, expedient, feasible, fortuitous, hopeful, hypothetical, imaginable, indeterminate, latent, no sweat*, obtainable, piece of cake*, potential, practicable, probable, promising, pushover*, realizable, setup, simple as ABC*, snap, thinkable, uncertain, viable, welcome, within reach, workable; SEE CONCEPTS 528,552,576

possibly [adv] *by chance; in some way*

at all, by any chance, by any means, conceivably, could be, God willing*, if possible, in any way, likely, maybe, not impossibly, peradventure, perchance, perhaps, probably, within realm of possibility; SEE CONCEPTS 544,552

post [n1] *upright support*

column, doorpost, leg, mast, newel, pale, palisade, panel, pedestal, picket, pile, pillar, pole, prop, rail, shaft, stake, standard, stilt, stock, stud; SEE CONCEPTS 440,445,470,479

post [n2] *job, employment*

appointment, assignment, berth, billet, office, place, position, situation; SEE CONCEPTS 351,362

post [n3] *lookout, station*

beat, locus, place, position, whereabouts; SEE CONCEPTS 198,321,439

post [n4] *mail service*

collection, delivery, mail, PO*, postal service, post office; SEE CONCEPTS 299,770

post [v] *situate, position*

assign, establish, locate, place, put, set, station; SEE CONCEPT 201

post [v2] *advise, inform*

acquaint, apprive, brief, clue, fill in, notify, put wise to, report, tell, warn, wise up; SEE CONCEPT 60

poster [n] *large paper advertisement*

affiche, announcement, banner, bill, billboard, broadside, handbill, notice, placard, public notice, sheet, sign, signboard, sticker; SEE CONCEPT 271

posterior [n] *behind of animate being*

back, backside, bottom, butt*, buttocks, can*, cheeks*, derriere, duff*, fanny*, hind part, keester*, moon*, rear, rear end, rump, seat, tail, tail end, tuchis*, tush*; SEE CONCEPT 392

posterior [adj1] *rear*

after, back, behind, dorsal, hind, hinder, hindmost, in back of, last, retral; SEE CONCEPTS 583,827

posterior [adj2] *subsequent*

after, coming after, ensuing, following, later, latter, next, postliminary, subsequential, succeeding; SEE CONCEPTS 585,799

posterity [n] *future generations*

breed, brood, children, descendants, family, heirs, issue, lineage, next generation, offspring, progeniture, progeny, scions, seed, stock, succeeding generations, successors, unborn; SEE CONCEPT 296

posthaste [adj/adv] *fast*

at once, breakneck*, directly, double-quick*, expeditious, flat-out*, fleet, fleetly, full tilt*, hastily, hasty, headlong, lickety-split*, pell-mell*, promptly, pronto, quick, quickly, rapid, rapidly, speedily, speedy, straightaway, swift, swiftly; SEE CONCEPTS 544,588,799

postmortem [n] *analysis after death*

autopsy, coroner's report, dissection, examination, necropsy, post*; SEE CONCEPTS 103,310

postmortem [adj] *following death*

future, later, posthumous, postmundane, postobit, post-obituary; SEE CONCEPT 799

postpone [v] *put off till later time*

adjourn, cool it*, defer, delay, give a rain check*, hang fire*, hold off, hold over, hold up, lay over, pigeonhole*, prorogue, put back, put on back burner*, put on hold, shelve, suspend, table; SEE CONCEPT 130

postulate [v] *suppose, figure*

advance, affirm, assert, assume, aver, estimate, guess, hypothesize, posit, predicate, premise, presuppose, propose, put forward, speculate, suppose, take for granted, theorize; SEE CONCEPTS 12,26

posture [n1] *stance, circumstance*

aspect, attitude, bearing, brace, carriage, condition, demeanor, deportment, disposition, mien, mode, phase, port, pose, position, positure, presence, set, situation, state; SEE CONCEPTS 657,723

posture [n2] *beliefs*

attitude, disposition, feeling, frame of mind, inclination, mood, outlook, point of view, sentiment, stance, standpoint; SEE CONCEPT 410

posture [v] *display an attitude*

affect, attitudinize, display, do a bit*, do for effect*, fake, fake it, make a show*, masquerade, pass for, pass off, playact, pose, put on airs*, put up a front*, show off*; SEE CONCEPTS 59,261

pot [n1] *container, cauldron*

basin, bowl, bucket, can, canister, crock, crucible, cup, jar, jug, kettle, mug, pan, pitcher, receptacle, saucepan, tankard, urn, vessel; SEE CONCEPT 494

pot [n2] *marijuana*

cannabis, grass*, hashish, maryjane*, weed*; SEE CONCEPT 307

potency [n] *effectiveness*

authority, birr, capability, capacity, command, control, dominion, efficacy, efficiency, energy, force, go*, hardihood, influence, juice*, kick*, might, moxie*, muscle*, pep, potential, power, puissance, punch, sinew*, snap, sock*, steam*, strength, sway, vigor, virtue, what it takes*, zap*, zing*, zip*; SEE CONCEPTS 411,676,732

potent [adj] *effective, powerful, forceful*

almighty, authoritative, ball of fire*, cogent, commanding, compelling, convincing, dominant, dynamic, efficacious, forcible, full-bodied, gogetter*, great, gutsy*, impressive, influential, lusty, mighty, persuasive, powerhouse, puissant, punchy, robust, spanking, stiff, strong, sturdy, telling, trenchant, useful, vigorous; SEE CONCEPTS 372,489,540

potential [n] *possibility for achievement*

ability, aptitude, capability, capacity, potentiality, power, the makings*, what it takes*, wherewithal; SEE CONCEPTS 650,706

potential [adj] *promising*

abeyant, budding, conceivable, dormant, embryonic, future, hidden, imaginable, implied, inherent, latent, likely, lurking, plausible, possible, prepatent, probable, quiescent, thinkable, undeveloped, unrealized, within realm of possibility; SEE CONCEPTS 528,552

po
po

potion [n] *concoction prepared for mental or physical effect*
aromatic, brew, cordial, cup, dose, draft, dram, draught, drink, elixir, libation, liquid, liquor, medicine, mixture, nip, philter, remedy, restorative, spirits, stimulant, tonic; SEE CONCEPTS 307,467

potpourri [n] *miscellany*
assortment, blend, collection, combination, combo, gallimaufry, goulash, hash, hodgepodge, medley, mélange, mishmash, mixed bag, mixture, motley, olio*, pastiche*, patchwork, salmagundi*, soup, stew; SEE CONCEPTS 260,432

pottery [n] *containers made from clay; clay art*
ceramics, crockery, earthenware, firing, glazing, porcelain, porcelainware, stoneware, terra cotta; SEE CONCEPTS 174,259,494

pouch [n] *soft container, often made of cloth or skin*
bag, pocket, poke, purse, receptacle, sac, sack; SEE CONCEPTS 446,450,494

pounce [n/v] *leap at; take by surprise*
ambush, attack, bound, dart, dash, dive, drop, fall upon, jump, snatch, spring, strike, surge, swoop, take unawares; SEE CONCEPTS 86,159,194

pound [n] *sixteen ounces/.454 kilograms of weight*
avoirdupois, pint, troy; SEE CONCEPT 795

pound [v1] *crush; beat rhythmically*
batter, belabor, bruise, buffet, clobber, comminute, drub, hammer, hit, malleate, palpitate, pelt, pestle, powder, pulsate, pulse, pulverize, pummel, stomp, strike, thrash, throb, thump, tramp, triturate, wallop; SEE CONCEPTS 150,186,189

pound [v2] *impress; make someone listen*
din, drive, drub, drum, grave, hammer, stamp; SEE CONCEPTS 14,49

pour [v] *be or make flowing*
cascade, cataract, course, crowd, decant, deluge, discharge, drain, drench, emit, flood, flow, give off, gush, inundate, issue, jet, let flow, proceed, rain, rill, roll, run, rush, sheet, shower, sluice, spew, spill, splash, spout, spring, stream, surge, swarm, teem, throng; SEE CONCEPTS 146,179,209

pout [n] *sad face*
frown, glower, long face, moue, sullen look; SEE CONCEPT 716

pout [v] *make a sad face; be sad*
be cross, be in bad mood*, be moody, be petulant, be sullen, frown, grouch, grump*, make a long face*, make a moue, mope, stick one's lip out*, sulk; SEE CONCEPTS 261,410

poverty [n] *want; extreme need, often financial*
abjection, aridity, bankruptcy, barrenness, beggary, dearth, debt, deficiency, deficit, depletion, destitution, difficulty, distress, emptiness, exiguity, famine, hardship, impecuniousness, impoverishment, inadequacy, indigence, insolvency, insufficiency, lack, meagerness, necessitousness, necessity, pass, paucity, pauperism, pennilessness, penury, pinch, poorness, privation, reduction, scarcity, shortage, starvation, straits, underdevelopment, vacancy; SEE CONCEPTS 335,709

poverty-stricken [adj] *in great need; financially poor*
bad off*, bankrupt, beggared, beggarly, broke*, destitute, dirt poor*, distressed, down-and-out*, hard up*, impecunious, impoverished, indigent, in dire circumstances, in want, moneyless, necessitous, needful, needy, penniless, penurious,

short*, stone broke*, stranded*, strapped*, unmoneyed, wanting; SEE CONCEPT 334

powder [n] *fine, loose grains made by crushing a solid*
crumb, dust, film, grain, grit, meal, particle, pounce, pulverulence, seed, talc; SEE CONCEPTS 471,831

powder [v] *crush into fine grains; sprinkle fine grains*
abrade, bray, comminute, cover, crumble, crunch, dredge, dust, file, flour, granulate, grate, grind, pestle, pound, pulverize, rasp, reduce, scatter, scrape, smash, strew, triturate; SEE CONCEPTS 186,222

powdery [adj] *consisting of fine, loose grains*
arenaceous, arenose, branny, chalky, crumbling, crumbly, dry, dusty, fine, floury, friable, grainy, granular, gravelly, gritty, impalpable, loose, mealy, pulverized, pulverulent, sandy; SEE CONCEPT 606

power [n1] *ability, competence*
aptitude, bent, capability, capacity, competency, dynamism, effectiveness, efficacy, endowment, faculty, function, gift, influence, potential, potentiality, qualification, skill, talent, turn, virtue; SEE CONCEPT 630

power [n2] *physical ability, capacity*
applied force, arm*, brawn, dynamism, energy, force, forcefulness, horsepower, intensity, mechanical energy, might, muscle*, omnipotence, potency, potential, puissance, sinew*, strength, vigor, vim, virtue, voltage, weight; SEE CONCEPTS 520,641,732

power [n3] *control, dominance*
ascendancy, authority, authorization, birthright, clout, command, connection, diadem, direction, domination, dominion, hegemony, imperium, influence, inside track*, jurisdiction, law, leadership, license, management, might, moxie*, omnipotence, paramountcy, predominance, prerogative, prestige, privilege, regency, right, rule, say-so*, sovereignty, steam, strength, strings*, superiority, supremacy, sway, warrant, weight*, wire*; SEE CONCEPTS 376,671

powerful [adj] *strong, effective*
able, all-powerful, almighty, authoritarian, authoritative, capable, cogent, commanding, compelling, competent, controlling, convincing, dominant, dynamic, effectual, efficacious, energetic, forceful, forcible, impressive, in control, influential, in the saddle*, mighty, omnipotent, overruling, paramount, persuasive, potent, preeminent, prevailing, puissant, robust, ruling, sovereign, stalwart, strapping*, strengthy, sturdy, supreme, telling, upper hand*, vigorous, weighty, wicked*, wieldy; SEE CONCEPTS 489,527, 540,574

powerfully [adv] *with energy, authority*
effectively, energetically, forcefully, forcibly, hard, intensely, mightily, severely, strongly, vigorously, with might and main; SEE CONCEPTS 540,544,569

powerless [adj] *weak; unable*
blank, chicken*, debilitated, defenseless, dependent, disabled, disenfranchised, etiolated, feeble, frail, gutless, helpless, impotent, incapable, incapacitated, ineffective, ineffectual, inert, infirm, out of gas*, paralyzed, passive, prostrate, subject, supine, tied, unarmed, unfit, vulnerable, wimp*, wishy-washy*; SEE CONCEPTS 489,527

powwow [n] *discussion*
confab*, confabulation, conference, consultation, council, get-together, huddle, meeting, palaver, parley, talk; SEE CONCEPTS 56,324,384

powwow [v] *discuss*
advise, confab*, confabulate, confer, consult, get together, go into a huddle*, huddle, meet, palaver, parley, talk, treat; SEE CONCEPT 56

practicable [adj] *within the realm of possibility*
accessible, achievable, applicable, attainable, doable, employable, feasible, functional, handy, open, operative, performable, possible, practical, serviceable, usable, useful, utile, utilizable, viable, workable; SEE CONCEPT 560

practical [adj1] *realistic, useful*
applied, both feet on the ground*, businesslike, commonsensical, constructive, doable, down-to-earth, efficient, empirical, experimental, factual, feasible, functional, handy, hard-boiled*, implicit, in action, in operation, matter-of-fact*, nuts and bolts*, operative, orderly, possible, practicable, pragmatic, rational, reasonable, sane, sensible, serviceable, sober, solid, sound, systematic, unidealistic, unromantic, usable, utile, utilitarian, virtual, workable, workaday, working; SEE CONCEPTS 533,542,560

practical [adj2] *experienced, proficient*
accomplished, cosmopolitan, effective, efficient, qualified, seasoned, skilled, sophisticated, trained, versed, vet*, veteran, working, worldly, worldly-wise; SEE CONCEPTS 326,527,528,678

practically [adv] *almost, nearly*
about, all but, approximately, as good as, as much as, basically, close to, essentially, for all intents and purposes*, fundamentally, in effect, in essence, morally, most, much, nearly, nigh, virtually, well-nigh; SEE CONCEPTS 531,772

practice [n1] *routine, usual procedure*
convenance, convention, custom, fashion, form, habit, habitude, manner, method, mode, praxis, proceeding, process, rule, system, tradition, trick, usage, use, usefulness, utility, way, wont, use; CONCEPT 688

practice [n2] *exercise, application*
action, assignment, background, discipline, drill, drilling, effect, experience, homework, iteration, operation, preparation, prepping, recitation, recounting, rehearsal, relating, repetition, seasoning, study, training, tune-up, use, work-out; SEE CONCEPTS 87,100,658

practice [n3] *business; clientele of business*
career, clients, patients, profession, vocation, work; SEE CONCEPTS 325,417

practice [v1] *repeat action to improve*
become seasoned, build up, discipline, do again, dress, dress rehearse*, drill, dry run*, exercise, go over, habituate, hone, iterate, polish, prepare, recite, rehearse, run through, shake-down*, sharpen, study, train, try out, tune up, walk through, warm up, work, work out; SEE CONCEPTS 87,100

practice [v2] *carry out; undertake*
apply, carry on, do, engage in, execute, follow, fulfill, function, live up to, observe, perform, ply, pursue, put into effect, specialize in, work at; SEE CONCEPTS 91,310,317,324

pragmatic [adj] *sensible*
businesslike, commonsensical, down-to-earth, efficient, hard, hard-boiled*, hardheaded*, logical,

matter-of-fact, practical, realistic, sober, unidealistic, utilitarian; SEE CONCEPTS 401,542

praise [n] *congratulations; adoration*
acclaim, acclamation, accolade, applause, appreciation, approbation, approval, big hand*, boost, bravo, celebration, cheer, cheering, citation, commendation, compliment, cry, devotion, encomium, esteem, eulogy, exaltation, extolment, flattery, glorification, glory, good word*, homage, hurrah, hymn, kudos*, laudation, obeisance, ovation, panegyric, pat on the back*, plaudit, puff*, rave, recognition, recommendation, regard, sycophancy, thanks, tribute, worship; SEE CONCEPTS 69,278

praise [v] *congratulate; adore*
acclaim, admire, adulate, advocate, aggrandize, applaud, appreciate, approve, bless, boost, bow down*, build up*, cajole, celebrate, cheer, cite, clap, commend, compliment, cry up*, dignify, distinguish, elevate, endorse, ennoble, eulogize, exalt, extol, flatter, give thanks, glorify, hail, honor, laud, make much of*, panegyrize, pay homage, pay tribute, proclaim, puff*, rave over, recommend, resound, reverence, root*, sanction, sing the praises*, smile on*, stroke*, tout, worship; SEE CONCEPT 69

praiseworthy [adj] *deserving congratulations, adoration*
admirable, commendable, creditable, estimable, excellent, exemplary, fine, gnarly, gone, honorable, keen, laudable, meritable, meritorious, pillar, salt of earth*, select, slick, stellar, swell, thankworthy, tough, worthy; SEE CONCEPTS 568,574

prance [v] *cavort; show off*
bound, caper, dance, flounce, foot it*, frisk, gambol, hoof it*, jump, leap, mince, parade, romp, sashay, skip, spring, stalk, step, strut, swagger, sweep, tread; SEE CONCEPTS 150,292,384

prank [n] *practical joke; frivolity*
antic, caper, caprice, escapade, fancy, fooling, frolic, gag, gambol, high jinks*, horseplay*, hotfoot*, lark, levity, lightness, monkeyshines*, play, put-on, rib*, rollick, roughhouse*, roughhousing*, rowdiness, shenanigans, shine*, skylarking*, spoof, sport, tomfoolery, trick, whim; SEE CONCEPTS 59,384

pray [v] *plead; call upon for help, answer*
adjure, appeal, ask, beseech, brace, commune with, crave, cry for, entreat, implore, importune, invocate, invoke, petition, recite, request, say, solicit, sue, supplicate, urge; SEE CONCEPTS 48,367

prayer [n] *pleading, especially with a deity; request for help, answer*
adoration, appeal, application, begging, benediction, beseeching, communion, devotion, entreaty, grace, imploration, imploring, imprecation, invocation, litany, orison, petition, plea, pleading, request, rogation, service, suit, supplication, worship; SEE CONCEPTS 48,367,662

preach [v1] *speak publicly about beliefs*
address, deliver, deliver sermon, evangelize, exhort, give sermon, homilize, inform, minister, mission, missionary, orate, prophesy, pulpiteer, sermonize, talk, teach; SEE CONCEPTS 51,285,367

preach [v2] *lecture, moralize*
admonish, advocate, blow, exhort, get on a soapbox*, harangue, pile it on*, preachify, sermonize, talk big*, urge; SEE CONCEPTS 51,75

preacher [n] *person who gives religious instruction*

clergy, cleric, clerical, divine, ecclesiastic, evangelist, evangelizer, minister, missionary, parson, pulpiter, reverend, revivalist, sermonizer; SEE CONCEPT 361

precarious [adj] *tricky, doubtful*

ambiguous, borderline, chancy, contingent, dangerous, delicate, dicey*, dubious, dynamite, equivocal, hairy*, hanging by a thread*, hazardous, iffy*, impugnable, indecisive, insecure, loaded, on thin ice*, open, out on a limb*, perilous, problematic, risky, rocky, rugged*, sensitive, shaky, slippery, ticklish, touch and go*, touchy, uncertain, unhealthy, unreliable, unsafe, unsettled, unstable, unsteady, unsure; SEE CONCEPTS 535,587

precaution [n] *carefulness; preventative measure*

anticipation, canniness, care, caution, circumspection, discreetness, discretion, foresight, forethought, insurance, protection, providence, provision, prudence, regard, safeguard, safety measure, wariness; SEE CONCEPTS 410,633,729

precede [v] *go ahead of in space, time, order*

announce, antecede, antedate, anticipate, be ahead of, come first, forerun, foreshadow, go before, go in advance, guide, harbinger, have a head start*, head, head up, herald, introduce, lead, light the way*, outrank, pace, pave the way*, pioneer, predate, pre-exist, preface, presage, rank, ring in*, run ahead, scout, take precedence, usher; SEE CONCEPTS 727,747,813,818

precedence [n] *highest in rank; first in order*

antecedence, anteposition, earliness, lead, precedency, precession, preeminence, preexistence, preference, prevenience, previousness, primary, priority, rank, seniority, superiority, supremacy; SEE CONCEPTS 671,727,747,818

precedent [n] *authoritative example*

antecedent, authority, criterion, exemplar, instance, model, paradigm; SEE CONCEPT 686

preceding [adj] *earlier, above*

above-mentioned, above-named, aforeknown, aforementioned, aforesaid, ahead of, antecedent, anterior, before, erstwhile, foregoing, forerunning, former, forward, front, head, heretofore, introductory, lead, leading, one time, other, past, pioneer, pioneering, precedent, precursive, precursory, preexistent, prefatory, preliminary, preparatory, prevenient, previous, prior, supra; SEE CONCEPTS 585,586,799,811,818

precept [n] *law, rule of behavior, action*

axiom, behest, bidding, byword, canon, command, commandment, decree, decretum, direction, doctrine, dogma, edict, formula, fundamental, guideline, injunction, instruction, law, mandate, maxim, motto, order, ordinance, prescript, principle, regulation, rule, saying, statute, tenet; SEE CONCEPTS 318,688

precious [adj1] *favorite, valued*

adored, beloved, cherished, darling, dear, dearest, idolized, inestimable, loved, pet, prized, treasured; SEE CONCEPTS 529,567

precious [adj2] *expensive; rare*

choice, costly, dear, exquisite, fine, high-priced, inestimable, invaluable, priceless, prizable, prized, recherché, rich, treasurable, valuable, worth a king's ransom*, worth eyeteeth*, worth one's weight in gold*; SEE CONCEPT 334

precious [adj3] *extremely sophisticated and picky*

affected, alembicated, artful, artificial, chichi*, choosy, dainty, delicate, fastidious, finicky, fragile, fussy, la-di-da*, nice, ostentatious, overnice, overrefined, particular, persnickety*, precieux, pretentious, refined, showy, stagy, studied; SEE CONCEPT 401

precipice [n] *face or brink of a rock, mountain*

bluff, cliff, crag, height, sheer drop, steep; SEE CONCEPTS 509,513

precipitate [v] *hurry, speed*

accelerate, advance, bring on, cast, discharge, dispatch, expedite, fling, further, hasten, hurl, launch, let fly, press, push forward, quicken, send forth, speed up, throw, trigger; SEE CONCEPTS 152,242,704

precipitation [n] *moisture in air or falling from sky*

cloudburst, condensation, drizzle, hail, hailstorm, heavy dew, precip*, rain, rainfall, rainstorm, sleet, snow, storm, wetness; SEE CONCEPTS 467,524,526

precipitous/precipitate [adj1] *fast, sudden; impulsive; initial*

abrupt, breakneck*, brief, frantic, gone off half-cocked*, harum-scarum*, hasty, headlong, heedless, hurried, ill-advised, impatient, impetuous, indiscreet, jump the gun*, madcap, off the hip*, off the top of head*, plunging, precipitant, quick, rapid, rash, reckless, refractory, rushing, subitaneous, swift, unanticipated, uncontrolled, unexpected, unforeseen, violent, willful, without warning; SEE CONCEPTS 229,401,542,588,799

precipitous [adj2] *steep, falling sharply*

abrupt, arduous, craggy, dizzy, dizzying, high, perpendicular, precipitate, sharp, sheer; SEE CONCEPTS 490,583,779

precis [n] *abridgment*

abstract, aperçu, compendium, condensation, digest, outline, pandect, résumé, rundown, sketch, summary, survey, syllabus, synopsis; SEE CONCEPT 283

precise [adj1] *exact, accurate*

absolute, actual, categorical, circumscribed, clear-cut, correct, decisive, definite, determinate, explicit, express, fixed, individual, limited, literal, narrow, nice, on the button*, on the money*, on the nose*, particular, proper, restricted, right, rigid, rigorous, specific, strict, stringent, unequivocal, very, well-defined; SEE CONCEPTS 535,557,653

precise [adj2] *meticulous, fastidious*

careful, ceremonious, choosy, exact, finicky, formal, fussy, genteel, inflexible, nice, particular, persnickety*, picky, priggish, prim, prissy, punctilious, rigid, scrupulous, stickling, stiff*, strict, stuffy, uncompromising; SEE CONCEPTS 401,542

precisely [adv] *exactly, just*

absolutely, accurately, as well, correctly, definitely, even, expressly, for a fact, for sure, just so, literally, no ifs ands or buts*, no mistake*, on the button*, on the money*, on the nose*, plumb, right, sharp, smack*, smack-dab*, specifically, square, squarely, strictly, sure, sure thing*, the ticket*, the very thing*, to a tee*, yes; SEE CONCEPTS 535,557

precision [n] *accuracy*

attention, care, carefulness, correctness, definiteness, definitiveness, definitude, exactitude, exactness, fidelity, heed, meticulousness, nicety, particularity, preciseness, rigor, sureness; SEE CONCEPTS 638,654

preclude [v] *inhibit; make impossible*
avert, cease, check, debar, deter, discontinue, exclude, forestall, forfend, hinder, impede, interrupt, make impracticable, obviate, prevent, prohibit, put a stop to, quit, restrain, rule out, stave off, stop, ward; SEE CONCEPTS 121,234

precocious [adj] *exceptionally smart, ahead of age in understanding*
advanced, aggressive, ahead of time*, beforehand, bold, brassy*, bright, cheeky*, cocky*, developed, early, flip*, flippant, forward, fresh, intelligent, mature, nervy, premature, presumptuous, pushy, quick, sassy*, smart-alecky*; SEE CONCEPT 402

preconception [n] *idea formed before event occurs or facts are received*
assumption, bias, delusion, illusion, inclination, notion, preconceived idea, predisposition, prejudgment, prejudice, prepossession, presumption, presupposition; SEE CONCEPT 689

precursor [n1] *something that indicates outcome or event beforehand*
forerunner, harbinger, herald, messenger, outrider, usher, vanguard; SEE CONCEPTS 70,278

precursor [n2] *something that precedes another*
ancestor, antecedent, antecessor, forebear, foregoer, forerunner, original, originator, parent, pioneer, predecessor, prototype; SEE CONCEPTS 648,727,828

predatory [adj] *eating, destroying for sustenance or without conscience*
bloodthirsty, carnivorous, depredatory, despoiling, greedy, hungry, hunting, marauding, pillaging, plundering, predacious, predative, preying, rapacious, raptorial, ravaging, ravening, thieving, voracious, vulturine, vulturous, wolfish; SEE CONCEPTS 401,406

predecessor [n] *something, someone that comes before*
ancestor, antecedent, antecessor, forebear, foregoer, forerunner, former, precursor, previous, prior, prototype; SEE CONCEPTS 414,828

predetermined [adj] *decided in advance*
agreed, arranged, calculated, cut and dried*, deliberate, destined, determined, doomed, fated, fixed, forestalled, foreordained, forethought, planned, prearranged, precogitated, predestined, premeditated, preordained, preplanned, proposed, set, settled, set up; SEE CONCEPT 548

predicament [n] *difficult situation*
asperity, bad news*, bind*, Catch-22*, circumstance, clutch, condition, corner*, crisis, deadlock, deep water*, dilemma, drag*, emergency, exigency, fix*, hang-up*, hardship, hole, hot water*, imbroglio, impasse, jam*, juncture, large order*, lot, mess*, muddle, pass, perplexity, pickle*, pinch, plight, position, posture, puzzle, quagmire, quandary, rigor, rough go*, scrape*, soup*, spot*, state*, strait, tall order* ticklish spot* tight situation* trouble, vicissitude; SEE CONCEPTS 388,674

predict [v] *express an outcome in advance*
adumbrate, anticipate, augur, be afraid, call, call it, conclude, conjecture, croak, crystal-ball* divine, envision, figure, figure out, forebode, forecast, foresee, forespeak, foretell, gather, guess, have a hunch*, hazard a guess*, infer, judge, make book*, omen, portend, presage, presume,

prognosticate, prophesy, psych out*, read, see coming*, see handwriting on wall*, size up*, soothsay, suppose, surmise, telegraph*, think, vaticinate; SEE CONCEPT 70

predictable [adj] *easy to foretell*
anticipated, calculable, certain, expected, foreseeable, foreseen, likely, prepared, sure, sure-fire*; SEE CONCEPTS 404,542,548

prediction [n] *declaration made in advance of event*
anticipation, augury, cast, conjecture, crystal gazing*, divination, dope, forecast, forecasting, foresight, foretelling, fortune-telling, guess, horoscope, hunch*, indicator, omen, palmistry, presage, prevision, prognosis, prognostication, prophecy, soothsaying, surmising, tip, vaticination, zodiac; SEE CONCEPTS 70,278,689

predilection [n] *inclination, preference toward something*
bent*, bias, cup of tea*, dish*, druthers*, fancy, flash, fondness, groove, inclining, leaning, liking, love, mindset*, partiality, penchant, predisposition, proclivity, proneness, propensity, taste*, tendency, thing*, type, weakness; SEE CONCEPTS 20,32,709

predispose [v] *influence to believe something*
activate, affect, animate, bend*, bias, cultivate, dispose, govern, impress, incline, indoctrinate, induce, inspire, lead, make expectant, make of a mind to*, prejudice, prepare, prime, prompt, stimulate, strike, sway, teach, urge; SEE CONCEPTS 12,14,26,68

predisposed [adj] *willing, inclined*
agreeable, amenable, biased, eager, enthusiastic, fain, given to, liable, likely, minded, partial, prone, ready, subject, susceptible; SEE CONCEPT 403

predisposition [n] *willingness, inclination*
bent*, bias, choice, cup of tea*, dish*, disposition, druthers*, flash, groove, leaning, likelihood, liking, option, partiality, penchant, potentiality, predilection, preference, proclivity, proneness, propensity, susceptibility, tendency, thing*, type, weakness; SEE CONCEPTS 20,32,410,709

predominant [adj] *ruling; most important*
absolute, all-powerful, almighty, arbitrary, ascendant, authoritative, capital, chief, controlling, directing, dominant, dominating, effective, efficacious, governing, holding the reins*, imperious, influential, leading, main, mighty, official, omnipotent, overbearing, overpowering, paramount, potent, predominate, preponderant, prevailing, prevalent, primary, prime, principal, prominent, reigning, sovereign, superior, superlative, supervisory, supreme, surpassing, transcendent, weighty; SEE CONCEPTS 568,574

predominate [v] *be the most important, noticeable*
carry weight*, command, dominate, domineer, get the upper hand*, govern, hold sway*, manage, outweigh, overrule, overshadow, preponderate, prevail, reign, rule, tell; SEE CONCEPTS 94,117,141

preeminent [adj] *most important; superior*
capital, chief, consummate, distinguished, dominant, excellent, foremost, incomparable, main, major, matchless, number one*, outstanding, paramount, peerless, predominant, principal, renowned, stellar, supreme, surpassing, towering, transcendent, ultimate, unequalled, unmatchable,

unrivalled, unsurpassable, unsurpassed; SEE CONCEPTS 568,574

preempt [v] *take over in place of another*
accroach, acquire, annex, anticipate, appropriate, arrogate, assume, bump, commandeer, confiscate, expropriate, obtain, seize, sequester, take, usurp; SEE CONCEPTS 121,142,234

preface [n] *introduction*
beginning, exordium, explanation, foreword, overture, preamble, preliminary, prelude, prelusion, proem, prolegomenon, prologue; SEE CONCEPT 270

preface [v] *introduce*
begin, commence, launch, lead, lead up to, open, precede, prefix, usher; SEE CONCEPTS 57,221

prefer [v] *favor; single out*
adopt, advance, aggrandize, be partial to, be turned on to, choose, cull, desire, elect, elevate, fancy, finger, fix upon, go for, incline, like better, mark, optate, opt for, pick, place, pose, present, promote, propone, proposition, propound, put, put forward, raise, select, suggest, tag, take, tap, upgrade, wish, would rather*, would sooner*; SEE CONCEPTS 20,41

preference [n1] *first choice*
alternative, choice, cup of tea*, desire, druthers*, election, favorite, flash*, groove, inclination, option, partiality, pick, predilection, prepossession, propensity, say, say so*, selection, top, weakness; SEE CONCEPTS 20,529,709

preference [n2] *favorable treatment*
advancement, advantage, elevation, favoritism, first place, precedence, preferment, prelation, pride of place, priority, promotion, upgrading; SEE CONCEPT 693

preferred [adj] *favorite, chosen*
adopted, approved, culled, decided upon, elected, endorsed, fancied, favored, handpicked, liked, named, picked, popular, sanctioned, selected, set apart, settled upon, singled out, taken, well-liked; SEE CONCEPTS 555,574

pregnant [adj1] *carrying developing offspring within the body*
abundant, anticipating, carrying a child, enceinte, expectant, expecting*, fecund, fertile, fraught, fruitful, gestating, gravid, heavy, hopeful, in family way*, parous, parturient, preggers*, productive, prolific, replete, teeming, with child*; SEE CONCEPTS 406,485

pregnant [adj2] *significant, meaningful*
charged, cogent, consequential, creative, eloquent, expressive, fecund, imaginative, important, inventive, loaded, momentous, original, pointed, redolent, rich, seminal, sententious, suggestive, telling, weighty; SEE CONCEPTS 267,567

prejudice [n] *belief without basis, information; intolerance*
ageism, animosity, antipathy, apartheid, aversion, bad opinion, bias, bigotry, chauvinism, contemptuousness, detriment, discrimination, disgust, dislike, displeasure, disrelish, enmity, foregone conclusion, illiberality, injustice, jaundiced eye, mindset*, misjudgment, narrow-mindedness, onesidedness, partiality, pique, preconceived notion, preconception, prejudgment, prepossession, racism, repugnance, revulsion, sexism, slant, spleen, tilt, twist, umbrage, unfairness, warp, xenophobia; SEE CONCEPT 689

prejudice [v] *influence another's beliefs without basis, information*
angle*, bend*, bias, blemish*, color*, damage, dispose, distort, harm, hinder, hurt, impair, incline, indoctrinate, injure, jaundice, mar, poison*, predispose, prejudge, prepossess, skew*, slant*, spoil, sway*, twist*, undermine, vitiate, warp*; SEE CONCEPTS 14,19

prejudicial [adj] *harmful, undermining*
bad, biased, bigoted, counterproductive, damaging, deleterious, detrimental, differential, disadvantageous, discriminatory, evil, hurtful, inimical, injurious, mischievous, nocuous, unfavorable, unjust; SEE CONCEPTS 537,545,570

preliminary [n] *introductory event; beginning*
first round, foundation, groundwork, initiation, introduction, opening, preamble, preface, prelims*, prelude, preparation, start; SEE CONCEPTS 828,832

preliminary [adj] *introductory, initial*
basic, elemental, elementary, exploratory, first, fundamental, inductive, initiatory, opening, pilot, preceding, precursory, prefatory, preparatory, preparing, primal, primary, prior, qualifying, readying, test, trial; SEE CONCEPTS 549,585,799

prelude [n] *beginning of event*
commencement, curtain-raiser*, exordium, foreword, intro*, introduction, overture, preamble, preface, preliminary, prelusion, preparation, proem, prolegomenon, prologue, start; SEE CONCEPTS 264,832

premature [adj1] *earlier in occurrence than anticipated*
a bit previous, abortive, early on, embryonic, forward, green*, immature, incomplete, inopportune, overearly, oversoon, precipitate, predeveloped, previous, raw*, soon, unanticipated, undeveloped, unfledged, unripe, untimely; SEE CONCEPTS 485,549

premature [adj2] *rash, impulsive*
half-baked*, half-cocked*, hasty, ill-considered, inopportune, jumping the gun*, overhasty, precipitate, previous, too soon, untimely; SEE CONCEPTS 401,542

premeditated [adj] *planned, intended*
advised, aforethought, calculated, conscious, considered, contrived, deliberate, designed, fixed, framed up, intentional, laid-out*, prepense, purposed, rigged*, set-up*, sewn-up*, stacked deck*, studied, thought-out, willful; SEE CONCEPTS 542,548

premier [adj] *leading; original*
arch, beginning, champion, chief, earliest, first, foremost, head, highest, inaugural, initial, main, opening, primary, prime, principal; SEE CONCEPTS 568,585

premiere [n] *original production*
beginning, debut, first night, first performance, first showing, opening, opening night; SEE CONCEPTS 263,832

premise [n] *hypothesis, argument*
apriorism, assertion, assumption, basis, evidence, ground, post, postulate, postulation, presumption, presupposition, proof, proposition, supposition, thesis; SEE CONCEPTS 529,689

premise [v] *hypothesize*
announce, assume, begin, commence, introduce, posit, postulate, predicate, presume, presuppose, start, state, suppose; SEE CONCEPTS 18,37

premises [n] *grounds and buildings*

bounds, campus, digs, establishment, fix, flat, hangout*, home, house, joint*, land, lay, layout, limits, neck of the woods*, office, pad, place, plant, property, real estate*, roof, scene, site, spot, terrace, turf, zone; SEE CONCEPTS *198,515*

premium [n] *bonus, prize*

appreciation, boon, bounty, carrot*, dividend, extra, fee*, gravy*, guerdon, meed, percentage, perk*, perquisite, plum*, recompense, regard, remuneration, reward, spiff*, stock, store, value; SEE CONCEPTS *337,344*

premium [adj] *excellent*

choice, exceptional, prime, select, selected, superior; SEE CONCEPT *574*

premonition [n] *feeling that an event is about to occur*

apprehension, apprehensiveness, feeling, feeling in bones*, foreboding, forewarning, funny feeling, handwriting on wall*, hunch, idea, intuition, misgiving, omen, portent, prenotion, presage, presentiment, sign, sinking feeling, suspicion, vibes, vibrations, warning, wind change*, winds*, winds of change*, worriment; SEE CONCEPTS *410,529,689,690*

preoccupied [adj] *busy; mentally caught up in something*

absent, absent-minded, absorbed, abstracted, airheaded*, asleep*, bemused, bugged*, daydreaming, deep*, distracted, distrait, engaged, engrossed, faraway, fascinated, forgetful, have on the brain*, heedless, hung up*, immersed, inconscient, intent, lost, lost in thought*, mooning*, moony*, oblivious, obsessed, rapt, removed, spellbound, spread out*, taken up, unaware, woolgathering*, wrapped-up*; SEE CONCEPT *403*

preparation [n1] *development, readiness*

alertness, anticipation, arrangement, background, base, basis, build-up*, construction, dry run*, education, establishment, evolution, expectation, fitting, foresight, formation, foundation, gestation, getting ready, groundwork, homework, incubation, lead time*, making ready, manufacture, measure, plan, precaution, preparedness, preparing, provision, putting in order, qualification, readying, rehearsal, rundown, safeguard, schoolwork, study, substructure, training, tryout, workout; SEE CONCEPTS *35,202,285*

preparation [n2] *something concocted, put together*

arrangement, blend, brew, composition, compound, concoction, confection, decoction, medicine, mixture, product, tincture; SEE CONCEPT *260*

preparatory [adj] *introductory, basic*

before, elementary, in advance of, in anticipation of, inductive, opening, precautionary, prefatory, preliminary, prelusive, prep*, preparative, previous, primary, prior to; SEE CONCEPTS *546,585*

prepare [v] *make or get ready*

adapt, adjust, anticipate, appoint, arrange, assemble, brace, build up, coach, concoct, construct, contrive, cook, develop, dispose, draw up, endow, equip, fabricate, fashion, fill in, fit, fit out, fix, form, formulate, fortify, furnish, gird, groom, lay the groundwork, make, make provision, make up, outfit, perfect, plan, practice, prime, produce, provide, put in order, put together, qualify, ready, settle, smooth the way*, steel*, strengthen, supply, train, turn out, warm up; SEE CONCEPTS *35,202*

prepared [adj] *ready in body or mind*

able, adapted, adjusted, all bases covered*, all set*, all systems go*, arranged, available, disposed, fit, fixed, framed, gaffed, groomed, handy, inclined, in order, in readiness, minded, of a mind, on guard*, planned, predisposed, prepped, primed, processed, psyched-up*, put up, qualified, rehearsed, rigged*, set, set-up, sewed-up, stacked, up*, up on*, willing, wired; SEE CONCEPTS *403,485,560*

preponderance [n] *great numbers; supremacy*

advantage, ascendancy, bigger half*, bulk, command, dominance, domination, dominion, extensiveness, greater part, lion's share*, mass, max*, mostest, power, predominance, prevalence, superiority, sway, weight; SEE CONCEPTS *671,687, 767*

prepossessed [adj] *made partial by initial impression*

biased, colored, inclined, jaundiced, one-sided, opinionated, partisan, predisposed, prejudiced, tendentious, unindifferent, warped; SEE CONCEPTS *403,542*

prepossessing [adj] *attractive, handsome*

alluring, amiable, appealing, attracting, beautiful, bewitching, captivating, charming, drawing, enchanting, engaging, fair, fascinating, fetching, good-looking, inviting, likable, lovable, magnetic, pleasant, pleasing, striking, taking, winning; SEE CONCEPTS *404,537*

preposterous [adj] *ridiculous, bizarre*

absurd, asinine, crazy, excessive, exorbitant, extravagant, extreme, fantastic, far-out*, foolish, harebrained*, impossible, incredible, insane, irrational, laughable, ludicrous, monstrous, nonsensical, out of the question*, outrageous, senseless, shocking, silly, stupid, taking the cake*, thick*, too much*, unbelievable, unreasonable, unthinkable, unusual, wacky*, wild; SEE CONCEPTS *529,548,555*

prerequisite [n] *condition, necessity*

essential, imperative, must, need, postulate, precondition, qualification, requirement, requisite, sine qua non; SEE CONCEPTS *646,709*

prerequisite [adj] *necessary*

called for, essential, expedient, imperative, important, indispensable, mandatory, necessitous, needful, obligatory, of the essence, required, requisite, vital; SEE CONCEPT *546*

prerogative [n] *right, privilege*

advantage, appanage, authority, birthright, choice, claim, droit, due, exemption, immunity, liberty, perquisite, sanction, title; SEE CONCEPT *376*

presage [n] *prediction, indication*

apprehension, apprehensiveness, augury, auspice, bodement, boding, forecast, foretoken, forewarning, harbinger, intimation, misgiving, omen, portent, premonition, prenotion, presentiment, prognostic, prognostication, prophecy, sign, warning; SEE CONCEPTS *410,529,689*

presage [v] *predict or have a feeling*

adumbrate, announce, augur, betoken, bode, divine, feel, forebode, forecast, forerun, foresee, foreshadow, foreshow, foretell, foretoken, forewarn, harbinger, herald, intuit, omen, point to, portend, preindicate, prognosticate, promise, prophesy, sense, signify, soothsay, vaticinate, warn; SEE CONCEPTS *34,70,118*

prescribe [v] *stipulate action to be taken*
appoint, assign, choose, command, decide, decree, define, designate, determine, dictate, direct, enjoin, establish, fix, guide, impose, lay down, ordain, order, pick out, require, rule, select, set, settle, specify, write prescription; SEE CONCEPTS *50,60,61,88*

prescription [n] *formula, medicine*
decree, direction, drug, edict, instruction, law, mixture, ordinance, preparation, prescript, recipe, regulation, remedy, rule; SEE CONCEPTS *274,307, 311,318*

presence [n1] *occupancy, attendance*
being, companionship, company, existence, habitation, inhabitance, latency, occupation, omnipresence, potentiality, residence, subsistence, ubiety, ubiquity, whereabouts; SEE CONCEPTS *407,518,710*

presence [n2] *appearance, demeanor*
address, air, aspect, aura, bearing, behavior, carriage, comportment, deportment, ease, look, mien, personality, poise, port, seeming, self-assurance, set; SEE CONCEPTS *411,673,716*

presence [n3] *closeness, vicinity*
immediate circle, nearness, neighborhood, propinquity, proximity; SEE CONCEPT *747*

presence [n4] *ghost*
apparition, manifestation, shade, specter, spirit, supernatural being, wraith; SEE CONCEPT *370*

presence [n5] *composure of mind*
acumen, alertness, aplomb, calmness, cool, coolness, imperturbability, levelheadedness, quickness, sangfroid, self-assurance, self-command, self-composure, poise, self-possession, sensibility, sobriety, watchfulness, wits; SEE CONCEPTS *410,657*

present [n1] *existing time*
here and now, instant, nonce, now, present moment, the time being, this day, this time, today; SEE CONCEPTS *802,807,815*

present [n2] *gift*
benefaction, benevolence, boon, bounty, compliment, donation, endowment, favor, gifting, giveaway, goodie*, grant, gratuity, handout, largess, lump, offering, stake, write-off; SEE CONCEPT *337*

present [adj1] *existing; at this time*
ad hoc, already, at this moment, begun, being, coeval, commenced, contemporaneous, contemporary, current, even now, existent, extant, for the time being, going on, immediate, in duration, in process, instant, just now, modern, nowadays, present-day, prompt, started, today, topical, under consideration, up-to-date; SEE CONCEPT *820*

present [adj2] *nearby, here*
accounted for, at hand, attendant, available, existent, in attendance, in view, made the scene*, near, on board, on deck, on hand, on-the-spot, ready, show up, there, there with bells on*, within reach; SEE CONCEPTS *539,583*

present [v1] *introduce; demonstrate*
acquaint, adduce, advance, allege, cite, declare, display, do, do the honors, exhibit, expose, expound, extend, fix up, get together, give, give an introduction, hold out, imply, infer, intimate, lay, make a pitch*, make known, manifest, mount, offer, open to view, perform, pitch, pose, produce, proffer, proposition, put forward, put on,

raise, recount, relate, roll out, show, stage, state, submit, suggest, tender, trot out; SEE CONCEPTS *66,261*

present [v2] *give, hand over*
award, bestow, come up with, confer, devote, donate, entrust, furnish, gift, give away, grant, hand out, kick in*, lay on*, offer, proffer, put at disposal, put forth; SEE CONCEPTS *67,108*

presentable [adj] *respectable; fit to be seen*
acceptable, attractive, becoming, decent, fit, good enough*, not bad*, okay*, passable, prepared, proper, satisfactory, suitable, tolerable; SEE CONCEPTS *558,579*

presentation [n] *performance; something given, displayed*
act, appearance, arrangement, award, bestowal, coming out, conferral, debut, delivering, delivery, demonstration, display, dog and pony show*, donation, exhibition, exposition, giving, introduction, investiture, knockdown*, launch, launching, offering, overture, pitch, present, production, proposal, proposition, reception, remembrance, rendition, representation, sales pitch*, show, staging, submission; SEE CONCEPTS *261,263,337*

presentiment [n] *anticipation, expectation*
apprehension, apprehensiveness, discomposure, disquietude, disturbance, fear, feeling, feeling in bones*, foreboding, forecast, forethought, funny feeling*, handwriting on wall*, hunch, intuition, misgiving, perturbation, premonition, prenotion, presage, sinking feeling, vibes*, worriment; SEE CONCEPTS *410,532,689*

presently [adv] *in a short while*
anon, before long, before you know it, by and by, directly, down the line*, down the pike*, down the road*, immediately, in a minute, in a moment, in a short time, now, nowadays, pretty soon, shortly, soon, today, without delay; SEE CONCEPT *820*

preservation [n] *maintenance, protection*
canning, care, conservancy, conservation, curing, defense, evaporation, freezing, guard, guardianship, keeping, perpetuation, pickling, preserval, refrigeration, safeguard, safeguarding, safekeeping, safety, salvation, saving, security, shield, storage, support, sustentation, tanning, upholding, ward; SEE CONCEPTS *134,170,202,257*

preserve [v] *care for, maintain; continue*
bottle, can, conserve, cure, defend, evaporate, freeze, guard, keep, keep up, mothball*, mummify, perpetuate, pickle, process, protect, put up, refrigerate, retain, safeguard, save, season, secure, shelter, shield, store, sustain, uphold; SEE CONCEPTS *134,170,202*

preserves [n] *thickened fruit prepared for storage and use as a condiment*
confection, confiture, conserve, extract, gelatin, jam, jell, jelly, marmalade, pectin, spread, sweet; SEE CONCEPTS *457,461*

preside [v] *be in authority*
administer, advise, be at the head of*, be in driver's seat*, call the signals*, carry on, chair, conduct, control, direct, do the honors, govern, handle, head, head up, keep, lead, manage, officiate, operate, ordain, oversee, pull the strings*, run, run the show*, sit on top of*, supervise; SEE CONCEPTS *94,117*

press [n1] *people or person working in communications*
columnist, correspondent, editor, fourth estate*,

interviewer, journalism, journalist, magazine, media, newspaper, newsperson, paper, periodical, photographer, publicist, publisher, reporter, writer; SEE CONCEPTS *280,349,356*

press [n2] *horde, large group*
bunch, crowd, crush, drove, flock, herd, host, mob, multitude, pack, push, swarm, throng; SEE CONCEPT *432*

press [n3] *strain, pressure*
bustle, confusion, demand, hassle, haste, hurry, rush, stress, urgency; SEE CONCEPTS *230,674*

press [v1] *push on with force*
bear down, bear heavily, bulldoze*, clasp, compress, condense, constrain, crowd, crush, cumber, depress, embrace, enfold, express, finish, flatten, force down, hold, hug, impel, iron, jam, level, mangle, mash, mass, move, pack, pile, pin down, ram, reduce, scrunch, shove, smooth, squash, squeeze, squish, steam, stuff, thrust, unwrinkle, weigh; SEE CONCEPTS *191,208*

press [v2] *pressure, trouble*
afflict, assail, beg, beset, besiege, buttonhole*, come at, compel, constrain, demand, depress, disquiet, enjoin, entreat, exhort, force, harass, implore, importune, insist on, lean on, oppress, petition, plague, plead, pressurize, push, railroad*, sadden, sell, squeeze, sue, supplicate, torment, urge, vex, weigh down, work on, worry; SEE CONCEPT *14*

pressing [adj] *important; urgent*
acute, burning, claiming, clamant, clamorous, compelling, constraining, critical, crucial, crying, demanding, dire, distressing, exacting, exigent, forcing, heat-on*, high-priority, hurry-up*, immediate, imperative, importunate, insistent, instant, life-and-death*, obliging, requiring, serious, vital; SEE CONCEPTS *548,568*

pressure [n1] *physical force, weight*
burden, compressing, compression, crushing, encumbrance, heaviness, load, mass, shear, squeeze, squeezing, strain, strength, stress, tension, thrust; SEE CONCEPTS *641,734*

pressure [n2] *demand, difficulty*
adversity, affliction, albatross*, burden, choke, clout, coercion, compulsion, confinement, constraint, crunch, discipline, distress, drag, duress, exigency, force, full court press*, hardship, hassle, heat, hurry, influence, inside track*, load, misfortune, necessity, obligation, persuasion, power, press, pressure cooker*, pull, requirement, strain, stress, sway, tension, trouble, unnaturalness, urgency, weight; SEE CONCEPTS *14,666,674,687*

pressure [v] *bother, urge*
come at, compel, constrain, drive, impel, insist, lean on*, politick, press, push, push around*, rush, sell, squeeze, twist arm*, work over*; SEE CONCEPTS *7,14,19,22*

prestige [n] *fame, influence*
authority, cachet, celebrity, consequence, control, credit, dignity, distinction, éclat*, eminence, esteem, fame, illustriousness, importance, kudos*, position, power, preeminence, prominence, prominency, rank, regard, renown, reputation, repute, standing, state, stature, status, sway, weight; SEE CONCEPTS *388,668*

prestigious [adj] *famous, influential*
celebrated, distinguished, eminent, esteemed, exalted, famed, great, illustrious, important, impos-

ing, impressive, notable, prominent, renowned, reputable, respected; SEE CONCEPTS *555,568*

presumably [adv] *likely, reasonably*
apparently, assumably, credible, doubtless, doubtlessly, hypothetically, in all likelihood, in all probability, indubitably, it would seem, most likely, on the face of it, presumptively, probably, seemingly, supposedly, surely, theoretically, unquestionably; SEE CONCEPTS *544,552*

presume [v1] *make assumption; believe*
assume, bank on*, be afraid, conclude, conjecture, consider, count on, depend, figure, gather, guess, infer, jump the gun*, posit, postulate, predicate, premise, presuppose, pretend, rely, speculate, suppose, surmise, take for granted, take it, think, trust; SEE CONCEPTS *12,26,28*

presume [v2] *dare; take the liberty*
go so far, have the audacity, impose, infringe, intrude, make bold, undertake, venture; SEE CONCEPT *87*

presumption [n1] *belief, hypothesis*
anticipation, apriorism, assumption, basis, chance, conjecture, grounds, guess, likelihood, opinion, plausibility, posit, postulate, postulation, premise, presupposition, probability, reason, shot, shot in the dark*, sneaking suspicion*, stab, supposition, surmise, suspicion, thesis; SEE CONCEPT *689*

presumption [n2] *forwardness, daring*
arrogance, assurance, audacity, boldness, brashness, brass, cheek*, chutzpah*, confidence, contumely, effrontery, gall, impudence, insolence, nerve, presumptuousness, rudeness, temerity; SEE CONCEPT *633*

presumptuous [adj] *self-confident*
arrogant, audacious, bold, cheeky*, conceited, confident, contumelious, egoistic, foolhardy, forward, fresh, insolent, overconfident, overfamiliar, overweening, pompous, presuming, pretentious, pushy, rash, rude, self-assertive, self-assured, self-satisfied, smug, supercilious, uppity*; SEE CONCEPTS *401,542*

pretend [v1] *fake, falsify*
act, affect, allege, assume, be deceitful, beguile, be hypocritical, bluff, cheat, claim, claim falsely, counterfeit, cozen, deceive, delude, dissemble, dissimulate, dupe, fake out*, feign, fish*, fool, fudge*, hoodwink*, impersonate, jazz*, jive*, lay claim*, let on*, make out*, malinger, masquerade, mislead, pass off*, pass oneself off as*, profess, purport, put on*, put up a front*, sham*, shuck and jive*, simulate, stonewall*, sucker*, whitewash*; SEE CONCEPTS *59,63*

pretend [v2] *play the part of*
act, assume the role, imagine, imitate, impersonate, make as if, make believe, make out like, make up, masquerade, mimic, play, playact, portray, pose, purport, put on a front*, put on airs*, put on an act*, represent, reproduce, suppose; SEE CONCEPTS *111,171,292,384*

pretended [adj] *alleged; imaginary*
affected, artificial, assumed, avowed, bluffing, bogus, charlatan, cheating, concealed, counterfeit, covered, dissimulated, factitious, fake, false, falsified, feigned, fictitious, impostrous, imposturous, lying, make-believe, masked, mock, ostensible, phony, pretend, professed, pseudo*, purported, put-on*, quack*, sham*, shammed*, simulated, so-called, spurious, supposed; SEE CONCEPTS *545,582*

pr
pr

pretense [n] *falsehood, affected show; cover*
act, acting, affectation, appearance, artifice, charade, claim, cloak, deceit, deception, display, dissimulation, double-dealing*, dumb act*, evasion, excuse, fabrication, facade, fakery, faking, falsification, feigning, gag, guise, insincerity, invention, make-believe, mask, masquerade, misrepresentation, misstatement, ostentation, posing, posturing, pretentiousness, pretext, routine, ruse, schtick*, semblance, sham*, shuffling, simulation, stall, stunt, subterfuge, trickery, veil, veneer, wile; SEE CONCEPTS 59,63,633,716

pretension [n1] *airs, snobbishness*
affectation, big talk*, charade, conceit, disguise, fake*, false front*, front, hypocrisy, ostentation, phony, pomposity, pretentiousness, put-on*, self-importance, show, showboat*, showiness, show-off, snobbery, splash*, vainglory, vanity; SEE CONCEPT 633

pretension [n2] *false claim, assertion of importance*
allegation, ambition, ambitiousness, aspiration, assumption, charade, declaration, demand, disguise, maintenance, make-believe, pageant, pretense, pretext, profession, title; SEE CONCEPTS 278,657

pretentious [adj] *snobbish, conceited*
affected, arty, assuming, aureate, big*, bombastic, chichi*, conspicuous, euphuistic, exaggerated, extravagant, feigned, flamboyant, flashy, flaunting, flowery, gaudy, grandiloquent, grandiose, highfaluting*, high-flown*, high-sounding*, hollow, imposing, inflated, jazzy*, la-di-da*, lofty, magniloquent, mincing, ornate, ostentatious, overambitious, overblown, pompous, puffed up*, put-on*, rhetorical, showy, specious, splashy, stilted, swank, too-too*, tumid, turgid, utopian, vainglorious; SEE CONCEPTS 401,542, 589

preternatural [adj] *unusual, abnormal*
aberrant, anomalous, atypical, deviant, deviative, extraordinary, ghostly, inexplicable, irregular, marvelous, miraculous, mysterious, odd, peculiar, strange, superhuman, superior, supermundane, supernatural, unaccountable, unearthly, unnatural, unrepresentative, untypical; SEE CONCEPT 564

pretext [n] *disguise; alleged reason*
affectation, alibi, appearance, bluff, cleanup, cloak, color*, coloring*, copout*, cover, cover story*, cover-up*, device, excuse, face, feint, fig leaf*, front, guise, mask, masquerade, plea, ploy, pretense, red herring*, routine, ruse, semblance, show, simulation, song and dance*, stall, stratagem, subterfuge, veil*; SEE CONCEPTS 59,661, 716

pretty [adj] *attractive*
appealing, beauteous, beautiful, boss*, charming, cheerful, cher*, comely, cute, dainty, darling, delicate, delightful, dishy*, dreamboat*, elegant, eyeful*, fair, fine, foxy*, good-looking, graceful, handsome, looker, lovely, neat, nice, picture, pleasant, pleasing, pulchritudinous, tasteful; SEE CONCEPT 579

pretty [adv] *considerable; somewhat*
a little, ample, fairly, kind of, large, moderately, more or less, much, notable, pretty much, quite, rather, reasonably, sizable, some, something, sort of, tolerably; SEE CONCEPTS 531,569

prevail [v] *dominate, control*
abound, beat, be common, be current, be prevalent, best, be usual, be victorious, be widespread, carry, come out on top*, command, conquer, domineer, exist generally, gain, get there, go great guns*, go places*, hit pay dirt*, luck out*, make it, make out, master, move out, obtain, overcome, overrule, predominate, preponderate, prove, reign, succeed, take off, triumph, win; SEE CONCEPTS 94,95,141

prevailing [adj] *general, dominant*
all-embracing, by the numbers*, catholic, common, comprehensive, current, customary, ecumenical, established, familiar, fashionable, influential, in style, in vogue, main, operative, ordinary, popular, predominant, predominating, preponderating, prevalent, principal, rampant, regnant, regular, rife, ruling, set, steady, sweeping, universal, usual, widespread, worldwide; SEE CONCEPT 530

prevail upon/prevail on [v] *persuade, influence*
affect, argue into, bring around, convince, crack, dispose, draw, get, get around, impress, incline, induce, promote, prompt, put across, ram down throat*, sell*, suck in*, sway, talk into, win over; SEE CONCEPT 68

prevalent [adj1] *accepted, widespread*
accustomed, common, commonplace, current, customary, established, everyday, extensive, faddy, frequent, general, habitual, in use, latest*, latest word*, leading edge*, natural, new, normal, now*, ongoing, popular, prevailing, rampant, regnant, regular, rife, run-of-the-mill*, state-of-the-art*, stylish, swinging, trendy, typic, typical, ubiquitous, universal, up-to-date, usual, with it*, wonted; SEE CONCEPTS 530,547,589

prevalent [adj2] *governing, superior*
ascendant, compelling, dominant, overbearing, paramount, powerful, predominant, predominate, preponderant, prevailing, regnant, ruling, sovereign, successful; SEE CONCEPTS 536,574

prevaricate [v] *deceive; stretch the truth*
beat around the bush*, beg the question*, belie, cavil, con, distort, dodge, equivocate, evade, exaggerate, fabricate, falsify, fib, fudge, hedge, invent, jive*, lie*, misrepresent, misspeak, palter, phony up*, put on*, quibble, shift, shuffle, tergiversate; SEE CONCEPT 63

prevent [v] *keep from happening or continuing*
anticipate, arrest, avert, avoid, baffle, balk, bar, block, check, chill*, cool, cork, counter, counteract, dam, debar, defend against, foil, forbid, forestall, forfend, frustrate, halt, hamper, head off, hinder, hold back, hold off, impede, inhibit, intercept, interdict, interrupt, keep lid on*, limit, nip in the bud*, obstruct, obviate, preclude, prohibit, put an end to, put a stop to, repress, restrain, restrict, retard, rule out, shut out, stave off, stop, thwart, turn aside, ward off; SEE CONCEPT 121

preview [n] *preliminary showing*
examination, preliminary study, research, show, sneak, sneak peek*, survey, viewing; SEE CONCEPTS 263,292,832

previous [adj1] *former, prior*
antecedent, anterior, earlier, erstwhile, ex, foregoing, one-time, past, precedent, preceding, quondam, sometime; SEE CONCEPTS 585,811, 818,820

previous [adj2] *premature*
ahead of, early, inopportune, overearly, oversoon,

precipitate, soon, too early, too soon, unfounded, untimely, unwarranted; SEE CONCEPTS *558,799*

previously [*adv*] *earlier*
ahead, already, ante, antecedently, at one time, away back, a while ago, back, back when, before, beforehand, erstwhile, fore, formerly, forward, heretofore, hitherto, in advance, in anticipation, in days gone by, in the past, long ago, once, one-shot, precedently, then, time was, until now; SEE CONCEPT *820*

prey [*n*] *target of attack*
casualty, chased*, dupe*, game, kill, loot, mark, martyr, mug*, pillage, quarry, quest, raven, spoil, sufferer, underdog, victim; SEE CONCEPTS *394,423*

prey on [*v*] *attack, terrorize*
blackmail, bleed, bully, burden, consume, depredate, devour, distress, eat, exploit, feed on, fleece, haunt, hunt, intimidate, live off, load, oppress, plunder, raid, seize, take advantage of, tax, trouble, victimize, weigh, worry; SEE CONCEPTS *14,86,169*

price [*n1*] *financial value*
amount, appraisal, appraisement, asking price, assessment, barter, bill, bounty, ceiling, charge, compensation, consideration, cost, damage, demand, disbursement, discount, dues, estimate, exaction, expenditure, expense, face value, fare, fee, figure, hire, outlay, output, pay, payment, premium, prize, quotation, ransom, rate, reckoning, retail, return, reward, score, sticker*, tab, tariff, ticket, toll, tune*, valuation, wages, wholesale, worth; SEE CONCEPT *329*

price [*n2*] *consequences of action*
cost, expense, penalty, sacrifice, toll; SEE CONCEPT *230*

price [*v*] *assess financial value*
appraise, cost, estimate, evaluate, fix, mark down, mark up, put a price on, rate, reduce, sticker, value; SEE CONCEPT *330*

priceless [*adj1*] *precious, irreplaceable*
beyond price, cherished, collectible, costly, dear, expensive, incalculable, incomparable, inestimable, invaluable, out-of-bounds*, out-of-sight*, prized, rare, rich, treasured, valuable, valued, without price, worth a king's ransom*, worth its weight in gold*; SEE CONCEPTS *334,568*

priceless [*adj2*] *extremely funny*
absurd, amusing, comic, droll, hilarious, humorous, killing, rib-tickling*, ridiculous, riotous, scream, sidesplitting; SEE CONCEPT *267*

prick [*n*] *small hole made by stab*
cut, gash, jab, jag, perforation, pinhole, prickle, puncture, stab, wound; SEE CONCEPT *309*

prick [*v*] *stab, perforate*
bore, cut, drill, enter, hurt, jab, lance, pierce, pink, punch, puncture, slash, slit, smart, spur, sting; SEE CONCEPT *220*

prickly [*adj1*] *thorny or difficult*
annoying, barbed, bothersome, brambly, briery, bristly, complicated, echinated, intricate, involved, knotty, nettlesome, pointed, sharp, spiny, stimulating, ticklish, tricky, troublesome, trying; SEE CONCEPTS *485,565*

prickly [*adj2*] *irritable, bad-tempered*
cantankerous, edgy, fractious, fretful, grumpy, irritable, peevish, petulant, snappish, touchy, waspish; SEE CONCEPT *401*

pride [*n1*] *self-esteem*
amour-propre, delight, dignity, ego, egoism, ego-

tism, ego trip, face, gratification, happiness, honor, joy, pleasure, pridefulness, repletion, satisfaction, self-admiration, self-confidence, self-glorification, self-love, self-regard, self-respect, self-satisfaction, self-sufficiency, self-trust, self-worth, sufficiency; SEE CONCEPT *411*

pride [*n2*] *arrogance, self-importance*
airs, assumption, big-headedness*, cockiness*, conceit, condescension, contumely, disdain, disdainfulness, egoism, egotism, haughtiness, hauteur, hubris, huff, immodesty, insolence, loftiness, narcissism, overconfidence, patronage, pragmatism, presumption, pretension, pretentiousness, proud flesh*, self-exaltation, self-love, smugness, snobbery, superbity, superciliousness, swagger, swelled head*, vainglory, vanity; SEE CONCEPT *633*

pride [*n3*] *treasure; best*
boast, choice, cream, elite, fat, flower*, gem*, glory, jewel*, pick, pride and joy*, prime, prize, top*; SEE CONCEPTS *446,668,689*

pride [*v*] *take pleasure in accomplishment*
be proud, boast, brag, congratulate, crow, exult, felicitate, flatter oneself, gasconade, glory in, hold head high, overbear, pique*, plume*, prance, preen, presume, puff up*, revel in, strut, swagger, swell, vaunt; SEE CONCEPTS *10,633*

priest [*n*] *man who is minister in Roman or Orthodox Catholic church*
clergyperson, cleric, curate, divine, ecclesiastic, elder, father, father confessor, friar, holy man, lama, man of God, man of the cloth*, monk, padre, pontiff, preacher, rector, vicar; SEE CONCEPT *361*

prim [*adj*] *particular, fussy*
blue nose*, ceremonial, ceremonious, choosy, cleanly, conventional, correct, dapper*, decorous, demure, fastidious, formal, genteel, good, goody-goody*, nice, nit-picking*, orderly, overmodest, polite, precise, priggish, prissy, proper, prudish, puritanical, rigid, shipshape*, spic-and-span*, spruce, stickling, stiff, straight, strait-laced, stuffy*, tidy, uncluttered, upright, Victorian, well-groomed, wooden*; SEE CONCEPTS *401,404*

primarily [*adv1*] *generally; for the most part*
above all, basically, chiefly, especially, essentially, fundamentally, generally, largely, mainly, mostly, on the whole, overall, predominantly, principally; SEE CONCEPTS *531,544,772*

primarily [*adv2*] *in the beginning*
at first, at the start, first and foremost, from the start, initially, in the first place, originally, primitively; SEE CONCEPTS *548,799*

primary/prime [*adj1*] *best, principal*
capital, cardinal, chief, crackerjack*, dominant, excellent, fab*, first, first-class*, greatest, heavy, highest, hot*, leading, main, number one*, paramount, primo*, state-of-the-art*, stellar, top, top-of-the-line*, tough*, world-class*; SEE CONCEPTS *567,574*

primary/prime [*adj2*] *earliest*
aboriginal, beginning, direct, first, firsthand, immediate, initial, original, pioneer, primal, primeval, primitive, primordial, pristine; SEE CONCEPTS *585,799*

primary/prime [*adj3*] *basic, fundamental*
basal, beginning, bottom, central, elemental, elementary, essential, first, foundational, introductory, meat-and-potatoes*, original, primitive, principal, radical, rudimentary, simple, three

pr
pr

R's*, ultimate, underivative, underived, underlying; SEE CONCEPTS 549,585

prime [n1] *best part of existence*
best, best days*, bloom, choice, cream*, elite, fat*, flower*, flowering*, height, heyday, maturity, peak, perfection, pink*, prize, spring, springtime, top, verdure, vitality, zenith; SEE CONCEPT 816

prime [n2] *beginning; spring*
adolescence, aurora, dawn, daybreak, dew, greenness*, juvenility, morn*, morning, opening, puberty, pubescence, springtime, start, sunrise, sunup, tender years*, vitality, youth, youthfulness; SEE CONCEPTS 817,832

prime [v] *get ready; prepare*
break in, brief, clue*, coach, cram, excite, fill in, fit, galvanize, groom, inform, innervate, make ready, motivate, move, notify, prep*, provoke, rehearse, stimulate, tell, train; SEE CONCEPTS 7,19,22,35,202

primeval [adj] *ancient*
earliest, early, first, old, original, prehistoric, primal, primary, primitive, primordial, pristine; SEE CONCEPT 799

primitive [adj1] *ancient, original*
archaic, basic, earliest, early, elementary, essential, first, fundamental, old, primal, primary, primeval, primordial, pristine, substratal, underivative, underived, underlying, undeveloped, unevolved; SEE CONCEPT 799

primitive [adj2] *barbaric, crude*
animal, atavistic, austere, barbarian, barbarous, brutish, childlike, fierce, ignorant, naive, natural, nonliterate, preliterate, raw, rough, rude, rudimentary, savage, simple, uncivilized, uncultivated, uncultured, underdeveloped, undeveloped, undomesticated, unlearned, unrefined, unsophisticated, untamed, untaught, untrained, untutored, vestigial, wild; SEE CONCEPTS 406,485

primordial [adj] *earliest*
basic, early, elemental, first, fundamental, original, prehistoric, primal, primary, prime, primeval, primitive, pristine, radical; SEE CONCEPT 799

primp [v] *beautify and dress nicely*
deck out*, dress up, fix up, get dressed up, groom, gussy up*, preen, prepare, slick*, smarten, spiff, spruce, titivate; SEE CONCEPTS 162,167,202

principal [n1] *person in charge of organization, often an educational one*
administrator, boss, chief, dean, director, exec*, head, key player*, lead, leader, preceptor, protagonist, rector, ruler, star, superintendent; SEE CONCEPTS 347,350

principal [n2] *original amount of property either owned or owed*
assets, capital, capital funds, money; SEE CONCEPT 332

principal [adj] *most important*
arch, capital, cardinal, champion, chief, controlling, crowning, dominant, essential, first, foremost, greatest, head, highest, incomparable, key, leading, main, mainline, major, matchless, maximum, outstanding, paramount, peerless, predominant, preeminent, premier, prevailing, primary, prime, prominent, second-to-none, sovereign, star, stellar, strongest, supereminent, superior, supreme, transcendent, unapproachable, unequaled, unparalleled, unrivaled; SEE CONCEPTS 568,574

principally [adv] *mainly*
above all, basically, before anything else, cardi-

nally, chiefly, dominantly, eminently, especially, essentially, first and foremost, first of all, for the most part, fundamentally, generally, importantly, in the first place, in the main, largely, materially, mostly, notably, particularly, peculiarly, predominantly, preeminently, prevailingly, prevalently, primarily, substantially, superlatively, supremely, to a great degree, universally, vitally; SEE CONCEPTS 531,544,772

principle [n1] *law, standard*
assumption, axiom, basis, canon, convention, criterion, dictum, doctrine, dogma, ethic, form, formula, foundation, fundamental, golden rule*, ground, maxim, origin, postulate, precept, prescript, principium, proposition, regulation, rule, source, theorem, truth, usage, verity; SEE CONCEPTS 318,688

principle/principles [n2] *belief, morality; morals*
attitude, character, code, conduct, conscience, credo, ethic, ethics, faith, ideals, integrity, opinion, policy, probity, rectitude, scruples, sense of duty, sense of honor, system, teaching, tenet, uprightness; SEE CONCEPTS 645,689

print [n] *publication; something impressed*
black-and-white*, book, characters, composition, copy, edition, engraving, face, font, impress, impression, imprint, indentation, issue, lettering, letters, lithograph, magazine, newspaper, newsprint, periodical, photograph, printed matter, stamp, type, typeface, typescript, typesetting, writing; SEE CONCEPTS 259,265,280

print [v] *produce writing, impression; reproduce publication*
calligraph, compose, disseminate, engrave, go to press, impress, imprint, issue, let roll, letter, mark, offset, publish, put to bed*, reissue, reprint, run off, set, set type, stamp, strike off; SEE CONCEPTS 174,203,205

prior [adj] *earlier*
above-mentioned, aforementioned, ahead, antecedent, anterior, before, foregoing, former, forward, past, precedent, preceding, preexistent, preexisting, previous; SEE CONCEPTS 811,812, 818,820

priority [n] *first concern*
antecedence, arrangement, crash project*, greatest importance, lead, order, precedence, preeminence, preference, prerogative, previousness, rank, right of way*, seniority, superiority, supremacy, transcendence; SEE CONCEPTS 532,668, 727

prison [n] *residence for incarcerating criminals*
bastille, can*, clink*, confinement, cooler*, dungeon, G*, guardhouse, jail, keep, lockup, pen*, penal institution, penitentiary, reformatory, slammer*, statesville*, stockade, up the river*; SEE CONCEPTS 439,449,516

prisoner [n] *person jailed for crime; person kept against their will*
captive, chain gang member, con, convict, culprit, detainee, hostage, internee, jailbird*, lag*, lifer*, loser*, tough*, yardbird*; SEE CONCEPT 412

prissy [adj] *particular and fussy*
epicene, fastidious, finicky, genteel, goody-goody*, goody-two-shoes*, overnice, pansified, persnickety, picky, precious, prim, prim and proper*, prudish, puritanical, sissified, sissy, squeamish, stickling, strait-laced, stuffy*, tight-laced*, Victorian; SEE CONCEPTS 401,404

privacy [n] *solitude, secrecy*
aloofness, clandestineness, concealment, confidentiality, isolation, one's space, penetralia, privateness, quiet, retirement, retreat, seclusion, separateness, separation, sequestration, solitude; SEE CONCEPTS 388,631,714

private [n] *lowest rank of person enlisted in armed service*
enlisted person, first-class*, GI, infantry, private soldier, sailor, second-class*, soldier; SEE CONCEPT 358

private [adj] *personal, intimate*
behind the scenes*, clandestine, closet*, close to one's chest*, confidential, discreet, exclusive, hushed, hush-hush*, independent, individual, inside, nonpublic, not open, off the record*, own, particular, privy*, reserved, secret, separate, special, under one's hat*, unofficial; SEE CONCEPTS 267,406

private [adj2] *hidden, isolated*
concealed, discreet, quiet, removed, retired, secluded, secret, separate, sequestered, solitary, withdrawn; SEE CONCEPTS 576,583

privilege [n] *right, due*
advantage, allowance, appanage, appurtenance, authority, authorization, benefit, birthright, boon, chance, charter, claim, concession, entitlement, event, exemption, favor, franchise, freedom, grant, immunity, liberty, license, opportunity, perquisite, prerogative, right, sanction; SEE CONCEPT 376

privileged [adj1] *favored, elite*
advantaged, entitled, honored, indulged, powerful, ruling, special; SEE CONCEPTS 334,574

privileged [adj2] *allowed, exempt*
authorized, chartered, eligible, empowered, entitled, excused, franchised, free, furnished, granted, immune, kosher*, legit*, licensed, okay*, okayed*, palatine, qualified, sanctioned, special, vested; SEE CONCEPT 548

privileged [adj3] *confidential, secret*
exceptional, for eyes only*, inside, not for publication, off the record*, on the QT*, privy, special, top secret, under one's hat*; SEE CONCEPT 267

privy [adj1] *secret*
buried, concealed, confidential, covert, hidden, hush-hush*, obscured, off the record*, personal, private, separate, shrouded, ulterior; SEE CONCEPTS 267,576

privy [adj2] *aware*
acquainted, apprised, cognizant, conscious, informed, in on*, in the know*, private, privileged, wise; SEE CONCEPT 402

prize [n1] *award, winnings*
accolade, acquirement, acquisition, advantage, blue ribbon*, bonus, bounty, cake*, capture, carrot*, championship, citation, crown, decoration, dividend, feather in cap*, first place*, gold*, gold star*, gravy*, guerdon, haul, honor, inducement, jackpot, laurel, loot*, medal, meed, payoff, pickings*, pillage, plum*, plunder*, possession, premium, privilege, purse, recompense, requital, reward, scholarship, spoil, spoils, stakes, strokes*, swag*, title, trophy, windfall; SEE CONCEPTS 337,344,693,710

prize [n2] *goal; best*
aim, ambition, choice, conquest, cream*, desire, elite, fat, flower*, gain, gold*, hope, pick, pride, prime, top*; SEE CONCEPTS 659,709

prize [adj] *best*
award-winning, champion, choice, cream*, elite, fat*, first-class*, first-rate*, outstanding, pick, prime, top, topnotch, winning; SEE CONCEPT 574

prize [v] *value highly*
appreciate, apprize, cherish, count, enshrine, esteem, guard, hold dear, rate, regard highly, set store by*, treasure; SEE CONCEPTS 10,32

probability [n] *likelihood of something happening*
anticipation, chance, chances, conceivability, contingency, credibility, expectation, feasibility, hazard, liability, likeliness, odds, outside chance*, plausibility, possibility, practicability, prayer, presumption, promise, prospect, reasonableness, shot, snowball's chance*, toss-up*; SEE CONCEPT 650

probable [adj] *likely to happen*
apparent, believable, credible, earthly, feasible, illusory, in the cards*, mortal, most likely, odds-on*, ostensible, plausible, possible, presumable, presumed, rational, reasonable, seeming; SEE CONCEPT 552

probably [adv] *likely to happen*
apparently, as likely as not, assumably, as the case may be, believably, dollars to doughnuts*, doubtless, expediently, feasibly, imaginably, in all likelihood, in all probability, like enough, maybe, most likely, no doubt, one can assume, perchance, perhaps, plausibly, possibly, practicably, presumably, presumptively, reasonably, seemingly, to all appearances; SEE CONCEPT 552

probe [n] *investigation*
delving, detection, examination, exploration, fishing expedition*, inquest, inquiry, inquisition, legwork*, probing, quest, research, scrutiny, study, third degree*; SEE CONCEPTS 31,103,216,290

probe [v] *explore, investigate*
ask, catechize, check, check out, check over, check up, delve into, dig, examine, eye, feel around, feel out, go into, inquire, interrogate, look into, look-see, penetrate, pierce, poke, prod, prospect, put out a feeler*, query, quiz, scrutinize, search, sift, sound, sound out, study, test, test the waters*, verify; SEE CONCEPTS 31,103,216

probity [n] *fairness, honesty*
equity, fidelity, goodness, honor, integrity, justice, morality, rectitude, righteousness, rightness, sincerity, trustworthiness, truthfulness, uprightness, virtue, worth; SEE CONCEPTS 411,645

problem [n1] *difficulty; bad situation*
botheration, box*, can of worms*, complication, count*, crunch*, dilemma, disagreement, dispute, disputed point, doubt, headache*, hitch*, hot water*, issue, mess*, obstacle, pickle*, point at issue*, predicament, quandary, question, scrape*, squeeze*, trouble, worriment; SEE CONCEPTS 666,674

problem [n2] *puzzle, question*
brainteaser*, bugaboo*, cliff-hanger*, conundrum, enigma, example, grabber*, illustration, intricacy, mind-boggler*, mystery, poser*, puzzler, query, riddle, sixty-four thousand dollar question*, stickler, stumper, teaser, twister; SEE CONCEPTS 529,532

problematic [adj] *open to doubt*
ambiguous, arguable, chancy, debatable, disputable, doubtful, dubious, dubitable, enigmatic, iffy*, indecisive, moot, open, precarious, problematical, puzzling, questionable, suspect,

tricky, uncertain, unsettled, up for grabs*; SEE CONCEPT 529

procedure [n] *process, system for accomplishing something*

action, agenda, agendum, channels, conduct, course, custom, daily grind*, fashion, form, formula, game plan*, gimmick, grind, idea, layout, line, maneuver, measure, method, mode, modus operandi, move, nuts and bolts*, operation, performance, plan, policy, polity, practice, proceeding, program, red tape*, routine, scheme, setup, step, strategy, style, the book*, the numbers*, transaction; SEE CONCEPT 6

proceed [v1] *physically or mentally carry on, carry out*

advance, continue, fare, get, get going, get on with, get under way*, go ahead, go on, hie, journey, make a start, march, move on, move out, pass, press on, progress, push on, repair, set in motion, travel, wend; SEE CONCEPTS 43,91

proceed [v2] *flow from; originate*

arise, come, derive, emanate, ensue, extend, follow, head, issue, pass, result, rise, spring, stem; SEE CONCEPTS 179,230,676

proceeding [n] *undertaking, course of action*

act, action, adventure, casualty, circumstance, come off, deed, exercise, experiment, go-down*, goings-on*, happening, incident, maneuver, measure, move, movement, occurrence, operation, performance, procedure, process, step, transaction, venture; SEE CONCEPTS 2,3

proceedings [n] *account, report of event*

affairs, annals, archives, business, dealings, documents, doings*, matters, minutes, records, transactions; SEE CONCEPT 271

proceeds [n] *earnings from business*

gain, gate, handle, income, interest, lucre, produce, product, profit, receipts, result, returns, revenue, reward, split, take, takings, till, yield; SEE CONCEPT 344

process [n] *method; series of actions to achieve result*

action, advance, case, channels*, course, course of action*, development, evolution, fashion, formation, growth, manner, means, measure, mechanism, mode, modus operandi, movement, operation, outgrowth, performance, practice, procedure, proceeding, progress, progression, red tape*, routine, rule, stage, step, suit, system, technique, transaction, trial, unfolding, way, wise, working; SEE CONCEPT 6

process [v] *subject to series of actions to achieve result*

alter, concoct, convert, deal with, dispose of, fulfill, handle, make ready, prepare, refine, take care of, transform, treat; SEE CONCEPT 204

procession [n] *parade, sequence*

advance, autocade, cavalcade, column, consecution, cortege, course, cycle, file, march, motorcade, movement, order, process, run, series, string, succession, train; SEE CONCEPTS 155,727

proclaim [v] *advertise, make known*

affirm, announce, annunciate, blast, blaze, blazon, broadcast, call, circulate, declare, demonstrate, disseminate, enunciate, evidence, evince, exhibit, expound, get on a soapbox*, give out, herald, illustrate, indicate, manifest, mark, ostend, pass the word*, profess, promulgate, publish, shoot off mouth*, shout out, show, sound off, spiel*, spout, spread it around*, stump*,

trumpet*, utter, vent, ventilate, voice; SEE CONCEPTS 49,60

proclamation [n] *advertisement, announcement*

broadcast, declaration, decree, edict, manifesto, notice, notification, promulgation, pronouncement, pronunciamento*, publication; SEE CONCEPTS 271,278

proclivity [n] *inclination, tendency*

bent*, bias, cup of tea*, disposition, druthers, facility, flash*, groove*, inclining, leaning, liableness, penchant, predilection, predisposition, proneness, propensity, thing for*, type, weakness; SEE CONCEPTS 20,32,411

procrastinate [v] *delay, put off doing*

adjourn, be dilatory, cool*, dally, dawdle, defer, drag, drag one's feet*, give the run around*, goldbrick*, hang fire*, hesitate, hold off, lag*, let slide, linger, loiter, pause, play a waiting game*, play for time*, poke*, postpone, prolong, protract, retard, shilly-shally*, stall, stay, suspend, tarry, temporize, wait; SEE CONCEPTS 121,237, 681

procreate [v] *reproduce*

beget, breed, conceive, create, engender, father, generate, get, give birth to, hatch, impregnate, make, mother, multiply, originate, parent, produce, progenerate, proliferate, propagate, sire, spawn; SEE CONCEPTS 173,251,374

procure [v] *acquire, obtain*

annex, appropriate, bring around, buy, buy out, buy up, come by, compass, cop*, corral, draw, earn, effect, find, gain, get, get hold of, grab, have, induce, land*, latch on to, lay hands on, make a haul*, manage to get*, persuade, pick up, prevail upon, promote, purchase, score, secure, solicit, wangle, win; SEE CONCEPTS 68,120,327

prod [v1] *poke at*

crowd, dig, drive, elbow, goose, jab, jog, nudge, press, prick, punch, push, shove; SEE CONCEPT 208

prod [v2] *urge, incite*

crowd*, egg on*, excite, exhort, goad, goose*, impel, instigate, jog memory, motivate, move, pique, prick, prompt, propel, provoke, push, remind, rouse, sic*, sound, spark, spur, stimulate, stir up, trigger, turn on; SEE CONCEPTS 7,19,22,242

prodigal [n] *person who spends a lot*

big spender*, compulsive shopper*, deep pockets*, dissipator, high roller*, profligate, spender, spendthrift, sport, squanderer, waster, wastrel; SEE CONCEPTS 348,412

prodigal [adj1] *wasteful*

dissipated, excessive, extravagant, immoderate, improvident, intemperate, lavish, profligate, reckless, spendthrift, squandering, wanton; SEE CONCEPTS 401,560

prodigal [adj2] *luxurious, profuse*

abundant, bounteous, bountiful, copious, exuberant, lavish, lush, luxuriant, moneyed, munificent, opulent, riotous, sumptuous, superabundant, teeming; SEE CONCEPTS 334,781

prodigious [adj1] *huge, enormous*

big, colossal*, fantastic, giant, gigantic, gross, Herculean*, immeasurable, immense, inordinate, jumbo*, king-size*, large, mammoth, massive, mighty, monstrous, monumental, mortal, stupendous, towering, tremendous, vast; SEE CONCEPTS 773,781

prodigious [*adj2*] *extraordinary, fabulous*
abnormal, amazing, astonishing, astounding, bad, exceptional, fab*, fantastic, heavy, impressive, marvelous, miraculous, out-of-this-world*, phenomenal, preternatural, remarkable, spectacular, staggering, startling, state-of-the-art*, striking, stupendous, surprising, unreal, unusual, utmost, wonderful; SEE CONCEPTS 567,572,574

prodigy [*n*] *person or thing that is extraordinary*
brain*, child genius, curiosity, enormity, freak*, genius, intellect, marvel, mastermind, miracle, monster, natural, one in a million*, phenomenon, portent, rare bird*, rarity, sensation, spectacle, stunner, talent, whiz*, whiz kid*, wizard, wonder, wonder child, wunderkind; SEE CONCEPTS 416,671,706

produce [*n*] *fruit and vegetables*
crop, fruitage, goods, greengrocery, harvest, outcome, outgrowth, outturn, production, yield; SEE CONCEPTS 426,429,431,457,461

produce [*v1*] *generate, create*
afford, assemble, author, bear, beget, blossom, breed, bring forth, bring out, build, come through, compose, conceive, construct, contribute, cultivate, deliver, design, develop, devise, effectuate, engender, erect, fabricate, fetch, flower, form, frame, furnish, give, give birth, give forth, imagine, invent, make, manufacture, multiply, offer, originate, parent, present, procreate, propagate, provide, put together, render, reproduce, return, show fruit, supply, turn out, write, yield; SEE CONCEPTS 173,205,251,374

produce [*v2*] *cause, effect*
beget, breed, bring about, draw on, engender, generate, get up, give rise to, hatch, induce, make, make for*, muster, occasion, provoke, result in, secure, set off, work up; SEE CONCEPT 242

produce [*v3*] *demonstrate, show*
advance, bring forward, bring to light, display, exhibit, offer, present, put forward, set forth, unfold; SEE CONCEPT 261

produce [*v4*] *put on a public performance*
act, come through, direct, do, exhibit, make, mount, percolate, perform, perk, play, present, pull off*, show, stage; SEE CONCEPTS 292,324

product [*n*] *result or goods created*
aftermath, amount, artifact, blend, brand, brew, by-product, commodity, compound, concoction, confection, consequence, contrivance, creation, crop, decoction, device, effect, emolument, fabrication, fruit, gain, handiwork, invention, issue, legacy, line, manufacture, merchandise, offshoot, outcome, outgrowth, output, preparation, produce, production, profit, realization, result, returns, spinoff, stock, synthetic, upshot, work, yield; SEE CONCEPTS 230,338

production [*n*] *creating of goods, result*
assembly, authoring, bearing, blossoming, construction, creation, direction, elongation, engendering, extention, fabrication, formulation, fructification, generation, giving, lengthening, making, management, manufacture, manufacturing, origination, preparation, presentation, producing, prolongation, protraction, provision, rendering, reproduction, return, staging, yielding; SEE CONCEPT 205

productive [*adj*] *fruitful, creative*
advantageous, beneficial, constructive, dynamic, effective, energetic, fecund, fertile, gainful, generative, gratifying, inventive, plentiful, producing, profitable, prolific, rewarding, rich, teeming, useful, valuable, vigorous, worthwhile; SEE CONCEPTS 537,542,560

productivity [*n*] *output, work rate*
abundance, capacity, fecundity, fertility, mass production, potency, production, productiveness, richness, yield; SEE CONCEPT 630

profane [*adj*] *immoral, crude, disrespectful of religion*
abusive, atheistic, blasphemous, coarse, dirty*, filthy*, foul, godless, heathen, idolatrous, impious, impure, indecent, infidel, irreligious, irreverent, irreverential, mundane, nasty, obscene, pagan, profanatory, raunchy, sacrilegious, sinful, smutty*, temporal, transient, transitory, unconsecrated, ungodly, unhallowed, unholy, unsanctified, vulgar, wicked, worldly; SEE CONCEPTS 267,401,545

profane [*v*] *defile, desecrate*
abuse, be evil, befoul, blaspheme, commit sacrilege, commit sin, contaminate, curse, cuss, damn, darn, debase, despoil, do wrong, flame, hoodoo*, misuse, mock, mudsling*, pervert, pollute, prostitute, put double whammy on*, revile, scorn, swear, talk dirty*, tar, trash, vice, violate, vitiate, voodoo*; SEE CONCEPTS 44,52,58,63

profanity [*n*] *foul language*
abuse, blasphemy, curse, cursing, cuss, cuss word, dirty language*, dirty name*, dirty word*, execration, four-letter word*, impiety, imprecation, irreverence, malediction, no-no*, obscenity, profaneness, sacrilege, swearing, swearword, taboo; SEE CONCEPTS 278,645

profess [*v*] *declare, assert*
acknowledge, act as if, admit, affirm, allege, announce, asseverate, aver, avouch, avow, blow hot air*, certify, claim, come out*, confess, confirm, constate, croon, cross heart*, depose, dissemble, fake, feign, get off chest* get on soapbox*, maintain, make out, open up*, own, own up*, predicate, pretend, proclaim, purport, say so*, sing*, soapbox*, spiel*, spout*, state, stump*, swear on bible*, swear up and down*, talk big*, vouch; SEE CONCEPTS 49,63

profession [*n1*] *line of work requiring academic or practical preparation*
art, avocation, berth, billet, biz*, business, calling, career, chosen work, concern, craft, dodge*, employment, engagement, field, game*, handicraft, lifework, line*, line of work*, métier, occupation, office, position, post, pursuit, rat race*, role, service, situation, slot*, specialty, sphere, thing*, trade, undertaking, vocation, walk of life*; SEE CONCEPT 360

profession [*n2*] *declaration*
acknowledgment, affirmation, assertion, attestation, avowal, claim, confession, pretense, statement, testimony, vow; SEE CONCEPT 278

professional [*n*] *person prepared for work by extended study or practice*
adept, artist, artiste, authority, brain*, egghead*, expert, hotshot*, old hand*, old pro*, old warhorse*, phenom, powerhouse, pro, proficient, pundit, shark, specialist, star, superstar, virtuoso, whiz*, whiz kid*, wizard; SEE CONCEPTS 347,348

professional [*adj*] *skilled, trained*
able, ace, acknowledged, adept, competent, crackerjack*, efficient, experienced, expert, finished, knowing one's stuff*, known, learned, li-

censed, on the ball*, polished, practiced, proficient, qualified, sharp, skillful, slick*, there*, up to speed*, well-qualified; SEE CONCEPTS 326,402,527,528

professor [n] *person who teaches college courses*
assistant, brain*, educator, egghead*, faculty member, fellow, instructor, lecturer, pedagogue, principal, prof*, pundit, quant*, rocket scientist*, sage, savant, teacher, tutor; SEE CONCEPT 350

proffer [v] *suggest, offer*
extend, gift, give, hand, hit on, hold out, make a pitch*, pose, present, propose, proposition, propound, submit, tender, volunteer; SEE CONCEPTS 66,67,75

proficiency [n] *ability, skillfulness*
accomplishment, advance, advancement, aptitude, chops, competence, dexterity, efficiency, expertise, expertness, facility, formula, green thumb*, headway*, knack*, know-how*, knowledge, learning, makings, mastery, moxie*, oil*, progress, right stuff*, savvy*, skill, stuff, talent, what it takes*; SEE CONCEPTS 409,630,706

proficient [adj] *able, skilled*
accomplished, adept, apt, capable, clever, competent, consummate, conversant, crack*, crackerjack*, drilled, effective, effectual, efficient, exercised, experienced, expert, finished, gifted, on the beam*, phenom, pro, qualified, savvy*, sharp, skillful, slick*, talented, trained, up to speed*, versed, whiz*, with it*; SEE CONCEPTS 402,527,528

profile [n1] *drawing of outline*
contour, delineation, figuration, figure, form, likeness, line, lineament, lineation, portrait, shadow, shape, side view, silhouette, sketch; SEE CONCEPTS 259,625

profile [n2] *description, characterization*
analysis, biography, character sketch, chart, diagram, review, sketch, study, survey, thumbnail sketch, vignette, vita; SEE CONCEPTS 268,283

profit [n] *gain*
accumulation, acquisition, advancement, advantage, aggrandizement, augmentation, avail, benefit, bottom line*, cleanup, earnings, emoluments, gate*, goods*, gravy*, gross, harvest, income, interest, killing, lucre, net, output, outturn, percentage, proceeds, product, production, receipt, receipts, remuneration, return, revenue, saving, skim*, split*, surplus, take*, takings*, turnout, use, value, velvet*, winnings, yield; SEE CONCEPTS 332,344,693

profit [v] *gain; get or give an advantage*
aid, avail, benefit, be of advantage, better, capitalize on, cash in on, clean up, clear, contribute, earn, exploit, help, improve, learn from, make a haul*, make a killing*, make capital, make good use of*, make it big*, make money, make the most of*, pay, pay off, promote, prosper, put to good use*, realize, reap the benefit*, recover, score, serve*, stand in good stead*, take advantage of, thrive, turn to advantage, use, utilize, work for; SEE CONCEPTS 110,124,330,693

profitable [adj] *advantageous; money-making*
assisting, beneficial, commercial, conducive, contributive, cost-effective, effective, effectual, favorable, fruitful, gainful, going*, good, instrumental, in the black*, lucrative, paid off, paying, paying well, practical, pragmatic, productive, remunerative, rewarding, self-sustaining, serviceable, successful, sustaining, sweet*, use-

ful, valuable, well-paying, worthwhile; SEE CONCEPTS 334,537,572

profligate [n] *person who is immoral*
debauchee, degenerate, dissipater, good-for-nothing*, lecher, libertine, nighthawk*, no-good*, old goat*, operator*, prodigal, rake, reprobate, roué, swinger, waster, wastrel; SEE CONCEPT 412

profligate [adj1] *immoral, corrupt*
abandoned, debauched, degenerate, depraved, dissipated, dissolute, iniquitous, lax, lewd, libertine, licentious, loose, promiscuous, reprobate, shameless, unprincipled, vicious, vitiated, wanton, wicked, wild; SEE CONCEPT 545

profligate [adj2] *wasteful*
extravagant, immoderate, improvident, lavish, prodigal, reckless, spendthrift, squandering; SEE CONCEPTS 334,401

profound [adj1] *intellectual, thoughtful*
abstruse, acroamatic, deep, difficult, discerning, enlightened, erudite, esoteric, heavy*, hermetic, informed, intellectual, intelligent, knowing, knowledgeable, learned, mysterious, occult, Orphic, penetrating, philosophical, recondite, reflective, sagacious, sage, scholarly, secret, serious, shrewd, skilled, subtle, thorough, weighty, wise; SEE CONCEPTS 402,529

profound [adj2] *bottomless*
abysmal, buried, cavernous, deep, fathomless, subterranean, yawning; SEE CONCEPT 777

profound [adj3] *intense; emotional*
abject, absolute, acute, consummate, deep, deeply felt, deep-seated, exhaustive, extensive, extreme, far-reaching, great, hard, heartfelt, heartrending, hearty, keen, out-and-out*, pronounced, sincere, thorough, total, utter; SEE CONCEPTS 403,531,569

profuse [adj] *abundant, excessive*
abounding, alive with*, ample, aplenty, bounteous, bountiful, copious, crawling with*, dime a dozen*, extravagant, extreme, exuberant, fulsome, galore, generous, immoderate, lavish, liberal, lush, luxuriant, no end*, openhanded, opulent, overflowing, plentiful, plenty, prodigal, profusive, prolific, riotous, sumptuous, superfluous, swarming, teeming, thick with*, unstinting; SEE CONCEPTS 762,781

progeny [n] *offspring*
begats, breed, children, descendants, family, get*, issue, kids*, lineage, posterity, progeniture, race, scions, seed, stock, young; SEE CONCEPTS 296,414

prognosis [n] *forecast*
cast, diagnosis, expectation, foretelling, guess, prediction, prevision, prognostication, projection, prophecy, speculation, surmise; SEE CONCEPTS 274,689

prognosticate [v] *predict, foretell*
adumbrate, augur, betoken, call it*, crystal-ball*, divine, forebode, forecast, foreshadow, harbinger, have a hunch*, herald, make book*, point to, portend, presage, prophesy, read, see coming*, soothsay, vaticinate; SEE CONCEPT 70

program [n1] *agenda, list*
affairs, appointments, arrangements, bill, bulletin, business, calendar, card, catalog, chores, curriculum, details, docket, happenings, index, lineup, listing, meetings, memoranda, necessary acts*, order of business*, order of events*, order of the day*, plan, plans, preparations, record,

schedule, series of events, slate, syllabus, things to do*, timetable; SEE CONCEPTS 281,283

program [n2] *scheme, plan*
course, design, instructions, line, order, plan of action, policy, polity, procedure, project, sequence; SEE CONCEPTS 274,660

program [n3] *performance in medium*
broadcast, presentation, production, show; SEE CONCEPT 263

program [v] *plan out; supply instructions*
arrange, bill, book, budget, calculate, compile, compute, design, draft, edit, engage, enter, estimate, feed, figure, formulate, get on line*, itemize, lay on, lay out, line up, list, map out, pencil in*, poll, prearrange, prioritize, process, register, schedule, set, set up, slate, work out; SEE CONCEPTS 36,60,84,384

progress [n] *advancement, gain*
advance, amelioration, anabasis, betterment, boost, break, breakthrough, buildup, course, dash, development, evolution, evolvement, expedition, flowering, growth, headway, hike, impetus, improvement, increase, journey, lunge, march, momentum, motion, movement, ongoing, pace, passage, process, procession, proficiency, progression, promotion, rate, rise, step forward, stride, tour, unfolding, voyage, way; SEE CONCEPTS 704,706

progress [v1] *move forward*
advance, continue, cover ground*, dash, edge, forge ahead, gain ground, get along, get on, go forward, keep going, lunge, make headway*, make strides*, move on, proceed, shoot, speed, travel; SEE CONCEPTS 149,159

progress [v2] *improve, advance*
ameliorate, become better, better, blossom, boost, develop, gain, grow, increase, make first rate, mature, shape up, straighten up, truck, turn over new leaf*, upgrade; SEE CONCEPT 700

progressive [adj] *liberal; growing*
accelerating, advanced, advancing, avant-garde*, bleeding-heart*, broad, broad-minded, continuing, continuous, developing, dynamic, enlightened, enterprising, escalating, forward-looking, go-ahead*, gradual, graduated, increasing, intensifying, left*, left of center*, lenient, modern, ongoing, onward, open-minded, radical, reformist, revolutionary, tolerant, up-and-coming*, up-to-date, wide; SEE CONCEPTS 542,544

prohibit [v] *make impossible; stop*
ban, block, bottle up*, box in*, bring to screeching halt*, constrain, cool*, cork*, debar, disallow, enjoin, forbid, forfend, freeze*, gridlock, halt, hamper, hang up*, hinder, hold up, impede, inhibit, interdict, jam up*, keep lid on*, kill, lock up, nix, obstruct, outlaw, pass on*, preclude, prevent, proscribe, put a lock on*, put a stopper in*, put chill on*, put down, put half nelson on*, restrain, restrict, rule out, shut out, spike*, stymie*, taboo*, throw cold water on*, tie up*, veto, zing*; SEE CONCEPTS 50,88,121,130,317

prohibited [adj] *forbidden*
banned, barred, closed down, contraband, crooked*, illegal, illicit, no-no*, not allowed, not approved, off limits*, out of bounds*, out of line*, proscribed, refused, restricted, shady*, taboo, verboten, vetoed, wildcat*; SEE CONCEPTS 554,576

prohibition [n] *ban, forbiddance*
bar, constraint, disallowance, don't*, embargo,

exclusion, injunction, interdict, interdiction, negation, no-no*, obstruction, off limits*, out of bounds*, prevention, proscription, refusal, repudiation, restriction, taboo, temperance, veto; SEE CONCEPTS 121,130,652,691

prohibitive [adj] *restrictive; beyond one's financial means*
conditional, excessive, exorbitant, expensive, extortionate, forbidding, high-priced, limiting, preposterous, preventing, prohibiting, proscriptive, repressive, restraining, sky-high*, steep*, suppressive; SEE CONCEPTS 334,554

project [n] *undertaking, work*
activity, adventure, affair, aim, assignment, baby*, blueprint*, business, concern, deal, design, enterprise, exploit, feat, game plan, intention, job, matter, occupation, outline, pet*, plan, program, proposal, proposition, scheme, setup, strategy, task, thing*, venture; SEE CONCEPTS 324,349,362

project [v1] *plan*
arrange, blueprint, calculate, cast, chart, conceive, contemplate, contrive, delineate, design, devise, diagram, draft, envisage, envision, estimate, extrapolate, feature, forecast, frame, gauge, image, imagine, intend, map out, outline, predetermine, predict, propose, purpose, reckon, scheme, see, think, vision, visualize; SEE CONCEPTS 28,36,37,70

project [v2] *bulge, hang out*
be conspicuous, beetle, be prominent, extend, hang over, jut, lengthen, overhang, poke, pop out, pout, prolong, protrude, protuberate, push out, stand out, stick out, stretch out, thrust out; SEE CONCEPT 747

project [v3] *throw, discharge*
cast, fling, heave, hurl, launch, pitch, propel, shoot, transmit; SEE CONCEPTS 179,222

projection [n1] *bulge, overhang*
bump, bunch, eaves, extension, hook, jut, knob, ledge, outthrust, point, prolongation, prominence, protrusion, protuberance, ridge, rim, shelf, sill, spine, spur, step, swelling; SEE CONCEPTS 471,509,513

projection [n2] *prediction*
calculation, computation, estimate, estimation, extrapolation, forecast, guess, prognostication, reckoning; SEE CONCEPTS 28,278

proliferate [v] *increase quickly*
breed, burgeon, engender, escalate, expand, generate, grow rapidly, multiply, mushroom*, procreate, propagate, reproduce, run riot*, snowball*; SEE CONCEPT 780

prolific [adj] *fruitful, productive*
abounding, abundant, bountiful, breeding, copious, creative, fecund, fertile, generating, generative, luxuriant, profuse, proliferant, rank, reproducing, reproductive, rich, spawning, swarming, teeming, yielding; SEE CONCEPTS 485,542

prolong [v] *extend, draw out*
carry on, continue, delay, drag one's feet*, drag out*, hold, hold up, increase, lengthen, let it ride*, make longer, pad*, perpetuate, protract, spin out*, stall, stretch, stretch out; SEE CONCEPTS 239,250

prominence [n1] *something that sticks out*
bulge, bump, cliff, conspicuousness, crag, crest, elevation, eminence, headland, height, high point, jutting, markedness, mound, pinnacle, projection,

promontory, protrusion, protuberance, rise, spur, swelling, tor; SEE CONCEPTS 513,836

prominence [n2] *distinction, outstandingness*
celebrity, eminence, fame, greatness, illustriousness, importance, influence, kudos*, name, notability, precedence, preeminence, prestige, rank, renown, reputation, salience, specialness, standing, top billing*, weight; SEE CONCEPT 668

prominent [adj1] *sticking out; conspicuous*
arresting, beetling, bulging, easily seen, embossed, extended, extrusive, eye-catching, flashy, hanging out, hilly, in the foreground, jutting, marked, noticeable, obtrusive, obvious, outstanding, projecting, pronounced, protruding, protrusive, protuberant, raised, relieved, remarkable, rough, rugged, salient, shooting out, signal, standing out, striking, to the fore, unmistakable; SEE CONCEPTS 485,583,619

prominent [adj2] *important; famous*
big-league*, big-name*, big-shot*, celebrated, chief, distinguished, eminent, famed, foremost, great, high-profile*, leading, main, notable, noted, notorious, outstanding, popular, preeminent, renowned, respected, top, underlined, VIP*, well-known, well-thought-of, world-class*; SEE CONCEPT 568

promiscuous [adj] *indiscriminately sexually active*
abandoned, debauched, dissipated, dissolute, easy*, fast*, immoral, indiscriminate, lax, libertine, licentious, loose*, of easy virtue, oversexed, profligate, pushover, unbridled, unchaste, undiscriminating, unrestricted, wanton, wild; SEE CONCEPTS 372,545

promise [n1] *one's word that something will be done*
affiance, affirmation, agreement, asseveration, assurance, avowal, betrothal, bond, commitment, compact, consent, contract, covenant, earnest, engagement, espousal, guarantee, insurance, marriage, oath, obligation, pact, parole, pawn, pledge, plight, profession, promissory note, sacred word, security, stipulation, swear, swearing, token, troth, undertaking, vow, warrant, warranty, word, word of honor; SEE CONCEPTS 71,278

promise [n2] *hope, possibility*
ability, aptitude, capability, capacity, encouragement, flair, good omen, outlook, potential, talent; SEE CONCEPTS 630,650

promise [v1] *give word that something will be done*
accede, affiance, affirm, agree, answer for, assent, asseverate, assure, bargain, betroth, bind, commit, compact, consent, contract, covenant, cross heart*, declare, engage, ensure, espouse, guarantee, hock*, insure, live up to*, mortgage, obligate, pass, pawn*, pledge, plight, profess, say so*, secure, stipulate, string along*, subscribe, swear, swear on bible*, swear up and down*, take an oath, undertake, underwrite, vouch, vow, warrant; SEE CONCEPT 71

promise [v2] *bring hope, possibility*
augur, bespeak, betoken, bode, denote, encourage, forebode, foreshadow, foretoken, give hope, hint, hold out hope*, hold probability, indicate, lead to expect, like, look, omen, portend, presage, seem likely, show signs of*, suggest; SEE CONCEPTS 118,650

promising [adj] *hopeful*
able, assuring, auspicious, bright, encouraging, favorable, gifted, happy, likely, lucky, propitious,

reassuring, rising, roseate, rosy, talented, up-and-coming; SEE CONCEPTS 406,548

promote [v1] *help, advance*
advertise, advocate, aid, assist, avail, back, befriend, benefit, bolster, boost, build up*, call attention to, champion, contribute, cooperate, cry*, develop, encourage, endorse, espouse, forward, foster, further, get behind, hype*, improve, nourish, nurture, patronize, plug*, popularize, propagandize, publicize, puff*, push, push for, recommend, sell, serve, speak for, speed, sponsor, stimulate, subsidize, succor, support, uphold, urge, work for; SEE CONCEPTS 49,110,324

promote [v2] *give a higher position in organization*
advance, aggrandize, ascend, better, dignify, elevate, ennoble, exalt, favor, graduate, honor, increase, kick upstairs*, magnify, move up, prefer, raise, skip, up*, upgrade; SEE CONCEPT 351

promotion [n1] *higher position in organization*
advance, advancement, advocacy, aggrandizement, backing, betterment, boost, break, breakthrough, buildup, bump, elevation, encouragement, ennoblement, exaltation, favoring, furtherance, go-ahead*, hike, honor, improvement, jump, jump up, lift, move up, preference, preferment, prelation, progress, raise, rise, step up, support, upgrade, upgrading; SEE CONCEPT 351

promotion [n2] *publicity*
advertising, advertising campaign, ballyhoo*, blurb*, buildup*, hard sell*, hoopla*, hype*, notice, pitch, pizzazz*, plug*, PR*, press*, press-agentry, promo*, propaganda, publicity, public relations, puff*, puffery*, pushing, squib*; SEE CONCEPTS 49,110,271,324

prompt [n] *hint*
cue, help, jog, jolt, mnemonic, prod, reminder, spur, stimulus, twit; SEE CONCEPT 274

prompt [adj] *early, responsive*
alert, apt, brisk, eager, efficient, expeditious, immediate, instant, instantaneous, on the ball*, on the button*, on the dot*, on the nose*, on time, precise, punctual, quick, rapid, ready, smart, speedy, swift, timely, unhesitating, vigilant, watchful, wide-awake, willing; SEE CONCEPTS 401,799

prompt [v] *incite, cue*
advise, aid, arouse, assist, bring up, call forth, cause, convince, draw, egg on*, elicit, evoke, exhort, get, give rise to, goad, help, help out, hint, impel, imply, indicate, induce, inspire, instigate, jog, mention, motivate, move, occasion, persuade, prick*, prod, propel, propose, provoke, refresh, remind, sic*, spur, stimulate, suggest, talk into, urge, win over; SEE CONCEPTS 68,242

promptly [adv] *immediately*
at once, directly, expeditiously, fast, flat-out*, fleetly, hastily, in nothing flat*, instantly, lickety-split*, like a shot*, now, on the dot*, on the double*, on time, PDQ*, posthaste, pronto, punctually, quickly, rapidly, right away, sharp, speedily, straightaway, swiftly, unhesitatingly; SEE CONCEPTS 544,799

promulgate [v] *make known*
advertise, announce, annunciate, broadcast, call, circulate, communicate, declare, decree, disseminate, drum, issue, make public, notify, pass the word*, proclaim, promote, publish, sound, spread, toot, trumpet; SEE CONCEPT 60

prone [*adj1*] *lying down*
decumbent, face down, flat, horizontal, level, procumbent, prostrate, reclining, recumbent, resupine, supine; SEE CONCEPT *583*

prone [*adj2*] *liable, likely*
apt, bent, devoted, disposed, exposed, fain, given, inclined, minded, open, predisposed, ready, sensitive, subject, susceptible, tending, willing; SEE CONCEPTS *542,552*

pronounce [*v1*] *produce words vocally*
accent, articulate, enunciate, phonate, say, sound, speak, stress, utter, verbalize, vocalize, voice; SEE CONCEPT *47*

pronounce [*v2*] *announce, declare*
affirm, assert, blast, call, decree, deliver, drum, judge, mouth, proclaim, say, sound off, spread around, trumpet, verbalize; SEE CONCEPT *49*

pronounced [*adj*] *distinct, evident*
arresting, assured, broad, clear, clear-cut, conspicuous, decided, definite, marked, notable, noticeable, obvious, outstanding, striking, strong, unmistakable; SEE CONCEPTS *535,576,619*

pronouncement [*n*] *declaration, statement*
advertisement, announcement, broadcast, decree, dictum, edict, judgment, manifesto, notification, proclamation, promulgation, pronunciamento*, publication, report, ukase; SEE CONCEPTS *271,274,278*

proof [*n1*] *evidence, authentication*
affidavit, argument, attestation, averment, case, certification, chapter and verse*, clincher*, clue, confirmation, corroboration, credentials, criterion, cue*, data, demonstration, deposition, documents, establishment, exhibit, facts, goods*, grabber*, grounds, information, lowdown*, nitty-gritty*, paper trail*, picture, reason, reasons, record, scoop*, score*, skinny*, smoking gun*, straight stuff*, substantiation, testament, testimony, trace, validation, verification, warrant, wherefore*, why*, whyfor*, witness; SEE CONCEPT *274*

proof [*n2*] *photographic print*
galley, galley proof, impression, page proof, pass, pull, repro, revise, slip, stereo, trial, trial print, trial proof; SEE CONCEPT *265*

prop [*n*] *support*
aid, assistance, brace, buttress, column, mainstay, post, shore, stanchion, stay, strengthener, strut, truss, underpinning; SEE CONCEPTS *440,470*

prop [*v*] *hold up or lean against*
bear up, bolster, brace, buoy, buttress, carry, maintain, rest, set, shore, stand, stay, strengthen, support, sustain, truss, underprop, uphold; SEE CONCEPTS *190,201*

propaganda [*n*] *information that is designed to mislead or persuade*
advertising, agitprop, announcement, brainwashing*, disinformation, doctrine, evangelism, handout, hogwash*, hype*, implantation, inculcation, indoctrination, newspeak, promotion, promulgation, proselytism, publication, publicity; SEE CONCEPT *278*

propagate [*v1*] *breed, reproduce*
bear, beget, engender, father, fecundate, fertilize, generate, grow, impregnate, increase, inseminate, make pregnant, mother, multiply, originate, procreate, produce, proliferate, raise, sire; SEE CONCEPT *374*

propagate [*v2*] *spread, make known*
broadcast, circulate, develop, diffuse, disperse, disseminate, distribute, proclaim, promulgate, publicize, publish, radiate, scatter, strew, transmit; SEE CONCEPTS *60,222*

propel [*v*] *throw; release into air*
actuate, drive, force, impel, launch, mobilize, move, press, push, send, set going, set in motion, shoot, shove, start, thrust; SEE CONCEPTS *208,221,222*

propensity [*n*] *inclination, weakness*
ability, aptness, bent*, bias, capacity, competence, disposition, flash, inclining, leaning, liability, partiality, penchant, predilection, predisposition, proclivity, proneness, susceptibility, sweet tooth*, talent, tendency, thing*, tilt*, yen; SEE CONCEPTS *20,411,630,709*

proper [*adj1*] *suitable*
able, applicable, appropriate, apt, au fait, becoming, befitting, capable, competent, convenient, decent, desired, felicitous, fit, fitting, good, happy, just, legitimate, meet, qualified, right, suited, true, useful; SEE CONCEPT *558*

proper [*adj2*] *mannerly, decent*
becoming, befitting, by the book*, by the numbers*, comely, comme il faut*, conforming, correct, decorous, demure, de rigueur*, genteel, in line, kosher*, moral, nice, polite, precise, priggish, prim, prissy, prudish, punctilious, puritanical, refined, respectable, right, seemly, solid, square*, stone, straight*, strait-laced*, stuffy*; SEE CONCEPTS *401,404*

proper [*adj3*] *conventional, correct*
absolute, accepted, accurate, arrant, complete, consummate, customary, decorous, established, exact, formal, free of error, on target*, on the button*, on the nose*, on the right track*, orthodox, out-and-out*, precise, right, unmistaken, usual, utter; SEE CONCEPTS *326,533*

proper [*adj4*] *individual, personal*
characteristic, distinctive, idiosyncratic, own, particular, peculiar, private, respective, special, specific; SEE CONCEPTS *549,557*

property [*n1*] *possessions, real estate*
acreage, acres, assets, belongings, buildings, capital, chattels, claim, dominion, effects, equity, estate, farm, freehold, goods, holdings, home, house, inheritance, land, means, ownership, plot, possessorship, premises, proprietary, proprietorship, realty, resources, riches, substance, title, tract, wealth, worth; SEE CONCEPTS *446,509,515,710*

property [*n2*] *characteristic, feature*
ability, affection, attribute, character, hallmark, idiosyncrasy, mark, peculiarity, quality, trait, virtue; SEE CONCEPTS *411,654*

prophecy [*n*] *prediction*
apocalypse, augury, cast, divination, forecast, foretelling, oracle, presage, prevision, prognosis, prognostication, revelation, second sight, soothsaying, vision; SEE CONCEPTS *70,278,689*

prophesy [*v*] *predict, warn*
adumbrate, augur, call*, call the turn*, crystal-ball*, divine, forecast, foresee, foretell, forewarn, have a hunch*, make book*, portend, predict, presage, prognosticate, psych it out*, see coming*, soothsay, vaticinate; SEE CONCEPT *70*

prophet [*n*] *person, thing that predicts future*
astrologer, augur, auspex, bard, clairvoyant, diviner, druid, evocator, forecaster, fortuneteller, haruspex, horoscopist, magus, medium, meteorologist, oracle, ovate, palmist, predictor, prog-

pr
pr

nosticator, prophesier, reader, seer, seeress, sibyl, soothsayer, sorcerer, tea-leaf reader, witch, wizard; SEE CONCEPTS 361,423

prophetic [adj] *telling of the future*
apocalyptic, augural, Delphian*, divinatory, fatidic, foreshadowing, mantic, occult, oracular, predictive, presaging, prescient, prognostic, prophetical, pythonic, sibylline, vaticinal, veiled; SEE CONCEPT 267

propitious [adj1] *full of promise; good, favorable*
advantageous, auspicious, beneficial, benign, brave, bright, dexter, encouraging, favoring, fortunate, happy, hopeful, lucky, opportune, pat*, promising, prosperous, rosy, seasonable, timely, toward, useful, well-timed; SEE CONCEPTS 548,560,572

propitious [adj2] *friendly*
benevolent, benign, favorably inclined, gracious, kind, nice, well-disposed; SEE CONCEPT 401

proponent [n] *person who advocates, supports cause*
advocate, backer, champion, defender, enthusiast, exponent, expounder, friend, partisan, patron, protector, second, seconder, spokesperson, subscriber, supporter, upholder, vindicator; SEE CONCEPTS 355,359,423

proportion [n1] *relative amount, size of part to whole*
admeasurement, amplitude, apportionment, breadth, bulk, capacity, cut, degree, dimension, distribution, division, equation, expanse, extent, fraction, magnitude, measure, measurement, part, percentage, portion, quota, rate, ratio, relationship, scale, scope, segment, share, volume; SEE CONCEPTS 730,783

proportion [n2] *balance between parts of whole*
agreement, congruity, correspondence, harmony, symmetry; SEE CONCEPTS 664,717

proportionate/proportional [adj] *balanced, corresponding*
commensurable, commensurate, comparable, comparative, compatible, consistent, contingent, correlative, correspondent, corresponding, dependent, equal, equitable, equivalent, even, in proportion, just, reciprocal, relative, symmetrical, uniform; SEE CONCEPTS 480,563

proposal [n] *suggestion, presentation for action*
angle, bid, big idea*, brain child*, design, feeler*, game plan*, idea, layout, motion, offer, outline, overture, pass, picture, pitch, plan, proffer, program, project, proposition, recommendation, scenario, scheme, setup, tender, terms; SEE CONCEPTS 271,324,662

propose [v1] *suggest, present for action*
adduce, advance, advise, affirm, ask, assert, broach, come up with*, contend, counsel, hit on*, hold out, introduce, invite, kibitz*, lay before*, lay on the line*, make a motion, make a pitch*, move for, name, nominate, offer, pose, prefer, press, proffer, propone, proposition, propound, put forward, put to, put up, recommend, request, set forth, solicit, speak one's piece*, spitball*, state, submit, tender, urge, volunteer; SEE CONCEPTS 66,75

propose [v2] *intend; have in mind*
aim, contemplate, design, have every intention, mean, mind, plan, purpose, scheme; SEE CONCEPTS 26,36

propose [v3] *ask for hand in marriage*
ask in marriage, fire the question*, get down on one knee*, make a proposal, offer marriage, pop the question*, press one's suit*; SEE CONCEPTS 48,297

proposition [n] *suggestion; scheme*
hypothesis, invitation, motion, overture, plan, premise, presentation, proffer, program, project, proposal, recommendation; SEE CONCEPTS 384, 662

proposition [v] *make suggestion, often improper*
accost, approach, ask, pose, prefer, propose, propound, put, solicit, suggest; SEE CONCEPTS 48,375

proprietor [n] *person who owns something*
freeholder*, front office, holder, land owner, meal ticket*, owner, possessor, proprietary, titleholder; SEE CONCEPTS 343,347

propriety [n1] *suitableness, appropriateness*
accordance, advisability, agreeableness, appositeness, aptness, becomingness, compatibility, concord, congruity, consonance, convenience, correctness, correspondence, decorum, ethicality, expedience, fitness, harmony, justice, legitimacy, meetness, morality, order, pleasantness, properness, recommendability, rectitude, respectability, rightness, seemliness, suitability; SEE CONCEPT 656

propriety [n2] *good manners*
accepted conduct, amenities, breeding, civilities, correctness, courtesy, decency, decorum, delicacy, dignity, etiquette, good behavior, good form, modesty, mores*, niceties, politeness, politesse, protocol, punctilio, rectitude, refinement, respectability, rules of conduct, seemliness, social conventions, scheme, social grace, the done thing*; SEE CONCEPTS 633,644

prosaic [adj] *unimaginative*
actual, banal, blah*, boring, clean, colorless, common, commonplace, dead*, diddly*, drab, dry, dull, everyday, factual, flat*, garden-variety*, hackneyed, ho-hum*, humdrum*, irksome, lackluster, lifeless, literal, lowly, lusterless, matter-of-fact, monotonous, mundane, nothing, nowhere, ordinary, pabulum*, pedestrian, platitudinous, plebeian, practicable, practical, prose, prosy, routine, square, stale, tame, tedious, trite, uneventful, unexceptional, uninspiring, vanilla*, vapid, workaday, yawn*, zero*; SEE CONCEPTS 267,537,547

proscribe [v] *condemn, exclude*
ban, banish, blackball*, boycott, censure, damn, denounce, deport, doom*, embargo, excommunicate, exile, expatriate, expel, forbid, interdict, ostracize, outlaw, prohibit, reject, sentence; SEE CONCEPTS 25,121,317

prose [n] *written, nonrhythmic literature*
book, composition, essay, exposition, fiction, nonfiction, speech, story, talk, text, tongue*, writing; SEE CONCEPTS 268,271

prosecute [v1] *bring action against in court*
arraign, bring suit, bring to trial, contest, do, haul into court*, indict, involve in litigation, law, litigate, prefer charges, pull up, put away*, put on docket, put on trial, see in court*, seek redress, sue, summon, take to court, try, turn on the heat*; SEE CONCEPT 317

prosecute [v2] *follow through, persevere*
carry on, carry through, conduct, continue, direct, discharge, engage in, execute, follow up, manage, perform, persist, practice, pursue, put

through, see through, wage, work at; SEE CON-
CEPT *91*

prospect [*n1*] *outlook for future*
anticipation, calculation, chance, contemplation,
expectancy, expectation, forecast, future, hope, in
the cards*, irons in the fire*, likelihood, odds,
opening, plan, possibility, presumption, probability, promise, proposal, thought; SEE CONCEPTS
689,693

prospect [*n2*] *landscape, vista*
aspect, lookout, outlook, overlook, panorama,
perspective, scape, scene, sight, spectacle, view,
vision; SEE CONCEPTS *509,628*

prospect [*v*] *look for; seek*
delve, dig, explore, go after, go into, inquire, investigate, look, look into, probe, search, sift, survey; SEE CONCEPT *216*

prospective [*adj*] *anticipated, potential*
about to be, approaching, awaited, coming, considered, destined, eventual, expected, forthcoming, future, hoped-for, imminent, impending,
intended, likely, looked-for, planned, possible,
promised, proposed, soon-to-be, to be*, to come;
SEE CONCEPTS *548,552*

prospectus [*n*] *details, outline of event*
announcement, catalogue, conspectus, design,
list, plan, program, scheme, syllabus, synopsis;
SEE CONCEPT *283*

prosper [*v*] *be fortunate; succeed*
advance, arrive, augment, batten, bear, bear fruit,
become rich, become wealthy, be enriched, benefit, bloom, blossom, catch on*, do well, do won-
ders*, fare well, fatten*, feather nest*, flourish,
flower, gain, get on*, get there*, go places*, go to
town*, grow rich, hit it big, hit the jackpot*, increase, make a killing*, make good*, make it*,
make mark*, make money, make out*, multiply,
produce, progress, rise, score*, strike it rich*,
thrive, turn out well, yield; SEE CONCEPT *706*

prosperity [*n*] *affluence, good fortune*
abundance, accomplishment, advantage, arrival,
bed of roses*, benefit, boom, clover, do, ease*,
easy street*, exorbitance, expansion, flying colors*, fortune, good, good times, gravy train*,
growth, high on the hog*, increase, inflation, interest, life of luxury*, luxury, opulence, plente-
ousness, plenty, prosperousness, riches, success,
successfulness, the good life*, thriving, velvet,
victory, wealth, welfare, well-being; SEE CON-
CEPTS *335,706*

prosperous [*adj1*] *successful, thriving*
affluent, blooming, booming, comfortable, doing
well, easy, flourishing, fortunate, halcyon, in clover*, in the money*, lousy rich, lucky, mainline*, moneyed, money to burn*, on top of heap*,
opulent, owning, prospering, rich, roaring, robust,
sitting pretty*, snug, substantial, upper-class*,
uptown, wealthy, well, well-heeled*, well-off,
well-to-do; SEE CONCEPTS *334,528*

prosperous [*adj2*] *promising, advantageous*
appropriate, auspicious, bright, convenient, desirable, favorable, felicitous, fortunate, good,
happy, lucky, opportune, profitable, propitious,
seasonable, timely, well-timed; SEE CONCEPTS
548,572

prostitute [*n*] *person who sells own abilities, talent, or name for inferior purpose*
betrayer, cheater, deceiver, gigolo, hustler, seducer; SEE CONCEPT *412*

prostitute [*v*] *to put one's talent to an unworthy
use*
abuse, cheapen, corrupt, debase, debauch, degrade, demean, deprave, devalue, misapply, misemploy, misuse, pervert, profane, vitiate; SEE
CONCEPTS *156,645*

prostrate [*adj1*] *flat, horizontal*
abject, bowed low, procumbent, prone, reclining,
recumbent, supine; SEE CONCEPT *583*

prostrate [*adj2*] *helpless*
beaten, defenseless, disarmed, impotent, open,
overcome, overpowered, overwhelmed, paralyzed, powerless, reduced, weak; SEE CONCEPT
542

prostrate [*adj3*] *tired, worn*
crippled, dejected, depressed, disarmed, drained,
drowned, exhausted, fagged*, fallen, frazzled*,
immobilized, incapacitated, inconsolable,
knocked over*, obedient, overcome, paralyzed,
pooped*, spent*, submissive, subservient, tuckered*, wearied, worn out; SEE CONCEPTS *406,485*

prostrate [*v1*] *fall on knees; submit*
abase, bow, bow down, cast before, cringe, fall at
feet, give in, grovel, kneel, kowtow*, obey, surrender; SEE CONCEPT *384*

prostrate [*v2*] *overwhelm; wear out*
bring low, cripple, debilitate, defeat, destroy, disable, disarm, drain, drown, exhaust, fatigue, fell,
floor, frazzle*, immobilize, impair, incapacitate,
knock over, level, mow*, overcome, overpower,
overthrow, overtire, overturn, paralyze, reduce,
ruin, sap, tire, tucker out*, weary, whelm, wreck;
SEE CONCEPTS *95,250,252*

protagonist [*n*] *person who takes the lead; central
figure of narrative*
advocate, central character, champion, combatant,
exemplar, exponent, hero, idol, lead, lead character, leader, mainstay, prime mover, principal,
standard-bearer, warrior; SEE CONCEPTS *352,
359,423*

protect [*v*] *take care of; guard from harm*
assure, bulwark, care for, champion, chaperon,
conserve, cover, cover all bases*, cover up, cushion, defend, fend, foster, give refuge, give sanctuary*, go to bat for*, harbor, hedge, insulate,
keep, keep safe, look after, preserve, ride shotgun
for*, safeguard, save, screen, secure, sentinel,
shade, shelter, shield, shotgun*, stand guard,
stonewall*, support, take under wing*, watch,
watch over; SEE CONCEPTS *96,134*

protection [*n*] *care, guardianship*
aegis, armament, armor, assurance, barrier,
buffer, bulwark, camouflage, certainty, charge,
conservation, cover, custody, defense, fix, guard,
guarding, insurance, invulnerability, preservation,
protecting, reassurance, refuge, safeguard, safekeeping, safety, salvation, screen, security, self-
defense, shelter, shield, stability, strength, surety,
tutelage, umbrella*, ward, wardship; SEE CON-
CEPTS *712,729*

protective [*adj*] *guarding, securing*
careful, conservational, conservative, covering,
custodial, defensive, emergency, guardian, insu-
lating, jealous, possessive, preservative, protecting, safeguarding, sheltering, shielding, vigilant,
warm, watchful; SEE CONCEPTS *542,550*

protest [*n*] *complaint, disapproval*
bellyache*, big stink*, blackball*, challenge,
clamor, declaration, demonstration, demur, demurral, difficulty, dissent, flak*, formal com-

pr
pr

plaint, grievance, gripe, grouse*, holler*, howl, kick*, knock*, march, moratorium, nix, objection, outcry, protestation, question, rally, remonstrance, remonstration, revolt, riot, stink*, tumult, turmoil; SEE CONCEPTS 52,54,300

protest [v] *complain, disapprove; argue against*
affirm, assert, asseverate, attest, avouch, avow, back-talk*, be against, be displeased by, blast*, buck, combat, constate, contend, cry out, declare, demonstrate, demur, disagree, except, expostulate, fight, holler, howl, insist, inveigh against, kick*, maintain, make a stink*, object, oppose, predicate, profess, put up a fight*, rebel, remonstrate, resist, revolt, say no*, sound off*, squawk*, take exception*, testify, thumbs down*; SEE CONCEPTS 46,52,54,300

protocol [n] *rules of conduct, behavior in certain situation*
agreement, code, compact, concordat, contract, conventions, courtesy, covenant, custom, decorum, etiquette, formalities, good form, manners, obligation, order, pact, politesse, propriety, p's and q's*, treaty; SEE CONCEPTS 684,688

prototype [n] *original, example*
ancestor, antecedent, antecessor, archetype, criterion, first, forerunner, ideal, mock-up*, model, norm, paradigm, pattern, precedent, precursor, predecessor, standard, type; SEE CONCEPT 686

protract [v] *extend, draw out*
continue, cool*, defer, delay, drag on*, drag out*, draw, elongate, hold off, hold up, keep going, lengthen, pad*, postpone, procrastinate, prolong, prolongate, put off, put on hold, spin out*, stall, stretch, stretch out; SEE CONCEPTS 237,239,250

protrude [v] *stick out*
beetle, bulge, butt out, come through, distend, extend, extrude, jut, jut out, obtrude, overhang, point, poke, pop, pouch, pout, project, shoot out, stand out, start, stick up, swell; SEE CONCEPTS 208,746

protuberance [n] *lump, outgrowth*
bulge, bump, excrescence, jut, jutting, knob, outthrust, process, projection, prominence, protrusion, swelling, tumor; SEE CONCEPTS 471,824

proud [adj 1] *pleased, pleasing*
appreciative, august, content, contented, dignified, eminent, fiery, fine, glad, glorious, gorgeous, grand, gratified, gratifying, great, greathearted, honored, illustrious, imposing, impressive, magnificent, majestic, memorable, noble, red-letter*, rewarding, satisfied, satisfying, self-respecting, spirited, splendid, stately, sublime, superb, valiant, vigorous, well-pleased; SEE CONCEPTS 403,572,574

proud [adj 2] *arrogant, self-important*
bloated, boastful, cavalier, cocky*, conceited, contemptuous, cool*, disdainful, dismissive, domineering, egotistic, egotistical, haughty, high-and-mighty*, high-handed*, huffy*, imperious, insolent, lofty, narcissistic, ostentatious, overbearing, pompous, presumptuous, pretentious, puffed up*, scornful, self-satisfied, sniffy*, snobbish, snooty*, stuck-up*, supercilious, superior, vain, vainglorious; SEE CONCEPTS 401,542

prove [v] *establish facts; put to a test*
add up, affirm, analyze, ascertain, assay, attest, authenticate, back, bear out, certify, check, confirm, convince, corroborate, declare, demonstrate, determine, document, end up, evidence, evince, examine, experiment, explain, find, fix, have a case*, justify, make evident, manifest, pan out*, result, settle, show, show clearly, show once and for all*, substantiate, sustain, test, testify, trial, try, turn out, uphold, validate, verify, warrant, witness; SEE CONCEPTS 57,118,138

proverb [n] *saying referring to common fact, knowledge*
adage, aphorism, apophthegm, axiom, byword, catch phrase, daffodil*, dictum, epigram, folk wisdom, gnome, maxim, moral, motto, platitude, precept, repartee, saw*, text, truism, witticism, word; SEE CONCEPTS 275,278

proverbial [adj] *conventional, traditional*
accepted, acknowledged, archetypal, axiomatic, current, customary, famed, familiar, famous, general, legendary, notorious, self-evident, time-honored, typical, unquestioned, well-known; SEE CONCEPT 530

provide [v1] *supply, support*
accommodate, add, administer, afford, arrange, bestow, bring, care, cater, contribute, dispense, equip, favor, feather*, feed, fit, fit out, fix up, fix up with, furnish, give, grant, hand over, heel*, impart, implement, indulge, keep, lend, line, look after, maintain, minister, outfit, prepare, present, procure, produce, proffer, provision, ration, ready, render, replenish, serve, stake, stock, stock up*, store, sustain, take care of, transfer, turn out, yield; SEE CONCEPTS 108,110,136,140

provide [v2] *determine, specify*
condition, lay down, necessitate, require, state, stipulate; SEE CONCEPTS 18,646

provident [adj] *careful, frugal*
canny, cautious, discreet, economical, expedient, far-sighted, foresighted, judicious, penny-pinching*, politic, prepared, prudent, sagacious, saving, shrewd, sparing, thrifty, tight, unwasteful, vigilant, well-prepared, wise; SEE CONCEPTS 334,401

providing/provided [conj] *as long as; with the understanding*
contingent upon, given, if, if and only if, in case, in the case that, in the event, on condition, on the assumption, on these terms, subject to, supposing, with the proviso; SEE CONCEPTS 544,546

province [n] *area of rule, responsibility*
arena, bailiwick, business, calling, canton, capacity, champaign, charge, colony, concern, county, demesne, department, dependency, district, division, domain, dominion, duty, employment, field, function, jurisdiction, line, office, orbit, part, post, pursuit, realm, region, role, section, shire, sphere, terrain, territory, tract, walk, work, zone; SEE CONCEPTS 198,349,362,508,532

provincial [adj] *countrified; limited*
bigoted, bucolic, country, hidebound, homegrown, homespun, insular, inward-looking, local, narrow, narrow-minded, parochial, pastoral, petty, rude, rural, rustic, sectarian, small-minded, small-town, uninformed, unpolished, unsophisticated; SEE CONCEPTS 403,549,589

provision [n1] *supplies, supplying*
accouterment, arrangement, catering, emergency, equipping, fitting out, foundation, furnishing, groundwork, outline, plan, prearrangement, precaution, preparation, procurement, providing, stock, store, supplying; SEE CONCEPTS 140,712

provision/proviso [n2] *stipulation, condition of agreement*
agreement, catch*, Catch-22*, clause, demand,

fine print*, joker*, kicker*, limitation, prerequisite, qualification, requirement, reservation, restriction, rider, small print*, specification, stipulation, strings*, term, terms; SEE CONCEPTS *270,684,711*

provisional [adj] *contingent, tentative*
conditional, dependent, ephemeral, experimental, interim, limited, makeshift, passing, pro tem, provisionary, provisory, qualified, rough-and-ready*, stopgap*, temporary, test, transient, transitional; SEE CONCEPTS *546,554,711*

provocation [n] *incitement, stimulus*
affront, annoyance, bothering, brickbat*, casus belli, cause, challenge, dare, defy, grabber*, grievance, grounds, harassment, incentive, indignity, inducement, injury, instigation, insult, irking, justification, motivation, offense, provoking, reason, taunt, vexation, vexing; SEE CONCEPTS *14,240,532*

provocative [adj1] *aggravating*
annoying, challenging, disturbing, exciting, galling, goading, heady, incensing, inciting, influential, inspirational, insulting, intoxicating, offensive, outrageous, provoking, pushing, spurring, stimulant, stimulating; SEE CONCEPT *529*

provocative [adj2] *sexually stimulating*
alluring, arousing, enchanting, erotic, exciting, heady, interesting, intoxicating, intriguing, inviting, seductive, sexy, stimulating, suggestive, tantalizing, tempting; SEE CONCEPTS *372,537*

provoke [v1] *make angry*
abet, abrade, affront, aggravate, anger, annoy, bother, bug*, chafe, enrage, exasperate, exercise, foment, fret, gall*, get*, get on one's nerves*, get under one's skin*, grate, hit where one lives*, incense, incite, inflame, infuriate, insult, irk, irritate, madden, make blood boil*, make waves*, nag, offend, perturb, pique, put out, raise, rile, roil, ruffle, set*, set on*, try one's patience*, upset, vex, whip up*, work into lather*, work up*; SEE CONCEPTS *7,19*

provoke [v2] *start, evoke; stimulate*
animate, arouse, awaken, begin, bestir, bring about, bring down, bring on, bring to one's feet*, build up, call forth, cause, challenge, draw forth, electrify, elicit, enthuse, excite, fire, fire up*, galvanize, generate, give rise to, incite, induce, inflame, innervate, inspire, instigate, kindle, lead to, make, motivate, move, occasion, pique, precipitate, prime, produce, promote, prompt, quicken, rally, rouse, roust, stir, suscitate, thrill, titillate, titivate, waken, whet; SEE CONCEPTS *7,19,22,221,242*

prowess [n1] *ability, skill*
accomplishment, address, adeptness, adroitness, aptitude, attainment, command, deftness, dexterity, excellence, expertise, expertness, facility, genius, mastery, readiness, sleight, talent; SEE CONCEPT *630*

prowess [n2] *bravery*
backbone*, boldness, courage, daring, dauntlessness, fearlessness, gallantry, grit*, guts*, heart*, heroism, intrepidity, mettle, moxie*, nerve, pluck, right stuff*, spunk, starch*, stomach*, stuff*, true grit*, valiance, valiancy, valor, valorousness, what it takes*; SEE CONCEPTS *411,633*

prowl [v] *move stealthily*
cruise, hunt, lurk, nose around*, patrol, range, roam, rove, scavenge, skulk, slink, snake, sneak, stalk, steal, stroll, tramp; SEE CONCEPT *151*

proximity [n] *nearness to something*
adjacency, appropinquity, closeness, concurrence, contiguity, contiguousness, immediacy, juxtaposition, propinquity, togetherness; SEE CONCEPT *747*

prudent [adj] *wise, sensible in action and thought*
advisable, canny, careful, cautious, circumspect, discerning, discreet, economical, far-sighted, frugal, hedging one's bets*, judgmatic, judicious, leery, playing safe*, politic, provident, reasonable, sagacious, sage, sane, sapient, shrewd, sound, sparing, tactical, thinking twice*, thrifty, vigilant, wary; SEE CONCEPTS *401,542*

prudish [adj] *shy and strict in behavior*
affected, artificial, austere, bigoted, conventional, demure, fastidious, finicky*, genteel, illiberal, mincing, narrow, narrow-minded, offish, overexact, overmodest, overnice, precise, pretentious, priggish*, prim, prissy*, proper, puritanical, rigid, rigorous, scrupulous, severe, simpering, square, squeamish*, starchy*, stern, stiff*, stilted, strait-laced, stuffy, uptight*, Victorian*; SEE CONCEPT *401*

prune [v] *trim; cut short*
clip, cut back, dock, eliminate, exclude, gut, knock off, lop, pare down, reduce, shape, shave, shear, shorten, skive, snip, thin; SEE CONCEPTS *137,176,236,247*

pry [v1] *interfere in someone else's business*
be a busybody*, be all ears*, be curious, be inquisitive, be nosy, bug*, ferret out, gape, gaze, hunt, inquire, intrude, investigate, listen in, meddle, nose, peek, peep, peer, poke, poke nose into*, ransack, reconnoiter, rubberneck*, search, snoop, spy, stare, tap, tune in on*, wiretap; SEE CONCEPTS *216,384,623*

pry [v2] *force or break open*
disengage, disjoin, divide, elevate, elicit, extort, extract, heave, hoist, jimmy, lever, lift, move, pick up, press, prize, pull, push, raise, rear, separate, take up, tear, tilt, turn, turn out, twist, uplift, upraise, uprear, wrest, wring; SEE CONCEPTS *196,206,211*

psalm [n] *song of praise*
canticle, celebration, chant, chorale, eulogy, hymn, paean, shout, verse; SEE CONCEPT *595*

pseudo [adj] *artificial, fake*
bogus, counterfeit, ersatz, false, imitation, mock, not genuine, not kosher*, not legit*, not real, phony, pirate, pretend, pretended, quasi*, sham*, simulated, spurious, wrong; SEE CONCEPT *582*

pseudonym [n] *false name*
AKA*, alias, ananym, anonym, assumed name, handle*, incognito*, nickname, nom de guerre, nom de plume, pen name, professional name, stage name, summer name*; SEE CONCEPTS *268,683*

psyche [n] *innermost self; personality*
anima, animus, character, ego, élan vital, essential nature, individuality, inner child, inner self, mind, pneuma, self, soul, spirit, spirituality, subconscious, true being; SEE CONCEPTS *410,411*

psychedelic [adj] *affecting the mind so as to produce vivid visions*
consciousness-expanding, crazy*, experimental, freaky*, hallucinatory, hallucinogenic, kaleidoscopic, mind-bending*, mind-blowing*, mind-changing, mind-expanding*, multicolored*, psychoactive, psychotomimetic, psychotropic, trip*; SEE CONCEPTS *529,537*

pr
ps

psychiatrist [n] *person who treats mental disorders*
analyst, clinician, doctor, psychoanalyst, psychologist, psychotherapist, shrink*, therapist; SEE CONCEPT 357

psychic [adj] *extrasensory in perception*
analytic, cerebral, clairvoyant, immaterial, impressible, impressionable, intellective, intellectual, mental, metaphysical, mystic, occult, preternatural, psychal, psychical, psychogenic, psychological, responsive, sensible, sensile, sensitive, sentient, spiritual, supernatural, supersensible, supersensitive, supersensory, supersensual, susceptible, susceptive, telekinetic, telepathic, transmundane, unworldly; SEE CONCEPTS 402, 403

psychobabble [n] *rhetoric using psychological-terms*
argot, buzzword, jargon, patter, pop psych*, psychospeak, self-help; SEE CONCEPT 275

psychological [adj] *concerning the mind*
cerebral, cognitive, emotional, experimental, imaginary, intellective, intellectual, in the mind, mental, psychical, subconscious, subjective, unconscious; SEE CONCEPTS 403,536

psychology [n] *study of the mind; emotional and mental constitution*
attitude, behaviorism, medicine, mental make-up, mental processes, personality study, psych*, science of the mind, therapy, way of thinking*, where head is at*; SEE CONCEPTS 349,360,410

psychopath [n] *person who is mentally deranged, often prone to hurt others*
antisocial personality, insane person, lunatic, mad person, maniac, mental case*, nutcase*, psycho*, psychotic, schizoid*, sociopath, unstable personality; SEE CONCEPT 412

psychotic [adj] *mentally deranged*
certifiable*, crazy, demented, distracted, flipped-out*, insane, lunatic, mad, manic-depressive, mental, non compos mentis, nuts*, off one's rocker*, over the edge*, psycho*, psychopathic, schizophrenic, sick, unbalanced, unhinged*; SEE CONCEPT 403

pub [n] *business where liquor and food are served*
after-hours joint*, ale house*, bar, barroom, beer joint*, drinkery, drinking establishment, gin mill*, inn, joint*, lounge, public house, roadhouse, saloon, taproom, tavern; SEE CONCEPTS 439,448,449

puberty [n] *young adulthood*
adolescence, awkward stage*, boyhood, girlhood, greenness*, high-school years, juvenescence, juvenility, potency, preadolescence, pubescence, spring*, springtide*, springtime*, teenage years, teens, youth, youthfulness; SEE CONCEPT 817

public [n] *people of community; people interested in something*
audience, bodies*, buyers, citizens, clientele, commonalty, community, country, electorate, everyone, followers, following, heads, masses, men and women, mob, multitude, nation, patrons, people, populace, population, society, suite, supporters, voters; SEE CONCEPTS 379,417

public [adj1] *community, general*
accessible, city, civic, civil, common, communal, conjoint, conjunct, country, federal, free, free to all, government, governmental, intermutual, metropolitan, municipal, mutual, national, not private, open, open-door, popular, social, state, universal, unrestricted, urban, widespread, without charge; SEE CONCEPTS 536,576

public [adj2] *known, acknowledged*
exposed, general, in circulation, notorious, obvious, open, overt, patent, plain, popular, prevalent, published, recognized, social, societal, usual, vulgar, widespread; SEE CONCEPTS 267, 530

publication [n1] *printing of written or visual material*
advertisement, airing, announcement, appearance, broadcast, broadcasting, communication, declaration, disclosure, discovery, dissemination, divulgation, issuance, issuing, notification, proclamation, promulgation, pronunciamento, publicity, public relations, publishing, reporting, revelation, statement, ventilation, writing; SEE CONCEPTS 60,274,292

publication [n2] *something printed for reading*
annual, book, booklet, brochure, handbill, information, issue, leaflet, magazine, news, newsletter, newspaper, pamphlet, periodical; SEE CONCEPT 280

publicity [n] *promotion of something, someone*
advertising, announcement, announcing, attention, ballyhoo*, big noise*, billing, blurb*, boost*, broadcasting, build-up*, clout*, commercial, currency, distribution, fame, handout, hoopla*, hype*, ink*, limelight*, noise*, notoriety, pitch, plug*, PR*, press, press-agentry, promo*, promulgation, propaganda, public notice, public relations, puff*, puffery*, pushing, réclame, release, report, scratch*, spotlight*, spread, write-up; SEE CONCEPTS 274,280,293

publicize [v] *make widely known; promote*
advance, advertise, announce, bill, billboard, boost*, broadcast, build up*, cry, drum*, extol, hard sell*, headline, hype*, immortalize, make a pitch for, pitch, play up*, plug*, press-agent, promulgate, propagandize, puff*, push, put on the map*, skywrite*, soft-sell*, splash, spot*, spotlight*, spread, tout, trumpet*, write up; SEE CONCEPTS 60,292,324

pucker [n] *wrinkle*
crease, crinkle, crumple, fold, furrow, plait, ruck, ruckle; SEE CONCEPT 754

pucker [v] *draw together; wrinkle*
cockle, compress, condense, contract, crease, crinkle, crumple, fold, furrow, gather, knit, purse, ruckle, ruck up, ruffle, screw up, squeeze, tighten; SEE CONCEPTS 185,219

pudgy [adj] *slightly fat*
chubby*, hefty, plump, plumpish, rotund, round, stout, thick-bodied, tubby*; SEE CONCEPTS 491,773

puerile [adj] *childish*
babyish, babylike, callow, foolish, green*, immature, inane, inexperienced, infantile, irresponsible, jejune, juvenile, naive, petty, ridiculous, silly, trivial, unfledged, ungrown, weak, young; SEE CONCEPTS 401,578,797

puff [n1] *blast of air*
breath, draft, drag, draught, draw, emanation, flatus, flurry, gust, pull, smoke, waft, whiff, wind, wisp; SEE CONCEPTS 437,524

puff [n2] *advertisement*
advertising, blurb*, boost*, buildup*, commendation, favorable mention, good word, hype*, laudation, plug*, praise, press-agentry, promo*,

promotion, publicity, puffery*, push*, sales talk, write-up; SEE CONCEPTS 69,278,324

puff [v1] *inhale or exhale air*
blow, breathe, distend, drag, draw, enlarge, fill, gasp, gulp, heave, huff, huff and puff*, inflate, pant, pull at, pull on, smoke, suck, swell, wheeze, whiff; SEE CONCEPTS 163,185,526

puff [v2] *publicize*
admire, advertise, ballyhoo*, blow up*, build, commend, congratulate, cry*, flatter, hype*, overpraise, plug*, praise, press-agent*, promote, push; SEE CONCEPTS 49,69

puffy [adj] *swollen*
billowy, bloated, blown, bulgy, distended, distent, enlarged, expanded, full, increased, inflamed, inflated, puffed up; SEE CONCEPT 485

pugnacious [adj] *belligerent*
aggressive, antagonistic, argumentative, bellicose, brawling, cantankerous, chip on shoulder*, choleric, combative, contentious, defiant, disputatious, have a bone to pick*, hot-tempered, irascible, irritable, itching to fight*, militant, petulant, pushing, pushy*, quarrelsome, ready to fight, rebellious, salty*, scrappy*, self-assertive, truculent, warlike; SEE CONCEPTS 401,542

pull [v1] *drawing something with force*
cull, dislocate, drag, evolve, extract, gather, haul, heave, jerk, lug, paddle, pick, pluck, remove, rend, rip, row, schlepp*, sprain, strain, stretch, take out, tear, tow, trail, truck, tug, twitch, uproot, weed*, wrench, yank; SEE CONCEPT 206

pull [v2] *attract*
draw, entice, get, lure, magnetize, obtain, pick up, secure, win; SEE CONCEPT 11

pull down [v] *destroy; knock over*
annihilate, bulldoze, decimate, demolish, destruct, dismantle, let down, lower, raze, remove, ruin, take down, tear down, wreck; SEE CONCEPT 252

pull in [v1] *arrest*
apprehend, bust, collar, detain, nab, nail, pick up, pinch, run in, take into custody; SEE CONCEPTS 90,317

pull in [v2] *attract, obtain*
absorb, bring in, clear, draw, draw in, earn, gain, gross, make, net, pocket, suck, take home*; SEE CONCEPT 120

pull off [v] *accomplish*
achieve, bring off, carry out, manage, score, score a success, secure, succeed, win; SEE CONCEPTS 91,706

pull out [v] *quit*
abandon, depart, evacuate, exit, get off, go, leave, retire, retreat, shove off, stop, stop participating, take off, withdraw; SEE CONCEPTS 119,121,195

pull through [v] *recover*
come through, get better, get over, improve, rally, ride out*, survive, triumph, weather*; SEE CONCEPTS 82,700

pull up [v] *stop, halt*
arrive, brake, bring up, come to a halt, come to a stop, draw up, fetch up, get there, haul up, pause, reach a standstill; SEE CONCEPTS 119,121,159

pulp [n] *flesh of plant, animal*
batter, curd, dough, grume, jam, marrow, mash, mush, pap, paste, pomace, poultice, sarcocarp, semisolid, soft part, sponge, triturate; SEE CONCEPTS 399,428

pulp [adj] *cheap, vulgar, especially regarding reading material*
lurid, mushy, rubbish, sensational, trash, trashy; SEE CONCEPT 267

pulp [v] *mash, pulverize*
bruise, coagulate, crush, gelatinate, macerate, squash, triturate; SEE CONCEPTS 208,219

pulpit [n] *structure from which sermon is given*
desk, lectern, platform, podium, rostrum, soapbox*, stage, stump*; SEE CONCEPTS 368,443

pulsate/pulse [v] *quiver, beat*
drum, fluctuate, hammer, oscillate, palpitate, pound, pump, roar, throb, thrum, thud, thump, tick, vibrate; SEE CONCEPTS 147,185

pulse [n] *rhythm, beat*
beating, oscillation, pulsation, stroke, throb, throbbing, vibration; SEE CONCEPTS 147,185

pulverize [v1] *smash by beating, crushing*
abrade, atomize, beat, bray, break up, buck, comminute, contriturate, crumble, crunch, crush, flour, fragment, fragmentalize, fragmentize, granulate, grate, grind, levigate, micronize, mill, mull, pestle, pound, powder, shatter, splinter, triturate; SEE CONCEPTS 186,219

pulverize [v2] *destroy*
annihilate, crush, decimate, defeat, demolish, destruct, dynamite, flatten, rub out*, ruin, shatter, smash, tear down*, vanquish, vaporize, wax, wreck; SEE CONCEPT 252

pump [v1] *draw or push out*
bail out, blow up, dilate, distend, draft, drain, draw, draw off, drive, drive out, elevate, empty, force, force out, inflate, inject, pour, push, send, siphon, supply, swell, tap; SEE CONCEPTS 142,206,208

pump [v2] *question relentlessly*
cross-examine, draw out, give the third degree*, grill, interrogate, probe, query, question, quiz, worm out of*; SEE CONCEPTS 48,53

pun [n] *play on words*
ambiguity, calembour, conceit, double entendre, double meaning, equivoque, joke, paronomasia, quibble, quip, witticism; SEE CONCEPTS 273,278

punch [n1/v1] *hit*
bash, belt, biff, blow, bop, box, buffet, clip, clout, cuff, dig, jab, jog, knock, lollop, nudge, one-two*, plug, plunk*, poke, prod, pummel, rap, shot, slam, slap, slug, smack, smash, sock, strike, stroke, thrust, thump, wallop; SEE CONCEPT 189

punch [n2] *energy, vigor*
bite, cogency, drive, effectiveness, force, forcefulness, impact, point, validity, validness, verve; SEE CONCEPTS 676,682

punch [v2] *perforate, prick*
bore, cut, drill, jab, pierce, poke, puncture, stab, stamp; SEE CONCEPT 220

punctilious [adj] *careful, finicky*
ceremonious, conscientious, conscionable, conventional, exact, formal, formalistic, fussy, good eye*, heedful, meticulous, nice, observant, overconscientious, overscrupulous, painstaking, particular, persnickety, precise, proper, punctual, right on*, scrupulous, strict; SEE CONCEPTS 401,542,557

punctual [adj] *on time*
accurate, careful, conscientious, conscionable, constant, cyclic, dependable, early, exact, expeditious, fussy, heedful, in good time*, meticulous, on schedule, on the button*, on the dot*, on

the nose*, painstaking, particular, periodic, precise, prompt, punctilious, quick, ready, recurrent, regular, reliable, scrupulous, seasonable, steady, strict, timely, under the wire*; SEE CONCEPTS 544,550,799

punctuate [v] *lay stress on*
accent, accentuate, break, divide, emphasize, interject, interrupt, intersect, intersperse, mark, pepper*, point, point up*, separate, sprinkle, stress, underline; SEE CONCEPTS 49,79,98,266

puncture [n] *hole, rupture*
break, cut, damage, flat, flat tire*, jab, leak, nick, opening, perforation, prick, slit, stab; SEE CONCEPTS 309,513,674

puncture [v1] *poke hole in*
bore, cut, cut through, deflate, drill, go down, go flat, knife, lacerate, lance, nick, open, penetrate, perforate, pierce, prick, punch, riddle, rupture; SEE CONCEPTS 137,220

puncture [v2] *deflate someone's idea, feelings*
blow sky high*, discourage, discredit, disillusion, disprove, explode, flatten*, humble, knock bottom out*, knock props from under*, poke full of holes*, shoot full of holes*, take down a peg*, take wind out of sails*; SEE CONCEPTS 7,19,54

pundit [n] *person who is authority*
auger, bookworm, brain*, buff, cereb*, cognoscenti, egghead*, expert, intellectual, learned one, philosopher, professor, savant, scholar, solon, teacher, thinker; SEE CONCEPTS 416,423

pungent [adj1] *highly flavored*
acid, acrid, aromatic, bitter, effluvious, hot, nosey*, odoriferous, peppery, piquant, poignant, racy, rich, salty, seasoned, sharp, snappy, sour, spicy, stinging, stinking*, strong, tangy, tart, whiffy*, zesty; SEE CONCEPT 613

pungent [adj2] *sharp, stinging in speech*
acrimonious, acute, barbed, biting, bitter, caustic, cutting, exciting, hot, incisive, keen, mordant, penetrating, peppery, piercing, poignant, pointed, provocative, racy, salt, salty, sarcastic, scathing, snappy, spicy, stimulating, stringent, telling, trenchant, zesty; SEE CONCEPT 267

punish [v] *penalize for wrongdoing*
abuse, attend to, batter, beat, beat up, blacklist, castigate, chasten, chastise, correct, crack down on*, cuff, debar, defrock, discipline, dismiss, do in, execute, exile, expel, fine, flog, give a going over*, give the works*, harm, hurt, immure, incarcerate, injure, knock about, lash, lecture, maltreat, misuse, oppress, paddle, rap knuckles*, reprove, rough up, scourge, sentence, slap wrist, spank, switch, teach a lesson, throw the book at*, train, whip; SEE CONCEPT 122

punishment [n] *penalty*
abuse, amercement, beating, castigation, chastening, chastisement, comeuppance, confiscation, correction, deprivation, disciplinary action, discipline, forfeit, forfeiture, gallows, hard work, infliction, just desserts*, lumps, maltreatment, mortification, mulct, ostracism, pain, penance, proof, punitive measures, purgatory, reparation, retribution, rod, rough treatment, sanction, sequestration, short shrift*, slave labor*, suffering, torture, trial, unhappiness, victimization, what for*; SEE CONCEPT 123

punitive [adj] *concerning punishment*
castigating, correctional, disciplinary, in reprisal, in retaliation, penal, punishing, punitory, retalia-

tive, retaliatory, revengeful, vindictive; SEE CONCEPT 319

puny [adj] *small, insignificant*
diminutive, feeble, fragile, frail, half-pint*, inconsequential, inferior, infirm, little, measly*, minor, niggling*, nothing, paltry, peanut*, peewee*, petty, picayune, piddling*, pint-sized*, runt, shrimp*, small-fry*, small time*, stunted, tiny, trifling, trivial, two-bit*, unconsequential, underfed, undersized, undeveloped, unsound, unsubstantial, weak, weakly, wee*, worthless, zero*, zilch*; SEE CONCEPTS 489,575,773

pupil [n] *person who is learning something*
adherent, attendant, beginner, bookworm*, brain*, catechumen, disciple, first-year student, follower, graduate student, junior, learner, neophyte, novice, satellite, scholar, schoolboy/girl, senior, sophomore, student, tenderfoot*, undergraduate; SEE CONCEPT 350

puppet [n] *person or toy manipulated by another*
creature, doll, dupe*, figurehead, figurine, instrument, jerk*, manikin, marionette, moppet, mouthpiece*, patsy*, pawn, pushover, schlemiel*, servant, soft touch*, stooge*, tool*, victim; SEE CONCEPTS 423,446

purchase [n] *possession obtained with money*
acquirement, acquisition, asset, bargain, booty*, buy, gain, investment, property, steal; SEE CONCEPTS 446,710

purchase [v] *buy, obtain*
achieve, acquire, attain, come by, cop*, deal in, earn, gain, get hold of, go shopping, invest, make a buy, make a purchase, market, patronize, pay for, pick up, procure, realize, redeem, secure, shop, shop for, take, take up, truck*, win; SEE CONCEPT 327

pure [adj1] *unmixed, genuine*
authentic, bright, classic, clear, complete, fair, flawless, kosher*, limpid, lucid, natural, neat, out-and-out*, pellucid, perfect, plain, plenary, pure and simple, real, simple, straight, total, transparent, true, twenty-four carat*, unadulterated, unalloyed, unclouded, undiluted, unmingled; SEE CONCEPT 485

pure [adj2] *clean, uncontaminated*
disinfected, germ-free, immaculate, intemerate, pasteurized, pristine, purified, refined, sanitary, snowy, spotless, stainless, sterile, sterilized, taintless, unadulterated, unblemished, undebased, unpolluted, unsoiled, unspotted, unstained, unsullied, untainted, untarnished, wholesome; SEE CONCEPT 621

pure [adj3] *virginal, chaste*
babe in woods*, blameless, celibate, clean, continent, decent, exemplary, fresh, good, guileless, honest, immaculate, inculpable, innocent, inviolate, irreproachable, kid, lily white*, maidenly, modest, pure as driven snow*, righteous, sinless, spotless, stainless, true, unblemished, unblighted, uncorrupted, undefiled, unprofaned, unspotted, unstained, unsullied, upright, virgin, virtuous, wet behind ears*, wide-eyed; SEE CONCEPT 372

pure [adj4] *absolute, utter*
blasted*, blessed*, complete, confounded, infernal*, mere, out-and-out, sheer, thorough, unmitigated, unqualified; SEE CONCEPTS 531,535

pure [adj5] *theoretical*
abstract, academic, philosophical, speculative, tentative, unproved; SEE CONCEPT 529

purely [adv] *simply, absolutely*
all, all in all, altogether, barely, completely, entirely, essentially, exactly, exclusively, in toto*, just, merely, only, plainly, quite, solely, totally, utterly, wholly; SEE CONCEPTS *531,544*

purge [n] *elimination, removal*
abolition, abstersion, catharsis, clarification, cleaning, cleanup, coup, crushing, disposal, disposition, ejection, eradication, evacuation, excretion, expulsion, expurgation, extermination, extirpation, liquidation, murder, purification, reign of terror*, suppression, witch hunt; SEE CONCEPTS *165,211,252*

purge [v] *rid of; clean out*
abolish, absolve, clarify, cleanse, clear, depurate, disabuse, dismiss, dispose of, do away with*, eject, eradicate, erase, excrete, exonerate, expel, expiate, expunge, exterminate, forgive, kill, liquidate, oust, pardon, prevent, purify, remove, rout out, shake out*, sweep out, unload, wash, wipe off map*, wipe out; SEE CONCEPTS *165,211,252*

purification [n] *freeing, cleansing*
ablution, absolution, atonement, baptism, bathing, catharsis, depuration, disinfection, distillation, expiation, expurgation, forgiveness, grace, lavation, laving, lustration, purgation, purge, purifying, rarefaction, rebirth, redemption, refinement, regeneration, salvation, sanctification, washing; SEE CONCEPTS *165,367*

purify [v] *free; make clean*
absolve, aerate, acrify, atone, chasten, clarify, clean, cleanse, clear, decontaminate, deodorize, depurate, deterge, disinfect, edulcorate, elutriate, exculpate, exonerate, expiate, filter, fumigate, lustrate, oxygenate, purge, rarify, redeem, refine, remit, sanctify, sanitize, shrive, sublimate, wash; SEE CONCEPTS *165,367*

purple [n/adj] *blue and red colors mixed together*
amaranthine, amethyst, bluish red, color, heliotrope, lavender, lilac, magenta, mauve, mulberry, orchid, perse, plum, pomegranate, reddish blue, violaceous, violet, wine; SEE CONCEPTS *618,622*

purport [n] *meaning, implication*
acceptation, aim, bearing, burden, connotation, core, design, drift, gist, heart, idea, import, intendment, intent, intention, matter, meat, message, nub, object, objective, pith, plan, point, purpose, score, sense, significance, significancy, signification, spirit, stuff, substance, tendency, tenor, thrust, understanding, upshot; SEE CONCEPTS *20,659,660,689*

purport [v] *assert, mean*
allege, betoken, claim, convey, declare, denote, express, imply, import, indicate, intend, maintain, point to, pose as, pretend, proclaim, profess, signify, suggest; SEE CONCEPTS *49,682*

purpose [n1] *intention, meaning, aim*
ambition, animus, aspiration, big idea*, bourn, calculation, design, desire, destination, determination, direction, dream, drift, end, expectation, function, goal, hope, idea, intendment, intent, mecca, mission, object, objective, plan, point, premeditation, principle, project, proposal, proposition, prospect, reason, resolve, scheme, scope, target, ulterior motive, view, whatfor*, where one's headed*, whole idea*, why and wherefore*, whyfor*, will, wish; SEE CONCEPTS *20,659, 660,689*

purpose [n2] *persistence, resolve*
confidence, constancy, determination, faith, firmness, resolution, single-mindedness, steadfastness, tenacity, will; SEE CONCEPTS *633,644*

purpose [n3] *use*
advantage, avail, benefit, duty, effect, function, gain, goal, good, mark, mission, object, objective, outcome, profit, result, return, target, utility; SEE CONCEPTS *658,694*

purpose [v] *intend, set sights on*
aim, aspire, bid for, commit, conclude, consider, contemplate, decide, design, determine, have a mind to*, have in view, intend, make up one's mind*, mean, meditate, mind, plan, ponder, propose, pursue, resolve, think to, work for, work toward; SEE CONCEPTS *18,36,87*

purposeful [adj] *resolved to do something*
bent, be out for blood*, bound, calculated, dead set on*, decided, deliberate, determined, firm, fixed, intense, intent, mean business*, obstinate, persistent, playing hard ball*, positive, purposive, resolute, settled, single-minded, stalwart, staunch, steadfast, steady, strong-willed, stubborn, teleological, tenacious, undeviating, unfaltering, unwavering; SEE CONCEPTS *326,403,542*

purposeless [adj] *useless, insignificant*
aimless, designless, desultory, drifting, empty, feckless, floundering, fustian, goalless, good-for-nothing*, haphazard, hit-or-miss*, indiscriminate, irregular, meaningless, motiveless, needless, nonsensical, pointless, purportless, random, senseless, uncalled for, undirected, unhelpful, unnecessary, unplanned, unprofitable, unpurposed, vacuous, wanton, worthless; SEE CONCEPTS *544,560*

purposely [adv] *intentionally*
advisedly, by design, calculatedly, consciously, deliberately, designedly, explicitly, expressly, knowingly, on purpose, prepensely, purposedly, willfully, with intent; SEE CONCEPTS *529,544*

purse [n1] *tote for carrying personal items*
bag, billfold, bursa, carryall, clutch, frame, handbag, hide, leather, lizard, moneybag, pocket, pocketbook, poke, pouch, receptacle, reticule, sack, wallet; SEE CONCEPTS *339,446,450,494*

purse [n2] *award; winnings*
coffers, exchequer, funds, gift, means, money, present, prize, resources, reward, stake, treasury, wealth, wherewithal; SEE CONCEPTS *337,344*

purse [v] *press together*
close, cockle, contract, crease, knit, pucker, ruffle, tighten, wrinkle; SEE CONCEPTS *185,208*

pursue [v1] *chase, follow*
accompany, attend, badger, bait, bird-dog*, bug, camp on the doorstep of*, chivy, dog*, fish*, give chase, go after, harass, harry, haunt, hound, hunt, hunt down, move behind, nose around*, oppress, persevere, persist, plague, play catch up*, poke around, prowl after, ride, run after, run down, scout out, search for, search high heaven*, search out, seek, shadow, stalk, tag, tail*, take out after*, trace, track, track down, trail; SEE CONCEPT *207*

pursue [v2] *have as one's goal*
aim for, aspire to, attempt, desire, go in for, go out for, have a go at, purpose, seek, strive for, try for, work for, work toward; SEE CONCEPTS *20,36*

pursue [v3] *persist, persevere*
adhere, apply oneself, carry on, conduct, continue, cultivate, engage in, hold to, keep on, maintain, perform, ply, practice, proceed, prosecute,

see through, tackle, wage, work at; SEE CONCEPTS *87,100,239*

pursue [*v4*] *seek social alliance with*
address, call, chase, chase after, court, date, go after, go for, pay attention, pay court*, play up to, rush*, spark, sue, sweetheart*, woo; SEE CONCEPT *384*

pursuit [*n1*] *chase, search*
following, going all out, hunt, hunting, inquiry, pursual, pursuance, pursuing, quest, reaching, seeking, stalk, tracking, trail, trailing; SEE CONCEPT *207*

pursuit [*n2*] *occupation, interest of person*
accomplishing, accomplishment, activity, biz*, business, calling, career, do*, employment, game*, go*, hang*, hobby, job, line*, occupation, pastime, pleasure, racket, thing*, undertaking, venture, vocation, work; SEE CONCEPT *349*

push [*n1*] *physical force*
advance, assault, attack, bearing, blow, butt, charge, drive, driving, effort, energy, exerting, exertion, forcing, impact, jolt, lean, mass, nudge, offensive, onset, poke, prod, propulsion, shove, shoving, straining, thrust, thrusting, weight; SEE CONCEPTS *200,208,641,724*

push [*n2*] *mental determination*
ambition, drive, dynamism, energy, enterprise, get-up-and-go*, go*, gumption*, guts*, initiative, pep, punch, snap, spunk, starch, vigor, vitality; SEE CONCEPTS *410,411*

push [*v1*] *thrust, press with force*
accelerate, bear down, budge, bulldoze*, bump, butt, crowd, crush against, depress, dig, drive, elbow, exert, force, gore, high pressure*, hustle, impel, jam, jostle, launch, lie on, make one's way*, move, muscle, nudge, poke, pour it on*, pressure, propel, put the arm on*, railroad*, ram*, rest on, shift, shoulder, shove, squash, squeeze, squish, steamroll*, stir, strain, strong-arm*; SEE CONCEPTS *200,208,243*

push [*v2*] *incite, urge*
bear down, browbeat, bulldoze*, coerce, constrain, dragoon, egg on*, encourage, exert influence, expedite, fire up*, goad, goose*, go to town on*, hurry, impel, influence, inspire, jolly, key up*, kid, lean on*, motivate, oblige, overpress, persuade, pour it on*, press, pressure, prod, push around, put the screws to*, put up to*, railroad*, sell on*, speed, speed up, spur, squeeze, steamroll*, strong-arm*, turn on*; SEE CONCEPTS *14,68,243*

push [*v3*] *advertise, promote*
advance, boost, cry up*, hype*, make known, plug*, propagandize, publicize, puff*; SEE CONCEPTS *49,324*

push off/push on [*v*] *leave; go to another place*
beat it*, continue, depart, exit, fare, get away, get lost*, go, go away, hie, hit the road*, journey, keep going, launch, light out, make oneself scarce*, make progress, pass, proceed, process, pull out, quit, repair, shove off, start, take off, travel, wend, withdraw; SEE CONCEPTS *195,704*

pushover [*n*] *something or someone easily influenced*
breeze, child's play*, chump*, cinch, duck soup*, easy game*, easy mark*, easy pickings*, fool, kid stuff*, picnic*, piece of cake*, setup, snap, soft touch*, stooge*, sucker, victim, walkover; SEE CONCEPTS *423,693*

pushy [*adj*] *aggressive, offensive*
ambitious, assertive, bold, brash, bumptious, forceful, loud, militant, obnoxious, obtrusive, officious, presumptuous, pushful, pushing, self-assertive; SEE CONCEPTS *401,404*

pussyfoot [*v*] *walk or act carefully*
avoid, beat around the bush*, be noncommittal, creep, dodge, equivocate, evade, glide, hedge, hem and haw*, lurk, prevaricate, prowl, shuffle, sidestep, sit on the fence*, skulk, slide, slink, slip, sneak, steal, tergiversate, tergiverse, tiptoe, tread warily, weasel*; SEE CONCEPTS *151,410*

put [*v1*] *position*
bring, concenter, concentrate, deposit, embed, establish, fasten, fix, fixate, focus, insert, install, invest, lay, nail, park, peg, place, plank, plank down, plant, plop, plunk, plunk down, quarter, repose, rest, rivet, seat, set, settle, situate, stick; SEE CONCEPT *201*

put [*v2*] *propose; express in words*
advance, air, bring forward, couch, express, formulate, forward, give, offer, phrase, pose, posit, prefer, present, propone, proposition, propound, render, set, set before, state, submit, suggest, tender, translate, transpose, turn, utter, vent, ventilate, word; SEE CONCEPTS *47,66,67*

put [*v3*] *commit, assign*
condemn, consign, constrain, doom, employ, enjoin, force, impose, induce, inflict, levy, make, oblige, require, set, subject, subject to; SEE CONCEPTS *14,242*

putative [*adj*] *commonly believed*
accepted, alleged, assumed, conjectural, hypothetical, imputed, presumed, presumptive, reported, reputed, supposed, suppositional, suppositious; SEE CONCEPT *529*

put away/put aside/put by [*v1/v*] *keep in reserve*
cache, deposit, keep, lay aside, lay away, lay by, lay in, put by, put out of the way, salt away*, save, set aside, squirrel away*, stockpile, store, store away*, stow away; SEE CONCEPTS *129,134*

put away [*v2*] *incarcerate*
certify, commit, confine, institutionalize, jail, lock up; SEE CONCEPT *317*

put away [*v3*] *consume*
devour, eat up, gobble*, gulp down, polish off*, punish, put down, shift, swill, wolf down*; SEE CONCEPT *169*

put away [*v4*] *kill*
assassinate, bury, cool*, cut off, destroy, dispatch, do away with, do in*, dust off*, execute, finish, inter, knock off*, liquidate, murder, plant, put down*, put out of its misery*, put to sleep*, slay, tomb; SEE CONCEPT *252*

put down [*v1*] *write into record*
enter, inscribe, jot down, log, record, set down, take down, transcribe, write down; SEE CONCEPT *79*

put down [*v2*] *subdue*
annihilate, crush, defeat, dismiss, extinguish, quash*, quell, reject, repress, silence, squash*, stamp out*, suppress; SEE CONCEPTS *95,252*

put down [*v3*] *comment negatively*
belittle, condemn, crush, decry, deflate, derogate, discount, dismiss, disparage, downcry, humiliate, minimize, mortify, opprobriate, reject, run down, shame, slight, snub, write off; SEE CONCEPT *54*

put-down [*n*] *nasty commentary*
cut*, dig*, disparagement, gibe*, humiliation, indignity, insult, jibe*, knock*, pan*, rebuff, sar-

casm, slight, sneer*, snub, suppression; SEE CONCEPTS 54,278

put off [v] *defer, delay*
adjourn, dally, dawdle, dillydally*, drag one's feet*, hold off, hold over, lag*, lay over, linger, loiter, poke*, postpone, prorogue, put back, reschedule, retard, shelve, stay, suspend, tarry, trail; SEE CONCEPTS 121,234

put on [v1] *pretend*
act, affect, assume, bluff, confound, confuse, counterfeit, deceive, don, fake, feign, make believe, masquerade, playact, pose, pull, put on a front, put on an act, sham, simulate, strike, take on, trick; SEE CONCEPT 59

put on [v2] *stage a performance*
do, mount, present, produce, show; SEE CONCEPT 292

put out [v1] *upset, irritate; inconvenience*
aggravate, anger, annoy, bother, burn, confound, discomfit, discommode, discompose, disconcert, discountenance, disoblige, displease, dissatisfy, disturb, embarrass, exasperate, gall, get*, grate, harass, impose upon, incommode, inflame, irk, nettle, perturb, provoke, put on the spot*, rile, roil, trouble, vex; SEE CONCEPTS 7,14,19

put out [v2] *extinguish fire*
blow out, douse, out, quench, smother, snuff out, stamp out; SEE CONCEPT 252

putrefy [v] *rot*
break down, corrupt, crumble, decay, decompose, deteriorate, disintegrate, go bad*, molder, putresce, spoil, stink, taint, turn; SEE CONCEPT 469

putrid [adj] *rotten, stinking*
bad, contaminated, corrupt, decayed, decomposed, fetid, foul, high, malodorous, moldered, nidorous, noisome, off, putrefied, rancid, rank, reeking, rotting, smelly, spoiled, strong, tainted, whiffy*; SEE CONCEPTS 485,598

putter [v] *dawdle*
doodle, fiddle, fritter, goof around*, loiter, mess, mess around*, niggle, poke*, potter*, puddle*, shuffle around, tinker*; SEE CONCEPTS 87,210

put up [v2] *accommodate guest*
bestow, billet, board, bunk, domicile, entertain, give lodging, harbor, house, lodge, make welcome, provide, quarter, take in; SEE CONCEPTS 324,384

put up [v2] *build, erect*
construct, fabricate, forge, make, put together, raise, rear, shape, uprear; SEE CONCEPT 168

puzzle [v1] *baffle, confuse*
addle, amaze, bamboozle*, beat, befog, befuddle, bemuse, bewilder, buffalo*, complicate, confound, discombobulate*, disconcert, distract, disturb, dumbfound, flabbergast, floor*, flummox, foil, frustrate, get to*, mystify, nonplus, obscure, perplex, pose, profundicate, psych out*, put off, rattle, snow*, stir, stumble, stump, throw; SEE CONCEPT 16

puzzle [v2] *wonder about*
ask oneself, brood, cudgel, marvel, mull over, muse, ponder, rack one's brains*, study, think about, think hard; SEE CONCEPT 17

puzzled [adj] *confused*
at a loss*, at sea*, baffled, bewildered, bollixed, clueless, come apart, come unzipped*, discombobulated*, dopey*, doubtful, floored*, foggy, fouled up*, hung up*, in a fog*, lost, loused up*, messed up*, mind-blown*, mixed up*, mucked up*, mystified, nonplussed, perplexed, rattled, screwed up*, shook, shook up, spaced out*, stuck, stumped, thrown, unglued*, without a clue; SEE CONCEPTS 403,690

puzzling [adj] *confusing*
abstruse, ambiguous, baffling, bewildering, beyond one, difficult, enigmatic, hard, incomprehensible, inexplicable, involved, knotty, labyrinthine, misleading, mystifying, obscure, perplexing, surprising, unaccountable, unclear, unfathomable; SEE CONCEPT 529

Q

quack [n] *person who pretends to be an expert*
actor, bum*, bunco artist, charlatan, cheat, con artist, counterfeit, counterfeiter, fake, faker, flimflammer*, four-flusher*, fraud, hoser*, humbug, impostor, mountebank, phony, playactor, pretender, pseudo*, put-on*, quacksalver*, sham, shammer*, shark*, sharp*, simulator, slicker*, whip*; SEE CONCEPT 412

quack [adj] *counterfeit*
bum*, dishonest, dissembling, fake, false, fraudulent, phony, pretended, pretentious, pseudo*, sham*, simulated, unprincipled; SEE CONCEPT 582

quaff [v] *drink down*
down, gulp, guzzle, imbibe, ingurgitate, partake, sip, sup, swallow, swig, swill, toss; SEE CONCEPT 169

quagmire [n1] *bad situation*
box*, corner*, difficulty, dilemma, entanglement, fix, hole*, imbroglio, impasse, involvement, jam, mire, morass, muddle, pass, perplexity, pickle*, pinch*, plight, predicament, quandary, scrape, trouble; SEE CONCEPTS 666,674

quagmire [n2] *bog*
fen, marsh, marshland, mire, morass, moss, quag, quicksand, slough, swamp; SEE CONCEPT 509

quail [v] *cower, shrink*
blanch, blench, cringe, droop, faint, falter, flinch, have cold feet*, quake, recoil, shake, shudder, start, tremble, wince; SEE CONCEPTS 35,149,195

quaint [adj1] *strange, odd*
bizarre, curious, droll, eccentric, erratic, fanciful, fantastic, freakish, freaky*, funny, idiosyncratic, laughable, oddball, offbeat, off the beaten track*, original, outlandish, peculiar, queer, singular, special, unusual, weird*, whimsical; SEE CONCEPTS 564,589

quaint [adj2] *old-fashioned; nostalgically attractive*
affected, ancient, antiquated, antique, archaic, artful, baroque, captivating, charming, colonial, curious, cute, enchanting, fanciful, Gothic*, ingenious, old-world, picturesque, pleasing, Victorian*, whimsical; SEE CONCEPTS 578,589,797

quake [n] *earthquake*
aftershock, convulsion, quaker, seism, shake, shock, temblor, tremblor, tremor; SEE CONCEPT 526

quake [v] *shake, vibrate*
convulse, cower, fluctuate, jar, jitter, move, pulsate, quail, quiver, rock, shiver, shrink, shudder, throb, totter, tremble, tremor, twitter, waver, wobble; SEE CONCEPT 152

qualification [n1] *ability, aptitude*
accomplishment, adequacy, attainment, attribute, capability, capacity, competence, eligibility, endowment, experience, fitness, goods, makings, might, qualifiedness, quality, skill, stuff, suitability, suitableness, what it takes*; SEE CONCEPT *630*

qualification [n2] *requirement, restriction*
allowance, caveat, condition, contingency, criterion, essential, exception, exemption, limitation, modification, need, objection, postulate, prerequisite, provision, proviso, requisite, reservation, stipulation; SEE CONCEPTS *646,652*

qualified [adj1] *able, skillful*
accomplished, adept, adequate, all around, au fait, capable, catechized, certified, competent, disciplined, efficient, equipped, examined, experienced, expert, fit, fitted, good, instructed, knowledgeable, licensed, practiced, pro*, proficient, proper, proved, quizzed, talented, tested, trained, tried, up to snuff*, up to speed*, vet*, veteran, war-horse*, wicked; SEE CONCEPT *527*

qualified [adj2] *limited, restricted*
bounded, circumscribed, conditional, confined, contingent, definite, determined, equivocal, fixed, guarded, modified, partial, provisional, reserved; SEE CONCEPT *554*

qualify [v1] *make or become ready, prepared*
authorize, capacitate, certify, check out, come up to snuff*, commission, condition, cut it*, earn one's wings*, empower, enable, endow, entitle, equip, fill the bill*, fit, get by*, ground, hack it*, make it*, make the cut*, make the grade*, measure up, meet, pass, pass muster*, permit, ready, sanction, score, suffice, suit, train; SEE CONCEPTS *99,630*

qualify [v2] *lessen, restrict*
abate, adapt, alter, assuage, change, circumscribe, diminish, ease, limit, mitigate, moderate, modify, modulate, reduce, regulate, restrain, soften, temper, vary, weaken; SEE CONCEPTS *240,698*

qualify [v3] *characterize, distinguish*
ascribe, assign, attribute, describe, designate, impute, individualize, individuate, mark, name, predicate, signalize, singularize; SEE CONCEPT *411*

quality [n1] *characteristic, feature*
affection, affirmation, aspect, attribute, character, condition, constitution, description, element, endowment, essence, factor, genius, individuality, kind, make, mark, name of tune*, nature, nature of beast*, parameter, peculiarity, predication, property, savor, sort, trait, virtue, way of it*; SEE CONCEPT *543*

quality [n2] *value, status*
arete, caliber, capacity, character, class, condition, distinction, excellence, excellency, footing, grade, group, kind, merit, perfection, place, position, preeminence, rank, repute, standing, state, station, stature, step, superbness, superiority, variety, virtue, worth; SEE CONCEPTS *346,378,668*

qualm [n] *nagging doubt*
agitation, anxiety, apprehension, compunction, conscience, demur, disquiet, foreboding, hesitation, indecision, insecurity, misdoubt, misgiving, mistrust, nervousness, objection, pang, perturbation, presentiment, regret, reluctance, remonstrance, remorse, scruple, suspicion, twinge, uncertainty, unease, uneasiness; SEE CONCEPTS *410,532*

quandary [n] *delicate situation*
bewilderment, bind, Catch-22*, clutch, corner*, difficulty, dilemma, double trouble*, doubt, embarrassment, hang-up*, impasse, mire, perplexity, pickle*, plight, predicament, puzzle, spot*, strait, uncertainty, up a tree*; SEE CONCEPTS *532,674,690*

quantity [n] *number or amount*
abundance, aggregate, allotment, amplitude, batch, body, budget, bulk, capacity, deal, expanse, extent, figure, greatness, length, load, lot, magnitude, mass, measure, multitude, part, pile, portion, profusion, quota, size, sum, total, variety, volume; SEE CONCEPT *787*

quarrel [n] *disagreement*
affray, altercation, argument, battle royal*, beef*, bickering*, brannigan*, brawl, breach, broil*, catfight*, combat, commotion, complaint, contention, controversy, difference, difference of opinion, difficulty, disapproval, discord, disputation, dispute, dissension, dissidence, disturbance, dust*, falling-out*, feud, fight, fisticuffs*, fracas, fray, fuss, hassle, misunderstanding, objection, rhubarb*, row, ruckus*, run-in, scrap, set-to*, spat, squabble, strife, struggle, tiff, tumult, vendetta, wrangle; SEE CONCEPTS *46,106*

quarrel [v] *disagree*
altercate, argue, battle, be at loggerheads*, bicker, brawl, break with, bump, carp, caterwaul, cavil, charge, clash, collide, complain, contend, contest, cross swords*, differ, disapprove, dispute, dissent, divide, embroil, fall out*, feud, fight, find fault, get tough with*, hassle, have it out*, have words*, lock horns*, mix it up*, object to, row, scrap, set to, spar, spat, squabble, strive, struggle, take exception, take on, tangle, vary, war, wrangle; SEE CONCEPTS *46,106*

quarrelsome [adj] *being disagreeable*
argumentative, bad-tempered, bellicose, belligerent, brawling, cantankerous, cat-and-dog*, choleric, churlish, combative, contentious, crabby*, cross, disputatious, dissentious, excitable, fiery, fractious, gladiatorial, hasty, have chip on shoulder*, hotheaded*, huffy, impassioned, irascible, irritable, litigious, ornery, passionate, peevish, pettish, petulant, pugnacious, querulous, ructious, snappy, tempestuous, thin-skinned*, touchy, truculent, turbulent, unruly, violent, war; SEE CONCEPTS *401,542*

quarry [n] *goal*
aim, chase, game, objective, prey, prize, quest, raven, victim; SEE CONCEPT *659*

quarter [n1] *one of four equal parts*
division, farthing, fourth, one-fourth, part, portion, quad, quadrant, quartern, section, semester, span, term, two bits*; SEE CONCEPT *835*

quarter [n2] *area, neighborhood*
barrio, bearing, direction, district, division, domain, ghetto, inner city, locality, location, neck of the woods*, old town, part, place, point, position, precinct, province, region, section, sector, side, skid row, slum, spot, station, stomping ground*, territory, turf, zone, zoo*; SEE CONCEPTS *508,512*

quarter [n3] *forgiveness*
clemency, compassion, favor, grace, leniency, lenity, mercy, pity; SEE CONCEPTS *410,633*

quarter [v1] *divide into four equal parts*
cleave, cut, cut up, dismember, fourth; SEE CONCEPT *98*

quarter [v2] *provide lodging*
accommodate, billet, board, bunk, canton, domicile, domiciliate, entertain, establish, harbor, house, install, lodge, place, post, put up, settle, shelter, station; SEE CONCEPT *140*

quarters [n] *place to live or sleep*
abode, accommodation, apartment, barracks, billet, cabin, cantonment, chambers, condo, cottage, digs*, domicile, dorm, dwelling, flat, fraternity, habitat, habitation, home, house, lodge, lodging, place, post, ranch, residence, room, roost*, shelter, sorority, station, tent; SEE CONCEPT *516*

quash [v1] *destroy, defeat*
annihilate, beat, crush, extinguish, extirpate, overcome, overthrow, put down, quell, quench, repress, scrunch*, snow under*, squash*, squish*, subdue, suppress, trash; SEE CONCEPTS *95,252*

quash [v2] *nullify, cancel*
abrogate, annul, black out*, bottle up*, clamp down on, cork up*, crack down on*, declare null and void*, discharge, dissolve, hush up*, invalidate, kill, negate, overrule, overthrow, put damper on*, put the lid on*, repeal, rescind, reverse, revoke, set aside, shut down, squelch, undo, vacate, veto, vitiate, void, watergate*; SEE CONCEPTS *121,234,266*

quasi [adj] *almost; to a certain extent*
apparent, apparently, fake, mock, near, nominal, partly, pretended, pseudo-*, seeming, seemingly, semi-, sham*, so-called, supposedly, synthetic, virtual, would-be*; SEE CONCEPT *582*

queasy [adj] *not feeling well; not comfortable*
anxious, bilious, concerned, fidgety, green around gills*, groggy, ill, ill at ease, indisposed, nauseated, pukish, qualmish, queer, restless, rocky*, sick, sick as a dog*, sickly, squeamish, troubled, uncertain, uncomfortable, under the weather*, uneasy, unwell, upset, worried; SEE CONCEPTS *314,403*

queer [adj1] *odd; abnormal*
anomalous, atypical, bizarre, crazy, curious, demented, disquieting, doubtful, droll, dubious, eccentric, eerie, erratic, extraordinary, fishy*, flaky*, fly ball*, freaky*, funny, idiosyncratic, irrational, irregular, kinky*, kooky*, mad, mysterious, oddball*, off the wall*, outlandish, outré, peculiar, puzzling, quaint, questionable, remarkable, shady, singular, strange, suspicious, touched, unbalanced, uncanny, uncommon, unconventional, unhinged, unnatural, unorthodox, unusual, wacky*, weird; SEE CONCEPTS *404,548,564*

queer [adj2] *not feeling well*
dizzy, faint, giddy, green*, ill, lightheaded, pukish*, qualmish, qualmy*, queasy*, reeling, sick, squeamish*, uneasy; SEE CONCEPT *314*

quell [v1] *defeat, suppress*
annihilate, conquer, crush, extinguish, hush up*, kill, overcome, overpower, put down, put the lid on*, queer, quench, shut down, silence, sit on, stamp out*, stifle, stop, subdue, subjugate, vanquish; SEE CONCEPTS *95,121,234*

quell [v2] *alleviate, calm*
allay, appease, assuage, check, compose, deaden, dull, ease, mitigate, moderate, mollify, pacify, quiet, reduce, silence, soothe, still; SEE CONCEPTS *7,22,110*

quench [v1] *destroy, extinguish*
annihilate, check, choke, crush, dampen, deci-

mate, demolish, destruct, dismantle, douse, end, kill, knock down, moisten, put down, put out, quash*, quell, raze, ruin, shatter, smother, snuff out*, stifle, suppress, wreck; SEE CONCEPTS *234,252*

quench [v2] *satisfy, especially thirst*
allay, alleviate, appease, assuage, content, cool*, glut, gorge, gratify, lighten, mitigate, moisten, relieve, sate, satiate, slake; SEE CONCEPTS *136,244*

querulous [adj] *grouchy, hard to please*
bearish, bemoaning, cantankerous, captious, carping, censorious, complaining, critical, cross, crying, deploring, discontented, dissatisfied, edgy, fault-finding, fretful, grousing, grumbling, grumbly, huffy* irascible, irritable, lamenting, out of sorts* peevish, petulant, plaintive, scrappy, snappy, sour, testy, thin-skinned* touchy, uptight, wailing, waspish, waspy, whimpering, whining, whiny; SEE CONCEPTS *401,542*

query [n] *demand for answers*
concern, doubt, dubiety, inquiry, interrogation, interrogatory, mistrust, objection, problem, question, questioning, reservation, skepticism, suspicion, uncertainty; SEE CONCEPTS *21,48,53,662*

query [v] *ask*
catechize, challenge, disbelieve, dispute, distrust, doubt, enquire, examine, hit up, impeach, impugn, inquire, interrogate, knock, mistrust, put out a feeler* question, quiz, suspect, test the waters*; SEE CONCEPTS *21,48,53*

quest [n] *search, exploration*
adventure, chase, crusade, delving, enterprise, examination, expedition, hunt, inquest, inquiry, inquisition, investigation, journey, mission, pilgrimage, prey, probe, probing, pursuit, pursuit, quarry, research, seeking, voyage; SEE CONCEPTS *48,103,216*

question [n1] *asking for answer*
catechism, examination, inquest, inquiring, inquiry, inquisition, interrogation, interrogatory, investigation, poll, Q and A*, query, questioning, third degree*, wringer*; SEE CONCEPTS *48,53*

question [n2] *controversy, doubt*
argument, challenge, confusion, contention, debate, demur, demurral, difficulty, dispute, dubiety, enigma, misgiving, mystery, objection, problem, protest, puzzle, query, remonstrance, remonstration, uncertainty; SEE CONCEPTS *666,674*

question [n3] *issue, point at issue*
discussion, motion, point, problem, proposal, proposition, subject, theme, topic; SEE CONCEPTS *532,690*

question [v1] *ask for answer*
ask about, catechize, challenge, cross-examine, enquire, examine, give the third degree*, go over, grill, hit*, hit up*, hold out for, inquire, interrogate, interview, investigate, knock*, make inquiry, petition, pick one's brains*, probe, pry, pump, put through the wringer*, put to the question*, query, quest, quiz, raise question, roast*, search, seek, show curiosity, solicit, sound out*, sweat it out of*, work over*; SEE CONCEPTS *48,53*

question [v2] *doubt*
call into question, cast doubt upon, challenge, controvert, disbelieve, dispute, distrust, hesitate, impeach, impugn, mistrust, oppose, puzzle over, query, suspect, suspicion, wonder about; SEE CONCEPT *21*

questionable [adj] *doubtful, uncertain*
ambiguous, apocryphal, arguable, contingent, controversial, controvertible, cryptic, debatable, disputable, dubious, dubitable, enigmatic, equivocal, fishy*, hard to believe, hypothetical, iffy*, indecisive, indefinite, indeterminate, moot, mysterious, obscure, occult, open to doubt, open to question, oracular, paradoxical, problematic, problematical, provisional, shady, suspect, suspicious, unconfirmed, undefined, under advisement, under examination, unproven, unreliable, unsettled, vague; SEE CONCEPTS 529,535

queue [n] *sequence*
chain, concatenation, echelon, file, line, order, progression, rank, row, series, string, succession, tail, tier, train; SEE CONCEPTS 432,727

quibble [n] *objection, complaint*
artifice, cavil, criticism, dodge, duplicity, equivocation, evasion, hair-splitter*, nicety, niggle*, nit-picker*, pretense, prevarication, protest, quiddity, quirk, shift, sophism, subterfuge, subtlety; SEE CONCEPTS 46,52

quibble [v] *disagree over minor issues*
altercate, argue over, argufy, avoid, bicker, blow hot and cold*, carp, catch at straws*, cavil, chicane, criticize, dispute, equivocate, evade, fence*, flip-flop*, hassle, have at it*, hem and haw*, hypercriticize*, make a big thing about*, nit-pick*, paralogize, pettifog*, pretend, prevaricate, put up an argument, set to, shift, spar, split hairs*, squabble, talk back, waffle, wrangle; SEE CONCEPTS 46,52

quick [adj1] *fast, speedy*
abrupt, accelerated, active, agile, alert, a move on*, animated, ASAP*, breakneck*, brief, brisk, cursory, curt, double time*, energetic, expeditious, expeditive, express, fleet, flying, going, harefooted*, hasty, headlong, hurried, immediate, impatient, impetuous, instantaneous, keen, lively, mercurial, move it, nimble, on the double*, perfunctory, posthaste, prompt, pronto*, rapid, snappy, spirited, sprightly, spry, sudden, swift, the lead out*, winged*; SEE CONCEPTS 544,588

quick [adj2] *smart*
able, active, acute, adept, adroit, all there, apt, astute, bright, canny, capable, clever, competent, deft, dexterous, discerning, effective, effectual, intelligent, keen, knowing, nimble-witted, on the ball*, perceptive, perspicacious, prompt, quick on the draw, quick on the trigger*, quick on the uptake*, quick-witted, ready, receptive, savvy*, sharp, sharp as a tack*, shrewd, skillful, slick, smart as a whip*, vigorous, whiz*, wired*, wise; SEE CONCEPT 402

quicken [v] *make faster; invigorate*
accelerate, activate, actuate, animate, arouse, awaken, dispatch, energize, excite, expedite, galvanize, goad, grow, hasten, hurry, impel, incite, increase, innervate, innerve, inspire, kindle, liven, make haste, motivate, move, pique, precipitate, promote, refresh, revitalize, revive, rouse, shake up, speed, spring, spur, step up, stimulate, stir, strengthen, urge, vitalize, vivificate, vivify; SEE CONCEPTS 7,19,22,250

quick-tempered [adj] *easily upset, angered*
choleric, cranky, cross, excitable, fiery, hot-tempered, impatient, impulsive, inflammable, irascible, irritable, passionate, peppery, petulant, quarrelsome, ratty, sensitive, short-tempered, shrewish, splenetic, temperamental, testy, waspish; SEE CONCEPTS 401,404

quick-witted [adj] *smart*
acute, agile, alert, apt, astute, brainy, bright, brilliant, canny, clever, facetious, humorous, intelligent, keen, knowing, nimble-witted, on the ball*, penetrating, penetrative, perceptive, prompt, quick, quick on the draw*, quick on the uptake*, ready, savvy*, sharp, sharp as a tack*, sharp-sighted, sharp-witted, shrewd, slick*, whiz*, wired*, wise, witty; SEE CONCEPTS 267,402

quiet [n] *calmness, silence*
calm, cessation, dead air*, ease, hush, lull, noiselessness, peace, quietness, quietude, relaxation, repose, rest, serenity, silence, soundlessness, speechlessness, still, stillness, stop, termination, tranquillity; SEE CONCEPTS 65,315,592,673,705

quiet [adj1] *without or with little sound*
buttoned up*, clammed up*, close, closemouthed, could hear a pin drop*, dumb, hushed, hushful, inaudible, low, low-pitched, muffled, mute, muted, noiseless, not saying boo*, peaceful, quiescent, quieted, reserved, reticent, secretive, silent, soft, soundless, speechless, still, stilled, taciturn, tight-lipped*, uncommunicative, unexpressed, unspeaking, unuttered, whist; SEE CONCEPTS 592,594

quiet [adj2] *calm, peaceful*
collected, contented, docile, fixed, gentle, halcyon, hushed, inactive, isolated, level, meek, mild, motionless, pacific, placid, private, remote, reserved, restful, retired, secluded, secret, sedate, sequestered, serene, shy, smooth, stable, stagnant, still, tranquil, unanxious, undisturbed, unexcited, unfrequented, unruffled, untroubled; SEE CONCEPTS 401,583,584,705

quiet [adj3] *simple, unobtrusive*
conservative, homely, inobtrusive, modest, plain, restrained, sober, subdued, tasteful, unassuming, unpretentious; SEE CONCEPT 589

quiet [v] *make silent, calm*
allay, ameliorate, appease, assuage, becalm, button one's lip*, calm down, can it, choke, clam up*, compose, console, cool it*, cool out*, dummy up*, fix up, gag, gratify, hold it down, hush, ice*, inactivate, lull, moderate, mollify, muffle, muzzle, pacify, palliate, patch things up*, please, quieten, reconcile, relax, satisfy, settle, shush, shut up, silence, slack, smooth, soften, soft-pedal*, soothe, square, squash, squelch, still, stroke, subdue, take the bite out of*, tranquilize; SEE CONCEPTS 126,244,266

quilt [n] *thick bedcovering made of patches*
batt, bedspread, blanket, comforter, counterpane, cover, coverlet, down, duvet, eiderdown, pad, patchwork, pouf, puff; SEE CONCEPTS 445,451, 473

quintessence [n] *essence, core*
apotheosis, bottom, distillation, epitome, essentiality, extract, gist, heart, kernel, last word, lifeblood, marrow, pith, quiddity, soul, spirit, stuff, substance, ultimate, virtuality; SEE CONCEPTS 682,826

quip [n] *witty communication, often verbal*
badinage, banter, bon mot, crack, drollery, gag, gibe, insult, jeer, jest, joke, mockery, offense, pleasantry, pun, repartee, retort, riposte, sally, satire, spoof, wisecrack, witticism; SEE CONCEPTS 273,278

quirk [n] *oddity of personality, way of doing something*

aberration, caprice, characteristic, conceit, crotchet, eccentricity, equivocation, fancy, fetish, foible, habit, humor, idée fixe, idiosyncrasy, irregularity, kink, knack, mannerism, peculiarity, quibble, singularity, subterfuge, trait, turn, twist, vagary, whim, whimsy; SEE CONCEPTS 411,644

quit [vl] *abandon, leave*

abdicate, blow*, book*, bow out, check out, cut out*, decamp, depart, desert, drop, drop out, evacuate, exit, forsake, get off, give up, go, go away from, hang it up*, leave flat*, leave hanging*, pull out, push off*, relinquish, renounce, resign, retire, run out on, surrender, take a walk*, take off, throw over*, vacate, walk out on, withdraw, yield; SEE CONCEPT 195

quit [v2] *stop doing something*

abandon, break off, call it a day*, call it quits*, cease, conclude, cut it out*, desist, discontinue, drop, end, get on the wagon*, give notice, give over*, give up, halt, hang it up*, kick over*, kick the habit*, knock off*, leave, leave off*, pack in*, quit cold, resign, retire, secede, sew up*, surcease, suspend, take the cure*, terminate, wind up*, withdraw, wrap up*; SEE CONCEPTS 119,234

quite [advl] *completely*

absolutely, actually, all, all in all, all told, altogether, considerably, entirely, fully, in all respects, in fact, in reality, in toto, in truth, just, largely, perfectly, positively, precisely, purely, really, thoroughly, totally, truly, utterly, well, wholly, without reservation; SEE CONCEPTS 531,582

quite [adv2] *to a certain extent*

considerably, fairly, far, moderately, more or less, pretty, rather, reasonably, relatively, significantly, somewhat, to some degree, very; SEE CONCEPTS 569,772

quiver [n] *shaking, vibration*

convulsion, flash, glimmer, glitter, oscillation, palpitation, pulsation, shake, shimmer, shiver, shudder, sparkle, spasm, throb, tic, tremble, tremor, twinkle; SEE CONCEPT 152

quiver [v] *shake, vibrate*

agitate, beat, convulse, dither, jitter, oscillate, palpitate, pulsate, pulse, quake, quaver, shiver, shudder, thrill, throb, tremble, tremor, twitter; SEE CONCEPT 152

quiz [n] *questioning, often in an organized academic setting*

blue book*, check, exam, examination, investigation, query, shotgun*, test; SEE CONCEPT 290

quiz [v] *question*

ask, catechize, check, cross-examine, examine, give the third degree*, grill*, inquire, interrogate, investigate, pick one's brains*, pump*, query, test; SEE CONCEPT 48

quizzical [adj] *appearing confused or curious*

amusing, aporetic, arch, bantering, derisive, disbelieving, eccentric, incredulous, inquiring, inquisitive, mocking, odd, probing, quaint, queer, questioning, sardonic, searching, show-me*, skeptical, supercilious, suspicious, teasing, unbelieving, unusual; SEE CONCEPTS 267,485

quota [n] *portion allotted to something*

allocation, allotment, allowance, apportionment, assignment, bite, chunk, cut, division, divvy*, end, lot, measure, meed, part, partage, percentage, piece, piece of action*, proportion, quantum, ration, share, slice, split; SEE CONCEPTS 768,835

quotation/quote [nl] *repetition of something spoken or written by someone*

citation, citing, cutting, excerpt, extract, passage, quote, recitation, reference, saying, selection; SEE CONCEPTS 274,278

quotation/quote [n2] *financial estimate*

bid, bid price, charge, cost, current price, figure, market price, price, price named, published price, quote, rate, stated price, tender; SEE CONCEPTS 274,332,784

quote [v] *repeat something spoken, written by another*

adduce, attest, cite, detail, excerpt, extract, instance, name, paraphrase, parrot, proclaim, recall, recite, recollect, reference, refer to, retell; SEE CONCEPTS 79,171

R

rabid [adj] *very angry; maniacal*

berserk, bigoted, bitten, corybantic, crazed*, crazy, delirious, deranged, enthusiastic, extreme, extremist, fanatical, fervent, flipped*, foaming at the mouth*, frantic, freaked out*, frenetic, frenzied, furious, hot*, infuriated, insane, intemperate, intolerant, irrational, keen, mad, mad-dog*, narrow-minded, nutty*, obsessed, overboard, poisoned, radical, raging, revolutionary, sick*, sizzling, smoking*, steamed up*, ultra, ultraist, violent, virulent, wild, zealous; SEE CONCEPT 403

race [nl] *pursuit, running, speeding*

chase, clash, clip, competition, contention, contest, course, dash, engagement, event, go, marathon, match, meet, relay, rivalry, run, rush, scurry, sprint, spurt; SEE CONCEPT 363

race [n2] *ethnic group*

blood, brood, clan, color, cultural group, culture, family, folk, house, issue, kin, kind, kindred, line, lineage, nation, nationality, offspring, people, progeny, seed, species, stock, strain, tribe, type, variety; SEE CONCEPT 380

race [n3] *stream, river*

branch, brook, creek, duct, gill, raceway, rill, rindle, rivulet, run, runnel, sluice, tide; SEE CONCEPT 514

race [v] *run, speed in competition*

boil, bolt, bustle, career, chase, compete, contest, course, dart, dash, fling, fly, gallop, haste, hasten, hie, hurry, hustle, lash, outstrip, plunge ahead, post, pursue, rush, scamper, scramble, scud, scuttle, shoot, skim, sprint, spurt, swoop, tear, whisk, wing; SEE CONCEPTS 150,363

racial [adj] *ethnic*

ancestral, ethnological, folk, genealogical, genetic, hereditary, lineal, national, phyletic, phylogenetic, tribal; SEE CONCEPT 549

racism [n] *prejudice against an ethnic group*

apartheid, bias, bigotry, discrimination, illiberality, one-sidedness, partiality, racialism, sectarianism, segregation, unfairness; SEE CONCEPT 689

rack [n] *frame, framework*

arbor, bed, box, bracket, counter, furniture, holder, ledge, perch, receptacle, shelf, stand, structure, trestle; SEE CONCEPTS 443,479

qu ra

rack [v] *torture; strain*
afflict, agonize, crucify, distress, excruciate, force, harass, harrow, martyr, oppress, pain, persecute, pull, shake, stress, stretch, tear, torment, try, wrench, wring; SEE CONCEPTS *7,19,246*

racket [n1] *commotion; fight*
agitation, babel, battle, blare, brawl, clamor, clangor, clash, clatter, din, disturbance, fracas, free-for-all*, fuss, hoo-ha*, hubbub*, jangle, noise, outcry, pandemonium, riot, roar, row, ruction, rumpus*, shouting, shuffle, squabble, squall, stir, to-do*, tumult, turbulence, turmoil, uproar, vociferation, wrangle; SEE CONCEPTS *65,106,230*

racket [n2] *criminal activity*
cheating, confidence game, con game, conspiracy, corruption, crime, dirty pool*, dishonesty, dodge, extortion, fraud, game, graft, illegality, illicit scheme, intrigue, lawlessness, lay, plot, push, scheme, shakedown, squeeze*, swindle, swindling, theft, trick, underworld; SEE CONCEPT *192*

racy [adj1] *energetic, zestful*
animated, bright, buoyant, clever, distinctive, entertaining, exciting, exhilarating, fiery, forceful, forcible, gingery, heady, keen, lively, mettlesome, peppery, piquant, playful, poignant, pungent, rich, salty, saucy*, sharp, snappy, sparkling, spicy, spirited, sportive, sprightly, stimulating, strong, tangy, tart, tasty, vigorous, vivacious, witty, zesty; SEE CONCEPTS *401,613*

racy [adj2] *risqué, vulgar*
bawdy, blue*, broad, erotic, immodest, indecent, indelicate, lewd, lurid, naughty, off-color*, purple*, shady*, smutty*, spicy*, suggestive, wicked; SEE CONCEPTS *267,545*

radiance [n1] *brightness, luminescence*
brilliance, effulgence, glare, gleam, glitter, glow, incandescence, light, luminosity, luster, resplendence, shine; SEE CONCEPT *620*

radiance [n2] *happiness*
delight, gaiety, joy, pleasure, rapture, warmth; SEE CONCEPT *633*

radiant [adj1] *bright, luminous*
beaming, brilliant, effulgent, gleaming, glittering, glorious, glowing, incandescent, lambent, lucent, lustrous, radiating, refulgent, resplendent, shining, sparkling, sunny; SEE CONCEPT *617*

radiant [adj2] *happy in appearance*
beaming, beatific, blissful, bright, cheerful, cheery, delighted, ecstatic, gay, glad, glowing, joyful, joyous, rapturous; SEE CONCEPT *401*

radiate [v] *give off; scatter*
afford, beam, branch out, broadcast, circulate, diffuse, disseminate, distribute, diverge, emanate, emit, expand, give out, gleam, glitter, illumine, irradiate, issue, light up, pour, proliferate, propagate, ramble, ramify, send out, shed, shine, shoot out, spread, spread out, sprinkle, strew, throw out, transmit, yield; SEE CONCEPTS *118,217,620,716*

radical [n] *person who advocates significant, often extreme change*
agitator, anarchist, avant-garde, extremist, fanatic, firebrand, freethinker, iconoclast, insurgent, insurrectionist, leftist, left-winger, militant, mutineer, nihilist, nonconformist, objector, pacifist, progressive, rebel, reformer, renegade, revolter, revolutionary, rioter, secessionist, subversive, ultraist; SEE CONCEPT *359*

radical [adj1] *fundamental, basic*
basal, bottom, cardinal, constitutional, deep-seated, essential, foundational, inherent, innate, intrinsic, meat-and-potatoes*, native, natural, organic, original, primal, primary, primitive, profound, thoroughgoing, underlying, vital; SEE CONCEPTS *546,549*

radical [adj2] *deviating by extremes*
advanced, anarchistic, complete, entire, excessive, extremist, fanatical, far-out*, freethinking, iconoclastic, immoderate, insubordinate, insurgent, insurrectionary, intransigent, lawless, leftist, militant, mutinous, nihilistic, progressive, rabid, rebellious, recalcitrant, recusant, refractory, restive, revolutionary, riotous, seditious, severe, sweeping, thorough, ultra, ultraist, uncompromising, violent, way out*; SEE CONCEPTS *403,529,542*

radio [n] *communication by electronic air waves*
AM-FM, CB, Marconi, radionics, radiotelegraph, radiotelegraphy, radiotelephone, radio-telephonics, receiver, shortwave, telegraphy, tele-phony, transmission, Walkman, wireless; SEE CONCEPT *279*

radius [n] *range, sweep*
ambit, boundary, compass, expanse, extension, extent, interval, limit, orbit, purview, reach, semidiameter, space, span, spoke; SEE CONCEPT *651*

raffish [adj] *unmindful of social conventions*
bohemian*, careless, casual, coarse, dashing, devil-may-care*, disreputable, fast*, gay, jaunty, rakish, sporty, tasteless, tawdry, unconventional, uncouth, vulgar, wild; SEE CONCEPT *401*

raffle [n] *lottery for a prize*
bet, betting, disposition, draw, drawing, flier*, gambling, game of chance, gaming, long odds*, lots*, numbers*, numbers game*, pool, random shot, speculation, stake, sweep, sweepstake, tossup*, wager, wagering; SEE CONCEPTS *363,364*

ragamuffin [n] *person who is poor, tattered*
beggar, bum*, gamin, guttersnipe*, hobo, loafer, orphan, scarecrow, street person, tatterdemalion*, tramp, urchin, vagabond, vagrant, waif, wastrel; SEE CONCEPTS *412,423*

rage [n1] *extreme anger*
acerbity, acrimony, agitation, animosity, apoplexy, asperity, bitterness, blowup*, bluster, choler, convulsion, dander, eruption, exasperation, excitement, explosion, ferment, ferocity, fireworks, frenzy, furor, fury, gall, heat*, hemorrhage, huff*, hysterics, indignation, ire, irritation, madness, mania, obsession, outburst, paroxysm, passion, rampage, raving, resentment, spasm, spleen, squall, storm, tantrum, temper, umbrage, uproar, upset, vehemence, violence, winging*, wrath; SEE CONCEPTS *410,657*

rage [n2] *something in vogue; popular notion*
caprice, chic, conceit, craze, crotchet, cry, dernier cri, enthusiasm, fad, fancy, fashion, freak, furor, happening, hot spot*, in*, in-spot*, in-thing*, last word*, latest*, latest thing*, latest wrinkle*, mania, mode, newest wrinkle*, now*, passion, style, thing*, up to the minute*, vagary, whim; SEE CONCEPTS *388,655*

rage [v] *be angry*
be beside oneself*, be furious, be uncontrollable, blow a fuse*, blow one's top*, blow up*, boil over*, bristle, chafe, champ at bit*, erupt, fly off the handle*, foam at the mouth*, fret, fulminate, fume, go berserk, have a fit, have a tantrum, let

off steam*, look daggers*, make a fuss over, overflow, rail at, rampage, rant, rant and rave*, rave, roar, scold, scream, seethe, snap at, splutter, steam, storm, surge, tear, throw a fit*, work oneself into sweat*, yell; SEE CONCEPTS *29,410*

ragged [adj] worn-out; in shreds

badly dressed, badly worn, battered, broken, contemptible, crude, desultory, dilapidated, dingy, disorganized, down at the heel*, fragmented, frayed, frazzled, full of holes*, in holes*, in rags, in tatters*, irregular, jagged, mean, moth-eaten, notched, patched, poor, poorly made, rent, rough, rugged, scraggy, seedy, serrated, shabby, shaggy, shoddy, shredded, tacky*, tattered, tatty*, threadbare, torn, uneven, unfinished, unkempt, unpressed, worse for wear*; SEE CONCEPT *485*

raging [adj] violent; mad

angry, at boiling point*, bent*, bent out of shape*, beside oneself*, blowing a gasket*, blowing one's top*, blustering, blustery, boiling mad*, boiling over*, enraged, fit to be tied*, frenzied, fuming, furious, going ape*, incensed, infuriated, irate, mad as a hornet*, on the warpath*, rabid*, ranting and raving*, raving, raving mad*, rough, seeing red*, seething, stormy, tempestuous, throwing a fit, turbulent, wild; SEE CONCEPTS *403,542*

raid [n] attack, seizure

arrest, assault, break-in, bust, capture, descent, foray, forced entrance, hit-and-run*, incursion, inroad, invasion, irruption, onset, onslaught, pull, reconnaissance, roundup, sally*, shootup*, sortie*, surprise attack, sweep, tipover*; SEE CONCEPTS *86,317*

raid [v] attack, pillage

assail, assault, blockade, bomb, bombard, breach, break in, charge, descend on, despoil, devastate, fall upon, fire on, forage, foray, harass, harry, heat, inroad, invade, knock off*, knock over*, lean against, lean on, loot, maraud, march on, overrun, pirate, plunder, rake, ransack, rifle, rob, sack, sally, sally forth, shell, slough, spoliate, storm, strafe, strike, sweep, swoop, tip over*, torpedo, waste; SEE CONCEPT *86*

rail/railing [n] post, pole along an edge

balustrade, banister, bar, barrier, fence, paling, rails, rest, siding; SEE CONCEPTS *443,479*

rail [v] criticize harshly

abuse, attack, bawl out*, berate, blast, castigate, censure, chew out*, complain, fulminate, fume, inveigh, jaw, objurgate, rant, rate, revile, scold, thunder, tongue-lash*, upbraid, vituperate, vociferate, whip; SEE CONCEPT *52*

rain [n] downpour of water or other substance

cat-and-dog weather*, cloudburst, condensation, deluge, drencher, drizzle, fall, flood, flurry, hail, heavy dew, liquid sunshine*, mist, monsoon, pour, pouring, precip*, precipitation, raindrops, rainfall, rainstorm, sheets, shower, showers, sleet, spate, spit, sprinkle, sprinkling, stream, sun shower*, torrent, volley*, wet stuff*, window washer*; SEE CONCEPT *526*

rain [v] drop water or other substance

bestow, bucket, come down in buckets*, deposit, drizzle, fall, hail, lavish, mist, patter, pour, shower, sleet, sprinkle, storm; SEE CONCEPT *526*

raise [n] increase in salary or position

accession, accretion, addition, advance, augmentation, boost, bump, hike, hold-up*, increment, jump, jump-up*, leg*, leg-up*, move-up*, promotion, raising, rise, step-up*; SEE CONCEPTS *344,351,763*

raise [v1] lift; build from the ground

boost, bring up, construct, elevate, erect, establish, exalt, heave, hoist, hold up, lever, lift, lift up, mount, move up, place up, promote, pry, pull up, put on its end, put up, rear, run up, set up, set upright, shove, stand up, take up, throw up, upcast, upheave, uplift, upraise, uprear; SEE CONCEPTS *168,196*

raise [v2] increase, augment

advance, aggravate, amplify, assemble, boost, build up, collect, congregate, congress, dignify, enhance, enlarge, escalate, exaggerate, exalt, fetch up, forgather, form, gather, get, goose*, goose up*, heighten, hike, hike up*, honor, inflate, intensify, jack up, jump, jump up, levy, look up, magnify, mass, mobilize, mushroom*, muster, obtain, perk up, pick up, promote, put up, pyramid, rally, recruit, reinforce, rendezvous, run up*, send through the roof*, shoot up, snowball*, strengthen, up; SEE CONCEPTS *236,244,245*

raise [v3] start up, motivate; introduce

abet, activate, advance, arouse, awaken, bring up, broach, cause, evoke, excite, foment, foster, incite, instigate, kindle, moot, motivate, provoke, put forward, resurrect, set, set on, stir up, suggest, whip up; SEE CONCEPTS *75,221*

raise [v4] nurture, care for

breed, bring up, cultivate, develop, drag up, fetch up, foster, group, grow, nourish, nurse, plant, produce, propagate, provide, rear, sow, suckle, support, train, wean; SEE CONCEPTS *253,257,295*

rake [v] scrape up, hoe

break up, clean up, clear, clear up, collect, comb, enfilade, examine, finecomb, fine-tooth-comb*, gather, grade, graze, grub, harrow, hunt, ransack, rasp, remove, rummage, scan, scour, scrape, scratch, scrutinize, search, smooth, sweep, weed; SEE CONCEPTS *109,165,178,216*

rakish [adj] charming and immoral

abandoned, chic, dashing, debauched, depraved devil-may-care*, dissipated, dissolute, fashionable, fast*, flashy, gay, jaunty, lecherous, licentious, loose*, natty, prodigal, profligate, raffish, saucy, sinful, smart, sporty, wanton, wild; SEE CONCEPTS *401,545*

rally [n1] celebrating meeting

assemblage, assembly, celebration, clambake*, convention, convocation, get-together, mass meeting, meet, pep rally, pow-wow*, session; SEE CONCEPTS *377,386*

rally [n2] turn for the better

comeback, improvement, recovery, recuperation, renewal, resurgence, revival, turning point; SEE CONCEPT *700*

rally [v1] reorganize, unite

arouse, assemble, awaken, bestir, bond together, bring together, bring to order, call to arms*, challenge, charge, collect, come about, come together, come to order, convene, counterattack, encourage, fire, gather, get together, inspirit, kindle, marshal, mobilize, muster, organize, reassemble, redouble, reform, refresh, regroup, rejuvenate, renew, restore, resurrect, resuscitate, revive, round up, rouse, summon, surge, urge, wake, waken, whet, wreak havoc*; SEE CONCEPTS *7,22,117,320*

rally [v2] revive; take a turn for the better

bounce back, brace up, come along, come around,

come from behind, enliven, get act together*, get back in shape*, get better, get second wind*, grow stronger, improve, invigorate, make a comeback, perk up, pick up, pull through, recover, recuperate, refresh, regain strength, shape up, snap out of it, surge, turn around, turn things around*; SEE CONCEPT 700

ram [v] *bang into; pack forcibly*
beat, butt, collide with, cram, crash, crowd, dash, dig, drive, drum, force, hammer, hit, hook, impact, jack, jam-pack, pack, plunge, poke, pound, run, run into, sink, slam, smash, stab, stick, strike, strike head-on, stuff, tamp, thrust, wedge; SEE CONCEPTS 189,208,209

ramble [n] *aimless walk*
constitutional, excursion, hike, perambulation, peregrination, roaming, roving, saunter, stroll, tour, traipse, trip, turn; SEE CONCEPTS 151,224

ramble [v1] *wander about; travel aimlessly*
amble, bat around*, be all over the map*, branch off, clamber, climb, cruise, depart, digress, divagate, diverge, drift, excurse, extend, fork, gad, gallivant, get sidetracked*, knock about*, knock around*, meander, perambulate, percolate, peregrinate, promenade, range, roam, rove, saunter, scramble, snake, sprangle, sprawl, spread, spreadeagle, straddle, straggle, stray, stroll, trail, traipse, turn, twist, walk, wind, zigzag; SEE CONCEPTS 151,154,581,692

ramble [v2] *talk aimlessly, endlessly*
amplify, babble, beat around bush*, be diffuse, blather, chatter, depart, descant, digress, divagate, diverge, drift, drivel, dwell on, enlarge, excurse, expatiate, get off the subject*, go astray, go off on tangent*, go on and on*, gossip, harp on, lose the thread*, maunder, meander, prose, protract, rant and rave*, rattle on*, stray, talk nonsense, talk off top of head*, talk randomly, wander; SEE CONCEPT 51

rambling [adj1] *disconnected, wordy*
circuitous, confused, desultory, diffuse, digressive, discursive, disjointed, incoherent, incongruous, irregular, long-winded, periphrastic, prolix; SEE CONCEPT 267

rambling [adj2] *sprawling, spread out*
at length, covering, gangling, here and there, irregular, random, scattered, spreading, straggling, strewn, trailing, unplanned; SEE CONCEPTS 485,772

rambunctious [adj] *loud, energetic*
boisterous, noisy, raucous, rough, rowdy, rude, termagant, tumultous/tumultuous, turbulent, unruly; SEE CONCEPT 542

ramification [n] *consequence, development*
bifurcation, branch, branching, breaking, complication, consequence, divarication, division, excrescence, extension, forking, offshoot, outgrowth, partition, radiation, result, sequel, subdividing, subdivision, upshot; SEE CONCEPTS 98,230,824

ramp [n] *incline*
access, adit, grade, gradient, hill, inclination, inclined plane, rise, slope; SEE CONCEPTS 443,757

rampage [n] *storm, violence*
binge, blowup, boiling point*, destruction, disturbance, ferment, fling, frenzy, fury, mad*, more heat than light*, orgy, rage, ruckus, splurge, spree, tear, tempest, tumult, turmoil, uproar, wingding; SEE CONCEPT 86

rampage [v] *go crazy; storm*
go berserk, rage, run amuck, run riot, run wild, tear; SEE CONCEPTS 86,384

rampant [adj] *uncontrolled, out of hand*
aggressive, blustering, boisterous, clamorous, dominant, epidemic, exceeding bounds, excessive, extravagant, exuberant, fanatical, flagrant, furious, growing, impetuous, impulsive, luxuriant, on the rampage, out of control, outrageous, pandemic, predominant, prevalent, profuse, raging, rampaging, rank, rife, riotous, spreading, tumultous/tumultuous, turbulent, unbridled, unchecked, uncontrollable, ungovernable, unrestrained, unruly, vehement, violent, wanton, widespread, wild; SEE CONCEPTS 544,554,772

rampart [n] *fortification, stronghold*
barricade, barrier, bastion, breastwork, bulwark, defense, earthwork, elevation, embankment, fence, fort, guard, hill, mound, parapet, protection, ridge, security, support, vallation, wall; SEE CONCEPTS 321,439,509

ramshackle [adj] *falling apart; in poor condition*
broken-down, crumbling, decrepit, derelict, dilapidated, flimsy, jerry-built*, rickety, shabby, shaky, tottering, tumble-down, unfirm, unsafe, unsteady; SEE CONCEPTS 485,488

rancid [adj] *rotten, strong-smelling*
bad, carious, contaminated, curdled, decomposing, disagreeable, disgusting, evil-smelling, feculent, fetid, foul, frowzy, fusty, gamy, high, impure, loathsome, malodorous, moldy, musty, nasty, nidorous, noisome, noxious, off, offensive, olid, polluted, putrefactive, putrefied, putrescent, putrid, rank, reeky, repulsive, sharp, smelly, sour, soured, stale, stinking, strong, tainted, turned, unhealthy, whiffy; SEE CONCEPTS 462,570,598,613

rancor [n] *bitterness, hatefulness*
acerbity, acrimony, animosity, animus, antagonism, antipathy, aversion, bad blood*, bile*, dudgeon, enmity, grudge, hardness of heart*, harshness, hate, hatred, hostility, ill feeling, ill will, malevolence, malice, malignity, mordacity, pique, resentfulness, resentment, retaliation, revengefulness, ruthlessness, spite, spitefulness, spleen, umbrage, uncharitableness, unfriendliness, variance, vengeance, vengefulness, venom, vindictiveness, virulence; SEE CONCEPTS 29,410,633

random [adj] *haphazard, chance*
accidental, adventitious, aimless, arbitrary, casual, contingent, designless, desultory, driftless, fluky, fortuitous, hit-or-miss*, incidental, indiscriminate, irregular, objectless, odd, promiscuous, purposeless, slapdash*, spot, stray, unaimed, unconsidered, unplanned, unpremeditated; SEE CONCEPTS 535,548,557

range [n1] *sphere, distance, extent*
ambit, amplitude, area, bounds, circle, compass, confines, diapason, dimension, dimensions, domain, earshot*, elbowroom*, expanse, extension, extensity, field, gamut, hearing, ken, latitude, leeway, length, limits, magnitude, matter, neighborhood, orbit, order, panorama, parameters, play, province, purview, radius, reach, realm, run, run of, scope, space, span, spectrum, sphere, spread, stretch, sweep, swing, territory, tune, vicinity, width; SEE CONCEPTS 651,743,745,756,761,788

range [n2] *order, series*
assortment, chain, class, collection, file, gamut,

kind, line, lot, rank, row, selection, sequence, sort, string, tier, variety; SEE CONCEPTS 727,769

range [v1] *order, categorize*
align, allineate, arrange, array, assort, bias, bracket, catalogue, categorize, class, classify, dispose, draw up, file, grade, group, incline, line, line up, pigeonhole*, predispose, rank; SEE CONCEPTS 84,158

range [v2] *wander, roam*
circumambulate, cover, cross, cruise, drift, encompass, explore, float, follow one's nose*, gallivant, globe-trot*, hit the road*, hit the trail*, make circuit, meander, pass over, ply, prowl, ramble, reach, reconnoiter, rove, scour, search, spread, straggle, stray, stroll, sweep, traipse, tramp, travel, traverse, trek; SEE CONCEPTS 151,224

range [v3] *extend; change within limits*
differ, diverge from, fluctuate, go, reach, run, stretch, vary, vary between; SEE CONCEPT 697

rangy [adj] *long and lean*
gangling, gangly, lanky, leggy, long-legged, long-limbed, reedy, skinny, spindling, spindly, thin, weedy; SEE CONCEPTS 491,779

rank [n1] *standing in a system, often a social one*
ancestry, authority, birth, blood, cachet, capacity, caste, circumstance, class, classification, condition, consequence, degree, dignity, distinction, division, echelon, estate, esteem, family, footing, grade, hierarchy, level, nobility, note, order, paramountcy, parentage, pecking order, pedigree, place, position, primacy, privilege, quality, reputation, seniority, situation, slot, sort, sovereignty, sphere, state, station, stature, status, stock, stratum, supremacy, type; SEE CONCEPTS 296,378, 388,744

rank [n2] *column, tier of individuals*
echelon, file, formation, group, hierarchy, line, queue, range, row, series, string; SEE CONCEPT 727

rank [adj1] *stinking, foul*
bad, dank, disagreeable, disgusting, evil-smelling, feculent, fetid, funky*, fusty*, gamy*, graveolent, gross*, high, humid, loathsome, mephitic, moldy, musty, nasty, nauseating, noisome, noxious, obnoxious, off, offensive, olid, pungent, putrescent, putrid, rancid, reeking, repulsive, revolting, smelly, sour, stale, strong, strong-smelling, tainted, turned; SEE CONCEPT 598

rank [adj2] *abundant, luxurious*
coarse, dense, excessive, extreme, exuberant, fertile, flourishing, fructiferous, grown, high-growing, junglelike, lavish, lush, luxuriant, overabundant, overgrown, productive, profuse, prolific, rampant, rich, semitropical, tropical, vigorous, wild; SEE CONCEPT 485

rank [adj3] *utter, absolute*
arrant, blatant, capital, complete, conspicuous, consummate, downright, egregious, excessive, extravagant, flagrant, glaring, gross, noticeable, outright, outstanding, perfect, positive, rampant, sheer, thorough, total, undisguised, unmitigated; SEE CONCEPTS 531,535

rank [adj4] *obscene, vulgar*
abusive, atrocious, coarse, crass, dirty, filthy, foul, gross, indecent, nasty, outrageous, raunchy, scurrilous, shocking, smutty, wicked; SEE CONCEPT 545

rank [v1] *line up; classify in system*
align, arrange, array, assign, assort, button

down*, class, dispose, establish, estimate, evaluate, fix*, give precedence, grade, include, judge, list, locate, marshal, order, peg, pigeonhole*, place, place in formation, position, put, put away, put down as, put down for, put in line, range, rate, regard, settle, size up, sort, tab, typecast, valuate, value; SEE CONCEPTS 37,84,158

rank [v2] *be worthwhile; have supremacy*
antecede, be classed, belong, be worth, come first, count among, forerun, go ahead of, go before, have the advantage, outrank, precede, stand, take the lead; SEE CONCEPTS 388,671

rankle [v] *annoy, irritate*
aggravate, anger, bother, chafe, embitter, exasperate, fester, fret, gall, get one's goat*, harass, hurt, inflame, irk, irritate, mortify, nettle, obsess, pain, pester, plague, rile, torment, vex; SEE CONCEPTS 7,14,19

ransack [v] *turn inside out in search; ravage*
appropriate, comb, despoil, explore, ferret, filch, go over with a fine-tooth comb*, go through, gut*, hunt, investigate, lay waste, leave no stone unturned*, lift, look all over for*, look high and low*, look into, loot, make off with*, maraud, overhaul, peer, pilfer, pillage, pinch, plunder, poach, probe, pry, purloin, raid, rake, rape, ravish, rifle, rob, rummage, rustle, sack, scan, scour, scrutinize, search, seek, seize, shake down*, sound, spoil, spy, steal, strip, take away, thieve; SEE CONCEPTS 103,139,142,216

ransom [n] *blackmail money paid for return of possession or person*
bribe, compensation, deliverance, expiation, liberation money, payment, payoff, price, redemption, release, rescue; SEE CONCEPT 344

ransom [v] *pay blackmail money for return of possession or person*
buy freedom of, buy out, deliver, emancipate, extricate, free, liberate, manumit, obtain release of, pay for release of, recover, redeem, regain, release, reprise, repurchase, rescue, save, set free, unchain; SEE CONCEPTS 127,131,341

rant [n] *yelling, raving*
bluster, bombast, diatribe, fustian, harangue, oration, philippic, rhapsody, rhetoric, rodomontade, tirade, vociferation; SEE CONCEPTS 44,49,52

rant [v] *yell, rave*
bellow, bloviate, blow one's top*, bluster, carry on, clamor, cry, declaim, fume, harangue, mouth, objurgate, orate, perorate, rage, rail, roar, scold, shout, sizzle*, soapbox*, sound off*, spiel*, spout*, storm*, stump*, take on*, vociferate; SEE CONCEPTS 44,49,52

rap [n1/v1] *hit quickly and lightly*
beat, blow, conk, crack, knock, lick, pat, strike, swat, swipe, tap, whack; SEE CONCEPT 189

rap [n2] *conversation*
causerie, chat, chin*, colloquy, confabulation, conference, deliberation, dialogue, discourse, discussion, prose, talk, ventilation, yarn; SEE CONCEPTS 56,266

rap [n3] *blame; criticism*
admonishment, admonition, censure, chiding, flak, knock, pan*, punishment, rebuke, reprimand, reproach, reproof, responsibility, sentence, swipe; SEE CONCEPTS 52,123,317

rap [v2] *talk casually; speak abruptly*
babble, bark, chat, chatter, chitchat, confabulate, converse, discourse, jabber, palaver, run off at the mouth*, spit, talk; SEE CONCEPTS 56,266

ra
ra

rap [v3] *criticize*

blame, castigate, censure, condemn, denounce, denunciate, knock*, pan*, reprehend, reprimand, reprobate, scold, skin, tick off*; SEE CONCEPT 52

rape [n] *defilement; a forced sexual assault*

abduction, abuse, criminal attack, depredation, despoilment, despoliation, forcible violation, maltreatment, molestation, pillage, plunder, plundering, rapine, spoliation, statutory offense, violation; SEE CONCEPTS 192,375

rape [v] *sexual assault by force; act of plunder*

abuse, attack, betray, compromise, corrupt, deceive, despoil, force, loot, molest, pillage, plunder, ransack, ruin, sack, seize, spoliate, violate; SEE CONCEPTS 192,375

rapid [adj] *very quick*

accelerated, active, agile, breakneck, brisk, double time, expeditious, expeditive, express, fast, fleet, fleet of foot*, flying, hasty, hurried, in nothing flat*, light-footed*, like a house on fire*, lively, mercurial, nimble, on the double*, precipitate, prompt, quick as a wink*, quickened, ready, really rolling*, screaming*, speedy, spry, swift, winged; SEE CONCEPTS 541,588,799

rapidity [n] *quickness*

acceleration, alacrity, bat, briskness, celerity, dispatch, expedition, fleetness, gait, haste, hurry, pace, precipitateness, promptitude, promptness, rapidness, rush, speed, speediness, swiftness, velocity; SEE CONCEPTS 755,805

rapidly [adv] *very quickly*

at speed, briskly, expeditiously, fast, flat out*, full tilt*, hastily, hurriedly, immediately, in a hurry, in a rush, in haste, lickety-split*, like a shot*, posthaste, precipitately, promptly, speedily, swiftly, with dispatch; SEE CONCEPTS 544,588,799

rapport [n] *understanding between people*

affinity, agreement, bond, compatibility, concord, cotton, empathy, good vibes*, good vibrations, groove, harmony, hitting it off*, interrelationship, link, relationship, same wavelength*, simpatico*, soul, sympathy, the groove*, togetherness, unity; SEE CONCEPT 388

rapprochement [n] *restoration of harmony*

agreement, cordiality, detente, friendliness, friendship, harmonization, harmony, reconcilement, reconciliation, reunion, softening; SEE CONCEPTS 384,388

rapt [adj] *absorbed, fascinated*

absent, absent-minded, abstracted, beguiled, bewitched, blissful, busy, captivated, carried away*, caught up in*, charmed, daydreaming, deep*, delighted, dreaming, ecstatic, employed, enamored, engaged, engrossed, enraptured, enthralled, entranced, gripped, happy, held, hung up*, hypnotized, immersed, inattentive, intent, involved, lost, oblivious, occupied, overwhelmed, preoccupied, rapturous, ravished, spellbound, taken*, transported, unconscious, wrapped*, wrapped up*; SEE CONCEPT 403

rapture [n] *extreme happiness and delight in something*

at-oneness*, beatitude, bliss, buoyancy, cheer, cloud nine*, communion, contentment, cool*, delectation, ecstasy, elation, elysium, enchantment, enjoyment, enthusiasm, euphoria, exaltation, exhilaration, felicity, gaiety, gladness, glory, good spirits, gratification, heaven, inspiration, joy, jubilation, nirvana, paradise, passion, pleasure, ravishment, rhapsody, satisfaction, seventh heaven*, spell, transport, well-being; SEE CONCEPTS 32,410

rare [adj1] *exceptional, infrequent*

attenuate, attenuated, deficient, extraordinary, few, few and far between*, flimsy, inconceivable, isolated, light, limited, occasional, out of the ordinary, rarefied, recherché, scanty, scarce, scattered, seldom, semioccasional, short, singular, sparse, sporadic, strange, subtile, subtle, tenuous, thin, uncommon, unfrequent, unheard of, unimaginable, unique, unlikely, unthinkable, unusual, unwonted; SEE CONCEPTS 530,576

rare [adj2] *precious, excellent*

admirable, choice, dainty, delicate, elegant, exquisite, extreme, fine, great, incomparable, invaluable, matchless, peerless, priceless, recherché, rich, select, superb, superlative, unique; SEE CONCEPT 574

rare [adj3] *not fully cooked*

bloody, half-cooked, half-raw, moderately done, nearly raw, not done, rarely done, red, undercooked, underdone; SEE CONCEPT 462

rarely [adv] *not often; exceptionally*

almost never, barely, extra, extraordinarily, extremely, finely, hardly, hardly ever, infrequently, little, notably, now and then, once in a while, once in blue moon*, on rare occasions, remarkably, scarcely ever, seldom, singularly, uncommon, uncommonly, unfrequently, unoften, unusually; SEE CONCEPTS 530,541

rascal [n] *person who is unprincipled, does not work hard*

beggar, blackguard, black sheep*, bully, bum, cad, cardsharp*, charlatan, cheat, delinquent, devil, disgrace, felon, fraud, good-for-nothing*, grafter, hooligan*, hypocrite, idler, imp, liar, loafer, mischief-maker, miscreant, opportunist, pretender, prodigal, profligate, recreant, reprobate, robber, rowdy, ruffian, scamp, scoundrel, sinner, skunk*, sneak*, swindler, tough*, tramp, trickster, varmint*, villain, wastrel, wretch; SEE CONCEPT 412

rash [n] *outbreak of disease or condition*

breakout, epidemic, eruption, flood, hives, pandemic, plague, series, spate, succession, wave; SEE CONCEPTS 230,306

rash [adj] *careless, impulsive*

adventurous, audacious, bold, brash, daring, determined, devil-may-care*, fiery, foolhardy, frenzied, furious, harebrained, hasty, headlong, headstrong, heedless, hotheaded, ill-advised, ill-considered, immature, impetuous, imprudent, incautious, indiscreet, injudicious, insuppressible, irrational, jumping to conclusions*, madcap, overhasty, passionate, precipitant, precipitate, premature, reckless, thoughtless, unguarded, unthinking, unwary, venturesome, venturous, wild; SEE CONCEPT 401

rasp [v] *grind, rub*

abrade, bray, excoriate, file, grate, irk, irritate, jar, pound, raze, rub, sand, scour, scrape, scratch, vex, wear; SEE CONCEPTS 7,19,186,215

rate [n1] *ratio, proportion*

amount, comparison, degree, estimate, percentage, progression, quota, relation, relationship, relative, scale, standard, weight; SEE CONCEPT 768

rate [n2] *fee charged for service, privilege, goods*

allowance, charge, cost, dues, duty, estimate, figure, hire, price, price tag, quotation, tab, tariff, tax, toll, valuation; SEE CONCEPTS 329,766

rate [n3] *speed, pace*
clip, dash, flow, gait, gallop, hop, measure, motion, movement, pace, spurt, tempo, time, tread, velocity; SEE CONCEPT 755

rate [v1] *judge, classify*
adjudge, admire, appraise, apprise, assay, assess, button down*, calculate, class, consider, count, deem, determine, esteem, estimate, evaluate, fix, grade, guess at, measure, peg, pigeonhole*, price, put away, put down as*, put down for*, rank, reckon, redline*, regard, relate to standard, respect, score, set at, size up*, stand in with, survey, tab*, tag, take one's measure, think highly of, typecast*, valuate, value, weigh; SEE CONCEPTS 12,37

rate [v2] *be entitled to*
be accepted, be favorite, be welcome, be worthy, deserve, earn, merit, prosper, succeed, triumph; SEE CONCEPTS 129,376,388

rather [adv1] *moderately*
a bit, a little, averagely, comparatively, enough, fairly, in a certain degree, kind of, more or less, passably, pretty, quite, ratherish, reasonably, relatively, slightly, some, something, somewhat, sort of, so-so*, tolerably, to some degree, to some extent; SEE CONCEPTS 544,548

rather [adv2] *significantly*
a good bit, considerably, noticeably, quite, somewhat, very, well; SEE CONCEPTS 544,772

rather [adv3] *preferably; instead*
alternately, alternatively, as a matter of choice, by choice, by preference, first, in lieu of, in preference, just as soon, more readily, more willingly, much sooner, sooner, willingly; SEE CONCEPT 529

ratify [v] *affirm, authorize*
accredit, approve, authenticate, bear out, bind, bless, certify, commission, confirm, consent, corroborate, endorse, establish, give stamp of approval*, go for*, license, okay*, rubber stamp*, sanction, sign, substantiate, uphold, validate; SEE CONCEPTS 50,88

ratio [n] *percentage, relation of part to whole*
arrangement, correlation, correspondence, equation, fraction, proportion, proportionality, quota, quotient, rate, relationship, scale; SEE CONCEPT 768

ration [n] *allotment of limited supply*
allowance, apportionment, assignment, bit, consignment, cut, distribution, division, dole, drag, food, helping, measure, meed, part, piece of action*, portion, provender, provision, quantum, quota, share, store, supply; SEE CONCEPTS 457,835

ration [v] *divide something into portions*
allocate, allot, apportion, assign, budget, conserve, control, deal, distribute, divvy*, divvy up*, dole, give out, issue, limit, measure out, mete, mete out, parcel, parcel out, proportion, prorate, quota, restrict, save, share; SEE CONCEPTS 98,140

rational [adj] *realistic; of sound mind*
all there*, analytical, balanced, calm, cerebral, circumspect, cognitive, collected, cool*, deductive, deliberate, discerning, discriminating, enlightened, far-sighted, impartial, intellectual, intelligent, judicious, knowing, levelheaded, logical, lucid, normal, objective, perspicacious, philosophic, prudent, ratiocinative, reasonable,

reasoning, reflective, sagacious, sane, sensible, sober, sound, stable, synthetic, thinking, thoughtful, together, well-advised, wise; SEE CONCEPT 402

rationale [n] *logic for belief, action*
account, excuse, explanation, exposition, grounds, hypothesis, justification, motivation, motive, philosophy, principle, raison d'être, rationalization, reason, reasons, song and dance*, sour grapes*, story*, the big idea*, theory, the whole idea*, whatfor*, why and wherefore*, whyfor*; SEE CONCEPT 661

rationalize [v] *make excuse; justify*
account for, apply logic, cop a plea*, cop out*, deliberate, elucidate, excise, excuse, explain away, extenuate, give alibi*, intellectualize, justify, make allowance, reason, reason out, reconcile, resolve, think, think through, vindicate; SEE CONCEPT 57

rattle [v1] *bang, jiggle*
bicker, bounce, clack, clatter, drum, jangle, jar, jolt, jounce, knock, shake, shatter, sound, vibrate; SEE CONCEPTS 65,152

rattle [v2] *talk aimlessly, endlessly*
babble, cackle, chat, chatter, clack, gab, gabble, gush, jabber, jaw, list, prate, prattle, reel off, run on, run through, yak; SEE CONCEPT 51

rattle [v3] *disconcert, upset someone*
abash, addle, bewilder, bother, confound, confuse, discombobulate, discomfit, discompose, discountenance, distract, disturb, embarrass, faze, flummox, frighten, get to*, muddle, nonplus, perplex, perturb, psych out*, put off, put out, put out of countenance, rattle one's cage*, scare, shake, throw, unnerve; SEE CONCEPT 16

raucous [adj1] *noisy, rough*
absonant, acute, atonal, blaring, blatant, braying, brusque, cacophonous, discordant, dissonant, dry, ear-piercing, grating, grinding, gruff, harsh, hoarse, husky, inharmonious, jarring, loud, piercing, rasping, sharp, squawking, stertorous, strident, thick, unharmonious, unmusical; SEE CONCEPTS 592,594

raucous [adj2] *rowdy*
boisterous, disorderly, intemperate, rambunctious, tumultuous/tumultuous, turbulent, unruly; SEE CONCEPT 401

ravage [v] *destroy, ransack*
annihilate, break up, capture, consume, cream*, crush, damage, demolish, desecrate, desolate, despoil, devastate, dismantle, disorganize, disrupt, exterminate, extinguish, forage, foray, gut, harry, impair, lay waste, leave in ruins, loot, overrun, overthrow, overwhelm, pillage, pirate, plunder, prey, prostrate, pull down, raid, rape, raze, rob, ruin, sack, seize, shatter, sink, smash, spoil, spoliate, stamp out, strip, sweep away, total*, trample, trash, waste, wreak havoc, wreck, wrest; SEE CONCEPTS 86,252

rave [v1] *talk endlessly*
babble, be delirious, bloviate, blow one's top*, carry on*, come unglued*, declaim, flip one's lid*, freak out*, fume, gabble, go ape*, go bananas*, go crazy, go mad, harangue, jabber, make a to-do*, mouth, orate, perorate, prate, prattle, rage, rail, rant, rattle on, roar, run amuck*, splutter, storm, talk wildly, thunder, wander; SEE CONCEPTS 51,54

rave [v2] *be very enthusiastic*
be delighted, be excited, be mad about, be wild

about, bubble*, carry on about*, cry up*, effervesce, enthuse, fall all over*, go on about*, gush, make a to-do*, praise, rhapsodize; SEE CONCEPTS 49,410

ravel [v] *come apart; unwind*
disentangle, free, loosen, make plain, smooth out, unbraid, unravel, unsnarl, untangle, untwine, untwist, unweave, unwind, weave out; SEE CONCEPTS 250,469

ravenous [adj] *very hungry; desirous*
avaricious, could eat a horse*, covetous, devouring, edacious, empty, famished, ferocious, gluttonous, grasping, greedy, insatiable, insatiate, omnivorous, predatory, rapacious, ravening, starved, starved to death*, starving, voracious, wolfish; SEE CONCEPT 406

ravine [n] *gap in earth's surface*
abyss, arroyo, break, canyon, chasm, clove, coulee, crevasse, crevice, cut, defile, ditch, fissure, flume, gorge, gulch, gulf, gully, notch, pass, valley, wash; SEE CONCEPTS 509,513

ravish [v1] *enchant*
allure, attract, bewitch, captivate, charm, delight, draw, enrapture, enthrall, entrance, fascinate, hold, hypnotize, magnetize, mesmerize, overjoy, please, spellbind, trance, transport; SEE CONCEPT 11

ravish [v2] *sexually assault*
abduct, abuse, force, rape, violate; SEE CONCEPTS 192,375

raw [adj1] *not cooked, prepared*
basic, bloody, callow, coarse, crude, fibrous, fresh, green, hard, immature, impure, native, natural, organic, rough, roughhewn, rude, unbaked, uncooked, undercooked, underdone, undressed, unfashioned, unformed, unfried, ungraded, unpasteurized, unprepared, unprocessed, unrefined, unripe, unsorted, unstained, untreated; SEE CONCEPTS 462,485

raw [adj2] *exposed, tender, referring to skin*
abraded, au naturel, blistered, bruised, chafed, cut, dressed, galled, grazed, naked, nude, open, pared, peeled, scraped, scratched, sensitive, skinned, sore, unclad, unclothed, uncovered, wounded; SEE CONCEPTS 406,485

raw [adj3] *inexperienced*
callow, fresh, green, ignorant, immature, inexperienced, new, unconversant, undisciplined, unpracticed, unseasoned, unskilled, untaught, untrained, untried, unversed, young; SEE CONCEPT 527

raw [adj4] *vulgar, nasty*
coarse, crass, crude, dirty, filthy, foul, gross, indecent, inelegant, low, mean, obscene, pornographic, rank, rough, rude, smutty, uncouth, unrefined, unscrupulous; SEE CONCEPTS 372,545

raw [adj5] *harsh, unpleasant, referring to weather*
biting, bitter, bleak, breezy, chill, chilly, cold, damp, freezing, piercing, wet, wind-swept, windy; SEE CONCEPT 525

ray [n] *beam; indication*
bar, blaze, blink, emanation, flash, flicker, gleam, glimmer, glint, glitter, hint, incandescence, irradiation, light, moonbeam, patch, pencil, radiance, radiation, scintilla, shaft, shine, spark, sparkle, streak, stream, sunbeam, trace, wave; SEE CONCEPTS 624,628

raze [v] *flatten, knock down; wipe out*
batter, blow down, bomb, break down, bulldoze, capsize, cast down, crash, decimate, delete, demolish, destroy, dynamite, efface, erase, expunge, extinguish, extirpate, fell, level, mow down, obliterate, overthrow, overturn, pull down, reduce, remove, rub out*, ruin, scatter, scratch out, smash, spill, strike out, subvert, tear down, tear up, throw down, topple, total, unbuild, undo, unmake, upset, wipe out, wrack, wreck, zap*; SEE CONCEPT 252

reach [n] *extent, range; stretch*
ability, ambit, capacity, command, compass, distance, extension, gamut, grasp, horizon, influence, jurisdiction, ken, latitude, magnitude, mastery, orbit, play, power, purview, radius, scope, spread, sweep, swing; SEE CONCEPTS 651,756

reach [v1] *arrive at*
arrive, attain, catch up to, check in, clock in*, come, come to, enter, gain on*, get as far as, get in, get to, hit, hit town*, land, make, make it, make the scene*, overtake, ring in*, roll in, show, show up, sign in, turn up, wind up at; SEE CONCEPT 159

reach [v2] *stretch to; touch*
approach, attain, buck, carry to, come at, come up to, contact, continue to, encompass, end, equal, extend to, feel for, get a hold of, get hold of, get to, go, go as far as, go on, go to, grasp, hand, hold out, join, lead, lunge, make, make contact with, overtake, pass, pass along, put out, roll on, seize, shake hands, shoot, span, spread, stand, strain, strike; SEE CONCEPTS 108,612,756

reach [v3] *attain; rise*
accomplish, achieve, amount to, arrive at, climb to, come to, drop, fall, gain, move, rack up*, realize, score, sink, win; SEE CONCEPTS 706, 763,780

reach [v4] *communicate with*
affect, approach, contact, get, get in touch, get through, get to, influence, keep in contact, keep in touch, maintain, move, sway, touch; SEE CONCEPTS 7,19,22,266

react [v] *respond; conduct oneself*
acknowledge, act, answer, answer back, backfire, be affected, behave, boomerang*, bounce back*, counter, echo, feel, function, get back at, give a snappy comeback*, give back, have a funny feeling*, have vibes*, operate, perform, proceed, rebound, reciprocate, recoil, recur, reply, return, revert, take, talk back, turn back, work; SEE CONCEPTS 45,633

reaction [n1] *response*
acknowledgment, answer, attitude, backfire, backlash, back talk*, boomerang*, comeback, compensation, counteraction, counterbalance, counterpoise, double-take*, echo, feedback, feeling, hit, kick, kickback, knee-jerk*, lip*, opinion, reagency, rebound, reception, receptivity, reciprocation, recoil, reflection, reflex, rejoinder, repercussion, reply, retort, return, reverberation, revulsion, sass*, snappy comeback*, take*, vibes*, wisecrack; SEE CONCEPTS 45,633

reaction [n2] *political conservativism*
backlash, backsliding, counterrevolution, obscurantism, regression, relapse, retreat, retrenchment, retrogression, right, right wing, status quo, Toryism, withdrawal; SEE CONCEPTS 300,689

reactionary [n] *person who is politically conservative*
bitter-ender*, counterrevolutionary, diehard*, hard hat*, intransigent, obscurantist, reactionist,

rightist*, right-winger, royalist, standpatter*, Tory*, traditionalist, ultraconservative; SEE CONCEPT 359

reactionary [adj] *conservative*
counterrevolutionary, die-hard*, obscurantist, old-line*, orthodox, regressive, retrogressive, right, rightist*, rigid, standpat*, tory*, traditional, traditionalistic; SEE CONCEPTS 529,542

read [v1] *look at and understand written word*
apprehend, bury oneself in*, comprehend, construe, decipher, dip into*, discover, flip through*, gather, glance, go over, go through, interpret, know, leaf through*, learn, make out*, perceive, peruse, pore over*, refer to, scan, scratch the surface*, see, skim, study, translate, unravel, view; SEE CONCEPT 72

read [v2] *express, state*
affirm, announce, assert, declaim, deliver, display, explain, expound, hold, indicate, mark, paraphrase, pronounce, recite, record, register, render, restate, say, show, speak, utter; SEE CONCEPT 266

readable [adj1] *understandable, legible*
clear, coherent, comprehensible, decipherable, distinct, explicit, flowing, fluent, graphic, intelligible, lucid, orderly, plain, precise, regular, simple, smooth, straightforward, tidy, unequivocal, unmistakable; SEE CONCEPTS 272,529

readable [adj2] *pleasurable to peruse*
absorbing, amusing, appealing, brilliant, clever, easy, eloquent, engaging, engrossing, enjoyable, entertaining, enthralling, exciting, fascinating, gratifying, gripping, ingenious, interesting, inviting, pleasant, pleasing, relaxing, rewarding, satisfying, smooth, stimulating, well-written, worthwhile; SEE CONCEPT 272

readily [adv] *quickly; effortlessly*
at once, at the drop of a hat*, cheerfully, eagerly, easily, facilely, freely, gladly, hands down*, immediately, in a jiffy*, in no time*, lightly, no sweat*, nothing to it*, piece of cake*, promptly, quick as a wink*, right away, slick as whistle*, smoothly, speedily, straight away, swimmingly, unhesitatingly, well, willingly, without delay, without demur, without difficulty, without hesitation; SEE CONCEPTS 544,820

readiness [n] *skill, eagerness*
address, adroitness, alacrity, aptness, deftness, dexterity, dispatch, ease, eloquence, expedience, expedition, facility, fitness, fluency, good will, handiness, inclination, keenness, maturity, preparation, preparedness, promptitude, promptness, prowess, quickness, rapidity, ripeness, sleight, volubility, willingness; SEE CONCEPTS 630,633, 678

reading [n] *interpretation of written word*
account, book-learning, commentary, conception, construction, edification, education, erudition, examination, grasp, impression, inspection, knowledge, learning, lesson, paraphrase, perusal, rendering, rendition, review, scholarship, scrutiny, study, translation, treatment, understanding, version; SEE CONCEPTS 72,271,274

ready [adj1] *prepared; available*
accessible, adjusted, all set, all systems go*, anticipating, apt, arranged, at beck and call*, at fingertips*, at hand, at the ready, champing at bit*, close to hand, completed, convenient, covered, equal to, equipped, expectant, fit, fixed for, handy, in line, in order, in place, in position, in

readiness, in the saddle*, near, on call, on hand, on tap*, on the brink*, open to, organized, primed, qualified, ripe, set, waiting, wired*; SEE CONCEPTS 560,576,799

ready [adj2] *willing, inclined*
agreeable, apt, ardent, disposed, eager, enthusiastic, fain, game, game for, glad, happy, keen, minded, predisposed, prompt, prone, psyched up*, wired*, zealous; SEE CONCEPTS 401,542

ready [adj3] *skillful, intelligent*
active, acute, adept, adroit, alert, apt, astute, bright, brilliant, clever, deft, dexterous, dynamic, expert, handy, keen, live, masterly, perceptive, proficient, prompt, quick, quick-witted, rapid, resourceful, sharp, skilled, smart; SEE CONCEPTS 402,527

ready [v] *prepare*
arrange, brace, brief, clear the decks*, equip, fill in, fit, fit out, fix, fortify, gear up*, get, get ready, get set, gird, keep posted*, let in on*, make, make ready, make up, order, organize, pave the way*, post, prep, provide, psych up*, put on to*, set, strengthen, warm up, wise up*; SEE CONCEPTS 35,60,202

real [adj] *genuine in existence*
absolute, actual, authentic, bodily, bona fide, certain, concrete, corporal, corporeal, de facto, embodied, essential, evident, existent, existing, factual, firm, heartfelt, honest, incarnate, indubitable, in the flesh*, intrinsic, irrefutable, legitimate, live, material, original, palpable, perceptible, physical, positive, present, right, rightful, sensible, sincere, solid, sound, stable, substantial, substantive, tangible, true, unaffected, undeniable, undoubted, unfeigned, valid, veritable; SEE CONCEPT 582

realistic [adj1] *sensible, matter of fact*
astute, businesslike, commonsense, down-to-earth, earthy, hard, hard boiled*, levelheaded, practical, pragmatic, pragmatical, prudent, rational, real, reasonable, sane, sensible, shrewd, sober, sound, unfantastic, unidealistic, unromantic, unsentimental, utilitarian; SEE CONCEPTS 403, 542,548

realistic [adj2] *genuine*
authentic, faithful, graphic, lifelike, natural, original, representational, representative, true, true to life, truthful; SEE CONCEPT 582

reality [n] *facts of existence*
absoluteness, actuality, authenticity, being, bottom line*, brass tacks*, certainty, concreteness, corporeality, deed, entity, existence, genuineness, how things are*, like it is*, materiality, matter, name of the game*, nuts and bolts*, object, palpability, perceptibility, phenomenon, presence, realism, realness, real world*, sensibility, solidity, substance, substantiality, substantive, tangibility, truth, validity, verisimilitude, verity, way of it*, what's what*; SEE CONCEPTS 689,725

realize [v1] *appreciate, become aware of*
apprehend, be cognizant of, become conscious of, catch, catch on*, comprehend, conceive, discern, envisage, envision, fancy*, feature*, get, get it*, get the idea*, get the picture*, get through one's head*, grasp, image, imagine, know, pick up*, recognize, see daylight*, take in*, think, understand, vision, visualize; SEE CONCEPT 15

realize [v2] *accomplish*
actualize, bring about, bring off*, bring to fruition, carry out, carry through, complete, consum-

mate, corporealize, do, effect, effectuate, fulfill, make concrete, make good*, make happen, materialize, perfect, perform, reify; SEE CONCEPT *91*

realize [*v3*] *gain, earn*
accomplish, achieve, acquire, attain, bring in, clear, get, go for*, make, make a profit, net, obtain, produce, rack up*, reach, receive, score*, sell for, take in, win; SEE CONCEPTS *120,124,330*

really [*adv*] *without a doubt*
absolutely, actually, admittedly, as a matter of fact, assuredly, authentically, beyond doubt, categorically, certainly, de facto, easily, for real*, genuinely, honestly, in actuality, indeed, indubitably, in effect, in fact, in point of fact, in reality, legitimately, literally, no ifs ands or buts*, nothing else but, of course, positively, precisely, surely, truly, undoubtedly, unmistakably, unquestionably, verily, well; SEE CONCEPTS *535,582*

realm [*n*] *area of responsibility or rule*
branch, compass, country, department, dimension, domain, dominion, empire, expanse, extent, field, ground, kingdom, land, monarchy, neck of the woods*, neighborhood, orbit, place, principality, province, purview, radius, range, reach, region, scope, sphere, state, stomping grounds*, sweep, territory, turf*, world, zone; SEE CONCEPTS *349,362,512,651*

reap [*v*] *collect, harvest*
acquire, bring in, come to have, crop, cull, cut, derive, draw, gain, garner, gather, get, get as a result, glean, ingather, mow, obtain, pick, pick up, pluck, procure, produce, profit, realize, receive, recover, retrieve, secure, strip, take in, win; SEE CONCEPTS *109,120,124,257*

rear [*n*] *back or end part*
afterpart, back, back door*, back end, back seat*, backside, behind, bottom, butt, buttocks, end, heel, hind, hind part, hindquarters, posterior, postern, rear end, rear guard, rearward, reverse, rump, seat, stern, tail, tail end, tailpiece, tush*; SEE CONCEPTS *825,827*

rear [*adj*] *back, end*
aft, after, astern, backward, behind, dorsal, following, hind, hinder, hindermost, hindmost, last, mizzen, posterior, postern, rearmost, rearward, retral, reverse, stern, tail; SEE CONCEPT *583*

rear [*v1*] *raise young*
breed, bring up, care for, cultivate, educate, foster, grow, nurse, nurture, propagate, train; SEE CONCEPT *295*

rear [*v2*] *lift, rise*
bring up, elevate, hoist, hold up, jump, leap, loom, pick up, raise, set upright, soar, spring up, support, take up, tower, turn up, uphold, uplift, upraise; SEE CONCEPTS *194,196,741*

rear [*v3*] *build*
construct, erect, fabricate, put up, raise, set up, uprear; SEE CONCEPT *168*

reason [*n1*] *mental analysis*
acumen, apprehension, argumentation, bounds, brain*, brains*, comprehension, deduction, dialectics, discernment, generalization, induction, inference, intellect, intellection, judgment, limits, logic, lucidity, marbles*, mentality, mind, moderation, propriety, ratiocination, rationalism, rationality, rationalization, reasonableness, reasoning, saneness, sanity, senses*, sensibleness, sound mind, soundness, speculation, understanding, wisdom, wit; SEE CONCEPTS *37,409*

reason [*n2*] *intention, aim*
antecedent, argument, basis, cause, consideration, design, determinant, end, goal, grounds, idea, impetus, incentive, inducement, motivation, motive, object, occasion, proof, purpose, rationale, root, spring, target, ulterior motive, warrant, wherefore*, why, why and wherefore*, whyfor*; SEE CONCEPT *659*

reason [*n3*] *explanation for an action*
account, apologia, apology, argument, case, cover, defense, excuse, exposition, ground, idea, justification, notion, proof, rationale, rationalization, song and dance*, sour grapes*, the whole idea*, vindication, whatfor*, wherefore*, why*, why and wherefore*, whyfor*; SEE CONCEPT *661*

reason [*v1*] *mentally analyze*
adduce, cerebrate, cogitate, conclude, contemplate, decide, deduce, deduct, deliberate, draw conclusion, draw from, examine, figure out, gather, generalize, infer, make out, philosophize, ratiocinate, rationalize, reflect, resolve, solve, speculate, study, suppose, syllogize, think, think through, thresh out, work out; SEE CONCEPT *37*

reason [*v2*] *argue, persuade*
bring around, contend, debate, demonstrate, discourse, discuss, dispute, dissuade, establish, expostulate, justify, move, point out, prevail upon, prove, remonstrate, show error of ways*, talk into, talk out of, urge, win over; SEE CONCEPTS *46,56,68*

reasonable [*adj1*] *moderate, tolerable*
acceptable, analytical, average, cheap, circumspect, conservative, controlled, discreet, equitable, fair, feasible, fit, honest, humane, impartial, inexpensive, judicious, just, justifiable, knowing, legit, legitimate, low-cost, low-priced, making sense, modest, objective, okay, plausible, politic, proper, prudent, rational, reflective, restrained, right, sane, sapient, sensible, sound, standing to reason*, temperate, understandable, unexcessive, unextreme, valid, within reason; SEE CONCEPTS *547,558*

reasonable [*adj2*] *intelligent, practical*
advisable, all there*, arguable, believeable, cerebral, clear-cut, cognitive, commonsensical, conscious, consequent, consistent, cool*, credible, in one's right mind*, judicious, justifiable, level-headed, logical, perceiving, percipient, plausible, ratiocinative, rational, reasoned, reasoning, reflective, sane, sensible, sober, sound, tenable, thoughtful, thought-out, together*, tolerant, unbiased, unprejudiced, well-advised, wise; SEE CONCEPT *402*

reasoning [*n*] *logic, interpretation*
acumen, analysis, apriority, argument, case, cogitation, concluding, corollary, deduction, dialectics, exposition, generalization, hypothesis, illation, induction, inference, interpretation, logistics, premise, proof, proposition, ratiocination, rationale, rationalizing, reason, syllogism, syllogization, thinking, thought, train of thought; SEE CONCEPTS *37,529*

reassure [*v*] *restore confidence to*
assure, bolster, brace, buoy, cheer, comfort, console, convince, encourage, give a lift*, give confidence, guarantee, hearten, inspire, inspirit, perk up, pick up*, put one's mind to rest*, relieve, snap one out of it*; SEE CONCEPTS *7,22*

rebate [*n*] *refund given to purchaser*
abatement, allowance, bonus, deduction, dis-

count, kickback, payback, reduction, reimbursement, remission, repayment, **subtraction**; SEE CONCEPT *344*

rebel [*n*] *person who does not obey*

agitator, anarchist, antagonist, apostate, demagogue, deserter, disectarian, dissenter, experientialist, experimenter, frondeur, guerrilla, heretic, iconoclast, independent, individualist, innovator, insurgent, insurrectionary, malcontent, mutineer, nihilist, nonconformist, opponent, overthrower, recreant, renegade, resistance, revolter, revolutionary, revolutionist, rioter, schismatic, secessionist, seditionist, separatist, subverter, traitor, turncoat; SEE CONCEPTS *359,412,423*

rebel [*adj*] *not obeying*

insubordinate, insurgent, insurrectionary, mutinous, rebellious, **revolutionary**; SEE CONCEPT *401*

rebel [*v*] *refuse to obey*

be insubordinate, boycott, break with*, censure, combat, come out against*, criticize, defy, denounce, disobey, dissent, drop out*, fight, get out of line*, insurrect, make waves*, mutiny, oppose, opt out*, overthrow, overturn, remonstrate, renounce, resist, revolt, riot, rise up*, rock the boat*, run amok*, secede, strike, take up arms, turn against, **upset**; SEE CONCEPTS *106,633*

rebellion [*n*] *disobedience; revolt*

apostasy, defiance, disobedience, dissent, heresy, insubordination, insurgence, insurgency, insurrection, nonconformity, revolution, rising, schism, **uprising**; SEE CONCEPTS *106,300,320,633*

rebellious [*adj*] *disobedient, unmanageable*

alienated, anarchistic, attacking, bellicose, contumacious, defiant, difficult, disaffected, disloyal, disobedient, disorderly, dissident, factious, fractious, iconoclastic, incorrigible, individualistic, insurgent, insurrectionary, intractable, mutinous, obstinate, pugnacious, quarrelsome, radical, rebel, recalcitrant, refractory, resistant, restless, revolutionary, rioting, riotous, sabotaging, seditious, threatening, treasonable, turbulent, ungovernable, unruly, **warring**; SEE CONCEPTS *401, 529,542*

rebuff [*n*] *turning away; ignoring*

brushoff*, check, cold shoulder*, cut, defeat, denial, discouragement, go-by*, hard time*, insult, kick in the teeth*, nix*, nothing doing*, opposition, rebuke, refusal, rejection, reprimand, repulse, slight, snub, thumbs down*, **turndown**; SEE CONCEPTS *30,278*

rebuff [*v*] *turn away; give the cold shoulder**

beat off, brush off, check, chide, cross, cut, decline, deny, disallow, discourage, dismiss, disregard, fend off, hold off, ignore, keep at a distance*; keep at arm's length*, keep at bay, lash out at, neglect, not hear of, oppose, pass up, push back, put in one's place*, put off, rebuke, refuse, reject, repel, reprove, repudiate, repulse, resist, send away, slight, snub, spurn, stave off, tell off*, turn down, **ward off**; SEE CONCEPTS *30,54*

rebuke [*n*] *reprimand; harsh criticism*

admonishment, admonition, affliction, bawling-out*, berating, blame, castigation, censure, chewing-out*, chiding, comeuppance, condemnation, correction, disapproval, dressing-down*, earful*, expostulation, going-over*, hard time*, kick in the teeth*, lecture, lesson, objurgation, ostracism, punishment, put-down, rap*, rating, rebuff, refusal, remonstrance, reprehension, reproach, reproof, reproval, repulse, row, scolding,

slap in the face*, snub, talking-to*, telling-off*, tongue-lashing*, **upbraiding**; SEE CONCEPTS *44,52,278*

rebuke [*v*] *reprimand; criticize harshly*

admonish, bawl out*, berate, blame, call on the carpet*, carp on, castigate, censure, chew out*, chide, climb all over*, dress down*, fry*, go after*, jawbone*, jump down one's throat*, jump on*, lay into*, lean on*, lecture, lesson, monish, oppose, pay, rake, read*, reprehend, reprimand, reproach, reprove, rip*, scold, sit on*, sound off*, take to task*, tear apart*, tell off*, tick off*, upbraid, **zap***; SEE CONCEPTS *44,52*

rebut [*v*] *argue against; prove wrong*

break, come back at, confound, confute, controvert, cross, defeat, deny, disconfirm, disprove, evert, fend off, get back at, hold off, invalidate, keep off, negate, negative, overturn, prove false, quash, refute, repel, repulse, stave off, take on, top, **ward off**; SEE CONCEPTS *46,54*

recalcitrant [*adj*] *disobedient, uncontrollable*

contrary, contumacious, defiant, fractious, indomitable, insubmissive, insubordinate, intractable, obstinate, opposing, radical, rebellious, refractory, resistant, resisting, stubborn, undisciplinable, undisciplined, ungovernable, unmanageable, unruly, untoward, unwilling, wayward, wild, willful, **withstanding**; SEE CONCEPT *401*

recall [*n1*] *remembrance*

anamnesis, memory, recollection, **reminiscence**, SEE CONCEPT *529*

recall [*n2*] *request for return*

annulment, cancellation, nullification, recision, repeal, rescindment, rescission, retraction, revocation, **withdrawal**; SEE CONCEPTS *662,685*

recall [*v1*] *remember*

arouse, awaken, bethink, bring to mind, call to mind, call up, cite, come to one, educe, elicit, evoke, extract, flash, flash on*, look back, mind, nail it down*, recollect, reestablish, reinstate, reintroduce, remind, reminisce, renew, retain, retrospect, revive, ring a bell*, rouse, stir, strike a note*, summon, think back*, think of, **waken**; SEE CONCEPT *40*

recall [*v2*] *ask for return of offending thing*

abjure, annul, call back, call in, cancel, countermand, discharge, dismantle, dismiss, disqualify, forswear, lift, nullify, palinode, recant, repeal, rescind, retract, reverse, revoke, suspend, take back, unsay, **withdraw**; SEE CONCEPTS *50,88, 131,143*

recant [*v*] *take back something said*

abjure, abnegate, abrogate, annul, apostatize, back down, back off, back out, backtrack*, call back, cancel, contradict, countermand, deny, dial back*, disavow, disclaim, disown, eat one's words*, forswear, go back on one's word*, nullify, recall, renege, renounce, repeal, repudiate, rescind, retract, revoke, take back, unsay, void, weasel out*, welsh*, withdraw, worm out of*; SEE CONCEPTS *25,266*

recapitulate [*v*] *go over something again*

epitomize, go over same ground*, go the same round*, outline, paraphrase, recap*, recount, rehash, reiterate, repeat, rephrase, replay, restate, review, reword, run over*, run through again*, summarize, sum up; SEE CONCEPT *266*

recede [*v*] *withdraw; diminish*

abate, back, close, decline, decrease, depart, die off, diminish, drain away, draw back, drop, dwin-

re
re

dle, ebb, fade, fall back, flow back, go away, go back, lessen, reduce, regress, retire, retract, retreat, retrocede, retrograde, retrogress, return, shrink, sink, subside, taper, wane; SEE CONCEPTS 195,698,776

receipt [n1] *acknowledgment of delivery*
cancellation, certificate, chit, counterfoil, declaration, discharge, letter, notice, proof of purchase, quittance, release, sales slip, slip, stub, voucher; SEE CONCEPTS 271,332

receipt [n2] *delivery of goods*
acceptance, accession, acquiring, acquisition, admission, admitting, arrival, getting, intaking, receiving, reception, recipience, taking; SEE CONCEPT 124

receipts [n] *money earned in business venture*
bottom line*, cash flow, comings in*, earnings, gain, gate, get*, gross, handle*, income, net, proceeds, profit, return, revenue, revenue stream, royalty, take*, take-in*, taking*; SEE CONCEPT 344

receive [v1] *accept delivery of something*
accept, acquire, admit, apprehend, appropriate, arrogate, assume, be given, be informed, be in receipt of, be told, catch, collect, come by, come into, cop*, corral*, derive, draw, earn, gain, gather, get, get from, get hands on*, get hold of*, grab, hear, hold, inherit, latch on to*, make, obtain, perceive, pick up, pocket*, procure, pull, pull down*, reap, redeem, secure, seize, snag*, take, take in, take possession, win; SEE CONCEPT 124

receive [v2] *endure, sustain*
bear, be subjected to, encounter, experience, go through, meet with, suffer, undergo; SEE CONCEPT 23

receive [v3] *take in guest or member*
accept, accommodate, admit, allow entrance, bring in, entertain, greet, host, induct, initiate, install, introduce, invite, let in, let through, make comfortable, make welcome, meet, permit, roll out red carpet*, shake hands*, show in, take in, usher in, welcome; SEE CONCEPTS 50,83,88,140

recent [adj] *current*
contempo*, contemporary, fresh, hot off the fire*, hot off the press*, just out*, late, latter, latter-day, modern, modernistic, neoteric, new, newborn, newfangled, novel, present-day, the latest*, today, up-to-date, young; SEE CONCEPTS 578, 797,820

recently [adv] *currently*
afresh, anew, freshly, in recent past, in recent times, just a while ago, just now, lately, latterly, new, newly, not long ago, of late, short while ago, the other day; SEE CONCEPT 820

receptacle [n] *container for disposal, storage*
bowl, box, holder, hopper, repository, vessel, wastebasket; SEE CONCEPT 494

reception [n1] *acceptance; acknowledgment*
accession, acquisition, admission, disposition, encounter, gathering, greeting, induction, introduction, meeting, reaction, receipt, receiving, recipience, recognition, response, salutation, treatment, welcome; SEE CONCEPTS 83,124,384

reception [n2] *celebratory party*
buffet, dinner, do*, entertainment, function, gathering, levee, matinee, soiree, supper, tea; SEE CONCEPT 383

receptive [adj] *open to new ideas*
acceptant, acceptive, accessible, alert, amenable,

approachable, bright, favorable, friendly, hospitable, influenceable, interested, observant, open, open-minded, open to suggestions, perceptive, persuadable, pushover*, quick on the uptake*, ready, recipient, responsive, sensitive, suggestible, susceptible, swayable, sympathetic, welcoming, well-disposed; SEE CONCEPT 404

recess [n1] *niche, corner*
alcove, ambush, angle, apse, bay, break, carrel, cavity, cell, closet, cove, cranny, crutch, crypt, cubicle, dent, depression, depths, embrasure, fork, heart, hiding place, hole, hollow, indentation, mouth, nook, opening, oriel, penetralia, reaches, retreat, secret place, slot, socket; SEE CONCEPTS 440,513

recess [n2] *break, interval in action*
break-off, breather*, breathing spell*, cessation, closure, coffee break*, cutoff, downtime*, halt, happy hour*, hiatus, holiday, interlude, intermission, interregnum, layoff, letup, lull, pause, respite, rest, stop, suspension, ten*, time-out, vacation; SEE CONCEPT 807

recess [v] *stop action*
adjourn, break off*, break up*, call time*, dissolve, drop, drop it, pigeonhole*, prorogate, prorogue, put on hold, rise, shake, sideline*, take a break, take a breather*, take five*, take ten*, terminate; SEE CONCEPTS 119,121

recession [n] *reversal of action; reduction of business activity*
bad times*, bankruptcy, big trouble*, bottom-out*, bust, collapse, decline, deflation, depression, downturn, hard times*, inflation, rainy days*, shakeout*, slide, slump, stagnation, unemployment; SEE CONCEPT 335

recipe [n] *directions, formula*
compound, ingredients, instructions, method, modus operandi, prescription, procedure, process, program, receipt, technique; SEE CONCEPT 274

reciprocal [adj] *exchanged, alternate*
changeable, companion, complementary, convertible, coordinate, correlative, corresponding, dependent, double, duplicate, equivalent, exchangeable, fellow, give-and-take*, interchangeable, interdependent, matching, mutual, reciprocative, reciprocatory, twin; SEE CONCEPTS 566,577

reciprocate [v] *exchange, alternate; equal*
barter, be equivalent, correspond, equal, feel in return, interchange, make up for*, match, pay one's dues*, recompense, render, repay, reply, requite, respond, retaliate, retort, return, return the compliment*, scratch one's back*, serve out, share, square, swap, swing, tit for tat*, trade, vacillate; SEE CONCEPTS 45,104,384

recital [n] *narrative, rendering*
account, concert, description, detailing, enumeration, fable, musical, musicale, narration, narrative, performance, portrayal, presentation, reading, recapitulation, recitation, recountal, recounting, rehearsal, relation, repetition, report, statement, story, tale, telling; SEE CONCEPTS 263,264

recitation [n] *reading to audience*
address, appeal, declaiming, delivery, discourse, discoursing, discussion, exercise, holding forth, lecture, monologue, narrating, narration, oration, passage, performance, piece, playing, proclamation, recital, recounting, rehearsal, rendering, re-

port, selection, soliloquizing, speaking, talk, telling; SEE CONCEPTS 72,263,266

recite [v] *read out loud; narrate*
account for, address, answer, chant, communicate, convey, declaim, delineate, deliver, describe, detail, discourse, dramatize, enact, enlarge, enumerate, expatiate, explain, give an account, give a report, give verbal account, hold forth, impart, interpret, itemize, mention, narrate, parrot*, perform, picture, portray, quote, recapitulate, recount, reel off*, rehearse, relate, render, repeat, reply, report, retell, soliloquize, speak, state, tell, utter; SEE CONCEPTS 55,57,72,266

reckless [adj] *irresponsible in thought, deed*
adventuresome, adventurous, any which way*, audacious, brash, breakneck, carefree, careless, daredevil, daring, desperate, devil-may-care*, fast and loose*, feckless, foolhardy, harebrained, hasty, headlong, heedless, helter-skelter, hopeless, hotheaded*, ill-advised, imprudent, inattentive, incautious, inconsiderate, indiscreet, kooky*, madcap, mindless, negligent, overventuresome, playing with fire*, precipitate, rash, regardless, temerarious, thoughtless, uncareful, venturesome, venturous, wild; SEE CONCEPTS 401,542

reckon [v1] *add up; evaluate*
account, appraise, approximate, calculate, call, cast, cipher, compute, conjecture, consider, count, count heads*, count noses*, deem, enumerate, esteem, estimate, figure, figure out, foot, gauge, guess, hold, judge, keep tabs*, look upon, number, place, put, rate, regard, run down, square, sum, surmise, take account of, tally, think of, tick off*, tot, total, tote*, tote up*, tot up, view; SEE CONCEPTS 37,764

reckon [v2] *suppose, imagine*
assume, bank on, bargain for, believe, be of the opinion, build on, conjecture, count on, depend on, expect, fancy, gather, guess, plan on, rely on, surmise, suspect, take, think, trust in, understand; SEE CONCEPTS 12,26

reckoning [n] *computation, account*
adding, addition, arithmetic, bad news*, bill, calculation, charge, check, ciphering, cost, count, counting, debt, due, estimate, estimation, fee, figuring, grunt*, invoice, IOU*, score, settlement, statement, summation, tab, working; SEE CONCEPT 331

recline [v] *lie down*
be recumbent, cant, heel, lay down, lean, lie, list, loll, lounge, repose, rest, slant, slope, sprawl, stretch, stretch out, tilt, tip; SEE CONCEPTS 154,201

recluse [n] *person who does not want social contact*
anchorite, ascetic, cenobite, eremite, hermit, monk, nun, solitaire, solitary, troglodyte; SEE CONCEPT 423

recluse/reclusive [adj] *hermitlike, unsociable*
antisocial, ascetic, cloistered, eremetic, hermetic, isolated, misanthropic, monastic, reserved, retiring, secluded, secluse, seclusive, sequestered, solitary, standoffish, withdrawn; SEE CONCEPTS 404,555

recognition [n1] *identification, acknowledgment*
acceptance, acknowledging, admission, allowance, apperception, appreciation, apprehending, assimilation, avowal, awareness, cognizance, concession, confession, consciousness, detection,

discovery, double take*, high sign*, identifying, memory, notice, noticing, perceiving, perception, realization, recall, recalling, recognizance, recollection, recurrence, remembering, remembrance, respect, salute, sensibility, tumble*, understanding, verifying; SEE CONCEPT 38

recognition [n2] *appreciation given*
acceptance, acknowledgment, approval, attention, credit, esteem, gratitude, greeting, honor, notice, pat on back*, pat on head*, plum*, puff*, puffing up*, pumping up*, rave, regard, renown, salute, strokes*; SEE CONCEPTS 10,337,689

recognize [v1] *identify*
admit, be familiar, button down*, descry, determinate, diagnose, diagnosticate, distinguish, espy, finger*, flash on*, know, know again, make*, make out, nail*, note, notice, observe, peg*, perceive, pinpoint, place, recall, recollect, remark, remember, ring a bell*, see, sight, spot, tab, tag, verify; SEE CONCEPT 38

recognize [v2] *acknowledge, understand; approve*
accept, admit, agree, allow, appreciate, assent, avow, be aware of, comprehend, concede, confess, grant, greet, honor, make, own, perceive, realize, respect, salute, sanction, see; SEE CONCEPT 15

recoil [v] *shrink away*
backfire, balk, blanch, blench, blink, carom, cringe, demur, dodge, draw back, duck, falter, flinch, hesitate, jerk, kick, pull back, quail, quake, react, rebound, reel, resile, shake, shirk, shrink, shudder, shy away, spring, start, step back, stick, stickle, swerve, tremble, turn away, waver, wince, withdraw; SEE CONCEPTS 150,194,195

recollect [v] *remember*
arouse, awaken, bethink, bring to mind, call to mind, cite, come to one, flash, flash on*, look back on mind, place, recall, recognize, remind, reminisce, retain, retrospect, revive, rouse, stir, summon, waken; SEE CONCEPT 40

recommend [v] *advise, approve*
acclaim, advance, advocate, applaud, back, be all for*, be satisfied with, celebrate, commend, compliment, confirm, counsel, endorse, enjoin, esteem, eulogize, exalt, exhort, extol, favor, front for*, glorify, go on record for*, hold up, justify, laud, magnify, plug*, praise, prescribe, prize, propose, put forward, put in a good word*, put on to*, sanction, second, speak highly of, speak well of, stand by, steer, suggest, think highly of, uphold, urge, value, vouch for; SEE CONCEPTS 10,75

recommendation [n] *advice, approval*
advocacy, approbation, blessing, certificate, character reference, charge, commendation, counsel, direction, endorsement, esteem, eulogy, favorable mention, good word*, guidance, injunction, instruction, judgment, letter of support, order, pass, plug*, praise, proposal, proposition, reference, sanction, steer*, suggestion, support, testimonial, tip, tribute, two cents' worth*, urging; SEE CONCEPTS 274,278

recompense [n] *something returned, paid back*
amends, atonement, bus fare*, compensation, cue, damages, emolument, expiation, gravy*, indemnification, indemnity, overcompensation, pay, payment, propitiation, quittance, recoupment, recovery, redemption, redress, remuneration, reparation, repayment, requital, restitution, retrieval, retrievement, return, reward, salvo, sat-

isfaction, solatium, sweetener*, tip, wages; SEE
CONCEPTS 340,344

recompense [v] *pay back, make restitution*
ante up*, atone, atone for, balance, comp*, compensate, cough up*, counterbalance, counterpoise, countervail, do business*, equalize,
expiate, fix, give satisfaction, grease*, indemnify,
make amends, make good*, make up for, offset,
overcompensate, pay, pay for, propitiate, put
out*, reciprocate, recoup, recover, redress, reimburse, remunerate, repay, requite, retaliate, retrieve, return, reward, satisfy, spring for, square*,
sweeten the pot*, swing for*, take care of; SEE
CONCEPTS 126,341

reconcile [v1] *make peace; adjust*
accommodate, accord, accustom, appease, arbitrate, arrange, assuage, attune, bring together,
bring to terms, bury the hatchet*, come together,
compose, conciliate, conform, cool*, coordinate,
fit, fix up, get together on, harmonize, integrate,
intercede, kiss and make up*, make matters up,
make up, mediate, mitigate, pacify, patch things
up*, patch up*, placate, propitiate, proportion,
reconciliate, rectify, re-establish, regulate, resolve, restore harmony, reunite, settle, suit, tune,
win over; SEE CONCEPTS 384,697

reconcile [v2] *resign oneself to something*
accept, accommodate, get used to*, make the best
of*, put up with*, resign, submit, yield; SEE CONCEPT 23

recondite [adj] *mysterious, obscure*
abstruse, academic, acroamatic, arcane, cabalistic, concealed, cryptic, dark, deep, difficult, esoteric, hard, heavy*, hermetic, hidden, involved,
little-known, mystic, mystical, occult, orphic, pedantic, profound, scholarly, secret; SEE CONCEPTS 529,576

reconsider [v] *think about again*
amend, change one's mind, consider again, correct, emend, go over, have second thoughts*, polish, rearrange, reassess, recheck, reevaluate,
reexamine, rehash, replan, rethink, retrace, review, revise, reweigh, rework, run through, see in
a new light*, sleep on, take another look, think
better of*, think over, think twice*, work over;
SEE CONCEPT 17

reconstruct [v] *reorganize, build up*
copy, deduce, doctor*, do up*, fix, fix up, make
over, modernize, overhaul, patch, piece together,
reassemble, rebuild, recast, recondition, reconstitute, recreate, reestablish, refashion, reform, regenerate, rehabilitate, rejuvenate, remake,
remodel, remold, renovate, reorient, repair, replace, reproduce, reshuffle, restore, retool, revamp, rework; SEE CONCEPTS 84,168,171

record [n1] *account of event or proceedings*
almanac, annals, archive, archives, chronicle,
comic book*, diary, directory, document, documentation, entry, evidence, file, history, inscription, jacket, journal, legend, log, manuscript,
memo, memoir, memorandum, memorial, minutes, monument, note, paper trail*, register, registry, remembrance, report, script, scroll, story,
swindle sheet*, testimony, trace, track record*,
transcript, transcription, witness, writing, written
material; SEE CONCEPTS 271,281

record [n2] *background, experience*
accomplishment, administration, career, case history, conduct, curriculum vitae, history, past be-

havior, performance, reign, studies, track record*,
way of life*, work; SEE CONCEPT 678

record [n3] *achievement*
ceiling, maximum; SEE CONCEPT 706

record [v1] *write down; store information*
book, can*, catalog, chalk up*, chronicle, copy,
cut, cut a track*, document, dub*, enroll, enter,
enumerate, file, indite, inscribe, insert, jot down,
keep account, lay down, list, log, make a recording, mark, mark down, matriculate, note, post,
preserve, put down, put in writing, put on file*,
put on paper*, put on tape*, register, report, set
down, tabulate, take down, tape, tape-record,
transcribe, video*, videotape, wax*, write in; SEE
CONCEPT 125

record [v2] *give evidence of*
contain, designate, explain, indicate, mark, point
out, point to, read, register, say, show; SEE CONCEPT 261

recount [v] *tell a story*
break a story*, convey, delineate, depict, describe, detail, echo, enumerate, give an account
of, itemize, narrate, picture, play back, portray,
recap*, recapitulate, recite, rehash, rehearse, relate, repeat, report, run by again*, run down*, run
through*, say again, state, tell, track, unload, verbalize; SEE CONCEPTS 55,266

recoup [v] *recover, make up for*
compensate, get back, get out from under*, get
well, make good, make redress for, make well,
redeem, refund, regain, reimburse, remunerate,
repay, repossess, requite, retrieve, satisfy, win
back; SEE CONCEPTS 124,126,342,700

recourse [n] *alternative*
aid, appeal, choice, expediency, expedient, help,
makeshift, option, refuge, remedy, resort, resource, shift, stand-by, stopgap, substitute, support, way out; SEE CONCEPTS 693,712

recover [v1] *find again*
balance, bring back, catch up, compensate, get
back, make good, obtain again, offset, reacquire,
recapture, reclaim, recoup, recruit, redeem, rediscover, regain, reoccupy, repair, replevin, replevy,
repossess, rescue, restore, resume, retake, retrieve, salvage, take back, win back; SEE CONCEPTS 120,183

recover [v2] *improve in health*
be out of woods*, better, bounce back*, come
around, convalesce, feel oneself again*, forge
ahead, gain, get back on feet*, get better, get in
shape, get out from under*, get over, get well,
grow, heal, increase, make a comeback*, mend,
overcome, perk up*, pick up, pull through, rally,
rebound, recuperate, refresh, regain one's health,
regain one's strength, rejuvenate, renew, restore,
return to form, revive, snap back*, sober up*,
start anew, take turn for better; SEE CONCEPTS
303,700

recreation [n] *sports, games, special interests*
amusement, avocation, ball*, disport, dissipation,
distraction, diversion, divertissement, ease, enjoyment, entertainment, exercise, festivity, field
day*, frolic, fun, fun and games*, game, hilarity,
hobby, holiday, jollity, laughs*, leisure activity,
mirth, pastime, picnic, play, playtime, pleasure,
R and R*, rec, refreshment, relaxation, relief, repose, rollick, sport, vacation; SEE CONCEPTS
363,364

recruit [n] *person beginning service*
apprentice, beginner, convert, draftee, enlisted

person, fledgling, GI*, greenhorn*, helper, initiate, learner, neophyte, newcomer, new person, novice, novitiate, plebe*, proselyte, rookie, sailor, selectee, serviceperson, soldier, tenderfoot*, trainee, volunteer; SEE CONCEPTS *348,358*

recruit [v] *gather resources*
augment, better, build up, call to arms, call up, deliver, draft, engage, enlist, enroll, fill up, find human resources, gain, impress, improve, induct, levy, mobilize, muster, obtain, procure, proselytize, raise, reanimate, recoup, recover, recuperate, refresh, regain, reinforce, renew, repair, replenish, repossess, restore, retrieve, revive, round up, select, sign on, sign up, store up, strengthen, supply, take in, take on, win over; SEE CONCEPTS *41,109,120,320*

rectify [v] *correct a situation; make something right*
adjust, amend, clean up, clean up act*, debug, dial back*, doctor, emend, fix, fix up, go over, improve, launder, make good*, make up for*, mend, pay one's dues*, pick up, put right, recalibrate, redress, reform, remedy, repair, revise, right, scrub, shape up, square, straighten out, straighten up, turn things around*; SEE CONCEPT *126*

recuperate [v] *improve in health*
ameliorate, be on the mend*, be out of the woods*, bounce back*, convalesce, gain, get back on one's feet*, get better, get well, heal, look up, make a comeback*, mend, perk up*, pick up, pull out of it*, pull through, rally, recover, regain health, snap out of it*, turn the corner*; SEE CONCEPTS *303,700*

recur [v] *happen again; repeat in one's mind*
be remembered, be repeated, come again, come and go, come back, crop up again*, haunt thoughts*, iterate, persist, reappear, recrudesce, reiterate, repeat, return, return to mind, revert, run through one's mind*, turn back; SEE CONCEPTS *3,242*

recurrent [adj] *repeating*
alternate, chain, continued, cyclical, frequent, habitual, intermittent, isochronal, isochronous, periodic, periodical, recurring, regular, reoccurring, repeated, repetitive, rolling; SEE CONCEPTS *541,544*

red [n/adj] *color of blood; shade resembling such a color*
bittersweet, bloodshot, blooming, blush, brick, burgundy, cardinal, carmine, cerise, cherry, chestnut, claret, copper, coral, crimson, dahlia, flaming, florid, flushed, fuchsia, garnet, geranium, glowing, healthy, inflamed, infrared, magenta, maroon, pink, puce, rose, roseate, rosy, rubicund, ruby, ruddy, rufescent, russet, rust, salmon, sanguine, scarlet, titian, vermilion, wine; SEE CONCEPTS *618,622*

redden [v] *blush, make rosy*
bloody, color, crimson, dye, encarmine, encarnadine, flush, glow, go red, mantle, paint, pink, pinken, rose, rouge, rubify, rubric, rubricate, ruby, ruddle, ruddy, rust, suffuse, tint, turn red; SEE CONCEPTS *250,469*

redeem [v1] *recover possession*
buy back, buy off, call in, cash, cash in, change, cover, defray, discharge, exchange, get back, make good, pay off, purchase, ransom, recapture, reclaim, recoup, regain, reinstate, repay, replevin, replevy, repossess, repurchase, restore, retrieve, settle, take in, trade in, win back; SEE CONCEPTS *104,131,327*

redeem [v2] *free; buy the freedom of*
deliver, disenthrall, disimprison, emancipate, extricate, liberate, loose, manumit, pay ransom, ransom, release, rescue, save, set free, unbind, unchain, unfetter; SEE CONCEPTS *127,327*

redeem [v3] *atone for; compensate*
abide by, absolve, acquit, adhere to, balance, carry out, compensate, counterbalance, counterpoise, countervail, defray, discharge, fulfill, hold to, keep, keep the faith*, make amends, make good, make up for, meet, offset, outweigh, perform, redress, rehabilitate, reinstate, restore, satisfy, save, set off; SEE CONCEPTS *91,126*

redress [n] *help, compensation*
aid, amendment, amends, assistance, atonement, balancing, change, conciliation, correction, cure, ease, indemnity, justice, offsetting, payment, quittance, recompense, rectification, reestablishment, reformation, rehabilitation, relief, remedy, remission, remodeling, renewal, repair, reparation, reprisal, requital, restitution, retribution, return, revision, reward, reworking, satisfaction, vengeance; SEE CONCEPTS *344,712*

redress [v] *change, rectify*
adjust, amend, annul, balance, cancel, compensate, correct, counteract, counterbalance, dial back*, ease, even out, frustrate, make amends, make reparation, make restitution, make up for, mend, negate, negative, neutralize, pay for, pay one's dues*, put right*, recalibrate, recompense, reform, regulate, relieve, remedy, repair, restore, revise, square, turn around, turn over new leaf*, turn things around*, vindicate; SEE CONCEPTS *126,697*

reduce [v1] *make less; decrease*
abate, abridge, bankrupt, bant, break, cheapen, chop, clip, contract, curtail, cut, cut back, cut down, debase, deflate, depreciate, depress, diet, dilute, diminish, discount, drain, dwindle, go on a diet*, impair, impoverish, lessen, lose weight, lower, mark down, moderate, nutshell, pare, pauperize, rebate, recede, roll back, ruin, scale down, shave, shorten, slash, slim, slow down, step down, take off weight, taper, taper off, tone down, trim, truncate, turn down, weaken, wind down; SEE CONCEPTS *137,236,240,247,698*

reduce [v2] *defeat*
bear down, beat down, break, bring, conquer, cripple, crush, disable, drive, enfeeble, force, master, overcome, overpower, ruin, subdue, subjugate, undermine, vanquish, weaken; SEE CONCEPT *95*

reduce [v3] *humble, humiliate*
abase, break, bring low, bump*, bust*, declass, degrade, demerit, demote, disgrade, disrate, downgrade, lower, take down a peg*; SEE CONCEPTS *7,19,384*

redundant [adj] *excessive; repetitious*
bombastic, de trop*, diffuse, extra, extravagant, inessential, inordinate, iterating, long-winded*, loquacious, oratorical, padded*, palaverous, periphrastic, pleonastic, prolix, reiterating, spare, supererogatory, superfluous, supernumerary, surplus, tautological, unnecessary, unwanted, verbose, wordy; SEE CONCEPTS *553,781*

reef [n] *underwater or partially submerged ledge*
atoll, bank, bar, beach, cay, coral reef, ridge,

rock, rock barrier, sand bar, shoal, skerry; SEE
CONCEPT *509*

reek [*n*] *strong odor*
effluvium, fetor, mephitis, smell, stench, stink;
SEE CONCEPT *600*

reek [*v*] *smell of; be characterized by*
be permeated by, be redolent of, emit, fume, give
off odor, have an odor, smell, smoke, steam,
stench, stink; SEE CONCEPT *600*

reel [*v*] *wobble; spin around*
bob, careen, falter, feel giddy, go around, lurch,
pitch, revolve, rock, roll, shake, stagger, stumble,
sway, swim, swing, swirl, teeter, titubate, totter,
turn, twirl, waver, weave, wheel, whirl; SEE CON-
CEPTS *151,153*

refer [*v1*] *mention*
accredit, adduce, advert, allude, ascribe, assign,
associate, attribute, bring up, charge, cite, credit,
designate, direct attention, excerpt, exemplify, extract, give as example, glance, hint, impute, indicate, insert, instance, interpolate, introduce,
invoke, lay, make allusion, make mention of,
make reference, name, notice, point, point out,
put down to, quote, speak about, speak of, specify, touch on; SEE CONCEPT *73*

refer [*v2*] *direct, guide*
commit, consign, deliver, hand in, hand over, introduce, pass on, point, put in touch, recommend,
relegate, send, submit, transfer, turn over; SEE
CONCEPTS *143,187*

refer [*v3*] *concern, apply*
answer, appertain, be about, be a matter of, bear
upon, be directed to, belong, be relevant, connect,
correspond with, cover, deal with, encompass,
have a bearing on, have reference, have relation,
have to do with, hold, include, incorporate, involve, pertain, point, regard, relate, take in, touch;
SEE CONCEPT *532*

refer [*v4*] *seek information*
advise, apply, commune, confer, consult, go,
have recourse, look up, recur, repair, resort, run,
turn, turn to; SEE CONCEPTS *72,216*

referee [*n*] *person who mediates, judges*
adjudicator, arbiter, arbitrator, conciliator, judge,
ref*, umpire; SEE CONCEPTS *348,366*

referee [*v*] *judge, mediate*
adjudge, adjudicate, arbitrate, umpire; SEE CON-
CEPT *18*

reference [*n1*] *remark, citation*
advertence, allusion, associating, attributing,
bringing up, connecting, hint, implication, indi-
cating, innuendo, insinuation, mention, mentioning, note, plug*, pointing out, quotation, relating,
resource, source, stating; SEE CONCEPT *278*

reference [*n2*] *testimonial of good character*
certificate, certification, character, credentials, endorsement, good word, recommendation, tribute;
SEE CONCEPTS *69,274*

reference [*n3*] *printed matter with information*
archives, cyclopedia, dictionary, encyclopedia,
evidence, source, thesaurus, writing; SEE CON-
CEPTS *271,280*

refine [*v1*] *purify*
clarify, cleanse, distill, filter, process, rarefy,
strain; SEE CONCEPT *165*

refine [*v2*] *perfect, polish*
better, civilize, clarify, cultivate, elevate, explain,
hone, improve, make clear, round, sleek, slick,
smooth, temper; SEE CONCEPT *244*

refined [*adj1*] *cultured, civilized*
aesthetic, civil, classy*, courteous, courtly, cultivated, delicate, discerning, discriminating, elegant, enlightened, exact, fastidious, fine,
finespun, genteel, gracious, high-brow*, high-
minded, nice, plush, polished, polite, posh, precise, punctilious, restrained, ritzy*, sensitive,
snazzy*, sophisticated, spiffy*, suave, sublime,
subtle, swanky*, tasteful, urbane, well-bred, well-
mannered; SEE CONCEPTS *401,555,589*

refined [*adj2*] *cleaned of impurities*
aerated, boiled down, clarified, clean, cleansed,
distilled, drained, expurgated, filtered, processed,
pure, purified, rarefied, strained, washed; SEE
CONCEPT *621*

refinement [*n1*] *cleansing*
clarification, cleaning, depuration, detersion, distillation, draining, filtering, processing, purification, rarefaction, rectification; SEE CONCEPT *165*

refinement [*n2*] *cultivation, civilization*
affability, civility, courtesy, courtliness, delicacy,
dignity, discrimination, elegance, enlightenment,
erudition, fastidiousness, fineness, fine point*, finesse, fine tuning*, finish, gentility, gentleness,
good breeding, good manners, grace, graciousness, knowledge, lore, nicety, nuance, polish, politeness, politesse, precision, sophistication, style,
suavity, subtlety, tact, taste, urbanity; SEE CON-
CEPTS *388,633,655*

reflect [*v1*] *give back*
cast, catch, copy, echo, emulate, flash, follow,
give forth, imitate, match, mirror, rebound, repeat, repercuss, reply, reproduce, resonate, resound, return, reverberate, reverse, revert, shine,
take after, throw back; SEE CONCEPTS *65,171,624*

reflect [*v2*] *think about*
cerebrate, chew*, cogitate, consider, contemplate,
deliberate, meditate, mull over, muse, ponder,
reason, ruminate, speculate, stew*, study, think,
weigh, wonder; SEE CONCEPTS *17,24*

reflect [*v3*] *demonstrate, indicate*
bear out, bespeak, communicate, display, evince,
exhibit, express, indicate, manifest, reveal, show;
SEE CONCEPT *261*

reflection [*n1*] *thought, thinking*
absorption, brainwork, cerebration, cogitation,
consideration, contemplation, deliberation, idea,
imagination, impression, meditation, musing, observation, opinion, pensiveness, pondering, rumination, speculation, study, view; SEE CONCEPTS
17,24

reflection [*n2*] *mirror image*
appearance, counterpart, duplicate, echo, idea,
image, impression, light, likeness, picture, representation, reproduction, shadow; SEE CONCEPT
628

reflection [*n3*] *criticism*
animadversion, aspersion, blame, censure, derogation, discredit, disesteem, imputation, obloquy,
reproach, slam, slur, stricture; SEE CONCEPT *52*

reflective [*adj*] *thoughtful*
cogitating, contemplative, deliberate, meditative,
pensive, pondering, reasoning, ruminative, speculative, studious; SEE CONCEPT *403*

reform [*v*] *correct, rectify*
ameliorate, amend, better, bring up to code*,
change one's ways*, clean up, clean up one's
act*, convert, correct, cure, emend, go straight*,
improve, make amends, make over, mend, rearrange, rebuild, reclaim, reconstitute, reconstruct,

redeem, refashion, regenerate, rehabilitate, remake, remedy, remodel, renew, renovate, reorganize, repair, resolve, restore, revise, revolutionize, rework, shape up, standardize, swear off, transform, turn over a new leaf*, uplift; SEE CONCEPTS *35,110,126,202*

refrain [n] *chorus of musical piece*
burden, melody, music, song, strain, theme, tune, undersong; SEE CONCEPTS *264,595*

refrain [v] *do without; keep from doing*
abstain, arrest, avoid, be temperate, cease, check, curb, desist, eschew, forbear, forgo, give up, go on the wagon*, halt, inhibit, interrupt, keep, leave off, not do, pass, pass up, quit, renounce, resist, restrain, sit out*, stop, take the cure*, take the pledge*, withhold; SEE CONCEPTS *121,681*

refresh [v] *make like new; give new life*
brace, breathe new life into, bring around, brush up, cheer, cool, enliven, exhilarate, freshen, inspirit, jog, modernize, prod, prompt, quicken, reanimate, recreate, regain, reinvigorate, rejuvenate, renovate, repair, replenish, restore, resuscitate, revitalize, revive, revivify, stimulate, update, vivify; SEE CONCEPTS *35,202,697*

refreshment [n] *small amount of food or drink*
bite, pick-me-up*, snack, spread, tidbit; SEE CONCEPT *457*

refrigerate [v] *chill, usually in storage*
air-condition, air-cool, cool, freeze, ice, keep cold, make cold; SEE CONCEPTS *202,255*

refuge [n] *place to hide, have privacy*
ambush, anchorage, asylum, cover, covert, den, escape, exit, expedient, fortress, harbor, harborage, haven, hideaway, hideout, hiding place, hole, home, immunity, ivory tower*, makeshift, opening, outlet, port, preserve, protection, recourse, resort, resource, retreat, safe place, sanctuary, security, shelter, shield, stopgap*, stronghold, way out*; SEE CONCEPTS *198,515*

refugee [n] *person running from something, often oppression*
alien, boat person*, castaway, defector, derelict, deserter, displaced person, DP*, emigrant, émigré, escapee, evacuee, exile, expatriate, expellee, foreigner, foundling, fugitive, homeless person, leper, maroon, outcast, outlaw, prodigal, renegade, runaway, stateless person; SEE CONCEPTS *359,413*

refund [n] *returned money*
acquittance, allowance, compensation, consolation, discharge, discount, give-back*, give-up*, kickback, money back, payment, rebate, reimbursement, remuneration, repayment, restitution, retribution, return, satisfaction, settlement; SEE CONCEPTS *340,344*

refund [v] *return money; rebate*
adjust, balance, compensate, give back, honor a claim, indemnify, make amends, make good*, make repayment, make up for, pay back, recompense, recoup, redeem, redress, reimburse, relinquish, remit, remunerate, repay, restore, reward, settle; SEE CONCEPT *341*

refurbish [v] *spruce up*
clean up, do up*, fix up, gussy up*, mend, modernize, overhaul, recondition, redo, reequip, refit, refresh, rehab, rehabilitate, rejuvenate, remodel, renew, renovate, repair, restore, retread, revamp, set to rights, spruce, update; SEE CONCEPTS *177,202*

refusal [n] *denial of responsibility; unwillingness*
abnegation, ban, choice, cold shoulder*, declension, declination, defiance, disallowance, disapproval, disavowal, disclaimer, discountenancing, disfavor, dissent, enjoinment, exclusion, forbidding, interdiction, knockback*, negation, nix*, no, nonacceptance, noncompliance, nonconsent, option, pass*, prohibition, proscription, rebuff, refutation, regrets, rejection, renouncement, renunciation, repudiation, repulse, repulsion, reversal, thumbs down*, turndown, veto, withholding, writ; SEE CONCEPTS *278,633*

refuse [n] *garbage*
debris, dregs, dross, dump, dust, hogwash*, junk, leavings, litter, muck, offal, rejectamenta*, remains, residue, rubbish, scraps, scum*, sediment, slop*, sweepings, swill, trash, waste, waste matter; SEE CONCEPT *260*

refuse [v] *deny; say no*
beg off, brush off*, decline, demur, desist, disaccord, disallow, disapprove, dispense with, dissent, dodge, evade, give thumbs down to*, hold back, hold off, hold out, ignore, make excuses, nix*, not budge, not budget, not buy*, not care to*, pass up, protest, rebuff, refuse to receive, regret, reject, repel, reprobate, repudiate, send off*, send regrets*, set aside*, shun, spurn, turn away, turn deaf ear to*, turn down, turn from, turn one's back on*, withdraw, withhold; SEE CONCEPTS *30,49,266*

refute [v] *prove false; discredit*
abnegate, argue against, blow sky high*, break, burn, burn down, cancel, cancel out, confute, contend, contradict, contravene, convict, counter, crush, debate, demolish, disclaim, disconfirm, dispose of, disprove, dispute, evert, explode, expose, gainsay, give the lie to*, give thumbs down to*, invalidate, negate, oppose, overthrow, parry, quash, rebut, reply to, repudiate, shoot down, shoot full of holes*, show up, silence, squelch, take a stand against, tear down*, top*; SEE CONCEPT *54*

regain [v] *get back, get back to*
achieve, attain, compass, gain, get out from under, get well, make well, reach, reach again, reacquire, reattain, recapture, reclaim, recoup, recover, recruit, redeem, repossess, retake, retrieve, return to, save, take back, win back; SEE CONCEPTS *120,124,131*

regal [adj] *fit for royalty*
august, glorious, imposing, kingly, magnificent, majestic, monarchial, monarchical, noble, proud, queenly, resplendent, royal, sovereign, splendid, stately, sublime; SEE CONCEPT *589*

regale [v] *throw a party; have fun*
amuse, delight, divert, entertain, feast, fracture, give a party, grab, gratify, have a get-together, laugh it up, nurture, party, please, ply, refresh, satisfy, serve, toss a party; SEE CONCEPTS *292,384*

regard [n1] *attention, look*
care, carefulness, cognizance, concern, consciousness, curiosity, gaze, glance, heed, interest, interestedness, mark, mind, note, notice, observance, observation, once-over*, remark, scrutiny, stare, view; SEE CONCEPTS *596,623,626,690*

regard [n2] *affection, good opinion*
account, appreciation, approbation, approval, attachment, care, cherishing, concern, consideration, curiosity, deference, devotion, esteem,

re
re

estimation, favor, fondness, homage, honor, interest, interestedness, liking, love, note, opinion, prizing, reputation, repute, respect, reverence, satisfaction, store, sympathy, thought, value, valuing, veneration, worship; SEE CONCEPTS 10,532,689

regard [n3] *feature, detail*
aspect, bearing, concern, connection, item, matter, particular, point, reference, relation, relevance, respect; SEE CONCEPTS 532,644

regard [v1] *look at; listen to*
advertise, attend, beam, behold, contemplate, eye, eyeball*, flash, gaze, get a load of*, give attention, heed, look on, mark, mind, note, notice, observe, overlook, pay attention, pipe*, pore over*, read, remark, respect, scan, scrutinize, see, spy, stare at, take into consideration, take notice of, view, watch, witness; SEE CONCEPTS 596,623,626

regard [v2] *believe, judge*
account, adjudge, admire, assay, assess, consider, deem, esteem, estimate, look upon, rate, reckon, respect, revere, see, suppose, surmise, think, treat, value, view; SEE CONCEPTS 10,12

regard [v3] *have something to do with*
apply to, bear upon, be relevant to, concern, have a bearing on, have to do with*, interest, pertain to, refer to, relate to; SEE CONCEPT 532

regardful [adj] *attentive, observant*
advertent, arrect, aware, careful, considerate, deferential, duteous, dutiful, heedful, intentive, mindful, observative, observing, respectful, thoughtful, watchful; SEE CONCEPT 401

regardless [adj] *indifferent, unconcerned*
behindhand, blind, careless, coarse, crude, deaf, delinquent, derelict, disregarding, heedless, inadvertent, inattentive, inconsiderate, insensitive, lax, listless, mindless, neglectful, negligent, nonobservant, rash, reckless, remiss, rude, slack, unfeeling, unheeding, uninterested, unmindful; SEE CONCEPT 401

regardless [adv] *despite everything*
against, although, anyway, aside from, at any cost, but, come what may, despite, distinct from, for all that, in any case, in spite of everything, leaving aside, nevertheless, no matter what, nonetheless, notwithstanding, without considering, without regard to; SEE CONCEPTS 544,548

regards [n] *best wishes*
commendations, compliments, deference, devoirs, good wishes, greeting, love, love and kisses*, remembrances, respects, salutation, salutations; SEE CONCEPT 278

regenerate [v] *breathe new life into*
change, exhilarate, inspirit, invigorate, produce, raise from the dead*, reanimate, reawaken, reconstruct, recreate, reestablish, refresh, reinvigorate, rejuvenate, renew, renovate, reproduce, restore, revive, revivify, uplift; SEE CONCEPTS 7,22,173,202,251

regime [n] *leadership of organization*
administration, dynasty, establishment, government, incumbency, management, pecking order*, reign, rule, system, tenure; SEE CONCEPTS 299,325

region [n] *area, domain; scope*
arena, bailiwick, belt, block, clearing, country, demesne, district, division, domain, dominion, environs, expanse, field, ghetto, ground, inner city, jungle, land, locale, locality, neck of

woods*, neighborhood, part, place, precinct, province, quarter, range, realm, scene, section, sector, shire, sphere, stomping ground*, suburb, terrain, territory, tract, turf*, vicinity, walk, ward, world, zone; SEE CONCEPTS 198,508,512

register [n] *list, record*
annals, archives, book, catalog, catalogue, chronicle, diary, entry, file, ledger, log, memorandum, registry, roll, roll call, roster, schedule, scroll; SEE CONCEPT 281

register [v1] *enter in list, record*
catalogue, check in, chronicle, enlist, enroll, file, inscribe, join, list, note, record, schedule, set down, sign on, sign up, sign up for, subscribe, take down, weigh in; SEE CONCEPTS 79,114,125

register [v2] *indicate, reveal*
be shown, bespeak, betray, disclose, display, exhibit, express, manifest, mark, point out, point to, read, record, reflect, say, show; SEE CONCEPT 261

register [v3] *make an impression*
come home to, dawn on, get through to, have an effect on, impress, sink in, tell; SEE CONCEPTS 7,19,22

regress [v] *return to earlier way of doing things*
backslide, degenerate, deteriorate, ebb, fall away, fall back, fall off, go back, lapse, lose ground, recede, relapse, retreat, retrogress, revert, roll back, sink, throw back, turn back; SEE CONCEPTS 633,698

regret [n] *upset over past action*
affliction, anguish, annoyance, apologies, apology, bitterness, care, compunction, concern, conscience, contrition, demur, disappointment, discomfort, dissatisfaction, dole, grief, heartache, heartbreak, lamentation, misgiving, nostalgia, pang, penitence, qualm, regretfulness, remorse, repentance, ruefulness, scruple, self-accusation, self-condemnation, self-disgust, self-reproach, sorrow, uneasiness, woe, worry; SEE CONCEPTS 21,410

regret [v] *be upset about*
apologize, be disturbed, bemoan, be sorry for, bewail, cry over*, cry over spilled milk*, deplore, deprecate, disapprove, feel remorse, feel sorry, feel uneasy, grieve, have compunctions*, have qualms*, kick oneself*, lament, look back, miss, moan, mourn, repent, repine, rue, weep, weep over; SEE CONCEPTS 21,410

regretful [adj] *sad, sorry*
apologetic, ashamed, attritional, compunctious, contrite, disappointed, mournful, penitent, remorseful, repentant, rueful, sorrowful; SEE CONCEPT 403

regrettable [adj] *unfortunate, wrong*
afflicting, calamitous, deplorable, dire, disappointing, distressing, dreadful, grievous, heartbreaking, ill-advised, lamentable, pitiable, pitiful, sad, shameful, unfavorable, unhappy, woeful; SEE CONCEPTS 548,571

regular [adj1] *normal, common*
approved, bona fide, classic, commonplace, correct, customary, daily, established, everyday, formal, general, habitual, lawful, legitimate, natural, normal, official, ordinary, orthodox, prevailing, prevalent, proper, routine, run-of-the-mill*, sanctioned, standard, time-honored, traditional, typic, typical, unexceptional, unvarying, usual; SEE CONCEPTS 530,533,547

regular [adj2] *orderly, consistent, balanced*
accordant, alternating, arranged, automatic, clas-

sified, congruous, consonant, constant, cyclic, dependable, efficient, established, even, exact, expected, fixed, flat, formal, harmonious, in order, invariable, level, measured, mechanical, methodical, momentary, ordered, organized, patterned, periodic, precise, probable, punctual, rational, recurrent, regulated, rhythmic, routine, serial, set, smooth, standardized, stated, steady, straight, successive, symmetrical, systematic, uniform; SEE CONCEPTS 326,544,566,585

regulate [v] *manage, organize*
adapt, adjust, administer, allocate, arrange, balance, classify, conduct, control, coordinate, correct, determine, direct, dispose, fit, fix, govern, guide, handle, improve, legislate, measure, methodize, moderate, modulate, monitor, order, oversee, pull things together*, put in order, readjust, reconcile, rectify, rule, run, set, settle, shape up*, square, standardize, straighten up, superintend, supervise, systematize, temper, time, true, tune, tune up*; SEE CONCEPTS 94,117

regulation [n1] *managing, organizing*
adjustment, administration, arrangement, classification, codification, control, coordination, direction, governance, governing, government, guidance, handling, management, moderation, modulation, reconciliation, regimentation, reorganization, settlement, standardization, superintendence, supervision, systematization, tuning; SEE CONCEPTS 94,117

regulation [n2] *rule, requirement*
bible, book, canon, chapter and verse*, code, commandment, decree, decretum, dictate, direction, edict, law, no-nos*, numbers, order, ordinance, precept, prescript, principle, procedure, reg*, standing order, statute; SEE CONCEPTS 318,688

rehabilitate [v] *renovate, adjust*
change, clear, convert, fix up, furbish, improve, make good*, mend, rebuild, reclaim, recondition, reconstitute, reconstruct, recover, redeem, reestablish, reform, refurbish, rehab*, reinstate, reintegrate, reinvigorate, rejuvenate, renew, restitute, restore, save; SEE CONCEPTS 35,126,134,202

rehash [v] *talk over again*
change, discuss, reiterate, repeat, rephrase, restate, reuse, rework, rewrite, say again, state differently; SEE CONCEPT 56

rehearsal [n] *preparation for performance*
call, description, drill, dry run*, experiment, going-over, practice, practice session, prep*, reading, readying, recital, recitation, recounting, rehearsing, relation, retelling, run-through, shakedown*, test flight*, trial balloon*, trial performance, tryout, workout; SEE CONCEPTS 264,292,363

rehearse [v] *prepare for performance*
act, depict, describe, do over, drill, dry run*, experiment, go over, go through, hold a reading*, hone, iterate, learn one's part, narrate, practice, ready, recapitulate, recite, recount, reenact, reiterate, relate, repeat, review, run lines, run through, study, take from the top*, tell, test, train, try out, tune up, walk through*, warm up, work out; SEE CONCEPTS 266,292,363

reign [n] *rule, dominion*
administration, ascendancy, command, control, dynasty, empire, hegemony, incumbency, influence, monarchy, power, regime, sovereignty, supremacy, sway, tenure; SEE CONCEPTS 198,376

reign [v] *have power over; prevail*
administer, be in power, be in the driver's seat*, be supreme, boss, command, dominate, domineer, govern, head up, helm, hold power, hold sway*, influence, manage, obtain, occupy, overrule, predominate, preponderate, rule, rule the roost*, run the show*, run things*, sit, superabound, wear the crown*; SEE CONCEPTS 117,298

reimburse [v] *pay back something owed*
balance, compensate, indemnify, make reparations, make up for, offset, pay, recompense, recover, refund, remunerate, repay, require, restore, return, square, square up; SEE CONCEPT 341

rein [n] *restraint, control*
bit, brake, bridle, check, curb, deterrent, governor, halter, harness, hold, line, restriction, strap; SEE CONCEPT 499

rein [v] *restrain, control*
bridle, check, collect, compose, cool, curb, halt, hold, hold back, limit, repress, restrict, simmer down, slow down, smother, suppress; SEE CONCEPT 130

reinforce [v] *strengthen, augment*
add fuel to fire*, add to, back up, beef up*, bolster, boost, build up, buttress, carry, emphasize, energize, enlarge, fortify, harden, heat up, hype, increase, lend a hand, multiply, pick up, pillar, prop, prop up, punch up, shore up, soup up*, stand up for, stiffen, stress, stroke, supplement, support, sustain, toughen, underline; SEE CONCEPTS 5,236,245,250

reinstate [v] *give back responsibility*
bring back, put back, put in power again, recall, redeem, reelect, reestablish, rehabilitate, rehire, reintroduce, reinvest, renew, replace, restore, return, revive; SEE CONCEPTS 351,384

reiterate [v] *say or do again*
come again, ditto*, double-check, echo, go over again, ingeminate, iterate, play back, recap*, recapitulate, recheck, rehash, renew, repeat, reprise, resay, restate, retell, rewarn, say again; SEE CONCEPTS 100,171,266

reject [v] *say no to*
burn*, cashier*, cast aside, cast off, cast out, chuck, decline, deny, despise, disallow, disbelieve, discard, discount, discredit, disdain, dismiss, eliminate, exclude*, give thumbs down to*, jettison, jilt, kill*, nix*, not buy*, pass by, pass on, pass up, put down, rebuff, refuse, renounce, repel, reprobate, repudiate, repulse, scoff, scorn, scout, scrap, second, shed, shoot down*, shun, slough, spurn, throw away, throw out, turn down, veto; SEE CONCEPTS 21,30,180

rejection [n] *denial, refusal*
bounce, brushoff*, cold shoulder*, disallowance, dismissal, elimination, exclusion, hard time*, kick in teeth*, nix*, no dice*, no go*, nothing doing*, no way*, pass*, rebuff, renunciation, repudiation, slap in the face*, thumbs down*, turndown, veto; SEE CONCEPTS 21,30,180

rejoice [v] *be very happy about something*
be glad, be overjoyed, celebrate, delight, enjoy, exult, feel happy, glory, joy, jump for joy, make merry, revel, triumph; SEE CONCEPT 410

rejuvenate [v] *make new again*
breathe new life into*, do, do up*, exhilarate, give face lift to*, give new life to, make young again, modernize, reanimate, reclaim, recondition, reconstruct, recover, refresh, refurbish, regenerate, rehab, reinvigorate, renew, renovate,

re
re

restitute, restore, retread, revitalize, revivify, spruce, spruce up*, update; SEE CONCEPTS 35,202

relapse [n] *deterioration, weakening*
backsliding, fall, fall from grace*, lapse, loss, recidivism, recurrence, regression, repetition, retrogression, return, reversion, setback, turn for the worse*, worsening; SEE CONCEPT 698

relapse [v] *deteriorate, weaken*
backslide, fail, fall, fall back, lapse, recidivate, be overcome, be overtaken, degenerate, fade, fail, fall, fall back, lapse, recidivate, regress, retrogress, revert, sicken, sink, slide back, slip back, suffer, turn back, worsen; SEE CONCEPT 698

relate [v1] *give an account of*
break a story*, chronicle, clue one in*, depict, describe, detail, disclose, divulge, express, get off one's chest*, give the word*, impart, itemize, lay it on the line*, let one's hair down*, narrate, particularize, picture, present, recite, recount, rehearse, report, retell, reveal, run down, run through, set forth, shoot the breeze*, sling*, spill, spill the beans*, spin a yarn*, state, tell, track, verbalize; SEE CONCEPT 55

relate [v2] *correlate, pertain*
affect, ally, appertain, apply, ascribe, assign, associate, bear upon, be joined with, be relevant to, bracket, combine, compare, concern, conjoin, connect, consociate, coordinate, correspond to, couple, credit, have reference to, have to do with, identify with, impute, interconnect, interdepend, interrelate, join, link, orient, orientate, pertain, refer, tie in with, touch, unite, yoke; SEE CONCEPT 532

related [adj] *connected, accompanying*
affiliated, agnate, akin, alike, allied, analogous, associated, cognate, complementary, concomitant, connate, connatural, consanguine, convertible, correlated, correspondent, dependent, enmeshed, fraternal, germane, incident, interchangeable, interconnected, interdependent, interrelated, intertwined, interwoven, in the same category, in touch with, joint, knit together*, like, linked, mutual, of that ilk, parallel, pertinent, reciprocal, relevant, similar, tied up; SEE CONCEPTS 487,573,577

relation [n] *connection, family connection*
affiliation, affinity, alliance, association, consanguinity, kin, kindred, kinship, kinsperson, liaison, propinquity, relationship, relative, sibling, similarity; SEE CONCEPTS 296,414,421,714

relationship [n] *connection; friendship*
accord, affair, affiliation, affinity, alliance, analogy, appositeness, association, bond, communication, conjunction, consanguinity, consociation, contact, contingency, correlation, dependence, dependency, exchange, homogeneity, hookup, interconnection, interrelation, interrelationship, kinship, liaison, likeness, link, marriage, nearness, network, parallel, pertinence, pertinency, proportion, rapport, ratio, relation, relativity, relevance, similarity, tie, tie-in, tie-up; SEE CONCEPTS 388,714

relative [n] *member of a family*
agnate, aunt, blood, brother-in-law, clansperson, cognate, connection, cousin, father, father-in-law, folk, folks, grandparents, great-grandparents, in-laws, kinsperson, mother, mother-in-law, nephew, niece, relation, sib*, sibling, sister-in-law, stepbrother, stepparent, stepsister, uncle; SEE CONCEPT 414

relative [adj1] *comparative, respective*
about, allied, analogous, approximate, associated, concerning, conditional, connected, contingent, corresponding, dependent, in regard to, near, parallel, proportionate, reciprocal, referring, related, relating to, reliant, with respect to; SEE CONCEPT 563

relative [adj2] *pertinent, applicable*
apposite, appropriate, appurtenant, apropos, contingent, dependent, germane, pertaining, referring, related, relevant; SEE CONCEPT 558

relatively [adv] *in or by comparison*
almost, approximately, comparably, comparatively, nearly, proportionately, rather, somewhat, to some extent; SEE CONCEPTS 544,772

relax [v1] *be or feel at ease*
breathe easy*, calm, calm down*, collect oneself, compose oneself, cool off*, ease off, feel at home, hang loose*, knock off*, laze, let oneself go*, lie down, loosen up, make oneself at home*, put one's feet up*, recline, repose, rest, settle back, simmer down*, sit around, sit back, soften, stop work, take a break*, take a breather*, take it easy*, take one's time*, take ten*, take time out*, tranquilize, unbend, unlax*, unwind; SEE CONCEPT 210

relax [v2] *diminish, lessen*
abate, ease, ease off, ebb, lax, let up, loose, loosen, lose speed, lower, mitigate, moderate, modify, modulate, reduce, relieve, remit, slack, slacken, slow, slow down, untighten, weaken; SEE CONCEPTS 240,698

relaxation [n] *entertainment; resting or recovering*
alleviation, amusement, assuagement, diversion, enjoyment, fun, leisure, loosening, mitigation, pleasure, reclining, recreation, refreshment, relief, repose, requiescence, rest; SEE CONCEPTS 210,292,363

relay [v] *pass on, transmit*
broadcast, carry, communicate, deliver, hand down, hand on, hand over, send, send forth, spread, transfer, turn over; SEE CONCEPT 143

release [n1] *delivery; dispensation*
absolution, acquittal, acquittance, charge, clemency, commute, deliverance, discharge, dispensation, emancipation, exemption, exoneration, floater, freedom, freeing, let-off*, liberation, liberty, lifeboat, lifesaver, manumission, relief, spring, turnout, walkout; SEE CONCEPTS 127,685

release [n2] *publication*
announcement, flash*, handout, issue, leak, news, notice, offering, proclamation, propaganda, publicity, story; SEE CONCEPTS 271,280

release [v] *let go, let out*
absolve, acquit, bail out, cast loose, clear, commute, deliver, discharge, disengage, dispense, drop, emancipate, exculpate, excuse, exempt, exonerate, extricate, free, give off, give out, go easy on, issue, leak, let off, let off steam*, let up on*, liberate, loose, loosen, manumit, open up, set at large, set free, set loose, spring, surrender, take out, turn loose, turn out, unbind, unchain, undo, unfasten, unfetter, unleash, unloose, unshackle, untie, vent, wipe slate clean*, yield; SEE CONCEPTS 50,60,88,127,143

relegate [v1] *assign, transfer*
accredit, charge, commend, commit, confide,

consign, credit, delegate, entrust, hand over, pass on, refer, turn over; SEE CONCEPTS *41,143*

relegate [v2] *banish, downgrade*
demote, deport, dismiss, displace, eject, exile, expatriate, expel, expulse, lag, ostracize, remove, throw out, transport; SEE CONCEPTS *30,121,211*

relent [v] *die down; let up*
acquiesce, be merciful, capitulate, cave in*, change one's mind, come around, comply, cool it*, cry uncle*, die away, drop, ease, ease off, ease up on*, ebb, fall, fold, forbear, give in, give quarter*, give some slack*, give up, give way, go along with, go easy on*, have mercy, have pity, lay back, let go, let it happen*, lighten up*, mellow out*, melt, moderate, quit, relax, say uncle*, show mercy, slacken, slow, soften, subside, wane, weaken, yield; SEE CONCEPTS *35,698,776*

relentless [adj1] *cruel, merciless*
adamant, bound, bound and determined, dead set on*, determined, dogged, ferocious, fierce, go for broke*, grim, hang in*, hang-tough*, hard, harsh, implacable, inexorable, inflexible, inhuman, mortal, obdurate, pitiless, remorseless, rigid, rigorous, ruthless, single-minded, stiff, stop at nothing, strict, stringent, unappeasable, unbending, uncompromising, undeviating, unflinching, unforgiving, unrelenting, unstoppable, unyielding, vindictive; SEE CONCEPT *401*

relentless [adj2] *continuous, neverending*
incessant, nonstop, persistent, pertinacious, punishing, sustained, tenacious, unabated, unbroken, unfaltering, unflagging, unrelenting, unrelieved, unremitting, unstoppable; SEE CONCEPTS *326,534,798*

relevant [adj] *appropriate; to the purpose*
accordant, admissible, ad rem, allowable, applicable, applicatory, apposite, appurtenant, apt, becoming, cognate, compatible, concerning, conformant, conforming, congruent, congruous, consistent, consonant, correlated, correspondent, fit, fitting, germane, harmonious, having direct bearing on, having to do with, important, material, on the button*, on the nose*, pat*, pertaining to, pertinent, pointful, proper, referring, related, relative, significant, suitable, suited to, to the point, weighty; SEE CONCEPT *558*

reliable [adj] *trustworthy*
candid, careful, certain, conscientious, constant, decent, decisive, definite, dependable, determined, devoted, faithful, firm, good, high-principled, honest, honorable, impeccable, incorrupt, loyal, okay, positive, predictable, proved, reputable, respectable, responsible, righteous, safe, sincere, solid, sound, stable, staunch, steadfast, steady, sterling, strong, sure, there, tried, tried-and-true*, true, true-blue*, true-hearted, trusty, unequivocal, unfailing, unimpeachable, upright, veracious; SEE CONCEPTS *535,542,544*

reliance [n] *confidence*
assurance, belief, credence, credit, dependence, faith, hope, interdependence, interdependency, stock, trust; SEE CONCEPT *689*

relic [n] *something saved from the past*
antique, antiquity, archaism, artifact, curio, curiosity, evidence, fragment, heirloom, keepsake, memento, memorial, monument, remains, remembrance, remembrancer, reminder, remnant, residue, ruins, scrap, souvenir, survival, testimo-nial, token, trace, trophy, vestige; SEE CONCEPT *446*

relief [n] *remedy, aid; relaxation*
abatement, allayment, alleviation, amelioration, appeasement, assistance, assuagement, balm, break, breather, cheer, comfort, comforting, consolation, contentment, cure, deliverance, diversion, ease, easement, extrication, fix, hand, happiness, help, let-up, lift, lightening, load off one's mind*, maintenance, mitigation, mollification, palliative, quick fix*, refreshment, release, remedy, remission, reprieve, respite, rest, restfulness, satisfaction, softening, solace, succor, support, sustenance; SEE CONCEPTS *681,712*

relieve [v1] *make less painful; let up on*
abate, allay, alleviate, appease, assuage, break, brighten, calm, comfort, console, cure, decrease, diminish, divert, dull, ease, free, interrupt, lighten, mitigate, moderate, mollify, palliate, qualify, quiet, relax, salve, slacken, soften, solace, soothe, subdue, take load off one's chest*, take load off one's mind*, temper, vary; SEE CONCEPTS *244,700*

relieve [v2] *help; give assistance*
aid, assist, bring aid, give a break*, give a hand*, give a rest, spell, stand in for, substitute for, succor, support, sustain, take over from, take the place of; SEE CONCEPT *110*

relieve [v3] *remove blame, responsibility*
absolve, deliver, discharge, disembarrass, disencumber, dismiss, dispense, excuse, exempt, force to resign, free, let off, privilege, pull, release, spare, throw out, unburden, yank*; SEE CONCEPTS *50,88,351*

religion [n] *belief in divinity; system of beliefs*
church, communion, creed, cult, denomination, devotion, doctrine, higher power, morality, myth, mythology, observance, orthodoxy, pietism, piety, prayer, preference, religiosity, rites, ritual, sacrifice, sanctification, sect, spirituality, spiritual-mindedness, standards, superstition, theology, veneration; SEE CONCEPTS *368,689*

religious [adj1] *concerning belief in divinity*
believing, born-again*, canonical, churchgoing, churchly, clerical, deistic, devotional, devout, divine, doctrinal, ecclesiastical, god-fearing, godly, holy, ministerial, moral, orthodox, pietistic, pious, pontifical, prayerful, priestly, pure, reverent, righteous, sacerdotal, sacred, sacrosanct, saint-like, saintly, scriptural, sectarian, spiritual, supernatural, theistic, theological; SEE CONCEPTS *536,545*

religious [adj2] *conscientious, scrupulous*
exact, faithful, fastidious, meticulous, punctilious, rigid, rigorous, steadfast, unerring, unswerving; SEE CONCEPT *538*

relinquish [v] *give up, let go*
abandon, abdicate, abnegate, back down, cast, cast off, cede, cut loose*, desert, discard, ditch*, drop, drop like hot potato*, drop out, dump*, forbear, forgo, forsake, forswear, hand over, kick, kiss good-bye*, lay aside, leave, opt out, quit, quit cold turkey*, release, renounce, repudiate, resign, retire from, sacrifice, shed, stand down, surrender, swear off*, take the oath*, take the pledge*, vacate, waive, withdraw, yield; SEE CONCEPTS *119,127,234*

relish [n] *great appreciation of something*
appetite, bias, delectation, diversion, enjoying, enjoyment, fancy, flair, flavor, fondness, gusto,

heart, leaning, liking, love, loving, palate, partiality, penchant, pleasure, predilection, prejudice, propensity, sapidity, sapor, savor, smack, stomach, tang, taste, zest; SEE CONCEPTS 20,32

relish [v] *look forward to; appreciate*
admire, be fond of, cherish, delight in, dig*, enjoy, fancy, go, go for*, like, luxuriate in, mind, prefer, revel in, savor, taste; SEE CONCEPT 32

reluctant [adj] *unenthusiastic, unwilling*
afraid, averse, backward, calculating, cautious, chary, circumspect, demurring, diffident, discouraged, disheartened, disinclined, grudging, hanging back, hesitant, hesitating, indisposed, involuntary, laggard, loath, opposed, queasy, recalcitrant, remiss, shy, slack, slow, squeamish, tardy, uncertain, uneager, wary; SEE CONCEPT 401

rely [v] *have confidence in*
await, bank, be confident of, believe in, be sure of, bet, bet bottom dollar on*, build, calculate, commit, confide, count, depend, entrust, expect, gamble on, have faith in, hope, lay money on*, lean, look, reckon, ride on coattails*, swear by*, trust; SEE CONCEPTS 12,26

remain [v] *stay, wait*
abide, be left, bide, bivouac, bunk*, cling, continue, delay, dwell, endure, freeze, go on, halt, hang, hang out, hold over, hold the fort*, hover, inhabit, keep on, last, linger, live, lodge, make camp, nest, outlast, outlive, pause, perch, persist, prevail, put on hold, remain standing, reside, rest, roost, sit out, sit through, sit tight*, sojourn, squat, stand, stay behind, stay in, stay over, stay put, stick around, stop, survive, tarry, visit, wait; SEE CONCEPTS 23,239,681,804

remainder [n] *balance, residue*
bottom of barrel*, butt, carry-over, detritus, dregs, excess, fragment, garbage, hangover*, heel, junk, leavings, leftover, obverse, oddment, odds and ends*, overplus, refuse, relic, remains, remnant, residuum, rest, ruins, salvage, scrap, stump, surplus, trace, vestige, waste, wreck, wreckage; SEE CONCEPTS 260,835

remark [n] *comment, observation*
acknowledgment, annotation, assertion, attention, back talk, bon mot*, cognizance, comeback, commentary, conclusion, consideration, crack*, declaration, elucidation, exegesis, explanation, explication, exposition, expression, gloss, heed, illustration, interpretation, mention, mind, note, notice, obiter dictum, observance, observation, opinion, point, recognition, reflection, regard, saying, statement, talk, thought, two cents' worth*, utterance, wisecrack, witticism, word; SEE CONCEPTS 51,278

remark [v] *notice and comment*
animadvert, behold, catch, commentate, crack*, declare, descry, espy, heed, make out, mark, mention, mouth off*, note, observe, pass comment, perceive, pick up on, reflect, regard, say, see, speak, spot, state, take note, take notice, utter, wisecrack; SEE CONCEPTS 38,51,626

remarkable [adj] *extraordinary, unusual*
arresting, arrestive, conspicuous, curious, distinguished, exceptional, famous, gilt-edged*, greatest, important, impressive, marked, miraculous, momentous, notable, noteworthy, noticeable, odd, outstanding, peculiar, phenomenal, preeminent, primo*, prominent, rare, salient, signal, significant, singular, smashing, solid, splashy*,

strange, striking, super, surprising, uncommon, uncustomary, unique, unordinary, unwonted, weighty, wicked*, wonderful, world class*, zero cool*; SEE CONCEPT 574

remedial [adj] *healing, restorative*
alleviative, antidotal, antiseptic, corrective, curative, curing, healthful, health-giving, invigorating, medicating, medicinal, purifying, recuperative, reformative, remedying, repairing, restitutive, restorative, sanative, sanatory, solving, soothing, therapeutic, tonic, treating, vulnerary, wholesome; SEE CONCEPT 537

remedy [n] *cure, solution*
antidote, assistance, biologic, corrective, counteractant, counteraction, counteractive, counteragent, countermeasure, counterstep, cure-all*, drug, elixir, fix, improvement, medicament, medicant, medicine, panacea, pharmaceutical, pharmacon, physic, pill, quick fix*, redress, relief, restorative, support, therapy, treatment; SEE CONCEPTS 307,311,693,712

remedy [v] *fix, cure*
aid, alleviate, ameliorate, amend, assuage, attend, change, clean up, clean up one's act*, control, correct, debug*, doctor, ease, fiddle with, fix up, go over, heal, help, launder, make up for, mitigate, palliate, pick up, put right, recalibrate, rectify, redress, reform, relieve, renew, repair, restore, revise, right, scrub, set right, set to rights*, shape up, solve, soothe, square*, square up*, straighten out, treat, upgrade; SEE CONCEPTS 126,212,310

remember [v] *keep in mind; summon into mind*
bear in mind, bethink, brood over, call to mind, call up, cite, commemorate, conjure up, dig into the past*, dwell upon, educe, elicit, enshrine, extract, fix in the mind, flash on*, get, go back, have memories, hold dear*, keep forever, know by heart*, learn, look back, memorialize, memorize, mind, nail down*, recall, recognize, recollect, refresh memory, relive, remind, reminisce, retain, retrospect, revive, revoke, ring a bell*, strike a note*, summon up, think back, treasure; SEE CONCEPT 40

remembrance [n1] *memory, recollection*
afterthought, anamnesis, flash*, flashback*, hindsight*, mental image, mind, recall, recognition, reconstruction, regard, reminiscence, retrospect, thought; SEE CONCEPTS 40,529

remembrance [n2] *gift, testimonial*
commemoration, favor, keepsake, memento, memorial, monument, present, relic, remembrancer, reminder, reward, souvenir, token, trophy; SEE CONCEPT 337

remind [v] *awaken memories of something*
admonish, advise, bethink, bring back to, bring to mind, call attention, call to mind, call up, caution, cite, emphasize, give a cue*, hint, imply, intimate, jog one's memory*, make one remember, make one think, mention, note, point out, prod, prompt, put in mind, recall, recollect, refresh memory, remember, reminisce, retain, retrospect, revive, stir up, stress, suggest, warn; SEE CONCEPTS 7,19,22,40,78

reminder [n] *warning, notice; keepsake*
admonition, expression, gesture, hint, indication, intimation, memento, memo, memorandum, memorial, note, notice, relic, remembrance, remembrancer, sign, souvenir, suggestion, token, trinket, trophy; SEE CONCEPTS 271,278,529

reminisce [v] *go over in one's memory*
bethink, call up, cite, hark back, live in the past, look back, mind, muse over, recall, recollect, remember, remind, retain, retrospect, review, revive, think back; SEE CONCEPTS *17,40*

reminiscent [adj] *suggestive of something in the past*
bringing to mind, evocative, implicative, mnemonic, nostalgic, recollective, redolent, remindful, similar; SEE CONCEPT *529*

remiss [adj] *careless, thoughtless*
any old way*, any which way*, asleep at switch*, asleep on job*, behindhand, culpable, daydreaming, defaultant, delinquent, derelict, dilatory, disregardful, fainéant, forgetful, heedless, inattentive, indifferent, indolent, lackadaisical, lax, lazy, neglectful, negligent, regardless, slack, slapdash, slipshod, sloppy, slothful, slow, tardy, uninterested, unmindful, woolgathering*; SEE CONCEPT *401*

remission [n1] *acquittal, pardon*
absolution, amnesty, discharge, excuse, exemption, exoneration, forgiveness, indulgence, mercy, pardon, release, reprieve; SEE CONCEPT *685*

remission [n2] *pause; lessening*
abatement, abeyance, alleviation, amelioration, break, decrease, delay, diminution, ebb, interruption, let-up, lull, moderation, reduction, relaxation, release, respite, suspension; SEE CONCEPTS *303,698,807*

remit [v1] *send, transfer*
address, consign, dispatch, forward, mail, make payment, pay, post, route, settle, ship, square, transmit; SEE CONCEPTS *217,341*

remit [v2] *stop, postpone*
abate, absolve, alleviate, amnesty, cancel, condone, decrease, defer, delay, desist, diminish, dwindle, ease up, excuse, exonerate, fall away, forbear, forgive, halt, hold off, hold up, intermit, mitigate, moderate, modify, modulate, pardon, prorogue, put off, reduce, relax, release, repeal, reprieve, rescind, respite, shelve, sink, slack, slacken, soften, stay, suspend, wane, weaken; SEE CONCEPTS *234,698*

remnant [n] *leftover part*
balance, bit, dregs, dross, end, end piece, excess, fragment, hangover*, heel, leavings, lees, leftovers, odds and ends*, orts, part, particle, piece, portion, remainder, remains, residual, residue, residuum, rest, rump, scrap, shred, strip, surplus, survival, vestige; SEE CONCEPTS *260,835*

remonstrate [v] *argue against*
animadvert, blame, censure, challenge, combat, complain, criticize, decry, demur, deprecate, disapprove, disparage, dispute, dissent, except, expostulate, fight, find fault, frown upon, inveigh, kick*, nag, object, oppose, pick at, protest, rain, recriminate, resist, scold, sound off*, take exception, take issue, withstand; SEE CONCEPTS *46,52,54*

remorse [n] *guilty or bad conscience*
anguish, attrition, compassion, compunction, contriteness, contrition, grief, guilt, pangs of conscience*, penance, penitence, penitency, pity, regret, remorsefulness, repentance, rue, ruefulness, self-reproach, shame, sorrow; SEE CONCEPTS *410,728*

remorseful [adj] *guilty, ashamed*
apologetic, attritional, chastened, compunctious, conscience-stricken, contrite, guilt-ridden, mournful, penitent, penitential, regretful, repentant, rueful, sad, self-reproachful, sorrowful, sorry; SEE CONCEPT *401*

remorseless [adj] *without guilt in spite of wrong-doing*
avaricious, barbarous, bloody, callous, cruel, fierce, forbidding, greedy, grim, hard, hard-bitten, hardened, hard-hearted, harsh, impenitent, implacable, inexorable, inhuman, inhumane, insensitive, intolerant, merciless, murderous, obdurate, pitiless, relentless, rigorous, ruthless, sanguinary, savage, shameless, sour, tough, tyrannical, uncompassionate, uncontrite, unforgiving, unmerciful, unregenerate, unrelenting, unremitting, unrepenting, unyielding, vindictive; SEE CONCEPT *401*

remote [adj1] *out-of-the-way; in the distance*
alien, back, backwoods, beyond, boondocks*, devious, distant, far, faraway, far-flung, far-off, foreign, frontier, godforsaken*, god-knows-where*, in a backwater*, inaccessible, isolated, lonely, lonesome, middle of nowhere*, obscure, off-lying, off the beaten path*, outlandish, outlying, private, removed, retired, secluded, secret, undiscovered, unknown, unsettled, wild; SEE CONCEPT *583*

remote [adj2] *irrelevant, unrelated*
abstracted, alien, alone, apart, detached, exclusive, extraneous, extrinsic, farfetched, foreign, immaterial, inappropriate, indirect, nongermane, obscure, outside, pointless, removed, strange, unconnected; SEE CONCEPTS *564,575*

remote [adj3] *unlikely, improbable*
doubtful, dubious, faint, implausible, inconsiderable, meager, negligible, off, outside, poor, slender, slight, slim, small; SEE CONCEPT *552*

remote [adj4] *cold, detached; unapproachable*
abstracted, aloof, casual, cool*, disinterested, distant, faraway, icy, incurious, indifferent, introspective, introverted, laid-back*, offish, putting on airs, removed, reserved, standoffish, stuck up, uncommunicative, unconcerned, uninterested, uninvolved, uppity, withdrawn; SEE CONCEPTS *401,404*

remove [v1] *lift or move object; take off, away*
abolish, abstract, amputate, carry away, carry off, cart off, clear away, cut out, delete, depose, detach, dethrone, dig out, discard, discharge, dislodge, dismiss, displace, disturb, do away with, doff, efface, eject, eliminate, erase, evacuate, expel, expunge, extract, get rid of, junk*, oust, pull out, purge, raise, relegate, rip out, separate, shed, ship, skim, strike out, take down, take out, tear out, throw out, transfer, transport, unload, unseat, uproot, wipe out*, withdraw; SEE CONCEPT *211*

remove [v2] *do away with; kill*
assassinate, blot out*, clear away, dispose of, do away with, do in*, drag, drag down, efface, eliminate, eradicate, erase, exclude, execute, expunge, exterminate, extirpate, get rid of, liquidate, murder, obliterate, purge, scratch, sterilize, take down, take out, waste*, wipe out*; SEE CONCEPTS *121,252*

remunerate [v] *compensate, reward*
accord, ante up*, award, dish out*, do business*, grant, guerdon, indemnify, pay, pay off, pay up, post, recompense, redress, reimburse, repay, requite, shell out*, spring for*, vouchsafe; SEE CONCEPT *341*

re
re

render [v1] *contribute*
cede, deliver, distribute, exchange, furnish, give, give back, give up, hand over, impart, make available, make restitution, minister, part with, pay, pay back, present, provide, relinquish, repay, restore, return, show, submit, supply, surrender, swap, tender, trade, turn over, yield; SEE CONCEPTS 108,140

render [v2] *show; execute*
act, administer, administrate, carry out, delineate, depict, display, do, evince, exhibit, give, govern, image, interpret, limn, manifest, perform, picture, play, portray, present, represent; SEE CONCEPTS 91,261

render [v3] *translate, explain*
construe, deliver, interpret, paraphrase, pass, put, reproduce, restate, reword, state, transcribe, transliterate, transpose, turn; SEE CONCEPTS 57,266

rendezvous [n1] *get-together*
affair, appointment, assignation, blind date, date, double date, engagement, heavy date*, matinee, meet, meeting, one night stand*, tête-à-tête, tryst; SEE CONCEPT 384

rendezvous [n2] *place for get-together*
gathering point, hangout*, haunt, love nest*, meeting place, purlieu, resort, spot, stomping ground*, venue, watering hole*; SEE CONCEPT 198

rendezvous [v] *meet, often secretly*
assemble, be closeted, be reunited, collect, come together, congregate, congress, converge, forgather, gather, get together, join up, meet behind closed doors*, meet privately, muster, raise, rally; SEE CONCEPT 384

rendition [n] *explanation; interpretation*
arrangement, construction, delivery, depiction, execution, interpretation, performance, portrayal, presentation, reading, rendering, transcription, translation, version; SEE CONCEPTS 263,278

renegade [n] *person who is rebellious*
abandoner, apostate, backslider, betrayer, defector, deserter, dissident, double-crosser*, escapee, exile, forsaker, fugitive, heretic, iconoclast, insurgent, mutineer, outlaw, rebel, recreant, refugee, runaway, schismatic, snake*, snake in the grass*, tergiversator, traitor, turnabout, turncoat; SEE CONCEPTS 359,412

renegade [adj] *rebellious*
apostate, backsliding, disloyal, dissident, heterodox, mutinous, outlaw, radical, reactionary, rebel, recreant, revolutionary, runaway, schismatic, traitorous, unfaithful, untraditional; SEE CONCEPTS 401,542

renew [v] *start over; refurbish*
begin again, brace, breathe new life into*, bring up to date*, continue, exhilarate, extend, fix up, freshen, gentrify, go over, mend, modernize, overhaul, prolong, reaffirm, reawaken, recommence, recondition, recreate, reestablish, refit, refresh, regenerate, rehabilitate, reinvigorate, rejuvenate, remodel, renovate, reopen, repair, repeat, replace, replenish, restate, restock, restore, resume, resuscitate, retread, revitalize, revive, spruce, stimulate, transform; SEE CONCEPTS 35,202,221

renounce [v] *abandon, reject*
abdicate, abjure, abnegate, abstain from, apostacize, arrogate, cast off, decline, defect, demit, deny, desert, disavow, discard, disclaim, disown, divorce oneself from*, drop out, dump*, eschew,

forgo, forsake, forswear, give up, leave flat*, leave off, opt out, quit, rat*, recant, reject, relinquish, repudiate, resign, sell out*, spurn, swear off, take the pledge*, tergiversate, tergiverse, throw off, throw over, toss over, turn, waive, walk out on, wash hands of*; SEE CONCEPTS 30,54,195

renovate [v] *fix up, modernize*
clean, cleanse, do*, do up*, face-lift*, gussy up*, make over, overhaul, reactivate, recondition, reconstitute, recreate, refit, reform, refresh, refurbish, rehabilitate, rekindle, remake, remodel, renew, repair, restore, resurrect, resuscitate, retread, retrieve, revamp, revitalize, revive, revivify, spruce, spruce up*, update; SEE CONCEPTS 168,177,202

renown [adj] *fame*
acclaim, celebrity, distinction, éclat, eminence, glory, honor, illustriousness, kudos, luster, mark, note, notoriety, preeminence, prestige, prominence, prominency, rep*, reputation, repute, stardom; SEE CONCEPT 668

renowned [adj] *famous*
acclaimed, celebrated, celebrious, distinguished, eminent, esteemed, extolled, famed, great, illustrious, in the limelight*, lauded, monster*, name*, notable, noted, of note, outstanding, praised, prominent, redoubted, signal, splashy, star, superstar, well-known; SEE CONCEPTS 568,574

rent [n1] *fee paid for use, service, or privilege*
hire, lease, payment, rental, tariff; SEE CONCEPT 329

rent [n2] *opening, split*
breach, break, chink, cleavage, crack, discord, dissension, division, faction, fissure, flaw, fracture, gash, hole, perforation, rift, rip, rupture, schism, slash, slit, tatter, tear; SEE CONCEPTS 513,665

rent [v] *pay or charge fee for use, service, or privilege*
allow the use of, borrow, charter, contract, engage, hire, lease, lend, let, loan, make available, put on loan, sublet, take it; SEE CONCEPTS 89,115

renunciation [n] *abandonment, rejection*
abdication, abjuration, abnegation, abstention, cancellation, denial, disavowal, disclaimer, eschewal, eschewing, forbearing, forswearing, giving up, rebuff, refusal, relinquishment, remission, renouncement, repeal, repudiation, resignation, sacrifice, self-abnegation, self-denial, self-sacrifice, spurning, surrender, veto, waiver, yielding; SEE CONCEPTS 30,54,195

repair [n] *restoration, fixing*
adjustment, darn, improvement, mend, new part, overhaul, patch, reconstruction, reformation, rehabilitation, replacement, substitution; SEE CONCEPTS 513,700,824

repair [v1] *fix, restore*
compensate for, correct, darn, debug*, doctor*, do up*, emend, fiddle with, give a face-lift*, heal, improve, make good, make up for, mend, overhaul, patch, patch up, put back together, put in order, put right, rebuild, recondition, recover, rectify, redress, reform, refresh, refurbish, rejuvenate, remedy, renew, renovate, restore, retread, retrieve, revive, right, settle, sew, square*, touch up; SEE CONCEPT 212

repair [v2] *leave; retire*
apply, betake oneself, fare, go, head for, hie, journey, move, pass, proceed, process, push on, re-

cur, refer, remove, resort, run, set off for, travel, turn, wend, withdraw; SEE CONCEPT 195

reparation [n] *compensation, amends*
adjustment, apology, atonement, damages, dues, emolument, expiation, indemnification, indemnity, making good, payment, penance, propitiation, quittance, recompense, redemption, redress, remuneration, renewal, repair, repayment, reprisal, requital, restitution, retribution, reward, satisfaction, settlement, squaring things*; SEE CONCEPTS 337,344,712

repartee [n] *pleasant conversation*
answer, badinage, banter, bon mot*, comeback, humor, irony, persiflage, pleasantry, quip, raillery, rejoinder, reply, response, retort, riposte, sally, sarcasm, satire, wit, witticism, wittiness, wordplay; SEE CONCEPTS 45,56,266

repay [v1] *give back money or possession*
accord, award, balance, compensate, indemnify, make amends, make restitution, make up for, offset, pay back, pay dues, rebate, recompense, refund, reimburse, remunerate, requite, restore, return, reward, settle up, square*; SEE CONCEPTS 131,341

repay [v2] *get even; obtain restitution for past injustice*
avenge, even the score, get back at, get revenge, make reprisal, pay back, reciprocate, requite, retaliate, return, return the compliment*, revenge, settle the score*, square accounts*; SEE CONCEPTS 7,19,246,384

repeal [n] *cancellation*
abolition, abrogation, annulment, invalidation, nullification, rescinding, rescindment, rescission, revocation, withdrawal; SEE CONCEPTS 121,318, 685

repeal [v] *declare null and void*
abolish, abrogate, annul, back out, backpedal*, blow, call off*, cancel, countermand, dismantle, invalidate, kill*, KO*, lift, nix*, nullify, opt out, recall, renig, rescind, reverse, revoke, scrub, set aside, shoot down, stand down, throw over, vacate, void, wash out, weasel out*, wipe out, withdraw, worm out*, X-out*, zap*; SEE CONCEPTS 50,88,121,317

repeat [n] *something done over; duplicate*
echo, recapitulation, reiteration, repetition, replay, reproduction, rerun, reshowing; SEE CONCEPT 695

repeat [v] *duplicate, do again*
chime, come again, din, ditto*, drum into*, duplicate, echo, go over again, hold over, imitate, ingeminate, iterate, make like*, occur again, play back, play over, quote, read back, reappear, recapitulate, recast, reciprocate, recite, reconstruct, recrudesce, recur, redo, refashion, reform, rehash*, rehearse, reissue, reiterate, relate, remake, renew, reoccur, replay, reprise, reproduce, rerun, resay, reshow, restate, retell, return, revert, revolve, rework*, run over, sing same old song*; SEE CONCEPTS 91,111,171

repeatedly [adv] *over and over again*
again, again and again, frequently, many a time, many times, much, oft, often, oftentimes, ofttimes, regularly, time after time, time and again; SEE CONCEPT 799

repel [v1] *push away; repulse*
beat back, beat off, brush off, buck, cast aside, chase away, check, confront, cool*, cut, decline, dismiss, disown, dispute, drive away, drive back,

drive off, duel, fend off, fight, force back, force off, give cold shoulder to*, hold back, hold off, keep at arm's length*, keep at bay*, keep off, kick, knock down, oppose, parry, push back, put down, put to flight, rebuff, rebut, refuse, reject, resist, stand up against, stave off, traverse, turn down, ward off, withstand; SEE CONCEPTS 30,208

repel [v2] *induce aversion*
disgust, give a pain in neck*, make sick*, offend, put off*, reluct, repulse, revolt, sicken, turn off*, turn one's stomach*; SEE CONCEPTS 7,19,303

repent [v] *ask forgiveness*
apologize, atone, be ashamed, be contrite, be sorry, bewail, deplore, feel remorse, have qualms, lament, reform, regret, relent, reproach oneself, rue, see error of ways*, show penitence, sorrow; SEE CONCEPTS 48,410

repentance [n] *feeling bad for past action*
attrition, compunction, conscience, contriteness, contrition, grief, guilt, penitence, penitency, regret, remorse, rue, ruth, self-reproach, sorriness, sorrow; SEE CONCEPTS 410,728

repercussion [n] *consequence*
backlash, chain reaction, echo, effect, fallout, feedback, flak*, follow-through*, follow-up, impact, imprint, influence, kickback*, mark, reaction, rebound, recoil, re-echo, result, reverberation, side effect, spinoff*, waves*; SEE CONCEPT 230

repertory [n] *collection*
bit, cache, depot, list, range, rep*, repertoire, repository, routine, schtick*, stock, stockroom, store, storehouse, stunt*, supply; SEE CONCEPTS 263,432,712

repetition [n] *duplication; doing again*
alliteration, broken record*, chant, chorus, copy, echo, encore, ingemination, iteracy, iterance, iteration, litany, paraphrase, periodicity, perseveration, practice, reappearance, recapitulation, recital, recurrence, redundancy, rehearsal, reiteration, relation, renewal, reoccurrence, repeat, repetitiousness, replication, report, reproduction, restatement, return, rhythm, rote, tautology; SEE CONCEPT 695

repetitious [adj] *wordy, tedious*
alliterative, boring, dull, echoic, iterant, iterative, long-winded, plangent, pleonastic, prolix, recapitulatory, redundant, reiterative, repeating, repetitive, resonant, tautological, verbose, windy; SEE CONCEPT 553

replace [v] *take the place of; put in place of*
alter, back up, change, compensate, displace, fill in, follow, front for*, give back, mend, oust, outplace, patch, pinch hit for*, put back, reconstitute, recoup, recover, redeem, redress, reestablish, refund, regain, reimburse, reinstate, repay, restitute, restore, retrieve, ring, ring in, shift, sit in, stand in, stand in lieu of, step into shoes of*, sub*, substitute, succeed, supersede, supplant, supply, swap places, take out, take over, take over from; SEE CONCEPTS 104,128,211,697

replenish [v] *fill, stock*
furnish, make up, provide, provision, refill, refresh, reload, renew, replace, restock, restore, stock, top; SEE CONCEPTS 140,209

replete [adj] *full, well-stocked*
abounding, abundant, alive, awash, brimful, brimming, charged, chock-full*, complete, crammed, crowded, filled, full up*, glutted, gorged, jammed, jam-packed, lavish, loaded, lux-

re
re

urious, overfed, overflowing, packed, plenteous, rife, sated, satiated, stuffed, swarming, teeming, thronged, well-provided; SEE CONCEPTS 483,740

replica [n] *duplicate*
carbon, carbon copy, chip off old block*, clone, copy, ditto*, dupe*, facsimile, flimsy*, imitation, likeness, lookalike, mimeo, mimic, miniature, model, photocopy, reduplication, repeat, replication, repro, reproduction, stat, Xerox*; SEE CONCEPTS 260,670,686

reply [n] *answer*
acknowledgment, antiphon, back talk*, comeback, counter, echo, feedback, knee-jerk reaction*, lip*, reaction, reciprocation, rejoinder, respond, response, retaliation, retort, return, riposte, sass*, snappy comeback*, vibes*, wisecrack; SEE CONCEPT 278

reply [v] *answer*
acknowledge, be in touch*, come back*, counter, echo, feedback, field the question*, get back to, react, reciprocate, rejoin, respond, retaliate, retort, return, riposte, shoot back*, squelch*, top*, write back; SEE CONCEPT 45

report [n1] *account, story*
address, announcement, article, blow by blow*, brief, broadcast, cable, chronicle, communication, communique, declaration, description, detail, digest, dispatch, handout, history, hot wire*, information, message, narration, narrative, news, note, opinion, outline, paper, picture, piece, precis, proclamation, pronouncement, recital, record, relation, release, résumé, rundown, scoop*, statement, summary, tale, telegram, tidings, version, wire, word*, write-up; SEE CONCEPTS 274,282, 283

report [n2] *gossip, talk*
advice, blow by blow*, buzz*, canard, chat, chatter, chitchat, comment, conversation, cry*, dirt*, earful, grapevine*, hash*, hearsay, intelligence, murmur, news, prating, rumble*, rumor, scandal, scuttlebutt*, small talk*, speech, tattle, the latest*, tidings, whispering, word*; SEE CONCEPTS 51,278

report [n3] *loud noise*
bang, blast, boom, crack, crash, detonation, discharge, explosion, reverberation, sound; SEE CONCEPT 595

report [n4] *reputation*
character, esteem, fame, name, regard, rep*, repute; SEE CONCEPT 388

report [v1] *communicate information, knowledge*
account for, advise, air, announce, bring word, broadcast, cable, circulate, cover, declare, describe, detail, disclose, document, enunciate, give an account of, give the facts, impart, inform, inscribe, itemize, list, make known, make public, mention, narrate, note, notify, pass on, present, proclaim, promulgate, provide details, publish, recite, record, recount, rehearse, relate, relay, retail, reveal, set forth, spread, state, summarize, telephone, tell, trumpet, wire, write up; SEE CONCEPT 60

report [v2] *present oneself*
appear, arrive, be at hand, be present, clock in*, come, get to, reach, show, show up, turn up*; SEE CONCEPT 159

reporter [n] *person who informs*
anchor, anchorperson, announcer, columnist, correspondent, cub*, editor, ink slinger*, interviewer, journalist, legperson*, newscaster,

newshound*, newsperson, newswriter, press person, scribe, scrivener, stringer, writer; SEE CONCEPTS 348,356

repose [n] *restfulness; calm*
ease, inaction, inactivity, leisure, peace, quiet, quietness, quietude, refreshment, relaxation, relaxing, renewal, requiescence, respite, rest, restoration, sleep, slumber, stillness, tranquillity; SEE CONCEPTS 410,681,720

repose [v] *relax; recline*
deposit, lay down, lie, lie down, loaf, loll, lounge, place, rest, settle, settle down, slant, sleep, slumber, stretch, stretch out, take it easy, tilt; SEE CONCEPTS 154,210

reprehensible [adj] *very bad; shameful*
amiss, blamable, blameworthy, censurable, condemnable, culpable, delinquent, demeritorious, discreditable, disgraceful, errant, erring, guilty, ignoble, objectionable, opprobrious, remiss, sinful, unholy, unworthy, wicked; SEE CONCEPT 571

represent [v1] *present image of; symbolize*
act as, act as broker, act for, act in place of, appear as, assume the role of, be, be agent for, be attorney for, be proxy for, betoken, body, buy for, copy, correspond to, do business for, emblematize, embody, enact, epitomize, equal, equate, exemplify, exhibit, express, factor, hold office, imitate, impersonate, mean, perform, personify, play the part, produce, put on, reproduce, sell for, serve, serve as, show, speak for, stage, stand for, steward, substitute, symbolize, typify; SEE CONCEPTS 87,317,682,716

represent [v2] *depict, show*
body forth, delineate, denote, describe, design, designate, display, draft, enact, evoke, exhibit, express, hint, illustrate, interpret, limn, mirror, narrate, outline, picture, portray, realize, relate, render, reproduce, run down, run through, sketch, suggest, track; SEE CONCEPTS 138,261

representative [n1] *person who acts in the stead of another*
agent, assemblyperson, attorney, commissioner, congressperson, councilor, councilperson, counselor, delegate, deputy, lawyer, legislator, member, messenger, proxy, rep*, salesperson, senator, spokesperson; SEE CONCEPTS 348,354

representative [n2] *typical example*
archetype, case, case history, embodiment, epitome, exemplar, illustration, instance, personification, sample, sampling, specimen, type; SEE CONCEPT 686

representative [adj] *characteristic, typical*
adumbrative, archetypal, classic, classical, delineative, depictive, emblematic, evocative, exemplary, ideal, illustrative, model, presentational, prototypal, prototypical, quintessential, rep*, symbolic, symbolical; SEE CONCEPTS 487,573

repress [v] *keep back, hold in*
black out*, bottle, chasten, check, collect, compose, control, cool*, cork*, crush, curb, gridlock*, hinder, hold back, inhibit, jam up, keep in, keep in check, keep under wraps*, kill*, lock, master, muffle, overcome, overpower, quash, quelch, quell, rein, restrain, shush, silence, simmer down*, smother, squelch, stifle, subdue, subjugate, suppress, swallow, throw cold water on*, tie up*; SEE CONCEPTS 121,130

reprieve [n] *relief of blame, responsibility*
abatement, abeyance, absolution, acquittal, alleviation, amnesty, anchor*, clearance, clemency,

commute, deferment, freeing, let-up*, lifeboat*, lifesaver*, mitigation, palliation, pardon, postponement, release, remission, respite, spring*, stay, suspension, truce; SEE CONCEPTS 318,685

reprieve [v] *relieve of blame, responsibility*
abate, absolve, allay, alleviate, amnesty, excuse, forgive, grant a stay, let go, let off, let off the hook*, let off this time*, let up on*, mitigate, palliate, pardon, postpone, remit, respite; SEE CONCEPTS 50,88,317

reprimand [n] *oral punishment*
admonishment, admonition, bawling out*, blame, calling down*, castigation, censure, chiding, comeuppance, dressing-down*, going over*, grooming, hard time*, lecture, piece of one's mind*, ragging*, rap*, rebuke, reprehension, reproof, scolding, slap on wrist*, talking-to, telling-off, tongue-lashing, what for*; SEE CONCEPTS 123,278

reprimand [v] *blame, scold*
admonish, call on the carpet*, castigate, censure, check, chew out*, chide, come down on*, criticize, denounce, dress down*, give piece of one's mind*, give the dickens*, lecture, lesson, light into*, lower the boom*, monish, rap, rebuke, reprehend, reproach, reprove, take to task*, tell off, tick off*, upbraid; SEE CONCEPTS 44,52

reprisal [n] *revenge*
avengement, avenging, counterblow, counterstroke, eye for an eye*, paying back, requital, retaliation, retribution, vengeance; SEE CONCEPT 384

reproach [n] *strong criticism; dishonor*
abuse, admonishment, admonition, blame, blemish, censure, chiding, condemnation, contempt, disapproval, discredit, disgrace, disrepute, ignominy, indignity, obloquy, odium, opprobrium, rap*, rebuke, reprehension, reprimand, reproof, scorn, shame, slight, slur, stain, stigma; SEE CONCEPTS 44,52,123,388

reproach [v] *find fault with*
abuse, admonish, blame, call down, call to task*, cavil, censure, chide, condemn, criticize, defame, discredit, disparage, give comeuppance*, give the devil*, jawbone*, lay on*, lesson, rake, ream, rebuke, reprehend, reprimand, reprove, scold, sit on*, take to task, trim, upbraid; SEE CONCEPTS 44,52

reproduce [v1] *make more copies of*
carbon*, clone, copy, do again, dupe*, duplicate, echo, emulate, engross, follow, imitate, knock off, manifold, match, mimeo*, mimeograph, mirror, parallel, photocopy, photograph, photostat, pirate, portray, print, reawaken, recount, recreate, redo, reduplicate, reenact, reflect, relive, remake, repeat, replicate, represent, reprint, restamp, revive, stereotype, transcribe, type, Xerox*; SEE CONCEPTS 111,171

reproduce [v2] *make something new; give birth*
bear, beget, breed, engender, father, fecundate, generate, hatch, impregnate, mother, multiply, procreate, produce young, progenerate, proliferate, propagate, repopulate, sire, spawn; SEE CONCEPTS 173,251,374

reproduction [n] *something duplicated; duplication*
breeding, carbon*, carbon copy, chip off old block*, clone, copy, ditto*, dupe*, facsimile, fake, flimsy, generation, imitation, increase, lookalike, mimeo*, mimeograph, mirror image*, mul-

tiplication, offprint, photocopy, photograph, Photostat, pic*, picture, portrayal, print, procreation, proliferation, propagation, recreation, reduplication, reenactment, renewal, replica, replication, reprinting, repro*, revival, stat, transcription, twin, Xerox*, X-ray*; SEE CONCEPTS 173,625,670,716

repudiate [v] *reject; turn one's back on*
abandon, abjure, apostatize, banish, be against, break with, cast, cast off, cut off, decline, default, defect, demur, deny, desert, disacknowledge, disapprove, disavow, discard, disclaim, dishonor, disinherit, dismiss, disown, dump, flush*, fly in the face of*, forsake, nix*, oust, rat*, recant, refuse, renounce, repeal, reprobate, rescind, retract, reverse, revoke, spurn, tergiversate, tergiverse, turn, turn down, wash one's hands of*; SEE CONCEPTS 13,21,30

repugnant [adj] *bad, obnoxious; hostile*
abhorrent, abominable, adverse, against, alien, antagonistic, antipathetic, averse, conflicting, contradictory, counter, creepy*, different, disagreeable, disgusting, distasteful, extraneous, extrinsic, foreign, foul, hateful, horrid, incompatible, inconsistent, inconsonant, inimical, in opposition, invidious, loathsome, nasty, nauseating, noisome, objectionable, odious, offensive, opposed, opposite, repellent, revolting, revulsive, sickening, unconformable, unfitted, unfriendly, vile; SEE CONCEPTS 401,564,571

repulse [n] *snub; rejection*
brush-off*, check, cold shoulder*, defeat, disappointment, failure, nix*, nothing doing*, rebuff, refusal, reverse, slap in the face*, spurning, thumbs down*, turndown; SEE CONCEPTS 388,674

repulse [v1] *push away*
beat off, brush off*, check, defeat, drive back, fend off, fight off, heave-ho*, hold off, keep off, kick in the teeth*, nix*, overthrow, push back, put down, rebuff, rebut, reject, repel, resist, set back*, stave off, throw back, ward off; SEE CONCEPTS 96,108

repulse [v2] *make sick*
disdain, disgust, disregard, give a pain*, rebuff, refuse, reject, reluct, repel, revolt, sicken, snub, spurn, turn down, turn off; SEE CONCEPTS 21,410

repulsion [n] *hatred, disgust*
abhorrence, abomination, antipathy, aversion, denial, detestation, disrelish, distaste, hate, horror, loathing, malice, rebuff, refusal, repugnance, repugnancy, resentment, revolt, revulsion, snub; SEE CONCEPT 29

repulsive [adj] *very disgusting, offensive*
abhorrent, abominable, animal*, creepy*, disagreeable, distasteful, forbidding, foul, gross, hateful, hideous, horrid, loathsome, nasty, nauseating, noisome, objectionable, obnoxious, odious, off-putting, pugnacious, repellent, revolting, sickening, sleazy*, ugly, undesirable, unpleasant, unsightly, vile; SEE CONCEPTS 529,571,579

reputable [adj] *worthy of respect*
acclaimed, celebrated, conscientious, constant, creditable, dependable, distinguished, eminent, esteemed, estimable, excellent, fair, faithful, famed, famous, favored, good, high-principled, high-ranking, honest, honorable, honored, illustrious, in high favor, just, legitimate, notable, of good repute, popular, prominent, redoubted, reliable, renowned, respectable, righteous, salt of the

re
re

earth*, sincere, straightforward, trustworthy, truthful, upright, well-known, well-thought-of; SEE CONCEPTS 545,567,574

reputation [n] *commonly held opinion of person's character*

acceptability, account, approval, authority, character, credit, dependability, distinction, éclat, eminence, esteem, estimation, fame, favor, honor, influence, mark*, name*, notoriety, opinion, position, prestige, privilege, prominence, rank, regard, reliability, renown, rep*, report, repute, respectability, standing, stature, trustworthiness, weight; SEE CONCEPTS 388,411,689

reputed [adj] *believed*

accounted, alleged, assumed, conjectural, considered, deemed, estimated, gossiped, held, hypothetical, ostensible, putative, reckoned, regarded, reported, rumored, said, seeming, supposed, suppositional, suppositious, supposititious, suppositive, suppository, thought; SEE CONCEPT 529

request [n] *question or petition*

appeal, application, asking, begging, call, commercial, demand, desire, entreaty, inquiry, invitation, offer, prayer, recourse, requisition, solicitation, suit, supplication; SEE CONCEPT 662

request [v] *ask for*

appeal, apply, beg, beseech, bespeak, call for, demand, desire, entreat, hit, hit up for*, hold out for*, hustle*, inquire, petition, pray, promote, put in for*, requisition, seek, solicit, sponge*, sue, supplicate, touch; SEE CONCEPT 53

require [v1] *need, want*

crave, depend upon, desire, feel necessity for, have need, hurting for, lack, miss, stand in need, wish; SEE CONCEPTS 20,646

require [v2] *ask, demand; necessitate*

assert oneself, beg, beseech, bid, call for, call upon, cause, challenge, claim, command, compel, constrain, crave, demand, direct, enjoin, entail, exact, expect, insist upon, instruct, involve, look for, obligate, oblige, order, postulate, push for, request, requisition, solicit, take; SEE CONCEPTS 53,646

required/requisite [adj] *necessary*

appropriate, called for, compulsatory, compulsory, condign, demanded, deserved, due, enforced, essential, imperative, imperious, indispensable, just, mandatory, needed, needful, obligatory, prerequisite, prescribed, recommended, right, rightful, set, suitable, unavoidable, vital; SEE CONCEPT 546

requirement/requisite [n] *necessity, want*

claim, compulsion, concern, condition, demand, desideratum, element, engrossment, essential, exaction, exigency, extremity, fulfillment, fundamental, imperative, lack, must, need, obligation, obsession, pinch, precondition, preliminary, preoccupation, prepossession, prerequisite, prescription, provision, proviso, qualification, sine qua non, specification, stipulation, terms, urgency, vital part; SEE CONCEPTS 646,709

requisition [n] *demand; application for need*

appropriation, call, commandeering, demand, occupation, request, seizure, summons, takeover; SEE CONCEPT 662

requisition [v] *ask for; apply for something needed*

buy, call for, challenge, claim, demand, exact, order, postulate, put dibs on*, put in for, request, require, solicit; SEE CONCEPTS 48,53

requite [v] *compensate, give in return*

indemnify, make, make amends, make good, pay, pay off, quit, reciprocate, recompense, redeem, redress, reimburse, remunerate, repay, respond, restitution, retaliate, return, revenge, reward, satisfy, settle; SEE CONCEPTS 126,131,341,384

rescind [v] *declare null and void*

abolish, abrogate, annul, back out of, backpedal*, backwater*, call off, cancel, countermand, crawl out of*, dismantle, forget, invalidate, lift, nix*, overturn, pull the plug*, quash, recall, remove, renege, repeal, retract, reverse, revoke, scrub*, set aside, void, wangle out*, weasel out*, X-out*; SEE CONCEPTS 121,234,317

rescue [n] *saving from danger*

deliverance, delivery, disembarrassment, disentanglement, emancipation, exploit, extrication, feat, heroics, heroism, liberation, performance, ransom, reclaiming, reclamation, recovering, recovery, redemption, release, relief, salvage, salvation, saving; SEE CONCEPT 134

rescue [v] *save from danger*

bail one out*, conserve, deliver, disembarrass, disentangle, emancipate, extricate, free, get off the hook*, get out, get out of hock*, give a break, hold over, keep, liberate, manumit, preserve, protect, pull out of the fire*, ransom, recapture, recover, redeem, regain, release, retain, retrieve, safeguard, salvage, save life of, set free, spring*, unleash, unloose; SEE CONCEPT 134

research [n] *examination, study*

analysis, delving, experimentation, exploration, fact-finding, fishing expedition*, groundwork, inquest, inquiry, inquisition, investigation, legwork*, probe, probing, quest, R and D*, scrutiny; SEE CONCEPTS 349,362

research [v] *examine, study*

analyze, consult, do tests, experiment, explore, inquire, investigate, look into, look up, play around with*, probe, read up on, scrutinize; SEE CONCEPTS 31,103

resemblance [n] *correspondence, similarity*

affinity, alikeness, analogy, birds of a feather*, carbon*, carbon copy, clone, closeness, coincidence, comparability, comparison, conformity, counterpart, double, facsimile, image, kinship, likeness, like of, look-alike, parallel, parity, peas in a pod*, ringer*, sameness, semblance, simile, similitude, spitting image*, two of a kind*, Xerox*; SEE CONCEPTS 664,670,716

resemble [v] *look or be like*

appear like, approximate, bear resemblance to, be similar to, be the very picture of*, bring to mind, coincide, come close to, come near, correspond to, double, duplicate, echo, favor, feature, follow, have earmarks of*, have signs of, match, mirror, parallel, pass for, relate, remind one of, seem like, simulate, smack of*, sound like, take after; SEE CONCEPTS 664,670,716

resent [v] *be angry about*

bear a grudge, begrudge, be in a huff*, be insulted, be offended by, be put off by*, be rubbed wrong way*, be vexed, dislike, feel bitter, feel sore*, frown at, get nose out of joint*, grudge, harbor a grudge*, have hard feelings*, object to, take amiss, take as an insult, take exception, take offense, take umbrage; SEE CONCEPTS 29,410

resentment [n] *hate, anger*

acerbity, acrimony, animosity, animus, annoyance, antagonism, bad feeling, bitterness, choler, cynicism, displeasure, dudgeon, exacerbation, exasperation, fog, fury, grudge, huff, hurt, ill feeling, ill will, indignation, ire, irritation, malice, malignity, miff, offense, outrage, passion, perturbation, pique, rage, rancor, rise, spite, umbrage, vehemence, vexation, wrath; SEE CONCEPTS 29,410

reservation [n1] *condition, stipulation*
catch, circumscription, demur, doubt, fine print*, grain of salt*, hesitancy, kicker*, provision, proviso, qualification, restriction, scruple, skepticism, string*, strings*, terms; SEE CONCEPTS 646,711

reservation [n2] *the act of holding something, or thing held for future use*
bespeaking, booking, exclusive possession, place, restriction, retaining, retainment, setting aside, withholding; SEE CONCEPT 710

reservation [n3] *habitat for large group*
enclave, homeland, preserve, reserve, sanctuary, territory, tract; SEE CONCEPTS 512,516

reserve [n1] *supply*
ace in hole*, assets, backlog, cache, capital, drop, emergency fund*, fund, hoard, insurance, inventory, nest egg*, plant, provisions, rainy day fund*, reservoir, resources, savings, stash*, stock, stockpile, store, wealth; SEE CONCEPTS 340,710,712

reserve [n2] *coolness of manner*
aloofness, backwardness, calmness, caution, coldness, constraint, coyness, demureness, diffidence, formality, inhibition, modesty, quietness, reluctance, repression, reservation, restraint, reticence, secretiveness, self-restraint, shyness, silence, suppression, taciturnity, uncommunicativeness, unresponsiveness; SEE CONCEPT 633

reserve [v1] *keep, hold back*
conserve, defer, delay, duck*, have, hoard, hold, keep back, keep out, lay up, maintain, plant, possess, postpone, preserve, put away, put by, put off, retain, save, set aside, squirrel*, squirrel away*, stash, stockpile, store, store up, stow away, withhold; SEE CONCEPT 129

reserve [v2] *hold for future use*
bespeak, book, contract, engage, prearrange, preengage, retain, schedule, secure; SEE CONCEPT 53

reserved [adj1] *silent, unsociable; constrained*
aloof, backward, bashful, cautious, ceremonious, close, close-mouthed, cold*, collected, composed, conventional, cool, demure, diffident, distant, eremitic, formal, frigid, gentle, icy*, mild, misanthropic, modest, noncommittal, offish, peaceful, placid, prim, quiet, reclusive, restrained, reticent, retiring, secretive, sedate, self-contained, serene, shy, soft-spoken, solitary, standoffish, taciturn, unapproachable, uncommunicative, uncompanionable, undemonstrative, unresponsive, withdrawn; SEE CONCEPTS 401,404

reserved [adj2] *held for future use*
appropriated, arrogated, booked, claimed, engaged, kept, laid away, limited, preempted, private, qualified, restricted, retained, roped off, set apart, set aside, spoken for, taken; SEE CONCEPTS 576,710

reservoir [n] *accumulation, repository*
backlog, basin, cistern, container, fund, holder, lake, nest egg*, pond, pool, receptacle, reserve, source, spring, stock, stockpile, storage, store, supply, tank, tarn; SEE CONCEPTS 514,712

reside [v] *live or exist in*
abide, be intrinsic to, be vested, bide, consist, continue, crash*, dig*, dwell, endure, hang one's hat*, inhabit, inhere, lie, locate, lodge, nest, occupy, park*, people, perch, populate, remain, rest with, roost, settle, sojourn, squat, stay, take up residence, tenant; SEE CONCEPTS 226,407

residence [n] *place for living*
abode, address, apartment, condo, co-op, domicile, dwelling, habitation, hall, headquarters, hole, home, homeplate*, house, household, inhabitancy, inhabitation, living quarters, lodging, manor, mansion, occupancy, occupation, palace, rack*, roof*, roost*, seat, settlement, villa; SEE CONCEPT 516

resident [n] *person living in a particular place*
citizen, denizen, dweller, habitant, householder, indweller, inhabitant, inmate, liver, local, lodger, native, occupant, resider, squatter, suburbanite, tenant, urbanite; SEE CONCEPT 413

residual [adj] *leftover*
balance, continuing, enduring, extra, lingering, net, remaining, surplus, unconsumed, unused, vestigal; SEE CONCEPTS 560,771

residue [n] *leftover part*
balance, debris, dregs, dross, excess, extra, garbage, heel, junk, leavings, leftovers, orts, parings, remainder, remains, remnant, residual, residuum, rest, scourings, scraps, scum, sewage, shavings, silt, slag, surplus, trash; SEE CONCEPTS 260,432

resign [v] *give up responsibility*
abandon, abdicate, bail out, bow out, capitulate, cease work, cede, demit, divorce oneself from, drop, drop out, end service, fold, forgo, forsake, give notice, give up the ship*, hand in resignation, hand over, hang it up*, leave, quit, relinquish, renounce, retire, secede, separate oneself from, sign off, stand aside, stand down, step down, surrender, terminate, throw in the towel*, turn over, vacate, waive, walk out, wash hands of*, yield; SEE CONCEPTS 119,195,351

resignation [n1] *relinquishment of responsibility*
abandonment, abdication, departure, giving up, leaving, notice, quitting, renunciation, retirement, surrender, tendering, termination, vacating, withdrawal; SEE CONCEPTS 119,195,351

resignation [n2] *endurance, passivity*
acceptance, acquiescence, compliance, conformity, deference, docility, forbearing, fortitude, humbleness, humility, longanimity, lowliness, meekness, modesty, nonresistance, patience, patientness, resignedness, submission, submissiveness, sufferance; SEE CONCEPTS 410,657

resigned [adj] *enduring, passive*
accommodated, acquiescent, adapted, adjusted, agreeable, amenable, biddable, calm, compliant, cordial, deferential, docile, genial, gentle, long-suffering, manageable, nonresisting, obedient, patient, peaceable, philosophical, pliant, quiescent, quiet, ready, reconciled, relinquishing, renouncing, satisfied, stoical, subdued, submissive, subservient, tame, tolerant, tractable, unassertive, unprotesting, unresisting, well-disposed, willing, yielding; SEE CONCEPTS 401,542

resilient [adj] *bouncy, flexible*
airy, buoyant, effervescent, elastic, expansive, hardy, irrepressible, plastic, pliable, quick to recover, rebounding, rolling with punches*, rub-

bery, snapping back, springy, stretchy, strong, supple, tough, volatile; SEE CONCEPTS *488,489*

resist [*v*] *withstand, oppose*
abide, abstain from, antagonize, assail, assault, battle, bear, brook, buck, check, combat, confront, contend, continue, counteract, countervail, curb, defy, die hard, dispute, duel, endure, fight back, forbear, forgo, hinder, hold, hold off, hold out against, keep from, leave alone, maintain, persevere, persist, prevent, put up a fight, refrain, refuse, remain, remain firm, repel, stand up to, stay, stonewall*, struggle against, suffer, thwart, traverse, turn down, weather, withstand; SEE CONCEPTS *23,35,96,106*

resistance [*n*] *fighting, opposition*
battle, blocking, check, combat, contention, counteraction, cover, defiance, detention, fight, friction, halting, hindrance, holding, impedance, impediment, impeding, intransigence, obstruction, parrying, protecting, protection, rebuff, refusal, retardation, safeguard, screen, shield, stand, striking back, struggle, support, warding off, watch, withstanding; SEE CONCEPTS *23,96,106,410*

resolute [*adj*] *determined, strong-willed*
adamant, bold, constant, courageous, dead set on*, decided, dogged, faithful, firm, fixed, immutable, inflexible, intent upon, intrepid, loyal, meaning business*, obstinate, persevering, persistent, persisting, purposeful, relentless, resolved, serious, set, settled, staunch, steadfast, steady, strong, stubborn, tenacious, true, unbending, unchanging, uncompromising, undaunted, unfaltering, unflagging, unflinching, unshakable, unshaken, unwavering, unyielding, valiant; SEE CONCEPTS *403,542*

resolution [*n1*] *determination, strong will*
aim, boldness, constancy, courage, dauntlessness, decidedness, decision, declaration, dedication, determination, doggedness, earnestness, energy, firmness, fixed purpose, fortitude, guts*, heart*, immovability, intent, intention, judgment, mettle, moxie*, obstinacy, perseverance, pluck, purpose, purposefulness, purposiveness, relentlessness, resoluteness, resolve, settlement, sincerity, spirit, spunk, staunchness, staying power, steadfastness, stubbornness, tenacity, verdict, willpower; SEE CONCEPTS *410,657*

resolution [*n2*] *answer, judgment*
analysis, assertion, breakdown, call, conclusion, decision, declaration, determination, dissection, elucidation, end, exposition, finding, interpretation, motion, nod, outcome, pay dirt*, presentation, proposal, proposition, quick fix*, recitation, recommendation, resolve, settlement, solution, solving, sorting out, ticket*, unravelling, upshot, verdict, working out; SEE CONCEPTS *18,230,274*

resolve [*n*] *decision, determination*
boldness, conclusion, courage, decidedness, design, earnestness, firmness, fixed purpose, intention, objective, project, purpose, purposefulness, purposiveness, resoluteness, resolution, steadfastness, undertaking, will, willpower; SEE CONCEPTS *410,659,689*

resolve [*v*] *make up one's mind; find solution*
agree, analyze, anatomize, answer, break, break down, choose, clear up, clinch*, conclude, deal with, decide, decipher, decree, design, determine, dissect, dissolve, elect, elucidate, fathom, figure, fix, intend, iron out*, lick, make a point of, pan

out*, pass upon, propose, purpose, puzzle out, remain firm, rule, settle, solve, take a stand, undertake, unfold, unravel, untangle, unzip*, will, work, work out, work through; SEE CONCEPTS *15,18,24*

resonant [*adj*] *vibrant in sound*
beating, booming, clangorous, consonant, deep, deep-toned, earsplitting, echoing, electrifying, enhanced, full, heightened, intensified, loud, mellow, noisy, orotund, plangent, powerful, profound, pulsating, pulsing, resounding, reverberant, reverberating, rich, ringing, roaring, round, sonorant, sonorous, stentorian, strident, thrilling, throbbing, thundering, thunderous; SEE CONCEPT *594*

resort [*n1*] *vacation place*
camp, fat farm*, hangout, harbor, haunt, haven, hideaway, hideout, holiday spot, hotel, hot spring*, inn, lodge, mineral spring, motel, park, purlieu, refuge, rendezvous, retreat, spa, spot, spring, stomping ground*, tourist center, tourist trap*; SEE CONCEPTS *198,516*

resort [*n2*] *alternative, recourse*
chance, course, device, expediency, expedient, hope, makeshift, opportunity, possibility, reference, refuge, relief, resource, shift, stopgap, substitute, surrogate; SEE CONCEPTS *693,712*

resort [*v*] *have recourse to; make use of*
address, affect, apply, avail oneself of, benefit by, bring into play, devote, direct, employ, exercise, fall back on, frequent, go, go to, haunt, head for, look to, make use of, put to use, recur, recur to, refer to, repair, run, take up, try, turn, turn to, use, utilize, visit; SEE CONCEPT *225*

resource [*n*] *supply drawn upon, either material or nonmaterial*
ability, appliance, artifice, assets, capability, capital, cleverness, contraption, contrivance, course, creation, device, expedient, fortune, hoard, ingenuity, initiative, inventiveness, makeshift, means, measure, method, mode, nest egg*, property, quick-wittedness, recourse, refuge, relief, reserve, resourcefulness, riches, shift, source, step, stock, stockpile, store, stratagem, substance, substitute, support, surrogate, system, talent, way, wealth, worth; SEE CONCEPTS *340,523,658,710,712*

resourceful [*adj*] *imaginative*
able, active, adventurous, aggressive, bright, capable, clever, creative, enterprising, ingenious, intelligent, inventive, original, quick-witted, sharp, talented, venturesome; SEE CONCEPT *402*

resources [*n*] *money, possessions, natural resources*
ace in hole*, assets, backing, bankroll, basics, belongings, budget, capital, collateral, effects, funds, holdings, income, kitty*, material goods, means, nest egg*, nut*, property, reserves, revenue, riches, savings, sock*, stuff, supplies, the goods*, ways and means*, wealth, wherewithal*; SEE CONCEPTS *340,446,523,710,712*

respect [*n1*] *admiration given by others*
account, adoration, appreciation, approbation, awe, consideration, courtesy, deference, dignity, esteem, estimation, favor, fear, homage, honor, obeisance, ovation, recognition, regard, repute, reverence, testimonial, tribute, veneration, worship; SEE CONCEPT *689*

respect [*n2*] *way, sense*
aspect, bearing, character, connection, detail,

facet, feature, matter, particular, point, reference, regard, relation; SEE CONCEPT 682

respect [v] *admire; obey*
abide by, adhere to, adore, appreciate, attend, be awed by, be kind to, comply with, defer to, esteem, follow, have good opinion of, have high opinion, heed, honor, look up to, note, notice, observe of, pay attention, recognize, regard, revere, reverence, set store by, show consideration, show courtesy, spare, take into account, think highly of, uphold, value, venerate; SEE CONCEPTS 10,32

respectable [adj1] *good, honest*
admirable, appropriate, august, becoming, befitting, comely, conforming, correct, creditable, decent, decorous, dignified, done, estimable, fair, honorable, mediocre, moderate, modest, nice, ordinary, passable, presentable, proper, redoubtable, redoubted, reputable, reputed, respected, satisfactory, seemly, sublime, suitable, tolerable, upright, venerable, virtuous, well-thought-of, worthy; SEE CONCEPT 572

respectable [adj2] *substantial, ample*
appreciable, considerable, decent, fair, fairly good, good, goodly, presentable, reasonable, sensible, sizable, tidy, tolerable; SEE CONCEPT 771

respectful [adj] *courteous, mannerly*
admiring, appreciative, civil, considerate, courtly, deferential, duteous, dutiful, gracious, humble, obedient, obeisant, polite, recognizing, regardful, regarding, reverent, reverential, self-effacing, solicitous, submissive, upholding, venerating, well-mannered; SEE CONCEPT 401

respective [adj] *particular, specific*
corresponding, each, individual, own, personal, relevant, separate, several, singular, various; SEE CONCEPT 556

respects [n] *good wishes*
best wishes, compliments, courtesies, deference, devoirs, greetings, kind wishes, regards, salaam*, salutations; SEE CONCEPT 278

respite [n] *pause, suspension in activity*
acquittal, adjournment, break, breath*, breather*, breathing space*, cessation, coffee break*, deadlock, deferment, delay, deliverance, discharge, downtime*, ease, exculpation, five*, forgiveness, halt, hiatus, immunity, intermission, interregnum, interruption, interval, layoff, leisure, letup*, lull, moratorium, pardon, postponement, protraction, recess, relaxation, release, relief, reprieve, rest, stay, stop, ten*, time, time out*, truce; SEE CONCEPTS 121,681,807

resplendent [adj] *bright, radiant*
beaming, blazing, brilliant, dazzling, effulgent, flaming, gleaming, glittering, glorious, glossy, glowing, gorgeous, irradiant, luminous, lustrous, magnificent, proud, refulgent, shining, shiny, splendid, splendiferous, splendorous, sublime, superb; SEE CONCEPTS 618,617

respond [v] *act in answer to something*
acknowledge, act in response, answer, answer back, behave, be in touch with, come back, come back at, come in, counter, feedback, feel for, field the question*, get back to*, get in touch, react, reciprocate, rejoin, reply, retort, return, talk back; SEE CONCEPTS 45,384

response [n] *answer, reaction*
acknowledgment, antiphon, back talk*, comeback, counter, double-take*, echo, feedback, hit, kickback*, knee-jerk reaction*, lip*, rejoinder,

reply, respond, retort, return, reverberation, riposte, sass*, snappy comeback*, vibes*, wisecrack; SEE CONCEPT 278

responsibility [n1] *accountability, blame*
albatross*, amenability, answerability, authority, boundness, burden, care, charge, constraint, contract, culpability, duty, encumbrance, engagement, fault, guilt, holding the bag*, importance, incubus, incumbency, liability, obligation, obligatoriness, onus, pledge, power, rap, restraint, subjection, trust; SEE CONCEPT 645

responsibility [n2] *maturity, trustworthiness*
ability, capableness, capacity, competency, conscientiousness, dependability, dependableness, efficiency, faithfulness, firmness, honesty, levelheadedness, loyalty, rationality, reliability, sensibleness, soberness, stability, steadfastness, trustiness, uprightness; SEE CONCEPTS 411,633

responsible [adj1] *accountable, in charge*
answerable, at fault, at the helm, authoritative, bonded, bound, bound to, carrying the load, censurable, chargeable, compelled, constrained, contracted, culpable, decision-making, devolving on, duty-bound, engaged, executive, exposed, fettered, guilty, hampered, held, high, important, in authority, in control, incumbent, liable, minding the store*, obligated, obliged, on the hook*, open, pledged, subject, susceptive, sworn to, tied, to blame, under contract, under obligation; SEE CONCEPT 545

responsible [adj2] *trustworthy, mature*
able, adult, capable, competent, conscientious, dependable, dutiful, effective, efficient, faithful, firm, levelheaded, loyal, qualified, rational, reliable, self-reliant, sensible, sober, sound, stable, steadfast, steady, tried, trusty, upright; SEE CONCEPTS 401,404

responsive [adj] *quick to react*
acknowledging, active, alive, answering, awake, aware, compassionate, conscious, forthcoming, impressionable, influenceable, kindhearted, open, passionate, perceptive, persuadable, reactive, receptive, replying, respondent, sensible, sensile, sensitive, sentient, sharp, softhearted, susceptible, susceptive, sympathetic, tender, warm, warmhearted; SEE CONCEPTS 401,542

rest [n1] *inactivity*
break, breather*, breathing space*, calm, calmness, cessation, coffee break*, comfort, composure, cutoff, downtime*, doze, dreaminess, ease, forty winks*, halt, holiday, hush, idleness, interlude, intermission, interval, leisure, letup*, lull, motionlessness, nap, pause, peace, quiescence, quiet, quietude, recess, recreation, refreshment, relaxation, relief, repose, respite, siesta, silence, sleep, slumber, somnolence, standstill, stay, stillness, stop, time off, tranquillity, vacation; SEE CONCEPTS 315,681,807

rest [n2] *remainder of something*
balance, bottom of barrel*, dregs, dross, excess, heel, leavings, leftovers, odds and ends*, orts, others, overplus, remains, remnant, residual, residue, residuum, rump, superfluity, surplus; SEE CONCEPTS 260,835

rest [n3] *base, foundation*
basis, bed, bottom, footing, ground, groundwork, holder, pedestal, pediment, pillar, prop, seat, seating, shelf, stand, stay, support, trestle; SEE CONCEPTS 442,825

re
re

rest [v1] *be calm; sleep*
be at ease, be comfortable, breathe, compose one-self, doze, dream, drowse, ease off, ease up, idle, laze, lean, let down, let up, lie by, lie down, lie still, loaf, loll, lounge, nap, nod, put feet up*, recline, refresh oneself, relax, repose, sit down, slack, slacken, slack off, sleep, slumber, snooze, spell, stretch out, take a break, take a nap, take five*, take it easy*, take life easy*, take ten*, take time out, unbend, unlax*, unwind, wind down; SEE CONCEPTS *210,315,681*

rest [v2] *lie, recline*
be quiet, be supported, lay, lean, lie still, loll, lounge, pause, prop, repose, roost, settle, sit, stand, stand still, stretch out; SEE CONCEPTS *154,681*

rest [v3] *depend, hinge*
base, be based, be contingent, be dependent, be founded, be seated on, be supported, be upheld, bottom, count, establish, found, ground, hang, lie, predicate, rely, reside, stay, turn; SEE CONCEPT *711*

restaurant [n] *business establishment serving food and drink*
bar, café, cafeteria, canteen, chophouse*, coffee shop, diner, dining room, dive*, doughnut shop, drive-in, eatery, eating house, eating place, fast-food place, greasy spoon*, grill, hamburger stand, hashery*, hideaway*, hotdog stand, inn, joint*, luncheonette, lunchroom, night club, outlet*, pizzeria, saloon, soda fountain, watering hole*; SEE CONCEPTS *439,448,449*

restitution [n] *compensation, repayment*
amends, dues, indemnification, indemnity, payment, quittance, rebate, recompense, redress, refund, reimbursement, remuneration, reparation, reprisal, requital, restoration, return, satisfaction, squaring things*; SEE CONCEPT *344*

restive [adj] *impatient, nervous*
agitated, balky, contrary, edgy, fidgety, fractious, fretful, froward, ill at ease, jittery, jumpy, nervy, obstinate, on edge, ornery*, perverse, recalcitrant, refractory, restless, stubborn, tense, uneasy, unruly, unyielding, uptight; SEE CONCEPTS *401,542*

restless [adj] *not content; moving about*
active, agitated, antsy*, anxious, bundle of nerves*, bustling, changeable, disturbed, edgy, fidgeting, fidgety, fitful, footloose*, fretful, hurried, ill at ease, inconstant, intermittent, irresolute, itchy*, jumpy, nervous, nomadic, on edge, perturbed, restive, roving, sleepless, spasmodic, strung out*, tossing and turning*, transient, troubled, turbulent, uneasy, unpeaceful, unquiet, unrestful, unruly, unsettled, unstable, unsteady, wandering, worried; SEE CONCEPTS *403,542,584*

restlessness [n] *constant motion; discontent*
activity, agitation, ailment, ants*, antsiness*, anxiety, bustle, disquiet, disquietude, disturbance, edginess, excitability, ferment, fitfulness, fretfulness, hurry, inconstancy, inquietude, insomnia, instability, jitters, jumpiness, movement, nervousness, restiveness, transience, turbulence, turmoil, uneasiness, unrest, unsettledness, worriedness; SEE CONCEPTS *410,657,748*

restore [v1] *fix, make new*
bring back, build up, cure, heal, improve, make healthy, make restitution, mend, modernize, reanimate, rebuild, recall, recondition, reconstitute, reconstruct, recover, redeem, reenforce, reerect, re-establish, refresh, refurbish, rehabilitate, reim-

pose, reinstate, reintroduce, rejuvenate, renew, renovate, repair, replace, rescue, retouch, revitalize, revive, revivify, set to rights, strengthen, touch up, update, win back; SEE CONCEPTS *126,212,244*

restore [v2] *give back*
hand back, put back, replace, return, send back; SEE CONCEPTS *131,232*

restrain [v] *keep under control; hold back*
arrest, bind, bottle up, box up, bridle, chain, check, choke back, circumscribe, confine, constrain, contain, control, cool*, cork*, crack down*, curb, curtail, debar, delimit, detain, deter, direct, fetter, gag, govern, guide, hamper, handicap, harness, hem in, hinder, hogtie*, hold, impound, imprison, inhibit, jail, keep, keep down, keep in line*, kill*, limit, lock up, manacle, muzzle, pinion, prevent, proscribe, pull back, repress, restrict, sit on, stay, subdue, suppress, tie down, tie up; SEE CONCEPTS *121,130,191*

restrained [adj] *calm, quiet*
bottled up, calm and collected, chilled, conservative, controlled, cool, corked up, discreet, in charge, in check, inobtrusive, laid-back*, mild, moderate, muted, on a leash*, plain, reasonable, reticent, retiring, self-controlled, shrinking, soft, steady, subdued, tasteful, temperate, unaffable, undemonstrative, under control, under wraps*, unexcessive, unexpansive, unextreme, unobtrusive, uptight, withdrawn; SEE CONCEPTS *401,542*

restraint [n1] *self-control*
abstemiousness, abstinence, caution, coercion, command, compulsion, confines, constraint, control, coolness, curtailment, economy, forbearance, grip, hindrance, hold, inhibition, limitation, moderation, prevention, repression, reserve, restriction, secretiveness, self-denial, self-discipline, self-government, self-possession, self-restraint, silence, suppression, unnaturalness, withholding; SEE CONCEPT *633*

restraint [n2] *limitation; something that holds*
abridgment, arrest, ban, bar, barrier, bondage, bridle, captivity, chains, check, command, confinement, constraint, cramp, curb, decrease, deprivation, detention, determent, deterrence, embargo, fetters, hindrance, impediment, imprisonment, instruction, interdict, limit, manacles, obstacle, obstruction, order, pinions, prohibition, reduction, rein, repression, restriction, rope, stop, stoppage, straitjacket, string*, taboo, weight; SEE CONCEPTS *5,666,674*

restrict [v] *confine, limit situation or ability to participate*
bind, bottle up, bound, chain, check, circumscribe, come down on, constrict, contain, contract, cool down, cramp, curb, decrease, define, delimit, delimitate, demarcate, demark, diminish, encircle, enclose, hamper, handicap, hang up, hem in, hold back, hold down, impede, inclose, inhibit, keep within bounds, keep within limits, moderate, modify, narrow, pin down, prelimit, put away, put on ice*, qualify, reduce, regulate, restrain, send up, shorten, shrink, shut in, surround, temper, tether, tie; SEE CONCEPT *130*

restriction [n] *limit*
ball and chain*, bounds, brake, catch, check, circumscription, condition, confinement, constraint, containment, contraction, control, cramp, curb, custody, demarcation, excess baggage*, fine print*, glitch*, grain of salt*, handicap, hang-

up*, inhibition, limitation, limits, lock*, no-no*, qualification, regulation, reservation, restraint, rule, small difficulty, stint, stipulation, stricture, string*, stumbling block*; SEE CONCEPTS 666,674

result [n] *effect brought about by something*
aftereffect, aftermath, arrangement, backwash*, by-product, close, completion, conclusion, consequence, consummation, corollary, creature, crop, decision, denouement, determination, development, emanation, end, ensual, event, eventuality, execution, finish, fruit*, fruition, harvest, issue, offshoot*, outcome, outcropping, outgrowth, payoff, proceeds, product, production, reaction, repercussion, returns, sequel, sequence, settlement, termination, upshot; SEE CONCEPT 230

result [v] *happen, develop*
accrue, appear, arise, attend, become of, be due to, come about, come forth, come from, come of, come out, conclude, culminate, derive, effect, emanate, emerge, end, ensue, eventualize, eventuate, finish, flow, follow, fruit, germinate, grow, happen, issue, occur, originate, pan out, proceed, produce, rise, spring, stem, terminate, turn out, wind up, work out; SEE CONCEPTS 4,119,242

résumé [n] *outline of experience*
abstract, bio*, biography, curriculum vitae, CV*, digest, epitome, précis, recapitulation, review, rundown, sum, summary, summation, summing-up, synopsis, vita, work history; SEE CONCEPTS 271,283

resume [v] *begin again*
assume again, carry on, come back, continue, go on, go on with, keep on, keep up, occupy again, pick up, proceed, reassume, recapitulate, recommence, recoup, regain, reinstitute, reoccupy, reopen, repossess, restart, retake, return to, take back, take up; SEE CONCEPTS 221,239

retain [v1] *hold on to physically or mentally*
absorb, bear in mind, cling to, clutch, contain, detain, enjoy, grasp, hand onto, have, hold, hold fast, husband, keep, keep in mind, keep possession, maintain, memorize, mind, own, possess, preserve, put away, recall, recognize, recollect, remember, reminisce, reserve, restrain, retrospect, save, withhold; SEE CONCEPTS 40,190,710

retain [v2] *hire*
commission, contract, employ, engage, maintain, pay, reserve; SEE CONCEPT 351

retaliate [v] *get even with someone*
even the score*, exact retribution, get, get back at, give and take*, make reprisal, pay, pay back, reciprocate, recompense, repay, requite, retrospect, return, return the compliment, revenge, revive, settle, square accounts*, strike back, take an eye for an eye*, take revenge, turn the tables on*, turn upon, wreak vengeance; SEE CONCEPTS 126,384

retard [v] *hinder, obstruct*
arrest, back off, baffle, balk, bog, bog down, brake, bring to screeching halt*, check, choke, choke off, clog, close off, crimp, dawdle, decelerate, decrease, defer, delay, detain, down, encumber, falter, fetter, flag, hamper, handicap, hang up, hesitate, hold back, hold up, impede, lessen, let up, loaf, loiter, mire, poke, postpone, reduce, retardate, set back, shut down, shut off, slacken, slow down, slow up, stall, take down; SEE CONCEPTS 121,130,190,240

reticent [adj] *secretive, quiet*
bashful, clammed up*, close, close-mouthed, dried up*, dummied up*, hesitant, mum, reserved, restrained, shy, silent, taciturn, tight-lipped, uncommunicative, unforthcoming, unspeaking, uptight*; SEE CONCEPTS 267,401

retire [v] *leave a place or responsibility*
absent oneself, decamp, deny oneself, depart, draw back, ebb, exit, fall back, get away, get off, give ground, give up work, give way, go, go away, go to bed, go to one's room*, go to sleep, hand over, hit the sack*, leave service, make vacant, part, pull back, pull out, recede, regress, relinquish, remove, repeal, rescind, resign, retreat, revoke, run along, rusticate, secede, seclude oneself, separate, sever connections, stop working, surrender, take off, turn in, withdraw, yield; SEE CONCEPTS 195,234,351

retiring [adj] *shy, undemonstrative*
backward, bashful, coy, demure, diffident, humble, meek, modest, nongregarious, not forward, quiet, rabbity, recessive, reclusive, reserved, restrained, reticent, self-effacing, shrinking, timid, timorous, unaffable, unassertive, unassuming, unexpansive, unsociable, withdrawing, withdrawn; SEE CONCEPT 401

retort [n] *snappy answer*
antiphon, back answer, back talk, comeback, cooler, counter, crack*, gag*, jape, jest, joke, lip*, parting shot*, quip, rejoinder, repartee, reply, reprisal, respond, response, retaliation, return, revenge, riposte, sally, snappy comeback*, topper*, wisecrack, witticism; SEE CONCEPT 278

retort [v] *answer*
answer back, come back at*, counter, crack*, rebut, rejoin, repay, reply, requite, respond, retaliate, return, riposte, sass*, shoot back*, snap back*, squelch*, talk back, top*; SEE CONCEPT 45

retract [v] *take back; renege on*
abjure, back, back down, back off, back out of, call off, cancel, change one's mind, countermand, deny, disavow, disclaim, disown, draw in, eat one's words*, eliminate, exclude, fall back, forget it, forswear, go back on, have change of heart*, nig*, pull back, pull in, recall, recant, recede, reel in*, renege, renounce, repeal, repudiate, rescind, retreat, retrocede, retrograde, reverse, revoke, rule out, sheathe, suspend, take back, take in, unsay, welsh*, withdraw; SEE CONCEPTS 25,49,119,697

retreat [n1] *departure*
ebb, evacuation, flight, retirement, withdrawal; SEE CONCEPTS 30,195

retreat [n2] *place one goes for peace*
adytum, ark, asylum, cell, cloister, convent, cover, covert, defense, den, habitat, harbor, haunt, haven, hermitage, hideaway, hiding place, ivory tower*, port, privacy, refuge, resort, retirement, safe house, safe place, sanctuary, seclusion, security, shelter, solitude; SEE CONCEPT 516

retreat [v] *pull back, go away*
abandon, avoid, back, back away, back down, back off, back out, backtrack, beat it, cave in, decamp, depart, disengage, draw back, ebb, elude, escape, evacuate, evade, fall back, fold, give ground, go, go along with, go back, hand over, hide, keep aloof, keep apart, lay down, leave, move back, opt out*, pull out, quail, quit, recede, recoil, reel, regress, relinquish, resign, re-

re
re

tire, retrocede, retrograde, reverse, run, seclude oneself, sequester, shrink, start back, turn tail*, vacate, withdraw; SEE CONCEPTS *30,195*

retribution [n] *payback for another's action*
avengement, avenging, comeuppance, compensation, counterblow, eye for an eye*, just desserts*, justice, punishment, reckoning, recompense, redress, repayment, reprisal, requital, retaliation, revanche, revenge, reward, satisfaction, vengeance, what for*; SEE CONCEPTS *123,126,384*

retrieve [v] *get back*
bring back, fetch, get back, reacquire, recall, recapture, reclaim, recoup, recover, recruit, redeem, regain, repair, repossess, rescue, restore, salvage, save, win back; SEE CONCEPTS *120,124,131*

retrospect [n] *afterthought*
hindsight, recollection, reconsideration, reexamination, remembering, remembrance, reminiscence, retrospection, review, revision, survey; SEE CONCEPTS *278,410*

return [n1] *coming again*
acknowledgment, answer, appearance, arrival, coming, entrance, entry, homecoming, occurrence, reaction, reappearance, rebound, recoil, recoiling, recompense, recompensing, recovery, recrudescence, recurrence, reestablishment, reinstatement, rejoinder, reoccurrence, replacement, repossession, restitution, restoration, restoring, retreat, reversion, revisitation; SEE CONCEPTS *4,695*

return [n2] *earnings, benefit*
accrual, accruement, advantage, avail, compensation, gain, gate, income, interest, lucre, proceeds, profit, reciprocation, recompense, reimbursement, reparation, repayment, requital, results, retaliation, revenue, reward, take*, takings, yield; SEE CONCEPTS *340,710*

return [n3] *answer*
antiphon, comeback, rejoinder, reply, respond, response, retort, riposte; SEE CONCEPT *278*

return [n4] *summary*
account, form, list, record, report, statement, tabulation; SEE CONCEPTS *283,331*

return [v1] *go back, turn back*
back up, bounce back, circle back, come again, come back, double back, go again, hark back to, move back, react, reappear, rebound, recoil, reconsider, recrudesce, recur, reel back, reenter, reexamine, reoccur, repair, repeat, retire, retrace steps, retreat, revert, revisit, revolve, rotate, turn, turn back; SEE CONCEPTS *159,242*

return [v2] *give back, send back*
bestow, carry back, convey, give, hand back, make restitution, pay back, put back, react, rebate, reciprocate, recompense, reestablish, refund, reimburse, reinsert, reinstate, remit, render, repay, replace, requite, reseat, restitute, restore, retaliate, roll back, send, take back, thrust back, toss back, transmit; SEE CONCEPTS *108,131,217*

return [v3] *earn*
bring in, cash in on*, clean up*, clear*, make, make a killing*, net, pay, pay dividend, pay off, repay, score, show profit, yield; SEE CONCEPT *330*

return [v4] *answer*
announce, arrive at, bring in, come back, come in, come to, communicate, declare, deliver, pass, rejoin, render, reply, report, respond, retort, state, submit; SEE CONCEPT *45*

reveal [v1] *disclose, tell*
acknowledge, admit, affirm, announce, avow, betray, break the news*, bring out into open*, bring to light*, broadcast, come out with, communicate, concede, confess, declare, divulge, explain, expose, get out of system*, give away, give out, give the low-down*, impart, inform, leak, let cat out of the bag*, let fall, let on, let out, let slip*, make known, make plain, make public, notify, proclaim, publish, put cards on table*, report, talk, tell, unfold, utter; SEE CONCEPT *60*

reveal [v2] *show, uncover*
bare, disclose, display, exhibit, expose, flash, lay bare, manifest, open, unclothe, unearth, unmask, unveil; SEE CONCEPT *138*

revel [n] *celebration, merrymaking*
bacchanal, carousal, carouse, debauch, festivity, frolic, gaiety, gala, high jinks*, jollification, jollity, merriment, party, reveling, revelment, saturnalia, skylarking*, spree, wassail, whoopee*; SEE CONCEPTS *292,377*

revel [v] *take pleasure; celebrate*
bask, blow off steam*, carouse, carry on, crow, cut loose*, delight, enjoy, fool around*, frolic, gloat, go on a spree*, indulge, kick up heels*, kid around*, lap up*, lark, let go*, let loose*, live it up*, luxuriate, make merry, paint the town*, rejoice, relish, riot, roister, roll, rollick, run around, savor, step out, thrive, wallow, whoop it up*; SEE CONCEPTS *292,377*

revelation [n] *disclosure, telling*
adumbration, announcement, apocalypse, betrayal, blow by blow*, break, broadcasting, clue, communication, cue, discovery, display, divination, divulgement, earful, exhibition, expose, exposition, exposure, eye-opener*, flash, foreshadowing, inspiration, leak, lightning bolt*, manifestation, news, oracle, proclamation, prophecy, publication, scoop*, showing, sign, the latest*, tip, uncovering, unearthing, unveiling, vision; SEE CONCEPTS *60,274*

revelry [n] *merrymaking*
carousal, carouse, celebration, debauch, debauchery, entertainment, festival, festivity, fun, gaiety, high jinks*, jollification, jollity, party, reveling, revelment, saturnalia, spree, whoop-de-do*, whoopla*; SEE CONCEPTS *377,384*

revenge [n] *retaliation for wrong, grievance*
animus, attack, avenging, avengment, counterblow, counterinsurgency, counterplay, eye for an eye*, fight, getting even*, ill will, implacability, malevolence, measure for measure, rancor, repayment, reprisal, requital, retribution, return, ruthlessness, satisfaction, sortie, spitefulness, tit for tat*, vengeance, vengefulness, vindictiveness; SEE CONCEPTS *86,122,384*

revenge [v] *retaliate for wrong, grievance*
avenge, be out for blood*, defend, even the score*, fight back, fix, fix one's wagon*, get, get back at, get even, give comeuppance, give just desserts*, hit back, justify, kick back, make reprisal, match, pay back, pay back in spades*, pay off, punish, reciprocate, redress, repay, requite, retort, return, return the compliment*, score, settle up, settle with, square, stick it to, take an eye for an eye*, turn the tables on*, venge, vindicate; SEE CONCEPTS *86,122,384*

revenue [n] *income, profit*
acquirement, annuity, bottom line*, cash flow, credit, dividend, earnings, emolument, fruits*, fund, gain, gate*, get*, gravy*, handle*, interest, means, net, pay, payoff, perquisite, proceeds, re-

ceipt, resources, return, reward, salary, split*, stock, strength, take*, takings*, wages, wealth, yield; SEE CONCEPTS 329,332,344

reverberate [v] *vibrate in sound*
echo, react, rebound, recoil, redound, re-echo, resound, ring; SEE CONCEPT 65

revere/reverence [v] *have a high opinion of*
admire, adore, apotheosize, appreciate, be in awe of, cherish, defer to, deify, enjoy, esteem, exalt, hold in awe, honor, look up to*, love, magnify, pay homage, prize, put on pedestal*, regard, respect, think highly of, treasure, value, venerate, worship; SEE CONCEPTS 10,32

reverence [n] *high opinion of something*
admiration, adoration, apotheosis, approbation, approval, awe, bow, deference, deification, devotion, devoutness, esteem, fealty, fear, genuflection, high esteem, homage, honor, love, loyalty, obeisance, obsequiousness, piety, praise, prostration, religiousness, respect, veneration, worship; SEE CONCEPTS 10,32

reverie [n] *daydream*
absent-mindedness, absorption, abstraction, castle-building*, castles in the air*, contemplation, detachment, dreaminess, dreaming, fantasy, fool's paradise*, head trip*, inattention, meditation, mind trip*, muse, musing, pensiveness, phantasy, pipe dream*, preoccupation, study, thought, trance, trip*, woolgathering*; SEE CONCEPTS 529,532

reverse [n1] *opposite*
about-face, antipode, antipole, antithesis, back, bottom, change of mind, contra, contradiction, contradictory, contrary, converse, counter, counterpole, flip-flop*, flip side*, inverse, other side, overturning, rear, regression, retrogression, retroversion, reversal, reversement, reversion, switch, turn, turnabout, turn around, turning, underside, verso, volte-face, wrong side; SEE CONCEPTS 665,697,738

reverse [n2] *bad luck; failure*
adversity, affliction, bath, blow, catastrophe, check, conquering, defeat, disappointment, hardship, misadventure, misfortune, mishap, repulse, reversal, setback, trial, turnabout, vanquishment, vicissitude; SEE CONCEPTS 674,679

reverse [v1] *turn upside down or backwards*
about-face*, back, backpedal*, backtrack, back up, capsize, double back*, evaginate, evert, exchange, flip-flop*, go back, go backwards, interchange, inverse, invert, move backwards, overturn, rearrange, retreat, revert, shift, switch, transfer, transplace, transpose, turn around, turn back, turn over, upend, upset; SEE CONCEPTS 158,213,697

reverse [v2] *cancel, change*
alter, annul, backpedal*, backtrack, convert, countermand, declare null and void*, dismantle, double back*, flip-flop*, invalidate, lift, modify, negate, nullify, overrule, overset, overthrow, overturn, quash, recall, renege, repeal, rescind, retract, revoke, set aside, turn around, turn the tables*, undo, upset; SEE CONCEPTS 13,234,697

revert [v] *return to an earlier, less-developed condition*
about-face*, backslide, change, come back, decline, degenerate, deteriorate, fall off the wagon*, flip-flop*, go back, hark back, inverse, invert, lapse, react, recrudesce, recur, regress, relapse, resume, retrograde, retrogress, return, take up

where left off*, throw back, transpose, turn, turn back; SEE CONCEPTS 13,385,698

review [n1] *examination, study*
analysis, another look*, audit, check, checkup, drill, file, fresh look*, inspection, march past*, once-over*, parade, procession, reassessment, recapitulation, reconsideration, reflection, report, rethink, retrospect, revision, scan, scrutiny, second look, second thought, survey, view; SEE CONCEPTS 24,103

review [n2] *critique; summary*
abstract, analysis, appraisal, article, assessment, blurb, book review, canvass, column, comment, commentary, criticism, discourse, discussion, dissertation, essay, evaluation, exposition, inspection, investigation, journal, judgment, magazine, mention, monograph, notice, organ, outline, pan*, periodical, recapitulation, redraft, reviewal, revision, study, synopsis, theme, thesis, treatise, write-up; SEE CONCEPTS 280,283

review [v1] *go over again*
analyze, brush up*, call to mind, check out, check thoroughly, debrief, go over, hash over*, look at again, look back on, polish up, reassess, recall, recap*, recapitulate, recollect, reconsider, reevaluate, reexamine, reflect on, rehash*, remember, rethink, revise, revisit, run over, run through, run up flagpole*, summon up, take another look, think over; SEE CONCEPT 103

review [v2] *criticize, scrutinize*
assess, bad-mouth*, correct, discuss, evaluate, examine, give one's opinion, inspect, judge, knock*, pan*, put down*, rave, read through, re-edit, revise, rip, skin alive*, slam*, study, swipe at*, take down*, trash*, weigh, write a critique, zap*; SEE CONCEPTS 49,52

revise [v] *correct, edit*
alter, amend, blue pencil*, change, clean up, compare, cut, debug, develop, emend, go over, improve, launder, look over, modify, overhaul, perfect, polish, recalibrate, recast, reconsider, redo, redraft, redraw, reexamine, rehash, reorganize, restyle, revamp, review, rework, rewrite, run through, scan, scrub, scrutinize, study, tighten, update, upgrade; SEE CONCEPTS 79,126,244

revision [n] *change; rewriting*
afterlight, alteration, amendment, correction, editing, emendation, homework, improvement, modification, overhauling, polish, recension, reconsideration, rectification, rectifying, redaction, redraft, reediting, reexamination, rescript, restyling, retrospect, retrospection, review, revisal, revise, updating; SEE CONCEPTS 79,126,244,700

revival [n] *rebirth, reawakening*
awakening, cheering, consolation, enkindling, freshening, invigoration, quickening, reanimation, recovery, recrudescence, regeneration, rejuvenation, renaissance, renascence, renewal, restoration, resurgence, resurrection, resuscitation, revitalization, revivification, risorgimento; SEE CONCEPTS 119,221

revive [v] *start again; bring back to life*
animate, arouse, awaken, bounce back*, breathe new life into*, brighten, bring around*, bring to*, cheer, come around*, come to life, comfort, console, encourage, energize, enkindle, enliven, exhilarate, gladden, inspirit, invigorate, make whole*, overcome, please, quicken, rally, reanimate, recondition, recover, refresh, rejuvenate,

re
rc

rekindle, relieve, renew, renovate, repair, restore, resurrect, resuscitate, revitalize, rouse, snap out of it*, solace, spring up*, strengthen, touch up*, wake up; SEE CONCEPTS 13,221,469,697

revoke [v] take back; cancel
abjure, abolish, abrogate, annul, back out of, backpedal*, call back, call off, countermand, counterorder, declare null and void*, deny, disclaim, dismantle, dismiss, disown, erase, expunge, forswear, invalidate, lift, negate, nix*, nullify, obliterate, quash*, recall, recant, remove, renounce, repeal, repudiate, rescind, retract, reverse, rub out*, scrub*, set aside, vacate, void, wipe out*, withdraw; SEE CONCEPTS 50,88, 121,234

revolt [n] uprising
defection, displeasure, insurgency, insurrection, mutiny, rebellion, revolution, rising, sedition; SEE CONCEPTS 106,300,320

revolt [v1] rebel, rise up against
arise, boycott, break, defect, defy, drop out, get out of line*, insurrect, make waves*, mutiny, oppose, opt out, overthrow, overturn, rebel, renounce, resist, riot, rock the boat*, strike, take up arms, turn against; SEE CONCEPTS 106,300,320

revolt [v2] disgust, nauseate
crawl*, gross out*, make flesh crawl*, make sick, offend, pain, reluct, repel, repulse, shock, sicken, turn off*, turn stomach*; SEE CONCEPTS 7,19

revolting [adj] disgusting, nauseating
abhorrent, abominable, appalling, awful, distasteful, foul, gross, horrible, horrid, loathsome, nasty, nauseous, noisome, obnoxious, obscene, offensive, repellent, repugnant, repulsive, rotten, shocking, sickening, sleazy*, vile; SEE CONCEPT 529

revolution [n1] drastic action or change, often in politics
anarchy, bloodshed, cabal, coup, coup d'état, crime, debacle, destruction, disorder, foment, golpe, guerrilla activity, innovation, insubordination, insurgency, metamorphosis, mutiny, outbreak, overthrow, overturn, plot, radical change, rebellion, reformation, reversal, revolt, rising, row, shake-up, shift, strife, strike, subversion, transformation, tumult, turbulence, turmoil, turnover, underground activity, unrest, upheaval, uprising, uproar, upset, violence; SEE CONCEPTS 106,300,320,697

revolution [n2] circuit around something
circle, circumvolution, cycle, gyration, gyre, lap, orbit, pirouette, reel, revolve, revolving, roll, rotation, round, spin, swirl, turn, turning, twirl, wheel, whirl; SEE CONCEPTS 436,484,738,792

revolve [v1] turn, circle
circumduct, go around, gyrate, gyre, orbit, roll, rotate, spin, turn around, twist, wheel, whirl; SEE CONCEPTS 147,738

revolve [v2] think about
consider, deliberate, meditate, mull over, muse, ponder, reflect, roll, ruminate, study, think over, turn over in mind; SEE CONCEPT 17

revulsion [n] disgust, hatred
abhorrence, abomination, aversion, detestation, dislike, distaste, hate, horror, loathing, recoil, repugnance, repulsion; SEE CONCEPT 29

reward [n] payment, prize
accolade, award, benefit, bonus, bounty, carrot*, comeuppance, compensation, crown*, cue, dividend, feather in cap*, fringe benefit, gain, gar-

land, goodies*, gravy*, grease*, guerdon, honor, just deserts*, meed, merit, perks*, plum*, premium, profit, punishment, recompense, remuneration, repayment, requital, retribution, return, salve, strokes*, sweetener*, tip, wages; SEE CONCEPTS 337,344

reward [v] pay; give prize
compensate, honor, recompense, remunerate, repay, requite, stroke*, sugarcoat*, take care of*, tip; SEE CONCEPTS 108,132,341

rewarding [adj] beneficial, pleasing
advantageous, edifying, fruitful, fulfilling, gainful, gratifying, productive, profitable, remunerative, satisfying, valuable, worthwhile; SEE CONCEPTS 548,572

rhetoric [n] wordiness; long speech
address, balderdash*, big talk*, bombast, composition, discourse, elocution, eloquence, flowery language, fustian, grandiloquence, hot air*, hyperbole, magniloquence, oration, oratory, pomposity, rant, verbosity; SEE CONCEPTS 51,277,278

rhetorical [adj] wordy; flowery in speech
articulate, aureate, bombastic, declamatory, eloquent, embellished, euphuistic, exaggerated, flamboyant, flashy*, florid, fluent, glib*, grand, grandiloquent, grandiose, high-flown, hyperbolic, imposing, inflated, magniloquent, mouthy, oratorical, ornate, ostentatious, overblown, overdone, overwrought, pompous, pretentious, showy, silver-tongued, sonorous, stilted, swollen, tumescent, tumid, turgid, verbose, vocal, voluble, windy*; SEE CONCEPT 267

rhyme [n] poetry in which lines end with like sounds
alliteration, beat, cadence, couplet, doggerel, half-rhyme, harmony, iambic pentameter, measure, meter, nursery rhyme, ode, poem, poesy, poetry, rhythm, rune, slant rhyme, song, tune, verse, vowel-chime; SEE CONCEPTS 278,595

rhythm [n] beat, accent of sound, music
bounce, cadence, cadency, downbeat, flow, lilt, measure, meter, metre, movement, pattern, periodicity, pulse, regularity, rhyme, rise and fall, swing, tempo, time, uniformity; SEE CONCEPT 595

ribald [adj] vulgar, obscene
base, bawdy, blue*, coarse, devilish, earthy, fast*, filthy*, foul-mouthed, gross*, indecent, indecorous, juicy, lascivious, lewd, licentious, lowdown and dirty, naughty, off-color, out of line*, purple*, racy, rascally, raunchy, raw*, risqué*, rogue, rough, rude, salacious, salty, scabrous, scurrilous, sly, smutty, spicy*, unbecoming; SEE CONCEPTS 267,401

rich [n] wealthy people or institutions
bountiful, haves*, landed, monied, nouveau riche, old money, upper class, upper crust*, well-to-do*; SEE CONCEPT 423

rich [adj1] having a lot of money
affluent, bloated, comfortable, easy, fat, filthy rich*, flush, gilded, in clover*, independent, in the money*, loaded*, made of money*, moneyed, opulent, plush, propertied, prosperous, rolling in it*, swimming, upscale, uptown, wealthy, well-heeled*, well-off*, well provided for*, well-to-do*, worth a million*; SEE CONCEPT 334

rich [adj2] abundant, well-supplied
abounding, ample, chic, classy, copious, costly, deluxe, elaborate, elegant, embellished, expensive, exquisite, extravagant, exuberant, fancy, fe-

cund, fertile, fine, fruitful, full, gorgeous, grand, high-class, lavish, lush, luxurious, magnificent, ornate, palatial, plenteous, plentiful, plush, posh, precious, priceless, productive, prolific, resplendent, ritzy*, smart, snazzy*, spiffy, splendid, stylish, sumptuous, superb, swank*, swanky*, swell*, valuable, well-endowed; SEE CONCEPTS 334,589,771

rich [adj3] *flavorful*
creamy, delicious, fatty, full-bodied, heavy, highly flavored, juicy, luscious, nourishing, nutritious, oily, satisfying, savory, spicy, succulent, sustaining, sweet, tasty; SEE CONCEPT 613

rich [adj4] *full in color or sound*
bright, canorous, deep, dulcet, eloquent, expressive, intense, mellifluous, mellow, resonant, rotund, significant, silvery, sonorous, strong, vibrant, vivid, warm; SEE CONCEPTS 406,594,618

rich [adj5] *very funny*
absurd, amusing, comical, diverting, droll, entertaining, farcical, foolish, hilarious, humorous, incongruous, laughable, ludicrous, odd, preposterous, queer, ridiculous, risible, side-splitting*, slaying*, splitting*, strange; SEE CONCEPTS 267,529

riches [n] *money and possessions*
abundance, affluence, assets, clover, fortune, gold, lap of luxury*, means, opulence, plenty, property, resources, richness, substance, treasure, wealth, worth; SEE CONCEPTS 335,340,446,710

rickety [adj] *unsound, broken-down*
broken, decrepit, derelict, dilapidated, feeble, flimsy, fragile, frail, imperfect, infirm, insecure, jerry-built*, precarious, ramshackle, rattletrap*, rocky, shaky, tottering, tottery*, tumble-down, unsteady, wavering, weak, wobbly; SEE CONCEPT 488

rid [v] *do away with; free*
abolish, clear, deliver, disabuse, disburden, disembarrass, disencumber, dump*, eject, eliminate, eradicate, expel, exterminate, extinguish, extirpate, fire, give the brush*, heave-ho*, junk*, kiss goodbye*, liberate, make free, purge, release, relieve, remove, roust, scrap, send packing*, shake off, shed, throw away, throw out, toss out, unburden, unload, uproot; SEE CONCEPTS 180,211

riddle [n] *brain-teaser*
bewilderment, brain-twister*, charade, closed book*, complexity, complication, confusion, conundrum, cryptogram, dilemma, distraction, doubt, embarrassment, enigma, entanglement, intricacy, knotty question*, labyrinth, maze, mind-boggler*, mystery, mystification, perplexity, plight, poser, predicament, problem, puzzle, puzzlement, quandary, question, rebus, sixty-four dollar question*, stickler*, strait, stumper*, teaser, tough nut to crack*, tough proposition, twister*; SEE CONCEPT 532

riddle [v] *perforate, permeate*
bore, corrupt, damage, honeycomb*, impair, infest, mar, pepper, pervade, pierce, pit, puncture, spoil; SEE CONCEPTS 156,220

ride [n] *journey, trip in vehicle*
airing, commute, drive, excursion, expedition, hitch, jaunt, joyride*, lift, outing, pick up*, run, spin, Sunday drive, tour, transportation, turn, whirl; SEE CONCEPT 224

ride [v1] *carry or be carried*
be supported, control, cruise, curb, direct, drift, drive, float, go, go with, guide, handle, hitch a

ride*, hitchhike, journey, manage, motor, move, post, progress, restrain, roll, sit, sit on, thumb a ride*, tool around*, tour, travel; SEE CONCEPTS 94,148,224

ride [v2] *dominate, oppress*
afflict, annoy, badger, bait, be arbitrary, be autocratic, berate, disparage, domineer, enslave, grip, harass, harry, haunt, hector, hound, override, persecute, rate, reproach, revile, scold, torment, torture, tyrannize, upbraid; SEE CONCEPTS 7,14,19

ridge [n] *raised part of solid*
backbone, chine, corrugation, crease, crinkle, elevation, esker, fold, furrow, hill, hogback, moraine, parapet, plica, pole, range, rib, rim, rimple, rivel, ruck, seam, spine, upland, wrinkle; SEE CONCEPTS 471,509,513

ridicule [n] *contemptuous laughter at someone or something*
badinage, banter, buffoonery, burlesque, caricature, chaff, comeback, contempt, derision, dig*, disdain, disparagement, farce, foolery, gibe, irony, jab*, jeer, laughter, leer, mockery, mordancy, needling, parody, parting shot*, persiflage, putdown*, put-on*, raillery, rally, razz*, rib*, roast*, sarcasm, sardonicism, satire, scorn, slam*, sneer*, swipe*, taunt, taunting, travesty; SEE CONCEPTS 54,59

ridicule [v] *make contemptuous fun of something or someone*
banter, caricature, cartoon, chaff, deflate, deride, expose, fleer, gibe, haze, humiliate, jape, jeer, jive, jolly, josh*, kid, lampoon, laugh at, make a fool of*, make a game of*, make a laughing-stock*, make fun of, mimic, mock, needle, pan*, parody, poke fun at*, pooh-pooh*, pull one's leg*, put down*, quiz, rag, rail at, rally, raz*, rib*, roast*, run down*, satirize, scoff, scorn, send up*, show up*, sneer, takeoff, taunt, travesty, twit, unmask; SEE CONCEPTS 54,59

ridiculous [adj] *stupid, funny*
absurd, antic, bizarre, comic, comical, contemptible, daffy*, derisory, droll, fantastic, farcical, foolheaded*, foolish, gelastic, goofy*, grotesque, harebrained*, hilarious, impossible, incredible, jerky*, laughable, ludicrous, nonsensical, nutty*, outrageous, preposterous, risible, sappy*, silly, slaphappy*, unbelievable, wacky*; SEE CONCEPTS 529,548,552

rife [adj] *overflowing*
abounding, abundant, alive, common, current, epidemic, extensive, frequent, general, many, multitudinous, numerous, pandemic, plentiful, popular, prevailing, prevalent, profuse, raging, rampant, regnant, replete, ruling, swarming, teeming, thronged, ubiquitous, universal, widespread; SEE CONCEPTS 771,772

rifle [v] *ransack*
burglarize, burgle, despoil, go through, grab, gut, loot, pillage, plunder, rip, rip off*, rob, rummage, sack, smash and grab*, strip, take, tip over*, trash*, waste*; SEE CONCEPT 139

rift [n1] *break, crack*
breach, chink, cleavage, cleft, cranny, crevice, fault, fissure, flaw, fracture, gap, hiatus, interruption, interval, opening, parting, rent, rima, rime, space, split; SEE CONCEPT 513

rift [n2] *difference of opinion*
alienation, breach, break, clash, disagreement, division, estrangement, falling out*, misunderstand-

re
ri

ing. quarrel, rupture, schism, separation, split;
SEE CONCEPTS 46,106,388

rig [n] *equipment*
accouterments, apparatus, equipage, fittings, fixtures, gear, machinery, outfit, paraphernalia,
tackle; SEE CONCEPT 496

rig [v1] *outfit, supply*
accouter, appoint, arm, array, attire, clothe, costume, dress, equip, fit out, furnish, gear, kit, provision, set up, turn out; SEE CONCEPTS
140,167,182

rig [v2] *arrange for certain outcome*
doctor, engineer, fake, falsify, fiddle with*, fix,
gerrymander*, juggle, manipulate, tamper with,
trump up*; SEE CONCEPTS 202,697

right [n1] *privilege*
advantage, appanage, authority, benefit, birthright, business, claim, comeuppance, desert, deserving, due, exemption, favor, franchise,
freedom, immunity, interest, liberty, license,
merit, permission, perquisite, power, preference,
prerogative, priority, title; SEE CONCEPT 376

right [n2] *justice, morality*
correctness, emancipation, enfranchisement, equity, freedom, good, goodness, honor, independence, integrity, lawfulness, legality, liberty,
morality, properness, propriety, reason, rectitude,
righteousness, rightness, straight, truth, uprightness, virtue; SEE CONCEPT 645

right [adj1] *fair, just*
appropriate, condign, conscientious, deserved,
due, equitable, ethical, fitting, good, honest, honorable, justifiable, lawful, legal, legitimate, merited, moral, proper, requisite, righteous, rightful,
scrupulous, stand-up*, suitable, true, upright, virtuous; SEE CONCEPT 545

right [adj2] *accurate, precise*
absolute, admissible, amen, authentic, bona fide,
complete, correct, exact, factual, faithful, free of
error, genuine, immaculate, indubitable, inerrant,
infallible, just, nice, on the money*, on the nose*,
out-and-out*, perfect, proper, punctilious, real,
right as rain*, righteous, right on*, rigorous, satisfactory, solemn, sound, strict, sure, thoroughgoing, true, undistorted, undoubted, unerring,
unmistaken, utter, valid, veracious, veridical, veritable, watertight*; SEE CONCEPTS 535,557,582

right [adj3] *appropriate, fitting*
acceptable, adequate, advantageous, all right, becoming, befitting, comely, comme il faut, common, condign, convenient, correct, decent,
decorous, deserved, desirable, done*, due, favorable, felicitous, fit, good, happy, ideal, merited,
nice, opportune, proper, propitious, requisite,
rightful, satisfactory, seemly, sufficient, suitable,
tolerable; SEE CONCEPTS 558,572

right [adj4] *sane, healthy*
all there, balanced, circumspect, compos mentis,
discerning, discreet, enlightened, far-sighted,
fine, fit, hale, in good health*, in the pink*, judicious, lucid, normal, penetrating, rational, reasonable, sound, unimpaired, up to par*, well,
wise; SEE CONCEPTS 314,403

right [adj5] *conservative politically*
die-hard*, old-line*, orthodox, reactionary, right
wing, traditionalistic; SEE CONCEPTS 529,689

right [adj6] *opposite of left*
clockwise, dexter, dextral, right-handed; SEE
CONCEPT 581

right [v] *fix, correct*
adjust, amend, balance, clean up, compensate for,
debug*, dial back*, doctor*, do justice, emend,
fiddle with*, fix up, go straight, launder, make up
for, mend, overhaul, patch, pick up, put in place,
put right, recalibrate, recompense, recondition, reconstruct, rectify, redress, repair, restore, reward,
scrub, set straight, settle, set upright, shape up,
sort out, square, straighten, straighten out, turn
around, vindicate; SEE CONCEPTS 126,212

right [adv1] *accurately, precisely*
absolutely, all the way, altogether, bang*, clear,
completely, correctly, entirely, exactly, factually,
fully, genuinely, just, perfectly, precisely, quite,
sharp, slap, smack-dab*, square, squarely, thoroughly, totally, truly, utterly, well, wholly; SEE
CONCEPTS 531,557,582

right [adv2] *appropriately, suitably*
acceptably, adequately, amply, aptly, becomingly, befittingly, fittingly, properly, satisfactorily, well; SEE CONCEPTS 558,572

right [adv3] *fairly, justly*
conscientiously, decently, dispassionately, equitably, ethically, evenly, honestly, honorably,
impartially, lawfully, legitimately, morally, objectively, properly, reliably, righteously, sincerely, squarely, virtuously, without bias, without
prejudice; SEE CONCEPT 545

right [adv4] *beneficially*
advantageously, exceedingly, extremely, favorably,
for the better, fortunately, highly, notably, perfectly, remarkably, to advantage, very, well; SEE
CONCEPTS 537,572

right [adv5] *directly, without delay*
at once, away, direct, due, first off, forthwith,
immediately, instanter, instantly, now, promptly,
quickly, right away, straight, straight away,
straightly, undeviatingly; SEE CONCEPT 799

righteous [adj] *good, honest*
angelic, blameless, charitable, commendable,
conscientious, creditable, deserving, devoted, devout, dutiful, equitable, ethical, exemplary, fair,
faithful, godlike, guiltless, holy, honorable, impartial, innocent, irreproachable, just, laudable,
law-abiding, matchless, meritorious, moral, noble, peerless, philanthropic, philanthropical,
praiseworthy, punctilious, pure, reverent, right-
minded, saintly, scrupulous, sinless, spiritual,
sterling, trustworthy, upright, virtuous, worthy;
SEE CONCEPT 545

rightful [adj] *legitimate*
applicable, appropriate, apt, authorized, befitting,
bona fide, canonical, card-carrying*, condign, deserved, due, ethical, fair, fit, fitting, holding water, honest, just, kosher*, lawful, legal, legit*,
merited, moral, moralistic, noble, official, on the
level*, on the up and up*, orthodox, permitted,
principled, proper, real, requisite, right, right-
minded, suitable, true, twenty-four carat*, valid,
virtuous; SEE CONCEPTS 545,558

rigid [adj] *stiff, strict, severe*
adamant, adamantine, austere, bullheaded,
changeless, chiseled*, dead set*, definite, determined, exact, firm, fixed, hard, hard-line*, harsh,
incompliant, inelastic, inexorable, inflexible, intransigent, invariable, locked in*, obdurate, rigorous, set, set in stone*, single-minded, solid,
static, stern, strait-laced*, stringent, tough nut to
crack*, unalterable, unbending, unbreakable, unchanging, uncompromising, undeviating, unmov-

ing, unpermissive, unrelenting, unyielding; SEE
CONCEPTS *403,534,535*

rigor [*n*] *strictness, exactness*

accuracy, affliction, asperity, austerity, conscientiousness, conventionalism, difficulty, exactitude, firmness, hardness, hardship, harshness, inclemency, inflexibility, intolerance, meticulousness, obduracy, ordeal, preciseness, precision, privation, punctiliousness, rigidity, roughness, severity, sternness, stiffness, stringency, suffering, tenacity, thoroughness, traditionalism, trial, tribulation, vicissitude, visitation; SEE CONCEPTS *638,654,666*

rigorous [*adj*] *severe; exact*

accurate, ascetic, austere, bitter, brutal, burdensome, correct, definite, dogmatic, exact, exacting, hard, harsh, inclement, inflexible, intemperate, ironhanded, meticulous, nice, onerous, oppressive, precise, proper, punctilious, right, rigid, rugged, scrupulous, stern, stiff, strict, stringent, uncompromising, unpermissive; SEE CONCEPTS *535,557,565*

rile [*v*] *anger, upset*

acerbate, aggravate, annoy, bother, bug*, disturb, exasperate, gall, get one's goat*, get under skin*, grate, inflame, irk, irritate, nettle, peeve, pique, provoke, put out*, roil, rub one the wrong way*, try one's patience*, vex; SEE CONCEPTS *7,19*

rim [*n*] *border; top edge*

band, brim, brink, brow, circumference, confine, curb, end, fringe, hem, ledge, limit, line, lip, margin, outline, perimeter, periphery, ring, skirt, strip, terminus, top, verge; SEE CONCEPTS *484,836*

ring [*n1*] *circle; circular object*

arena, band, brim, circlet, circuit, circus, enclosure, eye, girdle, halo, hoop, loop, ringlet, rink, round; SEE CONCEPTS *436,446*

ring [*n2*] *group participating together*

association, band, bloc, bunch, cabal, camp, cartel, cell, circle, clan, clique, coalition, combination, combine, corner, coterie, crew, crowd, faction, gang, in-group, junta, junto, knot, Mafia, mob, monopoly, organization, outfit, party, pool, push, racket, syndicate, troop, troupe, trust; SEE CONCEPTS *325,381*

ring [*n3*] *chime, bell-like noise*

buzz, call, clangor, clank, jangle, jingle, knell, peal, reverberation, tinkle, toll, vibration; SEE CONCEPT *595*

ring [*v1*] *encircle*

begird, belt, circle, circumscribe, compass, confine, enclose, encompass, gird, girdle, hem in, inclose, loop, move around, rim, round, seal off, surround; SEE CONCEPT *758*

ring [*v2*] *chime; make bell-like noise*

bang, beat, bong, buzz, clang, clap, jangle, jingle, knell, peal, play, pull, punch, resonate, resound, reverberate, sound, strike, tinkle, tintinnabulate, toll, vibrate; SEE CONCEPT *65*

rinse [*v*] *wash off, out*

bathe, clean, cleanse, dip, flush, soak, splash, wash, water, wet; SEE CONCEPTS *165,256*

riot [*n1*] *uprising, disorder*

anarchism, anarchy, branigan*, brawl, burst, commotion, confusion, distemper, disturbance, flap, fray, free-for-all*, fuss, hassle, lawlessness, misrule, mob, mob violence, protest, quarrel, racket, row, ruckus, ruction, rumble, rumpus, run-in, scene, shivaree, shower, snarl, stir, storm,

street fighting, strife, to-do*, trouble, tumult, turbulence, turmoil, uproar, wingding*; SEE CONCEPTS *106,300*

riot [*n2*] *very funny happening*

boisterousness, carousal, confusion, excess, extravaganza, festivity, flourish, frolic, high jinks*, howl*, jollification, lark, merrymaking, panic*, revelry, romp, scream*, sensation, show, sidesplitter*, skylark*, smash*, splash*, tumult, uproar, wow*; SEE CONCEPTS *384,386*

riot [*v*] *protest; cause an uproar*

arise, debauch, dissipate, fight, go on rampage, racket, rampage, rebel, revolt, rise, run riot*, stir up trouble*, take to the streets*; SEE CONCEPTS *106,300*

rip [*n*] *tear, cut*

cleavage, gash, hole, laceration, rent, slash, slit, split; SEE CONCEPTS *309,513*

rip [*v*] *tear, cut*

burst, claw, cleave, fray, frazzle, gash, hack, lacerate, rend, rive, score, shred, slash, slit, split; SEE CONCEPT *214*

ripe [*adj1*] *fully developed; experienced*

accomplished, adult, aged, completed, consummate, conditioned, enlightened, enriched, filled out, finished, fit, full, full-blown, full-fledged, fully grown, grown, grown-up, increased, informed, in readiness, judicious, learned, mature, matured, mellow, overdue, perfected, plump, prepared, prime, ready, ripened, sagacious, seasoned, skilled, skillful, sound, timely, usable, versed, well-timed, wise; SEE CONCEPTS *462,560,578,797*

ripe [*adj2*] *favorable, ideal*

auspicious, opportune, right, suitable, timely; SEE CONCEPT *558*

rip off [*v*] *rob; trick*

abuse, appropriate, bleed*, cheat, con*, cop*, defraud, dupe, exploit, filch*, fleece*, heist, impose on*, lift*, nab*, pilfer, pinch, plunder, ransack, relieve, rifle, skin*, soak*, stick*, swindle, swipe, thieve, use; SEE CONCEPTS *139,192*

rip-off [*n*] *trick; robbery*

cheat, con*, exploitation, fraud, gyp*, larceny, lift*, pinch*, purloining, racket*, steal, stealing, swindle, theft, thievery, thieving; SEE CONCEPTS *139,192*

rise [*n1*] *increase, improvement*

acceleration, accession, accretion, addition, advance, advancement, aggrandizement, ascent, augmentation, boost, breakthrough, climb, distention, doubling, enlargement, growth, heightening, hike, increment, inflation, intensification, intensifying, multiplication, piling up, progress, promotion, raise, stacking up, step-up, surge, swell, upgrade, upsurge, upswing, upturn, waxing; SEE CONCEPTS *700,780*

rise [*n2*] *movement upward; upward slope*

acclivity, ascension, ascent, climb, elevation, eminence, highland, hillock, incline, lift, mount, rising, rising ground, soaring, surge, towering, upland, upsurge; SEE CONCEPTS *166,738,752*

rise [*v1*] *get up; ascend*

arise, arouse, aspire, awake, be erect, be located, be situated, blast off*, bob up*, climb, come up, get out of bed, get steeper, get to one's feet*, go uphill, grow, have foundation, levitate, lift, mount, move up, pile out*, push up, reach up, rise and shine*, rise up, rocket, roll out*, rouse, scale, sit up, slope upwards, soar, sprout, stand

ri
ri

up, straighten up, surface, surge, surmount, sweep
upward, tower, turn out, up*, upspring; SEE CON-
CEPTS 154,166,738

rise [v2] *increase, grow*
accelerate, add to, advance, aggravate, arise, ascend, augment, billow, build, bulge, climb,
deepen, distend, double, enhance, enlarge, expand, go through the roof*, go up, heighten, improve, inflate, intensate, intensify, levitate, lift,
magnify, mount, move up, multiply, perk up, pick
up, pile up, raise, redouble, rouse, soar, speed up,
spread, stack up, swell, take off, upsurge, wax;
SEE CONCEPTS 700,780

rise [v3] *progress in business*
advance, be elevated, be promoted, better oneself,
climb the ladder*, flourish, get on, get somewhere*, go places*, progress, prosper, succeed,
thrive, work one's way up*; SEE CONCEPTS
351,704

rise [v4] *become apparent*
appear, arise, befall, begin, betide, chance, come,
crop up, dawn, derive, develop, emanate, emerge,
eventuate, fall out*, flare up, flow, go, happen,
head, issue, loom, occur, originate, proceed,
spring, stem, surface, transpire, turn up*; SEE
CONCEPTS 4,716

rise [v5] *rebel*
insurrect, mount, mutiny, resist, revolt, riot, take
up arms; SEE CONCEPT 106

risk [n] *chance taken*
accident, contingency, danger, exposedness, exposure, flyer*, fortuity, fortune, gamble, hazard,
header, jeopardy, liability, liableness, luck, openness, opportunity, peril, plunge, possibility, prospect, shot in the dark*, speculation, stab*,
uncertainty, venture, wager; SEE CONCEPTS
675,693

risk [v] *take a chance*
adventure, beard, be caught short*, brave, chance,
compromise, confront, dare, defy, defy danger,
encounter, endanger, expose to danger, face, gamble, go out of one's depth*, hang by a thread*,
hazard, imperil, jeopardize, jeopardy, leap before
looking*, leave to luck*, meet, menace, peril,
play with fire*, plunge, put in jeopardy, run the
chance, run the risk, skate on thin ice*, speculate,
tackle, take a flyer*, take a header*, take a
plunge*, take on*, take the liberty*, venture, wager; SEE CONCEPTS 87,100

risky [adj] *dangerous*
chancy, delicate, dicey*, endangered, fraught
with danger*, going for broke*, hairy*, hanging
by a thread*, hazardous, iffy*, insecure, jeopardous, long shot*, not a prayer*, off the deep end*,
on slippery ground*, on the spot*, on thin ice*,
out on a limb*, perilous, playing with fire*, precarious, rocky*, sensitive, speculative, ticklish,
touch-and-go*, touchy, treacherous, tricky, uncertain, unhealthy, unsafe, unsound, venturesome,
wicked, wide-open; SEE CONCEPT 548

risqué [adj] *improper, referring to sex*
amoral, bawdy*, blue*, breezy, crude, daring,
dirty, earthy, erotic, filthy*, foul, gross*, hot*,
immodest, immoral, indecent, indecorous, indelicate, indiscreet, inelegant, lewd, lurid, naughty,
obscene, off-base*, off-color, offensive, out-of-
line, provocative, purple*, racy, raw, ribald, salacious, salty, shady, sizzling, smart, smutty,

spicy*, suggestive, unrefined, vulgar, wanton,
warm, wicked, X-rated*; SEE CONCEPTS
267,545,548

rite [n] *ceremony, tradition*
act, celebration, ceremonial, communion, custom,
form, formality, liturgy, observance, occasion, ordinance, practice, procedure, ritual, sacrament,
service, solemnity; SEE CONCEPTS 377,386

ritual [n] *ceremony, tradition*
act, ceremonial, communion, convention, custom,
form, formality, habit, liturgy, observance, ordinance, practice, prescription, procedure, protocol,
red tape*, rite, routine, sacrament, service, solemnity, stereotype, usage; SEE CONCEPTS
386,634,688

rival [n] *person who opposes in competition*
adversary, antagonist, bandit, buddy, challenger,
competition, competitor, contender, contestant,
emulator, entrant, equal, equivalent, match, opponent, opposite number, peer; SEE CONCEPTS
348,366,423

rival [adj] *opposing*
battling, combatant, combating, competing, competitive, conflicting, contending, contesting, cutthroat, disputing, emulating, emulous, equal,
opposed, striving, vying; SEE CONCEPTS 542,564

rival [v] *oppose; be a match for*
amount, approach, approximate, bear comparison
with*, come near to*, come up to*, compare with,
compete, contend, contest, correspond, emulate,
equal, go after, go for, jockey for position*,
match, measure up to, meet, near, partake,
resemble, rivalize, scramble for, seek to displace,
tie, touch, vie with; SEE CONCEPTS 92,667

road [n] *path upon which travel occurs*
alley, artery, asphalt, avenue, back street, boulevard, byway, cobblestone, concrete, course,
crossroad, direction, drag*, dragway, drive, expressway, highway, lane, line, main drag*, parking lot*, parkway, passage, pathway, pavement,
pike, roadway, route, street, subway, terrace,
thoroughfare, throughway, thruway, track, trail,
turnpike, viaduct, way; SEE CONCEPT 501

roam [v] *wander about*
bum*, bum around*, drift, gad, gallivant, hike,
hit the road*, knock around*, meander, peregrinate, prowl, ramble, range, rove, saunter, straggle, stray, stroll, struggle along, traipse, tramp,
travel, traverse, trek, vagabond, walk; SEE CON-
CEPTS 151,224

roar [n1] *growl, howl*
barrage, bawl, bay, bellow, blast, bluster, boom,
clamor, clash, crash, cry, detonation, din, drum,
explosion, holler, outcry, reverberation, rumble,
shout, thunder, uproar, yell; SEE CONCEPTS
77,595

roar [n2/v2] *laugh loudly*
belly laugh, guffaw, hoot, howl, scream; SEE
CONCEPT 77

roar [v1] *growl, howl*
bark, bawl, bay, bellow, blast, bluster, boom,
brawl, bray, clamor, crash, cry, detonate, din,
drum, explode, holler, rebound, reecho, repercuss, resound, reverberate, roll, rout, rumble,
shout, sound, thunder, trumpet, vociferate, yell;
SEE CONCEPTS 64,77

rob [v] *steal, deprive*
abscond, appropriate, bereave, break into, burglarize, burgle, cheat, con, cop*, defalcate, defraud, despoil, disinherit, dispossess, divest, do

out of*, embezzle, filch*, heist, hijack, hold up*, hustle, liberate, lift*, loot, lose, mug, oust, peculate, pilfer, pillage, pinch, plunder, promote, purloin, raid, ransack, relieve, requisition, rifle, rip off*, roll*, sack*, scrounge, snitch*, stick up, strip, strong-arm*, swindle, swipe, take, thieve, withhold; SEE CONCEPTS *139,142,192*

robber [n] *person who steals*

bandit, brigand, buccaneer, burglar, cardsharper*, cat burglar, cattle thief*, cheat*, chiseler*, con artist, corsair, crook, desperado, despoiler, fence, forager, fraud, grafter, hijacker, holdup artist*, housebreaker, looter, marauder, mugger, operator, pickpocket, pilferer, pillager, pirate, plunderer, prowler, punk*, raider, rustler, safecracker, sandbagger*, second-story operator*, shoplifter, stealer, stickup, swindler, thief, thug; SEE CONCEPT *412*

robe [n] *gown, often for wearing at home*

bathrobe, cape, costume, covering, dress, dressing gown, frock, garment, habit, housecoat, kimono, mantle, muumuu, negligee, outfit, peignoir, vestment, wrapper; SEE CONCEPT *451*

robust [adj] *healthy, strong*

able-bodied, athletic, boisterous, booming, brawny, built, concentrated, fit, fit as fiddle*, flourishing, full-bodied, hale, hardy, hearty, hefty, husky, in fine fettle*, in good health, in good shape, in the pink*, live, lusty, muscular, peppy, potent, powerful, powerhouse, prospering, prosperous, roaring, rough, rugged, sinewy, snappy, sound, stout, strapping, sturdy, thriving, tiger*, tough, vigorous, well, wicked*, zappy*, zippy*; SEE CONCEPTS *314,489,613*

rock [n1] *stone*

bedrock, boulder, cobblestone, crag, crust, earth, gravel, lava, lodge, mass, metal, mineral, ore, pebble, promontory, quarry, reef, rubble, shelf, slab, slag; SEE CONCEPTS *470,474,477,478, 509,523*

rock [n2] *foundation*

anchor, bulwark, cornerstone, defense, mainstay, protection, Rock of Gibraltar*, strength, support; SEE CONCEPTS *442,712*

rock [v] *move back and forth*

agitate, billow, careen, concuss, convulse, falter, heave, jiggle, jog, jolt, jounce, lurch, move, oscillate, pitch, push and pull, quake, quaver, quiver, reel, roll, roll about, shake, shock, stagger, sway, swing, toss, totter, tremble, undulate, vibrate, wobble; SEE CONCEPTS *147,149*

rocky [adj1] *rugged, stony*

bouldered, craggy, flinty, hard, inflexible, jagged, lapidarian, lithic, pebbly, petrified, petrous, rockbound, rock-ribbed, rough, solid, stonelike; SEE CONCEPTS *485,604*

rocky [adj2] *unyielding, inflexible*

adamant, bloodless, firm, flinty, hard, impassible, insensate, insensible, insensitive, obdurate, pitiless, rocklike, rough, rugged, solid, steady, tough; SEE CONCEPT *401*

rocky [adj3] *doubtful, undependable*

dizzy, ill, rickety, shaky, sick, sickly, staggering, ticklish, tottering, tricky, uncertain, unreliable, unstable, unsteady, unwell, weak, wobbly; SEE CONCEPTS *314,488,489*

rod [n] *bar, pole*

baton, billet, birch, cane, cylinder, dowel, ingot, mace, pin, rodule, scepter, sceptre, shaft, slab,

spike, staff, stave, stick, strip, switch, wand; SEE CONCEPTS *436,470,479*

rogue [n] *person who deceives, swindles*

bad egg*, bad news*, blackguard*, black sheep*, charlatan, cheat, cheater, con artist, criminal, crook, defrauder, devil, fraud, heel*, hooligan*, lowlife*, mischief, miscreant, monstrosity, ne'er-do-well*, outlaw, problem*, rapscallion, rascal, reprobate, scalawag, scamp, scoundrel, swindler, trickster, villain; SEE CONCEPT *412*

role [n1] *impersonation of a character*

act, acting, appearance, aspect, bit, character, clothing, execution, extra, guise, hero, ingenue, lead, look, part, performance, personification, piece, player, portrayal, presentation, representation, seeming, semblance, show, star, stint, super, title, walk-on; SEE CONCEPTS *263,716*

role [n2] *duty, function*

act, bit, business, capacity, execution, game*, guise, job, office, part, piece, pose, position, post, posture, province, stint, task, what one is into*; SEE CONCEPTS *362,694*

roll [n1] *revolving, turning*

cycle, gyration, reel, revolution, rotation, run, spin, trundling, turn, twirl, undulation, whirl; SEE CONCEPTS *147,201*

roll [n2] *cylindrical object*

ball, barrel, bobbin, cartouche, coil, cone, convolution, cornucopia, cylinder, fold, reel, rundle, scroll, shell, spiral, spool, trundle, volute, wheel, whorl; SEE CONCEPT *436*

roll [n3] *list, roster*

annals, catalog, census, chronicle, directory, head count, index, muster, nose count*, register, roll call, schedule, scroll, table; SEE CONCEPT *281*

roll [n4] *growl, reverberation*

barrage, boom, booming, clangor, drone, drumbeat, drumming, echoing, grumble, quaver, racket, rat-a-tat*, resonance, roar, rumble, rumbling, thunder; SEE CONCEPT *595*

roll [v1] *revolve, turn; proceed smoothly*

alternate, be in sequence, bowl, circle, circumduct, coil, curve, drape, drive, eddy, elapse, enfold, entwine, envelop, flow, fold, follow, furl, go around, go past, gyrate, gyre, impel, pass, pirouette, pivot, propel, reel, rock, rotate, run, spin, spiral, succeed, swaddle, swathe, swing around, swirl, swivel, trundle, twirl, twist, undulate, wheel, whirl, wind, wrap; SEE CONCEPTS *147,201*

roll [v2] *spread out*

even, flatten, grind, level, press, pulverize, smooth; SEE CONCEPTS *137,208,250*

roll [v3] *thunder, reverberate*

bombinate, boom, cannonade, drum, echo, growl, grumble, hum, pattern, quaver, rattle, re-echo, resound, roar, ruffle, rumble, rustle, sound, trill, whirr; SEE CONCEPT *65*

roll [v4] *rock, sway*

billow, drift, flow, glide, heave, incline, jibe, lean, lumber, lurch, pitch, ramble, range, reel, roam, rove, run, stagger, stray, surge, swagger, swing, toss, tumble, undulate, waddle, wallow, wave, welter, yaw; SEE CONCEPTS *147,149*

rollicking [adj] *fun-loving, lively*

antic, boisterous, carefree, cavorting, cheerful, devil-may-care*, exuberant, frisky, frolicsome, glad, happy, hearty, jaunty, jovial, joyful, joyous, lighthearted, merry, playful, rip-roaring*, romping, spirited, sportive, sprightly; SEE CONCEPTS *401,548*

ri
ro

romance [n1] *love affair*
affair*, affair of the heart*, amour, attachment, courtship, enchantment, fascination, fling, flirtation, intrigue, liaison, love, love story, passion, relationship; SEE CONCEPTS 375,384

romance [n2] *fanciful story or narrative*
ballad, fairy tale, fantasy, fiction, idealization, idyll, legend, love story, lyric, melodrama, novel, story, tale, tear-jerker*; SEE CONCEPT 280

romance [n3] *adventure, flight of fancy*
charm, color, excitement, exoticness, fairy tale, fancy, fantasy, fascination, glamour, hazard, idealization, idyll, mystery, nostalgia, risk, sentiment, venture; SEE CONCEPT 673

romantic [adj] *sentimental, idealistic*
adventurous, amorous, bathetic, charming, chimerical, chivalrous, colorful, corny*, daring, dreamy, enchanting, erotic, exciting, exotic, extravagant, fairy-tale, fanciful, fantastic, fascinating, fond, glamorous, idyllic, impractical, lovey-dovey*, loving, maudlin, mushy*, mysterious, nostalgic, passionate, picturesque, poetic, quixotic, sloppy*, soppy*, starry-eyed, syrupy, tear-jerking*, tender, unrealistic, utopian, visionary, whimsical, wild; SEE CONCEPTS 403,542,548

romp [n] *fun; caper*
antic, cakewalk*, cavort, dance, escapade, frisk, frolic, gambol, hop, lark, leap, play, rollick, rout, skip, sport; SEE CONCEPTS 292,384

romp [v] *have fun, enjoy oneself*
caper, cavort, celebrate, cut capers*, cut up*, fool around*, frisk, frolic, gambol, go on the town*, kid around*, lark, let loose*, make merry, play, prance, revel, roister, rollic, skip, skylark, sport, whoop it up*; SEE CONCEPTS 292,384

room [n1] *space, range*
allowance, area, capacity, chance, clearance, compass, elbowroom, expanse, extent, latitude, leeway, license, margin, occasion, opening, opportunity, place, play, range, reach, rein, rope, scope, sway, sweep, territory, vastness, volume; SEE CONCEPTS 651,756

room [n2] *enclosed section of building designed for specific purpose*
accommodation, alcove, apartment, cabin, cave*, chamber, cubbyhole, cubicle, den, flat, flop*, joint*, lodging, niche, office, setup*, suite, turf, vault; SEE CONCEPT 448

roomy [adj] *having ample space*
ample, broad, capacious, commodious, extensive, generous, large, sizable, spacious, wide; SEE CONCEPT 583

root [n] *base, core*
basis, bedrock, beginnings, bottom, cause, center, crux, derivation, essence, essentiality, footing, foundation, fountain, fountainhead, fundamental, germ, ground, groundwork, heart, motive, nub, nucleus, occasion, origin, pith, provenance, provenience, quick, quintessence, radicle, radix, reason, rhizome, rock bottom*, seat, seed, soul, source, starting point, stem, stuff, substance, substratum, tuber, underpinning, well; SEE CONCEPTS 442,648,661,826,829

root [v] *dig and search*
burrow, delve, embed, ferret, forage, grub, grub up, hunt, ingrain, lodge, nose, place, poke, pry, rummage; SEE CONCEPT 178

rope [n] *cord, line*
braiding, cable, cordage, hawser, lace, lanyard, lariat, lasso, strand, string, tape, thread, twine; SEE CONCEPT 475

roster [n] *list of items, names*
agenda, catalog, head count, index, inventory, listing, muster, nose count*, program, record, register, roll, roll call, rota, schedule, scroll, table; SEE CONCEPTS 281,283

rosy [adj1] *pink, reddish in color*
aflush, blooming, blushing, colored, coral, deep pink, fresh, glowing, healthy-looking, high-colored, incarnadine, pale red, peach, red, red-complexioned, red-faced, roseate, rose-colored, rubicund, ruddy; SEE CONCEPT 618

rosy [adj2] *cheerful, hopeful*
alluring, auspicious, bright, encouraging, favorable, glowing, likely, optimistic, pleasing, promising, reassuring, roseate, rose-colored, sunny; SEE CONCEPTS 529,548

rot [n1] *corrosion, disintegration*
blight, canker, corrosion, decay, decomposition, deterioration, mold, putrefaction, putrescence; SEE CONCEPTS 469,698

rot [n2] *garbage, nonsense*
balderdash, bilge, bunk, claptrap, drivel, foolishness, guff, hogwash, hooey*, moonshine*, poppycock, rubbish, silliness, stuff and nonsense*, tommyrot; SEE CONCEPTS 278,529

rot [v] *corrode, deteriorate*
break down, corrupt, crumble, debase, debauch, decay, decline, decompose, degenerate, demoralize, deprave, descend, disimprove, disintegrate, fester, go bad*, go downhill*, go to pot*, languish, molder, perish, pervert, putrefy, retrograde, sink, spoil, stain, taint, turn, warp, waste away, wither, worsen; SEE CONCEPTS 240,469,698

rotary [adj] *turning*
encircling, gyral, gyratory, revolving, rotating, rotational, rotatory, spinning, vertiginous, vorticular, whirligig, whirling; SEE CONCEPTS 581,584

rotate [v1] *go around in circle*
circle, circumduct, circumvolve, gyrate, gyre, move, pirouette, pivot, reel, revolve, roll, spin, swivel, troll, trundle, turn, twirl, twist, waltz, wheel, whirl, whirligig, whirr; SEE CONCEPTS 147,738

rotate [v2] *alternate*
bandy, ensue, exchange, follow, follow in sequence, interchange, relieve, spell, succeed, switch, take turns; SEE CONCEPTS 104,697

rotten [adj1] *decayed, decaying*
bad, bad-smelling, corroded, corrupt, crumbled, crumbling, decomposed, decomposing, disgusting, disintegrated, disintegrating, fecal, feculent, festering, fetid, foul, gross, infected, loathsome, loud, mephitic, moldering, moldy, noisome, noxious, offensive, overripe, perished, polluted, purulent, pustular, putrescent, putrid, putrified, rancid, rank, rotting, smelling, sour, spoiled, stale, stinking, strong, tainted, touched, unsound; SEE CONCEPTS 462,485

rotten [adj2] *dishonest, immoral*
bent, bribable, contaminated, corrupt, crooked, debauched, deceitful, defiled, degenerate, depraved, dirtied, dishonorable, disloyal, faithless, filthy, flagitious, impure, mercenary, nefarious, perfidious, perverse, polluted, soiled, sullied, tainted, treacherous, unclean, untrustworthy, venal, vicious, villainous, vitiated; SEE CONCEPTS 404,545

rotten [*adj3*] *despicable, inferior, bad*
amiss, base, below par*, bruised, bum*, contemptible, crummy*, defective, deplorable, dirty, disagreeable, disappointing, diseased, displeasing, dissatisfactory, filthy, impaired, inadequate, injured, lousy*, low-grade, mean, nasty, poor, punk*, regrettable, rough, scurrilous, shaky, sorry, sour, substandard, unacceptable, unfortunate, unhappy, unlucky, unpleasant, unsatisfactory, unsound, vile, wasted, wicked, withering, wrong; SEE CONCEPTS *570,571,574*

rough [*adj1*] *uneven, irregular*
asperous, bearded, brambly, bristly, broken, bumpy, bushy, chapped, choppy, coarse, cragged, craggy, cross-grained, disheveled, fuzzy, hairy, harsh, jagged, knobby, knotty, nappy, nodular, not smooth, ridged, rocky, ruffled, rugged, scabrous, scraggy, shaggy, sharp, stony, tangled, tousled, tufted, unequal, uneven, unfinished, unlevel, unshaven, unshorn, woolly, wrinkled, wrinkly; SEE CONCEPTS *485,606*

rough [*adj2*] *stormy; not quiet*
agitated, blustering, blustery, boisterous, buffeting, cacophonous, choppy, coarse, discordant, dry, furious, grating, gruff, harsh, hoarse, husky, inclement, inharmonious, jarring, raging, rasping, raucous, rugged, squally, stridulent, tempestuous, tumultuous/tumultuous, turbulent, unmusical, wild; SEE CONCEPTS *525,592,594*

rough [*adj3*] *rude, impolite*
bearish, bluff, blunt, boisterous, boorish, brief, brusque, churlish, coarse, crass, crude, cruel, crusty, curt, discourteous, drastic, extreme, gross*, hairy*, hard, harsh, ill-mannered, improper, inconsiderate, indecorous, indelicate, inelegant, loud, loutish, mean, nasty, raw, rowdy, severe, sharp, short, tough, unceremonious, uncivil, uncouth, uncultivated, uncultured, unfeeling, ungracious, unjust, unmannerly, unpleasant, unpolished, unrefined, untutored, violent, vulgar; SEE CONCEPTS *267,401*

rough [*adj4*] *basic, incomplete*
austere, crude, cursory, formless, hard, imperfect, raw, rough-and-ready*, roughhewn, rudimentary, shapeless, sketchy, spartan, uncompleted, uncut, undressed, unfashioned, unfinished, unformed, unhewn, unpolished, unprocessed, unrefined, unwrought; SEE CONCEPT *531*

rough [*adj5*] *approximate*
amorphous, estimated, foggy, general, hazy, imprecise, inexact, proximate, rude, sketchy, uncertain, unprecise, vague; SEE CONCEPT *557*

rough out [*v*] *do preliminary design*
adumbrate, block out, chalk, characterize, delineate, draft, outline, plan, skeleton, sketch, suggest; SEE CONCEPTS *36,79,174*

rough up [*v*] *beat up*
bash, batter, hit, knock about, knock around, maltreat, mishandle, mistreat, roughhouse, slap around, thrash; SEE CONCEPTS *189,246*

round [*n1*] *globe, ball; semicircular area*
arc, arch, band, bend, bow, circle, circlet, curvation, curvature, curve, disc, disk, equator, eye, gyre, hoop, loop, orb, orbit, ring, ringlet, sphere, wheel; SEE CONCEPT *436*

round [*n2*] *cycle, stage*
ambit, beat, bout, circuit, circulation, circumvolution, compass, course, division, gyration, lap, level, performance, period, revolution, rotation, round trip, routine, schedule, sequence, series,

session, succession, tour, turn, wheel, whirl; SEE CONCEPTS *364,727,807*

round [*n3*] *unit of ammunition*
bullet, cartridge, charge, discharge, load, shell, shot; SEE CONCEPTS *498,500*

round [*adj1*] *ball-shaped; semicircular area*
annular, arced, arched, arciform, bent, bowed, bulbous, circular, coiled, curled, curved, curvilinear, cylindrical, discoid, disk-shaped, domical, egg-shaped, elliptical, globose, globular, looped, orbed, orbicular, orbiculate, oval, ringed, rotund, rounded, spherical, spheroid, spiral; SEE CONCEPT *486*

round [*adj2*] *complete*
accomplished, done, entire, finished, full, rounded, solid, unbroken, undivided, whole; SEE CONCEPT *531*

round [*adj3*] *full-bodied, ample in size*
chubby, expansive, fleshy, generous, large, plump, plumpish, pudgy*, roly-poly*, rotund, rounded, tubby; SEE CONCEPTS *491,773*

round [*adj4*] *resonant, rich in sound*
consonant, full, mellifluous, orotund, plangent, resounding, ringing, rotund, sonorous, vibrant; SEE CONCEPT *594*

round [*adj5*] *honest, direct*
blunt, candid, frank, free, outspoken, plain, straightforward, unmodified, vocal; SEE CONCEPT *267*

round [*v1*] *turn; encircle*
begird, bypass, circle, circulate, circumnavigate, compass, encompass, flank, gird, girdle, go around, gyrate, hem, pivot, revolve, ring, roll, rotate, skirt, spin, surround, wheel, whirl; SEE CONCEPTS *147,149,187*

round [*v2*] *make curved; remove angles*
arch, bend, bow, coil, convolute, crook, curl, curve, form, loop, mold, perfect, polish, recurve, refine, shape, sleek, slick, smooth, whorl; SEE CONCEPTS *184,202*

round [*adv1*] *approximate*
about, all but, almost, around, as good as, close to, in the neighborhood of, just about, most, near, nearly, practically, roughly; SEE CONCEPT *762*

roundabout [*adj*] *indirect*
ambiguous, circuitous, circular, circumlocutory, collateral, deviating, devious, discursive, evasive, meandering, oblique, obliquitous, periphrastic, taking the long way*, tortuous; SEE CONCEPTS *559,581,584*

round off [*v*] *finish*
bring to a close, cap, climax, close, complete, conclude, crown, culminate, finish off, settle, top off; SEE CONCEPT *234*

roundup [*n*] *collection, collation*
assembly, branding, gathering, herding, marshalling, muster, rally, summary, survey; SEE CONCEPTS *257,397*

round up [*v*] *collect, gather*
assemble, bring in, bring together, cluster, drive, group, herd, marshal, muster, rally; SEE CONCEPTS *109,257*

rouse [*v1*] *wake*
arouse, awake, awaken, call, get up, raise, rise, stir, wake up; SEE CONCEPT *250*

rouse [*v2*] *stimulate, excite*
aggravate, agitate, anger, animate, arouse, ask for it*, awaken, bestir, bug*, challenge, craze, deepen, disturb, enhance, enliven, exhilarate, fire up*, foment, galvanize, get going, heighten, in-

cite, inflame, innervate, innerve, instigate, intensate, intensify, key up*, kindle, magnify, make waves*, mount, move, needle, pep up*, pique, provoke, quicken, rally, redouble, rile, rise, startle, steam up*, stir, trigger, urge, vivify, wake, waken, wake up, whet, whip up*, work up; SEE CONCEPTS 7,22,244

rout [n] *overwhelming defeat*
beating, clobbering*, comedown, confusion, debacle, disaster, drubbing*, embarrassment, flight, hiding, overthrow, retreat, romp, ruin, shambles, shutout, thrashing, trashing*, upset, vanquishment, walkover*, washout*, waxing*, whipping; SEE CONCEPTS 95,119,363

rout [v] *defeat overwhelmingly*
bash, beat, blow out of water*, bulldoze*, bury*, chase, clean up on*, clobber, conquer, cream*, crush, cut to pieces*, destroy, discomfit, dispel, drive off, expel, finish*, hunt, kill*, lambaste*, larrup*, murder*, outmaneuver, overpower, overthrow, put to flight*, repulse, scatter, scuttle, shut out*, skunk*, subdue, subjugate, swamp*, torpedo*, total*, trounce, vanquish, wallop, wax*, whip, wipe off map*, wipe out*, worst, zap*; SEE CONCEPT 95

route [n] *path over which someone or something travels*
avenue, beat, beeline, byway, circuit, course, detour, digression, direction, divergence, itinerary, journey, line, meandering, passage, pavement, pike, plot, program, rambling, range, road, round, rounds, run, short cut, tack, track, trail, wandering, way; SEE CONCEPTS 501,660

route [v] *send along a path*
address, conduct, consign, convey, direct, dispatch, escort, forward, guide, lead, pilot, remit, see, shepherd, ship, show, steer, transmit; SEE CONCEPTS 187,217

routine [n] *habitual activity*
act, beaten path*, bit, channels, custom, cycle, daily grind*, drill, formula, grind*, groove*, habit, line, method, order, pace, pattern, piece, practice, procedure, program, rat race*, rote, round, rut, schtick*, spiel*, system, tack, technique, treadmill, usage, way, wont; SEE CONCEPTS 6,362,770

routine [adj] *habitual*
accepted, accustomed, chronic, conventional, customary, everyday, familiar, general, methodical, normal, ordinary, periodic, plain, quotidian, regular, seasonal, standard, typical, unremarkable, usual, wonted, workaday; SEE CONCEPTS 530,547,548

row [n1] *sequence, series*
bank, chain, column, consecution, echelon, file, line, order, progression, queue, range, rank, string, succession, tier, train; SEE CONCEPTS 432,727,744

row [n2] *fight, ruckus*
affray, altercation, bickering, brawl, castigation, commotion, controversy, dispute, disturbance, falling-out*, fracas, fray, fuss, knock-down-drag-out*, lecture, melee, noise, quarrel, racket, reprimand, reproof, riot, rumpus, run-in*, scrap*, set-to*, shouting match*, squabble, talking-to*, telling-off*, tiff, tongue-lashing*, trouble, tumult, uproar, words*, wrangle; SEE CONCEPTS 46,52,106

row [v1] *move boat with paddle*
drag, oar, paddle, pull, punt, sail, scud, scull, sky an oar, swim*; SEE CONCEPT 187

row [v2] *argue, fight*
bawl out, berate, bicker, brawl, call on the carpet*, dispute, jaw, quarrel, ream, scold, scrap, spat, squabble, tiff, tongue-lash*, wrangle; SEE CONCEPTS 46,106

rowdy [n] *person who is boisterous, noisy*
brawler, bully, hellion, hooligan, lout, punk, roughneck, ruffian, terror*, troublemaker; SEE CONCEPT 412

rowdy [adj] *boisterous, noisy*
disorderly, lawless, loud, loudmouthed, loutish, mischievous, obstreperous, rambunctious, raucous, rebellious, rough, roughhouse, rude, turbulent, unruly, uproarious, wild; SEE CONCEPT 401

royal [adj] *monarchical, grand*
aristocratic, august, authoritative, baronial, commanding, dignified, elevated, eminent, grandiose, high, high-born, honorable, illustrious, imperial, imposing, impressive, kingly, lofty, magnificent, majestic, noble, queenly, regal, regnant, reigning, renowned, resplendent, ruling, sovereign, splendid, stately, superb, superior, supreme, worthy; SEE CONCEPTS 549,574

rub [n1] *stroke, massage*
abrasion, attrition, brushing, caress, friction, grinding, kneading, pat, polish, rasping, scouring, scraping, shine, smear, smoothing, stroking, swab, swipe, wear, wipe; SEE CONCEPT 215

rub [n2] *difficulty, problem*
bar, catch, crimp, dilemma, drawback, hamper, hindrance, hitch, hurdle, impediment, obstacle, predicament, snag, stumbling block*, traverse, trouble; SEE CONCEPTS 666,674

rub [v] *stroke, massage*
abrade, anoint, apply, bark, brush, buff, burnish, caress, chafe, clean, coat, cover, curry, daub, erase, erode, excoriate, file, fray, fret, furbish, glance, glaze, gloss, grate, graze, grind, knead, mop, paint, pat, plaster, polish, put, rasp, scour, scrape, scrub, shine, slather, smear, smooth, spread, swab, triturate, wear, wear down, wipe; SEE CONCEPT 215

rubbish [n1] *garbage*
debris, dregs, dross, junk, litter, lumber, offal, refuse, rubble, rummage, scrap, sweepings, trash, waste; SEE CONCEPT 260

rubbish [n2] *nonsense*
balderdash, bilge*, bunkum, drivel, gibberish, hogwash, hooey*, poppycock, rot*, stuff and nonsense*, tommyrot; SEE CONCEPTS 230,278

ruddy [adj] *pinkish, blushing*
blooming, blowsy, bronzed, crimson, florid, flush, flushed, fresh, full-blooded, glowing, healthy, pink, red, red-complexioned, reddish, roseate, rosy, rubicund, ruby, sanguine, scarlet; SEE CONCEPT 618

rude [adj1] *disrespectful, rough*
abrupt, abusive, bad-mannered, barbarian, barbaric, barbarous, blunt, boorish, brusque, brutish, cheeky, churlish, coarse, crabbed, crude, curt, discourteous, graceless, gross, gruff, ignorant, illiterate, impertinent, impolite, impudent, inconsiderate, insolent, insulting, intrusive, loutish, low, obscene, offhand, peremptory, raw, savage, scurrilous, short, surly, uncivil, uncivilized, uncouth, uncultured, uneducated, ungracious, un-

mannerly, unpolished, unrefined, vulgar, wild; SEE CONCEPTS *267,401*

rude [*adj2*] *crude, primitive*

angular, artless, barbarous, callow, coarse, formless, fresh, green, ignorant, inartistic, inelegant, inexperienced, inexpert, makeshift, primal, raw, rough, roughhewn, roughly made, rudimental, rudimentary, shapeless, simple, uncivilized, unconversant, uncultivated, unfashioned, unfinished, unformed, unhewn, unpolished, unprocessed, unrefined, wild; SEE CONCEPTS *490,531*

rude [*adj3*] *sudden; approximate*

abrupt, guessed, harsh, imperfect, imprecise, inexact, in the ballpark*, proximate, rough, sharp, startling, stormy, surmised, turbulent, unpleasant, unprecise, violent; SEE CONCEPTS *557,799*

rudimentary [*adj*] *basic, fundamental*

abecedarian, basal, beginning, early, elemental, elementary, embryonic, immature, initial, introductory, larval, nuts-and-bolts*, primary, primitive, simple, simplest, uncompleted, undeveloped, vestigial; SEE CONCEPTS *546,549*

ruffle [*v1*] *mess up*

cockle, confuse, crease, crinkle, crumple, crush, derange, disarrange, discompose, dishevel, disorder, pucker, purse, rifle, rumple, tangle, tousle, wrinkle; SEE CONCEPT *158*

ruffle [*v2*] *upset, irritate*

abrade, agitate, anger, annoy, bluster, bother, browbeat, bully, chafe, confuse, cow*, disconcert, disquiet, disturb, excite, floor*, flummox, flurry, fluster, fret, fuddle, gall, get to*, harass, intimidate, irk, nettle, peeve, perturb, provoke, put off, put out, rattle, rattle one's cage*, shake up*, stir, stump, throw into tizzy*, torment, trouble, unsettle, vex, wear, worry; SEE CONCEPTS *7,14,19*

rugged [*adj1*] *bumpy, weathered*

asperous, broken, coarse, craggy, difficult, furrowed, harsh, hilly, irregular, jagged, leathery, lumpy, mountainous, ragged, rocky, rough, roughhewn, scabrous, scraggy, stark, uneven, unlevel, unpolished, unrefined, unsmooth, weatherbeaten, worn, wrinkled; SEE CONCEPTS *490,606*

rugged [*adj2*] *severe, violent*

bitter, brutal, difficult, hard, harsh, inclement, intemperate, rigorous, rough, stormy, tempestuous, turbulent; SEE CONCEPTS *525,537*

rugged [*adj3*] *uncouth, crude*

barbarous, blunt, boorish, churlish, graceless, ill-bred, loutish, rude, uncultured, unpolished, unrefined; SEE CONCEPT *401*

rugged [*adj4*] *difficult, rigorous*

arduous, demanding, exacting, formidable, hairy*, hard, harsh, heavy*, heavy sledding*, knotty*, laborious, large order*, mean, murder*, no picnic*, operose, rough, stern, strenuous, taxing, tough, trying, uncompromising, uphill*; SEE CONCEPTS *538,565*

rugged [*adj5*] *big, strong*

able-bodied, athletic, brawny, energetic, forceful, hale, hardy, healthy, husky, indefatigable, lusty, muscular, robust, sturdy, tough, unflagging, vigorous, well-built; SEE CONCEPTS *314,489*

ruin [*n*] *situation of devastation*

atrophy, bane, bankruptcy, bath, breakdown, collapse, confusion, crackup, crash, crumbling, damage, decay, defeat, degeneracy, degeneration, demolition, destitution, destruction, deterioration, dilapidation, disintegration, disrepair, dissolution, downfall, downgrade, extinction, failure, fall, havoc, insolvency, loss, nemesis, overthrow, ruination, skids*, subversion, the end*, undoing, waste, waterloo, wreck, wreckage; SEE CONCEPT *674*

ruin [*v*] *devastate, destroy*

bankrupt, beggar, botch, break, bring down, bring to ruin, bust, clean out, crush, decimate, deface, defeat, defile, demolish, deplete, deplore, depredate, desecrate, despoil, devour, dilapidate, disfigure, do in*, drain, exhaust, fleece, impoverish, injure, lay waste, maim, make a mess of, mangle, mar, mutilate, overthrow, overturn, overwhelm, pauperize, pillage, rape, ravish, raze, reduce, sack, shatter, smash, spoil, spoilate, total, use up, wipe out*, wrack, wreak havoc on, wreck; SEE CONCEPTS *234,246,252*

ruinous [*adj*] *disastrous, devastating*

annihilative, baleful, baneful, calamitous, cataclysmic, catastrophic, crippling, damaging, deadly, deleterious, depleting, dire, disastrous, draining, exhausting, extravagant, fatal, fateful, harmful, hurtful, immoderate, impoverishing, injurious, murderous, noxious, pernicious, shattering, suicidal, unfortunate, wasteful, withering, wrackful; SEE CONCEPTS *537,548,570*

ruins [*n*] *buildings that are dilapidated*

ashes, debris, destruction, detritus, foundation, relics, remains, remnants, residue, rubble, traces, vestiges, wreck, wreckage; SEE CONCEPTS *439,733*

rule [*n1*] *standard, principle of behavior*

aphorism, apothegm, assize, axiom, basis, brocard, canon, chapter and verse*, command, commandment, criterion, decorum, decree, decretion, dictum, direction, edict, etiquette, formula, fundamental, gnome, guide, guideline, keynote, key stone, law, maxim, model, moral, no-no's*, order, ordinance, precedent, precept, prescription, propriety, regimen, regulation, ruling, statute, tenet, test, the book*, the numbers*, truism; SEE CONCEPT *688*

rule [*n2*] *leadership of organization*

administration, ascendancy, authority, command, control, direction, domination, dominion, empire, government, influence, jurisdiction, power, regime, regnancy, reign, sovereignty, supremacy, sway; SEE CONCEPTS *299,376*

rule [*n3*] *method, way*

course, custom, formula, habit, normalcy, normality, order of things, policy, practice, procedure, routine; SEE CONCEPTS *6,647*

rule [*v1*] *govern, manage*

administer, be in authority, be in driver's seat*, be in power, bridle, command, conduct, control, crack the whip*, curb, decree, dictate, direct, dominate, domineer, guide, hold sway*, hold the reins*, keep under one's thumb*, lay down the law*, lead, order, overrule, predominate, preponderate, preside, prevail, regulate, reign, restrain, rule the roost*, run, run the show*, sit on top of*, sway, take over; SEE CONCEPTS *117,133,298*

rule [*v2*] *judge, decide*

adjudge, adjudicate, conclude, decree, deduce, determine, establish, figure, find, fix, gather, hold, infer, lay down, pass upon, postulate, prescribe, pronounce, resolve, settle, theorize; SEE CONCEPTS *18,81*

rule out [*v*] *exclude, reject*

abolish, avert, ban, bate, cancel, count out, debar,

deter, dismiss, eliminate, except, forbid, forestall, forfend, leave out, not consider, obviate, preclude, prevent, prohibit, proscribe, recant, revoke, stave off, suspend, ward off; SEE CONCEPTS 25,121

ruler [n] *historically, person who ruled an area*
baron, baroness, caesar, caliph, contessa, count, countess, crowned head, czar, czarina, dame, duchess, duke, dynast, emperor, empress, gerent, imperator, kaiser, khan, king, lady, lord, magnate, maharajah, maharani, majesty, mikado, mogul, monarch, oligarch, overlord, pasha, potentate, prince, princess, queen, rajah, rani, rex, royal, shah, sovereign, sultan, sultana, tycoon; SEE CONCEPT 422

ruler [n2] *tool for measuring or calculating length*
folding rule, measure, measuring stick, rule, slide rule, straightedge, T-square, yardstick; SEE CONCEPT 499

ruling [n] *judgment, decree*
adjudication, decision, directive, edict, finding, judgment, law, order, precept, pronouncement, resolution, rule, ukase, verdict; SEE CONCEPT 318

ruling [adj] *dominant, governing*
cardinal, central, commanding, controlling, leading, overriding, overruling, pivotal, regnant, reigning, sovereign, supreme, upper; SEE CONCEPT 574

ruling [adj2] *prevailing, main*
chief, current, dominant, pivotal, popular, predominant, preeminent, preponderant, prevalent, principal, rampant, rife, widespread; SEE CONCEPT 568

rumble [v] *growl, thunder*
boom, grumble, resound, roar, roll; SEE CONCEPT 65

ruminate [v] *think about seriously*
brainstorm*, brood, chew over, cogitate, consider, contemplate, deliberate, excogitate, figure, meditate, mull over, muse, ponder, rack one's brains*, reflect, revolve, stew about*, think, turn over, use one's head*, weigh; SEE CONCEPT 24

rummage [v] *ransack, search*
beat the bushes*, comb, backside, delve, dig out, disarrange, disarray, disorder, disorganize, disrupt, disturb, examine, explore, ferret out, fish, forage, grub, hunt, jumble, leave no stone unturned*, look high and low*, mess up, mix up, poke, rake, root, scour, search high heaven*, seek, shake, shake down, spy, toss, turn inside out*, turn upside down*; SEE CONCEPTS 158,216

rumor [n] *talk about supposed truth*
back-fence talk*, breeze*, bruit, canard, comment, cry, dispatch, earful*, fabrication, falsehood, fame, fiction, gossip, grapevine*, hearsay, hoax, innuendo, intelligence, invention, lie, news, notoriety, report, repute, rumble, scandal, scuttlebutt*, story, suggestion, supposition, tale, tattle, tidings, whisper, wire*; word; SEE CONCEPTS 274,277,278

rumor [v] *tell a supposed truth*
bruit, buzz*, circulate, gossip, noise about*, pass around, publish, report, say, talk, tattle, whisper; SEE CONCEPTS 49,54

rump [n] *bottom, posterior of animal or human*
back, backside, beam, behind, breech, bum*, butt, butt end, buttocks, can*, croup, derrière, duff*, fanny*, haunches, hind end, hindquarters, keister*, moon*, prat, rear, rear end, sacrum, seat, tail*, tail end, tush*; SEE CONCEPTS 392,825

rumple [v] *crush, wrinkle*
bedraggle, cockle, crease, crimp, crinkle, crumple, derange, dishevel, disorder, fold, mess up, muss up, pucker, ruck up, ruffle, screw up, scrunch, seam, tousle, wreathe; SEE CONCEPTS 137,219,250

run [n+] *fast moving on foot*
amble, bound, break, canter, dart, dash, drop, escape, fall, flight, gallop, jog, lope, pace, race, rush, scamper, scuttle, spring, sprint, spurt, tear, trot, whisk; SEE CONCEPTS 150,195

run [n2] *journey*
drive, excursion, jaunt, joy ride*, lift, outing, ride, round, spin, tour, travel, trip; SEE CONCEPT 224

run [n3] *sequence, course*
bearing, chain, continuance, continuation, continuity, current, cycle, drift, duration, endurance, field, flow, line, motion, movement, passage, path, period, persistence, progress, prolongation, round, route, season, series, spell, streak, stream, stretch, string, succession, swing, tendency, tenor, tide, trend, way; SEE CONCEPTS 721,727,738

run [v1] *move fast on foot*
abscond, amble, barrel, beat it*, bolt, bound, bustle, canter, career, clear out, course, cut and run*, dart, dash, decamp, depart, dog it*, escape, flee, flit, fly, gallop, go like lightning*, hasten, hie, hotfoot*, hurry, hustle, jog, leg it*, light out*, lope, make a break*, make off, make tracks*, pace, race, rush, scamper, scoot, scorch, scramble, scud, scurry, shag, shoot, skedaddle*, skip, skitter, smoke*, speed, spring, sprint, spurt, take flight, take off, tear, tear out, travel, trot, whisk; SEE CONCEPTS 150,195

run [v2] *move rapidly, flowingly*
bleed, cascade, course, deliquesce, diffuse, discharge, dissolve, drop, fall, flow, flux, fuse, glide, go, go soft, gush, issue, leak, leap, liquefy, melt, pass, pour, proceed, roll, sail, scud, skim, slide, spill, spin, spout, spread, stream, thaw, tumble, turn to liquid, whirl, whiz; SEE CONCEPT 146

run [v3] *operate, drive*
act, bear, carry, command, control, convey, go, govern, handle, manage, maneuver, move, perform, ply, propel, tick, transport, use, work; SEE CONCEPTS 225,680

run [v4] *manage, supervise*
administer, be in charge, be in driver's seat*, be in saddle*, boss, carry on, conduct, control, coordinate, direct, head, head up*, helm*, keep, lead, look after, operate, ordain, oversee, own, pull the strings*, regulate, ride herd on*, superintend, take care of*; SEE CONCEPT 117

run [v5] *continue, range*
be current, circulate, cover, encompass, extend, go, go around, go on, last, lie, move past, persevere, proceed, reach, spread, stretch, trail, vary; SEE CONCEPTS 651,721

run [v6] *attempt to be elected to public office*
be a candidate, challenge, compete, contend, contest, hit the campaign trail*, kiss babies*, oppose, politick, race, ring doorbells*, shake hands*, stand, stump, whistlestop*; SEE CONCEPT 300

run-around [n] *avoidance*
come-off, delay, detour, difficulty, diversion, elusion, escape, escaping, eschewal, evasion, inertia, postponement, roundabout, shunning; SEE CONCEPTS 30,121

runaway [n] *person who is trying to escape*
absconder, delinquent, deserter, escapee, escaper, fugitive, lawbreaker, maroon, offender, truant, wanted person; SEE CONCEPT 412

runaway [adj] *out of control*
delinquent, disorderly, escaped, fleeing, fugitive, loose, out of hand*, running, uncontrolled, wild; SEE CONCEPT 401

rundown [n] *summary*
briefing, outline, precis, recap*, recapitulation, report, résumé, review, run-through, sketch, synopsis; SEE CONCEPT 283

run down [v] *ridicule*
belittle, criticize, decry, defame, denigrate, depreciate, derogate, detract, diminish, disparage, dispraise, downcry, knock*, make fun of, opprobriate, revile, speak ill of, vilify; SEE CONCEPTS 52,54

run-down [adj] *shabby, in bad shape*
abandoned, beat-up, below par, broken-down, crumbling, debilitated, decrepit, derelict, deserted, desolate, dilapidated, dingy, dog-eared*, down-at-the-heel*, drained, enervated, exhausted, fatigued, forsaken, frowzy*, in a bad way*, neglected, old, out of condition, peaked, ramshackle, ratty*, rickety, seedy, shabby, tacky, tattered*, tired, tumble-down, uncared-for, under the weather*, unhealthy, untended, used up, weak, weary, worn-out; SEE CONCEPTS 314,485,570

rung [n] *notch, step*
bar, board, crossbar, crosspiece, degree, grade, level, rod, round, rundle, stage, tread; SEE CONCEPTS 471,744

run in [v] *arrest*
apprehend, bust, collar, cop*, detain, handcuff, jail, nab, pick up, pinch*, pull in, put the cuffs on*, take into custody, throw in jail*; SEE CONCEPTS 298,317

run-in [n] *argument*
altercation, bickering, brush, confrontation, contretemps, dispute, encounter, falling-out*, fight, hassle, quarrel, row, set-to*, skirmish, tussle; SEE CONCEPTS 46,106

running [n] *management of organization*
administration, care, charge, conduct, control, coordination, direction, functioning, handling, intendance, leadership, maintenance, operation, organization, oversight, performance, regulation, superintendency, supervision, working; SEE CONCEPT 117

running [adj] *continuous, flowing, operating*
active, alive, constant, cursive, dynamic, easy, effortless, executing, fluent, functioning, going, in action, incessant, in operation, in succession, live, moving, operative, perpetual, proceeding, producing, smooth, together, unbroken, unceasing, uninterrupted, working; SEE CONCEPTS 538,560,584

running [adv] *continually*
consecutively, continuously, night and day*, successively, together, unintermittedly, uninterruptedly; SEE CONCEPTS 482,798

run out [v] *fail, be exhausted*
be cleaned out*, be out of, cease, close, come to a close, depart, dissipate, dry up, end, exhaust, expire, finish, give out, go, have no more, have none left, lose, peter out*, stop, terminate, tire, waste, waste away, weaken, wear out; SEE CONCEPTS 105,699

runt [n] *very small person*
half-pint*, homunculus, Lilliputian, midget, peewee*, punk*, shrimp*; SEE CONCEPT 424

run through [v] *use up; waste*
blow, consume, dissipate, exhaust, expend, finish, fritter away, lose, spend, squander, throw away, wash up; SEE CONCEPT 156

rupture [n1] *break, split*
breach, burst, cleavage, cleft, crack, division, fissure, fracture, hernia, herniation, parting, rent, schism, tear; SEE CONCEPTS 309,513

rupture [n2] *disagreement, dissolution*
altercation, breach, break, break-up, bust-up*, clash, contention, detachment, disruption, disunion, division, divorce, divorcement, estrangement, falling-out, feud, hostility, misunderstanding, parting, partition, quarrel, rift, schism, separation, split, split-up*; SEE CONCEPTS 46,388

rupture [v1] *break open*
breach, burst, cleave, crack, disrupt, divide, erupt, fracture, hold, open, part, puncture, rend, rive, separate, sever, shatter, split, sunder, tear; SEE CONCEPTS 98,246,308

rupture [v2] *disagree; dissolve union*
break off, break up, come between, disjoin, disrupt, dissect, dissever, disunite, divide, divorce, part, separate, split, split up, sunder; SEE CONCEPTS 297,384

rural [adj] *country, not urban*
agrarian, agricultural, agronomic, Arcadian, backwoods, bucolic, countrified, farm, georgic, idyllic, natural, outland, pastoral, provincial, ranch, rustic, rustical, simple, sylvan, unsophisticated; SEE CONCEPT 583

ruse [n] *trick, deception*
angle, artifice, blind, booby trap*, curveball*, deceit, device, dodge, feint, gambit, game, game plan*, gimmick, hoax, imposture, jig*, maneuver, ploy, scenario, sham, shenanigans*, shift, stratagem, stunt, subterfuge, switch*, twist*, wile; SEE CONCEPTS 59,674

rush [n1] *hurry, speed*
blitz, charge, dash, dispatch, expedition, flood, flow, flux, haste, hastiness, hurriedness, precipitance, precipitancy, precipitation, race, scramble, stream, surge, swiftness, urgency; SEE CONCEPTS 145,748,818

rush [n2] *attack*
assault, blitz, charge, onslaught, push, storm, surge, violence; SEE CONCEPT 86

rush [v1] *hurry, speed*
accelerate, barrel, bolt, break, career, charge, chase, course, dart, dash, dispatch, expedite, fire up*, fleet, fling, flit, fly, get cracking*, get the lead out*, go like lightning*, haste, hasten, hotfoot*, hurry up, hustle, lose no time*, make haste, make short work of*, press, push, quicken, race, roll, run, scramble, scud, scurry, shake a leg*, shoot, speed up, sprint, step on gas*, streak, surge, tear, whiz*, zip*, zoom*; SEE CONCEPTS 91,150,152

rush [v2] *charge, attack*
capture, overcome, storm, surge, take by storm*; SEE CONCEPT 86

rust [n] *corrosion*
blight, corruption, decay, decomposition, dilapidation, mold, oxidation, rot, wear; SEE CONCEPTS 309,720

ru
ru

rust [v] *corrode*
decay, decline, degenerate, deteriorate, oxidize, stale, tarnish, wither; SEE CONCEPT 469

rustic [n] *person from the country, with little experience*
backwoodsperson, boor, country cousin*, countryperson, farmer, hayseed*, hick*, hillbilly, mountaineer, peasant, provincial, redneck*, rural, yokel*; SEE CONCEPT 413

rustic [adj1] *country, rural*
agrarian, agricultural, Arcadian, artless, austere, bucolic, countrified, homely, homespun, homey, honest, natural, outland, pastoral, picturesque, plain, primitive, provincial, simple, sylvan, unaffected, unpolished, unrefined, unsophisticated, verdant; SEE CONCEPTS 583,589

rustic [adj2] *crude, uncouth*
awkward, boorish, churlish, clodhopping, clownish, coarse, countrified, dull, foolish, graceless, ignorant, inelegant, loutish, maladroit, rough, rude, stupid, uncultured, uneducated, ungainly, unmannerly, unpolished, unsophisticated; SEE CONCEPT 401

rustle [n] *whisper, swish*
crackle, crepitation, crinkling, friction, noise, patter, ripple, rustling, sound, stir; SEE CONCEPT 595

rustle [v] *swish, whisper*
crackle, crepitate, crinkle, hum, murmur, patter, sigh, stir, tap, whir, whish, whoosh; SEE CONCEPT 65

rusty [adj1] *corroded*
decayed, oxidized, rust-covered, rusted; SEE CONCEPT 485

rusty [adj2] *out of practice; inexperienced*
deficient, impaired, neglected, not what it was*, sluggish, soft, stale, unpracticed, unqualified, weak; SEE CONCEPT 527

rut [n1] *groove, indentation*
furrow, gouge, hollow, pothole, rabbet, score, track, trench, trough; SEE CONCEPT 513

rut [n2] *routine of daily life*
circle, circuit, course, custom, daily grind*, dead end*, grind*, groove, habit, humdrum*, pace, pattern, performance, practice, procedure, rote, round, system, treadmill, usage, wont; SEE CONCEPTS 6,647

ruthless [adj] *mean, heartless*
adamant, barbarous, brutal, callous, cold, cold-blooded, cruel, cutthroat, dog-eat-dog*, feral, ferocious, fierce, grim, hard, hard-hearted, harsh, implacable, inexorable, inhuman, ironfisted, killer, malevolent, merciless, mortal, obdurate, pitiless, rancorous, relentless, remorseless, revengeful, sadistic, savage, severe, stern, stony, surly, unappeasable, unfeeling, unforgiving, unmerciful, unrelenting, unsympathetic, unyielding, vicious, vindictive, without pity; SEE CONCEPTS 401,404

S

sable [adj] *very dark in color*
black, dark, dusky, dusty, ebon, ebony, gloomy, inky, jet, jetty, murky, pitch-black, pitch-dark, raven, somber; SEE CONCEPT 618

sabotage [n] *damage*
demolition, destruction, disruption, impairment, injury, mischief, overthrow, subversion, subversiveness, treachery, treason, undermining, vandalism, wreckage, wrecking; SEE CONCEPTS 86,246,252

sabotage [v] *incapacitate, damage*
attack, block, bollix, break up, cripple, deep six*, destroy, disable, disrupt, do*, do in*, foul up*, frustrate, hamper, hinder, louse up*, mess up*, obstruct, put out of action, put out of commission*, screw up*, subvert, take out*, throw a monkey wrench into*, torpedo*, undermine, vandalize, wreck; SEE CONCEPTS 86,246,252

sack [v1] *remove from position of responsibility*
ax*, bounce*, can*, cashier, discharge, dismiss, drop, expel, fire, give a pink slip*, give marching orders*, give the boot*, kick out, send packing*, ship, terminate; SEE CONCEPT 351

sack [v2] *raid, plunder*
demolish, depredate, desecrate, desolate, despoil, destroy, devastate, devour, fleece, gut, lay waste, loot, maraud, pillage, ravage, rifle, rob, ruin, spoil, spoliate, strip, waste; SEE CONCEPTS 139,252

sacred [adj1] *holy, blessed*
angelic, cherished, consecrated, divine, enshrined, godly, hallowed, numinous, pious, pure, religious, revered, sacramental, saintly, sanctified, solemn, spiritual, unprofane, venerable; SEE CONCEPT 574

sacred [adj2] *protected*
dedicated, defended, guarded, immune, inviolable, inviolate, invulnerable, sacrosanct, secure, shielded, untouchable; SEE CONCEPT 587

sacrifice [v] *give up, let go*
cede, drop, endure, eschew, forfeit, forgo, immolate, kiss goodbye*, lose, offer, offer up, part with, renounce, resign oneself to, spare, suffer, surrender, waive, yield; SEE CONCEPTS 108,116

sacrilege [n] *irreverence*
blasphemy, crime, curse, desecration, heresy, impiety, mockery, offense, profanation, profaneness, profanity, sin, violation; SEE CONCEPT 645

sad [adj1] *unhappy, depressed*
bereaved, bitter, blue*, cheerless, dejected, despairing, despondent, disconsolate, dismal, distressed, doleful, down, downcast, down in dumps*, down in mouth*, forlorn, gloomy, glum, grief-stricken, grieved, heartbroken, heartsick, heavyhearted, hurting, in doldrums*, in grief, in the dumps*, languishing, low, low-spirited, lugubrious, melancholy, morbid, morose, mournful, out of sorts*, pensive, pessimistic, sick at heart*, somber, sorrowful, sorry, troubled, weeping, wistful, woebegone; SEE CONCEPT 403

sad [adj2] *unfortunate, distressing*
bad, calamitous, dark, dejecting, deplorable, depressing, disastrous, discomposing, discouraging, disheartening, dismal, dispiriting, dreary, funereal, grave, grievous, hapless, heart-rending, joyless, lachrymose, lamentable, lugubrious, melancholic, miserable, moving, oppressive, pathetic, pitiable, pitiful, poignant, regrettable, saddening, serious, shabby, sorry, tearful, tearjerking*, tragic, unhappy, unsatisfactory, upsetting, wretched; SEE CONCEPTS 529,548

sadden [v] *upset, depress*
break one's heart*, bring one down*, bum out*, cast down, dampen spirits, dash, deject, deplore,

desolate, discourage, dishearten, dispirit, distress, down, drag down*, grieve, make blue*, oppress, press, put a damper on*, put into a funk*, throw cold water on*, turn one off*, weigh down*; SEE CONCEPTS 7,19

sadistic [adj] *cruel, perverted*
barbarous, brutal, fiendish, perverse, ruthless, vicious; SEE CONCEPTS 542,545

sadness [n] *unhappiness, depression*
anguish, blahs*, bleakness, blue devils*, blue funk*, broken heart*, bummer, cheerlessness, dejection, despondency, disconsolateness, dismals*, dispiritedness, distress, dolefulness, dolor, downcastness, downer*, dysphoria, forlornness, funk, gloominess, grief, grieving, heartache, heartbreak, heavy heart*, hopelessness, letdown, listlessness, melancholy, misery, moodiness, mopes*, mournfulness, mourning, poignancy, sorrow, sorrowfulness, the blues*, the dumps*, tribulation, woe; SEE CONCEPT 410

safe [adj1] *free from harm*
buttoned up*, cherished, free from danger, guarded, home-free*, impervious, impregnable, in safety, intact, inviolable, invulnerable, maintained, okay*, out of danger, out of harm's way*, preserved, protected, safe and sound*, safeguarded, secure, sheltered, shielded, sitting pretty*, snug, tended, unassailable, undamaged, under lock and key*, under one's wing*, unharmed, unhurt, uninjured, unmolested, unscathed, unthreatened, vindicated, watched; SEE CONCEPT 587

safe [adj2] *not dangerous*
certain, checked, clear, competent, decontaminated, dependable, harmless, healthy, innocent, innocuous, innoxious, inoffensive, neutralized, nonpoisonous, nontoxic, pure, reliable, risk-free, riskless, secure, sound, tame, trustworthy, uninjurious, unpolluted, wholesome; SEE CONCEPTS 314,537,548

safe [adj3] *cautious, conservative*
calculating, careful, chary, circumspect, competent, considerate, dependable, discreet, gingerly, guarded, on safe side*, prudent, realistic, reliable, sure, tried and true*, trustworthy, unadventurous, wary; SEE CONCEPTS 401,542

safeguard [n] *protection*
aegis, armament, armor, buffer, bulwark, convoy, defense, escort, guard, screen, security, shield, surety, ward; SEE CONCEPT 712

safeguard [v] *protect*
assure, bulwark, conserve, cover, defend, ensure, fend, guard, insure, look after, preserve, ride shotgun*, save, screen, secure, shield, watch over; SEE CONCEPT 96

safety [n] *protection from harm*
assurance, asylum, cover, defense, freedom, immunity, impregnability, inviolability, invulnerability, refuge, safeness, sanctuary, security, shelter; SEE CONCEPT 729

safety net [n] *level of economic security guaranteed by government*
benefits, buffer, government aid, insurance, precaution, protective umbrella, safeguard, subsidy; SEE CONCEPT 344

sag [n] *drop, decline*
basin, cant, concavity, depression, dip, distortion, downslide*, downswing*, downtrend, downturn, droop, fall, fall-off, hollow, list, settling, sink,

sinkage, sinkhole, sinking, slant, slip, slump, tilt; SEE CONCEPTS 181,698,776

sag [v] *droop*
bag, bend, bow, bulge, cave in, curve, dangle, decline, dip, droop, drop off, fail, fall, fall away, fall off, flag, flap, flop, give way, hang, hang down, languish, lean, settle, sink, slide, slip, slump, swag, wilt; SEE CONCEPTS 181,698,776

saga [n] *story, often long*
adventure, chronicle, epic, legend, narrative, soap opera*, tale, yarn; SEE CONCEPT 282

sagacious [adj] *smart, judicious*
acute, apt, astucious, astute, cagey, canny, clear-sighted, clever, cool*, discerning, discriminating, far-sighted, foxy*, gnostic, heady, hip*, insightful, intelligent, keen, knowing, knowledgeable, perceptive, perspicacious, prudent, rational, sage, sapient, savvy*, sensible, sharp, shrewd, smooth, sophic, wise, witty; SEE CONCEPT 402

sail [v] *travel through water, air; glide*
boat, captain, cast anchor, cast off, cross, cruise, dart, drift, embark, flit, float, fly, get under way*, leave, make headway, motor, move, navigate, pilot, put to sea*, reach, run, scud, set sail, shoot, skim, skipper, skirr, soar, steer, sweep, tack, voyage, weigh anchor, wing; SEE CONCEPT 224

sailboat [n] *a boat propelled with wind by sailcloth*
bark, brig, brigantine, catamaran, craft, cutter, dory, gaff-rigged sailboat, galleon, galley, jack, ketch, pinnace, ragboat*, schooner, ship, skiff, sloop, Sunfish, tall ship, windjammer, wooden boat, yacht, yawl; SEE CONCEPT 506

sailor [n] *person who travels by sea*
able-bodied sailor, bluejacket*, boater, cadet, circumnavigator, deck hand, diver, hearty*, jack*, lascar*, marine, mariner, mate, middy, midshipman/woman, navigator, old salt*, pilot, pirate, salt*, sea dog*, seafarer, sea person, shellback*, shipmate, swab, swabber*, swabbie*, tar*, tarpaulin*, water dog*, windjammer*, yachter; SEE CONCEPTS 348,358,366

saintly [adj] *good, righteous*
angelic, beatific, blameless, blessed, devout, divine, god-fearing, godly, holy, pious, pure, religious, sainted, saintlike, seraph, sinless, upright, upstanding, virtuous, worthy; SEE CONCEPT 404

sake [n1] *benefit, gain*
account, advantage, behalf, consideration, good, interest, profit, regard, respect, welfare, well-being; SEE CONCEPT 693

sake [n2] *reason, objective*
aim, cause, consequence, end, final cause, motive, principle, purpose, score; SEE CONCEPTS 659,661

salary [n] *money paid for work done*
bacon*, bread*, earnings, emolument, fee, hire, income, pay, payroll, recompense, remuneration, scale, stipend, take, take-home*, wage, wages; SEE CONCEPT 344

sale [n] *exchange of object for money*
auction, barter, business, buying, clearance, closeout, commerce, consuming, deal, demand, disposal, dumping, enterprise, marketing, negotiation, purchase, purchasing, reduction, selling, trade, transaction, unloading, vending, vendition; SEE CONCEPTS 324,345

salient [adj] *noticeable, important*
arresting, arrestive, conspicuous, famous, impressive, intrusive, jutting, marked, moving, notable, obtrusive, obvious, outstanding, pertinent, pro-

jecting, prominent, pronounced, protruding, remarkable, signal, significant, striking, weighty; SEE CONCEPT 567

sallow [adj] *pale, unhealthy*
anemic, ashen, ashy, bilious, colorless, dull, greenish-yellow, jaundiced, muddy, pallid, pasty, wan, waxy, yellowish; SEE CONCEPT 618

saloon [n] *business establishment that primarily serves liquor*
alehouse, bar, barroom, beer joint*, cocktail lounge, dive*, drinkery, gin mill*, hangout*, joint*, night club, pub, public house, speakeasy, taproom, tavern, watering hole*; SEE CONCEPTS 439,448,449

salt away [v] *save, store up*
accumulate, amass, bank, cache, hide, hoard, invest, lay aside, lay away, put away, put by, put in the bank, save, save for rainy day*, set aside, spare, stash, stockpile; SEE CONCEPT 330

salty [adj1] *flavored with sodium chloride*
acrid, alkaline, brackish, briny, highly flavored, oversalted, pungent, saliferous, saline, salt, salted, saltish, sour; SEE CONCEPTS 462,613

salty [adj2] *spicy, colorful*
humorous, lively, piquant, pungent, racy, sharp, snappy, tangy, tart, witty, zestful; SEE CONCEPTS 401,589

salubrious [adj] *health-giving*
beneficial, good, healthful, healthy, hygienic, invigorating, salutary, sanitary, wholesome; SEE CONCEPTS 560,572

salute/salutation [n] *greeting, recognition*
address, bow, howdy*, kiss, obeisance, tribute, welcome; SEE CONCEPT 38

salute [v] *greet; honor*
accost, acknowledge, address, bow, call to, congratulate, hail, pay homage, pay respects, pay tribute, present arms, receive, recognize, snap to attention*, speak, take hat off to*, welcome; SEE CONCEPTS 38,69,320

salvage [v] *save, rescue*
deliver, get back, glean, ransom, reclaim, recover, redeem, regain, restore, retrieve, salve; SEE CONCEPT 134

salvation [n] *rescue, saving*
conservancy, conservation, deliverance, emancipation, escape, exemption, extrication, keeping, liberation, lifeline, pardon, preserval, preservation, redemption, release, reprieve, restoration, safekeeping, sustentation; SEE CONCEPT 134

salve [n] *ointment for relief of pain or illness*
aid, balm, cerate, counterirritant, cream, cure, dressing, emollient, help, liniment, lotion, lubricant, medication, medicine, remedy, unction, unguent; SEE CONCEPTS 311,466

same [adj1] *alike, identical*
aforementioned, aforesaid, carbon*, carbon-copy*, clone, coequal, comparable, compatible, corresponding, ditto*, double, dupe*, duplicate, equal, equivalent, indistinguishable, interchangeable, in the same manner, like, likewise, look-alike, related, same difference, selfsame, similar, similarly, synonymous, tantamount, twin, very, Xerox*; SEE CONCEPTS 487,566,573

same [adj2] *unchanging*
changeless, consistent, constant, invariable, perpetual, unaltered, unchanged, unfailing, uniform, unvarying; SEE CONCEPT 534

sameness [n] *likeness, similarity*
adequation, alikeness, analogy, equality, equivalency, identicalness, identity, indistinguishability, monotony, no difference, oneness, par, parity, predictability, repetition, resemblance, selfsameness, standardization, tedium, uniformity, union, unity, unvariedness; SEE CONCEPTS 667,670

sample [n] *example, model*
bit, bite, case, case history, constituent, cross section, element, exemplification, fragment, illustration, indication, individual, instance, morsel, part, pattern, piece, portion, representative, sampling, segment, sign, specimen, typification, unit; SEE CONCEPTS 686,835

sample [v] *taste, try*
examine, experience, experiment, inspect, partake, savor, sip, test; SEE CONCEPTS 103,616

sanctify [v] *hold in highest esteem*
absolve, anoint, bless, cleanse, consecrate, dedicate, deify, enshrine, glorify, hallow, purify, set apart, worship; SEE CONCEPTS 10,12

sanctimonious [adj] *self-righteous*
bigoted, canting, deceiving, false, goody-goody*, holier-than-thou*, hypocritical, insincere, pharisaical, pietistic, pious, preachy, self-satisfied, smug, stuffy, unctuous; SEE CONCEPTS 401,404

sanction [n1] *authorization*
acquiescence, allowance, approbation, approval, assent, authority, backing, confirmation, consent, countenance, encouragement, endorsement, fiat, go-ahead*, green light*, leave, nod, okay*, permission, permit, ratification, recommendation, seal of approval*, stamp of approval*, sufferance, support, word; SEE CONCEPT 685

sanction [n2] *embargo, punishment*
ban, boycott, coercive measure, command, decree, injunction, penalty, punitive measure, sentence, writ; SEE CONCEPT 123

sanction [v] *authorize, confirm*
accredit, allow, approve, back, bless, certify, commission, countenance, empower, endorse, get behind*, give the go-ahead*, give the green light*, give the nod*, go for*, license, okay*, permit, ratify, support, vouch for, warrant; SEE CONCEPTS 50,88

sanctuary [n1] *church; holiest room or area in religious building*
altar, chancel, holy place, sanctorium, sanctum, shrine, temple; SEE CONCEPTS 368,439,448

sanctuary [n2] *place to hide, be safe*
asylum, church, convent, cover, covert, defense, den, harbor, harborage, haven, hideaway, hideout, hole, hole-up*, ivory tower*, oasis, port, protection, refuge, resort, retreat, safe house, screen, shelter, shield; SEE CONCEPTS 515,516

sanctuary [n3] *safe place for wildlife*
asylum, conservation area, game refuge, harborage, national park, nature reserve, park, preserve, refuge, reserve, retreat, shelter; SEE CONCEPT 517

sane [adj] *mentally sound; reasonable*
all there*, balanced, both oars in water*, commonsensical, compos mentis, discerning, fair-minded, fit, having all marbles*, healthy, in one's right mind*, intelligent, judicious, levelheaded, logical, lucid, moderate, normal, of sound mind, oriented, playing with full deck*, prudent, rational, right, right-minded, sagacious, sage, sapient, self-possessed, sensible, sober, sound, steady, together*, well, wise; SEE CONCEPTS 314,402,403

sanguine [adj1] *happy; optimistic*
animated, assured, buoyant, cheerful, confident,

enthusiastic, expectant, hopeful, lively, positive, secure, self-assured, self-confident, spirited, undoubtful, upbeat; SEE CONCEPTS *403,542*

sanguine [*adj2*] *reddish; flushed*
bloody, florid, flush, glowing, red, rubicund, ruddy, scarlet; SEE CONCEPT *618*

sanitary [*adj*] *clean, germ-free*
healthful, healthy, hygienic, prophylactic, purified, salubrious, sanative, sterile, uncontaminated, uninfected, unpolluted, unsullied, wholesome; SEE CONCEPT *621*

sanity [*n*] *mental health; soundness of judgment*
acumen, balance, clear mind, common sense, comprehension, good judgment, healthy mind, intelligence, judiciousness, levelheadedness, lucidity, lucidness, marbles*, normality, prudence, rationality, reason, reasonableness, right mind*, sagacity, saneness, sense, sound mind, soundness, stability, understanding, wit; SEE CONCEPTS *409,410*

sap [*n*] *stupid person*
chump, dolt, dupe, fool, idiot, jerk, nitwit, patsy*, pigeon*, simpleton, sucker*, weakling; SEE CONCEPT *412*

sap [*v*] *squeeze out; weaken*
attenuate, bleed, blunt, cripple, debilitate, deplete, destroy, devitalize, disable, drain, enervate, enfeeble, erode, exhaust, impair, prostrate, rob, ruin, subvert, undermine, vitiate, wear down, wreck; SEE CONCEPTS *142,156,240,246*

sappy [*adj*] *foolish, sentimental*
absurd, balmy, bathetic, crazy*, drippy*, idiotic, illogical, insane, loony*, maudlin, mushy*, preposterous, silly, slushy*, soppy*, sticky*, stupid; SEE CONCEPTS *403,542*

sarcasm [*n*] *mocking remark*
acrimony, aspersion, banter, bitterness, burlesque, causticness, censure, comeback, contempt, corrosiveness, criticism, cut*, cynicism, derision, dig*, disparagement, flouting, invective, irony, lampooning, mockery, mordancy, putdown*, raillery, rancor, ridicule, satire, scoffing, scorn, sharpness, sneering, superciliousness, wisecrack; SEE CONCEPTS *52,54,277,278*

sarcastic [*adj*] *nasty, mocking in speech*
acerb, acerbic, acid, acrimonious, arrogant, austere, backhanded, biting, bitter, brusque, captious, carping, caustic, chaffing, contemptuous, contumelious, corrosive, cussed*, cutting, cynical, derisive, disillusioned, disparaging, disrespectful, evil, hostile, irascible, ironical, mean, mordant, needling, offensive, ornery*, salty, sardonic, satirical, saucy*, scorching, scornful, scurrilous, severe, sharp, smart-alecky*, snarling, sneering, taunting, trenchant, twitting, weisenheiming*; SEE CONCEPT *267*

satiate [*v*] *stuff, satisfy completely or excessively*
cloy, content, feed to gills*, fill, glut, gorge, gratify, indulge, jade, nauseate, overdose, overfill, pall, sate, saturate, slake, surfeit; SEE CONCEPTS *169,740*

satire [*n*] *ridicule intended to expose truth*
banter, burlesque, caricature, causticity, chaffing, irony, lampoon, lampoonery, mockery, parody, pasquinade, persiflage, play-on, put-on*, raillery, sarcasm, send-up*, skit, spoof, squib*, takeoff*, travesty, wit, witticism; SEE CONCEPTS *263,271,280*

satirical/satiric [*adj*] *mocking*
abusive, bantering, biting, bitter, burlesque, caus-

tic, censorious, chaffing, cutting, cynical, farcical, incisive, ironical, lampooning, mordant, paradoxical, parodying, pungent, ridiculing, sarcastic, sardonic, spoofing, taunting; SEE CONCEPT *267*

satisfaction [*n*] *giving or enjoying a state of comfort, content*
achievement, amends, amusement, atonement, bliss, cheerfulness, comfort, compensation, complacency, conciliation, contentedness, contentment, delight, ease, enjoyment, fulfillment, gladness, good fortune, gratification, happiness, indemnification, indulgence, joy, justice, peace of mind, pleasure, pride, propitiation, recompense, redress, refreshment, reimbursement, relief, reparation, repletion, resolution, reward, satiety, serenity, settlement, vindication, well-being; SEE CONCEPTS *344,410,720*

satisfactory [*adj*] *acceptable, sufficient*
adequate, all right, ample, A-OK*, appeasing, assuaging, assuasive, average, cogent, comfortable, competent, cool*, decent, delighting, enough, fair, fulfilling, good, good enough, gratifying, groovy*, passable, peachy*, pleasing, satisfying, solid, sound, sufficing, suitable, tolerable, unexceptional, up to snuff*, valid; SEE CONCEPTS *529,558,560*

satisfy [*v1*] *please, content*
amuse, animate, appease, assuage, befriend, brighten up, captivate, capture, cheer, cloy, comfort, conciliate, content, delight, do the trick*, elate, enliven, entertain, enthrall, exhilarate, fascinate, fill, fill the bill*, flatter, get by, gladden, glut, gorge, gratify, hit the spot*, humor, indulge, make merry, make the grade*, mollify, pacify, placate, propitiate, quench, rejoice, sate, satiate, score, sell, sell on, slake, suit, surfeit; SEE CONCEPTS *7,22*

satisfy [*v2*] *answer, persuade*
accomplish, appease, assuage, assure, avail, be adequate, be enough, be sufficient, come up to, complete, comply with, conform to, convince, dispel doubt, do, equip, fill, fulfill, furnish, get by, induce, inveigle, keep promise, make good, make the grade*, meet, observe, pass muster*, perform, provide, put mind at ease*, qualify, quiet, reassure, score, sell, serve, serve the purpose*, suffice, tide over*, win over; SEE CONCEPTS *108,140,656*

satisfy [*v3*] *pay, compensate*
answer, atone, clear up, disburse, discharge, indemnify, liquidate, make good*, make reparation, meet, pay off, quit, recompense, remunerate, repay, requite, reward, settle, square*; SEE CONCEPTS *126,341*

saturate [*v*] *drench, wet through*
bathe, douche, douse, imbue, immerse, impregnate, infuse, overfill, penetrate, percolate, permeate, pervade, sate, satiate, soak, sop, souse, steep, suffuse, transfuse, wash, waterlog; SEE CONCEPT *256*

saucy [*adj*] *disrespectful*
arch, audacious, bold, brash, brazen, cheeky*, combative, contumelious, flip*, flippant, forward, fresh, impertinent, impudent, insolent, intrusive, meddlesome, nervy, obtrusive, pert, presumptuous, rude, sassy, smart, smart-alecky*, smug, snippy*, volatile, weisenheiming*, wise; SEE CONCEPTS *267,401*

sa
sa

saunter [n] *stroll*
airing, amble, constitutional, promenade, ramble, turn, walk; SEE CONCEPT 151

saunter [v] *stroll along*
amble, ankle, dally, drift, linger, loiter, meander, mope*, mosey*, ooze*, percolate, promenade, ramble, roam, rove, sashay, stump, tarry, toddle, traipse, trill, wander; SEE CONCEPT 151

savage [adj] *wild, untamed*
aboriginal, ancient, archaic, barbarian, barbaric, bestial, brutal, brute, crude, earliest, feral, ferocious, fierce, first, fundamental, harsh, in a state of nature, lupine, native, natural, nonliterate, original, primary, primeval, primitive, primordial, pristine, rough, rude, rugged, rustic, simple, turbulent, unbroken, uncivilized, uncultivated, uncultured, undomesticated, unmodified, unrestrained, unspoiled, vicious; SEE CONCEPTS 401,485

savage [adj2] *cruel, vicious*
atrocious, barbarous, beastly, bestial, bloodthirsty, bloody, brutal, brutish, cold-blooded, crazed, demoniac, destructive, devilish, diabolical, fell, feral, ferine, ferocious, fierce, frantic, furious, grim, harsh, heartless, hellish, infernal, inhuman, inhumane, malevolent, malicious, merciless, murderous, pitiless, rabid, raging, rapacious, ravening, relentless, remorseless, ruthless, sadistic, truculent, unrelenting, violent, wolfish; SEE CONCEPTS 401,540,542

save [v1] *rescue*
bail out, come to rescue, defend, deliver, emancipate, extricate, free, get off the hook*, get out of hock*, give a break, liberate, pull out of fire*, ransom, recover, redeem, salvage, save one's neck*, set free, spring, unchain, unshackle; SEE CONCEPTS 127,134

save [v2] *economize; set money aside for later use*
amass, be frugal, be thrifty, cache, collect, conserve, cut corners*, deposit, economize, feather nest*, gather, hide away, hoard, hold, keep, lay aside, lay away, maintain, make ends meet*, manage, pile up, pinch pennies*, put by, reserve, retrench, roll back*, salt away*, save for rainy day*, scrimp, skimp, sock away*, spare, squirrel*, stash, stockpile, store, stow away, tighten belt*, treasure; SEE CONCEPTS 120,129,330

save [v3] *guard, protect*
conserve, defend, keep safe, keep up, look after, maintain, preserve, safeguard, screen, shield, sustain, take care of; SEE CONCEPTS 96,117

savings [n] *provision for future*
accumulation, ace in hole*, cache, fund, funds, gleanings, harvest, hoard, investment, kitty*, mattress full*, means, money in the bank, nest egg*, property, provision, provisions, rainy day fund*, reserve, reserves, resources, riches, sock, stake, stockpile, store; SEE CONCEPTS 335,340,446,710

savior [n] *person who redeems, aids in time of difficulty*
conservator, defender, deliverer, friend in need*, Good Samaritan*, guardian, guardian angel, hero, liberator, preserver, protector, rescuer, salvager, salvation; SEE CONCEPTS 370,416

savor [n1] *taste, flavor*
odor, piquancy, relish, salt, sapidity, sapor, scent, smack, smell, spice, tang, tinge, zest; SEE CONCEPT 614

savor [n2] *distinctive quality*
affection, attribute, character, characteristic, excitement, feature, flavor, interest, mark, property, salt, spice, trait, virtue, zest; SEE CONCEPTS 411,543

savor [v] *delight in, enjoy*
appreciate, experience, feel, gloat, know, like, luxuriate in, partake, relish, revel in, sample, sip, smack, smell, taste; SEE CONCEPTS 32,616

savory [adj] *pleasing, delicious in flavor*
agreeable, ambrosial, aperitive, appetizing, aromatic, dainty, decent, delectable, exquisite, fragrant, full-flavored, good, luscious, mellow, mouthwatering, palatable, perfumed, piquant, pungent, redolent, relishing, respectable, rich, sapid, savorous, scrumptious, spicy, sweet, tangy, tasty, tempting, toothsome, wholesome; SEE CONCEPT 613

say [v] *make declaration*
add, affirm, allege, announce, answer, assert, break silence*, claim, come out with, communicate, conjecture, convey, declare, deliver, disclose, divulge, do, estimate, express, flap*, gab*, give voice*, guess, imagine, imply, jaw, judge, lip*, maintain, make known, mention, opine, orate, perform, pronounce, put forth, put into words, rap*, read, recite, rehearse, relate, remark, render, repeat, reply, report, respond, reveal, rumor, speak, spiel*, state, suggest, tell, utter, verbalize, voice, yak*; SEE CONCEPTS 51,266

saying [n] *maxim, proverb*
adage, aphorism, apophthegm, axiom, byword, dictum, epigram, motto, precept, saw, statement, truism; SEE CONCEPT 278

scale [n1] *graduated system*
calibration, computation, degrees, extent, gamut, gradation, hierarchy, ladder, order, pecking order*, progression, proportion, range, ranking, rate, ratio, reach, register, rule, scope, sequence, series, spectrum, spread, steps, system, way; SEE CONCEPTS 651,744,770,788

scale [n2] *thin covering, skin*
film, flake, incrustation, lamina, layer, plate, scurf; SEE CONCEPTS 399,484

scale [v1] *ascend, climb*
clamber, escalade, escalate, go up, mount, surmount; SEE CONCEPT 166

scale [v2] *measure*
adjust, balance, calibrate, compare, compute, estimate, gauge, graduate, proportion, prorate, regulate, size; SEE CONCEPT 764

scamper [v] *run, dash*
bolt, dart, flee, fly, hasten, hie, hurry, light out, make off, race, romp, rush off, scoot, scurry, scuttle, shoot, skedaddle*, skip, speed, speed away, sprint, tear, trot, whip, zip*; SEE CONCEPT 150

scan [v] *look over, scrutinize lightly*
browse, check, consider, contemplate, dip into*, examine, flash*, flip through, give the once-over*, glance at, glance over, have a look-see*, inquire, investigate, leaf through*, look, look through, look up and down*, overlook, regard, riff, riffle, rumble, run over, run through, scour, search, size up, skim, study, survey, sweep, take a gander*, take stock of*, thumb through*; SEE CONCEPTS 103,623

scandal [n] *public embarrassment*
aspersion, backbiting, backstabbing, belittlement, calumny, crime, defamation, depreciation, detraction, dirty linen*, discredit, disgrace, dishonor,

disparagement, disrepute, dynamite, eavesdropping, gossip, hearsay, idle rumor, ignominy, infamy, mud, obloquy, opprobrium, reproach, rumor, scorcher, shame, sin, skeleton in closet*, slander, tale, talk, turpitude, wrongdoing; SEE CONCEPTS *278,645,674*

scandalous [*adj*] *disreputable*
atrocious, backbiting, calumnious, crying, defamatory, desperate, detracting, detractive, disgraceful, gossiping, heinous, ignominious, infamous, libelous, maligning, monstrous, odious, opprobrious, outrageous, red hot*, scurrilous, shameful, shocking, slanderous, traducing, unseemly, untrue, vilifying; SEE CONCEPT *545*

scant/scanty [*adj*] *inadequate*
bare, barely sufficient, close, deficient, exiguous, failing, insufficient, limited, little, meager, minimal, narrow, poor, rare, restricted, scrimpy, short, shy, skimpy, slender, spare, sparing, sparse, stingy, thin, tight, wanting; SEE CONCEPTS *766,767,789*

scapegoat [*n*] *person who takes blame for another's action*
dupe, goat*, mark*, patsy*, sacrifice, substitute, sucker, target, victim; SEE CONCEPT *412*

scar [*n*] *blemish from previous injury or illness*
blister, cacatrice, cicatrix, crater, defect, discoloration, disfigurement, flaw, hurt, mark, pockmark, scab, track, wound; SEE CONCEPT *580*

scar [*v*] *mark, hurt*
beat, blemish, brand, cut, damage, deface, disfigure, flaw, injure, maim, mar, pinch, score, scratch, slash, stab, traumatize; SEE CONCEPTS *7,19,137,176,246*

scarce [*adj*] *insufficient, infrequent*
at a premium, deficient, failing, few, few and far between*, in short supply, limited, occasional, rare, scant, scanty, seldom, seldom met with, semioccasional, short, shortened, shy, sparse, sporadic, truncated, uncommon, unusual, wanting; SEE CONCEPTS *541,789*

scarcely [*adv*] *barely*
hardly, imperceptibly, infrequently, just, just barely, only just, rarely, scantily, seldom, slightly; SEE CONCEPTS *541,789*

scare [*n*] *frightened state*
alarm, alert, fright, panic, shock, start, terror; SEE CONCEPTS *230,410*

scare [*v*] *frighten someone*
affright, alarm, awe, chill, daunt, dismay, freeze, give a fright, give a turn*, intimidate, panic, paralyze, petrify, scare silly*, scare stiff*, scare the pants off*, shake up*, shock, spook, startle, strike terror in, terrify, terrorize; SEE CONCEPTS *7,19,42*

scared [*adj*] *frightened*
afraid, aghast, anxious, fearful, having cold feet*, panicked, panicky, panic-stricken, petrified, shaken, startled, terrified, terror-stricken; SEE CONCEPT *403*

scary [*adj*] *frightening, terrifying*
alarming, bloodcurdling, chilling, creepy, eerie, hair-raising, hairy*, horrendous, horrifying, intimidating, shocking, spine-chilling, spooky, unnerving; SEE CONCEPTS *529,548*

scathing [*adj*] *nasty, critical in remarks*
belittling, biting, brutal, burning, caustic, cruel, cutting, harsh, mordacious, mordant, salty, sarcastic, scorching, scornful, searing, severe, sulphurous, trenchant, withering; SEE CONCEPT *267*

scatter [*v*] *strew, disperse*
besprinkle, broadcast, cast, derange, diffuse, disband, discard, disject, dispel, disseminate, dissipate, distribute, disunite, diverge, divide, expend, fling, intersperse, litter, migrate, part, pour, put to flight*, run away, scramble, separate, set, set asunder, sever, shatter, shed, shower, sow, spend, split up, spray, spread, sprinkle, sunder, take off in all directions*, throw around, throw out; SEE CONCEPTS *179,217,222*

scatterbrained [*adj*] *not thinking clearly*
birdbrained*, careless, dizzy, empty-headed*, featherbrained*, flighty, forgetful, frivolous, giddy, harebrained*, illogical, inattentive, irrational, irresponsible, madcap, silly, slaphappy*, stupid, thoughtless; SEE CONCEPT *402*

scenario [*n*] *master plan; sequence of events*
book, outline, pages, plot, résumé, rundown, scheme, sides, sketch, story line, summary, synopsis; SEE CONCEPTS *282,283,660*

scene [*n1*] *setting of a performance or event*
arena, backdrop, background, blackout, display, exhibition, flat, flats, landscape, locale, locality, location, mise en scène, outlook, pageant, picture, place, representation, scenery, seascape, set, setting, show, sight, site, spectacle, spot, stage, tableau, theater, view; SEE CONCEPTS *263,625,628*

scene [*n2*] *part of a dramatic performance*
act, bit, episode, incident, part, piece, routine, schtick, spot; SEE CONCEPT *264*

scene [*n3*] *display of emotion*
carrying-on*, commotion, confrontation, exhibition, fit, fuss, performance, row, tantrum, temper tantrum, to-do*, upset; SEE CONCEPT *633*

scene [*n4*] *field of interest*
arena, business, compass, culture, environment, field, milieu, setting, sphere, world; SEE CONCEPT *349*

scenery [*n*] *surroundings*
backdrop, decor, flat, flats, furnishings, furniture, landscape, mise en scène, neighborhood, properties, props, prospect, set, setting, spectacle, sphere, stage set, stage setting, terrain, view, vista; SEE CONCEPTS *263,628*

scenic [*adj*] *beautiful, picturesque*
breathtaking, dramatic, grand, impressive, panoramic, spectacular, striking; SEE CONCEPTS *485,579*

scent [*n*] *smell, aroma*
aura, balm, bouquet, essence, fragrance, incense, odor, perfume, redolence, spice, tang, track, trail, whiff; SEE CONCEPT *599*

scent [*v*] *detect, smell*
be on the track of*, be on the trail of*, discern, get wind of*, nose, nose out*, recognize, sense, sniff; SEE CONCEPTS *601,602*

schedule [*n*] *plan for one's time*
agenda, appointments, calendar, catalog, chart, diagram, docket, inventory, itinerary, lineup*, list, order of business, program, record, registry, roll, roster, sked*, table, timetable; SEE CONCEPTS *271,283,660*

schedule [*v*] *plan one's time*
appoint, arrange, be due, book, card, catalog, engage, get on line*, line up*, list, note, organize, pencil in*, program, record, register, reserve, set, set up, sew up*, slate, time, write in one's book*; SEE CONCEPTS *36,125*

sa
sc

scheme [n1] *course of action*
arrangement, blueprint, chart, codification, contrivance, design, device, diagram, disposition, draft, expedient, game plan, layout, order, ordering, outline, pattern, plan, presentation, program, project, proposal, proposition, purpose, schedule, schema, strategy, suggestion, system, tactics, theory; SEE CONCEPTS 271,625,660

scheme [n2] *plot, maneuver to get result*
action, angle*, brainchild*, cabal, conspiracy, covin, dodge*, frame-up*, game, game plan*, gimmick, hookup*, hustle, hype*, intrigue, layout, machination, picture*, pitch, ploy, practice, proposition, put-up job*, ruse, scenario, scene, setup*, shift*, story, stratagem, subterfuge, tactics, trick*, twist*; SEE CONCEPTS 59,645,660

scheming [adj] *deceitful, sly*
artful, calculating, conniving, crafty, cunning, designing, duplicitous, foxy, slippery, tricky, underhand, wily; SEE CONCEPT 542

scholar [n] *person who is very involved in education and learning*
academic, augur, bookish person, bookworm*, brain*, critic, disciple, doctor, egghead*, gnome*, grind*, intellectual, learned person, learner, litterateur, person of letters, philosopher, professor, pupil, sage, savant, schoolchild, scientist, student, teacher, tool, wise person; SEE CONCEPT 350

scholarly [adj] *academic*
bookish, cultured, educated, erudite, intellectual, learned, lettered, literate, longhair*, scholastic, schooled, studious, taught, trained, well-read; SEE CONCEPT 402

school [n1] *place, system for educating*
academy, alma mater, blackboard*, college, department, discipline, establishment, faculty, hall, halls of ivy*, institute, institution, jail*, schoolhouse, seminary, university; SEE CONCEPTS 287,289

school [n2] *persons receiving education*
academy, adherents, circle, class, clique, denomination, devotees, disciples, faction, followers, following, group, party, pupils, sect, set; SEE CONCEPTS 288,350

school [n3] *body of philosophy on subject*
belief, creed, faith, outlook, persuasion, school of thought, stamp*, way, way of life; SEE CONCEPTS 349,689

school [v] *teach*
advance, coach, control, cultivate, direct, discipline, drill, educate, guide, indoctrinate, inform, instruct, lead, manage, prepare, prime, show, train, tutor, verse; SEE CONCEPT 285

science [n] *methodical study of part of material world*
art, body of knowledge, branch, discipline, education, erudition, information, learning, lore, scholarship, skill, system, technique, wisdom; SEE CONCEPTS 274,349,360

scientific [adj] *systematic; discovered through experimentation*
accurate, clear, controlled, deductive, exact, experimental, logical, mathematical, methodical, objective, precise, sound; SEE CONCEPT 535

scintillating [adj] *bright, stimulating*
animated, brilliant, clever, dazzling, ebullient, exciting, flashing, gleaming, glimmering, glinting, glittering, lively, shining, smart, sparkling,

sprightly, twinkling, witty; SEE CONCEPTS 401,529,617

scion [n] *offshoot, descendant*
begotten, branch, brood, child, chip off old block*, graft, heir, heiress, issue, junior, offspring, progeny, seed, shoot, slip, sprout, successor, twig; SEE CONCEPTS 414,428

scoff [v] *make fun of; despise*
belittle, boo*, contemn, deride, dig at*, disbelieve, discount, discredit, disdain, flout, gibe, jeer, knock*, laugh at, make light of*, mock, pan*, poke fun at, pooh-pooh*, rag*, rally, reject, revile, ride, ridicule, scorn, show contempt, sneer, tease; SEE CONCEPT 54

scold [v] *find fault with*
abuse, admonish, asperse, berate, blame, castigate, cavil, censure, chasten, chide, criticize, denounce, disparage, dress down*, expostulate, give a talking-to*, jump on*, keep aft*, lay down the law*, lecture, light into*, nag, objurgate, preach, put down, rail, rake over the coals*, rate, ream, rebuke, recriminate, reprimand, reproach, reprobate, reprove, revail, take to task*, taunt, tell off*, upbraid, vilify, vituperate; SEE CONCEPTS 44,52,54

scoop [n1] *utensil, tool for shovelling*
bail, dipper, ladle, shovel, spade, spoon, trowel; SEE CONCEPTS 493,499

scoop [n2] *previously secret information that is suddenly public*
beat, exclusive, exposé, inside story*, news, revelation, sensation; SEE CONCEPT 274

scoop [v] *dig up; shovel*
bail, clear away, dig, dig out, dip, empty, excavate, gather, gouge, grub, hollow, lade, ladle, lift, pick up, remove, scrape, spade, sweep away, sweep up, take up; SEE CONCEPT 178

scope [n] *extent or range of something*
ambit, amplitude, area, breadth, capacity, compass, comprehensiveness, confines, elbow room*, extension, field, field of reference, freedom, fullness, latitude, leeway, margin, opportunity, orbit, outlook, play, purview, radius, reach, room, run, space, span, sphere, wideness; SEE CONCEPTS 651,739,788

scorch [v] *burn*
bake, blacken, blister, broil, char, cook, melt, parch, roast, scald, sear, seethe, shrivel, simmer, singe, stale, stew, swelter, wither; SEE CONCEPTS 249,255

score [n1] *total, points*
account, addition, aggregate, amount, average, count, final count, grade, mark, number, outcome, rate, reckoning, record, result, stock, sum, summary, summation, tab, tally; SEE CONCEPTS 364,784

score/scores [n2] *large group; a great number*
army, cloud, crowd, drove, flock, host, hundred, legion, lot, mass, million, multitude, myriad, rout, swarm, throng, very many; SEE CONCEPT 432

score [n3] *musical arrangement*
charts, composition, music, orchestration, transcript; SEE CONCEPT 262

score [n4] *obligation; account payable*
account, amount due, bill, charge, debt, grievance, grudge, injury, injustice, invoice, reckoning, statement, tab, tally, total; SEE CONCEPTS 332,645

score [v1] *achieve, succeed*
accomplish, amass, arrive, attain, chalk up*, connect, flourish, gain, gain advantage, get*, hit pay dirt*, impress, luck out*, make a killing*, make an impression*, make the grade*, notch, procure, prosper, pull off*, put over*, rack up*, reach, realize, secure, take the cake*, thrive, triumph, win; SEE CONCEPTS 704,706

score [v2] *keep count*
add, calculate, chalk up, count, enumerate, keep tally, rack up*, reckon, record, register, tally, total; SEE CONCEPTS 125,764

score [v3] *cut, nick*
cleave, crosshatch, deface, furrow, gash, gouge, graze, groove, indent, line, mark, mill, notch, scrape, scratch, serrate, slash, slit; SEE CONCEPTS 137,176

score [v4] *write a musical arrangement*
adapt, arrange, compose, orchestrate, set; SEE CONCEPTS 79,292

scorn [n] *contempt toward something*
contemptuousness, contumely, derision, despisal, despisement, despite, disdain, disparagement, disregard, jeering, mockery, ridicule, sarcasm, scoffing, scornfulness, slight, sneer, sport, taunting, teasing; SEE CONCEPTS 29,54

scorn [v] *hold in contempt; look down on*
abhor, avoid, be above, confute, consider beneath one*, contemn, defy, deride, despise, disdain, disregard, flout, gibe, hate, ignore, make fun of, mock, put down, refuse, refute, reject, renounce, repudiate, ridicule, run down*, scoff at, shun, slight, sneer, spurn, taunt, trash*, turn back on*, turn nose up at*; SEE CONCEPTS 21,30,52,54

scoundrel [n] *person who is deceptive and uncaring of others*
bad egg*, bad news*, blackguard*, black sheep*, caitiff, cheat, creep, crook, dastard, good-for-nothing*, heel, imp, incorrigible, lowlife*, maggot*, mischiefmaker, miscreant, ne'er-do-well*, rascal, reprobate, scalawag, scamp, thief, vagabond, villain, wretch; SEE CONCEPT 412

scour [v1] *clean, polish thoroughly*
abrade, brush, buff, burnish, cleanse, flush, furbish, mop, pumice, purge, rub, sand, scrub, wash, whiten; SEE CONCEPT 165

scour [v2] *search thoroughly*
beat, comb, ferret out, find, forage, go over with a fine-tooth comb*, grub, hunt, inquire, leave no stone unturned*, look for, look high and low*, look up and down*, rake, ransack, rout, rummage, seek, track down, turn inside out*, turn upside-down*; SEE CONCEPT 216

scourge [n] *plague, torment*
affliction, bane, correction, curse, infliction, misfortune, penalty, pest, pestilence, punishment, terror, visitation; SEE CONCEPTS 674,675

scourge [v] *beat, punish, often physically*
afflict, belt, cane*, castigate, chastise, curse, discipline, excoriate, flail, flog, harass, hit, horsewhip*, lambaste*, lash, penalize, plague, scathe, scorch*, tan*, terrorize, thrash, torment, trounce, wallop*, whale*, whip; SEE CONCEPTS 14,52,122,189

scout [n] *person who is searching, investigating*
advance, adventurer, detective, escort, explorer, guard, lookout, outpost, outrider, patrol, picket, pioneer, precursor, reconnoiterer, recruiter, runner, sleuth, spotter, spy, vanguard; SEE CONCEPTS 348,358

scout [v] *investigate, check out*
case, examine, explore, ferret, have a look-see*, hunt, inspect, look for, observe, probe, reconnoiter, run reconnaissance, rustle up*, search, seek, set eyes on*, spot, spy, stake out, survey, take in, track down, watch; SEE CONCEPTS 103,216,623

scowl [n] *frown*
black look*, dirty look*, evil eye*, glower, grimace; SEE CONCEPTS 185,716

scowl [v] *frown*
disapprove, glare, gloom, glower, grimace, look daggers at*, lour, lower, make a face*; SEE CONCEPT 185

scram [v] *leave quickly*
beat it*, clear out*, decamp, depart, disappear, get lost*, go away, hightail*, make oneself scarce*, make tracks*, scoot*, skedaddle*, take off, vamoose*; SEE CONCEPT 195

scramble [n] *mix-up, confusion*
clutter, commotion, competition, conglomeration, free-for-all*, hash*, hassle, hustle, jumble, jungle, litter, melee, mishmash, muddle, race, rat race*, rush, shuffle, struggle, tumble, tussle; SEE CONCEPTS 230,388,432

scramble [v] *race; get into position clumsily*
clamber, climb, contend, crawl, hasten, jockey for position*, jostle, look alive*, make haste, move, push, run, rush, scrabble, scurry, scuttle, strive, struggle, swarm, trek, vie; SEE CONCEPTS 87,150

scrap [n1] *tiny bit of something*
atom, bite, bits and pieces*, butt, castoff, chip, chunk, crumb, cutting, discard, end, fragment, glob, gob, grain, hunk, iota, jot, junk, leaving, leftover*, lump, mite, modicum, morsel, mouthful, odds and ends*, orts, pan, particle, piece, portion, remains, shred, slice, sliver, smithereen*, snatch, snippet, speck, stump, trace, waste; SEE CONCEPTS 831,835

scrap [n2] *argument, fight*
affray, battle, brawl, broil*, disagreement, dispute, tracas, fray, quarrel, row, scuffle, set-to*, squabble, tiff*, wrangle; SEE CONCEPTS 46,106

scrap [v1] *abandon; throw away*
abandon, break up, cast, chuck, consign to scrap heap*, demolish, discard, dismiss, dispense with, ditch, do away with*, drop, forsake, get rid of, jettison, junk, put out to pasture*, reject, retire, shed, slough, throw out, toss out, write off; SEE CONCEPTS 121,180

scrap [v2] *fight, argue*
battle, bicker, caterwaul, come to blows*, fall out, have shouting match*, have words*, quarrel, row, spat, squabble, tiff, wrangle; SEE CONCEPTS 46,106

scrape [n] *bad or embarrassing situation*
awkward situation, corner*, difficulty, dilemma, discomfiture, distress, embarrassment, fix*, hole*, jam*, mess*, pickle*, plight, predicament, tight spot*, trouble; SEE CONCEPT 674

scrape [v1] *scratch, remove outer layer*
abrade, bark, bray, chafe, clean, erase, file, grate, graze, grind, irritate, pare, peel, rasp, rub, scour, scuff, shave, skin, squeak, thin, triturate; SEE CONCEPTS 165,186,215

scrape [v2] *be very frugal*
cut it close*, get along, get by, pinch, save, scrimp, shave, skimp, stint, struggle; SEE CONCEPT 330

SC
SC

scratch [n] *small cut or mark*
blemish, claw mark, gash, graze, hurt, laceration, score, scrape; SEE CONCEPTS *309,513*

scratch [v1] *cut; make a mark on*
claw, damage, etch, grate, graze, incise, lacerate, mark, prick, rasp, rub, scarify, score, scrape, scrawl, scribble; SEE CONCEPTS *79,176*

scratch [v2] *cancel*
annul, delete, eliminate, erase, pull, pull out, strike, withdraw; SEE CONCEPT *121*

scrawl [v] *write erratically*
doodle, inscribe, scrabble, scratch, scribble, squiggle; SEE CONCEPT *79*

scrawny [adj] *unhealthily thin*
angular, bony, gaunt, lank, lanky, lean, raw-boned, scraggy, skeletal, skin-and-bones*, skinny, spare, undernourished, underweight; SEE CONCEPTS *490,491,773*

scream [n1] *outcry*
cry, high-pitched shout, holler*, howl, screech, shriek, wail, yell, yelp; SEE CONCEPT *595*

scream [n2] *person or thing that is very funny*
card*, character*, comedian, comedienne, comic, entertainer, guffaw*, hoot*, howl*, joker, laugh, panic*, riot, sensation, sidesplitter*, wit; SEE CONCEPTS *423,529*

scream [v] *cry out*
bawl, bellow, blare, caterwaul, holler*, howl, jar, roar, screak, screech, shout, shriek, shrill, sing out, squeal, voice, wail, yell, yip, yowl; SEE CONCEPT *77*

screen [n] *protection used in or as furniture, motion picture display*
awning, canopy, cloak, concealment, cover, covering, curtain, divider, envelope, guard, hedge, mantle, mask, net, partition, security, shade, shelter, shield, shroud, veil; SEE CONCEPTS *277,440,443,445,473*

screen [v1] *hide, protect*
adumbrate, blind, block out, bulwark, bury, cache, camouflage, cloak, close, conceal, cover, cover up, defend, disguise, ensconce, fend, guard, mask, obscure, obstruct, safeguard, seclude, secrete, secure, separate, shade, shadow, shelter, shield, shroud, shut off, shut out, shutter, stash, umbrage, veil, wall off; SEE CONCEPTS *96,188*

screen [v2] *examine and choose*
cull, eliminate, evaluate, extract, filter, gauge, grade, pick out, process, riddle, scan, select, separate, sieve, sift, sort, winnow; SEE CONCEPT *41*

screw [v1] *twist in*
spiral, tighten, turn, twine, wind, work; SEE CONCEPTS *85,160*

screw [v2] *twist, contort*
contract, crimp, crinkle, crumple, distort, pucker, rimple, ruck up, rumple, scrunch, wrinkle; SEE CONCEPT *219*

screw [v3] *pressure*
bilk, bleed, cheat, chisel, coerce, constrain, defraud, do*, exact, extort, extract, force, hold a knife to*, oppress, pinch*, pressurize, put screws to*, ream*, screw down*, squeeze, wrench, wrest, wring; SEE CONCEPTS *14,192*

screw up [v] *make a mess of*
blow, bobble, bollix*, botch, bungle, confuse, flub*, foul up, goof*, goof up*, louse, make hash of*, mess, mess up, mishandle, mismanage, muck up*, muddle, muff, queer, snafu*, spoil; SEE CONCEPT *101*

script [n1] *handwriting*
calligraphy, characters, chirography, fist, hand, letters, longhand, penmanship, writing; SEE CONCEPTS *79,284*

script [n2] *story for a performance*
article, book, copy, dialogue, libretto, lines, manuscript, playbook, scenario, text, typescript, words; SEE CONCEPTS *263,271*

scrounge [v] *beg, forage for*
bum, freeload, hunt, sponge, wheedle; SEE CONCEPTS *48,216*

scrub [v1] *clean with force*
abrade, brush, buff, cleanse, mop, polish, rub, scour, wash; SEE CONCEPT *165*

scrub [v2] *cancel*
abandon, abolish, abort, call off, delete, discontinue, do away with, drop, forget about, give up; SEE CONCEPTS *121,234*

scruffy [adj] *rough, bedraggled*
badly groomed, frowzy*, mangy*, messy, ragged, run-down, seedy, shabby, slovenly, tacky*, tattered, threadbare, ungroomed, unkempt, untidy; SEE CONCEPTS *485,589*

scrumptious [adj] *delicious*
ambrosial, appetizing, delectable, delightful, exquisite, heavenly, inviting, luscious, lush, magnificent, mouthwatering, rich, succulent, tasty, yummy; SEE CONCEPTS *529,613*

scruple [n] *misgiving, doubt*
anxiety, caution, censor, compunction, conscience, demur, difficulty, faltering, hesitancy, hesitation, pause, perplexity, qualm, reconsideration, reluctance, reluctancy, second thought*, squeamishness, superego, twinge, uneasiness; SEE CONCEPTS *532,690*

scruple [v] *balk, have misgivings*
be loath, be reluctant, be unwilling, boggle, demur, doubt, falter, fret, gag, have qualms, hesitate, question, shy, stick, stickle, stumble, think twice about*, vacillate, waver, worry; SEE CONCEPT *21*

scrupulous [adj] *extremely careful*
conscientious, conscionable, critical, exact, fastidious, fussy, heedful, honest, honorable, just, meticulous, minute, moral, nice, painstaking, particular, precise, principled, punctilious, punctual, right, rigorous, strict, thinking twice*, true, upright; SEE CONCEPTS *401,538,542*

scrutinize [v] *examine closely*
analyze, burn up, candle, canvass, case, check, check out, check over, comb*, consider, contemplate, dig, dissect, explore, eyeball*, get a load of*, go over with a fine-tooth comb*, inquire into, inspect, investigate, look over, overlook, peg*, penetrate, perlustrate, peruse, pierce, pore over, probe, put under a microscope*, scan, scope, scrutinate, search, sift, smoke*, stare, study, survey, take the measure of, view, watch, weigh; SEE CONCEPTS *24,103,623*

scrutiny [n] *close examination*
analysis, audit, close-up, eagle eye*, exploration, inquiry, inspection, investigation, long hard look*, perlustration, perusal, review, scan, search, sifting, study, surveillance, survey, tab*, the eye*, view; SEE CONCEPTS *24,103,623*

scuffle [n] *fight*
affray, brawl, broil, commotion, disturbance, fracas, fray, fuss*, go*, jump, mix-up, row, ruckus, ruction, rumpus, scrap, set-to*, shuffle, strife, tussle, wrangle; SEE CONCEPT *106*

scuffle [v] *fight*
clash, come to blows, contend, cuff, grapple, jostle, skirmish, struggle, tussle, wrestle; SEE CONCEPT *106*

sculpture [v] *form a three-dimensional art object*
carve, cast, chisel, cut, engrave, fashion, hew, model, mold, sculp, sculpt, shape; SEE CONCEPTS *137,174,184*

scum [n1] *superficial impurities, dirt*
algae, crust, dross, film, froth, residue, scruff, spume, waste; SEE CONCEPT *260*

scum [n2] *people who are bad, despicable*
curs*, dregs, lowest, mass, mob, proletariat, rabble, riffraff, rubbish*, scum of the earth*, trash*, unwashed, vermin; SEE CONCEPT *412*

scurrilous [adj] *foul-mouthed, vulgar*
abusive, coarse, contumelious, defamatory, dirty, filthy, foul, gross, indecent, infamous, insulting, invective, lewd, low, nasty, obscene, offending, offensive, opprobrious, outrageous, raunchy, ribald, salacious, scabrous, scandalous, shameless, slanderous, smutty*, truculent, vituperative, vituperatory, vituperous; SEE CONCEPTS *267,542,545*

scurry [v] *move along swiftly*
barrel, bustle, dart, dash, dust, fly, hasten, hop along, hurry, race, rip, run, rush, scamper, scoot, scud, scutter, scuttle, shoot, skim, sprint, step along, tear, whisk, zip*; SEE CONCEPT *150*

sea [n] *large body of water; large mass*
abundance, blue*, bounding main*, brine, briny*, briny deep*, Davy Jones's locker*, deep, drink*, expanse, lake, main, multitude, number, ocean, plethora, pond, profusion, sheet, splash*, surf, swell, waves; SEE CONCEPT *514*

seal [n] *authentication; stamp*
allowance, assurance, attestation, authorization, cachet, confirmation, imprimatur, insignia, notification, permission, permit, ratification, signet, sticker, tape, tie; SEE CONCEPTS *284,685*

seal [v1] *make airtight*
close, cork, enclose, fasten, gum, isolate, paste, plaster, plug, quarantine, secure, segregate, shut, stop, stopper, stop up, waterproof; SEE CONCEPTS *85,160*

seal [v2] *ensure, finalize*
assure, attest, authenticate, clinch, conclude, confirm, consummate, establish, ratify, settle, shake hands on*, stamp, validate; SEE CONCEPTS *234,324*

seam [n] *line where two objects are connected*
bond, closure, connection, coupling, gore, gusset, hem, joint, junction, juncture, pleat, stitching, suture, tuck, union; SEE CONCEPTS *452,471*

seamy [adj] *corrupt, unwholesome*
bad, dark, degraded, disagreeable, disappointing, disreputable, disturbing, low, nasty, rough, sordid, squalid, unpleasant; SEE CONCEPT *545*

sear [v] *dry, burn*
blight, brand, brown, burn up, cauterize, cook, dehydrate, desiccate, dry out, dry up, exsiccate, harden, parch, scorch, seal, shrivel, sizzle, tan, toast, wilt, wither; SEE CONCEPTS *170,249*

search [n] *seeking to find something*
chase, examination, exploration, fishing expedition*, frisking*, going-over*, hunt, inquest, inquiry, inspection, investigation, legwork*, perquisition, pursual, pursuance, pursuing, pursuit, quest, research, rummage, scrutiny, shakedown*, wild-goose chase*, witch hunt*; SEE CONCEPT *216*

search [v] *seek to find something*
beat, beat about, cast about, chase after, check, comb, examine, explore, ferret, forage, frisk, go in quest of, go over with a fine-tooth comb*, go through, grope, grub, gun for*, hunt, hunt for, inquire, inspect, investigate, leave no stone unturned*, look, look for, look high and low*, look over, poke into, probe, prospect, pry, quest, rake, ransack, rifle through, root, rummage, run down, scan, scour, scout, scrutinize, seek, shake down, sift, smell around, study, track down, turn inside out*, turn upside down*; SEE CONCEPT *216*

season [n] *time of year governed by annual equinoxes*
autumn, division, fall, interval, juncture, occasion, opportunity, period, spell, spring, summer, term, time, while, winter; SEE CONCEPT *814*

season [v1] *flavor food*
color, enliven, lace, leaven, pep, pepper, salt, spice; SEE CONCEPT *170*

season [v2] *acclimatize, prepare*
acclimate, accustom, anneal, climatize, discipline, fit, habituate, harden, inure, mature, qualify, school, steel, temper, toughen, train; SEE CONCEPTS *35,202*

seasonable [adj] *timely, appropriate*
apropos, apt, auspicious, convenient, favorable, fit, opportune, pertinent, propitious, prosperous, providential, relevant, seasonal, suitable, timeous, towardly, welcome, well-timed; SEE CONCEPT *558*

seasoning [n] *flavoring for food*
condiment, dressing, gravy, herb, pepper, pungency, relish, salt, sauce, spice, zest; SEE CONCEPTS *457,461*

seat [n1] *furniture for sitting, reclining*
bench, chair, chaise lounge, chesterfield, couch, davenport, lounge, loveseat, pew, recliner, settee, settle, stall, stool, wing chair; SEE CONCEPT *443*

seat [n2] *central location of organization*
abode, axis, capital, center, cradle, focal point, fulcrum, headquarters, heart, house, hub, location, mansion, nerve center, place, polestar, post, residence, site, situation, source, spot, station; SEE CONCEPT *198*

seat [n3] *base, foundation*
basement, basis, bed, bottom, cause, fitting, footing, ground, groundwork, rest, seating, support; SEE CONCEPT *442*

seat [n4] *rear end of animate being*
backside, behind, bottom, breech, derrière, duff*, fanny*, fundament*, keister*, posterior, rear, rear end, rump, tush*; SEE CONCEPTS *392,825,827*

seat [v] *place in furniture, position*
accommodate, deposit, establish, fix, hold, install, locate, lounge, nestle, perch, plant, put, roost, set, settle, sit, squat, take; SEE CONCEPTS *154,201,384*

secede [v] *pull away; split from*
abdicate, apostatize, break with, disaffiliate, leave, quit, resign, retire, retract, retreat, separate, withdraw; SEE CONCEPTS *119,298,384*

seclude [v] *isolate, hide*
blockade, boycott, cloister, closet, conceal, confine, cover, embargo, enclose, evict, immure, ostracize, quarantine, retire, screen, segregate, separate, sequester, shut off, withdraw; SEE CONCEPTS *121,135,188*

secluded [adj] *isolated, sheltered*
abandoned, alone, aloof, beleaguered, blockaded,

sc
se

cloistered, close, closet, confidential, covert, cut off, deserted, hermetic, hidden, incommunicado, insular, isolate, lonely, lonesome, off the beaten track*, out-of-the-way*, personal, private, quarantined, quiet, reclusive, remote, removed, reserved, retired, screened, secude, seclusive, secret, segregated, sequestered, shut off, shy, singular, solitary, tucked away*, unapproachable, unfrequented, uninhabited, unsociable, withdrawn; SEE CONCEPTS 401,576,583

seclusion [n] *isolation*
aloneness, aloofness, beleaguerment, blockade, concealment, desolation, detachment, hiding, privacy, privateness, quarantine, reclusion, reclusiveness, remoteness, retirement, retreat, seclusiveness, separateness, separation, sequestration, shelter, solitude, withdrawal; SEE CONCEPTS 135,188,388,631

second [n1] *shortest interval of time*
bat of an eye*, flash, instant, jiffy*, moment, nothing flat*, sec*, shake*, split second, twinkling*, wink; SEE CONCEPTS 803,821

second [n2] *support; duplicate*
assistant, backer, double, exponent, helper, placer, proponent, reproduction, runner-up, supporter, twin; SEE CONCEPTS 423,670

second [adj] *next; subordinate*
additional, alternative, another, double, duplicate, extra, following, further, inferior, lesser, lower, next, next in order, other, place, repeated, reproduction, runner-up, secondary, subsequent, succeeding, supporting, twin, unimportant; SEE CONCEPTS 575,585

second [v] *support, advance a suggestion*
aid, approve, assist, back, back up, encourage, endorse, forward, further, give moral support, go along with, promote, stand by, uphold; SEE CONCEPTS 298,324,384

secondary [adj1] *subordinate; less important*
accessory, alternate, auxiliary, backup, bush-league*, collateral, consequential, contingent, dependent, dinky*, extra, inconsiderable, inferior, insignificant, lesser, lower, minor, minor-league*, petty, relief, reserve, second, second-rate, small, small-fry*, small-time*, subject, subservient, subsidiary, substract, supporting, tributary, trivial, under, unimportant; SEE CONCEPTS 574,575

secondary [adj2] *derivative*
auxiliary, borrowed, consequent, dependent, derivate, derivational, derived, developed, eventual, indirect, proximate, resultant, resulting, secondhand, subordinate, subsequent, subsidiary, vicarious; SEE CONCEPT 549

second-rate/second-class [adj] *inferior, cheap*
cheap and dirty*, common, commonplace, déclassé, hack*, low-grade, low-quality, mean, mediocre, poor, shoddy*, substandard, tacky*, tawdry; SEE CONCEPTS 334,567,574

secrecy [n] *concealment*
clandestineness, confidence, confidentiality, covertness, dark, darkness, furtiveness, hiding, hush, isolation, mystery, privacy, reticence, retirement, seclusion, secretiveness, secretness, silence, solitude, stealth, suppression, surreptitiousness; SEE CONCEPT 631

secret [n] *something kept hidden, unrevealed*
cipher, classified information, code, confidence, confidential information, enigma, formula, key, magic number*, mystery, occult, oracle, pass-

word, privileged information, puzzle, skeleton in cupboard*, unknown; SEE CONCEPTS 274,631

secret [adj1] *hidden, unrevealed*
abstruse, ambiguous, arcane, backdoor, camouflaged, classified, cloak-and-dagger*, close, closet, clouded, conspiratorial, covered, covert, cryptic, dark, deep, disguised, enigmatical, esoteric, furtive, hush-hush*, mysterious, mystic, mystical, obscure, occult, on the QT*, out-of-the-way*, private, recondite, reticent, retired, secluded, shrouded, strange, undercover, underground, under wraps*, undisclosed, unenlightened, unfrequented, unintelligible, unknown, unpublished, unseen, veiled; SEE CONCEPTS 529,576

secret [adj2] *underhand, clandestine*
backdoor, backstairs, camouflaged, classified, close, confidential, covert, cryptic, discreet, disguised, dissembled, dissimulated, furtive, hush-hush*, in ambush, incognito, inside, restricted, secretive, sly, sneak, sneaky, stealthy, sub-rosa, surreptitious, top secret, unacknowledged, under false pretense*, underhanded, under-the-table*; SEE CONCEPTS 545,576

secrete [v1] *hide*
bury, cache, conceal, cover, cover up, deposit, disguise, ditch, ensconce, finesse, harbor, hide out, keep quiet, keep secret, keep to oneself, keep under wraps*, palm*, paper, plant, screen, seclude, secure, shroud, squirrel*, stash, stash away, stonewall*, stow, sweep under rug*, veil, whitewash*, withhold; SEE CONCEPTS 188,266

secrete [v2] *give off, emit*
discharge, emanate, excrete, extravasate, extrude, exude, perspire, produce, sweat; SEE CONCEPTS 146,179

secretive [adj] *uncommunicative*
backstairs*, buttoned up*, cagey, clammed up*, close, close-mouthed*, covert, cryptic, enigmatic, feline, furtive, hushed, in chambers*, in privacy*, in private, in the background*, in the dark*, on the QT*, reserved, reticent, silent, taciturn, tight-lipped*, undercover, unforthcoming, withdrawn, zipped*; SEE CONCEPTS 267,548

secretly [adv] *in hidden manner*
behind closed doors*, behind someone's back*, by stealth, clandestinely, confidentially, covertly, furtively, hush-hush*, in camera*, in confidence, in holes and corners*, in secret, insidiously, in strict confidence*, intimately, obscurely, on the QT*, on the quiet*, on the sly*, personally, privately, privily, quietly, slyly, stealthily, sub rosa, surreptitiously, underhandedly, under the table*, unobserved; SEE CONCEPTS 267,548

sect [n] *school of thought*
camp, church, communion, connection, creed, crew, cult, denomination, division, faction, faith, following, group, order, party, persuasion, religion, school, splinter group, team, wing; SEE CONCEPTS 381,382

sectarian [n] *person who is narrow-minded*
adherent, bigot, cohort, disciple, dissenter, dissident, dogmatist, extremist, fanatic, heretic, maverick, misbeliever, nonconformist, partisan, radical, rebel, revolutionary, satellite, schismatic, separatist, supporter, true believer, zealot; SEE CONCEPTS 359,423

sectarian [adj] *narrow-minded, exclusive*
bigoted, clannish, cliquish, dissident, doctrinaire, dogmatic, factional, fanatic, fanatical, hidebound,

insular, limited, local, nonconforming, nonconformist, parochial, partisan, provincial, rigid, schismatic, skeptical, small-town*, splinter; SEE CONCEPT *403*

section [*n*] *division, portion*
area, belt, bite, branch, category, chunk, classification, component, cross section, cut, department, district, drag, end, field, fraction, fragment, hunk, installment, locality, lump, member, moiety, parcel, part, passage, piece, precinct, quarter, region, sample, sector, segment, share, slice, slot, sphere, split, subdivision, territory, tier, tract, vicinity, zone; SEE CONCEPT *835*

sectional [*adj*] *localized, divided*
exclusive, factional, local, narrow, partial, regional, selfish, separate, separatist; SEE CONCEPTS *557,785*

sector [*n*] *area, subdivision*
category, district, division, part, precinct, quarter, region, stratum, zone; SEE CONCEPTS *508,835*

secular [*adj*] *not spiritual or religious*
civil, earthly, laic, laical, lay, material, materialistic, nonclerical, nonreligious, of this world*, profane, temporal, unsacred, worldly; SEE CONCEPTS *529,549*

secure [*adj1*] *safe*
defended, guarded, immune, impregnable, out of harm's way, protected, riskless, safe, sheltered, shielded, unassailable, undamaged, unharmed, SEE CONCEPT *587*

secure [*adj2*] *fastened, stable*
adjusted, anchored, bound, buttoned down*, fast, firm, fixed, fortified, immovable, iron, locked, nailed, safe and sound*, set, solid, solid as a rock*, sound, staunch, steady, strong, sure, tenacious, tight; SEE CONCEPT *488*

secure [*adj3*] *certain, definite*
able, absolute, assured, at ease, balanced, carefree, cinch, conclusive, confident, determined, easy, established, firm, hopeful, in the bag*, locked on*, nailed down*, on ice*, reassured, reliable, resolute, sanguine, self-assured, self-confident, settled, shoo-in*, solid, sound, stable, steadfast, steady, strong, sure, sure thing*, tried and true*, unanxious, undoubtful, well-founded; SEE CONCEPTS *403,535*

secure [*vl*] *obtain*
access, achieve, acquire, annex, assure, bag*, buy, capture, catch, chalk up*, cinch, come by, ensure, gain, get, get hold of, grasp, guarantee, have, hook, insure, land, lock, lock up, make sure, pick up, procure, rack up*, take, win; SEE CONCEPT *120*

secure [*v2*] *attach, tie up*
adjust, anchor, batten down, bind, bolt, button, button down, catch, cement, chain, clamp, clinch, close, fasten, fix, hitch, hook on, lash, lock, lock up, make fast, moor, nail, padlock, pinion, rivet, settle, tack, tie, tie down, tighten; SEE CONCEPTS *85,160*

secure [*v3*] *protect, make safe*
assure, bulwark, cover, defend, ensure, fend, guarantee, guard, insure, safeguard, screen, shield; SEE CONCEPT *96*

security [*n1*] *safety, protection*
aegis, agreement, armament, armor, asylum, bail, bond, care, collateral, compact, contract, covenant, cover, custody, defense, earnest, freedom, guarantee, guard, immunity, insurance, pact, pawn, pledge, precaution, preservation, promise,

protection, redemption, refuge, retreat, safeguard, safekeeping, safeness, safety measure, salvation, sanctuary, shelter, shield, surety, surveillance, token, ward, warrant; SEE CONCEPTS *712,729*

security [*n2*] *peace of mind*
assurance, calm, certainty, confidence, conviction, ease, freedom, positiveness, reliance, soundness, sureness, surety; SEE CONCEPT *410*

sedate [*adj*] *calm, collected*
cold sober*, composed, cool, cool as cucumber*, decorous, deliberate, demure, dignified, dispassionate, earnest, grave, imperturbable, laid-back*, no-nonsense, placid, proper, quiet, seemly, serene, serious, sober, solemn, somber, staid, steady, tranquil, unflappable, unruffled; SEE CONCEPTS *404,542*

sedative [*n*] *soothing agent, medicine*
analgesic, anodyne, barbiturate, calmant, calmative, depressant, dope*, downer, drug, hypnotic, knockout pill, medication, narcotic, nerve medicine, opiate, pacifier, pain-killer, pain pill*, quietive, sleeping pill, tranquillizer; SEE CONCEPT *307*

sedative [*adj*] *soothing*
allaying, anodyne, calmative, calming, lenitive, relaxing, sleep-inducing, soporific, tranquillizing; SEE CONCEPT *537*

sedentary [*adj*] *motionless, lazy*
desk, desk-bound, idle, inactive, seated, settled, sitting, sluggish, stationary, torpid; SEE CONCEPTS *542,584*

sediment [*n*] *solid residue from liquid solution*
debris, deposit, dregs, dross, gook*, grounds, gunk*, lees, matter, powder, precipitate, precipitation, residuum, settling, silt, slag, solids, trash, waste; SEE CONCEPT *260*

seduce [*vl*] *tempt, ensnare*
bait, beguile, betray, bribe, coax, deceive, decoy, delude, draw, entice, entrap, hook, induce, inveigle, invite, lead astray*, lead on*, lure, mislead, mousetrap*, persuade, pull, rope in, steer, string along*, sucker*, wheedle; SEE CONCEPT *11*

seduce [*v2*] *entice sexually*
allure, attract, beguile, captivate, charm, come on to*, enamour, entrance, sweep off one's feet*, tempt; SEE CONCEPT *375*

seductive [*adj*] *alluring, sexy*
attracting, attractive, beguiling, bewitching, captivating, charming, come-hither*, desirable, drawing, enchanting, enticing, fascinating, flirtatious, inviting, irresistible, magnetic, provocative, ravishing, siren, specious, tempting; SEE CONCEPTS *372,579*

see [*vl*] *perceive with eyes*
beam, be apprised of, behold, catch a glimpse of, catch sight of, clock*, contemplate, descry, detect, discern, distinguish, espy, examine, eye, flash, gape, gawk, gaze, get a load of*, glare, glimpse, heed, identify, inspect, lay eyes on*, look, look at, make out, mark, mind, note, notice, observe, pay attention to, peek, peep, peer, peg*, penetrate, pierce, recognize, regard, remark, scan, scope, scrutinize, sight, spot, spy, stare, survey, take notice, view, watch, witness; SEE CONCEPTS *590,626*

see [*v2*] *appreciate, comprehend*
appraise, ascertain, behold, catch, catch on, conceive, descry, determine, discern, discover, distinguish, envisage, envision, espy, experience, fancy, fathom, feature, feel, find out, follow, get,

se
se

get the drift*, get the hang of*, grasp, have, hear, imagine, investigate, know, learn, make out, mark, mind, note, notice, observe, perceive, ponder, realize, recognize, remark, study, suffer, sustain, take in, think, tumble, undergo, understand, unearth, view, visualize, weigh; SEE CONCEPTS 15,31,43

see [v3] *accompany, guide*
associate with, attend, bear company, call, come by, come over, conduct, consort with, date, direct, drop by, drop in, encounter, escort, go out with, go with, keep company with, lead, look up, meet, pilot, pop in, receive, route, run into, shepherd, show, speak to, steer, stop by, stop in, take out, usher, visit, walk; SEE CONCEPTS 187,227,384

see [v4] *visualize*
anticipate, conceive, divine, envisage, envision, fancy, feature, foresee, foretell, imagine, picture, realize, think, vision; SEE CONCEPT 12

seed [n1] *beginning, source*
berry, bud, cell, conceit, concept, conception, core, corn, ear, egg, embryo, germ, grain, image, impression, inkling, kernel, notion, nucleus, nut, ovule, ovum, particle, rudiment, semen, spark, sperm, spore, start, suspicion; SEE CONCEPTS 393,428,648

seed [n2] *children*
brood, descendants, heirs, issue, offspring, posterity, progenitor, progeny, race, scions, spawn, successors; SEE CONCEPT 414

seedy [adj] *run-down, dilapidated*
ailing, beat up, bedraggled, crummy*, decaying, decrepit, dingy, dog-eared*, down-at-the-heel*, drooping, droopy, faded, flagging, frowzy, gone to seed*, grubby, in a bad way*, mangy, messy, neglected, old, overgrown, poor, poorly, ragged, ratty, sagging, scruffy, shabby, sickly, sleazy*, slovenly, squalid, tacky, tattered, threadbare, tired, torn, unkempt, untidy, unwell, used up, wilted, wilting, worn; SEE CONCEPTS 485,570

seek [v1] *look for*
be after, beat the bushes*, bird-dog*, bob for, cast about, chase, comb, delve, delve for, dig for, dragnet, explore, fan, ferret out, fish, fish for*, follow, go after, gun for*, hunt, inquire, investigate, leave no stone unturned*, look about, look around, look high and low*, mouse*, nose*, prowl, pursue, quest, ransack, root, run after, scout, scratch, search for, search out, sniff out*, track down; SEE CONCEPT 216

seek [v2] *try, attempt*
aim, aspire to, assay, endeavor, essay, have a go at*, offer, pursue, strive, struggle, undertake; SEE CONCEPT 87

seek [v3] *ask, inquire*
beg, entreat, find out, invite, petition, query, request, solicit; SEE CONCEPT 48

seem [v] *appear; give the impression*
assume, be suggestive of, convey the impression, create the impression, give the feeling of*, give the idea of*, have the appearance of, have the aspects of, have the earmarks of*, have the features of, have the qualities of, hint, imply, insinuate, intimate, look, look as if, look like, look to be, make a show of, pretend, resemble, show, show every sign of, sound, sound like, strike one as being, suggest; SEE CONCEPT 543

seeming [adj] *apparent*
appearing, illusive, illusory, ostensible, outward,

professed, quasi-, semblant, specious, surface; SEE CONCEPTS 487,573

seemly [adj] *appropriate, suitable*
becoming, befitting, comme il faut, compatible, conforming, congenial, congruous, consistent, consonant, correct, decent, decorous, fit, fitting, in good taste, meet, nice, pleasing, proper, suited, timely; SEE CONCEPT 558

seep [v] *leak*
bleed, drain, drip, exude, flow, ooze, percolate, permeate, soak, sweat, transude, trickle, weep, well; SEE CONCEPTS 146,179

seethe [v] *be very angry*
be furious, be incensed, be livid, be mad, be on the warpath*, blow one's stack*, blow up*, boil, breathe fire*, bristle, burn, ferment, flare, flip, foam, foam at mouth*, froth, fume, hit the ceiling*, rage, see red*, simmer, smolder, spark, stew*, storm; SEE CONCEPTS 29,34

segment [n] *part of something*
articulation, bit, compartment, cut, division, member, moiety, parcel, piece, portion, section, sector, slice, subdivision, wedge; SEE CONCEPT 835

segregate [v] *discriminate and separate*
choose, close off, cut off, disconnect, dissociate, divide, insulate, island, isolate, quarantine, select, sequester, set apart, sever, single out, split up; SEE CONCEPTS 21,135,645

seize [v1] *grab, take*
appropriate, catch, catch hold of, clasp, clench, clinch, clutch, compass, embrace, enclose, enfold, envelope, fasten, grapple, grasp, grip, hang onto, hold fast, lay hands on*, lay hold of*, pinch, pluck, snag, snatch, squeeze, take hold of; SEE CONCEPTS 142,164,190

seize [v2] *abduct; take by force*
ambush, annex, apprehend, appropriate, arrest, arrogate, bag, bust, capture, carry off, catch, claw, clutch, commandeer, confiscate, conquer, exact, force, gain, get, grab, grasp, hijack, hook, impound, incorporate, kidnap, lift, nab, nail*, occupy, overcome, overpower, overrun, overwhelm, pick up, pounce, secure, snag, snare, spirit away*, subdue, take, take by storm*, take captive, take over, take possession of, throttle, trap, usurp, wrench; SEE CONCEPT 90

seizure [n1] *convulsive attack*
access, breakdown, convulsion, fit, illness, paroxysm, spasm, spell, stroke, throe, turn; SEE CONCEPT 308

seizure [n2] *capture, taking*
abduction, annexation, apprehension, arrest, bust*, collar*, commandeering, confiscation, drop, grab, grabbing, hook*, pinch*, seizing, snatch; SEE CONCEPT 90

seldom [adv] *infrequently*
a few times, every now and then, from time to time, hardly, hardly ever, in a few cases, inhabitually, irregularly, little, not often, not very often, occasionally, on and off, once in a blue moon*, once in a while, rarely, scarcely, scarcely ever, semioccasionally, sometimes, sporadically, uncommonly, unoften, unusually, whimsically; SEE CONCEPT 541

select [adj] *excellent, elite, preferable*
best, blue-chip*, boss*, choice, chosen, cool*, cream*, culled, delicate, discriminating, eclectic, elect, elegant, exclusive, exquisite, favored, first-class*, first-rate*, handpicked, limited, number

one*, pick, picked, posh, preferred, prime, privileged, rare, recherché, screened, selected, selective, special, superior, top, topnotch, tops*,
weeded*, winner, winnowed, world-class*; SEE
CONCEPTS 574,653

select [v] *pick out, prefer from among choices*
choose, cull, decide, elect, make, make a choice,
make a selection, mark, name, opt, optate, opt
for, peg*, pick, pin down, say so*, single out,
slot*, sort out, tab*, tag*, take, tap*, winnow;
SEE CONCEPT 41

selection [n] *preference from among choices*
alternative, choice, choosing, collection, culling,
draft, druthers*, election, excerpt, option, pick,
picking; SEE CONCEPT 529

selective [adj] *discriminating*
careful, choicy, choosy, discerning, discriminatory, eclectic, fussy, judicious, particular, persnickety*, picky, scrupulous, select; SEE
CONCEPTS 404,542

self-centered [adj] *absorbed with oneself*
egocentric, egoistic, egomaniacal, egotistic, egotistical, grandstanding, having a swelled head*,
independent, inward-looking, know-it-all*, narcissistic, on an ego trip*, self-absorbed, self-
indulgent, self-interested, self-involved, selfish,
self-seeking, self-serving, self-sufficient, stuck on
oneself*, wrapped up with oneself*; SEE CON-
CEPT 404

self-confident [adj] *secure with oneself*
assured, fearless, hotdog*, hotshot*, know-it-all*,
poised, sanguine, self-assured, self-reliant, sure
of oneself, undoubtful; SEE CONCEPT 404

self-conscious [adj] *insecure with oneself*
affected, anxious, artificial, awkward, bashful,
diffident, discomfited, embarrassed, ill-at-ease,
mannered, nervous, out of countenance, shamefaced, sheepish, shy, stiff, stilted, uncertain, uncomfortable, uneasy, unsure; SEE CONCEPTS
401,404

self-control [n] *willpower over one's actions*
abstemiousness, aplomb, balance, constraint, dignity, discipline, discretion, poise, repression, reserve, restraint, reticence, self-constraint, self-
discipline, self-government, sobriety, stability,
stoicism, strength of character; SEE CONCEPT 633

self-evident/self-explanatory [adj] *obvious*
apparent, axiomatic, clear, comprehensible, incontrovertible, inescapable, manifest, patently
true, plain, prima facie, undeniable, understandable, unmistakable, unquestionable, visible; SEE
CONCEPTS 529,548

selfish [adj] *thinking only of oneself*
egocentric, egoistic, egoistical, egomaniacal, egotistic, egotistical, greedy*, hoggish*, mean, mercenary, miserly, narcissistic, narrow, narrow-
minded, out for number one*, parsimonious,
prejudiced, self-centered, self-indulgent, self-
interested, self-seeking, stingy, ungenerous,
wrapped up in oneself*; SEE CONCEPTS 404,542

self-respect/self-esteem [n] *pride in oneself*
amour-propre, conceit, confidence, dignity, egotism, faith in oneself, morale, narcissism, self-
assurance, self-content, self-regard, self-
satisfaction, vanity, worth; SEE CONCEPTS
411,689

self-righteous [adj] *smug*
affected, canting, complacent, egotistical, goody-
goody*, holier-than-thou*, hypocritical, noble,
pharisaic, pietistic, pious, preachy, sanctimo-

nious, self-satisfied, superior; SEE CONCEPTS
401,542

self-satisfaction [n] *pride, contentment*
complacency, conceit, glow, peace of mind, self-
approbation, self-approval, self-pleasure, smugness; SEE CONCEPTS 410,689

self-satisfied [adj] *proud, content*
complacent, conceited, egotistic, flushed, pleased,
puffed up*, self-congratulatory, smug, vain; SEE
CONCEPTS 404,542

self-sufficient [adj] *able to take care of oneself*
arrogant, closed, competent, conceited, confident,
doing one's own thing*, efficient, egotistic,
haughty, independent, individual, on one's own,
out for number one*, self-confident, self-
dependent, self-sufficing, self-supported, self-
supporting, self-sustained, self-sustaining, smug,
unit; SEE CONCEPTS 334,404

sell [v] *exchange an object for money*
advertise, auction, bargain, barter, be in business*, boost, clinch the deal, close, close the deal,
contract, deal in, dispose, drum, dump, exchange,
handle, hawk, hustle, market, merchandise,
move, peddle, persuade, pitch, plug, puff*, push,
put across, put up for sale, retail, retain, snow,
soft sell*, soft soap*, spiel*, stock, sweet talk*,
trade, traffic, unload, vend, wholesale; SEE CON-
CEPT 345

sell/sell out [v2] *betray*
beguile, break faith, bunk, cross, deceive, deliver
up, delude, disappoint, double-cross*, fail, four-
flush*, give away, give up, mislead, play false,
rat on*, sell down the river*, stab in the back*,
surrender, take in, violate; SEE CONCEPTS 14,63

seller [n] *person who gives object in exchange for
money*
agent, auctioneer, businessperson, dealer, marketer, merchant, peddler, representative, retailer,
sales help, salesperson, shopkeeper, storekeeper,
trader, tradesperson, vendor; SEE CONCEPTS
347,348

semblance [n] *aura, appearance*
affinity, air, alikeness, analogy, aspect, bearing,
comparison, facade, face, false front*, feel, feeling, figure, form, front, guise, image, likeness,
mask, mien, mood, pose, pretense, resemblance,
seeming, show, showing, similarity, simile, similitude, simulacrum, veil, veneer; SEE CON-
CEPTS 673,716

semiotics [n] *study of signs as elements of communication*
langue, parole, pragmatics, semantics, sign systems, symbolism, syntactics; SEE CONCEPT 349

send [v1] *transmit, transfer through a system*
accelerate, address, advance, assign, broadcast,
cast, circulate, commission, commit, communicate, consign, convey, delegate, deliver, detail,
direct, dispatch, drop, emit, expedite, express,
fire, fling, forward, freight, get under way, give
off, grant, hasten, hurl, hurry off, impart, issue,
let fly, mail, post, propel, put out, radiate, relay,
remit, route, rush off, ship, shoot, televise, troll,
wire; SEE CONCEPTS 217,223

send [v2] *please*
charm, delight, electrify, enrapture, enthrall, enthuse, excite, intoxicate, move, please, ravish,
stir, thrill, titillate, turn on; SEE CONCEPTS
7,11,22

se
se

senile [adj] *failing in physical and mental capabilities due to old age*
aged, ancient, anile, decrepit, doddering, doting, enfeebled, feeble, imbecile, infirm, in second childhood*, old, senescent, shattered, sick, weak; SEE CONCEPTS 314,402,403

senior [n] *older person*
ancient, doyen, doyenne, elder, elderly person, first-born, golden-ager*, grandfather, grandmother, head, matriarch, old folk*, oldster*, oldtimer*, patriarch, pensioner, retired person, senior citizen; SEE CONCEPTS 414,424

senior [adj] *older or of higher rank*
chief, elder, higher, leading, major, more advanced, next higher, superior; SEE CONCEPTS 574,578,585,797

seniority [n] *rank in organization due to length of service*
advantage, antiquity, eldership, precedence, preference, priority, rank, ranking, standing, station, superiority; SEE CONCEPTS 671,727

sensation [n1] *feeling, perception*
awareness, consciousness, emotion, gut reaction*, impression, passion, response, sense, sensibility, sensitiveness, sensitivity, sentiment, susceptibility, thought, tingle, vibes*; SEE CONCEPTS 34,410,529

sensation [n2] *something wonderful or awe-inspiring*
agitation, bomb*, bombshell*, commotion, excitement, flash, furor, hit, marvel, miracle, phenomenon, portent, prodigy, scandal, stir, stunner, surprise, thrill, wonder, wow*; SEE CONCEPTS 293,529

sensational [adj1] *startling, exaggerated*
amazing, arresting, astounding, breathtaking, coarse, colored, conspicuous, dramatic, electrifying, emotional, excessive, exciting, extravagant, hair-raising, horrifying, juicy*, livid, lurid, marked, melodramatic, noticeable, outstanding, piquant, pointed, prominent, pungent, remarkable, revealing, rough, salient, scandalous, sensationalistic, shocking, signal, spectacular, staggering, stimulating, sultry, tabloid*, thrilling, vulgar, X-rated*; SEE CONCEPTS 267,537,545

sensational [adj2] *excellent, superb*
agitating, astonishing, breathtaking, cool*, dandy*, divine, dramatic, eloquent, exceptional, exciting, fabulous, first-class*, glorious, impressive, incredible, keen, marvelous, mind-blowing, most*, moving, out of this world*, smashing, spectacular, stirring, surprising, thrilling, zero cool*; SEE CONCEPT 574

sense [n1] *feeling of animate being*
faculty, feel, function, hearing, impression, kinesthesia, sensation, sensibility, sensitivity, sight, smell, taste, touch; SEE CONCEPT 405

sense [n2] *awareness, perception*
ability, appreciation, atmosphere, aura, brains, capacity, clear-headedness, cleverness, cognizance, common sense, consciousness, discernment, discrimination, feel, feeling, gumption*, imagination, impression, insight, intellect, intelligence, intuition, judgment, knowledge, mentality, mind, premonition, presentiment, prudence, quickness, reason, reasoning, recognition, sagacity, sanity, sentiment, sharpness, smarts*, soul, spirit, tact, thought, understanding, wisdom, wit; SEE CONCEPTS 33,409

sense [n3] *point, meaning*
acceptation, advantage, bottom line*, burden, core, definition, denotatiton, drift, gist, good, heart, implication, import, intendment, interpretation, logic, matter, meat*, meat and potatoes*, message, name of the game*, nature of the beast*, nitty-gritty*, nuance, nub, nuts and bolts*, punch line*, purport, purpose, reason, short, significance, significancy, signification, stuff, substance, thrust, understanding, upshot, use, value, worth; SEE CONCEPTS 668,682

sense [v] *become aware of*
anticipate, apperceive, appreciate, apprehend, believe, be with it, catch, catch on, catch the drift*, consider, credit, deem, dig*, discern, divine, feel, feel in bones*, feel in gut*, get the drift*, get the idea*, get the impression*, get the picture*, get vibes*, grasp, have a feeling*, have a hunch*, hold, know, notice, observe, perceive, pick up, read, realize, savvy*, suspect, take in, think, understand; SEE CONCEPT 34

senseless [adj] *silly, meaningless*
absurd, asinine, batty, crazy, daft, doublespeak*, double talk*, fatuous, flaky, foolish, idiotic, illogical, imbecilic, inane, incongruous, inconsistent, insignificant, irrational, ludicrous, mad, mindless, moronic, nonsensical, nutty, pointless, purportless, purposeless, ridiculous, simple, stupid, trivial, unimportant, unintelligent, unmeaning, unreasonable, unsound, unwise, wacky*, without rhyme or reason*; SEE CONCEPTS 548,558

sensibility [n] *responsiveness; ability to feel*
affection, appreciation, awareness, discernment, emotion, feeling, gut reaction*, heart*, insight, intuition, judgment, keenness, perceptiveness, rationale, sensation, sense, sensitiveness, sensitivity, sentiment, susceptibility, taste, vibes*; SEE CONCEPTS 409,410

sensible [adj] *realistic, reasonable*
all there*, astute, attentive, au courant, aware, canny, cognizant, commonsensical, conscious, consequent, conversant, cool*, discerning, discreet, discriminating, down-to-earth, far-sighted, having all one's marbles*, informed, in right mind, intelligent, judicious, knowing, logical, matter-of-fact, practical, prudent, rational, sagacious, sage, sane, sentient, shrewd, sober, sound, together, well-reasoned, well-thought-out, wise, witting; SEE CONCEPTS 402,542

sensitive [adj1] *impressionable*
acute, cognizant, conscious, delicate, easily affected, emotionable, emotional, feeling, fine, high-strung, hung up*, hypersensitive, impressible, irritable, keen, knowing, nervous, oversensitive, perceiving, perceptive, precarious, precise, psychic, reactive, receptive, responsive, seeing, sensatory, sensible, sensorial, sensory, sentient, supersensitive, susceptible, tense, ticklish, touchy, touchy feely*, tricky, tuned in*, turned on to*, umbrageous, understanding, unstable, wired*; SEE CONCEPT 403

sensitive [adj2] *easily hurt*
delicate, easily harmed, painful, sore, tender; SEE CONCEPT 406

sensitivity [n] *responsiveness to stimuli*
acuteness, affectibility, awareness, consciousness, delicacy, feeling, impressionability, nervousness, reactiveness, reactivity, receptiveness, sensation,

sense, sensitiveness, subtlety, susceptibility, sympathy; SEE CONCEPTS **405,410**

sensory [adj] *affecting animate nerve organs*
acoustic, afferent, audible, audiovisual, auditory, aural, auricular, clear, discernible, distinct, gustative, gustatory, hearable, lingual, neural, neurological, ocular, olfactive, olfactory, ophthalmic, optic, perceptible, phonic, plain, receptive, sensational, sensatory, sensible, sensual, sonic, tactile, visual; SEE CONCEPT **406**

sensual [adj] *physical, erotic*
animal, animalistic, arousing, bodily, carnal, debauched, delightful, epicurean, exciting, fleshly, heavy*, hedonic, hot*, lascivious, lecherous, lewd, libidinous, licentious, lustful, moving, pleasing, rough, sensuous, sexual, sexy, sharpened, steamy, stimulating, stirring, tactile, unchaste, unspiritual, voluptuous, X-rated*; SEE CONCEPTS **372,401**

sensuous [adj] *gratifying to senses*
carnal, epicurean, exciting, fleshly, fleshy, hedonistic, luscious, lush, luxurious, passionate, physical, pleasurable, pleasure-loving, pleasure-seeking, primrose, rich, self-indulgent, sensory, sensual, sensualistic, sumptuous, sybaritic, voluptuous; SEE CONCEPTS **372,537**

sentence [n] *punishing decree*
book, censure, clock, condemnation, considered opinion, decision, determination, dictum, doom, edict, fall, getup*, hitch, jolt, judgment, knock, order, penalty, pronouncement, punishment, rap*, ruling, sending up the river*, sleep, stretch, term, time, trick, vacation, verdict; SEE CONCEPT **318**

sentence [v] *decide punishment*
adjudge, adjudicate, blame, condemn, confine, convict, damn, denounce, devote, doom, impound, imprison, incarcerate, jail, judge, mete out, ordain, pass judgment, penalize, proscribe, punish, put away*, put on ice*, railroad*, rule, send to prison, send up the river*, settle, take the fall*, throw the book at*; SEE CONCEPTS **122,317**

sentiment [n] *emotion, belief*
affect, affectivity, attitude, bias, conception, conviction, disposition, emotionalism, eye, feeling, hearts and flowers*, idea, inclination, inclining, judgment, leaning, mind, opinion, overemotionalism, partiality, passion, penchant, persuasion, position, posture, predilection, propensity, romanticism, sensibility, sentimentality, slant, softheartedness, tendency, tender feeling, tenderness, thought, view, way of thinking; SEE CONCEPTS **32,410,689**

sentimental [adj] *emotional, romantic*
affected, affectionate, corny*, demonstrative, dewy-eyed, dreamy, effusive, gushing, gushy, idealistic, impressionable, inane, insipid, jejune, languishing, lovey-dovey*, loving, maudlin, moonstruck*, mushy*, nostalgic, overacted, overemotional, passionate, pathetic, rosewater*, saccharine*, sappy*, schmaltzy*, silly, simpering, sloppy*, slushy*, soapy*, soft, softhearted*, sugary*, sweet, syrupy*, tearful, tear-jerking*, tender, touching, vapid, visionary, weepy; SEE CONCEPTS **267,401,542**

separate [adj1] *disconnected*
abstracted, apart, apportioned, asunder, cut apart, cut in two, detached, disassociated, discrete, disembodied, disjointed, distant, distributed, disunited, divergent, divided, divorced, far between, free, independent, in halves, isolated, loose,

marked, parted, partitioned, put asunder, removed, scattered, set apart, set asunder, severed, sovereign, sundered, unattached, unconnected; SEE CONCEPT **577**

separate [adj2] *alone, individual*
apart, autonomous, detached, different, discrete, distinct, distinctive, diverse, free, independent, lone, one, only, particular, peculiar, several, single, sole, solitary, unique, various; SEE CONCEPTS **557,564**

separate [v1] *remove something from group; keep or set apart*
break, break off, cleave, come apart, come away, come between, detach, dichotomize, disconnect, disentangle, disjoin, disjoint, dissect, dissever, distribute, divide, divorce, intersect, part, rupture, sever, split, split up, sunder, uncombine, uncouple, undo; SEE CONCEPT **135**

separate [v2] *isolate, segregate*
assign, break up, classify, close off, comb, compartment, compartmentalize, cut off, discriminate, distribute, draw apart, group, insulate, interval, intervene, island, order, put on one side, rope off, seclude, sequester, sift, single out, sort, space, split up, stand between, winnow; SEE CONCEPTS **158,201**

separate [v3] *part company in a romantic relationship or marriage*
alienate, bifurcate, break it off*, break off, break up, decimbcile, depart, discontinue, disunify, disunite, diverge, divorce, drop, estrange, go away, go different ways*, go separate ways*, leave, part, pull out, split up, take leave, uncouple, unlink, untie the knot*; SEE CONCEPTS **297,384**

separately [adv] *alone, individually*
apart, clearly, definitely, disjointly, distinctly, independently, one at a time, one by one, personally, severally, singly, solely; SEE CONCEPTS **544,577**

separation [n] *being apart; break-up*
break, break-up, decimciling, departure, detachment, disconnection, disengagement, disjunction, disrelation, dissociation, dissolution, disunion, division, divorce, divorcement, embarkation, estrangement, farewell, gap, leave-taking*, parting, parting of the ways*, partition, pfftt*, rift, rupture, segregation, severance, split, split-up*; SEE CONCEPTS **135,195,297,388**

sequel [n] *follow-up*
aftereffect, aftermath, alternation, causatum, chain, close, closing, conclusion, consecution, consequence, continuation, development, effect, end, ending, epilogue, eventuality, finish, finishing, issue, order, outcome, part two*, payoff, progression, result, row, sequence, sequent, series, spin-off*, termination, train, upshot; SEE CONCEPTS **271,293,824,832**

sequence [n] *series, order*
arrangement, array, catenation, chain, classification, concatenation, consecution, consecutiveness, continuance, continuity, continuousness, course, cycle, disposition, distribution, flow, graduation, grouping, ordering, pecking order*, perpetuity, placement, procession, progression, row, run, sequel, skein, streak, string, subsequence, succession, successiveness, track, train; SEE CONCEPTS **721,727**

sequential [adj] *occurring in an order*
consecutive, constant, continuous, following, incessant, later, next, persistent, regular, sequent,

se
se

serial, steady, subsequent, subsequential, succedent, succeeding, successive; SEE CONCEPTS 482,548,585

sequester [v] *isolate, seclude*
cloister, close off, cut off, draw back, enisle, hide, insulate, island, secrete, segregate, separate, set apart, set off, withdraw; SEE CONCEPTS 90,188

serene [adj] *calm, undisturbed*
at peace, clear, collected, comfortable, composed, content, cool*, cool as a cucumber*, dispassionate, easy, easygoing, fair, halcyon, imperturbable, laid-back*, limpid, patient, peaceful, pellucid, phlegmatic, placid, poised, quiescent, quiet, reconciled, resting, satisfied, sedate, self-possessed, smooth, still, stoical, tranquil, undisturbed, unflappable, unruffled, untroubled; SEE CONCEPTS 401,485

serenity [n] *calm, peacefulness*
calmness, composure, cool, patience, peace, peace of mind, placidity, quietness, quietude, stillness, tranquillity; SEE CONCEPTS 633,673

serial [adj] *in continuing order*
consecutive, continual, continued, continuing, ensuing, following, going on, sequent, sequential, succedent, succeeding, successional, successive; SEE CONCEPTS 482,585

series [n] *order, succession*
alternation, arrangement, array, category, chain, classification, column, consecution, continuity, course, file, gradation, group, line, list, procession, progression, range, row, run, scale, sequel, sequence, set, skein, streak, string, suit, suite, tier, train; SEE CONCEPTS 721,727,769

serious [adj1] *somber, humorous*
austere, bound, bound and determined*, businesslike, cold sober*, contemplative, deadpan*, deliberate, determined, downbeat*, earnest, funereal, genuine, go for broke*, grave, grim, honest, intent, long-faced*, meditative, nononsense*, pensive, pokerfaced*, reflective, resolute, resolved, sedate, set, severe, sincere, sober, solemn, staid, steady, stern, thoughtful, unhumorous, unsmiling, weighty; SEE CONCEPTS 403,542

serious [adj2] *crucial, weighty*
arduous, dangerous, deep, difficult, far-reaching, fateful, fell, formidable, grave, grievous, grim, hard, heavy, important, laborious, major, meaning business*, meaningful, menacing, momentous, no joke*, no laughing matter*, of consequence, operose, out for blood*, playing hard ball*, pressing, severe, significant, smoking*, sobering, strenuous, strictly business*, threatening, tough, ugly, unamusing, unhumorous, urgent, worrying; SEE CONCEPTS 538,565,568

seriously [adv1] *not humorously*
actively, all joking aside*, cool it*, cut the comedy*, determinedly, down, earnestly, fervently, for real*, gravely, in all conscience, in all seriousness, in earnest, intently, passionately, purposefully, resolutely, sedately, simmer down*, sincerely, soberly, solemnly, sternly, straighten out, thoughtfully, vigorously, with a straight face*, with forethought, with sobriety, zealously; SEE CONCEPTS 535,542,544

seriously [adv2] *dangerously, critically*
acutely, badly, decidedly, deplorably, distressingly, gravely, grievously, harmfully, intensely, menacingly, perilously, precariously, quite, regrettably, severely, sorely, threateningly, very; SEE CONCEPTS 544,565,568

seriousness [n1] *humorlessness*
calmness, coolness, earnest, earnestness, gravity, intentness, sedateness, serious-mindedness, sincerity, sober-mindedness, sobriety, solemnity, staidness, sternness, thoughtfulness; SEE CONCEPTS 410,657

seriousness [n2] *danger; criticalness*
enormity, gravity, importance, moment, significance, urgency, weight; SEE CONCEPTS 668,675

sermon [n] *instructive speech with a moral*
address, advice, discourse, doctrine, exhortation, harangue, homily, lecture, lesson, moralism, pastoral, preach, preaching, preachment, tirade; SEE CONCEPTS 278,368

serrated [adj] *jagged*
denticulate, indented, notched, ragged, sawlike, sawtooth, saw-toothed, scored, serrate, serried, serriform, serrulate, toothed; SEE CONCEPT 486

servant [n] *person who waits on another*
assistant, attendant, cleaning person, dependent, domestic, drudge, help, helper, hireling, live-in, menial, minion, retainer, serf, server, slave; SEE CONCEPT 348

serve [v1] *aid, help; supply*
arrange, assist, attend to, be of assistance, be of use, care for, deal, deliver, dish up*, distribute, do for, give, handle, hit, minister to, nurse, oblige, play, present, provide, provision, set out, succor, wait on, work for; SEE CONCEPTS 110,136,140

serve [v2] *act, do*
accept, agree, attend, be employed by, carry on, complete, discharge, follow, fulfill, function, go through, hearken, labor, obey, observe, officiate, pass, perform, subserve, toil, work; SEE CONCEPT 91

serve [v3] *suffice; do the work of*
advantage, answer, answer the purpose, apply, avail, be acceptable, be adequate, be good enough, benefit, be of use, be useful, content, do, do duty as, fill the bill*, fit, function, make, profit, satisfy, service, suit, work, work for; SEE CONCEPTS 656,658

service [n1] *aid, help*
account, advantage, applicability, appropriateness, assistance, avail, benefit, business, check, courtesy, dispensation, duty, employ, employment, favor, fitness, indulgence, kindness, labor, maintenance, ministration, office, overhaul, relevance, serviceability, servicing, supply, use, usefulness, utility, value, work; SEE CONCEPTS 110,324,658

service [n2] *rite of a church*
ceremonial, ceremony, formality, function, liturgy, observance, ritual, sermon, worship; SEE CONCEPT 368

service [n3] *time in military service*
action, active duty, combat, duty, fighting, sting; SEE CONCEPTS 320,321

serviceable [adj] *useful, functional*
advantageous, aiding, assistive, beneficial, convenient, dependable, durable, efficient, handy, hardwearing, helpful, invaluable, operative, practical, profitable, usable, utile, utilitarian, valuable; SEE CONCEPT 560

servile [adj] *grovelling, subservient*
abject, base, beggarly, bootlicking, craven, cringing, despicable, eating crow*, eating humble pie*,

fawning, humble, ignoble, low, mean, obedient, obeisant, obsequious, passive, slavish, submissive, sycophantic, toadying, unctuous, unresisting; SEE CONCEPTS *401,404*

servitude [n] *slavery*
bondage, bonds, chains, confinement, enslavement, obedience, peonage, serfdom, serfhood, subjection, subjugation, thrall, thralldom, vassalage, yoke; SEE CONCEPTS *388,410*

session [n] *meeting, gathering*
affair, assembly, concourse, conference, discussion, get-together, hearing, huddle, jam session*, meet, period, showdown, sitting, term; SEE CONCEPTS *114,324*

set [n1] *physical bearing*
address, air, attitude, carriage, comportment, demeanor, deportment, fit, hang, inclination, mien, port, position, posture, presence, turn; SEE CONCEPT *757*

set [n2] *stage setting*
flats, mise en scène, scene, scenery, setting, stage set; SEE CONCEPT *263*

set [n3] *group, assortment*
array, assemblage, band, batch, body, bunch, bundle, camp, circle, clan, class, clique, clump, cluster, clutch, collection, company, compendium, coterie, crew, crowd, faction, gaggle, gang, kit, lot, mob, organization, outfit, pack, push, rat pack*, sect, series; SEE CONCEPTS *417,432,769*

set [adj1] *decided*
agreed, appointed, arranged, bent, certain, concluded, confirmed, customary, dead set on*, decisive, definite, determined, entrenched, established, firm, fixed, hanging tough*, immovable, intent, inveterate, ironclad, locked in*, obstinate, pat, pigheaded*, prearranged, predetermined, prescribed, regular, resolute, resolved, rigid, rooted, scheduled, set in stone*, settled, solid as a rock*, specified, stated, steadfast, stiff-necked, stipulated, stubborn, unflappable, usual, well-set; SEE CONCEPTS *535,542*

set [adj2] *firm, hardened; inflexible*
entrenched, fixed, hard and fast, hidebound, immovable, jelled, located, placed, positioned, rigid, settled, situate, situated, solid, stable, stiff, strict, stubborn, unyielding; SEE CONCEPT *488*

set [v1] *position, place*
affix, aim, anchor, apply, arrange, bestow, cast, deposit, direct, embed, ensconce, establish, fasten, fix, head, insert, install, introduce, lay, level, locate, lock, lodge, make fast, make ready, mount, park, plank, plant, plop, plunk, point, post, prepare, put, rest, seat, settle, situate, spread, station, stick, train, turn, wedge, zero in*; SEE CONCEPTS *201,202*

set [v2] *decide upon*
agree upon, allocate, allot, appoint, arrange, assign, conclude, decree, designate, determine, dictate, direct, establish, estimate, fix, fix price, impose, instruct, lay down, make, name, ordain, prescribe, price, rate, regulate, resolve, schedule, settle, specify, stipulate, value; SEE CONCEPT *18*

set [v3] *harden*
become firm, cake, clot, coagulate, condense, congeal, crystallize, fix, gel, gelate, gelatinize, jell, jellify, jelly, solidify, stiffen, thicken; SEE CONCEPT *250*

set [v4] *decline*
descend, dip, disappear, drop, go down, sink, subside, vanish; SEE CONCEPT *181*

set [v5] *start, incite*
abet, begin, commence, foment, initiate, instigate, provoke, put in motion, raise, set on*, stir up*, whip up*; SEE CONCEPT *221*

setback [n] *disappointment*
about-face*, backset, bath*, blow, bottom, check, comedown, defeat, delay, difficulty, drawing board*, flip-flop*, hindrance, hitch*, hold-up, impediment, misfortune, obstacle, rebuff, regress, regression, reversal, reversal of fortune, reverse, slowdown, stumbling block*, trouble, upset, whole new ballgame*; SEE CONCEPTS *388,674,679*

set back [v] *delay, hinder*
bog down*, decelerate, defeat, detain, embog, hang up*, hold up, impede, mire, retard, reverse, slow, slow down, slow up; SEE CONCEPT *130*

setting [n] *scene, background*
ambience, backdrop, context, distance, environment, frame, framework, horizon, jungle, locale, location, mise en scène, mounting, perspective, set, shade, shadow, site, stage set, stage setting, surroundings; SEE CONCEPTS *198,263*

settle [v1] *straighten out, resolve*
achieve, adjudicate, adjust, appoint, arrange, call the shots*, choose, cinch, clean up, clear, clear up, clinch, come to a conclusion, come to a decision, come to an agreement, complete, concert, conclude, confirm, decide, determine, discharge, dispose, end, establish, figure, fix, form judgment, judge, make a decision, make certain, mediate, nail down*, negotiate, order, pay, put an end to, put into order, reconcile, regulate, rule, satisfy, seal, set to rights, square, verify, work out; SEE CONCEPTS *18,126,341*

settle [v2] *calm, relieve*
allay, assure, becalm, compose, lull, pacify, quell, quiet, quieten, reassure, relax, sedate, soothe, still, tranquilize; SEE CONCEPTS *7,22,469*

settle [v3] *come to rest; fall*
alight, bed down, decline, descend, flop, immerse, land, lay, light, lodge, perch, place, plop, plunge, put, repose, roost, seat, set down, settle down, sink, sit, submerge, submerse, subside, touch down; SEE CONCEPT *181*

settle [v4] *make one's home*
abide, colonize, dwell, establish, hang up one's hat*, inhabit, keep house, live, locate, lodge, move to, park, put down roots*, reside, set up home, squat, take root*, take up residence; SEE CONCEPT *226*

settlement [n1] *decision, conclusion*
adjustment, agreement, arrangement, clearance, compact, compensation, completion, conclusion, confirmation, contract, covenant, deal, defrayal, determination, discharge, disposition, establishment, happy medium*, liquidation, pay, payment, payoff, quietus, reimbursement, remuneration, resolution, satisfaction, showdown, termination, trade-off, working out; SEE CONCEPTS *230,684*

settlement [n2] *community*
colonization, colony, encampment, establishment, foundation, habitation, hamlet, inhabitancy, occupancy, occupation, outpost, plantation, principality, residence; SEE CONCEPTS *512,515*

set up [v] *start*
arrange, assemble, back, begin, build, build up,

compose, constitute, construct, create, elevate, erect, establish, excite, exhilarate, found, inaugurate, initiate, inspire, install, institute, introduce, launch, make provision for, open, organize, originate, prearrange, prepare, put together, put up, raise, rear, stimulate, strengthen, subsidize, usher in; SEE CONCEPT 221

sever [v1] *cut apart*
bisect, carve, cleave, cut, cut in two, detach, disconnect, disjoin, dissect, dissever, dissociate, disunite, divide, part, rend, rive, separate, slice, split, sunder; SEE CONCEPTS 98,176

sever [v2] *dissociate*
abandon, break off, disjoint, dissolve, divide, divorce, put an end to, separate, terminate; SEE CONCEPTS 297,384

several [adj] *assorted, various*
a few, a lot, any, certain, considerable, definite, different, disparate, distinct, divers, diverse, handful, hardly any, indefinite, individual, infrequent, manifold, many, not many, numerous, only a few, particular, personal, plural, proportionate, quite a few, rare, respective, scant, scanty, scarce, scarcely any, separate, single, small number, some, sparse, special, specific, sundry; SEE CONCEPTS 564,762

severe [adj1] *uncompromising, stern*
astringent, austere, biting, caustic, close, cold, cruel, cutting, disapproving, dour, earnest, firm, flinty, forbidding, grave, grim, hard, hard-nosed*, harsh, inconsiderate, inexorable, inflexible, ironhanded, obdurate, oppressive, peremptory, pitiless, relentless, resolute, resolved, rigid, satirical, scathing, serious, sober, stern, stiff*, strait-laced*, strict, tight-lipped*, unalterable, unbending, unchanging, unfeeling, unrelenting, unsmiling, unsparing; SEE CONCEPTS 401,534, 542

severe [adj2] *difficult, harsh*
acute, arduous, ascetic, austere, bitter, bleak, consequential, critical, dangerous, dear, demanding, despotic, distressing, domineering, drastic, effortful, exacting, extreme, fierce, forbidding, grave, grim, grinding, hard, heavy, hefty, implacable, inclement, intemperate, intense, mordant, oppressive, overbearing, pitiless, punishing, rigorous, rugged, serious, sharp, sore, strenuous, stringent, taxing, toilsome, tough, tyrannical, unpleasant, unrelenting, violent, weighty, wicked; SEE CONCEPTS 565,569

severely [adv] *harshly*
acutely, badly, critically, dangerously, extremely, firmly, gravely, hard, hardly, intensely, markedly, painfully, rigorously, roughly, seriously, sharply, sorely, sternly, strictly, with an iron hand; SEE CONCEPT 569

sew [v] *prepare fabric for clothing, covering*
baste, bind, embroider, fasten, piece, seam, stitch, tack, tailor, work; SEE CONCEPT 218

sex [n1] *male or female gender*
femininity, manhood, manliness, masculinity, sexuality, womanhood, womanliness; SEE CONCEPT 648

sex [n2] *intercourse between animate beings*
birds and the bees*, coition, coitus, copulation, facts of life*, fornication, generation, intimacy, lovemaking, magnetism, procreation, relations, reproduction, sensuality, sexuality; SEE CONCEPT 375

sexual [adj] *concerning reproduction, intercourse*
animal, animalistic, bestial, carnal, erotic, fleshly, generative, genital, genitive, intimate, loving, passionate, procreative, reproductive, sensual, sharing, venereal, voluptuous, wanton; SEE CONCEPT 372

sexy [adj] *being erotically attractive to another*
arousing, come-hither*, cuddly, flirtatious, hot*, inviting, kissable, libidinous, mature, provocative, provoking, racy, risqué, seductive, sensual, sensuous, slinky*, spicy*, steamy*, suggestive, titillating, voluptuous; SEE CONCEPT 372

shabby [adj1] *broken-down; in poor shape*
bare, bedraggled, crummy, decayed, decaying, decrepit, degenerated, desolate, deteriorated, deteriorating, dilapidated, dingy, disfigured, disreputable, dog-eared*, faded, frayed, gone to seed*, mangy, meager, mean, miserable, moth-eaten, neglected, pitiful, poor, poverty-stricken, ragged, ramshackle, ratty, rickety, ruined, ruinous, run-down, scrubby, scruffy, seedy, shoddy, sleazy, slipshod, squalid, tacky, tattered, threadbare, tired, worn, worn-out, worse for wear*, wretched; SEE CONCEPT 485

shabby [adj2] *despicable*
beggarly, cheap, contemptible, despisable, dirty, disgraceful, dishonorable, disreputable, ignoble, ignominious, inconsiderate, inglorious, low, low-down, mean, mercenary, miserly, rotten, scummy, selfish, shady, shameful, shoddy, sordid, sorry, stingy, thoughtless, unkind, unworthy; SEE CONCEPTS 401,404

shade [n1] *dimness*
adumbration, blackness, coolness, cover, darkness, dusk, gloominess, obscuration, obscurity, penumbra, screen, semidarkness, shadiness, shadow, shadows, umbra, umbrage; SEE CONCEPT 620

shade [n2] *blind, shield*
awning, canopy, cover, covering, curtain, screen, veil; SEE CONCEPT 445

shade [n3] *color, hue*
brilliance, cast, saturation, stain, tinge, tint, tone; SEE CONCEPTS 620,622

shade [n4] *slight difference*
amount, cast, dash, degree, distinction, gradation, hint, nuance, proposal, semblance, soupçon, spice, streak, suggestion, suspicion, tincture, tinge, trace, variation, variety; SEE CONCEPT 665

shade [n5] *ghost*
apparition, bogey, haunt, manes, phantasm, phantom, revenant, shadow, specter, spirit, umbra, wraith; SEE CONCEPT 370

shade [v] *shut out the light*
adumbrate, be overcast, blacken, cast a shadow, cloud, cloud over, cloud up, conceal, cover, darken, deepen, dim, eclipse, gray, hide, inumbrate, mute, obscure, overshadow, protect, screen, shadow, shelter, shield, shutter, tone down, umbrage, veil; SEE CONCEPTS 250,526

shadow [n1] *darkness*
adumbration, cover, dark, dimness, dusk, gloom, obscuration, obscurity, penumbra, protection, shade, shelter, umbra, umbrage; SEE CONCEPTS 620,622

shadow [n2] *hint, suggestion*
breath, intimation, memento, relic, smack, suspicion, tincture, tinge, touch, trace, vestige; SEE CONCEPT 278

shadow [v1] *make dark*
adumbrate, becloud, bedim, cast a shadow, cloud, darken, dim, gray, haze, inumbrate, obscure, overcast, overcloud, overhang, overshadow, screen, shade, shelter, shield, umbrage, veil; SEE CONCEPT 250

shadow [v2] *follow secretly*
dog, keep in sight, pursue, spy on, stalk, tag, tail, trail, watch; SEE CONCEPT 207

shady [adj1] *dark, covered*
adumbral, bosky, cloudy, cool, dim, dusky, indistinct, leafy, out of the sun*, screened, shaded, shadowed, shadowy, sheltered, umbrageous, umbrous, under a cloud, vague; SEE CONCEPTS 485,617

shady [adj2] *disreputable, suspicious*
crooked, disgraceful, dishonest, dishonorable, dubious, fishy, ignominious, infamous, inglorious, notorious, questionable, scandalous, shabby, shameful, shifty, shoddy, slippery, suspect, suspicious, underhanded, unethical, unrespectable, unscrupulous, untrustworthy; SEE CONCEPT 545

shaggy [adj] *hairy, unkempt*
furry, hirsute, long-haired, ragged, rough, ruffled, rugged, uncombed, unshorn; SEE CONCEPT 485

shake [v1] *quiver, tremble*
agitate, brandish, bump, chatter, churn, commove, concuss, convulse, discompose, disquiet, disturb, dither, dodder, flap, flicker, flit, flitter, flourish, fluctuate, flutter, jar, jerk, jog, joggle, jolt, jounce, move, oscillate, palpitate, perturb, quail, quake, quaver, rattle, reel, rock, roil, ruffle, set in motion, shimmer, shimmy, shiver, shudder, stagger, stir up, succuss, sway, swing, totter, tremble, tremor, twitter, upset, vibrate, waggle, water, wave, whip, wobble; SEE CONCEPTS 150,152

shake [v2] *upset deeply*
appall, bother, consternate, daunt, discompose, dismay, distress, disturb, frighten, horrify, impair, intimidate, jar, knock props out*, make nervous*, move, rattle, throw, throw a curve*, undermine, unnerve, unsettle, unstring, upset, weaken, worry; SEE CONCEPTS 7,19

shake off [v] *lose by getting away*
clear, dislodge, drop, elude, get away from, get rid of, give the slip*, leave behind, remove, rid oneself of, throw off, unburden; SEE CONCEPTS 102,195

shake up [v] *upset, unsettle*
agitate, break with past*, cause revolution*, churn up*, clean out, clean up, clear out, disturb, liquidate, make a clean sweep*, mix, overturn, purge, remove, reorganize, rid, shock, stir up, turn upside down*; SEE CONCEPTS 14,324

shaky [adj1] *trembling*
all aquiver*, aquake, aquiver, ashake, faltering, fluctuant, infirm, insecure, jellylike, jerry-built*, jittery, nervous, not set, precarious, quaking, quivery, rattletrap, rickety, rocky, rootless, shaking, tottering, tottery, trembling, tremorous, tremulous, tumbledown, unfirm, unsettled, unsound, unstable, unsteady, unsure, vacillating, wavering, weak, wobbly, yielding; SEE CONCEPT 488

shaky [adj2] *doubtful*
dubious, indecisive, not dependable, not reliable, precarious, problematic, questionable, suspect, uncertain, unclear, undependable, unreliable, unsettled, unsound, unsteady, unsupported, unsure; SEE CONCEPT 535

shallow [adj1] *not deep*
cursory, depthless, empty, flat, hollow, inconsiderable, sand bar, shelf, shoal, slight, superficial, surface, trifling, trivial, unsound; SEE CONCEPTS 737,777

shallow [adj2] *unintelligent, ignorant*
cursory, empty, empty-headed, farcical, feather-brained, flighty, flimsy, foolish, frivolous, frothy, half-baked*, hollow, idle, inane, lightweight, meaningless, paltry, petty, piddling, puerile, simple, sketchy, skin-deep*, slight, superficial, surface, trifling, trivial, uncritical, unthinking, vain, wishy-washy*; SEE CONCEPT 402

sham [n] *hoax, trick*
burlesque, cant, caricature, cheat, counterfeit, cover-up, deceit, deception, facade, fake, fakery, false front, farce, feint, flimflam*, forgery, fraud, hypocrisy, hypocriticalness, imitation, impostor, imposture, jive*, mock, mockery, pharisaism, phoniness, pretend, pretense, pretext, pseudo*, put-on, sell, smoke*, snow job*, spoof, travesty, whitewash; SEE CONCEPTS 59,192

sham [adj] *artificial, counterfeit*
adulterated, affected, assumed, bogus*, dummy, ersatz*, fake, false, feigned, fictitious, forged, fraudulent, imitation, lying, make-believe, misleading, mock, phony, plaster*, pretend, pretended, pseudo*, simulated, so-called, spurious, substitute, synthetic, untrue; SEE CONCEPT 582

sham [v] *trick; pull a hoax*
act, affect, ape, assume, bluff, copy, counterfeit, create, do a number*, fake, fake it, feign, imitate, invent, lie, make like, mislead, mock, play possum*, pretend, put on, put up a front*, shuck and jive*, simulate, sucker*; SEE CONCEPTS 59,111, 171

shambles [n] *a mess*
anarchy, babel, bedlam, botch, chaos, confusion, disarray, disorder, disorganization, hash, havoc, hodge-podge, madhouse, maelstrom, mess-up, mix-up, muddle; SEE CONCEPTS 230,674

shame [n] *disgrace embarrassment*
abashment, bad conscience*, blot, chagrin, compunction, confusion, contempt, contrition, degradation, derision, discomposure, discredit, disesteem, dishonor, disrepute, guilt, humiliation, ignominy, ill repute, infamy, irritation, loss of face*, mortification, obloquy, odium, opprobrium, pang, pudency, remorse, reproach, scandal, self-disgust, self-reproach, self-reproof, shamefacedness, skeleton in the cupboard*, smear, stigma, stupefaction, treachery; SEE CONCEPTS 388,410

shame [v] *disgrace, embarrass*
abash, blot, confound, cut down to size*, debase, defile, degrade, disconcert, discredit, dishonor, give a black eye*, humble, humiliate, mortify, reproach, ridicule, shoot down*, smear, stain, take down*, take down a peg*; SEE CONCEPTS 7,14,19

shameful [adj] *atrocious; disreputable*
base, carnal, contemptible, corrupt, dastardly, debauched, degrading, diabolical, disgraceful, dishonorable, drunken, embarrassing, flagrant, heinous, humiliating, ignominious, immodest, immoral, impure, indecent, infamous, intemperate, lewd, low, mean, mortifying, notorious, obscene, opprobrious, outrageous, profligate, reprehensible, reprobate, ribald, scandalous, shaming, shocking, sinful, unbecoming, unclean, unwor-

se
sh

thy, vile, villainous, vulgar, wicked; SEE CON-
CEPTS *401,545,571*

shameless [*adj*] *corrupt, indecent*
abandoned, arrant, audacious, barefaced, bold,
brash, brassy, brazen, cheeky*, depraved, dissolute, flagrant, forward, hardened, high-handed*,
immodest, immoral, improper, impudent, incorrigible, insolent, lewd, outrageous, overbold, presumptuous, profligate, reprobate, rude, unabashed, unashamed, unblushing, unchaste, unprincipled, wanton; SEE CONCEPTS *401,545*

shape [*n1*] *form, structure*
appearance, architecture, aspect, body, build,
cast, chassis, circumscription, configuration, conformation, constitution, construction, contour,
cut, embodiment, figure, format, frame, guise,
likeness, lineation, lines, look, make, metamorphosis, model, mold, outline, pattern, profile,
semblance, shadow, silhouette, simulacrum,
stamp, symmetry; SEE CONCEPTS *436,754,757*

shape [*n2*] *condition, health*
case, estate, fettle, fitness, kilter, order, repair,
state, trim, whack*; SEE CONCEPTS *316,720*

shape [*v1*] *form, create*
assemble, block out, bring together, build, carve,
cast, chisel, construct, crystallize, cut, embody,
fabricate, fashion, forge, frame, hew, knead,
make, mint, model, mold, pat, pattern, produce,
roughhew, sculpture, sketch, stamp, streamline,
throw together*, trim, whittle; SEE CONCEPTS
137,184

shape [*v2*] *devise, plan*
accommodate, adapt, become, define, develop,
form, frame, grow, guide, modify, prepare, regulate, remodel, tailor, take form, work up; SEE
CONCEPT *36*

shapeless [*adj*] *formless*
abnormal, amorphic, amorphous, anomalous,
assymetrical, baggy, deformed, disfigured,
embryonic, ill-formed, inchoate, indefinite,
indeterminate, indistinct, invisible, irregular, malformed, misshapen, mutilated, nebulous, undeveloped, unformed, ungraceful, unmade, unshapely,
unstructured, unsymmetrical, vague, without
character, without form; SEE CONCEPTS *486,589*

shapely [*adj*] *well-proportioned*
balanced, beautiful, built, comely, curvaceous, elegant, full-figured, graceful, neat, pleasing, pro-
portioned, regular, rounded, sightly, statuesque,
sylphlike, symmetrical, trim, well-formed, well-
turned; SEE CONCEPTS *406,490*

share [*n*] *portion, allotment*
allowance, apportionment, bite, chunk, claim,
commission, contribution, cut, cut in, cut up, divide, dividend, division, divvy*, dose, drag*,
due, end, fifty-fifty*, fraction, fragment, halver,
helping, heritage, interest, lagniappe, lot, measure, meed, parcel, part, partage, percentage,
piece, pittance, plum, points, proportion, quantum, quota, quotient, quotum, rake-off*, ration,
segment, serving, slice, split, stake, taste,
whack*; SEE CONCEPTS *710,835*

share [*v*] *use in common with others*
accord, administer, allot, apportion, assign, be a
party to, bestow, cut the pie*, deal, dispense, distribute, divide, divide with, divvy*, divvy up*,
dole out, experience, give and take, give out, go
Dutch*, go fifty-fifty*, go halves*, go in with,
have a hand in, have a portion of, mete out, parcel
out, part, partake, participate, partition, pay half,

piece up, prorate, quota, ration, receive, shift,
slice, slice up, split, split up, take a part of, yield;
SEE CONCEPTS *98,100,384*

sharp [*adj1*] *knifelike, cutting*
aciculate, acuate, acuminate, acuminous, acute,
apical, barbed, briery, cuspate, cuspidate, edged,
fine, ground fine, honed, horned, jagged, keen,
keen-edged, knife-edged, needlelike, needle-
pointed, peaked, pointed, pointy, prickly,
pronged, razor-sharp, salient, serrated, sharp-
edged, sharpened, spiked, spiky, spiny, splintery,
stinging, tapered, tapering, thorny, tined, tipped,
unblunted, whetted; SEE CONCEPT *486*

sharp [*adj2*] *sudden*
abrupt, distinct, extreme, intense, marked; SEE
CONCEPTS *581,799*

sharp [*adj3*] *perceptive, quick-witted*
acute, adroit, alert, apt, astute, brainy, bright, brilliant, canny, clever, critical, cute, discerning, discriminating, fast, foxy*, having smarts*,
ingenious, intelligent, keen, knowing, nimble, nobody's fool*, not born yesterday*, observant, on
the ball*, original, penetrating, penetrative, quick,
quick on the trigger*, quick on the uptake*, ready,
resourceful, savvy*, sensitive, slick, smart, smart
as a tack*, subtle, wise; SEE CONCEPT *402*

sharp [*adj4*] *dishonest, deceitful*
artful, bent, crafty, cunning, designing, ornery,
salty, shady, shrewd, slick, slippery, sly, smart,
snaky, two-faced*, underhand, unethical, unscrupulous, wily; SEE CONCEPT *545*

sharp [*adj5*] *severe, intense*
acute, agonizing, biting, cutting, distinct, distressing, drilling, excruciating, fierce, keen, knifelike,
painful, paralyzing, penetrating, piercing, shooting, smart, sore, stabbing, stinging, violent; SEE
CONCEPTS *537,569*

sharp [*adj6*] *distinct, well-defined*
audible, clear, clear-cut, crisp, definite, explicit,
obvious, visible; SEE CONCEPT *535*

sharp [*adj7*] *stylish*
chic, classy, dashing, distinctive, dressy, excellent, fashionable, fine, first-class*, fly*, in style,
smart, snappy*, swank*, tony*, trendy; SEE CON-
CEPT *589*

sharp [*adj8*] *hurtful, bitter in speech*
acrimonious, angry, barbed, biting, caustic, cutting, double-edged, harsh, incisive, inconsiderate,
penetrating, peppery, piercing, pointed, pungent,
sarcastic, sardonic, scathing, severe, short, stabbing, stinging, tart, thoughtless, trenchant, unceremonious, ungracious, virulent, vitriolic; SEE
CONCEPT *267*

sharp [*adj9*] *having strong affect on animate senses*
acerbic, acid, acrid, active, astringent, austere,
bitter, brisk, burning, harsh, hot, lively, odorous,
piquant, pungent, sour, strong-smelling, suffocating, tart, vigorous, vinegary; SEE CONCEPTS
537,598,613

sharp [*adv*] *on time*
abruptly, accurately, bang, exactly, just, on the
button*, on the dot*, precisely, promptly, punctually, right, smack-dab*, square, squarely, suddenly; SEE CONCEPT *799*

sharpen [*v*] *make knifelike*
acuminate, dress, edge, file, grind, hone, make
acute, make sharp, put an edge on, put a point on,
sharp, stroke, strop, taper, whet; SEE CONCEPTS
137,250

shatter [v1] *break into small pieces*
blast, blight, burst, crack, crash, crunch, crush, dash, demolish, destroy, disable, exhaust, explode, fracture, fragment, fragmentalize, fragmentize, impair, implode, overturn, pulverize, rend, rive, ruin, scrunch, shiver, smash, smash to smithereens*, smatter, snap, splinter, splinterize*, split, torpedo*, total*, wrack up*, wreck; SEE CONCEPTS 246,252

shatter [v2] *hurt someone badly*
break a heart*, crush, destroy, devastate, dumbfound, rattle, ruin, upset; SEE CONCEPTS 7,19

shave [v] *cut outer covering off*
barber, brush, clip, crop, cut, cut back, cut down, decorticate, graze, kiss, make bare, pare, peel, plane, prune, shear, shingle, shred, skim, skin, slash, slice thin, sliver, strip, touch, trim; SEE CONCEPTS 137,162,176,202

shed [v] *cast off*
afford, beam, cashier, cast, diffuse, disburden, discard, doff, drop, emit, exude, exuviate, give, give forth, jettison, junk, let fall, molt, pour forth, radiate, reject, scatter, scrap, send forth, shower, slip, slough, spill, sprinkle, take off, throw, throw away, throw out, yield; SEE CONCEPTS 179,180,181,211

sheen [n] *brightness, shine*
burnish, finish, glaze, gleam, glint, gloss, luster, patina, polish, shimmer, shininess, wax; SEE CONCEPT 620

sheepish [adj] *shy, embarrassed*
abashed, ashamed, chagrined, diffident, docile, foolish, guilty, mortified, retiring, self-conscious, shamefaced, silly, tame, timid, timorous, uncomfortable; SEE CONCEPT 401

sheer [adj1] *abrupt, steep*
arduous, erect, headlong, perpendicular, precipitate, precipitous, sideling, upright; SEE CONCEPTS 490,581

sheer [adj2] *utter, absolute*
altogether, arrant, blasted, blessed, complete, confounded, downright, gross, infernal, out-and-out*, outright, perfect, pure, quite, rank, simple, single, thoroughgoing, total, unadulterated, unalloyed, undiluted, unmitigated, unmixed, unqualified; SEE CONCEPTS 531,535,544

sheer [adj3] *see-through, thin*
airy, chiffon, clear, cobwebby, delicate, diaphanous, filmy, fine, flimsy, fragile, gauzy, gossamer, lacy, limpid, lucid, pellucid, pure, slight, smooth, soft, tiffany, translucent, transparent; SEE CONCEPT 606

sheet [n] *coating, covering; page*
area, blanket, coat, expanse, film, foil, folio, lamina, layer, leaf, membrane, overlay, pane, panel, piece, plate, ply, slab, stratum, stretch, surface, sweep, veneer; SEE CONCEPTS 172,270,475,484

shelf [n] *jutting, flat area or piece*
bank, bracket, console, counter, cupboard, ledge, mantelpiece, mantle, rack, reef, ridge, rock, shallow, shoal; SEE CONCEPTS 445,509,513

shell [n] *structure; covering*
carapace, case, chassis, crust, frame, framework, hull, husk, integument, nut, pericarp, plastron, pod, scale, shard, shuck, skeleton, skin; SEE CONCEPTS 399,428,484

shell out [v] *give*
ante up, disburse, expend, fork over*, hand over, lay out, outlay, pay, pay for, pay out, spend; SEE CONCEPT 341

shelter [n] *protection, habitat*
apartment, asylum, cave, condo, co-op, cover, covert, crib*, defense, den, digs*, dwelling, guard, guardian, harbor, harborage, haven, hermitage, hide, hideaway, hideout, hole in the wall*, home, homeplate*, house, housing, hut, joint*, lodging, pad*, pen, port, preserve, protector, quarterage, rack, refuge, retirement, retreat, roof, roof over head*, roost*, safety, sanctuary, screen, security, shack, shade, shadow, shed, shield, tent, tower, turf, umbrella; SEE CONCEPTS 515,712

shelter [v] *provide safety, cover*
chamber, conceal, cover, cover up, defend, enclose, guard, harbor, haven, hide, house, lodge, preserve, protect, roof, safeguard, screen, secure, shield, surround, take care of, take in, ward, watch over; SEE CONCEPTS 134,188

shelve [v] *defer, postpone*
delay, dismiss, drop, freeze*, give up, hang up, hold, hold off, hold over, hold up, lay aside, mothball*, pigeonhole*, prolong, prorogue, put aside, put off, put on back burner*, put on hold, put on ice*, scrub*, sideline, slow up, stay, suspend, table, tie up, waive; SEE CONCEPT 121

shield [n] *protection*
absorber, aegis, armament, armor, buckler, buffer, bulwark, bumper, cover, defense, escutcheon, guard, mail, rampart, safeguard, screen, security, shelter, ward; SEE CONCEPTS 712,729

shield [v] *protect*
bulwark, chamber, conceal, cover, cover all bases*, cover up, defend, fend, give cover, give shelter, go to bat for*, guard, harbor, haven, house, ride shotgun*, roof, safeguard, screen, secure, shelter, shotgun*, stonewall*, take under one's wing*, ward off; SEE CONCEPTS 96,134

shift [n1] *switch, fluctuation*
about-face*, alteration, bend, change, changeover, conversion, deflection, deviation, displacement, double, fault, modification, move, passage, permutation, rearrangement, removal, shifting, substitution, switch, tack, transfer, transference, transformation, transit, translocation, turn, variation, veering, yaw; SEE CONCEPTS 213,697

shift [n2] *trick, stratagem*
artifice, contrivance, craft, device, dodge, equivocation, evasion, expediency, expedient, gambit, hoax, makeshift, maneuver, move, ploy, recourse, refuge, resort, resource, ruse, stopgap*, strategy, substitute, subterfuge, wile; SEE CONCEPTS 59,660

shift [n3] *time served doing work*
bout, go, period, spell, stint, time, tour, trick, turn, working time; SEE CONCEPT 802

shift [v] *switch, fluctuate*
about-face*, alter, blow hot and cold*, bottom out*, budge, change, change gears, cook*, deviate, dial back*, dislocate, displace, disturb, do up*, drift, exchange, fault, flip-flop*, hem and haw*, move, move around, move over, rearrange, recalibrate, relocate, remove, replace, reposition, ship, shuffle, slip, stir, substitute, swap places, swerve, switch over, tack, transfer, transmogrify, transpose, turn, turn around, turn the corner*, turn the tables*, vacillate, vary, veer, waffle, yo-yo*; SEE CONCEPTS 213,232,697

shifty [adj] *deceitful, untrustworthy*
cagey, collusive, conniving, contriving, crafty, crooked, cunning, devious, dishonest, dodging, duplicitous, elusive, equivocating, evasive, fly-

sh
sh

by-night*, foxy, fraudulent, furtive, insidious, lying, mendacious, prevaricative, prevaricatory, roguish, scheming, shady, shrewd, shuffling, slick, slimy*, slippery, sly, sneaky, treacherous, tricky, underhand, unhonest, unprincipled, untruthful, wily; SEE CONCEPTS 401,404

shimmer [n] *gleam*

blinking, coruscation, diffused light, flash, glimmer, glint, glisten, glitter, gloss, glow, incandescence, iridescence, luster, phosphorescence, scintillation, sheen, spangle, spark, sparkle, twinkle; SEE CONCEPTS 620,624

shimmer [v] *glisten*

blaze, coruscate, dance, flare, flash, gleam, glint, glow, jiggle, phosphoresce, scintillate, shimmy, shine, sparkle, twinkle; SEE CONCEPT 624

shine [n] *brightness; polish*

flash, glare, glaze, gleam, glint, glitz, gloss, lambency, light, luminosity, luster, patina, polish, radiance, rub, sheen, shimmer, show, sparkle; SEE CONCEPT 620

shine [v1] *give off or reflect light*

beam, bedazzle, blaze, blink, burn, dazzle, deflect, emit light, flare, flash, flicker, give light, glare, gleam, glimmer, glisten, glitter, glow, illuminate, illumine, incandesce, irradiate, luminesce, mirror, radiate, scintillate, shimmer, sparkle, twinkle; SEE CONCEPT 624

shine [v2] *polish, burnish*

brush, buff, buff up, finish, furbish, give a sheen, glance, glaze, gloss, make brilliant, put a finish on, put a gloss on, rub, scour, sleek, wax; SEE CONCEPT 202

shiny [adj] *bright, glistening*

agleam, burnished, clear, gleaming, glossy, lustrous, polished, satiny, sheeny, slick, sparkling, sunny; SEE CONCEPT 617

ship [v] *send, transport*

address, consign, direct, dispatch, drop, embark, export, forward, freight, go aboard, haul, move, put on board, remit, route, shift, ship out, smuggle, transfer, transmit; SEE CONCEPTS 148,217

shirk [v] *avoid, get out of responsibility*

bypass, cheat, creep, dodge, dog*, duck, elude, eschew, evade, fence, get around, goldbrick*, lie down on job*, lurk, malinger, parry, pussyfoot*, quit, shuffle off, shun, sidestep, skulk, slack, slink, slip, slough off, snake, sneak, steal; SEE CONCEPTS 30,59,681

shiver [v1] *shake, tremble*

be cold, dither, flutter, freeze, have the quivers, have the shakes, palpitate, quake, quaver, quiver, shudder, tremor, twitter, vibrate, wave; SEE CONCEPTS 152,185

shiver [v2] *shatter; break into small pieces*

burst, crack, fragment, fragmentalize, pash, rive, smash, smash to smithereens*, smatter, splinter, splinterize*; SEE CONCEPTS 246,252

shock [n] *complete surprise; blow*

awe, bombshell*, breakdown, bump, clash, collapse, collision, concussion, confusion, consternation, crash, distress, disturbance, double whammy*, earthquake, encounter, excitement, eye-opener*, hysteria, impact, injury, jarring, jolt, percussion, prostration, ram, scare, start, stroke, stupefaction, stupor, trauma, traumatism, turn, upset, whammy*, wreck; SEE CONCEPTS 33,309,529

shock [v] *completely surprise*

abash, agitate, anger, antagonize, appall, astound,

awe, bowl over*, daze, disgust, dismay, displease, disquiet, disturb, electrify, flabbergast, flood, floor*, give a turn*, hit like ton of bricks*, horrify, insult, jar, jolt, knock out*, nauseate, numb, offend, outrage, overcome, overwhelm, paralyze, revolt, rock, scandalize, shake, shake up, sicken, stagger, startle, stun, stupefy, throw a curve*, traumatize, unsettle; SEE CONCEPT 42

shocking [adj] *outrageous; very surprising*

abominable, appalling, atrocious, awful, burning, crying, desperate, detestable, direful, disgraceful, disgusting, disquieting, distressing, dreadful, fearful, formidable, foul, frightful, ghastly, glaring, hateful, heinous, hideous, horrible, horrific, horrifying, loathsome, monstrous, nauseating, odious, offensive, repulsive, revolting, scandalous, shameful, sickening, stupefying, terrible, ugly, unspeakable; SEE CONCEPTS 548,571

shoddy [adj] *in bad shape*

base, broken-down, cheap, cheesy*, common, dilapidated, dingy, discreditable, disgraceful, dishonorable, disreputable, gaudy, ignominious, inferior, inglorious, junky, makeshift, mean, not up to snuff*, paltry, plastic, poor, pretentious, run-down, scruffy*, second-rate*, seedy, shabby, shady, shameful, sleazy*, slipshod, tacky*, tawdry, trashy, unrespectable; SEE CONCEPTS 485,571

shoot [v1] *discharge a projectile, often to injure or kill*

bag*, barrage, blast, bombard, bring down, catapult, dispatch, drop the hammer*, emit, execute, expel, explode, fire, fling, gun, hit, hurl, ignite, kill, launch, let fly, let go with, loose, murder, open fire*, open up*, pick off*, plug, pop*, project, propel, pull the trigger, pump*, set off, throw lead*, torpedo, trigger, zap*; SEE CONCEPTS 179,246,252

shoot [v2] *dash*

boil, bolt, charge, chase, dart, flash, fling, fly, gallop, hotfoot*, hurry, hurtle, lash, pass, race, reach, run, rush, scoot, skirr, speed, spring, spurt, streak, tear, whisk, whiz; SEE CONCEPTS 150,152

shop [n] *place of retail business*

boutique, chain, deli, department store, emporium, five-and-dime, market, mill, outlet, showroom, stand, store, supermarket; SEE CONCEPTS 439,441,448,449

shop [v] *look for merchandise to buy*

buy, go shopping, hunt for, look for, market, purchase, try to buy; SEE CONCEPTS 327,330

shore [n] *waterside*

bank, beach, border, brim, brink, coast, coastland, embankment, lakeshore, lakeside, littoral, margin, river bank, riverside, sand, sands, seaboard, seacoast, seashore, shingle, strand, waterfront; SEE CONCEPT 509

shore [v] *reinforce*

bear up, bolster, brace, bulwark, buttress, carry, hold, prop, strengthen, support, sustain, underpin, upbear, uphold; SEE CONCEPTS 110,190

short [adj1] *abridged*

abbreviate, abbreviated, aphoristic, bare, boiled down, breviloquent, brief, compendiary, compendious, compressed, concise, condensed, curtailed, curtate, cut short, cut to the bone*, decreased, decurtate, diminished, epigrammatic, fleeting, in a nutshell*, laconic, lessened, little, momentary, not protracted, pithy, pointed, precise, sententious, short and sweet*, shortened, short-lived, short-term, succinct, summarized, summary, terse, undersized, unprolonged, unsustained; SEE CONCEPTS 267,272,798

short [adj2] *not tall*
abbreviated, chunky, close to the ground, compact, diminutive, little, low, not long, petite, pint-sized*, pocket, pocket-sized*, runty, sawed-off*, skimpy, slight, small, squat, squatty, stocky, stubby, stunted, thick, thickset, tiny, undersized, wee; SEE CONCEPTS 773,779,782

short [adj3] *insufficient*
deficient, exiguous, failing, inadequate, lacking, limited, low on, meager, needing, niggardly, poor, scant, scanty, scarce, short-handed*, shy, skimpy, slender, slim, sparse, tight, wanting; SEE CONCEPTS 527,560,762

short [adj4] *abrupt, discourteous*
bad-tempered, blunt, breviloquent, brief, brusque, curt, direct, gruff, impolite, inconsiderate, irascible, offhand, rude, sharp, short-spoken, short-tempered, snappy*, snippety*, snippy*, straight, terse, testy, thoughtless, unceremonious, uncivil, ungracious; SEE CONCEPTS 267,401

short [adj5] *crumbly*
brittle, crisp, crunchy, delicate, fragile, friable; SEE CONCEPT 462

short [adv] *abruptly*
aback, by surprise, forthwith, sudden, suddenly, unanticipatedly, unaware, unawares, unexpectedly, without delay, without hesitation, without warning; SEE CONCEPT 799

shortage [n] *deficiency*
curtailment, dearth, defalcation, deficit, failure, inadequacy, insufficiency, lack, lapse, leanness, paucity, pinch, poverty, scantiness, scarcity, shortfall, tightness, underage, want, weakness; SEE CONCEPTS 646,709,767

shortcoming [n] *weak point*
bug*, catch*, defect, deficiency, demerit, drawback, failing, fault, flaw, frailty, imperfection, infirmity, lack, lapse, sin, weakness; SEE CONCEPTS 411,666,674,679

shorten [v] *diminish, decrease*
abbreviate, abridge, blue pencil*, bob, boil down*, chop, clip, compress, condense, contract, curtail, cut, cut back, cut down, cut to the bone*, dock, edit, elide, excerpt, lessen, lop, make a long story short*, minimize, put in a nutshell*, reduce, retrench, shrink, slash, snip, trim; SEE CONCEPTS 137,236,240,247

short-lived [adj] *temporary*
brief, ephemeral, evanescent, fleeting, fugacious, fugitive, impermanent, momentary, passing, short, short-haul*, short-run, short-term, transient, transitory; SEE CONCEPT 798

shortly [adv] *right away*
anon, any minute now, before long, by and by, in a little while, presently, proximately, quickly, soon; SEE CONCEPT 820

short-sighted [adj] *unmindful of future consequences*
astigmatic, blind, careless, foolish, headlong, ill-advised, ill-considered, imperceptive, impolitic, impractical, improvident, imprudent, injudicious, myopic, near-sighted, rash, stupid, unsagacious, unwary; SEE CONCEPTS 401,542

shot [n1] *try, chance*
attempt, break, conjecture, effort, endeavor, fling*, go*, guess, occasion, opening, opportu-

nity, pop*, show, slap*, stab*, surmise, time, turn, whack*, whirl*; SEE CONCEPT 693

shot [n2] *discharge; ammunition*
ball, buckshot, bullet, dart, lead, lob, missile, pellet, projectile, slug, throw; SEE CONCEPT 498

shoulder [v1] *be responsible for*
accept, assume, bear, carry, take on, take upon oneself; SEE CONCEPT 23

shoulder [v2] *push, jostle*
bulldoze*, elbow, hustle, nudge, press, push aside, shove, thrust; SEE CONCEPT 208

shout [n] *loud outcry*
bark, bawl, bellow, call, cheer, clamor, cry, howl, hue, roar, salvo, scream, screech, shriek, squall, squawk, tumult, vociferation, whoop*, yammer*, yap*, yawp*, yell; SEE CONCEPTS 77,595

shout [v] *cry out loudly*
bawl, bay, bellow, call out, cheer, clamor, exclaim, holler*, raise voice, roar, scream, screech, shriek, squall, squawk, vociferate, whoop*, yammer*, yap*, yawp*, yell; SEE CONCEPT 77

shove [v] *push without gentleness*
boost, buck, bulldoze*, cram, crowd, dig, drive, elbow, hustle, impel, jab, jam, jostle, nudge, poke, press, prod, propel, shoulder, thrust; SEE CONCEPT 208

shove off [v] *leave quickly*
blow, clear out, depart, exit, get off, go, go away, pull out, push off, quit, run along, start out, take off, vamoose*; SEE CONCEPT 195

show [n1] *demonstration, exhibition*
appearance, array, display, expo*, exposition, fair, fanfare, fireworks, grandstand, manifestation, occurrence, pageant, pageantry, panoply, parade, pomp, presentation, program, representation, shine*, showboat*, showing, sight, spectacle, splash*, view; SEE CONCEPT 261

show [n2] *entertainment event*
act, appearance, burlesque, carnival, cinema, comedy, drama, entertainment, film, flick*, motion picture, movie, pageant, picture, play, presentation, production, showing, spectacle; SEE CONCEPTS 263,293

show [n3] *false front; appearance given*
affectation, air, display, effect, face*, front, grandstand play*, guise, illusion, impression, likeness, make-believe*, ostentation, parade, pose, pretense, pretext, profession, seeming, semblance, sham, shine*, showboat*, showing, simulacrum, splash*; SEE CONCEPTS 633,716

show [v1] *actively exhibit something*
afford, air, arrive, attend, bare, blazon, brandish, deal in, demonstrate, display, disport, exhibit, expose, flash, flaunt, flourish, lay bare, lay out, mount, offer, parade, present, produce, proffer, put on, reveal, sell, set out, showcase, show off, sport, spread, stage, streak, submit, supply, trot out, unfold, unfurl, unveil, vaunt, wave; SEE CONCEPT 138

show [v2] *passively exhibit something*
appear, arrive, assert, be visible, blow in, clarify, come, demonstrate, determine, disclose, discover, display, divulge, elucidate, emerge, establish, evidence, evince, explain, get, get in, illustrate, indicate, instruct, lay out, loom, make known, make out, make the scene*, manifest, mark, materialize, note, ostend, point, present, proclaim, project, prove, put in appearance, reach, register, reveal, show one's face*, show up, teach, testify to, turn up, unveil; SEE CONCEPT 261

sh
sh

show [v3] *grant*
accord, act with, bestow, confer, dispense, give; SEE CONCEPT *108*

show [v4] *accompany*
attend, conduct, direct, escort, guide, lead, pilot, route, see, shepherd, steer; SEE CONCEPTS *187,384*

showdown [n] *confrontation*
breaking point, clash, climax, crisis, culmination, exposé, moment of truth, unfolding; SEE CONCEPTS *388,674*

showoff [n] *person who brags about him- or herself*
boaster, braggadocio, braggart, egotist, exhibitionist, swaggerer, vulgarian; SEE CONCEPT *412*

show off [v] *flaunt; brag*
advertise, boast, brandish, demonstrate, display, disport, exhibit, expose, flash*, hand a line*, make a spectacle of, parade, spread out, swagger, trot out*; SEE CONCEPTS *49,261*

show up [v1] *arrive, attend*
appear, be conspicuous, be visible, blow in*, come, get, get in, make an appearance, put in appearance, reach, show, stand out, turn up; SEE CONCEPT *159*

show up [v2] *expose, embarrass*
belittle, convict, debunk, defeat, discover, discredit, highlight, invalidate, lay bare, mortify, pinpoint, put spotlight on*, put to shame*, reveal, shame, show in bad light*, uncloak, undress, unmask, unshroud, worst; SEE CONCEPTS *54,60*

showy [adj] *flamboyant, flashy*
classy, dashing, flash, garish, gaudy, glaring, histrionic, jazzy*, loud, luxurious, meretricious, opulent, ornate, ostentatious, overdone, overwrought, peacocky, pompous, pretentious, resplendent, screaming, sensational, snazzy*, splashy, splendiferous, sumptuous, swank*, tawdry, tinsel*, tony*; SEE CONCEPT *589*

shred [n] *tiny piece*
atom, bit, cantlet, crumb, fragment, grain, iota, jot, modicum, ounce, part, particle, rag, ray, ribbon, scintilla, scrap, shadow, sliver, smidgen, snippet, speck, stitch, tatter, trace, whit; SEE CONCEPT *831*

shred [v] *cut into ribbons*
cut, fray, frazzle, make ragged, reduce, shave, sliver, strip, tatter, tear; SEE CONCEPT *176*

shrewd [adj] *clever, intelligent*
acute, argute, artful, astucious, astute, brainy*, cagey, calculating, canny, crafty, cunning, cutting*, deep*, discerning, discriminating, far-sighted, foxy*, heady*, ingenious, inside, in the know*, judicious, keen, knowing, on the inside*, on top of*, penetrating, perceptive, perspicacious, piercing, probing, profound, prudent, quick-witted, sagacious, savvy*, sensible, shark, sharp, slick*, slippery*, sly, smart, smooth, streetwise, tricky, underhand, up on*, wily, wise, wised up*; SEE CONCEPTS *401,402*

shriek [n/v] *high-pitched scream*
blare, cry, howl, screech, shout, shrill, squawk, squeal, wail, whoop, yell; SEE CONCEPTS *77,595*

shrill [adj] *high-pitched, harsh in sound*
acute, argute, blaring, blatant, cacophonous, clanging, clangorous, deafening, discordant, ear-piercing, ear-splitting, high, metallic, noisy, penetrating, piercing, piping, raucous, screeching, sharp, strident, thin, treble; SEE CONCEPTS *592,594*

shrine [n] *tribute to a god, idol, or spirit*
altar, chapel, church, enshrinement, grave, hallowed place, holy place, mausoleum, reliquary, sacred place, sanctorium, sanctuary, sanctum, sepulcher, temple; SEE CONCEPTS *368,439,448*

shrink [v1] *become smaller*
compress, concentrate, condense, constrict, contract, decrease, deflate, diminish, drop off, dwindle, fail, fall off, fall short, grow smaller, lessen, narrow, reduce, shorten, shrivel, wane, waste, waste away, weaken, wither, wrinkle; SEE CONCEPTS *137,698,776*

shrink [v2] *recoil, shy away*
blench, boggle, contract, cower, cringe, crouch, demur, draw back, flinch, hang back, huddle, quail, recede, refuse, retire, retreat, scruple, shudder, slink, wince, withdraw; SEE CONCEPTS *188,195*

shrivel [v] *dehydrate, dry up*
burn, contract, desiccate, dwindle, fossilize, mummify, mummy, parch, scorch, sear, shrink, stale, welter, wilt, wither, wizen, wrinkle; SEE CONCEPTS *137,250,255*

shudder [v] *shake, quiver*
convulse, dither, gyrate, jitter, quake, shimmy, shiver, tremble, tremor, twitter, wave; SEE CONCEPTS *34,150,152*

shuffle [v1] *move along lazily*
drag, limp, muddle, pad, scrape, scuff, scuffle, shamble, straggle, stumble, trail; SEE CONCEPT *151*

shuffle [v2] *rearrange, mix up*
break the deck*, change, change the order, confuse, disarrange, disarray, discompose, dislocate, disorder, disorganize, disrupt, disturb, intermix, jumble, mess up*, shift; SEE CONCEPTS *158,363*

shun [v] *avoid, ignore*
bilk, cold-shoulder*, cut, decline, despise, disdain, ditch*, dodge, double, duck, elude, escape, eschew, evade, get around, give a wide berth*, give the runaround*, have no part of*, have nothing to do with*, hide out, keep away from, keep clear of, neglect, palm off*, pass up, refuse, reject, scorn, shake, shake off, shy, snub, stall, stand aloof from, stay shy of, steer clear of*, turn back on*; SEE CONCEPTS *30,384*

shut [v] *close*
bar, batten down*, cage, close down, close up, confine, draw, drop the curtain*, enclose, exclude, fasten, fold, fold up, imprison, lock, push, put to, seal, secure, shut down, slam, wall off; SEE CONCEPTS *85,121,160,206,208,324*

shut off/shut out [v] *exclude; screen*
bar, beleaguer, blockade, block out, close, conceal, cover, debar, discontinue, evict, fence off, hide, keep out, lock out, mask, obstruct, ostracize, refuse, seclude, shroud, veil; SEE CONCEPTS *25,121,188*

shut up [v] *be or make quiet*
bottle up*, choke, dry up*, dummy up*, fall silent, gag, hold tongue*, hush, keep trap shut*, muzzle, pipe down*, quiet, quieten, quit chattering, shush*, silence, soft-pedal*, still, stop talking; SEE CONCEPT *77*

shy [adj1] *quiet and self-conscious*
afraid, apprehensive, averse, backward, bashful, cautious, chary, circumspect, conscious, coy, demure, diffident, disinclined, distrustful, fearful,

hesitant, humble, indisposed, introvert, introverted, loath, loner, modest, nervous, recessive, reluctant, reserved, reticent, retiring, self-effacing, shamefaced, sheepish, shrinking, skittish, suspicious, timid, unassertive, unassured, uneager, uneffusive, unresponsive, unsocial, unwilling, wary; SEE CONCEPTS 401,404

shy [adj2] *lacking, failing*
deficient, inadequate, insufficient, scant, scanty, scarce, short, unsufficient, wanting; SEE CONCEPTS 546,762,789

sick [adj1] *not healthy, not feeling well*
ailing, bedridden, broken down, confined, debilitated, declining, defective, delicate, diseased, disordered, down, feeble, feverish, frail, funny*, green*, hospitalized, ill, impaired, imperfect, in a bad way*, incurable, indisposed, infected, infirm, in poor health, invalid, laid-up, lousy, mean, nauseated, not so hot*, peaked, poorly, qualmish, queasy, rickety, rocky, rotten, run down, sick as a dog*, suffering, tottering, under medication, under the weather*, unhealthy, unwell, weak, wobbly; SEE CONCEPT 314

sick [adj2] *morbid, gross*
black, ghoulish, macabre, morose, sadistic, sickly; SEE CONCEPTS 537,571

sick [adj3] *fed up, displeased*
blasé, bored, disgusted, jaded, revolted, satiated, tired, up to here with*, weary; SEE CONCEPT 403

sicken [v] *revolt, make ill*
affect, afflict, derange, disgust, disorder, gross out*, nauseate, offend, reluct, repel, repulse, turn, turn one's stomach*, unhinge, unsettle, upset; SEE CONCEPTS 14,246

sickening [adj] *disgusting, awful*
diseased, distasteful, foul, gross*, icky*, loathsome, nasty, nauseating, nauseous, noisome, offensive, putrid, repugnant, repulsive, revolting, rotten, stinking, stomach-turning, tainted; SEE CONCEPTS 529,571

sickly [adj1] *not healthy*
ailing, below par, bilious, cranky, delicate, diseased, down, dragging, faint, feeble, indisposed, infirm, in poor health, lackluster, laid-low, languid, low, mean, off-color*, out of action*, out of shape*, pallid, peaked, peaky, pining, poorly, rocky, run-down, seedy, sickish, unhealthy, wan, weak; SEE CONCEPT 314

sickly [adj2] *revolting*
bilious, cloying, insalubrious, mawkish, morbid, morose, nauseating, noisome, noxious, sick, unwholesome; SEE CONCEPTS 537,571

sickness [n] *ill or abnormal condition*
affection, affliction, ailment, bug*, complaint, condition, disease, diseasedness, disorder, ill, ill health, illness, indisposition, infirmity, malady, nausea, queasiness, syndrome, unhealth, unhealthfulness, unwellness; SEE CONCEPT 306

side [n1] *edge, exteriority of object*
aspect, attitude, border, bottom, boundary, direction, disposition, division, elevation, face, facet, flank, front, hand, haunch, jamb, lee, limit, loin, margin, part, perimeter, periphery, posture, quarter, rear, rim, sector, stance, stand, surface, top, verge, view, wing; SEE CONCEPTS 513,835

side [n2] *point of view*
angle, appearance, aspect, belief, direction, facet, hand, light, opinion, outlook, phase, position, slant, stand, standpoint, viewpoint; SEE CONCEPT 689

side [n3] *opposing person or view*
behalf, belligerent, camp, cause, combatant, competition, contestant, crew, enemy, faction, foe, interest, part, party, rival, sect, team; SEE CONCEPTS 301,365

side [adj] *minor; flanking*
ancillary, incidental, indirect, lateral, lesser, marginal, not the main, oblique, off-center, postern, roundabout, secondary, sidelong, sideward, sideways, sidewise, skirting, subordinate, subsidiary, superficial; SEE CONCEPT 575

sideways [adv] *to the edge, exteriority*
alongside, aside, aslant, aslope, athwart, broadside, crabwise, edgeways, indirectly, laterally, obliquely, side by side, sidelong, sidewards, slanting, slantingly, slantwise, sloping, to the side; SEE CONCEPTS 581,583

sift [v] *take out residue; remove impurities*
analyze, clean, colander, comb, delve into, dig into, drain, evaluate, examine, explore, fathom, filter, go into, go through, grade, inquire, investigate, look into, pan, part, pore over, probe, prospect, purify, riddle, screen, scrutinize, search, separate, sieve, size, sort, strain, winnow; SEE CONCEPTS 103,165

sigh [v1] *breathe out heavily*
blow, complain, cry, exhale, gasp, grieve, groan, howl, lament, moan, murmur, pant, respire, roar, sob, sorrow, sough, suspire, wheeze, whine, whisper, whistle; SEE CONCEPT 163

sigh [v2] *long for*
ache, crave, dream, hanker, hunger, languish, lust, mourn, pine, suspire, thirst, yearn; SEE CONCEPT 20

sight [n1] *ability to perceive with eyes*
afterimage, appearance, apperception, apprehension, eye, eyes, eyeshot, eyesight, field of vision, ken, perception, range of vision, seeing, view, viewing, visibility, vision; SEE CONCEPT 629

sight [n2] *spectacle*
display, exhibit, exhibition, outlook, pageant, parade, point of interest, scene, show, view, vista; SEE CONCEPTS 261,293

sight [n3] *horrifying person or thing*
blot, eyesore, fright, mess, monstrosity, ogre, ogress, scarecrow, slob, spectacle, tramp; SEE CONCEPTS 412,513

sight [v] *see*
behold, discern, distinguish, eyeball*, make out*, observe, perceive, spot, view, witness; SEE CONCEPT 626

sign [n1] *indication, evidence*
assurance, augury, auspice, badge, beacon, bell, caution, clue, divination, flag, flash, foreboding, foreknowledge, foreshadowing, foretoken, forewarning, gesture, giveaway, handwriting on wall*, harbinger, herald, high sign*, hint, light, manifestation, mark, nod, note, omen, portent, precursor, prediction, premonition, presage, presentiment, prognostic, proof, signal, suggestion, symbol, symptom, token, trace, vestige, warning, wave, whistle, wink; SEE CONCEPTS 274,529,673,689

sign [n2] *document with information; symbol*
badge, board, character, cipher, crest, device, emblem, ensign, guidepost, insignia, logo, mark, notice, placard, proof, representation, signboard, signpost, symbolization, token, type, warning; SEE CONCEPTS 271,284

sh
si

sign [v1] *write name*
acknowledge, authorize, autograph, confirm, endorse, initial, ink, inscribe, put John Hancock on*, put John Henry on*, rubber-stamp*, set one's hand to*, signature, subscribe, witness; SEE CONCEPT *79*

sign [v2] *motion to another*
beckon, express, flag, gesticulate, gesture, indicate, motion, signal, signalize, signify, use sign language, wave; SEE CONCEPT *74*

signal [n] *indication; authorization*
alarm, alert, beacon, bleep, blinker, cue, flag, flare, gesture, go-ahead*, green light*, high sign*, indicator, mark, Mayday*, movement, nod, okay*, omen, sign, SOS*, tocsin, token, wink; SEE CONCEPTS *74,284,529,685*

signal [adj] *extraordinary, outstanding*
arresting, arrestive, characteristic, conspicuous, distinctive, distinguished, eminent, exceptional, eye-catching, famous, illustrious, individual, marked, memorable, momentous, notable, noteworthy, noticeable, peculiar, prominent, pronounced, remarkable, renowned, salient, significant, striking; SEE CONCEPTS *568,574*

signal [v] *indicate; give a sign to*
beckon, communicate, flag, flash, gesticulate, gesture, motion, nod, semaphore, sign, signalize, warn, wave, wink; SEE CONCEPT *74*

significance [n1] *meaning*
acceptation, bottom line*, connotation, drift, force, heart, implication, import, intendment, kicker*, meat*, message, name of the game*, nature of the beast*, nitty-gritty*, nub, nuts and bolts*, point, punch line*, purport, score, sense, significancy, signification, stuff, understanding; SEE CONCEPT *682*

significance [n2] *importance*
authority, consequence, consideration, credit, excellence, gravity, import, impressiveness, influence, magnitude, matter, merit, moment, momentousness, perfection, pith, prestige, relevance, signification, virtue, weight, weightiness; SEE CONCEPT *668*

significant [adj1] *telling, meaningful*
cogent, compelling, convincing, denoting, eloquent, expressing, expressive, facund, forceful, heavy, important, indicative, knowing, meaning, momentous, powerful, pregnant, representative, rich, sententious, serious, sound, suggestive, symbolic, valid, weighty; SEE CONCEPTS *267,567*

significant [adj2] *important, critical*
big, carrying a lot of weight*, consequential, considerable, heavy, material, meaningful, momentous, notable, noteworthy, serious, substantial, vital, weighty; SEE CONCEPT *568*

signify [v1] *mean, indicate*
add up to, announce, bear, be a sign of, bespeak, betoken, carry, communicate, connote, convey, denote, disclose, evidence, evince, exhibit, express, flash, imply, import, insinuate, intend, intimate, manifest, matter, portend, proclaim, purport, represent, show, sign, spell, stand for, suggest, symbolize, talk, tell, wink; SEE CONCEPTS *55,266,682*

signify [v2] *be of importance*
be of consequence, be of significance, carry weight, count, import, matter, mean, weigh; SEE CONCEPT *668*

silence [n] *absence of sound, speech*
blackout, calm, censorship, dead air, death, dumbness, hush, hush-hush*, inarticulateness, iron curtain*, laconism, lull, muteness, noiselessness, peace, quiescence, quiet, quietness, quietude, quietus, reserve, reticence, saturninity, secrecy, sleep, speechlessness, still, stillness, sulk, sullenness, taciturnity, uncommunicativeness; SEE CONCEPT *65*

silence [v] *make or be quiet*
choke off*, clam, clam up*, close up, cool it*, cut off, cut short, dampen, deaden, decrease the volume, dry up*, dull, dumb, dummy up*, extinguish, gag, hold one's tongue*, hush, hush-hush*, hush one's mouth*, keep it down*, lull, muffle, mute, muzzle, overawe, pipe down*, quash, quell, quiet, quiet down, quieten, say nothing, shush*, shut up, sit on*, soft-pedal*, squelch, stifle, still, strike dumb*, subdue, suppress, tongue-tie*; SEE CONCEPT *266*

silent [adj1] *quiet; speechless*
bashful, buttoned up*, checked, clammed up*, close, closed up, closemouthed, curbed, dumb, dummied up*, faint, hush, hushed, iced*, inarticulate, incoherent, inconversable, indistinct, inhibited, laconic, mousy, mum, mute, muted, noiseless, nonvocal, not talkative, reserved, restrained, reticent, shy, silentious, soundless, still, struck dumb, taciturn, tongue-tied, unclear, uncommunicative, unheard, unsociable, unspeaking, voiceless, wordless, zipped*; SEE CONCEPT *594*

silent [adj2] *understood, implied*
aphonic, implicit, indescribable, inexpressible, nameless, tacit, unexpressed, unpronounced, unspoken, unuttered, unvoiced, wordless; SEE CONCEPT *267*

silhouette [n] *outline*
contour, delineation, etching, figuration, form, likeness, line, lineament, lineation, portrait, profile, shade, shadow, shape; SEE CONCEPTS *259,625*

silky [adj] *very smooth; like satin*
cottony, delicate, glossy, like silk, luxurious, plush, satiny, silk, silken, sleek, soft, tender, velvety; SEE CONCEPT *606*

silly [adj] *absurd, giddy, foolish*
asinine, balmy, brainless, childish, crazy, dippy*, dizzy*, empty, empty-headed*, fatuous, featherbrained*, flighty, foolhardy, frivolous, harebrained*, idiotic, ignorant, illogical, immature, imprudent, inane, inappropriate, inconsistent, irrational, irresponsible, ludicrous, meaningless, muddle-headed*, nitwitted, nonsensical, pointless, preposterous, puerile, ridiculous, senseless, sheepheaded*, simple, simple-minded, stupid, unintelligent, unreasonable, unwise, vacuous, witless; SEE CONCEPTS *401,403,542*

silver [adj] *shiny gray in color*
argent, argentate, bright, lustrous, pale, pearly, plated, resplendent, silvered, silvery, sterling, white; SEE CONCEPT *618*

similar [adj] *very much alike*
agnate, akin, allied, analogous, coincident, coincidental, coinciding, collateral, companion, comparable, complementary, congruent, congruous, consonant, consubstantial, correlative, corresponding, homogeneous, identical, in agreement, kin, kindred, like, matching, much the same, parallel, reciprocal, related, resembling, same, twin, uniform; SEE CONCEPTS *487,573*

similarity [n] *likeness, correspondence*
affinity, agreement, alikeness, analogy, approxi-

mation, association, closeness, coincidence, collation, community, comparability, comparison, concordance, concurrence, conformity, congruence, congruity, connection, correlation, dead ringer*, harmony, homogeneity, identity, interrelation, kinship, likes of, look-alike, parallel, parallelism, parity, peas in a pod*, proportion, reciprocity, relation, relationship, resemblance, sameness, semblance, simile, similitude, synonymity, two of a kind*; SEE CONCEPT *670*

simmer [v] *boil, smolder*
be agitated, be angry, be tense, be uptight*, bubble, burn, churn, cook, effervesce, ferment, fizz, fret, fricassee, fume, parboil, rage, seethe, smart, sparkle, stew, stir, warm; SEE CONCEPTS *35,170,410*

simple [adj1] *clear, understandable; easy*
child's play*, cinch*, clean, easy as pie*, effortless, elementary, facile, incomplex, intelligible, light, lucid, manageable, mild, no problem*, no sweat*, not difficult, picnic*, piece of cake*, plain, quiet, self-explanatory, simple as ABC*, smooth, snap*, straightforward, transparent, uncomplicated, uninvolved, unmistakable, untroublesome, walkover*; SEE CONCEPTS *529,538*

simple [adj2] *uncluttered, natural*
absolute, austere, classic, clean, discreet, elementary, folksy, homely, homey, humble, inelaborate, lowly, mere, modest, not complex, open and shut*, plain, pure, pure and simple*, rustic, sheer, single, Spartan, unadorned, unadulterated, unaffected, unalloyed, unblended, uncombined, uncomplicated, uncompounded, undecorated, unelaborate, unembellished, unfussy, unmitigated, unmixed, unornamented, unostentatious, unpretentious, unqualified, vanilla*; SEE CONCEPTS *562,589*

simple [adj3] *childlike, innocent*
amateur, artless, bald, basic, childish, direct, frank, green, guileless, honest, ingenuous, naive, naked, natural, plain, sincere, square, stark, trusting, unaffected, unartificial, undeniable, unexperienced, unpretentious, unschooled, unsophisticated, unstudied, unvarnished; SEE CONCEPTS *267,401,542*

simple [adj4] *feeble-minded; not intelligent*
amateur, asinine, backward, brainless, credulous, dense, dimwitted, dull, dumb, fat, feeble, foolish, green*, gullible, half-witted, idiotic, ignorant, illiterate, imbecile, inane, inexperienced, inexpert, insensate, mindless, moronic, nitwitted, obtuse, senseless, shallow, silly, simple-minded, slow, soft, soft-headed*, stupid, thick, uneducated, unintelligent, witless; SEE CONCEPT *402*

simplicity [n] *absence of complication, sophistication*
artlessness, candor, chastity, clarity, classicality, clean lines, clearness, directness, ease, easiness, elementariness, guilelessness, homogeneity, ingenuousness, innocence, integrity, lack of adornment, modesty, monotony, naiveté, naivety, naturalness, obviousness, openness, plainness, primitiveness, purity, restraint, severity, singleness, straightforwardness, uniformity, unity; SEE CONCEPTS *633,655,663*

simplify [v] *make easy, intelligible*
abridge, analyze, boil down, break down, break it down, chasten, clarify, clean it up*, clean up, clear up, cut down, cut the frills*, decipher, disentangle, disinvolve, draw a picture*, elucidate, explain, facilitate, get down to basics*, get to the meat*, hit the high spots*, interpret, lay out, let daylight in*, let sunlight in*, make clear, make perfectly clear, make plain, order, put in a nutshell*, put one straight*, reduce, shorten, spell out, streamline, unscramble; SEE CONCEPTS *57,110,261*

simply [adv1] *plainly, clearly*
artlessly, candidly, commonly, directly, easily, frankly, guilelessly, honestly, ingenuously, intelligibly, matter-of-factly, modestly, naturally, openly, ordinarily, quietly, sincerely, straightforwardly, unaffectedly, unpretentiously, without any elaboration; SEE CONCEPTS *544,562*

simply [adv2] *merely*
barely, but, just, only, purely, solely, utterly; SEE CONCEPTS *544,557*

simply [adv3] *absolutely, completely*
altogether, in fact, really, totally, unreservedly, utterly, wholly; SEE CONCEPTS *531,535*

simulate [v] *pretend, imitate*
act, act like, affect, ape, assume, bluff, borrow, cheat, concoct, copy, counterfeit, crib*, deceive, disguise, dissemble, do, do a take-off*, do like*, equivocate, exaggerate, fabricate, fake, favor, feature, feign, fence, gloss over, invent, knock off*, lie, lift, make believe, mimic, mirror, misrepresent, phony, pirate, play, playact, pose, prevaricate, put on*, put on an act*, replicate, reproduce, resemble, steal; SEE CONCEPTS *59,63,111,171*

simultaneous [adj] *happening at about the same time*
accompanying, agreeing, at the same time, coetaneous, coeval, coexistent, coexisting, coincident, coinciding, concurrent, concurring, contemporaneous, contemporary, dead heat*, in sync*, synchronal, synchronic, synchronous, with the beat*; SEE CONCEPTS *548,799*

sin [n] *illegal or immoral action*
anger, covetousness, crime, damnation, debt, deficiency, demerit, disobedience, envy, error, evil, evil-doing, fault, gluttony, guilt, immorality, imperfection, iniquity, lust, misdeed, offense, peccability, peccadillo, peccancy, pride, shortcoming, sinfulness, sloth, tort, transgression, trespass, ungodliness, unrighteousness, veniality, vice, violation, wickedness, wrong, wrongdoing, wrongness; SEE CONCEPTS *101,645*

sin [v] *commit illegal or immoral action*
backslide*, break commandment, break law, cheat, commit crime, deviate, do wrong, err, fall, fall from grace*, go astray*, lapse, live in sin, misbehave, misconduct, offend, sow wild oats*, stray, take the primrose path*, transgress, trespass, wallow in the mire*, wander; SEE CONCEPTS *101,375,645*

sincere [adj] *straightforward, honest*
aboveboard, actual, artless, bona fide, candid, dead-level*, dear, devout, earnest, faithful, forthright, frank, genuine, guileless, heartfelt, honest to God*, like it is*, meant, natural, no fooling*, no-nonsense*, on the level*, on the line*, on up and up*, open, outspoken, plain, pretensionless, real, regular, righteous, saintly, serious, square*, sure enough, true, true-blue*, trustworthy, twenty-four carat*, unaffected, undesigning, undissembled, unfeigned, unpretentious, up-front*, wholehearted; SEE CONCEPTS *267,401,542*

si
si

sincerely [adv] *seriously, honestly*
aboveboard, candidly, deeply, earnestly, frankly, from bottom of heart, genuinely, in all conscience, in all sincerity, ingenuously, in good faith, naturally, profoundly, really, truly, truthfully, wholeheartedly, without equivocation; SEE CONCEPTS 267,582

sincerity [n] *straightforwardness, honesty*
artlessness, bona fides, candor, earnestness, frankness, genuineness, good faith, goodwill, guilelessness, heart, honor, impartiality, innocence, justice, openness, probity, reliability, seriousness, sincereness, singleness, trustworthiness, truth, truthfulness, veracity, wholeheartedness; SEE CONCEPTS 633,657

sinful [adj] *immoral, criminal*
amiss, bad, base, blamable, blameful, blameworthy, censurable, corrupt, culpable, damnable, demeritorious, depraved, disgraceful, erring, evil, guilty, iniquitous, irreligious, low, morally wrong, reprehensible, reprobate, shameful, ungodly, unholy, unregenerate, unrighteous, vicious, vile, wicked, wrong; SEE CONCEPTS 545,548

sing [v1] *carry a tune with one's voice*
belt out*, burst into song*, buzz*, canary*, cantillate, carol, chant, chirp, choir, croon, descant, duet, groan*, harmonize, hum, hymn, intone, lift up a voice*, line out*, lullaby, make melody*, mouth, pipe, purr*, resound, roar, serenade, shout, singsong, solo, trill, troll, tune, vocalize, wait, warble, whine, whistle, yodel; SEE CONCEPTS 47,77,292

sing [v2] *tattle on someone*
betray, blow the whistle*, fink*, inform, peach*, rat*, snitch*, spill the beans*, talk, turn in; SEE CONCEPTS 60,317

singer [n] *person who can carry a tune*
accompanist, artist, artiste, chanter, chanteuse, choralist, chorister, crooner, diva, intoner, melodist, minstrel, musician, nightingale, serenader, soloist, songbird, songster, troubadour, vocalist, voice, warbler, yodeler; SEE CONCEPT 352

single [adj1] *alone, distinct*
distinct, distinguished, especial, exceptional, exclusive, individual, indivisible, isolated, lone, loner, not general, not public, odd, one, only, original, particular, peerless, personal, private, rare, restricted, secluded, separate, separated, simple, singled-out, singular, sole, solitary, special, specific, strange, unalloyed, unblended, uncommon, uncompounded, undivided, unique, unitary, unmixed, unrivaled, unshared, unusual, without equal; SEE CONCEPTS 564,577,762

single [adj2] *not married*
bachelor, companionless, divorced, eligible, free, living alone, loner, separated, sole, solo, spouseless, unattached, unfettered, unmarried, unwed; SEE CONCEPT 555

singly [adv] *individually*
apart, independently, one at a time, one by one, particularly, respectively, separately, severally; SEE CONCEPT 577

singular [adj1] *unique, odd*
atypical, avant-garde, bizarre, breaking new ground*, conspicuous, cool*, curious, eccentric, eminent, exceptional, extraordinary, loner, noteworthy, original, outlandish, out-of-the-way, outstanding, peculiar, prodigious, puzzling, queer, rare, remarkable, special, strange, uncommon, unimaginable, unordinary, unparalleled, unprecedented, unthinkable, unusual, unwonted, weird; SEE CONCEPT 564

singular [adj2] *alone, separate*
certain, definite, discrete, exclusive, individual, one, only, particular, respective, single, sole, solitary, solo, unique, unrepeatable; SEE CONCEPT 577

sinister [adj] *nasty, menacing*
adverse, apocalyptic, bad, baleful, baneful, blackhearted, corrupt, deleterious, dire, disastrous, dishonest, disquieting, doomful, evil, foreboding, harmful, hurtful, ill-boding, inauspicious, injurious, lowering, malefic, malevolent, malign, malignant, menacing, mischievous, obnoxious, ominous, pernicious, perverse, poisonous, portentous, threatening, unfavorable, unfortunate, unlucky, unpropitious, woeful; SEE CONCEPTS 401,548,571

sink [v1] *fall in, go under*
bore, bring down, capsize, cast down, cave in, couch, decline, demit, depress, descend, dig, dip, disappear, drill, drive, droop, drop, drown, ebb, engulf, excavate, fall, flounder, force down, founder, go down, go to the bottom, immerse, lay, let down, lower, overturn, overwhelm, plummet, plunge, put down, ram, regress, run, sag, scuttle, set, settle, shipwreck, slope, slump, stab, stick, stoop, submerge, subside, swamp, thrust, tip over, touch bottom, wreck; SEE CONCEPTS 181,213

sink [v2] *fall, decrease*
abate, collapse, diminish, drop, lapse, lessen, relapse, retrogress, slip, slump, subside, wane; SEE CONCEPTS 698,776

sink [v3] *deteriorate*
decay, decline, decrease, degenerate, depreciate, descend, deteriorate, die, diminish, disimprove, disintegrate, dwindle, fade, fail, flag, go downhill*, lessen, retrograde, rot, spoil, waste, weaken, worsen; SEE CONCEPTS 469,698

sink [v4] *be humble or humbled*
abase, bemean, be reduced to, cast down, debase, degrade, demean, humiliate, lower, stoop, succumb; SEE CONCEPTS 7,19,35

sinuous [adj] *winding, twisting*
anfractuous, circuitous, coiling, convoluted, crooked, curved, curvy, deviative, devious, flexuous, indirect, meandering, meandrous, serpentine, snaky*, supple, tortuous, twisting and turning*, undulating, vagrant; SEE CONCEPT 581

sip [v] *drink slowly*
drink in, extract, imbibe, partake, quaff, sample, savor, sup, swallow, taste, toss; SEE CONCEPT 169

sister [n] *female sibling*
blood sister, kin, kinsperson, relation, relative, twin; SEE CONCEPTS 414,415

sit [v1] *rest on one's behind*
bear on, be seated, cover, ensconce, give feet a rest*, grab a chair*, have a place, have a seat, hunker*, install, lie, park*, perch*, plop down*, pose, posture, put it there*, relax, remain, rest, seat, seat oneself, settle, squat, take a load off*, take a place, take a seat; SEE CONCEPTS 154,201

sit [v2] *hold a meeting*
assemble, be in session, come together, convene, deliberate, hold an assembly, meet, officiate, open, preside; SEE CONCEPTS 324,384

site [n] *place of activity*
fix, ground, habitat, hangout, haunt, home, lay,

layout, locale, locality, location, locus, mise en scène, plot, point, position, post, range, scene, section, situation, slot, spot, station, wherever, X marks the spot*; SEE CONCEPT 198

situation [n1] *place of activity*
bearings, direction, footing, latitude, locale, locality, location, locus, longitude, position, post, seat, setting, site, spot, stage, station, where, whereabouts; SEE CONCEPT 198

situation [n2] *circumstances, status*
ballgame*, bargain, capacity, case, character, condition, footing*, how things stack up*, like it is*, mode, picture, place, plight, position, posture, rank, scene, size of it*, sphere, stage, standing, standpoint, state, state of affairs, station, status quo*; SEE CONCEPTS 388,696

situation [n3] *employment status*
appointment, berth, billet, capacity, connection, employment, engagement, hire, job, office, place, placement, position, post, profession, spot, trade; SEE CONCEPTS 351,360,668

sizable [adj] *considerable, large*
ample, big, burly, capacious, comprehensive, decent, decent-sized, extensive, good, goodly, great, gross, hefty, husky, jumbo*, largish, major, massive, ponderous, respectable, sensible, spacious, strapping, substantial, tidy, voluminous, whopping*; SEE CONCEPT 781

size [n] *extent or bulk of some dimension*
admeasurement, amount, amplitude, area, bigness, body, breadth, caliber, capaciousness, capacity, content, diameter, dimensions, enormity, extension, extent, greatness, height, highness, hugeness, immensity, intensity, largeness, length, magnitude, mass, measurement, proportion, proportions, range, scope, spread, stature, stretch, substance, substantiality, tonnage, vastness, volume, voluminosity, width; SEE CONCEPTS 730,792

sizzle [v] *hiss, fry*
broil, brown, buzz, cook, crackle, fizz, fizzle, frizzle, grill, roast, sear, sibilate, spit, sputter, swish, wheeze, whisper, whiz; SEE CONCEPTS 65,170

skeleton [n] *structure of bones in animate being or supports in an object*
bones, bony structure, cage, design, draft, frame, framework, osteology, outline, scaffolding, sketch, support; SEE CONCEPTS 393,733

skeptic [n] *person who is leery, unbelieving*
agnostic, apostate, atheist, cynic, disbeliever, dissenter, doubter, doubting Thomas*, freethinker, heathen, heretic, infidel, materialist, misanthrope, misbeliever, nihilist, pagan, pessimist, profaner, questioner, rationalist, scoffer, unbeliever; SEE CONCEPTS 361,423

skeptical [adj] *disbelieving, leery*
agnostic, aporetic, cynical, dissenting, doubtful, doubting, dubious, freethinking, hesitating, incredulous, mistrustful, questioning, quizzical, scoffing, show-me*, suspicious, unbelieving, unconvinced; SEE CONCEPT 403

sketch [n] *drawing, outline*
account, adumbration, aperçu, blueprint, cartoon, chart, compendium, configuration, copy, delineation, depiction, description, design, diagram, digest, doodle, draft, figuration, figure, form, illustration, likeness, monograph, painting, picture, piece, plan, portrayal, precis, report, representation, rough, shape, skeleton, summary,

survey, syllabus, version, vignette; SEE CONCEPTS 268,283,625

sketch [v] *draw, outline*
adumbrate, block out*, blueprint*, chalk, characterize, chart, delineate, depict, describe, design, detail, develop, diagram, doodle, draft, lay out*, line, map out, paint, plan, plot, portray, represent, rough out*, skeleton, skeletonize, trace; SEE CONCEPTS 36,174

sketchy [adj] *rough, incomplete*
coarse, crude, cursory, defective, depthless, faulty, imperfect, inadequate, insufficient, introductory, outline, perfunctory, preliminary, rough, scrappy, shallow, skimpy, slight, superficial, uncritical, unfinished, vague; SEE CONCEPT 531

skid [v] *slide against will*
drift, glide, go into skid, move, sheer, skew, slip, slue, swerve, veer; SEE CONCEPT 152

skill [n] *ability, talent to do something*
accomplishment, address, adroitness, aptitude, art, artistry, cleverness, clout, command, competence, craft, cunning, deftness, dexterity, dodge*, ease, experience, expertise, expertism, expertness, facility, finesse, goods*, handiness, ingenuity, intelligence, job, knack*, know-how*, line, makings, moxie*, one's thing*, proficiency, prowess, quickness, readiness, right stuff*, savvy*, skillfulness, sleight, smarts*, stuff*, technique, trade, what it takes*; SEE CONCEPTS 409,630

skillful [adj] *able, talented*
accomplished, adept, adroit, a hand at*, apt, brainy, clever, competent, cool*, crack*, crackerjack*, dexterous, experienced, expert, good, handy, know*, learned, old*, on the ball*, practical, practiced, prepared, pretty, primed, pro*, professional, proficient, quick, ready, really into*, savvy*, seasoned, sharp, skilled, smart, smooth, there*, trained, tuned in*, versant, versed, vet*, veteran, well-versed, whiz, wicked*, wised up*; SEE CONCEPTS 402,527

skim [v1] *remove the top part*
brush, cream, dip, get the cream, glance, graze, ladle, ream, scoop, separate, shave, top; SEE CONCEPT 211

skim [v2] *glide over quickly, lightly*
brush, carom, coast, dart, float, fly, graze, kiss, ricochet, sail, scud, shoot, skate, skip, skirr, skitter, smooth along, soar, trip; SEE CONCEPTS 150,152

skim [v3] *look through cursorily*
browse, brush over, dip, examine, flip through, get the cream*, give the once-over*, glance, glance over, go once over lightly*, hit the high spots*, leaf through*, read, read swiftly, riff, riffle, run eye over*, scan, skip, thumb through*, turn the pages*; SEE CONCEPTS 72,103,623

skimp [v] *be cheap or frugal about*
be mean with, be sparing, cut corners*, make ends meet*, pinch, pinch pennies*, roll back, save, scamp, scant, scrape, screw, scrimp, slight, spare, stint, tighten one's belt*, withhold; SEE CONCEPT 330

skimpy [adj] *sparse, inadequate*
deficient, exiguous, failing, insufficient, meager, miserly, niggardly, poor, scant, scanty, scrimp, scrimpy, short, shy, spare, stingy, thin, tight, unsufficient, wanting; SEE CONCEPTS 334,762,789

si
sk

skin [n] *outer covering, especially of animate being*

bark, carapace, case, casing, coating, crust, cutis, derma, dermis, epidermis, fell, film, fur, hide, hull, husk, integument, jacket, membrane, outside, parchment, peel, pelt, rind, sheath, sheathing, shell, shuck, slough, surface, tegument, vellum; SEE CONCEPTS *392,428,484*

skin [v] *remove outer covering*

abrade, bare, bark, cast, cut off, decorticate, excoriate, exuviate, flay, gall, graze, hull, husk, lay bare, pare, peel, pull off, remove, rind, scale, scalp, scrape, shave, shed, shuck, slough, strip, trim; SEE CONCEPTS *176,211*

skinny [adj] *very thin*

angular, bony, emaciated, gaunt, lank, lanky, lean, like a rail*, malnourished, rawboned, scraggy, scrawny, skeletal, skin-and-bone*, slender, spare, twiggy, undernourished, underweight; SEE CONCEPTS *490,491*

skip [v1] *bounce or jump over*

bob, bolt, bound, buck, canter, caper, carom, cavort, dance, flee, flit, fly, frisk, gambol, glance, graze, hippety-hop*, hop, leap, lope, make off, prance, ricochet, run, scamper, scoot, skedaddle*, skim, skirr, skitter, spring, step, tiptoe, trip; SEE CONCEPTS *150,194*

skip [v2] *avoid, miss*

cut, desert, disregard, escape, eschew, flee, leave out, miss out, neglect, omit, pass over, pass up, play hooky*, run away, skim over, split; SEE CONCEPTS *30,681*

skirt [n1] *border, edge*

brim, brink, fringe, hem, margin, outskirts, perimeter, periphery, purlieus, rim, skirting, verge; SEE CONCEPTS *484,825*

skirt [n2] *ladies' garment that hangs from waist*

culottes, dirndl, dress, hoop, kilt, midi, mini, pannier, petticoat, sarong, tutu; SEE CONCEPT *451*

skirt [v1] *border; be on the edge*

bound, define, edge, flank, fringe, hem, lie along, lie alongside, margin, rim, surround, verge; SEE CONCEPT *751*

skirt [v2] *avoid; get around*

burke, bypass, circumnavigate, circumvent, detour, dodge, duck, elude, equivocate, escape, evade, hedge, ignore, sidestep, skip, steer clear of; SEE CONCEPTS *30,102,147*

skittish [adj] *very nervous*

agitable, alarmable, capricious, changeable, combustible, dizzy*, edgy, excitable, excited, fearful, fickle, fidgety, flighty, frivolous, giddy, harebrained, high-strung*, irresponsible, jumpy, lightheaded, lively, peppy, playful, restive, scatterbrained*, sensitive, spirited, undependable, unreliable, volative, whimsical, zippy*; SEE CONCEPT *401*

sky [n] *Earth's atmosphere*

azure, celestial sphere, empyrean, firmament, heavens, lid*, the blue*, upper atmosphere, vault, vault of heaven*, welkin, wild blue yonder*; SEE CONCEPT *437*

slab [n] *chunk of solid object*

bar, billet, bit, board, boulder, chip, cut, cutting, hunk, ingot, lump, muck, piece, plate, portion, rod, slice, stave, stick, stone, strip, wedge; SEE CONCEPTS *471,835*

slack [n] *looseness, excess*

give, leeway, play, room, slackening, slowdown, slow-up; SEE CONCEPTS *513,807*

slack [adj1] *loose, baggy; inactive*

dull, easy, feeble, flabby, flaccid, flexible, flimsy, inert, infirm, laggard, lax, leisurely, limp, not taut, passive, quaggy, quiet, relaxed, sloppy, slow, slow-moving, sluggish, soft, supine, unsteady, weak; SEE CONCEPTS *485,584,589*

slack [adj2] *lazy, negligent*

asleep on the job*, behindhand, careless, delinquent, derelict, dilatory, disregardful, dormant, dull, easy-going, faineant, idle, inactive, inattentive, indolent, inert, lackadaisical, lax, lethargic, neglectful, not busy, permissive, quiescent, quiet, regardless, remiss, slothful, slow, slow-moving, sluggish, stagnant, tardy; SEE CONCEPT *538*

slack/slacken [v] *do little or nothing; loosen*

abate, decrease, diminish, dodge, drop off, dwindle, ease, ease off, featherbed*, flag, goldbrick*, goof off*, idle, lax, lay back, lessen, let up, lie down on job*, loose, moderate, neglect, reduce, relax, release, shirk, slack off, slow down, taper, tire, untighten, wane; SEE CONCEPTS *210,681,698*

slam [n1] *loud noise from impact*

bang, bash, blast, blow, boom, burst, clap, crack, crash, ding, pound, smack, smash, whack, wham; SEE CONCEPTS *189,595*

slam [n2] *harsh criticism*

animadversion, aspersion, jab, obloquy, potshot*, slap*, slur*, stricture, swipe*; SEE CONCEPTS *52,278*

slam [v1] *throw or push very hard*

bang, bat, batter, beat, belt, blast, clobber, close, crash, cudgel, dash, fling, hammer, hit, hurl, knock, pound, shut, slap, slug, smash, strike, swat, thump, thwack, wallop; SEE CONCEPTS *189,208,222*

slam [v2] *criticize very harshly*

attack, castigate, damn, excoriate, flay, lambaste*, lash into*, pan, scathe, scourge, shoot down, slap, slash, vilify; SEE CONCEPTS *52,54*

slander [n] *scandalous remark*

aspersion, backbiting*, backstabbing*, belittlement, black eye*, calumny, defamation, depreciation, detraction, dirt*, dirty linen*, disparagement, hit*, libel, lie, misrepresentation, muckraking, mud*, mud-slinging*, obloquy, rap*, scandal, slam*, slime*, smear*, tale; SEE CONCEPTS *54,192,278*

slander [v] *make a scandalous remark*

asperse, assail, attack, backbite*, bad-mouth*, belie, belittle, besmirch, blacken name*, blaspheme, blister, blot, calumniate, cast a slur on, curse, damage, decry, defame, defile, denigrate, depreciate, derogate, detract, dishonor, disparage, give a bad name*, hit*, hurt, injure, libel, malign, muckrake, pan*, plaster, revile, roast*, run smear campaign*, scandalize, scorch, slam*, sling mud*, slur, smear, smirch, sneer, strumpet, sully, tarnish, tear down, traduce, vilify; SEE CONCEPTS *54,192*

slang [n] *casual dialect*

argot, cant, colloquialism, informal speech, jargon, lingo, neologism, patois, patter, pidgin, shoptalk, slanguage* street talk, vernacular, vulgarism, vulgarity; SEE CONCEPT *276*

slant [n1] *angle, slope*

camber, cant, declination, diagonal, grade, gradient, inclination, incline, lean, leaning, pitch, rake, ramp, tilt; SEE CONCEPT *738*

slant [n2] *particular opinion*

angle, attitude, bias, direction, emphasis, judgment, leaning, one-sidedness, outlook, point of view, predilection, predisposition, prejudice, prepossession, sentiment, side, standpoint, view, viewpoint; SEE CONCEPT 689

slant [v1] *angle off, slope*
aim, bank, beam, bend, bevel, cant, decline, descend, deviate, direct, diverge, grade, heel, incline, lean, level, lie obliquely, list, point, skew, splay, swerve, tilt, tip, train, veer; SEE CONCEPTS 201,738

slant [v2] *change to suit; distort*
aim, angle, bias, color, concentrate, direct, focus, influence, orient, point, prejudice, train, twist, warp, weight; SEE CONCEPTS 63,266

slap [n/v] *hard hit, often with hand*
bang, bash, blip, blow, box, buffet, bust, chop, clap, clout, crack, cuff, pat, percuss, poke, potch, punch, slam, smack, sock, spank, strike, swat, wallop, whack, wham; SEE CONCEPT 189

slash [v1] *cut*
carve, chop, gash, hack, incise, injure, lacerate, open up, pierce, rend, rip, score, sever, slice, slit, wound; SEE CONCEPTS 137,176

slash [v2] *reduce greatly*
abbreviate, abridge, clip, curtail, cut, cut back, cut down, drop, hack, lower, mark down, pare, retrench, shave, shorten; SEE CONCEPTS 236,240,247

slaughter [n] *killing*
annihilation, bloodbath, bloodshed, butchery, carnage, destruction, extermination, liquidation, massacre, murder, slaying; SEE CONCEPT 252

slaughter [v] *kill*
butcher, crush, decimate, defeat, destroy, do in*, exterminate, finish, liquidate, maim, mangle, massacre, murder, mutilate, overwhelm, rout, slay, stick, thrash, torture, total* trounce, vanquish, waste, wipe out*; SEE CONCEPT 252

slave [n] *person who serves, often under duress*
bondservant, captive, chattel, drudge, help, laborer, menial, peon, retainer, serf, servant, skivvy, subservient, thrall, toiler, vassal, victim, worker, workhorse; SEE CONCEPT 348

slave [v] *work very hard*
be servile, drudge, grind, grovel, grub, muck, plod, skivvy, slog, toil, work fingers to bone*; SEE CONCEPT 87

slavery [n] *state of working under duress or without freedom*
bondage, bullwork, captivity, chains* constraint, drudge, drudgery, enslavement, enthrallment, feudalism, grind, helotry, indenture, labor, menial labor, moil, peonage, restraint, serfdom, serfhood, servitude, subjection, subjugation, thrall, thralldom, toil, vassalage, work; SEE CONCEPTS 324,388

slay [v] *kill*
annihilate, assassinate, butcher, cut off, destroy, dispatch, do*, do away with, do in*, down*, eliminate, erase, execute, exterminate, finish, hit, knock off*, liquidate, massacre, murder, neutralize, put away*, rub out*, slaughter, snuff*, waste*; SEE CONCEPT 252

sleazy [adj] *disreputable*
base, broken-down, cheap, common, dilapidated, flimsy, limp, low, mean, paltry, poor, run-down, seedy, shabby, shoddy, sordid, squalid, tacky*, trashy, unsubstantial; SEE CONCEPTS 334,485,589

sleek [adj] *smooth, glossy*
glassy, glistening, lustrous, polished, satin, shiny, silken, silky; SEE CONCEPT 606

sleep [n] *suspension of consciousness*
bedtime, catnap, coma, dormancy, doze, dream, dullness, few z's*, forty winks*, hibernation, lethargy, nap, nod, repose, rest, sack time*, sandman*, shuteye*, siesta, slumber, slumberland*, snooze, torpidity, torpor, trance; SEE CONCEPT 315

sleep [v] *suspend consciousness*
bed down*, bunk*, catch a wink*, catch forty winks*, catnap, conk out*, cop some z's*, crash*, doze, dream, drop off*, drowse, fall asleep, fall out*, flop*, hibernate, hit the hay*, hit the sack*, languish, nap, nod, nod off, oversleep, relax, repose, rest, retire, sack out*, saw wood*, slumber, snooze, snore, take a nap, turn in*, yawn, zonk out*, zzz*; SEE CONCEPT 315

sleepy [adj] *tired, dull*
asleep, blah*, comatose, dopey*, dozy, draggy, drowsy, heavy, hypnotic, inactive, lethargic, listless, out*, out of it*, quiet, sleeping, sleepyhead*, slow, sluggish, slumberous, slumbersome, snoozy*, somnolent, soporific, torpid, yawning; SEE CONCEPTS 315,539

slender/slim [adj1] *thin, not heavy*
attenuate, beanpole*, beanstalk*, fine, insubstantial, lean, lithe, narrow, reedy, skeleton, skinny, slight, spare, stalky, stick, svelte, sylphlike, tenuous, threadlike, trim, twiggy, willowy; SEE CONCEPTS 490,491

slender/slim [adj2] *inadequate, flimsy*
bare, deficient, faint, feeble, fragile, inconsiderable, insufficient, little, meager, poor, remote, scant, scanty, scarce, short, shy, slight, small, spare, tenuous, thin, wanting, weak; SEE CONCEPTS 552,771

slice [n] *piece; share*
allotment, allowance, bite, chop, cut, helping, lot, part, piece of pie*, portion, quota, segment, sliver, thin piece, triangle, wedge; SEE CONCEPT 835

slice [v] *cut into portions, shares*
carve, chiv, cleave, dissect, dissever, divide, gash, hack, incise, pierce, segment, sever, shave, shred, slash, slit, split, strip, subdivide, sunder; SEE CONCEPTS 98,137,176

slick [adj1] *smooth, polished*
glossy, greasy, icy, lubricious, oily, oleaginous, shiny, sleek, sleeky, slippery, slithery, soapy; SEE CONCEPT 606

slick [adj2] *smart, clever*
adroit, cagey, canny, deft, dextrous, foxy, glib, knowing, meretricious, plausible, professional, quick, sharp, shrewd, skillful, sly, smooth, smooth-spoken, sophisticated, specious, streetwise*, unctuous, urbane, wise; SEE CONCEPTS 401,402

slide [v] *move smoothly; move down*
accelerate, coast, drift, drive, drop, fall, fall off, flow, glide, glissade, launch, move, move along, move over, propel, sag, scooch*, shift, shove, skate, skid, skim, slip, slither, slump, smooth along, spill, stream, thrust, toboggan, tumble, veer; SEE CONCEPTS 150,152

slight [n] *insult, disrespect*
affront, brush-off, call-down, cold shoulder*, contempt, cut, discourtesy, disdain, disregard, inattention, indifference, kick, neglect, put-down*,

sk
sl

rebuff, rejection, slap in the face*, snub; SEE CON-
CEPTS 30,384,529

slight [adj1] *insignificant, small*
fat, feeble, inconsiderable, insubstantial, meager,
minor, modest, negligible, off, outside, paltry,
petty, piddling, remote, scanty, slender, slim,
sparse, superficial, trifling, trivial, unessential,
unimportant, weak; SEE CONCEPTS 575,762,789

slight [adj2] *thin, small in build*
attenuate, broomstick*, dainty, delicate, feeble,
flimsy, fragile, frail, light, reedy, shadow, skeleton, skinny, slender, slim, spare, stick, twiggy;
SEE CONCEPTS 490,491

slight [v] *offend, insult*
affront, blink at, brush off, chill, contemn, cool*,
cut*, despise, discount, disdain, disparage, disregard, fail, flout, forget, give the brush*, give the
cold shoulder to*, ignore, make light of, neglect,
not give time of day*, omit, overlook, pooh-
pooh*, reject, scoff, scorn, show disrespect, shrug
off, skip, slur, sneeze at*, snub, treat with contempt, turn deaf ear to*, upstage; SEE CONCEPTS
7,19,30,384

slightly [adv] *a little*
hardly, hardly at all, hardly noticeable, imperceptibly, inappreciably, inconsiderably, insignificantly, kind of, lightly, marginally, more or less,
on a small scale, pretty, scarcely any, somewhat,
to some degree, to some extent; SEE CONCEPTS
544,772

slim [v] *lose weight*
diet, reduce, slenderize; SEE CONCEPT 202

slime [n] *muck, gelled waste*
fungus, glop*, goo*, gunk*, mire, mucus, mud,
ooze, scum, sludge; SEE CONCEPT 260

slimy [adj] *oozy, gooey*
clammy, glutinous, miry, mucky, mucous, mucu-
lent, muddy, scummy, viscous, yukky*; SEE CON-
CEPTS 485,621

sling [v] *throw or hang over*
bung, cast, catapult, chuck, dangle, fire, fling,
heave, hoist, hurl, launch, lob, peg, pitch, raise,
send, shoot, suspend, swing, toss, weight; SEE
CONCEPTS 181,222

slink/slither [v] *creep by*
coast, cower, glide, glissade, go stealthily, gumshoe*, lurk, meander, pass quietly, prowl, pussyfoot*, shirk, sidle, skitter, skulk, slick, slide, slip,
snake, sneak, steal, undulate; SEE CONCEPT 151

slip [n1] *error, goof*
blooper*, blunder, bungle, failure, fault, flub*,
fluff*, foul-up*, gaff, howler*, imprudence, indiscretion, lapse, misdeed, misstep, mistake,
muff*, omission, oversight, screw-up*, slip of the
tongue*, slip-up*, trip; SEE CONCEPT 101

slip [n2] *piece of paper*
label, leaf, page, sheet, sliver, strip, tag, ticket;
SEE CONCEPTS 270,475

slip [v1] *fall; glide*
drop, glissade, lose balance, lose footing, lurch,
move, shift, skate, skid, slick, slide, slither,
smooth along, totter, trip; SEE CONCEPTS 150,152

slip [v2] *err*
blunder, drop the ball*, flub*, fluff*, goof*, go
wrong, make a mistake, miscalculate, misjudge,
mistake, muff*, put foot in mouth*, slip up, stumble, trip; SEE CONCEPT 101

slippery [adj1] *smooth, slick*
glace, glassy, glazed, glistening, greasy, icy, like
a skating rink*, lubricious, lustrous, perilous, pol-

ished, satiny, silky, sleek, slimy, soapy, unctuous, unsafe, unstable, unsteady, waxy, wet; SEE
CONCEPT 606

slippery [adj2] *uncertain, unreliable*
cagey, changeable, crafty, cunning, devious, dishonest, duplicitous, elusive, evasive, false, fly-
by-night*, foxy, inconstant, insecure, mutable,
shifty, slick, slithery, smooth, sneaky, treacherous, tricky, two-faced*, unpredictable, unsafe,
unstable, unsteady, untrustworthy, variable; SEE
CONCEPTS 401,534,535

slipshod [adj] *careless; not well done*
bedraggled, botched*, disheveled, faulty, fly-by-
night*, fouled-up*, haphazard, imperfect, inaccurate, inexact, junky*, loose, messed-up, messy,
neglected, negligent, raunchy, screwed-up*,
scrubby*, scruffy*, shabby*, shoddy*, slapdash*,
sloppy, slovenly, tacky*, tattered, threadbare, unkempt, unmeticulous, unsystematic, unthorough,
untidy; SEE CONCEPTS 485,570,589

slit [n] *small opening, cut*
aperture, breach, cleavage, cleft, crack, crevice,
fissure, gash, hole, incision, rent, split, tear; SEE
CONCEPT 513

slit [v] *cut open*
gash, incise, knife, lance, pierce, rip, sever, slash,
slice, slot, split open, tear; SEE CONCEPT 176

sliver [n] *tiny piece, usually of wood or metal*
bit, flake, fragment, paring, shaving, shred, slice,
slip, snip, snippet, splinter, thorn; SEE CONCEPTS
471,831

slobber [v] *drool*
dribble, drip, drivel, froth, salivate, slabber,
slaver, water at the mouth; SEE CONCEPT 185

slogan [n] *motto*
byword, catchphrase, catchword, expression, idiom, jingle, phrase, proverb, rallying cry*, saying, shibboleth*, trademark*, war cry*,
watchword; SEE CONCEPT 278

slop [v] *splash; make a mess*
dash, drip, flounder, let run out, let run over, overflow, slosh, smear, smudge, spatter, spill, splatter, spray, wallow; SEE CONCEPT 250

slope [n] *slant, tilt*
abruptness, bank, bend, bevel, bias, cant, declination, declivity, deflection, descent, deviation,
diagonal, downgrade, gradient, hill, inclination,
incline, lean, leaning, obliqueness, obliquity,
pitch, ramp, rise, rising ground, shelf, skew,
steepness, swag, sway, tip; SEE CONCEPTS
738,757

slope [v] *slant, tilt*
angle, ascend, bank, bevel, cant, descend, dip,
drop, drop away, fall, heel, incline, lean, list,
pitch, rake, recline, rise, shelve, skew, splay, tip;
SEE CONCEPTS 201,738

sloppy [adj] *messy*
awkward, bedraggled, botched, careless, clumsy,
dingy, dirty, disheveled, inattentive, mediocre,
muddy, not clean, poor, slapdash, slipshod, slovenly, sludgy*, slushy*, splashy*, tacky*, unkempt, unthorough, untidy, watery, wet; SEE
CONCEPTS 531,603,621

slot [n] *opening, place*
aperture, channel, cut, groove, hole, niche, position, recess, slit, socket, space, time, vacancy;
SEE CONCEPT 513

slouch [v] *slump over*
be lazy, bend, bow, crouch, droop, lean, loaf,

loll, lounge, sag, stoop, wilt; SEE CONCEPTS *154,201*

slovenly [*adj*] *dirty, disordered*
bedraggled, botched, careless, dingy, disheveled, disorderly, dowdy, down-at-the-heel*, frowzy*, frumpy*, grody*, grubby, grungy*, heedless, icky*, loose, messed up*, messy, mussy, negligent, pigpen*, raunchy, seedy, slack, slapdash, sleazy*, slipshod, sloppy, tacky, topsy-turvy, unfastidious, unkempt, unthorough, untidy; SEE CONCEPTS *485,621*

slow [*adj1*] *unhurried, lazy*
apathetic, crawling, creeping, dawdling, delaying, deliberate, dilatory, disinclined, dreamy, drowsy, easy, gradual, heavy, idle, imperceptible, inactive, indolent, inert, lackadaisical, laggard, lagging, leaden, leisurely, lethargic, listless, loitering, measured, moderate, negligent, passive, phlegmatic, plodding, ponderous, postponing, procrastinating, quiet, reluctant, remiss, slack, sleepy, slothful, slow-moving, sluggish, snaillike, stagnant, supine, tardy, torpid, tortoiselike; SEE CONCEPTS *538,584,588*

slow [*adj2*] *behind, late*
backward, behindhand, belated, conservative, dead, delayed, detained, dilatory, down, draggy*, dull, gradual, hindered, impeded, inactive, lingering, long-delayed, long-drawn-out*, low, moderate, off, overdue, prolonged, protracted, reduced, slack, sleepy, sluggish, stagnant, stiff, tame, tardy, tedious, time-consuming, uneventful, unproductive, unprogressive, unpunctual; SEE CONCEPTS *529,537,548*

slow [*adj3*] *unintelligent*
backward, dense, dim, dimwitted, dull, dumb, dunce, imbecile, limited, moronic, obtuse, simple, slow on the uptake*, stupid, thick, unresponsive; SEE CONCEPT *402*

slow [*v*] *delay, restrict*
abate, anchor it, back-water*, bog down, brake, check, choke, curb, curtail, cut back, cut down, decelerate, decrease, detain, diminish, ease off, ease up, embog, handicap, hinder, hit the brakes*, hold back, hold up, impede, keep waiting, lag, lessen, let down flaps*, loiter, lose speed, lose steam*, mire, moderate, postpone, procrastinate, qualify, quiet, reduce, reduce speed, reef, regulate, rein in, relax, retard, retardate, set back, slacken, stall, stunt, temper, wind down; SEE CONCEPTS *130,234,250*

slowdown [*n*] *slacking off; gradual decrease*
arrest, deceleration, decline, delay, downtrend, downturn, drop, drop-off, falloff, freeze, inactivity, retardation, slack, slackening, slow-up, stagnation, stoppage, strike; SEE CONCEPTS *121,130*

sluggish [*adj*] *dull, slow-moving*
apathetic, blah*, comatose, dopey*, down, dragging, draggy*, drippy*, heavy, hebetudinous, inactive, indolent, inert, laid-back*, languid, languorous, leaden, lethargic, lifeless, listless, lumpish, mooney*, off, phlegmatic, pokey*, slack, sleepyheaded*, slothful, slow, sluggard, slumberous, stagnant, stiff, sullen, torpid, unresponsive; SEE CONCEPTS *401,584*

slumber [*n*] *sleep*
coma, dormancy, doze, drowse, forty winks*, inactivity, languor, lethargy, nap, repose, rest, sack time*, shut-eye*, snooze, stupor, torpor; SEE CONCEPT *315*

slump [*n*] *decline, failure*
bad period, bad times, blight, blue devils*, blue funk*, bottom, bust, collapse, crash, depreciation, depression, descent, dip, downer*, downslide*, downswing*, downtrend, downturn, drop, dumps*, fall, falling-off*, funk, hard times*, letdown*, low, rainy days*, recession, reverse, rut, sag, slide, slip, stagnation, the skids*, trough; SEE CONCEPTS *335,410,674*

slump [*v*] *decline, sink*
bend, blight, cave in, collapse, crash, decay, deteriorate, droop, drop, fall, fall off*, go down, go downhill*, go to ruin*, hunch, keel over, loll, pitch, plummet, plunge, reach new low*, sag, slide, slip, slouch, topple, tumble; SEE CONCEPTS *181,698,699,763*

slur [*n*] *insult*
accusation, affront, animadversion, aspersion, bar sinister*, black eye*, blemish, blot, blur, brand, brickbat*, calumny, dirty dig*, discredit, disgrace, dump, expose, hit, innuendo, insinuation, knock, obloquy, odium, onus, put-down*, rap*, reflection, reproach, slam, smear, stain, stigma, stricture, zinger*; SEE CONCEPTS *44,54,278*

slur [*v1*] *insult*
blacken, blemish, blister, blot, blow off*, brand, calumniate, cap, chop*, cut to the quick*, cut up*, defame, denigrate, detract, discredit, disgrace, dump on*, give a black eye*, hit where one lives*, insinuate, kick in the teeth*, libel, malign, miff, offend, push, put down*, reproach, roast*, scorch*, skin alive*, slander, slap in the face*, slight, smear*, snub, spatter, stain, tear down, traduce, vilify, zing*; SEE CONCEPTS *7,19,44,54*

slur [*v2*] *mumble words*
garble, mispronounce, miss, skip, stutter; SEE CONCEPT *47*

sly [*adj*] *clever, devious*
arch, artful, astute, bluffing, cagey, calculating, canny, captious, conniving, covert, crafty, crooked, cunning, deceitful, deceptive, delusive, designing, dishonest, dishonorable, dissembling, double-dealing, elusive, foxy, furtive, guileful, illusory, impish, ingenious, insidious, intriguing, mean, mischievous, plotting, roguish, scheming, secret, sharp, shifty, shrewd, slick, smart, smooth, sneaking, stealthy, subtle, traitorous, treacherous, tricky, underhand, unscrupulous, wily; SEE CONCEPTS *401,542*

smack [*n/v*] *strike, often with hand*
bang, blip, blow, box, buffet, chop, clap, clout, crack, cuff, hit, pat, punch, slap, snap, sock, spank, tap; SEE CONCEPT *189*

smack [*adv*] *directly, exactly*
accurately, bang*, clearly, just, plumb, pointblank*, precisely, right, sharp, square, squarely, straight; SEE CONCEPT *557*

small [*adj1*] *tiny in size, quantity*
baby, bantam, bitty*, cramped, diminutive, humble, immature, inadequate, inconsequential, inconsiderable, insufficient, limited, little, meager, microscopic, mini*, miniature, minuscule, minute, modest, narrow, paltry, petite, petty, picayune, piddling*, pint-sized*, pitiful, pocketsized*, poor, puny*, runty*, scanty, scrubby, short, shrimp*, slight, small-scale, stunted, teensy*, teeny, toy, trifling, trivial, undersized, unpretentious, wee*, young; SEE CONCEPTS *773,789*

small [*adj2*] *unimportant*
bush-league*, inadequate, inconsiderable, ineffec-

tual, inferior, insignificant, lesser, light, limited, lower, mean, minor, minor-league*, minute, narrow, negligible, paltry, petty, secondary, set, small-fry*, small-time*, trifling, trivial, unessential; SEE CONCEPT 575

small [adj3] narrow-minded, nasty
base, grudging, ignoble, illiberal, limited, little, mean, narrow, petty, selfish, set, vulgar; SEE CONCEPT 401

smart [adj1] intelligent
acute, adept, agile, alert, apt, astute, bold, brainy*, bright, brilliant, brisk, canny, clever, crafty, effective, eggheaded*, fresh, genius, good, impertinent, ingenious, keen, knowing, long-haired*, nervy, nimble, on the ball*, pert, pointed, quick, quick-witted, ready, resourceful, sassy, sharp, shrewd, skull, slick*, whiz*, wise; SEE CONCEPT 402

smart [adj2] stylish, fashionable
chic, dapper, dashing, dressed to kill*, elegant, exclusive, fine, fly*, in fashion, last word*, latest thing*, modish, natty, neat, snappy, spruce, swank, trendy, trim, well turned-out, with it*; SEE CONCEPT 589

smart [adj3] brisk; lively
active, bold, brazen, cracking, energetic, forward, good, jaunty, nervy, pert, quick, saucy, scintillating, spanking, spirited, sprightly, vigorous; SEE CONCEPTS 401,542

smart [v] hurt, pain
ache, be painful, bite, burn, prick, prickle, sting, suffer, throb, tingle; SEE CONCEPTS 246,728

smash [n1] collision; defeat
accident, bang, bash, blast, blow, boom, breakdown, breaking, breakup, burst, clap, collapse, crack, crack-up, crash, debacle, destruction, disaster, downfall, failure, pile-up, ruin, shattering, slam, smash-up, sock, wallop, welt, whack, wham, wreck; SEE CONCEPTS 674,675

smash [n2] great success
hit, knockout, sensation, wow*; SEE CONCEPT 706

smash [v1] break into pieces
bang, belt, blast, break to smithereens*, burst, clobber, collide, crack, crash, crush, demolish, disintegrate, fracture, fragment, hit, make mincemeat of*, pound, powder, pulverize, rive, scrunch, shatter, shiver, slam, slug, splinter, squash, squish, trash, wallop; SEE CONCEPTS 246,252

smash [v2] defeat, destroy
annihilate, break up, decimate, demolish, destruct, disrupt, lay in ruins*, lay waste*, overthrow, overturn, put out of action*, put out of commission*, raze, ruin, shatter, tear down, topple, trash, tumble, wreck; SEE CONCEPTS 95,252

smear [v1] rub on, spread over
apply, bedaub, besmirch, blur, coat, cover, dab, daub, defile, dirty, discolor, overlay, overspread, patch, plaster, slop, smudge, soil, spatter, spray, sprinkle, stain, sully, taint, tar, tarnish; SEE CONCEPTS 172,202,215

smear [v2] tarnish a reputation
asperse, bad-mouth*, befoul, besmirch, blacken, blackguard*, blister, calumniate, defame, defile, denigrate, discolor, drag through mud*, give a black eye*, hit*, libel, malign, pan*, poormouth*, rap*, rip up*, scorch*, slam*, slander, sling mud*, slur, sully, taint, traduce, vilify; SEE CONCEPTS 54,63

smell [n] odor
aroma, bouquet, emanation, essence, flavor, fragrance, incense, perfume, redolence, savor, scent, spice, stench, stink, tang, trace, trail, whiff; SEE CONCEPTS 590,599

smell [v1] perceive with the nose
breathe, detect, discover, find, get a whiff*, identify, inhale, nose, scent, sniff, snuff; SEE CONCEPTS 590,601,602

smell [v2] have an odor
be malodorous, funk*, reek, smell to high heaven*, stench, stink, whiff; SEE CONCEPT 600

smelly [adj] having a bad odor
evil-smelling, fetid, foul, foul-smelling, funky*, high, malodorous, mephitic, noisome, olid, putrid, rancid, rank, reeking, stinking, strong, strong-smelling, whiffy*; SEE CONCEPT 598

smile [v] put on a happy expression
beam, be gracious, express friendliness, express tenderness, grin, laugh, look amused, look delighted, look happy, look pleased, simper, smirk; SEE CONCEPT 185

smirk [n] sly smile
beam, grin, leer, simper, smug look, sneer; SEE CONCEPT 185

smoky [adj] hazy, sooty
begrimed, black, burning, caliginous, dingy, fumy, gray, grimy, messy, murky, reeking, silvery, smoke-colored, smoldering, thick, vaporous; SEE CONCEPTS 485,618

smolder [v] burn, simmer
boil, bubble, churn, consume, erupt, explode, ferment, fester, fulminate, fume, seethe, smoke, steam, stir; SEE CONCEPTS 35,249

smooth [adj1] level, unwrinkled; flowing
bland, continuous, creamy, easy, effortless, equable, even, flat, fluent, fluid, flush, frictionless, gentle, glassy, glossy, hairless, horizontal, invariable, lustrous, mild, mirrorlike, monotonous, peaceful, plain, planate, plane, polished, quiet, regular, rhythmic, rippleless, serene, shaven, shiny, silky, sleek, soft, soothing, stable, steady, still, tranquil, unbroken, undeviating, undisturbed, uneventful, uniform, uninterrupted, unruffled, untroubled, unvarying, velvety; SEE CONCEPTS 406,480,606

smooth [adj2] suave in behavior
agreeable, bland, civilized, courteous, courtly, facile, genial, glib, ingratiating, mellow, mild, persuasive, pleasant, polite, slick, smarmy*, unctuous, urbane; SEE CONCEPT 401

smooth [v1] make level
burnish, clear, even, flatten, flush, glaze, gloss, grade, iron, lay, level, make uniform, perfect, plane, polish, press, refine, round, sand, sleek, slick, varnish; SEE CONCEPTS 137,250

smooth [v2] make peace
allay, alleviate, appease, assuage, calm, comfort, cool*, ease, extenuate, facilitate, iron out, mellow, mitigate, mollify, palliate, pat, pave the way*, soften, stroke, take the edge off*, take the sting out*; SEE CONCEPTS 7,22

smother [v] extinguish; cover, hide
asphyxiate, choke, collect, compose, conceal, control, cool, cork, douse, envelop, heap, hush up*, inundate, keep back, kill, muffle, overwhelm, quash, quell, quench, rein, repress, restrain, shower, shroud, simmer down, snuff,

squelch, stamp out, stifle, strangle, suffocate, suppress, surround, throttle; SEE CONCEPTS *130,172,188,234*

smudge [n] *dirt smear*
blemish, blot, blur, macule, smut, smutch, soiled spot, spot; SEE CONCEPT *723*

smudge [v] *smear, dirty*
begrime, blacken, blotch, blur, daub, defile, foul, grime, mark, plaster, slop, smirch, soil, spatter, sully, taint, tarnish; SEE CONCEPT *254*

smug [adj] *pleased with oneself*
complacent, conceited, egoistic, egotistical, holier-than-thou*, hotshot*, pompous, priggish, puffed-up*, self-contented, self-righteous, self-satisfied, snobbish, stuck on oneself*, stuck-up*, stuffy, superior, vainglorious; SEE CONCEPTS *404,542*

smuggle [v] *transfer illegal goods*
bootleg, deal, export, hide, moonshine*, pirate, push, run, run contraband*, run rum*, snake in*; SEE CONCEPT *192*

smutty [adj] *obscene, vulgar*
bawdy, blue*, coarse, crude, dirty, filthy, foul, immoral, improper, indecent, indelicate, lewd, nasty, off-color, pornographic, prurient, racy, raunchy, raw, risqué, rough, salacious, salty, scatological, suggestive, X-rated*; SEE CONCEPTS *267,372,545*

snack [n] *tiny meal*
bite, bite to eat*, break, eats*, goodies*, grub*, light meal, lunch, luncheon, midnight snack, morsel, munch*, nibble, nosh*, pickings, piece, refreshment, tea, tidbit; SEE CONCEPTS *457,459*

snag [n] *complication in situation*
bar, barrier, blockade, brake, bug*, catch, Catch-22, clog, crimp, cropper, crunch, curb, difficulty, disadvantage, drag*, drawback, fix*, glitch, hamper, hitch, hold-up*, hole*, hurdle, impediment, inconvenience, knot, obstacle, obstruction, pickle*, problem, puzzler, scrape, spot, stumbling block, the rub*, tight spot*; SEE CONCEPTS *666,674*

snag [v] *catch on something*
hole, nail, rip, run into, tear; SEE CONCEPT *214*

snaky [adj1] *winding*
anfractuous, convoluted, entwined, flexuous, indirect, meandering, meandrous, serpentine, sinuous, tortuous, twisted, twisting, writhing, zigzag; SEE CONCEPT *581*

snaky [adj2] *devious, sly*
crafty, insidious, lurking, perfidious, slinking, sneaky, subtle, treacherous, venomous, vipery, virulent; SEE CONCEPT *401*

snap [n] *easy thing to accomplish*
breeze*, child's play*, cinch, duck soup*, ease, easy as pie*, kid stuff*, no problem, picnic*, pie*, smooth sailing*, soft touch*, walkover*; SEE CONCEPT *693*

snap [v1] *separate, break*
click, come apart, crack, crackle, fracture, give way, pop; SEE CONCEPTS *98,246*

snap [v2] *bite, seize*
bite at, catch, clutch, grab, grasp, grip, jerk, lurch, nip, snatch, twitch, yank; SEE CONCEPTS *90,191*

snap [v3] *speak sharply*
bark, flare, flash, fly off the handle*, get angry, growl, grumble, grunt, jump down throat*, lash out, retort, roar, snarl, snort, take it out on*, vent, yell; SEE CONCEPTS *54,77*

snappy [adj1] *nasty, irritable*
cross, disagreeable, edgy, fractious, hasty, huffy, petulant, quick-tempered, snappish, tart, testy, touchy, waspish; SEE CONCEPTS *267,401*

snappy [adj2] *fashionable*
chic, classy, dapper, dashing, fly*, in good taste, modish, natty, sharp, smart, stylish, swank*, tony*, trendy, up-to-the-minute, with style; SEE CONCEPT *589*

snappy [adj3] *fast*
abrupt, breakneck, expeditious, fleet, harefooted, hasty, immediate, instant, on-the-spot, quick, rapid, speedy, sudden, swift, unpremeditated; SEE CONCEPTS *588,799*

snare [n] *trap*
allurement, bait, booby trap*, catch, come-on*, deception, decoy, enticement, entrapment, inveiglement, lure, net, noose, pitfall, quicksand, seducement, temptation, trick, wire*; SEE CONCEPTS *529,674*

snare [v] *catch, trap*
arrest, bag*, corral*, decoy, enmesh, entangle, entrap, get hands on*, involve, land, lure, net, pull in, round up, seduce, seize, tempt, wire*; SEE CONCEPTS *11,90*

snarl [n] *complication, mess*
chaos, clutter, complexity, confusion, disarray, disorder, entanglement, intricacy, intricateness, jam, jungle, knot, labyrinth, maze, mishmash, morass, muddle, muss, skein, swarm, tangle, web; SEE CONCEPTS *663,666,674*

snarl [v1] *grumble*
abuse, bark, bluster, bully, complain, fulminate, gnarl, gnash teeth, growl, mumble, murmur, mutter, quarrel, show teeth, snap, threaten, thunder, yelp; SEE CONCEPT *77*

snarl [v2] *complicate, mess up*
confuse, embroil, enmesh, ensnarl, entangle, entwine, involve, muck, muddle, perplex, ravel, tangle; SEE CONCEPTS *16,158*

snatch [n] *small part*
bit, fragment, piece, smattering, snippet, spell; SEE CONCEPTS *264,832*

snatch [v] *grab away*
abduct, catch, clap hands on, clutch, collar*, gain, get fingers on*, grapple, grasp, grip, jerk, jump, kidnap, make off with, nab, nail*, pluck, pull, rescue, seize, snag, spirit away, steal, take, win, wrench, wrest, yank; SEE CONCEPTS *90,191*

sneak [n] *person who is very dishonest*
cheater, con artist, coward, cur, dastard, heel*, informer, louse, rascal, reptile, scoundrel, skunk*, slink*, snake*, snake in grass*, toad*, weasel*, wretch; SEE CONCEPT *412*

sneak [v] *move stealthily*
ambush, case, cheat, cower, crawl, creep, deceive, delude, evade, glide, gumshoe*, hide, lurk, mooch, move secretly, ooze, pad, pass, prowl, pussyfoot*, secrete, shirk, sidle, skulk, slide, slink, slip, slither, sly, smuggle, snake, snoop, spirit, steal, worm; SEE CONCEPTS *151,188*

sneaky [adj] *underhanded, dishonest*
base, contemptible, cowardly, deceitful, devious, disingenuous, double-dealing*, duplicitous, furtive, guileful, indirect, low, malicious, mean, nasty, recreant, secretive, shifty, slippery, sly, sneaking, snide, stealthy, surreptitious, tricky, underhand, unreliable, unscrupulous, untrustworthy, yellow*; SEE CONCEPTS *267,401,542*

sm
sn

sneer [v] *mock, condemn*
affront, belittle, burlesque, caricature, crack, curl one's lip at*, decry, deride, detract, disdain, disparage, dump, fleer, flout, gibe, gird, give Bronx cheer, grin, hold in contempt*, hold up to ridicule*, insult, jeer, jest, lampoon, laugh at, leer, look down on, put down, quip at, rally, rank out, ridicule, satirize, scoff, scorn, slam, slight, smile, sneeze at*, sniff at*, snigger, swipe, taunt, travesty, turn up one's nose*, twit, underrate; SEE CONCEPTS 30,52,54

snicker/snigger/sniggle [v] *laugh at mockingly*
chortle, chuckle, giggle, guffaw, hee-haw, smirk, sneer, teehee, titter; SEE CONCEPT 77

snide [adj] *hateful, nasty*
base, cynical, disparaging, hurtful, insinuating, malicious, mean, sarcastic, scornful, sneering, spiteful, unkind; SEE CONCEPT 401

sniff [v] *breathe in*
detect, inhale, inspire, nose, scent, smell, snift, snuff, snuffle; SEE CONCEPTS 601,602

snob [n] *person who looks down on others*
braggart, highbrow, name-dropper, parvenu, pretender, smarty pants*, stiff neck*, upstart; SEE CONCEPT 423

snobbish [adj] *stuck-up, conceited*
aloof, arrogant, condescending, egotistic, haughty, high-and-mighty*, high-flown*, high-hat*, ostentatious, overbearing, patronizing, persnickety*, pompous, pretentious, putting on airs*, remote, sniffy*, snippy*, snooty*, snotty*, supercilious, superior, swanky, tony*, uppish, uppity*; SEE CONCEPT 401

snoop [n] *person who noses around*
busybody, butt-in*, detective, eavesdropper, ferret, gumshoe*, meddler, peeping Tom*, pragmatist, pry, pryer, quidnunc, rubberneck*, scout, sleuth, snooper; SEE CONCEPTS 348,423

snoop [v] *nose around*
busybody*, interfere, intrude, meddle, mess with, mouse*, nose, peek, peep, peer, poke, poke nose in*, pry, snook, spy, stare; SEE CONCEPTS 216,384,623

snooze [n] *light sleep*
catnap, doze, forty winks*, nap, siesta, slumber; SEE CONCEPT 315

snooze [v] *sleep lightly*
catnap, doze, drop off, drowse, nap, nod off*, siesta, slumber, take forty winks*; SEE CONCEPTS 210,315

snore [v] *make sounds when sleeping*
breathe heavily, saw logs*, saw wood*, sleep, snort, snuffle, wheeze; SEE CONCEPTS 77,315

snub [v] *give someone the cold shoulder*
act cool*, boycott, brush off*, burr, censure, chill, cool, cut, cut dead*, disdain, disregard, duck, give the brush*, humble, humiliate, ice*, ice out*, ignore, look coldly upon, look right through*, mortify, neglect, not give time of day*, offend, ostracize, pass up, put down, put the chill on*, rebuff, scold, scorn, scratch, shame, shun, slight, slur, snob, swank, upstage; SEE CONCEPTS 30,54,384

snug [adj] *cozy, warm*
close, comfortable, comfy, compact, convenient, cushy, easeful, easy, homelike, homely, intimate, neat, restful, sheltered, snug as a bug in a rug*, soft, substantial, tight, trim, well-off; SEE CONCEPT 485

snuggle [v] *cuddle*
bundle, burrow, curl up, grasp, huddle, hug, nestle, nuzzle, snug, spoon; SEE CONCEPTS 190,201

soak [v] *drench, wet*
absorb, assimilate, bathe, damp, dip, drink, drown, dunk, flood, imbrue, immerge, immerse, impregnate, infiltrate, infuse, macerate, marinate, merge, moisten, penetrate, percolate, permeate, pour into, pour on, saturate, seethe, soften, sop, souse, steep, submerge, take in, wash, water, waterlog; SEE CONCEPT 256

soar [v] *climb, fly*
arise, ascend, aspire, escalate, glide, lift, mount, rise, rocket, sail, shoot, shoot up, skyrocket, top, tower, up, uprear, wing; SEE CONCEPTS 148,150

sob [v] *cry hard*
bawl, blub, blubber, boohoo*, break down, cry a river*, cry convulsively, cry eyes out*, howl, lament, shed tears, snivel, turn on waterworks*, wail, weep, whimper; SEE CONCEPTS 185,410

sober [adj] *not partaking of alcohol*
abstaining, abstemious, abstinent, ascetic, calm, clear-headed, cold sober*, continent, controlled, dry, moderate, nonindulgent, not drunk, on the wagon*, restrained, sedate, self-possessed, serious, steady, temperate, took the pledge*; SEE CONCEPT 401

sober [adj2] *calm, peaceful; dull*
abnegating, abstaining, calm, clear-headed, cold, collected, composed, constrained, cool, dark, disciplined, dispassionate, down-to-earth*, drab, earnest, eschewing, forgoing, grave, hard-boiled*, imperturbable, inhibited, levelheaded, low-key, lucid, no-nonsense, pacific, peaceful, plain, practical, quiet, rational, realistic, reasonable, reserved, restrained, sedate, serene, serious, severe, soft, solemn, somber, sound, staid, steady, subdued, toned down, unexcited, unimpassioned, unruffled; SEE CONCEPTS 401,542

so-called [adj] *supposed*
alleged, allegedly, commonly named, formal, nominal, ostensible, pretended, professed, purported, self-named, self-styled, soi-disant, supposed, titular, wrongly named; SEE CONCEPT 552

sociable [adj] *friendly, outgoing*
accessible, affable, approachable, close, clubby*, companionable, conversable, convivial, cordial, familiar, genial, good-natured, gregarious, intimate, neighborly, regular, social, warm; SEE CONCEPTS 401,555

social [adj] *public, friendly*
amusing, civil, collective, common, communal, communicative, community, companionable, convivial, cordial, diverting, entertaining, familiar, general, gracious, gregarious, group, hospitable, informative, mannerly, neighborly, nice, organized, pleasant, pleasurable, polished, polite, popular, public, sociable, societal; SEE CONCEPTS 536,555

socialize [v] *be friendly at gatherings*
associate, chum with*, club*, consort, entertain, fraternize, get about, get around, get together, go out, hang around with*, hang out, hobnob, join, keep company, league, make advances, make the rounds*, mingle, mix, pal around*, run with*, tie up with*; SEE CONCEPT 384

society [n1] *humankind, people*
association, camaraderie, civilization, commonality, commonwealth, community, companionship, company, comradeship, culture, friendship, gen-

eral public, humanity, jungle*, nation, population, public, rat race*, social order, world, zoo*; SEE CONCEPTS *379,417*

society [*n2*] *organization, institution*
alliance, association, circle, clan, clique, club, companionship, comradeship, corporation, coterie, gang, group, guild, hookup, institute, league, network, order, outfit, ring, sodality, syndicate, tie-in*, tie-up*, union; SEE CONCEPTS *381,387*

society [*n3*] *upper class of people*
aristocracy, beau monde*, beautiful people*, country set*, elite, flower*, gentry, glitterati*, haut monde, high society, jet set*, main line, patriciate, polite society, quality, smart set*, top drawer*, upper crust*, who's who*; SEE CONCEPTS *387,388,417*

sock [*n/v*] *hit hard*
beat, belt, bop, buffet, chop, clout, cuff, ding, nail, paste, punch, slap, smack, smash, soak, whack; SEE CONCEPT *189*

soft [*adj1*] *cushioned, squishy*
bendable, comfortable, comfy, cottony, cozy, creamy, cushiony, cushy, delicate, doughy, downy, ductile, easeful, easy, elastic, feathery, fine, flabby, fleecy, fleshy, flexible, flimsy, flocculent, flowing, fluffy, fluid, formless, furry, gelatinous, impressible, limp, malleable, moldable, mushy, pappy, pithy, plastic, pliable, pulpy, quaggy, rounded, satiny, silken, silky, smooth, snug, spongy, squashy, supple, thin, velvety, yielding; SEE CONCEPTS *488,606*

soft [*adj2*] *faint, temperate*
ashen, balmy, bland, caressing, comfortable, cool, cushy, delicate, diffuse, dim, dimmed, dulcet, dull, dusky, faint, gentle, hazy, lenient, light, low, low-key, mellifluous, mellow, melodious, mild, misty, murmured, muted, pale, pallid, pastel, pleasing, quiet, restful, shaded, smooth, sober, soothing, subdued, sweet, tinted, toned down, twilight [indicated], wan, whispered; SEE CONCEPTS *525,537,592,610*

soft [*adj3*] *compassionate*
affectionate, amiable, benign, courteous, easy, easy-going, effortless, gentle, gracious, indulgent, kind, kindly, lax, lenient, liberal, manageable, overindulgent, permissive, pitying, sensitive, sentimental, simple, spineless, sympathetic, tender, tender-hearted, undemanding, weak; SEE CONCEPT *401*

soft [*adj4*] *out of condition*
doughy, fat, flabby, flaccid, fleshy, formless, gone to seed*, limp, out of shape*, overindulged, pampered, untrained, weak; SEE CONCEPTS *314,485*

soft [*adj5*] *stupid*
daft, fatuous, feeble-minded, foolish, silly, simple, witless; SEE CONCEPT *402*

soften [*v*] *calm, soothe*
abate, allay, alleviate, appease, assuage, become tender, bend, cushion, diminish, disintegrate, dissolve, ease, enfeeble, give, knead, lessen, lighten, lower, mash, mellow, melt, mitigate, moderate, modify, moisten, mollify, palliate, qualify, quell, relax, relent, still, subdue, temper, tenderize, thaw, tone down, turn down, weaken, yield; SEE CONCEPT *250*

soggy [*adj*] *damp or soaking*
clammy, dank, dripping, heavy, humid, moist, mucky, muggy, mushy, pasty, pulpy, saturated,

soaked, sodden, soft, sopping, spongy, sticky, sultry, waterlogged; SEE CONCEPT *603*

soil [*n1*] *earth, dirt*
clay, dry land, dust, grime, ground, land, loam, soot, terra firma; SEE CONCEPT *509*

soil [*n2*] *land where one lives*
country, home, homeland, homestead, region, spread, terra firma; SEE CONCEPTS *198,510,511*

soil [*v*] *make dirty*
bedraggle, befoul, begrime, besmirch, contaminate, crumb, debase, defile, degrade, dirty, discolor, disgrace, foul, grime, maculate, mess, mess up, muck*, muck up*, muddy, muss*, muss up*, pollute, shame, smear, smudge, spatter, spoil, spot, stain, sully, taint, tar, tarnish; SEE CONCEPT *254*

sojourn [*n*] *brief travel; visit*
layover, residence, rest, stay, stop, stopover, tarriance, vacation; SEE CONCEPTS *224,226,227*

sojourn [*v*] *travel briefly; visit*
abide, dwell, inhabit, linger, lodge, nest, perch, reside, rest, roost, squat, stay, stay over, stop, tarry, vacation; SEE CONCEPTS *224,226,227*

solace [*n*] *comfort, peace*
alleviation, assuagement, condolement, condolence, consolation, pity, relief; SEE CONCEPTS *7,22,410*

solace [*v*] *give comfort, peace*
allay, alleviate, buck up, cheer, comfort, condole with, console, mitigate, soften, soothe, upraise; SEE CONCEPTS *7,22*

soldier [*n*] *person serving in military*
airforce member, cadet, cavalryperson, commando, conscript, draftee, enlisted person, fighter, GI*, Green Beret, guard, guerrilla, gunner, infantry, infantryperson, marine, mercenary, military person, musketeer, officer, paratrooper, pilot, private, rank, recruit, scout, selectee, serviceperson, soldier, soldier-at-arms, trooper, veteran, volunteer, warmonger, warrior; SEE CONCEPT *358*

sole [*adj*] *alone, singular*
ace, exclusive, individual, lone, one, one and only, onliest, only, only one, particular, remaining, separate, single, solitary, solo, unique, unshared; SEE CONCEPTS *555,564,577*

solely [*adv*] *only, alone*
barely, but, completely, entirely, exclusively, individually, merely, onliest, purely, simply, single-handedly, singly, singularly, totally, undividedly, wholly; SEE CONCEPTS *544,577*

solemn [*adj1*] *quiet, serious*
austere, brooding, cold sober*, deliberate, dignified, downbeat, earnest, funereal, glum, grave, heavy, intense, matter of life and death*, moody, no fooling*, no-nonsense*, pensive, portentous, reflective, sedate, sober, somber, staid, stern, thoughtful, weighty; SEE CONCEPTS *403,542*

solemn [*adj2*] *impressive, sacred*
august, awe-inspiring, ceremonial, ceremonious, conventional, devotional, dignified, divine, formal, full, grand, grave, hallowed, holy, imposing, impressive, magnificent, majestic, momentous, ostentatious, overwhelming, plenary, religious, reverential, ritual, sanctified, stately, venerable; SEE CONCEPT *574*

solicit [*v*] *plead for; try to sell*
accost, apply, approach, ask, beg, beseech, bespeak, bum, cadge, call, canvass, challenge, claim, come on to*, crave, demand, desire,

sn
so

drum*, drum up*, entreat, exact, go, hawk, hit on*, hit up*, hustle, implore, importune, inquire, mooch, panhandle, pass the hat*, peddle, petition, postulate, pray, promote, proposition, query, question, refer, request, require, requisition, resort, seduce, seek, sponge, steer, sue for, supplicate, touch, tout, turn, whistle for*; SEE CONCEPTS 53,345

solicitous [adj] worried
anxious, appetent, apprehensive, ardent, athirst, attentive, avid, beside oneself, careful, caring, concerned, devoted, eager, earnest, heedful, impatient, keen, loving, mindful, raring, regardful, tender, thirsty, troubled, uneasy, worried sick*, worried stiff*, zealous; SEE CONCEPT 403

solicitude [n] worry, anxiety
attention, attentiveness, care, compunction, concern, concernment, considerateness, consideration, disquiet, disquietude, heed, presentiment, qualm, regard, scruple, tender loving care*, TLC*, unease, uneasiness, watchfulness; SEE CONCEPT 410

solid [adj1] hard, dimensional
brick wall*, close, compact, compacted, concentrated, concrete, consolidated, dense, firm, fixed, heavy, hefty, hulk, hunk, husky, massed, material, physical, rock, rocklike, rooted, secure, set, sound, stable, strong, sturdy, substantial, thick, tight, unshakable; SEE CONCEPTS 483,604

solid [adj2] continuous, complete
agreed, brick wall*, consecutive, consentient, continued, firm, like a rock, regular, set in stone*, stable, steady, unalloyed, unanimous, unbroken, undivided, uninterrupted, united, unmixed; SEE CONCEPTS 482,488,531

solid [adj3] dependable, reliable
cogent, constant, decent, estimable, genuine, good, law-abiding, levelheaded, pure, real, satisfactory, satisfying, sensible, serious, sober, sound, stalwart, steadfast, trustworthy, trusty, upright, upstanding, valid, worthy; SEE CONCEPTS 401,534

solitary [adj] alone, single; unsociable
aloof, antisocial, cloistered, companionless, deserted, desolate, distant, eremetic, forsaken, friendless, hermitical, hidden, individual, introverted, isolated, lone, lonely, lonesome, lorn, misanthropic, offish, only, out-of-the-way*, particular, reclusive, remote, reserved, retired, secluded, separate, sequestered, singular, sole, solo, stag, standoffish, unaccompanied, unapproachable, unattended, uncompanionable, unfrequented, unique, unsocial, withdrawn; SEE CONCEPTS 555,577,583

solitude [n] aloneness
confinement, desert, detachment, emptiness, isolation, loneliness, loneness, lonesomeness, peace and quiet*, privacy, quarantine, reclusiveness, retirement, seclusion, separateness, silence, solitariness, waste, wasteland, wilderness, withdrawal; SEE CONCEPTS 388,673,714

solution [n1] answer, resolution
Band-Aid*, clarification, elucidation, explanation, explication, key, pay dirt*, quick fix*, result, solving, the ticket*, unfolding, unraveling, unravelment; SEE CONCEPTS 230,661,712

solution [n2] mixture of liquid and another substance
blend, compound, dissolvent, elixir, emulsion, extract, fluid, juice, mix, sap, solvent, suspension; SEE CONCEPTS 260,467

solve [v] answer, resolve
break*, clarify, clear up, construe, crack*, deal with, decide, decipher, decode, determine, disentangle, divine, do, elucidate, enlighten, explain, expound, fathom, figure out, find out, fix, get, get right, get to the bottom*, have, hit, hit upon*, illuminate, interpret, iron out*, lick*, make a dent*, make out*, pan out*, put two and two together*, puzzle, reason, settle, think out, unfold, unlock, unravel, unriddle, untangle, work, work out; SEE CONCEPTS 15,18,37

somber [adj] sad, depressing
black, bleak, blue*, caliginous, cloudy, dark, depressive, dim, dingy, dire, dismal, dispiriting, doleful, down, drab, dragged, dreary, dull, dusky, earnest, funereal, gloomy, grave, grim, hurting, joyless, lugubrious, melancholy, mournful, murky, no-nonsense, obscure, sad, sedate, sepulchral, serious, shadowy, shady, sober, solemn, sourpuss, staid, tenebrous, weighty; SEE CONCEPTS 403,485,529

somebody [n] person of fame, importance
celebrity, dignitary, heavyweight*, household name*, luminary, name*, notable, one, personage, person of note, public figure, so-and-so*, someone*, some person*, star, superstar, VIP*, whoever*; SEE CONCEPT 423

someday [adv] eventually
after a while, anytime, at a future time, finally, in a time to come, one day, one fine day*, one of these days, one time, one time or another, sometime, sooner or later, subsequently, ultimately, yet; SEE CONCEPTS 548,820

somehow [adv] by some means
after a fashion, anyhow, anyway, anywise, by hook or crook*, come what may*, in one way or another, in some such way, in some way, one way or another, somehow or another, somehow or other; SEE CONCEPT 544

something [n] entity
article, being, commodity, existence, existent, individual, object, substance, thing; SEE CONCEPT 433

sometimes [adv] every now and then
at intervals, at times, consistently, constantly, ever and again, every so often, frequently, from time to time, here and there, intermittently, now and again, now and then, occasionally, off and on, once in a blue moon*, once in a while, on occasion, periodically, recurrently; SEE CONCEPT 805

somewhat [adv] to some extent
adequately, a little, bearably, considerably, fairly, far, incompletely, in part, insignificantly, kind of, moderately, more or less, not much, partially, pretty, quite, rather, ratherish, significantly, slightly, some, something, sort of, to a degree, tolerably, well; SEE CONCEPTS 548,569,772

somewhere [adv] in, or at some place
about, any old place, around, around somewhere, elsewhere, here and there, in one place or another, kicking around*, parts unknown*, scattered, someplace, someplace or another, someplace or other, somewheres; SEE CONCEPT 583

song [n] melody sung or played with musical instrument
air, anthem, aria, ballad, canticle, carol, chant, chorale, chorus, ditty, expression, golden oldie*, hymn, lay, lullaby, lyric, melody, number,

oldie*, opera, piece, poem, psalm, refrain, rock, rock and roll, round, shanty, strain, tune, verse, vocal; SEE CONCEPTS 262,293,595

soon [adv] *in the near future*
anon, any minute now, before long, betimes, by and by, coming down the pike*, directly, early, ere long, expeditiously, fast, fleetly, forthwith, hastily, in a little while, in a minute, in a second, in a short time, in due time, in short order, instantly, in time, lickety-split*, on time, posthaste, presently, promptly, pronto, quick, quickly, rapidly, short, shortly, speedily; SEE CONCEPTS 548,798,820

soothe [v] *calm, ease*
allay, alleviate, appease, assuage, balm, becalm, butter up*, calm down, cheer, compose, console, cool, cool off*, dulcify, help, hush, lighten, lull, make nice*, make up, mitigate, mollify, pacify, patch things up*, play up to*, pour oil on*, quiet, quieten, relieve, settle, smooth down, soften, square, still, stroke, subdue, take the edge off*, take the sting out*, tranquilize, unburden, untrouble; SEE CONCEPTS 7,22,110,384

sophisticated [adj1] *cosmopolitan, cultured*
adult, artificial, been around, blasé, bored, citified, cool*, couth, cultivated, cynical, disenchanted, disillusioned, experienced, in, in the know*, into*, jaded, jet-set*, knowing, laid-back*, mature, mondaine, on to*, practical, practiced, refined, schooled, seasoned, sharp, skeptical, smooth, stagy*, streetwise, studied, suave, svelte, switched on*, uptown*, urbane, well-bred, wised up*, wise to*, with it*, worldly, worldly wise, world-weary; SEE CONCEPTS 401,404,589

sophisticated [adj2] *complex, advanced*
complicated, delicate, elaborate, highly developed, intricate, involved, knotty, labyrinthine, modern, multifaceted, refined, subtle; SEE CONCEPT 562

sophistication [n] *culture, style*
composure, elegance, finesse, poise, refinement, savoir faire, savoir vivre, social grace, tact, urbanity, worldliness, worldly wisdom; SEE CONCEPTS 388,633,655

sophomoric [adj] *inexperienced*
brash, foolish, naive, reckless, young; SEE CONCEPT 401

soporific [adj] *sleepy; sleep-inducing*
anesthetic, balmy, calming, deadening, dozy*, drowsy, dull, hypnotic, mesmerizing, narcotic, nodding, numbing, opiate, quietening, sedative, slumberous, snoozy*, somniferous, somnolent, soothing, tranquilizing; SEE CONCEPTS 537,539

sorcery [n] *black magic, witchcraft*
abracadabra*, alchemy, bewitchment, black art, charm, conjuring, devilry, divination, enchantment, evil eye, hocus-pocus*, hoodoo*, incantation, jinx, magic, mumbo-jumbo*, necromancy, spell, thaumaturgy, voodoo, witchery, witching, wizardry; SEE CONCEPTS 370,689

sordid [adj] *dirty, bad, low*
abject, avaricious, base, black, calculated, corrupt, covetous, debauched, degenerate, degraded, despicable, disreputable, dowdy, filthy, foul, grasping, grubby, ignoble, impure, low-down, mean, mercenary, miserable, miserly, nasty, poor, scurvy, seedy, selfish, self-seeking, servile, shabby, shameful, sleazy, slovenly, slum, slummy, small, small-minded, squalid, unclean,

uncleanly, ungenerous, venal, vicious, vile, wretched; SEE CONCEPTS 334,545,571

sore [adj1] *hurt physically*
abscessed, aching, acute, afflicted, annoying, bruised, burned, burning, chafed, critical, distressing, extreme, hurtful, hurting, inflamed, irritated, pained, painful, raw, reddened, sensitive, severe, sharp, smarting, tender, ulcerated, uncomfortable, unpleasant, vexatious; SEE CONCEPT 314

sore [adj2] *angry; hurt mentally*
afflicted, aggrieved, annoyed, annoying, critical, distressing, grieved, grieving, indignant, irked, irritated, pained, peeved, pressing, resentful, sensitive, smarting, stung, troubled, upset, urgent, vexed, weighty; SEE CONCEPT 403

sorrow [n] *extreme upset, grief*
affliction, agony, anguish, bad news*, big trouble*, blow, blues*, care, catastrophe, dejection, depression, distress, dolor, grieving, hardship, heartache, heartbreak, lamenting, melancholy, misery, misfortune, mourning, pain, rain*, regret, remorse, repentence, rue, sadness, suffering, trial, tribulation, trouble, unhappiness, weeping, woe, worry, wretchedness; SEE CONCEPT 410

sorrow [v] *be very upset, grieved*
agonize, bemoan, be sad, bewail, carry on, cry a river*, deplore, eat heart out*, grieve, groan, hang crepe*, lament, moan, mourn, regret, sing the blues*, sob, take on*, weep; SEE CONCEPTS 34,410

sorrowful [adj] *very upset; grieving*
affecting, afflicted, dejected, depressed, disconsolate, distressing, doleful, dolent, full of sorrow, grievous, heartbroken, heartrending, heavyhearted, hurting, in mourning, in pain, in sorrow, lamentable, lugubrious, melancholy, miserable, mournful, painful, piteous, plaintive, rueful, ruthful, sad, sick at heart*, singing the blues*, sorry, tearful, tear-jerking*, unhappy, woebegone, woeful, wretched; SEE CONCEPT 403

sorry [adj1] *remorseful, regretful*
apologetic, attritional, compunctious, conscience-stricken, contrite, guilt-ridden, melted, penitent, penitential, repentant, self-accusing, self-condemnatory, self-reproachful, shamefaced, softened, touched; SEE CONCEPTS 403,545

sorry [adj2] *sad, heartbroken*
bad, disconsolate, distressed, grieved, heavy-hearted, melancholy, mournful, pitiful, rueful, saddened, sorrowful, unhappy; SEE CONCEPT 403

sorry [adj3] *despicable, pathetic*
abject, base, beggarly, cheap, contemptible, deplorable, despisable, disgraceful, dismal, distressing, inadequate, insignificant, mean, miserable, paltry, piteous, pitiable, pitiful, poor, sad, scruffy*, scummy*, scurvy, shabby, shoddy, small, trifling, trivial, unimportant, vile, worthless, wretched; SEE CONCEPTS 485,529

sort [n] *type, variety*
array, batch, battery, body, brand, breed, category, character, class, clutch, denomination, description, family, genus, group, ilk, kind, likes, likes of*, lot, make, nature, number, order, parcel, quality, race, set, species, stamp, stripe, style, suite; SEE CONCEPT 378

sort [v] *place in order*
arrange, assort, button down*, catalogue, categorize, choose, class, classify, comb, cull, distribute, divide, file, grade, group, order, peg, pick, pigeonhole*, put down as, put down for, put in

SO
SO

order, put in shape, put to rights*, rank, riddle, screen, select, separate, sift, size up, systematize, tab, typecast, winnow; SEE CONCEPTS *84,158*

so-so [adj] *adequate, passable*
average, enough, fair, fairish, fair to middling*, indifferent, mediocre, medium, middling*, moderate, not bad*, okay*, ordinary, respectable, run-of-the-mill*, tolerable, undistinguished; SEE CONCEPTS *533,575*

soul [n1] *psyche, inspiration, energy*
anima, animating principle, animation, animus, ardor, bosom, bottom, breast, breath of life, cause, conscience, courage, disposition, ego, elan vital, essence, feeling, fervor, force, genius, heart, individuality, intellect, intelligence, life, marrow, mind, nobility, noumenon, personality, pith, pneuma, principle, quintessence, reason, recesses of heart*, secret self*, spirit, spiritual being, stuff, substance, thought, vital force, vitality, vivacity; SEE CONCEPTS *409,410,411*

soul [n2] *being*
body, character, creature, ghost, human being, individual, living soul*, man, mortal, person, personage, phantom, shadow, spirit, umbra, woman; SEE CONCEPT *389*

sound [n] *something heard or audible*
accent, din, harmony, intonation, loudness, melody, modulation, music, noise, note, pitch, racket, report, resonance, reverberation, ringing, softness, sonance, sonancy, sonority, sonorousness, static, tenor, tonality, tone, vibration, voice; SEE CONCEPT *595*

sound [adj1] *complete, healthy*
alive and kicking*, effectual, entire, firm, fit, flawless, hale, hearty, intact, in the pink*, perfect, right, right as rain*, robust, safe, sane, solid, stable, sturdy, substantial, thorough, total, unblemished, undamaged, undecayed, unhurt, unimpaired, uninjured, up to snuff*, vibrant, vigorous, vital, well, well-constructed, whole, wholesome, wrapped tight*; SEE CONCEPTS *314,488*

sound [adj2] *logical, reasonable*
accurate, advisable, all there*, cogent, commonsensical, consequent, convincing, cool*, correct, deep, exact, fair, faultless, flawless, got it together*, impeccable, intellectual, judicious, just, levelheaded, orthodox, precise, profound, proper, prudent, rational, reliable, responsible, right, right-minded, right-thinking, satisfactory, satisfying, sensible, sober, solid, telling, thoughtful, together*, true, trustworthy, valid, well-advised, well-founded, well-grounded, wise; SEE CONCEPTS *403,529,558*

sound [adj3] *accepted, established*
all there*, authoritative, canonical, dependable, fair, faithful, fly*, go*, hanging together*, holding together*, holding up*, holding up in wash*, holding water*, kosher*, legal, legit*, loyal, orthodox, proper, proven, received, recognized, reliable, reputable, safe, sanctioned, secure, significant, solid, solvent, stable, standing up*, tried-and-true*, true, valid, washing; SEE CONCEPTS *535,552,582*

sound [v1] *produce noise*
babble, bang, bark, blare, blow, boom, burst, buzz, cackle, chatter, clack, clang, clank, clap, clatter, clink, crash, creak, detonate, echo, emit, explode, hum, jabber, jangle, jar, moan, murmur, patter, play, rattle, reflect, resonate, resound, re-

verberate, ring, roar, rumble, shout, shriek, shrill, sing, slam, smash, snort, squawk, thud, thump, thunder, toot, trumpet, vibrate, whine, whisper; SEE CONCEPT *65*

sound [v2] *give the impression*
appear, appear to be, look, seem, strike as being; SEE CONCEPTS *543,716*

sound bite [n] *very brief broadcast statement*
blurb*, buzzword, clip, excerpt, fifteen minutes of fame*, newsbreak, news item, one-liner, outtake, photo opportunity, piece, slogan, snippet, spot news; SEE CONCEPT *277*

sour [adj1] *bad-tasting; gone bad*
acerb, acetic, acetose, acetous, acid, acidic, acidulated, acrid, astringent, bad, biting, bitter, briny, caustic, curdled, cutting, dry, fermented, green, keen, musty, peppery, piquant, pungent, rancid, salty, sharp, soured, sourish, stinging, tart, turned, unpleasant, unripe, unsavory, unwholesome, vinegary, with a kick*; SEE CONCEPTS *462,613*

sour [adj2] *in a bad mood*
acid, acrid, acrimonious, bitter, churlish, crabby, cynical, disagreeable, discontented, displeasing, embittered, grouchy, grudging, ill-natured, ill-tempered, irritable, jaundiced, on edge*, peevish, rotten, tart, ungenerous, unhappy, unpleasant, waspish; SEE CONCEPTS *403,542*

sour [v] *alienate*
acidify, curdle, disenchant, embitter, envenom, exacerbate, exasperate, make sour, spoil, turn, turn off; SEE CONCEPTS *14,250*

source [n] *beginning; point of supply*
antecedent, author, authority, authorship, begetter, birthplace, cause, commencement, connection, dawn, dawning, derivation, determinant, expert, father, fount, fountain, fountainhead, horse's mouth*, inception, informant, maternity, mother, onset, opening, origin, origination, originator, parent, paternity, provenance, provenience, rise, rising, root, specialist, spring, start, starting point, wellspring; SEE CONCEPT *648*

souse [v] *make very wet*
brine, deluge, dip, douse, drench, drown, duck, dunk, immerse, impregnate, marinate, pickle, preserve, seethe, soak, sop, steep, submerge, submerse, waterlog, wet; SEE CONCEPT *256*

souvenir [n] *keepsake from event*
gift, memento, memorial, relic, remembrance, remembrancer, reminder, token, trophy; SEE CONCEPTS *337,446*

sovereign [n] *supreme ruler*
autocrat, chief, czar, emperor, empress, king, leader, majesty, monarch, potentate, prince, princess, queen, ruler; SEE CONCEPT *354*

sovereign [adj] *dominant, effective*
absolute, ascendant, autonomous, chief, commanding, directing, effectual, efficacious, excellent, guiding, highest, imperial, independent, lofty, majestic, monarchal, monarchial, overbearing, paramount, predominant, predominate, preponderant, prevalent, principal, regal, regnant, reigning, royal, ruling, self-governed, supreme, unlimited; SEE CONCEPTS *536,568*

sovereignty [n] *domination*
ascendancy, ascendant, dominance, dominion, jurisdiction, preeminence, prepotence, prepotency, primacy, supremacy, supreme power, sway; SEE CONCEPT *299*

sow [v] *plant*
broadcast, disject, disseminate, drill, fling, grow, implant, inseminate, lodge, pitch, propagate, put in, raise, scatter, seed, strew, toss; SEE CONCEPTS 253,257

space [n1] *room, scope*
amplitude, area, arena, blank, breadth, capacity, compass, distance, elbowroom, expanse, expansion, extension, extent, field, gap, headroom, headway, infinity, interval, lacuna, leeway, location, margin, omission, play, range, reach, slot, spaciousness, sphere, spot, spread, stretch, territory, tract, turf, volume, zone; SEE CONCEPTS 739,746,756

space [n2] *time interval*
bit, duration, period, season, span, spell, stretch, term, time, while; SEE CONCEPT 807

spacious [adj] *extensive, expansive*
ample, big, boundless, broad, capacious, cavernous, comfortable, commodious, endless, enormous, extended, generous, great, huge, immense, infinite, large, limitless, roomy, sizable, uncrowded, vast, voluminous, wide, widespread; SEE CONCEPTS 481,482,774

span [n] *distance, duration*
amount, compass, extent, interval, length, measure, period, reach, space, spell, spread, stretch, term, time; SEE CONCEPTS 756,807,822

span [v] *stretch over*
arch, bridge, connect, cover, cross, extend, ford, go across, link, pass over, range, reach, traverse, vault; SEE CONCEPT 756

spank [v] *slap, usually on bottom*
belt, blip, box, buffet, cane, chastise, clobber, clout, cuff, flax, flog, hide, larrup*, lash, lather*, leather*, lick, paddle, punch, punish, put over one's knee*, smack, sock, tan*, tan one's hide*, thrash, trim, wallop, welt, whip, whup*; SEE CONCEPT 189

spare [adj1] *extra, reserve*
additional, backup, de trop, emergency, free, in excess, in reserve, in store, lagniappe, leftover, more than enough*, odd, option, over, supererogatory, superfluous, supernumerary, surplus, unoccupied, unused, unwanted; SEE CONCEPTS 771,824

spare [adj2] *thin; sparse*
angular, bony, economical, exiguous, frugal, gaunt, lank, lanky, lean, meager, modest, poor, rangy, rawboned, scant, scanty, scraggy, scrawny, shadow, skimpy, skinny, slender, slight, slim, sparing, sparse, stick, stilt, stingy, wiry; SEE CONCEPTS 490,491,771

spare [v1] *do or manage without*
afford, allow, bestow, dispense with, give, grant, part with, pinch, provide, put by, relinquish, salt away*, save, scrape, scrimp, short, skimp, stint, supply; SEE CONCEPT 129

spare [v2] *forgive; have mercy upon*
absolve, bail out, be lenient, be merciful, discharge, dispense, excuse, exempt, forbear, get off the hook*, get out of hock*, give a break*, give quarter to, go easy on*, leave, let go, let off*, pardon, pity, privilege from, pull out of the fire*, refrain from, release, relent, relieve from, save bacon*, save from, save neck*, spring; SEE CONCEPTS 50,88,134

sparing [adj] *careful, economical*
avaricious, canny, chary, close, cost-conscious, frugal, humane, mean, money-conscious, parsimonious, provident, prudent, saving, stewardly, stingy, thrifty, tight, tight-fisted, tolerant, ungiving, unwasteful, wary; SEE CONCEPTS 334,401

spark [n] *flash, trace*
atom, beam, fire, flare, flicker, gleam, glint, glitter, glow, hint, jot, nucleus, ray, scintilla, scintillation, scrap, sparkle, spit, vestige; SEE CONCEPTS 519,624,828,831

spark [v] *start, inspire*
animate, excite, kindle, precipitate, provoke, set in motion, set off, stimulate, stir, touch off, trigger; SEE CONCEPT 221

sparkle [n] *glitter, shine*
animation, brilliance, coruscation, dash, dazzle, élan, flash, flicker, gaiety, gleam, glimmer, glint, glitz, glow, life, panache, radiance, scintillation, shimmer, show, spark, spirit, twinkle, vim, vitality, vivacity, zap*, zip*; SEE CONCEPTS 411,624,628

sparkle [v] *glitter, shine*
beam, bubble, coruscate, dance, effervesce, fizz, fizzle, flash, flicker, gleam, glimmer, glint, glisten, glow, scintillate, shimmer, spark, twinkle, wink; SEE CONCEPT 624

sparse [adj] *very few and scattered*
dispersed, exiguous, few and far between, inadequate, infrequent, meager, occasional, poor, rare, scant, scanty, scarce, scrimpy, skimpy, spare, sporadic, thin, uncommon; SEE CONCEPTS 762,789

spasm [n] *twitch, fit*
access, attack, burst, contraction, convulsion, eruption, frenzy, jerk, outburst, pain, paroxysm, seizure, throe, yank; SEE CONCEPTS 185,728

spasmodic [adj] *twitching, erratic*
bits and pieces*, changeable, choppy, convulsive, desultory, fitful, fits and starts*, intermittent, irregular, jerky, on-again-off-again*, periodic, shaky, spastic, sporadic, spotty, spurtive, uncertain; SEE CONCEPTS 482,530,541

spatter [v] *splash, sprinkle*
bespatter, bestrew, broadcast, dash, daub, dirty, discharge, disperse, dot, douse, dribble, mottle, polka-dot, scatter, shower, slop, smudge, soil, spangle, speck, speckle, splutter, spot, spray, sputter, stipple, strew, swash, wet; SEE CONCEPTS 172,179,256

spawn [v] *produce*
bring forth, create, father, generate, give rise to, hatch, issue, make, mother, originate, parent, procreate, reproduce, sire; SEE CONCEPTS 173,251,374

speak [v1] *talk*
allege, articulate, assert, aver, blab*, break silence, chat, chew*, communicate, converse, convey, declare, deliver, descant, discourse, drawl, enunciate, expatiate, express, gab*, gas*, go*, jaw*, lip*, make known, make public, modulate, mouth, mumble, murmur, mutter, open one's mouth, perorate, pop off*, pronounce, put into words, rap*, say, shout, sound, speak one's piece*, spiel*, spill, state, tell, utter, verbalize, vocalize, voice, whisper, yak*, yakkety-yak*, yammer; SEE CONCEPTS 47,266

speak [v2] *address; give a lecture*
argue, declaim, descant, discourse, get across, harangue, hold forth, orate, pitch, plead, prelect, recite, sermonize, spiel*, spout*, stump, talk; SEE CONCEPTS 60,285

so
sp

speak out/speak up [v] *make one's position known*
assert, come out with, declare, have one's say*, insist, let voice be heard*, make oneself heard, make plain, say loud and clear*, sound off*, speak loudly, speak one's mind*, stand up for; SEE CONCEPTS 49,57

special [adj] *distinguished, distinctive; important in own way*
appropriate, best, certain, characteristic, chief, choice, defined, definite, designated, determinate, different, earmarked, especial, exceptional, exclusive, express, extraordinary, festive, first, gala, individual, limited, main, major, marked, memorable, momentous, out of the ordinary, particular, peculiar, personal, primary, proper, rare, red-letter*, reserved, restricted, select, set, significant, smashing*, sole, specialized, specific, uncommon, unique, unreal*, unusual; SEE CONCEPTS 557,564,567

specialist [n] *person who is an expert in a field*
ace, adept, authority, connoisseur, consultant, devotee, doctor, guru*, old hand*, old pro*, pro*, professional, pundit, sage, savant, scholar, technician, veteran, virtuoso; SEE CONCEPTS 347,357

specialize [v] *concentrate on specific area*
be into, develop oneself in, do one's thing*, go in for, have a weakness for*, limit oneself to, practice, practice exclusively, pursue, study intensively, train, work in; SEE CONCEPTS 91,324

specially [adv] *particularly*
distinctively, especially, expressly, in specie, specifically, uniquely; SEE CONCEPT 557

specialty [n] *distinctive feature; concentration*
career, claim to fame, cup of tea*, distinguishing feature, field of concentration, forte, game*, hobby, job, long suit*, magnum opus, major, masterpiece, minor, number, object of attention, object of study, occupation, pièce de résistance*, practice, profession, pursuit, racket*, special, speciality, special project, thing*, vocation, weakness, work; SEE CONCEPT 349

species [n] *class, variety*
breed, category, collection, description, division, group, kind, likes*, lot, nature, number, order, sort, stripe*, type; SEE CONCEPT 378

specific [adj] *particular, distinguishing*
bull's eye*, categorical, characteristic, clean-cut, clear-cut, cut fine*, dead on*, definite, definitive, different, distinct, downright, drawn fine, especial, exact, explicit, express, flat out*, hit nail on head*, individual, limited, on target, outright, peculiar, precise, reserved, restricted, right on, set, sole, special, specialized, straight-out, unambiguous, unequivocal, unique; SEE CONCEPTS 535,557,564

specifically [adv] *expressly, particularly*
accurately, categorically, characteristically, clearly, concretely, correctly, definitely, distinctively, especially, exactly, explicitly, in detail, indicatively, individually, in specie, minutely, peculiarly, pointedly, precisely, respectively, specially; SEE CONCEPTS 557,564

specification [n] *requirement, qualification*
blueprint, condition, designation, detail, item, particular, particularization, spec*, stipulation, term; SEE CONCEPTS 270,646

specify [v] *designate; decide definitely*
be specific, blueprint*, button down*, cite, come to the point, condition, define, detail, determine, draw a picture*, enumerate, establish, finger*,

fix, get down to brass tacks*, get to the point*, go into detail, indicate, individualize, instance, inventory, itemize, lay out, limit, list, make, mention, name, particularize, peg, pin down, point out, precise, put down, put finger on*, set, settle, show clearly, slot, specialize, specificate, specificize, spell out, stipulate, tab, tag, tick off; SEE CONCEPTS 18,57

specimen [n] *example, sample*
case, case history, copy, cross section, embodiment, exemplar, exemplification, exhibit, illustration, individual, instance, model, part, pattern, proof, representation, representative, sampling, sort, species, type, unit, variety; SEE CONCEPTS 686,831

specious [adj] *misleading*
apparent, apparently right, beguiling, captious, casuistic, colorable, credible, deceptive, delusive, empty, erroneous, fallacious, false, flattering, hollow, idle, illogical, inaccurate, incorrect, likely, nugatory, ostensible, ostentatious, plausible, presumable, presumptive, pretentious, probable, seeming, sophistic, sophistical, sophisticated, spurious, unsound, untrue, vain, wrong; SEE CONCEPTS 552,582

speck [n] *tiny bit*
atom, blemish, blot, crumb, defect, dot, fault, flaw, fleck, flyspeck, grain, iota, jot, mark, mite, modicum, molecule, mote, particle, point, shred, smidgen, speckle, splotch spot, stain, trace, whit; SEE CONCEPT 831

speckled [adj] *dotted*
brindled, dappled, flaked, flecked, freckled, mosaic, motley, mottled, particolored, patchy, peppered, punctate, spotted, spotty, sprinkled, stippled, studded, variegated; SEE CONCEPTS 485,618

spectacle [n] *something showy; exhibition*
comedy, curiosity, demonstration, display, drama, event, exposition, extravaganza, marvel, movie, pageant, parade, performance, phenomenon, play, production, representation, scene, show, sight, spectacular, tableau, view, wonder; SEE CONCEPTS 261,529

spectacular [adj] *wonderful, impressive*
amazing, astonishing, astounding, breathtaking, daring, dazzling, dramatic, eye-catching, fabulous, fantastic, grand, histrionic, magnificent, marked, marvelous, miraculous, prodigious, razzle-dazzle*, remarkable, sensational, splendid, staggering, striking, stunning, stupendous, theatrical, thrilling, wondrous; SEE CONCEPTS 529,537,574

spectator [n] *person who watches event*
beholder, bystander, clapper, eyewitness, fan, gaper*, gazer, kibitzer*, looker, looker-on, moviegoer, observer, onlooker, perceiver, playgoer, seer, showgoer, sports fan, standee, stander-by, theatergoer, viewer, watcher, witness; SEE CONCEPTS 366,423

speculate [v] *think about deeply and theorize*
beat one's brains*, brainstorm*, build castles in air*, call it, call the turn, cerebrate, chew over*, cogitate, conjecture, consider, contemplate, deliberate, dope*, dope out*, excogitate, figure, figure out*, guess, guesstimate*, have a hunch*, hazard a guess, head trip*, hypothesize, kick around*, meditate, muse, pipe-dream*, psych out*, read, read between lines*, reason, reflect, review, ruminate, run it up flagpole*, scheme, size up,

study, suppose, surmise, suspect, weigh, wonder; SEE CONCEPTS *17,24,28,37*

speculate [*v2*] *gamble, risk*
dare, hazard, make book*, margin up*, play, play the market*, plunge, pour money into*, spec*, stick neck out*, take a chance, take a flier*, take a fling*, venture, wildcat; SEE CONCEPTS *28,330,363*

speculation [*n1*] *theory, guess*
belief, brainwork*, cerebration, cogitation, conjecture, consideration, contemplation, deliberation, excogitation, guesstimate*, guesswork, hunch, hypothesis, meditation, opinion, reflection, review, shot, shot in the dark*, sneaking suspicion*, stab, stab in the dark*, studying, supposition, surmise, thinking, thought, weighing; SEE CONCEPTS *24,28,529,689*

speculation [*n2*] *risk, gamble*
backing, flier*, flutter, gambling, hazard, hunch, piece, plunge, right money*, risky business*, risky venture, shot, shot in the dark*, smart money*, spec*, speculative enterprise, stab*, venture, wager; SEE CONCEPTS *192,330,363*

speech [*n1*] *talk*
accent, articulation, communication, conversation, dialect, dialogue, diction, discussion, doublespeak*, double talk*, elocution, enunciation, expressing, expression, idiom, intercourse, jargon, language, lingo, locution, mother tongue, native tongue, oral communication, palaver, parlance, prattle, pronunciation, prose, speaking, spiel, tone, tongue, utterance, verbalization, vernacular, vocal expression, vocalization, vocalizing, voice, voicing; SEE CONCEPTS *47,266,276*

speech [*n2*] *formal talk to audience*
address, allocution, appeal, bombast, chalk talk*, commentary, debate, declamation, diatribe, discourse, disquisition, dissertation, eulogy, exhortation, harangue, homily, invocation, keynote, lecture, opus, oration, oratory, panegyric, paper, parlance, parley, pep talk*, pitch, prelection, recitation, rhetoric, salutation, sermon, spiel*, stump*, tirade, valedictory; SEE CONCEPTS *60,285*

speechless [*adj*] *without ability to talk*
aghast, amazed, aphonic, astounded, buttoned up*, clammed up*, close-mouthed, cool*, cool as cucumber*, dazed, dumb, dumbfounded, dumbstruck, inarticulate, mum, mute, not saying boo*, reserved, shocked, silent, taciturn, thunderstruck*, tight-lipped*, tongue-tied*, uncommunicative, unflappable, voiceless, wordless; SEE CONCEPT *267*

speed [*n*] *rate of motion, often a high rate*
acceleration, activity, agility, alacrity, breeze, briskness, celerity, clip, dispatch, eagerness, expedition, fleetness, gait, haste, headway, hurry, hustle, legerity, lick, liveliness, momentum, pace, precipitancy, precipitation, promptitude, promptness, quickness, rapidity, rapidness, readiness, rush, rustle, snap, steam, swiftness, urgency, velocity; SEE CONCEPT *755*

speed [*v*] *move along quickly*
advance, aid, assist, barrel, belt, bomb, boost, bowl over, career, cover ground*, cut along, dispatch, expedite, facilitate, flash, fly, further, gallop, gather momentum, gear up*, get a move on*, get moving, get under way, go all out*, go fast, go like the wind*, hasten, help, hightail*, hurry, impel, lose no time*, make haste, open up throt-

tle*, press on, promote, quicken, race, ride, run, rush, sail, spring, step on it*, tear, urge, whiz, zoom; SEE CONCEPTS *110,150,152*

speedy [*adj*] *fast, quick*
accelerated, agile, alacritous, breakneck, brisk, expeditious, express, fleet, harefooted, hasty, headlong, hurried, immediate, lissome, lively, nimble, precipitate, prompt, quick-fire, rapid, rapid-fire, ready, snappy, summary, supersonic, swift, ultrasonic, winged; SEE CONCEPTS *548,584,588*

spell [*n1*] *interval, period*
bit, bout, course, go, hitch, interlude, intermission, patch, relay, season, shift, space, stint, streak, stretch, term, time, tour, tour of duty, trick, turn, while; SEE CONCEPTS *807,817,822*

spell [*n2*] *magical aura over an entity*
abracadabra*, allure, amulet, bewitching, bewitchment, charm, conjuration, enchanting, enchantment, exorcism, fascination, glamour, hex, hexing, hocus-pocus*, incantation, jinx, magic, mumbo-jumbo*, rune, sorcery, talisman, trance, voodoo*, whack*, whammy*, witchery; SEE CONCEPTS *370,673,689*

spell [*n3*] *seizure*
access, attack, fit, illness, jag, paroxysm, spasm, stroke, throe, turn; SEE CONCEPTS *306,308*

spell [*v1*] *mean, imply*
add up to, amount to, augur, connote, denote, express, herald, import, indicate, intend, point to, portend, presage, promise, signify, suggest; SEE CONCEPTS *55,74,75*

spell [*v2*] *give rest, relief*
allow, breathe, free, lay off, lie by, release, relieve, stand in for, take over, take the place of; SEE CONCEPTS *83,110*

spellbound [*adj*] *enchanted, fascinated*
agape, amazed, bemused, bewildered, bewitched, breathless, captivated, caught up, charmed, enthralled, gripped, held, hooked, mesmerized, open-mouthed, petrified, possessed, rapt, transfixed, transported, under a spell; SEE CONCEPT *403*

spend [*v1*] *give, pay out*
absorb, allocate, ante up*, apply, bestow, blow*, cast away, come across, come through, concentrate, confer, consume, contribute, cough up*, defray, deplete, disburse, dispense, dissipate, donate, drain, drop, employ, empty, evote, exhaust, expend, foot the bill*, fritter, give, hand out, invest, lavish, lay out, liquidate, misspend, outlay, pay down, pay up, put in, run through, settle, shell out*, spring for*, squander, throw away, use, use up, waste; SEE CONCEPTS *156,169,225,341*

spend [*v2*] *use time; occupy*
consume, devote, drift, employ, fill, fool around*, fritter, go, idle, kill, laze, let pass, misuse, pass, put in, squander, waste, while away*; SEE CONCEPT *100*

spendthrift [*n*] *person careless with money*
big spender*, dissipater, high-roller*, improvident, imprudent, prodigal, profligate, spender, sport, squanderer, waster, wastrel; SEE CONCEPTS *348,353,423*

spent [*adj*] *used up, gone; tired out*
all in*, bleary, blown, burnt-out*, bushed, consumed, dead*, debilitated, depleted, disbursed, dissipated, dog-tired*, done-in*, down the drain*, drained, effete, enervated, exhausted, expended,

fagged, far-gone*, finished, had it*, limp, lost, played-out*, prostrate, ready to drop*, shattered, shot, thrown away, used, washed-up*, wasted, weakened, wearied, weary, worn out; SEE CONCEPTS 314,560,771

spew [v] *spit out*
belch, bring up, cascade, disgorge, eject, eruct, erupt, expel, flood, gush, heave, irrupt, puke*, regurgitate, scatter, spit, spit up, spread, spritz, throw up, urp*, vomit; SEE CONCEPTS 179,308

sphere [n1] *globular object*
apple*, ball, big blue marble*, circle, Earth, globe, globule, orb, pellet, pill, planet, rondure, round; SEE CONCEPTS 436,511

sphere [n2] *domain of influence*
bailiwick, capacity, champaign, circle, class, compass, demesne, department, dominion, employment, field, function, ground, jungle, jurisdiction, level, neck of the woods*, orbit, pale, position, precinct, province, range, rank, realm, scope, station, stomping ground*, stratum, terrain, territory, turf*, walk of life, zone; SEE CONCEPTS 349,388,658

spice [n] *flavor, zest*
aroma, color, excitement, fragrance, gusto, guts*, kick, pep, piquancy, pungency, relish, salt, savor, scent, seasoning, tang, zap*, zip*; SEE CONCEPTS 614,673

spicy [adj1] *pungent, flavorful*
ambrosial, appetizing, aromal, aromatic, distinctive, fiery, flavorsome, fragrant, fresh, herbaceous, highly seasoned, hot, keen, odoriferous, peppery, perfumed, piquant, poignant, racy, redolent, savory, scented, seasoned, snappy, spirited, sweet, tangy, tasty, zesty, zippy*; SEE CONCEPT 613

spicy [adj2] *off-color, vulgar*
breezy, broad, erotic, hot*, indelicate, racy, red hot*, ribald, risqué, salty*, scandalous, sensational, sophisticated, suggestive, titillating, unseemly, wicked, X-rated*; SEE CONCEPTS 267,372,545

spike [v] *pierce*
fasten, impale, lance, make fast, nail, pin, prick, skewer, spear, spit, stick, transfix; SEE CONCEPT 220

spill [v1] *slop, drop*
discharge, disgorge, dribble, drip, empty, flow, lose, overfill, overflow, overrun, overturn, pour, run, run out, run over, scatter, shed, spill over, splash, splatter, spray, sprinkle, spurt, squirt, stream, throw off, upset, well over; SEE CONCEPTS 179,181

spill [v2] *reveal*
betray, blab, blow, disclose, divulge, give away, inform, let the cat out of the bag*, mouth, squeal, tattle, tell; SEE CONCEPT 60

spin [n] *circular motion*
circuit, gyration, revolution, roll, rotation, spiral, turn, twist, whirl; SEE CONCEPT 748

spin [v] *go around, make go around*
gyrate, gyre, oscillate, pendulate, pirouette, purl, reel, revolve, rotate, spiral, swim, turn, twirl, twist, wheel, whirl; SEE CONCEPTS 150,152,218

spine [n] *backbone*
back, bone, chine, rachis, ridge, spinal column, vertebrae, vertebral column; SEE CONCEPTS 393,420

spineless [adj] *cowardly*
amoebalike*, faint-hearted, fearful, feeble, force-

less, frightened, gutless*, impotent, inadequate, ineffective, ineffectual, invertebrate, irresolute, lily-livered*, nerveless, pithless, soft, spiritless, squeamish, submissive, timid, vacillating, weak, weak-kneed, weak-willed, yellow*, yellow-bellied*; SEE CONCEPTS 401,542

spiral [n] *curled shape*
coil, corkscrew, curlicue, flourish, gyration, gyre, helix, quirk, screw, volute, whorl; SEE CONCEPT 436

spiral [adj] *curling, winding*
circling, circular, circumvoluted, cochlear, coiled, corkscrew, curled, helical, helicoid, radial, rolled, screw-shaped, scrolled, tendrillar, tortile, voluted, whorled, wound; SEE CONCEPT 486

spirit [n1] *soul, attitude*
air, animation, ardor, backbone*, boldness, breath, character, complexion, courage, dauntlessness, disposition, earnestness, energy, enterprise, enthusiasm, essence, fire, force, frame of mind, gameness, grit*, guts*, heart, humor, jazz*, life, life force, liveliness, mettle, mood, morale, motivation, nerve, oomph*, outlook, psyche, quality, resolution, resolve, sparkle, spunk*, stoutheartedness, substance, temper, temperament, tenor, vigor, vitality, vital spark, warmth, will, willpower, zest; SEE CONCEPTS 407,411

spirit [n2] *atmosphere, essence*
feeling, genius, gist, humor, intent, intention, meaning, purport, purpose, quality, sense, substance, temper, tenor, timbre, tone; SEE CONCEPTS 673,682

spirit [n3] *ghost*
apparition, eidolon, phantasm, phantom, poltergeist, shade, shadow, soul, specter, spook, sprite, supernatural being, umbra, vision, wraith; SEE CONCEPT 370

spirited [adj] *lively, vivacious*
active, alert, animate, animated, ardent, audacious, avid, bold, bouncy, brave, bright, burning, chirpy, courageous, dauntless, eager, effervescent, energetic, enthusiastic, fearless, fiery, full of life, game, gingery*, gritty, gutsy*, high-spirited, hot, hyper*, intrepid, jumping, keen, mettlesome, nervy, passionate, peppery, peppy, plucky, resolute, rocking, sharp, snappy, sparkling, sprightly, spunky, vigorous, zappy*, zealous, zesty, zingy*, zippy*; SEE CONCEPTS 404,542

spiritless [adj] *depressed*
apathetic, blah*, blue*, broken, cast down, dejected, despondent, disconsolate, dispirited, dopey*, down, downcast, downhearted, down in the dumps*, down in the mouth*, draggy, drippy, droopy, dull, enervated, flat*, flat tire*, inanimate, indifferent, lackadaisical, lackluster, languid, languishing, languorous, lifeless, limp, listless, low, melancholic, melancholy, mopy, slothful, subdued, submissive, tame, torpid, unconcerned, unenthusiastic, unmoved, zero*; SEE CONCEPTS 403,542

spiritual [adj] *religious, otherworldly*
airy, asomatous, devotional, discarnate, disembodied, divine, ethereal, extramundane, ghostly, holy, immaterial, incorporeal, intangible, metaphysical, nonmaterial, nonphysical, platonic, pure, rarefied, refined, sacred, supernal, unfleshly, unphysical; SEE CONCEPTS 536,582

spit [n] *saliva*
discharge, dribble, drool, slaver, spittle, sputum, water; SEE CONCEPT 467

spit [v] *eject saliva or substance*
discharge, drool, expectorate, hawk, hiss, sibilate, sizz, slobber, spatter, spew, splutter, spritz, sputter, throw out; SEE CONCEPTS 179,185

spite [n] *hateful feeling*
animosity, antipathy, bad blood*, contempt, despite, enmity, gall, grudge, harsh feeling, hate, hatred, ill will, malevolence, malice, maliciousness, malignity, peeve, pique, rancor, resentment, revenge, spitefulness, spleen, umbrage, vengeance, vengefulness, venom, vindictiveness; SEE CONCEPT 29

spite [v] *offend, hurt*
annoy, begrudge, beset, crab*, cramp style*, discomfit, gall, get even*, grudge, hang up*, harass, harm, injure, louse up*, needle, nettle, persecute, pique, provoke, put out*, upset the apple cart*, vex; SEE CONCEPTS 7,19,121

spiteful [adj] *hurtful, nasty*
accidentally on purpose*, angry, barbed, catty*, cruel, cussed*, despiteful, dirty, evil, hateful, ill-disposed, ill-natured, malevolent, malicious, malign, malignant, mean, ornery*, rancorous, snide, spleenful, splenetic, venomous, vicious, vindictive, waspish, wicked; SEE CONCEPTS 401,542

splash [n] *spattering, impact*
burst, dash, display, effect, patch, sensation, splurge, stir, touch; SEE CONCEPT 676

splash [v] *throw liquid*
bathe, bespatter, broadcast, dabble, dash, douse, drench, drown, get wet, moisten, paddle, plash, plunge, shower, slop, slosh, soak, sop, spatter, splatter, spray, spread, sprinkle, squirt, strew, throw, wade, wallow, wet; SEE CONCEPTS 222,256

splendid [adj1] *luxurious, expensive*
baroque, beaming, beautiful, bright, brilliant, costly, dazzling, elegant, fab*, fat*, flamboyant, glittering, glowing, gorgeous, grand, grandiose, imposing, impressive, lavish, lustrous, mad*, magnificent, magnifico, marvelous, ornate, plush, posh, radiant, refulgent, resplendent, rich, solid gold*, splashy, splendiferous, splendrous, sumptuous, superb, swanky*; SEE CONCEPTS 334,485,589

splendid [adj2] *excellent, illustrious*
admirable, brilliant, celebrated, distinguished, divine, eminent, exceptional, exquisite, fantastic, fine, first-class, glorious, gorgeous, grand, great, heroic, impressive, magnificent, marvelous, matchless, outstanding, peerless, premium, proud, rare, remarkable, renowned, resplendent, royal, splendiferous, splendorous, sterling, sublime, superb, superlative, supreme, transcendent, unparalleled, unsurpassed, very good, wonderful; SEE CONCEPTS 568,574

splendor [n] *radiance, glory*
brightness, brilliance, ceremony, dazzle, display, effulgence, gorgeousness, grandeur, luster, magnificence, majesty, pageant, pomp, refulgence, renown, resplendence, richness, show, solemnity, spectacle, stateliness, sumptuousness; SEE CONCEPTS 620,655,673

splice [v] *join, interweave*
braid, entwine, graft, hitch, interlace, intertwine, intertwist, knit, marry, mate, mesh, plait, tie, unite, weave, wed, yoke; SEE CONCEPT 193

splinter [n] *thin piece of solid*
bit, chip, flake, fragment, needle, paring, shaving, sliver, wood; SEE CONCEPTS 471,479,831

splinter [v] *break into thin, small pieces*
break to smithereeens*, burst, disintegrate, fracture, fragment, pash, rive, shatter, shiver, smash, split; SEE CONCEPT 246

split [n1] *opening*
breach, chasm, chink, cleavage, cleft, crack, damage, division, fissure, gap, rent, rift, rima, rimation, rime, rip, rupture, separation, slash, slit, tear; SEE CONCEPT 513

split [n2] *difference, disunion*
alienation, breach, break, break-up, discord, disruption, dissension, divergence, division, estrangement, fissure, fracture, partition, rent, rift, rupture, schism; SEE CONCEPTS 297,388

split [v1] *break up, pull apart*
bifurcate, branch, break, burst, cleave, come apart, come undone, crack, dichotomize, disband, disjoin, dissever, disunite, diverge, divide, divorce, fork, gape, give way, go separate ways, hack, isolate, open, part, part company, put asunder, rend, rip, rive, separate, sever, slash, slit, snap, splinter, sunder, tear, whack; SEE CONCEPTS 135,176,297

split [v2] *divide into parts*
allocate, allot, apportion, carve up, distribute, divide, divvy*, divvy up*, dole, go even-steven*, go fifty-fifty*, halve, mete out, parcel out, partition, share, slice, slice the pie*, slice up; SEE CONCEPT 98

splurge [v] *spend lavishly*
be extravagant, binge, celebrate, fling, give a party*, rampage, spread; SEE CONCEPTS 327,377

spoil [v1] *ruin, hurt*
blemish, damage, debase, deface, defile, demolish, depredate, desecrate, desolate, despoil, destroy, devastate, disfigure, disgrace, harm, impair, injure, make useless, mar, mess up*, muck up*, pillage, plunder, prejudice, ravage, wreck, smash, spoliate, squash, take apart, tarnish, trash*, undo, upset, vitiate, waste, wreck; SEE CONCEPTS 246,252

spoil [v2] *baby, indulge*
accommodate, cater to, coddle, cosset, favor, humor, kill with kindness*, mollycoddle*, oblige, overindulge, pamper, spoon-feed*; SEE CONCEPTS 14,136

spoil [v3] *decay, turn bad*
addle, become tainted, become useless, break down, crumble, curdle, decompose, deteriorate, disintegrate, go bad, go off, mildew, molder, putrefy, rot, taint, turn; SEE CONCEPTS 456,469

spoils [n] *possessions stolen or gained*
booty*, cut*, gain, goods, graft, hot goods*, loot, make*, pickings, pillage, plunder, prey, prize, squeeze, swag, take; SEE CONCEPTS 337,710

spoken [adj] *by word of mouth*
announced, articulate, communicated, expressed, lingual, mentioned, oral, phonetic, phonic, put into words, said, sonant, told, traditional, unwritten, uttered, verbal, viva voce, voiced; SEE CONCEPT 267

spokesperson [n] *person who communicates for another*
agent, champion, delegate, deputy, mediator, mouth, mouthpiece*, prolocutor, prophet, protagonist, representative, speaker, stand-in, substitute, talker; SEE CONCEPTS 348,354,359

sp
sp

spongy [adj] *cushioned, absorbent*
absorptive, cushiony, elastic, light, mushy, pappy, porous, pulpous, pulpy, resilient, rubbery, soft, springy, squishy, yielding; SEE CONCEPT 606

sponsor [n] *person who helps, promotes another*
adherent, advocate, angel*, backer, benefactor, godparent, grubstaker, guarantor, mainstay, patron, promoter, supporter, surety, sustainer, underwriter; SEE CONCEPTS 348,423

sponsor [v] *help, promote*
answer for, back, bankroll, be responsible for, finance, fund, grubstake, guarantee, patronize, put up money, stake, subsidize, vouch for; SEE CONCEPTS 110,341

spontaneous [adj] *impulsive, willing*
ad-lib*, automatic, break loose, casual, down, extemporaneous, extempore, free, free spirited, from the hip*, impetuous, impromptu, improvised, inevitable, instinctive, involuntary, irresistible, natural, offhand, off the cuff*, off top of head*, simple, unartful, unavoidable, unbidden, uncompelled, unconscious, unconstrained, uncontrived, uncontrolled, unforced, unintentional, unplanned, unpremeditated, unprompted, unsophisticated, unstudied, up front, voluntary; SEE CONCEPTS 401,542,548

spoof [n] *trick, mockery*
bluff, bon mot, burlesque, caricature, cheat, deceit, deception, fake, flim-flam*, game, hoax, imposture, jest, joke, lampoon, parody, phony, prank, put-on, quip, satire, sell, send-up*, sham, take-off, travesty, trickery, wisecrack; SEE CONCEPTS 59,273

spooky [adj] *frightening*
chilling, creepy, eerie, ghostly, mysterious, ominous, scary, spine-chilling, supernatural, uncanny, unearthly, weird; SEE CONCEPTS 529,537

sporadic [adj] *on and off*
bits and pieces*, desultory, few, fitful, fits and starts*, hit-or-miss*, infrequent, intermittent, irregular, isolated, occasional, on-again-off-again*, random, rare, scarce, scattered, seldom, semioccasional, spasmodic, spotty, uncommon, unfrequent; SEE CONCEPT 541

sport [n1] *recreational activity; entertainment*
action, amusement, athletics, ball, disport, diversion, exercise, frolic, fun, fun and games*, gaiety, game, games, pastime, physical activity, picnic, play, pleasure, recreation; SEE CONCEPT 363

sport [n2] *fun, joking*
antics, badinage, banter, derision, drollery, escapade, frolic, horseplay, jest, jesting, joke, jollification, jollity, kidding, laughter, merriment, mirth, mockery, mummery, nonsense, pleasantry, practical joke, raillery, scorn, teasing, tomfoolery, trifling; SEE CONCEPTS 59,273

sport [n3] *person who takes kidding*
buffoon, butt, jestee, joke, laughingstock, mock, mockery, object of derision, object of ridicule, plaything, target; SEE CONCEPT 423

sport [v] *display, wear*
be dressed in, don, exhibit, have on, model, show off; SEE CONCEPTS 167,261

sporting/sportive [adj] *playful and fair*
antic, coltish, considerate, devil-may-care*, frisky, frolicsome, full of fun*, game, gamesome, gay, generous, impish, jaunty, joyous, larkish, lively, merry, mischievous, reasonable, roguish,
rollicking, sportspersonlike, sprightly, square, wild; SEE CONCEPT 401

spot [n1] *mark, stain*
atom, blemish, blot, blotch, daub, discoloration, dollop, dram, drop, flaw, iota, jot, little bit, mite, molecule, mote, nip, particle, pimple, pinch, shot, smidgen, smudge, snort, speck, taint, whit; SEE CONCEPTS 284,831

spot [n2] *location*
hangout*, hole*, joint*, layout, locality, locus, office, pad, place, plant, point, position, post, roof, scene, seat, section, sector, site, situation, slot, station, wherever*, X*, X marks the spot*; SEE CONCEPT 198

spot [n3] *bad situation*
box*, corner*, difficulty, dilemma, fix, hole*, jam, mess, pickle*, plight, predicament, quandary, scrape, trouble; SEE CONCEPTS 666,674

spot [n4] *position in organization*
appointment, berth, billet, connection, job, office, place, post, responsibility, situation, station, work; SEE CONCEPTS 351,362

spot [v1] *mark, stain*
besmirch, bespatter, blot, blotch, dapple, dirty, dot, fleck, maculate, marble, mottle, pepper, pimple, soil, spatter, speck, speckle, splash, splotch, stipple, streak, stripe, stud, sully, taint, tarnish; SEE CONCEPTS 79,179

spot [v2] *see, recognize*
catch, catch sight of, descry, detect, determinate, diagnose, discern, discover, distinguish, encounter, espy, ferret out, find, identify, locate, make out, meet with, observe, pick out, pinpoint, place, point out, sight, trace, track, turn up; SEE CONCEPTS 38,183,626

spotless [adj] *very clean; innocent*
above reproach, blameless, chaste, clean, decent, faultless, flawless, gleaming, hygienic, immaculate, irreproachable, modest, pure, sanitary, shining, snowy, stainless, unblemished, undefiled, unimpeachable, unsoiled, unstained, unsullied, untarnished; SEE CONCEPTS 404,621

spotlight [n] *attention; bright beam of light*
center stage, fame, flashlight, floodlight, interest, light, limelight, notoriety, public attention, public eye, publicity; SEE CONCEPTS 388,624,668

spotlight [v] *focus attention on*
accentuate, draw attention, feature, floodlight*, give prominence, highlight, illuminate, limelight*, point up, publicize, put on center stage*; SEE CONCEPTS 261,292

spotty [adj] *blotchy, irregular*
desultory, erratic, flickering, fluctuating, not uniform, on-again-off-again*, patchy, pimply, spasmodic, sporadic, unequal, uneven; SEE CONCEPT 534

spouse [n] *one of a married couple*
better half*, bride, companion, groom, helpmate, husband, man, mate, partner, roommate, wife, woman; SEE CONCEPT 414

spout [v1] *spurt, emit*
cascade, discharge, eject, erupt, expel, exude, gush, jet, pour, roll, shoot, spill, spray, squirt, stream, surge; SEE CONCEPT 179

spout [v2] *talk forcefully*
boast, brag, chatter, declaim, expatiate, go on, gush, harangue, hold forth, orate, pontificate, ramble, rant, sermonize, shoot off one's mouth*, speechify, spellbind, spiel, vapor, yell; SEE CONCEPTS 49,51

sprawl [v] *sit or lie spread out*
drape, extend, flop, lie, lie spread-eagle*, loll, lounge, ramble, recline, sit, slouch, slump, spread, straddle, straggle, stretch, trail; SEE CONCEPT *201*

spray [n] *fine mist*
aerosol, atomizer, drizzle, droplets, duster, fog, froth, moisture, spindrift, splash, sprayer, sprinkler, vaporizer; SEE CONCEPTS *514,680*

spray [v] *sprinkle, diffuse*
atomize, drizzle, dust, scatter, shoot, shower, smear, spatter, splash, spritz, squirt, throw around; SEE CONCEPTS *179,256*

spread [n1] *expansion, development; extent*
advance, advancement, compass, diffusion, dispersion, dissemination, enlargement, escalation, expanse, extension, increase, period, profusion, proliferation, radiation, ramification, range, reach, scope, span, spreading, stretch, suffusion, sweep, term, transfusion, transmission; SEE CONCEPTS *651,704,721,788*

spread [n2] *outlay of food, meal*
array, banquet, blowout, dinner, feast, lunch, regale, repast; SEE CONCEPT *459*

spread [v1] *open or fan out*
arrange, array, be displayed, be distributed, bloat, branch off, broaden, cast, circulate, coat, cover, daub, develop, diffuse, dilate, disperse, diverge, enlarge, escalate, even out, expand, extend, flatten, flow, gloss, increase, lay, lengthen, level, lie, multiply, mushroom, open, outstretch, overlay, paint, pervade, prepare, proliferate, radiate, reach, roll out, set, settle, smear, sprawl, spray, stretch, strew, suffuse, swell, uncoil, unfold, unfurl, unroll, untwist, unwind, widen; SEE CONCEPTS *158,172,201*

spread [v2] *publicize*
advertise, blazon, broadcast, cast, circulate, declare, diffuse, disseminate, distribute, make known, make public, proclaim, promulgate, propagate, publish, radiate, scatter, shed, sow, strew, transmit; SEE CONCEPT *60*

spree [n] *wild activity*
bacchanalia, ball, bash, binge, caper, carousal, carouse, carousing, celebration, field day*, fling, frolic, high jinks*, high time*, jag, jamboree, junket, lark, merry-go-round*, orgy, party, rampage, revel, rip*, spending expedition, splurge, tear*; SEE CONCEPTS *327,377,384*

sprightly [adj] *fun, vivacious*
active, agile, airy, alert, animate, animated, blithe, bouncy, breezy, bright, brisk, cheerful, cheery, chipper, chirpy, clever, dapper, dashing, energetic, fairylike, frolicsome, gay, good, grooving, hyper, jaunty, jolly, joyous, jumping, keen, keen-witted, light, lively, nimble, peppy, perky, playful, quick, quick-witted, saucy, scintillating, smart, snappy, spirited, sportive, spry, swinging, zappy*, zingy*, zippy*; SEE CONCEPTS *401,404,542*

spring [n1] *jump, skip*
bounce, bounciness, bound, buck, buoyancy, elasticity, flexibility, give, hop, leap, recoil, resilience, saltation, springiness, vault; SEE CONCEPTS *194,731*

spring [n2] *season following winter*
blackberry winter*, budding, budtime, flowering, prime, seedtime, springtide, springtime, vernal equinox, vernal season; SEE CONCEPT *814*

spring [n3] *origin*
beginning, cause, consideration, fount, fountain, fountainhead, impetus, motive, root, source, stimulus, well, wellspring, whence; SEE CONCEPTS *648,661*

spring [n4] *body of rushing waters*
artesian well, baths, fountain, geyser, hot spring, hydrolysate, spa, thermal spring, watering place, wells; SEE CONCEPT *514*

spring [v1] *jump, skip*
bolt, bounce, bound, hippety hop*, hop, hurdle, leap, lop, lope, rebound, recoil, skitter, start, startle, trip, vault; SEE CONCEPT *194*

spring [v2] *originate, emerge*
appear, arise, arrive, be derived, be descended, begin, birth, burgeon, come, come into being, come into existence, come out, commence, derive, descend, develop, emanate, flow, grow, hatch, head, issue, loom, mushroom, proceed, rise, shoot up, start, stem, upspring; SEE CONCEPTS *105,302,373*

sprinkle [v] *scatter, disseminate*
baptize, christen, dampen, dot, dredge, dust, freckle, mist, moisten, pepper, powder, rain, shake, shower, smear, speck, speckle, spit, spot, spray, spritz, squirt, strew, stud; SEE CONCEPTS *179,222,256*

sprinkling [n] *hint, dash*
admixture, dust, dusting, few, handful, lick, mixture, powdering, scattering, several, smattering, sprinkle, strain, taste, tinge, touch, trace; SEE CONCEPT *831*

sprint [v] *run very fast*
dart, dash, go at top speed, hotfoot*, race, rush, scamper, scoot, scurry, shoot, tear, whiz; SEE CONCEPT *150*

sprout [v] *develop*
bud, burgeon, germinate, grow, push, shoot, shoot up, spring, take root, vegetate; SEE CONCEPT *257*

spruce [adj] *stylish, neat*
classy, clean, dainty, dapper, elegant, prim, smart, tidy, trim, well-groomed; SEE CONCEPT *589*

spruce up [v] *make neat, well-groomed*
brush, deck out*, dress up, fix up, groom, prim, primp, sleek, slick, smarten, tidy, titivate, wash; SEE CONCEPTS *162,167,202*

spry [adj] *active, vivacious*
agile, alert, brisk, energetic, fleet, full of pep, healthy, in full swing*, lithe, nimble, on the go*, prompt, quick, quick on the draw*, ready, robust, rocking, sound, spirited, sprightly, supple, vigorous; SEE CONCEPT *401*

spunk [n] *courage, nerve*
backbone, determination, doggedness, fortitude, gameness, grit*, gumption*, guts*, intestinal fortitude*, mettle, moxie*, pluck, resolution, spirit, toughness, true grit*; SEE CONCEPTS *411,633*

spur [n] *incitement, stimulus*
activation, actuation, catalyst, excitant, goad, goose*, impetus, impulse, incentive, incitation, inducement, motivation, motive, needle*, prick, stimulant, trigger, turn-on*, urge; SEE CONCEPT *661*

spur [v] *incite, prompt*
animate, arouse, awaken, countenance, drive, egg on*, exhort, favor, fire up*, goad, goose*, impel, instigate, key up, press, prick, prod, propel, push, put up to, rally, rouse, sic*, spark, stimulate, stir,

trigger, turn on, urge, work up; SEE CONCEPTS *14,68*

spurious [*adj*] *counterfeit, fake*
affected, apocryphal, artificial, assumed, bastard*, bent, bogus, bum, contrived, deceitful, deceptive, dummy*, ersatz, faked, false, feigned, forged, framed, illegitimate, imitation, make-believe, mock, phony, pirate, pretend, pretended, pseudo*, put-on*, sham*, simulated, specious, substitute, unauthentic, ungenuine, unreal; SEE CONCEPT *582*

spurn [*v*] *turn away; ignore*
air, contemn, cut, decline, despise, disapprove, disdain, dismiss, disregard, drop, dump, flout, flush*, give the cold shoulder*, hold in contempt, look down on*, nix*, not hear of*, pass by, rebuff, refuse, reject, reprobate, repudiate, repulse, scoff, scorn, slight, sneer, sneeze at*, snub, steer clear*, turn down, turn nose up at*; SEE CONCEPTS *21,30,384*

spurt [*n*] *burst of activity*
access, commotion, discharge, eruption, explosion, fit, jet, outburst, rush, spate, spritz, squirt, stream, surge; SEE CONCEPTS *1,119,179*

spurt [*v*] *erupt*
burst, emerge, flow, flow out, gush, issue, jet, ooze, pour out, shoot, spew, spout, spritz, squirt, stream, surge, well; SEE CONCEPT *179*

spy [*n*] *person who secretly finds out about another's business*
agent, detective, double agent, emissary, espionage agent, foreign agent, informer, inside agent, intelligencer, investigator, lookout, mole*, observer, operative, patrol, picket, plant*, scout, secret agent, secret service, sleeper, sleuth, snoop, spook, spotter, undercover agent, watcher; SEE CONCEPTS *348,412*

spy [*v*] *secretly follow, watch another's actions*
case, catch sight of, discover, examine, eyeball*, fish out*, get a load of*, glimpse, keep under surveillance, look for, meddle, notice, observe, peep, pry, recon*, reconnoiter, scout, scrutinize, search, set eyes on, shadow, sleuth, snoop, spot, stag, stake out, tail, take in, take note, trail, view, watch; SEE CONCEPTS *103,623*

squabble [*n*] *argument*
altercation, bickering, controversy, difference, difference of opinion, disagreement, dispute, feud, fight, flap*, fuss*, hassle, quarrel, row*, scene*, scrap*, set-to*, spat*, tiff*, words*, wrangle; SEE CONCEPT *46*

squabble [*v*] *argue*
argufy, bicker, brawl, clash, disagree, dispute, encounter, fall out*, fight, hassle, have words*, quarrel, quibble, row, scrap, spat, tiff*, wrangle; SEE CONCEPT *46*

squad [*n*] *team, crew*
band, battalion, company, division, force, gang, group, regiment, squadron, troop; SEE CONCEPTS *322,365,417*

squalid [*adj*] *poor, run-down*
abominable, base, broken-down, decayed, despicable, dingy, dirty, disgusting, disheveled, fetid, filthy, foul, grimy, gruesome, horrible, horrid, ignoble, impure, low, mean, miry, moldy, muddy, musty, nasty, odorous, offensive, poverty-stricken, ramshackle, reeking, repellent, repulsive, scurvy, seedy, shabby, shoddy, sloppy, slovenly, soiled, sordid, ugly, unclean, unkempt, vile, wretched; SEE CONCEPTS *334,485,570*

squander [*v*] *fritter away, use up*
be prodigal with, be wasteful, blow*, cash out*, consume, dissipate, expend, frivol, frivol away, go through, lavish, misspend, misuse, prodigalize, put out*, run through, scatter, spend, spend like water*, spring for*, throw away, throw money around*, trifle, waste; SEE CONCEPTS *156,225,327*

square [*n1*] *person who is old-fashioned, conventional*
antediluvian, conservative, diehard*, fuddy-duddy*, reactionary, stick-in-the-mud*, traditionalist; SEE CONCEPT *423*

square [*n2*] *municipal park*
area, center, circle, common, green, plaza, space, village green; SEE CONCEPT *509*

square [*adj1*] *honest, genuine*
aboveboard, decent, equal, equitable, ethical, even, fair, fair-and-square, impartial, impersonal, just, nonpartisan, objective, on-the-level, sporting, sportspersonlike, straight, straightforward, unbiased, unprejudiced, upright; SEE CONCEPTS *267,542*

square [*adj2*] *four-sided*
boxlike, boxy, equal-sided, equilateral, four-square, orthogonal, quadrate, quadratic, quadratical, rectangular, rectilinear, right-angled, squared, squarish; SEE CONCEPT *486*

square [*adj3*] *old-fashioned, conventional*
behind the times, bourgeois, button-down*, conservative, dated, orthodox, out-of-date, straight*, strait-laced*, stuffy*; SEE CONCEPTS *401,404*

square [*v1*] *correspond, agree*
accord, balance, check out, coincide, conform, dovetail*, fit, fit in, gee, harmonize, jibe, match, reconcile, tally; SEE CONCEPT *664*

square [*v2*] *pay off, satisfy*
balance, bribe, buy, buy off, clear, clear off, clear up, corrupt, discharge, fix, have, liquidate, make even, pay, pay up, quit, rig, settle, tamper with; SEE CONCEPT *341*

square [*v3*] *adapt, regulate*
accommodate, adjust, align, conform, even up, fit, level, quadrate, reconcile, suit, tailor, tailor-make*, true; SEE CONCEPTS *126,202*

squash [*v*] *compress*
annihilate, bear, bruise, crowd, crush, distort, extinguish, flatten, jam, kill, macerate, mash, pound, press, pulp, push, put down, quash, quell, scrunch, shut down, sit on, smash, squeeze, squish, stamp on, suppress, trample, triturate; SEE CONCEPTS *121,208,219*

squat [*adj*] *short and stocky*
broad, chunky, dumpy*, fat, heavy, heavyset, splay, thick, thick-bodied, thickset; SEE CONCEPTS *491,773,779*

squat [*v*] *lower body by bending knees*
bow, cower, crouch, hunch, hunker down, perch, roost, settle, sit, stoop; SEE CONCEPT *201*

squawk [*v1*] *make high-pitched, animal-like sound*
cackle, caw, crow, cry, hoot, screech, yap, yawp, yelp; SEE CONCEPTS *64,77*

squawk [*v2*] *gripe*
bellyache*, complain, kick up a fuss*, protest, raise Cain*, squeal, yammer; SEE CONCEPTS *52,54*

squeak [*v*] *make sharp, high-pitched sound*
cheep, creak, cry, grate, peep, pipe, scream, screech, scritch, shrill, sing, sound, squeal, talk, whine, yelp; SEE CONCEPTS *64,65*

squeal [n/v1] *yell in a loud and high-pitched manner*
bleat, cheep, creak, grate, howl, peep, rasp, scream, scream bloody murder*, screech, shout, shriek, shrill, squawk, wail, yelp, yip, yowl; SEE CONCEPTS 64,77

squeal [v2] *inform on*
betray, blab*, complain, protest, rat on*, sell down the river*, sing*, snitch*, squawk*, talk, tattle, tattletale*, tell; SEE CONCEPTS 54,60

squeamish [adj] *nauseated; finicky*
annoyed, captious, delicate, disgusted, dizzy, exacting, fastidious, fussy, hypercritical, mincing, particular, prim, prudish, puritanical, qualmish, queasy, queer, scrupulous, shaky, sick, sickly, sick to one's stomach*, strait-laced, unsettled, upset, vertiginous; SEE CONCEPTS 314,401,404

squeeze [n] *pressure, crushing*
clasp, clutch, congestion, crowd, crunch, crush, embrace, force, handclasp, hold, hug, influence, jam, press, restraint, squash; SEE CONCEPTS 219,674,687

squeeze [v1] *exert pressure on sides, parts of something*
bear, choke, clasp, clip, clutch, compress, contract, cram, crowd, crush, cuddle, embrace, enfold, force, grip, hold tight, hug, jam, jostle, nip, pack, pinch, press, quash, ram, scrunch, squash, squish, strangle, stuff, throttle, thrust, wedge, wring; SEE CONCEPT 219

squeeze [v2] *try to get money out of*
bleed*, bring pressure to bear, eke out, extort, extract, lean on*, milk*, oppress, pinch*, pressure, pressurize*, put screws to*, shake down*, wrench, wring; SEE CONCEPTS 53,192,347

squelch [v] *suppress, restrain*
black out, censure, crush, extinguish, kill, muffle, oppress, quelch, quench, repress, settle, shush, sit on, smother, squash, stifle, strangle, thwart; SEE CONCEPT 130

squint [v] *scrunch up eyes when viewing*
cock the eye, look, look askance, look cross-eyed, peek, peep, screw up eyes, squinch*; SEE CONCEPTS 185,623

squire [v] *accompany*
assist, attend, chaperon, companion, date, escort, serve; SEE CONCEPTS 384,714

squirm [v] *wiggle, fidget*
agonize, flounder, shift, skew, squiggle, toss, twist, wind, worm, wriggle, writhe; SEE CONCEPT 213

squirt [v] *squeeze out liquid*
eject, emit, flow, jet, pour, spatter, spit, splash, splur, spray, sprinkle, spritz, spurt, stream, surge; SEE CONCEPTS 179,256

stab [n1] *piercing cut*
ache, blow, gash, hurt, incision, jab, jag, pang, piercing, prick, puncture, rent, stick, thrust, transfixion, twinge, wound; SEE CONCEPT 309

stab [n2] *attempt*
attempt, crack*, endeavor, essay, fling*, go*, one's best*, shot*, try, venture, whack*, whirl*; SEE CONCEPT 87

stab [v] *puncture, pierce with sharp, pointed object*
bayonet, brand, carve, chop, cleave, clip, cut, drive, gore, hit, hurt, injure, jab, jag, knife, open up, penetrate, pierce, plow, plunge, prick, prong, punch, ram, run through, saber, shank, sink, slice, spear, stick, thrust, transfix, wound, SEE CONCEPT 220

stability [n] *resistance of some degree*
adherence, aplomb, assurance, backbone, balance, cohesion, constancy, dependability, determination, durability, endurance, establishment, firmness, immobility, immovability, maturity, permanence, perseverance, resoluteness, security, solidity, solidness, soundness, stableness, steadfastness, steadiness, strength, substantiality, support, toughness; SEE CONCEPTS 411,731

stabilize [v] *make or keep in steady state; make resistant to change*
balance, ballast, bolt, brace, buttress, counterbalance, counterpoise, equalize, fasten, firm, firm up*, fix, freeze*, maintain, ossify, poise, preserve, prop, secure, set, settle, stabilitate, steady, stiffen, support, sustain, uphold; SEE CONCEPTS 110,250

stable [adj] *constant, fixed; resistant*
abiding, anchored, balanced, brick-wall*, calm, deep-rooted, durable, enduring, equable, established, even, fast, firm, immutable, invariable, lasting, nailed, perdurable, permanent, poised, reliable, resolute, safe, secure, set, set in stone*, solid, solid as a rock*, sound, stabile, stalwart, stationary, staunch, staying put, steadfast, steady, stout, strong, sturdy, substantial, sure, together, tough, unalterable, unchangeable, unfluctuating, uniform, unvarying, unwavering, well-built, well-founded; SEE CONCEPTS 404,488

stack [n] *pile*
assemblage, bank, bundle, cock, drift, heap, hill, hoard, load, mass, mound, mountain, pack, pyramid, sheaf; SEE CONCEPTS 432,440,509

stack [v] *pile up*
accumulate, amass, bank up, cock, drift, heap, hill, load, mound, pile, rick, stockpile; SEE CONCEPTS 109,158

stadium [n] *arena for recreation or spectating*
amphitheater, athletic field, bowl, coliseum, diamond, field, garden, gymnasium, pit, ring, stade, strand; SEE CONCEPT 438

staff [n1] *employees of organization*
agents, assistants, cadre, cast, crew, deputies, faculty, force, help, officers, operatives, organization, personnel, servants, shop, teachers, team, workers, work force; SEE CONCEPT 325

staff [n2] *stick, usually for walking*
cane, club, pikestaff, pole, prop, rod, stave, walking stick, wand; SEE CONCEPTS 311,479

stage [n1] *level, period within structure or system*
date, degree, division, footing, grade, juncture, lap, leg, length, moment, node, notch, phase, plane, point, point in time, rung, standing, status, step; SEE CONCEPTS 727,744,816

stage [n2] *theater platform; theater life*
arena, boards*, Broadway, dais, drama, footlights, frame, legit*, limelight*, mise-en-scène, off-Broadway, play, scaffold, scaffolding, scene, scenery, set, setting, show biz*, show business, spotlight, stage set, staging, theater; SEE CONCEPTS 263,349,438,439,448

stage [v] *arrange, produce*
bring out, do, engineer, execute, give, mount, open, orchestrate, organize, perform, play, present, put on, show; SEE CONCEPTS 94,292

stagger [v1] *walk falteringly*
alternate, careen, dither, falter, halt, hesitate, lurch, overlap, pitch, reel, shake, stammer, step,

sway, swing, teeter, titubate, topple, totter, vacillate, waver, wheel, whiffle, wobble, zigzag; SEE CONCEPT *151*

stagger [v2] *astound, shock*
amaze, astonish, boggle, bowl over*, confound, consternate, devastate, dumbfound, flabbergast, floor*, give a shock, nonplus, overpower, overwhelm, paralyze, perplex, puzzle, shake, shatter, startle, strike dumb*, stump, stun, stupefy, surprise, take aback, take breath away*, throw off balance*; SEE CONCEPTS *7,19,42*

stagnant [adj] *motionless, dirty*
brackish, dead, dormant, filthy, foul, idle, immobile, inactive, inert, lifeless, listless, passive, putrid, quiet, sluggish, stale, standing, static, stationary, still, unmoving; SEE CONCEPTS *584,621*

stagnate [v] *deteriorate by lack of action*
constipate, decay, decline, fester, go to seed*, hibernate, idle, languish, lie fallow, not move, putrefy, rot, rust, stall, stand, stand still, stifle, stultify, trammel, vegetate; SEE CONCEPTS *698,748*

staid [adj] *restrained, set*
calm, cold sober*, collected, composed, cool, decorous, demure, dignified, earnest, formal, grave, no-nonsense*, quiet, sedate, self-restrained, serious, settled, sober, solemn, somber, starchy, steady, stuffy, weighty; SEE CONCEPTS *401,404*

stain [n] *spot of dirt, blot*
bar sinister*, black eye*, blemish, blot, blotch, blur, brand, color, discoloration, disgrace, dishonor, drip, dye, infamy, ink spot, mottle, odium, onus, reproach, shame, slur, smirch, smudge, spatter, speck, splotch, spot, stigma, tint; SEE CONCEPTS *230,622*

stain [v] *dirty, taint*
animalize, bastardize, besmirch, bestialize, blacken, blemish, blot, brutalize, color, contaminate, corrupt, daub, debase, debauch, defile, demoralize, deprave, discolor, disgrace, drag through the mud*, dye, mark, pervert, smear, smudge, soil, spot, sully, tar, tarnish, tinge, tint; SEE CONCEPTS *54,250,254*

stake [n1] *pole*
pale, paling, picket, post, rod, spike, stave, stick; SEE CONCEPTS *471,479*

stake [n2] *bet, wager*
ante, chance, hazard, peril, pledge, pot, risk, venture; SEE CONCEPTS *329,363*

stake [n3] *share, investment*
award, claim, concern, interest, involvement, prize, purse; SEE CONCEPTS *344,710,835*

stake [v] *bet, wager*
back, bankroll*, capitalize, chance, finance, gamble, game, grubstake*, hazard, imperil, jeopardize, lay, play, pledge, put, put on, risk, set, stake down, venture; SEE CONCEPTS *330,363*

stale [adj1] *old, decayed*
dried, dry, faded, fetid, flat, fusty, hard, insipid, malodorous, musty, noisome, parched, rank, reeking, smelly, sour, spoiled, stagnant, stenchy, stinking, tasteless, watery, weak, zestless; SEE CONCEPTS *462,485,598*

stale [adj2] *overused, out-of-date*
antiquated, banal, bent, cliché, clichéd, cliché-ridden, common, commonplace, corny*, dead, drab, dull, dusty, effete, flat, fusty, hackneyed, insipid, like a dinosaur*, mawkish, moth-eaten*,

out*, passé, past, platitudinous, repetitious, shopworn, stereotyped, threadbare, timeworn, tired, trite, unoriginal, well-worn, worn-out, yesterday's*, zestless; SEE CONCEPTS *267,578,589,797*

stalemate [n] *deadlock*
arrest, Catch-22*, check, delay, draw, gridlock, impasse, pause, standoff, standstill, tie; SEE CONCEPTS *230,807,832*

stalk [n] *stem of plant*
axis, bent, helm, pedicel, pedicle, reed, shaft, spike, spire, support, trunk, twig, upright; SEE CONCEPT *428*

stalk [v] *follow, creep up on*
ambush, approach, chase, drive, flush out, haunt, hunt, pace, pursue, shadow, stride, stride, tail, track, trail, walk up to; SEE CONCEPTS *149,159,749*

stall [v] *delay for own purposes*
arrest, avoid the issue*, beat around the bush*, brake, check, die, drag one's feet*, equivocate, fence, filibuster, halt, hamper, hedge, hinder, hold off, interrupt, not move, play for time*, postpone, prevaricate, put off, quibble, shut down, slow, slow down, stand, stand off, stand still, stay, still, stonewall*, stop, suspend, take one's time*, tarry, temporize; SEE CONCEPTS *121,234*

stalwart [adj] *strong, valiant*
athletic, bold, bound, bound and determined*, brave, brawny, brick-wall*, courageous, daring, dauntless, dead set on*, dependable, fearless, forceful, gutsy*, hanging tough*, hefty, husky, indomitable, intrepid, lusty, muscular, nervy*, powerhouse*, redoubtable, robust, rugged, sinewy, solid, spunky*, staunch, steamroller*, stout, stouthearted, strapping, sturdy, substantial, tenacious, tough, unafraid, undaunted, valorous, vigorous; SEE CONCEPTS *404,489*

stamina [n] *strength, vigor*
backbone*, endurance, energy, force, fortitude, grit*, guts*, gutsiness, heart, indefatigability, intestinal fortitude*, legs*, lustiness, moxie*, power, power of endurance, resilience, resistance, starch*, staying power, tolerance, toleration, vim, vitality, zip*; SEE CONCEPTS *411,732*

stammer [v] *stutter in speech*
falter, halt, hammer, hem and haw*, hesitate, jabber, lurch, pause, repeat, splutter, sputter, stop, stumble, wobble; SEE CONCEPTS *47,266*

stamp [n1] *impression, symbol, seal*
brand, cast, earmark, emblem, hallmark, impress, imprint, indentation, mark, mold, print, signature, sticker; SEE CONCEPTS *259,284*

stamp [n2] *character*
breed, cast, cut, description, fashion, form, ilk, kind, lot, mold, sort, stripe, type; SEE CONCEPT *411*

stamp [v1] *step on hard*
beat, clomp, clump, crush, stomp, stump, tramp, trample, tromp; SEE CONCEPT *149*

stamp [v2] *imprint; press mark on*
brand, cast, drive, engrave, etch, fix, grave, hammer, impress, infix, inscribe, letter, mark, mold, offset, pound, print; SEE CONCEPTS *79,174*

stampede [n] *rush of animals*
charge, chase, crash, dash, flight, fling, hurry, panic, rout, run, scattering, shoot, smash, tear; SEE CONCEPT *152*

stance [n] *position, posture*
attitude, bearing, carriage, color, deportment,

posture, say-so*, slant, stand, standpoint, viewpoint; SEE CONCEPTS *689,757*

stand [n1] *position, opinion*
angle, attitude, belief, carriage, determination, notion, poise, pose, sentiment, slant, sound, stance, standpoint, twist, two cents' worth*, view; SEE CONCEPT *689*

stand [n2] *base, stage*
board, booth, bracket, counter, dais, frame, gantry, grandstand, place, platform, rack, rank, staging, stall, station, support, table; SEE CONCEPTS *442,443*

stand [v1] *be or get upright*
be erect, be on feet, be vertical, cock, dispose, erect, jump up, locate, mount, place, poise, position, put, rank, rise, set, settle; SEE CONCEPT *201*

stand/stand for [v2] *endure, bear*
abide, allow, bear with, brook, cope, countenance, experience, handle, hang on, hold, last, live with, put up with, resign oneself to, stay the course*, stomach*, submit, suffer, support, sustain, swallow, take, tolerate, undergo, wear, weather, withstand; SEE CONCEPT *23*

stand [v3] *be in force, exist*
be located, belong, be situated, be valid, continue, endure, fill, halt, hold, last, obtain, occupy, pause, prevail, remain, rest, stay, stop, take up; SEE CONCEPT *758*

standard [n1] *guideline, principle*
archetype, average, axiom, barometer, beau ideal, belief, benchmark, canon, code, criterion, ethics, example, exemplar, fundamental, gauge, grade, guide, guideline, ideal, ideals, law, mean, measure, median, mirror, model, morals, norm, par, paradigm, pattern, principle, requirement, rule, rule of thumb*, sample, specification, test, touchstone, type, yardstick; SEE CONCEPT *688*

standard [n2] *flag*
banderole, banner, bannerol, color, colors, emblem, ensign, figure, insignia, jack, pennant, streamer, symbol; SEE CONCEPT *475*

standard [adj] *regular, approved*
accepted, authoritative, average, basic, boilerplate*, canonical, classic, common, customary, definitive, established, everyday, garden variety*, general, normal, official, orthodox, popular, prevailing, recognized, regulation, run-of-the-mill*, set, staple, stock, typical, usual, vanilla*; SEE CONCEPT *533*

standardize [v] *make regular, similar*
assimilate, bring into line, homogenize, institute, institutionalize, mass produce, normalize, order, regiment, stereotype, systematize; SEE CONCEPT *126*

stand for [v] *signify, mean*
answer for, appear for, betoken, denote, exemplify, imply, indicate, represent, signify, suggest, symbol, symbolize; SEE CONCEPT *682*

standing [n] *position, rank*
cachet, capacity, character, condition, consequence, credit, dignity, eminence, estimation, footing, place, prestige, reputation, repute, scene, situation, slot, state, station, stature, status, term; SEE CONCEPTS *388,727*

standing [adj] *permanent*
continuing, existing, fixed, perpetual, regular, repeated; SEE CONCEPT *551*

standoffish [adj] *cold, distant*
aloof, antisocial, cool, distant, eremitic, haughty, indifferent, misanthropic, reclusive, remote, reserved, solitary, unapproachable, uncompanionable, unsociable, withdrawn; SEE CONCEPTS *401,404*

stand out [v] *be conspicuous, prominent*
attract attention, be distinct, beetle, be highlighted, be striking, bulge, bulk, catch the eye, emerge, jut, loom, overhang, poke, pouch, project, protrude, stick out; SEE CONCEPT *716*

standstill [n] *stop*
arrest, cessation, check, checkmate, corner*, dead end*, deadlock, dead stop*, delay, gridlock, halt, hole, impasse, inaction, pause, stalemate, standoff, wait; SEE CONCEPTS *119,832*

staple [adj] *necessary, basic*
chief, essential, fundamental, important, in demand, key, main, popular, predominant, primary, principal, standard; SEE CONCEPT *546*

star [n] *person who is famous*
celebrity, draw*, favorite, headliner, hero, idol, lead, leading role, luminary, name, starlet, superstar, topliner*; SEE CONCEPTS *352,366*

star [adj] *famous, illustrious*
brilliant, capital, celebrated, chief, dominant, leading, main, major, outstanding, paramount, predominant, preeminent, principal, prominent, talented, well-known; SEE CONCEPT *568*

stare [v] *gape, watch*
beam*, bore*, eagle eye*, eye, eyeball*, fix, focus, gawk, gaze, glare, glim*, goggle*, lay eyes on*, look, look fixedly, ogle, peer, rivet, rubberneck*, take in; SEE CONCEPT *623*

stark [adj1] *utter, absolute*
abrupt, arrant, bald, bare, blasted, blessed, blunt, complete, confounded, consummate, downright, entire, firm, flagrant, gross, infernal, out-and-out*, outright, palpable, patent, pure, rank, severe, sheer, simple, stiff, unalloyed, unmitigated; SEE CONCEPTS *531,569*

stark [adj2] *bare, unadorned*
au naturel, austere, bald, barren, bleak, chaste, clear, cold, depressing, desolate, dreary, empty, forsaken, grim, harsh, naked, nude, plain, raw, severe, solitary, stripped, unclad, uncovered, undraped, vacant, vacuous, void; SEE CONCEPT *485*

start [n1] *beginning*
alpha*, birth, bow, commencement, countdown, dawn, dawning, day one*, derivation, embarkation, exit, first step, flying start*, foundation, inauguration, inception, initiation, jump-off, kickoff*, leaving, onset, opening, origin, outset, running start, setting out, source, spring, square one*, start-off, takeoff; SEE CONCEPTS *648,832*

start [n2] *advantage*
allowance, backing, break, bulge, chance, draw, edge, handicap, head start, helping hand, introduction, lead, odds, opening, opportunity, sponsorship, vantage; SEE CONCEPT *693*

start [n3] *flinch*
convulsion, jar, jump, scare, shock, spasm, turn, twitch; SEE CONCEPTS *150,194*

start [v1] *begin; come into existence*
activate, appear, arise, arouse, come into being, commence, create, depart, embark, engender, enter upon, establish, found, get going, get under way*, go ahead, hit the road*, inaugurate, incite, initiate, instigate, institute, introduce, issue, launch, lay foundation, leave, light, make a beginning, open, originate, pioneer, rise, rouse, sally forth, see light, set in motion, set out, set up,

st
st

spring, take first step*, take the plunge*, turn on;
SEE CONCEPTS 221,241

start [v2] *flinch*
blanch, blench, bolt, bounce, bound, buck, dart,
draw back, jerk, jump, jump the gun*, leap, quail,
recoil, shrink, shy, spring, squinch, startle,
twitch, wince; SEE CONCEPTS 150,194

startle [v] *frighten, surprise*
affright, agitate, alarm, amaze, astonish, astound,
awe, bolt, consternate, floor, fright, give a turn*,
jump, make jump, rock, scare, scare to death*,
shake up, shock, spook, spring, spring something
on*, stagger, start, stun, take aback, terrify, terrorize; SEE CONCEPTS 7,19,42

starving/starved [adj] *deprived of food*
could eat a horse*, craving, dehydrated, drawn,
dying, emaciated, empty, faint, famished, haggard, hungering, hungry, malnourished, peaked,
peckish, perishing, pinched, ravenous, skinny,
thin, underfed, undernourished, weakened; SEE
CONCEPTS 406,546

state [n1] *condition or mode of being*
accompaniment, attitude, capacity, case, category, chances, character, circumstance, circumstances, contingency, element, environment,
essential, estate, event, eventuality, fix, footing,
form, frame of mind, humor, imperative, juncture, limitation, mood, nature, occasion, occurrence, outlook, pass, phase, plight, position,
posture, predicament, prerequisite, proviso, reputation, requirement, shape, situation, spirits,
stand, standing, state of affairs, station, status,
stipulation, time, welfare; SEE CONCEPTS
410,639,696,701,720

state [n2] *dignity, grandeur*
cachet, ceremony, consequence, display, glory,
majesty, pomp, position, prestige, rank, splendor,
standing, stature, status, style; SEE CONCEPT 388

state [n3] *government, country*
body politic, commonwealth, community, federation, land, nation, republic, sovereignty, territory, union; SEE CONCEPTS 508,510

state [v] *declare, assert*
affirm, air, articulate, asseverate, aver, bring out,
chime in*, come out with, deliver, describe, elucidate, enounce, enumerate, enunciate, explain,
expound, express, give, give blow-by-blow*, give
rundown*, interpret, narrate, pitch, present, pronounce, propound, put, recite, recount, rehearse,
relate, report, say, set forth, speak, specify,
spiel*, tell, throw out*, utter, vent, ventilate,
voice; SEE CONCEPTS 49,51,55

stately [adj] *dignified, impressive*
august, ceremonial, ceremonious, conventional,
courtly, deliberate, elegant, elevated, formal, gallant, gracious, grand, grandiose, haughty, high,
highfalutin*, high-minded*, imperial, imperious, imposing, kingly, large, lofty, luxurious,
magnificent, majestic, massive, measured, monumental, noble, opulent, palatial, pompous, portly,
proud, queenly, regal, royal, solemn, stiff, sumptuous, superb, towering; SEE CONCEPTS
401,574,589

statement [n1] *declaration, assertion*
ABCs*, account, acknowledgment, affidavit, affirmation, allegation, announcement, articulation,
aside, asseveration, assurance, averment, avowal,
blow-by-blow*, charge, comment, communication, communiqué, description, dictum, ejaculation, explanation, make*, manifesto, mention,

narrative, observation, picture, presentation, presentment, proclamation, profession, protestation,
recital, recitation, relation, remark, report, run-
down, testimony, utterance, ventilation, verbalization, vocalization, voice, word; SEE CONCEPTS
271,274,278

statement [n2] *account of finances*
affidavit, audit, bill, budget, charge, invoice,
reckoning, record, report, score, tab; SEE CON-
CEPT 331

static [adj] *motionless, changeless*
at a standstill, constant, deadlocked, fixed, format, gridlocked, immobile, immovable, inactive,
inert, latent, passive, rigid, stabile, stable, stagnant, stalled, standing still, stationary, sticky,
still, stopped, stuck, unchanging, unfluctuating,
unmoving, unvarying; SEE CONCEPTS 534,584

station [n1] *headquarters, base*
base of operations, depot, home office, house, location, locus, main office, place, position, post,
seat, site, situation, spot, stop, terminal, whereabouts; SEE CONCEPT 198

station [n2] *social or occupational status*
appointment, business, calling, capacity, caste,
character, class, duty, employment, estate, footing, grade, level, occupation, order, place, position, post, rank, service, situation, sphere,
standing, state, stratum; SEE CONCEPTS
349,376,388

station [v] *place at a location*
allot, appoint, assign, base, commission, establish, fix, garrison, install, lodge, park, plant, post,
put, set; SEE CONCEPTS 50,88,201,320,351

stationary [adj] *not moving; fixed*
anchored, at a standstill, immobile, inert, moored,
motionless, nailed*, nailed down*, parked*, pat*,
permanent, stable, stagnant, standing, static,
stock-still, unmoving; SEE CONCEPTS 488,551

statue [n] *trophy or memorial*
bronze, bust, cast, effigy, figure, icon, image,
ivory, likeness, marble, piece, representation,
sculpture, simulacrum, statuary, statuette, torso;
SEE CONCEPT 259

statuesque [adj] *tall and dignifed*
beautiful, graceful, grand, imposing, majestic, regal, shapely, stately, trim, well-proportioned; SEE
CONCEPTS 579,589,779

stature [n] *importance*
ability, cachet, caliber, capacity, competence,
consequence, development, dignity, elevation,
eminence, growth, merit, position, prestige,
prominence, qualification, quality, rank, size,
standing, state, station, status, tallness, value, virtue, worth; SEE CONCEPTS 668,741

status [n] *rank*
cachet, caliber, capacity, character, condition,
consequence, degree, dignity, distinction, eminence, footing, grade, merit, mode, place, position, prestige, prominence, quality, rating,
renown, situation, stage, standing, state, station,
stature, worth; SEE CONCEPTS 388,668

statute [n] *rule, law*
act, assize, bill, canon, decree, decretum, edict,
enactment, measure, ordinance, precept, regulation; SEE CONCEPT 318

staunch [adj] *resolute, dependable*
allegiant, ardent, constant, faithful, fast, firm, inflexible, liege, loyal, reliable, secure, sound, stable, stalwart, steadfast, stiff, stout, strong, sure,

tough, tried-and-true, true, true-blue, trustworthy, trusty; SEE CONCEPTS *401,534,542*

stay [*n1*] *visit*
break, halt, holiday, sojourn, stop, stopover, vacation; SEE CONCEPT *227*

stay [*n2*] *hold, delay*
deferment, halt, pause, postponement, remission, reprieve, standstill, stop, stopping, suspension; SEE CONCEPTS *121,832*

stay [*n3*] *support, underpinning*
brace, buttress, column, hold, prop, reinforcement, shore, shoring, stanchion, truss, underpropping; SEE CONCEPTS *440,445*

stay [*v1*] *wait*
abide, bide, bunk, continue, dally, delay, endure, establish oneself, halt, hang, hang about, hang around, hang in, hang out, hold the fort*, hover, lag, last, linger, loiter, nest, outstay, pause, perch, procrastinate, put down roots*, remain, reprieve, reside, respite, roost*, settle, sit tight*, sojourn, squat, stand, stay out, stay put, stick around*, stop, sweat*, sweat it out*, tarry; SEE CONCEPTS *210,681*

stay [*v2*] *visit*
be accommodated, bide, dwell, live, lodge, put up, sojourn, stop, stop over, tarry; SEE CONCEPTS *226,227*

stay [*v3*] *hold in abeyance*
adjourn, arrest, check, curb, defer, delay, detain, discontinue, halt, hinder, hold, hold over, impede, intermit, interrupt, obstruct, postpone, prevent, prorogue, put off, shelve, stall, stop, suspend, ward off; SEE CONCEPT *121*

steadfast [*adj*] *loyal, steady*
abiding, adamant, allegiant, ardent, bound, changeless, constant, dedicated, dependable, enduring, established, faithful, fast, firm, fixed, immutable, immovable, inexorable, inflexible, intense, intent, loyal, never-failing, obdurate, persevering, relentless, reliable, resolute, rigid, single-minded, stable, staunch, stubborn, sure, tried-and-true*, true, true-blue*, unbending, unfaltering, unflinching, unmovable, unqualified, unquestioning, unswerving, unwavering, unyielding, wholehearted; SEE CONCEPTS *401,534,542*

steady [*adj1*] *stable, fixed*
abiding, brick-wall*, certain, changeless, constant, durable, enduring, equable, even, firm, immovable, never-failing, patterned, regular, reliable, safe, set, set in stone*, solid, solid as a rock*, stabile, steadfast, steady-going, substantial, sure, unchangeable, unchanging, unfaltering, unfluctuating, uniform, unqualified, unquestioning, unshaken, unvarying, unwavering; SEE CONCEPTS *488,534*

steady [*adj2*] *continuing*
ceaseless, confirmed, consistent, constant, continuous, equable, eternal, even, faithful, habitual, incessant, never-ending, nonstop, persistent, regular, rhythmic, stabile, stable, steady-going, unbroken, unfaltering, unfluctuating, uniform, uninterrupted, unremitting, unvarying, unwavering; SEE CONCEPT *798*

steady [*adj3*] *balanced, faithful in mind*
allegiant, ardent, calm, constant, cool, dependable, equable, fast, imperturbable, intense, level-headed, liege, loyal, poised, reliable, reserved, resolute, sedate, self-possessed, sensible, serene, serious-minded, settled, single-minded, sober,

staid, staunch, steadfast, unswerving, unwavering, wholehearted; SEE CONCEPTS *403,542*

steal [*v1*] *take something without permission*
abduct, appropriate, blackmail, burglarize, carry off, cheat, cozen, defraud, despoil, divert, embezzle, heist, hold for ransom, hold up, housebreak*, keep, kidnap, lift*, loot, make off with*, misappropriate, peculate, pilfer, pillage, pinch*, pirate, plagiarize, plunder, poach, purloin, ransack, remove, rifle, rip off*, run off with*, sack*, shoplift, snitch*, spirit away*, stick up*, strip, swindle, swipe, take, take possession of, thieve, walk off with*, withdraw; SEE CONCEPT *139*

steal [*v2*] *sneak around*
creep, flit, glide, go stealthily, insinuate, lurk, pass quietly, skulk, slide, slink, slip, snake, tiptoe; SEE CONCEPTS *151,207*

stealthy [*adj*] *quiet and secretive*
catlike, catty*, clandestine, covert, crafty, cunning, enigmatic, feline, furtive, hush-hush*, noiseless, private, secret, shifty, silent, skulking, slinking, sly, sneak, sneaking, sneaky, sub-rosa*, surreptitious, undercover, underhand, under wraps*, wily; SEE CONCEPTS *401,576*

steam [*n*] *energy*
beef, force, might, muscle, potency, power, puissance, sinew, strength, vigor, vim; SEE CONCEPT *633*

steel [*v*] *prepare oneself*
animate, brace, buck up*, cheer, embolden, encourage, fortify, gird, grit teeth*, harden, hearten, inspirit, make up one's mind*, prepare, rally, ready, reinforce, strengthen; SEE CONCEPT *35*

steep [*adj1*] *extreme in direction, course*
abrupt, arduous, breakneck, declivitous, elevated, erect, headlong, high, hilly, lifted, lofty, perpendicular, precipitate, precipitous, prerupt, raised, sharp, sheer, straight-up; SEE CONCEPT *581*

steep [*adj2*] *very expensive*
dizzying, excessive, exorbitant, extortionate, extreme, high, immoderate, inordinate, overpriced, stiff, towering, uncalled-for, undue, unmeasurable, unreasonable; SEE CONCEPTS *334,762*

steep [*v*] *let soak*
bathe, damp, drench, fill, imbue, immerse, impregnate, infuse, ingrain, invest, macerate, marinate, moisten, permeate, pervade, saturate, soak, sodden, sop, souse, submerge, suffuse, waterlog; SEE CONCEPT *256*

steer [*v*] *guide, direct on a course*
beacon, be in the driver's seat*, captain, conduct, control, drive, escort, govern, head for, helm, herd, lead, pilot, point, route, run, run things, see, shepherd, show, skipper*, take over, take the helm, take the reins; SEE CONCEPTS *94,187*

stem [*n*] *stalk of plant*
axis, branch, pedicel, pedicle, peduncle, petiole, shoot, stock, trunk; SEE CONCEPT *428*

stem [*v1*] *come from*
arise, be bred, be brought about, be caused, be generated, derive, develop, emanate, flow, head, issue, originate, proceed, rise, spring; SEE CONCEPT *648*

stem [*v2*] *prevent, stop*
arrest, bring to a standstill, check, contain, control, curb, dam, hinder, hold back, oppose, resist, restrain, stay, withstand; SEE CONCEPT *121*

stench [*n*] *foul odor*
fetor, funk*, malodor, mephitis, noisomeness, redolence, smell, stink*; SEE CONCEPTS *599,600*

step [n1] *pace of feet in walking*
footfall, footprint, footstep, gait, impression, mark, print, spoor, stepping, stride, trace, track, trail, tread, vestige, walk; SEE CONCEPT *149*

step [n2] *action, move*
act, advance, advancement, deed, degree, expedient, gradation, grade, level, maneuver, means, measure, motion, notch, phase, point, procedure, proceeding, process, progression, rank, remove, rung, stage, start; SEE CONCEPTS *1,832*

step [n3] *one level of stairs*
doorstep, gradation, notch, rest, round, run, rung, stair, tread; SEE CONCEPTS *440,445*

step [v] *move foot to walk*
advance, ambulate, ascend, dance, descend, go backward, go down, go forward, go up, hoof, mince, move backward, move forward, pace, prance, skip, stride, tiptoe, traipse, tread, trip, troop, walk; SEE CONCEPT *149*

step in [v] *become involved*
arrive, be invited, chip in*, come, enter, intercede, interfere, intermediate, interpose, intervene, lend a hand*, mediate, negotiate, take action; SEE CONCEPTS *100,324,384*

step up [v] *accelerate*
augment, boost, escalate, hasten, hurry, improve, increase, intensify, lift, quicken, raise, shake up, speed, speed up, up; SEE CONCEPTS *236,244,245*

stereotype [n] *idea held as standard, example*
average, boilerplate*, convention, custom, fashion, formula, institution, mold, pattern, received idea; SEE CONCEPT *686*

stereotype [v] *categorize as being example, standard*
catalogue, conventionalize, define, dub, institutionalize, methodize, normalize, pigeonhole*, regulate, standardize, systematize, take to be, typecast*; SEE CONCEPTS *38,49*

stereotyped [adj] *standard, conventional*
banal, clichéd, cliché-ridden, commonplace, corny*, dull, hackneyed, mass-produced, ordinary, overused, platitudinous, played out*, stale, standardized, stock, threadbare*, tired*, trite, unoriginal, well-worn, worn-out, worn thin; SEE CONCEPT *530*

sterile [adj] *unproductive, clean*
antiseptic, arid, aseptic, bare, barren, bleak, dead, decontaminated, desert, desolate, disinfected, dry, effete, empty, fallow, fruitless, futile, gaunt, germ-free, hygienic, impotent, infecund, infertile, pasteurized, sanitary, septic, sterilized, unfruitful, uninfected, unprofitable, unprolific, vain, waste, without issue; SEE CONCEPTS *485,621*

sterilize [v] *make clean or unproductive*
alter, antisepticize, asceptize, aseptify, autoclave, castrate, change, clean, decontaminate, desexualize, disinfect, emasculate, fix, fumigate, incapacitate, make sterile, neuter, pasteurize, purify, sanitize, spay; SEE CONCEPTS *231,250*

stern [adj] *serious, authoritarian*
ascetic, astringent, austere, bitter, bullheaded, by the book*, cruel, disciplinary, dyed-in-the-wool*, flinty, forbidding, frowning, grim, hang-tough*, hard, hard-boiled*, hard-core*, hardheaded*, hard-line*, hard-nosed*, hard-shell*, harsh, implacable, inexorable, inflexible, mortified, mulish, relentless, rigid, rigorous, rough, severe, steely, stiff-necked*, strict, stubborn, tough, unrelenting, unsparing, unyielding; SEE CONCEPTS *401,542*

stew [n1] *mixture, miscellany*
brew, goulash*, hash, jumble, medley, mélange, mishmash, mulligan*, olio*, pasticcio*, pie*, potpourri, salmagundi*, soup; SEE CONCEPTS *432,457,460,461*

stew [n2] *commotion; mental upset*
agitation, confusion, dither, flap, fretting, fuming, fuss, lather, pother, snit, sweat, tizzy, tumult, turbulence, turmoil, worry; SEE CONCEPT *410*

stew [v] *worry; steam*
boil, chafe, cook, fret, fume, fuss, pother, seethe, simmer; SEE CONCEPT *35*

stick [n] *pole, often wooden*
bar, bat, baton, billet, birch, bludgeon, board, branch, cane, club, cudgel, drumstick, ferrule, ingot, mast, rod, rule, ruler, shoot, slab, slat, staff, stake, stalk, stave, stem, strip, switch, timber, twig, wand, wedge; SEE CONCEPTS *470,479*

stick [v1] *adhere, affix*
attach, be bogged down, become embedded, become immobilized, bind, bond, braze, catch, cement, clasp, cleave, cling, cling like ivy*, clog, cohere, fasten, fix, freeze to, fuse, glue, hold, hold fast, hold on, hug, jam, join, linger, lodge, paste, persist, remain, snag, solder, stay, stay put, stick like barnacle*, stick together, unite, weld; SEE CONCEPTS *85,160*

stick [v2] *poke with pointed object*
dig, drive, gore, impale, insert, jab, penetrate, pierce, pin, plunge, prod, puncture, ram, run, sink, spear, stab, thrust, transfix; SEE CONCEPT *220*

stick [v3] *position, lay*
deposit, drop, establish, fix, install, place, plant, plonk, plunk, put, set, settle, store, stuff; SEE CONCEPT *201*

stick [v4] *endure*
abide, bear, bear up under, brook, get on with, go, grin and bear it*, last, persist, put up with, see through, stand, stay, stomach*, suffer, support, take, take it, tolerate, weather; SEE CONCEPT *23*

stick-in-the-mud [n] *person set in ways*
antediluvian, conservative, diehard*, fossil*, mossback*, old fogy*, reactionary; SEE CONCEPT *423*

stick out [v] *bulge*
beetle, come through, extend, extrude, jut, obtrude, outthrust, overhang, poke, pouch, pout, project, protend, protrude, push, show, stand out; SEE CONCEPT *751*

sticky [adj1] *gummy, adhesive*
agglutinative, clinging, gluey, glutinous, ropy, syrupy, tacky, tenacious, viscid, viscous; SEE CONCEPT *606*

sticky [adj2] *humid and hot*
clammy, close, dank, mucky, muggy, oppressive, soggy, sultry, sweltering; SEE CONCEPT *525*

sticky [adj3] *difficult, embarrassing*
awkward, delicate, discomforting, formidable, hairy*, hard, heavy*, knotty, laborious, nasty, operose, painful, rough, rugged, strenuous, thorny, tricky, unpleasant; SEE CONCEPT *565*

stiff [adj1] *hard, inflexible*
annealed, arthritic, benumbed, brittle, buckram, cemented, chilled, congealed, contracted, creaky, firm, fixed, frozen, graceless, hardened, immalleable, impliable, incompliant, indurate, inelastic, jelled, mechanical, numbed, ossified, petrified, refractory, resistant, rheumatic, rigid, set, solid, so-

lidified, starched, starchy, stark, steely, stiff as a board*, stony, taut, tense, thick, thickened, tight, unbending, unflexible, ungraceful, unsupple, unyielding, wooden; SEE CONCEPT 604

stiff [adj2] *formal, standoffish*
angular, artificial, austere, ceremonious, cold, constrained, forced, hardheaded, headstrong, inflexible, intractable, labored, mannered, obstinate, pertinacious, pompous, priggish, prim, punctilious, relentless, starchy, stilted, strong, stubborn, uneasy, ungainly, ungraceful, unnatural, unrelaxed, unrelenting, wooden; SEE CONCEPT 401

stiff [adj3] *difficult*
arduous, exacting, fatiguing, formidable, hard, laborious, tough, trying, uphill; SEE CONCEPT 565

stiff [adj4] *extreme, severe*
austere, brisk, cruel, drastic, exact, excessive, exorbitant, extravagant, great, hard, harsh, heavy, immoderate, inexorable, inordinate, oppressive, pitiless, potent, powerful, ruinous, sharp, steep, strict, stringent, strong, towering, unconscionable, undue, vigorous; SEE CONCEPTS 540,569

stiffen [v] *make or become harder*
anneal, benumb, brace, cake, candy, cement, chill, clot, coagulate, condense, congeal, crystallize, curdle, firm, fix, freeze, gel, harden, inflate, inspissate, jell, jelly, ossify, petrify, precipitate, prop, reinforce, set, solidify, stabilize, starch, steady, strengthen, tauten, tense, thicken; SEE CONCEPTS 137,250,469

stifle [v] *prevent, restrain*
asphyxiate, black out, bring to screeching halt*, burke, check, choke, choke back, clamp down*, clam up*, constipate, cork, cover up, crack down*, curb, dry up*, extinguish, gag, hold it down, hush, hush up, kill*, muffle, muzzle, prevent, put the lid on*, repress, restrain, shut up, silence, sit on*, smother, spike, squash, squelch, stagnate, stop, strangle, stultify, suffocate, suppress, torpedo*, trammel; SEE CONCEPTS 121,130,191

stigma [n] *shame*
bar sinister*, besmirchment, black mark*, blame, blemish, blot, brand, disfigurement, disgrace, dishonor, imputation, lost face*, mark, odium, onus, reproach, scar, slur, spot, stain, taint; SEE CONCEPTS 230,388,689

still [n] *quiet*
hush, noiselessness, peace, quietness, quietude, silence, soundlessness, still, stillness, tranquillity; SEE CONCEPTS 65,748

still [adj] *calm, motionless*
at rest, buttoned up*, clammed up*, closed, closemouthed, deathlike, deathly, deathly quiet, deathly still, fixed, halcyon, hushed, hushful, inert, lifeless, noiseless, pacific, peaceful, placid, restful, sealed, serene, silent, smooth, soundless, stable, stagnant, static, stationary, stock-still, tranquil, undisturbed, unruffled, unstirring, untroubled, whist; SEE CONCEPTS 584,594

still [v] *make quiet, motionless, calm*
allay, alleviate, appease, arrest, balm, becalm, calm, choke, compose, decrease volume, fix, gag, hush, lull, muffle, muzzle, pacify, quiet, quieten, settle, shush*, shut down, shut up, silence, slack, smooth, smooth over, soothe, squash, squelch, stall, stop, subdue, tranquilize; SEE CONCEPTS 7,22,65,121

still [conj] *however*
after all, besides, but, even, for all that, furthermore, howbeit, nevertheless, nonetheless, notwithstanding, still and all, though, withal, yet; SEE CONCEPT 544

stilted [adj] *artificial, pretentious*
affected, angular, aureate, bombastic, constrained, decorous, egotistic, euphuistic, flowery, forced, formal, genteel, grandiloquent, highflown, high-sounding, inflated, labored, magniloquent, mincing, overblown, pedantic, pompous, prim, rhetorical, sonorous, stiff, unnatural, wooden; SEE CONCEPTS 267,401

stimulant [n] *substance that invigorates*
analeptic, bracer, catalyst, drug, energizer, excitant, goad, impetus, impulse, incentive, incitation, incitement, motivation, motive, pick-me-up*, restorative, reviver, shot in the arm*, spark plug*, spur, stimulus, tonic, upper; SEE CONCEPTS 240,307,661

stimulate [v] *excite, provoke*
activate, animate, arouse, build a fire under*, commove, dynamize, elate, encourage, energize, enliven, exhilarate, fan, fire, fire up*, foment, foster, galvanize, get one going*, get one started*, goad, grab, hook, impel, incite, inflame, innervate, innerve, inspire, instigate, jazz*, juice*, key up*, motivate, move, perk, pique, prod, prompt, quicken, rouse, send, set up, spark, spirit, spur, steam up*, stir up*, support, trigger, turn on*, urge, vitalize, vivify, wake up*, whet, work up*; SEE CONCEPTS 14,242

stimulus [n] *provocation*
bang*, boost, catalyst, cause, charge, encouragement, eye-opener*, fillip, fireworks*, flash*, goad, impetus, impulse, incentive, incitation, incitement, inducement, instigation, invitation, kick*, motivation, motive, piquing, propellant, provocation, push, shot in the arm*, spur, stimulant, stimulation, sting*, turn-on*, urging; SEE CONCEPTS 240,307,661

sting [v] *prick, pain*
bite, burn, electrify, hurt, injure, inspire, needle, pique, poke, prickle, smart, tingle, wound; SEE CONCEPTS 220,246,313,728

stingy [adj] *penny-pinching, averse to spending money*
acquisitive, avaricious, chary, cheap, chintzy*, churlish, close, close-fisted, costive, covetous, curmudgeonly, economical, extortionate, frugal, grasping, greedy, grudging, ignoble, illiberal, ironfisted, mean, miserly, narrow, near, parsimonious, pennywise*, penurious, petty, pinchpenny*, rapacious, saving, scrimping, scurvy, selfish, skimping, sordid, sparing, thrifty, tightfisted, uncharitable, ungenerous, ungiving; SEE CONCEPTS 326,334,401

stink [n] *bad smell*
fetor, foulness, foul odor, malodor, noisomeness, offensive smell, stench; SEE CONCEPTS 599,600

stink [v1] *smell badly*
be offensive, be rotten, funk*, have an odor, offend, reek*, smell up, stink to high heaven*; SEE CONCEPT 600

stink [v2] *be lousy, bad*
be abhorrent, be detestable, be held in disrepute, be no good, be offensive, be rotten, have a bad name*, smell; SEE CONCEPTS 230,388

stint [n] *period of responsibility*
assignment, bit, chore, consignment, duty, job,

st
st

participation, quota, share, shift, spell, stretch, task, term, time, tour, turn, work; SEE CONCEPTS *362,807,822*

stint [v] *economize; hold back*
be frugal, begrudge, be parsimonious, be sparing, be stingy, confine, cut corners*, define, go easy on, grudge, limit, make ends meet*, penny-pinch*, pinch, restrain, roll back*, save, save for rainy day*, scrape, scrimp, skimp on*, sock away*, spare, squirrel*, stash, tighten belt*, withhold; SEE CONCEPT *330*

stipend [n] *payment for services*
allowance, award, consideration, emolument, fee, gratuity, hire, pay, pension, salary, take, wage; SEE CONCEPT *344*

stipulate [v] *decide on conditions*
agree, arrange, bargain, condition, contract, covenant, designate, detail, engage, guarantee, impose, insist upon, lay down, lay finger on, make, make a point, name, particularize, pin down, pledge, postulate, promise, provide, put down for, require, settle, slot, specificate, specificize, specify, spell out, state; SEE CONCEPTS *8,18,60*

stipulation [n] *condition of agreement*
agreement, arrangement, circumscription, clause, contract, designation, engagement, fine print*, limit, obligation, precondition, prerequisite, provision, proviso, qualification, requirement, reservation, restriction, settlement, sine qua non, small print*, specification, string attached*, term, terms; SEE CONCEPTS *270,318,684*

stir [n] *commotion, excitement*
activity, ado, agitation, backwash*, bustle, din, disorder, disquiet, disturbance, ferment, flap*, flurry, furor, fuss, movement, pandemonium, pother, racket, row, scene, to-do*, tumult, turmoil, uproar, whirl, whirlwind; SEE CONCEPTS *230,388*

stir [v1] *mix up, agitate*
beat, blend, disturb, flutter, mix, move, move about, quiver, rustle, shake, toss, tremble, whip, whisk; SEE CONCEPTS *158,170*

stir [v2] *incite, stimulate*
abet, actuate, add fuel to fire*, adjy*, affect, agitate, animate, arouse, awaken, bestir, challenge, craze, drive, electrify, energize, excite, feed the fire*, foment, galvanize, impel, inflame, inspire, kindle, make waves*, motivate, move, prompt, provoke, psych*, quicken, raise, rally, rile, rouse, roust, rout, set, spark, spook*, spur, stimulate, stir embers*, stir up, switch on, thrill, touch, trigger, urge, vitalize, wake, waken, whet, whip up*, work up*; SEE CONCEPTS *14,221*

stir [v3] *get up and going*
awake, awaken, bestir, be up and about, budge, exert, get a move on*, get moving, hasten, look alive, make an effort, mill about, move, rouse, shake a leg*, wake, waken; SEE CONCEPT *149*

stock [n1] *merchandise*
accumulation, array, articles, assets, assortment, backlog, cache, choice, commodities, fund, goods, hoard, inventory, nest egg*, produce, range, reserve, reservoir, selection, stockpile, store, supply, variety, wares; SEE CONCEPT *338*

stock [n2] *animals raised on a farm*
animals, beasts, cattle, cows, domestic, farm animals, flock, fowl, herd, hogs, horses, livestock, pigs, sheep, swine; SEE CONCEPTS *394,397*

stock [n3] *ancestry*
background, breed, clan, descent, extraction, family, folk, forebears, house, kin, kindred, line, lineage, line of descent, parentage, pedigree, race, species, strain, tribe, type, variety; SEE CONCEPTS *296,378*

stock [n4] *investment in company*
assets, blue chips, bonds, capital, convertible, funds, over-the-counter*, paper, property, share; SEE CONCEPT *332*

stock [n5] *estimation, faith*
appraisal, appraisement, assessment, confidence, count, dependence, estimate, evaluation, figure, hope, inventory, judgment, reliance, review, trust; SEE CONCEPTS *37,689,764*

stock [adj] *commonplace*
banal, basic, common, conventional, customary, dull, established, formal, hackneyed, normal, ordinary, overused, regular, routine, run-of-the-mill*, set, standard, staple, stereotyped, traditional, trite, typical, usual, worn-out; SEE CONCEPTS *530,547*

stock [v] *supply with merchandise*
accumulate, amass, carry, deal in, equip, fill, furnish, gather, handle, have, hoard, keep, keep on hand, lay in, provide, provision, put away, reserve, save, sell, stockpile, store, stow away, trade in; SEE CONCEPTS *140,182,324*

stocky [adj] *short and overweight; short and muscular*
chunky, corpulent, fat, heavyset, plump, solid, squat, stout, stubby, sturdy, thick, thickset; SEE CONCEPTS *491,773*

stodgy [adj] *dull, stuffy*
banausic, boring, dim, dreary, formal, heavy, labored, monotonous, pedantic, pedestrian, plodding, ponderous, staid, tedious, turgid, unexciting, unimaginative, uninspired, uninteresting, weighty; SEE CONCEPTS *401,404*

stoic/stoical [adj] *philosophic, calm*
aloof, apathetic, cool, cool as cucumber*, detached, dispassionate, dry, enduring, impassive, imperturbable, indifferent, indomitable, long-suffering, matter-of-fact, patient, phlegmatic, resigned, rolling with punches*, self-controlled, sober, stolid, unconcerned, unemotional, unflappable, unmoved; SEE CONCEPTS *401,404*

stolid [adj] *apathetic, stupid*
blunt, bovine, dense, doltish, dry, dull, dumb, heavy, impassive, inactive, indifferent, inert, lumpish, matter-of-fact, obtuse, passive, phlegmatic, slow, stoic, supine, unemotional, unexcitable, wooden; SEE CONCEPTS *401,402*

stomach [n1] *digestive organ of animate being; exterior abdominal region*
abdomen, belly, below the belt*, breadbasket*, gut, inside, insides, maw*, paunch, pot*, potbelly*, solar plexus, spare tire*, tummy*; SEE CONCEPTS *393,420*

stomach [n2] *appetite*
appetence, desire, inclination, mind, relish, taste, tooth; SEE CONCEPT *20*

stomach [v] *endure, tolerate*
abide, bear, bear with, bite the bullet*, brook, digest, grin and bear it*, live with*, put up with, reconcile oneself, resign oneself, stand, submit to, suffer, swallow, sweat, take, tolerate; SEE CONCEPT *23*

stone [n] *hard piece of earth's surface*
boulder, crag, crystal, gem, grain, gravel, jewel, metal, mineral, ore, pebble, rock; SEE CONCEPTS *474,477*

stony [adj] *hard, icy in appearance, response*
adamant, blank, callous, chilly, cold, cold-blooded, coldhearted, cruel, expressionless, firm, frigid, hard-boiled*, hardened, heartless, hostile, indifferent, inexorable, inflexible, merciless, obdurate, pitiless, rough, tough, uncompassionate, unfeeling, unforgiving, unrelenting, unresponsive, unsympathetic; SEE CONCEPTS *401,485*

stoop [n] *slouched posture*
droop, round shoulders, sag, slouch, slump; SEE CONCEPT *757*

stoop [v1] *bow down*
be bowed, bend, be servile, bow, cringe, crouch, descend, dip, duck, hunch, incline, kneel, lean, relax, sink, slant, squat; SEE CONCEPTS *181,201*

stoop [v2] *condescend; lower oneself to another*
accommodate, act beneath oneself, concede, debase oneself, deign, demean oneself, descend, favor, oblige, patronize, relax, resort, sink, thaw, unbend, vouchsafe; SEE CONCEPTS *35,384*

stop [n1] *end, halt; impediment*
bar, barricade, blank wall*, block, blockade, break, break off, brick wall*, cease, cessation, check, close, closing, conclusion, control, cutoff, desistance, discontinuation, ending, fence, finish, freeze*, grinding halt*, hindrance, layoff, letup, lull, pause, plug, roadblock*, screeching halt*, standstill, stay, stoppage, termination, wall; SEE CONCEPTS *240,832*

stop [n2] *visit; place of rest*
break, depot, destination, halt, rest, sojourn, stage, station, stay, stopover, termination, terminus; SEE CONCEPTS *198,227*

stop [v1] *bring or come to a halt or end*
be over, blow off*, break, break off, call it a day*, cease, close, cold turkey*, come to a standstill*, conclude, cool it*, cut off*, cut short, desist, discontinue, draw up, drop, end, finish, halt, hang it up*, hold, kill, pause, pull up, put an end to, quit, quit cold*, refrain, run its course*, scrub*, shut down, sign off*, stall, stand, stay, tarry, terminate, wind up*, wrap up*; SEE CONCEPTS *119,234,237*

stop [v2] *prevent, hold back*
arrest, avoid, bar, block, bottle, break, check, choke, choke off, clog, close, congest, cut off, disrupt, fill, fix, forestall, frustrate, gag, hinder, hush, impede, intercept, interrupt, muzzle, obstruct, occlude, plug, put a stop to, rein in, repress, restrain, seal, shut down, shut off, shut out, silence, stall, staunch, stay, stem, still, stopper, suspend, throw over, turn off, ward off; SEE CONCEPT *121*

stopgap [n] *temporary help*
Band-Aid*, expediency, expedient, improvisation, makeshift, pis aller*, recourse, refuge, resort, resource, shift, substitute, temporary expedient; SEE CONCEPT *712*

stopgap [adj] *temporarily helping*
Band-Aid*, emergency, expedient, impromptu, improvised, makeshift, practical, provisional, rough-and-ready*, rough-and-tumble*, substitute, temp, temporary, throwaway*; SEE CONCEPTS *551,560*

stoppage [n] *halt, curtailment*
abeyance, arrest, blockage, check, close, closure, cutoff, deduction, discontinuance, down, downtime*, hindrance, interruption, layoff, lockout, obstruction, occlusion, shutdown, sit-down, standstill, stopping, walkout; SEE CONCEPT *832*

store [n1] *collection, supply*
abundance, accumulation, backlog, cache, fount, fountain, fund, hoard, inventory, lode, lot, mine, nest egg*, plenty, plethora, provision, quantity, reserve, reservoir, savings, spring, stock, stockpile, treasure, wares, wealth, well; SEE CONCEPTS *432,710*

store [n2] *place for keeping supply*
arsenal, bank, barn, box, cache, conservatory, depository, depot, magazine, pantry, repository, reservoir, stable, storehouse, storeroom, tank, treasury, vault, warehouse; SEE CONCEPTS *439,441,448,494*

store [n3] *business establishment that sells goods*
boutique, chain store, convenience store, deli, department store, discount house, discount store, drugstore, emporium, five-and-dime*, five-and-ten*, grocery store, market, mart, outlet, repository, shop, shopping center, showroom, specialty shop, stand, storehouse, super*, superette*, supermarket; SEE CONCEPTS *325,439,448,449*

store [v] *collect and put aside*
accumulate, amass, bank, bin, bottle, bury, cache, can, cumulate, deposit, freeze, garner, hide, hive, hoard, hutch, keep, keep in reserve, lay away, lay up*, lock away, lock up, mothball*, pack, pack away, park, plant, put, put away, put by, put in storage, reserve, roll up, salt away*, save, save for rainy day*, sock away*, squirrel*, stash, stock, stockpile, treasure, victual, warehouse; SEE CONCEPTS *109,129*

storm [n1] *strong weather*
blast, blizzard, blow, cloudburst, cyclone, disturbance, downpour, gale, gust, hurricane, monsoon, precip*, precipitation, raining cats and dogs*, snowstorm, squall, tempest, tornado, twister, whirlwind, windstorm; SEE CONCEPT *526*

storm [n2] *commotion, turmoil*
agitation, anger, annoyance, assault, attack, barrage, blitz, blitzkrieg, bluster, bomb, bombardment, broadside, burst, bustle, cannonade, clamor, clatter, convulsion, disturbance, drumfire, furor, fury, fusillade, hail, hassle, hysteria, offensive, onset, onslaught, outbreak, outburst, outcry, passion, perturbation, pother, rabidity, racket, rage, rampancy, roar, row, ruction, rumpus, rush, salvo, squall, stir, strife, temper, tumult, upheaval, violence, volley; SEE CONCEPTS *86,230,674*

storm [v] *attack, rush*
aggress, assail, assault, beset, blow violently, bluster, breathe fire*, burn up, carry on*, charge, come at*, complain, drizzle, drop, fly, fume, go on, howl, pour, rage, rain, rant, rave, rip, roar, scold, set in, sizzle, sound off, spit, squall, stalk, steam up*, stomp, strike, take by storm*, take on*, tear, thunder*; SEE CONCEPTS *52,86,150,526*

stormy [adj] *rough (referring to weather)*
bitter, blowy, blustering, blustery, boisterous, cold, coming down*, damp, dirty, foul, frigid, furious, gusty, howling, menacing, murky, pouring, raging, raining cats and dogs*, rainy, riproaring*, roaring, savage, squally, stormful, storming, tempestuous, threatening, torrid, turbulent, violent, wet, wild, windy; SEE CONCEPT *525*

story [n1] *account, news*
adventure, allegory, anecdote, apologue, article, autobiography, beat, biography, book, chronicle, cliffhanger*, comedy, conte, description, drama,

epic, fable, fairy tale, fantasy, feature, fiction, folktale, gag, history, information, legend, long and short of it*, memoir, myth, narration, narrative, news item, nonfiction, novel, old saw*, parable, potboiler*, recital, record, relation, report, romance, saga, scoop*, sequel, serial, spiel*, tale, tragedy, version, yarn*; SEE CONCEPTS *270,274,282*

story [*n2*] *lie*
canard, cock-and-bull story*, fabrication, falsehood, falsity, fib, fiction, misrepresentation, prevarication, tale, untruism, untruth, white lie*; SEE CONCEPTS *278,282*

stout [*adj1*] *overweight*
big, bulky, burly, corpulent, fat, fleshy, heavy, obese, plenitudinous, plump, porcine, portly, rotund, substantial, thick-bodied, tubby, upholstered, weighty, zaftig*; SEE CONCEPTS *491,773*

stout [*adj2*] *strong, brawny*
able-bodied, athletic, hard, hardy, hulking, husky, indomitable, invincible, lusty, muscular, robust, stable, stalwart, staunch, strapping, sturdy, substantial, tenacious, tough, vigorous; SEE CONCEPTS *489,490*

stout [*adj3*] *courageous*
bold, brave, dauntless, fearless, gallant, heroic, intrepid, lionhearted, plucky, resolute, stalwart, undaunted, valiant, valorous; SEE CONCEPTS *403,542*

stow [*v*] *reserve, store*
bundle, deposit, load, pack, pack like sardines*, put away, secrete, stash, stuff, top off, tuck, warehouse*; SEE CONCEPT *209*

straggle [*v*] *wander, stray*
be late, dawdle, drift, lag, loiter, maunder, meander, poke, poke around, ramble, range, roam, rove, scramble, spread, straddle, string out, tail, trail; SEE CONCEPT *151*

straight [*adj1*] *aligned; not curved*
beeline*, collinear, consecutive, continuous, direct, erect, even, horizontal, in a line, in a row, inflexible, in line, invariable, level, like an arrow*, lineal, linear, near, nonstop, perpendicular, plumb, precipitous, frank, rectilineal, rectilinear, right, running, sheer, short, smooth, solid, square, straightforward, successive, through, true, unbent, unbroken, uncurled, undeviating, undistorted, uninterrupted, unrelieved, unswerving, upright, vertical; SEE CONCEPTS *482,486,581*

straight [*adj2*] *honest, fair*
aboveboard, accurate, authentic, bald, blunt, candid, categorical, decent, equitable, fair and square*, forthright, frank, good, honorable, just, law-abiding, moral, outright, plain, point-blank*, reliable, respectable, straightforward, summary, trustworthy, unqualified, upright; SEE CONCEPTS *267,542*

straight [*adj3*] *orderly*
arranged, correct, exact, in order, neat, organized, put to rights, right, shipshape*, sorted, tidy; SEE CONCEPTS *535,585*

straight [*adj4*] *unmixed*
concentrated, neat, out-and-out*, plain, pure, strong, thoroughgoing, unadulterated, undiluted, unmodified, unqualified; SEE CONCEPTS *462,621*

straight [*adj5*] *conventional, square*
bourgeois, buttoned-down*, conservative, orthodox, traditional; SEE CONCEPT *404*

straight [*adv1*] *immediately, directly*
as the crow flies*, at once, away, dead*, direct,

due, exactly, first off, forthwith, in direct line, instanter, instantly, lineally, now, point-blank*, right, right away, straightaway, straightforwardly, straightly, undeviatingly; SEE CONCEPTS *581,820*

straight [*adv2*] *honestly*
candidly, frankly, in plain English*, no holds barred*, no punches*, point-blank*; SEE CONCEPTS *267,544*

straighten [*v*] *put in neat or aligned order*
align, arrange, compose, correct, even, level, make plumb, make straight, neaten, order, put in order, put perpendicular, put straight, put to rights, put upright, put vertical, rectify, set to rights, smarten up*, spruce up*, tidy, unbend, uncoil, uncurl, unfold, unravel, unsnarl, untwist; SEE CONCEPTS *158,202,231*

straightforward [*adj1*] *honest*
aboveboard, barefaced*, candid, direct, forthright, frank, genuine, guileless, honorable, just, laid on the line*, level, like it is*, mellow*, open, outspoken, plain, plain-dealing*, pretenseless, right-on*, sincere, square-shooting*, straight, straight-arrow*, talking turkey*, truthful, unconcealed, undisguised, undissembled, undissembling, unequivocal, unvarnished, up front*, upright, upstanding, veracious; SEE CONCEPT *267*

straightforward [*adj2*] *simple, easy*
apparent, clear, clear-cut, direct, distinct, elementary, evident, manifest, palpable, patent, plain, routine, straight, through, unambiguous, uncomplicated, undemanding, unequivocal, uninterrupted; SEE CONCEPTS *535,538*

strain [*n1*] *pain, due to exertion*
ache, anxiety, bruise, brunt, burden, constriction, effort, endeavor, exertion, force, injury, jerk, pressure, pull, sprain, stress, stretch, struggle, tautness, tension, tensity, twist, wrench; SEE CONCEPT *728*

strain [*n2*] *ancestry*
blood, breed, descent, extraction, family, lineage, pedigree, race, species, stock; SEE CONCEPTS *296,380*

strain [*n3*] *suggestion, hint*
humor, manner, mind, shade, soupçon, spirit, streak, style, suspicion, temper, tendency, tinge, tone, touch, trace, trait, vein, way; SEE CONCEPTS *410,529,682*

strain [*n4*] *melody*
air, descant, diapason, lay, measure, song, tune, warble; SEE CONCEPTS *262,595*

strain [*v1*] *stretch, often to limit*
constrict, distend, distort, draw tight, drive, exert, extend, fatigue, injure, overexert, overtax, overwork, pull, push, push to the limit, rack, sprain, task, tauten, tax, tear, tighten, tire, twist, weaken, wrench; SEE CONCEPTS *156,206,208,313*

strain [*v2*] *work very hard*
bear down, endeavor, exert, go all out*, go for broke*, grind, hammer, hustle, labor, moil, peg away*, tug, push, strive, struggle, sweat, toil, try; SEE CONCEPT *87*

strain [*v3*] *filter*
exude, percolate, purify, refine, riddle, screen, seep, separate, sieve, sift; SEE CONCEPTS *135,202*

strain [*v4*] *cause mental stress*
distress, harass, hassle, irk, pain, pick at, push, stress, trouble, try; SEE CONCEPTS *7,19*

strained [*adj*] *forced, pretended*
artificial, at end of rope*, awkward, choked, constrained, difficult, embarrassed, false, farfetched,

hard put*, in a state*, labored, nervous wreck*, put, self-conscious, stiff, strung out*, taut, tense, tight, uncomfortable, uneasy, unglued, unnatural, unrelaxed, uptight, wired*, wreck*; SEE CONCEPTS 267,401

strait [n1] *crisis, difficulty*
bewilderment, bind, bottleneck*, choke point*, contingency, crossroad, dilemma, distress, embarrassment, emergency, exigency, extremity, hardship, hole*, mess*, mystification, pass, perplexity, pinch*, plight, predicament, rigor, squeeze*, turning point*, vicissitude, zero hour*; SEE CONCEPT 674

strait [n2] *water channel*
inlet, narrows, sound; SEE CONCEPT 514

strand [n] *fine thread*
fiber, filament, length, lock, rope, string, tress; SEE CONCEPTS 392,452,475

stranded [adj] *marooned, abandoned*
aground, ashore, beached, cast away, godforsaken*, grounded, helpless, high and dry*, homeless, left at the altar*, left in the lurch*, on the rocks*, out in left field*, passed up, penniless, run aground, shipwrecked, sidelined, sidetracked*, wrecked; SEE CONCEPT 577

strange [adj1] *deviating, unfamiliar*
aberrant, abnormal, astonishing, astounding, atypical, bizarre, curious, different, eccentric, erratic, exceptional, extraordinary, fantastic, far-out*, funny, idiosyncratic, ignorant, inexperienced, irregular, marvelous, mystifying, new, newfangled*, odd, oddball*, off, offbeat*, outlandish, out-of-the-way*, peculiar, perplexing, quaint, queer, rare, remarkable, singular, unaccountable, unaccustomed, uncanny, uncommon, unheard of, unseasoned, unusual, weird, wonderful; SEE CONCEPT 564

strange [adj2] *exotic, foreign*
alien, apart, awkward, detached, external, faraway, irrelevant, isolated, lost, new, novel, out of place, outside, remote, romanesque, romantic, unexplored, unfamiliar, unknown, unrelated, untried; SEE CONCEPTS 549,576

stranger [n] *person who is unfamiliar*
alien, drifter, foreign body, foreigner, guest, immigrant, incomer, interloper, intruder, itinerant person, migrant, migratory worker, new arrival, newcomer, outcomer, outlander, out-of-stater*, outsider, party crasher*, perfect stranger*, squatter*, transient, uninvited person, unknown, unknown person, visitor, wanderer; SEE CONCEPTS 413,423

strangle [v] *choke, stifle*
asphyxiate, gag, garrote/garrotte, inhibit, kill, muffle, quelch, repress, restrain, shush, smother, squelch, strangulate, subdue, suffocate, suppress, throttle; SEE CONCEPTS 130,191,252

strap [n] *long piece of material*
band, belt, harness, leash, strop, switch, thong, tie, whip; SEE CONCEPTS 471,475

strapped [adj] *destitute*
beggared, broke*, dirt poor*, flat*, fortuneless, impoverished, out of money, penniless, penurious, poor, stone-broke*; SEE CONCEPT 334

strapping [adj] *big and strong*
brawny, burly, hefty, hulk, hulking, hunk, husky, ox, powerful, powerhouse, robust, stalwart, stout, sturdy, tall, vigorous, well-built; SEE CONCEPTS 489,773

stratagem [n] *trick*
action, angle, artifice, bit*, booby trap*, brainchild*, con, deception, device, dodge, feint, gambit, game, game plan*, gimmick, grift, intrigue, layout, maneuver, method, pitch, plan, play, plot, ploy, pretext, proposition, racket, ruse, scenario, scene, scheme, setup, shift, slant, stall, story, subterfuge, switch, twist, wile; SEE CONCEPTS 59,660

strategic [adj1] *crucial*
cardinal, critical, decisive, imperative, important, key, necessary, vital; SEE CONCEPTS 546,567

strategic [adj2] *clever, calculated*
cunning, deliberate, diplomatic, dishonest, planned, politic, tricky; SEE CONCEPT 544

strategy [n] *plan of action*
action, angle, approach, artifice, blueprint*, brainchild*, craft, cunning, design, game, game plan*, gimmick, grand design, layout, maneuvering, method, plan, planning, policy, procedure, program, project, proposition, racket*, scenario, scene, scheme, setup, slant, story, subtlety, system, tactics; SEE CONCEPT 660

stray [adj] *abandoned, wandering*
devious, erratic, homeless, lost, roaming, roving, vagrant; SEE CONCEPT 583

stray [v1] *deviate, err*
circumlocute, depart, digress, divagate, diverge, do wrong, excurse, get off the subject*, get off the track*, get sidetracked*, go off on a tangent*, ramble, sin, wander; SEE CONCEPTS 101,266

stray [v2] *wander; get lost*
be abandoned, be lost, deviate, drift, err, gad*, gallivant, go all over the map*, go amiss, go astray, lose one's way, meander, ramble, range, roam, rove, straggle, swerve, traipse, turn, wander away, wander off; SEE CONCEPT 149

streak [n] *vein, line; small part*
band, bar, beam, dash, element, hint, intimation, layer, ray, ridge, rule, shade, slash, smear, strain, stream, strip, stripe, stroke, suggestion, suspicion, touch, trace; SEE CONCEPTS 436,628,657,727

streak [v] *make a line on*
band, dapple, daub, fleck, marble, slash, smear, spot, strake, striate, stripe, variegate, vein; SEE CONCEPT 250

stream [n] *small river*
beck, branch, brook, burn, course, creek, current, drift, flood, flow, freshet, race, rill, rindle, rivulet, run, runnel, rush, spate, spritz, surge, tide, torrent, tributary, watercourse; SEE CONCEPT 514

stream [v] *flow from*
cascade, continue, course, emerge, emit, flood, glide, gush, issue, move past, pour, roll, run, shed, sluice, spill, spout, spritz, spurt, surge; SEE CONCEPTS 146,179

street [n] *path upon which travel occurs*
artery, avenue, back alley*, boulevard, byway, court, dead end*, drag*, drive, highway, lane, parkway, passage, pavement, place, road, roadway, route, row, stroll, terrace, thoroughfare, track, trail, turf*, way; SEE CONCEPT 501

strength [n1] *stamina, mental or physical*
backbone, body, brawn, brawniness, brute force*, clout, courage, durability, energy, firmness, force, fortitude, hardiness, health, healthiness, lustiness, might, muscle, nerve, physique, pith, potency, pow*, power, powerhouse*, robustness, security, sinew, sock*, soundness, stability, stableness, stalwartness, steadiness, steamroller,

st
st

stoutness, strong arm*, sturdiness, substance, tenacity, toughness, verdure, vigor, vim, vitality, zip*; SEE CONCEPTS *410,732*

strength [n2] *intensity*
clout, cogency, concentration, depth, effectiveness, efficacy, energy, extremity, fervor, force, juice*, kick*, potency, power, resolution, spirit, vehemence, vigor, virtue; SEE CONCEPT *669*

strength [n3] *advantage, substance*
anchor, asset, body, burden, connection, core, gist, guts, in, intestinal fortitude, license, mainstay, meat, pith, purport, security, sense, strong point, succor, upper hand, weight, wire; SEE CONCEPTS *682,693*

strengthen [v1] *make more forceful, powerful*
add, add fuel to fire*, anneal, ascend, bolster, brace, build up, buttress, confirm, corroborate, empower, enhance, enlarge, establish, extend, fortify, harden, heighten, increase, intensify, invigorate, justify, make firm, mount, multiply, regenerate, reinforce, rejuvenate, renew, restore, rise, set up, sinew*, steel, step up, substantiate, support, sustain, temper, tone, tone up, toughen, wax*; SEE CONCEPTS *244,250*

strengthen [v2] *encourage, hearten*
animate, back, back up, bear out, bloom, brace, brace up, burgeon, carry weight, cheer, consolidate, embolden, enhearten, enliven, flourish, flower, fortify, gather resources, gird, give weight, harden, inspirit, invigorate, nerve, nourish, prepare, prosper, rally, ready, refresh, rejuvenate, restore, steel, substantiate, temper, thrive, toughen, uphold; SEE CONCEPTS *7,22,35*

strenuous [adj1] *difficult; requiring hard work*
arduous, demanding, effortful, energy-consuming, exhausting, hard, Herculean, laborious, mean, operose, taxing, toilful, toilsome, tough, tough going*, uphill*, wicked; SEE CONCEPT *538*

strenuous [adj2] *energetic, zealous*
active, aggressive, ardent, bold, determined, dynamic, eager, earnest, lusty, persistent, red-blooded, resolute, spirited, strong, tireless, vigorous, vital; SEE CONCEPTS *401,542*

stress [n1] *emphasis*
accent, accentuation, beat, force, import, importance, significance, urgency, weight; SEE CONCEPTS *65,668*

stress [n2] *physical or mental pressure*
affliction, agony, alarm, albatross*, anxiety, apprehensiveness, burden, clutch, crunch, disquiet, disquietude, distention, draw, dread, expectancy, extension, fear, fearfulness, ferment, flutter, force, hardship, hassle, heat, impatience, intensity, misgiving, mistrust, nervousness, nervous tension, oppression, overextension, passion, protraction, pull, restlessness, spring, strain, stretch, tautness, tenseness, tension, tensity, tightness, traction, trauma, trepidation, trial, urgency, worry; SEE CONCEPTS *410,720,728*

stress [v1] *accentuate, emphasize*
accent, belabor, dwell on, feature, harp on*, headline*, italicize*, lay emphasis on, make emphatic, play up, point up, repeat, rub in*, spot, spotlight*, underline*, underscore*; SEE CONCEPTS *49,68*

stress [v2] *put under physical or mental pressure*
afflict, burden, crunch, distend, force, fret, hassle, overdo, overextend, pull, put in traction*, put on trial*, spring, strain, stretch, tense, tense up*, traumatize, worry; SEE CONCEPTS *7,19,246,313*

stretch [n1] *expanse*
amplitude, area, branch, breadth, bridge, compass, dimension, distance, expansion, extension, extent, gamut, length, orbit, proliferation, purview, radius, range, reach, region, scope, space, span, spread, sweep, tract, wing; SEE CONCEPTS *651,721,746*

stretch [n2] *period of time*
bit, continuance, duration, extent, length, run, space, span, spell, stint, term, time, while; SEE CONCEPTS *807,822*

stretch [v] *extend, elongate*
amplify, branch out, bridge, burst forth, cover, crane, develop, distend, drag out, draw, draw out, expand, fill, go, grow, inflate, lengthen, lie out, magnify, make, make taut, make tense, open, overlap, pad, prolong, prolongate, protract, pull, pull out, pyramid, rack, range, reach, recline, repose, run, shoot up, span, spin out, spread, spread out, spring up, strain, string out, swell, tauten, tighten, unfold, unroll, widen; SEE CONCEPTS *137,250*

strict [adj1] *authoritarian*
austere, dead set*, disciplinary, dour, draconian*, exacting, firm, forbidding, grim, hard, hard-boiled*, harsh, iron-fisted*, no-nonsense*, oppressive, picky, prudish, punctilious, puritanical, rigid, rigorous, scrupulous, set, severe, square, stern, stickling, straight, strait-laced*, stringent, stuffy*, tough, unpermissive, unsparing, uptight*; SEE CONCEPTS *401,542*

strict [adj2] *accurate, absolute*
close, complete, exact, faithful, just, meticulous, particular, perfect, precise, religious, right, scrupulous, total, true, undistorted, utter, veracious, veridical; SEE CONCEPTS *535,557*

stride [v] *walk purposefully*
clump, drill, march, pace, parade, pound, stalk, stamp, stomp, striddle, stump, traipse, tramp, tromp; SEE CONCEPT *149*

strident [adj] *harsh, shrill*
blatant, boisterous, clamorous, clashing, discordant, grating, hoarse, jangling, jarring, loud, noisy, obstreperous, rasping, raucous, screeching, squawky, squeaky, stentorian, stertorous, stridulant, stridulous, unmusical, vociferant, vociferous; SEE CONCEPTS *592,594*

strife [n] *struggle, battle*
affray, altercation, animosity, argument, bickering, blowup, brawl, clash, combat, competition, conflict, contention, contest, controversy, difference, disagreement, discord, dispute, dissension, dissent, dissidence, disunity, emulation, faction, factionalism, fighting, friction, fuss, hassle, quarrel, rivalry, spat, squabble, squabbling, static, striving, tug of war*, variance, warfare, words*, wrangle, wrangling; SEE CONCEPTS *46,106,674*

strike [v1] *hit hard*
bang, bash, beat, boff, bonk, box, buffet, bump into, chastise, clash, clobber, clout, collide, conk*, crash, cuff*, drive, force, hammer, impel, knock, percuss, plant*, pop*, pound, pummel, punch, punish, run into, slap, slug, smack, smash into, sock, swat, thrust, thump, touch, wallop, whop*; SEE CONCEPT *189*

strike [v2] *make an impact*
affect, be plausible, carry, come to mind*, dawn on*, get*, have semblance, hit*, impress, influ-

ence, inspire, look, move, occur to, reach, register*, seem, sway, touch; SEE CONCEPTS 7,19,22,716

strike [v3] *find, discover*
achieve, arrive at, attain, catch, chance upon*, come across, come upon, dig up*, effect, encounter, happen upon*, hit upon*, lay bare*, light upon, open up, reach, seize, stumble across*, take, turn up*, uncover, unearth; SEE CONCEPTS 120,183

strike [v4] *devastate, affect*
afflict, aggress, assail, assault, attack, beset, deal a blow, excruciate, fall upon, harrow, hit, invade, martyr, rack, set upon, smite, storm, torment, torture, try, wring; SEE CONCEPTS 7,19

strike [v5] *walk out of job in protest*
arbitrate, be on strike, boycott, go on strike, hit the bricks*, hold out, mediate, mutiny, negotiate, picket, quit, refuse to work, resist, revolt, sit down*, sit in*, slow down, stick out, stop, tie up; SEE CONCEPT 351

strike out [v] *leave to begin new venture*
bear, begin, get under way*, head, initiate, light out*, make, set out, start, start out, take off*; SEE CONCEPT 195

striking [adj] *extraordinary; beautiful*
arresting, arrestive, astonishing, attractive, bizarre, charming, cogent, commanding, compelling, confounding, conspicuous, dazzling, distinguished, dynamite, electrifying, eye-catching, fascinating, forceful, forcible, handsome, impressive, jazzy*, lofty, marked, memorable, noteworthy, noticeable, out of the ordinary*, outstanding, powerful, prominent, remarkable, salient, showy, signal, singular, staggering, startling, stunning, surprising, telling, unusual, wonderful, wondrous; SEE CONCEPTS 574,579

string [n1] *long fiber*
cord, rope, strand, twine, twist; SEE CONCEPT 475

string [n2] *succession, series*
chain, consecution, echelon, file, line, order, procession, queue, rank, row, sequel, sequence, strand, tier, train; SEE CONCEPTS 727,769

string along [v] *play with; keep dangling*
bluff, coquet, dally, deceive, dupe, flirt, fool, hoax, lead on*, put one over on*, take for a ride*, toy, trifle, wanton; SEE CONCEPT 59

stringent [adj] *rigid, tight*
acrimonious, binding, brick-wall*, by the book*, by the numbers*, compelling, confining, convincing, dead set on*, demanding, draconian, drawing, dyed-in-the-wool*, exacting, forceful, hard, hard-nosed*, harsh, inflexible, ironclad, iron-fisted, picky, poignant, powerful, rigorous, rough, set, severe, stiff, strict, tough, unpermissive, valid; SEE CONCEPTS 401,535,569

stringy [adj] *long, thin*
fibrous, gangling, gristly, lank, lanky, muscular, reedy, ropy, sinewy, spindling, spindly, threadlike, tough, wiry; SEE CONCEPT 490

strip [n] *thin piece of material*
band, banding, bar, belt, billet, bit, fillet, ingot, layer, ribbon, rod, section, segment, shred, slab, slip, stick, stripe, swathe, tape, tongue; SEE CONCEPTS 471,834

strip [v] *bare, uncover*
decorticate, denude, deprive, despoil, dismantle, displace, disrobe, divest, empty, excorticate, expose, gut, hull, husk, lay bare, lift, peel, pillage,

plunder, ransack, ravage, remove, rob, scale, shave, shed, shuck, skin, slip out of, spoil, take off, tear, unclothe, undress, withdraw; SEE CONCEPT 211

stripe [n] *line, strip*
band, banding, bar, border, decoration, division, fillet, layer, ribbon, rule, streak, striation, stroke; SEE CONCEPTS 284,622

strive [v] *try for, exert oneself*
aim, assay, attempt, bear down, bend over backward*, break one's neck*, compete, contend, do one's best*, do one's utmost*, drive, endeavor, essay, fight, go after, go all out*, go for broke*, go for the jugular*, go the limit*, hassle, jockey*, knock oneself out*, labor, leave no stone unturned*, make every effort, moil, offer, push, scramble, seek, shoot for*, strain, struggle, sweat, tackle, take on, toil, try hard, tug*, work; SEE CONCEPT 87

stroke [n1] *accomplishment*
achievement, blow*, feat, flourish, hit*, move, movement; SEE CONCEPT 706

stroke [n2] *seizure*
apoplexy, attack, collapse, convulsion, fit, shock; SEE CONCEPTS 33,308

stroke [v] *pat lengthwise*
brush, caress, chuck, comfort, fondle, pet, rub, smooth, soothe, tickle; SEE CONCEPT 612

stroll [n] *lazy walk*
airing, breath of fresh air*, constitutional, cruise, excursion, promenade, ramble, saunter, turn; SEE CONCEPT 151

stroll [v] *walk along lazily*
amble, cruise, drift, gallivant, linger, make one's way*, mope, mosey*, promenade, ramble, roam, rove, sashay*, saunter, toddle, traipse, tramp, wander; SEE CONCEPT 151

strong [adj1] *healthy, powerful*
able, able-bodied, active, athletic, big, capable, durable, enduring, energetic, firm, fixed, forceful, forcible, hale, hard as nails*, hardy, hearty, heavy, heavy-duty*, in fine feather*, mighty, muscular, reinforced, robust, rugged, secure, sinewy, solid, sound, stable, stalwart, stark, staunch, steady, stout, strapping, sturdy, substantial, tenacious, tough, unyielding, vigorous, well-built, well-founded, well-made; SEE CONCEPTS 314,489,540

strong [adj2] *determined, resolute*
aggressive, brave, clear, cogent, courageous, dedicated, deep, eager, fervent, fervid, fierce, firm, forceful, gutsy*, handful*, hard-nosed*, independent, intelligent, intense, iron-willed, keen, mean, perceptive, plucky, potent, pushy, resilient, resourceful, sagacious, self-assertive, severe, staunch, steadfast, take charge*, tenacious, tough, unbending, uncompromising, unyielding, vehement, violent, wicked*, zealous; SEE CONCEPTS 403,542

strong [adj3] *distinct, unmistakable*
clear, clear-cut, cogent, compelling, convincing, effective, fast, firm, forceful, formidable, great, hard, influential, marked, mighty, overpowering, persuasive, potent, powerful, redoubtable, secure, sharp, sound, stiff, stimulating, telling, trenchant, urgent, weighty, well-established, well-founded; SEE CONCEPTS 535,537

strong [adj4] *extreme*
acute, draconian, drastic, forceful, intense, keen, severe, sharp, strict; SEE CONCEPT 569

st
st

strong [*adj5*] *forceful on the senses*
biting, bold, bright, brilliant, concentrated, dazzling, effective, fetid, full-bodied, glaring, hard, heady, high, highly flavored, highly seasoned, hot, inebriating, intoxicating, loud, malodorous, noisome, piquant, potent, powerful, pungent, pure, rancid, rank, rich, robust, sharp, spicy, stark, stimulating, stinking, straight, strong-flavored, undiluted, unmixed; SEE CONCEPTS *462,598,618*

stronghold [*n*] *refuge*
bastion, bulwark, castle, citadel, fastness, fort, fortification, fortress, garrison, keep, presidio, redoubt; SEE CONCEPTS *439,712*

structure [*n1*] *makeup, form*
anatomy, architecture, arrangement, build, complex, configuration, conformation, construction, design, fabric, fabrication, format, formation, frame, framework, interrelation, make, morphology, network, order, organization, skeleton, system, texture; SEE CONCEPT *733*

structure [*n2*] *building*
cage, construction, edifice, erection, fabric, house, pile, pile of bricks*, rockpile, skyscraper; SEE CONCEPT *439*

struggle [*n*] *hard try; fight to win*
attempt, battle, brush, clash, combat, conflict, contest, effort, encounter, endeavor, essay, exertion, free-for-all*, grind, hassle, jam, jump, labor, long haul*, pains*, roughhouse*, row, scramble, set-to*, skirmish, strife, striving, toil, trial, tussle, undertaking, work, wrangle; SEE CONCEPTS *87,106,674*

struggle [*v1*] *labor, work*
assay, attempt, bend over backwards*, break one's back*, break one's neck*, cope, dig, endeavor, exert oneself, give it one's best shot*, give the old college try*, go all out*, grind, hassle, have one's nose to grindstone*, hustle, make every effort*, offer, plug, plug away*, scratch, seek, slave, strain, strive, sweat, tackle, take a crack*, take a stab*, take on, toil, try, try one's hardest*, undertake, work like a dog*; SEE CONCEPT *87*

struggle [*v2*] *fight, wrestle*
battle, brawl, buck, bump heads*, compete, contend, contest, cross swords*, go up against*, grapple, hassle, lock horns*, put up a fight*, romp, rough-house*, row, scrap, scuffle, shuffle, slug, smack, tangle; SEE CONCEPT *106*

strut [*v*] *walk pompously*
flaunt, flounce, grandstand*, mince, parade, peacock*, play to audience, prance, put on airs*, sashay*, show off, stalk, stride, swagger, swank, sweep; SEE CONCEPTS *149,261*

stub [*n*] *stumpy end*
butt, counterfoil, dock, remainder, remnant, root, short end*, snag, stump, tag, tail, tail end*; SEE CONCEPTS *825,827*

stubborn [*adj*] *obstinate, unyielding*
adamant, balky, bullheaded, cantankerous, contumacious, cussed*, determined, dogged, firm, fixed, hardheaded, headstrong, inexorable, inflexible, insubordinate, intractable, mulish, obdurate, opinionated, ornery*, persevering, persistent, pertinacious, perverse, pigheaded*, rebellious, recalcitrant, refractory, relentless, rigid, self-willed, set in one's ways*, single-minded, steadfast, stiffnecked*, tenacious, tough, unbending, unman-

ageable, unreasonable, unshakable, untoward, willful; SEE CONCEPTS *401,404*

stubby [*adj*] *short and thick*
fat, heavyset, squat, stocky, stout, stumpy, thick-bodied, thickset; SEE CONCEPTS *491,773,779*

student [*n*] *person actively learning*
apprentice, disciple, docent, first-year student, grad, graduate, junior, learner, novice, observer, pupil, registrant, scholar, schoolchild, skill, sophomore, undergrad*, undergraduate; SEE CONCEPT *350*

studied [*adj*] *intentional*
advised, affected, aforethought, calculated, conscious, considered, deliberate, designed, examined, gone into, investigated, planned, plotted, premeditated, prepared, prepense, purposeful, reviewed, studious, thought-about, thoughtful, thought-out, thought-through, voluntary, well-considered, willful, willing; SEE CONCEPTS *538,548*

studious [*adj*] *scholarly, attentive*
academic, assiduous, bookish*, bookworm*, busy, careful, contemplative, diligent, eager, earnest, grubbing, hard-working, industrious, intellectual, learned, lettered, meditative, reflective, sedulous, serious, thoughtful, well-informed, well-read; SEE CONCEPTS *402,538*

study [*n*] *learning, analysis*
abstraction, academic work, analyzing, application, attention, class, cogitation, comparison, concentration, consideration, contemplation, course, cramming, debate, deliberation, examination, exercise, inquiry, inspection, investigation, lesson, meditation, memorizing, muse, musing, pondering, questioning, reading, reasoning, reflection, research, reverie, review, rumination, schoolwork, scrutiny, subject, survey, thought, trance, weighing; SEE CONCEPTS *31,103*

study [*v1*] *contemplate, learn*
apply oneself, bone up*, brood over, burn midnight oil*, bury oneself in*, coach, cogitate, consider, crack the books*, cram, dig*, dive into*, examine, excogitate, go into, go over, grind*, hit the books*, inquire, learn, learn the ropes*, lucubrate, meditate, mind, mull over, perpend, peruse, plug*, plunge, polish up*, ponder, pore over*, read, read up, refresh, think, think out, think over, tutor, weigh; SEE CONCEPT *31*

study [*v2*] *examine, analyze*
brainstorm*, canvass, case, check out, check over, check up, compare, deliberate, do research, figure, give the eagle eye*, inspect, investigate, keep tabs*, look into, peruse, read, research, scope, scrutinize, sort out, survey, view; SEE CONCEPT *103*

stuff [*n1*] *personal belongings*
being, effects, equipment, gear, goods, impedimenta, individual, junk*, kit, luggage, objects, paraphernalia, possessions, substance, tackle, things, trappings; SEE CONCEPTS *432,446*

stuff [*n2*] *essence, substance*
bottom, bottom line*, essentiality, heart, marrow*, matter, meat*, nitty-gritty*, nuts and bolts*, pith, principle, quintessence, soul, staple, virtuality; SEE CONCEPTS *668,682*

stuff [*n3*] *fabric*
cloth, material, raw material, textile, woven material; SEE CONCEPT *167*

stuff [*v*] *load with*
choke up, clog up, compress, congest, cram,

crowd, fill, fill to overflowing, fill to the brim, force, glut, gobble, gorge, gormandize, guzzle, jam, jam-pack*, overfill, overindulge, overstuff, pack, pad, push, ram, sate, satiate, shove, squeeze, stow, wad, wedge; SEE CONCEPTS 169,209

stuffy [adj1] close, oppressive
airless, breathless, confined, fetid, heavy, humid, muggy, stagnant, stale, stifling, suffocating, sultry, thick, unventilated; SEE CONCEPT 525

stuffy [adj2] old-fashioned, prim
arrogant, bloated, conventional, dreary, dull, fusty, genteel, humorless, important, magisterial, musty, narrow-minded, pompous, priggish, prim and proper*, prissy, prudish, puffy, puritanical, self-important, staid, stilted, stodgy, straitlaced*, uninteresting, Victorian*; SEE CONCEPTS 401,404

stumble [v1] slip, stagger
blunder, bumble, careen, err, fall, fall down, falter, flounder, hesitate, limp, lose balance, lumber, lurch, muddle, pitch, reel, shuffle, stammer, swing, tilt, topple, totter, trip, wallow, waver, wobble; SEE CONCEPTS 101,181

stumble [v2] happen upon
blunder upon*, bump, chance, chance upon*, come across, come up against, discover, encounter, fall upon, find, happen upon*, hit, light, light upon*, luck*, meet, run across, stub toe on*, tumble, turn up; SEE CONCEPTS 183,693

stump [n] end piece
butt, end, projection, stub, tail end, tip; SEE CONCEPTS 825,827

stump [v1] confuse, bewilder
baffle, bring up short, confound, dumbfound, foil, mystify, nonplus, outwit, perplex, puzzle, stagger, stick, stop, stymie; SEE CONCEPT 16

stump [v2] walk with deliberation
barge, clomp, clump, galumph, lumber, plod, stamp, stomp, stumble, trudge; SEE CONCEPT 149

stun/stupefy [v] amaze, shock
astonish, astound, bemuse, bewilder, blow away*, bowl over*, confound, confuse, daze, dumbfound, flabbergast, floor*, fog*, give a turn*, hit like ton of bricks*, knock out*, knock over*, knock unconscious, muddle, overcome, overpower, overwhelm, paralyze, petrify, rock*, shake up*, stagger, strike dumb*, surprise, take breath away*, throw a curve*; SEE CONCEPT 42

stunning [adj] beautiful, marvelous
beauteous, bonny, brilliant, comely, dazzling, devastating, excellent, fair, famous, fine, first-class*, first-rate*, gorgeous, great, handsome, heavenly, impressive, lovely, number one*, out of this world*, pretty, ravishing, remarkable, royal, sensational, smashing, spectacular, striking, superior, top, wonderful; SEE CONCEPTS 574,579

stunt [n] deed, trick
achievement, act, antic, caper, exploit, feat, feature, performance, sketch, skit, tour de force; SEE CONCEPTS 264,384

stunted [adj] kept from growing
bantam, diminutive, dwarf, dwarfed, dwarfish, half-pint*, little, measly, mite, peanut*, peewee*, pint-sized*, runted, runtish, runty, scrub, short, shot, shrimp*, small, small fry*, tiny, undergrown, undersized, wee*, yea big*, yea high*; SEE CONCEPTS 773,779

stupendous [adj] wonderful, amazing
astonishing, astounding, breathtaking, colossal, dynamite, enormous, fab*, fabulous, fantastic, fat*, gigantic, great, huge, marvelous, mind-blowing*, mind-boggling*, miraculous, monster, monumental, overwhelming, phenomenal, prodigious, radical*, smashing, spectacular, staggering, stunning, super, superb, surprising, terrific, titantic, too much*, tremendous, unreal*, utmost*, vast, wonderful, wondrous; SEE CONCEPTS 574,781

stupid [adj] not intelligent; irresponsible
brainless, dazed, deficient, dense, dim, doltish, dopey*, dull, dumb, dummy*, foolish, futile, gullible, half-baked*, half-witted*, idiotic, ill-advised, imbecilic, inane, indiscreet, insensate, irrelevant, irresponsible, laughable, loser*, ludicrous, meaningless, mindless, moronic, naive, nonsensical, obtuse, out to lunch*, pointless, puerile, rash, senseless, shortsighted, simple, simpleminded, slow, sluggish, stolid, stupefied, thick, thick-headed*, trivial, unintelligent, unthinking, witless; SEE CONCEPTS 402,548

stupor [n] daze, unconsciousness
amazement, anaesthesia, apathy, asphyxia, bewilderment, coma, dullness, fainting, hebetude, hypnosis, inertia, inertness, insensibility, languor, lassitude, lethargy, narcosis, numbness, petrifaction, sleep, slumber, somnolence, sopor, stupefaction, suspended animation, swoon, swooning, torpor, trance; SEE CONCEPTS 315,316

sturdy [adj] solid, durable
athletic, built to last*, bulky, determined, durable, firm, flourishing, hardy, hearty, hefty, hulking, husky, lusty, muscular, powerful, powerhouse*, resolute, robust, rugged, secure, solid, sound, stalwart, staunch, steadfast, stiff, stout, stouthearted, strapping, strong, strong-arm*, substantial, tenacious, tough, unyielding, vigorous, well-built, well-made; SEE CONCEPTS 314,488,489

stutter [v] speak haltingly
dribble, falter, hesitate, splutter, sputter, stammer, stumble; SEE CONCEPT 77

style [n1] fashion, manner
appearance, approach, bearing, behavior, carriage, characteristic, cup of tea*, custom, cut*, description, design, druthers*, flash*, form, genre, groove*, habit, hand, idiosyncrasy, kind, method, mode, number, pattern, peculiarity, rage*, sort, spirit, strain, technique, tenor, thing*, tone, trait, trend, type, variety, vein, vogue, way; SEE CONCEPTS 411,655

style [n2] fashionableness
chichi, comfort, cosmopolitanism, craze, dash, delicacy, dernier cri, dressiness, ease, élan, elegance, fad, flair, grace, grandeur, luxury, mode, panache, polish, rage, refinement, savoir-faire, smartness, sophistication, stylishness, taste, thing*, urbanity, vogue; SEE CONCEPTS 655,668

style [n3] way of speaking, writing, expressing oneself
diction, expression, mode of expression, phraseology, phrasing, treatment, turn of phrase*, vein, wording; SEE CONCEPT 276

style [v] name, title
address, baptize, call, christen, denominate, designate, dub, entitle, label, name, term; SEE CONCEPT 62

stylish [adj] fashionable
à la mode*, beautiful, chic, chichi*, classy, dap, dapper, dashing, dressed to kill*, dressed to the

st
st

teeth*, dressy, fly*, groovy*, high-class*, in, in
fashion, in the mainstream*, in vogue, jazzy*,
latest, mod*, modernistic, new, nifty, now*,
ostentatious, polished, pretentious, rakish, ritzy,
sassy*, sharp, showy, sleek, slick*, smart,
snappy*, snazzy*, swank*, swell, tony*, trendy,
upscale, up-to-date, uptown, urbane, voguish;
SEE CONCEPTS 579,589

stymie [v] frustrate, hinder
balk, block, choke off, confound, corner, crab*,
cramp, cramp one's style*, crimp, cut off, dead-
end*, defeat, foil, give the run around*, hang
fire*, hang up*, hold off, hold up, impede, mystify, nonplus, obstruct, pigeonhole*, prevent, put
on back burner*, put on hold, puzzle, shelve,
snooker*, stall, stonewall*, stump, throw a monkey wrench into*, thwart; SEE CONCEPTS 121,130

suave [adj] charming, smooth
affable, agreeable, bland, civilized, cordial, courteous, courtly, cultivated, cultured, diplomatic,
distingué, fulsome, genial, glib, gracious, ingratiating, obliging, oily*, pleasant, pleasing, polished, polite, politic, refined, smooth-tongued*,
sociable, soft*, soft-spoken, sophisticated, unctuous, urbane, well-bred, worldly; SEE CONCEPTS
401,404

subconscious [n] inner thoughts
essence, mind, psyche, soul, subconsciousness,
subliminal, subliminal self, submerged mind, un-
derconsciousness, undersense; SEE CONCEPT 410

subconscious [adj] innermost in thought
hidden, inmost, inner, intuitive, latent, mental,
repressed, subliminal, suppressed, unconscious;
SEE CONCEPT 529

subdivision [n] smaller entity of whole
class, community, development, group, lower
group, minor group, subclass, subsidiary, tract;
SEE CONCEPTS 513,835

subdue [v] keep under control; moderate
bear down, beat down, break, break in, check,
conquer, control, crush, defeat, discipline, dominate, drop, extinguish, gentle, get the better of*,
get the upper hand*, get under control, humble,
mellow, overcome, overpower, overrun, put
down, quash, quell, quench, quiet, quieten, reduce, repress, restrain, shut down, soften,
squelch, subjugate, suppress, tame, temper, tone
down, trample, triumph over, vanquish; SEE CON-
CEPTS 121,130,252

subdued [adj] quiet, controlled
chastened, crestfallen, dejected, dim, domestic,
domesticated, downcast, down in the mouth*,
grave, hushed, inobtrusive, low-key*, mellow*,
moderated, muted, neutral, out of spirits*, repentant, repressed, restrained, sad, serious, shaded,
sober, soft, softened, solemn, submissive, subtle,
tasteful, tempered, toned down, unobtrusive; SEE
CONCEPTS 401,403,594

subject [n1] issue, matter
affair, argument, business, case, chapter, class,
core, course, discussion, field of reference, gist,
head, idea, item, material, matter at hand, meat*,
motif, motion, motive, object, point, principal object, problem, proposal, question, resolution,
study, subject matter, substance, text, theme, theorem, thesis, thought, topic; SEE CONCEPTS
529,532,689

subject [n2] one under authority or control of another
case, client, customer, dependent, guinea pig*,

liege, national, patient, serf, subordinate, vassal;
SEE CONCEPTS 413,423

subject [adj] at the mercy of; answerable
accountable, apt, at one's feet*, bound by, captive, collateral, conditional, contingent, controlled, dependent, directed, disposed, enslaved,
exposed, governed, in danger of, inferior, liable,
likely, obedient, open, prone, provisional, ruled,
satellite, secondary, sensitive, servile, slavish,
sub*, subaltern, subjugated, submissive, subordinate, subservient, substract, susceptible, tentative,
tributary, under, vulnerable; SEE CONCEPTS
552,575

subjective [adj] emotional; based on inner experience rather than fact
abstract, biased, fanciful, idiosyncratic, illusory,
individual, instinctive, introspective, introverted,
intuitive, nonobjective, nonrepresentative, personal, prejudiced, unobjective; SEE CONCEPTS
529,542

subjugate [v] overpower, defeat
bear down, beat down, bring to heel*, bring to
knees*, coerce, compel, conquer, crush, enslave,
enthrall, force, hold sway, keep under thumb*,
kick around*, overcome, overthrow, put down,
quell, reduce, reel back in*, rule, rule over, subdue, suppress, tame, triumph, vanquish; SEE CON-
CEPTS 95,117,133

sublime [adj] great, magnificent
abstract, august, divine, dynamite, elevated, eminent, exalted, glorious, gorgeous, grand, heavenly, high, holy, ideal, imposing, lofty, majestic,
noble, outrageous, proud, resplendent, sacred,
spiritual, splendiferous, splendorous, stately, super, superb, the most*, too much*, transcendent,
transcendental; SEE CONCEPT 574

submerge [v] dunk in liquid
deluge, descend, dip, douse, drench, drown,
duck, engulf, flood, go down, go under, immerse,
impregnate, inundate, overflow, overwhelm,
plunge, sink, sound, souse, submerse, subside,
swamp, whelm; SEE CONCEPTS 181,256

submission [n] compliance
acquiescence, appeasement, assent, backing
down, bowing, capitulation, cringing, defeatism,
deference, docility, giving in, humbleness, humility, malleability, meekness, nonresistance, obedience, passivism, passivity, pliability, prostration,
recreancy, resignation, servility, subjection, submissiveness, submitting, surrender, tractability,
unassertiveness, yielding; SEE CONCEPT 633

submissive [adj] compliant
abject, accommodating, acquiescent, amenable,
bowing down, comfortable, complying, deferential, docile, domesticated, dutiful, giving-in*,
humble, ingratiating, lowly, malleable, meek, menial, nonresistant, nonresisting, obedient, obeisant, obeying, obsequious, passive, patient,
pliable, pliant, resigned, servile, slavish, subdued,
tame, tractable, uncomplaining, unresisting, yes*,
yielding; SEE CONCEPT 401

submit [v1] comply, endure
abide, accede, acknowledge, acquiesce, agree, appease, bend, be submissive, bow, buckle, capitulate, cave, cede, concede, defer, eat crow*, fold,
give away, give ground, give in, give way, go
with the flow*, grin and bear it*, humor, indulge,
knuckle, knuckle under*, kowtow*, lay down
arms, obey, put up with, quit, relent, relinquish,
resign oneself, say uncle*, stoop, succumb, sur-

render, throw in the towel*, toe the line*, tolerate, truckle, withstand, yield; SEE CONCEPT 23

submit [v2] *present, offer; argue for*
advance, advise, affirm, argue, assert, claim, commit, contend, hand in, make a pitch*, move, proffer, propose, proposition, propound, put, put forward, refer, state, suggest, table, tender, theorize, urge, volunteer; SEE CONCEPT 66

subordinate [n] *person or thing that serves another*
aide, assistant, attendant, dependent, deputy, flunky*, gofer*, helper, inferior, junior, peon, poor relation*, scrub*, second, second fiddle*, second string*, serf, servant, slave, subaltern, third string*, underling; SEE CONCEPTS 348,423

subordinate [adj] *lesser, supplementary*
accessory, adjuvant, ancillary, auxiliary, baser, below par, collateral, contributory, dependent, inferior, insignificant, junior, low, lower, minor, paltry, satellite, secondary, second-fiddle*, second-string*, smaller, sub, subaltern, subalternate, subject, submissive, subnormal, subservient, subsidiary, substract, tributary, under, underaverage, unequal; SEE CONCEPT 575

subscribe [v1] *pay for use; contribute*
advocate, ante up*, buy, chip in*, come through*, consent, donate, do one's part*, endorse, enroll, give, grant, ink*, make a deal*, offer, pitch in*, pledge, promise, put up*, register, second, set, sign, signature, sign up*, support; SEE CONCEPTS 129,341

subscribe [v2] *agree*
accede, acquiesce, advocate, approve, assent, autograph*, back, bless, boost, consent, cosign, countenance, ditto*, endorse, favor, get behind*, give stamp of approval*, give the go-ahead*, go along with*, hold with*, ink*, obey, okay*, put John Hancock on*, rubber-stamp*, sanction, sign, signature, support, take, undersign, underwrite, yes*; SEE CONCEPTS 10,50,88

subsequent [adj] *after*
consecutive, consequent, consequential, ensuing, following, later, next, posterior, postliminary, proximate, resultant, resulting, sequent, sequential, serial, subsequential, succeeding, successional, successive; SEE CONCEPTS 585,820

subsequently [adv] *afterward*
after, afterwards, afterwhile, at a later date, behind, by and by, consequently, finally, infra, in the aftermath, in the end, later, latterly, next; SEE CONCEPTS 585,820

subservient [adj1] *extremely compliant*
abject, acquiescent, a slave to*, at one's beck and call*, at one's mercy*, bootlicking, cowering, cringing, dancing, deferential, docile, fawning, ignoble, inferior, in one's clutches*, in one's pocket*, in one's power*, mean, menial, obeisant, obsequious, resigned, servile, slavish, subject, submissive, sycophantic, under one's thumb*; SEE CONCEPTS 401,404

subservient [adj2] *secondary, useful*
accessory, adjuvant, ancillary, appurtenant, auxiliary, bush-league*, collateral, conducive, contributory, flunky, helpful, inferior, instrumental, minor, serviceable, subordinate, subsidiary, supplemental, supplementary; SEE CONCEPTS 560,575

subside [v] *die down; decrease*
abate, cave in, collapse, decline, de-escalate, descend, die away, diminish, drop, dwindle, ease,

ease off, ebb, fall, let up, level off, lower, lull, melt, moderate, peter out*, quieten, recede, settle, sink, slacken, taper, wane; SEE CONCEPTS 181,698,776

subsidiary [adj] *secondary, helpful*
accessory, adjuvant, aiding, ancillary, appurtenant, assistant, assisting, auxiliary, backup, branch, collateral, contributory, cooperative, lesser, minor, serviceable, subject, subordinate, subservient, supplemental, supplementary, tributory, useful; SEE CONCEPTS 560,575

subsidize [v] *give money to get started*
angel*, back, bankroll*, contribute, endow, finance, fund, grubstake*, help, juice*, pick up the check*, pick up the tab*, prime the pump*, promote, put up the money for, sponsor, stake, support, underwrite; SEE CONCEPTS 110,341

subsidy [n] *money given to help another*
aid, alimony, allowance, appropriation, assistance, bequest, bonus, bounty, contribution, endowment, fellowship, financial aid, gift, grant, gratuity, help, honorarium, indemnity, payment, pension, premium, reward, scholarship, subsidization, subvention, support, tribute; SEE CONCEPTS 337,344

subsist [v] *keep going, living*
barely exist*, be, breathe, continue, eke out a living*, eke out an existence*, endure, exist, get along*, get by*, hang in*, hang on*, hang tough*, just make it*, last, live, make ends meet*, make it*, manage, move, remain, remain alive, ride out*, scrape by*, stay alive, stick it out*, stick with it*, survive, sustain; SEE CONCEPTS 23,330,407

subsistence [n] *provisions for survival*
affluence, aliment, alimentation, bread*, bread and butter*, capital, circumstances, competence, earnings, existence, food, fortune, gratuity, income, independence, keep, legacy, livelihood, living, maintenance, means, money, necessities, nurture, pension, property, provision, ration, resources, riches, salary, salt*, substance, support, sustenance, upkeep, victuals, wages, wealth, wherewithal; SEE CONCEPTS 446,457,646,710

substance [n1] *entity, element*
actuality, animal, being, body, bulk, concreteness, core, corpus, fabric, force, hunk, individual, item, mass, material, matter, object, person, phenomenon, reality, something, stuff, stuff, texture, thing; SEE CONCEPTS 433,478,523

substance [n2] *essence, meaning*
ABCs*, amount, basis, body, bottom, bottom line*, brass tacks*, burden, center, core, corpus, crux, drift, effect, essentiality, focus, general meaning, gist, gravamen, guts*, heart, import, innards, kernel, marrow, mass, matter, meat*, name of the game*, nitty-gritty*, nub, nuts and bolts*, pith, point, purport, quintessence, sense, significance, soul, staple, strength, stuff, subject, sum total*, tenor, theme, thrust, upshot, virtuality, way of it*; SEE CONCEPTS 682,689

substance [n3] *wealth*
affluence, assets, estate, fortune, means, property, resources, riches, worth; SEE CONCEPT 335

substantial [adj1] *important, ample*
abundant, big, big-deal*, bulky, consequential, considerable, durable, extraordinary, firm, generous, goodly, heavy, heavyweight, hefty, key, large, major-league*, massive, material, meaningful, momentous, plentiful, principal, serious, sig-

nificant, sizable, solid, sound, stable, steady, stout, strong, sturdy, superabundant, tidy, valuable, vast, weighty, well-built, worthwhile; SEE CONCEPTS 568,773,781

substantial [adj2] *material, real*
actual, card-carrying*, concrete, corporeal, existent, for real*, honest-to-god*, legit*, objective, phenomenal, physical, positive, righteous, sensible, solid, sure enough*, tangible, true, twenty-four-carat*, valid, visible, weighty; SEE CONCEPT 582

substantial [adj3] *rich*
affluent, comfortable, easy, opulent, prosperous, snug, solid, solvent, wealthy, well, well-heeled, well-off, well-to-do; SEE CONCEPT 334

substantially [adv] *to a large extent*
considerably, essentially, extensively, heavily, in essence, in fact, in reality, in substance, in the main, largely, mainly, materially, much, really; SEE CONCEPTS 569,772

substantiate [v] *back up a statement, idea*
actualize, affirm, approve, attest to, authenticate, bear out, check out, check up, complete, confirm, corroborate, debunk, demonstrate, establish, incarnate, justify, manifest, materialize, objectify, personify, prove, ratify, realize, reify, support, test, try, try on, try out, validate, verify; SEE CONCEPTS 49,138,317

substitute [n] *someone or something that takes the place of another*
agent, alternate, assistant, auxiliary, backup, changeling, delegate, deputy, dernier ressort*, double, dummy, equivalent, expediency, expedient, fill-in, ghost, ghost writer, locum, locum tenens, makeshift, pinch-hitter*, procurator, proxy, recourse, refuge, relay, relief, replacement, representative, reserve, resort, resource, stand-by, stand-in, stopgap*, sub*, succedaneum, successor, supplanter, supply, surrogate, symbol, temp*, temporary, temporary expedient, understudy, vicar; SEE CONCEPTS 423,712

substitute [adj] *alternative*
acting, alternate, alternative, another, artificial, backup, counterfeit, dummy, ersatz*, experimental, false, imitation, makeshift, mock, near, other, provisional, proxy, pseudo*, replacement, representative, reserve, second, sham, simulated, spurious, stopgap*, substitutive, supplemental, supplementary, supposititious, surrogate, symbolic, temporary, tentative, vicarial, vicarious; SEE CONCEPTS 560,575

substitute [v] *interchange, exchange*
act for, alternate, answer for, back up, be in place of, change, commute, cover for, deputize, displace, do the work of, double for, fill in for, fill one's position, go as, proxy, relieve, replace, serve in one's stead, spell, stand for, stand in for, sub*, supersede, supplant, swap, swap places with*, switch, take another's place, take over; SEE CONCEPTS 87,104

subtle [adj1] *nice, quiet, delicate*
attenuate, attenuated, deep, discriminating, ethereal, exquisite, faint, fine, finespun, hairline, hairsplitting, illusive, implied, inconspicuous, indirect, indistinct, inferred, ingenious, insinuated, mental, penetrating, profound, refined, slight, sophisticated, suggestive, tenuous, thin, understated; SEE CONCEPTS 537,544

subtle [adj2] *clever, cunning*
analytic, analytical, artful, astute, complex,

crafty, deep, designing, detailed, devious, dexterous, exacting, foxy, guileful, insidious, intriguing, keen, penetrating, perceptive, precise, ratiocinative, scheming, shrewd, skillful, sly, wily; SEE CONCEPT 402

subtract [v] *take away*
decrease, deduct, detract, diminish, discount, draw back, knock off, remove, take, take from, take off, take out, withdraw, withhold; SEE CONCEPTS 211,764

suburb [n] *neighborhood outside of but reliant on nearby large city*
bedroom community*, burb*, country, countryside, environs, fringe, hamlet, hinterland, outlying area, outpost, outskirts, precinct, purlieu, residential area, slub, suburbia, village; SEE CONCEPTS 508,512

subversive [adj] *rebellious, destructive*
incendiary, inflammatory, insurgent, insurrectionary, overthrowing, perversive, riotous, ruinous, seditious, treasonous, underground, undermining; SEE CONCEPT 401

subvert [v] *rebel, destroy*
capsize, contaminate, corrupt, debase, defeat, demolish, deprave, depress, extinguish, invalidate, invert, level, overthrow, overturn, pervert, poison, pull down, raze, reverse, ruin, sabotage, supersede, supplant, suppress, topple, tumble, undermine, upset, vitiate, wreck; SEE CONCEPTS 86,95,252

succeed [v1] *attain good outcome*
accomplish, achieve, acquire, arrive, avail, benefit, be successful, carry off*, come off*, conquer, distance, do all right*, do the trick*, earn, flourish, fulfill, gain, get, get to the top*, grow famous, hit*, make a fortune*, make good*, make it*, make out*, obtain, outdistance, outwit, overcome, possess, prevail, profit, prosper, pull off*, realize, reap, receive, recover, retrieve, score, secure, surmount, thrive, triumph, turn out*, vanquish, win, work, worst; SEE CONCEPTS 141,706

succeed [v2] *come after; take the place of*
accede, assume, be subsequent, come into, come into possession, come next, displace, ensue, enter upon, follow, follow after, follow in order, go next, inherit, postdate, replace, result, supersede, supervene, supplant, take over; SEE CONCEPTS 727,749,813

succeeding/successive [adj] *following*
alternating, consecutive, ensuing, following after, in a row, in line, next, next in line for, next in order, next off, next up, rotating, sequent, sequential, serial, seriate, subsequent, subsequential, succedent, successional; SEE CONCEPTS 585,811,812,818,820

success [n] *favorable outcome*
accomplishment, achievement, advance, arrival, ascendancy, attainment, bed of roses*, benefit, big hit*, boom*, clover*, consummation, do well, Easy Street*, éclat, eminence, fame, flying colors*, fortune, fruition, gain, good luck*, good times*, grand slam*, gravy train*, happiness, happy days*, hit, killing, lap of luxury*, laugher*, maturation, profit, progress, prosperity, realization, reward, savvy, sensation, snap, strike, successfulness, triumph, victory, walkaway*, walkover*, win; SEE CONCEPTS 693,706

successful [adj] *favorable, profitable*
acknowledged, advantageous, ahead of the game*, at the top*, at top of ladder*, auspicious,

bestselling, blooming, blossoming, booming, champion, crowned, efficacious, extraordinary, flourishing, fortuitous, fortunate, fruitful, happy, lucky, lucrative, moneymaking, notable, noteworthy, on track*, out in front*, outstanding, paying, prosperous, rewarding, rolling, strong, thriving, top, triumphant, unbeaten, undefeated, victorious, wealthy; SEE CONCEPT 528

succinct [adj] *brief, to the point*
blunt, boiled down*, breviloquent, brusque, compact, compendiary, compendious, concise, condensed, curt, cut to the bone*, in a nutshell*, in few words*, laconic, pithy, short, summary, terse; SEE CONCEPT 267

succulent [adj] *juicy, delicious*
divine, heavenly, luscious, lush, mellow, moist, mouthwatering, pulpy, rich, sappy, tasty, yummy*; SEE CONCEPTS 462,613

succumb [v] *die or surrender*
accede, bow, break down, buckle, capitulate, cave, cave in*, cease, collapse, croak, decease, defer, demise, depart, drop, eat crow*, expire, fall, fall victim to, flake out*, fold, give in, give into, give out, give up the ghost*, give way, go, go down, go under, knuckle, knuckle under*, meet waterloo*, pack it in*, pass, pass away, perish, quit, show white flag*, submit, take the count*, throw in the towel*, wilt, yield; SEE CONCEPTS 35,105,385

such [adj/conj] *aforementioned, specific*
aforesaid, akin, alike, analogous, comparable, corresponding, equivalent, like, parallel, said, similar, such a one, such a person, such a thing, suchlike, that, the like, this; SEE CONCEPT 557

sudden [adj] *unexpected; happening quickly*
abrupt, accelerated, acute, expeditious, fast, flash, fleet, hasty, headlong, hurried, immediate, impetuous, impromptu, impulsive, out of the blue*, precipitant, precipitate, precipitous, quick, quickened, rapid, rash, rushing, spasmodic, speeded, subito, swift, unforeseen, unusual; SEE CONCEPT 799

suddenly [adv] *unexpectedly*
aback, abruptly, all at once, all of a sudden, asudden, forthwith, on spur of moment*, quickly, short, sudden, swiftly, unanticipatedly, unaware, unawares, without warning; SEE CONCEPT 799

sue [v] *bring legal charges against*
accuse, appeal, beg, beseech, bring an action, charge, claim, claim damages, contest, demand, drag into court, enter a plea, entreat, file, file a claim, file suit, follow up, haul into court, have the law on, have up, indict, institute legal proceedings, litigate, petition, plead, prefer charges against, prosecute, pull up, put away, see in court, solicit, summon, supplicate, take out after, take to court; SEE CONCEPT 317

suffer [v1] *be in pain*
ache, agonize, ail, be affected, be at disadvantage, be convulsed, be handicapped, be impaired, be racked, be wounded, brave, complain of, deteriorate, droop, endure, experience, fall off, feel wretched, flag, get, go through, grieve, have a bad time*, hurt, languish, pain, sicken, smart, undergo, writhe; SEE CONCEPTS 308,313

suffer [v2] *endure, permit*
abide, accept, acquiesce, admit, allow, bear, bear with, bleed, bow, brave, brook, carry the torch*, concede, countenance, encounter, experience, feel, go through, have, hurt, indulge, know, let,

license, live with, put up with, receive, sanction, see, sit and take it, stand, stomach*, submit, support, sustain, swallow*, sweat*, take*, take it*, tolerate, undergo, wait out, yield; SEE CONCEPTS 23,83

suffering [n] *pain, agony*
adversity, affliction, anguish, difficulty, discomfort, distress, dolor, hardship, martyrdom, misery, misfortune, ordeal, passion, torment, torture; SEE CONCEPT 728

suffice [v] *be adequate, enough*
answer, avail, be good enough, be sufficient, be the ticket*, content, do, do the trick*, fill the bill*, get by, go over big*, hack it*, hit the spot*, make a hit*, make the grade*, meet, meet requirement, satisfy, serve, suit; SEE CONCEPT 713

sufficient [adj] *enough, adequate*
acceptable, agreeable, all right*, ample, aplenty, appreciate, comfortable, commensurable, commensurate, common, competent, copious, decent, due, galore, pleasing, plenteous, plentiful, plenty, proportionate, satisfactory, sufficing, tolerable, unexceptionable, unexceptional, unobjectionable; SEE CONCEPTS 558,560,771

suffocate [v] *choke*
asphyxiate, drown, smother, stifle, strangle; SEE CONCEPTS 163,246

suggest [v1] *convey advice, plan, desire*
advance, advise, advocate, broach, commend, conjecture, exhort, give a tip*, move, offer, plug*, pose, prefer, propone, propose, proposition, propound, put, put forward, put in two cents*, put on to something*, recommend, steer, submit, theorize, tip, tip off*; SEE CONCEPT 75

suggest [v2] *imply; bring to mind*
adumbrate, advert, allude, be a sign of, connote, cross the mind, denote, evoke, hint, indicate, infer, insinuate, intimate, lead to believe, occur, point, point in direction of, promise, put in mind of, refer, represent, shadow, signify, symbolize, typify; SEE CONCEPTS 74,682

suggestion [n1] *advice, plan*
advancement, angle, approach, bid, big idea*, bit*, brainchild*, charge, commendation, exhortation, game plan*, gimmick, hot lead*, idea, injunction, instruction, invitation, lead, motion, opinion, outline, pitch, presentation, proffer, proposal, proposition, recommendation, reminder, resolution, scheme, setup, sneaking suspicion*, steer*, submission, telltale, tender, testimonial, thesis, tip, tip-off*; SEE CONCEPTS 278,689

suggestion [n2] *hint, implication*
allusion, association, autosuggestion, breath, clue, connotation, cue, indication, inkling, innuendo, insinuation, intimation, notion, overtone, reminder, self-suggestion, shade, signification, smack, soupçon, strain, suspicion, symbol, symbolism, symbolization, symbology, telltale, thought, tinge, trace, undertone, vein, whisper, wind; SEE CONCEPT 529

suggestive [adj1] *signifying*
evocative, evocatory, expressive, giving an inkling*, indicative, intriguing, pregnant, redolent, reminreful, reminiscent, significative, symbolic, symptomatic; SEE CONCEPTS 267,529

suggestive [adj2] *dirty, vulgar*
bawdy, blue*, broad, erotic, immodest, improper, indecent, indelicate, obscene, off-color*, provocative, prurient, racy, ribald, risqué, rude, seduc-

tive, sexy, shady, tempting, titillating, unseemly, wicked; SEE CONCEPTS 372,545

suit [n1] *matching top and bottom clothing*
clothing, costume, dress, ensemble, getup*, gray flannel*, habit, livery, outfit, threads*, tuxedo, uniform, wardrobe; SEE CONCEPT 451

suit [n2] *legal action*
case, cause, lawsuit, litigation, proceeding, prosecution, trial; SEE CONCEPT 318

suit [n3] *appeal, request*
address, application, asking, attention, court, courtship, entreaty, imploration, imprecation, invocation, petition, plea, prayer, requesting, solicitation, soliciting, supplication, wooing; SEE CONCEPT 662

suit [v1] *be acceptable, appropriate*
accord, agree, answer, answer a need, become, befit, benefit, be proper for, beseem, be seemly, check, check out, conform, correspond, cut the mustard*, do, enhance, fill the bill*, fit, fit in, flatter, fulfill, get by, go, go together, gratify, harmonize, make the grade*, match, pass muster*, please, satisfy, serve, square, suffice, tally; SEE CONCEPT 656

suit [v2] *adapt, tailor*
accommodate, adjust, amuse, change, conform, entertain, fashion, fill, fit, fit in, gratify, modify, please, proportion, quadrate, readjust, reconcile, revise, satisfy, tailor-make*, toe the mark*; SEE CONCEPTS 126,697

suitable [adj] *appropriate, acceptable*
advisable, applicable, apposite, apt, becoming, befitting, commodious, condign, convenient, copacetic, correct, cut out for*, deserved, due, expedient, felicitous, fit, fitting, good, good enough*, handy, happy, in character, in keeping*, just, kosher*, legit*, meet, merited, nice, okay*, opportune, peachy, pertinent, politic, presentable, proper, reasonable, relevant, requisite, right, righteous, rightful, satisfactory, seemly, sufficient, suited, swell, up to snuff*, useful, user friendly; SEE CONCEPT 558

suite [n1] *set of rooms or furniture*
apartment, array, batch, body, chambers, collection, flat, group, lodging, lot, parcel, rental, series, set, tenement; SEE CONCEPTS 441,516

suite [n2] *entourage of people*
array, attendants, batch, body, clutch, cortege, court, escort, faculty, followers, group, lot, retainers, retinue, servants, set, staff, train; SEE CONCEPT 417

suite [n3] *series*
chain, concatenation, consecution, line, order, progression, row, scale, sequel, sequence, string, succession, train; SEE CONCEPT 727

suitor [n] *person who desires another*
admirer, beau, boyfriend, cavalier*, courter, date, follower, girlfriend, lover, man, paramour, supplicant, swain, woman, wooer; SEE CONCEPT 423

sulk [v] *pout*
be down in the mouth*, be in a huff*, be morose, be out of sorts*, be silent, brood, frown, gloom, glower, gripe, grouse, grump*, look sullen, lower, moon*, mope*, scowl, take on; SEE CONCEPTS 35,52

sullen [adj] *brooding, upset*
bad-tempered, cheerless, churlish, crabbed*, crabby*, cross, cynical, dismal, dour, dull, fretful, frowning, gloomy, glowering, glum, gruff, grumpy*, heavy, hostile, ill-humored, inert, irri-

table, malevolent, malicious, malign, mean, moody, morose, obstinate, ornery*, out of sorts*, peevish, perverse, pessimistic, petulant, pouting, pouty, querulous, saturnine, silent, somber, sour, sourpussed*, stubborn, sulking, sulky, surly, tenebrific, tenebrous, ugly, unsociable, uptight*; SEE CONCEPT 403

sultry [adj1] *hot and humid*
baking, broiling, burning, close, hot, mucky, muggy, oppressive, red-hot*, scorching, sizzling, smothering, soggy, sticky, stifling, stuffy, suffocating, sweltering, sweltry, torrid, wet; SEE CONCEPTS 525,605

sultry [adj2] *sensuous*
desirable, erotic, heavy*, hot*, lurid, passionate, provocative, seductive, sexy, steamy*, voluptuous, X-rated*; SEE CONCEPT 372

sum [n] *total*
aggregate, all, amount, body, bulk, entirety, entity, epitome, gross, integral, mass, quantity, reckoning, résumé, score, structure, summary, summation, sum total*, synopsis, system, tally, totality, value, whole, works*, worth; SEE CONCEPTS 432,784,787

summarily [adv] *without delay*
arbitrarily, at short notice, expeditiously, forthwith, immediately, on the spot, peremptorily, promptly, readily, speedily, swiftly, without waste; SEE CONCEPTS 544,799

summarize [v] *give a rundown*
abridge, abstract, boil down*, cipher, compile, condense, cut, cut back, cut down, digest, encapsulate, epitomize, get to heart*, give main points, inventory, outline, pare, precis, prune*, put in a nutshell*, recap*, recapitulate, rehash*, retrograde, review, run down*, run through*, shorten, skim, snip, sum, summate, sum up, synopsize, trim; SEE CONCEPTS 55,236,247

summary [n] *short statement of main points*
abbreviation, abridgment, abstract, analysis, apercu, brief, capitulation, case, compendium, condensation, conspectus, core, digest, epitome, essence, extract, inventory, long and short of it*, nutshell*, outline, pandect, precis, prospectus, recap*, recapitulation, reduction, rehash*, report, résumé, review, roundup, rundown, run-through, sense, skeleton*, sketch, sum and substance*, summing-up*, survey, syllabus, synopsis, version, wrap-up*; SEE CONCEPT 283

summary [adj] *concise, to the point*
arbitrary, boiled down*, breviloquent, brief, compact, compacted, compendiary, compendious, condensed, cursory, curt, hasty, in a nutshell*, laconic, perfunctory, pithy*, recapped, rehashed, run-down, run-through, short, short and sweet*, succinct, terse; SEE CONCEPTS 267,272

summer [n] *hot season of the year*
daylight savings time*, dog days*, heat, midsummer, picnic days*, riot time*, summer solstice, summertide, summertime, sunny season, vacation; SEE CONCEPT 814

summit [n] *top, crowning point*
acme, apex, apogee, capstone, climax, crest, crown, culmination, head, height, max, meridian, most, peak, pinnacle, roof, vertex, zenith; SEE CONCEPT 836

summon [v] *call to a place*
arouse, ask, assemble, beckon, beep, bid, call, call back, call for, call forth, call in, call into action, call together, call upon, charge, cite, com-

mand, conjure, convene, convoke, direct, draft, draw on, enjoin, gather, hail, invite, invoke, mobilize, motion, muster, order, petition, rally, recall, request, ring, rouse, send for, sign, signal, subpoena, toll; SEE CONCEPT 53

sumptuous [adj] luxurious, splendid
awe-inspiring, beautiful, costly, dear, deluxe, elegant, expensive, extravagant, gorgeous, grand, grandiose, imposing, impressive, lavish, luscious, luxuriant, magnificent, opulent, out of this world, palatial, plush, pompous, posh, prodigal, profuse, rich, ritzy*, splendiferous, superb, swank*, ultra*, upholstered; SEE CONCEPTS 334,485,574

sum up [v] form an opinion of; summarize
close, conclude, condense, digest, epitomize, estimate, examine, get the measure of, inventory, put in a nutshell*, recapitulate, review, size up, sum, synopsize, total; SEE CONCEPT 55

sundry [adj] miscellaneous
assorted, different, divers, manifold, many, quite a few, several, some, varied, various; SEE CONCEPTS 564,772

sunny [adj1] bright, clear (referring to weather)
brilliant, clarion, cloudless, fine, light, luminous, pleasant, radiant, rainless, shining, shiny, summery, sunlit, sunshiny, unclouded, undarkened; SEE CONCEPTS 525,617

sunny [adj2] happy
beaming, blithe, buoyant, cheerful, cheery, chirpy, genial, joyful, lighthearted, lightsome, optimistic, pleasant, smiling, sunbeamy; SEE CONCEPTS 401,542

sunrise [n] rise of sun above horizon
aurora, break of day*, bright, cockcrow*, dawn, dawning, daybreak, daylight, early bright*, light, morn, morning, sunup; SEE CONCEPT 810

sunset [n] fall of sun below horizon
close of day, crepuscular light, dusk, eve, evening, eventide, gloaming, nightfall, sundown, twilight; SEE CONCEPT 810

super [adj] excellent
cool*, divine, glorious, great, groovy*, hot*, incomparable, keen, magnificent, marvelous, matchless, neat, outstanding, peerless, sensational, smashing*, superb, terrific, topnotch, wonderful; SEE CONCEPT 574

superb [adj] excellent, first-rate
admirable, august, best, breathtaking, choice, elegant, elevated, exalted, exquisite, fine, glorious, gorgeous, grand, great, lofty, magnificent, majestic, marvelous, matchless, noble, optimal, optimum, outstanding, peerless, prime, proud, resplendent, solid, splendid, splendiferous, splendorous, standout, state-of-the-art*, stunning, sublime, super, superior, superlative, unrivaled, very best; SEE CONCEPT 574

supercilious [adj] arrogant, stuck-up
bossy, cavalier, cocky*, condescending, contemptuous, disdainful, egotistic, haughty, high-and-mighty*, imperious, insolent, lofty, nervy*, overbearing, patronizing, proud, putting on airs*, scornful, snobby, superior, uppity*, vainglorious; SEE CONCEPT 401

superficial [adj] without depth, detail
apparent, casual, cosmetic, cursory, depthless, desultory, empty, evident, exterior, external, flash, flimsy, frivolous, general, glib, half-baked*, hasty, hurried, ignorant, inattentive, lightweight, nodding, one-dimensional*, on the surface*, ostensible, outward, partial, passing,

perfunctory, peripheral, quick fix*, seeming, shallow, shoal, silly, sketchy, skin-deep*, slapdash*, slight, smattery, summary, surface, tip of the iceberg*, trivial, uncritical, warped; SEE CONCEPTS 557,777

superficially [adv] lightly; without care
apparently, at first glance, carelessly, casually, externally, extraneously, flimsily, frivolously, hastily, ignorantly, not profoundly, not thoroughly, once over lightly*, on the surface*, ostensibly, outwardly, partially, skim, to the casual eye*; SEE CONCEPTS 531,544

superfluous [adj] extra, unnecessary
abounding, de trop, dispensable, excess, excessive, exorbitant, expendable, extravagant, extreme, gratuitous, inessential, in excess, inordinate, lavish, leftover, needless, nonessential, overflowing, overmuch, pleonastic, profuse, redundant, remaining, residuary, spare, superabundant, supererogatory, superfluent, supernumerary, surplus, unasked, uncalled-for, unneeded, unrequired, unwanted, useless; SEE CONCEPTS 546,560,824

superintendent [n] person who oversees organization
administrator, boss, caretaker, chief, conductor, controller, curator, custodian, director, foreperson, governor, head, head person, inspector, manager, overseer, sitter, slave driver*, straw boss*, super*, supervisor, zookeeper*; SEE CONCEPT 347

superior [n] person higher or highest in rank
boss, brass*, CEO*, chief, chieftain, director, elder, exec*, executive, head, head honcho*, heavyweight*, higher-up*, key player*, leader, manager, principal, ruler, senior, supervisor, VIP*; SEE CONCEPT 347

superior [adj1] better, greater, higher; excellent
above, a cut above*, admirable, capital, choice, dandy, deluxe, distinguished, exceeding, excellent, exceptional, exclusive, expert, famous, fine, finer, first-class, first-rate, first-string*, five-star*, great, good quality, grander, higher-caliber, highclass, major, more advanced, more skillful, more worthy, of higher rank, over, overlying, paramount, predominant, preferable, preferred, premium, prevailing, primary, remarkable, senior, superhuman, superincumbent, surpassing, unrivalled; SEE CONCEPT 574

superior [adj2] arrogant, haughty
airy, bossy, cavalier, cocky*, condescending, cool, disdainful, high-and-mighty*, high-hat*, insolent, lofty, overbearing, patronizing, pretentious, proud, snobbish, stuck-up*, supercilious, uppity*, upstage*, wiseguy*; SEE CONCEPT 401

superiority [n] advantage, predominance
ahead, ascendancy, authority, better, bulge, dominance, edge, eminence, excellence, influence, lead, meliority, nobility, perfection, position, power, predomination, preeminence, preponderance, prestige, prevalence, pull, rank, spark, supremacy, top, transcendence, upper hand*, vantage, victory, whip hand*; SEE CONCEPT 671

superlative [adj] excellent, first-class
accomplished, all-time*, A-1*, best, capital, consummate, crack, effusive, exaggerated, excessive, extreme, finished, gilt-edge*, greatest, highest, hundred-proof*, inflated, magnificent, matchless, of highest order*, optimum, outstanding, peerless, standout*, superb, supreme, surpassing, tops*,

transcendent, unexcelled, unparalleled, unrivaled, unsurpassed, winning, world-class*; SEE CONCEPT 574

supernatural [adj] mysterious, not of this world
abnormal, celestial, concealed, dark, fabulous, fairy, ghostly, heavenly, hidden, impenetrable, invisible, legendary, metaphysical, miraculous, mystic, mythical, mythological, numinous, obscure, occult, paranormal, phantom, phenomenal, preternatural, psychic, rare, secret, spectral, superhuman, superior, supermundane, superordinary, supranatural, transcendental, uncanny, uncomprehensible, unearthly, unfathomable, unintelligible, unknowable, unknown, unnatural, unrevealed, unusual; SEE CONCEPT 582

supersede [v] take the place of; override
abandon, annul, desert, discard, displace, forsake, oust, outmode, outplace, overrule, reject, remove, replace, repudiate, set aside, succeed, supplant, supplement, suspend, take over, usurp; SEE CONCEPTS 128,141

superstition [n] belief in sign of things to come
false belief, fear, irrationality, notion, shibboleth*, unfounded fear; SEE CONCEPT 689

supervise [v] manage people, project
administer, be in charge*, be in driver's seat*, be in the saddle, be on duty, be responsible for, boss, call the play*, call the shots*, chaperon, conduct, control, crack the whip*, deal with, direct, handle, inspect, keep an eye on*, look after, overlook, oversee, preside over, quarterback*, ride herd on*, run, run the show*, run things*, sit on top of*, superintend, survey, take care of; SEE CONCEPT 117

supervision [n] management of people, project
administration, auspices, care, charge, conduct, control, direction, guidance, handling, instruction, intendance, oversight, running, superintendence, superintendency, surveillance; SEE CONCEPT 117

supervisor [n] person who manages people, project
administrator, boss, brass hat*, caretaker, chief, curator, custodian, director, executive, foreperson, head, inspector, manager, overseer, slave driver*, straw boss*, super*, superintendent, zookeeper*; SEE CONCEPT 347

supplant [v] displace, replace
back up, bounce, cast out, crowd, cut out, eject, expel, fill in, force, force out, front for, oust, outplace, overthrow, remove, ring, ring in, sit in, stand in, substitute, succeed, supersede, swap places with, take out, take over, take the place of, transfer, undermine, unseat, usurp; SEE CONCEPT 128

supple [adj] bendable
adaptable, agile, bending, ductile, elastic, flexible, graceful, limber, lissome, lithe, lithesome, malleable, moldable, plastic, pliable, pliant, resilient, rubber, springy, stretch, stretchy, svelte, willowy, wiry, yielding; SEE CONCEPTS 488,604

supplement [n] something added
added feature*, addendum, addition, additive, appendix, bell*, bells and whistles*, codicil, complement, continuation, extra, insert, option, postscript, pullout, rider, sequel, spin-off*, subsidiary; SEE CONCEPTS 270,824

supplement [v] add to
add fuel to fire*, augment, beef up*, build up, buttress, complement, complete, enhance, enrich,

extend, fill out, fill up, fortify, heat up*, improve, increase, jazz up*, pad*, punch up*, reinforce, step up, strengthen, subsidize, supply, top; SEE CONCEPTS 236,244,245

supplies [n] equipment, provisions
food, foodstuffs, items, material, materials, necessities, provender, rations, raw materials, replenishments, stock, store, stores; SEE CONCEPTS 446,451,457

supply [n] reserve of goods
accumulation, amount, backlog, cache, fund, hoard, inventory, number, quantity, reservoir, source, stock, stockpile, store, surplus; SEE CONCEPT 712

supply [v] furnish, provide, give a resource
afford, cater, cater to, come across with*, come through*, come up with, contribute, deliver, dispense, drop, endow, equip, feed, fill, find, fix up, fulfill, give with, grant, hand, hand over, heel*, kick in*, minister, outfit, pony up*, produce, provide, provision, purvey, put out, put up, replenish, satisfy, stake, stock, store, transfer, turn over, victual, yield; SEE CONCEPTS 107,140

support [n1] something that holds up structure
abutment, agency, back, backing, base, bed, bedding, block, brace, buttress, collar, column, cornerstone, device, flotation, foothold, footing, foundation, fulcrum, groundwork, guide, hold, lining, means, medium, pillar, platform, pole, post, prop, rampart, reinforcement, rest, rib, rod, shore, stake, stanchion, stave, stay, stiffener, stilt, substratum, substructure, sustentation, timber, underpinning; SEE CONCEPTS 440,442,445,471

support [n2] help, approval
aid, assist, assistance, backing, blessing, championship, comfort, encouragement, friendship, furtherance, hand, lift, loyalty, moral support, patronage, protection, relief, succor, sustenance; SEE CONCEPTS 10,110,388,712

support [n3] food, money, possessions for staying alive
alimentation, alimony, allowance, care, keep, livelihood, living, maintenance, necessities, nutriment, payment, provision, relief, responsibility, stock, stores, subsidy, subsistence, sustenance, upkeep, victuals; SEE CONCEPTS 340,446, 457,712

support/supporter [n4/n] person who helps another
adherent, advocate, ally, angel*, apologist, backbone, backer, benefactor, champion, cohort, comforter, confederate, coworker, defender, disciple, endorser, espouser, exponent, expounder, fan, follower, friend, helper, mainstay, maintainer, partisan, patron, pillar, preserver, prop, proponent, satellite*, second, sponsor, stalwart, stay, subscriber, supporter, sustainer, tower of strength*, upholder, well-wisher*; SEE CONCEPT 423

support [v1] hold up
base, be a foundation for, bear, bed, bolster, bottom, brace, buttress, carry, cradle, crutch, embed, found, ground, hold, keep from falling, keep up, mainstay, poise, prop, reinforce, shore, shore up, shoulder, stand, stay, strut, sustain, undergird, upbear, uphold; SEE CONCEPT 190

support [v2] take care of, provide for
angel*, attend to, back, bankroll*, be a source of strength*, bring up, buoy up, care for, chaperon, cherish, earn one's keep, encourage, feed, fi-

nance, fortify, foster, fund, give a leg up*, guard, keep, keep an eye on*, look after, maintain, make a living, nourish, nurse, pay expenses of, pay for, pick up the check*, prop, put up money for*, raise, set up, sponsor, stake, stiffen, strengthen, stroke, subsidize, succor, sustain, underwrite, uphold; SEE CONCEPTS *7,19,22,140,295,341*

support [*v3*] *defend, advocate belief*
abet, advance, agree with, aid, approve, assist, back, bear out, bolster, boost, boost morale, carry, champion, cheer, comfort, countenance, endorse, establish, forward, foster, get behind*, go along with, go to bat for*, help, hold, justify, keep up, maintain, plead for, promote, pull for, put forward, rally round, second, side with, stand behind, stand up for, stay, stick by*, stick up for*, substantiate, sustain, take one's side*, take the part of*, throw in one's lot with*, throw in with*, uphold, verify; SEE CONCEPTS *10,49,110*

support [*v4*] *endure*
abide, bear, bear with, brook, carry on, continue, countenance, go, go through, handle, keep up, live with*, maintain, put up with*, stand, stand for*, stay the course*, stick it out*, stomach*, submit, suffer, swallow*, sweat out*, take, tolerate, undergo, wait out; SEE CONCEPT *23*

suppose [*v1*] *assume, guess*
accept, admit, brainstorm, calculate, conjecture, cook up*, dare-say*, deem, divine, dream, estimate, expect, figure, go out on a limb*, grant, guess, guesstimate*, hazard a guess*, hypothesize, imagine, infer, judge, opine, posit, predicate, presume, presuppose, pretend, spark, speculate, surmise, suspect, take, take for granted, theorize, think, understand; SEE CONCEPT *28*

suppose [*v2*] *believe*
assume, be afraid, conceive, conclude, conjecture, consider, deem, dream, expect, fancy, feel, gather, have a hunch*, have sneaking suspicion*, hypothesize, imagine, judge, postulate, pretend, reckon, regard, suspect, swear by, take, take as gospel truth*, take stock in*, think, understand, view; SEE CONCEPT *12*

supposition [*n*] *guess, belief*
apriorism, assumption, condition, conjecture, doubt, guessing, guesstimate*, guesswork, hunch, hypothesis, idea, likelihood, notion, opinion, posit, postulate, postulation, premise, presumption, presupposition, rough guess*, shot in the dark*, sneaking suspicion*, speculation, stab in the dark*, suppose, surmise, suspicion, theory, thesis, view; SEE CONCEPT *689*

suppress [*v*] *restrain, hold in check*
abolish, annihilate, beat down, bottle, bring to naught, burke, censor, check, clamp, conceal, conquer, contain, cover up, crack down on, crush, curb, cut off, extinguish, hold back, hold down, hold in, interrupt, keep in, keep secret, muffle, muzzle, overcome, overpower, overthrow, put an end to, put down, put kibosh on*, put lid on*, quash, quell, quench, repress, shush*, silence, sit on*, smother, snuff out*, spike, squash*, stamp out*, stifle, stop, subdue, trample, withhold; SEE CONCEPTS *121,130,252*

supremacy [*n*] *total domination*
absolute rule, ascendancy, authority, command, control, dominance, dominion, driver's seat*, paramountcy, power, predominance, preeminence, preponderance, prepotence, primacy, principality,

sovereignty, superiority, supreme authority, sway, transcendence; SEE CONCEPTS *133,376*

supreme [*adj*] *greatest, principal*
absolute, best, cardinal, chief, closing, crowning, culminating, excellent, extreme, final, first, foremost, head, highest, incomparable, last, leading, marvelous, matchless, maximum, paramount, peerless, perfect, predominant, preeminent, prevailing, prime, sovereign, superb, superlative, surpassing, terminal, top, top-drawer*, towering, transcendent, ultimate, unequaled, unmatched, unparalleled, unsurpassable, unsurpassed, utmost; SEE CONCEPTS *568,574*

sure [*adj1*] *certain, definite*
abiding, assured, changeless, clear, confident, constant, convinced, convincing, decided, doubtless, enduring, firm, fixed, for a fact, free from doubt*, genuine, incontestable, incontrovertible, indisputable, indubitable, never-failing, persuaded, positive, real, satisfied, set, steadfast, steady, telling, unchangeable, unchanging, uncompromising, undeniable, unequivocal, unfailing, unfaltering, unqualified, unquestionable, unquestioning, unshakable, unshaken, unvarying, unwavering, valid; SEE CONCEPT *535*

sure [*adj2*] *physically stable*
fast, firm, fixed, safe, secure, solid, staunch, steady, strong; SEE CONCEPT *488*

sure [*adj3*] *inevitable*
assured, bound, certain, guaranteed, indisputable, ineluctable, inerrant, inescapable, infallible, irrevocable, surefire, unavoidable, unerring, unfailing; SEE CONCEPT *548*

sure [*adj4*] *self-confident*
arrogant, assured, certain, composed, confident, decided, decisive, positive, self-assured, self-possessed; SEE CONCEPT *401*

surely [*adv*] *without doubt*
absolutely, admittedly, assuredly, beyond doubt, beyond shadow of doubt*, certainly, clearly, come what may*, conclusively, decidedly, definitely, distinctly, doubtlessly, evidently, explicitly, fixedly, for certain, for real, indeed, indubitably, inevitably, inexorably, infallibly, irrefutably, manifestly, nothing else but, plainly, positively, rain or shine*, to be sure, undoubtedly, unequivocally, unerringly, unfailingly, unmistakably, unquestionably, unshakably, with certainty, without fail; SEE CONCEPT *535*

surface [*n*] *external part of something*
area, cover, covering, expanse, exterior, exteriority, externality, facade, face, facet, level, obverse, outside, peel, periphery, plane, rind, side, skin, stretch, superficiality, superficies, top, veneer; SEE CONCEPT *484*

surface [*adj*] *external*
apparent, covering, depthless, exterior, facial, outer, outside, outward, shallow, shoal, superficial, top; SEE CONCEPTS *485,583*

surface [*v*] *come to the top of*
appear, arise, come to light, come up, crop up, emerge, flare up, materialize, rise, transpire; SEE CONCEPTS *166,716*

surfeit [*n*] *excess*
bellyful*, excess, glut*, overabundance, overflow, overfullness, overindulgence, overkill, overmuch, overplus, plenitude, plethora, profusion, remainder, repletion, satiety, satisfaction, saturation, superabundance, superfluity, surplus, up to here*; SEE CONCEPT *740*

surfeit [v] *overfill*

cloy, cram, eat, fill, glut, gorge, jade, overfeed, overindulge, pall, sate, satiate, satisfy, stuff; SEE CONCEPTS 209,740

surge [n] *rush, usually of liquid*

billow, breaker, deluge, efflux, flood, flow, growth, gush, intensification, outpouring, rise, roll, surf, swell, upsurge, wave; SEE CONCEPTS 432,467,787

surge [v] *rush, usually in liquid form*

arise, billow, climb, deluge, eddy, flow, grow, gush, heave, mount, pour, ripple, rise, roll, sluice, stream, swell, swirl, tower, undulate, well forth; SEE CONCEPTS 146,179

surly [adj] *gruff, bearish*

boorish, brusque, churlish, cross, crusty, curmudgeonly, discourteous, dour, fractious, glum, grouchy, ill-mannered, ill-natured, irritable, morose, perverse, rude, saturnine, sulky, sullen, testy, ugly, uncivil, ungracious; SEE CONCEPT 401

surmise [n] *guess, conclusion*

assumption, attempt, conjecture, deduction, guesstimate*, guesswork, hunch, hypothesis, idea, inference, notion, opinion, possibility, presumption, sneaking suspicion*, speculation, supposition, suspicion, theory, thought; SEE CONCEPTS 529,689

surmise [v] *come to a conclusion*

assume, conclude, conjecture, consider, deduce, fancy, guess, guesstimate*, hazard a guess*, hypothesize, imagine, infer, opine, presume, pretend, regard, risk assuming, speculate, suppose, suspect, take a shot*, take a stab*, theorize, think, venture a guess; SEE CONCEPTS 18,28

surmount [v] *overcome, triumph over*

best, better, cap, clear, conquer, crest, crown, defeat, down, exceed, hurdle, leap, lick*, negotiate, outdo, outstrip, over, overpower, overtop, pass, prevail over, rise above, subdue, surpass, throw*, top*, vanquish, vault; SEE CONCEPTS 95,141

surpass [v] *outdo something or someone*

beat, best, better, cap, eclipse, exceed, excel, go beyond, go one better*, improve upon, outdistance, outgo, outmatch, outpace, outperform, outrank, outrival, outrun, outshine, outstep, outstrip, outweigh, override, overshadow, overstep, pass, put to shame*, rank*, surmount, top, tower, tower above*, transcend, trump*; SEE CONCEPT 141

surplus [n] *extra material*

balance, excess, overage, overflow, overkill, overmuch, overrun, overstock, oversupply, plethora, plus, remainder, residue, something extra, superabundance, superfluity, surfeit, surplusage, the limit, too much; SEE CONCEPTS 260,658,824

surplus [adj] *extra*

de trop, excess, in excess, leftover, odd*, over, remaining, spate, superfluent, superfluous, supernumerary, too much, unused; SEE CONCEPTS 560,781,824

surprise [n] *something amazing; state of amazement*

abruptness, amazement, astonishment, astoundment, attack, awe, bewilderment, bombshell*, consternation, curiosity, curveball*, disappointment, disillusion, eye-opener*, fortune, godsend*, incredulity, jolt*, kick*, marvel, miracle, miscalculation, phenomenon, portent, precipitance, precipitation, precipitousness, prodigy, rarity, revelation, shock, start, stupefaction,

suddenness, thunderbolt*, unexpected, unforeseen, whammy*, wonder, wonderment; SEE CONCEPTS 410,529

surprise [v1] *astonish; cause amazement*

amaze, astound, awe, bewilder, blow away*, bowl over*, cause wonder, confound, confuse, consternate, daze, dazzle, discomfit, disconcert, dismay, dumbfound, electrify, flabbergast, floor, jar, jolt, leave aghast, leave open-mouthed, nonplus, overwhelm, perplex, petrify, rattle, rock, shake up, shock, spring something on, stagger, startle, strike dumb*, strike with awe, stun, stupefy, take aback, take one's breath away*, throw a curve*, unsettle; SEE CONCEPT 42

surprise [v2] *sneak up on; catch*

ambush, burst in on, bushwhack*, capture, catch in the act*, catch off-balance*, catch off-guard*, catch red-handed*, catch unawares*, come down on, discover, drop in on, grab, grasp, lay for, lie in wait*, nab, seize, spring on, startle, take, take by surprise, waylay; SEE CONCEPTS 42,86

surrender [n] *giving up; resignation*

abandonment, abdication, acquiescence, appeasement, capitulation, cessation, dedition, delivery, giving way, relenting, relinquishment, renunciation, submission, succumbing, white flag*, yielding; SEE CONCEPTS 67,108,119,320

surrender [v] *give up; resign*

abandon, buckle under*, capitulate, cave in*, cede, commit, concede, consign, cry uncle*, deliver up, eat crow*, eat humble pie*, entrust, fall, fold, forego, give in, go along with, go down, go under, hand over, knuckle, knuckle under*, leave, let go, pack it in*, part with, play dead*, put up white flag*, quit, relinquish, renounce, roll over*, submit, succumb, throw in the towel*, toss it in*, waive, yield; SEE CONCEPTS 67,108,119,320

surreptitious [adj] *sneaky, secret*

clandestine, covert, fraudulent, furtive, hidden, hole-and-corner*, hush-hush*, on the QT*, on the sly*, private, skulking, slinking, sly, sneaking, stealthy, sub-rosa, unauthorized, undercover, underhand, under-the-table*, under wraps*, veiled; SEE CONCEPT 548

surrogate [n] *person or thing that acts as substitute*

agent, alternate, backup, delegate, deputy, expediency, expedient, fill-in, makeshift, pinch hitter*, proxy, recourse, refuge, replacement, representative, resort, resource, stand-in, stopgap*, sub*; SEE CONCEPTS 348,414,423

surround [v] *enclose, encircle something*

beleaguer, beset, besiege, blockade, border, bound, box in, circle, circumscribe, circumvent, close around, close in, close in on, compass, confine, edge, enclave, encompass, envelop, environ, fence in, fringe, gird, girdle, go around, hem in, inundate, invest, lay siege to, limit, loop, margin, outline, rim, ring, round, shut in, skirt, verge; SEE CONCEPT 758

surroundings [n] *environment*

ambience, atmosphere, background, climate, community, environs, home, location, medium, milieu, neighborhood, setting, vicinity; SEE CONCEPTS 198,673

surveillance [n] *close observation, following*

body mike*, bug*, bugging*, care, control, direction, eagle eye*, examination, eye, inspection, lookout, peeled eye*, scrutiny, spying, stakeout, superintendence, supervision, surveyance, tab*, tail*, tap*, track*, vigil, vigilance, watch, wire-tap; SEE CONCEPTS *103,298,749*

survey [n] *scrutiny, examination*
analysis, aperçu, audit, check, compendium, critique, digest, inquiry, inspection, outline, overview, pandect, perlustration, perusal, precis, review, sample, scan, sketch, study, syllabus, view; SEE CONCEPTS *37,103,197,271,291*

survey [v] *scrutinize, take stock of*
appraise, assay, assess, canvass, case, check, check out, check over, check up, contemplate, estimate, evaluate, examine, give the once over*, inspect, look over, look upon, measure, observe, overlook, oversee, plan, plot, prospect, rate, read, reconnoiter, research, review, scan, scope, scrutinize, set at, size, size up, stake out, study, summarize, superintend, supervise, take stock of*, test the waters*, valuate, value, view; SEE CONCEPTS *37,48,103,197,291*

survive [v] *continue to live*
bear, be extant, be left, carry on, carry through, come through, cut it, endure, exist, get on, get through, go all the way*, go the limit*, handle, hold out, keep, keep afloat, last, live, live down, live on, live out, live through, make a comeback*, make the cut*, outlast, outlive, outwear, persevere, persist, pull out of it*, pull through, recover, remain, remain alive, revive, ride out*, see through, stand up, subsist, suffer, sustain, tough it out*, weather, withstand; SEE CONCEPTS *23,239,407*

susceptible [adj] *exposed, naïve*
affected, aroused, be taken in, disposed, easily moved, easy, fall for, given, gullible, impressed, impressible, impressionable, inclined, influenced, liable, mark, movable, nonresistant, obnoxious, open, out on a limb*, persuadable, predisposed, prone, pushover, ready, receptive, responsive, roused, sensible, sensile, sensitive, sentient, sitting duck*, soft, stirred, subject, sucker*, suggestible, susceptive, swallow, swayed, tender, touched, tumble for*, vulnerable, wide open; SEE CONCEPTS *403,542*

suspect [adj] *doubtful*
doubtable, dubious, fishy*, incredible, open, problematic, pseudo*, questionable, ridiculous, shaky*, suspected, suspicious, thick*, thin*, unbelievable, uncertain, unclear, unlikely, unsure; SEE CONCEPTS *529,582*

suspect [v] *distrust; guess*
assume, be afraid, believe, conceive, conclude, conjecture, consider, disbelieve, doubt, expect, feel, gather, harbor suspicion*, have a hunch*, have doubt, have sneaking suspicion*, hazard a guess*, hold, imagine, mistrust, presume, reckon, smell a rat*, speculate, suppose, surmise, think, think probable, understand, wonder; SEE CONCEPTS *21,28*

suspend [v1] *hang from above*
append, attach, be pendent, dangle, depend, hang down, hang up, hook up, sling, swing, wave; SEE CONCEPTS *181,190*

suspend [v2] *delay, hold off*
adjourn, arrest, bar, break up, can, cease, check, count out, cut short, debar, defer, discontinue, eject, eliminate, exclude, file, halt, hang, hang fire*, hang up, hold up, inactivate, intermit, interrupt, lay aside, lay off, lay on the table*, lay over, omit, pigeonhole*, pink-slip*, postpone, procrastinate, prorogue, protract, put an end to,

put a stop to, put off, put on back burner*, put on hold, put on ice*, put on the shelf*, reject, retard, rule out, shelve, stave off, stay, waive, withhold; SEE CONCEPTS *119,121,130,351*

suspense [n] *anticipation*
anxiety, apprehension, chiller*, cliff-hanger*, cloak and dagger*, confusion, dilemma, doubt, eagerness, expectancy, expectation, grabber*, hesitancy, hesitation, impatience, indecision, indecisiveness, insecurity, irresolution, page-turner*, perplexity, potboiler*, tension, thriller*, uncertainty, wavering; SEE CONCEPTS *410,679*

suspension [n] *delay*
abeyance, abeyancy, adjournment, break, breather*, breathing spell*, cessation, coffee break*, concluding, conclusion, cutoff, deferment, disbarment, discontinuation, discontinuing, doldrums, dormancy, downtime*, end, ending, finish, five*, freeze, halt, heave-ho*, intermission, interruption, latency, layoff, letup, moratorium, pause, period, postponement, quiescence, quiescency, remission, respite, stay, stoppage, suspense, ten*, termination, time-out; SEE CONCEPTS *119, 807,832*

suspicion [n1] *doubt*
bad vibes*, chariness, conjecture, cynicism, distrust, dubiety, dubiosity, funny feeling*, guess, guesswork, gut feeling*, hunch, idea, impression, incertitude, incredulity, jealousy, lack of confidence, misgiving, mistrust, nonbelief, notion, qualm, skepticism, sneaking suspicion*, supposition, surmise, uncertainty, wariness, wonder; SEE CONCEPTS *532,689,690*

suspicion [n2] *hint, trace*
cast, glimmer, intimation, shade, shadow, smell, soupçon, strain, streak, suggestion, tinge, touch, whiff; SEE CONCEPTS *529,831*

suspicious [adj1] *distrustful*
apprehensive, cagey, careful, cautious, doubtful, green-eyed*, incredulous, in doubt, jealous, leery, mistrustful, not born yesterday* on the lookout*, questioning, quizzical, skeptical, suspect, suspecting, unbelieving, uptight*, wary, watchful, without belief, without faith, wondering; SEE CONCEPTS *403,542*

suspicious [adj2] *doubtful, fishy*
borderline, debatable, different, disputable, doubtable, dubious, equivocal, farfetched, funny*, irregular, not kosher*, open, open to doubt, open to question, out of line*, overt, peculiar, phony, problematic, queer, questionable, reaching, rings untrue*, shady, shaky*, suspect, too much*, uncertain, uncommon, unsure, unusual, won't wash*; SEE CONCEPTS *529,564*

sustain [v1] *keep up, maintain*
aid, approve, assist, back, bankroll, bear, befriend, bolster, brace, buoy, buttress, carry, comfort, confirm, continue, convey, defend, endorse, favor, feed, foster, go for, help, keep alive, keep from falling, keep going, lend a hand*, lug, nourish, nurse, nurture, pack, preserve, prolong, prop, protract, provide for, ratify, relieve, save, shore up, stand by, stick up for, supply, support, tote, transfer, transport, uphold, validate, verify; SEE CONCEPTS *110,140,190*

sustain [v2] *endure, experience*
abide, bear, bear up under, bear with, brook, digest, encounter, feel, go, hang in, have, know, live with*, put up with*, see, stand*, stand up to,

stomach*, suffer, take it, tolerate, undergo, withstand; SEE CONCEPTS 23,678

sustenance [n] *necessities for existence*
aid, aliment, bacon*, bread*, bread and butter*, comestible, daily bread*, eatables, edibles, food, keep, livelihood, maintenance, nourishment, nutrition, pap*, provender, provision, ration, refreshment, salt*, subsistence, support, victual, wherewithal; SEE CONCEPTS 340,446,457,709

svelte [adj] *thin and well-built*
graceful, lean, lissom, lithe, slender, slinky, smooth, sylphlike, willowy; SEE CONCEPTS 490,491

swagger [v] *show off; walk pompously*
bluster, boast, brag, brandish, bully, cock, flourish, gasconade, gloat, grandstand*, hector, look big*, lord, parade, parade one's wares*, peacock*, play to the crowd*, pontificate, prance, put on, put on airs*, sashay*, saunter, strut, swank*, swashbuckle*, sway, sweep, swell; SEE CONCEPTS 49,149,716

swallow [v1] *consume*
absorb, belt*, bolt*, chugalug*, devour, dispatch, dispose, down, drink, drop, eat, gobble, gulp, imbibe, ingest, ingurgitate, inhale, put away, quaff, sip, slurp, swig, swill, take, toss, wash down*, wolf; SEE CONCEPT 169

swallow [v2] *believe without much thought*
accept, be naive, buy, fall for; SEE CONCEPT 12

swamp [n] *wet land covered with vegetation*
bog, bottoms, everglade, fen, glade, holm, marsh, marshland, mire, moor, morass, mud, muskeg, peat bog, polder, quag, quagmire, slough, swale, swampland; SEE CONCEPT 509

swamp [v] *overwhelm, flood*
beset, besiege, crowd, drench, drown, engulf, inundate, overcrowd, overflow, overload, satiate, saturate, sink, snow*, submerge, submerse, surfeit, swallow up, upset, wash, waterlog, whelm; SEE CONCEPTS 146,179,641

swank/swanky [adj] *plush, stylish*
chichi*, classy, deluxe, exclusive, expensive, fancy, fashionable, flamboyant, flashy, glamorous, grand, lavish, luxurious, ostentatious, peacocky, plushy*, posh, pretentious, rich, ritzy*, sharp, showy, smart, snappy, splashy, sumptuous, tony*, trendy, with-it*; SEE CONCEPT 589

swap/swop [v] *exchange*
bandy, bargain, barter, change, interchange, substitute, switch, trade, traffic, truck; SEE CONCEPT 104

swarm [n] *large, moving group*
army, bevy, blowout, concourse, covey, crowd, crush, drove, flock, herd, horde, host, jam, mass, mob, multitude, myriad, pack, press, push, school, shoal, throng, troop, turnout; SEE CONCEPTS 397,417,432

swarm [v] *move forward as a group*
abound, be alive, be numerous, cluster, congregate, crawl, crowd, flock, flow, gather, gather like bees*, jam, mass, mob, move in a crowd, overrun, pullulate, rush together, stream, teem, throng; SEE CONCEPTS 113,114,159

swarthy [adj] *dark-complexioned*
black, brown, brunet, dark, dark-hued, darkish, dark-skinned, dusky, swart, tan, tawny; SEE CONCEPT 618

swat [v] *hit*
beat, belt, biff, box, buffet, clobber, clout, cuff,

ding, knock, slap, slug, smack, smash, sock, strike, wallop, whack; SEE CONCEPT 189

sway [n] *strong influence*
amplitude, authority, clout, command, control, dominion, empire, expanse, government, jurisdiction, mastery, might, power, predominance, range, reach, regime, reign, rule, run, scope, sovereignty, spread, stretch, sweep; SEE CONCEPTS 376,687

sway [v1] *move back and forth*
bend, blow hot and cold*, careen, fluctuate, hem and haw*, incline, lean, lurch, oscillate, pendulate, pulsate, rock, roll, stagger, swagger, swing, undulate, vibrate, wave, waver, weave, wobble, yo-yo*; SEE CONCEPTS 13,145,151

sway [v2] *influence, affect*
bias, brainwash, carry, conduct, control, crack*, direct, dispose, dominate, get*, govern, guide, hold sway over, hook, impact on, impress, incline, induce, inspire, lead by the nose*, manage, move, overrule, persuade, predispose, prevail on, put across, reign, rule, rule over, sell*, soften up*, strike, suck in*, touch, turn one's head*, twist one's arm*, whitewash*, win over, work on; SEE CONCEPTS 14,68,117

swear [v1] *declare under oath*
affirm, assert, attest, avow, covenant, cross one's heart*, depend on, depose, give one's word*, give witness, have confidence in, maintain, make an affidavit, pledge oneself, plight, promise, rely on, say so*, state, state under oath, swear by, swear to God*, swear up and down*, take an oath, testify, trust, vouch, vow, warrant; SEE CONCEPT 49

swear [v2] *speak profanely; be vulgar*
bedamn, be foul-mouthed, blaspheme, curse, cuss*, execrate, flame*, imprecate, take name in vain*, talk dirty*, use bad language*, utter profanity; SEE CONCEPTS 52,54

swearing [n] *foul language*
bad language*, blasphemy, cursing, cuss*, cussing*, dirty language*, dirty name*, dirty talk*, dirty word*, execration, expletives, four-letter word*, imprecation, malediction, no-no*, profanity, swearword; SEE CONCEPTS 54,276,278

sweat [n1] *body's perspiring*
diaphoresis, excretion, exudation, perspiration, steam, transudation; SEE CONCEPTS 185,467

sweat [n2] *hard work*
backbreaker*, chore, drudgery, effort, grind, labor, moil, slavery, task, toil, travail, work; SEE CONCEPTS 362,677

sweat [v1] *perspire*
break out in a sweat, drip, eject, exude, glow, ooze, secrete, seep, spout, swelter, transude, wilt; SEE CONCEPT 185

sweat [v2] *worry about; bear*
abide, agonize, be on pins and needles*, be on tenterhooks*, brook, chafe, endure, exert, fret, go, labor, lose sleep over*, stand, stay the course*, stick it out*, stomach*, suffer, take, toil, tolerate, torture, work hard; SEE CONCEPTS 23,35

sweaty [adj] *damp with perspiration*
bathed, clammy, covered with sweat, drenched, dripping, drippy, glowing, hot, moist, perspiring, perspiry, soaked, sticky, stinky, sweating, wet; SEE CONCEPT 406

sweep [n1] *range, extent*
ambit, breadth, compass, extension, latitude, length, orbit, purview, radius, reach, region,

scope, span, stretch, vista; SEE CONCEPTS
651,756,788

sweep [n2] *movement*
arc, bend, course, curve, gesture, move, play,
progress, stroke, swing; SEE CONCEPTS 145,748

sweep [v1] *brush off, away*
broom, brush, brush up, clean, clear, clear up,
mop, ready, remove, scrub, tidy, vacuum; SEE
CONCEPT 165

sweep [v2] *fly, glide*
career, fleet, flit, flounce, glance, hurtle, pass,
sail, scud, skim, tear, wing, zoom; SEE CONCEPTS
150,152

sweeping [adj] *wide-ranging*
across-the-board, all-around, all-embracing, all-
encompassing, all-inclusive, all-out, bird's-eye*,
blanket, broad, complete, comprehensive, exaggerated, exhaustive, extensive, full, general, global, inclusive, indiscriminate, out-and-out*,
overall, overdrawn, overstated, radical, thorough,
thorough-going, unqualified, vast, wall-to-wall*,
whole-hog*, wholesale*, wide; SEE CONCEPTS
531,772

sweet [n] *sugary food*
bonbon, candy, chocolate, confection, confectionery, confiture, delight, dessert, enjoyment, final
course, gratification, joy, pleasure, pudding,
snack, sugarplum, sweetmeat; SEE CONCEPTS
457,461

sweet [adj1] *sugary*
candied, candy-coated, cloying, delicious, honeyed, like candy, like honey, luscious, nectarous,
saccharine, sugar-coated, sugared, sweetened,
syrupy, toothsome; SEE CONCEPTS 462,613

sweet [adj2] *friendly, kind*
affectionate, agreeable, amiable, angelic, appealing, attractive, beautiful, beloved, charming,
cherished, companionable, considerate, darling,
dear, dearest, delectable, delicious, delightful,
dulcet, engaging, fair, generous, gentle, good-
humored, good-natured, heavenly, lovable, loving, luscious, mild, mushy, patient, pet, pleasant,
pleasing, precious, reasonable, saccharine, sweet-
tempered, sympathetic, taking, tender, thoughtful, treasured, unselfish, winning, winsome; SEE
CONCEPTS 401,404,542

sweet [adj3] *nice-smelling*
ambrosial, aromal, aromatic, balmy, clean, fragrant, fresh, new, perfumed, perfumy, pure, redolent, savory, scented, spicy, sweet-smelling,
wholesome; SEE CONCEPT 598

sweet [adj4] *nice-sounding*
dulcet, euphonic, euphonious, harmonious, mellifluous, mellow, melodic, melodious, musical,
orotund, rich, rotund, silver-tongued, silvery,
smooth, soft, sonorous, soothing, sweet-
sounding, tuneful; SEE CONCEPT 594

sweeten [v1] *add sugar*
add sweetening, candy, candy-coat, honey, make
sweet, make toothsome, mull, sugar, sugar-coat;
SEE CONCEPT 170

sweeten [v2] *make happy; appease*
alleviate, assuage, conciliate, mollify, pacify, placate, propitiate, soften up, soothe; SEE CONCEPTS
7,22

sweetheart [n] *person whom another loves*
admirer, beau, beloved, boyfriend, companion,
darling, dear, dear one, flame, girlfriend, heartthrob, honey*, inamorata, inamorato, love, love-
bird*, lover, one and only*, paramour, pet,

significant other, steady*, suitor, swain, sweet,
treasure*, truelove, valentine; SEE CONCEPTS
414,423

swell [n] *large increase, flow*
billow, crescendo, growth, ripple, rise, seat, surf,
surge, undulation, uprise, wave; SEE CONCEPT
780

swell [adj] *wonderful*
awesome, cool*, dandy*, deluxe, desirable, excellent, exclusive, fashionable, fine, fly*, grand,
groovy*, keen, marvelous, neat, nifty, plush,
posh, ritzy*, smart, stylish, super, terrific; SEE
CONCEPTS 548,574

swell [v] *become larger*
accumulate, add to, aggravate, amplify, augment,
balloon, become bloated, become distended, become swollen, be inflated, belly, billow, blister,
bloat, bulge, dilate, distend, enhance, enlarge, expand, extend, fatten, fill out, grow, grow larger,
heighten, increase, intensity, mount, plump,
pouch, pout, protrude, puff, puff up, rise, round
out, surge, tumefy, uprise, well up; SEE CON-
CEPTS 236,245,780

swelling [n] *physical growth; lump*
abscess, blister, boil, bruise, bulge, bump, bun-
ion, carbuncle, contusion, corn, dilation, distention, enlargement, hump, increase, inflammation,
injury, knob, knurl, node, nodule, pimple, pock,
protuberance, puff, puffiness, pustule, ridge, sore,
tumescence, tumor, wale, wart, weal, welt; SEE
CONCEPTS 306,309

sweltering [adj] *very hot*
airless, baking, broiling, burning, close, fiery, humid, oppressive, perspiring, scorching, sizzling,
stewing, sticky, stifling, stuffy, sultry, sweaty,
sweltry, torrid; SEE CONCEPT 605

swerve [v] *turn aside, often to avoid collision*
bend, deflect, depart, depart from, deviate, dip,
diverge, err, get off course, go off course, incline,
lurch, move, sheer, sheer off, shift, sideslip, sidestep, skew, skid, slue, stray, swing, tack, train
off, turn, veer, wander, waver, wind; SEE CON-
CEPTS 150,195,201

swift [adj] *very fast*
abrupt, alacritous, barrelling, breakneck, cracking*, double-quick*, expeditious, express, fleet,
fleet-footed*, flying, hasty, headlong, hurried, in
nothing flat*, like crazy*, like mad*, nimble, on
the double*, precipitate, prompt, pronto, quick,
rapid, ready, screaming, shaking a leg*, short,
short-lived, snappy*, spanking*, speedball*,
speedy, sudden, supersonic, unexpected, winged;
SEE CONCEPTS 588,799

swiftly/swift [adv] *very fast*
apace, double-quick*, expeditiously, flat-out*,
fleetly, full tilt*, hastily, hurriedly, in no time*,
posthaste, promptly, quick, quickly, rapidly,
speedily, without losing time*, without warning*;
SEE CONCEPTS 588,799

swim [v] *make way through water using arms, legs*
bathe, breast-stroke, crawl, dive, dog paddle,
float, freestyle, glide, go for a swim, go swimming, go wading, high-dive, move, paddle, practice, race, skinny-dip*, slip, stroke, submerge,
take a dip, wade; SEE CONCEPT 363

swimmingly [adv] *very well*
as planned, cosily, easily, effectively, effortlessly,
favorably, fortunately, happily, like a dream*,
like clockwork*, prosperously, quickly, satisfyingly, smoothly, successfully, well, with flying

colors*, with no trouble, without a hitch*; SEE CONCEPTS 528,544

swindle [n] *cheating, stealing*
blackmail, cheat, con, crooked deal*, deceit, deception, dirty pool*, double-cross*, double-dealing*, extortion, fake, fast one*, fast shuffle*, frame-up, fraud, hoax, hustle, imposition, imposture, knavery, racket*, rip-off*, scam, sell, shady deal*, shakedown, sham, sharp practice*, shell game*, sting, trick, trickery; SEE CONCEPTS 59,139,192

swindle [v] *cheat, steal*
bamboozle, beat*, bilk, clip*, con*, cozen, deceive, defraud, diddle*, do*, dupe, extort, fleece*, flimflam*, fool, frame*, fudge*, gouge*, gull*, hoodwink, overcharge, pluck, pull a fast one*, put one over on*, rip off*, rook, run a game on*, sandbag, scam, sell a bill of goods*, set up, shaft, stiff*, sting*, sucker, take for a ride*, take to the cleaners*, trick, trim*, victimize; SEE CONCEPTS 59,139,192

swindler [n] *person who cheats another*
absconder, backscratcher, charlatan, cheat, cheater, chiseler, clip, con artist, confidence artist, counterfeiter, crook, deceiver, defrauder, dodger, double-dealer, falsifier, forger, four-flusher*, fraud, gouger, grifter, impostor, mechanic, mountebank, operator, rascal, rook, scammer, scoundrel, shark, sharp, sharper, slicker, thief, trickster; SEE CONCEPT 412

swing [n] *moving back and forth*
beat, cadence, cadency, fluctuation, lilt, measure, meter, motion, oscillation, rhythm, stroke, sway, swaying, tempo, undulation, vibration; SEE CONCEPTS 65,748

swing [v] *move back and forth; be suspended*
avert, away, be pendent, curve, dangle, deflect, divert, flap, fluctuate, hang, lurch, oscillate, palpitate, pendulate, pitch, pivot, reel, revolve, rock, roll, rotate, sheer, shunt, suspend, sway, swerve, swivel, turn, turn about, turn on an axis, twirl, undulate, vary, veer, vibrate, volte-face, wag, waggle, wave, wheel, whirl, wiggle, wobble; SEE CONCEPT 145

swipe [n/v] *hit*
bash, blow, clip, clout, clump, cuff, knock, lash out, lick, rap, slap, smack, sock, strike, swat, wallop, wipe; SEE CONCEPT 189

swipe [v2] *steal*
appropriate, cop, filch, heist, hook, lift, make off with, nab, nick, pilfer, pinch, purloin, sneak, snitch; SEE CONCEPT 139

swirl [v] *spin around*
agitate, boil, churn, coil, crimp, crisp, curl, eddy, purl, roil, roll, snake, surge, swoosh*, twirl, whirl, whirlpool, whorl, wriggle; SEE CONCEPTS 145,738

swish [adj] *fashionable, elegant*
classy, deluxe, exclusive, grand, in, plush, posh, ritzy*, smart, stylish, sumptuous, swank, swell, tony*, trendy, with-it*; SEE CONCEPT 589

switch [n] *change, exchange*
about-face, alteration, change of direction, reversal, shift, substitution, swap, transformation; SEE CONCEPT 697

switch [v] *change, exchange*
change course, convert, deflect, deviate, divert, interchange, rearrange, replace, shift, shunt, sidetrack, substitute, swap, trade, turn, turnabout, turn aside, veer; SEE CONCEPTS 104,232,697

swivel [v] *spin around axis*
hinge, pirouette, pivot, revolve, rotate, swing around, turn, whirl; SEE CONCEPT 145

swollen [adj] *enlarged*
bloated, bulgy, distended, distent, inflamed, inflated, puffed, puffy, tumescent, tumid; SEE CONCEPT 485

swoop [v] *descend quickly*
dive, fall, plummet, plunge, pounce, rush, slide, stoop, sweep; SEE CONCEPTS 150,181

sycophant [n] *person who caters to another*
adulator, backscratcher*, backslapper*, bootlicker*, brownnoser*, doormat*, fan, fawner, flatterer, flunky*, groupie*, groveler, handshaker*, hanger-on*, lackey, minion, parasite, politician, puppet, slave; SEE CONCEPT 423

symbol [n] *letter, character, sign of written communication*
attribute, badge, denotation, design, device, emblem, figure, image, indication, logo, mark, motif, note, numeral, pattern, regalia, representation, stamp, token, type; SEE CONCEPT 284

symbolic [adj] *representative*
allegorical, characteristic, denotative, emblematic, figurative, indicative, indicatory, significant, suggestive, symptomatic, token, typical; SEE CONCEPT 267

symbolize [v] *represent; stand for*
betoken, body forth, connote, denote, emblematize, embody, epitomize, exemplify, express, illustrate, indicate, mean, mirror, personify, show, signify, suggest, symbol, typify; SEE CONCEPTS 74,138,682

symmetrical [adj] *well-proportioned*
balanced, commensurable, commensurate, equal, in proportion, proportional, regular, shapely, well-formed; SEE CONCEPTS 480,485,579

symmetry [n] *proportion*
agreement, arrangement, balance, centrality, conformity, correspondence, equality, equilibrium, equipoise, equivalence, evenness, finish, form, harmony, order, proportionality, regularity, rhythm, shapeliness, similarity; SEE CONCEPTS 716,717

sympathetic [adj1] *concerned, feeling*
affectionate, all heart*, appreciating, benign, benignant, caring, commiserating, compassionate, comprehending, condoling, considerate, having heart in right place*, interested, kind, kind-hearted, kindly, loving, pitying, responsive, sensitive, soft, softhearted, supportive, sympathizing, tender, thoughtful, understanding, vicarious, warm, warmhearted; SEE CONCEPT 542

sympathetic [adj2] *agreeable, friendly*
amenable, appreciative, approving, companionable, compatible, congenial, congruous, consistent, consonant, cool, down, encouraging, favorably disposed, having a heart*, in sympathy with, like-minded, on same wavelength*, open, open-minded, pro*, receptive, responsive, simpatico, tuned in*, vicarious, well-disposed, well-intentioned; SEE CONCEPTS 401,542,563

sympathize [v] *feel for, be compassionate*
ache, agree, appreciate, be in accord, be in sympathy, be kind to, be there for*, be understanding, bleed for*, comfort, commiserate, compassionate, comprehend, condole, emphathize, feel heart go out to*, go along with, grieve with, have compassion, identify with, love, offer consolation, pick up on, pity, relate to*, share another's sorrow,

show kindliness, show mercy, show tenderness, side with*, tune in*, understand; SEE CONCEPTS **34,110**

sympathy [n1] *shared feeling*
accord, affinity, agreement, alliance, attraction, benignancy, close relation, commiseration, compassion, concord, congeniality, connection, correspondence, empathy, feelings, fellow feeling, harmony, heart, kindliness, kindness, mutual attraction, mutual fondness, rapport, responsiveness, sensitivity, tenderness, understanding, union, unity, warmheartedness, warmth; SEE CONCEPTS **388,410,664**

sympathy [n2] *pity*
aid, cheer, comfort, commiseration, compassion, condolence, consolation, empathy, encouragement, reassurance, rue, ruth, solace, tenderness, thoughtfulness, understanding; SEE CONCEPTS **410,633**

symptom [n] *sign of illness or problem*
evidence, expression, index, indication, indicia, manifestation, mark, note, significant, syndrome, token, warning; SEE CONCEPTS **306,316**

syndicate [n] *group of business entities*
association, board, bunch, cabinet, cartel, chain, chamber, combine, committee, company, conglomerate, council, crew, gang, group, megacorp*, mob, multinational*, organization, outfit, partnership, pool, ring, trust, union; SEE CONCEPTS **323,325**

syndrome [n] *disease, condition*
affection, ailment, complaint, complex, diagnostics, disorder, infirmity, malady, problem, prognostics, sickness, sign, symptoms; SEE CONCEPTS **306,316,674**

synonymous [adj] *equivalent*
alike, apposite, coincident, compatible, convertible, correspondent, corresponding, equal, identical, identified, interchangeable, like, one and the same, same, similar, synonymic, tantamount; SEE CONCEPTS **487,573**

synopsis [n] *digest, summary*
abridgment, abstract, aperçu, breviary, brief, capsule, compendium, condensation, conspectus, epitome, outline, précis, recap*, résumé, review, rundown, run-through, sketch; SEE CONCEPT **283**

synthesis [n] *combining; combination*
amalgam, amalgamation, blend, building a whole, coalescence, composite, compound, constructing, construction, entirety, forming, fusion, integrating, integration, making one, organism, organization, structure, unification, union, unit, welding, whole; SEE CONCEPTS **113,837**

synthesize [v] *combine; make whole*
amalgamate, arrange, blend, harmonize, incorporate, integrate, manufacture, orchestrate, symphonize, unify; SEE CONCEPTS **113,205**

synthetic [adj] *artificial*
constructed, counterfeit, ersatz*, fabricated, factitious, fake, false, hokey*, made, makeshift, manufactured, mock, phony, plastic, unnatural; SEE CONCEPTS **485,582**

system [n1] *order, whole*
arrangement, classification, combination, complex, conformity, coordination, entity, fixed order, frame of reference, ideology, integral, integrate, logical order, orderliness, organization, philosophy, red tape*, regularity, rule, scheme, setup, structure, sum, theory, totality; SEE CONCEPTS **770,837**

system [n2] *method, plan*
arrangement, artifice, course of action, custom, definite plan, fashion, logical process, manner, methodicalness, methodology, mode, modus, modus operandi, operation, orderliness, orderly process, pattern, policy, practice, procedure, proceeding, process, regularity, routine, scheme, strategy, structure, systematic process, systematization, tactics, technique, theory, usage, way, wise; SEE CONCEPT **6**

systematic [adj] *orderly*
analytical, arranged, businesslike, complete, efficient, logical, methodic, methodical, ordered, organized, out-and-out*, precise, regular, standardized, systematized, thoroughgoing, well-ordered; SEE CONCEPTS **557,585**

systematize [v] *put in order*
arrange, array, contrive, design, devise, dispose, establish, frame, get act together, institute, make uniform, marshal, methodize, order, organize, plan, project, pull together, rationalize, regulate, schematize, shape up, standardize, straighten up, systemize, tighten up; SEE CONCEPTS **84,94**

T

tab [n1] *ticket, label*
bookmark, clip, flag, flap, holder, logo, loop, marker, slip, sticker, stop, strip, tag; SEE CONCEPTS **270,475**

tab [n2] *bill for service*
account, charge, check, cost, invoice, price, price tag, rate, reckoning, score, statement, tariff; SEE CONCEPT **329**

table [n1] *furniture upon which to work, eat*
bar, bench, board, buffet, bureau, console, counter, desk, dining table, dinner table, dresser, lectern, pulpit, sideboard, sink, slab, stand, wagon; SEE CONCEPT **443**

table [n2] *meal*
bill of fare, board, cuisine, diet, fare, food, meat and drink, menu, spread, victuals; SEE CONCEPT **459**

table [n3] *flatland*
flat, mesa, plain, plateau, tableland, upland; SEE CONCEPT **509**

table [n4] *diagram with columns of information*
agenda, appendix, canon, catalogue, chart, compendium, digest, graph, illustration, index, inventory, list, plan, record, register, roll, schedule, statistics, summary, synopsis, table of contents, tabulation; SEE CONCEPTS **283,625**

table [v] *postpone a proposition*
cool*, defer, delay, enter, hang*, hold off, hold up, move, pigeonhole*, propose, put aside, put forward, put off, put on back burner*, put on hold*, put on ice*, put on the shelf*, shelve, submit, suggest; SEE CONCEPTS **121,324**

tableau [n] *scene, often painted*
illustration, picture, representation, spectacle, view; SEE CONCEPTS **625,716**

tablet [n1] *sheaf of papers that are connected*
book, folder, memo pad, notebook, pad, quire, ream, scratch, scratch pad, sheets; SEE CONCEPT **475**

tablet [n2] *encapsulated medicine*
cake, capsule, dose, lozenge, medicine, pellet, pill, square, troche; SEE CONCEPT *307*

taboo [n] *something not allowed, permitted*
anathema, ban, disapproval, don't*, forbiddance, inhibition, interdict, law, limitation, no-no*, prohibition, proscription, regulation, religious convention, reservation, restraint, restriction, sanction, social convention, stricture, superstition, thou-shalt-not*; SEE CONCEPTS *532,688*

taboo [adj] *not allowed, permitted*
anathema, banned, beyond the pale*, disapproved, forbidden, frowned on*, illegal, off limits*, outlawed, out of bounds*, prohibited, proscribed, reserved, restricted, ruled out, unacceptable, unmentionable, unthinkable; SEE CONCEPT *548*

tabulate [v] *figure, classify*
alphabetize, arrange, catalogue, categorize, chart, codify, digest, enumerate, formulate, grade, index, list, methodize, order, range, register, systematize, tabularize; SEE CONCEPTS *84,764*

tacit [adj] *taken for granted; not said aloud*
alluded to, allusive, assumed, hinted at, implicit, implied, inarticulate, indirect, inferred, intimated, silent, suggested, undeclared, understood, unexpressed, unsaid, unspoken, unstated, unvoiced, wordless; SEE CONCEPTS *529,548*

taciturn [adj] *uncommunicative*
aloof, antisocial, brooding, clammed up*, close, close-mouthed*, cold, curt, distant, dour, dried-up*, dumb, laconic, mum, mute, quiet, reserved, reticent, sententious, silent, sparing, speechless, tight-lipped*, unexpressive, unforthcoming, withdrawn; SEE CONCEPTS *267,401*

tack [n1] *course of movement*
aim, alteration, approach, bearing, bend, deflection, deviation, digression, direction, double, echelon, heading, line, method, oblique course, path, plan, point of sail, procedure, set, shift, siding, sidling, sweep, swerve, switch, tactic, tangent, turn, variation, way, yaw, zigzag; SEE CONCEPTS *692,738*

tack [n2] *short pin for attaching*
brad, nail, point, pushpin, staple, thumbtack; SEE CONCEPT *475*

tack [v] *attach*
add, affix, annex, append, baste, fasten, fix, hem, mount, nail, paste, pin, sew, staple, stitch, tag, tie; SEE CONCEPTS *85,160,218*

tackle [n] *equipment for activity*
accouterment, apparatus, appliance, gear, goods, habiliments, hook, impedimenta, implements, line, machinery, materiel, outfit, paraphernalia, rig, rigging, tools, trappings; SEE CONCEPT *496*

tackle [v1] *make an effort*
accept, apply oneself, attack, attempt, bang away at*, begin, come to grips with*, deal with, devote oneself to, embark upon, engage in, essay, give a try*, give a whirl*, go for it*, launch, make a run at*, pitch into, set about, square off*, start the ball rolling*, take a shot at*, take in hand*, take on, take up, try, try on for size*, turn one's hand to*, turn to, undertake, work on; SEE CONCEPTS *87,100*

tackle [v2] *jump on and grab*
attack, block, bring down, bring to the ground*, catch, challenge, clutch, confront, down, grapple, grasp, halt, intercept, nail, put the freeze on*,

sack, seize, smear, stop, take, take hold of, throw, throw down, upset; SEE CONCEPTS *90,164,191*

tacky [adj] *cheap, tasteless*
broken-down, crude, dilapidated, dingy, dowdy, down-at-heel*, faded, frumpy*, gaudy, inelegant, mangy*, messy, nasty*, outmoded, out-of-date, poky*, ratty, run-down, seedy, shabby, shoddy, sleazy*, sloppy*, slovenly, stodgy, threadbare, unbecoming, unkempt, unstylish, unsuitable, untidy, vulgar; SEE CONCEPTS *485,589*

tact [n] *finesse, thoughtfulness*
acumen, acuteness, address, adroitness, amenity, aptness, care, common sense, consideration, control, courtesy, delicacy, delicatesse, diplomacy, discernment, discretion, discrimination, gallantry, good taste, head, horse sense*, intelligence, judgment, penetration, perception, perspicacity, poise, policy, politicness, presence, prudence, refinement, repose, savoir-faire, sensitivity, skill, smoothness, suavity, subtlety, tactfulness, understanding, urbanity; SEE CONCEPT *633*

tactful [adj] *thoughtful, careful*
adroit, aware, cautious, civil, considerate, courteous, deft, delicate, diplomatic, discreet, gentle, judicious, observant, perceptive, poised, polished, polite, politic, prudent, sensitive, skilled, skillful, suave, subtle, sympathetic, tactical, understanding, urbane, wise; SEE CONCEPT *401*

tactics [n] *strategy*
approach, campaign, channels, course, defense, device, disposition, generalship, line, maneuver, maneuvering, means, method, move, plan, plan of attack, ploy, policy, procedure, red tape*, scheme, stratagem, system, tack, technique, trick, way; SEE CONCEPT *660*

tactless [adj] *unthinking, careless*
awkward, blundering, boorish, brash, bungling, clumsy, crude, discourteous, gauche, gruff, harsh, hasty, impolite, impolitic, imprudent, inconsiderate, indelicate, indiscreet, inept, injudicious, insensitive, maladroit, misunderstanding, rash, rough, rude, sharp, stupid, thoughtless, uncivil, unconsiderate, undiplomatic, unfeeling, unkind, unperceptive, unpolished, unsubtle, unsympathetic, untactful, vulgar; SEE CONCEPT *401*

tag [n] *label, ticket*
badge, button, card, check, chip, docket, emblem, flap, ID*, identification, inscription, insignia, logo, mark, marker, motto, note, pin, slip, stamp, sticker, stub, tab, tally, trademark, voucher; SEE CONCEPTS *270,284,475*

tag [v1] *label; attach label*
add, adjoin, affix, annex, append, call, check, christen, designate, docket, dub, earmark, fasten, hold, identify, mark, name, nickname, style, tack, tally, tap, term, ticket, title, touch; SEE CONCEPTS *62,85,160*

tag [v2] *follow*
accompany, attend, bedog, chase, dog, heel, hunt, pursue, shadow, tail, trace, track, track down, trail; SEE CONCEPT *207*

tail [n] *end piece, part*
appendage, behind, butt*, buttocks, caudal appendage, conclusion, empennage, end, extremity, fag end*, hind end, hindmost part, hind part, last part, posterior, rear, rear end, reverse, rudder, rump*, stub, tag, tag end, tailpiece, train, tush*, wagger*; SEE CONCEPTS *392,825,827*

tail [v] *follow*
bedog, dog, eye*, hound, keep an eye on, pursue,

shadow, stalk, tag, track, trail; SEE CONCEPT 207

tailor [n] *person who sews clothing*
clothier, costumier, couturier, dressmaker, garment maker, needle worker*, outfitter, suit maker; SEE CONCEPT 348

tailor [v] *make to fit; adjust*
accommodate, adapt, alter, conform, convert, custom-make, cut, cut to fit, dovetail*, fashion, fit, make to order, modify, mold, quadrate, reconcile, shape, shape up, square, style, suit, tailor-make*; SEE CONCEPTS 126,202,218

taint [n] *contamination, corruption*
black mark, blemish, blot, contagion, defect, disgrace, dishonor, fault, flaw, infection, pollution, shame, smear, spot, stain, stigma; SEE CONCEPTS 230,388

taint [v] *dirty, contaminate; ruin*
adulterate, besmirch, blacken, blemish, blight, blot, blur, brand, break down, cast a slur, cloud, cook, corrupt, crud up*, crumble, cut, damage, debase, decay, decompose, defile, deprave, discolor, discredit, disgrace, dishonor, disintegrate, doctor, foul, give a bad name*, harm, hurt, infect, muddy, poison, pollute, putrefy, rot, shame, smear, soil, spike, spoil, stain, stigmatize, sully, tar, tarnish, trash*, turn, water, water down; SEE CONCEPTS 246,254,384

take [n] *profit*
booty*, catch, catching, cut, gate, haul*, holding, part, proceeds, receipts, return, returns, revenue, share, takings, yield; SEE CONCEPT 344

take [v1] *get; help oneself to*
abduct, accept, acquire, arrest, attain, capture, carry off, carve out, catch, clasp, clutch, collar*, collect, earn, ensnare, entrap, gain possession, gather up, get hold of, grab, grasp, grip, handle, haul in, have, hold, lay hold of, obtain, overtake, pick up, prehend, pull in, reach, reap, receive, secure, seize, snag, snatch, strike, take hold of, take in, win; SEE CONCEPTS 120,142

take [v2] *steal*
abduct, abstract, accroach, annex, appropriate, arrogate, borrow, carry off, commandeer, confiscate, expropriate, filch*, haul in, liberate, lift*, misappropriate, nab*, nail*, nip*, pick up, pinch*, pluck, pocket*, preempt, pull in, purloin, rip off*, run off with*, salvage, seize, sequester, snag, snare, snatch*, snitch*, swipe*, take in; SEE CONCEPT 139

take [v3] *buy; reserve*
book, borrow, charter, choose, cull, decide on, derive, draw, elect, engage, gain, get, hire, lease, mark, obtain, optate, opt for, pay for, pick, prefer, procure, purchase, rent, select, single out; SEE CONCEPTS 41,327

take [v4] *endure*
abide, accept, accommodate, bear, bear with, brave, brook, contain, give access, go, go through, grin and bear it*, hack*, hang in*, hang on*, hang tough*, hold, let in, live with, put up with, receive, ride out*, stand, stand for, stick it out*, stomach, submit to, suffer, swallow, take it, take it lying down*, take it on the chin*, tolerate, undergo, weather, welcome, withstand; SEE CONCEPT 23

take [v5] *consume*
devour, down, drink, eat, feed, feed on, imbibe, ingest, inhale, meal, partake of, swallow; SEE CONCEPT 169

take [v6] *accept, adopt; use*
accommodate, admit, appropriate, assume, be aware of, behave, bring, deal with, delight in, do, effect, enjoy, enter upon, execute, exercise, exert, experience, function, give access, have, include, let in, like, luxuriate in, make, observe, operate, perform, play, practice, put in practice, react, receive, relish, sense, serve, take in, treat, undertake, utilize, welcome, work; SEE CONCEPTS 100,124,225

take [v7] *understand*
accept, apprehend, assume, be aware of, believe, catch, compass, comprehend, consider, deem, expect, experience, feel, follow, gather, grasp, hold, imagine, interpret as, know, look upon, observe, perceive, presume, receive, reckon*, regard, see, see as, sense, suppose, suspect, take in, think, think of as; SEE CONCEPT 15

take [v8] *win; be successful*
beat, be efficacious, do the trick, have effect, operate, prevail, succeed, triumph, work; SEE CONCEPT 706

take [v9] *carry, transport; accompany*
attend, back, bear, bring, buck, cart, conduct, convey, convoy, drive, escort, ferry, fetch, go with, guide, gun, haul, heel, jag, journey, lead, lug, move, pack, piggyback*, pilot, ride, schlepp*, shoulder, steer, tote, tour, trek, truck, usher; SEE CONCEPTS 114,187,217

take [v10] *captivate, enchant*
allure, attract, become popular, bewitch, charm, delight, draw, entertain, fascinate, magnetize, overwhelm, please, wile, win favor; SEE CONCEPT 11

take [v11] *require*
ask, call for, crave, demand, necessitate, need; SEE CONCEPT 646

take [v12] *subtract*
deduct, discount, draw back, eliminate, knock off, remove, subtract, take away, take off, take out; SEE CONCEPTS 211,236,247

take [v13] *cheat, deceive*
bamboozle*, beat*, bilk, con, cozen, defraud, do*, dupe, fiddle, flimflam*, gull, hoodwink, pull a fast one*, swindle, take for a ride*, trick; SEE CONCEPTS 59,192

take [v14] *contract, catch*
be seized, come down with*, derive, draw, get, sicken with, take sick with; SEE CONCEPT 308

take down [v1] *write down*
inscribe, jot down, make a note of, minute, note, note down, put on record, record, set down, transcribe; SEE CONCEPT 125

take down [v2] *humble*
deflate, humiliate, let down, lower, mortify, pull down, put down, take apart; SEE CONCEPTS 7,19,52

take in [v1] *deceive, fool*
beguile, betray, bilk, bluff, cheat, con, defraud, delude, do*, double-cross*, dupe, flimflam*, four-flush*, gull, hoodwink, lie, mislead, pull wool over eyes*, swindle, trick; SEE CONCEPT 59

take in [v2] *understand*
absorb, assimilate, comprehend, digest, get, grasp, perceive, receive, savvy, see, soak up, take; SEE CONCEPT 15

takeoff [n1] *leaving*
ascent, climb, departure, hop, jump, launch, lift-off, rise, upward flight; SEE CONCEPTS 148,195,224

takeoff [n2] *mockery, satire*
burlesque, caricature, cartoon, comedy, imitation, lampoon, mocking, parody, ridicule, send-up, spoof, travesty; SEE CONCEPTS *111,263,292*

take off [v1] *leave; leave the ground*
ascend, bear, beat it, become airborne, begone, blast off, blow*, clear out*, decamp, depart, disappear, exit, get off, get out, go, go away, head, hightail*, hit the road*, hit the trail*, lift off, light out*, make*, pull out, quit, scram*, set out*, shove off*, soar, split, take to the air*, vamoose*, withdraw; SEE CONCEPTS *148,195,224*

take off [v2] *mock, satirize*
ape, burlesque, caricature, imitate, lampoon, mimic, parody, ridicule, send up, spoof, travesty; SEE CONCEPTS *111,273,292*

take on [v1] *assume, accept*
acquire, add, address oneself to, adopt, agree to do, annex, append, attempt, become, begin, come to have, commence, develop, embrace, employ, endeavor, engage, enlist, enroll, espouse, handle, have a go at*, hire, launch, put on, retain, set about, tackle, take in hand*, take up, take upon oneself*, try, turn, undertake, venture; SEE CONCEPTS *87,221*

take on [v2] *compete*
attack, battle, contend, contest, encounter, engage, face, fight, match, meet, oppose, pit, vie; SEE CONCEPT *92*

take up [v] *begin or start again*
adopt, assume, become involved in, carry on, commence, continue, embrace, engage in, enter, espouse, follow through, get off, go on, initiate, kick off, open, pick up, proceed, recommence, renew, reopen, restart, resume, set to, start, tackle, take on, tee off, undertake; SEE CONCEPTS *221,239*

tale [n1] *story*
account, anecdote, fable, fairy tale, fiction, folk tale, legend, myth, narration, narrative, novel, relation, report, romance, saga, short story, yarn; SEE CONCEPT *282*

tale [n2] *made-up story*
canard, chestnut*, clothesline*, cock-and-bull story*, defamation, detraction, exaggeration, fabrication, falsehood, falsity, fib, fiction, lie, misrepresentation, prevarication, rigmarole*, rumor, scandal, slander, spiel*, tall story*, untruism, untruth, yarn*; SEE CONCEPTS *278,282*

talent [n] *ability*
aptitude, aptness, art, a way with*, bent*, capability, capacity, craft, endowment, expertise, facility, faculty, flair, forte, genius, gift, green thumb*, head*, inventiveness, knack*, know-how*, nose*, power, savvy*, set, skill, smarts*, the formula*, the goods*, the right stuff*, thing*, turn*, what it takes*; SEE CONCEPT *630*

talk [n1] *speech, address to group*
allocution, chalk talk*, declamation, discourse, disquisition, dissertation, epilogue, exhortation, expatiation, harangue, homily, lecture, monologue, oration, peroration, prelection, recitation, screed, sermon, spiel*; SEE CONCEPTS *60,285*

talk [n2] *gossip*
allusion, badinage, banter, blather*, bombast, bunk*, buzz*, cant, chat, chatter, chitchat, conversation, cry, gab, grapevine*, hearsay, hint, hot air*, idle talk, innuendo, insinuation, jaw*, jive*, lip*, noise, nonsense*, palaver, persiflage, prose,

racket*, raillery, report, rot*, rubbish*, rumble*, rumor, scuttlebutt*, small talk, tête-à-tête, trash*, yarn*; SEE CONCEPTS *51,278*

talk [n3] *discussion*
argument, colloquy, conclave, confabulation, conference, consultation, conversation, deliberation, dialogue, earful, encounter, eyeball-to-eyeball*, huddle*, interlocution, interview, meeting, negotiation, palaver, parlance, parley, powwow*, seminar, spiel*, straight talk, symposium, ventilation, visit; SEE CONCEPT *56*

talk [n4] *communication with language*
argot, chatter, dialect, discourse, jargon, lingo, locution, parlance, patois, slang, speaking, speech, utterance, verbalization, vocalization, words; SEE CONCEPTS *47,65*

talk [v1] *produce words; inform*
articulate, babble, broach, chant, chat, chatter, comment on, communicate, confess, converse, describe, divulge, drawl, drone, express, flap one's tongue*, gab, gabble*, give voice to, gossip, influence, intone, notify, palaver, parley, patter, persuade, prate, prattle, pronounce, reveal, rhapsodize, run on*, say, sing*, soliloquize, speak, spill the beans*, spout, squeak*, squeal*, talk one's leg off*, tell, tell all*, use, utter, ventriloquize, verbalize, voice, yak*; SEE CONCEPTS *60,266*

talk [v2] *discuss with another*
argue, be in contact, canvass, carry on conversation, chew*, collogue, commune, confabulate, confer, confide, consult, contact, deliberate, dialogue, engage in conversation, exchange, go into a huddle*, groupthink*, have a meet*, hold discussion, huddle*, interact, interface, interview, join in conversation, keep in touch*, negotiate, network*, palaver, parley, reach out, reason, relate, thrash out*, touch*, touch base*, vent, visit; SEE CONCEPT *56*

talk [v3] *address group*
accost, deliver a speech, discourse, give a talk, give speech, harangue, hold forth, induce, influence, lecture, orate, persuade, pitch, prelect, sermonize, speak, spiel*, spout*, stump*, sway*; SEE CONCEPTS *60,285*

talkative [adj] *excessively communicative*
articulate, big-mouthed*, chattering, chatty*, effusive, eloquent, fluent, full of hot air*, gabby*, garrulous, glib, gossipy, long-winded*, loose-lipped*, loquacious, loudmouthed*, mouthy*, multiloquent, prolix, rattling, slick*, smooth*, talky, verbal, verbose, vocal, voluble, windy*, wordy; SEE CONCEPT *267*

tall [adj1] *high in stature, length*
alpine, altitudinous, beanstalk*, big, elevated, giant, great, high-reaching, lank, lanky, lofty, rangy, sizable, sky-high, skyscraping, soaring, statuesque, towering; SEE CONCEPTS *779,782*

tall [adj2] *exaggerated, unreasonable*
absurd, demanding, difficult, embellished, exorbitant, farfetched, hard, implausible, impossible, outlandish, overblown, preposterous, steep, unbelievable; SEE CONCEPTS *529,565*

tally [n] *count, record*
account, mark, poll, reckoning, running total, score, summation, tab, total; SEE CONCEPTS *283,787*

tally [v] *add up; count, record*
catalog, compute, enumerate, inventory, itemize, keep score, mark, mark down, number, numerate,

reckon, register, sum, tale, tell, total, write down; SEE CONCEPTS *125,764*

tame [*adj1*] *domesticated, compliant*
acclimatized, amenable, biddable, bridled, broken, busted, civilized, cultivated, disciplined, docile, domestic, fearless, gentle, gentle as a lamb*, habituated, harmless, harnessed, housebroken, kindly, manageable, meek, mild, muzzled, obedient, overcome, pliable, pliant, subdued, submissive, tractable, trained, unafraid, unresisting, yoked*; SEE CONCEPT *401*

tame [*adj2*] *dull, uninteresting*
bland, bloodless, boiled down*, boring, conventional, diluted, feeble, flat*, halfhearted, humdrum*, insipid, lifeless, limp, mild, monotonous, prosaic, routine, spiritless, tedious, unexciting, uninspiring, vapid, weak, wearisome, whitebread*, without punch*; SEE CONCEPTS *529,542,548*

tame [*v*] *domesticate, make compliant*
break, break in, break the spirit*, bridle, bring to heel*, bust, check, conquer, curb, discipline, domesticize, domiciliate, enslave, gentle, housebreak, house-train, humble, mitigate, mute, pacify, repress, restrain, soften, subdue, subjugate, suppress, temper, tone down, train, vanquish, water down*; SEE CONCEPTS *14,250*

tamper [*v1*] *interfere, alter*
busybody*, butt in*, change, cook, cut, damage, destroy, diversify, doctor, fiddle with*, fool, horn in*, interfere, interlope, interpose, intrude, irritate, manipulate, meddle, mess around with*, monkey around*, muck about*, phony up*, plant*, poke nose into*, spike*, tinker, vary, water*; SEE CONCEPT *232*

tamper [*v2*] *bribe*
buy, buy off, corrupt, fix, get to, have, influence, lubricate, manipulate, reach, rig, square*; SEE CONCEPT *192*

tan [*n/adj*] *light brown*
beige, biscuit, bronze, brown, brownish, buff, cream, drab, ecru, gold, khaki, leather-colored, natural, olive, olive-brown, saddle, sand, suntan, tawny, umber, yellowish; SEE CONCEPTS *618,622*

tang [*n*] *biting taste or odor*
aroma, bite, flavor, guts*, kick*, nip, piquancy, pungency, reek, relish, sapidity, sapor, savor, scent, smack*, smell, spiciness, tanginess, thrill, twang, zest, zip*; SEE CONCEPTS *599,600,614*

tangible [*adj*] *real, concrete*
actual, appreciable, corporeal, definite, detectable, discernible, distinct, embodied, evident, factual, gross, incarnated, manifest, material, objective, observable, obvious, palpable, patent, perceivable, perceptible, phenomenal, physical, plain, positive, sensible, solid, stable, substantial, tactile, touchable, verifiable, visible, wellgrounded; SEE CONCEPTS *529,582*

tangle [*n*] *knot, confusion*
coil, complication, entanglement, jam, jungle, labyrinth, mass, mat, maze, mesh, mess, mix-up, morass, muddle, rummage, skein, snag, snarl, twist, web; SEE CONCEPTS *230,674,720*

tangle [*v*] *knot, complicate*
catch, coil, confuse, derange, discompose, disorganize, drag into, embroil, enmesh, ensnare, entangle, entrap, foul up*, hamper, implicate, interlace, interlock, intertwist, interweave, involve, jam, kink, make a party to*, mat, mesh, mess up*, mix up*, muck up*, obstruct, perplex,

ravel, snarl, tie up, trap, twist, unbalance, upset; SEE CONCEPTS *112,190*

tantalize [*v*] *provoke, tease*
annoy, badger, baffle, bait, bedevil, beleaguer, charm, entice, fascinate, frustrate, gnaw, harass, harry, keep hanging*, lead on, make mouth water*, pester, plague, taunt, thwart, titillate, torment, torture, worry; SEE CONCEPTS *7,11,19,22*

tantamount [*adj*] *same*
alike, as good as, commensurate, duplicate, equal, equivalent, identical, indistinguishable, like, parallel, same as, selfsame, synonymous, uniform, very; SEE CONCEPTS *487,573*

tantrum [*n*] *fit*
anger, animosity, conniption, dander*, flare-up, hemorrhage*, huff*, hysterics, outburst, storm*, temper, temper tantrum, wax; SEE CONCEPTS *306,384*

tap [*n*] *faucet*
bibcock, cock, egress, hydrant, nozzle, petcock, spigot, spout, stopcock, valve; SEE CONCEPTS *445,464*

tap [*v1*] *hit lightly*
beat, bob, dab, drum, knock, palpate, pat, percuss, rap, strike, tag, thud, thump, tip, touch; SEE CONCEPT *189*

tap [*v2*] *pierce to drain*
bleed, bore, broach, draft, drain, draw, draw forth, draw off, draw out, drill, empty, lance, milk, mine, open, penetrate, perforate, pump, riddle, siphon, spear, spike, stab, unplug, unstopper, use, utilize; SEE CONCEPTS *142,230*

tape [*n*] *ribbon of material*
band, braid, edging, line, rope, strip; SEE CONCEPT *475*

tape [*v1*] *stick together with material*
bandage, bind, bond, fasten, hold together, rope, seal, secure, support, swathe, tie, tie up, truss, wire, wrap; SEE CONCEPTS *85,160*

tape [*v2*] *record sounds, sights*
audiotape, make a tape, register, tape-record, video, videotape; SEE CONCEPTS *125,292*

taper/taper off [*v*] *decrease to a point*
abate, bate, close, come to a point, die away, die out, diminish, drain, dwindle, fade, lessen, narrow, recede, reduce, rescind, subside, thin, thin out, wane, weaken, wind down; SEE CONCEPTS *137,698,776*

tardy [*adj*] *late*
backward, behindhand, belated, dawdling, delayed, delinquent, detained, dilatory, held up, hung up*, in a bind, jammed, laggard, loitering, not arrived, not done, overdue, procrastinating, retarded, slack, slow, sluggish, strapped for time*, too late, unpunctual; SEE CONCEPTS *542,548,799*

target [*n1*] *aim, goal*
ambition, bull's-eye*, destination, duty, end, function, ground zero*, intention, mark, object, objective, point, purpose, spot, use; SEE CONCEPT *659*

target [*n2*] *person as object of ridicule*
butt*, byword, game, mark*, pigeon*, prey, quarry, scapegoat*, scorn, sitting duck*, sport, victim; SEE CONCEPT *423*

tariff [*n*] *tax or fee*
assessment, charge, cost, duty, excise, impost, levy, price, price tag, rate, tab, tax, toll; SEE CONCEPT *329*

ta
ta

tarnish [v] *dirty, corrupt*

befoul, begrime, blacken, blemish, blot, contaminate, damage, darken, defame, defile, dim, discolor, disgrace, dull, embarrass, grime, harm, hurt, impair, injure, lose luster, lose shine, mar, muddy, pale, pollute, rust, slander, smear, smudge, soil, spoil, spot, stain, sully, taint, tar, vitiate; SEE CONCEPTS 246,254,469

tarry [v] *dawdle, delay*

abide, bide, dally, drag, drag one's feet*, dwell, filibuster, get no place fast*, goof around*, hang around*, hold the phone*, lag, linger, lodge, loiter, lose time, pause, poke, procrastinate, put off, remain, rest, sojourn, stall, stay, stick around, stop, stop over, tail, take one's time*, temporize, tool*, trail, visit, wait, warm a chair*; SEE CONCEPTS 35,151,210

tart [n] *pastry*

bun, Danish, eclair, fruit tart, pie, popover, roll, turnover; SEE CONCEPT 457

tart [adj] *bitter, sour in taste or effect*

acerb, acerbic, acetose, acid, acidulous, acrimonious, astringent, barbed, biting, caustic, cutting, dry, harsh, nasty, piquant, pungent, scathing, sharp, short, snappish, snappy, snippy, tangy, testy, trenchant, vinegary, wounding; SEE CONCEPTS 267,613

task [n] *job or chore, often assigned*

assignment, bother, burden, business, calling, charge, daily grind*, deadweight*, duty, effort, employment, enterprise, errand, exercise, fun and games*, function, gig*, grind*, grindstone*, headache*, job, labor, load, long row to hoe*, millstone*, mission, nuisance, occupation, office, onus, pain, project, province, responsibility, stint, strain, tax, toil, trouble, undertaking, vocation, work; SEE CONCEPTS 362,666

task [v] *assign, burden*

charge, encumber, entrust, exhaust, lade, load, oppress, overload, push, saddle, strain, tax, test, weary, weigh, weight; SEE CONCEPTS 14,112,666

taste [n1] *flavor of some quality*

aftertaste, aroma, bang*, bitter, drive, ginger, jolt, kick*, oomph*, palatableness, piquancy, punch*, relish, salt, sapidity, sapor, savor, savoriness, smack, sour, sting*, suggestion, sweet, tang*, wallop, zest, zing*, zip*; SEE CONCEPT 614

taste [n2] *tiny sample*

appetizer, bit, bite, canapé, chaw, dash, delicacy, drop, fragment, hint, hors d'oeuvre, morsel, mouthful, nip, sampling, sip, soupçon, spoonful, sprinkling, suggestion, swallow, tidbit, tincture, tinge, titbit, touch, trifle, whiff*, wink*; SEE CONCEPTS 458,835

taste [n3] *inclination, preference*

affection, appetence, appetite, attachment, bent*, comprehension, cup of tea*, desire, disposition, druthers*, fancy, fondness, gusto, heart, leaning, liking, palate, partiality, penchant, predilection, predisposition, prepossession, relish, soft spot*, stomach*, tendency, thing*, type, understanding, weakness, zest; SEE CONCEPTS 20,32,529,659

taste [n4] *capacity to sense flavor*

appetence, appetite, gout, gustation, palate, stomach, taste buds, tongue; SEE CONCEPTS 590,615

taste [n5] *judgment, propriety*

acumen, acuteness, aestheticism, appreciation, correctness, cultivation, culture, decorum, delicacy, discernment, discretion, discrimination, distinction, elegance, feeling, finesse, good taste, grace, nicety, penetration, perception, polish, politeness, refinement, restraint, style, susceptibility, tact, tactfulness, tastefulness; SEE CONCEPTS 388,411,655,689

taste [v1] *judge, try*

assay, bite, chew, criticize, differentiate, discern, distinguish, eat, enjoy, lick, nibble, partake, perceive, relish, sample, savor, sense, sip, test, touch, try, try the flavor of; SEE CONCEPTS 169,616

taste [v2] *experience*

appreciate, be exposed to, come up against, encounter, feel, have knowledge of, know, meet with, partake of, perceive, run up against, savor, undergo; SEE CONCEPT 678

tasteful [adj] *nice, refined*

aesthetically pleasing, artistic, beautiful, charming, chaste, classical, classy, cultivated, cultured, delectable, delicate, discriminating, elegant, esthetic, exquisite, fastidious, fine, graceful, gratifying, handsome, harmonious, in good taste, pleasing, plush, polished, posh, precise, pure, quiet, restrained, rich, savory, smart, snazzy*, spiffy*, splendiferous, stylish, subdued, swank*, tasty, unaffected, unobtrusive, uptown*; SEE CONCEPTS 529,574,589

tasteless [adj1] *without flavor*

big zero*, blah*, bland, boring, distasteful, dull, flat, flavorless, insipid, mild, nowhere*, pabulum*, plain, plain vanilla*, savorless, stale, tame, thin, unappetizing, uninspired, uninteresting, unpalatable, unpleasurable, unsavory, unseasoned, vanilla*, vapid, watered-down, watery, weak, without spice, zero*; SEE CONCEPT 613

tasteless [adj2] *cheap, vulgar*

artificial, barbaric, barbarous, coarse, crass, crude, flashy, foolish, garish, gaudy, graceless, hideous, impolite, improper, indecorous, indelicate, indiscreet, inelegant, loud, low, low-down, low-down-and-dirty*, makeshift*, off-color*, ornate, ostentatious, outlandish, pretentious, raunchy*, rough, rude, showy, stupid, tacky, tactless, tawdry, trivial, uncouth, unlovely, unpolished, unrefined, unseemly, unsightly, useless, wild; SEE CONCEPTS 401,570,589

tasty [adj] *delicious*

appetizing, delectable, delish*, divine, flavorful, flavorsome, flavory, full-flavored, good-tasting, heavenly, luscious, mellow, palatable, piquant, pungent, sapid, savory, scrumptious, spicy, sugar-coated, sweetened, tasteful, toothsome, toothy, yummy, zestful; SEE CONCEPT 613

tattle [v] *gossip; tell rumor*

babble, blab*, chat, chatter, give away, give the show away*, gossip, have a big mouth*, jabber, leak, noise, prate, prattle*, rumor, snitch, spill, spill the beans*, spread rumor*, squeal, talk, talk idly, tell on, tell tale*, yak*; SEE CONCEPTS 54,60

tattletale/tattler [n] *person who gossips, tells rumors*

bigmouth*, blabberer, blabbermouth*, busybody, canary*, fat mouth*, fink*, gossip, informer, rat*, rumormonger, scandalmonger, snitch*, squealer*, stool pigeon*, talebearer, taleteller, telltale*, tipster, troublemaker, whistleblower, windbag*; SEE CONCEPTS 412,423

taunt [n] *provocation; teasing*

backhanded compliment*, barb, brickbat*, censure, comeback, crack, cut, derision, dig, dirty dig*, dump, gibe, insult, jab, jeer, mockery, outrage, parting shot*, put-down*, reproach, ridicule, sarcasm, slam*, slap*, snappy comeback*, swipe*; SEE CONCEPTS 7,19,266

taunt [v] provoke, reproach; tease
affront, bother, deride, dig*, disdain, dump on*, flout, insult, jab*, jeer, lout, mock, offend, outrage, put down, quiz, rally, revile, ridicule, scoff at, scorn, scout, slam*, slap*, sneer, swipe at, tantalize, torment, twitter, upbraid; SEE CONCEPTS 7,19,54

taut [adj] rigid, tight
close, firm, flexed, snug, stiff, strained, stressed, stretched, tense, tightly drawn, trim, unyielding; SEE CONCEPTS 488,604

tavern [n] business establishment for serving drink, food
alehouse, bar, barroom, beer joint*, dive*, drinkery, gin mill*, grog shop*, honky tonk*, hostelry, hotel, inn, joint*, lodge, lounge, night spot, nineteenth hole*, pub, public house, roadhouse, saloon, speakeasy*, suds*, taphouse*, taproom, watering hole*; SEE CONCEPTS 439,448,449

tawdry [adj] cheap, tasteless
blatant, brazen, chintzy*, common, crude, dirty, flaring, flashy, flaunting, garish, gaudy, gimcrack, glaring, glittering, glitzy, jazzy, junky*, loud, meretricious, obtrusive, offensive, plastic, poor, raffish, screaming, showy, sleazy*, sporty, tacky*, tinsel, vulgar; SEE CONCEPTS 334,589

tax [n1] charge levied by government on property, income
assessment, bite*, brokerage, capitation, contribution, cost, custom, dues, duty, excise, expense, fine, giveaway*, imposition, impost, levy, obligation, pork barrel*, price, rate, salvage, tariff, tithe, toll, towage, tribute; SEE CONCEPT 329

tax [n2] burden
albatross*, charge, deadweight*, demand, difficulty, drain, duty, imposition, load, millstone*, onus, pressure, strain, task, weight; SEE CONCEPTS 362,666

tax [v1] levy charge on property, income
assess, charge, charge duty, demand, demand toll, enact, exact, exact tribute, extract, impose, lay an impost, rate, require contribution, tithe; SEE CONCEPT 298

tax [v2] burden
charge, cumber, drain, encumber, enervate, exhaust, lade, load, make demands on, oppress, overburden, overtax, overuse, overwork, press hard on, pressure, prey on, push, put pressure on, saddle, sap, strain, stress, stretch, task, tire, try, weaken, wear out, weary, weigh, weigh down, weigh heavily on, weight; SEE CONCEPTS 14,208,240

tax [v3] accuse
arraign, blame, censure, charge, criminate, impeach, impugn, impute, incriminate, inculpate, indict, reproach, reprove; SEE CONCEPT 44

taxing [adj] burdensome
demanding, difficult, disturbing, enervating, exacting, exigent, grievous, heavy, onerous, oppressive, punishing, sapping, stressful, tedious, tiring, tough, troublesome, trying, wearing, wearisome, weighty; SEE CONCEPT 565

teach [v] educate; instill knowledge
advise, brainwash*, break in*, brief, catechize, coach, communicate, cram, demonstrate, develop, direct, discipline, drill, edify, enlighten,

exercise, explain, expound, fit, form, give instruction, give lessons, give the facts, ground, guide, illustrate, imbue, impart, implant, improve mind, inculcate, indoctrinate, inform, initiate, instruct, interpret, lecture, nurture, open eyes*, polish up*, pound into*, prepare, profess, rear, school, sharpen, show, show the ropes*, train, tutor; SEE CONCEPT 285

teacher [n] person who educates
abecedary, adviser, assistant, coach, disciplinarian, educator, faculty member, guide, instructor, lecturer, mentor, pedagogue, preceptor, professor, pundit, scholar, schoolteacher, supervisor, teach*, trainer, tutor; SEE CONCEPT 350

team [n] group, crew
aggregation, band, body, bunch, club, company, contingent, duo, faction, foursome, gang, lineup, organization, outfit, pair, partners, party, rig, sect, set, side, span, squad, stable, string, tandem, trio, troop, troupe, unit, workers, yoke; SEE CONCEPTS 365,397,417

tear [n1] rip, cut
breach, break, crack, damage, fissure, gash, hole, imperfection, laceration, mutilation, rent, run, rupture, scratch, split, tatter; SEE CONCEPT 513

tear/tears [n2] droplets from eyes, often caused by emotion
blubbering*, crying, discharge, distress, drops, grieving, lachryma, lamentation, lamenting, moisture, mourning, pain, regret, sadness, sob, sob act*, sobbing, sorrow, teardrop, wailing, water, waterworks*, weep, weeping, weeps*, whimpering, woe; SEE CONCEPTS 185,467

tear [n3] wild action
bender, binge, bust, carousal, carouse, drunk, spree, wassail; SEE CONCEPTS 383,384

tear [v1] cut, rip an object
break, claw, cleave, crack, damage, divide, evulse, extract, fray, frazzle, gash, grab, impair, incise, injure, lacerate, mangle, mutilate, pluck, pull, pull apart, rend, ribbon, rift, rive, run, rupture, scratch, seize, separate, sever, shred, slash, slit, snatch, split, sunder, wrench, wrest, yank; SEE CONCEPTS 206,214

tear [v2] move very fast
boil, bolt, career, charge, chase, course, dart, dash, fling, fly, gallop, hurry, lash, race, run, rush, shoot, speed, spring, zoom; SEE CONCEPTS 150,152

tearful [adj] crying, very upset
bawling*, blubbering*, blubbery*, distressed, dolorous, in tears, lachrymose, lamentable, lamenting, moist, mournful, pathetic, pitiable, pitiful, poignant, sad, sniveling*, sobbing, sorrowful, teary, watery, weeping, weepy, wet, whimpering, woeful; SEE CONCEPTS 401,403

tease [v] aggravate, provoke
annoy, badger, bait, banter, be at, bedevil, beleaguer, bother, chaff, devil, disturb, dog*, gibe, give a hard time*, gnaw, goad, harass, harry, hector, importune, jive*, josh, lead on*, mock, needle*, nudge, pester, pick on*, plague, put down*, rag*, rally, razz*, rib*, ride, ridicule, roast*, send up*, slam, snap, sound, spoof, swipe at, tantalize, taunt, torment, vex, worry; SEE CONCEPTS 7,11,19,22

technical [adj] concerning details, mechanics
abstruse, high-tech*, industrial, mechanical, methodological, occupational, professional, re-

ta
te

stricted, scholarly, scientific, special, specialized, technological, vocational; SEE CONCEPT *536*

technique [n] *method*
address, approach, art, artistry, capability, capacity, course, craft, delivery, execution, facility, fashion, knack*, know-how*, manner, means, mode, modus, modus operandi, performance, procedure, proficiency, routine, skill, style, system, tactics, technic, touch, usage, way, wise; SEE CONCEPTS *6,630*

tedious [adj] *dull, monotonous*
annoying, arid, banal, boring, bromidic, drab, dragging, draggy*, dreary, drudging, dry, dull as dishwater*, dusty*, endless, enervating, exhausting, fatiguing, ho-hum*, humdrum, insipid, irksome, laborious, lifeless, long-drawn-out*, mortal, pabulum*, poky*, prosaic, prosy, slow, snooze*, soporific, tiresome, tiring, unexciting, uninteresting, vapid, wearful, wearisome; SEE CONCEPTS *529,548*

tedium [n] *dullness, monotony*
banality, boredom, deadness*, doldrums, drabness, dreariness, ennui, irksomeness, lack of interest, lifelessness, routine, sameness, tediousness, tiresomeness, wearisomeness, yawn*; SEE CONCEPTS *388,410,668*

teem [v] *be abundant, full*
abound, bear, be crawling with, be full of, be numerous, be plentiful, be prolific, brim, bristle, burst, burst at seams*, bustle, crawl, crowd, flow, grow, jam, overflow, overrun, pack, pour, pour out, produce, prosper, pullulate, rain, roll in, shower, superabound, swarm, swell, swim in, wallow in; SEE CONCEPTS *146,179,740*

teeming [adj] *abundant, full*
alive, brimful, brimming, bristling, bursting, chock-full, crammed, crawling, filled, fruitful, multitudinous, numerous, overflowing, packed, plentiful, populous, pregnant, replete, rife, swarming, thick, thronged; SEE CONCEPTS *481,483,774*

teeny/teensy [adj] *very small*
diminutive, Lilliputian, microscopic, miniature, minuscule, minute, teensy-weensy*, teeny-weeny*, tiny, wee, weeny*; SEE CONCEPTS *773,789*

teeter [v] *wobble back and forth*
balance, dangle, falter, flutter, lurch, pivot, quiver, reel, rock, seesaw, stagger, stammer, stumble, sway, teeter-totter*, topple, totter, tremble, tremble precariously, waver, weave, wiggle; SEE CONCEPT *145*

telegram [n] *message sent by coded radio signals*
buzzer, cable, cablegram, call, coded message, flash, radiogram, report, signal, summons, telegraph, telegraphic message, teletype, telex, wire; SEE CONCEPTS *269,271*

telepathy [n] *ability to know another's thoughts*
clairvoyance, ESP*, extrasensory perception, insight, mind-reading, parapsychology, premonition, presentiment, second sight*, sixth sense*, spiritualism, telepathic transmission, telesthesia, thought transference; SEE CONCEPTS *410,630*

telephone [v] *communicate through telephone system*
buzz*, call, call up, contact, dial, get back to*, get on the horn*, get on the line*, give a call, give a jingle*, give a ring*, make a call, phone, pick up*, put a call through*, ring, ring up, touch base with*; SEE CONCEPTS *225,266,269*

television [n] *visual and audio entertainment transmitted via radio waves*
audio, baby-sitter*, boob tube*, box*, eye*, idiot box*, receiver, small screen, station, telly*, tube, TV, TV set, vid*, video; SEE CONCEPTS *277,279,293,463*

tell [v1] *communicate*
acquaint, advise, announce, apprise, authorize, bid, break the news*, call upon, clue in*, command, confess, declare, direct, disclose, divulge, enjoin, explain, express, fill in*, give facts, give out, impart, inform, instruct, keep posted*, lay open*, leak, leave word, let in on*, let know, let slip*, level, make known, mention, notify, open up, order, proclaim, put before, recite, reel off*, report, represent, require, reveal, say, speak, spit it out*, state, summon, utter; SEE CONCEPT *266*

tell [v2] *narrate, describe*
chronicle, depict, express, give an account of, portray, recount, rehearse, relate, report, set forth, speak, state; SEE CONCEPT *55*

tell [v3] *understand, discern*
ascertain, be sure, clinch, comprehend, deduce, determine, differentiate, discover, discriminate, distinguish, divine, find out, identify, know, know for certain, learn, make out, perceive, recognize, see; SEE CONCEPT *15*

tell [v4] *carry weight*
count, have effect, have force, make presence felt, make presence known, militate, register, take effect, take its toll*, weigh; SEE CONCEPT *676*

tell [v5] *calculate*
compute, count, count one by one, enumerate, number, numerate, reckon, tale, tally; SEE CONCEPT *764*

telling [adj] *effective, significant*
cogent, considerable, conspicuous, convincing, crucial, decisive, devastating, effectual, forceful, forcible, important, impressive, influential, marked, operative, potent, powerful, satisfactory, satisfying, solid, sound, striking, trenchant, valid, weighty; SEE CONCEPTS *537,567*

tell off [v] *reprimand; criticize harshly*
berate, censure, chide, give piece of one's mind*, give tongue-lashing*, lecture, rail, rake over the coals*, rebuke, reproach, reprove, revile, scold, take to task*, tick off*, upbraid, vituperate; SEE CONCEPTS *44,52*

temerity [n] *nerve, audacity*
assurance, boldness, brass*, carelessness, daring, effrontery, foolhardiness, forwardness, gall, hardihood, hastiness, heedlessness, impertinence, impetuosity, imprudence, impudence, impulsiveness, indiscretion, intrepidity, intrusiveness, nerve, overconfidence, pluck, precipitancy, precipitateness, precipitation, presumption, rashness, recklessness, rudeness, thoughtlessness, venturesomeness; SEE CONCEPTS *411,633*

temper [n1] *state of mind*
atmosphere, attitude, attribute, aura, character, climate, complexion, condition, constitution, disposition, drift, frame of mind, humor, individualism, individuality, leaning, makeup, mind, mood, nature, orientation, outlook, peculiarity, personality, posture, property, quality, scene, soul, spirit, state, strain, style, temperament, tendency, tenor, thing*, timbre, tone, trend, type, vein, way; SEE CONCEPTS *410,411*

temper [n2] *angriness; bad mood*
acerbity, anger, annoyance, bad-humor, cantan-

kerousness, crossness, dander*, excitability, fit, fretfulness, furor, fury, grouchiness, heat*, hotheadedness, huffiness, ill-humor, impatience, irascibility, ire, irritability, irritation, miff, outburst, passion, peevishness, petulance, pugnacity, rage, resentment, sensitivity, short fuse*, slow burn*, snit, sourness, stew*, sullenness, surliness, tantrum, tartness, tear*, tiff, tizzy*, touchiness, wax; SEE CONCEPTS 29,410

temper [n3] *calmness*
calm, composure, cool, coolness, equanimity, good humor, moderation, poise, self-control, tranquility; SEE CONCEPTS 32,410

temper [v1] *calm, moderate*
abate, adjust, admix, allay, alleviate, assuage, chill out*, cool, cool out*, curb, dilute, ease, fine tune, lessen, make reasonable, mitigate, modulate, mollify, monkey around with*, pacify, palliate, relieve, restrain, revamp, soften, soft-pedal*, soothe, switch, take the bite out of*, take the edge off*, take the sting out of*, tone down, transmogrify, weaken; SEE CONCEPTS 7,22, 110,126

temper [v2] *harden*
anneal, bake, braze, cement, chill, congeal, dry, indurate, mold, petrify, set, solidify, starch, steel, stiffen, strengthen, toughen, toughen up; SEE CONCEPTS 250,726

temperament [n] *disposition, personality*
attitude, bent, capacity, cast, character, complexion, constitution, distinctiveness, ego, emotions, frame of mind, humor, idiosyncrasy, inclination, individualism, individuality, inner nature, intellect, kind, makeup, mentality, mettle, mood, nature, outlook, peculiarity, quality, soul, spirit, stamp, structure, susceptibility, temperament, tendency, turn, type, way; SEE CONCEPTS 410,411

temperamental [adj] *angry most of the time; moody*
captious, changeable, cussed*, easily upset, emotional, erratic, excitable, explosive, fickle, fiery, froward, headstrong, high-strung*, hotheaded*, hyper*, hypersensitive, impatient, in bad mood, inconsistent, irritable, mean, mercurial, neurotic, ornery, passionate, petulant, sensitive, thin-skinned*, ticklish, touchy, uncertain, undependable, unpredictable, unreliable, unstable, variable, volatile, willful; SEE CONCEPT 403

temperance [n] *self-restraint; abstinence*
abnegation, abstemiousness, asceticism, astringency, austerity, conservatism, constraint, continence, control, discretion, eschewal, forbearance, forgoing, frugality, golden mean*, happy medium*, measure, moderateness, moderation, moderatism, mortification, prohibition, prudence, reasonableness, refrainment, restraint, sacrifice, self-control, self-denial, self-deprivation, self-discipline, soberness, sobriety, stoicism, teetotalism, uninebriation, unintoxication; SEE CONCEPTS 410,633

temperate [adj1] *calm, moderate*
agreeable, balmy, checked, clement, collected, composed, conservative, constant, cool, curbed, discreet, dispassionate, equable, even, even-tempered, fair, gentle, levelheaded, medium, mild, modest, pleasant, reasonable, regulated, restrained, self-controlled, self-restrained, sensible, sober, soft, stable, steady, unexcessive, unextreme, unimpassioned, warm; SEE CONCEPTS 525,542,547

temperate [adj2] *controlled, sober*
abstemious, abstentious, abstinent, continent, moderate, restrained, self-restraining; SEE CONCEPT 401

temperature [n] *hotness, coldness of some degree*
body heat, calefaction, climate, cold, condition, degrees, febricity, feverishness, heat, incalescence, pyrexia, thermal reading, warmth; SEE CONCEPT 610

tempest [n] *wild storm; commotion*
blizzard, bluster, chaos, convulsion, cyclone, disturbance, ferment, furor, gale, hurricane, squall, tornado, tumult, typhoon, upheaval, uproar, wildness, windstorm; SEE CONCEPTS 230,526

tempestuous [adj] *wild, stormy*
agitated, blustering, blustery, boisterous, breezy, coarse, emotional, excited, feverish, furious, gusty, heated, hysterical, impassioned, intense, passionate, raging, rough, rugged, squally, storming, tumultuous/tumultuous, turbulent, unbridled, uncontrolled, unrestrained, violent, windy; SEE CONCEPTS 401,525,542

temple [n] *house of worship*
cathedral, chapel, church, holy place, house, house of God*, house of prayer*, mosque, pagoda, pantheon, place of worship, sanctuary, shrine, synagogue, tabernacle; SEE CONCEPTS 368,439

tempo [n] *beat, rhythm*
bounce, cadence, downbeat, measure, meter, momentum, pace, pulse, rate, speed, time, velocity; SEE CONCEPT 65

temporal [adj1] *material, worldly*
banausic, carnal, civil, earthly, earthy, fleshly, lay, materialistic, mortal, mundane, nonsacred, nonspiritual, physical, profane, secular, sensual, subcelestial, sublunary, terrestrial, unhallowed, unsacred, unsanctified, unspiritual; SEE CONCEPT 582

temporal [adj2] *momentary*
chronological, ephemeral, evanescent, fleeting, fugacious, fugitive, impermanent, momentary, of time, passing, short-lived, temporary, transient, transitory; SEE CONCEPT 799

temporary [adj] *lasting only a short while*
acting, ad hoc, ad interim, alternate, Band-Aid*, brief, changeable, ephemeral, evanescent, fleeting, for the time being*, fugacious, fugitive, impermanent, interim, limited, make-do*, makeshift*, momentary, mortal, overnight, passing, perishable, pro tem, pro tempore, provisional, provisory, shifting, short, short-lived, slapdash*, stopgap*, substitute, summary, supply, temp*, transient, transitory, unfixed, unstable, volatile; SEE CONCEPTS 551,798

tempt [v] *lure, entice*
allure, appeal to, attract, bait, butter up*, captivate, charm, coax, court, dare, decoy, draw, draw out, entrap, fascinate, honey*, hook*, incite, induce, influence, instigate, intrigue, inveigle, invite, lead on, make mouth water*, motivate, mousetrap*, move, oil, persuade, play up to, promote, provoke, risk, rouse, seduce, solicit, stimulate, tantalize, test, train, try, turn one's head*, wheedle, whet, woo*; SEE CONCEPTS 11,68

temptation [n] *lure, attraction*
allurement, appeal, attractiveness, bait, blandishment, coaxing, come-on*, decoy, draw, enticement, fancy, fascination, hankering, inducement, inveiglement, invitation, provocation, pull, se-

te
te

ducement, seduction, snare, tantalization, trap*, yen; SEE CONCEPTS 20,529,532,690,709

tempting [adj] alluring, inviting
appetizing, attractive, charming, divine, enticing, fascinating, fetching, heavenly, intriguing, luring, magnetic, mouth-watering*, provoking, rousing, scrumptious, seductive, tantalizing, yummy*; SEE CONCEPTS 462,529

tenable [adj] reasonable
arguable, believable, condonable, credible, defendable, defensible, excusable, impregnable, justifiable, maintainable, plausible, rational, reliable, secure, sound, strong, trustworthy, viable, vindicable, warrantable; SEE CONCEPTS 552,558

tenacious [adj1] strong, unyielding
adamant, bound, clinging, coherent, cohesive, determined, dogged, fast, firm, forceful, inflexible, intransigent, iron, meaning business*, mulish, obdurate, obstinate, persevering, persistent, persisting, pertinacious, possessive, purposeful, relentless, resolute, retentive, set, solid, spunky, stalwart, staunch, steadfast, stout, strong-willed, stubborn, sturdy, sure, tight, tough, true, unforgetful, unshakable, unswerving; SEE CONCEPTS 326,401,489,542

tenacious [adj2] sticky
adhesive, clinging, clingy, fast, firm, fixed, glutinous, gummy, inseparable, mucilaginous, resisting, retentive, secure, set, tacky, tight, viscid, viscose, viscous, waxy; SEE CONCEPTS 488,606

tenacity [n] diligence, stubbornness
application, backbone, chutzpah*, clock*, courage, determination, doggedness, firmness, grit, guts*, gutsiness*, guttiness*, heart*, inflexibility, intestinal fortitude*, intransigence, moxie*, nerve, obduracy, obstinacy, perseverance, persistence, pertinacity, resoluteness, resolution, resolve, spunk, starch*, staunchness, steadfastness, stick-to-itiveness*, stomach*, strength of purpose, true grit*, what it takes*, willfulness; SEE CONCEPTS 411,657

tenant [n] person who leases a place
addressee, boarder, dweller, holder, householder, indweller, inhabitant, leaseholder, lessee, lodger, occupant, occupier, possessor, renter, rent payer, resident, roomer; SEE CONCEPTS 348,423

tend [v1] be apt, likely
aim, bear, be biased, be conducive, be disposed, be inclined, be in the habit of, be liable, bend, be predisposed, be prejudiced, conduce, contribute, dispose, drift, favor, go, gravitate, have an inclination, have a tendency, head, impel, incline, influence, lead, lean, look, make for, move, move toward, point, redound, result in, serve to, trend, turn, verge on; SEE CONCEPTS 411,650

tend [v2] care for
accomplish, administer, attend, baby-sit, cater to, cherish, control, corral, cultivate, defend, direct, do, do for, feed, foster, guard, handle, keep, keep an eye on*, keep tabs on*, look after, maintain, manage, mind, minister to, nurse, nurture, oversee, perform, protect, ride herd on*, safeguard, see after, see to, serve, shepherd, shield, sit, superintend, supervise, take care of, take under wing*, wait on, watch, watch out for, watch over; SEE CONCEPTS 136,257,295

tendency [n1] inclination to think or do in a certain way
addiction, affection, bent*, bias, current, custom, disposition, drift, habit, impulse, inclining, leaning, liability, mind, mindset*, partiality, penchant, predilection, predisposition, proclivity, proneness, propensity, readiness, run, set, shift, slant, susceptibility, temperament, thing*, trend, turn, type, usage, way*, weakness; SEE CONCEPT 657

tendency [n2] direction of movement
aim, bearing, bent, bias, course, current, curve, drift, drive, heading, inclination, leaning, movement, purport, run, shift, tenor, trend, turn, turning, way; SEE CONCEPTS 692,738

tender [adj1] fragile, soft
breakable, dainty, delicate, effete, feeble, frail, supple, weak; SEE CONCEPTS 604,606

tender [adj2] young, inexperienced
callow, childish, childlike, green*, immature, impressionable, new, raw*, rookie*, sensitive, unripe, vernal, vulnerable, wet behind the ears*, youthful; SEE CONCEPTS 578,797

tender [adj3] affectionate, loving
all heart*, amorous, benevolent, bleeding-heart*, caring, charitable, commiserative, compassionate, considerate, demonstrative, emotional, evocative, fond, forgiving, gentle, humane, kind, lenient, lovey-dovey*, merciful, mild, moving, mushy*, poignant, responsive, romantic, sensitive, sentimental, soft, softhearted, solicitous, sympathetic, tenderhearted, thoughtful, ticklish, tolerant, touching, touchy, warm, warmhearted, yielding; SEE CONCEPTS 401,542

tender [adj4] painful, sore
aching, acute, bruised, delicate, hypersensitive, inflamed, irritated, oversensitive, raw, sensitive, smarting, thin-skinned, ticklish, touchy; SEE CONCEPTS 314,403,548

tenebrous [adj] dark, ominous
ambiguous, amphibological, caliginous, dim, dingy, dusk, dusky, equivocal, gloomy, lightless, murky, obscure, shadowy, shady, somber, sunless, uncertain, unclear, unexplicit, unilluminated, unintelligible, unlit, vague; SEE CONCEPTS 535,617

tenet [n] belief, principle
article of faith, assumption, canon, conception, conviction, credo, creed, doctrine, dogma, faith, impression, maxim, opinion, persuasion, position, precept, presumption, profession, rule, self-conviction, system, teaching, thesis, trust, view; SEE CONCEPTS 688,689

tenor [n1] meaning, intent
aim, body, burden, core, course, course of thought, current, direction, drift, evolution, gist, inclination, meat, mood, path, pith, purport, purpose, run, sense, stuff, substance, tendency, theme, tone, trend, way; SEE CONCEPTS 529,682

tenor [n2] high male voice
alto, countertenor, falsetto; SEE CONCEPT 65

tense [adj1] tight, stretched
close, firm, rigid, stiff, strained, taut; SEE CONCEPTS 485,604

tense [adj2] under stress, pressure
agitated, anxious, apprehensive, beside oneself*, bundle of nerves*, choked, clutched, concerned, edgy, excited, fidgety, fluttery, high-strung*, hung up*, hyper*, in a tizzy*, jittery, jumpy, keyed up*, moved, moving, nerve-racking, nervous, nervous wreck*, on edge, overanxious, overwrought, queasy, restive, restless, shaky, shot*, shot to pieces*, strained, stressful, strung out*, uneasy, unnerved, unquiet, up the wall*,

uptight*, white knuckled*, wired*, worried, worrying, wound up*, wreck*; SEE CONCEPTS *401,403,548*

tension [n1] *tightness*
astriction, balance, constriction, force, pressure, rigidity, stiffness, strain, straining, stress, stretching, tautness, tenseness, tensity; SEE CONCEPTS *723,726*

tension [n2] *mental stress*
agitation, antsiness*, ants in pants*, anxiety, apprehension, bad feeling*, brunt, concern, discomfort, disquiet, edginess, hostility, jitters*, jumps*, nail-biting*, nerves, nervousness, pins and needles*, pressure, restlessness, shakes*, strain, suspense, unease, uneasiness, worriment, worry; SEE CONCEPT *410*

tentative [adj1] *conditional, experimental*
acting, ad interim, conjectural, contingent, dependent, iffy*, indefinite, makeshift, not final, not settled, on trial, open for consideration, probationary, provisional, provisionary, provisory, speculative, subject to change, temporary, test, trial, unconfirmed, undecided, unsettled; SEE CONCEPTS *551,552*

tentative [adj2] *indefinite, uncertain*
backward, cautious, diffident, disinclined, doubtful, faltering, halting, hesitant, irresolute, reluctant, timid, undecided, unsure, vacillating, vacillatory, wobbly; SEE CONCEPTS *534,535,542*

tenuous [adj] *weak, thin*
aerial, airy, attenuate, attenuated, delicate, doubtful, dubious, ethereal, fine, flimsy, gossamer, insignificant, insubstantial, light, narrow, nebulous, questionable, rare, rarefied, reedy, shaky, sketchy, slender, slight, slim, subtle, twiggy; SEE CONCEPTS *489,491,575*

tenure [n] *time in position of responsibility*
administration, clamp, clasp, clench, clinch, clutch, dynasty, grasp, grip, hold, holding, incumbency, occupancy, occupation, ownership, possession, proprietorship, reign, resign, residence, security, tenancy, term; SEE CONCEPTS *287,816*

tepid [adj] *lukewarm*
apathetic, cool, disinterested, dull, halfhearted, indifferent, languid, lifeless, mild, milk-warm, moderate, slightly warm, spiritless, temperate, unenthusiastic, unlively, warm, warmish; SEE CONCEPTS *542,605*

term [n1] *description of a concept*
appellation, article, caption, denomination, designation, expression, head, indication, language, locution, moniker*, name, nomenclature, phrase, style, terminology, title, vocable, word; SEE CONCEPTS *275,683*

term [n2] *time period*
course, cycle, duration, go*, hitch*, interval, phase, quarter, season, semester, session, space, span, spell, standing, stretch, time, tour, turn, while; SEE CONCEPTS *807,822*

term [n3] *limit*
bound, boundary, close, conclusion, confine, confines, culmination, end, finish, fruition, limitation, terminus; SEE CONCEPTS *745,832*

term [v] *name something*
baptize, call, christen, denominate, describe, designate, dub, entitle, label, style, subtitle, tag, title; SEE CONCEPT *62*

terminal [n1] *end of road; limit*
boundary, depot, end, end of the line, extremity, station, termination, terminus; SEE CONCEPTS *198,745*

terminal [n2] *computer screen, computer input/output device*
cathode ray tube, CRT*, display, input device, monitor, screen, VDT*, video display; SEE CONCEPT *463*

terminal [adj] *final, deadly*
bounding, check out*, closing, concluding, eventual, extreme, fatal, hindmost, incurable, killing, lag, last, latest, latter, lethal, limiting, mortal, on way out*, period, ultimate, utmost; SEE CONCEPTS *314,548*

terminate [v] *stop, finish*
abolish, abort, achieve, adjourn, annul, bounce, bound, bring to an end, cancel, cease, close, come to an end, complete, conclude, confine, cut off, define, desist, determine, discharge, discontinue, dismiss, dissolve, drop, eliminate, end, expire, extinguish, fire, halt, issue, lapse, limit, perfect, prorogate, prorogue, put an end to, recess, restrict, result, run out, sack, scratch, scrub*, tether, ultimate, wind down, wind up*, wrap*, wrap up*; SEE CONCEPTS *119,121,234*

termination [n] *end*
abortion, ballgame*, cease, cessation, close, completion, conclusion, consequence, curtains*, cutoff*, desistance, discontinuation, effect, ending, end of the line*, expiry, finale, finis, finish, issue, kiss-off*, outcome, payoff*, period, result, stop, terminus, windup*, wrap-up*; SEE CONCEPTS *119,832*

terms [n1] *conditions, agreement*
charge, circumstances, conclusion, condition, details, fee, fine print*, items, nitty-gritty*, particulars, payment, points, premise, premises, price, provision, provisions, proviso, provisos, qualifications, rate, reservation, size of it*, small print*, specifications, stipulation, stipulations, strings*, treaty, understanding, what it is*; SEE CONCEPTS *270,318,684*

terms [n2] *status of relationship*
balance, equality, equivalent, footing, par, parity, position, relations, relationship, standing; SEE CONCEPT *388*

terrain [n] *landscape*
area, bailiwick, contour, country, domain, dominion, field, form, ground, land, profile, province, region, shape, soil, sphere, territory, topography, turf; SEE CONCEPTS *508,509*

terrestrial [adj] *earthly*
earthbound, earthlike, earthy, global, mundane, physical, profane, prosaic, secular, sublunary, subsolar, telluric, temporal, terrene, uncelestial, unspiritual, worldly; SEE CONCEPT *536*

terrible [adj] *bad, horrible*
abhorrent, appalling, atrocious, awe-inspiring, awesome, awful, beastly, dangerous, desperate, dire, disastrous, disturbing, dread, dreaded, dreadful, extreme, fearful, frightful, ghastly, gruesome, harrowing, hateful, hideous, horrendous, horrible, horrid, horrifying, inconvenient, loathsome, monstrous, obnoxious, odious, offensive, petrifying, poor, repulsive, revolting, rotten, serious, severe, shocking, unfortunate, unnerving, unpleasant, unwelcome, vile; SEE CONCEPT *571*

terribly [adv] *very*
awfully, badly, decidedly, desperately, discouragingly, disturbingly, drastically, dreadfully, exceedingly, extremely, fearfully, frightfully,

le
te

gravely, greatly, highly, horribly, intensely, markedly, mightily, much, notoriously, remarkably, seriously, staggeringly, thoroughly, unbelievably, unfortunately, unhappily; SEE CONCEPTS 569,570

terrific [adj1] intense
agitating, appalling, awesome, awful, deafening, disquieting, dreadful, enormous, excessive, extreme, fearful, fierce, formidable, frightful, gigantic, great, harsh, horrible, horrific, huge, immense, large, monstrous, severe, shocking, terrible, terrorizing, thunderous, tremendous, upsetting; SEE CONCEPT 569

terrific [adj2] wonderful
ace*, amazing, breathtaking, divine, excellent, fabulous, fantastic, fine, glorious, great, groovy*, hot*, keen*, magnificent, marvelous, outstanding, sensational, smashing*, stupendous, super, superb, swell, very good; SEE CONCEPT 572

terrify [v] scare
alarm, appall, awe, chill, dismay, freeze, fright, frighten, horrify, intimidate, paralyze, petrify, scare stiff*, scare the pants off of*, scare to death*, shock, spook, startle, strike fear into*, stun, stupefy, terrorize; SEE CONCEPTS 7,19,42

territory [n] domain, region
area, belt, block, boundary, colony, commonwealth, country, district, dominion, empire, enclave, exclave, expanse, extent, field, land, mandate, nation, neck of the woods*, neighborhood, province, quarter, section, sector, sphere, state, stomping grounds*, street, terrain, terrene, township, tract, turf*, walk, zone; SEE CONCEPTS 198,349,508

terror [n] intense fear
alarm, anxiety, awe, consternation, dismay, dread, fearfulness, fright, horror, intimidation, panic, shock, trepidation, trepidity; SEE CONCEPTS 27,690

terrorize [v] upset, threaten
alarm, appall, awe, bludgeon, browbeat, bulldoze*, bully, coerce, cow, dismay, dragoon, fright, frighten, hector, horrify, intimidate, menace, oppress, petrify, scare, scare to death*, shock, spook, startle, strike terror into*, strongarm*, terrify; SEE CONCEPTS 7,14,19

terse [adj] brief, short
abrupt, aphoristic, boiled down*, breviloquent, brusque, clear-cut, clipped, close, compact, compendiary, compendious, concise, condensed, crisp, cryptic, curt, cut to the bone*, elliptical, epigrammatic, exact, gnomic, in a nutshell*, incisive, laconic, lean, neat, pithy, pointed, precise, sententious, short and sweet*, snappy, succinct, summary, taut, to the point, trenchant; SEE CONCEPTS 267,272

test [n] examination, quiz
analysis, approval, assessment, attempt, blue book*, catechism, check, comp*, confirmation, corroboration, countdown, criterion, dry run*, elimination, essay, evaluation, exam, experiment, final, fling*, go*, inquest, inquiry, inspection, investigation, lick*, oral*, ordeal, pop quiz, preliminary, probation, probing, proof, questionnaire, scrutiny, search, shibboleth, standard, substantiation, touchstone*, trial, trial and error*, try, tryout, verification, yardstick*; SEE CONCEPTS 5,290

test [v] examine, quiz
analyze, assay, assess, check, confirm, demonstrate, experiment, experimentalize, give a tryout, inquire, investigate, look into, make a trial run, match up, prove, prove out, put to the test*, question, run idea by someone*, run it up a flagpole*, see how it flies*, see how wind blows*, send up a balloon*, shake down*, stack up, substantiate, try, try on, try on for size*, try out, validate, verify; SEE CONCEPTS 5,103,291

testament [n] tribute; last wishes
attestation, colloquy, confirmation, covenant, demonstration, earnest, evidence, exemplification, instrument, proof, testimonial, testimony, will, witness; SEE CONCEPT 318

testify [v] vouch for; give testimony
affirm, announce, argue, assert, attest, bear witness, bespeak, betoken, certify, corroborate, cross one's heart*, declare, demonstrate, depone, depose, evince, give evidence, give facts, give one's word*, indicate, make evident, mount, point to, prove, say so*, show, sing*, stand up for, state, swear, swear to, swear up and down*, token, warrant, witness; SEE CONCEPTS 49,317

testimonial [n] tribute
affidavit, appreciation, attestation, certificate, character, commemoration, commendation, confirmation, credential, degree, endorsement, evidence, homage, honor, indication, manifestation, memorial, memorialization, monument, ovation, plug*, proof, recommendation, reference, remembrance, salute, salvo, say-so*, show, sign, symbol, testament, testimony, token, voucher, witness; SEE CONCEPTS 49,278,318

testimony [n] declaration about truth; proof
affidavit, affirmation, attestation, avowal, confirmation, corroboration, data, demonstration, deposition, documentation, evidence, facts, grounds, illustration, indication, information, manifestation, profession, statement, submission, substantiation, support, testament, verification, witness; SEE CONCEPTS 49,278,318

testy [adj] irritable, touchy
annoyed, bad-tempered, cantankerous, captious, choleric, crabbed, cranky*, cross, crotchety, edgy, exasperated, fretful, grouchy, grumpy*, impatient, irascible, mean, ornery*, out of sorts, peevish, peppery, petulant, quarrelsome, quick-tempered, short-tempered, snappy*, splenetic, sullen, thin-skinned*, uptight*, waspish; SEE CONCEPTS 401,403,542

tether [n] fastening
binding, bond, chain, cord, fetter, halter, harness, lead, leash, picket, rope, shackle; SEE CONCEPT 475

tether [v] fasten
batten, bind, chain, fetter, leash, manacle, moor, picket, restrain, rope, secure, shackle, tie; SEE CONCEPTS 85,160

text [n1] subject matter of document
argument, body, consideration, content, contents, context, document, extract, fundamentals, head, idea, issue, line, lines, main body, matter, motify, motive, paragraph, passage, point, quotation, sentence, stanza, subject, theme, thesis, topic, verse, vocabulary, wording, words; SEE CONCEPTS 270,682

text [n2] book used in education
assignment, class book, course book, handbook, manual, reader, reference, reference book, required reading, schoolbook, source, syllabus, textbook, workbook; SEE CONCEPTS 280,287

texture [n] *characteristics of a surface*
arrangement, balance, being, character, coarseness, composition, consistency, constitution, disposition, essence, essentiality, fabric, feel, feeling, fiber, fineness, flexibility, form, framework, grain, intermixture, make, makeup, nap, nature, organization, pattern, quality, roughness, scheme, sense, smoothness, stiffness, strategy, structure, surface, taste, tissue, touch, warp, weave, web, woof; SEE CONCEPTS *611,673,682*

thank [v] *express gratitude*
acknowledge, be grateful, be indebted, be obligated, be obliged, bless, bow down*, give thanks, kiss*, praise, say thank you, show appreciation, show courtesy, show gratitude, smile on*; SEE CONCEPTS *60,69,76*

thankful [adj] *appreciative*
beholden, content, contented, grateful, gratified, indebted, much obliged, obliged, overwhelmed, pleased, relieved, satisfied; SEE CONCEPTS *401,403*

thankless [adj1] *unappreciated*
barren, disagreeable, distasteful, fruitless, futile, miserable, not worth it*, ungrateful, unpleasant, unprofitable, unrecognized, unrequited, unreturned, unrewarding, useless, vain, wretched; SEE CONCEPTS *538,548*

thankless [adj2] *unappreciative, inconsiderate (in behavior)*
careless, cruel, heedless, inappreciative, rude, self-centered, thoughtless, ungracious, ungrateful, unmindful, unthankful; SEE CONCEPT *401*

thanks [n] *spoken or written appreciation*
acknowledgment, benediction, blessing, credit, grace, gramercy, gratefulness, gratitude, praise, recognition, thankfulness, thanksgiving, thank you note; SEE CONCEPTS *60,69,278*

thaw [v] *unfreeze, warm*
become liquid, become soft, defrost, deliquesce, dissolve, flow, flux, fuse, liquefy, loosen, melt, mollify, open up, relax, relent, run, soften, unbend, warm up; SEE CONCEPTS *13,255,469*

theater/theatre [n] *stage, building for performance*
amphitheater, arena, assembly hall, auditorium, barn, boards*, cinema, coliseum, concert hall, deck, drama, drive-in, footlights, hall, hippodrome, house, locale, movie, movie house, oak*, odeum, opera house, playhouse, room, scene, show hall, site; SEE CONCEPTS *263,293,439,448*

theatrical [adj] *dramatic*
affected, amateur, artificial, campy*, ceremonious, comic, dramaturgic, exaggerated, ham*, hammy*, histrionic, legitimate, mannered, melodramatic, meretricious, operatic, ostentatious, pompous, schmaltzy*, show, showy, staged, stilted, superficial, theatric, thespian, tragic, unnatural, unreal, vaudeville; SEE CONCEPTS *401,536*

theft [n] *stealing*
annexation, appropriation, break-in, burglary, caper, cheating, crime, defrauding, deprivation, embezzlement, extortion, filch, fleece*, fraud, grab*, heist, holdup, hustle*, job*, larceny, lift*, looting, mugging, peculation, pilferage, pilfering, pillage, pinch*, piracy, plunder, purloining, racket*, rapacity, rip-off*, robbery, robbing, score*, shoplifting, snatch*, snitch*, steal, stickup, swindle, swindling, swiping*, thievery, thieving, touch*, vandalism; SEE CONCEPTS *139,192*

theme [n1] *idea, subject matter*
affair, argument, burden, business, case, head, keynote, leitmotif, line, matter, matter in hand, motif, motive, point, point at issue, problem, proposition, question, stuff, subject, text, thesis, thought, topic; SEE CONCEPTS *278,682,689*

theme [n2] *written composition*
article, description, dissertation, essay, exercise, exposition, manuscript, paper, report, statement, thesis; SEE CONCEPT *271*

then [adv1] *before; at another time*
again, all at once, anon, at that instant, at that moment, at that point, at that time, before long, formerly, later, next, on that occasion, soon after, suddenly, thereupon, when, years ago; SEE CONCEPT *799*

then [adv2] *therefore*
accordingly, consequently, ergo, from that time, from then on, from there on, hence, so, thence, thenceforth, thereupon, thus, whence; SEE CONCEPT *548*

theological [adj] *religious, concerning a god-centered philosophy*
apostolic, canonical, churchly, deistic, divine, doctrinal, ecclesiastical, metaphysical, scriptural, theistic; SEE CONCEPT *536*

theorem [n] *explanation based on hypothesis and experiments*
assumption, axiom, belief, deduction, dictum, doctrine, formula, fundamental, law, postulate, principium, principle, proposition, rule, statement, theory, thesis; SEE CONCEPTS *529,688,689*

theoretical [adj] *hypothetical*
abstract, academic, analytical, as a premise, assumed, codified, conjectural, contingent, formalistic, formularized, general, ideal, idealized, ideational, ideological, imaginative, impractical, instanced, intellectual, in the abstract, in theory, logical, metaphysical, notional, on paper*, pedantic, philosophical, postulated, presumed, problematical, pure, quixotic, speculative, suppositional, tentative, transcendent, transcendental, unearthly, unproved, unsubstantiated, vague; SEE CONCEPT *529*

theorize [v] *hypothesize*
conjecture, formulate, guess, project, propound, speculate, submit, suggest, suppose, think; SEE CONCEPT *43*

theory [n] *hypothesis, belief*
approach, argument, assumption, base, basis, belief, code, codification, concept, conditions, conjecture, doctrine, dogma, feeling, formularization, foundation, grounds, guess, guesswork, hunch, idea, ideology, impression, method, outlook, philosophy, plan, position, postulate, premise, presentiment, presumption, proposal, provision, rationale, scheme, shot*, speculation, stab*, supposal, suppose, supposition, surmise, suspicion, system, systemization, theorem, thesis, understanding; SEE CONCEPTS *529,689*

therapeutic [adj] *healing*
ameliorative, analeptic, beneficial, corrective, curative, good, remedial, restorative, salubrious, salutary, sanative; SEE CONCEPT *537*

therapy [n] *healing treatment*
analysis, cure, healing, medicine, remedial treatment, remedy, therapeutics; SEE CONCEPT *310*

thereafter [adv] *from that time forward*
after that, consequently, following, forever after, from that day forward, from that day on, from

te
th

there on, hereafter, thenceforth, thenceforward; SEE CONCEPT 799

therefore [adv] *as a result; for that reason*
accordingly, and so, consequently, ergo, for, forasmuch as, for this reason, hence, inasmuch as, in consequence, in that event, on account of, on the grounds, since, so, then, thence, therefrom, thereupon, thus, to that end, whence, wherefore; SEE CONCEPTS 230,676

thesaurus [n] *dictionary of synonyms and antonyms*
glossary, language reference book, lexicon, onomasticon, reference book, sourcebook, storehouse of words, terminology, treasury of words, vocabulary, word list; SEE CONCEPT 280

thesis [n1] *belief, assumption to be tested*
apriorism, contention, contestation, hypothesis, idea, line, opinion, point, posit, position, postulate, postulation, premise, presumption, presupposition, principle, proposal, proposition, sentiment, statement, supposition, surmise, theory, view; SEE CONCEPTS 529,689

thesis [n2] *written dissertation*
argument, argumentation, composition, discourse, disquisition, essay, exposition, memoir, monograph, monography, paper, research, theme, tractate, treatise; SEE CONCEPTS 271,287

thick [adj1] *deep, bulky*
blubbery, broad, bulky, burly, chunky, compact, concrete, consolidated, fat, firm, hard, heavy, high, husky, massive, obese, pudgy, solid, squat, stocky, stubby, stumpy, substantial, thickset, wide; SEE CONCEPTS 491,773

thick [adj2] *concentrated, dense*
caked, clabbered, close, clotted, coagulated, compact, compressed, concrete, condensed, congealed, consolidated, crowded, curdled, deep, firm, fixed, gelatinous, gloppy*, gooey, gummous, gummy, gunky*, heavy, impenetrable, impervious, jelled, jellied, opaque, ossified, ropy, set, sloppy, solid, solidified, stiff, syrupy, thickened, turbid, viscid, viscous, vitrified; SEE CONCEPTS 483,606

thick [adj3] *crowded, packed*
abundant, brimming, bristling, bursting, chockfull*, close, compact, compressed, concentrated, condensed, considerable, covered, crammed, crawling with*, dense, frequent, full, great, heaped, impenetrable, impervious, inspissated, like sardines*, localized, multitudinous, numerous, populated, populous, profuse, rank, replete, several, solid, swarming, teeming, tight; SEE CONCEPT 771

thick [adj4] *stupid*
blockheaded, boneheaded, brainless, dense, dim-witted, doltish, dopey*, dull, dumb, ignorant, insensitive, moronic, numbskulled, obtuse, slow, slow-witted, thickheaded; SEE CONCEPT 402

thick [adj5] *dense (referring to weather)*
cloudy, dull, foggy, heavy, impenetrable, indistinct, muddy, obscure, soupy*, turbid; SEE CONCEPT 525

thick [adj6] *friendly*
chummy*, close, confidential, cordial, devoted, familiar, hand in glove*, inseparable, intimate, on good terms; SEE CONCEPT 555

thick [adj7] *unreasonable*
excessive, flimsy*, implausible, improbable, inconceivable, incredible, thin*, too much*, unbelievable, unconvincing, unfair, unjust, unsubstantial; SEE CONCEPTS 529,548

thicken [v] *set; make more dense*
add, buttress, cake, clabber, clot, coagulate, condense, congeal, curdle, deepen, enlarge, expand, freeze, gel, grow thick, harden, inspissate, jell, jelly, ossify, petrify, reinforce, solidify, stiffen, swell, widen; SEE CONCEPTS 137,250,469

thief [n] *person who steals*
bandit, burglar, cat burglar, cheat, clip*, criminal, crook, defalcator, embezzler, heister*, highway robber, hijacker, holdup artist, housebreaker, kleptomaniac, larcener, larcenist, lifter*, moonlighter*, mugger, owl*, pickpocket, pilferer, pirate, plunderer, porch climber*, prowler, punk*, purloiner, robber, scrounger, shoplifter, sniper, spider*, stealer, stickup artist*, swindler; SEE CONCEPT 412

thieving/thievish [adj] *criminal*
crooked, cunning, dishonest, fraudulent, furtive, kleptomaniacal*, larcenous, light-fingered*, pilfering, piratic*, plunderous, predatory, rapacious, secretive, sly, spoliative, stealthy, sticky-fingered*; SEE CONCEPT 401

thin [adj1] *fine, light, slender*
attenuate, attenuated, beanpole*, beanstalk*, bony*, cadaverous, delicate, emaciated, ethereal, featherweight, fragile, gangling, gangly, gaunt, haggard, lank, lanky, lean, lightweight, meager, narrow, peaked, pinched, pole*, puny*, rangy, rarefied, rawboned, reedy, rickety, scraggy*, scrawny, shadow, shriveled, skeletal, skinny, slight, slim, slinky, small, spare, spindly, stalky*, starved, stick*, stilt*, subtle, threadlike, twiggy*, twiglike, undernourished, underweight, wan, wasted, wizened; SEE CONCEPTS 491,773

thin [adj2] *transparent, fine*
attenuate, attenuated, delicate, diaphanous, filmy, flimsy, gossamer, paper-thin, permeable, rare, rarefied, refined, see-through, sheer, slight, slim, subtle, subtle, tenuous, translucent, unsubstantial, wafer-thin, wispy; SEE CONCEPT 606

thin [adj3] *deficient, weak*
diluted, feeble*, flat*, flimsy*, implausible, improbable, inadequate, inconceivable, incredible, insubstantial, insufficient, lame, meager, poor, questionable, scant, scanty, scarce, scattered, shallow, sketchy, skimpy*, slight, sparse, stretched, superficial, thick*, transparent, unbelievable, unconvincing, unpersuasive, unsubstantial, untenable, vapid, weak-kneed*; SEE CONCEPT 771

thin [adj4] *diluted*
diffuse, dilute, dispersed, fine, light, rarefied, refined, runny, subtle, watery, weak, wishy-washy*; SEE CONCEPT 485

thin [v] *make diluted or less dense*
attenuate, cook, cut, cut back, decrease, delete, diminish, disperse, doctor, edit, emaciate, expand, extenuate, irrigate, lace*, needle*, prune, rarefy, reduce, refine, shave, spike, trim, water, water down, weaken, weed out; SEE CONCEPTS 137,250

thing [n1] *something felt, seen, perceived*
affair, anything, apparatus, article, being, body, business, circumstance, commodity, concept, concern, configuration, contrivance, corporeality, creature, device, element, entity, everything, existence, existent, fact, figure, form, gadget, goods, implement, individual, information, instrument, item, machine, material, materiality, matter, means, mechanism, object, part, person,

phenomenon, piece, point, portion, shape, situation, stuff, subject, substance, tool, word; SEE CONCEPT *433*

thing [*n2*] *act*
accomplishment, action, circumstance, deed, doing, duty, episode, event, eventuality, exploit, feat, happening, incident, job, movement, obligation, occasion, occurrence, phenomenon, proceeding, stunt, task, work; SEE CONCEPT *3*

thing [*n3*] *aspect, characteristic*
article, attribute, detail, element, facet, factor, feature, item, particular, point, property, quality, statement, thought, trait; SEE CONCEPTS *411,657,834*

thing/things [*n4*] *personal possessions*
apparel, attire, baggage, belongings, chattels, clothes, clothing, duds*, effects, equipment, gear, goods, habiliments, impedimenta, luggage, odds and ends*, paraphernalia, personal effects, personals*, property, raiment, stuff, trappings, tricks; SEE CONCEPTS *446,451*

thing [*n5*] *idea, obsession*
attitude, bee in bonnet*, craze, fad, fetish, fixation, hang-up*, idée fixe, impression, mania, notion, opinion, phobia, preoccupation, quirk, style, thought; SEE CONCEPT *529*

think [*v1*] *believe; anticipate*
assume, be convinced, comprehend, conceive, conclude, consider, credit, deem, determine, envisage, envision, esteem, estimate, expect, fancy, feature, feel, foresee, gather, guess, hold, image, imagine, judge, plan for, presume, project, realize, reckon, regard, see, sense, suppose, surmise, suspect, take, understand, vision, visualize; SEE CONCEPTS *12,26*

think [*v2*] *contemplate*
analyze, appraise, appreciate, brood, cerebrate, cogitate, comprehend, conceive, consider, deduce, deliberate, estimate, evaluate, examine, figure out, have in mind, ideate, imagine, infer, intellectualize, judge, logicalize, meditate, mull, mull over, muse, ponder, rack one's brains*, rationalize, reason, reflect, resolve, revolve, ruminate, sort out, speculate, stew*, stop to consider, study, take under consideration, turn over, use one's head*, weigh; SEE CONCEPTS *17,33,43*

think [*v3*] *remember*
call to mind, recall, recollect, reminisce; SEE CONCEPT *40*

thinkable [*adj*] *believable, feasible*
cogitable, comprehendible, comprehensible, conceivable, convincing, imaginable, likely, possible, practicable, practical, presumable, reasonable, supposable, within realm of possibility*, within the limits; SEE CONCEPT *529*

thirst [*n*] *craving (especially for liquid)*
appetite, aridity, desire, drought, dryness, eagerness, hankering, hunger, keenness, longing, lust, passion, thirstiness, yearning, yen; SEE CONCEPTS *20,709*

thirsty [*adj*] *dry, desirous (especially for liquid)*
agog*, anxious, appetent, ardent, arid, athirst, avid, bone-dry*, breathless, burning, cotton-mouthed*, craving, crazy for*, dehydrated, droughty, dry as dust*, dying for*, eager, greedy, hankering, hungry, impatient, inclined, itching for*, juiceless, keen, longing, lusting, parched, partial to, sapless, thirsting, waterless, wild for*, yearning; SEE CONCEPTS *403,603*

thorny [*adj1*] *sharp, pointed*
barbed, briery, bristling, bristly, prickly, spiked, spiky, spinous, spiny, stinging, thistly; SEE CONCEPT *485*

thorny [*adj2*] *difficult, problematic*
awkward, baffling, bothersome, formidable, harassing, hard, irksome, nettlesome, perplexing, prickly, severe, sticky, ticklish, tough, tricky, troublesome, trying, unpleasant, upsetting, vexatious, worrying; SEE CONCEPT *565*

thorough/thoroughgoing [*adj1*] *exhaustive*
absolute, all-embracing, all-inclusive, all-out*, all the way*, assiduous, blow-by-blow*, careful, circumstantial, clocklike, complete, comprehensive, conscientious, detailed, efficient, exact, from A to Z*, full, full-dress*, in-depth, intensive, itemized, meticulous, minute, painstaking, particular, particularized, plenty, royal, scrupulous, slam bang*, soup to nuts*, sweeping, tough, whole-hog*; SEE CONCEPTS *531,538*

thorough/thoroughgoing [*adj2*] *absolute, utter*
arrant, complete, consummate, downright, entire, out-and-out*, outright, perfect, pure, rank, sheer, straight-out*, total, unmitigated, unqualified; SEE CONCEPTS *531,535,557*

thoroughbred [*adj*] *pure, unmixed*
blood, full-blooded, graded, papered, pedigree, pedigreed, pure-blooded, purebred; SEE CONCEPT *549*

thoroughly [*adv1*] *exhaustively*
all, assiduously, carefully, completely, comprehensively, conscientiously, earnestly, efficiently, exceedingly, exceptionally, extremely, flat out*, from A to Z*, from top to bottom*, fully, hard, highly, hugely, in and out*, in detail, inside out*, intensely, intensively, meticulously, notably, painstakingly, remarkably, scrupulously, strikingly, sweepingly, through and through*, throughout, unremittingly, up and down*, very, whole hog*, wholly; SEE CONCEPTS *531,538*

thoroughly [*adv2*] *utterly*
absolutely, altogether, completely, downright, entirely, fully, perfectly, plumb, quite, totally, to the full, well, wholly, without reservation; SEE CONCEPTS *531,535,557*

though [*adv*] *however*
after all, all the same, for all that, howbeit, nevertheless, nonetheless, notwithstanding, still, still and all, withal, yet; SEE CONCEPT *544*

though [*conj*] *while*
albeit, allowing, although, but, despite, despite the fact, even if, even supposing, even though, granted, howbeit, if, much as, notwithstanding, when, whereas; SEE CONCEPT *544*

thought [*n1*] *formation of mental objects*
anticipation, apprehending, attention, brainwork, cerebration, cogitation, cognition, concluding, consideration, considering, contemplation, deducing, deduction, deliberation, deriving, discerning, heed, hope, ideation, inducing, inferring, introspection, intuition, judging, knowing, logic, meditation, musing, perceiving, rationalization, rationalizing, realizing, reasoning, reflection, regard, rumination, scrutiny, seeing, speculation, study, theorization, thinking, understanding; SEE CONCEPTS *17,43,409,410*

thought [*n2*] *idea, concept*
aim, anxiety, appreciation, aspiration, assessment, assumption, attentiveness, belief, brainchild*, brainstorm*, caring, compassion,

conception, concern, conclusion, conjecture, conviction, design, dream, drift, estimation, expectation, fancy, feeling, guess, hope, hypothesis, image, inference, intention, intuition, judgment, kindness, knowledge, notion, object, opinion, plan, premise, prospect, purpose, regard, reverie, solicitude, supposition, sympathy, theory, thinking, understanding, view, worry; SEE CONCEPT 529

thoughtful [adj1] *caring, mindful*
anxious, astute, attentive, aware, benign, canny, careful, cautious, charitable, chivalrous, circumspect, civil, concerned, considerate, cooperative, courteous, deliberate, diplomatic, discreet, friendly, gallant, gracious, heedful, helpful, indulgent, kind, kindly, mindful, neighborly, obliging, observant, observative, observing, polite, prudent, regardful, responsive, sensitive, social, solicitous, tactful, unselfish, wary, well-bred, well thought-out; SEE CONCEPTS 401,555

thoughtful [adj2] *contemplative, introspective*
absorbed, analytical, attentive, brainy*, calculating, cerebral, cogitative, deep, deliberative, discerning, earnest, engrossed, farsighted, grave, intellectual, intent, keen, levelheaded, logical, lost in thought*, meditative, melancholy, museful, musing, pensive, philosophic, pondering, preoccupied, rapt, rational, reasonable, reasoning, reflecting, reflective, retrospective, ruminative, serious, sober, studious, subjective, thinking, wise, wistful; SEE CONCEPTS 402,403,542

thoughtless [adj1] *inconsiderate*
antisocial, apathetic, asocial, blind, boorish, brash, deaf, discourteous, egocentric, hasty, heedless, hot-headed, impolite, inattentive, incautious, indelicate, indifferent, indiscreet, insensitive, listless, madcap, neglectful, negligent, primitive, rash, reckless, rude, self-centered, selfish, sharp, short, tactless, uncaring, unceremonious, unconcerned, undiplomatic, ungracious, unheeding, unkind, unmindful, unrefined; SEE CONCEPTS 401,555

thoughtless [adj2] *absent-minded, unobservant*
bovine, careless, confused, doltish, dull, empty-headed, flighty, foolish, heedless, ill-advised, ill-considered, imprudent, inadvertent, inane, inattentive, incomprehensible, inept, injudicious, irrational, irreflective, lamebrained*, loony*, mindless, neglectful, negligent, obtuse, puerile, rash, reckless, regardless, remiss, senseless, silly, stupid, undiscerning, unheeding, unmindful, unreasonable, unreasoning, unreflective, unthinking, vacuous, witless; SEE CONCEPTS 402,403,542

thrash [v] *flail about; beat*
batter, beat up, belabor, belt, birch, buffet, bury, cane, chasten, chastise, clobber, crush, defeat, flagellate, flog, jerk, kill, lambaste*, lick, maul, murder, overwhelm, paste, pelt, pitch, pound, pummel, punish, rout, rush, scourge, seesaw, slaughter, spank, stir, strike, surge, tan, tan one's hide*, thresh, toss, toss and turn*, trash, trim, trounce, wallop, wax*, whip, work over*, writhe; SEE CONCEPTS 95,189

threadbare [adj1] *worn, frayed*
beat up*, damaged, dilapidated, dingy, dog-eared, down-at-the-heel*, faded, frowzy*, impaired, injured, old, ragged, ratty*, run-down, scruffy, seedy, shabby, shopworn, tacky, tattered, timeworn, used, used-up, worn-out, worse for wear*; SEE CONCEPTS 485,606

threadbare [adj2] *trite, corny*
banal, bathetic, cliché, clichéd, cliché-ridden, common, commonplace, conventional, dull, everyday, familiar, hackneyed, imitative, motheaten*, musty, overused, poor, set, stale, stereotyped, stock, tedious, tired, uncreative, well-worn, worn-out; SEE CONCEPT 267

threat [n] *warning; danger*
blackmail, bluff, commination, fix, foreboding, foreshadowing, fulmination, hazard, impendence, intimidation, menace, omen, peril, portent, presage, risk, thunder, writing on the wall*; SEE CONCEPTS 278,675

threaten [v1] *warn, pressure*
abuse, admonish, augur, blackmail, bluster, browbeat, bully, caution, comminate, cow, enforce, flex muscles*, forebode, forewarn, fulminate, growl, intimidate, look daggers*, make threat, menace, portend, presage, pressurize, push around*, scare, scowl, shake fist at*, snarl, spook, terrorize, torment, walk heavy*; SEE CONCEPTS 7,19,78

threaten [v2] *endanger*
advance, approach, be dangerous, be gathering, be imminent, be in the air*, be in the offing*, be on the horizon*, brewing, come on, forebode, foreshadow, frighten, hang over*, impend, imperil, jeopardize, loom, overhang, portend, presage, put at risk, put in jeopardy, warn; SEE CONCEPTS 231,407

threatening [adj] *menacing, ominous*
aggressive, alarming, apocalyptic, at hand, baleful, baneful, black, bullying, cautionary, close, comminatory, dangerous, dire, fateful, forthcoming, grim, ill-boding, imminent, impendent, impending, inauspicious, intimidatory, looming, loury, lowering, lowery, minacious, minatory, near, overhanging, portending, portentous, scowling, sinister, terrorizing, ugly, unlucky, unpropitious, unsafe, upcoming, warning; SEE CONCEPTS 525,548,570

threshold [n] *opening; beginning*
brink, dawn, door, doorstep, doorway, edge, entrance, gate, inception, origin, outset, point, point of departure, sill, start, starting point, verge, vestibule; SEE CONCEPTS 440,513,648,832

thrift [n] *economy*
austerity, carefulness, economizing, frugality, parsimony, providence, prudence, saving, stinginess, thriftiness; SEE CONCEPT 335

thrifty [adj] *economical*
canny, careful, chary, cheap, chintzy*, close*, close-fisted, conserving, frugal, mean, parsimonious, penny-pinching, preserving, provident, prudent, saving, scrimpy*, sparing, steal, stingy*, tight*, unwasteful; SEE CONCEPTS 334,401

thrill [n] *sudden excitement*
adventure, bang*, blast, charge*, circus, fireworks, flash*, flush*, fun, good feeling, inspiration, kicks*, lift*, pleasure, refreshment, response, sensation, stimulation, tingle*, titillation, turn-on*, twitter*, upper*, wallop*; SEE CONCEPTS 32,529

thrill [v] *excite, stimulate*
animate, arouse, blow away*, delight, electrify, enchant, enthuse, fire up*, flush, flutter, galvanize, glow, go over big*, grab*, inspire, juice*, key up*, knock one's socks off*, move, palpitate, quicken, quiver, race one's motor*, rally, rouse, score, send, stir, stir up, tickle*, tingle*, titillate,

tremble, turn on*, wow*; SEE CONCEPTS 7,22

thrilling [adj] exciting

blood-tingling*, boss*, breathtaking, electrifying, enchanting, exquisite, fab*, fabulous, frantic, gripping, hair-raising*, large, mad, magnificent, mind-bending*, mind-blowing*, miraculous, overwhelming, rip-roaring*, riveting, rousing, sensational, shivering, stimulating, stirring, swinging, trembling, wild, wondrous, zero cool*; SEE CONCEPTS 548,572

thrive [v] do well

advance, arrive, batten, bear fruit, bloom, blossom, boom, burgeon, develop, flourish, get ahead*, get fat*, get on*, get places*, get there*, grow, grow rich, increase, make a go*, mushroom*, progress, prosper, radiate, rise, score*, shine, shoot up, succeed, turn out well, wax; SEE CONCEPTS 704,706

thriving [adj] successful

advancing, arrived, blooming, booming, burgeoning, cooking*, developing, doing well, flourishing, going strong*, growing, have it made*, have the wherewithal*, healthy, home free*, on top of heap*, progressing, prolific, prospering, prosperous, rich, roaring, robust, rolling*, sitting pretty*, wealthy; SEE CONCEPTS 334,528

throb [v] pulsate, beat

flutter, palpitate, pitpat, pound, pulse, resonate, thrill, thump, tingle, tremble, twitter, vibrate; SEE CONCEPTS 152,185

throng [n] large crowd

assemblage, assembly, bunch, collection, concourse, congregation, crush, drove, everybody, flock, gathering, horde, host, jam, mass, mob, multitude, pack, press, push, sellout, swarm; SEE CONCEPTS 417,432

throttle [v] choke

burke, control, gag, inhibit, silence, smother, stifle, strangle, strangulate, suppress; SEE CONCEPT 191

through [adj] done

buttoned up*, complete, completed, concluded, ended, finis*, finished, in the bag*, over, terminated, wound up*, wrapped up*; SEE CONCEPTS 531,548

through [adj2] direct

constant, free, nonstop, one-way, opened, rapid, regular, straight, straightforward, unbroken, unhindered, uninterrupted; SEE CONCEPTS 482,581

through [prep1] by way of

as a consequence, as a result, at the hand of, because of, by, by dint of, by means of, by reason, by the agency of, by virtue of, for, in consequence of, in virtue of, per, through the medium of, using, via, with, with the help of; SEE CONCEPT 544

through [prep2] between, during

about, by, clear, for the period, from beginning to end, in, in and out, in the middle, into, past, round, straight, throughout, within; SEE CONCEPTS 583,798

throughout [adj] during the whole of

all over, all the time, all through, around, at full length, completely, during, every bit, everyplace, everywhere, far and near, far and wide, for the duration, from beginning to end, from end to end, from one end to the other, from start to finish, from the start, from the word go*, high and low, in all respects, in every place, in everything, inside and out, on all accounts*, over, overall, right through, round, the whole time, through the whole

of, to the end, up and down; SEE CONCEPTS 482,531,798

throw [v1] propel something through the air

bandy, barrage, bombard, buck, bunt, butt, cant, cast, catapult, chuck, dash, deliver, discharge, dislodge, drive, fell, fire, flick, fling, fling off, flip, floor, force, heave, hurl, impel, lapidate, launch, let fly*, let go, lift, lob, overturn, overwhelm, peg, pellet, pelt, pepper, pitch, precipitate, project, push, put, scatter, send, shove, shower, shy, sling, splatter, spray, sprinkle, start, stone, strew, thrust, toss, tumble, unhorse, unseat, upset, volley, waft; SEE CONCEPT 222

throw [v2] confuse

addle, astonish, baffle, befuddle, bewilder, confound, disconcert, distract, disturb, dizzy, dumbfound, fluster, mix up*, throw off*, unsettle, upset; SEE CONCEPT 16

throw away [v1] dispose of

abandon, cast, cast off, chase, clear, discard, dismiss, dispense with, ditch*, drop*, dump*, eject, eliminate, evict, extrude, free oneself of, get rid of, jettison, junk*, lose, refuse, reject, rid oneself of, scrap*, shake off*, shed, shuck, slip, throw off, throw out, turn down, unburden; SEE CONCEPT 180

throw away [v2] waste

be wasteful, blow, consume, dissipate, fail to exploit, fritter, lose, refuse, reject, squander, trifle, turn down; SEE CONCEPT 156

throw off [v] elude, escape

abuse, deceive, evade, get away from, give the slip*, leave behind, lose, outdistance, outrun, shake off, trick; SEE CONCEPT 102

throw out [v] comment

bring forward, bring to light*, bring up, chime in*, come out with, declare, deliver, produce, reveal, say, state, suggest, tell, utter; SEE CONCEPT 51

throw over [v] abandon, leave

break up with, break with, desert, discard, drop, eighty-six*, finish with, forsake, jilt*, quit, renounce, split up with, walk out on*, SEE CONCEPTS 195,384

throw up [v1] vomit, be nauseous

be sick, bring up, disgorge, heave, puke*, regurgitate, retch, spew, spit up, upchuck*; SEE CONCEPTS 179,308

throw up [v2] build quickly

build overnight*, jerrybuild*, knock together*, patch, put together, roughcast, roughhew, run up*, slap together*, throw together*; SEE CONCEPT 168

thrust [n1] point of communication

burden, core, effect, gist, meaning, meat*, pith*, purport, sense, short, substance, upshot; SEE CONCEPT 682

thrust [n2] forward movement

advance, blitz, boost, drive, impetus, impulsion, jump, lunge, momentum, onset, onslaught, poke, pressure, prod, propulsion, punch, push, shove, stab, whack, wham; SEE CONCEPTS 208,222

thrust [v] push hard

advance, assail, assault, attack, bear down, boost, buck, butt, chuck, chunk, clip, clout, crowd, cut, dig, drive, elbow*, embed, fire, force, heave, hump, impale, impel, interject, jab, jam, jostle, lob, lunge, nick, nudge, peg, pierce, pitch, plunge, poke, pour it on*, press, prod, propel, punch, push forward, put, railroad*, ram, run, shove, sink, sling, smack, stab*, stick, toss, transfix, urge, wham*; SEE CONCEPTS 208,222

thud/thump [n/v] *dull crash; dull sound*
bang, beat, blow, clonk, clout, clump, clunk, fall, flutter, hammer, hit, knock, plop, poke, pound, pounding, pulse, rap, slap, smack, strike, throb, thunk*, thwack*, wallop*, whack*; SEE CONCEPTS 65,181,189

thunder [n] *crashing sound*
barrage, blast, boom, booming, cannonade, clap, cracking, crash, crashing, detonation, discharge, drumfire, explosion, fulmination, outburst, peal, pealing, roar, rumble, rumbling, thunderbolt, thundercrack, uproar; SEE CONCEPTS 524,595

thunder [v1] *boom, crash*
blast, clamor, clap, crack, deafen, detonate, drum, explode, peal, resound, reverberate, roar, rumble, storm; SEE CONCEPTS 65,521,526

thunder [v2] *yell at*
bark, bellow, curse, declaim, denounce, fulminate, gnarl, growl, rail, roar, shout, snarl, threaten, utter threat; SEE CONCEPTS 52,54

thus [adv1] *in this manner*
along these lines, as follows, hence, in kind, in such a way, in this fashion, in this way, just like that, like so, like this, so, thus and so, thus and thus, thusly, to such a degree; SEE CONCEPT 544

thus [adv2] *accordingly*
consequently, ergo, for this reason, hence, on that account, so, then, therefore, thereupon; SEE CONCEPT 544

thwart [v] *stop, hinder*
baffle, balk, beat, bilk, check, circumvent, confuse, counter, crab*, cramp, crimp, cross, curb, dash, defeat, disappoint, ditch, dodge, double-cross*, duck, foil, foul up*, frustrate, give the slip*, hold up, impede, louse up*, match, obstruct, oppose, outwit, pit, play off, prevent, queer*, restrain, ruin, scotch*, skin, snafu*, stymie, take down, take wind out of*, trammel, upset, upset one's apple cart*; SEE CONCEPTS 121,130

tic [n] *spasm*
contraction, fit, jerk, twitch; SEE CONCEPT 308

tick [n1] *clicking sound; one beat*
beat, blow, clack, click, clicking, flash, instant, metallic sound, minute, moment, pulsation, pulse, rap, second, shake, tap, tapping, throb, ticktock, twinkling, wink; SEE CONCEPTS 595,808,810

tick [n2] *checkmark*
check, cross, dash, flick, indication, line, mark, stroke, X*; SEE CONCEPT 284

tick [v] *click*
beat, clack, pulsate, tap, thump, ticktock; SEE CONCEPTS 65,189

ticket [n] *authorization on paper*
admission, badge, board, card, certificate, check, chit, coupon, credential, docket, document, invite, key, label, license, marker, note, notice, open sesame, paper, pass, passage, passport, password, permit, raincheck, receipt, record, slip, sticker, stub, tab, tag, token, voucher; SEE CONCEPTS 271,685

tickle [v] *make laugh*
amuse, brush, caress, convulse, delight, divert, enchant, entertain, excite, gratify, itch, pat, pet, please, stimulate, stroke, thrill, tingle, titillate, touch, vellicate; SEE CONCEPTS 7,22,612

ticklish [adj] *difficult, tricky*
awkward, capricious, chancy, changeable, critical, dangerous, delicate, fickle, inconstant, mercurial, nice, precarious, risky, rocky, sensitive, temperamental, thorny, touchy, trying, uncertain, unstable, unsteady, variable, volatile; SEE CONCEPTS 548,565

tidbit [n] *tiny portion*
bit, bite, delicacy, goody*, morsel, mouthful, snack, soupçon, titbit, treat; SEE CONCEPTS 458,835

tide [n] *flow, current*
course, direction, drag, drift, ebb, eddy, flood, flow, flux, movement, race, run, rush, sluice, spate, stream, tendency, torrent, trend, undercurrent, undertow, vortex, wave, whirlpool; SEE CONCEPT 514

tide over [v] *help along*
aid, assist, bridge the gap*, keep head above water*, keep one going, see through; SEE CONCEPT 110

tidings [n] *greetings, news*
advice, bulletin, communication, dirt, information, intelligence, message, report, word; SEE CONCEPT 274

tidy [adj1] *clean, neat*
apple-pie order*, businesslike, chipper*, cleanly, in good shape, methodical, neat as a pin*, ordered, orderly, shipshape*, sleek, snug, spick-and-span*, spruce, systematic, to rights*, trim, uncluttered, well-groomed, well-kept, well-ordered; SEE CONCEPTS 485,585,621

tidy [adj2] *considerable*
ample, fair, generous, good, goodly, handsome, healthy, large, largish, respectable, sizable, substantial, vast; SEE CONCEPTS 762,781

tidy [v] *make neat and orderly*
clean, clear the decks*, fix up, frame*, get act together*, groom, neaten, order, police, pull together, put in good shape, put in order, put in shape, put to rights*, shape up, spruce, spruce up*, straighten, straighten up, tauten, whip into shape*; SEE CONCEPT 250

tie [n1] *fastening*
attachment, band, bandage, bond, brace, connection, cord, fastener, fetter, gag, hookup, joint, knot, ligament, ligature, link, network, nexus, outfit, rope, strap, string, tackle, tie-in, tie-up, yoke, zipper; SEE CONCEPT 680

tie [n2] *deadlock*
dead heat*, draw, drawn battle*, equivalence, even game, level, photo finish*, push, stalemate, standoff; SEE CONCEPTS 364,667

tie [n3] *relationship*
affiliation, allegiance, association, bond, commitment, connection, duty, hookup, kinship, liaison, network, obligation, outfit, tie-in; SEE CONCEPT 388

tie [v1] *connect, interlace*
anchor, attach, band, bind, cinch, clinch, do up, fasten, gird, join, knot, lash, link, make a bow, make a hitch, make a knot, make fast, marry, moor, rivet, rope, secure, splice, tether, tie up, tighten, truss, unite, wed; SEE CONCEPTS 85,160,193

tie/tie up [v2] *hamper, hinder*
bind, clog, confine, curb, delay, entrammel, fetter, hog-tie*, hold, leash, limit, lock up, obstruct, restrain, restrict, shackle, stop, tie one's hands*, trammel; SEE CONCEPT 130

tie [v3] *equal*
balance, be even, be neck and neck*, be on a par,

break even*, deadlock*, draw, even up, keep up with, match, measure up, meet, parallel, rival, touch; SEE CONCEPTS *92,667*

tier [*n*] *level*
bank, category, class, course, echelon, file, grade, group, grouping, layer, league, line, order, pigeonhole*, queue, range, rank, row, series, story, stratum, string; SEE CONCEPTS *378,727,744*

tiff [*n*] *argument*
altercation, bad mood, bickering, difference, disagreement, dispute, falling-out*, fit, huff*, miff*, pet, quarrel, row*, run-in*, scrap, spat, squabble, sulk, tantrum, temper, words*, wrangle; SEE CONCEPTS *46,674*

tight [*adj1*] *close, snug*
bound, clasped, close-fitting, compact, constricted, contracted, cramped, crowded, dense, drawn, enduring, established, fast, firm, fixed, hidebound, inflexible, invulnerable, narrow, quick, rigid, secure, set, skintight, solid, stable, steady, stiff, strained, stretched, strong, sturdy, taut, tenacious, tense, thick, tightened, unbending, unyielding; SEE CONCEPTS *483,485*

tight [*adj2*] *sealed*
airtight, blind, blocked, bolted, choking, clumped, cramping, crushing, cutting, fast, fastened, firm, fixed, hermetic, hermetically sealed, impenetrable, impermeable, impervious, locked, nailed, obstructed, padlocked, pinching, plugged, proof, sealed, secure, short, shrunken, shut, skintight, slammed, smothering, snapped, sound, stopped up, tied, tied up, uncomfortable, watertight; SEE CONCEPTS *489,576*

tight [*adj3*] *stingy*
cheap, close, grasping, mean, miserly, parsimonious, penny-pinching, penurious, sparing, tightfisted; SEE CONCEPTS *334,401*

tight [*adj4*] *difficult, troublesome*
arduous, close, critical, dangerous, distressing, disturbing, exacting, hazardous, near, perilous, precarious, punishing, rough, sticky, tense, ticklish, tough, tricky, trying, upsetting, worrisome; SEE CONCEPTS *548,565*

tight [*adj5*] *intoxicated*
boozy*, buzzed*, drunk, drunken, high*, inebriated, loaded*, pickled*, plastered*, smashed*, stewed*, stoned*, tipsy, under the influence; SEE CONCEPTS *401,406*

tighten [*v*] *constrict*
bind, clench, close, compress, condense, congeal, contract, cramp, crush, fasten, fix, grip, harden, narrow, pinch, pressure, rigidify, screw, secure, squeeze, stiffen, strain, strangle, stretch, tauten, tense, toughen; SEE CONCEPTS *250,469,697*

till [*n*] *cash box*
box, cash drawer, cash register, kitty*, money box, safe, tray, treasury, vault; SEE CONCEPT *339*

till [*v*] *cultivate land*
dig, dress, farm, grow, harrow, hoe, labor, mulch, plant, plough, plow, prepare, raise crops, sow, tend, turn, turn over, work; SEE CONCEPTS *253,257*

tilt [*n1*] *lean, slope*
angle, cant, dip, drop, fall, grade, gradient, inclination, incline, leaning, list, pitch, rake, slant, slide; SEE CONCEPT *738*

tilt [*n2*] *fight*
attack, bout, clash, collision, combat, conflict, contest, duel, encounter, fracas, joust, meet, scrimmage, scuffle, set-to, skirmish, struggle,

tournament, tourney, tussle; SEE CONCEPT *106*

tilt [*v1*] *lean, slant*
bend, cant, careen, dip, heel, incline, list, lurch, pitch, rake, recline, seesaw, set at an angle, shift, slope, slouch, swag, sway, tip, turn, yaw; SEE CONCEPTS *147,149*

tilt [*v2*] *attack, fight*
break, charge, clash, combat, contend, cross swords*, duel, encounter, joust, overthrow, spar, thrust; SEE CONCEPT *106*

timber [*n*] *trees, wood*
balk, beam, board, boom, club, forest, frame, girder, grove, hardwood, log, mast, plank, pole, rafter, rib, stake, timberland, weald, woodland, wood lot, woods; SEE CONCEPTS *430,479*

time [*n1*] *temporal length of event or entity's existence, period*
age, allotment, bit, bout, chronology, clock, continuance, date, day, duration, epoch, era, eternity, extent, future, generation, go*, hour, infinity, instance, instant, interval, juncture, lastingness, life, life span, lifetime, many a moon*, moment, month, occasion, pace, past, point, present, season, second, shift, space, span, spell, stage, stint, stretch, tempo, term, tide, tour, turn, week, while, year; SEE CONCEPTS *801,806,809,819,823*

time [*n2*] *opportunity*
break, chance, heyday, look-in*, occasion, opening, peak, shot, show, squeak*; SEE CONCEPT *693*

timely [*adj*] *at the right time*
appropriate, auspicious, convenient, favorable, fit, fitting, in good time*, in the nick of time*, judicious, likely, meet, modern, now, opportune, pat, promising, prompt, proper, propitious, prosperous, punctual, seasonable, suitable, timeous, towardly, up-to-date, up-to-the-minute, well-timed, with it*; SEE CONCEPTS *558,799*

timid [*adj*] *shy*
afraid, ambivalent, apprehensive, badgered, bashful, browbeaten, bullied, capricious, cowardly, cowed, cowering, coy, daunted, demure, diffident, fainthearted, fearful, feeble, frightened, gentle, having cold feet*, humble, intimidated, irresolute, milquetoast, modest, mousy, nervous, pusillanimous, retiring, shaky, shrinking, shy, soft, spineless, spiritless, submissive, timid, timorous, trembling, unassertive, unassured, unnerved, vacillating, wavering, weak, yellow*; SEE CONCEPT *401*

tinge [*n1*] *color*
cast, colorant, coloration, coloring, dye, dyestuff, hue, nib, pigment, shade, stain, tincture, tint, tone, wash; SEE CONCEPT *622*

tinge [*n2*] *hint*
bit, dash, drop, intimation, nib, pinch, shade, smack, smattering, soupçon, sprinkling, strain, streak, suggestion, tincture, touch, trace; SEE CONCEPTS *529,831*

tinge [*v*] *color*
complexion, dye, imbue, impregnate, infiltrate, saturate, shade, stain, streak, suffuse, tincture, tint; SEE CONCEPT *250*

tingle [*v*] *feel tickled, itchy*
creep, get excited, have goose bumps*, itch, prickle, shiver, sting, thrill, throb, tickle, twitter; SEE CONCEPT *612*

tinker [*v*] *fiddle with*
dabble, doodle*, fix, mess*, mess with*, monkey*, muck about*, niggle*, play, play with, pud-

th
ti

dle, putter, repair, take apart, toy, trifle with; SEE CONCEPTS 87,212

tinkle [v] *jingle, ring*
chime, chink, chinkle, clink, ding, jangle, make bell sound, plink, sound, ting, tingle, tintinnabulate; SEE CONCEPT 65

tint [n] *shade of color*
cast, chroma, color, coloration, complexion, dash, dye, flush, glow, hint, hue, luminosity, pigmentation, rinse, stain, suggestion, taint, tinct, tincture, tinge, tone, touch, trace, wash; SEE CONCEPT 622

tint [v] *color with a certain shade*
affect, complexion, dye, influence, rinse, shade, stain, taint, tincture, tinge, touch, wash; SEE CONCEPT 250

tiny [adj] *very small*
bitsy*, bitty, diminutive, infinitesimal, insignificant, itsy-bitsy*, itty-bitty*, Lilliputian, little, microscopic, midget, mini*, miniature, minikin, minimum, minuscular, minuscule, minute, negligible, pee-wee*, petite, pint-sized*, pocket, pocket-size*, puny, slight, teensy*, teensy-weensy*, teeny*, trifling, wee, yea big*; SEE CONCEPTS 762,773,789

tip/tipoff [nl/n] *inside information*
bang*, bug*, buzz*, clue, cue, dope*, forecast, hint, in*, information, inkling, inside wire, knowledge, news, point, pointer, prediction, prompt, secret information, steer*, suggestion, two cents' worth*, warning, whisper, word, word of advice, word to the wise*; SEE CONCEPT 274

tip [n2] *very top*
apex, cap, crown, cusp, edge, end, extremity, head, nip, peak, point, stub, summit, tiptop, vertex; SEE CONCEPT 836

tip [n3] *gratuity paid*
compensation, fee, gift, handout, lagniappe, money, one-way*, perk, perquisite, pourboire, reward, small change, something*, sweetener; SEE CONCEPT 344

tip [vl] *knock over; cause to lean*
bend, cant, capsize, careen, dump, empty, heel, incline, lean, list, overset, overturn, pour, recline, shift, slant, slope, spill, tilt, topple, topple over, turn over, unload, upend, upset, upturn; SEE CONCEPTS 189,201,208

tip [v2] *give inside information*
advise, caution, clue, cue, forewarn, give a clue, give a hint, give the low-down*, hint, prompt, steer, suggest, tip off, warn; SEE CONCEPT 60

tipsy [adj] *inebriated*
addled, dazed, drunk, drunken, fuddled, happy, high*, intoxicated, irrigated*, lit*, loaded*, mellow, merry, stewed*, tight, unsteady, woozy; SEE CONCEPTS 401,406

tirade [n] *abuse, outburst*
anger, berating, censure, condemnation, denunciation, diatribe, dispute, fulmination, harangue, invective, jeremiad*, lecture, malediction, philippic*, ranting, revilement, screed, sermon, tongue-lashing*, vituperation; SEE CONCEPTS 44,54,278

tire [v] *exhaust, weary*
annoy, bore, burn out*, bush*, collapse, crawl, debilitate, deject, depress, disgust, dishearten, dispirit, displease, distress, drain, droop, drop, enervate, ennui, exasperate, fag, fail, faint, fatigue, flag, fold, give out, go stale, grow weary, harass, irk, irritate, jade, nauseate, overburden, overstrain, overtax, overwork, pain, pall, peter out*, poop out*, prostrate, put to sleep, sap, sicken, sink, strain, tax, vex, weaken, wear, wear down, wear out, weary, wilt, worry, yawn*; SEE CONCEPTS 13,14,469

tired [adj] *exhausted, weary*
all in*, annoyed, asleep, beat*, bored, broken-down, burned out*, collapsing, consumed, dead on one's feet*, distressed, dog-tired*, done for*, done in*, drained, drooping, droopy, drowsy, empty, enervated, exasperated, fagged, faint, fatigued, fed up*, finished, flagging, haggard, irked, irritated, jaded, narcoleptic, overtaxed, overworked, petered out*, played out*, pooped*, prostrated, run-down, sick of, sleepy, spent, stale, tuckered out*, wasted, weary, worn, worn out; SEE CONCEPTS 314,403,406

tireless [adj] *determined*
active, ball of fire*, eager, energetic, enthusiastic, grind, hard-working*, hyper*, incessant, indefatigable, industrious, jumping on, on the go*, perky, persevering, resolute, steadfast, strenuous, unflagging, untiring, unwearied, unwearying, vigorous; SEE CONCEPTS 538,542

tiresome [adj] *irritating, exasperating*
a bit much*, annoying, arduous, boresome, boring, burdensome, demanding, difficult, drag, dragging, drudging, dull, enervative, exacting, exhausting, fatiguing, flat, hard, heavy, hefty, ho-hum*, humdrum, irksome, jading, laborious, monotonous, nowhere, onerous, oppressive, strenuous, tedious, tired, tiring, too much*, tough, trying, uncool*, uninteresting, unrelieved, vexatious, wearing, wearisome, wearying, yawn*; SEE CONCEPTS 529,537,538

titillate [v] *excite, stimulate*
amuse, arouse, entertain, grab, grapple, hook, interest, palpate, provoke, switch on, tantalize, tease, thrill, tickle, tickle pink*, turn on; SEE CONCEPTS 7,11,22

title [nl] *heading, label*
appellation, banner, caption, close, description, head, headline, inscription, legend, name, rubric, salutation, sign, streamer, style, subtitle; SEE CONCEPT 283

title [n2] *name*
appellation, appellative, brand, cognomen, denomination, designation, epithet, handle*, honorific, label, moniker*, nom de plume, nomen, pseudonym, sobriquet, style, tab*, tag*, term; SEE CONCEPT 683

title [n3] *possession, laurel*
authority, championship, claim, commission, crest, crown, decoration, deed, degree, desert, dibs*, due, entitlement, holding, justification, license, medal, merit, ownership, power, prerogative, pretense, pretension, privilege, proof, ribbon, right; SEE CONCEPTS 376,710

title [v] *name*
baptize, call, christen, denominate, designate, dub, entitle, label, style, term; SEE CONCEPT 62

toast [n] *salutation when drinking alcohol*
acknowledgment, celebration, ceremony, commemoration, compliment, down, drink, health, honor, pledge, proposal, salute, sentiment, shingle, thanksgiving, tribute; SEE CONCEPT 278

toast [v] *brown with heat*
cook, crisp, dry, grill, heat, parch, roast, warm; SEE CONCEPT 170

to-do [n] *commotion, excitement*
agitation, bother, brouhaha*, bustle, clamor, disorder, disturbance, flap*, furor, fuss, hassle, hooha*, hoopla*, hubbub*, hurly-burly*, hurrah, performance, pother, quarrel, racket, ruction, rumpus, stir, tumult, turmoil, unrest, uproar, whirl; SEE CONCEPTS 230,674

together [adj] *composed*
calm, cool*, in sync*, stable, well-adjusted, well-balanced, well-organized; SEE CONCEPT 542

together [adv1] *as a group; all at once*
all together, as one, at one fell swoop*, closely, coincidentally, collectively, combined, commonly, concertedly, concomitantly, concurrently, conjointly, contemporaneously, en masse, hand in glove*, hand in hand*, in a body, in concert, in cooperation, in one breath*, in sync*, in unison, jointly, mutually, on the beat*, side by side, simultaneously, synchronically, unanimously, unitedly, with one accord, with one voice, with the beat; SEE CONCEPTS 538,544,548

together [adv2] *in a row*
consecutively, continually, continuously, in succession, night and day, one after the other, on end, running, successively, unintermittedly, without a break, without interruption; SEE CONCEPTS 482,585

toil [n] *hard work*
application, drudgery, effort, exertion, industry, labor, moil, nine-to-five*, occupation, pains*, sweat, travail; SEE CONCEPTS 100,362,677

toil [v] *work hard*
drive, drudge, grind, knock oneself out*, labor, moil, peg away*, plod, plug, push oneself, slave, strain, strive, struggle, sweat, tug, work, work like a dog*; SEE CONCEPTS 100,677

token [n] *indication, remembrance*
badge, clue, demonstration, earnest, evidence, expression, favor, gift, index, indicia, keepsake, manifestation, mark, memento, memorial, note, omen, pawn, pledge, presage, proof, relic, reminder, representation, sample, security, sign, significant, souvenir, symbol, symptom, trophy, warning, warrant; SEE CONCEPTS 284,337,529

tolerable [adj] *acceptable, good enough*
adequate, allowable, all right, average, bearable, better than nothing*, common, decent, endurable, fair, fairly good, fair to middling*, goodish*, indifferent, livable, mediocre, middling*, not bad*, okay*, ordinary, passable, presentable, respectable, run-of-the-mill*, satisfactory, so-so*, sufferable, sufficient, supportable, sustainable, tidy, unexceptionable, unexceptional, unimpeachable; SEE CONCEPTS 529,548

tolerance [n1] *open-mindedness*
altruism, benevolence, broad-mindedness, charity, clemency, compassion, concession, endurance, forbearance, freedom, good will, grace, humanity, indulgence, kindness, lenience, leniency, lenity, liberalism, liberality, liberalness, license, magnanimity, mercifulness, mercy, patience, permission, permissiveness, sensitivity, sufferance, sympathy, toleration, understanding; SEE CONCEPTS 410,657

tolerance [n2] *fortitude, grit*
endurance, guts*, hardiness, hardness, opposition, patience, resilience, resistance, stamina, staying power*, steadfastness, steadiness, strength, sufferance, toughness, vigor; SEE CONCEPT 732

tolerant [adj] *open-minded, easygoing*
advanced, benevolent, big, broad, broad-minded, catholic, charitable, clement, complaisant, condoning, easy on, easy with, excusing, fair, forbearing, forgiving, free and easy*, humane, indulgent, kindhearted*, lax, lenient, liberal, long-suffering*, magnanimous, merciful, patient, permissive, progressive, radical, receptive, soft, sophisticated, sympathetic, understanding, unprejudiced, wide; SEE CONCEPTS 403,542

tolerate [v] *allow, indulge*
abide, accept, admit, authorize, bear, bear with, blink at*, brook, condone, consent to, countenance, endure, go, go along with, have, hear, humor, live with, permit, pocket, put up with, receive, sanction, sit and take it*, sit still for*, stand, stand for, stay the course*, stomach*, string along, submit to, suffer, sustain, swallow*, take, tough out*, undergo, wink at*; SEE CONCEPTS 23,83

toll [n1] *fee*
assessment, charge, cost, customs, demand, duty, exaction, expense, impost, levy, payment, price, rate, tariff, tax, tribute; SEE CONCEPT 329

toll [n2] *damage, deaths*
casualties, cost, expense, inroad, loss, losses, penalty, price; SEE CONCEPT 230

toll [v] *ring out*
announce, bell, bong, call, chime, clang, knell, peal, signal, sound, strike, summon, warn; SEE CONCEPT 65

tomb [n] *burial place*
box, burial, burial chamber, catacomb, coffin, crypt, grave, mausoleum, monument, pit, sepulcher, trough, vault; SEE CONCEPT 305

tome [n] *large, scholarly book*
classic, great work, magnum opus, novel, opus, publication, reference book, schoolbook, textbook, title, tradebook, volume, work, writing; SEE CONCEPT 280

tone [n1] *pitch, volume*
accent, emphasis, force, inflection, intonation, modulation, resonance, strength, stress, timbre, tonality; SEE CONCEPT 65

tone [n2] *attitude, spirit*
air, approach, aspect, character, condition, current, drift, effect, expression, fashion, feel, frame, grain, habit, humor, manner, mind, mode, mood, movement, nature, note, quality, state of things, strain, style, temper, tenor, trend, vein; SEE CONCEPTS 655,673,682

tone [n3] *color*
blend, cast, coloration, hue, shade, tinge, tint, value; SEE CONCEPT 622

tone [n4] *condition of the body*
elasticity, health, healthiness, resiliency, strength, tonicity, tonus, vigor; SEE CONCEPT 316

tone down [v] *moderate*
chill out*, cloud, dampen, darken, deepen, dim, mitigate, modulate, play down, reduce, restrain, shade, sober, soften, soft-pedal*, subdue, temper; SEE CONCEPT 240

tongue [n] *language*
argot, articulation, dialect, discourse, expression, idiom, language, lingo, parlance, patois, speech, talk, utterance, vernacular, voice; SEE CONCEPT 276

tonic [n] *restorative drink, medicine*
analeptic, boost, bracer, conditioner, cordial, drug, fillip, invigorator, livener, pick-me-up*,

ti
to

pickup, refresher, restorative, roborant, shot in the arm*, stimulant, strengthener; SEE CONCEPT 307

too [adv1] *also*
additionally, along, as well, besides, further, furthermore, in addition, into the bargain, likewise, more, moreover, to boot, withal; SEE CONCEPTS 544,771

too [adv2] *excessively*
awfully, beyond, ever, exceptionally, exorbitantly, extremely, greatly, highly, immensely, immoderately, in excess, inordinately, notably, over, over and above, overly, overmuch, remarkably, strikingly, unconscionably, unduly, unreasonably, very; SEE CONCEPTS 569,772

tool [n1] *instrument used to shape, form, finish*
apparatus, appliance, contraption, contrivance, device, engine, gadget, gizmo*, implement, job, machine, means, mechanism, utensil, weapon, whatchamacallit*; SEE CONCEPT 499

tool [n2] *person who allows himself to be used*
accessory, accomplice, agent, auxiliary, chump*, creature, dupe, easy mark*, figurehead, flunky*, go-between, greenhorn*, hireling, idiot, intermediary, jackal, lackey, mark*, medium, messenger, minion, patsy*, pawn, peon, puppet, stooge, stool pigeon*, sucker*; SEE CONCEPTS 348,412,423

top [n1] *highest point*
acme, apex, apogee, cap, capital, ceiling, climax, cork, cover, crest, crown, culmination, cusp, face, fastigium, finial, head, height, high point, lid, limit, maximum, meridian, peak, pinnacle, point, roof, spire, stopper, summit, superficies, surface, tip, utmost, vertex, zenith; SEE CONCEPT 836

top [n2] *highest rank*
best, captain, chief, choice, cream, elite, first place, flower, head, lead, leader, pick, pride, prime, prize, utmost; SEE CONCEPT 668

top [adj] *best, most important; highest*
apical, capital, chief, crack, crowning, culminating, dominant, elite, excellent, fine, finest, first, first-class, first-rate, five-star*, foremost, greatest, head, lead, leading, loftiest, maximal, maximum, outside, paramount, preeminent, primary, prime, principal, ruling, sovereign, superior, supreme, tiptop*, top-drawer*, topmost, top-notch, upper, uppermost; SEE CONCEPTS 567,574,583

top [v1] *place on or reach highest part*
ascend, cap, climb, cloak, clothe, cover, crest, crown, face, finish, garnish, piggyback*, protect, reinforce, roof, scale, spread over, superimpose, surmount, tip; SEE CONCEPTS 172,201,750

top [v2] *surpass*
bash, beat, be first, best, better, blow away*, clobber*, eclipse, exceed, excel, fake out*, finagle*, fox*, go beyond, goose*, outdo, outfox, outshine, outstrip, overrun, run circles around*, shut out*, total*, transcend; SEE CONCEPTS 95,141

top [v3] *remove the upper part*
amputate, cream, crop, curtail, cut off, decapitate, detruncate, dock, file off, lop off, pare, pollard, prune, ream, scrape off, shave off, shear, shorten, skim, trim, truncate; SEE CONCEPT 211

topic [n] *subject matter*
affair, argument, business, case, division, field, head, issue, material, matter, matter in hand, moot point, motif, motion, motive, point, point in question, problem, proposition, question, resolution,

subject, text, theme, theorem, thesis; SEE CONCEPT 532

topical [adj1] *current*
contemporary, modern, newsworthy, nominal, popular, subjective, thematic, up-to-date; SEE CONCEPT 820

topical [adj2] *restricted, local*
confined, insular, limited, parochial, particular, regional, sectional; SEE CONCEPTS 557,583

topple [v] *fall or knock over; overthrow*
bring down, capsize, collapse, do a pratfall*, fall, falter, founder, go belly up*, go down, hit the dirt*, keel over, knock down, land, lose it*, lurch, nose-dive, oust, overbalance, overturn, pitch, plunge, slump, stagger, stumble, take a header*, teeter, tip over, totter, tumble, turn over, unhorse, unseat, upset; SEE CONCEPTS 95,147,181,208

topsy-turvy [adj] *mixed-up*
chaotic, cluttered, cockeyed, confused, disarranged, disheveled, disjointed, dislocated, disordered, disorderly, disorganized, downside-up*, inside-out, inverted, jumbled, littered, messy, muddled, overturned, pell-mell*, riotous, tangled, tumultous/tumultuous, unhinged, untidy, upended, upside-down, upturned; SEE CONCEPTS 485,548,585

torment [n] *severe mental distress*
affliction, agony, anguish, annoyance, bane, bother, excruciation, harassment, hell, irritation, misery, nag, nagging, nuisance, pain, pain in the neck*, persecution, pest, plague, provocation, rack, scourge, suffering, torture, trouble, vexation, worry; SEE CONCEPTS 410,728

torment [v] *be or make very upset*
abuse, afflict, agonize, annoy, bait, bedevil, bone, bother, break, crucify, devil, distress, drive bananas*, drive up the wall*, excruciate, give a hard time*, harass, harrow, harry, heckle, hound, hurt, irritate, mistreat, molest, nag, pain, persecute, pester, plague, play cat and mouse*, provoke, punish, put through wringer*, rack, rub salt in wound*, smite, tease, torture, trouble, try, vex, worry, wring; SEE CONCEPTS 7,19,313

torn [adj1] *cut open*
broken, burst, cleaved, cracked, damaged, divided, fractured, gashed, impaired, lacerated, mangled, ragged, rent, ripped, ruptured, severed, shabby, slashed, sliced, slit, snapped, split, wrenched; SEE CONCEPT 485

torn [adj2] *undecided*
divided, irresolute, of two minds*, split, uncertain, unsure, vacillating, wavering; SEE CONCEPTS 403,542

torpid [adj] *lazy, slow*
apathetic, benumbed, comatose, dopey*, dormant, drowsy, dull, faineant, heavy, hebetudinous, idle, inactive, indifferent, indolent, inert, lackadaisical, languid, languorous, latent, leaden, lethargic, listless, lymphatic, motionless, numb, paralyzed, passive, slothful, slow-moving, sluggish, slumberous, sodden, somnolent, stagnant, static, stupid, stuporous; SEE CONCEPTS 401,538

torrent [n] *heavy flow*
cascade, cataclysm, cataract, cloudburst, deluge, downpour, effusion, flood, flooding, flux, gush, inundation, niagara, outburst, overflow, pour, rush, shower, spate, stream, tide, waterfall; SEE CONCEPTS 146,179,526

torrid [adj1] *very hot*
arid, austral, blazing, blistering, boiling, broiling,

burning, dried, dry, fiery, heated, parched, parching, red-hot*, scalding, scorched, scorching, sizzling, stifling, sultry, sweltering, tropic, tropical; SEE CONCEPT 605

torrid [adj2] *sensuous*
ardent, blazing, burning, erotic, fervent, flaming, hot*, hot-blooded*, impassioned, intense, passionate, red-hot*, sexy, steamy*, sultry, white-hot*; SEE CONCEPT 372

tortuous [adj1] *very twisted*
anfractuous, bent, circuitous, convoluted, crooked, curved, flexuous, indirect, involute, labyrinthine, mazy, meandering, meandrous, roundabout, serpentine, sinuous, snaky, twisting, vermiculate, winding, zigzag; SEE CONCEPT 581

tortuous [adj2] *complicated*
ambiguous, convoluted, cunning, deceptive, devious, indirect, involute, involved, misleading, perverse, roundabout, tricky; SEE CONCEPT 562

torture [n] *severe mental or physical pain*
ache, affliction, agony, anguish, cruciation, crucifixion, distress, dolor, excruciation, impalement, laceration, martyrdom, misery, pang, persecution, rack, suffering, third degree*, torment, tribulation, twinge; SEE CONCEPTS 410,728

torture [v] *upset or hurt severely*
abuse, afflict, agonize, annoy, beat, bother, crucify, distress, disturb, excruciate, grill, harrow, impale, injure, irritate, lacerate, maim, mangle, martyr, martyrize, mistreat, mutilate, oppress, pain, persecute, rack, smite, torment, try, whip, wound, wring, wrong; SEE CONCEPTS 7,19,246,313

toss [n/v] *throw*
bung, cast, chuck, chunk, fire, fling, flip, heave, hurl, launch, lob, peg, pitch, project, propel, sling, twirl, wing; SEE CONCEPT 222

toss [v2] *move back and forth*
agitate, agonize, bob, buffet, disturb, flounder, heave, jiggle, joggle, jolt, labor, lurch, move restlessly, oscillate, pitch, rise and fall, rock, roll, seesaw, shake, squirm, stir, sway, swing, thrash, tumble, undulate, wallow, wave, wobble, wriggle, writhe; SEE CONCEPT 147

total [n] *whole*
aggregate, all, amount, body, budget, bulk, entirety, flat out*, full amount, gross, jackpot*, mass, quantity, quantum, result, sum, sum total*, tale, the works*, totality; SEE CONCEPTS 787,837

total [adj] *complete, thorough*
absolute, all-out, comprehensive, consummate, downright, entire, every, full, full-blown, full-scale, gross, inclusive, integral, out-and-out, outright, overall, perfect, plenary, positive, sheer, sweeping, thoroughgoing, totalitarian, unconditional, undisputed, unlimited, unlimited, unmitigated, unqualified, unreserved, unrestricted, utter, whole; SEE CONCEPTS 531,762

total [v] *add up*
add, aggregate, amount to, calculate, cast, come, come to, comprise, consist of, equal, figure, foot, mount up to, number, pile up, reach, reckon, result in, ring up*, run into, run to, stack up, summate, sum up, totalize, tote*, yield; SEE CONCEPT 764

totalitarian [adj] *dictatorial*
absolute, authoritarian, autocratic, communist*, despotic, fascistic, monolithic, Nazi*, one-party, oppressive, total, totalistic, tyrannical, undemocratic; SEE CONCEPT 536

totally [adv] *completely*
absolutely, all, all in all, altogether, comprehensively, consummately, entirely, exactly, exclusively, flat out*, full blast*, fully, in toto*, just, perfectly, quite, thoroughly, top to bottom*, unconditionally, unmitigatedly, utterly, wholeheartedly, wholly; SEE CONCEPT 531

totter [v] *move falteringly*
blunder, careen, dodder, falter, flounder, hesitate, lurch, quake, quiver, reel, rock, roll, seesaw, shake, shimmy, slide, slip, stagger, stammer, stumble, sway, teeter, topple, tremble, trip, walk unsteadily, waver, weave, wheel, wobble, zigzag; SEE CONCEPT 151

touch [n1] *physical contact*
blow, brush, caress, collision, communication, contact, contingence, crash, cuddling, embrace, feel, feeling, fondling, graze, grope, handling, hit, hug, impact, junction, kiss, lick, manipulation, nudge, palpation, pat, peck, perception, percussion, petting, push, rub, rubbing, scratch, shock, stroke, stroking, tactility, taction, tap, taste, touching; SEE CONCEPTS 590,608,612

touch [n2] *tiny amount*
bit, dash, detail, drop, hint, inkling, intimation, jot, pinch, scent, shade, smack, small amount, smattering, soupçon, speck, spot, streak, suggestion, suspicion, taste, tincture, tinge, trace, whiff; SEE CONCEPTS 529,831,832

touch [n3] *manner, method*
ability, acquaintance, adeptness, adroitness, approach, art, artistry, awareness, characteristic, command, communication, contact, deftness, direction, effect, facility, faculty, familiarity, finish, flair, hand, handiwork, influence, knack; mastery, skill, style, talent, technique, trademark, understanding, virtuosity, way; SEE CONCEPTS 6,630,655

touch [v] *make physical contact*
abut, adjoin, be in contact, border, brush, butt on, caress, come together, communicate, contact, converge, dab, examine, feel, feel up*, finger, finish, flick, glance, graze, grope, handle, hit, impinge upon, inspect, join, kiss, lay a finger on*, lick, line, manipulate, march, massage, meet, neighbor, osculate, palm, palpate, partake, pat, paw, percuss, pet, probe, push, reach, rub, scrutinize, sip, smooth, strike, stroke, suck, sweep, tag, tap, taste, thumb, tickle, tip, toy, verge; SEE CONCEPT 612

touch [v2] *have an effect on*
affect, arouse, carry, disturb, excite, feel out, get through to*, get to*, grab, impress, influence, inspire, make an impression*, mark, melt, move, quicken, soften, stimulate, stir, strike, strike a chord*, stroke, sway, tug at the heart*, upset; SEE CONCEPTS 7,19,22

touch [v3] *have to do with; regard*
affect, be a party to, bear on, bear upon, be associated with, belong to, center upon, concern, concern oneself with, consume, deal with, drink, eat, get involved in, handle, have to do with, interest, involve, partake of, pertain to, refer to, use, utilize; SEE CONCEPT 532

touch [v4] *make mention*
allude to, bring in, cover, deal with, discuss, go over, mention, note, refer to, speak of, treat; SEE CONCEPT 51

touch [v5] *compare with; correspond to*
amount, approach, be a match for*, be in the same

to
to

league*, be on a par*, come near, come to, come up to, equal, hold a candle to*, match, measure up, meet, parallel, partake of, rival, tie, verge on; SEE CONCEPT *561*

touched [*adj1*] *deeply moved emotionally*
affected, disturbed, grabbed*, impressed, melted*, softened, stirred, swayed, turned on by*, turned on to*, upset; SEE CONCEPTS *403,542*

touched [*adj2*] *crazy*
batty*, bizarre, bonkers*, cuckoo*, daft, eccentric, fanatic, flighty, insane, neurotic, not all there*, not right*, nuts*, nutty*, obsessed, out of one's mind*, peculiar, pixilated, queer, unhinged; SEE CONCEPTS *402,403*

touching [*adj1*] *affecting, moving emotionally*
compassionate, emotive, heartbreaking, heart-rending, impressive, melting, mind-blowing*, pathetic, piteous, pitiable, pitiful, poignant, responsive, sad, stirring, stunning, sympathetic, tear-jerking, tender, wistful; SEE CONCEPTS *529,537*

touch up [*v*] *fix up; improve*
amend, brush up, do up, enhance, finish off, give a face-lift*, gloss, make improvements, modify, patch up, perfect, polish, put finishing touches on*, remodel, renew, renovate, repair, retouch, revamp, rework, round off, tease*; SEE CONCEPTS *212,244*

touchy [*adj*] *easily offended*
bad-tempered, bundle of nerves*, cantankerous, captious, choleric, crabbed, cranky, cross, delicate, dicey*, grouchy, grumpy, hazardous, hypersensitive, irascible, irritable, jumpy*, mean, ornery*, oversensitive, peevish, perturbable, pettish, petulant, precarious, querulous, quick-tempered, risky, sensitive, splenetic, surly, temperamental, testy, thin-skinned*, ticklish*, tricky, unpredictable, unsafe, uptight*, volatile, wired up*, wound up*; SEE CONCEPTS *401,542,548*

tough [*n*] *person who is rowdy, mean*
bruiser, brute, bully, criminal, gangster, goon*, hood*, hoodlum, hooligan, punk*, rough*, roughneck, rowdy, ruffian, thug, villain; SEE CONCEPT *412*

tough [*adj1*] *sturdy, strong*
brawny, cohesive, conditioned, dense, durable, fibrous, firm, fit, flinty, hard, hard as nails*, hard-bitten*, hardened, hardy, healthy, indigestible, inflexible, leathery, lusty, mighty, molded, resilient, resistant, rigid, robust, rugged, seasoned, sinewy, solid, stalwart, steeled, stiff, stout, strapping, tenacious, tight, tough as nails*, unbreakable, unyielding, vigorous, withstanding; SEE CONCEPTS *314,489*

tough [*adj2*] *obstinate, rough*
adamant, arbitrary, callous, confirmed, cruel, desperate, drastic, exacting, ferocious, fierce, firm, fixed, hard, hard-bitten*, hard-boiled*, hard-line*, hard-nosed*, hard-shelled*, harsh, headstrong, immutable, inflexible, intractable, merciless, narrow, obdurate, pugnacious, refractory, resolute, ruffianly, ruthless, savage, severe, stern, stiff, strict, stubborn, taut, terrible, unalterable, unbending, uncompromising, uncontrollable, unforgiving, unmanageable, unyielding, vicious, violent; SEE CONCEPTS *403,542*

tough [*adj3*] *difficult, laborious*
arduous, backbreaking*, baffling, burdensome, demanding, effortful, exacting, exhausting, exigent, grievous, hairy*, handful*, hard, heavy, intractable, intricate, irksome, knotty*, labored, mean, no piece of cake*, onerous, oppressive, perplexing, puzzling, resisting, severe, stiff, strenuous, taxing, thorny, toilsome, troublesome, trying, unyielding, uphill*, weighty*, wicked; SEE CONCEPTS *538,565*

toughen [*v*] *harden*
acclimate, acclimatize, anneal, brutalize, climatize, develop, inure, make difficult, season, strengthen, temper; SEE CONCEPTS *202,250*

tour [*n*] *journey; stint*
bout*, circle tour*, circuit, course, cruise, excursion, expedition, getaway*, go*, hitch*, hop*, jaunt*, junket, outing, overnight*, peregrination, progress, road, round*, roundabout*, round trip, run, shift, spell, stretch, stump*, swing*, time, travel, trek, trick*, trip, turn, voyage, weekend, whistle-stop*; SEE CONCEPTS *81,224,807*

tour [*v*] *visit, journey*
barnstorm*, cruise, explore, globe-trot*, go on the road*, holiday*, hop*, jaunt, jet, junket, peregrinate, sightsee, stump*, swing*, take a trip, travel, vacation, voyage; SEE CONCEPTS *224,227*

tourist [*n*] *person who visits a place*
day-tripper, excursionist, globetrotter, jet-setter, journeyer, rubberneck*, sightseer, stranger, traveler, tripper*, vacationist, visitor, voyager, wayfarer; SEE CONCEPT *423*

tournament [*n*] *sporting competition*
clash, contest, duel, event, fight, games, joust, match, meet, meeting, series, sport, test, tilt, tourney; SEE CONCEPT *363*

tousled [*adj*] *disarrayed*
beat-up*, dirty, disarranged, disheveled, disordered, grubby*, messed-up*, messy, mussed-up*, ruffled, rumpled, sloppy, tangled, uncombed, unkempt; SEE CONCEPTS *485,589*

tout [*v*] *brag about, show off*
acclaim, ballyhoo*, boost, give a boost*, herald, laud, plug*, praise, proclaim, promote, publicize, push, steer, tip, tip off*, trumpet; SEE CONCEPTS *69,138*

tow [*v*] *pull along*
drag, draw, ferry, haul, lug, propel, push, trail, trawl, tug, yank; SEE CONCEPT *206*

toward/towards [*prep1*] *on the way to; near*
against, almost, approaching, close to, coming up, contra, en route, facing, for, fronting, headed for, in relation to, in the direction of, in the vicinity, just before, moving, nearing, nearly, not along, on the road to, over against, pointing to, proceeding, shortly before, to, via, vis-à-vis; SEE CONCEPT *586*

toward/towards [*prep2*] *concerning*
about, against, anent, apropos, as for, as to, for, in re, re, regarding, with regard to, with respect to; SEE CONCEPT *532*

tower [*n*] *very high building or building part*
belfry, castle, citadel, cloud buster*, column, fort, fortification, fortress, high rise*, keep, lookout, mast, minaret, monolith, obelisk, pillar, refuge, skyscraper, spire, steeple, stronghold, turret; SEE CONCEPTS *439,440*

tower [*v*] *rise above*
ascend, be above, dominate, exceed, extend above, look down, look over, loom, mount, overlook, overtop, rear, soar, surmount, surpass, top, transcend; SEE CONCEPTS *141,752*

towering [adj] *huge, excessive*
aerial, airy, colossal, elevated, extraordinary, extravagant, extreme, fantastic, gigantic, great, high, immoderate, imperial, imposing, impressive, inordinate, intense, lofty, magnificent, massive, mighty, monumental, outstanding, paramount, preeminent, prodigious, skyscraping, soaring, spiring, stately, stupendous, sublime, superior, supreme, surpassing, tall, towery, transcendent, tremendous, ultimate, undue, unmatchable, unmeasurable; SEE CONCEPTS 567,779

town [n] *incorporated community*
apple*, boondocks, borough, burg*, city, hamlet, metropolis, municipality, seat, sticks*, township, whistle-stop*; SEE CONCEPTS 507,508

toxic [adj] *poisonous*
baneful, deadly, harmful, lethal, mephitic, noxious, pernicious, pestilential, poison, septic, toxicant, venomous, virulent; SEE CONCEPT 537

toy [n] *entertainment article*
bauble, curio, doll, game, knickknack, novelty, plaything, trifle, trinket; SEE CONCEPT 446

toy [v] *play with*
amuse oneself, coquet, cosset, dally, dandle, fiddle, flirt, fool, fool around*, jest, lead on, mess around*, pet, play, play around, play games, sport, string along*, tease, trifle, wanton; SEE CONCEPT 384

trace [n] *evidence; small bit*
breath, crumb, dab, dash, drop, element, footmark, footprint, fragment, hint, indication, intimation, iota, jot, mark, memento, minimum, nib, nuance, particle, pinch, proof, record, relic, remains, remnant, scintilla, shade, shadow, shred, sign, slot, smell, smidgen, snippet, soupçon, speck, spoor, spot, sprinkling, strain, streak, suggestion, survival, suspicion, taste, tincture, tinge, tittle, token, touch, track, trail, tread, trifle, vestige, whiff, whisper; SEE CONCEPTS 529,831

trace [v1] *seek, follow*
ascertain, detect, determine, discern, discover, ferret out, find, hunt, perceive, pursue, run down, search for, shadow, smell out, spoor, spot, stalk, track, trail, unearth; SEE CONCEPTS 207,216

trace [v2] *draw around*
chart, copy, delineate, depict, duplicate, map, mark out, outline, record, reproduce, show, sketch; SEE CONCEPTS 79,174

track [n1] *mark, print made by something*
clue, footmark, footprint, footstep, groove, impress, impression, imprint, indication, memorial, monument, path, print, record, remains, remnant, rut, scent, sign, slot, spoor, step, symbol, token, trace, tract, trail, tread, vestige, wake; SEE CONCEPTS 513,628

track [n2] *path, way*
alley, artery, avenue, beaten path*, boulevard, clearing, course, cut*, drag*, footpath, highway, lane, line, orbit, passage, pathway, rail, rails, road, roadway, route, street, thoroughfare, track, trackway, trail, trajectory, walk; SEE CONCEPT 501

track/track down [v] *follow, pursue*
apprehend, beat the bushes*, be hot on the trail*, bird-dog*, bring to light*, capture, catch, chase, cover, dig up, discover, do, dog*, dog footsteps of*, draw an inference, expose, ferret out, find, go after, hunt, piece together, put together, run down, scout, shadow, smell out*, sniff out*,

stalk, stick to, tail, trace, trail, travel, traverse, unearth; SEE CONCEPTS 183,207,216

tract [n] *area, lot*
amplitude, belt, district, estate, expanse, extent, field, parcel, part, piece, plat, plot, portion, quarter, region, section, sector, spread, stretch, zone; SEE CONCEPTS 508,513

tractable [adj] *manageable*
acquiescent, amenable, biddable, complaisant, compliant, controllable, docile, ductile, facile, flexible, game, going along with*, governable, hanging loose*, malleable, meek, obedient, persuadable, plastic, pliable, pliant, putty in hands*, rolling with punches*, subdued, submissive, tame, tractile, willing, workable, yielding; SEE CONCEPTS 401,488,542

traction [n] *physical resistance, friction*
absorption, adherence, adhesion, constriction, contraction, drag, draught, drawing, grip, haulage, pull, pulling, purchase, resorption, strain, stress, stretch, suck, suction, towage; SEE CONCEPTS 731,748

trade [n1] *buying and selling*
barter, business, clientele, commerce, contract, custom, customers, deal, dealing, enterprise, exchange, industry, interchange, market, merchantry, patronage, public, sales, swap, traffic, transaction, truck; SEE CONCEPTS 324,327, 330,345

trade [n2] *profession, work*
art, avocation, business, calling, craft, employment, game, handicraft, job, line, line of work, métier, nine to-five*, occupation, position, pursuit, skill, thing*, vocation; SEE CONCEPTS 349,360

trademark [n] *logo, symbol*
brand, brand name, identification, initials, label, logo, logotype, mark, stamp, tag; SEE CONCEPTS 259,284

tradition [n] *established practice*
attitude, belief, birthright, conclusion, convention, culture, custom, customs, ethic, ethics, fable, folklore, form, habit, heritage, idea, inheritance, institution, law, legend, lore, mores, myth, mythology, mythos, opinion, practice, praxis, ritual, unwritten law, usage, wisdom; SEE CONCEPT 688

traditional [adj] *usual, established*
acceptable, accustomed, acknowledged, ancestral, classic, classical, common, conventional, customary, doctrinal, fixed, folk, habitual, historic, immemorial, long-established, old, oral, popular, prescribed, regular, rooted, sanctioned, taken for granted, time-honored, transmitted, universal, unwritten, widely used, widespread; SEE CONCEPTS 530,533

traffic [n1] *coming and going*
cartage, flux, freight, gridlock, influx, jam, movement, parking lot*, passage, passengers, rush hour, service, shipment, transfer, transit, transport, transportation, travel, truckage, vehicles; SEE CONCEPTS 224,505,770

traffic [n2] *buying and selling*
barter, business, closeness, commerce, communication, communion, connection, custom, dealing, dealings*, doings*, exchange, familiarity, industry, interchange, intercourse, intimacy, merchantry, patronage, peddling, relations, relationship, soliciting, trade, transactions, truck*; SEE CONCEPTS 330,335

to
tr

traffic [v] *buy and sell; do business*
bargain, barter, black-market*, bootleg*, connect with, contact, deal, deal in*, dicker, exchange, fence, handle, have dealings, have transaction, horse trade*, interact, interface, make a deal, market, moonshine*, negotiate, network, peddle, push, reach out, relate, shove, swap, touch, touch base*, trade, truck*, work out; SEE CONCEPTS *324,327,330,345*

tragedy [n] *disaster*
adversity, affliction, bad fortune, bad luck, blight, blow, calamity, cataclysm, catastrophe, contretemps, curse, curtains*, dole, dolor, doom, downer*, failure, hard knocks*, hardship, humiliation, lot, misadventure, mischance, misfortune, mishap, reverse, shock, struggle, the worst*, unluckiness, waterloo*, woe, wreck; SEE CONCEPTS *674,675*

tragic [adj] *catastrophic, very bad*
adverse, anguished, appalling, awful, calamitous, cataclysmic, crushing, deadly, deathly, deplorable, desolate, destructive, dire, disastrous, doleful, dreadful, fatal, fateful, forlorn, grievous, grim, hapless, harrowing, heartbreaking, heartrending, ill-fated, ill-starred, lamentable, miserable, mournful, painful, pathetic, pitiable, pitiful, ruinous, sad, shocking, sorrowful, terrible, unfortunate, unhappy, woeful, wretched; SEE CONCEPTS *548,571*

trail [n] *path, track*
aisle, beaten track*, byway, footpath, footprints, footsteps, groove*, mark, marks, pathway, road, route, rut, scent, spoor, stream, stroll, tail, trace, train, wake, way; SEE CONCEPT *501*

trail [v] *lag behind, follow*
bedog, bring up the rear*, chase, dally, dangle, dawdle, delay, dog*, drag, draggle, draw, droop, drop back, extend, fall back, fall behind, falter, flag, follow a scent*, halt, hang, hang back, hang down, haul, hunt, lag, linger, loiter, nose out*, plod, poke, poke along*, procrastinate, pull, pursue, shadow, shag, spook*, spoor, stalk, straggle, stream, string along*, tag along*, tail, take out after, tarry, tow, trace, track, traipse, trudge; SEE CONCEPTS *207,727,753*

train [n] *series*
alternation, appendage, caravan, chain, column, concatenation, consecution, convoy, cortege, course, court, entourage, file, following, gradation, line, order, procession, progression, retinue, row, run, scale, sequel, sequence, set, string, succession, suite, tail, thread, tier, track, trail, wake; SEE CONCEPTS *432,727*

train [v1] *prepare*
accustom, brainwash*, break in, care for, coach, cultivate, develop, discipline, drill, drum into, dry run*, educate, enlighten, equip, exercise, get a workout, get in shape, ground, grow strong, guide, habituate, harden, hone, improve, instruct, inure, make ready, mold, prime, qualify, rear, rehearse, run through, school, season, shape, sharpen, show the ropes*, study, tame, teach, tutor, update, warm up*, whip into shape*, wise up*, work out; SEE CONCEPTS *35,202,285*

train [v2] *aim at*
beam, bring to bear, cast, cock, direct, draw a bead*, focus, get in one's sights*, head, incline, lay, level, line up, point, slant, turn, zero in*; SEE CONCEPT *201*

training [n] *preparation*
background, basics, buildup, chalk talk*, coaching, cultivation, discipline, domestication, drill, education, exercise, foundation, grounding, groundwork, guidance, indoctrination, instruction, practice, preliminaries, preparation, principles, readying, schooling, seasoning, sharpening, teaching, tuition, tune-up*, tutelage, upbringing, warm-up*, workout*; SEE CONCEPTS *202,285, 678*

trait [n] *characteristic*
affection, attribute, birthmark, cast, character, custom, denominator, feature, habit, idiosyncrasy, lineament, manner, mannerism, mark, nature of the beast*, oddity, peculiarity, point, property, quality, quirk, savor, thing*, trick, virtue; SEE CONCEPTS *411,644,834*

traitor [n] *person who is disloyal*
apostate, backslider*, back-stabber*, Benedict Arnold*, betrayer, conspirator, deceiver, defector, deserter, double-crosser*, fink*, hypocrite, impostor, informer, intriguer, Judas*, miscreant, quisling, rebel, renegade, snake*, sneak*, snitch*, snitcher*, spy, squealer*, stool pigeon*, tattletale, traducer, treasonist, turncoat, two-timer*, whistle-blower*, wolf*; SEE CONCEPT *412*

tramp [n1] *person who is poor, desperate*
beggar, bum, derelict, down-and-out*, drifter, floater, hitchhiker, hobo, homeless person, loafer, outcast, panhandler, vagabond, vagrant, wanderer; SEE CONCEPT *412*

tramp [n2] *heavy walk*
cruise, excursion, expedition, footfall, footstep, hike, jaunt, march, ramble, saunter, slog, stomp, stroll, tour, traipse, tread, trek, turn, walking trip; SEE CONCEPTS *151,224*

tramp [v] *walk heavily*
crush, footslog, gallop, hike, hop, march, navigate, plod, pound, ramble, range, roam, rove, slog, stamp, stodge, stomp, stroll, stump, thud, toil, tour, traipse, trample, tread, trek, trip, tromp, trudge, walk over; SEE CONCEPTS *151,224*

trample [v] *walk forcibly over*
bruise, crush, encroach, flatten, grind, hurt, infringe, injure, override, overwhelm, pound, ride roughshod over*, run over, squash, stamp, step on, stomp, tramp, tread, tromp, violate; SEE CONCEPTS *137,208,246*

trance [n] *hypnotic state*
abstraction, coma, daze, dream, ecstasy, glaze, insensibility, muse, petrifaction, rapture, reverie, spell, study, stupor, transfixion, transfixture, unconsciousness; SEE CONCEPT *410*

tranquil [adj] *quiet, peaceful*
agreeable, amicable, at ease, at peace, balmy, calm, collected, comforting, composed, cool, easy, easygoing, even, even-tempered, gentle, halcyon, hushed, lenient, low, measured, mild, moderate, murmuring, pacific, paradisiacal, pastoral, patient, placid, pleasing, poised, possessed, quiet, reasonable, restful, sedate, sedative, serene, smooth, sober, soft, soothing, stable, still, tame, temperate, undisturbed, unexcitable, unexcited, unperturbed, unruffled, untroubled, whispering; SEE CONCEPTS *525,542,594*

tranquility [n] *peace, quiet*
ataraxia, calm, calmness, composure, coolness, equanimity, hush, imperturbability, imperturbation, law and order, order, peacefulness, placid-

ity, quietness, quietude, repose, rest, restfulness, sedateness, serenity, stillness; SEE CONCEPTS 65,673

tranquilize [v] *make calm, quiet*
balm, calm, calm down, compose, hush, lull, pacify, put at rest, quell, quiet, quieten, relax, sedate, settle one's nerves*, soothe, still, subdue, unruffle; SEE CONCEPTS 7,22,310

transact [v] *do business, carry out*
accomplish, button down*, button up*, buy, carry on, clinch, close, conclude, conduct, discharge, do*, effectuate, enact, execute, finish, handle, jell, manage, move, negotiate, operate, perform, prosecute, pull off, run with the ball*, see to, sell, settle, sew up*, take care of, TCB*, work out a deal*, wrap up*; SEE CONCEPTS 91,223,324, 330,706

transaction [n] *business dealing; undertaking*
act, action, activity, affair, agreement, bargain, bond, business, buying, compact, contract, convention, covenant, deal, deed, disposal, doings*, enterprise, event, execution, goings-on*, happening, intercourse, matter, negotiation, occurrence, pact, performance, play, proceeding, purchase, purchasing, sale, selling, step; SEE CONCEPTS 223,324,330,684

transcend [v] *go beyond; surpass*
beat, best, be superior, better, eclipse, exceed, excel, go above, leave behind, leave in the dust*, outdo, outrival, outshine, outstrip, outvie, overstep, overtop, rise above, top, transform; SEE CONCEPT 141

transcendent/transcendental [adj] *extraordinary, superior*
absolute, abstract, accomplished, beyond grasp, boundless, consummate, entire, eternal, exceeding, fantastic, finished, hypothetical, ideal, incomparable, infinite, innate, intact, intellectual, intuitive, matchless, obscure, original, otherworldly, peerless, perfect, preeminent, primordial, second to none*, sublime, supernatural, supreme, surpassing, theoretical, towering, transcending, transmundane, ultimate, unequalable, unequalled, unique, unparalleled, unrivalled, whole; SEE CONCEPT 574

transcribe [v] *transfer to another medium*
copy out, decipher, duplicate, engross, interpret, note, record, render, reprint, reproduce, rewrite, set out, take down, tape, tape-record, transfer, translate, transliterate, write out; SEE CONCEPTS 79,125,171

transfer [n] *change of possession*
alteration, assignment, conduction, convection, deportation, displacement, move, relegation, relocation, removal, shift, substitution, transference, translation, transmission, transmittal, transposition, variation; SEE CONCEPTS 108,143,217,223

transfer [v] *pass possession to*
assign, bear, bring, carry, cart, cede, change, consign, convert, convey, deed, delegate, deliver, dislocate, dispatch, dispense, displace, disturb, express, feed, ferry, find, forward, give, hand, hand over, haul, lug, mail, make over, metamorphose, move, pass on, pass the buck*, post, provide, relegate, relocate, remove, sell, send, shift, ship, shoulder, sign over, supply, taxi, tote, transfigure, translate, transmit, transmogrify, transmute, transplant, transport, transpose, turn over; SEE CONCEPTS 108,143,217,223,243

transfix [v1] *hold one's attention*
bewitch, captivate, enchant, engross, fascinate, hold, hypnotize, mesmerize, palsy, paralyze, petrify, rivet, root, spellbind, stop in one's tracks*, stop one dead*, stun; SEE CONCEPTS 11,14

transfix [v2] *pierce*
fix, impale, lance, nail down, penetrate, pin down, puncture, run through, skewer, skiver, spear, spike, spit, stick, transpierce; SEE CONCEPT 220

transform [v] *change completely*
alter, commute, convert, cook, denature, doctor, make over, metamorphose, mold, mutate, reconstruct, remodel, renew, revamp, revolutionize, shift gears*, sing different tune*, switch, switch over, transfer, transfigure, translate, transmogrify, transmute, transpose, turn around, turn over new leaf*, turn the corner*, turn the tables*; SEE CONCEPTS 232,697

transformation [n] *complete change*
about-face*, alteration, changeover, conversion, flip-flop*, metamorphosis, radical change, renewal, revolution, shift, switch, transfiguration, transmogrification, transmutation; SEE CONCEPT 697

transgression [n] *violation, misbehavior*
breach, breaking of the law, contravention, crime, defiance, disobedience, encroachment, erring, error, fault, infraction, infringement, iniquity, lapse, misdeed, misdemeanor, offense, overstepping, sin, slip, trespass, vice, wrong, wrongdoing; SEE CONCEPTS 101,192,645

transient/transitory [adj] *temporary, brief*
changeable, deciduous, emigrating, ephemeral, evanescent, flash, fleeting, flitting, fly-by-night*, flying, fugacious, fugitive, going by, impermanent, insubstantial, migrating, momentary, moving, passing, provisional, short, short-lived, short-term, temporal, transmigratory, unstable, vacating, volatile; SEE CONCEPT 798

transit [n] *transportation*
alteration, carriage, carrying, conveyance, crossing, infiltration, motion, movement, osmosis, passage, penetration, permeation, portage, shift, shipment, transfer, transference, transport, transporting, travel, traverse; SEE CONCEPTS 155,224

transition [n] *change, often major*
alteration, changeover, conversion, development, evolution, flux, growth, metamorphosis, metastasis, passage, passing, progress, progression, realignment, shift, transformation, transit, transmutation, turn, turning point, upheaval; SEE CONCEPT 697

translate [v1] *interpret, explain*
construe, convert, decipher, decode, do into, elucidate, explicate, gloss, make clear, metaphrase, paraphrase, put, render, reword, simplify, spell out, transcribe, transliterate, transpose, turn; SEE CONCEPTS 55,57

translate [v2] *change*
alter, commute, convert, metamorphose, transfigure, transform, transmogrify, transmute, transpose, turn; SEE CONCEPT 232

translation [n] *rewording; interpretation*
adaptation, construction, crib*, decoding, elucidation, explanation, gloss, key, metaphrase, paraphrase, reading, rendering, rendition, rephrasing, restatement, simplification, transcription, transliteration, version; SEE CONCEPTS 268,277,278

translucent [adj] *clear*
clear-cut, crystal, crystalline, diaphanous, glassy,

transmit [v] *communicate, send*
address, bear, bequeath, break, broadcast, carry, channel, conduct, consign, convey, diffuse, dispatch, disseminate, drop a line*, drop a note*, forward, funnel, give a call*, give a ring*, hand down, hand on, impart, instill, issue, mail, pass on, pipe, put on the air*, radio, relay, remit, route, send, send out, ship, siphon, spread, take, traject, transfer, transfuse, translate, transport; SEE CONCEPTS 217,266,292

transparent [adj1] *see-through*
cellophane, clear, crystal-clear, crystalline, diaphanous, filmy, gauzy, glassy, gossamer, hyaline, limpid, lucent, lucid, pellucid, permeable, plain, sheer, thin, tiffany, translucent, transpicuous, vitreous; SEE CONCEPTS 606,618

transparent [adj2] *obvious, understandable*
apparent, articulate, artless, candid, clear-cut, direct, distinct, distinguishable, easily seen, easy, evident, explicit, forthright, frank, guileless, honest, ingenuous, manifest, open, patent, perspicuous, plain, plain-spoken, recognizable, self-explanatory, sincere, straight, straightforward, unambiguous, undisguised, unequivocal, unmistakable, unsophisticated, visible; SEE CONCEPT 267

transpire [v1] *occur, happen*
arise, befall, betide, chance, come about, come to pass, develop, ensue, eventuate, fall out*, gel, go, occur, result, shake, take place, turn up; SEE CONCEPT 3

transpire [v2] *become known*
be disclosed, be discovered, be made public, break, come out, come to light, emerge, get out, leak; SEE CONCEPTS 261,266

transplant [v] *relocate*
displace, emigrate, graft, immigrate, move, readapt, recondition, remove, reorient, reset, resettle, revamp, shift, transfer, transpose, uproot; SEE CONCEPTS 213,310

transport [n1] *move, transfer*
carriage, carrier, carrying, carting, conveyance, conveying, conveyor, freightage, hauling, lift, movement, mover, moving, passage, removal, shipment, shipping, transference, transferring, transit, transportation, transporting, transshipment, truckage, vehicle; SEE CONCEPTS 155,503

transport [n2] *delight*
ardor, bliss, cloud nine*, ecstasy, enchantment, enthusiasm, euphoria, fervor, happiness, heaven, passion, rapture, ravishment, rhapsody, seventh heaven*; SEE CONCEPTS 32,410

transport [v1] *move, transfer*
back, bear, bring, carry, conduct, convey, ferry, fetch, haul, heel*, jag, lug, pack, piggyback*, remove, ride, run, schlepp*, ship, shoulder, take, tote, truck; SEE CONCEPTS 147,187,217

transport [v2] *exile*
banish, cast out, deport, displace, expel, expulse, oust, relegate, sentence; SEE CONCEPTS 211,317

transport [v3] *captivate, delight*
agitate, carry away, electrify, elevate, enchant, enrapture, entrance, excite, inflame, move, provoke, quicken, ravish, send, slay, spellbind, stimulate, stir, thrill, trance, uplight, wow; SEE CONCEPTS 7,22

transpose [v] *swap, switch*
alter, backtrack*, change, commute, convert, double back, exchange, flip-flop*, interchange, inverse, invert, metamorphose, move, put, rearrange, relocate, render, reorder, reverse, revert, shift, substitute, transfer, transfigure, transform, translate, transmogrify, transmute, turn, turn the tables*; SEE CONCEPTS 104,232,697

trap [n] *snare, trick*
allurement, ambuscade, ambush, artifice, bait, booby trap*, come-on*, conspiracy, deception, decoy, device, dragnet, enticement, feint, gambit, hook*, intrigue, inveiglement, lasso*, lure, machination, maneuver, net, noose, pitfall, plot, ploy, prank, quagmire, quicksand, ruse, seducement, snag*, stratagem, subterfuge, temptation, wile; SEE CONCEPT 674

trap [v] *catch, snare; trick*
ambuscade, ambush, beguile, box in*, circumvent, collar*, corner*, crimp*, deceive, decoy, dupe, enmesh, ensnare, entangle, entrap, fool, grab, hook, inveigle, land*, mousetrap*, nab, nail*, net, overtake, rope in*, seduce, snag, suck in*, surprise, take, tangle, trammel, trip up*; SEE CONCEPTS 59,90

trappings [n] *paraphernalia, equipment*
accouterment, adornment, apparel, appointment, decoration, dress, embellishment, finery, fitting, fixture, furnishing, gear, livery, ornament, panoply, personal effects, raiment, rigging, things, trimming; SEE CONCEPTS 446,451,496

trash [n1] *garbage*
debris, dregs, droppings, dross, excess, filth, fragments, junk, leavings, litter, oddments, odds and ends*, offal, pieces, refuse, residue, rubbish, rubble, rummage, scourings, scrap, scraps, scum*, sediment, shavings, sweepings, waste; SEE CONCEPTS 260,834

trash [n3] *ridiculous communication*
balderdash, bilge*, drivel, foolish talk, hogwash, inanity, malarkey*, nonsense, rot, rubbish, tripe, twaddle; SEE CONCEPT 278

trauma [n] *severe mental or physical pain*
agony, anguish, blow, collapse, confusion, damage, derangement, disturbance, hurt, injury, jolt, ordeal, outburst, shock, strain, stress, suffering, torture, traumatization, upheaval, upset, wound; SEE CONCEPT 728

travel [n] *journey*
biking, commutation, cruising, drive, driving, excursion, expedition, flying, globe-trotting*, hop*, junket, movement, navigation, overnight, passage, peregrination, ramble, ride, riding, sailing, seafaring, sightseeing, swing, tour, touring, transit, trek, trekking, trip, voyage, voyaging, walk, wandering, wanderlust, wayfaring, weekend; SEE CONCEPT 224

travel [v] *journey on a trip or tour*
adventure, carry, cover, cover ground, cross, cruise, drive, explore, fly, get through, go, go abroad, go camping, go into orbit*, go riding, hop*, jaunt, jet*, junket*, knock around, make a journey, make one's way, migrate, motor, move, overnight*, proceed, progress, ramble, roam, rove, sail, scour, set forth, set out, sightsee, take a boat, take a plane, take a train, take a trip, tour, transmit, traverse, trek, vacation, visit, voyage, walk, wander, weekend*, wend; SEE CONCEPT 224

traveler [n] *person who journeys*
adventurer, barnstormer*, bum*, commuter, displaced person, drifter, excursionist, expeditionist, explorer, floater, gadabout*, globetrotter, gypsy, haj, hiker, hobo, itinerant, jet-setter, journeyer, junketer, migrant, navigator, nomad, passenger, peddler, pilgrim, rambler, roamer, rover, sailor, seafarer, sightseer, tourist, tramp, transmigrant, trekker, tripper, trouper, truant, vagabond, vagrant, voyager, wanderer, wayfarer; SEE CONCEPTS 348,423

traverse [v1] *cross over; travel*
bisect, bridge, cover, crisscross, cross, cut across, decussate, do, go across, go over, intersect, move over, negotiate, pace, pass over, pass through, perambulate, peregrinate, ply, quarter, range, roam, span, track, transverse, travel over, tread, walk, wander; SEE CONCEPTS 147,201,692,750

traverse [v2] *resist, contradict*
balk, buck, check, combat, contest, contravene, counter, counteract, cross, deny, disaffirm, dispute, duel, fight, frustrate, gainsay, go against, hinder, impede, impugn, negate, negative, obstruct, oppose, repel, thwart, withstand; SEE CONCEPTS 54,121

travesty [n] *spoof, ridicule*
burlesque, caricature, distortion, exaggeration, farce, lampoon, lampoonery, mimicry, mock, mockery, parody, perversion, play, put-on*, roast*, satire, send-up*, sham*, takeoff*; SEE CONCEPTS 273,292

travesty [v] *ridicule, spoof*
ape, burlesque, caricature, deride, distort, imitate, lampoon, make a mockery of, make fun of, mimic, mock, parody, pervert, play on*, put on*, satirize, send up*, sham*, take off*; SEE CONCEPTS 273,292

treacherous [adj1] *dishonest, disloyal*
betraying, catchy, deceitful, deceptive, double-crossing*, double-dealing*, duplicitous, faithless, false, false-hearted, fly-by-night*, insidious, misleading, perfidious, recreant, shifty*, slick*, slippery*, snake in the grass*, traitorous, treasonable, tricky, two-faced*, two-timing*, undependable, unfaithful, unloyal, unreliable, untrue, untrustworthy; SEE CONCEPTS 401,404

treacherous [adj2] *dangerous*
alarming, chancy, deceptive, difficult, dissembled, faulty, hairy*, hazardous, icy*, insecure, jeopardous, menacing, misleading, ominous, perilous, precarious, risky, shaky, slippery, ticklish, tricky, undependable, unhealthy, unreliable, unsafe, unsound, unstable, wicked; SEE CONCEPTS 565,587

treachery [n] *disloyalty, dishonesty*
betrayal, bunco, corruption, dirty dealing*, dirty pool*, dirty trick*, dirty work*, disaffection, dodge, double-cross*, double-dealing*, duplicity, faithlessness, fake, falseness, fast shuffle*, flimflam*, grift, gyp*, infidelity, perfidiousness, perfidy, put-on*, racket*, recreancy, scam*, sellout, shell game*, skin game*, spoof, stab in the back*, sweet talk*, treacherousness, treason, two-timing*, whitewash*; SEE CONCEPTS 633,645

tread [n] *walk*
footstep, footsteps, gait, march, pace, step, stride, trace, track, tramp; SEE CONCEPTS 149,284

tread [v] *walk; bear down*
ambulate, crush, foot, hike, hoof, march, oppress, pace, plod, quell, repress, squash, stamp, stamp on, step, step on, stride, subdue, subjugate, suppress, traipse, tramp, trample, troop, trudge; SEE CONCEPT 149

treason [n] *disloyalty*
breach of faith, crime, deceit, deceitfulness, deception, disaffection, dishonesty, duplicity, faithlessness, lèse majesté, mutiny, perfidy, revolt, revolutionary, sedition, seditious act, seditiousness, subversion, traitorousness, treachery; SEE CONCEPTS 192,645

treasure [n] *prized possession or entity*
abundance, apple of one's eye*, cache, capital, cash, catch*, darling, find, fortune, funds, gem, gold, hoard, jewel, money, nest egg*, nonpareil, paragon, pearl*, pile*, plum*, pride and joy*, prize, reserve, riches, richness, store, treasure trove, valuable, wealth; SEE CONCEPTS 332,337,446,710

treasure [v] *hold dear*
adore, appreciate, apprize, cherish, conserve, dote on, esteem, guard, idiolize, love, preserve, prize, revere, reverence, save, value, venerate, worship; SEE CONCEPT 32

treasury [n] *place where money, valuables are kept*
archive, bank, bursar, bursary, cache, chest, coffer, damper, depository, exchange, exchequer, Fort Knox*, gallery, hoard, museum, register, repository, safe, storage, store, storehouse, strongbox, treasure house, vault; SEE CONCEPTS 339,439,449

treat [n] *pleasing entity or occurrence*
amusement, banquet, celebration, dainty, delicacy, delight, enjoyment, entertainment, feast, fun, gift, goody*, gratification, joy, party, pleasure, refreshment, satisfaction, surprise, sweet, thrill, tidbit; SEE CONCEPTS 457,529,693

treat [v1] *act, behave towards*
account, act with regard to, appraise, conduct, conduct oneself toward, consider, deal with*, employ, estimate, evaluate, handle, have business with*, have recourse to*, have to do with*, hold, look upon, manage, negotiate, play, rate, react toward, regard, respect, serve, take, use, value, wield; SEE CONCEPT 633

treat [v2] *doctor, medicate*
administer, apply treatment, attend, care for, cure, dose, dress, heal, medicament, minister to, nurse, operate, prescribe; SEE CONCEPT 310

treat [v3] *pay the bill for someone else*
amuse, blow, buy for, divert, entertain, escort, feast, foot the bill*, give, indulge, pay for, pick up the check*, pick up the tab*, play host*, provide, regale, satisfy, set up, spring for*, stake, stand*, take out, wine and dine*; SEE CONCEPTS 327,384

treat [v4] *be concerned with; discuss*
advise, approach, arrange, comment, confabulate, confer, consider, consult, contain, criticize, deal with, deliberate, discourse on, discuss, enlarge upon, explain, go into, interpret, manipulate, reason, review, speak about, study, tackle, talk about, think, touch upon, weigh, write about; SEE CONCEPTS 17,56

treatise [n] *written study of a subject*
argument, book, commentary, composition, discourse, discussion, disquisition, dissertation, essay, exposition, memoir, monograph, pamphlet, paper, review, script, thesis, tract, tractate, work, writing; SEE CONCEPTS 271,280

tr
tr

treatment [n1] *medical care*
analysis, cure, diet, doctoring, healing, hospitalization, medication, medicine, operation, prescription, regimen, remedy, surgery, therapeutics, therapy; SEE CONCEPT *310*

treatment [n2] *handling of entity, situation*
action towards, angle, approach, behavior towards, conduct, custom, dealing, employment, execution, habit, line, management, manipulation, manner, method, mode, modus operandi, practice, procedure, proceeding, processing, reception, strategy, usage, way; SEE CONCEPTS *117,633*

treaty [n] *agreement, contract*
accord, alliance, arrangement, bargain, bond, cartel, charter, compact, concord, concordat, convention, covenant, deal, entente, league, negotiation, pact, reconciliation, sanction, settlement, understanding; SEE CONCEPTS *684,685*

tree [n] *large plant enclosed in bark and shedding leaves*
forest, hardwood, pulp, sapling, seedling, shrub, softwood, stock, timber, wood, woods; SEE CONCEPT *430*

trek [n] *long journey*
expedition, footslog, hegira, hike, long haul, march, odyssey, peregrination, slog, tramp, travel, trip; SEE CONCEPT *224*

trek [v] *journey*
be on the move*, be on the trail*, foot, hike, hit the road*, march, migrate, plod, range, roam, rove, slog, traipse, tramp, travel, trudge, walk; SEE CONCEPT *224*

tremble [v] *shake, vibrate*
flutter, have the shakes*, jar, jitter, oscillate, palpitate, quake, quaver, quiver, rock, shiver, shudder, teeter, throb, totter, tremor, wobble; SEE CONCEPT *152*

tremendous [adj] *huge, overwhelming*
amazing, appalling, astounding, awesome, awful, blimp, colossal, cracking, deafening, dreadful, enormous, excellent, exceptional, extraordinary, fabulous, fantastic, fearful, formidable, frightful, gargantuan, gigantic, great, great big*, huge, humongous, immense, incredible, jumbo*, large, mammoth, marvelous, massive, mondo*, monstrous, monumental, prodigious, stupendous, super, terrible, terrific, titanic, towering, vast, whale*, whopper, whopping, wonderful; SEE CONCEPTS *574,773,781*

tremor [n] *shaking, shock*
agitation, earthquake, flutter, quake, quaking, quaver, quiver, quivering, ripple, shake, shiver, shivering, tremble, trembling, trepidation, upheaval, vibration, wobble; SEE CONCEPTS *145,526*

trench [n] *ditch, channel dug in earth*
arroyo, canal, cut, depression, dike, drain, drill, dugout, earthwork, entrenchment, excavation, fosse, foxhole, furrow, gorge, gulch, gully, gutter, hollow, main, moat, pit, rut, sink, trough, tube, waterway; SEE CONCEPTS *509,513*

trenchant [adj] *sarcastic, scathing*
acerbic, acid, acidulous, acute, astringent, biting, caustic, clear, clear-cut, crisp, critical, crushing, cutting, distinct, driving, dynamic, effective, effectual, emphatic, energetic, explicit, forceful, forcible, graphic, hurtful, impressive, incisive, intense, keen, mordant, penetrating, piquant, pointed, potent, powerful, pungent, razor-sharp*,

salient, salty*, sardonic, sententious, severe, sharp, significant, strong, tart, to the point, unequivocal, unsparing, vigorous, weighty, well-defined; SEE CONCEPTS *267,537*

trend [n1] *flow, current*
aim, bearing, bent, bias, course, direction, drift, inclination, leaning, movement, orientation, progression, run, swing, tendency, tenor, wind; SEE CONCEPTS *230,657,738*

trend [n2] *style, fashion that is in favor*
craze, cry, fad, furor, in-thing*, latest thing*, look, mode, newest wrinkle*, rage, thing*, vogue; SEE CONCEPT *655*

trendy [adj] *in fashion, style*
à la mode*, contemporary, fashionable, fly*, in, in vogue, latest, modish*, now*, popular, stylish, swank*, tony*, up-to-the-minute, voguish, with-it*; SEE CONCEPT *589*

trepidation [n] *anxiety, worry*
agitation, alarm, apprehension, blue funk*, butterflies*, cold feet*, cold sweat*, consternation, creeps*, dismay, disquiet, disturbance, dread, emotion, excitement, fear, fright, goose bumps*, horror, jitters, nervousness, palpitation, panic, perturbation, shock, terror, trepidity, uneasiness, worriment; SEE CONCEPT *27*

trespass [n] *invasion, offense*
breach, contravention, crime, delinquency, encroachment, entrenchment, error, evildoing, fault, infraction, infringement, iniquity, injury, intrusion, misbehavior, misconduct, misdeed, misdemeanor, obtrusion, poaching, sin, transgression, unlawful entry, violation, wrongdoing, wrongful entry; SEE CONCEPTS *101,192,645,691*

trespass [v] *infringe, offend*
butt in*, chisel in*, crash, crash the gates*, deviate, displease, do wrong by, encroach, entrench, err, horn in*, interlope, intrude, invade, kibitz*, lapse, meddle, misbehave, mix in, muscle in*, nose in*, obtrude, overstep, penetrate, poach, poke, sin, stick nose in*, transgress, violate, wrong; SEE CONCEPTS *101,159,192,384*

trial [n1] *test*
analysis, assay, attempt, audition, check, crack*, dry run*, effort, endeavor, essay, examination, experience, experiment, experimentation, fling*, go*, hassle*, investigation, lick*, probation, proof, R and D*, research and development, shakedown*, shot*, showcase*, stab*, striving, struggle, testing, test run, trial and error*, trial run, try, try on*, tryout, undertaking, venture, whack*, workout; SEE CONCEPTS *87,290,291*

trial [n2] *legal proceeding*
action, arraignment, case, citation, claim, contest, counterclaim, court action, court martial, cross-examination, habeas corpus, hearing, impeachment, indictment, lawsuit, litigation, prosecution, rap*, seizure, suit, tribunal; SEE CONCEPTS *317,691*

trial [n3] *trouble, big problem*
adversity, affliction, albatross*, anguish, annoyance, bane, blow, bother, burden, calvary, care, complication, cross to bear*, crucible*, difficulty, distress, drag*, grief, hardship, hard time*, hassle*, heartbreak, inconvenience, irritation, load, misery, misfortune, nightmare, nuisance, ordeal, pain, pain in the neck*, pest, plague, rigor, severe test, sorrow, suffering, thorn, tribulation, trying time*, unhappiness, vexation, vicissitude, visitation, woe, wretchedness; SEE CONCEPTS *674,728*

trial [adj] experimental
balloon, exploratory, pilot, preliminary, probationary, provisional, tentative, test, testing; SEE CONCEPTS 548,560

tribe [n] ethnic group; family
association, blood, caste, clan, class, division, dynasty, horde, house, ilk, kin, kind, kindred, lineage, people, race, seed, society, sort, stock, type; SEE CONCEPTS 296,380,421

tribulation [n] pain, unhappiness
adversity, affliction, albatross*, bad luck*, blow*, bummer*, burden, care, cross to bear*, crucible*, curse, difficulty, distress, double whammy*, downer*, drag*, grief, hard knock*, hard time*, headache*, heartache*, misery, misfortune, oppression, ordeal, persecution, rainy day*, reverse, sorrow, suffering, trial, trouble, vexation, visitation, woe, worry, wretchedness, wronging; SEE CONCEPTS 666,728

tributary [adj] secondary; branch
accessory, dependent, feeding, minor, satellite, shoot, side, sub, subject, subordinate, under; SEE CONCEPT 560

tribute [n] testimonial, praise
accolade, acknowledgment, applause, appreciation, citation, commendation, compliment, encomium, esteem, eulogy, gift, gratitude, honor, laudation, memorial, offering, panegyric, recognition, recommendation, respect, salutation, salvo; SEE CONCEPTS 69,278

trick [n1] deceit
ambush, artifice, blind, bluff, casuistry, cheat, chicanery, circumvention, con*, concealment, conspiracy, conundrum, cover, deception, decoy, delusion, device, disguise, distortion, dodge*, double-dealing, duplicity, equivocation, evasion, fabrication, fake, falsehood, feint, forgery, fraud, game, gimmick, hoax, illusion, imposition, imposture, intrigue, invention, machination, maneuver, perjury, plot, ploy, pretense, ruse, snare, stratagem, subterfuge, swindle, trap, treachery, wile; SEE CONCEPTS 59,645

trick [n2] prank, joke
accomplishment, antic, caper, catch, device, escapade, feat, frolic, funny business, gag*, gambol, jape, jest, lark, monkeyshine*, practical joke, put-on*, shenanigan*, sleight of hand, sport, stunt, tomfoolery; SEE CONCEPTS 59,273,384

trick [n3] expertise, know-how
ability, art, command, craft, device, facility, gift, hang, knack, method, secret, skill, swing, technique; SEE CONCEPT 630

trick [n4] characteristic, habit
crotchet, custom, foible, habitude, idiosyncrasy, manner, mannerism, peculiarity, practice, praxis, quirk, trait, usage, use, way, wont; SEE CONCEPTS 644

trick [n5] time working at something
bout, go*, hitch, shift, spell, stint, tour, turn; SEE CONCEPT 807

trick [v] fool; play joke on
bamboozle, catch*, cheat, con, deceive, defraud, delude, disinform, double deal*, dupe, fake, flimflam*, fool, gull, hoax, hocus-pocus*, hoodwink, impose upon, jive*, mislead, outwit, play for a fool*, pull wool over*, put one over on*, rook*, screw*, set up*, swindle, take for a ride*, take in*, throw, trap, victimize; SEE CONCEPT 59

trickery [n] deception, joke
bait and switch*, cheat, cheating, chicane, chica-

nery, con, deceit, dishonesty, dodge, double-cross*, double-dealing*, dupery*, fast shuffle*, flimflam*, fourberie, fraud, funny business*, guile, hoax, imposture, pretense, quackery, razzle-dazzle*, scam, sharp practice, shell game*, shenanigans*, snow job*, sting*, stunt, swindling, underhandedness; SEE CONCEPTS 59,645

trickle [v] run out
crawl, creep, distill, dribble, drip, drop, exude, flow, issue, leak, ooze, percolate, seep, stream, trill, weep; SEE CONCEPTS 146,179

tricky [adj1] complicated, difficult
catchy, complex, critical, delicate, intricate, involved, knotty*, perplexing, precarious, problematic, quirky, risky, rocky, sensitive, sticky, thorny, ticklish, touch-and-go*, touchy, undependable, unstable; SEE CONCEPT 562

tricky [adj2] deceptive, sly
artful, astute, cagey, catchy, clever, crafty, cunning, deceitful, deep, delusive, delusory, devious, dishonest, foxy, greasy*, guileful, insidious, intelligent, keen, misleading, scheming, shady, sharp, shifty, shrewd, slick*, slippery*, smooth, streetwise*, subtle, treacherous, wily, witted, wry; SEE CONCEPT 401

tried [adj] reliable
approved, certified, constant, demonstrated, dependable, faithful, proved, secure, staunch, steadfast, tested, tried-and-true*, true-blue*, trustworthy, trusty, used; SEE CONCEPT 535

trifle [n1] novelty item
bagatelle, bauble, bibelot, curio, gewgaw*, knick-knack, nothing*, novelty, objet d'art, plaything, toy, trinket, triviality, whatnot*; SEE CONCEPT 446

trifle [n2] very small amout
hit, dash, diddly*, drop, eyelash*, fly speck*, fraction, hint, jot, little, no big deal*, particle, picayune*, piece, pinch, shade, smack, soupçon, speck, spice, spot, squat, suggestion, suspicion, touch, trace; SEE CONCEPTS 668,831

trifle [v] toy with; mess around
amuse oneself, be insincere, coquet, dabble, dally, dawdle, dilly-dally*, doodle, fidget, flirt, fool, fool around*, fool with*, fribble*, fritter, futz around*, horse around*, idle, indulge in, lead on, loiter, lollygag*, lounge, mess with*, misuse, monkey, monkey with*, palter, philander, play, play games with*, play with, potter, putter, squander, string along*, toy, twiddle, use up, wanton, waste, waste time, wink at*; SEE CONCEPTS 210,292,363

trifling [adj] insignificant, worthless
banal, dinky*, empty, forget it*, frivolous, hollow, idle, idling, inane, inconsequential, inconsiderable, insipid, jejune, loitering, measly, minuscule, negligible, niggling*, no big deal*, no big thing*, nugatory, paltry, petty, picayune, piddling, puny, shallow, silly, slight, small, tiny, trivial, unimportant, vain, valueless, vapid; SEE CONCEPTS 575,789

trigger [v] cause to happen
activate, bring about, cause, elicit, generate, give rise to, produce, prompt, provoke, set in motion, set off, spark, start; SEE CONCEPT 242

trim [n1] decoration
adornment, border, edging, embellishment, frill, fringe, garnish, gingerbread*, ornamentation, piping, trimming; SEE CONCEPTS 475,824

tr
tr

trim [n2] *condition, health*
commission, fettle*, fitness, form, kilter*, order, repair, shape, situation, state, whack*; SEE CONCEPT 316

trim [adj1] *neat, orderly*
apple-pie order*, clean, clean-cut, compact, dapper, fit, in good shape, neat as a pin*, nice, shipshape*, slick, smart, snug, spick-and-span*, spruce, streamlined, symmetrical, tidy, to rights*, uncluttered, well-groomed; SEE CONCEPTS 485,621

trim [adj2] *shapely*
beautiful, clean, comely, fit, graceful, in fine fettle*, in good shape, sleek, slender, slick, slim, statuesque, streamlined, svelte, well-balanced, well-proportioned, willowy; SEE CONCEPTS 314,490,491

trim [v1] *cut shorter*
abbreviate, barber, blue pencil*, bob, boil down*, clip, crop, curtail, cut, cut back, cut down, dock, edit, even up, lop, mow, pare, pare down, plane, prune, put in a nutshell*, shave, shear, shorten, slice off, snip, tidy, truncate, whittle down*; SEE CONCEPTS 176,236,247

trim [v2] *decorate*
adorn, array, beautify, bedeck, beribbon, deck, dress, dress up, embellish, emblazon, embroider, garnish, ornament, prank, pretty up*, prink*, spangle, spruce up*; SEE CONCEPTS 162,177

trim [v3] *beat, defeat*
clobber, drub, lambaste, lick, smother, thrash, trounce, wax*, whip; SEE CONCEPT 95

trinket [n] *knickknack*
bagatelle, bauble, bead, bibelot, curio, doodad*, gadget, gewgaw*, gimcrack*, glass*, hardware, jewel, jewelry, junk, nothing*, novelty, objet d'art, ornament, plaything, rock*, sparkler*, stone, toy, trifle, whatnot*; SEE CONCEPT 446

trio/triple [n] *three of something*
leash, set of three, ternion, threesome, trey, triad, triangle, trilogy, trine, trinity, triplet, triplicate, triptych, triumvirate, triune, troika; SEE CONCEPTS 784,787

trip [n1] *journey, excursion*
cruise, errand, expedition, foray, hop*, jaunt, junket, outing, overnight, peregrination, ramble*, run, swing*, tour, travel, trek, voyage, weekend; SEE CONCEPT 224

trip [n2] *error, blunder*
bungle, fall, false move, false step, faux pas*, indiscretion, lapse, misstep, mistake, slip, stumble; SEE CONCEPTS 101,230

trip [v] *fall, err*
buck, canter, confuse, disconcert, fall, fall over, founder, frolic, go headlong*, go wrong, hop, lapse, lope, lose balance, lose footing, lurch, make a faux pas*, miscalculate, misstep, pitch, play, plunge, skip, slide, slip, slip on, slip up, sprawl, spring, stumble, throw off, topple, tumble, unsettle; SEE CONCEPTS 101,149

trite [adj] *silly, commonplace*
banal, bathetic, bromidic, chain, cliché, clichéd, common, cornball*, corny*, drained, dull, exhausted, familiar tune*, flat, hackneyed, hokey*, jejune, mildewed*, moth-eaten*, musty*, old hat*, ordinary, pedestrian, platitudinous, prosaic, ready-made, routine, run-of-the-mill*, set, shopworn, stale, stereotyped, stock, threadbare, timeworn, tired, uninspired, unoriginal, used-up,

vapid, warmed-over*, well-worn, worn, worn-out; SEE CONCEPTS 267,530

triumph [n1] *extreme happiness*
celebration, elation, exultance, exultation, festivity, joy, jubilance, jubilation, jubilee, merriment, pride, rejoicing, reveling; SEE CONCEPT 410

triumph [n2] *victory, achievement*
accomplishment, ascendancy, attainment, big hit*, big win*, cinch, clean sweep*, conquest, coup, feat, feather in cap*, gain, grand slam*, hit, hole in one*, homer*, pushover*, riot, score, sell, sensation, shoo-in*, smash-hit*, splash, success, sure bet*, sure thing*, surmounting, takeover, the gold*, tour de force*, vanquishing, vanquishment, walkover*, win; SEE CONCEPT 706

triumph [v1] *be very happy*
celebrate, crow, delight, exult, gloat, glory, jubilate, rejoice, revel, swagger; SEE CONCEPT 32

triumph [v2] *achieve, succeed*
beat the game*, beat the system*, best, blow away*, carry the day*, come out on top*, conquer, dominate, flourish, get last laugh*, overcome, overwhelm, prevail, prosper, sink, strike it big*, subdue, sweep, take it all*, take the cake*, thrive, trounce, vanquish, win, win hands down*, win out*; SEE CONCEPTS 95,141,706

triumphant [adj] *successful*
boastful, celebratory, champion, conquering, dominant, elated, exultant, glorious, happy, in the lead*, jubilant, looking good, lucky, on top, out front*, prizewinning, proud, rejoicing, swaggering, triumphal, unbeaten, undefeated, victorious, winning; SEE CONCEPT 528

trivia [n] *details*
fine points, memorabilia, minutiae, trifles, trivialities; SEE CONCEPTS 274,543

trivial [adj] *not important*
atomic, beside the point*, commonplace, diminutive, evanescent, everyday, flimsy, frivolous, immaterial, inappreciable, incidental, inconsequential, inconsiderable, insignificant, irrelevant, little, meager, mean, meaningless, microscopic, minor, minute, momentary, negligible, nonessential, nugatory, of no account, paltry, petty, piddling*, puny, scanty, skin-deep*, slight, small, superficial, trifling, trite, unimportant, valueless, vanishing, worthless; SEE CONCEPT 575

troop/troops [n] *group, often military*
armed forces, army, assemblage, assembly, band, body, bunch, collection, combatants, company, contingent, corps, crew, crowd, delegation, drove, fighting forces, flock, forces, gang, gathering, herd, horde, host, legion, military, multitude, number, outfit, pack, party, personnel, service personnel, soldiers, soldiery, squad, swarm, team, throng, troopers, troupe, unit; SEE CONCEPTS 322,417

trophy [n] *physical award*
blue ribbon*, booty, citation, crown, cup, decoration, gold*, gold star*, guerdon, keepsake, laurels, medal, memento, memorial, palm, prize, reminder, ribbon, souvenir, spoils*, token; SEE CONCEPT 337

tropical [adj] *warm and humid*
close, equatorial, hot, lush, steamy, sticky, stifling, sultry, sweaty, sweltering, torrid, tropic; SEE CONCEPTS 525,605

trot [v] *move along briskly*
amble, canter, go, hurry, jog, lope, pad, rack, ride, run, scamper, step lively; SEE CONCEPT 150

trot out [v] *bring forward*
brandish, bring up, come out with, display, disport, drag up, exhibit, expose, flash, flaunt, parade, recite, rehearse, reiterate, relate, repeat, represent, show, show off; SEE CONCEPT 138

trouble [n1] *annoyance, worry*
agitation, anxiety, bad news*, bind, bother, commotion, concern, danger, difficulty, dilemma, dire straits, discontent, discord, disorder, disquiet, dissatisfaction, distress, disturbance, grief, hang-up*, heartache, hindrance, hot water*, inconvenience, irritation, mess, misfortune, nuisance, pain, pest, pickle*, predicament, problem, puzzle, row, scrape, sorrow, spot, strain, stress, strife, struggle, suffering, task, torment, tribulation, tumult, unrest, vexation, woe; SEE CONCEPTS 532,674,675,690,728

trouble [n2] *something requiring great effort*
ado, attention, bother, bustle, care, concern, difficulty, effort, exertion, flurry, fuss, hardship, inconvenience, labor, pains, pother, rigor, strain, stress, struggle, thought, trial, while, work, worry; SEE CONCEPTS 666,677

trouble [n3] *bad health*
affliction, ailment, complaint, curse, defect, disability, disease, disorder, failure, illness, malady, malfunction, upset; SEE CONCEPT 316

trouble [v] *bother, worry*
afflict, agitate, ail, annoy, bug*, burden, burn up*, concern, discommode, discompose, disconcert, disoblige, disquiet, distress, disturb, drive up the wall*, flip out*, fret, get to, give a bad time*, give a hard time*, grieve, harass, harry, impose on, inconvenience, irk, irritate, make a fuss*, make a scene*, make waves*, pain, perplex, perturb, pester, plague, psych*, put out*, sadden, spook*, stir up, strain, stress, torment, try, upset, vex; SEE CONCEPTS 7,19

trouble [v2] *make an effort*
be concerned with, exert, go to the effort of, take pains*, take the time*; SEE CONCEPT 100

troublemaker [n] *person who causes a problem*
agent provocateur, agitator, bad actor*, firebrand*, gremlin*, heel*, hellion, incendiary, inciter, inflamer, instigator, loose cannon*, meddler, mischief-maker, nuisance, phony*, punk*, rabble-rouser*, rascal, recreant, smart aleck*, snake*, stormy petrel*, weasel*; SEE CONCEPT 412

troublesome [adj] *bothersome, worrisome*
alarming, annoying, arduous, burdensome, damaging, dangerous, demanding, difficult, disquieting, harassing, hard, heavy, importunate, inconvenient, infestive, intractable, irksome, irritating, laborious, mean, messy, murder, oppressive, painful, pesky, pestiferous, pestilential, problematic, refractory, repressive, rough, taxing, tiresome, tough, tricky, troublous, trying, ugly, ungovernable, unruly, uphill, upsetting, vexatious, vexing, wearisome, wicked, worrying; SEE CONCEPTS 529,565

trough [n] *gutter, depression*
canal, channel, crib, cup, dike, dip, ditch, duct, flume, furrow, gully, hollow, manger, moat, trench, watercourse; SEE CONCEPTS 509,513

trounce [v] *defeat overwhelmingly*
bash, beat, blank, bury, bust*, cap, clobber, conquer, cook one's goose*, crush, drub, dust*, fix one's wagon*, flog, hammer*, lambaste*, lather*, lick*, make mincemeat of*, murder, overcome, overwhelm, paste*, pommel*, put away*, rout, swamp, thrash*, total*, trash*, walk over*, wallop*, waste*, wax*, whip, win, wipe off the mat*; SEE CONCEPT 95

truce [n] *peaceful solution*
accord, agreement, amnesty, armistice, break, breather*, cease-fire, cessation, de-escalation, detente, halt, intermission, interval, letup, lull, moratorium, olive branch*, pause, peace, reconciliation, reprieve, respite, rest, stay, suspension, temporary peace, terms, treaty, white flag*, wind-down*; SEE CONCEPTS 230,298,684

truck [n1] *commerce, merchandise*
barter, business, buying and selling, commercial goods, commodities, communication, communion, connection, contact, dealings, exchange, goods*, intercourse, relations, stock, stuff*, trade, traffic, wares*; SEE CONCEPTS 324,330,338

truck [n2] *wheeled vehicle for hauling*
buggy*, car, carryall, crate*, dump, eighteen-wheeler*, four by eight*, four by four*, four-wheel drive*, freighter, jeep, lorry, pickup, rig*, semi*, van, wagon, wheels*; SEE CONCEPT 505

truck [v] *buy and sell*
bargain, barter, deal, deal in*, do business, exchange, handle, have dealings, negotiate, peddle, retail, swap, trade, traffic, transact, wholesale*; SEE CONCEPTS 324,327,345

truculent [adj] *belligerent, hateful*
abusive, aggressive, antagonistic, bad-tempered, barbarous, bellicose, browbeating, brutal, bullying, caustic, combative, contentious, contumelious, cowing, cross, defiant, ferocious, fierce, frightening, harsh, hostile, inhuman, inhumane, intimidating, invective, mean, militant, mordacious, mordant, obstreperous, opprobrious, ornery*, pugnacious, quarrelsome, rude, savage, scathing, scrappy, scurrilous, sharp, sullen, terrifying, terrorizing, trenchant, violent, vituperative, vituperous; SEE CONCEPTS 267,401

trudge [v] *walk heavily*
clump, drag oneself*, footslog, hike, lumber, march, plod, plug along*, schlepp*, slog, step, stumble, stump, traipse, tramp, tread, trek, wade; SEE CONCEPT 151

true [adj1] *real, valid; concordant with facts*
accurate, actual, appropriate, authentic, authoritative, bona fide, correct, dependable, direct, exact, factual, fitting, genuine, honest, indubitable, kosher*, lawful, legal, legitimate, natural, normal, on target*, perfect, precise, proper, pure, regular, right, rightful, sincere, straight, sure-enough*, trustworthy, truthful, typical, undeniable, undesigning, undoubted, unerring, unfaked, unfeigned, unquestionable, veracious, veridical, veritable, very, wash*; SEE CONCEPTS 267,535,582

true [adj2] *loyal*
allegiant, ardent, confirmed, conscientious, constant, creditable, dedicated, dependable, devoted, dutiful, estimable, faithful, fast, firm, high-principled, honest, honorable, just, liege, no lie*, on the up and up*, pure, reliable, resolute, right, right-minded, scrupulous, sincere, square, staunch, steadfast, steady, straight, strict, sure, true-blue*, truehearted, trustworthy, trusty, unaffected, undistorted, unfeigned, unswerving, up front*, upright, veracious, veridical, wholehearted, worthy; SEE CONCEPTS 267,401,542

tr
tr

true [adv] *honestly, accurately*
correctly, on target, perfectly, precisely, properly, rightly, truthfully, unerringly, veraciously, veritably; SEE CONCEPTS 267,535,544

truly [adv] *really, doubtlessly*
absolutely, accurately, actually, authentically, beyond doubt, beyond question, confirmedly, constantly, correctly, de facto, definitely, devotedly, exactly, factually, faithfully, firmly, genuinely, honestly, honorably, in actuality, in fact, in reality, in truth, legitimately, loyally, positively, precisely, reliably, righteously, rightly, sincerely, staunchly, steadily, surely, truthfully, unequivocally, veraciously, veritably, very, with all one's heart*, with devotion, without a doubt; SEE CONCEPTS 267,535,582

truncate [v] *shorten*
abbreviate, abridge, clip, crop, curtail, cut, cut off, cut short, lop, pare, prune, shear, top, trim; SEE CONCEPTS 137,236,247

trunk [n1] *body, core*
block, bole, butt, column, log, soma, stalk, stem, stock, thorax, torso; SEE CONCEPTS 392,428,826

trunk [n2] *long nose of animal*
beak, proboscis, prow, snoot*, snout; SEE CONCEPT 399

trunk [n3] *container, box*
bag, baggage, bin, case, chest, coffer, coffin, crate, foot locker, locker, luggage, portmanteau, suitcase, wardrobe; SEE CONCEPTS 494,502

trust [n1] *belief in something as true, trustworthy*
assurance, certainty, certitude, confidence, conviction, credence, credit, dependence, entrustment, expectation, faith, gospel truth*, hope, positiveness, reliance, stock, store, sureness; SEE CONCEPT 689

trust [n2] *responsibility, custody*
account, care, charge, duty, guard, guardianship, keeping, liability, moment, obligation, protection, safekeeping, trusteeship, ward; SEE CONCEPTS 376,645

trust [n3] *large company*
bunch, business, cartel, chain, combine, conglomerate, corporation, crew, crowd, gang, group, institution, megacorp*, mob, monopoly, multinational organization, outfit, pool, ring, syndicate; SEE CONCEPTS 323,325

trust [v1] *believe, place confidence in*
accredit, assume, be convinced, bet bottom dollar on*, bet on, build on, calculate on, confide in, count on, depend on, expect, gamble on, have faith in, hope, imagine, lay money on*, lean on, look to, place confidence in, place trust in, presume, reckon on, rely upon, suppose, surmise, swear by, take, take at face value*, think likely; SEE CONCEPT 12

trust [v2] *give to for safekeeping*
advance, aid, assign, command, commission, commit, confer, confide, consign, delegate, entrust, give over, grant, lend, let, let out, loan, make trustee, patronize, put into hands of, sign over, store, transfer, turn over; SEE CONCEPT 115

trustworthy/trusty [adj] *reliable, believable*
accurate, always there*, authentic, authoritative, convincing, credible, dependable, ethical, exact, honest, honorable, kosher*, levelheaded, mature, on the level*, on up and up*, open, plausible, principled, realistic, responsible, righteous, rock solid*, saintly, secure, sensible, solid, square, steadfast, straight, there*, to be trusted, tried,

tried-and-true*, true, true-blue*, trustable, truthful, unfailing, up-front*, upright, valid, veracious; SEE CONCEPTS 267,404,535

truth [n1] *reality, validity*
accuracy, actuality, authenticity, axiom, case, certainty, correctness, dope*, exactitude, exactness, fact, facts, factualism, factuality, factualness, genuineness, gospel*, gospel truth*, honest truth*, infallibility, inside track*, legitimacy, maxim, naked truth*, nitty-gritty*, perfection, picture, plain talk, precision, principle, rectitude, rightness, scoop, score, trueness, truism, truthfulness, unvarnished truth, veracity, verisimilitude, verity, whole story*; SEE CONCEPTS 278,638,725

truth [n2] *honesty, loyalty*
authenticity, candor, constancy, dedication, devotion, dutifulness, faith, faithfulness, fidelity, frankness, integrity, openness, realism, revelation, sincerity, uprightness, veridicality, verity; SEE CONCEPT 657

truthful [adj] *accurate, honest*
believable, candid, correct, exact, factual, faithful, forthright, frank, guileless, ingenuous, just, kosher*, legit*, like it is*, literal, on the level*, on the up and up*, open, outspoken, plainspoken, precise, real, realistic, reliable, righteous, scrupulous, sincere, square, straight, straightforward, true, true-blue*, trustworthy, truth-telling, unfeigned, unreserved, veracious, veritable; SEE CONCEPTS 267,542

try [n] *attempt*
all one's got*, best shot*, bid, crack*, dab, effort, endeavor, essay, fling*, go*, jab*, pop*, shot*, slap*, stab*, striving, struggle, trial, undertaking, whack*, whirl*; SEE CONCEPTS 87,677

try [v1] *attempt*
aim, aspire, attack, bear down, chip away at*, compete, contend, contest, do one's best*, drive for, endeavor, essay, exert oneself, go after, go all out*, go for, have a crack*, have a go*, have a shot*, have a stab*, have a whack*, knock oneself out*, labor, lift a finger*, make a bid, make an attempt, make an effort, make a pass at*, propose, put oneself out*, risk, seek, shoot for*, speculate, strive, struggle, tackle, undertake, venture, vie for, work, wrangle; SEE CONCEPT 87

try [v2] *experiment, test*
appraise, assay, check, check out, evaluate, examine, inspect, investigate, judge, prove, put to the proof*, put to the test*, sample, scrutinize, taste, try out, weigh; SEE CONCEPTS 103,291

try [v3] *bother, afflict*
agonize, annoy, crucify, distress, excruciate, harass, inconvenience, irk, irritate, martyr, pain, plague, rack, strain, stress, tax, tire, torment, torture, trouble, upset, vex, weary, wring; SEE CONCEPTS 7,19

try [v4] *bring before a judge*
adjudge, adjudicate, arbitrate, decide, examine, give a hearing, hear, judge, referee, sit in judgment; SEE CONCEPT 317

trying [adj] *difficult, bothersome*
aggravating, annoying, arduous, demanding, exacting, exasperating, exigent, fatiguing, hard, irksome, irritating, onerous, oppressive, pestilent, provocative, rough, severe, sticky, strenuous, stressful, taxing, tight, tiresome, tough, tricky, troublesome, upsetting, vexing, wearisome, weighty; SEE CONCEPTS 548,565

try on/try out [v] *evaluate, test*
appraise, audition, check out, demonstrate, experiment, fit, give a try, have a dry run*, have a fitting*, inspect, practice, probe, prove, put into practice, put to the test, sample, scrutinize, taste, try for size, wear; SEE CONCEPTS *103,167, 291,453*

tryst [n] *meeting during a love affair*
appointment, assignation, date, engagement, meet, meeting, rendezvous, union; SEE CONCEPTS *375,384*

tuck [v] *fold together*
constrict, contract, draw together, enfold, gather, hem, insert, make snug, pinch, plait, pleat, push, put in, seam, squeeze in, swaddle, wrap; SEE CONCEPTS *193,218*

tuft [n] *clump of strands of something*
bunch, cluster, collection, cowlick, feathers, group, knot, plumage, ruff, shock, topknot, tussock; SEE CONCEPTS *392,432,471*

tug [n/v] *quick pull*
drag, draw, haul, heave, jerk, lug, strain, toil, tow, traction, wrench, yank; SEE CONCEPT *206*

tuition [n] *education; education costs*
charge, expenditure, fee, instruction, lessons, price, schooling, teaching, training, tutelage, tutoring; SEE CONCEPT *287*

tumble [v] *fall or make fall awkwardly*
bowl down, bring down, descend, dip, disarrange, disarray, disorder, disturb, do a pratfall, down, drop, fall headlong*, flatten, floor, flop, go belly up*, go down, hit the dirt*, jumble, keel, keel over, knock down, knock over, level, lose footing, lose it*, mess up, nose-dive, pitch, plummet, plunge, roll, sag, skid, slip, slump, spill, stumble, take a header*, tip over, topple, toss, trip, unsettle, upset; SEE CONCEPTS *147,149,181*

tumor [n] *abnormal growth in animate being*
bump, cancer, carcinoma, cyst, lump, neoplasm, sarcoma, swelling, tumefaction; SEE CONCEPT *316*

tumult [n] *uproar, confusion*
ado, affray, agitation, altercation, babel, bedlam, brawl, clamor, commotion, convulsion, din, disorder, disturbance, dither, excitement, ferment, fight, fracas, fuss, hassle*, jangle, lather*, maelstrom, noise, outbreak, outcry, pandemonium, paroxysm, pother, quarrel, racket, riot, row, ruction, seething, stir, strife, turbulence, turmoil, unrest, unsettlement, upheaval, upturn, wildness; SEE CONCEPTS *230,674*

tumultuous/tumultous [adj] *confused; in an uproar*
agitated, boisterous, clamorous, disorderly, disturbed, excited, fierce, hectic, irregular, lawless, noisy, obstreperous, passionate, raging, rambunctious, raucous, restless, riotous, rowdy, rowdydowdy, rumbunctious, stormy, termagant, turbulent, unrestrained, unruly, uproarious, violent, vociferous, wild; SEE CONCEPT *548*

tune [n1] *melody, harmony*
air, aria, carol, chorus, composition, concert, consonance, descant, diapason, ditty*, harmony, jingle, lay, measure, melodia, motif, number, piece, song, strain, theme, warble; SEE CONCEPTS *264,595*

tune [n2] *agreement*
accord, chime, chorus, concert, concord, concordance, consonance, euphony, harmony, pitch, sympathy, unison; SEE CONCEPTS *670,714*

tune/tune up [v] *bring into harmony*
accommodate, adapt, adjust, attune, conform, coordinate, dial, fix, harmonize, integrate, modulate, pitch, proportion, reconcile, regulate, set, string, tighten; SEE CONCEPTS *65,126*

tunnel [n] *covered passageway*
adit, burrow, channel, crawl space, crawlway, crosscut, drift, hole, hole in the wall*, mine, passage, pit, shaft, subway, tube, underpass; SEE CONCEPTS *509,513*

tunnel [v] *dig a passage through*
burrow, excavate, mine, penetrate, sap, scoop out, undermine; SEE CONCEPT *178*

turbulent [adj1] *unsettled, raging (referring to weather)*
agitated, bitter, blustering, blustery, boiling, bumpy, choppy, coarse, confused, destructive, disordered, disturbed, fierce, foaming, furious, howling, inclement, moiling, noisy, restless, riotous, roaring, rough, ruffled, rugged, stirred up, stormful, storming, stormy, swirling, tempestuous, thunderous, tremulous, tumultuous/tumultuous, unstable, violent, wild; SEE CONCEPT *525*

turbulent [adj2] *rebellious, unmanageable*
agitated, anarchic, angry, bitter, boisterous, chaotic, demonstrative, destructive, disorderly, excited, fierce, fiery, foaming, insubordinate, lawless, mutinous, obstreperous, passionate, perturbed, quarrelsome, rabid, rambunctious, rampant, raucous, refractory, riotous, rough, roughhouse*, rowdy, rude, seditious, shaking, stern, storming, termagant, tumultuous/tumultuous, unbridled, uncontrolled, undisciplined, ungovernable, unruly, untamed, uproarious, vehement, violent, vociferous, wild; SEE CONCEPT *401*

turmoil [n] *chaos*
agitation, ailment, anxiety, anxiousness, bedlam, bustle, commotion, confusion, disorder, disquiet, disquietude, distress, disturbance, dither, ferment, flap*, flurry, free-for-all*, fuss, hassle*, hectic, hubbub*, lather*, mix-up, noise, pandemonium, pother, restiveness, restlessness, riot, row, ruckus, stir, strife, to-do*, topsy-turvy, trouble, tumult, turbulence, unrest, uproar, violence, whirl; SEE CONCEPTS *230,674*

turn [n1] *revolution, curving*
about-face, angle, bend, bias, bow, branch, change, changeabout, circle, circuit, circulation, circumvolution, corner, curve, cycle, departure, detour, deviation, direction, drift, flection, flexure, fork, gyration, gyre, heading, hook, pirouette, pivot, quirk, retroversion, reversal, reverse, reversion, right-about, roll, rotation, round, shift, spin, spiral, swing, tack, tendency, trend, turnabout, turning, twist, twisting, wheel, whirl, wind, winding, yaw; SEE CONCEPTS *198,738,754*

turn [n2] *sudden change*
alteration, bend, branch, crotch, deflection, departure, detour, deviation, digression, distortion, divarication, double, fork, modification, mutation, shift, tack, twist, variation, warp, yaw; SEE CONCEPT *697*

turn [n3] *chance, opportunity*
accomplishment, act, action, bit, bout, crack*, deed, favor, fling*, gesture, go*, go around*, move, period, round, routine, say*, service, shift, shot*, spell, stint, succession, time, tour, trick, try; SEE CONCEPT *693*

tr
tu

turn [n4] *walk, outing*
airing, circuit, constitutional, drive, excursion, jaunt, promenade, ramble, ride, saunter, spin, stroll; SEE CONCEPTS 147,224,363

turn [n5] *aptitude, knack*
affinity, aptness, bent, bias, bump, disposition, faculty, flair, genius, gift, head, inclination, leaning, predisposition, propensity, talent; SEE CONCEPTS 411,630

turn [n6] *scare*
attack, blow, fit, fright, jolt, seizure, shock, spell, start, surprise; SEE CONCEPTS 230,410

turn [v1] *revolve, curve*
arc, bend, circle, circulate, circumduct, come around, corner, cut, eddy, go around, go round, ground, gyrate, gyre, hang a left*, hang a right*, incline, loop, make a left, make a right, move in a circle, negotiate, orbit, oscillate, pass, pass around, pirouette, pivot, revolve, roll, rotate, round, spin, sway, swing, swivel, take a bend*, twirl, twist, vibrate, weave, wheel, whirl, wind, yaw; SEE CONCEPTS 147,201,738,748

turn [v2] *reverse; change course*
about-face, aim, alter, alternate, backslide, call off, capsize, change, change position, convert, curve, depart, detour, detract, deviate, digress, direct, diverge, double back, face about, go back, incline, inverse, invert, loop, move, pivot, rechannel, recoil, redirect, regress, relapse, retrace, return, revert, sheer, shift, shunt, shy away, sidetrack, subvert, sway, swerve, swing, swirl, switch, tack, transform, twist, upset, vary, veer, volte-face, wheel, whip, whirl, zigzag; SEE CONCEPTS 195,198,213

turn [v3] *adapt, fit*
alter, become, change, change into, come, convert, divert, fashion, form, get, go, grow into, metamorphose, modify, mold, mutate, pass into, put, refashion, remake, remodel, render, run, shape, transfigure, transform, translate, transmute, transpose, vary, wax; SEE CONCEPTS 232,697

turn [v4] *become sour or tainted*
acidify, become rancid, break down, crumble, curdle, decay, decompose, disintegrate, dull, ferment, go bad, molder, putrefy, rot, sour, spoil, taint; SEE CONCEPTS 456,469

turn [v5] *use; resort to*
adapt, address, appeal, apply, approach, bend, be predisposed to, devote, direct, employ, favor, give, go, have recourse, incline, lend, look, prefer, recur, repair, run, tend, throw, turn one's energies to*, turn one's hand to*, undertake, utilize; SEE CONCEPTS 100,225

turn [v6] *sicken*
derange, discompose, disgust, disorder, make one sick*, nauseate, revolt, unbalance, undo, unhinge*, unsettle, upset; SEE CONCEPTS 7,19,250

turn [v7] *change one's mind; defect*
apostatize, bring round, change sides, desert, go over, influence, persuade, prejudice, prevail upon, rat*, renege, renounce, repudiate, retract, talk into, tergiversate, tergiverse; SEE CONCEPTS 21,41,54

turn [v8] *twist a body part*
bruise, crick, dislocate, hurt, sprain, strain, wrench; SEE CONCEPT 246

turn down [v] *reject*
decline, disapprove, dismiss, rebuff, refuse, reprobate, repudiate, say no, scorn, spurn, throw out; SEE CONCEPTS 18,54

turn in [v] *go to bed*
bed, catch some z's*, flop*, go to sleep, hit the hay*, hit the sack*, lie down, nap, pile in, rest, retire, roll in; SEE CONCEPT 210

turning point [n] *crucial occurrence*
axis, change, climacteric, climax, contingency, crisis, critical moment, critical period, crossing, crossroads, crux, culmination, decisive moment, development, emergency, exigency, hinge, juncture, moment of truth*, pass, peak, pinch, pivot, shift, strait, transition, twist, zero hour*; SEE CONCEPTS 679,832

turn off [v1] *disgust*
alienate, bore, disenchant, disinterest, displease, irritate, lose one's interest, make one sick*, nauseate, offend, put off, repel, sicken; SEE CONCEPTS 7,19

turn off [v2] *stop from operating*
close, cut, cut out, douse, extinguish, halt, hit the switch*, kill*, log off, put out, shut, shut down, shut off, switch off, turn out, unplug; SEE CONCEPTS 121,234

turn on [v1] *excite, please*
arouse, attract, captivate, enchant, get started, initiate, introduce, show, stimulate, stir up, thrill, titillate, work up; SEE CONCEPT 11

turn on [v2] *start the operation of*
activate, begin, energize, get started, ignite, initiate, introduce, log on, put in gear, put on, set in motion, start up, switch on; SEE CONCEPT 221

turnout [n1] *group assembling for event*
assemblage, assembly, attendance, audience, congregation, crowd, gate, gathering, number, throng; SEE CONCEPT 417

turnout [n2] *amount produced*
aggregate, output, outturn, product, production, productivity, quota, turnover, volume, yield; SEE CONCEPTS 338,787

turn out [v1] *equip; produce*
accouter, appoint, arm, bear, bring out, build, clothe, dress, fabricate, finish, fit, fit out*, furnish, make, manufacture, outfit, process, put out, rig*, rig out*, yield; SEE CONCEPTS 167,205,234

turn out [v2] *get out of bed*
appear, arise, come, emerge, get up, pile out*, rise, rise and shine*, roll out*, show up, uprise, wake, wake up; SEE CONCEPT 159

turn over [v1] *give, transfer*
assign, come across with, commend, commit, confer, confide, consign, convey, delegate, deliver, entrust, feed, find, furnish, give over, give up, hand, hand over, pass on, provide, relegate, relinquish, render, supply, surrender, yield; SEE CONCEPTS 108,143

turn over [v2] *think about seriously*
consider, contemplate, deliberate, give thought to, meditate, mull over, muse, ponder, reflect on, revolve, roll, ruminate, think over, wonder about; SEE CONCEPTS 17,24

turn up [v1] *come, arrive*
appear, attend, blow in*, come, come in, enter, get, get in, make an appearance*, materialize, pop in*, punch in*, put in an appearance*, reach, roll in*, show, show up*, weigh in*; SEE CONCEPT 159

turn up [v2] *discover or be discovered*
become known, be found, bring to light*, catch, come across, come to light*, come to pass, crop

up, descry, detect, dig up*, disclose, encounter, espy, expose, find, hit upon*, learn, meet with*, pop up*, reveal, see, spot, track, track down*, transpire, uncover, unearth; SEE CONCEPTS *31,183*

tutor [*n*] *person who teaches another privately*
coach, educator, governor, grind, guardian, guide, instructor, lecturer, mentor, preceptor, private teacher, prof*, teach*, teacher; SEE CONCEPT *350*

tutor [*v*] *teach someone privately*
clue, coach, direct, discipline, drill, drum into*, edify, educate, guide, instruct, lay it out for*, lecture, let in on*, ready, school, train, update; SEE CONCEPT *285*

twilight [*n*] *onset of darkness at end of day*
afterglow, afterlight, crepuscular light, decline, dimness, dusk, early evening, ebb, end, evening, eventide, gloaming, half-light, last phase*, late-afternoon, night, nightfall, sundown, sunset; SEE CONCEPTS *810,832*

twin [*n*] *something exactly like another*
clone, companion, coordinate, corollary, counterpart, doppelgänger, double, duplicate, fraternal twin, identical twin, likeness, lookalike, match, mate, reciprocal, ringer*, Siamese twin; SEE CONCEPTS *414,664,670*

twin [*adj*] *duplicate, similar*
accompanying, bifold, binary, copied, corresponding, coupled, double, dual, duplicating, geminate, identical, joint, like, matched, matching, paired, parallel, same, second, selfsame, twofold, very same; SEE CONCEPTS *487,563,573*

twine [*n*] *rope, cord*
braid, coil, convolution, cordage, knot, snarl, string, tangle, thread, twist, whorl, yarn; SEE CONCEPT *475*

twine [*v*] *coil, twist together*
bend, braid, corkscrew, curl, encircle, enmesh, entangle, entwine, interlace, interweave, knit, loop, meander, plait, spiral, splice, surround, tangle, twist, undulate, weave, wind, wrap, wreathe; SEE CONCEPTS *147,201,742*

twinge [*n*] *sharp pain*
ache, bite, gripe, lancination, misery, pang, pinch, prick, shiver, smart, spasm, stab, stitch, throb, throe, tic, tweak, twist, twitch; SEE CONCEPT *728*

twinkle [*v*] *glimmer, shine*
blink, coruscate, flash, flicker, gleam, glint, glisten, glitter, glow, illuminate, light, light up, scintillate, shimmer, sparkle, wink; SEE CONCEPT *624*

twirl [*v*] *turn around circularly*
gyrate, gyre, pirouette, pivot, purl, revolve, rotate, spin, turn, twist, wheel, whirl, whirligig, wind; SEE CONCEPTS *150,152*

twist [*n1*] *curl, spin*
arc, bend, braid, coil, convolution, curlicue, curve, flourish, hank, helix, jerk, meander, plug, ply, pull, roll, spiral, swivel, torsion, turn, twine, undulation, warp, wind, wrench, yank, zigzag; SEE CONCEPTS *738,754*

twist [*n2*] *sudden development; oddity*
aberration, bent, change, characteristic, confusion, crotchet, eccentricity, entanglement, foible, idiosyncrasy, kink, knot, mess, mix-up, peculiarity, proclivity, quirk, revelation, screw up*, slant, snarl, surprise, tangle, trait, turn, variation; SEE CONCEPTS *411,832*

twist [*v1*] *curl, spin*
coil, contort, corkscrew, encircle, entwine, intertwine, rick, screw, spiral, sprain, squirm, swivel, turn, turn around, twine, twirl, warp, weave, wiggle, wind, wrap, wrap around, wreathe, wrench, wriggle, wring, writhe, zigzag; SEE CONCEPTS *80,147,184,201,206,738*

twist [*v2*] *misrepresent*
alter, belie, change, color, contort, distort, falsify, garble, misquote, misstate, pervert, warp; SEE CONCEPT *63*

twitch [*v*] *have a spasm*
beat, blink, clasp, clutch, flutter, grab, grasp, grip, jerk, jiggle, jump, kick, lug, lurch, nip, pain, palpitate, pluck, pull, seize, shiver, shudder, snap, snatch, squirm, tic, tremble, tug, twinge, vellicate, yank; SEE CONCEPTS *185,206*

tycoon [*n*] *person who has a lot of money, power*
administrator, big shot*, boss, business person, capitalist, captain of industry*, director, entrepreneur, executive, fat cat*, financier, industrialist, investor, magnate, mogul, wealthy person; SEE CONCEPT *347*

type [*n1*] *class, kind*
blazon, brand, breed, cast, category, character, classification, cut, description, feather, form, genre, group, ilk, likes, lot, mold, nature, number, order, persuasion, rubric, sample, sort, species, specimen, stamp, standard, strain, subdivision, variety, way; SEE CONCEPTS *378,411*

type [*n2*] *example, model*
archetype, epitome, essence, exemplar, original, paradigm, pattern, personification, prototype, quintessence, representative, sample, specimen, standard; SEE CONCEPT *686*

type [*n3*] *printed characters*
case, emblem, face, figure, font, point size, print, printing, sign, symbol; SEE CONCEPTS *79,284*

type [*v1*] *classify*
arrange, button down*, categorize, class, peg, pigeonhole*, put away, put down as, sort, standardize, stereotype, tab*, typecast; SEE CONCEPTS *18,84*

type [*v2*] *hit keys on machine to print document*
copy, dash off*, enter data, hunt-and-peck*, teletype, touch, touch-type, transcribe, typewrite, write; SEE CONCEPTS *79,199,203*

typical [*adj*] *usual, conventional*
archetypal, archetypical, average, characteristic, classic, classical, common, commonplace, emblematic, essential, everyday, exemplary, expected, general, habitual, ideal, illustrative, in character*, indicative, in keeping, matter-of-course*, model, natural, normal, old hat*, ordinary, orthodox, paradigmatic, patterned, prevalent, prototypal, prototypical, quintessential, regular, representative, standard, standardized, stock, suggestive, symbolic, typic, unexceptional; SEE CONCEPTS *530,533,547*

typify [*v*] *represent, characterize*
body forth, characterize, describe, emblematize, embody, epitomize, exemplify, feature, illustrate, incarnate, mean, mirror, model, personify, stand for, sum up, symbolize; SEE CONCEPTS *55,261,682*

tyranny [*n*] *dictatorship*
absolutism, authoritarianism, autocracy, coercion, cruelty, despotism, domination, fascism, high-handedness, imperiousness, monocracy, oligarchy, oppression, peremptoriness, reign of terror*,

tu
ty

severity, terrorism, totalitarianism, totality, unreasonableness; SEE CONCEPTS 299,301

tyrant [n] *person who dictates, oppresses*
absolute ruler, absolutist, authoritarian, autocrat, bully, despot, dictator, Hitler*, inquisitor, martinet, oppressor, slave driver*, Stalin*; SEE CONCEPTS 354,412

U

ubiquitous [adj] *ever-present*
all-over, everywhere, omnipresent, pervasive, ubiquity, universal, wall-to-wall*; SEE CONCEPT 530

ugly [adj1] *unattractive*
animal, appalling, awful, bad-looking, beastly, deformed, disfigured, foul, frightful, grisly, gross, grotesque, hard-featured, hideous, homely, horrid, ill-favored, loathsome, misshapen, monstrous, not much to look at*, plain, repelling, repugnant, repulsive, revolting, unbeautiful, uncomely, uninviting, unlovely, unprepossessing, unseemly, unsightly; SEE CONCEPT 579

ugly [adj2] *unpleasant, disagreeable*
base, despicable, dirty, disgusting, distasteful, filthy, foul, frightful, hideous, horrid, ignoble, low, low-down, mean, messy, monstrous, nasty, nauseous, noisome, objectionable, odious, offensive, pesky, repellent, repugnant, repulsive, revolting, scandalous, servile, shocking, sickening, sordid, sorry, terrible, troublesome, troublous, vexatious, vile, wicked, wretched; SEE CONCEPTS 403,571

ugly [adj3] *dangerous, threatening*
angry, bellicose, black, cantankerous, crabbed, crabby, dark, disagreeable, dour, evil, fell, forbidding, formidable, gloomy, glum, grave, grievous, major, malevolent, menacing, morose, nasty, obnoxious, ominous, pugnacious, quarrelsome, rough, saturnine, scowling, serious, sinister, spiteful, sullen, surly, treacherous, truculent, vicious, violent, wicked; SEE CONCEPTS 401,548

ulterior [adj] *secret; pertaining to a hidden goal*
ambiguous, buried, concealed, covert, cryptic, dark, enigmatic, equivocal, guarded, hidden, implied, obscure, obscured, personal, privy, remote, secondary, selfish, shrouded, under cover, under wraps*, undisclosed, undivulged, unexpressed, unsaid; SEE CONCEPTS 544,576

ultimate [adj1] *last, final*
capping, chips down*, closing, concluding, conclusive, decisive, end, eventual, extreme, far out*, farthermost, farthest, final curtain*, furthermost, furthest, hindmost, latest, latter, lattermost, most distant, terminal; SEE CONCEPTS 799,820

ultimate [adj2] *best, greatest*
extreme, highest, incomparable, max*, maxi*, maximum, most, paramount, preeminent, significant, superlative, supreme, surpassing, the most, topmost, towering, transcendent, unequalable, unmatchable, unsurpassable, utmost; SEE CONCEPTS 568,574

ultimate [adj3] *fundamental*
absolute, basic, categorical, elemental, empyreal, empyrean, primary, radical, sublime, transcendental; SEE CONCEPTS 535,546

ultimately [adv] *eventually*
after all, after a while, as a conclusion, at last, at long last, at the close, basically, by and by, climactically, conclusively, finally, fundamentally, hereafter, in conclusion, in consummation, in due time, in future, in the end, in the sequel, presently, sequentially, someday, sometime, somewhere, sooner or later, yet; SEE CONCEPT 820

ultra [adj] *extreme*
all out*, drastic, excessive, extremist, fanatical, far-out*, gone*, immoderate, outlandish, out of bounds*, outré, rabid*, radical, revolutionary, too much*; SEE CONCEPTS 562,569

umbrage [n] *personal displeasure*
anger, annoyance, chagrin, exasperation, fury, grudge, high dudgeon*, huff, indignation, injury, ire, irking, irritation, miff*, nettling*, offense, pique, provoking, rage, resentment, sense of injury, vexation, wrath; SEE CONCEPTS 29,410

umpire [n] *person who settles dispute*
adjudicator, arbiter, arbitrator, assessor, compromiser, inspector, judge, justice, mediator, moderator, negotiator, peacemaker, proprietor, ref*, referee, settler, ump*; SEE CONCEPTS 348,366,423

unable [adj] *not having talent, skill*
can't cut it*, can't hack it*, can't make the grade*, clumsy, helpless, hog-tied*, impotent, impuissant, inadequate, incapable, incapacitated, incompetent, ineffectual, inefficacious, inefficient, inept, inoperative, no can do*, no good*, not able, not cut out for*, not equal to*, not up to*, out of commission*, powerless, sidelined*, unfit, unfitted, unqualified, unskilled, weak; SEE CONCEPT 527

unabridged [adj] *not shortened*
complete, entire, full-length, intact, total, unabbreviated, uncondensed, uncut, unexpurgated, unshortened, whole; SEE CONCEPTS 267,531

unacceptable [adj] *not suitable or satisfactory*
below par*, damaged, disagreeable, displeasing, distasteful, exceptionable, half-baked*, ill-favored, improper, inadmissible, insupportable, lousy*, not up to snuff*, objectionable, obnoxious, offensive, reject, repugnant, unappealing, undesirable, uninviting, unpleasant, unsatisfactory, unwanted, unwelcome, won't do*; SEE CONCEPTS 529,558

unaccompanied [adj] *alone*
abandoned, a cappella*, apart, by oneself, deserted, detached, hermit, individual, isolate, isolated, lone, loner, odd, on one's own, removed, single, solitary, solo, stag, traveling light*, unattended, unescorted; SEE CONCEPTS 555,577

unaccountable [adj] *not explainable; mysterious*
arcane, astonishing, baffling, extraordinary, impenetrable, incomprehensible, inexplicable, inscrutable, mystic, odd, peculiar, puzzling, strange, uncommon, unexplainable, unfathomable, unheard-of, unintelligible, unknowable, unusual, unwonted; SEE CONCEPTS 529,564

unaccustomed [adj1] *not prepared, ready; new to*
green*, ignorant, incompetent, inexperienced, newcome, not given to*, not used to, novice, unacquainted, unfamiliar with, uninformed, uninstructed, unpracticed, unseasoned, unskilled, untaught, untrained, unused to, unversed in; SEE CONCEPTS 527,678

unaccustomed [adj2] *new, strange*
alien, altered, bizarre, different, eccentric, excep-

tional, exotic, foreign, imported, novel, outlandish, out of the ordinary, quaint, remarkable, singular, special, surprising, uncommon, unconventional, uncustomary, unexpected, unfamiliar, unknown, unorthodox, unprecedented, unusual, unwonted, variant; SEE CONCEPTS *547,564*

unadvised [*adj*] *not smart; careless*
brash, hasty, heedless, hot-headed, ignorant, ill-advised, imprudent, inadvisable, incautious, inconsiderate, indiscreet, injudicious, in the dark*, rash, reckless, thoughtless, unaware, unconsidered, undetermined, unknowing, unsuspecting, unwarned, unwary, unwise; SEE CONCEPTS *403,548*

unaffected [*adj*] *honest, unsophisticated*
artless, candid, direct, folksy*, forthright, frank, genuine, guileless, homey*, ingenuous, modest, naive, natural, plain, simple, sincere, single, spontaneous, straightforward, true, unartificial, unassuming, unpretentious, unschooled, unspoilt, unstudied, up front*; SEE CONCEPTS *401,404*

unaffected [*adj2*] *unchanged, unmoved*
aloof, callous, calm, casual, cold fish*, cool, easy-going, hard-boiled*, hard-hearted*, impassive, impervious, laid-back*, not influenced, proof, steady, thick-skinned*, unaltered, unconcerned, unexcited, unimpressed, uninfluenced, unresponsive, unruffled, unstirred, untouched; SEE CONCEPTS *542,548*

unanimous [*adj*] *in agreement; uncontested*
accepted, accordant, agreed, agreeing, as one, assenting, collective, combined, common, communal, concerted, concordant, concurrent, consensual, consentient, consistent, consonant, harmonious, homogeneous, in complete accord, like-minded, of one mind, popular, public, shared, single, solid, undisputed, undivided, unified, united, universal, unquestioned, with one voice*; SEE CONCEPTS *8,267,563*

unappetizing [*adj*] *distasteful*
flat, flavorless, grody*, gross, icky*, insipid, savorless, stinky, tasteless, unappealing, unattractive, uninteresting, uninviting, unpalatable, unpleasant, unsavory, vapid, yucky*; SEE CONCEPTS *462,529*

unapproachable [*adj1*] *unfriendly*
aloof, chilly*, cold, cool, distant, frigid, hesitant, inaccessible, remote, reserved, standoffish, uncommunicative, unsociable, withdrawn; SEE CONCEPTS *404,555*

unapproachable [*adj2*] *difficult to get to*
inaccessible, out of reach, out-of-the-way, remote, unattainable, unobtainable, unreachable; SEE CONCEPT *576*

unasked [*adj*] *voluntary*
arrogant, gratuitous, impudent, not asked, of one's own accord, overbearing, presumptuous, spontaneous, supererogatory, unbidden, uncalled-for, undemanded, undesired, uninvited, unprompted, unrequested, unsought, unwanted, unwelcome, voluntarily, willing, without prompting; SEE CONCEPTS *401,558*

unassuming [*adj*] *shy*
backward, bashful, diffident, humble, lowly, meek, modest, mousy*, plain, prim, quiet, reserved, retiring, self-effacing, simple, unambitious, unassertive, unobtrusive, unostentatious, unpretending, unpretentious; SEE CONCEPTS *401,404*

unauthorized [*adj*] *not sanctioned, permitted*
crooked*, dirty*, illegal, illegitimate, no-no*, off base*, out of bounds*, out of line*, over the line*, pirated, shady*, unapproved, unconstitutional, under the table*, unjustified, unlawful, unofficial, unsanctioned, unwarranted, wildcat*, wrongful; SEE CONCEPTS *319,548*

unavoidable [*adj*] *bound to happen*
certain, compulsory, fated, impending, ineluctable, ineludible, inescapable, inevasible, inevitable, inexorable, locked up*, necessary, obligatory, open and shut*, set, sure, unescapable; SEE CONCEPT *535*

unaware [*adj*] *ignorant*
blind, careless, caught napping*, daydreaming, deaf, deaf to*, doped*, forgetful, heedless, ignorant, in a daze*, inattentive, incognizant, inconversant, insensible, mooning, negligent, nescient, not all there*, not cognizant, oblivious, out cold*, out of it*, out to lunch*, spacey*, unacquainted, unconcerned, unconscious, unenlightened, unfamiliar, uninformed, uninstructed, unknowing, unmindful, unsuspecting, unwitting; SEE CONCEPT *402*

unawares [*adv*] *without warning; suddenly*
aback, abruptly, accidentally, by accident, by mistake, by surprise, carelessly, ignorantly, inadvertently, mistakenly, off guard, short, sudden, surprisingly, unconsciously, unexpectedly, unintentionally, unknowingly, unprepared, unready, unwittingly, without warning; SEE CONCEPTS *544,548,799*

unbalanced [*adj1*] *not even, stable*
asymmetric, asymmetrical, disproportionate, irregular, lopsided, not balanced, off-balance, shaky, top-heavy, treacherous, unequal, uneven, unstable, unsteady, unsymmetrical, wobbly; SEE CONCEPT *480*

unbalanced [*adj2*] *crazy; mentally disturbed*
batty*, daft, demented, deranged, eccentric, erratic, flaky*, freaky*, insane, irrational, kinky*, kooky*, lunatic, mad, nobody home*, non compos mentis*, not all there*, nutty*, out to lunch*, psychotic*, touched, troubled, unglued*, unhinged*, unscrewed*, unsound, unstable; SEE CONCEPT *403*

unbearable [*adj*] *very bad; too much*
a bit much*, enough, heavy-handed*, inadmissible, insufferable, insupportable, intolerable, last straw*, oppressive, unacceptable, unendurable, unsurpassable; SEE CONCEPTS *537,571*

unbecoming [*adj*] *improper, unsuitable*
awkward, clumsy, discreditable, gauche, ill-suited, inappropriate, inapt, incongruous, indecent, indecorous, indelicate, inept, maladroit, malapropos, offensive, rough, salacious, tacky*, tasteless, unattractive, unbefitting, uncomely, undue, unfair, unfit, unfitting, unflattering, ungodly, unhandsome, unlovely, unseasonable, unseemly, unsightly, unsuited, untimely, untoward, unworthy; SEE CONCEPTS *558,579,589*

unbelievable [*adj*] *beyond the imagination*
astonishing, beyond belief, cockamamie*, cock-eyed*, doubtful, dubious, far-fetched, fishy*, flaky*, flimsy*, for the birds*, full of holes*, harebrained*, implausible, impossible, improbable, incogitable, inconceivable, incredible, kooky*, lamebrained*, open to doubt, outlandish, past belief, phony, preposterous, questionable, reaching, scatterbrained*, screwy*, staggering, suspect, thick*, thin*, too much*, unconvincing, unimaginable, unsubstantial, unthinkable, weak,

ty
un

unbending [adj] rigid, tough

aloof, crisp, distant, do or die*, dug in*, firm, formal, hard as nails*, hard-line*, hold one's ground*, hold the fort*, hold the line*, incompliant, inelastic, inexorable, inflexible, intractable, locked in*, obdurate, obstinate, relentless, reserved, resolute, set in stone*, severe, single-minded, standing one's ground*, standing pat*, sticking to one's guns*, stiff, strict, stubborn, uncompromising, unflexible, unrelenting, unswayable, unyielding, uptight; SEE CONCEPTS 401,534,604.

unbiased [adj] not prejudiced

aloof, cold, disinterested, dispassionate, equal, equitable, even-handed, fair, honest, impartial, just, neutral, nondiscriminatory, nonpartisan, objective, on the fence*, open-minded, straight, unbigoted, uncolored, uninterested, unprejudiced; SEE CONCEPT 542

unblemished [adj] not flawed

chaste, clean, decent, faultless, flawless, immaculate, intact, modest, perfect, pure, sound, spotless, stainless, undamaged, undefiled, unflawed, unhurt, unimpaired, uninjured, unmarked, unmarred, unspotted, unstained, unsullied, untarnished, whole; SEE CONCEPTS 485,621

unbreakable [adj] strong, tough

adamantine, armored, brass-bound, durable, everlasting, firm, incorruptible, indestructible, infrangible, invulnerable, lasting, nonbreakable, perdurable, resistant, rugged, shatterproof, solid, tight, toughened, unshakable, unyielding; SEE CONCEPTS 488,489,798

unbroken [v] continuous, whole

ceaseless, constant, deep, endless, entire, even, fast, incessant, intact, perfect, perpetual, profound, progressive, regular, solid, sound, successive, total, undisturbed, unimpaired, uninterrupted, unremitting, unruffled, untroubled; SEE CONCEPTS 482,485,798

unburden [adj] get rid of

clear, confess, confide, disburden, discharge, disclose, disencumber, dispose of, divulge, dump, ease, empty, get off one's chest*, lay bare*, let hair down*, lighten, lose, out with it*, own, relieve, relinquish, reveal, shake, shake off*, tell all*, throw off, unbosom, unload; SEE CONCEPTS 60,211,244

uncanny [adj] very strange, unusual

astonishing, astounding, creepy, devilish, eerie, exceptional, extraordinary, fantastic, ghostly, ghoulish, incredible, inexplainable, inspired, magical, miraculous, mysterious, mystifying, preternatural, prodigious, queer, remarkable, scary, secret, singular, spooky, superhuman, supernatural, supernormal, supranormal, unearthly, unheard-of, unnatural, weird; SEE CONCEPTS 537,564

uncertain [adj] doubtful, changeable

ambiguous, ambivalent, chancy, conjectural, dubious, erratic, fitful, hanging by a thread*, hazy, hesitant, iffy*, incalculable, inconstant, indefinite, indeterminate, indistinct, insecure, irregular, irresolute, on thin ice*, precarious, questionable, risky, speculative, touch and go*, unclear, unconfirmed, undecided, undetermined, unfixed, unforeseeable, unpredictable, unreliable, unresolved, unsettled, unsure, up for grabs*, up in the air*, vacillating, vague, variable, wavering; SEE CONCEPTS 529,534,535

uncertainty [n] doubt, changeableness

ambiguity, ambivalence, anxiety, bewilderment, concern, confusion, conjecture, contingency, dilemma, disquiet, distrust, doubtfulness, dubiety, guesswork, hesitancy, hesitation, incertitude, inconclusiveness, indecision, irresolution, lack of confidence, misgiving, mistrust, mystification, oscillation, perplexity, puzzle, puzzlement, qualm, quandary, query, questionableness, reserve, scruple, skepticism, suspicion, trouble, uneasiness, unpredictability, vagueness, wonder, worry; SEE CONCEPTS 388,410,696

unchangeable [adj] constant, steadfast

changeless, continuing, firm, fixed, immovable, immutable, inalterable, inevitable, inflexible, invariable, irreversible, permanent, resolute, stable, strong, unalterable, unmodifiable, unmovable; SEE CONCEPT 534

unchanging [adj] constant, permanent

abiding, changeless, consistent, continuing, enduring, equable, eternal, even, fixed, immutable, imperishable, invariable, lasting, perpetual, rigid, same, stabile, static, unchanged, unfading, unfailing, unfluctuating, uniform, unvarying; SEE CONCEPTS 534,551,649

uncivilized [adj] wild, uncultured

barbarian, barbaric, barbarous, boorish, brutish, churlish, coarse, crass, crude, discourteous, disrespectful, gross, ill-bred, impertinent, impolite, loutish, mannerless, outrageous, philistine, primitive, rude, rugged, savage, unconscionable, uncontrolled, uncouth, uncultivated, uneducated, ungodly, unholy, unmannered, unpolished, unrefined, unsophisticated, vulgar, wicked; SEE CONCEPT 401

unclean [adj] dirty

bedraggled, befouled, besmirched, black, blurred, common, contaminated, corrupt, decayed, defiled, desecrated, dusty, evil, feculent, fetid, filthy, foul, grimy, impure, messy, muddy, nasty, polluted, profaned, putrescent, putrid, rancid, rank, rotten, sloppy, slovenly, smeared, smudged, soiled, sooty, sordid, spotted, squalid, stable, stained, stall, stinking, sullied, tainted, tarnished, unhealthful, vile; SEE CONCEPTS 529,537,583

uncomfortable [adj1] painful, rough

afflictive, agonizing, annoying, awkward, bitter, cramped, difficult, disagreeable, distressing, dolorous, excruciating, galling, grievous, hard, harsh, ill-fitting, incommodious, irritating, thorny, torturing, troublesome, vexatious, wearisome; SEE CONCEPTS 529,537,583

uncomfortable [adj2] distressed, upset

aching, angry, anguished, annoyed, awkward, chafed, cheerless, comfortless, confused, discomfited, discomposed, disquieted, disturbed, embarrassed, exhausted, fatigued, galled, harsh, hurt, ill at ease, in pain, miserable, nervous, pained, restless, self-conscious, smarting, sore, stiff, strained, suffering, tired, troubled, uneasy, vexed, weary, worn, wracked, wretched; SEE CONCEPTS 403,485

uncommitted [adj] free; not involved

cut loose*, don't care*, fence-sitting*, floating, free-spirited, laid-back*, middle ground*, middle of the road*, neutral, nonaligned, nonpartisan, on the fence*, restrained, unaffiliated, unattached, uninvolved, unpledged; SEE CONCEPTS 403,542

uncommon [*adj1*] *very different*
aberrant, abnormal, anomalous, arcane, bizarre, curious, eccentric, egregious, exceptional, exotic, extraordinary, extreme, fantastic, few, freakish, infrequent, irregular, nondescript, noteworthy, novel, odd, original, out of the ordinary, out of the way*, outré, peculiar, prodigious, queer, rare, remarkable, scarce, seldom, singular, sporadic, startling, strange, surprising, unaccustomed, unconventional, uncustomary, unfamiliar, unheard of, unique, unorthodox, unusual, weird; SEE CONCEPT 564

uncommon [*adj2*] *wonderful, exceptional*
distinctive, extraordinary, incomparable, inimitable, notable, noteworthy, outstanding, rare, remarkable, singular, special, superior, unimaginable, unique, unparalleled, unprecedented, unthinkable, unwonted; SEE CONCEPT 574

uncommonly [*adv*] *infrequently*
exceptionally, extra, extremely, hardly ever, in few instances, irregularly, not often, now and then, occasionally, oddly, on occasion, particularly, peculiarly, rarely, remarkably, scarcely ever, seldom, sporadically, strangely, unusually, very; SEE CONCEPT 541

uncommunicative [*adj*] *shy, silent*
aloof, buttoned up*, clammed up*, close, close-mouthed*, curt, distant, dried up*, evasive, guarded, hush-hush*, offish*, on the QT*, quiet, reserved, reticent, retiring, secretive, short, standoffish, taciturn, tight-lipped*, unapproachable, unresponsive, unsociable; SEE CONCEPT 267

uncompromising [*adj*] *stubborn*
brick-wall*, decided, determined, firm, hardcore*, hard-line*, inexorable, inflexible, intransigent, locked, obdurate, obstinate, pigheaded*, relentless, resolute, rigid, set in stone*, single-minded, steadfast, stiff-necked*, strict, strong, tough, unbending; SEE CONCEPTS 401,542

unconcerned [*adj*] *carefree; apathetic*
aloof, blind, blithe, callous, careless, cold, cool, deaf, detached, dispassionate, distant, easy, feckless, forgetful, hardened, hard-hearted, heedless, impassive, inattentive, incurious, indifferent, insensible, insensitive, insouciant, lackadaisical, lukewarm, negligent, neutral, nonchalant, oblivious, phlegmatic, relaxed, reserved, self-centered, serene, stony, supine, unbothered, uninterested, uninvolved, unmoved, unperturbed, unruffled, unsympathetic, untroubled, unworried; SEE CONCEPTS 403,542

unconditional [*adj*] *absolute, total*
actual, all out, assured, categorical, certain, clear, complete, decisive, definite, determinate, downright, entire, explicit, final, flat out, full, genuine, indubitable, no catch*, no fine print*, no holds barred*, no ifs ands or buts*, no kicker*, no strings*, open, out-and-out*, outright, plenary, positive, straight out, thorough, thoroughgoing, unconstrained, unequivocal, unlimited, unmistakable, unmitigated, unqualified, unquestionable, unreserved, unrestricted, utter, whole, wide; SEE CONCEPTS 531,535,544

unconscionable [*adj*] *immoral, immoderate*
amoral, barbarous, conscienceless, criminal, dishonest, excessive, exorbitant, extravagant, extreme, inordinate, knavish, outrageous, preposterous, sneaky, too much*, uncivilized, undue, unethical, unfair, ungodly, unholy, unjust, unprincipled, unreasonable, unscrupulous, wanton, wicked; SEE CONCEPTS 545,569

unconscious [*adj1*] *not awake; out cold*
benumbed, blacked out*, bombed*, cold*, comatose, dead to the world*, drowsy, entranced, feeling no pain*, flattened*, inanimate, in a trance, inert, insensate, insensible, knocked*, lethargic, numb, on the canvas*, out, out like a light*, palsied, paralyzed, passed out*, put away*, raving, senseless, stunned, stupefied, swooning, torpid, tranced, zonked*; SEE CONCEPTS 314,539

unconscious [*adj2*] *ignorant; automatic*
accidental, gut*, ignorant, inadvertent, inattentive, inherent, innate, instinctive, involuntary, latent, lost, reflex, repressed, subconscious, subliminal, suppressed, unaware, uncalculated, undeliberate, unheeding, unintended, unintentional, unmindful, unpremeditated, unrealized, unwitting; SEE CONCEPTS 542,544

uncontrollable [*adj*] *wild; carried away*
beside oneself, disorderly, excited, fractious, frantic, freaked, furious, headstrong, indocile, indomitable, insuppressible, insurgent, intractable, irrepressible, irresistible, lawless, like a loose cannon*, mad, obdurate, obstinate, recalcitrant, strong, stubborn, uncontainable, undisciplinable, undisciplined, ungovernable, unmanageable, unrestrainable, unruly, violent; SEE CONCEPT 401

unconventional [*adj*] *very different; odd*
anarchistic, atypical, avant-garde, beat, bizarre, crazy, eccentric, far-out*, freakish, freaky, free and easy*, idiosyncratic, individual, individualistic, informal, irregular, kinky*, kooky*, nonconformist, oddball*, offbeat, off the beaten track*, off the wall*, original, out in left field*, out of the ordinary, unceremonious, uncommon, uncustomary, unique, unorthodox, unusual, way-out*, weirdo*; SEE CONCEPT 564

uncouth [*adj*] *clumsy, uncultivated*
awkward, barbaric, boorish, cheap, clownish, clumsy, coarse, crass, crude, discourteous, disgracious, gawky, graceless, gross, heavy-handed, ill bred, ill mannered, impertinent, impolite, inelegant, loud, loud-mouthed, loutish, oafish, raunchy, raw, rough, rude, rustic, strange, tacky*, uncalled-for*, uncivil, uncivilized, uncultivated, ungainly, ungenteel, ungentlemanly, unpolished, unrefined, unseemly, vulgar; SEE CONCEPT 401

uncover [*v*] *reveal, disclose*
bare, betray, break, bring to light*, crack, denude, dig up*, disclose, discover, display, divulge, expose, give away, hit upon, lay bare, lay open, leak, make known, open, open up, reveal, show, strike, strip, stumble on, subject, tap, tell, tip one's hand*, unclothe, unearth, unmask, unveil, unwrap; SEE CONCEPTS 60,183,261

uncritical [*adj*] *casual, unfussy*
careless, cursory, easily pleased, imperceptive, imprecise, imprudent, inaccurate, indiscriminate, offhand, perfunctory, shallow, slipshod, superficial, undiscerning, undiscriminating, unexacting, uninformed, unperceptive, unselective, unthinking; SEE CONCEPT 542

undaunted [*adj*] *brave, bold*
audacious, coming on strong*, courageous, dauntless, fearless, fire-eating*, gallant, icy*, indomitable, intrepid, not discouraged, not put off*, resolute, spunky, steadfast, unafraid, unalarmed, unapprehensive, undeterred, undiscouraged, un-

dismayed, unfaltering, unflinching, unshrinking, valiant, valorous; SEE CONCEPT *401*

undecided [*adj*] *not sure, not definite*
ambivalent, betwixt and between*, blowing hot and cold*, borderline, debatable, dithering*, doubtful, dubious, equivocal, hemming and hawing*, hesitant, iffy*, indecisive, indefinite, in the middle*, irresolute, moot, of two minds*, on the fence*, open, pendent, pending, running hot and cold*, tentative, torn, undecided, unclear, uncommitted, undetermined, unfinished, unsettled, unsure, up in the air*, vague, waffling, wavering, wishy-washy*; SEE CONCEPTS *403,529*

undeniable [*adj*] *definite, proven*
actual, beyond doubt, beyond question, binding, certain, clear, compulsory, evident, for sure*, inarguable, incontestable, incontrovertible, indisputable, indubitable, irrefutable, manifest, necessary, no ifs and or buts*, obligatory, obvious, open and shut*, patent, positive, real, sound, sure, sure thing*, true, unanswerable, unassailable, undoubted, unquestionable; SEE CONCEPT *535*

undependable [*adj*] *irresponsible*
bum, capricious, careless, changeable, dubious, erratic, fickle, fly-by-night*, inconsistent, inconstant, indefinite, indeterminate, loose*, no bargain*, no-good*, treacherous, trick, tricky, trustless, unassured, uncertain, unpredictable, unreliable, unsafe, unsound, unstable, unsure, untrustworthy, variable; SEE CONCEPTS *401,535*

under [*adv1/prep1*] *below*
beneath, bottom, concealed by, covered by, down, downward, held down, inferior, lower, nether, on the bottom, on the nether side, on the underside, pinned, pressed down, supporting, to the bottom, underneath; SEE CONCEPTS *586,735,793*

under [*adv2/prep2*] *secondary*
amenable, belonging, collateral, consequent, corollary, dependent, directed, following, governed, included, inferior, in the power of, junior, lesser, low, lower, obedient, obeying, reporting, sub, subject, subjugated, subordinate, subsequent, subservient, subsidiary, substract, subsumed; SEE CONCEPTS *560,575,577*

undercover [*adj*] *secret, spy*
clandestine, concealed, confidential, covert, creep, furtive, hidden, hole-and-corner*, hush-hush*, incognito*, intelligence, on the QT*, private, stealth, stealthy, sub-rosa*, surreptitious, underground, underhand, underneath, under wraps*; SEE CONCEPTS *544,576*

undercurrent [*n*] *drift, pull*
atmosphere, aura, crosscurrent, direction, eddy, feeling, flavor, hint, inclination, indication, insinuation, intimation, murmur, overtone, propensity, riptide, sense, suggestion, tendency, tenor, tinge, trace, trend, underflow, undertone, undertow, vibes*, vibrations; SEE CONCEPTS *673,738*

underdog [*n*] *unlikely winner in a contest or struggle*
bottom dog, dark horse, longshot, out-of-towner*; SEE CONCEPTS *366,423*

underestimate [*v*] *minimize; rate too low*
belittle, deprecate, depreciate, disesteem, disparage, make light of*, miscalculate, miscarry, not do justice*, put down*, sell short*, slight, think too little of*, underrate, undervalue; SEE CONCEPTS *12,54,764*

undergo [*v*] *be subjected to*
abide, bear, bear up, bow, defer, encounter, endure, experience, feel, go through, have, know, meet with, put up with, see, share, stand, submit to, suffer, support, sustain, tolerate, weather, withstand, yield; SEE CONCEPT *23*

underground [*adj1*] *below the surface*
below ground, buried, covered, in the recesses, subterranean, subterrestrial, sunken, underfoot; SEE CONCEPT *583*

underground [*adj2*] *secret, subversive*
alternative, avant-garde, clandestine, concealed, covert, experimental, hidden, hush-hush*, on the QT*, on the sly*, private, radical, resistant, resistive, revolutionary, surreptitious, unbowed, unconventional, undercover, under wraps*, unusual; SEE CONCEPTS *564,576*

underhand [*adj*] *deceitful*
clandestine, concealed, crafty, crooked, cunning, deceptive, devious, dirty-dealing*, dishonest, dishonorable, double-crossing*, duplicitous, fraudulent, furtive, guileful, hush-hush*, indirect, insidious, oblique, on the QT*, on the quiet*, secret, secretive, shady, shifty, slippery*, sly*, sneaking, sneaky, stealthy, sub-rosa, surreptitious, treacherous, tricky, two-faced*, two-timing*, undercover, underhanded, under wraps*, unethical, unfair, unjust, unscrupulous, wily; SEE CONCEPTS *401,544*

underline [*v*] *emphasize; mark*
accentuate, bracket, call attention to, caption, check off, draw attention to, feature, give emphasis, highlight, indicate, interlineate, italicize, play up, point to, point up, rule, stress, underscore; SEE CONCEPTS *49,79*

underlying [*adj*] *fundamental, latent*
basal, basic, bottom, bottom-line*, cardinal, concealed, critical, crucial, elemental, elementary, essential, hidden, indispensable, intrinsic, lurking, necessary, needful, nitty-gritty*, nub, primary, prime, primitive, radical, root, substratal, veiled, vital; SEE CONCEPTS *546,549*

undermine [*v*] *weaken*
attenuate, blunt, clip one's wings*, corrode, cripple, debilitate, dig, dig out*, disable, eat away*, enfeeble, erode, excavate, foil, frustrate, hollow out, hurt, impair, knock the bottom out of*, mine, poke full of holes*, ruin, sabotage, sandbag*, sap, soften, subvert, threaten, thwart, torpedo*, tunnel, undercut, wear, whittle away, wreck; SEE CONCEPTS *14,240*

underneath [*adv/prep*] *below*
beneath, bottom, covered, lower, neath, nether, under; SEE CONCEPTS *586,735*

underprivileged [*adj*] *poor*
badly off*, depressed, deprived, destitute, disadvantaged, down and out*, handicapped, hapless, hard up*, have-not*, ill-fated, ill-starred, impoverished, indigent, in dire straits, in need, in want, needy, unfortunate, unlucky; SEE CONCEPT *334*

understand [*v1*] *appreciate, comprehend*
accept, apprehend, be aware, be conscious of, be with it*, catch, catch on, conceive, deduce, discern, distinguish, explain, fathom, figure out, find out, follow, get*, get the hang of*, get the idea*, get the picture*, get the point*, grasp, have knowledge of, identify with, infer, interpret, ken*, know, learn, make out*, make sense of, master, note, penetrate, perceive, possess, read, realize, recognize, register, savvy*, see, seize,

sense, sympathize, take in*, take meaning, tolerate; SEE CONCEPT 15

understand [v2] *think, believe*
accept, assume, be informed, concede, conceive, conclude, conjecture, consider, count on, deduce, expect, fancy, feel for, gather, guess, hear, imagine, infer, learn, presume, reckon, suppose, surmise, suspect, take for granted, take it, think; SEE CONCEPT 12

understanding [n1] *comprehension, appreciation*
acumen, apperception, apprehension, assimilation, awareness, decipherment, discernment, discrimination, grasp, grip, insight, intellect, intelligence, intuition, judgment, ken, knowing, knowledge, mastery, penetration, perception, perceptiveness, perceptivity, percipience, perspicacity, prehension, realization, reason, recognition, savvy, sense, sharpness, wit; SEE CONCEPT 409

understanding [n2] *belief*
acceptation, conception, conclusion, estimation, idea, import, impression, inkling, intendment, interpretation, judgment, knowledge, meaning, message, notion, opinion, perception, purport, sense, significance, significancy, signification, sympathy, view, viewpoint; SEE CONCEPTS 682,689

understanding [n3] *informal agreement*
accord, common view, concord, deal, handshake*, harmony, meeting of minds*, pact, SEE CONCEPT 684

understanding [adj] *accepting, tolerant*
compassionate, considerate, discerning, empathetic, forbearing, forgiving, generous, kind, kindly, patient, perceptive, responsive, sensitive, sympathetic; SEE CONCEPTS 401,542

understood [adj] *assumed, implicit*
accepted, appreciated, axiomatic, down pat*, implied, inferential, inferred, known, on to*, pat, presumed, roger*, tacit, taken for granted, undeclared, unexpressed, unsaid, unspoken, unstated, wise to, wordless; SEE CONCEPT 529

undertake [v] *attempt, engage in*
address oneself, agree, answer for, bargain, begin, commence, commit, commit oneself, contract, covenant, devote, embark, endeavor, enter upon, fall into, go about, go for, go in for, go into, guarantee, have a hand in*, have a try, hazard, initiate, launch, make a run at*, move, offer, pitch in, pledge, promise, set about, set in motion, set out, shoulder, stake, stipulate, tackle, take on, take the plunge*, take upon oneself, try, try out, venture, volunteer; SEE CONCEPTS 87,100

undertaking [n] *endeavor, attempt*
adventure, affair, business, deal, effort, engagement, enterprise, essay, experiment, game, happening, hassle, hazard, job, move, operation, outfit, play, project, proposition, pursuit, shop, striving, struggle, task, thing*, trial, try, venture, what one is into*, work; SEE CONCEPTS 87,324,349,362

undertone [n] *suggestion, whisper*
association, atmosphere, buzz, connotation, feeling, flavor, hint, hum, implication, low tone, mumble, murmur, mutter, overtone, rumor, tinge, touch, trace, undercurrent; SEE CONCEPTS 65,682

underwear [n] *clothing worn under outerwear*
bikini, boxers*, boxer shorts, bra, briefs, BVDs*, corset, drawers*, intimate things, jockeys, jockey shorts, lingerie, long johns, panties, shorts, skivvies*, smallclothes, underclothes, underclothing,

undergarment, underpants, undershirt, underthings, undies; SEE CONCEPT 451

underweight [adj] *thin*
angular, anorectic, bony, gangly, malnourished, puny, scrawny, shadow, skeleton*, skin and bones*, skinny, starved, stringbean*, undernourished, undersized; SEE CONCEPT 491

underworld [n] *criminal activity, element*
abyss, Cosa Nostra, criminals, felonry, gangland, gangsters, Mafia, mob*, organized crime, racket*, riffraff*, syndicate; SEE CONCEPTS 412,645

underwrite [v] *endorse, insure*
accede, agree to, angel*, approve, back, bankroll*, collateral, consent, countersign, endow, finance, float, fund, guarantee, help, initial, okay*, pay, provide, provide financing, sanction, seal, secure, sign, sponsor, stake, subscribe, subsidize, support; SEE CONCEPTS 50,88,110,341

undesirable [adj] *offensive, unacceptable*
abominable, annoying, bothersome, defective, disagreeable, disliked, displeasing, distasteful, dreaded, icky, inadmissible, incommodious, inconvenient, inexpedient, insufferable, loathed, loathsome, objectionable, obnoxious, offensive, outcast, out of place, rejected, repellent, repugnant, scorned, shunned, to be avoided, troublesome, unacceptable, unattractive, unlikable, unpleasing, unpopular, unsatisfactory, unsavory, unsought, unsuitable, unwanted, unwelcome, unwished for, useless; SEE CONCEPTS 529,570

undeveloped [adj] *immature*
abortive, backward, behindhand, embryonic, half-baked, ignored, inchoate, incipient, inexperienced, latent, potential, primitive, primordial, unactualized, underdeveloped, unevolved, unprogressive, untaught, untrained; SEE CONCEPTS 485,578,797

undisputed/undisputable [adj] *positive, accepted*
acknowledged, admitted, arbitrary, assured, authoritative, beyond question, certain, conclusive, decided, dogmatic, final, incontestable, incontrovertible, indisputable, indubitable, irrefutable, not disputed, positive, recognized, sure, tyrannous, unchallenged, uncontested, undeniable, undoubted, unequivocal, unerring, unquestioned; SEE CONCEPT 535

undivided [adj] *whole*
absorbed, circumspect, collective, combined, complete, concentrated, concerted, continued, deliberate, detailed, diligent, engrossed, entire, exclusive, fast, fixed, full, intense, intent, joined, lock stock and barrel*, minute, rigid, scrupulous, single, solid, steady, thorough, unanimous, unbroken, uncut, undistracted, unflagging, united, unswerving, vigilant, wholehearted; SEE CONCEPTS 482,531

undo [v1] *open*
disengage, disentangle, free, loose, loosen, release, unbind, unblock, unbutton, unclose, unfasten, unfix, unlock, unloose, unloosen, unravel, unshut, unstop, untie, unwrap; SEE CONCEPT 135

undo [v2] *nullify, invalidate*
abate, abolish, abrogate, annihilate, annul, break, bring down, bring to naught*, cancel, cramp*, craze, crimp*, decimate, defeat, demolish, destroy, have*, impoverish, injure, make waves*, mar, negate, neutralize, offset, outfox, outmaneuver, outsmart, overreach, overthrow, overturn, quash, queer*, raze, reverse, ruin, screw up*, shatter, skin*, smash, spoil, stymie*, subvert, un-

un
un

build, undermine, unsettle, upset, vitiate, wipe out*, wrack, wreck; SEE CONCEPTS *7,19,121,252*

undoing [*n*] *destruction, misfortune*
accident, adversity, affliction, bad luck, bad omen, bane, blight, blow, blunder, calamity, casualty, catastrophe, collapse, curse, defeat, destroyer, difficulty, disgrace, doom, downfall, error, failure, fault, faux pas, flaw, fumble, grief, humiliation, last straw*, misadventure, miscalculation, mischance, mishap, misstep, omission, overthrow, overturn, reversal, reverse, ruin, ruination, shame, slip, smash, stumble, subversion, trial, trip, trouble, visitation, weakness, wreck; SEE CONCEPTS *230,674,679*

undoubtedly [*adv*] *certainly*
assuredly, beyond question, beyond shadow of a doubt*, definitely, doubtless, easily, indeed, of course, really, surely, truly, undeniably, unmistakably, unquestionably, well, without doubt; SEE CONCEPT *535*

undress [*v*] *take off clothes*
denude, disarray, dismantle, disrobe, divest oneself, doff, get off, get out of, husk, peel, shed, shock, slip off, slip out of, strip, unattire, uncloak, unclothe, unmask; SEE CONCEPTS *211,453*

undue [*adj*] *excessive, unnecessary*
disproportionate, exceeding, exorbitant, extravagant, extreme, forbidden, illegal, ill-timed, immoderate, improper, inappropriate, inapt, indecorous, inept, inordinate, intemperate, needless, overmuch, sinister, too great, too much, unapt, uncalled-for, unconscionable, underhanded, undeserved, unfair, unfitting, unjust, unjustifiable, unjustified, unmeasurable, unreasonable, unseasonable, unseemly, unsuitable, untimely, unwarrantable, unwarranted; SEE CONCEPTS *546,558,569*

unduly [*adv*] *excessively*
disproportionately, ever, extravagantly, extremely, illegally, immensely, immoderately, improperly, indecorously, inordinately, out of proportion, over, overfull, overly, overmuch, too, underhandedly, unfairly, unjustifiably, unjustly, unnecessarily, unreasonably; SEE CONCEPTS *544,546,569*

undying [*adj*] *never-ending*
constant, continuing, deathless, eternal, everlasting, immortal, imperishable, indestructible, inextinguishable, infinite, interminable, perennial, permanent, perpetual, persistent, unceasing, undiminished, unended, unending, unfading; SEE CONCEPT *798*

unearth [*v*] *dig up*
ascertain, bring to light*, catch on*, delve, determine, discover, disinter, dredge up, excavate, exhibit, exhume, expose, ferret, find, find out, hear, hit upon, learn, reveal, root, see, see the light, show, spark, spotlight*, strike, stumble on, turn up, unbury, uncover, uproot; SEE CONCEPTS *178,183*

unearthly [*adj*] *supernatural; very strange*
abnormal, absurd, appalling, demonic, devilish, eerie, ethereal, extraordinary, fiendish, frightening, funereal, ghastly, ghostly, ghoulish, hair-raising, haunted, heavenly, hyperphysical, miraculous, nightmarish, not of this world, phantom, preternatural, ridiculous, scary, sepulchral, spectral, spooky*, sublime, superhuman, uncanny, ungodly, unholy, unreasonable, weird; SEE CONCEPTS *536,564,582*

uneasy [*adj*] *awkward, uncomfortable*
afraid, agitated, alarmed, all nerves*, anguished, anxious, apprehensive, bothered, constrained, discomposed, dismayed, disquieted, disturbed, edgy, fearful, fidgety, fretful, harassed, ill at ease, impatient, insecure, in turmoil, irascible, irritable, jittery, jumpy, nervous, on edge, on the qui vive, palpitant, peevish, perplexed, perturbed, precarious, restive, restless, shaken, shaky, strained, suspicious, tense, tormented, troubled, unquiet, unsettled, unstable, upset, vexed, worried, wrung; SEE CONCEPTS *403,548,690*

uneducated [*adj*] *lacking knowledge*
benighted, empty-headed, ignoramus, ignorant, illiterate, inerudite, know-nothing*, lowbrow*, uncultivated, uncultured, uninstructed, unlearned, unlettered, unread, unrefined, unschooled, untaught, untutored; SEE CONCEPT *402*

unemotional [*adj*] *not responsive*
along for the ride*, apathetic, blah*, callous, chill*, cold, coldhearted*, cool, deadpan, dispassionate, emotionless, flat, frigid, glacial, going with the flow*, hard-boiled*, hard-hearted*, heartless, impassive, indifferent, insensitive, laid-back*, listless, marble*, obdurate, passionless, phlegmatic, quiet, reserved, reticent, rolling with the punches*, thick-skinned*, uncompassionate, undemonstrative, unexcitable, unfeeling, unimpressionable, unresponsive, unsympathetic; SEE CONCEPTS *401,403*

unemployed [*adj*] *without a job*
at liberty*, between jobs*, closed down*, disengaged, down, fired, free, idle, inactive, jobless, laid off, leisured, loafing*, on layoff, on the bench*, on the dole*, on the shelf*, out of action*, out of a job, out of work, resting, unapplied, underemployed, unengaged, unexercised, unoccupied, unused, without gainful employment, workless; SEE CONCEPT *538*

unending [*adj*] *continuing*
amaranthine, ceaseless, constant, continual, continuous, endless, eternal, everlasting, immortal, incessant, infinite, interminable, never-ending, perpetual, steady, unceasing, uninterrupted, unremitting; SEE CONCEPTS *482,798*

unequal [*adj1*] *different*
differing, disparate, dissimilar, distant, divergent, diverse, incommensurate, like night and day*, mismatched, not uniform, odd, poles apart*, unalike, unequivalent, uneven, unlike, unmatched, unsimilar, variable, various, varying, weird*; SEE CONCEPT *564*

unequal [*adj2*] *not balanced; lopsided*
asymmetrical, disproportionate, ill-matched, inequitable, irregular, nonsymmetrical, off-balance, one-sided, overbalanced, unbalanced, uneven, unproportionate, unsymmetrical; SEE CONCEPT *480*

unequaled [*adj*] *supreme, pre-eminent*
alone, beyond compare, incomparable, inimitable, matchless, nonpareil, only, paramount, peerless, second to none*, surpassing, towering, transcendent, ultimate, unique, unmatched, unparagoned, unparalleled, unrivaled, unsurpassed, without equal; SEE CONCEPT *574*

unequivocal [*adj*] *definite, positive*
absolute, apparent, categorical, certain, clear, clear-cut, decided, decisive, direct, distinct, downright, evident, explicit, flat out*, incontestable, incontrovertible, indisputable, indubitable, manifest, no catch*, no fine print*, no holds

barred*, no ifs ands or buts*, no strings attached*, obvious, open and shut*, palpable, patent, plain, straight, straightforward, straight out, unambiguous, uncontestable, undeniable, undisputable, univocal, unmistakable, unquestionable; SEE CONCEPT 535

unerring [adj] accurate

certain, errorless, exact, faultless, impeccable, inerrable, inerrant, infallible, invariable, just, perfect, reliable, sure, true, trustworthy, unfailing; SEE CONCEPTS 535,574

unethical [adj] dishonest, immoral

cheating, corrupt, crooked, dirty*, dirty-dealing*, dishonorable, disreputable, double-crossing*, fake, fishy*, flimflam*, fly-by-night*, illegal, improper, mercenary, scam*, shady*, sharp*, slick*, slippery*, sneaky*, two-faced*, two-timing*, underhand, unfair, unprincipled, unprofessional, unscrupulous, wrong; SEE CONCEPT 545

uneven [adj] not smooth or balanced

asperous, asymmetrical, broken, bumpy, changeable, craggy, differing, discrepant, disparate, disproportionate, fitful, fluctuating, harsh, ill-matched, intermittent, irregular, jagged, jerky, leftover, lopsided, nonsymmetrical, notched, not flat, not level, not parallel, odd, off-balance, one-sided, overbalanced, patchy, remaining, rough, rugged, scabrous, scraggy, serrate, spasmodic, spotty, unbalanced, unequal, unfair, unlevel, unsmooth, unsteady, unsymmetrical, variable; SEE CONCEPTS 480,566,606

uneventful [adj] monotonous, dull

boring, common, commonplace, humdrum, inconclusive, indecisive, ordinary, prosaic, quiet, routine, tedious, unexceptional, unexciting, unfateful, uninteresting, unmemorable, unnoteworthy, unremarkable, unvaried; SEE CONCEPT 548

unexpected [adj] surprising

abrupt, accidental, amazing, astonishing, chance, electrifying, eye-opening*, fortuitous, from left field*, impetuous, impulsive, instantaneous, not bargained for*, not in the cards*, out of the blue*, payback, prodigious, staggering, startling, stunning, sudden, swift, unanticipated, unforeseen, unheralded, unlooked-for, unpredictable, unpredicted, wonderful; SEE CONCEPTS 544,548

unfailing [adj] certain, unchanging

absolute, assiduous, bottomless, boundless, ceaseless, come-through*, consistent, constant, continual, continuing, continuous, counted on, delivering, dependable, diligent, dyed-in-the-wool*, endless, eternal, faithful, inexhaustible, infallible, invariable, loyal, never-failing, persistent, reliable, rock solid*, same, solid, staunch, steadfast, straight, sure, surefire, there*, tried-and-true*, true, trustworthy, unflagging, unlimited, unrelenting; SEE CONCEPTS 534,535,538

unfair [adj] prejudiced, wrongful

arbitrary, bad, base, biased, bigoted, blameworthy, cheating, criminal, crooked, cruel, culpable, discreditable, discriminatory, dishonest, dishonorable, foul, grievous, illegal, immoral, improper, inequitable, inexcusable, iniquitous, injurious, low, mean, one-sided, partial, partisan, petty, shameful, shameless, uncalled-for, undue, unethical, unjust, unjustifiable, unlawful, unprincipled, unreasonable, unrightful, unscrupulous, unsporting, unwarranted, vicious, vile, wicked, wrong; SEE CONCEPTS 544,545,548

unfaithful [adj] disloyal, adulterous

adulterine, cheating, deceitful, double-crossing*, faithless, false, false-hearted, fickle, foresworn, inconstant, incontinent, moonlighting*, not true to, of bad faith, perfidious, philandering, recreant, shifty*, snaky*, sneaking, traitorous, treacherous, treasonable, two-faced*, two-timing*, unchaste, unreliable, untrue, untrustworthy, wicked; SEE CONCEPT 545

unfaltering [adj] steadfast

abiding, bent on, bound, bound and determined*, dead set on*, enduring, firm, going all the way*, indefatigable, meaning business*, mulish*, never-failing, persevering, pigheaded, resolute, set, steady, stiff-necked*, stubborn, sure, tireless, unfailing, unflagging, unflappable, unflinching, unqualified, unquestioning, unswerving, untiring, unwavering, wholehearted; SEE CONCEPTS 403,535,538

unfamiliar [adj1] different, strange

alien, anomalous, bizarre, curious, exotic, extraordinary, fantastic, foreign, little known, new, novel, obscure, original, outlandish, out-of-the-way*, peculiar, recondite, remarkable, remote, unaccustomed, uncommon, unexpected, unexplored, uninvestigated, unknown, unusual; SEE CONCEPT 564

unfamiliar [adj2] inexperienced; not knowing about

ignorant, incognizant, inconversant, not associated, not versed in, oblivious, out of contact, unaccustomed, unacquainted, unaware, unconversant, uninformed, uninitiated, uninstructed, unknowing, unknown, unpracticed, unskilled, unversed, unwitting; SEE CONCEPTS 402,678

unfathomable [adj1] bottomless

abysmal, boundless, deep, eternal, immeasurable, infinite, soundless, unending, unmeasured, unplumbed; SEE CONCEPTS 482,777

unfathomable [adj2] hard to believe; difficult to understand

abstruse, baffling, clear as mud*, deep, enigmatic, esoteric, heavy, impenetrable, incognizable, incomprehensible, indecipherable, inexplicable, obscure, profound, too deep*, uncomprehensible, ungraspable, unintelligible, unknowable; SEE CONCEPT 529

unfavorable [adj] very bad

adverse, antagonistic, calamitous, contrary, damaging, destructive, disadvantageous, discommodious, hostile, ill, ill-advised, improper, inadvisable, inauspicious, inconvenient, inexpedient, infelicitous, inimical, inopportune, late, low, malapropos, negative, objectionable, ominous, opposed, poor, regrettable, tardy, threatening, troublesome, unfit, unfortunate, unfriendly, unlucky, unpromising, unpropitious, unseasonable, unseemly, unsuited, untimely, untoward, wrong; SEE CONCEPTS 529,571

unfeeling [adj] hard-hearted, numb

anesthetized, apathetic, asleep, benumbed, brutal, callous, cantankerous, churlish, cold, cold-blooded, cold fish*, cold-hearted, crotchety, cruel, deadened, exacting, feelingless, hard, hardened, heartless, icy, inanimate, inhuman, insensate, insensible, insensitive, iron-hearted, merciless, obdurate, pitiless, ruthless, sensationless, senseless, severe, stony, surly, thick-skinned*, tough, unamiable, uncaring,

un
un

uncompassionate, uncordial, unemotional, unkind, unsympathetic; SEE CONCEPTS *314,403,542*

unfinished [*adj*] *not completed*
amateurish, bare, crude, cut short, dabbling, defective, deficient, dilettante, faulty, formless,
found wanting, fragmentary, half-baked*, half-
done*, immature, imperfect, incomplete, in the
making, in the rough*, lacking, natural, not done,
plain, raw, rough, roughhewn, shapeless, sketchy,
tentative, unaccomplished, unadorned, unassembled, uncompleted, unconcluded, under construction, undeveloped, undone, unexecuted,
unfashioned, unfulfilled, unperfected, unpolished,
unrefined, wanting; SEE CONCEPTS *485,531*

unfit [*adj1*] *not appropriate or suited*
below par*, can't make the grade*, debilitated,
decrepit, discordant, down, dragging, feeble,
flimsy, ill-adapted, ill-equipped, ill-suited, improper, inadequate, inapplicable, inappropriate,
incompatible, incongruous, incorrect, ineffective,
inexpedient, infelicitous, inharmonious, laid
low*, mistaken, not fit, out of element*, out of
place, out of shape, poorly, rocky*, unbecoming,
uncongenial, uncool, unhealthy, unlikely, unmeet, unpromising, unsuitable, unsuited, useless,
valueless; SEE CONCEPT *558*

unfit [*adj2*] *not ready*
amateur, awkward, blundering, bungling, bush
league*, butter-fingered*, clumsy, debilitated,
disqualified, feeble, heavy-handed, ill-equipped,
impotent, inadequate, incapable, incapacitated,
incompetent, ineffective, inefficient, ineligible,
inept, inexperienced, inexpert, maladjusted, maladroit, no good*, not cut out for*, not equal to,
not up to*, unable, unapt, unfitted, unhandy, unpracticed, unprepared, unproficient, unqualified,
unskilled, unskillful, untrained, useless, weak;
SEE CONCEPT *527*

unflagging [*adj*] *persistent*
active, assiduous, constant, diligent, dynamic, energetic, fixed, indefatigable, inexhaustible, persevering, staunch, steady, tireless, unceasing,
undeviating, unfailing, unfaltering, unrelenting,
unremitting, unretiring, untiring, unwearied; SEE
CONCEPTS *538,798*

unflappable [*adj*] *cool and calm*
collected, composed, deliberate, disimpassioned,
easy, impassive, imperturbable, level-headed,
nonchalant, relaxed, self-possessed, unruffled;
SEE CONCEPTS *401,542*

unfold [*v1*] *spread out*
disentangle, display, expand, extend, fan, fan out,
flatten, loosen, open, outspread, outstretch, reel
out, release, shake out, spread, straighten, stretch
out, unbend, uncoil, uncrease, uncurl, undo, unfurl, unravel, unroll, untwist, unwind, unwrap;
SEE CONCEPT *201*

unfold [*v2*] *make known*
announce, clarify, clear up, decipher, describe,
disclose, discover, display, divulge, dope out, elucidate, explain, explicate, expose, figure out, illustrate, present, publish, resolve, reveal, show,
solve, uncover, unravel; SEE CONCEPTS *55,261*

unfold [*v3*] *develop*
bear fruit, demonstrate, elaborate, evidence,
evince, evolve, expand, grow, manifest, mature;
SEE CONCEPT *704*

unforeseen [*adj*] *surprising*
abrupt, accidental, from left field*, not bargained
for*, out of the blue*, startling, sudden, surprise,

unanticipated, uncalculated, unexpected,
unlooked-for; SEE CONCEPTS *544,548*

unfortunate [*adj*] *unlucky, bad*
adverse, afflicted, broken, burdened, calamitous,
cursed, damaging, deplorable, desperate, destitute, disastrous, doomed, forsaken, hapless, hopeless, ill-fated, ill-starred, in a bad way*,
inappropriate, infelicitous, inopportune, jinxed,
lamentable, luckless, out of luck*, pained, poor,
regrettable, ruined, ruinous, shattered, star-
crossed*, stricken, troubled, unbecoming, unfavorable, unhappy, unpropitious, unprosperous,
unsuccessful, unsuitable, untoward, wretched;
SEE CONCEPTS *334,548,570*

unfounded [*adj*] *not based on fact*
baseless, bottomless, deceptive, fabricated, fallacious, false, foundationless, gratuitous, groundless, idle, illogical, mendacious, misleading, off-
base, spurious, trumped up*, uncalled-for,
unjustified, unproven, unreal, unsubstantiated, untrue, untruthful, unwarranted, vain, without basis,
without foundation; SEE CONCEPTS *267,582*

unfriendly [*adj*] *nasty, hostile*
acrimonious, against, alien, aloof, antagonistic,
antisocial, censorious, chilly, cold, combative,
competitive, conflicting, contrary, disaffected,
disagreeable, distant, estranged, grouchy, grudging, gruff, hateful, ill-disposed, inauspicious, inhospitable, inimical, malicious, malignant,
misanthropic, not on speaking terms*, opposed,
opposite, quarrelsome, sour, spiteful, surly, uncharitable, uncongenial, unfavorable, unneighborly, unpropitious, unsociable, vengeful,
warlike; SEE CONCEPTS *401,548*

ungodly [*adj1*] *not accepting a religious doctrine;
impious*
atheistic, blasphemous, corrupt, depraved, godless, improper, indecent, indecorous, indelicate,
irreligious, malevolent, profane, rough, sinful,
undecorous, unhallowed, unholy, unseemly, vile,
wicked; SEE CONCEPTS *542,545*

ungodly [*adj2*] *outrageous*
atrocious, barbarous, dreadful, horrendous, horrid, intolerable, nasty, shocking, unbelievable,
uncivilized, unconscionable, unearthly, unreasonable, unseemly; SEE CONCEPTS *529,548,570*

ungrateful [*adj*] *not appreciative*
careless, demanding, dissatisfied, faultfinding,
forgetful, grasping, grumbling, heedless, ingrate,
insensible, oblivious, self-centered, selfish, thankless, unappreciative, unmindful, unnatural, unthankful; SEE CONCEPT *401*

unguarded [*adj*] *thoughtless; unwary*
accessible, artless, candid, careless, casual, direct, foolhardy, frank, headlong, heedless, honest, ill-considered, impolitic, imprudent,
impulsive, incautious, indiscreet, ingenuous, naive, offhand, rash, spontaneous, straightforward,
unalert, uncircumspect, unconscious, undiplomatic, unpremeditated, unreflective, unthinking,
unvigilant, unwatchful, unwise, vulnerable, weak;
SEE CONCEPT *401*

unhappy [*adj1*] *sad*
bleak, bleeding*, blue*, bummed out*, cheerless,
crestfallen, dejected, depressed, despondent, destroyed, disconsolate, dismal, dispirited, down*,
down and out*, downbeat, downcast, down in the
mouth*, dragged, dreary, gloomy, grim, heavyhearted, hurting, in a blue funk*, in pain, in the
dumps*, let-down*, long-faced, low, melancholy,

mirthless, miserable, mournful, oppressive, put away*, ripped*, sad, saddened, sorrowful, sorry, teary, troubled; SEE CONCEPT 403

unhappy [adj2] *unfortunate, unlucky*
afflicted, cursed, hapless, ill-fated, ill-starred, luckless, misfortunate, troubled, untoward, wretched; SEE CONCEPT 548

unhealthy [adj1] *sick*
ailing, below par, debilitated, delicate, diseased, down, dragging, feeble, frail, ill, in a decline, infirm, in ill health, in poor health, invalid, laid low*, out of action*, out of shape, peaked, poorly, run-down, shaky, sickly, unsound, unwell, weak; SEE CONCEPT 314

unhealthy [adj2] *very bad in effect on well-being*
baneful, chancy, corrupt, corrupting, dangerous, degenerate, degrading, deleterious, demoralizing, detrimental, harmful, hazardous, insalubrious, jeopardous, morbid, nefarious, negative, noisome, noxious, perilous, perverse, poisonous, risky, rotten, treacherous, undesirable, unhealthful, unsanitary, unsound, unwholesome, villainous, virulent, wicked; SEE CONCEPTS 537,571

unheard-of [adj] *unique, obscure*
exceptional, inconceivable, little-known, nameless, new, novel, outlandish, preposterous, rare, shocking, singular, unbelievable, undiscovered, unfamiliar, unknown, unlikely, unprecedented, unrenowned, unsung, unusual; SEE CONCEPTS 564,576

unholy [adj1] *sacreligious*
base, blameful, corrupt, culpable, depraved, dishonest, evil, godless, guilty, heinous, immoral, impious, iniquitous, irreligious, irreverent, irreverential, profane, sinful, ungodly, unhallowed, unsanctified, vile, wicked; SEE CONCEPTS 542,548

unholy [adj2] *outrageous*
appalling, awful, barbarous, dreadful, horrendous, shocking, uncivilized, unearthly, ungodly, unnatural, unreasonable; SEE CONCEPT 537

unidentified [adj] *secret*
anonymous, mysterious, nameless, not known, pseudonymous, unclassified, unfamiliar, unknown, unmarked, unnamed, unrecognized, unrevealed; SEE CONCEPT 576

unification [n] *joining together*
affinity, alliance, amalgamation, coalescence, coalition, combination, concurrence, confederation, connection, consolidation, coupling, federation, fusion, hookup, interlocking, linkage, melding, merger, merging, union, uniting; SEE CONCEPTS 230,388

uniform [n] *coordinated outfit*
attire, costume, dress, garb, gown, habit, khaki*, livery, monkey suit*, OD*, olive drab*, regalia, regimentals, robe, stripes*, suit; SEE CONCEPT 451

uniform [adj1] *consistent*
compatible, consonant, constant, equable, even, fated, fateful, fixed, habitual, homogeneous, immutable, incorrigible, inflexible, invariable, irreversible, level, methodical, monolithic, normal, of a piece*, ordered, orderly, ossified, plumb, regular, reliable, rigid, smooth, stable, static, steady, straight, symmetrical, systematic, true, unalterable, unbroken, unchanging, undeviating, undiversified, unfluctuating, unmodifiable, unvarying, well-balanced, well-proportioned; SEE CONCEPT 534

uniform [adj2] *alike*
agnate, akin, analogous, comparable, consistent, consonant, correspondent, ditto*, double, equal, identical, like, mated, monotonous, parallel, same, same difference*, self-same, similar, treadmill*, undifferentiated, unvaried; SEE CONCEPTS 487,573

unimaginable [adj] *mind-boggling*
beyond wildest dreams*, doubtful, exceptional, extraordinary, fantastic, impossible, improbable, inapprehensible, incogitable, incomprehensible, inconceivable, incredible, indescribable, ineffable, not understandable, rare, singular, unbelievable, uncommon, unheard-of, unique, unknowable, unordinary, unthinkable; SEE CONCEPTS 529,548

unimaginative [adj] *dull, predictable*
banal, barren, bromidic, common, commonplace, derivative, dime a dozen*, dry, dull as dishwater*, flat, hackneyed, ho hum*, lifeless, matter-of-fact, ordinary, pabulum, pedestrian, prosaic, routine, square*, tame, tedious, trite, uncreative, uninspired, unoriginal, unromantic, usual, vanilla*, well-worn, zero*; SEE CONCEPTS 542,547,548

unimportant [adj] *of no real worth, value*
beside the point*, casual, frivolous, frothy, immaterial, inconsequential, inconsiderable, indifferent, insignificant, irrelevant, little, low-ranking, meaningless, minor, minute, negligible, nonessential, nothing*, nugatory, null, of no account, of no consequence, paltry, petty, picayune, second-rate*, shoestring*, slight, trifling, trivial, unnecessary, useless, worthless, zero*, zilch*, zip*; SEE CONCEPT 575

uninhibited [adj] *free and easy; without restraint*
audacious, candid, cut loose*, expansive, fancy-free*, footloose*, frank, free, hanging out*, informal, instinctive, liberated, natural, no holds barred*, off the cuff*, open, relaxed, spontaneous, unbridled, unchecked, unconstrained, uncontrolled, uncurbed, ungoverned, unhampered, unrepressed, unreserved, unrestrained, unrestricted, unself-conscious, unsuppressed; SEE CONCEPTS 267,401

uninspired [adj] *dull, unoriginal*
bromidic, commonplace, corny*, everyday, heavy-handed, humdrum, indifferent, old hat*, ordinary, phoned in*, ponderous, prosaic, stale, sterile, stock, uncreative, unexciting, unimaginative, unimpressed, uninspiring, uninteresting, uninventive, unmoved, yawn*; SEE CONCEPTS 542,547,548

unintelligible [adj] *not understandable*
ambiguous, equivocal, fathomless, Greek*, illegible, impenetrable, inarticulate, incognizable, incoherent, incomprehensible, indecipherable, indistinct, inexplicit, jumbled, meaningless, muddled, obscure, opaque, tenebrous, uncertain, unclear, unexplicit, unfathomable, ungraspable, unknowable, unreadable, vague; SEE CONCEPT 267

unintentional/unintended [adj] *not planned*
accidental, aimless, casual, chance, erratic, extemporaneous, fortuitous, haphazard, inadvertent, involuntary, purposeless, random, unconscious, undesigned, undevised, unexpected, unforeseen, unintended, unplanned, unpremeditated, unthinking, unthought, unwitting; SEE CONCEPTS 401,548

un
un

uninterested [adj] oblivious to
aloof, apathetic, blasé, bored, bored stiff*, casual, could care less*, detached, disinterested, distant, going through motions*, hard-hearted*, impassive, incurious, indifferent, listless, remote, thick-skinned*, turned off*, unconcerned, uncurious, uninvolved, unresponsive, weary, withdrawn; SEE CONCEPTS 401,403

uninteresting [adj] boring, uneventful
arid, banal, big yawn*, bromidic, common, commonplace, depressing, dismal, drab, dreary, dry, dull, dusty*, fatiguing, flat, ho hum*, humdrum, insipid, irksome, jejune, monotonous, nothing*, nowhere*, pedestrian, prosaic, prosy, soporific, stale, stupid, tedious, tired, tiresome, trite, unenjoyable, unentertaining, unexciting, uninspiring, wearisome; SEE CONCEPTS 529,548

uninterrupted [adj] continuing; unbroken
ceaseless, consecutive, constant, continual, continuous, direct, endless, interminable, nonstop, peaceful, perpetual, steady, straight, straightforward, sustained, through, unceasing, undisturbed, unending, unremitting; SEE CONCEPTS 482,798

union [n1] merger, joining
abutment, accord, agglutination, agreement, amalgam, amalgamation, blend, centralization, coadunation, combination, coming together, commixture, compound, concatenation, conciliation, concord, concurrence, confluence, congregation, conjunction, consolidation, correlation, coupling, fusion, harmony, hookup, incorporation, intercourse, joint, junction, juncture, meeting, melding, merging, mixture, seam, symbiosis, synthesis, tie-in, tie-up, unanimity, unification, unison, uniting, unity; SEE CONCEPTS 113,664,714

union [n2] group with shared interest, cause
alliance, association, brotherhood, club, coalition, confederacy, confederation, congress, employees, federation, guild, labor union, league, local, order, sisterhood, society, sodality, syndicate, trade union; SEE CONCEPTS 325,381

unique [adj1] alone, singular
different, exclusive, individual, lone, one, one and only*, onliest*, only, particular, rare, separate, single, solitary, solo, sui generis, uncommon, unexampled; SEE CONCEPTS 564,577

unique [adj2] one-of-a-kind; without equal
anomalous, best, exceptional, extraordinary, far-out*, incomparable, inimitable, matchless, most, nonpareil, novel, only, peerless, primo*, rare, singular, something else*, special, standout, strange, uncommon, unequaled, unexampled, unimaginable, unmatched, unparagoned, unparalleled, unprecedented, unreal, unrivaled, utmost, weird*; SEE CONCEPTS 564,574

unison [n] harmony
accord, accordance, agreement, alliance, community, concert, concord, concordance, conjunction, consent, consonance, cooperation, federation, league, reciprocity, sympathy, unanimity, union, unity; SEE CONCEPT 664

unit [n1] whole
assemblage, assembly, bunch, complement, crew, crowd, detachment, entirety, entity, gang, group, mob, one, outfit, ring, section, system, total, totality; SEE CONCEPTS 432,837

unit [n2] part
arm, block, component, constituent, detachment, detail, digit, element, factor, feature, fraction, in-

gredient, integer, item, joint, layer, length, link, member, module, piece, portion, section, segment, square, wing; SEE CONCEPT 834

unite [v] combine; join together
affiliate, ally, amalgamate, associate, band, band together, become one, blend, close ranks*, coadjute, coalesce, commingle, concur, confederate, conjoin, connect, consolidate, cooperate, couple, embody, fuse, gather together, hang together*, harden, hook up with, incorporate, intertwine, join, join forces, keep together, league, link, marry, meet, merge, mix, pool, pull together, relate, solidify, stay together, stick together, strengthen, throw in with*, unify, wed; SEE CONCEPTS 113,193

united [adj] combined; in agreement
affiliated, agreed, allied, amalgamated, assembled, associated, banded, coadunate, cognate, collective, concerted, concordant, confederated, congruent, conjoint, conjugate, conjunctive, consolidated, cooperative, corporate, federal, homogeneous, hooked up*, in accord, in cahoots*, incorporated, integrated, joined up, leagued, like-minded*, lined up*, linked, of one mind, of the same opinion, one, plugged in*, pooled, tied in, unanimous, undivided, unified, unitary; SEE CONCEPTS 563,577

unity [n] wholeness
accord, agreement, alliance, coadunation, combination, concord, concurrence, confederation, consensus, consent, consonance, entity, federation, harmony, homogeneity, homogeneousness, identity, individuality, indivisibility, integral, integrality, integrity, interconnection, oneness, peace, rapport, sameness, singleness, singularity, soleness, solidarity, synthesis, totality, unanimity, undividedness, unification, uniformity, union, unison; SEE CONCEPTS 664,714,837

universal [adj] worldwide, entire
accepted, all, all-embracing, all-inclusive, all-over, astronomical, broad, catholic, celestial, common, comprehensive, cosmic, cosmopolitan, customary, diffuse, ecumenical, empyrean, extensive, general, generic, global, multinational, mundane, omnipresent, planetary, prevalent, regular, stellar, sweeping, terrestrial, total, ubiquitous, undisputed, unlimited, unrestricted, usual, whole, widespread, worldly; SEE CONCEPTS 536,772

universe [n] everything in creation
cosmos, everything, macrocosm, natural world, nature, world; SEE CONCEPTS 370,511

unjust [adj] not fair
below the belt*, biased, fixed*, inequitable, influenced, low-down*, one-sided, partial, partisan, prejudiced, shabby*, underhand, undeserved, unfair, unforgivable, unjustified, unmerited, unrighteous, wrong, wrongful; SEE CONCEPT 545

unkempt [adj] shabby, sloppy
bedraggled, coarse, crude, dilapidated, dirty, disarranged, disarrayed, disheveled, disordered, grubby*, grungy*, messed up, messy, mussed up*, neglected, rough, rumpled, scruffy, shaggy, slipshod, slovenly, tousled, unclean, uncombed, unfastidious, ungroomed, unimproved, unneat, unpolished, untidy, vulgar; SEE CONCEPTS 485,621

unkind [adj] not nice
barbarous, brutal, cold-blooded, coldhearted, cruel, hard-hearted, harsh, hateful, heartless, inconsiderate, inhuman, inhumane, insensitive, ma-

levolent, malicious, malignant, mean, nasty, sadistic, savage, spiteful, thoughtless, uncaring, uncharitable, unfeeling, unfriendly, unsympathetic; SEE CONCEPT *401*

unknown [*adj*] *obscure, mysterious*
alien, anonymous, concealed, dark, desolate, distant, exotic, far, faraway, far-off, foreign, hidden, humble, incog*, incognito, little known, nameless, new, remote, secret, so-and-so*, strange, such-and-such*, unapprehended, unascertained, uncelebrated, uncharted, undiscovered, undistinguished, unexplained, unexplored, unfamiliar, unheard-of, unidentified, unnamed, unnoted, unperceived, unrecognized, unrenowned, unrevealed, unsung, untold, X*; SEE CONCEPT *576*

unlawful [*adj*] *against the law*
actionable, banned, bootleg*, criminal, flagitious, forbidden, illegal, illegitimate, illicit, improper, iniquitous, lawless, nefarious, outlawed, prohibited, taboo, unauthorized, under-the-counter*, unlicensed, wrongful; SEE CONCEPT *319*

unlike [*adj*] *different*
apples and oranges*, clashing, conflicting, contradictory, contrary, contrasted, discordant, disharmonious, disparate, dissimilar, dissonant, distant, distinct, divergent, diverse, far cry from*, heterogeneous, hostile, incompatible, incongruous, inconsistent, mismatched, not alike, offbeat, opposed, opposite, poles apart*, separate, unalike, unequal, unrelated, variant, various, weird; SEE CONCEPT *564*

unlikely [*adj*] *not probable*
absurd, contrary, doubtful, dubious, faint, implausible, improbable, inconceivable, incredible, not likely, out of the ordinary, outside chance, questionable, rare, remote, slight, strange, unbelievable, unconvincing, unheard-of, unimaginable, untoward; SEE CONCEPT *552*

unlimited [*adj*] *extensive, complete*
absolute, all-encompassing, all-out*, boundless, countless, endless, full, full-blown*, full-out*, full-scale, great, illimitable, immeasurable, immense, incalculable, incomprehensible, indefinite, infinite, interminable, limitless, measureless, no end of*, no end to*, no strings*, numberless, total, totalitarian, unbounded, unconditional, unconfined, unconstrained, unfathomed, unfettered, universal, unqualified, unrestrained, unrestricted, untold, vast, wide open; SEE CONCEPT *772*

unload [*v*] *take off; empty*
break bulk, cast, clear out, disburden, discharge, discommode, disencumber, disgorge, dump, get rid of, jettison, lighten, off-load, relieve, remove, rid, slough, take a load off, unburden, unlade, unpack, void; SEE CONCEPTS *180,211*

unlucky [*adj*] *unfortunate, doomed*
afflicted, bad break*, behind eight ball*, black, calamitous, cataclysmic, catastrophic, cursed, dire, disastrous, down on luck*, hapless, hard luck, ill-fated, ill-starred, inauspicious, luckless, miserable, ominous, out of luck, star-crossed*, tough luck, tragic, unfavorable, unhappy, unsuccessful, untimely, untoward; SEE CONCEPTS *529,548*

unmarried [*adj*] *not presently wed*
bachelor, eligible, husbandless, single, sole, spouseless, unattached, uncoupled, unwed, unwedded, widowed, wifeless; SEE CONCEPT *555*

unmerciful [*adj*] *cruel*
bestial, bloodthirsty, brutal, coldhearted, hard,

heartless, hurtful, implacable, inhumane, merciless, monstrous, pitiless, relentless, remorseless, ruthless, tyrannous, uncaring, unfeeling, unpitying, unrelenting, unsparing, vengeful, vindictive; SEE CONCEPT *401*

unmistakable [*adj*] *certain, definite*
apparent, clear, conspicuous, decided, distinct, evident, explicit, for certain, glaring, indisputable, manifest, no ifs ands or buts*, obvious, open and shut*, palpable, patent, plain, positive, pronounced, self-explanatory, straightforward, sure, transparent, unambiguous, unequivocal, univocal; SEE CONCEPT *535*

unmitigated [*adj*] *absolute, pure*
arrant, austere, clear-cut, complete, consummate, damned, downright, gross, intense, oppressive, out-and-out*, outright, perfect, persistent, rank, relentless, rigid, severe, sheer, simple, straightout*, thorough, thoroughgoing, unabated, unabridged, unadulterated, unalleviated, unbending, unbroken, undiluted, unmixed, unqualified, unrelieved, utter; SEE CONCEPTS *531,535,569*

unnatural [*adj*] *not regular; artificial*
aberrant, abnormal, affected, anomalous, assumed, bizarre, concocted, contrary, contrived, ersatz*, extraordinary, fabricated, factitious, false, feigned, forced, freakish, freaky, imitation, incredible, insincere, irregular, labored, made-up*, make-believe*, odd, outlandish, outrageous, perverse, perverted, phony, preposterous, pseudo*, put-on*, queer, staged, stiff, stilted*, strained, strange, studied, supernatural, synthetic, theatrical, unaccountable, uncanny, unconforming, unorthodox, unusual; SEE CONCEPTS *564,582*

unnecessary [*adj*] *not required*
accidental, additional, avoidable, beside the point*, casual, causeless, chance, dispensable, excess, exorbitant, expendable, extraneous, extrinsic, fortuitous, futile, gratuitous, haphazard, inessential, irrelevant, lavish, needless, noncompulsory, nonessential, optional, prodigal, profuse, random, redundant, supererogatory, superfluous, surplus, uncalled-for, uncritical, undesirable, unessential, unneeded, unrequired, useless, wanton, worthless; SEE CONCEPT *546*

unnerve [*v*] *upset, intimidate*
agitate, bewilder, bowl over*, buffalo*, chill*, confound, daunt, demoralize, disarm, discombobulate, disconcert, discourage, dishearten, dismay, dispirit, distract, enervate, enfeeble, floor*, fluster, frighten, get to*, give a turn*, intimidate, needle*, perturb, psych out*, rattle, ride, sap*, shake, spook, throw, throw off*, uncalm, undermine, unhinge, unsettle, weaken; SEE CONCEPTS *7,14,19*

unnoticed [*adj*] *ignored*
disregarded, glossed over, hidden, inconspicuous, neglected, overlooked, passed by, pushed aside, secret, unconsidered, undiscovered, unheeded, unobserved, unobtrusive, unperceived, unrecognized, unremarked, unremembered, unrespected, unseen, winked at; SEE CONCEPT *529*

unobtrusive [*adj*] *keeping a low profile*
humble, inconspicuous, low-key, low-profile, meek, modest, quiet, reserved, restrained, retiring, self-effacing, soft-pedaled*, subdued, tasteful, unassuming, unnoticeable, unostentatious, unpretentious; SEE CONCEPTS *401,548*

unorthodox [*adj*] *abnormal; other than accepted*
beatnik*, crazy*, different, dissident, eccentric,

un
un

far-out, flaky*, heretical, heterodox, irregular, kinky*, nonconformist, off the beaten path*, schismatic, sectarian, unconventional, uncustomary, unusual, unwonted, way-out*, weird*; SEE CONCEPT 564

unpaid [adj1] free, voluntary
contributed, donated, due, freewilled, gratuitous, honorary, unindemnified, unrewarded, unsalaried, volunteer; SEE CONCEPT 538

unpaid [adj2] not settled; taken without remuneration
delinquent, due, in arrears, mature, not discharged, outstanding, overdue, owing, past due, payable, undefrayed, unliquidated, unsettled; SEE CONCEPT 334

unparalleled [adj] superlative
all-time*, alone, beyond compare, champ*, champion, consummate, exceptional, greatest, incomparable, matchless, most, nonpareil, only, peerless, rare, single, singular, solid gold*, ten*, tops*, unequaled, unique, unmatched, unprecedented, unrivaled, winner, without equal, world-class*; SEE CONCEPT 574

unpleasant [adj] bad
abhorrent, bad news*, bad scene*, disagreeable, displeasing, distasteful, fierce, grody*, gross, hard-time*, icky*, irksome, lousy, nasty, objectionable, obnoxious, poisonous, repulsive, rotten, sour, troublesome, unacceptable, unattractive, uncool*, undesirable, unhappy, unlikable, unlovely, unpalatable, yucky*; SEE CONCEPTS 529,570

unpopular [adj] not liked or sought after
abhorred, avoided, creepy*, despised, detested, disesteemed, disfavored, disliked, drip*, dumpy*, execrated, gross*, loathed, loser*, lousy, nerdy*, obnoxious, ostracized, out, out of favor, rejected, scorned, shunned, unaccepted, unattractive, uncared for, undesirable, unloved, unvalued, unwanted, unwelcome, weird, wimpy*; SEE CONCEPTS 529,555

unprecedented [adj] exceptional, original
aberrant, abnormal, anomalous, bizarre, eccentric, exotic, extraordinary, fantastic, freakish, idiosyncratic, marvelous, miraculous, modern, new, newfangled, novel, odd, outlandish, out-of-the-way*, outré, preternatural, prodigious, remarkable, signal, singular, sui generis, uncommon, unexampled, unheard-of, unique, unparalleled, unrivaled, unusual; SEE CONCEPTS 549,564,574

unpredictable [adj] changeable
capricious, chance, chancy, dicey*, doubtful, erratic, fickle, fluctuating, fluky*, from left field*, hanging by a thread*, iffy*, incalculable, inconstant, random, touch and go*, touchy, uncertain, unforeseeable, unreliable, unstable, up for grabs*, variable, whimsical; SEE CONCEPT 534

unprejudiced [adj] fair
balanced, dispassionate, equal, equitable, even-handed, fair-minded, impartial, just, liberal, nondiscriminatory, nonpartisan, objective, open-minded, straight, unbiased, unbigoted, uncolored, uninfluenced; SEE CONCEPTS 319,401,542

unpretentious [adj] simple, honest
discreet, down, down home*, easy-going, folksy*, free-spirited, homey*, humble, inelaborate, laid-back*, lowly, modest, plain, prosaic, straightforward, unaffected, unambitious, unassuming, unbeautified, uncomplex, unembellished, unimposing, unobtrusive, unostentatious, unpre-

sumptuous, unspoiled, up front; SEE CONCEPTS 401,404

unprincipled [adj] corrupt
abandoned, amoral, bent*, cheating, conscienceless, crooked, deceitful, devious, dirty-dealing*, dishonest, dissolute, double-crossing*, double-dealing*, immoral, licentious, mercenary, praetorian, profligate, reprobate, shady, sly, stop-at-nothing*, tricky, two-faced*, two-timing*, unconscionable, underhand, unethical, unprofessional, unscrupulous, venal, wanton; SEE CONCEPT 545

unprofessional [adj] not done well or skillfully
amateur, amateurish, ignorant, improper, inadequate, incompetent, inefficient, inexperienced, inexpert, lax, negligent, nonexpert, unethical, unfitting, unsuitable, untrained, unworthy; SEE CONCEPTS 527,538

unqualified [adj1] not prepared, incompetent
amateur, bush, bush-league*, disqualified, ill-equipped, inadequate, incapable, incompetent, ineligible, inexperienced, not equal to, not up to*, unequipped, unfit, unfitted, unprepared, unskilled; SEE CONCEPT 527

unqualified [adj2] outright, absolute
abiding, blasted, blessed, categorical, certain, clear, complete, confounded, consummate, downright, enduring, entire, explicit, express, firm, flat out*, infernal, never-failing, no catch*, no ifs ands or buts*, out-and-out*, perfect, positive, rank, sheer, simple, steadfast, steady, sure, thorough, thoroughgoing, total, unadulterated, unalloyed, unconditional, unfaltering, unlimited, unmitigated, unreserved, unrestrained, unrestricted, utter, wholehearted, without reservation; SEE CONCEPTS 531,535

unquestionable [adj] definite; beyond doubt
absolute, accurate, authentic, bona fide*, certain, clear, cold, conclusive, dependable, down pat*, downright, established, faultless, flat*, flawless, for certain, genuine, incontestable, incontrovertible, indisputable, indubitable, irrefutable, manifest, no ifs ands or buts*, obvious, pat, patent, perfect, positive, real, reliable, self-evident, superior, sure, sure-enough, true, undeniable, undisputable, undoubted, unequivocal, unimpeachable, unmistakable, veritable, well-founded, well-grounded; SEE CONCEPTS 529,535

unreal [adj] fake, make-believe; hypothetical
aerial, artificial, chimerical, delusive, dreamlike, fabled, fabulous, false, fanciful, fictitious, fictive, figmental, hallucinatory, ideal, illusory, imaginary, imagined, immaterial, impalpable, insincere, insubstantial, intangible, invented, legendary, misleading, mock, mythical, nebulous, nonexistent, notional, ostensible, phantasmagoric*, pretended, reachy, romantic, seeming, sham*, storybook*, suppositious, supposititious, theoretical, unbelievable, unsubstantial, visionary; SEE CONCEPT 582

unrealistic [adj] not believable or practical
blue sky*, floating, gone*, half-baked*, impossible, impracticable, impractical, improbable, ivory-tower*, nonrealistic, nonsensical, not applicable, not sensible, on cloud nine*, quixotic, reachy, romantic, silly, starry-eyed, theoretical, unreal, unworkable; SEE CONCEPTS 552,560

unreasonable [adj] not logical or sensible
absurd, all wet*, arbitrary, biased, capricious, contradictory, erratic, fallacious, far-fetched,

foolish, full of hot air*, headstrong, illogical, incoherent, incongruous, inconsequential, inconsistent, invalid, irrational, loose, mad, nonsensical, off the wall*, opinionated, preposterous, quirky, reasonless, senseless, silly, stupid, thoughtless, unreasoned, vacant, wrong; SEE CONCEPTS 401,548

unreasonable [adj2] *extravagant; beyond normal limits*
absonant, arbitrary, costing an arm and a leg*, dear, excessive, exorbitant, extortionate, extreme, far-out*, illegitimate, immoderate, improper, inordinate, intemperate, out of bounds*, overkill*, overmuch, peremptory, posh, pricey*, senseless, steep*, stiff*, too great, too much, too-too*, uncalled-for*, unconscionable, undue, unfair, unjust, unjustifiable, unlawful, unrightful, unwarrantable, unwarranted, up to here*, way out*, wrongful; SEE CONCEPTS 334,762,771

unrelated [adj] *independent; different*
beside the point*, dissimilar, extraneous, inapplicable, inappropriate, irrelative, irrelevant, mismatched, nongermane, not germane, not kin, not kindred, not related, separate, unassociated, unattached, unconnected, unlike; SEE CONCEPTS 563,564

unrelenting [adj] *merciless*
bound, bound and determined, brick-wall*, ceaseless, constant, continual, continuous, cruel, dead set on*, endless, grim, hanging tough*, hardheaded*, implacable, incessant, inexorable, intransigent, iron-fisted, mortal, perpetual, persistent, pitiless, relentless, remorseless, rigid, ruthless, set, steady, stern, stiff, stiff-necked*, tenacious, tough, unabated, unbending, unbroken, unflinching, unremitting, unsparing, unwavering, unyielding; SEE CONCEPTS 401,548,798

unreliable [adj] *not trustworthy, not true*
capricious, deceitful, deceptive, delusive, disreputable, dubious, erroneous, fake, fallible, false, fickle, fly by night*, furtive, hallucinatory, hollow, implausible, inaccurate, inconstant, irresponsible, makeshift, meretricious, mistaken, pretended, pseudo*, questionable, sham, shifty, specious, treacherous, tricky, uncertain, unconvincing, undependable, underhand, underhanded, unfaithful, unsound, unstable, unsure, untrue, untrustworthy, vacillating, wavering, weak; SEE CONCEPTS 542,552,587

unresolved [adj] *uncertain; not settled*
betwixt and between*, changing, doubtful, faltering, hesitant, hesitating, hot and cold*, incomplete, indecisive, irresolute, moot, open to question*, pending, problematical, pussyfooting*, unanswered, unconcluded, undecided, undetermined, unfinished, unsettled, unsolved, up in the air*, vacillating, vague, waffling; SEE CONCEPTS 529,534

unrest [n] *state of agitation; disturbance*
altercation, anarchy, annoyance, anxiety, bickering, bother, chagrin, change, confusion, contention, controversy, crisis, debate, disaffection, discontent, discord, disease, disquiet, dissatisfaction, dissension, distress, dither*, ennui, grief, insurrection, irritation, malaise, moodiness, mortification, perplexity, perturbation, protest, quarrel, rebellion, restlessness, sedition, sorrow, strife, tension, tizzy*, trouble, tumult, turmoil, unease, uneasiness, uproar, upset, vexation, worry; SEE CONCEPTS 410,674

unruly [adj] *disobedient*
assertive, bawdy, disorderly, drunken, forward, fractious, headstrong, heedless, impervious, impetuous, imprudent, impulsive, incorrigible, inexorable, insubordinate, intemperate, intractable, lawless, mean, mutinous, obstreperous, opinionated, ornery, out of control, out of line*, perverse, quarrelsome, rash, rebellious, recalcitrant, reckless, refractory, restive, riotous, rowdy, turbulent, uncontrollable, ungovernable, unmanageable, unyielding, violent, wayward, wild, willful; SEE CONCEPT 401

unsafe [adj] *dangerous*
alarming, chancy, erratic, explosive, fearsome, hanging by a thread*, hazardous, insecure, on a limb*, on thin ice*, perilous, precarious, risky, shaky, slippery, threatening, ticklish*, touch and go*, touchy*, treacherous, uncertain, undependable, unreliable, unsound, unstable, untrustworthy; SEE CONCEPT 587

unsaid [adj] *not expressed or partially expressed*
implicit, implied, inferred, left to the imagination*, silenced, tacit, undeclared, understood, unexpressed, unspoken, unstated, unuttered, unvoiced, wordless; SEE CONCEPT 267

unsatisfactory [adj] *insufficient, inadequate*
amiss, bad, damaged, deficient, disappointing, disconcerting, displeasing, disquieting, distressing, disturbing, for the birds*, junky*, lame, mediocre, no good, not good enough, not up to par*, offensive, poor, regrettable, rotten, schlocky*, second, thin, unacceptable, undesirable, unsuitable, unwelcome, unworthy, upsetting, vexing, weak, wrong; SEE CONCEPTS 529,558,570

unsavory [adj] *revolting, sickening*
acid, bitter, bland, disagreeable, distasteful, dull, flavorless, gross*, icky*, insipid, lousy, nasty, nauseating, no good*, objectionable, obnoxious, offensive, rancid, rank, raunchy*, repellent, repugnant, repulsive, rough, sad, shady, sharp, shifty, sour, stinking, tart, tasteless, tough, unappetizing, unpalatable, unpleasant, wrong; SEE CONCEPTS 462,571,613

unscathed [adj] *not hurt*
in one piece*, safe, sound, unharmed, unhurt, uninjured, unmarked, unscarred, unscratched, untouched, whole; SEE CONCEPT 314

unscrupulous [adj] *immoral*
arrant, base, casuistic, conscienceless, corrupt, crafty, crooked, deceitful, degraded, degrading, disgraceful, dishonest, dishonorable, exploitative, illegal, improper, low-down*, mercenary, perfidious, petty, questionable, recreant, ruthless, scandalous, scheming, selfish, self-seeking, shady, shameless, shifty, sinister, slippery, sly, two-faced*, unconscientious, unconscionable, underhand, underhanded, unethical, unfair, unprincipled, unworthy, venal, wicked, wrongful; SEE CONCEPTS 401,545

unseemly [adj] *improper; in bad taste*
cheap, coarse, crude, discreditable, disreputable, inappropriate, inapt, incorrect, indecent, indecorous, indelicate, inelegant, inept, in poor taste, malapropos, malodorous, out of keeping, out of place, poor, raffish, rough, rowdy, rude, ruffian, tawdry, unapt, unbecoming, unbefitting, undignified, ungodly, unrefined, unsuitable, untoward, vulgar, wrong; SEE CONCEPTS 401,558

unseen [adj] *hidden*
concealed, curtained, dark, imaginary, imagined,

impalpable, impenetrable, imperceptible, inconspicuous, invisible, lurking, not in sight, obscure, occult, out of sight, shrouded, undetected, undiscovered, unnoticed, unobserved, unobtrusive, unperceived, unsuspected, veiled; SEE CONCEPT *576*

unselfish [*adj*] *kind, giving*
altruistic, benevolent, charitable, chivalrous, denying, devoted, disinterested, extroverted, generous, helpful, humanitarian, incorruptible, indulgent, liberal, loving, magnanimous, noble, open-handed, self-effacing, self-forgetting, selfless, self-sacrificing; SEE CONCEPTS *401,404*

unsettle [*v*] *bother, upset*
agitate, confuse, dement, derange, disarrange, disarray, discommode, discompose, disconcert, disorder, disorganize, displace, disquiet, disrupt, disturb, down, flurry, fluster, fuddle, get to*, jumble, needle, perturb, psych out*, put off, rattle, ruffle, rummage, sicken, spook, throw, throw off*, trouble, turn, unbalance, unhinge*, unnerve; SEE CONCEPTS *7,19,242*

unsettled [*adj1*] *bothered, upset*
active, agitated, antsy*, anxious, busy, changeable, changeful, changing, complex, complicated, confused, disorderly, disturbed, explosive, fidgety, fluid, flustered, inconstant, insecure, kinetic, mobile, mutable, on edge*, perilous, perturbed, precarious, rattled, restive, restless, shaken, shaky, shifting, shook up*, tense, thrown, ticklish, troubled, unbalanced, uncertain, uneasy, unnerved, unpeaceful, unpredictable, unquiet, unrestful, unstable, unsteady, variable, wavering, wobbling; SEE CONCEPTS *401,403*

unsettled [*adj2*] *not decided, taken care of*
betwixt and between*, clouded*, debatable, doubtful, dubious, dubitable, due, immature, in arrears, moot, open, outstanding, overdue, owing, payable, pendent, pending, problematic, uncertain, unclear, undecided, undetermined, unfixed, unpaid, unresolved, up for grabs*, waffling; SEE CONCEPTS *334,535*

unsightly [*adj*] *not pretty*
deformed, disagreeable, drab, dull, hideous, homely, horrid, lackluster, repulsive, revolting, ugly, unattractive, unpleasant, unprepossessing, unshapely; SEE CONCEPT *579*

unsociable [*adj*] *unfriendly*
aloof, antagonistic, brooding, cold, cool, distant, easy-going, hostile, inaccessible, inhospitable, introverted, laid-back*, nongregarious, recessive, reclusive, reserved, retiring, secretive, sensitive, shy, standoffish*, stuck-up*, timid, unapproachable, unbending, uncommunicative, uncongenial, unforthcoming, unneighborly, unsocial, uppity*, withdrawn; SEE CONCEPTS *401,555*

unsolicited [*adj*] *unasked for*
free, freewilled, gratis*, gratuitous, offered, spontaneous, uncalled-for*, undesirable, undesired, unforced, uninvited, unrequested, unsought, unwelcome, voluntary, volunteered; SEE CONCEPT *538*

unsophisticated [*adj*] *natural, simple*
artless, authentic, bush-league*, callow, childlike, clean, cornball*, corny*, crude, folksy, genuine, green*, guileless, homey*, inexperienced, ingenuous, innocent, kid*, naive, plain, pure, raw, rookie, straightforward, unadulterated, unaffected, unartificial, uncomplicated, uninvolved,

unrefined, unschooled, unstudied, untutored, unworldly, wide-eyed*; SEE CONCEPTS *401,548, 562*

unsound [*adj*] *not well; flimsy*
ailing, crazed, dangerous, decrepit, defective, delicate, demented, deranged, diseased, erroneous, fallacious, false, faulty, flawed, fragile, frail, ill, illogical, inaccurate, incongruous, incorrect, infirm, in poor health, insane, insecure, insubstantial, invalid, lunatic, mad, not solid, rickety, shaky, specious, tottering, unbacked, unbalanced, unhealthy, unhinged, unreliable, unsafe, unstable, unsteady, unsubstantial, unwell, weak, wobbly; SEE CONCEPTS *314,403,587*

unspeakable [*adj*] *very bad; beyond description*
abominable, alarming, appalling, atrocious, awful, beastly, beyond words, calamitous, detestable, dire, disgusting, dreadful, evil, execrable, fearful, frightening, frightful, heinous, horrible, horrid, incommunicable, inconceivable, indefinable, indescribable, ineffable, inexpressible, inhuman, loathsome, monstrous, nameless, obnoxious, odious, offensive, outrageous, overwhelming, preternatural, repellent, repugnant, repulsive, revolting, shocking, unbelievable, unimaginable, unutterable; SEE CONCEPTS *548,571*

unstable/unsteady [*adj*] *doubtful, weak*
ambiguous, borderline, capricious, changeable, dizzy, dubious, erratic, fickle, fitful, fluctuating, giddy, inconsistent, inconstant, insecure, irrational, lubricious, mercurial, mobile, movable, moving, mutable, not fixed, precarious, rickety, risky, rocky, sensitive, shaky, shifty, slippery, suspect, teetering, temperamental, ticklish, tricky, uncertain, unpredictable, unsettled, unsteady, untrustworthy, vacillating, variable, volatile, wavering, weaving, wiggly, wobbly; SEE CONCEPTS *488,534,542*

unsuitable [*adj*] *not proper, inappropriate*
clashing, disagreeable, discordant, discrepant, disparate, disproportionate, dissident, dissonant, ill-suited, improper, inadequate, inadmissible, inapposite, inappropriate, inapt, incompatible, incongruous, inconsistent, ineligible, infelicitous, inharmonious, interfering, irrelevant, jarring, malapropos, out of character*, out of keeping, out of place, senseless, unacceptable, unbecoming, unbefitting, uncalled-for, undue, unfit, unfitting, unmatched, unseasonable, unseemly, unsuited; SEE CONCEPT *558*

unsure [*adj*] *doubtful, insecure*
betwixt and between*, borderline, distrustful, dubious, fluctuant, fly-by-night*, hesitant, iffy*, in a quandary, indecisive, indeterminate, irresolute, lacking, mistrustful, open, problematic, rootless, shaky, skeptical, suspicious, touch and go*, unassured, uncertain, unclear, unconfident, unconvinced, undecided, undependable, unreliable, unstable, untrustworthy, untrusty, up for grabs*, vacillating, wavering, weak, wimpy*, wobbly; SEE CONCEPT *535*

unsuspecting [*adj*] *gullible*
confiding, credulous, easy, inexperienced, ingenuous, innocent, naive, off guard*, simple, swallowing, taken in*, trustful, trusting, unconscious, undoubting, unsuspicious, unwarned, unwary; SEE CONCEPTS *401,404*

unsympathetic [*adj*] *without agreement in feeling*
aloof, antipathetic, apathetic, aversive, callous,

cold, cold-blooded, cool, cruel, disinterested, frigid, halfhearted, hard, harsh, heartless, icy, indifferent, insensitive, lukewarm*, mean, nasty, obdurate, repellent, repugnant, stony, tough, uncompassionate, unconcerned, uncongenial, unemotional, unfeeling, unkind, unmoved, unpitying, unpleasant, unresponsive; SEE CONCEPTS 401,542

untangle [v] straighten out
clear up, disembroil, disencumber, disentangle, explain, extricate, put in order, solve, unravel, unscramble, unsnarl, untwist, unweave; SEE CONCEPT 126

unthinkable [adj] incredible, unusual
absurd, beyond belief, beyond possibility, exceptional, extraordinary, illogical, implausible, impossible, improbable, incogitable, inconceivable, insupportable, outlandish, out of the question*, preposterous, rare, singular, unbelievable, uncommon, unimaginable, unique, unlikely, unordinary, unreasonable; SEE CONCEPTS 564,582

unthinking [adj] careless
blundering, brutish, feckless, foolish, heedless, impulsive, inadvertent, inconsiderate, indelicate, insensitive, instinctive, mechanical, napping, negligent, oblivious, outrageous, rash, rude, selfish, senseless, tactless, thoughtless, uncaring, unconscious, undiplomatic, unknowing, unintended, unmeant, unmindful, unpremeditated, unreasoning, untactful, unwise, vacant, witless; SEE CONCEPT 401

untidy [adj] dirty, disorderly
bedraggled, careless, chaotic, cluttered, disarranged, disarrayed, disheveled, dowdy*, frowzy*, in disorder, jumbled, littered, mess, messy, mixed up*, muddled, rumpled, slapdash*, slipshod*, sloppy, slovenly, snarled, tacky*, tangled, topsy-turvy, tousled, uncombed, unfastidious, unkempt, unneat, unorderly, unsettled, upset; SEE CONCEPTS 589,621

until [prep] just before
as far as, before, before the coming, continuously, down to, in advance of, in expectation, prior to, till, to, up till, up to; SEE CONCEPT 820

untimely [adj] inappropriate
a bit previous*, abortive, anachronistic, awkward, badly timed, bright and early*, disagreeable, early, early bird*, early on, ill-timed, improper, inappropriate, inauspicious, inconvenient, inexpedient, inopportune, intrusive, malapropos, mistimed, out-of-date, overearly, oversoon, premature, previous, soon, too early, too late, undue, unfavorable, unfit, unfortunate, unlucky, unpropitious, unseasonable, unseemly, unsuitable, unsuited, wrong; SEE CONCEPTS 548,799

untiring [adj] determined, persevering
constant, continued, continuing, dedicated, devoted, dogged, eager beaver*, fireball*, firm, go-go*, grind*, hyper*, incessant, indefatigable, indomitable, inexhaustible, jumping, patient, perky, persistent, pertinacious, plodding, plugging, resolute, staunch, steady, strong, tenacious, tireless, unceasing, undeterred, unfailing, unfaltering, unflagging, unflinching, unremitting, unstinted, unswerving, unwavering, unwearied; SEE CONCEPT 538

untold [adj] very many; enormous
beyond measure, countless, gigantic, hidden, huge, immense, incalculable, indescribable, inexpressible, innumerable, innumerous, mammoth,

manifold, many, measureless, mighty, monstrous, multiple, multitudinous, myriad, numberless, private, prodigious, staggering, suppressed, titanic, uncountable, uncounted, undreamed of, unexpressed, unimaginable, unknown, unnumberable, unnumbered, unspeakable, unthinkable, vast; SEE CONCEPTS 529,762,781

untouched [adj] whole; not spoiled
clear, entire, flawless, fresh, good, immaculate, incorrupt, indifferent, in good condition, intact, out of danger, perfect, pure, safe and sound*, sanitary, secure, shipshape, sound, spotless, unaffected, unblemished, unbroken, unconcerned, undamaged, unharmed, unhurt, unimpressed, uninjured, unmarred, unmoved, unscathed, unstained, unstirred, untried, virgin, virginal, without a scratch; SEE CONCEPTS 403,485,621

untoward [adj1] troublesome
adverse, annoying, awkward, contrary, disastrous, disturbing, fractious, hapless, ill-starred, inauspicious, inconvenient, indocile, inimical, inopportune, intractable, irritating, luckless, misfortunate, perverse, recalcitrant, refractory, starcrossed, undisciplined, unfavorable, unfortunate, ungovernable, unhappy, unlucky, unmanageable, unpliable, unpropitious, unruly, untimely, unyielding, vexatious, wild; SEE CONCEPTS 542,548,570

untoward [adj2] improper; not suitable
improprietous, inappropriate, indecent, indecorous, indelicate, malodorous, out of place*, rough*, unbecoming, uncouth, unfitting, ungodly*, unseemly; SEE CONCEPTS 401,558

untroubled [adj] calm, peaceful
composed, cool, halcyon, hushed, placid, quiet, serene, steady, still, tranquil, unagitated, unconcerned, undisturbed, unflappable, unflustered, unperturbed, unruffled, unstirred, unworried; SEE CONCEPTS 403,548,594

untrue [adj] dishonest
apocryphal, cheating, counterfactual, deceitful, deceptive, delusive, deviant, disloyal, dissembling, distorted, erroneous, faithless, fallacious, false, fictitious, forsworn, hollow, imprecise, inaccurate, inconstant, incorrect, inexact, lying, meretricious, misleading, mistaken, off*, out of line*, perfidious, perjured, prevaricating, recreant, sham*, specious, spurious, traitorous, treacherous, two-faced*, unfaithful, unloyal, unsound, untrustworthy, untruthful, wide, wrong; SEE CONCEPTS 267,545,582

untrustworthy [adj] not dependable, unfaithful
capricious, conniving, crooked, deceitful, devious, dishonest, disloyal, dubious, fair-weather*, faithless, false, fickle, fink*, fly-by-night*, guileful, irresponsible, questionable, shady, sharp, shifty*, slippery, sneaky, treacherous, tricky, trustless, two-faced*, two-timing*, unassured, undependable, unfaithful, unreliable, unsafe, unsure, untrue, untrusty; SEE CONCEPTS 401,542,545

unusual [adj] different
abnormal, amazing, astonishing, atypical, awe-inspiring, awesome, bizarre, conspicuous, curious, different, distinguished, eminent, exceptional, extraordinary, far-out*, inconceivable, incredible, memorable, noteworthy, odd, out of the ordinary*, outstanding, phenomenal, prodigious, prominent, queer, rare, refreshing, remarkable, significant, singular, something else*,

special, strange, surprising, uncommon, unconventional, unexpected, unfamiliar, unique, unparalleled, unwonted, weird*; SEE CONCEPT 564

unusually [adv] *extremely*
almighty*, awful*, awfully, curiously, especially, extra, extraordinarily, mighty, oddly, peculiarly, plenty, powerful, rarely, real, really, remarkably, right, so, so much, strangely, surprisingly, terribly, terrifically, too much, uncommon, uncommonly, very; SEE CONCEPTS 544,569

unvarnished [adj] *plain, honest*
bare, candid, clean, folksy*, for real*, frank, genuine, homey*, naked, open, open and shut*, pure, pure and simple*, simple, sincere, stark, straight, straightforward, unadorned, unconcealed, undisguised, undissembled, unembellished, vanilla*; SEE CONCEPTS 267,582

unveil [v] *reveal*
bare, betray, bring to light*, come out, disclose, discover, display, divulge, expose, give away, lay bare*, lay open*, let it all hang out*, make known, make public, open, open up, show, spring, tell, tip one's hand*, unbosom, uncover; SEE CONCEPTS 60,138

unwarranted [adj] *not reasonable or right*
baseless, bottomless, foundationless, gratuitous, groundless, indefensible, inexcusable, uncalledfor, unconscionable, undue, unfair, unfounded, ungrounded, unjust, unjustifiable, unjustified, unprovoked, unreasonable, unwarrantable, wrong; SEE CONCEPTS 545,548,558

unwary [adj] *thoughtless, heedless*
brash, careless, credulous, hasty, ignorant, illadvised, impetuous, imprudent, incautious, inconsiderate, indiscreet, negligent, rash, reckless, unadvised, unalert, uncircumspect, unguarded, unprepared, unsuspecting, unsuspicious, unvigilant, unwatchful; SEE CONCEPTS 401,403

unwavering [adj] *consistent, unchanging*
abiding, brick-wall*, dead set on*, dedicated, determined, enduring, firm, fixed, intense, neverfailing, pat, regular, resolute, set, set in stone*, single-minded, solid, staunch, steadfast, steady, sure, undeviating, unfaltering, unflagging, unflappable, unqualified, unshakable, unshaken, unswerving, untiring; SEE CONCEPTS 488,535,542

unwelcome [adj] *not wanted, desired*
blackballed*, disagreeable, displeasing, distasteful, exceptionable, excess baggage*, excluded, ill-favored, inadmissible, left out in cold*, lousy, not in the picture*, objectionable, obnoxious, rejected, repellent, shut out, thankless, unacceptable, unasked, undesirable, uninvited, unpleasant, unpopular, unsought, unwanted, unwished-for; SEE CONCEPTS 529,555,570

unwieldy [adj] *awkward, bulky*
burdensome, clumsy, cumbersome, cumbrous, encumbering, gross, hefty, inconvenient, lumbering, massive, onerous, ponderous, uncontrollable, ungainly, unhandy, unmanageable, weighty; SEE CONCEPTS 562,781

unwilling [adj] *not in the mood*
afraid, against, against the grain*, averse, backward, begrudging, compelled, contrary, demurring, disinclined, disobliging, evasive, forced, grudging, hesitating, indisposed, indocile, involuntary, laggard, loath, malcontent, opposed, recalcitrant, refractory, reluctant, remiss, resistant, shrinking, shy, slack, slow, unaccommodating, uncheerful, uncooperative, uneager, unenthusias-

tic, uninclined, unobliging, unready, unwishful, wayward; SEE CONCEPTS 401,542

unwind [v1] *undo, untangle*
disentangle, free, loose, loosen, ravel, separate, slacken, unbend, uncoil, unfurl, unravel, unreel, unroll, untwine, untwist, unwrap; SEE CONCEPT 158

unwind [v2] *relax*
calm down*, ease off*, loosen up*, quiet down*, quieten, recline, rest, sit back*, slow down*, take a break*, take it easy*, wind down*; SEE CONCEPT 210

unwise [adj] *stupid, irresponsible*
childish, foolhardy, foolish, ill-advised, illconsidered, immature, impolitic, improvident, imprudent, inadvisable, inane, inappropriate, indiscreet, inept, injudicious, misguided, naive, rash, reckless, senseless, short-sighted, silly, thoughtless, undesirable, unfortunate, unintelligent, unsound, witless; SEE CONCEPTS 401, 402,548

unwitting [adj] *without fully realizing*
accidental, aimless, chance, comatose, forgetful, haphazard, ignorant, inadvertent, incognizant, inconversant, innocent, involuntary, numb, oblivious, senseless, unacquainted, unaware, unconscious, undesigned, unfamiliar, uninformed, uninstructed, unintended, unintentional, unknowing, unmeant, unmindful, unplanned, unsuspecting, unthinking; SEE CONCEPTS 401, 544,548

unworldly [adj1] *spiritual*
abstract, astral, celestial, daydreaming, daydreamy, dreamy, ethereal, extraterrestrial, fantastic, incorporeal, metaphysical, nonmaterialistic, otherworldly, religious, supersensory, transcendental, unearthly, unreal, visionary; SEE CONCEPTS 536,582

unworldly [adj2] *not sophisticated; inexperienced*
artless, babe in woods*, clean, corn-fed*, country, folksy*, green*, idealistic, ingenuous, innocent, naive, natural, raw*, simple, trusting, unaffected, unartificial, uncool, unschooled, unsophisticated, unstudied, wide-eyed*; SEE CONCEPTS 401,555,589

unworthy [adj] *not of value*
base, beneath, blamable, contemptible, degrading, disgraceful, dishonorable, disreputable, good-for-nothing, ignoble, improper, inappropriate, ineligible, inexcusable, no-account*, nogood*, not deserving, not fit, not good enough, nothing, not worth, offensive, out of place*, recreant, reprehensible, shameful, unbecoming, unbefitting, undeserving, unfit, unmerited, unseemly, unsuitable, valueless, vile, wretched, wrong; SEE CONCEPTS 404,558,571

unwritten [adj] *understood*
accepted, conventional, customary, oral, spoken, tacit, traditional, unformulated, unrecorded, unsaid, verbal, vocal, word-of-mouth; SEE CONCEPTS 267,533

unyielding [adj] *steadfast, resolute*
adamant, dead set on*, determined, firm, fixed, hard, hard-core*, hardheaded, hard-line*, hardnosed*, headstrong*, immalleable, immovable, implacable, impliable, inexorable, inflexible, intractable, locked in, merciless, mulish, obdurate, obstinate, pertinacious, pigheaded*, refractory, relentless, resolute, rigid, ruthless, single-minded, solid, staunch, stiff, stiff-necked, stubborn, tough,

unbending, uncompliant, uncompromising, unmovable, unrelenting, unswayable, unwavering; SEE CONCEPTS *401,542*

upbeat [*adj*] *cheerful*
buoyant, cheery, encouraging, favorable, fond, happy, heartening, hopeful, optimistic, positive, promising, rosy, sanguine; SEE CONCEPTS *403,572*

update [*v*] *bring up to date*
amend, modernize, refresh, refurbish, rejuvenate, renew, renovate, restore, revise; SEE CONCEPT *244*

upheaval [*n*] *major change*
about-face*, alteration, cataclysm, catastrophe, clamor, commotion, convulsion, disaster, disorder, disruption, disturbance, eruption, explosion, ferment, flip-flop*, new ball-game*, new deal*, outbreak, outburst, outcry, overthrow, revolution, shakeout*, stirring, switch, temblor, tremor, tumult, turmoil, turnaround, upturn; SEE CONCEPT *230*

uphill [*adj1*] *going up*
acclivous, ascending, climbing, mounting, rising, skyward, sloping upward, toward summit, up, uprising; SEE CONCEPT *581*

uphill [*adj2*] *difficult, laborious*
arduous, effortful, exhausting, grueling, hard, labored, operose, punishing, rugged, strenuous, taxing, toilsome, tough, wearisome; SEE CONCEPTS *538,565*

uphold [*v*] *maintain, support*
advocate, aid, assist, back, back up, bolster, boost, brace, buoy up, buttress, carry, champion, confirm, countenance, defend, elevate, encourage, endorse, help, hoist, hold to, hold up one's end*, justify, pick up, promote, prop, raise, rear, second, shore up, side with, stand by, stick by, stick up for*, sustain, take up, upbear, uplift, upraise, uprear, vindicate; SEE CONCEPT *110*

upkeep [*n*] *maintenance*
budget, conservation, costs, expenditure, expenses, keep, outlay, overhead, preservation, price, repair, running, subsistence, support, sustenance, sustentation; SEE CONCEPTS *117,344*

upper [*adj1*] *above*
high, higher, loftier, more elevated, overhead, top, topmost, uppermost, upward; SEE CONCEPT *583*

upper [*adj2*] *superior*
beautiful, elevated, elite, eminent, greater, important, more important; SEE CONCEPTS *555,567*

uppermost [*adj1*] *top*
apical, culminating, highest, loftiest, most elevated, topmost, upmost; SEE CONCEPT *583*

uppermost [*adj2*] *most important; chief*
best, big, boss, dominant, executive, foremost, greatest, high-up*, leading, main, paramount, predominant, preeminent, primary, principal, supreme, the most*, tops*, winner, world-class*; SEE CONCEPTS *568,632*

upright [*adj1*] *straight-up*
cocked, end on, end up, erect, on end, perpendicular, plumb, raised, sheer, standing, stand-up, steep, straight, upended, upstanding, upward, vertical; SEE CONCEPTS *581,583*

upright [*adj2*] *honorable, honest*
aboveboard, blameless, circumspect, conscientious, correct, equitable, ethical, exemplary, fair, faithful, good, high-minded, impartial, incorruptible, just, kosher*, legit*, moral, noble, principled, punctilious, pure, right, righteous, square, straight, straightforward, true, true-blue*, trustworthy, unimpeachable, up front*, virtuous; SEE CONCEPTS *404,545*

uprising [*n*] *disturbance*
insurgence, insurrection, mutiny, outbreak, rebellion, revolt, revolution, riot, upheaval; SEE CONCEPTS *106,674*

uproar [*n*] *commotion, pandemonium*
ado, babble, babel, bedlam, bickering, big scene*, brawl, broil*, bustle, chaos, clamor, clangor, clatter, confusion, din, disorder, flap*, fracas*, free-for-all*, furor, fuss, hassle, jangle, mayhem, melee, noise, outcry, racket, riot, roughhouse*, row, ruction, shivaree*, stink*, stir, strife, to-do*, tumult, turmoil, violence; SEE CONCEPTS *46,65,106,674*

uproot [*v*] *destroy; rip out of a place*
abate, abolish, annihilate, blot out, demolish, deracinate, dig up, displace, do away with*, eliminate, eradicate, excavate, exile, exterminate, extirpate, extract, move, overthrow, overturn, pull up, remove, root out, tear up, weed, weed out, wipe out; SEE CONCEPTS *147,178,211,252*

upset [*n*] *problem*
agitation, bother, complaint, defeat, destruction, disorder, disquiet, distress, disturbance, free-for-all*, goulash*, hassle, illness, malady, overthrow, queasiness, reverse, reversion, screw-up*, shake-up*, shock, sickness, stew*, subversion, surprise, tizzy*, trouble, turmoil, worry; SEE CONCEPT *674*

upset [*adj*] *disturbed, bothered*
agitated, all torn up*, amazed, antsy*, apprehensive, blue*, broken up*, bummed out*, capsized, chaotic, come apart*, confused, disconcerted, dismayed, disordered, disquieted, distressed, disturbed, dragged*, frantic, grieved, hurt, ill, in disarray, jittery, jumpy, low, muddled, overturned, overwrought, psyched out*, rattled, ruffled*, shocked, shook up*, sick, spilled, thrown, tipped over, toppled, troubled, tumbled, unglued*, unsettled, unzipped*, upside-down, worried; SEE CONCEPTS *403,485,570*

upset [*v1*] *disorder; knock over*
capsize, change, derange, disarray, disorganize, disturb, invert, jumble, keel over, mess up*, mix up, muddle, overset, overturn, pitch, put out of order, reverse, rummage, spill, spoil, subvert, tilt, tip over, topple, tumble, turn, turn inside-out*, turn topsy-turvy*, turn upside-down*, unsettle, upend, upturn; SEE CONCEPTS *147,208,213*

upset [*v2*] *bother, trouble*
adjy*, afflict, agitate, ail, bewilder, bug*, confound, cramp, craze, debilitate, derange, discombobulate*, discompose, disconcert, dismay, disquiet, distract, distress, disturb, egg on*, fire up*, flip*, flip out*, floor*, flurry, fluster, get to*, give a hard time*, grieve, incapacitate, indispose, key up*, lay up, make a scene*, make waves*, perturb, pick on*, pother, psych*, rattle, rock the boat*, ruffle, sicken, spook, stir up, throw off balance*, turn, turn on, unhinge*, unnerve, unsettle; SEE CONCEPTS *7,19*

upset [*v3*] *defeat*
beat, be victorious, conquer, get the better of*, outplay, overcome, overpower, overthrow, overturn, topple, triumph over, win; SEE CONCEPT *95*

upshot [*n*] *end result*
aftereffect, aftermath, burden, climax, completion, conclusion, consequence, core, culmination,

un
up

denouement, development, effect, end, ending, event, eventuality, finale, finish, gist, issue, meaning, meat*, outcome, payoff, pith*, purport, result, sense, sequel, substance, termination, thrust; SEE CONCEPTS 230,682

upside-down [adj] overturned, inverted
backward, bottom-side up, bottom up, confused, disordered, downside-up*, haywire*, helter-skelter*, in chaos, in disarray, jumbled, mixed-up, on head, reversed, tangled, topsy-turvy*, upended, wrong-side-up, wrong way; SEE CONCEPT 583

upstanding [adj] honorable
ethical, good, honest, incorruptible, moral, principled, straightforward, true, trustworthy, upright; SEE CONCEPT 545

uptight [adj] nervous
anxious, apprehensive, cautious, concerned, conventional, edgy, nervy, old-fashioned, on edge*, on the defensive*, restive, strict, tense, troubled, uneasy, withdrawn, worried; SEE CONCEPT 401

up-to-date [adj] current, modern
abreast, advanced, à la mode*, all the rage*, au courant, avant-garde, brand-new, contemporary, cutting edge*, dashing, expedient, faddish*, fashionable, fitting, hot*, in, in fashion, in-thing*, in vogue, modernistic, modish, neoteric, new, newest, newfangled, now*, opportune, popular, red-hot*, state-of-the-art*, stylish, suitable, timely, today*, trendy, up*, up-to-the-minute, with it*; SEE CONCEPTS 578,589,797,799

urban [adj] city
burghal, central, citified, civic, civil, downtown, inner-city, metropolitan, municipal, nonrural, oppidan, popular, public, town, village; SEE CONCEPT 536

urbane [adj] civilized
affable, balanced, bland, civil, cosmopolitan, courteous, cultivated, cultured, debonair, elegant, genteel, gracious, mannerly, metropolitan, obliging, poised, polished, polite, refined, smooth, sophisticated, suave, well-bred, well-mannered; SEE CONCEPT 401

urchin [n] mischievous youngster
brat*, cub, dickens*, gamin, imp, juvenile delinquent, punk*, pup*, ragamuffin, waif; SEE CONCEPT 423

urge [n] very strong desire
appetite, appetition, compulsion, craving, drive, druthers, fancy, fire in belly*, goad, impetus, impulse, incentive, itch*, longing, lust, motive, passion, pressure, stimulant, stimulus, sweet tooth*, weakness, wish, yearning, yen; SEE CONCEPTS 20,532

urge [v] beg, push for, encourage
adjure, advance, advise, advocate, appeal to, ask, attract, beseech, champion, charge, commend, compel, conjure, counsel, countenance, drive, egg on*, endorse, entreat, exhort, favor, fire up*, force, further, goad, hasten, impel, implore, incite, induce, influence, insist on, inspire, instigate, maneuver, move, plead, press, promote, prompt, propel, propose, push, put up to*, rationalize, recommend, request, sanction, solicit, speak for, spur, stimulate, support, tempt, wheedle; SEE CONCEPTS 68,75

urgent [adj] needing immediate attention
burning*, called-for, capital, chief, clamant, clamorous, compelling, critical, crucial, crying*, demanded, demanding, driving, essential, exigent, foremost, heavy*, hurry-up, immediate, impelling, imperative, important, importunate, indispensable, insistent, instant, leading, life and death*, momentous, necessary, paramount, persuasive, pressing, primary, principal, required, salient, serious, top-priority, touch and go*, touchy*, vital, wanted, weighty*; SEE CONCEPTS 548,568

usable [adj] available, working
accessible, adaptable, advantageous, applicable, at disposal, at hand, beneficial, consumable, convenient, current, employable, exhaustible, expendable, exploitable, fit, functional, good, helpful, in order, instrumental, open, operative, practicable, practical, profitable, ready, running, serviceable, subservient, unused, useful, utile, utilizable, valid, valuable, wieldy; SEE CONCEPTS 560,576

usage [n] habit, custom
acceptance, control, convention, currency, form, formula, habitude, handling, management, matter of course, method, mode, operation, practice, praxis, procedure, regime, regulation, rote, routine, rule, running, tradition, treatment, trick, use, way, wont; SEE CONCEPTS 6,658

use [n] application; employment
account, adoption, advantage, appliance, applicability, appropriateness, avail, benefit, call, capitalization, cause, convenience, custom, end, exercise, exercising, exertion, fitness, good, habit, handling, help, helpfulness, mileage, mobilization, necessity, need, object, occasion, operation, point, practice, profit, purpose, reason, relevance, service, serviceability, treatment, usability, usage, usefulness, utility, value, way, wear and tear*, wont, worth; SEE CONCEPTS 225,658,709

use [v] work with; consume
accept, adopt, apply, avail oneself of, bestow, bring into play*, bring to bear*, capitalize, control, do with, draw on, employ, exercise, exert, exhaust, expend, exploit, find a use, govern, handle, make do with*, make the most of*, make use, manage, manipulate, operate, play on, ply, practice, press into service*, put forth*, put into action, put to use, put to work, regulate, relate, run, run through, set in motion, spend, take advantage of*, turn to account, utilize, waste, wield, work; SEE CONCEPTS 169,225

useful [adj] beneficial, valuable
advantageous, all-purpose, applied, appropriate, brave, commodious, convenient, effective, favorable, fit, fruitful, functional, good, handy, helpful, instrumental, meet, of assistance, of service, of use, practicable, practical, pragmatic, profitable, proper, propitious, purposive, salutary, serviceable, subsidiary, suitable, suited, toward, utile, utilitarian, workaday, worthwhile; SEE CONCEPT 560

useless [adj] not working; not valuable
abortive, bootless, counterproductive, disadvantageous, dysfunctional, expendable, feckless, fruitless, futile, good-for-nothing*, hopeless, idle, impracticable, impractical, incompetent, ineffective, ineffectual, inept, inoperative, inutile, meaningless, no good, nonfunctional, of no use, pointless, profitless, purposeless, scrap, stupid*, unavailable, unavailing, unfunctional, unproductive, unprofitable, unpurposed, unusable, un-

workable, vain, valueless, waste, weak, worthless; SEE CONCEPT 560

user-friendly [adj] *easily operated*
accessible, adaptable, convenient, easy to use, feasible, foolproof, handy, manageable, practical, simple, straightforward, uncomplicated, useful, wieldy; SEE CONCEPTS 560,576

usher [n] *person who guides others to place*
attendant, conductor, doorkeeper, doorperson, escort, guide, herald, lead, leader, page, pilot, precursor; SEE CONCEPT 352

usher [v] *guide*
bring in, conduct, direct, escort, herald, inaugurate, initiate, institute, introduce, launch, lead, marshal, open the door, originate, pave the way*, pilot, precede, preface, receive, set up, show around, show in, show out, steer; SEE CONCEPTS 187,221

usual [adj] *common, typical*
accepted, accustomed, average, chronic, commonplace, constant, conventional, current, customary, cut-and-dried*, everyday, expected, familiar, fixed, frequent, garden variety*, general, grind, habitual, mainstream, matter-of-course, natural, normal, ordinary, plain, plastic, prevailing, prevalent, quotidian, regular, rife, routine, run-of-the-mill*, so-so*, standard, stock, typic, unremarkable, vanilla*, white bread*, wonted, workaday; SEE CONCEPTS 530,547

usually [adv] *for the most part*
as a rule, as is the custom, as is usual, as usual, by and large, commonly, consistently, customarily, frequently, generally, habitually, in the main, mainly, more often than not, mostly, most often, normally, now and again, now and then, occasionally, once and again, on the whole, ordinarily, regularly, routinely, sometimes; SEE CONCEPTS 530,541

usurp [v] *take over*
accroach, annex, appropriate, arrogate, assume, barge in*, butt in*, clap hands on*, commandeer, cut out, displace, elbow in*, get hands on*, grab, grab hold of, highjack*, infringe upon, lay hold of, muscle in*, preempt, seize, squeeze in, supplant, swipe, take, work in, worm in*, wrest; SEE CONCEPTS 142,384

utensil [n] *tool, usually for eating*
apparatus, appliance, contrivance, convenience, device, equipment, fork, gadget, implement, instrument, knife, silverware, spoon, tableware, ware; SEE CONCEPTS 493,499

utilitarian [adj] *practical*
commonsensical, down-to-earth, effective, efficient, functional, hard, hardheaded, matter-of-fact, nuts and bolts*, pragmatic, pragmatical, realistic, sensible, serviceable, unidealistic, unromantic, useful; SEE CONCEPT 560

utility [n] *serviceableness*
account, adequacy, advantage, advantageousness, applicability, appropriateness, avail, benefit, convenience, efficacy, efficiency, expediency, favor, fitness, function, point, practicality, productiveness, profit, relevance, service, serviceability, use, usefulness; SEE CONCEPT 658

utilize [v] *make use of*
advance, apply, appropriate, avail oneself of, bestow, employ, exercise, exploit, forward, further, handle, have recourse to, profit by, promote, put to use, resort to, take advantage of, turn to account, use; SEE CONCEPT 225

utmost [adj] *extreme, maximum*
absolute, all-out*, chief, complete, entire, exhaustive, farthest, final, full, furthermost, greatest, highest, last, last straw*, maximal, most, most distant, outermost, out of bounds*, outside, paramount, plenary, preeminent, remotest, sheer, supreme, thorough, thoroughgoing, too much*, too too*, top, topmost, total, ultimate, ultra*, unconditional, undiminished, unlimited, unmitigated, unqualified, unreserved, uttermost, whole, worst case*; SEE CONCEPTS 531,574,772

utopia [n] *ideal place and life*
Arcadia, bliss, dreamland, dreamworld, Eden, Elysian Fields*, Erehwon*, fairyland, Garden of Eden, heaven, land of milk and honey*, never-never land*, paradise, perfection, pie in the sky*, promised land*, seventh heaven*, Shangri-La*, wonderland; SEE CONCEPTS 370,689

utopian [adj] *imaginary, ideal*
abstract, airy, ambitious, arcadian, chimerical, dream, fanciful, fantasy, grandiose, hopeful, idealist, idealistic, ideological, illusory, impossible, impractical, lofty, otherworldly, perfect, pie-in-the-sky*, pretentious, quixotic, romantic, transcendental, unfeasible, visionary; SEE CONCEPTS 572,574,582

utter [adj] *outright, absolute*
all-fired*, arrant, blasted*, blessed*, blooming*, complete, confounded, consummate, downright, entire, flat-out*, infernal, out-and-out*, perfect, pure, sheer, stark, straight-out*, thorough, thoroughgoing, total, unmitigated, unqualified; SEE CONCEPTS 531,535

utter [v] *say, reveal*
affirm, air, announce, articulate, assert, asseverate, blurt, bring out, chime, chin*, come out with*, declaim, declare, deliver, disclose, divulge, ejaculate, enunciate, exclaim, express, give words to*, go, jaw*, lip*, make known, modulate, mouth*, mutter, proclaim, promulgate, pronounce, publish, put into words, recite, say, shout, speak, spiel*, state, talk, throw out, verbalize, vocalize, voice, whisper; SEE CONCEPTS 47,55

utterance [n] *revelation*
announcement, articulation, assertion, asseveration, declaration, delivery, discourse, ejaculation, expression, opinion, oration, peroration, pronouncement, rant, recitation, remark, reply, response, saying, sentence, speaking, speech, spiel, statement, talk, vent, verbalization, vocalization, vociferation, voice, word, words; SEE CONCEPTS 47,278

utterly [adv] *completely*
absolutely, all, all in all, altogether, entirely, exactly, extremely, fully, in toto, just, perfectly, plumb*, purely, quite, thoroughly, totally, to the core*, to the nth degree*, well, wholly; SEE CONCEPT 531

uttermost [adj] *extreme*
farthest, final, furthermost, furthest, last, outermost, outmost, remotest, utmost; SEE CONCEPTS 585,778

V

vacancy [n] *opening*
abstraction, blankness, desertedness, emptiness, gap, job, lack, opportunity, position, post, room,

up
va

situation, space, vacuity, vacuousness, vacuum, void, voidness; SEE CONCEPTS *513,516,693*

vacant [*adj1*] *empty; unoccupied*
abandoned, available, bare, clear, deserted, devoid, disengaged, free, idle, not in use, stark, tenantless, to let, unemployed, unengaged, unfilled, uninhabited, unlived in, untaken, untenanted, unused, void, without contents; SEE CONCEPTS *481,560,740,774*

vacant [*adj2*] *absent-minded; expressionless*
abstracted, blank, daydreaming, deadpan, dreaming, dreamy, empty-headed*, foolish, idle, inane, incurious, inexpressive, silly, stupid, thoughtless, unexpressive, unintelligent, unthinking, vacuous, vapid, witless; SEE CONCEPT *402*

vacate [*v*] *leave empty*
abandon, abrogate, annul, clear, depart, discharge, dissolve, empty, evacuate, give up, go away, leave, move out, move out of, part with, quash, quit, relinquish, renounce, rescind, retract, reverse, revoke, void, withdraw; SEE CONCEPTS *195,234*

vacation [*n*] *planned time spent not working*
break, breathing space*, day of rest, few days off*, fiesta, furlough, holiday, intermission, layoff, leave, leave of absence, liberty, long weekend*, R and R*, recess, recreation, respite, rest, sabbatical, spell, time off, two weeks with pay*; SEE CONCEPTS *363,807*

vaccinate [*v*] *give a shot to treat or prevent disease*
immunize, inject, inoculate, mitigate, prevent, protect, treat, variolate; SEE CONCEPT *310*

vacillate [*v*] *go back and forth*
alternate, be indecisive, be irresolute, change, change mind, dither, fence-straddle*, fluctuate, hedge, hem and haw*, hesitate, hover, oscillate, pause, pussyfoot around*, reel, rock, run hot and cold*, seesaw*, shilly-shally*, stagger, straddle, sway, swing, waffle, waver, whiffle*, yo-yo*; SEE CONCEPT *13*

vacuous [*adj*] *empty; unintelligent*
airheaded*, birdbrained*, blank, drained, dull, dumb, emptied, foolish, half-baked*, inane, lamebrained*, minus*, shallow, silly*, stupid, superficial, uncomprehending, unreasoning, vacant, void; SEE CONCEPT *402*

vacuum [*n*] *emptiness*
exhaustion, free space, gap, nothingness, rarefaction, space, vacuity, void; SEE CONCEPTS *513,740*

vagabond [*n*] *person who leads an unsettled life; traveler*
explorer, gypsy, haji, pathfinder, pilgrim, pioneer, rambler, rover, tourist, trailblazer, trekker, wanderer, wayfarer; SEE CONCEPT *423*

vagabond [*adj*] *unsettled; vagrant*
aimless, destitute, down-and-out*, drifting, errant, fancy-free*, fly-by-night*, footloose*, idle, itinerant, itinerate, journeying, mendicant, migratory, moving, nomadic, perambulant, perambulatory, peripatetic, prodigal, rambling, roaming, rootless, roving, sauntering, shifting, shiftless, straggling, stray, strolling, transient, travelling, unsettled, wandering, wayfaring, wayward; SEE CONCEPT *539*

vagrant [*n*] *person with no permanent home and often with no means of support*
drifter, floater, homeless person, itinerant, rolling stone*, street person, transient, wanderer; SEE CONCEPT *423*

vague [*adj*] *not definite or clear*
ambiguous, amorphous, amphibological, bewildering, bleary, blurred, cloudy, dark, dim, doubtful, dreamlike, dubious, enigmatic, equivocal, faint, fuzzy, generalized, hazy, ill-defined, impalpable, imprecise, indefinite, indeterminate, indistinct, inexplicable, lax, loose, misunderstood, muddy, nebulous, obscure, perplexing, problematic, puzzling, questionable, shadowy, superficial, tenebrous, uncertain, unclear, undetermined, unexplicit, unintelligible, unknown, unsettled, unspecified, unsure; SEE CONCEPTS *267,485,529*

vain [*adj1*] *egotistical*
arrogant, big-headed*, boastful, cocky*, conceited, egocentric, egoistic, haughty, high-and-mighty*, inflated, narcissistic, ostentatious, overweening, pleased with oneself*, proud, puffed up*, self-important, stuck-up*, swaggering*, swollen-headed*, vainglorious; SEE CONCEPTS *401,404*

vain [*adj2*] *futile, useless*
abortive, barren, bootless, delusive, delusory, empty, frivolous, fruitless, going nowhere*, hollow, idle, inefficacious, insignificant, in vicious circle*, misleading, not a prayer*, no-win*, nugatory, on a treadmill*, otiose, paltry, petty, pointless, profitless, puny, senseless, shuck, slight, sterile, time-wasting, trifling, trivial, unavailing, unimportant, unnotable, unproductive, unprofitable, valueless, void, worthless; SEE CONCEPTS *552,575*

valedictory [*adj*] *farewell*
departing, final, goodbye, last, parting, terminal; SEE CONCEPT *267*

valiant [*adj*] *brave*
adventurous, assertive, audacious, bold, brave, chivalrous, courageous, dauntless, fearless, fire-eating*, gallant, game, grand, great, gritty*, gutsy*, gutty*, heroic, high-spirited, indomitable, intrepid, lion-hearted, magnanimous, nervy*, noble, plucky*, powerful, puissant, redoubtable, self-reliant, spunky*, stalwart, steadfast, stout, stouthearted, strong-willed, unafraid, undaunted, undismayed, valorous, venturesome, venturous, vigorous, worthy; SEE CONCEPTS *401,404,538*

valid [*adj*] *right, genuine*
accurate, attested, authentic, authoritative, binding, bona fide, cogent, compelling, conclusive, confirmed, convincing, credible, determinative, efficacious, efficient, good, in force, irrefutable, just, kosher*, lawful, legal, legit*, legitimate, logical, official, original, persuasive, potent, powerful, proven, pure, solid, sound, stringent, strong, substantial, telling, tested, true, trustworthy, ultimate, unadulterated, unanswerable, uncorrupted, weighty, well-founded, well-grounded; SEE CONCEPTS *319,545,582*

validate [*v*] *ascertain the truth, authenticity of something*
approve, authenticate, authorize, bear out, certify, confirm, constitute, corroborate, endorse, give stamp of approval*, give the go-ahead*, give the green light*, give the nod*, John Hancock*, justify, legalize, legitimize, make binding*, make legal*, make stick*, okay*, ratify, rubber-stamp*, sanction, set seal on*, sign off on*, substantiate, verify; SEE CONCEPTS *50,88,317*

validity [*n*] *genuineness, lawfulness*
authority, cogency, effectiveness, efficacy, force, foundation, gravity, grounds, legality, legitimacy,

persuasiveness, point, potency, power, punch, right, soundness, strength, substance, validness, weight; SEE CONCEPTS 645,691,725

valley [n] *hollow in the land*
basin, bottom, canyon, channel, coulee, dale, dell, depression, dingle, glen, gorge, lowland, notch, plain, swale, trough, vale; SEE CONCEPTS 509,513

valor [n] *bravery*
backbone*, boldness, courage, dash*, defiance, derring-do*, determination, fearlessness, fight, firmness, fortitude, gallantry, grit*, guts*, hardihood, heart, heroism, indomitableness, intestinal fortitude*, intrepidity, invincibility, mettle, moxie*, nerve, pluck, prowess, resolution, sand*, spirit, spunk, starch*, stomach*, tenacity, valiance, valiancy; SEE CONCEPTS 411,633

valuable [n] *prized possession*
advantage, antique, asset, benefit, collectible, commodity, heirloom, nugget*, plum*, treasure; SEE CONCEPT 446

valuable [adj] *very important; priceless*
admired, appreciated, beneficial, cherished, collectible, costly, dear, esteemed, estimable, expensive, heirloom, held dear, helpful, high-priced, hot*, hot property*, important, in demand, inestimable, invaluable, of value, precious, prized, profitable, relevant, respected, scarce, serviceable, treasured, useful, valued, worthwhile, worthy; SEE CONCEPTS 334,560,568

value [n1] *financial worth*
amount, appraisal, assessment, charge, cost, equivalent, expense, market price, monetary worth, price, profit, rate; SEE CONCEPTS 335,336

value [n2] *advantage, worth*
account, bearing, benefit, caliber, condition, connotation, consequence, content, denotation, desirability, distinction, drift, eminence, esteem, estimation, excellence, finish, force, goodness, grade, help, implication, import, importance, interpretation, mark, marketability, meaning, merit, power, preference, profit, purpose, quality, regard, repute, sense, serviceableness, significance, state, stature, substance, superiority, use, usefulness, utility, valuation; SEE CONCEPTS 346,658,668,682

valve [n] *on-and-off device*
cock, faucet, flap, gate, hydrant, lid, pipe, plug, shutoff, spigot, stopper, tap; SEE CONCEPTS 445,464,499

vandal [n] *person who defiles property*
defacer, despoiler, destroyer, hoodlum, looter, mischief-maker, pillager, pirate, plunderer, ravager, thief; SEE CONCEPT 412

vanish [v] *disappear*
become invisible, be lost, clear, dematerialize, die, die out, dissolve, evanesce, evaporate, exit, fade, fade away, go away, melt; SEE CONCEPT 105

vanity [n] *conceit, egotism*
affectation, airs, arrogance, big-headedness*, conceitedness, display, ego trip*, narcissism, ostentation, pretension, pride, self-admiration, self-love, self-worship, show*, showing off*, smugness, vainglory; SEE CONCEPT 410

vanquish [v] *defeat soundly*
bear down, beat, conquer, crush, humble, overcome, overpower, overturn, overwhelm, put down, quell, reduce, repress, rout, subdue, subjugate, subvert, surmount, trample, triumph over; SEE CONCEPT 95

vapid [adj] *flat, dull*
bland, boring, colorless, dead*, driveling, flat, flat tire*, flavorless, inane, innocuous, insipid, jejune, least, lifeless, limp, milk-and-water*, milquetoast*, nothing, nowhere, stale, tame, tasteless, tedious, tiresome, unimaginative, uninspiring, uninteresting, unpalatable, vacant, vacuous, watery, weak, wishy-washy*, zero*; SEE CONCEPTS 529,537,575

vapor [n] *fumes, mist*
breath, condensation, dampness, dew, effluvium, exhalation, fog, gas, haze, miasma, moisture, reek, smog, smoke, steam; SEE CONCEPTS 437,524

variable [adj] *changing, changeable*
capricious, changeful, fickle, fitful, flexible, fluctuating, fluid, iffy*, inconstant, irregular, mercurial, mobile, mutable, protean, shifting, shifty, slippery*, spasmodic, temperamental, ticklish, uncertain, unequable, unsettled, unstable, unsteady, vacillating, volatile, waffling, wavering, yo-yo*; SEE CONCEPT 534

variance [n] *difference*
about-face*, argument, change, conflict, contention, deviation, difference of opinion, different strokes*, disaccord, disagreement, discord, discrepancy, dissension, dissent, dissidence, disunity, divergence, diversity, division, flip-flop*, fluctuation, incongruity, inconsistency, midcourse correction*, mutation, separation, severing, strife, sundering, switch, transmogrification, unharmoniousness, variation, variety; SEE CONCEPTS 388,665,697

variant [n] *derived form*
alternative, branch, development, exception, irregularity, modification, result, spinoff, variation, version; SEE CONCEPT 665

variant [adj] *different*
alternative, derived, differing, divergent, exceptional, modified, various, varying; SEE CONCEPT 564

variation [n] *difference; alternative*
aberration, abnormality, adaptation, alteration, bend, break, change, contradistinction, contrast, curve, deflection, departure, departure from the norm*, deviation, digression, discrepancy, disparity, displacement, dissimilarity, dissimilitude, distinction, divergence, diversification, diversity, exception, fluctuation, inequality, innovation, modification, mutation, novelty, shift, swerve, turn, unconformity, variety; SEE CONCEPTS 665,697

varied [adj] *different*
assorted, conglomerate, discrete, diverse, heterogeneous, indiscriminate, miscellaneous, mixed, motley, multifarious, separate, sundry, various; SEE CONCEPT 564

variety [n1] *difference*
array, assortment, change, collection, combo*, conglomeration, cross section, departure, discrepancy, disparateness, divergency, diversification, diversity, fluctuation, heterogeneity, incongruity, intermixture, many-sidedness, medley, mélange, miscellany, mishmash, mixed bag*, mixture, modification, multifariousness, multiplicity, potpourri, range, shift, soup, stew, variance, variation; SEE CONCEPTS 432,665

va
va

variety [n2] *type, sort*
assortment, brand, breed, category, character, class, classification, description, division, family, genus, grade, ilk, kidney, kind, make, nature, order, quality, race, rank, species, strain, stripe, tribe; SEE CONCEPT *378*

various [adj] *miscellaneous, differing*
all manner of*, assorted, changeable, changing, different, discrete, disparate, distinct, distinctive, diverse, diversified, heterogeneous, individual, legion, manifold, many, many-sided, multifarious, multitudinal, multitudinous, numerous, omnifarious, peculiar, populous, separate, several, sundry, unalike, unequal, unlike, variant, varied, variegated; SEE CONCEPTS *564,771*

varnish [v] *add a layer to; embellish*
adorn, coat, cover, decorate, enamel, finish, gild, glaze, gloss, japan, lacquer, luster, paint, polish, shellac, surface, veneer, wash, wax; SEE CONCEPTS *172,177*

vary [v] *change*
alter, alternate, assort, be unlike, blow hot and cold*, convert, depart, deviate, differ, digress, disagree, displace, dissent, divaricate, diverge, diversify, divide, fluctuate, hem and haw*, inflect, interchange, modify, mutate, part, permutate, range, separate, shilly-shally*, swerve, take turns, transform, turn, variegate, yo-yo*; SEE CONCEPT *697*

vast [adj] *very large; wide in range*
all-inclusive, ample, astronomical, big, boundless, broad, capacious, colossal, comprehensive, detailed, endless, enormous, eternal, expanded, extensive, far-flung, far-reaching, forever, giant, gigantic, great, huge, illimitable, immeasurable, immense, infinite, limitless, mammoth, massive, measureless, monstrous, monumental, never-ending, prodigious, prolonged, spacious, spread-out, stretched-out, sweeping, titanic, tremendous, unbounded, unlimited, voluminous, widespread; SEE CONCEPTS *772,773,781*

vault [n] *depository*
basement, box, can, catacomb, cavern, cellar, crib*, crypt, dungeon, grave, mausoleum, pit, repository, safe, safe-deposit box, sepulcher, strong room, tomb; SEE CONCEPT *494*

vault [v] *jump over; span*
arch, ascend, bend, bounce, bound, bow, clear, curve, hop, hurdle, leap, mount, negotiate, over, overleap, rise, soar, spring, surmount; SEE CONCEPTS *194,752*

veer [v] *change direction*
angle off, avert, bear, be deflected, bend, change, change course, curve, cut, deflect, depart, deviate, digress, dip, divagate, diverge, divert, drift, get around, make a left*, make a right*, pivot, sheer, shift, skew, skid, swerve, swing, swivel, tack, train off, turn, twist, volte-face*, wheel, whip, whirl; SEE CONCEPTS *148,150,213*

vegetable [n] *edible part of plant*
edible, green, greens, herb, herbaceous plant, legume, produce, root, salad, truck, yellow; SEE CONCEPT *431*

vegetate [v1] *be very passive*
be inert, decay, deteriorate, exist, go to pot*, go to seed*, hibernate, idle, languish, loaf*, pass time, stagnate, weaken; SEE CONCEPTS *210,698*

vegetate [v2] *grow, sprout*
bloom, blossom, bud, burgeon, germinate, shoot, spring, swell; SEE CONCEPTS *253,257*

vehement [adj] *passionate, opinionated*
angry, ardent, concentrated, delirious, desperate, eager, earnest, emphatic, enthusiastic, exquisite, fervent, fervid, fierce, fiery, forceful, forcible, frantic, furious, hearty, heated, hopped up*, hot*, hyper*, impassioned, impetuous, inflamed, intense, lively, on the make*, potent, powerful, pronounced, rabid, strong, terrible, vicious, violent, wild, zealous; SEE CONCEPTS *401,542*

vehicle [n1] *machine used for transportation*
agent, automobile, bicycle, boat, buggy, bus, cab, car, carrier, chariot, conveyance, crate*, jalopy*, jeep, mechanism, motorcycle, taxi, transport, truck, van, vector, wagon, wheels; SEE CONCEPT *503*

vehicle [n2] *means of attaining end*
agency, agent, apparatus, channel, expedient, implement, instrument, instrumentality, intermediary, means of expression, mechanism, medium, ministry, organ, tool, vector, way, ways and means*; SEE CONCEPTS *6,277,278,694,712*

veil [n] *disguise*
blind, cloak, coloring, cover, curtain, facade, false front, film, front, guise, mantilla, mask, screen, shade, shroud, veiling; SEE CONCEPTS *451,673*

veil [v] *hide*
beard*, blanket, camouflage, cloak, conceal, cover, cover up, curtain*, dim, disguise, drape, enclose, enfold, enshroud, envelop, finesse, invest, launder, mantle, mask, obscure, put up a front*, screen, secrete, shield, shroud, stonewall*, whitewash*, wrap; SEE CONCEPT *172*

vein [n1] *mood, tone*
attitude, bent, character, characteristic, complexion, dash, disposition, faculty, fashion, fettle, hint, humor, line, manner, mind, mode, nature, note, spice, spirit, strain, streak, style, suggestion, suspicion, tang, temper, temperament, tenor, tinge, touch, trace, turn, wave, way; SEE CONCEPTS *411,673,682*

vein [n2] *blood vessel*
capillary, course, current, duct, follicle, hair, lode, nerve, seam, stratum, streak, stripe, thread, venation; SEE CONCEPTS *393,420*

velocity [n] *speed*
acceleration, celerity, dispatch, expedition, fleetness, gait, haste, headway, hurry, impetus, momentum, pace, quickness, rapidity, rapidness, rate, swiftness, tempo; SEE CONCEPTS *755,792*

vendor [n] *person who sells wares*
businessperson, dealer, hawker, huckster*, merchant, outcrier, peddler, pitcher, traveler, traveling salesperson; SEE CONCEPT *348*

veneer [n] *pretense, front*
appearance, coating, cover, covering, disguise, exterior, facade, face, finish, gloss, guise, layer, leaf, mask, overlay, semblance, show, surface, window dressing*; SEE CONCEPTS *633,673,716*

veneer [v] *cover, overlay*
blanch, coat, extenuate, face, finish, gloss, palliate, plate, shellac, sugarcoat, surface, varnish, whiten, whitewash; SEE CONCEPT *172*

venerable [adj] *respected*
admirable, aged, august, dignified, esteemed, estimable, experienced, grand, grave, honorable, honored, imposing, matriarchal, noble, patriarchal, philosophical, revered, reverenced, reverend, sacred, sage, sedate, serious, stately,

venerated, wise, worshipful, worshipped; SEE CONCEPT 574

vengeance [n] *retaliation for another's act*
avengement, avenging, counterblow, evening of score*, eye for an eye*, getting even*, repayment, reprisal, requital, retribution, return, revenge, settling of score*, tit for tat*, vengefulness, wrath; SEE CONCEPTS 29,384

vengeful [adj] *retaliating; hating*
antagonistic, avenging, hostile, implacable, inimical, punitive, rancorous, relentless, retaliatory, revengeful, spiteful, unforgiving, vindictive; SEE CONCEPTS 401,542

venom [n] *poison; hating*
acidity, acrimony, anger, bane, bitterness, contagion, gall, grudge, hate, hatred, ill will, infection, malevolence, malice, maliciousness, malignity, rancor, spite, spitefulness, spleen, taint, toxin, virulence, virus; SEE CONCEPTS 29,399

venomous [adj] *poisonous; hateful*
accidentally on purpose*, antagonistic, baleful, baneful, catty*, cussed*, deadly, destructive, dirty, evil, hostile, lethal, malefic, malevolent, malicious, malign, malignant, mean, mephitic, noxious, ornery*, poisonous, rancorous, savage, spiteful, toxic, toxicant, vicious, vindictive, viperish, viperous, virulent, waspish; SEE CONCEPTS 537,542,544

vent [n] *outlet*
aperture, avenue, chimney, drain, duct, exit, flue, hole, opening, orifice, pipe, split, spout, ventilator; SEE CONCEPTS 440,464

vent [v] *let out; express*
air, assert, come out with, declare, discharge, drive out, emit, empty, express, give, give off, give out, issue, loose, pour out, provide escape, put, release, state, take out on*, throw off*, unleash, utter, ventilate, verbalize, voice; SEE CONCEPTS 49,51,179

ventilate [v] *air out; make known*
advertise, air, bring into the open, bring up, broach, broadcast, circulate, debate, deliberate, discourse, discuss, examine, express, free, give, go into, introduce, moot, publish, put, scrutinize, sift, state, take up, talk about, talk of, talk over, thresh out, vent, verbalize; SEE CONCEPTS 51,60

venture [n] *gamble, attempt*
adventure, baby*, chance, deal, endeavor, enterprise, essay, experiment, exploit, feat*, hazard, header, investment, jeopardy, peril, pet project*, project, proposition, pursuit, risk, setup*, shot*, spec*, speculation, stab*, stake, test, thing*, trial, undertaking, wager; SEE CONCEPTS 87,675

venture [v] *take a chance*
advance, assay, attempt, bet, brave, challenge, chance, dare, dare say*, defy, endanger, essay, experiment, expose, feel, front*, gamble, get down*, go out on a limb*, grope, have a fling at*, hazard, imperil, jeopardize, lay open, make a stab at*, make bold, play for, play the market*, presume, put in jeopardy*, put up*, risk, speculate, stake, stick one's neck out*, take a crack at*, take a flyer*, take a plunge*, try, try out, volunteer, wager; SEE CONCEPTS 87,330,363

venturesome [adj] *courageous*
adventurous, aggressive, audacious, bold, brave, daredevil, daring, enterprising, fearless, foolhardy, gutsy, intrepid, overbold, plucky, pushy, rash, reckless, resourceful, risky, spirited,

spunky, stalwart, stout, sturdy, temerarious, venturous; SEE CONCEPTS 401,548

veracious [adj] *true*
accurate, credible, dependable, direct, ethical, factual, faithful, frank, genuine, high-principled, honest, just, kosher*, legit*, like it is*, on the level*, on the line*, on the up and up*, open, reliable, right, righteous, straight-arrow*, straightforward, strict, true-blue*, trustworthy, truthful, undeceptive, up front*, valid, veridical; SEE CONCEPTS 267,545,582

veracity [n] *truth*
accuracy, actuality, authenticity, candor, correctness, credibility, exactitude, exactness, fact, fairness, fidelity, frankness, genuineness, gospel*, honest-to-god truth*, honesty, honor, impartiality, integrity, like it is*, openness, precision, probity, reality, real McCoy*, rectitude, rightness, sincerity, straight stuff*, trueness, truism, trustworthiness, truthfulness, uprightness, verisimilitude, verity, word*; SEE CONCEPTS 278,645

verbal [adj] *spoken*
exact, expressed, lingual, literal, oral, rhetorical, said, stated, told, unwritten, verbatim, word-for-word*, word-of-mouth*; SEE CONCEPT 267

verbatim [adj] *exactly*
accurately, direct, directly, literally, literatim, precisely, sic, to the letter*, word-for-word*; SEE CONCEPTS 267,535

verbiage [n] *repetition, wordiness*
circumlocution, expansiveness, floridity, long-windedness, loquacity, periphrase, periphrasis, pleonasm, prolixity, redundancy, tautology, verbosity; SEE CONCEPTS 278,695

verbose [adj] *wordy, long-winded*
bombastic, circumlocutory, diffuse, flowery, full of air*, fustian, gabby*, garrulous, grandiloquent, involved, loquacious, magniloquent, palaverous, periphrastic, pleonastic, prolix, redundant, repeating, repetitious, repetitive, rhetorical, talkative, talky*, tautological, tautologous, tedious, tortuous, windy*, yacking*; SEE CONCEPT 267

verdant [adj] *green, blooming*
flourishing, fresh, grassy, leafy, lush, verdurous; SEE CONCEPTS 485,618

verdict [n] *law judgment*
adjudication, answer, arbitrament, award, conclusion, decision, decree, deduction, determination, finding, opinion, ruling, sentence; SEE CONCEPT 318

verge [n] *extremity, limit*
border, borderline, boundary, brim, brink, edge, extreme, fringe, hem, lip, margin, point, rim, selvage, skirt, terminus, threshold; SEE CONCEPT 484

verge [v] *come near*
abut, adjoin, approach, be on the edge*, border, bound, brink on, butt on*, communicate, edge, end, fringe, gravitate toward, hem, incline, join, lean, line, march, margin, neighbor, outline, rim, skirt, surround, tend, touch, trench, trend; SEE CONCEPTS 657,749

verify [v] *confirm, validate*
add up*, attest, authenticate, bear out, certify, check, check out, check up, check up on*, confirm, corroborate, debunk, demonstrate, document, double-check, establish, eye*, eyeball*, find out, hold up, justify, make certain, make sure, pan out*, peg*, prove, settle, size*, size up*,

va
ve

stand up*, substantiate, support, test, try; SEE CONCEPTS 291,317

verisimilitude [n] *authenticity*
color, credibility, genuineness, likeliness, likeness, plausibility, realism, resemblance, semblance, show, similarity, virtual reality; SEE CONCEPT 725

veritable [adj] *authentic*
actual, bona fide, factual, for real*, genuine, indubitable, kosher*, legit*, real, true, undoubted, unquestionable, very; SEE CONCEPT 582

vernacular [n] *native language*
argot, cant, dialect, idiom, jargon, jive talk*, language, lingo*, lingua franca, native tongue, parlance, patois, patter, phraseology, slang, speech, street talk*, tongue; SEE CONCEPT 276

vernacular [adj] *native, colloquial*
common, dialectal, domesticated, idiomatic, indigenous, informal, ingrained, inherent, local, natural, ordinary, plebian, popular, vulgar; SEE CONCEPTS 267,549

versatile [adj] *adjustable, flexible*
able, accomplished, adaptable, adroit, all-around, all-purpose, ambidextrous, conversant, dexterous, elastic, facile, functional, gifted, handy, ingenuous, many-sided, mobile, multifaceted, plastic, pliable, protean, puttylike*, ready, resourceful, skilled, skillful, talented, variable, varied; SEE CONCEPTS 527,542

verse [n] *written composition*
ballad, epic, jingle, lay, lyric, ode, poem, poesy, poetry, rhyme, rune, song, sonnet, stanza; SEE CONCEPT 282

versed [adj] *experienced, informed*
abreast, accomplished, acquainted, au courant*, au fait*, competent, conversant, familiar, in the know*, knowledgeable, learned, practical, practiced, proficient, qualified, savvy, seasoned, skilled, trained, tuned in*, up*, up on*, versant, veteran, well-informed; SEE CONCEPTS 402, 403,527

version [n] *account of a happening*
adaptation, chronicle, clarification, condensation, construction, exercise, form, history, interpretation, narrative, paraphrase, portrayal, reading, redaction, rendering, rendition, report, restatement, rewording, side, simplification, sketch, statement, story, tale, transcription, translation, variant; SEE CONCEPT 282

vertex [n] *top*
acme, apex, apogee, cap, cope, crest, crown, culmination, extremity, fastigium, height, peak, pinnacle, roof, summit, tip, upper extremity, zenith; SEE CONCEPT 836

vertical [adj] *upright*
bolt upright, cocked, erect, on end, perpendicular, plumb, sheer, steep, straight-up, up-and-down, upward; SEE CONCEPTS 581,583

very [adj] *real, exact*
actual, appropriate, authentic, bare, bona fide, correct, especial, express, genuine, ideal, identical, indubitable, mere, model, perfect, plain, precise, pure, right, same, selfsame, sheer, simple, special, sure-enough, true, undoubted, unqualified, unquestionable, veritable, very same; SEE CONCEPTS 535,557

very [adv] *much, really; to a high degree*
absolutely, acutely, amply, astonishingly, awfully, certainly, considerably, dearly, decidedly, deeply, eminently, emphatically, exaggeratedly, exceedingly, excessively, extensively, extraordinarily, extremely, greatly, highly, incredibly, indispensably, largely, notably, noticeably, particularly, positively, powerfully, pressingly, pretty, prodigiously, profoundly, remarkably, substantially, superlatively, surpassingly, surprisingly, terribly, truly, uncommonly, unusually, vastly, wonderfully; SEE CONCEPTS 544,569,772

vessel [n1] *ship*
barge, bark, bateau, boat, bottom, bucket*, can*, craft, liner, ocean liner, steamer, tanker, tub*; SEE CONCEPT 506

vessel [n2] *container, bowl*
basin, kettle, pitcher, pot, receptacle, urn, utensil; SEE CONCEPT 494

vest [v] *authorize, entrust*
belong, bestow, confer, consign, empower, endow, furnish, invest, lodge, pertain, place, put in the hands of*, settle; SEE CONCEPTS 50,88

vestibule [n] *small room for arrivals*
antechamber, anteroom, doorway, entrance, entrance hall, entry, entryway, foyer, gateway, hall, hallway, lobby, narthex, porch, portal, portico; SEE CONCEPT 448

vestige [n] *sign, indication*
evidence, glimmer, hint, memento, print, relic, remainder, remains, remnant, residue, scrap, shadow, suspicion, token, trace, track; SEE CONCEPTS 260,284,673

veteran [n] *person with much experience; particularly in war*
expert, GI*, old guard*, old hand*, old pro*, old salt*, old soldier*, old-timer*, pro, shellback*, sourdough*, trouper, vet*, warhorse*; SEE CONCEPTS 358,423

veteran [adj] *experienced, seasoned*
adept, battle-scarred*, been around*, disciplined, exercised, expert, from way back*, hardened, inured, knows one's stuff*, long-serving, long-time, not born yesterday*, of the old school*, old, old-time, practical, practiced, pro*, proficient, skilled, sophisticated, steady, trained, up to speed*, versed, vet*, weathered, wise, wise to ways*, worldly; SEE CONCEPTS 402,527,678

veto [n] *refusal of permission*
ban, blackball*, declination, denial, embargo, interdict, interdiction, negative, nonconsent, prohibition; SEE CONCEPTS 81,121,298,685

veto [v] *refuse permission*
ban, blackball*, burn, cut, decline, defeat, deny, disallow, disapprove, discountenance, forbid, give thumbs down*, interdict, kill, negate, negative, nix*, not go for*, pass, pass by, pass on, prohibit, put down, refuse, reject, rule out*, shoot down*, throw away*, throw out*, thumbs down*, turn down; SEE CONCEPTS 50,81,88,121,298

vex [v] *distress, bother*
abrade, afflict, aggravate, agitate, anger, annoy, be at, chafe, depress, displease, disquiet, disturb, eat*, embarrass, exasperate, fret, gall*, get in one's hair*, get under one's skin*, give a bad time*, give a hard time*, grate on*, harass, harry, hassle, infuriate, irk, irritate, molest, needle, nettle, offend, peeve, perplex, pester, pique, plague, provoke, put out*, rasp, ride, rile, tease, tick off*, torment, trouble, turn off*, upset, worry; SEE CONCEPTS 7,19

vexatious [adj] *distressing, bothersome*
afflicting, aggravating, annoying, burdensome, disagreeable, disappointing, disturbing, exasper-

ating, irksome, irritating, mean, nagging, pesky*, provoking, teasing, tormenting, troublesome, troublous, trying, ugly, unpleasant, upsetting, wicked, worrisome, worrying; SEE CONCEPTS *529,537*

via [*prep*] *by way of*
along, as a means, by, by dint of, by means of, by this route, by virtue of, on the way, over, per, through, through the medium of, through this medium, with; SEE CONCEPT *544*

viable [*adj*] *reasonable, practicable*
applicable, doable, feasible, operable, possible, usable, within possibility, workable; SEE CONCEPTS *552,560*

vibrant [*adj1*] *alive, colorful*
active, animated, dynamic, electrifying, energetic, lively, peppy, responsive, sensitive, sound, sparkling, spirited, vigorous, virile, vital, vivacious, vivid, zesty*, zippy*; SEE CONCEPTS *401,618*

vibrant [*adj2*] *throbbing*
aquiver, consonant, oscillating, palpitating, pulsating, pulsing, quaking, quivering, resonant, resounding, reverberant, ringing, sonorant, sonorous, trembling; SEE CONCEPT *584*

vibrate [*v*] *shake, quiver*
beat, echo, fluctuate, flutter, jar, oscillate, palpitate, pulsate, pulse, quake, resonate, resound, reverberate, ripple, shiver, sway, swing, throb, tremble, tremor, undulate, wave, waver; SEE CONCEPTS *152,748*

vibration [*n*] *shaking, quivering*
beating, fluctuation, judder, oscillation, pulsation, pulse, quake, quiver, resonance, reverberation, shake, shimmy, throb, throbbing, trembling, tremor, vacillation, wave, wavering; SEE CONCEPTS *152,748*

vicarious [*adj*] *done or felt for, or on behalf of, another*
by proxy, commissioned, delegated, deputed, empathetic, eventual, imagined, indirect, pretended, secondary, substituted, substitutional, surrogate, sympathetic; SEE CONCEPTS *401,538*

vice [*n1*] *bad habit; sin*
carnality, corruption, debasement, debauchery, decay, degeneracy, depravity, evil, evildoing, ill, immorality, indecency, iniquity, lechery, lewdness, libidinousness, licentiousness, looseness, lubricity, lust, maleficence, malignance, offense, perversion, profligacy, rot, sensuality, squalor, transgression, trespass, venality, wickedness, wrong; SEE CONCEPTS *372,645*

vice [*n2*] *weakness*
blemish, defect, demerit, failing, fault, flaw, foible, frailty, imperfection, mar, shortcoming, weak point; SEE CONCEPTS *411,657,666*

vice versa [*adv*] *contrary, oppositely*
about-face*, again, contra, contrariwise*, conversely, far from it*, in reverse, on the contrary, the other way around*, turn about; SEE CONCEPTS *544,564*

vicinity [*n*] *local area*
around*, ballpark*, district, environment, environs, hood, locality, nearness, neck of the woods*, neighborhood, precinct, pretty near*, propinquity, proximity, purlieus, range, region, surroundings, territory, turf*, vicinage; SEE CONCEPTS *198,747*

vicious [*adj1*] *corrupt, wrong*
abandoned, abhorrent, atrocious, bad, barbarous, base, contaminated, cruel, dangerous, debased, degenerate, degraded, demoralized, depraved, diabolical, faulty, ferocious, fiendish, flagitious, foul, heinous, immoral, impious, impure, indecent, infamous, iniquitous, insubordinate, lewd, libidinous, licentious, miscreant, monstrous, nefarious, perverse, profligate, putrid, reprehensible, reprobate, rotten, savage, sinful, unprincipled, untamed, vile, villainous, violent, wicked, wild, worthless; SEE CONCEPTS *401,545,571*

vicious [*adj2*] *nasty, hateful*
backbiting*, beastly, bloodthirsty, brutal, cruel, cussed*, defamatory, despiteful, dirty*, evil, fierce, frightful, furious, horrid, intense, lousy*, malevolent, malicious, malign, mean, murderous, ornery*, poisonous, rancorous, rough, savage, slanderous, spiteful, tough, vehement, venomous, vindictive, violent, wicked; SEE CONCEPTS *267,401,542*

vicissitude [*n*] *change*
about-face*, alteration, alternation, diversity, flip-flop*, fluctuation, innovation, mid-course correction*, mutability, mutation, novelty, permutation, progression, reversal, revolution, shift, sport, switch, switchover, transposition, turnaround, uncertainty, ups and downs*, variation, variety; SEE CONCEPT *697*

victim [*n*] *someone or something sacrificed, preyed upon*
babe in woods*, butt, casualty, clown, dupe, easy make*, easy mark*, fatality, fool, gambit, gopher*, gudgeon*, gull, hireling, hunted, immolation, injured party, innocent, mark, martyr, patsy, pawn, pigeon*, prey, pushover*, quarry, sacrifice, scapegoat, sitting duck*, sitting target*, soft touch*, stooge*, sucker*, sufferer, underdog, wretch; SEE CONCEPTS *423,659*

victimize [*v*] *cheat, fool*
bamboozle*, burn*, chisel*, clip*, con, cozen, deceive, defraud, discriminate against, dupe, exploit, fleece, flimflam*, gull, have it in for*, hoax, hoodwink, immolate, persecute, pick on, pigeon*, prey on, rope in*, screw*, set up*, snow*, stack the deck*, stiff*, sting*, sucker*, swindle, take advantage of, trick, use; SEE CONCEPTS *14,59,192*

victor [*n*] *person who wins*
champ, champion, conquering hero*, conqueror, defeater, first*, gold medalist, greatest, hero, king, medalist, prizewinner, queen, subjugator, title holder, top*, top dog*, vanquisher, winner; SEE CONCEPTS *366,416*

victorious [*adj*] *successful, winning*
arrived, champion, conquering, on top, prizewinning, triumphant, vanquishing; SEE CONCEPT *528*

victory [*n*] *win, success*
achievement, advantage, ascendancy, bull's-eye*, clean sweep*, conquest, control, defeat, defeating, destruction, dominion, feather in cap*, gain, grand slam*, hit, hole in one*, killing*, laurels, mission accomplished*, overthrow, prize, subjugation, superiority, supremacy, sweep, the gold*, triumph, upper hand*, upset, winning; SEE CONCEPTS *95,671,706,832*

video [*n/adj*] *related to the televised image*
broadcast, canned*, music video, prerecorded, program, promotional film, recorded, taped, telegenic, television, TV; SEE CONCEPTS *277,293.*

ve
vi

videocassette [n] *magnetic tape on which video image is recorded*
cartridge, flick*, movie, recording, rental, vid*, videotape; SEE CONCEPTS *277,293,464.*

vie [v] *compete*
be rivals, buck, challenge, contend, contest, counter, go for*, go for broke*, go for the gold*, go for the jugular*, jockey for position*, match, oppose, pit, play, play off, push, rival, scramble for, strive, struggle, sweat; SEE CONCEPTS *92,363*

view [n1] *something that is seen*
appearance, aspect, composition, contour, design, field of vision, glimpse, illustration, landscape, look, opening, outline, outlook, panorama, perspective, picture, prospect, range of vision, representation, scene, seascape, show, sight, spectacle, stretch, tableau, vision, vista, way; SEE CONCEPT *628*

view [n2] *examination*
analysis, audit, check, contemplation, display, eyeball*, flash*, gander*, inspection, lamp*, look, look-see, perlustration, review, scan, scrutiny, sight, slant, squint*, survey, viewing; SEE CONCEPTS *24,103*

view [n3] *belief*
attitude, belief, close-up, concept, conception, consideration, conviction, deduction, eye*, feeling, impression, inference, judgment, judgment call*, mind, notion, opinion, persuasion, point of view, say-so*, sentiment, slant*, thought, twist, two cents' worth*, value judgment*, way of thinking; SEE CONCEPT *689*

view [v1] *look at*
beam, behold, canvass, check out*, check over, consider, contemplate, descry, dig*, discern, distinguish, eagle eye*, espy, examine, explore, eye*, feast eyes on*, flash*, gaze, get a load of*, inspect, lay eyes on, mark, notice, observe, perceive, pipe*, read, regard, rubberneck*, scan, scope, scrutinize, see, set eyes on, spot, spy, stare, survey, take in*, watch, witness; SEE CONCEPTS *623,626*

view [v2] *believe*
account, consider, deem, judge, look on, reckon, regard, think about; SEE CONCEPT *12*

viewpoint [n] *way of thinking*
angle, aspect, attitude, direction, estimation, eye*, frame of reference, ground, light, long view, outlook, perspective, point of observation, point of view, position, posture, respect, side, slant, stance, stand, standpoint, twist, two cents' worth*, vantage point, view; SEE CONCEPT *689*

vigilance [n] *carefulness*
acuity, alertness, attention, attentiveness, caution, circumspection, diligence, lookout, observance, surveillance, vigil, watch, watchfulness; SEE CONCEPTS *644,657*

vigilant [adj] *careful, watchful*
acute, agog, alert, anxious, attentive, aware, cautious, circumspect, guarded, keen, looking for, looking to, observant, on alert, on guard, on the ball*, on the job*, on the lookout, on the qui vive, on toes*, open-eyed*, sharp, sleepless, unsleeping, waiting on, wakeful, wary, wide-awake, with eyes peeled*, with weather eye open*; SEE CONCEPTS *401,542,576*

vigor [n] *power, energy*
ability, action, activity, agility, alertness, bang*, birr, bounce, capability, capacity, dash, drive, dynamism, endurance, enterprise, exercise, fire, force, get-up-and-go*, go*, hardiness, healthiness, intensity, juice*, kick*, liveliness, lustiness, might, nimbleness, moxie*, muscle*, nimbleness, pep*, pith, potency, puissance, punch*, push, quickness, snap*, sock, soundness, starch*, steam*, strength, tuck*, urgency, vehemence, vim, vitality, well-being, zing*, zip*; SEE CONCEPTS *316,411,732*

vigorous [adj] *energetic, powerful*
active, athletic, ball of fire*, bouncing, brisk, dashing, driving, dynamic, effective, efficient, enterprising, exuberant, flourishing, forceful, forcible, hale, hard-driving, hardy, healthy, hearty, intense, lively, lusty, mettlesome, peppy, persuasive, potent, red-blooded*, robust, rugged, snappy, sound, spanking, spirited, steamroller*, strapping, strenuous, strong, strong as an ox*, sturdy, take-charge*, take-over*, tough, vital, zealous, zippy*; SEE CONCEPTS *314,404,489*

vile [adj] *offensive, horrible*
abandoned, abject, appalling, bad, base, coarse, contemptible, corrupt, debased, degenerate, depraved, despicable, dirty, disgraceful, disgusting, evil, filthy, foul, horrid, humiliating, ignoble, immoral, impure, iniquitous, loathsome, low, mean, miserable, nasty, nauseating, nefarious, noxious, perverted, repellent, repugnant, repulsive, revolting, shocking, sickening, sinful, sleazy*, stinking*, ugly, vicious, vulgar, wicked, worthless, wretched; SEE CONCEPTS *529,545,571*

vilify [v] *criticize very harshly*
abuse, asperse, assail, attack, bad-mouth*, berate, blister, call down*, caluminate, censure, curse, cuss*, damn, debase, decry, defame, denigrate, denounce, dig*, disparage, dress down*, dump on*, give a black eye*, jinx, knock*, libel, malign, mistreat, mudsling*, pan*, put a whammy on*, put down*, rag on*, rap*, revile, rip up*, roast*, run down, scorch, skin alive*, slam*, slander, slur, smear*, speak ill of, tear down*, tear into*, traduce, vituperate, voodoo*; SEE CONCEPTS *44,52*

village [n] *small town*
center, crossroads, hamlet, suburb; SEE CONCEPT *507*

villain [n] *evil person*
antihero, blackguard*, brute, caitiff, creep*, criminal, devil, enfant terrible*, evildoer, heel, libertine, lowlife*, malefactor, mischief-maker*, miscreant, offender, profligate, rapscallion, rascal, reprobate, scoundrel, sinner, wretch; SEE CONCEPT *412*

vindicate [v] *prove one's innocence*
absolve, acquit, advocate, argue, assert, bear out, claim, clear, confute, contend, corroborate, defend, disculpate, disprove, do justice to, establish, exculpate, excuse, exonerate, free, free from blame, guard, justify, maintain, plead for, protect, prove, rationalize, refute, rehabilitate, second, shield, substantiate, support, uphold, warrant, whitewash*; SEE CONCEPTS *49,57,317*

vindictive [adj] *hateful, revengeful*
avenging, cruel, grim, grudging, implacable, malicious, malignant, merciless, rancorous, relentless, resentful, retaliatory, ruthless, spiteful, unforgiving, unrelenting, vengeful, venomous, wreakful; SEE CONCEPTS *401,542*

vintage [n] *crop, especially of wine*
collection, epoch, era, generation, grapes, harvest, origin, wine, year; SEE CONCEPT *429*

vintage [adj] superior
best, choice, classic, classical, excellent, mature, old, prime, rare, ripe, select, selected, venerable; SEE CONCEPTS 574,578,797

violate [v1] break a law, agreement
breach, contaminate, contravene, defy, disobey, disregard, disrupt, encroach, err, infract, infringe, meddle, offend, oppose, outrage, profane, resist, sacrilege, sin, tamper with, trample on, transgress, trespass, withstand; SEE CONCEPTS 101,192

violate [v2] rape, defile
abuse, assault, befoul, debauch, defile, desecrate, force, invade, outrage, pollute, profane, ravish, spoil; SEE CONCEPTS 246,375

violation [n1] breach; breaking of the law
abuse, break, breaking, contravention, encroachment, illegality, infraction, infringement, misbehavior, misdemeanor, negligence, nonobservance, offense, rupture, transgressing, transgression, trespass, trespassing, violating, wrong; SEE CONCEPTS 101,192

violation [n2] rape, defilement
assault, blasphemy, debasement, defacement, defacing, degradation, desecration, destruction, devastation, dishonor, invasion, mistreatment, outrage, pollution, profanation, rapine, ravishment, ruin, sacrilege, spoliation; SEE CONCEPTS 246,252,375

violence [n] extreme force, intensity
abandon, acuteness, assault, attack, bestiality, bloodshed, blowup, brutality, brute force, clash, coercion, compulsion, confusion, constraint, cruelty, destructiveness, disorder, disturbance, duress, ferocity, fervor, fierceness, fighting, flap, foul play, frenzy, fury, fuss, harshness, murderousness, onslaught, passion, power, raging, rampage, roughness, ruckus, rumble, savagery, severity, sharpness, storm, storminess, struggle, terrorism, tumult, turbulence, uproar, vehemence, wildness; SEE CONCEPTS 29,641,669,675

violent [adj1] destructive
agitated, aroused, berserk, bloodthirsty, brutal, coercive, crazy, cruel, demoniac, desperate, distraught, disturbed, enraged, fierce, fiery, forceful, forcible, frantic, fuming, furious, great, headstrong, homicidal, hotheaded*, hysterical, impassioned, impetuous, inflamed, intemperate, mad, maddened, maniacal, mighty, murderous, passionate, potent, powerful, raging, riotous, rough, savage, strong, uncontrollable, ungovernable, unrestrained, urgent, vehement, vicious, wild; SEE CONCEPTS 401,540,544

violent [adj2] severe, extreme
acute, agonizing, biting, blustery, coercive, concentrated, devastating, excruciating, exquisite, forceful, forcible, gale force*, great, harsh, immoderate, inordinate, intense, mighty, outrageous, painful, potent, powerful, raging, rough, ruinous, sharp, strong, tempestuous, terrible, tumultuous/tumultuous, turbulent, wild; SEE CONCEPTS 525,569

virgin/virginal [adj] brand-new, unused
first, fresh, idle, immaculate, initial, innocent, intact, modest, natural, new, original, primeval, pristine, pure, spotless, uncorrupted, undefiled, undisturbed, unmarred, unspoiled, unsullied, untapped, untested, untouched, untried, vestal; SEE CONCEPTS 372,560,578,797

virile [adj] potent, powerful
driving, energetic, forceful, generative, lusty, macho*, procreative, red-blooded*, reproductive, robust, sound, strong, vibrant, vigorous, vital; SEE CONCEPTS 372,401,404

virtual [adj] in essence
basic, constructive, essential, fundamental, implicit, implied, in all but name*, in conduct, indirect, in effect, in practice, potential, practical, pragmatic, tacit, unacknowledged; SEE CONCEPTS 487,537,544,573

virtually [adv] for all practical purposes
around, as good as, basically, effectually, essentially, for all intents and purposes*, fundamentally, give or take a little*, guesstimate*, implicitly, in all but name*, in effect, in essence, in substance, in the ballpark*, in the neighborhood*, morally, nearly, not absolutely, not actually, practically, something like*, upwards of*; SEE CONCEPTS 487,544,573

virtue [n] honor, integrity
advantage, asset, character, charity, chastity, consideration, credit, ethic, ethicality, ethicalness, excellence, faith, faithfulness, fineness, fortitude, generosity, goodness, good point*, highmindedness, hope, ideal, incorruptibility, innocence, justice, kindness, love, merit, morality, plus*, probity, prudence, purity, quality, rectitude, respectability, righteousness, temper, temperance, trustworthiness, uprightness, value, worth, worthiness; SEE CONCEPTS 411,645

virtuoso [n] person who is an expert
ace, adept, artist, artiste, authority, big league*, brain*, celebrity, champ*, champion, crackerjack*, dilettante, egghead, genius, hotshot*, hot stuff*, intelligent, magician, musician, natural*, no slouch*, old hand*, old pro*, performer, pro*, prodigy, professional, pundit, sharp*, star, superstar, whiz*, wizard; SEE CONCEPTS 348,352,416

virtuous [adj] good, ethical; innocent
blameless, celibate, chaste, clean-living, effective, effectual, efficient, excellent, exemplary, faithful, guiltless, high-principled, honest, honorable, incorruptible, inculpable, in the clear*, irreprehensible, kosher*, legit*, moral, moralistic, noble, on the level*, on the up and up*, praiseworthy, principled, pure, regular, righteous, rightminded, spotless, straight, true-blue*, unsullied, untainted, untarnished, up front*, upright, wholesome, without reproach, worthy; SEE CONCEPTS 401,545

virulent [adj1] poisonous, lethal
baneful, deadly, destructive, fatal, harmful, infective, injurious, malign, malignant, mephitic, pernicious, poison, septic, toxic, toxicant, unhealthy, unwholesome, venomous; SEE CONCEPTS 537,571

virulent [adj2] hostile
acrimonious, antagonistic, bitter, cutting, hateful, malevolent, malicious, rancorous, resentful, scathing, sharp, spiteful, splenetic, stabbing, unfriendly, venomous, vicious, vindictive, vitriolic; SEE CONCEPTS 267,542

viscous [adj] sticky, gummy
adhesive, clammy, gelatinous, gluey*, glutinous, gooey*, mucilaginous, ropy, slimy, stiff, syrupy, tenacious, thick, tough, viscid; SEE CONCEPT 606

visible [adj] apparent, seeable
arresting, big as life*, bold, clear, conspicuous, detectable, discernible, discoverable, distinguish-

vi
vi

able, evident, inescapable, in sight, in view, macroscopic, manifest, marked, not hidden, noticeable, obtrusive, obvious, ocular, open, out in the open*, outstanding, palpable, patent, perceivable, perceptible, plain, pointed, pronounced, revealed, salient, seen, signal, striking, to be seen, unconcealed, under one's nose*, unhidden, unmistakable, viewable, visual; SEE CONCEPTS 529,576,619

vision [n1] *ability to perceive with eyes*
eyes*, eyesight, faculty, optics, perceiving, perception, range of view, seeing, sight, view; SEE CONCEPT 629

vision [n2] *mental image, concept*
angle, aspect, astuteness, breadth of view, castles in the air*, conception, daydream, discernment, divination, dream, facet, fancy, fantasy, farsightedness, foreknowledge, foresight, head trip*, idea, ideal, ideality, imagination, insight, intuition, keenness, mental picture, muse, nightmare, outlook, penetration, perspective, phantasm, pie in the sky*, pipe dream*, point of view, prescience, retrospect, slant, standpoint, trip, understanding, view; SEE CONCEPTS 529,532,689

vision [n3] *apparition*
apocalypse, chimera, delusion, ecstasy, fantasy, ghost, hallucination, haunt, illusion, mirage, nightmare, oracle, phantasm, phantom, phenomenon, presence, prophecy, revelation, specter, spirit, spook, trance, warlock, wraith; SEE CONCEPTS 370,529

vision [n4] *very beautiful thing or person*
angel*, dazzler, dream, eyeful*, feast for the eyes*, perfect picture*, picture, sight, sight for sore eyes*, spectacle, stunner*; SEE CONCEPTS 424,529

visionary [n] *person who dreams, is idealistic*
castle-builder*, daydreamer, Don Quixote*, dreamer, enthusiast, idealist, mystic, prophet, romancer, romantic, seer, stargazer, theorist, utopian, zealot; SEE CONCEPTS 361,416

visionary [adj] *idealized, romantic*
abstracted, ambitious, astral, chimerical, daydreaming, delusory, dreaming, dreamy, exalted, fanciful, fantastic, grandiose, ideal, idealist, idealistic, illusory, imaginary, impractical, in the clouds*, introspective, lofty, musing, noble, otherworldly, pretentious, prophetic, quixotic, radical, speculative, starry-eyed*, unreal, unrealistic, unworkable, unworldly, utopian; SEE CONCEPTS 529,560,582

visit [n] *social call upon another*
appointment, call, evening, holiday, interview, sojourn, stay, stop, stopover, talk, tarriance, vacation, visitation, weekend; SEE CONCEPTS 226,227

visit [v1] *be a guest of*
call, call on, chat, come around, come by, converse, crash, drop by, drop in, drop over, dwell, frequent, go over to*, go to see*, hit, inspect, look around, look in on, look up, pay a call*, pay a visit to, play, pop in*, reside, see, sojourn, stay at, stay with, step in, stop by*, stop off*, swing by*, take in, talk, tarry, tour; SEE CONCEPTS 226,227

visit [v2] *bother, haunt*
afflict, assail, attack, avenge, befall, bring down on, descend upon, force upon, impose, inflict, pain, punish, smite, trouble, wreak, wreck; SEE CONCEPTS 7,14,19

visitor [n] *person temporarily in a foreign location*
caller, company, foreigner, guest, habitué, inspector, invitee, out-of-towner, transient, visitant; SEE CONCEPT 423

visual [adj] *able to be seen with eyes*
beheld, discernible, imaged, observable, observed, ocular, optic, optical, perceptible, seeable, seen, viewable, viewed, visible, visional; SEE CONCEPTS 485,576,619

visualize [v] *make a picture of in the mind*
anticipate, apprehend, bring to mind, call to mind, call up, conceive of, conjure up, create, divine, dream up, envisage, envision, fancy, feature, foresee, get the picture*, image, imagine, object, picture, reflect, see, see in the mind's eye*, think, view, vision; SEE CONCEPTS 17,34

vital [adj1] *essential*
basic, bottom-line*, cardinal, coal-and-ice*, constitutive, critical, crucial, decisive, fundamental, heavy*, imperative, important, indispensable, integral, key, life-or-death*, meaningful, meat-and-potatoes*, name, name-of-the-game*, necessary, needed, nitty-gritty*, prerequisite, required, requisite, significant, underlined, urgent; SEE CONCEPTS 546,567

vital [adj2] *lively*
animated, dynamic, energetic, forceful, lusty, red-blooded, spirited, strenuous, vibrant, vigorous, vivacious, zestful; SEE CONCEPT 401

vital [adj3] *alive*
animate, animated, breathing, generative, invigorative, life-giving, live, living, quickening; SEE CONCEPT 539

vitality [n] *energy, spirit*
animation, ardor, audacity, bang, being, bloom, bounce, clout, continuity, drive, endurance, existence, exuberance, fervor, force, get-up-and-go*, go, guts*, intensity, life, liveliness, lustiness, pep, pizzazz*, power, pulse, punch, robustness, snap, sparkle, spunk*, stamina, starch*, steam, strength, stuff*, venturesomeness, verve, vigor, vim, vivaciousness, vivacity, zest, zing*, zip*; SEE CONCEPTS 407,411,633

vitiate [v1] *cancel*
abate, abolish, abrogate, annihilate, annul, delete, deny, invalidate, negate, nullify, quash, recant, revoke, undermine, undo; SEE CONCEPTS 121,317

vitiate [v2] *hurt, corrupt*
blemish, blight, brutalize, contaminate, damage, debase, debauch, defile, deprave, deteriorate, devalue, harm, impair, injure, mar, pervert, pollute, prejudice, spoil, sully, taint, tarnish, violate, warp, water down, weaken; SEE CONCEPTS 246,250

vituperate [v] *criticize harshly*
abuse, accuse, asperse, bark at*, bawl out*, berate, blame, calumniate, castigate, censure, chew out*, condemn, curse, denounce, find fault, growl, insult, lambaste*, lash, malign, rail, rate, reproach, revile, rip into*, run down*, scold, smear, tear into*, tongue-lash*, traduce, upbraid, vilify, yell at*; SEE CONCEPTS 44,52,54

vivacious [adj] *lively, spirited*
active, alert, animate, animated, bouncy, brash, breezy, bubbling, cheerful, ebullient, effervescent, exuberant, frolicsome, full of life*, gay, happy, high-spirited, jolly, jumping, keen, lighthearted, merry, playful, rocking, scintillating, sparkling, sportive, sprightly, swinging, upbeat, vibrant, vital, zesty; SEE CONCEPTS 401,404

vivid [*adj*] *intense, powerful*
active, animated, bright, brilliant, clear, colorful, definite, distinct, dramatic, dynamic, eloquent, energetic, expressive, flamboyant, gay, glowing, graphic, highly colored, lifelike, lively, meaningful, memorable, picturesque, realistic, resplendent, rich, sharp, shining, spirited, stirring, striking, strong, telling, theatrical, true-to-life, vigorous; SEE CONCEPTS 537,569,618

vocabulary [*n*] *language of a person or people*
cant, dictionary, glossary, jargon, lexicon, palaver, phraseology, terminology, thesaurus, wordbook, word-hoard*, words, word-stock*; SEE CONCEPTS 276,280

vocal [*adj1*] *spoken*
articulate, articulated, choral, expressed, intonated, lyric, modulated, operatic, oral, phonetic, phonic, pronounced, put into words*, said, singing, sonant, sung, uttered, verbal, viva voce, vocalic, vocalized, voiced, vowel; SEE CONCEPTS 267,594

vocal [*adj2*] *extroverted about opinion*
articulate, blunt, clamorous, eloquent, expressive, facile, fluent, forthright, frank, free, free-spoken, glib, noisy, outspoken, plain-spoken, round, smooth-spoken, stentorian, strident, venting, vociferous; SEE CONCEPTS 267,404

vocalize [*v*] *put into words or song*
belt out*, canary*, chant, chirp, communicate, convey, croon, emit, enunciate, express, give out*, groan, impart, let out*, moan, pronounce, say, shout, sing, sound, speak, talk, utter, vent, verbalize, voice, warble, yodel; SEE CONCEPT 77

vocation [*n*] *life's work*
art, business, calling, career, craft, do*, dodge*, duty, employment, field, game, handicraft, job, lifework, line*, line of business*, métier, mission, nine-to-five*, occupation, office, post, profession, pursuit, racket*, role, thing*, trade, undertaking; SEE CONCEPTS 349,360

vociferous [*adj*] *loud, insistent*
boisterous, clamant, clamorous, distracting, loud-mouthed, noisy, obstreperous, ranting, shouting, shrill, strident, uproarious, vehement, vociferant; SEE CONCEPTS 267,592,594

vogue [*n*] *fashion; current practice*
chic, craze*, currency, custom, dernier cri, fad*, fashionableness, favor, in thing*, last word*, latest, mode, popularity, practice, prevalence, rage*, style, stylishness, thing*, trend, usage, use, way; SEE CONCEPT 655

vogue [*adj*] *fashionable*
faddy*, in*, latest, mod*, modish, now, popular, prevalent, rage*, state-of-the-art*, trendy, up-to-the-minute*, with it*; SEE CONCEPT 589

voice [*n1*] *expression, language*
articulation, call, cry, delivery, exclamation, inflection, intonation, modulation, murmur, mutter, roar, shout, song, sound, speech, statement, tone, tongue, utterance, vent, vocalization, vociferation, words, yell; SEE CONCEPTS 77,276

voice [*n2*] *opinion*
approval, choice, decision, expression, option, part, participation, preference, representation, right of free speech, say, say-so*, suffrage, vent, view, vote, vox populi, will, wish; SEE CONCEPTS 278,376

voice [*v*] *express opinion; put into words*
air, announce, articulate, assert, come out with*, cry, declare, deliver, divulge, emphasize, enunci-

ate, give expression, give utterance, inflect, intonate, modulate, present, proclaim, pronounce, put, recount, say, sound, speak, talk, tell, utter, vent, verbalize, vocalize; SEE CONCEPTS 49,51

void [*n*] *emptiness, want*
blank, blankness, cavity, gap, hole, hollow, lack, nihility, nothingness, nullity, opening, space, vacuity, vacuum; SEE CONCEPTS 513,646,709

void [*adj1*] *empty*
abandoned, bare, barren, bereft, clear, deprived, destitute, devoid, drained, emptied, free, lacking, scant, short, shy, tenantless, unfilled, unoccupied, vacant, vacuous, without; SEE CONCEPTS 481,583,740,774

void [*adj2*] *nullified, meaningless*
avoided, bad, dead, forceless, fruitless, ineffective, ineffectual, inoperative, invalid, negated, not viable, nugatory, null, null and void, set aside, sterile, unconfirmed, unenforceable, unfruitful, unratified, unsanctioned, unsuccessful, useless, vain, voided, worthless; SEE CONCEPT 560

void [*v1*] *get rid of; empty*
clear, deplete, discharge, dispose, drain, dump, eject, eliminate, emit, evacuate, flow, give off, go, pour, relieve, remove, throw out, vacate; SEE CONCEPTS 179,180

void [*v2*] *nullify, cancel*
abnegate, abrogate, annul, black out*, bleep*, blue pencil*, clean up, cut, declare null and void*, discharge, dissolve, drop*, gut*, invalidate, launder, rescind, sanitize, sterilize, take out, trim, vacate; SEE CONCEPTS 50,88,131,211

volatile [*adj*] *explosive, changeable*
airy, buoyant, capricious, effervescent, elastic, elusive, ephemeral, erratic, expansive, fickle, fleeting, flighty, flippant, frivolous, fugacious, fugitive, gaseous, gay, giddy, impermanent, imponderable, inconsistent, inconstant, light, lively, lubricious, mercurial, momentary, playful, resilient, short-lived, sprightly, subtle, temperamental, ticklish, transient, transitory, unsettled, unstable, unsteady, up-and-down, vaporous, variable, whimsical; SEE CONCEPTS 401,534

volition [*n*] *free will*
accord, choice, choosing, conation, desire, determination, discretion, election, option, preference, purpose, resolution, selection, will, willingness, wish; SEE CONCEPTS 20,41

volume [*n1*] *capacity, measure of capacity*
aggregate, amount, body, bulk, compass, content, contents, cubic measure, dimensions, extent, figure, mass, number, object, quantity, size, total; SEE CONCEPTS 719,740,794

volume [*n2*] *loudness of a sound*
amplification, degree, intensity, power, sonority, strength; SEE CONCEPTS 65,792

volume [*n3*] *book*
album, edition, publication, tome, treatise, version; SEE CONCEPT 280

voluminous [*adj*] *big, vast*
abundant, ample, billowing, bulky, capacious, cavernous, comprehensive, convoluted, copious, covering, expansive, extensive, full, great, large, legion, many, massive, multifarious, multitudinous, numerous, prolific, roomy, several, simple, spacious, sundry, swelling, various; SEE CONCEPTS 773,781

voluntarily [*adv*] *of one's own free-will*
at one's discretion, by choice, by preference, deliberately, freely, intentionally, of one's own ac-

vi
vo

cord*, on one's own, on one's own initiative*, optionally, spontaneously, willingly, with all one's heart*, without being asked, without prompting; SEE CONCEPTS *538,544*

voluntary [*adj*] *willing*
autonomous, chosen, deliberate, designful, discretional, elected, free, freely, free-willed, gratuitous, honorary, independent, intended, intentional, opted, optional, spontaneous, unasked, unbidden, uncompelled, unconstrained, unforced, unpaid, unprescribed, volitional, volunteer, willed, willful, wished, witting; SEE CONCEPTS *538,544*

volunteer [*v*] *offer to do something*
advance, bring forward, chip in*, come forward, do on one's own volition*, enlist, go in*, let oneself in for*, offer services, present, proffer, propose, put at one's disposal*, put forward, sign up, speak up, stand up, step forward, submit oneself, suggest, take bull by the horns*, take initiative*, take the plunge*, take upon oneself*, tender; SEE CONCEPTS *66,67*

voluptuous [*adj*] *given to sensual pleasure; pleasurable to the senses*
appealing, attractive, delightful, desirable, enticing, erotic, fleshly, hedonist, indulgent, lubricious, luxurious, pleasing, salacious, self-indulgent, sensuous, sexy, sybaritic, wanton; SEE CONCEPTS *372,485*

vomit [*v*] *disgorge*
be seasick*, be sick, bring up*, dry heave*, eject, emit, expel, gag*, heave*, hurl*, puke*, regurgitate, retch, ruminate, spew, spit up, throw up, upchuck*; SEE CONCEPTS *179,185,308*

voracious [*adj*] *very hungry, greedy*
avid, covetous, devouring, dog-hungry*, edacious, empty, gluttonous, gorging, grasping, gross, insatiable, omnivorous, piggy*, prodigious, rapacious, ravening, ravenous, sating, starved, starved to death*, starving, uncontrolled, unquenchable; SEE CONCEPTS *20,401*

vote [*n*] *decision or right to decide representation*
aye*, ballot, choice, franchise, majority, nay*, plebiscite, poll, referendum, secret ballot, show of hands*, suffrage, tally, ticket, will, wish, yea*, yes or no*; SEE CONCEPTS *300,376*

vote [*v*] *decide on representation*
ballot, cast ballot, cast vote, choose, confer, declare, determine, effect, elect, enact, enfranchise, establish, go to the polls*, grant, judge, opt, pronounce, propose, put in office*, recommend, return, second, suggest; SEE CONCEPTS *41,300*

vouch [*v*] *give assurance*
act as a witness, affirm, answer for, assert, asseverate, assure, attest to, avert, avow, back, bear testimony, be responsible for, certify, confirm, contend, corroborate, cosign, declare, get behind*, give an affidavit, guarantee, maintain, okay*, predicate, profess, prove, put forth, rubber-stamp*, say so*, sign for, sponsor, stand up for*, substantiate, support, swear to, swear up and down*, testify, uphold, verify, vow, warrant, witness; SEE CONCEPTS *49,71,317*

vow [*n*] *promise*
affiance, assertion, asseveration, oath, pledge, profession, troth, word of honor; SEE CONCEPTS *278,689*

vow [*v*] *make a solemn promise*
affirm, assure, consecrate, covenant, cross one's heart*, declare, dedicate, devote, give word of honor*, pledge, plight, promise, swear, swear up and down*, testify, undertake solemnly*, vouch, warrant; SEE CONCEPTS *71,297*

voyage [*n*] *journey, often by water*
boating, crossing, cruise, excursion, hop, jaunt, junket, overnight, passage, sail, swing, tour, travel, travels, trek, trip, weekend; SEE CONCEPTS *155,224*

vulgar [*adj1*] *rude, offensive*
base, blue*, boorish, cheap, coarse, common, contemptible, crude, dirty, disgusting, dishonorable, filthy, fractious, gross*, hard-core*, ignoble, impolite, improper, indecent, indecorous, indelicate, inferior, low, malicious, nasty, naughty, obscene, odious, off-color, profane, raw, repulsive, ribald, risqué, rough, rude, scatological, slippery, smutty, sneaking, soft-core*, sordid, suggestive, tasteless, tawdry, uncouth, unmannerly, unrefined, unworthy, villainous, X-rated*; SEE CONCEPTS *267,372,545*

vulgar [*adj2*] *common, general*
colloquial, conversational, dime a dozen*, everyday, familiar, garden variety*, low, native, ordinary, plastic, plebeian, popular, public, run-of-the-mill*, unrefined, vernacular; SEE CONCEPT *530*

vulnerable [*adj*] *open to attack*
accessible, assailable, defenseless, exposed, liable, naked, on the line*, on the spot*, out on a limb*, ready, sensitive, sitting duck*, sucker*, susceptible, tender, thin-skinned*, unguarded, unprotected, unsafe, weak, wide open*; SEE CONCEPTS *403,587*

W

wacky [*adj*] *acting crazy*
absurd, balmy, crazed, crazy, daft, demented, deranged, eccentric, erratic, foolish, hare-brained, insane, irrational, loony*, lunatic, mad, nuts*, nutty*, odd, preposterous, screwy*, silly, unpredictable, wild, zany*; SEE CONCEPTS *401,403*

wad [*n*] *ball of something*
back, block, boodle, bunch, bundle, chunk, clump, cushion, fortune, gathering, heap, hunk, lining, lump, mass, mint, nugget, packet, pad, pile, plug, pot, ream, roll, slew, stuff, tuft, wadding; SEE CONCEPTS *432,436*

waddle [*v*] *walk like a duck*
rock, shuffle, sway, toddle, totter, wiggle, wobble; SEE CONCEPT *151*

wade [*v*] *plod, often through water*
attack, attempt, bathe, drudge, fall to, ford, get feet wet*, get stuck in*, go for, initiate, jump in, labor, launch, light into, paddle, pitch in, set about, set to, splash, start, stumble, tackle, tear into*, toil, trek, walk, work through; SEE CONCEPTS *87,151*

waft [*v*] *carry*
bear, be carried, blow, carry, convey, drift, float, ride, transmit, transport; SEE CONCEPTS *147,217*

wag [*n*] *person who is very funny*
a million laughs*, card*, clown, comedian, comic, cutup*, droll*, farceur*, funny person, funster*, humorist, jester*, joker, jokester,

kibitzer*, kidder, life of the party*, madcap*, prankster, punster, quipster, show-off*, trickster, wisecracker, wit, zany; SEE CONCEPTS *416,423*

wag [v] *wiggle back and forth*
beat, bob, fish-tail*, flutter, lash, move side to side, nod, oscillate, quiver, rock, shake, shimmy, stir, sway, swing, switch, twitch, vibrate, waggle, wave; SEE CONCEPTS *150,152*

wage/wages [n] *earnings for work*
allowance, bacon*, bacon and eggs*, bread*, compensation, cut, emolument, fee, hire, pay, payment, price, receipts, recompense, remuneration, return, returns, reward, salary, share, stipend, sugar*, take*, take-home*; SEE CONCEPT *344*

wage [v] *carry on*
carry out, conduct, do, engage in, fulfill, make, practice, proceed with, prosecute, pursue, undertake; SEE CONCEPTS *91,100*

wager [n] *money or something gambled*
action, ante*, bet, challenge, chunk, fifty-fifty*, fighting chance*, flyer*, gamble, handle, hazard, hedge, hunch, long shot*, odds on*, outside chance*, parlay, play, pledge, plunge, pot*, risk, stake, toss-up, venture; SEE CONCEPTS *329,363,364*

wager [v] *bet money or something else in a gamble*
adventure, chance, gamble, game, hazard, hedge, hustle, lay, lay a wager, parlay, play, play the market*, pledge, plunge, put on*, put on the line*, put up, risk, set*, shoot*, shoot the works*, spec*, speculate, stake, take action, venture; SEE CONCEPTS *28,363*

waif [n] *lost or unclaimed person or thing*
castaway, dogie, drop*, fetch*, flotsam, foundling, homeless one, jetsam, orphan, ragamuffin, stray, urchin; SEE CONCEPT *423*

wail [v] *cry loudly*
bawl, bay, bemoan, bewail, carry on*, complain, cry the blues*, deplore, fuss, grieve, howl, jowl, keen, kick, lament, moan, mourn, repine, sob, squall, ululate, weep, whimper, whine; SEE CONCEPTS *77,185*

wait [n] *pause, delay*
down, downtime*, halt, hold*, hold-up, interim, interval, on hold*, rest, stay, time wasted*; SEE CONCEPT *807*

wait [v] *pause, rest*
abide, anticipate, await, bide, bide one's time*, cool it*, dally, delay, expect, fill time, foresee, hang*, hang around*, hang onto your hat*, hang out, hold back, hold everything*, hold on, hold the phone*, hole up*, keep shirt on*, lie in wait*, lie low*, linger, look for, look forward to, mark time*, put on hold*, remain, save it*, sit tight*, sit up for*, stall, stand by, stay, stay up for, stick around*, sweat it*, tarry, watch; SEE CONCEPTS *210,681*

wait on [v] *serve*
arrange, attend, care for, deal, deliver, help, minister, nurse, portion, ready, set, tend; SEE CONCEPTS *136,324*

waive [v] *give up; let go*
abandon, allow, cede, defer, delay, disclaim, disown, dispense with, forgo, grant, hand over, hold off, hold up, leave, neglect, postpone, prorogue, put off, refrain from, reject, relinquish, remit, remove, renege, renounce, reserve, resign, set aside, shelve, stay, surrender, suspend, table, turn over, yield; SEE CONCEPTS *121,234,317*

waiver [n] *giving up; letting go*
abandonment, abdication, disclaimer, foregoing, postponement, refusal, rejection, relinquishment, remission, renunciation, reservation, resignation, setting aside, surrender, tabling; SEE CONCEPTS *121,318,685*

wake [n1] *formal observance of a body before funeral*
deathwatch, funeral service, last rites, obsequies, rites, vigil, watch; SEE CONCEPTS *367,377*

wake [n2] *trail behind something*
aftermath, backwash, furrow, path, track, train, wash, wave; SEE CONCEPTS *753,824*

wake/waken [v1] *stop sleeping*
arise, awake, awaken, be roused, bestir, bring to life*, call, come to, get out of bed*, get up, nudge, open one's eyes*, prod, rise, rise and shine*, roll out, rouse, shake, stir, stretch, tumble out*, turn out, wake up; SEE CONCEPT *105*

wake/waken [v2] *excite, stimulate*
activate, animate, arouse, awaken, challenge, enliven, fire, fire up*, freshen, galvanize, grasp, jazz up*, key up*, kindle, notice, pep up*, provoke, quicken, rally, renew, rouse, see, steam up*, stir up, switch on*, understand, whet, zip up*; SEE CONCEPTS *7,14,22*

wakeful [adj] *alert, restless*
alive, astir, attentive, careful, heedful, insomniac, insomnious, observant, on guard, on the alert, on the lookout, on the qui vive, sleepless, unsleeping, vigilant, waking, wary, watchful, wide-awake; SEE CONCEPTS *539,542*

walk [n1] *brief travel on foot*
airing, carriage, circuit, constitutional, gait, hike, jaunt, march, pace, parade, perambulation, peregrination, promenade, ramble, saunter, schlepp*, step, stretch, stride, stroll, tour, traipse, tramp, tread, turn; SEE CONCEPTS *149,224*

walk [n2] *pathway*
aisle, alley, avenue, boardwalk, boulevard, bricks, bypath, byway, catwalk, cloister, course, court, crossing, esplanade, footpath, gangway, lane, mall, passage, path, pavement, pier, platform, promenade, road, sidewalk, street, track, trail; SEE CONCEPT *501*

walk [n3] *discipline*
area, arena, bailiwick, calling, career, course, domain, dominion, field, line, metier, profession, province, sphere, terrain, territory, trade, vocation; SEE CONCEPTS *349,360*

walk [v] *move along on foot*
advance, amble, ambulate, canter, escort, exercise, file, foot, go, go on foot*, hike, hit the road*, hoof it, knock about*, lead, leg*, locomote, lumber, march, meander, pace, pad, parade, patrol, perambulate, plod, prance, promenade, race, roam, rove, run, saunter, scuff, shamble, shuffle, slog, stalk, step, stride, stroll, strut, stump, take a walk, toddle, tour, traipse, tramp, travel on foot, traverse, tread, trek, troop, trudge, wander, wend one's way*; SEE CONCEPT *149*

wall [n] *obstruction, divider*
bank, bar, barricade, barrier, block, blockade, bulwark, curb, dam, embankment, enclosure, facade, fence, fortification, hindrance, hurdle, impediment, levee, limitation, palisade, panel, paneling, parapet, partition, rampart, restriction, retainer, roadblock, screen, side, stockade, stop, surface; SEE CONCEPTS *440,666*

vo
wa

wallop [n] *strong hit*
bash, belt, blow, bop, bump, clash, collision, crash, haymaker*, impact, jar, jolt, kick, percussion, punch, shock, slam, slug, smack, smash, thump, thwack*, whack; SEE CONCEPT *189*

wallop [v1] *beat, hit*
bam, bash, batter, belt, blast, boff, bop, buffet, bushwhack*, clobber*, drub*, hide, lambaste*, paste, pelt, plant one*, pound, pummel, punch, slam, slog, slug, smack, smash, sock, strike, swat, take out, tan*, thrash, thump, whack, wham, whomp, zap*; SEE CONCEPT *189*

wallop [v2] *defeat soundly*
beat, best, clobber*, crush*, drub*, lambaste*, lick*, rout, shellac*, thrash*, trim*, trounce, vanquish, whip*; SEE CONCEPT *95*

wallow [v1] *slosh around in*
bathe in, be immersed, blunder, flounder, get stuck, immerse, lie, loll, lurch, move around in, reel, roll, roll about, roll around in, splash around, sprawl, stagger, stumble, sway, toss, totter, tumble, wade, welter; SEE CONCEPTS *149,201*

wallow [v2] *become very involved in*
bask, delight, enjoy, glory, grovel, humor, indulge oneself, luxuriate, pamper, relish, revel, roll, rollick, spoil, take pleasure; SEE CONCEPT *384*

wan [adj] *colorless, weak*
anemic, ashen, ashy, bilious, blanched, bleached, bloodless, cadaverous, dim, discolored, faint, feeble, forceless, ghastly, haggard, ineffective, ineffectual, livid, pale, pallid, pasty, peaked, sickly, washed-out, waxen, white, worn; SEE CONCEPTS *314,618*

wand [n] *rod*
baton, caduceus, scepter, sprig, staff, stick, twig; SEE CONCEPTS *470,499*

wander [v1] *move about aimlessly*
aberrate, amble, circumambulate, circumlocute, circumnutate, cruise, deviate, divagate, diverge, drift, float, follow one's nose*, gad*, gallivant*, globe-trot, hike, hopscotch*, jaunt, maunder, meander, peregrinate, ramble, range, roam, roll, rove, saunter, straggle, stray, stroll, take to the road*, trail, traipse, tramp, trek, vagabond, walk the tracks*; SEE CONCEPTS *151,224*

wander [v2] *digress; get lost*
babble, depart, deviate, divagate, diverge, err, get off the track*, get sidetracked*, go astray*, go off on a tangent*, lose one's way, lose train of thought*, ramble, rave, shift, stray, swerve, talk nonsense*, veer; SEE CONCEPTS *101,266,665*

wanderer [n] *person who travels aimlessly*
adventurer, beachcomber, bum, drifter, explorer, floater, gad*, gadabout, gallivanter, globe-trotter, gypsy, itinerant, meanderer, nomad, pilgrim, rambler, ranger, roamer, rolling stone*, rover, straggler, stray, stroller, traveler, vagabond, vagrant, voyager; SEE CONCEPT *423*

wane [v] *diminish, lessen*
abate, atrophy, decline, decrease, die away, die down, die out, dim, draw to a close*, drop, dwindle, ease off, ebb, fade, fade away, fail, fall, fall short, let up, moderate, peter out*, relent, shrink, sink, slacken, slack off, subside, taper off, waste away, weaken, wind down*, wither; SEE CONCEPTS *698,776*

want [n1] *desire*
appetite, craving, demand, fancy, hankering, hunger, longing, necessity, need, requirement, thirst, wish, yearning, yen; SEE CONCEPT *20*

want [n2] *lack, need*
absence, dearth, default, defect, deficiency, destitution, exigency, exiguousness, famine, impecuniousness, impoverishment, inadequacy, indigence, insufficiency, meagerness, neediness, paucity, pauperism, penury, poorness, poverty, privation, scantiness, scarcity, shortage, skimpiness; SEE CONCEPTS *646,709*

want [v1] *desire*
ache, aspire, be greedy, choose, could do with*, covet, crave, desiderate, fancy, feel a need, hanker*, have ambition, have an urge for*, have a passion for*, have a yen for*, have eyes for*, hunger, incline toward*, itch for*, long, lust, need, pine, prefer, require, spoil for*, thirst, wish, yearn; SEE CONCEPT *20*

want [v2] *lack, need*
be deficient, be deprived of, be found wanting, be insufficient, be poor, be short of, be without, call for, demand, fall short in, have need of, miss, require, stand in need of, starve; SEE CONCEPT *646*

wanting [adj] *lacking, inadequate*
absent, away, bankrupt, bereft, burned out*, cooked*, cut off, defective, deficient, deprived, destitute, devoid, disappointing, empty, failing, faulty, gone, half-baked*, imperfect, incomplete, in default, inferior, less, minus, missing, needed, not good enough, not up to par*, omitted, out of gas*, patchy, poor, scant, scanty, scarce, short, shy, sketchy, substandard, too little too late*, unfulfilled, unsound; SEE CONCEPTS *531,546,560*

wanton [n] *profligate person*
debauchee, libertine, rake; SEE CONCEPTS *412,415,419*

wanton [adj1] *extravagant, lustful*
abandoned, fast*, lax, lewd, libertine, libidinous, licentious, outrageous, profligate, promiscuous, shameless, speedy*, unprincipled, unscrupulous, wayward, X-rated*; SEE CONCEPTS *372,401,545*

wanton [adj2] *cruel, malicious*
accidentally on purpose*, arbitrary, contrary, double-crossing*, evil, gratuitous, groundless, inconsiderate, malevolent, malicious, mean, merciless, motiveless, needless, ornery, perverse, senseless, spiteful, unasked, uncalled-for*, unfair, unjust, unjustifiable, unjustified, unprovoked, vicious, wayward, wicked, willful; SEE CONCEPT *401*

wanton [adj3] *careless*
capricious, changeable, devil-may-care*, extravagant, fanciful, fickle, fitful, fluctuating, free, frivolous, heedless, hot and cold*, immoderate, inconstant, intemperate, lavish, outrageous, prodigal, profuse, rash, reckless, spendthrift, spoiled, thriftless, unfettered, unreserved, unrestrained, up and down*, variable, volatile, wasteful, whimsical, wild; SEE CONCEPTS *534,542*

war [n] *armed conflict*
battle, bloodshed, cold war, combat, conflict, contention, contest, enmity, fighting, hostilities, hostility, police action, strife, strike, struggle, warfare; SEE CONCEPT *320*

war [v] *fight, battle*
attack, attempt, bombard, campaign against, challenge, clash, combat, contend, contest, differ, disagree, endeavor, engage in combat, go to war, kill, make war, march against, meet, murder, op-

pugn, shell, shoot, strive, struggle, take on, take the field against, take up arms, tug, wage war; SEE CONCEPTS *106,320*

ward [n1] *district*

area, canton, department, diocese, division, parish, precinct, quarter, territory, zone; SEE CONCEPTS *508,513*

ward [n2] *custody; person in one's custody*

adopted child, care, charge, child, client, dependent, foster child, godchild, guardianship, keeping, minor, orphan, pensioner, protection, protégé, protégée, pupil, safekeeping, trust; SEE CONCEPTS *414,691*

ward/ward off [v] *defend, guard*

avert, avoid, beat off, block, check, deflect, deter, divert, fend, foil, forestall, frustrate, halt, hold off, interrupt, keep at arm's length*, keep at bay*, keep off, obviate, parry, preclude, prevent, rebuff, rebut, repel, repulse, rule out, stave off, stop, stymie*, thwart, turn, turn aside, turn away; SEE CONCEPTS *96,134*

warden [n] *person who guards and manages*

administrator, bodyguard, caretaker, curator, custodian, deacon, dogcatcher, gamekeeper, governor, guard, guardian, jailer/jailor, janitor, keeper, officer, overseer, prison head, ranger, skipper, superintendent, watchdog, watchkeeper; SEE CONCEPT *347*

wardrobe [n] *clothes or furniture for storing clothes*

apparel, attire, buffet, bureau, chest, chiffonier, closet, clothing, commode, costumes, cupboard, drapes*, dresser, dry goods, duds*, ensembles, garments, locker, outfits, rags*, suits, threads*, toggery, togs, trousseau, trunk, vestments, weeds*; SEE CONCEPTS *443,451*

warehouse [n] *storage place*

barn, bin, depository, depot, distribution center, establishment, repository, shed, stash house, stockpile, stockroom, store, storehouse; SEE CONCEPTS *439,449*

wares [n] *merchandise for sale*

articles, commodities, goods, line, lines, manufactures, material, produce, product, products, range, seconds, stock, stuff, vendibles; SEE CONCEPT *338*

warfare [n] *armed conflict*

armed struggle, arms, battle, blows, campaigning, clash, combat, competition, contest, counterinsurgency, discord, emulation, fighting, hostilities, military operation, passage of arms, rivalry, strategy, strife, striving, struggle, tug-of-war*, war; SEE CONCEPT *320*

warlike [adj] *hostile, battling*

aggressive, attacking, bellicose, belligerent, bloodthirsty, combative, contending, contentious, contrary, fighting, gladiatorial, hawkish, inimical, martial, militant, militaristic, military, offensive, pugnacious, quarrelsome, ructious, soldierly, truculent, unfriendly, warmongering, warring; SEE CONCEPTS *401,548*

warm [adj1] *moderately hot*

balmy, broiling, clement, close, flushed, glowing, heated, hot, lukewarm, melting, mild, perspiring, pleasant, roasting, scorching, sizzling, snug, summery, sunny, sweating, sweaty, sweltering, temperate, tepid, thermal, toasty, warmish; SEE CONCEPT *605*

warm [adj2] *friendly, kind*

affable, affectionate, amiable, amorous, ardent, cheerful, compassionate, cordial, empathetic, fervent, genial, gracious, happy, heartfelt, hearty, hospitable, kindhearted, kindly, loving, pleasant, responsive, sincere, softhearted, sympathetic, tender, warmhearted, wholehearted; SEE CONCEPTS *267,401,404*

warm [adj3] *enthusiastic*

amorous, angry, animated, ardent, earnest, effusive, emotional, excitable, excited, fervent, fervid, glowing, gung-ho*, heated, hot*, intense, irascible, keen, lively, nutty*, passionate, spirited, stormy, vehement, vigorous, violent, zealous; SEE CONCEPTS *401,542*

warm [v] *heat up*

bake, chafe, cook, fix, heat, melt, microwave, prepare, put on the fire, thaw, toast, warm over, warm up; SEE CONCEPTS *170,255*

warn [v] *give notice of possible occurrence*

acquaint, address, admonish, advise, advocate, alert, apprise, caution, clue, clue in*, counsel, cry wolf*, deprecate, direct, dissuade, enjoin, exhort, fill in, forbid, forearm, forewarn, give fair warning, give the high sign*, give warning, guide, hint, inform, instruct, lay it out*, make aware, notify, order, post, predict, prepare, prescribe, prompt, put on guard, recommend, remind, remonstrate, reprove, signal, suggest, summon, tell, threaten, tip, tip off*, urge, wise up*; SEE CONCEPT *70*

warning [n] *notice of possible occurrence*

admonition, advice, alarm, alert, augury, caution, caveat, distress signal, example, exhortation, fore, foretoken, forewarning, guidance, handwriting on wall*, heads up*, hint, indication, information, injunction, intimation, lesson, look out*, Mayday*, notification, omen, portent, prediction, premonition, presage, recommendation, sign, signal, SOS*, suggestion, threat, tip, tip-off*, token, watch-it*, wink, word, word to the wise*; SEE CONCEPTS *78,274*

warning [adj] *cautionary*

admonishing, admonitory, cautioning, exemplary, exhortatory, monitorial, monitory, ominous, premonitory, threatening; SEE CONCEPT *267*

warp [v] *bend, distort*

bastardize*, brutalize, color, contort, corrupt, crook, curve, debase, debauch, deform, deprave, deviate, misrepresent, misshape, pervert, swerve, torture, turn, twist, vitiate, wind; SEE CONCEPTS *63,137,213,250*

warrant [n] *authorization*

accreditation, assurance, authentication, authority, basis, carte blanche, certificate, commission, credential, credentials, ducat, earnest, foundation, go-ahead*, green light*, guarantee, license, official document, okay*, pass, passport, pawn, permission, permit, pledge, right, sanction, security, shingle*, sticker, subpoena, summons, tag, testimonial, ticket, token, verification, warranty, word; SEE CONCEPTS *376,685*

warrant [v] *guarantee, justify, authorize*

affirm, answer for, approve, argue, assert, assure, attest, avouch, back, bear out, call for, certify, claim, commission, contend, declare, defend, delegate, demand, empower, endorse, ensure, entitle, excuse, explain, give grounds for, guarantee, guaranty, insure, license, maintain, necessitate, permit, pledge, privilege, promise, require, sanction, secure, sponsor, stand behind, state, stipulate, swear, take an oath*, undertake, underwrite,

wa
wa

uphold, vindicate, vouch for, vow; SEE CONCEPTS 50,57,71,88

warranty [n] *promise*
assurance, bail, bond, certificate, contract, covenant, guarantee, guaranty, pledge, security, surety, written promise; SEE CONCEPTS 684,685

warrior [n] *person who fights in combat*
battler, champion, combatant, conscript, enlisted person, fighter, fighting person, GI*, hero, serviceperson, soldier, trooper; SEE CONCEPT 358

wary [adj] *careful, cautious*
alert, attentive, cagey, calculating, canny, chary, circumspect, considerate, discreet, distrustful, doubting, frugal, gingerly, guarded, handling with kid gloves*, heedful, keeping on one's toes*, leery, on guard, on the lookout*, on the qui vive, provident, prudent, safe, saving, sly, sparing, suspicious, thinking twice*, thrifty, unwasteful, vigilant, walking on eggs*, watchful, watching one's step*, watching out, wide-awake; SEE CONCEPTS 401,403

wash [n1] *laundry, bath*
ablution, bathe, cleaning, cleansing, dirty clothes, laundering, rinse, scrub, shampoo, shower, washing; SEE CONCEPTS 451,514

wash [n2] *wave; water movement*
ebb and flow, eddy, flow, gush, heave, lapping, murmur, roll, rush, spurt, surge, surging, sweep, swell, swirl, swishing, undulation; SEE CONCEPT 748

wash [n3] *coloring*
coat, coating, film, layer, overlay, rinse, stain, suffusion, swab; SEE CONCEPT 475

wash [v1] *bathe, clean*
bath, brush up, bubble, cleanse, clean up, dip, do the dishes*, do the laundry*, douse, drench, float, freshen up*, fresh up*, hose, imbue, immerse, lap, launder, lave, moisten, rinse, scour, scrub, shampoo, shine, shower, slosh, soak, soap, sponge, starch, swab, take a bath*, take a shower*, tub, wash up*, wet, wipe; SEE CONCEPT 165

wash [v2] *be convincing*
be acceptable, bear scrutiny, be plausible, be reasonable, carry weight, convince, endure, hold up, hold water*, stand up*, stick*; SEE CONCEPT 676

waste [n1] *spending, use without thought*
decay, desolation, destruction, devastation, dilapidation, dissipation, disuse, exhaustion, expenditure, extravagance, fritter*, havoc, improvidence, lavishness, loss, lost opportunity*, misapplication, misuse, overdoing, prodigality, ravage, ruin, squander, squandering, unthriftiness, wastage, wastefulness; SEE CONCEPTS 156,252

waste [n2] *land that is uncultivated*
badlands, barren, bog, brush, brushland, bush, desert, dust bowl, fen, jungle, marsh, marshland, moor, quagmire, solitude, swamp, tundra, void, wasteland, wild, wilderness, wilds; SEE CONCEPT 509

waste [n3] *garbage, refuse*
debris, dreck, dregs, dross, excess, hogwash*, junk, leavings, leftovers, litter, offal, offscourings, rubbish, rubble, ruins, rummage, scrap, slop, sweepings, swill, trash; SEE CONCEPT 260

waste [v1] *spend or use without thought; dwindle*
atrophy, be of no avail*, blow, burn up, consume, corrode, crumble, debilitate, decay, decline, decrease, deplete, disable, disappear, dissipate, divert, drain, droop, eat away, ebb, emaciate,

empty, enfeeble, exhaust, fade, fritter away*, frivol away*, gamble away, gnaw, go to waste, lavish, lose, misapply, misemploy, misuse, perish, pour down the drain*, run dry, run through*, sap, sink, splurge, squander, thin, throw away, trifle away, undermine, wane, wear, wear out, wilt, wither; SEE CONCEPT 156

waste [v2] *ruin, destroy*
depredate, desecrate, desolate, despoil, devastate, devour, lay waste, pillage, rape, ravage, raze, reduce, sack, spoil, spoliate, wreak havoc; SEE CONCEPT 252

wasteful [adj] *not economical*
careless, cavalier, destructive, dissipative, extravagant, immoderate, improvident, incontinent, lavish, liberal, overdone, overgenerous, pound-foolish*, prodigal, profligate, profuse, reckless, ruinous, spendthrift, squandering, thriftless, uneconomical, unthrifty, wanton, wild; SEE CONCEPT 401

watch [n1] *clock worn on body*
analog watch, chronometer, digital watch, pocket watch, stopwatch, ticker*, timepiece, timer, wristwatch; SEE CONCEPT 463

watch [n2] *lookout*
alertness, attention, awareness, duty, eagle eye*, eye*, gander, guard, hawk, heed, inspection, notice, observance, observation, patrol, picket, scrutiny, sentinel, sentry, supervision, surveillance, tab, tout, vigil, vigilance, watchfulness, weather eye*; SEE CONCEPTS 134,623

watch [v1] *look at*
attend, case, check out, concentrate, contemplate, eagle-eye*, examine, eye*, eyeball*, focus, follow, gaze, get a load of*, give the once over*, have a look-see*, inspect, keep an eye on*, keep tabs on*, listen, look, mark, mind, note, observe, pay attention, peer, pipe*, regard, rubberneck*, scan, scope, scrutinize, see, spy, stare, take in, take notice, view, wait; SEE CONCEPT 623

watch [v2] *guard, protect*
attend, be on alert*, be on the lookout*, be vigilant*, be wary, be watchful, care for, keep, keep eyes open*, keep eyes peeled*, keep watch over, look after, look out, mind, oversee, patrol, pick up on, police, ride shotgun for*, superintend, take care of, take heed*, tend, wait; SEE CONCEPTS 134,623

watchful [adj] *on the lookout*
alert, all ears*, attentive, careful, cautious, chary, circumspect, glued*, guarded, heedful, hooked*, keen, not missing a trick*, observant, on guard, on one's toes*, on the ball*, on the job*, on the qui vive, on the watch, open-eyed, prepared, ready, see after, see to, suspicious, unsleeping, vigilant, wakeful, wary, while-awake, with eyes peeled*; SEE CONCEPT 401

watchkeeper [n] *person who guards, is on lookout*
caretaker, curator, custodian, detective, flagger, guard, keeper, lookout, observer, patrol, picket, police officer, ranger, scout, security guard, security officer, sentinel, sentry, signaller, spotter, spy, ward, warden, watch, watcher; SEE CONCEPT 348

water [n] *pure liquid hydrogen and oxygen*
Adam's ale*, aqua, aqua pura*, drink, H_2O, rain, rainwater, saliva, tears; SEE CONCEPT 467

water [v] *dampen; put water in*
baptize, bathe, damp, dilute, doctor, douse, drench, drool, flood, hose, imbue, inundate, irri-

gate, moisten, saturate, soak, sodden, souse, spatter, spray, sprinkle, steep, thin, wash, weaken, wet; SEE CONCEPT *256*

watery [*adj*] *liquid, diluted*
adulterated, anemic, aqueous, bloodless, colorless, damp, dilute, doused, flavorless, fluid, humid, insipid, marshy, moist, pale, runny, serous, sodden, soggy, tasteless, thin, washed, watered-down, waterlike, water-logged, weak, wet; SEE CONCEPTS *485,603,618*

wave [*n*] *sea surf, current*
bending, billow, breaker, coil, comber, convolution, corkscrew, crest, crush, curl, curlicue, drift, flood, foam, ground swell, gush, heave, influx, loop, movement, outbreak, rash, ridge, ripple, rippling, rocking, roll, roller, rush, scroll, sign, signal, stream, surge, sweep, swell, tendency, tide, tube, twirl, twist, undulation, unevenness, uprising, upsurge, whitecap, winding; SEE CONCEPTS *147,436,514*

wave [*v*] *move back and forth; gesture*
beckon, billow, brandish, coil, curl, direct, falter, flap, flourish, flow, fluctuate, flutter, fly, gesticulate, indicate, motion, move to and fro, oscillate, palpitate, pulsate, pulse, quaver, quiver, reel, ripple, seesaw, shake, sign, signal, stir, stream, surge, sway, swell, swing, swirl, swish, switch, tremble, twirl, twist, undulate, vacillate, vibrate, wag, waggle, waver, whirl, wield, wigwag*, wobble; SEE CONCEPTS *74,147,149*

waver [*v*] *shift back and forth; be indecisive*
be irresolute, be unable to decide*, blow hot and cold*, change, deliberate, dilly-dally*, dither, falter, flicker, fluctuate, halt, hedge, hem and haw*, hesitate, oscillate, palter, pause, pussyfoot around*, quiver, reel, run hot and cold*, seesaw*, shake, stagger, sway, teeter, totter, tremble, trim, undulate, vacillate, vary, waffle, wave, weave, whiffle, wobble, yo-yo*; SEE CONCEPTS *18,147,410*

wax [*v*] *become large, fuller*
augment, become, build, come, develop, dilate, enlarge, expand, fill out, get bigger, get to, grow, grow full, heighten, increase, magnify, mount, multiply, rise, run, swell, turn, upsurge; SEE CONCEPTS *704,780*

way [*n1*] *method, technique*
action, approach, contrivance, course, course of action, custom, design, expedient, fashion, form, groove*, habit, habitude, hang-up*, hook*, idea, instrument, kick, manner, means, measure, mode, modus, move, outline, plan, plot, policy, practice, procedure, process, scheme, shot, step, stroke, style, system, tack, thing*, usage, use, vehicle, wise, wont; SEE CONCEPT *6*

way [*n2*] *direction, route*
access, admission, admittance, advance, alternative, approach, artery, avenue, bearing, boulevard, byway, channel, course, distance, door, drag*, elbowroom, entrance, entrée, entry, extent, forward motion, gate, gateway, headway, highway, ingress, journey, lane, length, line, march, movement, opening, orbit, passage, path, pathway, progress, progression, ride, road, room, row, space, stone's throw*, street, stretch, tendency, thataway*, thoroughfare, track, trail, trend, walk; SEE CONCEPTS *501,738,739*

way [*n3*] *characteristic, habit*
aspect, behavior, circumstance, condition, conduct, consuetude, custom, detail, fashion, feature,

fettle, form, gait, groove, guise, habit, hook, idiosyncrasy, kick*, manner, nature, particular, personality, point, practice, praxis, respect, sense, shape, shot, situation, state, status, style, thing*, tone, trait, trick, usage, use, wont; SEE CONCEPT *411*

wayfaring [*adj*] *traveling*
drifting, gadabout, globe-trotting, itinerant, itinerate, jet-setting*, journeying, nomadic, perambulant, perambulatory, peripatetic, rambling, roving, rubbernecking*, vagabond, vagrant, voyaging, walking, wandering; SEE CONCEPT *401*

waylay [*v*] *intercept, ambush*
accost, ambuscade, assail, attack, box*, bushwhack*, catch, hold up, intercept, jump, lay for*, lie in wait, lurk, pounce on, prowl, set upon, skulk, slink, surprise, swoop down on*; SEE CONCEPTS *86,121*

wayward [*adj*] *contrary, unmanageable*
aberrant, arbitrary, balky, capricious, changeable, contumacious, cross-grained, delinquent, disobedient, disorderly, errant, erratic, fickle, flighty, fractious, froward, headstrong, immoral, inconstant, incorrigible, insubordinate, intractable, mulish, obdurate, obstinate, ornery*, perverse, rebellious, recalcitrant, refractory, restive, self-indulgent, self-willed, stubborn, uncompliant, undependable, ungovernable, unpredictable, unruly, unstable, variable, whimsical, willful; SEE CONCEPT *401*

weak [*adj1*] *not strong*
anemic, debilitated, decrepit, delicate, effete, enervated, exhausted, faint, feeble, flaccid, flimsy, forceless, fragile, frail, hesitant, impuissant, infirm, insubstantial, irresolute, lackadaisical*, languid, languorous, limp, makeshift, out of gas*, powerless, prostrate, puny, rickety, rocky*, rotten, senile, shaky, sickly, sluggish, spent, spindly, supine, tender, torpid, uncertain, undependable, unsound, unsteady, unsubstantial, wasted, wavering, weakened, weakly, wobbly; SEE CONCEPTS *314,488,489*

weak [*adj2*] *cowardly*
faint-hearted, fluctuant, frightened, hesitant, impotent, indecisive, ineffectual, infirm, insecure, irresolute, laid-back*, nerveless, nervous, palsied, powerless, shaky, soft, spineless, tender, timorous, uncertain, undependable, unreliable, unstable, unsure, vacillating, wavering, weak-kneed*, wimpy*, wishy-washy*, wobbly, zero*; SEE CONCEPTS *402,403,542*

weak [*adj3*] *faint, soft*
bated, dim, distant, dull, feeble, gentle, imperceptible, inaudible, indistinct, low, muffled, pale, poor, quiet, reedy, slight, small, stifled, thin, unaccented, unstressed, whispered; SEE CONCEPT *594*

weak [*adj4*] *deficient, feeble*
faulty, flabby, flimsy, forceless, green*, handicapped, hollow, immature, implausible, impotent, improbable, inadequate, incompetent, incomplete, inconceivable, inconclusive, incredible, ineffective, ineffectual, inept, invalid, lacking, lame, limited, pathetic, poor, raw, shaky, shallow, slight, slim, small, spineless, substandard, thick, thin, unbelievable, unconvincing, unprepared, unqualified, unsatisfactory, unsubstantial, unsure, untrained, wanting; SEE CONCEPTS *537,558,570*

wa
we

weak [adj5] *exposed, vulnerable*
accessible, assailable, defenseless, helpless, indefensible, unguarded, unprotected, unsafe, untenable, wide-open*, woundable; SEE CONCEPTS 576,587

weak [adj6] *watered-down*
dilute, diluted, insipid, milk-and-water*, runny, tasteless, thin, washy, waterish, watery, wishy-washy*; SEE CONCEPTS 462,485

weaken [v] *reduce the strength of*
abate, adulterate, break up, cripple, crumble, cut, debase, debilitate, decline, decrease, depress, devitalize, dilute, diminish, droop, dwindle, ease up, enervate, exhaust, fade, fail, faint, flag, give way, halt, impair, impoverish, invalidate, languish, lessen, limp, lose, lose spirit, lower, minimize, mitigate, moderate, reduce, relapse, relax, sap, slow down, soften, temper, thin, thin out, tire, totter, tremble, undermine, vitiate, wane, water down, wilt; SEE CONCEPTS 240,698

weakling [n] *person who has no strength*
baby, chicken*, chicken heart*, coward, cream puff*, crybaby, dotard, invertebrate, jellyfish*, misfit, pushover, wimp*, yellow belly*; SEE CONCEPTS 412,423

weakness [n] *defect, proneness*
Achilles heel*, appetite*, blemish, chink in armor*, debility, decrepitude, deficiency, delicacy, enervation, failing, faintness, fault, feebleness, flaw, fondness, fragility, frailty, gap, impairment, imperfection, impotence, inclination, inconstancy, indecision, infirmity, instability, invalidity, irresolution, lack, languor, lapse, liking, passion, penchant, powerlessness, predilection, proclivity, prostration, senility, shortcoming, soft spot*, sore point*, taste*, vice, vitiation, vulnerability; SEE CONCEPTS 411,674,732

wealth [n] *money, resources*
abundance, affluence, assets, belongings, bounty, cache, capital, cash, clover*, commodities, copiousness, cornucopia, dough*, estate, fortune, funds, gold, goods, hoard, holdings, lap of luxury*, long green*, lucre, luxuriance, luxury, means, opulence, pelf, plenitude, plenty, possessions, profusion, property, prosperity, prosperousness, revenue, riches, richness, security, stocks and bonds, store, substance, substantiality, treasure, velvet*, worth; SEE CONCEPTS 340,710

wealthy [adj] *rich; having a lot of money*
affluent, booming, comfortable, having it made*, independent, in the money*, loaded, made of money*, moneyed, of independent means, opulent, pecunious, prosperous, rolling in it*, substantial, upscale, well-heeled*, well-off*, well-to-do*; SEE CONCEPT 334

wear [n] *use, corrosion*
abrasion, attrition, damage, depreciation, deterioration, dilapidation, diminution, disappearance, employment, erosion, friction, impairment, inroads, loss, mileage, service, usefulness, utility, waste, wear and tear; SEE CONCEPTS 658,698

wear [v1] *be clothed in*
array, attire, bear, be dressed in, carry, clothe oneself, cover, display, don, draw on, dress in, effect, exhibit, fit out, get into, get on, harness, have on, put on, show, slip on, sport, suit up*, turn out*, wrap; SEE CONCEPTS 167,453

wear [v2] *corrode, use*
abrade, become threadbare, become worn, be worthless, chafe, consume, crumble, cut down,
decay, decline, decrease, deteriorate, diminish, drain, dwindle, erode, exhaust, fade, fatigue, fray, gall, go to seed*, graze, grind, impair, jade, overuse, overwork, rub, scrape, scrape off, scuff, shrink, tax, tire, use up, wash away, waste, wear out, wear thin, weary, weather; SEE CONCEPTS 156,225,240,698

wear [v3] *bother, undermine*
annoy, drain, enervate, exasperate, exhaust, fatigue, get the better of, harass, irk, pester, reduce, tax, vex, weaken, wear down, weary; SEE CONCEPTS 7,19

wear [v4] *endure*
bear up, be durable, hold up, last, remain, stand, stand up; SEE CONCEPT 23

weary [adj] *tired*
all in*, beat*, bone-tired*, bored, burned out*, bushed, dead*, dead tired*, discontented, disgusted, dog-tired*, done in*, drained, drooping, drowsy, enervated, exhausted, fagged, fatigued, fed up, flagging, had it*, impatient, indifferent, jaded, knocked out, out of gas*, overworked, pooped*, punchy*, ready to drop*, sick, sick and tired*, sleepy, spent*, taxed, wearied, wearing, wiped out*, worn out, zonked*; SEE CONCEPTS 314,403,485

weary [v] *make tired*
annoy, bore, burden, cause ennui, cloy, debilitate, depress, disgust, dishearten, distress, drain, droop, drowse, enervate, enfeeble, exasperate, exhaust, fade, fag, fail, fall off, fatigue, flag, glut, grow tired, harass, have had enough*, irk, jade, leave one cold*, lose interest, make discontented, nauseate, oppress, overwork, pain, plague, sap, sicken, sink, strain, take it out of*, tax, tire, tire out, try the patience of*, tucker out*, vex, weaken, wear down, wear out, weigh; SEE CONCEPTS 13,250,303

weather [n] *atmospheric conditions*
climate, clime, elements; SEE CONCEPTS 522,524

weather [v] *endure*
acclimate, bear the brunt of*, bear up against*, become toughened, brave, come through, expose, get through, grow hardened, grow strong, harden, make it, overcome, pull through, resist, ride out*, rise above*, season, stand, stick it out*, suffer, surmount, survive, toughen, withstand; SEE CONCEPTS 23,35,202

weave [v] *blend, unite; contrive*
braid, build, careen, complect, complicate, compose, construct, create, criss-cross, crochet, cue, entwine, fabricate, fold, fuse, incorporate, interfold, interlace, interlink, intermingle, intertwine, introduce, knit, knot, loop, lurch, make, make up, manufacture, mat, merge, mesh, move in and out, net, piece together, plait, ply, put together, reticulate, sew, snake, spin, splice, twine, twist, twist and turn, whip through, wind, wreathe, writhe, zigzag; SEE CONCEPTS 147,158

web [n] *netting*
cobweb, complexity, entanglement, fabric, fiber, filigree, gossamer, interconnection, interlacing, involvement, labyrinth, lacework, lattice, mat, matting, maze, mesh, meshwork, morass, net, network, plait, reticulation, screen, skein, snarl, tangle, texture, tissue, toil, trellis, warp, weave, webbing, weft, wicker, woof; SEE CONCEPTS 260,473

wed [v1] *marry*
become husband and wife, be married, couple,

espouse, get hitched*, get married, join, lead to
the altar, make one*, receive in marriage, say I
do*, take in marriage, tie*, tie the knot*, unite;
SEE CONCEPT *297*

wed [*v2*] *join, unite*
ally, associate, blend, coalesce, cojoin, combine,
commingle, connect, couple, dedicate, fuse, interweave, link, marry, merge, relate, unify, yoke;
SEE CONCEPTS *113,193*

wedding [*n*] *marriage rite*
bells*, bridal, espousal, hook, marriage, marriage
ceremony, matrimony, nuptial rite, nuptials, spousal, union, wedlock; SEE CONCEPT *297*

wedge [*n*] *solid piece, often triangular*
block, chock, chunk, cleat, cotter, cusp, keystone,
lump, prong, quoin, shim, spire, taper; SEE CON-
CEPTS *471,499*

weep [*v*] *cry*
bawl, bemoan, bewail, blubber*, boohoo*, break
down*, burst into tears*, complain, deplore, drip,
grieve, howl, keen, lament, let go*, let it out*,
mewl, moan, mourn, shed tears, snivel, sob,
squall, ululate, wail, whimper, yowl; SEE CON-
CEPTS *49,185*

weigh [*v1*] *measure heaviness*
counterbalance, have a weight of, heft, measure,
put in the balance, put on the scale, scale, tip the
scales at; SEE CONCEPT *103*

weigh [*v2*] *consider, contemplate*
analyze, appraise, balance, brainstorm*, deliberate, estimate, evaluate, examine, excogitate, give
thought to, hash over*, meditate, mind, mull over,
perpend, ponder, rate, reflect upon, rehash, sort
out, study, sweat*, think about, think out, think
over, track; SEE CONCEPT *24*

weigh [*v3*] *have influence*
be heavy, be important, be influential, be something, burden, carry weight, charge, count, cumber, cut, cut some ice*, import, impress, lade,
matter, mean, militate, press, pull, register, saddle, show, signify, stack up against* tax tell;
SEE CONCEPTS *7,19,22,237,682*

weigh down [*v*] *depress*
bear down, burden, cumber, get down, hold
down, oppress, overburden, overload, press, press
down, prey on, pull down, sadden, task, trouble,
weight, weigh upon, worry; SEE CONCEPTS *7,19*

weight [*n1*] *heaviness*
adiposity, avoirdupois, ballast, burden, density,
G-factor*, gravity, gross, heft, heftiness, load,
mass, measurement, net, ponderosity, ponderous-
ness, poundage, pressure, substance, tonnage;
SEE CONCEPT *795*

weight [*n2*] *something used to measure heaviness*
anchor, ballast, bob, counterbalance, counterpoise, counterweight, mass, pendulum, plumb,
plumb bob, poundage, pressure, rock, sandbag,
sinker, stone; SEE CONCEPTS *290,470*

weight [*n3*] *importance*
access, authority, clout, connection, consequence,
consideration, credit, effectiveness, efficacy, emphasis, forcefulness, forcibleness, impact, import,
influence, magnitude, moment, momentousness,
persuasiveness, pith, potency, power, powerfulness, prestige, pull, significance, signification,
substance, sway, value, weightiness; SEE CON-
CEPTS *668,682*

weight [*n4*] *burden*
albatross*, ball and chain*, charge, cumber, cumbrance, deadweight*, duty, encumbrance, excess

baggage*, load, millstone*, onus, oppression,
pressure, responsibility, strain, task, tax; SEE
CONCEPTS *532,674,679,690*

weighty [*adj1*] *heavy*
burdensome, cumbersome, cumbrous, dense, fat,
fleshy, hefty, massive, obese, overweight, ponderous, porcine, portly, stout; SEE CONCEPT *491*

weighty [*adj2*] *serious, important*
big, big deal*, consequential, considerable, critical, crucial, earnest, forcible, grave, heavy*,
heavyweight, life and death*, material, meaningful, momentous, no-nonsense*, portentous, sedate, severe, significant, sober, solemn, somber,
staid, substantial, underlined; SEE CONCEPTS
548,568

weighty [*adj3*] *troublesome, difficult*
backbreaking, burdensome, crushing, demanding,
exacting, exigent, grievous, onerous, oppressive,
superincumbent, taxing, tough, worrisome, worrying; SEE CONCEPTS *538,565*

weird [*adj*] *odd, bizarre*
awe-inspiring, awful, creepy*, curious, dreadful,
eccentric, eerie*, far-out*, fearful, flaky*,
freaky*, funky*, ghastly, ghostly, grotesque,
haunting, horrific, inscrutable, kinky*, kooky*,
magical, mysterious, occult, oddball*, ominous,
outlandish, peculiar, preternatural, queer, secret,
singular, spooky*, strange, supernal, supernatural, uncanny, uncouth, unearthly, unnatural; SEE
CONCEPTS *564,570*

welcome [*n*] *greeting*
acceptance, entertainment, entrée, friendliness,
handshake, hello, hospitality, howdy*, key to the
city*, ovation, reception, red carpet*, rumble*,
salutation, salute, tumble*; SEE CONCEPT *278*

welcome [*adj*] *gladly received*
acceptable, accepted, agreeable, appreciated,
cherished, congenial, contenting, cordial, delightful, desirable, desired, esteemed, favorable, genial, good, grateful, gratifying, honored, invited,
nice, pleasant, pleasing, pleasurable, refreshing,
satisfying, sympathetic, wanted, SEE CONCEPTS
555,572

welcome [*v*] *receive gladly*
accept, accept gladly, accost, admit, bid welcome,
embrace, entertain, flag*, greet, hail, hug, meet,
offer hospitality, receive, roll out red carpet*, salute, show in, take in, tumble*, usher in; SEE CON-
CEPTS *266,384*

weld [*v*] *bind, connect*
bond, braze, cement, combine, fix, fuse, join,
link, solder, unite; SEE CONCEPT *193*

welfare/well-being [*n*] *health and prosperity*
abundance, advantage, benefit, contentment, ease,
easy street*, euphoria, felicity, good, good fortune, happiness, interest, luck, profit, progress,
satisfaction, success, thriving; SEE CONCEPTS
316,693,706

well [*n*] *water hole*
abyss, bore, chasm, depression, derivation, fount,
fountain, fountainhead, geyser, hole, inception,
mine, mouth, origin, pit, pool, repository, reservoir, root, shaft, source, spa, spout, spring,
springs, watering place, wellspring; SEE CON-
CEPTS *509,513,514*

well [*adj1*] *healthy*
able-bodied, alive and kicking*, blooming, bright-
eyed*, bushy-tailed*, chipper*, fine, fit, flourishing, fresh, great, hale, hardy, hearty, husky, in
good health, in the pink*, right, right as rain*,

we
we

robust, sane, solid as a rock*, sound, strong, strong as an ox*, together, trim, up to par*, vigorous, whole, wholesome, wrapped tight*; SEE CONCEPT 314

well [adj2] *lucky, fortunate*
advisable, agreeable, bright, comfortable, fine, fitting, flourishing, good, happy, pleasing, profitable, proper, prosperous, providential, prudent, right, satisfactory, thriving, useful; SEE CONCEPTS 548,572

well [adv1] *happily, pleasantly; capably*
ably, accurately, adeptly, adequately, admirably, agreeably, attentively, capitally, carefully, closely, commendably, competently, completely, conscientiously, correctly, effectively, efficiently, excellently, expertly, famously, favorably, fully, in a satisfactory manner, irreproachably, nicely, proficiently, profoundly, properly, rightly, satisfactorily, skillfully, smoothly, soundly, splendidly, strongly, successfully, suitably, thoroughly, with skill; SEE CONCEPTS 527,528,544

well [adv2] *sufficiently*
abundantly, adequately, amply, appropriately, becomingly, by a wide margin, completely, considerably, easily, effortlessly, entirely, extremely, far, fittingly, freely, fully, greatly, heartily, highly, luxuriantly, plentifully, properly, quite, rather, readily, right, satisfactorily, smoothly, somewhat, substantially, suitably, thoroughly, very much, wholly; SEE CONCEPTS 558,772

well-bred [adj] *mannerly*
aristocratic, blue-blooded*, civil, considerate, courteous, courtly, cultivated, cultured, gallant, genteel, gentle, noble, patrician, polished, polite, refined, taught, trained, upper-crust*, urbane, well-behaved, well-mannered; SEE CONCEPTS 334,401

well-known [adj] *familiar, famous*
acclaimed, big, big name*, celeb*, celebrated, common, conspicuous, eminent, illustrious, important, infamous, in the limelight*, in the public eye*, known, large, leading, name, notable, noted, notorious, outstanding, popular, prominent, public, recognized, renowned, reputable, somebody, splashy, star, superstar, VIP*, widely known, WK*; SEE CONCEPT 568

well-off [adj] *successful, wealthy*
affluent, comfortable, easy, flourishing, flush, fortunate, loaded, lucky, moneyed, prosperous, rich, snug, substantial, thriving, well, well-to-do; SEE CONCEPT 334

welt [n] *red mark*
bruise, contusion, injury, mouse, ridge, scar, streak, stripe, wale, weal, wheal, wound; SEE CONCEPT 309

wet [n] *dampness, moisture*
clamminess, condensation, damp, drizzle, humidity, liquid, rain, rains, water, wetness; SEE CONCEPT 607

wet [adj] *damp, moist*
aqueous, clammy, dank, dewy, drenched, dripping, drizzling, foggy, humid, misty, moistened, muggy, pouring, raining, rainy, saturate, saturated, showery, slimy, slippery, slushy, snowy, soaked, soaking, sodden, soggy, sopping, soppy, soused, stormy, teary, teeming, water-logged, watery, wringing-wet; SEE CONCEPT 603

wet [v] *cause to become damp, moist*
bathe, damp, dampen, deluge, dip, douse, drench, drown, hose, humidify, imbue, irrigate, moisten, rinse, saturate, soak, sop, souse, splash, spray, sprinkle, steep, wash, water; SEE CONCEPTS 161,256

whack [n1/v] *hit*
bang, bash, bat, beat, belt, biff, box, buffet, clobber, clout, crack, cuff, ding*, lambaste*, nail, rap, slap, slug, smack, smash, sock, strike, thrash, thump, thwack*, wallop, wham*; SEE CONCEPT 189

whack [n2] *try, attempt*
bash, crack, fling, go, pop, shot, slap, stab, turn, whirl; SEE CONCEPT 87

wharf [n] *boat storage*
berth, breakwater, dock, jetty, landing, landing stage, levee, pier, quay, slip; SEE CONCEPT 439

wheedle [v] *talk into*
banter, blandish, butter up*, cajole, charm, coax, con, court, draw, entice, finagle, flatter, inveigle, kowtow*, lay it on*, oil*, persuade, seduce, snow*, soap*, soften up*, soft-soap*, spread it on*, sweeten up*, sweet-talk*, work on*, worm*; SEE CONCEPT 68

wheel [n] *circle, revolution*
caster, circuit, circulation, circumvolution, cycle, disk, drum, gyration, gyre, hoop, pivot, pulley, ratchet, ring, roll, roller, rotation, round, spin, trolley, turn, twirl, whirl; SEE CONCEPTS 436,464,502

wheel [v] *turn, rotate*
circle, gyrate, orbit, pirouette, pivot, reel, revolve, roll, spin, swing, swivel, trundle, twirl, whirl; SEE CONCEPT 147

wheeze [v] *breathe roughly, heavily*
buzz, catch one's breath, cough, gasp, hiss, murmur, pant, puff, rasp, sibilate, snore, whisper, whistle; SEE CONCEPTS 163,308

when [conj] *though*
albeit, although, at, at the same time, during, howbeit, immediately upon, just after, just as, meanwhile, much as, whereas, while; SEE CONCEPT 799

where [n] *place*
location, locus, point, position, site, situation, spot, station; SEE CONCEPT 583

where/wherever [adv] *at which point*
anywhere, everywhere, in whatever place, in which, to what end, to which, whereabouts, whither; SEE CONCEPT 583

whet [v1] *make sharp*
edge, file, finish, grind, hone, sharpen, strop; SEE CONCEPTS 137,250

whet [v2] *arouse, excite*
animate, awaken, challenge, enhance, incite, increase, kindle, pique, provoke, quicken, rally, rouse, stimulate, stir, wake, waken; SEE CONCEPTS 7,11,22

whiff [n] *smell of an odor*
aroma, blast, breath, dash, draught, flatus, fume, gust, hint, inhalation, odor, puff, scent, shade, smack, sniff, snuff, soupçon, trace, trifle, waft; SEE CONCEPTS 599,601,602

while [n] *time interval*
bit, instant, interim, meantime, moment, occasion, period, space, spell, stretch, time; SEE CONCEPTS 807,822

while [conj] *as long as*
although, at the same time, during, during the

time, in the time, throughout the time, whilst; SEE CONCEPT 799

while [conj2] *even though*
albeit, although, howbeit, much as, though, when, whereas; SEE CONCEPT 544

whim [n] *sudden idea*
caprice, conceit, craze, desire, disposition, dream, fad, fancy, fantasy, freak, humor, impulse, inclination, notion, passing thought, quirk, sport, thought, urge, vagary, vision, whimsy; SEE CONCEPTS 529,661

whimper [v] *cry softly*
bleat, blubber, complain, fuss, mewl, moan, object, pule, snivel, sob, weep, whine; SEE CONCEPTS 77,185

whimsical [adj] *playful, fanciful*
amusing, arbitrary, capricious, chancy, chimerical, comical, curious, dicey, droll, eccentric, erratic, fantastic, flaky*, freakish, funny, kinky*, mischievous, odd, peculiar, quaint, queer*, quizzical, singular, uncertain, unpredictable, unusual, waggish, wayward, weird*; SEE CONCEPTS 401,548

whine [n] *complaint, cry*
gripe, grouse, grumble, moan, plaintive cry, sob, wail, whimper; SEE CONCEPTS 54,77

whine [v] *complain, cry*
bellyache, carp, drone, fuss, gripe, grouse, grumble, howl, kick, mewl, moan, murmur, pule, repine, snivel, sob, wail, whimper, yowl; SEE CONCEPTS 54,77

whip [n] *length of material for hitting*
bat, belt, birch, bullwhip, cane, cat-o'-nine-tails, crop, goad, horsewhip, knout, lash, prod, push, rawhide, rod, ruler, scourge, strap, switch, thong; SEE CONCEPT 499

whip [v1] *hit repeatedly*
bash, beat, birch, bludgeon, cane, castigate, chastise, cudgel, drub, ferule, flagellate, flog, hide, larrup*, lash, lather*, punish, scourge, spank, strap, strike, switch, tan, thrash, trash, wallop, whale, whomp*; SEE CONCEPT 189

whip [v2] *defeat soundly*
beat, best, blast, clobber, conquer, drub, hammer*, kill*, lambaste, lick*, mop up*, outdo, overcome, overpower, overrun, overwhelm, put away*, rout, run circles around*, settle, steamroller*, subdue, take apart*, thrash, top, trim*, trounce, vanquish, wallop, wax*, whomp*, worst*; SEE CONCEPT 95

whip [v3] *dash, dart*
avert, deflect, dive, divert, flash, flit, fly, jerk, pivot, pull, rush, seize, sheer, shoot, snatch, surge, tear, turn, veer, wheel, whirl, whisk; SEE CONCEPTS 150,152

whip [v4] *agitate, stir up*
beat, blend, mix, whisk, work up; SEE CONCEPTS 152,170

whip up [v] *incite, excite*
abet, agitate, arouse, compel, disturb, drive, foment, goad, hound, inflame, instigate, kindle, prick, prod, provoke, push, raise, set, set on, spur, start, stir, stir up, urge, work up; SEE CONCEPTS 14,221

whirl [n1] *spin, revolution*
circle, circuit, circulation, circumvolution, flurry, gyration, gyre, pirouette, reel, roll, rotation, round, spin, surge, swirl, turn, twirl, twist, wheel, whir, whirlpool; SEE CONCEPTS 152,738

whirl [n2] *commotion, confusion*
ado*, agitation, bustle, clatter, daze, dither, ferment, flurry, fluster, flutter, furor, fuss, hubbub*, hurly-burly*, hurry, merry-go-round*, moil, pother, round, ruction, rush, series, spin, stir, storm, succession, tempest, tumult, turbulence, uproar, whirlwind; SEE CONCEPTS 230,388

whirl [n3] *attempt*
bash, crack, fling, go, pop, shot, slap, stab, try, whack*; SEE CONCEPT 87

whirl [v] *spin around*
circle, eddy, gyrate, gyre, pirouette, pivot, purl, reel, revolve, roll, rotate, swirl, swoosh, turn, turn around, twirl, twist, wheel, whir; SEE CONCEPT 152

whirlpool [n] *spinning water*
eddy, maelstrom, stir, undercurrent, undertow, vortex, whirl; SEE CONCEPT 514

whirlwind [adj] *very fast*
cyclonic, hasty, headlong, hurricane, impetuous, impulsive, lightning, quick, rapid, rash, short, speedy, swift, tornado; SEE CONCEPTS 588,798

whisk [v] *brush quickly; hasten*
barrel, bullet, dart, dash, flick, flit, flutter, fly, hurry, race, rush, shoot, speed, sweep, tear, whip, whiz, wipe, zip; SEE CONCEPT 152

whisper [n1] *rumor; information expressed in soft voice*
buzz*, confidence, disclosure, divulgence, gossip, hint, hum, hushed tone, innuendo, insinuation, low voice, mumble, murmur, mutter, report, secret, secret message, sigh, sighing, susurration, undertone, word; SEE CONCEPTS 274,278

whisper [n2] *trace, suggestion*
breath, dash, fraction, hint, shade, shadow, soupçon, suspicion, tinge, touch, whiff; SEE CONCEPTS 529,673,831

whisper [v] *speak softly*
breathe, buzz*, confide, gossip, hint, hiss, insinuate, intimate, mumble, murmur, mutter, say softly, say under one's breath*, sibilate, sigh, speak confidentially, spread rumor, susurrate, talk into someone's ear*, talk low, tell, tell a secret; SEE CONCEPTS 60,266

whistle [v] *make sharp, shrill sound*
blare, blast, fife, flute, hiss, pipe, shriek, signal, skirl, sound, toot, tootle, trill, warble, wheeze, whine, whiz*; SEE CONCEPTS 65,77

whit [n] *very tiny bit*
atom, crumb, dash, drop, fragment, grain, hoot*, iota, jot, little, mite, modicum, particle, piece, pinch, scrap, shred, speck, trace; SEE CONCEPTS 831,835

white [adj] *extremely pale; lacking color*
achromatic, achromic, alabaster, ashen, blanched, bleached, bloodless, chalky, clear, fair, frosted, ghastly, hoary, immaculate, ivory, light, milky, neutral, pallid, pasty, pearly, silver, silvery, snowy, transparent, wan, waxen; SEE CONCEPT 618

whiten [v] *make or become extremely pale*
blanch, bleach, blench, chalk, decolor, decolorize, dull, etiolate, fade, frost, grizzle, lighten, pale, silver, turn pale, white, whitewash; SEE CONCEPT 250

whitewash [v] *cover up the truth*
blanch, camouflage, conceal, exonerate, extenuate, gloss over, launder*, liberate, make light of*, paint, palliate, sugarcoat*, suppress, varnish, ve-

we
wh

neer, vindicate, white, whiten; SEE CONCEPTS 49,63

whittle [v] *cut away at; reduce*
carve, chip, consume, decrease, diminish, eat away, erode, fashion, form, hew, lessen, model, mold, pare, sculpt, shape, shave, trim, undermine, wear away; SEE CONCEPTS 176,184,236,247

whiz [n] *very intelligent person*
adept, expert, genius, gifted person, marvel, pro*, prodigy, professional, star, virtuoso, wonder; SEE CONCEPT 416

whiz [v] *move quickly by*
bullet, buzz, dart, flit, fly, hiss, hum, hurry, hurtle, race, speed, swish, whir, whirl, whisk, whoosh*, zip; SEE CONCEPT 150

whole [n] *total made up of parts*
aggregate, aggregation, all, amount, assemblage, assembly, being, big picture, body, bulk, coherence, collectivity, combination, complex, ensemble, entirety, entity, everything, fullness, gross, hook line and sinker*, integral, jackpot*, linkage, lock stock and barrel*, lot, lump, oneness, organism, organization, piece, quantity, quantum, result, sum, summation, sum total*, supply, system, the works*, totality, unit, unity, whole ball of wax*, whole enchilada*, whole nine yards*, whole shebang*; SEE CONCEPTS 432,635,837

whole [adj1] *entire, complete*
accomplished, aggregate, all, choate, completed, concentrated, conclusive, consummate, every, exclusive, exhaustive, fixed, fulfilled, full, full-length, gross, inclusive, in one piece, integral, outright, perfect, plenary, rounded, total, unabbreviated, unabridged, uncut, undivided, unexpurgated, unqualified, utter; SEE CONCEPT 531

whole [adj2] *unbroken, perfect*
complete, completed, developed, faultless, flawless, good, in good order*, in one piece*, intact, inviolate, mature, mint, plenary, preserved, replete, safe, ship-shape, solid, sound, thorough, together, undamaged, unharmed, unhurt, unimpaired, uninjured, unmarred, unmutilated, unscathed, untouched, without a scratch; SEE CONCEPTS 485,574

whole [adj3] *healthy*
able-bodied, better, cured, fit, hale, healed, hearty, in fine fettle, in good health, recovered, right, robust, sane, sound, strong, well, wholesome; SEE CONCEPT 314

wholehearted/whole-hearted [adj] *enthusiastic, sincere*
abiding, ardent, authentic, bona fide, candid, committed, complete, dedicated, determined, devoted, earnest, emphatic, enduring, fervent, frank, genuine, heartfelt, hearty, impassioned, never-failing, passionate, real, serious, steadfast, steady, sure, true, unfaltering, unfeigned, unqualified, unquestioning, unreserved, unstinting, unwavering, warm, zealous; SEE CONCEPTS 542,548,582

wholesale [adj] *all-inclusive*
broad, bulk, complete, comprehensive, extensive, far-reaching, general, in bulk, indiscriminate, in quantity, in the mass, large-scale, mass, overall, quantitative, sweeping, total, wide-ranging, widespread; SEE CONCEPTS 771,772

wholesome [adj] *healthy, decent*
all there, beneficial, clean, edifying, ethical, exemplary, fit, good, hale, healthful, health-giving, helpful, honorable, hygienic, in fine feather*, innocent, in the pink*, invigorating, moral, nice, normal, nourishing, nutritious, nutritive, pure, respectable, restorative, right, righteous, safe, salubrious, salutary, sane, sanitary, sound, strengthening, together, virtuous, well, worthy; SEE CONCEPTS 314,462,537,545

wholly [adv1] *completely, entirely*
all, all in all*, all the way*, altogether, comprehensively, from A to Z*, fully, heart and soul*, in every respect*, in toto, one hundred percent*, outright, perfectly, quite, roundly, thoroughly, top to bottom*, totally, utterly, well; SEE CONCEPTS 531,772

wholly [adv2] *exclusively*
individually, just, only, purely, solely, specifically, without exception; SEE CONCEPT 557

whoop [n/v] *hurrah*
bellow, boo, cheer, cry, cry out, holler, hoot, howl, jeer, scream, shout, shriek, squawk, yell; SEE CONCEPT 77

whopping [adj] *enormous*
big, colossal, extraordinary, gargantuan, giant, gigantic, great, huge, immense, large, mammoth, massive, mighty, monstrous, mountainous, prodigious, tremendous; SEE CONCEPTS 773,781

whorl [n] *spiral*
coil, corkscrew, curl, eddy, helix, swirl, twirl, twist, vortex, whirlpool; SEE CONCEPT 436

wicked [adj1] *corrupt, bad*
abandoned, abominable, amoral, arch, atrocious, bad news*, base, contemptible, debased, degenerate, depraved, devilish, dissolute, egregious, evil, fiendish, flagitious, foul, gross, guilty, heartless, heinous, immoral, impious, impish, incorrigible, indecent, iniquitous, irreligious, low-down, mean, mischievous, nasty, naughty, nefarious, profane, reprobate, rotten, scandalous, shameful, shameless, sinful, unethical, unprincipled, unrighteous, vicious, vile, villainous, wayward, worthless; SEE CONCEPTS 401,545

wicked [adj2] *destructive, troublesome*
acute, agonizing, awful, barbarous, bothersome, chancy, crashing, dangerous, difficult, distressing, dreadful, fearful, fierce, galling, harmful, hazardous, injurious, intense, mean, mighty, offensive, outrageous, painful, perilous, pesky, risky, severe, terrible, treacherous, troublous, trying, ugly, uncivilized, unconscionable, ungodly, unhealthy, unholy, unpleasant, unsound, vexatious; SEE CONCEPTS 537,565,571

wicked [adj3] *expert*
able, adept, adroit, au fait, capable, clever, competent, deft, good, masterly, mighty, outstanding, powerful, pretty, qualified, skillful, strong; SEE CONCEPT 527

wide [adj1] *expansive, roomy*
advanced, all-inclusive, ample, baggy, broad, capacious, catholic, commodious, comprehensive, deep, dilated, distended, encyclopedic, expanded, extensive, far-ranging, far-reaching, full, general, immense, inclusive, large, large-scale, liberal, loose, open, outspread, outstretched, progressive, radical, scopic, spacious, splay, squat, sweeping, tolerant, universal, vast, voluminous; SEE CONCEPTS 772,773,796

wide [adj2] *off-course*
astray, away, distant, far, far-off, inaccurate, off, off-target, off the mark, remote; SEE CONCEPTS 581,583

widen [v] *open up*
add to, augment, broaden, dilate, distend, enlarge, expand, extend, grow, grow larger, increase, multiply, open, open out, open wide, ream, spread, spread out, stretch, swell, unfold; SEE CONCEPTS 236,245,780

widespread [adj] *extensive*
across the board*, all over the place*, boundless, broad, common, comprehensive, current, diffuse, epidemic, far-flung, far-reaching, general, on a large scale, outspread, overall, pandemic, pervasive, popular, prevailing, prevalent, public, rampant, regnant, rife, ruling, sweeping, universal, unlimited, unrestricted, wall-to-wall*, wholesale; SEE CONCEPTS 530,536,772

width [n] *breadth, wideness of some amount*
amplitude, area, broadness, compass, cross measure, diameter, distance across, expanse, extent, girth, measure, range, reach, scope, span, squatness, stretch, thickness; SEE CONCEPTS 760,788,792

wield [v] *control, use*
apply, brandish, command, conduct, employ, exercise, exert, flourish, handle, have, have at one's disposal, hold, maintain, make use of, manage, maneuver, manipulate, operate, ply, possess, put to use, shake, swing, throw, utilize, wave, work; SEE CONCEPTS 94,147,225

wife [n] *married woman*
bride, companion, consort, helpmate, mate, monogamist, other half*, partner, roommate, spouse; SEE CONCEPTS 414,415

wiggle [n/v] *shake back and forth*
jerk, jiggle, shimmy, squirm, twist, twitch, wag, waggle, wave, worm, wriggle, writhe, zigzag; SEE CONCEPTS 80,150,152

wild [adj1] *untamed*
agrarian, barbarian, barbaric, barbarous, dense, desert, deserted, desolate, escaped, feral, ferocious, fierce, free, indigenous, lush, luxuriant, native, natural, neglected, overgrown, overrun, primitive, rampant, rude, savage, unbroken, uncivilized, uncultivated, undomesticated, uninhabited, untouched, vicious, waste; SEE CONCEPTS 406,583

wild [adj2] *disorderly, rowdy*
avid, berserk, boisterous, chaotic, crazed, crazy, eager, enthusiastic, extravagant, flighty, foolhardy, foolish, giddy, hysterical, impetuous, impracticable, imprudent, incautious, irrational, lawless, licentious, mad, madcap, noisy, nuts, outrageous, preposterous, profligate, rabid, rash, raving, reckless, riotous, rough, self-willed, turbulent, unbridled, uncontrolled, undisciplined, unfettered, ungovernable, unmanageable, unrestrained, unruly, uproarious, violent, wayward; SEE CONCEPT 401

wild [adj3] *intense, stormy*
blustering, blustery, choppy, disturbed, furious, howling, inclement, raging, rough, storming, tempestuous, turbulent, violent; SEE CONCEPTS 525,569

wilderness/wilds [n] *uninhabited area*
back country, back of beyond*, badland, barrens, boondocks, bush, desert, forest, hinterland, jungle, middle of nowhere*, outback, primeval forest, sticks*, waste, wasteland, wild; SEE CONCEPT 517

wile [n] *cunning*
angle, artfulness, artifice, cheating, chicane, chicanery, con*, contrivance, craft, craftiness, deceit, deception, device, dishonesty, dissimulation, dodge, feint, flimflam*, fraud, gambit, game, gimmick, guile, hoax, horseplay, imposition, little game*, lure, maneuver, monkey business*, monkeyshines*, plot, ploy, racket*, ruse, scam*, scheming, setup*, shenanigans*, skullduggery*, slant, slyness, stratagem, stunt, subterfuge, switch, trick, trickery, twist; SEE CONCEPTS 59,63

will [n1] *personal choice*
aim, appetite, attitude, character, conviction, craving, decision, decisiveness, decree, design, desire, determination, discipline, discretion, disposition, fancy, feeling, hankering, heart's desire*, inclination, intention, liking, longing, mind, option, passion, pining, pleasure, power, preference, prerogative, purpose, resolution, resolve, self-control, self-discipline, self-restraint, temperament, urge, velleity, volition, willfulness, willpower, wish, wishes, yearning; SEE CONCEPTS 20,411,659

will [n2] *last wishes; command*
bequest, bestowal, declaration, decree, device, directions, dispensation, disposition, estate, heritage, inheritance, insistence, instructions, legacy, order, property, testament; SEE CONCEPT 318

will [v1] *cause*
authorize, bid, bring about, command, decide on, decree, demand, determine, direct, effect, enjoin, exert, insist, intend, ordain, order, request, resolve; SEE CONCEPT 242

will [v2] *choose*
be inclined, crave, desire, elect, have a mind to*, incline, like, opt, please, prefer, see fit*, want, wish; SEE CONCEPT 20

will [v3] *give, bequeath to another*
bequest, confer, cut off, devise, disherit, disinherit, leave, legate, pass on, probate, transfer; SEE CONCEPTS 108,317

willful [adj1] *stubborn, obstinate*
adamant, bullheaded, contumacious, determined, dogged, fractious, froward, headstrong, inflexible, intractable, intransigent, mulish, obdurate, persistent, pertinacious, perverse, pigheaded, refractory, resolved, self-willed, stiffnecked, uncompromising, unyielding; SEE CONCEPTS 401,542

willful [adj2] *voluntary*
conscious, contemplated, deliberate, designed, intended, intentional, planned, premeditated, purposeful, studied, unforced, volitional, willed, willing, witting; SEE CONCEPTS 401,535

willing [adj] *agreeable, ready*
accommodating, active, amenable, cheerful, compliant, consenting, content, deliberate, desirous, disposed, eager, energetic, enthusiastic, fair, favorable, feeling, forward, game, go along with, happy, in accord with, inclined, in favor, intentional, in the mood, like-minded, obedient, one, pleased, predisposed, prepared, prompt, prone, reliable, responsible, tractable, unasked, unbidden, unforced, voluntary, well-disposed, willful, witting, zealous; SEE CONCEPTS 401,403,576

willpower [n] *personal determination*
discipline, drive, firmness, fixity, force, grit, resolution, resolve, self-control, self-discipline, self-government, self-restraint, single-mindedness, strength, will; SEE CONCEPT 411

wilt [v] *sag, fail*
become limp, break down, cave in, collapse, di-

wh
wi

minish, droop, drop, dry up, dwindle, ebb, fade, faint, flag, give out, languish, melt, mummify, shrivel, sink, succumb, wane, waste, waste away, weaken, wither, wizen; SEE CONCEPTS *181,427,469,699*

wily [*adj*] *crafty, clever*
arch, artful, astute, cagey, crazy like a fox*, crooked, cunning, deceitful, deceptive, deep, designing, foxy, greasy*, guileful, insidious, intriguing, knowing, sagacious, scheming, sharp, shifty, shrewd, slick*, slippery*, sly, smooth, sneaky, streetwise, tricky, underhanded; SEE CONCEPTS *401,545*

win [*n*] *victory*
accomplishment, achievement, conquest, gain, gold*, gold star*, kill*, killing*, pay dirt*, score, slam, success, sweep, triumph; SEE CONCEPTS *95,141,832*

win [*v1*] *finish first; succeed*
achieve, beat, be first, be victorious, carry the day*, come in first, conquer, edge, finish in front*, finish off, gain, gain victory, overcome, overwhelm, prevail, run circles around*, shut out*, sink*, take the prize, triumph, upset, walk away with*, walk off with*; SEE CONCEPTS *95,141,363*

win [*v2*] *achieve, obtain*
accomplish, acquire, annex, approach, attain, bag*, bring in, catch, collect, come away with*, derive, earn, effect, gain, get, harvest, have, make, net, pick up, procure, rack up*, reach, realize, receive, score, secure; SEE CONCEPTS *120,706*

win/win over [*v3*] *influence, persuade*
allure, argue into, attract, bring around, carry, charm, convert, convince, disarm, draw, get, induce, overcome, prevail upon, prompt, slay, sway, talk into, wow*; SEE CONCEPTS *11,68*

wince [*v*] *draw back*
back off, blanch, blench, cower, cringe, dodge, duck, flinch, grimace, jib, make a face*, quail, recoil, shrink, shy, start, swerve, turn; SEE CONCEPTS *154,185*

wind [*n1*] *air currents*
air, blast, blow, breath, breeze, chinook, cyclone, draft, draught, flurry, flutter, gale, gust, mistral, puff, tempest, typhoon, wafting, whiff, whirlwind, whisk, zephyr; SEE CONCEPT *524*

wind [*n2*] *warning, report*
babble, clue, cue, gossip, hint, hot air*, idle talk, inkling, intimation, notice, rumor, suggestion, talk, tidings, whisper; SEE CONCEPT *278*

wind [*v*] *bend, turn*
coil, convolute, corkscrew, cover, crook, curl, curve, deviate, distort, encircle, enclose, entwine, envelop, fold, furl, loop, meander, ramble, reel, roll, screw, slither, snake, spiral, swerve, twine, twist, weave, wrap, wreathe, wriggle, zigzag; SEE CONCEPTS *201,738*

winding [*adj*] *bending, turning*
ambiguous, anfractuous, circuitous, convoluted, crooked, curving, devious, flexuous, gyrating, indirect, intricate, involved, labyrinthine, mazy, meandering, roundabout, serpentine, sinuous, snaky, spiraling, tortuous, twisting, wriggly, zigzag; SEE CONCEPTS *581,584*

wind up [*v*] *finish*
be through with, bring to a close, clean up*, close, close down, come to the end, complete, conclude, determine, do, end, end up*, finalize, finish up,

halt, liquidate, settle, terminate, tie up loose ends*, wrap up*; SEE CONCEPT *234*

windy [*adj1*] *breezy*
airy, blowing, blowy, blustering, blustery, boisterous, brisk, drafty, fresh, gusty, raw, squally, stormy, tempestuous, wild, windswept; SEE CONCEPT *525*

windy [*adj2*] *talkative; boastful*
bombastic, diffuse, empty, garrulous, inflated, lengthy, long-winded, loquacious, meandering, palaverous, pompous, prolix, rambling, redundant, turgid, verbose, wordy; SEE CONCEPT *267*

wing [*n1*] *organ, device of flight*
aileron, airfoil, appendage, feather, pennon, pinion; SEE CONCEPTS *399,502*

wing [*n2*] *section; extension*
addition, adjunct, annex, arm, block, branch, bulge, circle, clique, coterie, detachment, division, ell, expansion, faction, group, part, projection, prolongation, protrusion, protuberance, section, segment, set, side, unit; SEE CONCEPTS *440,441,824,835*

wink [*n1/v*] *flutter, flick*
bat, blink, flash, gleam, glimmer, glitter, nictate, nictitate, sparkle, squinch, squint, twinkle; SEE CONCEPTS *185,624*

wink [*n2*] *moment*
flash*, instant, jiffy*, minute, second, shake*, split second*, twinkle*, twinkling*; SEE CONCEPTS *808,821*

winner [*n*] *someone or something that succeeds*
champ, champion, conquering hero, conqueror, first, hero, medalist, medalwinner, number one*, prizewinner, title-holder, top dog*, vanquisher, victor; SEE CONCEPTS *366,416*

winning/winsome [*adj*] *attractive, charming*
acceptable, adorable, agreeable, alluring, amiable, bewitching, captivating, cute, delectable, delightful, disarming, enchanting, endearing, engaging, fascinating, fetching, gratifying, lovable, lovely, pleasing, prepossessing, sweet, taking; SEE CONCEPTS *401,404*

winning [*adj2*] *triumphant*
champion, conquering, leading, successful, victorious; SEE CONCEPTS *528,632*

winter [*n*] *cold season of the year*
chill, cold, frost, Jack Frost*, wintertide, wintertime; SEE CONCEPT *814*

wintry [*adj*] *cold, snowy*
biting, bleak, brumal, chilly, cutting, desolate, dismal, freezing, frigid, frosty, frozen, harsh, hibernal, hiemal, icebox*, icy, raw, snappy, threedog night*; SEE CONCEPTS *525,605*

wipe [*v*] *brush, swab*
clean, clean off, clear, dry, dust, erase, mop, obliterate, remove, rub, sponge, take away, towel, wash; SEE CONCEPT *165*

wipe out [*v*] *destroy; get rid of*
abate, abolish, annihilate, black out, blot out, cancel, decimate, delete, efface, eliminate, eradicate, erase, expunge, exterminate, extinguish, extirpate, kill, massacre, obliterate, remove, root out, slaughter, slay, uproot, X-out*; SEE CONCEPT *252*

wiry [*adj*] *thin and strong*
agile, athletic, bristly, fibrous, lean, light, limber, muscular, ropy, sinewy, stiff, strapping, stringy, supple, tough; SEE CONCEPTS *490,491*

wisdom [*n*] *insight, common sense*
acumen, astuteness, balance, brains*, caution, circumspection, clear thinking, comprehension, dis-

cernment, discrimination, enlightenment, erudition, experience, foresight, good judgment, gumption*, horse sense*, information, intelligence, judgment, judiciousness, knowledge, learning, pansophy, penetration, perspicacity, poise, practicality, prudence, reason, sagacity, sageness, sanity, sapience, savoir faire, savvy*, shrewdness, solidity, sophistication, stability, understanding; SEE CONCEPT 409

wise [adj] intelligent, reasonable

astute, aware, calculating, careful, clever, cogitative, contemplative, crafty, cunning, discerning, discreet, educated, enlightened, erudite, experienced, foresighted, grasping, informed, insightful, intuitive, judicious, keen, knowing, knowledgeable, perceptive, perspicacious, politic, prudent, rational, reflective, sagacious, sage, sane, sapient, scholarly, sensible, sensing, sharp, shrewd, smart, sophic, sound, tactful, taught, thoughtful, understanding, wary, well-informed, witty; SEE CONCEPT 402

wish [n] desire

ambition, aspiration, choice, disposition, hankering, hope, hunger, inclination, intention, invocation, itch, liking, longing, pleasure, prayer, preference, request, thirst, urge, want, whim, will, yearning, yen; SEE CONCEPTS 20,709

wish [v] desire

aspire, beg, choose, command, covet, crave, desiderate, elect, entreat, envy, expect, fancy, hanker*, hope, hunger, invoke, itch, like, long, look forward to*, need, order, please, pray for, prefer, request, set one's heart on*, sigh for, solicit, spoil for*, thirst, want, will, yearn, yen; SEE CONCEPT 20

wishy-washy [adj] bland, dull

banal, characterless, cowardly, enervated, feeble, flat, flavorless, indecisive, ineffective, ineffectual, insipid, irresolute, jejune, languid, listless, mediocre, namby-pamby*, sapless, spiritless, tasteless, thin, vacillating, vapid, watered-down, watery, wavering, weak, weak-kneed*; SEE CONCEPT 404

wisp [n] strand

bit, lock, piece, shock, shred, snippet, string, thread, tuft, twist; SEE CONCEPTS 392,831

wistful [adj] daydreaming, longing

contemplative, desirous, disconsolate, dreaming, dreamy, forlorn, hopeless, meditative, melancholy, mournful, musing, nostalgic, pensive, plaintive, reflective, sad, thoughtful, wishful, yearning; SEE CONCEPT 403

wit [n1] humor

aphorism, badinage, banter, bon mot, burlesque, drollery, facetiousness, fun, gag, jest, jocularity, joke, lark, levity, pleasantry, practical joke, prank, pun, quip, raillery, repartee, sally, satire, trick, whimsicality, wisecrack, wittiness, wordplay; SEE CONCEPTS 59,273,411

wit [n2] person who is very funny

a million laughs*, banterer, card, comedian, comic, cutup*, epigrammatist, farceur, funster, gag person, humorist, jester, joker, jokesmith, jokester, life of the party*, madcap, punster, quipster, trickster, wag, wisecracker; SEE CONCEPTS 352,416

wit/wits [n3] judgment, intelligence

acumen, acuteness, astucity, astuteness, awareness, balance, brainpower, brains*, cleverness, common sense, comprehension, depth of perception, discernment, discrimination, esprit, grasp,

ingenuity, insight, keenness, lucidity, marbles*, mentality, mind, perception, perspicacity, practicality, prudence, rationality, reason, sagaciousness, sagacity, sageness, saneness, sanity, sapience, sense, shrewdness, soundness, understanding, wisdom; SEE CONCEPT 409

witch [n] person who casts spells over others

conjurer, enchanter, magician, necromancer, occultist, sorcerer; SEE CONCEPTS 361,412,415

witchcraft [n] spell-casting, magic

abracadabra*, bewitchment, black art, black magic, charisma, conjuring, divination, enchantment, hocus-pocus*, hoodoo*, incantation, jinx, magnetism, mumbo-jumbo*, necromancy, occult, occultism, sorcery, spell, thaumaturgy, voodoo, voodooism, whammy*, witchery, witching, wizardry; SEE CONCEPTS 367,370,689

withdraw [v1] remove something or someone from situation

abjure, absent oneself, back out, bail out, blow, book, bow out, check out, depart, detach, disengage, draw away, draw back, drop out, ease out, eliminate, exfiltrate, exit, extract, fall back, get away, get lost, get off, give ground, give way, go, keep aloof, keep apart, leave, make oneself scarce*, phase out, pull back, pull out, quail, quit, recede, recoil, retire, retreat, run along, secede, seclude oneself, shrink, switch, take a hike*, take away, take leave, take off, take out, vacate; SEE CONCEPTS 195,211

withdraw [v2] retract; declare void

abjure, abolish, abrogate, annul, ban, bar, call off, disavow, disclaim, dissolve, forswear, invalidate, nullify, quash, recall, recant, renege, renig, repress, repudiate, rescind, retire, reverse, revoke, stamp out, suppress, take back, unsay; SEE CONCEPTS 50,88,121,697

withdrawal [n] removal; retraction

abandonment, abdication, abjuration, alienation, departure, disavowal, disclaimer, disengagement, egress, egression, exit, exiting, exodus, extraction, marooning, palinode, recall, recantation, relinquishment, repudiation, rescission, resignation, retirement, retreat, revocation, revulsion, secession; SEE CONCEPTS 195,211,685

withdrawn [adj1] unsociable

aloof, aseptic, casual, cool, detached, disinterested, distant, incurious, indifferent, introverted, nongregarious, offish, quiet, recluse, reclusive, remote, reserved, restrained, retired, retiring, retreated, shrinking, shy, silent, solitary, standoffish, taciturn, timorous, uncommunicative, uncompanionable, unconcerned, uncurious, undemonstrative, unforthcoming, uninterested; SEE CONCEPT 401

withdrawn [adj2] hidden, remote

cloistered, departed, isolated, out-of-the-way, private, recluse, removed, retreated, secluded, solitary, taken out; SEE CONCEPT 583

wither [v] droop, decline

atrophy, become stale, blast, blight, collapse, constrict, contract, decay, deflate, desiccate, deteriorate, die, disintegrate, dry, dry up, fade, fold, languish, perish, shrink, shrivel, wane, waste, waste away, wilt, wizen; SEE CONCEPTS 427,698

withhold [v] keep back

abstain, bridle, check, clam up*, conceal, constrain, curb, deduct, deny, detain, disallow, dummy up*, hide, hold, hold back, hold down, hold out, hold out on, inhibit, keep, keep secret,

wi
wi

keep to oneself*, keep under one's hat*, keep under wraps*, kill, refrain, refuse, repress, reserve, resist, restrain, retain, sit on, spike, stop oneself, suppress; SEE CONCEPTS 35,121,188

within [adv] inside
in, in a period, indoors, inner, in reach, interior, inward, not beyond, not outside, not over; SEE CONCEPTS 586,772

without [adv] outside
after, beyond, externally, left out, on the outside, out, outdoors, out-of-doors, outwardly, past; SEE CONCEPTS 586,772

withstand [v] endure, bear
brace, brave, buck, combat, confront, contest, cope, cross, defy, dispute, duel, face, fight, fly in the face of*, grapple with, hang on*, hang tough*, hold off*, hold one's ground*, hold out*, oppose, prevail against, put up struggle*, put up with*, remain firm, repel, resist, ride out*, sit and take it*, stand, stand fast*, stand firm*, stand one's ground*, stand up against*, stand up to*, stick*, stick fast*, suffer, take, take it*, take on, thwart, tolerate, traverse, violate, weather, win out; SEE CONCEPTS 23,96

witness [n] person who observes an event
attestant, attestor, beholder, bystander, corroborator, deponent, eyewitness, gawker, looker-on, observer, onlooker, proof, rubbernecker*, signatory, signer, spectator, testifier, testimony, viewer, watcher; SEE CONCEPTS 355,423

witness [v1] observe
attend, be a witness, behold, be on hand*, be on the scene*, be present, eyeball*, flash on*, get a load of*, look on, mark, note, notice, perceive, pick up on, pipe*, read, see, sight, spot, spy, take in, view, watch; SEE CONCEPT 626

witness [v2] testify; authenticate
affirm, announce, argue, attest, bear out, bear witness, be a witness, bespeak, betoken, certify, confirm, corroborate, countersign, depone, depose, endorse, give evidence, give testimony, indicate, say under oath, sign, stand for, subscribe, vouch for; SEE CONCEPTS 49,50,88,317

witty [adj] funny and clever
amusing, bright, brilliant, campy*, crazy*, diverting, droll, entertaining, epigrammatic, facetious, fanciful, gay, humorous, ingenious, intelligent, jocose, jocular, joshing, keen, lively, original, penetrating, piercing, piquant, quick-witted, ridiculous, scintillating, screaming*, slapstick, sparkling, waggish, whimsical*; SEE CONCEPTS 267,542

wizard [n1] person who can perform magic
astrologer, augurer, clairvoyant, conjurer, diviner, enchanter, fortuneteller, hypnotist, magician, magus, medium, necromancer, occultist, palmist, seer, shaman, soothsayer, sorcerer, thaumaturge, warlock, witch; SEE CONCEPT 361

wizard [n2] person who is highly skilled
ace*, adept, artist, authority, crackerjack*, expert, genius, hot shot*, pro*, prodigy, professional, proficient, shark*, star, virtuoso, whiz*, whiz kid*, wiz*; SEE CONCEPTS 348,423

wizened [adj] dried, shriveled up
diminished, gnarled, lean, macerated, mummified, old, reduced, shrunk, shrunken, wilted, withered, worn, wrinkled; SEE CONCEPTS 485,603

wobble [v] stagger, quake
be unsteady, careen, falter, flounder, lurch, oscillate, quiver, reel, rock, roll, seesaw, shake,

shimmy, stumble, sway, swing, teeter, totter, tremble, vacillate, vibrate, waver, weave, wiggle; SEE CONCEPTS 150,152

wobbly [adj] shaky
fluctuant, insecure, precarious, rattletrap, rickety, rocky, teetering, tottering, unbalanced, uneven, unsafe, unstable, unsteady, unsure, vacillating, wavering, wavy, weak, wiggling; SEE CONCEPT 488

woe [n] suffering
adversity, affliction, agony, anguish, bemoaning, blues*, burden, calamity, care, cataclysm, catastrophe, curse, dejection, deploring, depression, disaster, distress, dole, drag, gloom, grief, grieving, hardship, headache*, heartache*, heartbreak, lamentation, melancholy, misadventure, misery, misfortune, pain, rain*, regret, rue, sadness, sorrow, tragedy, trial, tribulation, trouble, unhappiness, wretchedness; SEE CONCEPTS 410,532, 690,728

woebegone [adj] depressed, troubled
black, bleak, blue*, bummed out*, chapfallen, cheerless, crestfallen, dejected, despondent, disconsolate, dismal, dispirited, doleful, down, downcast, downhearted, down-in-the-mouth*, dreary, forlorn, gloomy, grief-stricken, grim, hangdog*, hurting, in pain*, long-faced*, low, lugubrious, melancholy, miserable, mournful, sad, shot down*, sorrowful, unhappy, woeful, wretched; SEE CONCEPT 403

woeful [adj] terrible, sad
afflicted, agonized, anguished, appalling, awful, bad, calamitous, catastrophic, cruel, deplorable, disappointing, disastrous, disconsolate, disgraceful, distressing, doleful, dreadful, feeble, gloomy, grieving, grievous, grim, heartbreaking, heartrending, heartsick, hopeless, inadequate, lamentable, lousy*, mean, miserable, mournful, paltry, pathetic, piteous, pitiable, pitiful, plaintive, poor, racked, rotten, shocking, sorrowful, sorry, tortured, tragic, unfortunate, unhappy; wretched; SEE CONCEPTS 548,571

wolf [v] consume sloppily and fast
bolt, cram, devour, gobble, gorge, gulp, guzzle, ingurgitate, pack, slop, slosh, stuff, swallow; SEE CONCEPT 169

woman [n] female human
aunt, daughter, gentlewoman, girl, girlfriend, grandmother, matron, mother, Ms./Miss/Mrs., niece, she, spouse, wife; SEE CONCEPTS 414,415

wonder [n1] amazement
admiration, astonishment, awe, bewilderment, concern, confusion, consternation, curiosity, doubt, fascination, fear, incredulity, jar, jolt, marveling, perplexity, perturbation, puzzlement, reverence, shock, skepticism, start, stupefaction, stupor, surprise, suspicion, uncertainty, wondering, wonderment; SEE CONCEPTS 410,532,690

wonder [n2] something that is amazing
act of God*, curiosity, cynosure, freak, marvel, miracle, nonpareil, oddity, phenomenon, portent, prodigy, rara avis, rarity, sensation, sight, spectacle, stunner*, wonderment; SEE CONCEPTS 529,687

wonder [v1] doubt; ponder
ask oneself, be curious, be inquisitive, conjecture, disbelieve, inquire, meditate, puzzle, query, question, speculate, think; SEE CONCEPTS 17,21

wonder [v2] be amazed
admire, be astonished, be awestruck, be con-

founded, be dumbstruck, be fascinated, be flabbergasted, be startled, be taken aback, boggle, gape, gawk, look aghast, marvel, stare; SEE CONCEPT 34

wonderful [adj] great, extraordinary
admirable, amazing, astonishing, astounding, awe-inspiring, awesome, brilliant, cool*, divine*, dynamite*, enjoyable, excellent, fabulous, fantastic, fine, groovy*, incredible, magnificent, marvelous, miraculous, outstanding, peachy*, phenomenal, pleasant, pleasing, prime, remarkable, sensational, something else*, staggering, startling, strange, stupendous, super, superb, surprising, swell, terrific, too much*, tremendous, unheard-of, wondrous; SEE CONCEPTS 529,574

wonk [n] excessive studier
bookworm, brain*, dweeb*, geek*, greasy grind*, grind*, grub*, nerd, poindexter, swotter*; SEE CONCEPT 350

woo [v] seek as romantic partner
address, aim for, beg, bill and coo*, butter up*, caress, charm, chase, court, cultivate, curry favor*, date, entreat, go steady, importune, keep company, make advances, make love, press one's suit with*, propose, pursue, run after, rush, seek in marriage*, seek the hand of*, set one's cap for*, solicit, spark*, spoon*; SEE CONCEPTS 297,375,384

wood/woods [n] forest
copse, grove, lumber, thicket, timber, timberland, trees, weald, woodland; SEE CONCEPTS 430,509,517

wooden [adj] made of timber
board, clapboard, frame, ligneous, log, peg, plant, slab, timber, timbered, woody; SEE CONCEPT 485

wooden [adj2] stiff, inflexible
awkward, bumbling, clumsy, gauche, gawky, graceless, heavy, heavy-handed, inelegant, inept, maladroit, obstinate, ponderous, rigid, stilted, unbending, ungainly, ungraceful, unhandy, unyielding, weighty; SEE CONCEPTS 488,542

word [n1] discussion
chat, chitchat*, colloquy, confab*, confabulation, consultation, conversation, discussion, talk, tête-à-tête; SEE CONCEPT 56

word [n2] statement
account, adage, advice, announcement, bulletin, byword, comment, communication, communiqué, declaration, directive, discourse, dispatch, expression, gossip, hearsay, information, intelligence, intimation, introduction, message, news, notice, pronouncement, proverb, remark, report, rumble, rumor, saw, saying, scuttlebutt, speech, talk, tidings, utterance; SEE CONCEPTS 274,278

word [n3] unit of language
concept, designation, expression, idiom, lexeme, locution, morpheme, name, phrase, sound, term, usage, utterance, vocable; SEE CONCEPT 275

word [n4] command
behest, bidding, charge, commandment, decree, dictate, edict, go-ahead*, green light*, injunction, mandate, order, signal, ukase, will; SEE CONCEPT 685

word [n5] promise
affirmation, assertion, assurance, commitment, declaration, engagement, guarantee, oath, parole, pledge, plight, solemn oath*, solemn word*, vow, warrant, word of honor; SEE CONCEPTS 71,278,689

word [n6] password
countersign, slogan, watchword; SEE CONCEPTS 684,685

wording [n] way of expressing a thought
choice of words, diction, language, locution, manner, mode, parlance, phraseology, phrasing, style, terminology, turn of phrase, wordage, words; SEE CONCEPTS 278,682

wordy [adj] talkative
bombastic, chatty*, diffuse, discursive, flatulent, gabby*, garrulous, inflated, lengthy, long-winded, loquacious, palaverous, pleonastic, prolix, rambling, redundant, rhetorical, tedious, turgid, verbose, voluble, windy*; SEE CONCEPT 267

work [n1] labor, chore
assignment, attempt, commission, daily grind*, drudge, drudgery, effort, elbow grease*, endeavor, exertion, functioning, grind, grindstone*, industry, job, moil, muscle, obligation, pains*, performance, production, push, salt mines*, servitude, slogging, stint, stress, striving, struggle, sweat*, task, toil, travail, trial, trouble, undertaking; SEE CONCEPTS 87,362,677

work [n2] business, occupation
activity, art, calling, commitment, contract, craft, do*, duty, employment, endeavor, gig*, grind*, industry, job, line, line of business, livelihood, métier, nine-to-five*, obligation, office, practice, profession, pursuit, racket*, responsibility, skill, slot*, specialization, swindle, task, thing*, trade, vocation, walk; SEE CONCEPTS 349, 351,360

work [n3] achievement
act, application, article, composition, creation, deed, end product, function, handicraft, handiwork, oeuvre, opus, output, performance, piece, product, production; SEE CONCEPTS 260,706

work [v1] be employed; exert oneself
apply oneself, be gainfully employed, buckle down*, carry on, dig, do a job, do business, drive, drudge, earn a living*, freelance, have a job, hold a job, hustle*, knuckle down*, labor, manage, manufacture, moil, moonlight*, nine-to-five it*, peg away*, plug away*, ply, punch a clock*, pursue, report, scratch, slave, slog*, specialize, strain, strive, sweat*, take on, toil, try; SEE CONCEPTS 100,351

work [v2] manipulate, operate
accomplish, achieve, act, behave, bring about, carry out, cause, contrive, control, create, direct, drive, effect, execute, force, function, go, handle, implement, manage, maneuver, move, perform, ply, progress, react, run, serve, take, tick, use, wield; SEE CONCEPTS 94,117,199,204

work [v3] cultivate, form
care for, dig, dress, farm, fashion, handle, knead, labor, make, manipulate, mold, process, shape, tend, till; SEE CONCEPTS 173,184,257

workable [adj] feasible
applicable, breeze*, cinch*, doable, duck soup*, easy, easy as pie*, exploitable, functional, no sweat*, piece of cake*, possible, practicable, practical, simple as ABC*, snap, usable, useful, viable, working; SEE CONCEPTS 538,552,560

worker [n] person who is employed
artisan, blue collar*, breadwinner, company person, craftsperson, employee, hand, help, laborer, nine-to-fiver*, operative, peasant, proletarian, serf, slave, stiff, toiler, trader, tradesperson, wage

wi
wo

earner, white collar*, working person, working stiff*; SEE CONCEPT 348

working [adj] *active, occupied*
alive, busy, dynamic, effective, employed, engaged, functioning, going, hot*, in a job, in force, in full swing, in gear, in process, laboring, live, moving, on fire*, on the job, on track*, operative, practical, running, useful, viable; SEE CONCEPTS 538,560

workout [n] *exercise, practice*
conditioning, constitutional, drill, rehearsal, routine, session, test, training, tryout, warm-up, work; SEE CONCEPTS 290,363

work out [v] *solve; satisfy*
accomplish, achieve, arrange, attain, be effective, bring off, clear, come out, come to terms*, complete, compromise, construct, contrive, develop, devise, elaborate, evolve, figure out, find out, finish, fix, form, formulate, get something done*, go, go well, handle, happen, manipulate, pan out*, plan, prosper, pull off*, put together, reach agreement, resolve, result, succeed, swing*, turn out, up, win; SEE CONCEPTS 706,713

work up [v] *stimulate*
agitate, animate, arouse, breed, cause, develop, engender, excite, generate, get up, hatch, improve, incite, induce, inflame, instigate, move, muster up, occasion, produce, rouse, spur, stir up; SEE CONCEPTS 14,242

world [n1] *planet, globe*
cosmos, creation, earth, heavenly body, macrocosm, microcosm, nature, sphere, star, terrene, universe; SEE CONCEPTS 511,770

world [n2] *class of existing beings*
class, division, everybody, everyone, group, humanity, humankind, human race, race, realm; SEE CONCEPTS 378,391

world [n3] *person's environment, experience*
ambience, area, atmosphere, business, domain, field, life, matters, memory, province, pursuits, realm, sphere, system; SEE CONCEPT 678

worldly [adj1] *material, nonreligious*
carnal, earthly, earthy, fleshly, human, lay, materialistic, mundane, natural, physical, practical, profane, secular, sublunary, telluric, temporal, terrene, terrestrial, ungodly; SEE CONCEPTS 536,582

worldly [adj2] *sophisticated, materialistic*
avaricious, been around, blasé, callous, cool*, cosmopolitan, covetous, disenchanted, grasping, greedy, hardened, knowing, opportunistic, power-loving, practical, self-centered, selfish, unprincipled, uptown*, urbane, worldly wise; SEE CONCEPT 401

worldwide [adj] *general*
catholic, common, comprehensive, cosmic, ecumenical, extensive, global, international, multinational, omnipresent, pandemic, planetary, ubiquitous, universal; SEE CONCEPT 536

worn/worn-out [adj] *used, tired*
beat, burned out*, bushed*, busted*, clichéd, consumed, depleted, destroyed, deteriorated, drained, drawn, effete, exhausted, fatigued, frayed, gone, hackneyed, had it*, haggard, jaded, kaput*, knocked out*, old, out of gas*, overused, overworked, pinched, played out*, pooped*, ragged, ruined, shabby, shot, spent, stale, tattered, the worse for wear*, threadbare, timeworn, tired out, totaled*, used up, useless, wearied,

weary, well-worn, wiped out, worn down, wrung out*; SEE CONCEPTS 485,560

worried [adj] *anxious, troubled*
afraid, apprehensive, beside oneself, bothered, clutched, concerned, distracted, distraught, distressed, disturbed, fearful, fretful, frightened, hung up*, ill-at-ease, nervous, on edge*, on pins and needles*, overwrought, perturbed, solicitous, tense, tormented, uneasy, upset, uptight, worried stiff*; SEE CONCEPT 403

worry [n] *anxiety, trouble*
anguish, annoyance, apprehension, bad news*, care, concern, disquiet, distress, disturbance, doubt, fear, headache*, heartache*, irritation, misery, misgiving, nag*, pain*, perplexity, pest, plague, presentiment, problem, torment, torture, trial, uncertainty, uneasiness, vexation, woe, worriment; SEE CONCEPTS 532,690

worry [v] *be or make anxious, troubled*
afflict, aggrieve, agonize, ail, annoy, attack, bedevil, beleaguer, beset, bite one's nails*, bother, brood, bug*, chafe, concern oneself, depress, despair, disquiet, distress, disturb, dun, feel uneasy, fret, gnaw at, goad, go for*, harass, harry, hassle, have qualms, hector, importune, irritate, needle, oppress, persecute, perturb, pester, plague, stew*, sweat out*, take on, tantalize, tear, tease, test, torment, torture, trouble, try, unsettle, upset, vex, wince, writhe, wrong; SEE CONCEPTS 7,14,19,410

worsen [v] *diminish, decay*
aggravate, corrode, damage, decline, degenerate, depress, descend, deteriorate, disintegrate, exacerbate, fall off, get worse, go downhill*, impair, lower, retrograde, retrogress, rot, sink; SEE CONCEPTS 240,698

worship [n] *honoring, glorification*
adoration, adulation, awe, beatification, benediction, chapel, church service, deification, devotion, exaltation, genuflection, glory, homage, honor, idolatry, idolization, invocation, laudation, love, offering, praise, prayer, prostration, regard, respect, reverence, rite, ritual, service, supplication, veneration, vespers; SEE CONCEPTS 69,367

worship [v] *honor, glorify*
admire, adore, adulate, bow down to, canonize, celebrate, chant, deify, dote on, esteem, exalt, extol, idolize, laud, love, magnify, offer prayers to, pay homage to, praise, pray to, put on a pedestal*, respect, revere, reverence, sanctify, sing, sing praises to*, venerate; SEE CONCEPTS 69,367

worth [n] *value, estimation associated with something*
account, aid, assistance, avail, benefit, caliber, class, consequence, cost, credit, desirability, dignity, equivalence, excellence, goodness, help, importance, mark, meaningfulness, merit, moment, note, perfection, price, quality, rate, significance, stature, use, usefulness, utility, valuation, virtue, weight, worthiness; SEE CONCEPTS 335,346

worthless [adj] *of no use; without value*
abandoned, abject, barren, base, bogus, cheap, contemptible, counterproductive, despicable, empty, futile, good-for-nothing*, ignoble, inconsequential, ineffective, ineffectual, inferior, insignificant, inutile, meaningless, mediocre, miserable, no-account*, no-good*, nothing, nugatory, paltry, pointless, poor, profitless, sterile, trashy, trifling, trivial, unavailing, unessential, unimportant, unproductive, unprofitable, unus-

able, useless, valueless, waste, wretched; SEE CONCEPTS 560,570,575

worthwhile [*adj*] *helpful*

advantageous, beneficial, constructive, estimable, excellent, gainful, good, important, invaluable, justifiable, lucrative, meritorious, money-making, paying, priceless, productive, profitable, remunerative, rewarding, serviceable, useful, valuable, worthy; SEE CONCEPTS 560,567,572

worthy [*adj*] *honorable, respectable*

aces*, admirable, A-1*, best, blameless, choice, commendable, creditable, decent, dependable, deserving, desirable, divine, estimable, ethical, excellent, exemplary, first-class*, first-rate*, good, honest, incorrupt, invaluable, laudable, meritorious, model, moral, noble, pleasing, praiseworthy, precious, priceless, pure, reliable, reputable, righteous, right-minded, salt of the earth*, satisfying, sterling, top-drawer*, top-notch*, true, trustworthy, upright, valuable, virtuous, winning, worthwhile; SEE CONCEPTS 545,567,572

wound [*n*] *injury*

anguish, bruise, cut, damage, distress, gash, grief, harm, heartbreak, hurt, insult, laceration, lesion, pain, pang, shock, slash, torment, torture, trauma; SEE CONCEPT 309

wound [*vl*] *cause bodily damage*

bruise, carve, clip*, contuse, cut, damage, ding*, gash, harm, hit, hurt, injure, irritate, lacerate, nick, open up, ouch*, pierce, rough up*, scrape, scratch, slash, slice, stick, total*; SEE CONCEPTS 137,246,313

wound [*v2*] *cause mental hurt*

bother, cut to the quick*, distress, disturb, do in*, dump on*, get*, grieve, hurt, hurt one's feelings, mortify, offend, outrage, pain, put down*, shake up*, sting, traumatize, trouble, upset; SEE CONCEPTS 7,14,19

wrangle [*n*] *fight, argument*

altercation, battle royal*, bickering, blow-off*, blowup*, branigan*, brawl, brouhaha*, clash, contest, controversy, disagreement, dispute, exchange, falling-out*, flap*, fracas, hassle, knockdown drag-out*, quarrel, row, ruckus*, ruction, rumble, rumpus, scene, set-to*, squabble, tiff; SEE CONCEPTS 46,106

wrangle [*v*] *fight, argue*

altercate, bicker, brawl, bump heads*, contend, cross swords*, disagree, dispute, fall out*, hassle, have at it*, have words*, lock horns*, pick a bone*, put up a fight, quarrel, quibble, row, scrap, spat, squabble, take on, tangle, tiff; SEE CONCEPTS 46,106

wrap [*n*] *clothing that is worn over for warmth*

blanket, cape, cloak, coat, cover, fur, jacket, mantle, shawl, stole; SEE CONCEPT 451

wrap [*v*] *surround with a covering*

absorb, bandage, bind, bundle, bundle up, camouflage, cloak, clothe, cover, drape, encase, encircle, enclose, enfold, envelop, fold, gift-wrap*, hide, immerse, invest, mask, muffle, pack, package, protect, roll up, sheathe, shelter, shroud, swaddle, swathe, twine, veil, wind; SEE CONCEPT 172

wrap up [*v*] *finish*

bring to a close, close, complete, conclude, determine, end, halt, polish off, terminate, wind up; SEE CONCEPT 234

wrath [*n*] *extreme anger*

acrimony, asperity, boiling point*, conniption*,

dander, displeasure, exasperation, flare-up, fury, hate, hatefulness, huff, indignation, ire, irritation, mad, madness, offense, passion, rage, resentment, rise, stew*, storm, temper, vengeance; SEE CONCEPTS 29,410

wrathful [*adj*] *very angry*

beside oneself, displeased, enraged, furious, heated, incensed, indignant, infuriated, irate, ireful, mad, on the warpath*, raging, storming; SEE CONCEPT 403

wreak [*v*] *force, cause*

bring about, carry out, create, effect, execute, exercise, force upon, inflict, unleash, vent, visit, work, wreck; SEE CONCEPT 242

wreath [*n*] *circular decoration*

band, bay, bouquet, chaplet, circlet, coronal, coronet, crown, festoon, garland, laurel, lei, loop, ring, ringlet; SEE CONCEPTS 259,260,429

wreck [*n*] *severe damage or severely damaged goods*

collapse, crash, crate, debacle, debris, derelict, destruction, devastation, disruption, fender bender*, heap*, hulk*, jalopy*, junk*, junker*, litter, mess, pile-up*, rear-ender*, relic, ruin, ruins, shipwreck, smashup*, total*, waste, wreckage; SEE CONCEPTS 260,674

wreck [*v*] *ruin, destroy*

bash, batter, beach, break, capsize, crack up*, crash, cripple, dash, decimate, demolish, devastate, dilapidate, disable, do in*, efface, founder, impair, injure, mangle, mar, mess up*, pile up*, put out of commission*, ravage, raze, run aground, sabotage, scuttle, shatter, shipwreck, sink, smash, smash up, spoil, strand, subvert, take apart, take out, tear up, torpedo*, total*, trash*, undermine, vandalize, wrack*, wrack up*; SEE CONCEPT 252

wrench [*v*] *jerk, force violently*

bend, coerce, compel, contort, dislocate, dislodge, distort, drag, exact, extract, pervert, pinch, pull, rend, rip, screw, sprain, squeeze, strain, tear, tug, tweak, twist, wrest, wring, yank; SEE CONCEPTS 80,206

wrestle [*v*] *struggle physically or mentally with something*

battle, combat, contend, endeavor, essay, exert, fight, grapple, grunt, scuffle, strain, strive, tangle, tussle, work; SEE CONCEPTS 17,191,208

wretched [*adj*] *terrible, very bad*

abject, afflicted, base, bummed, calamitous, cheap, contemptible, dejected, deplorable, depressed, despicable, disconsolate, distressed, dolorous, down, down-and-out*, downcast, faulty, flimsy, forlorn, gloomy, hapless, hopeless, hurting, inferior, in the pits*, low, low-down*, mean, melancholy, miserable, paltry, pathetic, pitiable, pitiful, poor, shabby, shameful, sordid, sorrowful, sorry, spiritless, tragic, unfortunate, unhappy, vile, weak, woebegone, woeful, worthless; SEE CONCEPTS 403,571

wriggle [*v*] *maneuver out of; wiggle*

convulse, crawl, dodge, extricate oneself, glide, jerk, jiggle, ooze, skew, slink, slip, snake, sneak, squirm, turn, twist, twitch, wag, waggle, worm, writhe, zigzag; SEE CONCEPTS 30,149

wring [*v*] *twist, contort*

choke, coerce, compress, draw out, exact, extort, extract, force, gouge, hurt, pain, pinch, pry, push, screw, shake down, squeeze, strain, strangle,

throttle, turn, wrench, wrest; SEE CONCEPTS *142,206,208*

wrinkle [n] *crinkle, fold*
contraction, corrugation, crease, crow's-foot*, crumple, depression, furrow, gather, line, pleat, plica, pucker, ridge, rimple, rumple, tuck; SEE CONCEPTS *418,513*

wrinkle [v] *crinkle, fold*
compress, corrugate, crease, crimp, crisp, crumple, furrow, gather, line, prune up, pucker, purse, rimple, ruck, rumple, screw up, scrunch, seam, shrivel, twist; SEE CONCEPTS *185,201*

writ [n] *court order*
command, decree, document, habeas corpus, mandate, paper, prescript, process, replevin, subpoena, summons, warrant; SEE CONCEPT *318*

write [v] *put language down on paper*
address, author, autograph, bang out*, chalk*, commit, communicate, comp*, compose, copy, correspond, create, dash off*, draft, draw up*, drop a line*, drop a note*, engross, formulate, ghost, indite, ink, inscribe, jot down, knock off*, knock out*, letter, note, note down*, pen, pencil, print, push a pencil*, put in writing, record, reproduce, rewrite, scrawl, scribble, scribe, scriven, set down, set forth, sign, take down, tell, transcribe, turn out, typewrite, write down, write up; SEE CONCEPTS *79,203*

write off [v] *devalue; forget about*
cancel, cross out, decry, depreciate, disregard, downgrade, give up, lower, mark down, shelve, take a loss on, underrate, undervalue; SEE CONCEPT *54*

writer [n] *person who composes with language*
author, biographer, columnist, contributor, correspondent, critic, dramatist, editor, essayist, freelancer, ghostwriter, journalist, newspaper person, novelist, person of letters, poet, reporter, screenwriter, scribbler, scribe, scripter, stenographer, stringer, wordsmith; SEE CONCEPTS *348,356*

writhe [v] *contort; toss back and forth*
agonize, bend, distort, jerk, recoil, squirm, struggle, suffer, thrash, thresh, twist, wiggle, wince, worm, wriggle; SEE CONCEPTS *80,150*

writing [n1] *on paper*
autograph, calligraphy, chirography, cuneiform, hand, handwriting, hieroglyphics, longhand, manuscription, print, scrawl, scribble, script, shorthand; SEE CONCEPTS *79,284*

writing [n2] *printed composition*
article, belles-lettres, book, discourse, dissertation, document, editorial, essay, letter, literature, manuscript, novel, ode, opus, pamphlet, paper, piece, play, poem, prose, publication, record, review, signature, theme, thesis, tract, treatise, work; SEE CONCEPT *271*

wrong [n] *offense, sin*
abuse, bad deed, bias, blunder, crime, cruelty, damage, delinquency, discourtesy, error, evil, faux pas, favor, foul play, grievance, harm, hurt, immorality, imposition, indecency, inequity, inhumanity, iniquity, injury, injustice, insult, libel, malevolence, miscarriage, misdeed, misdemeanor, misdoing, mistake, oppression, persecution, prejudice, sinfulness, slander, slight, spite, tort, transgression, trespass, turpitude, unfairness, vice, villainy, violation, wickedness, wrongdoing; SEE CONCEPT *645*

wrong [adj1] *incorrect*
amiss, askew, astray, at fault, awry, bad, counterfactual, defective, erratic, erring, erroneous, fallacious, false, faulty, fluffed, goofed*, inaccurate, in error, inexact, miscalculated, misconstrued, misfigured, misguided, mishandled, mistaken, not precise, not right, not working, off-target*, on the wrong track*, out, out of commission*, out of line*, out of order*, perverse, rotten*, sophistical, specious, spurious, ungrounded, unsatisfactory, unsound, unsubstantial, untrue, wide; SEE CONCEPTS *571,582*

wrong [adj2] *immoral, dishonest*
amoral, bad, base, blamable, blameworthy, blasphemous, censurable, corrupt, criminal, crooked, debauched, depraved, dishonorable, dissipated, dissolute, evil, felonious, illegal, illicit, indecent, iniquitous, naughty, profane, profligate, reprehensible, reprobate, risqué, sacrilegious, salacious, shady, sinful, smutty, unethical, unfair, ungodly, unholy, unjust, unlawful, unrighteous, vicious, wanton, wicked, wrongful; SEE CONCEPT *545*

wrong [adj3] *inappropriate, not suitable*
amiss, awkward, bad, disproportionate, funny, gauche, ill-advised, improper, inapt, incongruous, incorrect, indecorous, infelicitous, malapropos, misplaced, not done*, off-balance, rotten*, unacceptable, unbecoming, unconventional, undesirable, unfit, unfitted, unfitting, unhappy, unsatisfactory, unseemly, unsuitable; SEE CONCEPT *558*

wrong [adj4] *reverse, opposite*
back, inside, inverse, obverse; SEE CONCEPT *586*

wrong [v] *hurt, mistreat another*
abuse, aggrieve, cheat, damage, defame, discredit, dishonor, harm, hurt, ill-treat, impose upon, injure, malign, maltreat, misrepresent, mistreat, offend, oppress, outrage, persecute, take advantage of; SEE CONCEPTS *7,19,246,313*

wrong [adv] *astray*
afield, amiss, askew, badly, erroneously, inaccurately, incorrectly, mistakenly, unfavorably, wrongly; SEE CONCEPTS *544,548*

wrongful [adj] *evil, illegal*
blameworthy, criminal, dishonest, dishonorable, felonious, illegitimate, illicit, immoral, improper, lawless, reprehensible, unethical, unfair, unjust, unlawful, wicked; SEE CONCEPTS *319,545*

wry [adj] *sarcastic, distorted*
askew, aslant, awry, contorted, crooked, cynical, deformed, droll, dry, ironic, mocking, sardonic, twisted, uneven, warped; SEE CONCEPTS *267,581*

X

x-ray [n] *picture of inside a body*
actinism, cathode rays, encephalogram, fluoroscope, radioactivity, radiograph, refractometry, Roentgen rays, ultraviolet rays; SEE CONCEPT *311*

Y

yacht [n] *pleasure boat*
cabin cruiser, cruiser, ketch, racer, sailboat, sailing boat, sloop, yawl; SEE CONCEPT *506*

yak/yap [n/v] *talk a lot*
babble, blather, chat, chatter, clack, confabulate, gab, gossip, jabber, jaw*, prate, prattle, run on*, tattle, yammer; SEE CONCEPTS *51,266*

yank [v] *pull hard and fast*
draw, evulse, extract, hitch, jerk, lug, snap, snatch, tear, tug, twitch, vellicate, wrench; SEE CONCEPT *206*

yard [n] *grassy area around a structure*
backyard, barnyard, clearing, close, corral, court, courtyard, enclosure, fold, garden, grass, lawn, lot, patch, patio, playground, quadrangle, terrace; SEE CONCEPT *509*

yarn [n1] *fiber for knitting*
cotton fiber, flaxen thread, fleece, spun wool, thread, twist, wool; SEE CONCEPT *473*

yarn [n2] *story, often long and made-up*
adventure, alibi, anecdote, fable, fabrication, fairy tale, lie, line, narrative, potboiler*, prose, sea story*, song*, song and dance*, string*, tale, tall story*, tall tale; SEE CONCEPT *282*

yawn [v] *open mouth wide, often sign of fatigue*
catch flies*, divide, doze, drowse, expand, gap, gape, give, nap, part, sleep, snooze, spread, yaw, yawp*; SEE CONCEPTS *163,185*

yearly [adj] *every twelve months*
annual, annually, once a year, per annum, perennial, regularly, year by year, yearlong; SEE CONCEPTS *541,823*

yearn [v] *desire strongly*
ache, be desirous of, be eager for, be passionate, chafe, covet, crave, dream, hanker, have a crush on*, have a yen for, hunger, itch, languish, long, lust, pine, set one's heart on*, thirst, want, wish for; SEE CONCEPT *20*

years [n] *age, old age*
age, agedness, caducity, dotage, elderliness, generation, lifespan, lifetime, oldness, senescence, senility; SEE CONCEPT *715*

yell [n/v] *loud communication*
bawl, bellow, call, cheer, complain, cry, holler*, hoot, howl, lament, roar, scream, screech, shout, shriek, shrill, squawk, squeal, ululate, vociferate, wail, weep, whoop, yap, yelp, yip; SEE CONCEPTS *47,595*

yellow [n/adj1] *sunny color*
amber, bisque, blond, buff, chrome, cream, gold, ivory, lemon, saffron, sand, tawny; SEE CONCEPTS *618,622*

yellow [adj2] *cowardly*
chicken*, craven, deceitful, gutless, lily-livered*, low, offensive, pusillanimous, sneaking, treacherous, tricky, unethical, unprincipled; SEE CONCEPTS *267,401*

yelp [n/v] *short, high cry*
bark, hoot, howl, screech, yap, yip, yowl; SEE CONCEPT *64*

yen [n] *strong want*
craving, desire, hankering, hunger, itch, longing, lust, passion, thirst, urge, yearning; SEE CONCEPTS *20,709*

yes [adv] *agreed*
affirmative, all right*, amen, aye*, beyond a doubt, by all means, certainly, definitely, even so, exactly, fine, gladly, good, good enough, granted, indubitably, just so, most assuredly, naturally, of course, okay*, positively, precisely, surely, sure thing*, true, undoubtedly, unquestionably, very well, willingly, without fail, yea*, yep*; SEE CONCEPTS *535,572*

yesterday [n] *the day before today*
bygone, foretime, lang syne*, last day, not long ago, past, recently, the other day*; SEE CONCEPT *815*

yet [adv1] *up until now*
as yet, earlier, hitherto, prior to, so far, still, thus far, till, until now, up to now; SEE CONCEPT *820*

yet [adv2] *in spite of*
after all, although, at any rate, but, despite, even though, howbeit, however, nevertheless, nonetheless, notwithstanding, on the other hand, still, still and all, though, withal; SEE CONCEPT *544*

yet [adv3] *in addition*
additionally, along, also, as well, besides, further, furthermore, likewise, more, moreover, over and above*, still, still further, to boot*, too; SEE CONCEPT *548*

yet [adv4] *in the future*
after a while, at some future time, beyond this, even, eventually, finally, in due course, in the course of time, someday, sometime, sooner or later, still, ultimately; SEE CONCEPT *799*

yield [n] *production of labor*
crop, earnings, harvest, income, output, outturn, produce, profit, return, revenue, takings, turnout; SEE CONCEPTS *260,338*

yield [v1] *produce*
accrue, admit, afford, allow, beam, bear, blossom, bring forth, bring in, discharge, earn, furnish, generate, give, give off, hold out, net, offer, pay, proffer, provide, return, sell for, supply, tender, turn out; SEE CONCEPT *205*

yield [v2] *give in, surrender*
abandon, abdicate, admit defeat, back down, bend, bow, break, buy, call it quits*, capitulate, cave in, cede, collapse, come to terms*, crumple, defer, fold, fold up, give oneself over, give up, give way*, go, hand over, knuckle, knuckle under*, lay down arms*, leave, let go*, part with, relax, relent, relinquish, resign, sag, submit, succumb, suffer defeat, surrender, throw in the towel*; SEE CONCEPTS *14,18,35*

yield [v3] *grant, allow*
accede, accept, acknowledge, acquiesce, admit, agree, assent, bow, break, comply, concede, concur, consent, defer, fail, fit in, go along with*, go with the flow*, permit, play the game*, surrender, toe the line*, toe the mark*, waive; SEE CONCEPT *8*

yielding [adj1] *accommodating*
acquiescent, biddable, compliant, docile, easy, flexible, humble, nonresistant, obedient, passive, pliable, pliant, putty in one's hands, resigned, submissive, tractable; SEE CONCEPTS *401,404*

yielding [adj2] *soft, flexible*
elastic, malleable, mushy, pappy, plastic, pliable, pulpy, quaggy, resilient, spongy, springy, squishy, supple, tractable, tractile, unresisting; SEE CONCEPTS *488,606*

yoke [n] *bondage, bond*
burden, chain, coupling, enslavement, helotry, knot, ligament, ligature, link, nexus, oppression, peonage, serfdom, service, servility, servitude, slavery, tie; SEE CONCEPTS *513,677*

yoke [v] *bond together; join*
associate, attach, bracket, buckle, combine, conjoin, conjugate, connect, couple, fasten, fix, harness, hitch, link, secure, splice, strap, tack, tie, unite, wed; SEE CONCEPTS *85,160,193*

wr
yo

yokel [n] *person who is mired in local custom*
backwoods person, boor*, country cousin*, country person, hayseed*, peasant, rustic; SEE CONCEPT *413*

yonder [adv] *faraway*
away, beyond, distant, farther, further, remote, yon; SEE CONCEPTS *586,778*

young [n] *animate beings that are not mature*
babies, baby, brood, family, infants, issue, litter, little ones*, offspring, progeny; SEE CONCEPTS *394,414,424*

young [adj] *immature*
adolescent, blooming, blossoming, boyish, boy-like, budding, burgeoning, callow, childish, child-like, crude, developing, early, fledgling, fresh, girlish, girllike, green*, growing, half-grown, ignorant, inexperienced, infant, inferior, junior, juvenile, little, modern, new, newborn, newish, not aged, pubescent, puerile, punk, raw, recent, tender, tenderfoot*, undeveloped, undisciplined, unfinished, unfledged, unlearned, unpracticed, unripe, unseasoned, untried, unversed, vernal, youthful; SEE CONCEPTS *578,678,715,797*

youngster/youth [n/nl] *person before the age of maturity*
boy, chick*, cub*, fledgling, girl, junior, juvenile, juvenile delinquent*, kid*, lad, lass, pup, pupil, student, teenager, young person; SEE CONCEPTS *414,424*

youth [n2] *early period in life of animate being*
adolescence, awkward age, bloom, boyhood, childhood, girlhood, greenness, ignorance, immaturity, inexperience, innocence, juvenescence, minority, prime, puberty, salad days*, springtide, springtime of life, teens, tender age*, youthfulness; SEE CONCEPT *817*

youthful [adj] *new, immature*
active, adolescent, boyish, budding, buoyant, callow, childish, childlike, enthusiastic, fresh, full of life, girlish, green*, inexperienced, infant, juvenile, keen, pubescent, puerile, tender, underage, vernal, vigorous, young; SEE CONCEPTS *542,578,797*

yowl [n/v] *long, loud animate sound*
bawl, bay, caterwaul, cry, holler*, howl, mewl, scream, screech, squall, squeal, ululate, wail, whine, yell, yelp, yip; SEE CONCEPT *77*

yuppie [n/adj] *young upwardly mobile professional*
button-down, clone, conspicuous consumer, suit, three-piecer, urban professional, white-collar worker; SEE CONCEPT *348*

Z

zany [n] *person who is wildly funny*
buffoon, card*, clown, comedian, comic, cutup*, farceur, funny person, gag person, humorist, idiot, jester, joker, madcap*, moron, nut*, practical joker, prankster, screwball*, show-off, simpleton*, wag*, wisecracker*; SEE CONCEPTS *352,423*

zany [adj] *crazy, funny*
camp*, campy*, clownish, comical, dumb, eccentric, fool, foolish, goofy, hare-brained*, humorous, joshing, kooky*, loony*, madcap*,

nutty*, sappy*, wacky*, witty; SEE CONCEPTS *267,401*

zeal [n] *enthusiasm*
alacrity, ardor, bustle, determination, devotion, diligence, dispatch, drive, eagerness, earnestness, enterprise, fanaticism, fervor, fierceness, fire, gusto, hustle, inclination, initiative, intensity, intentness, keenness, mania, passion, perseverance, push, readiness, sincerity, spirit, stick-to-itiveness*, urgency, vehemence, verve, warmth, what-it-takes*, yen, zest; SEE CONCEPTS *32,410,411*

zealous [adj] *enthusiastic*
afire, antsy*, ardent, avid, burning, coming on strong*, dedicated, devoted, eager, earnest, fanatic, fanatical, fervent, fervid, fireball*, fired, frenetic, gung-ho*, hot*, impassioned, itchy*, keen, obsessed, passionate, possessed, pushy*, rabid, ripe, self-starting, spirited, wild-eyed*; SEE CONCEPTS *326,401,404*

zenith [n] *top*
acme, altitude, apex, apogee, cap, capper, capstone, climax, crest, crown, culmination, elevation, eminence, height, high noon*, high point, meridian, payoff*, peak, pinnacle, roof, summit, tiptop*, topper*, vertex; SEE CONCEPTS *706,832, 836*

zero [n] *nothing*
aught, blank, bottom, cipher, insignificancy, love*, lowest point, nada*, nadir, naught, nil*, nix*, nobody*, nonentity, nought, nullity, oblivion, ought, rock bottom*, scratch, shutout, void, zilch*, zip*, zot*; SEE CONCEPTS *407,784*

zero hour [n] *vital moment*
appointed hour*, climax, contingency, countdown, crisis, crossroad, D-day*, emergency, exigency, jumping-off point*, juncture, moment of truth*, pinch, strait, target, the time*, turning point*; SEE CONCEPTS *668,815,832*

zest [n1] *taste, flavor*
bite, body, charm, flavoring, ginger, guts*, interest, kick*, nip, piquancy, punch*, pungency, relish, salt, savor, seasoning, smack*, snap*, spice, tang, zap*, zip*; SEE CONCEPT *614*

zest [n2] *energy, gusto*
appetite, ardor, bliss, bounce, cheer, delectation, delight, eagerness, ecstasy, elation, enjoyment, enthusiasm, fervor, guts*, happiness, keenness, moxie*, passion, pep*, pleasure, relish*, satisfaction, zeal, zing*; SEE CONCEPTS *410,411*

zigzag [adj] *moving side to side*
askew, awry, bent, crinkled, crooked, devious, diagonal, erratic, fluctuating, inclined, indirect, irregular, jagged, meandering, oblique, oscillating, rambling, serrated, sinuous, sloping, snaking, tortuous, transverse, twisted, twisting, undulating, waggling, winding; SEE CONCEPT *581*

zip [n] *enthusiasm, energy*
brio, drive, get-up-and-go*, go*, gusto, life, liveliness, oomph*, pep, pizzazz*, punch, sparkle, spirit, verve, vigor, vim, vitality, zest, zing*; SEE CONCEPTS *411,633*

zip [v] *move about quickly*
bustle, dash, flash, fly, hasten, hurry, run, rush, shoot, speed, tear, waltz, whisk, whiz, zoom; SEE CONCEPT *150*

zone [n] *district*
area, band, belt, circuit, ground, realm, region, section, sector, segment, sphere, territory, tract; SEE CONCEPTS *508,513*

zoom [*v*] *move very quickly*
buzz, dart, dash, dive, flash, fly, hum, hurtle, outstrip, rip, rocket, rush, shoot, shoot up, sky-rocket, speed, streak, surge, tear, whirl, whiz, zip*; SEE CONCEPT *150*

ROGET'S 21ST CENTURY CONCEPT INDEX

HOW TO USE THE CONCEPT INDEX

Simply put, a thesaurus is a collection of words grouped according to idea. 17,000 words appear in the A to Z listings of *Roget's 21st Century Thesaurus* with over 450,000 synonyms to choose from. This selection alone would seem generous enough to satisfy the lexicographer's expectation of what a thesaurus should contain. But a wealth of new alternatives is created when we begin to think about the higher connections that can be made between words and ideas in the language. This is the purpose of *Roget's 21st Century's* Concept Index.

The Concept Index not only helps writers and thinkers to *organize* their ideas but leads them from those very ideas to

the words that can best express them. It is a semantic hierarchy of the most common concepts we use in American
English, as it is spoken and written today. 837 concepts are
classified according to their subject and usage, and are
grouped under ten general categories of interest: Actions,
Causes, Fields of Human Activity, Life Forms, Objects, the
Planet, Qualities, Senses, States, and Weights and Measures.

Each of *Roget's 21st Century Thesaurus*'s 17,000 main
entries is cross-referenced to any concept(s) to which it can
be related. For example, when you look up the entry for
"knowledgeable" in the A to Z listing, it is referenced to
concept #402. Turning in the index to concept #402, "attribute of intelligence," you will see over 100 other main
entries that are also related to this concept:

MAIN ENTRY

with synonym list as it appears in the A to Z listing

knowledgeable [*adj*] *aware, educated*,
abreast, acquainted, alert, appreciative, apprised,
au courant, au fait, brainy, bright, brilliant, clever,
cognizant, conscious, conversant, discerning, erudite, experienced, familiar, informed, insightful,
intelligent, in the know, knowing, learned, lettered,
omniscient, perceptive, plugged in*, posted, prescient, privy, quick-witted, sagacious, sage, savvy,
scholarly, sensible, sharp, smart, sophic, sophisticated, tuned-in*, understanding, versed, well-
informed, well-rounded, wise, with-it; SEE
CONCEPT *402*

CONCEPT

with collection of main entry words referenced to it in the index

402 attribute of intelligence: able, abreast, abstruse, academic, acute, adept, alert, amenable, analytic/analytical, appreciative, apt,
astute, awake, aware, backward, bewildered,
blank, blind, bright, brilliant, calculable,

canny, childish, clairvoyant, clear, clever, complex, childish, clairvoyant, clear, clever, clumsy, cognizant, coherent, common-sense, complex, comprehensible, conscious, considered, contemplative, conversant, creative, cunning, dark, deducible, deep, delirious, dense, designedly, dexterous, dim, discerning, dizzy, dopey, down-to-earth, dull, dumb, educated, efficient, elevated, empty, empty-headed, enlightened, erudite, experienced, expert, familiar, farsighted, fatuous, forgotten, frivolous, gifted, gullible, harebrained, hazy, idiotic, ignorant, illiterate, imbecile, impressionable, incisive, incomprehensible, inefficient, ineligible, inept, inexperienced, informed, ingenious, inquiring, inquisitive, insipid, intellectual, intelligent, intuitive, inventive, irrational, judicious, keen, knowing, knowledgeable, learned, logical, lucid, mental, mindful, mistaken, nimble, oblivious, observant, obtuse, omniscient, penetrating, perceptive, perspicacious, philosophical/philosophic, precocious, privy, professional, proficient, profound, psychic, quick, quick-witted, rational, ready, reasonable, resourceful, retarded, sagacious, sane, scatterbrained, scholarly, senile, sensible, shallow, sharp, shrewd, simple, skillful, slick, slow, smart, soft, stolid, studious, stupid, subtle, thick, thoughtful, thoughtless, touched, unaware, uneducated, unfamiliar, unwise, vacant, vacuous, versed, veteran, weak, wise

Any of these main entry words appearing together as attributes of intelligence in the Concept Index—from "astute" to "ingenious" to "perspicacious" to "veteran"—may be the one perfect word you are looking for. Or, intrigued by the associations the word "veteran" brings to mind, you could return to the A to Z listing to explore its synonyms:

veteran [*adj*] *experienced, seasoned*
adept, battle-scarred*, been around*, disciplined, exercised, expert, from way back*, hardened, inured, knows one's stuff*, long-serving, long-time, not born yesterday*, of the old school*, old, old-time, practical, practiced, pro, proficient, skilled, sophisticated, steady, trained, up to speed*, versed, vet*, weathered, wise, wise to ways*, worldly; SEE CONCEPTS *402,527,678*

Even further possibilities exist, when you realize that "veteran" is referenced to two additional concepts: #527, the quality of "ability" and #678, the state of "experience." Main entries are often referenced to as many as three or four different concepts.

Simple to use, the Concept Index becomes invaluable in the effort to turn an idea into a specific word. By linking together the main entries that share similar concepts, but may not be direct synonyms, the index makes possible creative semantic connections between words in our language, stimulating thought and broadening vocabulary.

Whether you begin by browsing through the Concept Index for ideas, or in the A to Z listing with a particular word in mind, you will find that *Roget's 21st Century Thesaurus* goes beyond traditional thesauri and synonym-finders to offer thousands of word choices through access to its unique Concept Index.

QUICK REFERENCE GUIDE TO CONCEPTS

Actions

CLASS OF

1 action: act, action, activity, behave, feat, spurt, step

2 event: affair, anything, be, event, eventuate, experience, fact, incident, milestone, move, movement, occasion, outbreak, pass, proceeding

3 occurrence: development, episode, occurrence, proceeding, recur, thing, transpire

4 occurrence with one participant: act, befall, behave, break, chance, coincidence, come, come off, deed, episode, fall out, fluke, go, happen, happening, intervene, occur, occurrence, result, return, rise

5 occurrence with two participants: boundary, limit, measure, obstruct, reinforce, restraint, test

6 series of related actions: channel, commit, disposition, elapse, form, instrument, maneuver, manner, means, mechanism, method, mode, path, pattern, policy, procedure, process, routine, rule, rut, system, technique, touch, usage, vehicle, way

COGNITIVE

7 affect: abandon, abase, affect, afflict, affront, aggravate, agitate, agonize, alarm, alienate, allay, alleviate, allure, anger, annoy, antagonize, appall/appal, appeal, appease, appeasement, arouse, arrest, assuage, attract, awaken, awe, baffle, bait, beckon, bedazzle, befuddle, beguile, beleaguer, bemuse, beset, besiege, bewitch, bias, bombard, bore, bother, brighten, bring down, bug, buoy (up), burden, captivate, chafe, chagrin, charm, cheer, chill, clear, cloud, comfort, complicate, compose, concern, console, content, cow, craze, cross, crucify, crush, dampen, dash, daunt, debase, deceive, deception, defame, deflate, degrade, delight, demean, demoralize, deprecate, depreciate, depress, disaffect, disappoint, disarm, discomfit, discomfort, discommode, discompose, disconcert, discountenance, disgust, dishearten, dismay, disoblige, disparage, displease, disquiet, distress, disturb, divert, double-cross, downgrade, draw, dwarf, electrify, elevate, embarrass, embitter, embroil, enamor, enchant, encourage, encouragement, encroach, endear, energize, enliven, enrage, enrapture, enthrall, entice, enticement, entrance, estrange, exacerbate, exasperate, excite, exercise, exhilarate, fail, fascinate, faze, ferment, flurry, fluster, fortify, freak, fret, frustrate, fulfill, gall, galling, galvanize, get, govern, grate, gratify, grieve, grip, gripe, harass, harm, harry, hearten, horrify, hound, hurt, impress, inflame, ingratiate, inspire, instigate, interest, intimidate, intrigue, invigorate, irk, irritate, jar, kindle, let down, lighten, lower, lull, madden, matter, menace, miff, mock, molest, mollify, mortify, move,

nag, needle, nerve, nettle, occupy, offend, oppress, outrage, pacify, pain, pall, peeve, pep up, perk up, persecute, perturb, pester, petrify, pick at/pick on, pique, placate, plague, please, prejudice, pressure, prime, prod, provoke, puncture, put out, quell, quicken, rack, rally, rankle, rasp, reach, reassure, reduce, regenerate, register, remind, repay, repel, revolt, ride, rile, rouse, ruffle, sadden, satisfy, scar, scare, send, settle, shake, shame, shatter, sink, slight, slur, smooth, solace, soothe, spite, stagger, startle, still, strain, strengthen, stress, strike, support, sweeten, take down, tantalize, taunt, tease, temper, terrify, terrorize, threaten, thrill, tickle, titillate, torment, torture, touch, tranquilize, transport, trouble, try, turn, turn off, undo, unnerve, unsettle, upset, vex, visit, wake/waken, wear, -weigh, weigh down, whet, worry, wound, wrong

8 agree: accede, accept, acceptance, accession, accord, acknowledge, acknowledgment, acquiesce, acquiescence, agree, align, assent, back, bear, cleave, cohere, comply, compromise, concur, consent, conspire, contract, covenant, draft, encourage, enlist, follow, give in/give up, go, go along/go along with, go by, grant, league, negotiate, stipulate, unanimous, yield

9 amuse: amuse, bait, divert, entertain, humor

10 approve: acquiesce, acquiescence, advocate, agree, applaud, appreciate, approbation, approval, approve, authorize, blessing, champion, concur, condone, countenance, defend, deference, endorse, envy, espouse, exalt, exculpate, excuse, exonerate, favor, go for, honor, idolize, league, nod, okay, overlook, pardon, pity, pride, prize, recognition, recommend, regard, respect, revere/reverence, reverence, sanctify, subscribe, support

11 attract: attract, fascinate, grip, interest, intrigue, inveigle, lure, mesmerize, pull, ravish, seduce, send, snare, take, tantalize, tease, tempt, titillate, transfix, turn on, whet, win/win over

12 believe: accept, acceptance, acknowledge, appreciate, appreciation, assume, authenticate, bank on, bear, believe, bleed, consider, convert, count on/count upon, credit, deem, disagree, embrace, esteem, expect, feel, forgive, glorify, glory, hold, imagine, infer, lean, make believe, misjudge, object, overrate, postulate, predispose, presume, rate, reckon, regard, rely, sanctify, see, suppose, swallow, think, trust, underestimate, understand, view

13 change conception: ache, alternate, awakening, caprice, catharsis, concession, conform, conformity, crack, crack up, fit, flare, fluctuate, give, go back/go back on, oscillate, perish, repudiate, reverse, revert, revive, sway, thaw, tire, vacillate, weary

14 compel: abet, alarm, attraction, badger, bait, bewilder, bind, brainwash, browbeat, brutality, bulldoze, bully, burden, coerce, coercion, come between, compel, confusion, conjure, constrain, constraint, convert, corrupt, dare, debauch, defeat, demoralize, deprave, discourage, disgrace, dispel, distract, domineer, duress, embitter, engross, enrage, enslave, entrance, excite, fan, fire, foment, force, freeze, frighten, galvanize, get back at, goad, grate, grind, harass, harassment, hassle, haunt, horrify, humble, humiliate, hurt, impel, impinge, imposition, incense, incite, inconvenience, inculcate, indoctrinate, induce, infest, inflame, intrude, inveigle, invigorate, jinx, jog, kindle, load, lumber, make, manipulate, meddle, mesmerize, mistreat, molest, motivate, nauseate, nerve, nettle, nonplus, oblige, offend, oppress, oppression, panic, paralyze, pervert, petrify, pique, plague, poison, pound, predispose, prejudice, press, pressure, prey on, provocation, push, put, put out, rankle, ride, ruffle, scourge, screw, sell/sell out, shake up, shame, sicken, sour, spoil, spur, stimulate, stir, sway, tame, task, tax, terrorize, tire, transfix, undermine, unnerve, victimize, visit, wake/waken, whip up, work up, worry, wound, yield

15 comprehend: appreciate, appreciation, apprehend, assimilate, catch, comprehend, conceive, decipher, deduce, deduction, derive, determine, differentiate, dig, digest, discern, discriminate, distinguish, do, draw, embrace, familiarize, fathom, feel, figure, follow, gather, get, grasp, hear, identify with, infer, know, make, make out, misapprehend, misconstrue, mistake, misunderstand, outwit/outsmart, penetrate, perceive, realize, recognize, resolve, see, solve, take, take in, tell, understand

16 confuse: confound, confuse, daze, dazzle, decoy, derange, disconcert, disrupt, distract, dumbfound, floor, fluster, foul up, get, hassle, humble, jumble, mix up, muddle, mystify, nonplus, obscure, overwhelm, perplex, perturb, puzzle, rattle, snarl, stump, throw

17 consider: absorb, ache, balance, begrudge, bleed, brood, buckle down, cogitate, commune, concentrate, consider, consult, contemplate, cook up, cram, daydream, deliberate, deliberation, devote, dream, dream up, dwell on/dwell upon, engross, entertain, envisage/envision, excogitate, eye, fancy, fantasize, focus, gnaw, grieve, harbor, heed, hide, immerse, marvel, meditate, mull, muse, occupy, picture, ponder, puzzle, reconsider, reflect, reflection, reminisce, retrospect, revolve, speculate, think, thought, treat, turn over, visualize, wonder, wrestle

18 decide: abnegation, adjudicate, adopt, adoption, appraisal, appraise, cancel, circumscribe, classification, classify, conclude, convict, count, credit, date, decide, dedicate, define, derive, destine, determine, disapprove, disavow, dispose of, distinguish, evaluate, falter, figure, fix, go along/go along with, go by, ground, group, hedge, impose, influence, intend, judge, make out, misjudge, moderate, ordain, plant, premise, provide, purpose, referee, resolution, resolve, rule, set, settle, solve, specify, stipulate, surmise, turn down, type, waver, yield

19 depress: abandon, abase, affect, afflict, affront, aggravate, agitate, agonize, alarm, alienate, anger, annoy, antagonize, appall/appal, appeal, arouse, arrest, awaken, awe, baffle, bait, befuddle, beguile, beleaguer, bemuse, beset, besiege, bias, bombard, bore, bother, bring down, bug, burden, chafe, chagrin, chill, cloud, complicate, concern, cow, craze, cross, crucify, crush, dampen, dash, daunt, debase, deceive, deception, defame, deflate, degrade, demean, demoralize, deprecate, depreciate, depress, disaffect, disappoint, disarm, discomfit, discomfort, discommode, discompose, disconcert, discountenance, disgust, dishearten, dismay, disoblige, disparage, displease, disquiet, distress, disturb, divert, double-cross, downgrade, draw, dwarf, embarrass, embitter, embroil, encroach, enrage, enthrall, entice, enticement, estrange, exacerbate, exasperate, excite, exercise, fail, faze, ferment, flurry, fluster, freak, fret, frustrate, gall, galling, get, govern, grate, grieve, gripe, harass, harm, harry, horrify, hound, hurt, impress, inflame, instigate, intimidate, irk, irritate, jar, let down, lower, madden, matter, menace, miff, mock, molest, mortify, move, nag, needle, nettle, occupy, offend, oppress, outrage, pain, pall, peeve, persecute, perturb, pester, petrify, pick at/pick on, pique, plague, prejudice, pressure, prime, prod, provoke, puncture, put out, quicken, rack, rankle, rasp, reach, reduce, register, remind, repay, repel, revolt, ride, rile, ruffle, sadden, scar, scare, shake, shame, shatter, sink, slight, slur, spite, stagger, startle, strain, stress, strike, support, take down, tantalize, taunt, tease, terrify, terrorize, threaten, torment, torture, touch, trouble, try, turn, turn off, undo, unnerve, unsettle, upset, vex, visit, wear, weigh, weigh down, worry, wound, wrong

20 desire: addiction, advance(s), affinity, aim, ambition, anger, appetite, aspiration, aspire, avid, behest, burn, care, covet, crave, craving, crush, cupidity, curiosity, dependence/dependency, desire, drool, eagerness, envy, expect, famished, fancy, fantasy, fascination, fish for, free will, goad, greed, hanker after/hanker for, hankering, hope, hunger, hungry, impulse, inclination, indulge, insatiable, interest, itch, lack, languish, lean, leaning, like, liking, long, longing, lust, mania, mind, miss, moon, mope, motivation, motive, need, nostalgia, notion, obsession, pant, penchant, pine, please, pleasure, predilection, predisposition, prefer, preference, proclivity, propensity, purport, purpose, pursue, relish, require, sigh, stomach, taste, temptation, thirst, urge, volition, voracious, want, will, wish, yearn, yen

21 doubt: begrudge, controvert, deplore, despair, disallow, disapprove, disbelief, disbelieve, discount, discountenance, discredit, dissent, distrust, doubt, frown, fume, grudge, hesitate, hesitation, mind, misgiving, mistrust, object, objection, oppose, query, question, regret, reject, rejection, repudiate, repulse, scorn, scruple, segregate, spurn, suspect, turn, wonder

22 elated: affect, allay, alleviate, allure, appeal, appease, appeasement, arouse, arrest, as-

nesse, fix, formulate, frame, hatch, intend, intrigue, invent, lay, lay out, machinate, maneuver, manufacture, mean, organize, outline, plan, plot, program, project, propose, purpose, pursue, rough out, schedule, shape, sketch

37 reason: analyze, cipher, clear up, conclude, construe, crack, criticize, date, decipher, dialectic, do, educe, equate, estimate, figure, forecast, gauge, generalize, induction, infer, judgment, logic, make, premise, project, rank, rate, reason, reasoning, reckon, solve, speculate, stock, survey

38 recognize: acknowledge, ascertain, come across, conjure up, crack, cut, detect, detection, diagnose, differentiate, discern, discriminate, distinguish, elude, encounter, familiarize, fathom, feel, identify, know, mark, perceive, pinpoint, place, recognition, recognize, remark, salute/salutation, salute, spot, stereotype

39 relate: ascribe, associate, association, categorize, class, classification, classify, codify, compare, comparison, contrast, correlate, equate, identify with, implication

40 remember: block out, forget, mind, recall, recollect, remember, remembrance, remind, reminisce, retain, retrospect, think

41 select: aim, allocate, allot, allow, appoint, appointment, assign, assignment, cast, choice, choose, cull, designate, designation, elect, election, excerpt, favoritism, finger, like, name, nominate, nomination, opt, pick, prefer, recruit, relegate, screen, select, take, turn, volition, vote

42 surprise: alarm, amaze, appall/appal, astonish, astound, awe, backfire, baffle, bedazzle, befuddle, bewilder, confound, daze, dazzle, deluge, dumbfound, electrify, flabbergast, frighten, jolt, overwhelm, petrify, scare, shock, stagger, startle, stun/stupefy, surprise, terrify

43 think: count, design, devise, envisage/envision, fancy, imagine, mint, occur, originate, picture, proceed, see, theorize, think, thought

COMMUNICATIVE

44 accuse: accuse, affront, arraign, bastardize, betray, betrayal, blame, blow up, charge, condemn, condemnation, decry, denounce, discredit, forswear, gripe, groan, grumble, heckle, humble, humiliate, impeach, implicate, impute, indict, indictment, invective, inveigh, malign, persecute, profane, rant, rebuke, reprimand, reproach, scold, slur, tax, tell off, tirade, vilify, vituperate

45 answer: acknowledge, agree, answer, counter, decline, denial, fill in, give in/give up, react, reaction, reciprocate, repartee, reply, respond, retort, return

46 argue: agitate, altercation, argue, argument, back talk, battle, beard, bicker, brawl, clash, conflict, confront, confrontation, confute, contend, contention, contest, contradict, contradiction, contravene, controversy, controvert, demur, deny, dicker, differ, difference, difficulty, disagree, disagreement, dispute, dissension, dissent, diverge, divide, encoun-

ter, expostulate, fall out, feud, fight, fracas, friction, fuss, haggle, hassle, imbroglio, maintain, misunderstanding, negate, object, objection, protest, quarrel, quibble, reason, rebut, remonstrate, rift, row, run-in, rupture, scrap, squabble, strife, tiff, uproar, wrangle

47 articulate: articulate, call, cry, delivery, diction, elocution, enunciate, exclaim, expression, hail, heckle, mumble, parrot, pipe, pronounce, put, sing, slur, speak, speech, stammer, talk, utter, utterance, yell

48 ask: accost, apologize, apology, appeal, application, apply, approach, ask, beg, beseech, canvass, catechize, charter, conjure, consult, consultation, crave, crawl, cross-examine, desire, entreat, examine, grill, hearing, implore, inquest, inquire, inquiry, interrogate, interview, investigate, investigation, invitation, invite, invocation, invoke, pester, petition, plead, poll, pray, prayer, propose, proposition, pump, query, quest, question, quiz, repent, requisition, scrounge, seek, survey

49 assert: accredit, acknowledge, advance, advocate, affirm, affirmation, allegation, allege, announce, announcement, ascribe, assert, assertion, attest, avow, bemoan, blow up, bluster, boast, brag, bravado, color, come clean, corroborate, crow, debunk, declaim, declaration, declare, defend, deny, dramatize, drum into, embellish, emphasize, establish, exclaim, exclamation, exult, generalize, gloat, glory, gloss, gush, impress, impute, insinuate, insist, intimate, justify, lay, level, magnify, maintain, mock, mockery, overrate, pass, play down, play up, plead, plug, point out, pound, proclaim, profess, promote, promotion, pronounce, puff, punctuate, purport, push, rant, rave, refuse, retract, review, rumor, show off, speak out/speak up, spout, state, stereotype, stress, substantiate, support, swagger, swear, testify, testimonial, testimony, underline, vent, vindicate, voice, vouch, weep, whitewash, witness

50 authorize: accede, accord, accredit, acknowledge, acknowledgment, acquit, affirm, aggrandize, appoint, appointment, approve, arm, assign, authorize, back, ban, bar, bear out, bless, blessing, certify, charter, commission, concession, consent, constitute, contract, countenance, countermand, crown, decree, dedicate, delegate, delegation, detail, disown, empower, enable, enact, endorse, enforce, enjoin, entitle, entrust, establish, exempt, fire, forgive, grant, induct, inflict, invest, invoke, lay, let, let off, license, make, name, negate, nod, nominate, nomination, nullify, okay, ordain, order, override/overrule, pardon, permission, permit, place, prescribe, prohibit, ratify, recall, receive, release, relieve, repeal, reprieve, revoke, sanction, spare, station, subscribe, underwrite, validate, vest, veto, void, warrant, withdraw, witness

51 comment: accost, acknowledge, add, air, annotate, aside, babble, badger, bemoan, brag, bravado, bring up, broach, circumlocution, comment, commentary, congratulate, conjecture, couch, critique, declaim, decline, deliver, discourse, enunciate, express, extemporize, greet, greeting, harangue, hearsay, interject, interrupt, jabber, jaw, observation, observe, preach, ramble, rattle, rave, remark, report, rhetoric, say, spout, state, talk, throw out, touch, vent, ventilate, voice, yak/yap

52 criticize: abuse, admonish, air, aspersion, assail, assault, attack, barb, baste, beef, belittle, berate, blast, browbeat, carp, castigate, censure, chasten, chastise, chew out, chide, come down on, complain, complaint, condemn, condemnation, confront, correct, cow, criticism, criticize, critique, crucify, cut, cut up, damn, debase, decry, denigrate, denounce, denunciation, deny, deprecate, depreciate, deride, derision, detract, detraction, diatribe, disapprove, disparage, disparagement, dress down, excoriate, flak, fulminate, fulmination, gainsay, gibe, gird, grievance, gripe, groan, grouch, grumble, hiss, humble, humiliate, impeach, impugn, insult, invective, inveigh, jaw, kick, knock, lambaste, lament, lash, lay into, lecture, malign, moan, mortify, mutter, nag, offense, pan, pick at/pick on, profane, protest, quibble, rail, rant, rap, rebuke, reflection, remonstrate, reprimand, reproach, review, row, run down, sarcasm, scold, scorn, scourge, slam, sneer, squawk, storm, sulk, swear, take down, tell off, thunder, vilify, vituperate

53 demand: ask, beckon, beg, behest, bid, bidding, bribe, call, challenge, charge, claim, command, countermand, crave, cross-examine, dare, decree, demand, dictate, direct, enjoin, entreat, exact, extort, extortion, grill, importune, impose, inflict, insist, instruct, interrogate, necessitate, obligate, order, petition, pump, query, question, request, require, requisition, reserve, solicit, squeeze, summon

54 deny: abuse, accusation, affront, aspersion, attack, backbiting, barb, belie, belittle, blacken, blame, blemish, calumny, confront, contradict, curse, damn, debase, defamation, defame, defile, demean, demur, denial, denigrate, deride, detract, detraction, dig, diminish, disclaim, discountenance, discredit, disgrace, dishonor, disown, disparage, disparagement, downgrade, embarrass, explode, flout, forswear, fulminate, fulmination, gainsay, gibe, gird, insult, invective, inveigh, jeer, lambaste, lament, laugh at, lecture, lip, malign, mimic, minimize, mortify, mouth, needle, oath, oppose, protest, puncture, put down, put-down, rave, rebuff, rebut, refute, remonstrate, renounce, renunciation, ridicule, rumor, run down, sarcasm, scoff, scold, scorn, show up, slam, slander, slur, smear, snap, sneer, snub, squawk, squeal, stain, swear, swearing, tattle, taunt, thunder, tirade, traverse, turn, turn down, underestimate, vituperate, whine, write off

55 describe: articulate, articulation, blab, define, denote, describe, detail, mean, narrate, narration, outline, paraphrase, phrase, portray, recite, recount, relate, signify, spell, state, summarize, sum up, tell, translate, typify, unfold, utter

56 discuss: argue, bargain, canvass, communicate, confer, conference, consult, debate, deliberate, deliberation, dialogue/dialog, discourse, discuss, discussion, gossip, huddle, intercede, interchange, jabber, jaw, negotiate, negotiation, powwow, rap, reason, rehash, repartee, talk, treat, word

57 explain: account for, admission, admit, annotate, cite, clarification, clarify, clear up, come clean, comment, concede, confide, confirm, construe, corroborate, declare, defense, define, demonstrate, detail, dilate, elaborate, elucidate, emphasize, enlighten, enumerate, evidence, excuse, expand, explain, explicate, expound, gloss, illuminate, illustrate, interpret, itemize, justify, let on, own, palliate, paraphrase, plea, preface, prove, rationalize, recite, render, simplify, speak out/speak up, specify, translate, vindicate, warrant

58 fabricate: aspersion, backbiting, belie, bluff, disprove, embroider, fabricate, impugn, profane

59 fool: affect, artifice, assume, bamboozle, banter, beguile, bilk, blow up, bluff, burn, cajole, charade, cheat, chicanery, circumvent, color, con, copy, corner, counterfeit, cross, deceit, deceive, deception, decoy, default, defraud, delude, disguise, dishonesty, dissemble, dissimulate, do, dodge, do out of, double-cross, double-dealing, dramatize, dupe, duplicity, elude, enmesh, ensnare, entangle, entrap, evasion, excuse, extort, fake, feign, fence, finesse, flatter, flattery, fleece, fool, fooling, forge, forgery, fraud, frolic, fudge, gag, game, garble, gimmick, hanky-panky, have, hoax, hocus-pocus, impersonate, imposition, imposture, inveigle, invent, juggle, kid, make believe, maneuver, masquerade, mimic, mince, mislead, mock, outwit/outsmart, overplay, palliate, pander, parody, play down, ploy, pose, posture, prank, pretend, pretense, pretext, put on, ridicule, ruse, scheme, sham, shift, shirk, simulate, spoof, sport, stratagem, string along, swindle, take, take in, trap, trick, trickery, victimize, wile, wit

60 inform: acknowledge, acquaint, address, advance, advertise, advise, allow, allude, allusion, announce, avow, bare, betray, betrayal, bill, blab, break, breathe, brief, briefing, broadcast, buzz, chronicle, circulate, clue, come out, come out with, confess, confession, convene, convey, cover, debunk, declare, define, deliver, detail, develop, dictate, disclose, divulge, enlighten, expose, exposure, feature, furnish, get across, give, give away, gossip, herald, hint, impart, inform, instruct, intimate, introduce, issue, leak, lecture, let on, notify, outing, pass, plug, post, prescribe, proclaim, program, promulgate, propagate, publication, publicize, ready, release, report, reveal, revelation, show up, sing, speak, speech, spill, spread, squeal, stipulate, talk, tattle, thank, thanks, tip, unburden, uncover, unveil, ventilate, whisper

61 instruct: bar, direct, educate, instruct, prescribe

62 label: attach, call, christen, define, designate, dub, entitle, identify, label, name, style, tag, term, title

63 lie: backbiting, belie, bunk, cant, casuistry, color, default, detraction, distort, distortion, duplicity, embroider, equivocate, equivocation, evasion, exaggerate, exaggeration, fabricate, fabrication, falsehood, falsify, feign, fib, fiction, fudge, garble, gloss, hoax, hypocrisy, invent, invention, juggle, libel, lie, malign, misinform, mislead, misrepresent/misquote, mock, obscure, pad, perjure, pervert, play down, pose, pretend, pretense, prevaricate, profane, profess, sell/sell out, simulate, slant, smear, twist, warp, whitewash, wile

64 **noise, animal:** bark, bay, call, cheep, chirp, howl, peep, roar, squawk, squeak, squeal, yelp

65 **noise-making:** bang, blare, blast, blow, boom, buzz, cadence, chant, chime, clank, clash, clatter, click, clink, clump, cough, crash, creak, crinkle, drone, drum, grumble, gurgle, harmony, hum, hush, inflection, jangle, jar, jingle, measure, meter, muffle, murmur, mute, patter, peal, pipe, pitch, play, quiet, racket, rattle, reflect, reverberate, ring, roll, rumble, rustle, silence, sizzle, sound, squeak, still, stress, swing, talk, tempo, tenor, thud/thump, thunder, tick, tinkle, toll, tone, tranquility, tune/tune up, undertone, uproar, volume, whistle

66 **offer:** allude, extend, lay, offer, pose, present, proffer, propose, put, submit, volunteer

67 **offer to give:** amends, apologize, apology, bid, bidding, come forward, concession, expiate, extend, furnish, offer, pose, present, proffer, put, surrender, volunteer

68 **persuade:** advance, argue, argument, assure, bend, bring around, budge, cajole, carry, coax, coerce, coercion, convince, disarm, discourage, dissuade, draw, drive, drum up, egg on, elicit, eloquence, entice, enticement, forward, get, goad, hammer away/hammer into, impel, induce, inducement, influence, ingratiate, invite, lead, lobby, maintain, motivate, negotiate, negotiation, occasion, persuade, persuasion, pitch, predispose, prevail upon/prevail on, procure, prompt, push, reason, spur, stress, sway, tempt, urge, wheedle, win/win over

69 **praise:** accent, acclaim, acclamation, accolade, accredit, adulation, aggrandize, applaud, applause, approbation, benediction, blarney, bless, champion, cheer, citation, commemorate, commend, commendation, compliment, congratulate, congratulations, consecrate, credit, crown, dedicate, dedication, deify, distinguish, elevate, elevation, endorse, enshrine, eulogize, eulogy, exalt, exaltation, extol, felicitate, flatter, flattery, further, glorify, hail, homage, kudos, laud, laurels, magnify, ovation, praise, puff, reference, salute, thank, thanks, tout, tribute, worship

70 **predict:** announce, anticipate, astrology, augur, augury, call, forebode, forecast, foreordain, foresee, foreshadow, foretell, oracle, precursor, predict, prediction, presage, prognosticate, project, prophecy, prophesy

71 **promise:** assurance, assure, avow, commitment, covenant, ensure, go back/go back on, guarantee, oath, pledge, portend, promise, vouch, vow, warrant, word

72 **read:** leaf, look up, narrate, narration, peruse, pore, read, reading, recitation, recite, refer, skim

73 **refer:** attach, attribute, drive at, instance, intend, mean, mention, oppose, point out, refer

74 **signal:** beckon, call, flag, gesture, gesture/gesticulate, hail, harbinger, hint, indicate, indication, nod, omen, page, sign, signal, spell, suggest, symbolize, wave

75 **suggest:** advice, advise, advocate, approach, ask, cajole, come up with, commend, connote, counsel, drum into, enlighten, exhort, exhortation, fish for, foreshadow, get at, guidance, guide, hint, imply, innuendo, insinuate, intimate, motion, move, nominate, nomination, pointer, pose, preach, proffer, propose, raise, recommend, spell, suggest, urge

76 **thank:** appreciate, gratitude, thank

77 **vocalize:** accent, air, bark, bawl, bellow, blare, cackle, caterwaul, chant, cheer, chortle, chuckle, clamor, croak, cry, drawl, drone, exclamation, giggle, groan, growl, grumble, hail, harmonize, hiss, howl, hum, laugh/laughter, laugh, moan, mumble, murmur, mutter, outcry, parrot, pipe, roar, scream, shout, shriek, shut up, sing, snap, snarl, snicker/snigger/sniggle, snore, squawk, squeal, stutter, vocalize, voice, wail, whimper, whine, whistle, whoop, yowl

78 **warn:** admonish, alert, bluster, caution, caveat, charge, defy, dissuade, enjoin, exhort, exhortation, forebode, foreboding, forecast, foretell, forewarn, page, portend, remind, threaten, warn, warning

79 **write:** abstract, address, annotate, autograph, chronicle, compile, compose, correspond, correspondence, cover, depict, dot, draft, draw, draw up, edit, endorse, engrave, engraving, enroll, extract, fill in, fleck, hand, inscribe, label, line, list, mark, notify, page, pen, picture, plot, point, punctuate, put down, quote, register, revise, revision, rough out, score, scratch, scrawl, script, sign, spot, stamp, trace, transcribe, type, underline, write, writing

GENERAL

80 **act abstractly:** freak, jerk, lurch, twist, wiggle, wrench, writhe

81 **act over an area:** decree, rule, tour, veto

82 **admit:** accede, accept, acquiesce, admit, allow, concede, concur, grant

83 **allow:** absolve, accord, acquit, admission, admit, allow, approve, authorize, capitulate, capitulation, contribute, defer, enable, entitle, excuse, exempt, grant, have, leave, let, let off, liberate, license, overlook, patronage, permission, permit, pity, receive, reception, spell, suffer, tolerate

84 **arrange:** adjust, alphabetize, antedate, arrange, arrangement, array, center, centralize, codify, collate, collocate, compile, concentrate, coordinate, derange, dispose, disrupt, distribute, disturb, divide, file, graduate, group, index, jumble, line, marshal, muddle, order, organization, organize, perplex, pile, place, program, range, rank, reconstruct, sort, systematize, tabulate, type

85 **attach:** adhere, adjoin, affix, anchor, annex, append, attach, batten, bind, bond, cement, chain, clamp, clasp, cling, cohere, connect, engage, fasten, fix, hitch, knot, latch, lock, moor, nail, paste, peg, pin, screw, seal, secure, shut, stick, tack, tag, tape, tether, tie, yoke

86 **attack:** aggression, ambush, assail, assault, attack, bashing, besiege, blast, blitz, bomb, bombard, brutality, burst, charge, combat, come at, coup d'état, descent, embroil, encounter, encroach, engage, fire, fix, foray, fray, go for, incursion, infest, inroad, insurrection, invade, invasion, lambaste, lay into, maraud, occupation, occupy, offensive, onset, onslaught, outbreak, overrun, overwhelm, pillage, plunder, pounce, prey on, raid, rampage, ravage, revenge, rush, sabotage, storm, subvert, surprise, waylay

87 **attempt:** adhere, angle for, answer, apply, assume, attempt, bid, bother, buckle down, campaign, chance, commit, counteract, counterbalance, crack, dabble, dare, defy, delve, dip into, direct, drill, drive, drudge, effort, emulate, endeavor, engage, enterprise, essay, exercise, exert, exertion, experiment, fiddle, function, further, go, hammer away/hammer into, hazard, hush, imitate, keep at, keep up, labor, mess around, monkey, offer, overdo, overplay, persevere, persist, plod, practice, presume, purpose, pursue, putter, represent, risk, scramble, seek, slave, stab, strain, strive, struggle, substitute, tackle, take on, tinker, trial, try, undertake, undertaking, venture, weak, whack, whirl, work

88 **authorize:** accede, accord, accredit, acknowledge, acknowledgment, acquit, affirm, aggrandize, appoint, appointment, approve, arm, assign, authorize, back, ban, bar, bear out, bless, blessing, certify, charter, commission, concession, consent, constitute, contract, countenance, countermand, crown, decree, dedicate, delegate, delegation, detail, disown, empower, enable, enact, endorse, enforce, enjoin, entitle, entrust, establish, exempt, fire, forgive, grant, induct, inflict, invest, invoke, lay, let, let off, license, make, name, negate, nod, nominate, nomination, nullify, okay, ordain, order, override/overrule, pardon, permission, permit, place, prescribe, prohibit, ratify, recall, receive, release, relieve, repeal, reprieve, revoke, sanction, spare, station, subscribe, underwrite, validate, vest, veto, void, warrant, withdraw, witness

89 **borrow:** borrow, charter, lease, let, rent

90 **capture:** apprehend, apprehension, arrest, bag, besiege, capture, catch, collar, commandeer, confinement, conquer, corner, coup d'état, custody, enslave, ensnare, entangle, entrap, expropriate, fetch, foray, get, grab, grasp, imprison, incarcerate, kidnap, nab, nail, net, occupation, occupy, pinch, pull in, seize, seizure, sequester, snap, snare, snatch, tackle, trap

91 **carry out:** accomplish, action, application, assure, avail, complement, complete, comply, conclude, contrive, discharge, do, duplicate, echo, effect, enact, execute, execution, fill, finalize, finish, follow, follow through, fulfill, hammer out, handle, hustle, implement, make, make out, manage, meet, mind, obey, observe, operate, perfect, perform, perpetrate, persist, practice, proceed, prosecute, pull off, realize, redeem, render, repeat, rush, serve, specialize, transact, wage

92 **compete:** bout, boxing, compete, competition, contend, contention, contest, opposition, pit, play, rival, take on, tie, vie

93 **contract:** catch, come down with, contract, get, incur

94 **control:** auspices, contain, contrive, deal/deal with, determine, deregulate, direct, discipline, dominate, domineer, harness, manage, moderate, monopolize, operate, overlook, predominate, preside, prevail, regulate, regulation, ride, stage, steer, systematize, wield, work

95 **defeat:** beat, best, confute, conquer, conquest, coup de grâce, crush, defeat, discomfit, edge, extinguish, finish, floor, lick, outdo, overcome, overpower, overrun, overtake, overthrow, overwhelm, prevail, prostrate, put down, quash, quell, reduce, rout, smash, subjugate, subvert, surmount, thrash, top, topple, trim, triumph, trounce, upset, vanquish, victory, wallop, whip, win

96 **defend:** beard, bulwark, convoy, counteract, counterbalance, cover, defend, ensure, fend, fend off, fight back/fight off, guard, protect, repulse, resist, resistance, safeguard, save, screen, secure, shield, ward/ward off, withstand

97 **demonstrate:** advertising, bear out, demonstrate, establish, evidence, exemplify, give, illustrate, imply

98 **divide:** allocate, apportion, bestow, bisect, cleave, disconnect, dismember, disrupt, dissect, distribute, distribution, divide, division, fork, fragment, halve, mete, part, partition, place, portion, punctuate, quarter, ramification, ration, rupture, sever, share, slice, snap, split

99 **enable:** allow, enable, implement, qualify

100 **engage in:** address, anticipate, apply, collaborate, dig in, drudge, embark on, exist, fall to, fare, fend for, fight, give, go about, go into, go on, grub, immerse, labor, make, participate, pitch in, plunge, ply, practice, pursue, reiterate, risk, share, spend, step in, tackle, take, toil, trouble, turn, undertake, wage, work

101 **err:** blunder, botch, bungle, butcher, compromise, err, error, fault, faux pas, flounder, frailty, fumble, gaffe, guilt, impropriety, inaccuracy, indiscretion, lapse, malpractice, miscalculate, mishandle/mismanage, misjudge, miss, misstep, mistake, neglect, overlook, oversight, screw up, sin, slip, stray, stumble, transgression, trespass, trip, violate, violation, wander

102 **escape:** abscond, avoid, avoidance, bail out, break, break out, bypass, circumvent, disappear, disappearance, dodge, duck, elude, equivocate, escape, eschew, evade, evasion, extricate, flee, flight, flinch, fly, getaway, get out, lose, make off, shake off, skirt, throw off

103 **examine:** analysis, analyze, assay, audit, authenticate, autopsy, case, check, compare, confirm, criticize, decompose, delve, dig,

evaluate, evaluation, examination, examine, experiment, explore, follow up, go into, go over, go through, grade, graduate, hearing, inspect, inspection, investigate, investigation, judgment, look into, measure, nose, observe, peer, peruse, pore, postmortem, probe, quest, ransack, research, review, sample, scan, scout, scrutinize, scrutiny, sift, skim, spy, study, surveillance, survey, test, try, try on/try out, view, weigh

104 exchange: alternate, amends, barter, commute, exchange, interchange, reciprocate, redeem, replace, rotate, substitute, swap/swop, switch, transpose

105 existential change: age, arise, awaken, awakening, begin, come from, date, demise, disappear, disappearance, dissipate, dissolution, dissolve, emerge, fade, form, go, go out, languish, materialize, originate, pass, perish, peter out, run out, spring, succumb, vanish, wake/waken

106 fight: altercation, battle, bout, box, brawl, brush, clamor, clash, combat, conflict, confrontation, contend, contention, contest, contravene, dispute, encounter, engage, engagement, faction, ferment, feud, fight, fight back/fight off, fighting, fracas, fray, free-for-all, friction, fuss, grapple, hassle, imbroglio, mayhem, melee, misunderstanding, oppose, opposition, quarrel, racket, rebel, rebellion, resist, resistance, revolt, revolution, rift, riot, rise, row, run-in, scrap, scuffle, strife, struggle, tilt, uprising, uproar, war, wrangle

107 fuel: charge, feed, fill, fuel, supply

108 give: administer, afford, allocate, allot, allow, apportion, atone, bear, bequeath, bestow, cast, cede, commend, commit, compensate, confide, consign, consignment, contribute, deal, deliver, delivery, descend, devote, disburse, disseminate, dole out, donate, drop off, emit, endow, entrust, finance, furnish, give, give away, hand out, hand over, impart, leave, mete, pass, pass off, present, provide, reach, render, return, reward, sacrifice, satisfy, show, surrender, transfer, turn over, will

109 group: aggregate, alloy, amass, bank, blend, bunch, cluster, collect, collection, commingle, compilation, compile, compound, concentrate, confluence, congregate, consolidate, consolidation, cull, distribution, flock, garner, gather, get together, group, heap, herd, muster, pick, pile, rake, reap, recruit, round up, stack, store

110 help: abet, aid, alleviate, assist, assistance, attend, baby, backing, bail out, befriend, benefit, bolster, boost, break, care, chip in, coddle, commiserate, contribute, convoy, cooperate, cooperation, cover, cultivate, cultivation, cure, defend, dispense, doctor, do for, ease, encourage, encouragement, facilitate, favor, fawn, forward, foster, free, further, furtherance, guarantee, guide, hand, help, hold, indulge, intercede, intervene, invigorate, keep, kindness, lavish, liberate, lift, lighten, mind, minister, nurse, nurture, oblige, patronage, patronize, pitch in, profit, promote, promotion, provide, quell, reform, relieve, serve, service, shore, simplify,

soothe, speed, spell, sponsor, stabilize, subsidize, support, sustain, sympathize, temper, tide over, underwrite, uphold

111 imitate: ape, imitate, mimic, mirror, mock, mockery, parallel, parody, pattern, pretend, repeat, reproduce, sham, simulate, takeoff, take off

112 involve: attack, coalesce, confuse, contain, cooperate, cooperation, count, devote, embody, embrace, enclose, encompass, enmesh, entangle, entrap, figure in, implicate, include, incorporate, interpolate, introduce, involve, mire, overdo, tangle, task

113 join: accompany, add, adhere, adjoin, affiliate, affix, alloy, amalgamate, annex, annexation, append, articulate, articulation, assemble, assembly, attach, band, bridge, butt, cleave, close, coalesce, cohere, combine, compound, connect, converge, couple, dovetail, embody, engage, fasten, fix, fuse, fusion, get together, graft, hitch, incorporate, integrate, intermingle, intersect, intertwine/interweave, introduce, join, knit, knot, lace, link, meeting, meld, merge, mesh, mix, pair, piece, pool, swarm, synthesis, synthesize, union, unite, wed

114 join socially: affiliate, align, assemble, associate, attach, attend, band, belong, bump into, call, cavort, chaperon, collect, collusion, confluence, congregate, consort, consultation, convene, convention, converge, convocation, couple, dalliance, dally/dally with, date, enroll, enter, escort, gather, group, hang about/hang around/hang out, huddle, integrate, intermingle, intertwine/interweave, join, league, link, matriculate, meet, mix, register, session, swarm, take

115 lend: finance, fund, invest, lease, lend, let, loan, pawn, rent, trust

116 lose: deliver, fall, forfeit, forget, leak, lose, misplace, omission, sacrifice

117 manage: adjust, administer, administration, boss, carry on, charge, compose, conduct, control, custody, deal/deal with, deregulate, direct, dispense, dispose, dominate, drill, economy, face, fare, farm, farming, fend for, get along, get by, get on, guide, handle, handling, head, lead, manage, management, marshal, monitor, officiate, operate, orchestrate, organization, overlook, oversee, oversight, predominate, preside, rally, regulate, regulation, reign, rule, run, running, save, subjugate, supervise, supervision, sway, treatment, upkeep, work

118 manifest: agree, comprehend, connote, embodiment, embody, emerge, exemplify, exude, give, indicate, loom, manifest, mirror, point, presage, promise, prove, radiate

119 modify an event: abide, advent, balk, birth, cancellation, cessation, close, closure, come on, come out, come up, coming, commence, complement, completion, conception, conclude, conclusion, culminate, dawn, desist, develop, discontinuance, disposal, embargo, end, ending, end up, ensue, entrance, expiration, expire, fall, finish, genesis, give in/give up, halt, knock off, lapse, lay off, matriculate, pass, pause, pull out, pull up, quit, recess, relinquish, resign, resignation, result, retract, revival, rout, secede, spurt, standstill, stop, surrender, suspend, suspension, terminate, termination

120 obtain: acquire, acquisition, amass, attain, capitalize, earn, gain, get, get at, get back, land, lay up/lay by, make, obtain, pick up, possess, procure, pull in, realize, reap, recover, recruit, regain, retrieve, save, secure, strike, take, win

121 prevent: abolish, abolition, abort, abrogate, abstain, adjourn, adjournment, anticipate, arrest, asphyxiate, avert, avoid, avoidance, baffle, balk, ban, banish, bar, birth control, block, bog down, brake, break, bridle, censor, cheat, check, choke, circumvent, clog, close, confine, constrain, constraint, contravene, cop out, counter, cripple, cross, curb, cut short, dash, defeat, defer, deferment/deferral, delay, deprivation, deprive, deter, discharge, discontinue, discourage, disqualify, dissolve, drop, drop out, encumber, exclude, exclusion, foil, forbear, forbid, forgo, freeze, frustrate, gag, halt, hesitate, hesitation, hinder, hold back/hold off, hold up, impede, incapacitate, inhibit, intercept, interfere, interference, interrupt, invalidate, jam, keep, kill, mire, muffle, muzzle, negate, negation, neutralize, nip, nullify, obstruct, obviate, occlude, omit, outlaw, override/overrule, paralyze, parry, pause, preclude, preempt, prevent, procrastinate, prohibit, prohibition, proscribe, pull out, pull up, put off, quash, quell, recess, refrain, relegate, remove, repeal, repress, rescind, respite, restrain, retard, revoke, rule out, run-around, scrap, scratch, scrub, seclude, shelve, shut, shut off/shut out, slowdown, spite, squash, stall, stay, stem, stifle, still, stop, stymie, subdue, suppress, suspend, table, terminate, thwart, traverse, turn off, undo, veto, vitiate, void, waive, waiver, waylay, withdraw, withhold

122 punish: avenge, chasten, chastise, correct, correction, discipline, evict, exile, expel, fine, pay, penalize, punish, revenge, scourge, sentence

123 punishment: blackmail, damage(s), discipline, eviction, fine, forfeit, lesson, punishment, rap, reprimand, reproach, retribution, sanction

124 receive: accept, acceptance, acquire, acquisition, bring in, come by, come in for, fetch, find, gain, have, inherit, make, object, profit, realize, reap, receipt, receive, reception, recoup, regain, retrieve, take

125 record: enroll, enter, enumerate, itemize, list, record, register, schedule, score, take down, tally, tape, transcribe

126 rectify: accommodate, amend, appease, appeasement, arbitrate, arbitration, atone, atonement, avenge, compensate, conclude, correct, correction, counteract, counterbalance, cover, cure, do up, edit, emend, equalize, expiate, fix, iron out, make up, mediate, mediation, mend, offset, overhaul, penance, placate, quiet, recompense, recoup, rectify, redeem, redress, reform, rehabilitate, remedy, requite, restore, retaliate, retribution, revise, revision, right, satisfy, settle, square, standardize, suit, tailor, temper, tune/tune up, untangle

127 release: acquittal, cede, clear, deliver, delivery, discharge, disentangle, dismiss, dismissal, emancipate, exculpate, exempt, exonerate, extricate, free, loose/loosen, ransom, redeem, release, relinquish, save

128 replace: change, fill in, follow, replace, supersede, supplant

129 reserve: allocate, assign, assignment, assumption, claim, clear, come by, deserts, deserve, designate, earmark, earn, engage, enroll, entitle, gain, intend, merit, put away/put aside/put by, rate, reserve, save, spare, store, subscribe

130 restrict: bar, barricade, bind, block, bound, boycott, brake, check, circumscribe, clog, cocoon, confine, constrain, constraint, constrict, constriction, control, cramp, curb, curtail, dam, deaden, defer, deferment/deferral, delay, disable, embargo, encumber, enjoin, enslave, expatriate, expel, expulsion, fetter, fetters, foil, forbear, forgo, gag, govern, grind, ground, hamper, handicap, harness, hem/hem in, hinder, hobble, hold back/hold off, hold up, impair, impede, imposition, inhibit, limit, matter, moderate, narrow, obligate, obstruct, postpone, prohibit, prohibition, rein, repress, restrain, restrict, retard, set back, slow, slowdown, smother, squelch, stifle, strangle, stymie, subdue, suppress, suspend, thwart, tie/tie up

131 return: deliver, fetch, hand over, ransom, recall, redeem, regain, repay, requite, restore, retrieve, return

132 reward: award, commend, confer, decorate, reward

133 rule: abdicate, accession, command, depose, deposition, dictatorship, displace, enforce, enforcement, govern, impose, oppress, rule, subjugate, supremacy

134 save: cocoon, conservation, conserve, deposit, guard, harbor, lay up/lay by, maintain, maintenance, pad, patrol, preservation, preserve, protect, put away/put aside/put by, rehabilitate, rescue, salvage, salvation, save, shelter, shield, spare, ward/ward off, watch

135 separate: abstract, analyze, appropriate, appropriation, assign, class, classification, classify, dedicate, detach, disaffect, disconnect, disengage, disentangle, dislocate, dismantle, dismember, disperse, disrupt, dissociate, divide, division, filter, fragment, gape, garner, glean, hoard, open, part, partition, seclude, seclusion, segregate, separate, separation, split, strain, undo

136 serve: accommodate, administer, board, bondage, cater, obey, oblige, pamper, pander, provide, quench, serve, spoil, tend, wait on

137 shape change: beat, bisect, bruise, carve, chip, chisel, cleave, clip, compact, crimp, crinkle, cut, desiccate, disfigure, disguise, distort, disturb, divide, do in, edge, elongate, enlarge, fatigue, file, flatten, fragment, gash, hack, lacerate, nick, notch, pierce, prune, puncture, reduce, roll, rumple, scar, score, sculpture, shape, sharpen, shave, shorten, shrink, shrivel, slash, slice, smooth, stiffen, stretch, taper/taper off, thicken, thin, trample, truncate, warp, whet, wound

138 **show:** advertising, bare, circulate, model, point, prove, represent, reveal, show, substantiate, symbolize, tout, trot out, unveil

139 **steal:** abduct, appropriate, appropriation, assume, bilk, break in, burglary, cheat, confiscate, copy, divest, do out of, embezzle, embezzlement, extort, extortion, filch, fleece, hold up, kidnap, knock off, larceny, lift, loot, maraud, milk, misappropriate, pilfer, pillage, pinch, plagiarism, plunder, poach, pocket, ransack, rifle, rip off, rip-off, rob, sack, steal, swindle, swipe, take, theft

140 **supply:** appoint, contribute, deal, deluge, dish out, dispensation, dispense, disseminate, distribute, distribution, divide, dole out, equip, feed, foster, fuel, furnish, glut, hand out, infuse, issue, keep, lend, maintain, make out, nourish, nurse, nurture, portion, provide, provision, quarter, ration, receive, render, replenish, rig, satisfy, serve, stock, supply, support, sustain

141 **surpass:** abound, beat, better, break, cap, conquer, eclipse, exceed, excel, flourish, get ahead, go by, lead, lick, outdo, outweigh, overtake, pass, predominate, prevail, succeed, supersede, surmount, surpass, top, tower, transcend, triumph, win

142 **take:** acquire, acquisition, arrogate, assume, assumption, broach, burn, commandeer, compass, confiscate, cull, deplete, deprivation, deprive, disarm, disarmament, divest, drain, draw, educe, elicit, exact, excerpt, expropriate, extract, filch, harvest, have, milk, nip, peel, pilfer, pocket, preempt, pump, ransack, rob, sap, seize, take, tap, usurp, wring

143 **transfer abstractly:** afford, bear, bring, commit, consign, consignment, conveyance, delegate, delegation, infect, recall, refer, relay, release, relegate, transfer, turn over

MOTION

144 **be moved:** earthquake, elapse, flop, hang, lap

145 **change of place:** flicker, motion, movement, passage, pop, rush, sway, sweep, swing, swirl, swivel, teeter, tremor

146 **flow:** flow, pour, run, secrete, seep, stream, surge, swamp, teem, torrent, trickle

147 **move:** bob, budge, careen, churn, circulate, circulation, contort, cruise, curl, curve, dandle, deflect, descend, descent, dislocate, dislodge, displace, dive, drift, drive, entwine, falter, fidget, flex, flourish, gyrate, haul, lean, loop, move, oscillate, overturn, paddle, pitch, pivot, pulsate/pulse, pulse, revolve, rock, roll, rotate, round, skirt, tilt, topple, toss, transport, traverse, tumble, turn, twine, twist, uproot, upset, waft, wave, waver, weave, wheel, wield

148 **move mechanically:** aviation, bank, carriage, carry, cart, drive, fly, haul, mobilize, navigate, operate, pack, park, ride, ship, soar, takeoff, take off, veer

149 **move oneself:** ascend, ascension, bend, constitutional, flap, flex, flounce, gad, gait, gallivant, gambol, go ahead, go for, gyrate, hike, jerk, motion, mount, move, negotiate, pace, pad, pass, patter, progress, quail, rock,

roll, round, stalk, stamp, step, stir, stray, stride, strut, stump, swagger, tilt, tread, trip, tumble, walk, wallow, wave, wriggle

150 **move oneself quickly:** barge in/barge into, beat, bolt, bounce, bustle, capsize, coast, course, dart, dash, flash, flee, flinch, flit, flutter, fly, gallop, glide, hasten, hurry, hurtle, hustle, jerk, jiggle, lurch, make off, march, plunge, pound, prance, race, recoil, run, rush, scamper, scramble, scurry, shake, shoot, shudder, skim, skip, slide, slip, soar, speed, spin, sprint, start, storm, sweep, swerve, swoop, tear, trot, twirl, veer, wag, whip, whiz, wiggle, wobble, writhe, zip, zoom

151 **move oneself slowly:** amble, crawl, creep, cruise, dalliance, dally, decline, drag, hobble, jog, knock about/knock around, lag, limp, linger, loiter, lumber, lurk, meander, plod, poke, prowl, pussyfoot, ramble, range, reel, roam, saunter, shuffle, slink/slither, sneak, stagger, steal, straggle, stroll, sway, tarry, totter, tramp, trudge, waddle, wade, wander

152 **move quickly:** advance, advancement, agitate, capsize, convulsion, course, discharge, dispatch, fall, flicker, flourish, flutter, hasten, jerk, jiggle, jostle, keel over, lurch, palpitate, plunge, precipitate, quake, quiver, rattle, rush, shake, shiver, shoot, shudder, skid, skim, slide, slip, speed, spin, stampede, sweep, tear, throb, tremble, twirl, vibrate, vibration, wag, whip, whirl, whisk, wiggle, wobble

153 **move slowly:** dangle, float, lag, reel

154 **position oneself:** arise, bow, cant, duck, get down, get off, get up, hover, huddle, hunch, kneel, lie, list, loll, lounge, mount, nestle, obeisance, perch, poise, pose, ramble, recline, repose, rest, rise, seat, sit, slouch, wince

155 **travelling:** lift, navigation, procession, transit, transport, voyage

PHYSICAL

156 **abuse:** abuse, charge, consumption, cop out, corrode, defile, dissipate, dope, enervate, exploit, force, frazzle, fritter, impinge, lose, malpractice, milk, misappropriate, mishandle/mismanage, mistreat, misuse, overdo, pervert, prostitute, riddle, run through, sap, spend, squander, strain, throw away, waste, wear

157 **anatomical change:** distend, flake, neuter

158 **arrange:** align, arrange, bundle, collate, coordinate, crease, deploy, dispose, file, group, indent, lay, lay out, mess up, mix up, muss, order, organize, position, range, rank, reverse, ruffle, rummage, separate, shuffle, snarl, sort, spread, stack, stir, straighten, unwind, weave

159 **arrive:** admission, advent, appear, appearance, approach, arrival, arrive, billow, board, come, come in, coming, cross, cruise, disembark, dock, embark, encroach, enter, entrance, foray, get, get back, get in, get on, go, go ahead, gravitate, immigrate, infiltrate, influx, insinuate, intrude, invade, invasion,

jaunt, land, light, loom, lunge, make, penetrate, permeate, pierce, pounce, progress, pull up, reach, report, return, show up, stalk, swarm, trespass, turn up, turn up

160 attach: adhere, adjoin, affix, anchor, annex, append, attach, batten, bind, bond, cement, chain, clamp, clasp, cling, cohere, connect, engage, fasten, fix, hitch, knot, latch, lock, moor, nail, paste, peg, pin, screw, seal, secure, shut, stick, tack, tag, tape, tether, tie, yoke

161 bathe: bath, bathe, clean, wet

162 beautify: adorn, adornment, bask, beautify, comb, decorate, decoration, doll up, embellish, enhance, fix up, flatter, furbish, groom, ornament, primp, shave, spruce up, trim

163 breathe: breath, breathe, draw, exhale, expire, gasp, heave, huff, inhale, pant, puff, sigh, suffocate, wheeze, yawn

164 catch: catch, field, intercept, seize, tackle

165 clean: bath, bathe, brush, catharsis, clarify, clean, cleanse, clear, disinfect, distill, do up, expurgate, filter, flush, furbish, gut, housework, lather, mop, purge, purification, purify, rake, refine, refinement, rinse, scour, scrape, scrub, sift, sweep, wash, wipe

166 climb: arise, ascend, ascension, ascent, climb, get on, mount, rise, scale, surface

167 clothe: array, attire, clothe, deck, disrobe, doll up, dress, dress up, garb, get on, ornament, outfit, primp, rig, sport, spruce up, stuff, try on/try out, turn out, wear

168 construct: build, compose, construct, construction, dismantle, erect, establish, fashion, forge, form, found, frame, make, modernize, pave, pitch, put up, raise, rear, reconstruct, renovate, throw up

169 consume: absorption, bolt, chew, consume, consumption, contract, corrode, crunch, demolish, deplete, devour, diet, digest, dig in, dine, dispatch, dissipate, draft, drink, eat, engulf, exhaust, fast, feast, feed on, finish, gargle, glut, gnaw, gobble, gorge, go through, graze, gulp, guzzle, imbibe, munch, nibble, nip, partake, peck, polish off, prey on, put away, quaff, satiate, sip, spend, stuff, swallow, take, taste, use, wolf

170 cook: bake, barbecue, baste, beat, boil, brew, broil, butcher, can, churn, coddle, cook, cure, distill, fix, flavor, foam, fry, grill, housework, knead, mash, pickle, preservation, preserve, sear, season, simmer, sizzle, stir, sweeten, toast, warm, whip

171 copy: ape, copy, counterfeit, duplicate, echo, emulate, follow, forge, forgery, imitate, imitation, mimic, mirror, multiply, parallel, parrot, pattern, pretend, quote, reconstruct, reflect, reiterate, repeat, reproduce, sham, simulate, transcribe

172 cover: blanket, bury, camouflage, coat, cover, daub, disguise, dissimulate, drape, dress, dust, engulf, envelop, face, finish, funeral, gild, glaze, insulate, inter, inundate, laminate, lap, line, mask, masquerade, muzzle, obscure, oil, overrun, paint, palliate, paper, pave, pervade, plate, sheet, smear, smother, spatter, spread, top, varnish, veil, veneer, wrap

173 create: bear, beget, breed, coin, come up with, compose, conceive, concoct, constitute,

construct, contrive, create, creation, design, draft, engineer, establish, establishment, fabricate, fashion, film, forge, form, formation, formulate, frame, generate, generation, hatch, improvise, institute, invent, make, make up, materialize, mint, mold, originate, piece, pioneer, procreate, produce, regenerate, reproduce, reproduction, spawn, work

174 create art: chart, compose, depict, dot, draw, engrave, engraving, etch, illustrate, impress, imprint, lay out, mount, outline, paint, photograph, picture, plot, portray, pose, pottery, print, rough out, sculpture, sketch, stamp, trace

175 create with effort: beat, forge, mold

176 cut: amputate, ax/axe, behead, bisect, carve, chisel, chop, cleave, clip, crop, cut, cut up, dent, dismember, dissect, dissection, engrave, engraving, etch, fell, gash, hack, knife, lacerate, mangle, mince, mutilate, nick, notch, pare, peel, pierce, pink, prune, scar, score, scratch, shave, shred, skin, slash, slice, slit, split, trim, whittle

177 decorate: adorn, adornment, decorate, decoration, embellish, embellishment, embroider, enhance, enrich, furnish, gild, modernize, ornament, paper, refurbish, renovate, trim, varnish

178 dig: bore, burrow, claw, dig, embed, excavate, excavation, exhume, grub, hollow, inter, mine, plant, plow, rake, root, scoop, tunnel, unearth, uproot

179 discharge: blast, blowout, blow up, bubble, burst, cascade, come from, deliver, detonate, discharge, drain, dribble, drop, effusion, eject, emanate, emanation, emission, emit, erupt, eruption, evacuate, excrete, expel, explode, explosion, express, exude, fire, flare, flood, flow, flush, gag, give off/give out, go off, gush, heave, impregnate, infest, infiltrate, influx, infuse, inject, inundate, issue, jet, launch, leak, mushroom, ooze, outbreak, overflow, overrun, pass, penetrate, percolate, permeate, pervade, pour, proceed, project, scatter, secrete, seep, shed, shoot, spatter, spew, spill, spit, spot, spout, spray, sprinkle, spurt, squirt, stream, surge, swamp, teem, throw up, torrent, trickle, vent, void, vomit

180 dispose: boot, buck, chuck, discard, disposal, dispose, dispose of, ditch, do away with, dump, jettison, kick out, reject, rejection, rid, scrap, shed, throw away, unload, void

181 drop: clatter, crash, crumble, decline, descend, descent, dip, dive, drip, droop, drop, duck, dump, fall, fell, flop, founder, fumble, go down, go under, ground, keel over, land, light, lower, percolate, pitch, plumb, plummet, plunge, sag, set, settle, shed, sink, sling, slump, spill, stoop, stumble, submerge, subside, suspend, swoop, thud/thump, topple, tumble, wilt

182 equip: arm, do up, equip, fit, furnish, gear, outfit, rig, stock

183 find: come across, detect, detection, discover, discovery, ferret out, find, find out, learn, locate, meet, pick up, pinpoint, recover, spot, strike, stumble, track/track down, turn up, uncover, unearth

184 form: arch, bend, bloat, braid, carve, chisel,

constitute, contort, crumple, curl, curve, fold, form, materialize, model, mold, pat, round, sculpture, shape, twist, whittle, work

185 gesture: bawl, beam, beat, belch, bite, bleed, blink, blow, chew, clap, drag, dribble, drivel, drool, excrete, expire, frown, gesture, gnaw, grimace, grin, gulp, itch, kink, kiss, laugh/laughter, laugh, lick, munch, nod, perspire, pucker, puff, pulsate/pulse, pulse, purse, scowl, shiver, slobber, smile, smirk, sob, spasm, spit, squint, sweat, tear/tears, throb, twitch, vomit, wail, weep, whimper, wince, wink, wrinkle, yawn

186 grind: abrasion, corrode, creak, crunch, file, frazzle, granulate, grate, grind, mash, mill, pound, powder, pulverize, rasp, scrape

187 guide: aviation, channel, conduct, convey, direct, divert, drive, ease, ferry, funnel, guide, infuse, inject, lay, lead, level, maneuver, marshal, mobilize, navigate, navigation, point, refer, round, route, row, see, show, steer, take, transport, usher

188 hide: ambush, balk, bury, cache, camouflage, cloak, conceal, concealment, cover, cower, cringe, cut, disguise, dissemble, dissimulate, eavesdrop, embed, ensconce, envelop, harbor, hide, isolate, lurk, mask, masquerade, obscure, palliate, screen, seclude, seclusion, secrete, sequester, shelter, shrink, shut off/shut out, smother, sneak, withhold

189 hit: applaud, applause, bang, baste, bat, batter, battery, beat, belt, blow, boot, box, buffet, bump, bunt, butt, chip, clap, clash, clatter, clip, clobber, club, collide, collision, concussion, crack, crash, crown, cuff, dash, deflect, dent, drive, drum, flog, glance, hail, hammer, hand, hit, impact, jab, jar, jostle, kick, knock, lash, lick, maul, nail, pat, peck, pelt, poke, pound, punch, ram, rap, rough up, scourge, slam, slap, smack, sock, spank, strike, swat, swipe, tap, thrash, thud/thump, tick, tip, wallop, whack, whip

190 hold: anchor, cling, clog, clutch, cradle, cuddle, dandle, dangle, embrace, fondle, grab, hold, hook, hug, nip, nuzzle, pin, prop, retain, retard, seize, shore, snuggle, support, suspend, sustain, tangle

191 hold forcefully: apprehend, brace, cage, captivity, clasp, clench, clinch, clutch, confinement, constrict, constriction, contain, cramp, dam, detain, detention, embrace, enfold, enslave, fetter, fetters, grapple, grasp, grip, gripe, harness, hold, imprison, incarcerate, leash, overpower, pen, press, restrain, snap, snatch, stifle, strangle, tackle, throttle, wrestle

192 illegal behavior: blackmail, bleed, breach, break, break in, bribe, bug, buy, cheat, conspire, contraband, contravene, crime, delinquency, depredation, disobey, entrench, extortion, fault, fix, fraud, graft, have, holdup, hold up, imposture, infraction, infringe, injustice, intrigue, jinx, kickback, knock off, larceny, libel, loot, mischief, misconduct, misdeed/misdemeanor, murder, offense, outrage, pick, pilfer, plagiarism, poach, racket, rape, ravish, rip off, rip-off, rob, screw, sham, slander, smuggle, specu-

lation, squeeze, swindle, take, tamper, theft, transgression, treason, trespass, victimize, violate, violation

193 join physically: link, mail, merge, mesh, mingle, mix, piece, pool, splice, tie, tuck, unite, wed, weld, yoke

194 jump: bounce, bound, clear, deflect, dive, flip, gallop, gambol, hop, hurdle, jump, leap, lunge, lurch, plunge, pounce, rear, recoil, skip, spring, start, vault

195 leave: abandon, abscond, back, blow, board, bolt, break, break out, clear out, cringe, dart, defection, depart, departure, desert, desertion, deviate, diaspora, digress, disappear, disappearance, dismount, distance, diverge, draw back, drop, ebb, egress, embark, evacuate, exit, exodus, fall back, farewell, flee, flight, fly, forsake, get along, get off, get out, go, goodbye, go off, go out, jaunt, jilt, leave, light out, make off, maroon, part, parting, pull out, push off/push on, quail, quit, recede, recoil, renounce, renunciation, repair, resign, resignation, retire, retreat, run, scram, separation, shake off, shove off, shrink, strike out, swerve, takeoff, take off, throw over, turn, vacate, withdraw, withdrawal

196 lift: boost, dip, elevate, heave, hoist, lift, pick up, pry, raise, rear

197 measure: balance, figure, measure, survey

198 move living quarters: anyplace, anywhere, approach, arena, battlefield, camp, colonization, cover, defect, defection, deport, deportation, destination, dominion, element, emigrate, empire, evict, eviction, exile, expatriate, expel, jurisdiction, landmark, locale/locality, location, lookout, migrate, move, neighborhood, outdoors, outside, point, position, post, premises, province, refuge, region, reign, rendezvous, resort, seat, setting, site, situation, soil, spot, station, stop, surroundings, terminal, territory, turn, vicinity, where

199 perform: fan, hit, perform, type, work

200 physical action: application, apply, drop, hit, hold, lift, push

201 position: aim, barricade, bow, cant, close, cock, coil, deposit, dial, dip, direct, disseminate, ensconce, entwine, fix, hang, indent, insert, install, installation, interpolate, intersperse, isolate, jut, lap, lay, lean, lie, list, lodge, loop, misplace, occlude, park, pile, pitch, place, plant, point, position, post, prop, put, recline, roll, seat, separate, set, sit, slant, slope, slouch, snuggle, sprawl, spread, squat, stand, station, stick, stoop, swerve, tip, top, train, traverse, turn, twine, twist, unfold, wallow, wind, wrinkle

202 prepare physically: acclimate, adjust, braid, brush, brush up, buff, bundle, burnish, coat, condition, disguise, doll up, domesticate, do up, dress, embalm, face, finish, fix up, formulate, fortify, gear, get, gild, glaze, gloss, grace, groom, habituate, housework, knit, lubricate, make up, modernize, modulate, orient, overhaul, pack, pad, pare, plaster, plate, polish, preparation, prepare, preservation, preserve, prime, primp, ready, reform, refresh, refrigerate, refurbish, regenerate, rehabilitate, rejuvenate, renew, renovate, rig, round, season, set, shave, shine, slim, smear,

Causes

ABSTRACT

228 affect: affect, cause, change, evoke
229 event that causes another: account, beginning, cause, origin, precipitous/precipitate
230 state of causation: adaptation, aftermath, amazement, anticlimax, armistice, astonishment, awe, backlash, backwash, bang, bedlam, bereavement, bind, blessing, bliss, blot, blunder, boom, bottom line, break, buildup, catharsis, certainty, change, chaos, check, coincidence, collapse, collision, comfort, complication, compromise, congestion, consequence, consternation, contamination, corollary, culmination, decay, deception, decomposition, decoy, degeneracy, degradation, descent, destruction, deterioration, disadvantage, disappointment, disarray, disorder, disposal, disrepair, dissipation, dissolution, effect, end, ending, error, event, eventuality, fall, flap, flurry, frailty, frenzy, fruit, fulfillment, furor, gaffe, headway, hubbub, huddle, impact, imperfection, impression, improvement, inaccuracy, infection, irony, issue, jinx, jitters, lapse, lather, mess, miscarriage, mistake, mix-up, morass, muddle, muss, nonsense, occurrence, outcome, outgrowth, payoff, phenomenon, portent, press, price, proceed, product, racket, ramification, rash, repercussion, resolution, result, rubbish, scare, scramble, settlement, shambles, solution, stain, stalemate, stigma, stink, stir, storm, taint, tangle, tempest, therefore, to-do, toll, trend, trip, truce, tumult, turmoil, turn, undoing, unification, upheaval, upshot, whirl
231 to be: alienate, animate, antagonize, awake, awaken, awakening, calm, cause, compound, energize, even, materialize, sterilize, straighten, threaten
232 to change: adapt, adjust, alter, alternate, assimilate, attune, cancel, change, commute, conversion, convert, co-opt, differentiate, distort, diversify, double back, equalize, expurgate, fashion, fit, fix, invert, modify, neutralize, offset, overturn, restore, shift, switch, tamper, transform, translate, transpose, turn
233 to change abstractly: demote, intensify, mitigate
234 to change an event: abbreviate, accelerate, acceleration, activate, actuate, adjourn, approach, arrest, bed, begin, break off, break up, build, cancel, cease, close, commence, complement, conclude, consummate, continue, crown, cut in, cut off, cut short, desist, determine, discontinue, dispatch, dispose of, disrupt, dissolve, end, enter, finish, foul up, graduate, halt, hurry, intervene, invalidate, kick, knock off, lay off, leave, leave off, lift, manipulate, nip, nullify, pause, pick up, preclude, preempt, put off, quash, quell, quench, quit, relinquish, remit, rescind, retire, reverse, revoke, round off, ruin, scrub, seal, slow, smother, stall, stop, terminate, turn off, turn out, vacate, waive, wind up, wrap up

235 to change cognitively: agree, change, concede, harden, lay
236 to change number or quantity: abbreviate, abridge, abstract, accumulate, add, addition, advance, aggrandize, alleviate, amplification, amplify, augment, blow up, boost, build, build up, commute, compress, condense, contract, curtail, cut, cut back, deduct, deepen, deflate, detract, digest, dilate, discount, double, downsize, draw out, enlarge, escalate, evolve, expand, extend, extension, fatten, hike, imbue, increase, inflate, jump, lengthen, lift, lower, magnify, modify, narrow, pare, prune, raise, reduce, reinforce, shorten, slash, step up, summarize, supplement, swell, take, trim, truncate, whittle, widen
237 to change or affect an event: delay, procrastinate, protract, stop, weigh
238 to change state of being: dispatch, do for
239 to continue: abide, bear, broaden, carry on, come, come back, continue, create, drag on/drag out, draw, drawl, draw out, dwell on/dwell upon, eke out, elongate, endure, extend, go, go on, hammer away/hammer into, hang on, hold, kill, lengthen, linger, perpetuate, persevere, persist, prolong, protract, pursue, remain, resume, survive, take up
240 to diminish: abate, adulterate, aggravate, aggravation, alloy, attenuate, blot, blunt, break, canker, cheapen, compound, compromise, cool, corrupt, cut, deaden, debase, debauch, debilitate, decay, decline, decrease, degrade, depress, disorder, doctor, downgrade, downsize, emasculate, enfeeble, fatigue, impair, imperil, let up, lower, minimize, mitigate, moderate, modify, muffle, mute, pale, provocation, qualify, reduce, relax, retard, rot, sap, shorten, slash, stimulant, stimulus, stop, tax, tone down, undermine, weaken, wear, worsen
241 to function: animate, begin, cause, start
242 to happen: accelerate, boomerang, breathe, bring, copy, engender, ensue, entail, eventuate, evoke, expedite, expedition, facilitate, follow, impel, incite, inconvenience, induce, inflict, influence, inspire, instigate, institute, intervene, make, motivate, move, muddle, necessitate, oblige, occasion, occur, orchestrate, pass, precipitate, prod, produce, prompt, provoke, put, recur, result, return, stimulate, trigger, unsettle, will, work up, wreak
243 to have: accent, give, push, transfer
244 to improve: advance, allay, ameliorate, amend, assuage, augment, augmentation, become, benefit, better, betterment, boost, brighten, bring about, brush up, civilize, confirm, contribute, cultivate, cure, dignify, enhance, enrich, freshen, garnish, help, improve, lift, lighten, magnify, mend, mollify, pad, perfect, perk up, polish, quench, quiet, raise, refine, relieve, restore, revise, revision, rouse, step up, strengthen, supplement, touch up, unburden, update
245 to increase quantity: accumulate, add, addition, advance, aggrandize, amplification, amplify, augment, augmentation, blow up,

boost, build, build up, deepen, dilate, double, draw out, enlarge, escalate, evolve, expand, extend, extension, fatten, hike, imbue, increase, inflate, jump, lengthen, lift, magnify, raise, reinforce, step up, supplement, swell, widen

246 to injure: abuse, afflict, asphyxiate, batter, battery, beat, blemish, bruise, chip, cost, cripple, crush, damage, debilitate, decay, deface, defile, deform, dent, desecrate, desecration, devastate, disable, disagree, discomfort, disfigure, endanger, expose, fragment, get back at, gripe, handicap, harm, hurt, impair, incapacitate, infect, injure, irritate, knife, lacerate, lay up, maim, mangle, mar, maul, mistreat, molest, mutilate, outrage, pain, paralyze, persecute, poison, pollute, rack, repay, rough up, ruin, rupture, sabotage, sap, scar, shatter, shiver, shoot, sicken, smart, smash, snap, splinter, spoil, sting, stress, suffocate, taint, tarnish, torture, trample, turn, violate, violation, vitiate, wound, wrong

247 to reduce quantity: abbreviate, abridge, abstract, alleviate, commute, compress, condense, contract, curtail, cut, cut back, deduct, deflate, detract, digest, discount, downsize, lessen, lower, minimize, modify, narrow, pare, prune, reduce, shorten, slash, summarize, take, trim, truncate, whittle

PHYSICAL

248 to break: collide, crack, crash, crumble, dash
249 to burn: arson, blaze, burn, char, conflagration, fire, flame, flare, glow, ignite, inflame, kindle, lick, light, parch, scorch, sear, smolder
250 to change physically: awake, bite, blacken, black out, bleach, blush, brighten, bruise, buttress, chip, color, compact, confirm, congeal, consolidate, corrode, crimp, crinkle, cross, darken, daub, debase, deepen, deform, dehydrate, desiccate, dilute, dim, discolor, disfigure, disorder, disorganize, distort, disturb, do in, douse, dry, dye, eclipse, edge, elongate, emasculate, enervate, exhaust, fade, fatigue, fatten, ferment, file, flatten, flush, fog, foul, gird, harden, hypnotize, intensify, jell, lay, level, light, lighten, loose/loosen, mark, melt, muzzle, neuter, numb, open, pacify, pale, petrify, prolong, prostrate, protract, quicken,

ravel, redden, reinforce, roll, rouse, rumple, set, shade, shadow, sharpen, shrivel, slop, slow, smooth, soften, sour, stabilize, stain, sterilize, stiffen, streak, strengthen, stretch, tame, temper, thicken, thin, tidy, tighten, tinge, tint, toughen, turn, vitiate, warp, weary, whet, whiten

251 to create: bear, beget, breed, conceive, concoct, constitute, construct, create, engineer, establish, fabricate, forge, form, generate, hatch, materialize, mint, mold, originate, piece, procreate, produce, regenerate, reproduce, spawn

252 to destroy: abolish, abolition, annihilate, annul, assassinate, batter, blight, bomb, break, bring down, bulldoze, burst, bust, butcher, carnage, clobber, collapse, consume, consumption, contaminate, coup de grâce, crucify, crumple, crush, cut down, damage, deface, demolish, demolition, depredation, desecrate, desecration, desolate, despoil, destroy, destruction, devastate, disintegrate, dismantle, disorganize, dispatch, dissolve, do away with, do for, do in, drown, end, endanger, enfeeble, eradicate, erode, erosion, execute, execution, expunge, exterminate, extinguish, extirpate, finish, hang, homicide, hunt, kill, knock off, level, liquidate, mangle, manslaughter, massacre, mess up, murder, obliterate, overthrow, paralyze, pervert, pillage, plunder, poison, prostrate, pull down, pulverize, purge, put away, put down, put out, quash, quench, ravage, raze, remove, ruin, sabotage, sack, shatter, shiver, shoot, slaughter, slay, smash, spoil, strangle, subdue, subvert, suppress, undo, uproot, violation, waste, wipe out, wreck

253 to grow: cultivate, develop, farm, farming, flower, plant, raise, sow, till, vegetate
254 to make dirty: adulterate, blur, clutter, contaminate, dirty, litter, mess up, pollute, smudge, soil, stain, taint, tarnish
255 to make hot or cold: air, boil, chill, cool, freeze, heat, melt, numb, parch, refrigerate, scorch, shrivel, thaw, warm
256 to make wet: absorb, absorption, dampen, deluge, dip, douse, drench, drivel, drool, drown, dunk, engulf, extinguish, immerse, moisten, oil, overflow, permeate, rinse, saturate, soak, souse, spatter, splash, spray, sprinkle, squirt, steep, submerge, water, wet

Fields of human activity

AGRICULTURE

257 action: agriculture, bed, bury, conservation, cross, cultivate, cultivation, culture, erosion, fertilize, gather, graft, harvest, preservation, raise, reap, roundup, round up, sow, sprout, tend, till, vegetate, work
258 organization: farm, grange

THE ARTS

259 art object: antique, antiquity, canvas, classic, coat, collage, composition, creation, decoration, depiction, design, dye, emblem, embroidery, enamel, etching, exhibit, figure, flourish, glaze, handicraft, illustration, image, insignia, knickknack, landscape, lattice, masterpiece, medium, model, monument, ornament, pattern, picture, piece, pigment, portrait, pottery, print, profile, silhouette, stamp, statue, trademark, wreath

260 created object: alloy, amulet, apparatus, ash(es), badge, brew, camouflage, capsule, card, change, cinder, composite, composition, compound, concoction, contrivance, creation, curiosity, debris, decoration, derivative, dip, discovery, embers, enamel, essence, fabrication, fake, fence, fertilizer, filth, foam, folder, formation, froth, fusion, fuzz, garbage, garland, gimmick, glass, grime, grit, grounds, half-breed, hash, hodgepodge, hook, huddle, hybrid, imitation, innovation, invention, junk, knickknack, lather, leftover, litter, mess, mix/mixture, novelty, oddity, odds and ends, offshoot, original, outgrowth, output, pack, pad, paper, pastiche, patchwork, pennant, potpourri, preparation, refuse, remainder, remnant, replica, residue, rest, rubbish, scum, sediment, slime, solution, surplus, trash, vestige, waste, web, work, wreath, wreck, yield

261 exhibition: appear, appearance, boast, brandish, demonstrate, demonstration, develop, display, exhibit, exhibition, expose, exposure, flash, flaunt, foreshadow, impress, look, loom, manifest, mark, mount, parade, peep/peer, personify, point out, portend, posture, pout, present, presentation, produce, record, reflect, register, render, represent, show, show off, sight, simplify, spectacle, sport, spotlight, strut, transpire, typify, uncover, unfold

262 musical instrument: accompaniment, arrangement, baton, bugle, compact disc, harmony, hymn, measure, medley, melody, meter, note, piece, score, song, strain

263 performance: anthem, aria, ballet, broadcasting, burlesque, carol, chant, character, comedy, composition, concert, drama, enactment, event, extravaganza, farce, impression, lampoon, medium, movie, music, opus, part, performance, piece, play, premiere, presentation, preview, program, recital, recitation, rendition, repertory, role, satire, scene, scenery, script, set, setting, show, stage, takeoff, theater/theatre

264 performance part: act, chorus, encore, epilogue, ovation, plot, prelude, recital, refrain, rehearsal, scene, snatch, stunt, tune

265 photograph: observe, photograph, portray, print, proof

COMMUNICATIONS

266 communication: address, ad-lib, answer, arrogate, audience, babble, back down, bewail, bid, build up, call, carry, censor, chat, chatter, circumlocution, colloquy, commune, communicate, communication, contact, conversation, converse, correspond, digress, discourse, divide, drivel, effusion, emit, exult, falter, gab, get, give, hush up, improvise, indicate, interact, intercourse, interplay, intervene, intrude, lecture, magnify, mince, monologue, oration, patter, punctuate, quash, quiet, rap, reach, read, recant, recapitulate, recitation, recite, recount, refuse, rehearse, reiterate, render, repartee, say, secrete, signify, silence, slant, speak, speech, stammer, stray, talk, taunt, telephone, tell, transmit, transpire, wander, welcome, whisper, yak/yap

267 communicative quality: abusive, acerbity, acid, acidulous, acrid, acrimonious, ad-lib, ambiguous, amusing, apologetic, articulate, artless, biting, bitter, bluff, blustful, boastful, bombastic, brazen, brief, broken, brusque, candid, captious, caustic, censorious, chatty, close, closemouthed, colloquial, communicative, complimentary, confidential, confidentially, convincing, courteous, crisp, critical, crude, cryptic, curt, cutting, cynical, debatable, defamatory, demonstrative, derisive, derogatory, descriptive, destructive, diffuse, direct, directly, disconnected, dishonest, disjointed, disrespectful, doctrinaire, dogmatic, droll, dry, effusive, eloquent, emphatic, encyclopedic, erroneous, et cetera, evasive, even, exaggerated, expansive, explanatory, explicit, expository, expressive, extemporaneous/extempory, facetious, fallacious, false, falsely, farcical, feeble, fictitious, figurative, filthy, firm, firsthand, flaming, flatulent, flimsy, florid, flowery, fluent, forceful, forcible, foreign, forensic, forthright, foul, fractious, frank, frankly, fresh, fulsome, funny, gabby, garrulous, genuine, glib, glowing, grandiloquent, graphic, gross, grouchy, groundless, gruff, guileless, hackneyed, harsh, hateful, heartfelt, heated, hollow, honest, humorous, hypocritical, idle, illogical, illustrative, imperative, imperious, implicit, implied, importunate, impromptu, improvised, imprudent, inarticulate, incisive, incoherent, indescribable, indicative, ineffable, inelegant, inexplicable, inflated, informative, ingenuous, inoffensive, insincere, insistent, insolent, ironic/ironical, jocular/jocose/jocund, jolly, keen, laconic, laudatory, laughable, legendary, legible, lengthy, libelous, literal, literally, literary, loose, loquacious, lurid, lying, malicious, malign, matter-of-fact, mean, meaningful, meaty, mendacious, misleading, mushy, musty, mythical/mythological, naked, nameless, narrative, natural, negative, noncommittal, oblique, obnoxious, obscene, offensive, offhand, oily, open, openly, opinionated, opprobrious, oracular, oral, outspoken, overblown, parting, pejorative, penetrating, peppery, persuasive, pithy, plain, poetic, poignant, pointed, pompous, ponderous, pornographic, pregnant, priceless, private, privileged, privy, profane, prophetic, prosaic, public, pulp, pungent, quickwitted, quizzical, racy, rambling, reticent, rhetorical, ribald, rich, risqué, rough, round, rude, sarcastic, satirical/satiric, saucy, scathing, scurrilous, secretive, secretly, sensational, sentimental, sharp, short, significant, silent, simple, sincere, sincerely, smutty, snappy, sneaky, speechless, spicy, spoken, square, stale, stilted, straight, straightforward, strained, succinct, suggestive, summary, symbolic, taciturn, talkative, tart, terse, threadbare, transparent, trenchant, trite, truculent, true, truly, trustworthy/trusty,

truthful, unabridged, unanimous, uncommunicative, unfounded, uninhibited, unintelligible, unsaid, untrue, unvarnished, unwritten,
vague, valedictory, veracious, verbal, verbatim, verbose, vernacular, vicious, virulent,
vocal, vociferous, vulgar, warm, warning,
windy, witty, wordy, wry, yellow, zany

268 description: deconstructionist, denotation,
depiction, description, design, exposition, expression, formula, gloss, hermeneutical, history, hyperbole, identification, illustration,
kudos, label, legend, name, news, nickname,
notation, obituary, outline, paraphrase, plan,
poem, poetry, portrait, profile, prose, pseudonym, sketch, translation

269 devices used for: alarm, computer, copy,
downlink, photocopy, telegram, telephone

270 document, part: addendum, advertisement,
amendment, appendix, article, banner, body,
chapter, clause, codicil, condition, entry, epilogue, excerpt, extract, feature, foreword,
introduction, item, label, leaf, legend, margin, obituary, passage, preface, provision/
proviso, sheet, slip, specification, stipulation,
story, supplement, tab, tag, terms, text

271 document, physical object: act, affidavit,
agreement, album, analysis, annal(s), annual, archive, article, balance sheet, bill,
book, bulletin, card, caricature, catalog/cata-
logue, certificate, chronicle, circular, commitment, compact, composition, concord,
constitution, contract, convention, corpus,
credentials, criticism, critique, declaration,
deed, deposition, digest, diploma, direc-
tion(s), directive, dispatch, dissertation,
docket, document, draft, drama, enclosure,
epistle, essay, explanation, exposition, facsimile, fiction, file, form, guarantee, history,
identification, injunction, journal, letter, life,
line, log, mail, material, memoir, memoran-
dum/memo, message, missive, monument,
narrative, note/notes, notice, opus, pact,
pamphlet, paper/papers, paper, pass, passport, patent, permit, petition, piece, plan, policy, poster, proceedings, proclamation,
promotion, pronouncement, proposal, prose,
reading, receipt, record, reference, release,
reminder, résumé, satire, schedule, scheme,
script, sequel, sign, statement, survey, telegram, theme, thesis, ticket, treatise, writing

272 document quality: readable, short, summary, terse

273 humorous tale: banter, chaff, crack, jest,
joke, kid, lampoon, levity, parody, pleasantry, pun, quip, spoof, sport, take off, travesty, trick, wit

274 information: advice, allusion, analysis, annotation, announcement, answer, broadcast,
bulletin, buzz, calendar, caution, caveat,
charge, clarification, clue, command, commitment, communication, confession, conjecture, construction, counsel, cybernetics,
data, declaration, definition, dictate, direc-
tion(s), directive, disclosure, dope, evidence,
excerpt, exhortation, explanation, exposé,
fact, facts, gossip, grounds, groundwork,
guidance, guide, herald, hint, hypermedia, illumination, information, instruction, intelligence, intimation, key, knowledge, lead,
learning, lesson, light, lore, material, mes-

sage, multimedia, news, notice, particular,
plug, point, pointer, prescription, prognosis,
program, prompt, pronouncement, proof,
publication, publicity, quotation/quote, reading, recipe, recommendation, reference, report, resolution, revelation, rumor, science,
scoop, secret, sign, statement, story, tidings,
tip/tipoff, trivia, warning, whisper, word

275 integral language parts: adjective, adverb,
antonym, aphorism, banality, barbarism, buzzword, byword, cant, catchword, clause, cliché, euphemism, expletive, figure of speech,
grammar, idiom, jargon, metaphor, neologism, nomenclature, phrase, proverb, psychobabble, term, word

276 language: adage, adieu, alphabet, code, dialect, diction, expression, grammar, jargon,
language, lexicon, lingo, nomenclature, patter, slang, speech, style, swearing, tongue,
vernacular, vocabulary, voice

277 media: advertisement, banner, correspondence, criticism, desktop publishing, dispatch, infomercial, memorandum/memo,
pen, rhetoric, rumor, sarcasm, screen, sound
bite, television, translation, vehicle, video,
videocassette

278 object used in: address, advertisement, alert,
analogy, anathema, answer, aphorism, approach, assertion, assurance, axiom, babble,
back talk, banner, banter, breath, bunk, call,
cant, catchword, chat, chatter, claim, cliché,
comeback, comment, commentary, commonplace, compliment, congratulations, contact,
contention, contradiction, controversy, correspondence, criticism, cry, cue, curse, decision, declaration, defense, definition,
derision, dialogue/dialog, dictum, digression,
disapproval, dispatch, disputation, dispute,
dissension, dissidence, dissonance, double
entendre, double-talk, drivel, edict, eloquence, embellishment, epigram, epilogue,
epitaph, equivocation, eulogy, euphemism,
exaggeration, exaltation, fabrication, falsehood, falsity, farewell, fib, figure of speech,
flak, fulmination, gab, gibberish, gibe, goodbye, gossip, grace, gratitude, grievance,
gripe, groan, guidance, harangue, hearsay,
hiss, hocus-pocus, hogwash, honor, implication, impropriety, indication, indignity, innuendo, instruction, insult, invective, invention,
invocation, irony, issue, knock, lament/lam-
entation, laurels, lecture, letter, lie, line, lip,
litany, malediction, maxim, meaning, mem-
orandum/memo, mention, missive, mockery,
monologue, moral, motion, motto, mouth,
negation, negative, notice, oath, obscenity,
observation, offense, offer, omen, oracle,
oration, order, outcry, overtone, overture,
password, patter, phrase, pitch, platform,
platitude, plea, pleasantry, pledge, portent,
praise, precursor, prediction, pretension,
proclamation, profanity, profession, projection, promise, pronouncement, propaganda,
prophecy, proverb, puff, pun, put-down,
quip, quotation/quote, rebuff, rebuke, recommendation, reference, refusal, regards, remark, reminder, rendition, reply, report,
reprimand, respects, response, retort, return,
rhetoric, rhyme, rot, rubbish, rumor, sarcasm, saying, scandal, sermon, shadow,

slam, slander, slogan, slur, statement, story, suggestion, swearing, tale, talk, testimonial, testimony, thanks, theme, threat, tirade, toast, translation, trash, tribute, truth, utterance, vehicle, veracity, verbiage, voice, vow, welcome, whisper, wind, word, wording

279 organization: media, newspaper, radio, television

280 publication: advertisement, almanac, anthology, article, authority, autobiography, bible, bill, biography, book, brochure, canon, cartoon, catalog/catalogue, dictionary, directory, edition, fiction, handbook, issue, journal, lexicon, literature, magazine, manual, memoir, newspaper, novel, organ, pamphlet, paper, periodical, press, print, publication, publicity, reference, release, review, romance, satire, text, thesaurus, tome, treatise, vocabulary, volume

281 record: annal(s), archive, calendar, itinerary, list, program, record, register, roll, roster

282 story: account, allegory, anecdote, biography, chronicle, epic, fable, fib, fiction, folklore, legend, lore, memoir, mystery, myth, mythology, narration, narrative, phenomenology, plot, poem, poetry, report, saga, scenario, story, tale, verse, version, yarn

283 summary: abbreviation, abridgement, abstract, agenda, annotation, bill, breakdown, brief, caption, citation, compendium, condensation, diagnosis, diary, directory, epitome, inventory, menu, moral, precis, profile, program, prospectus, report, résumé, return, review, roster, rundown, scenario, schedule, sketch, summary, synopsis, table, tally, title

284 symbol: arms, augury, autograph, badge, brand, capital, character, charm, check, code, crest, cue, device, dot, emblem, exponent, flag, fleck, flourish, hallmark, handwriting, harbinger, herald, impression, imprint, index, indication, insignia, label, landmark, lead, letter, line, mark, notation, note, numeral, script, seal, sign, signal, spot, stamp, stripe, symbol, tag, tick, token, trademark, tread, type, vestige, writing

EDUCATION

285 educate: address, break in, breed, care, catechize, coach, domesticate, drill, educate, education, form, groom, ground, illuminate, inculcate, indoctrinate, initiate, instill, instruct, instruction, lesson, preach, preparation, school, speak, speech, talk, teach, train, training, tutor

286 education level: class, grade, level

287 objects used in: class, college, course, dissertation, edification, education, erudition, lesson, lore, school, tenure, text, thesis, tuition

288 organization: academy, alma mater, class, college, enrollment, faculty, institute/institution, school

289 place of: academy, alma mater, class, college, school

290 test: assay, audition, criterion, dissection, drill, examination, exercise, experiment, index, inquest, inquiry, inspection, investiga-

tion, probe, quiz, test, trial, weight, workout

291 testing: fiddle, grade, pace, plumb, survey, test, trial, try, try on/try out, verify

ENTERTAINMENT

292 action: act, acting, amuse, amusement, antic, appear, arrange, bet, bill, broadcast, cruise, dance, diversion, dramatize, enact, enactment, entertain, featuring, feign, game, host, hype, impersonate, interpret, issue, overplay, pageant, parody, perform, play, prance, pretend, preview, produce, publication, publicize, put on, regale, rehearsal, rehearse, relaxation, revel, romp, score, sing, spotlight, stage, takeoff, take off, tape, transmit, travesty, trifle

293 object: auditorium, balloon, bet, broadcast, broadcasting, cinema, circus, comedy, distraction, drama, extravaganza, farce, film, fireworks, humor, lounge, medium, movie, news, nightclub, picture, publicity, sensation, sequel, show, sight, song, television, theater/theatre, video, videocassette

294 organization: band, cast, chorus, corps, ensemble, following, gallery

FAMILY

295 child raising: baby, baby-sit, breed, bring up, care, coddle, cradle, cultivate, form, foster, mind, nourish, nurse, nurture, pamper, raise, rear, support, tend

296 family: aristocracy, birth, blood, bride, bridegroom, brood, clan, class, consanguinity, court, descendant, descent, extraction, family, folk, genealogy, heritage, house, household, issue, kin, kindred, line, lineage, mate, offspring, origin, pedigree, people, posterity, progeny, rank, relation, stock, strain, tribe

297 marriage: annul, annulment, betroth, betrothal, couple, desert, desertion, divorce, elope, engage, engagement, espouse, estrange, estrangement, jilt, marriage, marry, match, mate, matrimony, nuptials, part, parting, propose, rupture, separate, separation, sever, split, vow, wed, wedding, woo

GOVERNMENT AND POLITICS

298 government action: abdicate, abolish, abolition, accession, administer, administration, amnesty, bust, colonization, command, depose, deposition, dethrone, displace, dominate, enact, enforce, enforcement, exile, expulsion, filibuster, legalize, override/overrule, pass, reign, rule, run in, secede, second, surveillance, tax, truce, veto

299 government organization: administration, ally, cabinet, capitalism, capitol, chamber, confederacy, congress, council, court, delegation, democracy, deregulation, dictatorship, direction, empire, fascism, government, house, jury, legislature, police/police officer, post, regime, rule, sovereignty, tyranny

300 political action: amnesty, arbitrate, arbitration, ballot, campaign, canvass, crusade, demonstrate, demonstration, displace, drive, drum up, elect, election, endorse, lobby, mutiny, nominate, nomination, patronage, picket, politics, poll, protest, reaction, rebellion, revolt, revolution, riot, run, vote

301 political organization: alliance, ballot, caucus, commonwealth, communism, confederacy, delegation, faction, fascism, machine, party, politics, side, tyranny

HEALTH

302 birth: bear, birth, breed, childbirth, conception, delivery, spring

303 change in: ache, black out, come down with, faint, fit, look up, mend, pull through, recover, recuperate, remission, repel, weary

304 death: abort, abortion, death, decease, demise, die, dissolution, end, expiration, expire, fatality, pass away, passing, perish

305 deathplace: cemetery, crypt, grave, graveyard, monument, tomb

306 disease: affliction, ailment, bacteria, blight, bug, cancer, canker, complaint, condition, contagion, contamination, cyst, disease, disorder, epidemic, germ, growth, illness, indigestion, infection, infirmity, microbe, pest, pimple, plague, rash, sickness, spell, swelling, symptom, syndrome, tantrum

307 drug: analgesic, anesthetic/anaesthetic, antidote, antiseptic, antitoxin, balm, capsule, contraceptive, cure, dope, dose, drug, medicine/medication, narcotic, nostrum, panacea, pill, poison, pot, potion, prescription, remedy, sedative, stimulant, stimulus, tablet, tonic

308 event: abort, abortion, ache, attack, catch, contract, convulsion, cough, cramp, crick, faint, gag, gargle, heal, massage, nauseate, palpitate, paroxysm, pass out, perk up, rupture, seizure, spell, spew, stroke, suffer, take, throw up, tic, vomit, wheeze

309 injury: abrasion, affliction, bite, blister, boil, bruise, concussion, contusion, cut, damage, defect, detriment, disability, disadvantage, disservice, fracture, gash, harm, injury, prick, puncture, rip, rupture, rust, scratch, shock, stab, swelling, welt, wound

310 medical action: alter, analyze, autopsy, bandage, castrate, cure, diagnose, dissection, doctor, dope, dress, drug, ease, examination, heal, inject, malpractice, massage, operate, operation, postmortem, practice, remedy, therapy, tranquilize, transplant, treat, treatment, vaccinate

311 medical instruments: bandage, cure, injection, lotion, matter, nostrum, ointment, panacea, prescription, remedy, salve, staff, x-ray

312 medical organization: asylum, clinic, hospital, madhouse, office

313 pain: ache, afflict, anesthesia/anaesthesia, discomfort, distress, gripe, harassment, harm, hurt, itch, pinch, sting, strain, stress, suffer, torment, torture, wound, wrong

314 quality of: able-bodied, ailing, anemic, bad, benign, better, burning, catching, clean, communicable, congenital, contagious, convalescent, crippled, curable, curative, delicate, disabled, diseased, dizzy, doddering, done in, drugged, drunk, dysfunctional, epidemic, excruciating, faint, febrile, fit, game, genetic, giddy, gory, groggy, haggard, hale, hardy, healthy, hearty, high, hurt, ill, immune, indisposed, inebriated, infectious, infirm, insane, invalid, irreparable, lame, light-headed, low, lusty, malignant, mental, morbid, nauseous, neurotic, normal, palsied, paralytic, peaked, pestilent/pestilential, poor, poorly, queasy, queer, right, robust, rocky, rugged, run-down, safe, sane, senile, sick, sickly, soft, sore, sound, spent, squeamish, strong, sturdy, tender, terminal, tired, tough, trim, unconscious, unfeeling, unhealthy, unscathed, unsound, vigorous, wan, weak, weary, well, whole, wholesome

315 sleep: anesthesia/anaesthesia, asleep, awake, coma, doze, drop off, hibernate, insomnia, lethargy, nap, nightmare, nod, quiet, rest, sleep, sleepy, slumber, snooze, snore, stupor

316 state of: ache, addiction, ailment, apoplexy, beat, collapse, complaint, condition, cough, debility, disability, dislocation, eating disorder, epidemic, faint, fatigue, fitness, form, gestation, hangover, health, hurt, hygiene, ill, immunity, insanity, lapse, malaise, maternity, nausea, neurosis, pain, paroxysm, pink, shape, stupor, symptom, syndrome, tone, trim, trouble, tumor, vigor, welfare/well-being

LEGAL

317 legal action: absolve, acquit, acquittal, action, adjudicate, adopt, adoption, annul, annulment, apprehend, apprehension, arraign, arrest, bequeath, book, bring, bust, charge, cite, collar, commute, condemn, condemnation, convict, conviction, counsel, covenant, cross-examine, cut off, decree, detain, detention, disinherit, enact, enforce, enforcement, evidence, excommunicate, exculpate, exonerate, extradite, hearing, impeach, imprison, incarcerate, indict, indictment, inherit, insure, jail, judge, leave, legalize, let off, lift, litigate, moderate, nab, nail, ordain, outlaw, override/overrule, pardon, pass, perjure, pick up, pinch, plead, practice, prohibit, proscribe, prosecute, pull in, put away, raid, rap, repeal, represent, reprieve, rescind, run in, sentence, sing, substantiate, sue, testify, transport, trial, try, validate, verify, vindicate, vitiate, vouch, waive, will, witness

318 objects used in legal practice: acquittal, act, affidavit, article, bail, bar, bench, bequest, bill, bond, brief, canon, case, claim, code, constitution, court, decree, deed, deposition, dictate, enactment, entreaty, evidence, indictment, injunction, inquest, institute, insurance, jury, law, lawsuit, legislation, libel, litigation, mandate, measure, ordinance, paper/papers, pardon, passage, patent, plea, pledge, precept, prescription, principle, regulation, repeal, reprieve, ruling, sentence, statute, stipulation, suit, terms, testament, testimonial, testimony, verdict, waiver, will, writ

319 **quality of law:** administrative, authoritarian, authoritative, autocratic, canonical, clear, constitutional, contraband, democratic, effectual, exempt, forensic, free, illegal, illegitimate, illicit, inadmissible, judicial, just, lawful, lawless, legal, legislative, legitimate, misbegotten, permissible, punitive, unauthorized, unlawful, unprejudiced, valid, wrongful

MILITARY

320 **military action:** action, aggression, barrage, blitz, blow up, campaign, conflict, contest, coup d'état, defeat, deploy, depose, deposition, descent, dethrone, disarm, disarmament, draft, engage, engagement, enlist, explode, explosion, fire, incursion, induct, induction, insurrection, invade, invasion, maneuver, mobilize, occupation, occupy, offensive, oppression, overthrow, rally, rebellion, recruit, revolt, revolution, salute, service, station, surrender, war, warfare

321 **object used by military:** armory, barracks, battery, battlefield, citadel, defense, draft, fort/fortress, magazine, post, rampart, service

322 **organization:** ally, army, artillery, battalion, brigade, cavalry, corps, defense, detachment, detail, enemy, fleet, force, legion, military, platoon, squad, troop/troops

MONETARY AND FINANCIAL AFFAIRS

323 **association:** association, board, cartel, conglomerate, establishment, federation, firm, industry, market/mart, merger, patronage, syndicate, trust

324 **business action:** advertise, advertising, annexation, appear, appointment, auction, aviation, cashier, commercialize, commission, conclave, conference, consultation, convene, convention, cry, deal, dealings, deficit spending, depression, dictate, discharge, dismiss, drudge, enterprise, exchange, export, farm, farming, fold, gathering, hold, hype, incorporate, intercourse, malpractice, management, manufacture/manufacturing, market, mediate, mediation, meet, meeting, merge, merger, monopolize, operation, patronage, patronize, pioneer, popularize, position, powwow, practice, produce, project, promote, promotion, proposal, publicize, puff, push, put up, sale, seal, second, service, session, shake up, shut, sit, slavery, specialize, step in, stock, table, trade, traffic, transact, transaction, truck, undertaking, wait on

325 **business organization:** agency, airport, association, bakery, bar, branch, bureau, bureaucracy, business, cartel, clientele, commerce, company, concern, conglomerate, corporation, council, direction, dispensation, enterprise, establishment, exchange, field, firm, house, industry, labor, mall, management, operation, outfit, partnership, per-

sonnel, practice, regime, ring, staff, store, syndicate, trust, union

326 **business quality:** accomplished, ambitious, businesslike, busy, careful, concentrated, diligent, discipline, eager, earnest, enterprising, grasping, greedy, methodical/methodic, miserly, orderly, painstaking, persistent, practical, professional, proper, purposeful, regular, relentless, stingy, tenacious, zealous

327 **buying:** buy, charge, lavish, lay out, order, patronize, pay, procure, purchase, redeem, shop, splurge, spree, squander, take, trade, traffic, treat, truck

328 **cost:** appraisal, cost, expense

329 **fee:** amount, bet, bill, bribe, charge, commission, damage(s), debt, duty, excise, expense, fare, fee, levy, obligation, overhead, pay, price, rate, rent, revenue, stake, tab, tariff, tax, toll, wager

330 **financial action:** assess, audit, bank, bargain, bet, bid, bidding, bill, bring, bring in, budget, bust, cash, charge, deduct, default, deficit spending, deposit, depress, depression, devalue, dicker, discount, earn, economize, economy, endorse, fail, frugality, gross, insure, invest, investment, levy, liquidate, net, pawn, pay, pinch, price, profit, realize, return, salt away, save, scrape, shop, skimp, speculate, speculation, stake, stint, subsist, trade, traffic, transact, transaction, truck, venture

331 **financial document:** account, agreement, book, coupon, reckoning, return, statement

332 **financial object:** account, adjustment, arrears, assessment, asset(s), backing, bail, balance, balance sheet, bargain, bill, budget, capital, cheap, draft, equity, fund, insurance, interest, investment, liability, loan, means, order, overhead, patronage, pawn, pay, pension, pledge, principal, profit, quotation/quote, receipt, revenue, score, stock, treasure

333 **financial organization:** bank, board, market/mart

334 **financial quality:** affluent, balanced, bankrupt, behind, broke, charitable, cheap, close, comfortable, commercial, complimentary, costly, dear, depressed, destitute, disadvantageous, down-and-out, due, economic, economical, exorbitant, expensive, extravagant, fat, financial, finished, fiscal, flush, free, frugal, gainful, generous, good, grasping, gratis, gratuitous, high, humble, impecunious, impoverished, improvident, indebted, indigent, inexpensive, insolvent, invaluable, lavish, liberal, liquid, low, lucrative, marketable, mean, miserly, modest, monetary, moneyed, moneymaking, munificent, narrow, needy, net, nominal, opulent, outstanding, overdue, owing, palatial, paltry, parsimonious, patrician, payable, penniless, plush, poor, posh, poverty-stricken, precious, priceless, privileged, prodigal, profitable, profligate, prohibitive, prosperous, provident, rich, second-rate/second-class, self-sufficient, skimpy, sleazy, sordid, sparing, splendid, squalid, steep, stingy, strapped, substantial, sumptuous, tawdry, thrifty, thriving, tight, underprivileged, unfortunate, unpaid, unreasonable, unsettled, valuable, wealthy, well-bred, well-off

335 **financial state:** afford, arrears, avarice, bankruptcy, boom, bring, circumstances, credit, cutback, default, deficit, depression, devalue, discount, economy, extravagance, fail, fortune, frugality, hyperinflation, inadequacy, inflation, living, misery, need, obligation, owe, panic, paucity, pile, pomp, poverty, prosperity, recession, riches, savings, slump, substance, thrift, traffic, value, worth

336 **financial value state:** cost, decline, expense, value

337 **gift:** acquisition, allowance, arrival, atonement, award, balm, benefit, bequest, bonus, boon, bounty, charity, citation, comfort, commendation, compensation, contribution, courtesy, decoration, diploma, dispensation, dividend, dole, donation, due, endowment, extravagance, find, fruit, gain, gem, gift, godsend, good, grant, gratuity, haul, heirloom, honor, indulgence, inheritance, laurels, legacy, loot, luxury, medal, memento, memorial, offering, plum, premium, present, presentation, prize, purse, recognition, remembrance, reparation, reward, souvenir, spoils, subsidy, token, treasure, trophy

338 **merchandise:** bargain, cargo, commodity, consignment, contraband, fabrication, freight, goods, hardware, harvest, haul, inventory, line, load, merchandise, order, product, stock, truck, turnout, wares, yield

339 **monetary container:** bag, bank, purse, till, treasury

340 **money:** advance, allowance, appropriation, asset(s), bill, bread, cash, change, chips, coin, contribution, currency, deposit, dollar, donation, endowment, estate, finances, financing, fund, funds, income, investment, loot, maintenance, means, mint, money, offering, pay, pile, pool, recompense, refund, reserve, resource, resources, return, riches, savings, support, sustenance, wealth

341 **money giving:** advance, blow, buy, compensate, disburse, discharge, endow, expend, finance, fritter, fund, invest, lavish, lay out, misappropriate, patronage, patronize, pay, play, ransom, recompense, refund, reimburse, remit, remunerate, repay, requite, reward, satisfy, settle, shell out, spend, sponsor, square, subscribe, subsidize, support, underwrite

342 **money taking:** bill, blackmail, bleed, clear, collect, extort, extortion, fine, fleece, recoup, squeeze

343 **ownership part:** hold, owner, possession, proprietor

344 **payment:** advance, alimony, bounty, collateral, commission, compensation, consideration, cut, deal, debt, deficit spending, deposit, disbursement, discharge, dividend, dole, draft, dues, earnings, equity, expenditure, expense, fee, financing, gain, graft, grant, gratuity, gross, income, installment, interest, kickback, outlay, pay, payment, penalty, pension, perk, pittance, premium, prize, proceeds, profit, purse, raise, ransom, rebate, receipts, recompense, redress, refund, reparation, restitution, revenue, reward, safety net, salary, satisfaction, stake, stipend, subsidy, take, tip, upkeep, wage/wages

345 **selling:** auction, bazaar, charge, handle, market, merchandise, peddle, sale, sell, solicit, trade, traffic, truck

346 **value state:** appreciation, benefit, decline, import, importance, mark, quality, value, worth

PROFESSIONS

347 **business manager:** administrator, banker, boss, businessperson, capitalist, captain, chief, commander, dealer, director, employer, entrepreneur, establishment, executive, farmer, financier, founder, head, landlord, leader, magnate, manager, master, merchant, mogul, notable, officer, official, overseer, owner, principal, professional, proprietor, seller, specialist, superintendent, superior, supervisor, tycoon, warden

348 **businessperson:** accountant, adjutant, adviser/advisor, agent, aid/aide, analyst, announcer, applicant, apprentice, arbitrator, archaeologist, architect, assistant, associate, astronaut, attendant, auditor, author, authority, aviator, baker, banker, barber, bearer, broker, builder, businessperson, butcher, buyer, caretaker, carpenter, cartoonist, cashier, chair, chairperson, clerk, client, collaborator, colleague, commuter, connection, consumer, cook, correspondent, courier, court, craftsperson, creator, critic, custodian, customer, dabbler, deputy, detective, drudge, emissary, employee, engineer, envoy, expert, farmer, fellow, financier, flyer, fortune-teller, fountainhead, friend, go-between, gourmet, groom, guard, guide, hack, hand, help, interior, informant/informer, intermediary, inventor, investigator, janitor, journalist, labor, liaison, machine, mariner, maverick, mediator, messenger, middle person, miser, model, monitor, negotiator, novice, opposition, page, partner, patron, picket, pilot, pioneer, playwright, poet, porter, prodigal, professional, recruit, referee, reporter, representative, rival, sailor, scout, seller, servant, slave, snoop, spendthrift, spokesperson, sponsor, spy, subordinate, surrogate, tailor, tenant, tool, traveler, umpire, vendor, virtuoso, watchkeeper, wizard, worker, writer, yuppie

349 **discipline:** affair, anatomy, anthropology, appointment, archaeology, architecture, arithmetic, art, astronomy, botany, career, cinema, communications, cybernetics, department, discipline, domain, employment, ergonomics, field, geography, hermeneutics, lifework, line, livelihood, logic, matter, occupation, orbit, passion, phenomenology, philosophy, poetry, position, press, project, province, psychology, pursuit, realm, research, scene, school, science, semiotics, specialty, sphere, stage, station, territory, trade, undertaking, vocation, walk, work

350 **educator:** academic, adviser/advisor, alumnus/alumna, brain, coach, college student, dean, disciplinarian, expert, faculty, fountainhead, genius, graduate, guru, instructor, intellectual, inventor, learner, master, mastermind, mentor, monitor, novice, principal, professor, pupil, scholar, school, student, teacher, tutor, wonk

351 **employment:** ax/axe, bounce, can, collaborate, commission, demote, discharge, dismiss, dismissal, earn, elevate, elevation, employ, employment, engage, fire, gross, hire, interview, job, kick out, labor, layoff, lay off, live, livelihood, living, make, occupation, office, oust, pay, picket, post, promote, promotion, raise, reinstate, relieve, resign, resignation, retain, retire, rise, sack, situation, spot, station, strike, suspend, work

352 **entertainer:** acrobat, actor, artist, ballet dancer, buff, character, comedian, comic, connoisseur, creator, director, fan, fanatic, fledgling, follower, freak, hero/heroine, host, idol, joker, luminary, magician, mimic, musician, name, notable, participant, personage/personality, player, protagonist, singer, star, usher, virtuoso, wit, zany

353 **financier:** accountant, banker, bearer, broker, financier, spendthrift

354 **government officer:** administrator, ally, ambassador, arbiter, authoritarian, authority, autocracy, conqueror, consul, delegate, deputy, despot, dictator, diplomat, disciplinarian, envoy, establishment, executive, exile, expatriate, figure, figurehead, governor, informant/informer, inhabitant, intermediary, justice, leader, legislator, liaison, master, minister, mogul, monarch, negotiator, officer, official, page, patrol, peacemaker, personage/personality, police/police officer, representative, sovereign, spokesperson, tyrant

355 **legal practitioner:** attorney, bench, beneficiary, consul, counsel, counselor, heir, investigator, judge, lawyer, officer, party, proponent, witness

356 **media person:** commentator, journalist, press, reporter, writer

357 **medical practitioner:** analyst, doctor, nurse, patient, physician, psychiatrist, specialist

358 **military person:** commander, conqueror, deserter, fighter, lookout, mercenary, militant, officer, patrol, private, recruit, sailor, scout, soldier, veteran, warrior

359 **politician:** advocate, ally, anarchist, apostate, apostle, applicant, arbitrator, backer, bigot, candidate, conservative, demagogue, diehard, diplomat, dissident, donor, extremist, fanatic, hostage, idealist, insurgent, militant, nonconformist, partisan, patron, picket, politician, proponent, protagonist, radical, reactionary, rebel, refugee, renegade, sectarian, spokesperson

360 **profession:** business, calling, career, craft, employment, finance, hacker, job, labor, lifework, line, livelihood, mission, occupation, place, position, profession, psychology, science, situation, trade, vocation, walk, work

361 **religious person:** acolyte, agnostic, angel, apostle, believer, chaplain, clergyperson, convert, creator, cynic, disciple, doubter, father, hermit, layperson, magician, minister, missionary, monk, nun, pagan, pastor, preacher, priest, prophet, skeptic, visionary, witch, wizard

362 **task:** affair, assignment, bee, berth, chore, commission, concern, drudgery, duty, effort, enterprise, errand, exercise, exertion, function, grind, groove, job, labor, mission, office, part, picnic, post, project, province, realm, research, role, routine, spot, stint, sweat, task, tax, toil, undertaking, work

RECREATION

363 **action:** aerobics/aerobic, angle, athletics, boating, bowl, boxing, bunt, chance, coach, competition, contest, cruise, dance, deal, defeat, dissipation, diversion, engage, event, exercise, fish, gamble, gambol, game, gymnastics, hike, hobby, hunt, keep up, lay, leisure, match, meet, meeting, mess around, oppose, pastime, pit, play, race, raffle, recreation, rehearsal, rehearse, relaxation, rout, shuffle, speculate, speculation, sport, stake, swim, tournament, trifle, turn, vacation, venture, vie, wager, win, workout

364 **objects used in:** amusement, avocation, bicycle, club, equipment, field, game, gymnasium, hobby, holiday, lap, point, pool, raffle, recreation, round, score, tie, wager

365 **organization:** conference, field, league, side, squad, team

366 **participants:** amateur, athlete, aviator, champion, coach, competitor, contestant, dabbler, entrant, entry, fan, fanatic, fighter, fledgling, follower, freak, hacker, mariner, master, name, opponent, opposition, participant, pedestrian, player, referee, rival, sailor, spectator, star, umpire, underdog, victor, winner

RELIGIOUS

367 **action:** anoint, baptism, baptize, bless, blessing, burial, bury, canonize, christen, communion, consecrate, dedicate, dedication, defect, deify, enshrine, excommunicate, inter, penance, pray, prayer, preach, purification, purify, wake, witchcraft, worship

368 **objects used in:** abbey, beads, bible, casket, cathedral, cemetery, church, cloister, coffin, convent, deity, denomination, divinity, faith, grace, holiness, invocation, litany, liturgy, monastery, pulpit, religion, sanctuary, sermon, service, shrine, temple

369 **organization:** church, clergy, congregation, cult, parish

370 **supernatural:** angel, apparition, black magic, deity, demon, devil, divinity, elf, eternity, fairy, ghost, god, heaven, hell, hereafter, incantation, magic, monster, paradise, phantom, presence, savior, shade, sorcery, spell, spirit, universe, utopia, vision, witchcraft

SEX AND REPRODUCTION

371 **attribute of gender:** female, femininity/feminine, male, masculinity/masculine

372 **attribute of sexuality:** adulterous, amatory, amorous, aphrodisiac, bisexual, carnal, celibate, chaste, close, desirable, erotic, femininity/feminine, fertile, fertility, fleshly, gay,

homosexual, hot, kinky, lascivious, lecherous, lewd, libidinous, licentious, loose, loving, masculinity/masculine, nasty, naughty, obscene, passion, passionate, pornographic, potent, promiscuous, provocative, pure, raw, seductive, sensual, sensuous, sexual, sexy, smutty, spicy, suggestive, sultry, torrid, vice, virgin/virginal, virile, voluptuous, vulgar, wanton

373 **birth:** bear, birth, breed, childbirth, conception, delivery, spring

374 **child bearing:** beget, deliver, delivery, fertilize, generate, generation, get, have, labor, multiply, procreate, produce, propagate, reproduce, spawn

375 **sex act:** affair, alter, assignation, birth control, caress, climax, cohabit, conception, copulate, coquet, couple, cuddle, dalliance, dally/dally with, debauch, deflower, enamor, fertilize, flirt, flirtation, fondle, hug, impregnate, intercourse, kiss, love, love affair, mate, molest, pass, paw, pet, proposition, rape, ravish, romance, seduce, sex, sin, tryst, violate, violation, woo

SOCIAL INTERACTIONS

376 **authority:** agency, agent, ascendancy/ascendency, auspices, authority, carte blanche, censorship, chair, chairperson, chief, choice, claim, clearance, cogency, command, connoisseur, control, curb, custody, dominance, domination, dominion, duty, ease, empire, franchise, immunity, impunity, independence, jurisdiction, justice, leadership, leave, office, option, permission, permit, power, prerogative, privilege, rate, reign, right, rule, station, supremacy, sway, title, trust, voice, vote, warrant

377 **celebration:** acclamation, affair, banquet, baptism, carnival, celebrate, celebration, commemorate, commemoration, commencement, entertain, fair, fanfare, feast, festival, festivity, fete, fiesta, gaiety, gala, keep, observance, observe, orgy, pageant, parade, pomp, rally, revel, revelry, rite, splurge, spree, wake

378 **class:** branch, brand, breed, caste, category, class, classification, cut, denomination, description, division, echelon, estate, family, form, genre/genus, gradation, grade, kind, manner, mob, model, mold, nature, nobility, order, position, quality, rank, sort, species, stock, tier, type, variety, world

379 **community:** colony, commune, community, constituency, country, folk, neighborhood, people, population, public, society

380 **ethnic group:** nationality, people, race, strain, tribe

381 **organization:** affiliate, affiliation, agency, apparatus, assembly, bar, brigade, coalition, combination, commission, committee, council, crew, crowd, department, federation, foundation, guild, institute/institution, league, membership, movement, network, organization, partnership, party, ring, sect, society, union

382 **part of a group:** chapter, division, plurality, sect

383 **party:** affair, blowout, dance, entertainment, festivity, gala, masquerade, orgy, party, reception, tear

384 **social action:** abuse, accept, advance(s), adventure, amends, amuse, appeal, appointment, associate, befriend, betray, bite, blooper, bounce, caper, carouse, cavort, cohabit, collaborate, commemorate, compel, conclave, conduct, consort, cool, coquet, court, cower, cultivate, cut up, disaffect, discriminate, disgrace, disobey, disorganize, dissociate, encounter, endanger, engagement, enjoy, entertain, entertainment, escapade, escort, estrange, excursion, faux pas, fawn, fete, fight, flirt, flirtation, flock, forsake, frequent, frisk, frolic, go together/go with, grovel, hanky-panky, haunt, hold, host, hubbub, induct, induction, infringe, insinuate, interfere, interference, interrupt, introduce, invitation, invite, jilt, kick out, know, kowtow, lose, love, make up, maroon, mask, meddle, mediate, mediation, meet, meeting, mingle, mishandle/mismanage, mutiny, network, obeisance, oblige, observance, observe, ostracize, overture, pander, part, parting, pass, patch up, patronize, penance, pick up, play, poke, popularize, powwow, prance, prank, pretend, program, proposition, prostrate, pry, pursue, put up, rampage, rapprochement, reception, reciprocate, reconcile, reduce, regale, reinstate, rendezvous, repay, reprisal, requite, respond, retaliate, retribution, revel, revelry, revenge, riot, romance, romp, rupture, seat, secede, second, see, separate, sever, share, show, shun, sit, slight, snoop, snub, socialize, soothe, spree, spurn, squire, step in, stoop, stunt, taint, tantrum, tear, throw over, toy, treat, trespass, trick, tryst, usurp, vengeance, wallow, welcome, woo

385 **social change:** breakup, civilize, give in/give up, revert, succumb

386 **social event:** adventure, assignation, ball, bee, benefit, binge, blast, bustle, caper, caricature, carnival, ceremony, clamor, clown, come between, conference, date, debut, display, dissipation, diversion, entertainment, escapade, exhibition, exposition, fair, feature, fiesta, fling, frolic, fun, function, funeral, gathering, inauguration, initiation, memorial, merriment/merrymaking, occasion, outing, parade, picnic, rally, riot, rite, ritual

387 **social organization:** association, band, circle, clan, class, clique, club, congregation, congress, crowd, cult, elite, entourage, faction, fellowship, following, gang, guild, league, legion, order, society

388 **social state:** amity, association, attendance, awkwardness, behind, belong, belonging, bigotry, bond, brand, breach, break, breeding, calm, camaraderie, care, caste, celebrity, celibacy, censorship, ceremony, circumstances, civilization, class, clutches, coherence, commotion, companionship, compatibility, complicity, concert, concord, conflict, conjunction, connection, consanguinity, consequence, contact, contempt, co-

operation, correlation, courtesy, courtship, credit, crunch, culture, dalliance, degree, detachment, difference, dignity, diplomacy, disaffection, disagreement, discord, disfavor, disgrace, disharmony, dishonor, disorder, dissociation, dissolution, distinction, disturbance, division, duty, ease, echelon, elite, eminence, enrollment, entertainment, entrée, entry, equality, estate, estrangement, excitement, face, fame, familiarity, favoritism, fellowship, feud, fidelity, footing, friendliness, friendship, frivolity, fun, furor, fuss, gaiety, genre/genus, gentility, get along, get on, glory, harmony, height, hospitality, housing, hubbub, humiliation, immunity, importance, infidelity, intimacy, intrigue, juncture, kick, laissez-faire, lapse, lather, league, level, liai-

son, liberty, love affair, luxury, marriage, match, men's movement, mirth, mourning, mutiny, name, network, nobility, nonsense, notch, notoriety, obligation, odium, onus, pandemonium, partnership, peace, pink, place, platitude, pleasure, polish, popularity, position, predicament, prestige, privacy, rage, rank, rapport, rapprochement, rate, refinement, relationship, report, reproach, repulse, reputation, rift, rupture, scramble, seclusion, separation, servitude, setback, shame, showdown, situation, slavery, society, solitude, sophistication, sphere, split, spotlight, standing, state, station, status, stigma, stink, stir, support, sympathy, taint, taste, tedium, terms, tie, uncertainty, unification, variance, whirl

Life forms

BEINGS

389 beings: being, body, cell, creation, creature, cur, egg, form, individual, life, organism, soul

390 former beings: body, cadaver, carcass/carcase, corpse

391 group of beings: band, flock, group, world

392 limb or appendage of: ankle, arm, back, backside, beak, behind, branch, bust, butt/buttocks, calf, chest, claw, digit, egg, extremity, eye, fiber, finger, flank, flesh, foot, freckle, germ, hair, hand, head, jaw, leg, limb, lip, member, mop, mouth, nose, posterior, rump, seat, skin, strand, tail, trunk, tuft, wisp

393 organ: abdomen, abdominal, bacteria, belly, blood, bone, bowels, brain, gut, heart, joint, mind, molecule, muscle, nucleus, seed, skeleton, spine, stomach, vein

BEINGS, ANIMAL

394 animal: adult, animal, beast, brute, buck, calf, cat, cattle, chicken, clam, cock, colt, cur, father, fawn, frog, game, goat, half-breed, hound, hybrid, litter, mongrel, monkey, monster, mother, parasite, pet, pig, prey, stock, young

395 bird: bird, chicken

396 fish: aquarium, aquatic

397 group of animals: drove, family, herd, horde, litter, pack, roundup, stock, swarm, team

398 insect: bee, bug, grub, pest

399 limb or appendage of: bill, chin, coat, crest, feather, fertilizer, fur, meat, mop, paunch, pelt, pulp, scale, shell, trunk, venom, wing

400 mammal: cat, dog, donkey, father, fawn, goat, hound, mother, pig

GENERAL CHARACTERISTICS

401 attribute of behavior: abstemious, acerbity, acid, acrid, acrimonious, active, adamant, ad-

olescent, affable, affected, affectionate, agreeable, agreeably, aimless, alive, aloof, amiable, amuck, animate, animated, anxious, apathetic, arbitrary, arch, ardent, argumentative, arrogant, artificial, assured, attentive, audacious, austere, authoritarian, avid, babyish, backward, bad, balky, barbarian, barbaric, barbarous, barefaced, beaming, beastly, belligerent, benevolent, big, bland, blindly, boisterous, bold, brash, brassy, brave, brazen, brittle, brusque, brutal, calculating, calm, cantankerous, capricious, carnivorous, casual, cautious, cavalier, chary, childish, chill, chivalrous, chummy, civil, clumsy, coarse, cocky/cocksure, collected, combative, comic/comical, common, compassionate, complacent, complaisant, composed, compulsive, concerned, conciliatory, condescending, considerate, constructive, contemptuous, contrary, contumacious, convivial, cool, cordial, correct, corrupt, country, courageous, courteous, courtly, covetous, cowardly, coy, crabby/crabbed, crafty, cranky, crass, craven, cross, crotchety, crude, cruel, crusty, cunning, daring, dark, dauntless, deaf, debonair, deceitful, decent, deceptive, decided, decorous, defensive, deferential, defiant, deliberate, deliberately, delicate, delightful, delinquent, delirious, demonstrative, demure, desperate, detached, devious, diffident, diplomatic, disagreeable, disarming, discourteous, discreet, disdainful, disgruntled, disingenuous, disinterested, disloyal, disobedient, disobliging, disorderly, dispassionate, disputatious, disrespectful, disruptive, dissipated, dissolute, distant, distraught, docile, doctrinaire, dogged, dolorous, domineering, doting, doubledealing, dour, eager, earnest, easy, ebullient, edgy, effeminate, effervescent, emotionless, enthusiastic, envious, epicurean, equable, equal, evasive, even, exacting, excitable, excited, exuberant, faithful, faithless, fake, false, falsely, fanatical, favorable, favorably, fawning, fearful, fearless, feigned, ferocious, fervent/fervid, feverish, fickle, fidgety, fiery, fighting, finicky, flagrant, flamboyant, flexible, flighty, flippant, flirtatious, flushed, foolhardy, foolish, foolishly, forceful, formal, forward, foxy, fractious, free, freely, fresh, fretful, frisky, frivolous, fulsome, fussy, genial, genteel, giddy, glacial, glowing, good, graceless, gracious, grandiose, grave, gritty, grouchy, gruff, grumpy, halfhearted, hard, hardhearted, haughty, headstrong, heartless, hearty, heedless, helpless, heroic, highstrung, hostile, hot, huffy, humane, humble, hypocritical, icy, idle, ill at ease, illmannered, ill-natured, impatient, impersonal, impertinent, impish, impolite, impolitic, importunate, impossible, impudent, impulsive, inactive, inclement, inconsiderate, inexorable, ingratiating, inhospitable, inhuman/inhumane, inimical, innocuous, insensitive, insidious, insolent, insubordinate, insurgent, intractable/intransigent, intrepid, invidious, irascible, irreconcilable, irrepressible, irreverent, irritable, jaded, jaundiced, jaunty, jovial, jubilant, jumpy, juvenile, keen, kind, kittenish, lax, lazy, lecherous, lenient, lethargic, level, liberal, licentious, lifeless, light, light-headed, listless, lively, lofty, loose, loquacious, loud, loving, lunatic, maladroit, malevolent, malicious, mannered, mannerly, martial, mawkish, mean, meek, menacing, mercenary, merciful, merciless, mercurial, mild, militant, mincing, mischievous, miscreant, miserly, modest, mousy, munificent, naive, narcissistic, nasty, natural, naughty, nefarious, neglectful, negligent, neighborly, nerveless, nervy, noble, nomadic, nonchalant, noncompliant, nonconformist, nonviolent, nosy, obdurate, obedient, obliging, obnoxious, obsequious, obstinate, obtrusive, odious, offhand, oily, orderly, ostentatious, overwrought, parental, parsimonious, partisan, passionate, pedantic, peevish, pent-up, peppery, peppy, peripatetic, perky, permissive, persistent, pert, perverse, petulant, philosophical/philosophic, pious, pitiless, placid, plaintive, playful, polite, politic, pompous, possessed, pragmatic, precious, precipitous/precipitate, precise, predatory, premature, presumptuous, pretentious, prickly, prim, prissy, prodigal, profane, profligate, prompt, proper, propitious, proud, provident, prudent, prudish, puerile, pugnacious, punctilious, pushy, quarrelsome, querulous, quick-tempered, quiet, racy, radiant, raffish, rakish, rash, raucous, ready, rebel, rebellious, recalcitrant, reckless, refined, regardful, regardless, relentless, reluctant, remiss, remorseful, remorseless, remote, renegade, repugnant, reserved, resigned, respectful, responsible, responsive, restive, restrained, reticent, retiring, ribald, rocky, rollicking, rough, rowdy, rude, rugged, runaway, rustic, ruthless, safe, salty, sanctimonious, saucy, savage, scintillating, scrupulous, secluded, self-conscious, self-righteous, sensual, sentimental, serene, servile, severe, shabby, shameful, shameless, sheepish, shifty, short, short-sighted, shrewd, shy, silly, simple, sincere, sinister, skittish, slick, slippery, sluggish, sly, small, smart, smooth, snaky, snappy, sneaky, snide, snobbish, sober, sociable, soft, solid, sophisticated, sophomoric, sparing, spineless, spiteful, spontaneous, sporting/sportive, sprightly, spry, square, squeamish, staid, standoffish, stately, staunch, steadfast, stealthy, stern, stiff, stilted, stingy, stodgy, stoic/stoical, stolid, stony, strained, strenuous, strict, stringent, stubborn, stuffy, suave, subdued, submissive, subservient, subversive, sunny, supercilious, superior, sure, surly, sweet, sympathetic, taciturn, tactful, tactless, tame, tasteless, tearful, temperate, tempestuous, tenacious, tender, tense, testy, thankful, thankless, theatrical, thieving/thievish, thoughtful, thoughtless, thrifty, tight, timid, tipsy, torpid, touchy, tractable, treacherous, tricky, truculent, true, turbulent, ugly, unaffected, unasked, unassuming, unbending, uncivilized, uncompromising, uncontrollable, uncouth, undaunted, undependable, underhand, understanding, unemotional, unflappable, unfriendly, ungrateful, unguarded, uninhibited, unintentional/unintended, uninterested, unkind, unmerciful, unobtrusive, unprejudiced, unpretentious, unreasonable, unrelenting, unruly, unscrupulous, unseemly, unselfish, unsettled, unsociable, unsophisticated, unsuspecting, unsympathetic, unthinking, untoward, untrustworthy, unwary, unwilling, unwise, unwitting, unworldly, unyielding, uptight, urbane, vain, valiant, vehement, vengeful, venturesome, vibrant, vicarious, vicious, vigilant, vindictive, violent, virile, virtuous, vital, vivacious, volatile, voracious, wacky, wanton, warlike, warm, wary, wasteful, watchful, wayfaring, wayward, well-bred, whimsical, wicked, wild, willful, willing, wily, winning/winsome, withdrawn, worldly, yellow, yielding, zany, zealous

402 attribute of intelligence: able, abreast, abstruse, academic, acute, adept, alert, amenable, analytic/analytical, appreciative, apt, astute, awake, aware, backward, bewildered, blank, blind, bright, brilliant, calculable, canny, childish, clairvoyant, clear, clever, clumsy, cognizant, coherent, common-sense, complex, comprehensible, conscious, considered, contemplative, conversant, creative, cunning, dark, deducible, deep, delirious, dense, designedly, dexterous, dim, discerning, dizzy, dopey, down-to-earth, dull, dumb, educated, efficient, elevated, empty, empty-headed, enlightened, erudite, experienced, expert, familiar, far-sighted, fatuous, forgotten, frivolous, gifted, gullible, harebrained, hazy, idiotic, ignorant, illiterate, imbecile, impressionable, incisive, incomprehensible, inefficient, ineligible, inept, inexperienced, informed, ingenious, inquiring, inquisitive, insipid, intellectual, intelligent, intuitive, inventive, irrational, judicious, keen, knowing, knowledgeable, learned, logical, lucid, mental, mindful, mistaken, nimble, oblivious, observant, obtuse, omniscient, penetrating, perceptive, perspicacious, philosophical/philosophic, precocious, privy, professional, proficient, profound, psychic, quick, quick-witted, rational, ready, reasonable, resourceful, sagacious, sane, scatterbrained, scholarly, senile, sensible, shallow, sharp, shrewd, simple, skillful, slick, slow, smart, soft, stolid, studious, stupid, subtle, thick, thoughtful, thoughtless, touched, unaware, uneducated, unfamiliar, unwise, vacant, vacuous, versed, veteran, weak, wise

403 attribute of mentality: abashed, absentee, absent-minded, absorbed, absorbing, accustomed, addled, affected, affectionate, afraid, aggrieved, aghast, agonizing, alert, amatory, amorous, angry, anxious, apathetic, appreciative, apprehensive, aspiring, assumed, attentive, automatic, averse, avid, bad, balmy, beaten, beholden, believable, bent, bewildered, bewitched, bigoted, black, bleak, blissful, blue, boiling, breathless, broad, broad-minded, broken, brokenhearted, buoyant, burning, calculating, captive, carnal, cautious, certain, cheerful, cheerless, chipper, circumspect, clairvoyant, clear, compassionate, complacent, concerned, confident, confused, conscious, contemplative, content, contented, contrite, crabby/crabbed, cranky, crazy, crestfallen, cross, crotchety, curious, cynical, daft, dearly, decided, dejected, delighted, delirious, demented, depressed, deranged, desolate, despairing, desperately, despondent, disaffected, disappointed, disbelieving, disconcerted, disconsolate, discontented/discontent, discouraged, discouraging, disenchanted, disgruntled, disgusted, disillusioned, disinclined, disinterested, disoriented, dispirited, dissatisfied, dissident, distraught, distressed, distrustful, doleful, dolorous, doubtful, down, downcast, downhearted, dumbfounded, ecstatic, elated, emotional, emotionless, enamored, engrossed, envious, excited, expectant, exultant, fascinated, fed up, festive, firm, flaming, flushed, foggy, forgetful, forgotten, forlorn, frantic, frenetic, fretful, frightened, frustrated, fulfilled, funereal, furious, gay, glad, gladly, gleeful, gloomy, grateful, greedy, grumpy, gut, half-baked, happily, happy, hard, headstrong, healthy, heavy, high, hopeful, hot, huffy, hurt, hysterical, ill at ease, impartial, impassioned, impressionable, inattentive, incensed, inconsolable, incredulous, indifferent, indignant, indiscriminate, infatuated, insane, insatiable, insecure, insular, intent, intently, interested, intolerant, intoxicated, invidious, irate, irrational, irresolute, irritable, jaundiced, jealous, jovial, joyful/joyous, joyless, jubilant, judicious, keen, lackadaisical, languid, lascivious, lethargic, levelheaded, livid, lonely, lonesome, longing, lost, low, lucid, lukewarm, lunatic, mad, malleable, manic/maniacal, melancholy, mental, merry, mindful, mindless, miserable, moody, morbid, morose, narrow, narrow-minded, negative, nerveless, nervous, neurotic, neutral, new age, noncommittal, normal, nostalgic, numb, nuts/nutty, objective, oblivious, observant, obsessed, opposed/opposing, overcome, overjoyed, overwrought, partial, penitent, pensive, pent-up, pessimistic, petty, platonic, predisposed, preoccupied, prepared, prepossessed, profound, proud, provincial, psychic, psychological, psychotic, purposeful, puzzled, queasy, rabid, radical, raging, rapt, realistic, reflective,

regretful, resolute, restless, right, rigid, romantic, sad, sane, sanguine, sappy, scared, sectarian, secure, senile, sensitive, serious, sick, silly, skeptical, solemn, solicitous, somber, sore, sorrowful, sorry, sound, sour, spellbound, spiritless, steady, stout, strong, subdued, sullen, susceptible, suspicious, tearful, temperamental, tender, tense, testy, thankful, thirsty, thoughtful, thoughtless, tired, tolerant, torn, touched, tough, ugly, unadvised, unbalanced, uncomfortable, uncommitted, unconcerned, undecided, uneasy, unemotional, unfaltering, unfeeling, unhappy, uninterested, unsettled, unsound, untouched, untroubled, unwary, upbeat, upset, versed, vulnerable, wacky, wary, weak, weary, willing, wistful, woebegone, worried, wrathful, wretched

404 attribute of personality: aboveboard, abrasive, adventurous, aggressive, airy, altruistic, amenable, amorphous, approachable, ardent, arrogant, artful, assertive, assuming, assured, audacious, august, bashful, belligerent, big, bitter, blasé, blessed, blithe, bloodless, boastful, bold, boorish, brash, bright, buoyant, busy, callous, calm, captious, carefree, catty, charitable, charming, chaste, cheerful, childlike, chill, chilly, choosy, churlish, clean, clear, clement, clinical, close, cocky/cocksure, co-dependent, cold, colorful, colorless, combative, conceited, confident, convivial, cool, courageous, coy, credulous, culpable, cursed, cute, dainty, dashing, decent, dedicated, deep, delicate, delightful, demonic/demoniac/demoniacal, demure, dependent, deserving, despicable, detached, determined, devious, die-hard, difficult, dignified, discriminating, dispassionate, disreputable, distant, docile, dynamic, easy, easygoing, effeminate, egocentric, egotistical/egoistic, elastic, enchanting, energetic, engaging, enterprising, exacting, exalted, excitable, exemplary, feckless, finicky, finished, flatulent, flirtatious, forbearing, fortunate, forward, foxy, free, fresh, frigid, fussy, gallant, game, garrulous, gauche, generous, genial, genteel, gentle, glacial, glib, good, good-humored, good-natured, green, gregarious, gritty, gutless, gutsy, happy-go-lucky, hardened, hardhearted, hard-nosed/hardheaded, hateful, heroic, high-strung, humble, icy, ill-natured, immaculate, immovable, impassive, imperturbable, impetuous, individual, indomitable, indulgent, inexperienced, infamous, inflexible, inherent, inhibited, innocent, insipid, insouciant, intolerant, intrinsic, inveterate, inviting, irresponsible, jaunty, kind, kindhearted, kindly, latent, lazy, liberal, lighthearted, likable, little, lovable, low, lowly, loyal, magnanimous, magnetic, mercurial, meritorious, mild, mincing, misanthropic, miserly, modest, narcissistic, native, natural, nice, noble, nonchalant, notorious, obedient, obliging, obsequious, obsessed, odd/oddball, odious, officious, opinionated, opprobrious, optimistic, outgoing, outspoken, overbearing, particular, patient, peculiar, peppy, perky, persistent, persnickety, personable, pert, philanthropic, picky, pigheaded, pliable, predictable, prepossessing, prim, prissy, proper, pushy, queer, quick-tempered, receptive, recluse/reclusive, remote, reserved, responsible, rotten, ruthless, saintly, sanctimonious, sedate, selective, self-centered, self-confident, self-conscious, selfish, self-satisfied, self-sufficient, servile, shabby, shifty, shy, smug, sophisticated, spirited, spotless, sprightly, square, squeamish, stable, staid, stalwart, standoffish, stodgy, stoic/stoical, straight, stubborn, stuffy, suave, subservient, sweet, treacherous, trustworthy/trusty, unaffected, unapproachable, unassuming, unpretentious, unselfish, unsuspecting, unworthy, upright, vain, valiant, vigorous, virile, vivacious, vocal, warm, winning/winsome, wishy-washy, yielding, zealous

405 essential property of life forms: awkwardness, body, complexion, dotage, fatigue, hygiene, physique, sense, sensitivity

406 essential quality of life forms: adult, alimentary, animal, athletic, awake, awkward, barefoot, bearded, blank, bodily, breathless, brunette/brunet, bushy, buxom, cadaverous, corpulent, curly, curvaceous, dark, decrepit, drowsy, empty, exhausted, expectant, expressionless, fair, famished, fleshy, florid, full, gaunt, glassy, haggard, hairless, hairy, high, human, hungry, imperceptible, inborn/inbred, infertile, innate, insensitive, intestinal/intestine, intoxicated, intrinsic, light, limber, lumbering, piercing, predatory, pregnant, primitive, private, promising, prostrate, ravenous, raw, rich, sensitive, sensory, shapely, smooth, starving/starved, sweaty, tight, tipsy, tired, wild

407 existential state: be, being, casualty, coexistence, endure, exist, existence, flesh, gone, live, loss, manage, matter, mortality, nature, none, nothing/nothingness, oblivion, outlast, presence, reside, split, stand, subsist, survive, threaten, vitality, zero

408 gender: female, femininity/feminine, gender, male, masculinity/masculine

409 intelligence: acquaintance, acumen, anticipation, appreciation, apprehension, aptitude, attention, awareness, bent, brain, capacity, clairvoyance, clarity, cleverness, cognizance/cognition, common sense, comprehension, conception, consciousness, craft, dark, darkness, delusion, depth, dexterity, education, efficiency, empathy, enlightenment, erudition, experience, expertise/expertness, familiarity, fancy, feeling, finesse, foresight, forte, genius, gift, grasp, grip, head, idiocy, ignorance, illumination, imagination, innocence, insight, intellect, intelligence, intuition, invention, judgment, knack, know-how, knowledge, learning, light, literacy, memory, mentality, mind, misconception, misunderstanding, observance, observation, originality, perception, proficiency, reason, sanity, sense, sensibility, skill, soul, thought, understanding, wisdom, wit/wits

410 mentality: absorption, abstraction, accession, ache, aggravation, agility, agonize, agony, alarm, alienation, alter ego, amazement, anger, anguish, anticipation, anxiety, apathy, application, assurance, astonishment, attention, attitude, attrition, avarice, awe, behalf,

belief, belonging, bigotry, bitterness, blues, boast, boredom, bosom, breakdown, breast, bristle, buoyancy/buoyance, capitulation, caprice, care, caution, censure, chagrin, cheer, clairvoyance, clemency, cogitation, collapse, comfort, compassion, complex, composure, compulsion, compunction, conception, concern, confusion, conquest, consideration, consolation, constancy, contemplation, content, contentment, contrition, conviction, corollary, credit, cult, curiosity, dark, darkness, daze, decision, defeat, deference, degradation, delight, delight in, delirium, delusion, dependence/dependency, depression, design, desolation, despair, desperation, difficulty, disability, disaffection, disappointment, discipline, discomfiture, discomfort, discontent, discouragement, discrimination, disgust, disinclination, dismay, disorder, displeasure, disquiet, dissatisfaction, distraction, distress, disturbance, doldrums, dolor, doubt, ease, ecstasy, elation, embarrassment, emotion, encouragement, enjoyment, ennui, envy, equanimity, euphoria, exaltation, exasperation, excitement, exhaustion, exhilaration, expectancy, expectation, exultation, fallacy, feeling, fever, firmness, fluster, fog, folly, forbearance, force, foresight, forethought, forgetfulness, fortitude, frazzle, free will, frenzy, fret, fright, frustration, fume, funk, furor, fury, gladness, glee, gloom, gratification, gratitude, grief, grieve, happiness, health, heart, heartbreak, heat, heaven, hesitation, hope, huff, humiliation, humor, hysteria, idiocy, imagination, impulse, indifference, indignity, insanity, insight, instability, introspection, ire, jitters, joy, kick, lament/lamentation, letdown, lethargy, levity, lunacy, malaise, mania, martyrdom, melancholy, merriment/merrymaking, mirth, mistake, monotony, mood, mope, morale, mourn, mourning, muddle, nausea, neglect, nerves, nervousness, neurosis, nostalgia, objection, oblivion, observance, observation, obsession, offense, optimism, originality, outlook, pain, panic, paradise, paroxysm, passion, pathos, peace, penance, penitence, perception, perspective, pessimism, pique, pity, pleasure, posture, pout, precaution, predisposition, premonition, presage, presence, presentiment, psyche, psychology, push, pussyfoot, qualm, quarter, rage, rancor, rapture, rave, regret, rejoice, remorse, repent, repentance, repose, repulse, resent, resentment, resignation, resistance, resolution, resolve, restlessness, retrospect, sadness, sanity, satisfaction, scare, security, self-satisfaction, sensation, sensibility, sensitivity, sentiment, seriousness, servitude, shame, simmer, slump, sob, solace, solicitude, sorrow, soul, state, stew, strain, strength, stress, subconscious, surprise, suspense, sympathy, tedium, telepathy, temper, temperament, temperance, tension, thought, tolerance, torment, torture, trance, transport, triumph, turn, umbrage, uncertainty, unrest, vanity, waver, woe, wonder, worry, wrath, zeal, zest

411 personality: aggression, ardor, arrogance, art, artifice, assumption, atrocity, attribute, audacity, backbone, bearing, being, best, bounce, bravery, buoyancy/buoyance, caliber, calm, candor, character, characteristic, charisma, charity, charm, complexion, compliance, conceit, confidence, constraint, courage, cultivation, dash, decision, dedication, demeanor, determination, dignity, disposition, disrepute, distinction, drive, effrontery, ego, egoism/egotism, élan, empathy, endowment, endurance, energy, enterprise, entity, essence, eye, failing, fiber, fight, fire, foible, forte, fortitude, frailty, gall, gallantry, generosity, geniality, gentility, go, goodness, good will/goodwill, greatness, grit, gumption, gusto, guts, heart, heroism, honor, humor, identity, idiosyncrasy, inclination, individuality, infamy, inhibition, initiative, innocence, integrity, kind, kink, laziness, life, loyalty, magnetism, makeup, manner, mark, martyrdom, mentality, mettle, mien, might, mold, mood, morale, morals, motivation, mystique, nature, nerve, notoriety, obedience, oddity, panache, patience, peculiarity, penchant, pep, perseverance, personality, pluck, point, possibilities, potency, presence, pride, probity, proclivity, propensity, property, prowess, psyche, push, qualify, quirk, reputation, responsibility, savor, self-respect/self-esteem, shortcoming, soul, sparkle, spirit, spunk, stability, stamina, stamp, style, taste, temerity, temper, temperament, tenacity, tend, thing, trait, trick, turn, twist, type, valor, vein, vice, vigor, virtue, vitality, way, weakness, will, willpower, wit, zeal, zest, zip

HUMANS

412 bad person: accessory, accomplice, addict, adversary, agitator, anarchist, antagonist, apostate, ass, assailant, assassin, authoritarian, bandit, barbarian, beggar, braggart, bum, bungler, burglar, cad, cannibal, captive, character, cheat, clod, clown, confederate, convict, criminal, critic, crook, culprit, cur, delinquent, demagogue, demon, derelict, deserter, desperado, despot, devil, dolt, dope, drone, dumbbell, dummy, dunce, enemy, exile, expatriate, failure, fake, felon, fiend, fighter, foe, fool, fraud, fugitive, gangster, glutton, good-for-nothing, gossip, grouch, hypocrite, idiot, imbecile, imp, impostor, incendiary, insurgent, interloper, intruder, joke, kook, liar, loafer, loser, lunatic, mad person, maniac, menace, mercenary, misanthrope, miscreant, miser, monster, murderer, nuisance, nut, oaf, ogre, outlaw, parasite, pawn, pervert, pessimist, pest, pill, prisoner, prodigal, profligate, prostitute, psychopath, quack, ragamuffin, rascal, rebel, renegade, robber, rogue, rowdy, runaway, sap, scapegoat, scoundrel, scum, showoff, sight, sneak, spy, swindler, tattletale/tattler, thief, tool, tough, traitor, tramp, troublemaker, tyrant, underworld, vandal, villain, wanton, weakling, witch

413 community group member: citizen, denizen, emigrant, foreigner, immigrant, inhabitant, local, migrant, native, newcomer, nomad, outsider, patriot, pioneer, plebeian, refugee, resident, rustic, stranger, subject, yokel

414 family member: ancestor, ancestry, antecedent(s), babe, baby, brother, child, descendant, domestic partner, father, fiancé/fiancée, forebearer, forerunner, guardian, heir, husband, hybrid, infant, issue, kid, kin, kindred, man, mother, nurse, occupant, offspring, orphan, owner, parent, partner, predecessor, progeny, relation, relative, scion, seed, senior, sister, spouse, surrogate, sweetheart, twin, ward, woman, young, youngster/youth

415 female: bachelor, bride, female, girl, girlfriend, mother, nymph, sister, wanton, wife, woman

416 good person: ace, angel, benefactor, expert, genius, hero/heroine, humanitarian, idealist, intellect, intellectual, intimate, missionary, peacemaker, pet, prodigy, pundit, savior, victor, virtuoso, visionary, wag, whiz, winner, wit

417 group of people: anybody, anyone, army, assemblage, attendance, audience, band, board, body, cadre, caucus, circle, civilization, class, clientele, clique, cloud, company, congregation, contingent, convention, corps, corpse, crew, crowd, crush, elite, enrollment, entourage, everybody/everyone, expedition, federation, field, flesh, following, force, gallery, gathering, horde, host, huddle, human, humankind, legion, masses, member, membership, mob, mortal, mortality, multitude, muster, outfit, pack, party, people, person, personnel, platoon, practice, public, set, society, squad, suite, swarm, team, throng, troop/troops, turnout

418 limb or appendage: ankle, beard, bosom, bottom, braid, breast, bristle, brow, cam, cheek, coiffure, curl, elbow, features, pore, wrinkle

419 male: bachelor, boy, boyfriend, bridegroom, brother, escort, father, groom, husband, lad, male, man, wanton

420 organ: backbone, blood, bone, brain, heart, muscle, spine, stomach, vein

421 racial group member: kin, kindred, relation, tribe

422 royalty: crown, monarch, noble

423 social group member: acquaintance, addict, admirer, adventurer, advocate, alien, alliance, alter ego, another, apprentice, aristocracy, aristocrat, arrival, assistant, associate, augur, auxiliary, bachelor, beatnik, beau, beggar, beginner, believer, beloved, benefactor, beneficiary, bigot, boor, bore, boyfriend, braggart, brute, buddy, buff, buffoon, bully, bum, bungler, busybody, butt, bystander, captive, casualty, celebrity, chaperon, character, chicken, chum, churl, civilian, clairvoyant, clod, clown, cohort, collaborator, colleague, comedian, comic, companion, company, competitor, comrade, confidant, connection, conquest, consort, convoy, correspondent, couch potato, coward, craven, crony, cynic, darling, date, dear, derelict, deserter, devotee, diehard, dilettante, disciple, disciplinarian, dissident, dolt, donor, dope, doubter, driver, drunk/drunkard, dumbbell, dummy, dunce, dupe, eccentric, emigrant, emissary, enthusiast, entrant, epicurean, equal, escort, exception, exile, expatriate, exponent, extremist, extrovert, eyewitness, failure, fan, father, favorite, fellow, fiancé/fiancée, fiend, figure, figurehead, flame, flirt, follower, fool, forerunner, fortune-teller, founder, freak, friend, gentleperson, girlfriend, go-between, gourmet, greenhorn, grouch, guardian, guest, guide, hanger-on, hedonist, herald, hermit, hostage, humanitarian, idealist, idol, inferior, informant/informer, interloper, intimate, introvert, intruder, jerk, jester, joke, joker, kook, layperson, liaison, local, loser, love, lover, luminary, machine, mad person, master, mate, maverick, mediator, miser, moron, mother, negotiator, neighbor, newcomer, noble, nobody/nonentity, nonconformist, notable, novice, nut, oddity/oddball, old hand, onlooker, original, outcast, outsider, pagan, pal, participant, partisan, partner, passenger, patrician, patron, pauper, peer, personage/personality, pessimist, philanderer, pill, pillar, plebeian, poet, prey, prophet, proponent, protagonist, pundit, puppet, pushover, ragamuffin, rebel, recluse, rich, rival, scream, second, sectarian, skeptic, snob, snoop, somebody, spectator, spendthrift, sponsor, sport, square, stick-in-the-mud, stranger, subject, subordinate, substitute, suitor, support/supporter, surrogate, sweetheart, sycophant, target, tattletale/

tattler, tenant, tool, tourist, traveler, umpire, underdog, urchin, vagabond, vagrant, veteran, victim, visitor, wag, waif, wanderer, weakling, witness, wizard, zany

424 traits: adolescent, adult, babe, baby, beauty, beginner, boy, brat, child, childish, dwarf, elder, eyeful, fledgling, freak, giant, girl, gnome, grown-up, infant, invalid, juvenile, kid, lad, midget, minor, nymph, runt, senior, vision, young, youngster/youth

PLANTS

425 flower: bloom, blossom, bouquet, flower
426 fruit: berry, fruit, produce
427 growth or death of: bloom, blossom, bud, develop, germinate, grow, growth, wilt, wither
428 part: bark, bough, branch, bud, fiber, flavoring, flower, foliage, fruit, grain, husk, juice, leaf, limb, log, nut, peel, pod, pulp, scion, seed, shell, skin, stalk, stem, trunk
429 plant: algae, bouquet, bramble, brush, bush, creation, crop, fertilizer, fossil, garland, grove, harvest, hedge, hybrid, nature, organism, plant, produce, vintage, wreath
430 tree: timber, tree, wood/woods
431 vegetable: produce, vegetable

Objects

ARTICLES, PHYSICAL

432 group of: accumulation, aggregate, amalgam, anthology, archive, armada, array, arsenal, assembly, assortment, backlog, bale, batch, battery, bevy, blend, body, bolt, bunch, bundle, cadre, canon, caravan, cavalcade, chain, clot, cloud, clump, cluster, clutter, collection, column, combination, compilation, complex, composite, compound, concentration, concoction, concourse, congestion, conglomeration, couple, crush, deluge, deposit, drift, drove, ensemble, everything, fleet, flock, fusion, group, hash, heap, herd, hodgepodge, host, huddle, jumble, junk, knot, litter, load, lot, lump, many, mass, medley, mélange, miscellany, mix/mixture, mob, mound, mountain, multitude, muster, number, odds and ends, pack, package, pair, parcel, party, patchwork, pile, pool, potpourri, press, queue, repertory, residue, row, score/scores, scramble, set, stack, stew, store, stuff, sum, surge, swarm, throng, train, tuft, unit, variety, wad, whole
433 object: anything, article, entity, fact, individual, loser, matter, object, something, substance, thing
434 part of: aspect, barb, carcass/carcase, compartment
435 place: asylum, barrier, base, center, depository, depot, dynasty, haunt, haven, heaven, hell, place

436 shape: angle, arc, arch, ball, bead, bend, bulb, bulge, check, circle, coil, cone, contortion, contour, convolution, corner, crescent, curl, curve, disk, dummy, effigy, elbow, globe, kink, knot, labyrinth, lap, line, loaf, loop, maze, mold, orb, orbit, outline, revolution, ring, rod, roll, round, shape, sphere, spiral, streak, wad, wave, wheel, whorl

ATMOSPHERE

437 air: air, atmosphere, billow, blast, breath, breeze, bubble, cloud, draft, dust, effervescence, firmament, fumes, lather, puff, sky, vapor

BUILDINGS, FURNISHINGS, POSSESSIONS

438 arena: aquarium, arena, bazaar, center, coliseum, dump, field, gymnasium, hall, stadium, stage
439 building: abbey, airport, architecture, archives, armory, arsenal, asylum, auditorium, bakery, bank, bar, barn, booth, building, cathedral, clinic, club, conservatory, construction, consulate, court, dock, domicile, edifice, embassy, enclosure, factory, food court, fort/fortress, fortification, framework, garage, gymnasium, hall, hangout, harbor,

hospital, hotel, house, inn, installation, institute/institution, jail, joint, mall, mansion, mill, monastery, motel, museum, nightclub, office, outlet, pavilion, pen, penitentiary, pier, plant, post, prison, pub, rampart, restaurant, ruins, saloon, sanctuary, shop, shrine, stage, store, stronghold, structure, tavern, temple, theater/theatre, tower, treasury, warehouse, wharf

440 building part: aisle, alcove, annex, archway, attic, awning, balcony, basement, bay, belfry, bleachers, booth, buttress, canopy, ceiling, cellar, chimney, chute, closet, column, concourse, corner, corridor, cranny, den, department, dome, door, egress, entrance, entry, exit, fireplace, floor, foyer, gallery, gate, gutter, hall, niche, nook, partition, passage/passageway, pillar, platform, pole, post, prop, recess, screen, stack, stay, step, support, threshold, tower, vent, wall, wing

441 business place: agency, annex, building, bureau, factory, foyer, hall, lobby, office, shop, store, suite, wing

442 foundation: backbone, base, basis, bed, bottom, core, foot, footing, foundation, frame, groundwork, rest, rock, root, seat, stand, support

443 furniture: altar, antique, banister, bed, bench, bleachers, booth, buffet, bunk, bureau, cabinet, can, chair, cot, couch, cradle, crib, cupboard, fireplace, furniture, mirror, partition, pen, perch, pier, platform, podium, pulpit, rack, rail/railing, ramp, screen, seat, stand, table, wardrobe

444 furniture accessory: bedding, bedspread, candlestick, canopy, chandelier, curtain, cushion

445 furniture part: gate, handle, knob, latch, ledge, picket, pivot, post, quilt, screen, shade, shelf, stay, step, support, tap, valve

446 personal item: adornment, album, amulet, backpack, beads, belongings, bracelet, briefcase, brooch, cache, cargo, chain, charm, contraceptive, curio, disguise, doll, equipment, favorite, fetish, gem, glasses, goods, handbag, jewel, jewelry, keepsake, knickknack, lotion, luggage, makeup, memento, novelty, odds and ends, pack, paraphernalia, plaything, pledge, pocketbook, possession, pouch, pride, property, puppet, purchase, purse, relic, resources, riches, ring, savings, souvenir, stuff, subsistence, supplies, support, sustenance, thing/things, toy, trappings, treasure, trifle, trinket, valuable

447 recreation area: cabaret, casino, hangout, landmark

448 room: alcove, apartment, attic, auditorium, bath, bathroom, bedroom, cell, cellar, chamber, den, enclosure, food court, foyer, gallery, hall, kitchen, lobby, loft, office, outlet, parlor, pub, restaurant, room, saloon, sanctuary, shop, shrine, stage, store, tavern, theater/theatre, vestibule

449 workplace: bakery, base, bazaar, brothel, bureau, business, cabaret, café, canteen, capitol, church, clinic, conservatory, consulate, dairy, depot, diner, dive, dump, embassy, emporium, establishment, exchange, factory, farm, field, food court, gallery, garage, hangout, hospital, hotel, inn, jail, joint, lounge, madhouse, mall, market/mart, mill, mine, motel, museum, nightclub, office, outlet, penitentiary, plant, port, prison, pub, restaurant, saloon, shop, store, tavern, treasury, warehouse

CLOTHING

450 accessory: bag, bandanna, belt, boot, buckle, cap, collar, mask, pocketbook, pouch, purse

451 clothing: apparel, armor, array, attire, bathing suit, blouse, cape, cloak, clothes/clothing, coat, costume, disguise, dress, ensemble, finery, frock, garb, garment, gear, glove, gown, habit, hat, jacket, masquerade, nightgown, outfit, pajamas, pants, quilt, robe, skirt, suit, supplies, thing/things, trappings, underwear, uniform, veil, wardrobe, wash, wrap

452 part: collar, crease, crown, patch, pocket, seam, strand

453 state of dress: bareness, try on/try out, undress, wear

FOOD AND DRINK

454 beverage: alcohol, ale, beverage, brew, coffee, draft, drink

455 beverage, alcoholic: beer, liquor

456 change in: curdle, spoil, turn

457 food: appetizer, batter, bite, bread, brew, broth, bun, candy, casserole, confection, cracker, delicacy, diet, dish, doughnut, fare, food, frankfurter, game, grub, hamburger, helping, leftover, loaf, maintenance, meat, morsel, nourishment, nurture, nutrition, pancake, pastry, preserves, produce, ration, refreshment, seasoning, snack, stew, subsistence, supplies, support, sustenance, sweet, tart, treat

458 food part: morsel, nibble, nip, pat, taste, tidbit

459 meal: banquet, barbecue, bite, board, buffet, diet, dinner, fare, feast, meal, picnic, plate, snack, spread, table

460 produced from animal: dish, food, frankfurter, game, grub, hamburger, loaf, meat, stew

461 produced from plant: dish, doughnut, food, loaf, pancake, pastry, preserves, produce, seasoning, stew, sweet

462 quality of: acerbity, alcoholic, baked, crusty, done, eatable, edible, effervescent, mellow, natural, nourishing, nutritious, perishable, rancid, rare, raw, ripe, rotten, salty, short, sour, stale, straight, strong, succulent, sweet, tempting, unappetizing, unsavory, weak, wholesome

MACHINES

463 machine: alarm, apparatus, appliance, brake, catapult, clock, computer, contrivance, device, engine, fan, furnace, gadget, installation, instrument, jet, machine, machinery, mechanism, model, plant, television, terminal, watch

464 **machine part:** anchor, antenna, axle, bank, cog, cushion, engine, gear, pivot, pointer, tap, valve, vent, videocassette, wheel

MATTER. CONDITIONS OF

465 **gas:** gas, jet
466 **gel:** balm, batter, clot, cream, dip, gum, lotion, ointment, ooze, paste, plaster, salve
467 **liquid:** alcohol, broth, cream, drop, enamel, eruption, essence, flow, fluid, froth, fuel, gush, jet, juice, liquid, matter, milk, moisture, ooze, paint, potion, precipitation, solution, spit, surge, sweat, tear/tears, water
468 **liquid part:** cream, drop, froth
469 **physical change:** attrition, bubble, clot, cloud, coagulate, coagulation, collapse, color, congeal, consolidation, contraction, crack, crumble, cry, darken, decay, decompose, degeneracy, degenerate, dehydrate, die, discolor, disintegrate, dissipate, dissolution, dissolve, distend, dry, eat, erode, evaporate, evaporation, exhaust, fade, fester, fizz, flake, flare, flatten, fluctuate, flush, foam, foul, fragment, give, glow, go out, grow, growth, harden, heat, jell, languish, metamorphose, metamorphosis, open, ossify, perspire, putrefy, ravel, redden, revive, rot, rust, settle, sink, spoil, stiffen, tarnish, thaw, thicken, tighten, tire, turn, wilt
470 **solid:** band, bar, barricade, barrier, baton, block, blockade, bolt, brace, bulge, cake, cast, clot, club, clump, cord, dam, deposit, fossil, glass, hedge, hunk, hurdle, ice, jump, lump, matter, mirror, monument, obstacle, obstruction, partition, pill, pole, post, prop, rock, rod, stick, wand, weight
471 **solid part:** arm, attachment, back, bar, beam, block, bolt, branch, chunk, chute, closure, corner, deposit, flap, hinge, hump, hunk, knob, knot, leg, ligature, link, lump, node/ nodule, nub, nugget, outgrowth, patch, plug, powder, projection, protuberance, ridge, rung, seam, slab, sliver, splinter, stake, strap, strip, support, tuft, wedge

MATTER. DIVISIONS OF

472 **chemical:** alkali, alkaline, ammonia, antiseptic
473 **fabric:** apparel, awning, bedding, blanket, canvas, carpet, cloth, fabric, flag, lace, nap, net, pad/padding, pennant, quilt, screen, web, yarn
474 **gem:** gem, jewel, rock, stone
475 **material:** appointment, binding, blanket, brace, cast, cement, cloak, coat, coating, glaze, glue, lace, leash, line, material, pad/ padding, pad, page, paint, paper, patchwork, pipe, plaster, plate, poison, pole, rope, sheet, slip, standard, strand, strap, string, tab, tablet, tack, tag, tape, tether, trim, twine, wash
476 **metallic:** alloy, armor, badge, can, chain, fence, iron, medal, metal, ornament

477 **mineral:** rock, stone
478 **natural element:** blaze, carbohydrate, cell, conflagration, embers, ferment, film, fire, flame, jewel, rock, substance
479 **wood:** beam, board, cane, coffin, fence, framework, log, paddle, perch, picket, pier, pole, post, rack, rail/railing, rod, splinter, staff, stake, stick, timber

MATTER, QUALITIES OF

480 **balance:** awkward, dizzy, even, lopsided, odd, proportionate/proportional, smooth, symmetrical, unbalanced, unequal, uneven
481 **capacity:** brimming/brimful, capacious, capacity, close, compact, congested, crowded, empty, full, packed, spacious, teeming, vacant, void
482 **continuity:** broken, connected, continuous, direct, disconnected, discontinuous, disjointed, dragging, durable, endless, entire, episodic, eternal, fitful, flowing, indelible, intermittent, lengthy, long, never-ending, nonstop, numberless, old, ongoing, patchy, perfect, running, sequential, serial, solid, spacious, spasmodic, straight, through, throughout, together, unbroken, undivided, unending, unfathomable, uninterrupted
483 **density:** airtight, anemic, close, compact, concentrated, congested, cramped, crowded, dense, devoid, fraught, full, hollow, impenetrable, packed, replete, solid, teeming, thick, tight
484 **exteriority:** adjunct, adornment, annex, border, bound/bounds, boundary, brink, buffer, circuit, circumference, compass, confines, corner, cover, crust, cushion, edge, exterior, extreme, extremity, face, fringe, hem, horizon, hull, husk, jacket, lip, margin, membrane, outer, outside, peel, perimeter, periphery, pod, revolution, rim, scale, sheet, shell, skin, skirt, surface, verge
485 **physical:** ablaze, acid, acute, adulterated, aesthetic/esthetic, agile, alimentary, antiseptic, atomic, austere, bad, bald, bare, barren, bearded, beautiful, bland, blank, bloody, blunt, brawny, broken, burning, caustic, clean, combustible, comfortable, corrugated, corrupt, cozy, crippled, crumbly, cuddly, curable, damaged, decayed, decrepit, deformed, deserted, desolate, devoid, dilapidated, diluted/dilute, dingy, dirty, disgusting, disheveled, disordered, disorderly, disorganized, disrepair, done in, drained, drawn, droopy, dusty, effervescent, enervated, erect, exhausted, expectant, exposed, failing, faint, fallow, fat, fatigued, fatty, fertile, filthy, fireproof, fit, flaccid, flaming, flammable, flexible, foamy, forked, formless, foul, fragile, frail, free, fresh, frothy, game, gaping, ghastly, ghostly, gnarled, good, green, grimy, grubby, gruesome, hardy, immature, impaired, impalpable, impervious, impotent, inchoate, inconspicuous, incorruptible, incurable, indistinct, infirm, inflammable, insubstantial, intact, invisible, irreparable, laden, leafy, lean, lifeless, liquid, livable, loathsome, loose, lusty, magnificent, malleable, mangy, marked, material, mature, mean,

messy, mild, miserable, mixed, muddy, muscular, naked, nasty, natural, neat, neutral, noxious, nude, oblique, obtuse, obvious, open, orderly, outstanding, palatial, palpable, palsied, paltry, paralytic, pathetic, peaceful, pendulous/pendent, perfect, perishable, perverted, physical, piteous, pitiful, placid, plain, pregnant, premature, prepared, prickly, primitive, prolific, prominent, prostrate, puffy, pure, putrid, quizzical, ragged, rambling, ramshackle, rank, raw, rocky, rotten, rough, run-down, rusty, savage, scenic, scruffy, seedy, serene, shabby, shady, shaggy, shoddy, slack, sleazy, slimy, slipshod, slovenly, smoky, snug, soft, somber, sorry, speckled, splendid, squalid, stale, stark, sterile, stony, sumptuous, surface, swollen, symmetrical, synthetic, tacky, tense, thin, thorny, threadbare, tidy, tight, topsy-turvy, torn, tousled, trim, unblemished, unbroken, uncomfortable, undeveloped, unfinished, unkempt, untouched, upset, vague, verdant, visual, voluptuous, watery, weak, weary, whole, wizened, wooden, worn/worn-out

486 shape: angular, baggy, beaten, bent, billowy, blunt, checkered, circular, concave, conical/conic, convex, crescent, crooked, curly, curved, deformed, dull, elliptical, flabby, flat, flush, gnarled, grotesque, kinky, malformed, oblong, obtuse, oval, round, serrated, shapeless, sharp, spiral, square, straight

487 similarity: akin, alike, analogous, approximate, closely, cognate, comparable, comparative, conformable, different, equal, equivalent, faithful, homogenous, identical, interchangeable, like, parallel, related, representative, same, seeming, similar, synonymous, tantamount, twin, uniform, virtual, virtually

488 stability: adhesive, adrift, brittle, choppy, doddering, ductile, durable, fast, firm, firmly, fixed, flexible, hard, immobile, immovable, insecure, limber, lithe, motionless, movable, moving, pliable, ramshackle, resilient, rickety, rocky, secure, set, shaky, soft, solid, sound, stable, stationary, steady, sturdy, supple, sure, taut, tenacious, tractable, unbreakable, unstable/unsteady, unwavering, weak, wobbly, wooden, yielding

489 strength: able-bodied, athletic, brawny, breakable, brute, durable, failing, feeble, firmly, flimsy, fragile, frail, full-bodied, hale, hardy, indestructible, indomitable, infirm, invincible, lame, leathery, lusty, mighty, muscular, potent, powerful, powerless, puny, resilient, robust, rocky, rugged, stalwart, stout, strapping, strong, sturdy, tenacious, tenuous, tight, tough, unbreakable, vigorous, weak

490 structure: airtight, airy, amorphous, baggy, bare, beaten, bleak, blind, budding, cavernous, clean-cut, clear, cleft, composite, conglomerate, craggy, crooked, curvaceous, curved, dainty, delicate, depressed, detached, diaphanous, ductile, elastic, emaciated, even, flabby, flat, flush, gaping, gaunt, hollow, incarnate, irregular, jagged, level, limp, oblique, plane, pointed, precipitous, rude,

rugged, scrawny, shapely, sheer, skinny, slender/slim, slight, spare, stout, stringy, svelte, trim, wiry

491 weight: bantam, beaten, buoyant, cadaverous, chubby, chunky, corpulent, dainty, emaciated, ethereal, fat, fine, fleshy, gargantuan, gaunt, giant, gigantic, haggard, heavy, hefty, lanky, lean, light, lightweight, lithe, meager, obese, overweight, plump, ponderous, portable, portly, pudgy, rangy, round, scrawny, skinny, slender/slim, slight, spare, squat, stocky, stout, stubby, svelte, tenuous, thick, thin, trim, underweight, weighty, wiry

TOOLS

492 cleaner: antiseptic, cleanser, deodorant, polish

493 cooking: barbecue, bowl, china, pan, plate, scoop, utensil

494 container: bag, baggage, barrel, basin, basket, bottle, bowl, box, briefcase, bucket, cabinet, cage, can, canteen, carton, case, cask, casket, cell, chamber, chest, coffer, coffin, container, crate, cup, dish, envelope, flask, glass, hamper, jar, jug, keg, kit, luggage, main, package, packet, pan, parcel, portfolio, pot, pottery, pouch, purse, receptacle, store, trunk, vault, vessel

495 cutting: blade, chisel, knife

496 equipment: equipment, gear, harness, installation, kit, outfit, pack, paraphernalia, plant, rig, tackle, trappings

497 grasping: bond, bridle, catch, clasp, curb

498 part: ammunition, hinge, hook, pivot, pointer, round, shot

499 tool: apparatus, ax/axe, blade, brace, broom, brush, cart, chain, chisel, clamp, club, conduit, connection, contrivance, device, drill, gadget, hardware, implement, instrument, key, knife, latch, lock, mop, organ, paddle, pen, pipe, rein, ruler, scoop, tool, utensil, valve, wand, wedge, whip

500 weapon: ammunition, armament(s), arms, artillery, atom bomb, baton, battery, bomb, bullet, catapult, cudgel, defense, explosive, fetters, gun, magazine, missile, nuclear weapon, round

TRANSPORTATION

501 object used for: access, alley, approach, artery, avenue, boulevard, bridge, career, channel, circuit, concourse, conduit, conveyance, course, crossing, detour, diversion, drain, duct, expressway, highway, intersection, line, passage/passageway, path, road, route, street, track, trail, walk, way

502 part, vehicle: anchor, bow, fender, handle, portal, trunk, wheel, wing

503 vehicle: caravan, conveyance, jet, transport, vehicle

504 vehicle, air: airplane, armada, balloon, craft, plane

505 vehicle, land: ambulance, automobile, bicycle, cab, car, cart, coach, hack, model, traffic, truck

506 vehicle, water: armada, barge, boat, canoe, craft, ferry, fleet, sailboat, vessel, yacht

The Planet

GEOGRAPHY

507 city: capital, center, city, town, village

508 geographic division: area, country, county, department, desert, district, dynasty, grounds, kingdom, land, outskirts, province, quarter, region, sector, state, suburb, terrain, territory, town, tract, ward, zone

509 land: abyss, avalanche, backwoods, bank, basin, bay, beach, bed, bluff, bog, canyon, cape, cave, cavern, clay, cliff, coast, compost, court, cove, crevice/crevasse, culvert, dirt, ditch, downgrade, drop, earth, elevation, eminence, excavation, expanse, farm, field, forest, fossil, frontier, garden, geography, glacier, glen, gorge, green, ground, gulf, gully, harbor, hill, horizon, inlet, island, land, landscape, lawn, lot, marsh, meadow, mine, mire, morass, mound, mountain, nature, outlook, parcel, park, pass, peak, pit, plain, plateau, plaza, plot, port, precipice, projection, property, prospect, quagmire, rampart, ravine, reef, ridge, rock, shelf, shore, soil, square, stack, swamp, table, terrain, trench, trough, tunnel, valley, waste, well, wood/woods, yard

510 nation: country, home, kingdom, land, nation, nationality, soil, state

511 planet: cosmos, Earth, environment, globe, moon, nature, planet, soil, sphere, universe, world

512 region: capital, colony, commonwealth, community, quarter, realm, region, reservation, settlement, suburb

513 section: aisle, alcove, backyard, barrier, bend, bed, belt, berth, blank, border, breach, brink, canyon, cavity, cell, chasm, clearance, clearing, cleavage, cleft, corner, country, county, court, crack, cranny, crevice/crevasse, crossing, den, depression, dip, ditch, edge, enclosure, excavation, expanse, fracture, frontier, furrow, gap, green, groove, gulf, gully, gutter, hem, hole, hump, interstice, lawn, leak, ledge, limit, lip, margin, marginal, mouth, niche, nook, notch, opening, outlet, outskirts, parcel, park, pass, patch, pit, plaza, plot, pocket, precipice, projection, prominence, puncture, ravine, recess, rent, repair, ridge, rift, rip, rupture, rut, scratch, shelf, side, sight, slack, slit, slot, split, subdivision, tear, threshold, track, tract, trench, trough, tunnel, vacancy, vacuum, valley, void, ward, well, wrinkle, yoke, zone

514 water: abyss, aquarium, aqueduct, arm, basin, bay, beach, billow, brine, brook, canal, cape, cascade, channel, coast, condensation, course, creek, current, deep, fountain, gulf, harbor, ice, inlet, lake, ocean, pond, pool, race, reservoir, sea, spray, spring, strait, stream, tide, wash, wave, well, whirlpool

HABITATS

515 habitat: abode, asylum, environment, habitat/habitation, harbor, haven, home, lair, land, oasis, paradise, place, premises, property, refuge, sanctuary, settlement, shelter

516 habitat, human: accommodations, address, apartment, asylum, barracks, berth, cabin, camp, castle, cloister, condominium, convent, cottage, domicile, dwelling, element, embassy, environs, estate, flat, grange, grounds, haunt, home, hotel, house, household, housing, hovel, hut, inn, jail, lodge, lodging, madhouse, mansion, monastery, motel, neighborhood, palace, penitentiary, prison, quarters, reservation, residence, resort, retreat, sanctuary, suite, vacancy

517 habitat, rural: barn, belt, burrow, cobweb, conservatory, dairy, desert, desolation, farm, field, forest, garden, grange, grove, jungle, lawn, sanctuary, wilderness/wilds, wood/woods

518 state of: domain, eco-rich, entrench, occupancy, occupation, presence

NATURAL RESOURCES

519 electricity: beam, current, spark

520 energy: electricity, energy, fuel, power

521 expression of energy: blast, blaze, boom, chill, combustion, concussion, crash, discharge, explosion, fire, flame, flash, freeze, noise, thunder

522 natural event: eclipse, effervescence, weather

523 resources: fuel, material, resource, resources, rush, substance

WEATHER

524 object connected with: avalanche, blast, breeze, chill, climate, cloud, cold, deluge, drift, film, flood, flurry, fog, frost, gale, gust, hail, haze, humidity, hurricane, mist, moisture, precipitation, puff, thunder, vapor, weather, wind

525 quality of: breezy, bright, clear, clement, close, cloudy, crisp, dirty, dismal, dreary, fair, fierce, fiercely, filmy, fine, foggy, furious, gentle, gloomy, gusty, hazy, heavy, humid, inclement, mild, misty, muggy, oppressive, overcast, raw, rough, rugged, soft, sticky, stormy, stuffy, sultry, sunny, temperate, tempestuous, thick, threatening, tranquil, tropical, turbulent, violent, wild, windy, wintry

526 type of: blizzard, blow, cloud, downpour, drizzle, earthquake, fog, gale, hail, hurricane, mist, precipitation, puff, quake, rain, shade, storm, tempest, thunder, torrent, tremor

Qualities

ABSTRACT

527 ability: able, accountable, adept, adroit, agile, artistic, awkward, barren, capable, commendable, competent, deft, dexterous, dilettante, disabled, effete, efficient, eligible, executive, experienced, expert, facile, feeble, gifted, good, great, handy, inapt, incapable, incompetent, inefficient, inept, inexperienced, master, masterful, neat, nimble, powerful, powerless, practical, professional, proficient, qualified, raw, ready, rusty, short, skillful, unable, unaccustomed, unfit, unprofessional, unqualified, versatile, versed, veteran, well, wicked

528 achievement: able, abortive, accomplished, ace, artful, attainable, complete, consummate, crack, defensible, done, effectual, efficacious, feasible, fine, finished, flourishing, forward, fruitful, fruitless, futile, gifted, great, obtainable, possible, potential, practical, professional, proficient, prosperous, successful, swimmingly, thriving, triumphant, victorious, well, winning

529 cognitive: academic, affective, afraid, afterthought, alternative, amicable, anathema, appalling, attractive, axiomatic, bad, bag, balm, bane, bearable, belief, black, boring, bothersome, breast, breathtaking, burdensome, cheering, chimera, comforting, comic/comical, comparison, complex, comprehensible, conceivable, considered, considering, corollary, crazy, daydream, deducible, deep, demonstrable, deplorable, depressing, derivable, desirous, detestable, dialectic, difficult, discouraging, disputable, disquieting, distasteful, doleful, doubtful, dream, dry, dull, elusive, enchanting, engrossing, enigmatic/enigmatical, enjoyable, entertaining, equivocal, esoteric, evident, exalted, exciting, exhilarating, explicit, fabulous, fanciful, fantasy, far-fetched, fascinating, favored, favorite, fearful, fetish, figment, flat, fleshly, forerunner, forgotten, foul, frightful/frightening, frightful, funny, ghastly, glad, golden, good, grating, half-baked, hallucination, harbinger, hard, harebrained, harrowing, hazy, heady, heartbreaking, heinous, heretical, hilarious, hopeless, horizon, horrible/horrendous/horrid, humorous, hypnotic, hypothetical, idea, ideal, idyllic, illogical, illusory/illusive, image, imaginable, imaginary, imaginative, impalpable, impenetrable, impression, inadvisable, incomprehensible, inconceivable, incredible, incredulous, indelible, inexplicable, inner, innovation, innovative, inscrutable, inside, insoluble, inspiration, instinct, insufferable, intelligible, interesting, intimate, intolerable, inviting, inward, irrational, irrefutable, irresistible, itch, jocular/jocose/jocund, joy, knotty, knowledge, known, lamentable, leery, left, liberal, liking, limit, loathsome, logical, loose, lucid, luminous, lure, mad, make-believe, mania, manifest, marvel, marvelous, matter, maud-

lin, maze, measurable, memorable, memory, metaphysical, miraculous, mirage, mistaken, mode, monotonous, moving, mysterious, mystic/mystical, naked, nauseous, new age, nondescript, nostalgic, note, noticeable, notion, obscure, observable, obsession, obvious, offensive, opaque, open, painful, palatable, palpable, panorama, pathetic, pedagogic, pedantic, perceptible, perspicuous, pesky, phantom, phenomenon, phobia, pick, piquant, piteous, pitiful, plain, plaintive, poignant, pointless, politically correct, ponderous, portent, precious, preference, premise, premonition, preposterous, presage, problem, problematic, profound, provocative, psychedelic, pure, purposely, putative, puzzling, questionable, radical, rather, reactionary, readable, reasoning, rebellious, recall, recondite, remembrance, reminder, reminiscent, repulsive, reputed, reverie, revolting, rich, ridiculous, right, rosy, rot, sad, satisfactory, scary, scintillating, scream, scrumptious, secret, secular, selection, self-evident/self-explanatory, sensation, shock, sickening, sign, signal, simple, slight, slow, snare, somber, sorry, sound, spectacle, spectacular, speculation, spooky, strain, subconscious, subject, subjective, suggestion, suggestive, surmise, surprise, suspect, suspicion, suspicious, tacit, tall, tame, tangible, taste, tasteful, tedious, temptation, tempting, tenor, theorem, theoretical, theory, thesis, thick, thing, thinkable, thought, thrill, tinge, tiresome, token, tolerable, touch, touching, trace, treat, troublesome, unacceptable, unaccountable, unappetizing, unbelievable, uncertain, uncomfortable, undecided, undesirable, unfathomable, unfavorable, ungodly, unimaginable, uninteresting, unlucky, unnoticed, unpleasant, unpopular, unquestionable, unresolved, unsatisfactory, untold, unwelcome, vague, vapid, vexatious, vile, visible, vision, visionary, whim, whisper, wonder, wonderful

530 commonality: accidental, antiquated, antique, automatic, banal, bourgeois, common, commonly, commonplace, conventional, current, customarily, customary, diffuse, dogmatic, dull, everyday, fair, familiar, frequent, frequently, general, generally, generic, habitual, hackneyed, infrequent, lay, less, little, mainly, much, musty, natural, occasional, occasionally, old, ordinarily, ordinary, pedestrian, popular, prevailing, prevalent, proverbial, public, rare, rarely, regular, routine, spasmodic, stereotyped, stock, traditional, trite, typical, ubiquitous, usual, usually, vulgar, widespread

531 completeness: absolutely, all-out, almost, altogether, blank, bodily, capsule, clean, complete, completely, comprehensive, conscientious, crowning, dead, deeply, deficient, definitive, demonstrative, done, downright, entire, entirely, every, exhaustive, fatal, final, finished, fulfilled, full, full-scale, fully, halfway, incomplete, inseparable, intact, integral, intensive, outright, over, partial, partially, partly, past, perfectly, piecemeal, plenary, practically, pretty, primarily, principally, profound, pure, purely, quite, rank, right, rough, round, rude, sheer, simply, sketchy, sloppy, solid, stark, superficially, sweeping, thorough/thoroughgoing, thoroughly, through, throughout, total, totally, unabridged, unconditional, undivided, unfinished, unmitigated, unqualified, utmost, utter, utterly, wanting, whole, wholly

532 concerned with: about, anxiety, appertain, apply, apropos, barrier, bear on/bear upon, beat, behalf, behind, belong, bother, bug, burden, business, care, challenge, charge, compulsion, concept, concern, consideration, conundrum, craze, debate, difficulty, discovery, disputation, disquiet, distraction, distress, ear, enigma, fancy, fascination, feeling, fixation, focus, guilt, hallucination, hang-up, heed, horror, include, interest, issue, keynote/keystone, matter, mystery, notice, notion, object, obstacle, obstruction, pain, paradox, part, particular, passion, peeve, pertain, pivot, place, presentiment, priority, problem, province, provocation, qualm, quandary, question, refer, regard, relate, reverie, riddle, scruple, subject, suspicion, taboo, temptation, topic, touch, toward/towards, trouble, urge, vision, weight, woe, wonder, worry

533 conformity: acceptable, adequate, admissible, befitting, classic, decent, formal, ideal, mediocre, medium, moderate, ordinary, orthodox, practical, proper, regular, so-so, standard, traditional, typical, unwritten

534 constancy: ambivalent, arbitrary, borderline, changeable, chronic, consistent, constant, continual, fickle, firmly, fitful, fluid, forever, formative, frozen, grim, halting, hesitant, immovable, immutable, impervious, incessant, inconsistent, indecisive, indestructible, indomitable, inexorable, insistent, intermittent, intractable/intransigent, invariable, inveterate, iron, irregular, irrevocable, monotonous, relentless, rigid, same, severe, slippery, solid, spotty, static, staunch, steadfast, steady, tentative, unbending, uncertain, unchangeable, unchanging, unfailing, uniform, unpredictable, unresolved, unstable/unsteady, variable, volatile, wanton

535 definiteness: absolute, absolutely, accurate, aimless, airtight, ambiguous, apparent, apparently, assured, automatic, canonical, categorical, certain, certainly, clean, clean-cut, clear-cut, clearly, close, complete, conclusive, concrete, conscious, controversial, debatable, decided, decidedly, decisive, definite, definitely, definitive, demonstrable, designedly, dicey, discernible, disordered, disorderly, disputable, distinct, doubtful, doubtless, dubious, easily, elective, emphatic, entirely, equivocal, erratic, especial, especially, evident, evidently, exact, exactly, experimental, explicit, express, expressly, factual, final, finally, finite, fixed, flat, formless, graphic, gross, guaranteed, haphazard, hard, hard-core, hesitant, illegible, impeccable, implicit, implied, inalienable, incalculable, incontrovertible, indecisive, indeed,

indefinite, indeterminate, indisputable, indistinct, inevitable, infallible, ingrained, intangible, irrefutable, irresolute, just, legible, limpid, main, marked, markedly, mere, moot, nebulous, necessarily, necessary, official, only, open, outright, overt, palpable, pat, peremptory, perfect, plain, positive, positively, precarious, precise, precisely, pronounced, pure, questionable, random, rank, really, reliable, right, rigid, rigorous, scientific, secure, seriously, set, shaky, sharp, sheer, simply, slippery, sound, specific, straight, straightforward, strict, stringent, strong, sure, surely, tenebrous, tentative, thorough/thoroughgoing, thoroughly, tried, true, truly, trustworthy/trusty, ultimate, unavoidable, uncertain, unconditional, undeniable, undependable, undisputed/undisputable, undoubtedly, unequivocal, unerring, unfailing, unfaltering, unmistakable, unmitigated, unqualified, unquestionable, unsettled, unsure, unwavering, utter, verbatim, very, willful, yes

536 domain: absolute, academic, administrative, agrarian, agricultural, aquatic, athletic, authoritative, autocratic, blessed, bridal, captive, celestial, chemical, city, civic, civil, classical, clerical, commanding, commercial, communal, confederate, constituent, country, democratic, dismal, domestic, drab, earthly, economic, fleshly, foreign, free, global, home, household, industrial, infernal, internal, international, itinerant, literary, local, marine/maritime, metropolitan, military, municipal, national, native, nautical/naval, nomadic, pedagogic, personal, prevalent, psychological, public, religious, social, sovereign, spiritual, technical, terrestrial, theatrical, theological, totalitarian, unearthly, universal, unworldly, urban, widespread, worldly, worldwide

537 effects: advisory, aphrodisiac, awesome, awry, bad, baleful, baneful, beastly, benign, bitter, bleak, bracing, bright, burning, calamitous, cogent, combustible, coming, consequent, convincing, corrective, corrosive, costly, cultural, curative, damaging, deadly, deathly, deep, defamatory, deleterious, demonstrative, desperate, destined, destructive, detrimental, dire, direful, disadvantageous, disagreeable, disastrous, disruptive, done for, doomed, dramatic, drastic, dread, dreadful, eclectic, ecumenical, eerie, effective, effectual, efficacious, embarrassing, emergent, entertaining, epidemic, exigent, expressive, extenuating, faint, fatal, fateful, favorable, favorably, fearful, fecund, fetching, fierce, fiercely, flat, fooled, forbidding, forcible, foreign, formative, formidable, fortunately, foul, fresh, frightful/frightening, fruitful, fruitless, fun, funereal, funny, furious, general, gentle, ghastly, ghostly, gloomy, good, gory, grateful, grave, greatly, grievous, grisly, gross, grotesque, harmful, harmless, harsh, healthful/healthy, heartbreaking, heavenly, helpful, hideous, highly, horrible/horrendous/horrid, hurtful, hypnotic, ill, ill-fated/ill-starred, imperceptible, imposing, incendiary, inconclusive, inconvenient, ineffective/ineffectual, inflammatory, influential, inimical, injurious, insipid, insufferable, intoxicating, invigorating, inviting, jazzy, juicy, lamentable, lethal, lovely, lucky, lurid, macabre, madly, magic/magical, magnetic, malign, memorial, menacing, mighty, mild, monstrous, morbid, mortal, moving, narcotic, nasty, neutral, noisome, nondescript, noticeable, nourishing, noxious, offensive, oppressive, outstanding, painful, pale, penetrating, peremptory, pernicious, persuasive, pesky, pestilent/pestilential, piercing, pleasing/pleasurable, poison/poisonous, prejudicial, prepossessing, productive, profitable, prosaic, provocative, psychedelic, remedial, right, rugged, ruinous, safe, sedative, sensational, sensuous, sharp, sick, sickly, slow, soft, soporific, spectacular, spooky, strong, subtle, telling, therapeutic, tiresome, touching, toxic, trenchant, unbearable, uncanny, uncomfortable, unhealthy, unholy, vapid, venomous, vexatious, virtual, virulent, vivid, weak, wholesome, wicked

538 efforts: ambitious, applied, assiduous, automated, automatic, concerted, conscientious, cooperative, difficult, diligent, employed, gladly, go-ahead, hard, heavy, idle, indolent, industrious, labored, laborious, laden, light, lightly, mindless, murderous, onerous, painstaking, persistent, religious, rugged, running, scrupulous, serious, simple, slack, slow, straightforward, strenuous, studied, studious, thankless, thorough/thoroughgoing, thoroughly, tireless, tiresome, together, torpid, tough, unemployed, unfailing, unfaltering, unflagging, unpaid, unprofessional, unsolicited, untiring, uphill, valiant, vicarious, voluntarily, voluntary, weighty, workable, working

539 existential: alive, almighty, animate, comatose, conscious, consist, dead, deadly, deceased, defunct, dormant, drowsy, dying, extant, extinct, fallen, fatal, immaterial, immortal, inanimate, incarnate, late, lifeless, live, living, lost, luxuriate, missing, nil, nonexistent, obsolete, out, perennial, present, sleepy, soporific, unconscious, vagabond, vital, wakeful

540 forcefulness: almighty, bang, blatant, bloody, brute, cumulative, desperate, driving, dynamic, effective, electric/electrical, fierce, fiercely, hard, insistent, invincible, madly, mightily, mighty, potent, powerful, powerfully, savage, stiff, strong, violent

541 frequency: annual, annually, casual, commonly, daily, hardly, nightly, occasional, occasionally, often, periodic, rapid, rarely, recurrent, scarce, scarcely, seldom, spasmodic, sporadic, uncommonly, usually, yearly

542 inclination: abrupt, accommodating, acquisitive, active, addicted, adrift, adventurous, affirmative, aggressive, agreeable, alive, aloof, ambitious, amicable, anxious, apt, arbitrary, arid, assiduous, base, beastly, benign, blindly, brisk, busy, careful, carefully, careless, casual, characteristic, charitable, cheap, co-dependent, cold-blooded, competitive, conducive, confirmed, conflicting, conservative, conspicuous, constant, contradictory, corporal, corporeal, correct,

crack, creditable, curious, decent, dedicated, deep, deliberate, deliberately, delicate, delicately, demanding, dependable, derelict, designing, determined, detestable, devoted, devout, dictatorial, die-hard, difficult, dilatory, diligent, dim, diplomatic, dirty, discriminating, disinclined, disingenuous, disposed, disputatious, distrustful, dogged, dogmatic, domestic, doubtful, dour, downtrodden, dull, dutiful, dynamic, eager, earnest, earthy, easy, economical, effervescent, effusive, elusive, emotional, emotionless, energetic, engaged, engrossed, enterprising, enthusiastic, equable, equal, equitable, errant, erratic, evasive, even, exact, exaggerated, exciting, execrable, exigent, exotic, expeditious, explosive, factious, fair, fairly, fallible, farcical, fast, fastidious, feckless, ferocious, fervent/fervid, fiery, firm, firmly, flexible, fluid, fly-by-night, fond, foolish, foolishly, forbearing, forced, fortunate, frantic, free, frenzied, fresh, frisky, frolicsome, funereal, gaily, gallant, gay, generous, gentle, genuine, gingerly, given to, gladly, go-ahead, godless, godly, good, gracious, grandiose, grasping, gratuitous, greedy, gross, guarded, guileless, gullible, gutless, gutsy, half-hearted, happily, happy-go-lucky, hard, hardcore, hardened, hard-nosed/hardheaded, harsh, hasty, headlong, heartless, hearty, helpless, hesitant, hospitable, hostile, humane, humanitarian, hurtful, hypocritical, hysterical, idle, ignoble, ignorant, imaginative, immersed, impartial, impassive, impatient, impersonal, impetuous, implacable, improper, improvident, imprudent, impulsive, inadvertent, inane, inattentive, incautious, indefatigable, indifferent, indignant, indiscriminate, indisposed, indolent, indulgent, inelegant, inert, infant/infantile, inflammatory, ingenuous, inhibited, innocent, inoffensive, inquiring, insecure, insidious, insincere, insouciant, intent, intolerant, intractable/intransigent, inventive, involved, irate, jaundiced, jealous, jolly, joyful/joyous, joyless, judicious, kind, kindhearted, kindly, kinky, lackadaisical, lackluster, languid, lax, lenient, levelheaded, lewd, liable, liberal, lifeless, light, lighthearted, live, lively, livid, loath, loud, loving, low, low-key, lukewarm, magnanimous, malevolent, malicious, malign, materialistic, maudlin, mawkish, mean, melodramatic, merciful, merciless, meretricious, methodical/methodic, meticulous, mindful, mushy, naive, narrow, narrow-minded, neat, neglectful, negligent, nerveless, nervous, neutral, nice, nonchalant, noncommittal, noncompliant, nonconformist, nonpartisan, obdurate, objective, objectively, oblivious, obnoxious, obstinate, obtrusive, occupied, odd/oddball, offhand, open, opposed/opposing, opprobrious, optimistic, overconfident, overwrought, pagan, parental, parochial, partial, particular, partisan, passionate, passive, patient, peaceful, peevish, penitent, peppery, perceptive, peremptory, perfunctory, persuasive, perverse, petulant, philanthropic, pigheaded, plastic, playful, pleasant, politically correct, pompous, ponderous, poor, practical, pragmatic, precipitous/precipitate, precise, predictable, premature, premeditated, prepossessed, presumptuous, pretentious, productive, progressive, prolific, prone, prostrate, protective, proud, prudent, pugnacious, punctilious, purposeful, quarrelsome, querulous, radical, raging, rambunctious, reactionary, ready, realistic, rebellious, reckless, reliable, renegade, resigned, resolute, responsive, restive, restless, restrained, rival, romantic, sadistic, safe, sanguine, sappy, savage, scheming, scrupulous, scurrilous, sedate, sedentary, selective, selfish, self-righteous, self-satisfied, sensible, sentimental, serious, seriously, set, severe, short-sighted, silly, simple, sincere, sly, smart, smug, sneaky, sober, solemn, sour, spineless, spirited, spiritless, spiteful, spontaneous, sprightly, square, staunch, steadfast, steady, stern, stout, straight, strenuous, strict, strong, subjective, sunny, susceptible, suspicious, sweet, sympathetic, tame, tardy, temperate, tempestuous, tenacious, tender, tentative, tepid, testy, thoughtful, thoughtless, tireless, together, tolerant, torn, touched, touchy, tough, tractable, tranquil, true, truthful, unaffected, unbiased, uncommitted, uncompromising, unconcerned, unconscious, uncritical, understanding, unfeeling, unflappable, ungodly, unholy, unimaginative, uninspired, unprejudiced, unreliable, unstable/unsteady, unsympathetic, untoward, untrustworthy, unwavering, unwilling, unyielding, vehement, vengeful, venomous, versatile, vicious, vigilant, vindictive, virulent, wakeful, wanton, warm, weak, wholehearted/whole-hearted, willful, witty, wooden, youthful

543 is an attribute of: appear, appearance, belong, quality, savor, seem, sound, trivia

544 manner: abominable, absurd, advisedly, aimless, although, anyhow, anyway, as, beautifully, blah, blind, breezy, broken, brutal, brutally, busily, businesslike, busy, by, calm, camp, casual, catchy, circuitous, circumspect, counter, covert, covertly, cumbersome, delicately, despite, dreary, easy, equable, ergo, even, foolish, foolishly, for, forcibly, forthwith, fortunately, freely, frenzied, frequently, gradual, gradually, grievous, grim, grisly, hastily, helter-skelter, how, however, ill-advised, immediately, immoderate, impersonal, impolitic, inadvertent, incautious, incidentally, indelicate, indirect, individually, instant, instantly, instinctive, intentional, intently, involuntary, irregularly, irresponsible, just, justly, kindly, lackadaisical, largely, leisurely, less, lightly, little, long, low-key, luckily, luxuriate, luxurious, madly, mainly, manual, markedly, mechanical, methodical/methodic, meticulous, mightily, misguided, misspent, moderately, monotonous, more, moreover, most, mostly, much, mutually, narrowly, naturally, necessarily, nevertheless, notwithstanding, objectively, of course, openly, otherwise, outwardly, over, overly, parenthetical, partially, pell-mell, perfectly, perfunctory, per se, personally, piecemeal, poorly, positively, possibly, posthaste, powerfully, presumably, primarily, principally, progressive, promptly,

providing/provided, punctual, purely, purposeless, purposely, quick, rampant, rapidly, rather, readily, recurrent, regardless, regular, relatively, reliable, separately, seriously, sheer, simply, slightly, solely, somehow, still, straight, strategic, subtle, summarily, superficially, swimmingly, though, through, thus, together, too, true, ulterior, unawares, unconditional, unconscious, undercover, underhand, unduly, unexpected, unfair, unforeseen, unusually, unwitting, venomous, very, via, vice versa, violent, virtual, virtually, voluntarily, voluntary, well, while, wrong, yet

545 morality: abandoned, answerable, astray, atrocious, bad, badly, bawdy, black, blasphemous, blue, broad, coarse, common, conscientious, contraband, corrupt, criminal, crooked, culpable, cunning, damnable, damned, dark, debauched, decadent, degenerate, demonic/demoniac/demoniacal, depraved, devilish, diabolic, dirty, disorderly, dissipated, dissolute, drunk, egregious, elevated, equitable, erotic, errant, ethical, evil, faithful, faithless, fast, faultless, fickle, filthy, flagrant, fleshly, fraudulent, frightful, good, gross, guileless, guiltless, guilty, heathen, heretical, holy, honest, ignoble, ill, illegal, illicit, immaculate, immoral, impious, improper, impure, incorruptible, indecent, indefensible, indelicate, inexcusable, infamous, infernal, inhuman/inhumane, innocent, insidious, insincere, Involved, irreproachable, just, justifiable, justly, lawful, lawless, lewd, liable, libidinous, licentious, loose, loyal, mischievous, miscreant, moral, nasty, naughty, nefarious, obscene, off-color, perverted, pornographic, prejudicial, pretended, profane, profligate, promiscuous, racy, rakish, rank, raw, religious, reputable, responsible, right, righteous, rightful, risqué, rotten, sadistic, scandalous, scurrilous, seamy, secret, sensational, shady, shameful, shameless, sharp, sinful, smutty, sordid, sorry, spicy, suggestive, unconscionable, unethical, unfair, unfaithful, ungodly, unjust, unprincipled, unscrupulous, untrue, untrustworthy, unwarranted, upright, upstanding, valid, veracious, vicious, vile, virtuous, vulgar, wanton, wholesome, wicked, wily, worthy, wrong, wrongful

546 necessity: absent, applied, auxiliary, bereft, binding, capital, chosen, collateral, component, compulsory, controversial, deciding, dependent, dire, discretionary, dispensable, elementary, enough, essential, expendable, extra, extraneous, famished, fresh, fundamental, gratuitous, imperative, inadequate, inapplicable, indebted, indispensable, insatiable, insufficient, integral, intrinsic, introductory, lacking, main, mandatory, marketable, meager, necessary, needless, nonessential, obligatory, preparatory, prerequisite, providing/provided, provisional, radical, required/requisite, rudimentary, shy, staple, starving/starved, strategic, superfluous, ultimate, underlying, undue, unduly, unnecessary, vital, wanting

547 normality: aberrant, abnormal, accepted, accustomed, all right, anomalous, astonishing, atypical, average, bizarre, characteristic, classic, common, conventional, curious, customarily, customary, disguised, eccentric, everyday, exorbitant, extreme, familiar, formal, general, generally, habitual, incidental, incongruous, irregular, lowly, macabre, mean, mediocre, medium, middle, middling, moderate, modest, mundane, natural, nondescript, normal, normally, ordinary, pedestrian, plain, prevalent, prosaic, reasonable, regular, routine, stock, temperate, typical, unaccustomed, unimaginative, uninspired, usual

548 **occurrence:** amusing, atrocious, ceremonial, ceremonious, chaotic, chronological, closed, coincident, coincidental, consequent, covert, covertly, crowning, cumulative, cursed, dangerous, dangerously, dark, desperate, didactic, dire, disagreeable, disastrous, disgusting, dismal, dramatic, droll, dull, egregious, embarrassing, empirical/empiric, endurable, enjoyable, ensuing, eventful, exciting, excruciating, exhilarating, exigent, exposed, express, festive, forbidden, forced, forcibly, forthcoming, fortuitous, foul, furious, furtive, futile, gala, gloomy, grateful, grave, grievous, gruesome, hairy, half-baked, hapless, happily, harrowing, hazardous, heavy, hectic, heinous, historic, historical, hopeful, hopeless, humdrum, hurried, ill-advised, ill-fated/ill-starred, ill-timed, imminent, impending, inane, inauspicious, incidental, inconclusive, inconvenient, incurable, indefensible, informal, insane, ironic/ironical, irregularly, jolly, joyful/joyous, joyless, juicy, lackluster, late, limit, lively, low-key, ludicrous, madcap, magic/magical, maiden, memorable, menacing, meritorious, merry, meteoric, miraculous, misguided, misleading, mostly, much, murderous, nasty, nearing, necessary, nefarious, nice, objectionable, offensive, ominous, oncoming, opportune, oppressive, outlandish, over, overall, overblown, overdue, partisan, peaceable, penal, pending, perilous, permissible, pernicious, pessimistic, pleasant, poignant, pointless, poor, predetermined, predictable, premeditated, preposterous, pressing, primarily, privileged, promising, propitious, prospective, prosperous, queer, random, rather, realistic, regardless, regrettable, rewarding, ridiculous, risky, risqué, rollicking, romantic, rosy, routine, ruinous, sad, safe, scary, secretive, secretly, self-evident/self-explanatory, senseless, sequential, shocking, simultaneous, sinful, sinister, slow, someday, somewhat, soon, speedy, spontaneous, studied, stupid, sure, surreptitious, swell, taboo, tacit, tame, tardy, tedious, tender, tense, terminal, thankless, then, thick, threatening, thrilling, through, ticklish, tight, together, tolerable, topsy-turvy, touchy, tragic, trial, trying, tumultuous/tumultuous, ugly, unadvised, unaffected, unauthorized, unawares, unbelievable, uneasy, uneventful, unexpected, unfair, unforeseen, unfortunate, unfriendly, ungodly, unhappy, unholy, unimaginable, unimaginative, uninspired, unintentional/unintended, uninteresting, unlucky, unobtrusive, unreasonable, unrelenting, unsophisticated, unspeakable, untimely,

untoward, untroubled, unwarranted, unwise, unwitting, urgent, venturesome, warlike, weighty, well, whimsical, wholehearted/whole-hearted, woeful, wrong, yet

549 **original:** aboriginal, ancestral, automated, automatic, bastard, born, built-in, classical, colonial, congenital, constitutional, counterfeit, derivative, domestic, essential, ethereal, ethnic, exotic, extraneous, extrinsic, foreign, from, genetic, hereditary, human, humble, ignoble, illegitimate, implicit, imported, inborn/inbred, indigenous, ingrained, inherent, innate, intimate, low, lowly, medieval, misbegotten, mortal, mystic/mystical, native, noble, organic, original, patrician, pedigree, plebeian, preliminary, premature, primary/prime, proper, provincial, racial, radical, royal, rudimentary, secondary, secular, strange, thoroughbred, underlying, unprecedented, vernacular

550 **peculiarity:** ablaze, adaptable, aggressive, airy, ashamed, austere, authoritative, babyish, born, characteristic, clement, closed, contemptible, continent, conventional, corny, craven, cultured, dead, defensive, dreadful, fastidious, forbidding, forceful, forgetful, gawky, gingerly, halting, laborious, laughable, leisurely, protective, punctual

551 **permanency:** abiding, always, chronic, endless, fixed, fleeting, fly-by-night, forever, fugitive, invincible, irrevocable, lasting, makeshift, passing, permanent, perpetual, standing, stationary, stopgap, temporary, tentative, unchanging

552 **probability:** absurd, accidental, alleged, apparent, apparently, attainable, chance, chancy, clearly, conceivable, contingent, convincing, credible, definitely, dicey, disposed, doubtless, dubious, earthly, easily, eventual, eventually, far-fetched, feasible, fishy, fluky, fortuitous, funny, groundless, hardly, hypothetical, ideal, iffy, illusory/illusive, imaginable, immune, implausible, impossible, impractical/impracticable, improbable, inconceivable, incredible, inevitable, insurmountable, intended, invalid, legendary, liable, likely, logical, marvelous, maybe, negligible, odd, off, optional, ostensible, out, outside, perhaps, plausible, possible, possibly, potential, preposterous, presumably, probable, probably, prone, prospective, remote, ridiculous, slender/slim, so-called, sound, specious, subject, tenable, tentative, unlikely, unrealistic, unreliable, vain, viable, workable

553 **repetition:** again, alternate, away, redundant, repeatedly, repetitious

554 **restrictiveness:** absolute, all, autonomous, beyond, binding, bound, bounded, boundless, captive, cloistered, concentrated, conditional, confined, exclusive, exclusively, exclusive of, exempt, finite, fixed, independent, independently, limited, narrow, numbered, oligarchic, permissible, prohibited, prohibitive, provisional, qualified, rampant

555 **social:** accommodating, allied, amorous, antisocial, aristocratic, awkward, bigoted, blameless, brotherly, burlesque, busy, chummy, civilian, clandestine, clannish, close, commemorative, companionable, com-

patible, congenial, conjugal, connubial, co-operative, cultural, dear, defenseless, depressed, difficult, dignified, disadvantageous, disaffected, disgraceful, dishonorable, elite, eminent, engaged, fallen, familiar, forsaken, friendless, friendly, frisky, gentle, homeless, hospitable, hot, important, inelegant, intimate, lonely, lonesome, marital, matrimonial, meddlesome, near, noble, nuptial, platonic, popular, preferred, prestigious, recluse/reclusive, refined, single, sociable, social, sole, solitary, thick, thoughtful, thoughtless, unaccompanied, unapproachable, unmarried, unpopular, unsociable, unwelcome, unworldly, upper, welcome

556 specialization: alone, circumstantial, express, expressly, finicky, respective

557 specificity: accurate, all right, approximate, careless, catholic, certain, closely, correct, definite, descriptive, detailed, exact, exactly, extra, fine, general, just, lax, limited, literal, literally, meticulous, minute, namely, nice, particular, particularly, pat, peculiar, perfect, photographic, precise, precisely, proper, punctilious, random, right, rigorous, rough, rude, sectional, separate, simply, smack, special, specially, specific, specifically, strict, such, superficial, systematic, thorough/thoroughgoing, thoroughly, topical, very, wholly

558 suitability: absurd, acceptable, accepted, accordingly, adequate, adequately, agreeable, all right, ample, amply, applicable, appropriate, apropos, apt, awkward, becoming, befitting, best, conformable, congruous, correct, correctly, cut out for, decent, decorous, de rigeur, discordant, done, down-to-earth, due, duly, eligible, enough, excusable, exorbitant, expedient, extreme, favorable, favorably, feasible, felicitous, fit, fitted, fitting, full-grown/full-fledged, fully, germane, good, granted, happy, improper, inadmissible, inadvisable, inapplicable, inappropriate, inapt, incongruous, incorrect, ineligible, inept, inopportune, just, justifiable, lame, legitimate, livable, meet, nice, objectionable, okay, old, orthodox, passable, pat, perfect, pertinent, presentable, previous, proper, reasonable, relative, relevant, right, rightful, ripe, satisfactory, seasonable, seemly, senseless, sound, sufficient, suitable, tenable, timely, unacceptable, unasked, unbecoming, undue, unfit, unsatisfactory, unseemly, unsuitable, untoward, unwarranted, unworthy, weak, well, wrong

559 transmission: infectious, passable, roundabout

560 usefulness: acting, adequately, barren, broken, convenient, damaged, dead, defective, defunct, dependable, derelict, desert, desirable, desolate, dilapidated, dissipated, drained, effective, effete, efficient, employed, enervated, excessive, exhausted, expedient, extravagant, faded, fallow, faulty, finished, fitted, fixed, fruitful, fruitless, functional, futile, good, handy, helpful, hollow, idle, impaired, impoverished, inactive, ineffective/ineffectual, inefficient, infallible, infertile, instead, instrumental, interim, invalid, irrelevant, leftover, live, living, lost, makeshift, misspent, null, obsolete, occupied, old,

open, operative, outmoded, practicable, practical, prepared, prodigal, productive, propitious, purposeless, ready, residual, ripe, running, salubrious, satisfactory, serviceable, short, spent, stopgap, subservient, subsidiary, substitute, sufficient, superfluous, surplus, trial, tributary, under, unrealistic, usable, useful, useless, user-friendly, utilitarian, vacant, valuable, viable, virgin/virginal, visionary, void, wanting, workable, working, worn/worn-out, worthless, worthwhile

COMPARATIVE

561 compared with: contrast, mark, touch

562 complexity: abstruse, artless, backward, bare, baroque, bilateral, blank, clarion, clear, complex, complicated, crude, cursory, elaborate, elementary, exaggerated, fancy, graphic, intricate, involved, modest, pellmell, simple, simply, sophisticated, tortuous, tricky, ultra, unsophisticated, unwieldy

563 correspondence: akin, allied, applicable, close, commensurate, concurrent, conformable, congruent, congruous, consistent, consonant, duplicate, harmonious, kindred, likewise, moderate, mutual, proportionate/proportional, relative, sympathetic, twin, unanimous, united, unrelated

564 difference: alien, altered, alternative, ambivalent, another, assorted, atypical, avantgarde, averse, bizarre, converse, curious, deviant, diametric/diametrical, different, differently, discordant, discrepant, discrete, disparate, disproportionate, dissimilar, dissonant, distinct, distinctive, divergent, diverse, eccentric, especial, especially, exceptional, extraordinary, fantastic, freakish, funny, heterogeneous, incompatible, inconsistent, individual, inverse, irreconcilable, manifold, miscellaneous, mixed, monstrous, motley, multiple/multifarious, new, novel, odd/oddball, offbeat, opposed/opposing, opposite, other, particular, peculiar, phenomenal, polar, preternatural, quaint, queer, remote, repugnant, rival, separate, several, single, singular, sole, special, specific, specifically, strange, sundry, suspicious, unaccountable, unaccustomed, uncanny, uncommon, unconventional, underground, unearthly, unequal, unfamiliar, unheard-of, unique, unlike, unnatural, unorthodox, unprecedented, unrelated, unthinkable, unusual, variant, varied, various, vice versa, weird

565 difficulty: agonizing, arduous, awkward, complicated, defective, deficient, delicate, demanding, easily, easy, effortless, facile, formidable, grueling, hard, heavy, inaccurate, insurmountable, knotty, laborious, murderous, onerous, ponderous, prickly, rigorous, rugged, serious, seriously, severe, sticky, stiff, tall, taxing, thorny, ticklish, tight, tough, treacherous, troublesome, trying, uphill, weighty, wicked

566 equivalence: alike, alternate, approximately, balanced, commensurate, comparable, comparative, coordinate, corresponding, disproportionate, duplicate, equal, equivalent, even, identical, indistinguishable, level, matching, mock, model, nearly, reciprocal, regular, same, uneven

567 importance: above, august, below, beneath, beneficial, central, chiefly, chosen, climactic/climacteric, collateral, component, conspicuous, costly, dear, dogmatic, elevated, essential, estimable, exclusive, front, fundamental, grave, high, holy, immediate, important, inferior, known, main, majestic, material, meaningful, noteworthy, noticeable, operative, precious, pregnant, primary/prime, prodigious, reputable, salient, second-rate/second-class, significant, special, strategic, telling, top, towering, upper, vital, worthwhile, worthy

568 importance, extreme: acute, basic, basically, beloved, best, better, big, blessed, bright, brilliant, burning, capital, cardinal, celebrated, chief, consequential, considerable, critical, crucial, deciding, dire, divine, dominant, earnest, eminent, exigent, fabled, famous, fatal, fateful, favored, favorite, first, foremost, glorious, grand, great, hallowed, head, historic, illustrious, immortal, influential, invaluable, key, legendary, major, master, momentous, monumental, necessary, notable, noted, noteworthy, oligarchic, outstanding, overriding, paramount, pet, pivotal, praiseworthy, predominant, preeminent, premier, pressing, prestigious, priceless, principal, prominent, renowned, ruling, serious, seriously, signal, significant, sovereign, splendid, star, substantial, supreme, ultimate, uppermost, urgent, valuable, weighty, well-known

569 intensity: acute, almighty, awfully, bad, badly, biting, blatant, bloody, concentrated, considerably, desperate, desperately, drastic, exceedingly, exquisite, extra, extreme, extremely, greatly, harsh, heavy, high, highly, immoderate, insanely, intense, mightily, most, notably, outrageous, powerfully, pretty, profound, quite, severe, severely, sharp, somewhat, stark, stiff, stringent, strong, substantially, terribly, terrific, too, ultra, unconscionable, undue, unduly, unmitigated, unusually, very, violent, vivid, wild

570 negative: adverse, affected, amiss, apocryphal, awful, awfully, bad, baleful, baneful, base, black, conflicting, creepy, cruel, damnable, damned, defiled, degenerate, deleterious, delinquent, deplorable, derogatory, despicable, detrimental, dire, direful, done for, egregious, empty, erroneous, evil, fallacious, false, faulty, fearful, filthy, grim, grisly, heinous, icky, ill, imperfect, inadequate, inauspicious, incendiary, incorrect, incorrigible, inexcusable, infamous, injurious, inordinate, insecure, lame, loathsome, miserable, misguided, misspent, negative, null, objectionable, off, poor, prejudicial, rancid, rotten, ruinous, run-down, seedy, slipshod, squalid, tasteless, terribly, threatening, undesirable, unfortunate, ungodly, unpleasant, unsatisfactory, untoward, unwelcome, upset, weak, weird, worthless

571 negative, extreme: abject, abominable, atrocious, awful, awfully, bad, badly, cursed, lousy, nasty, noisome, outrageous, pernicious, perverse, poorly, regrettable, reprehensible, repugnant, repulsive, rotten, shameful, shocking, shoddy, sick, sickening, sickly, sinister, sordid, terrible, tragic, ugly, unbearable, unfavorable, unhealthy, unsavory, unspeakable, unworthy, vicious, vile, virulent, wicked, woeful, wretched, wrong

572 positive: admirable, affirmative, agreeable, agreeably, all right, angelic, astonishing, auspicious, awesome, beloved, beneficial, benign, best, better, boss, comfort, comfortable, commendable, consummate, cool, decent, delicious, desirable, estimable, exceptional, exemplary, extraordinary, fabulous, fanciful, fantastic, faultless, favorable, favorably, fortunate, fortunately, fun, good, grateful, heavenly, idyllic, incredible, innocuous, interesting, luckily, lucky, magnificent, majestic, meritorious, merry, miraculous, nice, nifty, noble, opportune, pleasant, pleasing/pleasurable, positive, prodigious, profitable, propitious, prosperous, proud, respectable, rewarding, right, salubrious, terrific, thrilling, upbeat, utopian, welcome, well, worthwhile, worthy, yes

573 similarity: akin, alike, analogous, approximate, closely, cognate, comparable, comparative, conformable, different, equal, equivalent, faithful, homogenous, identical, interchangeable, like, parallel, related, representative, same, seeming, similar, synonymous, tantamount, twin, uniform, virtual, virtually

574 superiority: absolute, admirable, advanced, advantage, advisable, all right, all-time, arch, capital, cardinal, champion, chief, choice, chosen, classic/classical, coarse, commanding, correct, crack, dandy, definitive, delectable, delicate, deluxe, dependent, deplorable, dignified, distinctive, distinguished, divine, dominant, elegant, elite, eminently, enviable, especial, especially, excellent, exceptional, exemplary, exquisite, fantastic, fine, first-class/first-rate, flawless, glorious, golden, grand, great, head, holy, ideal, impeccable, imperative, imperfect, imperious, important, imposing, impressive, incomparable, ineffable, infallible, inferior, inimitable, irreproachable, irresistible, junior, laudable, leading, less, lofty, low, luscious, lush, luxuriant, luxurious, majestic, major, marvelous, matchless, maximum, menial, mint, modest, omnipotent, optimum, outstanding, paramount, peerless, perfect, perfectly, pet, phenomenal, poor, poorly, powerful, praiseworthy, predominant, preeminent, preferred, premium, prevalent, primary/prime, principal, privileged, prize, prodigious, proud, rare, remarkable, renowned, reputable, rotten, royal, ruling, sacred, secondary, second-rate/second-class, select, senior, sensational, signal, solemn, spectacular, splendid, stately, striking, stunning, stupendous, sublime, sumptuous, super, superb, superior, superlative, supreme, swell, tasteful, top, transcendent/transcendental, tremendous, ultimate, uncommon, unequaled, unerring, unique, unparalleled, unprecedented, utmost, utopian, venerable, vintage, whole, wonderful

575 unimportance: empty, expendable, frivolous, immaterial, inconsequential/inconsiderable, insignificant, irrelevant, lesser, lightweight, little, meaningless, menial, minor, minute, moderate, needless, negligible, nominal, nonessential, ordinary, peripheral, petty, piddling, puny, remote, second, secondary, side, slight, small, so-so, subject, subordinate, subservient, subsidiary, substitute, tenuous, trifling, trivial, under, unimportant, vain, vapid, worthless

PHYSICAL

576 accessibility: accessible, adaptable, approachable, arcane, available, bereft, blind, broad, clandestine, close, closed, concealed, confidential, confidentially, cryptic, dark, defenseless, depleted, discernible, dissipated, distant, dubious, engaged, enigmatic/enigmatical, esoteric, exposed, flagrant, furtive, glaring, graphic, hidden, hush-hush, illegible, impenetrable, inaccessible, incognito, inconspicuous, inner, inscrutable, inside, insoluble, known, latent, legible, lost, manifest, missing, mobile, mysterious, nameless, obscure, observable, obtainable, occult, open, optional, out, outward, outwardly, passable, patent, perceptible, permeable, plain, possible, private, privy, prohibited, pronounced, public, rare, ready, recondite, reserved, secluded, secret, stealthy, strange, tight, ulterior, unapproachable, undercover, underground, unheard-of, unidentified, unknown, unseen, usable, user-friendly, vigilant, visible, visual, weak, willing

577 accompaniment: abandoned, again, alone, along, also, and, attendant, complementary, concomitant, connected, deserted, each, en masse, en route, ensemble, et cetera, except, furthermore, incidental, including, isolated, joint, jointly, left, lone, mutually, odd, one, only, parenthetical, per se, personally, reciprocal, related, separate, separately, single, singly, singular, sole, solely, solitary, stranded, unaccompanied, under, unique, united

578 age: adolescent, advanced, afresh, aged, ancient, antediluvian, antiquarian, antiquated, antique, archaic, big, callow, childish, contemporary, crude, doddering, elder, elderly, fresh, full-grown/full-fledged, green, immature, immemorial, inchoate, infant/infantile, innovative, junior, juvenile, late, mature, medieval, mellow, mint, modern, modish, musty, new, newfangled, novel, old, older, old-fashioned, original, originally, outdated/out-of-date, outmoded, passé, puerile, quaint, recent, ripe, senior, stale, tender, undeveloped, up-to-date, vintage, young, youthful

579 appearance: adorable, aesthetic/esthetic, artistic, attractive, beautiful, becoming, comely, cosmetic, crisp, cute, dapper, deathly, decorative, delectable, desirable, disheveled, dressy, elegant, exquisite, fair, fancy, fashionable, fetching, fine, flawless, glamorous, glorious, good-looking, gorgeous, graceful, grotesque, handsome, hideous, homely, imperfect, irresistible, lovely, ornamental, ornate, picturesque, plain, presentable, pretty, repulsive, resplendent, scenic, seductive, statuesque, striking, stunning, stylish, symmetrical, ugly, unbecoming, unsightly

580 deformity: blemish, blot, blotch, chip, contortion, defect, deformity, dent, distortion, fault, flaw, frailty, freak, scar

581 direction: about, across, adrift, along, around, astern, astray, at, away, awry, backward, below, centrifugal, circuitous, counter, crooked, crosswise/crossways, devious, diagonal, diagonally, direct, directly, due, erect, errant, erratic, forked, forth, forward, haphazard, horizontal, indirect, inward, lateral, left, north, outgoing, outward, parallel, perpendicular, plane, plumb, ramble, right, rotary, roundabout, sharp, sheer, sideways, sinuous, snaky, steep, straight, through, tortuous, uphill, upright, vertical, wide, winding, wry, zigzag

582 genuineness: abstract, actual, actually, airy, alias, allegorical, apocryphal, apparent, apparently, artificial, arty, assumed, authentic, authoritative, baseless, believable, bogus, certain, circumstantial, colored, concrete, conjectural, counterfeit, credible, dark, deceptive, de facto, delusive, dogmatic, dreamy, effective, empirical/empiric, enigmatic/enigmatical, erroneous, ersatz, esoteric, ethereal, extant, factual, fake, fallacious, false, fantastic, far-fetched, feigned, fictitious, figurative, frank, fraudulent, genuine, good, groundless, hard, heartfelt, historical, hypothetical, illusory/illusive, imaginary, imitative, inaccurate, indisputable, intangible, invisible, irrefutable, just, legitimate, made-up, magic/magical, make-believe, matter-of-fact, metaphysical, mock, monstrous, mystic/mystical, mythical/mythological, nominal, nonexistent, occult, ostensible, ostensibly, palpable, phony, physical, plastic, positive, positively, pretended, pseudo, quack, quasi, quite, real, realistic, really, right, sham, sincerely, sound, specious, spiritual, spurious, substantial, supernatural, suspect, synthetic, tangible, temporal, true, truly, unearthly, unfounded, unnatural, unreal, unthinkable, untrue, unvarnished, unworldly, utopian, valid, veracious, veritable, visionary, wholehearted/wholehearted, worldly, wrong

583 location: aboard, about, abroad, absent, absentee, advance, aerial, agricultural, aground, airy, alone, ashore, astride, at, beached, center, central, civic, civil, cloistered, coastal, diffuse, down, everywhere, exterior, external, fixed, forward, from, front, here, horizontal, inside, insular, interior, isolated, lateral, leafy, left, lonely, low, middle, north, off, out, outdoor, outer, outlying, outside, outward, over, overseas, pastoral, penal, peripheral, perpendicular, polar, populous, posterior, precipitous, present, private, prominent, prone, prostrate, quiet, rear, remote, roomy, rural, rustic, secluded, sideways, solitary, somewhere, stray, surface, through, top, topical, uncomfortable, underground, upper, uppermost, upright, upside-down, vertical, void, where/wherever, wide, wild, withdrawn

584 **movement:** ambulatory, billowy, brisk, centrifugal, clumsy, destined, fleet, flowing, fluent, flying, frozen, fugitive, gawky, graceful, graceless, heavy, immobile, inactive, indolent, inert, itinerant, languid, leisurely, lethargic, lifeless, lightly, liquid, listless, lithe, lumbering, maladroit, migrant/migratory, mobile, motionless, movable, moving, nimble, nomadic, nonstop, outgoing, passive, pendulous/pendent, peripatetic, portable, quiet, restless, rotary, roundabout, running, sedentary, slack, slow, sluggish, speedy, stagnant, static, still, vibrant, winding

585 **order:** advance, advanced, alphabetical, avant-garde, bottom, center, chronological, collective, confused, consecutive, direct, disjointed, disorganized, first, following, fore, foregoing, foremost, former, formerly, forward, front, immediate, incipient, indiscriminate, initial, intermediate, internal, introductory, last, lastly/last, latter, leading, least, maiden, mean, median, methodical/methodic, next, older, on, onward/onwards, orderly, original, originally, past, pell-mell, pioneer, posterior, preceding, preliminary, premier, preparatory, previous, primary/prime, regular, second, senior, sequential, serial, straight, subsequent, subsequently, succeeding/successive, systematic, tidy, together, topsy-turvy, uttermost

586 **relative placement:** about, abreast, adjacent, adjoining, after, ahead, ajar, almost, along, alongside, amid/amidst, among, apart, approximate, around, aside, askew, behind, below, beneath, beside, between, bottom, by, close, cockeyed, contiguous, convenient, direct, down, elsewhere, en route, far, faraway, farther, farthest, furthest, gone, halfway, handy, hard, immediate, lower, near, nearby, next, on, overhead, parallel, preceding, toward/towards, under, underneath, within, without, wrong, yonder

587 **safety:** chancy, chary, perilous, precarious, sacred, safe, secure, treacherous, unreliable, unsafe, unsound, vulnerable, weak

588 **speed:** agile, cursory, expeditious, express, fast, fleet, gradual, gradually, hastily, hasty, headlong, hurried, instant, instantly, posthaste, precipitous/precipitate, quick, rapid, rapidly, slow, snappy, speedy, swift, swiftly/swift, whirlwind

589 **style:** adorable, bald, baroque, beautiful, becoming, bedraggled, black, bland, bold, bourgeois, brassy, casual, cheap, chic, class, classical, classy, conglomerate, contemporary, cosmopolitan, country, crude, cultural, cursory, dashing, distasteful, dowdy, dressy, elegant, exquisite, fashionable, fitted, flamboyant, flashy, floral, florid, flowery, formless, gaily, garish, gaudy, gay, generous, glamorous, glaring, gorgeous, graceful, grand, grandiose, graphic, homely, hot, humble, improvised, incognito, informal, ingenuous, innovative, jazzy, kinky, lavish, loud, lovely, lush, luxuriate, luxurious, marked, mean, mere, meretricious, modern, modish, naked, neat, new, newfangled, obsolete, old-fashioned, opulent, orderly, original, ornamental, ornate, ostentatious, outdated/out-of-date, outmoded, palatial, passé, picturesque, plain, plush, popular, posh, pretentious, prevalent, provincial, quaint, quiet, refined, regal, resplendent, rich, rustic, salty, scruffy, shapeless, sharp, showy, simple, slack, sleazy, slipshod, smart, snappy, sophisticated, splendid, spruce, stale, stately, statuesque, stylish, swank/swanky, swish, tacky, tasteful, tasteless, tawdry, tousled, trendy, unbecoming, untidy, unworldly, up-to-date, vogue

Senses

ASPECTS OF PERCEPTION

590 **physical:** burn, caress, hear, see, smell, taste, touch

AUDITORY

591 **attribute of hearing:** audible, deaf, distinct
592 **attribute of noise:** blatant, brassy, cacophonous, clarion, discordant, dissonant, grating, loud, noisy, piercing, quiet, raucous, rough, shrill, soft, strident, vociferous
593 **attribute of noise-making:** dumb, mute
594 **attribute of sound:** aloud, audible, blatant, brassy, cacophonous, clarion, deep, discordant, dissonant, dull, faint, full, gentle, grating, gruff, guttural, high, hoarse, hollow, husky, loud, low, mellow, melodious/melodic, muffled, musical, noiseless, noisy, off-key, piercing, quiet, raucous, resonant, rich, rough, round, shrill, silent, still, strident, subdued, sweet, tranquil, untroubled, vocal, vociferous, weak

595 **audible object:** acknowledgment, air, alert, anthem, aria, arrangement, ballad, bang, bell, blast, boom, buzz, carillon, carol, chant, clamor, clank, clap, clatter, click, clink, clump, crack, crash, delivery, din, dirge, discord, dissonance, drone, echo, gasp, groan, growl, gurgle, harmony, hiss, howl, hymn, inflection, jangle, melody, murmur, music, noise, peal, pop, psalm, refrain, report, rhyme, rhythm, ring, roar, roll, rustle, scream, shout, shriek, slam, song, sound, strain, thunder, tick, tune, yell
596 **hearing:** attend, bug, commiserate, eavesdrop, hear, listen, mind, monitor, regard
597 **sound perception:** hearing

OLFACTORY

598 **attribute of odor:** aromatic, astringent, fetid, fragrant, high, malodorous, musty, noisome, odorless, odorous, putrid, rancid, rank, sharp, smelly, stale, strong, sweet

599 object that can be smelled: aroma, bouquet, breath, incense, odor, perfume, scent, smell, stench, stink, tang, whiff

600 odor: fragrance, fumes, incense, perfume, reek, smell, stench, stink, tang

601 olfactory perception: breathe, inhale, nose, scent, smell, sniff, whiff

602 smelling: scent, smell, sniff, whiff

TACTILE

603 attribute of dryness: absorbent, arid, balmy, clammy, damp, dank, dry, filmy, fluid, humid, juicy, liquid, misty, moist, muggy, musty, oily, parched, sloppy, soggy, thirsty, watery, wet, wizened

604 attribute of hardness: adamant, concrete, downy, erect, firm, firmly, flaccid, hard, impenetrable, impervious, inflexible, iron, limp, mushy, permeable, plastic, rocky, solid, stiff, supple, taut, tender, tense, unbending

605 attribute of temperature: ablaze, arctic, balmy, benign, biting, bland, boiling, bracing, brisk, broiling, burning, chill, chilly, close, cold, cool, cozy, crisp, febrile, feverish, fiery, freezing, frigid, frosty, frozen, glacial, heated, hot, icy, lukewarm, polar, sultry, sweltering, tepid, torrid, tropical, warm, wintry

606 attribute of texture: abrasive, adhesive, beaten, bias, breakable, brittle, bushy, coarse, corrugated, cozy, craggy, creamy, crisp, crumbly, crusty, dainty, delicate, diaphanous, diluted/dilute, downy, elastic, ethereal, fibrous, filmy, fine, firm, fleecy, flimsy, fluffy, fuzzy, gauzy, gelatinous, glassy, glossy, gooey, gossamer, greasy, gritty, icy, irregular, jagged, lacy, leathery, lucid, matted, mottled, muddy, mushy, oily, opaque, paper, pasty, permeable, pointed, porous, powdery, rough, rugged, sheer, silky, sleek, slick, slippery, smooth, soft, spongy, sticky, tenacious, tender, thick, thin, threadbare, transparent, uneven, viscous, yielding

607 dryness: drought, evaporation, humidity, wet

608 tactile perception: feeling, itch, touch

609 tactile quality: excruciating, numb

610 temperature: cold, fever, frost, glow, heat, temperature

611 texture: consistency, delicacy, feel, fiber, finish, gloss, grain, mesh, nap, polish, texture

612 touching: brush, caress, dab, feel, finger, graze, grope, handle, itch, lick, manipulate, meet, monkey, nestle, nudge, nuzzle, pat, paw, pet, reach, stroke, tickle, tingle, touch

TASTING

613 attribute of taste: acerbity, acid, acidulous, acrid, appetizing, astringent, bad, bitter, bland, corrupt, delectable, delicious, distasteful, done, eatable, edible, full-bodied, hot, insipid, luscious, palatable, peppery, piquant, poignant, pungent, racy, rancid, rich, robust, salty, savory, scrumptious, sharp, sour, spicy, succulent, sweet, tart, tasteless, tasty, unsavory

614 taste: bite, bitterness, flavor, savor, spice, tang, taste, zest

615 taste perception: taste

616 tasting: bite, gargle, sample, savor, taste

VISUAL

617 attribute of brightness: ablaze, beaming, bold, bright, brilliant, clear, colorful, crystal, dark, dim, dingy, drab, dull, dusky, effulgent, faded, faint, glaring, gloomy, glossy, glowing, incandescent, lackluster, light, lucid, luminescent, luminous, lustrous, misty, murky, nebulous, obscure, opaque, radiant, resplendent, scintillating, shady, shiny, sunny, tenebrous

618 attribute of color: amber, anemic, beige, black, blond/blonde, bloodless, blue, bold, bright, bronze, brown, brunette/brunet, buff, cadaverous, cherry, clear, colored, colorful, colorless, crystal, dappled, dark, deathly, deep, drab, dusky, faded, fair, florid, flushed, gaudy, gay, gloomy, glowing, gold/golden, gray/grey, green, iridescent, jet, light, livid, mauve, milky, motley, mottled, mousy, muddy, multicolored, murky, neutral, opaque, orange, pale, pastel, pasty, peaked, pearly, purple, red, rich, rosy, ruddy, sable, sallow, sanguine, silver, smoky, soft, speckled, strong, swarthy, tan, translucent, transparent, verdant, vibrant, vivid, wan, watery, white, yellow

619 attribute of vision: appreciable, blind, clear, concealed, conspicuous, discernible, disguised, distinct, fuzzy, glaring, glassy, graphic, impalpable, invisible, lucid, myopic, prominent, pronounced, visible, visual

620 brightness: dark, darkness, gleam, glitter, gloom, gloss, glow, illumination, light, luster, night, overshadow, pall, polish, radiance, radiate, shade, shadow, sheen, shimmer, shine, splendor

621 clean: grimy, grubby, hygienic, immaculate, impeccable, impure, mangy, messy, neat, pure, refined, sanitary, slimy, sloppy, slovenly, spotless, stagnant, sterile, straight, tidy, trim, unblemished, unclean, unkempt, untidy, untouched

622 color: auburn, beige, blush, cast, color, complexion, decor, fade, flush, gloom, glow, hue, orange, pigment, pink, purple, red, shade, shadow, stain, stripe, tan, tinge, tint, tone, yellow

623 looking: attend, avert, browse, contemplate, contemplation, dip into, eye, face, fix, focus, gape, gawk, gaze, glance, glare, glimpse, glower, heed, inspect, leaf, leer, look, lookout, look out, mind, monitor, patrol, peek/peep, peer, point, pry, regard, scan, scout, scrutinize, scrutiny, skim, snoop, spy, squint, stare, view, watch

624 occurrence of light: beam, blink, bolt, cast, eclipse, flash, flicker, glance, glare, gleam, glimmer, glisten, glitter, glow, halo, illuminate, illumination, light, lighten, ray, reflect, shimmer, shine, spark, sparkle, spotlight, twinkle, wink

625 picture: arms, caricature, cartoon, chart, design, diagram, drawing, emblem, engraving, facsimile, figure, handwriting, impression, imprint, layout, map, model, outline, pattern, picture, plan, portrait, profile, reproduction, scene, scheme, silhouette, sketch, table, tableau

626 seeing: behold, distinguish, eye, gaze, make out, mark, meet, note, notice, observe, perceive, regard, remark, see, sight, spot, view, witness

627 visibility change: blur, clear, dim, fog

628 visible object: acknowledgment, alert, aspect, beacon, beam, blaze, buoy, cue, glance, glare, hallmark, halo, handwriting, light, mirage, model, outlook, panorama, prospect, ray, reflection, scene, scenery, sparkle, streak, track, view

629 visual perception: blindness, perspective, sight, vision

States

ABSTRACT

630 ability: ability, agility, artifice, artistry, awkwardness, bent, can, capability, capacity, competence, dexterity, disqualification, ease, efficiency, eloquence, endowment, expertise/expertness, facility, faculty, feebleness, flair, gift, hand, handicraft, head, inability, inclination, knack, know-how, league, literacy, master, mastery, mind, niche, performance, power, productivity, proficiency, promise, propensity, prowess, qualification, qualify, readiness, skill, talent, technique, telepathy, touch, trick, turn

631 accessibility: access, circulation, concealment, privacy, seclusion, secrecy, secret

632 be ahead: ahead, first, front, uppermost, winning

633 behavior: abandon, abstinence, acquit, acrimony, act, adultery, affectation, airs, alacrity, amenity, antithesis, apathy, arrogance, asperity, audacity, austerity, balance, barbarism, barbarity, bearing, behave, behavior, benevolence, betrayal, bitterness, bluster, brass, bravery, carriage, carry on, chastity, cheek, chivalry, coarseness, compassion, complaisance, condescend, condescension, condolence, conduct, cordiality, correctness, corruption, countenance, courage, courtesy, cruelty, culture, custom, cut, debauchery, deceit, decency, decorum, deference, defiance, demeanor, deportment, desperation, detachment, diffidence, diplomacy, dishonesty, disloyalty, disobedience, disregard, disrespect, dissidence, dissipation, distance, do, eagerness, earnestness, ebullience, effervescence, effrontery, endurance, enthusiasm, equanimity, equilibrium, etiquette, excess, excitement, exuberance, face, faithfulness, faithlessness, fanaticism, feint, fervor, firmness, flightiness, flippancy, folly, foolishness, forbearance, formality, freedom, frivolity, fuss, gall, geniality, grace, grit, grovel, haughtiness, heroism, honesty, honor, hostility, humility, hypocrisy, impatience, impertinence, indecency, indiscretion, insolence, irreverence, kindness, laziness, lethargy, license, lunacy, manhood/womanhood, manner, manners, mercy, misbehave, misbehavior, mischief, misconduct, misdeed/misdemeanor, moderation, modesty, mutiny, naïveté, nonconformity, nonsense, obedience, oblivion, observance, order, ostentation, outburst, pep, perseverance, piety, poise, polish, pose, precaution, presumption, pretense, pretension, pride, propriety, prowess, purpose, quarter, radiance, rancor, react, reaction, readiness, rebel, rebellion, refinement, refusal, regress, reserve, responsibility, restraint, scene, self-control, serenity, show, simplicity, sincerity, sophistication, spunk, steam, submission, sympathy, tact, temerity, temperance, treachery, treat, treatment, valor, veneer, vitality, zip

634 commonality: diffusion, frequency, ritual

635 completeness: bulk, complement, culmination, deficiency, entirety, finality, fullness, integrity, whole

636 conformity: adequacy, adhere, archetype, cohere, fidelity, par

637 constancy: consistency, constancy, continuance, instability, monotony

638 definiteness: accuracy, ambiguity, certainty, clarity, correctness, exactness, finality, precision, rigor, truth

639 exist in a condition: blame, condition, existence, state

640 extension: addition, continuation

641 forcefulness: clasp, clutches, dictatorship, efficacy, force, gravity, impact, impetus, impulse, intensity, kick, might, momentum, muscle, power, pressure, push, swamp, violence

642 made of: compose, have, inclusion, manifestation

643 make up: accompany, comprise, consist of, cover, form, include, make up

644 mannerism: air, attention(s), austerity, characterize, clemency, courtesy, custom, earmark, entity, fashion, foible, forgetfulness, habit, idiosyncrasy, manner, mannerism, mark, mien, mode, propriety, purpose, quirk, regard, trait, vigilance

645 morality: abandon, atrocity, blasphemy, coarseness, conscience, corruption, craft, debauchery, decadence, degeneracy, delinquency, depravity, dirt, disservice, enormity, environment, equality, equity, ethics/ethic, evil, excess, fairness, faithfulness, faithlessness, falsity, favoritism, fraud, good, goodness, good will/goodwill, greatness, guile, guilt, guise, holiness, honesty, honor, ideals, imposition, imposture, indecency, infamy, infidelity, infraction, iniquity, injustice, innocence, justice, liability, license, loyalty, misbehave, misbehavior, mischief, misconduct, misdeed/misdemeanor, morality, morals, obligation, obscenity, outrage, principle/principles, probity, profanity, prostitute, responsibility, right, sacrilege, scandal, scheme, score, segregate, sin, transgression, treachery, treason, trespass, trick, trickery, trust, underworld, validity, veracity, vice, virtue, wrong

646 **necessity:** absence, behoove, call for, dearth, defect, deficit, demand, do, do without, drought, enough, entail, essential, exigency/exigence, frill, go without, have, lack, mainstay, must, necessitate, necessity, need, obligate, oblige, paucity, prerequisite, provide, qualification, require, requirement/requisite, reservation, shortage, specification, subsistence, take, void, want

647 **normality:** aberration, abnormality, anomaly, average, eccentricity, gauge, norm, rule, rut

648 **origin:** ancestry, birth, bottom, counterfeit, cradle, derivation, derive from, emanate, emanation, extraction, femininity/feminine, fountain, germ, hail, head, heredity, heritage, home, inception, issue, masculinity/masculine, matrix, mortality, origin, parent, precursor, root, seed, sex, source, spring, start, stem, threshold

649 **permanency:** constant, fixed, forever, permanent, perpetual, unchanging

650 **probability:** absurdity, chance, contingency, credibility, eventuality, liability, likelihood, must, odds, possibilities, possibility, potential, probability, promise, tend

651 **range:** area, breadth, circulation, compass, continuation, degree, diffusion, dissemination, dissipation, distance, diversity, expanse, extent, gamut, go, jurisdiction, latitude, length, matter, overrun, panorama, play, radius, range, reach, realm, room, run, scale, scope, spread, stretch, sweep

652 **restrictiveness:** abbreviation, abridgement, autonomy, bar, block, blockade, bondage, captivity, constraint, curb, exemption, flexibility, prohibition, qualification

653 **specialization:** alone, circumstantial, express, precise, select

654 **specificity:** accuracy, correctness, exactness, model, point, precision, property, rigor

655 **style:** appeal, approach, artistry, behavior, clash, classic, classicism, cultivation, cut, dash, discrimination, elegance, fad, fashion, finish, frill, frippery, genre/genus, glamour, glitter, grace, look, mode, ostentation, polish, pomp, popularity, rage, refinement, simplicity, sophistication, splendor, style, taste, tone, touch, trend, vogue

656 **suitability:** absurdity, adequacy, agree, awkwardness, blend, consistency, correctness, do, expediency/expedience, fitness, propriety, satisfy, serve, suit

657 **tendency:** acrimony, alacrity, animation, aptitude, atrocity, care, charity, cultivation, dedication, defiance, determination, devotion, diligence, direction, discretion, dishonesty, disinclination, eagerness, earnestness, effervescence, enterprise, enthusiasm, equity, face, fairness, fashion, fervor, finesse, gallantry, generosity, grace, guile, gusto, guts, heat, hospitality, hostility, humility, hurry, hypocrisy, idleness, impatience, incline, indifference, indignation, indulgence, inertia, inhibition, initiative, kindness, liability,

mind, moderation, naïveté, neglect, nervousness, nonconformity, patience, pity, posture, presence, pretension, rage, resignation, resolution, restlessness, seriousness, sincerity, streak, tenacity, tendency, thing, tolerance, trend, trick, truth, verge, vice, vigilance

658 **usefulness:** agency, agent, convenience, efficiency, employment, expediency/expedience, good, help, makeshift, malfunction, medium, operation, practice, purpose, resource, serve, service, surplus, usage, use, utility, value, wear

COGNITIVE

659 **goal:** aim, ambition, aspiration, destination, dream, end, function, goal, intent/intention, mark, meaning, mission, object, objective, pleasure, point, prize, purport, purpose, quarry, reason, resolve, sake, target, taste, victim, will

660 **plan:** angle, approach, architecture, calculation, channel, chart, chicanery, collusion, complicity, concoction, conspiracy, contrivance, craft, deceit, design, device, diagram, diet, dispensation, disposition, dodge, draft, expediency/expedience, expedient, feint, form, gambit, game, gimmick, groundwork, idea, innovation, intrigue, invention, itinerary, layout, machination, maneuver, manner, method, move, plan, plot, policy, program, purport, purpose, route, scenario, schedule, scheme, shift, stratagem, strategy, tactics

661 **reason:** alibi, angle, asset, basis, benefit, blame, boon, cause, confirmation, essence, essential, excuse, explanation, footing, fuel, goad, grounds, groundwork, hypothesis, idea, impetus, incentive, inducement, inspiration, justification, keynote/keystone, lesson, meaning, message, motive, nub, occasion, origin, pretext, rationale, reason, root, sake, solution, spring, spur, stimulant, stimulus, whim

662 **request:** command, demand, desire, directive, edict, entreaty, petition, plea, prayer, proposal, proposition, query, recall, request, requisition, suit

COMPARATIVE

663 **complexity:** complexity, exaggeration, labyrinth, simplicity, snarl

664 **correspondence:** accord, answer, approximate, balance, clash, community, conform, conformity, connection, consonance, consort, correspond, correspondence, double, dovetail, duplicate, fit, flatter, go, go together/go with, harmonize, harmony, identity, jibe, likeness, make, match, mate, proportion, resemblance, resemble, square, sympathy, twin, union, unison, unity

665 **difference:** aberration, antithesis, assortment, contradict, contradiction, contrast, controversy, converse, depart, departure, deviate, deviation, differ, difference, digression, disagree, disagreement, discrepancy, disharmony, disparity, disproportion, dissension, dissent, dissimilarity, dissonance, distinction, diverge, divergence, diversity, eccentricity,

exception, foil, gap, gradation, grade, inequality, innovation, miscellany, multiculturalism, mutation, novelty, nuance, oddity, opposite, opposition, peculiarity, rent, reverse, shade, variance, variant, variation, variety, wander

666 **difficulty:** abomination, awkwardness, conundrum, deficiency, delay, disadvantage(s), downside, drawback, enormity, entanglement, facility, handicap, hindrance, hitch, impediment, labyrinth, limitation, matter, misery, muddle, obstacle, obstruction, plight, pressure, problem, quagmire, question, restraint, restriction, rigor, rub, shortcoming, snag, snarl, spot, task, tax, tribulation, trouble, vice, wall

667 **equivalence:** alternate, amount, balance, border on, cancel, cohere, coincide, coincidence, come up to, copy, correlation, counterpart, disproportion, duplicate, equal, equality, equate, equivalence, equivalent, image, make, match, model, par, parallel, parity, rival, sameness, tie

668 **importance:** accent, aspect, bearing, beauty, berth, best, celebrity, character, cipher, consequence, core, count, cream, crux, dignity, dominance, element, elevation, eminence, emphasis, essence, flower, forefront/foreground, fundamental, glory, grandeur, gravity, greatness, height, honor, import, importance, kernel, key, lead, magnitude, mark, matter, moment, name, nobility, nothingness, overshadow, peak, prestige, pride, priority, prominence, quality, renown, sense, seriousness, significance, signify, situation, spotlight, stature, status, stress, stuff, style, tedium, top, trifle, value, weight, zero hour

669 **intensity:** intensity, strength, violence

670 **similarity:** affinity, agree, analogy, community, consistency, equivalence, equivalent, identity, likeness, parallel, parity, replica, reproduction, resemblance, resemble, sameness, second, similarity, tune, twin

671 **superiority:** ascendancy/ascendency, distinction, elegance, eminence, excel, excellence, ideal, imperfection, importance, jewel, marvel, miracle, paragon, perfection, pick, power, precedence, preponderance, prodigy, rank, seniority, superiority, victory

OF BEING

672 **abstraction:** manifestation, oblivion

673 **aura:** air, allure, ambience, appeal, appearance, aspect, atmosphere, attribute, aura, background, being, blaze, celestial, charm, chorus, climate, cultivation, dash, dump, ease, environment, feel, feeling, flavor, glory, glow, kind, look, medium, milieu, monotony, mood, orbit, presence, quiet, romance, semblance, serenity, sign, solitude, spell, spice, spirit, splendor, surroundings, texture, tone, tranquility, undercurrent, veil, vein, veneer, vestige, whisper

674 **bad situation:** abortion, accident, adversity, affliction, anarchy, anticlimax, atrophy, backwash, bane, beaten, bedlam, bereavement, bind, blight, blooper, blow, brunt, calamity, casualty, cataclysm, catastrophe,

catch, chagrin, chaos, clamor, clog, clutter, cobweb, collapse, collision, comedown, commotion, complication, conflict, contamination, contempt, corner, crisis, crunch, curse, damage, deadlock, dearth, debacle, decay, decline, decomposition, deficiency, descent, detriment, devastation, difficulty, dilemma, disadvantage(s), disappointment, disaster, discomfiture, discouragement, disorganization, disrepair, disservice, distress, disturbance, downfall, downside, drag, drama, drawback, dud, duress, embarrassment, emergency, entanglement, error, exigency/exigence, eyesore, failing, fall, famine, ferment, fiasco, filth, fix, flap, flaw, flop, frenzy, friction, frustration, handicap, hang-up, hardship, harm, hassle, havoc, hell, hindrance, hitch, holdup, hole, hurdle, ill, impasse, imposture, impropriety, inadequacy, inconvenience, indiscretion, infirmity, injustice, jam, jump, kink, lapse, liability, limitation, load, lose, loss, madhouse, malfunction, matter, maze, mess, mire, misadventure, misery, misfortune/mishap, misstep, mix-up, muss, neglect, nightmare, nuisance, obstacle, obstruction, onus, oppression, ordeal, outrage, pall, pandemonium, pass, pell-mell, pest, pickle, pinch, pitfall, pity, plague, plight, poison, predicament, press, pressure, problem, puncture, quagmire, quandary, question, repulse, restraint, restriction, reverse, rub, ruin, ruse, scandal, scourge, scrape, setback, shambles, shortcoming, showdown, slump, smash, snag, snare, snarl, spot, squeeze, storm, strait, strife, struggle, syndrome, tangle, tilt, to-do, tragedy, trap, trial, trouble, tumult, turmoil, undoing, unrest, uprising, uproar, upset, weakness, weight, wreck

675 **danger:** calamity, cataclysm, corner, crunch, curse, danger, dilemma, disaster, emergency, fatality, hardship, hazard, ill, jeopardy, mayhem, menace, peril, poison, risk, scourge, seriousness, smash, threat, tragedy, trouble, venture, violence

676 **effect:** amount, attraction, because, cogency, combustion, cost, culmination, effectiveness, efficacy, feebleness, magnetism, potency, proceed, punch, splash, tell, therefore, wash

677 **effort:** concentration, cooperation, difficulty, diligence, direct, effort, exertion, force, go, groove, idleness, industry, plod, sweat, toil, trouble, try, work, yoke

678 **experience:** background, callow, career, culture, heritage, history, ignorance, lead (a life), life, live, maturity, mellow, memory, naive, naïveté, phenomenon, practical, readiness, record, sustain, taste, training, unaccustomed, unfamiliar, veteran, world, young

679 **fate:** accident, blessing, break, catch, chaff, chance, contingency, cost, demise, destiny, disadvantage, doom, downfall, dues, duty, fate, fluke, fortune, freak, future, godsend, good, jinx, judgment, limbo, lot, luck, misfortune/mishap, oblivion, outlook, payoff, penalty, pitfall, plague, portion, reverse, setback, shortcoming, suspense, turning point, undoing, weight

680 **function:** application, avail, bar, begin, bolt, cloak, closure, cord, cushion, decoy, deter-

rent, disguise, dump, gauge, operate, operation, run, spray, tie

681 inaction: abeyance, abide, asleep, bide, dalliance, dally, dawdle, doze, drag, fool around, forbear, forgo, hang, hesitate, hesitation, idleness, inertia, leisure, linger, loaf, loiter, lounge, neglect, nod, procrastinate, refrain, relief, remain, repose, respite, rest, shirk, skip, slack/slacken, stay, wait

682 meaning: ambiguity, connotation, content, context, cryptic, denotation, denote, double entendre, drift, drive at, emphasis, express, fiber, gist, imply, import, importance, light, matter, mean, meaning, meat, message, nature, nub, point, punch, purport, quintessence, represent, respect, sense, significance, signify, spirit, stand for, strain, strength, stuff, substance, suggest, symbolize, tenor, text, texture, theme, thrust, tone, typify, understanding, undertone, upshot, value, vein, weigh, weight, wording

683 name: alias, anonymous, denomination, designation, epithet, handle, name, nickname, nomenclature, pseudonym, term, title

684 of agreement: accord, agreement, alliance, armistice, arrangement, assent, bargain, bond, charter, chorus, coherence, coincidence, communion, compact, compliance, compromise, concert, concord, consensus, consent, contract, convention, covenant, deal, faction, meeting, negotiation, okay, order, pact, protocol, provision/proviso, settlement, stipulation, terms, transaction, treaty, truce, understanding, warranty, word

685 of authorization: approval, authority, certificate, confirmation, consent, credentials, decree, delegation, determination, dispensation, enactment, endorsement, enforcement, entrée, entry, exemption, fiat, finding forgiveness, go-ahead, grace, guaranty, indication, leave, license, mandate, negation, nod, order, pardon, pass, passage, passport, patent, permission, permit, recall, release, remission, repeal, reprieve, sanction, seal, signal, ticket, treaty, veto, waiver, warrant, warranty, withdrawal, word

687 of being an influence: bolt, contact, effect, effectiveness, fetish, gush, influence, instrument, leadership, leverage, muscle, orbit, persuasion, preponderance, pressure, sphere, squeeze, sway, wonder

688 of being a rule: authority, axiom, ban, basis, benchmark, canon, code, condition, convention, creed, criterion, custom, democracy, dictate, doctrine, dogma, edict, essence, ethics/ethic, fact, form, formality, formula, fundamental, gauge, generality, ideology, institute, keynote/keystone, law, line, measure, model, morals, norm, observance, parameter, philosophy, policy, practice, precept, principle, protocol, regulation, ritual, rule, standard, taboo, tenet, theorem, tradition

686 of being an example: archetype, case, classic, embodiment, epitome, example, exemplar, exponent, guide, ideal, illustration, instance, lesson, light, measure, model, norm, original, paradigm, paragon, pattern, picture, precedent, prototype, replica, representative, sample, specimen, stereotype, type

689 of belief: advocacy, ageism, allegiance, anticipation, aphorism, apparition, assumed, assumption, atheism, attitude, attrition, axiom, basis, belief, bias, black magic, capitalism, cause, chauvinism, church, commonplace, complaint, concept, conception, conclusion, confidence, conformity, conjecture, connotation, conscience, consensus, contention, conviction, credence, creed, cult, culture, decision, deduction, definition, delusion, democracy, denomination, dependence/dependency, derision, determination, diagnosis, dictum, disapproval, disbelief, discrimination, dissent, dissidence, dissonance, distrust, divinity, doctrine, dogma, doubt, estimate, estimation, ethics/ethic, evaluation, expectancy, expectation, eye, faith, faithfulness, fallacy, fanaticism, fantasy, fascism, fatalism, favor, feeling, fetish, foreboding, forgiveness, generality, gospel, grievance, guess, heresy, honor, hunch, hypothesis, idea, ideals, ideology, illusion, image, impression, incantation, induction, inkling, instinct, intimation, intuition, judgment, leaning, line, logic, magic, make-believe, maxim, mind, miracle, misconception, misgiving, motivation, motive, multiculturalism, nihilism, nonconformity, notion, objection, obsession, omen, opinion, optimism, oracle, outlook, perception, perspective, persuasion, pessimism, philosophy, piety, platform, position, preconception, prediction, prejudice, premise, premonition, presage, presentiment, presumption, pride, principle/principles, prognosis, prophecy, prospect, purport, purpose, racism, reaction, reality, recognition, regard, reliance, religion, reputation, resolve, respect, right, school, self-respect/self-esteem, self-satisfaction, sentiment, side, sign, slant, sorcery, speculation, spell, stance, stand, stigma, stock, subject, subsistence, suggestion, superstition, supposition, surmise, suspicion, taste, tenet, theme, theorem, theory, thesis, trust, understanding, utopia, view, viewpoint, vision, vow, witchcraft, word

690 of concern: afraid, aghast, alarm, anxiety, anxious, apprehension, burden, concern, conundrum, craze, difficulty, dismay, disquiet, distraction, distraught, distress, doubt, fascination, feeling, fixation, foreboding, frightened, guilt, hallucination, hang-up, horror, interest, jitters, jumpy, misgiving, mistrust, obsession, panic, passion, peeve, premonition, puzzled, quandary, question, regard, scruple, suspicion, temptation, terror, trouble, uneasy, weight, woe, wonder, worry

691 of law: abomination, annulment, autocracy, custody, exemption, freedom, independence, justice, laissez-faire, liberty, offense, order, peace, prohibition, trespass, trial, validity, ward

692 on a course: career, pitch, ramble, tack, tendency, traverse

693 opportunity: contingency, facility, fluke, freedom, handicap, hazard, hearing, interest, juncture, lead, leverage, luck, merit, miracle, occasion, odds, opening, opportunity, outlet, picnic, plus, possibility, preference, prize, profit, prospect, pushover, recourse, remedy,

resort, risk, sake, shot, snap, start, strength,
stumble, success, time, treat, turn, vacancy,
welfare/well-being

694 purpose: application, employment, help,
purpose, role, vehicle

695 repetition: boomerang, echo, repeat, repetition, return, verbiage

696 situation: case, circumstance, condition,
context, environment, experience, instance,
landmark, matter, medium, mystery, occurrence, point, position, situation, state, uncertainty

OF CHANGE

697 abstract: about-face, accommodation, adapt,
adaptation, adjust, adjustment, back down,
balance, deepen, depart, departure, deviate,
deviation, digress, digression, dip, diversify,
fluctuate, flux, get, interchange, metamorphose, metamorphosis, movement, mutation,
novelty, oscillate, range, reconcile, redress,
refresh, replace, retract, reverse, revive, revolution, rig, rotate, shift, suit, switch, tighten,
transform, transformation, transition, transpose, turn, variance, variation, vary, vicissitude, withdraw

698 diminish: abate, atrophy, come down, cut,
decline, decrease, degenerate, depreciate, deteriorate, deterioration, die, diminish, diminution, drain, drop, drop off, dwarf, dwindle,
ebb, erosion, evaporate, evaporation, fade,
fester, flag, go, go down, lapse, lessen, let
up, lull, mollify, peter out, plummet, qualify,
recede, reduce, regress, relapse, relax, relent,
remission, remit, revert, rot, sag, shrink,
sink, slack/slacken, slump, stagnate, subside,
taper/taper off, vegetate, wane, weaken,
wear, wither, worsen

699 fail: blow, bomb, comedown, decline, default, disappoint, disqualify, downfall, droop,
error, fail, failure, fall, fault, fizzle, flag,
flop, flounder, fold, founder, go, go down,
go under, miscarriage, miss, misstep, neglect, omission, overlook, run out, slump,
wilt

700 improve: accession, advance, advancement,
amendment, boom, boost, clear up, come
along, correction, develop, development, dignify, edification, elevate, embellish, embellishment, energize, expansion, furbish, grace,
improve, improvement, lift, look up, mend,
pay, pick up, progress, pull through, rally,
recoup, recover, recuperate, relieve, repair,
revision, rise

701 of state: acclimate, aging, alteration, alternate, approach, assimilate, backfire, become,
break out, change, come, come about, conversion, convert, co-opt, metamorphose,
metamorphosis, state

702 of structure: buckle, collapse, degenerate,
dissolve, flatten

703 organizational: adjournment, dissolution,
growth, merger

704 progress: advance, advancement, batten,
boom, breakthrough, breeze, bring off,
buildup, click, climax, coast, come on, consummate, course, develop, development, evolution, evolve, expansion, fare, flourish,

flower, form, fruition, furtherance, gestation,
get along, get on, go, go ahead, go far, grow,
growth, headway, inroad, jump, mature, mellow, mount, mushroom, passage, precipitate,
progress, push off/push on, rise, score,
spread, thrive, unfold, wax

705 unchanged: abeyance, calm, limbo, peace,
quiet

OF NEED OR ACHIEVEMENT

706 achievement: ability, accomplish, accomplishment, achieve, achievement, acme, action, apex, arrive, art, attain, attainment,
background, bloom, blossom, bring about,
bring off, carry, carry out, climax, clinch,
come at, comeback, come through, compass,
completion, conquer, conquest, consummate,
consummation, coup, craft, crown, deed, degree, discharge, distinction, doing, draw,
drive, effect, efficacy, excel, execute, execution, exercise, exploit, extreme, extremity,
failure, feat, find, finish, flair, flourish, fruition, fulfill, fulfillment, gain, get, get ahead,
gift, go far, go over, hammer out, hit, land,
manage, maximum, milestone, operate, pan
out, pass, perfect, perfection, performance,
pinnacle, potential, prodigy, proficiency,
progress, prosper, prosperity, pull off, pull
through, reach, record, score, smash, stroke,
succeed, success, take, thrive, transact, triumph, victory, welfare/well-being, win,
work, work out, zenith

707 lack: lack, loss, nothing/nothingness

708 mutual possession: communal, joint, mutual

709 need: addiction, affinity, bait, call, charge,
claim, craving, cupidity, dearth, default, de-
pendence/dependency, deprivation, desire,
exigency/exigence, famine, hankering, hope,
hunger, inadequacy, lack, longing, lust,
must, necessity, need, partiality, penchant,
poverty, predilection, predisposition, preference, prerequisite, prize, propensity, require-
ment/requisite, shortage, sustenance,
temptation, thirst, use, void, want, wish, yen

710 possession: abundance, acquisition, asset(s),
belongings, boast, buy, cache, capital, cash,
clutches, commodity, custody, deserts, desolation, division, domain, dominion, due, dynasty, enjoy, enjoyment, entrench, estate,
exuberance, fixtures, fortune, fund, funds,
gain, get, grasp, have, hoard, hold, keep, legacy, lot, monopolize, monopoly, occupancy,
occupation, own, ownership, plunder, possess, possession, presence, prize, property,
purchase, reservation, reserve, reserved, resource, resources, retain, return, riches, savings, share, spoils, stake, store, subsistence,
title, treasure, wealth

711 requirement: depend, hinge, provision/pro-
viso, provisional, reservation, rest

712 resource: amenity, arrival, ballast, bastion,
catalyst, comfort, convenience, edge, expe-
diency/expedience, expedient, facility, find,
guard, hoard, indulgence, luxury, mainstay,
maintenance, makeshift, medium, mine, momentum, nurture, option, organ, pillar, plum,

750 on: cover, on, pile, top, traverse

751 outside: band, edge, skirt, stick out

752 over: above, altitude, dominate, overhang, overlook, rise, tower, vault

753 sequential: line, trail, wake

754 shape: bag, conformation, curvature, cut, entwine, figure, fold, form, hollow, loop, pucker, shape, turn, twist

755 speed: celerity, dispatch, expedition, haste, hurry, pace, rapidity, rate, speed, velocity

756 spread: balloon, branch off/branch out, breadth, bridge, go, latitude, range, reach, room, space, span, sweep

757 structure: aperture, ascent, attitude, bag, beef, break, build, composition, condition, conformation, constitution, construction, crease, curvature, even, fabric, figure, fluid, form, frame, grade, gradient, makeup, physique, plane, ramp, set, shape, slope, stance, stoop

758 surrounding: circle, coil, compass, define, edge, encircle, enclose, encompass, fence, frame, gird, hedge, hem/hem in, mob, pen, ring, surround

759 touching: meet, neighbor, overlap

760 width: breadth, diameter, width

761 within a group: middle, range

Weights and measures

MATHEMATICS

762 attribute of a number: any, apiece, average, calculable, countless, dual, immeasurable, infinite, innumerable, just about, legion, less, light, limitless, manifold, many, mathematical, maximum, minimal, minimum, more, multiple/multifarious, multitudinous, myriad, nil, numberless, numeric/numerical, numerous, one, plentiful/plenty, plus, profuse, round, several, short, shy, single, skimpy, slight, sparse, steep, tidy, tiny, total, unreasonable, untold

763 change in number: accrue, appreciate, appreciation, deduction, discount, increase, increment, inflation, jump, peak, plummet, raise, reach, slump

764 mathematic reasoning: add, addition, appraise, arithmetic, average, balance, calculate, calculation, cast, computation, compute, count, enumerate, estimate, figure, gauge, measure, number, pace, page, reckon, scale, score, stock, subtract, tabulate, tally, tell, total, underestimate

765 numeric symbol: digit, fraction, number

766 numeric value: appraisal, count, couple, majority, maximum, peak, percentage, rate, scant/scanty

767 quantity: abundance, copiousness, enough, exuberance, greatness, overabundance, paucity, peak, plenty, plethora, preponderance, scant/scanty, shortage

768 ratio: quota, rate, ratio

769 series: array, chain, range, series, set, string

770 system: apparatus, automation, bureaucracy, business, capitalism, channel, circuit, commerce, communications, complex, cosmos, dispensation, file, finance, grammar, machinery, mail, method, net, network, pattern, post, routine, scale, system, traffic, world

QUANTIFIERS

771 attribute of quantity: about, additional, affluent, all, altogether, amply, below, best, better, big, bountiful, brimming/brimful, copious, depleted, disproportionate, double, dual, enough, excessive, exhausted, exiguous, extra, extravagant, extreme, extremely, few, flush, fraught, further, good, hardly, huge, inadequate, insufficient, just about, lacking, leftover, liberal, limited, limitless, lush, luxuriant, many, more, most, much, new, nil, other, outrageous, over, plus, residual, respectable, rich, rife, slender/slim, spare, spent, sufficient, thick, thin, too, unreasonable, various, wholesale

772 attribute of range: abysmal, all, all-out, barely, besides, beyond, blanket, bodily, bounded, boundless, broad, capacious, catholic, chiefly, comprehensive, cosmic, dead, dearly, deeply, different, diffuse, diverse, eclectic, ecumenical, encyclopedic, exhaustive, expansive, extended, extensive, far, far-reaching, full-scale, fully, general, generally, global, greatly, inclusive, increasingly, indiscriminate, international, largely, lower, mainly, mixed, moderately, more, moreover, most, mostly, motley, much, multiple/multifarious, only, overall, pervasive, practically, primarily, principally, quite, rambling, rampant, rather, relatively, rife, slightly, somewhat, substantially, sundry, sweeping, too, universal, unlimited, utmost, vast, very, well, wholesale, wholly, wide, widespread, within, without

773 attribute of size: angular, atomic, baby, bantam, better, big, brief, broad, burly, capacious, capsule, cavernous, chubby, chunky, commodious, compact, compendious, concise, corpulent, cramped, cumbersome, dwarf, enormous, extensive, fleshy, full, gargantuan, giant, gigantic, grand, great, gross, hearty, hefty, huge, husky, immeasurable, immense, imposing, impressive, incalculable, infinitesimal, inflated, laconic, large, little, major, mammoth, massive, microscopic, midget, mighty, miniature, minimal, minor, minute, monstrous, monumental, narrow, petite, pocket, portable, prodigious, pudgy, puny, round, scrawny, short, small, squat, stocky, stout, strapping, stubby, stunted, substantial, teeny/teensy, thick, thin, tiny, tremendous, vast, voluminous, whopping, wide

774 **capacity:** brimming/brimful, capacious, capacity, close, compact, congested, crowded, empty, full, packed, spacious, teeming, vacant, void

775 **change of quantity:** accession, allowance, develop, development, grow, growth

776 **decreasing:** attrition, contraction, cut, cutback, deduction, deflate, depreciate, diminish, diminution, drop, drop off, dwindle, fall, lessen, recede, relent, sag, shrink, sink, subside, taper/taper off, wane

777 **depth:** abysmal, deep, profound, shallow, superficial, unfathomable

778 **distance:** about, afar, away, beyond, contiguous, directly, distant, extreme, far, faraway, farther, farthest, furthest, immediate, last, near, nearby, off, onward/onwards, uttermost, yonder

779 **height:** alpine, elevated, giant, gigantic, high, lanky, lofty, long, low, midget, petite, precipitous, rangy, short, squat, statuesque, stubby, stunted, tall, towering

780 **increasing:** accretion, accrue, accumulation, amplification, boost, bulge, distend, enlarge, enlargement, expansion, gather, increase, increment, inflate, inflation, leap, mount, peak, proliferate, reach, rise, swell, wax, widen

781 **large:** abundant, aggregate, ample, appreciable, bulky, colossal, commodious, considerable, countless, excessive, extreme, extremely, exuberant, fantastic, far, generous, giant, gigantic, good, great, gross, handsome, handsomely, immeasurable, incalculable, infinite, inordinate, jumbo, large, lavish, legion, manifold, massive, maximum, mighty, monstrous, much, multitudinous, myriad, numberless, numerous, opulent, plentiful/plenty, prodigal, prodigious, profuse, redundant, sizable, stupendous, substantial, surplus, tidy, tremendous, untold, unwieldy, vast, voluminous, whopping

782 **length:** extended, high, lengthy, low, short, tall

783 **measurement:** degree, extent, mark, proportion

784 **number:** amount, digit, estimate, figure, number, numeral, pair, percentage, point, quotation/quote, score, sum, trio/triple, zero

785 **portion:** among, apart, asunder, fractional, fragmentary, gross, half, sectional

786 **quantity:** all, amount, array, avalanche, average, backlog, barrage, batch, buildup, bundle, calculation, cascade, cipher, deal, deluge, duo, excess, extravagance, few, figure, flood, flow, glut, gust, heap, lot, many, mass, measure, minimum, mint, myriad, number, overabundance, pile, pittance, plenty, plethora, quantity, sum, surge, tally, total, trio/triple, turnout

787 **range:** bound/bounds, breadth, compass, confines, expanse, extent, gamut, latitude, length, range, scale, scope, spread, sweep, width

788 **relative:** cumulative, empty, fairly, full, influx

789 **small:** compendious, diminutive, dinky, exiguous, few, handful, infinitesimal, least, less, light, little, low, marginal, meager, measly, microscopic, miniature, minimal, minimum, minor, minute, negligible, nominal,

one, outside, petite, piddling, scant/scanty, scarce, scarcely, shy, skimpy, slight, small, sparse, teeny/teensy, tiny, trifling

790 **unit of distance measure:** depth, distance, foot, inch, mile

791 **unit of height measure:** altitude, foot, height, inch, mile

792 **unit of measure:** acre, area, degree, dimensions/dimension, gauge, mass, measure, measurement, perimeter, revolution, size, velocity, volume, width

793 **unit of scalar measure:** above, abysmal, lesser, low, over, under

794 **unit of volume measure:** capacity, fill, volume

795 **unit of weight measure:** ounce, pound, weight

796 **width:** broad, cavernous, wide

TIME

797 **attribute of age:** adolescent, advanced, afresh, aged, ancient, antediluvian, antiquarian, antiquated, antique, archaic, big, callow, childish, contemporary, crude, doddering, elder, elderly, fresh, full-grown/full-fledged, green, immature, immemorial, inchoate, infant/infantile, innovative, junior, juvenile, late, mature, medieval, mellow, mint, modern, modish, musty, new, newfangled, novel, old, older, old-fashioned, original, originally, outdated/out-of-date, outmoded, passé, puerile, quaint, recent, ripe, senior, stale, tender, undeveloped, up-to-date, vintage, young, youthful

798 **attribute of duration:** ad infinitum, all-time, always, annual, awhile, brief, ceaseless, chronic, compact, concise, confirmed, constant, continual, continuous, dragging, endless, ephemeral, eternal, eternity, ever, everlasting, extended, fleeting, forever, fugitive, immortal, incessant, indefinitely, infinite, interminable, inveterate, laconic, lasting, lifelong, limitless, long, meteoric, momentary, never-ending, nonstop, old, ongoing, passing, perennial, permanent, perpetual, relentless, running, short, short-lived, soon, steady, temporary, through, throughout, transient/transitory, unbreakable, unbroken, undying, unending, unflagging, uninterrupted, unrelenting, whirlwind

799 **attribute of time:** actual, advance, afterward/afterwards, again, almost, already, antediluvian, anterior, at, behind, bottom, colonial, coming, concurrent, consecutive, dilatory, dire, due, duly, early, effective, ever, extemporaneous/extemporary, fast, felicitous, finally, foremost, forever, forthcoming, forward, frequently, gradual, gradually, hasty, hence, hereafter, hurried, immemorial, initial, instant, instantly, intermittent, irregular, irregularly, just about, last, lastly/last, late, later, latter, leisurely, meantime, meanwhile, meteoric, narrowly, never, next, nightly, nocturnal, old, old-fashioned, once, oncoming, originally, overdue, pell-mell, periodic, perpetual, posterior, posthaste, postmortem, preceding, precipitous/precipitate, preliminary, previous, primarily, primary/

prime, primeval, primitive, primordial, prompt, promptly, punctual, rapid, rapidly, ready, right, rude, sharp, short, simultaneous, snappy, sudden, suddenly, summarily, swift, swiftly/swift, tardy, temporal, then, thereafter, timely, ultimate, unawares, untimely, up-to-date, when, while, yet

800 date: anniversary, date

801 day: afternoon, almanac, anniversary, daily, date, day, ephemeral, evening, journal, morning, night, nightly, nocturnal, noon, time

802 definite period: date, day, holiday, instant, leave, morning, noon, present, shift

803 division of: day, minute, second

804 duration: brevity, continuance, continuation, course, duration, endurance, endure, eternity, extent, go, halt, length, remain

805 frequency: rapidity, sometimes

806 hour: afternoon, evening, morning, night, noon, time

807 indefinite period: age, antiquity, anytime, bit, bout, break, breath, continuance, convenience, downtime, era, future, generation, hiatus, history, infinity, interim, interlude, intermission, interruption, interval, lapse, leave, leisure, letup, lull, meantime, minute, moment, past, pause, period, present, recess, remission, respite, rest, round, slack, space, span, spell, stalemate, stint, stretch, suspension, term, tour, trick, vacation, wait, while

808 minute: flash, instant, jiffy, moment, tick, wink

809 month: almanac, calendar, gestation, lunatic, moon, time

810 part of a day: afternoon, dark, dawn, day, daybreak, daylight, dusk, evening, gloom, light, morning, night, nightfall, sunrise, sunset, tick, twilight

811 past or future: following, future, past, preceding, previous, prior, succeeding/successive

812 proximity: immediate, near, now, prior, succeeding/successive

813 relative order: follow, precede, succeed

814 season: autumn, season, spring, summer, winter

815 specific: anniversary, beginning, date, dawn, daybreak, instance, juncture, point, present, yesterday, zero hour

816 stage of existence: administration, age, childhood, cycle, day, era, generation, life, past, phase, prime, stage, tenure

817 stage of life form: adolescence, age, babyhood, childhood, cradle, cycle, landmark, life, lifetime, majority, maternity, old age, prime, puberty, spell, youth

818 temporal association: anachronism, clockwork, dispatch, elapse, eternity, fly, following, future, haste, pace, past, precede, precedence, preceding, previous, prior, rush, succeeding/successive

819 temporal object: anytime, clock, time

820 time relative to present: abrupt, after, ago, ahead, amid/amidst, anew, antecedent, back, before, beforehand, behind, belated, between, bygone, circa, coincident, contemporary, current, deferred, destined, directly, during, early, ensuing, erstwhile, eventual, eventually, final, first, following, fore, foregoing, former, formerly, forthwith, future, historical, immediate, immediately, imminent, impending, infant/infantile, instantaneous, just, lately, momentarily, near, nearing, new, newly, now, once, past, present, presently, previous, previously, prior, readily, recent, recently, shortly, someday, soon, straight, subsequent, subsequently, succeeding/successive, topical, ultimate, ultimately, until, yet

821 unit of time measure: day, flash, minute, second, wink

822 within a time period: interim, interval, period, span, spell, stint, stretch, term, while

823 year: almanac, anniversary, annual, annually, time, yearly

WHOLENESS OR DIVISION

824 added part: arm, attachment, auxiliary, complement, complementary, excess, extension, extra, fitting, flap, fresh, frill, frippery, furthermore, garnish, new, offshoot, outgrowth, protuberance, ramification, repair, sequel, spare, superfluous, supplement, surplus, trim, wake, wing

825 bottom part: fringe, rear, rest, rump, seat, skirt, stub, stump, tail

826 core part: base, bosom, bottom, constituent, core, crux, element, essential, filling/filler, focus, foundation, fundamental, germ, heart, hub, inner, interior, internal, kernel, marrow, meat, nub, nucleus, quintessence, root, trunk

827 end part: addendum, back, border, butt, end, point, posterior, rear, seat, stub, stump, tail

828 first part: appetizer, early, initial, introduction, lead, nucleus, overture, precursor, predecessor, preliminary, spark

829 main part: body, bulk, capital, chief, element, feature, flower, focus, fundamental, hulk, hull, main, majority, parcel, plurality, root

830 middle part: aisle, axis, axle, bowels, center, central, filling/filler, inner, inside, interior, intermediate, internal, joint, junction/juncture, mean, median, middle, midst, pivot

831 minor part: atom, bit, breath, chip, collateral, component, crumb, dash, detail, dot, drop, factor, feature, fiber, flake, fleck, flicker, glimmer, grain, grit, handle, iota, item, joint, lick, ligature, minimum, modicum, molecule, morsel, nibble, nip, node/nodule, particle, patch, peripheral, pinch, point, powder, scrap, shred, sliver, spark, specimen, speck, splinter, spot, sprinkling, suspicion, tinge, touch, trace, trifle, whisper, whit, wisp

832 of an event: chapter, close, conclusion, dawn, end, ending, finale, finality, finish, genesis, germ, head, height, highlight, inception, installation, interruption, last, leg, limit, meridian, onset, opening, orientation, origin, outbreak, overture, particular, peak, period, preliminary, prelude, premiere, preview, prime, sequel, snatch, stalemate, standstill, start, stay, step, stop, stoppage, suspension, term, termination, threshold, touch, turning point, twilight, twist, victory, win, zenith, zero hour

833 of an order: back, beginning, end, front, middle

834 part: accessory, accompaniment, attribute, component, constituent, counterpart, feature, member, part, phase, piece, strip, thing, trait, trash, unit

835 portion: accompaniment, addition, adjunct, allotment, ancillary, appendage, arm, bit, bite, branch, constituent, contents, dab, deal, division, dose, drop, end, excerpt, excess, extract, facet, factor, feature, fraction, fragment, front, half, ingredient, installment, interest, item, layer, link, little, lot, majority, mass, measure, member, morsel, parcel, pat-, percentage, piece, portion, quarter, quota, ration, remainder, remnant, rest, sample, scrap, section, sector, segment, share, side, slab, slice, stake, subdivision, taste, tidbit, whit, wing

836 top part: acme, alpine, apex, barb, brim, ceiling, citadel, climax, crest, crown, extreme, extremity, face, front, head, height, lid, maximum, meridian, peak, pinnacle, plug, point, prominence, rim, summit, tip, top, vertex, zenith

837 whole: all, amount, entirety, everything, gross, synthesis, system, total, unit, unity, whole